COMPRI
SWAHILI–ENGLISH
DICTIONARY

Kamusi kutoka EAEP

1. **My First Peak Dictionary** - *Njeru, M. na wengineo*

2. **Kamusi Yangu ya Kwanza** - *Ahmed Ndalu*

3. **Kamusi ya Methali za Kiswahili (Toleo Jipya)** - *Kitula King'ei na Ahmed Ndalu*

4. **Kamusi ya Semi za Kiswahili (Toleo Jipya)** - *Kitula King'ei na Ahmed Ndalu*

5. **Kamusi ya Vitendawili na Mafumbo** - *Ahmed Ndalu na H. Ikambili*

6. **Kamusi ya Visawe** - *M.A. Mohamed na S.A. Mohamed*

7. **Maneno Yanayotatanisha: *Kimaana na Kimatamshi*** - *Godson Maanga*

8. **Kamusi Angaza: *Kwa Shule za Msingi*** - *A. Ndalu*

9. **Comprehensive Swahili-English Dictionary** - *M. A. Mohamed*

COMPREHENSIVE SWAHILI–ENGLISH DICTIONARY

Mohamed A. Mohamed

**East African
Educational Publishers Ltd.**

Nairobi • Kampala • Dar es Salaam • Kigali

Kimetolewa na
East African Educational Publishers Ltd.
Brick Court, Mpaka Road/Woodvale Grove
Westlands, S.L.P. 45314
Nairobi-00100
KENYA.

Barua pepe: eaep@eastafricanpublishers.com
Tovuti: www.eastafricanpublishers.com

East African Educational Publishers Ltd.
S.L.P. 11542
Kampala
UGANDA.

Ujuzi Educational Publishers Ltd.
S.L.P. 32737, Kijito-Nyama
Dar es Salaam
TANZANIA.

East African Publishers Rwanda Ltd.
No 86 Benjamina Street
Nyarutarama Gacuriro, Gasabo District
S.L.P. 5151, Kigali
RWANDA.

Idhini ya kunakili © Mohamed A. Mohamed 2011

Kilichapishwa mara ya kwanza 2011

ISBN 978-9966-25-812-0

Kimepigwa chapa nchini Kenya na
English Press Ltd
S.L.P. 30127
Nairobi, KENYA

In

memory of

my two

greatest friends

Seif Mohamed Seif (El Mauly),

Dr. I. S. Ngozi

and my

beloved sister

Fatma Abdulla Mohamed

(Toti)

who all contributed

significantly to the

making of this

Dictionary

CONTENTS

Preface viii

Foreword ix

Acknowledgements xiii

Descriptive Chart showing how to use the Dictionary xiv

Guide to the Use of the Dictionary xviii

Abbreviations and Symbols used in the Dictionary xxxi

Bibliography 889

PREFACE

Comprehensive Swahili-English Dictionary is the latest publication of its kind. It offers the most current use of the language among Swahili speakers today. Users of this dictionary will be able to achieve a superior mastery of speech and the different forms of writing.

The dictionary has advanced the works of previous lexicographers who have written dictionaries similar in nature. These include the first English-Swahili dictionary published by Madan in 1894, followed later by Johnson's publications (1939) namely *A Standard Swahili-English Dictionary*, *A Standard English-Swahili Dictionary* and *Kamusi ya Kiswahili*. Later publications of this kind include *A Concise English-Swahili Dictionary* by R.A. Snoxall, *The Friendly Modern Swahili-English Dictionary* by Malaika, B., Kamusi ya Kiswahili Sanifu by Tuki (Institute of Kiswahili Research), *English-Swahili Pocket Dictionary* by J. Safari and H. Akida and more recently *English-Swahili Dictionary* by Tuki (Institute of Kiswahili Research).

Comprehensive Swahili-English Dictionary has more than 60,000 entries covering various fields. These include scientific, political, economic, linguistic and educational domains. The dictionary also contains illustrations and pictures which facilitate a quick understanding of the various headwords.

The wide selection of headwords in this dictionary, accompanied by a phonetic transcription is derived both from spoken and written sources. The former includes discussions with Swahili native speakers and the latter includes the use of existing dictionaries, Swahili newspapers and relevant materials in the various fields.

It should be noted that the author of this dictionary has tried his best to be gender neutral. In many cases, the use of "he" although very common in this dictionary, is meant to have generic reference, that is, without referring to a particular group.

The dictionary mainly targets a bilingual audience and will certainly be of invaluable benefit to students, teachers, experts and the public in general.

Professor Mohamed A. Mohamed
The State University of Zanzibar
2011

FOREWORD

The English language is not the oldest European source of loan words for Kiswahili, but English has become the biggest European source of loan words in Kiswahili. A new Swahili-English dictionary is probably needed every two decades. This version by Professor Mohamed A. Mohamed is particularly welcome because of its sophistication and linguistic sensitivity.

The oldest European source of loan words is probably Portuguese, following the early settlement of Portuguese adventurers along the East African coast. The most enduring physical monument to the Portuguese historic role along the Kenyan Coast is Fort Jesus in Mombasa, which was partly carved out of solid rock by the Portuguese in the 18th century. Fort Jesus was partly conquered by the Mazrui dynasty of Mombasa, and finally by the British as part of colonial Kenya. After Kenya's independence the Fort has now been converted into a national museum.

If this construction is the most enduring physical monument to Portugal, the most important linguistic contribution from Portugal is probably the Swahili word for *money*. The word *pesa* is arguably the most significant economic word in the Swahili language. It was born out of the Iberian world. Ironically, the word *pesa* is closer to Spanish than to Portuguese. The Mexican currency is the *peso* to the present day.

Household Swahili words which have persisted from Portuguese include *meza* (table), *shimizi* (a slip worn by a woman) and some other domestic nomenclature. The Swahili word for a Portuguese person is *Mreno*.

Metaphorically across the ages the word *Mreno* has also been used to mean *aristocrat*. As for the Portuguese word for *table* it was spelt *mesa*, rather than *meza*.

Next to the Portuguese language, German is the oldest European source of loan words for Kiswahili. This borrowing was triggered mainly by the German colonization of Tanganyika early in the 20th century, which ended after World War 1.

The Germans introduced their colonial subjects to formalized educational institutions. It is particularly appropriate that the word for *school* in Kiswahili is *shule*, drawn from its German version.

But, a far more important German impact on Kiswahili arose out of the German policy of deliberate cultural distance created between the rulers and the colonial subjects. German cultural arrogance early in the 20th century was based on the proposition that no African was good enough to speak German. This was in contrast to the French policy of assimilation, which was based on the belief that no African was good enough unless he or she spoke French.

For all the wrong reasons, German colonial policy in Tanganyika promoted Kiswahili as a language of administration and thereby reduced the need to teach the "natives" the German language. The German policy of cultural distancing was therefore unintended good news for the expansion of the Swahili language.

The French policy of assimilation, on the other hand, was detrimental to native cultures and traditions. The French language prospered in the colonies of France and Belgium, but often at the expense of the indigenous heritage. Loan words in Kiswahili from the French language came mainly through the linguistic impact of Belgium in the Congo (Kinshasa) and her influence in Rwanda and Burundi, where Kiswahili is still spreading. There was also early German influence in what was then called Ruanda-Urundi.

But by far the most extensive European lending to Kiswahili has come from the English language since the beginning of the 20th century. This dictionary is rich in examples of this cultural interaction. As a beneficiary of loan words, Kiswahili started by borrowing religious concepts from the Arabic language to the more recent phenomenon of borrowing scientific concepts from the English language. The loan words in religious expression began with the word *religion* itself. *Dini* has been widely distributed orally and in writing as the Swahili word for "religion", inherited from the Arabic language. Other East African languages have in turn borrowed the same word for religion in Luganda, Lunyoro/Lutoro, Kigiriama and others.

There are paradoxes in these exchanges, While the word for God *(Mungu)* is Bantu, the word for "Almighty" (Mwenye *ezi)* is partly Arabic.

The word for prophet in Kiswahili is *"Mtume",* which is Bantu, whereas the word for "angel" is *malaika,* borrowed from Arabic.

The verb "to pray" is Arabic *[kusali],* whereas the verb "to fast" *[kufunga]* is Bantu. Although originally the religion from which Kiswahili was borrowing was Islam, the outreach of the language extended to Christianity. The Arabic language became a source of Christian concepts, as well as Islamic. Shared concepts between Islam and Christianity which are borrowed from Arabic include *malaika* (angel), *shetani* (satan), *roho* (soul).

Also borrowed from Arabic by Kiswahili are such crucial Christian concepts as *msalaba* (the cross), *mtakatifu* (saint) and the verb "to crucify" *(sulubisha).*

But if the story of Kiswahili is a transition from dependency on *religion* for loan words to depending upon *science,* where does the science come in? If the religious loan words had been borrowed mainly from Arabic, the scientific loan words arrived much later through the impact of the English language.

This dictionary confronts the gradual encroachment of European scientific words into the verbal heritage of Kiswahili. Standard Kiswahili is already resigned to translating the word "science" into *sayansi* and the word "technology" into *teknolojia*. Related "Swahinglish" words include *telegrafu, telegramu* and *televisheni.*

Another East African professor called Muhammad — Professor Muhammad Hyder Emeritus in Zoology from the University of Nairobi — has also engaged in Swahilizing essential English words needed in Swahili discourse. In the 20th century Kiswahili needed more and more words about dangerous diseases afflicting African populations. and the causes and cures of those diseases. These medical words which have transitioned from English to Kiswahili include *malaria* and *kansa.*

In counting beyond thousands, Kiswahili has had to resort to the big numbers of European languages — *milioni, bilioni* and *trilioni*.

Swahili counting up to a thousand has relied greatly on verbalized Arabic numerals. While the English language depends on Arabic numerals when *written* as numbers, Kiswahili relies more on actual Arabic words *ten, twenty, thirty, forty* — up to *one hundred (mia)*. Even onwards to the Arabic word for a thousand *(alfu)*.

Although the Swahili word for "vehicle" *(gari)* has been borrowed from Indian languages, the Swahili word for lorry *(lori)* and helicopter *(helikopta)* come directly from English.

The science of politics has borrowed heavily from Arabic, but the more recent ideological concepts like "democracy" *(demokrasia)* and communism *(ukomunisti)* have had to be borrowed from European ideological concepts.

While the history of Kiswahili is indeed a narrative from religious discourse to the new secular and scientific European wealth of concepts, the biggest contributors of words to Kiswahili have continued to be Bantu coastal languages of East Africa, on the one hand, and the impact of Islam and the Arabic language, on the other.

A dictionary like this one whets our appetites about the richness and diversity of words in Kiswahili and how that heritage relates to other Bantu languages, to European languages and to the wide-ranging penetration of Arabic.

CONCLUSION

It is already clear that Europe is the mother of the most influential language in human history — English. It is conceivable that East Africa is the mother of the most influential *African* language in history — Kiswahili. The success of English has already been accomplished and is globally self-evident. The success of Kiswahili is a work in progress — an African language of great expansionist potential, but still in the making. Great culture leaders like the Nigerian, Wole Soyinka, the first African winner of the Nobel Prize for Literature (1986), has already recommended that Kiswahili should be taught throughout the African continent. The theoretical possibility of Kiswahili being adopted as a continental African language in another century is already being taken seriously. Universities abroad wishing to teach at least one African language have repeatedly been drawn to Kiswahili as the pre-eminent indigenous language of Africa.

There is one paradox in any comparison between the success of the English language and the success of Kiswahili. The ultimate triumph of the English language has been because its native speakers [the English and Anglo-Americans] became a world-force and empire-builders. In contrast, the ultimate triumph of Kiswahili has been because its native speakers became, by the middle of the 20th century, politically marginal in East Africa, and posing almost no threat to other language-groups on the continent. Tanzania and Kenya could adopt Kiswahili as the main language of national business partly because the Swahili people as a cultural group were no major political threat to the Kikuyu or Luo of Kenya or to the major so-called "tribes" of Tanzania. These other groups could therefore embrace Kiswahili without worrying about giving undue political advantage to the native speakers of a rival language.

In Nigeria, resistance to the adoption of Hausa as a national language has been mainly because the Hausa are already very powerful even without the promotion of their language as a national medium.

The global success of the English language is a tribute to the role of cultural imperialism in world affairs. The regional success of Kiswahili is partly a tribute to the reassuring quality of the marginality of the Waswahili. English expanded because of the power of its native speakers. Kiswahili has expanded partly because of the relative powerlessness of the Swahili people.

What English and Kiswahili have had in common is a readiness to borrow from other languages and to learn from other civilizations. We have indicated that Arabic has been to Kiswahili what Latin has been to the English language — a great source of loan words and the provider of the original alphabet. Kiswahili used to be written primarily in the Arabic orthography until British colonialism promoted the Latinisation of the Swahili alphabet. On the other hand, English had adopted the Latin alphabet hundreds of years earlier — and has continued to express itself through the Roman orthography, to the present day.

The history of Kiswahili has been a transition from depending heavily on Arabic for religious and moral concepts and then move on towards depending more recently on the English language for concepts in science, technology and ideology.

Both English and Kiswahili have borrowed extensively from other languages. In the case of English, the range of loan words have come not only from Latin and Greek, but also from French, German, Arabic and Indian languages. English words borrowed directly from Kiswahili include the word *safari* (in the sense of hunting trip). English words shared with Kiswahili but both of them borrowed from Arabic include the word *tariff* in English and the word *taarifa* in Kiswahili. The scientific word *alcohol* in English *(alkoholi* in Kiswahili) are both ironically borrowed from Arabic *(alquhl)*.

Earliest Swahili borrowings from European languages were from Portuguese and German, as we have indicated. But English has more recently been by far the main European contributor to Kiswahili. French has also been important to the Congolese and Rwandan dialects of Kiswahili.

Apart from Arabic, Middle Eastern languages which have affected Kiswahili have included Farsi (Persian) and Ottoman Turkish.

A dictionary about ONE single language is a cultural guide but a bilingual one is partly a cultural conversation between the two languages, and a linguistic exchange across space and time.

This dictionary by Professor Mohamed A. Mohamed is both a cultural guide to Kiswahili, and a cultural conversation between two influential languages in this 21st century. The dictionary is bound to both enrich linguistic education and help promote dialogue between civilizations. More significant is the fact that this dictionary that contains an up-to-date repertoire of lexical words emanating from various disciplines, will surely benefit the different users of the language. To mention a few, words such as mchakato 'process', wembezi, 'funnel chest', utandawazi, 'globalization', uchakachuaji, 'adulteration/malpractice', kiseyeye, 'gingivitis' and a host of others will be new to a number of Swahili speakers. It is my sincere hope and wish that this dictionary will travel across space and time and benefit a global audience of students, teachers and the general public.

Professor Ali A. Mazrui

ACKNOWLEDGEMENTS

Writing a comprehensive dictionary of this kind is definitely an onerous task. Therefore I would be thankless if I did not mention all the services of the people who made this dictionary comprehensive in the true sense of the word. To begin with, I would like to express my profound gratitude to Dr. Henry Chakava, the Chairman of East African Educational Publishers for commissioning, reviewing and facilitating the publishing of this work. In addition, I would like to express my sincere gratitude to the late Dr. Ibrahim S. Ngozi of the Islamic University in Uganda, who spent countless days reading and exchanging views with me on all the drafts of my manuscript. His constructive criticisms and suggestions cannot be summarized. Then there are Mr. Ahmed Mgeni of Zanzibar and the late Mr. Khamis Akida, a former research fellow of the Institute of Kiswahili Research, University of Dar es Salaam, who all spent their valuable time exchanging views with me on many complex Swahili headwords that have been incorporated into this dictionary.

I would also like to express my deep appreciation to the team of lexicographers, editors, proofreaders and designers who made accomplishing of this dictionary possible.

Lexicographers

I would wish to express my sincere thanks to the following lexicographers for their input and patience in making this dictionary a comprehensive piece of reference.

Prof. H. M. Mwansoko	Prof. M. M Mulokozi	Prof. Abdul Aziz Lodhi
Prof. J. S. Mdee	Dr. Said A. Vuai	Prof. Aboud A. O
Mrs. Ramla Hemed Mbarouk		

Editors

The writing, compiling and reviewing of this dictionary would not have taken shape without the editorial input of the following editors.

Prof. Kimani Njogu	Dr. Paul M. Musau	Dr. Wadi Wamitila
Dr. John Habwe	Dr. Angeline Kioko	Mr. Kiarie Kamau
Mr. Peter Nyoro	Mrs. Lilian Dhahabu	Mr. Kirimi Mitambo

Proofreaders

Dr. Tayya Timammy	Dr. Hassan Babusa	Mr. Shullam Nzioka

Designers

Mr. Walex Nkonge	Mrs. Anne Mungai	Mr. Simon Kago
Mr. Frank Katee	Mrs. Cynthia Mwanza	Mrs. Serah Muchai

Other Professionals

Apart from the lexicographers, editors, proofreaders and designers, I would like to appreciate the input of the following professionals and friends.

Mr. Seif Mohamed Mauly	Dr. Mohamed S. Jiddawi	Dr. Hassan A. attasi
Mrs. Josefrieda G. Pereira	Dr. Narimand Jiddawi	Mr. Muumin
Mr. Mohamed S. Mohamed	Mr. Saleh Yahya	Mr. Said Juma
Mrs. Catherine A. Mwakosya	Mr. Yussuf Salum Yusuf	Dr. Z. Gaya
Mrs. Fatma Abdulla Toti	Mr. Vifii S. Makoti	Dr. Omar S. Omar

Professor Mohamed A. Mohamed

DESCRIPTIVE CHART SHOWING HOW TO USE THE DICTIONARY

headword and pronunciation	mpambe n (wa-)	1. master of ceremonies; a person who is dressed up in finery and is supposed to give information on a function such as that of a wedding; equerry: *Mpambe wa spika*, sergeant-at-arms. 2. a person fond of decorating himself or herself. 3. bridesmaid. 4. bodyguard, aide-de-camp.	meanings are separated by numbers
homographs	bodi[1] (ma-)	body; the part of an automobile truck, etc. that holds the load or passengers; part of a vehicle that is not the chassis. (Eng)	words with the same spelling but used differently because of the difference in meaning
	bodi[2] n (n)	board, committee, council: *Bodi ya wakurugenzi*, the board of directors. *Bodi ya wadhamini*, the board of trustees. *Bodi ya uhariri*, editorial board. (Eng)	
synonyms	tadi n (n)	rudeness, discourteousness, impoliteness: *Meneja alionyesha tadi kwa wafanyakazi wake*, the manager was rude to his workers. (cf *ujeuri, ufidhuli*)	words with similar or related meanings
parts of speech	kusudi[1]	(also *kusudio*) n (ma-) aim, goal, purpose, intent, objective: *Kusudio lake halieleweki*, his goal is not understood. (cf *nia, lengo*) (Ar)	words of the same form but with different parts of speech
	kusudi[2] adv.	intentionally, deliberately, purposely: *Amemchokoza ndugu yake kusudi*, he has teased his brother deliberately. (cf *makusudi*) (Ar)	
	kusudi[3] conj	in order that, so that: *Amekwenda shuleni kusudi aonane na mwalimu*, he has gone to school in order to see his teacher. (cf *ili*) (Ar)	

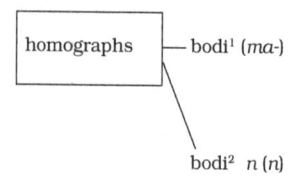

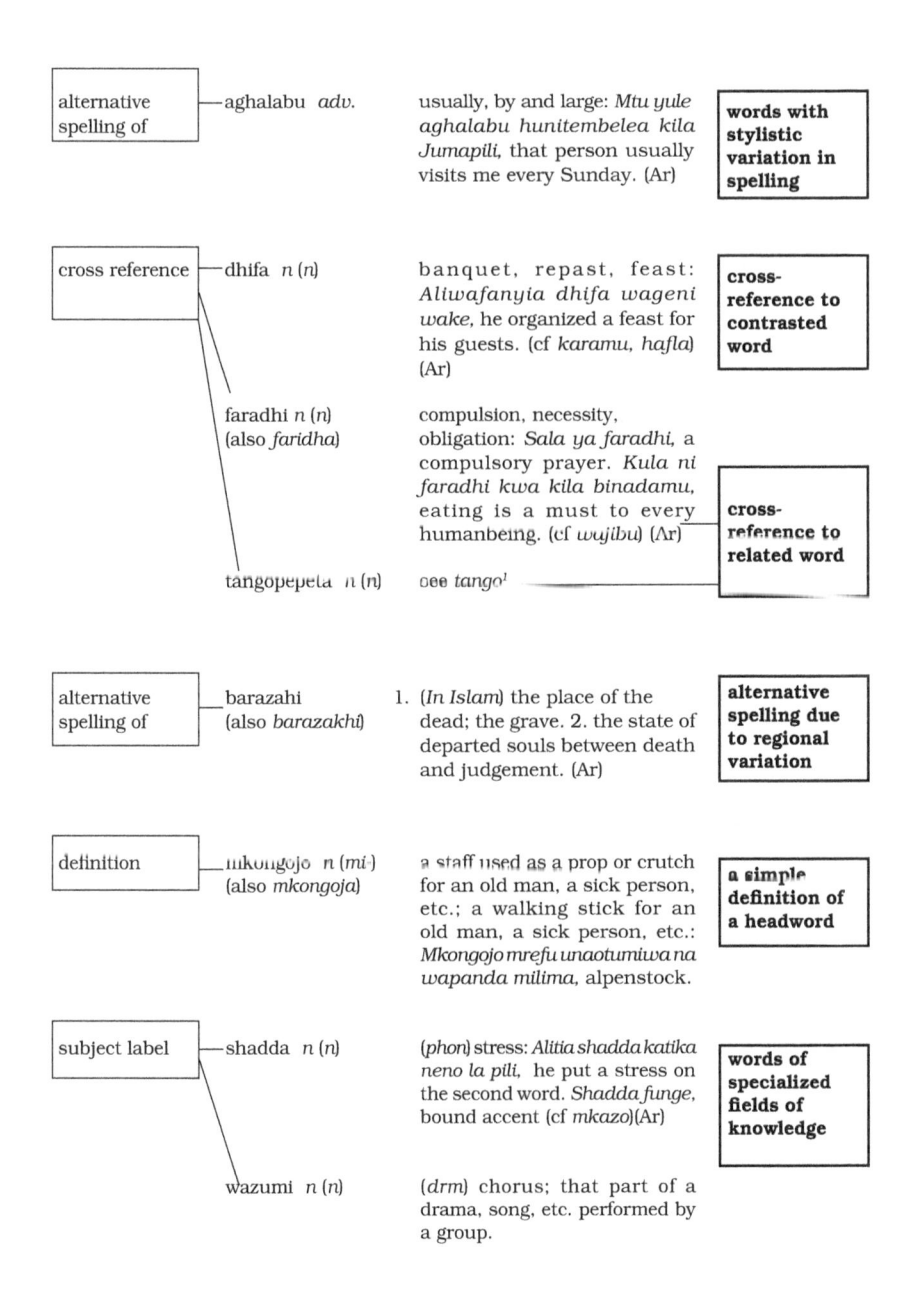

alternative spelling of	aghalabu *adv.*	usually, by and large: *Mtu yule aghalabu hunitembelea kila Jumapili*, that person usually visits me every Sunday. (Ar)	**words with stylistic variation in spelling**
cross reference	dhifa *n (n)*	banquet, repast, feast: *Aliwafanyia dhifa wageni wake*, he organized a feast for his guests. (cf *karamu, hafla*) (Ar)	**cross-reference to contrasted word**
	faradhi *n (n)* (also *faridha*)	compulsion, necessity, obligation: *Sala ya faradhi*, a compulsory prayer. *Kula ni faradhi kwa kila binadamu*, eating is a must to every humanbeing. (cf *wujibu*) (Ar)	**cross-reference to related word**
	tangopepeta *n (n)*	see *tango¹*	
alternative spelling of	barazahi (also *barazakhi*)	1. (*In Islam*) the place of the dead; the grave. 2. the state of departed souls between death and judgement. (Ar)	**alternative spelling due to regional variation**
definition	mkongojo *n (mi-)* (also *mkongoja*)	a staff used as a prop or crutch for an old man, a sick person, etc.; a walking stick for an old man, a sick person, etc.: *Mkongojo mrefu unaotumiwa na wapanda milima*, alpenstock.	**a simple definition of a headword**
subject label	shadda *n (n)*	(*phon*) stress: *Alitia shadda katika neno la pili*, he put a stress on the second word. *Shadda funge*, bound accent (cf *mkazo*)(Ar)	**words of specialized fields of knowledge**
	wazumi *n (n)*	(*drm*) chorus; that part of a drama, song, etc. performed by a group.	

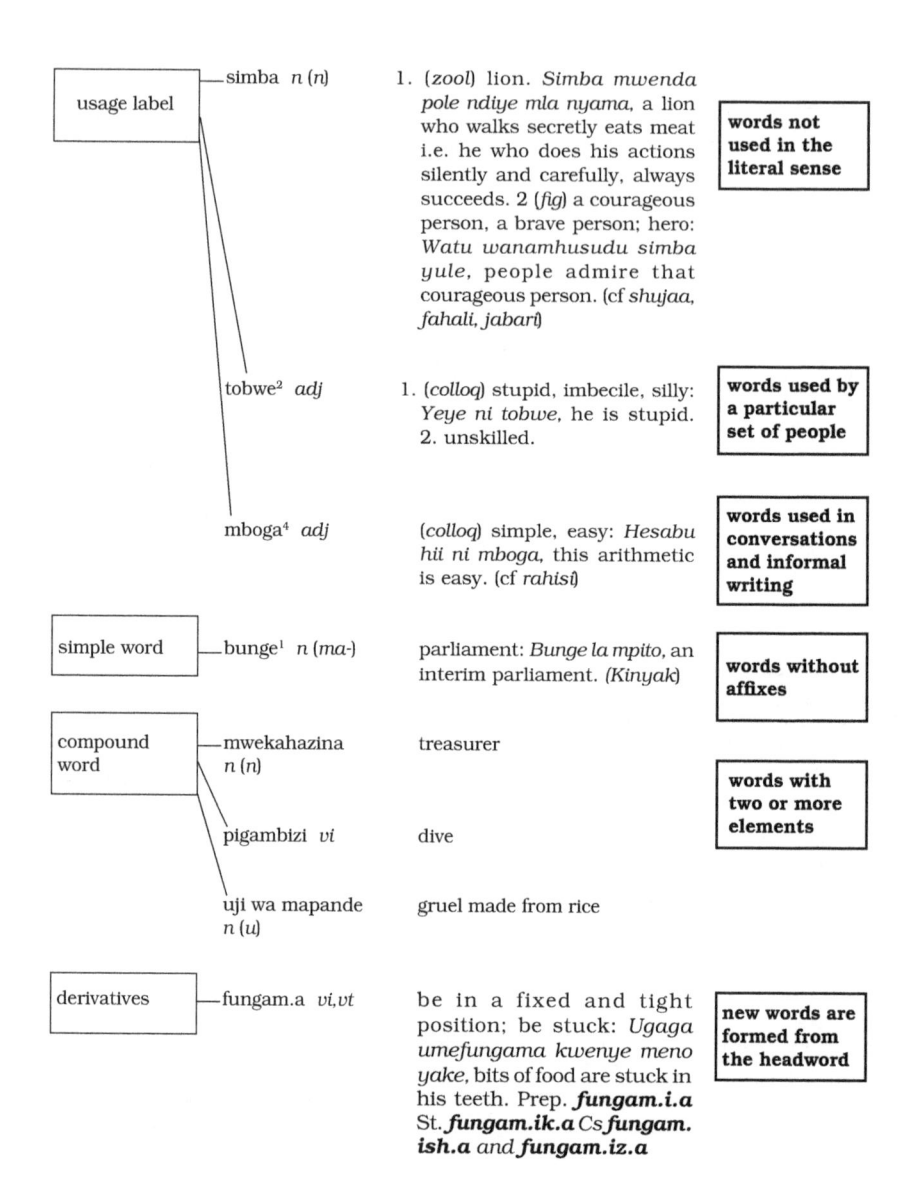

Category	Headword	Definition	Label description
usage label	simba *n (n)*	1. (*zool*) lion. *Simba mwenda pole ndiye mla nyama*, a lion who walks secretly eats meat i.e. he who does his actions silently and carefully, always succeeds. 2 (*fig*) a courageous person, a brave person; hero: *Watu wanamhusudu simba yule*, people admire that courageous person. (cf *shujaa, fahali, jabari*)	words not used in the literal sense
	tobwe[2] *adj*	1. (*colloq*) stupid, imbecile, silly: *Yeye ni tobwe*, he is stupid. 2. unskilled.	words used by a particular set of people
	mboga[4] *adj*	(*colloq*) simple, easy: *Hesabu hii ni mboga*, this arithmetic is easy. (cf *rahisi*)	words used in conversations and informal writing
simple word	bunge[1] *n (ma-)*	parliament: *Bunge la mpito*, an interim parliament. (*Kinyak*)	words without affixes
compound word	mwekahazina *n (n)*	treasurer	words with two or more elements
	pigambizi *vi*	dive	
	uji wa mapande *n (u)*	gruel made from rice	
derivatives	fungam.a *vi,vt*	be in a fixed and tight position; be stuck: *Ugaga umefungama kwenye meno yake*, bits of food are stuck in his teeth. Prep. ***fungam.i.a*** St. ***fungam.ik.a*** Cs ***fungam.ish.a*** and ***fungam.iz.a***	new words are formed from the headword

idiomatic expression	jongoo *n* (*ma-*)	1. (*zool*) millipede. *Jongoo panda*, a large millipede. 2. (*idm*) *Tupa jongoo na mti wake*, forget; abandon sth completely. (*syn*) *Jongoo hapandi mtungi*, gay, homosexual. (cf *hanithi*, *shoga*)	expressions with specialized meanings
proverb	kibindo *n* (*ki-vi*)	a fold of the loincloth used as a kind of pocket for carrying things; a knot in the waistcloth used as a pocket. (*prov*) *Hamadi kibindoni, silaha iliyo mkononi*, a reserve is always useful because of the need that may arise at a later stage.	words that express some obvious truth or familiar experience
saying	mata² *n* (*ma-*)	bow (of an arrow) (*syn*) *Washindwao ni waume na mata*, defeat is not a strange thing. Even those who are brave have been defeated.	words of usu shorter forms that express same obvious truth or familiar experience
collocation	hamu *n* (*n*) (also *hamumu*)	1. anxiety, desire, craving, ardour: *Ana hamu ya kutaka kuoa*, he is anxious to get married. *Hana hamu ya kula*, he is not keen to eat. (cf *shauku, uchu, kiu*) 2. (*idm*) *Hamu na ghamu*, be very eager, be very anxious e.g. *Ana hamu na ghamu juu ya jambo lile*, he is very anxious about that matter. (Ar)	words that appear together in usage

GUIDE TO THE USE OF THE DICTIONARY

The following information is provided to assist the dictionary user when he is looking for a particular word or information.

This dictionary, like all other dictionaries has headwords that are arranged alphabetically. A headword is a word that is alphabetically listed in the dictionary and printed in bold letters in order to catch the eye of a dictionary user when he is looking for a particular word. It can be a simple or a compound word.

Simple word

A simple word, as it implies, is simple in form. It has no affixes. Some examples of simple words used in this dictionary include *bahili*, 'miser', *chetezo*, 'thurible', *godoro*, 'mattress' and *shughuli*, 'activity'. All simple words have been entered as headwords.

Compound word

A compound word is a combination of two or more separate words that operate as a single word and possesses its own meaning. Here are a few examples of compound words used in this dictionary.

bata mzinga	n (n)	turkey
kifunguamimba	n (ki-vi)	first-born child
katibu mtendaji	n (n)	executive secretary
mshika bendera	n (wa-)	linesman

In this dictionary, compounds have been treated as headwords or as run-ons to a headword which constitute the first element of the compound word. For example:

ulaji   *n (u)*   1. act (method, etc.) of eating. 2. the maximum capacity a person can eat. 3. food. (cf *chakula*) 4. used in the expression: *Ulaji-rushwa*, bribing, bribery.(cf *ufisadi*)

The dictionary user has to distinguish between compound words that have a fixed form and those that are merely phrases. For example, *mwenyekiti*, 'chairman' is listed as a headword because it is a compound word whereas *mwenye mali* has not been listed as a headword because it is a mere phrase. It is a mere phrase which can be combined with other qualifiers to produce constructions such as *mwenye mali nyingi*, 'a person having a lot of wealth'. In addition, the phrase '*mwenye mali*' is made up of two free morphemes but in the case of a compound word, the constituents elements forming the compound word are not 'free' because they are either attached together or sometimes hyphenated.

Homographs

Main entries that are spelt alike but are different in meaning and origin are called *homographs* as in the case of *panda*, 'fork', *panda*, 'forked', *panda*, 'bugle', *panda*, 'temple', *panda*, 'climb', 'mount' and *panda*, 'grow', 'plant'. In this dictionary, homographs are entered in separate blocks and are marked by superscript numbers immediately following boldface spelling.

panda[1]	n(n)	1. bifurcation, fork; the act of dividing into two parts or branches: *Njia panda*, crossroads, crossways. 2. catapult, sling-shot (cf *manati, fyata*)
panda[2]	adj	bifurcated, forked.
panda[3] (also *parapanda*)	n(n)	bugle; an animal's horn used as a musical instrument in local dances and for sounding information: *Piga panda*, blow a a bugle (cf *baragumu, rewa, pembe*)
panda[4]	n(ma-)	temple; the two flat areas at the sides of the forehead.
panda[5]	vt	1. climb, mount, ascend, go up. (cf *kwea, paraga*) 2. board, go on board, enter: *Amepanda meli*, he has boarded the ship. *Panda farasi*, mount a horse; ride a horse. 3. (of mountain, etc.) be steep: *Mlima ule umepanda*, that mountain is steep. 4. (of price) go up; increase in number, amount, etc.: *Bei ya kahawa imepanda*, the price of coffee has gone up. (cf *ongezeka*) 5. (idms) *Panda cheo*, rise up in position. *Panda kichwa*, become big-headed. 6. (of a vessel) run ashore; run aground e.g. *Jahazi limepanda mwamba kwenye tindo la matope*, the dhow has run aground on a mud bank. Prep. **pand.i.a** St. **pand.ik.a** Cs. **pand.ish.a** Ps. **pand.w.a** Rp. **pand.an.a**
pand.a[6]	vt	1. grow, plant, sow, seed: *Amepanda chai*, he has grown tea. (cf *otesha, sia, melesha*) 2. bet, bid: *Unaweza kupanda kwa bei yoyote?* Can you bet any amount? Prep. **pand.i.a** St. **pand.ik.a** Cs. **pand.ish.a** Ps. **pand.w.a** Rp. **pand.a.n.a**

The part of speech of each homograph is given. This is important because this system assists the reader in finding a particular word and thus, simplifies one's search.

In some homographs as in the case of the word *taa*, an attempt has been made to distinguish their meanings by the use of the aspirated symbol. Thus, we can have this kind of arrangement:

taa[1]	n(n)	lamp: *Taa ya kandili*, lantern. *Taa ya karabai*, pressure lamp. *Taa ya kibatari*, a small oil lamp. *Washa taa*, turn on the light/lights. *Zima taa*, turn off the light/lights.
taa[2]	n (n)	skate, ray; a kind of fish of the families *Gymnuridae, Rajidae* and *Dasyatidae*, having a broad flat body and a short spineless whiplike tail with two dorsal fins. *Taa chui*, manta ray. *Taa usinga*, sting ray. *Taa kilimawe*, electric ray.

taa[3] n (n) obedience, loyalty, respect: *Lazima uonyeshe taa kwa Mwenyezi Mungu,* you must show obedience to God. (cf *utii, unyenyekevu*) (Ar)

taa[4] *adj* exalted, sacred, holy (Ar)

PARTS OF SPEECH

Labels

Parts of speech labels are given in this dictionary in English. The following labels, which are classified according to the traditional grammar system, are seen throughout the dictionary.

n	noun
vt	transitive verb
vi	intransitive verb
adj	adjective
adv	adverb
prep	preposition
conj	conjunction
pron	pronoun
interj	interjection

In addition, the following labels have also been used:

In most cases, if an entry word belongs to more than one part of speech, then it is given a separate block and is marked by a superscript number as in the case of homographs:

kusudi[1] (also *kusudio*) n (*ma-*) aim, goal, purpose, intent, objective: *Kusudio lake halieleweki,* his goal is not understood. (cf *nia, lengo*) (Ar)

kusudi[2] *adj* intentionally, deliberately, purposely: *Amemchokoza ndugu yake kusudi,* he has teased his brother deliberately. (cf *makusudi*) (Ar)

kusudi[3] *conj* in order that, so that: *Amekwenda shuleni kusudi aonane na mwalimu,* he has gone to school in order to see his teacher. (cf *ili*) (Ar) sihir.i¹   vt   bewitch, hex. *Alimsihiri jirani yake na hatimaye akafariki*, she bewitched her neighbour and in the end, he died. Prep. **sihir.i.a** St. **sihir.ik.a** Cs. **sihir.ish.a** Ps. of Prep. **sihir.iw.a** Rp. of Prep. **sihir.i.an.a** (cf *roga, cheza, anga*) (Ar)

sihiri²   n (n)   witchcraft, sorcery: *Anaamini sana mambo ya sihiri*, he believes very much in witchcraft. (cf *uramali, uchawi, amali, ulozi*) (Ar)

In this dictionary, all verbs have their final suffix separated from the root by a small dot as can be seen above.

Noun class labels

Each entry of noun class labels has been put into brackets. In some cases, however, an irregular form of plural form of a particular entry is also given. This has been placed on the right side of the part of speech labels:

wano¹   n (*ma-*)   the shaft of a spear or an arrow or a harpoon. (cf *mpini*)

wano²   n (*ma-*)   a stick used along with three others for arresting a thicf. (cf *kibano*)

waraka¹ (pl *nyaraka*) n (*u*)   1. letter, epistle, missive (cf *barua*) 2. document, certificate, record 3. invoice, bill of sale. (cf *ankra*) (Ar)

waraka² (pl *nyaraka*) n (*u*)   a small piece of paper, used for rolling tobacco to make cigarettes; cigarrette paper. (cf *chupri*) (Ar)

ukwenje (pl *kwenje*) n (*u*)   noise, shout. (cf *ukemi*)

The inclusion of Noun class labels is meant to assist the dictionary user who may not be sure of the appropriate plural form of a particular entry. This system is also meant to help new language learners of Swahili in line with the principals of concordial agreements.

Cross-reference

Cross-reference are notes that direct the reader from one headword to another. They are used for the purpose of drawing one's attention to other words that share similar meanings. The use of cross-references is therefore an important strategy in dictionary work as it gives the dictionary user additional information on a given word. Furthermore, it helps the user to discover new words previously unknown and as a result, increases the user's vocabulary. Words which are cross-referenced in this dictionary are:

1. words which have the same or nearly the same meaning with headwords.

    mapigano n (ma-)   fight, fighting, battle: *Mapigano ya barabarani*, street fighting. *Mapigano ya karibu*, infighting. (cf *kondo, vita, ugomvi*)

    pupa n (n)   haste, rush, hurry: *Ana pupa sana akifanya kazi*, he is very hasty at work. (*prov*) *Mtaka yote kwa pupa, hukosa yote*, whoever wants everything will get nothing i.e. don't look for everything at one time; look for one and when you get it, look for another and so on.

Here, the abbreviated form cf is given to show the words that are to be cross-referenced with the headword.

2. words with variant forms of spelling.

    msobemsobe (also mzobemzobe) adv   1. haphazardly, disorderly: *Aliifanya kazi yangu msobemsobe*, he did my work haphazardly. (cf *hobelahobela, ovyoovyo*) 2. forcefully, by compulsion: *Alilima msobemsobe kufuatia amri kutoka kwa bwana wake*, he cultivated by force following an order from his master.

    tangu.a (also *tengua*) vt   invalidate, revoke, annul, repeal: *Tangua ndoa*, annul a marriage. *Tangua sheria*, rescind a law. *Tangua udhu*, make ablution null and void. *Tangua saumu*, break a fast. *Tangua ahadi*, break a promise. *Tangua urafiki*, break off a friendship. Prep. **tangu.li.a** St. **tangu.k.a** Cs. **tangu.z.a** Ps. of Prep. **tangu.liw.a** Rp. **tangu.an.a** (cf *haramisha, batilisha, vunja*)

Here again, we find that the words *msobemsobe* and *tangua* are cross-referenced with their alternative spellings *mzobemzobe* and *tengua* respectively.

3. words and their synonyms.

    tangopepeta n (ma-)   see *tango*[1]

Derivatives

A derivative is a word formed by adding affixes to the base form of a given word. In Swahili, it is quite possible to find a vast number of derived forms simply by adding certain prefixes and suffixes to the base word. Derived forms especially among verbs, have been included in this dictionary as run-in entries. The appropriate label of the derived verb is listed and in some cases, the meaning and usage is also given.

pambu.a *vt* 1. remove ornaments, make-up, etc.; remove decorations; disfigure, deface: *Biharusi alijipambua sherehe zilipomalizika,* the bride removed her make-up when the celebrations were over. 2. *(naut)* open the sail from the main yard of the vessel. Prep. ***pambu.li.a*** St. ***pambu.k.a*** Cs. ***pambu.sh.a*** Ps. of Prep ***pambu.liw.a*** Rp. ***pambu.an.a***

In some cases, an attempt has been done to make a derivative operate as a headword when it carries a special meaning different from the base form. For example, in the case of *funga*, close, bind, etc, we can have a derivative *fungama*, "be in a fixed and tight position", "be stuck", etc. Yet the derivative *fungama* appears as a headword in this dictionary because it carries a specialized meaning which is different from its base form. So, unlike other Swahili dictionaries, this dictionary emphasizes those words that have special meanings by treating them in separate blocks. Thus, in the case of *fungama*, we can have this kind of entry:

fungama *vi, vt* be in a fixed and tight position; be stuck: *Ugaga umefungama kwenye meno yake,* bits of food are stuck in his teeth. Prep. ***fungam.i.a*** St. ***fungam.ik.a*** Cs ***fungam.ish.a*** and ***fungam.iz.a***

In addition to derivatives, this dictionary also shows the derivational suffixes of each base word, which operate in line with the principles of vowel harmony. The following is an illustration of this kind of arrangement:

rus.a *vt* seduce, lure; tempt someone to have sexual intercourse: *Alimrusa msichana mrembo,* he seduced a glamorous girl. Prep. ***rus.i.a*** St. ***rus.ik.a*** Cs. ***rus.ish.a*** Ps. ***rus.w.a*** Rp. ***rus.an.a*** (cf *tongoza*)

pep.a *vi* totter, stagger, reel, sway: *Mlevi alikuwa anapita njiani kwa kupepa,* the drunkard was tottering on the street. (cf *yumbayumba, pepesuka*) 2. lose strength, vigour, vitality, speed, etc. Prep. ***pep.e.a*** St. ***pep.ek.a*** Cs. ***pep.esh.a*** Ps. ***pep.w.a*** (cf *pepesuka, yumbayumba*)

tamb.a *vt* narrate, tell, account: *Ni hodari katika kutamba hadithi za kale,* he is good at narrating ancient tales. Prep. ***tamb.i.a*** St. ***tamb.ik.a*** Cs. ***tamb.ish.a*** Ps. ***tamb.w.a*** (cf *simulia, elezea*)

og.a (also *koga*) *vi* bathe; take a bath: *Amekwenda msalani kuoga,* he has gone to the bathroom to take a bath. Prep. ***og.e.a*** St. ***og.ek.a*** Cs. ***og.esh.a*** Ps. of Cs. ***og.esh.w.a***

The derivational suffixes are italicized next to the root of the verb. It will be noted that in some cases, there is a double form of the derived verb as in the case of *ona*, 'see' where the prepositional form is *onea*, 'see', 'feel', etc, with (for, at, etc) and the double prepositional form is *onelea*, which has almost the same meaning as *onea*.

Headwords with more than one meaning

This dictionary consists of many words with more than one meaning and each meaning is given a number as shown below:

ubichi   n (u)   1.   greenness, rawness, freshness. 2. moistness, dampness. (cf *umajimaji*) 3. (of meat, etc) rawness, uncookedness. 4. immaturity, inexperience.

Here, the most common or most basic meanings are always given first. These are later followed by those which are less common or carry applied meanings. Finally, if there are idioms, proverbs or sayings, they are listed as run-on entries. In some limited cases, proverbs and the like have their meanings listed first accompanied by their paraphrases. For example:

mkakasi   n (mi-)   a fine soft tree but useless for timber. (*prov*) *Uzuri wa mkakasi, ukipata maji basi,* even though someone may be good in education, appearance, etc. he may have certain weaknesses and these can smear his reputation, etc.

Definitions

Definitions are explanations that define the meaning of a particular word. This dictionary has given short and simple explanations of the different headwords. For example:

mkale   n (wa-)   1. an experienced person of past events. (cf *mhenga*) 2. an old person: *Watu wengi wanamheshimu mkale yule,* many people respect that old person. (cf *mzee*) 3. a senior citizen. 4. a conservative person; diehard. (cf *mhafidhina*)

mkambala   n (mi-)   a medium-sized tree with thorny trunk and branches. *Acacia nigrescens.*

In some cases, synonyms are given in place of definitions:

rungu   n (ma-)   knobkerrie, club, cudgel, bludgeon: *Askari alitumia rungu kumpiga mwizi,* the policeman used a club to beat the thief. (cf *gongo, kibarango*)

rushwa   n (n)   bribe, kickback: *Kula rushwa,* take a bribe. *Pokea rushwa,* receive a bribe. *Toa rushwa,* give a bribe; offer a bribe. (cf *hongo, chai*) (Ar)

tali.i[1]   vt   revise, review: *Mwanafunzi aliyatalii masomo yake,* the student revised his lessons. Prep. **tali.i.a** St. **tali.k.a** Cs. **tali.sh.a** Ps. **tali.w.a** (cf *durusu*) (Ar) tali.i²   vt   visit, tour: *Wageni waliitalii nchi yetu*, the tourists visited our country. Prep. ***tali.i.a*** St. ***tali.k.a*** Cs. ***tali.sh.a*** Ps. ***tali.w.a*** (cf *zuru*) (Ar)

Idiomatic Expressions

An idiom is an expression which functions as a single unit and whose meaning cannot be worked out from its separate parts.

How to Locate Idioms

In this dictionary, idioms are not entered as headwords but as run-ons to the headwords. Like proverbs, idioms are also paraphrased in this dictionary. To locate an idiom, the dictionary user has to read the bracketed symbol (*idm*), which is usually numbered and italicized as shown here below:

udi   n (n)   1.   aloe wood; aromatic substance which derives from the heartwood of a special form. 2. (*idm*) *Kwa udi na uvumba*, in any possible means; by hook or by crook. (Ar)

An attempt has been made in this example to explain the meaning of the idiomatic expression by way of sentence construction.

Proverbs and Sayings

A proverb is a short expression that expresses some obvious truth or familiar experience. A saying however, is generally shorter that a proverb. However, the two share in common the didactic nature of each. Both use indigenous examples to teach a particular society.

How to Locate Proverbs and Sayings

The proverb and the saying also function usually as run-ons to the headword. To locate a proverb and a saying, the dictionary user simply needs to read the bracket symbols (*prov*) and (*syn*) respectively, which are abbreviated forms for the two of them. In the case of a proverb, it is first written in Swahili and is preceded by the abbreviated form. A literal translation is then given and finally an attempt is made in most cases to reveal the deeper meaning of the proverb. Likewise, a saying also follows the same procedure. The following is a brief illustration of how proverbs and sayings are organized in this dictionary:

ambari   n (n)   ambergris: (*prov*) *Ukiona zinduna, ambari i papo*, if you see amber, ambergris is following behind i.e. if you see so and so, then his close friend is following behind. (Ar)

mtashi   n (wa-)   a person who is need of sth very badly; beggar. (*syns*) *Mtashi hana haya*, a person who is in badly need of sth is shameless i.e if you are in need of sth very badly, you will beg. *Mtashi hana kinyongo; ajapo waswa, hakomi,* a beggar who is in need will continue to beg even if he is advised not to do so.

Synonyms

Synonyms are also included for the reader's information. Many of them are listed at the end of each entry and are labelled with a *cf,* meaning cross-reference. Even though these synonyms have similar or closely related meanings to the headword, they are not always interchangeable with one another. The entry for *sagua,* 'mock', 'ridicule', etc. thus explains the point below:

sagu.a   *vt, vi*   mock, ridicule; make fun of: *Watoto wadogo waliwasagua walemavu,* the small children mocked the crippled. Prep. **sagu.li.a** St. **sagu.lik.a** Cs. **sagu.lish.a** Ps. of Prep. **sagu.liw.a** Rp. **sagu.an.a** (cf *tania, dhihaki*)

Field Labels

Labels for specialized fields of knowledge and activity appear in brackets in italicized forms. These labels are given in abbreviated forms. The use of these labels helps the dictionary user to quickly find the special sense or senses he or she is seeking.

shadda   *n (n)*   stress: *Alitia shadda katika neno la pili,* he put stress on the second word. *Shadda funge,* bound accent (cf *mkazo*) (Ar)

wazumi   *n (u)*   lunacy, insanity, madness: *Tia wazimu,* make mad. *Fanya wazimu,* become mad. *Ingiliwa na wazimu* go mad. (cf *wehu, kichaa, uafkani*)

changamano   *n (n)*   (*gram*) complex: *Kikundi changamano,* complex group ...

The full forms of these abbreviations are given in the beginning of the dictionary under the title "Abbreviations and Symbols Used in this Dictionary."

Status of Words

The dictionary has listed many words operating as headwords. However, some of these words are used in special situations and for specific audiences. Here are the labels that have been used in this dictionary:

slang *(sl)*   This label refers to words which are outside the conventional or standard usage of a language and are thus only used by a particular set of people such as teenagers, popgroups, soldiers, etc. In that sense, slang is often referred to as 'in-group language'.

archaic *(arch)*   a word that has ceased to be used.

figurative *(fig)*   a word that is used in an imaginative or figurative way in the sense that it is not used in its original, usual, literal or exact sense or reference.

colloquial	a word that is thought to be characteristic of informal settings. This word should not be regarded as substandard or illiterate.
vul	the term applies to words that are thought to be indecent or obscene when used before ordinary people. Mostly, the taboo words are regarded as vulgar.

Scientific names of plants, animals, birds, fish and insects

The commonly used names of plants, animals, birds, fish and insects are entered in English. Their scientific name appears in italics. In a few cases, the commonly used name does not appear. This omission is a result of the author's inability to find the correct name from an expert in the field.

Almost all the names of plants, animals, birds and insects have been given Modern Latin or Latinized names by biologists in accordance with the rules as prescribed by international codes of zoological and botanical nomenclature. In most cases, the names of these living things have been systematically classified into the category or taxa of family and sometimes genus.

The scientific name of every species of those living things is an italicized binomial that consists of the genus followed by the uncapitalized specific name or epithet:

tuku	n (n)	sky emperor; a kind of salt water fish with a red blotch on the forehead. *Lethrinus mahsena*.
mdengu	n (mi-)	chick pea; an erect annual plant which bears a small edible bean or pick, used extensively for making cakes, curries, etc. *Cicer arietinum*.

Etymology

This dictionary gives the etymologies for a number of the vocabulary entries. These etymologies are bracketed at the end of each entry.

The etymology give the language from which the Swahili word was derived. This specific component of etymology has been incorporated into this dictionary because it is believed that insights into the current usage of a word can be gained from a full knowledge of the word's history and that a better understanding of the language generally can be achieved from knowing how words are related to other words in Swahili and to other words in other languages. Additionally, it is significant to the user in understanding the cultural influences other languages have had on Swahili. For example, by looking at the etymology of a word, one would find that because of historical and religious reasons, there has been mass borrowing from Arabic. Borrowing from English to Swahili is attributed mainly to political factors as the British were at one time the colonial rulers of the Swahili-speaking areas. Borrowed words from German and Portuguese are both political and historical. At one short time in history, the Germans ruled Tanganyika, known as Mainland Tanzania today. Thus, it is logical that Swahili has borrowed such words as *shule* for 'school' and *Mdachi* for 'Dutch'.

The arrival of Portuguese in East Africa also prompted certain words to be borrowed from their language. Hence, Swahili has borrowed household words such as *meza*, 'table' and *roda* for 'sheave or a pulley'.

The Swahili language has also borrowed from the Persian (Iranian) and Indian languages for purely historical and commercial reasons. With the arrival of these ethnic groups in East Africa and the subsequent intermarriages with the indigenous peoples of the area, the borrowing of words from different languages continued.

In quite limited cases, there has been borrowing from Turkish and indigenous languages such as Kinyakyusa and Kinyamwezi. This is evident if we take a glance in words such as afande, 'sir', 'master' in the case of Turkish language and bunge, 'parliament', ikulu, 'state house' in the case of certain indigenous languages in Tanzania. Although the tendency now is to borrow words mostly from indigenous languages, there is still an attempt to borrow words from other languages such as English and Arabic for technological, administrative, economic and religious reasons.

It should be remembered that in this dictionary, some of the words given can have their root in more than one language. A good example is a case of words such as bunduki, 'gun' where the source languages can be both Persian and Hindi. Another example is bamia, 'okra', 'lady's fingers' where the source languages can be Persian and Arabic. It is difficult to know exactly which one among the two relevant languages is the real 'source'. More research is necessary before one can come at a definite conclusion. All we can say for the time being is that two or more other languages can be a source for a particular Swahili word.

Pronunciation

Pronunciation refers to the way a certain sound or sounds are produced. Unlike articulation, which refers to the actual production of speech sounds in the mouth, pronunciation stresses more the way sounds are perceived by the hearer.

The aspect of pronunciation is very important in language learning. The truth of the matter is that effective language learning involves both the mastery of the spoken and written forms of the language. Thus, this dictionary, unlike other previous works, has incorporated a pronunciation component to assist the language learner articulate correct forms of the language. Although Swahili is more regular than English or some other languages in terms of stress pattern (since stress usually operates at penultimate level), difficulties still arise in nasalized words which carry more than one meaning. Here, language learners of Swahili usually find it difficult to pronounce each word appropriately. This dictionary has therefore taken note of the problems of language learners and has consequently provided solutions for them. All pronunciations of those particular words are shown using special signs in the headword.

mbuni[1]	n (n)	ostrich
mbuni[2]	n (mi-)	coffee plant

The phonetic transcription of these words above will facilitate the smooth learning of the correct pronunciation of those nasalized words.

In some cases, difficulties in terms of pronunciation also arise in Swahili in a cluster of sounds of two or more but pronounced as a single phoneme:

ndama	n (n)	calf
njama	n (n)	intrigue, gimmick, ploy

mwag.a	vi, vt	spill
shumndwa	n (n)	hyena

Even in some Swahili words containing a nasalized sound / / [ng'], pronunciation also becomes a problem to foreign language learners in the following:

ombe	n (n)	cow
atuka	vi	relinquish power, authority, etc.

This dictionary makes use of a syllabic peak in certain nasalized words, notably those beginning with *m* and *n* sounds.

The author has given only a few examples to those words that carry a syllabic peak although a lot of other words share the same characteristic.

ti	n	tree
ta	n (n)	wax

Here, a small line is put before the nasalized sound to show that it is a syllabic consonant, that is to say, the nasalized sound is in the nucleus of a syllable.

Stress

Stress is a force that is given to a particular word or syllable. A stress word or syllable is produced by using more air from the lungs and is often on a higher pitch and has a longer duration. That is to say, the vowel appears to be longer.

The syllable that is stressed is shown with a stressmark /'/. For instance, the word tembea, 'walk', 'visit' has a stress mark on the second syllable.

Since stress in Swahili generally operates at penultimate level, this dictionary has avoided putting stress marks on all the headwords. Again, it should be noted that stress in some loan words in Swahili is not regular. A word, like lazima, 'must' can have a stress mark on the first or on the second syllable. Nevertheless, an attempt has been made in this dictionary to show stress in some of the homographs:

barabara[1]	n (n)		road, highway
barabara[2]	adv		okay, alright
ala[1]	n (n)		case, sheath, scabbard
ala[2']	n (n)	1.	tool, implement, instrument: *Ala za muziki*, musical instruments. 2 (gram) *Ala za matamshi*, organs of speech.
àla![3]	interj.		an exclamation of surprise, annoyance, impatience, etc. (cf *do! lo!*)

Collocation

Certain words in some languages tend to appear together with other words. Thus, collocation refers to the habitual co-occurrence of individual lexical items. For example, the word *heshima*, 'respect' collocates with *taadhima*, honour. That is why, we have expressions such as *kwa heshima na taadhima*, 'with respect and honour'.

This dictionary, to a large extent, makes use of collocation as a strategy for explaining the meanings of different entries.

bandia	*adj*	fake, bogus, not genuine: *Waraka bandia*, a fake document.
potofu	*adj*	misleading, wrong, bad: *Dhana potofu*, a misleading idea. *Mtazamo potofu*, a misleading outlook.
-tukufu	*adj*	sacred, holy, glorious, honourable: *Kuran tukufu*, the Holy Koran. *Rais Mtukufu*, his/her the excellency the president. *Siku tukufu*, a sacred day. (cf *adhimu, takatifu*)

Abbreviations and Symbols Used in this Dictionary

adj	adjective	Ger	German
adv	adverb	Gh	Ghanaian
agric	agriculture	Gir	Giriama
agron	agronomy	Gr	Greek
amplic	amplicative	gram	grammar
anat	anatomy	gram part	grammatical particle
Ar	Arabic	Guj	Gujarati
arch	archaic	Heb	Hebrew
astron	astronomy	Hind	Hindi
aux	auxiliary	idm (s)	idiom (s)
bot	botany	interj	interjection
cf	compare	interrog	interrogative
Chin	China	It	Italian
com	commerce	Jap	Japanese
conj	conjunction	ki-vi	singular–plural form of the noun
cop	copular		
Cs	causative	Kich	Kichaga (an indigenous language in Tanzania)
dim	dimunitive	Kik	Kikuyu (an indigenous language in Kenya)
drm	drama		
Eng	English	Kinyak	Kinyakyusa (an indigenous language in Tanzania)
engin	engineering	Kinyam	Kinyamwezi (an indigenous language in Tanzania)
esp	especially		
fig	figurative; figuratively	Kip	Kipare (an indigenous language in Tanzania)
Fr	French	Lat	Latin
geog	Geography	leg	legal
geol	Geology	lit	literature

mi-	plural form of the noun	prov	proverb
ma-	plural form of the noun	Ps	Passive
math	mathematics	rel mark	relative marker
mech	mechanics	rel pron	relative pronoun
med	medicine	rel	religion
Mly	Malay	Rp	Reciprocal
monet	monetary	Rs	Russian
morph	morphology	sby	somebody
mus	music	sem	semantics
n	N class noun	Sik	Sikh
n	noun	sl	slang
naut	nautical usage	Sp	Spanish
PA	PA or Mahali class (pa-)	St	Stative
part	particle	Stc	Static
Pers	Persian	sth	something
phon	phone, phoneme, phonology	syn	saying
		trigon	Trigonometry
phon	phonology	Turk	Turkish
phon	phonetics	u	U class noun
physiol	physiology	usu	usually
pl	plural	vi	verb intransitive
poet	poetry	vt	verb transitive
Port	Portugal	vul	vulgar
prep	preposition	wa-	plural form of the noun
pron	pronoun	zool	Zoology

A

A, a /a/ 1. the first letter of the Swahili alphabet. 2. a low-back vowel.
aa! (also *ahaa*) *interj* an exclamation of wonder, pleasure, pain, acquiescence or dissent; ah!
aalam *adj* (of God) omniscient; all-knowing: *Allahu aalam*, God is all-knowing. (Ar)
aalamina *n* (n) all creatures. (Ar)
aali¹ *adj* good, superior, first-rate, tip-top: *Anapika chakula aali siku hizi*, she cooks good food these days (cf *bora, adhima*) (Ar)
aali² *n* (n) see *ali*
aalimu¹ *n* (n) (pl *ulamaa*) 1. a Muslim scholar, a Muslim authority. 2. scholar, savant, authority, pundit. (Ar)
aalimu² *adj* learned, erudite, scholarly, knowledgeable: *Yeye ni mwanafalsafa aalimu*, he is a knowledgeable philosopher. (Ar)
aathari *n* (n) relics, antiques, ancient ruins. (Ar)
aazi *adj* see *azizi¹* and *azizi²*
abaa *interj* an exclamation for calling attention to a friend; hey! hallo! (cf *ohaa!, aisee!*)
abadani *adv* (used only with the negatives) not at all, never: *Kijana huyu hanywi pombe abadani*, this young man never drinks beer. (cf *kamwe, hasha*) (Ar)
abadari *interj* (*naut*) an expletive used in a sailing vessel to alert all the crew and the passengers to get prepared for any danger.
abadi *adv* forever, always, permanently. (Ar)
abakusi *n* (n) abacus; a frame with beads or balls sliding back and forth on wires or in slots.

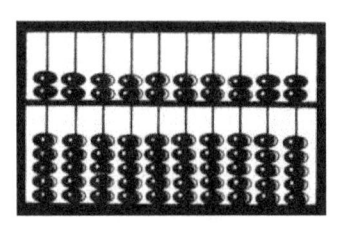

abakusi

abdi *n* (n) 1. servant. 2. human being. (Ar)
abedari¹ *n* (n) a sheave or a large block or pulley used in a canoe, dhow, etc (cf *roda, henza*)
abedari² *interj* see *habedari*
abee *interj* see *bee*
abinusi *n* (n) see *abunusi*
abir.i¹ *vt* sail, travel, navigate: *Aliabiri kwenye mashua*, he travelled by boat. Prep. ***abiri.a*** St. ***abir.ik.a*** Cs. ***abir.isha*** Ps. ***abiri.w.a*** Rp. of Prep ***abir.i.an.a*** (cf *safiri*) (Ar)
abir.i² *vt* foretell, predict, foresee: *Aliabiri kwamba mvua itanyesha leo*, he predicted that it would rain today. Prep. ***abir.i.a*** St. ***abir.ik.a*** Cs. ***abir.ish.a*** Ps. ***abir.iw.a*** Rp. of Prep ***abir.i.an.a*** (cf *bashiri*) (Ar)
abir.i³ *vt* learn from experience, etc.: *Kutokana na kifo cha wazee wake, ameabiri kwamba maisha ni magumu*, following the death of his parents, he has learnt that life is difficult. Prep. ***abir.i.a*** St. ***abir.ik.a*** Cs. ***abir.ish.a*** Ps. ***abir.iw.a***
abiria *n* (n) passenger (cf *msafiri*)
abjadi *n* (n) alphabet (cf *abtathi*) (Ar)
ablauti *n* (n) ablaut; patterned changes of base vowels in related words to show changes in tense, meaning, etc., as

1

in the Indo-European languages (Ex: drink (- *nywa*) drank, drunk) (Eng)

abra *n* (*n*) chance, opportunity, time: *Hajapata abra ya kuimaliza kazi yangu*, he has not got the chance to complete my work. (cf *fursa*) (Ar)

abtad.i (also *abutadi*) *vt* begin, start (Ar)

abtali (also *abutali*) *n* (*n*) warriors, fighters (Ar)

abtathi *n* (*n*) alphabet letters (cf *abjadi*)

abu *n* (*n*) father (cf *baba*) (Ar)

abud.u[1] *vt* 1. worship; pay homage to: *Anamwabudu Mungu*, he worships God. 2. idolize; make an idol. 3. respect, adore, love: *Mtumishi yule anamwabudu sana tajiri wake*, that servant respects his boss very much. Prep. *abud.i.a* St. *abud.ik.a* Cs. *abud.ish.a* Ps. of Prep *abud.iw.a* Rp. of Prep *abud.i.an.a* (cf *nyenyekea, tii.*)

abudu[2] *n* (*n*) puppet, marionette, dolly. (cf *karagosi, bandia*) (Ar)

abunusi (also *abinusi*) *n* (*n*) ebony: *Samani za abunusi*, ebony furniture.

abunuwasi *n* (*n*) a trickster figure in Arabic fables (Ar)

abutadi *n* (*n*) see abtadi

abutali *n* (*n*) see abtali.

abuwabu *n* (*n*) doors (Ar)

abwabu *n* (*n*) see *abuwabu*.

abwe *interj* an exclamation for praising a silly thing; wow! (*ebo*).

abyadhi[1] (also *baidhati*) *adj* white (Ar)

abyadhi[2] *n* (*n*) dominoes; a kind of dice

ach.a[1] (also *wacha*) *vt* 1. leave, leave off, stop. *Acha kucheza kamari*, stop gambling. 2. allow, permit: *Alimwacha mtoto wake afanye atakavyo*, she allowed her son to do as he pleased. (cf *ruhusu*) 3. forgive, pardon, release: *Nilimkamata mwizi wa mifuko na kisha nikamwachilia*, I arrested a pick-pocket and later released him. (cf *samehe*) 4. abandon, forsake, neglect: *Kuku aliwaacha watoto wake*, the hen neglected her chicks. 5. divorce, separate from: *Amemwacha mkewe*, he has divorced his wife. 6. give conditions, order, information, etc. to a particular person while being away: *Aliacha maagizo kwa jirani zake*, she left a message with his neighbours. 7. leave sth behind: *Aliacha mali nyingi alipokufa*, he left behind a lot of wealth when he died. 8. be disengaged, resign: *Ameacha kazi*, he has resigned from work. 9. pass over sth: *Acha nyumba ile mkono wa kushoto kisha uende moja kwa moja mpaka kwa hilo jengo*, pass that house on the left side and then go straight until you reach the building. 10. (*idm*) *Acha mkono*, die e.g. *Alituacha mkono zamani*, he died a long time ago Prep. *ach.i.a* St. *ach.ik.a* Cs. *ach.ish.a*, Ps. *ach.w.a* Rp. *ach.an.a* Ps. of Prep. *ach.iw.a*

acha[2] *interj* an exclamation for surprise and happiness e.g. *Acha wee!* incredible!

achali *n* (*n*) see *achari*

acham.a *vi* gape, gawk, gawp, goggle, stare; be open-mouthed, show astonishment: *Mbona unaachama?* Why are you gawping? Prep. *acham.i.a* St. *acham.ik.a*

achan.a[1] *vi* see *acha*

achan.a[2] *vi* (*n*) (of a road, etc.) fork; divide into two parts or more. *Njia imeachana*, the road forks.

achan.a[3] *vi* be separated, be divorced; *Ali na Hadija sasa wameachana*, Ali and Hadija are now divorced. Prep. *achan.i.a* St. *achan.ik.a* Cs. *achan.ish.a*

achari (also *achali*) *n* (*n*) pickles (Hind)

ache *interj* Usually *Ache wana*, an exclamation for expressing happiness or wishing good luck to someone esp. during wedding, initiation rites, etc.

achili.a *vt* acquit, discharge: *Mahakama ilimwachilia huru mshtakiwa*, the court acquitted the accused. Prep.

achili.li.a St. **achili.ik.a** Cs. **achili.ish.a** Ps. **achili.w.a** Rp. **achili.an.a**

achish.a *vt* stop sby from doing sth: *Achisha ziwa*, wean a child. *Achisha kazi*, terminate sby from employment. Prep. **achish.i.a** St. **achish.ik.a** Ps **achish.w.a** Rp. **achish.an.a**

ada *n* (*n*) 1. custom, tradition: *Ada za harusi*, marriage customs. 2. habit, practice: *Ana ada ya kuchelewa kazini kila siku*, he is in the habit of reporting to work late every day. (*prov*) *Ada ya mja hunena, muungwana ni kitendo*, public opinion says "a gentleman is judged by his actions" i.e. actions speak louder than words. 3. present given on such occasions as during wedding, etc. 4. fee: *Ada ya uhamisho*, transfer fee. (Ar)

adaa *n* (*n*) (In Islam) a prayer or a fast which is performed at the proper time in the islamic religion. (Ar)

adabu *n* (*n*) 1. respect, courtesy, good manners. (cf *heshima, utiifu*) 2. punishment: *Tia adabu*, punish. (Ar)

Adamu *n* (*n*) Adam; the first prophet. (cf *binaadamu, mwanaadamu*) (Ar)

adana *n* (*n*) (*mus*) a musical instrument like banjo. (Ar)

adapta *n* (*n*) adaptor (Eng)

adawa *n* (*n*) enmity (cf *uadui*)

adeade *n* (*n*) bodily weakness.

adesi *n* (*n*) (*bot*) lentils (cf *dengu*) (Hind)

adha *n* (*n*) inconvenience, nuisance, annoyance. (cf *taabu, usumbufu*) (Ar)

adhabu *n* (*n*) 1. punishment, penalty, discipline. (cf *adabu, marudio*) 2. persecution, torment. (Ar)

adhama *n* (*n*) 1. majesty, honour, esteem, distinction: *Lilikuwa jambo la adhama kwa wanariadha wetu kupata medali za dhahabu kwenye mashindano*, it was to the glory of our athletes to get gold medals in the competitions. (cf *fahari, heshima*) 2. glory, excellence, courtliness: *Adhama ya Mwenyezi Mungu*, the glory of God. (cf *utukufu, utakatifu*) 3. administration, authority: *Adhama ya mkuu wa mkoa ilikuwa inayumbayumba*, the administration of the regional commissioner was unstable. 4. pride, ostentation: *Alifanya harusi ya adhama*, he held an ostentatious wedding. (cf *fahari*) (Ar)

adhana *n* (*n*) (in Islam) the call of a muezzin to pray (Ar)

adharusi *n* (*n*) 1. fighting, skirmish. 2. battle, war. (cf *vita, mapigano*) (Ar)

adhib.u *vt* 1. punish, penalise, chastise: *Serikali itawaadhibu wale wanaovunja sheria*, the government will punish law-breakers. 2. torment, harass: *Akiniadhibu, basi mimi nitaripoti kwa wazee wake*, if he harasses me, I will report the matter to his parents. Prep. **adhib.i.a** St. **adhib.ik.a** Cs. **adhib.ish.a** Ps. of Prep. **adhib.iw.a** Rp. of Prep. **adhib.i.an.a** (cf *sumbua, tesa*) (Ar)

adhifari *n* (*n*) 1. an unpleasant human body or animal odour. 2. perspiration of the armpit. (cf *gugumo, kutuzi*) (Ar)

adhimish.a *vt* 1. commemorate, celebrate, honour, observe, mark: *Nchi yetu iliadhimisha miaka thelathini ya kupatikana kwa uhuru*, our country celebrated thirty years of independence. 2. glorify, dignify. Prep. **adhimish.i.a**, St. **adhimish.ik.a**. Ps. **adhimish.w.a** Rp. of Prep. **adhimish.i.an.a**

adhimisho *n* (*ma-*) commemoration, celebration, observance. (Ar)

adhimu[1] *adj* exalted, prestigious, honourable: *Kulikuwa na sherehe adhimu mtaani hivi karibuni*, there was a glorious celebration in the neighbourhood recently. (cf *tukufu, takatifu*) (Ar)

adhimu[2] *adj* bountiful, plenty, much: *Alikuwa na mali adhimu*, she had much wealth. (cf *tele*) (Ar)

adhin.i *vi* (in Islam) call to public prayers by a muezzin: *Alipoadhini, waumini walikimbilia msikitini*, when he gave the

A

adhini.a¹

call to prayers, the faithful rushed to the mosque. Prep. *adhin.i.a* St *adhin.ik.a* Cs. *adhin.ish.a* Ps *adhin.iw.a* Rp. of Prep. *adhin.i.an.a* (Ar)

adhini.a¹ *vi* see *adhini*

adhini.a² *vt* used in Islamic cultures in the expression: *Adhinia mtoto*, pray for a newly-born child. (Ar)

adhir.i *vt* see *aziri*

adhirik.a *vi* be disgraced, be discredited: *Aliadhirika hadharani*, he became disgraced in public. (cf *fedheheka, aibika*)

adhuhuri (also *dhuhuri*) *n (n)* 1. noontime, noon; time between noon and 3.00p.m 2. Islamic prayer during this time. (Ar)

ad.i *vt* see sby off; accompany a visitor part of the way: *Nilimuadi mgeni wangu kwenye kituo cha basi*, I saw my guest off at the bus-stand. Prep. *ad.i.a* St *ad.ik.a* Cs *ad.ish.a* Ps. *ad.iw.a* (cf *sindikiza, aga*) (Ar)

adia *n (n)* present, gift, reward: *Aliniletea adia nzuri kutoka ng'ambo*, he sent me a lovely present from abroad. (cf. *zawadi, hidaya*) (Ar)

adibik.a *vi* get moral training. Prep. *adibik.ia* St *adibik.ik.a*

adibish.a *vt* make sby get moral training. Prep *adibish.i.a* St. *adibish.ik.a* Ps. *adibish.w.a* Rp. *adibish.an.a*

adib.u¹ *vt* teach good manners: *Mzee alimwadibu binti yake jinsi ya kuwashughulikia wageni*, the parent taught his daughter how to attend to guests. Prep. *adib.i.a* St. *adib.ik.a* Cs. *adib.ish.a* Ps. of Prep. *adib.i.w.a* Rp. *adib.i.an.a* (Ar)

adibu² *adj* 1. decorous, polished, well-behaved, respectful: *Yeye ni kijana adibu anayependwa sana mtaani*, he is a well-behaved young person who is liked very much in the neighbourhood. (cf *telekevu*) 2. polite, civil. (Ar)

adid.i *vt, vi* 1. count, enumerate. 2. prepare, arrange; clear the decks. Prep. *adid.i.a* St. *adid. ik.a* Cs. *adid.ish.a*

adinasi

Ps. of Prep. *adid.iw.a* Rp. of Prep. *adid.i.an.a* (cf *andaa, tayarisha*) (Ar)

adili¹ *n (ma-)* 1. justice, righteousness, rectitude, impartiality: *Hakimu alitumia maadili alipowahukumu washtakiwa*, the magistrate exercised impartiality in trying the accused. (cf *uadilifu*) 2. moral training, moral teachings: *Shule yetu inaipa umuhimu mkubwa kipengele cha maadili*, our school attaches great importance to ethical training. (Ar)

adili² *adj* right, impartial, righteous, just: *Yeye ni hakimu adili*, he is an impartial judge. (Ar)

adil.i³ *vt* judge impartially, be impartial: *Mkuu wa wilaya anasifika sana katika kuadili shughuli mbalimbali za wilaya*, the district commissioner is reknown for impartially conducting district matters. Prep. *adil.i.a* St. *adil.ik.a* Cs *adil.ish.a* Ps. of Prep. *adil.iw.a* (Ar)

-adilifu *adj* moral, righteous, incorruptible: *Kiongozi mwadilifu*, a righteous leader. *Daktari Ngozi alikuwa kijana mwadilifu*, Dr. Ngozi was a righteous youth. (Ar)

adilish.a *vt* elevate, moralize. Prep. *adilish.i.a* St. *adilish.ik.a* Ps. *adilish.w.a*

adimik.a *vi* be scarce, be rare, be unobtainable: *Mchele umeadimika*, rice has become scarce. Prep. *adimik.i.a* (cf *potea, ghalika*) (Ar)

adimish.a *vt* cause sth to be scarce or unobtainable. Prep. *adimish.i.a* St *adimish.ik.a* Rp. *adimish.an.a*

adimu *adj* rare, scarce: *Huu si msimu wa maembe na ndiyo maana, yamekuwa adimu*, this is not the season for mangoes, and that is why, they are in short supply. (cf *kidogo*) (Ar)

adinasi (also *wadinasi*) *n (n)* 1. a person of noble birth: *Baadhi ya shule katika Uingereza zinapendwa na kina adinasi*, some of the schools in Great

adinati

Britain are favoured by the children of noble birth. 2. human being, person: *Kila adinasi ana kasoro zake*, every person has his weaknesses. (Ar)

adinati *adj* glorious, exalted. (cf *tukufu*)

admari *n* (*ma-*) see *admirali*

admeri *n* (*ma-*) admiral; naval officer of high rank. (Eng)

adrenalini *n* (*n*) adrenalin; a kind of chemical produced in the body. (Eng)

adresi *n* (*n*) see *anuwani*

adu.a *vt, vi* 1. make an offering to the spirits: *Aliadua kwa kutoa vyakula*, he made an offering to the spirits by giving food. 2. exorcise, exsufflate; drive out an evil eye; prepare a charm against the effects of the evil eye: *Mganga alimwadua shetani kutoka kwenye nyumba*, the sorcerer exorcised a ghost from the house. Prep. **adu.li.a** St. **adu.lik.a** Cs **adu.lish.a** Rp. **adu.an.a** Ps. of Prep. **adu.liw.a** Rp. of Prep. **adu.li.an.a** (cf *tambika*) (Ar)

adui *n* (*ma-*) 1. enemy, adversary, foe: *Adui aliihujumu nchi yetu*, the enemy attacked our country. *Adui Llahi*, the enemy of God (Ar) (cf *hasimu*) 2. opponent, contender, rival: *Aliwashinda maadui wote kwenye mashindano*, he defeated all other contenders in the race. 3. anything that hampers progress: *Umaskini ni adui mkubwa wa maendeleo ya nchi yetu*, poverty is a great impediment to the progress of our country. (Ar)

advansi *n* (*n*) an advance payment. (cf *rubuni*) (Eng)

afa *n* (*ma-*) jinx; a person or thing that causes a misfortune: *Yeye ni afa na ndiyo sababu ya sisi kupata majanga*, he is a jinx and that is why, we are suffering from misfortunes. (Ar)

afaalek (also *afanalek*) *interj* good gracious, good heavens; an expletive of surprise, etc. (cf *lahaula*)

afadhali *adv* 1. rather, preferable, by choice: *Afadhali kupumzika kuliko kuhangaika bureubure*, it is better to relax than to wander aimlessly. (cf *bora*) 2. better: *Yeye alikuwa anaumwa, lakini sasa amepata afadhali*, he was sick but now he is better. (Ar.)

afanalek *interj* see *afaalek*

afandi[1] *n* (*ma-*) sir, master. The word *afande* is a sign of respect used by soldiers and policemen towards their superiors. (Turk)

afandi[2] *n* (*ma*) (*vul*) sodomite; a person who practices sodomy. (cf *basha*) (Turk)

afik.i (also *wafiki*) *vt, vi* 1. agree with, concur with: *Mimi nililiafiki shauri lake la kufungua zahanati kijijini*, I agreed with his suggestion to open a dispensary in the village. (cf *kubali*) 2. suit, fit, become, satisfy: *Mtindo huu mpya wa kunyoa nywele utawaafiki vijana wa sasa*, this new hairstyle will suit today's young people. Prep. **afik.i.a** St. **afik.ik.a** Ps. **afik.iw.a** Rp. **afik.i.an.a** (cf *pendeza*) (Ar)

afikian.a *vi* to agree with: concur, conform: *Mtazamo wake unaafikiana na malengo yetu*, his viewpoint concurs with our objectives. (cf *patana*)

afisa *n* (*ma-*) see *ofisa*

afisi *n* (*ma-*) see *ofisi*

afiuni *n* (*n*) see *afyuni*

afkani[1] *n* (*n*) lunatic, maniac; a deranged person. (cf *punguani, mwehu*) (Ar)

afkani[2] *adj* mad, insane, lunatic: *Akili afkani*, deficient in intelligence. (Ar)

afkani[3] *n* (*n*) (*med*) heart attack; myocardial infarction. (cf *kimoyomoyo*) (Ar)

Afrika *n* (*n*) (*geog*) Africa. (Eng)

afrikanaizesheni *n* (*n*) africanisation; the policy of giving indigenous Africans positions in all sectors of the economy. (Eng)

afriti *n* (*ma-*) 1. devil, djinn; an evil spirit, an evil genius: *Inasemekana kwamba katika nyumba ile kuna afriti*, it is said that in that house there is an evil spirit. 2. a wicked person, an evil person; reprobate. (cf *mwovu, fisadi*) 3. rogue, trickster; a deceitful person, a cunning person: *Mfanyabiashara mmoja katika kijiji chetu ni afriti,* one business man in our village is a rogue. (Ar)

afu[1] *n* (*ma-*) (*bot*) a wild jasmine flower used in perfumes or for scenting tea. (Ar)

af.u[2] *vt* 1. (usu. of God) forgive, pardon: *Mungu atayaafu makosa yake,* God will forgive his sins. 2. cure, redeem: *Mungu ataniafu na maradhi niliyo nayo,* may God cure me the illness I am suffering from. 3. save, rescue, preserve: *Mungu atakuafu,* God may protect you. Prep. **afu.li.a** St. of Prep. **afu.lik.a** Ps. of Prep. **afu.liw.a** Rp. **afu.an.a** (cf *hifadhi, linda*) (Ar)

afu[3] *n* (*ma-*) 1. (of God) pardon; God's forgiveness. 2. cure, recovery. 3. save, rescue. 4. protection, safeguard. (Ar)

afua *n* (*n*) recovery, recuperation, convalescence, return to health: *Mgonjwa wangu sasa ameanza kupata afua,* my patient is now recuperating. (*prov*) *Afua ni mbili kufa na kupona,* deliverance is of two kinds, dying or getting better. (cf *uzima*) (Ar)

afueni *n* (*n*) (of a patient) recovery to health: *Mgonjwa bado hajapata afueni,* the patient has not yet recovered (Ar)

afwaji *n* (*n*) 1. a group of people. 2. army; an armed group of people. (cf *kikosi, jeshi*) (Ar)

afya[1] *n* (*n*) 1. health. (cf *siha, ria*) 2. strength: *Hana afya,* he is not strong. (cf *nguvu, zihi*) (Ar)

afya[2] *interj* an expression used as a sign of physical fitness when someone sneezes: *Afya! Kua kama mgomba,* Be healthy! Grow to become like a banana plant! (Ar)

afya[3] *interj* an exclamation used by children in persuading one another to do an action: *Afya! Tukacheze mpira,* hurry up! let us go play football.

afyuni (also *afiuni*) *n* (*n*) opium, dope. (cf *kasumba, majuni*) (Ar)

ag.a *vt, vi* 1. ask for permission: *Aliniaga alipokwenda hospitali,* she asked for my permission when she went to hospital. 2. bid goodbye, take leave of, say goodbye; bid farewell to. 3. say a last farewell e.g. when someone is dying or when people are not sure of meeting again. In that context, the expression usually used is *aga dunia* or *toa buriani.* Prep. **ag.i.a** St. **ag.ik.a** Pt. **ag.w.a** Rep. **ag.an.a**

aga.a *vi* 1. slip out, get away: *Nilimshika ndege lakini mara akaniagaa,* I held the bird but it immediately slipped out of my hands. (cf *ponyoka*) 2. be spilt, be scattered: *Maziwa yameagaa,* the milk has spilt. Prep. **aga.lik.a** Cs. **aga.lish.a**

agan.a[1] *vi* see *aga*

agan.a[2] *vi* make pact, agree mutually, strike a bargain: *Waliagana kushirikiana kwa hali na mali,* they agreed to cooperate mutually by all means. Prep. **agan.i.a** St. **agani.k.a** Cs. **agan.ish.a** Ps. **agan.w.a**

agano *n* (*ma-*) agreement, contract, mutual understanding: *Agano lake lina mashaka sana,* his promise is open to much doubt. (cf *ahadi, mapatano*) 2. promise (cf *ahadi*)

Agano *n* (*n*) Testament. *Agano Jipya,* the New Testament. *Agano la Kale,* the Old Testament.

aghalabu *adv* usually, by and large; *Mtu yule aghalabu hunitembelea kila Jumapili,* that person usually visits me every Sunday. (Ar)

agi.a[1] *vt* see *aga*

agi.a[2] *vt* suit, gratify; satisfy one's needs: *Sera zake za nyumbani hazikumwagia binti yake,* his domestic policies did not please his daughter. St. **agi.k.a** Cs. **agi.sh.a** (cf *pendeza, furahisha*)

agiz.a (also *agizia*) *vt, vi* direct, instruct, give instructions. Prep. ***agiz.i.a***, St. ***agiz.ik.a*** Cs. ***agiz.ish.a*** Ps. ***agiz.w.a*** Ps. of Prep. ***agiz.iw.a***. Rp. ***agiz.an.a***
agizi *n* (*n*) (*gram*) imperative: *Sentensi agizi*, imperative sentence.
agizi.a[1] *vt* see *agiza*
agizi.a[2] *vt* order sth: *Shule yetu imeagizia yunifomu mpya kutoka kwenye kiwanda*, our school has ordered new uniforms from the factory. St. ***agizi.k.a*** Cs. ***agizi.sh.a*** Ps. ***agizi.w.a*** Rp. ***agizi.an.a***
agizo *n* (*ma-*) 1. directive, order, instruction (cf *amri, sharti*) 2. guideline, directive: *Agizo la rais*, a presidential directive (cf *maagizo*)
ago[1] (also *rago*) *n* (*n*) encampment, camp.
ago[2] *n* (*ma-*) (*anat*) thigh: *Alimpakata mtoto wake agoni*, she cradled her child on the thigh. (cf *paja, kiga*)
Agosti *n* (*n*) August (Eng)
agronomia *n* (*n*) (*agron*) agronomy; the science and economics of crop production. (Eng)
agu.a *vt* 1. foretell, prophesy, predict: *Jana niliagua kwamba mvua itanyesha na kweli imenyesha*, yesterday I predicted that it would rain and indeed it has. (cf *bashiri, tabiri*) 2. treat medically; exorcise, disenchant; prepare a charm against the effects of the evil eye: *Mganga alimwagua mgonjwa wetu*, the sorcerer exorcised our patient. Prep. ***agu.li.a*** St. ***agu.lik.a*** Cs ***agu.li.sh.a*** Ps of Prep ***agu.liw.a*** Rp. of Prep. ***agu.li.an.a*** (cf *tibu, ganga*)
aguzi *n* (*ma-*) 1. prediction, prophecy, divination; interpretation of dreams: *Aguzi lake la kushinda katika bahati nasibu limesibu*, his prediction that he would win the lottery has come true. (cf *utabiri, tafsiri*) 2. service usually of giving medicine: *Aguzi lililo bora kwa mgonjwa ni kumpa dawa*, the best service for a patient is to give him medicine.

ah! *interj* an exclamation of disgust over sth (cf *lo! ka!*)
ahaa *interj* see *aa*
ahadharau[1] *adj* green (Ar)
ahadharau[2] *n* (*n*) green colour (Ar)
ahadi[1] *n* (*n*) 1. promise, pledge, assurance: *Timiza ahadi*, keep a promise. *Vunja ahadi*, break a promise. *Ahadi hewa*, empty promise. (*prov*) *Ahadi ni deni*, a promise is a debt i.e. never break a promise. 2. agreement, covenant, contract: *Pande mbili ziliweka ahadi kukomesha mapigano*, the two sides agreed to stop the fighting. (Ar)
ahadi[2] *n* (*n*) death; end of life: *Imeshatimia ahadi yake*, his life has come to an end. (cf *mauti*.) (Ar.)
ahali[1] *n* (*n*) 1. wife: *Ahali yangu anapika vizuri*, my wife cooks well. (cf *mke*.) 2. family, relatives: *Ahali yangu ni kubwa*, my family is large. (Ar)
ahali[2] *n* (*n*) used in the expression: *Ahali L-Badri*, the disciples of Prophet Muhammad, who fought in the holy war of *Badr* against the non-believers.
ahamaru[1] (also *ahamari*) *adj* red: *Rangi ahamaru*, red colour. (Ar)
ahamaru[2] (also *ahamari*) *n* (*n*) red colour. (Ar)
ahasi *adj* especially, particularly, in particular: *Wanafunzi wale ni watundu ahasi yule mkubwa wao kabisa*, those students are extremely naughty especially the oldest of them. (Ar)
ahera (also *akhera*) *n* (*n*) 1. life after death. 2. doomsday, day of judgement (cf *kuzimu, jongomeo*) (Ar)
aheri (also *ahiri, akhiri*) *n* (*n*) 1. the end: *Toka awali hadi aheri*, from first to last, from beginning to end. (cf *mwisho, kikomo*) 2. the final offer in business; bargain price: *Aheri yako ni shilingi ngapi?* What is your best price? (Ar)

A ahi

ahi (also *yakhe, yakhi*) *n* (*n*) see *yakhe*
ahid.i *vt, vi* promise, pledge; Prep. *ahid.i.a* St. *ahid.ik.a* Cs. *ahid.ish.a* Ps. of Prep. *ahid.iw.a* Rp. of Prep. *ahid.i.an.a*
ahiri[1] *vt* see *aheri*
ahir.i[2] *vt* see *ahirisha*
ahirish.a (also *ahiri, akhirisha*) *vt* 1. postpone, defer: *Waliuahirisha mkutano*, they postponed the meeting, 2. delay, cause to wait. Prep. *ahiri.sh.i.a* St. *ahiri.sh.ik.a* Ps. *ahiri.sh.w.a* Rp. of Prep *ahiri.sh.i.an.a*
ahmari *adj* see *ahmaru*
ahsante[1] (also *asante*) *n* (*n*) gratitude, thanks: (*prov*) *Ahsante ya punda ni mashuzi*, the gratitude of a donkey is like the breaking of wind i.e gratefulness is sometimes met by ungratefulness. (cf *shukrani*) (Ar)
ahsante[2] (also *asante*) *interj* an exclamation of gratitude, approval, etc. for an action that has been done: *Ahsante kwa kunitunzia mtoto wangu!* Thank you for looking after my child! (Ar)
ahueni (also *hueni*) *n* (*n*) better condition after illness (cf *ashikali, nafuu*) (Ar)
aibik.a *vi* be humiliated, be disgraced, be put to shame. Prep. *aibik.i.a* St. *aibik.ik.a* Cs. *aib.ish.a* (cf *fedheheka, dharaulika*)
aibish.a *vi* disgrace, embarass, discredit: *Aliniaibisha hadharani*, he disgraced me in public. Prep. *aibish.i.a* St. *aibish.ik.a* Ps. *aibi.sh.w.a*. Rp. *aibish.an.a*
aibu *n* (*n*) 1. disgrace, shame, debasement, scandal (cf *fedheha, izara, nazaa*) 2. defect, weakness: *Hata kama yeye ni kijana mwema, lakini pia ana aibu zake*, even though he is a good young man, he has his weaknesses. (cf *dosari, walakini*) (Ar)
aidha (also *waidha*) *conj* besides, furthermore, in addition: *Yeye ni tajiri; aidha anapenda watu*, he is rich; in addition, he loves people (cf *tena, kisha*) (Ar)

ajabu[2]

aidh.i *vt* advice, counsel. (cf *nasihi, shauri*) (Ar)
aidini *n* (*n*) iodine (Eng)
aila *n* (*n*) 1. family, relatives, kinsfolk. (cf *familia, ukoo*) 2. a group of people with common interests, beliefs, etc.; clique, coterie, fraternity: *Anaongoza aila kubwa ya waumini*, he heads a large fraternity of believers. (Ar)
ail.i *vt* blame, accuse, reprimand. Prep. *ail.i.a* St. *ail.ik.a* Cs. *ail.ish.a* Ps. Prep *ail.i.w.a* Rp. of Prep *ail.i.an.a* (cf *shutumu, karipia*) (Ar)
aili *n* (*n*) mistake, censure, blame. (*prov*) *Msema pweke hakosi; haijui ailiye*, One who expresses his/her opinion does not realize its fault, i.e. It is not right to judge a person for speaking out their opinion; to them the opinion has no fault.
aimi! *interj* oh me!
aina *n* (*n*) brand, variety, category: *Aina za maneno*, parts of speech.
aineaine *adv* see *hainehaine*
ain.i (usu *ainisha*) *vt* classify, specify, categorise, group. Prep. *ain.i.a* St. *ain.ik.a* Cs. *ain.ish.a* Ps. of Prep. *ain.iw.a* Rp. of Prep. *ain.i.an.a* (cf *tofautisha*)
ainish.a (also *aini*) *vt* classify, categorise, specify, breakdown: *Ainisha ngeli za nomino hizi*, classify these nouns. Prep. *ainish.i.a* St. *ainish.ik.a* Ps *ainish.w.a* Rp *ainish.an.a*
ainisho *n* (*ma*-) classification, specification, categorization.
aisee! *interj* an exclamation for calling attention to someone; hey! hallo! (cf *ohaa! abaa!*) (Eng)
ajaa *n* (*n*) miracle, marvel; work of wonder. (cf *ajabu*)
ajabi.a *vt* be dumbfounded, be astonished; wonder. St. *ajabi.k.a* Cs. *ajabi.sh.a* Ps. *ajabi.w.a* Rp. *ajabi.an.a*
ajabu[1] *n* (*n*) miracle, marvel, surprise. (Ar)
ajabu[2] *adv* extremely, terribly, incredibly, exceedingly: *Kulikuwa na mvua kubwa*

ajali   **akali¹**

ajabu, it was raining terribly. (cf *sana, mno*)

ajali *n* (*n*) accident, tragedy, mishap: *Alifariki kwa ajali ya ndege*, he died in a plane crash. (*prov*) *Ajali haina kinga*, fate has no prevention i.e. if God has written in his book that you will die on a particular day, then you will die (cf *mkosi, msiba*)

ajari *n* (*n*) overtime, *Malipo ya ajari*. overtime payment.

ajemi *n* (*n*) 1. see *uajemi*. 2. a kind of thin, flat and unleavened bread from India. *Mkate wa ajemi*, bread of this kind. (Pers)

ajenda *n* (*n*) agenda, programme, schedule, plan: *Ajenda ya siri*, hidden agenda (cf *ratibu, mada*) (Eng)

ajenti *n* (*n*) agent, representative. (cf *mwakilishi, wakulu*)

ajibu¹ *adj* wonderful, superb, remarkable: *Kazi ajibu*, a superb piece of work. (Ar)

ajibu² *adv* wonderfully, amazingly, fantastically: *Alivaa ajibu*, he dressed superbly. (Ar)

ajih.i *vt* visit a person living at a distant place; call upon: *Alimwajihi mjomba wake wakati wa likizo*, he visited his uncle during the vacation. Prep. **ajih.i.a** St. **ajih.ik.a** Cs. **ajih.ish.a** Ps. of Prep. **ajih.iw.a** Rp. of Prep. **ajih.i.an.a** (cf *zuru, tembelea*) (Ar)

ajila *n* (*n*) haste, speed, urgency: *Alifanya kazi kwa ajila*, she did the work hastily. (cf *haraka*) (Ar)

ajili¹ *n* (*n*) cause, reason, sake: *Kwa ajili ya*, because of; for the sake of: *Alikufa kwa ajili yenu*, he died for your sake. (Ar)

ajil.i² *vt* hurry, rush: *Aliajili ili amuwahi daktari kwenye zahanati yake*, she hurried in order to meet the doctor in time at his dispensary. St. **ajil.ik.a** Cs. **ajil.ish.a** (cf *harakisha*)

ajinabi¹ *n* (*n*) foreign, alien: *Yeye ni ajinabi*, he is a foreigner. 2. stranger. (Ar)

ajinabi² *adj* 1. foreigner, alien: *Mtu ajinabi*, a foreign person. (Ar)

ajinabia *adj* foreign, strange: *Mavazi ajinabia*, foreign dresses. *Mila ajinabia*, foreign cultures. (Ar)

ajinani *n* (*n*) see *jini*

ajira *n* (*n*) employment, work: *Ajira kamili*, full employment (cf *kazi*) (Ar)

ajir.i *vt* employ, hire. Prep. **ajir.i.a** St. **ajir.ik.a** Cs. **ajir.ish.a** Ps. of Prep. **ajir.iw.a**, be employed, be hired. Rp. of Prep. **ajir.i.an.a** (Ar)

ajiz.i¹ *n* (*n*) lethargy, sluggishness, slowness: *Ana ajizi sana katika kufanya kazi*, he is very slow at work. *Fanya ajizi*, be lazy (Ar)

ajizi² *adj* lazy, indolent, slothful: *Mtu ajizi*, a lazy person (Ar)

ajiz.i³ *vt* be lazy or negligent: *Alipewa kazi kuifanya lakini akawa analujizi*, he was given work to do but he kept on delaying it. Prep **ajiz.i.a** St. **ajiz.ik.a** Cs. **ajiz.ish.a** Ps. of Prep. **ajiz.iw.a** (cf *chelewa, tepeta*) (Ar)

ajmaina *n* (*n*) (*poet*) all people. (Ar)

ajua *n* (*n*) a chess game played on a board with two rows of holes in which pebbles are put.

ajuza *n* (*n*) a very old woman; crone: *Ajuza mtabiri*, sibyl. *Ajuza msumbufu*, harridan (cf *bikizee*) (Ar)

ajwadi *adj* glorious, majestic, dignified: *Nyumba ajwadi*, a prestigious house. (cf *adhimu*)

ajwari *adj* invalid, null and void, inoperative.

ak.a¹ *vt* 1. build (by using stones, bricks and mortar); do masonry work (cf *jenga*) 2. fence by using stones, poles, barbed wire, etc: *Alikiaka kiwanja chake*, he fenced his plot. Prep. **ak.i.a** St. **ak.ik.a** Cs. **ak.ish.a** Ps. **ak.w.a**

aka² *interj* 1. an exclamation of surprise; oh! (cf *ala! lo!*) 2. an exclamation for denial; never! no way!

akademia *n* (*n*) academy (Eng)

akali¹ *n* (*n*) a little, a few: *Akali ya vitu*, a few things. (Ar)

9

akali² *adv* approximately, fewer than, scarcely any: *Kwa akali, watu kama elfu walifika kwenye mazishi*, in approximation, a thousand people attended the funeral. (Ar)

akania¹ *n (n)* bridle (Ar)

akani.a² *vt* lead a horse by means of a bridle. St. *akani.k.a* Cs. *akani.sh.a* Ps. *akani.w.a* Rp. *akani.an.a* (Ar)

akarabu *n (n)* see *akrabu*

akari *n (n)* intoxicating liquor, alcoholic drink. (Ar)

akaunti *n (n)* account: *Akaunti ya akiba*, savings account. *Akaunti ya amana*, deposit account. *Akaunti ya hundi*, current account. *Akaunti ya malipo*, charge account. (Eng)

akdi *n (n)* see *akidi*

-ake *adj pron* possessive adjectival root for the third person singular meaning *his, her,* and *its*. This root takes different forms depending on the nominal class of the word in question: *Mtumishi wake*, his/her servant. *Embe yake ni tamu*, her mango is sweet.

akhera *n (n)* see *ahera*

akhiri *n (n)* 1. see *aheri*. 2. *(idm) Akhiri zaman*, in the olden days

akhiyari¹ *adj* better than, superior: *Chungwa hili ni akhiyari kuliko lile*, this orange is better than that one. (Ar)

akhiyari² *n (n)* superiority, excellence.

akhiyari³ *n (n)* good people.

aki.a *vt* gulp down; swallow without chewing: *Mlafi alikiakia chakula*, the glutton gulped down the food. Prep. *aki.li.a* St. *aki.lik.a* Cs. *aki.sh.a* Ps. *aki.w.a* (cf *bwakia, bwia, bugia*)

akiba *n (n)* reserve, savings: *Benki ya akiba*, a savings bank. *Weka akiba*, make a saving. *(prov) Akiba haiozi*, a reserve never goes bad i.e. a reserve will always be handy. (cf *limbiko*) (Ar)

akida (old use in Tanganyika) *n (n)* 1. head of the army. 2. an official assistant of the district officer during the colonial period. 3. an office messenger.

akid.i¹ (also *akdi*) *n (n)* marriage, matrimony: *Alifunga akidi*, he got married (cf *ndoa*) (Ar)

akid.i² *vi* 1. suffice, be sufficent, satisfy: *Chakula kilichopikwa kwa ajili ya wageni kiliweza kuakidi*, the food which was cooked for the guests was sufficient. (cf *tosha, kifu*) 2. finish, complete: *Ameakidi kula wali jikoni*, he has finished eating rice in the kitchen. (cf *pua, maliza*) 3. adulterate, contaminate, pollute: *Aliyaakidi maziwa*, he contaminated the milk. Prep. *akid.i.a* St. *akid.ik.a* (Ar)

akidi³ *n (n)* quorum (Ar)

akidu *n (n)* a contract worker: *Yeye ni akidu aliyeajiriwa kufundisha somo la kilimo*, he is a contract worker employed to teach agriculture. (Ar)

akifi.a *vt* entrust with property, money, etc. to the appropriate people: *Aliwaakifia warithi wa mali ya marehemu*, he entrusted the wealth to the rightful heirs. Prep. *akifi.k.a* Cs. *akifi.sh.a* Ps. *akifi.w.a* Rp. *akifi.an.a.*

akifish.a *vt, vi* stop, prevent, prohibit: *Alituakifisha tusimnunulie vitu sokoni*, she forbade us to buy things for her at the market. Prep. *akifish.i.a* St. *akifish.ik.a* Ps. *akifish.w.a* Rp. *akifish.an.a* (cf *komesha, zuia*)

akif.u *vt* see *wakifu*

akika (also *akiki*) *n (n)* 1. a feast held when a baby is eight days old or held perhaps later. 2. a funeral feast for a child in case it dies before his haircut. 3. the goat slain at the feast of the first hair-cutting of the child. (Ar)

akiki¹ *n (n)* 1. see *akika*. 2. a prayer recited at a funeral service of a child for whom *akika* ritual was not performed. (Ar)

akiki² *n (n)* a kind of red stone which is used for making rings, earrings, etc; cornelian, ruby. (Ar)

akiki³ *n (n)* torrent, alluvion, gully. (cf *mvo, mfo, mvuo*)

akili *n* (*n*) 1. intelligence, intellect, ingenuity: *Akili taahira*, mental retardation, *Akili ya kuzaliwa*, native intelligence. *Akili timamu*, sanity. 2. ability, discretion, judgement. (cf *uwezo, uamuzi, uteuzi*) 3. trick, ruse; a clever plan: *Fanya akili*, use one's brains; exercise intelligence. (*prov*) *Akili ni mali*, wits are wealth. i.e. intelligence is an asset. (Ar)

akilili *n* (*n*) (*astron*) the three stars in the middle or front of a crab.

akina *n* (*n*) a group of people of similar status, sex, interest, etc.: *Akina yahe*, common people. *Akina sisi*, we the like of us.

akiolojia *n* (*n*) archaelogy (Eng)

akisani *n* (*n*) parts of sth. (Ar)

akis.i *vt* 1. reflect, reverberate, echo: *Kioo kiliuakisi uso wake*, the mirror reflected his face. 2. reflect, manifest, exhibit: *Tabia yake inaakisi waziwazi kiburi chake*, her behaviour clearly reflects her arrogance. Prep. **akis.i.a** St. **akis.ik.a** Cs. **akis.ish.a** Ps. of Prep. **akis.iw.a** Rp. of Prep. **akis.i.an.a**

-ako *adj, pron* possessive adjectival root for the second person singular, *your, yours*. Its form is determined by the nominal class of the noun: *Mtoto wako*, your child. *Wazo lako*, your suggestion.

akraba *n* (*n*) relatives: *Akraba za kuukeni*, maternal relatives. *Akraba za kuumeni*, paternal relatives. (cf *jamaa, ahili*) (Ar)

akrabu[1] *n* (*n*) 1. hand of a clock. 2. (*astron*) Scorpion; the eighth sign of the Zodiac.

akrabu[2] *n* (*n*) (*naut*) on the side of: *Akrabu magharibi*, on the western side. *Akrabu mashariki*, on the eastern side. (Ar)

akrama *adj* glorious, illustrious, dignified: *Viongozi akrama wa dini*, dignified religious leaders. (cf *tukufu, jalili*) (Ar)

akronimi *n* (*n*) acronym; a word formed from the first letter of a group of words e.g. U.N.O. that is, United Nations Organization. (Eng)

akselereta *n* (*n*) accelerator (Eng)

akthari *n* (*n*) 1. majority, a great number: *Akthari ya wanavijiji hawa ni wavuvi*, the majority of these villagers are fishermen. (cf *wingi*) 2. assembly, congregation, gathering. (Ar)

aku.a *vt* 1. jump unexpectedly; 2. grab, snatch, seize: *Mwizi wa mifuko aliuakua mkoba wa mtalii*, the pickpoket snatched the tourist's purse. 3. attack sby verbally; affront: *Mbona anapenda kuakua watu hadharani?* Why does he like to affront people in public? 4. invade, assault, assail, raid. Prep. **aku.li.a** St. **aku.lik.a** Cs. **aku.lish.a** Ps. of Prep. **aku.liw.a** Rp. **aku.an.a** (cf *kamata, rukia, shika*. (cf *ingilia, jidukiza*)

akwami *n* (*n*) a crowd of people. (Ar)

ala[1] (pl. *nyala* or *maala*) *n* (*n*) sheath, scabbard, case: *Ala ya kisu*, a knife's sheath. (cf *uo, mfuko*) (Ar)

ala[2] *n* (*n*) 1. tool, implement, instrument: *Ala za muziki*, musical instruments. 2. (*gram*) *Ala za matamshi*, organs of speech. (Ar)

ala[3] *interj* an exclamation of surprise, annoyance, impatience, etc.; oh! (cf *do! lo!*)

alaa[1] *interj* an exclamation indicating one has understood the issues under discussion; I see!

alaa[2] *adv* used in the expression: *Alaa kulihali*, by all means.

ala ala (also *halahala*) *adv* 1. an expression of emphasizing a particular thing; don't forget, don't miss (to attend) *Ala ala na maagizo tuliyokupa hivi karibuni*, don't forget the instructions we gave you recently. 2. with care; carefully, politely: *Ala ala na jirani zako*, treat your neighbours carefully.

alaka (also *mlahaka*) *n* (*n*) rapport, understanding; good relationship. (Ar)

alama *n* (*n*) 1. sign, mark, signal: *Alama za barabarani*, road signs. *Alama mpaka*,

A

alamina

boundary marker. *Alama kapa*, dummy element. *Alama za kiisimu*, linguistic notations. *Alama saidizi*, diacritic marker. *Alama matumizi*, usage label. *Alama za kiarudhi*, prosodic signs. *Tia alama*, put a sign. 2. marks, scores: *Alipata alama nyingi kwenye mtihani*, he scored well in the examination. (cf *maksi*) 3. seal. 4. speck, smudge, splotch. 5. stigma. 6. vestige. 7. index. (Ar)

alamina *n* (*n*) all creatures. Used in the expression: *Rabbil alamina*, God of all creatures. (Ar)

alamsiki *interj* (used at night times) goodnight; goodbye. (Ar)

alamu *n* (*n*) 1. flag. 2. signal of warning or danger. (Ar)

alasiri (also *laasiri*) *n* (*n*) 1. afternoon; the time between 3.00 pm and evening 2. the afternoon prayer performed by Muslims. (Ar)

alau *conj* see *walau*

alawensi *n* (*n*) allowance. (Eng)

albino *n* (*n*) 1. albino; a person with a congenital absence of pigmentation in the skin, eyes, etc. 2. any animal or plant lacking in pigment. (Eng)

aleikum *pron* (*n*) all of you: *Salamu aleikum*, peace be with you all. (Ar)

aleluya (also *haleluya*) *interj* a word or an exclamation for expressing happiness or joy: *Aleluya Kristo amefufuka!* Hurrah, Christ has resurrected! Christ is risen!

alfa *n* (*n*) 1. alpha; the first letter of the Greek alphabet (A, α) 2. the beginning of anything used in the expression: *Alfa na Omega*, Alpha and Omega, that is, the beginning and the end.

alfabeti *n* (*n*) the alphabet. (cf *abtathi*, *abjadi*)

alfafa *n* (*n*) bandage tied to a circumcised penis. (cf *kata*, *kizingatine*)

alfajiri *n* (*n*) 1. dawn, day break, sunrise: *Alfajiri kuu*, the main dawn. *Alfajiri mbichi*, the early morning between 3.00 am and 5.00 am 2. the early morning

alifu¹

prayer perfomed by Muslims. (Ar)

alfeni (also *elfeni*) *adj*, *n* (*n*) two thousands. (Ar)

alfia *n* (*n*) see *halfiya*

alfu *adj*, *n* see *elfu* (Ar)

alhaji (also *haji*) *n* a Muslim man who went to Mecca to perform pilgrimage; hadji, hajji, haji.

alhamdu *n* (*n*) see *fatiha*

alhamdulilah *n* (*n*) 1. (in Islam) all praise be to God. This is an expression of gratitude or happiness. It is sometimes used to express sorrow. 2. (*fig*) better, okay: *Nchi yetu sasa imekuwa alhamdulilah*, our country has now become better. (Ar)

alhamisi *n* (*n*) Thursday (Ar)

alhani *n* (*n*) see *lahani*

alhasili *adv*, *conj* 1. infact, as a matter of fact: *Mpishi alipika wali, mchuzi mboga, uji; alhasili, vyakula vilikuwa vitamu sana*, the cook cooked rice, vegetables, curry, gruel; infact, it was all delicious. 2. like, as, just as similar to: *Hucheza michezo mingi alhasili kandanda na hoki*, he plays many games like soccer and hockey. 3. in short, in brief, in a nutshell: *Alhasili, sherehe zetu zilienda vizuri sana*, in short, our celebrations went well. (cf *kwa ufupi, kwa muhtasari*) (Ar)

ali¹ *n* (*n*) descendants, offspring, offshoots. (cf *dhuria, aila*) (Ar)

ali² *adj* 1. prestigious, remarkable, impressive: *Nyuso ali*, shining faces. 2. glorious, dignified: *Alikuwa kiongozi ali*, he was a dignified leader. (cf *tukufu*) (Ar)

ali.a¹ *vi* put marks on the body usu by flogging. Prep. **ali.li.a** St. **ali.k.a** Cs. **ali.sh.a**

ali.a² 1. dry fish by using fire or sun: *Aliwaalia samaki kwa kutumia moto*, he dried the fish by using fire. 2. arrange fish on a wooden or iron frame. Prep. **ali.li.a** St. **ali.k.a** Cs. **ali.sh.a**

alifu¹ *n* (*n*) the first letter of the Arabic

alphabet (Ar)

alif.u² *vt* author; write a book: *Alialifu kitabu cha tamthiliya*, he wrote a play. Prep. **alif.i.a** St. **alif.ik.a** Cs. **alif.ish.a** Ps. of Prep **alif.iw.a** Rp. of Prep. **alif.i.an.a** (cf *andika*) (Ar)

alik.a¹ (also *alisha*) *vi* click, crack, crackle: *Mashini za kupigia chapa zilikuwa zikialika sana*, the typewriters were clacking busily. Prep **alik.i.a** St. **alik.ik.a** Cs **alik.ish.a** Ps **alik.w.a** Rp **alik.an.a** (cf *tatalika, data*)

alik.a² *vt* 1. invite, call, be invited. (cf *karibisha, ita*) 2. announce, inform, summon: *Alika vita*, summon to a battle. Prep. **alik.i.a** St. **alik.ik.a** Cs. **alik.ish.a** Ps **alik.w.a** Rp. **alik.an.a** (cf. *tangaza*)

alik.a³ (also *alisa*) *vt* confine a person (say in a house) for medical treatment; restrict, tie down: *Wazee walimwalika binti yao*, the parents confined their daughter indoors. *Alimwalika mgonjwa*, he confined the patient for medical treatment. Prep. **alik.i.a** St. **alik.ik.a** Cs. **alik.ish.a** Ps. **alik.w.a** Rp. **alik.an.a**

alika⁴ *n* (*n*) a young man/woman who has undergone initiation rites.

alikali *n*(*n*) a bandage tied to a circumcized penis. (*kizingatine*)

alik.i *vt* hang sth, suspend, hook up: *Amelialiki koti lake kwenye chango*, he has hung his coat on the hook. Prep. **alik.i.a** St. **alik.ik.a** Cs. **ali.sh.a** Ps. **alik.w.a** (cf *angika, ning'iniza, tundika*)

alimradi *adv, conj* see *ilimradi*.

alimu *n* (*n*) pundit, scholar, savant; a learned person. *Yeye ni alimu katika taaluma ya uhandisi*, he is a scholar in the field of engineering. (cf *mjuzi, stadi*) (Ar)

alish.a¹ *vi* see *alika¹*

alish.a² *vt* crack, make a crack; make an explosive sound: *Upepo mkali uliualisha ukuta wa nyumba ile*, the strong wind cracked the wall of that house. Prep. **alish.i.a** St. **alish.ik.a** Ps **alish.w.a** Rp. **alish.an.a**

alizeti *n* (*n*) 1. sunflower plant or seed, whose flowers are large and yellow. 2. the flower of this plant.

aljebra *n* (*n*) Algebra (Ar)

alkemia *n* (*n*) alchemy; a medieval form of chemistry (Eng)

Allah *n* (*n*) Almighty God: *Allahu Akbar*, God is Great. *La ilahi ila Allah*, there is no God but God. (cf *Mola, Mwenyezi-Mungu*)

Allah Allah *n* (*n*) see *Ala Ala* (Ar)

Allahuma *interj* Oh God! (Ar)

almari *n* (*n*) a chest of drawers; commode. (cf *dawati*) (Port, Hind)

almanusra *adv* narrowly: *Almanusra aanguke*, he narrowly fell down.

almaria *n* (*n*) embroidery of a hem. (Port)

almasi *n* (*n*) 1. diamond: *Mgodi wa almasi*, diamond field. 2. a precious thing like of that kind.

almuradi *adv. conj* see *ilimradi*

alofoni *n* (*n*) (*phon*) allophone (Eng)

alomofu *n* (*n*) (*morph*) allomorph (Eng)

altare *n* (*n*) (in Christianity) altar (Eng)

alumini *n* (*n*) (*chem*) aluminium (Eng)

aluminiamu *n* (*n*) aluminium (Eng)

alumnasi *n* (*n*) alumnus; a graduate of a school, college, etc. (Lat)

alwaridi *n* (*n*) see *halwaridi*

alwatani *n* (*n*) nationalist (Ar)

ama¹ (also *ima*) *conj* either... or: *Ama wewe au yeye ni wa kulaumiwa*, either you or him is to be blamed. (Ar)

ama² *interj* an exclamation of wonder; oh! (cf *ala!*)

am.a³ *vt* annex, affix, attach, connect: *Aliama ghorofa ya pili kwenye jengo lake*, he annexed a second floor to his building. Prep. **am.i.a** St. **am.ik.a** Cs. **am.ish.a** Ps. **am.w.a** Rep. of Prep. **am.i an.a** (cf *ambata*)

ama.a *vi* (of a cloth) be dry after being wet or washed: *Nililifua shati langu asubuhi lakini sasa limeamaa*, I washed my shirt in the morning but now it is dry. Prep. **ama.li.a** St.

ama.k.a Cs. *ama.sh.a*
amali[1] *n* (*n*) charm; witchcraft, sorcery. (cf *hirizi, sihiri*) (Ar)
amali[2] *n* (*n*) 1. action, deed: *Mtu wa amali njema*, a person of good deeds. (cf *matendo, vitendo*) 2. work, business, occupation: *Amali yake ni kuvua samaki*, his business is fishing. (Ar)
amana[1] *n* (*n*) deposit, security; a thing entrusted to someone: *Nimeiweka amana yake*, I have kept aside what he has entrusted to me. *Weka amana*, make a deposit, give a security. (Ar)
amana[2] *n* (*n*) money kept in a bank
amani *n* (*n*) peace, security. (*prov*) *Amani haipatikani ila kwa ncha ya upanga*, peace is never obtained except by fighting.
amani.a *vt* see *tumaini*
amara[1] *n* (*n*) urgent work, pressing business: *Alikuwa na amara na ndiyo maana, hakuweza kuzungumza na mimi vizuri njiani*, he had an urgent business and that is why he could not talk to me comfortably on the street. (Ar)
amara[2] *n* (*n*) assistance, aid: *Haja amara?* Is there anything I can do for you? (cf *msaada, auni*) (Ar)
amari *n* (*n*) (*naut*) hawser; a large rope or a small cable often made of steel for anchoring, mowing or towing a ship.
amb.a[1] *v* 1. speak, say: *Wambaje?* What do you say? (cf *sema, eleza*) 2. slander, abuse; speak against: *Mimi simpendi kwa vile anapenda kuamba watu*, I don't like him because he likes slandering people. Prep. *amb.i.a* St. *amb.ik.a* Cs. *amb.ish.a* Ps. *amb.w.a* Rp. *amb.an.a*
amba[2] *adv* perhaps, maybe: *Amba atafika wiki ijayo*, he will probably come next week. (cf *labda, pengine*)
amba[3] *interj* an exclamation of acceptance; acknowledgement of a particular issue; exactly.
amba[4] *pron* a relative stem denoting *who, which, where, when*.
amba.a *vt* 1. skirt past; pass near sth without actual contact: *Alikiambaa chombo gatini*, he made the vessel pass near the harbour. 2. stay away from; escape: *Aliambaa hatari*, he escaped the danger. Prep. *amba.li.a* St. *amba.lik.a* Cs. *amba.z.a* Ps. *amba.w.a* Rp. *amba.n.a*
ambalasi *n* (*n*) see *ambalansi*
ambalansi (also *ambalasi*) ambulance; a specially equipped vehicle for carrying the sick or wounded (Eng)
ambari *n* (*n*) ambergris: (*prov*) *Ukiona zinduna, ambari i papo*, if you see amber, ambergris is following behind i.e. if you see so and so, then his close friend is following behind. (Ar)
ambat.a *vt, vi* adhere to, cleave to, cling to, hold fast: *Ulimi wake uliambata kaakaani*, her tongue got her stuck to palate. *Alimwambata rafiki yake*, he clung to his friend. Prep. *ambat.i.a* St. *ambat.ik.a* Cs. *ambat.ish.a* Ps. *ambat.w.a*
ambatan.a *vt, vi* cling; cleave or stick together: *Vijana wale wawili wameambatana sana*, those two young people are very close. Prep. *ambatan.i.a* St. *ambatan.ik.a* Cs. *ambatan.ish.a* Ps. of Prep. *ambatan.ish.w.a*
ambatano *n* (*ma-*) appendage, attachment, union, cohesion. (cf *fungamano, shikamano*)
ambatish.a *vt* attach, fasten: *Aliziambatisha hojaji zake kwenye tasnifu*, he attached his questionnaire to the thesis. Prep. *ambatish.i.a* St. *ambatish.ik.a* Ps. *ambatish.w.a*
ambi.a *vt* 1. tell sby sth; inform: *Aliniambia kwamba mkutano umeahirishwa*, he informed me that the meeting has been postponed. 2. bid; *Fanya unavyoambiwa*, do as you are bidden. Prep. *ambi.li.a* St. *ambi.lik.a* Cs. *ambi.li.z.a* Ps. *ambi.w.a*, Rp. *ambi.an.a* (cf *arifu, juvya*)
ambik.a[1] *vt* 1. set a fish-trap out of nets or dried stalks during low tide: *Aliambika wavu wake kwa ustadi*, he

ambik.a²

set his fishing trap skillfully. 2. hook a bait: *Aliambika ili apate samaki*, he hooked a bait to catch fish. Prep. ***ambik.i.a*** St. ***ambik.ik.a*** Cs. ***ambik.ish.a*** Ps. ***ambik.w.a*** Rp. ***ambik.an.a*** Rp. of Prep. ***ambik.i.an.a***

ambik.a² *vt* soak in water, drench: *Aliambika nguo zake kwenye maji ya moto*, he soaked his clothes in hot water. Prep. ***ambik.i.a*** St. ***ambik.ik.a*** Cs ***ambik.ish.a*** Ps. ***ambik.w.a*** Rp of Prep ***ambik.i.an.a*** (cf *roweka, tosa*)

ambik.a³ *vt* meddle, intrude: *Alijiambika mambo yasiyomhusu*, he intruded into other people's affairs. (*idm*) *Kavaa kinu kajiambika mchi*, he is completely finished financially, etc. Prep. ***ambik.i.a*** St. ***ambik.ik.a*** Cs. ***ambik.ish.a*** Ps ***ambik.w.a*** Rp. ***ambik.an.a*** (cf *jiingiza, dukuza.*)

ambilik.a *vi* (of a person) be approachable; be ready to listen to advice.

ambis.a *vt* see *ambisha*. Prep. ***ambis.i.a*** St. ***ambis.ik.a*** Ps. ***ambis.w.a***

ambish.a (also *ambisa*) *vt* 1. (*naut*) put a boat alongside another esp by bringing a small boat alongside a big one: *Aliambisha mashua*, he brought the boat alongside another. 2. affix; add a linguistic element to a word or root: *Ambisha mwanzo*, prefix. *Ambisha kati* infix. *Ambisha mwisho*, suffix.

ambizan.a *vi* confer with sby on/about sth.

ambo¹ *n* (*n*) gum, glue, paste (cf *sheresi, ambwa*)

ambo² *n* (*n*) a contagious disease; epidemic.

ambrosi *n* (*n*) 1. ambrosia; the food of the gods and immortals. 2. anything that tastes or smells delicious. (Eng)

ambu.a¹ *vt* 1. remove, peel off: *Ambua gome*, peel off the bark. *Ambua ngozi*, shed skin (cf *bandua, bambua*) 2. (*fig*) get, gain· *Hakuna alichoambua ingawa alikuwa akienda shuleni kila siku*, he has gained nothing although he was going to school everyday. *Aliambua*

ami.a

patupu, he did not get anything. Prep. ***ambu.li.a*** St. ***ambu.lik.a*** Cs. ***ambu.sh.a*** Ps. of Prep. ***ambu.liw.a*** Rp. ***ambu.an.a*** (cf *fanikiwa*)

ambu.a² *vt* lift, elevate, raise, hoist: *Anapenda kuambua vyuma*, he likes weightlifting. Prep. ***ambu.li.a.*** St. ***ambu.lik.a*** Cs. ***ambu.sh.a*** Ps. of Prep. ***ambu.liw.a*** (cf *nyanyua, inua*)

ambukiz.a *vt* 1. infect, be infectious, be contagious: *Magonjwa ya kuambukiza*, contagious diseases. 2. (*fig*) (of a person's habit) be infected, be influenced: *Ana tabia ya kuropokwaropokwa na sasa ameshamwambukiza rafiki yake*, she has the habit of prattling and now she has infected her friend. Prep. ***ambukiz.i.a*** St. ***ambukiz.ik.a*** Ps. ***ambukiz.w.a*** Rp. ***ambukiz.an.a***

ambukizo *n* (*n*) see *maambukizo*

ambulansi (also *ambalasi*) *n* (*n*) ambulance (Eng)

ambuli.a¹ *vt* win: *Chama chao hakikuambulia kitu wakati wa uchaguzi mdogo*, their party did not win anything in the by-election. St. ***ambuli.k.a*** Cs. ***ambuli.sh.a*** Ps. of Prep. ***ambuli.w.a***

ambuli.a² *vt* see *ambua¹* and *ambua²*

amdelahane (also *mderahani*) *n* (*n*) a kind of soft cloth.

ameta *n* (*n*) (*elect*) ammeter; an instrument for measuring the strength of an electric current in terms of amperes. (Eng)

amfibia *n* (*n*) amphibia (Lat)

ami *n* (*n*) (also *amu*) 1. paternal uncle. 2. (*fig*) hedonist; a leisure-minded person. (Ar)

ami.a *vt* protect plantation or garden usu by making noises to frighten destructive birds and animals: *Aliliamia shamba lake kwa kuwafukuza ndege na wanyama wabaya*, he protected his plantation by scaring off dangerous birds and animals. Prep. ***ami.li.a*** St. ***ami.lik.a*** Cs. ***ami.sh.a*** Cs. of Prep. ***ami.lish.a*** Ps. of Prep. ***ami.liw.a*** Rp. ***ami.an.a***

amid.i *vt, vi* 1. decide, intend: *Aliamidi kwenda zake*, he decided to go away (cf *amua*) 2. depend, rely, count on: *Aliishi kwa kumwamidi ndugu yake*, he lived by relying on his brother. Prep. *amid.i.a* St. *amid.ik.a* Cs. *amid.ish.a* Ps. of Prep. *amid.iw.a* Rp. of Prep. *amid.i.an.a*

amikto *n* (*n*) 1. (in Christianity) amice; an oblong white linen cloth worn about the neck and shoulders by a priest at Mass. 2. an almuce. (Lat)

amil.i *vt* 1. work, manage, be occupied: *Anaamili kwenye kiwanda*, he is working in a factory. 2 do business: *Anaamili katika kuuza samaki*, he is in the business of selling fish. 3. take part in an evil deed: *Anaamili katika kuiba vitu vya majirani zake siku hizi*, he is involved in stealing his neighbours' belongings these days. Prep. *amil.i.a* St. *amil.ik.a* Cs. *amil.ish.a*. Ps. of Prep. *amil.iw.a* Rp. of Prep. *amil.i.an.a* (Ar)

amin (also *amina*) *interj* amen; so be it! may be it so! so it is! The expression is usually used at the end of a prayer or to express approval (Ar)

amina *interj* see *amin*

amin.i[1] *vt, vi* 1. believe, trust; have faith in. 2. have faith in sth, put confidence in: *Mimi sitamkopesha mtu yule pesa zozote kwa vile simwamini*, I will not lend that person any money because I don't trust him. 3. have faith in God and follow religious teachings: *Nimemwamini Mwenyezi Mungu*. I believe in God. Prep. *amin.i.a* St. *amin.ik.a* Cs. *amin.ish.a* Ps. of Prep. *amin.iw.a* Rp. of Prep. *amin.i.an.a* (Ar)

amini[2] *n* (*n*) a person bound to one by blood; sworn friend/relative: *Kaka wa amini*, blood brother. (Ar)

amini[3] *adj* see *aminifu*

-aminifu (also *amini*[3]) *adj* faithful, honest, dependable: *Mtu mwaminifu*, an honest person.

aminik.a *vi* be trustworthy, be acceptable.

Prep. *aminik.i.a* St. *aminik.ik.a*

aminish.a *vt, vi* 1. see *amini*[1]. 2. venture, dare, risk, brave: *Aliaminisha kusafiri kwa jahazi*, he dared to travel by dhow. Prep. *aminish.i.a* St. *aminish.ik.a* Ps. *aminish.w.a* Rp. *aminish.an.a* (cf *jasirisha, diriki, thubutu*)

amir.i[1] *vt* start, begin, launch: *Aliamiri shule ya binafsi kijijini*, he started a private school in the village Prep. *amir.i.a* St. *amir.ik.a* Cs. *amir.ish.a* Ps. of Prep. *amir.iw.a*. Rp. of Prep. *amir.i.an.a* (cf *asisi, anza*) (Ar)

amiri[2] *n* (*ma-*) commander, leader: *Amiri jeshi*, military commander. (Ar)

amirik.a *vt* be firm, be strong: *Uchumi wa nchi yetu umeamirika*, the economy of our country has become stronger. Prep. *amirik.i.a* St. *amirik.ik.a* Cs. *amir.ish.a*

amirish.a *vt* strengthen, consolidate, reinforce: *Rais ameuamirisha ulinzi wake*, the president has strengthened his personal guard. Prep. *amirish.i.a* St. *amirish.ik.a* Ps. *amirish.w.a* Rp. *amirish.an.a*

amis.a *vt* confine a girl at her monthly period. Prep. *amis.i.a* St. *amis.ik.a* Cs. *amis.ish.a* Ps. *amis.w.a* Rp. *amis.an.a*

amk.a *vi* 1. wake up, get up. (cf *zinduka*) 2. (*fig*) be awakened, be conscious, be clever, be aware: *Watu sasa wameamka na kwa hivyo, wanadai haki zao*, the people are now more awakened, and so are demanding their rights. Prep. *amk.i.a* St *amk.ik.a* (cf *erevuka, janjaruka*)

amki.a[1] (also *amkua*) *vt* salute, greet. Prep. *amki.li.a* St. *amki.lik.a* Ps. *amki.w.a* Rp. *amki.an.a* (cf *salimia, lahiki*)

amki.a[2] *vt* come before: *Walikuja usiku wa kuamkia Ijumaa*, they came in the early dawn of Friday

amku.a *vt* see *amkia*[1] Prep. *amku.li.a* St. *amku.lik.a* Cs. *amku.lish.a* Ps. *amku.liw.a* Rp. *amku.an.a*

amonia *n (n) (chem)* ammonia (Eng)
ampia (also *ampere*) *n (n)* ampere: *Ampia meta*, ampere meter. (Eng)
amplifaya *n (n) (elect)* amplifier (Eng)
ampere *n (n)* see *ampea*
amrawi *n (n)* see *hamrawi*
amri *n (n)* 1. command, order, directive: *Amri kumi za Mungu*, the Ten commandments. (cf *agizo, sharti*) 2. authority, rule, administration, order, will: *Amri ya serikali*, the government's order. *Amri ya Mungu*, the will of God. *Amri ya kutotembea usiku*, curfew. (Ar)
amrish.a *vt* command, give orders: *Kamanda aliamrisha wanajeshi wake wasonge mbele*, the commander ordered his soldiers to move forward. Prep. **amrish.i.a** St. **amrish.ik.a** Ps. **amrish.w.a** Rp. **amrish.an.a**
amsh.a *vt* 1. awaken sby: *Nilikuwa nimelala lakini sasa ameniamsha*, I was asleep but now he has awakened me. (*prov*) *Aliyelala usimwamshe*, don't wake up someone who is asleep, i.e. do not wake up sby who has not realized his rights, etc. 2 arouse, activate, stimulate. Prep. **amsh.i.a** St. **amsh.ik.a** Ps. **amsh.w.a** Rp. **amsh.an.a**
amu *n (n)* see *ami*
amu.a *vt, vi* 1. decide, determine, resolve: (cf *hukumu, azimu*) 2. arbitrate, reconcile, compromise: *Aliwaamua vijana wawili*, he arbitrated between two young people. Prep. **amu.li.a** St. **amu.lik.a** Ps. of Prep. **amu.liw.a**, Rp. **amu.an.a** Rp. of Prep. **amu.li.an.a** (cf *suluhisha*) (Ar)
amuali *n (n)* riches; plenty of wealth. (cf *mali nyingi*)
amuata *adj* dead
amur.u *vt* command, direct, commission, instruct. Prep. **amur.i.a** St. **amur.ik.a** Cs. **amur.ish.a** Ps. of Prep. **amur.iw.a**, Rp. of Prep. **amur.i.an.a** (cf *shurutisha, lazimisha*) (Ar)
amw.a *vt* suck, take in. (*prov*) *Ukikosa la mama hata la mbwa huamwa*, if you miss the breast of the mother, go even for that of a dog i.e. a second-rated thing is better than nothing. Prep. **amw.i.a** St. **amw.ik.a** Cs. **amw.ish.a** Ps. **amw.a** (cf *nyonya*)
amz.a *vt* greet someone in the morning: *Aliniamza nilipokuwa ninakwenda kazini*, he greeted me in the morning when I was going to work. Prep. **amz.i.a** St. **amz.ik.a** Cs. **amz.ish.a** Ps. **amz.w.a** Rp. **amz.an.a**
ana *n (n) (idm)*: *Ana kwa ana*, face to face
anagramu *n (n)* anagram; a word or phrase made from another by rearranging its letters e.g. *kasa*, sea-turtle - *saka*, hunt (Eng)
-anana *adj* gentle, soft, smooth: *Upepo mwanana*, a gentle breeze: *Maji mwananu*, calm water
anasa *n (n)* 1. luxury, self-indulgence, enjoyment: *Anapenda mambo ya anasa*, he likes luxuries (cf *raha*) 2. affluence, wealth. (cf *ukwasi, utajiri*) (Ar)
anatomia *n (n)* 1. anatomy; the science of the morphology or structure of animals or plants. 2. any detailed analysis.
anda.a *vt* prepare, ready, organize. Prep. **anda.li.a** St. **anda.lik.a** Cs. **anda.lish.a** Ps. of Prep. **anda.liw.a** Rp. of Prep. **anda.li.an.a** (cf *tayarisha*)
andalio *n (ma-)* see *maandalio*
andam.a *vt, vi* 1. follow up, be next in order, succeed in order: *Mwezi umeandama*, the new moon has sighted. (cf *fuata*) 2. begin, start: *Kufunga kumeandama*, fasting has started. (cf *anza*) 3. chase, pursue, fly after, run after, follow up: *Polisi walimwandama jambazi mafichoni mwake*, the police chased the thug to his hideout. Prep. **andam.i.a** St. **andam.ik.a** Cs. **andam.ish.a** Ps. **andam.w.a** Rp. **andam.an.a** (cf *fuata*)

andaman.a *vi* demonstrate; march; go in procession: *Wafanyakazi waliandamana mpaka kwa waziri,* the workers staged a procession to the minister. Prep. ***andaman.i.a*** St. ***andaman.ik.a*** Cs. ***andaman.ish.a.*** Ps. ***andaman.w.a***

andamano *n* (*n*) see *maandamano*

-andamizi *adj* tending to follow the next in order: senior, *Mhadhiri mwandamizi,* a senior lecturer. *Mtafiti mwandamizi,* a senior research fellow. *Waziri mwandamizi,* a senior minister. *Mhasibu mwandamizi,* a senior accountant. *Kiongozi mwandamizi,* a senior leader. *Mrakibu mwandamizi,* a senior superintendent. *Mshauri mwandamizi,* a senior adviser

andasa *n* (*n*) vivacity, animation, liveliness. (cf *furaha*)

andazi *n* (*ma-*) a kind of doughnut deep fried in oil.

andik.a[1] *vt* write, inscribe, chronicle; jot sth down. Prep. ***andik.i.a*** St. ***andik.ik.a*** Cs. ***andik.ish.a*** Ps. ***andik.w.a*** Rp. of Prep. ***andik.i.an.a*** (cf *rasimu*)

andik.a[2] *vt* arrange, prepare, set in order, lay out: *Andika meza,* set the table. *Alituandikia chakula,* he served us the food. Prep. ***andik.i.a*** St. ***andik.ik.a*** Cs. ***andik.ish.a*** Ps. ***andik.w.a*** (cf *andaa, panga*)

andik.a[3] *vt* used in the expression: *Andika tashtiti,* satirize

andikish.a[1] *vt, vi* see *andika*[1] and *andika*[2]

andikish.a[2] *vt, vi* register, enrol; recruit: *Aliandikisha kupiga kura,* he registered to vote. Prep. ***andikish.i.a*** St. ***andikish.ik.a*** Ps. ***andikish.w.a*** Rp. ***andikish.an.a*** (cf *rajisi, sajili*)

andiko *n* (*n*) see *maandishi*

andishi[1] *n* (*n*) see *maandishi*

andishi[2] *adj* written: *Fasihi andishi,* written literature.

andis.i[1] *vi, vt* 1. meditate, ponder; think deeply: *Alikuwa akiandisi juu ya mambo mengi,* he was pondering over many issues. (cf *waza*) 2. guide, direct; show how to do sth: *Aliniandisi jinsi ya kuutumia mtambo,* he showed me how to use the equipment. Prep. ***andis.i.a*** St. ***andis.ik.a*** Cs. ***andis.ish.a*** Ps. of Prep. ***andis.iw.a*** Rp. of Prep. ***andis.i.an.a*** (cf *elekeza*) (Ar)

andis.i[2] *vi* be animated, be vivacious, be blissful, be happy: *Huandisi anapopata habari nzuri,* he becomes happy when he gets good news. Prep. ***andis.i.a*** St. ***andis.ik.a*** Cs. ***andis.ish.a*** Ps. of Prep. ***andis.iw.a*** Rp. of Prep. ***andis.i.an.a*** (cf *furahi, farajika*)

anemia *n* (*n*) (*med*) anaemia; a deficiency in the number of red blood cells. (Eng)

anga[1] *n* (*n*) 1. outer space, sky, upper atmosphere: *Anga la samawati,* blue sky. *Anga za kimataifa,* international circles. 2. the heavens.

ang.a[2] *vi* 1. hang, hover, levitate: *Kima alikuwa anaanga kwenye tawi la mti,* the monkey was hanging from the branch of a tree. St. ***ang.ik.a*** Cs. ***ang.ish.a*** Ps. ***ang.w.a*** Rp. ***ang.an.a***

ang.a[3] *vt* bewitch at night time: *Alikuwa akiwaanga majirani zake,* he was bewitching his neighbours during the night. Prep. ***ang.i.a*** St. ***ang.ik.a*** Cs. ***ang.ish.a*** Ps. ***ang.w.a*** Rp. ***ang.an.a*** Rp. of Prep. ***ang.i.an.a***

ang.a[4] (also *wanga*) *vt* count, calculate, compute. Prep. ***ang.i.a*** St. ***ang.ik.a*** Cs. ***ang.ish.a*** Ps. ***ang.w.a*** Rp. ***ang.an.a*** Rp. of Prep. ***ang.i.an.a***

ang.a[5] *vt* (*naut*) keep guard: *Baharia alivyanga vyombo vyake baharini,* the sailor kept guard on his vessels during the night. Prep. ***ang.i.a*** St. ***ang.ik.a*** Cs. ***ang.ish.a*** Ps. ***ang.w.a*** Rp. ***ang.an.a*** Rp. of Prep. ***ang.i.an.a***

anga[6] *adj* see *angavu*

anga.a *vi* shine, glow, glitter: *Viatu vyake vinaangaa baada ya kutiwa rangi,* his shoes are shining after having been polished. Cs. ***anga.z.a*** shine: *Mwezi huangaza usiku,* the moon shines at night.

angaang.a *vt* examine, scrutinise, investigate, check: *Niliyaangaanga mananasi dukani kabla sijaamua kuyanunua*, I examined the pineapples keenly in the shop before I decided to buy them.

angalao *conj* see *angalau*

angalau (*angalao, angao*) *conj* although, even though: *Nipatie maziwa angalau kidogo tu*, Give me some milk, however little.

angali.a *vi* 1. look at, watch, see, observe, notice: *Alikuwa anaangalia mechi ya mpira*, he was watching a football match. (cf *tazama*) 2. examine, think, imagine: *Angalia jinsi ya kufika kule*, think how you will reach there. (cf *fikiri*) 3. be aware, take care, be careful, watch out, look out. *Angalia! Kuna jiwe mbele yako*, watch out! There is a stone in front of you. 4. guard, protect, look after, watch over: *Mlinzi aliiangalia nyumba yangu nilipokuwa safarini*, the guard looked after my house when I was away. 5. take special note (of): *Angalia kwa makini*, nota bene; note well St. **angali.k.a** Cs. **angali.sh.a** Ps. **angali.w.a** Rp. **angali.an.a** (cf. *tunza, linda*)

-angalifu *adj* careful, discreet, thoughtful, cautious: *Mwanasiasa mwangalifu*, a thoughtful politician. (cf *makini, hadhiri*)

angalili.a *vt* foretell; consult a soothsayer; read palms. St. **angalili.k.a** Cs. **angalili.sh.a** Ps. **angalili.w.a** Rp. **angalili.an.a** (cf *tabiri, bashiri*)

angam.a *vi* hang, suspend, swing: be in mid-air: *Popo alikuwa akiangama kwenye tawi la mti*, the bat was hanging from the branch of a tree Prep. **angam.i.a** St. **angam.ik.a** Cs. **angam.ish.a** (cf *ning'inia*)

angami.a *vi* 1. perish, be wiped out, be destroyed: *Watu wengi waliangamia kwenye ajali ya ndege*, many people perished in the plane crash. 2. be in entanglement, be in embroilment, be in danger, be in trouble. 3. suffer a loss, lose, be losing, run at a loss. Prep. **angami.li.a** St. **angami.k.a** Cs. **angami.z.a** Ps. of Cs. **angami.z.w.a**

angamiz.a *vt* destroy, annihilate, demolish, wipe out, ruin: *Mafuriko yaliwaangamiza wanavijiji*, the floods wiped out the villagers. Prep **angamiz.i.a** St. **angamiz.ish.a** Cs. **angamiz.ish.a** Ps **angamiz.w.a** Rp **angamiz.an.a**

angao *conj* see *angalau*

angas.a[1] *vt* arrest, catch, grab, seize, clutch: *Askari alimwangasa mwizi*, the policeman arrested a thief. Prep. **angas.i.a** St. **angas.ik.a** Cs. **angas.ish.a** Ps. **angas.w.a** Rp. of Prep. **angas.i.an.a** (cf *zuia, kamata*)

angas.a[2] *vt* chase, pursue: *Niliwaangasa mbuzi kutoka kwenye shamba langu*, I chased the goats from my farm. Prep. **angas.i.a** St. **angas.ik.a** Cs. **angas.ish.a** Ps. **angas.w.a** Rp. of Prep. **angas.i.an.a** (cf *fukuza, furusha*)

angat.a (also *tungata*) *vt* carry sth esp on the shoulders; take; bear a load: *Aliiangata mizigo yake*, he carried his loads on the shoulders. Prep. **angat.i.a** St. **angat.ik.a** Cs. **angat.ish.a** Ps. **angat.w.a** Rp. **angat.an.a** (cf *beba, chukua*)

-angavu *adj* 1. transparent, pellucid, limpid. 2. bright, clear, white: *Maji mangavu*, clear water. 3. clever, intelligent, quick-witted: *Mwanafunzi mwangavu*, an intelligent student. (cf *fahamivu*)

angaz.a *vt, vi* 1. see *angaa*. 2. fix attention on sth: *Angaza macho*, fix the eyes. 3. remain awake the whole night: *Aliangaza usiku kucha*, he stayed awake the whole night. 4. (*fig*) enlighten, illuminate, throw light on: *Nilikuwa sielewi juu ya jambo lile lakini sasa ameniangaza*, I was unclear about that issue but now she has enlightened me. Prep. **angaz.i.a** St. **angaz.ik.a** Ps. **angaz.w.a** Rp. **angaz.an.a**

ange *adv* alertly, vigilantly, ready; carefully: *Jeshi lilikaa ange*, the army was on full alert.

angem.a *vi* despair; be depressed: *Aliangema alipokosa kazi*, he became depressed when he failed to get a job. Prep. **angem.e.a** St. **angem.ek.a** Cs. **angem.esh.a** Ps. **angem.w.a** (cf *sirima*)

angik.a *vt, vi* hang up; suspend sth especially against a wall, tree, etc: *Aliliangika shati lake kabatini*, he hung up his shirt in the cupboard. Prep. **angik.i.a.** St. **angik.ik.a** Cs. **angik.ish.a** Ps. **angik.w.a** Rp. of Prep. **angik.i.an.a** (cf *ning'iniza*)

Anglikana *n (n)* Anglican (Eng)

ango.a *vi* give an illuminating light; dazzle. Prep. **ango.le.a** Cs. **ango.lek.a** Cs. **ango.lesh.a** Ps. **ango.lew.a** Rp. **ango.an.a**

-angu *adj, pron* my, mine. The root takes different forms depending on the class of the word in question: *Mzee wangu*, my parent. *Kikombe changu*, my cup. *Kengele yangu*, my bell.

angu.a *vt* 1. throw down, knock down, take down: *Aliangua embe*, he knocked down the mangoes. (cf *tungua, popoa*) 2. hatch out, incubate, brood: *Kuku ameangua mayai*, the hen has hatched her eggs. 3. prune, chop off, cut off: *Aliangua kucha zake*, she clipped her finger nails. 4. (*idms*) *Angua kilio*, break out wailing. *Angua kicheko*, burst out laughing. *Angua ndoto*, predict, foretell. Prep. **angu.li.a** St. **angu.lik.a** Cs. **angu.lish.a** Ps. **angu.liw.a** Rp. **angu.an.a** Rp. of Prep. **angu.li.an.a** (cf *pogoa, pelea*)

anguk.a *vt, vi* 1. fall down, collapse, drop: *Mtoto alianguka kutoka kwenye mti*, the child fell from a tree. (cf *poromoka*) 2. (*fig*) lose as in a business; be ruined, fall, go down, decline: *Biashara yake imeanguka*, his business has declined. (cf *poromoka*) 3. fail, flop, flunk: *Ameanguka kwenye mtihani*, he has failed the examination. Prep. **anguk.i.a** St. **anguk.ik.a** Cs. **angu.sh.a** Ps. **anguk.w.a** Rp. **anguk.an.a** (cf *shindwa*)

anguki.a *vi* 1. see *anguka* 2. apologise, beg, pardon, ask pardon: *Alimwangukia mwalimu wake kwa kosa alilolifanya*, he apologised to his teacher for the mistake he had made. 3. fall into: *Aliangukia kwenye kidimbwi*, he fell into the pond. Ps. **anguki.w.a** Rp. **anguki.an.a** (cf *taradhia*)

anguko *n* (pl *ma-*) downfall, collapse: *Anguko la serikali limewahuzunisha raia*, the collapse of the government has saddened the citizens.

angus.a *vt, vi* hurry, hasten, quicken: *Nilimpa kazi kuifanya na akaangusa kuimaliza*, I gave him work to do and he hurried to complete it. Prep. **angus.i.a** St. **angus.ik.a** Cs. **angus.ish.a** Rp. of Prep. **angus.i.an.a**

angush.a *vt* 1. see *anguka*. 2. topple, overthrow: *Waasi waliiangusha serikali*, the rebels overthrew the government. 3. (*syn*) *Angusha mtu*, let someone down: *Mbona umeniangusha?* Why are you letting me down? Prep. **angush.i.a** St. **angush.ik.a** Ps. **angush.w.a**

ani.a *vt* see *wania*

anik.a *vt* set out to dry in the sun or air; expose to sun or air: *Anika nguo zenu*, hang out your clothes to dry. Prep. **anik.i.a** St. **anik.ik.a** Cs. **anik.ish.a** Ps. **anik.w.a** Rp. of Prep. **anik.i.an.a**

aninia *n* (n) (*zool*) shrike; a conspicuously coloured medium-sized bird (family *Laniidae*) with a strong hooked bill. (cf *kipwe, tiva*)

anis.i[1] (*also taanisi*) *vt, vi* please, gratify, delight: *Maonyesho yaliwaanisi watazamaji*, the show pleased the audience. (cf *pendeza*) Prep. **anis.i.a** St. **anis.ik.a** Cs. **anis.ish.a** Ps. of Prep. **anis.iw.a** Rp. of Prep. **anis.i.an.a**

anisi[2] *adj* pleasant, luxurious, exciting: *Tamasha anisi*, an exciting festival. (Ar)

anjali n (n) waist belt: *Anjali ya ngozi*, leather belt.

anjaz.a vt 1. stretch, extend, spread: *Anjaza nguo hii mezani*, spread this cloth on the table. (cf *tandaza*) 2. annex, widen, tauten, extend: *Anjaza jengo hili*, extend this building. Prep. **anjaz.i.a** St. **anjaz.ik.a** Cs. **anjaz.ish.a** Ps. **anjaz.w.a**

ankara n (n) invoice, bill of sale. (Hind)

anna n (n) a one-sixteenth of a rupee, which is the coinage of India. (Hind)

ansari n (pl *ma-*) humanitarian; helper, Samaritan. (Ar)

Antaktiki n (n) (*geog*) Antarctic (Eng)

anthropolojia n (n) anthropology; the study of the human race esp of its origins, development, etc. (Eng)

antifona n (n) 1. antiphon. 2. anything composed for responsive chanting or singing. (Eng)

antiseptiki n (n) antiseptic (Eng)

anu.a vt take sth away from the sun, rain, etc.: *Umeanua nguo zako?* Have you taken off your clothes from the drying lines? Prep. **anu.li.a** St. **anu.lik.a** Cs. **anu.sh.a** Ps. of Prep. **anu.liw.a** Rp. of Prep. **anu.an.a**

anuai adj see *anuwai*

anuani n (n) see *anwani*

anuk.a vi clear up; stop raining: *Kumeanuka sasa*, it has now stopped raining.

anuwai (*anwai, anuai*) adj various, diverse, varied: *Kuna rangi anuwai za taa katika jengo hili*, there are lights of different colours in this building. (cf *tofauti*)

anwai adj see *anuwai*

anwani n (n) address (of a letter): *Andika anwani yako*, write your address. (cf *adresi*) (Ar)

anz.a vt, vi start, begin, commence: *Alianza kulia bila ya sababu*, she started crying for no reason. Prep. **anz.i.a** St. **anz.ik.a** Cs. **anz.ish.a** Ps. **anz.w.a** Ps. of Cs. **anz.ish.w.a** (cf *asisi, zindua*)

anzali n (n) ne'er-do-well, good-for-nothing; a despicable person: *Usiandamane na anzali yule*, don't associate yourself with that good-for-nothing fellow. (Ar)

anzish.a vt 1. see *anza*. 2. establish, set up: *Walianzisha chama cha ushirika*, they set up a co-operative society. Prep. **anzish.i.a** St. **anzish.ik.a** Ps. **anzish.w.a**

-ao adj, pron possessive adjectival root for the third person *their, theirs*. Its form depends on the class of the word in question: *Mtumishi wao*, their servant, *Mlango wao*, their door. *Shamba lao*, their farm.

aorta n (n) (*anat*) aorta; the main artery of the body, carrying blood from the heart. (Eng)

ap.a vt, vi swear, take an oath: *Waziri aliapa kwamba ataitumikia nchi kwa dhati*, the minister swore that he would serve the country sincerely. Prep. **ap.i.a** St. **ap.ik.a** Cs. **ap.ish.a** Ps. of Cs. **ap.ish.w.a** Rp. of Prep. **ap.i.an.a**

apish.a vt swear; administer an oath: *Rais alimwapisha waziri wake*, the president swore in his minister. Prep. **apish.i.a** St. **apish.ik.a** Ps. **apish.w.a** Rp. **apish.an.a**

apiz.a vt, vi curse; maledict, damn, execrate: *Mzazi alimwapiza mwanawe*, the parent cursed her son. Prep. **apiz.i.a** St. **apiz.ik.a** Ps. **apiz.w.a** Rp. **apiz.an.a** (cf *laani*)

apizo n (*ma-*) curse, imprecation (cf *laana*)

apostrofi n (*ma-*) apostrophe; the mark (') denoting possession, etc. (Eng)

aprikoti n (*ma-*) (*bot*) apricot (Eng)

Aprili n (n) April (Eng)

aproni (also *eproni*) n (n) apron; a protective or sometimes decorative garment worn over the front of the body and tied around the waist. (Eng)

apu.a vt, vi 1. break an oath. 2. retract an oath; recant an oath. *Daada ya* *mwezi kupita, waziri aliapua kiapo chake kwa rais,* after one month had elapsed, the minister recanted his oath of allegiance to the president. *Kuapa na kuapua,* vowing and then retracting the oath.

Arabuni *n (n)* see *Uarabuni*

arachia *n (n) (bot)* Fever plant; a heavily-branched perennial herb up to six feet tall with aromatic leaves. *Ocimum viride.*

araka *n (n)* arrack; sweet strong alcoholic drink in the Middle East usu made from rice, molasses, or coconut milk. (Eng)

araknida *n (n)* arachid (Eng)

arba *adj* see *aruba*

arbatashara *adj* see *arubatashara*

arbuni (also *rubuni*) *n (n)* advance payment, down payment; deposit (cf *kishanzu*)

ardhi *n (n)* 1. land, ground, soil. (cf *konde, shamba*) 2. earth, universe, world: *Usilete balaa katika ardhi hii,* don't bring mischief on this land. (cf *dunia*)

ardhia *n (n) (naut)* wharfage, port tax. (Ar)

ardhilhali (also *ardhilihali*) *n (n)* 1. application for employment, etc; admission to a school, etc.: *Alituma ardhilhali yake ya kuomba kazi katika shirika letu,* he sent in his job application to our corporation. (cf *ombi*) 2. resolution, declaration: *Mkutano ulipitisha ardhilhali nyingi,* the meeting passed many resolutions. (cf *azimio*) (Ar)

arhani *n (n)* see *arihani*

ari *n (n)* zeal, enthusiasm, initiative, spirit. (cf *ghera, shime*)

aria *n (n)* part, section, segment (cf *sehemu*)

ariani *adv* nakedly (cf *uchi*)

aridha *n (n)* job application. (cf. *ardhilhali*)

aridh.i *vt* annoy, disturb. Prep. ***aridh.i.a*** St. ***aridh.ik.a*** Cs. ***aridh.ish.a*** Ps. ***aridh.iw.a*** Rp. ***aridh.i.an.a*** (Ar)

aridhilihali *n (n)* see *ardhilhali*

arifi.a *vt* bid cards; state the number of tricks or points one expects to make before playing cards. Prep. ***arifi.li.a*** St. ***arifi.k.a*** Cs. ***arifi.sh.a*** Ps. ***arifi.w.a***

arif.u[1] (also *taarifu*) *vt, vi* inform, tell, notify, declare. Prep. ***arif.i.a*** St. ***arif.ik.a*** Cs. ***arif.ish.a*** Ps. ***arif.iw.a***, Rp. ***arif.i.an.a*** (cf *eleza, sema, habarisha*)

arifu[2] (also *alifu*) *adj* knowledgeable, well-read, erudite: *Alikuwa mwanasiasa arifu,* he was a knowledgeable politician. (cf *bahri, mjuzi*) (Ar)

arifiwa *adj* see *arifu*[1]

arihami (also *arhami*) *n (n)* maternal relatives: *Yeye anawapenda arihami zake,* he likes his relatives on his mother's side. (Ar)

arijojo *adv* 1. go astray, out of control: *Kishada kimekwenda arijojo,* the kite is out of control. 2. stray; away from the right path: *Mwanamke yule amekwenda arijojo kwa sababu ni malaya,* that woman has strayed because she is a prostitute.

ariki (also *ark*) *n (n)* essence: *Ariki ya vanila,* vanilla essence.

arkadia *n (n)* arcadia (Eng)

arki *n (n)* see *ariki*

arkiaskofu *n (n)* archbishop (Eng)

armade *n (n)* armada; a large number of ships or aircrafts. (Eng)

arobaini *adj* see *arubaini*

arshi[1] *n (n)* compensation given for physically injuring a person or causing one to bleed: *Walitoa arshi kwa kumwuumiza jirani yao,* they paid compensation for physically injuring their neighbour. (Ar)

arshi[2] *n (n)* 1. God's throne 2. imperial throne; royal throne. (Ar)

arteri *n (n)* see *ateri*

aruba (also *arba*) *adj n (n)* four (cf *nne*) (Ar)

arubaini (also *arobaini, arbaini*) *adj* 1. forty. 2. commemoration held within

forty days after sby's death. 3. a period of forty days after a woman has given birth. (Ar)
arubatashara (also *arbatashara*) *adj* fourteen
arubausitini *n* (*n*) a kind of card game, the winner of which must score over sixty points. (Ar)
arubii *adv* quick, fast, rapid: *Alikwenda mwendo wa arubii ili aliwahi gari la moshi*, he went fast in order to catch the train. (Ar)
arudhi *n* (*n*) (*poet*) prosody; the study of poetic metre and the art of versification.
arufu *n* (*n*) mane; the long hair growing from the top or sides of the neck of certain animals like horse, etc.
arusi *n* (*n*) see *harusi*
arzaki *n* (*n*) plural of *riziki*, plenty of fortune; providence; necessities of life. (Ar)
as.a¹ (also *wasa*) *vt* 1. forbid, prohibit, warn. 2. stop, prevent: *Alimwasa mwanawe kunyonya alipofika miaka miwili*, she stopped her baby suckling when it reached two years old. Prep. **as.i.a** St. **as.ik.a** Cs. **as.ish.a** Ps. **as.w.a** Rp. **as.an.a** (cf *kataza*) (Ar)
asa² *conj* see *asaa*
asa³ (also *wasa*) *n* (*n*) staff; a walking-stick.
asaa (also *asa*) *conj* maybe; incase: *Asaa, akafika mjomba kesho*, let us hope my uncle comes tomorrow. (Ar)
asadi *n* (*n*) 1. lion. 2. (*fig*) a gallant person; hero/heroine. (Ar)
asali *n* (*n*) honey: *Asali ya miwa*, sugar-cane syrup. *Asali ya tembo*, syrup made by boiling palm wine. *Asali ya nyuki*, bee honey. (*prov*) *Fuata nyuki ule asali*, follow the bee that you may eat honey i.e. follow someone who is useful in many respects so that you may gain from him something. (Ar)
asante¹ *n* (*n*) see *ahsante*

asante² *interj* see *ahsante*
asasi¹ *n* (*n*) the beginning; source; basis of sth: *Asasi ya kuchelewa kwangu jana inatokana na shida ya usafiri*, the reason why I came to work late yesterday was due to lack of transport. (cf *chanzo, asili*) (Ar)
asasi² *n* (*n*) institution: *Asasi ya ndoa*, the marriage institution.
asbestosi *n* (*n*) asbestos (Eng)
asfari *adj* yellow (cf *manjano*) (Ar)
ashakum (also *hashakum*) *adv* a word used before mentioning sth vulgar or offensive (Ar)
ashara *adj* ten (cf *kumi*) (Ar)
asharati *n* (*n*) see *asherati*
ashekali *adj* better condition after illness; healthy, fit, well: *Mgonjwa anajiona ashekali leo*, the patient is feeling much better today. (cf *nafuu, ahueni*)
asherati (also *asharati, hasherati*) *n* (*n*) adulterer, lecher, prostitute. (cf *mzinifu, mzinzi*) (Ar)
ashik.i¹ *vt* have a great passion for sth; be infatuated; be addicted to, be mad about: *Kijana yule anaashiki mchezo wa gofu*, that young person is mad about golf. Prep. **ashik.i.a** St. **ashik.ik.a** Cs. **ashik.ish.a** Ps. of Prep. **ashik.iw.a** Rp. of Prep. **ashik.i.an.a** (Ar)
ashiki² *n* (*ma-*) fan, aficionado, devotee: *Yeye ni ashiki wa mpira*, he is a football fan. (cf *mshabiki, mraibu, mpenzi*) (Ar)
ashiki³ *n* (*n*) libido, lust (cf *uchu, hamu*) (Ar)
ashirafu *adj* glorious, dignified, noble: *Anatokana na aila ashirafu*, he comes from a noble family. (cf *tukufu*) (Ar)
ashiri.a *vt* 1. signal; give a signal, make signal to; indicate: *Aliashiria kwamba alikuwa anaondoka*, he signalled that he was leaving. (cf *konyeza*) 2. wink, blink. St. **ashiri.k.a** Cs. **ashiri.sh.u**

Ps. ***ashiri.w.a*** Rp. ***ashiri.an.a*** (cf. *onyesha*) (Ar)
ashiya *n* (*n*) evening (Ar)
ashuhuri (pl of *shahri*) *n* (*n*) months (Ar)
as.i[1] *vt* disobey, defy, disregard, ignore, flout, rebel: *Askari waliasi*, the soldiers rebelled. (cf *huni, goma*) Prep. ***as.i.a*** St. ***as.ik.a*** Cs. ***as.ish.a*** Ps. ***as.iw.a*** Rp. ***as.i.an.a*** (cf *halifu*) (Ar)
asi[2] *n* (*n*) see *mwasi*
asi[3] *adj* disobedient, defiant, non-compliant
asidi *n* (*n*) (*chem*) acid: *Asidi radikali*, acid radical. (cf *tindikali*) (Eng)
asighari *adj* small, little: *Yeye ni mtoto asighari*, he is a small child for his age. (Ar)
asilani (also *asili*[1]) *adv* (used in a strict negative context) never, not at all: *Mimi sijawahi kula viazi vikuu asilani*, I have never eaten yams. (cf *abadan, kamwe*) (Ar)
asili[1] *adv* see *asilani*
asili[2] *n* (*n*) 1. origin, source, lineage: *Sielewi asili ya neno hili*, I don't know the etymology of this word. (*syn*) *Hana asili wala fasili*, he is a nobody. (cf *chanzo*) 2. behaviour, manners, conduct: *Ana asili mbaya*, he has bad manners. (cf *tabia, mwenendo*) 3. ground, reason, base: *Asili ya suitafahamu hizi haieleweki*, the grounds for these misunderstandings are inexplicable. (cf *chanzo*) 4. fundamental. 5. property. 6. (*math*) denominator e.g. in 5/8, eight is the denominator (Ar)
asili[3] *adj* original, primary, first: *Babu asili*, original material, original cloth. (Ar)
asil.i[4] *vt*. adopt; take into one's family through legal means and raise as one's child: *Msamaria mwema alimwasili mtoto yatima*, a good Samaritan adopted an orphan. Prep. ***asil.i.a*** St ***asil.ik.a*** Cs ***asil.ish.a*** Ps. of Prep. ***asil.iw.a*** Rp ***asil.an.a***

asilia *adj* original, indigenous, natural: *Miti asilia*, indigenous trees. (cf *asili*) (Ar)
asilikumi *n* (*n*) decimal; one tenth. (cf *desimali*)
asilimia *n* (*n*) percent: *Asilimia arobaini*, forty percent. *Asilimia kumi*, ten percent. (Ar)
asira[1] *n* (*n*) war captive, prisoner. (cf *mateka*)
asira[2] *n* (*n*) residue (Ar)
asiria[1] *adj* modern, up-to-date: *Anapenda kuvaa nguo asiria*, she likes to wear modern clothes. (Ar)
asiria[2] *n* (*n*) a modern person, a sophisticated person, a stylish person. (Ar)
asis.i *vt* found, establish, originate, begin: *Aliasisi chama kipya*, he set up a new party. Prep. ***asis.i.a*** St. ***asis.ik.a*** Cs. ***asis.ish.a*** Ps. of Prep. ***asis.iw.a***. Rp. of Prep. ***asis.i.an.a*** (cf *anzisha*)
asiya *n* (*n*) 1. a portion or part of a thing; piece. 2. sign, symptom.
asiyeona *n* (*n*) a blind person. (cf *kipofu*)
askari *n* (*n*) 1. soldier. 2. guard: *Askari polisi*, policeman. *Askari jela*, warden. *Askari wa mgambo*, militia man. *Askari wa kukodiwa*, mercenary soldier. *Askari kanzu*, a plain-clothes policeman. *Askari wa usalama*, a security policeman. *Askari wa usalama barabarani*, traffic officer. (Ar)
askirimu *n* (*n*) ice cream (Eng)
askofu *n* (*ma-*) bishop: *Askofu mkuu*, archbishop. (Eng)
asmini (also *asumini*) *n* (*n*) (*bot*) jasmine. *Shada la asmini*, a bunch of jasmine. (Ar, Pers)
aspireta *n* (*n*) aspirator (Eng)
aspirini *n* (*n*) aspirin (Eng)
asteaste *adv* slowly, carefully: *Alizichukua sahani asteaste ili zisivunjike*, he carefully carried the plates so that they would not break. (cf *polepole*) (Guj)
asteroidi *n* (*n*) asteroid (Eng)
astrolabu *n* (*n*) astrolabe; an instrument used by early astronomers to measure

the altitude of stars, planets, etc. (Eng)

asubuhi *n* (*n*) morning. *Asubuhi na mapema*, early in the morning. *Tangu asubuhi hadi jioni*, from morning until evening. (Ar)

asumini *n* (*n*) see *asmini*

asusa *n* (*n*) snacks or bites; food such as groundnuts, cashewnuts, roasted meat and fried potatoes usu eaten with alcoholic drinks such as beer, spirit, etc.

asuwadi *adj* black (colour) (Ar)

atami.a (also *otamia*) *vt, vi* incubate, sit on and hatch eggs. Prep. ***atami.li.a*** St. ***atami.k.a*** Cs. ***atami.ish.a*** Ps. ***atami.w.a*** Rp. ***atami.an.a***

ateri (also *arteri*) *n* (*n*) (*anat*) artery; any of the tubes carrying blood from the heart to all parts of the body. (Eng)

athari *n* (*n*) 1. mark, spot, dot; *Chui ana athari kwenye mwili wake*, the leopard has spots on its body. (cf *alama*) 2. scar, mark, injury, wound: *Ana athari ya kisu kwenye paji la uso*, he has a knife's mark on the forehead. 3. trauma, impact, psychological disturbance: *Kifo cha mumewe kililleta athari kubwa kwake*, her husband's death traumatised her. (cf *mguso*) 4. deficiency, defect, blemish. 5. influence, effect, impact, weight: *Fikira zake za ujamaa zililleta athari kubwa juu ya sera ya uchumi wa nchi*, his socialist ideas greatly influenced the economic policies of the country. (Ar)

athir.i¹ *vt* 1. damage, hurt, destroy, ruin. 2. act on, have an effect on: *Dawa ile inaathiri moyo*, that medicine has an effect on the heart. Prep. ***athir.i.a*** St. ***athir.ik.a*** Cs. ***athir.ish.a*** Ps. ***athir.iw.a*** Rp. ***athir.i.an.a*** (Ar)

athir.i² *vt* influence, affect, sway: *Tabia yake nzuri imeniathiri sana*, his good behaviour has influenced me a lot. Prep. ***athir.i.a*** St. ***athir.ik.a*** Cs. ***athir.ish.a*** Ps. of Prep. ***athir.iw.a*** Rp. of Prep. ***athir.i.an.a*** (cf *vutia, gusa*) (Ar)

ati *interj* 1. an exclamation that calls someone to pay attention, hey! *Ati wewe!* I say you! 2. an exclamation expressing doubt over sth: *Hah! Ati leo sikukuu*. Oh! Is today really a holiday? 3. an exclamation expressing contempt: *Ati hata wewe unataka kuingia mambo ya siasa!* Even you want to join politics!

atia *n* (*n*) 1. gift, present. (cf *zawadi*) 2. talent: *Ana atia ya kuandika mashairi*, he has a talent for writing poems. 3. characteristic, trait, attribute: *Hasira nyingi ni atia mbaya*, excessive anger is a bad trait. (Ar)

atiati *n* (*n*) hesitation, temporization.

atib.u *vt* censure, reprimand, condemn: *Alimwatibu mumewe mbele za watu*, she scolded her husband in public. Prep. ***atib.i.a*** St. ***atib.ik.a*** Cs. ***atib.ish.a*** Ps. of Prep. ***atib.i.w.a*** Rp. of Prep. ***atib.i.an.a*** (cf *laumu, kemea*) (Ar)

atifali *n* (*n*) babies (Ar)

atik.a *vt* transplant: *Aliatika mimea yake kwenye ardhi yenye rutuba*, he transplanted his seedlings in a fertile land. Prep. ***atik.i.a*** St. ***atik.ik.a*** Cs. ***atik.ish.a***. Ps. ***atik.w.a*** Rp. of Prep. ***atik.i.an.a*** (cf *kitia, pandikiza*)

atikal.i *vi* understand, know, comprehend, learn (cf *fahamu*) (Ar)

atil.i *vt* waste time: *Wakati ni mali, si vizuri kuuatili*, time is precious; it is not good to waste time. Prep. ***atil.i.a*** St. ***atil.ik.a*** Cs. ***atil.ish.a*** Ps. of Prep. ***atil.iw.a*** Rp. of Prep. ***atil.i.an.a***

atilik.a *vi* 1. be deformed, be disfigured, be incapacitated, be disabled: *Uso wake uliatilika baada ya kuungua vibaya*, his face was disfigured after suffering from severe burns. 2. be destroyed, be ruined, be wrecked. Prep. ***atilik.i.a*** St. ***atilik.ik.a*** Cs. ***atilik.ish.a***

Atlantiki *n* (*n*) (*geog*) Atlantic: *Bahari ya Atlantiki*, Atlantic Ocean. (Eng)

atlasi¹ *n* (*n*) atlas (Eng)

atlasi² *n* (*n*) satin; a kind of cloth mainly of silk that is glossy on the front and dull on the back.

atomi *n* (*n*) see *atomu*

atomiki *adj* atomic: *Bomu la atomiki*, atomic bomb. (Eng)

atomu (*also atomi*) *n* (*n*) 1. (*chem, phys*) any of the smallest particles of an element that combine with similar particles of other elements to form a compound; atom. 2. a tiny particle of anything; atom, jot.

atu.a *vt* surprise, flabbergast, shock: *Kifo cha ghafla cha jirani yangu kimeniatua*, the sudden death of my neighbour has shocked me Prep. ***atu.li.a*** St. ***atu.lik.a*** Cs. ***atu.sh.a*** and ***atu.lish.a*** Ps. of Prep. ***atu.liw.a*** Rp. ***atu.an.a*** (cf *shtua, shangaza, fadhaisha*)

au *conj* or: *Kula chakula hiki au kile*, eat this food or that one. (cf *ama*) (Ar)

au.a *vt* 1. survey, inspect: *Aliliaua shamba kabla ya kulinunua*, he inspected the farm before buying it. (cf *kagua, tazama*) 2. mark the boundaries, etc.; demarcate: *Aliziaua konde yake*, he marked the boundaries of his field. (cf *pima*) 3. track, trail, follow, pursue: *Aliaua nyayo za jambazi*, he followed up the tracks of the thug. 4. yield, produce, give fruits: *Shamba lake limeaua vizuri*, his farm has produced good fruits. 5. purify a woman after childbirth or menstruation; cleanse: *Walimwaua msichana yule mara tu baada ya kuzaa*, they cleansed that girl immediately after she delivered a baby. Prep. ***au.li.a*** St. ***au.k.a*** Cs. ***au.sh.a*** and ***au.z.a*** Ps. of Prep. ***au.liw.a*** Rp. ***au.an.a*** (cf *toharisha*)

audhubilahi *interj* 1. an expletive used by Muslims to supplicate God for his protection against evil by Satan. 2. an expletive used to express surprise. It carries the meaning of *Would you believe it!* (Ar)

auk.a¹ *vi* (of firewood or coal) be burning; *Makaa yameauka*, the charcoal is burning. Prep. ***auk.i.a*** St. ***auk.ik.a*** Cs. ***auk.ish.a***

auk.a² *vt* 1. reach the stage of a set period: *Yule mama ameshauka arubaini*, the woman has completed the forty-day period after giving birth. 2. start work on a new ground: *Ameiauka ardhi yake kwa ajili ya msimu wa mvua*, he has started clearing his land ready for the rainy season. Prep. ***auk.i.a*** St. ***auk.ik.a*** Cs. ***auk.ish.a*** Ps. ***auk.w.a***. Prep. Rp ***auk.an.a***

auk.a³ *vt, vi* develop, improve, promote: *Anajaribu sana kuiauka biashara yake*, he is trying his best to promote his business. 2. reach the stage of bearing fruit: *Mipapai yangu sasa imeauka*, my pawpaw trees have reached the fruit-bearing stage. Prep. ***auk.i.a*** St. ***auk.ik.a*** Cs. ***auk.ish.a*** Ps. ***auk.w.a*** Rp. ***auk.an.a***

aula *adj* better, superior: *Si aula kwangu kuwasema wengine*, it is not good for me to backbite others. (Ar)

auladi *n* (*n*) male children. (cf *wavulana*) (Ar)

aun.i¹ (*also awini*) *vt, vi* aid, assist. Prep. ***aun.i.a*** St. ***aun.ik.a*** Cs. ***aun.ish.a*** Ps. of Prep. ***aun.iw.a*** Rp. of Prep. ***aun.i.an.a*** (cf *saidia*) (Ar)

auni² (*also muawana*) *n* (*n*) assistance, aid, help. (cf *msaada, amara*) (Ar)

aunsi *n* (*n*) ounce (Eng)

aushi¹ *n* (*n*) life: *Hajala chakula hiki aushi yake*, he has never eaten this food before in his life. (cf *maisha*) (Ar)

aushi² *adj* permanent, long-lasting, enduring: *Nguo za aushi*, durable clothes. *Vyombo vya aushi*, long-lasting dishes. (Ar)

aviz.a *vt, vi* aid, assist, help: *Aviza masikini*, help the poor. Prep. ***aviz.i.a*** St. ***aviz.ik.a*** Cs. ***aviz.ish.a*** Ps. ***aviz.w.a*** Rp. ***aviz.an.a***

avy.a *vi* 1. abort. 2. squander: *Anapenda kuavya pesa zake*, he likes to squander his money. (cf *badhiri*)

aw.a *vi* trickle, sweat, drop; flow gently: *Nimetembea sana na sasa jasho* limeniawa, I have walked a lot and now I am dripping with sweat. Prep. *aw.i.a* St. *aw.ik.a* Cs. *aw.ish.a* Ps. of Prep. *aw.iw.a* Rp. of Prep. *aw.i.an.a* (cf *churuzika, tiririka*)

awali[1] *n (n)* first, beginning, start. (*prov*) *Awali ni awali, awali mbovu hakuna*, a beginning is a beginning, there is no beginning which is bad i.e. the assistance you get at the beginning however small it may be, is better than the one which comes later. (Ar)

awali[2] *adj* first, initial, beginning: *Mtu wa awali kufika hapa alikuwa dada yako*, the first person to arrive here was your sister. (Ar)

awali[3] *adv* initially, at the outset: *Awali tulikuwa na wahadhiri wachache lakini sasu wameongezeka*, initially, we had few lecturers but now they have increased in number (Ar)

awamu *n (n)* phase, term (Ar)

awesia *n (n)* (*naut*) a small one-or two-masted ship of the *Wasuri* (from Oman) with a perpedicular stem and stern but now, no longer functioning. (Ar)

awin.i *vt, vi* see *auni*

aya[1] *n (n)* a section of the text or holybook esp the Holy Koran; verse

aya[2] *n (n)* paragraph.

ayale *n (n)* (*zool*) hart, stag; a male of the European red deer especially after its fifth year

ayali *n (n)* family, kinsfolk (cf *dhuria, ahli*) (Ar)

ayami *n (n)* used in the expression: *Siku ayami*, many days (Ar)

ayari *n (n)* liar, rogue, impostor (cf *tapeli, mwongo, laghai*) (Ar)

azali *adj* eternal (cf *milele, daima*) (Ar)

azama *n (n)* see *hazama*

azim.a[1] *vt* borrow; lend, Prep. *azim.i.a* St. *azim.ik.a* Cs. *azim.ish.a* Ps. *azim.w.a* Rp. *azim.an.a* (cf *kopa*)

azima[2] *n (n)* charm, talisman, amulet (cf *talasimu, hirizi*) (Ar)

azima[3] (also *azma*) *n (n)* intention, aim, objective: *Azima yangu ni kuwa mhandisi*, my aim is to become an engineer. (cf *kusudio, nia, lengo*) (Ar)

azimio *n (ma)* 1. intention, purpose. 2. declaration, announcement: *Azimio la Arusha*, Arusha declaration.

azim.u[1] *vt, vi* prepare a charm: *Mganga aliazimu ili amgangue mgonjwa wake*, the medicineman prepared a charm to treat his patient. Prep. *azim.i.a* St. *azim.ik.a* Cs. *azim.ish.a* Ps. *azim.w.a* Rp. of Prep. *azim.i.an.a* (Ar)

azim.u[2] (also *azimia*) *vt, vi* intend, decide, resolve. Prep. *azim.i.a* St. *azim.ik.a* Cs. *azim.ish.a* Ps. of Prep. *azim.iw.a* Rp. of Prep. *azim.i.an.a* (cf *kusudia, nuia, dhamiri*) (Ar)

azir.i (also *adhiri*) *vt* disgrace, vilify, slander, degrade: *Aliniaziri kwa kunidai pesa zake hadharani*, he disgraced me by asking for his money in public. Prep. *azir.i.a* St *azir.ik.a* Cs *azir.ish.a* Ps. of Prep. *azir.iw.a* Rp. of Prep. *azir.i.an.a* (cf *komoa, fedhehi*) (Ar)

azizi[1] *n (n)* a valuable thing; rarity; precious thing. (Ar)

azizi[2] *adj* precious, valuable, venerated, worthy of respect: *Yeye ni mtu azizi*, he is a highly esteemed person. (Ar)

azizi[3] (also *laazizi*) *n (n)* darling, lover. (cf *laazizi, mpenzi, hababi*) (Ar)

azma *n (n)* see *azima*[3]

azmamu *n (n)* (pl. of *zimamu*), bridle. (Ar)

B

B, b /b/ 1. the second letter of the Swahili alphabet. 2. a voiced bilabial stop.
ba n (n) abbrev. of *baba*, father.
baa¹ (also *balaa, balwa, beluwa*) n (n) disaster, calamity, evil (cf *janga, maafa*) 2. an ill-omened person, a portentous person; jinx (cf *mkosi, kisirani, nukusi*) (Ar)
baa² n (n) bar (Eng)
baa³ n (n) a kick by a person who is asleep.
baada adv after, afterwards. (*prov*) *Baada ya dhiki, faraja*, after hardships comes relief. (Ar)
baadaye adv later on, afterwards, subsequently. (cf *kisha, halafu*) (Ar)
baadhi n (n) 1. some, portion, section: *Baadhi ya watu*, some people 2. (usu used in pl) borders, suburbs, sides, neighbourhoods, outskirts: *Yeye anaishi katika baadhi za ng'ambo*, he lives in the outskirts. (cf *upande, janibu*) (Ar)
baadia n (n) (in Islam) an optional prayer after the obligatory one is prayed.
baalagha n (n) 1. hyperbole; a deliberate exaggeration for effect, not meant to be taken literally. 2. rhetoric: *Maswali ya baalagha*, rhetorical questions.
baasili n (n) see *bawasiri*.
baath.i (also *buathi*) vt 1. resurrect: *Siku ya kubaathiwa*. the day of resurrection. (cf *fufua*) 2. be given prophethood: *Kubaathiwa kwa mtume*, the prophet's bestowal of prophethood. Prep. **baath.i.a** St. **baath.ik.a** Cs. **baath.ish.a** Ps. of Prep. **baath.iw.a** (Ar)
baba¹ n (n) 1. father, a male parent: *Baba Mtakatifu*, Roman Pope. *Baba wa Taifa*, the Head of State. 2. adult; a grown-up person: *Yeye si mtoto tena bali ni baba*, he is not a child now but a grown-up. 3. a name given as a show of respect and love.

bab.a² vt bind tightly, close firmly: *Aliubaba mlango*, he closed the door firmly. Prep. **bab.i.a** St. **bab.ik.a** Cs. **bab.ish.a** Ps. **bab.w.a**
baba mkwe n (n) father-in-law (cf *hau*)
babadu.a (also *babatua, babatoa*) vt 1. twist apart, wrap, yank, wrench, disfigure, turn: *Alimbabadua kuku na baadaye akamkaanga*, he wrenched the fowl and then roasted it. (cf *nyonga, songonyoa*) 2. remove the scum, crust, film, layer etc. of anything; detach: *Aliubabadua utandu wa maziwa*, he removed the scum of the milk. Prep. **babadu.li.a** St. **babadu.k.a** and **babadu.lik.a** Cs. **babadu.sh.a** Ps. of Prep. **babadu.liw.a**.
-babaifu adj muddle-headed, mystified, confused: *Mtu mbabaifu*, a confused person.
babaik.a vi 1. speak or answer incoherently due to fear, etc. (cf *gugumia, goteza*) 2. talk in delirium; talk in one's sleep. (cf *weweseka, hohosa*) 3. be confused, be baffled; be puzzled: *Sijui kilichomsibu kwani ninamwona anababaika tu*, I don't know what has happened to him because I find him quite confused. Prep. **babaik.i.a** St. **babaik.ik.a** Cs. **babaik.ish.a,** Ps. of Prep. **babaik.iw.a** Rp. of Prep. **babaik.i.an.a** cause to confuse. (cf *paparika, mahanika*)
babaiko n (n) confusion, bafflement, perplexity: *Babaiko la mwizi*, the confusion of the thief. (cf *hangaiko, fazaa, sumbuko*)
babaish.a¹ vi confuse, confound, puzzle: *Ulinibabaisha katika maelezo yako*, you confused me in your explanation. Prep. **babaish.i.a** St. **babaish.ik.a** Ps. **babaish.w.a** Rp. **babaish.an.a**
babaish.a² vi, vt 1. earn a living in a haphazard and non-professional way; do sth without actually possessing

the necessary professional skills; fumble: *Yeye si daktari; alikuwa anababaisha tu,* he is not a doctor but rather a quack. (cf *babia, bambanya*) 2. prevaricate, shrug off: brush sth aside, be flighty, be inattentive: *Nieleze jambo gani hasa lililotokea; usiwe unababaisha,* tell me exactly what happened; do not prevaricate. Prep. *babaish.i.a* St. *babaish.ik.a* Ps. *babaish.w.a* Rp. *babaish.an.a* (cf *beregeza, pambaniza*)

-babaishaji *adj* bogus, deceitful, spurios: *Viongozi wababaishaji,* bogus leaders.

babaje *n* (*n*) (*zool*) sea hare; a large sea slug (Genus *Aplysia*) with a rudimentary internal shell and a prominent pair of tentacles(cf *kojojo*)

babak.a *vt, vi* argue, dispute, debate, moot: *Anapenda kubabaka ovyoovyo,* he likes to argue for nothing. Prep. *babak.i.a* St. *babak.ik.a* Cs. *babak.ish.a* Ps. of Prep. *babak.iw.a* Rp. of Prep. *babak.i.an.a* (cf *shindana*)

Babakrismasi *n* (*n*) Father Christmas

babas.a *vi* be puzzled, be confused: *Akiulizwa maswali, hubabasa,* if he is asked questions, he gets puzzled. Prep. *babas.i.a* St. *babas.ik.a* Cs. *babas.ish.a* Ps. *babas.w.a*

babat.a *vt* tap; strike sth gently as a metal-worker hits a metal to make it thin: *Mhunzi alilibabata bati ili atengeneze taa ya kibati,* the blacksmith hit the metal gently to make a tin lamp. Prep. *babat.i.a* St. *babat.ik.a* Cs. *babat.ish.a* Ps. *babat.w.a* Rp. *babat.an.a* (cf *pigapiga, nyoosha*)

babatan.a[1] *vt* see *babata*

babatan.a[2] *vi* be stuck together: *Skonzi zilikuwa zimebabatana,* the scones were sticking to each other. Prep. *babatan.i.a* St. *babatan.ik.a* Cs. *babatan.ish.a*

babatiz.a *vt, vi* confuse; perplex: *Mpira ulimbabatiza golikipa,* the ball confused the goalkeeper. Prep. *babatiz.i.a* St. *babatiz.ik.a* Cs. *babatiz.ish.a* Ps. *babatiz.w.a*

babatu.a *vt* see *babadua* Prep. *babatu.li.a* St. *babatu.k.a* Cs. *babatu.sh.a* Ps. of Prep. *babatu.li.w.a*

babe *n* (*ma-*) a hefty person; giant.

babewana (also *babewatoto*) *n* (*n*) (*zool*) verreaux's eagle owl. *Bubo lacteus.*

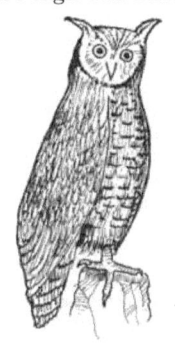

babewana

babewatoto *n* (*n*) see *babewana.*

babi.a *vt, vi* work on sth in a haphazard and non-professional way; fumble, bungle, botch: *Yeye si mhunzi; anababia tu kazi yenyewe,* he is not a metal worker; he is merely working on the job as an amateur rather than as a professional. (cf *babaisha, bambanya*)

babu[1] *n* (pl *ma-*) 1. grandfather. 2. an old man. (cf *shaibu*) 3. (usu) *mababu,* ancestors: *Mababu zetu,* our ancestors. 4. an expression used by women when calling one another.

babu[2] *n* (*n*) (*med*) a kind of a child's sickness which makes him or her undergo diarrhoea. (cf *mashuku*)

babu[3] *n* (*n*) a kind of cloth: *Babu pana,* a cloth that is thicker or twice the width of the usual kind and is of better quality. *Babu mdogo,* the cloth that is the opposite of *Babu pana.*

babu⁴ *n* (*n*) a male adviser in women's traditional dance.

babu⁵ *n* (*n*) 1. door. 2. chapter of a book; division, section. (Ar)

babu.a *vt* 1. strip off skin; bruise skin as with heat, fire, hot water or illness; scald. (cf *ambua, chubua*) 2. burn sth without actually cooking it properly: *Hakuzipika keki vizuri; kwa kweli, alizibabua tu,* he did not bake the cakes properly; as a matter of fact, he burnt them. Prep. ***babu.li.a*** St. ***babu.k.a*** and ***babu.lik.a*** Cs. ***babu.lish.a*** Ps. of Prep. ***babu.liw.a*** Rp. ***babu.an.a***

babuk.a *vi* be scalded, be disfigured: *Uso wake wote umebabuka,* her face is scalded. Prep. ***babuk.i.a*** St. ***babuk.ik.a***

-babuzi *adj* corrosive: *Kutu ni babuzi,* rust is corrosive.

bacha *n* (*n*) niche, alcove; recess or hollow in a wall. (cf *shubaka*)

bada *n* (*n*) stiff porridge prepared from fermented cassava flour.

badala (also *badili*) *adv* used with *ya* to mean 'instead of': *Badala ya yeye, alikuja mwakilishi wake,* instead of him, his representative came.

badamu *n* (*n*) (*bot*) almond (cf *lozi*) (Hind)

badani¹ *n* (*n*) the front or back piece of a *kanzu,* a long sleeved garment worn by men. (cf *kimo*) (Ar)

badani² *n* (*n*) the body of a human or an animal; trunk. (cf *mwili, kiwiliwili*)

badeni *n* (*n*) see *bedeni*

badhir.i *vt* squander, misuse, misspend, be a spendthrift: *Ukimpa pesa atazibadhiri,* if you give him money, he will squander it. Prep. ***badhir.i.a*** St. ***badhir.k.a*** Cs. ***badhir.ish.a*** Ps. of Prep. ***badhir.iw.a*** Rp. of Prep. ***badhir.i.an.a*** (cf *avya*) (Ar)

-badhirifu *adj* extravagant, spendthrift, wasteful: *Alikuwa mtu mbadhirifu,* he was an extravagant person.

badia *n* (*n*) see *bajia*

badil.i¹ *vt, vi* 1. change, alter, modify: *Ilibidi aibadili tabia yake mbovu ya kudharau watu,* it was necessary for her to change her bad habit of despising people. 2. exchange, change: *Badili fedha,* change money into smaller denominations or another currency. (*prov*) *Bura yangu sibadili kwa rehani,* my inferior dress of my size is better than another one of superior quality, but does not fit me i.e. It is better to have sth bad of your own that is useful to you than to have another one of superior quality of someone's else that is of no use to you. Prep. ***badil.i.a*** St. ***badil.ik.a*** Cs. ***badil.ish.a***. Ps. of Prep. ***badil.iw.a*** Rp. of Cs. ***badil.ish.an.a*** (Ar)

badili² (also *badala*) *n* (*n*) substitute, alternate, replacement; a thing given in exchange. (Ar)

-badilifu *adj* 1. changeable, alterable; liable to change: *Majira yamekuwa mabadilifu,* the seasons have changed. 2. erratic, capricious, whimsical, inconsistent: *Mwanasiasa badilifu,* an erratic politician.

badiliko *n* (*ma-*) transformation, change, alteration, modification: *Badiliko la hali ya hewa,* change of weather. *Badiliko la hali,* change of state. *Badiliko la umbo,* physical change. *Badiliko la sera ya serikali,* change of government's policy.

badilish.a *vt* exchange: *Alizibadilisha pesa za kigeni mara alipowasili nchini,* he exchanged the foreign currency immediately he arrived in the country. Prep. ***badilish.i.a*** St. ***badilish.ik.a*** Ps. ***badilish.w.a*** Rp. ***badilish.an.a***

badilisho *n* (*ma-*) transformation; change of state: *Badilisho la maumbile,* the transformation of the body.

badiri *n* (*n*) 1. different kinds of miracles. 2. the phase of the moon when it is seen to be fully illuminated; full moon (cf *mwezi mpevu*)

badiria *n* (*n*) see *halbadiri*

bado *adv* 1. not yet, not ready. The adverb *bado* is frequently used with the *-ja-* particle in what is known as the "Not-Yet-Tense": *Yeye bado hajaondoka*, he has not yet left. 2. till now, still, hitherto: *Bado yuko kwenye kikao*, he is still in the session. (Ar)

bafe *n* (*n*) (*zool*) puff adder; a large African snake which hisses or puffs loudly when irritated. *Bitis arietans*. (cf *kifutu*)

bafe

bafta (also *bafuta*) *n* (*n*) calico; any of several kinds of cotton cloth.

bafu *n* (*n*) 1. bathroom, washroom. 2. bath-tub.

bafuta *n* (*n*) see *bafta*

baghairi *n* (*n*) see *bighairi*

baghala[1] *n* (*n*) mule (cf *nyumbu*) (Ar)

baghala[2] *n* (*n*) (*naut*) a kind of two-masted dhow with a square ornamental stern and oblique curved stern. (Ar)

baghami[1] *n* (*n*) fool, imbecile, simpleton. (cf *mjinga, mpumbavu*) (Ar)

baghami[2] *adj* stupid, silly, dull-witted: *Yeye ni baghami*, he is stupid. (Ar)

baghau *adj* wicked, evil, infamous.

bagia *n* (*n*) see *bajia*

bagu.a *vt* 1. separate, disengage, put apart. (cf *tenga*) 2. discriminate, segregate: *Anabagua watu kidini*, he discriminates people along religious lines. Prep. *bagu.li.a* St. *bagu.k.a* and *bagu.lik.a*. Cs. *bagu.sh.a* and *bagu.lish.a* Ps of Prep. *bagu.liw.a* Rp. *bagu.an.a* Rp. of St. *bagu.k.an.a*

bahaimu (also *bahimu*) *n* (*n*) 1. an animal with four legs: *Mbuzi ni bahaimu*, a goat is a four-legged animal. 2. a brainless person, a witless person, a foolish person; good-for-nothing, *Yeye ni bahaimu na si ajabu, watu wengi wakawa wanamcheka*, he is good-for-nothing and so it is not surprising that many people laugh at him. (Ar)

bahaluli *n* (*n*) imbecile, idiot, fool. (cf *mjinga, mpumbavu*) (Ar)

bahamali *n* (*n*) see *bahameli*

bahameli (also *bahamali, mahameli*) *n* (*n*) a rich fabric of silk, rayon, nylon, etc. having a soft thick pile; velvet (cf *kiludhu*)

bahari *n* (*n*) 1. sea, ocean: *Bahari ya Hindi*, the Indian Ocean. *Bahari ya Shamu*, the Red sea. *Bahari ya Kati*, the Mediterranean sea. *Bahari Nyeusi*, the Black Sea. 2. (*fig*) vast, big, immeasurable. (*prov*) *Elimu ni bahari*, knowledge is vast. *Ana bahari ya nyumba*, he has a big house. *Usawa wa bahari*, sea level. 3. erudite, scholar, expert; a knowledgeable person: *Yeye ni bahari katika elimu ya mitishamba*, he is an expert in the discipline of herbs. (cf *aalimu*[1]) 4. a terminal syllable that appears repetitive in all the last line of *utenzi*, an epic poem. (Ar)

baharia *n* (*ma-*) sailor, mariner, seaman. (cf *mwanamaji*) (Ar)

bahasa *adj* cheap, inexpensive, low-price: *Bei bahasa*, cheap prices. (cf *rahisi*) (Ar)

bahasha *n* (*n*) 1. envelope: *Nilinunua bahasha ili niitie barua yangu*, I bought an envelope to put my letter in it. 2. satchet, bag, packet, bundle: *Niliona bahasha ya nguo njiani*, I saw a bundle of clothes on the street. (cf *furushi*) (Turk)

bahashik.a *vt, vi* 1. be misdirected, be obsessed, be intoxicated: *Mtu yule umebahashika katika mambo ya anasa*, that person is intoxicated by the pleasures of life. 2. be nonplussed, be dumbfounded, be astonished, be astounded: *Alibahashika aliposikia kwamba ameanguka kwenye mtihani,* she was nonplussed when she heard that she had failed the examination. Prep. **bahashik.i.a** St. **bahashik.ik.a** Cs. **bahashik.ish.a** Ps. **bahashik.w.a** (Ar)

bahashishi (also *bakshishi*) *n* (*n*) 1. tip, baksheesh. (cf *zawadi, hidaya*) 2. gratuity, douceur: *Licha ya mshahara wake wa mwezi, alipewa pia bahashishi,* apart from his normal monthly wage, he was also given gratuity. (Pers)

bahati *n* (*n*) luck, fortune, chance. (*prov*) *Asiye na bahati habahatiki,* an unlucky person will never be lucky. (Ar)

bahati nasibu *n* (*n*) lottery (Ar)

bahatik.a *vi* be lucky, be fortunate. (Ar)

bahatish.a *vt* 1. guess, speculate. 2. hazard, risk: *Alibahatisha kujiunga na vyama vya upinzani,* he took the risk of joining the opposition parties. Prep. **bahatish.i.a** St. **bahatish.ik.a** Ps. **bahatish.w.a** Rp. of Prep. **bahatish.i.ana** (Ar)

bahatisho *n* (*n*) speculation, venture, mission, attempt.

bahau (also *bahauu*) *n* (*n*) fool, imbecile, idiot. (cf *bozi, fala*)

bahauu *n* (*n*) see *bahau*

bahili[1] *adj* (*n*) stingy, parsimonious, mean, miserly: *Mtu bahili,* a miserly person. (Ar)

bahili[2] *n* (*n*) niggard, miser, skinflint. (cf *mchoyo*)

bahimu *n* (*n*) see *bahaimu*

ba.i[1] *vt* 1. elect someone to give him the leadership: *Wajumbe wote walimbai kuwa mwenyekiti wa chama,* all the delegates elected him as the chairman of the party. 2. support someone for an action; advocate: *Nilimbai katika kitendo alichotaka kukifanya,* I supported him in the action he wanted to take. Prep. **ba.i.a** St. **ba.ik.a** Cs. **ba.ish.a** Ps. of Prep. **ba.i.w.a** and **ba.i.liw.a** Rp. of Prep. **ba.i.an.a**

bai[2] *n* (*ma-*) see *buibui*[2]

baibui *n* (*ma-*) see *buibui*[2]

baidhati (also *abyadhi*) *adj* 1. white: *Msichana baidhati,* a white girl. 2. attractive, beautiful, glamorous, good-looking: *Mwanamke baidhati,* a beautiful woman. (Ar)

baidi[1] *adj* far, distant, remote, at a distance: *Yeye ni ndugu wa baidi,* he is a distant relative. (cf *mbali*) (Ar)

baidi[2] *adv* afar, far away, a long way off: *Anaishi baidi na hapa,* he lives far away from here. (cf *mbali*) (Ar)

baidik.a *vi* be separated, be apart, be aloof: *Amebaidika na jamaa zake,* he has remained aloof from his relatives. Prep. **baidik.i.a** St. **baidik.ik.a** Cs. **baidik.ish.a** (Ar)

baina *prep* 1. between: *Kuna suitafahamu baina yako na yeye,* there is a misunderstanding between you and her. 2. among, amid: *Walizigawa nazi kumi kumi baina yao,* they divided the coconuts in tens among themselves. 3. inter, across: *Baina ya mataifa,* across nations. (Ar)

bain.i (also *bainisha*) *vt* 1. expound, clarify, explicate, interpret: *Aliweza kuibaini maana ya methali,* he was able to explain the meaning of the proverb. (cf *fafanua, onyesha*). 2. recognize, realize, understand. Prep. **bain.i.a** St. **bain.ik.a** Cs. **bain.ish.a** Ps. of Prep. **bain.iw.a** Rp. of Prep. **bain.i.an.a** (cf *tambua, fahamu*) (Ar)

-bainifu *adj* evident, manifest, obvious, palpable, clear: *Jambo lenyewe limekuwa bainifu na ndiyo sababu ya sisi kuliunga mkono,* the thing itself has become evident and that is why we supported it.

bainik.a *vi* be discovered, be noticed, be found: *Imebainika kwamba yeye alisema uwongo,* it has been discovered that he lied. Prep. **bainik.i.a** St. **bainik.ik.a**

bainish.a *vt* differentiate, distinguish: *Aliweza kubainisha kwa ufasaha kati ya haki na dhuluma*, he was able to differentiate skillfully between right and wrong. Prep. ***bainish.i.a*** St. ***bainish.ik.a*** Ps. ***bainish.w.a*** Rp. ***bainish.an.a***

bairi *n (n)* camel (cf *ngamia, jamali*) (Ar)

baisani *n (n)* bison (Eng)

baiskeli (also *baisikili*) *n (n)* bicycle (Eng)

baisikili *n (n)* see *baiskeli*

baiti *n (n)* house: *Baiti Mal*, the house of wealth i.e. a treasure which preserves the property owned by Muslims. (cf *nyumba*) (Ar)

bajeti *n (n)* budget: *Bajeti ya mwaka*, annual budget. *Bajeti nakisi*, deficit budget. (Eng)

bajia (also *badia, bagia*) *n (n)* bhajia; a small cake usu flat, of mixed beans and pepper fried in a batter and eaten mostly with chutney. (Hind)

Bajuni *n (n)* some of the Swahili inhabitants of the North Coast of Kenya.

baka[1] (also *baku*) *n (ma-)* scar, spot, birthmark; mark on the body (cf *alama, doa, paku*)

baka[2] *n (n)* (*med*) ringworm; a skin disease, esp of children or animals producing red round patches. (cf *choa*)

bak.a[3] *vt* 1. grab, apprehend, seize, snatch: *Nilimbaka nzi*, I grabbed a fly. (cf *kamata, shika*) 2. rape: *Jambazi alimbaka msichana mdogo*, the thug raped a small girl. Prep. ***bak.i.a*** St. ***bak.ik.a*** Cs. ***bak.ish.a*** Ps. ***bak.w.a*** Rp. ***bak.an.a***

bakaa (also *bakaya*) *n (n)* 1. leftovers, remnants, remains, balance: *Bakaa za chakula*, the food's leftovers. 2. balance (of money). (Ar)

bakalhadi *n (n)* (*med*) gentian; a kind of medicine which comes from a sap of a special tree and is used to cure certain illnesses such as abdominal pains, gas stomach, and paralysis. (Ar)

bakari *n (n)* (*zool*) cow (cf *ng'ombe*) (Ar)

bakarikichwa *n (n)* (*zool*) bullhead; a kind of marine fish that has a large head covered with bony plates and spines.

bakaya[1] *n (n)* see *bakaa*

bakaya[2] *n (n)* 1. (*zool*) a kind of hyena fond of living near water. 2. a small hyena.

bak.i[1] (also *bakia*) *vi* 1. remain, be left over: *Kilichobaki ni kidogo*, what remains is a small amount. 2. remain behind, go nowhere, stay; *Wengine walibaki nyumbani*, others stayed at home. Prep. ***bak.i.a*** Cs. ***bak.ish.a*** and ***bak.iz.a*** Ps. of Prep. ***bak.iw.a*** Prep. of Cs. ***bak.iz.i.a*** (Ar)

baki[2] *n (ma-)* 1. left-overs, remainder, remnant, debris: *Mabaki ya ndege iliyoputa ajali*, the debris of the plane crash. 2. (*math*) remainder, difference; balance left in accounting; quantity left after subtraction or division. (Ar)

baki[3] *adj* used in the idiomatic expression: *Mtu baki*, a distant person; unconnected; unrelated.

baki.a *vi* see *baki*

bakish.a *vt* fail to complete sth; leave behind: *Aliubakisha wali aliokuwa akiula*, he left behind some rice which he was eating. Prep. ***bakish.i.a*** St. ***bakish.ik.a*** Ps. ***bakish.w.a*** Rp. of Prep. ***bakish.i.an.a***

bakiz.a *vt* leave behind sth; retain a part: *Bakiza chakula*, leave behind some food. Prep. ***bakiz.i.a*** St. ***bakiz.ik.a*** Ps. ***bakiz.w.a*** Rp. of Prep. ***bakiz.i.an.a*** (cf *saza*)

bako *n (n)* 1. the palm of the hand. 2. a measure by using the palm of the hand; handful: *Alinipa bako tatu za korosho*, he gave me three handfuls of cashewnuts.

bakoli *n (n)* 1. buckle; a clasplike ornament as for shoes (Eng)

bakora *n (n)* 1. a walking-stick with a crooked handle: *Bakora ya mdomo*, a stick with a crooked handle. 2. a stroke with a stick of this kind. 3. a fee given by a father to an expert when

bakteria / **bambakofi**

placing his son under apprenticeship. (cf *ufito*) 4. a kind of doughnut usu with printed edges.
bakteria *n* (*n*) very small things that are related to plants, some of which may cause disease; bacteria. (cf *kijimea*, *kijasumu*) (Eng)
baku *n* (*n*) see *baka*
baku.a *vt* 1. snatch, grab; take sth by force: *Aliubakua mkoba wa msichana*, he snatched the girl's purse. 2. strike: *Alinibakua makofi*, he slapped me. Prep. **baku.li.a** St. **baku.lik.a** Cs. **baku.lish.a** Ps. of Prep. **baku.liw.a** Rp **baku.an.a** (cf *nyakua*)
bakuli *n* (*ma-*) bowl; a large round container: *Bakuli la mchuzi*, curry bowl.
bakunja *n* (*ma-*) 1. imbecile, simpleton, idiot. 2. used in the idiomatic expression: a) *Kumteka mtu bakunja*, fool sby, b) *Kumteka mtu bakunja*, catch someone by surprise performing a bad action.
balaa *n* (*n*) see *baa*[1]
baladi[1] *n* (*n*) see *biladi*
baladi[2] *n* (*n*) an eloquent person. (Ar)
balagha *n* (*n*) rhetoric; the study of the technique of using language effectively 2. an eloquent person. (Ar)
balaghamu (also *balghamu*) *n* (*n*) (*med*) phlegm, sputum; saliva usu mixed with mucus from the respiratory tract and ejected from the mouth: *Ugonjwa wa balaghamu*, illness caused by sputum. (*idm*) *Toa balaghamu zako*, cool down your tempers. (Ar)
balari *n* (*n*) a kind of chisel. (cf *patasi*) (Pers)
balasi *n* (*n*) a large water-jar with a narrow neck.
balbu *n* (*n*) bulb (Eng)
balegh.e[1] (also *balehe*) *vi* reach the age of puberty; be matured. Prep. **balegh.e.a** St. **balegh.ek.a** Cs. **balegh.esh.a** (Ar)
baleghe[2] *n* (*n*) a person who has reached the age of puberty.

balghamu *n* (*n*) see *balaghamu*
bali[1] *conj* but, on the contrary, on the other hand: *Yeye si Mzungu bali ni Mhindi*, he is not a European but an Indian. (Ar)
bal.i[2] *vi* be unconcerned; a verb used to emphasize that someone is not bothered at all about an issue: *Hajali wala habali*, he is not bothered at all.
bali[3] *n* (*n*) ear-ring (Hind)
balia *n* (*n*) calamity, misfortune. (Ar)
balighish.a *vt* convey greetings, messages, etc.: *Nilizibalighisha salamu kwa jamaa zake*, I conveyed the greetings to her relatives. Prep. **balighish.i.a** St. **balighish.ik.a** Ps. **balighish.w.a** Rp. **balighish.an.a** (Ar)
balozi *n* (*ma-*) 1. ambassador, high commissioner. 2. (esp in Tanzania) ten-cell leader, headman. (Turk)
balungi *n* (*ma-*) 1. (*bot*) shaddock, pomelo; a large, yellow pear-shaped citrus fruit resembling a grapefruit. 2. grape-fruit (Pers)
baluni *n* (*ma-*) baloon (cf *puto*, *puritangi*) (Eng)
balwa *n* see *baa*[1]
bamb.a[1] *vt* 1. arrest, catch, apprehend, seize: *Askari alimbamba mwizi kichochoroni*, the policeman caught the thief in the alley. (cf *kamata*) 2. block, clog: *Wanamazingara waliibamba barabara*, the environmentalists clogged the road. Prep. **bamb.i.a** St. **bamb.ik.a** Cs. **bamb.ish.a** Ps. **bamb.w.a** Rp. **bamb.an.a** (cf *zuia*, *ziba*)
bamba[2] *n* (*n*) 1. a strip of metal. 2. a flat thin piece of anything: *Bamba la chuma*, hoop-iron. *Bamba la upanga*, the flat blade of a sword. *Bamba la kisu*, the flat blade of a knife, 3. bumper. 4. shell or scale of a fish. (cf *gamba*)
bamba[3] *n* (*n*) counsel, affair.
bambakofi *n* (*n*) (*bot*) fruits with two colours: red at the head and black at the tail.

34

bambalio *n* (*n*) worry, anxiety, uneasiness, trouble: *Tangu asikie kupotea kwa nduguye, amekuwa na bambalio*, since having heard that his brother got lost, he has been in a state of uneasiness. (cf *wasiwasi, wahaka*)

bambam *adj* (*colloq*) alright, okay. (cf *sawa*)

bambany.a *vt* 1. repair a bungled job; mend a spoiled work: *Mtengenezaji viatu alivibambanya viatu vyangu*, the cobbler repaired my spoiled shoes. 2. do a job in a haphazard, unprofessional way; fumble: *Aliibambanya kazi aliyopewa*, he did a job that was given to him in an unprofessional way. Prep. **bambany.i.a** St. **bambany.ik.a** Cs. **bambany.ish.a** Ps, **bambany.w.a** Rp. **bambany.an.a** (cf *babia, babaisha*)

bambatu.a *vt* tear apart, detach, unfasten, separate: *Aliubambatua ukwaju kabla ya kuula*, he detached the tamarind before eating it. Prep. **bambatu.li.a** St. **bambatu.k.a** Cs. **bambatu.sh.a** Ps. of Prep. **bambatu.liw.a** Rp. **bambatu.an.a**

bambik.a *vt, vi* soak in water; drench, imbue, sop, wet: *Alizibambika nguo zake chafu kwenye ndoo*, she soaked her dirty clothes in the bucket. Prep. **bambik.i.a** St. **bambik.ik.a** Cs. **bambik.ish.a** Ps. **bambik.w.a** (cf *ambika*)

bambo[1] *n* (*ma-*) 1. an iron instrument which is usu grooved and pointed and is used for drawing samples of rice, corn, etc. from a sack: *Piga bambo*, draw sth such as rice from a sack by using a scoop. 2. a kind of walking-stick.

bambo[2] *n* (*ma-*) 1. a kind of a long strip of plaited palm leaves from the leaves of *mwaa*, used for making coarse mats, baskets, etc. 2. a basket made from this kind of plaited palm leaves, used for holding corn and grain.

bambu.a *vt* strip off, peel off, pare, flay; *Aliubambua muhogo wake kabla ya kuupika*, he peeled off his cassava before cooking it. Prep. **bambu.li.a** St. **bambu.k.a** Ps. of Prep. **bambu.liw.a** Rp. **bambu.an.a** (cf *ambua, bandua*)

bambuti *n* (*n*) (*zool*) balloon porcupine fish; a kind of fish (family *Diodontidae*) with many spines. (cf *kitewatewa, nungu*)

bamia (*bot*) okra, lady's fingers. (cf *binda*) (Pers, Ar)

bamiz.a *vt, vi* 1. slam, bang, batter: *Alikibamiza kiti sakafuni*, he banged the chair on the floor. 2. thrash, trounce; beat soundly: *Waliibamiza timu yetu kwa mabao mengi*, they trounced our team by many goals. (cf *nyuka*) Prep. **bamiz.i.a** St. **bamiz.ik.a** Ps. **bamiz.w.a** Rp. **bamiz.an.a** (cf *nyuka*)

bamvua[1] *n* (*n*) springtide ; the tide occurring at or shortly after the new and full moon. It is usu the highest tide of the month.

bamvua[2] *n* (*n*) (*zool*) lamprey; an insect that bores into the flesh of fishes to suck their blood.

ban.a *vt* 1. squeeze, press, compress. (cf *finya, kaba*) 2. arrest, apprehend, catch: *Polisi wanaweza wakambana pindi akijaribu kutoroka*, the police can apprehend him if he tries to escape. (cf *nasa, kamata*) 3. close tightly; shut; *Aliubana mlango*, she shut the door. (cf *funga*) 4. (*idm*) *Bana matumizi*, cut down expenses. Prep. **ban.i.a** St. **ban.ik.a** Cs. **ban.ish.a** Ps. **ban.w.a** Rp. **ban.an.a**

banan.a *vt* be packed tightly together; be squeezed together: *Abiria walibanana kwenye basi*, the passengers were packed tightly together in the bus. Prep. **banan.i.a** St. **banan.ik.a** Cs. **banan.ish.a**

banang.a *vt* spoil work; botch, bungle, muff: *Ukimpa kazi ataibananga tu*, if you give him work, he will just bungle it. Prep. **banang.i.a** St. **banang.ik.a** Cs. **banang.ish.a** Ps. **banang.w.a** Rp. **banang.an.a** (cf *vuruga, haribu*)

banati *n* (*n*) girl, damsel. (cf *msichana, gashi, binti*) (Ar)
banawasi *n* (*n*) see *abunuwasi*
banda *n* (*ma-*) 1. shed, barn, shack, outhouse, outbuilding, lean-to: *Banda la ng'ombe,* cattle shed. *Banda la kuku,* hen's shed. *Banda la farasi,* stable. *Banda la gari,* garage, *Banda la ndege,* air-shed; hangar. 2. a kind of makeshift house. 3. the roof of a house.
bandali *n* (*n*) bundle; a number of things tied, wrapped or otherwise held together. (cf *robota*) (Eng)
bandama *n* (*n*) (*anat*) spleen (cf *wengu*)
bandari *n* (*n*) 1. harbour, port: *Bandari huria,* free port. 2. a town with a harbour. 3. a present given to sailors by their boss before he goes on a long journey: *Shali bandari,* presents given for this purpose. (Pers)
bandeji (also *bendaji*) *n* (*n*) bandage (Eng)
bandi *n* (*n*) 1. tack; a stitch of the coarser kind of sewing: *Piga bandi,* baste, tack. 2. width.
bandia[1] *n* (*n*) 1. doll, puppet, toy soldier. (cf *mwanasesere, karagosi*) 2. sth fake or not genuine, false: *Noti bandia,* fake note; counterfeit. *Cheti bandia,* fake certificate.
bandia[2] *adj* fake, bogus, not genuine: *Waraka bandia,* a fake document.
bandik.a[1] *vt, vi* 1. fasten to, attach, stick on, put on: *Bandika stampu,* put a stamp on. (cf *gandisha, shikamanisha*) 2. load, put on, lift sth on to another: *Aliubandika mzigo mabegani,* he put the load on his shoulders. 3. (*fig.*) be attached to a person; follow him about: *Amejibandika kwa jirani yake,* he has attached himself to his neighbour. *Bandika mtu jina,* nickname sby. Prep. ***bandik.i.a*** St. ***bandik.ik.a*** Cs. ***bandik.ish.a*** and ***bandik.iz.a*** Ps. ***bandik.w.a*** Rp. ***bandik.an.a*** (cf *ambatana*)
bandik.a[2] *vt* clear a debt by instalments or bit by bit: *Mdaiwa alilibandika deni lake,* the debtor cleared his debt bit by bit. Prep. ***bandik.i.a*** St. ***bandik.ik.a*** Cs. ***bandik.ish.a*** Ps. ***bandik.w.a*** Rp ***bandik.an.a***
bandiko *n* (*ma-*) attachment, fastening; the act of sticking sth on.
bandu *n* (*ma-*) a chip of wood; a splinter of wood. (*prov*) *Bandu bandu humaliza gogo,* chip chip finishes the log, i.e. constant dripping wears away a log.
bandu.a *vt* detach, unfasten, remove, disengage: *Aliibandua karatasi ukutani,* he removed a paper from the wall. Prep. ***bandu.li.a*** St. ***bandu.k.a*** and ***bandu.lik.a*** Cs. ***bandu.lish.a*** Ps. ***bandu.liw.a*** Rp. ***bandu.an.a*** Rp. of Prep. ***bandu.li.an.a*** (cf *gandua*)
banduk.a *vi* be detached, be peeled off: *Plasta imebanduka mguuni,* the plaster has detached from the leg Prep. ***banduk.i.a*** St. ***banduk.ik.a*** Cs. ***banduk.ish.a*** (cf *ganduka*)
banduru *n* (*n*) (*naut*) bilge; a place in a ship's hold where dirty water is bailed out. (cf *ngama*)
bangaiz.a *vt* maintain a living by doing different types of small casual jobs. Prep. ***bangaiz.i.a*** St. ***bangaiz.ik.a*** Cs. ***bangaiz.ish.a*** Ps ***bangaiz.w.a***
bang'ang'a *n* (*n*) (*zool*) a wild animal of the civet cat family.
bangaya *n* (*n*) (*naut*) a vessel's hull under construction.
bangaza[1] *n* (*n*) a person who keeps watch the whole night; watchman.
bangaz.a[2] *vi* leave the door open in expectation of sth: *Alibangaza usiku kucha akimsubiri mgeni wake,* he left the door open the whole night in expectation of his guest. Prep. ***bangaz.i.a*** St. ***bangaz.ik.a*** Cs. ***bangaz.ish.a***
bange *n* (*n*) (*zool*) a kind of fish with a pungent odour
bangi *n* (*n*) hashish, bhang. (cf *hashishi*) (Hind)
bangili *n* (*n*) bangle, armlet, bracelet (Hind)
bango[1] *n* (*ma-*) placard, poster.
bango[2] *n* (*ma-*) mudguard, fender (cf *madigadi*)

bango³ n (ma-) (bot) the stem of a coconut leaf.
bango⁴ n (ma-) board: *Jalidi kwa bango*, bind in cloth boards.
bangu¹ n (n) war, fighting, clash, hostility: *Shamiri bangu*, start the war. *Cheza bangu*, precipitate the war.
bangu² n (n) used in the expression: *Liwa bangu*, be deceived, be fooled.
bangu.a vt shell a nut like that of a groundnut, cashewnut, etc.: *Alizila karanga huku akizibangua*, he ate the groundnuts while shelling them. Prep. **bangu.li.a** St. **bangu.k.a** and **bangu.lik.a** Cs. **bangu.lish.a** Ps. of Prep. **bangu.liw.a** Rp. of Prep. **bangu.li.an .a** (cf *vunja*, *pasua*)
banguko n (ma-) avalanche.
banguzi n (n) ulcer; an incurable disease. (cf *dondandugu*)
bangwa n (ma-) a house under construction; an unfinished construction. (cf *boma*)
bani.a¹ vt see *bana*
bani.a² vt, vi become stingy, be miserly: *Mtu yule anabania sana pesa zake*, that person does not spend his money freely. St. **bani.k.a** Cs. **bani.sh.a** Ps. of Prep. **ban.iw.a** Rp. of Prep. **ban.i.an.a** (cf *zuia*)
Baniani n (ma-) Hindu; a follower of Hinduism.
-banifu adj unpaid, outstanding: *Ana deni banifu la shilingi milioni moja*, she has an outstanding debt of one million shillings.
banik.a¹ vt see *bana*
banik.a² vt grill; set to roast meat or fish on fire by using sticks. Prep. **banik.i.a** St. **banik.ik.a** Cs. **banik.ish.a** Ps. **banik.w.a** Rp. **banik.an.a** (cf *choma*)
banio n (ma-) see *bano*
banj.a vt, vi 1. crack, crackle, split, break off: *Alizibanja njugu*, he cracked the nuts. (cf *tema*, *vunja*, *kata*) 2. hit, beat, strike: *Alikibanja sana chuma mpaka kikavunjika*, he hit the iron hard several times until it broke down. Prep. **banj.i.a** St. **banj.ik.a** Cs. **banj.ish.a** Ps. **banj.w.a** Rp. **banj. an.a**
banjo n (n) (mus) banjo; a kind of stringed musical instrument with a long neck and a round body.

banjo

banju.a vt (colloq.) defeat, thrash, beat: *Tuliibanjua timu yao*, we defeated their team. Prep. **banju.li.a** St. **banju.k.a** Cs. **banju.sh.a** Ps. of Prep. **banju.liw.a** Rp. **banju.an.a** (cf *nyuka*)
banka n (n) a folding bed of a soldier.
bano (also *banio*) n (ma-) cramp, clamp, vice. (cf *gango*)
bantamu n (n) bantom: *Uzito wa bantamu*, bantom weight. (Eng)
banu.a¹ vt, vi unfasten, untighten, undo: *Aliubanua mlango*, he unfastened the door. Prep. **banu.li.a** St. **banu.k.a** and **banu.lik.a** Cs. **banu.lish.a** Ps. **banu.liw.a** Rp. **banu.an.a** (cf *legeza*)
banu.a² vt remove meat or fish from its stick split. Prep. **banu.li.a** St. **banu.k.a** and **banu.lik.a** Cs. **banu.liw.a** Rp. **banu.an.a**
Banyani n (ma-) see *Baniani*
banz.a vt, vi hide, slink, sidle: *Alijibanza nyuma ya miti ili watu wasimwone*, he hid himself behind the trees so that people could not see him. Prep. **banz.i.a** St. **banz.ik.a** Cs. **banz.ish.a** Ps. **banz.w.a** Rp. **banz.an.a** (cf *ficha*)
bao¹ (also *ubao*) n (n) 1. board, plank, beam. 2. platform, dais, stage.
bao² n (ma-) 1. a playing-board for chess, draughts, cards, etc.: *Cheza bao*, play chess. 2. the game itself; checkers, draughts.

bao³ n (ma-) a divining board. Also called *ramli* and *kibunzi*: *Piga bao*, consult a diviner.

bao⁴ n (ma-) goal, score: *Funga bao*, score a goal. *Bao la kuongoza*, a leading goal. *Bao la kufutia machozi*, a lone goal. (cf *goli*, *dungu*)

bapa n (ma-) a flat or slightly rounded surface. *Bapa la kisu*, the flat blade of a knife. *Bapa la uso*, broad forehead or broad cheek.

bara n (ma-) 1. continent; land in general: *Bara la Afrika*, the continent of Africa. 2. hinterland, the mainland, interior: *Tanzania bara*, Tanzania mainland. 3. land as opposed to sea: *Bara Hindi*, Indian ocean.

bara'bara¹ n (n) 1. highway, roadway. 2. mainroad.

ba'rabara² adv perfectly, precisely, accurately: *Aliifanya kazi yangu barabara*, he did my work perfectly. (cf *sawasawa*, *vizuri*)

ba'rabara³ adj perfect, good, precise.

baradhuli n (n) 1. an impudent, insolent or a disrespectful person. (cf *mfidhuli*) 2. simpleton, idiot, fool. (cf *mjinga*, *mpumbavu*) 3. gay, homosexual. (cf *hanithi*, *shoga*) (Ar)

barafu n (n) ice: *Reli za barafu*, ice skate. (Ar)

baragumu n (n) a horn used in traditional dances for giving signals or information and sounded by blowing through a hole near the small end; horn, bungle, trumpet. (cf *parapanda*, *gunda*)

baraguz.a vi shrug off, prevaricate, brush sth aside: *Kila akiulizwa swali, hupenda kujibaraguza*, whenever he is asked a question, he likes to prevaricate. Prep. **baraguz.i.a** St. **baraguz.ik.a** Cs. **baraguz.ish.a** Ps. **baraguz.w.a** (cf *gangaiza*, *pambaniza*)

barai n (n) (naut) see *baraji*

baraji (also *barai*) n (n) (naut) tripping line which is attached to aft arm of the main yard, coming down and serving to adjust the position thereof in some of the ship's manoeuvres e.g. take the yard from the weather side to the lee side (in convent land craft). (Ar)

baraka n (n) 1. blessing. 2. abundance, prosperity, riches, affluence, wealth: *Mwaka jana, kulikuwa na baraka ya chakula*, there was plenty of food last year. (cf *neema*) 3. abundance of anything: *Ana baraka ya majumba*, he has many houses. *Ana baraka ya watoto*, he has many children. (Ar)

barakala n (ma-) sycophant, flatterer, fawner. (cf *shawishi*)

barakinya n (n) (naut) a two-masted ship with square sails; brig, schooner. (Port)

barakoa n (n) a kind of veil worn by some women to cover the face down to the mouth, except the eyes. (cf *dusumali*, *utaji*, *shiraa*) (Ar)

baramaki n (ma-) 1. a person pretending to know sth while in fact he does not know; quack, charlatan, mountebank: *Yeye si tabibu hasa; ni baramaki tu*, he is not a real doctor; he just pretends to know about medicine i.e. he is just a quack. 2. rogue, trickster, impostor. (cf *mjanja*) (Pers and Ar)

barangeni (also *burangeni*) n (n) (naut) a kind of dhow with two colours or with a white stripe. (Pers)

barare n (n) see *parare*

barasati (also *baresati*) n (n) a kind of coloured dress.

barasi (also *balasi*) n (n) (med) vitiligo; a skin disorder that causes loss of pigment with light-coloured patches on the skin. (cf *mbalanga*, *manawa*) (Ar)

baraste n (n) a well-constructed road. (Ar)

barawai n (n) see *mbayuwayu*

barawaji n (n) a kind of cloth like a silk shawl which is worn round the waist. (Ar)

baraza n (n) 1. verandah, porch, gallery.

2. council: *Baraza la Chuo Kikuu*, University Council. *Baraza la Usalama*, Security Council. *Baraza la Mawaziri*, the Council of Ministers. 3. assembly; a meeting of people usu for conversation 4. lawcourt; a court of law: *Baraza la mahakimu*, a court of judges. 5. college: *Baraza la makadinali*, Sacred College; College of Cardinals; the body of Cardinals of the Roman Catholic Church responsible for the election of Pope. 6. sitting, session: *Baraza refu*, a long session. (Ar)

barazahi (also *barazakhi, barzakhi*) *n* (*n*) 1. (*In Islam*) the place of the dead; the grave. 2. the state of departed souls between death and judgement. (Ar)

barazakhi *n* (*n*) see *barazahi*

bardani *n* (*n*) a weighing machine without anything in it; tare. (Ar)

bar.i[1] *vi* (usu used in the reflexive form) avoid, escape: *Alijibari na hatari*, he escaped the danger. (cf *kwepa, epa*)

bar.i[2] *vt* push off a canoe from the shore; steer ship: *Alibari mashua yake ilipokuwa kwenye hatari*, he steered his boat away from danger. Prep. *bar.i.a* St. *bar.ik.a* Cs. *bar.ish.a* Ps. *bar.iw.a* (cf *tanua*) (Ar)

bari[3] *n* (*n*) (*chem*) barium (Eng)

baridi[1] *n* (*n*) 1. cold, chill: *Vita baridi*, cold war. *Mgomo baridi*, go-slow at work. (cf *mzizimo*) 2. atmospheric condition of coldness usu found in swampy areas or after it has rained in a particular place e.g. inside a building. 3. a kind of disease namely, paralysis: *Baridi yabisi*, rheumatism. (cf *kiharusi*) 4. gentleness, mildness calmness, coolness: *Maneno baridi*, gentle words. 5. sweetness, freshness, deliciousness: *Maji baridi*, fresh water. *Sigara baridi*, menthol cigarettes; mild cigarettes. (Ar)

baridi[2] *adj* 1. ice, cold, frosty, chilly. 2. cool, calm, quiet: *Wewe ni mtu baridi*, you are cool. 3. withdrawn, impassive, not cheerful: *Mapokezi yalikuwa baridi*, the reception was. (Ar)

barik.i[1] *vt* 1. bless, prosper, glorify, dignify: *Mungu aibariki Afrika*, may God bless Africa. 2. christen, baptize. Prep. *barik.i.a* St. *barik.ik.a* Cs. *barik.ish.a* Ps. of Prep. *barik.i.w.a* (Ar)

barik.i[2] *vi* suffice; be sufficient, be adequate: *Chakula kimebariki*, the food is sufficient. Prep. *barik.i.a* St. *barik.ik.a* Cs. *barik.ish.a* Ps. of Prep. *barik.iw.a* (cf *tosha, kifu*) (Ar)

bariki.a *vt* (of a salesman or an auctioneer) sell sth to someone at a reasonable price: *Mwenyeduka alimbarikia nguo mteja wake*, the shopkeeper sold clothes to his customer at a reasonable price. St. *barik.ik.a* Cs. *bariki.sh.a* Ps. *bariki.w.a* Rp. *barik.i.an.a*

bariyo *n* (*n*) last evening's meal left-overs. (cf *mwiku, kiporo*) (Ar)

bariz.i *vi* (of people) relax; sit out of doors and chat: *Wazee wale hubarizi barazani saa za jioni*, those old people sit and chat on the verandah in the evenings. 2. sit out in the cool; get some fresh air. Prep. *bariz.i.a* St. *bariz.ik.a* Cs. *bariz.ish.a* Ps. *bariz.iw.a* (Ar)

barizian.a *vi* face one another in a battle; confront each other in a war: *Pande mbili zinazopingana zilibariziana*, the two opposing sides faced one another in the battle. Prep. *barizian.i.a* St. *barizian.ik.a* Cs. *barizian.ish.a*

barkoa *n* (*n*) (*zool*) dragonfly; a kind of insect which feeds mostly on flies, mosquitoes, etc while in flight (cf *kereng'ende*)

barobaro *n* (*ma*-) see *barubaru*

barua *n* (*n*) letter, epistle, missive, despatch: *Barua pepe*, E-mail. *Barua za ndege*, air mail. *Barua ndogo*, chit. (cf *waraka, hati*)

barubaru *n* (*ma*-) teenage boy, youth, youngster.

baruti n (n) explosive, gunpowder, dynamite. (Turk)
barzakhi n (n) see *barazahi*
basbasi¹ n (n) chillies (cf *pilipili*)
basbasi² (also *basibasi*) n (n) (*bot*) the inner husk of a nutmeg; mace. (Ar)
basha¹ n (*ma-*) 1. the king in a suit of playing cards. Also called *mzungu wa nne* since it scores four. 2. (*arch*) head of policemen or warships. (Pers)
basha² n (*ma-*) a male homosexual; sodomite, bugger. (cf *afandi, mfiraji, mende*) (Pers)
bashala n (n) (*naut*) a kind of dhow.
bashasha (also *bashashi*) n (n) 1. cheerfulness, humour, joyfulness. (cf *furaha, uchangamfu*) 2. a cheerful or a jolly person. (cf *mchangamfu, mcheshi*)
bashashi n (n) see *bashasha*
bashir.i vt 1. predict, prophecy: *Alibashiri kwamba mvua itanyesha kesho*, he predicted that it would rain tomorrow. (cf *tabiri, agulia*) 2. divine, read palms: consult a fortune teller: *Mganga alibashiri kuwa mke wangu atazaa mtoto mwanamke*, the soothsayer divined that my wife would have a baby girl. 3. proclaim religious news; annunciate. Prep. **bashir.i.a** St. **bashir.ik.a** Ps. of Prep. **bashir.iw.a** Rp. **bashir.i.an.a** (Ar)
basi¹ *interj* used to ask someone to keep quiet. It carries the equivalent meanings of "That is enough," "That will do," "Stop that," etc. (cf *nyamaza, wacha*)
basi² *conj* so, then, therefore. The word *basi* is usu used in narratives and conversations: *Basi watu wote wakazama mtoni*, so all people drowned in the river. (Ar)
basi³ n (n) end, final: *Alikuja kukopa pesa kwangu na hiyo ndiyo ikawa basi*, he came to borrow money from me and that was the end. (cf *mwisho*)
basi⁴ n (*ma-*) bus (cf *matwana*) (Eng)

basibasi n (n) see *basbasi*
basmati n (n) a kind of pishori rice. (Hind)
bastola n (n) pistol (Pers)
basua n (n) bafflement, perplexity, bewilderment; confusion of the mind: *Ana basua sana leo na sijui kitu gani kimemsibu*, he is confused today and I don't know what has happened to him. (cf *hangaiko, wasiwasi, wahaka*)
bata n (*ma-*) (*zool*) duck: *Bata bukini*, a Madagascan duck. *Bata mzinga*, turkey. *Bata kibwenzi*, tufted duck. (cf *salili*)
batabat.a¹ *vi* waddle, toddle; walk flat-footed like a duck. (cf *matamata*)
batabata² *adj* having a flat level: *Ana miguu ya batabata*, she is flat-footed.
batalioni n (n) battalion (Eng)
batamzinga n (n) see *bata*
batara n (n) arrogance, vanity, pride. (cf *majivuno*) (Ar)
batela (also *betela*) n (*ma-*) (*naut*) a kind of sailing vessel with one perpendicular mast and a narrow prow and a lofty poop deck. (Port and Hind)
bati n (*ma-*) 1. tin, block tin. 2. galvanised iron. 3. metal roofing sheet.
batil.i¹ *vt* invalidate, nullify, revoke. Prep. **batil.i.a** St. **batil.ik.a** Cs. **batil.ish.a** Ps. of Prep. **batil.iw.a** Rp. of Prep. **batil.i.an.a** (cf *tangua, haramisha*) (Ar)
batili² *adj* invalid, ineffective, not binding: *Ndoa ile ni batili*, that marriage is invalid. (Ar)
batili³ n (n) invalidity, nullity, voidness: *Haki hushinda batili*, justice triumphs over wrongdoing.
-batilifu *adj* void, invalid, ineffective: *Mkuu wa kituo alitangaza kuwa uchaguzi wa pale mahali ulikuwa batilifu*, the returning officer announced that the election of that place was null and void. (Ar)
batilik.a *vi* be null and void, be invalid, be ineffective: *Sheria ile sasa imebatilika*, that law is now invalid.
batilish.a *vt* annul, abrogate, nullify,

revoke: *Bunge lilibatilisha sheria inayohusiana na rushwa*, parliament abrogated the law concerning corruption. Prep. ***batilish.i.a*** St. ***batilish.ik.a*** Ps. ***batilish.w.a*** Rp. ***batilish.an.a***

batini[1] *n (n) (anat)* abdomen, belly, stomach: *Maradhi mengi yanatokana na batini ya mtu*, most diseases emanate from someone's belly. (cf *tumbo*) (Ar)

batini[2] *n (n) (fig)* innermost thoughts or intentions: *Ana batini sana na kwa hivyo, hawezi kukupa siri yake*, he is an introvert so he cannot confide in you. (Ar)

batinilhuti *n (ma-)* 1. *(astron)* Pisces; the twelfth sign of the Zodiac. (cf *samaki*) 2. a shining star used as a decoration on a piece of cloth. 3. Andromeda (Ar)

batiz.a *vt* baptize. Prep. ***batiz.i.a*** St. ***batiz.ik.a*** Ps. ***batiz.w.a*** Rp. ***batiz.an.a*** (Eng)

batizo *n (ma-)* a place where a person is baptized.

batli *n (n) (naut)* a ship's logbook.

bato *n (ma-)* a ringworm on the head. (cf *paku, punye*)

batobato[1] *n (ma-)* 1. an open flat place, 2. a place where dancing takes place; dancing place.

batobato[2] *n (ma-)* coloured spots or stripes on an animal or on an insect.

batobato[3] *n (ma-)* a walk like that of a duck: *Mtu mwenye batobato*, a person walking like a duck.

batu.a *vi* waddle, toddle, wobble; walk unsteadily as a duck or child does: *Mtoto mdogo yule anabatuabatua*, that small child is toddling. Prep. ***batu.li.a*** St. ***batu.k.a*** Cs. ***batu.sh.a*** (cf *demadema*)

batuk.a *vi* chat loudly, talk loudly, speak loudly: *Akizungumza hubatuka*, when he speaks, he does it loudly. Prep. ***batuk.i.a*** St. ***batuk.ik.a*** Cs. ***batuk.ish.a***

batuli *n (n)* virgin (with special reference to the virgin Mary and Fatma, daughter of the Prophet Mohammad. (Ar)

bau.a *vi* urinate. Prep. ***bau.li.a*** St. ***bau.k.a*** and ***bau.lik.a*** Cs. ***bau.lish.a*** Ps. of Prep. ***bau.liw.a*** Rp. of Prep. ***bau.li.an.a*** (cf *kojoa, tabawali*)

baunsa *n (ma-)* henchman; a strong loyal supporter of a leader, etc. esp out of self-interests.

baura *n (n) (naut)* anchor with two flukes. Also called *nanga ya baura;* bower. (cf *nanga*)

bavu[1] *n (u)* see *ubavu*

bavu[2] *n (ma-) (usu mabavu)* force, strength: *Utawala wa mabavu*, iron fist rule.

bawa (see also *ubawa*) *n (u)* 1. the wing of a bird or an insect. 2. anything resembling or which does the work of a wing: *Bawa la eropleni*, the wing of an aeroplane.

bawaba *n (n)* hinge; a metal part which makes a door, gate, lid, etc.

bawabu *n (ma-)* doorman, doorkeeper, house porter. (Ar)

bawasiri (also *bawasili*) *n (n) (med)* piles, haemorrhoids (cf *puru, futuri, kikundu*) (Ar)

bawe *n (ma-)* a kind of coral rock. (cf *tumbawe*)

bawib.u *vt* divide oth into sections or chapters: *Aliubawibu mswada wake*, he divided his manuscript into different chapters. Prep. ***bawib.i.a*** St. ***bawib.ik.a*** Cs. ***bawib.ish.a*** Ps. of Prep. ***bawib.iw.a*** Rp. of Prep. ***bawib.i.an.a*** (Ar)

-baya *adj* bad, wicked, evil, unpleasant: *Mtu mbaya*, a wicked person. *Sifa mbaya*, bad trait. (cf *dhaifu, tule, makuruhi*)

bayana[1] *n (n)* clear evidence; testimony, exhibit: *Mwendeshaji mashtaka aliwasilisha kisu chenye damu kama bayana ya kumtia hatiani mshtakiwa*, the prosecutor presented a blood-stained knife as an exhibit to implicate the accused. (cf *ushahidi*) (Ar)

bayana² *adv* openly, conspicuously, vividly, obviously: *Alionyesha bayana chuki zake juu yangu,* he openly showed his animosity against me. (cf *waziwazi, dhahiri*) (Ar)

bayana³ *adj* clear, real, vivid. (Ar)

bayani *n* (*n*) eloquence, oratory, expressiveness; gift of the gab, command of speech: *Ana kipawa cha bayani,* he is a talented orator.

bayogesi *n* (*n*) (*chem*) biogas; gaseous fuel, esp methane, produced by the fermentation of organic matter.

bayokemia *n* (*n*) (*bot*) biochemistry (Eng)

bazazi *n* (*ma-*) 1. swindler, conman, duper. (cf *laghai, mdanganyifu*) 2. rambler, roamer. (cf *mzururaji*) (Ar)

bazoka *n* (*n*) bazooka; a short-range tubular rocket-launcher used against tanks. (Eng)

beb.a *vt* carry sth on the back, shoulders, hip or on the head: *Alimbeba mtoto begani,* she carried a child on the shoulders. Prep. **beb.e.a** St. **beb.ek.a** Cs. **beb.esh.a** Ps. **beb.w.a** Rp. **beb.an.a** Rp. of Prep. **beb.e.an.a** (cf *chukua*)

bebe *n* (*ma-*) (*anat*) rib: *Ametoka mabebe,* he is so thin that you can see his ribs.

bebedu.a *vt* see *bibidua*

beberu¹ *n* (*ma-*) 1. billy-goat, he-goat. 2. (*fig*) a strong man. 3. (*fig*) a person who gives off a bad smell.

beberu² *n* (*ma-*) imperialist, colonialist.

bebes.a *vi* (esp of a he-goat, sheep, etc.) bleat; make a sound like these animals. Prep. **bebes.e.a** St. **bebes.ek.a** Cs. **bebes.esh.a**

bebesh.a *vt* cause sby to carry luggage, etc.: *Alinibebesha mzigo mzito,* he made me carry a heavy load. Prep. **bebesh.e.a** St. **bebesh.ek.a** Ps. **bebesh.w.a** Rp. **bebesh.an.a**

bedani *n* (*ma-*) see *behedani*

bedeni (also *badeni*) *n* (*ma-*) (*naut*) a kind of Southern Arabian double-ended sailing vessel of between 20 and 50 tons with a perpendicular sharp stern and high rudder-head. (Ar)

Bedui *n* (*ma-*) 1. Bedouin; a member of the nomadic people living in tents in the desert. 2. a ruthless person, a cruel person; brute. (Ar)

bee (also *abee, beka*) *interj* a response used by women.

bega *n* (*ma-*) 1. (*anat*) shoulder. 2. (*idm*) *Bega kwa bega,* working close together; be hand in glove; in close cooperation: *Wanafanya kazi bega kwa bega katika maeneo yote,* they work in close cooperation in all areas. 3. neck and neck; nip and tuck: *Awali, wanariadha walikuwa wakishindana bega kwa bega lakini baadaye, mmoja akawa anaongoza,* at first, the athletes were neck and neck, but later, one of them took the lead.

begi *n* (*ma-*) handbag, bag. (Eng)

behedani (also *bedani*) *n* (*n*) a kind of sticky substance used by women for dressing their hair; lacquer. (Pers)

behewa¹ *n* (*ma-*) 1. an inner courtyard surrounded by buildings and open to the air; roofless inner court. 2. storehouse, magazine, godown, warehouse. (cf *ghala, bohari*) (Ar)

behewa² *n* (*ma-*) train compartment, carriage: *Behewa la abiria,* passengers' compartment. *Behewa la chakula,* buffet car. (Ar)

behewa³ *n* (*n*) a kind of ornament.

bei *n* (*n*) 1. price, cost, charge: *Piga bei,* sell sth. *Patana bei,* negotiate the price. *Tia bei,* fix price for sth. 2. value, worth, usefulness: *Bidhaa zake hazina bei,* his goods are worthless.

beja *vt* see *beza*

beji *n* (*n*) badge (cf *tepe*) (Eng)

beka¹ *interj* see *bee*

beka² *n* (*ki-vi*) (*bot*) a kind of sweet potato.

beki *n* (*ma-*) a defender in a soccer game. (Eng)

beku (also *paku*) *n* (*ma-*) an old worn-out sifting basket.

beku.a¹ *vt* 1. drive away, parry, ward off, keep off: *Aliwabekua nzi*, he drove away the flies. 2. pass a ball to another; receive and return a ball or blow: counteract, hit back: *Mchezaji aliupata mpira na baadaye akaubekua vizuri kwa mwenzake*, the player received the ball and later passed it well to his team mate. Prep. *beku.li.a* St. *beku.lik.a* Cs. *beku.lish.a* Ps. of Prep. *beku.liw.a* Rp. *beku.an.a*

beku.a² *vt* level off sth in a full measure; knock off overflowing contents from a full measure: *Aliubekua mchele kwenye kipimo*, she levelled off the overflowing rice measure. Prep. *beku.li.a* St. *beku.lik.a* Cs. *beku.lish.a* Ps. of Prep. *beku.liw.a* Rp. *beku.an.a*

beku.a³ *vt* ignore, neglect, disregard, snub: *Kwa vile ana mali nyingi, hupenda kuwabekua watu*, because he has a lot of wealth, he likes snubbing people. Prep. *beku.li.a* St. *beku.lik.a* Cs. *beku.lish.a* Ps. of Prep. *beku.liw.a* Rp. *beku.an.a*

beku.a⁴ *vt* snatch, grab, seize; take sth away by force: *Majambazi walizibekua kamera za watalii*, the thugs snatched the tourists' cameras. Prep. *beku.li.a* St. *beku.lik.a* Cs. *beku.lish.a* Ps. of Prep. *beku.liw.a* Rp. *beku.an.a*

belele *adv* excessively, abundantly, to the brim, copiously: *Vyakula vipo belele kwenye harusi*, there is food in abundance at the wedding. (cf *pomoni, tele*)

beleng.a *vi* swagger, prance, show off; walk arrogantly: *Kidosho yule hupenda kujibelenga njiani*, that beautiful girl likes to swagger in the street. (cf *hanja, tamba*)

beleshi *n* (*ma*-) shovel, spade. (cf *sepetu, shepe*)

belewasi *n* (*n*) (*zool*) a kind of ape.

belghamu *n* (*n*) see *halghamu*

beluwa *n* (*n*) see *baa¹*

bemb.a *vi* 1. interlope, pry, snoop; inquire into a person's affairs secretly: *Si vizuri kubemba mambo ya watu*, it is not good to pry into other people's affairs. (cf *dadisi, peleleza*) 2. seduce, entice, beguile: *Alimbemba msichana mrembo*, he seduced a glamorous girl. Prep. *bemb.e.a* St. *bemb.ek.a* Cs. *bemb.esh.a* Ps. *bemb.w.a* Rp. *bemb.an.a* (cf *tongoza, shawishi*)

bembe *n* (*ma*-) dainty dishes sent to someone as a present. (cf *kombe, soro*)

bembe.a¹ (also *pembea*) *vi* swing, oscillate, rock: *Kiti cha kubembea*, a child's swing/rocking chair. Prep. *bembe.le.a* St. *bembe.k.a* Cs. *bembe.sh.a* and *bembe.z.a* (cf *ning'inia, wayawaya*)

bembea² (also *pembea*) *n* (*ma*-) swing, seesaw.

bembej.a *vt* see *pembeja* Prep. *bembej.e.a* St. *bembej.ek.a* Ps. of Prep. *bembej.ew.a* Rp. *bembej.an.a*

bembelez.a *vt* 1. pacify, calm; sooth a child, etc. (cf *tuliza, burudisha*) 2. coax; wheedle, cajole: *Nilimbembeleza baba yangu aniruhusu kwenda kwenye maonyesho*, I coaxed my father into allowing me to go to the show. (cf *tafadhalisha, rai*) 3. (*idm*) *Bembeleza macho*, put on a coaxing expression, usu between men and women to signal love, affection, etc. Prep. *bembelez.e.a* St. *bembelez.ek.a* Ps. *bembelez.w.a* Rp. *bembelez.an.a*

-bembezi *adj* sultry, sensual; displaying or expressing smouldering passion: *Macho mabembezi*, sultry eyes.

ben.a *vt, vi* fold, turn up. Prep. *ben.e.a* St. *ben.ek.a* Cs. *ben.esh.a* Ps. *ben.ew.a* (cf *pinda*)

benchi *n* (*n*) 1. bench. 2. carpenter's table. 3. (in sports) *Benchi ya ufundi*, technical bench. (Eng)

bondeji *n* (*n*) see *bandeji*

bendera *n* (*n*) flag: banner; *Pandisha bendera*, hoist a flag. (*prov*) *Bendera*

hufuata upepo, a flag follows wind i.e. someone may support a policy not according to principles but according to other motives. (cf *beramu*) (Port)
bendi *n* (*n*) see *beni*
bene *n* (*n*) scapegoat, fall guy. (cf *msingiziwa*)
beneti *n* (*n*) bayonet (cf *singe*) (Eng)
bengi *n* (*n*) see *benki*
beni (also *bendi*) *n* (*n*) 1. a band of musicians. 2. a band played by people who sometimes dance in the streets. (Eng)
benibeni *adv* askew, awry, sideways: *Mipango yake ilikwenda benibeni*, his plans went awry. (cf *msobemsobe, kombo, kivoloya*)
benju.a *vt* reduce the length of a dress by hemming: *Mshoni aliibenjua miguu ya suruali yangu badala ya kuikata*, the tailor reduced the length of my trousers by hemming. Prep. *benju.li.a* St. *benju.k.a* Cs. *benju.lish.a* Ps. of Prep. *benju.liw.a*
benki (also *bengi*) *n* (*n*) bank: *Benki ya Dunia*, the World Bank. *Benki kuu*, central bank. *Benki ya damu*, blood bank (Eng)
benu.a (also *binua*) *vt, vi* protrude, project, bulge, stick out: *Anapotembea, hubenua kifua chake*, when he walks, he sticks his chest out. Prep. *benu.li.a* St. *benu.k.a* Cs. *benu.sh.a* Ps. of Prep. *benu.liw.a* (cf *nyanya, kubaza*)
benzini *n* (*n*) benzene (Eng)
bepari *n* (*ma-*) 1. capitalist, tycoon, magnate: *Bepari uchwara*, petty bourgeois. 2. investor: *Yeye in bepari maarufu aliyeweka rasilimali zake kwenye kampuni mbalimbali*, he is a well-known investor who has invested in different companies. (cf *mwekezaji*) 3. exploiter. (Hind)
ber.a[1] *vt* see *beza*
bera[2] *n* (*n*) a small box for keeping in matches, cigarettes or small things.

beramu *n* (*n*) flag, banner. (cf *bendera*) (Port)
beregez.a *vt, vi* brush aside, shrug off, be neglectful, be inattentive; pretend not to understand or be concerned in an affair: *Waziri alipoulizwa swali nyeti, aliberegeza*, when he was asked a sensitive question, the minister shrugged it off. Prep. *beregez.e.a* St. *beregez.ek.a* Cs. *beregez.esh.a* Ps. *beregez.w.a* (cf *bereuza, pambaniza, gangaiza*)
beresati *n* (*n*) see *barasati*.
bereu *n* (*n*) 1. grease mixed with lime, used for caulking dhow to prevent the water from "seeping in." (cf *deheni*) 2. thick tar. (Port)
bereuz.a *vt, vi* brush aside, shrug off. Prep. *bereuz.i.a* St. *bereuz.ik.a* Cs. *bereuz.ish.a* Ps. *bereuz.w.a*
beseni *n* (*ma-*) basin (Eng)
besera *n* (*n*) the frame of a mosquito net; poles or rods of a bedstead on which the mosquito net is hung. (Hind)
bet.a[1] *vt* curve, twist, crook, bend: *Beta kidole*, bend a finger. *Barabara ile imebeta*, that road twists and turns. Prep. *bet.e.a* St. *bet.ek.a* Cs. *bet.esh.a* Ps. *bet.w.a* Rp. *bet.an.a* (cf *pinda, kunja*)
bet.a[2] *n* (*n*) beta; the second brightest star in a constellation: *Miali ya beta*, beta rays. (Eng)
betela *n* see *batela*
beti *n* (*n*) stanzas; plural of *ubeti*, verse.
betili *n* (*n*) (*naut*) a two-masted vessel and its hull resembles *bedeni*, a kind of sailing vessel.
betri *n* (*n*) 1. battery. 2. radio cell, torch cell, etc. (Eng)
betua[1] *vt* (in soccer, etc.) 1. cut, punt: *Mchezaji aliubetua mpira*, the player punted the ball. 2. fold, turn up (cf *pinda, bana*) 3. distort, twist: *Usijaribu kuibetua lugha*, don't try to distort a language. Prep. *betu.li.a* St. *betu.k.a* Cs. *betu.sh.a* Ps. of Prep. *betu.liw.a* Rp. *betu.an.a*

betu.a²

betu.a² *vt* fold, clasp, bend. Prep. **betu.li.a** St. **betu.k.a** Cs. **betu.sh.a** Ps. of Prep. **betu.liw.a** Rp. **betu.an.a**

beu.a *vt* scorn, shun, disregard, ignore: *Simpendi mtu yule kwa vile huwabeua watu wa chini*, I don't like that person because he shuns low-class people. Prep. **beu.li.a** St. **beu.lik.a** Ps. of Prep. **beu.liw.a** Rp. **beu.an.a** (cf *dharau, puuza*)

bez.a (also *bera*) *vt* scorn, ignore, discredit, flout: *Alipewa amri kuzitekeleza lakini akazibeza*, he was given orders to follow but he ignored them. Prep. **bez.e.a** St. **bez.ek.a** Cs. **bez.esh.a** Ps. **bez.w.a** Rp. **bez.an.a** (cf *dharau, bera*)

bezo *n* (*ma-*) a scornful word or action: *Mabezo yake kwa watu yatamharibia jina lake*, his scornful attitude towards people will smear his name. (cf *mapuuza*)

bi *n* (*ma-*) 1. abbreviation form of *bibi*. see *bibi*. 2. an unmarried woman; spinster.

bia¹ *n* (*n*) partnership, cooperation: *Changa bia*, share expenses. *Gawa bia*, share out equally. *Kula bia*, feed together, each one bringing his own food, or each paying towards the cost. *Nunua bia*, purchase jointly.

bia² *n* (*n*) beer (Eng)

biabi.a *vt, vi* be diligent, be active, work hard; work with a will: *Mwanafunzi yule anabiabia sana kwenye masomo yake*, that student works very hard in his studies. (cf *jitahidi, hangaika*)

biarusi *n* (*ma-*) see *biharusi*

biashara *n* (*n*) business, trade, commerce (*prov*) *Biashara haigombi*, business entails bargaining. *Biashara ya jumla*, wholesale trade. *Biashara ya rejareja*, retail business. *Biashara haramu*, illegal business. *Biashara ya machinga*, vendor trade.

bibi¹ *n* (*ma*) grandmother. (cf *nyanya*)

bibi² (also *bi*) *n* (*ma-*) 1. a term of respectful reference and address to a woman;

bid.i

lady, Mrs. Ms. Miss: *Bibi Mary*, Ms Mary, Miss Mary. *Bibi arusi*, the bride. 2. wife. 3. mistress, courtesan, concubine. 4. the queen in a pack of playing cards. Also called *Mzungu wa pili*.

bibidu.a (also *bebedua, bibitua*) *vt* pout; thrust out and turn down the lower lip as a sign of contempt or derision: *Aliponiona tu, akaubibidua mdomo wake*, when she had just seen me, she thrust out her lower lip and turned it down as a sign of contempt. Prep. **bibidu.li.a** St. **bibidu.k.a** Cs. **bibidu.sh.a** Ps. of Prep. **bibidu.liw.a** Rp **bibidu.an.a**

Biblia *n* (*n*) The Bible. (Eng)

bibliografia *n* (*n*) bibliography (Eng)

bibo *n* (*bot*) cashew apple; the fruit of a cashew nut tree. (cf *kanju*)

-bichi *adj* 1. raw, unripe, fresh: *Embe mbichi*, raw mango. 2. uncooked: *Nyama mbichi*, raw meat. 3. damp, dewy, wettish, watery, wet: *Nguo mbichi*, wet clothes. 4. immature, unripe, beginning early: *Msichana mbichi*, an immature girl. *Alfajiri mbichi*, at the crack dawn.

bidaa *n* (*n*) (in Islam) innovation; the tendency to perfom a particular new practice in religion purely out of excessive fanatism without following the principles. (Ar)

bidhaa *n* (*n*) 1. goods, merchandise, vendibles: *Bidhaa kutoka nje*, imports. *Bidhaa zinazotoka ndani*, exports. 2. capital: *Sina bidhaa nzima wala mbovu*, I have no capital. 3. outcome (usu bad): *Yote yaliyonipata ni bidhaa ya ujinga wangu*, all that happened to me is due to my ignorance. (Ar)

bidhori *adv* forcefully, by force, involuntarily: *Wezi walilichukua gari yake bidhori*, the thieves took his car by force.

bid.i *vt* (used with a dummy subject) be obliged, be obligatory, be compelled, be necessary: *Ilibidi nimsaidie*, I was obliged to help her. St. **bid.ik.a**

bidii *n* (*n*) effort, exertion, attempts, trouble: *Hana bidii katika kazi yake*, he shows no effort in his work. (cf *juhudi, jitihada*) (Ar)

bidiish.a *vt, vi* take special pains; put efforts in one's work: *Anajibidiisha katika kazi zake*, she puts effort in her work. Prep. **bidiish.i.a** St. **bidiish.ik.a** Ps. **bidiish.w.a** Rp. **bidiish.an.a**

bigany.a *vt* garner, gather, accumulate, collect: *Alizibiganya taka zote kwenye jaa na kuzichoma*, he gathered all the refuse in the dunghill and burned them. Prep. **bigany.i.a** St. **bigany.ik.a** Cs. **bigany.ish.a** Ps. **bigany.w.a** Rp. **bigany.an.a** (cf *kusanya, somba*)

bighairi (also *ghairi*) *adv* 1. used in the expression: *Bighairi ya*, without, in the absence of. 2. apart from: *Bighairi ya madaktari, hata wafanyakazi wengine wameongezewa mshahara*, apart from doctors, the salaries of all other workers have even gone up. (Ar)

bigij.a *vt* squeeze, press, pinch, compress: *Aliyabigija machungwa ili anitengenezee glasi moja ya kinywaji kitamu*, he squeezed the oranges in order to make a glass of juice for me. Prep. **bigij.i.a** St. **bigij.ik.a** Cs. **bigij.ish.a** Ps. **bigij.w.a** Rp. **bigij.an.a** (cf *ming'inya*)

bigili *n* (*ma-*) 1. a fort constructed with stones, surrounding a farm. 2. a wooden fort kept for bull before dancing them. 3. a wooden fort kept for women to cheer the bullfight game.

bih.i *vt* forgo dowry or debt: *Msichana alibihi mahari yake kwa sababu alimpenda sana mchumba wake*, the girl forwent all of her dowry because she loved her bridegroom very much. Prep. **bih.i.a** St. **bih.ik.a** Cs. **bih.ish.a** (cf *samehe*) (Ar)

bikari *n* (*n*) a pair of compass: *Chora kwa kutumia bikari*, draw by using a compass. (Ar)

bikira¹ *n* (*ma-*) virgin, vestal, maiden. (cf *mwanamwari*) (Ar)

bikira² *adj* 1. vestal, chaste, maidenly: *Msichana bikira*, a chaste girl. 2. unused: *Ardhi bikira*, an unused land. (Ar)

bikir.i *vt* deflower, defile, deprive virginity. Prep. **bikir.i.a** St. **bikir.ik.a** Cs. **bikir.ish.a** Ps of Prep **bikir.iw.a**

bikizee *n* (*n*) a very old woman; crone, hag. (cf *ajuza*)

bila *prep* 1. without, beyond, not having: *Aliimaliza kazi bila ya msaada wowote*, he completed the work without any assistance. (*prov*) *Mali bila daftari, hupotea bila habari*, if you don't account for your money, you end up being bankrupt. (cf *pasipo*) 2. (sports) zero, nil. (Ar)

biladi (also *baladi*) *n* (*n*) town (Ar)

biladia *adj* pertaining to a town: *Watu wa biladia*, town people. (Ar)

bilahi *interj* By God. (Ar)

bilashi (also *bileshi*) *adv* 1. irrationally, for no reason, for nothing: *Alinikemea bilashi*, he scolded me for no reason. 2. gratuitously, freely: *Mwenye duka alinipa matunda bilashi*, the shopkeeper gave me fruits free of charge. (Ar)

bilauri *n* (*n*) a glass for drinking; tumbler. (Ar)

bilda *n* (*n*) (*astron*) Sagittarius; the ninth sign of the zodiac, which the sun enters about November 23. (cf *mshale*) (Ar)

bildi¹ (also *bilidi*) *n* (*n*) (*naut*) plumb, plummet: *Tia bildi*, take soundings. (Ar)

bildi² (also *bilidi*) *n* (*n*) the weight of a clock; pendulum.

bileshi *adv* see *bilashi*

bili *n* (*n*) bill, invoice, account. (cf *ankra*) (Eng)

biliadi *n* (*n*) billiards (Eng)

bilidi *n* (*n*) see *bildi*¹ and *bildi*²

bilikuli *adv* never, at no time, not any time: *Yeye hajawahi kunitembelea bilikuli*, he has never visited me. (cf *asilani, katu*) (Ar)

bilingani *n* (*n*) see *biringani*
bilioni *n* (*n*) 1. billion. 2. (formerly in Great Britain,) a million millions. (Eng)
bilisi *n* (*n*) see *ibilisi*
biliwili[1] (also *mbiliwili, mbelewele*) *n* (*n*) (*zool*) linnet; a kind of fish.
biliwili[2] *n* (*n*) (*bot*) Turkey blossom; a slender trailing plant, commonly found on seashores in parts of the tropics. *Tribulus cistoides*. (cf *mbiliwili, mbigili*)
billahi *interj* an expression of oath; in the name of God.
bilula (also *bulula, bulule*) *n* (*n*) tap, cock; tap for a barrel, pipe, etc. (Ar)
bima *n* (*n*) 1. insurance: *Shirika la bima, insurance corporation. Bima ya maisha*, life insurance. 2. lottery. (cf *bahati nasibu*) (Hind)
bimb.a *vt* dandle; rock a child, etc. Prep. *bimb.i.a* St. *bimb.ik.a* Cs. *bimb.ish.a* Ps. of Prep. *bimb.iw.a*
bimbashi *n* (*n*) (*arch*) sergeant (cf *koplo*) (Turk)
bimbirish.a[1] *vt* see *bimbiriza*
bimbirish.a[2] *vt* push forcefully: *Aliubimbirisha mlango*, he pushed the door forcefully. Prep *himbirish.i.a* St. *bimbirish.ik.a* Ps. *bimbirish.w.a* Rp. *bimbirish.an.a* (cf *sukuma*)
bimbiriz.a (also *bimbirisha*) *vt* flare up strongly; set on fire: *Mkulima alilibimbiriza biwi lake*, the farmer set the rubbish heap on fire. Prep. *bimbiriz.i.a* St. *bimbiriz.ik.a* Cs. *bimbiriz.ish.a* Ps. *bimbiriz.w.a* Rp. *bimbiriz.an.a*
bimkubwa *n* (*ma-*) 1. (*colloq*) an old woman. 2. a respectful name given to a mother.
bin *n* (*n*) son of. (Ar)
binaadamu *n* (*n*) human being, human, individual, person: *Kila binaadamu ana udhaifu wake*, every human being has his weaknesses. (cf *mja, mwanadamu*) (Ar)

binafsi *adv* personally; as a person, from one's own viewpoint: *Mimi binafsi sikubaliani naye*, I personally don't agree with him. (Ar)
binafsish.a (also *nafsisha*) *vt* privatise: *Kiwanda cha sukari kilibinafsishwa*, the sugar factory was privatized. Prep. *binafsish.i.a* St. *binafsish.ik.a* Ps. *binafsish.w.a*
binamu *n* (*n*) cousin; son of paternal uncle. (Ar)
binda *n* (*ma-*) (*bot*) okra, lady's fingers. (cf *bamia*)

binda

bindo *n* (*n*) 1. that part of the loincloth which is tied to the waist or stomach. 2. fold of the loincloth which has been put on.
bingiri.a *vi* swirl, whirl, eddy; roll over: *Alipopigwa ngumi, alibingiria chini*, when he was punched, he rolled over on the floor. Prep. *bingir.i.a* St. *bingir.ik.a* Cs. *bingir.ish.a* (cf *fingirika*)
bingirish.a *vt* roll: *Alijibingirisha sakafuni*, he rolled himself on the floor. Prep. *bingirish.i.a* St. *bingirish.ik.a* Ps. *bingirish.w.a* Rp. *bingirish.an.a*
bingwa *n* (*ma-*) 1. expert, authority, pundit, specialist. (cf *mtaalamu*) 2. master, champion; a talented person, a skilful person, a clever person.
bin.i *vt* forge, counterfeit, commit forgery: *Alifungwa kwa kosa la kubini sahihi ya*

mkurugenzi wa fedha, he was jailed for forging the signature of the director of finance. Prep. *bin.i.a* St. *bin.ik.a* Cs. *bin.ish.a* Ps. of Prep. *bin.iw.a* Rp. of Prep. *bin.i.an.a* (Ar)

binti *n* (*ma-*) 1. daughter. (cf *biti*) 2. girl, maid. (cf *msichana*) (Ar)

binu.a *vt, vi* see *benua*

binuk.a *vi* become bent/crooked.

biny.a *vt* squeeze, pinch, compress: *Mlango ulikibinya kidole chake*, he nipped his finger in the door. Prep. *biny.i.a* St. *biny.ik.a* Cs. *biny.ish.a* Ps. *biny.w.a* Rp. *biny.an.a* (cf *kaba, minya*)

binzari *n* (*n*) see *bizari*

biri[1] *n* (*n*) 1. (*bot*) tobacco leaf for rolling up cigarettes and used by some Indians. 2. a kind of cigarette made from tobacco leaves. (Hind)

biri[2] *interj* an exclamation for forbidding someone not to do sth; let him try it. (cf *jaribu, thubutu*)

biriani (also *birinzi*) *n* (*n*) a kind of cooked rice mixed with fried steak, ghee and spices. (Pers)

birigiji *n* (*n*) 1. a kind of cloth of a light brownish yellow colour. 2. light brownish yellow colour.

birika *n* (*ma-*) 1. kettle, water-jug; a large metal vessel for holding water. 2. teapot.

birimbi (also *mbirimbi*) *n* (*n*) (*bot*) averrhoa; a kind of cucumber-shaped fruit, waxy to the touch, greenish-yellow when ripe.

biring.a *vt* knock down, fling down, throw down: *Bondia alimbiringa mpinzani wake*, the boxer knocked his opponent down. Ps. *biring.i.a* St. *biring.ik.a* Cs. *biring.ish.a* Ps. *biring.w.a* Rp. *biring.an.a*

biringani (also *biringanya*) *n* (*n*) (*bot*) eggplant; a kind of large, edible, purple, white or red fruit used as a vegetable, which may be either boiled, fried or cooked.

biringanya *n* (*n*) see *biringani*

biringi.a *vi* roll down; rotate about its axis lengthwise: *Kama watoto, wao walipenda kubiringia kwenye kilima kile*, as children, they liked to roll down on that hill. (cf *bingiria*)

birinzi *n* (*n*) see *biriani*

birisi *n* (*n*) (*zool*) a kind of non-poisonous snake with a very small mouth; ground blind snake. Typhlopidae.

bisbisi (also *bisibisi*) *n* (*n*) screwdriver (Hind)

bish.a[1] *vt* knock at the door; Prep. *bish.i.a* St. *bish.ik.a* Ps. *bish.w.a* Rp. *bish.an.a* (cf *gonga*)

bish.a[2] *vt, vi* 1. dispute, refute, deny, challenge: *Anabisha kuwa dunia ni mviringo*, he denies that the world is round. (cf *kataa, pinga*) 2. argue, debate: *Yeye anapenda kubisha kila unalomwambia*, he likes to argue over whatever you tell him. Prep. *bish.i.a* St. *bish.ik.a* Ps. *bish.w.a* Rp. *bish.an.a* (cf *shindana, hoji*)

bish.a[3] *vt* (*naut*) tack; beat to windward; steer to windward: *Alikibisha chombo*, he tacked the vessel. Prep. *bish.i.a* St. *bish.ik.a* Ps. *bish.w.a*

bishara *n* (*n*) good news: *Alinipa bishara kuwa serikali imenikubalia ombi langu la kutaka kwenda kusoma ng'ambo*, he gave me the good news that the government had assented to my request to go abroad for studies. (Ar)

bishaushi (also *shausi*) *n* (*n*) (old use in former Tanganyika) sergeant.

-bishi *adj* argumentative, contentious, wranglesome: *Mtu mbishi*, an argumentative person. (cf *-shindani*)

bisi *n* (*n*) popcorn; roasted Indian corn; parched Indian corn. (Ar)

bisibisi *n* (*n*) see *bisbisi*

biskoti *n* (*n*) see *biskuti*

biskuti (also *biskoti*) *n* (*n*) biscuit (Eng)

bismillahi[1] *n* (*n*) 1. (in Islam) in the name of God. 2. the beginning of anything. (Ar)

bismillahi[2] *interj* an exclamation of anticipating an unpleasant affair. (Ar)

bitana *n* (*n*) any thin material which is used for lining a garment usu a coat or trousers. (Ar)

biti[1] *n* (*ma-*) daughter: *Aza biti Mohamed* means Aza, the daughter of Mohamed. (cf *binti*)

biti[2] *n* (*n*) musical beat: *Ongoza biti*, lead the musical beat. (Eng)

bitimrembo *adj* light green.

-bivu *adj* ripe, mellow: *Tunda bivu*, a ripe fruit. (cf *tosa, komavu*)

biwi *n* (*n*) rubbish heap; refuse heap in a garden, etc.

bizari (also *binzari*) *n* (*n*) (*bot*) curry powder, turmeric, dill: *Bizari nene*, a thick dill. *Bizari nyembamba*, a thin dill. (Ar)

bizimu *n* (*n*) 1. metallic button for fastening a belt. 2. buckle, broch, clasp, fastener. (Ar)

blangeti (also *blanketi*) *n* (*n*) blanket (Eng)

blanketi *n* (*n*) see *blangeti*

blauzi *n* (*n*) blouse. (Eng)

bloki *n* (*n*) block; a large building of offices, flats, etc. (Eng)

bluu *n* (*n*) see *buluu*

bob.a *vt* truss, bind, fasten, secure, bundle: *Wezi walimboba mlinzi kwa kamba*, the robbers trussed the guard up with a rope. Prep. **bob.i.a** St. **bob.ik.a** Ps. **bob.w.a** Rp. **bob.an.a** (cf *kaza, baba, funga*)

bobari *n* (*n*) a tool used by a carpenter for cutting grooves in wood; gouge. (cf *ngabu, sokondo*)

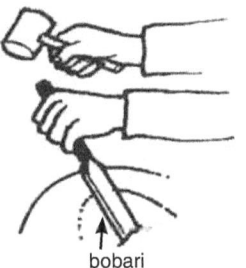

bobari

bobe.a *vt, vi* 1. be immersed in, be engrossed in, be absorbed in: *Amebobea katika mchezo wa kamari*, he is immersed in gambling. (cf *topea, komaa*) 2. (*fig*) be well-versed in, be well-qualified: *Amebobea katika fani ya ushairi*, he is well-versed in the field of poetry. Prep. **bobe.le.a** St. **bobe.lek.a** Cs. **bobe.sh.a** Ps. **bobe.w.a**

bobo *n* (*n*) 1. any huge tree. 2. imbecile, simpleton; a stupid person. 3. nonsense; useless words.

boboj.a *vi* prattle, blaster; talk nonsense, talk without thinking. Prep. **boboj.e.a** St. **boboj.ek.a** Cs. **boboj.esh.a** (cf *ropoka*)

bobok.a *vi* blather, twaddle; talk without thinking, talk nonsense: *Ana tabia ya kuboboka husu ukilewa*, he has the habit of prattling especially when he is drunk. Prep. **bobok.e.a** St. **bobok.ek.a** Cs. **bobok.esh.a** Ps. **bobok.w.a** (cf *ropoka, payuka*)

bobot.a *vt* hit, beat, strike, smack, slap: *Alimbobota rafiki yake usoni*, he slapped his friend on the face. Prep. **bobot.e.a** St. **bobot.ek.a** Cs. **bobot.esh.a** Ps. **bobot.w.a** Rp. **bobot.an.a** (cf *piga, buta*)

boboto.a *vt* see *babadua*

bobwe *n* (*n*) (*zool*) a mixture of different types of small fish.

bocho *n* (*n*) (*zool*) electric ray; a kind of fish (family *Torpedinadae*) with an ovate body and whip-like tail.

boda *n* (*ma-*) 1. a pupil in a boarding school; boarder. 2. a boarding school: *Kaa boda*, stay in a boarding school. *Shule ya boda*, a boarding school. (cf *bweni, dahalia, gane*) (Eng)

bodi[1] *n* (*ma-*) body; the part of an automobile truck, etc. that holds the load or passengers; part of a vehicle that is not the chassis. (Eng)

bodi[2] *n* (*n*) board, committee, council: *Bodi ya wakurugenzi*, the board of directors. *Bodi ya wadhamini*, the board of trustees. *Bodi ya uhariri*, editorial board. (Eng)

bodwe *n* (*ma-*) (*bot*) bottle-gourd; a kind of gourd, long and thin, and white inside its shell. (cf *mung'unye*)

boflo (also *bofulo*) *n* (*n*) a kind of big bread made from wheat flour, which contains yeast and then baked.

bofulo *n* (*n*) see *boflo*

bofy.a *vt* 1. press, push: *Aliibofya kengele ili awaite wafanyakazi wa kike waje kumhudumia*, she pressed the bell in order to call the stewardesses to serve her. 2. click: *Bofyabofya*, double click. Prep. ***bofy.e.a*** St. ***bofy.ek.a*** Cs. ***bofy.esh.a*** Ps. ***bofy.w.a*** Rp. ***bofy.an.a*** (cf *bonyeza, binya*)

boga *n* (*ma-*) (*bot*) pumpkin, marrow.

bogi *n* (*ma-*) carriage of a train; bogey. (Eng)

bogo.a *vt* see *pogoa*

bohad.i *vt* (*naut*) lengthen the sheet (rope of a main sail of a vessel). Prep. ***bohad.i.a*** St. ***bohad.ik.a*** Cs. ***bohad.ish.a*** Ps. of Prep. ***bohad.iw.a***

bohari *n* (*ma-*) warehouse, storehouse, godown. (cf *ghala*) (Hind)

Bohora *n* (*ma-*) a follower of Shia sect called *Bohora*. (Guj)

boi *n* (*ma-*) house servant, domestic servant, waiter, attendant. (Eng)

boji *n* (*n*) a kind of local intoxicating liquor made from maize husks. (Ar)

boji.a *vt, vi* tiptoe, stalk; walk stealthily: *Tuliwabojia adui majeruhi mafichoni mwao*, we stalked the wounded enemies to their lair. St. ***boji.k.a*** Cs. ***boji.sh.a*** Ps. ***boji.w.a*** Rp. ***boji.an.a*** (cf *nyatia, nyemelea*)

boko[1] *n* (*ma-*) gourmand, glutton; a voracious person.

boko[2] *n* (*n*) see *bokoboko*[2]

boko.a[1] *vt* 1. penetrate, bore, drill: *Mafuko walibokoa ukuta wa nyumba ya udongo*, the moles bored through the wall of the mud house. 2. bore, penetrate: *Alibokoa kwenye kundi la watu*, he bore his way through a crowd of people. Prep. ***boko.le.a*** St. ***boko.k.a*** and ***boko.lek.a*** Cs. ***boko.z.a*** (cf *penya, pita*)

boko.a[2] *vt* get a bumper harvest; reap a good harvest; obtain a plentiful harvest: *Alibokoa korosho nyingi mwaka jana*, he harvested a lot of cashew nuts last year. Prep. ***boko.le.a*** St. ***boko.k.a*** and ***boko.lek.a***

bokoboko[1] *n* (*n*) a particular dish of mixed type of food containing wheat flour, meat and ghee.

bokoboko[2] (also *boko*) *n* (*n*) (*bot*) a kind of banana which is very soft when cooked. (cf *makojozi, ngazija*)

bokoboko[3] *n* (*n*) (*bot*) a kind of sugarcane with soft outer part.

bokok.a[1] *vi* be gluttonous, be ravenous, be voracious, be open-mouthed: *Yeye amebokoka kwa vile hupenda kuhudhuria karamu nyingi hata kama hajaalikwa*, he is gluttonous because he likes to attend many feasts even if not invited. Prep. ***bokok.e.a*** St. ***bokok.ek.a*** Cs. ***bokok.esh.a*** Ps. ***bokok.w.a***

bokok.a[2] *vi* 1. (of eyes, flesh of a bone, etc., due to sickness, fear, etc.); bulge, protrude: *Macho yalimbokoka alipovamiwa na wezi nyumbani kwake*, her eyes bulged out when she was attacked by thieves at her house. 2. be emaciated, be enfeebled, be enervated: *Amebokoka kutokana na maradhi ya maze mrefu*, she is emaciated by the long illness. Prep. ***bokok.e.a*** St. ***bokok.ek.a*** Cs. ***bokok.esh.a***

bokor.a *vt* snatch, grab, plunder; take away by force: *Majambazi waliibokora saa yangu ya mkono*, the thugs snatched my wristwatch. Prep. ***bokor.e.a*** St. ***bokor.ek.a*** Cs. ***bokor.esh.a*** Ps. ***bokor.w.a*** Rp. ***bokor.an.a*** (cf *nyang'anya, pora, pokonya*)

bokozi *n* (*n*) (*zool*) amphipod; a small crustacean of the order *Amphipoda* having a laterally-compressed body with no carapace. They are found in a diversity of habitats, from the upper shore to great depths, free-living or in self-constructed tubes or inside sponges or ascidians. *Afrigitanopsis paguri*

boksi   **bonde**   **B**

bokozi

boksi *n* (*ma-*) box (Eng)
bokwa *n* (*ma-*) (*bot*) a kind of pawpaw.
bolamvuvi *n* (*n*) see *bowelamvuvi*
boli *n* (*n*) soccer (Eng)
bolingo *n* (*ma-*) a kind of dance originating from former Zaire.
bolti *n* (*n*) bolt; a screw with no point. (Eng)
boma[1] *n* (*n*) 1. stockade, parados, outerwall, earthwork. (cf *faja, ua*) 2. fort, redoubt, citadel, castle. (cf *ngome, buruji*)
boma[2] *n* (*ma-*) headquarters of the German administration in their former colonies.
bomba *n* (*n*) 1. pipe, hose, conduit, duct. 2. smokestack; a chimney of a house or ship. 3. watertap, spigot. 4. syringe. 5. hosepipe, waterpump; a pump for drawing water. Also called *bomba la kuvutia maji*. 6. loudspeaker, microphone. 7. *Bomba la kupulizia*, sprayer. 8. packet: *Bomba la tumbaku*, tobacco packet. *Bomba la nyuki*, a swarm of bees.
bombo[1] *n* (*n*) shorts; short trousers: *Anapenda kuvaa bombo*, he likes to wear shorts. (cf *kaptura*)
bombo[2] *n* (*n*) influenza, grippe, flu, cold. (cf *kamasi, mafua*)
bombo[3] *n* (*n*) (*zool*) a long tailed male bird which feeds on grass, millet, rice, etc.
bombomu[1] *n* (*ma-*) machinegun.
bombomu[2] see *bomu*
bombwe[1] *n* (*ma-*) 1. sculpture, carving. 2. ornamentation in a plaited leafstrip.

bombwe[2] *n* (*ma-*) potsherd
bombwe[3] *n* (*n*) (*zool*) grub, maggot, jigger; a kind of larva. (cf *funza, buu*)
bomla *n* (*n*) (*zool*) monitor lizard; a large water lizard, (family *Varanidae*) which can warn the presence of crocodiles. (cf *burukenge, kenge*)
bomo.a *vt* 1. demolish, raze, tear down, pull down. (cf *jengua, pomoa*) 2. wreck, destroy, scuttle, ruin: *Ameibomoa mipango yangu*, he has wrecked my plans. 3. (*colloq*) discredit sby; besmirch. Prep. **bomo.le.a** St. **bomo.k.a** Cs. **bomo.lesh.a** Ps. of Prep. **bomo.lew.a** Rp. **bomo.an.a** (cf *vuruga, pangua*)
bomoko *n* (*ma-*) 1. the broken part of a house, etc. 2. the ruins of a house or a deserted town; debris
bomu[1] *n* (*ma-*) 1. bomb: *Bomu la atomiki*, atomic bomb. (cf *kombora*) 2. Molotov cocktail; a type of simple bomb filled with gasoline, etc. and wrapped in a saturated rag or plugged with a wick, ignited and hurled as an antitank grenade. 3. (*fig*) conundrum, riddle. (Eng)
bomu[2] *n* (*ma-*) 1. the sound of a large deep sounding drum. 2. a particular kind of traditional drum: *Bomu la gogo*, a large drum with a deep booming sound. 3. a particular old style of drumming.
bomu[3] *n* (*ma-*) see *bumu*
bom.u[4] *vt* 1. bombard, shell, blitz: *Adui aliubomu mji*, the enemy shelled the town. 2. lambast, castigate, lash, vilify: *Alinibomu hadharani*, he slandered me in public. Prep. **bom.i.a** St. **bom.ik.a** Cs. **bom.ish.a** Ps. of Prep. **bom.iw.a** Rp. of Prep. **bom.i.an.a** (Eng)
bonanza *n* (*n*) bonanza (Eng)
bonasi *n* (*n*) bonus: *Bonasi ya kuendesha bila ajali*, no claim bonus (cf *mukafaa*) (Eng)
bonde *n* (*ma-*) 1. valley, dale, depression, *Bonde la ufa*, rift valley. 2. valley separated by a river: *Bonde la mto*, river valley.

bondia *n* (*ma-*) pugilist, boxer. (cf *mpiganaji ndondi*)

bondo *n* (*ma-*) unproperly cooked rice.

boneti *n* (*n*) (of a vehicle) bonnet; the hinged metal part of a motor vehicle body that provides access to the engine. (Eng)

bong.a *vt* bore or make holes in grain or wood as insects do; burrow: *Dumuzi waliubonga mtama,* the mealybugs made holes in the millet. Prep. **bong.e.a** St. **bonge.k.a** Cs. **bong.esh.a** Ps. **bong.w.a** Rp. **bong.an.a**

bonge *n* (*ma-*) 1. chunk, lump, wad: *Bonge la barafu,* a chunk of ice. *Bonge la nyama,* a hunk of meat. *Bonge la udongo,* a clump of earth. 2. used to emphasize the largeness of sth: *Bonge la gari,* a huge car. *Bonge la kazi,* a challenging job. *Bonge la mtu,* a gigantic person. *Bonge la matope,* ball of mud

bongo¹ (also *ubongo*) *n* (*n*) 1. brain. 2. marrow. 3. intelligence, intellect, brain: *Ana bongo kali,* he is very intelligent. (*idms*) *Chemsha bongo,* riddles. *Piga bongo,* ponder, meditate.

bongo² *n* (*n*) 1. brain. 2. bongo drum (Eng)

bong'o.a *vi* stoop; bend down such that the buttocks stick out. Prep. **bong'o.le.a** St. **bong'o.k.a** and **bong'o.lek.a** Cs. **bong'o.lesh.a** (cf *furama*)

bono *n* (*ma-*) (*zool*) a kind of fish.

bont.a *n* (*ma-*) see *bunta*

bonye.a *vi* dent, indent, push in, press in: *Sehemu ya mbele ya gari yangu imebonyea,* the bonnet of my car is dented. St. **bony.ek.a** and **bony.esh.a** Ps. **bony.ew.a** Cs. **bonye.z.a**.

bonyez.a *vt* 1. dent, indent, press on/in: *Aliibonyeza kengele,* he pressed the bell. 2. (*colloq*) give sby some information that he does not know about it. Prep. **bonyez.e.a** St. **bonyez.ek.a** Cs. **bonyez.esh.a** Ps. **bonyez.w.a** Rp. **bonyez.an.a**

bop.a *vt* 1. poke or touch gently a soft thing e.g. a ripe fruit, an abscess, etc.: *Aliyabopa maembe mabivu yale,* he poked those ripe mangoes gently. (cf *tofya, tomasa*) 2. be soft after touching a fruit, etc.: *Aliyabopa matunda yangu na sasa yamekuwa laini,* he poked my fruits and now they have gone soft. 3. sink in; become hollow as in the case of cheeks; be sunken, be dented; hollow: *Mashavu yake yamebopa kutokana na uzee,* her cheeks are sunken because of old age. Prep. **bop.e.a** St. **bop.ek.a** Cs. **bop.esh.a** Ps. **bop.w.a** Rp. **bop.an.a**

bopo *n* (*ma-*) 1. the act of pressing in a fruit, etc.: *Bopo la mapapai la mteja lilimkasirisha mwenyeduka,* the pressing in of the pawpaws by the customer annoyed the shopkeeper. 2. an impression made by pressing in: dent, hollow; *Pamefanya bopo katika tunda nililolitomasa,* there is an impression left on the fruit I had touched gently. 3. mud, marsh, swamp: *Nililikanyaga bopo wakati wa usiku,* I treaded on the mud at night. 4. pond, pool, water-hole.

bora¹ *adj* excellent, first-rate, good, super, of the first order: *Nguo bora,* excellent clothes. *Chakula bora,* good food. *Bora afya,* (there is nothing like) good health.

bora² *conj* better than, best, more desirable: *Bora afya kuliko mali,* health is better than wealth.

boresh.a *vt, vi* improve, develop, ameliorate, better: *Serikali inataka kuboresha sekta za uchumi nchini,* the government wants to improve the economic sectors in the country. Prep. **boresh.e.a** St. **boresh.ek.a** Ps. **boresh.w.a** Rp. **boresh.an.a** (cf *endeleza*)

boresho *n* (*ma-*) improvement, progress, development.

bori¹ *n* (*ma-*) clay bowl of a hookah pipe. (cf *toza, kiko*) (Pers)

bori² n (*ma-*) an elephant tusk; ivory.
boribo n (*ma-*) (*bot*) a kind of big mango with a red colour around the stalk.
boriti n (*ma-*) 1. roof pole, rafter, beam; thick pole of the mangrove. (*prov*) *Kila boriti ina mwandamizi*, every roof pole has a prop, i.e. where there is a successful person, there is an initiator for him. 2. girder: *Boriti la chuma cha pua*, steel girder.
borohoa n (*n*) a kind of relish comprising of beans or green grams pounded into a paste of thick broth like gruel and used alongside rice or stiff porridge. (cf *kihembe*) (Pers)
boromali n (*n*) (*zool*) a kind of fish of rockod (groupers) type. (family *Serranidae*)
borong.a vt wreck, destroy, bungle, ruin: *Aliiboronga mipango yangu*, he wrecked my plans. Prep. **borong.e.a** St. **borong.ek.a** Cs. **borong.esh.a** Ps. **borong.w.a** Rp. **borong.an.a** (cf *haribu*, *vuruga*)
borongo¹ n (*ma-*) muddle, mess, bungle; a badly done job: *Alinifanyia kazi ya borongo*, he did a bad job for me.
borongo² adj see *borongoboringo*
borongoboringo (also *borongo*) adj disorderly, chaotic, disorganized, muddled: *Mambo yake yamekuwa borongoboringo*, his affairs are chaotic.
bosa¹ (also *boso*) n (*n*) (*naut*) a piece of rope tied on an anchor to keep it in place aboard the ship.
bos.a² vt (*naut*) try to find out the condition of sth that is inside the water by shaking the rope tied with it. Prep. **bos.e.a** St. **bos.ek.a** Cs. **bos.esh.a** Ps. **bos.w.a** Rp. **bos.an.a**
bosho.a vt tear into pieces; rip, rend, reave, rive: *Aliiboshoa barua yangu baada ya kuisoma*, she tore my letter into shreds after reading it. Prep. **bosho.le.a** St. **bosho.k.a** and **bosho.lek.a** Cs. **bosho.sh.a** Ps. of Prep. **bosho.lew.a** (cf *chana, rarua*)

boshori n (*n*) a woollen hat usu used against wind and extreme cold. (Ar)
bosi n (*ma-*) 1. boss, manager. (cf *kiongozi, mkuu*) 2. employer. (cf *mwajiri, tajiri*)
boso n (*n*) (*naut*) see *bosa*
botania n (*n*) (*naut*) botany (Eng)
botanish.a vt botanize, Prep. **botanish.i.a** St. **botanish.ik.a** Ps. **botanish.w.a** (Eng)
boti n (*n*) (*naut*) boat, vessel: *Motaboti*, motorboat. (Eng)
botimpao n (*naut*) hydroplane
-bovu adj 1. (*naut*) bad, rotten, putrid, decayed, decomposed: *Yai bovu*, a rotten egg. (cf *tule, -baya*) 2. worthless, useless, weak; unfit for work or service: *Mzee yule ni mbovu*, that old person is weak. (of *dhaifu, hafifu*)
bowelamvuvi n (*n*) see *bwelamvuvi*
buya n (*n*) (*naut*) 1. buoy (cf *cholozo*) 2. used in the expression: *Weka boya*, keep one waiting but fail to appear.
boza¹ n (*n*) see *buzaa*
boza² n (*ma-*) see *bozi*
bozi (also *boza, bozibozi*) n (*n*) 1. a disoriented person; a confounded person. 2. simpleton, nincompoup, fool: *Yeye ni bozi*, he is a fool. (cf *mjinga, mpumbavu*)
bozibozi n (*n*) see *bozi*
bradha (also *bruda*) n (*n*) brother; a male member of a religious group esp a monk. (Eng)
braketi n (*n*) bracket; a pair of signs (), [ ] used to enclose a word or words inserted for explanation. (cf *parendesi, mabano*) (Eng)
brandi n (*n*) cognac, brandy; a strong alcoholic drink made from wine. (Eng)
brashi n (*n*) see *burashi*
breki¹ n (*n*) brake: *Piga breki*, apply brakes; put on the brakes. *Shika breki*, apply brakes. *Tia breki*, brake. *Funga breki*, brake. *Breki za dharura*, emergency brakes. *Breki za upepo*, air brakes. (Eng)

breki² *n* (*n*) break, recess, respite; a pause for rest between events: *Wakati wa breki,* breaktime. (cf *mapumziko*) (Eng)

brigadea *n* (*ma-*) brigadier: *Brigadia jenerali,* brigadier-general. (Eng)

brigedi *n* (*n*) brigade; a large group of soldiers in the army. (Eng)

briji *n* (*n*) (*mus*) bridge; a small part of a stringed musical instrument, which is used to keep the strings stretched. (Eng)

bronki (also *bruchi*) *n* (*n*) brooch. (Eng)

bruchi *n* (*n*) see *bronki*

bruda *n* (*n*) see *bradha*

bu (also *fu*) *interj* an exclamation used to emphasize the action of falling: *Kuanguka bu!* fall down as a waterfall.

bua¹ (also *ubua*) *n* (*n*) (*bot*) the main stem of a plant or millet or maize; stalk, trunk.

bua² *adj* light, unheavy, weightless: *Gunia lile la pamba ni bua,* that sack of cotton is weightless.

bua ³ *n* (*ma-*) an iron rod for stoking fire in a furnace; poker.

buabu.a *vt* hew, chop: *Aliibuabua miti katika bustani yake,* he cut the trees a little from the top in his garden.

buathi *n* (*n*) see *baathi*

buba (also *mbuba*) *n* (*med*) yaws; a tropical skin disease caused by a spirochaete. *Treponema pertenue.*

bubu¹ (also *bubwi*) *n* (*ma-*) 1. a dumb person, a mute person. 2. a reticent person; a taciturn person; a close-mouthed person; a silent person.

bubu² *adj* silent, quiet.

bubu³ *n* (*ma-*) (*bot*) a flower that has not blossomed.

bubujik.a *vi* 1. bubble out, foam up, boil up; burst forth in a flood: *Kitoweo kilikuwa kinabubujika chunguni,* the stew was boiling in the pot. (cf *foka, jiajia*) 2. (*fig*) prattle, blather, twaddle; talk nonsense, talk without thinking:

Mwanasiasa yule hupenda kububujika kwenye jukwaa, that politician likes prattling on the platform. Prep. **bubujik.i.a** St. **bubujik.ik.a** Cs. **bubujik.ish.a** Ps. **bubujik.w.a** (cf *ropoka, payuka*)

bubujiko (also *mbubujiko*) *n* (*ma-*) 1. water or tears, etc coming out in large quantities from a spring of water, eyes, etc: *Bubujuko la machozi,* a burst of tears (cf *chemchemi*) 2. gibbering, blather: *Bubujiko la mlevi,* the drunkard's gibbering.

buburush.a *vt, vi* push, shove, trundle, drive: *Mchuuzi aliububurusha mkokoteni wake barabarani,* the hawker trundled his cart on the road. Prep. **buburush.i.a** St. **buburush.ik.a** Ps. **buburush.w.a** Rp. **buburush.an.a** (cf *vuta, sukuma*)

bubut.a¹ *vt* knock down, hit, strike, throw down: *Mwanamasumbwi alimbubuta mpinzani wake,* the boxer knocked down his opponent. Prep. **bubut.i.a** St. **bubut.ik.a** Cs. **bubut.ish.a** Ps **bubu.t.w.a** Rp. **bubut.an.a** (cf *buta, piga*)

bubut.a² *vt* chew hard grain without opening your mouth. Prep. **bubut.i.a** St. **bubut.ik.a** Cs. **bubut.ish.a** Ps. **bubut.w.a** Rp. **bubut.an.a**

bubwi *n* (*ma-*) see *bubu*

bucha¹ *n* (*ma-*) butcher, meat cutter. (Eng)

bucha² *n* (*ma-*) butchery, slaughter-house. (Eng)

buchari *n* (*ma-*) a kind of a big knife. (cf *sime, shembea*) (Hind)

buchuru *n* (*n*) a broken marble. (cf *bachu, pachu*)

buda *n* (*ma-*) 1. a very old person. 2. a toothless person or a person who has few teeth. (cf *kibogoyo*) 3. an old elephant without a tusk or having born without it.

budaa¹ *n* (*n*) flour balls in porridge.

buda.a² *vi* become lumpy as of porridge that is not sufficiently cooked.

Prep. ***buda.li.a*** St. ***buda.ik.a*** and ***buda.lik.a*** Cs. ***buda.ish.a*** Ps. of Prep. ***buda.liw.a***

budhara *n* (*n*) extravagance, prodigality, lavishness: *Budhara yake ya kila mara imemfukarisha*, his frequent extravagance has impoverished him. (Ar)

budi *n* (*ma-*) alternative, way out, escape. Usually the word *budi* is used with negative forms *kuwa na*, to have, e.g. *Sina budi*, I have no alternative; I must. (Ar)

bufuu *n* (*ma-*) an empty shell: *Bufuu la kichwa*, skull. *Bufuu la nazi*, an empty coconut shell. (cf *bupu, bupuru*)

bug.a *vt* 1. pick or seek the remnants in a harvested farm: *Aliibuga konde yangu na kupata mahindi mengi*, he picked up a lot of maize out of my already-harvested field. 2. sponge, scrounge, bum, cadge: *Ananiaibisha kwa tabia yake ya kubuga vyakula kwa rafiki zake*, he disgraces me for scrounging for food off his friends. Prep. ***bug.i.a*** Cs. ***bug.ish.a*** Ps of Prep. ***bug.iw.a*** (cf *doea, rondea*)

buge[1] *n* (*ma-*) a person without a finger or a toe.

buge[2] *n* (*ma-*) muncher; a person fond of munching or nibbling at items of food all the time.

-buge[3] *adj* having the habit of throwing items of food into one's mouth while eating. (*syn*) *Mtu mbuge hawezi nyumba*, a person fond of eating all the time cannot stay in a house or manage a household.

bughudha *n* (*n*) 1. insinuation, slander, revilement, innuendo: *Nilimripoti kwa wazee wake kwa vile alikuwa akiniletea bughudha kila mara*, I reported him to his parents because he was slandering me every now and again. (cf *masengenyo*) 2. unpleasant words: *Sikuweza kuzihimili bughudha zake*, I was not able to bear his unpleasant words. 3. hatred, animosity, ill-feeling: *Yeye ni mtu wa bughudha sana*, he is a person full of hatred. (cf *chuki*) (Ar)

bughudh.i (also *bughudhu*) *vt* slander, vilify, vilipend, revile, defame: *Mimi simpendi kutokana na tabia yake ya kubughudhi watu*, I don't like him because of his behaviour of reviling people. Prep. ***bughudh.i.a*** St. ***bughudh.ik.a*** Cs. ***bughudh.ish.a*** Ps. of Prep. ***bughudh.iw.a*** Rp. of Prep. ***bughudh.i.an.a*** (cf *sengenya, simanga*) (Ar)

bughudh.u *vt* see *bughudhi*

bugi[1] *n* (*n*) a kind of soporific magic used by thieves, believed to cause deep sleep or make doors open.

bugi[2] *n* (*n*) a kind of Swahili traditional dance.

bugi.a *vt* 1. take a mouthful of sth. (cf *bwia, bwakia, akia*) 2. gulp down, eat ravenously, eat greedily: *Njaa ilipomshika, akaenda jikoni na kubugia chakula chote*, when he felt hungry, he went to the kitchen and gulped down all the food. Prep. ***bugi.li.a*** St. ***bugi.k.a*** Cs. ***bugi.sh.a*** and ***bugi.z.a*** Ps. ***bugi.w.a***

bugu[1] *n* (*ma-*) a thick kind of withy used as a cord or a rope in building or for plaiting baskets, etc.

bugu[2] *n* (*ma-*) dissatisfaction, dislike, displeasure, bitterness: *Watu wale wana bugu sana kutokana na jinsi kiongozi wao anavyoendesha mambo ya chama*, those people are very dissatisfied with the way their leader is running party affairs.

buguik.a *vi* spurt, spout, gush, shoot out: *Petroli ilikuwa ikibuguika kwenye paipu iliyopasuka*, the petrol was spouting out from the broken pipe. Prep. ***buguik.i.a*** St. ***buguik.ik.a*** Cs. ***buguik.ish.a*** Ps. ***buguik.w.a*** (cf *foka, pukutika, bonga, pukusa*)

buguj.a *vt, vi* (*of insects*) bore a hole in grain or in wood. Prep. ***buguj.i.a*** St. ***buguj.ik.a*** Cs. ***buguj.ish.a*** Ps. ***buguj.w.a*** Rp. ***buguj.an.a*** (cf *bungua, bonga, pukusa*)

buheri *adv* with prosperity, with good life, with strength: *Buheri wa afya*, with health and strength. (Ar)

buhumu *n* (*ma*-) lungs (cf *pafu, yavuyavu*)
buhuri *n* (*ma*-) 1. smoke obtained by burning incense or by boiling medicine roots in water to make vapour; incense smoke 2. incense such as gum, frankincense, aloe wood, etc. (Ar)
bui[1] *n* (*ma*-) (*zool*) a large hairy spider with a poisonous bite; tarantula.

bui

bui[2] (also *buye*) *n* (*n*) a children's game like blindman's buff or hide-and-seek in which the seeker is blindfolded. (cf *kizuizi*)
bui[3] *n* (*ma*-) friend, companion, sidekick. (cf *rafiki, mwenzi*)
bui[4] *n* (*ma*-) see *buibui*[2]
buibui[1] *n* (*ma*-) (*zool*) spider: *Utando wa buibui*, spider's web.
buibui[2] (also *bui, baibui*) *n* (*ma*-) purdah; a veil usu black used by Moslems and some Hindus to seclude or hide their women from strangers.
buju.a *vt* stone; remove or squeeze out a stone or kernel in a fruit: *Nilizibujua tende nilipokuwa ninazila*, I stoned the dates as I was eating them. Prep. ***buju.li.a*** St. ***buju.k.a*** and ***buju.ik.a*** Cs. ***buju.ish.a*** Ps. of Prep. ***buju.i.w.a*** (cf *pujua*)
buka[1] *n* (*n*) grief, distress, affliction, grievance: *Ameingiwa na buka tangu kufa kwa baba yake mwaka jana*, he has been filled with grief since his father died last year. (cf *majonzi, huzuni*)
buka[2] *adj* fierce, ferocious, vicious, wild: *Simba buka*, a fierce lion. *Chui buka*, a fierce leopard.

buki *n* (*n*) (*anat*) kidney (cf *figo, nso*)
bukrata *n* (*n*) see *bukurata*
bukta *n* (*ma*-) shorts for sports. (Eng)
buku[1] *n* (*ma*-) (*zool*) a long-tailed rat that lives underground and has many hairs; giant rat.

buku

buku[2] *n* (*ma*-) (common in Zanzibar and Pemba) book. (cf *daftari*) (Eng)
buku.a[1] *vt, vi* study diligently before examinations, study hard; swot: *Alibukua masomo yake wakati mtihani ulipokaribia*, he studied hard when the examination was approaching. Prep. ***buku.li.a*** St. ***buku.k.a*** and ***buku.lik.a*** Cs. ***buku.lish.a***
buku.a[2] *vt* divulge a secret, scandal, etc; reveal, disclose, leak: *Anapenda kubukua siri za watu*, he likes revealing other people's secrets. Prep. ***buku.li.a*** St. ***buku.k.a*** Cs. of Prep. ***buku.lish.a*** Ps. of Prep. ***buku.liw.a*** Rp. ***buku.an.a*** (cf *fichua, gundua*)
buku.a[3] *vt* cut sth at a joint. Prep. ***buku.li.a*** St. ***buku.lik.a*** Cs. ***buku.lish.a*** Ps. ***buku.liw.a***
bukurata (also *bukrata*) *n* (*n*) morning (cf *asubuhi*) (Ar)
bulangeti *n* (*ma*-) see *blangeti*
bulbul *adj* see *bulibuli*[2]
buldani *n* (*n*) towns (Ar)
buldoza *n* (*ma*-) bulldozer (Eng)

buldoza

buli *n* (*ma-*) kettle, tea-pot, cistern. (cf *birika*) (Port)

bulibuli[1] *n* (*mi-*) a kind of white, embroidered skull cap. (Ar)

bulibuli[2] (also *bulbul*) *adj* nice, good, pleasant, attractive: *Ana tabia bulibuli*, she has good manners.

bulima *n* (*n*) (*naut*) bowsprit; a large tapered spar extending forward from the bow of a sailing vessel.

bulula *n* (*n*) see *bilula*

bulule *n* (*n*) see *bilule*

bulungu *n* (*ma-*) see *balungi*

bulungutu *n* (*ma-*) wad

buluu (also *bluu*) *n* (*n*) 1. blue colour. 2. a blue pigment or dye. (Eng)

bumba[1] *n* (*ma-*) cluster, packet, parcel, package, sheaf: *Bumba la tumbaku*, a packet of tobacco. *Bumba la nyuki*, a cluster of bees. *Bumba la makaratasi*, a sheaf of papers. *Bumba la noti*, a sheaf of notes. (cf *bunda, furushi*)

bumb.a[2] *vt* do sth without possessing the necessary professional skills; fumble, mess up (cf *burunga*) Prep. **bumb.i.a** St. **bumb.ik.a** Cs. **bumb.ish.a**

bumbo *n* (*n*) (*zool*) lizard fish; a brightly coloured sea fish of the *Synodontidae* family having a fusiform body, large mouth with canineform teeth along margins of both jaws, found on muddy bottoms from 20 to 200 metre depth. *Saurida undosquamis*.

bumbuaz.a *vt* discomfort, disconcert; make sby confused in his explanation, etc. Prep. **bumbuaz.i.a** St. **bumbuaz.ik.a** Ps. **bumbuaz.w.a** Rp. **bumbuaz.an.a**

bumbuazi *n* (*n*) utter perplexity, total amazement, complete bewilderment: *Amepigwa na bumbuazi*, he is filled with complete perplexity. *Shikwa na bumbuazi*, be perplexed. (cf. *butaa, fadhaa*)

bumbura *n* (*n*) (*zool*) a kind of saltwater fish resembling a rock cod.

bumburuk.a *vi* 1. be startled and run away as in the case of birds, etc.; be frightened away: *Alirusha jiwe na mara njiwa wakabumburuka*, he hurled a stone and immediately, the pigeons flew away. (cf *kurupuka, vumburuka*) 2. wake up in fear: *Nilibumburuka niliposikia kelele za 'mwizi'*, I woke up in fear when I heard someone shouting 'thief'. Prep. **bumburuk.i.a** St. **bumburuk.ik.a** Cs. **bumburuk.ish.a**

bumburush.a *vt* startle, scare away. Prep. **bumburush.i.a** St. **bumburush.ik.a** Ps. **bumburush.w.a** Rp. **bumburush.an.a**

bumbwi (also *bwimbwi*) *n* (*n*) rice flour mixed with sugar, scraped coconut, a little water or coconut juice and yeast and eaten without being cooked. (cf *kiqodo*)

bumia *n* (*n*) (*naut*) beam forming stern posts and shore stem of a dhow and fastened to the keel, *mkuku*, and carrying the rudder-post.

bumu[1] (also *bomu*) *n* (*n*) (*naut*) a kind of old dhow.

bumu[2] *n* (*n*) see *bundi*

bumunda *n* (*ma-*) a kind of dumpling or fritter made from ripe bananas and baked flour. Sometimes the millet flour is mixed with ghee and then made into balls.

bunda[1] *n* (*ma-*) parcel, bale, pack. bundle: *Bunda la noti*, a bundle of notes. *Bunda la karatasi*, a bundle of papers; ream. (cf *furushi, topa*)

bund.a[2] *vt* beat recklessly; hit, smack. Prep. **bund.i.a** St. **bund.ik.a** Cs. **bund.ish.a** Ps. **bund.w.a** (cf *buta*)

bundi (also *bumu*) *n* (*ma-*) (*zool*) owl (cf *babewatoto*)

bunduki *n* (*n*) gun, rifle: *Piga bunduki*, fire a gun. *Elekeza bunduki*, aim or point at a gun. *Bunduki ya mrao*, a matchlock gun. *Bunduki ya jiwe au ya gumegume au ya gobari*, a flintlock gun. *Bunduki ya kushindiliwa au ya fataki*, a muzzle-loading gun. *Bunduki* ya midomo miwili (au mitutu miwili), a double-barrelled gun. *Bunduki ya kukunja,* a sporting gun, a hinged gun. *Bunduki ya korofindo,* a breech-loading rifle. *Bunduki ya upepo,* air gun. *Mtutu wa bunduki,* the barrel of a gun. (Hind and Pers)

bunga¹ *n (n)* simpleton, imbecile, fool, idiot. (cf *mpumbavu, bozi, zuzu*)

bunga² *adj* stupid, silly, dull: *Mtu bunga,* a stupid person.

bungala *n (n)* kinds of rice, bananas and sugarcane: *Mchele bungala,* Bengal rice. *Ndizi bungala,* thick bananas. *Muwa bungala,* sugarcane with black bark.

bunge¹ *n (ma-)* parliament: *Bunge la mpito,* an interim parliament. *(Kinyak)*

bunge² *n (ma-)* a secret plan to do sth.

bungo¹ *n (ma-) (bot)* rubber vine; the fruit of a rubber vine tree *(Landolphia florida),* which is pear-shaped, smooth and apricot-coloured when ripe and containing about a dozen of seeds covered with sticky pulp.

bungo² (also *bungu, bunzi*) *n (n)* 1. *(zool)* mud wasp. 2. carpenter bee. 3. mason wasp; a kind of wasp that builds mud cakes in twigs, stones and walls or nests in holes, in the ground or in stems. 4. a kind of caterpillar, 'scaly-winged' that can do considerable harm to both field and stored crops.

bungo³ *n (n)* a vessel like a small bowl or small cooking-pot.

bungu¹ *n (ma-)* see *bungo²*

bungu² *n (n)* see *bunju*

bungu.a *vt* bore holes in grain, timber, etc. as insects do: *Wadudu wamezibungua mbaazi zangu,* the insects have bored into my pigeon-peas. Prep. ***bungu.li.a*** St. ***bungu.ik.a*** Cs. ***bungu.sh.a*** Ps. of Prep. ***bungu.liw.a*** (cf *buguja, toboa*)

bunguu *n (ma-)* a large earthenware dish for serving up food or squeezing out coconut juice. (cf *kibia, mkungu*)

buni¹ *n (n) (bot)* coffee berry, coffee beans. (Ar)

bun.i² *vt* 1. construct, compose, contrive: *Walizibuni hadithi za kusisimua,* they composed interesting stories. (cf *jenga, aka*) 2. invent, discover, fabricate: *Ameyabuni maneno tu,* he has just invented the words. *Amebuni mbinu mpya,* he has invented new techniques. Prep. ***bun.i.a*** St. ***bun.ik.a*** Cs. ***bun.ish.a*** Ps. of Prep. ***bun.iw.a*** Rp. of Prep. ***bun.i.an.a*** (Ar)

bun.i³ *vt (naut)* build a vessel: *Alibuni meli,* he built a ship. Prep. ***bun.i*** St. ***bun.ik.a*** Cs. ***bun.ish.a*** Ps. of Prep. ***bun.iw.a*** Rp. of Prep. ***bun.i.an.a***

-bunifu *adj* creative, imaginative, inventive: *Waandishi wabunifu,* creative writers.

bunju *n* (also *bungu*) *(zool)* pufferfish, blowfish, toby; a kind of poisonous fish of the *Tetraodontidae* family with a circumglobal and inflatable body, capable of expanding the body by swallowing water or air, found usu in tropical and temperate waters, *Diodon holacanthus.*

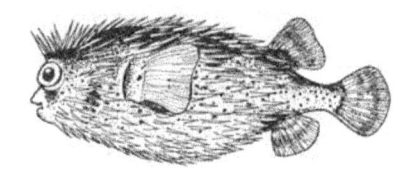

bunju

bunta (also *buntwa*) *n (ma-)* 1. *(naut)* landing-stage, harbour, pier. (cf *gati*) 2. ship building-yard.

buntwa *n (ma-)* see *bunta*

bunuwasi *n (n) abunuwasi*

bunzi¹ *n (ma-)* see *bungo²*

bunzi² (also *gunzi*) *n (ma-)* maize cob.

bupu (also *bupuru*) *n (ma-)* 1. an empty shell of a coconut: *Bupu la nazi,* an empty coconut shell. *Bupu la kichwa,* skull. (cf *fuvu, fuu*) 2. an empty thing: *Kichwa chake ni bupu,* he is not intelligent; he is dull.

bupuru *n* (*ma*-) see *bupu*

bura *n* (*n*) a kind of Muscat cloth. (*prov*) *Bura yangu sibadili na rehani,* something of poor quality that I own is better than one of superior quality that belongs to someone else. (cf *kitambi*)

buraa *n* (*n*) forgiveness of debt, dowry, obligation, etc.: *Kama buraa haingetolewa, bwana harusi angeshindwa kutoa mahari,* if the dowry was not forgiven, the bridegroom would have failed to pay it. (Ar)

buraha *n* (*n*) happiness, ease, comfort, relief, peace: *Anaishi kwa furaha na buraha,* he lives happily. (Ar)

burah.i *vi* 1. rest, relax, unwind; take one's case: *Daadu yu kufanya kazi kwa masaa mengi, akaenda kwake kuburahi,* after working for so many hours, he went to his place to take a rest. (cf *pumzika*) 2. (of a patient) recover, recuperate, convalesce; return to health: *Ameanza kuburahi baada ya kuugua takriban mwaka mmoja.* he has started to recuperate after being sick for almost one year. Prep. **burah.i.a** St. **burah.ik.a** Cs. **burah.ish.a** (cf *pona*) (Ar)

bura.i *vt* forgive a dowry, debt, etc.; renounce a claim: *Niliburai deni lake,* I forgave his debt. Prep **bura.i.a** St. **bura.ik.a** Cs. **bura.ish.a** Ps. of Prep. **bura.i.w.a** Rp. **bura.i.an.a** (cf *bihi*) (Ar)

burangani *n* (*n*) (*naut*) see *barangeni.*

burashi (also *brashi*) *n* (*n*) 1. brush, broom, besom: *Burashi ya nywele,* hair brush. (cf *ufagio*) 2. toothbrush. (Eng)

burda *adv* comfortably, happily. (Ar)

burdai *n* (*n*) see *burudai*

burdani (also *burudani*) *n* (*n*) entertainment, play, sport. (Ar)

bure[1] *adj* 1. gratuitous, gratis, free of charge, without payment: *Kazi bure,* unpaid work. (cf *bwerere, chewale*) 2. useless, worthless, valueless: *Maneno ya bure,* useless words, foolish words. *Bure ghali,* good-for-nothing. 3. for no good reason, without reason: *Bure bilashi,* without any reason at all, *Unawasimanga watu bure,* you speak ill of people for nothing.

bure[2] *adv* 1. gratuitously, free of charge 2. worthlessly, in vain, uselessly, fruitlessly: *Juhudi zake za kutafuta uhamisho zilikwenda bure,* his efforts to get a transfer were in vain. 3. meaninglessly, unsoundly, unreasonably, without reason: *Alinitukana bure,* he insulted me for nothing.

burhani *n* (*n*) see *buruhani*

buri *n* (*n*) (*zool*) a small elephant tusk when it begins to grow. (cf *kalasha*)

buriani *n* (*n*) 1. farewell; last words esp of people going for a long journey; bon voyage. *Peana buriani,* exchange farewell. (cf *maagano*) 2. forgiveness, pardon.

buru *n* (*n*) a kind of gourd for preparing butter. (cf *tungu*)

burubuku *n* (*n*) metal coins written in Arabic script used in the 17th century in certain coastal areas of Kenya such as Mombasa, Lamu and Pate.

burudai (also *burdai*) *n* (*n*) a kind of a special eulogy of Prophet Muhammad compiled by a prominent poet, "Al Bushiri".

burudani *n* (*n*) see *burdani*

burud.i *vi* be cool, be calm, be serene: *Ingawa alighadhibika mwanzoni, lakini sasa ameburudi,* even though he was angry at the beginning, he has now cooled down. Prep. **burud.i.a** St. **burud.ik.a** Cs. **burud.ish.a** (cf *poa, tulia*)

burudik.a *vi* refresh oneself; entertain oneself. Prep. **burudik.i.a** St. **burudik.ik.a** Cs. **burudik.ish.a**

burudish.a *vt* be entertaining, be comforting: *Anajiburudisha kwa kunywa vinywaji vya aina mbalimbali*, he is refreshing himself by taking various kinds of drinks. Prep. *burudish.i.a* St. *burudish.ik.a* Ps. *burudish.w.a* Rp. *burudish.an.a*

burug.a[1] *vt* see *buruga*. Prep. *burug.i.a* St. *burug.ik.a* Cs. *burug.ish.a* Ps. *burug.w.a*

burug.a[2] *vt* 1. till; level down the soil after ploughing or digging in order to prepare for planting: *Mkulima aliuburuga udongo kwa ajili ya msimu unaokuja*, the farmer levelled the soil in order to prepare for the forthcoming sowing season. 2. mix together by stirring when preparing food. Prep. *burug.i.a* St. *burug.ik.a* Cs. *burug.ish.a* Ps. *burug.w.a* Rp. *burug.an.a*

buruhani (also *burhani*) *n* (*n*) (In Islam) divine power. (cf *makarama, karama*) (Ar)

buruji[1] *n* (*n*) battlement, fortification; indented parapet of a fort. (Ar)

buruji[2] *n* (*n*) minaret, tower. (Ar)

buruji[3] *n* (*n*) 1. bugle. 2. a person in charge of blowing a bugle; bugler. (Ar)

buruji[4] *n* (*n*) the places underneath an enclosure in shallow waters behind which, fish traps are set.

buruji[5] *n* (*n*) the stars' path. (Ar)

buruma *n* (*ma-*) hookay, narghile; an oriental tobacco pipe with a long flexible tube such that it draws water in a vase or bowl and cools it.

buruma

burung.a *vt* 1. knead bread, dough, clay, etc. into balls: *Mpishi aliuburunga unga wa kufanyia mkate*, the cook kneaded the bread dough into balls. (cf *finyanga*) 2. botch, bungle; do sth haphazardly. Prep. *burung.i.a* St. *burung.ik.a* Cs. *burung.ish.a* Ps. *burung.w.a* Rp. *burung.an.a* (cf *vuruga, boronga*)

burungutu *n* (*ma-*) a bundle of things tied together.

burur.a (also *buruta*) *vt* drag along; haul, hale, lug, pull: *Hamali alikuwa akiburura mkokoteni*, the porter was dragging a pushcart, Prep. *burur.i.a* St. *burur.ik.a* Cs. *burur.ish.a* Ps. *burur.w.a* Rp. *burur.an.a* (cf *kokota, sukuma*)

burut.a *vt* see *burura*

buruz.a *vt* 1. drag, lead astray, mislead: *Kiongozi alitaka kuwaburuza wafuasi wake*, the leader wanted to lead his followers astray. 2. send: *Walitishia kuiburuza tume ya uchaguzi mahakamani*, they threatened to send the election commission to appear before the court of law. Prep. *buruz.i.a* St. *buruz.ik.a* Cs. *buruz.ish.a* Ps. *buruz.w.a* Rp. *buruz.an.a*

busa *n* (*n*) kick, push. (cf *msukumo, kibega*)

busara *n* (*n*) prudence, wisdom, sound judgement, common sense, intelligence: *Busara ni kitu azizi*, wisdom is a precious thing. (Ar)

busati *n* (*ma-*) a kind of mat made of stalks or rice plants or wheat usu used in mosques, etc. (Ar)

busha *n* (*ma-*) (*med*) hydrocele; a collection of fluid in a cavity of the body particularly in the scrotum. (cf *mshipa, pumbu*) (Port)

bushashi *n* (*n*) 1. a kind of thin white paper. 2. a thin white light muslin used to make a dress or used as a kind of shawl worn around shoulders; tiffany. (Ar)

bushati *n* (*ma-*) bush shirt; a round bottom shirt. (Eng)

bushura n (n) happiness, joy, gladness. (cf *furaha*) (Ar)
bushuti n (n) a long cloak worn by some men, decorated with gold threadwork around the back and the chest and usu worn during official functions. (cf *jojo*) (Ar)
bustani n (ma-) 1. garden, orchard: *Bustani ya biashara*, market garden. *Bustani ya mimea*, botanical garden. 2. park, recreation ground. (Ar)
bus.u[1] vt, vi kiss, smooch. Prep. **busi.a** St. **bus.ik.a** Cs. **bus.ish.a** Ps. of Prep. **bus.iw.a** Rp. of Prep. **bus.i.an.a**
bus.u[2] n (n) kiss; a caress with the lips.
busur.i vt, vi observe, be careful, be alert, keep watch: *Lazima ubusuri na wezi siku hizi*, you must be wary of thieves these days. Prep. **busur.i.a** St. **busur.ik.a** Cs. **busur.ish.a** Ps. of Prep. **busur.iw.a** Rp. of Prep. **busur.i.an.a** (cf *tahadhari*) (Ar)
but.a vt (colloq) beat, hit, strike, smack: *Mzazi alimbuta mwanawe kwa kosa la nidhamu*, the parent beat his son for misconduct. Prep. **but.i.a** St. **but.ik.a** Cs. **but.ish.a** Ps. **but.w.a** Rp. **but.an.a** (cf *piga, bobota*)
butaa (also *butwaa*) n (n) utter perplexity, total amazement, complete bewilderment, helpless confusion, astonishment: *Pigwa na butaa*, be perplexed. (cf *bumbuazi, fadhaa*)
buti[1] n (ma-) 1. (naut) a coastal vessel with one slightly curved mast, upright stem, square stern and of 20-60 tons. 2. a type of a dhow in Lamu, Kenya.
buti[2] n (n) boot (Eng)
buti[3] n (n) a traditional coastal dance in East Africa performed usu by young people of both sexes. The performers and drummers make a circle and one of them dances in the middle and before he leaves the arena, he or she touches one of the performers who follows suit.
buti[4] n (ma-) (of a car) boot (Eng)
-butu adj 1. blunt, dull, rounded, not sharp: *Kisu kibutu*, a blunt knife.

Pembe butu, obtuse angle. (cf *gutu*) 2. dull, unintelligent, witless, stupid: *Yeye ni butu*, he is dull.
butu.a vt 1. dull, blunt; take the edge off, make blunt: *Amelibutua jambia langu*, he has blunted my dagger. 2. (sports) kick wildly. Prep. **butu.li.a** St. **butu.k.a** Cs. **butu.sh.a** Ps. of Prep. **butu.liw.a** Rp. **butu.an.a** (cf *senega*)
butwaa n (n) see *butaa*
buu![1] interj Be quiet! Silence! Make less noise: *Enyi watoto buu!* You children be silent!
buu[2] n (n) (zool) maggot, jigger, larva, chrysalis; a kind of worm. (cf *pupa*)
buuwambe n (n) (zool) a parasitic mite which burrows under the skin and causes rash or skin disease called scabies. *Sarcoptes scabies*.
buye[1] n (n) see *buu*[2]
buye[2] n (n) obstruction, obstacle. (cf *kizuizi*)
buyu n (n) 1. (bot) fruit of a baobab tree; monkey-bread. 2. a calabash or gourd for drinking water, etc.
buz.a[1] vi booze; drink alcohol: *Mtu yule anapenda kubuza*, that person likes to booze. (Eng)
buza[2] n (n) a kind of intoxicating liquour prepared from honey.
bwabwaj.a[1] vi prattle, blather, talk foolishly. Prep. **bwabwaj.i.a** St. **bwabwaj.ik.a** Cs. **bwabwaj.ish.a** (cf *payuka, ropoka*)
bwabwaj.a[2] vi pass urine in bed; wet the bed: *Mtoto alibwabwaja*, the child wetted the bed. Prep. **bwabwaj.i.a** St. **bwabwaj.ik.a** Cs. **bwabwaj.ish.a** (cf *bwata, ropoka*)
bwacha n (n) (bot) amaranthus; spinach. (cf *mchicha*)
bwachi n (n) (naut) lower part of a beach. (cf *pwaji*)
bwag.a vt 1. (bot) throw down, drop. (cf *angusha*): *Alinibwaga chini*, he threw me down. 2. (colloq) defeat: *Kiongozi alimbwaga mpinzani wake*, the leader

defeated his opponent. 3. (*idms*) *Bwaga matusi*, insult someone incessantly. *Bwaga moyo*, rest the mind; be cheerful. *Bwaga mzigo*, drop a load on the ground. *Bwaga mtwae*, recklessly, chaotically, disorderly e.g. *Alivaa nguo bwaga mtwae*, he wore clothes in a disorderly manner. *Bwaga zani*, cause disorder, cause chaos. *Bwaga mbali*, forget. *Bwaga manyanga*, quit, resign. Prep. **bwag.i.a** St. **bwag.ik.a** Cs. **bwag.ish.a** and **bwagi.z.a** Ps. **bwag.w.a** Rp **bwag.an.a**

bwagaz.a *vi* sprawl on the ground anywhere; throw oneself down anywhere; spraddle: *Alipojiona amechoka, akajibwagaza*, when he felt tired, he simply sprawled on the ground. Prep **bwagaz.i.a** St. **bwagaz.ik.a** Cs. **bwagaz.ish.a**

bwagik.a *vi* 1.sit idly; sit without nothing to do. (cf *pweteka*) 2. be despondent, be disheartened. Prep. **bwagik.i.a** St. **bwagik.ik.a** Cs. **bwagik.ish.a** (cf *angema*)

bwaki.a *vt* take a mouthful of sth hurriedly; gulp down: *Alizibwakia njugu mawe zote*, he ate all the ground nuts in a hurry. Prep. **bwaki.li.a** St. **bwaki.lik.a** Cs. **bwaki.sh.a** Ps. **bwaki.w.a** (cf *bugia, akia*)

bwaku.a (also *bwakura*) *vt* snatch away, grasp; take by force: *Alikibwakua kitabu changu nilipokuwa ninakisoma*, he snatched my book while I was reading it. Prep. **bwaku.li.a** St. **bwaku.lik.a** Cs. **bwaku.lish.a** Ps. of Prep. **bwaku.liw.a** Rp. of Prep. **bwaku.li.an.a** (cf *pokonya, pekua*)

bwakur.a *vt* see *bwakua*. Prep. **bwakur.i.a** St. **bwakur.ik.a** Cs. **bwakur.ish.a** Ps. **bwakur.w.a** Rp. **bwakur.an.a**

bwalo *n* (*ma-*) dining-hall

bwambwa *n* (*ma-*) 1. anything that is degenerating or crumbling but can be used at least for a while. 2. a bad vessel; something defective.

bwambwara *n* (*ma-*) anything unfit to be used at all; a useless thing.

bwamkubwa *n* (*ma-*) 1. an old man. (cf *shaibu, buda*) 2. reference to father as a sign of respect.

bwana[1] *n* (*ma-*) 1. Sir, Mr: *Bwana mdogo*, a person of the next rank deserving respect. *Bwana shamba*, agricultural officer, farm officer. 2. husband: *Bwana harusi*, bridegroom. 3. employer, master. (cf *tajiri, bosi*) 4. the Lord: *Bwana Mungu*, Almighty God.

bwana[2] *interj* 1. an exclamation for calling someone to listen; hey! e.g. *Bwana ee*, listen please, may I have your attention. 2. an exclamation used to surprise someone.

bwanaharusi *n* (*ma-*) see *bwana*[1]

bwanashamba *n* (*ma-*) see *bwana*[1]

bwanyenye *n* (*ma-*) 1. bourgeois; a propertied person. 2. a well-to-do person from town. 3. parasite, leech, sponge. (cf *kupe*) 4. an excessively corpulent person.

bwat.a[1] *vi* prattle, blather, babble; talk nonsense: *Badala ya kuzungumza vizuri, yeye hubwata*, instead of talking distinctly, he babbles. Prep. **bwat.i.a** St. **bwat.ik.a** Cs. **bwat.ish.a** Ps. **bwat.w.a** Rp. **bwat.an.a** (cf *bwabwaja, ropoka*)

bwat.a[2] *vt* throw down sth; drop sth and smash it: *Alikibwata kikombe changu*, he dropped my cup and it smashed. Prep. **bwat.i.a** St. **bwat.ik.a** Cs. **bwat.ish.a** Ps. **bwat.w.a** Rp. **bwat.an.a** (cf *bwaga*)

bwawa *n* (*ma-*) 1. swamp, pool, bog, quagmire: *Bwawa la kuogelea*, swimming pool. *Bwawa la samaki*, pond. 2. wash. (cf *josho*)

bwege *n* (*ma-*) imbecile, simpleton, fool, idiot. (cf *mpumbavu, juha, fala*)

bweha *n* (ma-) see *mbweha*

bwek.a *vi* bay, bark, yelp. Prep. **bwek.e.a** St. **bwek.ek.a** Cs. **bwek.esh.a** Ps. **bwek.w.a** (cf *gumia*)

bweko *n* (*ma-*) bow-wow; the sound of a dog.

bwelamvuvi (also *bolamvuvi, bowelamvuvi*) *n* (*n*) cigar wrasse; a kind of fish (family *Labridae*) with a very elongate and slightly compressed body with a pair of canine teeth anteriorly in jaws, typically found in sea grasses or dense beds of algae. *Cheilio inermis*.

bwelasuti *n* (*ma-*) overalls; a loose-fitting coat-like garment worn usu over other clothing to protect against dirt and wear. (cf *ovaroli, msurupwenye*)

bwende *n* (*ma-*) an old piece of cloth worn around the loins by people of both sexes while working on a farm. (cf *demu*)

bweni *n* (*ma*) dormitory, hostel: *Bweni la wasichana*, girls' dormitory.

bwenzi *n* (*ma*) a tuft of hair left on the head; quiff. (cf *shungi, denge, sunzu*)

bwerere[1] *n* (*n*) 1. trash, rubbish; a valueless thing: *Alikwenda dukani kununua vitu vya bwerere*, he went to the shop to buy useless things. 2. free of charge, without payment: *Alipewa chakula cha bwerere*, he was given free food.

bwerere[2] *adv* gratuitously; free of charge: *Chakula kilitolewa bwerere*, the food was given free of charge. (cf *horera*)

bwes.a *vt* tear, rip, rend, pull apart. Prep. **bwes.e.a** St. **bwes.ek.a** Cs. **bwes.esh.a** Ps. **bwes.w.a**

bweshu *n* (ma-) a cheerless person; bête noire (cf *mkimwa*)

bwet.a[1] *n* (*ma-*) a special drawer for keeping in money. (Port)

bweta[2] *n* (*ma-*) a small chest; a small coffer; a small box such as a cash-box, jewel box, etc. (Port)

bwet.a[3] *vt, vi* pant, puff, breathe: *Alikimbia masafa marefu na ndiyo maana sasa anabweta*, he ran for a long distance and that is why he is now panting. Prep. **bwet.e.a** St. **bwet.ek.a** Cs. **bwet.esh.a** Rp. of Prep. **bwet.e.an.a** (cf *tweta, hema*)

bwete *adj* dormant: *Volkano bwete*, a dormant volcano.

bwetek.a *vi* be idle, be inactive: *Badala ya kufanya kazi, akabweteka*, instead of working, he became inactive. Prep. **bwetek.e.a** Cs. **bwetek.esh.a** Ps. **bwetek.w.a** (cf *dereka*)

bwi.a[1] *vt* take a mouthful of pieces of food such as nuts, rice, etc. hurriedly: *Aliibwia keki mpaka ikamalizika yote*, he ate the cake in a hurry until he finished all of it. Prep. **bwi.li.a** St. **bwi.lik.a** Cs. **bwi.lish.a** Ps. **bwi.w.a** Rp. **bwi.an.a** (cf *bugia, akia*)

bwi.a[2] *vt* apprehend, seize, arrest, nab: *Polisi walimbwia jambazi*, the police arrested the thug. Prep. **bwi.li.a** St. **bwi.lik.a** Cs. **bwi.lish.a** Ps. **bwi.w.a** Rp. **bwi.an.a** (cf *gwia, kamata*)

bwiki.a *vt, vi* be obsessed, be infatuated, be over-indulged: *Chakula kilimbwikia mgeni na kwa hivyo, akaomba nyongeza*, the guest was obsessed with the food and so he wanted some more. Prep. **bwiki.li.a** St. **bwiki.lik.a** Cs. **bwiki.lish.a**

bwiko *n* (*ma-*) 1. (*med*) Dupuytren's contracture; flexion deformity involving usu fourth and fifth fingers due to the contracture of the palm of the hand. *Palmar fascitis*. 2. the stiffness of fingers.

bwiko

bwimbwi *n* (*n*) 1. see *bumbwi*. 2. popcorn flour mixed with sugar or honey,

CH

Ch, ch /tʃ/ 1. the third letter of the Swahili alphabet. 2. a voiceless postal alveolar affricate.

ch.a[1] *vt, vi* dread, fear; be scared, be afraid of, be in awe of: (*prov*) *Ukicha kusemwa, hutatenda jambo,* if you are afraid of what people might say, you will never do anything. *Mcha Mungu si mtovu,* who obeys God is on the right path. Prep. ***ch.e.le.a*** St. ***ch.ek.a*** Cs. ***ch.esh.a*** Ps. of Prep. ***ch.ew.a*** Rp. of Prep. ***ch.e.an.a***

ch.a[2] *vi* dawn, lighten; grow light: *Kumekucha,* it is dawn. The expression is also used in political gatherings when a speaker wants to mobilize people for a particular cause.

cha[3] *prep* a Swahili word of preposition for nouns of ki-vi class. The grammatical particle carries the meaning of "*of*" in English.

chaa[1] *n (n)* a group of people cultivating together; co-farmers.

chaa[2] *n (n)* (*zool*) pursemouth, silver biddy; a kind of fish of the *Gerreidae* family with silvery sides, compressed, slender or deep body with large scales, and found in sandy shallows of tidal creeks, lagoons and coral reefs and near beaches.

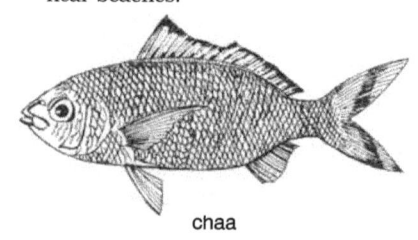

chaa

chaa[3] *n (n)* corral, pen, kraal. (cf *zeriba, dewa, faja*)

chaa[4] *n (n)* (*bot*) seed-bed, nursery. (cf *kitalu*)

chaa[5] *adj* white, glittering.

chaawe *n (n)* pebble (cf *tumbawe, fufuwele*)

chabang.a *vt* thrash, hit, beat, thwack: *Mzazi alimchabanga bintiye,* the parent beat his daughter. *Tuliichabanga timu yao kwa magoli mengi,* we thrashed their team by many goals. Prep. ***chabang.i.a*** St. ***chabang.ik.a*** Cs. ***chabang.ish.a*** Ps. ***chabang.w.a*** Rp. ***chabang.an.a*** (cf *nyuka, tandika, banjua*)

chach.a[1] *vt, vi* ferment; go sour, go bad: *Pombe imechacha,* the beer has fermented. Prep. ***chach.i.a*** St. ***chach.ik.a*** Cs. ***chach.ish.a*** (cf *haribika, oza*)

chach.a[2] *vt, vi* 1. rage; boil over, be wild, be angry, seethe with indignation; *Baba alichacha baada ya gari yake kuibiwa,* my father got angry after his car was stolen. (cf *hamaki, udhika*) 2. (*fig*) be vigorous, be intensified: *Vita vimechacha,* the war has intensified. Prep. ***chach.i.a*** St. ***chach.ik.a*** Cs. ***chach.ish.a*** (cf *rindima*)

chach.a[3] *vi* (*naut*) be rough, be churning: *Bahari imechacha,* the sea is rough. Prep. ***chach.i.a*** St. ***chach.ik.a*** Cs. ***chach.ish.a*** Ps. of Prep. ***chach.iw.a*** (cf *chafuka*)

chach.a[4] *vt, vi* show spirit or vigour after a period of laxness or abstinence; become more active: *Jirani yangu amechacha kunywa pombe,* my neighbour has intensified his beer drinking. Prep. ***chach.i.a*** St. ***chach.ik.a*** Cs. ***chach.ish.a*** (cf *chaga, chachawa, charuka*)

chacha[5] *n (n)* (*bot*) aquatic grass; grass growing in swampy areas.

chacha[6] *n (n)* a style of dancing.

chacha[7] *n (ma-)* a drying rack; a raised stage for drying grain, etc. (cf *kichaga*)

chach.a[8] *vt* be in financial difficulties. Prep. *chach.i.a* St. *chach.ik.a* Cs. *chach.ish.a*

chachacha *n* (*n*) a kind of musical dance of quick steps.

chachafy.a *vt* put pressure on sby: *Mtoto alimchachafya mzee wake ili amnunulie baiskeli*, the child pressurized his parent in order to buy him a bicycle. *Mchezaji alichachafya ngome ya wapinzani*, the player put pressure on the defence of the opposite team. Prep. *chachafy.i.a* St. *chachafy.ik.a* Cs. *chachafy.ish.a* Ps. of Prep. *chachafy.iw.a* Rp. *chachafy.an.a* (cf *chagiza*)

chachag.a (also *chachata*) *vt* wash clothes by dabbing on the board esp in the case of delicate fabrics: *Alizichachaga nguo zake za nailoni*, he washed his nylon clothes by gently beating them. Prep. *chachag.i.a* St. *chachag.ik.a* Cs. *chachag.ish.a* Ps. *chachag.w.a* (cf *chanyata, chachata*)

chachama.a *vt,vi* stand firm, be firm, be intransigent, be unyielding: *Serikali imechachamaa kuhusu uagizaji wa bidhaa duni kutoka nje*, the government has stood firm on the importation of low-class goods. Prep. *chachama.li.a* St. *chachama.lik.a* Cs. *chachama.lish.a* Ps. of Prep. *Chachama.liw.a* Rp. of Prep. *chachama.li.an.a* (cf *shikilia, ng'ang'ania*)

chachamu.a *vt* provoke, infuriate, exacerbate, anger, exasperate, vex; *Alinichachamua baada ya kuligonga gari langu*, he angered me after knocking into my car. St. *chachamu.k.a* Cs. *chachamu.sh.a* Ps. of Prep. *chachamu.liw.a* Rp. *chachamu.an.a* (cf *ghadhibisha, kasirisha*)

chacharik.a (also *chachatika*) *vi* 1. be restless, be uneasy, be fretful, be unstable: *Amekuwa akichacharika kutokana na maumivu ya tumbo*, he has been restless due to abdominal pains. 2. be busy, be occupied: *Wamechacharika na maandalizi ya sherehe za uhuru*, they are busy with the preparations of celebrations of independence. (cf *hangaika*)

chachat.a *vt* see *chachaga*

chachatik.a[1] *vi* see *chacharika*

chachatik.a[2] *vi* 1. (of blood or nerves) tingle, tickle: *Mwili wake ulichachatika baada ya mimi kuigusa pua yake na unyoya*, his body tickled after I touched his nose with a feather. 2. (of fat, etc. boiling in a frying pan) sizzle: *Mafuta yalipochachatika, akatumbukiza maandazi kwenye kikaango*, when the cooking fat sizzled, he put the doughnuts in the frying pan, Prep. *chachatik.i.a* St. *chachatik.ik.a* Cs. *chachat.ish.a*

chachatik.a[3] *vi* (of glass, etc) break into pieces. Prep. *chachatik.i.a* St. *chachatik.ik.a* Cs. *chachat.ish.a*

chachaw.a[1] *vi* 1. jump about with pleasure or for joy: *Nilipoambiwa kuwa nimefaulu vizuri kwenye mtihani, nilichachawa*, when I was told that I had passed the examination very well, I jumped about with joy. (cf *rukaruka*) 2. insist or be adamant about sth: *Alichachawa sana kwa baba yake mpaka hatimaye akakubali kumnunulia baiskeli*, after much insistence, his father finally agreed to buy him a bicycle. Prep. *chachaw.i.a* St. *chachaw.ik.a* Cs. *chachaw.ish.a* Rp. *chachaw.an.a* (cf *chaga, charuka*)

chachaw.a[2] *vi* prickle, tingle, smart, itch: *Kidonda mguuni mwake kilikuwa kimechachawa*, the wound on his leg was smarting. Prep. *chachaw.i.a* St. *chachaw.ik.a* Cs. *chachaw.ish.a* Rp. *chachaw.an.a* (cf *chonyota*)

chachawiz.a *vt,vi* interrupt or drown someone's speech by making noise thus causing an uproar: *Alinichachawiza nilipokuwa ninazungumza,* he interrupted me by making noise when I was talking. Prep. ***chachawiz.i.a*** St. ***chachawiz.ik.a*** Ps. ***chachawiz.w.a,*** Rp. ***chachawiz.an.a*** (cf *hanikiza, dakiza*)

chachawizo *n* (*ma-*) 1. uproar, tumult, pandemonium, confusion, trouble: *Usilete chachawizo hapa,* do not cause chaos here. (cf *kelele, fujo, ghasia*) 2. difficulty, trouble, problem: *Mtu yule anapenda kuwaletea machachawizo majirani zake,* that person likes causing problems for his neighbours. (cf *matata, udhia*)

chache[1] (also *kifumbo*) *n* (*n*) (*zool*) a kind of marine fish of the *Albulidae* family having an elongate cylindrical body with silvery cycloid scales, a naked head, and which is found in shallow waters over sandy and muddy bottoms; bonefish. *Albula vulpes.*

chache

-chache[2] *adj* few, not many, a handful of: *Watu wachache,* few people. (cf *haba, kidogo*)

chache[3] *adv* rarely, seldom: *Anakuja kwangu mara chache,* he rarely comes to my place.

chachi *n* (*n*) aunt (cf *shangazi*)

chachish.a[1] *vt* provoke, exasperate, anger. Prep. ***chachish.i.a*** St. ***chachish.ik.a*** Ps. ***chachish.w.a***

chachish.a[2] *vt* make sth turn sour; sour: *Aliuchachisha mchuzi,* she made the curry sour. Prep. ***chachish.i.a*** St. ***chachish.ik.a*** Ps. ***chachish.w.a***

chachu[1] *n* (*n*) yeast, leaven, ferment: *Alitia chachu katika pombe,* he put yeast in the beer. (cf *hamira*)

chachu[2] *n* (*n*) a thing that speeds up another thing or causes exasperation, etc.; catalyst: *Chachu ya maendeleo,* a catalyst for development.

chachu.a *vt* cause fermentation; leaven, sour: *Aliuchachua mchuzi,* he soured the curry. Prep. ***chachu.li.a*** St. ***chachu.k.a*** Cs. ***chachu.sh.a*** Ps. of Prep. ***chachu.liw.a*** (cf *dodesha, ozesha*)

chachuk.a *vi* ferment; go bad; go/turn sour. Prep. ***chachuk.i.a*** St. ***chachuk.ik.a*** Cs. ***chachuk.ish.a***

chachuli *n* (*n*) (*zool*) a young monkey.

chadi *n* (*n*) see *jadi*

chafi (also *tafi, tasi*) *n* (*n*) (*zool*) spinefoot, rabbit fish; a kind of fish of the *Siganidae* family having a compressed ovate body, covered with very small scales and which is found in coral and rock reefs.

-chafu *adj* 1. dirty, soiled, unclean: *Nguo chafu,* dirty clothes. 2. obscene, indecent, immoral: *Vitendo vichafu,* obscene actions. *Lugha chafu,* obscene language.

chafu.a *vt* 1. dirt, soil, pollute, spoil. (cf *haribu, pondaponda*) 2. ruin, destroy, wreck, foul up (cf *fuja, vuruga*) 3. vex, annoy, hurt, disturb: *Alimchafua moyo,* he annoyed her. Prep. ***chafu.li.a*** St. ***chafu.k.a*** Cs. ***chafu.sh.a*** *Amechafusha mazingira,* he has polluted the environment. Ps. of Prep. ***chafu.liw.a*** Rp. ***chafu.an.a*** (cf *kasirisha, chukiza*)

chafuk.a[1] *vi* see *chafua*

chafuk.a[2] *vi* 1. be upset: *Tumbo lake limechafuka,* she has an upset stomach. 2. be churning, be rough: *Bahari ilichafuka jana,* the sea was rough yesterday. 3. (of a person) be angry, be rough, be unstable: *Yeye* *amechafuka sana siku hizi*, he is very angry these days. Prep. ***chafuk.i.a*** St. ***chafuk.ik.a*** Cs. ***chafu.sh.a***

chafuko *n* (*ma-*) see *machafuko*

chafuo¹ *n* (*n*) act of dirtying, scuttling or disturbing sth.

chafuo² *n* (*n*) (*zool*) tsetsefly (cf *mbung'o, pange*)

chafya *n* (*n*) sneeze: *Piga/Enda chafya*, sneeze (cf *chemua*)

chag.a *vt, vi* 1. take up one's work, etc. vigorously: *Anazichaga kazi zake siku hizi*, he does his work with vigour these days. 2. persist, continue: *Sherehe za harusi zilichaga usiku kucha*, the wedding celebrations were in full swing for the whole night. (cf *endelea*) 3. form a habit, begin a habit: *Mamba amechaga kuua watu mtoni*, the crocodile has formed the habit of killing people at the river. (cf *zoea*) 4. spread, be prevalent: *Kipindupindu kimechaga kijijini*, cholera has spread in the village. (cf *enea*) Prep. ***chag.i.a*** St. ***chag.ik.a*** Cs. ***chag.iz.a***

chaga.a *vi* work hard. Prep. ***chaga.li.a*** St. ***chaga.lik.a*** Cs. ***chaga.sh.a***

chagaw.a *vt* cause an evil spirit to mount on the head. Prep. ***chagaw.i.a*** St. ***chagaw.ik.a*** Cs. ***chagaw.ish.a*** (cf *pagawa*)

chagina *n* (*n*) see *jagina*

chagiz.a *vt* insist, pester, importune, dun: *Alinichagiza nimlipe fedha zake*, he insisted that I should pay back his money. Prep. ***chagiz.i.a*** St. ***chagiz.ik.a*** Ps. ***chagiz.w.a*** Rp. ***chagiz.an.a***

chagizo¹ (*pl vy-*) *n* (ki-vi) (*gram*) adjunct, adverbial (cf *kielezi*)

chagizo² (*pl vy-*) *n* (*vi-*) insistence, pressure, arm twisting, annoyance: *Ameleta chagizo jingi kwa serikali*, he has put a lot of pressure on the government. (cf *kero, usumbufu, shinikizo*)

chago¹ (also *mchago, uchago*) *n* (*n*) part of the edge of the bed towards which the head is directed; headboard.

chago² *n* (*n*) see *chwago*

chagu.a *vt, vi* 1. choose the right thing and keep aside the wrong one 2. discriminate; choose unfairly, be unfair; treat people differently: *Anapenda kuchagua watu wa kabila lake*, he likes choosing people of his own tribe. 3. choose, elect, select: *Mchagua jembe si mkulima*, a good farmer does not choose a hoe, i.e. persons should not be choosing excessively any particular issue. 4. pick grit from rice, etc.; sort: *Alichagua mchele kabla ya kuupika*, she picked grit from rice before cooking it. Prep. ***chagu.li.a*** St. ***chagu.lik.a*** Ps. of Prep. ***chagu.liw.a*** Rp. ***chagu.an.a*** (cf *pembua*)

chaguo *n* (*ma-*) selection, choice: *Mgombea yule ndiye chaguo la watu wengi*, that contender is the choice of many people.

-chaguzi *adj* fastidious, choosy, dainty: *Mtu mchaguzi*, a choosy person.

chai (also *mchago, uchago*) *n* (*n*) 1. tea: *Chai ya mkandaa*, black tea. *Chai ya rangi*, tea without milk. *Chai ya mkono mmoja*, tea with no bites. *Chai ya masalo*, tea with many ingredients. 2. tea leaves. 3. bribe, kickback: *Toa chai*, bribe. (cf *hongo, rushwa*) 4. tip, bakshesh. (Hind, Pers)

chaja *n* (*n*) charger; an apparatus used to charge storage batteries. (Eng)

chaji¹ *n* (*n*) charge: *Chaji umeme*, electrical charge. *Chaji tuli*, static charge. (Eng)

chaj.i² *vt* charge; accuse someone usu before a court of law. Prep. ***chaj.i.a*** St. ***chaj.ik.a*** Cs. ***chaj.ish.a*** Ps. of Prep. ***chaj.iw.a***. (cf *shutumu, shtaki*) (Eng)

chaj.i³ *vt* charge; store electricity in a battery. Prep ***chaj.i.a*** St ***chaj.ik.a*** Cs ***chaj.ish.a*** Ps of Prep ***chaj.iw.a*** (Eng)

chaj.i⁴ *vt* charge, set a price: *Mwenyeduka alinichaji pesa nyingi kwa kumeka bidhaa zangu katika bohari lake*, the shopkeeper charged me a lot of money for storing my goods in his warehouse. Prep. *chaj.i.a* St. *chaj.ik.a* Cs. *chaj.ish.a* Ps. of Prep. *chaj.iw.a*

chaji[5] *n* (*n*) electrical charge. (Eng)

chaji[6] (*pl vy*) *n* (ki-vi) supper (cf *kilalio*)

chaka[1] *n* (*ma-*) (*bot*) thicket, brier, bramble, undergrowth; a clump of trees.

chaka[2] *n* (*n*) the hot season; that is, between December and February.

chaka.a *vi* (*n*) be worn out, wear-out, get old, be decrepit; age: *Gari yangu sasa imechakaa*, my car is now worn-out. Prep. *chaka.li.a* Cs. *chaka.z.a*. (cf *zeeka, dhoofika*)

chakaazi *n* (*n*) (*bot*) milk bush; a leafless much-branched succulent tree up to 30 feet tall with inconspicuous small yellow-green flowers and trilocular fruits, which is used in medicine, as a fish poison and as a protective hedge. *Euphorbia tirucalli*.

chakach.a[1] *vi* 1. rustle as in the case of dry leaves, paper, silk, etc., whoosh, swish, make slight sounds: *Majani yalichakacha kutokana na upepo,* the leaves rustled in the breeze. 2. pound, grind, pulverize; crush into powder, pulp, etc. in a mortar: *Alivichakacha vitunguu saumu kwenye kinu,* she ground garlic in the mortar. Prep. *chakach.i.a* St. *chakach.ik.a* Cs. *chakach.ish.a* Ps. *chakach.w.a* (cf *twanga, ponda, funda*)

chakacha[2] *n* (*n*) (*bot*) dry leaf of the betel plant (cf *tumbaku kavu*)

chakacha[3] *n* (*n*) (*mus*) a kind of famous women's traditional dance in the coastal parts of East Africa.

chakachaka *adv* hurriedly, quickly, fast, hastily, speedily: *Nilimpa kazi yangu jana na akaifanya chakachaka,* I gave him my work yesterday and he did it hurriedly. (cf *upesiupesi, haraka, chapuchapu*)

chakachu.a *vt* adulterate; render sth poor in quality by adding another substance of inferior ingredients. Prep. *chakachu.li.a* St. *chakachu.lik.a* Cs. *chakachu.lish.a* Ps *chakachu.liw.a*

chakapu *n* (*n*) (*zool*) a kind of wild cat. (cf *ngawa*)

chakaramu[1] *n* (*ma-*) lunatic, maniac, madman; an eccentric person: *Yeye ni chakaramu,* he is a madman. (cf *afkani, majununi*) (Hind)

chakaramu[2] *adj* insane, crazy, mad, outlandish: *Mtu chakaramu,* a crazy person. (Hind)

chakari[1] *n* (*ma-*) hangman, public executioner, electrocutioneer.

chakari[2] *adv* completely, extremely, totally: *Amelewa chakari,* he is totally drunk. *Usingizi umemjaa chakari,* he is fast asleep. (cf *chopi*)

chakarish.a *vt* 1. startle as in the case of an animal or bird; scare off, frighten: *Kelele za wasasi ziliwachakarisha wanyama,* the noise from the hunters scared off the animals. 2. make a rustling sound; swoosh, swish: *Mnyama aliuchakarisha mkia wake,* the animal swished its tail. Prep. *chakarish.i.a* St. *chakarish.ik.a* Ps. *chakarish.w.a* Rp. *chakarish.an.a*

chakavu *adj* decrepit, worn-out, time-worn, old: *Gari chakavu,* an old car. *Mitambo chakavu,* worn-out machines. (cf *kachara*)

chakaz.a[1] *vt* beat, defeat, thrash: *Timu yetu iliwachakaza mabingwa wa sasa,* our team beat the current champions. Prep. *chakaz.i.a* St. *chakaz.ik.a* Cs. *chakaz.ish.a* Ps. *chakaz.w.a* Rp. *chakaz.an.a* (cf *banjua, nyuka, bamiza, chapa*)

chakaz.a[2] *vt* cause sth to wear down. Prep. *chakaz.i.a* St. *chakaz.ik.a* Cs. *chakaz.ish.a* Ps. *chakaz.w.a* Rp. *chakaz.an.a*

chake *adj, pron* form of *-ake*, meaning his, hers, its: *Kitabu chake,* his book, her book. *Chake ni changu,* his is mine.

chakeleti *n* (*n*) see *chakleti*

chaki[1] (also *choki*) *n* (*n*) chalk: *Mwalimu alitumia chaki ubaoni*, the teacher used a piece of chalk on the blackboard. (Eng)

chaki[2] *n* (*n*) (*idm*) *Pembe za chaki*, a secret place.

chaki[3] (*zool*) *n* (*n*) a generic name for a small common ant which bites.

chakleti[1] (also *chokeleti*) *n* (*n*) chocolate (Eng)

chakleti[2] (also *chokeleti*) *n* (*n*) colour of chocolate; dark brown colour. (cf *hudhurungi, kahamia*) (Eng)

chako *adj, pron* form of *-ako*, your, yours: *Kiti chako*, your chair. *Chako na chetu ni kimoja*, yours and ours is one.

chaku.a *vt* see *chakura*

chakubimbi *n* (n) see *sakubimbi*

chakula (*pl vy-*) *n* (*ki-vi*) 1. food, diet: *Chakula cha asubuhi*, breakfast. *Chakula cha mchana*, lunch. *Chakula cha jioni*, supper. *Chakula cha usiku*, dinner. *Chakula cha nguruwe*, slop: *Chakula bora*, food with complete nutrients. *Chakula kikuu*, main dish. 2. feast, banquet, repast (cf *karamu, hafla*)

chakur.a (also *chakua*) *vt, vi* 1. search around to get sth that is hidden or missing. (cf *tafuta, pekua, pekechua*) 2. scratch with the feet as a fowl or a horse or a dog does with its hooves; paw the ground. 3. disarrange, displace, disorder, disorganize; put out of order. Prep. ***chakur.i.a*** St. ***chakur.ik.a*** Cs. ***chakur.ish.a*** Ps. ***chakur.w.a*** (cf *pangua, vuruga*)

chale[1] *n* (*n*) (*zool*) sea urchin; a kind of fish with long movable spines, and is considered to be poisonous.

chale[2] (also *chali*) *n* (*n*) clown, comedian, humourist, joker: *Yeye ni chale kwa vile ni hodari wa kuchekesha watu*, he is a comedian because he is good at making people laugh. (cf *damisi, chepe*)

chale[3] (also *chali*) *adj* humorous, funny, comic: *Yeye ni chale*, she is humorous. (cf *chepe, damisi*)

chale[4] *n* (*n*) tattoo, incision, gash, tribal marks. (cf *gema, tojo, nembo, taruma*)

chali[1] *n* (*n*) see *chale*[2] and *chale*[3]

chali[2] *n* (*n*) (*zool*) speckled snapper; a kind of generally bluish or greenish fish of the *Lutjanidae* family with a yellowish hue dorsally, and is found solitarily or in small aggregations over coral or rocky reefs; speckled snapper. *Lutjanus rivulatus*.

chali[3] (also *chani*) *adv* on the back: *Lala chali*, lie on the back. (cf *tani*)

chalo *n* (*n*) sugarcane farm.

chama[1] (*pl vy-*) *n* (*ki-vi*) party, society, association, guild, league, union; *Chama cha siasa*, political party. *Vyama vya ushirika*, cooperative societies.

cham.a[2] *vt* move to a new place. Prep. ***cham.i.a*** St. ***cham.ik.a*** Cs. ***cham.ish.a*** (cf *hama*)

chamb.a[1] (also *tamba*) *vi* wash one's genitals; wash one's behind: *Alikwenda msalani kuchamba*, he went to the toilet to wash his genitals. (*prov*) *Kuchamba kwingi ni kuondoka na mavi*, to wash your genitals from time to time is to leave behind your faeces, i.e don't be too inquisitive otherwise you will get answers that are not satisfactory. Prep. ***chamb.i.a*** St. ***chamb.ik.a*** Cs. ***chamb.ish.a*** Ps. ***chamb.w.a*** (cf *sogona, sosona, kokona*)

chamb.a[2] *vt* vituperate, affront, offend, berate, insult: *Alinichamba burebure mbele za watu wote*, he insulted me in public for nothing. Prep. ***chamb.i.a*** St. ***chamb.ik.a*** Cs. ***chamb.ish.a*** Ps. ***chamb.w.a*** Rp. ***chamb.an.a*** (cf *tukana, tusi, nyonyoa*)

chambarare *n* (*naut*) a sailing vessel of moderate dimensions.

chambega *n* (*n*) conman, trickster,

mountebank, deceiver. (cf *tapeli*)

chambembe *n* (*n*) (*anat*) sternum, breastbone; a bone which joins the ribs.

chambi (also *chamvi*) *n* (*n*) the act of approaching an opposite partner usu in a special local dance: *Peana chambi*, approach a partner of the opposite sex.

chambilecho *n* (*ki-vi*) as said, written by: *Chambilecho Kwame Nkrumah "Uhuru wa Ghana peke yake hauna maana mpaka uwe umejumuishwa kabisa na uhuru wote wa Bara la Afrika,"* as was said by Kwame Nkrumah, "the liberation of Ghana is meaningless unless it is linked up with the total liberation of Africa."

chambish.a *vt* torture, torment, persecute, agonize: *Askari jela waliwachambisha wafungwa*, the wardens tortured the prisoners. Prep. ***chambish.i.a*** St. ***chambish.ik.a*** Ps. ***chambish.w.a***. Rp. ***chambish.an.a*** (cf *tesa, adhibu*)

chambo (pl *vy-*) *n* (*ki-vi*) 1. a bait for catching fish, etc. (cf *dagaa, daa*) 2. a bait for catching animals. (*prov*) *Mtego bila ya chambo, haunasi*, a trap without a bait does not catch anything i.e. to succeed, motivation is necessary for success. 3. a person or thing that serves as an instrument of achieving one's needs, goals, etc.; anything used as a bait to achieve some goals, etc.

chambochambo *n* (*n*) bank, rim, edge, margin: *Alisimama kwenye chambochambo ya mto*, he stood on the bank of the river. (cf *ukingo, terebesha, pambizo, mbago*)

chambu.a[1] (also *chamvua, shamvua*) *vt* 1. clear; process for use; pick the grit from the grain, etc.; *Aliuchambua mchele*, she picked the grit from the rice. (cf *pembua*) 2. clean cotton, grains, vegetables, etc.; separate the wheat, etc. from the chaff; winnow: *Alizichambua karafuu*, he cleaned the cloves by removing the husks. 3. analyse, review, criticize, critique: *Aliichambua riwaya yangu*, he reviewed my novel. Prep. ***chambu.li.a*** St. ***chambu.lik.a*** Cs. ***chambu.lish.a*** Ps. of Prep. ***chambu.liw.a*** Rp. ***chambu.an.a*** (cf *hakiki*)

chambu.a[2] (also *chamvua, shamvua*) *vt* correct the mistakes of someone; pull apart. *Aliuchambua udhaifu wa rafiki yake*, he pulled apart the weaknesses of his friend. Prep. ***chambu.li.a*** St. ***chambu.lik.a*** Cs. ***chambu.lish.a*** Ps. of Prep. ***chambu.liw.a***

chamburo *n* (*n*) jeweller's pliers or tongs. (cf *nyamburo*)

chamchela *n* (*n*) 1. whirlwind, hurricane, cyclone, windstorm: *Pepo za chamchela*, cyclone, typhoon; circling winds. (cf *kimbunga, tufani*) 2. a place that is not inhabited because of fear of evil spirits caused by a whirlwind.

chamk.a *vi* 1. (of an illness, headache, etc.) recur, relapse, occur again: *Ugonjwa wa shurua ulichamka katika kijiji chetu*, measles recurred in our village. 2. (of a disease, sore, etc.) spread, be contagious: *Kipindupindu kimechamka*, cholera has spread. (cf *enea*) 3. dispense, scatter: *Mkutano ulipomalizika, watu wakachamka*, when the meeting ended, the people dispersed. Prep. ***chamk.i.a*** St. ***chamk.ik.a*** Cs. ***chamk.ish.a*** Ps. ***chamk.w.a***

chamkano (pl *vy*) *n* (*ki-vi*) 1. a group of people dispersing: *Niliiona chamkano baada ya mechi ya mpira kumalizika*, I saw a group of people dispersing after the football match. 2. split, division: *Chamkano kwenye klabu limewaathiri wanachama sana*, the division in the club has affected the members very much. 3. dispersal, scattering, dispersing.

chamko *n* (*n*) 1. outbreak or the recurrence of a disease or illness like fever: *Kumekuwa na chamko ya ugonjwa wa kuharisha mashambani*, there has been an outbreak of diarrhoea in the countryside. 2 spreading, scattering, dispersing: *Chamko la ugonjwa wa kipindupindu*, the spread of cholera.

championi *n* (*ma-*) champion, winner, victor. (cf *bingwa*) (Eng)

chamshakinywa (also *chamsha*) (*ki-vi*) breakfast. (cf *staftahi*, *kiamshakinywa*, *kifunguakinywa pia chamsha*)

chan.a¹ *vt* (*n*) tear, rip, pull apart: *Alizichana nguo zangu mpya*, she tore my new clothes. Prep. **chan.i.a** St. **chan.ik.a** Cs. **chan.ish.a** Ps. **chan.w.a** Rp. of Prep. **chan.i.an.a** (cf *pasua*, *rarua*)

chan.a² *vt* (*n*) comb; straighten esp hair with a comb: *Chana nywele*, comb hair, Prep. **chan.i.a** St. **chan.ik.a** Cs. **chan.ish.a** Ps. **chan.w.a** Rp. of Prep. **chan.i.an.a**

chana³ *n* (*ki-vi*) a piece of ginger or turmeric.

chan.a⁴ *n* (*n*) see *chane¹*

chanda¹ (*pl vy-*) *n* (*ki-vi*) 1. finger, toe. 2. (*idm*) *Chanda na pete*, hand in glove, very close: *Watu wale wawili ni chanda na pete*, those two people are very close.

chanda² (*pl vy-*) *n* (*ki-vi*) (*bot*) coconut leaf. (cf *kuti*)

chandalua (*pl vy-*) *n* (*ki-vi*) see *chandarua*

chandarua (also *chandalua*) (*pl vy-*) *n* (*ki-vi*) 1. mosquito net. 2. tarpaulin; a sheet of hard material used to make tents, etc. 3. the roof of a motor vehicle

chande *n* (*ki-vi*) (*pl vy-*) (*zool*) harvest spider, harvest man.

chando¹ *n* (*ki-vi*) a certain kind of dance in which the partners of both sexes meet in the ring and after dancing for a short period, they return to their positions.

chando² *n* (*n*) the first circumcised boy in a circumcision school. (cf *kiranja*)

chane¹ (also *chana*) *n* (*n*) the pedical or the fruit stem of a banana plant; a bunch of bananas: *Nilinunua chane moja ya ndizi*, I bought one pedical of bananas. (cf *shuke*, *kole*, *mkono*)

chane² (also *chana*) *n* (*n*) a slip of leaf used in plaiting mats and chords.

chang.a¹ *vt*, *vi* 1. contribute, donate: *Changa pesa*, collect money by voluntary contributions. (cf *kusanya*) 2. (*idm*) *changa bia*, contribute jointly. 3. (of cards) *Changa karata*, shuffle, ruffle; mix a set of playing cards, Prep. **chang.i.a** St. **chang.ik.a** Cs. **chang.ish.a** and **chang.iz.a** Ps. **chang.w.a**

chang.a² *vt*, *vi* hurt, ache, throb, pain: *Misuli yake inamchanga*, his muscles are aching. Prep. **chang.i.a** St. **chang.ik.a** Cs. **chang.ish.a**

-changa³ *adj* young, immature, underdeveloped, unripe: *Taifa changa*, a young nation. *Embe changa*, unripe mango. *Mimba changa*, young pregnancy. *Mtoto mchanga*, a baby.

chang'aa *n* (*n*) moonshine alcohol; a kind of strong intoxicating liquor like brandy. (cf *gongo*, *moshi*, *piwa*)

changaman.a *vi* 1. be mixed-up: *Vitu vyote vimechangamana chumbani*, all things are mixed up the in the room. 2. cooperate, work together; work side by side: *Wanavijiji wale huchangamana kijijini mwao*, those villagers work together in their village. (cf *shirikiana*, *shikamana*) 3. be adjoining, be abutting, be bordering, be adjacent, be beside: *Hoteli yake imechangamana na pwani*, his hotel is adjacent to the shore.

changamano *n* (*ma-*) 1. mixture; state of being mixed of what has been put together: *Changamano la wanafunzi wa makabila mbalimbali limeleta udugu kati yao*, the bringing together of students of different ethnic backgrounds has brought harmony among them. (cf *mchanganyiko*)

2. cooperation, collaboration, teamwork: *Changamano la viongozi wa siasa wa vyama tofauti limeleta umoja nchini*, the cooperation among political leaders of various parties has brought unity to the country. (cf *mshikamano, fungamano, ushirikiano*) 3. adjoining, adjacency: *Changamano la hoteli yake na ufukoni limewavutia watalii*, the adjacency of his hotel to the beach has attracted tourists. 4. (*gram*) complex: *Kikundi changamano*, complex group. *Sentensi changamano*, complex sentence. *Tungo changamano*, complex construction.

-changamfu *adj* vivacious, cheerful, humorous, jovial. *Kiongozi mchangamfu*, a cheerful leader.

changamk.a *vi* be cheerful, be lively, be in good spirits: *Hajachangamka tangu baba yake alipofariki*, he has not been cheerful since his father died. Prep ***changamk.i.a*** St ***changamk.ik.a*** Cs ***changamk.ish.a***. Ps of Prep ***changamk.w.a*** (cf *terema, furahika, chanjamaa*)

changamko *n* (ma-) cheerfulness, humour, good spirits: *Changamko lake limemletea kupendwa na watu wengi*, his humour has made him acquire many friends.

changamoto *n* (ma-) challenge, impetus, stimulus, appeal: *Ametoa changamoto kali kwa washairi*, he has posed a great challenge to the poets. (cf *kichocheo, mvuto*)

changamsh.a *vt* gladden, exhilarate, enliven, stimulate: *Mazungumzo yake mazuri yalituchangamsha sana*, her excellent talks stimulated us a great deal. Prep ***changamsh.i.a*** St ***changamsh.ik.a*** Ps ***changamsh.w.a*** Rp ***changamsh.an.a***

changamsho[1] *n* (ma-) sth that thrills; thriller: *Tamasha lile lilikuwa changamsho*, that festival was a thriller.

changamsho[2] *n* (ma-) challenge, impetus, stimulus, appeal (cf *changamoto*)

changanu.a *vt* 1. separate what is mixed; strip off: *Aliuchanganua ukwaju ili atengeneze kinywaji*, he stripped off the tamarind in order to make a drink. (cf *tenganisha*) 2. review, analyse: *Aliyachanganua machapisho yangu*, he reviewed my publications. Prep ***changanu.li.a*** St ***changanu.lik.a*** Cs ***changanu.lish.a*** Ps of Prep ***changanu.liw.a*** Rp ***changanu.an.a*** (cf *chambua, pambanua*)

changany.a *vt, vi* 1. mix, put together; form into one mass: *Alichanganya maziwa na maji*, he mixed milk with water. 2. mix, muddle, confuse, confound, perplex: *Maelezo yake yalituchanganya*, his statement confused us. *Pasi yake iliwachanganya mabeki*, his pass confused the defenders. 3. used in various expressions: *Changanya macho*, glance, peep, look. *Changanya maneno*, confuse the utterances. *Changanya mambo*, spoil the plans; wreck the plans. *Changanya miguu*, go fast on foot. Prep ***changany.i.a*** St. ***changany.ik.a*** Cs. ***changany.ish.a*** and ***changany.iz.a*** (rarely used) Ps. ***changany.w.a***

changanyik.a *vi,vt* be mixed together, mingle: *Kabila zile mbili hazitaki kuchanganyika*, those two tribes don't want to mingle. Prep ***changanyik.i.a*** St. ***changanyik.ik.a***

changanyikiw.a *vi, vt* be confused, be muddled up; *Mtu yule amechanganyikiwa siku hizi*, that person is confused these days.

changanyiko *n* (mi-) see *mchanganyiko*

changish.a (*mi-*) raise money, etc; collect contribution. Prep. ***changish.i.a*** St. ***changish.ik.a*** Ps. ***changish.w.a*** Rp. ***changish.an.a***

changanyo *n* (mi-) see *mchanganyo*

changarawe *n* (n) gravel, grit; small stones.

changi.a *vt* 1. contribute towards sth: *Wanavijiji wengi walichangia fedha nyingi katika ujenzi wa zahanati,* many villagers contributed a lot of money to the construction of a dispensary. 2. increase conditions already existing; contribute: *Makosa yake pia yamechangia kusambaratika kwa chama,* his mistakes have also contributed to the disintegration of the party.

changizo *n (n)* 1. contribution, donation; raising of funds: *Wanachama walitoa changizo yao kuisaidia klabu,* the members gave their donations to help the club. 2. members' fees to a club, party, etc; membership fees.

chango[1] *n (n)* see *mchango*[?]

chango[2] (also *uchango*) *n (mi-)* 1. gut; small intestines. (cf *uchengelele, ujengelele*) 2. a kind of an abdominal disease. 3. intestinal worm, intestinal parasite

chango[3] *n (n)* (*anat*) womb; umbilical cord.

chango[4] (pl *vy-*) *n (ki-vi)* peg, rail, hook; a hanger for suspending sth. (cf *kulabu, kijiti*)

changu[1] *n (n)* (*zool*) emperor, snapper; a kind of sea fish. There are several species of this fish e.g. *Changu chole,* thumb print monocle bream. *Changu fimbo,* green job fish. *Changu doa,* thumb print emperor. *Changu mdomo,* long face snapper. *Changu ndizi,* thumb print emperor. *Changu tewa,* spangled emperor. *Changu mdomo nyamvi,* variegated emperor.

changu[2] *adj, pron* see *-angu,* mine: *Kitabu changu,* my book. *Changu na chake si kimoja,* mine and his is not the same.

changu.a *vt* 1. separate, part, dismember: *Alivichangua vitunguu kutoka kwenye furushi la vitu alivyovinunua sokoni,* he separated the onions from the bundle of things he bought at the market. (cf *tenga*) 2. disarrange, disorganize, dislocate, mix: *Alivichangua vitabu vyangu nilivyovipanga awali,* he mixed my books which I had arranged earlier. (cf *pangua, tengua*) 3. dismember or cut up parts of an animal for food: *Aliichangua nyama ya mbuzi kabla ya kuigawa kwa watu mbalimbali,* he dismembered the mutton before it was distributed to different people. *Changua msitu,* cut down trees in a forest to prepare for cultivation. Prep. ***changu.li.a*** St. ***changu.lik.a*** Cs. ***changu.lish.a*** Ps. of Prep. ***changu.liw.a***

changudoa *n (n)* (*colloq*) street walker; a prostitute on the prowl.

chani[1] (also *chanui*) *n (n)* 1. (*zool*) sea porcupine, porcupine fish; a spiny globe fish.

chani[2] 1. low tide area. 2. a particular area for controlling fish-traps.

chanik.a[1] *vi* be torn, be ripped, be rent. Prep. ***chanik.i.a*** St. ***chanik.ik.a*** Cs. ***chanik.ish.a*** (cf *pasuka*)

chanik.a[2] *vi* become very fat/obese. Prep. ***chanik.i.a*** St. ***chanik.ik.a*** Cs. ***chanik.ish.a*** (cf *nenepa*)

chanikiwiti *n (n)* light green colour. (cf *bitimarembo*)

chanj.a[1] *vt* split, hew, chop: *Chanja kuni,* split logs for firewood; Prep. ***chanj.i.a*** St. ***chanj.ik.a*** Cs. ***chanj.ish.a*** Ps. ***chanj.w.a*** (cf *pasua, tema, kata*)

chanj.a[2] *vt* vaccinate, make an incision, make a tatoo: *Alichanja chale,* he made incisions. Prep. ***chanj.i.a*** St. ***chanj.ik.a*** Cs. ***chanj.ish.a*** Ps. ***chanj.w.a*** Rp. ***chanj.an.a*** Rp. of Prep. ***chanj.i.an.a*** (cf *toja*)

chanja[3] *n (n)* 1. gird iron; drying rack for meat etc 2. ceiling.

chanja[4] *n (n)* bicycle carrier.

chanja[5] *n (n)* pieces of wood set aside to start fire. (cf *chagaa*)

chanja[6] *vt* play in the rain. Prep. ***chanj.i.a*** St. ***chanj.ik.a*** Cs. ***chanj.ish.a***

chanj.a[7] *vt* cut fish into two pieces.

Prep. *chanj.i.a* St. *chanj.i.a* Cs. *chanj.ish.a* Ps. *chanj.w.a*
chanjaa *n (ma-)* an open space that has not been cultivated; plateau.
chanjagaa *n (n) (zool)* stalk-eyed ghost crab; a kind of crab of robust body living in burrow in the littord fringe of sandy beaches. Its adults have elongated straight horns above eyes (cf *chwago, kayakaya, chago*)

chanjagaa

chanjama.a *vi* be cheerful, be in good spirits: *Alichanjamaa baada ya kuzawadiwa,* he became cheerful after being given a gift. (cf *changamka*)
chanjamaji *n (ki-vi)* see *maganga*
chanjari (also *sanjari*) *adv* abreast, side by side: *Tulifuatana chanjari mpaka gatini,* we went side by side until we reached the port. (cf *sawa*)
chanjian.a *vt* make an incision in each other in the process of making a sworn friendship.
chanjo *n (n)* 1. gash, incision, cut. 2. vaccination: *Chanjo ya kinga,* innoculation. *Chanjo dhidi ya kifaduro,* vaccination against whooping cough.
chano (pl vy-) *n (ki-vi)* a flat round wooden platter with a low rim, used to serve food. (cf *fuo*)
chansela *n (n)* chancellor: *Chansela wa chuo kikuu,* chancellor of a university. (Eng)
chanu.a[1] *vt* comb out, tease. Prep. *chanu.li.a* St. *chanu.k.a* Cs. *chanu.sh.a* Ps. of Prep. *chanu.liw.a* (cf *fumua, shonoa*)
chanu.a[2] *vi* (of flowers) blossom, bloom, flower: *Maua yamechanua,* the flowers have blossomed. Prep. *chanu.li.a* St. *chanu.k.a* Cs. *chanu.sh.a* Ps. of Prep. *chanu.liw.a* (cf *papatua, fumbuka*)
chanu.a[3] *vi* widen a space that is narrow/squeezed. Prep. *chanu.li.a* St. *chanu.k.a* Cs. *Chanu.sh.a* Ps. of Prep. *chanu.liw.a*
chanuo (also *shanuo*) *n (ki-vi)* 1. a large wooden comb. 2. anything used to comb hair.
chanya *adj* positive: *Ana mtazamo chanya kuhusu lugha za Kiafrika,* he has a positive attitude towards African languages. 2. hopeful: *Fikira chanya,* hopeful thoughts.
chanyat.a[1] *vt* (of bananas, cassava and other kinds of food) slice up: *Aliuchanyata muhogo na kisha akauchemsha,* he sliced the cassava and then boiled it. Prep. *chanyat.i.a* St. *chanyat.ik.a* Cs. *chanyat.ish.a* Ps. *chanyat.w.a* (cf *lenga, buabua, checha*)
chanyat.a[2] *vt* wash clothes by beating them gently: *Alizichanyata nguo zake chafu,* he washed his dirty clothes by beating them gently. Prep. *chanyat.i.a* St. *chanyat.ik.a* Cs. *chanyat.ish.a* Ps. *chanyat.w.a* Rp. of Prep. *chanyat.i.an.a* (cf *chachaga*)
chanyati.a[1] *vi* swagger, swing; walk boastfully: *Alichanyatia mbele ya vipusa,* he swaggered infront of the beautiful girls. (cf *tamba, wika*)
chanyati.a[2] *vi* walk stealthily; slink, pussyfoot, tiptoe: *Alichanyatia mpaka kitandani alikolala mtoto,* she tiptoed up to the bed where the child slept. Prep. *chanyati.li.a* St. *chanyati.k.a* Cs. *chanyati.sh.a* (cf *nyata, nyapa, nyemelea*)
chanyatia[3] *n (n) (zool)* mudskipper; any group of fishes that are able to leave the water for a time and that skip over the mudflats and even climb mangroove roots in search of food.
chanzo (pl vy-) *n (ki-vi)* 1. source, root, basis, cause: *Chanzo cha ugomvi*

wao hakijulikani, the cause of their conflict is unknown. *Vyanzo vya maji*, sources of water (cf *asili, sababu, kiini, chimbuko*) 2. *(phon)* *Chanzo-sauti*, sound wave.

chao¹ *adj, pron* see *-ao* meaning *their, theirs: Kikapu chao*, their basket.

chao² *n (n) (naut)* a piece of wood in a slipway; roller. (cf *wenzo, mwao, nyenzo*)

chap.a¹ *vt* 1. beat, hit, strike, thwack, slap: *Alimchapa kibao*, he struck him a blow. (cf *piga, buta, charaza, twanga*) 2. used in various idiomatic expressions: *Chapa kazi*, work hard. *Chapa maji*, get drunk. *Chapa miguu*, walk; go on foot. Prep. *chap.i.a* St. *chap.ik.a* Cs. *chap.ish.a* Ps. *chap.w.a* Rp. *chap.an.a*

chap.a² *vt* 1. print: *Aliyachapa maandishi yake yaliyoandikwa kwanza kwa mkono*, he printed his writing which was first handwritten. 2. thrash, beat, trounce: *Waliichapa timu yetu kwa magoli mengi*, they thrashed our team by many goals. Prep. *chap.i.a* St. *chap.ik.a* Cs. *chap.ish.a* Ps. *chap.w.a* Rp. *chap.an.a* (cf *nyuka, bamiza*)

chapa³ *n (n)* 1. trademark, brand. 2. tag, earmark, hall-mark. 3. emblem, badge, mark.

chapa⁴ *n (n)* print: *Chapa ya kwanza*, first print.

chapa⁵ *adj* see *chapachapa*

chapachapa (also *chapa, chepechepe*) *adj* soggy, drenched, soaked, wet, wringing wet: *Nilitoka nje wakati wa mvua na nikarowa chapachapa*, I went out in the rain and got drenched. (cf *chege, majimaji*)

chapanya *n (n) (zool)* mole snake. *Pseudaspis cana*.

chapasi¹ *adj* active, diligent: *Mtu chapasi*, an active person.

chapasi² *adj* humorous, cheerful.

chapati *n (n)* a flat thin unleavened bread, usu of wheat-flour baked in a hot dry skillet; chapati. (Ind)

chapaunga *n (n)* novice; a person inexperienced in an occupation, activity, etc.

chapik.a *vi* booze excessively. Prep. *chapik.i.a* St. *chapik.ik.a* Cs. *chap.ish.a*

chapish.a *vt* publish: *Mswada huu baadaye utachapishwa*, this manuscript will later on be published. Prep. *chapish.i.a* St. *chapish.ik.a* Ps. *chapish.w.a* Rp. of Prep. *chapish.i.an.a*

chapisho *n (ma-)* publication: *Lile ni chapisho lake la tatu*, that is his third publication.

chapo *n (ma-)* eggwhisk

chapu.a *vt* 1. (of a drum) beat harder and faster: *Aliichapua ngoma kwa ufundi*, he beat the drum harder and skillfully. 2. accelerate, speed up, hurry up, hasten, quicken: *Chapua miguu*, walk quickly. Prep. *chapu.li.a* St. *chapu.k.a* Cs. *chapu.sh.a* Ps. of Prep *chapu.liw.a* (cf *harakisha, kazana*)

chapuchapu *adv* fast, quickly, hastily, speedily: *Alikwenda chapuchapu mpaka nyumbani kwake*, he walked home hastily. (cf *upesiupesi, haraka, mbiombio*)

chapuk.a¹ *vi* 1. distance oneself; stay aloof: *Alikuwa zamani akishirikiana sana na rafiki zake lakini siku hizi amechapuka*, in the past, he associated very closely with his friends but these days he has distanced himself. 2. accelerate, hurry, hasten; *Chapuka kwani tunachelewa*, hurry up because we are getting late. Prep. *chapuk.i.a* St. *chapuk.ik.a* Cs. *chapuk.ish.a* (cf *jitenga*)

chapuk.a² *vi* (esp of food) be well-flavoured, be well-seasoned. Prep. *chapuk.i.a* St. *chapuk.ik.a* Cs. *chapuk.ish.a*

chapuki.a *vi* 1. be savoury, be delectable, be luscious, be palatable, be tasty, be flavoursome: *Chakula cha leo kimechapukia*, today's food is palatable. (cf *kolea, noga*) 2. cheer,

CH   chapuo

acclaim, applaud: *Mashabiki walikuwa wanamchapukia mshindi*, the fans were cheering the winner. 3. get sexual satisfaction.

chapuo *n* (*n*) a small two-headed drum. (cf *vumi*)

chapuz.a[1] *vt* accelerate; hasten; increase speed. Prep. ***chapuz.i.a*** St. ***chapuz.ik.a*** Cs. ***chapuz.ish.a*** Ps. ***chapuz.w.a*** Rp. of Prep. ***chapuz.i.an.a***

chapuz.a[2] *vt* plan, organize: *Waliichapuza mikakati yao*, they organized their strategies. Prep. ***chapuz.i.a*** St. ***chapuz.ik.a*** Cs. ***chapuz.ish.a*** Rp. of Prep. ***chapuz.i.an.a*** (cf *jipanga*)

chapuzo *n* (*ma-*) a song that facilitates an activity.

chapwa *adj* 1. unpalatable, unsavoury, flavourless, tasteless; unpleasant to the taste: *Chakula hiki ni chapwa*, this food is tasteless. (cf *dufu*) 2. (of events, etc) boring, dull.

charahani (pl *vy-*) *n* (*ki-vi*) see *cherehani*

charang.a *vt* 1. cut into small parts, tear apart: *Walimcharanga kwa visu*, they cut him into pieces with knives. (cf *chinyanza*) 2. (*colloq*) beat, thrash, defeat: *Timu yao iliwacharanga mabingwa wa sasa*, their team defeated the reigning champions. Prep. ***charang.ia*** St. ***charang.ik.a*** Cs. ***charang.ish.a*** Ps. ***charang.w.a*** (cf *bamiza, nyuka*)

charaz.a *vt* 1. play well a musical instrument: *Alikicharaza kinanda*, he played the banjo well. 2. swing to the beat; dance to the beat: *Alicharaza vizuri kwenye dansi*, he really moved to the beat in the dance. 3. do anything without pause or with vigour: *Walicharaza kandanda*, they played soccer skillfully. *Aliicharaza baiskeli yake*, he rode his bicycle skillfully. *Alikicharaza cherehani*, he worked with a sewing-machine skillfully. 4. beat in a football match, etc.; *Walitucharaza magoli mengi*, they beat

chau.a

us by many goals. *Charaza viboko*, whip, beat by stick. Prep. ***charaz.i.a*** St. ***charaz.ik.a*** Cs. ***charaz.ish.a*** Ps. ***charaz.w.a*** Rp. ***charaz.an.a*** (cf *bamiza, nyuka*)

charo (pl *vy-*) *n* (*ki-vi*) caravan, convoy; a company of travellers. (cf *kafila, msafara*)

charu.a (also *charura*) *vt* 1. tease, hassle, pester, bother: *Nilimcharua mpaka akahamaki*, I teased her until she became angry. (cf *chokoza, tafiri*) 2. bully, dismay, distress, sadden: *Anapenda kuwacharua wadogo zake*, he likes bullying his juniors. Prep. ***charu.li.a*** St. ***charu.k.a*** Cs. ***charu.sh.a*** Ps. of Prep. ***charu.liw.a*** Rp. ***charu.an.a*** (cf *huzunisha, sikitisha*)

charuk.a *vi* 1. erupt, burst forth, split open: *Amecharukwa na akili*, he has gone mad. (cf *chacha, chaga chachawa*) 2. become naughty, become defiant, be disobedient: *Mtoto wake amecharuka siku hizi*, his child has become naughty these days. Prep. ***charuk.i.a*** Ps. ***charuk.w.a***

chat.a[1] *vt* 1. buzz: *Nyuki walikuwa wakichata karibu na maua*, the bees were buzzing near the flowers. 2. be happy, be joyful: *Alichata alipopata mtoto*, she was happy when she got a baby. (cf *furahi, furahia*)

chata[2] *n* (*n*) a chartered plane. (Eng)

chati[1] *n* (*n*) chart: *Chati ya hali ya hewa*, weather chart. (Eng)

chati[2] *n* (*n*) trick, fraud, sham, deception: *Alinifanyia chati*, he tricked me. (*idms*) *Panda chati*, become more famous. *Kwa chati*, with care. (cf *ghalati, ghiliba, hadaa, udanganyifu*)

chatne *n* (*n*) chutney; a relish made of fruits, spices, herbs, vinegar, salt, etc (Hind)

chatu (also *satu*) *n* (*n*) (*zool*) python

chau.a *vt* disarrange, unsettle, disorganize. Prep. ***chau.li.a*** St. ***chau.k.a*** Cs. ***chau.lish.a*** Ps. of Prep ***chau.liw.a***

76

chauchau¹ *n* (*n*) bribe, kickback, graft. (cf *chai, rushwa*)
chauchau² *adj* chaotic, jumbled, unplanned.
chavua *n* (*n*) pollen
chawa *n* (*n*) louse. (*prov*) *Kidole kimoja hakivunji chawa*, one finger does not kill a louse i.e. Unity is strength.
chawe *n* (*ma-*) a kind of coral rock. (cf *tumbawe, fufuwele*)
chawu *n* (*n*) a pit for burying in fiborous coconut husks
chaza (also *shaza*) *n* (*n*) (*zool*) oyster (Pers)

chaza

chazi *n* (*n*) (*bot*) liana; a climbing, woody, tropical plant growing around tree trunks, *Cissus rotundifolia*.
chazo *n* (*n*) (*zool*) a kind of sea fish which is used as a bait to catch sea-turtle.
che¹ *n* (*n*) (*idm*) morning: *Walilinda duka mpaka che*, they guarded the shop until morning.
che² *n* (*n*) walkover: *Ushindi wa che*, a walkover victory.
cheameni *n* (*ma-*) 1. chairperson; chairman (cf *mwenyekiti*) 2. leader of a political party, club, etc. (Eng)
chech.a¹ *vt* (of cassava, pawpaw, banana, etc.) slice up, cut into pieces: *Alizichecha ndizi na kisha akazipika*, he sliced the bananas and then cooked them. Prep. ***chech.e.a*** St. ***chech.ek.a*** Cs. ***chech.e.sh.a*** Ps. ***chech.w.a*** Rp. ***chech.an.a*** (cf *kata*)
chech.a² *vt* forbid, prohibit, taboo: *Mzee alinichecha kunywa pombe*, my parent forbade me to drink beer. Prep. ***chech.e.a***, St ***chech.ek.a*** Ps ***chech.w.a*** Rp ***chech.an.a*** (cf *kataza*)

chech.a³ *vt* dig up the earth by using a plough, hoe, etc. on a farm: *Aliichecha konde yake ili kutayarisha kupanda*, he dug his field to prepare for planting. Prep. ***chech.e.a*** St. ***chech.ek.a*** Cs. ***chech.esh.a*** Ps. ***chech.w.a*** Rp. ***chech.an.a***
cheche¹ *n* (*n*) 1. slice; a small piece of anything that has been sliced such as cassava, etc.: *Zile ni cheche za muhogo*, those are slices of cassava. 2. spark: *Cheche ya moto*, spark of fire. 3. agility, sharpness: *Mchezaji alionyesha cheche zake pale alipofunga magoli yote matatu*, the player showed his agility by scoring all the three goals.
cheche² *n* (*n*) see *kicheche*
cheche³ *n* (*n*) (*zool*) tarpon; a kind of large silvery fish (family *Megalopidae*) with very large scales, a deeper body and found in coastal pelagic areas, entering lagoons and estuaries. Oxeye

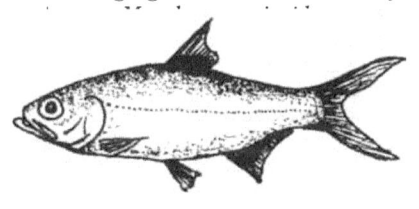

cheche

cheche⁴ *n* (*n*) collective responsibility: *Tulimpa baba yetu cheche juu ya jambo lile*, we gave our father the responsibility of handling that affair. (cf *jukumu, dhamana*)
cheche⁵ *n* (*n*) a word used by children to explain good or new clothes: *Vaa cheche*, wear good or new clothes.
cheche.a (also *chechemea*) *vi* limp, hobble; walk lamely: *Mchezaji alipoumia, alichechea hadi nje ya kiwanja*, when the player got injured, he limped off the field. Cs. ***cheche.sh.a*** and ***cheche.z.a*** (cf *guchia, chopea*)
chechele *n* (*n*) 1. forgetfulness, oblivion,

lapse of memory: *Alichukuliwa na chechele kwenda kusali,* he forgot to go to pray. (cf *mghafala, usahaulifu*) 2. (*idms*) *Kanyaga chechele,* lose one's way. *Liwa na chechele,* lose ones' way. *Chukuliwa na chechele,* forget 3. a small insect which if stepped on, supposedly causes one to lose one's way or wits.

checheme.a (also *chechea*) *vi* limp, hobble. Prep. **checheme.le.a** St. **checheme.k.a** Cs. **checheme.sh.a** (cf *guchia, chopea*)

chechemu.a *vt* motivate, arouse, stimulate, encourage, inspire: *Alituchechemua kwenda kuzuru mbuga za wanyama,* he encouraged us to visit the game reserves. Prep. **chechemu.li.a** St. **chechemu.k.a** Cs. **chechemu.sh.a** Ps. of Prep. **chechemu.liw.a** Rp. **chechemu.an.a** (cf *shajiisha, raghibu, motisha*)

chechesh.a (also *checheza*) *vt* 1. pamper, coddle; treat a child with too much kindness: *Alimchechesha mtoto wake na hatimaye, akalala,* she coddled her child to sleep. (cf *bembeleza*) 2. assist someone to walk. Prep **chechesh.e.a** St. **chechesh.k.a** Ps. **chechesh.w.a**

chechevu *n* (*n*) hiccup (cf *kwikwi, kekevu*)

chee *adj* simple, easy.

cheg.a[1] *vt* 1. shave hair, cut hair: *Alikwenda kwa kinyozi kuchega nywele,* he went to the barber to have his hair cut. 2. cut down ripe cereals on a farm for harvest: *Aliwaajiri vibarua shambani kuchega mpunga,* he hired labourers to harvest rice on the farm. Prep. **cheg.e.a** St. **cheg. esh.a** Ps. **cheg.w.a** Rp. **cheg.an.a**

chega[2] *n* (*n*) (*bot*) bhang

chegam.a[1] *vt.vi* 1. intrigue, machinate, manipulate, plot: *Alitaka kunichegama lakini niliweza kuipangua mipango yake,* he wanted to plot against me but I was able to spoil his plans. 2. confront, face, set face to face: *Alimchegama adui yake,* he confronted his enemy. Prep. **chegam.i.a** St. **chegam.ik.a** Cs. **chegam.ish.a** Ps. **chegam.w.a** Rp. **chegam.an.a** (cf *kabili, sogelea*)

chegam.a[2] (also *egemea*) *vt, vi* lean on a wall, etc.; *Nilichegama ukutani niliposikia nina kizunguzungu,* I leaned on the wall when I felt giddy. Prep. **chegam.i.a** St. **chegam.ik.a** Cs. **chegam.ish.a** Ps. **chegam.w.a**

-chege[1] *adj* 1. not properly cooked: *Alikula viazi vichege,* he ate potatoes that had not been cooked properly. 2. lax, remiss, slack, negligent: *Alikuwa mtumishi mchege,* he was a lax servant.

-chege[2] *adj* 1. soggy, sodden, limp, moist, watery: *Huo ni muhogo mchege,* that is watery cassava. (cf *cherema*) 2. wet, watery: *Nguo chege,* wet clothes. (cf *chapachapa*)

-chege[3] *adj* stupid, foolish, inane, absurd: *Hilo ni wazo chege,* that is an absurd suggestion.

chege[4] *n* (*n*) see *tege*

chegele *n* (*n*) looseness, flaccidity: *Mzigo huu usiufunge kwa chegele,* do not tie this luggage loosely. (cf *mchegeleko*)

chego *n* (*n*) see *gego*

cheichei *n* (*n*) a form of greeting used by children.

chek.a *vi* laugh, smile, grin Prep. **chek.e.a** St. **chek.ek.a** Cs. **chek. esh.a** Ps. **chek.w.a** Rp. **chek.an.a** (cf *chata, kenua, furahi*)

chekea (also *chokea*) *n* (*n*) sty; an inflammed swelling on the edge of the eyelid. (cf *sekenene*)

chekeamwezi *n* (*n*) (*zool*) water-dikkop, stone curlew, water thicknee; a kind of bird with long legs and a long bill. *Burhinus vermiculatus.* (cf *kipila, sulula*)

chekech.a[1] (also *chichita, chinyita*) *vt* 1. sift, sieve, winnow. (cf *chunga*) 2. pick

the grit; sort: *Aliuchekecha mtama*, he picked the grit from the millet. Prep. *chekech.e.a* St. *chekech.ek.a* Cs. *chekech.esh.a* Ps. *chekech.w.a*
chekech.a² *vt* ponder; think carefully before making a decision. Prep. *chekech.e.a* St. *chekech.ek.a* Ps. *chekech.w.a*
chekeche (also *chekecheke*) *n* (*n*) sieve, sifter (cf *chungio*)
chekechea¹ *n* (*n*) (*zool*) lesser seed-cracker: a kind of bird which is reddish on the head and underparts and one that inhabits dense shrub along wooded streams.
chekechea² *n* (*n*) (*zool*) young birds; chicks (cf *makinda*)
chekechea³ *n* (*n*) children not exceeding five years. *Skuli ya chekechea*, nursery school.
chekecheke *n* (*n*) see *chekeche*
chekehukwa *n* (*n*) (*zool*) stone curlew
chekele.a *vt* rejoice at, smile at: *Unachekelea nini?* What are you rejoicing at? Prep. *chekele.le.a* St. *chekele.k.a* Cs. *chekele.sh.a*
chekesh.a *vt* cause sby to laugh: *Alinichekesha mno kwa hadithi zake za kiajabuajabu*, he caused me to laugh so much because of his strange stories. Prep. *chekesh.ek.a* St. *chekesh.ek.a* Ps. *chekesh.w.a* Rp. *chekesh.an.a*
chek.i¹ *vt* check, inspect. Prep. *cheki.a* St. *chek.ik.a* Ps. of Prep. *chek.iw.a* Rp. of Prep. *chek.i.an.a* (cf *kagua*). (Eng)
cheki² *n* (*n*) cheque. *Cheki wazi*, open cheque. *Cheki fungwa*, closed cheque (cf *hundi*) (Eng)
cheko (also *mcheko*) *n* (*n*) risibility, laugh, laughter, laughing.
chekwa (also *chekwachekwa*) *adv* to the brim, in abundance, cock-full: *Sukari iko chekwa madukani*, sugar is in abundance at the shops. (cf *tele*, *pomoni*)
chekwachekwa *adv* see *chekwa*
chele.a¹ *vt, vi* be apprehensive about;

fear for: *Ninachelea kuondoka sasa hivi*, I am apprehensive about leaving now. (cf *ogopa*, *hofu*)
chele.a² *vi, vt* disembark, descend, debark.
cheleko *n* (*n*) 1. (*naut*) the upper part of the prow in a canoe. 2. the keel of a boat or ship. (cf *mkuki*, *mastamu*)
cheleo¹ *n* (*ma-*) see *macheleo*
cheleo² *n* (*ma-*) procrastination, tardiness, delay. (cf *ukawio*, *uchelewaji*)
chelew.a¹ *vt, vi* delay, be late. Prep. *chelew.e.a* St. *chelew.ek.a* Cs. *chelew.esh.a* and *chelew.ez.a*. Rp. of Prep. *chelew.esh.an.a* (cf *kawia*, *limatia*, *taahari*)
chelewa² *n* (*n*) hangover; unpleasant physical effects following the heavy use of alcohol.
chelewa³ *n* (*n*) a kind of rattle made by stones or dry seeds in a tin and used in special dances
chelewa⁴ *n* (*n*) (*bot*) vein; any of the bundles of vascular tissue that form the framework of a leaf blade.
chelewesh.a *vt* cause sby to be late; delay sby. Prep. *chelewesh.e.a* St. *chelewesh.ek.a* Ps. *chelewesh.w.a* Rp. *chelewesh.an.a* (cf *kawiza*)
chelez.a¹ *vt* keep or leave sth for a purpose; leave sth for a purpose: *Alicheleza ndoo kisimani ili achote maji baadaye*, he left the bucket in the well in order to fetch water later. Prep. *chelez.e.a* St. *chelez.ek.a* Cs. *chelez.esh.a* Ps. *chelez.w.a*
chelez.a² *vt* (*naut*) unload cargo from a ship, dhow, etc.: *Makuli walicheleza shehena kutoka kwenye meli*, the porters unloaded cargo from the ship. Prep. *chelez.e.a* St. *chelez.ek.a* Cs. *chelez.esh.a* Ps. *chelez.w.a*
chelez.a³ *vi* stay awake all night: *Mlinzi alicheleza kulilinda duka langu*, the watchman stayed awake all night guarding my shop. Prep. *chelez.e.a* St. *chelez.ek.a* Cs. *chelez.esh.a* Ps. *chelez.w.a* (cf *kesha*)

chelez.a[4] *vt, vi* (esp of underground stems such as those of cassava and potato tubers) grow thick, be swollen, become swollen: *Mihogo yake ilicheleza kutokana na hifadhi ya wanga*, his cassava became swollen because of storage of starch. *Rafiki yako amecheleza siku hizi kwa starehe alizo nazo*, your friend has become fat these days owing to his lifestyle. Prep. *chelez.e.a* Cs. *chelez.esh.a* Ps. *chelez.w.a*

chelezo[1] (pl *vy-*) *n* (*ki-vi*) anything that causes a delay

chelezo[2] (pl *vy-*) *n* (*ki-vi*) grindstone; a revolving stone disk for sharpening bladed tools or shaping and polishing things. (cf *cherehe*)

chelezo[3] (pl *vy-*) *n* (*ki-vi*) buoy, life-buoy, float, raft. 2. a place where sailing vessels are repaired. (cf *gudi*)

chemba[1] (pl *vy-*) *n* (*ki-vi*) private place, secret place: *Walikwenda chemba ili wazungumze siri yao*, they went into a private place to discuss their secret. (cf *faragha*) (Eng)

chemba[2] *n* (*n*) (*phon*) cavity: *Chemba pua*, nasal cavity. *Chemba cha kinywa*, oral cavity. *Chemba koromeo*, pharyngeal cavity. *Chemba mapafu*, pulmonic cavity. (Eng)

chembe[1] (also *tembe*) *n* (*n*) 1. particle, grain, bit, piece: *Chembe ya mchanga*, a particle of sand. *Chembe ya nafaka*, a grain of corn. (cf *punje, tete*) 2. used with a negative particle to express complete absence of sth: *Hana akili hata chembe*, he has no wits.

chembe[2] *n* (*n*) used in the expression: *Chembe cha moyo*, solar plexus; pit of the stomach.

chembe[3] *n* (*n*) the head of an arrow or spear.

chembechembe *n* (*ki-vi*) 1. vestige: a trace or mark of sth that once existed. 2. used in: *Chembechembe za damu*, blood cells.

chembelele *n* (*n*) very small pieces of bread, cake, sweets, etc.; crumbs.

chembeu[1] *n* (*n*) 1. caulking chisel. 2. a chisel for poking out copra. (cf *patasi*)

chembeu[2] *n* (*n*) (*zool*) moonfish, monies; a kind of fish of the family *Monodactylidae* with a deep and compressed body covered with small deciduous scales and which is usu silvery or yellow, found in deeper coastal waters in reef areas, sometimes entering estuaries. *Monodactylus argenus; Monodactylus falciformis*.

chemchemu *n* (*n*) a spring of water

chemk.a *vi* 1. boil, bubble up, seeth, simmer or stew. (cf *pwaga, tokota*) 2. (*fig*) be boiling: *Damu yake inachemka*, his blood is boiling. 3. be angry, be furious, be annoyed: *Akikaripiwa, huchemka damu*, whenever he is blamed, he gets angry. Prep. *chemk.i.a* St. *chemk.ik.a* Cs. *chem.sh.a* Ps. of Cs. *chem.sh.w.a* (cf *ghadhibika, kasirika*)

chemni *n* (*n*) lamp chimney; chimney of an oil lamp used to shield the flame. (cf *tungi*) (Eng)

chemsh.a *vt* 1. boil, seethe: *Aliuchemsha muhogo*, he boiled the cassava. 2. cook sth without putting coconut juice or oil. Prep. *chemsh.i.a* St. *chemsh.ik.a* Ps. *chemsh.w.a*

chemshabongo *n* (*n*) 1. puzzle. 2. crossword puzzle.

chemu.a *vi* sneeze. Prep. *chemu.li.a* St. *chemu.lik.a* Cs *chemu.z.a* Ps. of Prep. *chemu.liw.a*

chenene *n* (*n*) (*zool*) a kind of field cricket that usu feeds on plants and often bores or makes holes in clothing and linen.

cheneo (also *kieneo*) *n* (*n*) area, extent (cf *eneo*)

chenet.a *vi* itch, tingle, prick, irritate: *Kidonda kilikuwa kinacheneta*, the sore was itching. (cf *washa, chona, chonyota*)

chenezo (also *kienezo*) (pl *vy-*) *n* (*ki-vi*) tape measure, tape-line, ruler, etc.; measuring instrument

chenga[1] *n* (*n*) (*zool*) a kind of fish with a round shape and a flat head.

cheng.a[2] *vt* 1. cut, lop e.g. heads of millet, stalks of wheat, etc.: *Aliuchenga*

cheng.a³   **cherehe**   **CH**

mpunga kondeni, he cut the heads of rice in the field. (cf *kata*) 2. chop trees in order to make firewood or for construction purposes; lop, cut: *Niliichenga mikoko kwa ajili ya kupata kuni za kupikia,* I chopped the mangroove trees for making firewood. Prep. **cheng.e.a** St. **cheng.ek.a** Cs. **cheng.esh.a** Ps. **cheng.w.a** (cf *kata, tema, chanja, pasua*)

cheng.a³ *vt, vi* 1. dodge, duck, swerve. Prep. **cheng.e.a** St. **cheng.ek.a** Cs. **cheng.esh.a** Ps **cheng.w.a** Rp. **cheng.an.a**

chenga⁴ *n* (*n*) 1. (in football, etc.) dodge, duck, dribble: *Piga chenga,* dodge, duck, dribble e.g. *Alinipiga chenyu na baadaye akafunga goli,* he dribbled past me and later scored a goal. 2. (*idm*) *Piga chenga ya mwili,* deceive. (cf *laghai, tapeli*)

chenga⁵ *n* (*n*) chip, crumb; a small piece of grain e.g. of rice, millet, maize: *Chenga za mchele,* grains of rice.

chenge¹ *n* (*n*) (*bot*) a forest that has been cleared away and burnt. (cf *mtema*)

chenge² *n* (*n*) bonfire; a large fire built out of doors.

chengechenge *n* (*n*) pieces, crumbs, morsels, slices: *Mtumishi wangu aliyukulu mapapai chengechenge,* my servant cut the pawpaws into tiny pieces. (cf *chembechembe, vipande-vipande*)

chengeu *n* (*n*) lamp cover.

chengo¹ *n* (*ki-vi*) 1. (rare) house, residence; a person's dwelling or village. 2. camp, bivouac; a place where a caravan rests. (*prov*) *Mtu akifika chengo cha mtu, humtegemea,* when you are a visitor, you are at the mercy of the host.

chengo² *n* (*n*) a mixture of small fish; minnow.

cheni *adv* erect, upright: *Simama cheni,* stand upright. (cf *wima*)

chenj.i¹ *vt, vi* change money; give or receive money in exchange for money of a different type: *Alitaka kuchenji pesa zake kwangu,* he wanted me to change his money. Prep. **chenj.i.a** St.

chenj.ik.a Cs. **chenj.ish.a** Ps. of Prep. **chenj.iw.a** Rp. of Prep. **chenj.i.an.a** (Eng)

chenji² *n* (*n*) the balance of money when the amount rendered is larger than the amount due. (cf *bakaa*) (Eng)

chenji³ *n* (*n*) interval, interlude, intermission; a short period of time separating the parts of a football game, film, etc. (cf *mapumziko*) (Eng)

chenu *adj, pron* your, yours: *Kitabu chenu,* your book. *Chenu na chake ni kimoja,* yours and his is the same.

chenza *n* (*n*) (*bot*) tangerine; a variety of orange with reddish-yellow colour and rough skin:

cheo¹ (pl *vy-*) *n* (*ki-vi*) 1. measure, size: *Mshoni alichukua cheo changu cha suruali,* the tailor took my trousers' measurements. (cf *kipimo*) 2. rank, position, status, grade: *Amepandishwa cheo kazini kwake,* he has been promoted at his place of work. (cf *wadhifa, hadhi*)

cheo² (pl *vy-*) *n* (*ki-vi*) 1. a rod of iron, brass or ivory used as a wand by a medicineman when he intends to exorcise spirits or look for lost things. 2. a board used for plaiting *ukili,* a leaf-strip of the wild-date palm. 3. a stake that is used for husking coconuts. (cf *kifullu, kifuo*)

chepe *n* (*ma-*) 1. an inconsiderate and mannerless person; an impudent person: *Yeye ni chepe na kwa hivyo, usifanye urafiki naye,* he is impudent, so don't befriend him. (cf *safihi*) 2. clown, humourist: *Rafiki yako ni chepe,* your friend is a clown. (cf *chale, damisi*)

chepechepe *n* (*n*) see *chapachapa*

chepeo (also *chapeo, chepeu*) *n* (*n*) stetson; a kind of hat with a wide edge standing out round the head usu worn by cow-boys.

cherehani (also *charahani*) *n* (*ki-vi*) sewing-machine. (Pers)

cherehe (pl *vy-*) *n* (*ki-vi*) grindstone; a revolving stone disk for sharpening bladed tools (cf *chelezo*)

chereko n (n) joy in a wedding celebration or any other activity; jubilation: *Kulikuwa na chereko nyingi wakati wa harusi yake*, there was a lot of jubilation during his wedding. (cf *nderemo, vifijo, ramsa, furaha*)

cherema (also *chelema*) adj (used of certain foods such as cassava and potatoes) pulpy, soggy, soppy, sodden, watery: *Nilinunua muhogo cherema*, I bought pulpy cassava i.e. cassava that is soft and contains moisture. (cf *majimaji*)

cherewa[1] n (n) epic narrative; a special game where the audience listens to the songs of a narrative sung by singers.

cherewa[2] n (n) 1. thin sticks of coconut leaves that have been used for making fishing baskets or brooms. 2. left-over palmleaves that have been plaited.

-cheshi adj humorous, cheerful, vivacious, jovial: *Kijana mcheshi*, a cheerful young man.

chesi[1] n (n) chess; a game played on a chessboard by two players (cf *sataranji*) (Eng)

chesi[2] n (n) (zool) a kind of a small gazelle

chete (also *kete*) (pl vy-) n 1. market day; a special day in a week on which a market is held in a division: *Kwenye tarafa yetu, chete hufanyika kila Jumamosi*, in our division, the market is held every Saturday. (cf *gulio*) 2. market place; a place where the market is held.

chetezo (vy-) n (ki-vi) thurible; a vessel, often of earthenware used to burn incense or sweet-smelling aromatic substances.

cheti (pl vy-) n (ki-vi) 1. note, memo: *Nilimpelekea cheti*, I sent her a note. 2. certificate, testimonial, affidavit, letter of recommendation: *Amepoteza cheti chake cha kuzaliwa*, he has lost his birth certificate. 3 receipt, acknowledgement: *Nilimpa mteja cheti chake*, I gave the customer his receipt. (cf *stakabadhi*) (Hind)

chetu adj pron. our, ours, used for a ki-vi class nouns.

cheu[1] n (n) muncher; a person who keeps on chewing food, etc.

cheu[2] adj having the habit of chewing food, etc: *Yeye ni cheu*, he is in the habit of chewing a lot.

cheu.a vi 1. burp, belch; chew the cud: *Mtoto aliponyonya maziwa, mara akaanza kucheua*, when the baby sucked milk from the breast, it immediately began to belch. (cf *kovyoka, teuka, tapika*) 2. regurgitate, surge back, rush back, flow back: *Wanyama wake hucheua chakula chao ili kuvilisha vitoto vyao*, his animals regurgitate their food to feed their young ones. Prep. ***cheu.li.a*** St. ***cheu.k.a*** Cs. ***cheu.sh.a*** Ps. of Prep. ***cheu.liw.a***

cheuk.a vi be belched. Prep. ***cheuk.i.a*** St. ***cheuk.ik.a***

cheuzi[1] n (n) see *jozi*

cheuzi[2] adj burping, belching.

chewa[1] n (n) used in morning greetings: *Chewa?* how are you this morning?

chewa[2] n (n) easterly maritime winds.

chewa[3] n (n) (zool) rockcod, grouper; a kind of saltwater fish (family *Serranidae*), having small scales and which is usu found in tropical and subtropical seas, ranging from shallow coastal waters to moderate depths. Red mouth rockcod. *Aethaloperca rogaa*.

chewa

chewale adv 1. gratuitously; free of charge, without payment: *Alipewa* *chakula chewale hotelini*, he was given food free of charge at the hotel. (cf *bwerere, bure*) 2. *without much effort; easily*. (cf *kirahisi*)

chez.a *vt, vi* 1. play, sport. (cf *laabu*) 2. idle, loaf, loll, lounge, laze; be idle: *Wakati wote anacheza tu; hataki kufanya kazi yeyote*, he is always idle; he doesn't want to do any work. (cf *mangamanga, zurura*) 3. dance. 4. tremble (because of fear, sickness, etc.): *Mwili wote unamcheza kutokana na homa kali*, his whole body is trembling due to acute fever. 5. drill as soldiers: *Wanajeshi walikuwa wanacheza kwata*, the soldiers were drilling. 6. ridicule, mock, deride: *Nilimcheza na akahamaki*, I mocked him and he got angry (cf *dhihaki, tania*) 7. bewitch, becharm, put a spell on: *Mchawi alimcheza jirani yake*, the magician bewitched his neighbour. (cf *roga, anga, sihiri*) 8. understand sth very well; master: *Kijana yule anazicheza karata*, that young man has mastered the art of playing cards. 9. commit adultery; fornicate: *Anapenda kucheza na wake za watu*, he likes committing adultery with other men's wives. 10. used as a warning: *Usicheze na moto*, don't play with fire. 11. used in the expressions: *Cheza patapotea*, gamble. *Cheza ngoma goya*, do a useless job. *Chezea shere*, ridicule, mock. *Cheza na wembe*, do a hazardous thing. Prep. **chez.e.a** St. **chez.ek.a** Cs. **chez.esh.a** Ps. **chez.w.a** Rp. **chez.an.a** Rp. of Prep. **chez.e.an.a**

chibuku *n (n)* brew from maize, millet, beans, etc.

chicha[1] *n (n)* 1. grated coconut; the white nutty part of a coconut after it has been grated out or scraped and then squeezed. 2. leese; the thick substance found at the bottom of a local alcoholic bottle

chicha[2] *n (n) (med)* smegma; a cheese-like sebaceous secretion that accumulates under the foreskin or around the clitoris. (cf *pumba*)

chich.a[3] *vt, vi* surrender, back down/off: *Jeshi lilichicha baada ya kushindwa vibaya vitani*, the army surrendered after being badly beaten in the war. Prep. **chich.i.a** St. **chich.ik.a** Cs. **chich.ish.a** (cf *kai*)

chicha[4] *adj* drunk, intoxicated.

chichi *n (n) (naut)* fish; the side of a vessel facing the mainland.

chichiri *n (n)* 1. bribe, kickback, graft: *Alipokea chichiri kutoka kwenye kampuni za nje*, he received bribes from the overseas companies. (cf *chai, rush*wa, *chauchau*) 2. a small quantity of sth: *Alinipa chakula chichiri*, he gave me a small quantity of food.

chichit.a *vt* see *chekecha*

chifu *n (ma-)* 1. chief. (cf *mtemi, mkama, mangi*) 2. a government official in charge of a location or area. (Eng)

chigi *n (n) (zool)* manikin; a gregarious little bird feeding on grass seeds and on the ground like sparrows. There are several species of it e.g. *Chigi mkuu*, magpie manikin. *Chigi madoa*, bronze manikin. *Chigi rangi mbili*, black and white manikin.

chika *n (n) (bot)* a tall perennial herb esp found in Ethiopia with stems up to 12 feet tall.

chikich.a (also *tikita*) *vt* cut with a blunt knife: *Alichikicha nyama ya ng'ombe*, he cut the beef with a blunt knife. Prep. **chikich.i.a** St. **chikich.ik.a** Cs. **chikich.ish.a** Ps. **chikich.w.a** (cf *keketa*)

chikichi *n (n) (bot)* the fruit of an oil palm tree, *mchikichi*.

chikichiki *adv* see *kichikichi*

chiku *n (n)* see *chiriku*

chikwaya *n (n) (zool)* a kind of bird.

chila *n (n)* a pancake of rice flour and coconut cream.

chilumbo *n (ki-vi)* debate, discussion, symposium: *Kulikuwa na chilumbo katika shule yetu kati ya wanafunzi* *mbalimbali*, there was a debate in our school between different students. (cf *mjadala, mdahalo, malumbano*)

chimb.a[1] *vt* 1. dig, excavate, hollow out. 2. swot; study hard for examination: *Yeye huchimba sana karibu ya mtihani*, he swots a lot when the examinations are near. Prep. **chimb.ia** St. **chimb.ik.a** Cs. **chimb.ish.a** Ps. **chimb.w.a** Ps. of Prep. **chimb.iw.a** (cf *bekua, fyoma*)

chimb.a[2] *vt* (*fig*) cause trouble for sby; cause misfortune to someone; cause discord; cause ill feeling: *Alimchimba mzee wake kwa kumgombanisha na majirani*, he caused trouble for his parent by making him clash with the neighbours. *Alinichimba kazini na hatimaye, nikafukuzwa*, he created discord for me at my place of work and in the end, I was dismissed. (*prov*) *Mchimba kisima, huingia mwenyewe*, he who digs a well enters himself i.e. he who creates troubles for others, creates trouble for himself. Prep. **chimb.i.a** St. **chimb.ik.a** Cs. **chimb.ish.a** Ps. **chimb.w.a** Rp. **chimb.an.a**

chimbi.a *vt* bury in a hole Ps **chimbi.w.a**

chimbo *n* (*ma-*) mine, pit.

chimbu.a *vt* dig out, dig up, unearth, exhume: *Walilichimbua kaburi ili wamtoe maiti*; they dug out the grave to exhume the corpse. Prep. **chimbu.li.a** St. **chimbu.k.a** Cs. **chimbu.sh.a** Ps. of Prep. **chimbu.liw.a** (cf *fukua, zua, zikua*)

chimbuko *n* (*ma-*) source, origin, cause, basis: *Chimbuko la tetesi hizi halijajulikana bado*, the source of these rumours is not yet known. (cf *asili, chanzo*)

chimbule *n* (*n*) (*zool*) a kind of bird

chimvi (also *mchimvi, timvi*) *n* (*n*) mischief-maker, trouble-maker: *Watu wote wanamwogopa kwa vile yeye ni chimvi*, all people are scared of him because he is a trouble-maker. (cf *fatani, mzabizabina, afriti*)

chin.a[1] *vi* (of sth like food) be overdue; remain beyond the usual time thus causing sth to go stale: *Samaki wangu wamechina baada ya kuwekwa kwa muda mrefu*, my fish have gone bad after being kept for so long. Prep **chin.i.a** (cf *doda, selelea*)

chin.a[2] *vt, vi* 1. fail to get sth one desires: *Nilikwenda kutafuta sukari mjini lakini nikachina*, I went to look for sugar in town but I failed to find it. 2. be late: *Alichina kwenda shuleni na kwa hivyo, mwalimu wake akampiga*, he was late to go to school and so the teacher flogged him. (cf *chelewa, limatia*)

china[3] *adv* meanwhile, while: *Alikuwa akitembea china akizungumza*, he was walking while talking.

chingirish.a *vt* pour liquid gently out of a vessel in order to leave the sediment: *Alizichingirisha kunde kwenye bakuli*, he poured the liquid out of the bowl gently after washing the cowpeas. Prep. **chingirish.i.a** St. **chingirish.ik.a** Ps. **chingirish.w.a** Rp. of Prep. **chingirish.i.an.a** (cf *gida*)

chini[1] *adv* 1. down, downstairs, underfoot, on the ground. (cf *ardhini*) 2. at the bottom, under, underground: *Wapigambizi waliuona mwili wa marehemu chini katika mabaki ya meli*, the divers found the body of the deceased under the ship's wreckage. 3. used in the expressions: e.g. *Chini ya uongozi*, under the leadership. *Chini ya himaya*, under the protection. 4. below the sex organs. (cf *utupu, uchi*)

chini[2] *n* (*pa*) floor (cf *sakafu*) nakedness; man's or woman's genitals. (cf *utupu, uchi*)

chinj.a[1] *vt* 1. (of animals) slaughter, butcher. 2. (of people) kill brutally; butcher: *Watu wa sehemu ile waliwachinja wenzi wao kutokana na vita vya wenyewe kwa wenyewe*, the people on that side butchered their colleagues following the civil war. Prep. *chinj.i.a* St. *chinj.ik.a* Cs. *chinj.ish.a* Ps. *chinj.w.a* Rp. *chinj. an.a* (cf *ua*)

chinj.a² *vt* (*fig*) overcharge, profiteer: *Alinichinja niliponunua mchele dukani kwake*, he overcharged me when I bought rice at his shop. Prep. *chinj.i.a* St. *chinj.ik.a* Cs. *chinj.ish.a* Ps. *chinj.w.a* Rp. *chinj.an.a* (cf *langua*)

chinj.a³ *vt* level or size the clay while kneading; mould: *Alikichinja chungu alipokuwa anakifinyanga*, she moulded the pot while she was making it. Prep. *chinj.i.a* St. *chinj.ik.a* Ps. *chinj.w.a*

chinjio *n* (*ma-*) a slaughtering place, slaughterhouse

chinjo¹ *n* (*ma-*) slaughtering, butchering.

chinjo² *adj* short, small: *Anapenda kuwaa suruali chinjo*, he likes to wear short trousers. (cf *fupi*)

chinjo³ *n* (*n*) a small piece of sth; slice, portion: (*Prov*) *Mkataa chinjo hupata mtanda*, he who refuses to receive sth small may miss everything eventually.

chinyang.a *vt* cut into small pieces. Prep. *chinyang.i.a* St. *chinyang.ik.a* Cs. *chinyang.ish.a* Ps. *chinyang.w.a*

chinyango *n* (*ki-vi*) gobbet; a piece or fragment of meat ready for cooking.

chinyit.a *vt* see *chekecha* Prep. *chinyit.i.a* St. *chinyit.ik.a* Cs. *chinyit.ish.a* Ps. *chinyit.w.a*

chipsi *n* (*n*) chips; long thin pieces or fragments of potatoes that are fried and usu eaten hot. Also called *French fries*. (Eng)

chipu *n* (*ma-*) (*bot*) a branch that has sprung on the trunk.

chipu.a *vt, vi* 1. sprout, bud, germinate, begin to grow: *Kunde zangu zimeanza kuchipua*, my cowpeas have started to grow. (cf *ota*, *mea*) 2. prod, poke, stir up e.g. fire, coal, etc.: *Niliuchipua*

moto ili uweze kuwaka vizuri, I poked the fire so that it could burn stronger. Prep. *chipu.li.a* St. *chipu.k.a* Cs. *chipu.z.a* (cf *chechea*)

chipubodi *n* (*n*) chipboard; a paste board made from discarded paper. (Eng)

chipuk.a *vi* 1. be sprouted, be sprung, bud, shoot up. 2. start again: *Ugomvi wao umechipuka tena*, their quarrel has started again. Prep. *chipuk.i.a* St. *chipuk.ik.a* Cs. *chipuk.ish.a*

chipukizi *n* (*ma-*) 1. shoot of a plant; young plant: *Nina mimea chipukizi katika bustani yangu*, I have new shoots in my garden. 2. sprout; a new growth from a stump of a tree, bud, etc. 3. youngster, youth: *Vijana chipukizi*, young men. *Waandishi chipukizi*, budding writers.

chir.a¹ (also *chura*) *vt* harm a baby by not making it observe the taboos.

chir.a² *n* (*ma-*) curse, imprecation. (cf *laana*)

chir.a³ *vt* get cursed, be damned.

chiri.a *vt* jinx, ill-omen; put an evil spell on sby: *Walitaka kuichiria mipango yangu*, they wanted to jinx my plans.

chiriku (also *chiku*) *n* (*n*) 1. (*zool*) yellow-crowned canary. *Serinus canicollis*; a thick billed seed-eating song bird of the *Fringillidae family*; finch. 2. a garrulous/talkative person. (cf *ngebe*, *mlimi*)

chirimiri *n* (*n*) bribe, kickback, graft: *Alitoa chirimiri ili apandishwe cheo*, he gave a bribe in order to be promoted. (cf *chai*, *rushwa*, *mrungura*)

chiririk.a *vi* see *tiririka*

chiriwa (also *chirwa*) *n* (*n*) (*med*) a disease of the skeletal system, chiefly affecting children, resulting from absence of the normal effect of vitamin D; rickets. (cf *nyongea*)

-chirizi *adj* trickling: *Yale yalikuwa machozi machirizi kutoka mashavuni mwake*, those were tears trickling down from her cheeks.

chirizik.a (also *churuzika*) *vi* trickle,

sprinkle; flow gently: *Damu ilikuwa ikichirizika kutoka kwenye kidonda chake*, blood was trickling from his wound. Prep. ***chirizik.i.a*** St. ***chirizik.ik.a*** Cs. ***chirizik.ish.a*** (cf *tiririka, tona, dondoka, vuja*)

chirwa *n* (*n*) see *chiriwa*

chizi[1] *n* (*n*) cheese (cf *jibini*) (Eng)

chizi[2] *n* (ma-) 1. an amusingly odd person, a weird person; eccentric: *Chizi yule haaminiki*, that weird person cannot be trusted. (cf *damisi, chepe*) 2. a slightly crazy person: *Rafiki yako ni chizi*, your friend is slightly crazy. (cf *chakaramu, hazimtoshi*)

cho[1] *n* (*n*) the whole night: *Kesha cho*, all the night.

cho[2] *interj* an expletive of wonder. (cf *do! lo!*)

choa *n* (*n*) (*med*) ringworm; a skin disease characterized by itching and the formation of red patches, often on the head. 2. blotch on the head or skin; mark, spot: *Ana choa mwilini mwake aliyozaliwa nayo*, he has a congenital mark on his body. (cf *paku, punje, buka, doa*)

chobe.a *vt* make suggestive bodily movements towards one's dancing partner. Prep. ***chobe.le.a*** St. ***chobe.lek.a*** Cs. ***chobe.sh.a*** Ps. ***chobe.w.a*** Ps. of Prep. ***chobe.lew.a*** Rp. ***chobe.an.a*** (cf *kobea*)

choch.a[1] *vt* 1. poke, prod, stir up e.g. an animal, insect in a hole, etc.: *Alimchocha nyoka kwa fimbo yake kuhakikisha kuwa amekufa*, he prodded at the snake with his stick to find out if it was dead. (cf *dunga, choma*) 2. (*fig*) drink a lot of alcohol; booze: *Yeye huichocha pombe siku za Jumamosi*, he goes on the booze every Saturday.

choch.a[2] *n* (*n*) (*bot*) a fleshy black edible berry from the tree, *Mchocha*.

choche.a[1] *vt* see *chocha*

choche.a[2] *vt* 1. stir up an animal or insect; provoke: *Aliwachochea nyuki na baadaye, wakamwuma*, he provoked the bees and later they stung him. (cf *chokoza, chafua*) 2. arouse, instigate, incite, excite: *Alituchochea tufanye fujo*, he incited us to create chaos. Prep. ***choche.le.a*** St. ***choche.lek.a*** Cs. ***choche.z.a*** Ps. ***choche.w.a***. Rp. ***choche.an.a***

choche.a[3] *vt* pluck a fruit by using a stick: *Aliyachochea maembe mabivu kutoka kwenye mti*, he picked the ripe mangoes from the tree by using a stick. Prep. ***choche.le.a*** St. ***choche.lek.a*** Cs. ***choche.z.a*** Ps. ***choche.w.a*** (cf *chuma, tunda*)

choche.a[4] *vt* poke at the wick of a lamp. Prep. ***choche.le.a*** St. ***choche.lek.a*** Cs. ***choche.z.a*** Ps. ***choche.w.a***

-chochole *adj* poor, penurious: *Mtu chochole*, a poor person. (cf *fakiri, masikini*)

chochot.a (also *chonyota*) *vi* smart, sting, prick, itch: *Aliponitia spiriti, kidonda changu kilizidi kuchochota*, when he applied spirit to my wound, it stung even more. Prep. ***chochot.e.a*** St. ***chochot.ek.a*** Cs. ***chochot.esh.a*** Ps. ***chochot.w.a*** (cf *cheneta, washa*)

chochote *adj, pron* any

chogoe *n* (*ki-vi*) 1. a small hooked or forked stick or pole for plucking fruits. (cf *kingoe, ngowe, ngoweko*) 2. club; a variously shaped stick or bat used to strike the ball in such games as golf.

chok.a[1] *vi* 1. be exhausted, be weary, be tired. (cf *legea, nyong'onyea*) 2. be weary of a person or thing: be tired of sby or sth thus lose all the love one had had before: *Amechoka na mimi na sijui kwa nini*, he is tired of me and I don't know why. 3. be worn-out, be eaten away, be old: *Baiskeli yake imechoka na ndiyo maana, inamletea matatizo mengi*, his bicycle is old, and that is why it is giving him so many problems. (cf *zeeka*) Prep. ***chok.e.a*** St. ***chok.ek.a*** Cs. ***chok.esh.a*** and ***chok.ez.a*** Rp. ***chok.an.a***

choka² n (n) (zool) a kind of snake with stripes on it; a striped snake
chokaa n (n) lime obtained by the action of heat on limestone, shells and other materials: *Paka chokaa*, whitewash. *Choma chokaa*, burn the lime.
chokea n (n) see *chekea*
choki¹ n (n) see *chaki*
choki² n (n) (bot) a kind of liana with white yellowish flowers, woody fruits and seeds that are covered with brown-coloured hairs.
chokiro n (n) a tuft of black and white hair on the head. (cf *shore, shungi, bwenzi*)
choko¹ adj used in the expression: *Roho choko*, voracious behaviour.
choko² n (n) see *choroko*
choko.a (also *chokora*) vt poke out with a pointed instrument, finger, etc. usu at a hard substance; pick out, jab: *Alichokoa meno yake*, he poked out his teeth. Prep. ***choko.le.a*** St. ***choko.lek.a*** Cs. ***choko.lesh.a*** Ps. of Prep. ***choko.lew.a*** Rp. of Prep. ***choko.le.an.a*** (cf *pekecha*)
chokochoko n (n) 1. incitement, provocation, discord: *Anapenda kuleta chokochoko kati yetu*, he likes to create discord between us. 2. dispute, row, wrangle: *Chokochoko kati ya mke na mumewe sasa zimewatenganisha*, the disputes between the wife and her husband have now led to their separation. (cf *fitina, utesi, ugomvi*)
chokoleti n (n) chocolate (Eng)
chokomeo n (n) a deeply hidden place: *Amekwenda chokomeo kuficha zana zake*, he has gone deep inside to hide his implements. (cf *chokoro*)
chokomez.a (also *sokomeza*) vt stuff in, cram, jam: *Alizichokomeza mbata zangu kwenye gunia*, he crammed my copra into the sack. Prep. ***chokomez.e.a*** St. ***chokomez.ek.a*** Cs. ***chokomez.esh.a*** Ps. ***chokomez.w.a*** Rp. ***chokomez.an.a*** (cf *sheheneza,*

shindilia)
chokono.a vt harass, hassle, taunt: *Nilimchokonoa mpaka hatimaye akanitukana*, I taunted him so much that he finally insulted me. (cf *udhi, kera*)
chokor.a¹ vt see *chokoa*
chokora² (also *chokra*) n (n) 1. street boy/girl, youth; a youngster who is poor and homeless: *Chokora yule ni mrefu*, that boy is tall (cf *mvulana, kijana*) 2. a domestic worker doing small things in a kitchen. (Guj)
chokowe n (n) (zool) a kind of sea bird.
chokoz.a vt, vi 1. tease, fool around, provoke: *Ukimchokoza mwendawazimu yule, atakupiga tu*, if you tease that madman, he will just beat you. (cf *kasirisha, charua*) 2. muddle, mess up: *Aliyachokoza mambo yetu*, he messed up our affairs. Prep. ***chokoz.e.a*** St. ***chokoz.ek.a*** Cs. ***chokoz.esh.a*** Ps. ***chokoz.w.a*** Rp. ***chokoz.an.a*** (cf *chafua, vuruga*)
-chokozi adj provocative, irksome.
chokra n (n) see *chokora²*
chole¹ n (n) see *changu*
chole² n (n) (zool) lilac-breasted roller; a kind of large-headed medium-sized bird (family *Coraciidae*) with tawny-brown or greenish-brown underparts and rich lilac throat and breast. *Coracias caulata*.
chom.a¹ vt 1. pierce, stab, prick. (cf *dunga, dopoa*) 2. (fig) pain, hurt, offend: *Maneno yake yamenichoma sana*, his words have hurt me very much. (cf *umiza*) 3. (parts of the body) hurt, pain, smart Prep. ***chom.e.a*** St. ***chom.ek.a*** Cs. ***chom.esh.a*** Ps. ***chom.w.a*** Rp. ***chom.an.a***
chom.a² vt 1. burn, scorch, scald; set on fire. (cf *unguza*) 2. treat someone with radioactivity, heat, etc.: *Mwaguzi alimchoma mgonjwa kwa miale*, the nurse gave the patient radio-therapy. Prep. ***chom.e.a*** St. ***chom.ek.a*** Cs.

chom.esh.a Ps. **chom.w.a** Rp. **chom. an.a**
chombo (pl *vy-*) *n* (*ki-vi*) 1. tool, implement, utensil, instrument. 2. furniture. (cf *samani*) 3. gold ornament for a woman e.g. bangle, ring, etc. 4. utensil, household item e.g. bowl, plate, etc. 5. sailing-vessel; ship, dhow, boat, etc.; (*prov*) *Chombo hakiendi ila kwa nyenzo,* a vessel does not go without strategy. 6. used in various expressions: *Chombo cha serikali,* government agency. *Vyombo vya habari,* mass media. *Vyombo vya dola,* the state organs. *Vyombo vya sheria,* legal channels e.g. courts of law.
chome.a *vt* put kapok or cotton in a cloth or sack in order to stuff mattresses, sleeping bags, etc.: *Aliichomea pamba kwenye vitambaa vya mito,* he put cotton in the pillow cases. Prep. **chome.le.a** St. **chome.lek.a** Cs. **chome.lesh.a** Ps. of Prep. **chome. lew.a**
chomek.a[1] *vi* see *choma*
chomek.a[2] *vt* insert, stick into, put into: *Alichomeka kisu kiunoni mwake,* he stuck a knife into his girdle. Prep. **chomek.ek.a** Ps. **chomek.w.a** Rp. **chomek.an.a** (cf *penyeza*)
chomek.ea *vt* 1. replace an old thing with a new one esp in the case of putting new pieces of thatch into an old roof; rethatch, tuck into: *Aliyachomekea makuti ya paa la nyumba yake,* he rethatched the roof of his house. 2. stop up the cracks of window frames, pipes, etc.; caulk: *Wavuvi waliichomekea mashua yao,* the fishermen caulked their boat. 3. stick into, tuck in, insert; *Chomekea shati,* tuck in a shirt in a trouser. St. **chomek.ek.a** Cs. **chomek.ez.a** Ps **chomek.w.a** Rp. **chomek.an.a** (cf *karabati*)
chomeko *n* (*n*) a kind of buried witchcraft that is harmful if someone steps over it. (cf *sihiri*)

chomeo[1] *n* (*ma-*) frying pan, saucepan. (cf *kikaango, kari*)
chomeo[2] *n* (*ma-*) an iron frame for roasting meat; skewer
chomo[1] *n* (*ma-*) 1. slug; the fused refuse or dross separated from a metal in the process of smelting. 2. (*syn*) *Ruka chomo,* jump into the water.
chomo[2] *n* (*ma-*) stab, prick: *Chomo la kisu,* the stab of a knife.
chomo[3] *n* (*ma-*) used in the expression: *Ruka chomo,* dive; jump into the sea, river, etc.: *Aliruka chomo katika bwawa la kuogelea,* he dived into the swimming pool.
chomo.a *vt* 1. draw out, extract, pull out, remove. *Alichomoa jambia,* he unsheathed a dagger. 2. exorcise spirits: *Alichomoa pepo kichwani,* he exorcised a ghost from his head. 3. take sth from someone slyly: *Alinichomoa shilingi mia,* he took one hundred shillings from me cunningly. 4. pickpocket; steal from the pockets of someone: *Alikichomoa kipochi cha msichana,* he stole the girl's purse. Prep. **chomo.le.a** St. **chomo.k.a** and **chomo.lek.a** Cs. **chomo.z.a** Ps. of Prep. **chomo.lew.a** Rp. **chomo.an.a** (cf *poka, chopoa, baka, iba*)
chomok.a *vi* 1. (esp of sth) come out of its original place: *Mguu wa meza umechomoka,* the leg has come out. 2. dash, rush: *Mwanariadha alichomoka mara tu kengele ilipolia,* the athlete dashed immediately when the bell rang. (cf *kimbia*) 3. (esp of a bad activity) become common: *Wizi wa mifukoni umechomoka siku hizi,* pickpocketting has become common these days Prep. **chomok.e.a** St. **chomok.ek.a** Cs. **chomok.esh.a**
chomoz.a[1] *vt* see *chomoa*
chomoz.a[2] *vi* (of the sun) appear, rise: *Jua limechomoza,* the sun has risen. Prep. **chomoz.e.a** St. **chomoz.ek.a** Cs. **chomoz.esh.a** (cf *tokeza*)

chonda¹ n (n) distress, sorrow, grief. (cf *huzuni, sikitiko*)
chonda² n (n) jealousy, envy. (cf *wivu*)
chondo¹ (pl *vy-*) n (*ki-vi*) 1. a kind of large local xylophone. (cf *marimba*) 2. a local drum for sounding some information regarding death, meeting, etc.
chondo² (pl *vy-*) n (*ki-vi*) (*zool*) a kind of mollusc; barnacle.
chondo³ (pl *vy-*) n (*ki-vi*) 1. a kind of wide-mouthed basket usu carried by women for putting in vegetables, etc. 2. a small traveller's bag.
chong.a¹ vt 1. sharpen, whet; put an edge on; make keen. 2. carve, whittle; shape with a cutting instrument: *Alichonga sanamu, he carved out a statue*. (cf *tengeneza, kereza*) 3. (*idms*) *Chongu ulimi*, be insolent, be smart-mouthed. *Chonga mzinga*, make the beehive. 4. dash, dart, bolt, sprint, run away: *Mwanariadha alichonga vizuri kwenye mashindano*, the athlete sprinted well in the competition. (cf *kimbia*) Prep. *chong.e.a*. St. *chong.ek.a* Cs. *chong.esh.a* Ps. *chong.w.a*
chong.a² vi (of a coconut) stop bearing fruits. Prep. *chong.e.a* St. *chong.ek.a* Cs. *chong.esh.a* Ps. *chong.w.a*
chonganish.a vt set some people at odds. Prep. *chonganish.i.a* St. *chonganish.ik.a* Ps. *chonganish.w.a* Rp. *chonganish.an.a* (cf *chochea*)
chonge¹ n (n) 1. a sharp-pointed tooth on either side of the upper jaw and lower jaw; a canine tooth; cuspid. 2. a sharp pointed rock.
chonge² n (n) deformation of a coconut caused by a sucking bug. (cf *pashongo*)
chonge.a vt, vi 1. report against, inform against: *Alinichongea kwa mwalimu wetu wa darasa kwamba nilimpiga*, he reported me to our classteacher that I had beaten him. (cf *fitini, ripoti*) 2. cause disaster or misfortune: *Ulevi ulimchongea na sasa hana kazi tena*,

drinking brought misfortune upon him and now he is without a job. Prep. *chonge.le.a* St. *chonge.k.a* Cs. *chonge.sh.a* Ps. *chonge.w.a* Rp. *chonge.an.a* (cf *dhuru, hasirisha*)
chongezi n (n) innuendo (cf *kijembe*)
chongo¹ n (n) 1. the condition of being one-eyed 2. a mono-eyed person.
chongo² n (n) hump, hunch; a rounded protruding lump as the fleshy mass on the back of a camel, etc: *Mtu yule ana chongo mgongoni*, that person is hunch-backed. (cf *kibyongo, nundu, kijongo, kiduvya*)
chongo³ n (*zool*) red-fronted Tinkerbird; a kind of bird (family *Capitonidae*) with blackish underparts. *Pogoniulus pusilus*. (*tongo*)
chongo.a vt 1. sharpen, whet; put an edge on: *Aliuchongoa upanga wake*, he sharpened his sword (cf *pisha, noa*) 2. used in the expression: *Chongoa kikaango*, round off a cooking-pan. Prep. *chongo.le.a* St. *chongo.k.a* Cs. *chongo.lesh.a* Ps. of Prep. *chongo.lew.a* Rp. of Prep. *chongo.le.an.a*
chongoe n (n) (*zool*) a kind of large fish of *Carangidae* family.
chongok.a vi be sharpened, be whetted: *Kisu kimechongoka*, the knife is sharpened. Prep. *chongok.e.a* St. *chongok.ek.a* Cs. *chongesh.w.a*
chonji n (n) see *chonjo*
chonjo (also *chonji, chonza*) n (n) 1. tell-tale; an act of reporting someone: *Alinitilia chonjo kwa baba yangu*, he reported me to my father. (cf *fitina*) 2. used in the expression: *Kaa chonjo*, be alert, be vigilant.
chonjomo.a vt stir up, incite, foment, instigate. Prep. *chonjomo.le.a* St. *chonjomo.k.a* Cs. *chonjomo.sh.a* Ps. of Prep. *chonjomo.lew.a* Rp. *chonjomo.an.a*
chonot.a vt, vi see *chonyota¹*
chonyot.a¹ (also *chochota, chonota*) vt, vi 1. hurt, wound, pain; *Maneno yake yalinichonyota*, his words hurt me. (cf

umiza, tonesha) 2. smart, itch, sting, hurt, burn: *Kidonda kilinichonyota nilipotiwa spiriti na daktari*, my sore smarted when the doctor applied medicine to it. Prep. ***chonyot.e.a*** St. ***chonyot.ek.a*** Cs. ***chonyot.esh.a*** Ps. ***chonyot.w.a*** (cf *washa, changa, wanga*)

chonyot.a² (also *nyonyota*) *vi* drizzle, sprinkle, fall in drops: *Mvua ilikuwa inachonyota*, it was drizzling. Prep. ***chonyot.e.a*** St. ***chonyot.ek.a*** Cs. ***chonyot.esh.a*** (cf *nyunya, dondoka*)

chonza¹ *n* (*n*) see *chonjo*

chonza² *n* (*n*) uproar, confusion, pandemonium, chaos: *Kuna chonza hapo nje ya duka*, there is chaos outside the shop. (cf *ghasia, fujo, zahama*)

choo¹ (pl *vy-*) *n* (*ki-vi*) 1. toilet, bathroom, restroom, lavatory. (cf *msala*) 2. faeces, excrement, stool: *Choo kikubwa*, excrement. *Choo kidogo*, urine. *Funga choo*, be constipated. *Pata choo*, have a motion.

choo² *n* (*n*) (*zool*) a kind of brownish worm dug up on the muddy part of a shore and used as a kind of bait. (cf *chowe*)

chooko *n* (*n*) see *choroko*

chop.a¹ *vt* 1. scoop, ladle, lade; get little at a time with a hand or an instrument: *Alizichopa njugu za kukaanga kwenye mfuko*, he scooped some roasted groundnuts out of the bag. (cf *chota, danga*) 2. vend, hawk, retail; sell things in retail; trade in a small way: *Huchopa bidhaa zake mtaani mwetu kila Jumamosi*, he sells his goods in our neighbourhood every Saturday. Prep. ***chop.e.a*** St. ***chop.ek.a*** Cs. ***chop.esh.a*** Ps. ***chop.w.a*** Rp. of Prep. ***chop.an.a*** (cf *chuuza*)

chopa² (also *topa*) *n* (*ma-*) bundle, bale, lump, stack: *Chopa la udongo*, a lump of clay. *Chopa la kuni*, a bundle of firewood. (cf *bunda, furushi, mzigo*)

chop.a³ *vt* penetrate one's fingers in a soft place. Prep. ***chop.e.a*** St. ***chop.ek.a*** Cs. ***chop.esh.a*** Ps. ***chop.w.a*** Rp. of Prep. ***chop.e.an.a***

chope.a¹ *vi* limp, hobble; walk lamely: *Aliumia na ndiyo maana sasa anachopea*, he got injured that is why he is now limping. Prep. ***chope.le.a*** St. ***chope.k.a*** Cs. ***chope.sh.a*** (cf *chechea, guchia, pecha*)

chope.a² *vt, vi* tread on the mud; walk through mud: *Alichopea upande ule kwa vile ilinyesha sana jana*, he trod over there because it rained heavily yesterday. Prep. ***chope.le.a*** St. ***chope.k.a*** Cs. ***chope.sh.a***

chopea³ *n* swamp, fog, marsh; muddy place, spongy ground: *Ukipita kwenye chopea, utatumbukia*, if you walk on a muddy place, you will sink in the mire. (cf *kidimbwi*)

chopek.a¹ *vt* cook haphazardly: *Alichopeka chakula kwa vile alikuwa na haraka*, he made a mess of the cooking, because he was in such a hurry. 2. soak, wet down: *Alizichopeka mbaazi kabla ya kuzipika*, he soaked the pigeon peas before cooking them. Prep. ***chopek.e.a*** St. ***chopek.ek.a*** Cs. ***chopek.esh.a*** Ps. ***chopek.w.a*** (cf *roweka, ambika*)

chopek.a² *vt* slot in, put in: *Alichopeka mguu wake kwenye kiatu*, he put his foot into the shoe. Prep. ***chopek.e.a*** St. ***chopek.ek.a*** Cs. ***chopek.esh.a*** Ps. ***chopek.w.a*** (cf *chomeka, tia*)

chopi¹ *adv* lamely; in a limping manner: *Alianguka na sasa anaenda chopi*, he fell down and now he limps.

chopi² *adv* (used usu in the context of boozing) excessively, extremely: *Alilewa chopi*, he was very drunk

chopo.a (also *shopoa*) *vt* 1. pull out sth from a bundle; snatch out, take out: *Alichopoa kuni kutoka kwenye tita*, he pulled out a few sticks of firewood from the bundle. (cf *vuta, toa*) 2. snatch out forcefully sth which is stuck:

Alichopoa mwiba kutoka mguuni, he pulled out a thorn from the foot. 3. snatch away, seize by surprise, take away suddenly: *Niliichopoa kofia ya rafiki yangu nilipomwendea kwa nyuma*, I snatched away the cap of my friend when I came up behind him. 4. steal from people's pockets; pickpocket: *Mwizi alizichopoa pesa za mtalii mfukoni mwake*, the thief pickpocketted the tourist's money. Prep. *chopo.le.a* St. *chopo.k.a* Cs. *chopo.sh.a* Ps. of Prep. *chopo.lew.a* Rp. *chopo.an.a* (cf *iba, pora, poka, baka*)

chor.a *vt, vi* 1. scribble, scrawl, doodle; write sth meaninglessly. *Mtoto mdogo alikichora kitabu changu chote*, the kid scribbled all over my book. (cf *andika*) 2. draw, sketch, engrave: *Aliichora picha ya makumbusho*, he drew the museum's picture. 3. draw lines without a specific order. 4. erase writings by crossing them. Prep. *chor.e.a* St. *chor.ek.a* Cs. *chor.esh.a* Ps. *chor.w.a*

choroa *n (n)* (*zool*) oryx

choroko (also *choioko*) *n (n)* (*bot*) green grams; small dark green peas. (cf *pojo*)

chorombozi *n (ki-vi)* a present given to someone who has found sth that had been lost: *Nilimpa chorombozi baada ya kuniokotea njiani pasipoti yangu*, I gave him a reward for picking up my lost passport. (cf *kiokosi, utotole, bahashishi*)

chot.a *vt* 1. ladle, scoop up; take a little at a time with the hand or with an instrument. (cf *teka*) 2. used in the expression: *Chota akili*, investigate skillfully someone's ideas or feelings. Prep. *chot.e.a* St. *chot.ek.a* Cs. *chot.esh.a* Ps. *chot.w.a* Rp. *chot.an.a* Rp. of Prep. *chot.e.an.a*

chotara *n (ma-)* 1. mongrel, hybrid, half-cast, cross-breed; a half-breed person: *Yeye ni chotara*, he is a half-cast. (cf *suriama, mahuluti, shombe, hafukasti*) 2. (*bot*) a plant from two different offsprings; hybrid. (Ar)

chote *adj, pron* form of *-ote*, all: *Chakula chote*, all the food. *Chote ni changu*, all is mine.

chote.a *vt* see *chota*

choti *n (n)* a compound made by stakes dug to the ground; wooden fence.

choto *n (n)* 1. piece, bit; a small part of sth that has been scooped up: *Choto hili la sukari halitanitosha*, this scoop of sugar will not suffice me. 2. the act, method, etc. of scooping sth.

chovy.a[1] *vt* plunge, douse; dip in water or other liquid: *Aliichovya kalamu kwenye kidau cha wino*, he dipped the pen into the inkpot. Prep. *chovy.e.a* St. *chovy.ek.a* Cs. *chovy.esh.a* Ps. *chovy.w.a* Rp. *chovy.an.a*

chovya[2] *n (n)* (*med*) oedema; an abnormal accumulation of fluid in cells, tissues or cavities of the body resulting in swelling. (cf *shova*)

chovya[3] *n (n)* counterfeit; a falsified thing that has been coated or plated to make it appear new. (cf *bandia*)

chovyo *n (ki-vi)* a small hooked or forked stick or pole, used for pulling down branches of trees, etc. (cf *kingoe*)

choyo (also *uchoyo*) *n (n)* 1. avarice, greediness, meanness, stinginess: *Inaelekea kwamba yeye ana choyo kwa sababu hamsaidii yeyote*, it seems that he is greedy because he does not assist anyone. (cf *uroho, ukavu, ubahili*) 2. miser, skinflint; a greedy person: *Yeye ni choyo*, he is a miser.

chozi[1] *n (ma-)* teardrop, tear, droplet: *Alitokwa na machozi*, she burst into tears.

chozi[2] (also *kichozi*) *n (n)* 1. (*zool*) sunbird; a small brightly coloured tropical

CH chu.a¹   chuchu¹

song bird (family *Nectariniidae*) with a slender curved bill and is well-known for eating honey obtained from the flowers. 2. a kind of bird that drinks palm wine.

chu.a¹ *vt* 1. massage forcefully; rub, rub down. (cf *kanda, sugua*) 2. (*fig*) deceive someone with fine words; con, coax: *Alinichua na hatimaye nikakubali kumkopesha pesa*, he deceived me with his fine words and in the end, I agreed to lend him money. Prep. ***chu.li.a*** St. ***chu.lik.a*** Ps. of Prep. ***chu.liw.a*** Rp. ***chu.an.a*** (cf *danganya, hadaa*)

chua² (also *chuya*) *n* (*n*) (*bot*) rice chaff; refuse of rice.

chuan.a *vt* compete, contest: *Timu mbili zilichuana vikali*, the two teams competed vigorously. (cf *umana, menyana, pambana*)

chub *interj* see *chup*

chubu.a *vt, vi* bruise; graze the skin: *Alipoanguka, alijichubua*, when he fell down, he bruised himself. Prep. ***chubu.li.a*** St. ***chubu.k.a*** Cs. ***chubu.lish.a*** Ps. of Prep. ***chubu.liw.a*** Rp. ***chubu.an.a*** (cf *chuma, ambua*)

chubuko *n* (*mi-*) 1. a bruised part. 2. bruise, abrasion, wound.

chubuw.a *vt, vi* sip, drink slowly: *Aliichubuwa soda*, he sipped the soda. Prep. ***chubuw.i.a*** St. ***chubuw.ik.a*** Cs. ***chubuw.ish.a*** Ps of Prep. ***chubuw.iw.a***

chubwi *n* (*n*) 1. plummet, plumb; a leadweight hung at the end of a line to determine the depth of the water or whether a wall, etc., is vertical (cf *timazi, bildi*) 2. a leadweight attached to a fishing-line; sinker, bob, plumb. 3. plop; an expletive describing the sound of sth that has fallen in the water: *Alianguka chubwi*, he fell down with a splashing sound in water.

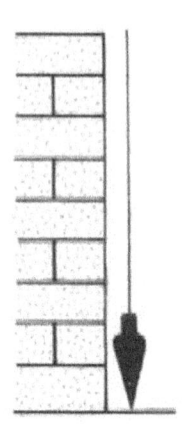

chubwi

chuch.a *vt* knock down sth with a stone, stick, etc.: *Aliyachuchua maembe mengi kutoka kwenye mwembe*, he knocked down a number of mangoes from the mango tree. Prep. ***chuch.i.a*** St. ***chuch.ik.a*** Cs. ***chuch.ish.a*** Ps. ***chuch.w.a*** Rp. of Prep. ***chuch.i.an.a*** (cf *popoa, angua, vurumisha*)

chuchi.a *vt* 1. sway; move to and from: *Watoto wa shule walichuchia vichwa vyao walipokuwa wanaimba*, the school children swayed their heads when they were singing. (cf *tikisika, tetemeka*) 2. used in calling the spirits into the head: *Chuchia pepo*, call the spirits or cause it to mount to the head; conjure. 3. used of a child when it intends to sleep: *Chuchia mtoto*, rock a baby. Ps. ***chuchi.w.a*** Rp. ***chuchi.an.a***

chuchio *n* (*ma-*) 1. the act of moving to and fro; *Chuchio la wale waimbaji lilinivutia*, the swaying of the singers attracted me. 2. the act of calling a spirit in exorcism or in seance; conjuration.

chuchu¹ *n* (*ma-*) teat; nipples of a breast, tit. (cf *titi, ziwa, kilembwe, tombo*)

chuchu² n (n) coward, yellow belly; a person who shrinks from fear or danger: *Hawezi kumkabili maiti yeyote kwa vile yeye ni chuchu,* he can't face a corpse because he is a coward. (cf *hawafu, mteke*)
chuchu.a vt lift sby so as to raise his height. Prep. *chuchu.li.a* St. *chuchu.k.a* Cs. *chuchu.lish.a*
chuchuk.a vi 1. grow up, become tall: *Yeye amechuchuka haraka,* she has grown up fast. 2. grow up slowly and with difficulties; be stunted: *Kwa vile mtoto yule ameugua kwa muda mrefu, anachuchuka kwa shida sasa,* since that child has been ill for such a long time, he is now growing slowly and with difficulties. Prep. *chuchuk.i.a* St. *chuchuk.ik.a* Cs. *chuchuk.ish.a*
chuchuli adv shoulder high, very high, high up: *Mshindi alibebwa chuchuli,* the victor was carried shoulder high. (cf *danadana, kitikiti*)
chuchuma.a vi squat on the hunches or heels; crouch, hunker: *Mlinzi alichuchumaa karibu na moto,* the watchman squatted down by the fire. Prep. *chuchuma.li.a* St. *chuchuma.ik.a* Cs. *chuchuma.lish.a* and *chuchuma.z.a* (cf *chutama, tutama*)
chuchumi.a vi stand on tiptoe; tiptoe: *Alitembea chumbani kwa kuchuchumia ili asimwamshe mtoto,* he tiptoed into the room to avoid waking up the baby. St. *chuchumi.k.a* Cs. *chuchumi.sh.a* Ps. *chuchumi.w.a* Rp. *chuchumi.an.a*
chuchunge (also *mususu*) n (n) half-beak; a sword-fish having a sail-like dorsal fin, and which is found in off-shore waters chiefly in areas of rich submerged vegetation. (cf *mchumbururu*)
chudere (also *mwanambee*) n (n) first born. (of *kifingyuamimba*)
chugachug.a¹ vi be uneasy, be worried: *Mgonjwa alichugachuga baada ya kusikia kwamba atafanyiwa operesheni,* the patient became worried after learning that he would be operated on. Prep. *chugachug.i.a* St. *chugachug.ik.a* Cs. *chugachug.i.sh.a* (cf *tayataya, vanga, hangaika*)
chugachuga² n (n) clumps of threads hanging on the bottom parts of women's dresses.
chuguu n (n) a white-ant hill; an ant-heap. (cf *kisuguu*)
chuguz.a vt beat on the drum hard; sound the drum hard: *Baada ya mavuno, wakulima walichuguza ngoma usiku kucha,* after the harvest, the farmers beat the drums hard the whole night. Prep *chuguz.i.a* St. *chuguz.ik.a* Cs. *chuguz.ish.a* Ps. *chuguz.w.a* Rp. of Prep. *chuguz.i.an.a*
chui n (n) 1. leopard. 2. (fig) a brutal or cruel person; brute: *Yeye ni chui na kwa hivyo, kila mmoja anamwoqopa,* he is a brute and so everyone is afraid of him. (cf *habithi, gwagu, thakili*)
chuj.a vt, vi 1. filter, strain: *Aliichuja chai,* he strained the tea. (cf *safisha*) 2. filter, purify: *Aliichuja asali,* he removed dirt from the honey (cf *safisha*) 3. strain; squeeze milk, water, etc.: *Alilichuja tui,* she strained the grated coconut pulp. 4. screen, choose, select: *Aliyachuja maombi yote ya kazi,* he screened all the applications for employment. Prep. *chuj.i.a* St. *chuj.ik.a* Cs. *chuj.ish.a* Ps. *chuj.w.a* Rp. *chuj.an.a* (cf *chagua*)
chujio n (ma-) strainer, siever, sifter, filter: *Alinunua chujio la chai,* he bought a tea filter. (cf *kifumbu, kumto, kung'uto*)
chuju.a vt 1. cause the colour of sth to fade by washing it with water, etc.: *Aliichujua suruali yake kwa kuifua vibaya,* he faded the colour of his trousers by washing it badly. (cf *fifisha, paua, pararisha*) 2. dilute: *Aliuchujua uji wake,* he diluted his gruel by adding in a lot of water. Prep. *chuju.li.a* St. *chuju.k.a* Cs. *chuju.sh.a* Ps. of Prep.

93

chuju.liw.a (cf *zimua*)
chujuk.a *vi* (of colour, etc.) fade out, wash out: *Rangi ile imechujuka*, that colour has washed out. Prep. ***chujuk.i.a*** St. ***chujuk.ik.a***
chuka[1] *n* (*n*) wart, pimple, pustule. (cf *chunjua, dutu, sagamba*)
chuk.a[2] *vt, vi* 1. lose colour when washed. 2. lose flavour by being dried or soaked in water. 3. (of behaviour) change. Prep. ***chuk.i.a*** St. ***chuk.ik.a*** Cs. ***chu.sh.a***
chuki *n* (*n*) 1. hatred, animosity, rancour, dislike. (cf *uhasama, upasi, uneni*) 2. words of hatred, discord: *Yeye anapenda kuleta chuki kati yetu*, he likes to bring discord between us. 3. sulkiness, sullenness, crossness, anger: *Ana chuki moyoni*, he has anger in his heart.
chuki.a *vt* hate, abhor, loathe, detest, dislike: *Yeye anachukia kila kitu*, he hates everything. Prep. ***chuki.li.a*** St. ***chuki.k.a*** Cs. ***chuki.z.a*** Ps. ***chuki.w.a*** Rp. ***chuki.an.a*** (cf *sumia, zia, mena*)
chukio *n* (*ma-*) abhorrence, detestation, hatred: *Chukio lake juu yetu sisi halina msingi*, his abhorrence towards us is baseless. (cf *karaha, uchukivu*)
chukiz.a *vt* 1. be hateful, be disgusting: *Inachukiza kuona watoto wadogo siku hizi wanaomba pesa*, it is disgusting to see small children are begging for money these days. 2. be unattractive, be repulsive: *Uso wake unachukiza*, her face is unattractive. Prep. ***chukiz.i.a*** St. ***chukiz.ik.a*** Ps. ***chukiz.w.a*** Rp. ***chukiz.an.a***
chukizo *n* (*ma-*) object of hate; a thing which causes an offence or hatred, etc.
chuku *n* (*n*) 1. a cupping horn: *Piga chuku*, cup by using a horn. 2. (*idm*) *Piga chuku*, exaggerate.
chuku.a *vt* 1. carry, take; bear a load. 2. take, bring: *Alikwenda kuchukua maembe yangu dukani*, he went to bring my mangoes from the shop.

3. steal, rob: *Amechukua pesa zangu*, he has stolen my money. 4. receive: *Chukua pesa hizi*, take this money. (cf *pokea*) 5. tolerate, bear, stand: *Mke yule anachukua maudhi mengi ya mumewe*, that woman bears a lot of hardships from her husband. (cf *stahamili, vumilia*) 6. last, endure, continue, take: *Kazi yako itachukua muda mfupi kumalizika*, your work will take a short time to be completed. (cf *dumu, endelea*) 7. suit, fit, match: *Nguo zile alizozivaa zinamchukua*, those clothes he wears fit him well. (cf *pendeza, kaa*) 8. cost, amount to, be worth: *Jengo hili la maktaba limechukua mamilioni ya shilingi kujenga*, this library building has cost millions of shillings to build. 9. (of vessel, measure, etc.) hold, contain, have capacity for: *Chombo hiki kinachukua galoni tano za maji*, this vessel holds five gallons of water. 10. take care of; support, maintain, sustain: *Yeye anamchukua mzee wake*, he maintains his parent. 11. used in various expressions: *Chukua mimba*, be pregnant. *Chukua sheria mkononi*, take the law into one's hands. *Chukua kibubusa*, take secretly/to a secret location. *Chukua hatua*, take steps, take measures (used usu at meetings) *Chukua nafasi*, take the opportunity. *Chukua vipimo*, take measurements. *Chukua kisokoni*, catch someone unawares; catch someone by surprise. Prep. ***chuku.li.a*** St. ***chuku.lik.a*** Cs. ***chuku.lish.a*** and ***chuku.z.a*** Ps. of Prep. ***chuku.liw.a*** Rp. ***chuku.an.a***
chukuan.a *vi* 1. be alike, be compatible: *Vazi lake limechukuana na tukio lenyewe*, his dress fits the occasion. 2. tolerate each other: *Bwana yule na mkewe wanachukuana*, that man and his wife tolerate each other.
chukuchuku *n* (*n*) a kind of relish prepared hurriedly.
chukulia[1] *vi* see *chukua*
chukuli.a[2] *vt, vi* 1. endure, tolerate, bear with: *Anamchukulia sana bibi yake*

chukuzan.a   **chun.a**   **CH**

kwa vile ni mzee, he tolerates a lot of the behaviour of his grandmother because she is old. St. ***chuku.lik.a*** e.g. *Rafiki yako hachukuliki*, your friend takes no advice. 2. believe, accept, take for granted: *Alichukulia kwamba mawazo yake na yangu ni mamoja*, he took it for granted that his ideas and mine are the same. St. ***chuku.lik.a***

chukuzan.a *vt* 1. carry in turns: W*apagazi wale walikuwa wakichukuzana mizigo*, those porters were carrying the loads in turn. 2. accompany each other in the sense that each one is compelling the other to go with him: W*alichukuzana mpaka kwa mkuu wa wilaya ili awatatulie matatizo yao*, they accompanied each other to the district commissioner in order to solve their problems. Prep. ***chukuzan.i.a***

chule *n* (*n*) encrustations of salt water; deposits from salt water found on the body of someone who has taken a swim. (cf *chunyu*)

chuma¹ (pl *vy-*) *n* (*ki-vi*) 1. iron, a piece of iron: *Chuma cha pua*, steel. *Mabamba ya chuma*, harpoon iron; sheets of iron, etc. *Pao* or *fito za chuma*, iron rods; *hars* of iron. *Chuma cha noti*, a tuning fork. *Chuma cha fuuwe*, anvil. *Chuma mfuo*, wrought iron. *Chuma udongo*, cast iron. 2. (*fig*) a strong person; a mighty person; a reliable person: *Yeye ni chuma na kwa hivyo, kila mmoja anamwogopa*, he is a strong person and so everyone is scared of him. 3. (*fig*) skinflint, niggard, miser: *Yeye ni chuma ingawa ana mali nyingi*, he is a miser although he has a lot of wealth. 4. a weapon esp pistol or gun (cf *silaha*) 5. a frying pan for baking pancakes, etc.

chuma² *adj* 1. strong, mighty: *Mtu chuma*, a strong person. 2. (*colloq*) miserly, stingy, niggardly: *Mwanamke chuma*, a stingy woman.

chum.a³ *vt* pluck, pick, cull, gather, reap: *Alichuma mapera kwenye shamba langu*, he plucked guavas from my farm. Prep. ***chum.i.a*** St. ***chum.ik.a*** Cs. ***chum.ish.a*** Ps. ***chum.w.a*** Rp. of Prep. ***chum.i.an.a*** (cf *tungua, chochea, tunda*)

chum.a⁴ *vt* earn, make a profit: *Anachuma pesa nyingi kwenye biashara yake mpya*, he earns a lot of money from his new business. Prep. ***chum.i.a*** St. ***chum.ik.a*** Cs. ***chum.ish.a*** Ps. ***chum.w.a***

chumba¹ (pl *vy-*) *n* (*ki-vi*) room: *Chumba cha kulala*, bedroom. *Chumba cha kulia*, dining room. *Chumba cha maiti*, mortuary. *Chumba cha mikutano*, board room. *Chumba cha wageni*, guest room. *Chumba giza*, a special room where electronic rays are removed.

chumba² (pl *vy-*) *n* (*ki-vi*) 1. the base of a carpenter's plane 2. the slit in the base of a plane. 3. standard, form: *Tuko katika chumba cha tatu*, he is in standard three. (cf *darasa*)

chumbi.a *vt* affiance, betroth; propose marriage to a young woman: *Nilimchumbia binti wa jirani*, I proposed marriage to my neighbour's daughter on his behalf. St. ***chumbi.k.a*** Cs. ***chumbi.sh.a*** Ps. ***chumbi.w.a*** Rp. ***chumbi.an.a***

chumo *n* (*n*) 1. a fruit, etc. that has been plucked from a tree. 2. sth that has been obtained from trade or work such as income. (cf *pato*) 3. source of getting work or profit.

chumu *n* (*n*) fortune, luck, happy chance (cf *bahati njema*)

chumvi *n* (*n*) 1. salt: *Chumvi ya maziwa*, lactate. (cf *munyu*) 2. saltness: *Maji ya chumvi*, salt water; brine. 3 used in the expressions: *Tia chumvi*, exaggerate. *Kula chumvi*, be old.

chumwi *n* (*n*) a special kind of cowrie or shell that is used in special games such as draughts (checkers). (cf *kete, kaure*)

chun.a *vt* 1. (of an animal) skin; flay:

CH   chung.a¹   chunguli.a

Alimchuna kondoo, he skinned the sheep. (cf *chunua, bambua*) 2. (*idms*) *Chuna jogoo*, be circumcized. *Chuna ngozi*, fuck; have sexual intercourse. *Chuna uso*, feel relaxed. Prep. **chun.i.a** St. **chun.ik.a** Cs. **chun.ish.a** Ps. **chun.w.a**

chung.a¹ *vt* 1. herd, graze animals. (cf *lisha*) 2. watch, protect, take care of: *Alilichunga begi langu nilipokwenda msalani*, he took care of my bag when I went to the toilet. (cf *angalia, tazama*) 3. supervise, oversee, watch over: *Mkurugenzi aliwachunga wafanyakazi wake watatu*, the director supervised his three employees. 4. help a sick man on the road; assist a sick man on the road: *Nilimchunga mgonjwa barabarani*, I assisted a sick man on the road. 5. (of a religious leader) shepherd a faithful: *Kasisi anawachunga waumini wa kanisa lake*, the clergyman shepherds the faithful of his church. Prep. **chung.i.a** St. **chung.ik.a** Cs. **chung.ish.a** Ps. **chung.w.a** Rp. **chung.an.a**

chung.a² *vt* winnow, sift, sieve, strain: *Aliuchunga unga wake*, she sifted her flour. Prep. **chung.i.a** St. **chung.ik.a** Cs. **chung.ish.a** Ps. **chung.w.a**

chungi.a *vt* 1. be afraid, be scared. 2. watch out, beware, be alert. 3. remain silent at a place. St. **chungi.k.a** Cs. **chungi.sh.a** Ps. **chungi.w.a** Rp. **chungi.an.a**

chungio *n* (*ma-*) sifter, sieve, strainer: *Hutumia chungio kuchunga mchele wake*, he uses a sieve to sift his rice. (cf *chekeche, chekecheke*)

-chungu¹ *adj* 1. bitter, acid, tart, sour: *Tunda hili ni chungu*, this fruit is bitter. *Dawa hii ni chungu kama shubiri*, this medicine is as bitter as aloes. 2. painful, unpleasant, tormenting: *Yale yalikuwa matokeo machungu*, those were bitter experiences.

chungu² (pl *vy-*) *n* (*ki-vi*) clay cooking pot: *Chungu meko*, a cooking pot and its stones is an expression resembling 'from hand to mouth'.

-chungu³ *adj* plenty, abundant, much: *Ana mali chungu nzima*, she has a lot of wealth.

chungu⁴ *n* (*n*) common black ant. (cf *mchwa, majimoto*)

chungu⁵ *n* (*n*) pimple, pustule, spot: *Ana chungu usoni*, he has pimples on his face. (cf *chunusi, kibuja*)

chungu.a¹ *vt* 1. investigate, scrutinize, probe, look into: *Polisi wanachungua chanzo cha kifo*, the police are investigating the cause of the death. (cf *peleleza, dadisi*) 2. meddle, snoop, pry, intrude: *Anapenda kuchungua mambo ya watu wengine*, he likes to snoop into the affairs of other people. (cf *jiingiza*) Prep. **chungu.li.a** St. **chungu.lik.a** Cs. **chungu.z.a** Ps. of Prep. **chungu.liw.a** Rp. **chungu.an.a**

chungu.a¹ *vt* sieve, sift, strain, winnow. Prep. **chung.li.a** St **chungu.lik.a** Cs. **chungu.z.a** Ps. **chungu.liw.a** Rp. of Prep. **chungu.li.an.a**

chunguchungu¹ *adv* abundantly, copiously, fully, to the brim: *Watu walijaa chunguchungu kwenye chumba cha mkutano*, people were packed in the conference room. (cf *pomoni, tele*)

chunguchungu² *n* (*n*) (*zool*) a kind of red ant. (cf *majimoto, koyokoyo*)

chunguli.a *vt, vi* 1. examine carefully, watch closely: *Alimchungulia sana mtuhumiwa*, he watched the suspect closely. (cf *angalia, chunga*) 2. watch secretly: *Aliwachungulia wageni kwenye tundu ya mlango*, he watched the visitors secretly through the key-hole. 3. look quickly; glance: *Alikichungulia chungu upesi jikoni kama kinachemka*, she looked quickly at the pot in the kitchen to see if it was boiling. St. **chunguli.k.a** Cs. **chunguli.sh.a** Ps. **chunguli.w.a** Rp. **chunguli.an.a**

chunguz.a *vt* 1. examine, inspect. 2. research, investigate: *Mtafiti alijaribu kuchunguza athari za utapiamlo*, the researcher tried to investigate the effects of malnutrition. Prep. ***chunguz.i.a*** St. ***chunguz.ik.a*** Ps. ***chunguz.w.a*** Rp. ***chunguz.an.a***

chungwa *n* (*ma-*) (*bot*) orange; a kind of fruit from a sweet orange tree, *Citrus simensis*.

chuni[1] *n* (*n*) (*zool*) a kind of water bird

chuni[2] *n* (*n*) provocation; the act of telling someone sth repeatedly in order to provoke him; perversity: *Kwa vile nilimshikia chuni, akanitukana*, since I kept on provoking him, he insulted me. (cf *stihizai, inadi*)

chunjua *n* (*n*) wart; a small hard tumorous growth on the skin.

chuno *n* (*mi-*) the act of skinning; flaying.

chunu.a *vt* scrap off the skin; flay: *Alimchunua kuku kabla ya kumpika*, he scrapped off the chicken before cooking it. Prep. ***chunu.li.a*** St. ***chunu.lik.a*** Cs. ***chunu.lish.a*** Ps. of Prep. ***chunu.liw.a*** Rp. of Prep. ***chunu.li.an.a*** (cf *chuna, ambua, bambua*)

chunusi[1] (also *chinusi*) *n* (*n*) (*zool*) an animal believed to be living in the sea and also believed to have drowned people.

chunusi[2] *n* (*n*) pimple, acne, pustule: *Uso wake umejaa chunusi*, her face is full of pimples. (cf *kijiwe, dutu, kidudusi*)

chunyu *n* (*n*) 1. encrustation of salt: *Ardhi hii ina chunyu*, this earth contains salt. 2. deposit from salt water found on the body of someone who has taken a swim. (cf *chule*)

chuo[1] (pl *vy-*) *n* (*ki-vi*) 1. college; an institution of higher learning: *Chuo cha kilimo*, agricultural college. *Chuo cha ufundi*, technical college. *Chuo cha uhazili*, secretarial college. *Chuo cha ardhi*, land institute. *Chuo kikuu*, university. *Chuo kikuu huria*, an open university.

Chuo cha jeshi, military academy. 2. a place where children go to learn the Holy Koran; a koranic school: *Enda chuoni*, go to a koranic school. (cf *madrasa*) 3. a book on Islam written in Arabic language. 4. marriage, matrimony. *Hiki ni chuo chake cha tatu*, this is her third marriage. (cf *ndoa*)

chuo[2] (pl *vy-*) *n* (*ki-vi*) a kind of caulking chisel for removing coconuts.

chup (also *chub*) *interj* shush; an expletive of scorn or anger asking someone to keep quiet. (cf *nyamaza! us!*)

chupa[1] *n* (*n*) bottle: *Chupa ya chai*, thermos flask.

chupa[2] *n* (*n*) (*anat*) amnion; the innermost membrane of a woman; amniotic membrane. (*idm*) *Vunja chupa*, break the amniotic membrane.

chup.a[3] *vt* 1. jump down, dash off, spring, leap, hop: *Alichupa mpaka chini kutoka ghorofa ya pili*, he jumped from the second floor. (cf *ruka*) 2. jump from one branch of a tree to another: *Kima alichupa kutoka tawi moja la mti hadi la pili*, the monkey jumped from one branch of a tree to another. Prep. ***chup.i.a*** St ***chup.ik.a*** Cs. ***chup.ish.a*** Ps. ***chup.w.a*** Ps. of prep. ***chup.iw.a*** (cf *kiuka, tambuka*)

chup.a[4] *vi* shrink, contract, shorten; lessen in size: *Suruali yake sasa imechupa baada ya kufuliwa sana*, his trousers have now shrunk after being washed repeatedly. St. ***chup.ik.a*** Cs. ***chup.ish.a*** (cf *fupika, punguka*)

chupi *n* (*n*) underwear, undergarment. (cf *koro*)

chupi.a *vt* 1. jump into a moving vehicle, etc.; rush and then jump into a vehicle, etc: *Alilichupia basi kwa ufundi*, he dashed off and then jumped into the bus skillfully. (cf *dakira, rukia*) 2. seize or arrest suddenly: *Polisi waliwachupia wezi waliokuwa wakitaka kuvunja duka*, the police arrested by surprise the thieves who wanted to break the shop. Prep. ***chupi.li.a*** St. ***chupi.k.a*** Cs. ***chupi.sh.a*** Ps. ***chupi.w.a*** Rp. ***chupi.an.a*** (cf *kamata*)

chupio *n* (*n*) hair clip; hair pin

chupuchupu *adj* narrowly: *Aliponea chupuchupu*, he escaped narrowly (cf *almanusra*)

chura[1] (pl *vy-*) *n* (*ki-vi*) (*zool*) frog

chura[2] *adj* (usu used in children's games) last, hindmost: *Yeye alikuwa chura katika mashindano ya riadha*, he was the last in the athletics' competition (cf *mwisho*)

chura[3] *n* (*n*) see *chira*

chur.a[4] *vt* 1. bring ill-omen cast a spell over sby; bewitch: cause ill luck to sby; bewitch: *Alimchura jirani yake*, he bewitched his neighbour. 2. do an extraordinary thing: *Alichura kwa kujaribu kula wali kwa kidole kimoja*, he did an extraordinary thing by trying to eat rice with one finger. Prep. ***chur.i.a*** St. ***chur.ik.a*** Cs. ***chur.ish.a*** Ps. ***chur.w.a***

chura[5] *n* (*ki-vi*) toilet cleaner, sewage attendant. (cf *topasi*)

churachur.a *vi* walk nervously here and there. Prep. ***churachur.i.a*** St. ***churachur.ik.a*** Cs. ***churachur.ish.a***

-churo *adj* ill-omened, ill-starred, ill-fated: *Mtu mchuro*, an ill-omened person; jinx.

churupuk.a *vi* 1. slip from the hand or grasp: *Alipokuwa anakata majani, panga lilichurupuka mikononi mwake*, when he was cutting the grass, the slasher slipped from his hands. (cf *chopoka, ponyoka*) 2. flee, get away; escape from a trap esp in the case of animals: *Ndege wake alichurupuka kwenye tundu*, his bird slipped out of the cage. Prep. ***churupuk.i.a*** St. ***churupuk.ik.a*** Cs. ***churupuk.w.a*** (cf *chopoka, kimbia*)

churur.a *vi* trickle, sprinkle, flow gently: *Maji yalikuwa yanachurura kutoka kwenye nguo zilizoanikwa*, the water was trickling from the clothes that were set to dry. Prep. ***churur.i.a***
St. ***churur.ik.a*** Cs. ***churur.ish.a*** and ***churur.iz.a*** Ps. ***churur.w.a*** (cf *dondoka, tiririka*)

chururu[1] *adj* watery, soppy, serous: *Mchuzi chururu*, watery curry.

chururu[2] *n* (*n*) an excessive leaking of water. (*prov*) *Chururu si ndo-ndo-ndo*, it is better to get something small everyday than to get only once in large quantity.

chururu[3] *n* (*n*) (*zool*) a small predatory spider (genus *Araneae*) with fang-like jaws that have poison for killing and one that dwells in a nest made underground.

chururuchururu *interj* an ideophone expressing the movement of water when it is trickling.

churusi *n* (*n*) wood chisel. (cf *balari, turusi, patasi*)

churuz.a *vt* see *chuuza*

churuzik.a *vi* see *chirizika*

chusa (pl *vy-*) *n* (*ki-vi*) a harpoon used for catching large fish.

chush.a[1] *vt, vi* annoy, irritate, disgust: *Vitendo vyake vinachusha*, his actions are disgusting. Prep. ***chush.i.a*** St. ***chush.ik.a*** Ps. ***chush.w.a*** Rp. ***chush.an.a*** (cf *udhi, sumbua*)

chush.a[2] *vt* wet sth inorder to reduce the degree of its acidity or bitterness. Prep. ***chush.i.a*** St. ***chush.ik.a*** Ps. ***chush.w.a*** Rp. ***chush.an.a***

chushi *adj* disgusting, annoying.

chutam.a *vi* crunch; squat: *Mtoto alichutama alipokuwa anakunya*, the child crunched when he was defecating. Prep. ***chutam.i.a*** St. ***chutam.ik.a*** Cs. ***chutam.ish.a*** Ps. ***chutam.w.a*** (cf *tutama, chuchumaa*)

chuuz.a[1] (also *churuza*) *vt* hawk wares; have a small business; sell small items; vend, retail, peddle: *Anachuuza bidhaa zake sokoni*, he hawks his wares at the market. Prep. ***chuuz.i.a*** St. ***chuuz.ik.a*** Cs. ***chuuz.ish.a*** Ps. ***chuuz.w.a*** Rep. of Prep. ***chuuz.i.an.a***

chuuz.a[2] *vt* sell sth of a commodity at a high price. Prep ***chuuz.i.a*** St. ***chuuz.***

ik.a Cs. ***chuuz.ish.a*** Ps. ***chuuz.w.a*** Rp. of Prep. ***chuuz.i.an.a***

chuya *n* (*n*) see *chua*²

chuz.a *vt* 1. select, choose, cull, pick: *Alichuza mayai mazima dukani*, he selected good eggs at the shop. (cf *chagua, teua*) 2. filter, strain, refine, purify: *Aliichuza chai*, she strained the tea. (cf *chuja*)

chw.a *vi* be sunset: *Jua limekuchwa*, the sun has set. *Kumekuchwa*, it is after sunset. Prep. ***chw.e.a*** Ps. of Prep. ***chw.ew.a***

chwago (also *chago, furo*) *n* (*n*) (*zool*) stalk-eyed ghost crab (cf *kayakaya, furo, chanjagaa*)

chwechwe *n* (*n*) callus; a kind of tissue which grows on a stem of a tree to recover the damage.

D

D, d /d/ 1. the fourth letter of the Swahili alphabet. 2. a voiced alveolar stop.

daa *n (n) (zool)* a kind of worm found on the muddy part of a shore, and used by fishermen as a bait. (cf *choo*)

daathar.i *vt* 1. jeopardize, endanger, threaten: *Waendeshaji magari wa mwendo wa kasi wanadaathari maisha ya watu*, motorists who drive very fast jeopardize peoples' lives. (cf *angamiza, hatarisha*) 2. invalidate, nullify, annul: *Bunge liliidaathari sheria iliyopitishwa mwaka jana*, parliament annulled the law which was passed last year. Prep. **daathar.i.a** St. **daathar.ik.a** Cs. **daathar.ish.a** Ps. of Prep. **daathar.iw.a**. Rp. of Prep. **daathar.i.an.a** (cf *batilisha*) (Ar)

daawa¹ *n (n)* 1. law suit, litigation, legal claim: *Mdai amekwenda mahakamani kusikiliza daawa yake*, the claimant has gone to the court to hear his lawsuit. (cf *mashtaka*) 2. misunderstanding, discord, disharmony, dispute: *Daawa iliyokuwapo kati ya watu wale wawili imewafanya sasa watengane*, the misunderstanding that existed between those two people has now estranged them.(cf *utesi*) (Ar)

daawa² *n (n)* (in Islam) a system of inculcating certain attributes to an adherent of a particular religion so as to be converted. (Ar)

daba¹ *n (ma-)* see *dubu*

daba² *n (ma-)* see *debe*

dabali¹ *adv* double, twice. (Eng)

dabali² *n (n)* a kind of cloth whose breadth has a double size to that of the normal one. (Eng)

dabir.i¹ *vt* plan, organise, arrange in order: *Yeye huzidabiri shughuli zake vizuri*, she plans her activities well. Prep. **dabir.i.a** St. **dabir.ik.a** Cs. **dabir.ish.a** Ps. of Prep. **dabir.iw.a** Rp. of Prep. **dabir.i.an.a**

dabir.i² *vt* pry, snoop; spy into private affairs or matters, be curious about other's affairs: *Anapenda kudabiri mambo ya watu*, he likes to snoop into other people's affairs. Prep. **dabir.i.a** St. **dabir.ik.a** Cs. **dabir.ish.a** Ps. of Prep. **dabir.iw.a** Rp. of Prep. **dabir.i.an.a** (cf *tafuta, chunguza, peleleza*)

dabir.i³ *vt* examine, heed, observe, pay attention: *Utayadabiri mambo yote niliyokuambia?* Will you pay attention to all that I have told you? Prep. **dabir.i.a** St. **dabir.ik.a** Cs. **dabir.ish.a** Ps. of Prep. **dabir.iw.a** Rp. of Prep. **dabir.i.an.a** (cf *zingatia*)

dabir.i⁴ *vt* escape; run away from someone because of fear: *Kuwaona tu, akawadabiri*, as soon as he saw them, he escaped them. Prep. **dabir.i.a** St. **dabir.ik.a** Cs. **dabir.ish.a** Ps. of Prep. **dabir.iw.a** Rp. of Prep. **dabir.i.an.a** (cf *kimbia, toroka*)

dab.u *vt* 1. manage, control: *Ali hakuweza kuidabu kazi aliyopewa*, Ali could not manage the work he was assigned to do. (cf *weza, mudu*) 2. terrify, horrify, threaten: *Mimi simdabu lakini ninampa ukweli*, I am not threatening him but I am telling him the truth. Prep. **dab.i.a** St. **dab.ik.a** Cs. **dab.ish.a** Ps. **dab.w.a** Ps. of Prep. **dab.iw.a** Rp. of Prep. **dab.i.an.a** (cf *tisha*)

dabwadabwa (also *debwedebwe*) *adj* watery, soggy, soppy: *Wali wa dabwadabwa*, watery rice.

-dachi *adj* German: *Lugha ya Kidachi*, German language.

dachia *n (n) (zool)* heifer; a female animal capable of begetting offsprings. (cf *mtamba*)

dada (also *dade*) *n (n)* 1. sister: *Dada wa kambo*, step sister. 2. an elder sister. 3. any female relative. 4. a term of respect given to a girl or woman.

dadavu.a *vt* unravel, disentangle, untangle, figure out: *Nilikuwa na matatizo mengi lakini sasa nimeyadadavua*, I had a lot of problems but now I have solved them. Prep. **dadavu.li.a** St. **dadavu.k.a** Cs. **dadavu.sh.a** Ps. of Prep. **dadavu.liw.a** Rp. **dadavu.an.a** (cf *tatua, zongoa*)

dade *n* (*n*) see *dada* Elder sister or brother) A name that younger person use when calling or refering to elder sister/ brother.

dadis.a *vt* tie or wrap a loin-cloth or other material round one's waist as women do when they intend to dance or work: *Mwanamke alijidadisa kanga huku akicheza ngoma kwa ufundi*, the woman tied a "khanga" round her waist and danced artistically. Prep. **dadis.i.a** St. **dadis.ik.a** Cs. **dadis.ish.a** Ps. **dadis.w.a** Rp. of Prep. **dadis.i.an.a**

dadis.i *vt* 1. pry, be inquisitive, be curious: *Acha kudadisi mambo ya watu*, stop prying into the affairs of other people. (cf *chunguza, peleleza*) 2. investigate, enquire, probe: *Makachero waliyadadisi mauaji yaliyotokea mitaani*, the detectives investigated the deaths which had occurred in the neighbourhoods. Prep. **dadis.i.a** St. **dadis.ik.a** Cs. **dadis.ish.a** Ps. of Prep. **dadis.iw.a** Rp. of Prep. **dadis.i.an.a** (cf *chunguza, peleleza*)

dado *n* (*n*) see *dadu*

dadu (also *dado*) *n* (*n*) die, dice; a small marked cube used in games of chance: *Dadu za barafu*, ice cubes. (cf *dhumna*)

dafi (also *dafu*) *n* (*n*) tambourine, timbrel (cf *tari, kigoma*) (Ar)

dafina *n* (*n*) 1. treasure. 2. treasure-trove; treasure such as gold, bullion, etc. found hidden or buried, when the original owner is not known. (cf *hazina*) 3. an unexpected present: *Rais aliwapa masikini dafina alipokuwa anaelekea nyumbani*, the president gave gifts to the poor people on his way home. (Ar)

dafrao (also *dafrau, dafurao*) *n* (*n*) 1. head-on collision; face to face confrontation: *Alipigwa dafrao*, he was hit by a car. 2. accident, casualty: *Alikuwa chanzo cha dafrao iliyowaua watu wengi*, he was the cause of the accident which killed many people. 3. fenders used to prevent damage to the hull in collision or contact with other vessels such as ships, etc.: *Piga dafrau*, damage by contact.

dafrau *n* (*n*) see *dafrao*

daftari *n* (*ma-*) 1. exercise book: *Daftari la mazoezi*, exercise book. 2. ledger; cashbook, journal. *Daftari la matukio*, diary. *Daftari la wapiga kura*, voters' book. *Daftari la kudumu la wapiga kura*, permanent voters' book. (*prov*) *Mali bila ya daftari, hupotea bila ya habari*, property without a book goes missing without knowing i.e. expenses without being recorded in a book disappear quickly without knowing.

dafu¹ *n* (*n*) see *dafi*

dafu² *n* (*ma-*) 1. an unripe coconut fruit containing water used for drinking, and which has a soft layer of nutty edible substance: *Dafu la uramberambe*, a kind of very young green coconut which is beginning to form a soft layer of nutty subtance in the shell. *Tonga la dafu*, semi-hard nut of a coconut, i.e. the nutty substance has become thick and tough. *Maji ya dafu*, coconut milky fluid. 2. (*idm*) *Fua dafu*, manage, be able e.g. *Mbele yangu, hafui dafu*, I have excelled him in every respect.

dafurao *n* (*n*) see *dafrao*

dagaa *n* (*n*) 1. (*zool*) sardines, herrings; a kind of small ocean fish of *Clupeidae* and *Engraulidae* families preserved in tightly packed cans for eating purposes. *Dagaa papa*, pilchard. *Dagaa mcheli*, short head anchovy. *Dagaa suli*, spotted sardinella. 2. (*fig*) a despised person or thing, bastard.

dagaapapa *n* (*n*) (*zool*) pilchard; a small,

101

salt water fish of the herring family.
daghadagha *n* (*n*) worry, anxiety, perplexity, concern. (cf *wahaka, wasiwasi*) (Ar)
dagla (also *degle*) *n* (*n*) a kind of a long coat which is well-ornamented with gold braid or thread. (Hind)
dago *n* (*n*) a fisherman's camp near a beach or on the sand at a high-water mark.
dahalia *n* (*n*) dormitory, hostel. (cf *bweni*)
dahari[1] *adv* 1. always, everytime, at all times, on every occasion, constantly: *Watumishi hawa dahari wanachelewa kazini*, these servants always report late for work. 2. formerly, in the past: *Watu wale walikuwa dahari wakulima*, in the past, those people were farmers. (cf *zamani*) (Ar)
dahari[2] *n* (*n*) aeon, eon; an extremely long, indefinite period of time.
dahil.i[1] *vt* 1. enquire, interrogate, investigate: *Askari waliwadahili majirani kuhusu ule wizi wa nguvu*, the policemen interrogated the neighbours regarding the violent robbery. (cf *dadisi*) 2. interfere, meddle, intrude, pry, snoop; poke one's nose in: *Usijaribu kudahili mambo ya watu*, don't try to meddle in other people's affairs. Prep. **dahil.i.a** St. **dahil.ik.a** Cs. **dahil.ish.a** Ps. of Prep. **dahil.iw.a** Rp. of Prep. **dahil.i.an.a** (cf *jiingiza*) (Ar)
dahili[2] *n* (*n*) 1. income, revenue, returns: *Kila siku, dahili ya biashara yangu kutoka duka hili ni takriban shilingi elfu kumi*, every day, I get an income of almost ten thousands from this shop. (cf *pato, chumo*) 2. salary, wages: *Dahili yangu kazini ni ndogo*, I get a low salary at my place of work. (Ar)
dahu.a *vt* repeat the earlier statements or words: *Wasemaji walidahua mmoja baada ya mwingine mambo yaleyale kwenye mkutano*, the speakers said the same thing one after another at the meeting. Prep. **dahu.li.a** St. **dahu.k.a** Cs. **dahu.lish.a** Ps. of Prep.

dahu.liw.a Rp. **dahu.an.a** (Ar)
dai[1] *n* (*ma-*) 1. claim, allegation, assertion: *Dai lake la kiwanja halina msingi*, his claim for the plot is baseless. 2. (*law*) *Dai kingani*, counter claim. (cf *kilio, lalamiko*) 3. rumour. (cf *uvumi*) (Ar)
da.i[2] *vt* 1. claim, demand: *Alinidai pesa zake*, he claimed his money from me. 2. claim, allege, assert: *Wachezaji wanadai kwamba rifarii alipendelea*, the players allege that the referee was biased. (cf *shikilia*) 3. used in the other expressions: *Dai talaka*, ask for divorce. *Dai urithi*, claim for inheritance. Prep. **da.i.a** St. **da.ik.a** Ps. of Prep. **da.iw.a** Rp. of Prep. **da.i.an.a** (Ar)
daima[1] *adv* always, forever, incessantly, at all times: *Vijana wale wawili daima wanagombana*, those two young men always quarrel. (cf *azali*) (Ar)
daima[2] *adj* permanent, everlasting, long lasting, durable: *Maisha ya daima*, everlasting life. (Ar)
dainamo *n* (*n*) dynamo; a machine for changing mechanical energy into electrical energy (Eng)
daini *n* (*n*) (*phys*) dyne; the unit of force in the cgs system. i.e. the amount of force that imparts to a mass of one gram on acceleration of one centimeter per second per second (Eng)
dak.a[1] *vi* 1. catch, snatch, grab, grasp: *Golikipa aliudaka mpira kwa ufundi*, the goalkeeper caught the ball skillfully. (cf *nyaka*) 2. (*idm*) *Daka maneno*, interrupt someone speaking; inteject. Prep. **dak.i.a** St. **dak.ik.a** Cs. **dak.ish.a** and **dak.iz.a** Ps. **dak.w.a** Rp. **dak.an.a**
daka[2] *n* (*ma-*) see *danga*
daka[3] *n* (*ma-*) niche, alcove, recess, nook. (cf *kishubaka*)
dakawa *n* (*n*) 1. (*naut*) tow-line, tow rope; a rope tied between two canoes so that the one at the front pulls the one behind: *Vuta dakawa*, pull the tow rope 2. a rope to haul cargo.

daki.a vt 1. jump into (on, to, over,etc.); step over, as of a threshold, log, pool of water, muddy place, etc. *Alilidakia gogo*, he jumped over a log. (cf *rukia, chupia*) 2. jump into a vehicle when in motion: *Baadhi ya abiria wanapenda kuyadakia magari hata kama yanaenda kwa kasi*, some of the passengers like jumping into vehicles even when they are going fast. 3. do sth in a hurry. Prep. ***daki.li.a*** St. ***daki.lik.a*** Cs. ***daki.z.a*** Ps. ***daki.w.a***

dakika n (n) minute; *Dakika tano*, five minutes: *Dakika hii*, this minute. (Ar)

dakiz.a vt interrupt, meddle, object; *Alinidakiza nilipokuwa nikizungumza*, he interrupted me when I was talking Prep. ***dakiz.i.a*** St. ***dakiz.ik.a*** Ps. ***dakiz.w.a*** Rp. ***dakiz.an.a***

dakizo n (ma-) 1. interference, objection, interruption: *Madakizo mengi ya watu yalitufanya kuyawacha mazungumzo yetu*, the many interruptions from people caused us to abandon our conversation. 2. intrusion; the act of forcing oneself in a place without permission, invitation or welcome: *Alibezwa kwenye hafla kwa sababu ya madakizo yake ya mara kwa mara*, he was snubbed at the reception because of his frequent intrusions. (cf *umbelembele, utosha*)

daktari n (ma-) 1. medical doctor: *Daktari wa macho*, oculist, opthalmologist; eye doctor, eye specialist. *Daktari wa meno*, dentist. *Daktari wa mifugo*, veterinarian; veterinary doctor. (cf *tabibu, mganga*) 2. a person who has received the highest university degree: *Daktari wa Falsafa*, Doctor of Philosophy. *Daktari wa Sayansi*, Doctor of Science. (Eng)

daku n (n) (in Islam) a late night meal during the fasting of the Holy month of Ramadan.

daku.a vi prattle, blather, jabber; gossip randomly, talk nonsense: *Anapenda kudakua mbele za watu*, he likes to talk nonsense in public. Prep. ***daku.li.a*** St. ***daku.lik.a*** Cs. ***daku.liz.a*** Ps. of Prep. ***daku.liw.a*** Rp. ***daku.an.a***

daladala n (ma-) (used in Tanzania) public vehicle, used for carrying passengers, usu making frequent stops; urban shuttle vehicle. (cf *matatu*)

dalali[1] n (ma-) auctioneer, broker: *Dalali yule hakuuza bidhaa zote*, that auctioneer did not auction off all the articles. (cf *mnadi*) (Ar)

dalali[2] n (ma-) 1. agent, representative. 2. pawnbroker, money-lender. (Ar)

dalasini (also *mdalasini*) n (mi-) (bot) cinammon. *Cinnamomum zeylanicum.*

dalhini adv see *dalihini*

dali n (n) end, conclusion, ending. (cf *kikomo, mwisho, tamati*)

dalia n (n) aromatic yellow mixture or powder used by women for personal adornment and which is also put on the shroud during the preparation of a dead body for burial.

dalihini (also *dalhini*) adv quickly, fast, rapidly, speedily: *Mtumishi aliupeleka dalihini ujumbe kwa baba*, the servant sent the message quickly to my father. (cf *chapuchapu, haraka*) (Ar)

dalili n (n) 1. sign, symptom, indication: *Hukuna dalili yoyote kwamba mvua itanyesha leo*, there is no sign at all that it will rain today. (prov) *Dalili ya mvua ni mawingu*, the sign of rain is clouds i.e. a big incident has normally got its indications. (cf *ishara, alama*) 2. mark, spot; the track or trail of an animal, etc. *Hapa pana nyayo za binadamu na mbwa; hii ni dalili kwamba vitu hivi viwili vilipita*, I can see here there are human footprints and those of dogs; this is an indication that these two things passed. (Ar)

dalji n (n) 1. (used of a horse or donkey) trot, amble; 2. swaggering walk, graceful walk: *Kwenda dalji*, walk pompously; walk gracefully. (Ar)

dalki n (n) see *telki*

daluga (*also daruga*) *n* (*n*) 1. spikes 2. (in soccer) *Piga mtu daluga*, kick sby.

dama *n* (*n*) draughts, checkers; a game played on a table by two players using 24 round pieces on a chequered board. (Port)

dambra *n* (*n*) (*naut*) cabin hold; a private room on a ship, as a bedroom or office.

dambwa *n* (*ma-*) a secret place where the arrangements for circumcision rites are made.

damir.i *vt*, *vi* spoil, wreck, ruin, scuttle, destroy: *Anapenda kuidamiri mipango yetu*, he likes wrecking our plans. Prep. **damir.i.a** St. **damir.ik.a** Cs. **damir.ish.a** (cf *angamiza*, *haribu*) (Ar)

damirik.a *vi* be devastated, be spoilt, be ruined: *Hamisi amedamirika siku hizi*, Hamisi is spoilt these days. Prep. **damirik.i.a** St. **damirik.ik.a** Cs. **damirik.ish.a** (cf *angamia*) (Ar)

damisi[1] *adj* cheerful, vivacious, jovial: *Mtu yule anapendwa na majirani kwa vile ni damisi*, that person is liked by the neighbours because he is cheerful. (Ar)

damisi[2] *n*(*n*) 1. a cheerful person, a light-hearted person. 2. an argumentative person; wrangler: *Usishindane na damisi*, don't argue with an argumentative person. (cf *mshindani*, *mbishi*) 3. clown, jester, buffoon. (Ar)

damk.a *vi* wake up early in the morning, wake up at dawn: *Itanibidi kudamka kesho kwa vile ndege yangu inaondoka asubuhi*, I will be obliged to wake up at dawn tomorrow because my plane leaves early morning. Prep. **damk.i.a** St. **damk.ik.a** Cs. **damk.ish.a** Ps. **damk.w.a** (cf *jihimu*)

dampo *n* (*ma-*) dump; a place where refuse is dumped. (Eng)

damu[1] *n* (*n*) blood: *Hara damu*, have dysentery. *Ingia damu*, menstruate. *Toka na damu*, bleed. *Tokwa na damu*, be bleeding. *Hana damu*, he is not healthy. *Upungufu wa damu*, anaemia, *Damu menyu*, pure blood. (Ar)

damu[2] *n* (*n*) kin, stock, family, breed: *Watu wenye damu moja*, relatives. *Ndugu wa damu*, relative. (*prov*) *Damu ni nzito kuliko maji*, blood is thicker than water. *Pandisha damu*, be angry. (Ar)

danadana[1] (*also danedane*) *adv* 1. high up, shoulder high, very high: *Alichukuliwa danadana*, he was carried high up. (cf *chuchuli*) 2. jubilantly, elatedly, joyfully: *Tuliusherehekea ushindi wetu danadana*, we celebrated our victory jubilantly. (Ar)

danadana[2] *n* (*n*) the state of sitting comfortably; the state of sitting with legs wide apart: *Sikuweza kukaa danadana kwenye basi kwa vile abiria walijaa pomoni ndani*, I was not able to sit comfortably in the bus as it was so full of passengers.

danadana[3] *n* (*n*) 1. (in soccer) dribbling. 2. cheating sby: *Piga danadana*, dodge sby so that you don't pay him now.

dand.a *vt*, *vi* 1. step over, pass over, jump over, cross: *Nilipofika matopeni, nikadanda kwa uangalifu ili nisije kuchafua viatu vyangu*, when I reached at the muddy place, I crossed carefully to avoid getting my shoes dirty. 2. jump on sth such as a vehicle when in motion: *Alisita kudanda kwenye basi lile ili asije kuanguka*, he hesitated to jump into the bus for fear of falling. Prep. **dand.i.a** St. **dand.ik.a** Cs. **dand.ish.a** Ps. of Prep. **dand.w.a** Rp. of Prep. **dand.i.an.a** (cf *rukia*, *chupia*)

dandala *n* (*n*) (*zool*) little egret; a kind of small white bird with black legs and conspicuous yellow toes and a black bill. *Egretta garzette*. (cf *yangeyange*)

dandalo[1] (*also ndolindoli*) *n* (*n*) a kind of coastal dance performed by local men holding sticks. (cf *tokomire*)

dandalo[2] *n* (*n*) shaft, post, pole, pier. (cf *nguzo*)

dandi.a *vt* travel in a vessel illegally. 2. jump into a moving vehicle, etc. (cf *rukia*) 3. work in a place informally. St. *dandi.k.a* Cs. *dandi.sh.a* Ps. *dandi.w.a* Rp. *dandi.an.a*

danedane[1] *n* (*n*) see *danadana*[1]

danedane[2] *n* (*n*) a street dance usu of the Aga Khan disciples performed by rows of people facing each other holding sticks with each person on one side striking the stick held by another on the opposite side as they move along singing. (Guj)

danga[1] (also *daka*) *n* (*ma-*) 1. (*bot*) white yam; 2. an unripe fruit e.g. coconut. 3. (*idm*) *Dunga la mwana*, a well-brought up young man.

dang.a[2] *vt* 1. scoop up, ladle; take a little at a time with the hand or with an instrument: *Danga maji*, take a little water, scoop up water, say in a bucket, etc. (cf *chota*) 2. hunt for sth which is not easily available: *Alikwenda kudanga sukari lakini hakufanikiwa*, he went to the shops to look for sugar but he did not succeed. Prep. *dang.i.a* St. *dang.ik.a* Cs. *dang.ish.a* Ps. *dang.w.a*

danga[3] *n* (*n*) (*zool*) the first milk of animals after giving birth; beestings; colostrum.

dangany.a *vt* deceive, hoodwink, swindle, beguile, defraud, cheat. Prep. *dangany.i.a* St. *dangany.ik.a* Cs. *dangany.ish.a* Ps. *dangany.w.a* Rp. *dangany.an.a* (cf *hadaa, ghilibu*)

-danganyifu *adj* deceitful, guileful, sly, untruthful, insincere: *Mfanyabiashara mdanganyifu*, a deceitful businessman.

dangirizi *n* (*ma-*) dungarees, jeans, overalls. (Eng)

dango *n* (*ma-*) target, objective

danguro *n* (*ma-*) a house of prostitution; brothel, bordello, whorehouse. (Port)

dansa (also *dansi*, *densi*) *n* (*n*) modern dance: *Rafiki yangu huenda kucheza dansa kila Jumamosi*, my friend goes dancing every Saturday. (Eng)

dansi *n* (*n*) see *dansa*

danzi *n* (*n*) (*bot*) seville orange; a kind of sweet or sour orange, the latter being used for marmalade and for cleaning floors and brass.

dapa (also *tapa*) *n* (*n*) (*bot*) the broad leaf of Deleb or Palmyra palm. (cf *tapa*)

dapi.a *vi* 1. jump from one branch of a tree to another as men or animals do e.g. *Yule kima anadapia kwenye matawi ya mti*, the monkey jumps from one branch of a tree to another. 2. walk swaggeringly; walk pompously or flamboyantly. Prep. *dapi.li.a* St. *dapi.lik.a* Cs. *dapi.z.a* Ps. *dapi.w.a*

dar.a *vt* 1. touch gently; palm, finger: *Nilimdara paka wangu*, I touched my cat gently. 2. tempt or test sby or sth. Prep. *dar.i.a* St. *dar.ik.a* Cs. *dar.ish.a* Ps. *dar.w.a* Rp. *dar.an.a*

daraba[1] *n* (*n*) (*naut*) a lavatory in a dhow' gunwale surrounding a hull. (cf *kipwi*) (Ar)

daraba[2] *n* (*n*)(*naut*) the top edge on the side of an outrigger canoe.

darabi *n* (*n*) (*bot*) rose apple; a kind of round fruit with a fleshy rose-scented pericarp surrounding a central seed. (cf *gulabi*) (Pers)

darahani *n* (*n*) journey star; a star which is very close to the moon. (Ar)

darahima (also *dirhamu*) *n* (*n*) money, currency, cash. (cf *fedha, fulusi*) (Ar)

daraja[1] *n* (*ma-*) 1. bridge. 2. staircase, stairs. (cf *ngazi*) (Ar)

daraja[2] *n* (*n*) rank, position, grade, status: *Amepandishwa daraja*, he has been promoted; he has been given a higher grade. *Karafuu zimegawanywa katika daraja mbalimbali*, the cloves have been divided into different grades. *Daraja hatua*, class interval. *Daraja modi*, modal class. (cf *cheo, wadhifa*) (Ar)

daraja[3] *n* (*n*) dock, jetty, pier, breakwater, sea wall: *Jahazi ilipotia nanga, abiria wakateremka kupitia kwenye daraja*, when the dhow anchored, the passengers descended via the jetty. (cf *gati*) (Ar)

daraja⁴ *n* (*ma-*) size, measure, dimension: *Siwezi kuivaa nguo hiyo kwa vile si daraja yangu*, I cannot wear that dress because it is not of my size. (cf *kiasi, kadiri*) (Ar)

daraja⁵ *n* (*n*) a mark or rating given to a student on a particular task; grade.

darasa *n* (*ma-*) 1. standard, class: *Yeye yuko darasa la tatu*, he is in standard three. (cf *chumba*) 2. lesson, practice, exercise: *Nimemaliza kulifanya darasa la sita*, I have completed exercise six. 3. subject, discipline, study; course of study: *Mimi silipendi darasa la Kiingereza*, I don't like the English subject. 4. instructions, usu Islamic, given in a Koranic school, or in another special place or mosque. (Ar)

daraya *n* (*n*) see *deraya*

dari¹ *n* (*ma-*) 1. ceiling, attic, upper storey; 2. balcony. (Pers and Ar)

dari² *n* (ma-) (*naut*) the front or back part of a sailing vessel e.g. dhow, canoe, etc. each of which has a plank to sit or put things on.

darii *n* (*n*) see *deraya*

darij.i *vt* 1. put in order; arrange in order: *Mtumishi wangu hudariji vitu vya nyumba vizuri*, my servant puts the household items in order. (cf *panga, rusu, safidi*) 2. act on a plan or implement sth step by step: *Mkurugenzi anadariji mpango wa kuboresha uchumi wa nchi*, the director is implementing the plan to improve the country's economy. Prep. ***darij.i.a*** St. ***darij.ik.a*** Cs. ***darij.ish.a*** Ps. of Prep. ***darij.iw.a*** Rp. of Prep. ***darij.i.an.a***

Darisalama *n* (*n*) Dar es Salaam; a major city in Tanzania. (Ar)

daris.i *vt, vi* see *durusu*, Prep. ***daris.i.a*** St. ***daris.ik.a*** Cs. ***daris.ish.a*** Ps. of Prep. ***daris.iw.a*** (Ar)

darizi¹ *n* (*n*) 1. embroidery: *Kanzu ya darizi*, an embroidered garment. 2. incision marks. (Ar)

dariz.i² (also *tarizi*) *vt, vi* embroider; do decorative needlework: *Mtu yule anapenda kuzidarizi kanzu zake ili zipate kupendeza*, that person likes to embroider his clothes so as to make them look attractive. Prep. ***dariz.i.a*** St. ***dariz.ik.a*** Cs. ***dariz.ish.a*** Ps. of Prep. ***dariz.iw.a*** Rp. of Prep. ***dariz.i.an.a*** (cf *nakshi*) (Ar)

darubini *n* (*n*) telescope, binoculars: *Darubini akisi*, reflecting telescope (Pers)

darumeti *n* (*n*) (*naut*) ceiling or interior planking brought crosswise against the ribs and running fore-and-aft in a dhow or other vessel. (Ar)

darzeni *n* (*n*) see *dazani*

dasi¹ *n* (*n*) (*naut*) 1. bolt-rope; edge of a sail sewn on a rope in order to make the sail strong. Used for either, *Dasi ya bara*, on the upper side. *Dasi ya chini*, on the lower side. *Dasi ya joshini/Dasi ya demani*, on the lower and broader ends. 2. thread used in making sails. (Pers)

dasi² *n* (*n*) (*vet*) mange; a parasitic disease affecting donkeys characterized by intense itching, lesions and a loss of hair, etc. (Pers)

dasili (also *ghasili*) *n* (*n*) powder made of the dried and powdered leaves of *mkunazi*, Chinese date or jujube tree, used as a detergent for a skin disease. (Ar)

dasta¹ *n* (*n*) see *deste*

dasta² *n* (*n*) duster; a thing that removes writing from a chalkboard. (cf *kifutio*) (Eng)

dasturi¹ *n* (*n*) see *desturi*

dasturi² (also *desturi*) *n* (*ma-*) (*naut*) movable bowsprit in function half way between sprit and boom; a large log laid across a ship, dhow, etc acting as a ballast (Ar)

dat.a¹ *vi* 1. crackle, snap, click: *Moto unadata jikoni*, the fire is crackling in the kitchen. 2. slip; fail to achieve sth; miscarry, go wrong: *Alimtafuta*

dat.a²

sana mtoto wake sokoni lakini alidata, she searched hard for her child at the market but she did not find her. Prep. ***dat.i.a*** St. ***dat.ik.a*** Cs. ***dat.ish.a*** Ps. ***dat.w.a.*** Rp. ***dat.an.a*** (cf *noa, shindwa*).

dat.a² *vi* be stuck, be jammed, be bogged down: *Nilipita kwenye matope na kisha gari yangu ikadata*, I passed through a muddy place and then my car got stuck. Prep. ***dat.i.a*** St. ***dat.ik.a*** Cs. ***dat.ish.a*** Ps. ***dat.w.a*** Rp. ***dat.an.a***

data³ *n (n)* data; facts or information used for a particular purpose: *Data ghafi*, raw data. *Data yu vikundi*, grouped data. (Eng)

datam.a *vi* cower, cringe; move backwards in fear, etc.: *Alidatama kutokuwa na baridi kali*, he cowered because of excessive coldness. (cf *jikunyata*)

dati.a *vi* walk pompously or majestically; swagger: *Alidatia alipopita hapa*, he swaggered when he passed here. Prep. ***dati.li.a*** St. ***dati.ik.a*** Cs. ***dati.ish.a***

datsi *n (n)* darts; a game in which a number of small, pointed missiles are thrown at a target.

dau¹ *n (ma-) (naut)* sail boat; a fishing vessel usu under 20 tons. (*prov*) *Dau la mnyonge haliendi joshi*, a poor man's voice is usu not listened to by those in power. (Ar)

dau² *n (ma-)* wager; the money or thing to be won in gambling.

dawa¹ *n (n)* 1. medication, medicament, drug: *Dawa ya kuharisha*, purgative, laxative. *Dawa ya mitishamba*, herbal medicine. *Dawa ya kulevya*, narcotics. *Dawa ya meno*, tooth paste. *Dawa ya usingizi*, sleeping pill. 2. chemical: *Dawa ya mbu*, a chemical for killing mosquitoes; mosquito killer. *Dawa ya uwongo*, nostrum. *Dawa ya panya*, a chemical for killing rats. *Dawa ya mseto*, anti-malaria combination therapy 3. (*fig*) panacea, remedy, treatment, solution: *Dawa yao ni kuwaongezea mshahara*, the solution is to increase their salaries. (Ar)

dawa² *n (n)* talisman, amulet, charm; a consecrated object believed to have magical powers of protection against evil. (cf *hirizi, talasimu*) (Ar)

dawa.a *vi (n)* see *duwaa*

dawamu *adv* always, forever, constantly. Sometimes the word *dawamu* (with *daima*) is used to give emphasis: *Watu hawa wamekuwa daima dawamu vinyozi*, these people have always been barbers. (Ar)

dawati *n (n)* 1. desk, writing desk. (cf *deski*) 2. drawer, davenport. 3. inkpot. (Ar)

Dayani (also *Dayanu*) *n (n)* (one of the names of God) Rewarder, Compensator. (Ar)

Dayanu *n (n)* see *Dayani*

dayosisi *n (n)* diocese. (Eng)

dazani (also *dazeni, darzani*) *n (n)* dozen: *Yapange mayai kwa dazani*, arrange the eggs in dozens. (Eng)

dazeni *n (n)* see *dazani*

debe *n (ma-)* tin can; a small metal can: *Debe la maji*, a tin can containing water. (Ar)

debwani *n (n)* 1. a kind of loin-cloth. 2. a red or brown striped cloth, usu of silk, worn on the head as a turban. (cf *rehani*)

debwedebwe *n (n)* see *dabwadabwa*

dede *adv* totteringly; the standing up of a baby which is just learning to stand independently: *Simama dede*, stand uncertainly as a baby does; stand totteringly.

defa *n (n)* time, occasion: *Alipiga defa tatu*, he struck thrice.

dege¹ (also *degedege*) *n (n) (med)* infantile convulsions caused by birth injury or a developmental defect of the brain.

dege² *n (n) (zool)* a kind of moth (of Order *Lepidoptera*) which is a scaly-winged insect whose caterpillars may cause considerable damage to field crops and stored products.

dege³ (also *degedege*) *n* (*n*) a look of envy that is believed to cause misfortune e.g. abdominal pains or a stare at a person eating sth that is believed to cause the thing to drop on the ground. This is believed by some people to be a kind of evil eye from someone who is keen to get the food (cf *zongo, husuda*)

dege⁴ *n* (*n*) the sickness of children believed to be caused through the action of Satan. It occurs suddenly without warning and a child may die if attacked. (cf *mnyama, babe watoto, mdudu*)

degedege *n* (*n*) see *dege¹* and *dege³*

dege la watoto *n* (*ma-*) (*bot*) fern; a flowerless seedless vascular plant. *Pteris longifolia*. (cf *kangaga*)

degi *n* (*n*) a very large brass pot for cooking food during a feast; large brass cooking pot. (cf *marigedi*)

degle *n* (*n*) see *dagla*

deheni¹ *n* (*n*) a mixture of chalk and camel fat, used to whiten either boards of hull planking or quickwork, to protect it against rust: *Tia deheni*, apply this kind of substance. (cf *bereu*) (Ar)

dehen.i² *vt* 1. apply/smear ointment, etc 2. careen; turn a ship on its side esp for cleaning or repairing. Prep. **dehen.i.a** St. **dehen.ik.a** Cs. **dehen.ish.a** Ps. of Prep. **dehen.iw.a** Rp. of Prep. **dehen.i.an.a** (Ar)

dek.a *vt* 1. (of a child) behave in a manner calculated to induce elders to pamper him: *Mtoto yule anadeka sana mbele ya wazee wake*, that child likes to be pampered by his parents. 2. be conceited, be haughty, be arrogant: *Anadeka kwa vile ana mali adhimu*, he is arrogant because he has a lot of wealth. 3. hope to get sth from sby whom you are sure he could help. Prep. **dek.e.a** St. **dek.ek.a** Cs. **dek.ez.a** Ps. **dek.w.a** Ps. of Cs. **dek.ez.w.a**. (cf *ringa, jitapa*)

dekani (also *dekoni*) *n* (*n*) deacon; a church official who is below a priest in rank. (Eng)

dekez.a *vt* pamper, cosset, coddle: *Mama alimdekeza bintiye*, the mother pampered her daughter. Prep. **dekez.e.a** St. **dekez.ek.a** Ps. **dekez.w.a** Rp. **dekez.an.a**

dekoni *n* (*n*) see *dekani*

dek.i¹ *vt* mop the floor, wash the floor. Prep. **dek.i.a** St. **dek.ik.a** Cs. **dek.ish.a** Ps. **dek.iw.a**

deki² *n* (*n*) (*naut*) deck; the outside part of a ship. (Eng)

dekio *n* (*ma-*) mop; a household implement used for moping the floor, etc.

deku.a (also *dengua*) *vt* 1. bring sth down with one shot e.g. a bird with a stone, a fruit off a tree with a stone or stick: *Alilidekua papai kwa jiwe*, he brought down the pawpaw with a stone. 2. hit sth suddenly and from the sideways: *Alimdekua ndege aliyekuwa akiruka angani lakini hakuanguka*, he hit the bird from the side but it did not fall down. 3. (*idm*) *Dekua kichwa*, take off a head. Prep. **deku.li.a** St. **deku.lik.a** Cs. **deku.lish.a** Ps. of Prep. **deku.liw.a**. Rp. **deku.an.a**

dele (also *mdele*) *n* (*n*) a long pot made of brass or other metal, used for holding coffee.

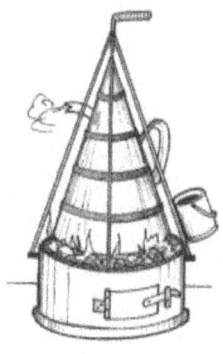

dele

delta *n* (*n*) delta; a deposit of sand and soil, usu triangular formed at the mouth of some rivers: *Delta ya Nile*, Nile Delta. (Eng)

dem.a[1] *vi* 1. toddle, dodder; walk unsteadily like a baby when it starts walking: *Mtoto wangu mdogo ameanza kudema*, my little baby has started to toddle. 2. totter along, limp, hobble, hitch; walk lamely: *Mwanamke mgonjwa alikuwa akidema hospitalini katika wadi yake*, the sick woman was limping in her hospital ward. Prep. *dem.e.a* St. *dem.ek.a* Cs. *dem.esh.a* (cf *chuchumia, guchia*)

dema[2] (also *lema*) *n* (*ma-*) wickerwork fishtrap: *Macho ya dema*, the holes of the wickerwork fish trap. *Utanga wa dema*, the upper and lower parts of the wickerwork fish trap.

demadem.a *vt* (*naut*) toddle, dodder. Prep. *demadem.e.a* St. *demadem.ek.a* Cs. *demadem.esh.a*

demani *n* (*n*) 1. (*naut*) a rope of main sail of a local vessel to which the sheet is attached. 2. that side of the ship that corresponds with the position of the sail. It may be either port or starboard; it corresponds to lee-side; leeward. 3. an order to the helmsman to fall away towards the lee. 4. the wind that blows from the sea. 5. the end of the south monsoon, from mid-August until November or sometimes from April to October. (cf *kipupwe*) (Ar)

demografia *n* (*n*) demography: *Demografia ya kiisimu*, linguistic demography. (Eng)

demokrasia *n* (*n*) democracy (Eng)

demu *n* (*ma-*) 1. an old worn-out piece of cloth. 2. a rag which was used in the past by women round the loins or breasts when working in a field. (cf *bwende*)

dend.a[1] *vt* beg slyly; want sth cunningly: *Huja kwangu kudenda pesa lakini sitampa tena*, he comes to me to beg for money slyly but I will not give him again. Prep. *dend.e.a* St. *dend.ek.a* Cs. *dend.esh.a* Ps. *dend.w.a* Rp. *dend.an.a*. (cf *doea, nyenga*)

denda[2] *n* (*ma-*) saliva which comes from the mouth when someone is asleep; drool, dribble, spittle. (cf *dovuo, ute, uderere*)

denge[1] *n* (*n*) a mode of shaving the hair leaving a tuft on top of the head. (cf *sekini, panja*)

denge[2] *n* (*n*) 1. (*idm*) *Denge la mbuzi*, a male goat. 2. a goat pen built on poles raised off the ground.

dengelua *n* (*n*) a kind of local brew prepared from sugarcane.

dengu *n* (*n*) (*bot*) lentils; small edible seeds shaped like biconvex lenses, and usu imported from India. *Lens culinaris*. (cf *adesi*) (Pers)

dengu.a[1] *vt* see *dekua*. Prep. *dengu.li.a* St. *dengu.lik.a* Cs. *dengu.lish.u* Ps. of Prep. *dengu.liw.a* Rp. *dengu.an.a*

dengu.a[2] *vt* shave the head on one side and leave the other side: *Niliamua kuzipunguza nywele sehemu zote badala ya kuzidengua*, I decided to shave the whole head a little instead of just one side. Prep. *dengu.li.a* St. *dengu.k.a* and *dengu.lik.a* Cs. *dengu.lish.a* Ps. of Prep. *dengu.liw.a* Rp. *dengu.an.a*

dengu.a[3] (also *nengua*) *vi* 1. limp, hobble; walk lamely: *Akitembea, hudengua kutokana na ajali ya gari aliyoipata*, if he walks, he limps because of the car accident he had had. 2. dance artistically: *Binti yake alidengua kwenye tamasha*, her daughter danced artistically at the festival. 3. twist one's hips. Prep. *dengu.li.a* St. *dengu.lik.a* Cs. *dengu.lish.a* Ps. of Prep. *dengu.liw.a*

dengu.a[4] *vt* scoop the upper scum of sth such as water, curry, etc. Prep. *dengu.li.a* St. *dengu.lish.a* Ps. of Prep. *dengu.liw.a* (cf *angua*)

deni *n* (*ma-*) 1. debt, debit: *Lipa deni*, pay a debt. *Deni fisa*, a debt that has been written off. *Deni viza*, a bad debt.

2. promise, pledge, assurance, word. (*prov*) *Ahadi ni deni*, a promise needs to be fulfilled. (Ar)

densi *n* (*n*) see *dansi*

depo *n* (*n*) 1. depot; a place where vehicles are kept. 2. depot, godown, storehouse, warehouse: *Depo ya mafuta*, petroleum depot. 3. a police training centre. (Eng)

deraya (also *daraya, dereya, diridi*) *n* (*n*) cuirass, armour, armour plate: *Magari ya deraya*, armoured vehicles.

dereli (also *drili*) *n* (*n*) a kind of cloth used for making trousers.

dererek.a[1] *vi* trickle, trill, drip; flow gently; fall in drops like thick oil: *Mafuta yaliderereka kutoka kwenye kikaango*, the cooking oil trickled from the frying pan. Prep. **dererek.e.a** St. **dererek.ek.a** Cs. **dererek.esh.a** Ps. **dererek.w.a** (cf *tiririka*)

dererek.a[2] *vt* do work lazily. Prep. **dererek.e.a** St. **dererek.ek.a** Cs. **dererek.esh.a** Ps. **dererek.w.a** (cf *bweteka*)

derereko *n* (*ma-*) an act of working lazily.

dereva (also *dreva*) *n* (*ma-*) 1. driver, chauffeur. 2. coachman, whip. 3. (*colloq*) a leader, director. (cf *muongozaji*) (Eng)

dereya *n* (*n*) see *deraya*

deri *n* (*n*) dairy; a place where milk, butter, cheese and eggs are sold (Eng)

des.a *vi* brag, vaunt, boast, show off: *Kijana yule anadesa kwa vile ana sura nzuri*, that young man boasts because he is handsome. Prep. **des.e.a** St. **des.ek.a** Cs. **des.esh.a** Ps. **des.w.a**. (cf *ringa, jivuna*).

Desemba (also *Disemba*) *n* (*n*) December; the twelfth month of the year. (Eng)

desimali *n* (*n*) decimal; a decimal system, based on the number 10. (cf *asilikumi*) (Eng)

deski *n* (*ma-*) desk; a writing-desk. (cf *dawati*) (Eng)

deste (also *dasta*) *n* (*ma-*) a container for serving *halua* (Turkish delight), a kind of candy. (Ar)

desturi[1] (also *dasturi*) *n* (*n*) 1. custom, practice, habit: *Ni desturi yake kufokea watu hadharani*, it is his habit to reprimand people in public. *Kwa desturi*, usually. 2. custom, habit, tradition: *Desturi za watu hawa ni kuvaa vilemba*, the custom of these people is to wear turbans. (cf *mazoea, tabia, desturi*) (Ar and Pers)

desturi[2] *n* (*n*) (*naut*) bowsprit

dete *n* (*n*) see *detepwani*

detepwani (also *dete*) *n* (*n*) (*zool*) pied kingfisher; a kind of coraciform bird (family *Alcedinidae*) with a crested head and an entirely black plumage, a relatively long white tail and spotted underparts. *Ceryle rudis*.

deu.a[1] *vt* treat with scorn, ignore, snub, disregard: *Huyu mtu ana madharau mengi kwa vile hukudeua ukimwuliza kitu*, this person possesses a strong scornful attitude because he ignores you when you ask him something. Prep. **deu.li.a** St. **deu.lik.a** Cs. **deu.lish.a** Ps. of Prep. **deu.liw.a**. Rp. **deu.an.a** (cf *dharau*)

deu.a[2] *vt* (of a pot, etc.) remove from the fire; take off: *Alikideua chungu cha kupikia baada ya chakula kuiva*, she removed the cooking-pot from the fire after the food was ready. Prep. **deu.li.a** St. **deu.lik.a** Cs. **deu.lish.a** Ps. of Prep. **deu.liw.a** Rp. of Prep. **deu.li.an.a** (cf *ipua*)

deuli *n* (*n*) 1. a waistband of silk, cloth, etc., used to tighten a dagger round the waist. 2. pall, shroud, winding-sheet; a cloth spread over for covering a coffin. (cf *sabaiya*)

dezo *n* (*n*) sth obtained free of charge.

dhaa *n* (*n*) worry, anxiety, trouble, concern: *Ana dhaa juu ya matokeo yake ya mtihani*, she is worried about her examination results. (cf *wasiwasi, wahaka*) (Ar)

dhabihu¹ n (n) 1. a ritual sacrifice; a thing offered or animal killed for an offering to God or spirits. 2. a place of ritual sacrifice. 3. abattoir, slaughterhouse, slaughterpen, butchery.
dhabih.u² vt offer a ritual sacrifice: *Wanavijiji walidhabihu kwa kutoa mbuzi watatu na ng'ombe wawili,* the villagers offered a ritual sacrifice by giving three goats and two cows. Prep. **dhabih.i.a** St. **dhabih.ik.a** Cs. **dhabih.ish.a** Ps. of Prep. **dhabih.iw.a** (Ar)
dhahabu n (n) gold; *Dhahabu bandia,* pinch beck; an alloy of copper and zinc used to imitate gold in cheap jewellery. (Ar)
dhahania n (n) abstraction, supposition, pipe dream: *Nomino dhahania,* abstract noun. (Ar)
dhahiri¹ adj clear, plain, obvious, evident: *Ni dhahiri kuwa kila binaadamu atakufa,* it is obvious that every human being will die. (cf *wazi, bayana*) (Ar)
dhahiri² adv clearly, plainly, evidently, vividly: *Inaonyesha dhahiri kuwa yeye ni mtu mwema,* it shows clearly that he is a nice person. (cf *waziwazi*) (Ar)
dhahiri shahiri adv (used for emphasis) very clearly, very vividly: *Taarifa ile inaonyesha dhahiri shahiri kwamba si ya kweli,* that statement shows very clearly that it is false. (Ar)
dhaifu adj 1. weak, feeble, ailing: *Amekuwa dhaifu sana baada ya kupata homa kali,* he has become very weak after being ill with acute fever. 2. poor, inferior, mean, weak: *Basi lake dhaifu haliwezi kubeba abiria wengi,* his weak bus cannot take many passengers. 3. wicked, mean, bad: *Ana roho dhaifu,* he is wicked. (Ar)
dhakari n (n) (anat) penis (cf *uboo, mboo, uume*) (Ar)
dhalala¹ n (n) depravity, immorality, perversion. *Kiongozi wa dini aliye na dhalala anafaa akebehiwe,* a religious leader who is sunk in depravity should be condemned (ridiculed). *Kufa dhalala bilhuda,* die without possessing good deeds. (cf *upotevu, uharibifu*) (Ar)
dhalala² n (n) disdain, scorn, contempt: *Mtu mwenye dhalala nyingi aghalabu huonyesha ujinga wake,* a person who is very contemptuous usually shows his ignorance. (cf *dharau, masimango*) (Ar)
dhalala³ adv pointlessly, senselessly; without any reason: *Alinitukana dhalala,* he insulted me for no reason. (Ar)
dhalili¹ adj wretched, abject, low, poor: *Yeye ni mtu dhalili na kwa hivyo si rahisi kukusaidia,* he is a poor man and so it is not easy for him to help you. (cf *dhuli*) (Ar)
dhalili² n (n) wretch; a person who is poor; have-not, pauper. (cf *masikini*)
dhalilish.a vt humiliate, humble, bring down: *Anajidhalilisha kwa kuwaomba watu pesa,* he is humiliating himself by begging money from people. Prep. **dhalilish.i.a** St. **dhalilish.ik.a** Ps. **dhalilish.w.a** Rp. **dhalilish.an.a** (cf *nyanyasa, nyongesha, hakirisha*) (Ar)
dhalimu¹ (also *mdhalimu*) n (ma-) 1. an oppressive or brutal person; tyrant, brute: *Raia hawampendi kiongozi yule kwa vile ni dhalimu,* the citizens do not like that leader because he is a tyrant. 2. a fraudulent person; rogue, scoundrel: *Mimi sinunui vitu kutoka kwa dhalimu kama yeye,* I don't buy things from a rogue like him. (Ar)
dhalimu² adj 1. oppressive, brutal, ruthless, merciless: *Yeye ni mwajiri dhalimu na ndiyo maana wafanyakazi wanamchukia,* he is an oppressive employer and that is why the workers hate him. 2. dishonest, fraudulent, unscrupulous: *Yule ni mfanyabiashara dhalimu,* that is a dishonest businessman. (Ar)
dhamana n (n) 1. bail, bond, surety;

Mshtakiwa alitolewa nje kwa dhamana, the accused was released on bail. 2. guarantee, pledge, assurance: *Mimi nilimwekea rafiki yangu dhamana ili aweze kukopeshwa pesa na benki*, I gave a guarantee for my friend to be lent money by the bank. (Ar)

dhamani *n* (*n*) the end of the South monsoon which begins from April to October. (cf *demani*) (Ar)

dhambi *n* (*n*) 1. sin, blasphemy; religious offence: *Vitabu vitakatifu vinasema kwamba zinaa ni dhambi*, the holy books say that adultery is a sin. (cf *dhunubu*) 2. (in sports) fault, foul: *Golikipa alifanya madhambi katika eneo la hatari*, the goalkeeper committed a foul in the penalty area. (cf *kosa*) (Ar)

dhamin.i[1] *vt* 1. guarantee, stand surety: *Niliweka hati ya kumiliki ili niweze kumdhamini mjomba wangu anayetaka mkopo kutoka benki*, I surrendered my title deed as a guarantee for a loan from the bank for my uncle. 2. give bail, go bail for, put bond for: *Alimdhamini ndugu yake mahakamani kwa kutoa shilingi milioni moja ili aachiliwe*, he paid one million shillings at the court to bail his brother out. 3. mortgage; give sby legal right to take possession of a house, land, etc. as a security for payment of money lent: *Niliidhamini mali yangu yote kwa mkopo niliouchukua*, I mortgaged all my assets for the loan I had taken. 4. sponsor: *Warsha ilidhaminiwa na shirika la kimataifa*, the workshop was sponsored by an international organisation. Prep. **dhamin.i.a** St. **dhamin.ik.a** Cs. **dhamin.ish.a** Ps. of Prep. **dhamin.iw.a**. Rp. of Prep. **dhamin.i.an.a** (Ar)

dhamini[2] *n* (*n*) see *mdhamini*

dhamira (also *dhamiri*) *n* (*n*) 1. goal, objective, purpose, aim, motive: *Dhamira yake hasa ilikuwa ni kukukashifu*, his real aim was to disgrace you. (cf *lengo, kusudio*. 2. theme, subject, topic, matter: *Dhamira ya tamthilia hii ni uzalendo*, the theme of this play is nationalism. 3. (*gram*) *Dhamira arifu*, declarative mood, indicative mood, fact mood. *Dhamira tegemezi*, subjunctive mood. *Dhamira lazimishi*, objective mood. (Ar)

dhamiri.a *vt* intend, plan, propose: *Anadhamiria kukusaidia*, he intends to help you. Prep. **dhamiri.li.a** St. **dhamiri.k.a** Cs. **dhamiri.sh.a** Ps. **dhamiri.w.a** Rp. **dhamiri.an.a.** (cf *kusudia, nuia*)

dhamma *n* (*n*) see *dhumma*

dhana *n* (*n*) 1. concept, idea, notion, thought: *Dhana potofu*, a misleading idea. (cf *wazo*) 2. suspicion, doubt, disbelief: *Hakuna uhakika kuwa yeye ameiba; hiyo ni dhana tu*, there is no proof that he has stolen; that is just a suspicion. (cf *shaka, tuhuma*) (Ar)

dhan.i *vt, vi* think, suppose, believe, presume: *Kwa nini unadhani kwamba shangazi yako hatafika leo?* Why do you think that your aunt will not arrive today? Prep. **dhan.i.a** St. **dhan.ik.a** Cs. **dhan.ish.a** Ps. of Prep. **dhan.iw.a** Rp. of Prep. **dhan.i.an.a**. (cf *shuku, tuhumu*) (Ar)

dhani.a[1] *vt, vi* see *dhani*

dhani.a[2] *vt, vi* imagine, think: *Alidhania kwamba wewe ulikuwa unatuzuga tu*, he thought that you were only deceiving us. Prep. **dhani.li.a** St. **dhani.k.a** Cs. **dhani.sh.a** Ps. **dhani.w.a** Rp. **dhani.an.a** (cf *fikiria*)

dhara *n* (*ma-*) harm, loss, damage, ruin: *Vitendo viovu kama hivyo vitaleta madhara nchini*, harmful deeds like those will bring harm to the country. (cf *hasara*) (Ar)

dharau[1] *n* (*ma-*) scorn, negligence, contempt: *Mtu yule ana madharau*, that person is contemptuous. (cf *bezo, mapuuza*) (Ar)

dhara.u[2] *vt* 1. ignore, neglect, disregard,

dharba

snub: *Kila aambiwalo afanye, hudharau*, everything he is told to do, he ignores. 2. despise, scorn; treat with contempt Prep. ***dharau.li.a*** St. ***dharau.lik.a*** Cs. ***dharau.lish.a*** Ps. of Prep. ***dharau.liw.a*** Rp. of Prep. ***dharau.li.an.a*** (cf *beza, beua, puuza*) (Ar)

dharba *n* (*n*) see *dharuba*

dhariri *n* (*n*) radiation: *Daktari alitumia dhariri kwa kumtibu mgonjwa wake wa kensa*, the doctor used radiation to treat his patient suffering from cancer. (cf *mnururisho*) (Ar)

dharuba[1] (also *dharba*) *n* (*n*) blow, stroke, hit, slap: *Alipopigwa dharuba moja ya kiganja cha mkono shavuni, akaanguka palepale*, when he got a slap on the cheek, he fell down immediately. (cf *pigo*) (Ar)

dharuba[2] *n* (*n*) (also *dharba, dhoruba*) hurricane, storm, cyclone, typhoon: *Dharuba kali ilipotokea, miti mingi ikaanguka*, when the cyclone occurred, many trees fell. (cf *chamchela, kimbunga*)

dharura *n* (*n*) 1. emergency, urgency, the unexpected: *Mkutano wa dharura*, an emergency meeting. *Kikao cha dharura*, an emergency session. 2. reason, cause, excuse, problem: *Dharura ya mimi kwenda kule ilikuwa ni kuonana na daktari*, the reason I went there was to see a doctor. (cf *udhuru, sababu*) (Ar)

dhati *n* (*n*) 1. sincerity, ingeniousness: *Aliniletea salamu zake za dhati*, she sent me her sincere greetings. (cf *roho, nia, imani*) 2. innermost, self: *Mimi kwa dhati yangu nisingemruhusu mwanafunzi yule darasani wakati alikuwa ameshachelewa*, I personally would not have agreed to allow that student to stay in the class while he was already late. 3. habit, behaviour (Ar)

dhiba *n* (*n*) reinforcements, fortifications, beefing-up forces. (Ar)

dhibit.i *vt* control, manage, monitor,

dhihirik.a   **D**

censor: *Anamdhibiti mumewe vizuri*, she controls her husband well. *Polisi wamedhibiti vitendo vya wizi katika mtaa wetu*, the police have controlled activities of theft in our neighbourhood. Prep. ***dhibit.i.a*** St. ***dhibit.ik.a*** Cs. ***dhibit.ish.a*** Ps. of Prep. ***dhibit.iw.a*** Rp. of Prep. ***dhibit.i.an.a*** (cf *zuia, chunga, linda*) (Ar)

dhidi *prep* centre, against, opposed to, in opposition, hostile to : *Alifanya vitendo viovu dhidi ya serikali*, he committed evil deeds against the government. (cf *kinyume*) (Ar)

dhifa *n* (*n*) banquet, repast, feast: *Aliwafanyia dhifa wageni wake*, he organized a feast for his guests. (cf *karamu, hafla*) (Ar)

dhihaka *n* (*n*) ridicule, mock, joke, sarcasm, ridicule, jest: *Ukimfanyia rafiki yako dhihaki nyingi, basi hatimaye ataudhika*, if you play so many jokes on your friend, he will ultimately be annoyed. (cf *mzaha, masihara, utani*) (Ar)

dhihak.i *vi, vt* joke, jest, fool around: *Walikuwa wakimdhihaki kuwa ameshinda katika bahati nasibu*, they were fooling him that he had won the lottery. Prep. ***dhihak.i.a*** St. ***dhihak.ik.a*** Cs. ***dhihak.ish.a*** Ps. of Prep. ***dhihak.iw.a*** Rp. of Prep. ***dhihak.i.an.a***. (cf *tania, kejeli*) (Ar)

dhihir.i *vt* manifest, exhibit, prove, demonstrate, become evident: *Imedhihiri kuwa yeye ni mkosa*, it has become evident that he is guilty. (*prov*) *Kweli ikidhihiri, uwongo hujitenga*, truth will always prevail where there is injustice. Prep. ***dhihir.i.a*** St. ***dhihir.ik.a*** Cs. ***dhihir.ish.a*** Ps. of Prep. ***dhihir.iw.a***. (cf *bainika, fahamika*) (Ar)

dhihirik.a *vt, vi* become evident, become clear: *Imedhihirika kwamba yeye alikuwa si raia*, it has become evident that she was not a citizen.

Prep. **dhihirik.i.a** St. **dhihirik.ik.a** Cs. **dhihirik.ish.a** (cf *bainika, tambulikana*)

dhihirish.a *vt* exhibit, clarify, verify, evince; show clearly: *Maneno yake yanadhihirisha kuwa yeye si mwaminifu*, his words show clearly that he is not honest. Prep. **dhihirish.i.a** St. **dhihirish.ik.a** Ps. **dhihirish.w.a** Rp. **dhihirish.an.a**

dhihirisho *n* (*n*) proof, verification, testimony, confirmation: *Kwa vile yeye haji shuleni kila siku, hili ni dhihirisho kwamba yeye hana haja na elimu*, the fact that he does not come to school regularly is a proof that he is not interested in getting education. (cf *thibitisho, elezo*)

dhi.i[1] *vt* 1. enervate, pine away, weaken, enfeeble, debilitate: *Mwili wake ulidhii kutokana na maradhi ya muda mrefu*, he was enervated by his long illness. (cf *dhoofu, konda*) 2. languish, suffer; experience hardship: *Wanavijiji walidhii miezi kadha kutokana na ukosefu wa vitu muhimu*, the villagers suffered for some months following the shortage of essential commodities. Prep. **dhi.li.a** St. **dhi.ik.a** Cs **dhi.ish.a** Ps. **dhi.iw.a** (cf *teseka, sumbuka*)

dhii[2] *n* (*n*) gauntness, emaciation, haggardness, witherdness: *Ugonjwa wa muda mrefu ulimletea dhii katika mwili wake*, his long illness made his body gaunt. (cf *udhaifu*) (Ar)

dhiik.a *vi* undergo hardships; be tormented, be distressed. Prep. **dhiik.i.a**

dhiish.a *vt* distress, torment, afflict; inflict suffering upon sby/sth: *Alimdhiisha jirani yake bila ya sababu*, he tormented his neighbour for no reason. Prep. **dhiish.i.a** St. **dhiish.ik.a** Ps. **dhiish.w.a** Rp. **dhiish.an.a**

dhiki[1] *n* (*n*) 1. distress, difficulty, affliction, hardship: *Watu wamo katika dhiki kwa vile hawana uhuru wa kusema nchini*, people are in hardships because they don't have freedom of expression in the country. (*prov*) *Baada ya dhiki, faraji*, after difficulties comes happiness. (cf *shida, taabu*) 2. lack of basic needs. (Ar)

dhik.i[2] *vt, vi* 1. distress, hassle, disturb, bother, pester, trouble: *Utamdhiki rafiki yako ikiwa utaendelea kumkopa pesa mara kwa mara*, you will hassle your friend if you keep on borrowing from him frequently. Prep. **dhik.i.a** St. **dhik.ik.a** Cs. **dhik.ish.a** Ps. **dhik.iw.a** Rp. **dhik.i.an.a**. (cf *sumbua, taabisha*)

dhikir.i[1] (also *dhukuru*) (in Islam) *vi, vt* (of a group of people) recite rhythmically and repeatedly the name of God in sing-song: *Waislamu walikutana na baadaye kudhikiri*, the Muslims assembled and later participated in a sing-song manner. Prep. **dhikir.i.a** St. **dhikir.ik.a** Cs. **dhikir.ish.a** Ps. **dhikir.iw.a** (Ar)

dhikiri[2] *n* (*n*) (in Islam) a rhythmic recitation of the name of God by a group of people in sing-song over and over again (Ar)

dhila *n* (*ma-*) (usu pl *madhila*) agony, wretchedness, misery, hardship: *Watu wale hawana raha kwa vile nchi yao imejaa madhila*, those people are not happy because their country is full of hardships. (Ar)

Dhilhaji (also *Dhulhija*) *n* (*n*) the twelfth month in the Islamic calendar. (Ar)

dhil.i[1] *vt, vi* 1. torture, torment, trouble, disturb: *Yule mwajiri anamdhili mfanyakazi wake kwa kumpa kazi ngumungumu*, the employer torments his worker by giving him arduous work. (cf *tesa, taabisha, sumbua*) 2. vilify, humiliate, disgrace, humble: *Haifai kumdhili mkeo kwa kumpiga kadamnasi*, it is not good to humiliate your wife publicly. Prep. **dhil.i.a** St. **dhil.ik.a** Cs. **dhil.ish.a** Ps. of Prep. **dhil.iw.a** Rp. of Prep. **dhil.i.an.a**. (cf *tweza, kashifu*) (Ar)

dhili² *n* (*n*) shadow, shade. (cf *kivuli*) (Ar)
dhilifu *adj* poor, simple, inferior: *Mkulima dhilifu*, a poor farmer. (cf *hakiri, maskini*) (Ar)
Dhilkaadi (also *Dhulkaadi*) *n* (*n*) the eleventh month in the Islamic calendar. (Ar)
dhima *n* 1. role, function, obligation, responsibility: *Sisi sote tuna dhima katika jamii zetu*, we all have responsibilities in our societies. (cf *kazi, jukumu*) 2. (accounts) debt.
dhiraa *n* (*n*) cubit; a measure of length from elbow to finger tip; *Dhiraa konde*, half a yard.
dhoofik.a *vi* become weak/feeble; lose strength; deteriorate: *Hali yake inazidi kudhoofika*, her health continues to deteriorate. Prep. *dhoofik.i.u* St. *dhoofik.ik.a* Cs. *dhoofik.ish.a* (cf *konda, atilika*)
dhoofish.a *vt* weaken, enfeeble, debilitate, emaciate, enervate, vitiate: *Mtoto mtundu yule amemdhoofisha mama yake*, that naughty child has enfeebled his mother. Prep. *dhoofish.i.a* St. *dhoofish.ik.a* Ps. *dhoofish.w.a* Rp. *dhoofish.an.a* (cf *atili*)
dhoof.u *vi* be weakened, be enfeebled, be debilitated, be enervated: *Alidhoofu kwa ajili ya ugonjwa*, he was enervated because of illness. Prep. *dhoof.i.a* St. *dhoof.ik.a* Cs. *dhoof.ish.a*
dhoruba (also *dharba, dharuba*) *n* (*n*) storm, hurricane, blizzard. (Ar)
dhuha *n* (*n*) 1. the period between the rising of the sun and noon. 2. (in Islam) the optional prayer prayed during this time not less than two and not exceeding 12 *rakaas*. (Ar)
dhuhuri *n* (*n*) see *adhuhuri*
dhuk.u *vt* taste, savour, relish: *Akipika chakula chochote, hukidhuku*, if she cooks any food, she tastes it. Prep. *dhuk.i.a* St. *dhuk.ik.a* Cs. *dhuk.ish.a* (cf *onja*) (Ar)

dhukuria *n* (*n*) sons
dhukur.u¹ *v* see *dhikiri¹*
dhukur.u² *vt* 1. remember, recollect, recall: *Hawezi kudhukuru siku aliyooa*, he can't remember the day he got married. (cf *kumbuka*) 2. mention, speak of; imagine: *Alikuwa anadhukuru moyoni kwamba kama angekuwa tajiri, angekwenda ng'ambo kusoma*, he was imagining that if he were rich, he would have gone overseas to study. (cf *taja, nena*) 3. examine, scrutinize, check: *Inafaa uidhukuru hali yenyewe kabla hujachukua hatua yoyote*, it is necessary for you to examine the situation before you take any steps. Prep. *dhukur.i.a* St. *dhukur.ik.a* Cs. *dhukur.ish.a* Ps. of Prep. *dhukur.iw.a* (cf *taamuli, zingatia, tafakari*) (Ar)
Dhulifikari *n* (*n*) see *Dhulifukari*
Dhulhaji *n* (*n*) see *Dhilhaji*
dhuli *n* (*n*) a poor person; have-not, pauper: *Yeye ni dhuli kwa vile hana pesa hata za kununulia nguo*, he is a poor person since he does not even have the money to buy clothes. (Ar)
Dhulifukari (also *dhulfikari*) *n* (*n*) the name of the sword used by Imam Ali during the war. (Ar)
Dhulkaadi *n* (*n*) see *Dhilkaadi*
dhul.u *vt* (*arch*) come to light, be discovered, become known. Prep. *dhul.i.a* St. *dhul.ik.a* Cs. *dhul.ish.a* (cf *julikana, dhihirika*)
dhuluma *n* (*n*) injustice, unfairness, oppression: *Alimfanyia kitendo cha dhuluma kwa kumchukulia mali yake yote*, he did him an injustice by taking all of his property. (cf *uonevu*) (Ar)
dhulum.u *vt* 1. persecute, torment, harass, oppress: *Wakoloni waliwadhulumu wananchi kwa kuwawekea sheria kali*, the colonialists oppressed the citizens by imposing strict laws upon them. (cf *tesa, onea*) 2. plunder, confiscate; take by force, treat unjustly: *Mwenyeduka alimdhulumu mteja wake*

kwa kumlangua, the shopkeeper treated his customer unjustly by overcharging him. Prep. ***dhulum.i.a*** St. ***dhulum.ik.a*** Cs. ***dhulum.ish.a*** Ps. of Prep. ***dhulum.iw.a*** Rp. of Prep. ***dhulum.i.an.a***

dhumma *n* (*n*) an Arabic vowel written above a consonant in a word to give an equivalent meaning of "u" in the Swahili language vowel system or pronounced like the *u* as in *bull* (Ar)

dhumna (also *dumma*) *n* (*n*) dominoes; a game of dice; a game played with a set of 28 dominoes. (cf *dadu, domino*) (Ar)

dhunubu *n* (*n*) sins (cf *dhambi*) (Ar)

dhuria *n* (*n*) descendants, offsprings, offshoots: *Dhuria wangu*, my children. (cf *kizazi*) (Ar)

dhur.u *vt* 1. harm, mar, damage, ruin: *Usishiriki katika biashara ya mihadarati kwa vile jambo hili linaweza hatimaye likakudhuru*, don't get involved in the business of selling narcotics for it can ultimately ruin your life. (cf *haribu, umiza, hasiri*) 2. harm: *Alikuwa akinywa kahawa nyingi na baadaye ikamdhuru*, he used to drink a lot of coffee and later, it harmed him. Prep. ***dhur.i.a*** St. ***dhur.ik.a*** Cs. ***dhur.ish.a*** Ps. of Prep. ***dhur.iw.a*** Rp. of Prep. ***dhur.i.an.a***. (Ar)

dhurub.u *vt* clobber; hit hard, hit severely. Prep. ***dhurub.i.a*** St. ***dhurub.ik.a*** Cs. ***dhurub.ish.a*** Ps. of Prep. ***dhurub.iw.a***. Rp. of Prep. ***dhurub.i.an.a*** (cf *piga*) (Ar)

dia (also *jizia*) *n* (*n*) 1. wergeld; fine for murder; money or things given by someone as a sort of compensation to the victim to atone for the killing. 2. fees paid by a foreigner to a country for his protection. (Ar)

dibaji[1] *n* (*n*) preface; an introductory statement appearing at the beginning of a book. (cf *utangulizi*) (Ar)

dibaji[2] *n* (*n*) a kind of good material which is woollen or silky.

didimi.a (also *dudumia*) *vi, vt* 1. submerge, submerse; sink in water or mud: *Ardhi yote imedidimia kwa mvua ya siku mbili*, the whole land is sunk because of the two days' rain. (cf *zama*) 2. (of business, etc.) dwindle, wane, decline: *Biashara yake inadidimia siku hizi*, his business is declining these days. Prep. ***didimi.li.a*** St. ***didimi.k.a*** Cs. ***didimi.sh.a*** and ***didimi.z.a***. (cf *anguka, angamia*)

didimiz.a *vt* 1. submerge; cause to sink in water, etc. 2. cause a loss or damage; ruin: *Kwa kweli, viongozi wale wanaudidimiza uchumi wa nchi yao*, as a matter of fact, those leaders are ruining the economy of their country (cf *poromosha*). 3. oppress, suppress: *Serikali yoyote isijaribu kuwadidimiza raia zake*, any government should not try to suppress its citizens. (cf *kandamiza*) Prep. ***didimiz.i.a*** St. ***didimiz.ik.a*** Ps. ***didimiz.w.a*** Rp. ***didimiz.an.a***

difensi *n* (*n*) 1. (in sports) defence of a goal. 2. football players at the back position guarding the goal. (cf *ngome*) (Eng)

difriza *n* (*n*) deep freezer; a freezer for quick-freezing and storing food. (Eng)

difu[1] *n* (*n*) a piece of the bone of a camel or ox used in the past by some school children as a writing board.

difu[2] *n* (*n*) (*bot*) the fibre binding the young leaves around the growing stem.

difu[3] *n* (*n*) differential; differential gear. (Eng)

digali *n* (*n*) (*bot*) the stem of a hookah tobacco pipe. (cf *shilamu, bori*) (Ar)

diglosia *n* (*n*) diglosia; a situation where two varieties of language co-occur in a speech community and each one is used for different purposes. (Eng)

digrii[1] *n* (*n*) degree; a unit of measurement for angles or temperature: *Digrii 50*, 50 degrees. (Eng)

digrii² n (n) degree; academic title; rank or grade given by a university or college to someone who has done and passed an examination, written a thesis successflly, etc.: *Digrii ya B.A.*, Bachelor of Arts degree. *Digrii ya jumla*, general degree. (Eng)

diko (also *liko*) n (ma-) a landing place; jetty, pier: *Chombo kimetia nanga katika diko ili kipakue kago*, the vessel has anchored at the jetty in order to unload the cargo.

dikodiko n (n) a thick coconut gravy.

dikoni n (n) (in Christianity) deacon (Eng)

dikrii n (n) 1. decree, ordinance, regulation, order: *Ilipitishwa dikrii kwamba watu wasitoke nje buula ya saa mbili za usiku*, it was decreed that people should not go out after eight o'clock at night. (cf *sheria*) 2. conditions, terms, provisions: *Dikrii za ardhi*, land terms. *Dikrii za biashara ndogo ndogo*, small business terms. (Eng)

dikteta n (ma-) 1. dictator; a person who rules a country by despotic or cruel ways. 2. a person who behaves in an autocratic manner; dictator. (Eng)

dila n (n) a vessel for bailing water out of a boat; bailing scoop. (cf *upo, zila*) (Ar)

dim.a vi (esp in cricket) field; play in the field: *Timu yetu ilikuwa ikidima*, our team was fielding. Prep. **dim.i.a** St. **dim.ik.a** Cs. **dim.ish.a** Ps. **dim.w.a** Rp. of Prep. **dim.i.an.a**

dimba¹ n (n) soccer, football. (cf *soka, kandanda*)

dimba² n (ma-) a land that is recultivated after it had been left fallow; a recultivated fallow.

dimba³ n (ma-) 1. the entrance in which the initiates go in for the circumcision rites. 2. the place or camp in which the initiates are put in the circumcision rites. 3. (idm) *Fungua/Funga dimba*, open/close an event.

dimbani adv in the playing ground: *Timu yao inashuka dimbani leo*, their team is playing today.

dimbwi n (ma-) pool, puddle, plash; standing water.

dinari n (n) gold or silver coin used in some Arab countries such as Kuwait, Jordan, Algeria, etc.; dinar. (Ar)

dind.a vt 1. oppose, resist, defy, object: *Mwalimu mkuu aliwataka wanafunzi warejee kwenye masomo yao lakini wakadinda*, the headmaster wanted the students to return to their classes but they defied. (cf *pinga, kinza*) 2. be tight, be taut, be firm, stand firm: *Mtumishi alidinda alipoambiwa hatapewa nyongeza ya mshahara*, the servant was firm when he was told that there was no pay rise. 3. (of a penis) be erect. Prep. **dind.i.a** St. **dind.ik.a** Cs. **dind.ish.a** Ps. **dind.w.a** Rp. **dind.an.a** (cf *disa, simika*)

dindi n (n) see *lindi*

dindi.a¹ vi (of land) be dented, sink down: *Nilianguka nilipopita mahala pale kwa vile sehemu ile ilikuwa imedindia*, I fell down when I passed that place because that area was depressed. (cf *titia, dulu*) Prep. **dindi.li.a** St. **dindi.k.a** Cs. **dindi.sh.a**

dindi.a² vi bend a little and raise up esp while playing traditional dance; stoop in a local dance: *Wanawake walikuwa wakidindia walipokuwa wakicheza ngoma*, the women were bending themselves and raising up when they were taking part in a traditional dance. Prep. **dindi.li.a** St. **dindi.k.a** Cs. **dindi.sh.a**

dingi n (n) (colloq) old man, father.

dini n (n) religion, worship, creed. (Ar)

dinosau n (n) 1. dinosaur; a large frightening animal that lived in the past but is now extinct. 2. (colloq) a person or thing that is no longer useful or effective (Eng)

dio *n* (ma-) a bird's nest.
diploma *n* (n) diploma: *Diploma katika elimu*, diploma in education. *Diploma katika uhandisi*, diploma in engineering. (Eng)
diplomasia *n* (n) 1. diplomacy; the conducting of relations between nations: *Chuo cha diplomasia*, college of diplomacy. *Diplomasia ya vitisho*, gunpoint diplomacy. 2. skill in doing this; diplomacy. (Eng)
dipu *n* (n) animal dip. (cf *josho*) (Eng)
dira¹ *n* (n) 1. a directional compass; a mariner's compass. 2. an instrument for drawing circles, measuring distances on maps, etc. 3. (fig) vision, direction; target: *Chama chochote cha siasa lazima kiwe na dira*, any political party must have a sense of direction. (Ar)
dir.a² *vt* snip, clip; cut or shave hair: *Nilikwenda dukani jana kwa kinyozi kuzidira nywele zangu*, I went to the barber's shop yesterday to have my hair cut. Prep. ***dir.i.a*** St. ***dir.ik.a*** Cs. ***dir.ish.a*** Ps. ***dir.w.a*** Rp. ***dir.an.a***
dirab.u *vt* twine (with the fingers); weave, interlace, knit: *Mtumishi alizidirabu nyuzi zangu*, the servant wove threads for me. Prep. ***dirab.i.a*** St. ***dirab.ik.a*** Cs. ***dirab.ish.a*** Ps. of Prep. ***dirab.iw.a*** Rp. of Prep. ***dirab.i.an.a*** (cf *sokota, pota*) (Ar)
diradir.a *vt* waffle, hedge; hide between words; hem and haw; beat around the bush; use evasive statements: *Nilipomwuliza swali nyeti, akaanza kudiradira tu*, when I asked him a sensitive question, he started to beat around the bush. Prep. ***diradir.i.a*** St. ***diradir.ik.a*** Cs. ***diradir.ish.a***
direki *n* (n) (*naut*) two thick ropes used for a yard in a dhow; halyard. (cf *hansa*)
dirhamu¹(also *darahamu*) *n* (n) currency used in certain Arab states like Dubai, Abudhabi and Yemen. (Ar)

dirhamu² (also *darahimu*) *n* (n) money, currency. (cf *pesa*) (Ar)
dirii *n* (n) see *deraya*
diriji *n* (n) Swahili-speaking people's traditional dance of playing with walking sticks or swords.
dirik.a *vt* meet, encounter: *Sikuwahi kudirika naye kwenye mkutano*, I was not able to meet him at the meeting. Prep. ***dirik.i.a*** St. ***dirik.ik.a*** Cs. ***dirik.ish.a*** Ps. ***dirik.w.a*** Rp. ***dirik.an.a***. (cf *kutana*)
dirik.i *vt, vi* 1. manage, succeed, be able: *Kutokana na shughuli nyingi, sikudiriki kumtembelea rafiki yangu*, because of the pressure of work, I was unable to visit my friend. (cf *wahi, weza*) 2. be stable in one place: *Nimediriki katika kijiji hiki kwa miaka mingi*, I have remained in this village for many years. 3. be in time to take action before the situation gets out of hand: *Wazima moto walidiriki kuwaokoa wanawake na watoto waliokuwa ndani ya nyumba iliyokuwa ikiungua*, the firemen were just in time to save the women and children from the house which was on fire. 4. venture, dare, try: *Alikuwa anawatukana majirani na mimi nikadiriki kumkataza asifanye hivyo*, he was insulting the neighbours and I ventured to stop him doing it. Prep. ***dirik.i.a*** St. ***dirik.ik.a*** Cs. ***dirik.ish.a*** Ps. of Prep. ***dirik.iw.a***
dirisha *n* (ma-) 1. window, aperture. 2. (idm) (in sports) *Dirisha dogo la usajili*, minor registration. (Pers)
diriz.i¹ *vt* (of a traditional dance, etc.) lead, guide: *Tuliwachia wanawake wawili wakidirizi ngoma*, we let the two women lead the traditional dance. Prep. ***diriz.i.a*** St. ***diriz.ik.a*** Ps. ***diriz.w.a*** Rp. ***diriz.an.a***
dirizi² *n* (n) see *deraya*
diro *n* (n) a place where people meet and eat together; public eating place.
dis.a *vi* (of a penis) be erect. Prep. ***dis.i.a*** St. ***dis.ik.a*** Cs. ***dis.ish.a*** Ps. ***dis.w.a*** (cf *dinda*)

Disemba *n* (*n*) see *Desemba*
dishi *n* (*n*) 1. basin. (cf *beseni*) 2. (*colloq*) food. 3. dish; a bowl-shaped aerial with which signals are transmitted to or received from a communications satellite. 4. (*electron*) dish; a dish antenna (Eng)
Disii *n* (*ma-*) District Commissioner; an administrative head in charge of a district. (Eng)
diskaunti *n* (*n*) discount (Eng)
disketi *n* (*n*) diskette (Eng)
disko *n* (*n*) disco, discotheque. (Eng)
dispensari *n* (*n*) dispensary, clinic; a small hospital. (Eng)
divai *n* (*n*) wine (cf *mvinyo*) (Eng)
divisheni[1] *n* (*n*) division: *Timu yetu iko katika divisheni ya pili*, our team is in the second division. (Eng)
divisheni[2] *n* (*n*) division; a particular section of a country, city, etc. defined for administrative or political purposes. (cf *tarafa*) (Eng)
divu *n* (*n*) divergence
diwali *n* (*n*) (in Hinduism); a Hindu religious festival commemorating the victory of Lord Rama, one of the three of the incarnations of the Hindu god esp the seventh. The festival is usually marked by a display of fireworks in the evenings, offerings and prayers in temples etc. and marks the beginning of the financial year in India. (Hind)
diwani[1] *n* (*n*) 1. councillor. 2. minister; adviser esp to the president. (Ar)
diwani[2] *n* (*n*) 1. anthology of a poet; collected works of a poet or poets: *Diwani ya Mnyapala*, anthology of Mnyapala. (Eng)
dizeli *n* (*n*) diesel. (Eng)
dizi *n* (*n*) (*zool*) blackspot emperor; a kind of fish of the *Lethrinidae* family, which is easily recognized by the dark area on the side of its body. *Lethrinus harak.*
do *interj* 1. an exclamation of wonder; oh! (cf *lo!*) 2. an exclamation of disgust, disapproval, etc.; Damn! To hell!

doa *n* (*ma-*) 1. stain, blot, blemish, taint, blotch, spot: *Doa la rangi*, a paint spot. *Doa la mafuta*, a greasy spot. (cf *alama, baka*) 2. (*fig*) defect, weakness, weak point, drawback: *Rafiki yako ameingia doa kwa kushirikiana na wahuni*, your friend has tarnished his name by associating himself with hooligans. (cf *ila, dosari*)
dobi *n* (*ma-*) launderer, washer, laundryman, laundrywoman. *Dobi yule anafua nguo vizuri*, that launderer washes clothes well. (Hind)
dod.a *vi* 1. putrefy, decay, rot; go stale, go bad: *Siwezi kuipika nyama hii kwa vile imedoda*, I can't cook this meat because it has gone bad. 2. (esp of a commodity) remain for long without being used or bought causing it to get spoiled: *Bidhaa za mwenyeduka zilidoda dukani kwa vile zilikuwa ghali*, the shopkeeper's goods remained in the shop for a long time because they were expensive. 3. try to get sth and fail: *Alihangaika sana kutafuta kazi lakini akadoda*, he restlessly looked for a job but he failed to get it. (cf *noa*) 4. lag, trail, struggle, dawdle; fall behind: *Rafiki zake Jane wanaendelea vizuri darasani lakini yeye mwenyewe amedoda*, Jane's friends are progressing well in the class but she herself is trailing behind. Prep. **dod.e.a** Cs. **dod.esh.a** Ps. of Prep. **dod.ew.a** (cf *bakia, selelea*)
dod.a[2] *vi* trickle, drip, plash; follow gently: *Maji yalikuwa yanadoda kutoka kwenye paa la nyumba*, the water was trickling from the roof of the house. Prep. **dod.e.a** Cs. **dod.esh.a** Ps. of Prep. **dod.ew.a** (cf *dondoka, tona*)
dod.a[3] *n* (*n*) great calmness (cf *utulivu*)
dodi *n* (*ma-*) 1. fine wire of brass, copper or iron. 2. a bracelet of fine wire, hair or thread worn by a woman around the neck, legs or arms.
dodo *n* (*ma-*) 1. (*bot*) a very large kind of mango known as *embe dodo*. 2. a fine breast usu of a young woman.

3. a bit of sand that can penetrate into your eye.

dodoki *n* (*ma-*) (*bot*) the fruit of a loofah, *Luffa acutangula*. When dry, it is used for rubbing one's body during bathing.

dodos.a¹ *vt, vi* 1. drawl, twang; hesitate on speech or writing: *Katika zoezi la kusoma hakupata alama nzuri kwa sababu alikuwa anadodosa*, in the reading exercise, she did not get good marks because she was drawling. (cf *gugumiza*) 2. interview, cross-examine, cross-question, interrogate, grill: *Alijaribu kunidodosa katika mambo yasiyomhusu*, he tried to cross-question me on matters that did not concern him. Prep. **dodos.e.a** St. **dodos.ek.a** Cs. **dodos.esh.a**. Ps. **dodos.w.a** Rp. **dodos.an.a** (cf *hoji, ulizauliza*)

dodos.a² *vt* 1. hammer, batter, pound, beat: *Alikuwa anakidodosa kipande cha chuma ili akinyooshe*, he was hammering a piece of iron in order to straighten it. 2. scrape, grate. Prep. **dodos.e.a** St. **dodos.ek.a** Cs. **dodos.esh.a** Ps. **dodos.w.a** (cf *kwangura, kwangua*)

-dodosi *adj* critical, censorious: *Mhakiki mdodosi*, a censorious reviewer.

doe.a *vt, vi* 1. scrounge, sponge on, cadge: *Hudoea chakula sikuzote kwa rafiki zake*, he is always scrounging food off his friends. (cf *pandia, rondea*) 2. spy, reconnoitre, scout, pry, snoop; meddle into other people's affairs: *Nilimfukuza nyumbani kwa vile anapenda kudoea mambo ya watu*, I expelled him from my house because he likes to snoop into other people's affairs. Prep. **doe.le.a** St. **doe.lek.a** Cs. **doe.sh.a** Ps. **doe.w.a** Rp. **doe.an.a** (cf *peleleza, doya*)

doezi (also *mdoezi*) *n* (*n*) scrounger, sponger, cadger; a person who borrows from and lives off others.

-dogo *adj* 1. small, little, young: *Mtoto mdogo*, a small child. *Ndugu mdogo*, a young brother. *Kanzu ndogo*, small dress. 2. few, little: *Watu kidogo*, few people. *Maji kidogo*, little water.

dogori *n* (*n*) 1. a kind of a big drum with one drumhead. 2. a kind of dance used in the exorcism of spirits.

dogosh.a *vt* see *dogoza*

dogoz.a (also *dogosha*) *vt* make sth small; belittle. Prep. **dogoz.e.a** St. **dogoz.ek.a** Ps. **dogoz.w.a** Rp. **dogoz.an.a** (cf *dhalilisha, dharau*)

dohani¹ *n* (*n*) 1. (*bot*) smoke (cf *moshi*) 2. chimney. (Ar)

dohani² *n* (*ma-*) a long big basket for carrying fruits and other things. (Ar)

dohani³ *n* (*n*) 1.(*bot*) a kind of corn like millet. 2. a kind of quality honey usu used for medicine. *Asali dohani*, a kind of pure honey. *Shubiri dohani*, a kind of pure bitter aloe. (Ar)

dokez.a *vt, vi* 1. hint, allude, suggest; mention indirectly: *Alidokeza kwangu kuwa ataoa mwakani*, he hinted to me that he would get married next year. (cf *funulia*) 2. apply a small quantity such as medicine, liquid, etc.: *Alidokeza maziwa kwenye kahawa yangu*, he put some milk in my coffee. Prep. **dokez.e.a** St. **dokez.ek.a** Cs. **dokez.esh.a** Ps. **dokez.w.a** Rp. **dokez.an.a**

dokezi *n* (*ma-*) see *dokezo*

dokezo (also *dokezi*) *n* (*ma-*) hint, clue, tip, inkling: *Dokezo pana*, broad hint, *Dokezo la wazi*, clear hint. (cf *fununu*)

doko.a¹ *vt* 1. break off a little portion; pick off a bit; take a pinch: *Mtumishi alikidokoa chakula changu mezani*, the servant pinched my food from the table. (cf *nyonyora*) 2. snaffle, pilfer, filch: *Mama aliweka vyakula vitamu jikoni lakini ndugu zangu wadogo wakawa wanavidokoa*, my mother kept delicacies in the kitchen but my young brothers kept filching them. Prep. **doko.le.a** St. **doko.lek.a** Cs. **doko.z.a** Ps. of Prep. **doko.lew.a**

Rp. of Prep. *doko.le.an.a* (cf *nyofoa, mega*)

doko.a² *vt* 1. touch sby gently so as to attract his attention. 2. touch the tail of an ox pulling a cart so as to hasten speed. Prep. *doko.le.a* St. *doko.lek.a* Cs. *doko.lez.a* Ps. of Prep. *doko.le.an.a*

dola¹ *n* (*ma-*) empire, nation, kingdom, sovereign state: *Jumuiya ya Madola*, Commonwealth of Nations. (Ar)

dola² *n* (*n*) dollar; American or Canadian currency or any other country using a dollar as its currency. (Eng)

dole *n* (*ma-*) (*bot*) one banana removed from the bunch or pedicel; a single banana in a duster

doli *n* (*n*) puppet, doll. (cf *mwanasesere*)

Dominika *n* (*n*) (In Christianity) Sunday (Eng)

domino *n* (*n*) dominoes (cf *dhumna*) (Ar)

domo *n* (ma-) conversation, chat, talk: *Piga domo*, chat. *Domo kaya*, chatterbox, blabber; a person who lets others' secrets. (*prov*) *Domo kaya samli kwa mwenye ng'ombe*, a person's bad habit looks good to himself just like profit gained from ghee by the owner of a cow.

don.a¹ (also *donoa*) *vt* 1. peck at, nibble; take small bites, pick up bit by bit as a bird does when it eats food: *Ndege walikuwa wanadona mawele*, the birds were pecking at bulrush millet. 2. eat food in small quantities: *Mtoto wangu alikidona chakula na kisha akakiacha*, my child ate the food in small quantities and left it there. Prep. *don.e.a* St. *don.ek.a* Cs. *don.esh.a* Ps. *don.w.a* Rp. *don.an.a*

dona² *n* (*n*) (*bot*) maize flour. (cf *sembe*)

donda *n* (*ma-*) 1. a large sore; ulcer: *Donda ndugu*, a spreading ulcer; a kind of ulcer that takes a long time to heal. 2. (*fig*) sth that cannot be treated easily.

dondakoo *n* (*ma-*) (*med*) diphtheria; a serious infectious disease of the throat that causes difficulty in breathing.

dondo *n* (*ma-*) 1. a large tiger cowrie shell, used by tailors for smoothing down seams to a good surface. 2. starch, chalk, etc 3. (*zool*) a kind of crab which is not edible and lives in eulittoral muddy banks of creeks: *Kaa dondo*, a crab of this kind.

dondo.a¹ *vt* 1. pick out bit by bit; pick out grain by grain as fowls do: *Mpishi aliudondoa mtama na kutoa takataka ndani yake kabla hajaupika*, the cook sorted out the millet grain by grain before cooking it. (cf *okotaokota*) 2. pick out sth one by one: *Alividondoa vijiti vya gamba la kibiriti*, she picked up matches of the matchbox. 3. quote, cite: *Alidondoa aya moja kutoka katika kitabu cha kitaaluma*, he quoted a paragraph from an academic book. Prep. *dondo.le.a* St. *dondo.lek.a* Cs. *dondo.lesh.a* Ps. of Prep. *dondo.lew.a* Rp. *dondo.an.a*

dondo.a² *vt* remove insects from the body: *Dondoa chawa*, remove lice from the body. *Dondoa kupe*, remove tick from an animal. Prep. *dondo.le.a* St. *dondo.lek.a* Cs. *dondo.lesh.a* Ps. of Prep. *dondo.lew.a* Rp. *dondo.an.a*

dondoandume *n* (*ma-*) an effeminate person; a person characterized by womanish qualities. (cf *msagaliwa*)

dondok.a *vi* 1. drip down, flow gently; trickle, sprinkle: *Maji yalikuwa yanadondoka*, the water was dripping down. (cf *tiririka, tona*) 2. slip out, slide out, glide: *Kikombe kilimdondoka mkononi*, the cup slipped out of her hand. 3. fall in love, love, be infatuated: *Mate yalimdondoka alipomwona msichana mrembo*, he drooped when he saw a beautiful girl. Prep. *dondok.e.a* Cs. *dondo.sh.a* Ps. *dondok.w.a* Ps. of Prep. *dondok.ew.a* Rp. of Prep. *dondok.e.an.a*

dondoo¹ *n* (*ma-*) 1. extract, quotation, excerpt, selection: *Alinisomea dondoo moja kutoka kwenye riwaya*, he read to me one quotation from the novel. 2. minutes of a meeting or item of an agenda: *Waliyajadili madondoo kadha kwenye mkutano uliopita,* they discussed certain minutes of the previous meeting.

dondoo² *n* (*ma-*) baiting for fish; act of catching bait.

dondoo³ *n* (*ma-*) fornication, adultery; irregular sexual intercourse; promiscuity.

dondora *n* (*ma-*) (zool) a kind of hornet or stinging fly, also known as "large paper wasp" that builds paper nests and feeds its larvae on pieces of chewed-up caterpillars.

dondoro *n* (*ma-*) (*zool*) steinbok; a kind of small slim, reddish and slender antelope with a short conical head, a thick sleek coat and long legs, and which usu lives on flat plains. *Raphicerus campestris.*

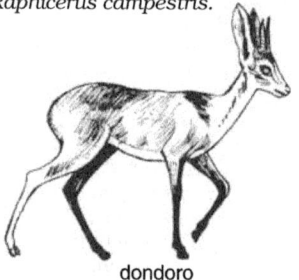

dondoro

done.a (also *donyea*) *vt* 1. kiss a child: *Alimdonea mtoto kama ishara ya kuonyesha mapenzi,* he kissed a child as a sign of affection for him. 2. kiss, lick; touch the lips: *Alimdonea mkewe,* he kissed his wife. St **done.k.a** Cs **done.sh.a** Ps **done.w.a** Rp **done.an.a** (cf *nonea, busu*)

donge *n* (ma-) 1. lump, ball, chunk: *Donge la uzi,* a ball of thread. *Donge la damu,* blood clot. *Donge la sukari,* a lump of sugar. *Donge la barafu,* a chunk of ice. (cf *bonge, tufe*) 2. (*colloq*) money, salary, income: *Amepata donge nono kubwa leo kutoka kwenye bahati nasibu,* he has received a lot of money today from the lottery.

dongoa *n* (ma-) dry clay exuding from a building.

dono.a *vt* see *dona¹* Prep. **dono.le.a** St. **dono.lek.a** Cs. **dono.lesh.a** Ps. of Prep. **dono.lew.a** Rp. **dono.an.a**

donye.a *vt* see *donea* Cs. **donye.sh.a** Ps. **donye.w.a** Rp. **donye.an.a**

dopa *n* (*ma-*) thimble; a small cap of metal, plastic, etc. that fits on a finger and pushes the needle during sewing. (cf *simbo*)

dopo.a *vt* make a hole with a thimble, etc.; perforate, pierce: *Nilimpelekea mjomba vifaranga kwenye sanduku ambalo nililidopoa,* I sent chicks to my uncle in a perforated box. Prep. **dopo.le.a** St. **dopo.k.a** Cs. **dopo.sh.a** Ps. of Prep. **dopo.lew.a** Rp. **dopo.an.a** (cf *toboa*)

dorati *n* (*n*) a precious stone.

doria¹ *n* (*n*) patrol, guarding: *Askari wa doria,* police patrol. (Hind)

doria² *n* (*n*) white muslin; a kind of white light cloth. (Hind)

doria³ *n* (*n*) a kind of food consisting of a mixture of cereals and sliced cassava.

doriani *n* (*ma-*) (*bot*) durian; an oval, spiny edible fruit like a jackfruit with an abominably offensive odour like that of rotten eggs. (Hind)

doro *adj* (*colloq*) tasteless, dull, boring, run-of-the-mill: *Mahala doro,* a dull place.

doror.a¹ *vi* salivate; drip saliva like someone who is in sleep, etc.: *Mzee yule alidorora alipokuwa amelala,* that old man dribbled when he was asleep. Prep. **doror.e.a** St. **doror.ek.a** Cs. **doror.esh.a**

doror.a² *vi* putrefy, decay; get stale, go bad: *Samaki wake wamedorora,* his fish have gone bad. Prep. **doror.e.a** St. **doror.ek.a** Cs. **doror.esh.a** (cf *china, doda*)

doror.a³

doror.a³ *vi* (of conversation, etc.) lose animation/liveliness. Prep. **doror.e.a** St. **doror.ek.a** Cs. **doror.esh.a**

dosari *n* (*n*) 1. flaw, fault, defect, weakpoint, weakness, imperfection: *Yeye ni mtu mzuri lakini ana dosari zake*, he is a good person but he has his weaknesses. (cf w*alakini, udhaifu*) 2. disgrace, shame, dishonour, infancy: *Vitendo vyake viovu vitaileta dosari familia yake*, his evil deeds will disgrace his family. (cf *aibu, fedheha*) (Ar)

dot.a *vt* (of fish) eat the bait. (cf *dona*)

doti *n* (*n*) set of two pieces of materials such as khanga.

doto *n* (*ma-*) spot, sparkle, mark.

dovuo *n* (*n*) saliva which drips from some people while they are asleep; dribble. (cf *udenda, uderere*)

doy.a *vt, vi* 1. reconnoitre, spy, scout; watch secretly, go as a spy: *Adui alizidoya nguvu za nchi ya jirani*, the enemy spied on the strength of a neighbouring country. (cf *peleleza, jasusi, duhushi*) 2. sponge on, cadge, scrounge: *Anapenda kudoya vyakula kwa majirani*, he likes to scrounge food from the neighbours. Prep. **doy.e.a** St. **doy.ek.a** Cs. **doy.ez.a** Ps. of Prep. **doy.ew.a** Rp. **doy.an.a** (cf *doea, rondea*)

drafti *n* (*n*) checkers; a game of draughts (Eng)

drama *n* (*n*) drama (Eng)

dramumeja *n* (*ma-*) drummajor; a sergeant who leads a military band or one who precedes it when it plays on parade. (Eng)

dreva *n* (*n*) see *dereva*

drili¹ *n* (*ma-*) see *dereli*

drili² *n* (*n*) drill; physical training, workout, physical exercises: *Wanajeshi walifanya drili*, the soldiers drilled. (cf *kwata*) (Eng)

dua *n* (*n*) prayer, supplication, invocation: *Walimwomba dua Mwenyezi Mungu ili wapate mvua*, they prayed to God for rain. (*idm*) *Pigwa dua*, be cursed.

dudi.a **D**

(*prov*) *Dua ya kuku haimpati mwewe*, a fowl's prayer does not reach a hawk, i.e. a tryrant or an oppressor does not bother if he is cursed. (Ar)

duala *n* (*n*) see *duwala*

duara¹ (also *duwara*) *n* (*n*) 1. circle, roundlet, roundel; a round object: *Mimi nimelichora duara hilo*, I have drawn that circle. (cf *mviringo*) 2. aureola; a border of light or radiance enveloping the head of a figure represented as holy. (Ar.)

duara² (also *duwara*) *adj* spherical, circular, global: *Umbo la duara*, a circular shape. (Ar)

duaradufu *n* (*n*) (*maths*) ellipse

duazi *n* (*n*) see *duwazi*

duba¹ *n* (*n*) see *dubu*

dub.a² *vi* be partly full: *Glasi ya maji imeduba*, the glass of water is partly full. Prep. **dub.i.a** St. **dub.i.k.a** Cs. **dub.ish.a**

dubu *n* (*ma-*) 1. (*zool*) bear; a large heavy animal with thick rough fur. 2. simpleton, imbecile, idiot, fool: *Yeye ni dubu kwani ukimweleza chochote, haelewi*, he is a fool because if you explain this or that to him, he will not understand. (cf *juha, zugezuge, jahili*) (Ar)

dubwana *n* 1. leviathan, monster, ogre; a giant: *Nilipoluona lile dubwana, nilitishika*, when I saw the monster, I became frightened. 2. an unknown thing, animal, etc. (cf *nyangarika*)

dubwasha *n* (*ma-*) a worthless or an unknown thing, etc.; thingamajig, trash.

dude *n* (*ma-*) 1. a general term referring to any object of which one does not know its name: *Dude gani hilo?* What object is that? 2. used to refer to a person or object that is despised and therefore does not need to be called by its name; bastard.

dudi.a *vt* fill sth with air; inflate: *Alidudia kibofu*, he filled a balloon with air. Prep. **dudi.li.a** St. **dudi.lik.a** Cs. **dudi.lish.a** Ps. **dudi.liw.a** Rp. **dudi.li.an.a**

123

duduik.a *vi* (because of disease, etc.) be disfigured, be defaced: *Aliduduika na maradhi ya siku nyingi*, he was disfigured following the long illness. Prep. **duduik.i.a** St. **duduik.ik.a** Cs. **duduik.ish.a** Ps. **duduik.w.a** (cf *ambuka*)

duduish.a *vt* cause to be disfigured. Prep. **duduish.i.a** St. **duduish.ik.a** Ps. **duduish.w.a** Rp. **duduish.an.a**

dudumi *n* (*ma-*) a big horn

dudumi.a[1] *vt, vi* see *didimia*

dudumi.a[2] *vt* perforate by force; bore a hole: *Alikidudumia kibao kwa kutumia msumari na nyundo*, he made a hole in a piece of wood by using a nail and a hammer. Prep. **dudumi.li.a** St. **dudumi.k.a** Cs. **dudumi.sh.a** and **dudumi.z.a** Ps. **dudumi.w.a** (cf *toboa*)

dudumi.a[3] (also *gugumia*) *vt, vi* gulp down, swig; drain one's glass: *Niliyadudumia maji baada ya kutembea masafa marefu*, I gulped down the water after walking for a long distance. Prep. **dudumi.li.a** St. **dudumi.k.a** Cs. **dudumi.sh.a** and **dudumi.z.a** Ps. **dudumi.w.a** Rp. **dudumi.an.a** (cf *kukumia*)

dudumizi *n* (*ma-*) (*zool*) White-Browed Coucal; a kind of bird which has a long broad grey tail with a black bill and head and chestnut wings. *Centropus superciliosus.*

dudumizi

duduvule *n* (*ma-*) (*zool*) wood borer; a white stinging insect with a red head belonging to *Cerambycidae* or *Buprestidae* family, and which stays in the trees and eat the trees.

dufi *n* (*ma-*) (*zool*) a kind of sea tortoise.

dufu[1] *adj* 1. tasteless, insipid, unpalatable: *Chakula dufu*, an unpalatable food. 2. valueless, worthless, useless: *Mtu dufu*, a useless person.

dufu[2] *n* (*n*) a kind of small circular single-headed hand drum with a stretched skin on one side and usu having jingling metal discs; tambourine. (cf *tari*)

-dugi *adj* blunt, dull, round: *Kisu kidugi*, a blunt knife. *Penseli dugi*, a blunt pencil.

dugik.a[1] *vi* be blunt, be dull, be unsharpened: *Kisu changu kimedugika*, my knife is blunt. Prep. **dugik.i.a** St. **dugik.ik.a** Cs. **dugik.ish.a**

dugik.a[2] *vt, vi* rattle, clatter, jingle: *Tulizisikia glasi zikidugika ndani ya trei*, we heard the glasses rattling in the tray. Prep. **dugik.i.a** St. **dugik.ik.a** Cs. **dugik.ish.a**

dugu *n* (*ma-*) a kind of round mat for drying food or other things.

dugud.a *vt, vi* 1. shake sth inside another thing: *Aliiduguda sarafu iliyoko ndani ya chupa*, he shook the coin which was inside the bottle. 2. tremble very much because of cold, etc. Prep. **dugud.i.a** St. **dugud.ik.a** Cs. **dugud.ish.a** Ps. **dugud.w.a** Rp. **dugud.an.a**

duhuli *n* (*n*) (in business) capital

duhush.i (also *duhusi*) *vt* spy, look for, search out: *Ndege ilipelekwa mipakani kuduhusi nguvu za adui*, the plane was sent to the borders to monitor and assess the enemy's strength. Prep. **duhush.i.a** St. **duhush.ik.a** Cs. **duhush.ish.a** Ps. **duhush.w.a** Ps. of Prep. **duhush.iw.a** Rp. of Prep. **duhush.i.an.a** (cf *doya, jasisi*)

duhus.i vt see *duhushi*

dui n (n) see *duwi*

dui.a vt, vi curse, damn, denounce, blast: *Mzee alimduia mwanawe kutokana na utundu wake*, the parent cursed her son because of his naughtiness. Prep. ***dui.li.a*** Cs. ***dui.z.a*** Ps. ***dui.w.a*** Rp. ***dui.an.a*** (cf *apiza, laani*)

duio n (ma-) curse, damnation, denunciation: *Duizo la wazee wake litamtia katika shida kubwa*, his parents' curse will cause him great problems. (cf *laana, apizo*)

duka n (ma-) shop, boutique: *Duka la dawa*, pharmacy. *Duka la nyama*, a butcher's shop. *Duka la viatu*, a shoe shop. *Duka la jumla*, wholesale shop. *Duka la rejareja*, retail shop. *Duka la maziwa*, dairy.

dukiz.a (also *dukisa*) vt 1. enter a place without being invited, force one's way into a place; intrude, gatecrash; *Alijidukiza kwenye karamu ingawa hakualikwa*, he forced his way into the reception although he was not invited. (cf *doea, pandia*) 2. sneak into a place; skulk, slink: *Paka alijidukiza jikoni na kuila nyama yote*, the cat sneaked into the kitchen and ate all the meat. 3. eavesdrop; listen secretly to a private conversation. 4. participate in sth that does not concern you. (cf *jitia*) Prep. ***dukiz.i.a*** St. ***dukiz.ik.a*** Cs. ***dukiz.ish.a*** Ps. ***dukiz.w.a*** Rp ***dukiz.an.a***

dukizi n (ma-) 1. eavesdropping, overhearing: *Watu walimlaani kutokana na dukizi zake*, the people cursed him because of his eavesdroppings. (cf *umbea, upelelezi*) 2. eavesdropper, gossip-monger, wiretapper: *Yeye ni dukizi na ndiyo maana watu hawampendi*, he is an eavesdropper and that is why people don't like him. (cf *mpelelezi, mdoya*) 3. a person who participates in sth that does not concern him.

duko (also *kiduko*) n (ma-) a deaf person: *Ilibidi nizungumze naye kwa kelele kwa vile yeye ni duko*, I was obliged to talk to him loudly because he is deaf. (cf *kiduko, kiziwi*)

duku.a vt, vi nudge; push or poke gently esp, with the elbow, in order to draw one's attention to sth: *Nilimdukua kwenye mbavu*, I nudged him in the ribs. Prep. ***duku.li.a*** St. ***duku.lik.a*** Cs. ***duku.lish.a*** Ps. of Prep. ***duku.liw.a***

dukuduku (also *dungudungu*) n (ma-) anxiety, uneasiness, worry: *Ana dukuduku sana juu ya matokeo ya mtihani wake*, he is very worried about the outcome of his examination. (cf *fundo, daghadagha, wasiwasi*)

dulabu n (n) spindle; a thin pointed rod used for spinning wool into thread by hand (Ar)

duma[1] n (n) (*zool*) cheetah; a long-legged African animal of the cat family which runs quite fast.

duma

dum.a[2] vt (esp in times of war) capture, catch. Prep. ***dum.i.a*** St. ***dum.ik.a*** Cs. ***dum.ish.a*** Ps. ***dum.w.a***

duma.a vi 1. be stunted in growth, be dwarfed; be thwarted: *Rafiki yake amedumaa labda kwa sababu ya utapiamlo*, his friend is stunted possibly because of malnutrition. (cf *sinyaa, finyua, via*) 2. (*fig*) be weak in the head; be dull, lack intelligence: *Mtu yule amedumaa*, that person is dull. *Uchumi wa nchi jirani umedumaa*, the economy of the neighbouring country is stagnant. Prep. ***duma.li.a*** Cs. ***duma.za***

dumaz.a *vt* stunt the growth of sth; inhibit, stifle, impede: *Walijaribu bila ya mafanikio kuyadumaza maendeleo ya wanavijiji*, they tried unsuccessfully to stifle the development of the villagers. Prep. ***dumaz.i.a*** St. ***dumaz.ik.a*** Cs. ***dumaz.ish.a*** Ps. ***dumaz.w.a*** Rp. ***dumaz.an.a***

dumbi *n* (*ma-*) dust (cf *vumbi*)

dumbwara *n* (*n*) see *zumbururu*

dumbwi *n* (*n*) gully in the beach. (cf *mfumbi, jimbu*)

dume *n* (*ma-*) 1. a male animal: *Farasi dume*, stallion. *Ngombe dume*, bull. *Punda dume*, jackass. *Bata dume*, drake. 2. (*fig*) valiant, hero, gallant, stalwart; a brave man: *Yeye ni dume kwelikweli kwani anaweza kumkabili mtu yeyote*, he is a real hero because he can face anyone. (cf *shujaa*) 3. (in card playing) king; a playing card having a conventionalized picture of a king on it. (cf *ree*)

dumi.a *vt* use water in small quantities esp in times of hardships: *Kwa vile kulikuwa na uhaba wa maji kijijini, ilibidi wanavijiji wayadumie*, since there was a scarcity of water in the village, the villagers had to use it in small quantities. Prep. ***dumi.li.a*** St. ***dumi.k.a*** Cs. ***dumi.z.a*** Ps. ***dumi.w.a***

dumiliz.a *vi* make blood friendship by mutual incisions: *Walidumiliza ili kukuza uhusiano wao*, they made a blood tie by mutual incisions in order to strengthen their relationship. Prep. ***dumiliz.i.a*** St. ***dumiliz.ik.a*** Cs. ***dumiliz.ish.a*** Ps. ***dumiliz.w.a*** Rp. ***dumiliz.an.a***

dumna *n* (*n*) see *dhumna*

dumish.a *vt* maintain, sustain, keep: *Lazima tudumishe umoja wetu*, we must maintain our unity. Prep. ***dumish.i.a*** St. ***dumish.ik.a*** Ps. ***dumish.w.a*** Rp. ***dumish.an.a***

dum.u[1] *vi* 1. last, endure, continue: *Trekta langu limedumu kwa miaka mingi*, my tractor has lasted for many years. 2. continue, remain, stay long: *Ameweza kudumu kazini*, he has managed to stay in that job for long. Prep. ***dum.i.a*** St. ***dum.ik.a*** Cs. ***dum.ish.a*** (cf *fululiza, fuliza*)

dumu[2] (also *mdumu*) *n* (*ma-*) pitcher, beaked jug, can. (cf *jagi*)

dumuzi *n* (*n*) (*zool*) corn borer; a moth whose larvae feeds upon corn and other plants.

dund.a (also *duta*) *vt* 1. beat on, knock, bang, tap: *Anaidunda ngoma*, he is beating the drum. (cf *piga*) 2. (of a ball) bounce, rebound, spring back after hitting a hard surface: *Aliudunda mpira mara mbili*, he bounced the ball twice. 3. pound with a mortar; pulverize, thresh: *Anadunda kunde katika kinu*, he is pounding cowpeas in the mortar. 4. (*fig*) beat severely: *Jeshi la uvamizi lilidundwa vibaya*, the invading army was beaten severely. 5. fail to accomplish sth after great efforts; backfire, boomerang: *Mipango yake ilidunda*, her plans backfired. Prep. ***dund.i.a***, St. ***dund.ik.a*** Cs. ***dund.ish.a*** Ps. ***dund.w.a*** Rp. ***dund.an.a***.

dundadund.a *vi* pulsate, beat, throb: *Moyo wake ulikuwa unadundadunda*, his heart was throbbing. Prep. ***dundadund.i.a*** St. ***dundadund.ik.a*** Cs. ***dundadund.ish.a*** Ps. ***dundadund.w.a*** Rp. ***dundadund.an.a***

dundiz.a (also *dundukiza, dunduliza*) *vt* 1. save up, place aside, save a bit at a time: *Anadundiza pesa zake katika benki*, he is keeping his savings in a bank. 2. accumulate, gather, collect, assemble, mass: *Anadundiza stempu za zamani*, he is collecting old stamps. Prep. ***dundiz.i.a*** St. ***dundiz.ik.a*** Cs. ***dundiz.ish.a*** Ps. ***dundiz.w.a*** Rp. ***dundiz.an.a*** (cf *limbikiza, tunduiza*)

dundu¹ n (ma-) bundle, package, parcel: *Alinunua dundu la nguo*, he bought a bundle of clothes. (cf *mtumba, furushi*)

dundu² n (ma-) (zool) scavenging beetle; a kind of insect (family *Scarabaedae*) which feeds on animal dung and carrion. (cf *tutamavi, tuta*)

dundu³ n (ma-) a dried gourd of large pumpkin used for storing water and other kinds of liquids. (cf *ndau, kibuyu, tungu*)

dunduka n (n) a stage in the coconut between becoming a coconut and before it becomes ripe.

dundukiz.a¹ vi see *dundiza*

dundukiz.a² vi begin to ripen: *Maembe yameanza kudundukiza mtini*, the mangoes have started to ripen on the tree.

dunduliz.a (also *dundiza, dunduiza*) vt 1. accumulate; collect little by little: *Anadunduliza pesa zake ili anunue gari*, he is accumulating his money in order to buy a car. 2. do odd jobs in order to survive. Prep. **dunduliz.i.a** St. **dunduliz.ik.a** Ps. **dunduliz.w.a** Rp. of Prep. **dunduliz.i.an.a**

dundumio n (n) (anat) larynx, gullet (cf *koromeo, kongomeo, kuu*)

dung.a¹ vt pierce, inject, perforate: *Msichana amedunga masikio yake*, the girl has pierced her ears. Prep. **dung.i.a** St. **dung.ik.a** Cs. **dung.ish.a** Ps. **dung.w.a** Rp. **dung.an.a** (cf *toboa, tunga, choma*)

dunga² n (n) a big bamboo basket with a cover on it; covered bamboo basket.

dunga³ n (n) sorcery, witchcraft, witchery, magic, wizardry: *Piga dunga*, do witchcraft. (cf *uchawi, sihiri*)

dung.a⁴ vt focus on, aim at, target on. Prep. **dung.i.a** St. **dung.ik.a** Cs. **dung.ish.a** Ps. **dung.w.a** Rp. **dung.an.a**

dung.a⁵ vt chase sby/sth; pursue, run after. Prep. **dung.i.a** St. **dung.ik.a** Cs. **dung.ish.a** Ps. **dung.w.a** Rp. **dung.an.a**

dunge n (n) (bot) a cashew apple while it is in the green and unripe stage.

dungu n (n) 1. watchtower, look-out; a stage or platform raised from the ground and usu with a roof, used by a watchman guarding against the destruction of crops by birds and animals. (cf *kilindo, kilingo*) 2. bench; a judge's seat in a court of law: *Hakimu alikaa katika dungu lake ili aihukumu kesi*, the judge sat on his bench in order to try the case. 3. (in sports) goal, score: *Alifunga dungu*, he scored a goal. 4. (idm) *Dungu la eropleni*, cockpit.

dungu.a vt shoot, shoot down, bring down; *Waasi waliidungua ndege ya adui*, the rebels shot down the enemy's plane. Prep. **dungu.li.a** St. **dungu.k.a** Cs. **dungu.lish.a** Ps. of Prep. **dungu.liw.a**

dungudungu¹ n (n) 1. used to describe anything of unusual quality or shape; prodigy, marvel, wonder, curiosity: *Gari lile ni dungudungu kwani kila mtu analiangalia akiliona*, that vehicle is an extraordinary one because every person glances at it when he sees it. 2. a disfigured person, a deformed person. 3. anything badly constructed. e.g. house.

dungudungu² n (n) see *dukuduku*

dungumaro n (n) 1. a kind of evil spirit. (cf *pepo, punga*) 2. a local dance used to expel such a spirit. 3. anything that is very heavy and big.

dungusi kakati n (bot) cactus; any of various succulent spiny usually leafless plants having variously coloured, often showy flowers with numerous stamens and petals.

duni adj inferior, mean, poor, wretched: *Mtu duni*, an inferior person. *Hali duni*, abject condition. *Maisha duni*, wretched life. (cf *dhaifu, hafifu*)

dunia *n* (n) 1. world, universe, earth: *Dunia ni kubwa*, the world is big. *Kiingereza kinazungumzwa takriban dunia nzima*, English is spoken almost all over the world. 2. life: *Fariki dunia*, die. (cf *maisha*) (Ar)

dunish.a *vt* 1. degrade, cheapen, lower: *Serikali imedunisha bei ya vitu vingi*, the government has lowered the prices of many items. (cf *teremsha*) 2. disgrace, dishonour, discredit, belittle, humiliate, humble: *Alitudunisha mbele ya kila mtu*, he humiliated us in front of everybody. Prep. **dunish.i.a** St. **dunish.ik.a** Ps. **dunish.w.a** Rp. **dunish.an.a** (cf *aibisha, fedhehesha*)

dunzi *n* (n) see *mdunzi*

duodeni *n* (n) (anat) duodenum; the first section of the small intestine, between the stomach and the jejunum. (Eng)

dup.a *vt* 1. step over as in the case of a log, etc.; leap, jump over: *Nililidupa gogo lililokuwa mbele yangu*, I leaped over the log which was in front of me. (cf *kiuka, dakia*) 2. lean, rest heavily on: *Alidupa juu ya kochi lake*, he leaned on his coach. Prep. **dup.i.a** St. **dup.ik.a** Cs. **dup.ish.a** Ps. **dup.w.a** Rp. **dup.an.a** (cf *lemea*)

dura (also *duri*) *n* (n) (zool) parrot (cf *kasuku*) (Ar)

duri[1] *n* (n) see *dura*

duri[2] *n* (n) pearl (cf *lulu*) (Ar)

dur.u[1] *vt, vi* 1. go round, circle round, move around: *Aliuduru uwanja wa mpira mara mbili*, he went round the football pitch two times. 2. take a turn: *Sungusungu waliduru katika kuilinda bandari*, the militia patrolled the harbour by turns. Prep. **dur. i. a** St. **dur. ik. a** Cs. **dur. ish.a** Ps. of Prep. **dur.iw.a** Rp. of Prep. **dur.i.an.a** (Ar)

duru[2] *n* (n) turn, round, shift, circle: *Sasa ni duru yangu kuzungumza*, now it is my turn to talk. *Ile ilikuwa duru ya mwisho ya mashindano*, that was the last round of the competition. *Yeye ni mwanasiasa maarufu katika duru za kimataifa*, he is a prominent politician in international circles. *Duru za kidiplomasia*, diplomatic circles. *Duru za kishushushu*, intelligence sources. (cf *mzunguko*) (Ar)

durufu *n* (n) tarpaulin; a ground sheet or cover of heavy cloth used for making a tent, etc. (cf *turubali, tonobari*). (Ar)

dururi *n* (n) pearls (cf *lulu*)

durus.i *vt, vi* see *durusu*

durus.u (also *durusi*) *vt, vi* 1. study: *Alikidurusu kitabu chake cha kemia maktabani*, he studied his chemistry book in the library. (cf *soma, jifunza*) 2. revise a lesson, etc.: *Niliyadurusu masomo yangu kabla ya mtihani*, I revised my lessons before the examination. Prep. **durus.i.a** St. **durus.ik.a** Cs. **durus.ish.a** Ps. of Prep. **durus.iw.a** (Ar)

dus.a (also *dusia*) *vt, vi* scrounge, sponge on: *Amezoea kudusa kwa rafiki zake*, he is used to scrounging food off his friends. Prep. **dus.i.a** St. **dus.ik.a** Cs. **dus.ish.a** Ps. **dus.w.a** (cf *pandia, rombeza*)

dusi.a *vt, vi* see *dusa*

dusumali *n* (n) a kind of coloured handkerchief or scarf worn by some women on the head. (cf *ushungi, utaji, barakoa*) (Pers)

dut.a[1] *vt* see *dunda*

duta[2] *n* (ma-) elevator, upslope. (cf *kilima, mwinuko*)

dutu[1] *n* (ma-) anthill, ant-heap (cf *kisuguu, kichuguu*)

dutu[2] *n* (ma-) 1. shape, appearance, structure. 2. wart, spot, pimple, speck. 3. any other blemish. (anat) gland. (cf *tezi*)

dutu[3] *n* (ma-) a book esp a big one; a big volume of a book. (cf *buku, daftari*)

dutu[4] *n* (ma-) 1. substance. 2. a big horn blown to signal the departure of a sailing vessel at the harbour: *Piga dutu*, blow a horn. (cf *baragumu*)

dut.u[5] *vi* protrude, extrude, project: *Mwavuli wake ulidutu kutoka kwenye furushi la nguo*, his umbrella protruded from a bundle of clothes. Prep. ***dut.i.a*** St. ***dut.ik.a*** Cs. ***dut.ish.a*** Ps. ***dut.w.a*** Rp. ***dut.an.a*** (cf *tokeza, kubaza, benua*)

duvi[1] *n* (*ma-*) a kind of conch blown by sailors to signal the departure of their sailing vessels from the harbour: *Piga duvi*, blow the conch.

duvi[2] *n* see *uduvi*

duwa.a (also *duala*) *vi* be dumbfounded, be flabbergasted, be stunned: *Niliduwaa niliposikia kuwa Mary ameachwa*, I was stunned when I heard that Mary is divorced. Prep. ***duwa.li.a*** St. ***duwa.lik.a*** Cs. ***duwa.lish.a*** and ***duwa.z.a*** Ps. of Prep. ***duwa.liw.a*** (cf *shangaa, tunduwaa*) (Ar)

duwara[1] *n* (*n*) see *duara*[1]

duwara[2] *adj* see *duara*[2]

duwaz.a *vt* nonplus, astonish, flabbergast, stun: *Habari ile ilituduwaza sote*, that information stunned all of us. Prep. ***duwaz.i.a*** St. ***duwaz.ik.a*** Cs. ***duwaz.ish.a*** Ps. ***duwaz.w.a*** Rp. ***duwaz.an.a***

duwazi (also *duazi*) *n* (*n*) (*med*) arthritis; a lasting disease causing the inflammation of one or more joints, characterized by swelling, warmth, pain restriction or motion, etc.

duwi (also *dui, kikande*) *n* (*n*) (*zool*) starry triggerfish; a kind of brightly coloured tropical fish (family *Balistidae*) often with numerous blue spots on back having a prominent first dorsal fin with two or three spines. (cf *goma*)

duzi[1] *n* (*n*) 1. eavesdropper, gossip-monger, snooper: *Yeye ni duzi kwani mara kwa mara hunyemelea mambo ya majirani zake*, he is an eavesdropper because he frequently goes to spy on his neighbours. 2. backbiter, slanderer. (Ar)

duzi[2] *n* (*n*) (*zool*) tomcat, wildcat. (cf *pakashume*)

E

E, e/e/ 1. represents the fifth letter of the Swahili alphabet. 2. represents the sound of *E* or *e* and is classified as a mid-front unrounded vowel.
e¹ *interj* What is it?
e² *interj* an interjection for assent; yes, okay, alright. (cf *ndiyo! naam! hasa!*)
e³ *interj* I say, you! You there! This is an expression for calling sby or to call attention.
ebo *interj* This is an exclamation of surprise, indignation, contempt, etc. The interjection is generally used to children and inferiors. (cf *a! ah! abwe!*)
Ebola *n* (n) (*med*) Ebola viral disease; a severe infectious disease characterised by fever, muscle aching, diarrhoea, sore throat, etc. (Eng)
ebos *interj* an exclamation employed to call attention to sth that is eccentric, etc.
ebu (also *hebu*) *interj* 1. an exclamation employed to call attention: *Ebu njoo*, do come. (cf *tafadhali*) 2. Let me pass; make room for me; allow passage for me: *Ebu nipite*, allow me to pass. (cf *simile! abadari!*) (Ar)
eda *n* (n) (for Muslim women) a period when a woman remains unmarried and under the care of the husband's relatives after divorce or husband's death: *Alipokufa mumewe, mwanamke yule alikaa eda*, when her husband died, that woman got into seclusion. (Ar)
edaha *n* (n) a sacrifice or an offering made to appease the spirits of the dead. (cf *sadaka, kafara*) (Ar)
edashara *adj* eleven: *Watu edashara*, eleven people. (Ar)
edeni (also *adani*) *n* (n) Eden: *Bustani ya Edeni*, the garden of Eden. (cf *pepo, paradiso, paradisi*) (Ar)
edita *n* (ma-) editor (cf *mhariri*) (Eng)

eé *interj* 1. an exclamation of contempt for calling to sby. (cf *wewe! we!*) 2. an exclamation of sarcasm, ridicule, etc. uttered to a person. 3. an exclamation of invocation: *Ee Mola!* O God! *Ee Bwana!* O Lord!
egam.a *vt, vi* be in a leaning position; be in a resting position; be in a reclining position. Prep. *egam.i.a* St. *egam.ik.a* Cs. *egam.ish.a* Ps. of Prep. *egam.iw.a* Rp. of Prep. *egam.i.an.a*
egem.a *vt, vi* 1. approach, come near to sth, come close, draw near, draw close. (*idm*) *Egema pwani*, come near the edge of the sea. *Ni hatari kwa yeyote kuegema gati ili kutaka kuvua samaki*, it is dangerous for anyone to come close to the harbour in order to fish. (cf *kurubia, sogea*) 2. confront sby, encounter, brave, meet face to face: *Alimwegema adui yake*, he confronted his enemy. 3. depend on, rely on. Prep. *egem.e.a* St. *egem.ek.a* Cs. *egem.esh.a* Ps. *egem.w.a* Rp. *egem.an.a*
egeme.a¹ *vt* see *egema*
egeme.a² *vt* lean/rest on against: *Aliegemea ukuta*, he rested against the wall. Prep. *egeme.le.a* St. *egeme.k.a* Cs. *egeme.sh.a* and *egeme.z.a* Ps. *egeme.w.a* Rp. *egeme.an.a*
egemeo *n* (ma-) an object placed beneath or against a structure to keep it from falling or shaking; prop e.g. handrail, support, beam: *Maegemeo ya paa la nyumba*, props for the roof of a house.
egemez.a *vt* repose, support, rest: *Aliegemeza kichwa chake ukutani*, he rested his head against the wall. Prep. *egemez.e.a* St. *egemez.ek.a* Ps. *egemez.w.a* Rp. *egemez.an.a*
egesh.a *vt, vi* 1. park: *Aliegesha gari lake karibu na njia kuu*, she parked her car near the main road. 2. move a boat; moor a vessel near the shore

and anchor it or attach to any object: *Nahodha aliegesha meli karibu na maji haba*, the captain anchored the ship near shallow waters. Prep. *egesh.e.a* St *egesh.ek.a* Ps *egesh.w.a* Rp. of Prep. *egesh.e.an.a*

egesho *n* (*ma-*) parking place: *Egesho la magari madogo*, car park.

egi *n* (*n*) (*phys*) erg; a unit used to measure work or energy. (Eng)

ehaa *interj* a shout or call for attention to a distant person. The interjection is often used by fishermen. (cf *aisee! abaa! halo! ohii!*)

ehee *interj* an exclamation of assent or anxiety of the hearer to see that the conversation is clear and should thus progress. It carries the equivalent meanings of *Yes! Well! That is it!* (cf *sawa! ndivyo!*)

ehu.a *vt* see *wehua* Prep. *ehu.li.a* St *ehu.k.a* Cs. *ehu.sh.a* Ps. of Prep. *ehu.liw.a* Rp. *ehu.an.a* (cf *pisa, renga*)

eka (also *ekari*) *n* (*n*) acre; a unit for measuring land of 4840 square yards or 4050 square metres: *Wana eka 100 za shamba*, they own 100 acres of farm land. (Eng)

ekari *n* (n) see *eka*

Ekaristi *n* (*n*) (in Christianity) Eucharist; the Christian Sacrament in which Christ's last supper was commemorated by the consecration of bread and wine. (Eng).

-ekevu *adj* see *elekevu*

ekseli *n* (*n*) axle: *Ekseli hawilishi*, driving axle. (Eng)

eksirei *n* (*n*) x-ray; a type of radiation that can pass through objects that are not transparent (Eng)

eku.a *vt, vi* break down, break up; dismantle, destroy: *Anataka kuuekua mlango wako*, he wants to break your door. Prep *eku.li.a* St. *eku.k.a* and *eku.lik.a* Cs. *eku.sh.a* and *eku.lish.a* Ps. of Prep. *eku.liw.a* (cf *bomoa, vunja*)

ekumini *n* (*n*) (in Christianity) ecumenism; the principles or practice of promoting cooperation or better understanding among different religious faiths. (Eng)

-ekundu *adj* red, reddish; the colour of blood or fire: *Ua jekundu*, a red flower. (cf *ahamaru, ahamari*)

ekzosi *n* (*n*) (*engine*) exhaust pipe. (Eng)

ela *conj* (*arch*) see *ila*

elani *n* (*n*) see *ilani*

ele.a[1] (also *olea*) *vi* float, buoy, remain on waters: *Chombo kinaelea*, the vessel is floating. St. *ele.k.a* Cs. *ele.z.a*

ele.a[2] *vt, vi* nauseate, sicken: *Moyo unanielea*, I feel nauseous; I feel sick. St. *ele.k.a* Cs. *ele.z.a*

ele.a[3] *vt* be intelligible, be clear, be comprehensible, be understood: *Maneno yako yote yamenielea*, I have understood all your words. St. *ele.k.a* Cs. *ele.z.a* Ps. *ele.w.a*. (cf *tambua, pulika, fahamu, jua*)

elek.a *vt* carry a child on the hip; carry a child shoulder high: *Mama alikuwa amemweleka mtoto wake*, the mother was carrying her child shoulder high. Prep. *elek.e.a* St. *elek.ek.a* Cs. *elek.esh.a* Ps. *elek.w.a* Rp. *elek.an.a* (cf *yongoa*)

eleke.a (also *lekea*) *vt* 1. face towards, be directed towards, turn on one side: *Elekea upande ule*, face that side. (cf *kabili*) 2. be headed for, head towards: *Aelekea kusini*, he is heading towards south. 3. tend to, incline to, seem; show a tendency: *Yaelekea yule msichana atapata mtoto leo*, it seems that the girl will give birth today. St. *eleke.k.a* Cs. *eleke.z.a* Ps. *eleke.w.a* Rp. *eleke.an.a* (cf *onyesha, onekana*)

-elekevu (also *ekevu*) *adj* 1. obedient, servile, compliant: *Mtumishi mwelekevu*, an obedient servant. 2. bright, talented, nimble, deft: *Seremala mwelekevu*, a talented carpenter. 3. honest, upright, truthful: *Mfanyabiashara mwelekevu*, an honest businessman.

elekez.a¹ (also *lekeza*) *vt* guide, direct; give directions, show sby the way: *Fulani amenielekeza jinsi ya kufika nyumbani kwako*, so and so has given me directions as how to reach to your home. Prep. *elekez.e.a* St. *elekez.ek.a* Ps. *elekez.w.a* Rp. *elekez.an.a* (cf *agiza*)

elekez.a² *vt* aim at, target on, direct sth at: *Alielekeza bunduki yake kwa yule mnyama*, he directed his gun at the animal. Prep. *elekez.e.a* St. *elekez.ek.a* Ps. *eleke.w.a* Rp. *elekez.an.a*

elekezi *adj* (*gram*) (of a verb) transitive: *Kitenzi elekezi*, transitive verb.

elektromita *n* (*n*) (*elect*) electrometer (Eng)

elektroni *n* (*n*) (*phys*) electron (Eng)

elektroniki *n* (*n*) (*phys*) electronics (Eng)

elektroskopu *n* (*n*) electroscope (Eng)

eleme.a (also *lemea*) *vt, vi* 1. rest heavily upon, lie on top of; lean: *Mbona unaelemea juu ya bega langu?* Why are you leaning on my shoulder? 2. disappear; recede from view, go away: *Sijui kwa nini ameelemea ghafla*, I don't know why he has suddenly disappeared. (cf *tokomea, toweka*) 3. depend on, rely on, lean on: *Nchi yetu inaelemea sana kwenye sekta ya utalii*, our country depends heavily on the tourism sector. 4. run somewhere for safety. Prep. *eleme.le.a* St. *eleme.k.a* Cs. *eleme.z.a* (cf *tegemea, tumainia*)

elementi *n* (*n*) (*chem*) element (Eng)

elemew.a *vi* 1. be overwhelmed, be overpowered. (cf *zidiwa*) 2. be busy, be occupied: *Ameelemewa na kazi*, he is overworked.

eleveta *n* (*n*) elevator (cf *lifti*) (Eng)

elew.a *vt, vi* understand, comprehend: *Unaelewa chochote anachozungumza?* Do you understand anything he is talking about? Prep. *elew.e.a* St. *elew.ek.a* Cs. *elew.esh.a* Rp. *elew.an.a* (cf *maizi, tanabahi, jua*)

elewan.a *vt* 1. negotiate, compromise: *Jaribu kuelewana na mwenyeduka*, try to negotiate with the shopkeeper. 2. understand one another: *Pande mbili sasa zinaelewana kwenye mazungumzo*, the two sides now understand one another at the talks. Prep. *elewan.i.a* Cs. *elewan.ish.a* (cf *fahamiana*)

elewek.a *vt* be understood, be comprehensible, be clear: *Taarifa ile inaeleweka*, that statement is clear. *Maneno yako hayaeleweki*, your words are incomprehensible. Prep. *elewek.e.a* St. *elewek.ek.a* Cs. *elewek.esh.a*

elewesh.a *vt* explain to sby sth that he does not understand; elucidate, clarify; throw light on sby: *Alinielewesha mpaka nikafahamu*, he explained to me until I understood. Prep. *elewesh.e.a* St. *elewesh.ek.a* Ps. *elewesh.w.a* Rp. *elewesh.an.a*

elez.a *vt* explain, illustrate, explicate: *Eleza kwa ufupi faida za mnazi*, explain in brief the advantages of a coconut tree. Prep. *elez.e.a* St. *elez.ek.a* Ps. *elez.w.a* Rp. *elez.an.a* (cf *fahamisha, fafanua*).

eleze.a *vt, vi* narrate on; describe, St. *eleze.k.a* Ps. *eleze.w.a* Rp. *eleze.an.a*

elfeni *adj, n* (*n*) see *alfeni*

elfu *adj, n* (*n*) see *alfu*

elimik.a *vi* be educated. Prep. *elimik.i.a* St. *elimik.ik.a*

elimish.a *vt* educate, train, instruct: *Anawaelimisha watoto wake vizuri*, she is educating her children well. Prep. *elimish.i.a* St. *elimish.ik.a* Ps. *elimish.w.a* Rp. *elimish.an.a* (cf *fundisha, funza*)

elimu (also *ilimu*) *n* (*n*) 1. education, knowledge, learning, scholarship, teaching: *Elimu viumbe*, biology. *Elimu-jamii*, sociology. *Elimu-madini*, mineralogy. *Elimu uzazi*, gynaecology. *Elimu lafudhi*, accentology. *Elimu-miamba*, lithology; the study of rocks.

(cf *mafunzo, masomo*) 2. experience, wisdom, common sense, intelligence, sound judgement: *Yeye ni mlezi mwenye elimu kubwa*, he is a patron with great experience. (cf *maarifa, hekima, busara, akili*) (Ar)

-ema *adj* 1. good, virtuous, upright, righteous: *Mtu mwema*, a good person. (cf *zuri, bulibuli, sheshi, taibu*) 2. acceptable, suitable, apt, appropriate: *Mawaidha mema*, good advice. 3. attractive, charming, pleasing. (*prov*) *Chema chajiuza, kibaya chajitembeza*, a good thing never asks for publicity but a bad one does.

-emalshani *n* (*n*) (*chem*) emulsion; a colloid in which both phases are liquids. (Eng)

-embamba *adj* 1. slender, slim, lean, thin: *Mtu mwembamba*, a slim person. (cf *dhaifu*) 2. light, weightless, thin, unheavy, weak, ethered, gossamer: *Uji mwembamba*, thin gruel. *Pombe nyembamba*, weak beer. (cf *sahali*) 3. narrow, slender, thin: *Njia nyembamba*, a narrow path. *Mto mwembamba*, a narrow river. (cf *finyu, kabibu*) 4. thin, slender: *Nguo nyembamba*, thin cloth. (cf *laini, teketeke*)

embe *n* (*n*) (*bot*) mango. The different kinds of mangoes are *dodo, boribo, shomari, kisukari, bungala,* etc. These varieties differ in colour, shape, etc.

embwe *n* (*n*) a kind of glue: *Embwe ya mbuyu*, sticky sap of a baobab tree. (cf *pombwe*)

emew.a *vi, vt* be puzzled, be confused, be bewildered: *Mtu yule sasa ameemewa, hajui lolote la kufanya*, that person is now confused, he does not know what to do next. (cf *fazaika, changanyikiwa*)

end.a (also *enenda*) *vi* 1. go, leave, depart. 2. progress, proceed, go: *Mambo yangu yanaenda vizuri*, my affairs are progressing well. (*prov*) *Mwamba ulijua huenda na jua*, he who likes to talk only without doing anything will not succed or prosper. (cf *stawi, endelea*) 3. operate, function, work: *Mtambo huu unaenda kwa kutumia umeme*, this machine operates on electricity. 4. disappear, vanish; go away, fade away: *Mfanyabiashara wa rejareja ameenda zake hivi punde*, the retailer has just gone away. 5. sell well: *Mayai yako yanaenda vizuri hapa*, your eggs are selling well here. 6. fornicate, copulate; commit coition or sexual intercourse: *Kwenda kuzini hakupendezi*, it is no good to commit coition. (cf *zini, tembea*) 7. (*colloq*) die, pass away: *Ameenda*, he has passed away. 8. (*idms*) *Enda chafya*, sneeze. *Enda mwayo*, yawn. *Enda haja*, go to a toilet to relieve oneself. *Enda segemnege*, be in disarray, be spoilt. *Enda sare*, draw as in sports. *Enda sambamba*, walk together, go together. *Enda joshi*, sail ahead. *Enda mrama*, pitch and toss. *Enda pecha*, stagger. *Enda shoti*, go at a trot. *Enda zake*, go his way or go her way. (cf *ondoka, uka*) Prep. **end.e.a,** St **end.ek.a** Cs. **end.esh.a** Ps. of Prep. **end.ew.a** Rp. **end.an.a** Rp. of Prep. **end.e.an.a**

endapo *conj* if, incase, provided: *Endapo atafika kesho, tutaanza kusherehekea ushindi wetu,* if he arrives tomorrow, we shall start celebrating our victory. (cf *iwapo, kama, ikiwa, pindi*)

ende.a *vt* 1. approach sby, go to sby: *Tulimwendea kwa ushauri*, we went to him for advice. 2. go for (in, by, etc.) *Niliuendea mtama wangu*, I went to fetch my millet. (cf *shughulikia*) Prep. **ende.le.a** St. **ende.k.a** Cs. **ende.sh.a** Ps. **ende.w.a**

endekez.a (also *tendekeza*) *vi* pamper, cosset; let sby esp a child have his own way so much and pampering him to such an extent that the results could be disastrous: *Ana tabia ya kumwendekeza sana binti yake* kwa kuwa anampenda, she has the habit of excessively pampering her daughter because she loves her. Prep. **endekez.e.a** St. **endekez.ek.a** Cs. **endekez.esh.a** Ps. **endekez.w.a**. Rp. **endekez.an.a** (cf *ridhia*)

endele.a *vi* 1. progress, advance, proceed: *Kesi yake inaendelea vizuri mahakamani*, her case is proceeding well at the court. (cf *enda, songambele*) 2. prosper, flourish, thrive, boom: *Uchumi wa nchi yetu unazidi kuendelea*, the economy of our country continues to boom. (cf *stawi*) 3. keep on, continue, go on, hang on, *Utaendelea kuishi katika nyumba yangu?* Would you continue to live in my house? St. **endele.k.a** Cs. **endele.z.a**

endelevu *adj* continuous, progressive: *Mipango endelevu*, continuous programmes.

endelez.a[1] *vt* see *endelea*. Ps. **endele.z.w.a**

endelez.a[2] *vt* 1. cause to develop/flourish; promote: *Rais mpya anaendeleza sera ile ile ya ubepari*, the new president continues to promote the same capitalist policy. 2. study/educate more: *Anajaribu kujiendeleza siku hizi*, he is trying to get more education these days. 3. (a) spell a word b) complete: *Endeleza sentensi hii*, complete this sentence. Prep. **endelez.e.a** St. **endelez.ek.a** Cs. **endelez.esh.a** Ps. **endelez.w.a**

endesh.a *vt* 1. drive, chauffer: *Anaendesha gari yake kwa spidi kubwa*, he is driving his car very fast. 2. have diarrhoea; have looseness of the bowels: *Tumbo linaniendesha sana*, I am suffering very much from diarrhoea. (cf *hara*) 3. (*fig*) pester, torment, disturb, vex, bother: *Ananiendesha mara kwa mara na kwa hivyo, sina raha*, he is bothering me from time to time and so, I am not happy. (cf *taabisha, sumbua, ghasi, kera*)

ene.a *vi* 1. be extended, spread out, fit in, have space: *Habari imeenea kila mahala kwamba karibu utaoa*, the news that you are soon to be married has spread everywhere. 2. be sufficient, be full. *Chakula kitaenea*, the food will be sufficient. (cf *kidhi, tosha*) 3. be abundant, be plentiful: *Maembe yameenea siku hizi*, mangoes are abundant these days Cs. **ene.z.a** Ps. of Cs. **ene.z.w.a**. (cf *tapakaa, shamiri, vavagaa*)

enema *n* (*n*) 1. (*med*) enema; medical treatment in which liquid is forced into a person's rectum in order to clean out the bowels. 2. liquid used in this treatment. (Eng)

enend.a *vi* see *enda*

enenz.a *vt* 1. inspect, survey, examine: *Mkaguzi alilienenza shamba langu*, the surveyor inspected my farm. (cf *kagua, tazama, angalia*) 2. measure, gauge, mark off, mark out: *Alienenza urefu na upana wa shamba lake*, he measured the length and breadth of his farm. Prep. **enenz.e.a** St. **enenz.ek.a** Cs. **enenz.esh.a** Ps. **enenz.w.a**. Rp. **enenz.an.a**

eneo *n* (*ma-*) 1. area, space, zone: *Eneo la mjini*, the town area. *Eneo lahaja kijiografia*, dialect area. *Maeneo ya uhusiano*, areas of cooperation. *Maeneo huru*, free zones. *Eneo la viwanda*, industrial estates. *Eneo la makazi*, housing estate. 2. sphere of influence. 3. discipline, field, topic, area: *Utafiti wake unajikita katika eneo pana*, his research focuses on a wide topic. (cf *taaluma, mada, uwanja, uga*)

-enevu *adj* spreading everywhere.

enez.a *n* (*n*) spread, propagate, diffuse: *Usieneze habari za uwongo*, don't spread lies Prep. **enez.e.a** St. **enez.ek.a** Ps. **enez.w.a**

-enezi *adj* having the means to spread; having the capacity to spread: *Katibu mwenezi*, publicity secretary.

eng.a¹ *vt* slice up (cassava etc.), split up: *Mpishi anaenga mhogo jikoni*, the cook is slicing cassava in the kitchen. Prep. **eng.e.a** St. **eng.ek.a** Cs. **eng.esh.a** Ps. **eng.w.a**. Rp. **eng.an.a** (cf *kata, tema, chenga*).

eng.a² (also *engaenga¹*) *vt* 1. cosset, pamper, coddle; treat sby esp a child with kindness and tenderness: *Mama yule anapenda sana kumwenga mwanawe*, that mother likes to pamper her child very much. Prep. **eng.e.a** St. **eng.ek.a** Cs. **eng.esh.a** Ps. **eng.w.a** Rp. **eng.an.a**

eng.a³ *vt* watch, look. Prep. **eng.e.a** St. **eng.ek.a** Cs. **eng.esh.a** Ps **eng.w.a** Rp. **eng.an.a**.

engaeng.a¹ (also *enga*) *vt* see *enga²*

engaeng.a² *vi* hesitate: be confused, be perplexed: *Mbona unaengaenga ninapokuuliza maswali?* Why are you hesitating when I ask you questions? Prep. **engaeng.e.a** St. **engaeng.ek.a** Cs. **engaeng.esh.a** Rp. **engaeng.an.a** (cf *suasua, sita, kwama*)

engaeng.a³ *vi* be on the verge of crying; be near to tears: *Mtoto ataka kuengaenga*, the child is about to cry. Prep. **engaeng.e.a** St. **engaeng.ek.a**

engu.a *vt* 1. skin, scoop off; take scum off, remove froth of cream: *Anaengua maziwa*, he is skimming the cream from the milk. *Anaengua tui*, he is skimming milk from the grated coconut. 2. strip sby of sth; dislodge: *Rais alimwengua makamu wake*, the president dislodged his deputy. Prep. **engu.li.a** St. **engu.lik.a** Cs. **engu.sh.a** Ps. of Prep. **engu.liw.a** Rp. **engu.an.a**.

enhe *interj* an exclamation of assent or of supporting sth; Yes, that is right!

-enu *adj, pron* possessive adjectival root for the second person plural meaning "your." This root takes different forms depending upon the nominal class of the word in question.

-enye *adj* having, with, possessing, in a state or condition of. This adjective is always followed by a noun or a verbal noun e.g. *Mvulana mwenye miguu mirefu*, a boy having long legs. *Mwizi mwenye kudanganya watu*, a thief who deceives people.

-enyewe¹ *adj* himself, herself, itself, etc. This is a reflexive marker: *Yeye mwenyewe alikosea*, he himself erred. *Wao wenyewe walipika chakula*, they themselves cooked the food. Sometimes the adjective is used with the *-ji-* particle in reflexive verbs e.g. *Ulijiumiza mwenyewe*, you hurt yourself.

-enyewe² *n (n)* owner, proprietor, possessor: *Mwambie mwenyewe akukodishe nyumba*, tell the owner to rent the house to you. *Hii ni mali ya mwenyewe*, this is somebody's property. (*cf mmiliki*)

enyi *interj* an exclamation of second person plural meaning "You there"; "I say you". The full form is *ee nyinyi!*

enz.a¹ *vt* measure, mark off, mark out: *Enza urefu na upana wa chumba*, measure the length and breadth of the room. Prep. **enz.e.a** St. **enz.ek.a** Cs. **enz.esh.a** Ps. **enz.w.a** Rp. **enz.an.a**. (cf *pima, enenza*)

enz.a² follow, accompany. Prep. **enz.e.a** St. **enz.ek.a** Cs. **enz.esh.a** Ps. **enz.w.a** Rp. **enz.an.a** (cf *fuata*)

enzi¹ *n (n)* 1. reign, dynasty, rule, might: *Kiti cha enzi*, throne. (cf *utawala, mamlaka*) 2. period, era, time, term, age: *Wakati wa enzi za wafalme wa zamani wa Kiingereza*, during the period of the ancient British kings. *Enzi ya mawe*, Stone Age. *Enzi za kati*, Middle Ages. *Enzi ya barafu*, Ice Age. (cf *wakati, kipindi*) (Ar)

enz.i² *vt* adore, exalt, esteem, praise, honour, respect: *Mimi ninawaenzi sana waimbaji watatu wale*, I admire very much those three singers. *Lazima nchi yetu iwaenzi mashujaa wake*, our country must honour her heroes. Prep.

135

enz.i.a St. **enz.ik.a** Cs. **enz.ish.a** Ps. of Prep. **enz.iw.a** Rp. **enz.i.an.a** (cf *sifu, heshimu*) (Ar)

ep.a (also *hepa, kwepa*) *vt* 1. flinch, avoid, swerve, escape: *Waliweza kuiepa hatari ile*, they managed to escape that danger. 2. avoid meeting someone; dodge. Prep. **ep.e.a** St. **ep.ek.a** Cs. **ep.esh.a** Ps. **ep.w.a** Rp. **ep.an.a** (cf *kimbia, epuka, futahi*)

-epesi *adj* 1. weightless, slight, unheavy (in weight), light (in weight): *Mzigo mwepesi*, a light load. (cf *sahali, bua*) 2. quick, agile, swift: *Mwanariadha mwepesi*, a fast athlete. *Mtu huyu ni mwepesi katika kupika*, this person is quick at cooking. 3. easy, simple: *Kazi nyepesi*, simple work.

Epifania *n* (*n*) (in Christianity) Epiphany; a Christian festival held on January 6, commemorating in the Western church, the manifestation of Christ to the Magi and the baptism of Jesus.

eproni *n* (*n*) see *aproni* (Eng)

epsiloni *n* (*n*) epsilon; the fifth letter of the Greek alphabet. (E, e) (Lat)

epu.a (also *ipua*) *vt* 1. remove from the fire sth like a pot; take off: *Aliepua chungu mekoni*, she removed a pot from the hearth. 2. save sby from danger; rescue: *Alitaka kuwaepua mateka*, he wanted to rescue the hostages. Prep. **epu.li.a** St. **epu.k.a** and **epu.lik.a** Cs. **epu.sh.a** Ps. of Prep. **epu.liw.a** Rp. **epu.an.a** (cf *opoa, okoa, topoa*)

epuk.a[1] *vt, vi* avoid, refrain; distance oneself from: *Mwepuke mtu huyo*, avoid that person. Prep. **epuk.i.a** St. **epuk.ik.a** Cs. **epuk.ish.a** Ps. **epuk.w.a** Rp. **epuk.an.a** (cf *jitenga*)

epuk.a[2] *vt, vi* (esp of food) be ready to be removed from the fire for eating. Ps. **epuk.i.a** St. **epuk.ik.a** Cs. **epuk.ish.a** Ps. **epuk.w.a** Rp. **epuk.an.a**

epuu *interj* an exclamation used to discourage sby from doing or believing in sth.

-erevu *adj* shrewd, clever, astute, intelligent: *Mwanasiasa mwerevu*, a shrewd politician. (cf *hodari, mahiri*)

erevuk.a *vi* become mature, become conscious or wise: *Hotuba zake za uzalendo zimetufanya tuerevuke kisiasa*, his patriotic speeches have made us politically more mature. Prep. **erevuk.i.a** St. **erevuk.ik.a** Cs. **erevuk.ish.a**

erevush.a *vt* prime sby; make sby aware of the true facts or circumstances; enlighten: *Ameweza kunierevusha hatari zilizopo*, he has managed to enlighten me of the prevailing dangers. Prep. **erevush.i.a** St. **erevush.ik.a** Ps. **erevush.w.a** Rp. **erevush.an.a**

eria *n* (*n*) antenna, aerial; a piece of equipment made of wire or metal rods for receiving or sending radio and television signals. (Eng)

eriali *n* (*n*) antenna, aerial. (Eng)

eropleni *n* (*n*) aeroplane (cf *ndege*) (Eng)

eskaleta *n* (*n*) escalator (Eng)

Esia *n* (*n*) Asia: *Kontinenti ya Asia*, the continent of Asia.

eti *interj* see *ati*

etimolojia *n* (*n*) etymology; the study of the sources and development of words. (Eng)

-etu *adj, pron* the possessive root of first person plural, meaning ours, our: *Kazi yetu*, our work. *Nyumba yetu*, our house.

etuk.a *vi* be astonished, be surprised Prep. **etuk.i.a** St. **etuk.ik.a** Cs. **etuk.ish.a** (cf *shangaa*)

eu.a *vt* exorcise; purify by rituals, remove magic spell: *Mama alitaka kumweua mtoto wake mara tu baada ya kuzaliwa*, the mother wanted to exorcise her baby immediately after it was born. Prep. **eu.li.a** St. **eu.lik.a** Cs. **eu.sh.a** Ps. of Prep. **eu.liw.a** Rp. **eu.an.a** (cf *safisha, takasa*)

-eupe *adj* 1. white colour: *Amevaa nguo nyeupe*, he has dressed in white.

2. clean, white, spotless. 3. clean, pure: *Maji ni meupe*, the water is clear. 4. clean, good, decent: *Moyo wake ni mweupe*, he has a good heart. 5. empty: *Kapu jeupe*, an empty basket.

eush.a *vt* separate, differentiate, discriminate. Prep. ***eush.i.a*** St. ***eush.ik.a*** Ps. ***eush.w.a*** Rp. ***eush.an.a***

-eusi *adj* 1. black colour: *Rangi nyeusi*, black colour. 2. bad, evil, sinister, wicked: *Roho yake ni nyeusi*, he is wicked.

ewa *interj* see *hewaa*

ewe (also *ee*) *interj* 1. an exclamation of surprise, fear, etc.: *Ewe angalia kule!* Oh, look at! Oh, watch out! (cf *ala!, abo!*) 2. an exclamation made when calling out. Usually the interjection carries contemptuous overtones. It has the equivalent meanings of "You there," "I say you."

ezek.a[1] *vt* roof; thatch usu with grass, reeds, rushes, straws, leaves or coconut palm leaves known as *makuti*: *Mfanyakazi ataezeka karibuni paa la nyumba yangu*, the worker will soon thatch the roof of my house. Prep. ***ezek.e.a*** St. ***ezek.ek.a*** Cs. ***ezek.esh.a*** Ps. ***ezek.w.a*** Rp. of Prep. ***ezek.e.an.a*** (cf *vimba*)

ezek.a[2] *vt* beat, hit, slap, smack: *Mwalimu wako atakuezeka makofi kama hutaenda shuleni kesho*, your teacher will slap you if you don't go to school tomorrow. Prep. ***ezek.e.a*** St. ***ezek.ek.a*** Cs. ***ezek.esh.a*** Ps. ***ezek.w.a*** Rp. of Prep. ***ezek.e.an.a*** (cf *piga, papata*)

ezi *n* (n) might, power, authority: *Mwenyezi Mungu*, God Almighty. (Ar)

ezu.a *vt* unroof, unthatch; strip a roof; uncover the rafters: *Anataka kuliezua paa la nyumba*, he wants to take off the roof of the house. Prep. ***ezu.li.a*** St. ***ezu.lik.a*** Cs. ***ezu.sh.a*** Ps. of Prep. ***ezu.liw.a***. Rp. of Prep. ***ezu.li.an.a*** (cf *vimbua*)

F

F, f /f/ 1. the sixth letter of the Swahili alphabet. 2. a voiceless labio-dental fricative.

fa.a vi 1. die, decease: *Alikufa kwa njaa*, he died of hunger. 2. lose strength, come to the end, be finished: *Gari lake limekufa*, his car is finished. 3. be numbed: *Mkono wake umekufa ganzi*, his arm has gone numb. 4. (*idms*) *Kufa kiofisa*, continue to perform a task despite the existence of problems. *Kufa kingoto*, bear the difficulties without complaining. *Kufa kiungwana*, experience difficulties without complaining. *Kufa kwa kihoro*, die with great sadness. *Kufa maji*, die after being drowned. (*prov*) *Heri kufa macho kuliko kufa moyo*, it is better for the eyes to die than the heart i.e. it is better to meet an expected calamity than an unexpected one. 5. (*colloq*) love someone very much: *Anakufa kwa msichana yule*, he loves that girl very much. Prep. ***f.i.a*** Cs. ***f.ish.a*** Ps. of Prep. ***f.iw.a*** Rp. of Prep. ***f.i.an.a***

fa.a vt,vi 1. be useful, be fitting, be of avail, be proper: *Jembe hili litanifaa ingawa ni kuukuu*, this hoe will be useful to me although it is old. Frequently, the verb *faa* is used with the dummy subject "I" e.g. *Inafaa umsaidie ndugu yako*, it is fitting that you help your brother. *Haifai kufanya masihara mengi*, it is not good to make lots of jokes. Prep. ***fa.li.a*** Ps. of Prep. ***fa.liw.a*** Rp. ***fa.an.a*** give mutual assistance, be of use to each other e.g. *Marafiki wale wawili wanafaana*, those two friends help one another. (cf *saidia*, *tosha*) 2. assist, help: *Yeye alinifaa wakati wa dhiki*, he assisted me while I was in difficulty. (cf *saidia*, *aviza*) 3. attract, fit: *Nguo yake inakufaa*, her dress fits you. (cf *pendeza*) 4. suit, match, befit,

fit: *Pea ile ya viatu inakufaa*, that pair of shoes fits you. (cf *tosha*) 5. prosper, flourish, thrive: *Mimea hii inafaa kwenye hali ya hewa yenye baridi*, these plants flourish in a cold climate. Prep. ***fa.li.a*** Ps. of Prep ***fa.liw.a*** Rp. ***fa.an.a*** (cf *stawi*)

fadhaa (also *fazaa*) n (n) perplexity, confusion, dismay: *Shikwa na fadhaa*, be perplexed. (cf *dukuduku*)

fadhaik.a vi see *fazaika*

fadhaisha vt see *fazaisha*

fadhila n (n) see *fadhili*[1]

fadhili[1] (also *fadhila*) n (n) 1. kindness, favour, goodness: *Mtu yule alinifanyia fadhili kubwa na kwa hivyo sitamsahau*, that person did to me great favour and so I will not forget him. (cf *jamala*, *wema*, *hisani*) 2. gratitude, thanks: *Mtu yule hana fadhili*, that person is ungrateful. (*prov*) *Fadhili ya punda mashuzi*, the gratitude of a donkey is the breaking of wind i.e. kindness is sometimes reciprocated by an ungrateful gesture. (Ar)

fadhil.i[2] vt do a kindness to sby, be favourable to: *Rafiki yangu alinifadhili wakati nilipokuwa katika shida*, my friend assisted me when I was in difficulty. Prep. ***fadhil.i.a*** St. ***fadhil.ik.a*** Ps. ***fadhil.iw.a*** be sponsored, be entertained e.g. *Mkutano wao ulifadhiliwa na shirika lisilo la kiserikali*, their conference was sponsored by a private organization. Rp. ***fadhil.i.an.a*** (cf *tajamali*, *kirimu*) (Ar)

fadhili[3] *adj* better than, more acceptable, excelling: *Nyumba hii ni fadhili kuliko yake*, this house is better than his. (cf *bora*, *ahsani*) (Ar)

fafanu.a vt clarify, elucidate, explicate, explain, disambiguate; make clear: *Serikali ilifafanua msimamo wake kuhusu suala la wakimbizi*, the

fafaruk.a government clarified its position on the question of refugees. Prep. **fafanu.li.a**: make clear to e.g. *Alinifafanulia taarifa yake*, he clarified his statement. St. **fafanu.k.a** and **fafanu.lik.a** be clear, be intelligible. Cs. **fafanu.z.a** and **fafanu.sh.a** Ps. of Prep. **fafanu.liw.a**, be clarified. Rp. of Prep. **fafanu.li.an.a** (cf *fasiri, eleza*).

fafaruk.a *vi* 1. shake, flutter, twitch; move with a sudden rapid movement: *Alimchinja kondoo na mara akaanza kufafaruka*, he slaughtered the sheep and immediately it started to twitch. (cf *paparika, papatika*) 2. prattle, blather, gabble; talk nonsense: *Alifafaruka kwa sababu alilewa sana*, he prattled because he was very drunk. Prep. **fafaruk.i.a** St. **fafaruk.ik.a** Cs. **fafaruk.ish.a** (cf *ropoka, boboja*)

fagi.a (also *fyagia*) *vt,vi* 1. (of brush, broom, etc.) sweep, whisk, brush: *Alifagia chumba changu na sasa kimekuwa safi*, he swept my room and now it is clean. Prep. **fagi.li.a** St. **fagi.lik.a**, be swept e.g. *Chumba changu kinafagilika*, my room can be swept. Cs. **fagi.lish.a** and **fagi.z.a** Ps. **fagi.w.a** Rp. **fagi.an.a** (cf *komba, pea*). 2. sweep away all the things: *Majambazi waliingia nyumba ya jirani na kufagia kila kitu kilichomo ndani*, the thugs raided the neighbour's house and took away everything that was inside. Prep. **fagi.li.a** St. **fagi.lik.a** Cs. **fagi.lish.a** and **fagi.z.a** Ps. **fag.iw.a** be swept. Rp. **fagi.an.a**

fagositi *n* (n) (*physiol*) phagocyte (Eng)

fahali¹ *n* (n) 1. bull. (cf *ng'ombe dume*) 2. valiant, gallant, paladin, hero; a brave person. (*prov*) *Fahali wawili hawakai zizi moja*, two bulls cannot stay together in the same kraal i.e. an activity or an affair cannot be performed by two people of the same rank since they will quarrel. (cf *shujaa, jabari*)

fahali² *adj.* courageous, brave: *Mwanajeshi fahali*, a courageous soldier. (Ar)

fahami.a *vt, vi* lie on the back, lie on the side, lie on the stomach. Prep. **fahami.li.a** Ps. **fahami.w.a**

fahamian.a *vt,vi* be knowing each other, understand each other, be acquainted with each other: *Vijana wale wanafahamiana*, those youths understand each other. (cf *elewana*)

fahamik.a *vi* 1. be known, be famous: *Kiongozi yule anafahamika sana kwa watu*, that leader is very well-known among the people. 2. be understood, be familiar: *Utata ule haufahamiki*, that problem is incomprehensible.

fahamish.a *vt* 1. explain, inform, cause to know: *Alinifahamisha kuwa atapata uhamisho karibuni*, he informed me that he would get a transfer quite soon. *Jaribu kunifahamisha faida za mkarafuu*, try to explain to me the advantages of a clove tree. 2. introduce sby: *Tafadhali nifahamishe huyu rafiki yako*, please introduce me to your friend. Prep. **fahamish.i.a** St. **fahamish.ik.a** Ps. **fahamish.w.a** Rp. **fahamish.an.a**

-fahamivu *adj* intelligent, acute, astute, brainy, clever: *Mwalimu alimpa zawadi mwanafunzi mfahamivu*, the teacher gave a present to the intelligent student. (cf *arifu, angavu*)

faham.u¹ *vt,vi* 1. understand, comprehend, know, perceive, apprehend, absorb: *Yeye anafahamu vizuri juhudi zote nilizozichukua*, he understands well all the efforts I have taken. (cf *elewa, tambua*) 2. beware, take notice, be conscious: *Fahamu kuwa hapa mtaani kuna wezi wengi*, beware that here in the neighbourhood, there are a lot of thieves. 3. realize, discover: *Sasa amefahamu kwamba kitendo alichokifanya si kizuri*, he has now realized that the thing he did was not good. Prep. **faham.i.u** St.

F   fahamu²   faini¹

faham.ik.a Cs. *faham.ish.a* Ps. of Prep. *faham.iw.a* Rp. *faham.i.an.a* (cf *tahadhari*) (Ar)

fahamu² *n* (*n*) comprehension, understanding, apprehension, knowledge: *Fahamu yake ni ndogo katika mambo mengi ya kidunia*, his understanding of many world affairs is quite lilited. 2. memory, recollection: *Hana fahamu nzuri*, he has no good memory. 3. consciousness, cognition; *Amepoteza fahamu*, he has lost consciousness. (cf *akili, utambuzi*) (Ar)

faharasa (also *faharisi*) *n* (*n*) 1. a table of contents of a book and its pages. 2. index; an alphabetical list of names or topics referred to in a book, etc. usu arranged at the end. (cf *sherehe*) (Ar)

fahari¹ (also *ufahari*) *n* (*n*) 1. pride, arrogance, conceit, braggadocio, vanity: *Yeye ni mtu mwenye fahari sana kwa vile ana mali nyingi*, he is very proud because he has a lot of wealth. (cf *kiburi, majisifu*) 2. splendour, glory, prestige, eminence, grandeur, ostentation: *Anapenda maisha ya fahari*, he likes a life of grandeur. (cf *utukufu, makuu*) (Ar)

fahari² *adj* 1. proud, gratified, pleased, snobbish, boastful: *Anaona fahari kusikia kwamba bintiye amefaulu vizuri kwenye mtihani*, she is proud to learn that her daughter has passed the examination well. 2. luxurious, enjoyable: *Maisha ya fahari*, ostentatious living. (Ar)

faharisi *n* (*n*) see *faharasa*

fahir.i *vi* 1.(usu *fahirish.a*) take pride in sth. 2. live in grandeur; live in enjoyable life. Prep. *fahir.i.a* St. *fahir.ik.a* Cs. *fahir.ish.a*

fahirish.a *vi* see *fahiri*. Prep. *fahirish.i.a* St. *fahirish.ik.a* Ps. *fahirish.w.a* Rp. *fahirish.an.a*

fahiwati *n* (*n*) meaning, message. (Ar)

fahuwa (also *fauwa*) *conj* (used to mean the following expressions) all the same, it makes no difference: *Akija asije, kwangu fahuwa*, if he comes or not, it makes no difference. (Ar)

faida *n* (*n*) 1. profit, gain, interest: *Anapata faida kubwa katika biashara yake ya kuuza vipuri*, he gets a big profit from his business of selling spare parts. *Faida halisi*, net profit. *Faida ya jumla*, gross profit. *Faida halisi*, profit margin. *Kugawana faida*, profit sharing. 2. benefit, asset, use, advantage: *Faida za mnazi ni kubwa*, the advantages of a coconut tree are many. (Ar)

faid.i *vt,vi* 1. profit, benefit, get profit from: *Nimefaidi sana kwa kuishi pamoja naye kwa muda wa miaka miwili*, I have benefitted a lot by staying with him for two years. 2. be pleased, feel happy: *Nilifaidi mno na mazungumzo yake*, I felt very happy with his conversation. Prep. *faid.i.a* St. *faid.ik.a* Cs. *faid.ish.a* Ps. of Prep. *faid.iw.a* Rp. of Prep. *faid.i.an.a*. (Ar)

faidik.a *vt, vi* profit/benefit from; be profiting/benefitting from. Prep. *faidik.i.a* St. *faidik.a* Cs. *faidk.ish.a*

fail.i¹ *vt* file; put papers or letters in a file: *Mhazili wangu hapendi kufaili barua za idara*, my secretary does not like filing departmental letters. Prep. *fail.i.a* St. *fail.ik.a* Cs. *fail.ish.a* Ps. of Prep. *fail.iw.a* Rp. of Prep. *fail.i.an.a* (Eng)

faili² *n* (*ma-*) file, folder. (cf *jalada*) 2. a collection of papers, cards, etc. for reference. (cf *jalada*) (Eng)

fainali *n* (*n*) last steps or stages in a sports tournament, etc. *Robo fainali*, quarter final. *Nusu fainali*, semi-final. (cf *mwisho, hatima*) (Eng)

faini¹ *n* (*n*) fine, mulct, amercement, penalty fees: *Alitozwa faini ya shilingi elfu kumi kwa kuendesha gari kwa kasi sana*, he was fined ten thousands

fain.i² .... **falahi F**

shillings for speeding. *Piga faini*, be fined. (cf *haka*) (Eng)

fain.i² *vt* fine, mulct, amerce; impose a fine upon: *Hakimu alimfaini mjomba kwa kuegesha gari barabarani*, the magistrate fined my uncle for parking his car on the highway. Prep. *fain.i.a* St. *fain.ik.a* Cs. *fain.ish.a* Ps. of Prep. *fain.iw.a* e.g. *Nilifainiwa shilingi elfu ishirini kwa kuendesha gari usiku bila ya taa*, I was fined twenty thousand shillings for driving at night without lights. Rp. *fain.i.an.a* (Eng)

faitik.a (also *fautika*) *vi* delay, procrastinate, temporize, be late: *Timu yetu ya mpira ilifaitika kufika uwanjani*, our football team arrived late at the pitch. Prep. *faitik.i.a* St. *faitik.ik.a* Cs. *faitik.ish.a* (cf *chelewa, kawia*)

faitish.a *vt* cause to be late; delay. Prep. *faitish.i.a* St *faitish.ik.a* Ps. *faitish.w.a*

faja *n* (*ma-*) 1. kraal, pen, corral, coop; an enclosure or fence for keeping animals. *Katika faja lake, kuna ng'ombe wengi*, in his pen, there are many cattle. (cf *zeriba, dewa*) 2. an enclosure attached to a house and usu fenced with sticks at the back. (cf *ua, boma, uga*)

fajaa¹ *n* (*n*) sudden death: *Alipatwa na fajaa baada ya gari lake kupinduka*, she died unexpectedly after her car overturned. (cf *mauti*)

fajaa² *adv* suddenly, abruptly, unawares: *Alikufa fajaa*, he died suddenly. (cf *ghafla*) (Ar)

faka *n* (*n*) peace of mind; tranquility, calmness.

fakachi *n* (*n*) 1. illwill, invidiousness spleen, gall, pique, hostility: *Watu wengi hawampendi kutokana na fakachi zake za mara kwa mara*, many people don't like him because of his frequent hostilities. (cf *fitina, uhasama*) 2. jealousy, envy, enviousness, green-eyed monster: *Majirani wanamsema kwa ajili ya fakachi zake kwa yeyote yule aliyebarikiwa*, the neighbours speak ill of him because of his jealousy towards anyone who has prospered. (cf *husuda, wivu*)

fakaifa (also *fakefu*) *adv* let alone, not to mention: *Wewe huna mali na bado unawasaidia masikini, fakaifa yeye mwenye utajiri mkubwa*, you are not rich and yet you help poor people, let alone him with immense wealth. (cf *seuze, sembuse*) (Ar)

fakami.a *vt* eat voraciously, eat hurriedly; gluttonize, gormandize. Prep. *fakami.w.a* St. *fakami.k.a* Cs. *fakami.w.a* Rp. *fakami.an.a*

fakefu *adv* see *fakaifa*

fakiri¹ (also *fukara*) adj poor, impecunious, penurious, impoverished, penniless: *Yeye ni fakiri sana kwani hana hata pesa za kununulia nguo*, she is very poor because she does not even have the money to buy clothes. (cf *maskini*) (Ar)

fakiri² (also *fukara*) *n* (*n*) pauper, beggar; a poor person: *Yeye ni fakiri na kwa hivyo, inafaa tumsaidie*, he is poor and we should therefore help him.

fakirik.a *vi* see *fukarika* (Ar)

faksi (*n*) 1. fax; *Aliipeleka barua yake kwa faksi*, he sent his letter by fax. 2. a machine for faxing; fax machine. (cf *kipepesi*) (Eng)

fala *n* (*n*) imbecile, noodle, nincompoop, simpleton, mooncalf, fool: *Yeye ni fala na ndiyo maana anauliza maswali ya kiupuuzi*, he is a fool and that is why he is asking silly questions. (cf *mpumbavu, bwege*)

falada *n* (*n*) see *faladi*

falad.i (also *falada*) *vi* sing. (cf *imba*) (Ar)

falahi *n* (*n*) 1. peasant, farmer. (cf *mkulima*) 2. a worker whose capital derives purely from his own efforts e.g. by working

falaki¹ n (n) 1. astronomy; the scientific study of stars, moon, etc. (cf *unajimu*) 2. astrology; the study of the positions of the stars and movements of the planets on the understanding that they influence human affairs: *Piga falaki*, read the omens by watching and observing the stars; read horoscope. Also it means 'take time to consider sth' (cf *unajimu*) 4. skies (cf *mbingu*) (Ar)

falaki² n (n) (*astron*) orbit; the path followed by a planet, star, moon, etc. round another body. (Ar)

falau adv 1. had it been, if it were, if only: *Falau asingekuja kwetu jana, ingebidi tumpigie simu*, if he had not come to our place yesterday, we would have been obliged to phone him. (cf *lau kama, laiti, angaa*) 2. better: *Falau angekuwa kama wewe kwani anatumia pesa zake ovyoovyo*, it would be better if he were like you because he is misusing his money. (Ar)

falaula adv were it not, had it not been: *Falaula si msaada wake, ningekuwa katika dhiki sana*, were it not for his assistance, I would have been in difficulties. (cf *laiti*) (Ar)

fali (also *feli*) n (n) 1. portent, omen: *Tazama feli*, augur; see in the stars. 2. luck, fate, chance either good or bad: *Usimtie fali mbaya*, don't bring him bad luck; don't jinx him. (cf *sudi, bahati*)

faliji n (n) paralysis; a disease that makes someone have partial or complete loss of temporary function of some part or all of the body. (cf *kiharusi, ganzi, subiani*) (Ar)

falka¹ n (n) (*naut*) 1. hold; a place in a ship where cargo is kept. 2. hold in a *dau*, canoe. 3. hatch; a covering in a ship's deck through which cargo is lowered or raised. (Ar)

falka² n (n) a piece of cloth sewn to make a sail. (Ar)

falsafa n (n) 1. philosophy: *Falsafa ya maisha*, the philosophy of life. *Falsafa ya maadili*, moral philosophy. *Falsafa ya maumbile*, natural philosophy. 2. a particular system of principles for the conduct of life required for a human being. *Falsafa ya mtu yule kuhusu maisha ni kutaka watu wote waishi kwa amani*, the philosophy of that person calls for people to live together in harmony. 3. wisdom, sagacity, judiciousness; reach of thought. (cf *busara, hekima*) 4. used in various contexts: *Falsafa ya lugha*, linguistic philosophy. *Falsafa ulingano*, anomalism. *Falsafa asili*, naturalism (Gr)

faluda n (n) agar-agar; a kind of dessert made from seaweed, and used as a base for bacterial cultures, as a laxative, in jellied and preserved foods, etc. (Ar)

famasia n (n) pharmacy (Eng)

familia n (n) 1. family; father, mother and children: *Ana familia kubwa*, he has a large family. *Familia kubwa* (*ukoo*), extended family. *Familia ya kiini*, nuclear family. 2. all people at home. (Eng)

fan.a vt,vi succeed, turn out well: *Sherehe yake ya kuzaliwa ilifana*, her birthday celebration turned out well. Prep. **fan.i.a** St. **fan.ik.a** Cs **fan.ish.a** Ps. of Prep. **fan.iw.a** (cf. *faulu, stawi*)

fanaka n (n) prosperity, success, prosperousness: *Nchi yetu imepata fanaka kutokana na juhudi za raia wake*, our country has achieved prosperity due to the hardwork on the part of its citizens. *Heri na fanaka*, blessings and prosperity. (cf *usitawi*)

fanan.a vt,vi resemble, look like, be similar to, seem like, appear like: *Yeye anafanana na mjomba wake*, he resembles his uncle. Prep. **fanan.i.a** Cs. **fanan.ish.a** compare, liken; make like e.g. *Aliifananisha kazi yake na yako*, he compared his work and yours. (cf *landana, lingana, shabihiana*)

142

fanani *n (n)* 1. actor 2. composer of poems, novels, music, etc.; artist. (cf *msanii*)

fananish.a 1. compare, liken, equate: *Mwalimu alinifananisha na mwanawe katika masuala mengi*, the teacher compared me and his son on many issues. (cf *linganisha*) 2. confuse sby. Prep. ***fananish.i.a*** St. ***fananish.ik.a*** Ps. ***fananish.w.a*** Rp. ***fananish.an.a***

fani[1] *n (n)* 1. field of study, area of study: *Yeye amebobea katika fani ya ushairi*, he is well-versed in the field of poetry. 2. form; style of writing: *Alizingatia fani na maudhui kwenye riwaya*, he examined form and content in the novel. (Ar)

fani[2] *n (n)* degree, size, extent (cf *kiasi, kiwango*)

fanicha *n (n)* furniture (cf *samani*) (Eng)

fanid.i *vt* select by comparing: *Aliweza kufanidi vizuri vitambaa vilivyo bora na vile vilivyo duni*, he was able to select successfully by comparing high-quality materials with inferior ones. Prep. ***fanid.i.a*** St. ***fanid.ik.a*** Cs. ***fanid.ish.a*** Ps. of Prep. ***fanid.iw.a*** Rp. of Prep. ***fanid.i.an.a*** (Ar)

faniki.a *vt* be successful at, turn out well

fanikio *n (ma-)* see *mafanikio*

fanikish.a *vt* ensure success; accomplish sth: *Chama tawala kiliahidi kufanikisha maendeleo ya uchumi nchini*, the ruling party pledged to bring success in economic development in the country. Prep. ***fanikish.i.a*** St. ***fanikish.ik.a*** Ps. ***fanikish.w.a*** Rp. ***fanikish.an.a***

fanikiw.a *vi* 1. get sth that you have been looking for; achieve, accomplish, succeed: *Nilikuwa nikitafuta mchele kila duka na sasa nimefanikiwa*, I was looking for rice in every shop and now I have found it. 2. prosper, thrive, flourish, grow: *Amefanikiwa sana katika maisha yake*, he has prospered very much in his life. (*cf. stawi*.)

fanusi *n (n)* lantern, lamp, hurricane lamp. (cf *kandili*) (Ar)

fanusi

fany.a (also *fanza*) *vt* 1. do, make: *Fanya kazi vizuri*, do a good job. *Fanya shauri*, make a decision; consider. 2. be involved, be engaged, be doing: *Anafanya biashara siku hizi*, he is doing business these days. (cf *jishughulisha*) 3. compel, force, let, cause; bring about a result: *Fanya aende*, let him go, make him go. 4. allow to happen, give spontaneous vent to, esp of the feelings: *Fanya huzuni*, be sorry. *Fanya hasira*, be angry. *Fanya fahari*, be proud, be conceited. *Fanya mzaha*, joke, make fun. 5. suppose, consider, think, make an imagination, regard as: *Ulinifanya mimi mpumbavu*, you made me a fool. 6. (*idms*) *Fanya hima*, make haste. *Fanya haraka*, hurry. *Fanya karamu*, feast; hold a banquet. *Fanya mvi*, become grey-haired. *Fanya shaka*, become suspicious. *Fanya upara*, become bald. *Fanya usaha*, suppurate, fester. *Fanya ufa*, crack. *Fanya taksiri*, err, make a mistake. *Fanya kibyongo*, become hunched. *Fanya rabsha*, cause chaos. *Fanya tashtiti*, ridicule, mock. Prep. ***fany.i.a*** St. ***fany.ik.a*** Cs. ***fany.ish.a*** Ps. ***fany.w.a*** Rp. ***fany.an.a***.

fanyi.a *vt* illtreat: *Fanyia kiburi*, defy. *Fanyia mzaha*, ridicule. *Fanyia uchawi*, bewitch. St. **fanyi.k.a** Cs. **fanyi.z.a** Ps. **fanyi.w.a** Rp. **fanyi.an.a**

fanyiz.a vt compose, mend: *Fanyiza upya*, renovate. Prep. ***fanyiz.i.a*** St. ***fanyiz.ik.a*** Ps. ***fanyiz.w.a*** Rp. of Prep. ***fanyiz.i.an.a***

fanz.a vt see *fanya*

fara¹ n (n) see *furi*

fara² n (n) the rim of a vessel (Ar)

faradhi¹ (also *faridha*) n (n) compulsion, necessity, obligation: *Sala ya faradhi*, a compulsory prayer. *Kula ni faradhi kwa kila binadamu*, eating is a must to every humanbeing. (cf *wajibu*) (Ar)

faradhi² n (n) haunt, abode, sojourn; a place of rest. (Ar)

faradhi³ n (n) death (cf *kifo*, *mauti*)

faradhish.a vt compel, force. Prep. ***faradhish.i.a*** St. ***faradhish.ik.a*** Ps. ***faradhish.w.a*** Rp. ***faradhish.an.a*** (cf *lazimisha*)

faragha¹ n (n) 1. privacy, seclusion, secrecy: *Mahala pa faragha*, a private place. *Neno la faragha*, a private matter. (cf *siri*, *hombo*) 2. time, free time, opportunity: *Kuwa na faragha*, have free time. (cf *wasaa*, *nafasi*) (Ar)

faragha² (usu *faraghani*) adv aside, privately, secretly: *Alinipeleka faraghani*, he took me aside.

faragu.a vi vaunt, brag, boast, show off: *Anapenda kujifaragua*, he likes to show off. Prep. ***faragu.li.a*** St. ***faragu.k.a*** Cs. ***faragu.sh.a*** Ps. of Prep ***faragu.liw.a*** Rp. ***faragu.an.a***

faraja (also *fariji*) n (n) comfort, relief, solace, consolation, easement: *Pata faraja*, get comfort. (*prov*) *Baada ya dhiki, faraja*, every cloud has a silver lining i.e. after adversities comes happiness. (Ar)

faraji n (n) see *faraja*

faraka¹ n (n) 1. separation, split, disengagement: *Faraka kati ya wanachama limeiathiri sana klabu yao*, the split between the members has seriously affected their club. (cf *utengano*) 2. division, section, part. (cf *sehemu*, *fungu*) (Ar)

faraka² n (n) a comb-like instrument, used for keeping threads apart. (Ar)

farakan.a vi 1. be estranged, be parted, be separated, be severed: *Mke na mumewe sasa wamefarakana*, the wife and her husband are now estranged. Prep. **farakan.i.a** St. **farakan.ik.a** Cs. **farakan.ish.a** (cf *tengana*, *tofautiana*, *hitilafiana*) 2. rupture, burst, break (Ar)

farakano n (ma-) 1. separation, estrangement, disunion, parting: *Farakano kati yao limeathiri watoto wao vibaya*, the estrangement between them has adversely affected their children. (cf *utengano*) 2. division, partition, rupture, split, disassociation: *Farakano kati ya wanachama limesababishwa na ukabila*, the division between the members has been caused by tribalism. (cf *tofauti*, *hitilafu*) (Ar)

farakish.a vt estrange, alienate, antagonize. Prep. ***farakish.i.a*** St. ***farakish.ik.a*** Ps. ***farakish.w.a*** Rp. ***farakish.an.a***

faranga n (n) 1. currency used in France, Belgium, Switzerland and other countries which are under their rule. 2. money, currency. (Fr)

farangi n (n) (*med*) syphilis; an infectious disease passed on by sexual contact from one person to another. (cf. *kaswende*, *sekeneko*)

Faransa adj. French: *Lugha ya Kifaransa*, French language. *Utamaduni wa Kifaransa*, French culture. [Fr]

farao n (ma-) see *Firauni*

farashani n (n) verandah (cf *veranda*)

farasi¹ n (n) (*zool*) horse: *Mpanda farasi*, a horseman. (*prov.*) *Mpanda farasi wawili, hupasuka msamba*, one who mounts two horses splits in two i.e. he who tackles two things at the same time, cannot succeed. (Ar).

farasi² n (n) 1. (in joinery) crossbar, tie-beam. 2. trestle, saw-horse. 3. bicycle frame. (Ar)

farasila (also *frasila*) n (n) a measure of weight of 35 or 36 pounds; 16 kilogrammes. (Ar)

faridh.i vt be compelled, be forced, be obliged, be pressurized, be hustled: *Ilinifaridhi kumsaidia mtu yule kwa sababu alikuwa katika dhiki*, I was obliged to help that person because he was in difficulties. Prep. ***faridh.i.a*** St. ***faridh.ik.a*** Cs. ***faridh.ish.a***. Ps. of Prep. ***faridh.iw.a***. Rp. of Prep. ***faridh.i.an.a*** (cf *shurutika, lazimika*) (Ar)

faridi[1] adj extraordinary, unique: unequalled; one of a particular kind: *Mungu ni faridi*, God is unique. (cf *pweke, wahidi*) (Ar)

faridi[2] n (n) (ling) item· *Faridi kifonolojia*, phonological item. *Faridi sarufi*, grammatical item. *Faridi na mpangilio*, item and arrangement. *Faridi na mfanyiko*, item and process. (Ar)

farij.i vt console, comfort, relieve, solace: *Alikwenda kwao kuwafariji wafiwa*, he went to their home to console the bereaved. Prep. ***farij.i.a*** St. ***farij.ik.a*** e.g. *Amefarijika kabisa*, he is quite consoled. Ps. of Prep. ***farij.iw.a***, be consoled e.g. *Majeruhi walifarijiwa na majirani*, the wounded were consoled by the neighbours. Rp. of Prep. ***farij.i.an.a*** (cf *liwaza, tuliza*) (Ar)

farijik.a vi be consoled, be soothed, be comforted. Prep. ***farijik.i.a*** St. ***farijik.ik.a*** Cs. ***farijik.ish.a***

farik.i vi 1. die, pass away, expire, cease to live: *Alifariki dunia papo hapo baada ya kugongwa na gari*, he died instantly after being knocked down by a car. (cf *fa*) 2. part company, etc; depart from, defect: *Alifariki kutoka chama chetu*, he defected from our party. Prep. ***farik.i.a*** St ***farik.ik.a*** Cs. ***farik.ish.a*** Ps. of Prep. ***farik.iw.a*** (cf *tenga, acha*) (Ar)

farikian.a vt be at loggerheads, be at odds, be feuding, be outraged. (cf *farakana*)

farikumu n (n) (naut) a triangular thwart over the gunwales in the bows and stern of a sailing vessel e.g. *mtepe* (cf *fundo, mtendikani*)

Farisayo n (n) a disciple of one of the Jewish religious denominations. (Pers)

farisha n (n) see *mfarisha*

farish.i vt 1. lay out cloth esp on bed. 2. spread out, lay out Prep. ***farish.i.a*** St. ***farish.ik.a*** Ps. ***farish.iw.a***. Rp. ***farish.an.a*** (Ar)

farisi n (n) 1. a good horseback rider: *Katika mapigano ya kishujaa kati ya mafarisi wawili, mmoja aliumia vibaya*, during gallant fighting between two horseback riders, one of them was badly injured. 2. expert, specialist, master: *Yeye ni farisi katika mieleka*, he is an expert in wrestling. (cf *bingwa, stadi*) (Ar)

faroma n (n) see *faruma*

faru (also *kifaru*) n (n) (zool) rhinoceros

faruma n (n) a block on which to put caps after being washed so as to prevent them from shrinking or sometimes losing their shape. (Ar)

farumi n (n) (naut) see *farumu*

farumu (also *farumi*) n (n) 1. (naut) ballast in a vessel; any heavy material used to stabilize a vessel. (cf *shehena, uzito*) 2. weight. 3. cargo. (Ar)

fasaha adj eloquent, articulate, silver-tongued, well-spoken: *Alizungumza lugha fasaha*, he spoke with eloquence. (Ar)

fashini[1] n (n) (naut) 1. a block of wood which is fastened to the stem post as well as a stern post in a vessel such as dhow. 2. the part in front of a dhow in which the ribs meet or are attached.

fashini[2] (also *fesheni*) n (n) vogue; a current style of haircut, mode of dress, etc. (Eng)

fasihi[1] n (n) literature: *Fasihi andishi*, written literature. *Fasihi simulizi*, oral literature. *Fasihi pendwa*, popular literature. *Fasihi mapokeo*, traditional literature.

145

fasihi² *adj* (of language) elegant, proper, excellent. (Ar)

fasiki *n* (ma-) lecher, libertine, rake, roue`, rake, debauchee, harlot; a profligate person, an immoral person: *Mimi siwezi kufanya urafiki na fasiki yule*, I can't befriend that immoral person. (cf *asherati, mzinzi, mzinifu*) (Ar)

fasil.i¹ *vt* 1. interpret, elaborate, elucidate, explicate, explain: *Aliifasili ndoto yangu*, he interpreted my dream. 2. define, translate (cf *tafsiri*) Prep. *fasil.i.a* St.. *fasil.ik.a* Cs. *fasil.ish.a* Ps. *fasil.iw.a* Rp. of Prep. *fasil.i.an.a*. (cf *fafanua, pambanua*) (Ar)

fasil.i² *vt* 1. classify genre, text, etc: *Mwalimu alifasili fasihi katika tanzu tatu*, the teacher classified literature into three genres. 2. cut out a garment: *Mshoni alikifasili kitambaa ili ashone kanzu*, the tailor cut the material in order to make a dress. 3. unravel, unwind, disentangle, solve, resolve: *Aliweza kufasili tatizo lake*, he was able to solve his problem. Prep. *fasil.i.a* St. *fasil.ik.a* Cs. *fasil.ish.a* Ps. of Prep. *fasil.iw.a* Rp. of Prep. *fasil.i.an.a* (cf *tanzua, tatua*) (Ar)

fasili³ *n* (n) 1. genre, style, fashion, brand: *Kumeibuka fasili mpya ya ushairi katika Kiswahili*, a new genre has emerged in Swahili poetry. (cf *utanzu, chipukio*) 2. good condition: *Hana asili wala fasili*, he has neither root nor offshoot i.e. he is in poor condition. (Ar)

fasili⁴ *n* (n) paragraph, verse, text, passage, excerpt: *Aliisoma fasili kwa uangalifu*, he read the text carefully. (cf *para, aya*) (Ar)

fasiri⁵ *n* (n) definition, interpretation, translation. (cf *tafsiri*) (Ar)

fasir.i¹ (also *tafsiri*) *vt, vi* 1. translate; change speech or writing from one language into another: *Aliifasiri riwaya ya Kiingereza kwa Kifaransa*, he translated an English novel into French. (cf *tarjumi*) 2. interpret, elaborate, elucidate: *Siwezi kuifasiri ndoto yako*, I can't interpret your dream. Prep. *fasir.i.a*. St. *fasir.ik.a* Cs. *fasir.ish.a* Ps. of Prep. *fasir.iw.a* Rp. of Prep. *fasir.i.an.a* (cf *fafanua, eleza*) (Ar)

fasiri² *n* (n) comment, remark.

faslu *n* (n) chapter, section, part: *Faslu ya tano ya kitabu*, the fifth chapter of a book (cf *mlango, sura*) (Ar)

fataha *n* (n) the Arabic vowel written on top of an alphabet letter to represent the vowel *a*. (Ar)

fataki *n* (n) 1. cartridge. 2. capgun, crackers, fireworks; a little paper percussion cap, used in times of celebrations, etc. (Ar)

fatani *n* (ma-) liar, cheat, hypocrite, deceiver. (cf *mdhabidhabina, mnafiki*)

fatashi *adj* inquisitive, snoopy, prying curious. (cf *-pelelezi, jasusi*)

fatiha (*alhamdu*) *n* (n) Literally, it means 'an opening one' or a prelude of the first chapter of the Holy Quran also called the 'Surat L-Hand' or the 'Chapter of Praise: *Piga fatiha*, recite the "fatiha" (Ar)

fatiish.a *vt* investigate, pry, enquire, snoop, search for: *Kijana yule anapenda kufatiisha mambo ya watu*, that young man likes to snoop into other people's affairs. Prep. *fatiish.i.a* St. *fatiish.ik.a* Ps. *fatiish.w.a* Rp. *fatiish.an.a* (cf *peleleza, chungua*) (Ar)

fatika¹ (also *fatka*) *n* (n) (*naut*) a piece of sail cloth. (cf *taya*)

fatika² *n* (n) (*med*) hernia. (cf *ngiri*) (Ar)

fatuma *n* (n) (*colloq*) a large stone used by thieves to break houses in order to steal.

fatundu *n* (n) see *fukundi*

fatuwa (also *fetwa*) *n* (n) a religious or judicial sentence or decree pronounced by a *mufti*, a religious scholar. (Ar)

fauka (also *foko*) *adv* (used in the expression) *Fauka ya*, apart from, besides, in addition: *Fauka ya kuwa amenitusi, sasa anataka kuniibia vitu vyangu*, apart from the fact that he has insulted me, he now wants to steal my things. (cf *zaidi ya*) (Ar)

faul.u *vt, vi* succeed, win, accomplish: *Alifaulu vizuri kwenye shindano la kuogelea*, he won the swimming competition quite well. Prep. ***faul.i.a*** St. ***faul.ik.a*** Cs. ***faul.ish.a*** (cf. *fanikiwa, fuzu*) (Ar)

fauwa *conj* see *fahuwa*

fawidh.i *vt* 1. delegate, entrust: *Nilimfawidhi shangazi watoto wangu tuliposafiri*, I entrusted my aunt with the care of my children when we were away. (cf *kabidhi*) 2. delegate power or responsibilities to someone on your behalf; commission: *Rais alifawidhi kwa naibu wake masuala muhimu ya nchi*, the president commissioned his deputy to make decisions on important issues of state. Prep. ***fawidh.i.a*** St. ***fawidh.ik.a*** Cs. ***fawidh.ish.a*** Ps. of Prep. ***fawidh.iw.a***. Rp. of Prep. ***fawidh.i.an.a*** (Ar)

fawitik.a *vi* see *faitika*

fazaa (also *fadhaa*) *n* (*n*) perplexity, confusion, bewilderment, worry, trouble: *Shikwa na fazaa*, be perplexed. *Aliingiwa na fazaa aliposikia kwamba shamba lake lote limeungua*, he was filled with bewilderment when he heard that his whole farm was on fire. (cf *dukuduku, wasiwasi*) (Ar)

fazaik.a (also *fadhaika*) *vi* be perplexed, be bewildered, be confused, be worried: *Nilifazaika nilipopata habari kuwa mama yangu amepondwa na gari*, I became confused when I heard that my mother was knocked down by a car. Prep. ***fadhaik.i.a*** St. ***fadhaik.ik.a*** Cs. ***fadhaik.ish.a*** (cf *papatika, hangaika*) (Ar)

fazaish.a (also *fadhaisha*) *vt* perplex, confuse, startle, baffle, confound: *Alinifazaisha kwa vitendo vyake vya kutukana watu ovyoovyo*, he startled me by his actions of insulting people haphazardly. Prep. ***fazaish.i.a*** St. ***fazaish.ik.a*** Ps. ***fazaish.w.a*** Rp. ***fazaish.an.a***

Februari *n* (*n*) February; the second month of the year. (Eng)

fedha *n* (*n*) 1. silver; a soft whitish precious metal: *Rangi ya fedha*, silver colour. *Sinia ya fedha*, a silver metal tray. 2. money, currency, finance: *Fedha taslimu*, cash money. *Fedha za kigeni*, foreign currency. *Fedha za kukirimu*, entertainment allowance. *Wizara ya fedha*, ministry of finance. (*prov*) *Fedha fedheha*, money is a disgrace. i.e. Money can put you into a very embarassing situation if you crave for it. 3. capital. (Ar)

fedhaluka *n* (*n*) 1. a kind of red bead: *Ushanga wa fedhaluka*, a shiny semi-transparent kind of bead. 2. a kind of red coral. (cf *marijani*) (Ar)

fedheha *n* (*n*) disgrace, shame, dishonour, degradation, scandal: *Ilikuwa fedheha kwa waziri yule kufikishwa mahakamani kwa kosa la rushwa*, it was a disgrace for that minister to be taken to court on charges of corruption. (cf *aibu, kashfa*) (Ar)

fedheh.e (also *fedhehi*) *vt* disgrace, dishonour, shame, degrade, debase: *Ameifedhehe familia yake kwa kuiba*, he has disgraced his family by stealing; his family has been disgraced by his stealing. Prep. ***fedheh.e.a*** St. ***fedheh. ek.a***, be disgraced, be dishonoured e.g. *Alifedheheka na kashfa ile*, he was disgraced by that scandal. Cs. ***fedheh. esh.a***, Ps ***fedheh.ew.a*** be disgraced Rp. ***fedheh.e.an.a*** (cf *aibisha, tweza*) (Ar)

fedhehek.a vi see *fedhehe*

fedhehesh.a vt disgrace sby, humiliate sby; dishonour, besmirch, abase: *Utamfedhehesha kila mmoja ikiwa utaamua kutenda kitu kibaya*, you will disgrace everyone if you decide to do that evil thing. Prep. ***fedhehesh.e.a*** St. ***fedhehesh.ek.a*** Ps. ***fedhehesh.w.a*** Rp. ***fedhehesh.an.a***.

fedheh.i vt see *fedhehe*

fedhuli adj see *fidhuli*

fee adv. see *fefefe*

fefe n (n) (bot) 1. a kind of long perennial grass up to 6 feet tall usu found on black cotton soils and sometimes used as thatching grass. *Hyparrhenia rufa*. 2. long coarse grass; lalang, reed.

fefefe (also fee) adv completely, totally, entirely, outrightly: *Kuanguka tu kutoka kwenye nyumba, kijana akafa fefefe*, after falling from the house, the young man died outrightly. (cf *kabisa*)

feki n (n) fake: *Barua feki*, a fake letter. (Eng)

felefele n (n) (bot) a kind of wild millet or grass used as famine food.

felegi n (n) see *feleji*

feleji (also *felegi*) n (n) steel of superior quality used for making a sword: *Upanga wa feleji*, a long straight double-edged sword. (Pers)

felet.i vt 1. let go, discharge; procure the release of someone after clearing his debt or paying fees: *Nilimfeleti rafiki yangu baada ya kukamatwa na polisi*, I procured the release of my friend after he was arrested by the police. (cf *burai, samehe*) 2. abscond, flee, bolt, elope, escape, run away: *Mfungwa alifeleti kutoka gerezani*, the prisoner escaped from prison. (cf *kimbia, toroka*) (Ar)

fel.i[1] vt, vi fail in a test or an examination: *Alifeli vibaya kwenye mtihani*, he failed badly in the examination. Prep. ***fel.i.a*** St. ***fel.ik.a*** Cs. ***fel.ish.a*** cause to fail e.g. *Usiambatane naye kwa vile anaweza kukufelisha mtihani*, do not associate with him because he can make you fail in the examination Ps. of Cs. ***feli.sh.w.a*** e.g. *Alifelishwa na mwalimu kwenye mtihani*, the teacher made her fail the examination. Rp. of Prep. ***fel.i.an.a***, fail in large numbers e.g. *Wanafunzi wanafeliana tu katika somo la hesabu*, the students fail in large numbers in mathematics. (cf *noa, anguka*) (Eng)

fel.i[2] vt 1. catch a person in a shameful act; catch red-handed: *Nilimfeli kijana yule akifanya mapenzi na mke wa watu*, I caught that young man red-handed flirting with somebody's wife. (cf *fumania, goga*) 2. ridicule, deride, mock, tease: *Usijaribu kunifeli kwa vile mimi ni mtu mzima*, don't ridicule me as I am an adult Prep. ***fel.i.a*** St. ***fel.ik.a*** Cs. ***fel.ish.a*** Ps. of Prep. ***fel.iw.a*** Rp. of Prep. ***fel.i.an.a*** (cf *kebehi*)

feli[3] n (n) see *fali*

feli[4] n (n) misdeed, evil deed, bad act: *Lazima aache feli zake*, he must abandon his evil deeds. *Feli mbaya*, jinx, ill-luck, misfortune (cf *nuhusi, mkosi*)

fenesi n (ma-) (bot) jackfruit; a large heavy fruit with numerous oval seeds, whose nuts are good for eating when boiled or roasted. (Hind)

feni n (ma-) fan; a device used to allow a current of air to move around. (Eng)

ferdausi n (n) see *firdausi*

feri n (n) ferry; boat, hovercraft, etc. that carries people and goods across the sea, etc. (cf *kivuko, pantoni*) (Eng)

feruwili (also *friweli, firiwili*) n (n) (usu in a bicycle, etc.) a device in the rear hub that allows the rear wheel to go on turning when the pedals have stopped; free wheel. (Eng)

feruzi n (n) 1. a semi-precious stone with a greenish blue colour; turquoise. 2. greenish blue colour. (Ar)

fesheni n (n) see *feshini*

fetwa *n* (*n*) see *fatwa*
feuli *n* (*n*) (*naut*) room underneath the poop, used generally to keep cargo or luggage. (cf *banduru, falka*) (Ar)
fezi *n* (*n*) phase, stage: *Mpango ule umetayarishwa katika fezi tatu,* that plan has been arranged in three phases. (Eng)
fi *adv* on, with, by, etc.: *Nane fi nane,* eight times eight. This is usu expressed by *Nane mara Nane.* (cf *mara*) (Ar)
fi.a *vt* 1. die at a particular place: *Alifia Mombasa,* he died in Mombasa. 2. love sby/sth excessively. Prep. *fi.li.a* St. *fi.lik.a* Cs *fi.lish.a*
fich.a vt,vi 1. hide, conceal, veil, shroud, screen, cover up: *Alikificha kitabu changu kwenye mtoto wa meza,* he hid my book in the drawer. *Anaficha ukweli,* he is hiding the truth. 2. conceal; refuse to explain, inform or show: *Anaificha aibu yake,* he is concealing his shame. (*prov*) *Mficha uchi hazai,* he who conceals his nakedness will not bear a child. i.e. he who hides his problems will not get assistance from anyone. Prep. *fich.i.a* St. *fich.ik.a* Cs. *fich.ish.a* Rp. *fich.an.a* Rp. *fich.an.a.* (cf *ondosha, sitiri*)
ficham.a *vi* be in the state of being hidden: *Ua limefichama,* the flower has not blossomed. Prep. *ficham.i.a* St. *ficham.ik.a* Cs. *ficham.ish.a* (cf *jificha*)
fichaman.a *vi* disappear completely; recede from view; vanish from sight: *Niliiona mwanzoni ndege ya kijeshi ikiruka angani lakini sasa imefichamana,* at first, I saw an army plane flying in the sky, but now it has disappeared. Prep. *fichaman.i.a* St. *fichaman.ik.a* Cs. *fichaman.ish.a* (cf *toweka.*)
fichik.a *vi* be in state of hiding; be capable of being hidden. Prep. *fichik.i.a* St. *fichik.ik.a* Cs. *fichik.ish.a*

ficho *n* (*ma-*) 1. concealment, hiding, covering, ensconcing, sanctuary: *Ficho la mwanasiasa kwenye ubalozi limetushangaza,* the politician's sanctuary in the embassy has amazed us. (cf *hifadhi, kimbilio*) 2. cover-up of a scandal, etc.
fichu.a[1] *vt* uncover, reveal, expose, divulge: *Nilimpa siri lakini akaifichua,* I told her a secret but she revealed it. Prep. *fichu.li.a* St. *fichu.k.a* and *fichu.liw.a* Ps. of Prep. *fichu.liw.a* be exposed, be revealed e.g. *Siri yake imefichuliwa,* his secret has been revealed Rp. *fichu.an.a* Rp. of Prep. *fichu.li.an.a* expose each other's secrets e.g *Wanapenda kufichuliana siri zao,* they like to expose each other's secrets. (cf *gubua*)
fichu.a[2] *vt* give a present so as to see a bride or a baby. Prep. *fichu.li.a* St. *fichu.k.a* and *fichu.lik.a* Rp. *fichu.an.a* Rp. of Prep. *fichu.li.an.a*
fichuo *n* (*ma-*) 1. a gift that is given to the bride by the bridegroom after he sees her for the first time after their marriage. 2. a gift that is given to a girl on reaching puberty or boy when he comes out of a circumcision school. 3. exposure, disclosure, revelation, unmasking: *Fichuo la mpango wa kutaka kumwua rais, limewafanya watu kadha wa kadha kukamatwa,* the exposure of the plot to assassinate the president has led to the arrest of a number of people. (cf *funuo*)
fidhuli[1] (also *fedhuli*) *adj* 1. rude, insolent, impolite, discourteous: *Anaweza hata kukukashifu hadharani kwa vile yeye ni mfidhuli,* he can even discredit you in public as he is rude. 2. arrogant, conceited. (cf *safihi*) (Ar)
fidhuli[2] (also *fedhuli*) *n* (*n*) a rude person, an insolent person; reprobate: *Yeye ni fidhuli,* he is a rude person. 2. snob, show-off. (cf *safihi, jeuri*) (Ar)

fidhulik.a vi bluster, strut; be arrogant, be conceited, be insolent, be rude: *Alikuwa akifidhulika mbele za watu*, he was blustering in public. Cs. ***fidhuli.sh.a***, cause to bluster. (cf *takabari*) (Ar)

fid.i vt,vi 1. compensate, ransom; pay ransom for: *Kampuni ilimfidi mfanyakazi wake aliyeumia*, the company compensated its injured worker. 2. assist, help, suit: *Alinipa viatu na vikanifidi*, she gave me shoes and they helped me. Prep. ***fid.i.a*** St. ***fid.ik.a*** Cs. ***fid.ish.a*** Ps. of Prep. ***fid.iw.a*** Rp. of Prep. ***fid.i.an.a*** (cf *faa, tosheleza*) (Ar)

fidi.a[1] vt, vi compensate, offset, recompense

fidia[2] n (n) compensation, ransom, remuneration; money paid as compensation or damages: *Fidia ya mfanyakazi*, the workman's compensation. *Toa fidia*, compensate. (cf *dia*) (Ar)

fidik.a vt cover, shield, shelter; put a covering on: *Alikifidika chakula mezani ili nzi wasiingie*, she covered the food on the table in order to protect it against flies. Prep. ***fidik.i.a*** St. ***fidik.ik.a*** Cs. ***fidik.ish.a*** Ps. ***fidik.w.a*** Rp. ***fidik.an.a*** (cf *funika*.)

fidla n (n) (mus) fiddle, violin. (Eng)

fidla

fido n (n) a stick used for reading palms or seeing in the stars.

fidu.a (also *fudua*) vt 1. uncover, unveil, unmask, unsheathe, unwrap, undress: *Aliwafunika watoto kwa mabedshiti na baadaye akawafidua*, she covered the children with bedsheets and later, she uncovered them. (cf *funua*) 2. unstitch, unseam, unweave, unravel: *Aliishona suruali yangu vibaya lakini baadaye akaamua kuifidua*, he stitched my trousers badly but later he decided to unstitch it. Prep. ***fidu.i.a*** St. ***fidu.k.a*** and ***fidu.lik.a*** Cs. ***fidu.sh.a*** Ps. of Prep. ***fidu.liw.a***. Rp. ***fidu.an.a*** (cf *shona, funua*) 3. used sometimes to mean the act of unsheathing the foreskin of a male organ.

fifi adj 1. inferior, poor, paltry, trifling, gimcrack; possessing little value: *Karafuu fifi zile haziwezi kupata bei nzuri katika soko la dunia*, those poor quality cloves cannot fetch a good price in the world market. (cf *hafifu, duni, ghafi*) 2. weak; tending to lose lustre, originality, etc.; be past its best: *Nilinunua redio yangu miaka kumi iliyopita na sasa imekuwa fifi*, I bought my radio ten years ago and now it is past its best.

fifi.a vi, vt 1. fade, blench, blanch, die out: *Baada ya kulifua shati langu mara nyingi, rangi yake sasa imefifia*, after having washed my shirt many times, it's colour has now faded. 2. become weak, lose strength; pine: *Baada ya kuumwa kwa miezi mingi, sasa amefifia*, after being sick for many months, he has now become weak. Prep. ***fifi.li.a*** St. ***fifi.k.a*** Cs. ***fifi.lish.a*** Ps. ***fifi.w.a***. (cf *konda, dhoofu*)

fifiliz.a vt 1. (*fig*) shrug off, brush aside sth, be inattentive, pretend not to understand or be concerned in an affair: *Nilipokuwa nikimweleza habari, akawa anafifiliza tu*, when I was explaining to her the point, she was just inattentive. 2. cheat for

figa¹

personal benefit usu during counting. *Alikuwa anafifiliza wakati alipokuwa anatuhesabia pesa*, he was cheating when he was counting the money for us. 3. (of colour) dilute, wipe out, cause to fade away. Prep. ***fifiliz.i.a*** St. ***fifiliz.ik.a*** Cs. ***fifiliz.ish.a*** Ps. ***fifiliz.w.a*** Rp. ***fifiliz.an.a*** (cf *danganya, ghilibu*)

figa¹ *n (ma-)* one of the three stones used for supporting a cooking pot over a fire; cooking stone: *Hakuweza kupika vizuri kwa vile figa moja lilikuwa limekosekana*, he could not cook properly because one of the stones was missing.

figa² *n (n)* shape, form: *Figa ya msichana*, the girl's figure. (Eng)

figau (also *figua*) *n (n)* (*naut*) a cooking place in a dhow, etc.

figili *n (n)* (*bot*) a kind of radish whose root and leaves are used as vegetables and eaten alongside food; white radish. (Ar)

figo *n (n)* (*anat*) kidney (cf *nso, buki*)

fihi (also *fii*) *n (n)* jealousy, spite, envy, bitterness, rivalry, discord, squabble, trouble: *Mtu yule anaweza kukuwekea fihi jını yako kama umepata kazi nzuri*, that person can feel jealous of you if you get a good job. (cf *wivu, husuda*) (Ar)

fii *n (n)* see *fihi*

fiili *n (n)* action, act, deed, effort. (cf *kitendo*) (Ar)

fik.a¹ *vi* 1. arrive, come to reach, show up, turn up, get in: *Alifika mapema kwenye kituo cha basi*, he arrived early at the bus station. (cf *wasili*) 2. attend, be present at, go to: *Alifika kwenye mkutano*, he attended the meeting. (cf *hudhuria*) 3. be ready, be in time (for), finally come, finally arrive: *Wakati umefika kwa sisi sote kushirikiana pamoja*, the time has come for all of us to cooperate. (cf *timu, timia*) 4. reach the required point: *Maji yalifika katika kiwango cha halijoto*, the water reached the required temperature. Prep. ***fik.i.a*** St. ***fik.ik.a*** Cs. ***fik.ish.a*** Ps. ***fik.w.a***

fika² *adv.* completely, fully, entirely, totally: *Nilielewa fika hotuba ya waziri*, I understood completely the minister's speech (cf *kabisa*)

fikara *n (n)* see *fikira*

fiki.a *vi* 1. put up; lodge, reside: *Umefikia hoteli gani?* At which hotel have you put up? 2. arrive, reach: *Kitabu kile kilinifikia kwa njia ya posta*, that book reached me through post. Prep. ***fiki.li.a*** St. ***fiki.k.a*** Cs. ***fiki.sh.a*** Ps. ***fiki.w.a*** Rp. ***fiki.an.a*** (cf *wasili*)

fikich.a (also *fikinya*) *vt, vi* 1. rub hard; crumble in the fingers: *Fikicha macho*, rub the eyes 2. husk grain, etc. with the hands; crumble in the hands; rub hard: *Alizifikicha njugu za kukaanga*, he rubbed hard the roasted groundnuts in the hands. Prep. ***fikich.i.a*** St. ***fikich.ik.a*** Cs. ***fikich.ish.a*** Ps. ***fikich.w.a*** Rp. ***fikich.an.a*** (cf *pukusa*)

fikiny.a *vt, vi* see *fikicha*

fikira (also *fikara, fikra* *n (n)* 1. thought, meditation, consideration: *Yeye yumo katika fikira nyingi*, he is deep in thought. (cf *wazo*) 2. idea, suggestion, opinion, view, viewpoint, position: *Alitoa fikira nzuri kwenye mkutano*, he gave good ideas at the meeting. (cf *rai, shauri*) (Ar)

fikir.i (also *fakari*) *vt,vi* 1. think, ponder, meditate, cogitate, consider: *Alifikiri juu ya matatizo ya ulimwengu sana*, he considered world problems seriously. (cf *waza*) 2. think uncertainly; suggest, assume, presume, suppose: *Unafikiri kuwa uliuacha mzigo wako kwenye basi?* Do you think you left your luggage in the bus? (cf *dhani*) Prep. ***fikir.ia*** St. ***fikir.ik.a*** Cs. ***fikir.ish.a*** Ps. ***fikir.iw.a*** Rp. of Prep. ***fikir.i.an.a.*** (Ar)

fikiri.a vt consider, cogitate, think: *Fikiria vibaya*, misjudge. *Fikiria kwa mpango wa mantiki*, ratiocinate. St. *fikiri.k.a* Cs. *fikiri.sh.a* Ps. *fikiri.w.a*

fikirish.a vt preoccupy, absorb. Prep. *fikirish.i.a* St. *fikirish.ik.a*

fikish.a vt 1. deliver, convey, send: *Fikisha salamu zangu kwa mjomba*, send my greetings to my uncle. (cf *wasilisha*) 2. cause to reach, cause to deliver: *Aliufikisha mzigo kwa mwenyewe*, he managed to deliver the luggage to the owner Prep. *fikish.i.a* St. *fikish.ik.a* Ps. *fikish.w.a* Rp. *fikish.an.a*

fikra n (n) see *fikira*

fila n (n) wickedness, iniquity, evil, vice: Used in the expression *Lila na fila havitangamani*, good and evil cannot go together. (cf *ubaya*) (Ar)

filamu n (n) 1. camera film. 2. movie, film; moving picture, motion picture. (Eng)

fileti n (n) fillet (*sarara, steki*) (Eng)

filhali adv see *filihali*

filifili¹ n (n) carpenter's square.

filifili² n (n)(*bot*) spices of different kinds of pepper. (Ar)

filihali (also *filhali*) adv immediately, instantly, at once, forthwith, without delay: *Walitaka kumfukuza kazi filihali*, they wanted to sack him immediately. (cf *ajilani, hapohapo*) (Ar)

filimbi (also *firimbi*) n (n) flute, whistle. (cf *kipenga, kikorombwe*)

filis.i vt 1. make bankrupt; impoverish, pauperize: *Walimfilisi baada ya kuuza hisa zake zote katika kampuni*, they made him bankrupt after selling all his shares in the company. 2. sell up a person's goods for debt, distrain upon goods of someone; bankrupt: *Aliwafilisi baada ya kuuza bidhaa zao zote kutokana na madeni mbalimbali*, he bankrupted them after selling all their goods due to indebtedness. 3. win a person's money during gambling,
card-playing, etc.: *Alimfilisi rafiki yake baada ya kumshinda kwenye mchezo wa kamari*, he bankrupted his friend after defeating him in gambling. Prep. *filis.i.a* St. *filis.ik.a* Cs *filis.ish.a* Ps. of Prep. *filis.iw.a* Rp. of Prep. *filis.i.an.a*. (Ar)

filisik.a vi be bankrupt, be impoverished. Prep. *filisik.i.a* St. *filisik.ik.a* Cs. *filisik.ish.a* (cf *parama*)

filolojia n (n) philology; the scientific analysis of written records and literary texts. (Eng)

filosofia n (n) philosophy (cf *falsafa*) (Gr)

fimbi n (n) (*zool*) a kind of bird with a dusky red bill and blackish-brown underparts, wings and a tail as well as a white breast and abdomen; crowned hornbill. *Tockus alborminatus* (cf *kwembe*)

fimbo n (n) 1. stick, staff, cane, wand, rode: *Alimpiga mtoto wake kwa fimbo*, he beat his child with a stick. (*prov*) *Fimbo ya mbali haiui nyoka*, a distant stick does not kill a snake i.e. a distant weapon does not have any impact on something. 2. walking-stick. (cf *asaa, mkongojo*)

fing.a¹ vt protect by charm as in the case of a house against thieves, against someone's jealousy, etc.: *Mganga aliwapa dawa ya kujifinga dhidi ya uhasidi*, the traditional doctor gave them some medicine to protect themselves against jealousy. Prep. *fing.i.a* St. *fing.ik.a* Cs *fing.ish.a* Ps. *fing.w.a* Rp. *fing.an.a* (cf *kaga*)

fing.a² vt put a heavy object on a light one so as to prevent it from moving. Prep. *fing.i.a* St. *fing.ik.a* Cs. *fing.ish.a* Ps. *fing.w.a* Rp. *fing.an.a*

finge n (n) obstruction, impediment. (cf *kikwazo, pingamizi*)

finginy.a (also *pinginya, vinginya*) vi 1. writhe, squirm, wiggle, wriggle, shimmy; move from side to side with rapid short movements: *Nilimwona*

fingirik.a   **fir.a²**   **F**

nyoka akijifinginya, I saw a snake wriggling. (cf *finginyika, nyekenya, jinyonga*) 2. wiggle, wriggle; shake the hips and backside during dancing or walking: *Mwanamke alikuwa akijifinginya kwenye ngoma*, the woman was shaking her hips during dancing. Prep. *finginy.i.a* St. *finginy.ik.a* Cs *finginy.ish.a* Ps *finginy.w.a* Rp. *finginy.an.a*

fingirik.a *vi* roll round, swirl, twirl, twiddle; go round and round like a grinding-stone: *Alianguka kwenye kilima huku akifingirika*, he fell on the hill rolling round and round. Prep. *fingirik.i.a* St. *fingirik.ik.a* Cs *fingirik.ish.a* (cf *bingiria, piringita*)

fingo *n (mw-)* charm to prevent thieves going into a house; charm against evil, etc, *Aluweku fingo katika mlango wa nyumba yake ili aepukane na ubaya*, she placed a charm to protect herself against evil. *Linda kwa fingo*, protect with charm against evil. (cf *kago, kafara*)

finik.a *vt* see *funika*

finingi *n* (n) (*zool*) gizzard; the second stomach of a bird. (cf *firigisi.*)

finy.a *vt* 1. pinch, nip, vellicate, twitch; press with the fingers or nails: *Alinifinya na mimi nikatoka damu kidogo*, he pinched me and I bled a little. (cf. *minya.*) 2. squeeze, press, compress, constrict, pinch; hold as in a vice: *Viatu vipya hivi vinanifinya*, these new shoes pinch me. Prep. *finy.i.a* St. *finy.ik.a* Cs *finy.ish.a* Ps *finy.w.a* Rp. *finy.an.a* (cf *bana.*) 3. (*idm*) *Finya uso*, scowl, grimace, frown, glower, glare; look daggers. (cf *kasirika, ghadhibika*)

finya.a *vi* 1. pucker, shrivel, wrinkle, crumple, crinkle, draw up; gather into wrinkles, pine away: *Uso wa mtu yule umefinyaa kwa vile ni mzee*, that person's face has wrinkled because of old age. 2. be stunted in growth; be dwarfed. (cf *via, sinyaa, dumaa*) Prep. *finya.i.a* St. *finya.ik.a* Cs. *finya.ish.a* Ps. *finya.w.a* (cf *konda, sinyaa*)

finyag.a *vt* crush/pound sth with your feet. Ps. of Prep. *finyag.i.a* Cs. *finyag.ish.a* Ps. *finyag.iw.a* Rp. *finyag.an.a*

finyang.a¹ *vt* 1. make pottery; knead clay with feet or hands to form a firm smooth paste; make vessels of clay: *Alivifinyanga vyungu*, he kneaded the pots. (cf *burunga, viringa*) 2. knead, mould; press and stretch watery stuff into a particular form or shape: *Aliifinyanga tonge ya wali na kuitia kinywani*, she moulded a lump of rice and stuffed it into his mouth. Prep. *finyang.i.a* St. *finyang.ik.a* Cs. *finyang.ish.a* Ps. *finyang.w.a*

finyang.a² *vt* hit hard, strike, thwack, smite: *Walimfinyanga vibaya*, they hit him hard. Prep. *finyang.i.a* St. *finyang.ik.a* Cs. *finyang.ish.a* Ps. *finyang.w.a*, be hit hard. (cf *tubisha, kong'ota*)

finyiliz.a *vt, vi* put/sit in a narrow space. Prep. *finyiliz.i.a* St. *finyiliz.ik.a* Cs. *finyiliz.ish.a* Ps. *finyiliz.w.a* (cf *jekenyeza*)

finyo *n* (*ma-*) pinch, pinching, nip: *Finyo la kucha kwenye paja*, a nail's pinch on the thigh.

finyu *adj* narrow, slender, constricted, slim, gracile: *Njia finyu*, a narrow road. *Maana finyu*, a narrow meaning. *Mtazamo finyu*, narrow-minded outlook.

fio *n* (n) bit (of a horse, donkey, etc); cantle. (cf *hatamu, lijamu, zimamu*)

fir.a¹ *vt* sodomize sby or an animal; commit sodomy. Prep. *fir.i.a* St. *fir.ik.a* Cs. *fir.ish.a* Ps. *fir.w.a* Rp. *fir.an.a* (cf *lawiti, kaza*)

fira² (also *firi*) *n* (n) (*zool*) black necked spitting cobra; a usu blackish cobra,

F firaka   fisi

which has the ability to discharge well- directed twin jets of venom into the eye of an aggressor. *Naja nigricollis.* (cf *swila, koboko-mate*)

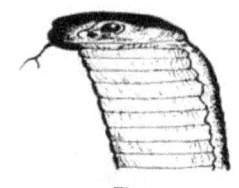

Fira

firaka *n* (*n*) (*anat*) penis (cf *uume, uboo, dhakari, mboo*) (Ar)

firangi *n* (*n*) (*med*) measles (cf *shurua, ukambi*)

firanji *n* (*n*) (*med*) yaws; an infectious tropical disease caused by spirochete. (cf *buba*)

firari[1] *n* (*n*) a victim of sodomy; a passive agent in sodomy; sby who is sodomized.

firari[2] *adv* hurriedly, quickly, swiftly. (cf *upesi, haraka*)

firar.i[3] *vt* (*naut*) serve a rope in a vessel. Prep. *firar.i.a* St. *firar.ik.a* Cs. *firar.ish.a* Ps. of Prep. *firar.iw.a* Rp. of Prep. *firar.i.an.a*

firashi *n* (*n*) see *mfarisha*

Firauni *n* (*n*) 1. Pharaoh; the title of ancient Egyptian rulers. 2. (*fig*) an evil person, a wicked person; reprobate: *Yule ni firauni na ndiyo maana watu wanamkwepa*, he is an evil person and that is why, people avoid him. (*prov*) *Ukistaajabu ya Musa, utayaona ya Firauni*, if you are astonished at Moses's deeds, you will be more astonished at Pharaoh's i.e. if you fear a lesser evil, you may see a worser one. (Ar)

firdausi (also *ferdausi*) *n* (*n*) (in Islam) the best place in heaven; the best abode of God. (cf *pepo, janna*) (Pers and Ar)

firi *n* (*n*) see *fira*[2]

firid.i *vi* be aromatic; smell nice. Prep. *firid.i.a* St. *firid.ik.a* Cs *firid.ish.a* (Ar)

firigis.a *vt, vi* 1. roll sby/sth on the ground forward and backward: *Alimfirigisa kwenye manyasi*, he rolled him over on the grass. 2. dirty oneself with mud, sand, clay, etc.: *Watoto walikuwa wakijifirigisa matopeni*, the children were making themselves dirty with mud. 3. beat someone; hit someone; *Walimfirigisa*, they hit him. Prep. *firigis.i.a* St. *firigis.ik.a* Cs. *firigis.ish.a* Ps. *firigis.w.a* Rp. *firigis.an.a*.

firigisi *n* (*n*) (*anat*) gizzard. (cf *firingi*) (Ar)

firikombe *n* (*n*) see *furukombe*

firimbi *n* (*n*) see *filimbi*

fisadi *n* (*n*) 1. lecher, libertine, rake, rogue; an immoral person: *Watu hawampendi fisadi yule*, people don't like that lecher. (cf *guberi, mwovu*) 2. firebrand, incendiary, rabble-rouser: *Fisadi aliwagombanisha marafiki wawili*, the firebrand caused two friends to quarrel. (cf *mfitini, fatani*) 3. a destructive person, a malicious person; reprobate: *Yeye ni fisadi kwa sababu alikwenda kuchoma nyumba ya jirani yake*, he is a destructive person because he torched his neighbour's house. 4. (used esp in Kenya) a corruptible person; *Fisadi papa*, hugely corrupt person. (cf *mharibifu*) (Ar)

fish.a *vt* 1. kill, cause death (cf *ua*) 2. discourage: *Kauli ya kufisha*, discouraging statement. 3. quench Prep. *fish.i.a* St. *fish.ik.a* Ps. *fish.w.a* Rp *fish.an.a*

fisi *n* (*n*) 1. (*zool*) hyena: *Fisi madoa*, spotted hyena. *Fisi miraba*, stripped hyena. (cf *bakaya, shumundwa*) 2. (*syn*) a cunning person: *Yeye ni fisi*, he is cunning. *Fisi za fisi*, be craving for sth that you can't achieve.

154

fisid.i vt 1. destroy, ruin, misuse, misspend: *Alirithi pesa nyingi lakini akazifisidi zote,* he inherited a lot of money but he misused all of it. (cf *badhiri, haribu*) 2. instigate, incite, foment, brew, fire up; stir a quarrel: *Aliwafisidi majirani zake wawili na hatimaye kuwafarakisha,* he instigated a quarrel between his two neighbours and ultimately caused them to part. Prep. *fisid.i.a* St. *fisid.ik.a* Cs. *fisid.ish.a* Ps. of Prep. *fisid.iw.a* Rp. of Prep. *fisid.i.an.a* (cf *chochea, fitini*) (Ar)

fisimaji n (n) (zool) otter; a swimming fish-eating animal with beautiful thick brown fur.

fitina[1] n (n) intrigue, calumny, discord, animosity, hostility. *Anapenda kuleta fitina kati ya rafiki zake,* he likes to cause hositility amongst his friends. (cf *uadui, chuki*) (Ar)

fitina[2] n (n) inciter, firebrand, incendiary (cf *mgombanishi, mchochezi*) (Ar)

fitin.i (also *fitinisha*) vt cause discord, bring disharmony; play one person off against the other: *Aliwafitini ndugu wawili,* he played one brother off against the other. Prep. *fitin.i.a* St. *fitin.ik.a* Cs. *fitin.ish.a* stir up mischief, make trouble e.g. *Usijaribu kufitinisha watu,* don't stir up conflicts between people. Ps. of Prep. *fitin.iw.a* Rp. of Prep. *fitin.i.an.a* (cf *gombanisha, tetanisha*) (Ar)

fitinish.a vt see *fitini.* Prep *fitinish.i.a* St. *fitinish.ik.a* Ps. *fitinish.w.a* Rp. *fitinish.an.a*

fitiri (also *fitri*) n (n) (in Islam) alms given by Muslims to the poor and needy people towards the end of fasting of the month of Ramadan or just before the prayers marking the end of that fasting. (Ar)

fitri n (n) see *fitiri*

fiw.a vi see *fa*

fiwi n (n) (*bot*) lima bean; a variety of bean that comes from a tree that has pinkish-purple or yellowish-white flowers and broad pods. (cf *njegere*)

fizikia n (n) physics: *Fizikia ya vitendo,* practical physics.

flamingo n (n) (zool) flamingo (cf *korongo*)

flamingo

flotila n (n) 1. dockyard, shipyard. 2. pontoon. (Eng)

foda n (n) fodder, provender; dry food for livestock. (Eng)

fofofo adv (used to emphasize the state while someone is asleep or dead): *Amekufa fofofo,* he is absolutely dead. *Amelala fofofo,* he has slept like a log,

fofomo.a vt boil over; flow over the sides of a container in boiling: *Mwanamke alikifofomoa chakula wakati wa kupika mhongo,* the woman boiled over the food when she was cooking cassava. Prep. *fofomo.le.a* St. *fofomo.k.a* Cs. *fofomo.lesh.a* Ps. of Prep *fofomo.lew.a* (cf *fufurisha*)

fok.a vi 1. rise as in the case of milk when it is overboiling; soar, shoot up, swell: *Maziwa kwenye birika yalikuwa yanafoka yalipochemka,* the milk in the kettle was swelling as it boiled over. (cf *bubujika, miminika*) 2. spurt out as in the case of water from a broken pipe or a holed canoe; squirt, gush, spout: *Maji yalikuwa yanafoka*

F fokasi

kutoka kwenye bomba lililopasuka, the water was squirting from the broken pipe. 3. rave, fulminate, rant, bluster, thunder: *Alinifokea hadharani*, he raved at me in public. Prep. ***fok.e.a***, Cs. ***fok.esh.a*** Ps. ***fok.w.a*** Ps. of Prep. ***fok.ew.a*** Rp. of Prep.. ***foke.an.a*** (cf *ghadhibika, hamaki*)

fokasi *n* (*n*) focus (Eng)

foke.a *vt* rave at, rage at: *Alinifokea burebure*, he raved at me for nothing. Prep. ***foke.le.a*** St. ***foke.k.a*** Cs. ***foke.sh.a*** Ps. ***foke.w.a*** Rp. ***foke.an.a***

foko[1] *adv* see *fauka*

foko[2] *adv* to the brim, chokeful, filled to the top: *Nilijaza maji foko kwenye ndoo*, I filled the bucket with water to the brim. (cf *tele, fukuchi*)

foko[3] *n* (*n*) forklift, forklift truck; a small vehicle used for lifting and lowering heavy goods. (Eng)

fola *n* (*n*) a gift given by a person who holds a baby for the first time.

foleni *n* (*n*) queue, row; line of persons: *Piga foleni*, line up. *Niliona foleni ndefu ya watu wakinunua mchele*, I saw a long queue of people buying rice. (cf *mistari, msururu, mlolongo*)

folio *n* (*n*) (*com*) folio (Eng)

foliti (also *foriti*) *n* (*n*) a children's game of chasing among themselves; tag, chase.

fomaika *n* (*n*) formica (Eng)

fomu[1] *n* (*n*) a printed form; a paper with spaces in it to answer questions and give other relevant information: *Fomu za kuingia shule*, admission forms to schools. *Fomu za kuombea kazi*, application forms. *Jaza fomu*, fill out a form. *Fomu za tenda*, tender forms. (Eng)

fomu[2] *n* (*n*) see *kidato*

fomu[3] *n* (*n*) condition, shape: *Mchezaji yumo katika fomu nzuri*, the player is in good shape. (Eng)

fomu[4] *n* (*n*) a long wooden seat usu without a back; bench, form.

fondogoa *n* (*n*) see *fondogoo*

fondogoo (also *fondogoa*) *n* (*n*) 1. the smell of mould. 2. the smell of fermenting flour. (cf *uvundo*)

fonetiki *n* (*n*) phonetics: *Fonetiki masikizi*,auditory phonetics. *Fonetiki matamshi*, articulatory phonetics. *Fonetiki majaribio*, instrumental phonetics, *Fonetiki maabara*, laboratory phonetics, experimental phonetics. (Eng)

foni *n* (*n*) (*phon*) phone; the smallest segment of sound in a stream of speech. (Eng)

fonimu *n* (*n*) (*phon*) phoneme; any one of the smallest distinctive speech sounds in a language that brings a change of meaning between words. For example, the 'p' in *pika* 'cook' and 'f' in *fika* 'arrive' represent two different phonemes. *Fonimu ambatani*, compound phoneme. *Fonimu kipandesauti*, segmental phoneme. *Fonimu visawe*, diagraph. (cf *kitamkwa*) (Eng)

fonolojia *n* (*n*) (*phon*) phonology; a branch of linguistics which studies the sound systems of a language: *Fonolojia arudhi*, prosodic phonology. *Fonolojia zalishi*, generative phonology. (Eng)

fonti *n* (*n*) (in Christianity) font; a basin for holy water in a church (Eng)

foo *adv*. see *fofofo*

fora[1] *n* (*n*) success, victory, win: *Tia fora, excel*. e.g. *Alitia fora kwenye mashindano ya kuogelea*, he excelled in the swimming competition.

fora[2] *adv* exceedingly, extremely, very: *Mchezaji wetu wa mbele alitia fora*, our forward player was outstanding. (Ar)

foriti see *foliti*

formali *n* (*n*) see *foromali*

forodha *n* (*n*) 1. customs office, customs house: *Idara ya forodha*, customs department. 2. Normally, the word *forodhani* is commonly used to refer to places where goods are unladen from ships, etc; harbour, port: *Alikwenda forodhani kupokea mizigo yake*, he

foromali went to the harbour to collect his cargo. (cf *bandari*) (Ar)

foromali (also *formali*) *n* (*n*) (*naut*) main yard of a ship, dhow, etc. (Ar)

foronya *n* (*n*) pillow case, cushion cover: *Foronya ya kiti*, antimacassar. (Port)

forosadi (also *fursadi*) *n* (*n*) (*bot*) mulberry; the edible fruit of mulberry tree (*Morus alba*), which is sweet, pleasant flavoured and blackish resembling the fruit of a jujube-tree. (Ar)

forot.a *vi, vt* 1. oversleep; sleep past the intended time for waking up: *Kwa vile alichoka sana jana, aliuforota usingizi*, since he was very tired yesterday, he overslept. 2. snore in one's sleep: *Akilala, huforota*, if he sleeps, he snores. Prep. *forot.e.a* St. *forot.ek.a* Cs. *forot.esh.a* (cf *koroma, korota*)

fosi *n* (*n*) force, energy, strength: *Walitumia fosi kuuvunja mlango*, they used force to break the door. (cf *nguvu, mabavu*) (Eng)

foto *n* (*n*) photograph (Eng)

foto.a *vt* photograph; take a picture of. Prep. *foto.le.a* St. *foto.k.a* Cs. *foto.lesh.a* Ps. of Prep *foto.lew.a* Rp. of Prep *foto.le.an.a*

fotografia *n* (*n*) photography (Eng)

fotostati *n* (*n*) photostat (Eng)

fowadi *n* (*n*) (in sports) a forward player; one of the attacking players in a team: *Fowadi laini*, forward line. (Eng)

frasila *n* (*n*) see *farasila*

fremu *n* (*n*) 1. frame; a frame for fitting or holding a picture. 2. the main support of which sth is built and that gives the thing its shape. *Fremu ya baiskeli*, bicycle frame. *Fremu ya dirisha*, window frame. 3. (*syn*) a thin emaciated person. (Eng)

friji *n* (*ma*-) fridge, refrigerator (cf *jokofu, jirafu*) (Eng)

frikiki *n* (*n*) (in football, etc.) free kick: *Mchezaji alipiga frikiki*, the player took a free kick. (Eng)

friweli *n* (*n*) see *feruwili*

friza *n* (*n*) deep freezer (Eng)

fu *interj* see *bu*

fu.a[1] *vt* forge, beat on, hammer out, strike: *Alifua chuma*, he forged an iron. *Alifua fedha*, he forged silver. *Alifua shaba*, he forged brass. *Alifua jembe*, he forged a hoe-blade. Prep. *fu.li.a* St. *fu.lik.a* e.g. *Madini yanafulika*, the metal can be forged. Cs. *fu.lish.a* and Ps. *fu.liz.a* Ps. of Prep *fu.liw.a*, be forged e.g. *Chuma kilifuliwa*, the iron was forged. Rp. of Prep. *fu.li.an.a*

fu.a[2] *vt, vi* 1. wash clothes by means of a soap and water usu on a board or stone: *Hufua nguo zake kila Jumapili*, he washes his clothes every Sunday. 2. (*idms*) *Fua tanga*, wash corpse's clothes. *Fua kisima*, clean the well by removing the dirty water. Prep. *fu.li.a*, wash for. St. *fu.lik.a*, be washable Cs. *fu.lish.a* and *fu.liz.a* Ps. of Prep. *fu.liw.a* Rp. of Prep. *fu.li.an.a*

fu.a[3] *vt* husk coconuts by dashing them on a pointed stake: *Mfanyakazi alizifua nazi zote*, the worker husked all the coconuts on a pointed stake. Prep. *fu.li.a* St. *fu.lik.a* Cs. *fu.lish.a* Ps. of Prep. *fu.liw.a* Rp. of Prep. *fu.li.an.a*

fu.a[4] *vt* (*idms*) *Fua dafu*, manage, succeed: e.g. *Alishindana na mimi katika mbio za mita 100 lakini hakufua dafu kwangu*, he ran against me in the 100 metres race, but he could not beat me. *Fua maji*, 1. bail water out of a vessel e.g. canoe, dhow, etc. 2. wipe out water that has spilt by using a rag, sack, etc.

fua[5] *n* (*n*) 1. a shallow wooden bowl for hand washing or dishing up food. 2. a round wooden tray with raised rim used for washing clothes

fua[6] *n* (*n*) a kind of coffee-coloured substance found in the roots of trees, used for dyeing plaited leaf-stripes of the wild date palm.

fuadi *n* (*n*) 1. heart (cf *moyo*) 2. (*fig*)

darling, sweet, honey, sweetheart. (cf *habibi*) (Ar)

fuam.a *vi* see *furama*. Prep. ***fuam.i.a*** St. ***fuam.ik.a*** Cs. ***fuam.ish.a*** and ***fuam.iz.a*** Ps. of Prep. ***fuam.i.w.a*** Rp. of Prep. ***fuam.i.an.a***

fuanda *n* (*n*) (*zool*) a kind of shark-like fish of the *Rhinobatidae* family with an elongated body and stout tail and which is found in all warm to cool continental seas; guitar fish

fuas.a *vt* 1. imitate, copy, emulate; follow as an example: *Usifuase tabia zake*, don't follow his habits. (cf *iga*) 2. follow; walk behind, go after: *Alimfuasa mpaka shuleni*, he followed her to school. Prep. ***fuas.i.a*** St. ***fuas.ik.a*** Cs. ***fuas.ish.a*** Ps. ***fuas.w.a*** Rp. ***fuas.an.a*** (cf *andamana*)

fuat.a *vt, vi* 1. follow, go after, go behind, walk behind, tread behind: *Mwanangu alinifuata sokoni kununua vitu*, my child followed me to the market to buy things. (cf *andama*) 2. copy, imitate, follow: *Amefuata tabia ya mjomba wake*, he is imitating the habits of his uncle. (cf *iga*) 3. obey, observe, comply, respect: *Amewafuata sana wazee wake kwa vile anakubali kila anachoamrishwa*, he obeys very much his parents with whatever he is being told. 4. (*idms*) *Fuata nyayo*, follow in the footsteps e.g. *Kijana yule anafuata nyayo za wazee wake*, that young man is following the footsteps of his parents. *Fuata sheria*, abide by the law; comply with the law: observe the law e.g. *Jaji anafuata sheria*, the judge is observing the law. 5. go side by side, be concomitant. (*provs*) *Bendera hufuata upepo*, a flag follows the wind i.e. a person is obliged to follow the trend of events according to the prevailing circumstances. *Mwana hufuata kisogo cha nina*, a child follows the back of the head of his mother i.e. a child follows in the footsteps of his mother. *Maji hufuata mkondo*, water follows current, i.e. a person follows the steps or examples of his colleagues. *Fuata nyuki ule asali*, follow the bees so that you may eat honey. i.e. follow good or wise people so that you may gain from them.

fuatan.a *vt* go with sby; accompany sby: *Nilifuatana naye mpaka sokoni*, I went with him to the market. (cf *ongozana*)

fuatano *n* (*ma-*) following, succession: *Mafuatano ya sauti*, melody, tune.

fuati.a *vt, vi* pursue, follow up, go after: *Lazima tulifuatilie suala lile*, we must pursue that issue. Prep. ***fuati.li.a*** St. ***fuati.k.a*** Cs. ***fuati.sh.a*** Ps. ***fuati.w.a*** Rp. of Prep. ***fuati.li.an.a***

fuatili.a *vt, vi* 1. follow up, pursue *Amelifuatilia ombi lake la kutafuta kazi*, he has made a follow-up of his application for employment. 2. investigate, probe. St. ***fuatili.k.a***, be followed up. Cs. ***fuatili.sh.a*** Ps. ***fuatili.w.a***, Rp. ***fuatili.an.a*** (cf *chunguza*)

fuatish.a *vt* 1. trace a drawing, line or letters; make a copy 2. imitate, emulate. Prep. ***fuatish.i.a*** St. ***fuatish.ik.a*** Ps. ***fuatish.w.a*** Rp. ***fuatish.an.a***

fuatundu *n* (*n*) see *fukundi*

fuawe[1] *n* (*n*) anvil; an iron or steel block which metal objects are hammered into shapes.

fuawe[2] *n* (*n*)(*anat*) incus; a small anvil-shaped bone in the middle ear.

fucham.a *vt, vi* 1. hide, conceal, veil, shroud: *Alivifuchama viatu vyangu nilivyokuwa nikivitafuta*, he hid my shoes which I was looking for. (cf *ficha*) 2. embrace sth as when a husband hugs his wife or when a hen lies on her chicks: *Mke alimfuchama mumewe*, the wife embraced her husband. *Kuku alikuwa ameyafuchama mayai yake*, the hen was incubating her eggs. Prep. ***fucham.i.a*** St. ***fucham.***

fuchu.a

ik.a Cs. ***fucham.ish.a*** Ps of Prep ***fucham.iw.a***

fuchu.a *vt* pluck out hair, feathers, wool, etc.: deplume, displume, denude, strip bare: *Niliyafuchua manyoya ya kuku wangu,* I plucked the feathers of my hen. Prep. ***fuchu.li.a,*** St. ***fuchu.lik.a*** and ***fuchu.k.a*** Cs. ***fuchu.sh.a*** Ps. of Prep. ***fuchu.liw.a*** Rp. ***fuchu.an.a*** (cf *nyonyoa*)

fudifudi (also *fulifuli, kifudifudi*) *adv* on the face; with face downwards: *Nililala kifudifudi,* I slept face downwards.

fudikiz.a[1] *vt* (also *funikiza*) invert, transpose; turn upside down, turn topsy-turvy, turn turtle, reverse position of: *Alilifudikiza bakuli,* he inverted the bowl, Prep. ***fudikiz.i.a*** St. ***fudikiz.ik.a*** Ps. ***fudikiz.w.a,*** be inverted e.g. *Kikombe kilifudikizwa,* the cup was inverted. Rp. **fudikiz.an.a** (cf *pindua*)

fudikiz.a[2] *vt* spread a scent; diffuse a scent: *Manukato ya msichana mrembo yalifudikiza alipopita hapa,* the scent of the beautiful girl spread out when she passed here. Prep. ***fudikiz.i.a*** St. ***fudikiz.ik.a*** Ps. ***fudikiz.w.a*** Rp. **fudikiz.an.a** (cf *hinikiza*)

fudo *n* (*n*) 1. a container holding 4 kilograms of sth like grain. 2. a bag from tree fibres holding more than 1 kilogram.

fudu *n* (*ma-*) (*anat*) an uncircumcized penis.

fudu.a *vi* see *fidua*

fufu *n* (*n*) see *fuu*

fufu.a *vt, vi* 1. resurrect, resuscitate, reanimate; raise from the dead: *Mungu atawafufua viumbe vyote,* God will resurrect all creatures. (cf *baathi, huisha*) 2. restore, revive, enliven, reactivate: *Ingawa timu yetu ya mpira imekufa, lakini tutajaribu kuifufua,* even though our football team is now dormant, we will try to revive it. *Serikali inataka kufufua uchumi*

fufuta[2]

wake, the government wants to revive its economy. *Fufua desturi,* restore traditions. Prep. ***fufu.li.a*** St. ***fufu.k.a*** Cs. ***fufu.sh.a*** Ps. of Prep. ***fufu.liw.a*** Rp. ***fufu.an.a*** (cf *rudisha*)

fufuk.a *vi* 1. come to life again be resurrected: *Binaadamu wote watafufuka,* all humanbeings will be resurrected 2. (*fig*) resurface: *Mgogoro wa ardhi umefufuka tena katika eneo lao,* land dispute has resurfaced in their area. Prep. ***fufuk.i.a*** St. ***fufuk.ik.a*** Cs. ***fufuk.ish.a***

fufuma.a *vi* 1. be dumbfounded, be nonplussed, be perplexed, be astonished: *Alifufumaa aliposikia kwamba mwanawe ametiwa korokoroni,* she was dumbfounded when she heard that her son had been sent to prison. 2. cower, cringe, crouch, quail; lie prone, fall on one's knees: *Alifufumaa kwa baridi,* he cowered because of the cold. Prep. ***fufuma.li.a*** St. ***fufuma.k.a*** Cs. ***fufuma.z.a*** and ***fufuma.sh.a*** (cf *jikunja, datama, jikunyata*)

fufumavu *adj* dejected, sulky, dull, cheerless: *Mtu fufumavu,* a cheerless person; splenetic, sourpuss.

fufurik.a (also *fufuka*) *vi* (of liquids) overflow because of overboiling: *Chai ilifufurika mekoni,* the tea overflowed on the stove. Prep. ***fufurik.i.a*** St. ***fufurik.ik.a*** Cs. ***fufur.ish.a,*** cause to overflow. (cf *fofomoka, mwagika, mwaika*)

fufut.a[1] *vt* hit hard, beat severely: *Mzee alimfufuta bintiye kutokana na ukosefu wa nidhamu,* the parent beat his daughter severely for misconduct. Prep. ***fufut.i.a*** St. ***fufut.ik.a*** Cs. ***fufut.ish.a*** Ps. ***fufut.w.a*** Rp. ***fufut.an.a*** (cf *kung'uta, bumuta*)

fufuta[2] *n* (*ma-*) blow, hit, slap, thwack, smack: *Tulilisikia fufuta la mwanafunzi,* we heard the student's slap. (cf *buta*)

fufutende *adj* tepid, lukewarm, summery, balmy, blood-warm: *Maji haya ni fufutende*, this water is lukewarm.

fufuwele *n* (n) a white coral rock which is in the intermediate stage between coral and rock; soft coral rock. (cf *tumbawe, chawe*)

fug.a *vt* 1. domesticate; breed, tame animals, raise animals, rear animals: *Fuga kuku*, raise chickens. *Fuga mbuzi*, raise goats. *Fuga ng'ombe*, raise cattle. 2. let sth or a situation to continue: *Fuga nywele*, keep long hair. *Fuga nguvu*, relax. *Fuga ndevu*, keep a beard. *Fuga ndani*, zero grazing. *Fuga nguvu*, relax, rest. *Fuga majani*, leave all the grass for special use. *Fuga maradhi*, remain uncured e.g. *Alifuga maradhi kwa muda mrefu na baadaye akafa*, he remained uncured for a long time and later died. Prep. *fug.i.a* St.. *fug.ik.a* Cs. *fug.ish.a* Ps. *fug.w.a* Rp. *fug.an.a*

fugo *n* (*ma-*) breeding, domestication, rearing: *Fugo la batamzinga*, the breeding of turkeys.

fuj.a *vt, vi* 1. spoil, ruin, destroy, wreck: *Aliifuja mipango yetu*, he wrecked our plans. (cf *haribu*) 2. squander, misuse, misspend: *Akipewa pesa kutumia, kijana yule huzifuja*, if he is given money to spend, that young man misuses it. Prep. *fuj.i.a* St. *fuj.ik.a* Cs. *fuj.ish.a* Ps. *fuj.w.a* Rp. *fuj.an.a* Rp. of Prep. *fuj.i.an.a* (cf *badhiri*)

fujo *n* (n) 1. disorder, riot, chaos, unrest, disturbance, tumult: *Alifanya fujo dukani na polisi ikamkamata baadaye*, he caused chaos at the shop and the police arrested him later on. (cf *ghasia, sokomoko*) 2. mess, disorderliness, disarrangement, mix-up: *Kazi ya fujo*, messy work.

fuk.a¹ *vi, vt* emit smoke; give out smoke: *Kuni zile zinafuka moshi*, those sticks of firewood emit smoke. Prep. *fuk.i.a* St. *fuk.ik.a* Cs. *fuk.iz.a* and *fuk.ish.a*, cause to give out smoke, fumigate, cense, burn with incense e.g. *Walimfukiza maiti kwa udi*, they fumigated the corpse with aloe-wood. *Alinifukiza udi*, she fumigated me with aloe wood Ps. *fuk.w.a*

fuka² *n* (n) a thin kind of gruel with ingredients of rice, sugar, honey, black pepper, ginger, cardamon, etc which is given to a woman after her delivery, supposedly to clean her abdomen.

fuka.a *vi* (of colour, etc) 1. fade, blanch; be worn-out, be corroded, be degenerated, be eaten away: *Gari lake limefukaa*, his car is worn-out. (cf *chakaa, pauka*) 2. tingle with excitement. 3. lose voice. Prep. *fuka.li.a* St. *fuka.k.a* Cs. *fuka.z.a* Ps of Prep *fuka.liw.a*

fukara *n* (*n*) see *fakiri¹* and *fakiri²*

fukarik.a (also *fakirika*) *vi* become impoverished, become impecunious, become poor; go to ruin: *Alifukarika baada ya kuifuja mali yake*, he became impoverished after squandering his wealth. Prep. *fukarik.i.a* St. *fukarik.ik.a* Cs. *fukarik.ish.a*, (cf *wamba, ruzu*) (Ar)

fukarish.a *vt* impoverish; reduce to poverty. Prep. *fukarish.i,a* St. *fukarish.ik.a* Ps. *fukarish.w.a* Rp. *fukarish.an.a*

fuki.a *vt* 1. fill in a hole, grave, etc.; fill up: *Walilifukia kaburi*, they filled up the grave. Prep.. *fuki.li.a* St. *fuki.lik.a*, be filled in, be capable of being filled in e.g. *Shimo linafukilika kwa mchanga*, the hole can be filled in with sand. Ps. *fuki.w.a* Rp. *fuki.an.a* (cf *zika*) 2. bury, hide in the ground: *Alifukia pesa nje ya nyumba yake*, she buried the money outside her house. Prep. *fuki.li.a* St. *fuki.lik.a* Ps. *fuki.w.a* Rp. *fuki.an.a*

fukiz.a *vt, vi* 1. see *fuka¹*. 2. exorcise; drive out an evil spirit by incantations, etc.: *Mganga alimfukiza mgonjwa aliyepagawa na pepo*, the sorcerer exorcised a patient who was possessed by an evil spirit. Prep. *fukiz.i.a* St. *fukiz.ik.a* Cs *fukiz.ish.a* Ps. *fukiz.w.a* Rp. *fukiz.an.a* (cf *buhurisha*)

fukizo n (*ma-*) 1. censing, fumigation, inhalation. 2. fumigant; a medicine used in fumigating.

fuko[1] n (*ma-*) (*zool*) mole; a small burrowing insect-eating mammal resembling a rat.

fuko

fuko[2] n (*ma-*) excavation

fuko[3] n (*ma-*) a hatching place for a hen; chicken hatchery.

fuko[4] n (*ma-*) 1. clan, tribe, family. (cf *kizazi, ayali, ukoo*) 2. *Fuko la uzazi*, uterus, womb.

fukombe n (*n*) see *furukombe*

fuku.a vt 1. unearth, dig out, dig up, exhume, disinter: *Aliufukua mhogo*, he dug out the cassava. Prep. *fuku.li.a* St. *fuku.lik.a* Cs. *fuku.lish.a* Ps. of Prep *fuku.liw.a*, be dug out, be exhumed e.g. *Maiti ilifukuliwa*, the corpse was exhumed. Rp. *fuku.an.a* Rp. of Prep.. *fuku.li.an.a* (cf *zikua, chimbua*) 2. devise, invent: *Alifukua mtindo mpya wa kunyoa nywele*, he invented a new style of hair cutting. Prep. *fuku.li.a* St. *fuku.lik.a* Cs. *fuku.lish.a* Ps. *fuku.liw.a* Rp. *fuku.an.a*

fukufuku[1] n (*n*) incitement, instigation, formentation, provocation: *Majirani wawili walitenganika kutokana na fukufuku zake*, the two neighbours were estranged by his incitements. (cf *chokochoko, uchochezi*)

fukufuku[2] n (*n*) (*bot*) a fruit from *mfukufuku*, a kind of small tree whose leaves are rounded at the apex. The fruit is borne, several together on woody stalks. The root of the fruit is used locally in the preparation of a lotion for the treatment of yaws; saxifragaceace.

fukufuku[3] n (*ma-*) stench, stink, reek; bad smell (cf *ufundo*)

fukundi (also *futundu, fuatundu*) n (*n*) a kind of fish with a deep red coloration (family *Lutjanidae*) with a moderately elongate to deep body and ctenoid scales, and which is found in most warm seas throughout the world; Emperor red snapper.

fukuo n (*ma-*) 1. excavation, digging, exhumation: *Fukuo la maiti*, the corpse's exhumation. 2. excavation; a hole dug out.

fukusi n (*n*) (*zool*) borer; an insect that bores holes in trees, fruits, etc.

fukut.a[1] (also *vukuta*) vi 1. itch, tingle, prickle, smart, prick: *Kidonda chake kinafukuta kwa vile alikitia spiriti*, his wound is smarting because he applied spirit to it. 2. (of fire) burn without showing a blaze or a flame; glow: *Moto unafukuta*, the fire is burning without a blaze. 3. (of conflict, etc.) be simmering, be boiling; *Mqogoro katika chama chao sasa umefukuta*, the conflict in their party is now simmering. Prep *fukut.i.a* St. *fukut.ik.a* Cs. *fukut.ish.a* Ps *fukut.w.a* Rp *fukut.an.a* (cf *rindima*)

fukut.a[2] (also *vukuta*) vt stoke up a fire, with bellows during metal work, etc.: *Mhunzi aliufukuta moto katika kalibu*, the metal worker stoked up the fire at the furnace. Prep. *fukut.i.a* St. *fukut.ik.a* Cs. *fukut.ish.a* Ps. *fukut.w.a* Rp. *fukut.an.a* (cf *vuvia, puliza*)

fukut.a[3] vt (of grain) become small pieces during pounding. Prep. *fukut.i.a* St *fukut.ik.a* Cs. *fukut.ish.a* Ps. *fukut.w.a* Rp. *fukut.an.a*

fukuto (also *vukuto*) *n* (*n*) 1. sweat, perspiration; heat of the body: *Jua kali lilinileteafukuto*, the hot sun made me sweat. (cf *joto, hari, mwako*) 2. uneasiness, irritation, distress, agony, affliction, vexation: *Ana fukuto moyoni mwake kwa sababu hana uhakika kama atafuzu kwenye mtihani*, he is uneasy in his heart because he is not sure if he will pass the examination. 3. waterskin. (cf *kiribi*)

fukuz.a *vt* 1. chase away, pursue, run after, fly after: *Mbwa alimfukuza paka wangu*, the dog chased my cat. Prep. ***fukuz.i.a***, chase away e.g. *Nilimfukuzia mbali mwizi*, I chased away the thief. St. ***fukuz.ik.a*** Cs. ***fukuz.ish.a*** Ps. ***fukuz.w.a***, be chased away e.g. *Alifukuzwa na mbwa mkali*, he was chased by a fierce dog. Rp. ***fukuz.an.a***, chase one another, run after each other e.g. *Watoto walikuwa wanafukuzana walipokuwa wanacheza*, the children were chasing one another when they were playing. (cf *winga, andama*) 2. banish, expatriate, deport, expel: *Serikali ilimfukuza jasusi nchini*, the government expelled the spy from the country. Prep. ***fukuz.i.a*** St. ***fukuz.ik.a*** Cs. ***fukuz.ish.a*** Ps. ***fukuz.w.a***, be deported, be sacked e.g. *Amefukuzwa kazini*, he has been sacked from work. Rp. ***fukuz.an.a***

fulama *vi* see *furama*

fulana *n* (*n*) flannel, undervest, undershirt. (Eng)

fulani[1] *n* (*n*) a word representing the name of a person; an unnamed or unspecified person; so- and so-.

fulani[2] *adj* having a word representing the name of a person; unnamed, unspecified: *Mtu fulani*, an unspecified person.

fuli *adv* hurriedly, quickly, rapidly: *Alikuja kwangu fuli*, he came to me hurriedly. (cf *upesi, haraka*)

fulifuli[1] *adv* see *fudifudi*

fulifuli[2] *adv* fast, quickly, speedily, promptly: *Alienda shuleni fulifuli*, he went to school quickly. (cf *upesiupesi, haraka*)

fuliz.a *vt, vi* see *fululiza*

fululiz.a (also *fuliza, fuuza*) *vt, vi* continue, persist, keep on: *Alifululiza kwenda kazini wiki yote ingawa alikuwa mgonjwa*, he kept on going to work for the whole week even though he was sick. Prep. ***fululiz.i.a***, keep on doing without pause; persist. St. ***fululiz.ik.a*** Cs. ***fululiz.ish.a*** Ps. ***fululiz.w.a*** Rp. ***fululiz.an.a***

fulusi[1] *n* (*n*) money, currency, cash (cf *pesa, fedha*) (Ar)

fulusi[2] *n* (*n*) a kind of fish of the Coryphaenidae family with elongate compressed body and numerous teeth and often a beaklike snout, common in tropical waters but sometimes caught near land; dolphin fish. Common dolphin fish, *Coryphaena hippurus*

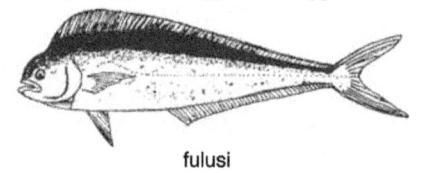

fulusi

fum.a[1] *vt, vi* weave, knit, crochet, twine, lace: *Aliifuma sweta nzuri*, he knitted a good sweater. Prep. ***fum.i.a***, knit for (with, etc) St. ***fum.ik.a*** Cs. ***fum.ish.a*** Ps. ***fum.w.a***, be knitted e.g. *Kanzu imefumwa*, the garment has been knitted. Rp. ***fum.an.a*** Rp. of Prep. ***fum.i.an.a*** (cf *shona*)

fum.a[2] *vt* spear with a sharp instrument e.g. spear, arrow, etc.; spear, lacerate, stab: *Msasi alimfuma nguruwe mwitu kwa mkuki*, the hunter speared the wild pig. (*prov*) *Kulenga si kufuma*, to aim is not necessarily to hit i.e. to aim to do sth does not necessarily mean that you would do it successfully. Prep. ***fum.i.a*** St. ***fum.ik.a*** Cs. ***fum.ish.a*** Ps. ***fum.w.a*** Rp. ***fum.an.a***

fum.a³ (also *fumania*) *vt* 1. catch someone unaware; catch someone by surprise; discover someone in the act of doing sth wrong; catch red-handed: *Nilimfuma mtumishi wangu akiiba nguo nyumbani*, I caught my servant red-handed stealing clothes at home. 2. catch someone red-handed in the act of doing sex: *Alimfuma akifanya mapenzi na mke wa watu*, he caught him red-handed flirting with somebody's wife. Prep. *fum.i.a* St. *fum.ik.a* Cs. *fum.ish.a* Ps. *fum.w.a* Rp. *fum.an.a* (cf *fumania*)

fum.a⁴ *vi (naut)* (of the tide) go out; ebb: *Maji yanafuma*, the tide is ebbing.

fuma⁵ *adj* (of a fruit) having a bad shape.

fuman.a *vi* interweave, interlace, intertwine.

fumani.a *vt* 1. catch sby red-handed; catch sby in the act of doing sth wrong. 2. catch sby committing adultery. Prep. *fumani.li.a* St. *fumani.k.a* Cs. *fumani.sh.a* and *fumani.z.a* Ps. *fumani.w.a* Rp. *fumani.an.a*

fumanizi *n (n)* 1. the act of discovering someone doing a wrongful act. 2. allegations connected with the act of doing a wrongful thing e.g. committing adultery: *Fumanizi zao zilifikishwa kwenye baraza la watu wazima*, their allegations connected with adultery were brought before the council of elders. 3. anything caught by surprise e.g. food which is found by someone from outside while it is the process of being eaten by other people: *Chakula fumanizi*, food which is being eaten when a guest suddenly arrives. *Hali fumanizi*, he will not eat the food when he finds that other people are eating at the time he arrives at the place.

fumatiti *n (n) (zool)* a bird of the nightjar family.

fumb.a¹ *vt, vi* close, shut: *Fumba macho*, close the eyes. *Fumba kinywa*, shut the mouth. *Fumba miguu*, put the legs together. Prep. *fumb.i.a* St. *fumb.ik.a* e.g. *Ua limefumbika*, the flower is closed. Cs. *fumb.ish.a* Ps. *fumb.w.a*, be closed up. Rp. *fumb.an.a,* close together e.g. *Walifumbana macho*, they closed each other's eyes. St. of Cs. *fumb.am.a,* be dazed, be light-headed e.g. *Akili yake imefumbama*, he is dull.

fumb.a² *vt* use unintelligible language; speak in riddles: *Alifumba maana ili nisielewe anachozungumza*, he spoke in riddles so that I would not understand what he was talking about. Prep. *fumb.i.a* St. *fumb.ik.a* Cs. *fumb.ish.a* Ps. *fumb.w.a* Rp. *fumb.an.a*

fumba³ *n (ma-)* 1. a matting-bag used for sleeping or for burying corpses; a burial mat doubled lengthwise and the ends are sewn. (cf *kishupi*) 2. a kind of plaited basket for picking up cloves. (cf *tumbi*)

fumba⁴ *n (ma-)* lump, clod, dump, chunk, handful, fistful: *Fumba la unga*, a fistful of flour.

fumba⁵ *n (ma-)* pad; the foot or footprint of certain animals such as a cat, dog, wolf, fox, etc. (cf *wayo*)

fumb.a⁶ *vt* reconnect two things that have parted. Prep. *fumb.i.a* St. *fumb.ik.a* Cs. *fumb.ish.a* Ps. *fumb.w.a* Rp. *fumb.an.a*

fumbam.a¹ *vi* be dazed, be confused, be bewildered: *Alifumbama baada ya kuzabwa kibao*, he became dazed after being slapped.

fumbam.a² *vi* lie down in order to spring; crouch: *Paka alifumbama ili amrukie panya*, the cat crouched in order to spring on the rat.

fumbat.a *vt* clutch in the hand; clasp, grab, grasp: *Aliufumbata mti kwa hofu ya simba*, he clasped the tree for fear of the lion. *Amezifumbata pesa mkononi*, he has grasped the money in his hand. (*prov*) *Konzi ya maji haifumbatiki*, a fistful of water cannot be grasped i.e. a secret thing cannot remain in secrecy forever. Prep. *fumbat.i.a* St. *fumbat.ik.a* Cs *fumbat.ish.a* Ps *fumbat.w.a* Rp. *fumbat.an.a*

fumbatio *n* (*n*) (*anat*) abdomen (cf *tumbo*)

fumbato *n* (*ma-*) 1. clasp, grip, clutch, clench, claw: *Aliitia noti kwenye fumbato*, he clasped the note. (*prov*) *Fumbato haliumizi mkono*, a clasp does not hurt a hand i.e. you will not fail to control anything that totally belongs to you. 2. the size of something that can be clasped at the hand.

fumbi[1] *n* (*ma-*) 1. terrace; a raised mound of earth with sloping sides. 2. stream: *Fumbi lile lilikuwa linashuka polepole hapo bondeni*, that stream was running slowly along the valley.

fumbi[2] *n* (*ma-*) a leader of the girls undergoing initiation rites. (cf *chando*, *kiranja*)

fumbi.a *vt* 1. see *fumbi*[2] 2. (*idm*) *Fumbia macho*, connive; secretly allow sth immoral, illegal, etc. to occur:*Serikali ililifumbia macho suala lile*, the government connived at that issue.

fumbo[1] *n* (*ma-*) 1. mystery, puzzle, problem, enigma: *Fumbo jina*, cryptonym; a name with a deep hidden meaning. 2. proverb, parable, riddle, conundrum: *Ongea kwa mafumbo*, speak in parables. *Piga fumbo*, speak in parables. *Jina la fumbo*, code name. (*prov*) *Fumbo humfumba mjinga, mwerevu akatambua*, a parable mystifies simpleton, a wise person recognizes it i.e. even though it is possible to find someone concealing the motive about what he really intends to tell or do to his colleague, that motive may have already been recognized by his friend.

fumbo[2] *n* (*n*) the position of a leader.

fumbu *n* (*ma-*) an unopened bud of a flower. (cf *tumba*)

fumbu.a *vt* 1. disclose. reveal, divulge: *Aliifumbua siri yangu*, he disclosed my secret. (cf *fichua*) 2. unclose, open: *Fumbua macho*, open the eyes. *Fumbua mdomo*, open the mouth. *Fumbua fumbo*, unravel a riddle. Prep. *fumbu.li.a* St. *fumbu.k.a* Cs. *fumbu.lish.a* Ps. of Prep *fumbu.liw.a* Rp. *fumbu.an.a* (cf *fungua*)

fumbwe *n* (*n*) 1. a kind of small bird with black, chestnut and buff plumage and long drooping tail feathers in the case of a male; paradise Whydah. *Steganura paradisaesa*. 2. (*syn*) *Kuwa fumbwe*, to have many women.

fume *n* (*ma-*) a person wounded by a spear.

fumi (also *pumi*) *n* (*n*) (*zool*) a kind of fish of *Aridae* family with long barbels and usu with sharp spines on the head and which is found in marine brackish and fresh water of warm temperate and tropical continental coasts; catfish. (cf *hongwe*)

fumi

fumk.a *vi* see *fumuka*

fumo[1] *n* (*n*) an old rank of a king.

fumo[2] *n* (*ma-*) a kind of broad tipped spear.

fumu.a *vt* 1. unstitch, unweave, unseam, undo: *Aliifumua sweta*, he unstitched the sweater. (cf *shonoa*, *shojoa*) 2. undo, untie: *Alizifumua nywele*, he undid the hair. *Alilifumua paa*, he unthatched the roof. *Aliufumua moto*, he pulled the fire to pieces. 3. (in sports) (*colloq*) kick: *Alifumua shuti kali*, he kicked a hard shot. 4. (fig) dismantle: *Meneja aliufumua mfumo wote wa kuajiri wafanyakazi*, the manager dismantled the entire system of recruiting workers. Prep. *fumu.*

li.a St. ***fumu.k.a*** and ***fumu.lik.a*** Cs. ***fumu.lish.a*** Ps. of Prep ***fumu.liw.a*** Rp. ***fumu.an.a*** (cf *chomoa, chopoa, toa*)

fumuk.a *vi* (also *fumka*) 1. become unsewn, become unstitched, be unravelled: *Nguo yake imefumuka*, her dress has become unstitched. 2. (*fig*) erupt, rapture, explode: *Mapigano yamefumuka mipakani*, fighting has erupted at the border.

fumukan.a *vi* be scattered, be dispersed: *Baada ya kumalizika mkutano, watu wakafumukana*, after the meeting had ended, people dispersed: Prep. ***fumukan.i.a*** Ps. ***fumukan.w.a*** (cf *tawanyika*)

fumukano *n* (*ma-*) dispersion, scattering, spread: *Fumukano la watu*, the dispersion of people. (cf *mtawanyiko*)

fumvu *n* (n) (*zool*) red-eyed dove; a kind of brownish-grey dove with a black collar on the hindneck. *Streptopelia semitorquara*. (cf *tutu*)

fund.a[1] *vt* pound, bruise, thresh, triturate, comminute, bray, pulverize; crush sth e.g. corn into powder esp in a mortar: *Aliifunda tangawizi kwenye kinu*, he pounded the ginger in the mortar. Prep. ***fund.i.a*** St. ***fund.ik.a*** Cs. ***fund.ish.a*** Ps. ***fund.w.a***, be pounded, e.g. *Mhogo ulifundwa*, the cassava was pounded. Rp. ***fund.an.a*** (cf *twanga, ponda*)

fund.a[2] *vt, vi* teach a child household and tribal matters; rear a child in the traditional way: *Alimfunda bintiye kufuata mwenendo mzuri*, she taught her daughter to have good behaviour. Prep. ***fund.i.a*** St. ***fund.ik.a*** Cs. ***fund.ish.a*** and ***fun.z.a*** Ps. ***fund.w.a*** Rp. ***fund.an.a*** (cf *fundisha, elimisha, lea*)

funda[3] *n* (n) (*anat*) the inside of the cheek; buccal mucosa.

funda[4] *n* (*ma-*) large mouthful; gulp; *Piqa mafunda ya maji*, take large gulps of water; take large mouthfuls of water.

fundabeka *n* (*ma-*) (*anat*) thigh bone; femur.

fundarere (also *vundarere*) *n* (n) (*zool*) a kind of snake.

fundi *n* (*ma-*) 1. a person skilled in an art, craft or profession: *Fundibomba*, plumber. *Fundi mwashi*, stone mason. *Fundi rangi*, painter. *Fundi mchundo*. a basic technician. *Fundi seremala*, carpenter. *Fundi stadi*, craftsman. *Fundi wa saa*, watch repairer. *Fundi sanifu*, technician. 2. expert, specialist: *Yeye ni fundi katika muziki*, he is an expert in music. (cf *bingwa, mtaalamu*)

fundi.a (also *fundira*) *vt, vi* take a large mouthful esp of food or water i.e. until the cheeks are distended: *Alikula chakula kwa kufundia*, he took a large mouthful of food. Prep. ***fundi.li.a*** St. ***fundi.k.a*** Cs. ***fundi.sh.a*** Ps. ***fundi.w.a*** Rp. ***fundi.an.a***

fundik.a[1] *vt, vi* 1. tie sth in a knot. 2. form a bud of a flower. Prep. ***fundik.i.a*** St. ***fundik.ik.a*** Cs. ***fundik.ish.a***

fundik.a[2] *vi* plait hair Prep. ***fundik.i.a*** St. ***fundik.ik.a*** Cs. ***fundik.ish.a*** (cf *bundika*)

fundira *vt, vi* see *fundia*

fundish.a *vt, vi* 1. teach, instruct, educate: *Mwalimu alitufundisha Kiingereza*, the teacher taught us English. (cf *somesha, elimisha*) 2. train, coach, teach: *Alinifundisha kuogelea*, he taught me how to swim. *Mbwa walifundishwa kutambua mihadharati*, the dogs were trained to detect drugs. 3. discipline, guide, direct, lead, teach: *Mzee alimfundisha mtoto wake mwenendo mzuri*, the parent taught his son good behaviour. Prep. ***fundish.i.a*** St. ***fundish.ik.a*** Ps. ***fundish.w.a*** Rp. ***fundish.an.a***. (cf *onyesha, elekeza*)

fundisho (also *funzo*) *n* (*ma-*) 1. teaching, lesson, instruction: *Lile lilikuwa fundisho la sayansi*, that was a science lesson. (cf *somo, darasa*) 2. direction, guidance, advice: *Fundisho* *lake lilitusaidia*, his advice helped us. (cf *mwelekezo*) 3. lesson, punishment: *Fundisho lile halitasahaulika*, that punishment will never be forgotten. (cf *adabu, onyo, somo*)

fundo[1] *n* (*ma-*) 1. joint, knot, junction, point of union, joint: *Fundo la mkono*, wrist. *Fundo la mguu*, ankle. 2. knot; anything that has swollen because of being tied with other things: *Fundo la nguo*, clothes tied in a knot. *Fundo la uzi*, knot in the thread. *Fundo la muwa*, knot in a sugarcane tree. 3. purse, usu made up of a knotted piece of waist cloth. (*prov*) *Siku ya mashaka, fundo*, for the day of difficulties, a purse i.e. if someone has reserved something for the future it can assist him when he is in hardships.

fundo[2] (also *mfundo*) *n* (*ma-*) bitterness, resentment, illfeeling: *Ana fundo la moyo*; he is resentful; he is bitter. (cf *kinyongo, hasira, chuki*)

fundo[3] *n* (*ma-*) (*naut*) crossbeam i.e. a beam which fixes the mast to the keel in a vessel. (cf *farikumu*)

fundu.a *vt* untie, uncork, unplug, unfasten; undo a knot, etc.: *Aliifundua chupa*, he uncorked the bottle. (cf *zibua, fidua*) 2. germinate, sprout, pullulate, burgeon, shoot up: *Vitunguu vimefundua*, the onions have germinated. 3. explain, elaborate, explicate, expound: *Aliifundua habari ambayo sikuielewa*, he elaborated on the information which I did not understand. Prep. ***fundu.li.a*** St. ***fundu.lik.a*** Cs. ***fundu.sh.a*** and ***fundu.z.a*** Ps. of Prep. ***fundu.liw.a*** Rp. ***fundu.an.a.*** (cf *eleza, fahamu*)

fung.a[1] *vt* 1. close, lock, shut, seal: *Funga mlango*, close the door. *Funga dirisha*, shut the window. *Funga bahasha*, seal up the envelope. 2. fasten, tie, wrap: *Aliifunga mizigo*, he tied the loads. *Aliifunga furushi*, he wrapped the parcel. Prep. ***fung.i.a*** St. ***fung.ik.a*** Cs. ***fung.ish.a*** Ps. ***fung.w.a*** Rp. ***fung.an.a***

fung.a[2] *vt* (in a game, etc.) win, overcome: *Tuliwafunga magoli mengi*, we beat them by many goals. Prep. ***fung.i.a*** St. ***fung.ik.a*** Cs. ***fung.ish.a*** Ps. ***fung.w.a,*** be overcome, be beaten e.g. *Timu yao ilifungwa kwa mabao mawili*, their team was beaten by two goals. Rp. ***fung.an.a,*** score a goal on each other's side e.g. *Walikuwa wamefungana magoli matatu*, they had a three-goal draw. (cf *shinda*)

fung.a[3] *vt* decide upon, resolve, embark on: *Alifunga kuoa mke wa tatu*, he decided to marry a third wife. Prep. ***fung.i.a*** St. ***fung.ik.a*** Cs. ***fung.ish.a*** Ps. ***fung.w.a*** Rp. ***fung.an.a***

fung.a[4] *vi* (in for religious reason, etc.) fast, go hungry: *Alifunga katika mwezi wa Ramadhan*, he fasted during the month of Ramadan. Prep. ***fung.i.a*** St. ***fung.ik.a*** Cs. ***fung.ish.a*** Ps. ***fung.w.a*** Rp. ***fung.an.a***

fung.a[5] *vt* (*idms*) *Funga choo*, fail to get bowel movement because of constipation; be constipated e.g. *Baada ya kula mikate mikavu, akafunga choo*, after eating dry loaves, he suffered from constipation. *Funga safari*, set on a journey, start on a trip. *Funga virago*, pack up and go. *Funga ndoa*, wed; get married e.g. *Alifunga ndoa jana*, he got married yesterday. *Funga mdomo*, silence someone who is talking free. *Funga kibwebwe*, work hard. *Funga kisaki*, tie properly e.g. a load. *Funga nira*, put effort in a job, etc. *Funga tumbo*, be unable to release bowels. Also (of a woman) stop begetting children.

funga[6] *n* (*n*) fasting, fast: *Yumo katika funga*, he is in fast. (cf *saumu*)

fungam.a *vi, vt* be in a fixed and tight position; be stuck: *Ugaga umefungama kwenye meno yake*, bits of food are stuck in his teeth. Prep. *fungam.i.a* St. *fungam.ik.a* Cs *fungam.ish.a* and *fungam.iz.a*

fungaman.a *vt* be linked, be allied, be interwoven, be interlocked, be interrelated: *Nchi zisizofungamana*, non-aligned countries. *Nchi yetu haijafungamana na upande wowote*, our country is not allied to any side. Prep. *fungaman.i.a.* St. *fungaman.ik.a* Cs. *fungaman.ish.a*

fungamanish.a *vt* link, connect, associate: *Nchi zilizoendelea hufungamanisha msaada na haki za binaadamu kwa nchi zinazoendelea*, developed countries link aid to developing countries with human records. Prep. *fungamanish.i.a* St. *fungamanish.ik.a* Ps. *fungamanish.w.a* Rp. *fungamanish.an.a*

fungamano *n* (*ma-*) alliance, pact, coalition, union, league, tie: *Lile lilikuwa fungamano la kisiasa*, that was a political union. (cf *umoja, ambatano*)

fungan.a *vi* be locked together: *Milango imefungana*, the doors have locked together. 2. (in sports) scoring equally on each other's side: *Timu hizi zimeshafungana kwa magoli mawili kwa mawili*, these two teams have already scored two goals equally on each side. 3. (of clouds) be thick.

fungany.a *vt* pack one's things for a journey: *Aliifunganya mizigo yake*, he packed his luggage. Prep. *fungany.i.a* St. *fungany.ik.a* Cs. *fungany.ish.a* Ps. *fungany.w.a* (cf *fungasha*)

funganyumba *n* (*n*) (*bot*) a much-branched shrub or small tree with scattered spines and small dense spikes of pink and yellow flowers, used in medicine as an antidote to scorpion and snake-bites. *Dichrostactys glomerata*.

fungash.a¹ *vt* 1. tie together, usu of one boat towing another; drag, tug, pull: *Mashua yake iliharibika na baadaye tukaifungasha na yangu*, his boat stopped working and later, we tied it to my boat. 2. trail, tug, tow; pull by a rope or chain: *Lori ilikuwa imeifungasha trela*, the lorry was towing the trailer. Prep. *fungash.i.a* St. *fungash.ik.a* Ps. *fungash.w.a* Rp. *fungash.an.a* 3. (*syn*) (of a woman) have big buttocks e.g. *Mtu yule amefungasha*, that person has big buttocks; that person has a big bottom.

fungash.a² *vt* 1. pack one's things for a journey. (cf *funganya*) 2. walk majestically with a woman. Prep. *fungash.i.a* St. *fungash.ik.a* Ps. *fungash.w.a* Rp. *fungash.an.a*

fungi.a *vt* bar, ban, confine, lock: *Amenifungia mlango*, he has locked me. Prep. *fungi.li.a* St. *fungi.k.a* Cs. *fungi.sh.a* Ps. *fungi.w.a*

fungate *n* (*n*) 1. honeymoon. 2. week; seven days

fungo¹ *n* (*ma-*) 1. fast; a period of fasting: *Fungo la mwezi wa Ramadhani*, the fasting of the month of Ramadan. 2. an act of closing or shutting; closure, blockage, locking. (cf *ufungaji*) 3. share: *Alipata fungo kubwa alipoingia ubia na rafiki zake*, he received a lion's share when he entered partnership with his friends.

fungo² *n* (*n*) (*zool*) civet cat; a cat-like, flesh-eating animal with black spots on the body, thick legs and two black collars on neck. *Viverra civetta*.

fungo

fungo³ *n* (*n*) local medicine made from the roots of *ndago*, nutgrass, believed to make a child's teeth firm. 2. magic protection against evil. (cf *zindiko*)

fungu¹ *n* (*ma-*) 1. share, lump, piece, portion: *Fungu la fedha*, a portion of money. *Fungu la nyama*, a portion of meat. *Fungu zima*, the whole pile. 2. shoal, ridge, sandbank, reef, sandbar, coral reef: *Niliona fungu la mchanga baharini*, I saw a sandbank in the ocean. 3. used in the expression: *Mafungu ya mchanga*, flowers put on a grave; wreath. 4. a verse of prose, a bar of music. 5. (*idm*) *Vunja fungu*, visit a grave after forty days to make a valedictory offering. 6. share, dividend: *Nilinunua fungu kubwa katika kampuni*, I bought a big share in the company. 7. a sum of money set aside for a specific use e.g. transport allowance, printing stationery, etc. 8. section, paragraph, part: *Fungu la tatu la sheria*, section three of the law. 9. group, assembly, pile: *Fungu la nyanya*, a pile of tomatoes. *Fungu tenzi*, verbal group, verb cluster. *Fungu la maneno*, phrase, group. 10. *Fungu visiwa*, archipelago; a group or chain of many islands.

fungu² *n* (*n*) an ornamental plant of the Amaranth family with red or yellow flower heads, and its leaves and stems are used as a vegetable;Cock's comb *Celosia argentea*

fungu.a *vt* 1. release, set free: *Walimfungua mfungwa*, they released the prisoner. 2. unfasten, undo, open: *Fungua mlango*, open the door. (cf *shindua*) 3. inaugurate, open: *Waziri aliifungua hospitali*, the minister opened the hospital. 4. open, unfold: *Fungua mkono*, open the hand. Prep. *fungu.li.a* St. *fungu.k.a* and *fungu.lik.a* Cs. *fungu.lish.a* and *fungu.z.a* Ps. of Prep. *fungu.liw.a* Rp. *fungu.an.a* (cf *fumbua*) 5. (*idms*) *Fungua dimba*, (a) start a football game. (b) *Fungua mimba*, deliver the first baby. *Fungua macho*, be vigilant, be awakened, e.g. *Tulidanganywa kwa muda mrefu lakini sasa tumefungua macho*, we were cheated for a long time but now we are enlightened. *Fungua kinywa*, breakfast; eat the morning meal. *Fungua mkono*, give money.

funguli.a *vt* 1. allow sby to get in or out; let out 2. open sth for sby. St. *funguli.k.a* Cs. *funguli.sh.a* Ps. *funguli.w.a*

fungule *n* (*n*) the fee or payment given to a sorcerer/medicineman. (cf *mafungu*)

fungutenzi *n* (*ma-*) (*gram*) verbal group, verbal cluster. (cf *kikunditenzi*)

funik.a (also *finika*) *vt* 1. cover, protect, conceal, disguise: *Alikifunika chakula kwa sahani*, she covered the food with a plate. *Alikifunika chungu*, he put a lid on the cooking pot. Prep. *funik.i.a* St. *funik.ik.a* Cs. *funik.i.z.a* Ps. *funik.w.a* Rp. *funik.an.a* (*prov*) *Funika kombe mwanaharamu apite*, cover the platter and let the bastard pass by i.e. Don't disclose anything to an irresponsible person. (cf *ficha, sitiri*) 2. (*idm*) *Funika maneno*, speak obscurely. e.g. *Alifunika maneno kwa hofu kwenye mkutano*, he spoke obscurely due to fear at the meeting.

funikiz.a *vt* see *fudikiza*¹

funo *n* (*n*) (*zool*) a small African antelope of the *Cephalophus* genus with small spike-like short horns, growing straight back along the plane of the head; red duiker. *Cephaphlus natalensis* (cf *mindi*)

funo

funu.a *vt* 1. uncover, expose, bare, lay open, undo: *Alikifunua chakula kilichowekwa mezani*, he uncovered

funuk.a   **furaha** **F**

the food which was put on the table. (cf *zibua, fudua*) 2. expound, explicate, elucidate, explain, clarify: *Aliifunua maana ya sentensi*, he explained the meaning of the sentence. (cf *fasiri, eleza*) 3. spread, stretch, extend: *Ndege alizifunua mbawa zake*, the bird stretched its wings. Prep. ***funu.li.a*** St. ***funu.k.a*** and ***funu.lik.a*** Ps. of Prep. ***funu.liw.a*** Rp. ***funu.an.a***

funuk.a *vi* be uncovered, be opened out: *Maua yanafunuka*, the flowers are opening. Prep. ***funuk.i.a*** St. ***funuk.ik.a*** Cs. **funuk.ish.a**

fununu *n* (*n*) gossip, grapevine, rumour, hearsay: *Nilisikia fununu kwamba mjomba atapata uhamisho kwenye kazi yake ya sasa*, I heard a rumour that my uncle would get a transfer from his present job, (cf *penyenye, tetesi, uvumi*)

funutu (also *tunutu, matundu*) *n* (*ma-*) (*zool*) 1. young grasshopper. 2. small locust.

funz.a[1] *vt, vi* teach esp moral values; inculcate, instruct, educate: *Mzazi alimfunza mwanawe mwenendo mzuri*, the parent instructed her child on how to conduct himself well. (*prov*) *Asiyefunzwa na mamaye hufunzwa na ulimwengu*, he who is not taught by his mother will be taught by the world i.e. he who does not listen to his parent's advice will suffer in the end.

funza[2] *n* (*n*) (*zool*) maggot, grub, larva, chigger, jigger. (cf *tekenya, bombwe, buu*)

funzo *n* (*ma-*) 1. instruction, teaching: *Nilipendezwa na funzo lake*, I was impressed by his instruction. (cf *somo*) 2. lesson, warning, punishment: *Lile lilikuwa funzo kwake kwani sasa hachelewi tena shuleni*, that was a lesson for him because now he does not go to school late. (cf *fundisho, adabu*)

fuo[1] *n* (*ma-*) 1. a place where clothes are washed; launderette, utility room, laundry. (cf *madobini, chanoni*) 2. washing, laundering: *Fuo la tatu liliniwezesha kuisafisha vizuri fulana yangu*, the third wash enabled me to get my flannel clean.

fuo[2] *n* (*ma-*) scum, froth, foam, lather, spume, suds: *Fuo la sabuni*, soap lather.

fupaja *n* (*n*) (*anat*) femur, thigh-bone. (cf *fundabeka*)

fupanyonga *n* (*ma-*) (*anat*) pelvis

-fupi *adj* 1. short, little, small: *Mtu mfupi*, a short person. *Masafa mafupi*, short distance. 2. brief, concise, succinct, short: *Taarifa fupi*, a short statement.

fupish.a (also *fupiza*) *vt* 1. summarize, epitomize, synopsize, shorten: *Aliifupisha hotuba yangu*, he shortened my speech. (cf *kasiri*) 2. resolve a conflict, etc.: *Waliufupisha ugomvi wao kwa wazee*, they resolved their conflict through the elders. Prep. ***fupish.i.a*** St. ***fupish.ik.a*** Ps. ***fupish.w.a*** Rp. of Prep ***fupish.i.an.a*** (cf *suluhisha*)

fupiz.a *vt* see *fupisha*

fur.a *vt, vi* 1. swell, dilate, bloat, puff out: *Uso wake ulifura baada ya kupigwa ngumi sana*, his face became swollen after being punched hard. Prep. ***fur.i.a*** St. ***fur.ik.a*** Cs. ***fur.ish.a*** Ps. ***fur.w.a*** Rp. ***fur.an.a***. 2. (*fig*) swell with anger, seethe with indignation, boil over; rage: *Uso wa mwalimu ulifura kwa hasira baada ya mwanafunzi kumwaibisha darasani*, the face of the teacher went red with rage after the student discredited him in the class. Prep. ***fur.i.a*** St. ***fur.ik.a*** Cs. ***fur.ish.a*** Ps. ***fur.w.a*** Rp. ***fur.an.a*** (cf *ghadhibika, hamaki, kasirika*)

furaha *n* (*n*) 1. happiness, pleasure, joy, gaiety, gayness: *Yeye yumo katika furaha kwa vile mkewe amepata mtoto*, he is happy because his wife has delivered a baby. (cf *uchangamfu, buraha*) 2. satisfaction, complacence, contentment: *Pato lake la wastani limemfanya kuwa katika furaha*, his average income has made him be contented. (cf *utoshelevu*) 3. enjoyment, pleasure, leisure, entertainment, luxury: *Anaishi maisha ya furaha*, he lives a luxurious life. (cf *raha*) (Ar)

furah.i (also *furahika*) *vi* 1. rejoice, be happy, be joyful, be glad: *Alifurahi kusikia kwamba nimeoa*, he was pleased to hear that I had got married. (cf *changamka, terema*) 2. be contented, be comfortable, be satisfied: *Mtu yule hufurahia kila anachopewa*, that person is contented with whatever he is given. 3. enjoy, entertain, take pleasure in: *Hufurahi anapokunywa pombe*, he enjoys drinking beer. Prep. *furah.i.a* St. *furah.ik.a* Cs. *furah.ish.a* Ps. *furah.iw.a* Rp. of Prep *furah.i.an.a* (Ar)

furahi.a *vt* 1. rejoice for (at, in, etc.): *Tulifurahia sana ushindi wake*, we were overjoyed at his victory. 2. enjoy: *Unafurahia kunywa kahawa?* Do you enjoy drinking coffee? Prep. *furahi.li.a* St. *furahi.k.a* Cs *furahi.sh.a* Ps. of Prep *furahi.w.a* Rp. of Prep *furahi.an.a*

-furahifu *adj* 1. cheerful, joyous, mirthful, vivacious, joyful, happy: *Mtu mfurahifu*, a cheerful person. (cf *karamshi*) 2. contented, satisfied, gratified: *Yeye ni msichana mfurahifu*, she is a contented girl. (cf *maridhia*) 3. leisurely, leisure-minded: *Vijana wafurahifu*, leisure-minded young people. (Ar)

furahish.a *vt, vi* 1. delight, gladden, please: *Masihara yake yalitufurahisha*, his jokes pleased us. 2. ravish, enrapture: *Uzuri wake ulinifurahisha*, I was ravished by her beauty. (cf *vutia*) 3. flatter: *Anapenda kukufurahisha*, he likes to flatter you. Prep. *furahish.ia* St. *furahish.ik.a* Ps. *furahish.w.a* Rp. *furahish.an.a*

furam.a (also *fuama, fulama*) *vi* bend forwards with the upper part of the body; stomach forwards: *Alifurama*, he bent forwards with the upper part of the body. Prep. *furam.i.a* St. *furam.ik.a* Cs. *furam.ish.a* Ps. *furam.w.a* Rp. of Prep *furam.i.an.a* (cf *bongoa, inika*)

furi *adj* brimful, filled-up, filled to the brim, filled to the capacity: *Maziwa yalijaa furi kwenye jagi*, the jug was filled to the brim with milk.

furik.a *vi* overflow, run over, overspill, flood: deluge, overrun: *Mto ulifurika*, the river was flooded. Prep. *furik.i.a* St. *furik.ik.a* Cs. *furik.ish.a* Ps. *furik.w.a*. (cf *miminika, mwaika*)

furiko *n* (*ma-*) inundation, deluge, flood: *Mafuriko ya mto yalileta maafa makubwa*, the river floods caused great disaster. (cf *gharika*)

Furkani *n* (*n*) the Holy Koran (Ar)

furo *n* (*n*) see *chwago*

fursa *n* (*n*) occasion, chance, opportunity: *Kupata fursa*, to have an opportunity. *Alipochaguliwa kuwa mkurugenzi, alitumia fursa ile kuwaajiri watu wa kabila lake*, when he was appointed as the director, he used that chance to employ people of his tribe. (cf *nafasi, wasaa*) (Ar)

fursadi *n* (*n*) (*bot*) mulberry; the edible fruit from mulberry tree and shrub. (Ar)

furu *n* (*n*) (*bot*) a small black fruit, about the size of cherries from *mfuru, Vinex cuneata*, a kind of tree.

-furufu *adj* cheerful, joyous, mirthful, vivacious, charming: *Akizungumza huonekana mfurufu*, when he talks, he is cheerful. (cf *karamshi*)

furufuru *n* (*n*) 1. confusion, disorder, turmoil, tumult, chaos: *Ukosefu wa umeme ulileta furufuru mjini*, electricity power failure caused confusion in the town. (cf *zogo, fujo*) 2. cloud, haze, mist: *Alishindwa kuendesha gari kwa kasi kutokana na furufuru iliyozagaa*, he was unable to drive the car fast because of the pervading mist.

furuk.a *vi* 1. grow up, develop: *Amefuruka haraka ingawa ni mdogo,* he has grown up fast even though he is young. (cf *kua*) 2. be cheerful, be lively, be in good spirits: *Amefuruka kwa vile wazee wake wamemnunulia baiskeli,* he is in good spirits because his parents have bought him a bicycle. Prep. ***furuk.i.a*** St. ***furuk.ik.a*** Cs. ***furuk.ish.a*** (cf *changamka, karamka*)

furukobe *n* (*ma-*) see *furukobe*

furukombe (also *furukobe*) *n* (*ma-*) 1. (*zool*) a large diving bird of prey of the hawk family with long wings, a slightly crested head, blue-grey legs, and which is nearly always seen near water; osprey. *Pandion haliaetus.* 2. land tortoise.

furukombe

furukut.a *vt, vi* 1. wiggle, squirm, wriggle, writhe, fidget; twist and turn; roll from side to side due to sickness, excitement, nightmare, etc.: *Alikuwa akifurukuta kitandani kutokana na maumivu makali,* she writhed on the bed in agony. (cf *garagara*) 2. escape forcefully from the hands of someone; struggle to be free; fight one's way to be free: *Alijaribu kufurukuta aliposhikwa na askari kanzu,* he fought his way free when he was caught by plainclothed policemen. 3. throb, beat, pulse, pulsate, palpitate: *Moyo wake ulikuwa ukifurukuta kutokana na wasiwasi mwingi,* her heart was throbbing with excessive anxiety. Prep. ***furukut.i.a*** St. ***furukut.ik.a*** Cs. ***furukut.ish.a*** Ps. ***furukut.w.a*** (cf *pwita, tuta, tweta*)

furukuto *n* (*ma-*) wriggling, squirming, restlessness; tossing and turning: *Furukuto la mgonjwa kwa usiku wote lilitutia wasiwasi,* the patient's restlessness throughout the night worried us. (cf *ugaagaaji*)

furungu¹ *n* (*ma-*) (*bot*) a large round yellow citrus fruit with aromatic pulp and a sweetish sour taste; shaddock, pomelo. (Pers)

furungu² *n* (*ma-*) an anklet usu of silver. (cf *mtali, kugesi*) (Pers)

furush.a *vt* chase away, pursue, run after, drive away: *Niliwafurusha ndege kutoka kwenye konde yangu,* I drove the birds away from my field. Prep. ***furush.i.a*** St. ***furush.ik.a*** Ps. ***furush.w.a*** Rp. ***furush.an.a*** (cf *fukuza, winda*)

furushi *n* (*ma-*) bundle, packet, parcel, package: *Furushi la nguo,* a bundle of clothes. (cf *tumba, rundo*) (Ar)

furutile *n* (*n*) sisal mill; sisal processing machine; decorticator.

fus.a¹ *vt* 1. soften by gentle beating; tenderise: *Aliifusa nyama kabla ya kuipika,* he beat the meat to tenderise it before cooking. 2. attack, assault, pounce: *Homa ya malaria ilimfusa vibaya,* malaria attacked him badly. 3. abuse,slur, insult, vituperate, vilipend, affront: *Walimfusa mbele ya mwalimu mkuu,* they insulted him in front of the headteacher. Prep. ***fus.i.a*** St. ***fus.ik.a*** Ps. ***fus.w.a*** Rp. ***fus.an.a*** (cf *tukana*)

fus.a² *vi* 1. (an explosion of air like that of a burst ball or tyre) burst: *Tulicheza mechi na katikati ya mchezo, mpira ukafusa,* we played the match and in the middle of the game, the ball burst. 2. fart noiselessly; break wind without noise: *Alifusa baada ya kulu dengu,* he broke wind after eating lentils. Prep.

F   fus.a³   futa⁶

fus.i.a, St. *fus.ik.a* Cs. *fus.ish.a* Ps. *fus.w.a* (cf *sura, shuta*) (Ar)

fus.a³ *vt* make bankrupt; impoverish: *Alizifusa pesa zake kutokana na kushindwa kwake kwenye mchezo wa kamari*, he became impoverished following his gambling losses. Prep. *fus.i.a* St. *fus.ik.a* Ps. *fus.w.a* Rp. *fus.an.a* (cf *futa*)

fusah.i *vt* nulify, invalidate, rescind, annul, repeal, abrogate, revoke: *Bunge liliifusahi sheria*, parliament repealed the law. Prep. *fusah.i.a* St. *fusah.ik.a* Cs. *fusah.ish.a* Ps. *fusah.iw.a*. (cf *batilisha, tangua*) (Ar)

fusho *n* (*ma-*) 1. fumigant, incense. 2. gun powder.

fusi *n* (*ma-*) mud or clay of walls, etc of a house that has fallen or become demolished; rubble: *Alifunikwa na fusi jengo lilipoanguka*, he was buried alive by the rubble when the building collapsed.

fusi.a *vt, vi* fill a hole; fill in the foundation of a house: *Mwashi alifusia msingi wa jengo langu kwa simenti na kokoto*, the mason filled the foundation of my building with cement and concrete. Prep. *fusi.li.a* St. *fusi.k.a* Cs. *fusi.sh.a* Ps. *fusi.w.a* Rp. *fusi.an.a*

fusik.a *vi* 1 be contused, be bruised; be injured without breaking the skin: *Mkono wake ulifusika alipoanguka chooni*, his arm was contused when he fell in the toilet. 2. stagger, wobble Prep. *fusik.i.a* St. *fusik.ik.a* Cs. *fusik.ish.a*(cf *tetereka, teseka*)

fuska *n* (*n*) 1. bad character; mischievousness: *Usilete fuska yako hapa*, don't show your mischievousness here. 2. adultery. (cf *uzinzi, zinaa*)

fusuli *n* (*n*) totality, length and breadth, everything, fullness, completeness, alpha and omega: *Kwa fusuli*, in details, in full. *Shahidi alitoa maelezo yake mahakamani kwa fusuli*, the witness gave her evidence in court in full. (Ar)

fususi *n* (*n*) gem; a kind of precious stone cut and polished for use as a jewel. (Ar)

fut.a¹ *vt* 1. clean up, sweep, scour, rub, wipe off: *Futa vumbi*, wipe off the dust. *Futa machozi*, wipe away tears. *Futa kamasi*, wipe the nose. (cf *pangusa*) 2. erase, rub, wipe off: *Aliyafuta maandishi kwenye ubao wa kuandikia*, he rubbed off the writing on the blackboard. (cf *pangusa*) 3. invalidate, repeal, abrogate, rescind: *Bunge liliifuta sheria*, parliament repealed the law. Prep. *fut.i.a* St. *fut.ik.a* Cs. *fut.ish.a* Ps. *fut.w.a* Rp. *fut.an.a* (cf *tengua*) 4. used in other expressions: *Futa mawazo*, stop thinking. *Futa mashtaka*, withdraw a suit, etc e.g. *Aliyafuta mashtaka yake mahakamani juu ya matokeo ya uchaguzi*, he withdrew his petition from court following the election results.

fut.a² *vt* unsheathe, extract; draw a sword, knife, etc.: *Aliufuta upanga*, he unsheathed the sword. Prep. *fut.i.a* St. *fut.ik.a* Cs. *fut.ish.a* Ps. *fut.w.a*, be unsheathed. Rp. *fut.an.a* Rp. of Prep *fut.i.an.a* (cf *chomoa, vura, chopoa*)

fut.a³ *vt* (*naut*) bail water out of a vessel: *Aliyafuta maji kutoka kwenye ngalawa*, he bailed water out of a canoe. Prep. *fut.i.a* St. *fut.ik.a* Cs. *fut.ish.a* Ps. *fut.w.a* Rp. of Prep. *fut.i.an.a*

fut.a⁴ *vt* (in gambling, etc.) win all of sby's money; clean him out: *Alimfuta rafiki yake kwenye mchezo wa kamari*, he scooped his friend's money while gambling Prep. *fut.i.a* St. *fut.ik.a* Cs. *fut.ish.a* Ps. *fut.w.a* Rp. *fut.an.a*

fut.a⁵ *vi* fall, plummet, go down, drop down: *Ukuta ulifuta*, the wall fell down. Prep. *fut.i.a* St. *fut.ik.a* Cs. *fut.ish.a* Ps. *fut.w.a*

futa⁶ (also *songwe, nachungu*) *n* (*n*) (*zool*) a kind of big short snake with long poisonous front teeth that open

172

and close; black-mouthed snake. *Dendroaspis polylepis*

fut.a⁷ *vt, vi* 1. boycott, eschew, spurn, avoid, reject, elude, stay away: *Alifuta kufanya kazi kwangu siku ya Jumapili,* he avoided working at my place on Sundays. 2. hate, abhor, dislike. Prep. ***fut.i.a*** St. ***fut.ik.a*** Cs. ***fut.ish.a*** Ps. ***fut.w.a*** (cf *chukia*)

futa⁸ *n* (*n*) hatred, animosity, rancour, antipathy, dislike: *Yeye ni mtu mwenye futa sana,* he is a person full of hatred. (cf *chuki*)

futa⁹ *n* (*ma-*) 1. fat, lard, grease, tallow. (cf *shahamu*) 2. obesity, corpulence, fatness. (cf *kitambi*)

futafut.a *vt, vi* flap; flutter as someone is slaughtering a chicken or as someone sometimes is dying: *Kuku akaanza kufutafuta baada ya kuchinjwa,* the hen began to flutter after it was slaughtered. Prep. ***futafut.ia*** St. ***futafut.ik.a*** Cs. ***futafut.ish.a*** Ps. ***futafut.w.a*** Rp. ***futafut.an.a***

futah.i¹ *vi* escape or run away from danger or difficulty: *Raia wengi walifutahi kutokana na vita vya wenyewe kwa wenyewe katika nchi ya jirani,* many citizens fled their homes following the civil war in the neighbouring country, Prep. ***futah.i.a*** St. ***futah.ik.a*** Cs. ***futah.ish.a*** Ps. of Prep. ***futah.iw.a*** Rp. of Prep ***futah.i.an.a*** (cf *dabiri, feleti, kimbia*) (Ar)

futahi² *n* (*n*) 1. luck, luckiness, good fortune: *Ilikuwa futahi kwa yeye kushinda katika bahati nasibu,* it was just good luck for him to win the lottery. (cf *bahati njema*) 2. victory, success, triumph: *Futahi zake kwenye mtihani hazikutegemewa,* his success in the examination was not expected. (cf *ushindi*) (Ar)

futari *n* (*n*) 1. (in Islam) the first food taken in the evening after fasting the whole day. 2. food like cassava, bananas, etc taken during this period.

futi¹ *n* (*ma-*) knee: *Maji ya mafuti,* water up to the knees. (cf *goti*) (Eng)

futi² *n* (*n*) 1. foot; a measure of twelve inches. 2. measuring tape. (cf *futikamba*) (Eng)

futi.a *vt, vi* seize someone, etc. abruptly and by falling on him; jump on sby: *Mwizi alimfutia msafiri na kumwibia mkoba wake,* the thief jumped on a traveller and stole her purse. Prep. ***futi.li.a*** St. ***futi.lik.a*** Cs. ***futi.sh.a*** Ps. ***futi.w.a*** Rp. ***futi.an.a***

futik.a *vt, vi* 1. put in the pocket, stick in the belt or wallet; insert, tuck: *Alizifutika pesa zake kibindoni,* he tucked his money in the loin-cloth. (cf *chomeka*) 2. be erased, be wiped out, be cleaned: *Maandishi haya hayafutiki,* these writings cannot be erased. Prep. ***futik.i.a*** St. ***futik.ik.a*** Cs. ***futik.ish.a*** Ps. ***futik.w.a***

futikamba *n* (*n*) tape measure.

futile *n* (*n*) a ship building industry. 2. a pier for ferry-boats.

fut.u¹ *vi* 1. get lost, be missing, be lost: *Kitabu chake kilifutu darasani,* his book got lost in the class. (cf *potea*) 2. forget; slip one's mind: *Alifutu kunilipa pesa zangu,* he forgot to pay my money. Prep. ***futu.li.a*** St. ***futu.k.a*** Cs. ***futu.sh.a*** (cf *sahau*) (Ar)

fut.u² *vi* resolve, solve, settle; *Alilifutu tatizo lake,* he solved his problem. Prep. ***futu.li.a*** St. ***futu.k.a*** Cs. ***futu.sh.a*** (cf *tatua*) (Ar)

futu.a¹ *vt* 1. take out, pull out, draw out, extract, pluck out, unsheathe: *Aliyafutua manyoya ya kuku,* he plucked out the hen's feathers. 2. take out what is inside; extract, remove: *Alikifutua kibofu cha ng'ombe,* he removed the bladder of an ox. 3. undo a bundle, girdle, etc.: *Alilifutua furushi lake la nguo,* he undid his bundle of clothes. (cf *fungua*) 4. reveal, expose, divulge, disclose; bring to light: *Aliifutua kashfa katika wizara,* he exposed the ministry's scandal. Prep. ***futu.li.a*** St. ***futu.k.a*** and ***futu.***

lik.a Cs. ***futu.lish.a*** Ps. of Prep. ***futu.liw.a*** be revealed e.g. *Siri ilifutuliwa*, the secret was revealed, Rp. ***futu.an.a*** Rp. of Prep. ***futu.li.an.a***

futu.a² *vt* magnify, enlarge, bloat, greaten, expand, inflate: *Mtoto alikifutua kibofu chake kwa kukipuliza*, the child inflated his balloon by blowing it up. Prep. ***futu.li.a*** St. ***futu.k.a*** and ***futu.lik.a*** Cs. ***futu.lish.a*** Ps. of Prep. ***futu.liw.a*** Rp. ***futu.an.a*** Rp. of Prep ***futu.li.an.a*** (cf *tunisha*)

futuk.a *vi* 1. be annoyed because of sby's utterances; be indignant, be angry: *Nilifutuka kwa sababu alinitukana*, I became annoyed because he insulted me. (cf *chukia*) 2. reject sth due to anger, etc.; spurn: *Alifutuka zawadi niliyompa kwa sababu nilimwudhi hivi karibuni*, he spurned the present I gave him because I had annoyed him recently. 3. expand, swell, dilate, inflate: *Mpira ulifutuka baada ya kutiwa pumzi*, the ball inflated after being filled with air. (cf *vimba*) 4. go or leave quickly and suddenly: *Tulipokuwa tunamlaumu, akafutuka*, when we were blaming him, he went quickly and suddenly. 5. (of sth in one's pocket, etc.) project, stick out, distend, protrude: *Kitovu chake kimefutuka*, his navel has projected. Prep. ***futuk.i.a*** St ***futuk.ik.a*** Cs. ***futuk.ish.a*** Ps. ***futuk.w.a*** Rp. ***futuk.an.a***

futuri¹ *n* (*n*) a short span used as a measure from the tip of the thumb to the tip of the finger. (cf *shubiri*)

futuri² (also *futuru*) *n* (*n*) (*med*) haemorrhoids, piles; swollen veins near the anus. (cf *mjiko, bawasiri, kikundu*)

futuru¹ *n* (n) see *futuri²*

futur.u² *vt, vi* (in Islam) take first meal after a day of fasting: *Alichelewa kufuturu*, he was late to break his fast. Prep. ***futur.i.a*** St. ***futur.ik.a*** Cs. ***futur.ish.a*** Ps. of Prep ***futur.i.w.a*** Rp. of Prep. ***futur.i.an.a***

fututa *n* (n) hot water, oil and a piece of cloth used to massage the body of an injured person.

futuza *n* (n) 1. (*anat*) the urinary bladder of a male animal with which children play. (cf *jambizi*) 2. balloon, airship. (cf *purutangi*)

fuu¹ (also *fufu*) *n* (*ma-*) (*bot*) a small black berry eaten by children and which comes from *mfuu* (*Vitex cuneata*), a kind of tree, up to 30 feet high; black plum. *Vitex doriana* sweet.

fuu² (also *fuvu*) *n* (*ma-*) an empty shell; skull, cranium. (cf *bupuru*)

fuu³ *n* (n) see *kisagaunga*

fuuz.a *vt, vi* see *fululiza*

fuvu n (ma-) see *fuu²*

fuwa.a *vi* shrivel, pucker, shrink, be dwarfed; be stunted in growth: *Yeye ana umri mkubwa ingawa amefuwaa*, he is grown up even though he is a dwarf. (cf *dumaa, via*)

fuwak.a (also *fwaka*) *vi* (of liquid, gas, electric current, etc.) discharge. Prep. ***fuwak.i.a*** St. ***fuwak.ik.a*** Cs. ***fuwak.ish.a***

fuwawe (also *fuwe*) *n* (n) pebble; a small smooth stone found on the sea shore. (cf *tumbawe*)

fuwe *n* (ma-) see *fuwawe*

fuwele *n* (n) crystal: *Fuwele owevu*, liquid crystal. *Fuwele duchu*, microcrystalline. (cf *tumbawe*)

fuz.a *vi* persist, continue: *Mvua ilifuza kunyesha kwa siku tatu*, the rain continued for three days. Prep. ***fuz.i.a*** St. ***fuz.ik.a*** Cs. ***fuz.ish.a*** Ps. ***fuz.w.a*** Rp. ***fuz.an.a***. (cf *fuliza, fululiza, endelea*)

fuzi *n* (ma-)(*anat*) shoulder tip. (cf *bega*)

fuz.u *vi, vt* succeed, win, triumph, pass, get through: *Alifuzu kwenye mtihani wake*, he passed his examination. Prep. ***fuz.i.a*** St. ***fuz.ik.a*** Cs. ***fuz.ish.a***. (cf *faulu, shinda*) (Ar)

fwak.a *vi* see *fuwaka*

fyand.a *vt* 1. bruise one's finger, foot, etc. because of being pinched by a door, window, etc.; hurt, stab: *Alikifyanda kidole chake alipokuwa anafunga dirisha*, her finger was bruised when she was closing the window. 2. crush, squash, pound. (cf *ponda*) Prep. *fyand.i.a* St. *fyand.ik.a* Cs. *fyand.ish.a* Ps. *fyand.w.a* Rp. *fyand.an.a*

fyat.a¹ *vt* tuck sth between the legs, thighs, etc.: *Alilifyata shati lake baina ya miguu yake*, he tucked his shirt between his legs. (cf *futika*) 2. hold one's tongue; be quiet. be silent: *Aliufyata ulimi wake wakati mzee wake alipokuwa anamkaripia*, she held her tongue when her parent was scolding her. (cf *sukutu*) 3. flog, whip, flail, thrash; beat someone with a stick, etc.: *Mwalimu alifyata mwanafunzi kwa ukosefu wa nidhamu*, the teacher flogged the student for misconduct. 4. (*idm*) *Fyata mkia*, withdraw out of fear; stop doing sth out of fear. Prep. *fyat.i.a* St. *fyat.ik.a* Cs. *fyat.ish.a* and *fyat.iz.a* Ps. *fyat.w.a* (cf *chapa*, *tandika*)

fyata² *n* (*n*) slingshot, catapult. (cf *manati*, *panda*)

fyatu.a *vt* spring a trap, etc.; release a spring, trigger, etc.; let go suddenly of anything that has been gripped; shoot: *Alifyatua risasi moja kwenye bastola yake*, he shot one bullet from his pistol. *Fyatua matofali*, make bricks. Prep. *fyatu.li.a* St. *fyatu.k.a* and *fyatu.lik.a* e.g. *Mtego wake ulifyatuka*, his trap sprung off. Cs. *fyatu.lish.a* Ps of Prep. *fyatu.liw.a*, be triggered off.

fyatuka *vi* go off suddenly. *Bunduki imefyatuka*, the spring of a gun has gone suddenly.

fyatuko (also *mfyatuko*) *n* (*ma-*) the sudden release of a spring, trap, etc. (cf *fyatuo*)

fyatuo (also *mfyatuo*) *n* (*ma-*) the triggering off of sth e.g. gun, bow, trap, etc.; shoot. (cf *fyatuko*)

fyek.a (also *fyekua¹*) *vt* 1. mow; clear away weeds and undergrowth; cut away grass or bush: *Fyeka mwitu*, make a clearing in a forest. *Alifyeka majani kwenye bustani yangu*, he cut down the grass in my garden. 2. (*fig*) exterminate or drive away an enemy during a war, etc.: *Wananchi walimfyeka mkoloni*, the nationalists drove away the colonialists. Prep. *fyek.e.a* St. *fyek.ek.a* Cs. *fyek.esh.a* Ps. *fyek.w.a* Rp. *fyek.an.a*

fyeko *n* (*ma-*) 1. the act of clearing away weeds and undergrowth. 2. the place cleared; cleared ground: *Anataka kupanda mhogo kwenye fyeko lile*, he wants to grow cassava in that clearing. 3. slash, stroke: *Baada ya mafyeko kadha, nyasi zilimalizika*, after several slashes, the reeds disappeared. 4. things cleared away; a heap of mowed grass or undergrowth.

fyeku.a¹ *vt* see *fyeka*

fyeku.a² *vt* 1. throw up sand behind oneself when running: *Walifyekua mchanga walipokuwa wanakimbia*, they threw up sand behind them when they were running. 2. move fast. Prep. *fyeku.li.a* St. *fyeku.lik.a* Cs. *fyeku.lish.a* Ps. of Prep. *fyeku.liw.a* Rp. *fyeku.an.a*

fyekur.a *vt* see *fyekuza*

fyekuz.a (also *fyekura*) *vt* move sth near with a foot. Prep. *fyekuz.i.a* St. *fyekuz.ik.a* Cs. *fyekuz.ish.a*

fyeruk.a *vi* become angry, become annoyed: *Alifyeruka nilipomlaumu*, she became angry when I scolded her. Prep. *fyeruk.i.a* St. *fyeruk.ik.a* Cs. *fyeruk.ish.a* (cf *hamaki*, *kasirika*)

fyo.a¹ *vt* see *fyua¹*

fyo.a² *vt, vi* see *fyosa*

fyok.a *vt, vi* see *fyonza*

fyokoch.a *vt, vi* (used in the context of sports) win, succeed: *Alifyokocha* kwenye mbio za magari, he won in motor racing Prep. ***fyokoch.e.a*** St. ***fyokoch.ek.a*** Ps. ***fyokoch.w.a*** Rp. ***fyokoch.an.a***

fyom.a *vt* read, study: *Anafyoma kitabu*, he is reading a book. Prep. ***fyom.e.a*** St. ***fyom.ek.a*** Cs. ***fyom.esh.a*** Ps. ***fyom.w.a*** Rp. of Prep. ***fyom.e.an.a*** (cf *soma*)

fyond.a *vt, vi* see *fyonza*

fyongo *adj* off-target, off-course.

fyony.a *vi* express contempt or displeasure over someone by curling the upper lips; tut: *Alinifyonya mimi burebure*, he tutted at me for no reason. Prep. ***fyony.e.a*** St. ***fyony.ek.a*** Cs. ***fyony.esh.a*** Ps. ***fyony.w.a*** Rp. ***fyony.an.a*** (cf *sonya*)

fyonz.a (also *fyonda, fyoka*) *vt, vi* suck, absorb, draw into: *Mtoto mchanga alilifyonza ziwa la mama yake*, the baby sucked its mother's breast. Prep. ***fyonz.e.a*** St. ***fyonz.ek.a*** Cs. ***fyonz.esh.a*** Ps. ***fyonz.w.a***, be sucked e.g. *Tamutamu ilifyonzwa na mtoto*, the sweet was sucked by the child. Rp. ***fyonz.an.a***

fyonzi *adj* (of cotton wool, blotting paper etc.) absorbent; capable of absorbing moisture, light rays, etc.

fyos.a (also *fyoa, fyoza*) *vt, vi* 1. deceive someone with rudeness; hoodwink, cheat, swindle: *Alinifyosa kwa kunipa noti bandia*, he cheated me by giving me a fake note. 2. lie; tell falsehood, stretch the truth. (cf *danganya, hadaa*) Prep. ***fyos.e.a*** St. ***fyos.ek.a*** Cs. ***fyos.esh.a*** Ps. ***fyos.w.a*** Rp. ***fyos.an.a*** (cf *ongopa*)

-**fyosi** (also *fyozi*) *adj* abusive, arrogant, scornful, contemptuous, impolite: *Yeye ni mfanyabiashara mfyosi*, he is an arrogant businessman.

fyoto *interj* an exclamation of contempt, anger, etc. expressed to someone to try to do sth if he could dare do it; You try! Just you dare! (cf *mawe! thubutu!*)

fyoto.a *vt, vi* speak with arrogance audacity, etc.; challenge: *Alifyotoa kwangu kama ningethubutu kumtukana*, he challenged me to insult him.

fyoz.a *vt, vi* see *fyosa*

fyozi *adj* see *fyosi*

fyu.a[1] (also *fyoa*) *vt* cut the ear of the millet or rice, wheat, etc.: *Alifyua mashuke ya mtama wakati yalipopevuka*, he cut the ear of the millet when they were ripe. Prep. ***fyu.li.a*** St. ***fyu.lik.a*** Cs. ***fyu.lish.a*** Ps. of Prep ***fyu.liw.a*** Rp. of Prep ***fyu.li.an.a***

fyu.a[2] *vt* ridicule, scorn, disdain, revile: *Alinifyua hadharani*, he ridiculed me in public. Prep. ***fyu.li.a*** St. ***fyu.k.a*** Cs. ***fyu.lish.a*** Ps. of Prep ***fyu.liw.a*** Rp. ***fyu.an.a*** (cf *tania, kebehi*)

fyuk.a *vi* (of a snare, etc.) go off, be sprung, be triggered off: *Mtego ulifyuka*, the snare sprung off. Prep. ***fyuk.i.a*** St. ***fyuk.ik.a*** Cs. ***fyuk.ish.a***

fyuzi *n* (*n*) (of electricity, etc.) 1. fuse: *Fyuzi katriji*, cartridge fuse. 2. (*syn*) *Amekatika fyuzi*, he is mad. (Eng)

G

G, g /g/ 1. the seventh letter of the Swahili alphabet. 2. a voiced velar stop.

gaaga.a (also *galagala, garagara*) *vt,vi* writhe; twist and turn, toss and turn, roll from side to side: *Alikuwa akigaagaa kitandani kutokana na ugonjwa wa saratani,* she was writhing on the bed because of cancer. Prep. ***gaaga.li.a*** St. ***gaaga.lik.a*** Cs. ***gaaga.z.a*** and ***gaaga.lish.a*** (cf *furukuta*)

gabadini *n (n)* a kind of cloth usu used for making trousers, suits, coats, etc.; gabardine. (Eng)

gadi[1] *n (n)* prop, pole, support. It is used to prevent keeled ships from lying over at low tide: *Tia magadi,* shore up. (cf *mwega*)

gadi[2] *n (n)* 1. guard, sentry, sentinel; a soldier or guard. 2. a period on guard: *Shika gadi,* be on guard: *Askari alishika gadi kutwa nzima,* the sentinel was on guard for the whole day. (Eng)

gadim.u *vt* shore up with *magadi*; buttress. Prep. ***gadim.i.a*** St. ***gadim.ik.a*** Cs. ***gadim.ish.a*** Ps of Prep. ***gadim.iw.a*** Rp. of Prep. ***gadim.i.an.a*** (Ar)

gae[1] *n (ma-)* a large potsherd of glass or cooking pot; a large piece of earthenware; crock: *Bakuli langu limevunjika na sasa limebaki magae manne,* my bowl is broken and now lies in four pieces. (*prov*) *Mfinyanzi hulia gaeni,* a potter eats from a potsherd i.e. a person can possess much wealth, yet he may fail to make use of it in a proper way.

gae[2] *n (ma-)* a container which has embers for a patient to warm himself.

gafi *adj* see *ghafi*.

gafu.a (also *gofua*) *vt, vi* emaciate, weaken, eat away: *Maradhi ya saratani yalimgafua vibaya,* cancer had emaciated her badly. St. ***gafu.k.a*** Cs. ***gafu.sh.a*** (cf *kondesha, sononesh.a*)

gaga *n (ma-)* 1. tartar on the teeth and similar incrustations: *Hapigi mswaki kila siku na ndio maana, ana magaga kwenye meno,* he does not brush his teeth regularly and that is why, he has a lot of tartar on his teeth. 2. a large scab; a large dry crust formed over a wound as it heals.

gagadu.a *vt* chew sth hard; masticate sth hard; munch: *Niliposhikwa na njaa, nikaanza kuzigagadua tosi,* when I felt hungry, I started munching on slices of toasts. Prep. ***gagadu.li.a*** St ***gagadu.k.a*** Cs. ***gagadu.sh.a*** and ***gagadu.z.a*** Ps. of Prep ***gagadu.liw.a*** (cf *tafuna*)

gagaik.a *vi* be confused, be perplexed. Prep. ***gagaik.i.a*** St. ***gagaik.ik.a*** Cs. ***gagaik.ish.a*** (cf *babaika*)

gagamiz.a *vt, vi* penetrate forcefully; enter with force: *Ingawa furushi la nguo lilijaa, nilijaribu sana kugagamiza nguo chache ili nazo zipelekwe kwa dobi,* even though the bundle of clothes was full and tight, I tried my best to force in a few more items so that they could also be sent to the laundry. Prep. ***gagamiz.i.a*** St. ***gagamiz.ik.a*** Cs. ***gagamiz.ish.a*** Ps. ***gagamiz.w.a*** Rp. ***gagamiz.an.a*** (cf *kokomeza, penyeza*)

gagazi *n (ma-)* roasted fish.

gagulo *n (ma-)* petticoat, slip; a woman's undergarment which hangs from the waist downwards. (cf *kirinda*)

gaham.u[1] *vi* go on strike; refuse to do sth: *Walimu wamegahamu kwa sababu wanataka nyongeza ya mshahara,* the teachers have gone on strike because they want a pay rise. Prep. ***gaham.i.a***

St. **gaham.ik.a** Cs. *gaham.ish.a* Ps. of Prep. *gaham.iw.a* Rp. of Prep. *gaham.i.an.a* (cf *goma*)
gaham.u² *vt* deny sth abruptly. Prep. *gaham.i.a* St. *gaham.ik.a* Cs. *gaham.ish.a* Ps. of Prep. *gaham.iw.a* Rp. of Prep. *gaham.i.an.a*
gai.a *vt* give sby sth voluntarily: *Alinigaia fedha nyingi*, he gave me a lot of money. St. *gai.ka* Cs. *gai.sh.a* Ps. *gai.w.a* Rp. *gai.an.a*
gaidi¹ *n* (*ma-*) robber, bandit, terrorist: *Gaidi alimwibia mtalii pesa nyingi*, the robber stole a lot of money from a tourist. *Magaidi walilipua bomu katika ubalozi nchini*, the terrorists exploded a bomb at the embassy in the country. (cf *mnyang'anyi*) (Ar)
gaidi² *n* (*ma-*) guide (Eng)
gaj.a *vt, vi* 1. speak indistinctly, speak without being understood; mumble: *Nilimwambia atoe taarifa vizuri kwa vile alikuwa akigaja maneno tu*, I told him to articulate his statement because he was just mumbling. 2. confuse, bewilder, puzzle: *Maneno yake ya mafumbomafumbo yalinigaja*, his enigmatic words baffled me. Prep. *gaj.i.a* St *gaj.ik.a* Cs *gaj.ish.a* Ps *gaj.w.a* Rp *gaj.an.a*
galacha *n* (*n*) expert, pundit, specialist: *Yeye ni galacha katika vipengele mbalimbali vya lugha*, he is an expert in the different aspects of the language (cf *stadi, fundi, gwiji*)
galagal.a¹ *vt* see *gaagaa*
galagala² *n* (*n*) (*med*) chicken pox; a disease common amongst children distinguished by a light fever and itchy red spots on the skin. (cf *tetekuwanga*)
galagala³ *n* (*n*) see *wayo³*
galani *n* (*n*) see *galoni*
galasha *n* (*ma-*) matchbox
gale *n* (*n*) see *ugale*
gali *n* (*n*) galley proofs (Eng)
galimu *n* (*n*) (*zool*) male camel.

galme (also *galmi*) *n* (*n*) 1. (*naut*) a kind of small sail in a dhow; a mizzen sail. 2. mizzen mast; a small second mast in a large dhow. (Ar)
galmi *n* (*n*) see *galme*
galoni *n* (*n*) gallon (Eng)
gamba *n* (*ma-*) scale of a fish or bark of a tree, etc.; the cover of a book, etc.; outer covering: *Gamba la mti*, the bark of a tree. *Gamba la kobe*, tortoise shell. *Gamba la kitabu*, book cover
gambera *n* (*ma-*) 1. an assistant to a hunter; a person who carries guns for a hunter: *Wawindaji wengi hufuatana na magambera wanapokwenda kuwinda wanyama wa porini*, many hunters are accompanied by their assistants when they go to hunt wild animals. 2. leader, guide, director. 3. pander, pimp, whore-monger, flesh-peddler. (cf *kuwadi*)
gambra *n* (*n*) (*naut*) dhow's entry.
gambusi¹ *n* (*ma-*) (*mus*) lute; a kind of an old stringed musical instrument related to the guitar, but having a long neck and an almost oval back and usu with four strings that are plucked or strummed with the fingers.

gambusi

gambusi² *n* (*n*) (*zool*) fish; a kind of small fresh water fish.
gamti¹ *n* (*n*) (*bot*) a kind of brown rice.
gamti² *n* (*n*) a kind of unbleached calico. (cf *marekani*)

gamu¹ *n* (*n*) an official reception parade.
gamu² *n* (*n*) gum, glue. (cf *gundi, gluu*) (Eng)
gamu³ *n* (*n*) awe, fear. (cf *hofu, woga*)
gana¹ *n* (*ma-*) a kind of rolled tobacco.
gana² *n* (*n*) hundred (cf *mia*)
ganda¹ *n* (*ma-*) (*bot*) the rind of a fruit, the skin of a fruit; integument, peel, shuck: *Ganda la limau*, lemon rind. *Ganda la chungwa*, orange rind.
gand.a² *vi* curdle, coagulate, clot; be frozen: *Gundi imeganda kwenye stempu*, the glue has coagulated on the stamp. *Maziwa yameganda*, the milk has curdled. Prep. **gand.i.a** St. **gand.ik.a** Cs. **gand.ish.a**, freeze; Ps. **gand.w.a** St, **gand.am.a**, be stuck, be frozen, be coagulated; be in a condition of sticking together. Rp. **gand.an.a** (cf *kwama, nasa*)
gand.a³ *vt, vi* 1. stick to, clasp, cleave to: *Amemganda shingoni*, he has clasped him round the neck. 2. remain behind: *Sote tulikwenda Uingereza lakini yeye kaganda huko hadi leo*, we all went to Britain but he remained behind to date. Prep. **gand.i.a** St. **gand.ik.a** Cs. **gand.ish.a** Ps. **gand.w.a** Rp. **gand.an.a** (cf *bakia, selelea*)
gandalo *n* (*ma-*) cleft stick or tree used as a stock for imprisoning culprits; wooden fetter. (cf *mkatale*)
gandam.a¹ *vi* see *ganda*². Prep. **gandam.i.a** St. **gandam.ik.a** Cs. **gandam.ish.a gandam.w.a** Rp. **gandam.an.a**
gandam.a² *vt, vi* 1. depend on, rely, count in: *Hataki kufanya kazi; anataka tu kuwagandama wazazi wake*, he doesn't want to work; he just wants to depend on his parents. 2. lean. Prep. **gandam.i.a** St. **gandam.ik.a** Cs. **gandam.ish.a** Ps. **ganda.mw.a** Rp. **gandam.an.a**
gandami.a *vt* 1. lean; rest on sby/sth without exerting pressure. (cf *egemea*) 2. involve in sth that does not concern you; meddle. St. **gandami.k.a** Cs.

gandami.sh.a Ps. *gandami.w.a* Rp. *gandami.an.a* (cf *ingilia*)
gandamiz.a (also *kandamiza*) *vt, vi* 1. press on, press heavily on: *Alinigandamiza mimi chini na nikawa siwezi kufanya lolote*, he pressed me heavily on the ground and I was helpless. (cf *bana, lalia*) 2. oppress, tyrannize, repress: *Wakoloni waliwagandamiza wananchi kwa muda mrefu*, the colonialists oppressed the nationalists for a long time. Prep. **gandamiz.i.a** St. **gandamiz.ik.a** Ps. **gandamiz.w.a** Rp. **gandamiz.an.a** (cf *kandamiza*)
gandi¹ *n* (*n*) sheet; a kind of calico worn as a loincloth: *Shuka ya gandi*, the loincloth of this kind.
gandi² *n* (*n*) a kind of knife having different uses.
gandish.a *vt* bind, coagulate, stick: *Niliigandisha gundi kulika stempu*, I stuck glue on the stamp. Prep. **gandish.i.a** St. **gandish.i.k.a** Ps **gandish.w.a** Rp **gandish.an.a**
gando *n* (*ma-*) 1. (*zool*) chela nipper; the pincerlike claw of a crab or lobster. 2. the tooth of a crab. (*prov*) *Kaa akiinua gando, mambo yamekatika*, a person who is used to scrounge things off his friends, etc. will not leave the place if he is in need of those things and if he leaves, it means that he has already obtained those things.
gandu.a *vt* unfasten, disjoin, pull away: *Aliigandua picha kwenye ukuta*, he detached the picture from the wall. Prep. **gandu.li.a** St. **gandu.k.a** Cs. **gandu.lish.a** Ps. of Prep. **gandu.liw.a** Rp. **gandu.an.a** (cf *bandua, ondoa*)
gane *n* (*ma-*) hostel, dormitory; the sleeping quarters of young unmarried boys and girls. (cf *bweni*)
ganeti *n* (*n*) (*naut*) garnet; a hoisting tackle for loading cargo (Eng)
gang.a *vt, vi* 1. cure, heal; effect a cure: *Daktari aliweza kuyaganga maradhi*

G gangaiz.a — gao

yake vizuri, the doctor was able to cure her disease effectively. 2. *(fig)* repair, mend, patch up, fix: *Fundi wa magari aliliganga gari langu*, the mechanic repaired my car. Prep. ***gang.i.a*** St. ***gang.ik.a*** Cs. ***gang.ish.a*** Ps. ***gang.w.a*** Rp. ***gang.an.a*** (cf *tengeneza*)

gangaiz.a *vt, vi* prevaricate, brush aside, be inattentive; pretend not to understand or be concerned in an affair: *Nilimwuliza kwa nini hakuja kazini jana lakini badala ya kunipa jibu sahihi, akawa anagangaiza*, I asked him why he did not come to work yesterday but instead of giving me a precise answer, he brushed my question aside. Prep. ***gangaiz.i.a*** St. ***gangaiz.ik.a*** Ps. ***gangaiz.w.a*** Rp. ***gangaiz.an.a*** (cf *jiberegeza, jipurukusha*)

gangamal.a *vt* persist, insist. Prep. ***gangamal.i.a*** St. ***gangamal.ika*** Cs. ***gangamal.iz.a*** Ps. of Prep. ***gangamal.iw.a*** Rp. of Prep. ***gangamal.i.an.a***

gange[1] *n (ma-)* a kind of limestone or soft chalky rock.

gange[2] *n (n)* job, work, employment: *Amepata gange karibuni*, he has found a job recently. (cf *kazi*)

gango[1] *n (ma-)* 1. treatment, healing, cure: *Gango la mgonjwa*, the treatment of a patient. (cf *matibabu*) 2. repair, mending, fixing up: *Baiskeli yangu imeharibika na sasa inataka kufanyiwa gango la haraka*, my bicycle is out of order and now it needs to be repaired immediately. 3. patch, joint, splice, joining.

gango[2] *n (ma-)* vice, cramp, clamp; a metal bar with both ends bent to a right angle for holding together pieces of timber and used usu by a carpenter.

gango[3] *n (ma-)* residue of unkempt dried dirt on the skin, etc. (cf *gago*)

gangiri *n (n)* lace

gangrini *n (n) (med)* gangrene; localized death and decay of tissue due to an interrupted blood supply, etc. (Eng)

gangu.a *vt* 1. undo sth that is being repaired or healed: *Nilikuwa nikiliganga gari moja lakini rafiki yako akaja kuligangua*, I was repairing a car but your friend came and undid all my work. 2. save, rescue; get out of a difficulty: *Daktari alimgangua mgonjwa mahututi*, the doctor saved a critically ill patient. 3. remove a magic spell. Prep. ***gangu.li.a*** St. ***gangu.lik.a*** Cs. ***gangu.lish.a*** Ps. of Prep. ***gangu.liw.a*** Rp. of Prep. ***gangu.an.a***

gani *adj* interrogative word meaning What? What kind of? What sort of? *Mtu gani alifika hapa jana?*: What kind of person arrived here yesterday? *Sababu gani ukacheleua juzi?* What was the reason for your being late the day before yesterday?

ganja[1] *n (ma-) (naut)* a type of a two-masted vessel.

ganja[2] *n (n)* rolled-up marijuana

ganjo *n (ma-)* a deserted village or town: *Alihiari kuishi kwenye ganjo ili aepukane na kero za watu mbalimbali*, he opted to live in a deserted place to avoid being bothered by different people. (cf *tongo, mahame*)

ganz.a *vi* falter, stutter, stammer; speak in a hesitating or lazy manner: *Tulimwuliza lakini hakutujibu mara moja; akawa anaganza tu*, we asked him but he did not reply us immediately; he began to stutter. Prep. ***ganz.i.a*** St. ***ganz.ik.a*** Cs. ***ganz.ish.a*** Ps. ***ganz.w.a*** (cf *gugumiza*)

ganzi *n (n)* 1. (usually used with the verb *fa*, die), numbness, insentience, deadness: *Mguu wangu umekufa ganzi*, my leg has gone numb. *Meno yako yamefanya ganzi*, your teeth are set on edge. 2. paralysis, insentience (cf *kibibi, faliji, kiharusi*)

gao *n (ma-)* the palm of the hand; a handful, a fistful: *Alinipatia gao moja* *la mtama*, he gave me a handful of millet. (cf *konzi, ukufi, chopa*)

gaogao (also *gaugau, gayogayo*) *n* (*n*) (*zool*) flounder, turbot; a kind of flat fish of the families *Bothidae* and *Psettodidae*, caught for food and which is found in all tropical and temperate seas; Disc flounder. *Bothus myriaster.*

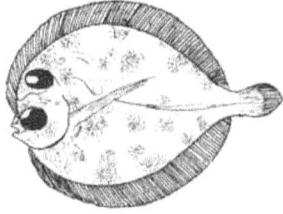

gaogao

garagar.a *vt, vi* writhe, squirm, roll from side to side. Prep. *garagar.i.u* St. *garagar.ik.a* (cf *gaagaa, biringia, furukuta*)

garagaz.a *vt* 1. cause or make to roll over. 2. discredit: *Mwanasiasa alifanikiwa kuigaragasa serikali bungeni*, the political succeeded in discrediting the government in the parliament. 3. thrash, whip, defeat: *Timu yao ilikigaragaza vibaya kikosi chetu*, their team badly defeated our eleven (cf *tandika, bamiza, sasambua*) Prep. *garagaz.i.a* St. *garagaz.ik.a* Cs. *garagaz.ish.a* Ps. *garagaz.w.a* Rp. *garagaz.an.a*

garasa (also *garasha*) *n* (*ma-*) a playing card that has no value in a particular game; a valueless playing card. (cf *gamba*)

garasha *n* (*ma-*) see *garasa*

garegare *n* (*n*) a person who is unstable.

gari *n* (*ma-*) any vehicle on wheels; cart, wagon, car, etc. *Gari la wazima moto*, fire brigade vehicle. *Gari la wagonjwa*, ambulance. *Gari la moshi*, train. *Gari la ng'ombe*, oxcart. (Hind)

gashi *n* (*ma-*) (*colloq*) girl, lass; a young female: *Wagashi wa siku hizi wanapenda kuvaa nguo za kisasa*, modern girls like to wear modern clothes. (cf *msichana*)

gasketi *n* (*n*) (*engin*) gasket; a piece or ring of rubber, metal, etc. placed around a piston or point to make it leak-proof (Eng)

gastronomia *n* (*n*) gastronomy; the science or art of good eating. (Eng)

gati *n* (*ma-*) pier, wharf, dock, quay: *Gati letu linahimili meli nyingi*, our dock is capable of allowing many ships to moor. (Hind)

gaugau *n* (*ma-*) (*zool*) a kind of bird.

gauk.a *vi* see *geuka* Cs. **gau.z.a**

gauni *n* (*ma-*) 1. a woman's dress; 2. gown, dress. (Eng)

gauz.a *vt* see *geuza*

gavana *n* (*ma-*) 1. governor: *Gavana mkuu*, governor general. 2. governor; a representative of a president or leader of a country in a particular region. 3. head, manager, governor: *Gavana wa Benki ya Tanzania*, the Governor of the Bank of Tanzania. (Eng)

gaw.a[1] *n* (*n*) (*zool*) night jar; a night bird of the *Caprimulgidae* family having a long tail and long wings. (cf *kirukanjia, kipasuasanda*)

gaw.a[2] (also *gawanya*) *vt* 1. distribute, deal out. 2. divide among, divide up: *Alizigawa pesa zote kwa wale vijana watatu*, he divided all the money between the three young men. Prep. *gaw.i.a* St. *gaw.ik.a* Cs. *gaw.ish.a* Ps. *gaw.iw.a* Rp. *gaw.an.a* (cf *kasimu*)

gawadi *n* (*ma-*) pimp, panderer, pander, procurer, whore-monger. (cf *fisadi kuwadi*)

gawadi.a (also *kuwadia*) *vt* pimp for sb; pander, procure, solicit: *Alihusika katika kugawadia wenzake*, he was involved in pimping for his colleagues. Prep. *gawadi.li.a* St. *gawadi.k.a* Cs. *gawadi.sh.a* Ps. *gawadi.w.a* Rp. *gawadi.an.a* (cf *tongoza*)

gawany.a see *gawa*[2]. Prep. *gawany.i.a*

G

St. *gawany.ik.a* Cs. *gawany.ish.a* Ps. *gawany.w.a* Rp. *gawany.an.a*

gawanyik.a *vt* be divided, be divisible: *Nambari hii haiwezi kugawanyika kwa tatu*, this number cannot be divided by three. Prep. *gawanyik.i.a* St. *gawanyik.ik.a* Cs. *gawany.ish.a* Ps. *gawanyik.w.a* Rp. *gawanyik.an.a*

gawi.a *vt* distribute to, allocate, assign, divide among: *Walitugawia kazi*, they divided work for us. St. *gawi.k.a* Cs. *gawi.sh.a* Ps. *gawi.w.a* Rp. *gawi.an.a*

gawio¹ *n* (*ma-*) a gift of God; talent, endowment: *Mungu amempa gawio la kuelewa mambo mengi mara moja*, God has given him the gift of understanding many things quite quickly. (cf *kipaji*)

gawio² *n* (*ma-*) 1. dividend, share. 2. sharing, apportionment; division: *Gawio la pesa*, the sharing of money.

gawo *n* (*ma-*) 1. share, dividend, portion: *Baba yetu aligawa mali kati yetu na gawo langu likawa shamba*, our father distributed property amongst us and my share was a plantation. (cf *sehemu, fungu*)

gay.a *vi* be occupied, be disturbed, be concerned, be busy with: *Anagaya sana kutafuta kazi*, he is very busy looking for a job. Prep. *gay.i.a* St. *gay.ik.a* Cs. *gay.ish.a* Ps. of Prep. *gay.iw.a* (cf *sumbuka, hangaika*)

gayagaya *n* (*ma-*) a kind of mat used for lolling on, resting, etc; sleeping mat, reed mat. (cf *mkeka, kibacha*)

gayogayo *n* (*n*) see *gaogao*

gaz.a *vt* hesitate, falter. Prep. *gaz.i.a* St. *gaz.ik.a* Cs. *gaz.ish.a* Ps. *gaz.w.a* (cf *sita*)

gazeti *n* (*ma-*) gazette, newspaper: *Gazeti la serikali*, government newspaper. *Gazeti pendwa*, popular newspaper. (cf *jarida*) (Eng)

ge.a *vt* 1. throw away, discard: *Mtoto alikigea kishada chake*, the child threw away his kite. (cf *tupa*) *Gea macho*, glance, glimpse. 2. leave behind, abandon, forsake: *Walivigea vitu vyao baada ya kuvamiwa na majambazi*, they left their things behind after being attacked by thugs. 3. disappear, vanish; recede from view: *Ndege wangu alikuwemo kwenye tundu lakini sasa amegea*, my bird was in the nest but now it has disappeared. Prep. *ge.le.a* St. *ge.lik.a* Cs. *ge.sh.a* and *ge.z.a* Ps. *ge.lew.a* Rp. *ge.an.a* (cf *toweka*)

gegedu *n* (*ma-*) (*anat*) cartilage (cf *tishu*)

gegenu *n* (*ma-*) (*zool*) soldier termite. This is a large fierce ant (family *Termitidae*) which has a white body and a red head.

gegereka *n* (*ma-*) (*zool*) crustacean; any of a class of anthropods including shrimps, crabs, barnacles and lobsters that generally live in the water and breathe through gills.

gego (also *chego, jego*) *n* (*ma-*) molar tooth.

geisha *n* (*n*) geisha; a Japanese girl trained in singing. (Jap)

geji *n* (*n*) gauge; an instrument for measuring the amount or level of sth e.g the amount of oil in an engine, steam pressure, etc. (Eng)

gele *adj* raw, unripe.

geli¹ *n* (*n*) a child's game like tip-cat; a child's stick game.

geli² *n* (*n*) a large knife

gem.a¹ *vt* tap a tree or fruit, etc. to get its sap esp getting palm wine from a coconut tree: *Gema tembo*, tap palm wine. (*prov*) *Mgema akisifiwa tembo hulitia maji*, if the palm tapper is praised because of his palm wine, he dilutes it with water i.e. if someone is praised a lot, he finally becomes swollen-headed.

gema² *n* (*ma-*) gash, incision, slit: *Yeye ana magema mwilini kutokana na matibabu aliyoyapata*, he has deep cuts due to medical treatment he has received. (cf *tojo, chale, nembo*)

gema³ *n* (*ma-*) downward slope; declension, escarpment: *Alipokuwa anateremka kwenye gema, alianguka,* while going down the declension, he fell. (cf *korongo, genge*)

gemu.a *vt* open a tap of a coconut tree in a calabash or gourd to get sap. Prep. ***gemu.li.a*** St. ***gemu.k.a*** Cs. ***gemu.sh.a*** Rp. of Prep. ***gemu.liw.a***

gendaeka *n* (*ma-*) (*zool*) a big male baboon. (cf *koogwe, mwenda, jendaweka*)

genderi *n* (*ma-*) (*bot*) sugar cane.

gendi *n* (*ma-*) nipper

genge¹ *n* (*ma-*) 1. den, grotto, cave, hollow, cavern: *Wanyama mbalimbali wanaishi katika magenge,* different animals live in the dens. (cf *pango, shimo*) 2. cliff, precipice, escarpment: *Aliukurubia ukingo wa genge,* he approached the edge of the cliff. (cf *korongo, gema*) 3. bank of a sea or lake.

genge² *n* (*ma-*) 1. gang, clique, company: *Niliona genge la watu likitokea upande wa kusini,* I saw a group of people coming from the south. 2. a group of workers working in the same place: *Genge la mabaharia,* a group of sailors. *Genge la vibarua,* a gang of labourers. 3. makeshift kiosks near construction sites or places of work. 4. hawkers' market; vendors' stall.

-geni *adj* 1. foreign, alien: *Lugha ya kigeni,* a foreign language. *Lugha ngeni,* a foreign language. 2. strange, exotic, outlandish, queer: *Tabia ya kigeni,* strange behaviour. *Jambo geni,* strange affair 3. new, recent, modern: *Neno geni,* a new word. *Habari geni,* new information.

gere *n* (*n*) jealousy, envy, bitterness: *Onea gere,* feel jealous. (cf *ngoa, wivu, kijicho*)

gereji *n* (*ma-*) garage (Eng)

gerek.a *vt* cook food for a short time. Prep. ***gerek.e.a*** St. ***gerek.ek.a*** Cs. ***gerek.esh.a*** Ps. ***gerek.w.a*** (cf *injika*)

geresh.a¹ *vt, vi* deceive, hoodwink, swindle: *Hataki kunipa pesa zangu; siku zote ananigeresha tu,* she doesn't want to pay back my money; she always deceives me. Prep. ***geresh.e.a*** St. ***geresh.ek.a*** Ps. ***geresh.w.a*** Rp. ***geresh.an.a*** (cf *danganya*)

geresh.a¹ *n* (*n*) deceit, deception, hypocrisy. (cf *udanganyifu*)

gereza *n* (*ma-*) prison, jail, (cf *jela*) (Port)

gerigeri (also *geri*) *adv* at the corner, beside.

gesi *n* (*n*) gas: *Gesi asilia,* natural gas. *Gesi amilifu,* active gas. *Gesi bwete,* inert gas. *Gesi makaa,* coal gas. *Gesi ya sumu,* poison gas. (Eng)

gestapo *n* (*n*) Gestapo; the secret state police in Nazi Germany. (Ger)

geti *n* (*n*) gate, entrance, opening. (Eng)

-geugeu *adj* whimsical, fickle; capricious, unpredictable: *Mtu wa kigeugeu,* a fickle person. *Mambo ya kigeugeu,* unpredictable matters.

geuk.a (also *gauka*) *vi, vt* 1. be altered, be changed, be transferred: *Hali ya hewa iligeuka jana,* the weather changed yesterday. 2. change position, turn oneself, turn around: *Aligeuka upande huu na nikamwona,* he turned around to this side and I saw him. Prep. ***geuk.i.a*** St. ***geuk.ik.a***

geuki.a *vt, vi* 1. turn to (from, towards, for, etc.): *Aligeukia upande wa kushoto,* he turned to the left. 2. betray, turn against: *Alikuwa akinipenda lakini sasa amenigeukia,* he used to like me very much but now he has turned against me. St. ***geuk.ik.a*** Ps. ***geuk.iw.a*** Rp. ***geuk.i.an.a***

geuko *n* (*ma-*) change, alteration, transformation: *Geuko la hali ya hewa,* change of weather. *Mageuko ya kisiasa,* political changes. (cf *badiliko, geuzo*)

geuz.a (also *gauza*) *vt* 1. change, transform, modulate, modify: *Lazima ugeuze tabia yako,* you must change your behaviour. 2. turn the other

G

way round: *Alikuwa amevaa shati lakini alikuwa ameligeuza,* he wore a shirt but he wore it inside out. Prep. ***geuz.i.a*** St. ***geuz.ik.a*** Ps. ***geuz.w.a*** Rp. ***geuz.a.na***

geuzi[1] *n* (*ma-*) (usu in pl) change, transformation: *Mageuzi ya kimapinduzi,* revolutionary changes, radical changes. *Mageuzi ya kisiasa,* political changes. (cf *badiliko*)

geuzi[2] *adj* changeable, changing, variable.

geuzo *n* (*ma-*) change, alteration, shifting: *Geuzo la mkuu wa wilaya,* the change of a district commissioner. (cf *badiliko*)

gez.a *vt* 1. imitate, copy, follow: *Aliligeza kila jambo zuri rafiki yake alilolifanya,* he copied every good deed his friend had done. (cf *iga*) 2. try, attempt: *Niligeza kumhamasisha kutafuta kazi lakini akakataa,* I tried to motivate him to look for work, but he refused. (cf *jaribu*) 3. compare, contrast: *Aliizigeza tabia za ndugu hawa wawili,* he compared the characters of these two brothers. (cf *fananisha, linganisha*) Prep. ***gez.e.a*** St. ***gez.ek.a*** Cs. ***gez.esh.a*** Ps. ***gez.w.a*** Rp. ***gez.an.a***

gezo *n* (*ma-*) idea, viewpoint, opinion: *Sisi tumempa gezo letu; itakuwa ni vizuri kwake kama atalizingatia,* we have given her our opinion; it will be best if she heeds it. (cf *wazo*)

ghadhabu *n* (*n*) anger, rage, wrath: *Fanya ghadhabu,* be raged. *Alihutubia kwa ghadhabu juu ya shida za wanavijiji,* he spoke in anger over the plight of the villagers. (cf *hamaki, hasira*) (Ar)

ghadhibik.a *vi* be annoyed, be furious, be enraged: *Mwanafunzi alighadhibika kwa vile alikemewa na mwalimu wake,* the student was annoyed because he was scolded by his teacher. Prep. ***ghadhibik.i.a*** St. ***ghadhibik.ik.a*** Cs. ***ghadhibik.ish.a*** (cf *hamaki, kasirika*)

ghadhibish.a *vt* infuriate, madden, enrage, anger, incense: *Alinighadhibisha bure,* he enraged me for nothing. Prep. ***ghadhibish.i.a*** St. ***ghadhibish.ik.a*** Ps. ***ghadhibish.w.a*** Rp. ***ghadhibish.an.a*** (cf *hamakisha, kasirisha*)

ghafi[1] (also *gafi*) *adj* raw, unprocessed: *Mali ghafi,* raw materials.

ghafi[2] *n* (*n*) gross weight (Ar)

ghafilik.a *vi* 1. forget; cease to remember, be taken unawares: *Alighafilika kunipigia simu,* he forgot to phone me. (cf *pitiwa, sahau*) 2. overlook, ignore, be neglectful: *Nilimwambia aifanye kazi lakini labda alighafilika,* I told him to do the job but probably he overlooked it. Prep. ***ghafilik.i.a*** St. ***ghafilik.ik.a*** Cs. ***ghafilik.ish.a*** (cf *sahau, pitiwa*) (Ar)

ghafla (also *ghafula*) *adv* suddenly, abruptly, all of a sudden: *Alitokea ghafla,* he appeared suddenly. (cf *fajaa*) (Ar)

ghafula *adv* see *ghafla*

ghafuri *adj* (of God's attributes) forgiving, remissive, absolving.

ghaibu *n* (*n*) absence, memory; a thing not seen because it is distant: *Aliisoma Kurani kwa ghaibu,* he read the Koran from memory; he recited the Koran. (Ar)

ghaidhi[1] *n* (*n*) anger, wrath, fury: *Ana ghaidhi za hali ya juu,* he has a bad temper. (cf *hamaki, hasira*) (Ar)

ghaidhi[2] *n* (*n*) determination, intention, purpose: *Hana ghaidhi ya kuoa tena,* he has no intention of remarrying. (cf *nia, kusudu*)

ghair.i[1] *vi* change one's mind, alter plan; do sth unexpected, sudden or surprising: *Alikuwa kwanza anataka kuitembelea Ubelgiji lakini sasa ameghairi,* at first, she wanted to visit Belgium but now she has changed her mind. Prep. ***ghair.i.a*** St. ***ghair.ik.a*** Cs. ***ghair.ish.a*** (cf *badili*) (Ar)

ghairi[2] (also *bighairi*) *prep* 1. (used with *ya*) without regard to, apart from:

ghairish.a   **gharama   G**

Ghairi ya yote yale niliyokueleza, mzee naye pia atakupa maelezo yake, apart from what I have told you, my father will also give you his explanation. (cf *mbali, bila*) 2. except, without. (Ar)

ghairish.a *vt* postpone, defer, delay: *Alighairisha safari yake*, he postponed his journey. Prep. ***ghairish.i.a*** St. ***ghairish.ik.a*** Ps. ***ghairish.w.a***

ghala *n* (*ma-*) storehouse, storeroom, warehouse: *Ghala ya silaha*, armoury. *Magunia yote yenye mbata yamewekwa kwenye ghala*, all the sacks containing copra have been put in the warehouse. (cf *stoo, bohari*) (Ar)

ghala mbegu *n* (*n*) (*bot*) cotyledon; the first single leaf or one of the first pair of leaves produced by the embryo of a flowering plant.

ghalati¹ *n* (*n*) error, mistake, falsehood, lie, distortion: *Aliwasilisha kwangu hesabu ya ghalati ya mauzo yote ya bidhaa zetu*, he presented me with false accounts of the sale of our goods. (cf *uongo, kosa*) (Ar)

ghalat.i² *vt* delay, temporize. Prep. ***ghalat.i.a*** St. ***ghalat.ik.a*** Cs. ***ghalat.ish.a*** Ps. ***ghalat.iw.a*** (cf *sita*)

ghali *adj* expensive, dear, high-priced: *Sukari imekuwa ghali siku hizi*, sugar has become expensive these days. (Ar)

ghalibu *adv* see *aghalabu*

ghalik.a *vi* 1. be rare, occur scarcely: *Msimu huu si wa machungwa na ndiyo maana yameghalika*, this is not the season for oranges and that is why, they are scarce. 2. be dear, be costly: *Vitambaa vimeghalika siku hizi kwa vile vingi vinaagizwa kutoka nje*, textile materials are expensive these days because so many of them are imported. Prep. ***ghalik.ia*** St. ***ghalik.ik.a*** Cs. ***ghalik.ish.a*** (Ar)

ghalish.a *vt* raise the price of sth; make sth dear. Prep. ***ghalish.i.a*** St. ***ghalish.ik.a*** Ps. ***ghalish.w.a***

ghamm.a *vi* be unique, be peculiar, be exceptional. Prep. ***ghamm.i.a*** St. ***ghamm.ik.a*** Cs. ***ghamm.ish.a*** Ps. ***ghamm.w.a*** (Ar)

ghamidha *n* (*n*) haste, hurry, rush (cf *haraka, pupa*)

ghamu¹ *n* (*n*) grief, sorrow, remorse: *Ana ghamu nyingi kutokana na kifo cha mjomba wake*, he is in deep sorrow following the death of his uncle. *Tia ghamu*, grieve. *Ingiwa na ghamu*, be grieved. (cf *jitimai, huzuni, majonzi*) (Ar)

ghamu² *n* (*n*) anxiety, eagerness, desire: *Ana ghamu ajabu kuhusu matokeo yake ya mtihani*, he is very anxious about his examination results. (cf *shauku, hamu*) (Ar)

ghan.i¹ *vi, vt* sing, melodize: *Akighani, kila mmoja huchangamka*, when he sings, everyone cheers up. Prep. ***ghan.i.a*** St. ***ghan.ik.a*** Ps. of Prep. ***ghan.iw.a*** Rp. of Prep. ***ghan.i.an.a*** (cf *imba*) (Ar)

ghani² *n* (*n*) song, melody (Ar)

ghanima¹ *n* (*n*) prosperity, success, progress, advancement: *Nchi yetu imepata ghanima tangu kuunyakua uhuru*, our country has made progress since attaining independence. (cf *neema, maendeleo, usitawi*) (Ar)

ghanima² *n* (*n*) captives, prisoners of war: *Ghanima wa vita waliteswa vibaya katika magereza*, the prisoners of war were treated badly in the prisons. (Ar)

gharadhi¹ *n* (*n*) aim, intention, ambition: *Imekuwa gharadhi yangu kuwasaidia masikini walio katika shida*, it has been my ambition to help those poor people who are in difficulties. (cf *kusudio, nia, lengo*) (Ar)

gharadhi² *n* (*n*) ostentation, pomposity, haughtiness, pompousness: *Yeye si mgeni wa gharadhi*, he is not a stranger to pomposity (cf *makuu*) (Ar)

gharama *n* (*n*) cost, price, worth, value, expense, charge, expenditure: *Hizi ndizo gharama zake alizotumia kununulia vitabu*, these are his expenses for the books he bought. (Ar)

G

gharika (also *gharikisho*) n (ma-) 1. flood, deluge. (cf *furiko*) 2. destruction, extinction, desolation: *Kumetokea gharika la tembo katika baadhi ya sehemu za dunia*, there has been an extinction of the elephants in some parts of the world. (cf *maangamizo*)

gharik.i vi 1. be flooded, be inundated: *Roho nyingi zilighariki kutokana na mafuriko ya maji*, a number of lives were lost following the floods. (cf *furika*) 2. be devastated, be destroyed, be ruined: *Roho kadha wa kadha zilighariki kutokana na vita vya wenyewe kwa wenyewe*, many lives were devastated following the civil war. (cf *angamia, teketea*) Prep. **gharik.i.a** St. **gharik.ik.a** Cs. **gharik.ish.a** Ps. of Cs. **gharik.ish.w.a** (Ar)

ghariki.sh.a vt deluge, flood, inundate. Prep. **gharikish.i.a** St. **gharikish.ik.a** Ps. **gharikish.w.a** Rp. **gharikish.an.a**

gharikisho n (ma-) see *gharika*

gharimi.a vt defray, finance, pay for: *Shirika la kigeni linataka kuugharimia mradi wetu*, a foreign organisation wants to finance our project. St. **gharimi.k.a** Cs. **gharimi.sh.a** Ps. **gharimi.w.a** Rp. **gharimi.an.a** (cf *lipia*)

gharim.u vi cost, be worth, sell for: *Nguo zake zinagharimu pesa nyingi*, his clothes cost a lot of money. Prep. **gharim.i.a**, St. **gharim.ik.a** Cs. **gharim.ish.a** Ps. of Prep. **gharim.iw.a** Rp. of Prep. **gharim.i.an.a** (cf *wakifu*) (Ar)

ghashi[1] n (n) deception, deceit, fabrication: *Hiyo si noti ya halali; hiyo ni ghashi*, that is not a legal tender note; it is fake. (cf *hadaa, ujanja*) (Ar)

ghashi[2] adj deceptive, fake, fraudulent: *Hayo mafuta mazuri ni ghashi; mimi sitayanunua*, that perfume is not genuine; I will not buy it. (Ar)

ghashi[3] n (n) (med) dirt from wound, abscess, etc.; discharge. (Ar)

ghas.i vt pester, bother, disturb, perturb: *Alinighasi sana nilipokuwa ninasoma*, he disturbed me a lot while I was reading. Prep. **ghas.i.a** St. **ghas.ik.a**, Cs. **ghas.ish.a** Ps. of Prep. **ghas.iw.a** Rp. of Prep. **ghas.i.an.a** (cf *sumbua, kera*) (Ar)

ghasia n (n) 1. pandemonium, brawl, commotion, chaos, turmoil: *Usilete ghasia hapa*, do not cause chaos here. (cf *fujo, zahama*) 2. problem, difficulty.

ghasili[1] n (n) see *dasili*

ghasil.i[2] vt wash, clear, cleanse. Prep. **ghasil.i.a** St. **ghasil.ik.a** Ps. **ghasil.iw.a** Rp. **ghasil.i.an.a** (cf *osha, suuza*) (Ar)

ghawazi n (n) money (cf *hela, fedha, pesa*) (Ar)

ghaya[1] adv extremely, exceedingly, very: *Alifurahi ghaya aliposikia kwamba amefaulu mtihani vizuri*, she was extremely happy to learn that she had passed the examination well. (cf *sana*) (Ar)

ghaya[2] n (n) end, extremity, limit. (*ukomo, mwisho*) (Ar)

ghazi[1] n (n) 1. war, fighting, hostilities. 2. an expert fighter: *Yeye alikuwa ghazi katika vita*, he was an expert fighter in the war. 3. valiant, hero; a brave person: *Maghazi wa kuendesha gari walishiriki kwenye mashindano ya kila mwaka*, brave drivers took part in the annual rally competition. (cf *shujaa, simba*) (Ar)

ghazi[2] n (n) steam, air

ghera[1] n (n) zeal, determination, enthusiasm: *Wana ghera kubwa ya kutaka kuanzisha miradi mbalimbali nchini*, they have great determination to start different projects in the country. (cf *kani, moyo*) (Ar)

ghera[2] n (n) jealousy, envy. (cf *wivu, choyo*)

ghib.u[1] vi disappear, be lost, recede from view: *Alighibu kwa siku nyingi na sijui alikwenda wapi*, he disappeared for a long time and I don't know where he went. Prep. *ghib.i.a* St. *ghib.ik.a* Cs. *ghib.ish.a* Prep. of Ps *ghib.iw.a* (cf *potea, adimika*) (Ar)

ghibu² *adv* (*idm*) *Kusoma kwa ghibu*, read by heart; recite.

ghila *n* (*n*) income derived from harvesting (crops): *Tunapata ghila ya shilingi milioni moja kwa mwezi kutokana na mauzo ya chai*, we get an income of one million shillings per month from the sale of tea. (Ar)

ghiliba *n* (*n*) deception, trick, subterfuge, hypocrisy: *Ghiliba anazonifanyia mara kwa mara zitamharibia jina lake*, the tricks he frequently employs on me will tarnish his name. (cf *hadaa, udanganyifu, magube*) (Ar)

ghilib.u *vt* delude, hoodwink, swindle, deceive: *Alitughilibu kwa muda mrefu kwa kujifanya mtu mwema*, he deceived us for a long time by pretending to be a nice person. Prep. *ghilib.i.a* St. *ghilib.ik.a* Cs. *ghilib.ish.a* Ps. of Prep. *ghilib.iw.a*, Rp. of Prep. *ghilib.i.an.a* (cf *laghai, danganya, hadaa*) (Ar)

ghoba *n* (*ma-*) cave, cavern, den (cf *pango*)

ghofira *n* (*n*) pardon, absolution; forgiveness of sins, remission of sins: *Ghofira ya dhambi zetu*, the forgiveness of our sins. (cf *msamaha*) (Ar)

ghofir.i *vt* absolve, forgive, pardon: *Mungu hughofiri madhambi ya waja wake*, God forgives the sins of his beings. Prep. *ghofir.i.a* St. *ghofir.ik.a* Ps. of Prep. *ghofir.iw.a* (cf *samehe*) (Ar)

ghorofa *n* (*n*) upper floor, storey: *Ghorofa ya tatu*, third floor. *Nyumba ya ghorofa sita*, a house with six floors. (cf *roshani*) (Ar)

ghoshi *vt* see *ghushi*

ghuba *n* (*n*) gulf, bay; an inlet of the sea: *Ghuba ya Ajemi*, the Persian Gulf. (cf *hori*) (Ar)

ghubari *n* (*ma-*) 1. nimbus; raincloud.

(cf *ufurufuru*) 2. dust, powder, dirt. (cf *vumbi*) (Ar)

ghulamu (also *galamu*) *n* (*n*) 1. a young man, a young boy: *Siku hizi baadhi ya ghulamu, hawawaekei heshima wakubwa zao*, these days, some of the young people do not respect their elders. (cf *kijana*) 2. the knave in a suit of playing cards; the Jack. (cf *dume*) (Ar)

ghuma *n* (*n*) debacle; a sudden disastrous collapse or defect.

ghumiw.a *vi* 1. faint, lose consciousness, pass out: *Alisimama sana juani na hatimaye, akaghumiwa*, he stood for a long time in the sun and in the end, he fainted. (cf *zirai*) 2. be dumbfounded, be astounded, be taken aback: *Nilighumiwa nilipomwona kijana mmoja wa kiume kavaa nguo za kike*, I was astounded when I saw a young man wearing women's clothes. Prep. *ghumiw.i.a* St. *ghumiw.ik.a* Cs. *ghumiw.ish.a* (cf *fazaika, shangaa, duwaa*)

ghunna *n* (*n*) (*phon*) a voiced sound.

ghur.i *vt* cheat, deceive, beguile: *Alinighuri kwa kuniuzia saa yake mbovu*, he cheated me by selling me his faulty watch. Prep. *ghur.i.a* St. *ghur.ik.a*, Cs. *ghur.ish.a* Ps. of Prep *ghur.iw.a* Rp. of Prep *ghur.i.an.a* (cf *danganya, ghilibu*) (Ar)

ghururi *n* (*n*) 1. deception, trick, falsehood: *Dunia ina ghururi nyingi na kwa hivyo, tutahadhari*, the world is full of deceptions and so we should take care. (cf *ghiliba, ghashi, hadaa*) 2. self-conceit, arrogance, haughtiness, vanity: *Ana ghururi nyingi kutokana na mali aliyo nayo*, he is very arrogant because of his wealth. (cf *majivuno, kiburi*) (Ar)

ghush.i¹ *vt, vi* 1. adulterate, falsify, defile: *Mwenye-duka ameyaghushi maziwa yake kwa kuchanganya na maji*, the shopkeeper has adulterated his milk with water. 2. deceive, hoodwink, swindle: *Usinighushi mara kwa mara kwani ninaelewa wazi kwamba wewe ni muongo*, don't keep deceiving me now and again because I know very well you are a liar. (cf *danganya, ghilibu*) 3. forge: *Mshitakiwa alighushi nyaraka za kampuni*, the accused forged the company's documents. Prep. ***ghush.i.a*** St. ***ghush.ik.a*** Cs. ***ghush.ish.a*** Ps. of Prep. ***ghush.iw.a*** Rp. of Prep. ***ghush.i.an.a***

ghushi² *adj* adequate, sufficient: *Aliweka chakula ghushi sahanini*, he put sufficient food on the plate.

ghusub.u *vt* take by force, compel, force, coerce, press: *Alinighusubu kumfanyia kazi yake*, he forced me to do his work. Prep. ***ghusub.i.a*** St. ***ghusub.ik.a*** Cs. ***ghusub.ish.a*** Ps. of Prep. ***ghusub.iw.a*** Rp. of Prep. ***ghusub.i.an.a*** (cf *shurutisha*) (Ar)

gia *n* (*n*) free gear (Eng)

gid.a *vt* 1. pour liquid gently out of a vessel in order to leave the sediment; let liquid flow gently: *Niliyagida maji kwenye sufuria yenye wali kutoka mekoni*, I poured the water slowly from the saucepan containing rice from the hearth. 2. fetch little water from a well. Prep. ***gid.i.a*** St. ***gid.ik.a*** Cs. ***gid.ish.a*** Ps. ***gid.w.a*** Rp. of Prep. ***gid.i.an.a***

gidamu (also *gulamu,kadamu*) *n* (*n*) 1. lace of a sandal; a small leather thing in a sandal 2. (*naut*) fore end of bows; the bow of a dhow (Ar)

gilasi (also *glasi*) *n* (*n*) glass: *Anataka kunywa gilasi moja ya maji*, he wants to drink a glass of water. (cf *bilauri*) (Eng)

gilid.i *vt* adorn a book cover: *Nilikigilidi kitabu changu*, I adorned the cover of my book. Prep. ***gilid.i.a*** St. ***gilid.ik.a*** Cs. ***gilid.ish.a*** Ps. of Prep ***gilid.iw.a*** Rp. of Prep. ***gilid.i.an.a***

giligilani *n* (*n*) (*bot*) coriander seed used in flavouring curry and food (Ar)

giligili *n* (*n*) fluid

gilotini *n* (*n*) guillotine; an instrument for beheading by means of a heavy blade dropped between two grooved uprights.

gilotini

gimba (also *kimba*) *n* (*n*) body, figure, physique, shape, form: *Ana gimba zuri*, he has a good body. (cf *umbo*)

gimbi¹ *n* (*n*) millet beer. (cf *pombe*)

gimbi² *n* (*ma-*) physique, figure, body, shape.

gin.a *vt* (of sby's fatness) be increasing. Prep. ***gin.i.a*** St. ***gin.ik.a*** Cs. ***gin.ish.a***

gingi *n* (*n*) (*naut*) bollard; a strong post on a dock, for holding a hawser fast

ginginiza *vt* see *gingiza*

ginginizo see *gingizo*

gingiri *n* (*ma-*) cutlet; a small slice of meat from the ribs or leg for frying or broiling

gingis.a *vt* mistreat the second wife in order to tire her and then make her ask for a divorce; taunt a co-wife: *Mume alimgingisa mkewe mpaka ikabidi aombe talaka*, the husband mistreated his second wife to the point where she had to ask for divorce. Prep. ***gingis.i.a*** St. ***gingis.ik.a*** Cs. ***gingis.ish.a*** Ps. ***gingis.w.a*** Rp. ***gingis.an.a***

gingiz.a (also *ginginiza*) *vt* harass, hector, pester; bother someone persistently in order to annoy them: *Alitugingiza mpaka tukaamua tupahame mahala*

gingizo   **-gofu²**   **G**

petu, he pestered us until we decided to vacate our place. Prep. ***gingiz.i.a*** St. ***gingiz.ik.a*** Cs. ***gingiz.ish.a*** Ps. ***gingiz.w.a*** Rp. ***gingiz.an.a*** (cf *sumbua, taabisha*)

gingizo (also *ginginizo*) *n* (*n*) hassle, nuisance, annoyance. (cf *kero*)

ging'ingi (also *giningi*) *n* (*n*) the headquaters of wizards.

giniz.a *vt* answer a call; respond, reply: *Niliitwa na nikaginiza*, I was called and responded. Prep. ***giniz.i.a*** St. ***giniz.ik.a*** Cs. ***giniz.ish.a*** Ps. ***giniz.w.a*** Rp. ***giniz.an.a*** (cf *itika, jibu*)

giridi *n* (*n*) see *gridi*

gita¹ (also *gitaa*) *n* (*ma-*) (*mus*) guitar; a kind of a six-stringed musical instrument: *Piga gita*, play the guitar. (Eng)

git.a² *vi* hesitate, pause, resist: *Nilitaka kumpiga lakini mara nikagita*, I wanted to beat him but then I hesitated. Prep. ***git.i.a*** St. ***git.ik.a*** Cs. ***git.ish.a*** Ps. ***git.w.a***

gitaa *n* (*ma-*) see *gita¹*

giza¹ (also *kiza*) *n* (*n*) **1.** darkness, gloom: *Tia giza*, darken. *Giza tororo*, blackest night, darkest night. *Macho yangu yaona giza*, my eyes are dim. **2.** (*fig*) ignorance, blindness, darkness, unenlightenment: *Sisi hatuelewi mipango yako; bado tuko katika giza*, we don't understand your plans; we are still in darkness. (cf *ujinga*)

giza² *adj* dark, lightless: *Hapa ni giza*, here it is dark.

glakoma *n* (*n*) see *glukoma*

glasi *n* (*n*) see *gilasi*

glavu (also *glovu*) *n* (*ma-*) glove (Eng)

globu *n* (*n*) see *glopu*

glopu (also *balbu, globu*) *n* (*n*) bulb, globe, electric lamp. (Eng)

glovu *n* (*ma-*) see *glavu*

glukoma (also *glakoma*) *n* (*n*) (*med*) glaucoma; a disease of the eye characterized by pressure within and hardening of the eyeball. (Eng)

glukojeni *n* (*n*) glucagon. (Eng)

glukosi *n* (*n*) glucose (Eng)

gluu *n* (*n*) glue. (cf *ambo, sherisi, gundi*) (Eng)

gobagob.a *vi* be gnarled, be curled, be twisted, be gnared, be curved: *Mnazi ule umegobagoba*, that coconut tree is gnarled. Prep. ***gobagob.e.a*** St. ***gobagob.ek.a*** Cs. ***gobagob.esh.a***

gobo.a (also *koboa*) *vt* **1.** break off with the hand, etc. as in the case of a maize cob: *Nilizigoboa chembe za mahindi kutoka kwenye gunzi lake*, I broke off grains of maize from the cob with my fingers. (cf *pukuchua, kokoa*) **2.** clean cotton, cloves, etc. by picking off the stalks; *Tulizigoboa karafuu kwenye kinu chetu*, we cleaned the cloves by picking off the stalks in our mill. **3.** strip off as of bark of a tree; pare, hull: *Niliyagoboa magome ya mti uliokuwa na matawi machache sana*, I stripped off the bark of a tree that had very few branches. **4.** extract, pull out: *Aliigoboa misumari kwenye kipande cha ubao*, he extracted nails from a piece of wood. Prep. ***gobo.le.a*** St. ***gobo.k.a*** and ***gobo.lek.a*** and Cs. ***gobo.lesh.a*** Ps. of Prep. ***gobo.lew.a*** Rp. ***gobo.an.a*** (cf *tabua, konyoa*)

gobori *n* (*ma-*) muzzle-loading gun; muzzle loader; musket (cf *korofindo, bunduki*)

gobwe *n* (*n*) knock-knees; a condition of knees in which the legs bend inward so that knees knock together or touch each other in walking.

godoro *n* (*ma-*) mattress (Hind)

goe *vt* see *ngoeka*

gofia *n* (*n*) (*naut*) a pulley that is attached to a rope (*henza*) which hoists the sail in a local sailing vessel. (cf *kapi, roda, abedari*)

gofu¹ *n* (*n*) **1.** building ruin: *Gofu la nyumba*, a ruined house. (cf *hame, bomoko*) **2.** (*idm*) *Gofu la mtu*, a thin emaciated person.

-gofu² *adj* emaciated, broken down, in ruins.

189

gofu³ *n* (*n*) 1. golf game. 2. a small hard white ball in the game of golf.

gofu.a *vt, vi* emaciate, atrophy; dry out, wear out the strength of: *Maradhi ya muda mrefu yalimgofua vibaya sana hata yakafanya asiweze kutembea,* her long illness had terribly emaciated her so much that she could hardly walk. Prep. *gofu.li.a* St. *gofu.k.a* Cs. *gofu.sh.a* Ps. *gofu.w.a* Rp. *gofu.an.a* (cf *kondesha, dhoofisha*)

gog.a¹ *vt* 1. take sby by surprise, catch unawares; startle: *Nilimgoga mtumishi wangu akila chakula changu jikoni,* I caught my servant unawares eating my food in the kitchen. (cf *fuma*) 2. fatigue, tire, weary, jade, bore, irritate, irk, vex: *Makosa yake ya mara kwa mara yamenigoga sana,* her frequent mistakes have irked me a lot. Prep. *gog.e.a* St. *gog.ek.a* Cs. *gog.esh.a* Ps. *gog.w.a* Rp *gog.an.a* (cf *chukiza, chusha*)

gog.a² *vt* 1. discover stollen property. 2. discover sth which is hunted after great hardships and a long duration. Prep. *gog.e.a* St. *gog.ek.a* Cs. *gog.esh.a* Ps. *gog.w.a* Rp. *gog.an.a*

gogadima *n* (*n*) a kind of a thick-branched shrub with recurved stipular spines bearing globuse fruits. *Capparis corymbosa.*

gogeni *n* (*n*) an expert in a particular field.

gogi *n* (*n*) pomposity, boastfulness, pompousness: *Anapenda kutia gogi mbele za watu,* he likes to display pomposity in front of the people. (cf *mashobo, maringo, madaha*)

gogo *n* (*ma-*) log; the trunk of a tree when felled: *Gogo la mnazi,* the log of a coconut tree.

gogomoa *vi* gargle, rinse out. Prep. *gogomo.le.a* St. *gogomo.k.a* Cs. *gogomo.sh.a*

gogoo¹ *n* (*n*) the inclination of a husband to love a woman whom he has divorced or a wife to love a husband whom she got divorced from: *Shikwa na gogoo,* love for one's divorced spouse.

gogoo² *n* (*ma-*) 1. cleft stick or tree used as a kind of stick for imprisoning people; wooden fetter. 2. yoke (cf *mkatale*)

gogot.a¹ (also *gota*) *vt* 1. knock at, hammer at, tap, hit. 2. hit a tree continuously like a bird when it wishes to drill a hole; peck Prep. *gogot.e.a* St. *gogot.ek.a* Cs. *gogot.ez.a* Ps. *gogot.w.a* Rp. *gogot.an.a*

gogota² (also *gongomola, kigogota, kigongo'ta, kigotagota, king'ota*) *n* (*n*) (*zool*) woodpecker; a kind of a bird of the *Picidae* family, having a chisel-shaped bill, used for drilling holes in barks to get insects.

gogota

gogotez.a *vt, vi* 1. stumble over words; falter, stammer: *Kwa vile alikuwa na hofu, akawa anagogoteza maneno alipokuwa anahutubia,* as he had fear, he faltered when he was speaking. 2. emphasize, accentuate, stress: *Waliongea kwa kugogoteza mambo muhimu,* they talked stressing important matters. Prep. *gogotez.e.a* St. *gogotez.ek.a* Ps. *gogotez.w.a* Rp. *gogotez.an.a*

goigoi¹ *n* (*n*) idler, laggard, sluggard, loafer: *Ukiwa goigoi, utakuwa hupendi*

goigoi²

kufanya kazi, if you are an idler, you will not like to work. (cf *mkunguni, mzembe*)

goigoi² *adj* lazy, indolent, slothful, sluggish: *Usinileete mtumishi goigoi kunifanyia kazi nyumbani*, don't bring me a lazy servant to work for me at home. (cf *-legevu*)

goigoi³ *n* (*n*) a kind of a dance used in the exorcism of spirits. (cf *pungwa*)

gojo *n* (*ma-*) (*zool*) mythical hyena; a kind of animal like a hyena with a long shaggy tail common in traditional stories.

gok.a¹ *vi* see *gooka*

goka² *n* (*ma-*) a coconut whose milk is decreasing and beginning to decay; spoiled coconut

goko *n* (*n*) tibia, shinbone; the front bone in the leg below the knee. (cf *muundi*)

gole¹ (also *golegole*) *n* (*n*) 1. phlegm, sputum; mucus of the nose, expectorated matter. (cf *balghamu, kamasi*) 2. expectoration or saliva of whale.

gole² *n* (*n*) a pellet of opium prepared for smoking.

gole³ *n* (*n*) the crop of a bird.

gole⁴ *n* (*n*) used in the expression: *Mkate wa gole*, a kind of bread cooked with steam; steamed bread.

golegole¹ *n* (*n*) see *goregore*

golegole² see *gole¹*

goli *n* (*n*) 1. (in sports) goal, score: *Goli la kuibia*, off-side goal. *Mchezaji alifunga magoli mengi*, the player scored many goals. (cf *bao, dungu*) 2. the area between two goal posts where the ball must go for a point to be gained: *Nguzo ya goli*, goalpost. *Mstari wa goli*, goalline. *Golini*, goal mouth. (Eng)

goligoli *n* (*n*) see *goregore*

golikipa (also *kipa*) *n* (*ma-*) goalkeeper. (Eng)

gololi *n* (*n*) 1. marble, pellet; a ball-bearing of cycles, motor-cars, etc. 2. (*anat*) testicle. (Pers)

gom.a¹ *vt* go on strike, boycott, refuse; be firm in demanding one's rights. Prep. *gom.e.a*, protest, strike against e.g. *Wanachama wa klabu wanagomea kufanyika kwa uchaguzi kwa mara ya pili*, the club members are protesting against holding elections for the second time. St. *gom.ek.a* Cs. *gom.esh.a* Ps. *gom.w.a* Ps. of Prep. *gom.ew.a* Rp. of Prep. *gom.e.an.a* (cf *susa, kataa*)

goma² *n* (*n*) 1. a kind of coastal dance usu played by men who wear white *kanzu* and carry sticks which they throw forward and back to their shoulders and at the same time make short steps slowly; coastal stick-dance. 2. a big drum.

goma³ *n* (*n*) (*zool*) starry trigger fish; a type of hard-skinned fish. (cf *kibande*)

gomb.a¹ *vt* 1. scold, chide. (cf *karipia*) 2. gainsay, forbid, prohibit, taboo: *Ilibidi nimgombe ndugu yangu asilewe kwa vile alikuwa akileta fujo mtaani*, I was obliged to tell my brother not to drink because he was causing chaos in the neighbourhood. Prep. *gomb.e.a* St. *gomb.ek.a* Cs. *gomb.ez.a* Ps. *gomb.w.a* Rp. *gomb.an.a* (cf *kataza*)

gomba² *n* (*ma-*) (*bot*) a strong fibre from a banana plant.

gombakanzu *n* (*n*) (*bot*) a perennial mat grass that grows in sand near the sea shore used as a good fodder. *Stenotaphrum demidiatum*.

gombakofi *n* (*n*) (*bot*) a kind of a large long-stalked sagittate leaf.

gomban.a *vi* quarrel, squabble, altercate, argue: *Aligombana na mkewe kwa kosa la upuuzi*, he quarrelled with his wife for a trivial mistake. Prep. *gomban.i.a* St. *gomban.ik.a* Cs. *gomban.ish.a* Ps. of Prep. *gomban.iw.a* Rp. of Prep. *gomban.i.an.a*

gombanish.a *vt* cause a strife between two or more people; cause an antagonism between two or more people. Prep. *gombanish.i.a* St. *gombanish.ik.a*

G

Ps. *gombanish.w.a* Rp. *gombanish.an.a* (cf *chonganisha*)

gombe.a[1] *vt* see *gomba*[1]

gombe.a[2] *vt* 1. argue (for, against, at, etc.) press a claim: *Alikemewa kwa sababu alikugombea*, he was scolded because he stood up for you. 2. compete. 3. contest, vie: *Utagombea ubunge safari hii?* Will you contest for a parliamentary seat this time? Prep. *gombe.le.a* St. *gombe.k.a* Cs. *gombe.sh.a* Ps. *gombe.w.a*

gombea[3] *n* (n) (*naut*) rustling of gentle waves on the shores; sound of small sea waves which are approaching the shore.

gombez.a *vt* scold, forbid, reprimand: *Gombeza mtoto mtundu*, scold a naughty child St. *gombez.ek.a* Ps. *gombez.w.a* Rp. *gombez.an.a* (cf *kataza, zuia*)

gombo[1] *n* (*ma-*) a leaf or page of a book. (cf *ukurasa*)

gombo[2] *n* (n) a kind of traditional dance performed to appease the spirits and is still done by some people of the East African Coast e.g. during the eclipse of the moon.

gombo[3] *n* (n) (*mus*) a kind of musical instrument related to the guitar; lute.

gombo.a *vt* see *komboa*

gomboro *n* (n) bursal disease; a kind of a disease affecting chickens and turkeys. The disease is caused by a virna virus of serotype 1, which makes the birds to become listless and depressed, pale and huddling.

gomdra *n* (n) sliding-door. (cf *mlango telezi*)

gome[1] *n* (*ma-*) a tree bark; the tough external covering of tree trunks and branches: *Niliyaambua magome ya mti*, I stripped off the bark of a tree.

gome[2] *n* (*ma-*) money, currency, cash. (cf *pesa, fedha*)

gome[3] *n* (n) (*zool*) the shell of a snail.

-gomvi *adj* hostile, quarrelsome, troublesome, cantakerous, aggressive: *Mvulana mgomvi*, a quarrelsome boy.

gona[1] *n* (n) (*zool*) a kind of salt water fish.

gon.a[2] *vi* take deep sleep; slumber; lie down: *Aligona asubuhi yote siku ya Jumamosi kwa vile kulikuwa hakuna kazi*, he slept the whole of Saturday morning because there was no work. Prep. *gon.e.a* St. *gon.ek.a* Cs. *gon.ez.a*

gon.a[3] *vt, vi* 1. catch sby by surprise in the act of doing sth wrong. 2. catch sby committing adultery.

gonasokola (also *gonosokola*) *n* (n) a herb or shrub with alternate leaves. (cf *mtata*)

gonda *n* (n) (*zool*) a two-striped skink; a kind of lizard with an elongate body, smooth scales and short legs. (cf *mjusi-islamu, koakoa*)

gondi *n* (*ma-*) (*zool*) the claw of a crab, lobster, etc. (cf *gando*)

gone.a *vt* remain for so long in a particular place as in the case of a student who is repeating the same class now and again; repeat: *Mwanafunzi yule amegonea darasa la tatu kwa muda wa miaka minne*, that pupil has repeated standard three for four years. Prep. *gone.le.a* St. *gone.k.a* Cs. *gone.sh.a* and *gon.e.z.a* (cf *sogonea*)

gonezi[1] *n* (n) sleep, rest, repose. (cf *usingizi*)

gonezi[2] *n* (*ma-*) dozer; a person who keeps on dozing when he sits down.

gong.a[1] *vt* 1. hit, knock, strike: *Anagonga mlango*, he is knocking the door. *Anagonga kengele*, he is striking the bell. 2. (*idm*) *Gonga mwamba*, fail to work e.g. *Juhudi zake ziligonga mwamba*, his efforts failed. Prep. *gong.e.a* strike for (with, at, etc) e.g. *Alitugongea kengele*, he rang the bell for us. St. *gong.ek.a* Cs. *gong.esh.a* Ps. *gong.w.a*, Rp. *gong.an.a* (cf *gota, piga*)

gonga² n (n) a kind of women's local dance for joy.

gongan.a vi 1. bump, collide, clash, bang; come into collision: *Gari mbili ziligongana jana*, two vehicles collided yesterday. 2. (of ideas, etc.) clash, collide: *Mawazo ya wajumbe yanaonekana kugongana*, the opinions of the delegates seem to clash. Prep. **gongan.i.a** St. **gongan.ik.a** Cs. **gongan.ish.a**

gonganish.a vt cause two things or more to collide/knock each other or one another: *Alizigonganisha glasi mbili*, he caused two glasses to knock each other. Prep. **gonganish.i.a** St. **gonganish.ik.a** Ps. **gonganish.w.a** Rp. **gonganish.an.a**

gonge.a¹ vt see *gonga*

gonge.a² vt (in card playing) signal to; make signal to a playmate (with, for, etc.): *Alinigongea kwenye mchezo wa karata*, he signalled to me while playing cards. Prep. **gonge.le.a** St. **gonge.k.a** Cs. **gonge.sh.a** Ps. **gonge.w.a** Rp. **gonge.an.a** (cf *ashiria, pigia*)

gongean.a vi (in soccer, etc) pass to each other: *Wachezaji walikuwa wakigongeana vizuri*, the players were passing the ball to each other quite well.

gongo¹ n (ma-) 1. club, cudgel, bludgeon; a heavy stick. (cf *rungu*) 2. an instrument used for knocking.

gongo² n (n) home brew; a kind of local brewed spirit. (cf *tende, piwa, moshi*)

gongo³ n (n) a seam in a cloth: *Gongo nene*, a large projecting seam.

gongo⁴ n (n) a hump of a camel. (cf *nundu*)

gongo⁵ n (n) used in the expression: *Gongo la mwitu*, a thick forest. *Gongo la mlima*, a broad hill.

gongo⁶ n (ma-) elevation

gongome.a¹ vt 1. hammer into, pound into, drive with blows as in the case rivets, nails, pegs, etc.: *Aligongomea misumari ukutani*, he hammered nails into the wall. (cf *pigilia, kongomea*) 2. compress, ram (into), compact, stuff, squeeze, astringe, press together: *Aligongomea furushi la nguo ili azitie ndani zile chache zilizobakia*, he pressed together a bundle of clothes so that the few remaining could go in. Prep. **gongome.le.a** St. **gongome.k.a** and **gongome.lek.a** Cs. **gongome.z.a** Ps. **gongome.w.a** Rp. **gongome.an.a** (cf *shindilia, sukumiza*)

gongome.a² vt put a heated metal on the ground to cool: *Alikigongomea chuma kimoto kwa kukitumbukiza kwenye maji baridi*, he put the heated metal into the cold water in order to cool it. Prep. **gongome.le.a** St. **gongome.k.a** and **gongome.lek.a** Cs. **gongome.sh.a** and **gongome.z.a** Ps. **gongome.w.a** Rp. **gongome.an.a** (cf *poza*)

gongomola n (n) see *gogota²*

gong'ot.a vt see *kong'ota*. Prep. **gong'ot.e.a** St. **gong'ot.ek.a** Cs **gong'ot.esh.a** Ps. **gong'ot.w.a** Rp. **gong'ot.an.a**

gong'otez.a vt emphasize a particular point during a sermon: *Mhubiri aligong'oteza umuhimu wa kumcha Mungu*, the preacher emphasized the importance of fearing God. Prep. **gong'otez.e.a** St. **gong'otez.ek.a** Cs. **gongo'tez.esh.a** Ps. **gong'otez.w.a** Rp. **gong'otez.an.a**

gong'oto.a vi hatch out eggs: *Kuku wangu wamegong'otoa leo*, my hens have hatched today. Prep. **gong'oto.le.a** St. **gong'oto.k.a** Cs. **gong'oto.sh.a** Ps. **gong'oto.w.a** (cf *totoa*)

goniometa n (n) goniometer; an instrument for measuring crystal angles esp of solid bodies. (Eng)

-gonjwa adj sick, ill, ailing, unhealthy: *Mtu mgonjwa*, a sick person.

gonosokola n (n) see *mtata*

gony.a¹ vt cause to sleep esp in the case of pacifying spirits of the dead: *Gonya koma*, appease spirits of ancestors.

G gony.a² — goto.a¹

Prep. **gony.e.a** St. **gony.ek.a** Cs. **gony.esh.a** Ps. **gony.w.a** Ps. of Prep. **gony.e.an.a** (cf *tambika*)

gony.a² *n* (*ma-*) dust from charcoal smoke, used to make antimony.

gook.a¹ *vi* retch violently, keck violently; gag, dry-heave, be nauseated, vomit: *Aligooka kutokana na homa kali ya malaria aliyokuwa nayo*, she retched violently from an acute bout of malaria. Prep. **gook.e.a** St. **gook.ek.a** Cs. **gook.esh.a** Ps. **gook.w.a** (cf *kokomoka, kovyoka*)

gooka² *n* (*n*) (*bot*) a fallen spoiled coconut.

gook.a³ *vt, vi* (of a branch of a tree) bend down due to the weight of the fruits on it. Prep. **gook.e.a** St. **gook.ek.a** Cs. **gook.esh.a** Ps. **gook.w.a** (cf *gotama, poogoka*)

gora *n* (*n*) a pair of *khanga*.

goregore (also *golegole*) *n* (*n*) (*zool*) a kind of slender highly glossed black-green bird with a long graduated tail, a slightly curved red bill and red legs; green wood hoopoe (Kabelaar). *Phoeniculus purpureus*.

gori *n* (*n*) a children's game of snatching a ball and then running with it. (cf *naga*)

goromwe¹ (also *gorong'ondo, gorong'ondwe*) *n* (*n*) (*zool*) a kind of tree lizard

goromwe² *n* (*n*) lizard fish; a kind of small brightly coloured sea fish (*Synodontidae* family) with a slender body, lizard-like head and a large mouth with canine form teeth along margins of both jaws.

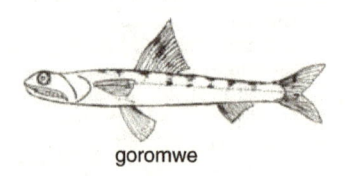

goromwe

gorong'ondo¹ *n* (*ma-*) see *goromwe¹*

gorong'ondo² *n* (*ma-*) (*zool*) the leg of a cow or any other animal.

gorong'ondwe *n* (*ma-*) see *goromwe¹*

got.a¹ *vt* knock, beat, rap, strike, whack, tap, thwack, bang: *Aligota mlango wangu mara tatu lakini mimi sikuwepo ndani*, he knocked at my door three times but I was not there. Prep. **got.e.a** St. **got.ek.a** Cs. **got.esh.a** and **got.ez.a** Ps. **got.w.a** Rp. **got.an.a** (cf *gonga*)

got.a² *vt, vi* end, finish, complete: *Alitaka mgogoro wetu ugote haraka*, he wanted our dispute to end as soon as possible. Prep. **got.e.a** St. **got.ek.a** Cs. **got.esh.a** and **got.ez.a** Ps. **got.w.a** (cf *isha, koma*)

gota³ *vi* get stuck: *Aligota katika jambo lile*, he got stuck on that issue. Prep. **got.e.a** St. **got.ek.a** Cs. **got.esh.a** and **got.ez.a** Ps. **got.w.a** Rp. **got.an.a**

gote.a *vt* doze, drowse, nap, catnap: *Mwanafunzi yule hugotea darasani*, that student dozes in the class. Prep. **gote.le.a** St. **gote.lek.a** Cs. **gote.z.a** Ps. of Prep. **gote.lew.a**. (cf *sinzia*)

goti *n* (*ma-*) 1. (*anat*) knee, patelar region: *Pia ya magoti*, knee cap. *Piga magoti*, kneel down, genuflect. 2. (*idm*) *Piga magoti*, surrender, yield, give up b) apologize; ask for pardon.

goto *n* (*n*) arrogance, pomposity, haughtiness, vanity, snobbery, conceit: *Msichana yule anatia goto mno kwa vile yeye ni mzuri*, that girl is very arrogant because she is beautiful. (cf *mikogo, majivuno, maringo*)

goto.a¹ *vt, vi* 1. summarize, abstract, epitomize, synopsize, sum up: *Nimekusudia kuigotoa hotuba yote ya waziri na nitakupa muhtasari wake baadaye*, I have decided to summarize the whole speech of the minister and I will give you its synopsis later. 2. conclude, finish, complete, round off: *Amegotoa kazi zake hivi punde na sasa anataka kuondoka*, he has just finished his work and now he

goto.a² wants to go. (cf *maliza*) 3. inform, notify: *Alinigotoa kwamba safari yake imevunjika*, he informed me that his trip was cancelled. Prep. **goto.le.a** St. **goto.lek.a** Cs. **goto.lesh.a** Ps. of Prep. **goto.lew.a** (cf *juvya*)

goto.a² *vt* introduce sby: *Gotoa mtoto*, introduce a child. Prep. **goto.le.a** St. **goto.lek.a** Cs. **goto.lesh.a** Ps. of Prep. **goto.lew.a** (cf *tambulisha*)

govi *n* (*n*) 1. (*anat*) prepuce, foreskin; the fold of skin covering the glands of a penis. (cf *ushungi*) 2. an uncircumcised penis. (cf *fudu, zunga*)

goy.a¹ *vt* take hold of anything e.g. fruit on a tree, etc. using a forked or hooked stick so as to pick it: *Nilipoyaona maembe mabivu kwenye mwembe, nikayayuyu*, when I saw ripe mangoes on the mango tree, I picked them by using a hooked stick. Prep. **goy.o.a** St. **goy.ek.a** Cs. **goy.esh.a** Ps. **goy.w.a** Rp. of Prep **goy.e.an.a** (cf *ngoeka*)

goya² *n* (*n*) pomposity, haughtiness, arrogance: *Yeye hawezi kukuamkia kwa vile anagoya sana*, he cannot greet you because he is full of arrogance. (cf *maringo*)

goya³ *n* (*n*) 1. joke, derision, ridicule. (cf *mzaha, dhihaka, utani*) 2. play, humour.

goya⁴ *adj* useless, fruitless; for no good cause, in vain: *Cheza ngoma goya*, be in vain e.g. *Alijitahidi sana kwenye masomo yake lakini alikuwa anacheza ngoma goya*, he worked very hard in his studies but it was all in vain.

gozi *n* (*n*) soccer, football: *Mwana gozi*, soccer player. (cf *kandanda, soka*)

gozo *n* (*n*) tobacco which has been dried, and used for rolling into cigarettes. (cf *biri, sonyo*)

grafiti *n* (*n*) graffiti; an inscription, drawing, etc. crudely scratched or scribbled on a wall or other public place. (cf *kibonzo*) (Eng)

gramatoni (also *gramfoni, gramofoni*) *n* (*n*) gramophone, record-player: *Sahani ya gramafoni*, gramophone record. (cf *santuri*) (Eng)

gramfoni *n* (*n*) see *gramafoni*

gramu *n* (*n*) a weight of 1000 milligrams or 100 centigrams. (Eng)

gredi *n* (*n*) grade, position, status, rank: *Karafuu zimepangwa katika gredi mbalimbali*, the cloves have been arranged in different grades. (cf *cheo, hadhi*) (Eng)

grife *n* (*n*) slate stone.

grisi (also *girisi*) *n* grease (Eng)

gruneti (also *guruneti*) *n* (*n*) hand grenade. (Eng)

gu.a *vt, vi* peel, skin, flay, strip: *Aliligua chungwa kwa kutumia kisu kikali*, he peeled the orange by using a sharp knife. Prep. **gu.li.a** St. **gu.lik.a** Cs. **gu.lish.a** Ps. of Prep **gu.liw.a** (cf *menya*)

Guatemala *n* (*n*) (*geog*) Guatemala; a country in Central America, south and east of Mexico.

gube (usu *magube*) *n* (*ma-*) trick, subterfuge, deceit, gimmick, deception: *Anataka kunifanyia magube lakini mimi nishaelewa vitimbi vyake*, he wants to employ deception against me but I have already seen his intrigues. (cf *ujanja, hila*)

guberi¹ *n* (*ma-*) 1. prostitute, whore, harlot, slut. (cf *malaya, mkware*) 2. swindler, conman, crook, trickster. (cf *tapeli*)

guberi² *n* (*ma-*) 1. colonizer, imperialist. (cf *beberu, mkoloni*) 2. lecher, adulterer, womanizer, whoremonger. (cf *gawadi, kuwadi, fisadi*)

guberi³ *adj* lecherous, adulterous, lustful: *Yeye ni guberi kwelikweli*, he is really lecherous. (cf *fisadi*)

gubeti *n* (*n*) (*naut*) prow of a dhow or other marine vessel. (cf *njeli*) (Ar)

gubi *n* (*ma-*) (*bot*) the fibrous sheath of a coconut palm. (cf *kozi*)

gubigubi (also *kubikubi*) *adv* all covered up; covered from head to foot: *Alijifunika gubigubi*, she covered herself from head to foot.

gubik.a (also *kubika*) *vt, vi* cover up completely; be all covered up. Prep. ***gubik.i.a*** St. ***gubik.ik.a*** Cs. ***gubik.iz.a*** Ps. ***gubik.w.a***, be covered up, be overshadowed e.g *Mkutano uligubikwa na migogoro ya nchi za wanachama*, the meeting was overshadowed by the conflicts of the member states. Rp. ***gubik.an.a*** (cf *funika*)

gubiko[1] *n* (*ma-*) 1. lid, cover, cap, stop, stopper. 2. state of being covered completely. 3. secret matter; sth covered.

gubiko[2] *n* (*ma-*) presents given to a traditional ruler for allowing a caravan to make a stop in his area.

gubiti[1] *n* (*n*) caramel; a kind of sweetmeat of long pieces of sticks of boiled sugar, milk, etc, liked very much esp by children. (Pers)

gubiti[2] *n* (*n*) (*zool*) the leg of a sea-turtle or a land tortoise. (Pers)

gubu *n* (*n*) annoyance, hassle, trouble, nuisance, pester; affliction resulting from interfering into other people's affairs, etc.: *Mtu mwenye gubu*, grumbler. (cf *ghasia, fujo*)

gubu.a *vt* reveal, divulge, disclose, expose; *Yeye anapenda kugubua siri za watu*, he likes to disclose the secrets of other people. Prep. ***gubu.li.a*** St. ***gubu.lik.a*** Cs. ***gubu.lish.a*** Ps. of Prep ***gubu.liw.a*** Rp. ***gubu.an.a***

guchi.a *vi* limp, hobble; walk lamely: *Siku hizi, rafiki yako anapotembea, huguchia*, these days, when your friend walks, he limps. Prep. ***guchi.li.a*** St. ***guchi.k.a*** Cs. ***guchi.sh.a*** Ps. ***guchi.w.a*** (cf *chechea, chechemea*)

gud.a[1] *vi* sound like the dry contents of a coconut when shaken; rattle, clatter: *Nilipoitikisa nazi, maji yaliguda ndani*, when I shook the coconut, it rattled inside. Prep. ***gud.i.a*** St. ***gud.ik.a*** Cs. ***gud.ish.a*** Ps. ***gud.w.a*** (cf *lia*)

guda[2] (also *gudi*) *n* (*n*) (*naut*) dock, pier, wharf, jetty, jutty, mole. (cf *gati*)

gudamu *n* (*n*) see *gidamu*

gude[1] *n* (*n*) (*zool*) White-Browed Coucal; a mainly chestnut plumaged bird with a long broad grey tail. (cf *shundi, kiota, dudumizi*)

gude[2] *n* (*n*) see *msharasi*

gudulia *n* (*n*) jug, pitcher, ewer, jar; *Gudulia la maji*, water jug. (cf *kasiki*) (Ar)

gugu *n* (*n*) 1. (*bot*) weed, undergrowth; underwood; a wild plant of no value: *Gugu bahari*, laminaria. 2. a heap of rubbish.

gugum.a *vi* tremble because of severe cold or heat. Prep. ***gugumi.li.a*** St. ***gugumi.k.a*** Cs. ***gugumi.sh.a*** Ps. ***gugumi.w.a*** Rp. ***gugumi.an.a***

gugumi.a[1] *vt, vi* 1. gulp down, guzzle, drain one's glass: *Jinsi alivyokuwa na kiu hata akagugumia chupa nzima ya maji baridi*, he was so thirsty that he gulped down a whole bottle of cold water. 2. swig; swallow with a gurgling sound: *Aligugumia pombe takriban usiku wote*, he swigged beer almost the whole night. Prep. ***gugumi.li.a*** St. ***gugumi.k.a*** Cs. ***gugumi.sh.a*** and ***gugumi.z.a*** Ps. ***gugumi.w.a*** Rp. ***gugumi.an.a***

gugumi.a[2] *vi* 1. stutter, stammer; falter in speaking: *Alipotoa hotuba kwenye jukwaa alikuwa akigugumia*, when he was delivering a speech from the platform, he was stammering. 2. withstand hardships. Prep. ***gugumi.lia*** and ***gugumi.z.a*** St. ***gugumi.k.a*** Cs. ***gugumi.sh.a*** Ps. ***gugumi.w.a*** Rp. ***gugumi.an.a***

gugumo *n* (*n*) body odour; armpit odour, the smell of perspiration from the armpit. (cf *kutuzi, kikwapa*)

gugumua *n* (*n*)(*bot*) reed grass with somewhat spiny leaf-tips and heads of white or buff flowers growing in swamps and on the margins of rivers and lakes. The stems are used for arrow-shafts, hut building, matting, etc. (cf *gwatemala*)

gugun.a¹ (also *gugunya*) *vt* gnaw, nibble, peck, bite, chew: *Mbwa alikuwa akiguguna mfupa*, the dog was gnawing at a bone. Prep. **gugun.i.a** St. **gugun.ik.a** Cs. **gugun.ish.a** Ps. **gugun.w.a** Rp. **gugun.an.a** (cf *ng'wenya, ng'ota, ngwegwenye, bebenya, tafuna*)

gugun.a² *vt* pester, molest, annoy, hector, disturb: *Alikuja kuniguguna wakati nilipokuwa ninasinzia*, he came to disturb me while I was dozing. Prep. **gugun.i.a** St. **gugun.ik.a** Cs. **gugun.ish.a** Ps. **gugun.w.a** Rp. **gugun.an.a** (cf *sumbua, kera*)

guguny.a *vt* see *guguna¹*

gugurush.a (also *gurugusha*) *vt* 1. (of a movement like that of a rat, etc.) rustle, rattle, chatter: *Upepo mkali ulikuwa unayagugurusha majani*, the strong wind was causing the leaves to rustle. 2. revolve, spin; twirl round like a grinding stone: *Alikuwa anazigugurusha funguo kwenye vidole vyake*, he was twirling keys round his fingers. (cf *zungusha*) 3. drag, haul, pull: *Alikuwa anaugugurusha mti ulioanguka upande wa barabarani*, he was dragging the fallen tree off the road. Prep. **gugurush.i.a** St. **gugurush.ik.a** Ps. **gugurush.w.a** Rp. **gugurush.an.a** (cf *burura, kokota*)

guguta *n* (*ma-*) cob of maize with the grains removed; grainless maize cob. (cf *gurunzi, bunzi*)

gui.a *vt* 1. see *gwia* 2. (*fig*) overtake as of darkness e.g. *Aligwiwa na giza*, he was overtaken by darkness. Prep. **gui.li.a** St. **gui.lik.a** Cs. **gui.z.a** Ps. **gui.w.a**

gulabi *n* (*ma-*) (*bot*) litchi, lychee; a fruit consisting of a single seed surrounded by a rough nutlike shell and sweet edible raisinlike pulp.

gulagula *n* (*n*) simpleton, imbecile, idiot, fool: *Yeye ni gulagula*, he is a fool. (cf *baradhuli, mjinga*)

gulamu *n* (*n*) see *ghulamu*

gulegule *n* (*n*) (*zool*) a kind of fish like a dolphin; porpoise-like fish.

gulio *n* (*ma-*) mart; open market, market town, trading centre; a place for buying and selling things. (cf *soko*)

gum.a (also *gumia*) *vi, vt* growl, bark, roar, gnarl, thunder: *Mbwa aliguma wakati watoto walipomchokoza*, the dog growled when the children provoked it. Prep. **gum.i.a** St. **gum.ik.a** Cs. **gum.ish.a** Ps. of Prep. **gum.iw.a** Rp. of Prep. **gum.i.an.a**

gumba¹ *n* (*ma-*) (*anat*) thumb: *Kidole gumba*, the thumb.

gumba² *n* (*n*) famine, starvation; large-scale food shortage.

gumba³ *adj* sterile, infertile, barren: *Mtu gumba*, a sterile person.

gumbizi *n* (*n*) giddiness, vertigo, dizziness. (cf *kisunzi, kisulisuli, kizunguzungu*)

gumbu *n* (*n*) 1. the calabash of a wild cucumber plant. 2. a kind of musical instrument made out of a calabash.

gumea (*ma-*) the leader of a local dance in the ceremony of exorcising spirits.

gumegume¹ *n* (*n*) a flint gun.

gumegume² *n* (*n*) a worthless person; trash, good-for-nothing.

gumi *n* (*n*) a fist.

gumi.a *vt* growl, groan, snarl, gnarl. Prep. **gumi.li.a** St. **gumi.k.a** Cs. **gumi.lish.a** Ps. **gumi.w.a** Rp. **gumi.an.a**

gumio *n* (*n*) see *mgumio*

-gumu *adj* 1. hard, difficult, intricate: *Tatizo gumu*, an intricate problem. 2. solid, tough, firm, strong: *Chuma ni kigumu*, iron is strong. 3. stingy, niggardly, parsimonious, mean: *Yeye ni mgumu kwani hatumii pesa zake ovyo*, he is stingy as he doesn't spend his money carelessly. *Wekea ngumu*, deprive someone the opportunity of benefitting from sth. 4. stubborn, obdurate, unyielding: *Jirani yako ni mtu mgumu kwa sababu hukataa ushauri wowote anaopewa*, your neighbour is stubborn because she rejects any advice that is given to her.

197

gumzo *n* (*ma-*) chat, conversation, talk. (cf *soga, porojo, mazungumzo*)

gun.a *vi, vt* croak, grunt, mutter, murmur; speak in an undertone: *Aliguna alipoambiwa kuwa likizo yake imeahirishwa*, he grunted when he was told that his leave has been postponed. Prep. **gun.i.a** St. **gun.ik.a** Cs. **gun.ish.a** Ps. **gun.w.a** (cf *nung'unika*)

gunda[1] *n* (*n*) 1. a horn used for blowing and usu made from wood or ivory; bull-horn. (cf *siwa, baragumu*) 2. siren (cf *pembe, king'ora, paipu*)

gunda[2] *n* (*n*) a big farm of not less than 50 acres. (cf *shunda*)

gunda[3] *n* (*n*) voluntary work, voluntary service: *Kazi ya gunda*, voluntary work. (cf *msaragambo, harambee*)

gundi[1] *n* (*n*) 1. glue, gum-paste for sticking things; rubber solution. (cf *sherisi*) 2. wheat flour mixed with water for making cigarettes. (Hind)

gundi[2] *n* (*ma-*) (*anat*) knee (cf *goti*)

gundish.a *vt* paste, gum; glue, bind, bond. Prep. **gundish.i.a** St. **gundish.ik.a** Ps **gundish.w.a** Rp. of Prep. **gundish.i.an.a**

gundu.a *vt* 1. discover, invent; find out a problem, fact, etc.: *Niligundua kwamba taarifa yake si kweli*, I discovered that his statement was not true. (cf *ng'amua, maizi*) 2. catch; discover someone in the act of doing wrong: *Aligundua kwamba mkewe alikuwa akifanya mapenzi na rafiki yake*, he found out that his wife was flirting with his friend. Prep. **gundu.li.a** St. **gundu.lik.a** Cs. **gundu.lish.a** Ps. of Prep **gundu.liw.a** Rp. **gundu.an.a** (cf *fumania*)

gung.a[1] *vt* 1. cure, heal; treat medically: *Madaktari waliweza kuyagunga maradhi yake*, the doctors were able to cure his disease. 2. keep a taboo; restrain oneself from eating certain foods for health reasons: *Kwa vile ana ugonjwa wa kisukari, mgonjwa yule sasa anagunga*, because he is a diabetic patient, he is now eating specific types of food. Prep. **gung.i.a** St. **gung.ik.a** Cs. **gung.ish.a** Ps. **gung.w.a** Rp. **gung.an.a**

gung.a[2] *vt* warn, caution, alert: *Nilimgunga asisafiri usiku*, I warned him not to travel at night. Prep. **gung.i.a** St. **gung.ik.a** Cs. **gung.ish.a** Ps. **gung.w.a** Rp. **gung.an.a** (cf *onya*)

gung.a[3] *vt* overcome temptations; control oneself against temptations: *Mcha Mungu yule anavigunga vishawishi vingi*, that pious person overcomes many temptations. Prep. **gung.i.a** St. **gung.ik.a** Cs. **gung.ish.a** Ps. **gung.w.a** Rp. **gung.an.a**

gung.a[4] *vt* wheedle, coax, cajole: *Alimgunga baba yake ampe fedha*, he wheedled his father into giving him some money. Prep. **gung.ia** St. **gung.ik.a** Cs. **gung.ish.a** Ps. **gung.w.a** Rp. **gung.an.a** (cf *bembeleza, engaenga*)

gunge *n* (*ma-*) expert, pundit, specialist; a highly proficient person usu in witchcraft activities: *Yule ni gunge anayesifika sana katika mambo ya uchawi*, he is an expert who is reknown in matters of sorcery. (cf *fundi, bingwa*)

gungu[1] *n* (*ma-*) an old kind of traditional dance performed by Swahili-Speaking people.

gungu[2] *n* (*ma-*) a barren land.

gungu[3] *n* (*ma-*) (*anat*) pelvic bone; sacrum. (cf *gungunyo*)

gungumk.a *vi* be dry, be parched, be descicated: *Mahindi yaligungumka kutokana na jua kali*, the maize plants were parched from the hot sun. *Gundi imegungumka*, the glue is dry. Prep. **gungumk.i.a** St. **gungumk.ik.a** Cs. **gungumk.ish.a** Ps. **gungumk.w.a**

gungwi *n* (*n*) a children's game of jumping with one foot. (cf *kideku, kungu*)

guni[1] *n* (*n*) a carpenter's spokeshave.

guni[2] *n* (*n*) (*poet*) a free verse as opposed to a rhymed verse: *Shairi lenye guni*, a free verse poem; a blank verse poem. (cf *dosari, kasoro*) (Hind)

guni³ *n* (*n*) defect, shortcoming, imperfection. (cf *dosari, kasoro*) (Hind)
gunia *n* (*n*) gunny sack; a sack cloth chiefly used for packing potatoes, rice, copra, cloves, etc. (Hind)
gunjam.a *vi* sleep in place for a short time; repose, rest: *Alikuwa amechoka na ndiyo maana amegunjama*, he was tired and that is why he is resting for a while. Prep. *gunjam.i.a* St. *gunjam.ik.a* Cs. *gunjam.ish.a*
guno (also *ngumo*) *n* (*n*) whimper, grumble, whine, undertone, complaint.
gunyu.a *vt* scald Prep. *gunyu.li.a* St. *gunyu.k.a* Cs. *gunyu.lish.a* Ps of Prep. *gunyu.liw.a*
gunyuk.a *vi* be scalded; be burnt because of boiling water or steam. Prep. *gunyuk.i.a* St. *gunyuk.ik.a* Cs. *gunyuk.ish.a* Ps. *gunyuk.w.a* (cf *chubuku, gwajuka*)
gunzi *n* (*n*) grainless maize cob (cf *guguta, bunzi*)
guoguo *n* (*ma-*) hawker (*mchuuzi*)
gur.a *vt, vi* 1. migrate, resettle; move one's place to another dwelling. 2. separate with sby because of conflict, etc. Prep. *gur.i.a* St. *gur.ik.a* Cs. *gur.ish.a* Ps. *gur.w.a* Rp. *gur.an.a* (cf *hama, haji*)
guro *n* (*n*) migration, resettlement; movement from one place to another (cf *uhamaji*)
guru¹ *n* (*n*) pundit, expert, authority, scholar. (Hind)
guru² *n* (*n*) a coarse, unrefined kind of dark-coloured lumpy sugar made from sugarcane: *Sukari guru*, dark-coloured unrefined sugar
gurudumu *n* (*ma-*) 1. wheel. 2. used in the expression: *Gurudumu la maendeleo*, the wheel of progress e.g. *Serikali imekusudia kusukuma gurudumu la maendeleo katika sekta zote za kiuchumi*, the government is determined to steer the wheel of progress in all economic sectors. (Pers)

gurufu¹ *n* (*n*) bend; a curve or turn in a road. (cf *korosi, kona*)
gurufu² *n* (*n*) highway, main road, main street. (cf *baraste, barabara*)
guruguru¹ *n* (*ma-*) 1. (*zool*) burrowing skink; a kind of lizard found beneath rocks, humus and fallen trees. 2. a kind of sole which is good for eating

guruguru

guruguru² *n* (*ma-*) thunder: *Guruguru lilipovuma, mvua ikaanza kunyesha*, after the thunderbolt, it started raining.
gurugush.a¹ *vt* see *gugurusha*
gurugush.a² *vt* bungle, botch, muddle; spoil work, do job improperly: *Nilimpa kazi afanye lakini akaigurugusha*, I gave him work to do but he bungled it. Prep. *gurugush.i.a* St. *gurugush.ik.a* Ps. *gurugush.w.a* Rp. *gurugush.an.a* (cf *boronga, vurunda*)
gurugush.a³ *vt, vi* shake, jiggle: *Alizigurugusha betri kwenye tochi*, he jiggled the batteries in a torch. Prep. *gurugush.i.a* St. *gurugush.ik.a* Ps. *gurugush.w.a* Rp. *gurugush.an.a*
guruguz.a *vt* 1. remove the husks by pounding in a mortar or grinding them: *Aliziguruguza ngano kwenye kinu*, he removed the husks of wheat by pounding in a mortar. 2. chew sth with insufficient number of teeth; suck: *Bikizee alikiguruguza kipande cha mkate*, the old woman chewed a piece of bread with insufficient number of teeth. Prep. *guruguz.i.a* St. *guruguz.ik.a* Ps. *guruguz.w.a* Rp. *guruguz.an.a* (cf *mung'unya, mumunya*)
gururu *n* (*n*) thick milk; butter milk; fermented milk; sour milk. (cf *mtindi*) (Ar)

gurus.a *vt* be in the habit of turning down every fiancee on flimsy grounds: *Kijana yule kwa kweli hataki kuoa; kazi yake ni kuwagurusa mabinti tu,* that young man doesn't really want to get married; his habit is just to turn down girls on flimsy grounds. Prep. *gurus.i.a* St. *gurus.ik.a* Cs. *gurus.ish.a* Ps. *gurus.w.a* Rp. *gurus.an.a*

gurut.a *vt* mangle; squeeze or dry clothes through the rollers of a mangling machine: *Baada ya kuzifua nguo zangu, niliziguruta,* after washing my clothes, I mangled them. Prep. *gurut.i.a* St. *gurut.ik.a* Cs. *gurut.ish.a* Ps. *gurut.w.a*

guruto *n* (*ma-*) mangling machine.

gus.a *vt* 1. touch, thumb, hold; handle with the fingers. (cf *shika*) 2. beat slightly: *Ukinigusa tu, nitakuadhibu,* If you beat me slightly, I will punish you (cf *piga*). 3. (*fig*) influence, move, arouse: *Hotuba yake kali ilinigusa sana,* his powerful speech moved me very much. (cf *athari*) Prep. *gus.i.a* St. *gus.ik.a* Cs. *gus.ish.a* Ps. *gus.w.a* Rp. *gus.an.a* (cf *athiri*)

gusi.a *vt* hint, allude, suggest: *Msemaji aligusia swala la rushwa nchini,* the speaker hinted on the issue of corruption in the country. St. *gusi.k.a* Cs. *gusi.sh.a* Ps. *gusi.w.a* Rp. *gusi.an.a*

gus.u *vt* refuse to do sth that you initially accepted; boycott, decline: *Kiongozi wa wafanyakazi aligusu kuacha mgomo wao,* the trade union leader refused to abandon their strike. Prep. *gus.i.a* St. *gus.ik.a* Cs. *gus.ish.a* Ps. of Prep. *gus.iw.a* Rp of Prep. *gus.i.an.a*

gut.a[1] *vi* shout, bawl, yell, cry out: *Msasi aliguta alipokuwa hatarini,* the hunter bawled when he was in danger. Prep. *gut.i.a* St. *gut.ik.a* Cs. *gut.ish.a* Ps. *gut.w.a* Rp. *gut.an.a*

gut.a[2] *vt* butt, gore; push as of an ox: *Ng'ombe dume alimguta mkulima mpaka akafa,* the bull butted the farmer until he died. Prep. *gut.i.a* St. *gut.ik.a* Cs. *gut.ish.a* Ps. *gut.w.a* Rp. *gut.an.a*

gutu[1] *adj* blunt, dull, unsharpened: *Kisu gutu,* a blunt knife.

gutu[2] *adj* broken off, mutilated: *Mkono gutu,* stump of a mutilated arm.

gutu[3] *n* (*n*) stump, trunk. stem, stalk: *Gutu la mnazi,* the trunk of a coconut tree having no crown.

gutu.a *vt* 1. frighten, horrify, terrify: *Kelele nyingi kali za majirani zilimgutua mgeni wangu,* the loud noises by my neighbours startled my guest. (cf *shitua, tisha*) 2. startle, surprise, astound, shock, stun: *Alinigutua aliponieleza kifo cha ghafla cha mwalimu wangu,* he shocked me when he broke the news of the sudden death of my teacher. Prep. *gutu.li.a* St. *gutu.lik.a* Cs. *gutu.sh.a* Ps of Prep. *gutu.liw.a* Rp. *gutu.an.a* (cf *staajabisha*)

gutuk.a *vi* be startled, be stunned, be shocked: *Aligutuka aliposikia sauti nyingi mtaani,* he was startled when he heard a lot of noise from the neighbourhood. Prep. *gutuk.i.a* St. *gutuk.ik.a* Cs. *gutuk.ish.a*

gutuz.a *vt* awaken sby who is asleep inorder to alert him of danger. Prep. *gutuz.i.a* St. *gutuz.ik.a* Cs. *gutuz.ish.a* Ps. *gutuz.w.a*

guu[1] *n* (*ma*) 1. a big leg. (*prov*) *Asiyesikia la mkuu huvunjika guu,* he who does not listen to the chief will cut his leg, i.e. he who does not listen to his elder's advice will suffer. 2. (*idm*) *Tia guu,* block someone; obstruct: *Amenitilia guu kwenye maombi yangu ya kazi serikalini,* he has blocked me in my application for employment in the government service.

guu[2] *n* (*ma*) (*naut*) pegs connecting outrigger boom with floats in a canoe.

gw.a vi (arch) fall down. Prep. *gw.i.a* St. *gw.ik.a* Cs. *gw.ish.a* Ps. *gw.iw.a* (cf *anguka, poromoka*)

gwadu adj sour

gwaduk.a vi produce saliva into the mouth when eating sth that causes sourness e.g. raw mangoes, tamarind, etc. Prep. *gwaduk.i.a* St. *gwaduk.ik.a* Cs. *gwaduk.ish.a* Ps. *gwaduk.w.a*

gwafu.a vt 1. show the teeth and snarl usu in anger as in the case of a dog: *Mbwa aligwafua*, the dog snarled. 2. seize and bite suddenly: *Mbwa aliugwafua mguu wa kijana mmoja*, the dog suddenly attacked a young man and bit his leg. Prep. *gwafu.li.a* St. *gwafu.k.a*

gwagu n (ma-) 1. (zool) a large tomcat; a half-wild cat. (cf *ngawa*) 2. an indisciplined person, a recalcitrant person; rebel. 3. brute; a cruel person, a ruthless person, a merciless person.

gwajuk.a vi be scalded, be abraded, be excoriated. Prep. *gwajuk.i.a* St. *gwajuk.ik.a* Cs. *gwajuk.ish.a* (cf *babuka, gunyuka, chubuka*)

gwanda 1. a garment like a smock or short *kanzu* reaching to the knees and is made of calico, occasionally worn by men. (cf *pindi, chepe, vulia*) 2. a worthless garment; a useless garment. 2. smock; a loose shirt like a garment worn to protect the clothes.

gwara n (ma-) see *gwaru*

gwaraz.a vt grind; make a grinding sound: *Gwaraza meno*, grind the teeth. Prep. *gwaraz.i.a* St. *gwaraz.ik.a* Cs. *gwaraz.ish.a*

gwaride n (ma-) military parade; drill: *Wanajeshi walifanya gwaride*, the soldiers conducted a parade. (cf *paredi*) (Ar)

gwaru[1] (also gwara) n (n) a coin of 5, 10, or 20 cents.

gwaru[2] n (n) (bot) cluster bean; pods which are used for curries.

gwase n (n) (zool) warthog; wild pig. (cf *mbango, ngiri*)

gwase

gwat.a vt entrap sby with the foot; hook sby with the foot; trip sby up: *Alimgwata rafiki yake kwenye michezo ya mieleka*, he tripped his friend up during wrestling. Prep. *gwat.i.a* St. *gwat.ik.a* Cs. *gwat.ish.a* Ps. *gwat.w.a* Rp. *gwat.an.a*

gwatemala n (bot) reed grass with somewhat spiny leaf tips. (cf *gugumua*)

gwato n (ma-) 1. crutch; a stick with a piece that fits under the arm for supporting someone who has walking problems. 2. stilt; one of a pair of poles with supporting pieces for the feet, which allows a person to walk raised above the ground. 3. prop; a rigid support esp that of a piece of wood used to prevent sth from falling.

gway.a vi, vt tremble to speak, etc. because of fear, cold, weakness, etc.; shudder, quiver, quaver, shake: *Aligwaya alipowaona polisi wakiingia nyumbani kwake*, she trembled when she saw policemen entering her house. Prep. *gway.i.a* St. *gway.ik.a* Cs. *gway.ish.a* Ps. *gway.w.a* (cf *tetemeka, tetema*)

gwaz.a¹ *vi* 1. stutter, stammer; falter in speaking because of fear, sickness, etc.; *Jirani yangu aligwaza baada ya kutishwa na majambazi*, my neighbour faltered in speaking after being threatened by thugs. 2. prevent, stop, impede, block: *Alijaribu kuyagwaza maendeleo ya kijijini*, he tried to impede the development of the village. Prep. *gwaz.i.a* St. *gwaz.ik.a* Cs. *gwaz.ish.a* Ps. *gwaz.w.a* (cf *zuia*)

gwaz.a² *vt* scrape grass: *Aligwaza manyasi katika bustani yangu*, he slashed grass in my garden. Prep. *gwaz.i.a* St. *gwaz.ik.a* Cs. *gwaz.ish.a* Ps. *gwaz.w.a* (cf *lima*)

gwechu *n* (*n*) an old worn-out utensil; an old worn-out item: *Nilikunywa maziwa katika glasi iliyokuwa gwechu*, I drank milk from a glass that was old and worn-out.

gwegweny.a *vt* gnaw with front teeth; nibble, peck; take small bites: *Mbwa alikuwa anagwegwenya mfupa*, the dog was gnawing at the bone. Prep. *gwegweny.e.a* St. *gwegweny.ek.a* Cs. *gwegweny.ez.a* Ps. *gwegweny.w.a* Rp. *gwegweny.an.a* (cf *guguna*)

gweny.a *vt* chop with an axe or an adze: *Mkulima aliugwenya mti ili apate magome*, the farmer chopped the tree with an axe in order to get the bark. Prep. *gweny.e.a* St. *gweny.ek.a* Cs. *gweny.esh.a* Ps. *gweny.w.a*

gwi.a (also *bwia*) *vt* 1. catch, hold, grasp, grab, claw, seize: *Askari alimgwia jambazi*, the policeman arrested the thug. (cf *nasa, shika, kamata*) 2 (*fig*) overtake as of darkness; fall: *Giza lilimgwia*, he was overtaken by darkness. Prep. *gwi.li.a* St. *gwi.k.a* Cs. *gwi.z.a* Ps. *gwi.w.a* Rp. *gwi.an.a* (cf *angukia*)

gwiji¹ *n* (*ma-*) 1. an expert, usu in medicine; ace; specialist, authority, mavin, adept. 2. valiant soldier, a brave soldier: *Mjomba ni gwiji aliyepigana Vita vya Pili vya Dunia*, my uncle is a brave soldier who fought in the Second World War.

gwiji² *adj* 1. clever, intelligent, ingenious, skillful: *Yeye ni dereva gwiji*, he is a skillful driver. 2. brave, valiant: *Wao ni askari jeshi gwiji*, they are brave soldiers.

gwish.a *vi* (of an ewe) give birth to lambs; lamb.

H

H, h /h/ 1. the eighth letter of the Swahili alphabet. 2. It is a glottal fricative.

ha *interj* an expletive used for showing surprise. (cf *oh!, do!*)

haba¹ *adj* 1. insufficient, rare, scarce, short of: *Maji haba*, insufficient water. *Chakula haba*, insufficient food. (*prov*) *Haba na haba hujaza kibaba*, little and little fills the measure i.e. Something small you possess at the moment will one day become big and help you at the time when the need arises. (cf *kidogo*) 2. skimpy, meagre, scant, few: *Siku haba*, few days.

haba² *n* (*n*) the rolling up of cigarettes: *Alitaka sigara haba tatu*, he wanted three rolled-up cigarettes.

haba³ *n* (*n*) bhang, hashish, opium. (cf *bangi, kasumba*)

hababi (also *hababu*) *n* (*n*) 1. lord, master, sir. 2. darling, sweetheart, beloved, honey: *Hababi wangu ni mama*, my beloved is my mother. (cf *mpenzi*) (Ar)

habatilmuluk *n* (*n*) a kind of laxative. (Ar)

hababu *n* (*n*) see *hababi*

hababuu *n* (*n*) a person of noble birth.

habari¹ *n* (*n*) 1. news, information, report: *Habari za kimataifa*, international news. *Habari za kuaminika*, reliable information. *Habari motomoto*, hot news. 2. (used in greetings): *Habari gani?* How are you? (Ar)

habari² *interj* an expression of greeting.

habarish.a *vt* inform, apprise, notify: *Alinihabarisha mambo mengi*, he informed me a lot of things. Prep. **habarish.i.a** St. **habarish.ik.a** Ps **habarish.w.a** Rp. **habarish.an.a** (cf *juvya, arifu*)

habasoda *n* (*n*) (*med*) black seed; a kind of medicine used for abdominal pains, etc. (Ar)

habedari (also *abedari*) *interj* an exclamation of warning *usu* used by porters when they want to pass or unload cargo. Beware! Make way! (cf *simile! heria!*) (Pers)

Habeshi (also *Uhabeshi*) *n* (*n*) (*geog*) Ethiopia (Ar)

habi *interj* an expletive used by a person whose evil spirit has mounted to the head and is now furious and begins to hit against himself here and there. (cf *tulia!*)

habibi *n* (*ma-*) darling, sweetheart. (cf *mpenzi*)

habithi *n* (*ma-*) 1. a wicked person, an evil person, a malicious person; brute. (cf *katili*) 2. a deceitful person, a crafty person; cheat, inveigler. (cf *mjanja, mdanganyifu*) (Ar)

habta *n* (*n*) (*naut*) anchor (cf *nanga, baura*)

hada.a¹ *vt* deceive, swindle, cheat, hoodwink: *Alinihadaa kwa kunipa noti bandia*, he cheated me by giving me a fake note. Prep. **hada.i.a** St. **hada.ik.a** Cs. **hada.ish.a** Ps. of Prep. **hada.iw.a** Rp. **hada.an.a** (cf *danganya, ghilibu, laghai*) (Ar)

hadaa² *n* (*n*) deceit, trickery, hypocrisy: (*prov*) *Dunia hadaa, Ulimwengu shujaa*, a deceiving world. *Usinifanyie hadaa*, don't cheat me. (cf *ghiliba, hila, ujanja*) (Ar)

hadaa³ *adj* deceitful, deceiving, insincere, untrustworthy.

hadhara *n* (*n*) 1. used in the expression: *Mkutano wa hadhara*, a public meeting, a public gathering. 2. a crowd of people, a multitude of people: *Mkutano wa jana ulikuwa wa hadhara*, yesterday's meeting was a public one. 3. in public: *Alimtukana hadhara ya watu*, she insulted him in public. (cf *jahara*)

hadharani *adv* publicly, openly: *Alinipiga hadharani*, he beat me in public. (cf *kadamnasi*) (Ar)

hadhar.i¹ (also *tahadhari*) *vi* be cautious, be alert, be on guard: *Lazima utahadhari na wezi siku hizi,* you must be careful with thieves these days. (cf *angalia, tazama*) (Ar)

hadhari² (also *tahadhari*) *n* (*n*) caution, alertness, care: *Mfanyakazi wangu ana hadhari anapoosha vyombo,* my worker is very careful when he is washing dishes. (cf *uangalifu, makini*) (Ar)

hadhi *n* (*n*) status, dignity, prestige, reputation, respect: *Hadhi ya utu,* human dignity. *Shushia hadhi,* disparage, discredit. (cf *heshima, utukufu, staha, ukubwa, cheo*) (Ar)

hadhira *n* (*n*) audience (Ar)

hadhir.i¹ *vt* lecture, talk, speak: *Alihadhiri juu ya uzazi wa majira,* he lectured on family planning. Prep. **hadhir.i.a** St. **hadhir.ik.a** Cs. **hadhir.ish.a** Ps. of Prep. **hadhir.iw.a** Rp. of Prep. **hadhir.i.an.a** (cf *hutubu*) (Ar)

hadhiri² *adj* vigilant, alert, attentive, watchful: *Yeye ni hadhiri,* he is very alert (cf *makini, nabihi*) (Ar)

hadhirina *n* (*n*) the audience, the invited, those in attendance (Ar)

hadi¹ *conj* 1. until, up to: *Alikusubiri hapa tangu asubuhi hadi mchana,* he waited for you since morning until afternoon. (cf *mpaka, lama*) 2. extremely, very, too far: *Nimefurahi hadi nikaanguka,* I was extremely happy to the point of falling. (cf *mpaka*) (Ar)

hadi² *n* (*n*) (*maths*) modulus

hadia *n* (*n*) present, gift, favour. (cf *zawadi, tunzo*) (Ar)

hadidi¹ *n* (*n*) 1. iron. (cf *chuma*) 2. (*idm*) *Hadidi za marejeo,* terms of reference. (Ar)

hadidi² *adj* strong, mighty, powerful, firm: *Mtu hadidi,* a strong person. (cf *madhubuti, kabili*) (Ar)

hadimu *n* (*n*) 1. servant, attendant: *Hadimu wake anafanya kazi vizuri,* his servant works quite well. (cf *mtumishi*) 2. a forced servant. (cf *abdi*) (Ar)

hadithi¹ *n* (*n*) 1. account, description: *Hadithi ya safari yake ni ya kusikitisha,* the account of his journey is sorrowful. (cf *kisa, ngano*) 2. fiction, tale, story: *Ile ilikuwa hadithi ya kubuni,* that was a fiction. 3. Prophet's Mohammad's traditions. (Ar)

hadith.i² (also *hadithia*) *vt, vi* narrate; give an account of. Prep. **hadith.i.a** St. **hadith.ik.a** Ps. **hadith.iw.a** Rp. **hadith.i.an.a** (cf *simulia, elezea*) (Ar)

hadubini *n* (*n*) microscope. (cf *maikroskopu, darubini*)

hae¹ *interj* 1. an expletive of sorrow; alas! oh: *Hae! Mungu wangu!* Oh, my God! 2. a rejoinder from an audience during story-telling, riddles, etc.

hae² *interj* see **hai²**

hafidhi *n* (*n*) note book, diary (Ar)

hafidhi² *n* (*n*) a person who knows by heart the whole of the Holy Koran.

hafifish.a *vt* deprecate, devaluate; render insignificant: *Aliihafifisha thamani ya gari yake mpya ili kukwepa ushuru mkubwa wa forodha,* he depreciated the value of his new car in order to avoid heavy customs duty (cf *dunisha, hakirisha*) (Ar)

hafifisho *n* (*ma-*) depreciation, devaluation: *Hafifisho la sarafu ya nchi liliwaumiza raia,* the devaluation of the country's currency hurt the citizens. (Ar)

hafifu *adj* 1. poor, inferior, second-rate: *Nguo hii ni hafifu,* this dress is inferior (cf *duni*) 2. light, unheavy, weightless: *Mzigo wake ulikuwa hafifu,* his luggage was light. (Ar)

hafla *n* (*n*) reception, party, banquet, get-together: *Tulifanya hafla kuisherehekea harusi yake,* we held a reception to celebrate his wedding. (cf *dhifa, karamu*) (Ar)

hafubeki *n* (*ma*) (in soccer, etc.) half-back player: *Hafubeki wa kulia,* half back right. (Eng)

hafukasti *n (ma-)* half-caste, crossbreed, hybrid; a half-breed person: *Yeye ni hafukasti wa Kiarabu na Kizungu,* he is a half-caste of Arab and European blood. (cf *suriama, chotara, shombe*) (Eng)

hafutaimu *n (n)* half time; the rest period between halves of a football game, basketball game, etc. (Eng)

hagali *n (n)* a special rope usu worn by male Bedouins and other Arabs around the head to support a turban; agal. (Ar)

hah.a *vt, vi* 1. gorge, gormandize, gluttonize; eat ravenously, eat hastily: *Alikuwa akihaha kwa vile yeye ni mroho,* he was eating ravenously as he is greedy. (cf *lapa, papia*) 2. pant, puff; breathe quickly and with great difficulty: *Alihaha baada ya kukimbia,* he panted after running fast. (cf *hema, pwita, tweta*) 3. be uneasy, be worried, be perplexed: *Alihaha baada ya kufukuzwa kazini,* he became perplexed after being sacked from work. (cf *hangaika*) 4. speak incoherently due to fear, etc: *Alihaha baada ya polisi kumsaili juu ya mauaji,* he spoke incoherently after being grilled by the police on the murder. 5. be enraged/angry over a small issue. Prep. *hah.i.a* St. *hah.ik.a* Cs. *hah.ish.a* Ps. *hah.w.a*

hai[1] *adj* 1. alive, living, live, animate: *Yeye yu hai ingawa mahututi,* she is alive although very sick. 2. active, robust, energetic: *Chama chetu kiko hai,* our party is active. (Ar)

hai[2] (also *hae*[2]) *interj* an expletive of intention to soothe sth so that it does not persist.

haiba (also *heba*) *n (n)* 1. eye appeal, attractiveness: *Yeye ni mke mwenye haiba sana,* she is an attractive wife. (cf *urembo, uzuri*) 2. good manners: *Kijana yule ana haiba sana,* that young person is well-mannered. (cf *adabu*) 3. honesty, integrity: *Keshia wetu ni mtu mwenye haiba,* our cashier is an honest person. (cf *uaminifu*) (Ar)

haibiskasi *n (n)* (*bot*) hibiscus; a tropical plant with large, brightly coloured flowers. (Eng)

haibridi *n (n)* hybrid (Eng) (cf *mahuluti*)

haidhuru *conj* it doesn't matter, never mind, no harm: *Haidhuru ikiwa mimi nitaikosa ile kazi,* it doesn't matter if I will miss the job. (cf *si neno, potelea mbali*)

haidroliki *n (n)* hydrolics (Eng)

haijambo *conj* it is better; it is manageable. (Ar)

haika *interj* an exclamation of acceptance of calm statements from a spirit; yes, okay, we hear that (Ar)

haikahaika *n (n)* see *hekaheka*

haikamishna *n (n)* the head of the embassy of a Commonwealth country; high commissioner. (cf *balozi*) (Eng)

hailigwa *adj* (of food) forbidden, prohibited, inedible.

haima (also *hema*) *n (n)* (*naut*) tent roofing over quarter deck of a dhow; awning.

hainehaine (also *aineaine*) *interj* an expletive of encouragement esp in the act of lifting heavy objects (cf *hoberahobera*)

haini[1] *n (n)* 1. traitor, renegade, turncoat, defector, betrayer: *Yule anayesaliti nchi yake ni haini,* he who betrays his country is a traitor. (cf *msaliti*) 2. cheater, deceiver, duper: *Usimwamini haini yule,* don't trust that duper. (cf *mdanganyifu*) (cf *asi*) 3. reprobate, tyrant, scoundrel. (cf *dhalimu*) (Ar)

hain.i[2] *vt* betray; deceive. *Aliihaini nchi yake,* he betrayed his country. Prep. *hain.i.a* St. *hain.ik.a* Cs. *hain.ish.a* Ps. of Prep. *hain.iw.a* Rp. of prep *hain.i.an.a*

haipotenyusi *n (n)* (*maths*) hypotenuse; the side of a right-angled triangle opposite the right angle. (cf *kiegana*)

H haja — hakimu

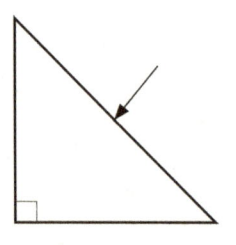

haipotenyusi

haja *n (n)* 1. need, want, necessity: *Kuna haja ya kuita mkutano wa dharura*, it is necessary to call for an emergency meeting. 2. reason, ground. 3. call of nature: *Enda haja kubwa*, excrete, defecate. *Enda haja ndogo*, urinate.

haji (also *alhaji*) *n (n)* pilgrim, a Muslim who went to Mecca to perform pilgrimage. (Ar)

hajir.i (also *hujuru*) *vt, vi* 1. emigrate, migrate, expatriate oneself, move away: *Aliihajiri nchi yake kwa majonzi*, he migrated from his country with grief. 2. part with others; split, separate. Prep. *hajir.i.a* St. *hajir.ik.a* Cs. *hajir.ish.a* Ps. of Prep. *hajir.iw.a* (cf *gura, hama*) (Ar)

hajivale *n (n)* (*zool*) African harrier hawk, gymnogene; a kind of bird with a long wide black tail and a broad white band. *Polyboroides radiatus*. (cf *shakevale*)

hajja *n (n)* a word of respect given to a woman pilgrim.

haka *n (n)* fine, forfeit; compensation for breach of rules of a club, guild, etc.: *Alitoa haka kwa kumpiga mwanakijiji*, he paid a fine for beating a villager. (cf *fidia, dia*)

hakahak.a *vt* wander; do sth like an amateur: *Aliihakahaka kazi yangu kwani yeye si fundi*, he did my job like an amateur as he is not an expert. Prep. *hakahak.i.a* St. *hakahak.ik.a* Cs. *hakahak.ish.a* (cf *babaisha*)

haki *n (n)* 1. right, just claim: *Haki za kunakili*, copyright. *Haki za binaadamu*, human rights. *Haki za mfalme*, royal prerogatives. *Haki za kupiga kura*, suffrage. 2. justice, fairness, impartiality, fair play: *Hakimu aliendesha kesi kwa haki*, the judge tried the case with impartiality. (cf *uadilifu, usawa*) 3. property: *Ilikuwa haki yangu*, it was my property. (cf *mali*) (Ar)

hakika¹ *n (n)* certainty, surety, actuality, truth: *Ana hakika nalo*, he is sure of it. (cf *uhalisi, yakini*) (Ar)

hakika² *adv* certainly, surely, truly, indeed, really, in fact, in truth: *Hakika, yeye si mtu mwaminifu*, truly, he is not an honest person. (cf *hakika*) (Ar)

hakik.i *vt, vi* 1. verify, ascertain, investigate, review critically, criticize, appraise: *Alikwenda kuihakiki ripoti ya jinai*, he went to verify the criminal report. (cf *chunguza, peleleza*) 2. review, critique: *Aliyahakiki maandishi yangu*, he reviewed my publications. Prep. *hakik.i.a* St. *hakik.ik.a* Cs. *hakik.ish.a* Ps. of Prep. *hakik.iw.a* Rp. of Prep *hakik.i.an.a* (cf *chambua, kosoa*) (Ar)

hakikish.a¹ *vt, vi* see *hakiki*

hakikish.a² *vt, vi* confirm, certify, affirm, prove: *Hakikisha kwanza kama habari yenyewe ni kweli*, confirm first if the information is correct. Prep. *hakikish.i.a* St. *hakikish.ik.a* Ps. *hakikish.w.a* Rp. of Prep. *hakikish.i.an.a* (cf *thibitisha*)

hakikishi.a *vt* certify to, prove to. St. *hakikishi.k.a* Ps. *hakikishi.w.a* Rp. *hakikishi.an.a*

hakikisho *n (n)* verification, confirmation, assurance, affirmation: *Alimpa hakikisho kwamba hatamtusi tena*, he gave her an assurance that he would not insult her again. (cf *ikirari, uthibitisho, ushahidi, yakini*) (Ar)

hakimiliki *n (n)* copyright (Ar)

hakimu *n (ma-)* 1. judge, magistrate: *Hakimu mkaazi*, resident magistrate. *Hakimu mfawidhi*, principal magistrate.

206

Hakimu mkuu, chief magistrate: *Hakimu wa wilaya*, district magistrate. *Hakimu mkuu mkaazi*, senior resident magistrate. (cf *jaji, kadhi*) 2. arbitrator, negotiator, arbiter: *Alikuwa hakimu hodari aliyeweza kusuluhisha ugomvi wao*, he was a skilful arbitrator who was able to settle their dispute. (cf *mwamuzi, msuluhishi, mpatanishi*) (Ar)

hakir.i[1] *vt, vi* discredit, debase, disgrace, dishonour, mortify, demean: *Alimhakiri mjomba wake hadharani*, he discredited his uncle in public. Prep. **hakir.i.a** St. **hakir.ik.a** Cs. **hakir.ish.a** Ps. of Prep. **hakir.iw.a** Rp. of Prep. **hakir.i.an.a** (cf *aibisha, tweza*) (Ar)

hakiri[2] *adj* 1. abject, debased, poor, inferior: *Yeye ni hakiri kwani anaishi maisha ya dhiki*, he is poor as he lives a difficult life. (cf *duni, dhalili*) 2. humble; an expression used in the closing lines of a letter to someone who is quite respected: *Mtumishi wako hakiri*, your humble servant. (cf *alhakiri*) (Ar)

hakiri[3] *n (n)* a debased person; an inferior person.

hal.a *vt* elope with sby's wife; abduct sby's wife: *Alimhala mke wa jirani yake*, he abducted his neighbour's wife. Prep. **hal.i.a** St. **hal.ik.a** Cs. **hal.ish.a** Ps. of Prep **hal.iw.a** Rp. **hal.an.a**

halabati *n (n)* (*zool*) halibut; a large edible flat fish (Eng)

halafa[1] *n (n)* 1. rebellion, mutiny, revolt, disobedience. (cf *uasi, uhalifu*) 2. misunderstanding, disagreement, discord. (cf *tofauti, hitilafu*) (Ar)

halafa[2] *n (n)* oath, vow, avowal. (cf *kiapo*) (Ar)

halafu *adv* later, subsequently, next: *Halafu, ukaanguka chini*, later, he fell down. (cf *baadaye, kisha*) (Ar)

halahala *n (n)* promptly, at once, immediately. (Ar)

halaiki *n (n)* 1. multitude, crowd: *Niliona halaiki ya watu mkutanoni*, I saw a crowd of people at the meeting. (cf *umati, umma*) 2. a school game of drilling. (Ar)

halali[1] *adj* legal, lawful, constitutional: *Haikuwa halali kwa yeye kuwekwa kizuizini*, it was not lawful for him to be detained. (Ar)

halali[2] *n (n)* right, just claim: *Hii ilikuwa halali yako*, this was your right. (cf *haki, ustahiki*) (Ar)

halalik.a *vi* 1. be legal, be lawful, be constitutional: *Ilihalalika kwa yeye kuwekwa rumande*, it was lawful for him to be detained. 2. be permissible, be allowable. Cs. **halalik.ish.a** Ps. of Prep. **halalik.iw.a** (Ar)

halalish.a[1] *vt* see *halalika*

halalish.a[2] *vt* legalize, legitimize; make legal: *Dini ya Kiislamu haijahalalisha kula nyama ya nguruwe*, the Islamic religion has not legalized the eating of pork. Prep. **halalish.i.a** St. **halalish.ik.a** Ps. **halalish.w.a** Rp. **halalish.an.a**

halambe (also *harambe*) *interj* 1. an expletive used for encouraging people to push a heavy object collectively. 2. forcefully, collectively: *Halambee, halambee*, forcefully, enthusiastically.

halani *adv* 1. immediately, instantly, at once, right away: *Aliitwa halani na meneja wake*, he was called immediately by his manager. (cf *mara moja, ajilani*) 2. there and then, in a moment. (cf *papo hapo*) (Ar)

halasa *n (n)* (*naut*) sailors' wages i.e. amount of money that is due to sailors after subtracting debts from shares. (Ar)

halbadiri (also *badiria*) *n (n)* (in Islam) a special recitation based on the battle of "Badr" in Islamic history, now commonly used to bring curse or spell on someone who has done sth harmful to another: *Soma halbadiri*, recite the curse of this kind. (Ar)

halelenji n (n) see *halilungi*
haleluya interj see *aleluya*
halfiya (also *alfiya*) n (n) an official turban that was worn by councillors.
hali[1] n (n) 1. condition, state, situation, stage; state of affairs: *Hali ya hewa*, weather condition. 2. (of health) state, condition: *Hali yake si nzuri*, her condition is not good. (cf *siha, afya, rai*) 3. (gram) aspect, tense: *Hali endelevu*, continuous aspect. 4. economic position or condition of sby/sth. (Ar)
hali[2] (also *ilhali*) conj whereas, while, seeing that: *Kwa nini alifanya vile hali anajua hairuhusiwi?* Why did he do that when he knows it is forbidden? *Aliondoka hali anatabasamu*, he left here smiling. (cf *ilhali*) (Ar)
halibari n (n) (naut) cyclone, windstorm, tornado, hurricane, storm: *Kulikuwa na halibari iliyozamisha jahazi*, there was a cyclone that sank the dhow. (cf *tufani, kimbunga, chamchela*) (Ar)
halib.u vt darken; become black/dark: *Jua limemhalibu*, the sun has darkened him. Prep. ***halib.i.a*** St. ***halib.ik.a*** Ps. of Prep. ***halib.iw.a*** (cf *sawidi*) (Ar)
halifa n (n) 1. (In Islam) caliph; a supreme religious ruler, a title commonly used to the four successors of Prophet Muhammad. 2. a leader of some traditional dances esp. those of *pungwa*, a kind of exorcising dance. 3. a leader of a religious sect. (Ar)
halif.u[1] vt, vi 1. transgress, flout, disobey, break the law: *Alihalifu sheria za nchi*, he transgressed the laws of the land. 2. defy, oppose, resist: *Aliihalifu amri yao*, he defied their order. Prep. ***halif.i.a*** St. ***halif.ik.a*** Cs. ***halif.ish.a*** Ps. of Prep. ***halif.iw.a*** Rp. of Prep. ***halif.i.an.a*** (cf *asi, pinga*) (Ar)
halif.u[2] vt,vi bequeath, will, dower; leave behind wealth, etc esp at death: *Alizihalifu mali nyingi kwa watoto wake*, she bequeathed a lot of wealth to her children. Prep. ***halif.i.a*** St. ***halif.ik.a*** Cs. ***halif.ish.a*** Ps. of Prep. ***halif.iw.a*** (cf *rithisha, achia*) (Ar)

halijoto n (n) temperature: *Halijoto kali*, high temperature. *Halijoto chini*, low temperature.
halili[1] n (n) a beloved person, a respectable person: *Wanamkumbuka sana kwa vile yeye ni halili*, they remember him very much because he is a beloved person. (cf *mpenzi*) (Ar)
halili[2] adj respectable, admirable: *Mtu halili*, a respectable person. (Ar)
halili[3] (also *tahalili*) n (n) (in Islam) a prayer for the dead by reciting the name of God for a fixed number of times. (Ar)
halili.a vt 1. used in the expression: *Halilia mbwewe*, recite God's names while counting small beads fixed in a rosary. 2. recite by saying that there is no deity but God.
halilungi (also *helelenji*) n (n) 1. pellet, a small pill. 2. medicine used to dilute laxative during production; antidiarrhoea.
halimtumwa (bot) a kind of sweet potato which is yellow inside; yellowish sweet potato.
halis.i[1] vt, vi 1. be worth, value, cost: *Kabati hili halihalisi shilingi elfu arobaini*, this cupboard is not worth forty thousand shillings. (cf *stahili, stahiki*) 2. be appropriate, be suitable, be fitting: *Haihalisi kwa yeye kufanya kitendo kiovu kama kile*, it is not befitting for him to do an evil deed of that kind. Prep. ***halis.i.a*** St. ***halis.ik.a*** Cs. ***halis.ish.a*** (cf *faa, pendeza*) (Ar)
halisi[2] adj real, actual, authentic: *Yeye ni ndugu yangu halisi*, he is my real (blood) brother. (cf *hasa, thabiti*) (Ar)
haliudi n (n) 1. (bot) agarwood, eaglewood, aloewood; a resinous fragrant and highly valuable heartwood produced by *Aquilaria malaccensis* and other species used as a medicine to treat nervous disorders and also used for spiritual purposes. 2. a good perfume

halizeti

oil used especially by some women in some cultures to scent clothes. (Ar)

halizeti n (n) see halzeti

halkumu n (n) (anat) jugular vein; any blood vessel that carries blood from some part of the body back towards the heart. (cf *vena*) (Ar)

halmaria n (n) see almaria

halmashauri n (n) board, council, committee: *Halmashauri ya shule*, school board. *Halmashauri ya wakurugenzi*, board of directors. *Halmashauri ya jiji*, city council. *Halmashauri ya manispaa*, municipal council. *Halmashauri kuu*, central committee. (cf *bodi*, *shura*, *kamati*) (Ar)

halo¹ interj hello; an expletive used in greeting, or to attract attention or to answer a telephone call, etc.: *Halo, unaweza kunisikia?* Hallo, can you hear me?

halo² n (n) nimbus; a dark grey rain-bearing cloud.

halua n (n) Turkish delight; sweatmeat made of flour, sugar, etc.: *Halua ya lozi*, Turkish delight containing almonds. (Ar)

halula n (n) 1. (*med*) struma, goitre; cellulitis of the neck; swelling of the neck due to the enlargement of the thyroid gland. (cf *mlezi*) 2. caries; a disease involving the decay of teeth. (cf *mange*) (Ar)

haluli n (n) laxative, purgative; any medicine that causes the bowels to empty: *Haluli ya chumvi*, sulphate of magnesia; Epsom salts. (cf *msahala*) (Ar)

halumbe interj an expletive used for emphasis during the pulling of a heavy object, thus *Halambe, halumbe*.

halwaridi (also *lawaridi*) n (n) 1. (*bot*) oto rose; the flower of usu red, pink, white or yellow colour with a sweet scent and having strong prickly stems. 2. perfume made from this flower; attar. (Ar)

hamanik.a

halzeti (also *halizeti*) n (n) olive oil. Also called *Mafuta ya halzeti*.

ham.a¹ vt, vi 1. change habitation; move away: *Alihama kutoka nyumba hii mwezi uliopita*, he moved from this house last month. 2. emigrate, migrate, expatriate oneself, move away: *Ameuhama watani wake*, he has emigrated from his country. Prep. *ham.i.a* St. *ham.ik.a* Cs. *ham.ish.a* Ps. *ham.w.a* Rp. *ham.an.a* Rp. of Prep. *ham.i.an.a* (cf *hajiri*, *gura*)

hama² n (n) hammer; a part of a gunlock that strikes the primer or percussion cap when the trigger is pulled.

hamadi interj 1. an expletive used to console someone when for example, he stumbles. (*prov*) *Hamadi kibindoni silulu mkononi*, a bird in the hand is worth two in the bush. i.e. something is better than nothing. 2. an expletive used by someone who happens to pick up sth usu valuable. 3. an expression used in introducing a new but related topic; incidentally: *Alinifuata nyumbani kwangu, hamadi mimi nikawa sipo*, he followed me to my house and incidentally, I was not there.

hamak.i¹ vi be angry, be enraged: *Alihamaki alipokemewa*, he became annoyed when he was scolded. Prep. *hamak.i.a* St. *hamak.ik.a* Cs. *hamak.ish.a* Ps. of Prep. *hamak.iw.a* Rp. of Prep. *hamak.i.an.a* (cf *ghasi*, *udhi*) (Ar)

hamaki² n (n) temper, anger, vexation (cf *hasira*, *ghadhabu*) (Ar)

hamali n (n) 1. porter. (cf *mpagazi*, *mchukuzi*, *kuli*) 2. freight, load: *Gari la hamali*, a push-cart. (Ar)

hamamu¹ n (n) (*zool*) pigeon (cf *njiwa*) (Ar)

hamamu² n (*ma-*) bathtub. (cf *bafu*)

hamanik.a vi 1. be worried, be uneasy, *Alihamanika alipogundua kwamba binti yake hajarejea nyumbani*, she became worried when she discovered

209

that her daughter had not returned home. (cf *haha, hangaika*) 2. be busy, be occupied, be uneasy: *Alihamanika kutokana na kazi nyingi za nyumbani*, she was occupied by too much housework. 3. be excited because of seeing a beautiful girl; be infatuated after seeing a beautiful girl: *Alihamanika kwa uzuri wake*, he was infatuated by her beauty. Prep. **hamanik.i.a** St. **hamanik.ik.a** Cs. **hamanik.ish.a,** disturb, perturb

hamanish.a *vt* disturb, perplex, confuse: *Alinihamanisha nilipokuwa ninaandika barua*, he disturbed me when I was writing a letter. Prep. **hamanish.i.a** St. **hamanish.ik.a** Ps. **hamanish.w.a** Rp. **hamanish.an.a** (cf *sumbua, kera*)

hamasa *n (n)* motivation, willpower, firmness: *Alinitia hamasa nisome*, he filled me with motivation to learn. (cf *ghera, jazba, ari*) (Ar)

hamasish.a *vt, vi* motivate, encourage, inspire: *Mwanasiasa aliwahamasisha wanavijiji kushiriki kikamilifu katika miradi ya maendeleo*, the politician encouraged the villagers to participate fully in the development projects. Prep. **hamasish.i.a** St. **hamasish.ik.a** Ps. **hamasish.w.a** Rp. **hamasish.an.a** (cf *shajiisha, raghibu*) (Ar)

hambarar.a *vi, vt* prattle, twaddle, tattle; talk nonsense: *Akizungumza, hupenda kuhambarara*, when she talks, she likes to prattle. Prep. **hambarar.i.a** St. **hambarar.ik.a** (cf *ropoka*)

hambe *n (n)* imbecile, simpleton, dullard, nincompoop, idiot, fool, silly: *Yeye ni hambe*, he is a fool. (cf *bozi, zuzu, mpumbavu*)

hamdi[1] (also *hamdu*) *n (n)* praise, laudation, (cf *sifa*) (Ar)

hamd.i[2] (also *himidi*) *vt, vi* praise, extol. Prep. **hamd.i.a** St. **hamd.ik.a** Cs. **hamd.ish.a** Ps. of Prep. **hamd.iw.a** Rp. of Prep **hamd.i.an.a** (cf *sifu*) (Ar)

hamdia *n (n)* the style of wearing *kanzu*, a long-sleeved calico robe, and trousers together with a coat and an embroidered skull-cap or tarboosh (Ar)

hamdu see *hamdi*[1]

hame *n (ma-)* a deserted place; a deserted village or town. (cf *gofu,ganjo*)

ham.i *vt* 1. protect, defend. 2. protect a plantation or garden usu by making noises to frighten destructive birds and animals; scare: *Nililihami shamba langu dhidi ya ndege waharibifu*, I protected my farm by scaring off destructive birds. 3. advocate, defend, support, assist: *Wakili wangu alinihami mahakamani wakati wa mahojiano na mwendesha mashtaka*, my lawyer defended me at the court during cross-examination with the prosecutor. (cf *tetea*) Prep. **ham.i.a** St. **ham.ik.a** Cs. **ham.ish.** a Ps. of Prep. **ham.iw.a** Rp. of Prep. **ham.i.an.a** (cf *tetea, saidia*) (Ar)

hami.a[1] *vt* see *hama*

hami.a[2] *vt* immigrate, move to, settle: *Sasa amehamia katika nyumba mpya*, now, he has moved to a new house. St. **hami.k.a** Cs. **hami.sh.a** Ps. **hami.w.a**

hami.a[3] *vt* attack, assault, raid: *Majambazi walilihamia duka lake*, the thugs raided his shop. Prep. **hami.li.a** St. **hami.k.a** Ps. **hami.w.a** Rp. **hami.an.a** (cf *hujumu, vamia*) (Ar)

hamil.i *vi* conceive; become pregnant with (a child) Prep. **hamil.i.a** St. **hamil.ik.a** Cs. **hamil.ish.a**

hamio *n (ma-)* new settlement, new residence: *Hamio lake limeleta uhasama mkubwa kwa majirani*, his new residence has brought a lot of animosity with the neighbours. (Ar)

hamira *n (n)* yeast, ferment: *Alitia hamira kwenye unga alipokuwa anatengeneza maandazi*, he added yeast to the dough while preparing doughnuts. *Hamira ya unga*, baking powder.

Hamira ya mpika pombe, brewer's yeast. (cf *chachu, kiumisho*) (Ar)

hamish.a¹ *vt* see *hama*

hamish.a² *vt* 1. confine a virgin girl indoors: *Walimhamisha binti yao alipovunja ungo*, they confined their daughter indoors when she reached the age of puberty. (cf *alika, alisa*) 2. confine a sick person indoors for medical treatment: *Tulimhamisha mgonjwa wetu baada ya kupata kipindupindu*, we confined our patient after contacting cholera. Prep. **hamish.i.a** St. **hamish.ik.a** Ps. **hamish.w.a** Rp. **hamish.an.a** (cf *alika, alisa*)

hamish.a³ *vt* shift from; move sby/sth. *Aliwahamisha wapangaji wake*, he shifted his tenants to another place. Prep. **hamish.i.a** St. **hamish.ik.a** Ps. **hamish.w.a** Rp. **hamish.an.a**

hamishik.a *vi* be movable. Prep. **hamishik.i.a** St. **hamishik.ik.a**

hamna¹ *verb form* there isn't, there is not, there are not, there is nothing: *Hamna mchele madukani leo*, there is no rice at the shops today.

hamna² *n (n)* idiot, imdecile. (cf *mpumbavu*)

hamna³ *adv (syn) Tolewa hamna*, lose all the pieces in a game of draughts.

hamnazo¹ *n (n)* used in the expressions: *Jitia hamnazo*, or *Jifanya hamnazo*, pretend not to notice.

hamnazo² *n (n)* a lunatic person, a crazy person: *Usimchokoze kwa vile yeye ni hamnazo*, don't tease him because he is crazy. (cf *chizi, afkani*)

hamrawi (also *amrawi*) *n (n)* (*naut*) a line slung from one end of the yard to be operated together with the *baraji* and serving to adjust the position of the yard with relation to the main direction of the ship. (Ar)

hamsa *adj, n (n)* five: *Hamsa elfu*, five thousand. (cf *tano*) (Ar)

hamsini¹ *adj, n (n)* fifty: *Hamsini na mbili*, fifty two. (Ar)

hamsini² *n (n)* used in the expression: *Alipita na hamsini zake*, he passed here minding his own business.

hamu (also *hamumu*) *n (n)* 1. anxiety, desire, craving, ardour: *Ana hamu ya kutaka kuoa*, he is anxious to get married. *Hana hamu ya kula*, he is not keen to eat. (cf *shauku, uchu, kiu*) 2. (*idm*) *Hamu na ghamu*, be very eager, be very anxious e.g. *Ana hamu na ghamu juu ya jambo lile*, he is very anxious about that matter. (Ar)

hamuma *n (n)* (*colloq*) imbecile, idiot, fool. (cf *mpumbavu*)

hamumi *n (n)* a kind of tobacco for smoking, used with a hookah pipe. (Ar)

hamumu *n (n)* see *hamu*

hamustashara *n (n)* fifteen (Ar)

hanali *n (n)* north (cf *kaskazi*)

hanamu¹ *adv* obliquely, askant, slantwise: *Kata hanamu*, cut obliquely. *Mstari wa hanamu*, an oblique line. (cf *mshazari*) (Ar)

hanamu² *n (n)* 1. (*naut*) oblique cutwater in *dau*, a special kind of canoe. *Hanamu ya chombo*, the cutwater of a vessel. *Hanamu ya ubao*, the sloping edge, bevel, etc. of a board. 2. hypotenuse; the longest side of a right-angled triangle. (Ar)

hanchifu *n (n)* handkerchief (cf *hanjiku, leso*) (Eng)

handaki *n (ma-)* 1. trench, channel. (cf *kuo*) 2. ditch, furrow. (cf *mtaro*) 3. hole, pit. (cf *shimo*)

handeki *interj* an expletive signalling the feeling of success. (cf *hobe*)

hando¹ *n (ma-)* copper or silver vessel similar to earthenware waterjar having a narrow circular opening at the top usu used by Indians for carrying and storing water.

hando² *n (ma-)* a kind of broad doughnut which looks like *chapati* but is hard.

hando³ *n (ma-)* a woman's dress resembling a skirt, worn by certain tribes in Kenya.

hangahanga¹ *adv* shoulder high, high up: *Walimchukua mshindi hangahanga*, they carried the victor shoulder high. (cf *kitikiti, danadana*)

hangahang.a² *vt* carry shoulder high, carry high up: *Vijana wawili walimhangahanga askari majeruhi*, the two young men carried the wounded soldier shoulder high. Prep. *hangahang.i.a* St. *hangahang.ik.a* Cs. *hangahang.ish.a*

hangaik.a *vi* 1. be uneasy, be perplexed, be confused, be worried, be busy: *Alihangaika sana kumtafuta mgeni wake*, he was very busy looking for his guest. Prep. *hangaik.i.a* Ps. of Prep. *hangaik.iw.a* Rp. of Prep. *hangaik.i.an.a* (cf *taabika, shughulika, mahanika*)

hangaiko *n* (*ma-*) anxiety, disquiet, uneasiness, worry, trouble: *Yeye yumo katika hangaiko kubwa juu ya kupotelewa na mwanawe*, he is in great anxiety about the loss of his child. (cf *shughuliko, mahana*)

hangaish.a¹ *vt* see *hangaika*

hangaish.a² *vt* trouble, bother, disturb: *Kwa nini unanihangaisha sana?* Why are you bothering me a lot? Prep. *hangaish.i.a* St. *hangaish.ik.a* Ps. *hangaish.w.a* Rp. *hangaish.an.a* (cf *taabisha*)

hangale *n* (*n*) (*bot*) a banana which has been baked. (cf *mkologwe*)

hangamaji *n* (*n*) (*naut*) a sailor's shanty sung during the night.

hangue *n* (*n*) see *hangwe*

hangungu *n* (*ma-*) 1. a short calico robe. 2. a worthless garment. (cf *gwanda*)

hangwe (also *hangue*) *n* (*n*) a hooked stick, etc. for pulling down fruit from a tree or flowers. (cf *kyovyo, kingoe, upembo*)

han.i *vt* condole with, grieve, lament, bleed for, weep for; pay a visit of condolence (to): *Alikwenda kwa wafiwa kuwahani*, he went to the bereaved to offer his condolences. Prep. *han.i.a* St. *han.ik.a* Cs. *han.ish.a* Ps. of Prep. *han.iw.a*, be condoled, be offered condolences e.g. *Wafiwa walihaniwa na watu wengi*, the bereaved were offered condolences by many people. Rp. of Prep. *han.i.an.a* (cf *taazia*) (Ar)

hanikiz.a (also *hinikiza*) *vt, vi* 1. outtalk, shout-down; interrupt someone speaking: *Kelele za yule msemaji zilihanikiza ukumbi wote*, the speaker's high-pitched voice filled the entire hall. (cf *dakiza, binikiza*) 2. diffuse smoke of incense, etc.: *Alipokuwa anajifukiza, alihanikiza chumba chote kwa ubani*, when she was applying incense to herself, she filled the whole room with the scent of aloewood. Prep. *hanikiz.i.a* St. *hanikiz.ik.a* Cs. *hanikiz.ish.a* Ps. *hanikiz.w.a* Rp *hanikiz.an.a*

hanithi¹ *n* (*ma-*) 1. an impotent person; a person unable to perform a sexual act. 2. gay, homosexual, sodomite. (cf *msenge, shoga*) 3. fool, idiot, imbecile. (cf *mpumbavu*) (Ar)

hanithi² *n* (*ma-*) a woman who does not get sexual pleasure during intercourse; a frigid woman. (Ar)

hanithi³ (also *kihanisi*) *n* (*n*) (*zool*) giant herring, ten pounder; a kind of salt water fish (family *Elopidae*) with an elongate body and oval in cross section. *Elops machanata*.

hanja¹ *n* (*n*) a brownish chewing gum.

hanj.a² *vi, vt* 1. roam, range, meander, wander: *Kijana yule anapenda kuhanja mitaani*, that young man likes to roam in the neighbourhood. (cf *zurura, randa*) 2. swagger, strut, swash, prance, carouse; walk in a proud or boastful manner: *Binti mzuri alikuwa akihanja njiani*, the beautiful girl was strutting up and down the street. Prep. *hanj.i.a* St. *hanj.ik.a* Cs. *hanj.ish.a* Ps. *hanj.w.a* (cf *tamba, belenga*) (Ar)

hanjamu¹ *n* (*n*) lust, sexual desire: *Hanjamu zake juu ya msichana zilimtia wazimu*, his lust for the girl drove him mad.

hanjamu² *n* (*n*) boasting speech, hot air, bravado: *Mimi siziogopi hata kidogo hanjamu zako*, I am not at all scared of your bravado. (cf *makeke, ndaro, machachari*) (Ar)

hanjari *n* (*n*) scimitar; a short curved sword with an edge on the convex side and usu used by Arabs, Turks, etc. (cf *sime, jambia*) (Ar)

hansa (also *direki*) *n* (*n*) (*naut*) two thick ropes in the main yard of a dhow. (cf *henza*)

hansadi *n* (*n*) Hansard; record of debates in British, Canadian and Australia parliaments. (Eng)

hanuni *n* (*n*) (*bot*) the flowers of a henna plant, *Lawsonia inermis*. (Ar)

hanzua *n* (*n*) 1. a kind of sword dance. 2. a kind of small drum with its skin stretched on both sides; a two-headed drum. (cf *tari, shela*) (Ar)

hao *adj pron* demonstrative marker for *m-wa* pl nouns.

hapa *adv, pron* here, this place.

hapana *neg verb form* 1. an expletive used as a negative in rejoinder; no. 2. there is nothing, there is none; no: 3. an expletive used to forbid someone doing sth; no, don't: *Hapana ruhusa kupita hapa*, it is forbidden to pass here.

hapo *adv* 1. used with reference to a place; there, at that place, away from the speaker: *Alikaa kimya hapo*, he sat there quietly. 2. Used with reference to time in expressions such as: *Hapo kale*, once upon a time, in the olden days. *Tangu hapo*, from long ago, over so long. *Hapo hapo*, immediately, at once. *Hapo zamani*, in the past, long time ago. *Hapo awali*, in the beginning. *Hapo atakapofika*, once she arrives. 3. used with reference to circumstances in conditional constructions such as: *Akikataa, hapo mlaumu*, if he refuses, then you can blame him.

har.a¹ (also *harisha*) *vi* 1. have diarrhoea; have looseness of the bowels: *Alihara damu*, he had dysentery i.e. he passed blood with the stool. *Hiyo ni dawa ya kuhara*, that is a laxative. Prep. **har.i.a** St. **har.ik.a** Cs. **har.ish.a** e.g. *Dawa hiyo inaharisha*, that drug causes diarrhoea. Rp. **har.i.an.a** 2. (*idm*) fear, be afraid: *Anamhara mkewe sana*, he is very afraid of his wife. (cf *endesha*)

hara² *n* (*n*) district of a town; suburbs. The word is seldom used except with a locative e.g. *Anaishi harani*, he lives in the district. (cf *kitongoji, mtaa*)

har.a³ *vt* acknowledge, admit the superiority of sby in sth: *Ninamhara Ahmed kwa kuongea lugha fasaha*. I admit that Ahmed is good in speaking the language eloquently. Prep. **har.i.a** St. **har.ik.a** Cs. **har.ish.a** Ps. of Prep. **har.iw.a** Rp. of Prep. **har.i.an.a**

harabu¹ *n* (*n*) vandal, ruffian, thug, mugger: *Tunamwogopa kwa vile yeye ni harabu*, we fear him because he is a vandal. 2. a naughty person, a prankish person, an impish person: *Yeye ni mtoto harabu*, he plays childish pranks; he is a naughty child. (Ar)

harabu² *adj* 1. destructive, vicious, injurious: *Mtu harabu*, a destructive person. 2. impish, prankish, naughty: *Mtoto harabu*, a naughty child; scamp. (*prov*) *Nazi mbovu harabu nzima*, a bad coconut spoils others i.e one bad person may affect negatively others. (Ar)

haradali *n* (*n*) (*bot*) mustard; a kind of yellow seed prepared as a paste and used as a pungent seasoning for foods or as a counter-irritant in medicine.

harage *n* (*ma-*) see *haragwe*

haragwe (also *harage*) *n* (*ma-*) (*bot*) a kind of bean from a climbing plant; haricot bean, French bean, kidney bean.

haraja *n* (*n*) see *harija*

haraka¹ *n* (*n*) haste, speed, swiftness: *Fanya haraka* (*sing*) make haste,

H

hurry up. *Fanyeni haraka* (pl), hurry up. (*prov*) *Haraka haraka haina baraka*, hurry hurry has no blessing. i.e. too much hurry on sth can bring bad results. (Ar)

haraka² *adv* hurriedly, hastily, quickly, speedily: *Aliondoka hapa haraka*, he left here hurriedly. (cf *upesi*, *chapuchapu*) (Ar)

harakati *n* (*n*) 1. struggle, fight, challenge: *Harakati za ukombozi*, liberation struggle. 2. activity, commotion, rush, scramble, bustle: *Kuna harakati nyingi hapo gatini kwa sababu abiria wengi sana wanasafiri*, there is hustle and bustle at the port because many passengers are travelling. (cf *kazi*, *shughuli*) (Ar)

harakish.a *vt, vi* expedite, accelerate, hasten, push, urge: *Aliniharakisha kuimaliza kazi yake*, he hastened me to complete his work. Prep. ***harakish.i.a*** St. ***harakish.ik.a*** Ps. ***harakish.w.a*** Rp. ***harakish.an.a*** (cf *himiza*, *sahilisha*) (Ar)

haram¹ *n* (*n*) pyramid (cf *piramidi*) (Ar)

haram² *n* (*n*) the sacred area in Mecca surrounding the Al-Kaaba. (Ar)

harambee *n* (*n*) see *halambee*

haramia *n* (*ma-*) 1. pirate, sea-robber, sea-rover, sea dog, freebooter. (cf *mnyang'anyi*) 2. brigand, outlaw, thug, bandit, gangster. (cf *jambazi*, *jangili*) (Ar)

haramish.a (also *harimisha*) *vt* illegalize; make illegal or unlawful: *Dini ya Kiislamu imeharamisha ulaji wa nyama ya nguruwe*, the Islamic religion has illegalized the eating of pork. Prep. ***haramish.i.a*** St. ***haramish.ik.a*** Ps. ***haramish.w.a*** Rp. ***haramish.an.a*** (cf *kataza*)

haramu *adj* 1. illicit, illegitimate, forbidden, unlawful, illegal, unauthorized. (*prov*) *Funika kawa mwana haramu apite*, don't disclose anything in the presence of illegitimate children who are considered to be troublesome. 2. profane, blasphemous, unlawful, desecrative.

harara *n* (*n*) 1. heat, hotness, warmth, prickly heat. (cf *joto*, *hari*, *fukuto*) 2. anger, enmity, ill temper: *Usimchokoze kwa vile yeye ni mtu wa harara*, don't tease him because he is a person of temper. 3. (*med*) heat rash, miliaria; an acute skin disease resulting from inflammation of the sweat glands, as from exposure to heat, and characterized by small white or red eruptions: *Mwili wake umefanya harara*, his body has heat rash. 4. excoriation; an abrasive or tearing injury to the surface of the body; scratch mark. (cf *michubuko*) (Ar)

harashi *adj* used in the expression: *Mwanaharashi*, a mannerless child; a cursed child. (Ar)

hari *n* (*n*) heat, hotness, warmth. (cf *joto*, *fukuto*) (Ar)

hari.a *vt* (*naut*) see *heria*

-haribifu *adj* 1. destructive, ruinous, corrupted, malicious, harmful: *Mtu mharibifu*, a malicious person. (cf *harabu*) 2. prodigal, wasteful, spendthrift. (cf *mbadhirifu*) (Ar)

haribik.a *vi* be spoiled, be damaged: *Maziwa yameharibika*, the milk is spoiled Prep. ***haribik.i.a*** St. ***haribik.ik.a*** Cs. ***haribik.ish.a***

harib.u *vt, vi* 1. destroy, damage, demolish, spoil: *Aliiharibu gari yangu*, he damaged my car. (cf *bananga*, *vuruga*) 2. cause miscarriage, have a miscarriage; miscarry: *Mwanamke aliharibu mimba*, the woman had a miscarriage. Prep. ***harib.i.a*** St. ***harib.ik.a*** Cs. ***harib.ish.a*** Ps. of Prep. ***harib.iw.a*** Rp. of Prep. ***harib.i.an.a*** (Ar)

harija¹ *n* (*n*) expenditure, expense, outlay of money: *Harija yake ya nyumbani imeongezeka siku hizi*, his home expenses have increased these days. (cf *matumizi*) (Ar)

harija² *n* (*n*) endless unfounded arguments: *Kijana yule ana harija sana,* that young person is very unnecessarily argumentative. (Ar)
harij.i *vt, vi* expend, disburse, spend: *Alihariji pesa nyingi alipolazwa hospitalini,* he spent a lot of money when he was hospitalized. Prep. ***harij.i.a*** St. ***harij.ik.a*** Cs. ***harij.ish.a*** Ps. of Prep ***harij.iw.a*** Rp of Prep ***harij.i.an.a*** (cf *gharimu, tumia*) (Ar)
harima *n* (*ma-*) see *harimu²*
harimish.a *vt, vi* see *haramisha* (Ar)
harimoni *n* (*n*) (*mus*) harmonica; a small rectangular wind instrument. (cf *kodiani*)

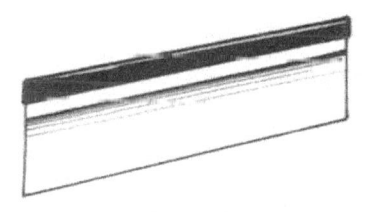

harimoni

harimu¹ *n* (*ma-*) see *maharimu*
harimu² (also *harima*) *n* (*ma-*) 1. woman. 2. wife. (cf *mke*) (Ar)
hario *interj* hurray, hooray, repeated; an exclamation of joy or approval. (cf *huree*)
harioe *interj* (*naut*) an exclamation of chant when a ship is seen to be approaching a harbour; hip hip hurray!
hariri¹ *n* (*n*) silk: *Nguo ya hariri,* silk dress (Ar)
hariri² *adj* used in the expression: *Mtu hariri,* a polite person, a gentle person. (Ar)
harir.i³ *vt* edit, revise: *Aliuhariri mswada wangu,* he edited my manuscript. Prep. ***harir.i.a*** St. ***harir.ik.a*** Cs. ***harir.ish.a*** Ps. of Prep. ***harir.iw.a*** Rp of Prep. ***harir.i.an.u***
harish.a¹ *vi* see *hara¹*

harish.a² *vt* purge; cause a person to empty the bowels. Prep. ***harish.i.a*** St. ***harish.ik.a*** (cf *endesha*)
harisho *n* (*n*) excessive frequency and looseness of bowel movement; diarrhoea
harita *n* (*n*) (*bot*) the round black hard seeds of a soap berry tree, the husks of which are used for washing clothes, esp woollens and silks; soapberry.
haro *n* (*n*) a farming machine for breaking up and levelling plowed ground, covering seeds, etc.; harrow. (cf *kaltiveta*) (Eng)

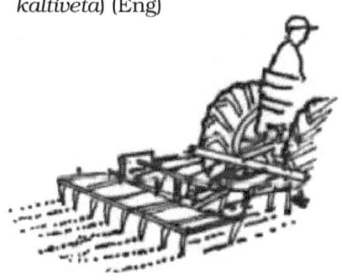

haro

harubu *n* (*n*) 1. war, fight, conflict. (cf *vita, kondo, kigambo, kitali*) 2. hardship, distress, affliction, difficulty: *Kazi za harubu,* arduous work, difficult work. (cf *shida, taabu*) (Ar)
harufu *n* (*n*) scent, odour, smell, effluvium. (cf *riha, rihi*) (Ar)
harusi (also *arusi*) *n* (*n*) 1. wedding, marriage, nuptials. 2. (*idm*) *Harusi imejibu,* the girl has proved to be a virgin at consummation. 3. wedding ceremony. 4. happiness. (*prov*) *Kukopa harusi, kulipa matanga,* borrowing is easy but repaying is difficult. (Ar)
has.a¹ *vt* perform rituals to appease the dead; make offering to propitiate the spirits of the dead: *Hasa koma,* perform rituals of this kind. Prep. ***has.i.a*** St. ***has.ik.a*** Cs. ***has.ish.a*** Ps. ***has.w.a*** (cf *tambika*)

hasa² *adv* especially, particularly, exactly.
hasada¹ *n* (*n*) powdered millet gruel; sorghum porridge. (cf *sima*)
hasada² *n* (*n*) see *husuda*
hasaisi *n* (*n*) 1. bad things/ affairs; evil, wickedness. (cf *maovu*) 2. bad situation.
hasama *n* (*n*) see *uhasama*
hasanati good deeds. (Ar)
hasara 1. loss in business: *Amepata hasara katika biashara yake mpya*, he has experienced losses in his new business. (cf *nakisi*) 2. ruin, damage, loss. (cf *maafa*) 3. destruction, damage: *Gari yake mpya ilipata hasara baada ya kugongwa na basi*, his new car was damaged after being hit by a bus. 4. (*naut*) loss at sea; sea wreckage. (*prov*) *Hasara humfika mwenye mabezo*, he who ignores sth pays a heavy price later on.
hasha *interj* 1. used as a very emphatic negative to mean *No Way!, Certainly not, By no means*, (cf *hapana*) 2. co-occurs with other words to strengthen the concept of negation: *La hasha*, by no means at all. *Hasha lilah*, by God, I didn't do it (Ar)
hashakum (also *ashakum*) *interj* a word used to ask pardon before a speaker intends to mention sth that may seem disgusting, offensive, etc to someone else; pardon me for what I am going to say. (cf *samahani, kumradhi*) (Ar)
hasharati *n* (*n*) see *asherati*
hashir.i¹ *vt* assemble people in a particular place. Prep. **hashir.i.a** St. **hashir.ik.a** Ps. of Prep **hashir.iw.a** Rp of Prep. **hashir.i.an.a** (cf *kusanya*) (Ar)
hashiri² *n* (*n*) a gathering of people esp during the day of resurrection.
hashir.i³ *vt* rape, fuck; have sex with a male or female: *Alifungwa miaka saba kwa kumhashiri msichana*, he was sentenced to seven years for raping a girl. Prep. **hashir.i.a** St. **hashir.ik.a** Ps. of Prep. **hashir.iw.a** (cf *jamii, lawiti*) (Ar)
hashishi *n* (*n*) hashish; a narcotic drug formed from the hemp plant and used for smoking or chewing. (cf *kasumba, afyuni*) (Ar)
hasho *n* (*ma-*) 1. (*naut*) a piece of wood or iron used as a patch in a sailing vessel. 2. a piece of wood or cloth used as a patch or caulker: *Tia hasho*, caulk.
hashuo¹ *n* (*ma-*) sby's favourite place; residence, dwelling place, home. (cf *maskani, makao*)
hashuo² *n* (*ma-*) ostentation; showy display of wealth, knowledge, etc.
has.i¹ *vt* castrate, emasculate, asexualise; remove the testicles of a male or an animal. Prep. **has.i.a** St. **has.ik.a** Cs. **has.ish.a** Ps. or Prep. **has.iw.a** Rp of Prep. **has.i.an.a** (cf *hanithisha*) (Ar)
hasi² *adj* negative: *Athari hasi*, negative effect. *Mtazamo hasi*, negative attitude. (Ar)
hasibu *vi* see *hesabu¹*
hasidi¹ *n* (*ma-*) 1. an envious person, a jealous person. (cf *mwivu*) 2. a destructive person, a malicious person. (cf *fisadi*) (Ar)
hasid.i² *vt, vi* see *husudu*
hasik.a *vi* be annoyed, be vexed, be irked, be irritated. Prep. **hasik.i.a** St. **hasik.ik.a** Cs. **hasik.ish.a** (cf *ghadhibika*) (Ar)
hasimu¹ *n* (*ma-*) 1. enemy, adversary, antagonist: *Hasimu wa kisiasa*, political enemy. (cf *adui*) 2. a quarrelsome person, a wranglesome person; wrangler (cf *mtesi*) (Ar)
hasim.u² (also *husumu*) *vt* 1. quarrel, squabble, dispute: *Jirani yangu amenihasimu bure*, my neighbour has quarrelled with me for no reason. 2. split, part, break friendship: *Nimemhasimu mke wangu baada ya kugombana naye*, I have parted from my wife after quarrelling with her. Prep. **hasim.i.a** St. **hasim.ik.a** Cs.

hasim.ish.a Ps. of Prep. **hasim.iw.a** Rp. of Prep. **hasim.i.an.a** (Ar)

hasira *n* (*n*) wrath, rage, anger, bad temper. (*prov*) *Hasira hasara*, anger brings damage. (cf *mafutu, kiruu, ghadhabu*) (Ar)

hasir.i *vt* harm, hurt, spoil, damage. Prep. **hasir.i.a** St. **hasir.ik.a** Cs. **hasir.ish.a** Ps. of Prep **hasir.iw.a**, Rp of Prep **hasir.i.an.a** (cf *haribu, umiza*) (Ar)

hasirik.a *vi* be hurt, be harmed, be hard hit. Prep. **hasirik.i.a** St. **hasirik.ik.a** Cs. **hasirik.ish.a**

hasua *n* (*n*) testicles (cf *korodani, kende*) (Ar)

hasusa *n* (*n*)(*anat*) see *asusa*

hata¹ *conj* 1. until, up to: *Anasubiri hata lini?* Until when is he going to wait? 2. even: *Kaa na mimi hata siku moja*, stay with me even for a day. 3. even if, although: *Hata akija na mzee wake usikubali*, even if he comes with his parent, don't agree. (cf *ingawa, ijapokuwa*) 4. co-occurs with other words in the negative context. (Ar)

hata² *interj* an expletive used to show that this is not the case; not at all! not so! *Unamjua mtu yule?* Do you know that person? *Hata!* Not at all! (Ar)

hata³ *adv* as far as, completely, totally: *Mzee yule hana subira hata kidogo*, that old man is not patient at all. (cf *kabisa*) (Ar)

hatabu *n* (*n*) fuel (cf *fueli*) (Ar)

hatamu *n* (*n*) 1. bridle; a head harness for guiding a horse, made up of a headstall, bit and reins. 2. (*idm*) *Shika hatamu*, lead; assume leadership. (Ar)

hatamu

hatari *n* (*n*) danger, peril, hazard, jeopardy: *Mtu wa hatari*, a dangerous person. (cf *janga, ponza*) (Ar)

hatarish.a (also *hatirisha*) *vt* endanger, risk, jeopardize, venture, imperil: *Alihatarisha maisha yake kwa kumwokoa mtoto yule*, he risked his life for saving that child. Prep. **hatarish.i.a** St. **hatarish.ik.a** Ps. **hatarish.w.a** Rp **hatarish.an.a** (cf *ponza, hizi*) (Ar)

hatarishi *adj* dangerous, hazardous: *Mazingira hatarishi*, dangerous environment.

hataza *n* (*n*) legal document forbiding the work of sby not to be copied by someone else. (Ar)

hati *n* (*n*) 1. document, certificate, form: *Hati ya kusafiria*, travelling document. *Hati ya maombi*, application form. *Hati ya nyumba*, title deed. *Hati ya mzigo*, bill of lading. *Hati ya madai*, demand note. *Hati ya bima*, insurance policy. *Hati bandia*, fake document. *Hati ya mashtaka*, plaint. *Hati ya kiapo*, affidavit. *Hati ya hisa*, share certificate. *Hati ya upekuzi*, search warrant. 2. instrument, memorandum, treaty: *Hati ya makubaliano*, memorandum of understanding. *Hati ya utambulisho*, credentials; letter of credence. *Hati ya kurithi; mkataba*, instrument of accession, instrument of ratification. *Hati ya mamlaka kamili*, instrument of full power. *Hati ya urafiki*, treaty of friendship. 3. script: *Hati za Kiarabu*, Arabic scripts. *Hati ya mkono*, handwriting e.g. *Ana hati nzuri*, he has good handwriting. (cf *mwandiko*) (Ar)

hatia *n* (*n*) guilt, fault: *Mshtakiwa alipatikana na hatia ya jinai*, the accused was found guilty of a criminal offence. *Alitiwa hatiani*, he was found guilty. (Ar)

hatibu *n* (*ma-*) 1. preacher, speaker: *Hatibu alizungumza kwa ufasaha mkubwa*, the speaker talked with great eloquence. 2. (*arch*) adviser. (Ar)

H

hatihati *n* (*n*) 1. anxiety, trouble, uneasiness, worry: *Aliingia na hatihati aliposikia kwamba mwanawe amewekwa rumande*, she was in a state of uneasiness when she heard that her son had been detained. (cf *wasiwasi,wahaka*) 2. suspicion, doubt, mistrust. (cf *tuhuma*) (Ar)

hatima *n* (*n*) the end of sth; conclusion, fate: *Hatima yake itajulikana leo*, his fate will be known today. (cf *mwisho, tamati*) (Ar)

hatimaye *adv* finally, lastly, at last, in the end (cf *mwishoni, mwishowe*) (Ar)

hatimiliki *n* (*n*) title deed: document or certificate of ownership.

hatimkato *n* (*n*) shorthand

hatinafsi *n* (*n*) 1. favouritism, nepotism: *Mkurugenzi huwapandisha vyeo wafanyikazi wake kwa hatinafsi*, the director promotes his workers by favouritism. (cf *upendeleo*) 2. egoism, selfishness, self-consideration: *Yeye ana hatinafsi kwani hajali maslahi ya watu wengine*, he is selfish because he does not care about the welfare of other people. (Ar)

hatirish.a *vt* see *hatarisha*

hatua *n* (*n*) 1. pace in walking; step, stride: *Alisogea hatua tatu mbele*, he moved three steps forward. 2. (*fig*) progress, development, stage: *Hatua ya mpito*, transitional stage. *Piga hatua*, make progress. (cf *maendeleo*) 3. opportunity, chance, time: *Atakuja tu apatapo hatua*, she will definitely come if she gets time. *Vuta hatua*, speed up. (*prov*) *Safari ni hatua*, for someone to do sth, it needs time. 4. step, action: *Hatua kali*, drastic steps. (Ar)

hau *n* (*ma-*) 1. maternal uncle, mother's uncle. 2. father in-law. (cf *baba mkwe*)

hauli *n* (*n*) (in Islam) an assembly of people who commemorate the death of someone after one year has elapsed; memorial. (Ar)

hawa *adj, pron* pl of *huyu*, these.
hawaa[1] *n* (*ma-*) see *hawara*
hawaa[2] *n* (*n*) zeal, ardour, fervour: *Hawaa ya nafsi*, personal excitement. (cf *matamanio, ashiki, nyege*) (Ar)
hawaa[3] desire (*ashiki etc*)

hawafu *n* (*n*) 1. coward, craven; a person who runs away from danger, etc: *Hawafu aliogopa kumkaribia mgonjwa aliyekuwa anakufa*, the coward feared to approach a sick person who was dying. 2. cowardice, timidity, cravenness, scare: *Ana hawafu sana juu ya matokeo ya kesi inayomkabili ndugu yake*, he is very scared of the results of the case which his brother faces. (cf *hofu, woga*) (Ar)

hawaiji *n* (*n*) too many desires; a lot of desires. (Ar)

hawaji *n* (*n*) (*bot*) curry powder; "turmeric". (cf *bizari*) (Ar)

hawala *n* (*n*) cheque, draft: *Hawala ya fedha*, money order. *Hawala ya posta*, postal order. *Hawala za serikali*, treasury bills. (cf *cheki, hundi, drafti*). (Ar)

hawara (also *hawaa*) *n* (*n*) prostitute, harlot, whore, slut; a loose woman: *Alijifanya hawara ili aweze kuwakidhi watoto wake*, she prostituted herself in order to support her children. (*kimada, kahaba, fasiki*) (Ar)

hawil.i *vt, vi* transfer, shift, move, change: *Hawili mwajiriwa*, transfer an employee. Prep. **hawil.i.a** St. **hawil.ik.a** Cs. **hawil.ish.a** Ps. of Prep. **hawil.iw.a** Rp. of Prep. **hawil.i.an.a** (Ar)

hawilish.a *n* (*n*) transfer, convey, subrogate: *Alihawilishia fedha zake kupitia benki*, he transferred his money through the bank. St. **hawilish.ik.a** Ps. **hawilish.w.a** Rp. **hawilish.an.a** (*cf hawili*)

hawilisho *n* (*ma-*) 1. a transferred thing. 2. transfer, change, shift, relocation: *Hawilisho la mfanyakazi yule lilimchukiza*, the transfer of that worker displeased him. (cf *uhamishaji*) (Ar)

hawinde *n* (*ma-*) pauper, destitute person: *Marafiki humsaidia kijana yule kwa sababu ni hawinde*, friends help that young man because he is a poor man. (cf *mkata, masikini, fakiri*)

haya[1] *n* (*n*) 1. shyness; a person's attitude of feeling shy because of his past misdeeds which may become known to others. 2. shyness; a person's attitude to refrain from doing sth because of too much respect given to another person say of higher authority, status, etc 3. shame, disgrace, dishonour: *Ona haya*, feel shameful. *Tia haya*, disgrace. *Hana haya*, she is shameless. 4. attitude of refraining from seeing sby's face: *Huya za uso; uso wa haya*, shyness.

haya[2] *interj* 1. an expletive of speeding up or calling to action or effort for sth; Come on! Step out! Make haste! 2. an expletive of accepting of what has been said; okay. (cf *nimesikia*) 3. an exclamation of driving out sby in a rude manner. (cf *ondoka*)

haya[3] *adj, pron* used as a demonstrative marker of proximity for *ma-* class countable and uncountable plural nouns; these: *Haya machungwa*, these oranges. *Haya maji*, this water.

hayati *n* (*n*) 1. the deceased, the departed: *Hayati mama yangu*, my late mother. 2. lifetime: *Wakati wa hayati yake*, during his lifetime. (*prov*) *Si hayati si mamati*, he is not alright, he is not alive and he is not dead; he is ill. (cf *maisha*) (Ar)

hayawani *n* (*ma-*) 1. animal, beast, brute. (cf *mnyama*) 2. a stupid person, a shameless person: *Yeye ni hayawani kwa vile aliropokwa ovyo hadharani*, he is a stupid person because he talked nonsense in public. (cf *bahaimu, mpumbavu*) 3. a wicked person, a vicious person; reprobate, scoundrel: *Mimi simpendi hayawani yule*, I don't like that scoundrel. (cf *mwovu, fisadi*) (Ar)

hayo *adj, pron* used as a demonstrative marker of non-proximity for *ma-* class countable and uncountable plural nouns: *Hayo maneno*, those words. *Hayo mananasi*, those pineapples.

haz.a *vt, vi* forbid sby from doing sth; prohibit, warn, advise: *Tulimhaza asiwabughudhi wazee wake lakini hakusikia*, we advised him not to pester his parents but he did not listen. Prep. **haz.i.a** St. **haz.ik.a** Cs. **haz.ish.a** Ps. **haz.w.a** Rp **haz.an.a** (cf *onya, asa, kataza*)

hazahaz.a *vt* conceal a secret, information, etc.; hide, keep, cover up: *Muungwana yule hupenda kuhazahaza siri za watu*, that gentleman likes to keep the secrets of other people. Prep. **hazahaz.i.a** St. **hazahaz.ik.a** Cs. **hazahaz.ish.a** Ps. **hazahaz.w.a** Rp **hazahaz.an.a** (cf *ficha*)

hazama (also *azama*) *n* (*n*) 1. lady's nose ornament, lady's nose ring. (cf *kishaufu*) 2. a nose-ring of an animal such as an ox. (cf *shemere*) (Ar)

hazina *n* (*n*) 1. treasure, riches, valuables, wealth. *Mweka hazina*, treasurer. *Hazina ya bunduki*, gun safe. 2. exchequer, treasury. 3. hidden treasure. (cf *dafina*) (Ar)

hazin.i[1] *vt* 1. stash; put or hide away money, valuables, etc. in a secret or safe place: *Alizihazini pesa zangu katika kasha la chuma*, he stashed my money in a safe. 2. serve as a treasurer. Prep. **hazin.i.a** St. **hazin.ik.a** Cs. **hazin.ish.a** Ps. of Prep. **hazin.iw.a** Rp of Prep. **hazin.i.an.a**

hazini[2] *n* (*ma-*) treasure

he *interj* 1. an exclamation of warning someone. 2. an exclamation of expressing surprise, disgust or disapproval over sth: *He! Kutwa kucha ananisema kwa ubaya tu*, Hey! Day and night he is speaking against me. 3. a scornful word for calling someone. *He! Njoo upande huu*, Hey! you come on this side.

heba *n (n)* see *haiba*
hebo *interj* an expletive of surprise, etc.; oh!: *Hebo! Wewe huoni?* Oh! Can't you see?
hebu (also *ebu*) *interj* 1. an expletive for calling attention; I say! e.g. *Hebu njoo*, I say, you come. 2 an expletive for asking someone to allow passage; make room for me; allow passage for me: *Hebu nipishe!* Allow me to pass. (cf *nipishe, sumile, abedari*)
hedashara (also *hideshara*) *n (n)* eleven; *Watu hedashara*, eleven people. (Ar)
hedaya *n (n)* see *hidaya*
hedhi *n (n)* catamenia, menstruation, menses: *Kuwa na hedhi*, menstruate. *Kukatika hadhi*, menopause. (Ar)
hedikota *n (n)* headquarters (cf *makao-makuu*) (Eng)
hedimasta *n (ma-)* headmaster; the male headteacher of a school. (Eng)
hedimistresi *n (ma-)* headmistress; the female headteacher of a school. (Eng)
hekaheka (also *heikaheika*) *n (n)* 1. confusion, pandemonium, chaos, disorder: *Huko kwenye mnada, kuna hekaheka nyingi*, at the auction, there is a lot of turmoil. (cf *fujo, ghasia*) 2. salvo, applause, cheering; shouts of encouragement such as in games: *Kulikuwa na hekaheka nyingi jana kwenye michuano ya kandanda*, there was a lot of cheering yesterday at the football tournament. (cf *pirikapirika*) 3. bustle, hustle; a lot of activities, work, etc.: *Nilikuwa katika hekaheka ya kutayarisha safari yangu ya kwenda ng'ambo*, I was in a state of hustle and bustle preparing for my trip overseas.
hekalu *n (n)* synagogue, temple. (Ar)
hekaya (also *hikaya*) *n (n)* 1. fable, tale: *Hekaya za Isopo*, Aesop's fables. 2. phenomenon; exciting or remarkable incident: *Alinihadithia hekaya zilizomfika katika safari yake*, he told me about the exciting incidents of his travels. (cf *kioja, maajabu*) (Ar)

hekemu.a[1] *vt, vi* stretch oneself as one wakes up or gets up from a cramped position, etc.: *Alipoamka, alijihekemua kabla hajaenda msalani*, when he woke up he stretched himself before going to the bathroom. Prep. **hekemu.li.a** St. **hekemu.k.a** Cs. **hekemu.sh.a** Ps. of Prep. **hekemu.liw.a** (cf *jinyongoa, jibenua, jinyoshanyosha*)
hekemu.a[2] *vi* sneeze Prep. **hekemu.li.a** St. **hekemu.k.a** (cf *chemua*)
hekima (also *hikima*) *n (n)* 1. wisdom, sagacity: *Yeye ni mtu mwenye hekima sana*, he is a person of great wisdom. (cf *busara, akili*) 2. gambit, trick, tactic: *Alitumia hekima kunishawishi kujiunga na chama chao*, he employed gambits to get me join their party. (cf *ujanja*) (Ar)
heko[1] *interj* an expletive of congratulating someone; Congratulations! Well done! *Toa heko*, congratulate. *Alinipa heko*, he congratulated me.
hekta *n (n)* hectare; a unit of surface measure in the metric system equivalent to 10,000 square metres. (Eng)
hela[1] *n (n)* (*colloq*) used in informal contexts; money, currency. (Ger)
hela[2] *interj* Allow me to pass! (cf *sumile! hebu!*)
helelez.a *vt* ignore; leave alone someone to sort out his own problems and thus render no service to him: *Ingawa tulimwelezea matatizo yetu, lakini akatuheleleza*, even though we explained to him our problems, he ignored us. Prep. **helelez.i.a** St. **helelez.ik.a** Ps. **helelez.w.a** Rp **helelez.an.a**
heliamu *n (n)* (*chem*) helium; a kind of colourless gas used in low-temperature work for inflating baloons, etc. (Eng)
helikopta *n (n)* helicopter (Eng)
helmeti *n (n)* 1. helmet; a strong covering to protect the head during war by soldiers. 2. a special covering worn by

hema¹   **hero**

people who might crack their heads in accidents or at work as in the case of motorcyclists, firemen, miners, etc. (Eng)

hema¹ *n (ma-)* wigwam, tepee, yurt, tent: *Piga hema,* pitch a tent. *(turubali)* (Ar)

hem.a² *vt* 1. pant, wheeze. (cf *kukuta, tweta)* 2. rest, relax, take a rest: *Alitaka kuhema kidogo kwenye kochi,* he wanted to rest a little on the coach. Prep. **hem.e.a** St. **hem.ek.a** Cs. **hem.esh.a** Ps. **hem.w.a** (cf *puma*)

heme.a¹ *vi* 1. be busy, be engrossed: *Hakuweza kuonana na mimi jana kwa vile kazi nyingi zilimhemea,* he could not see me yesterday because he was engrossed in his work. 2. be entangled with problems, etc. *Hana raha siku hizi kwa sababu matatizo mengi ya nyumbani yamemhemea,* he is not happy these days because he is entangled with many domestic problems. Prep. **heme.le.a** St. **heme.lek.a** Ps. **heme.w.a** Rp **heme.an.a**

hemea² *vi* see *hemera*

hemer.a (also *hemea*) *vi* emigrate because of difficulties; go searching for food because of difficulties. *Wakimbizi walihemera nchi za jirani kutokana na vita vya wenyewe kwa wenyewe,* the refugees emigrated to the neighbouring countries due to in-country fighting. Prep. **hemer.e.a** St. **hemer.ek.a** Cs. **hemer.esh.a** Ps. **hemer.w.a** Rp **hemer.an.a**

hemk.a *vt* be ecstatic, be inspired. Prep. **hemk.i.a** St. **hemk.ik.a** Cs. **hemk.ish.a**

hemofilia *n (n)* (med) haemophilia; a medical condition in which the ability of the blood to clot is severely reduced causing the sufferer to bleed severely from a small injury. (Eng)

henezi¹ *n (n)* gentleness, steadiness, calmness: *Nilisema naye kwa henezi na akanisikiliza,* I talked to him calmly

and he listened to me. (cf *upole, taratibu)*

henezi² *vt* slowly

henza (also *heza) n (n)* (naut) a rope or tackle used for raising or lowering a flag, sail, etc.; halyard. (cf *jarari*) (Ar)

henzirani *n (n)* see *hinzirani*

hep.a (also *epa, kwepa*) *vt, vi* 1. flinch, swerve, escape: *Dereva wangu alilihepa kifundi shimo kwenye barabara kuu,* my driver skilfully avoided the pothole on the highway. (cf *jiepusha*) 2. avoid meeting someone: *Nilipomwona kwa mbali, nilimhepa ili tusikutane naye,* when I saw him far away, I dodged him. Prep. **hep.e.a** St. **hep.ek.a** Cs. **hep.esh.a** Ps. **hep.w.a** Rp **hep.an.a**

hereni *n (n)* see *hirini*

heri¹ *n (n)* 1. goodness, kindness: *Alifanya jambo la heri kuwasaidia watoto yatima,* he did a good thing to help the orphans. 2. happiness, blessedness, prosperity, fortune: *Yeye ni mtu wa heri,* he is a virtuous person. 3. used in other expressions: *Heri ya sikukuu,* happy holiday. *Kwa heri,* (sing) goodbye. *Kwa heri ya kuonana,* goodbye until we meet again. *Kwa herini,* (pl) goodbye. (Ar)

heri² *adj* better, preferable. *(prov) Heri nusu ya shari kuliko shari kamili,* better half a disaster than a complete one i.e. it is better to face part of a problem rather than the whole of it. (Ar)

heria¹ *interj* an expression used by winch and crane workers as well as porters to alert someone so as to allow them to pass. (cf *simile, habadari!, heria!)* (Port)

heri.a² *vt (naut)* anchor; drop anchor. Prep. **heri.li.a** St. **heri.k.a** Cs. **heri.sh.a** (Port)

herini (also *hereni, hirini) n (n)* earring (cf *bali, kipuli*) (Hind)

hero *n (n)* a small wooden dish or container used for serving food. (cf *tasa*)

221

heroe *n* (*n*) (*zool*) greater flamingo; a tropical tall water bird (family Phoenicopteridae) with long legs, webbed feet, long neck, broad beak and bright pink or red feathers.

heroe

heroini *n* (*n*) heroin; a powerful illegal drug made from morphine.
herufi (*also harufi*) *n* (*n*) 1. a letter of the alphabet. *Herufi za Kiarabu*, Arabic characters. *Herufi jozi*, diagraph. 2. script, handwriting (Ar)
hesab.u[1] (*also hisabu*) *vt, vi* 1. total, add up, sum, compute. 2. count, reckon: *Hesabu mayai haya*, count these eggs. 3. estimate: *Alihesabu kuwa wageni zaidi ya mia watafika kwenye karamu yake*, he estimated that more than one hundred guests would attend his banquet. (cf *kadiria*) 4. assume, suppose: *Tulihesabu kwamba kutokuja kwake kwenye mkutano ni ushahidi wa upinzani dhidi yetu sisi*, we assumed that his absence from the meeting was a manifestation of opposition against us. Prep. **hesab.i.a** St. **hesab.ik.a** Cs. **hesab.ish.a** Ps. of Prep. **hesab.iw.a** Rp of Prep. **hesab.i.an.a** (cf *fikiria, dhania, chukulia*) (Ar)
hesabu[2] (*also, hisabu*) *n* (*n*) 1. total, sum, addition. 2. account, bill, arithmetic: *Kitabu cha hesabu*, an account book. *Taka hesabu*, demand an account. *Weka hesabu*, keep an account. *Fungua hesabu*, open an account. *Sawazisha hesabu*, square up, calculate, work a sum. *Maelezo ya mahesabu*, statements of accounts. *Hesabu za kichwani*, mental arithmetic. *Hamisha hesabu*, transfer an account. *Hesabu za kukisia*, an estimated account. *Hesabu ya idadi ya watu*, census. (cf *sensa*) *Hesabu endelezi*, arithmetic progression. (Ar)
hesabu[3] (*also hisabu*) *n* (*n*) (in Islam) punishment or reward in the hereafter for deeds or misdeeds done on earth. (Ar)
heshima (*also hishima*) *n* (*n*) 1. honour, respect, dignity. (cf *cheo, daraja*) 2. respect, reverence: *Ana heshima sana kwa watu*, he has a lot of respect to people. *Hana heshima*, he has no respect, he is disrespectful. *Weka heshima*, have respect. *Vunja heshima*, disrespect. (*syn*) *Heshima ni kitu cha bure*, respect costs nothing. (cf *staha*) 3. a thing given to someone as a token of respect: *Alipewa ngao kama heshima kutokana na uongozi wake bora*, he was given a shield as a token of respect for his good leadership.
heshim.u *vt, vi* 1. respect, revere, esteem: *Lazima uwaheshimu walimu wako*, you must rspect your teachers 2. adore, idolize, worship, love: *Wao wanamheshimu mtu yule kama Mungu wao*, they adore that person like their god. Prep. **heshim.i.a** St. **heshim.ik.a** Ps. of Prep. **heshim.iw.a** Rp. of Prep **heshim.i.an.a** (cf *tukuza, thamini, enzi*) (Ar)
hesi *n* (*n*) 1. thread of a screw. etc.: *Msumari wa hesi*, screw. 2. (*anat*) helix; the folded rim of cartilage around the outer ear.
hewa *n* (*n*) weather, air, atmosphere: *Hewa kanieneo*, air pressure. *Hewa nzuri*, nice weather. *Hewa mbaya*, bad weather, *Hewa safi*, clean air. *Punga hewa*, get some fresh air. *Badilisha*

hewa, go for a change in weather. (cf *anga, mbingu*) (Ar)

hewaa (also *ewa*) *interj* an exclamation of assent and approval by different categories of people. It usu carries the meanings of "just so," "that is right," and "yeah": (cf *barabara!*)

hewala *interj* an exclamation of acceptance; I agree. (*prov*) *Hewala si utumwa*, acceptance of order or instruction from someone does not cause servitude or capitulation.

heza[1] *n* (*n*) (*naut*) see *henza*

hez.a[2] *vt* give sby a job so that he has a hard time doing it; "challenge": *Kwa vile yeye ni majigambo, nilimheza kwa kumpa kazi kabambe*, since he is boastful, I gave him a hard time by giving him a tough job. Prep. *hez.e.a* St. *hez.ek.a* Cs. *hez.esh.a* Ps. *hez.w.a* Rp *hez.an.a* (cf *komoa, chagiza*)

hi *interj* an exclamation of surprise, horror, etc. (cf *lo! do! cho!*)

hiana *n* (*n*) 1. meanness; the attitude of preventing others from using what you have in hand. (cf *uchoyo, ubahili*) 2. unjust treatment, injustice, unfairness: *Nilifanyiwa hiana kazini kwangu*, I was given unjust treatment at my place of work (cf *dhuluma, uonevu*) (Ar)

hiar.i[1] *vt* choose, prefer, opt. Prep. *hiar.i.a* St. *hiar.ik.a* Cs. *hiar.ish.a* Ps. of Prep. *hiar.iw.a* (cf *chagua, pendelea*) (Ar)

hiari[2] *n* (*n*) choice, wish, volition, option: *Hiari yako*, it is your wish; it is up to you; do as you please. *Hiari yangu*, it is my wish, (*prov*) *Hiari yashinda utumwa*, voluntary work is better than forced labour. (Ar)

hiba *n* (*n*) gift, present; souvenir as a sign of affection: *Alipotoka ng'ambo, aniniletea kitabu kama hiba yangu*, when he came from overseas, he brought me a book as a present. (cf *atia, zawadi, hadia*) (Ar)

hib.u *vt* love, like, hold dear: *Anamhibu mkewe*, he loves his wife. Prep. *hib.i.a* St. *hib.ik.a* Cs. *hib.ish.a* Ps. of Prep. *hib.iw.a* Rp of Prep. *hib.i.an.a* (cf *penda*) (Ar)

hicho *adj, pron* used as a demonstrative marker of nonproximity for ki-vi class sing nouns meaning "that": *Hicho kitabu*, that book.

hidashara *n* (*n*) see *hedashara*

hidaya[1] *n* (*n*) righteousness, uprightness, virtuousness: *Mwenyezi Mungu amempa hidaya kwani mtu yule ni Mcha Mungu*, God has led him on the right path because that person is pious. (cf *uongofu*) (Ar)

hidaya[2] *n* (*n*) gift given to someone as a sign of affection; present usu sth costly or wonderful. (Ar)

hid.i *vt* lead sby to the right way: *Awali alikuwa kijana matata, lakini baadaye Mungu alimhidi*, in the beginning, he was a troublesome young man, but later God led him to the right path. Prep. *hid.i.a* St. *hid.ik.a* Cs. *hid.ish.a* Ps. of Prep. *hid.iw.a* Rp of Prep. *hid.i.an.a* (cf *ongoa*) (Ar)

hidrojini (also *haidrojeni*) *n* (*n*) (*chem*) hydrogen (Eng)

hieroglifu *n* (*n*) hieroglyph; a picture or symbol representing a word, syllable or sound used by the ancient Egyptians and others instead of alphabetic letters. (Eng)

hifadh.i[1] *vt* 1. conserve, preserve, safeguard, store. 2. learn by heart; memorize: *Alilihifadhi shairi lote*, he memorized the whole poem. Prep. *hifadh.i.a* St. *hifadh.ik.a* Cs. *hifadh.ish.a* Ps. of Prep. *hifadh.iw.a* Rp of Prep. *hifadh.i.an.a* (Ar)

hifadhi[2] *n* (*n*) protection, conservation, preservation: *Hifadhi ya kisiasa*, political asylum. *Hifadhi ya udongo*, soil conservation. *Hifadhi ya mazingira*, environmental protection. *Hifadhi ya wanyama*, game reserve. *Hifadhi ya taifa*, National Park. *Hifadhi za nyaraka*, archives. *Walimweka chini ya*

H

hifadhi ya polisi, they kept him under police custody. (cf *himaya, usalama*) (Ar)

hifadhi³ *n (n) (math)* conversion; a change in the form of a quantity or an expression without a change in the value: *Hifadhi ya momenta*, conversion of momentum. (cf *ubadilishaji*)

hii *adj* used as a demonstrative of proximity for n class sing and mi- class pl nouns; this, these: *Meza hii*, this table. *Miti hii*, these trees.

hija *n (n)* (in Islam) a pilgrimage to the holy place of Mecca: *Enda hija*, go for a pilgrimage. (Ar)

hijabu¹ *n (n) (med)* the inflammation and bleeding of gums; gingivitis. (cf *kiseyeye*) (Ar)

hijabu² *n (n)* a woman's garment worn by some Muslims and Hindus covering their bodies and faces; purdah. (Ar)

hijabu³ *n (n)* a kind of local medical treatment that protects someone against evil: *Yeye alitaka kufanyiwa hijabu*, he wanted to be treated medically against evil. (Ar)

hij.i *vt, vi* make pilgrimage to Mecca. Prep. *hij.i.a* St. *hij.ik.a* Cs. *hij.ish.a* Ps. of Prep. *hij.iw.a* Rp of Prep. *hij.i.an.a* (Ar)

hijra *n (n)* (in Islam) Hegira; the forced journey of Prophet Muhammad from Mecca to Medina in 622 A.D.

hikaya *n (n)* see *hekaya*

hiki *adj, pron* used as a demonstrative marker of proximity for ki-vi class sing noun: *Kitabu hiki*, this book.

hikima *n (n)* see *hekima*

hila *n (n)* trick, intrigue, scheme, plan: *Yeye ni mtu wa hila nyingi*, he is a person of many tricks. (cf *ujanja, ghiliba, makri*) (Ar)

hilaki *n (n)* calamity, tragedy: *Ile ilikuwa hilaki ya kweli kwa vile abiria wengi walikufa maji*, that was a real disaster because many passengers were drowned. (cf *maangamizi, uangamizaji*) (Ar)

hilali *n (n)* crescent; the new moon. (cf *mwezi mchanga, mwezi kongo*) (Ar)

hili *adj, pron* used as a demonstrative of proximity for ma- class sing. nouns; this: *Hili tango*, this cucumber.

hiliki¹ *n (n) see iliki*

hilik.i² *vi* 1. be destroyed, be ruined, perish, vanish: *Ng'ombe wake walihiliki kutokana na mvua kubwa*, his cattle perished following the downpour. St. *hilik.ik.a* Cs. *hilik.ish.a* Ps. of Prep. *hilik.iw.a* Rp of Prep. *hilik.i.an.a* (cf *teketea, angamia, potea*) (Ar)

hilo *adj, pron* used as a demonstrative of non-proximity for ma- class sing nouns: *Hilo neno*, that word.

hima¹ *adv* quickly, hastily, in a hurry: *Fanya hima*, do sth fast; make haste. (cf *chupuchupu, upesi, haraka*) (Ar)

hima² *n (n)* effort, pain, push, stress: *Ana hima sana katika kazi yake*, he puts a lot of effort in his work. (cf *bidii, juhudi*) (Ar)

hima³ *vi* (used in parades) halt e.g. *Shoto kulia, Shoto kulia, hima*, left right, left right, halt.

himahima *adv* fast, quickly, speedily.

himaya *n (n)* 1. protection, safety, guardianship: *Tulikuwa chini ya himaya ya Kiingereza*, we were under British protection. (cf *mamlaka, utawala*) 2. jurisdiction: *Himaya yake*, area under his jurisdiction. (Ar)

himid.i¹ *vt* (in Islam) praise, esp. God: *Tunamhimidi Mwenyezi Mungu kwa fadhila zote anazotupa*, we praise God for all the kindness that he bestows upon us. Prep. *himid.i.a* St. *himid.ik.a* Cs. *himid.ish.a* Ps. of Prep *himid.iw.a* Rp of Prep *himid.i.an.a* (cf *shukuru*) (Ar)

himidi² (also *hamdi*) *n (n)* praise, extolment. (cf *sifa*) (Ar)

himila *n (n)* pregnancy, gestation. (cf *ujauzito, mimba*) (Ar)

himil.i *vt, vi* 1. bear, withstand, support: *Mashua hii haiwezi kuhimili uzito wa* *abiria*, this canoe cannot bear the weight of the passengers. (cf *beba, tuta*) 2. be pregnant: *Mkewe amehimili*, his wife is pregnant. 3. bear, withstand; endure hardships: *Aliyahimili matatizo mengi ya mumewe*, she endured many hardships from her husband. (*prov*) *Nyumba ya udongo haihimili vishindo*, a clay house cannot withstand great shocks i.e. a weak person cannot endure great hardships. Prep. **himil.ia** St. **himil.ik.a** Cs. **himil.ish.a** Ps. of Prep. **himil.iw.a** Rp of Prep. **himil.i.an.a** (Ar)

himiz.a *vt* 1. encourage, urge: *Alinihimiza nisome udaktari*, he encouraged me to study medicine. 2. plead for quick action; hasten, expedite. *Alituhimiza tuimalize kazi yake kabla jua halijakuchwa*, he hastened us to complete his work before sunset. Prep. **himiz.i.a** St. **himiz.ik.a** Ps. **himiz.w.a** Rp **himiz.an.a**

himu *vt* see *jihimu*

hina *n* (*n*) 1. (*bot*) leaves of a henna plant used by women to stain the finger nails, palms of the hand and soles of the feet. 2. henna; a dye extracted from the leaves of this plant.

hindi *n* (*ma-*) a collection of maize grains in a cob.

hin.i *vt, vi* 1. betray; act treacherously: *Aliihini nchi yake*, she betrayed her country. (cf *saliti*) 2. refuse to give; keep back; withhold: *Ametuhini pesa zetu*, he has refused to give us our money. Prep. **hin.i.a** St. **hin.ik.a** Cs. **hin.ish.a** Ps. of Prep. **hin.iw.a** Rp of Prep. **hin.i.an.a** (cf *nyima*) (Ar)

hinik.a *vt, vi* see *inika*

hinikiz.a *vt, vi* see *hanikiza*

hino *adj, pron* (used in some parts of Kenya), this

hinzirani (also *henzirani*) *n* (*n*) 1. a thin kind of cane from a plant, *mhinzirani*, usu used for beating esp children 2. a long thin piece of stick; lath (cf *upapi*) (Ar)

hinziri (also *hanziri*) *n* (*n*) 1. (*zool*) pig, swine, hog. (cf *nguruwe*) 2. a person regarded as acting or behaving like a pig; swine. (Ar)

hiponimi *n* (*n*) (*sem*) hyponym; a word of more specific meaning than a general or superordinate term applicable to it (Ex: *mbuzi*, 'goat' is a hyponym of 'animal'). (Eng)

hiponimia *n* (*n*) (*sem*) hyponymy; the relation between a specific word and a general or superordinate term applicable to it. (Eng)

hipotenyusi *n* (*n*) (*math*) hypotenuse; the side of a right-angled triangle opposite the right angle.

hir.i *vi* (of a girl) reach the age of puberty: *Amehiri sasa*, she has now reached the age of puberty. Prep. **hir.i.a** St. **hir.ik.a** Cs. **hir.ish.a** Ps. of Prep. **hir.iw.a** (cf *vunja ungo*)

hirimia *vt* determine, intend: *Amehirimia kununua gari*, he has decided to buy a new car. (cf *kusudia, nuia*)

hirimu *n* (*n*) 1. age; period of life esp between ten and twenty five. 2. contemporary; one of the same age; living or happening in the same period of time: *Yeye ni hirimu yangu*, he is my contemporary. (cf *rika, mkeketo*) 3. youth, sprig, *Yeye ni hirimu mwenye adabu sana*, he is a well-mannered young man.

hirini *n* (*n*) see *herini*

hirizi *n* (*n*) amulet, talisman, charm. (cf *kago, azima*) (Ar)

hisa *n* (*n*) 1. a part or portion that belongs or is alloted to a particular person; share, portion, lot: *Hisa yake katika mirathi ilikuwa nyumba moja tu*, his share in the inheritance was only one house. 2. dividend; *Hisa ya rajua*, deferred share. *Hisa mgawanyo*, distributive share. *Hisa ya kawaida*, ordinary share. *Hisa maalum*, preference share. *Bei ya hisa*, share price. *Ameweka hisa zake*

katika shirika la ndege, he has put his shares in the airline. (cf *fungu*) 3. (*math*) quotient; the number obtained when one is divided by another.
hisabati *n* (*n*) mathematics (Ar)
hisab.u[1] see *hesabu*[1]
hisabu[2] see *hesabu*[2]
hisabu[3] see *hesabu*[3]
hisani *n*(*n*) kindness, courtesy, gentleness: *Alitufanyia hisani nyingi*, he did us many favours. (*prov*) *Hisani haiozi*, a good deed is always remembered. (cf *jamala, wema, fadhila*) (Ar)
hishima *n* (*n*) see *heshima*
hishim.u *vt* see *heshimu*
his.i[1] *vt* 1. sense, feel, perceive: *Anahisi njaa*, he feels hungry. *Anahisi baridi*, he feels cold. 2. think, recognise, feel: *Anahisi kwamba hatua uliyoichukua ilikuwa sawa*, he thinks that the action you had taken was proper. Prep. **his.i.a** St. **his.ik.a** Cs. **his.ish.a** Ps. of Prep. **his.iw.a** Rp of Prep. **his.i.an.a** (cf *dhania, fikiri*) (Ar)
hisi[2] (also *hisia*) *n* (*n*) 1. feeling, sense, sensation: *Binaadamu ana hisi tano*, human beings have five senses. 2. sentiment, feeling: *Hana hisia juu ya matakwa ya wananchi*, he has no feelings on the aspirations of the people. 3. love, affection: *Hana hisia juu ya mumewe*, she has no love for her husband. (cf *mapenzi, mahaba*) (Ar)
hisia *n* (*n*) see *hisi*[2]
Hispania (also *Uhispania*) *n* (*n*) Spain (Eng)
histogramu *n* (*n*) (*math*) histogram (Eng)
historia *n*(*n*) 1. history. (cf *salua, mapisi*) 2. account, narration, story: *Alinipa historia ndefu juu ya safari yake*, he gave me a long account of his journey. (cf *hadithi*) (Ar)
hitaj.i (also *hitajia*) *vt* require, desire, be in need: *Wanahitaji msaada*, they need assistance. Sometimes, used as impersonal or with a dummy subject e.g. *Inahitaji kuwepo ushirikiano mzuri kati yao*, there needs to be a close cooperation between them. Prep. **hitaj.i.a** St. **hitaj.ik.a** Ps. of Prep. **hitaj.iw.a** Rp of Prep. **hitaj.i.an.a** (cf *taka, tamani*) (Ar)
hitaji.a *n* (*n*) see *hitaji*
hitar.i[1] *vt* choose, opt, select: *Alihitari kuishi sehemu za shamba*, she preferred to live in the rural areas. Prep. **hitar.i.a** St. **hitar.ik.a** Ps. of Prep **hitar.iw.a** (cf *chagua, hiari*) (Ar)
hitari[2] *n* (*n*) choice, option, selection: *Hitari iko kwake*, the choice lies with him. (Ar)
hitari[3] *n* (*n*) (*math*) permutation (Ar)
hitilafian.a *vi* 1. differ, vary, be different: *Ingawa vijana wale ni ndugu lakini wanahitilafiana sana kitabia*, even though those two young men are brothers, they differ very much in character. (cf *tofautiana*) 2. be at loggerheads; wrangle, bicker, squabble, feud: *Waliachana baada ya kuhitilafiana kwa mambo ya upuuzi*, they got divorced over trivial issues. St. **hitilafian.ik.a** Cs. **hitilafian.ish.a** Ps. of Prep. **hitilafian.iw.a** (cf *zozana, kosana, gombana*) (Ar)
hitilafu (also *ihtilafu*) *n* (*n*) 1. difference, contrast: *Kuna hitilafu kubwa katika uzalishaji mali wa shule hizi mbili*, there is a big difference in production between these two schools. (cf *tofauti*) 2. defect, fault: *Saa yake ina hitilafu*, his watch is defective. (cf *kasoro, dosari*) 3. squabble, feud, differences: *Majirani walijaribu kusuluhisha hitilafu zetu*, the neighbours tried to solve our differences. (cf *tofauti, ugomvi, suitafahamu*) (Ar)
hitima *n* (*n*) 1. (in Islam) a special service involving the recitation of Koran held before but usu after a funeral.

hitimish.a

2. the total number of 30 chapters constituting the Holy Qoran. (Ar)

hitimish.a *vt* 1. conclude, end: *Mwenyekiti aliuhitimisha mjadala*, the chairman concluded the discussion. 2. (in Islam) conduct a special service held in honour of the dead person. Prep. **hitimish.i.a** St. **hitimish.ik.a** Ps. **hitimish.w.a** Rp of Prep. **hitimish.i.an.a**

hitimisho *n* (*ma-*) conclusion, end, termination; final stage.

hitim.u *vt, vi* 1. complete Koranic education in a religious school: *Mtoto wake amehitimu chuoni*, his child has completed Koranic education in the school. (cf *maliza*) 2. (usu *hitimisha*) conclude, end: *Walihitimisha mulunga*, they concluded the period of mourning. 3. graduate from a school, college, etc. *Amehitimu katika Chuo Kikuu cha Australia*, she has graduated from the University of Australia. Prep. **hitim.i.a** St. **hitim.ik.a** Cs. **hitim.ish.a** Ps. of Prep. **hitim.iw.a** (Ar)

hiut.a *vt* play and win a class game. Prep. **hiut.i.a** St. **hiut.ik.a** Cs. **hiut.ish.a** Ps. of Prep. **hiut.iw.a**

hivi[1] *adj, pron* used as a demonstrative of proximity for ki-vi class pl nouns; these: *Vitabu hivi*, these books. *Hivi ni vyako*, these are yours.

hivi[2] *adv* in this way, in this manner, accordingly: *Nataka ufanye hivi*, I want you to do this in this way.

hivyo[1] *adj, pron* used as a demonstrative of non-proximity for ki-vi class pl nouns; those: *Vikapu hivyo*, those baskets.

hivyo[2] *conj* therefore, hence, thus, in that way. *Yeye haji kesho kufanya kazi hapa; hivyo, itakubidi uje wewe kesho*, he will not come tomorrow to work here; hence, you will be obliged to come tomorrow.

hivyo[3] *adv* in that very manner, in the manner already described: *Fanya hivyo*, do that way. *Hivyo ndivyo ilivyo*, that is how it is. *Hivyo sivyo ilivyo*, that is not the way it is. *Je si hivyo?* Is that not so? *Usifanye hivyo kama yeye*, don't do that like him; don't do it that way like he did.

hivyo[4] *interj* an expletive of surprise indicating that sth is the reverse of what was expected or thought; you don't say. (cf *alaa, kumbe*)

hiyo *adj, pron* used as a demonstrative of nonproximity for n class singular and u- class pl nouns; that, those: *Kamba hiyo*, that rope. *Hiyo ni yangu*, that is mine.

hizaya *n* (*n*) 1. curse, damnation: *Mwana hizaya*, a cursed person. (cf *laana*) 2. shame, disgrace: *Ilikuwa hizaya tupu kwa mwanafunzi yule kumtukana mwalimu wake*, it was a sheer disgrace for that student to insult his teacher. (cf *aibu, fedheha*) (Ar)

hizi[1] *adj, pron* used as a demonstrative of proximity for n and u- classes pl nouns; these: *Siku hizi*, these days.

hiz.i[2] *vt, vi* 1. outrage, disgust, sicken: *Alinihizi kutokana na vitendo vyake viovu*, he outraged me for his evil deeds. (cf *kirihi*) 2. disgrace, dishonour, debase, vilify, discredit, shame. *Alituhizi mbele ya watu kwa lugha yake chafu*, he disgraced us in public with his filthy language. (cf *kashifu, aibisha, fedhehesha*) 3. hazard, imperil, jeopardise, risk, endanger: *Atakuhizi ukikubali kushirikiana naye katika mpango ule*, he will expose you to danger if you agree to cooperate with him in his plan. Prep. **hiz.i.a** St. **hiz.ik.a** Cs. **hiz.ish.a** Ps. of Prep **hiz.iw.a** Rp of Prep. **hiz.i.an.a** (cf *ponza*) (Ar)

hizo *adj, pron* used as a demonstrative of non-proximity for n and u- classes pl nouns; those: *Zawadi hizo*, those presents. *Kuta hizo*, those walls.

ho *interj* an expletive of stopping sth.

227

H

hobe *interj* an expletive of gratitude or ingratitude from a speaker: *Hobe! Mungu ametupa kila la heri*, Thanks! God has given us all the prosperity. (cf *handeki*)

hobelahobela *n (n)* 1. shoulder high: *Mshindi alibebwa hobelahobela*, the victor was carried shoulder high. (cf *juujuu*) 2. disorderly, chaotically, haphazardly. (cf *segemnege, shelabela*) 3. by using one's own hands: *Makuli walikuwa wakipakua na kupakia mizigo bandarini hobelahobela*, the coolies were offloading and loading the cargo at the port by using their hands.

hodari¹ *adj* 1. clever, intelligent: *Yeye ni mwanafunzi hodari*, he is an intelligent student. (cf *mahiri*) 2. experienced, polished, well-versed, knowledgeable: *Wewe ni hodari katika kazi yako*, you are experienced in your work. (cf *bingwa*) 3. artful, crafty, slick, shrewd, guileful, wily, cunning: *Wao ni hodari katika kulaghai watu*, they are shrewd in deceiving people. 4. powerful, mighty, strong: *Alikuwa hodari kwa vile aliweza kumkabili mpinzani wake kishujaa*, he was strong because he could face his opponent bravely. (Ar)

hodari² *n (n)* 1. a clever person, an intelligent person. 2. an experienced person. 3. a crafty person.

hodh.i¹ *vt* hoard, store, stock. Prep. **hodh.i.a** St. **hodh.ik.a** Cs. **hodh.ish.a** Ps. of Prep. **hodh.iw.a** Rp of Prep. **hodh.i.an.a** (cf *miliki*) (Ar)

hodhi² *n (n)* 1. property, wealth, treasure: *Hodhi zake hazina mnunuzi*, his stock does not have a buyer. (cf *mali*) 2. a plot of land belonging to sby. (Ar)

hodhi³ *n (n)* bathtub, footbath, water tank; a large vessel for holding water. (cf *bafu*) (Ar)

hodi¹ *interj* an expletive used as a polite request before someone enters a house or a room; May I come in?

hodi² *n (n)* a call-word to announce someone's presence: *Piga hodi*, knock at the door. *Bisha hodi*, knock at the door.

hodiya *n (n)* work song; a folk song sung by workers as in the fields, etc. with a marked rhythm. The song is used to encourage workers to do well while performing a difficult job collectively.

hof.u *vt* fear, cower, dread; be afraid, be scared, be worried: *Mwanasiasa alihofu juu ya usalama wake*, the politician feared for his safety. Prep. **hof.i.a** St. **hof.ik.a** Cs. **hof.ish.a** Ps. of Prep. **hof.iw.a** Rp. of Prep. **hof.i.an.a** (cf *ogopa, chelea*) (Ar)

hofu² *n (n)* 1. fear, dread, fright, worry: *Radi ilimtia hofu*, thunder instilled fear in him. (cf *woga, ukunguru*) 2. a thing that makes someone frightened: *Ameingiwa na hofu*, he is filled with fear. *Ameshikwa na hofu*, he is filled with fear. *Alifanya hofu*, he felt frightened.

hohehahe (also *hahehohe*) *n (n)* a destitute person, a poor person: *Hohehahe wanapata shida sana duniani*, the destitutes face a lot of hardships in the world. (*syn*) *Hohehahe jungu la mavi na mkorogwe*, a poor person is a recipient of all the bad things in the world. (cf *fukara, mkata, masikini*)

hoho *n (n)* (*bot*) red pepper: *Pilipili hoho*, red pepper. *Mkate wa hoho*, bread flavoured with pepper. (cf *pilipili, kichaa*)

hohos.a *vt, vi* talk in sleep; talk unconsciously: *Alihohosa usingizini kutokana na homa kali*, he talked in his sleep due to acute fever. Prep. **hohos.e.a** St. **hohos.ek.a** Cs. **hohos.esh.a** Ps. **hohos.w.a** (cf *weweseka*)

hoi *adj* fatigued, weary, worn-out: *Yeye yu hoi kutokana na shughuli nyingi*, he is tired due to pressure of work. (cf *taabani*)

hoihoi *n (n)* rejoicing, ululation, festivity, jubilation: *Kulikuwa na hoihoi nyingi harusini*, there was a lot of ululations at the wedding. (cf *vigelegele, vifijo*)

hoja *n (n)* 1. argument, point: *Jenga hoja*, make an argument. *Hoja yake haina msingi*, his argument is baseless. *Alitoa hoja nzuri*, he put forward a strong argument. 2. truth, fact: *Hiyo ndiyo hoja*, that is the truth. 3. suggestion, idea, opinion: *Alitoa hoja kwamba wafanyakazi waongezewe mshahara*, he put forward the suggestion that the salaries of the workers should be increased. (cf *wazo, fikira*) 4. query, statement: *Hakimu alimwuliza mshtaki kama ana hoja yoyote kwa mshtakiwa*, the judge asked the plaintiff if he had any statement to make on the accused. 5. recommendation, motion: *Hoja za serikali*, government's recommendations. *Hoja za kamati*, the committee's motions (Ar)

hojaji *n (n)* questionnaire: *Mtafiti alizitayarisha hojaji zake vizuri*, the researcher prepared his questionnaire well. (cf *kidadisi*)

hojatama *n (n)* (*math*) induction

hoj.i *vt, vi* 1. question, quiz, interrogate, query, interview: *Walimhoji kablu ya kumwajiri kazini*, they interviewed him before employing him. (cf *uliza, saili*) 2. cross-examine, cross-question: *Wakili alimhoji shahidi juu ya ushahidi alioutoa*, the lawyer cross-examined the witness on the evidence he gave. Prep. **hoj.i.a** St. **hoj.ik.a** Cs. **hoj.ish.a** Ps. of Prep. **hoj.iw.a** Rp of Prep. **hoj.i.an.a** (Ar)

hok.a *vt, vi* compete, contest, battle: *Walihoka kishujaa kwenye mashindano ya farasi*, they competed bravely in the horse race. Prep. **hok.i.a** St. **hok.w.a** Cs. **hok.ish.a** Ps. **hok.ik.a** (cf *shindana, menyana*)

hoki¹ *n (n)* hockey; a game played by two teams of eleven players each using sticks and a ball. (Eng)

hoki² *n (n)* baton; a slender stick used by a bandmaster. (cf *kome*)

hoko (also *huka*) *n (n)* hookah pipe. (cf *kikokoro, buruma*) (Eng)

holela *adv* see *horera*

holwaho *interj* an expletive of disgrace expressed by a speaker to someone who has done a horrible thing. (cf *loo!, lahaula!*)

homa *n (n)* 1. fever, feverishness: *Homa ya matumbo*, typhoid. *Homa ya mapafu*, pneumonia. *Homa ya manjano*, yellow fever. *Homa ya vipindi*, intermittent fever, recurrent fever. *Homa ya malaria*, malaria fever. *Homa ya papasi*, tick fever; an acute febrile disease caused by *Richettsia* and transmitted by ticks, producing high fever, cough and rash. *Homa ya uti wa mgongo*, meningitis. *Homa ya mafua ya ndege*, bird flu. *Homa ya bonde la ufa*, Rift valley fever. *Ana homa kali sana*, he is down with fever; he is suffering from a high fever. *Ameshikwa na homa*, he is suffering from fever. *Homa ya mafua ya nguruwe*, swine flu. 2. a feeling of sickness caused by a high temperature. (Ar)

hombo¹ *n (n)* (*zool*) a lot of fish: *Kulikuwa na hombo la samaki sokoni*, there was a lot of fish at the market.

hombo² *adj* abundant, copious: *Yalikuja machungwa hombo kutoka shambani*, a lot of oranges came from the farm. (cf *tele, pomoni*)

hombo³ *n (n)* secret; a private thing: *Fanya hombo*, make a secret. *Fuga hombo*, make a secret. *Weka hombo*, keep a secret. (cf *siri*)

hombwe *n (n)* (*zool*) escargot; a kind of snail of edible variety.

homo.a *vt* enjoy eating soft delicious food: *Anapenda kuhomoa vitu vitamu*, he likes to eat delicious things. 2. soften the food by overcooking: *Aliupika sana mhogo mpaka akauhomoa*, he overcooked the cassava until it became mushy. Prep. **homo.le.a** St. **homo.k.a**

H — homofoni / honi

Cs. *homo.sh.a* Ps. of Prep *homo.lew.a* Rp *homo.an.a*

homofoni n (n) homophone; words which have the same pronunciation but differ in meaning. e.g. *-zuri* 'good'; *zuri*, 'perjury' (Eng)

homografu n (n) homograph; a word that has the same spelling as another but has a different meaning e.g. *kamba*, 'rope'; *kamba*, 'prawn'. (Eng)

homoni n (n) hormone (Eng)

homonimu n (n) homonym; a word that has the same sound and spelling as another but is different in meaning e.g. *bárabara*, 'exactly'; *barábara*, 'road' (Eng)

homu n (n) a continuous windy weather.

honda n (n) a kind of a vehicle with two wheels.

hondohondo n (n) (*zool*) grey hornbill; a kind of bird (family *Bucerotidae*) with a huge and curved bill and grey chest and throat. *Tockus nasutus*.

hong.a vt 1. bribe, corrupt, buy off: *Alimhonga ofisa wa uhamiaji ili apate pasipoti*, he bribed the immigration officer in order to get a passport. 2. give a present to a male or female in order for someone to acquiesce to make love: *Mvulana alimhonga kidosho*, the boy gave a present to a glamorous girl in order to induce her to make love. Prep. *hong.e.a* St. *hong.ek.a* Cs. *hong.esh.a* Ps. *hong.w.a* Rp *hong.an.a*

honge.a (also *hongera*) vt, vi congratulate, compliment: *Nilimhongea kwa kuoa*, I congratulated him on getting married. Prep. *honge.le.a* St. *honge.lek.a* Cs. *honge.z.a* e.g. *Tulimhongeza binti yake kwa kuzaa*, we congratulated his daughter on giving birth. Ps. *honge.w.a*

honger.a[1] vt, vi see *hongea* Prep. *hongere.a* St. *honger.ek.a* Ps. *honger.w.a* Rp *honger.an.a*

hongera[2] n (n) congratulations, compliments. (cf *pongezi*)

hongera[3] interj an exclamation used for congratulating someone on his success, luck, etc.: *Hongera kwa kupandishwa cheo!* Congratulations on being promoted!

hongez.a vt reward, recompense, prize; give sby a present for an achievement made: *Alimhongeza kwa kumwokotea kikoba chake*, she rewarded him for finding her purse. Prep. *hongez.e.a* St. *hongez.ek.a* Ps. *hongez.w.a* Rp. *hongez.an.a* (cf *zawadia*, *tunza*, *tuza*)

hongo[1] n (n) 1. customary presents given to local chiefs in the former Tanganyika for permission to pass through 2. bribe, kickback. (cf *chai*, *rushwa*) 3. money paid to seduce a woman: *Ingawa msichana alipewa hongo, alikataa katakata*, even though the girl was given money to seduce her, she refused it completely.

hongo[2] n (n) (*zool*) green Mamba snake. *Dendroaspis angusticeps*.

hongo

hongwe n (n) (*zool*) catfish; a kind of scaleless fish (family *Ariidae*) with long barbels and usu with sharp spines. (cf *fumi*)

honi n (n) 1. horn; an apparatus usu fixed to a car or bicycle and used for sounding a warning signal: *Alipiga honi ya gari kwa nguvu*, he blew the horn of the car forcefully. 2. hoot; sound made by a vehicle's horn. 3. siren, honk: *Honi ya polisi*, police siren. *Honi ya ambulansi*, an ambulance siren. (cf *king'ora*, *sero*) (Eng)

honoraria *n* (*n*) honorarium (cf *sharafu*) (Eng)

honyo.a *vt* eat food lavishly because it is free of charge; eat food lavishly without payment: *Alivihonyoa vyakula kochokocho*, he helped himself to a variety of dishes free of charge. Prep. ***honyo.le.a*** St. ***honyo.lek.a*** Cs. ***honyo.lesh.a*** Ps. of Prep. ***honyo.lew.a*** Rp *honyo.an.a*

honza *n* (*n*) an arrow whose shaft is made from a stalk of millet and with a sharpened wooden head.

horera (also *holela*) (*adj*) 1. gratuitously, free of charge: *Masikini alipewa chakula horera*, the poor man was given food free of charge. (cf *bwerere*) 2. awry, disorderly: *Mipango yake ilikwenda horera*, her plans went awry. (cf *segemnege*, *shelabela*, *ovyoovyo*)

hori[1] *n* (*n*) bay, gulf, creek, inlet; arm of the sea: *Meli ilipita kwenye hori*, the ship passed through the gulf. (cf *ghuba*)

hori[2] *n* (*n*) (*naut*) a kind of a canoe, with raised stem and stern; a ship's boat; dingy. (cf *dingi*, *mtumbwi*)

hori[3] *n* (*n*) a vessel for feeding animals.

hospitali (also *spitali*) *n* (*n*) hospital, clinic. (Eng)

hosteli *n* (*n*) 1. hostel, boarding school. (cf *dakhalia*, *bweni*) 2. boarding-house, guest-house, motel, lodging.

hostie *n* (*n*) (in Christianity) host; the bread that is blessed and eaten at Holy Communion: *Hostie takatifu*, sacred host.

hot.a *vt* 1. treat a woman so that she bears children: *Mganga alimhota mwanamke mmoja ili apate kuzaa*, the medicineman treated a woman so that she could bear children. 2. treat a child medically so that his teeth grow quickly: *Alimhota mtoto ili meno yake yaweze kuota upesi*, he treated the child so that his teeth could grow fast. Prep. ***hot.i.a*** St. ***hot.ik.a*** Cs. ***hot.ish.a*** Ps. ***hot.w.a*** Rp of Prep. ***hot.e.an.a***

hoteli *n* (*n*) 1. restaurant, hotel, inn, motel: *Hoteli ya anasa*, luxury hotel. 2. guest house, hospice, boarding house.

hoto *n* (*n*) 1. local medicine used for treating a woman so as to conveive; fertility medicine. 2. local medicine used to treat a child so that his teeth grow. (cf *hoza*)

hotuba (also *hutuba*) *n* (*n*) speech, address: *Alitoa hotuba ya ufasaha*, he gave an eloquent speech. (cf *mawaidha*)

hovyo see *ovyo*

howa[1] *interj* an expletive used to sooth a child which is crying; hush! Quiet!

howa[2] *n* (*n*) (*zool*) domesticated animals that are suitable for charity purposes.

hoza *n* (*n*) herbal medicine prepared for children who are teething.

hozahoz.a *vt*, *vi* comfort someone who has undergone some problems; assuage, placate, sooth: *Alinihozahoza baada ya kusikia kwumba nimefiwa*, he comforted me after learning that I had been bereaved. Prep. ***hozahoz.i.a*** St. ***hozahoz.ik.a*** Ps. ***hozahoz.w.a*** Rp ***hozahoz.an.a*** (cf *liwaza*)

hua *n* (*n*) (*zool*) red-eye dove; a kind of brownish-grey dove (family Columbidae) with a black collar on the hindneck. *Streptopelia semitorquata*.

huba *n* (*n*) 1. love, romance, affection: *Huba zake kwa mkewe hazielezeki*, his love for his wife is beyond description. (cf *mapenzi*, *nyonda*) 2. nepotism, favouritism: *Meneja ana huba kwa wafanyakazi wa kabila lake*, the manager favours workers of his tribe. (cf *hatinafsi*, *upendeleo*) (Ar)

hubir.i *vt*, *vi* 1. preach, evangelize:

Alihubiri kwa ufasaha na kuweza kuwavutia waumini wengi, he preached eloquently and managed to attract many faithfuls. 2. lecture, talk: *Alihubiri juu ya uhusiano wa kimataifa*, he lectured on international relations. 3. advocate, support: *Mwanasiasa alihubiri chuki kwenye matamshi yake*, the politician advocated hatred in his utterances, Prep. *hubir.i.a* St. *hubir.ik.a* Cs. *hubir.ish.a* Ps. of Prep *hubir.iw.a* Rp. of Prep. *hubir.i.an.a* (Ar)

hududi[1] *n* (*n*) (*math*) range; the set of distinct values that may be taken on by any given function.

hududi[2] *n* (*n*) condition (cf *sharti*)

hudihudi *n* (*n*) (*zool*) hoopoe; a kind of bird (family *Pupidae*) with a long curved bill and an erectile crest. (Ar)

hudhuri.a *vt* attend, be present at, go to: *Alihudhuria kikao cha dharura*, he attended an emergency session. St. *hudhur.i.a* Cs. *hudhur.ish.a* Ps. *hudhur.iw.a* (cf *fika, wasili*) (Ar)

hudhurio *n* (*ma-*) attendance, presence: *Hudhurio lake la darasani lilimfurahisha mwalimu*, his attendance in the class pleased the teacher. (Ar)

hudhurish.a *vt* present, submit: *Balozi alihudhurisha karatasi zake mbele ya rais*, the ambassador presented his papers before the president. Prep. *hudhurish.i.a* St. *hudhurish.ik.a* Ps. *hudhurish.w.a* Rp *hudhurish.an.a*

hudhurungi *n* (*n*) 1. light brown colour; tan, puce. 2. light brown cotton cloth used for making *kanzu* e.g. *Hudhurungi madafu, Hudhurungi maskati*. (Ar)

huduma *n* (*n*) service, aid, assistance; *Huduma ya kwanza*, first aid. *Huduma za umma*, public utility. *Huduma muhimu*, important service. *Huduma teleksi*, telex service. 2. subsistence needs. (Ar)

hudum.u *vt* service, serve, attend to. Prep. *hudum.i.a* St. *hudum.ik.a* Cs. *hudum.ish.a* Ps. of Prep. *hudum.iw.a* Rp of Prep. *hudum.i.an.a* (cf *tumikia*) (Ar)

huenda *adv* probably, perhaps, mayhap, maybe: *Huenda mjomba akafika kesho*, perhaps my uncle will arrive tomorrow. (cf *labda, pengine*)

hueni *n* (*n*) see *ahueni*

hu.i *vt* revive, resuscitate, animate; rise from the dead: St. *hu.ik.a* Cs. *hu.ish.a* Ps. of Prep. *hu.iw.a* Rp. of Prep. *hu.i.an.a* (cf *baathi, fufua*)

huish.a *vt* rise from the dead; resuscitate, reanimate. 2. revive, renew: *Lazima tuuhuishe uchumi wetu*, we must revive our economy. Prep. *huish.i.a* St. *huish.ik.a* Ps. *huish.w.a* Prep. of Prep. *huish.i.an.a* (cf *fufua, endeleza*)

hujaji *n* (*ma-*) (in Islam) a pilgrim of Mecca; a person who travels to Mecca to perform a pilgrimage. (Ar)

hujambo[1] *verb form* How are you? Are you well? The word *hujambo* is used to salute someone in order to know the condition of his health.

hujambo[2] *n* (*n*) (of health) improvement, progress: *Mgonjwa wake amepata hujambo*, his patient's health has improved. (cf *afueni, ashekali*)

hujuma *n* (*n*) attack, onslaught, assault: *Adui alifanya hujuma yetu sisi wakati wa usiku*, the enemy carried out an attack against us at night. (cf *shambulio, vamio*) (Ar)

hujum.u *vt, vi* 1. attack, invade, assault, raid: *Waliihujumu nchi yetu kwa kutupa makombora*, they attacked our country by missiles. (cf *shambulia*) 2. sabotage, subvert, undermine. Prep. *hujum.i.a* St. *hujum.ik.a* Cs. *hujum.ish.a* Ps. of Prep. *hujum.iw.a* Rp of Prep. *hujum.i.an.a* (cf *vuruga, fisidi*) (Ar)

huka *n* (*n*) 1. bellows; a device used by goldsmiths and silversmiths for blowing fires. 2. see *hoko*.

huko[1] *adv* used as a demonstrative marker of nonproximity to indicate the dimension of "indefiniteness"; there: *Anaishi huko*, he lives there.

huko² *pron Huko kuna nyoka*, over there, there are snakes.

huku¹ *adv* used as a demonstrative marker of proximity to indicate the dimension of "definiteness"; *Amekuja huku sasa hivi*, he has come on this side just now.

huku² *pron* here, on this side; hereabouts.

huku³ *conj* while, meanwhile; of an action performed simultaneously: *Alikuja huku akilia*, she came while crying.

hukum.u¹ *vt, vi* 1. judge, adjudge, adjudicate, try; listen to litigation and pass a sentence: *Hakimu aliihukumu kesi kwa uadilifu*, the judge tried the case impartially. 2. decide; exercise authority, rule, etc.: *Rais anawahukumu ratu wote nchini*, the president exercises full authority over all the citizens in the country. Prep. **hukum.i.a** St. **hukum.ik.a** Cs. **hukum.ish.a** and **hukum.iz.a** Ps. of Prep. **hukum.iw.a** Rp of Prep. **hukum.i.an.a** (Ar)

hukumu² *n (n)* 1. judgement, sentence. (cf *maamuzi, utatuzi*) 2. order, command, regulation, authority: *Hukumu ya serikali*, government's order. *Mwenye hukumu*, the person with authority. (Ar)

hulka (also *huluka*) *n (n)* character, temperament: *Ana hulka mbaya*, he has a bad character. (cf *desturi, mwenendo*) (Ar)

hul.u *vt, vi* stop, cease: *Amehulu kuja hapa*, he has stopped coming here. Prep. **hul.i.a** St. **hul.ik.a** Cs. **hul.ish.a** (cf *acha, koma*) (Ar)

huluka see *hulka*

huluk.u *vt* (of God) create: *Mwenyezi Mungu amehuluku viumbe vyote*, God has created all creatures. Prep. **huluk.i.a** St. **huluk.ik.a** Ps. of Prep. **huluk.iw.a**

hulut.i *vt* mix, blend, compound. Prep. **hulut.i.a** St. **hulut.ik.a** Cs. **hulut.ish.a** Ps. of Prep. **hulut.iw.a** Rp of Prep. **hulut.i.an.a** (cf *changanya*)

humo¹ *adv* used as a demonstrative marker of nonproximity to indicate the dimension of "withinness"; inside, there, in that place, in there: *Panya ameingia humo*, the rat has gone in there.

humo² *pron* in there, there inside: *Humo mna maji*, there is water in there.

humra *n (n)* (*med*) a) menorrhagia; abnormally heavy and prolonged menstrual periods. b) polynomerrhoea; the occurrence of menstrural circles of greater than usual frequency.

humu¹ *adv* used as a demonstrative marker of proximity to indicate the dimension of "withinness"; inside here, in this place: *Mjusi ameingia humu*, the lizard has gone in here.

humu² *pron* inside here, in this place. *Humu mna magunia*, there are sacks in here.

humusi *n (n)* one fifth: *Humusi ya wanavijiji hawakupiga kura*, one fifth of the villagers did not vote. (Ar)

hunde *adj* hideous, unhandsome.

hundi *n (n)* cheque: *Hundi za wasafiri*, travellers' cheques. *Kitabu cha hundi*, cheque book. *Hundi za posta*, postal orders. *Funga hundi*, cross a cheque. (cf *hawala, cheki*)

hun.i *vt, vi* 1. desert, abandon: *Amekihuni kijiji chake*, he has abandoned his village. 2. be vagabond, be disobedient: *Mvulana yule amehuni siku hizi*, that boy has become a vagabond these days. 3. wander about aimlessly; roam; range; rove: *Amekuwa anahuni mitaani sasa kwa vile alifukuzwa kazini*, he is now roaming about in the neighbourhood because he was dismissed from work. (cf *zurura*) 4. rebel, defect, renege, betray: *Alikuwa katika chama chetu cha siasa lakini sasa amekihuni*, he belonged to our political party before but now he has abandoned it. (cf *asi, halifu*) 5. leave off going, coming, etc.; cease, stop:

Amehuni kuja nyumbani kwangu, he has ceased coming to my home. Prep. **hun.i.a** St. **hun.ik.a** Cs. **hun.ish.a** Ps. of Prep. **hun.iw.a** (cf *acha*)

huntha *n* (*n*) bisexual, hermaphrodite; a person or animal having both male and female organs. (Ar)

huree *interj* an expletive of applause; hurray. (cf *riboribo*)

huri see *huru*

huria[1] *n* (*n*) freedom, liberty; permission to do as one wishes: *Amempa binti yake huria na sasa anahukumu na kufanya atakalo*, she has given her daughter complete freedom and now she does as she wishes. (cf *uhuru*) (Ar)

huria[2] *adj* free, liberated: *Anajifanya yeye mtu huria*, she makes herself a free person. (Ar)

huru[1] (also *huri*) *adj* (of a country) free, liberated, independent: *Nchi iko huru*, the country is free. (Ar)

huru[2] *adj* (of slave, etc.) emancipated, free: *Mtumwa huru*, a free slave.

hurulaini *n* (*ma-*) sylph, houri, pure-eyed virgins; the beautiful nymph of paradise. (Ar)

huruma *n* (*n*) compassion, mercy, sympathy; consideration, soft-heartedness: *Kiongozi yule hana huruma*, that leader is merciless. (cf *imani, kite, upole*) (Ar)

hurumi.a *vt, vi* have mercy on, have pity on; pity: *Niliwahurumia sana wale majeruhi kwenye ajali ya ndege*, I pitied very much the casualties of the plane crash. St. **hurumi.k.a** Ps. **hurumi.w.a** Rp **hurumi.an.a** (cf *awaza, sikitika*) (Ar)

hurunzi *n* (*n*) see *kurunzi*

husik.a *vt* 1. be involved in, be concerned with: *Anahusika na kashfa ile*, he is involved in that scandal. 2. be applicable, apply. Prep. **husik.i.a** Rp **husik.an.a**

husikan.a *vi husikana na*, be concerned with, be relevant to: *Mtu yule hahusikani hata chembe*, that person is not concerned at all. Prep. **husikan.i.a**

husish.a *vt* integrate, associate, link, connect: *Usihusishe vitu hivi kwa vile viko tofauti*, don't associate these two things as they are quite different. Prep. **husish.i.a** St. **husish.ik.a** Ps. **husish.w.a** Rp **husish.an.a** (cf *fungamanisha, nasibisha*)

husisho *n* (*n*) (*math*) function: *Husisho endelevu*, continuous function. *Husisho piabambo*, hyperbolic function. *Husisho polinomia*, polynomial function. *Husisho wiano*, rational function. *Husisho ambatika*, one-to-one function.

hus.u[1] *vt, vi* 1. (of blood relationship) be related: *Ananihusu*, he is related to me. 2. concern, relate to, pertain to: *Mambo yale hayanihusu*, those matters don't concern me. Prep. **hus.i.a** St. **hus.ik.a** Cs. **hus.ish.a** Rp of Prep. **hus.i.an.a** (Ar)

hus.u[2] *vt, vi* give share, apportion. Prep. **hus.i.a** St. **hus.ik.a** Cs. **hus.ish.a** Ps. of Prep. **hus.iw.a** Rp of Prep **hus.i.an.a** (Ar)

husuda (also *uhasidi*) *n* (*n*) jealousy, envy, enviousness: *Ana husuda sana kwa wale wanaopata ufanisi*, he harbours envy towards those who are successful. (cf *choyo, wivu, kijicho*) (Ar)

husud.i *vt, vi* see *husudu*

husud.u (also *husudi*) 1. envy, begrudge, be jealous of. 2. admire, esteem, laud, extol; be mad about: *Marafiki wanalihusudu gari langu jekundu jipya*, my friends admire my new red car. *Wanamhusudu msichana yule*, they admire that girl. Prep. **husud.i.a** St. **husud.ik.a** Cs. **husud.ish.a** Ps. of Prep. **husud.iw.a** Rp of Prep. **husud.i.an.a** (cf *penda, sifu*) (Ar)

husuma *n* (*n*) feud, enmity, quarrel: *Husuma kati yake na mkewe sasa imewatenganisha*, the enmity between him and his wife has now estranged them. (cf *uadui, ugomvi, mzozo*) (Ar)

husum.u vt, vi see *hasimu*
husuni[1] n (n) fort, citadel, castle: *Tulijenga husuni dhidi ya maadui*, we built the fort against the enemies. (cf *ngome, buruji*)
husuni[2] n (n) virtuousness, goodness: *Husuni khatima*, good ending of one's life.
husur.u vt, vi 1. siege, blockade, encompass, surround: *Adui aliuhusuru mji wote*, the enemy besieged the whole town. 2. oppress, persecute. Prep. *husur.i.a* St. *husur.ik.a* Cs. *husur.ish.a* Ps. of Prep. *husur.iw.a* Rp of Prep. *husur.i.an.a* (cf *zunguka, zingia*) (Ar)
hususa[1] (also *hususan*) adv exactly, especially, particularly: *Wao huuifuata hususan wanapokuwa na matatizo*, they come to me especially when they are in difficulties. (cf *hasa, zaidi*) (Ar)
hususa[2] (also *hususan*) adj special, exact, precise: *Yale ndiyo hususa maneno yake*, those are his exact words. (*hasa*)
hususan[1] adv see *hususa*[1]
hususan[2] adj see *hususa*[2]
hutuba n (n) see *hotuba*
hutubi.a vt, vi lecture on (to, etc.); *Mhadhiri aliwahutubia juu ya umasikini duniani*, the lecturer lectured on world poverty. Prep. *hutubi.li.a* St. *hutubi.k.a* Cs. *hutubi.sh.a* Ps. *hutubi.w.a* Rp *hutubi.an.a*
hutub.u vt, vi 1. lecture, address, talk, speak: *Alihutubu juu ya ukiritimba wa matajiri*, he lectured on the monopoly of the rich. (cf *hubiri, zungumza*) 2. (in Islam) preach; spread the word of God: *Shekhe atahutubia msikitini leo*, the cleric will preach in the mosque today.

Prep. *hutub.i.a* St. *hutub.ik.a* Cs. *hutub.ish.a* Ps. of Prep. *hutub.iw.a* Rp of Prep. *hutub.i.an.a* (Ar)
huu adj, pron used as a demonstrative marker of proximity for mi- and u- classes singular nouns; this: *Mwavuli huu*, this umbrella. *Ukuta huu*, this wall.
huwa verb form it is, it becomes, he is, she is, they are.
huyo adj, pron used as a demonstrative marker of nonproximity for wa- class singular nouns; that: *Mkulima huyo*, that farmer. *Mbwa huyo*, that dog.
huyu adj, pron used as a demonstrative marker of proximity for wa- class sing nouns; this: *Mtu huyu*, this person. *Huyu ana mkia mrefu*, this one has a long tail.
huzuni n (n) melancholy, grief, sorrow, distress, sadness, dejection. (cf *simanzi, majonzi, jitimai*) (Ar)
huzunik.a vi, vt 1. be grieving, be sorry, be distressed. (cf *sikitika*) 2. be humiliated, be disgraced. Prep. *huzunik.i.a* Cs. *huzun.ish.a*
huzunik.i.a vt bemoan, grieve for (at, about, etc.) St. *huzunik.ik.a* Cs. *huzunik.ish.a* Ps. *huzunik.iw.a*
huzunish.a vt, vi 1. sudden, depress, dishearten: *Kifo chake cha ghafla kilituhuzunisha*, his sudden death saddened us. (cf *sikitisha*) 2. disgrace, discredit, belittle: *Vitendo vyake viovu vinatuhuzunisha*, his evil deeds disgrace us. Prep. *huzunish.i.a* St. *huzunish.ik.a* Ps. *huzunish.w.a* Rp *huzunish.an.a* (cf *aibisha, fedhehesha*)

I

I, i /I/ 1. the ninth letter of the Swahili alphabet. 2. represents the sound of I or i̩ and is a high-front unrounded vowel.

ib.a *vt* steal, embezzle, pilfer, finger: *Wezi waliiba mali nyingi*, the thieves stole a lot of property. Prep. ***ib.i.a*** St. ***ib.ik.a*** Cs. ***ib.ish.a*** Ps. ***ib.w.a*** Rp. ***ib.an.a*** steal each other's property. Rp. of Prep. ***ib.i.an.a*** (cf *jepa, kwepua, pora, pokoa*)

ibada *n* (*n*) 1. religious worship; service: *Pale ni pahala pa kufanyia ibada*, that is a place of worship. 2. habit, custom, practice, fashion, style: *Imekuwa ibada kwake kuvuta sigara*, it has become a habit for him to smoke cigarettes. (cf *mazoea, hulka*) (Ar)

iban.a *vt* coquette; flirt secretly with sby's wife or husband or between a husband and a woman; commit adultery. (cf *zini*)

ibara *n* (*n*) paragraph, section, part, clause: *Soma ibara ya tano ya katiba*, read section five of the constitution. (cf *aya, kifungu*) (Ar)

ibilisi (*also bilisi*) *n* (*ma-*) 1. satan, devil. 2. an evil person, a vicious person; fiend, ogre, monster. (Ar)

ibra[1] (*also ibura*) *n* (*n*) 1. miracle, marvel; a supernatural event; sth wonderful: *Ilikuwa ibra kwa yeye kuokoka*, it was a miracle for him to escape. (cf *muujiza, shani, kioja, ajaa*) 2. lesson, advice, warning: *Ajali niliyoipata ilikuwa ibra kwangu*, the accident I had was a lesson to me. (cf *fundisho, somo* (Ar)

ibra[2] *n* (*n*) a drawing compass. (cf *bikari*) (Ar)

Ibrahimu *n* (*n*) (in Christianity) the first patriarch and ancestor of the Hebrews; (in Islam) the prophet and a close friend of Allah.

ibu.a *vt, vi* fish out; take out sth from the water. Prep. ***ibu.li.a*** St. ***ibu.k.a*** Cs. ***ibu.sh.a*** Ps. of Prep. ***ibu.liw.a***

ibuk.a[1] *vt, vi* see *ibua*

ibuk.a[2] *vt, vi* emerge, spring up, resurface: *Mwanasiasa ameibuka kutoka mafichoni*, the politician has resurfaced from hiding. *Timu iliibuka mshindi*, the team emerged as winners. Prep. ***ibuk.i.a*** St. ***ibuk.ik.a*** Cs. ***ibuk.ish.a***

ichengu *n* (*n*) (*naut*) boom of an outrigger canoe; a long pole that supports a sail in a canoe.

idadi *n* (*n*) total sum, total number: *Idadi ya wanawake*, the total number of women. (cf *jumla*) (Ar)

idara *n* (*n*) department, division, section: *Idara ya elimu*, department of education. *Idara ya misitu*, department of forestry. (cf *kitengo, sehemu*)

idhaa *n* (*n*) 1. radio broadcast: *Idhaa ya BBC*, radio broadcast from BBC. 2. radio station, broadcasting station; voice.

idhilali *n* (*n*) 1. tribulation, oppression, persecution: *Kuna idhilali nyingi duniani*, there is a lot of oppression in the world. (cf *mateso, dhiki*) 2. poverty, penury: *Maisha ya idhilali yamemkosesha raha*, the life of poverty has deprived him of happiness. (cf *umasikini, ufukara*) (Ar)

idhin.i[1] *vt, vi* permit, sanction, allow, assent to, authorize: *Ofisa wa uhamiaji aliidhini nipewe hati ya kusafiria*, the immigration officer authorized that I be given a passport. Prep. ***idhin.i.a*** St. ***idhin.ik.a*** Cs. ***idhin.ish.a***. Ps. of Prep. ***idhin.iw.a*** Rp. of Prep. ***idhin.i.an.a*** (cf *ruhusu*) (Ar)

idhini[2] *n* (*n*) consent, assent, permission: *Mzazi alitoa idhini ya kumwozesha binti yake*, the parent gave his consent for his daughter to be married. (cf *ridhaa, ruhusa, kibali*) (Ar)

idhinish.a[1] *vt see idhini*[1]

idhinish.a[2] *vt* permit, approve, assent, sanction, authorize: *Shekhe aliidhinisha ndoa yao*, the Sheik sanctioned their marriage. Prep. *idhinish.i.a* St. *idhinish.ik.a* Ps. *idhinish.w.a* Rp. *idhinish.an.a*

Idi *n* (*n*) Muslim Festival: *Idd ul Fitr* or *idi ndogo*, the festival after the end of the fasting month of Ramadan. *Idd ul Hajj* or *Idi Kubwa*, the festival to commemorate the religious festival after performing pilgrimage.

idili *n* (*n*) effort, diligence, industry: *Huonyesha lilli katika kazi yake*, he shows diligence in his work. (cf *bidii, jitihada*) (Ar)

idiogramu *n* (*n*) 1. ideogram; a graphic symbol representing an object or idea without expressing, as in a phonetic system, the sound that forms its name. 2. a symbol representing an idea rather than a word (Ex: 4,÷, +,)

ifaki *n* (*n*) reconvert; change.

ifu[1] (*ma-*) 1. ashes of burnt material. 2. residue, remnant, remainder. (cf *bakio, salio*)

ifu[2] *n* (*ma-*) usu prefixed ma- or bi (*Maifu, Biifu* or *Bimaifu*) a name of respect given to a lady of noble descendants of Prophet Muhammad.

ify.a *vt* vex, torment, provoke: *Mtoto aliwaifya wazee wake kwa utovu wa adabu*, the child displeased his parents for misbehaviour. Prep. *ify.i.a* St. *ify.ik.a* Cs. *ify.ish.a* (cf *chukiza*)

ig.a (also *igiza*) *vt* 1. copy, imitate, follow: *Ni vizuri kuiga matendo mazuri*, It is good to imitate good deeds. (cf *fuasa, fuata, geza*) 2. mimic, ape, monkey, parrot: *Yeye ni hodari wa kumwiga mwalimu wake anavyozungumza*, he is good at imitating the way his teacher talks. (*prov*) *Ukimwiga tembo kunya utapasuka mwaramba*, if you imitate an elephant how to defecate, the outlet of your shit will burst i.e if you imitate how others live, etc., you will eventually be in trouble. Prep. *ig.ia*. St. *ig.ik.a* Cs. *ig.iz.a* Ps. *ig.w.a* Rp. *ig.an.a* (cf *tabii, fuata*)

igiz.a *vt* imitate, impersonate: *Mchezo wa kuigiza*, play. Prep. *igiz.i.a* St. *igiz.ik.a* Cs. *igiz.ish.a* Ps. *igiz.w.a* Rp *igiz.an.a*

igizo *n* (*ma-*) imitation, drama, dramatization, play: *Sanaa ya maigizo*, play.

igrotati *n* (*n*) 1. aegrotat; a certificate stating that a university student is too ill to attend an examination. 2. a degree or other qualification obtained in such circumstances; aegrotat. (Eng)

ihiramu *n* (*n*) 1. garments of the pilgrim, one of the two seamless clothes usu white, worn by Muslim pilgrims from the shoulder and the other to the waist and to the legs when performing pilgrimage in Mecca esp during the days of "Minna" and "Arafat" when goats and sheep are slaughtered. 2. an intention to perform pilgrimage either during the major one or during the minor one i.e. *Umra* (Ar)

ihisani *n* (*n*) see *hisani*

ijapo (also *japo*) *conj* although, albeit, notwithstanding: *Yeye ni mkarimu ijapo masikini*, he is generous though poor. (cf *ingawa, ijapokuwa*)

ijapokuwa *conj* even if, though: *Ijapokuwa gari langu ni kongwe, lakini linaweza kukimbia*, although my car is old, it can run fast. (cf *ingawa, ijapo*)

ijara *n* (*n*) 1. (in Islam) payment given to a person to perform a pilgrimage or to fast or to say prayers on behalf of a deceased person. 2. wages, payment: *Nilimpa fundibomba ijara kunitengenezea mfereji wangu*, I paid the plumber his charges for repairing my tap. 3. wharfage, port dues, port

I ijaza

fees: *Watalii walitoa ijara kwa kutia nanga bandarini,* the tourists paid the port dues at the harbour. (Ar)

ijaza (also *ijazi*) *n* (*n*) permission to do sth esp of religious nature; consent, authority: *Amepewa ijaza ya kufasiri vitabu vya dini kwa Kiswahili,* he has been given authority to translate theological works into Kiswahili. (cf *kibali, ruhusa, idhini*) (Ar) 2. acknowledgement

ijazi *n* (*n*) an ecstasy to do sth of religious nature. (Ar)

Ijumaa *adv, n* (*n*) Friday: *Ijumaa Kuu,* Good Friday. *Swala ya Ijumaa,* Friday prayers. (Ar)

ik.a[1] *vt* put sth, somewhere; place, set, lay: *Aliwiika vikombe juu ya rafu,* he put the cups on the shelf. Prep. ***ik.i.a***, St. ***ik.ik.a***, Cs. ***ik.ish.a*** and ***ik.iz.a*** e.g. *Aliniikisha vitabu mezani,* he made me put the books on the table. Ps. ***ik.w.a*** Rp. of Prep. ***ik.i.an.a*** (cf *weka, tua*)

ik.a[2] *vi* see *wika.* Prep. ***ik.i.a*** St. ***ik.ik.a***

ikabu *n* (*n*) punishment, penalty, retribution: *Ukiwafanyia maovu wenzako, utapata ikabu kwa Mwenyezi Mungu,* if you do evil to others, you will suffer divine retribution. (cf *rada, taabu, adhabu, malipo*) (Ar)

ikama[1] *n* (*n*) (in Islam) a second calling usu by a muezzin to begin prayers. (Ar)

ikama[2] *n* (*n*) resident permit; permission to stay in a foreign country for a specified period: *Amepata ikama,* she has got her resident's permit. (cf *viza*) (Ar)

ikama[3] *n* (*n*) requirements/needs to maintain a family. (Ar)

ikhlasi *n* (*n*) 1. integrity, probity, rectitude, honesty, sincerity: *Ikhlasi ni sifa njema,* sincerity is a virtue. *Tulimpa pongezi zetu za ikhlasi kwa kufaulu kwake kwenye mtihani,* we gave him our sincere congratulations for his success in the examination. (cf

iko

unyofu, ususuani, ukweli) 2. the name of the chapter 112 of the Holy Koran describing the oneness of God. (Ar)

ikibali *n* (*n*) 1. permission, consent, assent, sanction: *Waliingia kwenye kiwanja bila ya ikibali ya mwenyewe,* they entered the grounds without the owner's permission. 2. endorsement, acceptability. (cf *ridhaa, ruhusa*) (Ar)

ikirahi (also *ikrahi*) *n* (*n*) disgust, odium, displeasure, dislike: *Alionyesha ikirahi yake juu ya mipango yetu,* he showed that he was displeased with our plans. (cf *chukizo*) (Ar)

ikirari[1] (also *ikrari*) *n* (*n*) 1. confession, admission: *Ikirari yake juu ya mauaji yalimpeleka gerezani,* his confession of the murder sent him to prison. (cf *ungamo*) 2. word of confession. 3. proof, evidence, verification, validation: *Kuna ikirari yoyote kwamba dunia ni mviringo?* Is there any proof that the world is round? (cf *ushahidi, yakini, uthibitisho*) (Ar)

ikirari[2] *n* (*n*) certainty, assurance, surety: *Hana ikirari kama atasafiri kesho,* he is not sure if he will travel tomorrow. (cf *ushahidi, uhakika*) (Ar)

ikisiri *n* (*n*) elaboration, analysis. (cf *ufafanuzi, sherehe*)

ikitisadi *n* (*n*) see *iktisadi*

ikiwa *conj* if, in case: *Ikiwa atapata kazi, ataniarifu,* if he gets a job, he will inform me. (cf *kama, pindipo, iwapo, endapo*)

ikiz.a *vt, vi* lay across, spread over, set in position from side to side, place across: *Waliikiza boriti katika dari yangu,* they placed the beams across my ceiling. 2. arrange (cf *panga*) Prep. ***ikiz.i.a*** St. ***ikiz.ik.a*** Cs. ***ikiz.ish.a*** Ps. ***ikiz.w.a*** Rp. of Prep. ***ikiz.i.an.a***

iko *verb form* it is, there are. This verb form refers to the n class singular. and mi- class pl nouns e.g. *Kengele iko mezani,* the bell is on the table. *Mikate iko hapa,* the loaves are here.

238

ikoje (*interj*) (with reference to work, etc.) How is it? How does it go?

ikolojia *n* (*n*) ecology; the study of relationships between living organisms and their environment. (Eng)

ikrahi *n* (*n*) see *ikirahi*

iktisadi (also *ikitisadi*) *n* (*n*) 1. economics: *Iktisadi ya kilimo*, agricultural economics. *Iktisadi ya elimu*, economics of education. *Iktisadi ya nchi*, a country's economy. (cf *uchumi, pato*) 2. frugality, thrift. (Ar)

ikulu *n* (*n*) 1. state house: 2. a gigantic building; mansion: *Matajiri wengi wanaishi katika ikulu*, many rich people live in mansions. (cf *kasri*) (Kinyam)

ikwinoksi *n* (*n*) equinox (Eng)

ikweta *n* (*n*) equator: (cf *istiwai*) (Eng)

ila[1] *conj* except, save, with the exception of: *Majirani wote walikuja mazikoni ila yeye*, all the neighbours came for the funeral except him. (cf *thama, isipokuwa*) (Ar)

ila[2] *n* (*n*) 1. defect, weak point, weakness: *Yeye ni kijana mzuri lakini ana ila zake*, he is a good young man but he has his weaknesses. (*prov*) *Kizuri hakikosi ila*, a good thing never possesses its defects. (cf *dosari, kasoro*) 2. (*phon*) *Ila matamshi*, speech defect, speech disorder. (Ar)

ile *adj, pron* a demonstrative marker of non-proximity for n- class sing and mi- class pl nouns; that, those: *Kengele ile*, that bell. *Mikoba ile*, those bags. *Ile si yako*, that is not yours.

Ilahi *n* (*n*) Almighty God: *Mwenye kumwamini Ilahi, huomba maghufira kutoka kwake*, he who believes in God asks for mercy from him. (cf *Mwenyezi-Mungu, Mola*) (Ar)

ilani (also *elani*) *n* (*n*) 1. warning, notice, summon: *Ilani ya serikali*, government notice. (cf *tangazo*) 2. manifesto: *Ilani ya chama*, party manifesto. *Ilani ya uchaguzi*, election manifesto. (Ar)

ilhali (also *ilihali, hali*) *conj* while, on the contrary: *Mbona ulikwenda mjini ilhali ulijua kwamba kulikuwa hakuna mtu yeyote nyumbani?* Why did you go to town while you knew that there was nobody at home? (Ar)

ilhamu *n* (*n*) afflatus; divinely inspired intuition; the ability to recognize issues through God's inspiration: *Hiyo ni ilhamu kutoka kwa Mwenyezi Mungu*, that is divinely inspired intuition. (Ar)

ili *conj* in order that, so that: *Alikuja nyumbani kwangu ili apate kuonana na mimi*, he came to my house so that he could see me. (cf *kusudi*)

ilihali *conj* see *ilhali*

iliki (also *hiliki*) *n*(*n*) (*bot*) cardamom; a kind of cultivated seed used in medicine and as a kind of spice in making curries, cooking rice, etc. (Hind)

ilimradi (also *almuradi, mradi*) *conj* provided, on condition that, as long as: *Wanaweza kuazima gari langu ilimradi wanalitunza*, they can borrow my car provided they take care of it.

ilimu *n* (*n*) see *elimu*

iliy.a *vt* visit. Prep. **iliy.i.a** St. **iliy.ik.a** Cs. **iliy.ish.a** Ps. of Prep. **iliy.iw.a** Rp **iliy.an.a**

im.a[1] *vi* stand up, get up, rise to one's feet: *Ima mbele yangu*, stand in front of me. Prep. **im.i.a** St. **im.ik.a** Cs. **im.ish.a** Ps. **im.w.a** (cf *inuka*) (Ar)

im.a[2] *conj* see *ama*

imafaima *adj* come what may; let it be: *Kule kuna hatari lakini mimi nitakwenda imafaima*, there is danger there, but come what may, I will go.

imamu *n* (*n*) 1. Imam; the leader of a prayer in a mosque. 2. Imam; any of the various Muslim leaders and rulers e.g. *Imam Shafi*.

imani *n* (*n*) 1. faith, belief, creed, confidence: *Raia hawana imani na serikali yao*, the citizens have no faith in their government. *Imani potofu*, misguided belief. 2. ideology. 3. compassion, piety, sympathy, mercy: *Lazima umwonee imani rafiki yako*, you must show sympathy to your friend. (cf *huruma, upole*) (Ar)

imara[1] *n (n)* strength, firmness, stability: *Jeshi letu ni imara*, our armed forces are in a firm state. (cf *umadhubuti*) (Ar)

imara[2] *adj* 1. rigid, firm, strong, stable, solid: *Nchi yetu iko imara*, our country is stable. (cf *madhubuti, thabiti*). 2. true, veritable, accurate: *Habari ile ni imara*, that information is accurate. (cf *sahihi*) (Ar)

imarik.a *vi* be firm, be solid, be strong: *Jeshi letu limeimarika*, our armed forces have become strong. Prep. **imarik.i.a** St. **imarik.ik.a** Cs. **imarik.ish.a** (cf *tengenea, stawi*) (Ar)

imarish.a *vt* 1. strengthen, consolidate, make firm: *Mfalme anataka kuimarisha utawala wake*, the king wants to consolidate his rule. (cf *kuza, neemesha*) (cf *dumisha, stawisha*) 2. make sth last longer or prosperous. Prep. **imarish.i.a** St. **imarish.ik.a** Ps. **imarish.w.a** Rp. **imarish.an.a** (Ar)

imb.a *vt, vi* chant, sing: *Anaimba vizuri*, she sings well. *Imba kwa madoido*, yodel. Prep. **imb.i.a** St. **imb.ik.a** Cs. **imb.ish.a** Ps. **imb.w.a** Rp. **imb.an.a**

imbisha *vt* cause singing, direct singing. Prep. **imbish.i.a** St. **imbish.ik.a** Ps. **imbish.w.a** Rp. **imbish.an.a**

imbua *vt* see *limbua*

imla *n (n)* dictation (Ar)

inadi *n (n)* perversity, provocation, pique, vexation: *Usinifanyie inadi mara kwa mara*, don't show perversity towards me so often. (cf *inda*) (Ar)

inam.a *vi* 1. bend forwards, lean forward; crouch, stoop, slope: *Inama na okota pesa zako*, stoop and pick up your money (cf *nema, furama*) 2. be stunned, be astounded: *Aliinama baada ya kuhukumiwa kifungo cha maisha*, he was stunned after being sentenced to life imprisonment. 3. obey, respect, comply. (*prov*) *Mtaka cha mwunguni sharti ainame*, whoever wants to succeed in any activity e.g. business, studies, etc., must be prepared to work hard. Prep. **inam.i.a** St. **inam.ik.a** Cs. **inam.ish.a** Ps. of Prep. **inam.i.w.a** Rp of Prep. **inam.i.an.a**

inami.a *vi* 1. stoop; bend to show humility: *Mtumishi alimwinamia bwana wake*, the servant stooped before his master. 2. depend, rely. *Familia nzima inamwinamia yeye*, the whole family depends on him. 3. feel sad, be dejected, be low-spirited: *Alijiinamia baada ya kukataliwa kufanya uchumba na msichana mrembo*, he felt sad after being rejected to make courtship with a beautiful girl. St. **inami.k.a** Cs. **inami.sh.a** Ps. **inami.w.a** Rp **inami.an.a**

inamish.a *vt* tilt, slope, incline: *Inamisha chombo hicho ili niweze kutia mafuta*, tilt that vessel so that I can pour oil in it. Prep. **inamish.i.a** St. **inamish.ik.a** Ps. **inamish.w.a** Rp **inamish.an.a**

inchi *n (n)* inch (Eng)

inda *n (n)* 1. fussiness, pestering, fretting: *Mkwe wangu ana inda sana*, my in-law is given to a lot of pestering. (cf *inadi, kero*) 2. spite, grasping, insensitivity; unconcern for others: *Majirani wanamsema sana bibi yule kwa sababu ya inda zake*, the neighbours speak ill of that lady because of her spite.

inde *n (n)* (*bot*) guinea grass; a perennial tussock grass up to five feet tall, sometimes used for thatching, and the inflorescences are made into hand brooms. *Panicum maximum.*

inde

indhari *n (n)* warning, caution, admonition, precaution: *Amepata indhari kutoka kwa mwajiri wake*, he has received a warning from his employer. (cf *onyo, tahadhari*) (Ar)

indiketa *n (n)* indicator (Eng)

inesha *n (n)* inertia (Eng)

ing.a[1] *vt* drive away esp birds, chase. Prep. *ing.i.a* St. *ing.ik.a* Cs. *ing.ish.a* Ps. of Prep. *ing.iw.a* Rp. of Prep. *ing.i.an.a* (cf *winga*)

ing.a[2] *vt, vi* pass at a place without any definite purpose. Prep. *ing.i.a* St. *ing.ik.a* Cs. *ing.ish.a* Ps. of Prep. *ing.iw.a* Rp *ing.an.a*

ingawa *conj* even if, although, albeit, though, supposing that: *Ingawa kulinyesha sana jana, tuliweza kutoka nje*, though it rained heavily yesterday, we managed to go out. (cf *ingawaje, ijapokuwa*)

ingawaje *conj* even if, although. (cf *ingawa, ijapokuwa*)

-ingi *adj* much, many, copious, abundant. *Ana kazi nyingi*, he has a lot of work.

ingi.a *vt, vi* 1. enter, go in, get in, come in: *Aliingia chumbani kwa haraka*, he entered the room hurriedly. 2. join, unite, associate: *Utaingia katika chama chetu?* Will you join our party? 3. penetrate, pierce, pass through: *Mwiba uliingia unyayoni mwake*, the thorn pierced through his foot. (cf *penya, bokoa, pita*) 4. tumble, fall into: *Panya aliingia mtegoni*, the rat fell into the trap. 5. participate, take part in, engage in: *Ameingia katika shughuli za uvuvi siku hizi*, he is engaged in fishing activities these days. 6. (*idms*) *Ingia hasara*, make a loss. *Ingia nyumbani*, consummate. *Ingia ubia*, enter into partnership. *Ingia mwakani*, start a new year. *Ingia mwezini*, menstruate; discharge blood, etc from the uterus, usu once a month. *Ingia mafa*, inherit the deceased brother's wife property. *Ingia bahari si yako*, try things you cannot cope with. Prep. *ingi.li.a* St. *ingi.lik.a* Cs. *ingi.z.a* Ps. *ingi.w.a* Rp. *ingi.an.a*

ingili.a *vt, vi* 1. meddle, interfere, intervene, intrude: *Kwa nini unaingilia mambo ya watu wengine?* Why are you meddling in other people's affairs? (cf *jidukiza, jipenyeza*) 2. arbitrate, reconcile, mediate, settle, intervene, negotiate: *Mzee yule aliingilia ugomvi kati ya mke na mume*, that old man intervened in the dispute between husband and wife. (cf *suluhisha, patanisha*) 3. intervene, arrest: *Aliyaingilia kati mambo yetu na kuyasuluhisha*, he intervened in our affairs and settled them. 4. have sexual intercourse: *Ingilia mwanamke*, have sexual intercourse with a woman. St. *ingili.k.a* Ps. *ingili.w.a* Rp *ingili.an.a*

ingilian.a *vt* 1. interact; *Wanafunzi lazima waingiliane na walimu*, students must interact with teachers. 2. be connected, be related: *Mambo haya yanaingiliana*, these issues are related.

-ingine *adj* 1. other, additional: *Watoto wengine*, other children. 2. another:

I ingiz.a   intifada

Nipe kitabu kingine, give me another book. 3. different, dissimilar: *Bora ununue kalamu nyingine,* it is better to buy a different pen.

ingiz.a *vt* 1. admit, let into: *Aliwaingiza wanafunzi wapya shuleni,* he admitted new students to the school. 2. import: *Mfanyabiashara ameingiza bidhaa kutoka Ujapani,* the businessman has imported goods from Japan. Prep. *ingiz.i.a* St. *ingiz.ik.a* Ps. *ingiz.w.a* Rp. *ingiz.an.a*

ingizo *n (ma-)* book entry.

ini *n (ma-) (anat)* liver. Also used in the meaning as *moyo,* heart. 2. *(idm) Maneno yake yananikata maini,* his words cut me to the heart.

inik.a *vt* 1. put down, rest, place: *Inika mzigo,* put down the load. *Inika gunia la viazi kwenye mkeka,* put a sack of potatoes down on the mat. 2. tilt, turn: *Inika kichwa,* tilt the head; hang down the head because of grief or shame. 3. bend down: *Inika tawi la mti,* bend down the branch of a tree in order to get the fruit. (cf *inamisha*) Prep. *inik.i.a* St. *inik.ik.a* Cs. *inik.iz.a* and *inik.ish.a* Ps. *inik.w.a* Rp. *inik.an.a*

injekta *n (n)* injector; a person or thing that injects, as a device for injecting fuel into a combustion chamber, etc. (Eng)

injik.a *vt* put a cooking pot, etc. on the fire or on the stove to cook; heat: *Injika chungu kwa vile moto ni mkali,* put the cooking pot on the fire because the fire is ready. Prep. *injik.i.a* St. *injik.ik.a* Cs. *injik.iz.a* Ps. *injik.w.a* Rp of Prep *injik.i.an.a*

Injili *n (n) (rel)* Gospel: *Injili ya kale,* Old Testament. (Ar)

injini *n (n)* engine: *Injini ya gari,* car engine. *Injini mvuke,* steam engine. *Injini joto,* heat engine. *Injini ya mwako wa ndani,* internal combustion engine. *Injini reli,* locomotive. *Injini ya dizeli,* diesel engine. (Eng)

injinia engineer: *Injinia wa umeme,* electrical engineer. *Injinia wa ujenzi,* civil engineer. (cf *mhandisi*) (Eng)

inkishafi *n (n)* 1. revelation; a disclosure of information by a person himself. (cf *udhihirishaji*) 2. the name of a famous classical Swahili epic. (Ar)

inna *n (n)* 1. a word borrowed from Arabic, used to emphasize a particular issue under discussion. 2. truth, fact, reality, actuality. (Ar)

insafu *n (n)* discipline, integrity, probity: *Fanya insafu,* show uprightness. *Kuwa na insafu,* have integrity. *Mtu yule hana insafu hata kidogo,* that person does not have any integrity at all. (cf *unyofu, ususuani*) (Ar)

insani (also *insi*) *n (n) (poet)* human being; a male or female. (cf *binaadamu, mtu, mahuluki*) (Ar)

insha *n (n)* essay, composition: *Insha ya kubuni,* situational composition. *Insha ya maelezo,* expository essay, descriptive essay. *Insha ya malumbano,* argumentative essay. (cf *utungo*) (Ar)

inshallah *adv* God willing. A common expression used usu by Muslims if they intend to do sth whether they are sure of the outcome or not. It carries the equivalent meaning of "If God wishes": *Inshallah, kesho nitasafiri,* if God wishes, I will travel tomorrow. (Ar)

insi (also *insani*) *n (n)* human being; a male or female. (cf *mwanadamu, binaadamu, mtu*)

inspekta (also *spekta*) *n (ma-)* inspector: *Inspekta wa polisi,* police inspector. (cf *mkaguzi, msimamizi, mwangalizi*) (Eng)

insulini *n (n)* insulin (Eng)

intidhamu *n (n)* discipline, order, control. (cf *nidhamu*) (Ar)

intifada *n (n)* rebellion, insurrection, uprising: *Wapalestina walifanya intifada dhidi ya utawala wa Kiyahudi,* the Palestinians organized a revolt against Jewish rule. (cf *upinzani, uasi*) (Ar)

inu.a *vt, vi* lift, raise, elevate, hoist, heave, raise up: *Inua mkono wako,* raise up your arm. *Inua hicho kiti,* lift that chair. Prep. **inu.li.a** St. **inu.k.a**, get up, stand up, e.g. *Inuka haraka,* stand up immediately. Cs. **inu.lish.a** Ps. **inu.liw.a**, be lifted, be carried e.g. *Aliinuliwa kwa vile mguu wake umeteteraka,* he was lifted because his leg got dislocated. Rp. **inu.an.a**, lift one another. (cf *nyanyua*)

inuka *vi* see *inua*

inuki.a *vt, vi* 1. tend to, become; seem, appear, look: *Anainukia kuwa mtoto mwenye akili,* he seems to becoming an intelligent child. (cf *kua, ondokea*) 2. begin to prosper, begin to flourish, rise up: *Ameinukia vizuri tangu kuingia katika biashara,* he has started to prosper since he entered business, (cf *stawi, ongokewa, chipukia*) 3. recover, convalesce, recuperate: *Shangazi yake sasa anainukia vizuri baada ya kuugua sana,* his aunt is now recovering well after a long illness. Prep. **inuki.li.a** St. **inuki.k.a** Cs. **inuki.sh.a** Rp **inuki.an.a** (cf *pongea, ondokea*) 4. increase in weight.

inz.a *vt, vi* seek, search, look for: *Mchungaji aliwatnzu ng'ombe wake waliopotea,* the herdsman looked for his lost cattle. 2. follow, go behind, go after: *Anawainza mbuzi wake,* he is following his goats. Prep. **inz.i.a** St. **inz.ik.a** Cs. **inz.ish.a** Ps. **inz.w.a** Rp. **inz.an.a** (cf *tafuta*) 3. (*syn*) Inza pumvi, relax, rest. (cf *pumzika*)

iodini *n* (*n*) (*chem*) iodine

ipi[1] *n* (*n*) the palm of the hand extended or upturned; slap. (cf *kibao, kofi*)

ipi[2] *n* (*n*) (*naut*) carved ornamental board on bows for a vessel above the eye and on the stern quarter.

ipi[3] *adj, pron* which, what: *Kitabu kipi?* Which book? *Kalamu ipi?* Which pen? *Kipi kinakukera?* What is bothering you?

irabu *n* (*n*) (*phon*) vowel. *Irabu nyuma,* back vowel. *Irabu funge,* blocked vowel, checked vowel. *Irabu msingi,* cardinal vowel. *Irabu kati,* central vowel. *Irabu finye,* closed vowel. *Irabu unganishi,* connecting vowel. *Irabu mbele,* front vowel. *Irabu nusu chini,* half-open vowel. *Irabu nusu juu,* half-closed vowel. *Irabu juu,* high vowel. *Irabu kati,* middle vowel. (cf *vokali*) (Ar)

isha[1] *n* (*n*) 1. (in Islam) obligatory night prayer operating approximately between 7.30 p.m. and before dawn: *Sala ya isha,* "isha" prayers. 2. the time after "magharib" (evening) prayers. (Ar)

ish.a[2] (also *kwisha*) *vt, vi* 1. end, finish, come to an end: *Mjadala umeisha,* the debate has ended. (cf *timu, malizika*) 2. die, pass away, finish, overwhelm: *Alipigana nao na akawaisha wote,* he fought against them and finished them off. (cf *maliza*) 3. go bankrupt; become financially ruined, Prep. **ish.i.a** St. **ish.ik.a** Cs. **ish.iz.a** (seldom used) (cf *filisika, anguka*)

ishara (also *taashira*) *n* (*n*) sign, symptom, clue: *Hakuna ishara yoyote kwamba mvua itanyesha leo,* there is no sign at all that it will rain today. (cf *kielekezi, alama, dalili*) (Ar)

ish.i *vt, vi* 1. live, domicile, stay, reside: *Anaishi karibu na soko,* he lives near the market. (cf *kaa, keti*) 2. last, endure, persist: *Kanzu hii haitaishi sana,* this dress will not last long. (cf *dumu*) 2. live a good or bad life: *Anaishi vizuri,* he lives a good life. (cf *dumu*) Prep. **ish.i.a** St. **ish.ik.a** Ps. **ish.iw.a**

ishi.a *vt* end up, finish: *Jambazi yule ameishia jela,* that thug has ended up in prison. Prep. **ishi.li.a** (cf *malizika*)

ishirini *adj, n* (*n*) twenty: *Wanafunzi ishirini,* twenty students. (Ar)

ishiw.a *vt* be broke, be bankrupt: *Ameishiwa fedha*, he is broke, *Ameishiwa na nguvu*, he is weak. (cf *malizikiwa*)

isi (*also nsi*) *n* (*n*) fish (cf *samaki*)

isimu[1] *n* (*n*) 1. name, appelation (cf *jina*) 2. linguistics: *Isimu nafsia*, psycholinguistics. *Isimu fafanuzi*, descriptive linguistics. *Isimu jamii*, sociolinguistics. *Isimu elekezi*, prescriptive linguistics. *Isimu amali*, pragmatic linguistics. *Isimu uamilifu*, functional linguistics. *Isimu jumulifu*, general linguistics. *Isimu matumizi*, applied linguistics. *Isimu historia*, historical linguistics. *Isimu wakati*, diachronic linguistics. *Isimu viziada lugha*, paralinguistics. *Isimu viumbe hai*, bio-linguistics. *Isimu mambo leo*, synchronic linguistics. *Isimu lugha nyingi*, dialinguistics. *Isimu linganishi*, comparative linguistics. *Isimu linganuzi*, contrastive linguistics. *Isimu kokotozi*, computational linguistics. *Isimu shule*, pedagogical linguistics. *Isimu miundo*, structural linguistics. *Isimu anthropolojia*, anthropological linguistics. (cf *lughawiya*)

isimu[2] (*ismu*) *adj* emphatic negation; an expletive used to emphasize the act of denying sth: *Nilikwenda dukani lakini kulikuwa hakuna isimu ya mtu*, I went to the shop but there was no one. (Ar)

isingekuwa *conj* if it were not for, had it not been, were it not: *Isingekuwa yeye, mimi nisingekuja hapa*, had it not been for him, I would not have come here.

isipokuwa *conj* except, but, with the exception of: *Wafanyakazi wote waligoma isipokuwa wachache*, all the workers went on strike except a few (cf *ila*, *thama*)

isitoshe *conj* furthermore, besides, in addition: *Yeye hana mali; isitoshe hana watoto*, he does not have wealth in addition, he does not have children.

Islamu *n* (*n*) 1. see *Uislamu*. 2. a follower of Islamic religion.

isotopu *n* (*n*) (*chem*) isotope; any of the two or more forms of chemical elements with different atomic weight and different nuclear properties.

Israfili *n* (*n*) (in Islam), the angel of trumpet; the angel who will blow the last trumpet to mark the end of the world. (Ar)

Issa *n* (*n*) (in Islam) the apostle of Allah who is fatherless; (in Christianity) he is known as Jesus Christ, who is the founder of Christian religion.

istiara *n* (*n*) allegory; a story in which people, things, etc. have a hidden or symbolic meaning: *Taswira ya mtu aliyefunikwa kitambaa machoni akiwa na mezani, ni kielelezo cha kiistiiari cha kuonyesha haki*, the blindfolded figure with scales is an allegory of justice. (Ar).

istiari *n* (*n*) metaphor; a figure of speech containing an implied comparison in which a word or phrase is applied to an object or action to which it is not literally applicable (e.g. *Yeye alikuwa simba katika vita vyenyewe*, he was a hero in the battle.

istihaki *n* (*n*) privilege; advantage given to a particular group of people. (Ar)

istihizai *n* (*n*) see *stihizai*

istiimari imperialism, foreign domination: *Istiimari ni kitu cha kale*, imperialism is the thing of the past. (cf *ubeberu*, *ukoloni*) (Ar)

istilahi *n* (*n*) lexicon, terminology: *Istilahi sanifu*, nomenclature. *Istilahi za Kiswahili zinazidi kuongezeka kila siku*, the Swahili terminology continues to increase every day. (Ar)

istiskaa[1] *n* (*n*) (in Islam) Islamic prayer for rain. (Ar)

istiskaa[2] *n* (*n*) (*med*) dropsy; a disease formed by the executive accumulation of watery fluid under the skin or organs. (cf *jongo*)

istiwai *n* (*n*) (*geog*) equator (cf *ikweta*)

it.a *vt*, *vi* 1. call, summon, shout, cry out: *Mwalimu aliliita jina lako*, the teacher called your name. 2. invite, request, ask: *Ita watu nyumbani*, invite people home. Prep. *it.i.a* St. *it.ik.a* Cs. *it.ish.a* Ps. *it.w.a* Rp. *it.an.a*

itabir.i examine, scrutinize, look into: *Jaribu kuitabiri kazi yake*, try to examine his work. Prep. *itabir.i.a* St. *itabir.ik.a* Cs. *itabir.ish.a* Ps. of Prep. *itabir.iw.a* (cf *zingatia*)

itakad.i *vt, vi* see *itakidi*

itakid.i (*also itakadi*) *vt, vi* believe, trust: have faith in: *Unaitakidi kila anachosema?* Do you believe in everything he says? Prep. *itakid.i.a* St. *itakid.ik.a* Cs. *itakid.ish.a* Ps. of Prep. *itakid.iw.a* Rp. of Prep. *itakid.i.an.a* (cf *amini, sadiki*) (Ar)

italiki *n* (*n*) italics: *Mfano ule umewekwa katika italiki*, that example has been put in italics. (Eng)

ithibati *n* (*n*) evidence, truth, validation, proof: *Ithibati kwa upande wa mashtaka haina nguvu*, the evidence from the prosecution is weak. (cf *uthibitisho, ushahidi*)

iti *adv* down, under, below: *Kaa iti*, sit down. (cf *chini*)

itibari *n* (*n*) trust, faith, esteem, respect, confidence: *Baadhi ya wenye maduka hawana itibari na wateja wao*, some of the shopkeepers have no confidence in their customers. (cf *imani, muamana*) (Ar)

itifaki *n* (*n*) 1. agreement, accord, consensus, harmony, mutual understanding: *Haijapatikana itifaki yoyote mpaka sasa kati ya wajumbe kwenye mkutano*, there is no consensus so far among the delegates at the meeting. (cf *maafikiano, mapatano*) 2. protocol: *Adabu za itifaki*, protocol standards. (Ar)

itik.a *vi* reply, respond: *Aliitwa na akaitika*, he was called and he responded. Prep. *itik.i.a* St. *itik.ik.a* Cs. *itik.ish.a* (cf *itikia*)

itikadi *n* (*n*) 1. faith, belief, trust, confidence: *Raia wana itikadi kwa viongozi wao*, the citizens have faith in their leaders. (cf *imani*) 2. ideology, philosophy, viewpoint, opinion: *Itikadi ya chama chetu inasisitiza umoja*, our party's ideology stresses unity. (cf *fikira, wazo*) (Ar)

itikafu *n* (*n*) (in Islam) an assembly held inside a mosque, intended to perform different activities for a special period.

itiki.a¹ *vi* accept an invitation. St. *itik.ik.a* Cs. *itik.ish.a* Ps. *itik.iw.a* Rp. of Prep. *itik.i.an.a*

itiki.a² *vt* 1. sing a chorus line of a song. 2. used in the expression: *Harusi imeitikia*, the consummation has proved that the girl is a virgin. Prep. *itiki.li.a* St. *itiki.k.a* Cs. *itiki.sh.a* Ps. *itiki.w.a* Rp. *itiki.an.a*

itiko *n* (*ma-*) 1. response, answer, reaction: *Ombi letu la kutaka msaada lilipata itiko zuri*, our appeal for aid received a good response. (cf *mwiitiko, ukubalifu*) 2. answer, reply, retort, rejoinder.

itilo *n* (*n*) (*naut*) a big rope in sailing vessels tied from both sidea of the yard to the mast (cf *baraji, hamrawi*). (cf *baraji, hamrawi*)

itish.a *vi* 1. summon, call: *Itisha mkutano*, call a meeting. 2. request for sth to be brought; *Itisha faili*, call for a file. Prep. *itish.i.a* St. *itish.ik.a* Ps. *itish.w.a* Rp. *itish.an.a*

ito *n* (*n*) (*naut*) eye ornament (oculus) on bows of a dhow, canoe without outriggers (*dau*) and boat.

itw.a *vi* be called; be entitled: *Ninaitwa Juma*, I am called Juma.

iv.a (also *wiva*) *vi* 1. be ripe, get ripe; mature: *Tunda hili limeiva*, this fruit is ripe. (cf *komaa, pea*) 2. (of food) be cooked: *Chakula kimeiva*, the food is cooked. 3. (of affairs, etc.) be finalized; be ready: *Mambo yake yameiva*, his matters are finalized. 4. (of boil) be ready to burst: *Jipu lake limeiva*, her boil is about to burst. Prep. ***iv.i.a*** St. ***iv.ik.a*** Cs. ***iv.ish.a***

ivu *n* (*ma-*) see *jivu*

iwapo *conj* if, when, provided, on condition, in case of: *Iwapo una nafasi, twende mkutanoni*, if you have time, let us go to the meeting. (cf *kama, endapo, ikiwa*)

iweje *verb form* How can it be?: *Iweje yeye akutukane?* how can it be that he insults you?

iz.a *vt* reject, refuse, decline: *Aliiza shauri langu*, he rejected my suggestion. Prep. ***iz.i.a*** St. ***iz.ik.a*** Cs. ***iz.ish.a*** Ps. ***iz.w.a*** Rp. ***iz.an.a*** (cf *kana, kataa*)

izara (also *idhara*) *n* (*n*) disgrace, shame, scandal: *Matendo yake mabaya yamemletea izara tupu*, her evil deeds have brought her utter disgrace. (cf *aibu, fedheha*) (Ar)

Izraili[1] (also *ziraili*) *n* (*n*) (in Islam) the angel of death; the angel responsible for taking out the souls of all people. (cf *nduli*) (Ar)

Izraili[2] (also *Israeli*) *n* (*n*) (*geog*) Israel; the Jewish state in the Middle East. (Ar)

izu *n* (*ma-*) banana (cf *ndizi*)

J

J, J /j/ 1. the tenth letter of the Swahili alphabet. 2. a voiced affricate.

j.a¹ *vi* come, arrive, move towards, close in: *Akija, atanipa zawadi yangu, if he comes, he will give me my present.* Prep. **j.i.a** St. **j.ik.a** Cs. **j.ish.a** Ps. of Prep. **j.iw.a**, be approached. (cf *wasili, fika*)

ja² *conj* like, as, as if: *Anafanya mambo ja mtoto mdogo,* he is doing things like a small child. (cf *kama, kana*)

ja.a¹ *vt, vi* 1. (of liquid) brim; become full, be full: *Mtungi umejaa maji,* the jar is full of water. 2. be plentiful, abound, swarm, be everywhere: *Nzi wamejaa kote,* the flies are everywhere. 3. (fig) become fat, become stout: *Mtu yule amejaa kwa kula nyakula nya mafuta,* that person has become fat because of eating fatty foods. Prep. **ja.li.a** St. **ja.lik.a** Cs. **ja.z.a** and **ja.liz.a** Ps. **ja.w.a** Rp. **ja.an.a** and **ja.li.an.a**

jaa² (also *jalala*) *n* (*ma-*) 1. dunghill, dump, garbage, rubbish heap, dustheap, junkyard: *Tupa taka kwenye jaa,* throw the rubbish on the dunghill. 2. (*syn*) *Ukubwa ni jaa,* headship is like a dustbin i.e. if anything goes wrong in an organisation, etc., all the blame will go to the leader.

jaa³ *n* (*ma-*) north (cf *kaskazini*)

jaa⁴ *n* (*ma-*) jar; a container made of glass, stone or earthenware. (cf *dumu*)

jaala *n* (*n*) divine grace; grace of God. (cf *majaaliwa*) (Ar)

jaali.a *vt* see *jalia*

jabali *n* (*ma-*) 1. a huge rock; boulder, crag, tor: *Walishindwa kuliondosha jabali lile,* they were unable to remove that huge rock. (cf *mwamba*) 2. rocky hill, rocky mountain: *Nililipanda jabali kwa taabu,* I climbed the rocky hill with difficulty. (cf *kilima*) (Ar)

jabara *n* (*n*) a local doctor's technique of treating joints when they are dislocated: *Jirani yangu ni bingwa katika matibabu ya jabara,* my neighbour is an expert in the local treatment of joints or broken bones. (cf *uhazigi*) (Ar)

Jabari¹ *n* (*n*) 1. The Almighty God (cf *Subhana, Rabi, Rabana*) 2. a supreme ruler, a supreme chief. (Ar)

jabari² *n* (*ma-*) 1. valiant, hero; a brave person, a fearless person, lionheart: *Jabari alikufa vitani,* the hero died in the war. (cf *shujaa, kijogoo, jagina*) 2. brute; a violent person, an oppressive person, a ruthless person 3. a proud person; a conceited person. (cf *dhalimu*) (Ar)

jabiri *n* (*n*) (used in the expression): *Kikoi cha jabiri,* a woven loincloth. (Ar)

jadhba *n* (*n*) see *jazba*

jadhibik.a (also *jazibika*) *vi* be excited. Prep. **jadhibik.i.a** St. **jadhibik.ik.a** Cs. **jadhibik.ish.a** (Ar)

jadhibish.a *vt* see *jazibisha*

jadi *n* (*n*) pedigree, genealogy, lineage: *Mafunzo ya jadi,* traditional studies. *Ngoma za jadi,* traditional dances. *Wana jadi moja,* they have a common ancestral line. (cf *nasaba, ukoo*)

jadidi¹ *adj* new, modern, recent: *Nguo jadidi,* new clothes. (Ar)

jadidi² *adv* firmly, resolutely, steadfastly: *Mwanasiasa alisimama jadidi katika suala la haki za binaadamu,* the politician stood firm on the question of human rights. (cf *imara, kidete*) (Ar)

jadidifu *adj* alternative: *Nishati jadidifu,* alternative energy. (cf *mbadala*) (Ar)

jadil.i *vt, vi* debate, discuss: *Bunge lilijadili kwa kirefu suala la rushwa nchini,* the parliament discussed corruption in the country at length. Prep. **jadil.i.a** St. **jadil.ik.a** Ps. of Prep. **jadil.iw.a** Rp. of Prep. **jadil.i.an.a** (Ar)

jadilian.a vt, vi discuss among one another.
jadweli n (n) see *jedwali*
jagi n (ma-) jug, pitcher: *Jagi la maji*, water jug *Jagi la maziwa*, milk jug. (cf *dumu*) (Eng)
jagina[1] (also *chagina*) n (ma-) gallant, valiant, hero; a brave person, a man of courage: *Mwanajeshi alikuwa jagina katika vita*, the soldier was a hero in the war. (cf *jabari, shujaa*)
jagina[2] n (ma-) crook, conman, swindler. (cf *tapeli, guberi*)
jagwa n (n) (zool) jaguar, a large yellowish cat with black spots. (Port)
jaha n (n) 1. honour, glory, esteem, respect: *Yeye ni mtu aliyepata jaha kutoka kwa watu mbalimbali*, he is a person who has been honoured by different people. *Ametunukiwa jaha na rais*, he has been honoured by the president.(cf *utukufu, heshima, staha*) 2. luck, fluke, fortune, windfall: *Nyota ya jaha*, the star of luck. (cf *bahati, sudi, futahi*)
jahabu[1] n (n) (naut) dry dock, dock yard. (cf *gudi*) (Ar)
jahab.u[2] vt (naut) shore up a vessel above the high-water line for repairs or painting. Prep. *jahab.i.a* St. *jahab.ik.a* Cs. *jahab.ish.a* Ps. of Prep. *jahab.iw.a* (Ar)
jahanamu n (n) (in Islam) gehenna, hell; a place where sinners and unbelievers are doomed to eternal punishment after death. (cf *motoni*) (Ar)
jahara[1] adv conspicuously, openly, publicly, vividly: *Ametoa jahara maelezo yake*, he has explained his points publicly. (cf *waziwazi*) (Ar)
jahara[2] n (n) loudness, noise: *Akizungumza, huzungumza kwa jahara*, when he talks, he does it loudly. (Ar)
jahazi n (ma-) (naut) dhow (cf *safina*) (Ar)

jahi n (n) (geog) north pole.
jahili[1] n (ma-) idiot, fool, imbecile, simpleton; a stupid person. (cf *mpumbavu, baradhuli, mjinga*) (Ar)
jahili[2] n (ma-) illiterate, unschooled, uneducated: *Yeye ni jahili; hajui kusoma wala kuandika*, he is illiterate; he can neither read nor write. (Ar)
jahili[3] adj cruel, ruthless, brutal: *Kijana yule ni jahili*, that young man is ruthless. (cf *katili, habithi*)
jahimu n (n) (in Islam) one of the types of hellfire. (cf *jahanamu*) (Ar)
jaja n (n) (bot) a perennial herb with stems up to 8 feet long with small, yellow, blue, mauve or lilac flowers. *Aneilema acquinoctiale*.
jaji n (ma-) 1. judge: *Jaji mkuu*, chief justice. *Jaji kiongozi*, principal judge. *Jaji mfawidhi*, judge in charge of a zone. *Jaji wa mahakama ya rufaa*, justice of appeal. 2. arbiter, arbitrator, mediator, negotiator: *Yule jaji aliusuluhisha ugomvi kati ya pande mbili*, the arbiter resolved the conflict between the two sides. (cf *msuluhishi, mpatanishi*) (Eng)
jakamoyo n (n) 1. distress, restlessness, uneasiness, anxiety. (cf *dukuduku, wasiwasi, wahaka*) 2. bother, hassle, harrassment, pester: *Usinitie jakamoyo kila mara*, don't keep on bothering me now and again. (cf *kero, usumbufu*)
jaketi n (n) jacket: *Jaketi la kubana*, doublet. *Jaketi okozi, jaketi la kuokolea*, life jacket. (Eng)
jalada n (ma-) 1. the cover of a book. 2. file, folder: *Huzitia barua zangu zote katika jalada*, I put all my letters in a file (cf *faili*) 3. used in the expression: *Jalada la hati*, dossier; a collection of documents concerning a particular person or matter. (Ar)
jalala[1] see *jaa*[2]
jalala[2] n (n) His Majesty: *Jalala Sultan*, His Majesty the Sultan. (Ar)

jalalati n (n) Her Majesty: *Jalalati Malkia*, Her Majesty the Queen. (Ar)

Jalali[1] n (n) 1. (in Islam) the Glorious Almighty God; God of glory. (cf *Jalia*) 2. majesty: *Jalali mfalme*, His majesty the King. *Jalali malkia*, Her majesty the Queen. (Ar)

jalali[2] adj honourable, distinguished, noble, illustrious. (Ar)

jalbosi n (n) see *jaribosi*

jal.i[1] vt, vi care about, be concerned; heed: *Mwalimu yule hujali sana kazi za wanafunzi wake*, that teacher cares a lot about his students' work. (cf *sikiliza, hisi*) 2. respect, venerate, revere: *Mimi ninakujali sana kutokana na uaminifu wako*, I respect you a lot because of your integrity. Prep. *jal.i.a* St. *jal.ik.a* Cs. *jal.ish.a* Ps. of Prep. *jal.iw.a* Rp. of Prep. *jal.i.an.a* (cf *tii, heshimu, stahi*) (Ar)

jali[2] n (ma-) (in card playing) the ace or the seventh card in a pack of cards in a special game where the victor is identified if he gets a score of sixty one and over. (cf *ree, seti*)

jali.a[1] (also *jaalia*) vt 1. (esp of God) make it possible; assist, wish; *Mungu akinijalia, nitakupitia nyumbani kesho*, if God wishes, I will call on you at home tomorrow. 2. grant, empower, enable. Prep. *jali.i.a* St. *jali.k.a* Cs. *jali.sh.a* Ps. of Prep. *jali.w.a* Rp of Prep. *jali.an.a* (cf *wezesha, saidia*) (Ar)

Jalia[2] n (n) (in Islam) one of the names of Almighty God. (Ar)

jalid.i[1] vt bind a book; colligate a book: *Alilijalidi daftari lake ili lipate kudumu*, he bound his book so that it could last long. Prep. *jalid.i.a* St. *jalid.ik.a* Cs. *jalid.ish.a* Ps. of Prep. *jalid.iw.a* Rp of Prep. *jalid.i.an.a* (Ar)

jalid.i[2] vt whip, scourge, lash, flog, birch: *Nilimjalidi mwanangu kwa ukosefu wa nidhamu*, I flogged my son for lack of discipline. Prep. *jalid.i.a* St. *jalid.*

ik.a Cs. *jalid.ish.a* Ps. of Prep. *jalid.iw.a* Rp. of Prep *jalid.i.an.a*

jalidi[3] n (n) 1. black frost; severe frost that blackens growing plants: *Udongo jalidi*, permafrost. 2. severe cold; frigidity. (cf *baridi kali*)

jaliko n (ma-) 1. invitation, call, request: *Nilipata jaliko la harusi ya rafiki yangu*, I got an invitation to my friend's wedding. 2. a group of women who invite others for a wedding or for other functions. 3. act of confining sby indoors while undergoing treatment. 4. act of confining an initiate for giving him the teachings.

jalili adj dignified, noble, eminent: *Mwanachuoni jalili*, an eminent scholar. (cf *adhimu, tukufu*) (Ar)

jaluba[1] n (ma-) rice paddy, rice field. (Ar)

jaluba[2] n (ma-) snuffbox; a small ornamental box of metal, used for keeping a chewing mixture. (cf *uraibu, mfuraha*) (Ar)

jama interj see *jamani*

jamaa 1. people of the same family. (cf *aila, familia*) 2. relatives, clansmen, kinsman, kinsfolk: *Mimi nina jamaa wengi*, I have many relatives. (cf *akrabu, ahali*) 3. friends, comrades: *Jamaa wengi walifika mazikoni*, many friends came to the funeral. 4. a person of unknown or unmentioned name. (Ar)

jamadari (also *jemadari*) n (ma) see *jemadari* (Ar)

jamala n (n) 1. courtesy, civility, kindness, good manners, good behaviour: *Mtu yule hana jamala hata kidogo*, that person does not have courtesy at all. 2. boon, comfort. (cf *hisani, fadhila*)

jamali[1] n (n) camel (cf *ngamia*) (Ar)

jamali[2] (also *jamili*) adj beautiful, attractive, good-looking, handsome: *Msichana jamali*, a beautiful girl. (cf *taibu, sheshe*) (Ar)

jamanda n (ma-) a large basket fitted with a cover; hamper.

jamani (also *jama*) *interj* an exclamation used to attract attention to people in case of danger, fear, etc.: Hey! Listen here! *Jamani! Kuna moto ndani ya nyumba yangu*, Hey! there is a fire in my house. (cf *nyungwa!*)

jamati (also *jamatkhana*) n (n) 1. mosque. Normally used by Indian Muslims of the Ismailia sect. 2. a place of worship for various functions e.g. marriage ceremony. (Hind)

jamatkhana n (n) see *jamati*

jamb.a *vi* fart; break wind. Prep. ***jamb.i.a*** St. ***jamb.ik.a*** Cs. ***jamb.ish.a*** Ps. ***jamb.w.a*** Ps. of Prep. ***jamb.iw.a*** Rp. of Prep. ***jamb.i.an.a*** (cf *shuta, fusa*)

jambakoti n (ma-) tabard

jambazi n (ma-) 1. conman, crook, swindler, cheat, criminal: *Jambazi sugu*, a hardened criminal. *Usimwamini jambazi yule*, don't trust that conman. (cf *mdanganyifu, laghai*) 2. armed robber, gangster, thug. (cf *haramia*) (Pers)

jambeni n (ma-) a cross-cut saw. It is a large saw and is used by two people for cutting the logs, etc.

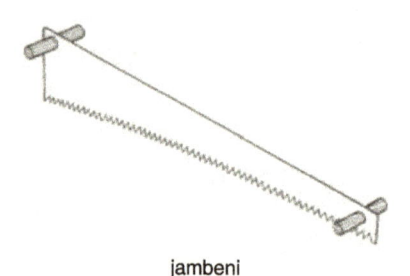

jambeni

jambia n (ma-) poniard, dagger: *Waarabu wa Omani aghalabu huvaa jambia kiunoni*, Omani Arabs normally wear a dagger at the waist. (cf *hanjari, sime*) (Ar)

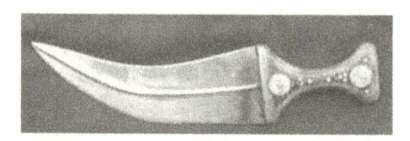

jambia

jambik.a *vt* wear a dress by passing it under one of the armpits and then tying it on the other shoulder. Prep. ***jambik.i.a*** St. ***jambik.ik.a*** Cs. ***jambik.ish.a*** Ps. ***jambik.w.a*** Rp. ***jambik.an.a***

jambo n (ma-) 1. information, report, news: *Je, amekuja na jambo gani?* What news has he brought? (cf *taarifa, ripoti*) 2. affair, matter, issue: *Mambo ya ndani*, home affairs. *Mambo ya nchi za nje*, foreign affairs. (cf *neno, tamko, mkasa*)

jambwe *interj* an expletive of ridicule, disdain, etc.; pooh: *Huyu jambwe amekaa bure tu hapa*, pooh! this fool is just sitting idly here.

jamdani n (n) white brocade; a kind of white cloth used for decorating women's dresses. (cf *ribini*) (Pers)

jamhuri n (n) 1. republic: *Jamhuri ya Muungano*, United Republic. 2. a multitude of people, a crowd of people. *Jamhuri ya watu ilionekana katika mazishi ya jirani yangu*, a large crowd of people was seen at the funeral of my neighbour. (cf *umati, halaiki*) (Ar)

jamia[1] n (n) a big mosque. (Ar)

jamia[2] n (n) a multitude of people; a large number of people: *Jamia kuu ilihudhuria sherehe ya harusi*, many people attended the wedding ceremony. (cf *halaiki, umati*) (Ar)

jamid.i[1] *vt* (of glue, blood, etc.) become hard; coagulate, congeal, clot, get frozen: *Maji yamejamidi*, the water has frozen. Prep. ***jamid.i.a*** St. ***jamid.ik.a*** Cs. ***jamid.ish.a*** Ps. of Prep. ***jamid.iw.a*** (cf *ganda*) (Ar)

jamidi² *adj* hard, solid, solidified: *Gundi imekuwa jamidi*, the glue has hardened. (cf *gumu*) (Ar)

jamii¹ *n* (*n*) society, community, association: *Jamii yetu inakusudia kuleta maendeleo*, our community intends to bring development. (cf *jumuiya*) (Ar)

jamii² *n* (*n*) 1. group, crowd: *Kuna jamii ya wafanyakazi nje wakingojea malipo yao*, there is a group of workers outside waiting for their payment. (cf *kundi*) 2. brand, breed, species, genus, class. (Ar)

jami.i³ *vt* have sexual intercourse with a woman; fuck. Prep. *jami.i.a* St. *jami.ik.a* Cs. *jami.tsh.a* Ps. of Prep. *jami.iw.a* Rp. of Prep. *jami.an.a* copulate (cf *zini, tomba*) (Ar)

jamian.a *vi* see *jamii³*

jamii⁴ *adv* together, in unison, as a group. (Ar)

jamili *adj* see *jamali²*

jamu¹ *n*(*n*) (of food) jam (Eng)

jamu² *adj* abundant, many.

jamvi *n* (*ma-*) 1. grass mat; a piece of floor mat made of plaited strips of leaf, used in mosques, funerals, marriage ceremonies, etc. 2. special concrete floor of a building. 3. special cultural fine paid to the elders of a council. 4. (*idms*) *Kunja jamvi*, wind up business or an activity. *Lipa jamvi*, pay costs of running a case. *Jamvi la wageni*, prostitute.

jana¹ *n* (*n*) yesterday: *Mwaka jana*, last year. *Mwezi jana*, last month.

jana² *adv* yesterday: *Alifika hapa jana*, he arrived here yesterday.

jana³ (*also chana, zana*) (*ma-*) (*zool*) bee grub. (cf *toto la nyuki*)

janaa (*also junaa*) *n* (*n*) disgrace, shame, dishonour, degradation: *Vitendo vyake viovu vimeiletea familia yake janaa*, his evil deeds have brought disgrace to his family. (cf *aibu, fedheha*) (Ar)

janaba *n* (*n*) defilement usu caused by coition or masturbation; maculation caused by coition or fornication which according to Islam is removed by taking a complete bath (cf *manii, hedhi*) (Ar)

janabi *n* (*n*) mister, sir, master, your honour; a word of respect. (cf *bwanamkubwa*)

jando *n* (*n*) 1. initiation or circumcision rites. (cf *ukumbi, unyago*) 2. a group of young men attending circumcision rites.

janga¹ *n* (*ma-*) difficulty, calamity, tragedy, disaster, misfortune: *Usituletee janga hapa*, don't create difficulties for us here. (*prov*) *Mchuma janga hula na wa kwao*, a person who causes a misfortune ends up with his people or relatives i.e. a person who commits something bad ends up disgracing his family or relatives. (Ar) (cf *balaa, zani, shida*)

jang.a² *vt, vi* complain, moan, grumble, mutter. Prep. *jang.i.a* St. *jang.ik.a* Cs. *jang.ish.a*

jangili (*also jangiri*) *n* (*ma-*) 1. rogue, thug: *Unadhani itakuwa rahisi kumkamata jangili yule?* Do you think it will be easy to arrest that rogue? 2. a cruel person; brute. (cf *haramia*)

janghi *n* (*ma-*) see *jangili*

janguo (*also jangusho*) *n* (*ma-*) 1. the season of knocking down dry coconuts; the coconut season: *Janguo limefika lakini wakwezi bado hawajapatikana*, the season of knocking down coconuts has arrived but the coconut climbers are not yet available. 2. the knocking down of dry coconuts. 3. (*idm*) payday: *Jana ilikuwa janguo*, yesterday, was payday.

jangusho *n* (*ma-*) see *janguo*

jangwa *n* (*ma-*) 1. desert. 2. wilderness, waste, barren ground.

jani *n* (*ma-*) 1. leaf; a blade of grass: *Jani la mgomba*, banana leaf. *Jani mchanganyiko*, compound leaf. *Jani changa*, leaflet. 2. a kind of plant like reeds.

janibu n (n) side, flank, place: *Anaishi katika janibu ya mashariki ya mji*, he lives in the eastern side of the town. (cf *jiha, sehemu, upande*)

-janja[1] adj sly, deceitful, crafty, wily, artful, cunning, shrewd: *Usimwamini mtu yule kwa vile ni mjanja sana*, don't trust that person because he is very sly.

janja[2] n (n) intrigue, gambit, machination, device. (cf *magube, ujanja*)

janja[3] (*zool*) snapper: a kind of percoid fish (family *Lutjanidae*) with moderately elongate to deep body and ctenoid scales, inhabiting most warm seas. (cf *tembo*)

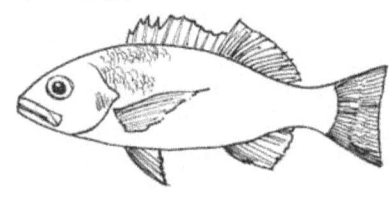

janja
Black spot snapper. *Lutjanus ehrenbergii*.

janjaruk.a vi become shrewd, wise up, get smart: *Huwezi kumdanganya tena kwani sasa amejanjaruka*, you can't deceive him anymore because he has now become shrewd. Prep. **janjaruk.i.a** St. **janjaruk.ik.a** Cs. **janjaruk.ish.a** (cf *erevuka, karamka*)

janjuzi n (n) (used in the phrase) *Janja na janjuzi*, a clever rogue.

janna n (n) (*poet*) paradise, heaven: *Ukifanya matendo mazuri duniani, utaingia katika janna*, if you do good deeds in this world, you will go to paradise. (cf *pepo*) (Ar)

Januari n (n) January (Eng)

japo *conj* even if, although, though. (short form of *ijapokuwa, ingawa*)

jarabati adj proof, tested, tried: *Dawa jarabati*, a tested medicine. (Ar)

jaraha n (ma-) see *jeraha*

jaramandia n (n) a bag for keeping arms.

jaramba n (n) (*colloq*) warm-up: *Piga jaramba*, warm-up; make preparations.

jarari[1] n (ma-) (*naut*) main part of a halyard connecting *henza* (thicker rope) and its block (*gofia*) with the *abedari* (pulley). (Ar)

jarari[2] n (ma-) drawer: *Niliziweka funguo zangu katika jarari*, I put my keys in the drawer. (cf *almaru, dawati, saraka*) (Ar)

jari n (n) impetus, momentum, drive; urge to do sth.

jaribio n (ma-) 1. attempt, plan, trial, experiment: *Jaribio la kutaka kuiangusha serikali halikufaulu*, the attempt to overthrow the government did not succeed. (cf *mpango, njama*) 2. exercise, lesson: *Jaribio la tano*, exercise five. 3. test, quiz. 4. temptation 5. (*math*) *Jaribio la dhanio*, test of hypothesis. (Ar)

jaribosi (also *jalbosi*) n (ma-) coloured tinfoil or paper used for decorating the rolls of paper worn by some women as earings. (Ar)

jarib.u vt, vi 1. attempt, try, endeavour, test: *Walijaribu bila ya mafanikio kuipindua serikali*, they attempted unsuccessfully to overthrow the government. (cf *geza, pindana, pirikana*) 2. venture, dare, hazard: *Alijaribu kumwua simba kwa mkuki*, he tried to kill a lion with a spear. Prep. **jarib.i.a** St. **jarib.ik.a** Cs. **jarib.ish.a** Ps. of Prep. **jarib.iw.a** Rp. of Prep. **jarib.i.an.a** (cf *thubutu, diriki*) (Ar)

jarida n (ma-) journal, newspaper, tabloid, periodical: *Jarida la Afrika*, Africa journal (cf *gazeti*)

jarife n (ma-) dragnet, seine: *Wavuvi hupenda kutumia majarife katika baadhi ya siku*, fishermen like to use dragnets on some days. (cf *juya, kimia*) (Ar)

jasadi (also *jisadi*) *n* (*n*) body, physique, figure: *Yeye ni mtu mwenye jasadi kubwa,* he is a person of large physique. (cf *kiwiliwili, umbo*) (Ar)

jasara *n* (*n*) see *ujasiri*

jasho *n* (*ma-*) 1. sweat, heat, perspiration: *Ukikimbia sana, utatokwa na jasho jingi,* if you run hard, you will sweat a lot. 2. effort, hard work. *Jasho la mtu,* a person's efforts. (*sym*) *Usile jasho la mwenzio,* don't be a parasite i.e. don't depend upon others. (cf *taabu, nguvu*)

jasi[1] *n* (*n*) gypsum; a kind of mineral used as a fertilizer. (Ar)

jasi[2] *n* (*n*) an ornament worn in the lobe of an ear. (cf *kipuli, kipini*) (Ar)

jasir.i[1] *vt, vi* venture, risk, wager, dare, gamble: *Alijasiri kwenda kupigana vitani,* he dared to go to war. Prep. *jasir.i.a* St. *jasir.ik.a* Cs. *jasir.ish.a* (cf *thubutu*) (Ar)

jasiri[2] *adj* bold, courageous, daring, fearless: *Yeye ni mwanajeshi jasiri,* he is a courageous soldier. (*shujaa*) (Ar)

jasirish.a *vt* venture, dare. Prep. *jasirish.i.a* St. *jasirish.ik.a* Ps. *jasirish.w.a* Rp. *jasirish.an.a*

jasis.i *vt* spy on, scout, reconnoitre: *Adui alijasisi shughuli za kijeshi za nchi yetu,* the enemy spied on the military activities of our country. 2. explore carefully. Prep. *jasis.i.a* St. *jasis.ik.a* Cs. *jasis.ish.a* Ps. of Prep. *jasis.iw.a* Rp. of Prep. *jasis.i.an.a* (cf *peleleza, dodosa*)

jasusi *n* (*ma-*) spy; secret agent: *Jasusi aliweza kuzipata siri za serikali,* the spy managed to obtain the government's secrets. *Jasusi wa shughuli za viwanda,* industrial spy (cf *shushushu, mpelelezi*) (Ar)

java *n* (*n*) bog; a wet, spongy ground.

jawabu[1] *n* (*ma-*) reply, answer, rejoinder, response: *Alitoa jawabu sahihi,* he gave an accurate response. (cf *jibu, itikio*) (Ar)

jawabu[2] *n* (*n*) (*mus*) a refrain in 'taarab' music.

jaz.a[1] *vt* fill; make full, congest, cram: *Jaza maji katika tangi,* fill water in a tank. Prep. *jaz.i.a* St. *jaz.ik.a* Ps. *jaz.w.a* Rp. *jaz.an.a*

jaz.a[2] (also *jazi*) *vt* 1. (esp of God) reward, requite, repay: *Mungu atakujaza heri,* God will reward you with grace. (cf *lipa*) 2. (esp of God) punish someone for his evil deeds: *Mungu anawajaza watu waovu,* God punishes the evil doers. Prep. *jaz.i.a* St. *jaz.ik.a* Ps. *jaz.w.a* Rp *jaz.an.a* (Ar)

jazan.a *vi* be crowded, be congested, be crammed: *Watu walijazana kwenye mkutano wa kisiasa,* people were crowded at the political rally.

jazanda *n* (*n*) (*lit*) image, impression.

jazba (also *jadhba, jaziba*) *n* (*n*) emotion, fanaticism, ecstasy, afflatus: *Mtu yule ana jazba sana katika mambo ya kidini,* that person is full of religious fanaticism. (cf *taasubi, hamasa*) (Ar)

jazi[1] *n* (*n*) see *jaza*[2]

jazi[2] (also *jezi*) *n* (*n*) 1. knitted sweater, jersey; a close fitting pullover sweater or shirt worn by athletes, etc. (Eng)

jazi[3] (also *jezi*) *n* (*n*) a kind of music with a strong beat; jazz. (Eng)

jazibik.a (also *jadhibika*) *vt, vi* be filled with fanaticism, be filled with ecstasy; become ecstatic, be emotional: *Kijana yule ana tabia ya kujazibika,* that young man is fanatic by nature. Prep. *jazibik.i.a* St. *jazibik.ik.a* Cs. *jazibik.ish.a* (cf *hamasika, raghibika*)

jazila *n* (*n*) a measurement of weight of grain equivalent to about 350 - 360 lbs. (cf *mzo*) (Ar)

jazo *n* (*ma-*) nimiety, excess, surplus, extra: *Niliponunua machungwa mengi, mwenye duka alinipa jazo,* when I bought a lot of oranges, the shopkeeper gave me some extra ones. (cf *ziada, nyongeza*)

jazua *n* (*n*) 1. present, reward, gift 2. a present usu of gold given by the bridegroom to his bride if he finds her to be a virgin. (cf *ukonavi, kipamkono, kipakasa*) (Ar)

je *interrog particle* 1. (used to introduce a question) *Je, hujambo?* How are you? *Je, unaumwa?* Are you sick? Sometimes the particle is suffixed to the verb *Ulikwendaje?* How did you go? (cf *nini, jinsi gani*)

jebu *n* (*ma-*) an ornament usu of silver or gold worn by women; a braid passing over the head and hanging under the chin; pendant. (cf *ukaya, kigwe*) (Hind)

jedhamu leprosy (cf *ukoma*) (Ar)

jedwali (also *jadweli*) *n* (*n*) table, chart: *Jedwali kaida*, periodic table. *Jedwali la marudio*, frequency table. *Jedwali la kuzidisha*, multiplication table.

jefule *n* (*n*) 1. roughness, ungentleness, disorderliness, rudeness; brutal behaviour: *Tumemtoa jefule zake*, we have rid him of his roughness. (cf *jeuri, ukorofi*) 2. trouble, noise, turbulence, chaos: *Kwa nini alituletea jefule hapa?* Why did he cause chaos to us here? (cf *fujo, ghasia*)

jego *n* (*ma-*) see *chego*

jeje.a *vt* scorn, snub, ignore. Prep. **jeje.le.a** St. **jeje.k.a** Cs. **jeje.sh.a** Ps. **jeje.w.a** Rp. **jeje.an.a**

jekejeke *n* (*n*) 1. excessive perspiration; excessive sweat: *Ametokwa na jekejeke mwilini*, he is soaking with sweat. 2. nuisance, bother, annoyance, affliction: *Jekejeke zake hazistahamiliki*, his nuisance is unbearable. *Ona jekejeke*, feel uncomfortable. (cf *udhia, usumbufu*)

jeki *n* (*n*) jack; an apparatus for lifting a heavy object such as a car, off the ground. (cf *gulamu*) 2. (*idm*) *Tia/piga jeki*, assist someone on a specific issue. (Eng)

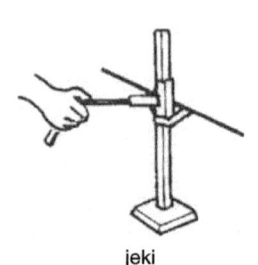

jeki

jela *n* (*n*) jail, prison, penitentiary: *Alikaa jela kwa muda wa miaka mitatu*, he stayed in prison for three years. (cf *gereza*) (Eng)

jelebi (also *chelebi*) *n* (*n*) a round confection made from wheat flour mixed with sugar. (Pers)

jelezi *n* (*n*) nausea, regurgitation, regorging: *Alipata jelezi baada ya kula samaki wengi*, he felt nauseous after eating a lot of fish. (cf *kichefuchefu, kigegezi*)

jeli *n* (*n*) jelly, blancmange. (Eng)

jemadari (also *jamadari*) *n* (*n*) marshall: *Jemadari mkuu*, field marshall. (Hind, Pers)

jembe *n* (*ma-*) hand hoe: *Jembe la plau*, plough blade. *Jembe la trekta*, tractor blade. *Jembe la kusukuma*, Dutch blade. (*prov*) *Mchagua jembe si mkulima*, a person who chooses a particular hoe is not a farmer i.e. if you are in need of sth, don't be too choosy. (cf *shilanga, ngwamba*)

jembetezo *n* (*ma-*) mattock

jembetezo

jemi *n* (*n*) see *ajemi*

jenerali *n* (*ma-*) (*mil*) general; army officer: *Meja jenerali*, major general. *Brigadia jenerali*, brigadier general. (Eng)

jenereta *n* (*ma-*) generator: *Jenereta ya umeme*, electricity generator. *Jenereta ya mkondo maradufu*, double current generator. (Eng)

jeneza *n* (*ma-*) 1. bier, a frame on which a dead body is carried or placed before the burial: *Jeneza lile lina maiti ya rafiki yangu*, in that bier, lies the body of my friend. (cf *tusi*) 2. coffin, casket.

jeng.a *vt* 1. build, construct, assemble, erect: *Alijenga nyumba kubwa*, he built a big house. (cf *aka, unda, tengeneza*) 2. (*fig*) strengthen, build, consolidate: *Wananchi wameamua kulijenga taifa lao*, the citizens have decided to build their nation. 3. help shy acquire sth e.g. promotion, position etc.; groom, ground. *Mwajiri anamjenga rafiki yake ili baadaye awe mkurugenzi wa shirika*, the employer is grooming his friend to become the future company director. 4. make, build: *Jenga hoja*, make an argument; make one's point. *Jenga imani*, have faith. Prep. *jeng.e.a* St. *jeng.ek.a* Cs. *jeng.esh.a* Ps. *jeng.w.a* Rp. *jeng.an.a*

jongek.a *vi* be constructible; be capable of being constructed. *Nyumba ile haijengeki kwa sababu ya ukosefu wa fedha*, that house cannot be constructed because of lack of funds. Prep. *jengek.e.a* St. *jengek.ek.a*

jengelele (also *chengelele*) *n* (*n*) 1. (*anat*) small intestine (cf *chango*) 2. uncircumcized penis. (cf *dhakari*)

jengo *n* (*ma-*) building, edifice, structure, construction: *Jengo lile ni makao makuu ya chama chetu*, that building is the headquarters of our party. *Jengo la ukumbusho*, monument. *Jengo la duara*, rotunda.

jengu.a *vt* 1. demolish, raze, tear down, pull down: *Alivijengua vibanda vibovu*, he demolished the old huts. (cf *bomoa, poromoa*) 2. (*fig*) spoil plans, wreck plans: *Alijengua mipango yangu*, he wrecked my plans. Prep. *jengu.li.a* St. *jengu.k.a* and *jengu.lik.a* Cs. *jengu.sh.a* Ps. of Prep. *jengu.liw.a* Rp. *jengu.an.a* (cf *haribu, tibua*)

jeraha (also *jaraha*) *n* (*ma-*) 1. wound, injury, hurt: *Ana jeraha kubwa mguuni*, he has a big wound on the leg. (cf *kidonda, kaga*) 2. (*fig*) trauma, impact, influence, effect: *Tukio lile limeleta jeraha kubwa katika siasa yetu*, that incident has made a big impact in our politics. (cf *athari*) (Ar)

jerikeni *n* (*n*) jerrycan; a large can for holding liquids esp gasoline. (Eng)

jerontolojia *n* (*n*) gerontology; the scientific study of the process of aging and the problems surrounding aging people. (Eng)

jeruh.i (also *juruhi*) *vt* 1. wound, injure, hurt: *Alimjeruhi mdogo wake kwa kumpiga sana*, he hurt his younger brother by beating him severely. (cf *umiza*) 2. hurt, pain, wound (psychologically): *Matusi yake yaliujeruhi moyo wangu*, his insults wounded my heart. Prep. *jeruh.i.a* St. *jeruh.ik.a* Cs. *jeruh.ish.a* Ps. of Prep *jeruh.iw.a* Rp. of Prep. *jeruh.i.an.a* (cf *athiri, gusa, choma, umiza*) (Ar)

jeshi *n* (*ma-*) 1. army, battalion; armed forces: *Jeshi la anga*, air force. *Jeshi la maji*, naval force. *Jeshi la nchi kavu*, infantry. *Jeshi la mgambo*, the people's militia. *Serikali ya kijeshi*, military government. *Jeshi la Kujenga Taifa*, National Service. *Jeshi la Wananchi*, the defence force. *Jeshi la Wokovu*, The Salvation Army. *Jeshi la ulinzi*, defence force. 2. troop, band, company, gang, team, crowd: *Kuna jeshi la watu huko nje*, there is a big crowd outside. (cf *kikosi, kikundi, umati*) (Ar)

jeni (also *jini*) *n* (*n*) gene; a unit inside a cell which consists of a particular quality in a living thing that has been passed on from its parents.

jeta[1] *n* (*n*) 1. (*zool*) barnacle; a

conspicuous thick heavy shellfish (family Gryphaeidae) which collects in large numbers on rocks, wharves, etc in the shallow sublittoral. 2. sluggard, idler, laggard; a lazy person: *Jeta hapendi kufanya kazi yoyote*, the idler does not like to do any work. (cf *mzembe*)

jet.a² *vt* 1. (of a child, etc.) behave in a manner calculated to induce elders to pamper someone: *Mtoto yule anajeta sana*, that child likes to be pampered very much. (cf *deka, nyeta*) 2. depend on, rely on, count on: *Msichana huyu ananyjeta dada yake katika kulipiwa karo ya shule*, this girl depends on her sister for the payment of school fees. (cf *tumainia, tegemea*) 3. brag, boast, vaunt, crow, show off: *Anajeta sana siku hizi kwa vile amenunua gari mpya*, he is boasting a lot these days because he has bought a new car. Prep. *jet.e.a* St. *jet.ek.a* Cs. *jet.esh.a* Ps. *jet.w.a* Rp. of Prep. *jet.e.an.a* (cf *jivuna, jinata*)

jeti¹ *n* (*n*) jet; an aircraft powered by a jet engine. (Eng)

jeti² *n* (*n*)(*min*) jet; a hard black variety of lignite, sometimes used in jewellery.

jeuri¹ (also *jauri, ujeuri*) *n* (*n*) 1. rudeness, insolence, impoliteness: *Fanya jeuri*, show rudeness; be rude. *Toa jeuri*, show rudeness, be rude. (cf *usafihi, ufidhuli*) 2. arrogance, conceit, pride, vanity, haughtiness: *Mtu yule ana jeuri sana*, that person is very arrogant. (cf *kiburi, maringo*)

jeuri² (also *jauri*) *adj* 1. rude, insolent, impolite: *Yeye ni mwajiri mjeuri*, he is a rude employer. (cf *safihi*) 2. arrogant, conceited, snobbish, high-and-mighty: *Yeye ni mtaalamu mjeuri*, he is an arrogant scholar. (Ar)

jezi¹ *n* (*n*) see *jazi²*

jezi² *n* (*n*) see *jazi³*

jiachi.a *vt* forget oneself.

jiaji.a *vi* spurt out, gush, jet: *Maji yalikuwa yanajiajia kutoka kwenye paipu iliyopasuka*, the water was spurting out from a broken pipe. (cf *bubujika, foka*)

jiamin.i *vt, vi* be self-confident, trust oneself: *Anajiamini sana katika kupika*, he is very self-confident in cooking. Prep. *jiamin.i.a* Cs. *jiamin.ish.a* (Ar)

jiaminish.a *vt* 1. dare, venture, risk: *Alijiaminisha kuogelea upande ule*, he dared to swim on that side. 2. prove to be loyal to others. Prep. *jiaminish.i.a*

jiamuli.a *vt, vi* judge or decide sth for oneself: *Lazima uwashauri wenzako; usijiamulie mambo yote mwenyewe*, you must consult your colleagues; don't decide everything by yourself.

jianda.a *vt, vi* prepare oneself: *Ameshughulika siku hizi akijiandaa kwa mtihani wake*, he is busy these days preparing himself for his examination. Prep. *jianda.li.a* (cf *jitayarisha*)

jiandikish.a *vt* enrol; register oneself: *Alijiandikisha kupiga kura*, he registered to vote. Prep. *jiandikish.i.a*

jibaidish.a *vi* stay aloof, seclude oneself; disassociate. Prep. *jibaidish.i.a*

jibanz.a *vt, vi* 1. hide oneself, conceal oneself; skulk, sneak, lurk: *Alijibanza ili nisimwone*, he hid himself so that I would not see him. Prep. *jibanz.i.a* (cf *jificha*)

jibar.i *vi* stay away from, keep one's distance: *Jibari hapo kwani gari sasa linakuja*, stay away from there because a vehicle is now coming. Prep. *jibar.i.a* (cf *jitenga, jibanza*)

jibini *n* (*n*) cheese (cf *chizi*) (Ar)

jibod.a *vi, vt* brag, boast.

jibodo.a *vi, vt* boast, brag, vaunt, show off: *Yeye anapenda kujibodoa mbele za watu*, he likes to show off in public. Prep. *jibodo.le.a* (cf *jigamba, jifutua, jisifu*)

Jibrili n (n) (in Islam) the angel who revealed the Koran to Prophet Mohammad; (in Christianity) the archangel who foretold the coming of Jesus to the virgin Mary; Gabriel.
jib.u[1] *vt, vi* answer, reply, retort, rejoin: *Jibu suala langu vizuri*, answer my question properly. Prep. *jib.i.a* St. *jib.ik.a* Cs. *jib.ish.a* and *jib.iz.a* Ps. of Prep. *jib.iw.a* Rp. of Prep. *jib.i.an.a* (cf *itikia, itika*) (Ar)
jibu[2] n (ma-) answer, rejoinder, response: *Alitoa jibu la haraka*, he gave a quick response. (cf *jawabu*) (Ar)
jicheke.a *vi* titter; laugh under one's breath.
jicho n (ma-) 1. (anat) eye: *Jicho lake linamuuma*, his eye is paining him. (cf *ozi*) 2. (*idms*) *Tupa jicho*, cast a glance. *Jicho kwa jicho*, an eye for an eye; reprisal (cf *tumba*) 2. (*bot*) bud of a flower when it is about to open: unopened bud of a flower. 3. (*naut*) eye ornament or oculus on a sailing vessel.
jichungu.a *vi* introspect; examine one's own thoughts or feelings.
jidab.a *vt* boast, brag, crow, vaunt. Prep. *jidab.i.a* (cf *jigumba, jicifu*)
jida.i *vt, vi* pretend; disguise oneself as, purport to be: *Alijidai kwamba yeye anafahamu masomo sana kuliko wenzake*, he pretended that he understood the subjects better than his colleagues. Prep. *jida.i.a* (cf *jifanya*)
jidangany.a *vi* deceive oneself. Prep. *jidangany.i.a*
jidhalilish.a *vi* eat humble pie; lower oneself; stoop, condescend: *Usijidhalilishe mbele ya mkubwa wako*, don't lower yourself before your boss. Prep. *jidhalilish.i.a*
jidhamini *vi* pledge oneself, sponsor oneself.
jidhil.i *vi* grovel; act obsequiously in order to obtain favour or forgiveness.

jidukiz.a *vt* interfere in other people's affairs; meddle, interlope, intrude. Prep. *jidukiz.i.a* (cf *ingilia*)
jielimish.a *vi, vt* self-educate Prep. *jielimish.i.a*
jiendeleza *vi* improve oneself, better oneself: *Alijiendeleza kielimu*, he improved himself academically.
jieliz.a *vt, vi* express one's opinion. Prep. *jielez.e.a*
jifaharish.a *vt* pride oneself; preen. Prep. *jifaharish.i.a*
jifany.a *vt, vi* pretend to be, disguise oneself as, purport to be: *Alijifanya mwehu*, he pretended to be insane. Prep. *jifany.i.a* Cs. *jifany.ish.a* (cf *jidai*)
jifaragu.a *vt* 1. pretend to be knowledgeable. 2. boast, brag. Prep. *jifaragu.li.a* Cs. *jifaragu.lish.a* (cf *jifaharisha*)
jifarij.i *vi* console oneself. Prep. *jifarij.i.a*
jifich.a *vi* hide, lurk, conceal oneself: *Alijificha kwenye kichaka*, he hid himself in the bush. Prep. *jifich.i.a*
jifikiri.a *vi* introspect; look into ones own mind, feeling, etc.
jifisid.i *vi* ruin oneself. Prep. *jifisid.i.a*
jifu n (n) 1. carcass; dead body of an animal: *Jifu lile linanuka*, that carcass is stinking. (cf *mzoga, mfu*) 2. anything that is unstable.
jifundish.a (also *jifunza*) *vt* self-educate, teach oneself, self-teach; study by oneself: *Alijifundisha mwenyewe namna ya kuendesha baiskeli*, she taught herself how to ride a bicycle. Prep. *jifundish.i.a*
jifundu.a *vt* give money. Prep. *jifundu.li.a*
jifung.a *vt, vi* 1. get oneself into a fix e.g. *Amejifunga kwa kuutia sahihi mkataba*, he has fixed himself by signing the contract. 2. avoid child-bearing: *Alijifunga kwa kutumia dawa*, she avoided child bearing by contraception. 3. (*idm*): *Jifunga*

J

kibwebwe a) work hard, pull one's socks b) gird one's loins.
jifungi.a *vi* (used in the expression) *Jifungia ndani*, remain indoors.
jifungu.a *vi, vt* give birth: *Alijifungua mtoto mwanamume*, she gave birth to a baby boy. Prep. ***jifungu.li.a***
jifunz.a¹ *vt* see *jifundisha*
jifunz.a² *vt, vi* learn from an experience; learn a lesson: *Kuna mengi ya kujifunza katika dunia hii*, there is a lot to learn from this world. Prep. ***jifunz.i.a***
jifurahish.a *vi* have fun, indulge oneself; have a good time: *Kijana yule anapenda kujifurahisha kwa mambo ya anasa*, that young man likes to indulge himself in luxuries. Prep. ***jifurahish.i.a***
jifutu.a *vt, vi* brag, boast, vaunt, show off: *Anapenda kujifutua kwamba yeye ni mzuri*, she likes to brag that she is beautiful. Prep. ***jifutu.li.a*** Cs. ***jifutu.sh.a*** (cf *jigamba, jisifu*)
jifya *n* (*ma-*) one of the three cooking stones used to support a cooking-pot; fire brick, hearth stone. (*prov*) *Jifya moja haliinjiki chungu*, one cooking stone does not carry a cooking-pot i.e. Unity is strength.
jigamb.a *vt, vi* brag, boast, show off: *Haifai kujigamba mbele za watu*, it is not good to boast in public. Prep. ***jigamb.i.a*** (cf *jibodoa, jifutua*)
jigambo *n* (*ma-*) a self-praise poem.
jigeuz.a *vt* sham; assume the appearance of sth. Prep. ***jigeuz.i.a***
jigija *n* (*n*) dark black thing; pitched black substance.
jigombo.a *vt* see *jikomboa*
jiha *n* (*n*) 1. direction: *Amesafiri jiha ya mashariki*, he has travelled eastwards. (cf *upande, janibu*) 2. viewpoint, stand, angle, perspective, point of view: *Kwa jiha hii*, in this perspective. (Ar)
jihada.a *vt* deceive oneself. (cf *jidanganya*)
jihadhar.i *vt* beware, be cautious, take care: *Jihadhari na wezi*, beware of thieves! Prep. ***jihadhar.i.a*** Cs. ***jihadhar.ish.a*** (cf *tahadhari*) (Ar)
jihadi *n* (*n*) jihad; holy war: *Ukombozi wa nchi yetu ulikuwa vita vya jihadi*, the liberation of our country was a holy war. (Ar)
jihamasish.a *vt* self-motivate; motivate oneself to do or achieve sth because of one's own enthusiasm or interest without pressure from others: *Lazima tujihamasishe katika shughuli zetu mbalimbali*, we must motivate ourselves in different activities. Prep. ***jihamasish.i.a*** St. ***jihamasish.ik.a*** Ps. ***jihamasish.w.a*** Rp. ***jihamasish.an.a***
jiham.i *vt, vi* protect oneself, defend: *Nchi ilijihami kijasiri*, the country defended itself bravely. Prep. ***jiham.i.a*** Cs. ***jiham.ish.a*** (cf *jikinga*) (Ar)
jihim.u (also *himu*) *vi* wake up early in the morning; get up early in the morning; rise with the sun: *Nikijihimu kesho, nitasafiri kwa ndege ya asubuhi*, if I wake up at dawn tomorow, I will travel on the morning flight. Prep. ***jihim.i.a*** Cs. ***jihim.ish.a***
jihin.i *vt, vi* deprive oneself of, deny oneself; abnegate: *Ana pesa lakini anajihini kula chakula kizuri*, he has money but he denies himself of eating good food. Prep. ***jihin.i.a*** Cs. ***jihin.ish.a*** (cf *jinyima*) (Ar)
jihis.i *vt* feel oneself bad or good about sth: *Alijihisi vibaya kwa kushindwa kuniazima gari lake*, he felt bad for failing to lend me his car. Prep. ***jihis.i.a***
jihusish.a *vi* be involved in, be connected to: *Alijihusisha katika miradi mbalimbali*, he involved himself in various projects. Prep. ***jihusish.i.a*** (cf *shughulikia*)
jiinami.a *vt, vi* be depressed; be bent down because of depression, etc.: *Alijiinamia kwa huzuni*, he bowed down with grief. Cs. ***jiinam.ish.a***
jiingiz.a *vt* indulge in; obtrude upon/on:

Anapenda kujiingiza katika mambo yangu, he likes to obtrude on my affairs. Prep. ***jiingiz.i.a***

jiinik.a *vi* sleep on one's side: *Watu wengine wanapenda kujiinika*, some people like to sleep on their side.

jiji *n* (*ma-*) metropolis, city: *Jiji la Dar es Salaam*, the city of Dar es Salaam.

jik.a *vt, vi* strain oneself as a woman in labour at childbirth or as a fowl lays an egg or like a person defecating: *Kuku alijika ili azae yai*, the fowl strained itself to lay an egg. Prep. ***jik.i.a*** St. ***jik.ik.a*** Cs. ***jik.ish.a***

jikalifish.a *vt* force oneself to do sth: *Usijikalifishe kuifanya kazi yangu*, don't force yourself to do my work. Prep. ***jikalifish.i.a*** (cf *jilazimisha*)

jikamu.a *vt* strain oneself.

jikaz.a *vi* be bold; take a grip on oneself: *Alijikaza licha ya matatizo yenyewe*, he took a grip on himself despite the problems. (*idm*) *Jikaza kisabuni*, persevere despite the problems confronting you. Prep. ***jikaz.i.a*** (cf *himili, vumilia*)

jike[1] *n* (*ma-*) 1. a female animal; a female bird: *Mbuzi jike*, she-goat. *Ng'ombe jike*, cow. 2. (*derog*) craven, recreant, coward: *Ingawa yeye ana nguvu sana lakini ni jike*, even though he is very strong, he is a coward. (cf *hawafu, chuchu*)

jike[2] *n* (*n*) (in card playing) seven; a playing card with seven pips, which has a value of ten points in a game where one needs sixty one points or more to win.

jikedume *n* (*ma-*) hoyden, tomboy; a girl who behaves like a boisterous boy.

jiketu.a *vt, vi* brag, boast; boast of a quality that you don't really possess; *Amekuwa akijiketua kwa majirani kwamba ni mganga*, he has been boasting to his neighbours that he is a medicine man. Prep. ***jiketu.li.a***

jikim.u *vt, vi* support oneself, self-maintain, pay one's expenses: *Alijikimu alipokuwa anasoma ng'ambo*, he supported himself when he was studying abroad. (cf *jiendesha*)

jikina.i *vt, vi* be self-contented. Prep. ***jikina.i.a*** St. ***jikina.ik.a*** Cs. ***jikina.ish.a*** (cf *ridhika*)

jiking.a *vt* fend, protect: *Lazima tujikinge na ugonjwa wa kipindupindu*, we must protect ourselves against cholera. Prep. ***jiking.i.a*** Cs. ***jiking.ish.a***

jikit.a *vi, vt* 1. boast, vaunt, show off: *Alipojikita, rafiki zake wakampuuza*, when he boasted, his friends ignored him. 2. hold firmly 3. focus, rest: *Utafiti wake umejikita katika eneo pana*, his research is focused on a broad area. Prep. ***jikit.i.a***

jiko *n* (*ma-*) 1. cooking place, fireplace, kitchen. 2. (*idms*) *Pulu jiko*, marry. *Kazi ya kijungu jiko*, work that enables you to get food only. 3. a cooking vessel: *Jiko la umeme*, electric cooker. *Jiko la stima*, stove. 4. (*naut*) caboose

jikokot.a *vt* drag oneself, trudge, plod, crawl: *Alipoumia, alianza kujikokota*, when he got injured, he started to crawl. Prep. ***jikokot.e.a*** Cs ***jikokot.esh.a*** (cf *jikongoja*)

jikomb.a *vt* ingratiate oneself with superiors in order to fulfill one's interests: *Anapenda kujikomba kwa wakubwa zake kazini*, he likes to ingratiate himself with his seniors at the work place. (cf *jipendekeza*)

jikombo.a (also *jigomboa*) *vt* liberate oneself: *Wananchi walijikomboa kutokana na utawala wa kigeni*, the people liberated themselves from foreign domination. Prep. ***jikombo.le.a***

jikongoj.a *vi* 1. traipse; move or walk wearily or reluctantly (cf *jivuta*) 2. falter, stagger; move unsteadily: *Uchumi katika nchi yetu umekuwa ukijikongoja*, the economy in our country has been moving unsteadily. Prep. ***jikongoj.e.a***

259

J

(cf *jikokota, suasua*)

jikosh.a *vi* evade blame; restore one's image. Prep. *jikosh.e.a*

jikoso.a *vt* self correct. Prep. *jikoso.le.a*

jikunj.a *vi, vt* fold oneself/itself 2 (*fig*) be in a state of melancholy, fear, etc; cringe; cower (cf *jikunyata*)

jikunyat.a *vt, vi* cower, cringe; flinch,shrink back as in fear, cold, etc. *Alijikunyata kwa baridi kali*, he cringed himself because of severe cold. Prep. *jikunyat.i.a* St. *jikunyat.ik.a* Cs. *jikunyat.ish.a* (cf *jikunya*)

jikusur.u *vt* try hard to do sth. Prep. *jikusur.i.a* St. *jikusur.ik.a* Cs. *jikusur.ish.a*

jikwa.a *vi* stumble, trip.

jilab.i *vi* boast oneself in public; brag, vaunt. Prep. *jilab.i.a*

jilind.a *vi* defend oneself; fend. Prep. *jilind.i.a* Cs. *jilind.ish.a*

jilio *n* (*ma-*) coming, advent: *Jilio lake kwangu halikutarajiwa*, his coming to my place was unexpected. (cf *ujio, mjo*)

jilis.i (also *julusi*) *vi* sit down, seat oneself: *Alijilisi kwenye mkeka*, he sat on the mat. Prep. *jilis.i.a* St. *jilis.ik.a* Cs. *jilis.ish.a* Ps. of Prep. *jilis.iw.a* (cf *kaa, keti*)

jimamas.a *vi* treat with contempt; pretend not to know or understand: *Anajimamasa kila nikimwambia anirejeshee vitabu vyangu*, he becomes inattentive whenever I tell him to return my books. Prep. *jimamas.i.a* Cs. *jimamas.ish.a* (cf *babaisha, jibarauza, gangaiza*)

jimbi[1] *n* (*ma-*) rooster, cock; a male fowl: *Jimbi liliwika*, the cock crowed. (cf *jogoo, kikwara*)

jimbi[2] *n* (*ma-*) (*bot*) taro; eddo. *Colocasia antiquorum*

jimbo[1] *n* (*ma-*) 1. province, state, region: *Jimbo la magharibi*, western province (election) 2. constituency: *Jimbo la uchaguzi*, constituency.

jimbo[2] *n* (*ma-*) herbal medicine made from leaves, used for bathing newly-born babies so as to give them good health.

jimbu *n* (*ma-*) rain water trench. (cf *mfumbi, dimbwi*)

jina *n* (*ma-*) 1. name: *Jina la kupanga*, pen name. *Jina la kupachika/la utani*, nickname. *Jina la msimbo*, code name. *Jina kamili*, full name. *Jina la ukoo*, surname. *Pata jina*, get a name. 2. (*gram*) noun: *Jina dhahania*, abstract noun. *Jina la mguso*, concrete noun. *Jina la pekee*, proper noun (cf *nomino*)

jinadhifish.a *vi* preen; dress up or adorn oneself. Prep. *jinadhifish.i.a*

jinad.i *vt* brag, boast, vaunt, show off: *Yeye anapenda kujinadi mbele ya watu*, he likes to boast himself in public. (cf *jigamba, jisifu*)

jinai *n* (*n*) crime, felony: *Kesi ya jinai*, criminal case. *Kosa la jinai*, criminal offence. *Mashtaka ya jinai*, criminal charge. (Ar)

jinak.i *vt, vi* 1. brag, boast, show off: *Ni kweli kwamba muungwana hajinaki?* Is it true that a gentleman never boasts? 2. exonerate; free oneself from blame for a wrongdoing or fault. Prep. *jinak.i.a* Cs. *jinak.ish.a* (cf *jisifu, jibodoa*)

jinakolojia *n* (*n*) (*med*) gynaecology; the branch of medicine dealing with the specific functions, diseases, etc. of women. (Eng)

jinamizi *n* (*ma-*) nightmare; bad dream: *Jana usiku, nilipata jinamizi*, I had a nightmare last night. (cf *kabusi*)

jinasibish.a *vi* relate oneself with sby/sth. Prep. *jinasibish.i.a*

jinat.a *vi* be conceited, be arrogant, be proud: *Haifai kujinata mbele za watu*, it is not good to be conceited in public. Prep. *jinat.i.a* Cs. *jinat.ish.a* (cf *jitwaza, jibodoa*)

jini[1] *n* (*ma-*) 1. genie; a spirit or goblin with strange powers. 2. brute, devil; a wicked person: *Usiambatane na jini*

jini²

yule, don't associate with that devil. (cf *guberi, mwovu*) (Ar)

jini² *n* (*n*) see *jeni*

jino *n* (*ma-*) (pl *meno*) 1. (*anat*)tooth: *Jino la juu*, upper tooth. *Jino la nyuma*, back tooth; molar. *Jino la mbele*, incisor. *Jino la utoto*, milk tooth. *Meno ya bandia*, dentures; artificial teeth. 2. toothlike part, as on a saw, fork, rake, gearwheel, etc.; tine, prong, cog (of a wheel), plug (of tobacco), etc.: *Jino la msumeno*, the tooth of a saw. *Jino zima la tumbaku*, a whole plug of tobacco. 3. an infection of the gums and tooth sockets, characterized by the formation of pus and, usu, by loosening of the teeth; pyorrhoea: *Ameshikwa na jino*, he has pyorrhoea. (cf *kimenomeno*)

jino.a *vi, vt* be well-trained for a particular thing: *Timu yetu imejinoa vizuri kwa ajili ya msimu mpya wa ligi unaokuja*, our team is well-trained for the forthcoming league season. Prep. *jino.le.a*

jinsi *n* (*n*) 1. method, way, kind, procedure: *Jinsi gani?* How? What way? *Yeye haelewi jinsi ya kujaza fomu*, he does not know how to fill the form. (The word *jinsi* is frequently used with the relative particle of manner -vyo- e.g. *Nieleze jinsi ulivyopika wali huu*, explain to me how you cooked the rice. 2. sex. (Ar)

jinsia *n* (*n*) 1. gender, sex: *Jinsia ya kiume*, masculine gender. *Jinsia ya kike*, feminine gender. *Suala la jinsia*, gender question. 2. ethnicity, tribe (Ar)

jinusurish.a *vt* save one's life. Prep. *jinusurish.i.a*

jinyim.a *vi, vt* deny, abnegate; deprive oneself of sth which gives pleasure, etc. *Anajinyima kula vyakula vizuri kwa sababu ya ubahili wake*, he denies himself good food because of his stinginess.

jipim.a

jinyong.a *vi* hang oneself; take one's own life. *Jinyonganyonga*, squirm, wriggle. Prep. *jinyong.e.a* Cs. *jinyong.esh.a*

jinyosh.a *vi* stretch oneself; lie. Prep. *jinyosh.e.a*

jio¹ *n* (*ma-*) coming, approach: *Jio la usiku*, the approach of the night.

jio² *adv, n* (*n*) evening (cf *jioni, alasiri*)

jiofizikia *n* (*n*) geophysics (Eng)

jiografia *n* (*n*) geography: *Jiografia ya kimaumbile*, physical geography. (Eng)

jiolojia *n* (*n*) geology (Eng)

jiometri (also *jometri*) *n* (*n*) geometry (Eng)

jion.a *vi* (*n*) be arrogant, be conceited, be proud: *Mtu yule anajiona sana*, that person is very arrogant. Prep. *jion.e.a* Cs. *jion.esh.a* (cf *ringa, jinata, takabari*)

jiondo.a *vt, vi* secede, disassociate: *Walijiondoa kwenye mashindano*, they disassociated from the tournament. Prep. *jiondo.le.a* Cs. *jiondo.sh.a*

jioni *n* (*n*) afternoon (cf *jio, alasiri*)

jionyesh.a *vi* (*ma-*) manifest oneself, reveal oneself, show off: *Anapenda kujionyesha*, he likes to show off. Prep. *jionyesh.e.a*

jipang.a *vi, vt* 1. stand in a line, etc. 2. prepare oneself in a particular task; brace oneself (for sth); *Serikali imejipanga upya katika juhudi za kuboresha uchumu wa nchi*, the government has braced it self afresh in its effort to develop the country's economy. Prep. *jipang.i.a* St. *jipang.ik.a*

jipendekez.a *vi, vt* ingratiate oneself: *Yeye siku zote hujipendekeza kwa wakubwa*, he always ingratiates himself with big bosses. Prep. *jipendekez.e.a* Cs. *jipendekez.esh.a*

jipim.a *vt* introspect; evaluate oneself: *Timu yao ilijipima nguvu kwa kucheza mechi chache*, their team organized few trial matches as a test of strength. Prep. *jipim.i.a* Cs. *jipim.ish.a*

jipindu.a *vi* summersault; make an acrobatic movement. Prep. ***jipindu.li.a*** Cs. ***jipindu.sh.a***

jipongez.a *vi* congratulate oneself, plume oneself. Prep. ***jipongez.e.a***

jipu[1] *n* (*ma-*) abscess, boil, blain, furuncle: *Nina jipu mguuni*, I have a boil on my leg. *Jipu lake limetumbuka*, his boil has burst. (cf *tambazi*)

jipu[2] *n* (*n*) jeep; heavy duty automotive vehicle. (Eng)

jira[1] *n* (*bot*) cumin seed. *Cumminum cyminum*. (cf *uzile*) (Hind)

jira[2] *n* (*n*) (*math*) axis: *Jira kuu*, principal axis. *Jira mlalo*, abscissa. *Jira wima*, ordinate.

jirafu *n* (*ma-*) fridge, refrigerator. (cf *jokofu, friji*)

jirani[1] *n* (*ma-*) neighbour (Ar)

jirani[2] *adv* near, adjacent: *Anaishi jirani*, he lives near. (cf *karibu*) (Ar)

jir.i *vi* occur, happen take place: *Wizi wa kutumia nguvu hujiri sana wakati wa usiku katika jiji letu*, robbery with violence commonly occurs at night in our city. Prep. ***jir.i.a*** St. ***jir.ik.a*** Cs. ***jir.ish.a*** Ps. of Prep. ***jir.iw.a*** (cf *tokea, tendeka*)

jiriwa *n* (*n*) 1. vice, clamp, brace; wooden or iron vice for holding things. 2. trap, snare: *Ameingia katika jiriwa*, he has fallen into a trap. (Ar)

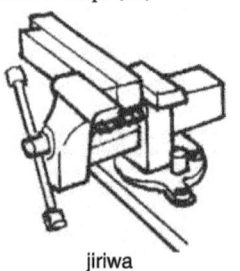

jiriwa

jis.a *vi* 1. converse esp at night; talk esp at night: *Rafiki yangu anapenda kujisa baada ya kula chakula cha usiku*, my friend likes to hold conversation after dinner. 2. talk esp after sleeping time; confabulate. 3. console: *Tangu kufiwa na mumewe, tumekuwa tukijaribu kumjisa nyumbani kwake*, since her husband's death, we have been trying to console her at her home. Prep. ***jis.i.a*** St. ***jis.ik.a*** Cs. ***jis.ish.a*** Ps. of Prep. ***jis.iw.a*** (cf *liwaza*)

jisadi *n* (*n*) see *jasadi*

jisaha.u *vi, vt* forget oneself because of thinking of sth that has earlier prevailed in your mind, etc.: *Amejisahau kwamba yuko kama mgeni hapa*, he has forgotten that he is like a visitor here. *Alijisahau na kukipiga kikombe bila ya kujua*. She forgot herself and kicked the cup inadvertently. Prep. ***jisahau.li.a*** Cs. ***jisahau.lish.a***

jisaidi.a *vi* 1. go (to the toilet), to relieve oneself: *Alimpeleka mtoto mdogo chooni kujisaidia*, he took a small child to the toilet to relieve himself. 2. do sth good for oneself. (Ar)

jisalimish.a *vi* surrender, give up: *Alijisalimisha kwa majeshi ya uvamizi*, he surrendered to the invading army. Prep. ***jisalimish.i.a***

jishughulish.a *vi, vt* be occupied, be busy, be engaged; engross oneself: *Amejishughulisha na kazi ya uvuvi*, he has busied himself in fishing. (Ar)

jishush.a *vi* stoop, condescend; humble oneself. Prep. ***jishush.i.a***

jisib.u *vt* curse oneself of sth. Prep. ***jisib.i.a*** (cf *jiapiza, jiokota*)

jisif.u *vt, vi* brag, boast, flaunt, show off: *Anajisifu bure*, he is boasting for nothing. Prep. ***jisif.i.a***

jisiki.a *vt* feel oneself; be in the mood: *Anajisikia vibaya*, he feels unwell. *Hajisikii vizuri*, he doesn't feel well.

jisimu *n* (*ma-*) body, physique, figure: *Ana jisimu kubwa*, he has a huge body. (cf *maumbile, umbo*) (Ar)

jisingizi.a *vt* sham, pretend, malinger: *Alijisingizia kwamba alikuwa mgonjwa*, he pretended that he was sick.

jisu *n* (*ma-*) a big knife used for tapping palm trees.

jitahid.i   **jitwaz.a** **J**

jitahid.i *vi, vt* do one's best; work hard: *Anajitahidi katika masomo yake*, he is working hard in his studies. (cf *pindana, kazana*) (Ar)

jitanib.u *vt, vi* 1. avert, escape, dodge, get rid of: *Dereva alijitanibu na hatari kwa umahiri*, the driver averted the accident skilfully. (cf *jiepusha*) 2. isolate oneself. (cf *jitenga*) Prep. *jitanib.i.a* St. *jitanib.ik.a* Cs. *jitanib.ish.a* (cf *epa, kwepa*) (Ar)

jitap.a *vi, vt* brag, boast, show off: *Anajitapa siku hizi kwa vile amepata shahada*, he is boasting these days because he has a degree. Prep. *jitap.i.a* (cf *jisifu, jibodoa*)

jitawal.a *vt, vi* be independent, have self-control: *Nchi ikijitawala inapata bendera yake*, if a country becomes independent, it gets its own flag. Prep. *jitawal.i.a*

jitegeme.a *vi, vt* be self-reliant, be self-sufficient: *Nchi yetu inafuata sera ya kujitegemea*, our country pursues upon a policy of self-reliance.

jiteng.a *vi* secede from, isolate, stay aloof: *Haifai nchi kujitenga na jumuiya ya kimataifa*, it is not good for a country to isolate itself from the international community.

jiti.a *vt* 1. meddle, intrude, interfere, pry, snoop. *Kwa nini anajitia katika mambo yasiyomhusu?* Why does he interfere in matters that don't concern him? (cf *jiingiza, jidukiza*) 2. pretend: *Anajitia hamnazo*, he pretends to be mad.

jitihada (also *jitihadi*) *n* (*n*) effort, endeavour, industriousness: *Mtu yule huonyesha jitihada sana katika kazi yake*, that person puts a lot of effort into his work. (cf *bidii, juhudi*) (Ar)

jitihadi *n* (*n*) see *jitihada*

jitikis.a *vi* move one's body. Prep. *jitikis.i.a* Cs. *jitikis.ish.a* (cf *jitukusa*)

jitimai *n* (*n*) grief, sorrow, distress: *Kifo cha mama yangu kilinitia katika jitimai kubwa*, my mother's death caused me a great deal of distress. (cf *simanzi,* *huzuni*) (Ar)

jito.a *vt, vi* remove oneself from, pull out; retire, withdraw: *Timu yetu ilijitoa katika mashindano*, our team pulled out of the tournament. Prep. *jito.le.a* Cs. *jito.z.a*

jitokez.a *vt, vi* 1. protrude, jut out, stick out: *Shati lake limejitokeza nje kiunoni*, his shirt has stuck out at the waist. 2. emerge, develop; come to the front: *Taasisi yao ilijitokeza kusaidia watu walemavu*, their institution came out to help handicapped people. Prep. *jitokez.e.a* Cs. *jitokez.esh.a*

jitoshelez.a *vt, vi* be self-sufficient, be adequate: *Nchi yetu inajitosheleza katika sekta nyingi*, our country is self-sufficient in many sectors.

jitu *n* (*ma-*) (amplic of *mtu*) ogre, monster, giant: *Jitu la kike*, giantess.

jituk.a *vt, vi* be startled, be astounded, be astonished: *Alijituka mara tu aliposikia kelele za "mwizi!" "mwizi!"* he was startled when he heard cries of "thief!" "thief!"

jitukus.a *vi* move one's body. Prep. *jitukus.i.a* Cs. *jitukus.ish.a* (cf *jitikisa*)

jitum.a *vi* 1. exert oneself a lot: *Anapenda kujituma*, he likes to exert himself a lot. 2. be dedicated: *Yule mfanyakazi amejituma kazini*, the employee is dedicated to his work. *Lazima uwe na moyo wa kujituma*, you must have a spirit of working hard.

jitwali.a usurp, arrogate, expropriate; take on oneself; assume a burden, etc.: *Kiongozi wa jeshi amejitwalia madaraka nchini*, the head of the army has taken for himself the leadership of the country.

jitwaz.a *vt, vi* brag, boast, show off: *Tangu kushinda katika bahati nasibu, amekuwa anajitwaza tu*, since he won the lottery, he has become boastful. Prep. *jitwaz.i.a* Cs. *jitwaz.ish.a* (cf *jisifu, jibodoa*)

jitwez.a *vi* stoop, condescend. Prep. *jitwez.e.a* Cs. *jitwez.esh.a*
jiu.a *vi* commit suicide; take one's own life. Prep. *jiu.li.a* Cs. *jiu.lish.a*
jiuliz.a *vt, vi* wonder by oneself: *Alijiuliza mwenyewe kwa nini alikuwa anaonewa*, he wondered why he was being bullied. Prep. *jiuliz.i.a*
jiung.a *vt, vi* join, associate: The verb *jiunga* is always followed by the particle *na* e.g. *Alijiunga na timu yetu ya mpira*, he joined our football team. Prep. *jiung.i.a* Cs. *jiung.ish.a* (cf *ingia*)
jiuzul.u *vi, vt* resign, abdicate: *Rais amejiuzulu*, the president has resigned. (cf *ng'atuka*) Prep. *jiuzul.i.a* Cs. *jiuzul.ish.a* (Ar)
jivi[1] (also *jizi*) *n* (*ma-*) (amplic of *mwizi*) a notorious thief; a habitual thief.
jivi[2] *n* (*ma-*) a wild hog. (cf *ngiri, mbogo*)
jivii *n* (*n*) gentian-violet
jivu *n* (*ma-*) ash
-jivujivu *adj* grey, ash colour: *Amevaa shati la rangi ya kijivujivu*, he has worn a grey shirt.
jivuli[1] *n* (*ma-*) shadow (cf *kivuli*)
jivuli[2] *n* (*n*) (*zool*) sea urchin. a kind of small black sea animal with a hard spiny body. (*Echinodermata*)
jivun.a *vi, vt* brag, boast; show off, be proud. Prep. *jivun.i.a* Cs. *jivun.ish.a* (cf *ringa, jisifu, jinata*)
jivut.a *vi* traipse; walk or move wearily or reluctantly. Prep. *jivut.i.a* Cs. *jivut.ish.a* (cf *jikongoja*)
jiwe *n* (*ma-*) 1. stone: *Jiwe la kusagia*, millstone. *Jiwe la mizani*, weighing stone. *Jiwe la msingi*, cornerstone. *Jiwe la thamani*, a jewel. *Nyumba ya mawe*, stone house. *Shoka la mawe*, stone axe. *Zama za zana za mawe*, Stone Age. 2. battery, cell: *Jiwe la kiberiti*, a flint for a lighter. 3. weight of a balance.
jiwez.a *vt, vi* be fit; be all right, be able to do without help: *Yeye anajiweza kifedha*, he is all right financially.
jizatit.i *vt, vi* prepare oneself for; brace oneself up: be ready for sth: *Jeshi lao limeanza kujizatiti kwa vita*, their army has started to brace itself for the war. Prep. *jizatit.i.a* Cs. *jizatit.ish.a* (cf *jitayarisha*) (Ar)
jizi *n* (*ma-*) see *jivi*
jizia (also *jizya*) *n* (*n*) tax or special payment made by non-Muslims to an Islamic government in return for their personal security and individual rights. (Ar)
jizoez.a *vt, vi* acquaint oneself, accustom oneself: get into a habit. *Usijizoeze kunywa kahawa kila mara*, don't get into the habit of drinking coffee every time. Prep. *jizoez.e.a* Cs. *jizoez.esh.a*
jizui.a *vt* control oneself, exercise self-control: *Anajizuia na anasa za dunia*, he exercises self-control over worldly pleasures. Prep. *jizui.li.a*
jizya *n* (*n*) see *jizia*
jodari *n* (*n*) (*zool*) tuna; a large ocean fish (family *Scombridae*) with elongated and fusiform body, moderately compressed in some genera and having a pointed snout. Dogtooth tuna. *Gymnosarda unicolor*.

jodari

joga *n* (*n*) coward, craven.
jogoo *n* (*ma-*) 1. (*zool*) cock, rooster; a male fowl. *Mlio wa jogoo*, cock-a-doodle-doo. *Jogoo lawika*, the cock crows. (*prov*) *Jogoo la shamba haliwiki mjini*, a country cock does not crow in town i.e. you cannot do as you wish in a foreign country. *Jogoo la kwanza*, midnight at 2.00 a.m. *Jogoo la pili*,

dawn at 4.00 a.m. *Jogoo wa mtaa*, a male prostitute. (cf *kikwara, jimbi*) 2. (*fig*) valiant, lion-heart; a brave person: *Watu wengi wanamwogopa jogoo yule*, many people are scared of that brave person (cf *shujaa, jabari*)

johari *n* (*n*) jewel, gem; a precious stone: *Mlango wa kasri ya mfalme umepambwa na majohari ya aina kwa aina*, the entrance to the king's palace is inset with jewels of various kinds. (*prov*) *Johari za mtu ni mbili, akili na haya*, the most precious qualities of a man are these two: intelligence and modesty. (cf *kito*) (Ar)

joho *n* (*ma-*) 1. a black woollen cloth. 2. a man's long loose robe which is richly embroidered along the neck and in front and which is normally worn by some Arabs and some wealthy people; mantle: *Joho lenye mkanda*, ulster. *joho la wanawake*, pelisser. (Ar)

joka *n* (*ma-*) (*zool*) a big snake; dragon.

joko *n* (*ma-*) oven, kiln, furnace: *Joko la mdukizo*, induction furnace. *Joko mfyuko*, blast furnace. *Joko la aki umeme*, electric arc furnace. *Joko rindimaji*, reverberatory furnace. (cf *oveni, tanu, tanuri*)

jokofu *n* (*ma-*) fridge, refrigerator. (cf *jirafu, frijt*)

jometri (also *jiometri*) *n* (*n*) geometry: *Jometri endelezi*, geometrical progression. *Jometri mstari*, linear geometry. *Jometri ya majira*, coordinate geometry. *Jometri ya uchambuzi*, analytic geometry.(Eng)

jonge.a *vt, vi* come near, draw near, come close; approach, advance: *Jongea hapa ili nipate kukunong'oneza*, come close so that I can whisper to you. Prep. **jonge.le.a** St. **jonge.lek.a** Cs. **jonge.z.a** Ps. **jonge.w.a** (cf *sogea, karibia*)

jongele.a *vt, vi* move near sth; approach.

jongo¹ *n* (*ma-*) seam obtained as a result of sewing: *Jongo nene*, a large projecting seam.

jongo² *n* (*ma-*) (*med*) an ailment accompanied by progressive pains in the joints and swollen legs, usu occurring when it is cloudy; rheumatoid arthritis.

jongomeo *n* (*n*) doomsday, judgement day; the day of resurrection, the next world. (cf *ahera*)

jongonene *n* (*n*) see *jongo¹*

jongoo *n* (*ma-*) 1. (*zool*) millipede. *Jongoo panda*, a large millipede. 2. (*idm*) *Tupa jongoo na mti wake*, forget; abandon sth completely. (*syn*) *Jongoo hapandi mtungi*, gay, homosexual. (cf *hanithi, shoga*)

jongoobahari *n* (*ma-*) (*zool*) sea cucumber; a cucumber-shaped echinoderm of the class *Holothuroidea* which has a thick wormlike body with tentacles around the mouth.

jongoobahari

jopo *n* (*ma-*) 1. panel, board, committee: *Jopo la wataalamu*, a panel of experts. (cf *paneli*) 2. gang; a group of people having assembled together.

jora *n* (*ma-*) a bale of calico material which is about 30 yards: *Nimenunua majora mengi ya vitambaa*, I have bought many bales of calico material. (Hind)

jore¹ *n* (*n*) (*zool*) broad-billed roller; a small thicket bird (family *Coraciidae*) with a conspicuous yellow bill and blackish wings. *Eurystomus glaucurus*.

jore² (also *jori*) *n* (*n*) a kind of card game.

joshi¹ *n* (*n*) 1. (*naut*) the windward side of a vessel. 2. the forward corner of a sail with rope attaching it to either bowspirit or prow. 3. the speed of a vessel.

joshi² *adv* 1. fast, quickly, rapidly, swiftly: *Enda joshi,* sail closer to the wind. 2. go fast. (*prov*) *Dau la mnyonge haliendi joshi,* because a poor man's resources are limited, he cannot go far in terms of achieving prosperity, etc. (Ar)

josho *n* (*n*) 1. animal dip; dipping trough. (cf *dipu*) 2. special bath.

joto *n* (*n*) 1. heat, hotness: *Joto fichu,* latent heat. *Joto nururifu,* radiant heat. 2. sweat, perspiration. (cf *jasho, jekejeke*) 3. (*fig*) anger, temper: *Ana joto jingi,* he has a bad temper.

jouli *n* (*n*) (*elect*) joule; the unit of work or energy in the mks system. (Eng)

joya *n* (*n*) spongy substance in the shell of a coconut when it wants to grow: *Joya la nazi,* either the substance or the nut. (*prov*) *Nyumba yangu ni joya, atakaye huingia,* my house is free, anyone who wants to come in is welcome. (*syn*) *Kama joya,* smooth and soft.

joyo *n* (*n*) kernel, germ, core; the central part of a grain or seed or anything else and usu. it is soft: *Joyo la muhogo,* the kernel of a cassava.

jozi *n* (*n*) 1. pair, duo, couplet, doublet: *Jozi ya viatu,* a pair of shoes. 2. (in card playing) a whole pack of cards. 3. (*gram*) *Jozi linganuzi,* contrastive pair. *Jozi semantiki,* semantic pair. *Jozi mlinganuo finyu,* minimal pair. (Ar)

jua¹ *n* (*n*) sun, sunlight: *Jua kali,* hot sun, hot weather. *Jua utosini,* noon.

ju.a² *vt, vi* know, understand, comprehend, realize: *Yeye anakujua,* he knows you. Prep. *ju.li.a,* know for (at, in, etc.), e.g. *Julia hali,* greet sby. St. *ju.lik.a* Cs. *ju.lish.a, ju.vy.a* and *ju.z.a* Rp *ju.an.a,* know each other e.g. *Watu wale wanajuana,* those people know each other. (cf *fahamu, elewa*)

juakali¹ (*n*) 1. artisanship; informal workmanship: *Kazi ya juakali,* artisan workmanship. 2. self employment.

juakali² *n* (*n*) hardships of life.

juan.a *vt* see *jua*

juba¹ *n* (*ma-*) jellaba, burnoose, a long cloak with a hood worn by Arabs, etc. (cf *mfuria*) (Ar)

juba² *n* (*ma-*) a mortising chisel. (cf *patasi, balari, turusi*)

jubilii *n* (*n*) jubilee; a special anniversary, especially a 25th or 50th one. (Eng)

jubuni *adj* elated, joyful, jubilant, jovial.

jubur.u *vt* compel, urge, coerce: *Alinijuburu kuifanya kazi yake upya,* he forced me to do his work all over again. Prep. *jubur.i.a* St. *jubur.ik.a* Cs. *jubur.ish.a* Ps. of Prep. *jubur.iw.a* Rp. of Prep. *jubur.i.an.a* (cf *lazimisha, kalifisha*) (Ar)

judo *n* (*n*) judo; a form of ju-jistu developed as a sport and a means of self defence without the use of weapons. (Jpn)

jugum.u *vt* discredit, belittle, humiliate: *Walitujugumu mbele za watu,* they humiliated us in public. Prep. *jugum.i.a* St. *jugum.ik.a* Cs. *jugum.ish.a* Ps. of Prep. *jugum.iw.a* Rp. of Prep. *jugum.i.an.a* (cf *kashifu, umbua*)

jugwe *n* (*n*) tug of war game: *Vuta jugwe,* pull the rope in this game.

juha *n* (*ma-*) fool, simpleton, imbecile, idiot. (cf *jura, mpumbavu, mjinga*)

juhudi *n* (*n*) 1. diligence, effort, pains: *Haonyeshi juhudi yoyote katika masomo yake,* he does not put any effort in his work. (cf *bidii, hima*) 2. arduous work, vigorous work. (cf *sulubu*) (Ar)

juilish.a *vt* see *julisha*

juisi juice (Eng)

juju *n* (*n*) juju; magic charm or fetish used by some West African tribes. (cf *uchawi*) (Hausa)

jukumu *n* (*ma-*) 1. responsibility, duty, obligation, burden: *Ana jukumu la kuwaangalia wazee wake,* he has an obligation of looking after his parents. (cf *dhima, wajibu*) 2. liability, accountability: *Mimi siwezi kula pesa*

jukwaa   **junaa**   **J**

za yatima kwa vile ninaogopa jukumu kwa Mwenyezi Mungu, I can't take away money meant for the orphans as I am accountable to God. (cf *lawama*) (Hind)

jukwaa *n* (*ma-*) stage, platform, dais, podium: *Kasisi alihutubia kutoka kwenya jukwaa*, the priest delivered a speech from the platform. (cf *kilingo, kilili, ulingo*)

julai *n* (*n*) July (Eng)

julfa *n* (*n*) chignon; a knot or coil of hair worn at the back of the neck.

julikan.a *vi* be known, be famous e.g. *Wewe unajulikana sana*, you are well-known. Prep. *julikan.i.a*

julish.a (also *juilisha*) *vt* inform, make known. *Alinijulisha alipokuwa tayari kusafiri*, he informed me when he was ready to travel. Prep. *julish.i.a* St. *julish.ik.a* Ps. *julish.w.a* Rp. *julish.an.a* (cf *arifu*)

juludi *n* (*ma-*) skin of a human being.

julus.i *vt, vi* see *jilisi*. Prep. *julus.i.a* St. *julus.ik.a* Cs. *julus.ish.a* Ps. of Prep *julus.iw.a* (Ar)

juma *n* (*ma*) week: *Juma lijalo,* next week. *Juma lililopita,* last week. *Juma zima,* the whole week (cf *wiki*) (Ar)

Jumamosi *n* (*n*) Saturday

Jumanne *n* (*n*) Tuesday

Jumapili *n* (*n*) Sunday

Jumatano *n* (*n*) Wednesday

Jumatatu *n* (*n*) Monday

jumba *n* (*ma-*) 1. building, mansion: *Jumba la mfalme,* palace. *Jumba la rais,* president's house; presidential palace; state house 2. a place where birds, insects like grubs, etc. live; nest, *Jumba la mishale,* sheathe, quiver, arrow-case. *Jumba la maonyesho/michezo,* theatre

jumbe *n* (*ma-*) chief, headman, leader: *Jumbe wa mtaa wetu ni mtu mzuri,* the headman of our neighbourhood is a good person. (cf *mudiri, mudewa*)

jumbereru *n* (*n*) (*zool*) a kind of fish.

jumbo *n* (*n*) physique; physical structure of a body: *Ana jumbo la kupendeza,* he has an attractive physique. (cf *tambo, gimba, kimba*)

jumla *n* (*n*) 1. sum, total, aggregate, altogether. 2. wholesale, in lots: *Anauza nguo kwa jumla,* he is selling clothes on wholesale. (Ar)

jumlish.a *vt, vi* add up, sum up, total: *Jumlisha idadi ya vitu hivi,* add the total number of these things. Prep. *jumlish.i.a* St. *jumlish.ik.a* Ps. *jumlish.w.a* Rp. *jumlish.an.a* (Ar)

jumlisho *n* (*ma-*) summation (Ar)

jumu[1] *n* (*ma-*) a kind of a big knife without a handle. (cf *ukengele*)

jumu[2] *n* (*ma-*) a kind of a big basket that has not been properly weaved and whose use is generallly short-lived; big straw basket.

jumuia (also *jumuiya*) *n* (*n*) association, union, community: *Jumuia ya wanamuziki,* an association of musicians. *Jumuia ya Madola,* the Commonwealth of Nations. *Jumuia ya Afrika ya Mashariki,* the East African Community. *Jumuia ya Uchumi ya Ulaya,* European Economic Community. *Jumuia ya Kimataifa,* international community. (Ar)

jumuik.a *vt, vi* be united, join together; assemble: *Wananchi walijumuika kuadhimisha sikukuu ya wafanyakazi,* the people gathered to celebrate workers' day. Prep. *jumuik.i.a*

jumuish.a *vt* include, encompass, bring together, generalize. *Muungano huu unajumuisha vyama mbalimbali vya ushirika,* this federation brings together different cooperatives. *jumuish.ik.a* Ps. *jumuish.w.a* Rp. *jumuish.an.a*

jumuisho *n* (*ma-*) generalization, conclusion, finalization. (Ar)

jumuiya *n* (*n*) see *jumuia*.

junaa *n* (*n*) disgrace, shame, dishonour: *Alikuwa hana junaa alipokuwa anaomba hadharani,* he had no shame

267

when he went begging in public. (cf *aibu, fedheha*) (Ar)
jungu *n* (*ma-*) a large cooking pot.
Juni *n* (*n*) June (Eng)
junju (also *sunzu*) *n* (*n*) quiff; a large tuft of hair left on the forehead: *Kijana yule anapenda kuweka junju la nywele kwenye paji la uso,* that young man likes to keep a large tuft of hair on the forehead. (cf *shore, chokiro*)
Jupita¹ *n* (*n*) (*astron*) Jupiter, the largest of the planets and the fifth from the sun. (cf *Mushtari*) (Eng)
Jupita² *n* (*n*) (in Roman tradition) the king and the ruler of the Olympian gods; Jupiter. (Eng)
jura *n* (*ma-*) imbecile, idiot, simpleton, fool: *Ukiwa jura, watu wanaweza kukudharau,* if you are a fool, people can despise you. (cf *juha, mjinga, mpumbavu*)
jurawa *n* (*n*) (*zool*) grey-headed sparrow; a mantle tawny brown bird (family *Ploceidae*) without striking and with bright rufous rump and shoulders as well as grey head. *Passer griseus.* (cf *shorewanda*)
jusur.u *vt, vi* dare, venture, risk: *Alijusuru kumkabili adui,* he dared to confront the enemy. Prep. *jusur.i.a* St. *jusur.ik.a* Cs. *jusur.ish.a*
jut.a¹ *vt, vi* regret, repent, lament: *Anajuta sasa kwa kuliuza shamba lake,* he now regrets for selling his farm. Prep. *jut.i.a* St. *jut.ik.a* Cs. *jut.ish.a* Ps. *jut.w.a* Rp. of Prep. *jut.i.an.a* (cf *sikitika. huzunika*)
juta² *n* (*n*) conman, scoundrel. (cf *tapeli*)
juti.a *vt* regret or do without; rue: *Unajutia nini?* What are you regretting?
juto *n* (*ma-*) regret, repentance, remorse, sorrow: *Utajuta juto la mjukuu ukifanya kitendo kile,* you will suffer deep regret if you do that. (*prov*) *Majuto ni mjukuu, mwishowe huja kinyume,* you must

think before you decide to take an action; otherwise you would come to regret it afterwards.
juu¹ *adv* above, up, atop, on top, overhead, upstairs: *Anaishi juu,* he lives upstairs. (*prov*) *Aliye juu mngoje chini,* he who occupies a top position at work can fall any day. **2.** used in the expression: *Juu yako,* resting on you, dependent upon you. *Juu yake,* resting upon him. *Juu yangu,* resting on me e.g. *Huna amri juu yangu,* you have no authority over me. **3.** used in the expressions: *Juu juu,* a) superficially e.g. *Alifanya kazi juu juu,* he did the work superficially b) be excited, be alarmed e.g. *Moyo wake u juu juu,* he is excited. **4.** (*idms*) *Kuja juu,* get very angry, *Juu chini,* upside down. *Fanya juu chini,* do everything possible.
juu² *prep* **1.** (with *ya*) of, from, on, about, concerning: *Mimi siwezi kuingilia juu ya jambo lile,* I can't interfere on that issue. *Shuka juu ya ngamia,* dismount from the camel. **2.** against, over, in opposition: *Walileta hujuma juu ya ardhi ya adui,* they carried out an invasion of the enemy's territory. **3.** in addition, besides: *Juu ya haya, kuna mengi mengineyo ambayo nitakueleza siku nyingine,* in addition to this, there are many others that I will explain to you next time.
juujuu *adv* superficially, tangentially, outside: *Alinieleza juujuu jinsi alivyomshinda mpinzani wake,* he explained to me superficially how he defeated his opponent.
-juvi *adj* haughty, arrogant, supercilious: *Kijana mjuvi,* an arrogant young man.
juvy.a *vt, vi* inform, apprise, notify, acquaint. (cf *elewesha, julisha, elimisha*)
juya *n* (*ma-*) dragnet, fishnet of seine type: *Juya lilimsaidia kupata samaki*

wengi, the dragnet enabled him to get a lot of fish.

juzi[1] *n* (*ma-*) 1. the day before yesterday: *Mwaka juzi*, the year before last. *Juzijuzi*, recently; a few days ago. 2. lately, recently: *Nimemwona mjomba wangu hivi juzi*, I have seen my uncle recently.

juzi[2] *adv* the day before yesterday: *Alikuja juzi*, he came the day before yesterday.

-juzi[3] *adj* learned, erudite, knowledge: *Mtu mjuzi*, a learned person; erudite.

juzijuzi *n*, *adv* see *juzi*[1]

juz.u *vt* befit, suit; be fitting, be proper, be the duty of: *Inakujuzu wewe kusali hapa*, it is proper for you to say your prayers here. *Haijuzu hata kidogo kumsengenya rafiki yako*, it is not proper at all for you to speak ill of your friend. Prep. ***juz.i.a*** St. ***juz.ik.a*** Cs. ***juz.ish.a*** (cf faa, pasa) (Ar)

juzuu *n* (*ma-*) 1. a chapter of the Holy Koran. 2. a volume of a book; tome. (Ar)

K

K, k /k/ 1. the eleventh letter of the Swahili alphabet. 2. a voiceless velar stop.

ka¹ *interj* an expletive of surprise for sth that has occurred; gosh! (cf *lo! ah!*)

ka² *tense prefix* (*gram*) a tense prefix denoting consecutiveness of actions, etc: *Alikwenda dukani akanunua machungwa, kisha akatoweka*, he went to the shop and bought oranges and then disappeared.

kaa¹ (*also mkaa*) *n* (*ma-*) 1. a piece of charcoal. 2. a piece of wood that is still burning; smouldering firewood; ember: *Makaa ya moto*, live embers.

kaa² *n* (*n*) 1. (*zool*) crab; a sea-animal with four pieces of pincers as legs and a flattish shell: *Kaa koko/gabe*, mangrove or mud crab. (*Scylla serrata*) *Kaa maweni*, rock crab. (*Grapsus tenuicrustatus*) 2. (*astron*) Cancer; the fourth sign of the zodiac, which the sun enters about 22nd June

kaa

ka.a³ *vi* 1. sit, remain, rest: *Kaa kwenye kiti*, sit on the chair. 2. live, stay, reside: *Anakaa karibu na mlima*, he lives near the mountain. 3. last, be long-lived: *Baskeli yangu imekaa miaka mingi*, my bicycle has lasted for many years. 4. fit, match: *Nguo hiyo imekukaa vizuri*, the dress fits you well. (cf *pendeza*, *chukua*) 5. stay, wait: *Alikuja hapa jana na kukaa kutwa nzima*, he came here yesterday and stayed the whole day. 6. (*idms*) *Kaa doria*, patrol, guard. *Kaa chonjo*, be alert, be vigilant. *Kaa ange*, remain firm, *Kaa mbumbumbu*, be stunned, be taken aback. *Kaa tuli*, remain silent. *Kaa tutwe*, be taken aback. *Kaa kimya*, keep quiet. *Kaa eda*, remain in seclusion for a specified period of time for a Muslim woman after her husband's death.

Kaaba *n* (*n*) Kaabah; a sacred stone building in the Great Mosque in Mecca towards which Muslims turn their faces when praying; it contains a black stone supposedly given to Abraham by the angel Gabriel. (Ar)

kaakaa¹ *n* (*ma-*) (*anat*) palate; roof of the mouth: *Kaakaa gumu*, hard palate. *Kaakaa laini*, soft palate.

kaakaa² *n* (*ma-*) (*med*) whitlow; an infection of pulp of the finger tip usu from a deep prick. (cf *kaka*)

kaang.a¹ *vt, vi* sauté, fry: *Kaanga samaki*, fry the fish. *Mayai ya kukaanga*, fried eggs. Prep. **kaang.i.a** St. **kaang.ik.a** Cs. **kaang.ish.a** Ps. **kaang.w.a,**

kaanga² *n* (*ma-*) (*bot*) the tough leathery sheath of coconut flower-stem (cf *karara*)

kaango *n* (*ma-*) grid iron

kab.a¹ *vt* 1. strangle, throttle, choke: *Kaba mtu roho*, strangle someone; seize by the throat. (cf *songa*, *kaza*) 2. pin someone down; insist on someone to do sth until he complies with it: *Walimkaba mpaka akalipa deni lao*, they were behind his neck until he cleared their debt. Prep. **kab.i.a** St. **kab.ik.a** Cs. **kab.ish.a** Ps. **kab.w.a** Rp. **kab.an.a** (cf *chagiza*)

kaba² *n* (*n*) used in the expression: *Hana kaba ya ulimi*, he cannot keep a secret.

kaba³ n (n) lining of the *kanzu* sewn on neck and shoulders so that the garment does not get torn quickly.

kababu n (n) meat ball, shish kebab (Hind)

kabaila¹(*also kabaili*) n (n) 1. aristocrat, silk-stocking: (cf *bwanyenye, lodi*) 2. head, chief. 3. a well-known person in a particular place; an important person in a particular place (Ar)

kabaila²(*also kabaili*) n (ma-) 1. exploiter. 2. feudalist, landowner. (Ar)

kabaili n (ma-) see *kabaila¹* and *kabaila²*.

Kabaka n (n) the traditional ruler of a Baganda of Uganda.

kabaku n (ma-) a brutal woman.

kabambe adj 1. intensive, solid: *Mpango kabambe*, an intensive programme. (cf *kabambe, shadidi*) 2. strong, stable: *Kampeni kabambe*, strong campaign (cf *madhubuti*)

kabari¹ n (n) a wedge of wood or iron, used to split logs, wood, etc. (Ar)

kabari² n (n) (*idms*) *Piga/Tia kabari*, strangle someone. (Ar)

kabati n (ma-) cupboard: *Kabati la ukutani la jikoni*, kitchen cupboard. (Eng)

kabechi (*also kabechi*) n (ma-) see *kabichi*.

kabibu adj narrow and straight. (cf *finyu*)

kabichi (*also kabeji*) n (n) (*bot*) cabbage (Eng)

kabidh.i¹ vt, vi 1. entrust to, handover: *Nilimkabidhi fedha zake*, I handed over his money. 2. receive, take: *Kabidhi vitu vyako hivi*, receive these things of yours. Prep.. **kabidh.i.a** St. **kabidh.ik.a** Cs. **kabidh.ish,a** Ps. of Prep. **kabidh.iw.a** Rp. of Prep. **kabidh.i.an.a** (cf *pokea, chukua*) (Ar)

kabidhi² n (n) used in the expression: *Kabidhi wasii*, public trustee. (Ar)

kabidhi³ adj 1. thrifty, frugal, economical, saving: *Mke kabidhi*, a thrifty housewife.

2. stingy, miserly: *Bepari kabidhi*, a stingy tycoon. (cf *bahili*) (Ar)

kabila n (ma-) 1. race, tribe, ethnic group: *Nchi yetu ina makabila mengi*, our country has many tribes. (cf *ukoo*) 2. variety, type,species: *Kuna makabila mbalimbali ya samaki changu*, there are different species of a snapper. (*jamii*) (Ar)

kabil.i¹ (also *kabilisha*) vt 1. face, front on: *Nyumba yake inaikabili shule ya msingi*, his house faces a primary school. 2. stand up to face bravely; confront: *Walimkabili adui kijasiri*, they faced the enemy bravely. Prep. **kabil.i.a** St. **kabil.ik.a** Cs. **kabil. ish.a** Ps. of Prep. **kabil.iw.a** Rp. of Prep. **kabil.i.an.a** (cf *pambana, menyana*) (Ar)

kabili² (also *kabiri*) n (n) clarinettist; a person who plays a clarinet. (Ar)

kabili³ n (n) a brave person; a person of courage or mettle; hero. (Ar)

kabili⁴ adj courageous, brave: *Mwanajeshi kabili*, a brave soldier. (cf *hodari*)

kabilian.a vt confront, face; *Unaweza kukabiliana naye kwenye mjadala?* Can you confront him in the debate?

kabilish.a¹ vt see *kabili¹*.

kabilish.a² vt present, give, forward; *Kabilisha barua*, forward a letter. *Kabilisha moyo*, resolve, decide. Prep. **kabilish.i.a** St. **kabilish.ik.a** Ps. **kabilish.w.a** (Ar)

kabiri¹ n (n) see *kabili²*.

kabiri² adj exalted, magnificent: *Yeye ni mfalme kabiri*, he is an exalted monarch. (cf *adhimu*) (Ar.)

kabisa¹ adv 1. completely, totally: *Ukikaa hapa mbele, utakuja kuniudhi kabisa*, if you sit here infront, you will disturb me totally. 2. very, extremely. *Kweli kabisa*, very true. 3. never, not all: *Sitaki kabisa kumwazima gari yangu mtu yule*, I don't want at all to lend that person my car. (cf *kamwe, abadan*) 4. first, prior to, immediately: *Lipa*

kabisa pesa kabla sijakupa mayai, pay first before I give you the eggs. (cf *palepale, papohapo*) (Ar)

kabisa² *interj* never, not at all, absolutely not. (cf *katu, kamwe, abadan*)

kabla¹ *conj* before, previously: *Itachukua muda kabla hatujapatiwa matokeo*, it will take sometime before we are given the results (Ar.)

kabla² *prep* before: *Alifika kabla ya mimi*, he arrived before me (Ar.)

kabla³ *adv* before, in *adv*ance, ahead: *Ungenieleza kabla*, you should have told me before. (Ar)

kabobo *n (n)* 1. high tide in the sea. 2. (*syn*) *Nakabobo huuandaa*, even the rich get poor.

kabohidrati *n (n)* (*chem*) carbodydrate. (Eng)

kabonati *n (n)* (*chem*) carbonate. (Eng)

kaboni¹ *n (n)* 1. (*chem*) carbon; a non metallic chemical element. 2. a stick of carbon used in an arch lamp. (Eng)

kaboni² *n (n)* a sheet of carbon paper; carbon. (Eng)

kaboni-dioksidi *n (n)* (*chem*) carbon dioxide. (Eng)

kabrasha *n (ma-)* meeting document; pamphlet.

kabsa *n (n)* a bell or a trumpet blown to signal danger, etc. in the army, police, etc. (Ar)

kabuli¹ *n (n)* God's accepatance of an invocation. (Ar)

kabuli² (also *kubuli*) *n (n)* a dish of cooked rice mixed with ghee, raisins, cinnamon, etc; pilaf (cf *pilau*)

kabumbu *n (n)* soccer, football. (cf *kandanda, soka, futiboli*)

kabureta *n (n)* carburettor; the part of an engine which mixes fuel and air producing the gas which burns in the engine to provide power for a vehicle or machine. (Eng)

kaburi *n (ma-)* 1. grave, tomb: *Kaburi kubwa*, mausoleum 2. (*idm*) *Chungulia kaburi*, be on the verge of dying. (Ar)

kaburu *n (ma-)* 1. Boer, Afrikaanar. 2. settler (cf *mlowezi*)

kabusi *n (n)* nightmare. (cf *jinamizi*)

kabuti *n (ma-)* see *kaputi*.

kabwela *n (ma-)* 1. plebeian, commoner; a person of low status socially. 2. proletariat. (cf *mlalahoi*)

kabwiri *n (n)* (*zool*) a special kind of herring.

kach.a¹ *vi, vt* 1. insist on, be intransigent, be firm: *Mtoto yule amekacha kwani kila unalomwambia afanye, anakataa*, that child is intransigent because whatever he is told to do, he refuses. (cf *shupaa, chachamaa*) 2. (of food, etc.) be dry, be hard: *Mkate wake umekacha*, his bread has become hard. (cf *yabisika*) 3. be numbed: *Mikono yangu imekacha kwa baridi*, my hands have become numb from the cold. 4. coagulate, thicken: *Damu polepole ilikacha pembezoni mwa jeraha*, blood slowly coagulated round the edges of the injury. 5. (*colloq.*) abandon, forsake, leave: *Mchezaji aliikacha timu yake*, the player abandoned his team. Prep. **kach.i.a** St. **kach.ik.a** Cs. **kach.ish.a** Ps. **kach.w.a** Rp. **kach.an.a**

kachara² *n (n)* a collection of used worn-out things.

kacha³ *interj*. an onomatopoeic expression used to emphasize the falling down of sth light e.g. branch of a tree; *Limeanguka kacha!* It has fallen down producing a sound like that of a falling branch or twig.

kachara¹ *n (n)* refuse, trash, rubbish: *Ondosha kachara hizi na kisha kazitupe mbali*, remove this rubbish and then throw it far away. (cf *taka*)

kachara² (also *katara*) *adj* 1. worn-out, decrepit, old: *Baskeli yake sasa imekuwa kachara*, his bicycle has now become worn-out. (cf *chakavu*) 2. be lacking fat; lean *Alinunua nyama kachara*, he bought lean meat.

kachero n (ma-) 1. detective, secret agent. (cf *shushushu*) 2. plainclothes policeman/woman; undercover police.
kachira n (n) a kind of container made from bamboo stalks, used for carrying things such as fruits, fish, chickens, etc; bamboo basket. (cf *tenga, susu*)
kachiri[1] n (n) a children's game in which a child would jump with both legs together forwards and backwards.
kachiri[2] n (n) a kind of mashed food made from a mixture of rice, grain and lentils.
kachu n (n) cachou; an astringent reisonous substance used in medicine, tanning, dyeing, etc (Eng)
kachumbari n (n) a kind of relish made from a mixture of fresh onions, tomatoes, cucumber, lemons or limes, etc together with salt and chillies
kada[1] n (n) cadre (Eng)
kada[2] n (n) category: *Chama kilichojumuisha watu wa kada mbalimbali*, the party that incorporated people of different categories.
kadamish.a vt see *kadimisha* Prep. *kadamish.i.a* St. *kadamish.ik.a* Ps. *kadamish.w.a* Rp. *kadamish.an.a*
kadamnasi adv in public, infront of: *Walimkebehi msichana mrembo kadamnasi ya watu*, they ridiculed a beautiful girl in public. (cf *hadharani*) (Ar)
kadamu[1] n (n) see *gidamu*.
kadamu[2] adj see *kadimu*.
kadari (also *kudura, takdiri*) n (n) God's omnipotence and predestination; God's will. (Ar)
kadeti n (n) cadet: *Kadeti wa jeshi la majini*, naval cadet (Eng)
kadha[1] (also *kadhaa*) adj 1. certain, various : *Watu kadha*, certain people 2. (idm) *Kadha wa kadha*, many, plenty.
kadha[2] adj, n (in Islam) prayer or fast that is performed after its usual time has elapsed
kadhaa adj see *kadha*[1]
kadhabu n (n) see *kidhabu*

kadhalika adv likewise, furthermore: *Yeye ameleta fujo hapa na wewe kadhalika*, he has brought chaos here and you also have done the same. *Kadhalika na kadhalika*, et cetera. (cf *pia, tena, vilevile*) (Ar)
kadhi n (ma-) 1. Muslim judge; cadi. 2. magistrate, judge. (cf *hakimu, jaji*) (Ar)
kadhia n (n) happening, affairs, incident. (cf *jambo, tukio, mkasa*) (Ar)
kadhibish.a (also *kidhibisha*) vt belie, disprove; prove a person to be in error or false: *Tulimpa ukweli wetu lakini yeye akatukadhibisha hadharani baadaye*, we gave him our facts but he belied us in public later on. Prep. *kadhibish.i.a* St. *kadhibish.ik.a* Ps. *kadhibish.w.a* Rp. *kadhibish.an.a* (cf *susuaza, kunusha*) (Ar)
kadhib.u (also *kidhibu*) vt lie, cheat, deceive, Prep. *kadhib.i.a* St. *kadhib.ik.a* Cs. *kadhib.ish.a* Ps. of Prep. *kadhib.iw.a* Rp. of Prep. *kadhib.i.an.a* (cf *hadaa, danganya*) (Ar)
kadhongo n (n) bribe (cf *mrungura, rushwa, chai*)
kadi[1] n (n) 1. card; thick stiff paper: *Kadi ya posta*, postal card 2. invitation card: *Kadi ya harusi*, wedding invitation card 3. identity card: *Kadi ya uanachama*, membership card. 4. (in sports) card: *Kadi manjano*,yellow card. *kadi nyekundu*, red card. (Eng)
kadi[2] n (n) caddy; an attendant who carries clubs, etc. for a player. (Eng)
kadibodi n (n) cardboard. (Eng)
kadimish.a (also *kadamisha*) vt send in advance; precede, forward. Prep. *kadimish.i.a* St. *kadimish.ik.a* Ps. *kadimish.w.a* Rp. *kadimish.an.a* (cf *tangulia*)
kadimu (also *kadamu*) adj ancient, old. (cf *kongwe*) (Ar.)
kadinali (also *kardinali*) n (ma-) cardinal. (Eng)
kadir.i[1] vt see *kadiria*
kadiri[2] (also *kadri*) n (n) 1. capacity, strength: *Kula kadiri yako*, eat

according to your capacity; Eat your fill (cf *nguvu, uwezo*) 2. rank, position: *Kaa pahala pa kadiri yako*, sit at a place of your status 3. approximation: *Kadiri ya watu ishirini walialikwa katika karamu*, approximately twenty people were invited at the reception. (cf *kiasi*) 4. value, cost. (Ar)

kadiri[3] (also *kadri*) *adj* as much as, in so far as: *Chukua kadiri unavyoweza*, take as much as you can.

kadiri.a (also *kadiri*) *vt* 1. estimate, approximate: *Walikadiria hasara iliyopatikana*, they estimated the incurred loss. (cf *kisia*) 2. think, ponder: *Alilikadiria wazo langu*, he pondered over my suggestion. St. **kadiri.k.a** Cs. **kadiri.sh.a** Ps. **kadiri.w.a** Rp. **kadiri.an.a** (cf *fikiri, taamuli, tafakuri, zingatia*) (Ar.)

kadirifu *adj* 1. calculating. 2. careful, considerate: *Yeye ni mtu kadirifu*, he is a considerate person. 3. moderate, temperate, average. (Ar)

kadirio *n* (*ma-*) see *makadirio*

kaditama *n* (*n*) (usu used in letter writing, etc.) final, end. (cf *mwisho*)

kadogo *adj* very little, small: *Mtoto kadogo*, a very small child.

kadri *n* (*n*) see *kadiri*[2] and *kadiri*[3]

kafala *n* (*n*) bail, surety, guarantee. (cf *dhamana*)

kafani *n* (*n*) burial cloth, shroud; a cloth covering a dead body for burial. (cf *sanda*) (Ar)

kafara *n* (*n*) 1. a kind of religious offering to serve as a sort of compensation for an obligatory thing that was not performed. 2. a sacrifice made to avert evil or disaster: *Toa kafara*, make a sacrifice of this kind; make an offering. *Chinja kafara*, slaughter an animal as a sacrifice. *Piga/Soma kafara*, make/ recite a curse or spell on someone who has done an evil thing. (Ar)

kafeni *n* (*n*) caffeine (Eng)

kafeteria *n* (*n*) cafeteria (Eng)

kafi[1] (also *kahafi*) *n* (*n*) 1. the top cover of a cap; a skull-cap top 2. a piece of round cloth which is cut for use as a top cover for a cap.

kafi[2] *n* (*ma-*) paddle, oar: *Piga kafi*, paddle; use an oar.

kafila *n* (*n*) caravan, convoy. (cf *msafara, charo*) (Ar)

kafin.i *vt* shroud; wrap a dead body in a shroud: *Walimkafini maiti*, they shrouded the corpse. Prep. **kafin.i.a** St. **kafin.ik.a** Cs **kafin.ish.a** Ps. of Prep. **kafin.iw.a** (Ar)

kafiri *n* (*ma-*) 1. pagan, a person who holds no religious belief. (*prov*) *Kafiri akufaaye si islamu asiyekufaa*, it is better to have a person who does not belong to any religion but is of use to you than to have a person who has a religion but is of no use to you. (cf *mpagani* 2. (*colloq*) a fantastic player.

kaftani *n* (*n*) 1. a long loose ceremonial cloak or outer garment with a girdle given by some kings to ambassadors or important people; caftan. 2. a long loose garment which resembles a coat. 3. a long outer garment worn on other clothes by women. (Ar)

kafu.a *vt* strip off grains of seeds, etc. by beating; thresh: *Mkulima aliyakafua mashuka ya mpunge*, the farmer threshed the stalks of the rice. Prep. **kafu.li.a** St. **kafu.lik.a** Cs. **kafu.lish.a** Ps. of Prep. **kafu.liw.a**

kafuki.a *vi* yell, scream: *Msichana alikafukia aliponyang'anywa mkoba wake*, the girl screamed when her purse was snatched Prep. **kafuki.li.a** St. **kafuki.k.a** Cs. **kafuki.sh.a** (Ar) (cf *lalama*)

kafuri *n* (*n*) (*chem*) camphor; strong-smelling white substance used in medicine: *Kafuri maiti*, camphor.

kaga[1] *n* (*n*) abscess, ulcer, sore. (cf *kidonda, uvimbe, donda*)

kag.a[2] *vt* protect by a magic charm, talisman, etc. *Kaga shamba*, protect a plantation by a charm. Prep. **kag.i.a**

St. ***kag.ik.a*** Cs. ***kag.ish.a*** Ps. ***kag.w.a*** Rp. ***kag.an.a*** (cf *zindika*)

kago[1] *n* (*ma-*) a magic charm to avert any evil; amulet, talisman. (cf *hirizi, zindiko, sihiri*)

kago[2] *n* (*n*) cargo, freight. (cf *shehena, mizigo*) (Eng)

kagu.a *vt* inspect, examine, probe, audit: *Mhasibu mkuu alizikagua hesabu*, the chief accountant audited the accounts. *Afisa kilimo alilikagua shamba*, the agricultural officer inspected the farm. Prep. ***kagu.li.a*** St. ***kagu.lik.a*** Cs. ***kagu.lish.a*** Ps. of Prep. ***kagu.liw.a*** Rp. ***kagu.an.a*** (cf *angalia, cheki*)

kahaba *n* (*ma-*) prostitute, harlot, whore. (cf *mzinzi, malaya, hawara*) (Ar)

kahafi *n* (*n*) see *kafi*[1]

kaharabu *n* (*n*) 1. thick yellowish beads made from hard glue. 2. amber. (Pers)

Kahari[1] *n* (*n*) (in Islam) one of the names of God; the Powerful. (Ar)

kahari[2] *n* (*n*) compulsion, force. (cf *ulazimishaji*) (Ar)

kahati *n* (*n*) calamity, disaster or catastrophe e.g. famine, epidemic disease, etc.

kahawa *n* (*n*) 1. coffee; 2. (*bot*) seed or berry from the plant, *mbuni*. (Ar)

kahawia *adj* brown. (Ar)

kahini[1] *n* (*ma-*) see *kuhani*

kahini[2] (also *kuhani*) *n* (*ma-*) 1. soothsayer, fortune teller. (cf *mnajimu*) 2. magician, conjurer, sorcerer. (cf *mchawi*) 3. crook, swindler, cheat, conman. (cf *laghai, ayari, mjanja*) 4. an oppressive person, a brutal person; brute, boor. (cf *bedui, habithi*) (Ar)

kahir.i *vt* coerce, compel, urge: *Wananchi walimkahiri rais ajiuzulu*, the people forced the president to resign. Prep. ***kahir.i.a*** St. ***kahir.ik.a*** Cs. ***kahir.ish.a*** Ps. of Prep. ***kahir.iw.a*** Rp. of Prep. ***kahir.i.an.a*** (cf *shurutisha, lazimisha*)

ka.i *vi* surrender, give up: *Adui alikai*, the enemy surrendered Prep. ***ka.li.a*** St. ***ka.ik.a*** Cs. ***ka.ish.a*** (cf *chicha*)

kaida *n* (*n*) habit, custom, convention (cf *taratibu, tabia, mwenendo*) (Ar)

kaid.i *vt, vi* be obstinate, defy, be stubborn: *Mwanafunzi alifukuzwa shuleni kwa kukaidi sheria kadha*, the student was expelled from school for defying certain rules. Prep. ***kaid.i.a*** St. ***kaid.ik.a*** Cs. ***kaid.ish.a*** Ps. of Prep. ***kaid.iw.a*** Rp. of Prep. ***kaid.i.an.a*** (cf *kinza, bisha, asi*) (Ar)

-kaidi *adj* stubborn, obstinate: *Mtoto mkaidi*, a stubborn child. (cf *shupavu*) (Ar)

kaifa[1] *n* (*n*) report, news, account, exposition: *Alinipa kaifa ya safari yake*, he gave me an account of his journey. (cf *habari, maelezo, taarifa*) (Ar)

kaifa[2] (also *fakaifa, kafu, sebuse*) *adv* let alone, not to mention: *Alimsaidia mtu wa mbali kaifa wewe*, he helped a distant person let alone you. (*prov*) *Mwana wa yungi hulewa kaifa wa kilimwengu*, a person in his lifetime cannot undergo difficulties forever. (cf *sembuse, seuze*)

kaimati *n* (*n*) a small cake of dried batter usu containing flour, syrup and other filling; fritter.

kaimu[1] *n* (*ma-*) 1. an acting official; a person designated to take over the duties of a specified position before he is fully confirmed: *Kaimu waziri mkuu*, acting prime minister. *Kaimu balozi*, charge d'affaires. *Kaimu mfalme*, viceroy. 2. deputy; a person designated to perform the functions of a particular head of an institution who is away. (Ar)

kaim.u[2] *vt* act as an acting official over the duties of a specified position before someone is fully confirmed: *Rais alimteua waziri wake kukaimu wizara ya viwanda*, the president appointed his minister to be the acting minister for the ministry of industry. Prep. **kaim.i.a** St. **kaim.ik.a** Cs. **kaim.ish.a** Ps. of Prep. **kaim.iw.a.** Rp. of Prep. **kaim.i.an.a**

kaimu³ *n* (*ma-*) exorcist, a person who exorcises spirits. (Ar)

kaini *adj* 1. cruel, ruthless. (cf *habithi, katili*) 2. rude: *Yeye ni mtu kaini*, he is a rude person. (cf *safihi*)

Kaizari *n* (*n*) Caesar, Kaiser. (Eng)

kajayeye *n* (*n*) (*bot*) a kind of sweet cassava.

kajekaje (also *kayekaye*) *n* (*n*) (*naut*) small ropes used to fasten the sail to the main yard in a sailing vessel.

kaji *n* (*n*) (*zool*) a kind of a big lobster; giant lobster.

kaka¹ *n*(*ma-*) 1. elder brother. 2. a name used to show respect or to joke when calling a male friend. (cf *ghulamu, barubaru*)

kaka² *n* (*ma-*) an empty shell usu of a matchbox or fruit: *Kaka la kibiriti*, the matchbox shell. (cf *ganda, bupuru, fuvu*)

kaka³ *n* (*n*) (*med*) whitlow; a painful pus-producing infection at the end of a finger or toe near the nail. (cf *kaakaa*)

kakakaka *adj* 1. hurriedly, hastily: *Shughuli za mazishi zilienda kakakaka*, the funeral rites went on hurriedly. (cf *chapuchapu, upesiupesi*) 2. violently, noisily: *Maandamano ya wafanyakazi yalifanyika kakakaka*, the workers' demonstrations were done in a violent manner.

kakakuona *n* (*n*) (*zool*) cape pangolin; a kind of toothless scaly mammal with a small head, a long broad tail and no external ears and which is found in Africa and Asia. It feeds on ants and termites and is able to roll into a ball when attacked.

kakakuona

kakama.a *vt, vi* 1. (of body, etc.) be stiff, be rigid: *Mwili wake ulipokakamaa, daktari alipata shida kumpiga mgonjwa shindano*, when his body became stiff, the doctor had difficulty injecting the patient (cf *kazana*) 2. (of bread, etc) be hard, be stony, be solid Prep. **kakama.li.a** St. **kakama.k.a** Cs. **kakama.z.a** Ps. **kakama.w.a** Rp. **kakama.n.a** (cf *kauka, gungumka*)

-**kakamavu** *adj* 1. determined, tenacious, steadfast: *Kamanda wa jeshi aliwataka askari wake kuwa wakakamavu*, the army commander wanted his soldiers to be firm. (cf *imara, madhubuti*) 2. hard, strong, solid: *Nyama kakamavu hii haikatiki*, this hard meat cannot be cut.

kakami.a *vi* make great effort to get sth; be determined to get sth. St. **kakami.k.a** Cs. **kakami.sh.a** (cf *kamia*)

kakamiz.a *vt* coerce, force. Prep. **kakamiz.i.a** St. **kakamiz.ik.a** Ps. **kakamiz.w.a** (cf *lazimisha, kahiri, shurutisha*)

-**kakamizi** *adj* stubborn, obstinate. (cf *sugu*)

kakamk.a *vi* go all-out; strain oneself to do some difficult task. e.g. lifting a heavy load. Prep. **kakamk.i.a** St. **kakamk.ik.a** Cs. **kakamk.ish.a** Ps. **kakamk.w.a**

kakamu.a *vt* work tirelessly to achieve sth: strain oneself; make a muscular effort to achieve sth: *Timu ilijikakamua na hatimaye kufanikiwa kusawazisha magoli mawili*, the team worked itself tirelessly and eventually equalized the two goals. Prep. *kakamu.li.a* St. *kakamu.k.a*

kakao *n* (*n*) 1. (*bot*) cocoa seeds. 2. cocoa crop. 3. flour from these seeds. 4. a drink made from these seeds. (Eng)

kakarakakara (also *kakara*) *n* (*n*) 1. pandemonium, chaos, turbulence: *Kakarakakara ilitokea njiani wakati mwizi aliyetaka kuiba gari, alikamatwa*, pandemonium occurred in the street when a thief who wanted to steal a car was caught. (cf *vurumai, mtafaruku*) 2. bustle, hubbub: *Mji wote uko katika kakarakakara kutokana na sherehe mbalimbali*, the whole city is bustling with celebrations. (cf *pirikapirika*)

kakasi *adj* tart, aciduous.

kakat.a *vt* eat voraciously; eat gluttonously: *Naona unaukakata wali*, I can see you are eating rice voraciously. Prep. *kakat.i.a* St. *kakat.ik.a* Ps. *kakat.w.a*

kakatu.a¹ *vt* break down sth hard esp with the teeth: *Alilikakatua hindi la kuchoma*, he broke the roasted maize cob with his teeth. Prep. *kakatu.li.a* St. *kakatu.k.a* Cs. *kakatu.sh.a* Ps. of Prep. *kakatu.liw.a*

kakatu.a² *vt* weed; remove weed in a field. Prep. *kakatu.li.a* St. *kakatu.k.a* Cs. *kakatu.sh.a* Ps. of Prep. *kakatu.liw.a*

kakawan.a *vi* 1. insist on sth, be persistent. (cf *shupaa*) 2. be strong, be well-knit: *Amekakawana baada ya kufanya mazoezi kabambe*, he has become strong after doing strenuous exercises. Prep. *kakawan.i.a* St. *kakawan.ik.a* Cs. *kakawan.ish.a* Ps. *kakawan.w.a*

kaki¹ *n* (*ma-*) thin hard-baked bread with pores in it; bread-stick pores.

kaki² *n* (*n*) a khaki material which is used for making shorts, trousers, etc. *Rangi ya kaki*, the colour of the dried leaves. (Hind, Pers)

kakindi *n* (*n*) (*bot*) a slender erect herb with white flowers about an inch in diameter, semi-parasitic on the root of the grasses.

kala¹ *n* (*n*) see *ukosi*

kala² (also *kara*) *n* (*n*) (*zool*) a kind of wild cat frequently fond of eating chicks. (cf *njuzi, kalakonje*)

kalabi *n* (*n*) 1. (*med*) hydrophobia; an abnormal fear of drinking fluids, esp that of a person with rabies, because of painful spasms when trying to swallow. 2. rabies.

kalachapa *n* (*n*) print-out

kalafat.i¹ (also *kalfati*) *vt* caulk; make a boat, dhow, etc. watertight by filling the seams or cracks with oakum, tar, etc: *Waliukalafati mtumbwi*, they caulked the canoe. Prep. *kalafat.i.a* St. *kalafat.ik.a* Cs. *kalafat.ish.a* Ps. *kalafat.iw.a* Rp. of Prep. *kalafat.i.an.a* (Ar)

kalafati² *n* (*n*) oakum; caulking material usu cotton and greese: *Tia kalafati*, caulk. (Ar)

kalakonje *n* (*ma-*) (*bot*) a kind of wild cat fond of eating chicks. (cf *njuzi*)

kalamari *n* (*n*) (*biol*) calamary. (Eng)

kalamini *n* (*n*) calamine; a pink powder consisting of zinc carbonate and ferric oxide, used to make a soothing lotion, etc. (Eng)

kalamu *n* (*n*) 1. pen: *Kalamu ya risasi*, pencil, *kalamu ya wino*, ink pen 2. (*idm*) *Pigwa kalamu*, be dismissed from work, be sacked e.g. *Alipopigwa kalamu, alirudi vijijini kulima*, when he was sacked from work, he returned to the villages to do farming. (Ar)

kalasha *n* (*n*) tusk of an elephant or other animal, and is smaller than *buri*. (Ar)

kalasi *n* (*ma-*) (*naut*) a kind of sailing vessel.

kalasia (also *karasia*) *n* (*ma-*) a kind of small round copper vase with a narrow neck and broad below, used for keeping water, milk, etc.; copper vase. (Ar)

Kalasinga *n* (*ma-*) Sikh (Sik)

kale¹ *n* (*n*) 1. ancientness, antiquity: *Kale ipi?* How ancient? 2. past history.

kale² *adj* ancient, old: *Mambo ya kale*, ancient issues. *Watu wa kale*, ancient people. (*prov*) *Mavi ya kale hayaachi kunuka*, old excrement cannot stop stinking, i.e. an old evil cannot be forgotten. *Hapo kale*, in the past.

kalenda *n* (*n*) calendar. (Eng)

kalfat.i *vt* see *kalafati*

-kali *adj* 1. stern, fierce, strict: *Mbwa mkali*, a fierce dog 2. sharp: *Kisu kikali*, a sharp knife 3. sour, bitter: *Chungwa kali*, bitter orange 4. severe; *Baridi kali*, severe cold 5. stern, cross: *Onyo kali*, stern warning.

kali.a *vt* 1. sit on: *Amekalia kiti chako*, he has sat on your chair 2. delay purposely: *Ameikalia barua yangu ya kuomba kazi*, he has purposely delayed my application for employment. Prep. ***kali.li.a*** St. ***kali.k.a*** Cs. ***kali.sh.a*** Ps. ***kali.w.a*** Rp. ***kali.an.a***

kalibu¹ *n* (*n*) 1. mould; a hollow container 2. a mould for casting concrete such as for drain-pipes, etc. (cf *subu*) 3. a heating pot or furnace 4. a mould for making bells (Ar)

kalib.u² *vt* mould; shape a soft substance into a particular form or object Prep. ***kalib.i.a*** St. ***kalib.ik.a*** Cs. ***kalib.ish.a*** Ps. of Prep. ***kalib.iw.a*** (Ar)

kalid.i¹ *vt* 1. spin threads with the fingers in order to strengthen them: *Kinu cha kukalidi*, spinning machine. 2. wrap oneself with sth such as cloth: *Mgonjwa alikalidi bendeji mguuni*, the patient wrapped a bandage round his foot. Prep. ***kalid.i.a*** St. ***kalid.ik.a*** Cs. ***kalid.ish.a*** Ps. of Prep. ***kalid.iw.a*** Rp. of Prep. ***kalid.i.an.a*** (cf *vika*) (Ar)

kilid.i² *vt* follow the laws of another religion abandoning temporarily the current ones you have. (Ar) Prep. ***kalid.i.a*** St. ***kalid.ik.a*** Cs. ***kalid.ish.a*** Ps. of Prep. ***kalid.iw.a*** Rp. of Prep. ***kalid.i.an.a***

kalifish.a *vi*,*vt* see *kalifu*. Prep. ***kalifish.i.a*** St. ***kalifish.ik.a*** Ps. ***kalifish.w.a*** Rp. ***kalifish.an.a***

kalif.u (also *kalifisha*) *vi, vt* compel, force: *Usijikalifu kunifanyia karamu*, don't take trouble to hold a party for me. *Mbona unajikalifisha?* Why are you bothering yourself? Prep. ***kalif.i.a*** St. ***kalif.ik.a*** Cs. ***kalif.ish.a*** Ps. of Prep. ***kalif.iw.a***

kaligrafia *n* (*n*) calligraphy (Eng)

kaliko *n* (*n*) calico (Eng)

kalili *adj* little, small, few: *Watu kalili*, few people.(Ar)

kalima *n* (*n*) statement, word, utterance (cf *tamko, kauli, neno*) (Ar)

kalipso *n* (*n*) calypso (Eng)

kalisi¹ *n* (*n*) (*chem*) calcium (Eng)

kalisi² *n* (*n*) calyx; outer covering pod (Eng)

kalisi³ *n* (*n*) (in Christianity) chalice; the cup for the wine of Holy Communion (Eng)

kalivari *n* (*n*) (in Christianity) calvary; the place near Jerusalem where the crucifixion of Jesus took place (Eng)

kalkulasi *n* (*n*) (*math*) calculus: *Kalkulasi tenguo*, differential calculus (Eng)

kalomeli *n* (*n*) (*chem*) calomel; mercurous chloride; a white powder formerly used as a purgative (Eng)

kalori *n* (*n*) (*chem*) calorie (Eng)

kaltiveta *n* (*n*) cultivator; a farming machine for loosening the earth and destroying weeds around growing plants (cf *haro*) (Eng)

kaltiveta

kalunguyeye *n* (*n*) (*zool*) hedgehog; a small insect eating mammal with a

kalvati

shaggy coat and sharp spines on the back.

kalunguyeye

kalvati *n (n)* culvert; a drain or covered channel that crosses under a road, etc. (Eng)

kama¹ *adv, prep* 1. like, as if, such as, as: *Yeye ni mrefu kama wewe*, he is tall like you. 2. used for emphasis when it co-occurs with *nini*, *Ndogo kama nini*, so small that it is impossible to say what it is like. *Mbaya kama nini*, inexpressibly bad 3. used to approximate things: *Watu kama hamsini*, around fifty people. 4. used in the expression: *Kama kwamba*, as if, as though. *Unanitukana kama kwamba mimi ni mtoto mdogo*, you are insulting me as if I am a small child. 5. rather than, as compared with: *Afadhali kujitawala kama kutawaliwa*, it is better to govern onself than to be governed by sby else (cf *kuliko*) 6. used with the relative particle of manner *-vyo-* and the verb: *Kama alivyosema*, as he said.

kama² *conj* (used in conditional sentences) if, provided, whether, supposing: *Kama atakuja kesho, nitampa pesa zake*, if he comes tomorrow, i will give him his money. (cf *pindi, endapo, ikiwa*)

kam.a³ *vt* 1. milk esp a cow: *Kama ng'ombe*, milk the cow. *Kama mbuzi*, milk the goat. 2. (*fig*) squeeze out, wring out, strangle, wrench: *Kama mkono*. wrench an arm. *Kama koo*, strangle a throat. *Kama nguo*, wring out the clothes Prep. *kam.i.a* St. *kam.ik.a* Cs. *kam.ish.a* Ps. *kam.w.a* Rp. *kam.an.a* (cf *bana, finya, kaba*)

kamambe¹ *n(ma-)* a muscular person, usu a courageous one

kamambe² *adj* big, intensive, strong: *Kampeni kamambe*, intensive campaign. *Nyumba kamambe*, a big house.

kamanda *n(ma-)* commander; *Kamanda wa jeshi*, army commander (Eng)

kamandoo *n (ma-)* commando (Eng)

kamani¹ *n (n)* the mainspring of a watch or clock. (Pers)

kamani² *adj* very, exceedingly: *Nzuri kamani*, very good. *Tamu kamani*, very sweet.

kamari *n (n)* a game of chance played for getting money or some other stake; gambling: *Cheza kamari*, gamble. (Ar)

kamasi¹ *n (n) (mod)* snot, nasal mucus: *Futa kamasi*, wipe the nose. *Vuta kamasi*, sniffle. *Penga kamasi*, blow the nose.

kamasi² *n (n) (bot)* a fruit from a shrub or tree (*Cordia sp*) with alternate leaves.

kamat.a¹ *vt* 1. arrest, apprehend, catch: *Walimkamata mwizi*, they arrested the thief. (cf *shika, bamba*) 2 take: *Kamata hizi pesa*, take this money 3. hold firmly: *Kamata usukani huu*, hold this steering wheel firmly. 4. (*idms*) *Kamata kikutu*, hold very firmly. *Kamata roho*, have self control. Prep. *kamat.i.a* St. *kamat.ik.a* Cs. *kamat.ish.a* Ps. *kamat.w.a* Rp. *kamat.an.a*

kamata² *n (n) (med)* deadly diseases e.g. influenza, pneumonia

kamati *n (n)* committee: *Kamati ya sungusungu*, vigilance committee. *Kamati ya utendaji*, steering committee. *Kamati ya matumizi*, committee of supply. *Kamati ya dharura*, adhoc committee. *Kamati ya kudumu*, standing committee. *Kamati teule*, select committee (Eng)

kamba¹ *n (n)* 1. rope, cord, string. (*prov*) *Ukuukuu wa kamba si upya ukambaa*, an old thing is more precious than new one and therefore one should try to respect it more 2. (of shoes) lace, line. 3. (*idm*) *Kata kamba*, a) despond, lose hope b) die, escape, run away: (cf *toroka, kimbia*) *Kamba ya mbuzi*, a very slim and depressed person.

kamba² (also *mkamba*) *n* (*n*) (*zool*) prawn.

kamba

kambadokozi *n* (*n*) (*zool*) mantis shrimp, mantis crab; this is a shrimp-like crustacean with movable stalked eyes and a pair of jointed grasping appendages.

kambakoche (also *kambamti*) *n* (*n*) (*zool*) lobster; a kind of edible sea crustacean with compound eyes, long antennae and five pairs of legs, the first pair of which are modified into large, powerful pincers.

kambakoche

kambamti *n* (*n*) see *kambakoche*

kambarau¹ *n* (*n*) 1. a rope to take the weight off a spar 2. crane, winch, derrick; a large apparatus for lifting and moving heavy objects 3. (*naut*) an extra rope in a vessel, used for assisting a dhow during a strong wind.

kambarau² *n* (*n*) elevator, lift (cf *lifti*)

kambare *n* (*n*) (*zool*) a kind of freshwater catfish with broad flat head, fleshy feelers and barbels

kambaremamba *n* (*n*) (*zool*) lungfish; a kind of freshwater fish resembling a catfish found in basins of Lakes Victoria and Tanganyika. *Protopterus aethiopicus*. (cf *kamongo*)

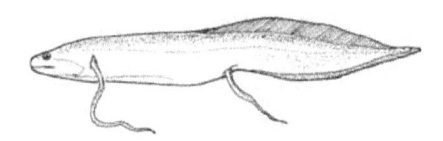

kambaremamba

kambi¹ *n* (*ma-*) 1. camp: *Piga kambi*, set up a camp. *Vunja kambi*, break a camp; decamp. *Kambi za wakimbizi*, refugee camps. (cf *ago, chengo, kigono*) 2. military camp 3. camp, side, block: *Kambi ya upinzani*, opposition camp.

kambi² *n* (*n*) (*biol*) cambium (Eng)

kambirani *interj* an expletive used to show insensitivity of what may happen; Come what may! So what! Who cares! (cf *potelea mbali, lolote liwe, vinani*)

kambisi (also *karambisi, karambizi*) *n* (*n*) (*zool*) caranx, scad: a kind of food fish with small scales, usu cycloid and a moderate mouth, and which is found in reef habitats.

kambo *n* (*n*) step relation: *Baba wa kambo*, step father. *Mama wa kambo*, step mother.

kambriki *n* (*n*) cambric; a very fine thin linen (Eng)

kamandegere *n* (*n*) (*zool*) springhare; a large burrowing rodent resembling a miniature kangaroo, with a rabbit-like head and a long bushy tail.

kamandegere
kambu¹ *n (n)* a parent who has not born you.
kambu² *n (n) (bot)* offspring.
kame *adj* dry, arid: *Ardhi imekuwa kame*, the land has become dry
kamera *n (n)* camera: *Kamera otomatia*, automatic camera. *Kamera tobwe*, pinhole camera. *Kamera akisi*, reflex camera. *Kamera ya televisheni*, television camera. (Eng)
kami.a *vt, vi* 1. determine, intend, resolve; be anxious to do sth. *(prov) Mkamia maji hayanywi*, he who is overzealous on sth may not necessarily get it 2. be insistent in demanding sth. 3. revenge, avenge: *Walimkamia kwa kuchoma moto nyumba yake*, they took revenge on him by burning his house Prep. *kami.li.a* St. *kami.k.a* Cs. *kami.sh.a* Ps. *kami.w.a* Rp. *kami.an.a*
kamian.a *vi* be anxious to do sth: *Mchezo wa kukamiana*, a game intended to prove one's might.
kamil.i¹ *vt* see *kamilisha*. Prep. *kamil.i.a* St. *kamil.ik.a* Cs. *kamil.ish.a* Ps. *kamil.iw.a* (Ar)
kamili² *adj* exact, perfect : *Hesabu kamili*, complete figure. (Ar)
-kamilifu *adj* exact, perfect.: *Hakuna mtu aliye mkamilifu*, there is no one who is perfect. (Ar)
kamilik.a *vi* be perfect, be faultless, be complete: *Je binaadamu amekamilika?* Is a human being perfect? Prep. *kamilik.i.a* St. *kamilik.ik.a* Cs.

kamilik.ish.a (cf *timizika*) (Ar)
kamilio *n (ma-)* strong determination; strong intent; forceful insistence
kamilish.a *vt* finalise, complete, perfect: *Ameikamilisha sasa mipango yake ya kwenda kusoma ng'ambo*, he has now finalized his arrangements to go overseas for studies. Prep. *kamilish.i.a* St. *kamilish.ik.a* Ps. *kamilish.w.a* Rp. *kamilish.an.a* (Ar)
kamisaa *n (n)* commissar : *Kamisaa wa siasa*, political commissar. *Kamisa wa jeshi*, military commissar (Eng)
kamishna *n (ma-)* 1. commissioner, delegate, representative 2. a public official of high office: *Kamishna wa polisi*, commissioner of police. *Kamishna wa pato la kodi*, commissioner of income tax. (Eng)
kamisi *n (n)* chemise, a woman's undergarment somewhat like a loose, short slip. (cf *shimizi*) (Eng)
kamo *n (n)* filter, sifter; palm leaves strainer (cf *kung'uto, chujio*)
kamongo *n (n) (zool)* lungfish (cf *kambaremamba*)
kampaundi *n (n)* compound (Eng)
kampeni¹ *n (n)* campaign : *Piga kampeni*, campaign; conduct a campaign. *Fanya kampeni*, organize a campaign. (Eng)
kampen.i² *vt* campaign, induce, persuade. Prep. *kampen.i.a* St. *kampen.ik.a* Cs. *kampen.ish.a* Ps. of Prep. *kampen.iw.a* Rp. of Prep. *kampen.an.a*
kampuni *n (n)* 1. company, firm: *Kampuni ya binafsi*, private company. *Kampuni tanzu*, subsidiary company. (cf *shirika*) 2. company; a group of policemen or sailors. 3. any other kind of group. association, etc (cf *kikosi*) (Eng)
kamsa *n (n)* siren, alarm; signal, sound, etc that is a warning of danger such as fire: *Piga kamsa*, make an alarm. (Ar)
kamu.a *vt* 1. squeeze out, wring out, compress: *Kamua nguo*, wring out wet clothes (cf *minya, bana, binya*) 2. dun; wring money, be insistent in

demanding money: *Mdai alimkamua mdaiwa*, the creditor dunned the debtor. Prep. **kamu.li.a** St. **kamu.lika** Cs. **kamu.lish.a** Ps. of Prep. **kamu.liw.a** Rp. **kamu.an.a**

kamukunji *n* (*n*) a gathering of people for a particular cause e.g demonstrating against a government, etc because of some injustice. (Kik)

kamusi *n* dictionary: *Kamusi ndogo ya mfukoni*, pocket dictionary (Ar)

kamuzi *n* (*n*) wringer, mangle; a machine or device for squeezing out water or other liquid from wet clothes (cf *gumto*)

kamwe *adv* 1. (always used with a negative particle preceding) never, by no means: *Sipendi kamwe kitu kile*, I don't like that thing at all (cf *abadan, asilani*) 2. used to give emphasis on an exclamative word: *Ala! Anakupiga na kofi kamwe*, Oh, he is beating you with a real slap.

kan.a[1] *vt* deny, disown, renounce: *Mshtakiwa alikana shtaka mbele ya hakimu*, the accused denied the charge before the magistrate. Prep. **kan.i.a** St. **kan.ik.a** Cs. **kan.ish.a** Ps. **kan.w.a**, be denied Rp. of Prep. **kan.i.an.a** (cf *kataa*)

kana[2] *n* (*n*) (*naut*) tiller; a bar or handle for turning a boat's rudder (cf *mkombo*)

kana[3] *conj* used with *kwamba*, to mean 'as if': *Anasema polepole kana kwamba sauti imemkauka*, he speaks slowly as if his voice has dried.

kana[4] *n* (*n*) money given to a captain of a sailing vessel as a reward for looking after the vessel.

kanadi (also *kunadi*) *n* (*n*) (*zool*) kingfish, mackerel; a kind of edible fish (family Scombridae) with an elongate body and fusiform, covered with moderate-sized scales, and which is found in coastal waters.

kanadi

Queen mackerel. *Scomberomorus plurilineatus*.

kanadili (also *kanandile*) *n* (*ma-*) (*naut*) a projection outside the railing on the port quarter of a dhow, used as a closet. (Ar)

kanali *n* (*ma-*) (*mil*) colonel: a high ranking military officer above lieutenant colonel and below a brigadier general. (Eng)

kanandile *n* (*ma-*) see *kanadili*.

kanchiri *n* (*n*) brassiere; bra (cf *sidiria*) (Ar)

kand.a[1] *vt* 1. massage; knead part of the body, etc usu with the hands so as to stimulate circulation: *Kanda mwili*, massage the body. (cf *chua*) 2. knead: *Kanda unga*, knead the dough. *Kanda udongo*, knead the clay. Prep. **kand.i.a** St. **kand.ik.a** Cs. **kand.ish.a** Ps. **kand.w.a** Rp. **kand.an.a**

kanda[2] *n* (*ma-*) a big bag of plaited matting, usu used for storing grain, dates, cloves, etc (cf *bambo, kapu, peto*)

kanda[3] *n* (*n*) fee paid to a medicineman (cf *kiingia pori*)

kanda[4] *n* (*n*) 1. (pl of *ukanda*,) zone 2. (pl of *ukanda*,) tape: *Kanda ya kaseti*, cassete tape.

kanda[5] *n* (*ma-*) 1. cheat, swindler, conman (cf *laghai, ayari*) 2. a misguided person; a perverted person 3. gay, homosexual (cf *hanithi*)

kanda[6] *n* (*n*) tape for a radio/video cassette

kandambili *n* (*n*) flip-flop, sandals. (cf *malapa*)

kandamiz.a *vt, vi* 1. see *gandamiza* 2. oppress, suppress: *Serikali iliwakandamiza raia*, the government oppressed the citizens. Prep **kandamiz.i.a** St. **kandamiz.ik.a,** be oppressed. Cs. **kandamiz.ish.a** Ps. **kandamiz.w.a** Rp. **kandamiz.an.a**

kandamizi *adj* oppressive, brutal, harsh: *Sheria kandamizi*, oppressive laws

kandamuda *n* (*n*) time zone

kandanda *n* (*n*) soccer, football (cf *soka, gozi, kabumbu*)
kandarasi *n* (*n*) 1. contract 2. see *kondrati*. (Eng)
kande *n* (*n*) 1. food. 2. food of mixed grain consisting of maize, millet, kidney beans, etc (cf *pure*)
kandi.a *vt* lambaste, attack, criticize: *Kocha aliwakandia wachezaji kwa ukosefu wa nidhamu*, the coach criticized the players for lack of discipline. Prep. **kandi.li.a** St. **kandi.k.a** Cs. **kandi.sh.a** Ps. **kandi.w.a** Rp. **kandi.an.a**
kandik.a *vt* 1. plaster a house with clay. 2. beat, hit: *Kandika makofi*, slap. *Kandika bakora*, flog, whip. Prep. **kandik.i.a** St, **kandik.ik.a** Cs. **kandik.ish.a** Ps. **kandik.w.a** Rp. **kandik.an.a**
kandili *n* (*n*) lantern (cf *fanusi*) (Ar)

kandili

kandirinya¹ *n* (*n*) 1. kettle, teapot (cf *birika*) 2. a special kettle made from silver or copper, used for washing hands before or after a feast. (Port)
kandirinya² *n* (*n*) (*bot*) bitter cassava
kando¹ *n* (*n*) (of the sea, river, etc) edge, bank, coast.: *Kando ya mto*, the bank of a river.
kando² *adv* aside: *Simama kando*, stand aside. (*prov*) *Aliye kando haangukiwi na mti*, he who stays aside will not be fallen by a tree i.e he who keeps away from an evil, etc will always be safe. (cf *pembeni, upande*)
kanga¹ *n* (*n*) (*zool*) (originally imported from Guinea) guinea fowl; a domestic fowl with a featherless head, rounded body and dark feathers spotted with white. *Numida meleagris*.
kanga² *n* (*n*) a piece of gaily decorated thin cotton wrap worn by women around their waist and printed with border and message; khanga.
kang.a³ *vt* see *kanza*. Prep. **kang.i.a** St. **kang.ik.a** Cs. **kang.ish.a** Ps. **kang.w.a**
kangaga *n* (*n*) 1. (*bot*) tall coarse reeds or grasses which grow around lakes, marshes, etc. 2. a fern with fronds up to $3^{1}/_{2}$ feet high or sometimes more, growing clumps. in walls or rocky places in the salt marshes on the coast. *Pteris vittata*.

kangaga

kangaichi *adj* (used with reference to fruits like mangoes, etc) raw, unripe: *Maembe haya ni kangaichi*, these mangoes are unripe. (cf *bichi*)
kangaja¹ *n* (*n*) (*bot*) a variety of mandarine, orange with a deep, reddish-yellow colour and segments that are easily separated; tangerine.
kangaja² *n* (*n*) (*zoo*) a kind of edible tropical sea fish (family *Acanthuridae*), usu brightly coloured having very small scales and with one or more movable scapel-like spines on either side of the base of the tail; surgeon fish.
kangaja³ *n* (*n*) (*bot*) a tussock herb with stems up to 3 feet with greenish flower spikes. *Cyperus rotundus*. (*prov*)

Mambo ni kangaja, huenda yakaja, incidents are small tangerines and that they may come i.e. an unexpected thing may happen unexpectedly.

kangambili[1] *n (n)* (*zool*) red bug, cotton red bug; a kind of red and black ant (family *Pyrrhocoridae*) living in certain trees such as baobab and cotton. The bugs are major pests of cotton in most parts of Africa and Asia. The stainers inject fungal spores of the genus *Nematospora* into the cotton boll and cause the staining.

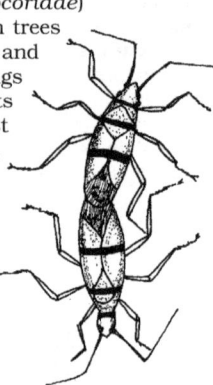

Kangambili (red bug.)

kangambili[2] *n (n)* a kind of a woman's khanga dress worn by someone when she is at home.

kangany.a *vt* baffle, obfuscate, puzzle, confuse, bewilder; *Amenikanganya na sasa sijui la kufanya*, he has confused me and now I don't know what to do. Prep. **kangany.i.a** St. **kangany.ik.a** Cs. **kangany.ish.a** Ps. **kangany.w.a,** Rp. **kangany.an.a** (cf *babaisha, tatiza*)

kangara *n (n)* a kind of local brew made from the sprouts of maize or bullrush millet and fermented with finger millet (*ulezi*) and then sweetened with sugar or honey.

kangaruu *n (n)* (*zool*) kangaroo (Eng)

kangat.a *vt* insist on sth; beseech persistently, be firm: *Mtoto wangu alikangata kwamba nimnunulie mwanasesere*, my child insisted that I buy for her a doll. Prep. **kangat.i.a** St. **kangat.ik.a** Cs. **kangat.ish.a** Ps. **kangat.w.a** Rp. **kangat.an.a** (cf *shikilia, ng'ang'ania.*)

kang'at.a (*also keng'eta*) *vi, vt* feel great pain or ache inside the bones due to sickness, etc: *Goti lake lilikuwa likimkang'ata*, his knee was paining him a lot. Prep. **kang'at.i.a** St. **kang'at.ik.a** Cs. **kang'at.ish.a** Ps. **kang'at.w.a** Rp. **kang'at.an.a** (cf *keng'eta*)

kangu *n (n)* (*zool*) a kind of fish belonging to the families of *Labridae* and *Sacridae*.

kani[1] *n (n)* obstinancy, stubbornness, firmness: *Shika kani*, be obstinate. *Jambo lenye kani*, a thing that is hard to deal with.

kani[2] *n (n)* force, energy; *Kani sumaku*, magnetic force. *Kani ya mvutano*, the force of gravity. *Kani ya nyuklia*, nuclear force. *Kani kinzani*, resisting force. *Kani kitovu*, centripetal force. *Kani pewa*, centrifugal force (Ar)

kani[3] *n (n)* (*naut*) division of hold in a boat. *Kani ya omo*, division of a prow. *Kani ya tezi*, division of a stern.

kani[4] *n (n)* an expletive used during a wedding celebration or any other joyful function: *Kugea kani*, move here and there joyfully as in a wedding celebration.

kania *n (n)* (*med*) a special kind of herbal medicine whose roots are used for treating cramps.

kanieneo *n (n)* pressure: *Kanieneo damu*, blood pressure. *Kanieneo maji*, water pressure. *Kanieneo mzizi*, root pressure. *Kanieneo hewa*, air pressure. *Kanieneo sanifu*, standard pressure (cf *shinikizo*)

kaniki *n (n)* dark blue calico or cotton wrap, usu worn by some women in place of *khanga* esp during work, as in farming.

kanisa   *mhudumu wa kanisa = deacon*   kanzi²   **K**

kanisa *n* (*ma-*) 1. church: *Kanisa kuu la dayosisi*, cathedral; abbey. *Kanisa la Anglikana*, the Anglican church. *Ibada ya kanisa*, church service. 2. Christian community.

kanivali *n* (*n*) (in Christianity) carnival (Eng)

kanja *n* (*ma-*) 1. (*bot*) plaited coconut palm leaf. 2. a mat made of strips of palm leaves.

kanju¹ *n* (*n*) 1. starch (cf *uwanga*) 2. gruel, porridge

kanju² *n* (*n*) (*bot*) cashew apple (cf *bibo*)

kano¹ *n* (*n*) (*anat*) tendon; a strong band of tissue that joins muscle fibres and the bone.

kano² *n* (*n*) nihilism; the rejection of all religious and moral principles, often in the belief that life is meaningless.

kanopi *n* (*n*) canopy (Eng)

kansa (*also kensa*) *n* (*n*) cancer. *Kansa ya mapafu*, lung cancer. *Kansa ya matiti*, breast cancer. *Kansa ya koo*, throat cancer. *Kansa ya kibofu cha mkojo*, prostrate cancer. (cf *saratani*) (Eng)

kanta *n* (*n*) a colouring matter solution for restoring hair; hair colour restorer.

kantara *n* (*n*) (rarely used) wooden bridge (cf *ulalo, mtatago*) (Ar)

kantini *n* (*n*) canteen, refectory. (Eng)

kanu *n* (*n*) (*zool*) a genet related to the civet cat and of the family *Genette commune*, having proportionately long legs and a short face and a well-haired tail, almost bushy with 9-10 dark rings and a whitish tip; common genet.

kanu

kanuni *n* (*n*) rule, regulation, principle. *Kanuni za chama*, party's rules. *Kanuni za tafsiri*, translation rules. *Kanuni geuza maumbo*, transformation rules. *Kanuni mkufu*, chain rules. (Ar)

kanush.a *vt* refute, confute, deny: *Alilikanusha tamko lake*, he refuted his statement. Prep. **kanush.i.a** St. **kanush.ik.a** Ps. **kanush.w.a**, Rp. **kanush.an.a** (cf *kana, pinga, susuage, iza, kataa*).

kanwa *n* (*ma-*) see *kinywa*.

kany.a *vt* forbid, prohibit, prevent: *Alimkanya mtoto wake kutukana watu*, he forbade his child to insult people. Prep. **kany.ia** St. **kany.ik.a** Cs. **kany.ish.a** Ps. **kany.w.a**, Rp. **kany.an.a** (cf *kataza, zuia*).

kanyag.a *vt* 1. tread on, trample on: *Alikanyaga matope*, he treaded on mud. (cf *vyoga*) 2. (*fig*) beat hard, hit hard: *Walimkanyaga burebure*, they hit him hard for no reason. (cf *dunda, bumunda*) 3. bully, oppress. *Alimkanyaga yule mtoto mdogo*, he bullied that small child. 4 (*idms*) *Kanyaga chechele*, lose one's way, be disorientated. *Kanyaga mambo*, (a) succeed in a particular issue, etc (b) hide sth. Prep. **kanyag.i.a** St. **kanyag.ik.a** Cs. **kanyag.ish.a** Ps. **kanyag.w.a** Rp. **kanyag.an.a**.

kanyagio *n* (*ma-*) 1. (*zool*) the foot of a slaughtered cow, goat or sheep. 2. pedal; a lever that drives a machine e.g. bicycle when pressed down by the foot.

kanyakanya *n* (*n*) pandemonium, chaos, confusion. (cf *vurungu, kitahanani*)

kanz.a (*also kanga*) *vt* warm up food, body, etc. *Alilikanza chakula chake*, she warmed up her food. Prep. **kanz.i.a** St. **kanz.ik.a** Cs. **kanz.ish.a** Ps. **kanz.w.a** Rp. **kanz.an.a**.

kanzi¹ *n* (*n*) 1. treasure: *Wafukuaji waligundua kanzi ya dhahabu*, the excavators discovered golden treasure (cf *kasiki, hazina*) 2. anything valuable such as property or goods.

kanzi² *n* (*n*) a dish made from rice, maize, green gram, meat, chilies and ghee.

kanzi³ *n* (*n*) data bank; a large repository of computer data on a particular topic. (cf *databenki*)

kanzu *n* (*n*) 1. men's long robe usu white or yellowish brown: *Kanzus* are distinguished as follows. *Kanzu ya mfuto*, plain common one. *Kanzu ya ziki*, with white stitching at the neck. *Kanzu ya kazi*, with ornamental stitching. *Kanzu ya melimeli*, white thin cloth; muslin. 2. a woman's garment. (cf *rinda, gauni*)

kapa¹ *adv* 1. used in the game of cards: *Kwenda kapa*, go away conquered; fail completely. 2. (*gram*) zero: *Mofimu kapa*, zero morpheme symbolized by ø as in *chungwa*, 'orange'. *Kiambishi kapa*, zero affix.

kapa² *n* (*n*) 1. waistcoat; a sleeveless jacket. (cf *kizibao, nusukoti*) 2. a measurement in dress from one shoulder to another.

kapa³ *n* (*n*) a section of the sea coast which is muddy and where mangrove trees grow; mangrove swamp.

kapani *n* (*n*) spring balance. (Pers)

kapeli *n* (*n*) (*bot*) carpel; the female reproductive organ of a flower. (Eng)

kapera *n* (*ma-*) bachelor, celibate: *Kijana yule bado ni kapera*, that young man is still a bachelor. *Kula kapera*, eat in a restaurant while you have a wife at home. (cf *mseja*)

kapi¹ *n* (*ma-*) husk, chaff, bran; the skin or husk of grains of wheat, rice, oats, etc: *Kapi la mpunga*, the husk of rice. *Kapi la mahindi*, the husk of maize. *Kapi la ngano*, the husk of wheat.

kapi² *n* (*n*) pulley (cf *roda*)

kapilari *n* (*n*) capillary: *Msukumo wa kapilari*, capillary repulsion. (Eng)

kapile *n* (*n*) 1. cooked food of any description, sold in the market. 2. potatoes when eaten together with fried peanuts.

kapo *n* (*n*) couple (Eng)

kapolojia *n* (*n*) (*bot*) carpology; the study of the structure of fruits and seeds. (Eng)

kapteni *n* (*n*) 1. a captain in the army. 2. a captain of a ship or an aircraft (cf *nahodha*) 3. leader of a sports team e.g. football, hockey, cricket, etc. (Eng)

kaptura *n* (*n*) shorts (cf *bondo*)

kapu *n* (*ma-*) a large basket: *Kapu la taka*, a waste basket.

kapungu *n* (*n*) (*zool*) a kind of shark

kaputa *n* (*n*) a kind of dance, used in the exorcism of spirits.

kaputi¹ *n* (*n*) 1. see *nusukaputi*. 2. day-dream.

kaputi² *n* (*n*) corpse, dead body. (cf *maiti, mfu*)

kaputi³ *n* (*ma-*) 1. overcoat; a heavy coat worn over the usual clothing against cold, etc.

kaputula *n* (*n*) (*med*) diarrhoea (cf *kuhara*)

kara¹ *n* (*ma-*) see *karaa*

kara² *n* (*ma-*) see *kala²*

kara³ *n* (*ma-*) a splinter of wood; a chip of wood; a slice of fruit e.g. cassava; *Kara la muhogo*, a slice of cassava. (cf *kichane, kibanzi, cheche*)

karaa (*also kara*) *n* (*ma-*) a big passage of Koran with many verses in it but is smaller than a paragraph. (Ar)

karabai *n* (*ma-*) 1. pressure lamp. 2. acetylene lamp. (Ar)

karabai

karabat.i *vt* rehabilitate, repair: *Serikali itakarabati barabara nyingi*, the government will repair many roads.

karabini   **karandinga**   **K**

Prep. **karabat.i.a** St. **karabat.ik.a** Cs. **karabat.ish.a** Ps. of Prep. **karabat.iw.a** Rp. of Prep. **karabat.i.an.a**

karabini *n* (*n*) carbine; a rifle with a short barrel (Eng)

karadha *n* (*n*) loan, credit: *Ofisi ya karadha*, loan office. *Shirika lilikubali kunipa karadha kwa ajili ya miradi yangu*, the corporation agreed to give me an interest free loan for my projects. (cf *mkopo*) (Ar)

karafuu *n* (*n*) (*bot*) clove: *Karafuu maiti*, camphor. *Mafuta ya karafuu*, clove oil. (Ar)

karagosi *n* (*ma-*) 1. puppet, dolly. (cf *mwanasesere, abudu*) 2. (*fig*) stooge, puppet; a person whose actions are controlled by another. (cf *kibaraka, kitimbakwiri*) 3. comedian; a person who entertains others by behaving in a comic way.

karaha (*also kiraha*) *n* (*n*) disgust, distaste, abhorrence: *Ni karaha kujamba mbele za watu*, it is disgusting to fart in public (cf *maudhi, makuruhi, kero*) (Ar)

karai *n* (*ma-*) 1. a large metal basin, used for frying things e.g. doughnuts. 2. a metal basin used by masons for carrying cement or sand.

karakana *n* (*ma-*) see *karakhana*

karakhana (also *karakana*) *n* (*ma-*) workshop for repairs, manufacture, etc.; factory: *Karakhana yao inakarabati matrekta*, their workshop repairs tractors. *Karakhana ya reli*, railway yard. (Pers)

karama *n* (*n*) gift esp from god given to a person; talent given to a person because of his keen devotion to God; God's blessings given to a person. (cf *kipaji*) (Ar)

karamala *n* (*n*) a flat tool for smoothing or spreading cement, plaster, etc.; float, trowel. (Pers)

karamala

karamamba *n* (*n*) (*zool*) juvenile grunter, cock grunter; a juvenile salt-water fish of olive or silvery colour, used as an excellent food fish.

karambisi *n* (*n*) see *kambisi*

karambizi *n* (*n*) see *kambisi*

karameli *n* (*n*) caramel (Eng)

karamk.a *vi* 1. be too sharp, be quick-witted, be clever: *Hawezi tena kukudanganya kwani sasa umekuramka*, he can't deceive you again because you are now too sharp. (cf *erevuka*) 2. be cheerful, be jovial, be lively, be active: *Amekaramka baada ya kusikia kwamba mkewe amepata mtoto*, he has become cheerful after hearing that his wife has had a baby. Prep. **karamk.i.a** St. **karamk.ik.a** Cs. **karam.sh.a** Ps. **karamk.w.a** (cf *changamka*)

karamshi *adj* 1. sly, cunning, crafty: *Yeye ni mfanyabiashara karamshi*, he is a cunning businessman. 2. cheerful, humorous, charming: *Watu wanayapenda mazungumzo yake kwa vile yeye ni kijana karamshi*, people like his conversations because he is a youth of humorous nature. (cf *bashasha*)

karamu *n* (*n*) 1. party, banquet, feast, reception: *Aliwafanyia karamu kubwa wageni wake*, he hosted a big reception for his guests (cf *dhifa, hafla*) 2. (in sports) (Used in the expression): *Karamu ya magoli*, many goals e.g *Timu yao ilivuna karamu ya magoli jana*, their team got many goals yesterday. (Ar)

karandinga *n* (*n*) a police van for carrying culprits.

287

K

karanga *n* (*n*) 1. (*bot*) groundnut/peanut plant. *Arachis hypogaea.* 2. groundnut, peanut. 3. *Karanga mwitu,* a perennial prostrate herb with lax few-flowered racemes of white or pale mauve flowers and sticky jointed pods. *Desmodium adscendens.*

karani *n* (*n*) office clerk: *Karani mkuu,* chief clerk. *Karani wa baraza la mawaziri,* clerk to the cabinet. *Karani wa bunge,* clerk to the National Assembly. (Pers)

karantini *n* (*n*) quarantine; a place where persons, animals or plants having contagious diseases, insect pests, etc. are kept in isolation, or beyond which they may not travel. (Eng)

karara[1] *n* (*n*) 1. (*bot*) the matured sheath of coconut inflorescence. 2. sisal husk.

karara[2] *n* (*n*) a kind of sweet doughnut made from flour and sugar, and which is fried by using ghee or cooking oil and later dipped in syrup.

karasa *n* (*n*) (*zool*) a small mongoose-like animal, fond of stealing and eating fowls.

karasia *n* (*n*) see *kalasia*

karata *n* (*n*) playing cards. *Piga karata,* shuffle the cards. *Cheza karata,* 1) play the cards. *Gawa karata,* deal the cards. *Changanya karata,* shuffle. *Kata karata,* cut the cards. 2) (*idm*) *Cheza karata,* handle a situation skilfully. (Port)

karatasi *n* (*n*) paper: *Karatasi ya mafuta,* oil paper. *Karatasi jarabati,* galley proof. *Karatasi kaushio,* blotting paper. *Karatasi kaboni,* carbon paper. *Karatasi yenye anwani,* letter-head. *Karatasi ya kura,* ballot paper, *Karatasi ya barua,* letter paper. *Karatasi za magazeti,* newsprint. *Karatasi zenye mistari,* lined papers.

kardinali *n* (*n*) see *kadinali*

karela *n* (*n*) 1. (*bot*) a perennial climbing plant with dark yellow flowers and containing cucumber-like fruits of brilliant orange colour, which are eaten when young. *Memordica charantia.* 2. a kind of vegetable obtained from this plant. (Hind)

kareti *n* (*n*) karate; an oriental system of unarmed combat using the hands and feet to deliver and block blows, widely practised as a sport.

karia[1] *n* (*n*) carrier; the second seat of a bicycle, etc. used for carrying a person, luggage, etc. (Eng)

karia[2] *n* (*n*) village (cf *kijiji*) (Ar)

karibi.a *vt, vi* approach, come near : *Adui aliukaribia mji,* the enemy approached the town. St. *karibi.ik.a* Cs. *karibi.sh.a* Ps *karib.iw.a* Rp *karibi.an.a* (cf *sogelea, jongelea*)

karibian.a *vi* be close to each other; be close to one another. (Ar)

karibiano *n* (*ma*-) 1. approach, nearing: *Karibiano la timu yetu kupata ushindi liliwafurahisha mashabiki,* the nearing of our team to clinch victory pleased the fans. 2. good understanding; good relationship: *Vijana wale wawili wana makaribiano mazuri,* those two young men have got good understanding. (Ar)

karibish.a[1] *vt* see *karibia*

karibish.a[2] *vt* 1. welcome; greet sby on his arrival: *Rais alimkaribisha mgeni wake alipowasili uwanja wa ndege,* the president welcomed his guest when he arrived at the airport. 2. invite someone to a party; request someone to start eating at a party, etc.: *Aliwakaribisha wageni kula mara tu chakula kilipowekwa mezani,* he requested his guests to start eating as soon as the food was laid on the table. Prep. *karibish.i.a* St. *karibish.ik.a* Ps. *karibish.w.a* Rp. *karibish.an.a*

karibisho *n* (*ma*-) 1. welcome 2. invitation

karibu[1] *adj* near, not distant: *Nyumba yake iko karibu,* his house is near. (Ar)

karibu[2] *adv* 1. almost, nearly: *Alikuwa karibu ashinde kwenye mbio,* he almost won the race. (cf *takriban*) 2. (of time, etc.) almost, nearly, about: *Ni karibu saa nne sasa hivi*, it is almost ten o'clock now. 3. about, approximately: *Karibu watu mia walikufa katika ajali ya ndege*, approximately hundred people died in the plane crash. (Ar)

karibu³ *interj* 1. welcome. 2. (in bidding farewell) come again; an expletive of respect used as a kind of response when someone is bidding farewell to someone else. (Ar)

karibuni *adj* recently, soon: *Watalii wale wamewasili hapa hivi karibuni*, those tourists have arrived here recently. (Ar)

karidh.i *vt* lend someone money without giving him interest: *Kampuni yao ilinikaridhi shilingi milioni tatu ili ninunue gari*, their company gave me a free interest loan of three million shillings to buy a car. Prep. **karidh.i.a** St. **karidh.ik.a** Cs. **karidh.ish.a** Ps. of Prep. **karidh.iw.a** Rp. of Prep. **karidh.i.an.a** (cf *bidi*) (Ar)

kariha *n* (*n*) 1. disgust, abhorrence, dislike: *Kutema mate ovyovyo ni kariha*, to spit indiscriminately is disgusting (cf *chukizo*) 2. obligation, necessity; obligatory thing: *Kuwatii wazee wako ni kariha*, to obey your parents is a necessity. (Ar)

karii *n* (*ma-*) 1. reciter of the Holy Koran, esp *tajuwidi*. 2. reviewer; a person who reviews plays, novels, etc. 3. good luck. (Ar)

karikopwa *n* (*n*) a kind of stiff white cloth, which is not attractive.

Karima *n* (*n*) one of the names of God, the Generous.

karimu¹ *n* (*ma-*) a generous person; an open-handed person: *Ingawa yeye ni masikini, lakini ni karimu*, even though he is poor, he is generous. 2. philanthropist, benefactor: *Karimu yule aliwasaidia masikini wengi*, that philanthropist helped many poor people. (Ar)

karimu² *adj* 1. generous, magnanimous, open-handed: *Mtu mkarimu*, a generous person. 2. philanthropic, aidful, helpful: *Wao ni wafadhili karimu*, they are helpful donors.

karina *n* (*n*) euphemism; an expletive or group of words used to explain a particular concept by using different words from those used in the original version: *Alikuja hapa na kutoa lulu*, he came here and delivered a pearl i.e. he came here and delivered good words. (cf *tasifida*)

karipi.a *vt* objurgate, berate, chide, scold, censure, reprove; rebuke severely: *Wazazi walimkaripia binti yao*, the parents scolded their daughter. St. **karipi.k.a** Cs. **karipi.sh.a** Ps. **karipi.w.a** Rp. **karipi.an.a** (cf *kemea, shutumu*)

karipio *n* (*ma-*) blame, censure, reprimand, scolding: *Karipio lake kwa wanawe halina msingi*, his scolding towards his children is baseless. (cf *kemeo, uaili*)

karir.i *vt* reiterate, emphasize, underscore, stress: *Waziri alikariri umuhimu wa mshikamano nchini*, the minister stressed the importance of unity in the country. 2. recite, rehearse: *Watoto walilikariri shairi*, the children recited the poem. Prep. **karir.i.a** St. **karir.ik.a** Cs **karir.ish.a** Ps. of Prep. **karir.iw.a** Rp. of Prep. **karir.i.an.a** (Ar)

karisaji *n* (*n*) 1. arrears; unpaid and overdue debts. 2. payment of an old debt: *Alinipa karisaji niliyokuwa ninamdai*, he cleared the old debt he owed me. (Pers)

karisi *n* (*n*) (*med*) caries; progressive decay of a bone or of a tooth. (Eng)

karne (also *karni*) *n* (*n*) century: *Karne ya sasa*, the present century. *Karne iliyopita*, the previous century. (Ar)

karni *n* (*n*) see *karne*

karo¹ n (n) 1. honorarium, fees, presents, etc. that a pupil gives to his teacher so that he can be taught. 2. school fees. (Ar)
karo² n (n) 1. sink, wash basin. 2. septic tank.
karoti n (n) (bot) carrot (Eng)
karotine n (n) (chem) carotene; an orange or red plant pigment found in carrots and other plant structures. (Eng)
karua n (ma-) 1. a sailor from the sailing-vessels of India. 2. a community of Indians making and selling pottery.
karwe n (n) (zool) a kind of stingray fish having a poisonous sting. (cf *nyenga, katwe*)
kasa n (n) (zool) sea turtle: *Kasa duvi*, loggerhead turtle (*Caretta Caretta*). *Kasa ngamba*, hawks bill turtle. (*Eretmochelys imbricata*) *Kasa kigome*, olive kidley turtle. (*Lepidochelys olivacea*)

kasa

kasabu¹ n (n) a kind of ornament resembling a brocade, that is a rich gold cloth with gold thread embroidery. (Ar)
kasabu² n (n) a stick fixed to the ground as a marker for competing runners who reach first position; post marking finishing line. (cf *mfunda*)
kasama¹ n (n) oath, vow. (cf *kiapo*) (Ar)
kasama² n (n) 1. (naut) beak-like prow of a ship, dhow, etc. representing a camel head. 2. prow, stern. (Ar)
kasama³ n (n) fault in plaiting mats, etc. (Ar)
kasarobo n (n) see *kasorobo*
kaseni n (n) casein; the main protein present in milk and in coagulated form in cheese used in plastics, glues, etc. (Eng)

kaseti n (n) cassette (Eng)
kasha n (ma-) chest, safe, box: *Aliweka vitu vyake vya dhahabu katika kasha*, she kept her gold things in the chest (cf *bweta, ndusi*)
kashab.i vt squeeze sugarcane in order to make sugar, etc. Prep. **kashab.i.a** St **kashab.ik.a** Cs **kashab.ish.a** Ps. of Prep **kashab.iw.a** Rp. of Prep. **kashab.i.an.a** (Pers)
kashabu¹ n (n) a wooden cord, which draws the thread of the web apart in weaving and embroidering. (Ar)
kashabu² n (n) a kind of coloured bead, often of silver or gold form. (Ar)
kashata¹ n (n) a confection of sugar paste with almonds or other nuts, and sometimes, fruit; nougat.
kashata² n (n) tread; the grooved face of a tire for added traction.
kasheshe n (n) a bizarre incident; saga: *Kasheshe ya kisiasa ilimwaibisha waziri*, the bizarre political incident disgraced the minister.
kashfa (also *kashifa*) n (n) scandal, chagrin: *Waziri alijiuzulu kutokana na kashfa katika wizara yake*, the minister resigned over a scandal in his ministry. (cf *aibu, fedheha*) (Ar)
kashida n (n) a kind of shawl, usu worn by Muslim religious leaders. (cf *shali*) (Ar)
kashifa n (n) see *kashfa*
kashif.u vt 1. vilify, discredit, disgrace, slander, defame: *Alimkashifu mzee wake mbele za watu*, he discredited his parent in public. (cf *fedhehesha, tehemu, aziri*) 2. reveal secrets of someone; divulge, disclose: *Ukimwambia siri zako, atazikashifu tu*, if you tell him your secrets, he will just disclose them. Prep. **kashif.i.a** St. **kashif.ik.a** Cs. **kashif.ish.a** Ps. of Prep. **kashif.iw.a** Rp. of Prep. **kashif.i.an.a** (cf *fichua, funua*) (Ar)
kashikashi n (n) hard time: *Mchezaji alimpa kashikashi golikipa wetu*, the player gave our goalkeeper a hard time.

kashimiri *n* (*n*) a fine carded wool obtained from goats of Kashmir and Tibet; cashmere. (Hind)

kasi[1] *n* (*n*) 1. speed, velocity: *Kasi husianifu*, related speed. *Kasi pambanuzi*, critical speed. *Aliendesha gari kwa kasi*, he drove the car at great speed. (cf *spidi*) 2. effort: *Anaifanya kazi yake kwa kasi*, he does his work with effort. (cf *bidii*, *hima*) (Ar)

kasi[2] *n* (*n*) (*idm*) *Tia kasi uzi*, twist the thread forcibly in order to make a fishing-line, etc. (Ar)

kasia *n*(*ma*-) oar: *Piga kasia*, row. *Vuta kasia*, row; propel a boat, etc. on water by using oars.

kasiba *n* (*n*) barrel of a gun: *Mdomo kama kasiba*, a small round mouth like the barrel of a gun. (Ar)

kasida *n* (*n*) 1. a poem, usu used to eulogize prophets, religious leaders, etc. 2. any composition intended to praise a person. (Ar)

kasidi *adj* deliberate, intentional. (Ar)

kasiki[1] *n* (*ma*-) cask; a large earthen waterjar. (Eng, Port)

kasiki[2] *n* (*n*) a long loose outer garment, worn by a Christian priest; cloak.

kasimile *n* (*n*) the first thick juice squeezed from a grated coconut; coconut cream (Ar)

kasim.u *vt* 1. divide, apportion: *Mahakama iliikasimu mali ya warithi wa marehemu katika mafungu matatu*, the court divided the property of the deceased into three parts. 2. delegate responsibility. Prep. **kasim.i.a** St. **kasim.ik.a** Cs. **kasim.ish.a** Ps. of Prep. **kasim.iw.a** Rp. of Prep. **kasim.i.an.a** (cf *gawa*, *gawanya*) (Ar)

kasimwelekeo *n* (*n*) velocity

kasino *n* (*n*) casino (Eng)

kasirani *n* (*n*) see *kisirani*

kasir.i *vt* 1. cause to be angry; provoke, annoy, enrage: *Mtoto alimkasiri baba yake kwa kutomtii*, the child enraged his father by disobeying him. (cf *ghasi*, *udhi*) 2. shorten words, prayers, etc.: *Alizikasiri sala zake alipokuwa safarini*, he shortened his prayers during his journey. Prep. **kasir.i.a** St. **kasir.ik.a** Cs. **kasir.ish.a** Ps. of Prep. **kasir.iw.a** Rp. of Prep. **kasir.i.an.a** (cf *fupisha*) (Ar)

kasirik.a *vi* be angry, be annoyed: *Alikasirika nilipomlaumu*, he became annoyed when I blamed him. Prep. **kasirik.i.a** St. **kasirik.ik.a** Cs. **kasirik.ish.a** Ps. of Prep. **kasirik.iw.a** Rp. of Prep. **kasirik.i.an.a** (cf *ghadhibika*, *hamaki*)

kasirish.a *vt* annoy, irritate, enrage: *Wanafunzi walimkasirisha mwalimu wao*, the students annoyed their teacher. Prep. **kasirish.i.a** St. **kasirish.ik.a** Ps. **kasirish.w.u** Rp. **kasirish.an.a** (cf *chukiza*, *hamakisha*, *udhi*)

kasisi *n* (*ma*-) priest, chaplain: *Kasisi mkuu*, arch deacon. (cf *padri*) (Ar)

kaskazi *n* (*n*) 1. north; northerly direction: *Anatoka upande wa kaskazini*, he comes from the north. 2. north moonson; northernly wind. (cf *kibla*)

kaskazini[1] *n* (*n*) north

kaskazini[2] *adv* on the northern side: *Alienda kaskazini*, he went to the north.

kasma *n* (*n*) 1. share, division. (cf *fungu*) 2. financial allocation; vote. (Ar)

kasoko *n* (*n*) crater (cf *zaha*)

kasoro[1] *n* (*n*) defect, fault, imperfection: *Saa hii ina kasoro*, this watch is defective. (cf *dosari*, *ila*, *upungufu*) (Ar)

kasoro[2] *prep* except, without: *Watu wote walihudhuria mkutano kasoro yeye*, all the people attended the meeting except him. (cf *ila*, *isipokuwa*) (Ar)

kasorobo *adj* see *kasrobo*

kasra (also *kisira*) *n* (*n*) vowel /i/ in Arabic script.

kasri *n* (*n*) 1. palace; stately residence. 2. mansion, manor; a large prestigious house. (Ar)

kasrobo (also *kasorobo*) *adj* quarter: *Ni saa tano kasrobo*, it is a quarter to eleven. (Ar)
kastabini (also *kustabini*) *n* (*n*) thimble; a small cap of metal, plastic, etc. that pushes the needle in sewing (cf *subana, tondoo*) (Ar)
kastadi *n* (*n*) (*bot*) custard (Eng)
kasuku¹ *n* (*n*) 1. (*zool*) parrot. 2. (*idm*) *kikasuku*, by rote e.g. *Anasoma kikasuku*, he is learning by rote.
kasuku² *n* (*n*) claw hammer. (cf *nyundo.*)

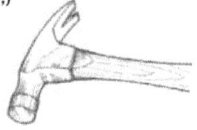

kasuku

kasula (also *kazula*) *n* (*n*) cassock; an outer garment worn by clergymen, choristers, etc.
kasumba *n* (*n*) 1. opium. 2. (*fig*) brainwashing. 3. (*fig*) outdated mentality; hangover: *Ana kasumba za kikoloni*, he has colonial hangovers.
kaswende *n* (*n*) (*med*) syphilis (cf *sekeneko*)
kat.a¹ *vt* 1. cut, cut off, cut across: *Aliukata ubao*, he cut the board. (cf *tema*) 2. reduce, deduct, cut, divide: *Kata mshahara*, cut one's pay; reduce salary or wages. *Kata tawi*, cut the branch. *Kata mkono*, cut the arm; amputate. 3. (*idms*) *Kata notisi*, give out summons. *Kata rufaa*, appeal a court sentence. *Kata tikiti*, buy a ticket. *Kata kiu*, quench the thirst. *Kata leseni*, get a licence. *Kata ini*, hurt one's feelings deeply. *Kata njia*, cross the road. *Kata kona*, turn a corner. *Kata roho*, die. *Kata shauri*, decide. *Kata tamaa*, despond, despair. *Kata urafiki*, break friendship. *Kata kuni*, cut firewood. *Kata mguu*, stop going to a particular place. *Kata kauli*, interrupt someone before he finishes to speak on a point. Prep. **kat.i.a** St.
kat.ik.a Cs. **kat.ish.a** Ps. **kat.w.a** Rp. **kat.an.a**
kata² (also *kataa*) *n* (*n*) ward; a political unit. (cf *mtaa*)
kata³ *n* (*n*) dipper, scoop, ladle; a calabash used as a ladle for drinking or dipping water from a container.
kata⁴ *n* (*n*) 1. a round pad usu of leaves, grass or a folded strip of cloth placed on the head when carrying a load, etc. 2. a long wrapped rope. 3. the dressing put on the child after circumcision to prevent it from being knocked. (cf *pimbili, alfafa, kizingatine*) 4. charm. (cf *hirizi, kago*)
kata⁵ *n* (*n*) a piece of folded gauze, compressed cotton, etc. used as a dressing or protection on a wound, etc.; pad. (cf *alfafa*)
kat.a⁶ *vt* reach the end: *Kata mbele*, stop. Prep. **kat.i.a** St. **kat.ik.a** Cs. **kat.ish.a** Ps. **kat.w.a** Rp. **kat.an.a**
kataa¹ *n* (*n*) see *kata²*
kata.a² *vt, vi* 1. deny, reject: *Alikataa tuhuma ile*, he denied that allegation. (cf *kana, kanusha*) 2. refuse, decline, disagree: *Walikataa kunisaidia*, they refused to help me. Prep. **kata.li.a** St. **kata.lik.a** Cs. **kata.z.a** Ps. of Prep. **kata.liw.a** Rp. **kata.an.a**
katakata *adj* emphasis given to sth when denying it: *Alilikataa katakata shauri langu*, he refused my suggestion completely. (cf *kabisa*)
katalogi *n* (*n*) catalogue (Eng)
katani *n* (*n*) see *kitani*
katapila *n* (*ma-*) caterpillar tractor. (Eng)
katara *n* (*n*) jalopy; a dilapidated old automobile; an old worn-out vehicle (cf *mkweche, ngongongo*)
kataupepo *n* (*n*) propeller blade.
-katavu *adj* contumacious, recalcitrant, obstinate, stubborn: *Mzazi amechoka na mwanawe kwa vile ni mkatavu*, the parent is tired of his son because he is stubborn. (cf *shupavu*)
katayo *n* (*n*) denial, refusal.
kataz.a *vt* forbid, prohibit, inhibit:

katazo

Alimkataza mwanawe asiende kuoga pwani, she forbade her son to go to swim at the sea. Prep. **kataz.i.a** St. **kataz.ik.a** Cs. **kataz.ish.a** Ps. **kataz.w.a** Rp. **kataz.an.a** (cf *zuia, iza*)

katazo *n (ma-)* forbiddance, prohibition, interdiction: *Katazo lake liliwaudhi wanafunzi,* his forbiddance angered the students. (cf *marufuku*)

kategoria *n (n)* category (Eng)

katakisimu (also *katekisimu*) *n (n)* (in Christianity) catechism; a handbook of questions and answers for teaching the principles of a religion. (Eng)

katekista *n (n)* catechist (Eng)

katheta *n (n)* a slender tube, used to drain fluids from the bladder; catheter. (Eng)

kathodi *n (n)* cathode (Eng)

kati[1] *adv* centre, middle: *Kaa kati;* sit in the middle.

kati[2] *n (n)* 1. centre, middle: *Kati na kati,* average. *Kati moja,* concentric. *Kati ndani,* incentre. 2. *(math)* median; a straight line joining one vertex of a triangle to the midpoint of the opposite side.

kati[3] *prep* used with *ya* to mean 'between' 'centre' etc.: *Kuna tofauti kubwa kati ya ndugu hawa wawili,* there is a big difference between these two brothers.

kati[4] *adj* centre, middle, medium: *Huu ni mstari wa kati,* this is the middle line.

katiba *n (n)* constitution: *Katiba ya mpito,* interim constitution. (Ar)

katibu *n (n)* secretary: *Katibu mkuu,* secretary general. *Katibu mtendaji,* executive secretary. *Katibu myeka,* private secretary. *Katibu muhtasi,* personal secretary. *Katibu mwandalizi,* social secretary. *Katibu mwenezi,* publicity secretary. *Katibu shakhsiya,* personal secretary.

katika *prep* 1. (with reference to time) in, at, whilst, on, during: *Meneja yuko katika likizo,* the manager is on leave. 2. (with reference to place)

katu[1]

at, in, into, towards, at: *Kuna watu wengi katika mtaa huu,* there are many people in this neighbourhod. 3. (in general) in, at: *Aliishi katika dhiki,* he lived in difficulties. *Watu wengi walikufa katika ajali ya ndege,* many people died in the plane crash. 4. In reference to, about, as to; as regards: *Katika habari ile,* with reference to that information.

katikati[1] *adv* in the middle: *Weka katikati,* put in the middle.

katikati[2] *n (n)* middle, centre: *Katikati hii haiko mbali na wewe,* this centre is not far from you.

katikiro *n (ma-)* 1. messenger. (cf *mesenja, tarishi*) 2. the traditional ruler, second in hierachy in Bukoba and Buganda.

katili *adj* cruel, brutal, ruthless: *Rais alikuwa katili,* the president was cruel. (Ar)

katishano *n (n)* intersection.

katiti[1] *adj* small, little, minute: *Alinipa chumvi katiti,* he gave me little salt.

katiti[2] *adv* in a very small degree; not heavily: *Mvua ilinyesha katiti,* it rained lightly; it did not rain heavily.

katiz.a *vt* 1. interrupt, intrude, cut off: *Alinikatiza nilipokuwa ninazungumza,* he interrupted me when I was talking. 2. shorten, postpone: *Amekatiza safari yake kwa sababu ya usalama,* he has shortened his journey for security reasons. 3. take a short cut. Prep. **katiz.i.a** St. **katiz.ik.a** Cs. **katiz.ish.a** Ps. **katiz.w.a** Rp. **katiz.an.a**

katizo *n (ma-)* 1. interruption, intrusion. 2. shortening, postponement.

katmiri *n (n)* see *kotmiri*

kato *n (ma-)* 1. cut, slash. 2. mark left after cutting. (cf *keyo*)

Katoliki *adj* Catholic: *Kanisa la Katoliki,* Catholic church. (Eng)

katoni (also *katuni*) *n (ma-)* carton (Eng)

katoto *n (n) (colloq)* infant

katu[1] *n (n)* a kind of dark-red gum, used mainly for chewing with betel. (Hind)

293

katu² *adv* never, not at all, absolutely not: *Yeye alisisitiza kwamba katu hataifanya kazi ile,* he stressed that he would never do that work. (cf *asilani, kamwe, abadan*) (Ar)

katu.a *vt* clear up grass, weeds, etc.; cultivate: *Alikatua magugu katika shamba lake,* he cleared up the weeds in his farm. Prep. **katu.li.a** St. **katu.lik.a** Cs. **katu.lish.a** Ps. of Prep. **katu.liw.a** Rp. of Prep. **katu.li.an.a**

katuni¹ *n* (*n*) see *katoni*

katuni² *n* (*ma-*) cartoon; an amusing drawing in a newspaper, etc. (cf *kibonzo*) (Eng)

katushi *n* (*n*) cartouche; a scroll-like ornament or tablet, esp as an architectural feature. (Eng)

kauk.a *vi* 1. be dry, dry up; be parched: *Mto umekauka,* the river is dry. *Nguo nilizozianika juani sasa zimekauka,* the clothes I hanged in the sun are now dry. 2. (cf voice, blood, etc.) be dry: *Sauti yake imekauka,* his voice has become hoarse. *Damu imekauka katika kidonda chake,* the blood on his wound has clotted. 3. (of corpse, joints, etc.) become hard, become stiff; be hard, be stiff, etc.: *Mwili wake umekauka,* his body has become stiff. Prep. **kauk.i.a** Cs. **kauk.ish.a** Ps. **kauk.w.a** Ps. of Prep. **kauk.iw.a** Rp. of Prep. **kauk.i.an.a.**

kaukau *n* (*n*) crisp

kauki.a *vi* 1. be dry, be parched. 2. be emaciated, be thin. (cf *konda*)

kaukian.a *vi* 1. be stone dry; be as stiff as a board: *Siwezi kula mkate huu kwa vile umekaukiana,* I can't eat this bread because it is stone dry. 2. (of a person, etc.) be absolutely stiff because of illness, thoughts, etc.: *Mtu yule amekaukiana baada ya kuugua kwa muda mrefu,* that person has become absolutely stiff after suffering from a long illness. 3. used in the expression: *Askari wamekaukiana,* the policemen have become vigilant. Prep. **kaukian.i.a**

kauleni *n* (*n*) 1. weathercock; a double-faced person; a two-tongued person; a two-faced person: *Kwa nini unamwamini kauleni yule?* Why do you trust that double-faced person? 2. a whimsical person; a fickle person; a flighty person, an untrustworthy person; weathercock: *Yeye ni kauleni,* he is a fickle person. (cf *ndumakuwili, lumbwi*) (Ar)

kauli *n* (*n*) 1. view, opinion, comment: *Kuna kauli mbili katika suala lile,* there are two views on that issue. (cf *fikira, wazo*) 2. promise, pledge: *Alinipa kauli yake kwamba ataimaliza kazi yangu haraka,* he gave me his pledge that he would finish my work soon. (cf *ahadi*) (Ar)

kaulimbiu *n* (*n*) an expression of encouraging people to do a particular thing.

kauma *n* (*n*) see *kaumu*

kaumu (also *kauma*) *n* (*n*) group, crowd, multitude. (cf *jumuiya*) (Ar)

kaunda *n* (*n*) safari suit.

kaumwa *n* (*n*) (*bot*) calumba root; root of the *mkaumwa* tree (*Jateorhiza palmata*), used for making medicine for dysentry and abdominal ailments.

kaunta *n* (*n*) counter; a long table board, etc. as in a shop for the display and sale of goods, etc. (Eng)

kaure (also *kauri*) *n* (*n*) see *kauri*

kauri (also *kaure*) *n* (*n*) 1. cowrie shell. (cf *simbi, kete*) 2. porcelain. (Hind)

kausa *n* (*n*) see *kausha²*

kaush.a¹ *vt* 1. dry up sth: *Aliikausha nyama,* he dried out the meat. 2. (*fig*) (of money) wipe sby out. Prep. **kaush.i.a** St. **kaush.ik.a** Ps. **kaush.w.a** Rp. **kaush.an.a**

kausha² (also *kausa*) *n* (*n*) an ill-omened person; a person who brings bad luck; jinx: *Bora asipewe kazi kuifanya kausha yule,* it is better not to give work to that jinx. (cf *kisirani, mkorofi*)

kauta *n* (*n*) (*zool*) dust, grit. (cf *vumbi*)
kauzu[1] *n* (*n*) (*zool*) dry sardines of fresh water.
kauzu[2] *n* (*n*) a brazen-faced person; a shameless person; an impudent person; cocky, smart alec: *Yeye ni kauzu na ndiyo maana anapenda kuropokwa hadharani,* he is a brazen-faced person and that is why he likes to prattle in public. (cf *mpujufu*)
-**kavu** *adj* 1. dry, parched, waterless: *Nguo kavu,* dry clothes. *Mahindi makavu,* dry maize. 2. barren, unproductive, infertile: *Mahala pakavu,* a barren place. 3. (*fig*) sly, crafty, deceitful: *Mtu mkavu,* a deceitful person.
kavukavu *adj* without a glove, etc.: *Mabondia walitwangana kavukavu,* the boxers fought each other without gloves.
kawa[1] *n* (*ma-*) a straw woven conical-shaped dish cover. (*syn*) *Tulingane sawasawa kama sahani na kawa,* let us be to each other as a dish and its cover i.e. let us live in harmony. *Kawa la ukili,* a dish cover of plaited leaves from the wild date palm.
kaw.a[2] *vi* see *kawia*
kawaida[1] *n* (*n*) custom, habit, practice: *Ni kawaida yake kupiga kelele,* it is his habit to talk loudly. *Si kawaida kwake kuchelewa kazini,* it is not usual for him to report to work late (cf *desturi, mazoea*) (Ar)
kawaida[2] *n* (*n*) (*math*) algorithm; any special method of solving a certain kind of specific, the repetitive calculations used in finding the greatest common divisor of two numbers.
kawi *n* (*n*) energy (cf *nishati*)
kawi.a (also *kawa*) *vt, vi* delay, linger, be late: *Alikawia kufika katika kituo cha basi,* he was late in reaching the bus stand. Prep. **kawi.li.a** Cs **kawi.lish.a** and **kawi.z.a** (cf *chelewa*)

kaya *n* (*n*) 1. village: *Hii ni kaya kubwa,* this is a big village. (cf *kijiji*) 2. household, homestead: *Ile ni kaya yao, au sivyo?* That is their homestead, isn't it? (Ar)
kayakaya[1] *n* (*n*) (*zool*) stalk-eyed ghost crab; a kind of sea animal of the crab family, living on the banks of the sea. (cf *chanjagaa, furo, chwago*)
kayakaya[2] *n* (*n*) 1. (*naut*) reef point in *mtepe* sail. 2. points with which sail is bent to the yard.
kayaki *n* (*n*) kayak; an Eskimo canoe made of skins. (Eng)

kayaki

kayamba *n* (*n*) rattle; dry grain, etc. shaken inside a flat case of reeds during dancing or singing.

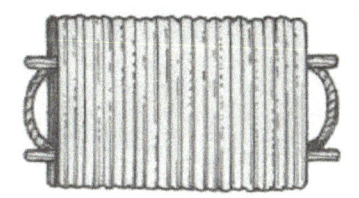

kayamba

kayaya[1] *n* (*n*) jubilation, celebration, euphoria, happiness: *Nilizisikia kayaya za harusi kwa mbali,* I heard wedding celebrations from a distance. (cf *sherehe, shamrashamra*)

kayaya² *adv* an expletive used to emphasize an action of sth; exceedingly, excessively: *Anakula kayaya*, he eats a lot. (cf *mno, sana*)

kayekaye *n (n) (naut)* ropes used to lash head of sail to the yard.

kaz.a¹ *vt* 1. tighten, fasten; make fast: *Ikaze kamba hii*, tighten this rope. *Aliukaza mzigo*, he tightened the luggage. 2. *(idms) Kaza kamba*, work tirelessly. *Kaza miguu*, walk fast. *Kaza mwendo*, walk fast. *Kaza roho*, endure, tolerate. Prep. ***kaz.i.a*** St. ***kaz.ik.a*** Cs. ***kaz.ish.a*** Ps. ***kaz.w.a*** Rp. ***kaz.an.a***

kaz.a² *vt (colloq)* fuck, screw; have sex with a male or a female partner. Prep. ***kaz.i.a*** St. ***kaz.ik.a*** Cs. ***kaz.ish.a*** Ps. ***kaz.w.a*** Rp. ***kaz.an.a***.

kazan.a¹ *vi* see *kaza¹* and *kaza²*

kazan.a² *vi* be firm, be determined; make a united effort: *Kazana au utanichelewesha*, speed up or you will delay me. *Mwanasiasa yule amekazana katika kupigania haki za wananchi*, that politician is firm in fighting for the rights of the citizens. Prep. ***kazan.i.a*** Cs. ***kazan.ish.a*** (cf *kakamaa, pania*)

kazani.a *vt, vi* insist on sth: *Alikazania kulipwa fidia*, he insisted on getting compensation.

kazi¹ *n (n)* work, labour, job: *Kazi ya mkono*, handiwork, manual work. *Kazi ya kikoa*, team work. *Kazi bure*, wasted work. *Kazi motomoto*, serious work. *Kazi ya kijungu jiko*, hand to mouth existence. *Kazi ya hiari*, voluntary work. *Kazi ya papara*, hasty work. *Kazi ya shokoa*, forced labour. *Kazi ya sulubu*, arduous work. *Kazi ya ziada*, extra work. (cf *shughuli*) 2. habit, custom, practice: *Kazi yake ni kupiga domo tu*, his habit is just to talk. *(provs) Kazi mbi si mchezo mwema*, it is better to try sth than to leave it undone. *Kazi isiyo faida kutenda si ada*, it is useless to engage in a work that is not beneficial to you.

kazi² *n (n)* 1. decoration. 2. embroidery.

kazi.a *vt* emphasize, accentuate: *Alikazia suala la mshikamano katika hotuba yake*, in his speech he stressed the issue of unity. Cs. ***kazi.sh.a*** Ps. ***kazi.w.a***

kazu.a *vt* untie, loosen, slacken. *Aliikazua kamba kwenye mzigo*, he loosened the rope in the load. Prep. ***kazu.li.a*** St. ***kazu.k.a*** Cs. ***kazu.sh.a*** Ps. ***kazu.liw.a*** (cf *legeza, fungua*)

kazula *n (n)* see *kasula*

keba (also *kebar*) *interj* an expletive of joy as during a wedding ceremony, etc; hurray!

kebeh.i¹ *vt* ridicule, vilify, disgrace: *Walimkebehi mzee mmoja bila ya sababu*, they ridiculed an old man for no reason. Prep. ***kebeh.i.a*** St. ***kebeh.ik.a*** Cs. ***kebeh.ish.a*** Ps. of Prep. ***kebeh.iw.a*** Rp. of Prep. ***kebeh.i.an.a*** (cf *tukana*) (Ar)

kebehi² *n (n)* humiliation, degradation.

kebo (also *kebu*) *n (n)* 1. cable; a thick heavy rope, often of wire strands. 2. cable gram; a message sent by undersea cable. (Eng)

kebu¹ *n (n)* see *kebo*

kebu² *n (n)* taxi cab. (Eng)

kechapu *n (n)* ketchup (Eng)

keche *interj* an expletive used to show the noise resulting from the breaking of sth: *Kuvunjika keche*, break with the noise produced.

kechek.a *vi* be broken into pieces; be shattered: *Sahani yangu ilikecheka ilipoanguka chini*, my plate got shattered when it fell down. Prep. ***kechek.e.a*** St. ***kechek.ek.a*** (cf *vunjika*)

kechekeche *interj* an expletive used to show the terrible state or condition of breaking of sth into pieces i.e. *Bakuli lake lilivunjika kechekeche*, her bowl broke in pieces. (cf *kabisakabisa*)

kedekede *adj* plenty, abundant: *Alipewa sifa kedekede*, he was given a lot of praise.

kedi¹ *n (n)* 1. bad behaviour: *Mbona*

ana kedi za kike? Why does he have womanish mannerisms? 2. wile, gimmick, trick, craft: *Kedi zake zilimtia matatani*, her wiles put her into problems. (cf *hila, ujanja*) (Ar)

kedi² *n (n)* arrogance, vanity, pride: *Mali nyingi ya wazee wake imemfanya kuwa na kedi*, his parents' enormous wealth, has made him to become arrogant. (cf *kiburi, majivuno*) (Ar)

keekee *n (n)* see *kekee¹*

kefle (also *kefule*) *interj* 1. an expletive of indignation expressed by a speaker who curses someone else. (cf *sefle!*) 2. an expletive of wonder. (cf *loo! do!*) (Ar)

kefu (also *fakaifa, kaifa*) *adv* let alone, not to mention: *Yeye aliweza kununua gari mpya kefu wewe mwenye mali udhumu*, he was able to buy a car let alone you who is very wealthy. (cf *fakaifa, sembuse, seuze*)

kefule *interj* see *kefle*

kefy.a¹ *vt, vi* 1. wink, blink the eye; shut and open the eye: *Alikefya jua lilipompiga*, he blinked his eyes as the sunlight shone on him. 2. ignore, despise: *Ana tabia ya kukefya watu kwa sababu ya kisomo chake*, he has the habit of despising people because of his education. Prep. **kefy.e.a** St. **kefy.ek.a** Cs. **kefy.esh.a** Ps. **kefy.w.a** Rp. **kefy.an.a** (cf *kebehi, beza, dharau*)

kefy.a² *vt* annoy, disturb: *Ukiendelea kuwakefya wanafunzi wenzako, mwalimu atakupiga*, if you continue to annoy your fellow students, the teacher will beat you. Prep. **kefy.e.a** St. **kefy.ek.a** Cs. **kefy.esh.a** Ps. **kefy.w.a** Rp. **kefy.an.a** (cf *ghasi, udhi*)

kejekeje *adj* (of luggage, etc.) loose, slack, infirm: *Mzigo wako ulifunguka kwa sababu ulikuwa kejekeje*, your luggage unfastened itself because it was loose. (cf *chegechege*)

kejel.i¹ *vt, vi* ridicule, deride; be sarcastic,

fool someone: *Walipomkejeli, alihamaki*, when they fooled him, he became annoyed. Prep. **kejel.i.a** St. **kejel.ik.a** Cs. **kejel.ish.a** Ps. of Prep. **kejel.iw.a**, be ridiculed e.g. *Alikejeliwa hadharani*, he was ridiculed in public. Rp. of Prep. **kejel.i.an.a** (cf *tania, dhihaki*) (Ar)

kejeli² *n (n)* sarcastic expression; irony, derision. *Kejeli zake ziliwaudhi watu wengi*, his sarcastic remarks annoyed many people. (Ar)

kekee¹ (also *keekee*) *n (n)* drill; a boring tool: *Kekee kifua*, breast drill. *Kekee umeme*, electric drill.

kekee² *n (n)* bracelet, armlet. (cf *kikuku, timbi, bangili*)

kekesu.a *vt* cut the flesh instead of the rind or the outer layer of a fruit during peeling. Prep. **kekesu.li.a** St. **kekesu.k.a** Cs. **kekesu.sh.a** Ps. of Prep. **kekesu.liw.u**

keket.a *vt* 1. chew sth tough or hard; gnaw: *Alikuwa akikeketa barafu*, he was chewing the ice. 2. have severe abdominal pains: *Tumbo lilikuwa likimkeketa takriban usiku wote*, he suffered sharp pains for almost the whole night. 3. cut sth hard or tough with a blunt tool: *Aliukeketa ubao kwa msumeno mbutu*, he cut the wood by using a blunt saw. 4. circumcise esp a woman: *Kukeketa wasichana ni marufuku katika jamii zetu*, to circumcise girls is forbidden in our societies. Prep. **keket.e.a** St. **keket.ek.a** Cs. **keket.esh.a** Ps. **keket.w.a** Rp. **keket.an.a**

kekevu *n (n)* hiccup, hiccough. (cf *chechevu*)

keki *n (n)* cake: *Keki ya malai*, gateau. *Keki ya rusu*, layer cake. (Eng)

kelbu¹ *n (n)* dog (cf *mbwa*) (Ar)

kelbu² *interj* an insult to a person who misbehaves likening his behaviour to that of a dog; you dog!

kele *n (n)* hustle and bustle.

kelele¹ *n (n)* 1. noise, shout: *Piga kelele*, shout; make noise. *Acha kelele*, stop the noise. 2. chaos, confusion, disorder: *Palikuwa na kelele nyingi nje mwizi alipokamatwa*, there was a lot of chaos outside when the thief was caught. (cf *ghasia, fujo*)

kelele² *interj* an expletive used to make someone stop making noise; Be quiet! Silence!

kem.a *vt, vi* 1. cry loudly because of illness, pain, etc.; groan in pain: *Alikema kwa sababu ya maradhi yake*, she groaned because of her illness. 2. shout. Prep. **kem.e.a** St. **kem.ek.a** Cs. **kem.esh.a** and **kem.ez.a** Ps. **kem.w.a**

kemb.a *vt* strip off the skin of a fruit, vegetable, etc.; peel, pare: *Alizikemba ndizi kabla hajazipika*, he pared the bananas before cooking them. Prep.. **kemb.e.a** St. **kemb.ek.a** Cs. **kemb.esh.a** Ps. **kemb.w.a** (cf *menya, goboa*)

keme.a *vt* censure, scold, blame: *Mzazi alimkemea mwanawe kwa kosa la nidhamu*, the parent scolded his son for misconduct. St. **keme.k.a** Cs. **keme.z.a** Ps. **keme.w.a** Rp. **keme.an.a** (cf *karipia, gombeza*)

kemia *n (n)* chemistry: *Kemia ogania*, organic chemistry. *Kemia sanisi*, synthetic chemistry. (Eng)

kemkemu *adv* full, copiously, plentifully, abundantly: *Machungwa yamejaa kemkemu madukani*, the oranges are in abundance at the shops. (cf *mzo, teletele*) (Ar)

kemikali *n (n)* chemical; any substance used in or obtained by a chemical process: *Elementi kemikali*, chemical element. (Eng)

kenda *adj, n* nine: (prov) *Kenda karibu ya kumi*, nine is near ten, i.e. when you are on the verge of completing a task, it is good to finish it.

kende *n (ma-) (anat)* testicles (cf *korodani, hasua*)

kenek.a *vt* distil. Prep. **kenek.e.a** St. **kenek.ek.a** Cs. **kenek.esh.a** Ps. **kenek.w.a** Rp. **kenek.an.a**

keng.a¹ *vt* 1. bamboozle, delude, deceive, cheat, hoodwink: *Walimkenga mwenye duka kwa kumpa noti bandia*, they deceived the shopkeeper by giving him fake notes. Prep. **keng.e.a** St. **keng.ek.a** Cs. **keng.esh.a** Ps. **keng.w.a** Rp. **keng.an.a** (cf *hadaa, ghilibu*) 2. look, watch. (cf *tazama, angalia*)

kenga² *adj* (of a fruit) properly unripe.

kenge (also *mburukenge*) *n (n) (zool)* monitor lizard; a large flesh-eating lizard (family *Varanidae*) of Africa, Asia and Australia and its name is given on the notion that it can warn the presence of crocodiles. (cf *uru, bomla*)

kenge.a *vt* protect, defend. St. **kenge.k.a** Cs. **kenge.sh.a** Ps. **kenge.w.a** Rp. **kenge.an.a**

kengee *n (ma-)* used in the expression: *Kengee ya jua*, ray of the sun during morning and afternoon making the eyes to become blurred.

kengele *n (n)* 1. bell: *Kengele ya umeme*, electric bell. *Piga kengele*, ring a bell. 2. a thing that gives a sound like a bell: *Kengele ya baiskeli*, bicycle bell. *Kengele ya mlango*, doorbell.

kengemek.a *vt* censure, scold, rebuke, reprimand: *Meneja alimkengemeka mfanyakazi wake kwa kuchelewa kazini*, the manager rebuked his worker for reporting to work late. Prep. **kengemek.e.a** St. **kengemek.ek.a** Ps. **kengemek.w.a** (cf *shutumu, laumu*)

keng'et.a *vt* see *kang'ata²*. Prep. **keng'et.e.a** Ps. **keng'et.w.a**.

kengeu.a *vt* misguide, debauch, pervert; backslide sby: *Vijana watukutu walimkengeua rafiki yao*, the naughty young men debauched their friend. Prep. **kengeu.li.a** St. **kengeu.k.a** Cs. **kengeu.sh.a** Rp. **kengeu.an.a** (cf *potoa*)

kengewa *n (n) (zool)* kestrel; a kind of hawk (family *Falconidae*) with sharply

kengeza

pointed wings and a short, curved notched beak.
kengeza *n* (*ma-*) squint, cross-eye: *Macho makengeza*, squinted eyes. (*prov*) *Ukipenda chongo huita kengeza*, love sees no defects.
kengo *n* (*n*) trick, deceit, fraud: *Alishtakiwa kwa sababu ya kengo zake za kuiba pesa katika benki*, he was prosecuted because of his tricks to steal money from the bank. (cf *hila, udanganyifu*)
kensa *n* (*n*) see *kansa*
kenu.a *vi* 1. show the teeth while smiling; grin: *Alikenua meno*, he grinned. (cf *kenya*) 2. draw back the lips and show the teeth in scorn; grin: *Waliikenua midomo yao kwangu kama ishara ya dharau*, they grinned at me as a kind of contempt. Prep. ***kenu.li.a*** St. ***kenu.k.a*** Cs. ***kenu.sh.a*** Ps. of Prep. ***kenu.liw.a*** Rp. ***kenu.an.a***
kenyekenye *adv* absolutely, entirely, categorically: *Mshtakiwa alilikataa kosa kenyekenye*, the accused categorically denied the charge. (cf *katakata, kabisa*)
kepteni *n* (*n*) see *kapteni*
ker.a *vt* upset, disturb, irritate, vex: *Nini kinakukera?* What is disturbing you? Prep. ***ker.e.a*** St. ***ker.ek.a*** Cs. ***ker.esh.a*** Ps. ***ker.w.a*** Rp. ***ker.an.a*** (cf *ghasi, udhi*)
kerek.a *vi* be annoyed, be vexed. Prep. ***kerek.e.a*** Cs. ***kerek.esh.a*** Ps. ***kerek.w.a*** (cf *udhika, kirihika*)
kereket.a *vt, vi* 1. cause an irritating sensation esp in the tongue or throat; have a rough taste: *Koo lake linamkereketa kwa sababu ya kutafuna tambuu*, his throat has an irritating sensation because of chewing betal leaves. 2. (*fig*) disturb, annoy, vex, irritate: *Mtoto alimkereketa bubu yake alipokosa kununuliwa baiskeli*, the child disturbed his father when he failed to buy a bicycle for him.

kero

Prep. ***kereket.e.a*** St. ***kereket.ek.a*** Cs. ***kereket.esh.a*** Ps. ***kereket.w.a*** (cf *udhi, ghasi*)
keremkeremu *n* (*n*) (*zool*) bee eater; a medium-sized bird of brilliant plumage, having a long decurved bill and which is fond of eating bees, wasps, etc.
kereng'ende[1] (also *kereng'enje*) (*zool*) grey breasted spurfowl; a chicken-like terrestrial bird with a bare orange throat. (cf *kware*)
kereng'ende[2] *n* (*n*) (*zool*) dragonfly; a predacious insect with biting mouthparts, which is strongly built and swift-flying.

kereng'ende

kereng'enje *n* (*n*) see *kereng'ende*[1]
kerez.a *vt* 1. gnash: *Kereza meno*, gnash the teeth. 2. lathe. 3. saw: *Aliukereza ubao wake kwa msumeno*, he sawed his piece of wood. Prep. ***kerez.e.a*** St. ***kerez.ek.a*** Cs. ***kerez.esh.a*** Ps. ***kerez.w.a*** Rp. ***kerez.an.a***
kerezo[1] *n* (*n*) lathe; a machine for shaping an article of wood, metal, etc.
kerezo[2] *n* (*n*) the snoring of a very sick person such as the one on the verge of dying; a sound that sometimes comes from the throat of a dying person caused by breath passing through mucus; death-rattle. (cf *kororo*)
kero *n* (*n*) annoyance, vexation, irritation: *Wewe umechoka na kero zake, au sivyo?* You are tired of his disturbances, aren't you? 2. problem, difficulty: *Wanavijiji walimweleza waziri kero zao*, the villagers explained to the minister their problems. (cf *maudhui, adha, usumbufu*)

299

K   kerosini   kiaga

kerosini *n* (*n*) kerosene, paraffin. (Eng)
kes.a *vi* (cf rain) stop raining; cease: *Mvua imekesa hivi punde*, it has just stopped raining. Prep. ***kes.e.a*** St. ***kes.ek.a*** Cs. ***kes.esh.a*** (cf *pusa*)
kesh.a[1] *vi* stay awake at night, keep vigil; remain awake at night; stay up at night: *Wasiwasi ulimfanya akeshe*, anxiety kept him awake the whole night. Prep. ***kesh.e.a*** St. ***kesh.ek.a*** Ps. ***kesh.w.a*** Rp. ***kesh.an.a***
kesha[2] (also *mkesha*) *n* (*n*) the act of spending a night for a particular activity such as in celebration, etc.: night watch, vigil: *Siku ya kesha ya mwisho*, the last night of a formal mourning.
keshi *n* (*n*) cash payment. (Eng)
keshia *n* (*n*) cashier (Eng)
kesho[1] *n* (*n*) 1. tomorrow. 2. the day of resurrection; doomsday.
kesho[2] *adv* tomorrow: *Atasafiri kesho*, he will travel tomorrow.
keshokutwa *n* (*n*) the day after tomorrow.
kesi *n* (*n*) case, lawsuit: *Kesi ya jinai*, criminal case. *Kesi ya kashfa*, libel case. *Kesi ya madai*, civil case. *Kesi ya uhaini*, treason case. (Eng)
ket.a *vt* knock sby down; hit sby until he falls down: *Alimketa mpinzani wake kwenye ndondi*, he knocked down his opponent in boxing. Prep. ***ket.e.a*** St. ***ket.ek.a*** Cs. ***ket.esh.a*** Ps. ***ket.w.a*** Rp. ***ket.an.a***
kete[1] *n* (*n*) 1. a small kind of cowrie; dice (cf *domino, namu*) 2. anything like cowrie used in the game of checkers (draughts): *Meno kama kete*, teeth like cowries.
kete[2] *adv* noiselessly, quietly, calmly, coolly: *Wiki hii nzima imekuwa kete*, the whole of this week has been quiet (cf *kimya, shwari*)
kete[3] *n* (*ki-vi*) see *chete*
ket.i *vt, vi* 1. sit down; take a seat: *Keti juu ya kiti*, sit on the chair. (cf *kaa*) 2. live, dwell, reside: *Anaketi ng'ambo*, he lives abroad. Prep. ***ket.i.a*** St. ***ket.ik.a*** Cs. ***ket.ish.a*** Ps. of Prep. ***ket.iw.a*** Rp. of Prep. ***ket.i.an.a*** (cf *ishi*)
keto *adj* (of sea, etc.) deep: *Maji katika ziwa lile yako keto*, that lake is deep. (cf *kina*)
keu *n* (*n*) a stroke made with an axe; chop.
keu.a *vt* 1. straighten a building pole, etc. by means of cutting a notch and then putting a small piece of wood between the cuts: *Wajenzi waliikeua miti iliyopindana*, the masons straightened the bent poles. 2. oil, lubricate; supply with oil: *Bibi yangu aliikeua miguu yake*, my grandmother oiled her legs. Prep. ***keu.li.a*** St. ***keu.lik.a*** Ps. of Prep. ***keu.liw.a***
keuk.a *vt* see *kiuka*. Prep. ***keuk.i.a*** St. ***keuk.ik.a*** Cs. ***keuk.ish.a*** Ps. of Prep. ***keuk.iw.a*** Rp. of Prep. ***keuk.an.a***
khaa *interj* an expletive for expressing anger or contempt.
khalifa *n* (*ma-*) caliph, calif. (Ar)
kia[1] *n* (*ki-vi*) door-bar, latch. (cf *komeo, pingo, kiwi*)
kia[2] *n* (*ki-vi*) (*anat*) a joint of a leg or arm: *Kia cha mwili*, a joint of the body.
ki.a[3] *vt* (of a log, pool of water, etc.) step over, jump over: *Alilimkia gogo*, he jumped over the log. Prep. ***ki.li.a*** St. ***ki.lik.a*** Cs. ***ki.lish.a*** Ps. of Prep. ***ki.liw.a*** Rp. of Prep. ***ki.an.a*** (cf *chupa, kiuka*)
kiada *adv* 1. in an orderly manner; properly, systematically: *Huyafanya mambo yake kiada*, he conducts his affairs systematically. *Kitabu cha kiada*, a book written in an orderly manner. 2. distinctly (cf *sawasawa*) (Ar)
kiaga *n* (*n*) promise, assurance, pledge: *Alinipa kiaga lakini hakuitekeleza*, he gave me a promise but he did not fulfill it. (cf *ahadi, miadi*)

kiagizo *n (ki-vi) (math)* operator; a symbol or function denoting an operation (e.g. x,+)

kiaka *n (ki-vi)* a piece of wood that protects the roof of a house and stands on the top of the beams of the house.

kiaki.a *vi* be uneasy, be unsettled, be restless, be disturbed: *Alikiakia wakati wa harusi ya mwanawe*, he was restless during the wedding of her daughter Prep. **kiaki.li.a** St. **kiaki.k.a** Cs. **kiaki.sh.a** (cf *hangaika, piapia, shughulika*)

kiali *n (ki-vi)* flame rising from the fire; tongue of the fire: *Moto ulipokuwa mkali, viali vilikuwa vingi*, when the fire was strong, the flames were many. (cf *kimota*)

kiama *n (n) (rel)* the day of resurrection; doomsday. (cf *jongomeo, kuzimu*) (Ar)

kiambajengo *n (ki-vi) (gram)* constituent: *Ngeli kiambajengo,* constituent class. *Sentensi kiambajengo,* constituent sentence.

kiambata *n (ki-vi)* accompaniment; anything that accompanies sth else.

kiambatisho *n (ki-vi)* 1. appendix in a book, etc.: *Mzamili aliviweka viambatisho mwisho wa tasnifu yake,* the postgraduate student attached the appendices at the end of his thesis. (cf *faharasa*) 2. enclosure; accompanying document.

kiambato *n (ki-vi)* 1. *(law)* appurtenance; an additional, subordinate right or privilege 2. ingredient.

kiambaupishi *n (ki-vi)* cooking ingredient.

kiambaza (also *kiwambaza*) *n (ki-vi)* wall (cf *ukuta*)

kiambishi *n (ki-vi)* affix: *Kiambishi awali,* prefix. *Kiambishi kati,* infix. *Kiambishi tamati,* suffix.

kiambizi *n (ki-vi)* oriel; bay window; a large window built out from a wall and resting on a bracket or a corbel.

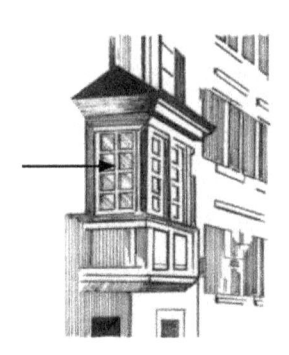

kiambizi

kiambo *n (ki-vi)* village: *Kiambo kile kina watu wengi,* that village has many people. (cf *kijiji*)

kiamshahamu *n (ki-vi)* aperitif; an alcoholic drink taken before a meal to stimulate the appetite.

kiamshakinywa *n (ki-vi)* see *kifungua-kinywa*

Kiamu[1] *n (n)* a dialect of Swahili, spoken on Lamu island and the adjacent mainland to the south.

kiamu[2] (also *kisimamo*) *n (n)* (in Islam) the period of standing up during *Maulidi* celebration, i.e. commemorations of the birthday of Prophet Muhammad.

kiamu[3] *n (ki-vi)* good handling.

kiana *n (ki-vi)* a large earthenware lid usu used during cooking, etc. (cf *bunguu, kibia*)

kianga *n (ki-vi)* a burst of light or sunshine after it has rained. (cf *uchesa, uchaaza, kichesa*)

kiangamacho *n (ki-vi)* a present given for finding sth that has been lost. (cf *machorombozi, utotole, kiokosi*)

kiangazi *n (ki-vi)* the season when the sun is strongest between the rainy seasons; the hot season; the dry season.

kiango *n (ki-vi)* a small frame or bracket hung on a wall for holding a lamp; lamp holder.

kiangulio *n (ki-vi)* incubator (cf *kitotoa, kianguzi*)

kianio *n (ki-vi)* rung, riser, step. (cf *daraja, kipandio*)

kianzio *n (ki-vi)* initial capital.

kianzo¹ *n (ki-vi)* a piece of wood used for starting to weave mats, carpets, etc. (cf *uteo, kiwao, kielezi*)

kianzo² *n (ki-vi)* introduction, foreword. (cf *utangulizi*)

kiapo *n (ki-vi)* 1. oath: *Fanya/Kula kiapo*, take an oath. *Lisha kiapo*, administer an oath. *Kiapo cha spika*, the speaker's oath of allegiance. (cf *kasama, yamini*) 2. a promise given to keep a secret. 3. charm, used as a protection against theft, etc. (cf *zindiko*)

Kiarabu *n (n)* Arabic (Ar)

kiarifa *n(ki-vi)* (*gram*) predicate; that part of a sentence after the subject, consisting of a verb, complement, etc.: *Kiarifu ambatani*, compound predicate.

kiashirio *n (ki-vi)* indicator, sign, marker: *Viashirio vya maendeleo ya kiuchumi*, indicators of economic development.

kiasi¹ *n (n)* 1. average, moderation: *Mtu wa kiasi*, a person of moderation; an average person. 2. about, approximately: *Kiasi cha watu sitini walifika kwenye harusi*, about sixty people attended the wedding. 3. amount, price, extent: *Kiasi fulani*, a certain amount. *Kiasi cha kuridhisha*, satisfactory amount. *Kwa kiasi fulani*, to a certain extent. 4. (*math*) numerator in arithmetic. For example, in 2/3, 2 is the numerator and 3 is the denominator. (cf *kigawanyo*) 5. quantity: *Kiasi cha umeme*, quantity of electricity. *Kiasi mchanganyiko*, compound quantity. (Ar)

kiasi² *adv* a little, not much: *Alinipa kiasi*, he gave me a little. (Ar)

kiasi³ *adj* enough, sufficient: *Walinipa fedha kiasi*, they gave me enough money. (Ar)

kiasi⁴ *n (ki-vi)* bullet (cf *risasi*) (Ar)

kiathiri *n (ki-vi)* a thing that influences sth else; influence. (Ar)

kiatu *n (ki-vi)* shoe, sandal: *Kiatu cha ngozi*, leather sandal. *Kiatu cha mti*, a kind of wooden clog worn indoors. *Kiatu cha makubadhi*, leather sandals adorned on some of its sides. *Kiatu cha malapa*, open sandals easily slipped on the foot, esp one for indoor wear; slipper. *Kiatu cha mtarawanda*, wooden clog. (*prov*) *Baniani mbaya kiatu chake dawa*, a Hindu can be a bad person but his shoes are a remedy i.e. you may regard someone badly and yet covet his things.

kiazi *n (ki-vi-)* (*bot*) sweet potato: *Kiazi kikuu*, yam. *Kiazi cha kizungu*, Irish potato.

kiazi sukari *n (ki-vi)* (*bot*) sugar beet. *Kiazi kitamu*, sweet potato.

kibaazi *n (ki-vi)* 1. (*bot*) a short-lived perennial plant up to 15 feet tall with racemes of white or reddish-mauve pea-like flowers and fairly large hairy pods, whose fresh green stems and leaves are used as a fish poison. *Tephrosia vogelii*. 2. a perennial herb up to 3 feet with small white pea-like flowers and small flat dark brown hairy pods. *Tephrosia noctiflora*. 3. a perennial semi-prostrate herb with pinkish-mauve flowers, grey leaves and grey-brown woolly pods. *Tephrosia ehrenbergiana*. 4. an annual or short-lived perennial herb up to 3 feet tall with dense spikes of small yellow pea-like flowers and pods. *Crotalaria emarginata*. 5. *Kibaazi mwitu*, a shrub or small tree with leathery grey-green leaves and yellow flowers in short terminal racemes and small sausage shaped fruits which split open exposing a number of bright red seeds, whose twigs are used as tooth brushes. *Cadaba farinosa*.

kibaba *n (ki-vi)* 1. an old measure of about 700 grams. 2. a measure to weigh grain, etc.

kibabe *adv* heroically, fearless: *Alifanya kazi kibabe*, he did the work fearlessly.

kibadala n (ki-vi) 1. (arch) pronoun. 2. alternative, variant.

kibafte n (ki-vi) see kibafute

kibafute (also kibafte) n (ki-vi) children's game of guessing what is hidden in the hand.

kibago n (ki-vi) stool, seat. (cf kigoda, kibao, stuli)

kibahaluli[1] n (ki-vi) 1. a small oil lamp. (cf kibatari) 2. a small torch of twisted grass or paper spill as the one used for lighting a tobacco pipe, etc.

kibahaluli[2] n (ki-vi) see bahaluli

kibainishi n (ki-vi) (gram) determiner, article: Kibainishi fiche, indefinite article. Kibainishi halisi, definite article. (Ar)

kibajebanje n (ki-vi) see kitatange

kibaka n (ki-vi) 1. pickpocket. 2. rapist.

kibali n (ki-vi) permit, permission, approval: Serikali ilimpa kibali cha kuagizia gari kutoka ng'ambo, the government gave him permission to import a car from abroad. (cf idhini)

kibama n (ki-vi) a kind of cake or bread made from flour and bananas.

kibamba n (ki-vi) a beautiful girl; beauty. (cf kimanzi, kisura)

kibanawasi n (ki-vi) see abunuwasi

kibanda n (ki-vi) hut, shed, shack, booth: Kibanda cha simu, telephone booth. Kibanda cha makuti, a hut thatched with coconut leaves. Kibanda cha kuku, a hen's coop; a poultry shed.

kibango n (ki-vi) (naut) a cross beam which fixes the mast of a dhow to the keel. (cf farikumu, bunta, fundo)

kibaniko (also mbano, ubano) n (ki-vi) a spit for roasting or drying fish or meat; skewer.

kibanio (also kibano) n (ki-vi) clip; an object such as a metal, used for holding things tightly together: Kibanio cha nywele, hair clip. Kibanio cha nguo, clothes' clip. Kibanio cha kaa la moto, fire tongs. (cf boi)

kibano n (ki-vi) see kibanio

Kibantu n (ki-vi) Bantu language.

kibanzi n (ki-vi) splinter; a chip of wood: Kibanzi cha ukuni, firewood splinter. (syn) Amemsakama kama kibanzi cha ukuni, he is disturbing him persistently. (cf kidondo)

kibao[1] n (ki-vi) writing slate; signboard. (cf sleti, ubao)

kibao[2] n (ki-vi) a small frameless sitting board not exceeding 15 centimetres; stool. (cf kigoda, kibago)

kibao[3] n (ki-vi) 1. a small card, board, etc. used for a special purpose: Kibao cha uzi, a card of thread. Kibao cha kusukumia mikate, a board for kneading dough to make bread like that of chapati; spinboard. 2. a square board used in making a mold for concrete bricks; moldboard. 3. an instrument with a serated edge for grating coconut; coconut grater. 4. an old hat/cap.

kibao[4] n (ki-vi) a smack on the face with the palm of the hand; slap: Alipigwa kibao, he was slapped. (cf kofi)

kibao[5] adj (colloq) many, much: Nimeona watu kibao leo, I have seen a lot of people today. Tuna matatizo kibao siku hizi, we have many problems these days.

kibao[6] n (ki-vi) hit song.

kibapara[1] n (ki-vi) pauper; a poor person: Kibapara yule anaishi kwa dhiki, that pauper lives in hardships. (cf hohehahe, fukara, masikini)

kibapara[2] n (ki-vi) a kind of small old cap.

kibapara[3] n (ki-vi) an old garment.

kibaraka n (ki-vi) 1. stooge, puppet, henchman: Wananchi waliwalaani vibaraka, the nationalists cursed the stooges. (cf karagosi, haini, kitimbakwiri) 2. servant, worker: Kibaraka wake anapata mshahara mzuri, his servant gets a good salary. 3. villain.

kibaramwezi n (ki-vi) see kibirinzi

kibarango[1] n (ki-vi) a small stout club; a small cudgel. (cf kimangare, kigongo)

kibarango[2] n (ki-vi) a piece of cassava which is still not soft in a prepared cassava dish.

kibarara (*zool*) aardvark; a burrowing African mammal that feeds on ants and termites and which is squat and heavy with a long, sticky tongue and an elongate head, ending in a round pig-like snout. (cf *mhanga*)

kibarara

kibarua *n* (*ki-vi*) 1. a day labourer; a worker paid on a daily basis; a casual labourer. 2. a temporary job. 3. task, duty, job: *Kiongozi atakuwa na kibarua kigumu cha kuleta amani katika eneo zima*, the leader will have a difficult task of bringing peace to the whole region.
kibatali *n* (*ki-vi*) see *kibatari*
kibatari (also *kibatali*) *n* (*ki-vi*) a small oil lamp with a wick. (cf *kibahaluli*)
kibavu (also *mabavu*) *n* (*n*) force: *Walitumia kibavu kumnyang'anya gari yake*, they used force to take away his car. (cf *ubavu, kiwavu, nguvu*)
kibawanta *n* (*ki-vi*) (*zool*) a kind of small bird with a long brown tail and a slightly crested head and brown underparts; speckled mouse-bird. *Colius striatus*. (cf *kuzumburu*)
kibe (also *kibemasa*) *n* (*n*) 1. a children's game of hide-and-seek. (cf *mwajificho*) 2. noise, shout, yell. (cf *ukelele*)
kibeberu[1] *n* (*n*) body odour; an unpleasant odour resulting from the perspiration of the human body. (cf *gugumo, kikwapa, kutuzi*)
kibeberu[2] *n* (*ki-vi*) (*zool*) rush. *Scirpus. sp.*
kibedi *n* (*n*) trick, deceit, deception: *Mwenye duka alimfanyia kibedi mnunuzi*, the shopkeeper played tricks on the buyer. (cf *hila, ujanja, udanganyifu*)

kibemasa *n* (*n*) see *kibe*
kibendo *n* (*ki-vi*) a small piece of sth; slice: *Kibendo cha mkate*, a slice of bread. *Kibendo cha keki*, a slice of cake. (cf *kinugu, ubale*)
kiberenge[1] *n* (*ki-vi*) 1. trolley; a small locomotive, used for sisal plantation work. (cf *toroli, kigarimoshi*) 2. trolley, railway handcar; a light locomotive used on a railway line.
kiberenge[2] *n* (*ki-vi*) prostitute, harlot; a loose woman. (cf *kahaba, malaya, fasiki*)
kiberiti *n* (*ki-vi*) see *kibiriti*
kibete (also *kibeti*) *n* (*ki-vi*) lilliputian, manikin, dwarf, midget; a very small person or animal: *Kibete yule amekuwa kivutio kwa watalii*, that dwarf has become an attraction to tourists. (cf *kibushuti, mbilikimo, kidurango, kibirikizi*)
kibeti[1] *n* (*ki-vi*) see *kibete*
kibeti[2] *n* (*ki-vi*) purse, wallet. (cf *pochi, kikoba*)
kibia *n* (*ki-vi*) 1. an earthenware bowl for serving food. 2. an earthenware cooking pot. (cf *mkungu, bunguu*)
kibibi[1] *n* (*ki-vi*) an expletive of respect used for calling or mentioning a girl.
kibibi[2] *n* (*ki-vi*) a kind of sweet doughnut made from watery rice flour.
kibibi[3] *n* (*n*) numbness or paralysis of short duration: *Shikwa na kibibi*, be numbed. (cf *ganzi, kiharusi*)
kibibi[4] *n* (*ki-vi*) an old woman; crone, hag. (cf *ajuza*)
kibindo *n* (*ki-vi*) a fold of the loincloth used as a kind of pocket for carrying things; a knot in the waistcloth used as a pocket. (*prov*) *Hamadi kibindoni, silaha iliyo mkononi*, a reserve is always useful because of the need that may arise at a later stage.
kibiongo *n* (*ki-vi*) see *kibyongo*
kibiri *n* (*ki-vi*) a piece of cigarette left after it has been smoked; butt, stub. (cf *kichungi*)

kibirikizi[1] *n (ki-vi)* 1. a horn used for giving signals or information; bugle: *Piga kibirikizi*, bugle; make a proclamation by using a bugle. (cf *mbiu, rewa, baragumu*) 2. a person incharge of blowing the horn.
kibirikizi[2] *n (ki-vi)* midget, manikin, dwarf; a very small person. (cf *mbilikimo, kibushuti, kibete*)
kibirikizi[3] *n (ki-vi)* 1. pimp, pander, panderer, whoremonger. (cf *kuwadi, gambera*) 2. instigator, intriguer, inciter, telltale, firebrand: *Kibirikizi aliwagombanisha majirani wawili*, the instigator caused discord between the two neighbours. (cf *sabasi, mfitini*) 3. liar, duper, cheater. (cf *mwongo, kidhabi*)
kibiringo *n (ki-vi)* spool; a child's toy made out of palm fronds and is kept down so that it is blown by the wind.
kibirinzi (also *kibaramwezi, kititia*) *n (ki-vi)* windmill toy; a child's toy made out of coconut palm fronds fixed to the end of a piece of the midriff.
kibiriti[1] (also *kiberiti*) *n (ki-vi)* matchbox: *Kibiriti cha chuma*, lighter. *Kibiriti cha baruti/Kibiriti cha ganda*, regular matchbox. (Ar)
kibiriti[2] *n (ki-vi)* a kind of medicine, used for treating pimples or skin eruptions.
kibiritingoma[1] *n (ki-vi)* 1. prostitute. (cf *malaya*) 2. short dress; miniskirt.
kibiritingoma[2] *n (ki-vi)* a house with a room, kitchen, toilet and a store.
kibiritiupele *n (ki-vi)* a kind of medicine, used for the treatment of scabies.
kibisi *n (ki-vi) (zool)* grebe; a diving waterbird with a long neck, lobed toes and almost no tail.
kibla (also *kibula*) *n (n)* 1. the northern direction upon which Muslims turn to for prayers. 2. the front part in the mosque locating the leader of the prayer i.e. "Imam". (cf *mihirabu*) 3. north. (Ar)

kibobwe *n (ki-vi)* see *kibwebwe*
kibofu *n (ki-vi)* 1. bladder, bag: *Kibofu cha mkojo*, urinary bladder. 2. balloon.
kibogoshi *n (ki-vi)* 1. the small bag made of skin for keeping money, cosmetics, etc.; leather bag. (cf *kibegi*) 2. a leather bag for putting in milk.
kibogoyo *n (ki-vi)* a toothless person or a person with a few teeth. (cf *buda*)
kiboko *n (ki-vi)* 1. *(zool)* hippopotamus 2. a fat person. 3. rawhide; a whip, formerly used for inflicting judicial punishment on offenders now replaced by a cane. (cf *mjeledi, ubati*) 4. a small zigzag ornamental stitch embroidered in silk on a *kanzu* around the neck. 5. *(idm) Kiboko yake*, a person or thing that has no parallel with sth else; an unmatched person or thing e.g *Yeye alikuwa kiboko cha viongozi wengine wote waliobakia*, he was unmatched among all other remaining leaders.
kibole *n (ki-vi) (med)* appendix; a small blind-ended tube attached to the intestine: *Kibole mnyolo*, vermiform appendix; an outgrowth of an organ esp a small sacklike appendage extending from the caecum of the large intestine. (cf *kidole tumbo*)
kiboleini *n (ki-vi) (med)* a small hydrocele; a small swelling of the scrotum. (cf *kibusha, kipumbu*)
kibonde *n (ki-vi)* 1. a small valley. 2. (in sports) *(fig)* a weak team: *Timu yetu ilipangiwa kucheza na vibonde*, our team was arranged to play against weak teams.
kibonge[1] *n (ki-vi)* see *kidonge*
kibonge[2] *n (ki-vi)* the name that you share with other members of your family; surname.
kibonge[3] *n (ki-vi)* a fat and strong person.
kibonyezo *n (ki-vi)* dent
kibonzo *n (ki-vi)* cartoon (cf *kikaragosi, katuni*)
kibua[1] *n (ki-vi)* anything light in weight

kibua² *n* (*ki-vi*) see *bua¹*

kibua³ *n* (*ki-vi*) (*zool*) a kind of fish belonging to the families of *Carangidae, Caesionidae and Scombridae* families; Indian mackerel, scad, fuselier.

kibubusa *adv* 1. incognito, secretly, stealthily, clandestinely: *Aliingia kibubusa chumbani*, he entered the room stealthily. (cf *kisirisiri, kimyakimya*) 2. without giving an opportunity to dispute.

kibubutu *n* (*ki-vi*) 1. stump; the part of sth such as a tree which is left after most of it has been removed: *Alibakisha kibubutu baada ya kuukata mti*, he left a stump after cutting down the tree. 2. stump; that part of a limb or tail of an animal that has been left after the rest has been cut off, broken off, etc.

kibudu¹ *adv* 1. (*idm*) *kufa kibudu*, die a natural death. 2. die without leaving a child; die childless.

kibudu² *n* (*ki-vi*) an animal dead body; carcass. (cf *mzoga, nyamafu*)

kibuhuti *n* (*n*) grief someone undergoes because of the death of someone else or loss of sth, etc.; sorrow, distress, anguish, agony: *Shikwa na kibuhuti*, be filled with distress. (cf *simanzi, majonzi*)

kibuja *n* (*ki-vi*) pimple, acne. (cf *chungu, kijiwe, chunusi*)

kibula *n* (*ki-vi*) see *kibla*

kibuluu *n* (*n*) (*bot*) a kind of cassava.

kibumba *n* (*ki-vi*) packet (cf *kifurushi, kichopa*)

kibumbu *n* (*ki-vi*) (*anat*) a woman's groin.

kibunju¹ *n* (*ki-vi*) a small child.

kubunju² *n* (*ki-vi*) water pond.

kibunzi¹ (also *kiburunzi*) *n* (*ki-vi*) the eve of the Swahili year, commemorated by the Swahilis and other people in the coast.

kibunzi² *n* (*ki-vi*) a sanded board, used for predicting future events, etc.; divine board.

kibunzi³ *n* (*ki-vi*) a children's game of sitting down and stretching legs, and one child sings and then passes his arms in the legs of his mates.

kibunzi⁴ *n* (*ki-vi*) a cob of maize. (cf *gumzi*)

kibunzi⁵ *n* (*ki-vi*) bait; a small piece of fish attached to a fishing line in order to attract the big one.

kiburi *n* (*ki-vi*) conceit, arrogance, vanity, pride. (cf *majivuno, ghururi, ndweo*) (Ar)

kiburudisho *n* (*ki-vi*) 1. anything that entertains: *Tulifurahi na kiburudisho chao cha muziki*, we enjoyed with their musical entertainment. 2. refreshment: *Alinikirimu kwake kwa viburudisho*, he entertained me at his place with refreshments.

kiburunzi *n* (*ki-vi*) see *kibunzi¹*

kibusha *n* (*ki-vi*) (*med*) a small hydrocele (cf *kiboleini*)

kibushuti *n* (*ki-vi*) lilliputian, dwarf, midget, manikin (cf *kisaka, mbilikimo*)

kibuyu *n* (*ki-vi*) a small round bowl made of the dry pumpkin, used for storing liquids, e.g. water, milk, etc. and also snuff; gourd, calabash. (cf *tungu, kitoma*)

kibwagizo *n* (*ki-vi*) 1. chorus; the last line in a stanza which is repeated in a poem. 2. refrain; a phrase or verse repeated at intervals in a song or poem. (cf *kipokeo, mkarara, kiitikio*)

kibwando *n* (*ki-vi*) (*bot*) a kind of okra-like green leafy plant used as a vegetable. (cf *sasa*)

kibwebwe (also *kibobwe*) *n* (*ki-vi*) 1. a broad strip of cloth, usu calico, khanga, etc. worn tightly round the waist esp by women and which is used as a kind of support during work, local dances (*ngoma*), etc.; girdle, sash, belly band, cummerbund. 2. (*idm*) *Kujifunga kibwebwe*, work diligently; get down to work.

kibwengo *n* (*ki-vi*) 1. a kind of evil spirit

kibweshu said to live in the sea, and is said to mock fishermen who fish at night. 2. one of the numerous kinds of local dances used in the exorcism of spirits.

kibweshu (also *kibweshuna*) *n* (*ki-vi*) bastard; a person or anything regarded with contempt, pity, etc.

kibweshuna *n* (*ki-vi*) see *kibweshu*

kibwiko¹ *n* (*ki-vi*) 1. (*med*) congenital deformity of the hand or foot characterized by a misshapen or twisted, often clublike appearance; club hand, club foot, talipes. 2. a person or animal suffering from this kind of deformity. (cf *kikono*)

kibwiko² *n* (*ki-vi*) a small hole made in a lump of food e.g. cooked maize flour, etc. during eating or during mixing it with curry.

kibyongo *n* (*ki-vi*) 1. humpback, hunchback; a deformed back. (cf *nundu*) 2. humpback, hunchback; a person having a humped back.

kicha *n* (*ki-vi*) 1. a bundle of palm leaf strips, vegetables, etc. 2. a bunch of keys.

kichaa¹ (also *mkichaa*) *n* (*ki-vi*) 1. insanity, madness, lunacy: *Kichaa cha mbwa*, rabies *Kichaa cha ng'ombe*, mad cow disease. (cf *wazimu, umajununi*) 2. a mad person; lunatic, maniac: *Watoto walikuwa wanamchokoza kichaa*, the children were teasing a mad person. (cf *afkani, chakramu*)

kichaa² (also *kichala*) *n* (*ki-vi*) a cluster of fruits; a bunch of fruits. (cf *kocha, kikonyo, kishada*)

kichaa³ *n* (*ki-vi*) (*bot*) a kind of red pepper.

kichaani *n* (*ki-vi*) (*bot*) an erect rather rigid annual parasitic herb of 6 to 18 inches tall with terminal spikes of crimson, scarlet, pink or white flowers. *Striga elegans*.

kichaazi *n* (*ki-vi*) (*bot*) a kind of banana.

kichaga¹ *n* (*ki-vi*) a kind of store for storing or drying grain, etc.; drying rack, bed slat. (cf *chaga, uchaga*)

kichaga² *n* (*ki-vi*) a broken rope that is tied in a bunch of leaves.

kichaka¹ (also *kiyaka*) *n* (*ki-vi*) 1. a piece of wood inserted in a twisted pole, used to straighten the pole. 2. a piece of wood used to support the roofing pole.

kichaka² *n* (*ki-vi*) (*bot*) a thick growth of shrubs, underbrush or small trees; thicket. (*kitua, kituka*)

kichala (*ki-vi*) see *kichaa²*

kichane¹ *n* (*ki-vi*) a small splinter of wood. (cf *kibanzi, kidondo*)

kichane² *n* (*ki-vi*) (*bot*) a bunch of bananas.

kichanio *n* (*ki-vi*) a kind of knife used for splitting leaves for plaiting; splitting knife.

kichapo *n* (*ki-vi*) thrash, defeat, beating: *Timu ilipokea kichapo cha pili kwa mfululizo*, the team was defeated for the second time consecutively. (cf *kisago, kipigo*)

kichapuzi *n* (*ki-vi*) accelerator

kichea *n* (*n*) 1. dawn. 2. the spreading of skies after the clouds have gone. (cf *kichesa*)

kicheche (also *cheche*) *n* (*ki-vi*) (*zool*) zorilla, polecat; a small stripped black and white weasel-like mammal, found in the drier parts of Africa. *Ictonyx striatus*.

kicheche

kichefuchefu (also *kitefetefu*) *n* (*ki-vi*) a feeling of sickness in the stomach with an impulse to vomit; nausea. (cf *jelezi, kigegezi*)

kichekesho *n* (*ki-vi*) 1. farce, comedy. 2. joke, jest, fun. (cf *masihara, mzaha*)

kicheko *n* (*ki-vi*) laughter, laugh, smile: *Angua kicheko*, burst out laughing.

kichele (also *kichelele*) *adj* 1. easily run, easily understood. *Hesabu za kichele*, easily understood sums. 2. bare, naked: *Mwendawazimu alitoka nje uchi kichele*, the madman went out stark naked. 3. small: *Fedha za kichele*, small change. 4. transparent.

kichelele *adj* see *kichele*

kichelema¹ (also *kicherema*) *n* (*ki-vi*) (of potatoes, cassava, etc.) watery condition when cooked instead of being floury: *Muhogo kichelema*, watery cassava.

kichelema² (also *kicherema*) *n* (*ki-vi*) a piece of soap left after the whole bar has been used. (cf *panza*)

kicherema *n* (*ki-vi*) see *kichelema¹* and *kichelema²*.

kichi (also *zumbulu*) *n* (*ki-vi*) (*zool*) kingfisher; a kind of coraciform bird (family *Alcedinidae*) usu bright coloured having a large crested head and a short tail and usu feeds on fish.

kichikichi (also *chikichiki*) *adv* by a blunt knife: *Aliikata nyama kichikichi*, he used a blunt knife to cut the meat.

kichimbachimba *n* (*ki-vi*) see *kitindamimba*

kichimbakazi *n* (*ki-vi*) a kind of messenger spirit; fairy.

kichinichini *adv* 1. underhanded, stealthily, furtively, surreptitiously, secretly: *Alihama hapa kichinichini*, he shifted from here secretly. (cf *kisirisiri*) 2. by theft: *Alivichukua kichinichini viatu vya mwenye duka*, he stole the shopkeeper's shoes.

kichinjaudhia *n* (*ki-vi*) (*bot*) a kind of perennial prostrate or scandent herb with reddish-purple flowers and opposite ovate leaves, used for the treatment of headaches. *Dissotis rotudinfolia*.

kicho *n* (*ki-vi*) respect, awe, reverence: *Mtoto yule ana kicho kwa wazee wake*, that child has respect for his parents. *Walii ana kicho kwa Mwenyezi Mungu*, the pious person awes God. (cf *uoga, hofu*)

kichocheo *n* (*ki-vi*) 1. (usu of iron) an instrument for stirring a fire; poker. 2. (*fig*) anything that motivates such as a present, etc.; incentive, impetus: *Matendo yake yalikuwa kichocheo katika harakati za ukombozi*, his actions served as an incentive towards the liberation struggle. (cf *changamoto*) 3. matter or issue that motivates.

kichocho *n* (*ki-vi*) (*med*) bilharzia, schistosomiasis; a kind of tropical disease caused by worms in the blood and bladder. (cf *bilhazia, kisalisali*)

kichochoro *n* (*ki-vi*) alleyway, waylane, backstreet, byway: *Kichochoro funge*, blind alley. (cf *usita, ususu*)

kichogo *n* (*ki-vi*) see *kisogo*

kichokoo¹ *n* (*ki-vi*) spur; any of various pointed devices worn on the heel by horsemen and used to urge the horse forward.

kichokoo² (also *kichokonoo*) *n* (*ki-vi*) toothpick; a slender printed instrument esp that of wood for dislodging food particles from and between the teeth.

kichomanguo (also *kishomanguo*) *n* (*ki-vi*) 1. (*bot*) black jack; an annual herb with yellowish flowers and little barbed spiny seeds that readily adhere to and penetrate clothing. *Bidens pilosa*. 2. a perennial tussuck grass up to 18 inches long with strongly awned glumes. *Heteropogon contortus*.

kichomi *n* (*ki-vi*) pang; sharp pain resulting from injection, etc.: *Alipata kichomi baada ya kupigwa sindano*, he felt a sharp pain after being injected. (cf *maumivu, uchungu*)

kichomozo *n* (*ki-vi*) (*bot*) bud of a plant: *Kichomoza kwapa*, auxiliary bud.

kichopa *n* (*ki-vi*) packet. (cf *kifurushi, kidurusi, kishirazi, kibumba*)

kichozi *n* (*ki-vi*) see *chozi*²
kichubuzi *n* (*ki-vi*) abrasive; a substance used for polishing, etc. such as sandpaper for smoothing wood.
kichuguu *n* (*ki-vi*) anthill. (cf *kingulima, kidurusi, kishirazi, kisuguu*)
kichujio *n* (*ki-vi*) strainer, sieve, sifter. (cf *kifumbo, king'uto*)
kichungi *n* (*ki-vi*) cigarette filter.
kichusi *n* (*ki-vi*) a small roof of a house usu situated in front and back of the house; rooflet.
kichwa *n* (*ki-vi*) 1. (*anat*) (of human, animal, etc.) the head. 2. leader: of a society, etc. (cf *kiongozi*) 3. the principal thing, headline, heading, etc. *Kichwa cha habari*, headline of a paper, speech, etc. *Kichwa cha garimoshi*, train engine. 4. (*idms*) *Kichwa kikubwa*, arrogance, pride. *Vimba kichwa*, be arrogant. *Kichwa kigumu*, dullness, stupidity. *Kichwa bupu*, lack of intelligence. *Kichwa maji*, obstinacy. *Kichwa kizito*, dull in understanding.
kichwamgomba *adj* falling head over heels; somersault: *Ameanguka kichwamgomba*, he has fallen head over heels.
Kidachi *adj, n* (*arch*) German (cf *Kijerumani*) (Eng)
kidadisi (also *hojaji*) *n* (*ki-vi*) questionnaire
kidahizo *n* (*ki-vi*) catchword, headword; a word which is written at the beginning of a description of its meaning as in dictionaries. (cf *kitomeo*)
kidaka (also *kidanga*) *n* (*ki-vi*) 1. (*bot*) a small nut of a coconut; coconut nutlet. 2. (*idm*) *Tia kidaka cha mdomo*, silence sby. 3. the young mango before having its seeds.
kidakatonge *n* (*ki-vi*) (*anat*) uvula, epiglottis. (cf *kilimi, kimio*)
kidanga *n* (*ki-vi*) see *kidaka*
kidani *n* (*ki-vi*) necklace; neck ornament.
kidari *n* (*ki-vi*) (of men, animals, etc.) chest, breast, thorax: *Nyama ya kidari*, breast meat; brisket. *Amekuja kidari nje*, he has come with his chest exposed. (Ar)
kidato *n* (*ki-vi*) 1. the cut made on the coconut tree to enable a climber to swarm up without any difficulty. 2. rung of a ladder. 3. (in education) form, standard, class. (cf *darasa*) 4. (*phon*) pitch; the degree of highness or lowness of speaking, etc.
kidau¹ (also *kidawati*) *n* (*ki-vi*) inkwell, inkpot. (cf *kidawa*)
kidau² *n* (*ki-vi*) (*zool*) a kind of small long-bodied tropical sea fish (family Hemiramphidae) with a greatly extended lower jaw and a short upper jaw; half beak.
kidawati *n* (*ki-vi*) see *kidau*¹
kidazi *n* (*ki vi*) baldness; hairlessness condition: *Ana kidazi kichwani*, he is bald. (cf *kipara, upara*)
kidedea *n* (*ki-vi*) (*colloq*) victor, winner, hero: *Timu inayozuru iliibuka kidedea*, the visiting team emerged as the winner. (cf *mshindi*)
kidei (also *kideri*) *n* (*ki-vi*) see *kideri*
kidekwa *n* (*ki-vi*) a bed whose legs are loose.
kideri *n* (*ki-vi*) (*med*) Newcastle disease, Ranikhet disease, pseudofowl pest; it is an acute highly contagious viral disease of domestic poultry, pigeons, turkeys and occasionally of other birds characterized by gastro-intestinal, respitory and nervous signs.
kidete *adv* firmly, strongly, steadfastly. *Wananchi wamesimama kidete katika kupigania haki zao*, the people have stood firm in the fight for their rights. (cf *imara*)
kidevu *n* (*ki-vi*) (*anat*) chin
kidhabu (also *kadhabu*) *n* (*ki-vi*) liar, fibber, fibster: *Usimwamini kidhabu yule*, don't trust that liar. (cf *mwongo*) (Ar)
kidh.i¹ *vt* satisfy, fulfill, grant: *Siwezi kuzikidhi haja zake*, I can't satisfy his demands. Prep. **kidh.i.a** St **kidh.ik.a** Cs. **kidh.ish.a** Ps. of Prep. **kidh.iw.a**

Rp. of Prep. **kidh.i.an.a** (Ar)
kidh.i[2] *vt* (in Islam) compensate a prayer, fast, etc. when the time is overdue: Prep. **kidh.i.a** St. **kidh.ik.a** Cs. **kidhi.sh.a** Ps. of Prep. **kidh.iw.a** Rp. of Prep. **kidh.i.an.a** (Ar)
kidhibish.a *vt* see *kadhibisha*
kidhib.u *vt* see *kadhibu*
kidigi *adj* very small: *Huyu ni mtoto kidigi*, this is a small child. (cf *kidinya*)
kidimbwi *n* (*ki-vi*) puddle
kidimu *n* (*ki-vi*) (*zool*) a kind of fowl with naturally ruffled feathers and very long legs; a featherless fowl. (cf *nungu, kidiku, kinyanyavu*)
kidimumsitu *n* (*ki-vi*) (*bot*) a wild citrus fruit tree. *Citrus sp.*
kidindia *adv* continuously, endlessly. Used in the expression: *Mvua ilinyesha kidindia*, it rained for a long time without stopping. (cf *mfululizo*)
kidingapopo[1] *n* (*n*) (*med*) dengue fever; the recurrence of a disease transmitted by mosquitoes and characterized by severe pains in the joints and back, fever, and rash. (cf *homa vipindi*)
kidingapopo[2] *n* (*ki-vi*) telltale, tattler, talebearer.
kidingapopo[3] *n* (*ki-vi*) a kind of a game of lying upside down; somersault.
kidinindi *adv* firmly, steadfastly: *Askari alimshika mwizi kidinindi*, the policeman held the thief firmly. (cf *kinying'inya, imara*)
kidinya *adj* very small, very little: *Yule ni ndege kidinya*, that is a very small bird. (cf *kidigi*)
kidiri *n* (*ki-vi*) (*zool*) bush squirrel; a small climbing animal with a long bushy tail and thick fur. (cf *kuchakulo*)

kidiri

kidogo[1] *adj* small, little, tiny, few: *Watu kidogo*, few people. *Maji kidogo*, little water. *Chakula kidogo*, little food.
kidogo[2] *adv* a little, not much: *Andika kidogo*, write a little. *Kula kidogo*, eat a little.
kidogokidogo *adv* slowly, bit by bit: *Aliyamimina maji kidogokidogo*, he poured water bit by bit. 2. in a small amount.
kidogori *n* (*ki-vi*) bongo drum
kidokezi[1] (also *kidokezo*) *n* (*ki-vi*) hint, clue, inkling.
kidokezi[2] (also *kidokozi*) *n* (*ki-vi*) (*zool*) a kind of fish.
kidokezo *n* (*ki-vi*) see *kidokezi*[1]
kidoko *n* (*ki-vi*) cluck, click: *Piga kidoko*, produce sound as a result of contact between the lips and the tongue; smack the lips.
kidokozi[1] *n* (*ki-vi*) see *kidokezi*[2]
kidokozi[2] *n* (*ki-vi*) pilfer, filcher; a person fond of taking small things of little value usu without permission.
kidokwa *n* (*ki-vi*) sound that comes out from the inside air.
kidole *n*(*ki-vi*) finger: *Kidole cha kati*, middle finger. *Kidole kikubwa*, middle finger. *Kidole cha mguu*, toe. *Kidole cha mwisho*, little finger. *Kidole gumba*, the thumb. *Kidole cha shahada*, forefinger. *Kidole cha pete*, ring finger. (*prov*) *Kidole kimoja hakivunji chawa*, one finger does not kill a louse i.e. unity is strength.
kidoletumbo *n* (*ki-vi*) (*med*) appendix (cf *kibole*)
kidomo *n* (*ki-vi*) a fastidious person with regards to eating; choosy in eating food; gourmet, epicure; a dainty eater. (cf *machagu, mbeuzi*)
kidomodomo *n* (*ki-vi*) 1. backbiter, slanderer. (cf *msimbuliaji*) 2. telltale, firebrand, rabble-rouser, inciter. (cf *sabasi, mfitini*)
kidonda *n* (*ki-vi*) wound, sore: *Kidonda cha tumbo*, ulcer.
kidondo (also *kidondoo*) *n* (*ki-vi*) tinder; a bit of dry easily flammable material,

used for starting a fire. (cf *kibanzi*)

kidonge[1] *n* (*ki-vi*) 1. pill, tablet, capsule. 2. anything that has swollen in the body; swelling, inflammation. 3. anything that is usu small and round.

kidonge[2] *n* (*ki-vi*) spool of thread; cotton reel: *Kidonge cha uzi*, a spool of thread.

kidongo *n* (*ki-vi*) clay (cf *kinamo, kinongo*)

kidosho *n* (*ki-vi*) 1. a beautiful girl; beauty: *Wavulana wengi wanampenda kidosho yule*, many boys love that beautiful girl. (cf *kipusa*) 2. a small bird.

kidotia (also *kiloilu*) *n* (*ki vi*) a child's cap. (cf *kofia*)

kidoto[1] *n* (*ki-vi*) a special bandage of cloth fastened over a camel's eyes while working a mill or travelling in a desert; blinker, blinder.

kidoto[2] *n* (*ki-vi*) a small container like a bowl made out of plaited palm leaves, used for drinking, etc.

kidoto[3] *n* (*ki-vi*) spot, speck, mark. (cf *paku*)

kidu[1] *n* (*ki-vi*) (*naut*) a small hole in a canoe, dhow, etc. into which the mast is placed; mastbank. (cf *kinyunga, kiwida*)

kidu[2] *n* (*ki-vi*) 1. a small hole into which children play marbles or participate in gambles. 2. a small hole in the game of draughts or checkers.

kidu[3] *n* (*ki-vi*) spot, speck, mark. (cf *paku*)

kidubini *n* (*ki-vi*) micro-organism.

kidubwana (also *kidubwasha, kidubweshu*) *n* (*ki-vi*) gimcrack, thingamajig, thingummy, trash; a small thing whose identity is unknown or unimportant: *Mtoto wangu mdogo alikuwa akichezea kidubwana*, my small child was playing with a thingamajig. (cf *kinyangarika*)

kidubwasha *n* (*ki-vi*) see *kidubwana*

kidubweshu *n* (*ki-vi*) see *kidubwana*

kidudumtu *n* (*ki-vi*) telltale, tattler, scandal monger.

kidudusi *n* (*ki-vi*) pimple on the face; spot, pustule: *Ana vidudusi usoni*, he has pimples on the face. (cf *chunusi, dutu, kijiwe*)

kidugu *adv* on brotherly basis: *Alinisaidia kidugu*, he helped me as a brother.

kiduhushi *n* (*ki-vi*) gossiper, snoop, busybody, meddler, talebearer: *Kiduhushi yule atazifichua siri zako*, that talebearer will disclose your secrets. (cf *kilimilimi, mdaku*)

kidukari *n* (*ki-vi*) (*zool*) aphid: a small homopterous insect (family *Alphididae*) which is familiar to most farmers due to the harm it causes to many different kinds of cultivated plants.

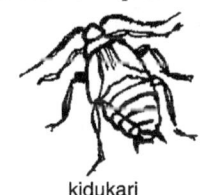

kidukari

kiduko *n* (*ki-vi*) see *kiziwi*

kidumbwi *n* (*ki-vi*) see *dimbwi*

kidunavi[1] *n* (*ki-vi*) a short person; *Mtu huyu amekuwa kidunavi kutokana na utapiamlo*, this child is stunted because of malnutrition. (cf *mbilikimo*)

kidunavi[2] *n* (*ki-vi*) a short thing.

kidundumavi *n* (*ki-vi*) (*anat*) coccyx; a small, triangular bone at the lower end of the vertebral column. (cf *kifandugu, kitonoko*)

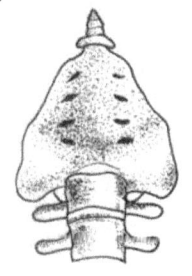

kidundumavi

kidunundu *n (ki-vi)* 1. *(zool)* a kind of fish like a small box with a long mouth, fleshy lips. and moderate teeth; boxfish. (cf *kibuyu*) 2. *(syn) Mfupi kama kidunundu*, as short as this kind of fish.

kidurango *n (ki-vi)* a very short person; lilliputian, manikin, dwarf, midget: *Kidurango hawezi kuigusa rafu ile*, the dwarf cannot touch that shelf. (cf *mbilikimo, kibeti*)

kidurasi (also *kidurusi*) *n (ki-vi)* see *kidurusi*

kidurusi *n (ki-vi)* anthill (cf *kichuguu, kishirazi*)

kidusi¹ *n (ki-vi)* 1. an unusual smell or odour of anything. 2. the smell or odour of a fish or a wild animal. (cf *uvungu*)

kidusi² *n (ki-vi)* scrounger, sponger: a person fond of visiting people's houses to take food, etc.

kiduta *n (ki-vi)* rising ground; knoll, mound, hillock. (cf *gongo*)

kidutu *n (ki-vi)* wart, blackhead.

kiduva (also *kiduvya*) *n (ki-vi)* hunchback, humpback. (cf *kibyongo*)

kiduvya *n (ki-vi)* see *kiduva*

kiegama *n (ki-vi) (geom)* hypotenuse

kiegemeo *n (ki-vi)* pole, pop. (cf *nguzo, mwimo*)

kielekezi (also *kielekezo*) *n (ki-vi)* hint, clue, sign; signal: *Kielekezi hiki kinatufahamisha kwamba eneo lote lina mwenyewe*, this sign shows that the whole area has an owner. (cf *ishara, kidokezo*)

kielekezo *n (ki-vi)* 1. illustration, diagram, model, example: *Kielekezo kile kimechorwa vizuri*, that diagram has been well drawn. (cf *kifani*) 2. evidence, index, proof, indication: *Ushindi ule katika uchaguzi mdogo ni kielekezo kwamba chama chetu kina nguvu nchini*, that victory in the by-election is an index that our party is strong in the country.

kielelezo *n (ki-vi)* 1. exhibit; *Upande wa mashtaka ulionyesha mahakamani nguo zilizoibiwa kama kielelezo*, the prosecution showed the stolen clothes in court as exhibits. 2. illustration, explanation: *Kielelezo chake cha kisa chenyewe hakiridhishi*, his illustration of the incident is unsatisfactory. (cf *kizibiti*)

kielezi¹ (also *kisifa*) *n (ki-vi) (gram)* adverb: *Aliondoka kimyakimya*, he left quietly. Here, the word *kimyakimya* is an adverb.

kielezi² (also *kielezo*) *n (ki-vi)* 1. anything that gives an explanation of sth; illustration: *Kielezi chake hakieleweki*, his explanation is not clear. 2. indication, index: *Kufuzu kwake ni kielezi kwamba yeye ni hodari*, her success is an index that she is intelligent. 3. picture, drawing, chart: *Kielezi hiki kinapendeza*, this drawing is impressive. 4. beginning: *Kielezi chake hakijulikani*, its beginning is unknown. 5 a piece of wood used for starting to plait mats, carpets, etc. (cf *kianzo*)

kielezo *n (ki-vi)* see *kielezi²*

kiendelezo *n (ki-vi)* continuation; a thing that serves as a support to continue a struggle, etc.

kieneo *n (ki-vi)* see *cheneo*

kienezo *n (ki-vi)* see *chenezo*

kienge *n (ki-vi)* a heap of palm leaves or dry sticks, used to gather honey or kill "safari" ants.

kienyeji¹ *adj* indigenous, native, local: *Lugha za kienyeji*, indigenous languages. *Wakunga wa kienyeji*, local midwives.

kienyeji² *adv* casually, unofficial way: *Usifanye mambo kienyeji*, don't do things casually.

kienzo *n (ki-vi)* 1. model, example, pattern, measurement: *Mshoni aliishona suruali yangu bila ya kuchukua vienzo sahihi*, the tailor sewed my trousers without taking proper measurements. (cf *kilingo*) 2. decoration, adornment: *Wanawake walitia vienzo usoni mwao*, the women put decorations on their faces. (cf *bombwe*)

kifaa *n* (*ki-vi*) instrument, appliance, equipment, implement, apparatus: *Vifaa vya nyumbani*, household appliances. *Hivi ni vifaa vya mwashi*, these are the mason's implements (cf *kitendeakazi*, *chombo*, *ala*)

kifaduro *n* (*ki-vi*) (*med*) an acute infectious disease usu affecting children marked by a mucous discharge from the nose and later causes repeated attacks of coughing followed by a whoop; whooping cough; pertussis.

kifafa *n* (*ki-vi*) (*med*) epilepsy; a condition of the brain which causes a person to lose consciousness for a short time or to move in a violent way.

kifai *adv* steadfastly, firmly, solidly: *Maradhi yalimbana kifai*, the disease affected him firmly. (cf *mno*, *barabara*)

kifabakazi *n* (*ki-vi*) (*bot*) Nandi Flame tree; a much-branched tree up to 40 feet tall with large brilliant scarlet flowers, woody pods, and has roughly pinnate leaves, and is often planted as an avenue and shade tree. *Sputhodea nilotica*.

kifandugu *n* (*ki-vi*) (*anat*) coccyx; a small, triangular bone at the end of the vertebral column. (cf *kidundumavi*, *kitokono*)

kifani (*also kifano*) *n* (*n*) match, equal: *Bila kifani*, incomparable, matchless. *Hakuna kifani cha mtu yule*, there is no match for that person. (cf *mfano*, *mithili*)

kifano (*also kifani*) *n* (*n*) 1. match, equal, resemblance: *Nyumba hii ni kifano cha ile ya pale*, this house resembles that one. (cf *mfano*) 2. picture (cf *sura*)

kifaranga *n* (*ki-vi*) (*zool*) chick; a young chicken or bird.

Kifaransa *adj*, *n* (*ki-vi*) French language. (Fr)

kifaru *n* (*ki-vi*) 1. (*zool*) rhinoceros. 2. military tank.

kifaungo *n* (*ki-vi*) see *kiforongo*

kifendege *n* (*ki-vi*) a signal cry or call made by blowing into the hands or fingers. (cf *kifenenge*, *kikorombwe*)

kifenenge *n* (*ki-vi*) see *kifendege*

kificho[1] *n* (*ki-vi*) furtively, secretly, stealthily, quietly: *Adui aliingia nchini kwa kificho*, the enemy entered the country secretly. (cf *kisirisiri*, *kinyemela*, *kibubusa*)

kificho[2] *n* (*ki-vi*) a secret place. (cf *sitara*)

kifimbo[1] *n* (*ki-vi*) (*zool*) a kind of sea fish (family *Albulidae*) having an elongate cylindrical body with silvery cycloid scales; bonefish.

kifimbo[2] *n* (*ki-vi*) a round long piece of wood used in kneading dough for making doughnuts or *chapati*.

kifirimbi *n* (*ki-vi*) whistle. (cf *filimbi*, *kipenga*)

kifo *n* (*ki-vi*) death, demise: *Kifo chake ni pigo kubwa kwa taifa*, his death is a big blow to the nation. (cf *mauti*)

kifoli *n* (*ki-vi*) click produced by a combination of middle finger and the thumb. (cf *kipwe*)

kiforongo (also *kifauongo*, *kifaurongo*) *n* (*ki-vi*) 1. (*bot*) Sensitive Plant; a scandent perennial woody herb with thorny stems, compound leaves crowded at the end of the leaf stalks and small heads of pinkish purple flowers. *Mimosa pudica*. 2. Sensitive Woodsorrel; an annual herb 3 to 12 inches tall with compound leaves in a rosette and small yellow or pale pink flowers. *Biophytum sensitivum*. 3. an insect which causes death when touched.

kifu[1] *n* (*ki-vi*) a dead thing. (cf *mzoga*, *mfu*)

kifu[2] *n* (*ki-vi*) fill, satisfaction: *Amekula kifu yake*, he has eaten his fill. (cf *kiasi*, *kadiri*) (Ar)

kif.u[3] *vt* satisfy, suffice, satiate; be sufficient: *Maamuzi yake yaliwakifu* *wanachama*, his decisions satisfied the members. Prep. **kif.i.a** St. **kif.ik.a** Cs. **kif.ish.a** Ps. of Prep. **kif.iw.a** (cf *kidhi, tosheleza, ridhisha*) (Ar)

kif.u⁴ *vt* save someone from an evil: *Mungu alimkifu na ile balaa*, God saved him from the calamity. Prep. **kif.i.a** St. **kif.ik.a** Cs. **kif.ish.a** Ps. of Prep. **kif.iw.a** (cf *epusha*)

kifua *n (ki-vi)* 1. *(anat)* breast, bosom, chest. 2. *(med)* tuberculosis: *Kifua kikuu*, pulmonary tuberculosis. 3. bravery, gallantry: *Ana kifua*, he is brave. (cf *ujasiri*) 4. perseverance, patience.

kifuasi¹ *n (ki-vi)* 1. sth which follows behind sth else. 2. even number such as 2, 4, 6, ... (cf *shufwa*)

kifuasi² *n (ki-vi)* a kind of a bullet that can be tracked when it falls down.

kifudifudi (also *fudifudi*) *adv* with face downwards, on the face: *Alilala kifudifudi*, he slept face down.

kifufumkunye (also *n (ki-vi) kifufunkunye*) a worthless issue; an unknown thing: *Anapenda kujishughulisha na vifufumkunye*, he likes to engross himself in worthless issues.

kifufunkunye *n (ki-vi)* see *kifufumkunye*

kifuka *n (ki-vi) (bot)* an erect herb up to 5 feet tall with much-branched panicles of numerous heads of small white or reddish blue daisy-like flowers. *Vernonia cinerea*.

kifukizo (also *kifukizio*) *n (ki-vi)* 1. incense burner. 2. incense; aromatic substance used in some religious ceremonies. (cf *mafusho, buhuri*) 3. fumigant; a substance used for treating sth contaminated or infected.

kifukizio *n (ki-vi)* see *kifukizo*

kifuko *n (ki-vi)* a small clay water jar; a small clay water pot.

kifukofuko *n (ki-vi) (zool)* the silky or fibrous case which the larvae of certain insects spin about themselves to shelter them during the pupa stage; cocoon.

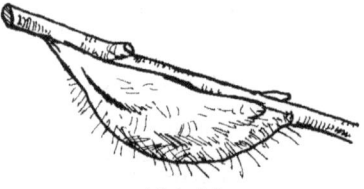

kifukofuko

kifuku *n (ki-vi)* 1. the hot rainy season i.e. when the air is very humid and causes people to perspire a lot. 2. long rains. (cf *masika*)

kifukulile *n (ki-vi) (zool)* shy crab, boxcrab; a kind of crab of molted greyish-green colour and lives in various soft substrates in enlittoral and shallow sublittoral often burrowing in sand. *(ellapa hepatica)* (cf *mswele*)

kifukusi *n (ki-vi) (zool)* a kind of weevil (family *Curculionidae*) which constitutes the destructive pests of stored cereals in warmer parts of the world. The insect often starts to infest the commodity in the field and later carries it in the storage; maize weevil.

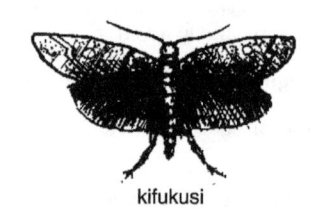

kifukusi

kifulio *n (ki-vi)* a pointed stake fixed in the ground for unhusking coconuts. (cf *cheo, kifuo*)

kifulizwa *n (ki-vi)*) continuant

kifumanzi *n (ki-vi)* ankle bell. (cf *njuga*)

kifumbu *n (ki-vi)* a small straw utensil having many meshed or perforated openings, used to filter coconut juice; coconut strainer/sieve/sifter. (cf *kung'uto, kichujio*)

kifumbuzi n (ki-vi) see kivumbasi
kifumufumu n (ki-vi) (bot) a kind of cassava.
kifundi[1] adv skilfully, cleverly, artistically, masterly, brilliantly: *Alifunga goli kifundi*, he scored the goal skilfully.
kifundi[2] n (ki-vi) (bot) a section in the cassava that has begun to dry and its colour is becoming brown.
kifundiro n (ki-vi) 1. a thing made from sth else; product. 2. goods produced from a factory; manufactured goods.
kifundo n (ki-vi) 1. body joint: *Kifundo cha mguu*, ankle. *Kifundo cha mkono*, wrist. 2. a kind of swelling or protuberance like an abscess that protrudes on the body; nodule, lump. 3. a small knot. 4. (bot) node; that part or joint of a stem from which a stem starts to grow.
kifungambuzi (also *kichungambuzi*) n (ki-vi) (bot) crow-feet grass; an annual or short-lived perennial tussock grass up to 12 inches long, common in waste places esp near villages. *Eleusine indica*.
kifungio (ki-vi) lock
kifungo n (ki-vi) 1. stud, brooch, buckle. 2. button. 3. prison sentence: *Alipata kifungo cha miaka sita*, he was given a six month sentence. 4. bracket sign () 5. same level: *Watu wale wako katika kifungo kimoja*, those people are in the same level. 6. fasting, fast. (cf *saumu*)
kifungu n (ki-vi) 1. a small heap; a small pile: *Kifungu hiki cha kuni ni chake*, this small heap of firewood belongs to him. 2. section: *Taarifa yote inapatikana katika kifungu cha ibara ya tano*, all the information is found in section five of the clause. (cf *ibara*)
kifungua n (ki-vi) used in different expressions: *Kifungua kopo*, a thing like a knife, used to open a tin or can; tin opener. *Kifungua mkoba*, first payment given to a medicine man.

kifunguakinywa (ki-vi) breakfast: *Kifunguakinywa chake kila siku ni chai na mkate*, his daily breakfast is tea and bread.
kifungua kopo n (ki-vi) see *kifungua*
kifungua mimba n (ki-vi) the firstborn child: *Dada yangu alikuwa kifungua mimba katika familia yetu*, my sister was the firstborn child in our family. (cf *mwanambae*)
kifungua mkoba n (ki-vi) initial consultation fee.
kifungulio n (ki-vi) opener: *Kifungulio hiki ni cha soda*, this opener is for soda bottles. (cf *kifungua*)
kifuniko n (ki-vi) lid, cover, cap, top, cork, stopper; anything that covers. (cf *kizibo, mfuniko*)
kifuo n (ki-vi) a pointed stake fixed in the ground for unhusking coconuts. (cf *cheo, kifulio*)
kifurushi n (ki-vi) a bundle of sth: *Kifurushi cha nguo*, a bundle of clothes.
kifusi (also *fusi*) n (ki-vi) 1. debris of demolition; rubble. 2. clay for building a house.
kifuta n (ki-vi) 1. the condition of someone experiencing pain in one's throat as if he has eaten some oily stuff stuck in the gullet; heartburn. 2. fat, lard, grease, tallow. (cf *shahamu*)
kifuta jasho n (ki-vi) 1. recompense; sth given or done in return for something else. 2. sth given or done to make up for a loss, injury, etc; compensation, recompense.
kifuta machozi n (ki-vi) compensation: *Alistahiki kupewa kifuta machozi kwa sababu aliumia wakati wa kazi*, he deserved compensation because he got injured during work.
kifutio n (ki-vi) eraser, rubber. (cf *raba, dasta*)
kifutu n (ki-vi) (zool) puff-adder; a most dangerous snake in Africa, whose prey consists usu of rodents. *Bitis arietans*. (cf *bafe, kipili*)
kifuu[1] (also *kifuvu*) n (ki-vi) an empty

coconut shell.
kifuu² *n (ki-vi) (zool)* a fish bone like that of a cuttlefish: *Kifuu cha ngisi*, cuttle fish bone.
kifuu³ *n (ki-vi)* a person with little intelligence.
kifuutundu *n (ki-vi)* a person whose earnings don't grow.
kifuvu *n (ki-vi)* see *kifuu¹*
kifyefye *n (ki-vi)* 1. a strip of palm leaf. 2. a very skinny person; a person who has lost a lot of weight.
kifyonzavumbi *n (ki-vi)* an electric sweeping brush which absorbs all the dust and refuse when used; vacuum cleaner.
kifyonzaji *n (ki-vi)* see *kifyonzi*
kifyonzi *n (ki-vi)* sucker, a person or thing which sucks.
kiga *n (ki-vi) (anat)* the thigh of an animal or person; ham.
kigae *n (ki-vi)* 1. roof-like potsherd; roof tile. 2. a broken piece of glass, etc.; potsherd.
kigaga *n (ki-vi)* 1. a veil of a wound when it is almost about to heal; scab. 2. crust of food left in a pot. (cf *ukoko*) 3. dry hard scale, etc. shed by the skin on the nose after someone had flu: *Kigaga cha pua*, dry hard scale of this kind.
kigagazi *n (ki-vi)* see *kigegezi*
kigambo *n (ki-vi)* war (cf *bangu, kondo*)
kigandamizo *n (ki-vi)* a pad for wounds.
kigango *n (ki-vi)* outstation; a post or station in a remote or unsettled area.
kiganja *n (ki-vi)* 1. the palm of the hand. (cf *kitanga*) 2. a stroke resulting from the palm of the hand.
kigano *n (ki-vi)* tale, fable, story. (cf *ngano*)
kigaro *n (ki-vi)* a meeting of the people intended to discredit someone or even hurt him physically.
kigasha *n (ki-vi) (anat)* forearm; the part of the arm between the elbow and the wrist.

kigawa *n (ki-vi) (math)* divider
kigawanyi *n (ki-vi) (math)* dividend
kigawanywa *n(ki-vi) (math)* dividend
kigawanyo *n (ki-vi) (math)* divisor
kigawe *n (ki-vi)* 1. factor: *Kigawe cha nguvu*, power factor. *Kigawe cha usalama*, safety factor. 2. multiple: *Kigawe kidogo cha shirika*, least common multiple. *Kigawe shirika*, common multiple.
kigawo *n (ki-vi) (math) Kigawo kikubwa cha shirika*, highest common factor. (cf *gawio*)
kigegezi (also *kigagazi*) *n (ki-vi)* 1. a feeling of sickness in the stomach prompting someone to vomit; nausea: *Nilipata kigegezi niliposikia harufu mbaya ya chakula*, I was filled with nausea after scenting bad food. (cf *kinyezi, kinyaa, kichefuchefu, jelezi*) 2. a feeling of sea sickness causing the stomach to be unstable while travelling in a vessel; nausea. 3. the condition of refusing to accept sth because you feel it is dirty.
kigego (also *kijego*) *n (ki-vi)* 1. a child who develops his upper teeth first or born with the teeth already grown or born in an abnormal manner. (cf *ngengemea, kamange*) 2. a person who does not listen to advice, etc.; an obstinate person; recalcitrant.
kigelegele (also *ugelegele*) *n (ki-vi)* a high pitched shrill, used usu by women as a sign of joy, triumph, etc.; ululation: *Nilivisikia vigelegele vya wanawake kwenye sherehe za harusi*, I heard women's ululations at the wedding celebrations.
kigeregenja *n (ki-vi)* see *kigereng'enza*
kigereng'enza *(ki-vi)* (also *kigeregenja*) a very small broken piece of a glass, pot, etc; potsherd. (cf *kigae, gae*)
kigesi *n (ki-vi)* see *kugesi*
kigeugeu *n (ki-vi)* a double-faced person, a two-faced person; weathercock, chameleon, hypocrite: *Wewe unamwamini kigeugeu yule, au sivyo?*

You trust that chameleon, don't you? (cf *kauleni, kimbaumbau*)

kigezo *n* (*ki-vi*) 1. yardstick, criterion: *Kigezo fulani kilitumiwa kupima umahiri wa wanafunzi*, a certain yardstick was used to measure the students' intelligence (cf *kipimo*) 2. clothes' pattern; a pattern for making clothes. (*ruwaza, sampuli*) 3. a measuring rod.

kigingi *n* (*ki-vi*) 1. a tent peg or a similar peg or stake used for teethering an animal, holding sth, etc. 2. (*fig*) obstacle, hindrance: *Chama kimeshinda vigingi vingi*, the party has overcome many obstacles.

Kigiriki *n* (*ki-vi*) Greek language. (cf *Kiyunani*)

kigoda *n* (*ki-vi*) a small three-legged stool: *Alikaa kwenye kigoda*, he sat on a small three-legged stool. (cf *stuli*)

kigodo *n* (*ki-vi*) rice flour dough mixed with sugar and grated coconut. (cf *bumbwi*)

kigoe (also *kingoe, kigovya*) *n* (*ki-vi*) 1. a small hooked or forked stick or pole used for pulling down branches of trees in order to pluck fruits. 2. golf-stick, golf-club.

kigogo *n* (*ki-vi*) 1. trunk: *Kigogo cha mti*; the trunk of a tree. 2. (*fig*) mogul, bigwig, stalwart; an important and influential person: *Kigogo cha chama tawala*, ruling party stalwart. *Kigogo cha soka*, soccer giant.

kigogota *n* (*ki-vi*) see *gogota*²

kigoli (also *kigori*) *n* (*ki-vi*) a young girl before reaching puberty; a pre pubescent girl.

kigoma *n* (*ki-vi*) tambourine, timbrel. (cf *dafi, rika, tari*)

kigombegombe¹ *n* (*ki-vi*) (*zool*) cowfish; a kind of trunkfish (family *Ostraciidae*) with horn-like processes on the head.

kigombegombe² *adv* by knees and hands: *Alitambaa kigombegombe*, he walked by using knees and hands.

kigongo¹ *n* (*ki-vi*) hunchback, humpback. (cf *kibyongo*)

kigongo² *n* (*ki-vi*) cudgel, bludgeon: *Alitumia kigongo kumpiga mwizi*, he used a cudgel to beat the thief. (cf *rungu*)

kigong'ondo *n* (*ki-vi*) a kind of click or sound produced by hitting sth in order to find out the condition of that thing e.g. hitting a coconut with a coin to find out if it is a good one; testing a coconut by tapping.

kigong'ota *n* (*ki-vi*) see *gogota*²

kigono *n* ((*ki-vi*) camp, encampment, bivouac: *Waliweka kigono chao karibu na mto*, they set up their camp near the river. (cf *ago, kambi*)

kigori *n* (*ki-vi*) see *kigoli*

kigosho *n* (*ki-vi*) 1. a hooked or curved thing used to hang clothes; coat hanger. 2. anything that is bent, abnormal, deformed, etc.: *Kigosho cha mkono*, a deformed arm or one that is bent due to accident, disease, etc. *Kigosho cha mguu*, a deformed leg or one that is bent.

kigotagota *n* (*ki-vi*) see *gogota*²

kigovya *n* (*ki-vi*) see *kigoe*

kigozikucha (also *kikuchia*) *n* (*ki-vi*) hangnail; a bit of torn or cracked skin hanging at the side or base of a fingernail.

kigubiko *n* (*ki-vi*) (*anat*) eyelid, palpebra; either of two folds of skin and muscle that can be closed over the exposed portion of the eye-ball.

kigugumizi *n* (*ki-vi*) 1. stammer, stutter; speaking in jerks or gulps.; stumbling in speech: *Kigugumizi chake kinamfanya asizungumze kwa wepesi*, his stammer causes him not to speak with ease. 2. obstacle, impediment. (cf *kitata*) 3. hesitance. hesitation, indecision: *Nilimwambia ahame kutoka nyumba yangu lakini akaonyesha kigugumizi*, I told him to move from my house but he was hesitant.

kigumba *n* (*ki-vi*) 1. the head of an arrow or spear. 2. the head of a cock.

317

kigumugumu n (ki-vi) (zool) six stripe soap fish; a kind of fish belonging to *Grammistidae* family. *Grammistes sexlineatus*. (cf *kitumbaku*)

kiguru (also *kiguu*) n (ki-vi) a crippled person; a lame legged person.

kiguruwe n (ki-vi) (bot) a kind of a short banana tree which produces a large stem or pedical of bananas.

kiguu n (ki-vi) see *kiguru*

kighushi n (ki-vi) adulterant; a substance that debases something else by adding inferior material.

kigwaru[1] n (ki-vi) (med) a growth, said to be like a wart or pimple on the clitoris of a woman, and which is believed to make the woman childless or if she has children, they die at birth or when they are still young; tubercle (cf *kisukuma, kinyakazi*)

kigwaru[2] n (ki-vi) women's initiation dance played in Kilwa island inside the house to avoid men watching it.

kigwe n (ki-vi) 1. a woman's ornament of string, braid, etc. worn around the neck. (cf *jebu*) 2. a band worn around the neck of an animal so that it does not get lost or does not mix itself with other groups. 3. a band of medicine worn around a child's leg or arm.

kigwena n (ki-vi) 1. a secret meeting held to inflict injury, evil, etc. against someone; intrigue, conspiracy, machination. 2. a meeting held to deliberate on sth good. (syn) *Nendeni kigwena*, go and discuss privately sth good.

kihalua (also *nyangushi*) n (ki-vi) (zool) an excellent good fish (family *Carangidae*) having an elongated body, found in offshore reefs; blackbanded trevally. *Seriolina nigrofasciata*.

kihame n (ki-vi) a deserted place; an abandoned village or town: *Sehemu ile sasa imekuwa kihame*, that place has now become deserted. (cf *mahame, ganjo*)

kihami n (ki-vi) (elect) insulator

kiharara[1] n (ki-vi) tax, levy (cf *kodi*)

kiharara[2] n (ki-vi) (zool) badger, antbear, aardvark. (cf *muhanga, loma*)

kiharara[3] n (ki-vi) (bot) a kind of tree resembling beef-wood.

kiharusi n (ki-vi) (med) paralysis, apoplexy, stroke. *Amepata ugonjwa wa kiharusi*, he has suffered from paralysis. (cf *ganzi, baridi*)

kihembe n (ki-vi) a kind of relish comprising beans or green grams pounded into a paste.

kihenge n (ki-vi) barn

kiherehere n (ki-vi) 1. anxiety, worry, perplexity, uneasiness: *Aliingiwa na kiherehere aliposikia uvumi kwamba polisi watakuja kumkamata*, he was filled with anxiety when he heard a rumour that the police would come to arrest him. (cf *wasiwasi, wahaka*) 2. palpitation.

kihero n (ki-vi) a small wooden tray, used for serving food. (cf *chano*)

kihil.i vt skin an animal and remove innards. Prep. **kihil.i.a** St. **kihil.ik.a** Cs. **kihil.ish.a** Ps. of Prep. **kihil.i.w.a** Rp. of Prep. **kihil.i.an.a**

Kihindi n (ki-vi) Hindi language. (Hind)

kihoda n (ki-vi) abortifacient; a drug or device that causes abortion.

kihodhi n (ki-vi) (anat) gland; any organ or specialized group of cells that separates certain elements from the blood, for use in the body or for excretion.

kihongwe n (ki-vi) (zool) a kind of wild donkey. (cf *kirongwe*)

kihori n (ki-vi) see *hori*

kihoro n (ki-vi) great grief because of bereavement or great loss of property, etc.; distress, anguish: *Pata kihoro*, be in distress. *Toa kihoro*, cause to be in distress. *Alipata kihoro baada ya kufiwa na mkewe*, he was in profound grief after his wife's death. (cf *huzuni, simanzi*)

kihunzi n (ki-vi) mysterious language

which is intended to make others not to understand it: *Mwanasiasa mwanagenzi alitumia kihunzi alipokuwa anahutubia mkutano wa hadhara*, the inexperienced politician used mysterious language when he was addressing a public meeting. (cf *kiwizi*, *kinyuma*)

kihusishi *n* (*ki-vi*) (*gram*) preposition e.g. *Anaishi na shangazi yake*, she lives with her aunt. Here, the word 'na' 'with' is a preposition. *Kihusishi sahili*, simple preposition. *Kihusishi changamano*, complex preposition.

kiila *n* (*ki-vi*) a word used to refute the first statement; negation: *Wanasema kwamba alizama baharini, kiila alinusurika*, they say that he drowned, on the contrary, he survived.

kiima *n* (*ki-vi*) (*gram*) subject: *Yeye ni mwalimu*, he is a teacher. Here, *yeye*, 'he' is the subject of the sentence. *Kiima cha muundo*, grammatical subject. *Kiima mantiki*, logical subject, psychological subject.

kiimbo *n* (*ki-vi*) intonation: *Kielezo cha kiimbo*, intonation pattern. *Kiimbo cha kupanda*, rising intonation. *Kiimbo cha kushuka*, falling intonation.

kiimla *adv* dictatorially: *Walitawala nchi kiimla*, they ruled the country dictatorially.

kiinamizi *n* (*ki-vi*) the portion of meat given to a slaughterer as his reward.

Kiingereza *n* (*ki-vi*) English language: *Anaipenda lugha ya Kiingereza*, he likes the English language.

kiingilio *n* (*ki-vi*) 1. entry fee for special activities e.g. sports, cinema, show, etc.: *Kiingilio katika sinema sasa kimeongezwa*, the entry fee for the cinema has now gone up. 2. entry fee for admission to a club, society, etc.; membership fee, *Kiingilio cha kuwa mwanachama katika klabu yetu huenda kikupunguzwa*, membership fee to our club may be reduced.

kiingizi *n* (*ki-vi*) (*gram*) interjection; an exclamative word or phrase. (cf *kihisishi*)

kiini *n* (*ki-vi*) 1. heart, core, nucleus; stone: *Kiini cha mti*, the heart of a tree. *Kiini cha kokwa*, the core of a seed. 2. essence: *Kiini cha jambo*, the essence of the matter; the gist of the matter. (cf *chanzo*) 3. a three-month pregnancy; foetus. 4. yolk; the yellow, principal substance of an egg.

kiinikizo *n* (*ki-vi*) 1. a heavy load (cf *shehena*) 2. bribe, kickback: *Alifungwa kwa kumpa kiinikizo askari wa polisi*, he was imprisoned for giving a bribe to a policeman. (cf *mrungura*, *hongo*, *rushwa*)

kiinilishe *n* (*ki-vi*) food nutrient.

kiinimacho *n* (*ki-vi*) 1. juggling, optical illusion; magic tricks used by someone for the purpose of deceiving or cheating: *Mchawi aliwadanganya watu kwa kutumia kiinimacho*, the conjurer deceived people by using optical illusion. (cf *mazingaombwe*) 2. (*fig*) camouflage, cover-up, disguise.

kiinitete *n* (*ki-vi*) (*biol*) embryo

kiinitoni *n* (*ki-vi*) (*phonet*) accent

kiinuamgongo *n* (*ki-vi*) 1. money given to a worker due to retirement because of old age, ill-health, etc; pension, gratuity: *Mfanyakazi huyu sasa amepewa kiinuamgongo chake*, this worker has now been given his gratuity. 2. a reward given for good service; tip: *Polisi walimpa kiinuamgongo kwa kufanikiwa kumkamata mwizi*, the police gave him a tip for arresting the thief. (cf *zawadi*, *bahashishi*)

kiitikio *n* (*ki-vi*) refrain; a phrase or verse repeated at intervals in a song or poem, as after each stanza: *Walishiriki kwa shauku katika kiitikio*, they joined enthusiastically in the refrain (cf *kibwagizo*, *kipokeo*, *mkarara*)

kijaa *n* (*ki-vi*) a round machine made from two stones, used for grinding grain; grain grinder.

kijakazi[1] *n* (*ki-vi*) (*zool*) angel fish; a small

brightly coloured tropical marine fish (family *Pomacanthidae*) that lives in shallow coral reef areas. The fish is said to have a compressed body and a small mouth with brist-like, generally tricuspid, teeth.

kijakazi² *n (ki-vi) (bot)* a kind of banana.

kijakazi³ *n (ki-vi)* see *mjakazi*

kijalizo *n (ki-vi)* 1. *(gram)* complement; sth added to complete a whole sentence, etc. In the sentences, *Yeye ni mrefu*, 'he is tall' and *Mimi nimekuwa mwenyekiti*, 'I have become the chairman,' the words *mrefu*, 'tall' and *mwenyekiti* 'chairman' are complements. (cf *kikamilisho, kitimizo, yambwa*) 2. anything added to complete another thing.

kijaluba *n (ki-vi)* casket; a small box or chest, for holding valuables, etc. (cf *kibweta*)

kijambia *n (ki-vi)* a gusset of a shirt or *kanzu*, used to make the garment stronger, etc.

kijana *n (ki-vi)* 1. a young man; adolescent, youth: *Umoja wa vijana*, youth union. 2. adult.

kijani *adj* green: *Amenunua gari la rangi ya kijani*, he has bought a green car.

kijaraha *n (ki-vi)* a small wound. (cf *kidonda*)

kijarida *n (ki-vi)* newsletter

kijasumu *n (ki-vi)* see *bakteria*

kijego *n (ki-vi)* see *kigego*

kijembe¹ *n (ki-vi)* razor

kijembe² *n (ki-vi)* innuendo, sarcasm: *Piga kijembe*, make an unpleasant innuendo to someone. (cf *masengenyo*)

Kijerumani *n (ki-vi)* see *Kidachi*

kijibwa *n (ki-vi)* 1. a small dog. 2. lackey, stooge, puppet: *Yeye alikuwa kijibwa cha wakoloni*, he was a colonialist stooge. 3. *(zool)* antlion. (cf *kifukufuku, kitukutuku*)

kijicho *n (ki-vi)* jealousy, envy, illwill: *Rafiki yako hajaonyesha kijicho kwa wenzake*, your friend has shown no envy towards others. (cf *ngoa, gere, wivu, uhasidi*)

kijiji *n (ki-vi)* 1. village, hamlet. (cf *kitongoji*) 2. socialist village; "ujamaa village."

kijijumba *n (ki-vi)* micro-organism

kijiko *n (ki-vi)* spoon: *Kijiko cha chai*, teaspoon. *Kijiko cha meza*, tablespoon. *Kijiko cha supu*, soup spoon. (cf *kikamshi*)

kijimbi msitu *n (ki-vi) (zool)* a kind of bird (family *Alcedimidae*) with a red bill and bluish-grey back; mangrove kingfisher. *Halcyon senegaloides*.

kijimea *n (ki-vi)* bacteria (cf *baktiria*)

kijimo *n (ki-vi)* dwarf, manikin, midget; a very short person. (cf *kibirikizi, kidurango, mbilikimo*)

kijineno *n (ki-vi)* a puny matter; a childish remark.

kijinga¹ *adv* foolishly, stupidly: *Alifanya mambo yake kijinga*, he conducted his affairs foolishly.

kijinga² *n (ki-vi)* firebrand: *Kijinga cha moto*, a burning stick.

kijingwi *n (ki-vi)* a hoe that remains very small after being used for digging, etc.

kijino *n (ki-vi)* a kind of small fishlike white bait.

kijinsia *adv* sexually: *Mwanamke alidhalilishwa kijinsia*, the woman was sexually molested.

kijisitu *n (ki-vi)* grove; a group of trees without undergrowth.

kijitabu *n (ki-vi)* pamphlet, brochure. (cf *kabrasha*) (Ar)

kijiti *n (ki-vi)* twig, peg; a small stick: *Kijiti cha kibiriti*, matchstick.

kijito *n (ki-vi)* stream, creek, affluent.

kijitu *n (ki-vi)* manikin, dwarf.

kijivu¹ *n (ki-vi)* the handle of a carpenter's drill.

kijivu² (also *kijivujivu*) *adj* grey: *Kanzu ya kijivu*, grey colour dress.

kijivujivu *adj* see *kijivu²*

kijiwe¹ *n (ki-vi)* a small stone.

kijiwe² *n (ki-vi)* pimple, acne: *Uso wake umejaa vijiwe*, his face is full of pimples (cf *chunusi*)

kijogoo¹ *n (ki-vi) (zool)* a kind of fish

(family *Scorpaenidae*) with poisonous fin spines that can cause very painful wounds; stingfish.

kijogoo² *n* (*ki-vi*) 1. valiant; a very brave person: *Mwanajeshi yule ni kijogoo, that soldier is valiant.* (cf *simba, nyamaume*) 2. womanizer.

kijogoo³ *n* (*ki-vi*) (*zool*) a small cock; cockerel. (cf *pora*)

kijogoo⁴ *n* (*ki-vi*) (*zool*) mussel; a kind of bivalve mollusk, often found attached to rocky surfaces or sides of ships. Mussels of this group are technically known as "Mytillidae Mussels." Many of their species are edible. They are generally elongate, oval or triangular, thin and light-weight.

kijongo *n* (*ki-vi*) see *kibyongo*

kijulanga *n* (*ki-vi*) a young man of less than twelve years old; youth: *Kijulanga huyu yuko darasa la sita*, this young man is in standard six. (cf *kijana*)

kijumbamshale *n* (*ki-vi*) (*zool*) swallow; a kind of small swift-flying insect-eating bird (family *Hirundinidae*) having a forked tail and a short bill with wide gape. (cf *saramala, mbayuwayu*)

kijumbe¹ *n* (*ki-vi*) 1. a special secret messenger: *Nilizipata habari zile kwa kijumbe, I got that news from the messenger.* (cf *mjumbe*) 2. a person in charge of arranging marriages for others; matchmaker, marriage broker: *Kijumbe alifanikiwa kumtafutia rafiki yangu mchumba,* the matchmaker succeeded in securing a fiancee for my friend.

kijumbe² *n* (*ki-vi*) a person in charge of blowing a horn in the villages or neighbourhood; bugler. (cf *mpigambiu*)

kijumlisho *n* (*ki-vi*) (*math*) addend; a number or quality to be added to another. (cf *kiongezewa*)

kijungujiko *n* (*ki-vi*) (*econ*) subsistence

kijusi¹ *n* (*ki-vi*) defilement, defloration: *Alifungwa kwa kosa la kijusi*, he was imprisoned for charges of defilement. (cf *unajisi*)

kijusi² *n* (*ki-vi*) bad odour, unpleasant odour; stink: *Ananuka kijusi kwa vile hajaoga kwa siku nyingi*, he has an unpleasant odour because he has not taken a bath for a long time. (cf *kikwapa, ujaka*)

kijusi³ *n* (*ki-vi*) a four-month old pregnancy; foetus. (cf *kilenge*)

kijuujuu *adv* cosmetically, superficially; on the surface: *Aliifanya kazi yangu kijuujuu,* he did my work superficially. (cf *kiholela, ovyoovyo*)

kikaango *n* (*ki-vi*) frying-pan (cf *kaango*)

Kikae *n* (*ki-vi*) 1. one of the Swahili spoken dialects in Makunduchi (Zanzibar South) e.g. *Kikae cha Makunduchi*, Makunduchi dialect. *Kikae cha Tumbatu*, Tumbatu dialect 2. Old Swahili: *Kikae cha Shungwaya*, Old Swahili of Shungwaya.

kikakakaka *adv* hurriedly, quickly, fast: *Alikuja hapa kikakakaka*, he came here hurriedly. (cf *upesi, haraka*)

kikalio *n* (*ki-vi*) anything used to sit on, e.g. stool, chair, praying mat, etc. 2. anything that is put down so that another can be put on top of it.

kikamilisho *n* (*ki-vi*) (*gram*) complement. (cf *kijalizo*)

kikamulio *n* (*ki-vi*) an instrument used to squeeze fruits in order to extract juice; squeezer, juicer: *Alitumia kikamulio kukamua machungwa,* he used a juicer to extract juice from the oranges. (cf *kiminyio*)

kikanda *n* (*ki-vi*) parcel, packet.

kikande *n* (*ki-vi*) (*zool*) triggerfish; any of the brightly coloured tropical fish (family *Balistidae*) having a prominent first dorsal fin with two or three spines.

kikanusho *n* (*ki-vi*) contrapositive

kikanza *n* (*ki-vi*) anything that is used to warm up other things; warmer.

kikao *n* (*ki-vi*) 1. a sitting place for someone e.g. verandah, etc. 2. society, club, mess. (cf *chama*) 3. session; meeting. *Kikao cha dharura*, emergency session.

kikapu *n* (*ki-vi*) a small basket: *Kikapu cha ukindu*, a basket made from the leaves of the wild date palm.

kikaramba *n* (*ki-vi*) a contemptible name given to an ageing person; an old person; dotard.

kikarwe *n* (*ki-vi*) see *karwe*

kikausho *n* (*ki-vi*) 1. anything that is used to dry other things; drier. 2. used in the expression: *Kikausho cha wino*, blotting paper; blotter. (cf *rishafu*)

kikaza (also *kikazo*) *n* (*ki-vi*) a thing like a screw which tightens, strengthens or holds together two things.

kikazio *n* (*ki-vi*) a thing like a screwdriver that is used to tighten; tightener.

kikazo[1] *n* (*ki-vi*) see *kikaza*

kikazo[2] *n* (*ki-vi*) tightening up; strengthening: *Weka kikazo katika mlango*, put sth to tighten the door.

-kike *adj* womanish, femalelike: *Mambo ya kike*, womanish affairs.

kikero *n* (*ki-vi*) a lady's nose ornament; a lady's nose ring or pendant. (cf *hazama*, *kishaufu*)

kiki *n* (*ki-vi*) kick: *Piga kiki mpira*, kick a ball. *Aliachia kiki kali nje ya eneo la adhabu*, he fired a hard shot outside the penalty area. (Eng)

kikiki *adv* firmly, steadfastly: *Funga mlango kikiki*, fasten the door firmly. (cf *imara*, *barabara*)

kikikiki *interj* an expletive of a sound resulting from the shaking of sth.

kikingio *n* (*ki-vi*) anything that protects someone against danger, etc.; shield, bulwark, defence: *Mwanajeshi alikamata kikingio wakati wa vita*, the soldier held a shield during the war.

kikiri *n* (*ki-vi*) pushing and shoving: *Kulikuwa na kikiri nyingi wakati abiria walipokuwa wanajaribu kupanda basi*, there was a lot of pushing and shoving as the passengers tried to board the bus. (cf *kukurukakara*)

kikirik.a *vt* push and shove; jostle one another: *Alikikirika kwenye msongamano wa watu*, he pushed and shoved his way in a crowd. Prep. **kikirik.i.a** St. **kikirik.ik.a** Cs. **kikirik.ish.a** Ps. **kikirik.w.a** Rp. **kikirik.an.a**

kiko[1] *n* (*ki-vi*) 1. tobacco pipe, briar (cf *toza*, *mtemba*) 2. hookah pipe; narghile.

kiko[2] *n* (*ki-vi*) (*anat*) elbow (cf *kisugudi*)

kik.o[3] *cop. v* (of ki-vi class singular noun) is here, is there: *Kitabu chako kiko pale*, your book is there.

kikoa *n* (*ki-vi*) 1. an association of people who work collectively or in turns or each person works on his particular day for the benefit of his colleagues: *Kikoa cha wakulima*, an association of farmers. *Kikoa cha mabaharia*, an association of sailors. 2. a meal eaten in common provided by those who join in it: *Kula kikoa*, have meals in common such that each participant meets the expenses or prepares the meal. 3. a football team. 4. field.

kikocha *n* (*ki-vi*) (*bot*) a bunch of fruits in a branch of a tree. (cf *kocha*)

kikohozi *n* (*ki-vi*) cough.

kikoi *n* (*ki-vi*) a white loin cloth with coloured border in cotton or silk; man's fringed sarong. (cf *shuka*)

kikojozi *n* (*ki-vi*) a person usu a child who wets his bed; bed-wetter (cf *mkojozi*)

kikoko *n* (*ki-vi*) crust of food left in a pot. (cf *kigaga*)

kikokoro[1] *n* (*ki-vi*) hookah pipe; narghille, hubble-bubble. (cf *hoko*, *buruma*)

kikokoro[2] *n* (*ki-vi*) coconut nutlet. (cf *kidaka*)

kikokotoa *n* (*ki-vi*) calculator

kikombe[1] *n* (*ki-vi*) 1. a cup for drinking tea, coffee, etc.: *Kikombe cha kahawa*, coffee cup. *Kikombe cha chai*, tea cup. 2. trophy; a prize usu a silver cup awarded in a sports contest or in other competitions.

kikombe[2] *n* (*ki-vi*) hub; the centre part of a wheel, etc. fastened to the axle or turning on it. (cf *habu*)

kikombe³ *n (ki-vi)* cap insulator.
kikombo¹ *n (ki-vi)* scraper: *Kikombo pembe tatu,* triangular scraper.
kikombo² *n (ki-vi)* anything that has a bend in it; curve, hem, arch, vault. (cf *pindo, tao*)
kikombo³ *adv* in a crooked way, in an irregular way; incomprehensibly: *Maneno ya kikombo,* incomprehensible words.
kikome *n (ki-vi) (bot)* shoot, sprout.
kikomo¹ *n (ki-vi)* 1. end, conclusion: *Maonyesho ya biashara yalifikia kikomo chake jana,* the trade fair came to an end yesterday. (cf *hatima, mwisho*) 2. limit, boundary: *Majirani wamechoka na uhuni wake ambao umefikia kwenye kikomo,* the neighbours are tired of his hooliganism which has reached its limit. (cf *kilele*)
kikomo² *n (ki-vi)* used in the expression: *Kikomo cha uso,* forehead. (cf *kipaji cha uso*)
kikomunisti *adj* communist: *Siasa ya kikomunisti,* communist policy.
kikonde *n (ki-vi) (bot)* a kind of banana.
kikongo *n (ki-vi)* horn
kikongwe *n (ki-vi)* an aged person: *Bibi yule ni kikongwe,* that lady is an old woman. (cf *shaibu, ajuza*)
kikono¹ *n (ki-vi)* used in the following expression: *Kikono cha mlingoti,* masthead. *Kikono cha omo,* the extreme point of the prow. *Kikono cha demani,* the small second rope of a sail.
kikono² *n (ki-vi)* a person with a defective arm; a person with a stump of an arm. (cf *kibwiko*)
kikono³ *n (ki-vi)* living room, lounge. (cf *kipesa, kibesa, sebule*)
kikontena *n (ki-vi)* container; a thing that can hold food, etc (Eng)
kikonyo *n (ki-vi)* stalk, bunch: *Kikonyo cha karafuu,* clove-stalk. *Kikonyo cha ndizi,* a bunch of bananas
kikonzo *adv* for a long time.
kikope *n (ki-vi) (med)* an inflammatory disease of the eye; cellulitis of the eyelid. (cf *chokea*)
kikopesa *n (ki-vi)* a small store of a house, usu used for keeping things; roofed verandah.
kikopo *n (ki-vi) (idm) Mtoto wa kikopo,* ruffian, vagabond, hooligan.
kikopwe *n (ki-vi)* see *kilopwe*
kikora *n (ki-vi)* the stem of the *muwaa* i.e. dwarf palm. (*Hyphaene parvina*)
kikore *n (ki-vi)* a new plantation or garden.
kikorokoro *n (ki-vi)* knick-knack, gimcrack.
kikorombwe *n (ki-vi)* signal cry or call made by blowing into the hands or through the fingers. (cf *kifenenge, kifedenge*)
kikorombwezo *n (ki-vi)* infrastructure (cf *miundombinu*)
kikoromeo *n (ki-vi) (anat)* larynx, thyroid. (cf *kuungo, zoloto, kongomeo*)
kikosi¹ *n (ki-vi)* back of the neck; nape: *Vunja kikosi,* break the nape.
kikosi² *n (ki-vi)* brigade, squad, band, troop, unit: *Kikosi cha wazima moto,* a brigade of firemen. *Kikosi cha mabaharia,* a band of sailors. *Kikosi cha kuzuia fujo,* Field Force Unit (FFU). *Kikosi cha ujenzi,* building brigade. (cf *chaa*)
kikota *n (ki-vi)* a kind of thin flat knife without a point; a tipless knife. (cf *ubamba*)
kikotama (also *kotama*) *n (ki-vi)* a kind of thin, curved broad-bladed knife, used in getting palm wine, etc
kikoto *n (ki-vi)* a kind of whip usu of plaited grass leaf strips or bark fibre. (cf *koto*)
kikotoo *n (ki-vi)* 1. calculator. 2. *Kikotoo elezi,* side rule.
kikotozi *n (ki-vi)* calculator: *kikotozi mezani,* desk calculator.
kikotwe *n (ki-vi) (zool)* a juvenile fish (family *Carangidae*) with a generally silvery body, paler below and which is found in coral and rocky reef areas

in shallow coastal waters; subnose pompano. (cf *kotwe*)

kikowe *n (ki-vi)* (*zool*) a kind of fish belonging to snapper group (*Lutjanidae*) family.

kikuba *n (ki-vi)* a kind of ornament made of aromatic herbs such as jasmine, etc. worn usu around the neck by some women.

kikuchia *n (ki-vi)* see *kigozikucha*

kikuku *n (ki-vi)* 1. armlet, bracelet, anklet; a kind of ornament worn on the arm or leg. (cf *kekee, kipingo, timbi*) 2. stirrup; a ring with a flat bottom hung by a strap from a saddle and used as a foot rest. 3. a holder or handle of a manhole cover, etc.

kikukusi *n (ki-vi)* (*naut*) severe wind that causes things to fall down quickly.

kikuli *n (ki-vi)* fright, horror, dread, fear: *Alishikwa na kikuli alipomwona simba*, he was filled with fear when he saw a lion. (cf *hofu, woga*)

kikumbo *n (ki-vi)* push, shove, jostling: *Mchezaji alipigwa kikumbo karibu na goli*, the player was given a push near the goalpost. (cf *kibega, busa*)

kikunazi *n (ki-vi)* a kind of thick short stick, used for fighting, killing fish, etc.

kikundi *n (ki-vi)* 1. group, band, crowd: *Kikundi cha wanamuziki*, a band of musicians. *Kikundi cha wataalamu*, a group of scholars. *Kikundi cha shinikizi*, pressure group. (cf *kikosi*) 2. (*gram*) group, phrase: *Kikundi husishi*, prepositional group. *Kikundi vumishi*, adjectival group. 3. (*math*) a collection of elements with an associative rule for combination of elements in which the product of any two elements is in the set, every element in the set has an inverse, and a unit (or identity) element is contained in the set; group.

kikundu *n (ki-vi)* (*med*) piles, haemorrhoids. (cf *bawasiri, futuru*)

kikungu *n (ki-vi)* (*naut*) crossbeam (*fundo*) in *mtepe* (a kind of sailing vessel) to which the sheets are fastened.

kikunjajamvi *n (ki-vi)* a communal fee given to local councils in the form of money, etc.

kikuta *n (ki-vi)* 1. a rectangular or circular object. 2. a small wall.

kikuto¹ *n (ki-vi)* (*zool*) spotted hyena; a kind of a large powerfully built hyena with a massive head, large eyes, short rounded ears, and which is entirely spotted. *Crocuta crocuta*.

kikuto² *n (ki-vi)* a thing that has been rolled over; roller: *Kikuto cha mkeka*, a mat that has been rolled over.

kikwakwa *n (ki-vi)* loud laughter.

kikwapa¹ *n (ki-vi)* unpleasant odour of the armpit; unpleasant odour of the underarm; armpit odour. (cf *gugumo, kibeberu*)

kikwapa² armpit hair

kikwapa³ *n (ki-vi)* (*bot*) a sprout in a plant.

kikwara *n (ki-vi)* cock, rooster. (cf *jogoo*)

kikware *n (ki-vi)* see *kware*

kikwaru *n (ki-vi)* 1. cock's spur. 2. (in soccer) a foul by a player at the back; back foul.

kikwata *n (ki-vi)* 1. (*bot*) a much-branched thorny shrub or small tree up to 15 feet tall with leaves, two to four pairs of pinnae and leaflets in pairs, and has white strongly scented flowers. The tree is a good fuel. *Acacia mellifera*. 2. a prickly much-branched tree up to 40 feet tall with recurved spines arranged in threes at the leaf nodes. *Acacia Senegal*.

kikwazo *n (ki-vi)* 1. obstacle, hindrance, impediment, obstruction: *Walimwekea vikwazo ili asipige kura*, they placed obstacles before him so that he could not vote. (cf *kizuizi*) 2. sanction: *Vikwazo vya kiuchumi viliwekewa nchi ya jirani*, economic sanctions were imposed on the neighbouring country. 3. barrier, road-block: *Polisi waliweka vikwazo barabarani ili kuzicheki gari zilizoingia nchini kiholela*, the police put road-blocks on the road to check those vehicles which were entering the country illegally.

kikwekwe (also *kikwikwi*) *n* (*ki-vi*) midget, dwarf; a very short person or thing: *Kikwekwe yule amekuwa kivutio kwa watalii*, that dwarf has become tourists' attraction. (cf *kidunavi, kibushuti*)

kikwemo *n* (*ki-vi*) a hoarse sound like that of a patient suffering from asthma; wheeze. (cf *mkwemo*)

kikweukweu *n* (*ki-vi*) (also *kikwifukwifu*) sobbing; weeping aloud with a catch or break in the voice and short gasping breaths: *Mtoto alishikwa na kikweukweu alipopigwa na mwalimu*, the child began sobbing when he was beaten by the teacher.

kikwezeo *n* (*ki-vi*) dais

kikwezo *n* (*ki-vi*) land stage.

kikwi¹ *n* (*n*) one thousand. (cf *elfu*)

kikwi² *adj* numerous, many: *Niliwaona watu kikwi kwenye mazishi*, I saw numerous people at the funeral.

kikwi³ *n* (*ki-vi*) a kind of a small breed made of rice.

kila¹ *adj* (used of singular nouns only) every, each: *Kila siku*, every day. *Kila uchao*, every new dawning. *Kila kukicha*, every day, day by day. *Kila binadamu anakosa*, every human being errs. (Ar)

kila² *adv* whenever, wherever: *Kila nikimwona, ananikwepa*, whenever I see him, he avoids me. *Kila aendako anakutana na watu wengi asiowajua*, wherever he goes, he meets people whom he doesn't know. (Ar)

kilabu *n* (*ki-vi*) club, association. (Eng)

kilachi (also *klachi*) *n* (*ki-vi*) clutch: *Kilachipewa*, centrifugal clutch. (Eng)

kilainisho *n* (*ki-vi*) 1. lubricant. 2. (*phon*) liquid sound i.e. [l] and [r]. (cf *kimiminiko*)

kilaji *n* (*ki-vi*) 1. food. 2. anything that eats, corrodes, etc. (Ar)

kilalanungu *n* (*ki-vi*) (*bot*) a perennial herb with creeping stems, cordate ever-green leaves and white flower spathes, growing on the floor of evergreen forests at low altitudes. *Callopsis volkensii.*

kilalio *n* (*ki-vi*) 1. dinner. (cf *chajio*) 2. bedding; matresses, bed clothes, etc.

kilalo *n* (*ki-vi*) left-overs; food left over from the previous evening until the next day (cf *kiporo, mwiku, uporo*)

Kilatini *n* (*ki-vi*) Latin (Eng)

kile *adj*, *pron* (used with ki-vi class nouns) that: *Kitabu kile*, that book. *Kile kiko mbali*, that is far.

kilegesambwa *n* (*ki-vi*) (*anat*) kneecap; patella. (cf *pia ya goti*)

kileja *n* (*ki-vi*) a kind of sweet meat made from wheat flour or rice mixed with sugar and other ingredients.

kilele *n* (*ki-vi*) 1. peak, summit: *Alifika kwenye kilele cha mlima*, he reached the peak of the mountain. 2. (*fig*) climax, acme: *Sherehe za harusi zilifikia kilele chake jana*, the wedding celebrations reached their climax yesterday. 3. (*phon*) *Kilele cha msikiko*, peak of prominence.

kilelecha (also *kileleta*) *n* (*ki-vi*) the topmost part of the summit: *Hakuweza kufika kwenye kilelecha alipokuwa anaupanda mlima*, he could not reach the topmost part of the summit when he was climbing the mountain.

kileleta *n* (*ki-vi*) see *kilelecha*

kilema *n* (*ki-vi*) 1. lameness, maim; physical deformity: *Ana kilema cha mguu*, he has a crippled leg. 2. a lamed person: *Yeye hawezi kutembea vizuri kwa vile ni kilema*, he can't walk properly because he is lame. (*prov*) *Achekaye kilema hafi hakijamfikia*, he who laughs at a cripple will not die before being crippled. Do not laugh those who are passing through misfortunes.

kilemba *n* (*ki-vi*) turban: *Piga kilemba*, wear a turban. *Vaa kilemba*, wear a turban. *Vunja kilemba*, take off a turban. 2. cock's comb; crest (cf *unju, shungi*) 3. (*fig*) gratuity at the end of a job, apprenticeship, course of teaching, etc. 4. fee given to the uncles of the wife during wedding. 5. bribe, kickback, key money i.e. additional money to the rent and usual charges, sometimes demanded before a person is allowed to occupy a flat or a house. (cf *mrungura*) 6. (*idm*) *Kilemba cha ukoka*, flattery.

kilemba

kilembwe[1] *n* (*ki-vi*) nipples of a breast; teat, tit. (cf *nyato, chuchu*)

kilembwe[2] *n* (*ki-vi*) the season of fruits.

kilembwe[3] *n* (*ki-vi*) great-great-grandchild. (cf *kirembwe*)

kilembwe[4] *n* (ki-vi) (*bot*) a piece of coconut palm leaf used to weave a large basket of palm fronds. (cf *pogoo*)

kilembwekeza *n* (*ki-vi*) the child of a great great-grandchild. (cf *kinying'inya*)

kilemeanembo *n* (*ki-vi*) (*bot*) an erect of scandent shrub with dark green oval opposite evergreen leaves and clusters of small white flowers in the axils of the leaves. *Cremaspora africana.*

kilendo *n* (*ki-vi*) (*zool*) a kind of fish.

kilenge[1] *n* (*ki-vi*) a four-month old pregnancy; foetus. (cf *kijusi*)

kilenge[2] *n* (*ki-vi*) children's game played by throwing pieces of sticks.

kileo[1] *n* (*ki-vi*) intoxicant, liquor. (cf *ulevi*)

kileo[2] *n* (*ki-vi*) 1. anything that motivates someone because of being used to it. 2. anxiety of sth.

kilete (also *kileti*[1]) *n* (*ki-vi*) 1. (*naut*) strut in the outrigger of *ngalawa*, a small canoe (cf *mbera*) 2. (*naut*) thole pin; a pin, typically one of a pair, fitted to the gunwale of a rowing boat and on which an oar pivots.

kileti[1] *n* (*ki-vi*) see *kilete*

kileti[2] *n* (*ki-vi*) (*naut*) a hole in the gunwale of a vessel such as a boat so as to keep the loop of the rope, used as a rowlock. (cf *shalaka*)

kilifi *n* (*ki-vi*) (*naut*) deep waters in the sense of safe anchorage. (cf *kilindi, kina*)

kilihafu (also *kisafu*) *n* (*ki-vi*) the first stomach of an animal; maw, paunch, rumen. (cf *kisahafu*)

kilili *n* (*ki-vi*) 1. a bedstead for carrying a person high up: *Harusi ya kilili*, the marriage whereby a bridegroom is carried on a bedstead during honeymoon days. 2. pulpit: *Alisimama kwenye kilili alipokuwa anahutubia,* he stood on the pulpit when he was preaching. (cf *mimbari, kijukwaa*)

kilima *n* (*ki-vi*) 1. hill: *Kilima kikali,* steep hill. 2. mound, knoll, hummock, monticule.

kilimbikizi *n* (*ki-vi*) anything that accomodates something else: **kilimbikizi umeme,** accumulator; a large rechargable electric cell.

kilimbili *n* (*ki-vi*) (*anat*) elbow (cf *kiwiko*)

kilimbilimbi *n* (*ki-vi*) (*anat*) part of the arm between the hand and the arm; forearm. (cf *kigasha*)

kilimbo *n* (*ki-vi*) hill (cf *kilima*)

kilimi[1] *n* (*ki-vi*) uvula (cf *kidakatonge, kimio*)

kilimi[2] *n* (*ki-vi*) a thin strip of some flexible substance as cane, placed against the opening of the mouthpiece of certain wind instruments, as the clarinet; reed. (cf *nari, mtapi*)

kilimia *n* (*ki-vi*) (*astron*) the Pleiades; a cluster of stars in the constellation system.

kilimilimi *n* (*ki-vi*) 1. gossiping, tale-bearing, rumour-mongering: *Watu watasitasita kukupa siri zao kwa* *sababu ya tabia yako ya kilimilimi*, people will hesitate telling you their secrets because of your rumour-mongering behaviour. (cf *udaku, umbeya*) 2. gossiper, rumour-monger, busybody, eavesdropper: *Mbona kilimilimi yule anayaingilia mambo ya watu wengine?* Why is that gossiper meddling in other people's affairs? (cf *mdaku, mbeya*)

kilimo *n (ki-vi)* 1. agriculture, farming: *Kilimo bora*, good crop husbandry. *Kilimo cha mchanganyiko*, intercropping. *Kilimo cha mseto*, agroforestry; mixed farming. *Kilimo shadidi*, intensive farming. *Kilimo endelezi*, sustainable agriculture. *Kilimo hai*, organic farming. *Kilimo cha umwagiliaji*, farming by irrigation. (cf *zaraa*) 2. crop production: *Kilimo cha pamba*, cotton production. *Kilimo cha nazi*, coconut production. 3. farming season: *Kilimo cha mwaka*, annual farming. *Kilimo cha kufa na kupona*, farming as a matter of life and death introduced in 1974 by former President of Tanzania, Dr. Julius K. Nyerere.

kilindachozi *n (ki-vi) (bot)* a cluster of flowers at the tip of a banana bunch.

kilindaua *n (ki-vi) (bot)* bract; a modified leaf, growing at the base of a flower or on its stalk.

kilindi *n (ki-vi)* deep waters, deep channel; deep: *Watu wengi walifariki kwenye kilindi kile wakati meli ilipozama*, many people died in those deep waters when the ship sank (cf *shumbi, kilifi, kina*)

kilindo[1] *n (ki-vi)* 1. a container made from the bark of a tree, used for keeping things e.g. tobacco. 2. a container made from skin, used for keeping honey.

kilindo[2] *n (ki-vi)* 1. guarding of crops against dangerous animals. 2. vigilance; the state, action, etc. of keeping careful watch.

kilinge *n (ki-vi)* 1. a traditional place where spirits are exorcised in order to treat the clients. 2. a place for dancing, playing cards, etc. 3. an undesirable decision; indecisiveness. (cf *kitendawili*)

kilingo[1] *n (ki-vi)* see *ulingo*

kilingo[2] *n (ki-vi)* a garment sent to a tailor in order to make another one of similar measurements for someone; pattern, model, sample: *Kilingo cha shati*, a model for a shirt. *Kilingo cha suruali*, a model for a pair of trousers. (cf *cheo, kipimo*)

kilinzi *n (ki-vi)* a strap of beads capable of being worn round the wrist.

kilio *n (ki-vi)* 1. cry, shout, scream: *Kilio cha mbwa*, dog's cry; bark. 2. crying, weeping; act (method, etc) of crying, weeping, etc. *Kilio chake kilitushtua*, her crying startled us. 3. funeral: *Palikuwa na kilio kwenye nyumba ya jirani*, there was a funeral in the neighbour's house. (*prov*) *Kwa mwoga kwenda kicheko, kwa shujaa kwenda kilio*, to a coward is laughter but to a valiant is a cry i.e. those who are cowards and don't go to the war front are not killed and that brings happiness and laughter to their families but the valiants who go to the front and get killed suffer tragedy. 4. (*fig*) cry, voice, aspiration: *Kilio cha wananchi kiliishtua serikali*, the voice of the people shocked the government.

kilo[1] *n (ki-vi)* a weight of 1000 grams.

kilo[2] *n (ki-vi)* a person who doesn't understand properly how to operate a motor machine.

kiloaka *n (ki-vi)* (also *kiloaka*) (*zool*) cloaca; the cavity into which both the intestinal and genitourinary tracts empty in reptiles, birds, amphibians and many fishes. (Eng)

kilogramu *n (n)* kilogram: *Kilogramu moja ya mchele*, one kilogram of rice (Eng)

kilolita *n* (*n*) kilolitre
kilometa *n* (*n*) (also *kilomita*) kilometre: *Yale ni masafa ya kilometa kumi*, that is the distance of ten kilometres. *Kilometa za mraba*, square kilometres. (Eng)
kilomita *n* (*n*) see *kilometa*
kiloo *n* (*ki-vi*) hardcore; a rough character, a hard character; a person who is able to endure hardships, etc. *Kiloo kama yeye anaweza kuvumilia matatizo mengi*, a hard character like him can endure many hardships. (cf *sugu*, *kuduku*)
kilopwe *n* (*ki-vi*) (also *kikopwe*) (*bot*) an annual herb with twining or trailing stem, heart-shaped leaves and dense heads of blue flowers. *Jacquemontia capitata*.
kilosaiko *n* (*n*) kilocycle, kilohertz; one thousand hertz. (Eng)
kilotazi *n* (*n*) kilobytes (Eng)
kilotia *n* (*n*) see *kidotia*
kilovolti *n* (*n*) kilovolt (Eng)
kilowati *n* (*n*) kilowatt: *Kilowati saa*, kilowatt hour. (Eng)
kilua[1] *n* (*ki-vi*) (*bot*) a kind of sweet scented, yellow and crimson flower from the *Anuonaceae* family, used for making garlands, etc.
kilua[2] *n* (*ki-vi*) a kind of traditional dance performed by women who decorate themselves on their faces.
kiludhu *n* (*ki-vi*) a rich fabric of silk, rayon, nylon, etc. with a soft, thick pile; velvet. (cf *mahameli*)
kilumwe *n* (*n*) (*med*) high blood pressure; hypertension: *Ana ugonjwa wa kilumwe*, he has high blood pressure.
kiluwiluwi[1] *n* (*ki-vi*) 1. (*zool*) larva or maggot; the growth stage of a fly, mosquito or an insect which undergoes "complete metamorphosis." Larva hatches from an insect egg and changes into a pupa from which an adult emerges. 2. tadpole; the larva of certain amphibians, as frogs and toads.

kiluwiluwi[2] *n* (*ki-vi*) (*zool*) plover; a kind of small or medium-sized wading bird (family *Charadriidae*) having a thick-looking neck, a short tail and long, painted wings.
kiluwiri *n* (*ki-vi*) (*zool*) land rail, corn crake; a duck-like fresh water bird of the (family *Rallidae*)
kima[1] *n* (*n*) (*zool*) monkey
kima[2] *n* (*ki-vi*) rate, price, amount, value: *Kima cha chini*, minimum rate. *Kima cha juu*, maximum rate. *Kima cha vifo*, mortality rate. *Kima cha chini cha mshahara*, minimum wage.
kima[3] *n* (*n*) mincemeat, mincesauce: *Mchuzi wa kima*, gravy made from mincemeat.
kimachomacho *adv* openly, vividly, plainly: *Aliniibia kimachomacho*, he stole from me openly. (cf *waziwazi*, *bayana*)
kimada *n* (*ki-vi*) mistress, odalisque, concubine: *Weka/Wekwa kimada*, cohabit. (cf *hawara*)
kimagamaga *adv* astride, astraddle: *Alikwenda kimagamaga*, he walked astride.
kimagendo *adv* illegally, illicitly: *Alishtakiwa kwa kuingiza bidhaa kimagendo*, he was sued for importing goods illegally.
kimako *n* (*ki-vi*) astonishment, surprise: *Alitutia sote kimako kwa kuvaa nguo za kike*, he filled us with astonishment by wearing woman's clothes. (cf *mshangao*, *buta*)
kimakosa *adv* by mistake: *Alifukuzwa kazini kimakosa*, he was sacked from work by mistake.
kimanda[1] *n* (*ki-vi*) (also *kiwanda*) omelette; Spanish omelette.
kimanda[2] *n* (*ki-vi*) a spot of dirt on a piece of cloth.
kimanda[3] *n* (*ki-vi*) an oath or trial in which the parties are given bread to eat, the guilty person is considered not to be able to swallow the bread.

kimangare *n (ki-vi)* a kind of weapon like a club used usually by African tribes like Maasais, etc. (cf *kirungu*)

kimangari *n (ki-vi)* (also *kimanjari*) 1. (*bot*) an annual or perennial herb with rose coloured flowers, parasitic on the roots of grasses. *Ramphicarpa veronicaefolia*. 2. a perennial herb up to 4 feet tall with much-branched corymbs of very small purple daisy-like flowers. *Ethulia conyzoides*.

kimanzi *n (ki-vi)* beauty; a beautiful woman: *Wavulana wengi wamevutika na kimanzi yule*, many boys are attracted to that beautiful woman. (cf *kisura, kibamba*)

kimao *n (ki-vi)* see *kimau*

kimasomaso¹ *n (n)* used in the expression: *Kujitoa kimasomaso*, conceal oneself so as to look innocent because of the unusual things one has done e.g. *Alijitoa kimasomaso alipohisi kwamba maovu yake yamegunduliwa*, he pretended to be innocent when he felt that his evil deeds were discovered.

kimasomaso² *n (ki-vi)* a person with an evil or jealous eye: *Kimasomaso yule hatapendelea wewe upate*, that jealous person will not like to see you get something. (cf *hasidi*)

kimatu *n (ki-vi)* (also *mutumutu*) (*zool*) a young locust belonging to family *Acrididae*. When it is a few years old, the locust gathers in bands and begins to move in swarms feeding in plants belonging to the grass family. (cf *tunutu*)

kimau *n (ki-vi)* (also *kimao*) a tunic without collar or nape.

kimavi cha kuku *n (ki-vi)* (*bot*) a perennial weed with opposite leaves and heads of mauve daisy-like flowers.

kimba¹ *n (ma-)* corpse, dead body: *Hicho ni kimba cha binadamu*, that is a dead human body.

kimba² *n (ma-)* a lump of tard of a human being or animal; a heap of dung of a human being or animal; faeces, excrement. (cf *mavi, kinyesi*)

kimba³ *n (ki-vi)* see *gimba*

kimbaombao¹ *n (ki-vi)* see *kimbaumbau¹*

kimbaombao² *n (ki-vi)* see *kimbaumbau²*

kimbaumbau¹ *n (ki-vi)* (also *kimbaombao*) a very slim tall person.

kimbaumbau² *n (ki-vi)* (also *kimbaombao*) weathercock, chameleon; a fickle person; a person who is not stable in his decisions, etc.: *Mbona unamwamini kimbaumbau yule?* Why do you trust that chameleon? (cf *kigeugeu*)

kimbelembele *n (n)* 1. busybody, meddler: *Kimbelembele yule amejiingiza katika shughuli zote za shule*, that busybody has interfered in all the school's activities. 2. meddlesomeness; the act of meddling in other people's affairs: *Majirani hawampendi kwa sababu ya tabia yake ya kimbelembele*, the neighbours don't like him because of his meddlesome behaviour. (cf *ushawishi*)

kimbi.a *vt, vi* 1. run, sprint: *Mwanariadha alikimbia vizuri*, the athlete ran well. 2. get rid of someone; avoid, avert: *Anajaribu kunikimbia*, he is trying to avoid me. Prep. **kimbi.li.a** St. **kimbi.lik.a** Cs. **kimbi.za** Ps. **kimbi.w.a** Rp. **kimbi.an.a**

kimbili.a *vt* 1. run after sby/sth: *Alimkimbilia yule kijana aliyesahau saa yake*, he ran after the young man who forgot his watch. 2. seek refuge: *Mwanasiasa alikimbilia ubalozini*, the politician sought refuge in the embassy. St. **kimbil.ik.a** Ps. **kimbil.iw.a** Rp. of Prep. **kimbil.i.an.a**

kimbilio *n (ki-vi)* a place of refuge or protection; sanctuary, hide out: *Kimbilio la hifadhi ya kisiasa*, political asylum. *Muuaji alikwenda kwenye kimbilio lake baada ya kuua*, the murderer went to his hide-out after committing murder. (cf *mafichoni*)

kimbimbi *n (ki-vi)* goose-flesh, goose pimples; a roughened condition of the skin in which the papillae are erected, caused by cold, fear, etc (cf *unyenyefu, mtambalio*)

kimbiz.a vt 1. send sby hurriedly to a place: *Majirani walimkimbiza mjamzito hospitalini*, the neighbours rushed a pregnant woman to hospital. 2. chase, pursue, fly after: *Polisi walilikimbiza gari la wahalifu*, the police chased after the criminal's car. 3. make sth run faster: *Dereva alilikimbiza gari letu*, the driver was driving our car very fast. Prep. **kimbiz.i.a** St. **kimbiz.ik.a** Ps. **kimbiz.w.a** Rp. **kimbiz.an.a**, run for dear life e.g. *Wanawake walikimbizana moto uliporipuka*, the women ran for dear life when fire broke out.

kimboya n (ki-vi) a kind of dish made from a ground mixture of cassava and greengrams or peas.

kimbu n (ki-vi) valley (cf *bonde*)

kimbunga n (ki-vi) cyclone, typhoon, hurricane, whirlwind: *Kimbunga kilipotokea kisiwani, watu wengi wakafariki*, when the cyclone occurred in the island, many people died. (cf *tufani*)

kimbugimbugi n (ki-vi) (bot) crow feet grass; an annual or short-lived perennial grass up to 1 foot tall, much liked by stock and its small seeds are eaten in time of famine. *Dactyloctenium aegyptium*.

kimburu n (ki-vi) (zool) a wild cat of the size and features of a domestic cat with a proportionately long tail and indistinct dark vertical stripes and spots; wild cat. *Felis libyca*.

kimburu

kimchango n (ki-vi) (zool) mite

kimchezo adv in form: *Mchezaji hakuwa katika hali nzuri kimchezo*, the player was not in good form.

kimea n (ki-vi) (bot) 1. malt grain sprout. 2. any plant growing on water or very wet earth.

kimeamaji n (ki-vi) (bot) any plant growing on water or very wet earth.

kimelea n (ki-vi) 1. (bot) plant parasite; plant fungus. 2. (fig) a person depending upon others for livelihood, etc.; parasite: *Usiwe kimelea katika jamii yako*, don't be a parasite in your society.

kimeng'enya n (ki-vi) (chem) enzyme

kimeng'enyawanga n (ki-vi) (biol, chem) amylase; an enzeme that helps change starch into sugar; it is found in saliva, panecratic juice, etc.

kimeng'enyenza n (ki-vi) (chem) coenzyme

kimenomeno[1] n (n) (med) pyorrhoea; an infection of the gums and tooth sockets, characterized by the formation of pus, etc. (cf *hijabu, kiseyeye*)

kimenomeno[2] adv with great difficulties.

kimeta n (ki-vi) (vet) anthrax; an infectious disease of wild and domesticated animals esp cattle and sheep.

kimetameta n (ki-vi) (also *kimetemete*) (zool) firefly, glow-worm; these are beetles of the *Lampyridae* family and are named for the brilliant light they produce. Larvae of the glow-worms and fireflies feed mainly on snails and slugs. The adults take little or no food at all (cf *kimulimuli*)

kimete n (ki-vi) see *kimeto*

kimetemete n (ki-vi) see *kimetameta*

kimeto (also *kimete*) n (ki-vi) anything that sparkles, glitters, etc. *Kimeto cha jua*, the sparkling radiance of sun. *Kimeto cha upanga*, the glitter of the sword.

kimia n (ki-vi) 1. a casting net. 2. a cloth

made by netting; lace work.
kimiminiko *n* (*ki-vi*) lateral sound. (cf *kilainisho*)
kimiani *adv* (of sports) in the net: *Mchezaji aliweka bao kimiani kwa ufundi*, the player put the ball in the net skilfully.
kimio *n* (*ki-vi*) 1. (*anat*) uvula (cf *kilimi*, *kidakatonge*) 2. epiglottis.
kimo¹ *n* (*ki-vi*) height: *Kimo cha mtu*, a person's height. *Kimo hanamu*, slant height. *Ana kimo kirefu*, he is tall. (cf *badani*)
kimo² *n* (*ki-vi*) the front or back piece of a *kanzu*, men's long robe.
kim.o³ *cop.v* (of ki-vi class singular nouns) is in, is inside: *Kitabu kimo kwenye mtoto wa meza*, the book is in the drawer.
kimombo *n* (*n*) see *Kiingereza*
kimondo¹ *n* (*ki-vi*) (also *kimwomdo*) shooting star, meteor, falling star; bolide.
kimondo² *n* (*ki-vi*) simpleton, imbecile, idiot, fool: *Kimondo yule haelewi chochote darasani*, that idiot does not understand anything in the class. (cf *mjinga*, *juha*)
kimondo³ *n* (*ki-vi*) pandemonium, chaos, confusion, disorder: *Kimondo kilitokea wakati abiria alipompiga ngumi kondakta*, confusion broke out when a passenger punched the conductor. (cf *ghasia*, *fujo*)
kimono *n* (*ki-vi*) a kind of woman's garment originating from Japan.
kimori *n* (*ki-vi*) apron; a garment of cloth, leather, etc. worn over the front part of the body, used usu to protect one's clothes. (Kich)
kimota *n* (*ki-vi*) the spark of a fire. (cf *kiali*)
kimoyomoyo *adv* by heart, in the heart; quietly: *Alilisoma shairi kimoyomoyo*, he read the poem quietly. *Aliwaza kimoyomoyo jinsi ya kumshinda adui*, he pondered quietly how to overcome the enemy.

Kimrima *n* (*ki-vi*) the Swahili dialect spoken in the Mainland, Dar es Salaam and coastal regions.
kimshazari *adv* diagonally: *Aliupita uwanja kimshazari*, he crossed the ground diagonally.
kimsingi *adv* primarily, basically; in principle: *Kimsingi*, *wazo lako limekubaliwa*, in principle, your suggestion has been accepted.
Kimtang'ata *n* (*ki-vi*) a southern Swahili dialect spoken along a twenty kilometre stretch South of Tanzania, that is around Tanga.
kim.u¹ *vt* (in Islam) recite a shortened version of the muezzin's call to prayer just before the prayers: *Kimu sala*, recite in this manner. Prep. **kim.i.a** St. **kim.ik.u** Cs. **kim.ish.a** Ps or Prep. **kim.iw.a** Rp. of Prep. **kim.i.an.a** (Ar)
kim.u² *vt* supply food, clothing, etc; look after, maintain, provide: *Anamkimu mkewe vizuri*, he looks after his wife well. Prep. **kim.i.a** St. **kim.ik.a** Cs. **kim.ish.a** Ps. of Prep. **kim.iw.a** Rp. of Prep. **kim.i.an.a** (Ar)
kim.u³ *vt* erect, build.
kimuhemuhe *n* (*ki-vi*) restlessness, fret, worry, anxiety: *Kimuhemuhe kilianza kati ya timu mbili kablu ya mechi kuanza*, a state of anxiety began between the two teams before the match.(cf. *kiherehere*, *wasiwasi*)
kimulimuli *n* (*ki-vi*) 1. (*zool*) firefly, glow-worm. (cf *kimetameta*) 2. flash: *Kimulimuli cha radi*, a flash of lightning. 3. vehicle flasher. 4. siren of a police vehicle or ambulance.
kimungu *n* (*ki-vi*) see *kivunjajungu*
kimuyemuye *n* (*ki-vi*) anxiety, worry, trouble, uneasiness: *Ana kimuyemuye kikubwa cha mtihani wake unaokuja*, he has a lot of anxiety over his forthcoming examination. *Ona kimuyemuye*, have anxiety; get worried. (cf *wahaka*, *wasiwasi*)

Kimvita n (ki-vi) a northern dialect of Swahili spoken in Mombasa.

kimw.a vt 1. be tired of doing the same thing again and again; become weary: *Amekimwa na kula chakula hicho hicho kila siku*, he is tired of eating the same food again and again everyday. 2. be in the habit of getting annoyed if asked to do sth.

kimwana n (ki-vi) darling, beloved.

kimweko n (ki-vi) anxiety

kimwondo n (ki-vi) see *kimondo*[1]

kimya[1] n (n) quietness, silence, stillness: (prov) *Kimya kingi kina mshindo mkuu*, much silence has a mighty noise i.e. silence is a powerful weapon. (cf *utulivu, ushwari*)

kimya[2] adv silently, quietly: *Kaa kimya*, remain silent. (cf *baridi, shuwari*)

kimya[3] adj quiet, calm: *Mtoto mkimya*, a quiet child.

kina[1] adj used to refer to a group of similar category, etc.: *Kina mama*, womenfolk. *Kina yahe*, the common people.

kina[2] n (ki-vi) (poet) rhyme: *Mshairi alitumia vina tofauti*, the poet used different rhymes. (cf *mizani*)

kina[3] n (ki-vi) depth: *Kina cha bahari*, a deep place in the sea. *Wanasiasa walilizingatia suala la uchafuzi wa mazingira kwa kina*, the politicians examined the issue of environmental pollution in depth.

kin.a[4] verb form (of ki-vi class singular nouns) it has: *Kikombe hiki kina mkono mrefu*, this cup has a long handle.

kinaa n (ki-vi) satisfaction, satiety, content: *Yeye ni kijana mwenye kinaa*, he is a young man who is contented. (cf *utoshelevu*)

kinaganaga adv see *kinagaubaga*

kinagaubaga (also *kinaganaga*) adv 1. openly, plainly, clearly: *Mfungwa alieleza kinagaubaga masaibu yaliyomkuta gerezani*, the prisoner described openly the hardships he met in prison. (cf *waziwazi*) 2. personally: *Eleza kinagaubaga*, explain personally. *Sema kinagaubaga*, speak personally.

kinagiri n (ki-vi) an ornament usu of gold like a large bead bored through the middle and worn on a chain.

kina.i vt, vi 1. be satiated, be contented, be self-satisfied: *Nimemkinai rafiki yangu*, I am content with my friend i.e. I have complete faith in him. (cf *tosheka*) 2. (of food, etc.) be disgusted, be surfeited, have loathing: *Amekinai chakula anachopewa kila siku*, he is disgusted with the food he is given everyday. Prep. **kina.i.a** St. **kina.ik.a** Cs. **kina.ish.a** Ps. of Prep. **kina.iw.a** Rp. of Prep. **kina.i.an.a** (Ar)

-kinaifu adj contented, self-satisfied, satiated, gratified: *Mtu mkinaifu*, a contented person. (Ar)

kinaish.a vi cloy, satiate: *Chakula kile kimenikinaisha*, that food has cloyed me. Prep. **kinaish.i.a** St. **kinaishik.a** Ps. **kinaish.iw.a**

kinamasi[1] n (ki-vi) 1. sludge, mucilage, slime; slimy substance or fluid: *Meza ile ilikuwa na kinamasi*, that table had slime on it. 2. marsh, bog, morass; wet slippery oil: *Mbuga yenye kinamasi*, murshy park.

kinamasi[2] n (ki-vi) shame, disgrace. (cf *aibu, fedheha*)

kinamo[1] adj flexible, pliable: *Mti wa kinamo*, a pliable tree or stick.

kinamo[2] n (ki-vi) flexibility, pliability, plasticity.

kinamu n (ki-vi) clay: *Kinamujoto*, fire clay; a type of clay that is able to withstand intense heat.

kinana n (ki-vi) (bot) a kind of yam.

kinanasi n (ki-vi) (bot) a perennial herb with grass-like leaves. *Anthericum sp.*

kinanda n (ki-vi) 1. (mus) a kind of musical instrument such as banjo or guitar: *Kinanda cha mdomo*, mouth organ. *Kinanda cha msumeno*, a musical instrument whose ends resemble the ends of a cutting saw. *Kinanda cha mkono,* harmonica. 2. gramophone.

kinara[1] *n (ki-vi)* candlestick (Hind)

kinara[2] *n (ki-vi)* embroidery worked in silk around the neck of a robe or garment i.e. the collar of a *kanzu.* (Hind)

kinara[3] *n (ki-vi) (arch)* 1. chairman, leader. (cf *kiongozi)* 2. (esp in sports) leader in a competition, etc.: *Vinara wa ligi kuu,* leaders in the premier league.

kinara[4] *n (ki-vi)* a place like a hut used for addressing a public meeting or for holding "Maulidi" celebrations i.e. celebrations marking the birthday of Prophet Muhammad; scaffold, stage.

kinasaba *adj* ancestral, genealogical.

kinasasauti *n (ki-vi)* tape recorder. (cf *tepurekoda)*

kinaya[1] *n (ki-vi)* insolence, pride, arrogance: *Unafanya hivyo kwa kinaya tu,* you are only doing that out of arrogance. (cf *kiburi)*

kinaya[2] *n (ki-vi)* provocation, joke, fun, mockery, ridicule: *Unamfanyia kinaya rafiki yako burebure,* you are ridiculing your friend for nothing (cf *inadi, stihizai)* (Ar)

kinaya[3] *n (ki-vi)* match, equivalent, equal: *Bila kinaya,* without a match; matchless, incomparable. (cf *mfano)*

kinda[1] *n (ma-)* 1. *(zool)* chick: *Kinda la ndege,* a young bird. *Kinda la farasi,* foal. (cf *mwanafarasi)* 2. a young tree: *Mnazi mkinda,* a young coconut tree. 3. a young man; adolescent, youth. *Kinda yule anapenda kuvaa nguo nzuri,* that young man likes to wear good clothes. (cf *kijana, ghulamu, barubaru)*

kind.a[2] *vt* see *kinza*

kindakindaki[1] *adj* 1. genuine, proper, original, pure. 2. aristocratic; of noble birth: *Yeye ni mwanakijiji kindakindaki,* he is a villager of noble birth.

kindakindaki[2] *adv* up in the air, high up; aloft: *Alibebwa kindakindaki,* he was carried shoulder high. (cf *juujuu)*

kindani *n (ki-vi)* the inside part of a fruit beginning to ripen. 2. ill feeling, bitterness, resentment, umbrage. (cf *chuki)*

kindanindani *adv* secretly, covertly, privately: *Alioa kindanindani,* he got married secretly. (cf *kisirisiri)*

kindengereka *n (ki-vi)* an insignificant thing; thingamajig, thingummy, trash. (cf *kinyangarika, kidubwana)*

kindi *n (n) (zool)* tree squirrel; tree-dwelling rodent (family *Sciuridae)* with heavy fur and a long, bushy tail. Red-legged sun-squirrel. *Heliosciurus rufobrachium.*

kindi

kindumbwendumbwe *n (n)* 1. apprehension, worry, anxiety, uneasiness, nervousness: *Mgonjwa aliingia katika kindumbwendumbwe baada ya kusikia kwamba atafanyiwa operesheni,* the patient suffered nervousness after learning that she would be operated on. (cf *wahaka, wasiwasi)* 2. a drama performed upon a child who has wetted the bed by covering with the clothes and the mat he has wetted, and then soiling his face with charcoal whilst booing songs are sung against him. 3. sports contest. (cf *pambano, mtanange, kipute)*

kinega *n (ki-vi) (zool)* bee-eater; a medium-sized slim bird of brilliant plumage. (cf *kiogajivu)*

kinegwa n (ki-vi) (zool) martin; a kind of bird of the swallow family having a short bill with a wide gape.

kinegwe n (ki-vi) 1. (zool) a young shark. 2. small dried sharks.

kinembe n (ki-vi) (anat) clitoris (cf kisimi)

kinena n (ki-vi) (anat) pubic region; pubis; mons-veneris

king.a[1] vt, vi 1. protect, defend, shield, prevent: *Mwanajeshi alijikinga na hujuma*, the soldier defended himself from an attack. 2. trap rain water, etc. in a vessel: *Aliyakinga maji ya mvua kwenye ndoo*, he trapped the rainwater in the bucket. Prep. **king.i.a** St. **king.ik.a** Cs. **king.ish.a** and **king.iz.a** Ps. **king.w.a** Rp. **king.an.a**

kinga[2] n (n) defence, protection, shield, prevention: *Ile ni dawa ya kinga*, that is a preventive medicine.

kinga[3] n (n) immunity: *Kinga ya kidiplomasia*, diplomatic immunity. *Kinga ya kujipatia*, acquired immunity. *Kinga fufumavu mnemba*, passive artificial immunity. *Chanjo ya kinga*, innoculation. *Kinga mnemba amilifu*, active immunity.

kinga[4] n (ki-vi) a piece of burning wood; firebrand. (prov) *Kinga na kinga ndiyo moto uwakapo*, firebrand and firebrand, causes fire to burn, i.e. when people work together for a particular objective, success is obtained.

kingaja n (ki-vi) 1. the back of the hand. 2. armlet or bracelet of seeds, beads, etc. worn by women.

kingalingali adv on the back, face upwards: *Lala kingalingali*, lie on the back. *Anguka kingalingali*, fall backwards. (cf kichalichali)

kingam.a vt, vi lie across, block, barricade, obstruct: *Gogo limeikingama njia*, the log has blocked the road. Prep. **kingam.i.a** e.g. *Nyoka alinikingamia njiani*, the snake stopped me on the road. Cs. **kingam.ish.a**, frustrate, block, stop altogether. Ps. **kingam.w.a** Rp. **kingam.an.a**

kingamaji n (ki-vi) dike, levee; an embankment or dam made to prevent flooding by the sea or by a river.

kingamwili n (n) body immunity: *Ukosefu wa kinga mwilini*, deficiency in body immunity.

kinganga n (ki-vi) (mus) a kind of small drum.

king'ang'anizi n (ki-vi) a person who does not want to abandon his position, etc.: *Ving'ang'anizi wa madaraka*, people who don't abandon their positions in power.

kingio n (n) 1. lamp-cover, lampshade. 2. a vessel for preserving sth probably for later use.

kingis.a vt carry a load with difficulties because of its weight: *Ijapokuwa alikuwa dhaifu, lakini aliukingisa mzigo wangu mpaka chumbani*, even though he was weak, he managed to carry my luggage to the room with difficulty. Prep. **kingis.i.a** St. **kingis.ik.a** Cs. **kingis.ish.a** Ps. **kingis.wa** Rp. **kingis.an.a**

kingo[1] n (n) 1. threshold, door-sill; a length of wood, masonry, etc. along the bottom of a doorway. 2. edge, end: *Kingo za dunia*, ends of the earth.

kingo[2] n (n) (med) cataract; an eye disease causing partial or total blindness. (cf mtoto wa jicho)

kingoe n (ki-vi) see kigoe

king'ong'o[1] n (ki-vi) speaking nasally as with the nose pinched; nasal sound: *Ana king'ong'o*, he speaks through his nose.

king'ong'o[2] n (ki-vi) a person who speaks nasally.

king'onyo n (ki-vi) 1. (zool) a young larva immediately after ecdysis takes place, a stage of hypermetamorphosis in some insects. 2. dirt from refuse or from insects.

king'ora n (ki-vi) siren (cf sero, kamsa, honi)

king'ota n (ki-vi) see gogota[2.]

kingoto *n* (*n*) used in the expression: *Kufa kingoto*, die in silence; suffer in silence; endure hardships without complaining.

Kingozi *n* (*n*) one of the early Swahili dialects spoken in Northern Kenya, namely Malindi and Pate.

kingubwa *n* (*n*) see *kingungwa*

kingungwa *n* (*ki-vi*) (also *kingubwa*) (*zool*) a large spotted hyena with a broad and massive head with large eyes and short rounded ears; spotted hyena. *Crocuta crocuta*. (cf *shundwa*, *kikuto*)

kingulima *n* (*ki-vi*) anthill (cf *kichuguu*)

kingwagu[1] *n* (*ki-vi*) addict; a person addicted to some habit, especially to the use of a narcotic drug

kingwagu[2] *n* (*ki-vi*) addiction; the condition of being addicted to narcotic drugs.

Kingwana *n* (*n*) Swahili dialect spoken in Eastern Congo.

kingwangwa *n* (*n*) sth that is overweight.

kining'ina *n* (*ki-vi*) see *kinying'inga*

kinofu *n* (*ki-vi*) a piece of steak.

kinokera *n* (*ki-vi*) (*zool*) a gazelle-like animal.

kinongo[1] *n* (*ki-vi*) (*bot*) a perennial more or less-branched herb up to four feet tall with sense spikes of small white or yellow–white woolly flowers. The dried flowers are used for stuffing local pillows. *Aerva lanata*.

kinongo[2] *n* (*ki-vi*) clay (cf *kinamo*)

kinoo[1] *n* (*ki-vi*) whetstone

kinoo[2] *n* (*ki-vi*) an ingot or bar of soap.

kinu *n* (*ki-vi*) 1. mortar. 2. milling/processing machine: *Kinu cha moshi*, steam mill. *Kinu cha mkono*, hand mill. 3. wheel-cap

kinubi *n* (*ki-vi*) 1. (*mus*) Nubian harp; lyre. 2. a kind of banjo of more than one string.

kinukajio *n* (*m-mi*) (*bot*) Marvel of Peru; Four-O'clock; an errect perennial herb up to three feet tall with ovate or ovate-cordate ocuminate leaves, whose seeds and roots are poisonous.

kinukamito[1] *n* (*ki-vi*) (*bot*) a plant with poisonous roots.

kinukamito[2] *n* (*ki-vi*) 1. a person who constantly keeps on divorcing and remarrying. 2. a flirtatious person.

kinundu *n* (*ki-vi*) nodule

kinungu *n* (*ki-vi*) piece: *Kinungu cha nyama*, a piece of meat.

kinyaa *n* (*ki-vi*) 1. filth; anything which causes a feeling of disgust e.g. excrement. 2. the disgust felt by a person because of anything filthy: *Ona kinyaa*, be disgusted.

kinyago *n* (*ki-vi*) 1. mask. 2. laughing-stock; a person or thing made the object of ridicule. 3. carving.

kinyakazi *n* (*ki-vi*) (*med*) Bartholinitis; inflammation, sometimes with abscess formation of a vulvovaginal (Bartholin) gland; a wart on the clitoris of a woman. (cf *kigwaru*, *kisukumi*)

kinyambuo *n* (*ki-vi*) (*gram*) derivative

kinyamkela *n* (*ki-vi*) a kind of evil spirit, believed to be dwelling in the baobab trees and other big trees.

kinyangalee *n* (*ki-vi*) peak e.g. of a hill, mountain, tree, etc.

kinyang'anyiro *n* (*ki-vi*) competition, race, scramble, contest, struggle: *Kulikuwa na kinyang'anyiro cha uongozi katika chama tawala*, there was a struggle for leadership in the ruling party. *Timu yao ilishiriki katika kinyang'anyiro cha ubingwa wa soka nchini*, their team participated in the competition for soccer championship in the country. *Kinyang'anyiro cha urais*, presidential race.

kinyangarika *n* (*ki-vi*) thingummy, thingamajig, gimcrack, trash; an insignificant thing. (cf *kidubwasha*)

kinyanyavu *n* (*ki-vi*) (*zool*) a kind of fowl with very long legs and a featherless neck. (cf *nungunungu*, *mangisi*)

kinyemela *adv* furtively, secretly, surreptitiously, quietly: *Walilipata eneo la ardhi kinyemela*, they acquired the plot surreptitiously. (cf *kisirisiri*)

kinyemi *n* (*n*) a good thing; an attractive/interesting thing. (*prov*) *Kipya kinyemi ingawa kidonda*, a new thing is a source of joy even if it is a sore i.e. a new thing even if it is defective is better than an old one, and so people would like to keep it.

kinyenyezi (*also unyenyezi*) *n* (*n*) 1. goosebumps, gooseflesh; a roughened condition in which the skin is temporarily raised into little lumps caused by cold, fear, etc.: *Nilihisi kinyenyezi kama ambaye nimetambaliwa na kiwavi*, I got goosebumps as if a caterpillar has crawled on my skin. 2. dazzle, glare; blindness from glare: *Kinyenyezi kile kilisababishwa na taa za mbele za gari*, that dazzle was caused by the headlights of the car.

kinyerenyere *adv* 1. gently, quietly, slowly: *Nyoka alitambaa kinyerenyere*, the snake creeped quietly. (cf *polepole, taratibu*) 2. severely.

kinyesi *n* (*ki-vi*) faeces, excrement. (cf *kutu, mavi*)

kinyevu *n* (*ki-vi*) see *kinyevunyevu*

kinyevunyevu (*also kinyevu*) *n* (*ki-vi*) dampness, humidity, moisture: *Hicho ni kinyevunyevu cha ganda la ndizi mbivu*, that is the moisture from the skin of ripe bananas.

kinyezi *n* (*ki-vi*) the condition of feeling nauseous because of seeing dirt, etc.; nausea, upset stomach: *Nilihisi kinyezi nilipoyaona matapishi njiani*, I experienced nausea when I saw some vomit on the road.

kinying'inya (*also kining'ina*) *n* (*ki-vi*) great great grandchild. (cf *kilembwekeza*)

kinyiriri *n* (*ki-vi*) (*biol*) spermatozoon; the male germ cell, found in semen, which penetrates the ovum or egg of the female to fertilize it.

kinyo *n* (*ki-vi*) anus (cf *mkundu*)

kinyonga *n* (*ki-vi*) 1. chameleon. 2. (*fig*) weathercock; a fickle person; a changeable person: *Usiyaamini maneno ya kinyonga yule*, don't trust the words of that weathercock (cf *lumbwi, kigeugeu*)

kinyongo[1] *n* (*ki-vi*) grudge, bile, antipathy, bitterness, ill humour: *Aliifanya kazi yangu kwa kinyongo*, he did my work with some reluctance. *Ameniwekea kinyongo tangu nilipomkosa*, he has harboured some grudge against me since I wronged him. (cf *chuki*) 2. feeling of loneliness; solitude, aloneness: *Ona kinyongo*, feel lonely. (cf *kivumvu, upweke*)

kinyongo[2] *n* (*ki-vi*) a small piece of tobacco. (cf *kishusa*)

kinyota *n* (*ki-vi*) asterisk

kinyozi *n* (*ki-vi*) 1. barber, hairdresser. 2. (*fig*) a person who cheats in business; fraud, swindler: *Mwenye duka yule ni kinyozi*, that shopkeeper is a swindler.

kinyumba *adv* used in the expression: *Weka kinyumba*, keep a mistress; cohabit.

kinyume[1] *n* (*ki-vi*) antonym, opposite, reverse: *Kinyume cha 'taabu' ni 'raha'*, the antonym of 'hardship' is 'happiness'. *Kinyume na*, contrary to e.g. *Mambo haya yametokea kinyume na tulivyotarajia*, these affairs have occurred contrary to our expectactions.

kinyume[2] *n* (*ki-vi*) used in the expression: *Endea kinyume*, go against someone; betray. (cf *tapeli, danganya, hadaa*)

kinyumenyume *adv* backwards: *Alikuja kinyumenyume*, he came backwards.

kinyungi *n* (*ki-vi*) (*med*) mastitis; inflammation of the breast or udder.

kinyunya *n* (*ki-vi*) flour usu of wheat or rice mixed with water to make a kind of doughnut; dough.

kinyunyuzi *n* (*ki-vi*) sprayer

kinyutinyuti *adv* stealthily, quietly, slowly: *Nyoka alitembea kwenye majani kinyutinyuti*, the snake crawled on the grass quietly. (cf *kimyakimya*)

kinywa *n (ki-vi)* mouth (cf *mdomo*)
kinywaji *n (ki-vi)* beverage, drink: *Kinywaji baridi*, soft drink. *Kinywaji kikali*, intoxicant.
kinyweleo *n (ki-vi) (anat)* pore of the skin; sweat duct, skin follicle.
kinyweo *n (ki-vi)* drinking vessel.
kinz.a *vt, vi* 1. oppose, resist, object, contradict: *Alikinza burebure hoja zangu zote*, he opposed all my arguments for no reason. 2. obstruct, impede: *Aliikinza miradi ya maendeleo*, he obstructed the development projects. Prep. **kinz.i.a** St. ***kinz.ik.a*** Cs. ***kinz.ish.a*** Ps. ***kinz.w.a*** Rp. ***kinz.an.a*** (cf *pinga*)
kinzamimba *n (ki-vi)* contraceptive (cf *kingamimba*)
-kinzani *adj* obstructive, opposing, contradictory, antagonistic: *Yeye alikuwa mwanasiasa mkinzani*, he was an antagonistic politician. (cf *-kaidi*)
kinzano *n (ma-)* obstruction, hindrance, impediment, opposition, antagonism: *Kinzano lao halikuleta faida yoyote*, their opposition did not bring any benefit. (cf *pingamizi*)
kiogajivu *n (ki-vi) (zool)* blue roller; a kind of tropical bluish bird (family *Coraciidae*) that rolls and tumbles in flight and hops clumsily on the ground. (cf *kinega*)
kioja *n (ki-vi)* miracle, marvel, oddity, wonder: *Kupona kwake kulikuwa ni kioja kitupu*, his survival was a sheer miracle. (cf *ajabu, shani, ibra*)
kiokamikate *n (ki-vi)* pan; a wire metal vessel used in cooking.
kiokosi *n (ki-vi)* a reward given for sth lost. (cf *kiangazamacho, utotole*)
kiokote *n (ki-vi)* orphan: *Inafaa umsaidie kiokote yule*, it is fitting that you help that orphan. (cf *yatima*)
kioleza *n (ki-vi)* buoy esp one that indicates the place of anchor; float, raft. (cf *chelezo, boya*)
kiomo[1] *n (ki-vi)* a platform in a plantation. (cf *ulingo*)
kiomo[2] *n (ki-vi)* tip, apex, peak: *Kiomo cha nchi*, headland. *Kiomo cha chombo*, extremity of prow.
kioneshi *n (ki-vi)* see *kionyeshi*
kiongezo *n (ki-vi)* supplement, addition, increment (cf *kijalizo*)
kiongozi *n (ki-vi)* 1. leader, chief: *Waziri kiongozi*, chief minister. *Naibu kiongozi*, deputy leader. *Kiongozi wa upinzani*, leader of the opposition. *Kiongozi mtendaji*, function head. *Kiongozi wa kiroho*, spiritual leader. 2. anything that guides such as a buoy, guide, manual, textbook, etc.: *Nahodha wa jahazi alikuwa akifuata kiongozi ili chombo chake kisikwame*, the captain of the dhow was following the buoy so that his vessel did not go aground. *Kiongozi cha mitaala*, curriculum guide.
kiongwe *n (ki-vi)* see *kihongwe*
kionjamchuzi *n (ki-vi)* a pointed tuft of beard on the lower lip and chin; imperial, goatee.
kionjo *n (ki-vi)* temptation, test, trial, tribulation; hardship, suffering, etc. that tries one's endurance: *Unadhani mwanamke yule anaweza kuvumilia vionjo vya maisha?* Do you think that woman can bear the trials of life? (cf *mtihani, jaribio*)
kionyeshi (also *kioneshi*) *n (ki-vi) (gram)* demonstrative marker; deictic marker e.g. *hiki*, 'this' and *kile*, 'that'
kioo[1] *n (ki-vi)* 1. mirror, glass: *Kioo bapa*, plane mirror. *Kioo ukungu*, tinted glass. *Kioo mbonyeo*, concave mirror. *Kioo tufe*, spherical mirror. 2. *(fig)* reflection, mirror: *Kioo cha lugha ni utamaduni wake*, the reflection of a language is its culture.
kioo[2] *n (ki-vi)* fish hook. (cf *ndoana*)
kiookuzi *n (ki-vi)* magnifier
kiopoo *n (ki-vi)* anything like a pole or stick with a fork or hook, etc. used for taking up, fishing up, etc. as from a well or a pit. (cf *upembo, ngoeka*)
kioski *n (ki-vi)* kiosk (Eng)

kiota *n* (*ki-vi*) nest, roost. (cf *tundu*)
kiotezi *n* (*ki-vi*) radicle; the root part. (cf *kitungamzizi*)
kiowevu *n* (*ki-vi*) liquid
kipa[1] (also *golikipa*) *n* (*ma-*) goalkeeper: *Kipa wa akiba*, reserve goalkeeper (Eng).
kipa[2] *n* (*ki-vi*) (*anat*) elbow (cf *kisugudi, kiwiko*)
kipaa[1] *n* (*ma-*) see *paa*[5]
kipaa[2] *n* (*ki-vi*) house division; room: *Nyumba yangu ina vipaa vitano*, my house has five rooms.
kipachikwa *n* (*ki-vi*) inset; a small picture or map set within the border of a larger one.
kipafumaji *n* (*ki-vi*) aqualung; a kind of self-contained underwater breathing apparatus.
kipagio *n* (*ki-vi*) see *kipago*
kipago (also *kipagio*) *n* (*ki-vi*) rung of a ladder; a step in a staircase. (cf *kidato, kipandio*)
kipaimara *n* (*ki-vi*) (in Christianity) confirmation: *Sakramenti ya kipaimara*, the sacrament of confirmation.
kipaji[1] *n* (*ki-vi*) aptitude, bent, talent, endowment; divine gift: *Ana kipaji cha kuweza kuimba hadharani*, he has the natural bent for singing in public. (cf *kipawa, upaji*)
kipaji[2] *n* (*ki-vi*) a mark, usu round on the forehead. (cf *kinundu*)
kipakasa *n* (*ki-vi*) a present given to a bride by the bridegroom on the day of marriage. (cf *jazua, kipamkono*)
kipaku *n* (*ki-vi*) fleck
kipalio *n* (*ki-vi*) 1. an instrument used for scraping the scales of a fish; fish scraper. 2. an instrument or equipment like tongs used in the kitchen, for picking up pieces of burning charcoal.
kipambio *n* (*ki-vi*) grill; a device with several parallel bars of thin metal for roasting meat, etc.
kipamkono *n* (*ki-vi*) a present given to the bride by the bridegroom on the day of marriage. (cf *kipakasa, jazua*)

kipandauso *n* (*ki-vi*) (*med*) migraine; a type of intense, periodically returning headache.
kipande[2] *n* (*ki-vi*) 1. piece, hunk: *Kipande cha nyama*, a piece of meat. *Kipande cha sabuni*, a piece of soap (cf *sehemu, kibendo*) 2. distance: *Kutoka hapa mpaka mjini ni kipande*, from here to town is a big distance (cf *masafa*) 3. (*idms*) *Kipande cha mtu*, a gigantic person. *Kipande cha nyumba*, a huge house. 4. work done on monthly basis: *Kazi ya kipande*, work done on a monthly basis.
kipande[2] *n* (*ki-vi*) a children's game which uses a pointed piece of wood and a bat.
kipandikizi *n* (*ki-vi*) graft
kipandikizo *n* (*ki-vi*) (*bot*) seedling planted from a nursery, etc.
kipandio *n* (*ki-vi*) means of travelling.
kipando[1] *n* (*ki-vi*) (esp in Zanzibar) vehicle
kipando[2] *n* (*ki-vi*) crops that are grown in a field.
kipanga *n* (*ki-vi*) (*zool*) kite; a kind of bird (*family Falconnidae*) with grey plumage and feeds largely on insects, chicks, etc.
kipapai *n* (*ki-vi*) a kind of black witchcraft, used to harm someone or make him disappear from a place: *Pigwa kipapai*, bewitched by this kind of black witchcraft.
kipapasi (also *papasi*) *n* (*ki-vi*) (*zool*) antenna
kipapatiko *n* (*ki-vi*) a little flapping object of a bird, hen or duck; wing.
kipara *n* (*ki-vi*) 1. baldness; hairless condition. 2. hairless head. 3. a person who is bald: *Watoto walimcheka kipara yule*, the children laughed at that person with a bald head.
kipashamoto *n* (*ki-vi*) chafing dish.
kipashio *n* (*ki-vi*) (*gram*) unit: *Kipashio sahili*, simple unit. *Kipashio tata*, complex unit. *Kipashio lafudhi*,

kipasuasanda   **kipepeo²**   **K**

accented unit. *Kipashio kiinitoni*, accentual unit.

kipasuasanda *n (ki-vi)* (*zool*) nightjar; a kind of nocturnal insectivorous bird (family *Camprimulgidae*) with a small weak bill but a huge gape, large eyes, tiny feet and long wings. (cf *kirukanjia, mramba*)

kipatasi *n (ki-vi)* bradawl; a hand boring tool similar to a small, sharpened screw driver.

Kipate *n (ki-vi)* a Swahili dialect spoken in Pate Island, located in Kenya.

kipato *n (ki-vi)* income, earning; money obtained from salary, business, etc.: *Kipato cha chini*, low income. *Kipato chake ni kidogo*, his income is meagre. (cf *chumo, vuno, dahili*)

kipaumbele *n (ki-vi)* priority: *Serikali imeipa kipaumbele sekta ya kilimo*, the government has given priority to the agricultural sector.

kipawa *n (ki-vi)* bent, talent; divine's gift. (cf *upaji, kipaji*)

kipazasauti *n (ki-vi)* loudspeaker (cf *spika, bomba*)

kipekecho *n (ki-vi)* a whisk for whipping eggs, etc.; blender.

kipele *n (ki-vi)* (*med*) pastule, pimple, scab: *Ana vipele usoni*, he has pimples on his face. (cf *chunusi*)

kipeleleza-nyambizi *n (ki-vi)* sonar, asdic; an apparatus for finding submarines, depths, etc.

kipemba¹ *n (ki-vi)* see *kitamli¹*

Kipemba² *n (ki-vi)* Swahili dialect spoken in Pemba Island of Tanzania.

kipembe *n (ki-vi)* nook

kipendo *n (ki-vi)* see *kipenzi*

kipenga *n (ki-vi)* whistle: *Piga kipenga*, whistle; make a whistle. (cf *firimbi, kikorombwe*)

kipengee (also *kipengele*) *n (ki-vi)* 1. excuse, pretext, evasion: *Anatafuta kipengee tu cha kutohudhuria mkutano wetu*, he is just looking for an excuse to absent himself from our meeting. 2. aspect, item: *Walilizingatia suala la uzalendo katika vipengee vyake mbalimbali*, they examined the question of nationalism in its different aspects.

kipengele *n (ki-vi)* see *kipengee*

kipenyo *n (ki-vi)* diameter: *Kipenyo cha parabola*, diameter of a parabola. *Kipenyo cha piadufu*, diameter of a parabola.

kipenzi (also *kipendo*) *n (ki-vi)* darling, dear, honey, sweetheart: *Kipenzi chake ni mkewe*, his darling is his wife. (cf *mwandani, muhibu*)

kipeo¹ *n (ki-vi)* a vessel made from the baobab fruit or bottle gourd (calabash cucumber) used for drinking water, gruel, etc.; gourd. (cf *kibuyu*)

kipeo² *n (ki-vi)* (*maths*) index power, exponent e.g. 4^2 means 4 to the power of 2=16. *Kipeo cha pili cha namba*, squared root of a number. *Kipeo cha tatu cha namba*, cube root of a number. *Kipeo cha upindaji*, refractive index. *Kipeo cha witri*, odd power.

kipeo³ *n (ki-vi)* climax: *Kipeo cha hadithi*, climax of the story.

kipepeo¹ *n (ki-vi)* (*zool*) butterfly; *Kipepeo mweupe*, cabbage butterfly. (cf *nzigunzigu*)

kipepeo² *n (ki-vi)* (*zool*) a kind of tropical reef fish belonging to the families of *Drepanidae* and *Monodactylidae* having an oval and compressed body covered with cycloid scales; sickle-fish, moony. Spotted sickle fish. *Drepane punctata*.

kipepeo

kipepeo³ (also *upepeo*) (*ki-vi*) fan, punkah operator.
kipepesi *n* (*ki-vi*) fax (cf *faksi*)
kiperea *n* (*ki-vi*) (*naut*) a small canoe usu used to carry two people.
kipete *n* (*ki-vi*) a hinged metal fixed to a suitcase, door or window for opening or closing and is secured by a pin, bolt, etc.; hasp, ferrule. (cf *kipingwa*)

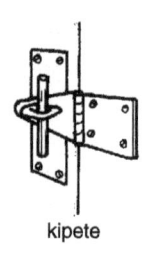

kipete

kipeto *n* (*ki-vi*) 1. a bag or matting-sack for carrying things such as grain, sand, etc. 2. bundle, package, parcel: *Kipeto cha barua*, a bundle of letters. (cf *kifurushi*) 3. a small box. (cf *kisanduku*)
kipeuo *n* (*ki-vi*) (*math*) root: *Kipeuo cha pili*, square root. *Kipeuo mraba*, square root. *Kipeuo cha mlingano*, root of congruency.
kipi¹ *n* (*ki-vi*) (*zool*) spur of a bird. (cf *kikwaru*)
kipi² *adj, pron* (for ki-vi class sing nouns) which: *Kipi kinakukera?* Which thing is bothering you? *Kitabu kipi?* which book?
kipia¹ *n* (*ki-vi*) the top of a mountain or fort or tower; apex, pinnacle.
kipia² *n* (*ki-vi*) (*zool*) a kind of fish of the *Tetraodontidae* family.
kipia³ *n* (*ki-vi*) leaves that are used to colour fishing lines in order to preserve them, making them become dark-reddish brown: *Piga kipia*, colour the fishing line.
kipigi (also *kipiki*) *n* (*ki-vi*) a small stick used to throw up into a tree in order to knock down fruits.
kipigo *n* (*ki-vi*) blow, shot, stroke: *Walimpiga kipigo kikubwa*, they dealt him a good blow. *Kufa kwake ni kipigo kikubwa kwa taifa zima*, his death is a big blow to the nation. (cf *kichapo*) 2. an act, method, etc. of bewitching.
kipiki *n* (*ki-vi*) see *kipigi*
kipila *n* (*ki-vi*) (*zool*) stone curlew, water dikkop. (cf *chekeamwezi*)
kipilipili *adj* used in the expression: *Nywele za kipilipili*, kinky hair; a kind of hair growing in small tufts.
kipimahewa *n* (*ki-vi*) barometer
kipimajoto *n* (*ki-vi*) calorimeter, thermometer.
kipimamavune *n* (*ki-vi*) strain gauge
kipima kasi *n* (*ki-vi*) speedometer (cf *spidometa*) (Eng)
kipima mtiririo *n* (*ki-vi*) flux meter.
kipima mvua *n* (*ki-vi*) raingauge.
kipima pembe *n* (*ki-vi*) protractor.
kipima pembe bapa *n* (*ki-vi*) plane table.
kipima ramani *n* (*ki-vi*) map measurer.
kipima rangi *n* (*ki-vi*) colourmeter
kipima upepo *n* (*ki-vi*) wind gauge.
kipima utego *n* (*ki-vi*) an instrument used to measure the distance in a gun; telescopic sight.
kipimio (also *kipimo*) *n* (*ki-vi*) 1. scale: *Kipimio cha muziki*, musical scale. *Kipimio cha namba*, number scale. *Kipimio sare*, uniform scale. *Kipimio upepo*, wind scale. 2. size, measurement.
kipimo (*ki-vi*) 1. see *kipimio*. 2. degree, size, measurement: *Kipimo mstari*, linear measurement. *Kipimo kiowevu*, liquid measure. *Kipimo ujazo*, cubic measure. *Kipimo cha suruali*, the measurements of a trouser. *Vipimo vya ndani*, inside measurements. *Kipimo cha urefu*, measurement of the length. *Kipimo cha upana*, measurement of the breadth.

kipindi¹ *n (ki-vi)* 1. *(idms) Kufa kipindi*, die naturally of an animal, e.g. *Nilimwona paka amekufa kipindi*, I saw a cat which died naturally. 2. an animal which has died a natural death; carcass. (cf *mzoga*)

kipindi² *n (ki-vi)* period; portion of time, often indefinite, characterized by certain events, processes, etc.: *Kipindi cha nyuma*, previously. *Kipindi kijacho*, the coming period. *Kipindi cha swala*, prayer period. *Kipindi cha somo*, lesson period. *Kipindi cha penduli*, period of the pendulum.

kipindupindu *n (ki-vi) (med)* cholera (cf *waba*)

kipingamizi *n (ki-vi)* obstruction, blockage, drawback, obstacle, hindrance: *Waliwiweka vipingamizi mbalimbali katika maendeleo yetu*, they placed various obstructions to our developments. (cf *kizuizi, kikwazo*)

kipingili *n (ki-vi)* see *pingili*

kipingo *n (ki-vi) (naut)* wooden peg or bolt to fasten, shroud, or anchor on the gunwale.

kipingwa *n (ki-vi)* door-bar, latch. (cf *komeo*)

kipini *n (ki-vi)* 1. a small pin. 2. a jewelled nose pin.

kipinzi *n (ki-vi)* refractor

kipipa *n (ki-vi)* keg: *Kipipa cha bia*, beer keg.

kipira *n (ki-vi)* 1. carpenter moulding plane. 2. a projecting moulding.

kipiri *n(ki-vi)(zool)* night viper; a nocturnal snake with a very poisonous venom. (*causus*)

kipitishi *n (ki-vi)* see *kipitishio*

kipitishio (*also kipitishi*) *n (ki-vi)* (*phys*) conductor of heat, electricity, etc.: *Kipitishio cha radi*, lightning conductor.

kipito *n (ki-vi)* a narrow strait.

kipleftl *n (ki-vi)* traffic circle, round about. (Eng)

kip.o¹ *cop. v* (used of singular ki-vi class nouns) is: *Kikombe chako kipo hapa*, your cup is here.

kipo² *n (ki-vi) (bot)* a small ovoid-globose fruit of rubbervine family. *Landolphia kirkii*.

kipochi *n (ki-vi)* a small bag. (cf *kibegi*)

kipodozi *n (ki-vi)* cosmetics.

kipofu *n (ki-vi)* a blind person: *Kipofu yule anaishi kwa dhiki*, that blind person lives in hardships. (cf *asiyeona*)

kipokeo *n (ki-vi)* 1. (in Islam) chorus, praise song 2. refrain. (cf *mkarara, kibwagizo, kiitikio*)

kipooza *n (ki-vi)* 1. a decayed fruit that loses its normal taste such as that of a mango, banana, etc. 2. a paralysed organ of a body: *Mkono wake umekuwa kipooza*, his arm is paralysed. 3. a paralysed person.

kipopo¹ *adv (idm) Piga/Pigwa kipopo*, be beaten by a large number of people together; be lynched e.g. *Mwizi alipigwa kipopo na hatimaye akafa*, the thief was lynched. (cf *kitutu*)

kipopo² *n (ki-vi)* part of the brain where cognition takes place; cognitive region.

kiporo (*also uporo*) *n (ki-vi)* night left-over food; food left over from evening until the next day. (cf *uporo, banyo, mwiku*)

kipozahewa *n (ki-vi)* a machine for cooling air.

kipozamataza *n (ki-vi) (zool)* lark; a kind of ground living songbird (family *Alaudidae*) with a heavy bill: *Kipozamataza kibenzi chekundu*, red-capped lark.

kipozi *n (ki-vi)* condenser

kipozo *n (ki-vi)* reserve, conservation, relaxant, soother. (cf *kitulizo*)

kipukusa¹ *n (ki-vi)* anything that has fallen from a tree e.g. leaves.

kipukusa² *n (ki-vi) (med)* bubonic plague disease.

kipukusa³ *n (ki-vi) (zool)* powder post beetle; a narrow, elongate flattened parallel-sided beetle (family *Lyctidae*) which bores into seasoned timber and conifers. It is termed so on the account of the larval habit of burrowing into hardwood until nothing is left but a fine powder.

kipukusa⁴ *n (ki-vi) (bot)* silk; a kind of widely distributed bananas in the tropics having short fingers which are inclined to be astringent unless fully ripe.

kipukusa⁵ *n (ki-vi)* rhino horn.

kipuli *n (ki-vi)* a small ornament worn on the ear; earring. (cf *herini*)

kipumulio *n (ki-vi)* respirator

kipungu¹ *n (ki-vi) (zool)* a kind of an eagle.

kipungu² *n (ki-vi)* see *pungu²*

kipunguo *n (ki-vi) (naut)* ropes sewn horizontally across the matting sail of *mtepe*, (a kind of sailing vessel) for reinforcement.

kipunguzo *n (ki-vi)* 1. a reduction from a usual or listed price; discount: *Nilipata kipunguzo kwa mwenye duka niliponunua mayai mengi,* I got a discount from the shopkeeper when I bought many eggs. 2. deducted money used to clear part of the debt at regular times over a specified period; instalment: *Kipunguzo kwenye mshahara wangu kiliathiri vibaya matumizi,* the money deducted from my salary affected adversely the expenditure.

kipupwe *n (ki-vi)* 1. winter, cold season 2. the wind blowing during this period. 3. winter

kipura *n (ki-vi) (zool)* a small bronze winged dove; lemon dove

kipure *n (ki-vi)* see *pure*

kipuri *n (ki-vi)* spare part: *Bei ya vipuri vya magari imepanda siku hizi,* the price of spare parts for motor vehicles has gone up these days.

kipusa¹ *n (ki-vi)* 1. the tusk of the rhinocerus when not fully grown. 2. *(colloq)* a beautiful girl: *Wavulana wengi wanampenda kipusa yule,* many boys like that beautiful girl. (cf *kidosho*)

kipusa² *n (ki-vi)* a precious thing that is hardly found.

kipute *n (ki-vi) (colloq)* contest, competition. (cf *mtanange, pambano*)

kipwa *n (ki-vi)* rock or dry patch left by a receding tide; shallow waters.

kipwe¹ *n (ki-vi) (zool)* shrike; a kind of shrill-voiced bird (family *Laniidae*) having a strong hooked bill and conspicuously coloured plumage and a long tail. (cf *tiva, aninia*)

kipwe² *n (ki-vi)* click; a slight sharp sound produced by contact of the middle finger and the thumb, when calling someone, etc.

kipwepwe *n (ki-vi) (med)* a condition of the skin causing red spots or blotches and thought to be caused by mites; lice bite.

kipwi *n (ki-vi) (naut)* gunwale surrounding a hull, a lavatory in a dhow. (cf *daraba*)

kiraa *n (ki-vi)* a style of Koran recitation. (Ar)

kirago¹ *n (ki-vi)* journey or expedition on foot: *Ilinibidi kwenda kirago upande ule kwa vile usafiri ulikuwa taabu,* I was obliged to go there on foot because transport was difficult.

kirago² *n (ki-vi)* 1. grass mat. 2. a worn-out mat. 3. *(idm) Funga virago,* pack up and go.

kiraha *n (n)* see *karaha*

kirai *n (ki-vi) (gram)* phrase: *Kirai elezi,* adverbial phrase. *Kirai nomino,* nominal phrase. *Kirai andamizi,* absolute phrase. (Ar)

kiraka *n (ki-vi)* patch in a cloth; darn: *Tia nguo kiraka,* patch clothes. *Nguo ya kiraka,* patched clothes. 2. *(colloq)* amendment, change: *Katiba yao imejaa viraka,* their constitution is full of amendments (cf *badiliko*).

kirambamchuzi n (ki-vi) goatee
kiranga n (ki-vi) sexual mania. (cf *uasherati, umalaya*)
kiranja n (ki-vi) 1. the first boy circumcised in a group, who is also considered to be a leader of the group. (cf *fumbi, chando*) 2. school prefect: *Yeye ni kiranja mkuu katika shule yetu*, he is the head prefect in our school.
kirasa n (ki-vi) (med) furuncle, boil; a localized pyogenic infection originating in a hair follicle.
kirehani n (ki-vi) (bot) a kind of sweet potato.
kirejeshi n (ki-vi) (gram) relative marker; relative particle: *Mtu aliyepita hivi punde ni mjomba wangu*, the person who has just passed is my uncle. Here, the relative marker is *ye* in the construction *aliyepita*, 'who has passed.'
Kireno n (ki-vi) Portuguese language.
kir.i vt, vi confess, acknowledge, admit: *Mshtakiwa alikiri kosa lake*, the accused confessed his crime. Prep. **kir.i.a** St. **kir.ik.a** Cs. **kir.ish.a** Ps. of Prep. **kir.iw.a** Rp. of Prep. **kir.i.an.a** (cf *ungama, kubali*) (Ar)
kiriba n (ki-vi) wineskin, waterskin; a bag made from the skin of an animal, used for carrying water and sometimes used for blowing fire in metal work: *Kiriba cha tumbo*, stomach bulging beneath the navel. (Ar)
kiribahewa n (ki-vi) air pocket.
kirih.i vt loath, detest, execrate; feel disgusted: *Kutema mate ovyo ovyo kutawakirihi watu*, to spit indiscriminately will disgust the public. Prep. **kirih.i.a** St. **kirih.ik.a** Cs. **kirih.ish.a** Ps. of Prep. **kirih.iw.a** Rp. of Prep. **kirih.i.an.a** (cf *chukiza, udhi*) (Ar)
kirimba[1] n (ki-vi) (of a bird or animal) cage: *Kuku wuliwekwa kwenye kirimba*, the fowls were kept in the cage. (cf *tundu*)

kirimba[2] n (ki-vi) the top or bottom piece of the frame of a door or window; lintel, sill. (cf *linta*)
kirimbi n (ki-vi) iron saw.
kirim.u vt feast, entertain, banquet; treat generously: *Aliwakirimu wageni wake vizuri*, he feasted his guests properly. Prep. **kirim.i.a** St. **kirim.ik.a** Cs. **kirim.ish.a** Ps. of Prep. **kirim.iw.a** Rp. of Prep. **kirim.i.an.a** (Ar)
kirinda n (ki-vi) a woman's undergarment which hangs from the waist down; petticoat, underskirt. (cf *gagro*)
kirini n (ki-vi) see *kreni*
kiritimb.a vt monopolize; gain control over business, etc.: *Mfanyabiashara yule anajaribu kuukiritimba uagizaji wa bidhaa*, that businessman is trying to monopolize import trade. Prep. **kiritimb.i.a** St. **kiritimb.ik.a** Cs. **kiritimb.ish.a** Ps. **kiritimb.w.a** Rp. **kiritimb.an.a**
kiroboto[1] n (ki-vi) (zool) a household flea; this is a small wingless insect which is found in human dwellings. Commonly found fleas include cat flea (*Ctenocephalides felis*), dog flea (*Ctenocephalides canis*) and human flea (*pulex irritans*). Household fleas cause irritation by their bites and are intermediate hosts of the cat and dog; tapeworm. (cf *kitumbi*)
kiroboto[2] n (ki-vi) 1. mercenary. 2. a special name given to a mercenary in oral literature.
kirohoroho adv quietly, secretly, discreetly: *Aliingia chumbani kirohoroho*, he entered the room quietly. (cf *kisirisiri, kinyemela*)
kiroja n (ki-vi) see *kioja*
kirudufu n (ki-vi) mimeograph
kirugu[1] n (ki-vi) 1. the wall-plate of a house; the top of a wall or of a cement roof. 2. height of a wall of a house.
kirugu[2] n (ki-vi) part of the body which

is swollen e.g. abscess, boil. (prov) *Mwana wa ndugu kirugu mjukuu mwanangu,* the son of a brother is on the top of a mountain and the grandson is also like that i.e. Don't rely upon the son of your brother when it comes to help. And when it comes to a grandson, the situation is worse.

kirugu³ *n (ki-vi)* cassava flour. (cf *bada*)

kirukamito *n (ki-vi)* see *kinukamito*

kirukanjia¹ *n (ki-vi)* 1. a restless person who cannot remain in one place. 2. a woman who cannot stay with a man; a woman on the make; prostitute.

kirukanjia² *n (ki-vi) (zool)* nightjar; a kind of bird of the *Caprimulgidae* family. (cf *gawa, mpasuasanda*) 2. *(zool)* a small rat with a long mouth.

kirumbizi¹ *n (ki-vi)* see *kurambiza*

kirumbizi² (also *kiumbizi*) *n (ki-vi)* a kind of dance in which the dancers fight by using sticks; stick fight dance.

kirungu *n (ki-vi)* a small club, a small knob-kerry; truncheon, knobstick, baton, cudgel. (cf *kigongo*)

Kirusi *n (ki-vi)* Russian language. (Rs)

kirusu *n (ki-vi)* a mixture of a kind of local brew made from millet gruel (*makomba*) and the sprouting seeds, malt. (*kimea*)

kirutubisho *n (ki-vi)* nutrient

kiruu *n (ki-vi)* fury, anger, rage. (cf *hamaki*)

kisa *n (ki-vi)* 1. event, incident, episode, account: *Alinielez kisa chote kilichomfika,* he gave me an account of all that had happened to him. (cf *mkasa, tukio*) 2. story, account, tale: *Alituhadithia visa vya mashimo ya Mfalme Suleiman,* he narrated to us the stories of King Solomon's mines. 3. reason, cause: *Walimpiga bila ya kisa,* they beat him without reason. *Kisa cha kuuawa kwake bado kinachunguzwa,* the cause of his murder is still being investigated. (cf *sababu, usuli*) 4. issue, matter: *Yeye anafanya kisa kikubwa,* he has made it a big issue. (Ar)

kisaa¹ *n (ki-vi)* any kind of cloth for wearing, etc. (cf *nguo*) (Ar)

kisaa² *n (ki-vi)* remnant, residue, remains (cf *sazo*) (Ar)

kisaa³ *adv* clockwise (Ar)

kisadifu (*biol*) gene (cf *jeni*) (Ar)

kisafu *n (ki-vi)* see *kilihafu*

kisaga¹ *n (ki-vi)* a dry measure of about a quart, equivalent to 1.4kg.

kisaga² *n (ki-vi) (zool)* bean weevil, bean bruchid; a kind of insect (family *Bruckidae*) which feeds on legume grains including beans, chickpeas, cowpeas, pigeon peas and many others. Most common species include the cowpea weevil, pea beetle, etc.

kisagalima *n (ki-vi)* a worn hoe which has become small through much use; worn-out hoe. (cf *kiserema*)

kisagaunga (*zool*) Burrowing sand crab; a kind of crab having a carapice with carapice prominent lateral spines. *Matuta lunaris.*

kisago *n (ki-vi)* (esp in sports) thrash, beating: *Timu yao ilipata kisago kikubwa,* their team got a good beating (cf *kipigo, kichapo*)

kisahani *n (ki-vi)* (esp in sports) thrash, beating: *Timu yao ilipata kisago kikubwa,* their team got a good beating.

kisahani *n (ki-vi)* 1. saucer; a small round shallow dish esp one with an indentation used to hold a cup. 2. anything like a saucer used in sports like a discus.

kisaka *n (ki-vi)* lilliputian, dwarf, midget, manikin; a very short person: *Watoto wanapenda kumchokoza kisaka yule,* the children like to tease that dwarf. (cf *kibushuti, kidurango, mbilikimo*)

kisaki *adv (idm) Funda kisaki,* fasten tightly, fix firmly e.g. *Aliufunga kisaki mzigo wake,* he fastened his luggage firmly.

kisalatamtaa *n (ki-vi)* see *salata*

kisalisali¹ *n (ki-vi) (med)* gonorrhoea (cf *kisonono*)

kisalisali² n (ki-vi) (zool) blood fluke; a tropical flatworm of the genus *Schistosoma*, which causes bilharzia in human and also affects other mammals and birds.

kisamaki n (ki-vi) 1. a piece of wood kept on the threshold of a door or window, usu used to prevent them from shutting; door stop. 2. (naut) one of the planks of a transo stern.

kisambare n (ki-vi) (bot) an annual glabrous weed of about 1 foot or less in height with a carpet of pretty blue flowers and slender triangular stems. *Lobelia fervens*.

kisambu (also *kisamvu*) n (ki-vi) (bot) vegetable made from the leaves of the cassava plant.

kisanamu n (ki-vi) miniature

kisanduku n (ki-vi) a small box used for keeping money raised usu from contribution; money box, piggy bank. (cf *kibweta*)

kisanga n (ki-vi) 1. pandemonium, trouble, confusion: *Kisanga kilitokea ndani ya basi baada ya abiria kugoma kulipa nauli*, confusion occurred inside the bus when a passenger refused to pay for his fare. 2. a misfortune which has fallen upon a person; disaster, tragedy.

kisangati n (ki-vi) miser, niggard, skinflint: *Ingawa yeye ana mali nyingi, lakini ni kisangati*, even though he has a lot of wealth, he is a miser. (cf *bahili, mchoyo*)

kisango n (ki-vi) divining board. (cf *kimbuzi, mbuzi*)

kisarambe n (ki-vi) a song which has eleven syllables in a line with a caesura (a break or pause on a line of verse) after the sixth syllable.

kisarawanda n (ki-vi) a white cloth spread on the bed on the night of marriage, used to ascertain the virginity of the bride.

kisasi n (ki-vi) reprisal, vengeance: *Lipiza kisasi*, take vengeance. *Wekea kisasi*, lay up vengeance. *Ondoa kisasi*, get rid of vengeance.

kisasili n (ki-vi) myth

kisawe n (ki-vi) synonym; a word or phrase that means exactly or nearly the same as another word or phrase in the same language e.g *ruka*, 'jump' and *chupa*, 'hop'. (cf *sinonimu*)

kisebusebu n (ki-vi) 1. sby pretending to lack interest in sth but actually he is interested: *Yeye ni kisebusebu*, he pretends to have no desire for help while he actually needs it. 2. (syn) *Kisebusebu na kiroho papo*, he who wants sth though pretending to lack interest in it is firm in the sense that he will not abandon his desire at all.

kisengenye (also *kitengenya*) n (ki-vi) (zool) kittlitz's plover; a kind of bird of the *Charadriidae* family having dusky grey-brown underparts with blackish shoulders and a white forehead band. *Charadrius pecuarius*.

kisengesenge adv backwards: *Mtoto alikuwa anakwenda kisengesenge*, the child was moving backwards. (cf *kimgongomgongo, kinyumenyume*)

kiserema n (ki-vi) an old worn-out hoe. (cf *kisagalima*)

kiseyeye n (ki-vi) (med) gingivitis; inflammation of the gums characterized by plaque around the necks of the teeth and the development of dental calculus. (cf *upacha, hijabu*)

kisha adv then, subsequently, later, next, finally: *Alikuja hapa asubuhi na kisha akaondoka*, he came here in the morning and then left. (cf *halafu, baadaye*)

kishada n (ki-vi) 1. child's kite. (cf *tiara*) 2. bunch, cluster, string: *Kishada cha maua*, a bunch of flowers. *Kishada cha shanga*, a string of beads. (cf *kicha, kishuke*) (Ar)

kishamia n (ki-vi) a cloth used to cover people who perform a special activity e.g. when Muslims bury a dead body. (Ar)

345

kishanzu n (ki-vi) downpayment, advance payment: *Toa kishanzu*, give advance payment. *Weka kishanzu*, keep advance payment. (cf *arbuni, advansi*)

kisharifu n (ki-vi) (*zool*) pygmy kingfisher; a kind of bird (family *Alcedinidae*) having a red bill and a short tail with ultramarine-blue crown and underparts. *Ispidina picta*. (cf *kizamiadagaa*)

kishaufu n (ki-vi) lady's nose ornament; lady's nose ring. (cf *hazama, kikero*)

kishawishi n (ki-vi) 1. temptation: *Vijana wanatakiwa wajizuie na vishawishi vya dunia*, the young are required to resist worldly temptations. 2. incentive, inducement: *Mwenye duka alinipa bure paketi ya sigara kama kishawishi*, the shopkeeper gave me a free packet of cigarettes as an incentive. (cf *kivutio*)

kishazi n (ki-vi) 1. string: *Kishazi cha samaki*, a string of fish. 2. (*gram*) clause: *Kishazi huru*, an independent clause. *Kishazi tegemezi*, a dependent clause, subordinate clause. *Kishazi vumishi*, adjectival clause. *Kishazi ingizwa*, interjected clause. *Kishazi kikuu*, main clause, principal clause. *Kishazi nomino*, nominal clause. *Kishazi sharti*, conditional clause, hypothetical clause. *Kishazi bebwa*, embedded clause. *Kishazi chopekwa*, inserted clause. *Kishazi banwa*, parenthetical clause. *Kishazi ambatani*, co-ordinate clause. *Kishazi ongezi*, additive clause. *Kishazi sababu*, causal clause. *Kishazi thibitishi*, confirmatory clause.

kishepe n (ki-vi) garden trowel.

kisheta[1] n (ki-vi) lilliputian, midget, dwarf, manikin; a very short person. (cf *kibushuti, kidurango, mbilikimo*)

kisheta[2] adj crippled, lame: *Amekuwa kisheta tangu kuzaliwa kwake*, he has been crippled since birth.

kisheti n (ki-vi) a kind of fried fritter, dried and then dipped in the syrup, and usu served to guests, etc.

kishikani n (ki-vi) adhesive; an adhesive substance like glue.

kishikizi n (ki-vi) holder, stopper: *Kishikizi cha mlango*, door stopper. *Kishikizi cha sigara*, a cigarette holder.

kishikizo[1] n (ki-vi) fastener, buckle. (cf *kifungio*)

kishikizo[2] n (ki-vi) anything that is used to secure sth firmly e.g. button; fastener: *Shati lake linakosa kishikizo kimoja*, his shirt misses one button. (cf *kifungo*)

kishiko n (ki-vi) handle

kishimo n (ki-vi) burrow

kishina[1] n (ki-vi) stump; the lower end of a tree or plant remaining in the ground after most of the trunk or stem has been cut off. (cf *kisiki*)

kishina[2] n (ki-vi) a kind of dance played by the Swahilis during celebrations or a misfortune.

kishina[3] n (ki-vi) counterfoil; the stub of a cheque, receipt, etc. kept as a record of the transaction.

kishindo n (ki-vi) 1. bang, crash, sound: *Nilisikia kishindo kikubwa cha mti ulioanguka nje*, I heard a loud sound of a felled tree outside. 2. chaos, pandemonium, disorder; *Kishindo kilitokea baada ya mwizi kukamatwa akiiba gari*, confusion ensued when the thief was caught red-handed stealing a car. (cf *vurugu, zogo, ghasia, fujo*) 3. restiveness, fussiness, recalcitrance, unruliness, disobedience: *Mtoto wangu alinifanyia vishindo nilipokataa kumpa pesa*, my child showed fussiness to me when I refused to give him money. (cf *machachari, matata*) 4. used in the expression: *Ushindi wa kishindo*, an overwhelming victory.

kishingo n (ki-vi) crick; a painful muscle spasm or cramp in the neck, back, etc.

kishinzi n (ki-vi) termite-hill (cf *kisuguu, kingulima*)

kishirazi n (ki-vi) anthill; a nest in the form of a mound built by ants or termites. (cf *kichuguu, kingulima*)

kishogo n (ki-vi) see kisogo
kishoka n (ki-vi) hatchet
kishomanguo n (ki-vi) see kichomanguo.
kishoroba n (ki-vi) a narrow strip of anything usu of land; a narrow space; lane, corridor: *Alilima kishoroba*, he cultivated a narrow strip of land.
kishubaka n (ki-vi) bay, ledge, niche, rill.
kishungi n (ki-vi) forelock
kishupi n (ki-vi) a kind of matting bag used for sleeping or for burying corpses. (cf *fumba*)
kishutuo n (ki-vi) see kisutuo
kishusha magendo n (ki-vi) antifreeze
kishwara n (ki-vi) (naut) oar grommet; a ring of rope or metal, used to hold an oar in place, etc. (cf *kileti, shalaka*) (Ar)
kis.i¹ vt, vi 1. consider critically; estimate, predict: *Alikisi kwamba uchumi wa nchi utatengenea baadaye*, he predicted that the country's economy would improve afterwards. 2. imagine, envisage, contemplate. Prep. **kis.i.a** St. **kis.ik.a** Cs. **kis.ish.a** Ps. of Prep. **kis.iw.a** Rp. of Prep. **kis.i.an.a** (Ar)
kisi² n (n) kiss: *Piga kisi*, kiss (Eng)
kis.i³ vt 1. (naut) change the course of a ship, etc. by turning its head to the wind. 2. change sail over tack. Prep. **kis.i.a** St. **kis.ik.a** Ps. of Prep. **kis.iw.a**
kisi.a vt estimate, conjecture, guess: *Unaweza kukisia watu wangapi watafika kwenye harusi yako?* Can you guess how many people will attend your wedding? Prep. **kisi.li.a** St. **kisi.k.a** Cs. **kisi.sh.a** Ps. **kisi.w.a** Rp. **kis.i.an.a**
kisiasa¹ adj political: *Mfungwa wa kisiasa*, political detainee. *Hifadhi ya kisiasa*, political asylum. *Jinai ya kisiasa*, political offence. (Ar)
kisiasa² adv politically: *Amekomaa kisiasa*, he is matured politically. (Ar)
kisibiti n (ki-vi) cumin; spicy strong-smelling seed used to give flavour to food: *Mboga za kisibiti*, cumin caraway seed.
kisifa adv see kielezi¹
kisigino n (ki-vi) heel: *Kisigino chake kinamwuma*, his heel is paining. (cf *kifundo*)
kisiki n (ki-vi) 1. stump of a felled tree; trunk of a fallen tree. (cf *kishina*) 2. the remaining part of a tooth after it has been extracted.
kisima n (ki-vi) 1. well. (prov) *Mchimba kisima huingia mwenyewe*, he who digs a well will fall into it himself i.e. he who causes trouble to others will find that the trouble will fall to himself. 2. a well for tapping an underground supply of oil, gas, etc. *Kisima cha mafuta*, oil well.
kisimamleo n (ki-vi) (bot) a succulent perennial herb with fleshy leaves and spicate racemes of crimson and yellow tubular flowers. The leaves are roasted and the mucilage from them is put on swellings of the body to reduce them. *Aloe* (sp)
kisimamo n (ki-vi) see kiamu²
kisimati (also *kismati*) n (ki-vi) good luck, fortune: *Mtu yule hana kisimati katika maisha yake*, that person has no luck in his life. (cf *bahati, chunu, fuluki*)
kisimi n (ki-vi) (anat) clitoris (cf *kinembe*)
kisingizio n (ki-vi) excuse, pretext, pretense, feint; alleged reason: *Alitafuta kisingizio tu cha kutokuja karamuni*, he merely looked for an excuse for not attending the party. (cf *dharura, kiongopeo*)
kisio¹ n (ki-vi) see makisio
kisio² n (ki-vi) extra stuff that is added in a kind of medicine that is cooked or pounded.
kisira n (ki-vi) a kind of bread like *chapati*, but is broader and thinner than *chapati*.
kisirani n (ki-vi) 1. misfortune, bad luck, mishap, jinx, hex, ill-omen: *Aliniletea kisirani kazini kwangu*, he jinxed me

347

at my place of work. (cf *mkosi, nuhusi*) 2. a person causing misfortune, evil eye, etc.; jinx: *Unajua kwamba kisirani yule hapendwi na watu?* Do you know that jinx is not liked by people? (cf *kausa, mkorofi*) (Ar)

kisirisiri *adv* furtively, secretly, surreptitiously, stealthily: *Aliingia nchini kisirisiri*, he entered the country secretly. (cf *kinyemela, kibubusa, kichinichini*)

kisiwa *n (ki-vi)* isle, island. (cf *jazira*)

kisimati *n (ki-vi)* see *kismati*.

kismati (also *kisimati*) *n (ki-vi)* good luck.

kisogo *n (ki-vi) (anat)* the back of the neck; nape.

kisoka *adv* in soccer: *Kisoka, yeye ni mchezaji mzuri*, in soccer, he is a good player.

kisokoto *n (ki-vi)* a kind of dance used in the exorcism of spirits; exercising dance.

kisombo *n (ki-vi)* a dish made of beans and cassava, etc. pounded or smashed up into a thick soup or paste.

kisomo *n (ki-vi)* 1. basic education: *Kisomo cha watu wazima*, adult education. *Kisomo chake kiliwanufaisha wanavijiji*, his education benefitted the villagers. (cf *elimu*) 2. (in Islam) prayer congregation held for a special purpose e.g. to pray for the dead.

kisongo *n (ki-vi)* 1. act (mode, means, etc) of twisting, etc.; twist. 2. *(med)* tourniquet; a device for stopping the flow of blood or for controllng circulation of blood to some spot.

kisonono *n (ki-vi) (med)* gonorrhoea (cf *kisalisali*)

kisoshalisti *n (ki-vi)* socialist, socialistic: *Nchi za kisoshalisti*, socialist countries.

kisra[1] *n (ki-vi)* a name given to the rank of the ancient kings of Persia. (Pers)

kisra[2] *n (ki-vi)* see *kasra*

kistari *n (ki-vi)* hyphen (cf *alama*)

kisu *n (ki-vi)* 1. knife: *Kisu cha kukunja*,

pocket knife. *Kisu fugutu*, pallete knife. 2. *(syn) Kisu cha uamu*, commission given to the cousins of the bride because of their relative being taken away.

kisua *n (ki-vi)* see *kiswa*

kisufugutu *n (ki-vi)* see *kisu*

kisugudi *n (ki-vi)* elbow: *Piga kisugudi*, push sby to one side with the elbow. (cf *kipa*)

kisuguru *n (ki-vi)* callus; a localized thickening and enlargement of the borny layer of the skin. (cf *suguru, sagamba*)

kisuguu *n (ki-vi)* termite hill. (cf *kichuguu*)

kisukari[1] *n (ki-vi) (bot)* a kind of thin sweet banana which can be eaten without being cooked.

kisukari[2] *n (n) (med)* diabetes

kisukio *n (ki-vi)* an instrument for steaming milk in order to get yoghurt; milkshaker. (cf *tungu*)

kisukuku *n (ki-vi)* fossil

kisukuma *n (ki-vi)* see *kisukumi*

kisukumi *n (ki-vi)* inflammation of Bartholin's glands on the vulva of the vagina due to infection; Bartholin's abscess; bartholinitis. (cf *kigwaru, kinyakazi*)

kisuli *n (ki-vi)* see *kisulisuli*

kisulisuli[1] (also *kisuli*) *n (ki-vi)* giddiness, dizziness: *Aliposhikwa na kisulisuli akakaa kitako*, when he experienced giddiness, he sat down. *Alishikwa na kisulisuli wakati shinikizo la damu lilipoteremka chini*, he experienced giddiness when the blood pressure went down. (cf *kizunguzungu, kisuli*)

kisulisuli[2] *n (ki-vi) (zool)* cotton stink bug; a kind of foul smelling insect (family *Pentatomidae*) of yellow and red colour, which eats cotton and its branches.

kisulisuli[3] *n (ki-vi)* a tailless kite; whirligig.

kisulisuli[4] *n (ki-vi)* a strong wind that is blowing.

kisura *n (ki-vi)* 1. beauty; a lovely looking

kisuse

girl; a pretty girl: *Kisura yule hutembea kwa madaha*, that pretty girl walks gracefully. (cf *kimanzi, kibamba*) 2. romantic nickname among youths.

kisuse *n (ki-vi) (zool)* shiny burrowing scorpion, yellow legged scorpion. This is a medium-sized have-built scorpion with large pedipalps. *Opistophthalmus glabrifrons*.

kisutu *n (ki-vi)* a kind of *khanga*, women's cotton wrapper, used very much during weddings and which has many decorations on it.

kisutuo (also *kishutua*) *n (ki-vi)* food given after communal work.

kisuunzi *n (ki-vi)* giddiness, dizziness: *Daima hushikwa na kisuunzi unaposafiri melini*, he always experiences giddiness when he travels in a ship. (cf *kizulizuli*)

kiswa (also *kisira*) *n (ki-vi)* a garment that carries respect, worn by religious people. (Ar)

Kiswahili *n (n)* Kiswahili language: *Kiswahili ni lugha ya Kibantu*, Swahili is a Bantu language.

kit.a¹ *vi* 1. (of penis, etc.) be erect, be firm, stand firm. 2. stick firmly in the ground: *Kita mkuki*, stick a spear upright in the ground. *Mwiba umemkita kooni mwake*, the thorn has stuck in his throat. Prep. **kit.i.a** St. **kit.ik.a** Cs. **kit.ish.a** Ps. **kit.w.a** Rp. **kit.an.a**

kita² *n (ki-vi)* see *vita*

kitaaluma¹ *adv* academically: *Amebobea kitaaluma*, he is well-grounded academically. (Ar)

kitaaluma² *adj* academic: *Mambo ya kitaaluma*, academic affairs.

kitabakero *n (ki-vi) (med)* ampoule; a small, sealed glass container for one dose of a sterile medicine to be injected hypodermically.

kitabu *n (ki-vi)* 1. book: *Kitabu cha kiada*, textbook. *Kitabu cha ziada*, supplementary book. *Kitabu cha cheki*, cheque book. *Kitabu cha hadithi*, story book. 2. school. 3. used in the expression e.g. *Mchezaji wetu alifungua kitabu cha magoli katika dakika za mwisho*, our player went on a goal scoring spree in the dying minutes.

kitadali *n (ki-vi) (bot)* an annual or perennial erect or prostrate herb with reddish-green leaves and clusters of small yellowish green flowers. *Euphorbia hirta*.

kitafunio *n (ki-vi)* snack, bite, nosh: *Nilimkuta akila vitafunio*, I saw him eating snacks.

kitahanaa *n (ki-vi)* pandemonium, confusion, chaos. (cf *kizaazaa*)

kitaji *n (ki-vi) (mus)* clarinet

kitaji

kitakasa *n (ki-vi) (med)* a small elephantisis. (cf *kitende*)

kitakataka *n (ki-vi)* a particle of dust; a speck of dust: *Kitakataka kiliniingia machoni*, a speck of dust entered my eye.

kitaifa¹ *adv* nationally: *Kitaifa, mchango wake ni mkubwa*, at national level, his contribution is enormous. (Ar)

kitaifa² *adj* national: *Habari za kitaifa*: national news.

kitakizo¹ *n (ki-vi)* headboard; end-piece at the head and foot for a local bedstead. (cf *mbwegu*)

kitakizo² *n (ki-vi)* a short mangroove pole supporting a ceiling of a house.

kitako¹ *n (ki-vi)* bicycle's carrier; seat of a bicycle.

kitako² *n (ki-vi) (anat)* rump, the buttocks; a person's bottom.

kitako³ *adv* down, on the base: *Kaa kitako*, sit down.

kitako⁴ n (ki-vi) a period of long duration for sitting in a place.
kitala¹ n (ki-vi) council of a local chief. (cf *baraza*)
kitala² n (ki-vi) see *kitara¹*
kitale n (ki-vi) 1. young coconut in the stage of development. (cf *nazi changa*) 2. its coconut shell which is edible.
kitali n (ki-vi) war, fighting: (*syn*) *Hanjamu nusu ya kitali*, a threat is half-way to war. (Ar)
kitalifa¹ n (ki-vi) distance: *Pana kitalifa kirefu baina ya hapa na pale*, there is a long distance from here to there. (cf *umbali, masafa*)
kitalifa² n (ki-vi) a small plaited leaf package of Turkish delight, *halua*. (cf *kitopa*)
kitalifa³ adv far, afar, far off.
kitalu (also *kitaru*) n (ki-vi) 1. walled garden, courtyard: *Kuna miti aina kwa aina katika kitalu hiki*, there are different kinds of trees in this walled garden. (cf *kiunga*) 2 a seedling that can be later transplanted. 3. a plot for building houses. (cf *ploti*)
kitambaa (also *kitambara*) n (ki-vi) 1. cloth; material made by weaving cotton, wool, etc.: *Alinunua kitambaa ili ashone kanzu*, she bought some cloth in order to sew it to make a frock. 2. a piece of small cloth used for a particular purpose: *Kitambaa cha meza*, table cloth. *Kitambaa cha kupangusia vyombo*, dishcloth. *Kitambaa cha mkono*, handkerchief. *Kitambaa cha kichwa*, headcloth; a cloth used for head wear.
kitambara n (ki-vi) see *kitambaa*
kitambi¹ n (ki-vi) a kind of loin-cloth, usu woven with thick threads and which is used as a dress or as a kind of turban, etc.
kitambi² n (ki-vi) 1. obesity, potbelly, beerbelly: *Ota kitambi*, develop obesity. *Fanya kitambi*, develop obesity. *Kuwa na kitambi*, have an obesity.

kitambo¹ adv a while ago, a short time ago, a short spell: *Aliondoka kitambo*, he left a short time ago.
kitambo² n (ki-vi) some period or distance: *Kutoka hapa mpaka kijijini kwao ni kitambo*, from here to their village is some distance.
kitambulishi n (ki-vi) label
kitambulisho n (ki-vi) identity card, identification paper: *Hakuwa na kitambulisho chochote alipovuka mpaka*, he did not have any identity card when he crossed the border.
kitamkwa n (ki-vi) (*phon*) phoneme; the minimal unit in the sound system of a language. (cf *kipandesauti, fonimu*)
kitamle n (ki-vi) see *kitamli*
kitamli (also *kitamle*) n (ki-vi) 1. a kind of a short coconut tree, the nuts of which are only used for drinking. 2. a kind of coconut, namely *dafu*, obtained from this tree.
kitana n (ki-vi) comb (cf *shanuo*)
kitanda¹ n (ki-vi) bed: *Kitanda cha mayowe*, a local bed made with ropes strung in a wooden frame. *Kitanda cha kufumia*, a weaving loom; weaver's loom.
kitanda² n (ki-vi) coffin, casket, bier. (cf *tusi, jeneza*)
kitandawili n (ki-vi) see *kitendawili*
kitandi n (ki-vi) cot; a bed for a small child, usu with sides to prevent the child from falling.
kitanga¹ n (ki-vi) 1. a circular mat, used for praying, drying food, etc. 2. the palm of the hand: *Kitanga cha mkono*, the palm of the hand. (cf *kiganja*) 3. the scale or pan of a balance. *Kitanga cha mizani*, the scale or pan of a balance.
kitanga² n (ki-vi) a place where a client is taken during the exorcism of spirits.
kitanga³ (also *kitangara*) n (ki-vi) halo; a ring of light that seems to encircle the sun, moon or other luminous body.
kitangara n (ki-vi) see *kitanga³*
kitange n (ki-vi) (*bot*) a kind of fish (family Scorpaenidae) of chiefly tropical seas

kitango ... having poisonous rays on the dorsal, anal and ventral fins; scorpion fish.

kitango n (ki-vi) a lace used to fasten together the mattresses during sewing it.

kitangu n (ki-vi) nursery; a place where young trees or other plants are raised for transplanting, etc.: *Kitangu cha mnazi*, a nursery of coconut trees. *Kitangu cha mpunga*, rice bed/garden. (cf *kitalu*)

kitanguakimbunga n (ki-vi) anticyclone

kitangulizi[1] n (ki-vi) 1. a person or thing that precedes as in the case of an appetizer during eating; starter: *Katika chakula cha mchana cha jana, kitangulizi kilikuwa ni cha supu*, in yesterday's lunch, the starter was soup. 2. precursor, harbinger: *Ghasia ndogondogo zilikuwa kitangulizi cha mapinduzi yaliyotokea baadaye katika nchi ya jirani*, the minor disturbances were a harbinger to the subsequent revolution that occurred in the neighbouring country. 3. advance payment, downpayment. (cf *kishangu, rubuni*)

kitangulizi[2] n (ki-vi) odd number. (cf *witiri*)

kitanguo n (ki-vi) anything that causes annulment of sth.

kitani (also *katani*) n (ki-vi) flax, linen, fibre.

kitano n (ki-vi) (arch) a coin of 5 cents.

kitanzi n (ki-vi) noose, loop: *Tia kitanzi*, put a loop. *Jitia kitanzi*, hang oneself.

kitapa n (ki-vi) a small leather bag.

kitapitapi n (ki-vi) electric ray; a kind of fish whose electric organs can produce a powerful and dangerous shock when it is disturbed. (cf *taa kilimawe*)

kitapo (also *mtapo*) n (ki-vi) bodily shivering because of cold, fear, illness, etc.: *Alishikwa na kitapo alipokuwa na homa kali*, he got the shivers when he had acute malaria. (cf *mtetemeko*)

kitara[1] n (ki-vi) see *kitala*

kitara[2] (cf *kitala*) n (ki-vi) a heavy cavalry sword with a slightly curved blade used in parades, etc.; sabre. (cf *hanjari*) (Hind)

kitara[3] n (ki-vi) a specified area used to dry seeds or different kinds of cereals.

kitaru[1] n (ki-vi) see *kitalu*

kitaru[2] n (ki-vi) a kind of a trap for catching animals. (cf *fyuka, mfyuka*)

kitasa n (ki-vi) built-in lock.

kitasi n (ki-vi) woven fruit basket. (cf *pakacha*)

kitata[1] n (ki-vi) splint; a flat piece of wood, metal, etc. strapped to an arm, leg, etc. which is used as a support for a broken bone so that the bone stays in the right position while it is healing.

kitata[2] n (ki-vi) stammer, stutter. *Ana kitata*, he has a stammer. (cf *kigugumizi*)

kitatange n (ki-vi) 1. (zool) a kind of small fish (family *Chaetodontidae*), which forms the habit of listening to its partners in the trap and then craftily runs away from it; butterfly fish. 2. (fig) inciter, firebrand, rabble-rouser: *Kitatange yule amewafitinisha marafiki wawili*, that inciter has antagonized two friends. (cf *mchochezi, mfitini*)

kitatanishi n (ki-vi) anything which causes a mystery.

kitawanya n (ki-vi) distributor: *Kitawanya mwanga*, light distributor. *Kitawanya nuru*, light distributor.

kitaya n (ki-vi) yoke (cf *nira*)

kite[1] n (ki-vi) groan, snort: *Piga kite*, groan, snort. (cf *mgumio*)

kite[2] n (ki-vi) mercy, compassion, pity, lenience: *Hana kite kwa binadamu wenzake*, he has no mercy towards his fellow beings. (cf *imani, huruma*)

kitefu n (ki-vi) see *kichefuchefu*

kitefute n (ki-vi) (anat) zygomatic bone, cheek-bone, molar bone. (cf *kiluku, kituguta*)

kitegauchumi *n* (*ki-vi*) investment: *Waliweka vitegauchumi vyao katika sekta ya uvuvi*, they put their investments in the fishing sector.

kitema *n* (*ki-vi*) old-worn clothes; rags. (cf *utambaa*)

kitembe (also *kithembe*) *n* (*ki-vi*) lisp; speech defect for sounds "s" and "z" where they are pronounced as 'th' and "dh" respectively e.g. the word *sita*, 'six' is pronounced as *thita*: *Ana kitembe*, he has a lisp. *Piga kitembe*, speak with a lisp.

kitembo *n* (*ki-vi*) rate, level, degree, grade, rank, standard: *Kitembo cha juu cha elimu kinastahili kuheshimiwa*, a high standard of education needs to be respected. (cf *kiasi, kiwango, stahili*)

kitembwe[1] *n* (*ki-vi*) vegetable fibre from the leaves of sisal, banana and pineapple trees.

kitembwe[2] *n* (*ki-vi*) see *tembo*[3]

kitendawili (also *kitandawili*) *n* (*ki-vi*) 1. riddle, conundrum; a problem or puzzle in the form of a question, statement, etc. so that some ingenuity is needed to solve or answer it: *Kitendawili*, a riddle; (reply) *Tega*, try me. 2. (*fig*) riddle, mystery, enigma: *Nani atakayeshinda kesho, imekuwa kitendawili kwa timu zote mbili*, who will win tomorrow has become a riddle to both teams.

kitende[1] *n* (*ki-vi*) (*med*) part of the leg or arm that is swollen because of a disease; elephantiasis. (cf *kitakasa*)

kitende[2] *n* (*ki-vi*) abode, residence; a person's home , surroundings, etc. (cf *maskani, mastakimu*)

kitendo *n* (*ki-vi*) 1. deed, action, act: *Kitendo cha haramu*, an illegal act. *Kitendo chake kinaweza kuhatarisha usalama wetu*, his action can endanger our safety. (cf *tendo*) 2. (*gram*) verb. (cf *kitenzi*)

kitendwa *n* (*ki-vi*) (*gram*) object, complement. (cf *yambwa*)

kitenge *n* (*ki-vi*) a woman's wrap of quality printed cloth in various colours and designs with distinctive borders; kitenge: *Amevaa kitenge*, she has dressed in a kitenge.

kitengele[1] *n* (*ki-vi*) (*anat*) the hand of a person; *Alitumia vitengele vya mkono kufua nguo zake*, he used his hands to wash his clothes. (cf *kiganja*)

kitengele[2] *n* (*ki-vi*) stripe; band of colour, etc. (cf *mlia*)

kitengele[3] *n* (*ki-vi*) a small round disk of cloth or leather, used to make mattresses.

kitengenya *n* (*ki-vi*) see *kisengenya*

kitengo *n* (*ki-vi*) production unit, section: *Kitengo cha elimu*, education unit. *Kitengo cha utafiti*, research unit.

kitenzi[1] *n* (*ki-vi*) (*gram*) verb: *Kitenzi saidizi*, auxiliary verb. *Shada la kitenzi*, verb cluster. *Kitenzi kishirikishi*, copular verb. *Kitenzi sababishi*, causative verb. *Kitenzi sharti*, conditional verb. *Kitenzi ghairi*, irregular verb. *Kitenzi jirejee*, reflexive verb, *Kitenzi elekezi*, transitive verb. *Kitenzi kielekezi*, intransitive verb.

kitenzi[2] *n* (*ki-vi*) miracle, marvel; act or an event of wonder. (cf *kituko*)

kitete *n* (*ki-vi*) cowardice, fear, awe: *Kitete chake kilisababishwa na ugeni wa makazi yake mapya*, his cowardice was caused by his new place of residence. (cf *woga, uoga*)

kitetefya *n* (*ki-vi*) anything that is soft e.g. flour: *Baada ya kusagwa, ngano ikawa kitetefya*, after being milled, the wheat became soft. (cf *kitepetepe*)

kitewatewa *n* (*ki-vi*) (*zool*) a kind of porcupine.

kithembe *n* (*ki-vi*) lisp; the act or speech defect in which 's' is pronounced like 'th' in 'thick' and 'z' is pronounced like 'th' in 'this.'

kithir.i *vi* excel, increase; grow beyond the limit: *Vitendo vyake viovu vimekithiri*

kiti¹   **kititi³**   **K**

siku hizi, his evil deeds have increased these days. Prep. **kithir.i.a** St. **kithir.ik.a** Cs. **kithir.ish.a** Ps. of Prep. **kithir.iw.a** (cf *zidi*)

kiti¹ *n (ki-vi)* 1. chair: *Kiti cha henzirani*, cane chair. *Kiti cha enzi*, throne. (cf *ufalme, utawala*) 2. a person who is being exorcised. 3. a place of residence of an administrator, chief, etc.

kiti² *n (ki-vi) (naut)* deck planking; floor underneath the roofing of the penthouse in a *mtepe*, a kind of sailing vessel.

kiti cha pweza *n (ki-vi) (zool)* sea star, star fish; a marine echinoderm of the class *Asteroidea* which has a thick, often spiny body with five arms extending from a central disk.

kiti cha pweza

kiti.a *vt* transplant, replant: *Mkulima alikitia mimea yake kwenye eneo lenye rutuba zaidi*, the farmer transplanted his seedlings in a more fertile area. Prep. **kiti.li.a** St. **kiti.k.a** Cs. **kiti.sh.a** Ps. **kit.i.w.a** Rp. **kiti.an.a** (cf *pandikiza, atika*)

kitiahamu *n (ki-vi)* appetizer

kitiba *n (ki-vi)* custom, manners, habit, character: *Mtoto yule ana kitiba kibaya*, that child has bad manners. (cf *desturi, tabia, mwenendo*) (Ar)

kitibegi *n (ki-vi)* kit-bag (Eng)

kitikiti *adv* shoulder high, high up: *Mshindi alibebwa kitikiti*, the victor was carried shoulder high.

kitimbakwiri *n (ki-vi)* 1. a person who is looking after his interests without regard for basic principles or interests of the public; opportunist: *Wananchi walimlaani kitimbakwiri yule*, the people denounced that opportunist. 2. traitor: *Kitimbakwiri aliihini nchi yake*, the traitor betrayed his country. (cf *kijibwa, kibaraka*)

kitimbi *n (ki-vi)* intrigue, plot, conspiracy, machination, gimmick; dirty trick: *Walimfanyia vitimbi vingi*, they carried many intrigues against him. (cf *njama, hila*)

kitimiri¹ *n (ki-vi)* see *kotmiri*

kitimiri² *n (ki-vi)* a name of a bad evil spirit. (Ar)

kitimutimu *n (ki-vi)* contest, competition, tournament, showdown: *Kitimutimu cha kombe la Dunia*, World cup tournament. *Washindi wa kitimutimu*, winners of the tournament (cf *pambano, mtanange*) 2 excitement, fever: *Kitimutimu cha uchaguzi*, election fever (cf *patashika, vuguvugu*)

kitindamimba *n (ki-vi)* the last born child of a woman. (cf *kichinjamimba, mziwanda, kifungamimba*)

kitindio *n (ki-vi)* a pair of tweezers.

kitini *n (ki-vi)* hand-out

kitisho *n (ki-vi)* terror, threat, intimidation: *Kitisho chake hakikuwaogopesha wanavijiji*, his threat did not frighten the villagers. (cf *ogofya*)

kitita *n (ki-vi)* pile, bundle; a large quantity: *Kitita cha pesa*, a large quantity of money. *Kitita cha kuni*, a bundle of firewood. *Kitita cha madeni*, a large amount of debt. *Kitita cha silaha*, a large quantity of weapons.

kititi¹ *n (ki-vi) (geol)* an area of subsidence.

kititi² *adv* upright, perpendicular, straight up: *Mnazi umesimama kititi*, the coconut tree stands upright. (cf *wima*)

kititi³ *adv* unexpectedly, suddenly, without any arrangement: *Nilikutana naye njiani kititi*, I met him on the way unexpectedly.

353

kititia n (ki-vi) see *kibirinzi*
kitivo n (ki-vi) 1. a fertile land. (cf *mboji*) 2. a prosperous place in a city, village, etc. where everything is available. 3. university faculty: *Kitivo cha sayansi*, faculty of science. *Kitivo cha sheria*, faculty of law.
kito[1] n (ki-vi) gemstone; a precious stone. (cf *johari*)
kito[2] n (ki-vi) a children's game of hiding things and looking for them; hide and seek game.
kitobo (also *kitobwe*) n (ki-vi) a small hole. (cf *tundu*)
kitobwe[1] n (ki-vi) see *kitobo*
kitobwe[2] n (ki-vi) a small area on the ground where is mud; marsh, bog, swamp.
kitobonya (also *kitobosha*) n (ki-vi) a kind of fritter, usu round made from wheat and flour and fried and then dipped in the syrup. (cf *kipopoo*)
kitobosha n (ki-vi) see *kitobonya*
kitokono n (ki-vi) (*anat*) a small triangular bone at the lower end of the vertebral column; coccyx (cf *kifandugu*)
kitoma[1] n (ki-vi) dipper, gourd; a dried hollowed-out shell made from pumpkin, used as a drinking cup, etc. (cf *kibuyu*)
kitoma[2] n (ki-vi) (*anat*) testicle, scrotum. (cf *pumbu, korodani*)
kitoma[3] n (ki-vi) cavity, hole. (cf *tundu, kitobo*)
kitomeo n (ki-vi) (of a dictionary, etc.) headword and its entries. (Ar)
kitonge n (ki-vi) small rounded mass or small lump or ball of food like rice taken in the fingers and eaten by the local people. (cf *kinyunya*)
kitongo[1] n (ki-vi) (zool) a kind of small bird of the *Pogoniulus* family.
kitongo[2] n (ki-vi) sideways, obliquely.
kitongoji n (ki-vi) a very small village; hamlet: *Wanaishi katika kitongoji chenye wakaazi wema*, they live in a small village which has good inhabitants. (cf *kijiji*) (Ar)

kitongoo n (ki-vi) (zool) surgenfish; a kind of edible salt-water fish. (family *Acanthuridae*)
kitopa n (ki-vi) a small plaited leaf package of Turkish delight. (cf *kitalifa*)
kitope n(ki-vi) a kind of black fertile soil.
kitoria (also *kipo*) n (ki-vi) (*bot*) a kind of edible smooth pear-shaped fruit of the *mtoria* tree. (*Landolphia petersiana*) (cf *kipo*)
kitororo n (ki-vi) (zool) Zanzibar golden-rumped barbet. *Pogoniulus bilineatus*.
kitotoa n (ki-vi) incubator (cf *kiangulio*)
kitotoria n (ki-vi) (*bot*) a very ripe small mangoe.
kitovu n (ki-vi) 1. incubator, navel, umbilicus; umbilical cord. 2. the mark left after the umbilical cord has been cut and become dry. 3. centre, origin, cradle; *Kitovu cha graviti*, centre of gravity. *Kitovu cha mvutano*, centre of gravity. *Kitovu cha ning'inizo*, centre of suspension. *Kitovu cha jambo*, the essence of the matter. *Nchi ile ilikuwa kitovu cha usambazaji wa mihadarati*, that country was the centre of the spread of narcotics. *Kitovumbegu*, hilum; the scar on a seed marking the point of attachment to its seed vessel.
kitoweo n (ki-vi) a side dish of the main food such as fish, poultry, etc.; relish: *Samaki ni kitoweo kizuri cha wali*, fish is a good side dish for rice. (cf *kitoweleo*)
kitu[1] n (ki-vi) thing: *Anauza vitu vingi dukani*, he sells a lot of things at the shop. *Kitu muhimu sana duniani ni utu*, the most important thing in the world is humanity. *Si kitu*, it is okay. It doesn't matter. *Hapana kitu*, there is nothing.
kitu[2] n (ki-vi) wealth, property: *Hana kitu*, he has no wealth. (syn) *Kitu kilivunja nguu na milima ikalala*, wealth reached the summit and the

mountain succumbed i.e. someone who is wealthy can also bribe his way through.
kitua¹ *n (ki-vi) (bot)* a kind of cassava plant with thin leaves and its seedling is grey.
kitua² *n (ki-vi)* a small bush; copse, coppice. (cf *kitua, kichaka*)
kitubio *n (ki-vi)* 1. (in Christianity) penance; a sacrament involving the confession of sin, repentance, etc. 2. a place for performing penance. (Ar)
kituguta *n (ki-vi) (anat)* molar bone, cheek-bone. (cf *kitefute, kituku*)
kituka *n (ki-vi) (bot)* a dense growth of small trees or bushes; thicket, copse, coppice. (cf *kitua, kichaka*)
kituko *n (ki-vi)* unusual event or incident; a moving incident generally unusual; a bizarre incident; freak, abnormality, uniqueness: *Kituko kile kilimshangaza kila mtu*, that unusual incident surprised everyone. (cf *kioja, ibra, ajabu*)
kituku *n (ki-vi) (anat)* molar bone, cheek-bone, zygomatic bone. (cf *kitefute, kituguta*)
kitukutuku *n (ki-vi) (zool)* a large-jawed larva (family *Myrmeleontidae*) which constructs cone-shaped pits. to catch ants, spiders, etc. on which it feeds; antlion.
kitukuu (also *mtukuu*) *n (ki-vi)* great-great-grand child.
kitulizo *n (ki-vi)* consolation, sedative, relaxant; anything that comforts you, relieves pain, etc. (cf *kipozo*)
kitumbaku *n (ki-vi) (zool)* six stripe soap fish; a kind of salt water fish (family *Grammistidae*) having dark brown body with yellow stripes. (cf *kigumugumu*)
kitumbi *n (ki-vi) (zool)* a kind of small larva. (cf *kiroboto*)
kitumbua *n (ki-vi)* a kind of small round fritter made from rice flour and fried in fat or ghee.
kitunda *n (ki-vi)* chess pawn; any of the pieces, used in the game of chess. (cf *sataranji*)
kitundu *n (ki-vi)* aperture, eyehole, pinhole, orifice, interstice.
kitunga¹ *n (ki-vi)* a kind of tarboosh; fez.
kitunga² *n (ki-vi)* a kind of basket with a cover and a handle; covered straw basket.
kitungule *n (ki-vi) (zool)* rabbit (cf *sungura*)
kitunguu *n (ki-vi) (bot)* onion; *Kitunguu maji*, green onion. *Kitunguu thaumu/saumu*, garlic.
kituo¹ *n (ki-vi)* 1. stopover; a brief stop or stay at a place during the cause of a journey. (cf *ago, kambi*) 2. halt; the final destination of a person. 3. stop, stand, station: *Kituo cha basi*, bus stop. *Kituo cha polisi*, police station. *Kituo cha usalama*, police station. *Kituo cha uchunguzi*, observation post. *Kituo cha matangazo*, broadcasting station. *Kituo cha jeshi*, army unit. *Kituo cha redio*, radio station. *Kituo cha kupigia kura*, polling station. *Kituo cha afya*, health centre.
kituo² *n (ki-vi)* (in writing) full stop, period, pause: *Mwalimu alimtaka mwanafunzi atumie vituo baada ya kila sentensi*, the teacher wanted the student to use a full stop after each sentence.
kituo³ *n (ki-vi)* security, peace, calmness, tranquility: *Kumekuwa hakuna kituo katika nchi ile*, there has been no tranquility in that country. (cf *umakini, utulivu*)
kitumitumi *n (ki-vi)* anything that gives out a rumbling sound e.g. volcano e.g. *Kitumitumi cha volkano kiliwashtua wanavijiji*, the rumbling of the volcano shocked the villagers. (cf *kitututu*)
kitutu *adv (idm) Pigwa kitutu*, be beaten by a large number of people e.g. *Mwizi alipigwa kitutu katika mtaa wetu*, the thief was beaten by a large number

of people in our neighbourhood. (cf *kipopo*)

kitututu *n* (*ki-vi*) motorbike, motor scooter. (cf *vespa, pikipiki*)

kitwea *n* (*ki-vi*) solitude, loneliness: *Amekuwa akiishi katika kitwea tangu kufa kwa mkewe*, he has been living in loneliness since the death of his wife. (cf *kivumvu, upweke, ukiwa*)

kitwitwi *n* (*ki-vi*) (*zool*) common sandpiper. *Actitis hypoleucos*. (cf *kiulimazi*)

kiu *n* (*ki-vi*) 1. thirst: *Ona kiu*, feel thirsty. *Kata kiu*, quench the thirst. *Sikia kiu*, feel the thirst. 2. desire for sth; eagerness, anxiety, zeal: *Ana kiu ya kutaka kwenda kusoma ng'ambo*, he is eager to go overseas for studies. (cf *uchu, hamu*)

kiua¹ *n* (*ki-vi*) (*zool*) a kind of fish of the *Tetradontidae* family.

kiua² *n* (*ki-vi*) ornamental eye-let hole; a hole made in embroidering white skull caps.: *Kifua ya kiua*, white-skull cap.

kiuamwitu *n* (*ki-vi*) (*bot*) a kind of small wild tree with scented flowers, used in medicine.

kiuasumu *n* (*ki-vi*) antidote, antipoison, counterpoison.

kiuavijasumu *n* (*ki-vi*) antibiotic; a drug that is used to kill bacteria and cure infections.

kiubabe *adv* gallantly, bravely: *Alipigana kiubabe kwenye vita*, he fought gallantly in the war. (cf *kijasiri*)

kiufundi *adj* skilfully: *Alifunga goli kiufundi*, he scored the goal skilfully.

kiuk.a (also **keuka**) *vt* 1. jump over, step over, leap over: *Alilikiuka gogo*, he stepped over the log. (cf *ruka*) 2. infringe, usurp, violate: *Kiuka sheria*, violate the law. *Kiuka mpaka*, transgress. *Wanavijiji walikiuka mila zao*, the villagers violated their customs. Prep. **kiuk.i.a** St. **kiuk.ik.a** Cs. **kiuk.ish.a** Ps. **kiuk.w.a** Rp. **kiuk.an.a**

kiulimazi *n* (*ki-vi*) (*zool*) common sandpiper. *Actitis hypoleucos*. (cf *kitwitwi*)

kiumambuzi *n* (*ki-vi*) (*zool*) writhing skink, burrowing skink; a kind of lizard that lives in burrows beneath rocks, humus and fallen trees. *Riopa sundevallii*.

kiumbe *n* (*ki-vi*) being, creature e.g. human being, animal, bird, fish, etc.; any animate thing: *Kila kiumbe kitakufa*, every creature will die.

kiumbizi *n* (*ki-vi*) see *kirumbizi²*

kiume¹ *adv* manly, bravely: *Alipigana kiume*, he fought bravely.

kiume² *adj* male, manly: *Mtoto wa kiume*, a male child, a baby boy.

kiunda¹ *n* (*ki-vi*) a kind of round trap made like a hedge.

kiunda² *n* (*ki-vi*) (*med*) a kind of disease affecting your back or knees making someone unable to straighten himself properly; flexion deformity.

kiunga¹ *n* (*ki-vi*) 1. orchard, shaded garden: *Kuna miti mingi katika kiunga hiki*, there are many trees in this orchard. (cf *kitalu, bustani*) 2. suburbs, outskirts: *Anaishi kiungani*, he lives in the outskirts.

kiunga² *n* (*ki-vi*) (*zool*) a kind of saltwater fish resembling wrasse.

kiunganishi *n* (*ki-vi*) (*gram*) conjunction e.g. *na* "and"; *lakini*, 'but', etc.: *Kiunganishi tegemezi*, subordinating conjunction. *Kiunganishi ambatano*, coordinating conjunction. *Kiunganishi wiani*, correlative conjunction.

kiungo¹ *n* (*ki-vi*) joint of a body: *Kiungo cha mwili*, a part of the body. *Kiungo badi*, lap joint. *Kiungo liwato*, butt joint. *Viungo vyake vimeachana*, his joints have come apart.

kiungo² *n* (*ki-vi*) sth which seasons, gives a taste to food e.g. spice, salt, onion, etc.; seasoning: *Mpishi alitia viungo vingi kwenye mchuzi*, the cook put many seasonings in the food; seasoner.

Kiunguja *n* (*ki-vi*) A Zanzibar dialect which is regarded as standard form of Swahili.

kiungulia *n (ki-vi)* pyrosis, heartburn, waterbrash; a burning sensation beneath the breastbone resulting from indigestion. *Shikwa na kiungulia,* feel symptoms of heartburn e.g. *Alishikwa na kiungulia baada ya kula chakula chenye pilipili,* he felt heartburn after eating a chilly dish.

kiuno¹ *n (ki-vi)* 1. waist; the part just above the hips: *Chezesha kiuno,* shimmy the hips; shake the hips. 2. *(idm) Vunja kiuno,* tire someone.

kiuno² *n (ki-vi)* concrete foundation.

kiunza *n (ki-vi)* a board used to protect a corpse when rested in the grave; burial board. (cf *kiwamba*)

kiunzi *n (ki-vi)* 1. *(naut)* a ship's hull under construction. 2. planking. 3. (in races) hurdle: *Wanariadha waliviruka viunzi,* the athletes jumped over the hurdles. 4. door frame.

kiunzi

kiupenyo *n (ki-vi)* aperture

kiva¹ *n (ki-vi)* the mouth of a wicker fish trap that a fish gets into it. (cf *kiambio, kipwa*)

kiva² *n (ki-vi)* unity (cf *umoja*)

kivangatio *n (ki-vi)* confusion, chaos, pandemonium, disorder: *Kivangatio kilitokea uwanjani wakati mchezaji mmoja alipompiga ngumi rifarii,* pandemonium broke out on the playground when a player punched the referee. (cf *vurumai, fujo, ghasia*)

kivazi *n (ki-vi)* 1. style of dressing: *Kivazi chake kinampendeza,* his style of dressing fits him. (cf *uvaaji*) 2. clothes, costumes.

kivi¹ *n (ki-vi)* see *kiwi⁵*

kivi² *n (ki-vi)* see *kiwiko*

kivi³ *n (ki-vi)* a bar of wood set against a door inside used for fastening, etc.; latch. (cf *kia, komeo*)

kivimbe¹ *n (ki-vi)* the circumference as of a tree trunk or person's waist; girth: *Kivimbe cha mti,* the girth of a tree.

kivimbe² *n (ki-vi)* a small swelling; protuberance.

kivo¹ *n (ki-vi)* surplus, excess, extra: *Kanipimia kibaba cha mchele na kivo,* he has measured for me a kilogram of rice and an extra weight. (cf *ziada, nyongeza*)

kivo² *n (ki-vi)* an empty shell of a coconut; coconut shell. (cf *kijuu*)

kivoloya *adv* haphazardly, carelessly, disorderly: *Alizitumia pesa zake kivoloya,* he spent his money carelessly. (cf *ovyoovyo*)

kivuko (also *kivusha*) *n (ki-vi)* 1. crossing, bridge, ferry; anything which puts one across a place: *Kivuko cha mguu,* pedestrian crossing. 2. act of crossing a river, etc.: *Kivuko kile kilisababisha vifo vingi kwa abiria,* that ferry crossing caused many deaths to the passengers.

kivukomilia *n (ki-vi)* pedestrian crossing.

kivuli *n (ki-vi)* 1. shadow: *Alipumzika kwenye kivuli,* he rested in the shadow. *(prov) Kivuli cha mvumo huwafunika waliye mbali,* the shadow of a Deleb palm provides shelter for those who are far away i.e. a well-off person can help people who are not part of his family. (syn) *Amekaa katika kivuli cha mumewe,* she has lived with her children without getting married again after her husband's death. 2. *(idm)*

Kula kivuli, ruin someone behind his back. 3. (*fig*) ghost, apparition.

kivuligiza *n* (*ki-vi*) umbra; the dark cone of shadow projecting from a planet or satellite on the side facing the sun.

kivumanyuki *n* (*ki-vi*) (*bot*) a kind of almost stalkless plant having leaves upto to $4\frac{1}{2}$ inches long and $1\frac{3}{8}$ inches broad with star-like flowers, which are lilac to purplish, with a pale centre. *Pentas puprurea*.

kivumanzi *n* (*ki-vi*) a small bell, such as the one used for fastening around the neck of domesticated animals such as cat, cow, goat, etc. (cf *njuga, mbugi, msewe*)

kivumbasi *n* (*ki-vi*) (*bot*) a kind of annual herb with a strong and pleasant aromatic odour, having leaves and seeds which are used as a pot herb, as a medicine for abdominal pains and as a mosquito repellent when the dried plant is burnt. *Ocimum sp*.

kivumbi *n* (*ki-vi*) 1. confusion, chaos, pandemonium, disorder: *Kivumbi kilitokea wakati askari polisi walipowatawanya waandamanaji kwa bomu la machozi*, chaos broke out when policemen dispersed the demonstrators with tear-gas. (cf *ghasia, fujo*) 2. a big contest: *Kulikuwa na kivumbi wakati timu mbili maarufu zilipomenyana vikali uwanjani*, there was a big contest when the two prominent teams in the country fought bitterly on the ground. (cf *pambano, mtanange*)

kivumishi *n* (*ki-vi*) (*gram*) adjective: *Kivumishi arifu*, predicative adjective. *Kivumishi onyeshi*, demonstrative adjective. *Kivumishi milikishi*, possessive adjective. *Kivumishi linganishi*, comparative adjective. (cf *sifa*)

kivumvu *n* (*ki-vi*) reclusion, reclusiveness: solitude affecting someone resulting esp after the death of someone else esp wife or husband: *Amekuwa na kivumvu tangu kufiwa na mumewe hivi karibuni*, she has been in a state of solitude since her husband's death recently. (cf *kitwea, ukiwa, upweke*)

kivunde *n* (*ki-vi*) gruel made from cassava flour which has been steeped until fermentation has begun: *Unga wa kivunde*, cassava flour of this kind.

kivunga *n* (*ki-vi*) a long thick crop of hair, tied together; ponytail: *Msichana yule anapenda kuweka kivunga kichwani*, that girl likes to keep a long thick crop of hair on her head.

kivunge *n* (*ki-vi*) envelope; sth that covers or wraps another thing.

kivunjajungu (also *vunjajungu*) *n* (*ki-vi*) (*zool*) mantis; praying mantis; hottentot god. This is a kind of slender, elongate insect like a grasshopper (family *Mantidae*) which feeds mainly on other insects and grasps their prey with stout, spiny forelegs often held up together as in praying. The mantises are found mainly in tropical and sub-tropical countries.

kivunjajungu

kivuno *n* (*ki-vi*) harvest, profit. (*prov*) *Ganda la mua la jana, chungu kama kivuno*, the skin of yesterday's sugarcane is a whole harvest to an ant i.e. a small thing that a person gets may be regarded as a big one by him simply because he is not used to getting things.

kivusho *n* (*ki-vi*) see *kivuko*

kivutavumbi *n* (*ki-vi*) hoover

kivutio *n* (*ki-vi*) incentive, stimulus: *Serikali imeweka vivutio fulani kwa wawekezaji kutoka nje*, the government has kept certain incentives for the investors from outside. *Mchezaji wetu wa kiungo alikuwa kivutio kwa* *watazamaji*, our midfield player was a centre of attraction in the eyes of the spectators. *Kivutio cha utalii*, tourists' attraction. (cf *motisha*)

kivuvu *n* (*ki-vi*) (*zool*) fruitfly; a kind of small fly whose larvae feed on fruits and vegetables.

kivyazi *n* (*ki-vi*) see *kizazi*

kivyere *n* (*ki-vi*) son's or daughter's parent in-law.

-kiwa[1] *adj* 1. solitary, alone: *Amekuwa mkiwa siku hizi*, he has become lonely these days. 2. poor: *Inafaa umsaidie kwa vile yeye ni mkiwa*, it is fitting that you help him because he is poor. (cf *masikini*)

kiwa[2] *n* (*ki-vi*) a small island; islet.

kiwaa *n* (*ki-vi*) 1. blurred vision; bad sight: *Ana kiwaa*, he has bad vision. (cf *gizu, utusitusi*) 2. unclear situation.

kiwakilishi *n* (*ki-vi*) (*gram*) pronoun: *Kiwakilishi nafsi*, personal pronoun. *Kiwakilishi milikishi*, possessive pronoun. *Kiwakilishi rejeshi*, relative pronoun. (cf *kibadala, kijina*)

kiwambaza *n* (*ki-vi*) see *kiambaza*

kiwambo *n* (*ki-vi*) 1. drumhead; the membrane stretched over the open end or ends of a drum. 2. diaphragm: *Kiwambo cha sikio*, eardrum. 3. a thing that assists a baby that begins to walk. 4. screen: *Kiwambo cha makuti*, a screen of coconut leaves.

kiwamwitu *n* (*ki-vi*) (*bot*) a kind of tree or shrub with many branches and which forms a thicket.

kiwanda[1] *n* (*ki-vi*) see *kimanda*[1]

kiwanda[2] *n* (*ki-vi*) factory, industry: *Kiwanda cha sabuni*, soap factory. *Kiwanda cha sukari*, sugar factory. *Kiwanda cha karatasi*, paper mill. (cf *karakhana*)

kiwanda[3] (*usu viwanda*) *n* (*ki-vi*) two sticks used to tie threads during weaving, etc.

kiwanda[4] *n* (*ki-vi*) a place where hoes and knives are made.

kiwango *n* (*ki-vi*) 1. amount, rate, measure, level, point. *Kiwango cha barafu*, ice point. *Kiwango cha kuchemka*, boiling point, *Kiwango cha kuganda*, freezing point, *Kiwango cha kuyeyuka*, melting point. *Kiwango cha riba*, interest rate. *Kwa kiwango kikubwa*, in large measure. 2. (in Islam) quantity which is normally provided as a religious offering: *Pesa zake hazijafikia kiwango cha kutoa zaka*, his money has not reached the quantity to offer alms. 3. rank, status, dignity, standard, position: *Wanafunzi walifikia kiwango cha juu cha elimu*, the students attained a high standard of education. (cf *cheo*)

kiwangwa *n* (*ki-vi*) cowrie shell used as an ornament.

kiwanja (also *uwanja*) *n* (*ki-vi*) ground, field: *Kiwanja cha mpira*, football ground. *Kiwanja cha ndege*, airfield, airport. *Kiwanja cha nyumba*, plot of a house. (cf *uga, kiwara*)

kiwara *n* (*ki-vi*) 1. plain; a large piece of ground. 2. unfertile land; grassland. (cf *mbuga*)

kiwavi *n* (*ki-vi*) 1. (*bot*) a perennial herb with long slender twining stems and stinging hairs. *Tragia furialis*. 2. (*zool*) a large hairy kind of larva whose hairs irritate very much if they penetrate the skin of someone; caterpillar. (cf *kiwaviwavi*)

kiwe[1] *n* (*ki-vi*) milestone, grinding-stone (cf *komango*)

kiwe[2] *n* (*ki-vi*) 1. the problem of not seeing at night; night blindness: *Macho yake yameingia kiwe*, his eyes cannot see at night. 2. pimple, acne. (cf *chunusi, kipele*)

kiweko *n* (*ki-vi*) base, holder, pedestal, stand, support. (cf *msingi, kitako*)

kiwele *n* (*ki-vi*) (*zool*) udder; milk gland of a female animal.

kiweo *n* (*ki-vi*) limb. (*prov*): *Mwana akinyea kiweo hakikatwi*, if a child defecates on a limb, the limb should not be amputated. e.g. One should not use heavy or stern punishment to solve a simple problem. (cf *paja, ago*)

kiwera *adv* in large quantities.

kiwete *n* (*ki-vi*) a disabled person; a

crippled person; lame, cripple.
kiweto *n (ki-vi)* a hen that does not lay eggs; non-layer.
kiwewe *n (ki-vi)* bafflement, bewilderment, anxiety; confusion resulting from an unpleasant experience, etc. *Aliingiwa na kiwewe aliposikia kwamba polisi wanamtafuta*, he was filled with anxiety when he learnt that the police were looking for him. (cf *kizaazaa, wasiwasi*)
kiwi[1] *n (ki-vi)* bar of wood set against a door inside as a kind of fastening, etc.; door fastener; dowel. (cf *komeo, kia*)
kiwi[2] (also *kiwiwi*) *n (ki-vi)* dazzle, glare: *Kiwi cha macho*, blindness from glare; the state of being dazed i.e. the state of being unable to see clearly. 2. (*idm*) *Tia mtu kiwi*, deceive someone.
kiwi[3] *n (ki-vi)* greediness, voracity, gluttony: *Kiwi chake kimemtia aibu*, his gluttonous behaviour has put him into shame. (cf *uroho*)
kiwi[4] *n (ki-vi)* (*zool*) a tailless New Zealand bird with underdeveloped wings, hair-like feathers and a long slender bill; kiwi.
kiwi[5] *n (ki-vi)* the dark fluid emitted by a cuttlefish in order to protect itself from being seen by its enemies.
kiwida *n (ki-vi)* (*naut*) a small hole in a dhow in which the mast is placed; mast-bank. (cf *kiyunga, kidu*)
kiwiko (also *kiko, kivi*) *n (ki-vi)* (*anat*) elbow.
kiwili *n (ki-vi)* a gathering of people usu for farming purposes where local beer or food is served: *Kiwili cha pombe*, a gathering of this kind for the purpose of drinking beer.
kiwiliwili *n (ki-vi)* (*anat*) body, trunk: *Kiwiliwili chake ni kipana*, his body is large.
kiwindu *n (ki-vi)* (*naut*) anchor and rope used to keep the ship's stern facing the beach: *Nanga ya kiwindu*, an anchor for this purpose. *Kamba ya kiwindu*, a rope for this purpose.
kiwiwi *n (ki-vi)* see *kiwi*[2]

Kiyahudi *n (ki-vi)* Jewish language.
kiyaka *n (ki-vi)* see *kichaka*[1]
kiyama *n (ki-vi)* the day of resurrection; the general resurrection of all the dead; doomsday: *Viumbe vyote vitafufuliwa siku ya kiama*, all creatures will be resurrected on doomsday. (cf *jongomeo*) (Ar)
kiyana *n (ki-vi)* an earthenware dish, used for cooking.
kiyeye *n (ki-vi)* (*med*) sensitivity of teeth; a condition caused by painful sensation of the teeth when exposed or in contact with hot or cold elements such as food, air, etc. (cf u*kakasi*)
kiyeyusho *n (ki-vi)* solvent
kiyoga *n (ki-vi)* (*bot*) a little mushroom. (cf *kuwu, uyoga*)
kiyombo *n (ki-vi)* clothes made from the pounded bark of a tree; bark cloth.
kiyoyozi *n (ki-vi)* air conditioner.
Kiyunani *n (ki-vi)* old Greek Koine; ancient Greek.
kiyunga *n (ki-vi)* mast-bank (cf *kiwida, kida*)
kiyuyu *n (ki-vi)* (*shrub*) a shrub up to 15 feet high with fleshy green branches and leaves which contain a milky juice, used as fish poison and for the treatment of boils or abscesses. *Synadenium carinatum*. (cf *chakazi, utupa*)
kiza (also *giza*) *n (ki-vi)* darkness: *Kiza tororo*, complete darkness.
kizaazaa *n (ki-vi)* confusion, chaos, pandemonium, turmoil, uproar: *Kizaazaa kilizuka wakati mchezaji alipompiga ngumi golikipa wetu*, confusion broke out when a player punched our goalkeeper (cf *patashika, kiherehere, fujo, ghasia*)
kizabizabina *n (ki-vi)* scandalmonger; a person who gossips maliciously and spreads scandals.
kizalia[1] *n (ki-vi)* offspring
kizalia[2] *n (ki-vi)* 1. inherited disability/defect. 2. birthmark.
kizamiadagaa *n (ki-vi)* (*zool*) malachite kingfisher; a kind of bird (family

Alcedindae) having a conspicuous blue and black barred crest, a white throat with rufous cheeks and underparts and which largely feeds upon small fish and dragon fly larvae. *Alcedo cristata*. (cf *kisharifu, mtilili, mdiria*)

kizao *n* (*ki-vi*) see *uzazi*

kizazi (also *kivyazi*) *n* (*ki-vi*) 1. offspring; childbearing: *Ana kizazi kikubwa*, she has many offsprings. *Funga kizazi*, stop childbearing. 2. uterus: *Mlango wa kizazi*, cervix; the neck of the womb. 3. clan: *Watu hawa ni wa kizazi kimoja*, these people are of the same clan. 4. generation: *Kizazi kijacho kitaongezeka*, the future generation will increase.

kizezele *n* (*ki-vi*) (*zool*) yellow-vented bulbul; a kind of bird (family *Pycnonotidae*) having greyish brown underparts and a black head which is slightly crested. *Pycnonotus barabatus*.

kizibao *n* (*ki-vi*) sleeveless waistcoat: *Amevaa kizibao leo*, he has worn a sleeveless waistcoat today.

kizibiti *n* (*ki-vi*) court exhibit: *Upande wa mashtaka ulitoa kizibiti mahakamani*, the prosecution produced an exhibit at the court.

kizibo *n* (*ki-vi*) stopper, cork: *Chupa hii haina kizibo*, this bottle does not have a stopper. (cf *kifuniko*)

kizidishi *n* (*ki-vi*) multiplier

kizidisho *n* (*ki-vi*) multiple: *Kizidisho shirika*, common multiple.

kizigeu *n* (*ki-vi*) (*math*) coefficient; a number or symbol multiplied with a variable or an unknown quantity in an algebraic term, as in 6 in the term 6x or x in the term x (y + z)

kizimba *n* (*ki-vi*) 1. barred cage; cage of a hen or animal. 2. the dock in a courtroom.

kizimbwi *n* (*ki-vi*) 1. (*naut*) anchorage; a place to anchor. (cf *bandari*) 2. the edge of a shelf.

kizimio *n* (*ki-vi*) ash-tray.

kizimwili *n* (*ki-vi*) 1. (*bot*) kernel smut, black smut; a plant disease caused by basidiomycetous fungi that enter the flowers and infect them with black spores which usually break into a fine powder. These spores can literally be found in every field where rice has been grown. 2. (*syn*) *Mweusi kama kizimwili*, as black as a kernel smut.

kizinda *n* (*ki-vi*) (*anat*) hymen, maiden head; the thin mucuous membrane that normally closes part of the opening of the vagina in a virgin: *Vunja kizinda*, break the hymen; break the virginity. *Weka kizinda*, preserve virginity. *Kizinda kisichobikiriwa*, unbroken hymen.

kizingatine *n* (*ki-vi*) a dressing which is put on the wound after circumcision in order to prevent it from being knocked; dressing of circumcision wound. (cf *ulfafa, kata*)

kizingiti *n* (*ki-vi*) 1. threshold; a piece of wood forming the bottom of a doorway. 2. barrier reef covered at high tide. 3. (*fig*) stumbling block, obstruction: *Wekea kizingiti*, block someone e.g. *Walimwekea vizingiti ili asiweze kusafiri*, they placed obstructions to prevent him from travelling. (cf *kikwazo, kizuizi, pingamizi*)

kizingo[1] *n* (*ki-vi*) curve, bend; the turning of a road or river. (cf *tao, pindo*)

kizingo[2] *n* (*ki-vi*) dustless sand from the seashore, used for building purposes.

kizio[1] *n* (*ki-vi*) half of anything round; hemisphere: *Kizio cha nazi*, half of a coconut. *Kizio cha chenza*, half of a tangerine.

kizio[2] *n* (*ki-vi*) (*math*) unit, base: *Kizio cha mnato*, unit of viscosity. *Kizio cha seti*, unit of sets. *Kizio cha ujazo*, cubic unit. *Kizio cha uvutano*, gravitational unit.

kizito *n* (*ki-vi*) (*colloq*) a very influential person; nabob, nob, bigwig. *Taasisi nyingi zinamheshimu Dr. Omar kwa vile yeye ni kizito*, many institutions respect Dr. Omar because he is a bigwig.

kiziwi *n* (*ki-vi*) a deaf person: *Ataweza kusikia vizuri na yeye ni kiziwi?* Can he hear properly while he is a deaf person? (cf *kiduko*)

kizuianoki *n* (*ki-vi*) (*engin*) antiknock; a substance added to the fuel of internal combustion engines to do away with or reduce noise resulting from top rapid combustion. (Eng)

kizuizi *n* (*ki-vi*) obstacle, barrier, impediment, stumbling-block: *Polisi waliweka vizuizi barabarani ili kuzichunguza gari zilizoibiwa*, the police set up roadblocks to check the stolen cars. *Wakoloni waliweka vizuizi vingi ili kuzuia maendeleo ya nchi*, the colonialists put up many impediments to prevent the country's development. (cf *pingamizi, kikwazo, kizingiti*)

kizuizini *adv* in detention: *Serikali imemweka kizuizini*, the government has put him in detention. (cf *korokoroni, ndani*)

kizuizui *n* (*ki-vi*) 1. a cloth used in blind man's buff. 2. a children's game like blind man's buff or hide-and-seek in which a blindfolded player has to catch and identify another.

kizuka *n* (*ki-vi*) (in Islam) a widow living in seclusion for a specific period of time after her husband's death.

kizuli *n* (*ki-vi*) see *kizunguzungu*

Kizungu[1] *n* (*ki-vi*) English language: *Anazungumza Kizungu vizuri*, he speaks English well.

kizungu[2] *adj* European: *Mtoto wa Kizungu*, European child.

kizungumkuti *n* (*ki-vi*) mystery, riddle, enigma: *Kizungumkuti cha silaha za maangamizi bado kinayahangaisha mataifa makubwa*, the mystery concerning weapons of mass destruction still plagues major powers.

kizunguzungu (also *kizuli*) *n* (*ki-vi*) dizziness, giddiness: *Alishikwa na kizunguzungu alipotazama chini kutoka juu ya jengo*, he experienced giddiness when he looked down from the top of the building. (cf *kimulimli, kisunzi*)

kizushi (also *mzushi*) *n* (*ki-vi*) 1. intruder, interloper, meddler: *Kwa nini kizushi yule hupenda kuingilia mambo yangu?* Why does that meddler like to interfere in my private affairs? (*prov*) *Mwana wa mtu kizushi, akizuka zuka naye*, a human being is a revolutionist; if he emerges, go with him i.e. if there is no clue at all as to what one may do against you, best follow all his movements. (cf *mdaku, mdukizo*) 2. liar, concocter, fabricator, cheater: *Usimwamini kizushi yule*, don't trust that liar. (cf *mnafiki, fatani*) 3. novelty, phenomenon.

kizuu[1] *n* (*ki-vi*) food like gruel made from grounded unripe maize and later squeezed; porridge of soft raw maize.

kizuu[2] *n* (*ki-vi*) a messenger of evil spirit, said to be employed by witches and wizards to serve in their houses in the form of a rat and kill people by devouring their lives.

kizuu[3] ghost

klabu[1] (also *kilabu*) *n* (*n*) 1. a group of people associated for a common purpose or mutual advantage; club: *Klabu ya usiku*, night club. 2. the building used by such a group. (Eng)

klabu[2] *n* (*n*) a place where beer is sold and drank: *Klabu ya pombe*, beer club. (Eng)

klachi *n* (*n*) clutch (Eng)

klempu *n* (*n*) clamp (Eng)

kliniki *n* (*n*) clinic (Eng)

kloraidi *n* (*n*) (*chem*) chloride (Eng)

klorini *n* (*n*) (*chem*) chlorine (Eng)

klorofili *n* (*n*) chlorophyll (Eng)

klorofomu *n* (*n*) (*med*) chloroform (Eng)

ko[1] *cop. verb* (of place) be here, be there: *Uko wapi?* Where are you? *Niko hapa*, I am here.

ko[2] *pron* (rel. pron. of place) where: *Sielewi alikokwenda*, I don't know

where he has gone.
koa¹ *n* (*ma-*) a band of thin metal made from copper or brass, etc. worn as an ornament on the necks or arm: *Koa la fedha*, a silver armlet.
koa² *n* (*ma-*) 1. (*zool*) snail, slug: *Ute wa koa*, the slime of a snail (cf *konokono*) 2. the shell of a snail or of an oyster.
koa³ *n* (*ma-*) a kind of fish-trap consisting of a fence of upright sticks fastened together and used to prevent fish from escaping.
ko.a⁴ *vi* 1. be sharp: *Kisu kile kinakoa*, that knife is sharp. 2. (of food or conversation) be pleasing, be pleasant, be attractive. Prep. **ko.le.a,** be pleasant e.g. *Mazungumzo haya yamekolea*, these conversations are pleasant. St. **ko.ek.a** Cs. **ko.z.a** Ps. **ko.lew.a,**
koakoa *n* (*ma-*) see *gonda*
koambili *adj* bivalve
koana *n* (*n*) see *kowana*
kobe *n* (*ma-*) 1. tortoise. 2. (*colloq*) name applied to a person who does not fast during the month of Ramadan for no concrete reasons.
kobeamiti *n* (*ma-*) (*zool*) a kind of bird of prey like a hawk which carries off chicks.
kobo.a *vt* see *goboa*
kobwe¹ *n* (*ma-*) (*bot*) a kind of French beans like cowpeas.
kobwe² *n* (*ma-*) (*zool*) a kind of insect like snail.
kobwe³ *n* (*ma-*) (*idm*) *Piga kobwe*, clap with hollowed hands or with the hands on the biceps.
kobwe⁴ *n* (*ma-*) 1. (*med*) exomphalos, exumbilication, omphalocele; congenital eventration at the umbilicus; herniation of some of the abdominal contents into the umbilical cord at birth. 2. umbilical hernia.
kocha *n* (*ma-*) (in sports) coach: *Kocha wa mpira*, football coach. *Kocha wa riadha*, athletics' coach. *Kocha wa kimataifa*, international coach. *Kocha wa kudumu*, permanent coach. (Eng)
koche¹ *n* (*ma-*) (*bot*) the edible fruit of *mkoche* dwarf palm (*Hyphaene crinita*), which is polished brown, closely resembling the ginger nut fruit. (cf *koma*)
koche² *n* (*ma-*) (*zool*) a class of prawns: *Kamba koche*, a class of prawns of this kind.
kochi *n* (*ma-*) couch, sofa, divan: *Amekaa katika kochi*, he has sat on the couch. (cf *sofa*) (Eng)
kochimili *n* (*n*) cochineal; a red dye made from the dried bodies of female cochineal insects. (Eng)
kocho¹ *n* (*n*) a barbed spear with a line attached to it, used for spearing whales or other large sea animals; harpoon. (cf *mbuda*)
kocho² *n* (*n*) underwear, underdress. (cf *chupi*)
-kocho³ *adj* (*colloq*) clever, expert: *Yeye ni mkocho katika kucheza gololi*, he is good at playing marbles.
kochokocho *adv* abundantly, copiously; in large quantities: *Samaki wamevuliwa kochokocho leo*, fish have been caught in large quantities today. (cf *tele, tupu*)
kodeini *n* (*n*) (*chem*) codein (Eng)
kodeksi *n* (*n*) codex (Eng)
kod.i¹ *vt* rent, live, lease: *Amelikodi gari hili*, he has hired this car. Prep. **kod.i.a** St. **kod.ik.a** Cs. **kod.ish.a** rent out, hire out e.g. *Anataka kunikodisha nyumba yake*, he wants to rent me his house. Ps. **kod.iw.a**, be rented, be hired. Ps. of Cs. **kod.ish.w.a,** be rented e.g. *Nyumba hii haijakodishwa kwa mtu yeyote*, this house has not been rented to anyone. (cf *panga*) (Pers, Hind)
kodi² *n* (*n*) rent, tax, levy, duty: *Kodi ya mapato*, income tax. *Kodi ya kichwa*, poll tax. *Kodi ya mauzo*, sales tax. *Kodi ya nyumba*, house rent. *Kodi ya forodha*, customs duty. *Kodi ya*

starehe, entertainment tax. *Kodi ya nyongeza*, Valued Added Tax. *Kodi ya kutia nanga*, harbour duty. *Kodi ya maendeleo*, development tax. *Kodi ya mtaji*, capital levy. *Lipa kodi*, pay rent. *Piga kodi*, tax someone. (Pers, Hind)

kodiani *n(n)* (*mus*) accordion; a musical instrument with keys, metal reeds, and a set of bellows controlled by the player's hands. (Eng)

kodiani

kodish.a *vt* see kodi¹ Prep. **kodish.i.a** St. **kodish.ik.a** Ps. **kodish.w.a** Rp. **kodish.an.a**

kodo *n* (*ma-*) (*anat*) testicles (cf *kende hasua, korodani*)

kodo.a *vt* (*idm*) *Kodoa macho*, stare at; gawk, gaze. Prep. **kodo.le.a**, stare at e.g. *Alinikodolea macho kwa dakika chache*, he stared at me for a few minutes. St. **kodo.lek.a** Cs. **kodo.lesh.a** Ps. of Prep. **kodo.lew.a** (*tumbua*)

kodrai *n* (*n*) corduroy; a kind of trousers made from this heavy cotton fabric(Eng)

kodwa (also *kodwe*) *n* (*n*) 1. a children's game of throwing small stones and putting them into small holes. 2. small stones like cashewnuts or like the seeds of *komwe*, used for this kind of game.

kodwe *n* (*n*) see *kodwa*

koek.a *vt* 1. pluck fruit, etc. by using a forged or hooked stick on its end: *Alikoeka mapapai kwenye kiunga changu*, he plucked pawpaws by using a hooked stick in my walled garden. Prep. **koek.e.a** St. **koek.ek.a** Cs. **koek.esh.a** Ps. **koek.w.a** 2. (*idm*) *Koeka mwari*, is used of *somo*, an initiation instructor, to make definite arrangements so that an initiate will be under her own command and not somebody else.

kofi¹ *n* (*ma-*) slap: *Piga kofi*, slap; box the ear. (cf *kibao*)

kofi² *n* (*ma-*) clapping of the hands; applause: *Watazamaji walikuwa wakiwapigia makofi washindi*, the spectators were applauding the victors.

kofi³ *n* (*n*) a kind of dance used in the exorcism of spirits from a patient; exorcising dance.

kofia *n* (*n*) cap, fez, hat: *Kofia ya kitunga*, a kind of tarboosh. *Kofia ya bulibuli*, a white embroidered skull-cap. *Kofia ya kiaskofu*, mitre. *Kofia ya viua*, an ordinary cap with small holes in it. *Kofia ya mdongea*, a white cap made by a sewing machine. *Vaa kofia*, wear a cap. *Vua kofia*, take off a cap.

kog.a¹ see *oga¹*

kog.a² *vi* boast usu in public; flaunt, brag, vaunt, show off: *Anapenda kujikoga hadharani*, he likes to boast about himself in public. Prep. **kog.e.a** St. **kog.ek.a** Cs. **kog.esh.a** Ps. **kog.w.a** Rp. **kog.an.a**

koga³ *n* (*n*) mould, blight, mustiness; dirt of the body usu resulting from a dress that has been constantly worn: *Fanya koga*, get mouldy. *Ingia koga*, get mouldy. *Amevaa shati hilo kwa hilo na sasa limemea koga*, he has constantly worn the shirt and now it has become dirty.

kogo¹ *n* (*n*) (*anat*) the back part of the head; occiput. (cf *kichogo*)

kogo² (also *ukogo*) *n* (*ma-*) a string of beads worn by some women around their loins. (cf *kondavi, utunda*)

kohli *n* (*n*) a kind of cosmetic preparation used as an antimony for eye make-up; kohl. (Ar)

koho *n* (*n*) (*zool*) vulturine fish eagle; a mainly white bird of prey with black scapulars and secondaries and a black band across its white tail. *Gypohierax angolensis.*

koho.a *vi* cough: *Ameanza kukohoa kwa sababu ya kuvuta sigara nyingi*, he has started coughing because of excessive smoking. Prep. **koho.le.a** St. **koho.leka** Cs. **koho.z.a**, cause to cough e.g. *Ugoro huu unakohoza sana*, this snuff causes a lot of coughing.

kohoo *n* (*ma-*) see *kohozi*

kohozi (also *kohoo*) *n* (*ma-*) (*med*) sputum, phlegm. (cf *balaghamu*)

koikol¹ *n* (*ma-*) see *goigoi*³

koikoi² *n* (*ma-*) (*zool*) a kind of bird with a long neck, long legs and a long tapered bill.

koja¹ *n* (*ma-*) a wreath of flowers, etc. worn around somebody's neck, as a kind of ornament or present: *Biharusi alivalishwa koja la maua*, the bride was garlanded with a wreath of flowers.

koja² *n* (*ma-*) a kind of metal pot.

kojo.a *vi* urinate: *Anakojoa sana kwa sababu ana ugonjwa wa kisukari*, he urinates very much because he has diabetes. Prep. **kojo.le.a** St. **kojo.lek.a** Cs. **kojo.z.a** e.g *Mama alikwenda chooni kumkojoza mtoto wake*, the mother went to the toilet to assist her child to urinate. Ps. of Prep. **kojo.le.wa** Rp. of Prep. **kojo.le.an.a** (cf *tabawali*)

kojojo (also *kojozi*) *n* (*ma-*) (*zool*) sea hare (cf *babaje*)

kojokojo *n* (*ma-*) (*zool*) see *zongapingu*.

kojozi¹ *n* (*ma-*) see *kojojo*

kojozi² *n* (*ma-*) (*bot*) a kind of squashy banana, which is said to cause much urine.

kojozi³ *n* (*n*) idiot, simpleton, fool. (cf *mjinga, baradhuli*)

-kok.a *vt* used in the expression: *Koka moto*, get fuel for fire, set on fire. Prep. **kok.e.a** St. **kok.ek.a** Cs. **kok.esh.a** Ps. **kok.w.a** Ps. of Prep. **kok.ew.a** Rp. of Prep. **kok.e.an.a**

kokeni *n* (*n*) cocaine (Eng)

koko¹ (also *kokwa*) *n* (*n*) (*bot*) nut or stone of a fruit.

koko² *n* (*n*) 1. see *mkoko*. 2. a kind of undergrowth such as that one found in a mangrove swamp.

-koko³ *adj* stray, wandering: *Mbwa koko*, a stray dog.

koko.a¹ *vt* sweep up rubbish; collect rubbish, dust, etc.: *Alizikokoa taka zote*, she collected all the rubbish. Prep. **koko.le.a** St. **koko.lek.a** Cs. **koko.lesh.a** Ps. of Prep. **koko.lew.a** (cf *komba, zoa, fagia*)

koko.a² *vt* strip the grains off a cob of maize; husk the grains off a cob of maize: *Aliyakokoa mahindi baadaye akayaanika juani*, she stripped the grains of maize from their cobs and later dried them in the sun. Prep. **koko.le.a** St. **koko.k.a** Cs. **koko.z.a** Ps. of Prep. **koko.lew.a** (cf *pukuchua*)

kokoko *n* (*n*) (*zool*) slimy; a kind of salt water fish (family *Leiognathidae*) with a compressed slimy body, frequently caught by seine nets and prawn trawlers.

kokome.a *vt* fix sth firmly with a wedge, etc.; fix sth in its place: *Aliukokomea mpini kwenye jembe lake*, he fixed the handle firmly into its hoe. Prep. **kokome.le.a** St. **kokome.k.a** Cs. **kokome.sh.a** **kokome.z.a** Ps. **kokome.w.a**

kokomez.a *vt* force or squeeze sth into a space that is narrow or full of other things; stuff, cram. Prep. **kokomez.e.a** St. **kokomez.ek.a** Cs. **kokomez.esh.a** Ps. **kokomez.w.a** Rp. of Prep. **kokomez.e.an.a**

kokomo.a *vi* 1. force out sth violently from the mouth; retch violently: *Mtoto aliukokomoa mwiba wa samaki kooni mwake*, the child forced out the fish bone violently from his throat. 2. (*fig*) blurt out, burst out: *Aliikokomoa siri yake hadharani*, she blurted out her secret in public. Prep. *kokomo.le.a* St. *kokomo.k.a* Cs. *kokomo.sh.a* Ps. of Prep. *kokomo.lew.a* Rp. *kokomo.an.a*

kokon.a *vi* (of a dog, etc.) clean its hindquarters on the ground against grass, leaves, etc. after evacuation: *Mbwa alikokona baada ya kwenda haja*, the dog cleaned its hindquarters on the ground against grass after evacuation. Prep. *kokon.e.a* St. *kokon.ek.a* Cs. *kokon.esh.a* Ps. *kokon.w.a*

kokonek.a *vi* 1. make a shrill cry like a hen; cluck: *Kuku alikokoneka alipotaka kutaga*, the hen clucked when it wanted to lay eggs. 2. fear, be afraid: *Mwenye duka alikokoneka alipoona kwamba wezi wamemzunguka*, the shopkeeper became afraid when he found that the thieves had surrounded him. Prep. *kokonek.e.a* St. *kokonek.ek.a* Cs. *kokonek.esh.a* (cf *ogopa*)

kokono.a *vt* scrape out, scratch; remove a coating, crust or anything adhering whether solid or liquid: *Aliukokonoa ukoko kwenye chungu cha wali*, he scrapped the crust from the rice pot. Prep. *kokono.le.a* St. *kokono.lek.a* Cs. *kokono.sh.a* Ps. of Prep. *kokono.lew.a* (cf *kwangura, kwangua*)

kokonya.a *vt* see *kukunyaa*

kokot.a *vt* hull, drag, draw, pull, tug: *Kokota gari*, drag a cart. *Kokota gogo*, drag a log. *Kokota maneno*, articulate with difficulty; speak with difficulty; drawl words. *Kokota roho*, breathe with difficulty. *Kokota kazi*, work slowly. Prep. *kokot.e.a* St. *kokot.ek.a* Cs. *kokot.ez.a* Ps. *kokot.w.a* Rp. *kokot.an.a* (cf *vuta, burura, buruta*)

kokote *adv, pron* anywhere: *Anataka kuishi kokote mjini*, he wants to live anywhere in town.

kokotez.a *vt* drawl, twang; speak slowly prolonging the vowel sounds. Prep. *kokotez.e.a* St. *kokotez.ek.a* Cs. *kokotez.esh.a* Ps. *kokotez.w.a* Rp. *kokotez.an.a*

kokoto *n* (*n*) gravel, pebble, grit; small stones: *Walitumia kokoto kuikarabati barabara kuu*, they used pebbles to repair the main road. (cf *changarawe*)

kokoto.a[1] *vt* calculate, compute: *Unakokotoa nini?* What are you computing? Prep. *kokoto.le.a* St. *kokoto.k.a* Cs. *kokoto.sh.a* Ps. of Prep. *kokoto.lew.a* Rp. of Prep. *kokoto.le.an.a*

kokoto[2] *vt* take or get sth in large quantities. Prep. *kokoto.le.a* St. *kokoto.k.a* Cs. *kokoto.sh.a* Ps. *kokoto.lew.a* Rp. *kokoto.an.a*

kokteli *n* (*n*) cocktail (Eng)

kokwa *n* (*n*) (*bot*) kernel; nut of a fruit, stone of a fruit: *Kokwa za tende*, the stones of the dates. *Kokwa za maembe*, the stones of the mangoes. *Kokwa za papai*, the pips of the pawpaw.

kola *n* (*n*) collar (Eng)

kole[1] (also *mkole*) *n* (*ma-*) (*bot*) branch of a coconut palm, date palm and oil palm trees.

kole[2] *n* (*ma-*) a person arrested in place of a brother who has committed an offence such as murder or in debt and has absconded: *Shika kole*, arrest a person of this kind.

kole.a *vi* 1. be flavoursome, be tasty, be properly seasoned: *Chumvi imekolea katika mchuzi*, the salt is tasting lightly in the curry. 2. (of dye, etc.) be properly dyed: *Kitambaa hiki rangi yake imekolea*, this cloth is well dyed. 3. (*fig*) be palatable, be good, be progressing well: *Moto huu umekolea*, this fire burns well. *Soga hili limekolea*, this conversation has become lively. St. *kole.k.a* Cs. *kole.z.a* Ps. *kole.w.a*

kolego *n* (*n*) see *koleo*[1]

kolekole *n* (*n*) (*zool*) a kind of fish (family Carangidae) having an elongate or compressed body with small scales, usu cycloid; scad, caranx, trevally.

koleo¹ (also *kolego*) *n* (*n*) 1. pincers, pliers, tongs: *Koleo rekebifu*, adjustable pliers. (*prov*) *Kuzima koleo si mwisho wa uhunzi*, cooling the tongs is not the end of the job i.e. a person who stops from a certain habit or occupation does not mean he has changed. 2. a notch in an arrow held on the string with fingers.

koleo² *n* (*n*) shovel, spade. (cf *sepetu, shepe, beleshi*)

kolez.a¹ *vt* clear a debt on behalf of a debtor: *Alilikoleza deni lote la rafiki yake*, he cleared all his friend's debt. Prep. ***kolez.e.a*** St. ***kolez.ek.a*** Cs. ***kolez.esh.a*** Ps. ***kolez.w.a***

kolez.a² *vt* 1. season food. 2. make fire burn up. Prep. ***kolez.c.a*** St. ***kolez.ek.a*** Ps. ***kolez.w.a*** Rp. ***kolez.an.a*** Rp. of Prep. ***kolez.e.an.a***

koli *n* (*n*) 1. (*naut*) ship's papers, crew list, etc 2. a metal vessel used to store the ship's documents/papers.

koliflawa *n* (*n*) (*bot*) cauliflower (Eng)

kololo *n* (*n*) uneasiness, disquiet, restlessness, anxiety: *Amekuwa katika kololo tangu mwanawe kutiwa korokoroni*, she has been in a state of restlessness since her son was detained. (cf *wasiwasi, dukuduku*)

koloni *n* (*ma-*) colony: *Koloni la Kiingereza*, British colony. (Eng)

kolw.a¹ *vt* be tired of sth, be exhausted of sth: *Amekolwa na maisha ya mjini*, he is tired of town life. Prep. ***kolw.e.a*** St. ***kolw.ek.a*** Cs. ***kolw.esh.a*** (cf *choshwa, kimwa*)

kolw.a² *vt* be better off, prosper. Prep. ***kolw.e.a*** St. ***kolw.ek.a*** Cs. ***kolw.esh.a***

koma¹ *n* (*n*) (*bot*) a kind of edible fruit of *mkoma*, which is dwarf or hyphaene palm. see also *mkoma*. (cf *koche*)

koma² *n* (*n*) (in writing) punctuation mark(,) indicating a slight pause or break between parts of a sentence or clause; comma. (cf *mkato*) (Eng)

kom.a³ *vt* cease, desist, stop; come to an end. *Amekoma kusema uwongo siku hizi*, he has stopped telling lies these days. Prep. ***kom.e.a*** St. ***kom.ek.a*** Cs. ***kom.esh.a*** (cf *sita, isha, malizika*)

koma⁴ *n* (*n*) the spirit of the dead person, believed to exist in the grave or in other special traditional place: *Gonya koma*, make offering to propitiate the spirits of the dead. (cf *mzimu*)

koma.a¹ *vi* 1. (of fruits) be fully ripe, be mature: *Tunda hili limekomaa*, this fruit is ripe. (cf *pevuka, iva*) 2. (of persons) become matured with respect to intelligence, etc.: *Kijana yule amekomaa kiakili*, that young man is mentally mature. Cs. ***koma.z.a***

koma.a² *vi* suffer from leprosy Cs. ***kamaz.a***

komafi *n* (*n*) (*bot*) a kind of globular fruit containing a large number of angular seeds from a much-branched shrub or tree *mkomafi*. *Xylocarpus granatum*.

komakanga *n* (*n*) (*zool*) a black and white finch that lives very much in big forests.

komamanga *n* (*ma-*) (*bot*) pomegranate; a kind of globular fruit with many seeds and is derived from the tree *mkomamanga*. (*Punica granatum*)

komang.a *vt* shake off by beating a mat, carpet, etc. usu with a stick to remove dust: *Aliukomanga mkeka kwa vile ulikuwa na vumbi jingi*, he beat the mat with a stick because it had a lot of dust. Prep. ***komang.i.a*** St. ***komang.ik.a*** Cs. ***komang.ish.a*** Ps. ***komang.w.a*** Rp. ***komang.an.a*** (cf *kung'uta*)

komango *n* (*ma-*) a circular stone, used for grinding things; grinding stone. (cf *kurugo*)

komaz.a *vt* force to mature. Prep. ***komaz.ik.a*** Cs. ***komaz.ish.a*** Ps. ***komaz.w.a*** Rp. ***komaz.an.a*** (cf *pevusha*)

komb.a¹ *vt* 1. scrape out food such as honey, curry, etc. stuck in a cooking vessel; hollow out, wipe clean: *Mpishi aliikomba samli kwenye bukuli*, the cook scraped out the ghee stuck in the bowl. 2. make someone unable to pay his debts; bankrupt, impoverish: *Walimkomba kijana yule kwenye mchezo wa kamari*, they bankrupted that young man in gambling. Prep. *komb.e.a* St. *komb.ek.a* Cs. *komb. esh.a* Ps. *komb.w.a* Rp. *komb.an.a*

komba² *n (n) (zool)* galago, bushbaby; a kind of nocturnal lemur-like mammal having a long bushy tail and large eyes.

komba

komba³ *n (n) (zool)* a kind of saltwater fish (family *Haemulidae*) having a fairly compressed body with moderate or small scales. The fish is said to "grunt" when removed from water; grunter, sweetlips, rubber-lips. (cf *kowe*)

kombaiko *n (ma-)* see *kombamwiko²*

kombaini *n (n)* (in sports) combined players taken from different teams to form a single team: *Timu ya kombaini*, combined team. (Eng)

kombamoyo *n (n)* 1. a long thin straight pole, used as a rafter in the construction of the roof of a house. 2. wall plate.

kombamwiko¹ *n (ma-) (zool)* a kind of bird of the *Columbidae* family, which belongs to doves and pigeons.

kombamwiko² (also *kombaiko*) *n (ma-) (zool)* cockroach (cf *mende*)

kombania *n (n)* a group of soldiers; battalion, squadron. (cf *kikosi*)

kombati *n (n)* see *ukombati*.

kombe¹ *n (ma-)* 1. anything that is hollow e.g. cooking pot. 2. *(anat)* collarbone, clavicle; a bone connecting the breastbone with the shoulder-blade. (cf *mtulinga*) 3. an egg-like big earthenware plate, usu used in public functions when the invited are served. 4. trophy, cup: *Kombe la Dunia*, World Cup. *Kombe la Mataifa ya Afrika*, Africa Cup of Nations. (cf *kikapu*)

kombe² *n (n) (zool)* cockle; an edible burrowing bivalve mollusk of the family *Cardidae* having rounded or heart shaped shells with radiating ribs. (cf *chaza*)

kombe³ *n (n) (bot)* a creeping plant, whose poison is used at the point of an arrow.

kombe⁴ *n (ma-)* medicine made by using saffron ink written on plates, etc. with Koranic verses, and later the verses are cleaned with water and then given to the patient to drink; Koranic medical drink.

kombe⁵ *n(ma-)* the food of the bridegroom.

kombeo *n (ma-)* a sling made from rope, fibre, cloth, etc. and is used for throwing stones (cf *teo, kumbwewe*)

kombo¹ *adv* astray, afield, off course; off the track: *Mipango yake imeenda kombo*, his plans have gone astray. (cf *segemnege, shoto, shaghalabaghala*)

kombo² *adj* curved, bent: *Mstari huu ni kombo*, this line is curved.

kombo.a (also *gomboa*) *vt* 1. emancipate, liberate, free: *Wananchi waliikomboa nchi yao*, the people liberated their country. 2. redeem, ransom; pay off a debt to obtain the release of a person or property: *Alikikomboa kidani chake kutoka kwenye duka la rehani*, she redeemed her necklace from the pawn shop. Prep. *kombo.le.a* St. *kombo.k.a* and *kombo.lek.a* Cs. *kombo.z.a* Ps. of Prep. *kombo.lew.a* Rp. *kombo.an.a*

komboli *n (n) (anat)* cochlea; the spiral shaped part of the internal ear.

kombora *n (ma-)* 1. missile, grenade: *Kombora la masafa mafupi*, short range missile. *Kombora la masafa* *marefu*, long range missile. 2. (in soccer) a hard shot: *Mchezaji alipiga kombora mpaka wavuni*, the player kicked a hard short to the net.

kome¹ *n (n)* 1. a long staff or rod used in special functions e.g. in local dances. 2. a staff or rod used by a Muslim preacher during Friday and "Idd" prayers'; scepter. 3. staff/rod of power, authority, etc.

kome² *n (n)* 1. (*zool*) rock shell; a shell belonging to the family of *Muricidae* which has heavy spined varices on whorls and lives around shallow sheltered reefs 2. tulip shell; an elongate shell (family *Fasciolaridae*) with tall spires and long siphonal canals and lives in seagrass beds.

kome³ *n (n)* a creeping plant, whose poison is used at the point of an arrow. (cf *kombe*)

kome.a¹ *vt* bolt; fasten a door with a piece of wood, iron rod, etc.; fasten sth e.g. a door with a latch of wood: *Komea mlango*, fasten the door with a latch. Prep. *kome.le.a* St. *kome.lek.a* Cs. *kome.lesh.a* Ps. *kome.w.a* Rp. *kome.an.a* (cf *shindilia*)

kome.a² *vt, vi* finish, end, terminate: *Mwandishi alikomoa pale alipokuwa anaiandika hadithi*, the writer ended there when he was writing the story Prep. *kome.le.a* St. *kome.lek.a* Cs. *kome.lesh.a* Ps. *kome.w.a* Rp. *kome.an.a*

komeo¹ *n (ma-)* a latch of wood, iron rod, etc for fastening a door, window, etc; bolt, bar, batch. (cf *kipingwa, kiwe, kia*)

komeo² *n (n)* (*naut*) creek; entrance of a creek or firth; a narrow inlet of the sea. (cf *hori*)

komiti *n (n)* see *kamiti*

komo *n (ma-)* a protruding forehead.

komo.a *vt* 1. unbar, unbolt; remove the bar, bolt, etc on a door, window, etc.: *Aliukomoa mlango*, he unbarred the door. 2. humiliate, discredit:

Alinikomoa hadharani, she discredited me in public. Prep. *komo.le.a* St. *komo.k.a* Cs. *komo.z.a* Rp. of Prep. *komo.lew.a* Rp. *komo.an.a*

komo.a² *vt* free a person from an evil spirit. Prep. *komo.le.a* St. *komo.k.a* Cs. *komo.z.a* Ps. of Prep. *komo.lew.a* Rp. *komo.an.a* (cf *opoa, chuchia*)

komoni *n (n)* local brew made of bran and malt, which is popular in Southern regions of Tanzania.

komoo *n (ma-)* 1. exorcism. 2. humiliation. 3. act of freeing a person from an evil spirit. (cf *chuchio*)

kompyuta *n (n)* computer: *Kompyuta tarakimu*, digital computer. (cf *tarakilishi*)

kumunyo *n (n)* (in Christianity) rite of communion.

komwe *n (n)* the seed of a tree *mkomwe*, used as counters in playing games such as draughts, etc. (cf *kite, namu*)

kona¹ *n (n)* a place where a road, etc. is bent; corner: *Kona ya nyumba*, the corner of a house.

kona² *n (n)* 1. (in soccer, etc.) the corner of a football game or of any other relevant sport. 2. corner kick: *Piga kona*, make a corner kick. 3. (*colloq*) a place where a person performs his illicit sexual activities; brothel.

kond.a *vt* get thin, grow thin; lose weight; be emaciated: *Mtoto yule amekonda kwa sababu ya utapiamlo*, that child has grown thin because of malnutrition. Prep. *kond.e.a* St. *kond.ek.a* Cs. *kond.esh.a*, make thin and weak e.g. *Vitendo vyako viovu vitamkondesha mama yako*, your evil deeds will thin down your mother. (cf *dhoofu, dhii*)

kondakta *n (ma-)* conductor; a person who has the charge of the passengers and collects fares on a bus, train, etc. (*utingo*) (Eng)

kondari *n (n)* see *kundari*

konde¹ *n (ma-)* biff, fist, punch: *Piga konde*, strike with a biff. *Bondia alimpiga makonde mengi mpinzani* wake, the boxer threw away many punches on his opponent. 2. (*idm*) *Piga moyo konde*, take courage; make a bold resolve. 3. the palm of the hand. (cf *kitanga*) 4. used in the expression: *Piga konde la nyuma*, bribe someone; offer a bribe to someone.

konde² *n* (*n*) a cultivated field: *Amelima vitu vingi katika konde yake*, he has cultivated many things in his field.

konde³ *interj* (*colloq*) an expression of calling to a person working in a farm before greeting him.

konde⁴ *n* (*n*) (*colloq*) wife (cf *mke*)

kondensa *n* (*n*) condenser: *Kondensa geugeu*, variable condenser. (Eng)

kondesh.a *vt* see *konda*. Prep. **kondesh.e.a** St. **kondesh.ek.a** Cs. **kondesh.w.a** Rp. **kondesh.an.a**

kondo¹ *n* (*n*) 1. used in the expression: *Kondo ya nyuma*, placenta; an organ within the uterus lining the womb during pregnancy by which the foetus is nourished. (cf *kuu*) 2. the period of a woman's rest after giving birth.

kondo² *n* (*n*) (*arch*) war, strife. (cf *vita, bangu*)

kondo³ *n* (*n*) good health.

kondomu *n* (*n*) condom (Eng)

kondoo *n* (*n*) 1. (*zool*) sheep: *Mwana kondoo*, lamb. *Kondoo jike*, ewe. *Nyama ya kondoo*, mutton. 2. (*idm*) *Kuinama kama kondoo*, remain silent. 3. used in the expression: *Mwana wa kondoo*, a name used by Christians to refer to Jesus Christ.

kondrati *n* (*n*) contract: *Amepewa kondrati ya kujenga mabweni*, he has been given a contract to build hostels. (cf *mkataba*) (Eng)

konea *n* (*n*) (*anat*) cornea; the transparent layer which covers and protects the outer part of the eye (Eng)

kong.a¹ *vi* be old, grow old; age: *Mtu yule anatembea kwa taabu kwa vile amekonga*, that person walks with difficulty because he is ageing. Prep. **kong.e.a** St. **kong.ek.a** Cs. **kong.esh.a** Ps. **kong.w.a** Rp. of Prep. **kong.e.an.a** (cf *zeeka*)

kong.a² *vt* drink a little water in order to quench thirst; take a sip of water to quench thirst: *Alikunywa maji baridi kuikonga kiu yake*, he drank cold water to quench his thirst. (cf *burudisha*) *Konga moyo*, refresh oneself. Prep. **kong.e.a** St. **kong.ek.a** Cs. **kong.esh.a** Ps. **kong.w.a**

kong.a³ *vt* assemble people or things for a particular purpose; amass, accumulate: *Afisa kilimo aliwakonga wanavijiji ili awaonyeshe mbinu mpya za ulimaji*, the agricultural officer assembled the villagers in order to show them new farming techniques. Prep. **kong.e.a** St. **kong.ek.a** Cs. **kong.esh.a** Ps. **kong.w.a** Rp. **kong.an.a**

kongaman.a *vt* (of scholars, etc.) reach a consensus at a symposium, etc. on a particular issue: *Wanasiasa wamekongamana kwamba demokrasia lazima ikuzwe katika nchi za Kiafrika*, the politicians have reached a consensus that democracy must be promoted in African countries. Prep. **kongaman.i.a** St. **kongaman.ik.a** Cs. **kongaman.ish.a** Rp. of Prep. **kongaman.i.an.a**

kongamano¹ *n* (*ma-*) symposium, colloquium; a conference organized for the discussion of some particular issue: *Kongamano la kimataifa*, international symposium. *Kongamano la madaktari litafanyika kutathmini maendeleo ya tiba ya UKIMWI*, the doctors' symposium will be held to evaluate progress in the cure of AIDS.

kongamano² *n* (*ma-*) consensus on a particular issue.

kongany.a *vt* heap, gather: *Alikuwa akikonganya kuni msituni*, he was gathering firewood in the bush. Prep. **kongany.i.a** St. **kongany.ik.a** Cs. **kongany.ish.a** Ps. **kongany.w.a** Rp. **kongany.an.a** (cf *kusanya*)

kongo¹ *n* (*n*) (*anat*) ulna; one of the two forearm bones. 2. radius; the other of the forearm bones.

kongo² *adj* used in the expression: *Mwezi kongo*, crescent moon.

kongo.a¹ *vt* uproot, extract; draw out: *Kongoa misumari*, extract the nails. *Kongoa jino*, extract the tooth. *Kongoa pembe*, extract the elephant's task. Prep. *kongo.le.a* St. *kongo.k.a* and *kongo.lek.a* Cs. *kongo.lesh.a* Ps. of Prep. *kongo.lew.a* Rp. *kongo.an.a* (cf *ng'oa*)

kongo.a² *vt* make sth to become old. Prep. *kongo.le.a* St. *kongo.k.a* and *kongo.lek.a* Cs. *kongo.lesh.a* Ps. *kongo.lew.a* Rp. *kongo.an.a*

kongoj.a *vi* 1. walk feebly like an old man; totter, stagger: *Mzee yule alikuwa akijikongoja barabarani*, that old man was tottering along the road. 2. walk by using a cane, walking stick, etc.: *Baba aghalabu hujikongoja anapotembea*, my father usually walks with the help of a stick. Prep. *kongoj.e.a* St. *kongoj.ek.u* Cs. *kongoj.esh.a* Ps. *kongoj.w.a*

kongole *n* (*n*) thanks, gratitude.

kongome.a (also *gongomea*) *vt* nail; fasten sth with nails: *Seremala alilikongomea sanduku lake kwa misumari*, the carpenter nailed his wooden box. Prep. *kongome.le.a* St. *kongome.lek.a* Cs. *kongome.z.a* Ps. *kongome.w.a* Rp. *kongom.an.a*

kongomeo¹ *n* (*ma-*) 1. an instrument used for fastening a door, etc. such as a piece of wood, etc.; fastener. 2. fastening; act of fastening a door, etc.

kongomeo² *n* (*n*) (*anat*) larynx, gullet. (cf *koromeo, zoloto*)

kongoni¹ *n* (*n*) (*zool*) hartebeest; a kind of large antelope with a reddish-brown coat and long curved horns.

kongoni

kongoni² *interj* an expletive used for welcoming someone; welcome! (cf *karibu*)

kongoo *n* (*n*) a collection of writings.

kongoro *n* (*n*) (*zool*) ox foot; the foot of a slaughtered bull, goat or sheep. *Supu ya makongoro*, oxfoot soup.

kongosho *n* (*n*) (*anat*) pancreas; a large elongate gland situated behind the stomach, which helps the digestion of food.

kong'ot.a¹ *vt* 1. (of the skin, metal, etc.) beat in order to make even; straighten a skin, metal, etc.: *Aliikong'ota ngozi ya mnyama ili atengeneze ngoma*, he straightened the animal skin in order to use it for making a drum. 2. punish by beating: *Mwalimu alimkong'ota mwanafunzi kwa ukosefu wa nidhamu*, the teacher punished the student for misconduct by beating him. Prep. *kong'ot.e.a* St. *kong'ot.ek.a* Cs. *kong'ot.esh.a* Ps. *kong'ot.w.a* Rp. *kong'ot.an.a* (cf *adhibu*)

kongot.a² *vt* knock sth such as a coconut to find out if it is good inside: *Aliikongota nazi ili ajue kama ni nzima*, he knocked the coconut to find out if it was a good one. Prep. *kongot.e.a* St. *kongot.ek.a* Cs. *kongot.esh.a* Ps. *kongot.w.a* Rp. *kongot.an.a* (cf *piga*)

kongoti *n* (*ma-*) (*zool*) stork; a kind of bird of the *Ciconiidae* family, having a long neck and bill and related to the herons. 2. a kind of play in which one of the players dresses up as a stork, by means of grass, sticks, etc.; stilt dance. 3. stilt game; a play used by acrobats, etc using a pair of poles fitted with a footrest somewhere along its length and used for walking with the feet above the ground.

kongowe.a *vt* 1. greet someone meekly; greet someone submissively; greet someone with excessive humility: *Aliwakongowea wazee wake alipowasili nyumbani*, she greeted her parents submissively when she arrived home. (cf *nyenyekea*) 2. welcome someone with openheartedness: *Niliwakongowea wageni wangu kwenye dhifa*, I welcomed my guests warmly at the reception. Prep. *kongowe.le.a* St. *kongowe.k.a* Cs. *kongowe.sh.a* Ps. *kongowe.w.a* Rp. *kongowe.an.a* (cf *karibisha*)

kongwa¹ *n* (*n*) (*bot*) the seed or nut of a fruit within the shell or stone; kernel. (cf *konde, kokwa*)

kongwa² *n* (*n*) (*bot*) a blue-flowered herb, found in damp places amongst grass, used as a vegetable and as an antidote for hot water ants (*majimoto*). *Commelina zambesica*.

kongwa³ *n* (*ma-*) a forged stick in which a slave was secured in the past with an iron-cross pin round the neck; slave yoke.

kongwa⁴ *n* (*ma-*) a rock or a place where fish hide themselves. (cf *pango, koma*)

kongwe¹ *n* (*n*) used in the expression: *Toa kongwe*, lead in singing; give a lead; start a song.

kongwe² *n* (*n*) 1. (*bot*) hair herb with stems up to 8 feet long and covered with hooked hairs, bearing elliptical leaves and yellow flowers and is used medicinally for colds. *Aneilema acquinoctiale*. 2. a perennial herb up to 3 feet tall with linear lanceolate leaves and panicle of small blue or dull purple flowers. *Aneilema sinicum*.

-kongwe³ *adj* old, worn-out, aged, ancient, outdated: *Gari langu limekuwa kongwe*, my car has become worn-out. *Yeye amekuwa mkongwe siku hizi*, he has become old these days.

koni¹ *n* (*n*) (*zool*) a small animal like a bush-baby. (cf *ndere*)

koni² *n* (*n*) (*bot*) a kind of fruit from *mkoni*, a kind of tree.

koni³ *n* (*n*) cone; a kind of ice cream. (Eng)

konje *n* (*n*) (*zool*) a kind of wild cat frequently fond of eating chicks. (cf *njuzi, kala, kalakonje*)

konokono¹ *n* (*n*) (*zool*) snail, slug: *Konokono wasio na magamba*, sea hare. (cf *koa*)

konokono² *n* (*n*) (*bot*) custard apple-like fruit: *Konokono mwitu*, wild custard apple-like fruit.

konsonanti *n* (*n*) (*phon*) consonant: *Konsonanti mlolongo*, consonant cluster. *Msogeo konsonanti*, consonant shift. *Konsonanti ghuna*, voiced consonant. *Konsonanti hafifu*, voiceless consonant. (Eng)

konstebo *n*(*n*) constable (Eng)

kontena *n* (*n*) container, crate box, etc.; a thing that contains or can contain sth. (Eng)

kontinenti *n* (*n*) continent: *Kontinenti la Afrika*, the African continent. *Kontinenti la Amerika*, the American continent. (Eng)

kontrakta *n* (*n*) contractor (Eng)

kontua *n* (*n*) contour (Eng)

konyagi *n* (*n*) Tanzania gin, cognac.

konyez.a¹ *vt, vi* wink; give sby a sign, make a covert sign to: *Alinikonyeza tuondoke*, he winked at me to leave. Prep. *konyez.e.a* St. *konyez.ek.a* Cs. *konyez.esh.a* Ps. *konyez.w.a* Rp. *konyez.an.a,* wink at each other. (cf *kupia*)

konyeza² *n* (*n*) (*zool*) caterpillar (cf *kiwavi*)

konyezo *n* (*ma-*) blink, wink, suggestion: *Konyezo ni moja katika mikakati ya mawasiliano ya lugha*, wink is one of the strategies of language communication.

konyo.a *vt* 1. pluck off as in the case of maize, etc. from its cob; break off, tear off: *Mtoto aliyakonyoa mahindi kutoka kwenye mabuu*, the child plucked off the maize from its cobs. 2. separate a fruit from its stalk: *Niliyakonyoa maembe kutoka kwenye matawi yake*, I separated mangoes from their branches. Prep. *konyo.le.a* St. *konyo.k.a* and *konyo.lek.a*

Cs. *konyo.lesh.a* Ps. of Prep. *konyo.lew.a* Rp. *konyo.an.a*

konzi¹ *n* (*ma-*) closed fist: *Piga konzi*, rap with the knuckles on the head by using a closed fist. *Gota konzi*, rap with the knuckles.

konzi² *n* (*n*) a fistful, a handful; as much as can be taken up in the fist with the fingers nearly closed: *Konzi ya maji haijanitoa kiu yangu*, a fistful of water has not quenched my thirst. (cf *ukufi*)

koo¹ *n* (*n*) 1. (*anat*) trachea, windpipe. (cf *umio, kikoromeo, koromeo*) 2. (*med*) laryngitis; the inflammation of the larynx often characterized by the temporary loss of voice.

koo² *n* (*ma-*) 1. (*zool*) a breeding bird or animal: *Koo la kuku*, a breeding fowl. *Koo la mbuzi*, a breeding goat. 2. (*sl*) mistress, paramour.

koongo¹ *n* (*ma-*) a hole dibbled or dug with a hoe for planting seeds; a planting hole.

koongo² *n* (*ma-*) see *korongo*

koongo³ *interj* an expletive signalling the sighting of the moon.

kopa¹ *n* (*ma-*) 1. a slice of dried cassava. 2. a slice of dried bananas.

kopa² *n* (*ma-*) (in card playing) hearts; a suit of playing cards shaped like a heart and marked in red symbols.

kop.a³ *vt* borrow money, etc.; get a loan: *Alikopa pesa nyingi kutoka benki*, he borrowed a lot of money from the bank. Prep. *kop.e.a* St. *kop.ek.a* Cs. *kop.esh.a*, lend, loan e.g. *Mwenye duka alimkopesha mteja wake sukari*, the shopkeeper lent his customer some sugar, i.e. the shopkeeper gave sugar to his customer on a credit basis. Ps. *kop.w.a* Rp. *kop.an.a*

kop.a⁴ *vt* swindle, cheat, defraud; get sth on false pretences: *Mwenye duka alimkopa mnunuzi*, the shopkeeper swindled the customer. Prep. *kop.e.a* St. *kop.ek.a* Cs. *kop.esh.a* Ps. *kop.w.a* Rp. *kop.an.a* (cf *punja*)

kope *n* (*n*) the burnt end of the wick of a lamp or candle.

kopes.a *vt* shut and open the eyes; flutter the eyes: *Kopesa macho*, blink the eyes; wink. Prep. *kopes.e.a* St. *kopes.ek.a* Cs. *kopes.esh.a* Ps. *kopes.w.a* Rp. *kopes.an.a*

kopesh.a *vt* see *kopa*³. Prep. *kopesh.e.a* St. *kopesh.ek.a* Ps. *kopesh.w.a* Rp. *kopesh.an.a*

kop.i¹ *vt* copy; make or do sth in imitation of (something or person) Prep. *kop.i.a* St. *kop.ik.a* Cs. *kop.ish.a* Ps. of Prep. *kop.iw.a* Rp. of Prep. *kop.i.an.a* (cf *iga, nakili*) (Eng)

kopi² *n*(*n*) copy, duplicate, replica (cf *nuskha, nakala*) (Eng)

kopi³ *vt* make a copy or copies of a piece of writing,etc, reproduce, duplicate, replicate. Prep *kop.i.a* St. *kop.ik.a* Cs. *kop.ish.a* Rp. *kop.i.an.a* (cf *nakili*) (Eng)

koplo *n* (*ma-*) corporal (Eng)

kopo *n* (*ma-*) 1. tin, can: *Samaki wa kopo*, tinned fish. *Nyama ya kopo*, tinned meat. *Kopo la utaboshaji*, overflow can. 2. gutter; rainspout 3. (*idm*) *Mtoto wa kikopo*, hooligan.

kopo.a¹ *vt* (of the skin of reptiles, etc.) slough off; shed off skin: *Nyoka aliikopoa ngozi yake kuukuu*, the snake sloughed off its old skin. Prep. *kopo.le.a* St. *kopo.k.a* and *kopo.lek.a* Cs. *kopo.lesh.a* Ps. of Prep. *kopo.lew.a* Rp. *kopo.an.a*

kopo.a² *vt* beget a child; deliver a child; give birth: *Dada yangu alikopoa watoto pacha*, my sister gave birth to twins. Prep. *kopo.le.a* St. *kopo.k.a* and *kopo.lek.a* Cs. *kopo.lesh.a* Ps. of Prep. *kopo.lew.a* Rp. *kopo.an.a*

kopok.a *vi* come out forcefully. Prep. *kopok.e.a* St. *kopok.ek.a* Cs. *kopok.esh.a*

koramu *n* (*n*) quorum (cf *akidi*) (Eng)

kore¹ *n*(*n*) plantation, garden; a cultivated field. (cf *shamba*)

kore² *n* (*n*) (*zool*) a kind of grey bird with a crest; tufted grey bird. (cf *shore*)

koridoo *n* (*n*) corridor (Eng)
korija *n* (*ma-*) (used in selling strings of beads, lengths of cloths, etc.) set of twenty; score: *Mwenye duka alinionyesha korija moja la vitambaa,* the shopkeeper showed me a score of cloths. (Hind)
koroboi[1] (also *karabai*) *n* (*n*) a small oil lamp without a chimney.
koroboi[2] *n* (*n*) (*bot*) a kind of succulent banana. (cf *bokooko, tovu*)
koroboi[3] *n* (*n*) a kind of rifle.
korodani *n* (*n*) (*anat*) testicles, scrotum. (cf *kende, hasua, pumbu*)
-korofi[1] *adj* destructive, nasty, troublesome, ill-omened: *Yeye ni mtu mkorofi,* he is a troublesome person. (cf *matata*) (Ar)
korof.i[2] *vt, vi* see *korofisha*
korofindo *n* (*n*) musket; muzzle-loading gun. (cf *gobori*)
korofish.a (also *korofi*) *vt, vi* 1. hassle, harass, hector, disturb: *Kijana yule anapenda kukorofisha watu,* that young man likes to harass people. Prep. **korofish.i.a** St. **korofish.ik.a** Ps. **korofish.w.a** Rp. **korofish.an.a** e.g. *Marafiki wale wawili haweshi kukorofishana,* those two friends often get into each other's nerves. (cf *udhi*) 2. distrupt, mess, wreck: *Ingawa alitaka kuikorofisha mipango yangu, hakufanikiwa,* even though he wanted to disrupt my plans, he did not succeed. Prep. **korofish.i.a** St. **korofish.ik.a** Ps. **korofish.w.a** Rp. **korofish.an.a** (cf *chafua, haribu, vuruga*) (Ar)
korog.a *vt* 1. stir: *Aliukoroga uji,* she stirred the gruel. 2. (*fig*) mess sth; stir up a strife, etc.; cause, discord, etc.: *Mtu yule anaweza kuikoroga mipango yako,* that person can mess up your plans. Prep. **korog.e.a** St. **korog.ek.a** Cs. **korog.esh.a** Ps. **korog.w.a** Rp. **korog.an.a** (cf *vuruga*)
korokoro[1] *n* (*ma-*) lottery (cf *bahati nasibu*)
korokoro[2] *n* (*ma-*) see *makorokoro*
korokoro[3] *n* (*n*) jail, prison: *Tia makorokoroni,* put someone in the lock-up. (cf *gereza*)
korokoroni[1] *adv* in the lock-up.
korokoroni[2] *n* (*ma-*) godown's watchman, warehouse's watchman, storehouse's watchman.
korola *n* (*n*) (*bot*) corolla; the petals or inner floral leaves of a flower.
korom.a[1] *vi* snore: *Alikuwa akikoroma takriban usiku wote,* he was snoring almost the whole night. Prep. **korom.e.a** St. **korom.ek.a** Cs. **korom.esh.a** Ps. **korom.w.a** e.g. *Sauti ilikoromwa,* the noise was snored Rp. of Prep. **korom.e.an.a**(cf *korota, forota*)
koroma[2] *n* (*ma-*) (of a coconut) be unripe or its milk beginning to dry and thus unfit for use: *Nazi koroma,* a coconut of this kind. (*prov*) *Mchagua nazi hupata koroma,* he who chooses a coconut gets an unripe one i.e. he who becomes too choosy eventually gets a wrong or bad thing.
koromeo *n* (*ma-*) (*anat*) larynx, gullet. (cf *dudumio, kongomeo, koo*)
korona[1] *n* (*ma-*) sisal pulping mill.
korona[2] *n* (*n*) (*monet*) krona; the monitoring unit and a coin of Sweden. (Lt)
korongo[1] *n* (*n*) 1. (*zool*) stork; a large-long-legged bird. (cf *kongoti*) 2. a tall person.
korongo[2] *n* (*ma-*) (*geol*) gulley; a channel of small valley esp one cut by heavy rainwater. (cf *genge, gema*)
kororo[1] *n* (*ma-*) (*zool*) crested guinea-fowl; a kind of bird having lax black crest, black plumage with bluish-white spots above and below as well as cobalt blue and red on the upper neck. *Guttera pucherani.*
kororo[2] *n* (*ma-*) 1. dewlap; a loose field of skin hanging from the throat of cattle and certain animals. (cf *shambwalele*) 2. (*med*) goitre; an enlargement of the thyroid gland. (cf *tezi*)

korosho¹ *n* (*n*) (*bot*) cashew nut. (Port)
korosho² *n* (*n*) (*naut*) projecting rudder ornament in *mtepe*, a kind of sailing vessel.
korosi *n* (*n*) 1. road bend. 2. reasons for evading the truth.
korot.a *vi* 1. sleep beyond the limit: *Korota usingizi*, sleep for long hours. 2. snore, snort: *Akilala hukorota*, when he sleeps, he snores. Prep. *korot.e.a* St. *korot.ek.a* Cs. *korot.esh.a* Ps. *korot.w.a* Rp. *korot.an.a*
korowez.a¹ *vt* make work more difficult than it is supposed to be; increase the difficulty of a task; complicate: *Wafanyakazi wote wanaichukia tabia yake ya kukoroweza*, all the workers hate his tendency to make work unnecessarily difficult. Prep. *korowez.e.a* St. *korowez.ek.a* Cs. *korowez.esh.a* Ps. *korowez.w.a* Rp. *korowez.an.a*
korowez.a² *vt* (of person, ball, etc) catch, arrest, apprehend: *Askari walimkoroweza jambazi mafichoni mwake*, the policemen arrested the thug in his hideout. Prep. *korowe.z.e.a* St. *korowez.ek.a* Cs. *korowez.esh.a* Ps. *korowez.w.a* (cf *kamata, data*)
korti *n* (*n*) a court of law: *Korti ya rufani*, appeal court. *Korti ya mataifa*, international court. (cf *mahakama*) (Eng)
kos.a¹ *vt, vi* 1. be mistaken; err, offend: *Umekosa*, you have erred. *Ulimkosa rafiki yako*, you offended your friend. 2. violate, transgress; break law. *Alikosa kwa kuvuka mpaka bila ya hati*, he broke the law by crossing the border without a document. 3. miss a target, miss a mark: *Alijaribu kumlenga ndege kwa panda lakini akamkosa*, he tried to aim at the bird with a catapult but he missed it. 4. fail to get sby/sth; lack: *Anakosa mapenzi ya mkewe*, he misses his wife's love. *Alikwenda kununua sukari dukani lakini akakosa*, he went to buy sugar in the shop but he failed to get it. Prep. *kos.e.a* St. *kos.ek.a* Cs. *kos.esh.a* Ps. *kos.w.a* Rp. *kos.an.a*
kosa² *n* (*ma-*) mistake, error, fault: *Fanya kosa*, make a mistake. *Sahihisha makosa*, correct mistakes. (*prov*) *Kosa la kwanza haliachi mke*, first mistake does not warrant a divorce i.e. the first mistake by someone can be forgiven.
kosakosa *n* (*n*) near miss: *Baada ya kosakosa nyingi, timu yetu ilifanikiwa hatimaye kufunga goli*, after so many near misses, our team finally scored a goal.
kosan.a *vi* 1. miss each other: *Bora umsubiri hapa kwani ukiondoka sasa, mnaweza mkakosana*, it is better that you wait for him here because if you leave now, you might miss each other. 2. quarrel; treat each other badly; not be on good terms; have a falling out: *Marafiki wale wawili wamekosana siku hizi*, those two friends have wronged each other these days. Prep. *kosan.i.a* St. *kosan.ik.a* Cs. *kosan.ish.a,* cause someone to be at loggerheads with someone else e.g. *Alitaka kunikosanisha na wazee wangu*, he wanted to alienate me from my parents.
kose.a *vt* 1. do sth incorrectly: *Wewe umekosea; usingemwambia vile*, you have done the wrong thing; you should have not told him like that. 2. offend: *Kosea adabu mtu*, offend sby. Prep. *kose.le.a* St. *kose.k.a* Cs. *kose.sh.a* Ps. *kose.w.a*
-kosefu *adj* 1. incorrect. 2. lacking, deficient: *Mkosefu wa adabu*: lacking in manners.
kosek.a *vi* be missing, be lacking.
kosekan.a *vt* be missing, be lacking: *Mlango wa nyuma unakosekana katika nyumba hii*, the rear door is missing in this house.
kosesh.a¹ *vt* lead astray; cause someone to do sth wrong: *Alinikosesha hesabu*, he caused me to get the

calculation wrong. 2. deprive sby sth; *Walinikosesha haki yangu ya kupiga kura*, they deprived me of my right to vote. Prep. ***kosesh.e.a*** St. ***kosesh.ek.a*** Ps. ***kosesh.w.a*** Rp. ***kosesh.an.a***

kosh.a¹ (also *osha*) *vt* 1. wash. 2. cleanse clean, absolve; free someone from blame, etc: *Jikosha*, Prep. ***kosh.e.a*** St. ***kosh.ek.a*** Ps. ***kosh.w.a***. Rp. ***kosh.an.a***

kosh.a² *vt* please, gratify, gladden: *Mazungumzo yake yalinikosha*, his conversation pleased me. Prep. ***kosh.e.a*** St. ***kosh.ek.a*** Ps. ***kosh.w.a*** Rp. ***kosh.an.a*** (cf *furahisha, ridhisha*)

koshi *n* (*ma-*) slippers without the back part. (cf *sapatu, sandali*) (Pers)

kosi *n* (*ma-*) (*naut*) a piece of iron or rope kept on the edge of a vessel fixed to a peg and used to row an oar.

kosini *n* (*n*) (*trigon*) cosine; the ratio between the side adjacent to a given acute angle in a right-angled triangle and the hypotenuse. (Eng)

koso.a *vt* criticize, correct. *Anapenda kukosoa watu*, he likes to criticise people. Prep. ***koso.le.a*** St. ***koso.lek.a*** Cs. ***koso.lesh.a*** Ps. of Prep. ***koso.lew.a*** Rp. ***koso.an.a*** (cf *rekebisha*)

kota¹ *n* (*ma-*) crook, bend; crooked condition: *Kota la miguu*, crooked legs. (cf *pindo*)

kota² *n* (*ma-*) (*bot*) sweet stalks of a kind of millet chewed like a sugarcane. (cf *bua*)

kot.a³ *vt* 1. use grappling iron tongs for holding an object: *Alilikota kaa la moto*, he used a crooked iron to hold the ember. 2. apprehend, seize, arrest: *Polisi walimkota jambazi*, the police arrested a thief. Prep. ***kot.e.a*** St. ***kot.ek.a*** Cs. ***kot.esh.a*** Ps. ***kot.w.a*** (cf *kamata, shika*)

kot.a⁴ (also *ota*) *vt* warm oneself: *Kota moto*, warm oneself. *Kota jua*, bask in the sun.

kota⁵ *n* (*n*) town quarter.

kotama *n* (*n*) a short curved broad bladed knife, used usu in getting palm wine. (cf *upumba, ramba*)

kote¹ (also *kotekote*) *adv* everywhere, on all sides: *Kote kuna watu*, there are people everywhere. *Kote duniani*, all over the world.

kote² (also *kotekote*) *pron* everywhere, all over: *Kote ni kuchafu*. Everywhere it is dirty.

kotekote¹ *adv* see *kote¹*

kotekote² *pron* see *kote²*

koti *n* (*ma-*) coat: *Koti la mvua*, raincoat. *Koti la baridi*, overcoat. (Eng)

kotia *n* (*ma-*) (*naut*) a two-mast dhow with transom stern and raking stem originating from Kutch and North West India.

kotiledoni *n* (*n*) (*bot*) cotyledon; a simple embryonic leaf in seed bearing plants.

kotmiri¹ (also *kitmiri*) *n* (*n*) (*bot*) a kind of annual herb having a strong smelling seedlike fruit, used in flavoring food, liqueurs, etc.; coriander. *Coriandrum sativum.*

kotmiri² *n* (*n*) a name of a bad evil spirit.

koto¹ *n* (*n*) a gift given by a father to a teacher when the parent's child is admitted in a Koranic school.

koto² *n* (*n*) (*naut*) a large hook, used for catching sharks; shark hook.

koto³ *n* (*n*) 1. crooked behaviour; unreformed behaviour. 2. (of trees, hair, etc.) twisted, curved, kinky: *Nywele za koto*, kinky hair.

koto⁴ *n* (*n*) forced labour; forced work; involuntary work, compulsory work.

koto⁵ *n* (*n*) herbal medicine used in drinking to treat abdominal pains.

koto⁶ *n* (*n*) a whip covered with coir or leaves of dwarf palm.

kotokoto *n* (*n*) overtime payment: *Alipokea kotokoto yake baada ya kufanya kazi zaidi ya masaa ya kawaida*, he received his overtime payment after working outside the regular hours.

kotwe¹ n (n) (zool) white-backed duck; a kind of duck with a white back when it is in flight, and resides only on inland waters, often small dams. *Thalassornis leuconotus*. (cf *salili*)

kotwe² n (n) (zool) a kind of salt-water fish (family *Leiognathidae*) having a compressed slim body with small scales and a very protracticle mouth; whipfin ponyfish.

kova n (n) (zool) a kind of snail. (cf *koachi*)

kovu n (n) scar: *Ana kovu usoni*, he has a scar on the face. (prov) *Mwenye kovu usimtaraji kupoa*, one with a scar, don't think he has healed i.e. don't trust somebody who was your old enemy.

kowana (also *koana*) n (n) (zool) a kind of saltwater fish (family *Nemipteridae*), having an oblong or elongated body with ctenoid scales covering the body and most of the head; threadfin bream.

kowe n (n) (zool) a kind of saltwater fish (family *Haemulidae*) with a fairly compressed body and moderate or small scales; grunter, sweet-lips., rubber-lips. (cf *komba*)

koy.a¹ vi rest and rejoice at getting sth or achieving some object; relax, be relieved: *Karibu utakoya maana serikali itakurejeshea nyumba yako*, you will soon rest because the government will give you back your house. Prep. **koy.e.a** St. **koy.ek.a** Cs. **koy.esh.a** Ps. **koy.w.a**

koya² n (ma-) dental calculus; tartar.

koyo¹ n (n) (med) pre-eclampsia; a disorder occurring late in pregnancy characterized by excessive fluid retention, high blood pressure, etc.

koyo² (also *koyokoyo*) n (n) (zool) a kind of bird of the *Ploceidae* family.

koyokoyo¹ n (n) see *koyo²*

koyokoyo² n (n) (zool) a kind of red ant. (cf *majimoto*)

kozi¹ n (n) a course of studies: *Amechukua kozi ya uwalimu*, he has taken a teaching course. (cf *mafunzo*) (Eng)

kozi² n (n) (bot) the fibrous sheath of the coconut palm. (cf *gubi*)

kozi³ n (n) (zool) falcon; a kind of hawk-like bird (family *Falconidae*) having a short curved notched bill and long pointed wings.

kozi⁴ n (n) a row of blocks built in a wall of a house.

Kremlini n (n) Kremlin (Eng)

kreni n (n) crane (cf *kambarau*, *slingi*) (Eng)

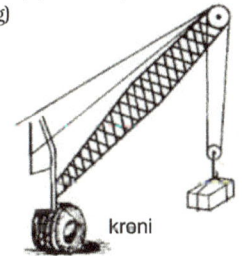

kreni

kreti n (n) crate (Eng)

kriketi n (n) cricket (Eng)

krioli n (n) (ling) creole; a mothertongue formed from the contact of a European language with local languages esp African languages spoken by slaves.

Krismasi n (n) Christmas: *Sikukuu ya Krismasi*, Christmas holiday. *Mkesha wa Krismasi*, Christmas eve. *Wimbo wa Krismasi*, Christmas carol. (Eng)

Kristo (also *Kristu*) n (n) Christ

Kristu n (n) see *kristo*

krokei n (n) croquet (Eng)

kromiamu n (n) (chem) chromium (Eng)

kromu n (n) (chem) chrome (Eng)

kronolojia n (n) chronology (Eng)

krosi¹ n (n) (in football, etc.) cross; a kick made across the sides of a pitch: *Mchezaji alitoa krosi maridadi*, the player gave a good cross pass. (Eng)

krosi² n (n) road bend.

ku verb form (gram) infinitive marker in Swahili language: *Kufika tu darasani, akaanza kupiga kelele*, immediately after he had arrived in the class, he started to make noise.

K ku.a   kuda²

ku.a vi 1. (*of age*) grow, develop: *Amekuwa haraka*, she has grown up fast. (*prov*) *Mtoto umleavyo ndivyo akuavyo*, as you bring up a child, so he will be i.e. if you bring up a child well, he will be good and vice versa. 2. (of height, etc.) become tall, flourish, be developing: *Miti hii imekua vizuri*, these trees have developed well. *Kijana huyu ni mdogo lakini amekua mrefu upesi*, this boy is young but he has grown tall quickly. 3. (of intelligence) grow; be matured: *Mwanafunzi yule amekua kiakili*, that student is mentally mature. Prep. *ku.lia* Cs. *ku.z.a*

kuba n (*ma-*) 1. cupola; a small dome found on a roof. 2. a grave built in with a wall; tomb.

kubadhi (also *makubadhi*) n (*ma-*) a kind of sandal with a small ornamental leather on the front usu worn by Muslims when they go to mosque for prayers. (Pers)

kubal.i vt, vi 1. confess, admit, accept, agree: *Alikubali kuwa yeye ni mkosa*, he admitted that he was wrong. *Mwajiri alikubali kutuongezea mshahara*, the employer agreed to raise our salary. (cf *kiri*) 2. permit, allow, agree: *Amekubali kunikodisha nyumba yake*, he has agreed to rent his house to me. Prep. *kubal.i.a* St. *kubal.ik.a* Cs. *kubal.ish.a* Ps. of Prep. *kubal.iw.a* Rp. of Prep. *kubal.i.an.a* (cf *ruhusu*) (Ar)

kubalian.a vi agree among each other: *Wamekubaliana kuunda chama cha ushirika*, they have agreed to form a co-operative society. (cf *afikiana*)

kubalik.a vi be acceptable: *Ushahidi wake haukubaliki*, his evidence is not acceptable. Prep. *kubalik.i.a* St. *kubalik.ik.a* Cs. *kubal.ish.a*

kubaz.a vi (of a sail, etc.) swell out, belly out, expand: *Viatu vyangu sasa vimekubaza baada ya kuvaliwa na mtu mwenye miguu mipana*, my shoes have now expanded after being worn by a person with broad feet. Prep. *kubaz.i.a* St. *kubaz.ik.a* Cs. *kubaz.ish.a* Ps. *kubaz.w.a*

kubikubi adv see *gubigubi*

kubl.a vi drink sth without a stop. Prep. *kubl.i.a* St. *kubl.ik.a* Cs. *kubl.ish.a* Ps. of Prep. *kubl.iw.a*

kubo n (n) (*zool*) long-tailed fiscal shriek; a kind of bird with black underparts merging to grey on lower back and rump, a white wingbar and a very long completely black tail. *Lanius cabanisi*. (cf *tiva*)

kubuh.u vt be used to performing sth; be accustomed to doing sth: *Amekubuhu kutembea usiku na lolote utakalomwambia, hasikii*, he is used to roaming about at night and whatever you tell him, he will not listen to it. (cf *zoea*) Prep. *kubuh.ia* St. *kubuh.ik.a* Cs. *kubuh.ish.a* (cf *zoea*)

kubuli n (n) see *kabuli²*

-kubwa adj 1. (of things) big, large: *Nyumba yake ni kubwa*, his house is big 2. (of a person, etc.) grown-up: *Mtoto wako amekuwa mkubwa*, your child has become grown-up. 3. important, significant, big: *Amepewa cheo kikubwa*, he has been given a big position. *Amelifanya neno kuwa kubwa*, he has made the issue an important one. (cf *muhimu*)

kucha adv the whole night: *Mgonjwa hakulala takriban usiku kucha*, the patient did not sleep almost the whole night.

kuchakulo n (n) (*zool*) African bush squirrel. (cf *kidiri*)

kuchi n (*ma-*) (*zool*) a kind of red rooster fond of fighting.

kud.a¹ vt roll up one's clothes beyond the thighs; turn up one's clothes beyond the thighs: *Alikuda nguo yake alipotaka kupita matopeni*, she turned up her dress when he wanted to cross over the mud. Prep. *kud.i.a* St. *kud.ik.a* Cs. *kud.ish.a* Ps. *kud.w.a* Rp. *kud.an.a*

kuda² n (n) payment given as a kind

kuda³ of compensation to meet cultural obligations because of wrongdoing. (cf *haka*)

kuda³ *n* (*n*) the habit of getting annoyed on flimsy grounds.

kudhumani *n* (*n*) pomegranate (cf *komamanga*)

kudra *n* (*n*) the right to be fined because of not treating a person with the respect to which he is entitled.

kudu¹ *n* (*n*) 1. worthiness of blame because of not treating a person with the respect to which he is entitled. 2. fine paid by an initiate to his instructor for lack of respect.

kudu² *n* (*n*) (*zool*) a kind of fish of the *Luthrinidae* family.

kuduku *n* (*n*) recalcitrant; an obstinate person, a difficult person; a hard character. (cf *kiloo, sui*)

kudukuda *n* (*n*) the last victory in a children's game.

kudura *n* (*n*) (used only of God) divine will: *Nchi yetu imepata neema kwa kudura za Mwenyezi Mungu*, our country has achieved prosperity by divine will. (cf *makadira, majaaliwa*) (Ar)

Kudusi *n* (*n*) one of the names of Almighty God referring to one who is infallible: *Maliki Kudusi*, the Holy God, the glorified God. (Ar)

kufu *n* (*n*) equal level in age, position, etc; resemblance of people in terms of age, importance, position, etc.: *Yeye hawezi kufunga ndoa naye kwa vile si mtu wa kufu yake*, he cannot get married to her because he is not of her equal level. (cf *laiki*) (Ar)

kufuli *n* (*ma-*) lock, padlock. (Ar)

kufur.u¹ *vt* 1. blaspheme; speak evil of God, sacred things, etc.: *Alimkufuru Mwenyezi Mungu*, he spoke evil of God. 2. speak ill of religion after being preached to; blaspheme: *Aliikufuru dini yetu*, he blasphemed our religion. Prep. **kufur.i.a** St. **kufur.ik.a** Cs. **kufur.ish.a** Ps. of Prep. **kufur.iw.a** Rp. of Prep. **kufur.i.an.a** (Ar)

kufuru² *n* (*n*) 1. sacrilage, blaspheme; profane or contemptuous speech against God, sacred things, etc. 2. despise of religion. (Ar)

kugesi (also *kigesi*) *n* (*n*) an anklet worn by a woman as a kind of ornament. (cf *mtali, furungu*) (Pers)

kuhani *n* (*n*) 1. Jewish priest. 2. soothsayer, fortune-teller: *Kuhani amepata umaarufu katika kazi yake ya kutazamia*, the soothsayer has gained eminence in his work of predicting things. (cf *mtabiri, mpiga ramli*) (Ar)

kuhusu *conj., prep* concerning, about, regarding: *Aliandika shairi kuhusu maisha yake*, she wrote a poem about her life.

kui *n* (*n*) (*zool*) terapon; a kind of saltwater fish (family *Teraponidae*) with a slightly compressed oblong body, having small scales and lives in inshore waters and sometimes brackish waters (cf *ngagu*)

kujiamini *n* (*ku*) confidence, hope: *Walicheza mechi kwa kujiamini*, they played the match with confidence. (cf *matumaini*)

kuju *n* (*ma-*) a kind of sieve made from coconut husks; coconut husk sieve.

kuke *n* (*n*) sea refuse consisting of small leaves, sticks, weeds, etc. that end up in the shore when they are swept away by the waves, etc.; effluent.

kukeni (also *kuukeni*) *adv* on the female side: *Anahusiana na mimi kwa upande wa kuukeni*, he is related to me on the female side i.e. mother's side.

kuko¹ *n* (*n*) a ridge made around a farm to block the flow of water; dike; dyke.

kuko² *adj, adv, n* 1. there, that: *Kuimbakuko kunapendeza*, singing that way is good. *Kuko huko*, in that very place. 2. used with *-je*. as a verb form: *Kukoje?* How are things? How is that place?

kuku¹ *n* (*n*) (*zool*) hen, chicken: *Nyama ya kuku*, chicken meat. *Koo la kuku*, breeding fowl. (*prov*) *Kuku mgeni hakosi kamba mguuni*, a foreign hen is easily recognized by the rope it is tied i.e. a person in a foreign country is easily recognized by his appearance, behaviour, etc.

kuku² *adv* on this side, this, here: *Kuku huku*, in this very place. (cf *hukuhuku*)

kukumi.a¹ *vt* swallow hastily or greedily and in large amounts some liquid stuff such as water, tea, etc.; gulp, guzzle: *Aliikukumia chai yake na kisha akatoka haraka*, he gulped down his tea and left hurriedly. Prep. ***kukumi.li.a*** St. ***kukumi.k.a*** Cs. ***kukumi.z.a*** Ps. ***kukumi.w.a*** (cf *gugumia*)

kukumi.a² *vt* invade suddenly. Prep. ***kukumi.li.a*** St. ***kukumi.k.a*** Cs. ***kukumi.z.a*** Ps. ***kukumi.w.a*** (cf *vamia*)

kukunya.a *vi* (of body, etc.) be hard, become stiff: *Mwili wake ulikukunyaa kutokana na ukosefu wa chakula bora*, his body had stiffened because of lack of good food. Prep. ***kukunya.i.a*** St. ***kukunya.ik.a***

kukurik.a¹ *vi* 1. skitter around, bustle about: *Amekuwa akikukurika siku hizi tangu kufikiwa na wageni nyumbani kwake*, she has been bustling these days since the arrival of guests at her home. 2. be impatient, lose patience. Prep. ***kukurik.i.a*** St. ***kukurik.ik.a*** Cs. ***kukuri.sh.a*** (cf *tukutika*)

kukurik.a² *vi* (esp of heart) throb. Prep. ***kukurik.i.a*** St. ***kukurik.ik.a*** Cs. ***kukuri.sh.a***

kukurukakara *n* (*n*) hustle and bustle; commotion, turmoil: *Kukurukakara za uchaguzi*, election turmoil. *Kuna kukurukakara hapo nje baada ya mwizi kukamatwa*, there is commotion outside after the thief has been caught. (cf *kikiri, patashika*)

kukus.a *vt* push forcefully: *Aliukukusa mlango*, he pushed the door forcefully. Prep. ***kukus.i.a*** St. ***kukus.ik.a*** Cs. ***kukus.ish.a*** Ps. ***kukus.w.a*** Rp. ***kukus.an.a***

kukut.a *vt* 1. (of cloth, etc.) shake off a wet thing such as a cloth after wringing it out: *Aliikukuta suruali yake kabla ya kuanika*, he shook off water from his trousers before hanging it. (cf *kung'uta*) 2. (of dust, etc.) shake off dust from sth like a carpet by beating it with a stick, etc.; dust: *Alilikukuta zulia ili kuondosha vumbi*, he dusted the carpet with a stick. 3. pant for breath; gasp, puff: *Alianza kukuta baada ya kukimbia*, he started to pant after running. Prep. ***kukut.i.a*** St. ***kukut.ik.a*** Cs. ***kukut.ish.a*** Ps. ***kukut.w.a*** (cf *tweta, puma*)

kukuta.a *vi* (of leaves, clothes, etc.) be dry because of excessive sun; wither, shrivel up, pucker: *Mimea yangu imekukutaa kwa sababu ya ukosefu wa mvua*, my plants have shrivelled up for lack of rain. Prep. ***kukuta.li.a*** St. ***kukuta.k.a*** Cs. ***kukuta.z.a*** (cf *gugutaa, kacha*)

kukuziwa *n* (*n*) (*zool*) African moorhen; a kind of bird having white flank streaks, a red bill with a yellow tip and green legs. *Gallinula chloropus*.

kulabu *n* (*n*) 1. a hooked instrument, used for plaiting, tailoring, etc.; crotchet, peg, hook. 2. a small anchor with four flukes; grapnel, grappling iron. 3. a kind of a small blacksmith's scissors with a hook.

kulastara *n* (*n*) (*zool*) heron; a kind of wading gregarious bird (family Ardeidae) with a long neck, long legs and a long tapered bill, living along marshes and river banks; black-headed heron. *Ardea melanocephala*.

kulateni *n* (*n*) amount of water exceeding 240 litres. (Ar)

kula.u *vt* 1. insist on sth. 2. refuse to budge.

kule¹ *adv, n, pron* form of *-le*, there, over there, in that place: *Kuna ghasia kule*, there is chaos over there.

kule² *n* (*n*) (*zool*) a kind of fish.

kulehemu *n* (*n*) soldering (Ar)

kuleksi *n* (*n*) culex (Eng)

380

kul.i¹ *vt* speak, say, utter. (cf *sema*) (Ar)
kuli² *n* (*ma-*) docker, coolie, stevedore, longshoreman; a person who works on a waterfront loading and unloading ships, etc.: *Makuli wamegoma bandarini*, the coolies have gone on strike at the harbour. (cf *hamali*) (Eng)
kulia¹ *n* (*n*) right hand: *Mkono wa kulia*, right hand side. (cf *kumeni, yamini*)
kulia² *adv* on the right side, to the right side, at the right side: *Amesimama kulia*, he has stood on the right side.
kulihali *adv* whatever the case, in all circumstances, by all means: *Nenda ukamtazame mjomba na kulihali usisahau kumpa salamu zangu*, go and see my uncle and whatever the circumstances, don't forget to convey my greetings. (Ar)
kuliko¹ *adv* (used for comparison) than: *Yeye ni mfupi kuliko dada yake*, she is shorter than her sister.
kuliko² *adv* where there is: *Kuliko na sherehe za harusi ni wapi?* Where are the wedding celebrations? (cf *kwenye*)
kulikoni *interj* What is wrong? What is happening?
kulul.a¹ *vt* sweep, clean, bail out, clear out: *Aliyakulula maji kutoka kwenye ngalawa*, he bailed the water out of the canoe. Prep. *kulul.i.a* St. *kulul. ik.a* Cs. *kulul.ish.a* Ps. *kulul.w.a* (cf *ondoa, safisha*)
kulul.a² *vt* excel, surpass, beat: *Wanafunzi wa shule yetu wamekulula katika kutunga mashairi*, the students from our school have excelled in composing poems. Prep. *kulul.i.a* St. *kulul.ik.a* Cs. *kulul.ish.a* Ps. *kulul.w.a* Rp. *kulul.an.a* (cf *zidi*)
kulul.a³ *vt* drink a mouthful of anything that is liquid esp when someone is thirsty, etc.; gulp, swig: *Aliukulula uji alipokuwa na njaa*, she drank a mouthful of gruel when she was hungry. Prep. *kulul.i.a* St. *kulul.ik.a* Cs. *kulul.ish.a* Ps. *kulul.w.a*

kululu (also *kururu*) *n* (*ma-*) a large kind of cowrie that has little value. It is used in the expression: *Fulani amepata kululu*, so-and-so has got something that has no value at all.
kulungu (also *kungu*) *n* (*n*) (*zool*) a kind of bushbuck.
kuma *n* (*n*) (*anat*) vagina
kumba¹ *n* (*ma-*) (*bot*) a whole coconut leaf with its fronds plaited all along each side of the central rib, and used for fencing, roofing, etc.
kumb.a² *vt* 1. push, shove, jostle, press: *Walinikumba kwenye kundi la watu*, they pushed me in the midst of the crowd. 2 collect, gather: *Alizikumba taka zote*, he collected all the refuse. 3. squander; spend extravagantly; be a spendthrift: *Aliyakumba mali yote aliyorithi*, he squandered all the wealth he inherited. 4. deceive, cheat: *Mfanya-biashara alimkumba mteja*, the businessman cheated the customer. 5. bail out water as from a canoe, etc.: *Aliyakumba maji kutoka kwenye mashua*, he bailed out water from the boat. Prep. *kumb.i.a* St. *kumb.ik.a* Cs. *kumb.ish.a* Ps. *kumb.w.a* (cf *futa*)
kumba³ *n* (*n*) a kind of drum of the evil spirit from Mozambique.
kumba⁴ *n* (*n*) (*zool*) a kind of fish of the tilapia family. (cf *bulibuli*)
kumba.a *vi* be stunted, be dwarfed; grow with difficulties, etc: *Mtoto yule amekumbaa kwa sababu ya utapiamlo*, that child is stunted because of malnutrition. Cs. *kumba.z.a* (cf *dumaa, via*)
kumbaga.a *vi* appear in a place unexpectedly.
kumbakumba¹ *interj* an expletive used to show the magnitude of sth: *Yale si maradhi; yale ni kumbakumba*, that is not an illness; that is a real disease.
kumbakumba² *n* (*n*) 1. a random collection of items esp in a hurried manner because of war, etc.: *Watu walichukua vitu vyao kwa*

kumbakumba na kukimbilia nchi jirani kwa sababu ya vita, people collected their things hurriedly and fled to the neighbouring country because of war. 2. sth that affects the majority of the people. 3. a person who takes things indiscriminately.

kumban.a *vi* 1. jostle one another, tussle with. 2. encounter difficulties, etc. *Alikumbana na matatizo mengi*, he encountered many difficulties. Prep. ***kumban.i.a*** St. ***kumban.ik.a*** Cs. ***kumban.ish.a***

kumbati *n* (*n*) see *ukombati*

kumbati.a *vt* cuddle, embrace, hug; take into one's arms: *Alimkumbatia mkewe*, he embraced his wife. Prep. ***kumbati.li.a*** St. ***kumbati.k.a*** Cs. ***kumbati.sh.a*** Ps. ***kumbati.w.a***, be embraced. Rp. ***kumbati.an.a***, embrace each other e.g. *Mgeni na mwenyeji wake walikumbatiana kwenye uwanja wa ndege*, the guest and his host embraced each other at the airport.

kumbe *interj, conj* 1. an expletive used to express surprise over pleasant or unpleasant things happening in reverse of what was expected or thought; you don't say: *Kumbe! Alimwacha mkewe; Mimi sikufikiria kwamba atafanya hivyo*, you don't say! He divorced his wife; I didn't think he would do so. (cf *alaa, ala*) 2. a word expressing the contrariness of things or situations; whereas, while, on the contrary: *Alitueleza kwamba atahudhuria mkutano; kumbe, alikuwa anatudanganya*, he told us that he would attend the meeting; on the contrary he was just deceiving us. (cf *ilhali*)

kumbi[1] (also *kumbesa, kumvi*) *n* (*ma-*) (*bot*) the fibrous outer sheath of a coconut, etc.: *Kumbi la nazi*, the fibrous husk of a coconut.

kumbi[2] *n* (*ma-*) 1. circumcision school; a place where young boys undergo circumcision. 2. a place where secret affairs connected with circumcision are organised. 3. a shed where circumcised young men are kept.

kumbikumbi *n* (*n*) (*zool*) winged termite; a kind of termite (family *Termitidae*) which usu swarms out of the nest during the long rains and finds new colonies. A winged termite is a nutritious delicacy sought by many tribes throughout tropical Africa. (cf *ngumbi*)

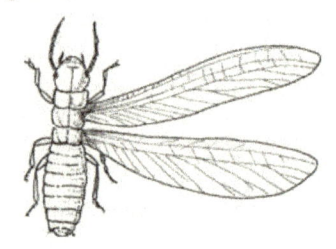

kumbikumbi

kumbo[1] *n* (*n*) a sudden push; shove: *Piga kumbo*, shove someone. (cf *kikumbo, busa*)

kumbo[2] *n* (*ma-*) wholesale collection of people or things at a go; swoop: *Wachezaji kamari wote walichukuliwa kumbo moja*, all the gamblers were arrested in one swoop. (cf *mkupuo*)

kumbu[1] *n* (*n*) (*zool*) sardines (cf *babwe, dagaa*)

kumbuk.a *vt* remember, collect, recall: *Unakumbuka uliweka wapi funguo zako?* Can you remember where you kept your keys? Prep. ***kumbuk.i.a*** St. ***kumbuk.ik.a*** Cs. ***kumbuk.ish.a*** Ps. ***kumbuk.w.a,*** be remembered e.g. *Utakumbukwa takriban na kila mtu kwa sababu ya wema wako*, you will be remembered by almost everyone because of your kindness. Rp. ***kumbuk.an.a*** (cf *tanabahi, dhukuru*)

kumbukizi *n* (*ma-*) 1. commemoration, memorial. 2. ideas about a person or an event of the past.

kumbuko *n* (*ma-*) recollection

kumbukumbu *n* (*n*) 1. remembrance, commemoration. memory, memorial: *Serikali ilifanya kumbukumbu ya kuadhimisha siku ya wale waliokufa vitani*, the government organized a memorial service for those who died in the war. 2. souvenir, records, minutes: *Wanachama walijadili kwanza kumbukumbu za mkutano uliopita*, the party members first discussed the minutes of the previous meeting. 3. used in the expression: *Kumbukumbu ya Torati*, the Book of Deuteronomy. *Kumbukumbu za kihistoria*, annals.

kumbush.a *vt* remind, prompt; jog the memory: *Binti yangu alinikumbusha nimnunulie mwanasesere*, my daughter reminded me to buy for her a doll. Prep. *kumbush.i.a* St. *kumbush.ik.a* Ps. *kumbush.w.a* Rp. *kumbush.an.a*

kumbusho *n* (*ma-*) 1. memorial; anything, such as monument, trustfund, holiday, etc, intended to celebrate or honour the memory of a person or an event. 2. reminder, souvenir, momento, keepsake: *Zawadi yako hii itakuwa kumbusho la urafiki wetu*, your present will serve as a reminder of our friendship.

kumbwaya[1] *n* (*n*) 1. (*mus*) a big three-legged drum which makes great noise when sounded. 2. a kind of a dance played in a circle. (cf *pungwa, kuro*)

kumbwaya[2] *n* (*n*) a sleeveless vestment that does not fit properly on the body; tunic.

kumbwe *n* (*n*) snack; a small quantity of food for eating.

kumbwewe *n* (*n*) a sling made from rope, fibre, etc., used for throwing stones, etc.; catapult. (cf teo, *kombeo, kumbawe*)

kumi *adj, n* (*n*) ten: *Vitabu kumi*, ten books. (*prov*) *Kenda karibu ya kumi*, nine is near ten i.e. when someone is nearing the end of a task, he should complete it even though he may be tired.

kumoja[1] *adv* one kind, one sort: *Kwao kumoja*, their place is the same. *Kazi zao hazina kumoja*, their occupations are not all of the one kind.

kumoja[2] *n* (*n*) sameness, same place, same direction.

kumradhi (also *kunradhi*) *interj* an expletive used for seeking pardon from someone; pardon me. (cf *samahani*)

kumt.a *vt* 1. shake off, shake out; dust: *Alikumta vumbi kwenye nguo yake*, she shook off the dust from her dress. 2. hit, beat, flog. Prep. *kumt.i.a* St. *kumt.ik.a* Cs. *kumt.ish.a* Ps. *kumt.w.a* (cf *kukuta, kung'uta*)

kumto *n* (*ma-*) see *kung'uto*

kumulasi *n* (*n*) heap, pile, cumulus, mass. (Eng)

kumvi[1] *n* (*ma-*) see *kumbi*[1]

kumvi[2] *n* (*ma*) (*bot*) husk, chaff; the fibrous husk or sheath of various seeds esp grains of rice, wheat, etc. (cf *kapi*)

kun.a[1] *vt, vi* 1. scratch, scrape: *Kuna kichwa*, scratch the head. *Kuna ngozi*, scratch the skin. 2. grate coconut meat: *Kuna nazi*, extract the nutty part from the coconut shell by using a special instrument. Prep. *kun.i.a* e.g. *Mbuzi ya kukunia nazi*, coconut grater. St. *kun.ik.a* Cs. *kun.ish.a* Ps. *kun.w.a* Rp. of Prep. *kun.i.an.a*

kun.a[2] *verb form* there is, there are: *Kuna kelele nyingi nje*, there is a lot of noise outside. *Kuna nini?* What is happening? What is the matter? *Kunako*, where there is. (*prov*) *Kunako moshi kuna moto*, where there is smoke, there is fire i.e. every happening has a source.

kunadi *n* (*n*) see *kanadi*

kunazi *n* (*n*) (*bot*) Chinese date; a small edible brown or yellow fruit with a slightly sub-acid flavour, from the tree known as *mkunazi, jujube*. (*Zizyphus jujube*) (Pers)

kunda[1] *n* (*ma-*) (*bot*) green vegetable resembling spinach. (cf *mchicha*)

kunda[2] *n* (*ma-*) (*zool*) speckled pigeon;

a pigeon with vinous chestnut back, white-spotted wing-coverts and a pale grey rump when in flight. *Columba guinea.*

kunda.a *vi* be stunted, be dwarfed; shrivel: *Mtoto huyu amekundaa,* this child is stunted. *Mimea yangu imekundaa kwa sababu ya ukame,* my plants have shrivelled because of drought. Prep. **kunda.li.a** St. **kunda.lik.a** Cs. **kunda.lish.a** (cf *dumaa, via, bundia*)

kundaji *n (mi-)* see *mkundaji*

kundavi (also *kundavi*) *n (n)* a broad belt of beads strung in a pattern, worn by some around their loins; waist beads belt.

kunde *n (n) (bot)* cowpea; a kind of bean produced by the plant *mkunde.* (*Vigna unguiculata*)

kundi *n (ma-)* group, flock, crowd, swarm, herd, etc.: *Kundi la wanamuziki,* a group of musicians. *Kundi la nyuki,* a swarm of bees. *Kundi la ng'ombe,* a herd of cattle. *Wanafunzi walikuja makundi makundi,* the students came in droves.

kunga¹ *n (n)* secret matters considered unfit for public discussion such as sex and marriage. (*prov*) *Mambo ya nyumbani ni kunga,* house matters are confidential i.e. don't let house matters go to the public.

kunga² *n (n) (bot)* a kind of vegetable, family of egg plants.

kung.a³ *vi* train a person esp a child moral values. Prep. **kung.i.a** St. **kung.ik.a** Cs. **kung.ish.a** Ps. **kung.w.a** Rp. **kung.an.a**

kung.a⁴ *vt* sew the hem of a carpet. Prep. **kung.i.a** St. **kung.ik.a** Cs. **kung.ish.a** Ps. **kung.w.a** Rp. **kung.an.a**

kunge¹ *n (ma-)* see *ukungu¹*

kunge² (also *kurungu*) *n (n) (bot)* the hard centre of a tree trunk; heartwood, duramen. (cf *ngarange*)

kunge³ *n (n)* a hard stone used to smoothen the surface of pottery during kneading.

kungfu *n (n)* kung fu; a Chinese system of self defence like karate but emphasizing circular rather than linear movements. (Chin)

kungu¹ *n (n) (bot)* an edible brilliant reddish fruit when ripe from the tree *mkungu* (*Terminalia catappa*), containing one seed somewhat resembling the sweet almond in flavour and is very popular with local children; tropical almond, wild almond, Indian almond.

kungu² *n (n)* see *kulungu*

kungu³ *n (n) (zool)* a kind of fish (family Lutjanidae) which is generally dark brown dorsally with a strong reddish hue, particularly on cheeks and lower half of sides; two-spot red snapper, river bream. *Lutjanus bohar.*

kungu⁴ *n (n)* a large cooking pot.

kungu⁵ *n (n)* a kind of children's game of walking with one foot. (cf *kidete*)

kungugu¹ *n (n)* heavy mist; heavy fog or haze: *Alishindwa kuendesha gari kwa sababu ya kungugu,* he was unable to drive the car fast because of the heavy fog. (cf *vundevunde*)

kungugu² *n (n)* restless sleeping. (cf *ulalavi*)

kungugu³ *n (n)* a kind of black cowrie with white spots.

kunguia *n (n)* see *kunguwia*

kunguma *n (n) (bot)* an edible oval fleshy fruit from the *mkunguma* (*Sorindeia obtusifoliolata*), a glaborous tree with alternate pinnate leaves.

kungumanga *n (n) (bot)* nutmeg; a kind of fleshy fruit resembling nectarines in size and appearance from the tree *mkungumanga.* (*Myristica fragrans*)

kunguni *n (n)* 1. (*zool*) bedbug; a kind of insect which sucks blood. 2. (*syn*) *Fulani ana damu ya kunguni,* so and so has the blood of a bedbug. i.e. so and so is unlucky.

kunguru¹ *n (n) (zool)* pied crow; a kind of bird which is generally black with a white breast and a white crescent on the back of the neck. *Corvus albus*. (*prov*) *Kunguru mwoga hukimbiza ubawawe*, a timid crow tries to evade its wing i.e. it is important that we should try to avoid issues that can bring problems to us.

kunguru² *n* (*n*) a kind of checked cotton material.

kung'ut.a¹ (also *kumta*) *vt* 1. remove dust esp from furniture, carpets, etc. by using a stick, etc.; dust, shake off: *Alilikung'uta jamvi lake lenye vumbi*, he dusted his mat. 2. hold a garment with both ends and then shake it off repeatedly to remove the extra drops. of water after washing it. 3. (*fig*) beat severely: *Mwalimu alimkung'uta mwanafunzi*, the teacher beat the student severely. 4. refuse bail. Ps. **kung'ut.i.a** St. **kung'ut.ik.a** Cs. **kung'ut.ish.a** Ps. **kung'ut.w.a** Rp. **kung'ut.an.a** (cf *nyuka, charaza, chapa*)

kung'uta² *n* (*n*) (*med*) hookworm disease. (cf *safura*)

kung'uto *n* (*ma-*) a kind of circular straw strainer, used for tossing and winnowing grain, etc.; colander, sieve, strainer, riddle.

kunguwa.a (also *kwaa*) *vt, vi* stumble the foot against a stone, log, etc.; trip: *Nilikikunguwaa kisiki kwenye kiza*, I stumbled against the stump in the dark. (*prov*) *Heri kujikunguwaa guu kuliko kujikunguwaa ulimi*, it is better to stumble with the toe than with the tongue i.e. one should not talk things that may endanger him. Prep. **kunguwa.li.a** St. **kunguwa.lik.a** Cs. **kunguwa.li.sh.a** (cf *kwaa*)

kunguwia (also *kunguia*) *n* (*n*) a kind of Swahili women's dance involving the wearing of a coloured dress and the use of umbrellas.

kungwi *n* (*ma-*) a person usu a woman who initiates young brides into the ways of married life. She also advises young girls how to cope with menstruation, etc.; initiation marriage instructor. (cf *somo*)

kunj.a¹ *vt* 1. fold, bend, furl, tangle, wrap: *Kunja uzi*, tangle the thread. *Kunja shati*, fold the shirt. *Kunja gazeti*, fold the newspaper, *Kunja mbawa*, fold the wings. (*prov*) *Kambare mkunje angali mbichi*, fold the catfish when it is fresh, i.e. strike the iron while it is hot; in other words, make haste to rectify a spoiled situation before it is too late. Prep. **kunj.i.a** St. **kunj. ik.a** Cs. **kunj.ish.a** Ps. **kunj.w.a** Rp. **kunj.an.a** e.g. *Ipige pasi nguo hii kwa vile imekunjana*, iron this garment because it is wrinkled. St. **kunj.am.a** Rp. of St. **kunj.am.an.a**, be folded, be wrinkled, be frown, e.g *Uso wake umekunjamana*, his face is frowned (cf *nepa, nesa, pinda*) 2. (*idm*) *Kunja uso*, scowl, frown, grimace; knit the eyebrows. *Kunja jamvi*, finalize an issue.

kunj.a² *vt* finish the distance with vigour. Prep. **kunj.i.a** St. **kunj.ik.a** Cs. **kunj. ish.a** Ps. **kunj.w.a** Rp. **kunj.an.a**

kunjaman.a *vi* see *kunja*. Prep. **kunjaman.i.a** St. **kunjaman.ik.a** Cs. **kunjaman.ish.a**

kunju *n* (*mi-*) see *mkunjo*

kunju.a *vt* unfold, uncoil, unbend, unfurl, open: *Alilikunjua jamvi*, he unfolded the mat. *Alilikunjua tanga*, he unfolded the sail. *Kunjua uso*, smooth the brows. *Kunjua mkono*, open your hand. Prep. **kunju.li.a** St. **kunju.k.a** Cs. **kunju.lish.a** Ps. of Prep. **kunju. liw.a**, be unfolded. Rp. **kunju.an.a** (cf *tandaza, nyoosha*)

-kunjufu *adj* affable, kind, genial, pleasant, good: *Ana moyo mkunjufu*, he has a good heart; he is kind-hearted. (cf *furahifu*)

kunradhi *adv* see *kumradhi*

kuntu¹ *adv* precisely, exactly: *Maneno yako ni kuntu*, your words are precise. (cf *hasa, kabisa, ndivyo*)

kuntu² *interj* an expletive of complete approval over sth.

kununu *n* (*ma-*) (*bot*) empty husk of grain; spike of grain: *Kununu la mawele,* a spike of bullrush millet with no grain in it. (cf *pepe, kapi, suke*)

kunusi *n* (*n*) badluck, ill-luck, bad omen, evil spell; jinx: *Alitaka kuniletea kunusi kazini kwangu,* he wanted to put a jinx on me at my place of work. (cf *mkosi, balaa, nuksi*) (Ar)

kunut.i *vi* (in Islam) invoke God while performing *usu* dawn prayers after rising up from the bowing position. Prep. **kunut.i.a** St **kunut.ik.a** Cs. **kunut.ish.a** Ps. of Prep. **kunut.iw.a** (Ar)

kunya.a *vi* 1. wrinkle, crease, cringe: *Alikunyaa kwa aibu,* he cringed in disgrace. 2. pucker, wither, shrivel up: *Mimea yake ilikunyaa kwa jua kali,* his plants withered in the hot sun. Prep. **kunya.li.a** St. **kunya.lik.a** Cs. **kunya.z.a**

kunyanzi *n* (*ma-*) 1. (of old people, etc.) fold, wrinkle: *Mzee yule ana kunyanzi usoni mwake,* that old person has wrinkles on his face.

kunyasi *n* (*n*) astringent; a substance that causes the contraction of body tissues, typically used to protect the skin and to reduce bleeding from minor abrasions.

kunyat.a *vi* (*usu* used with reflexive *JI*) *Jikunyata,* bend oneself down and forward because of fear, cold, embarrassment, pain, etc.; cower, cringe, wince, hunch over, shrink, double up: *Alijikunyata kwa baridi,* he doubled up with cold. Prep. **kunyat.i.a** St. **kunyat.ik.a** Cs. **kunyat.ish.a** Ps. **kunyat.w.a**

kunyu.a (also *kunyura*) *vt* 1. scratch the skin hard until there is an abrasion: *Alijikunyua baada ya kutafunwa na mbu,* he scratched himself hard after being bitten by mosquitoes. (cf *chubua*) 2. break off a piece of sth with teeth; cut a piece with teeth: *Watoto wadogo waliukunyua mkate,* the small children bit off the bread. 3. call secretly, give a sign secretly; signal: *Walinikunyua niondoke,* they signalled to me to leave. Prep. **kunyu.li.a** St. **kunyu.lik.a** Cs. **kunyu.lish.a** Ps. of Prep. **kunyu.liw.a** Rp **kunyu.an.a**

kunyur.a *vt* see *kunyua*

kuo¹ *n* (*ma-*) rut, furrow, trench, hollow, hole: *Makuo ya kuku,* holes scratched by fowls. (cf *handaki*)

kuo² *n* (*ma-*) 1. a bed or row of seedlings, etc. 2. a plot of ground marked out by a furrow or line drawn on the ground, and given to a person to cultivate. (cf *ngwe, mraba*)

kupa¹ *n* (*ma-*) (*naut*) one of the side pieces that form a pulley enclosing a sheave.

kupa² *n* (*ma-*) (*bot*) reeds of sugarcane that have been dried and used for thatching a house. *Nyumba ya makupa,* a thatched house of this kind.

kupaa *n* (*n*) (in Christianity) Ascension: *Kupaa Bwana,* Ascension Day; the 40th day after Easter when the Ascension of Christ into heaven after the resurrection is celebrated in the Christian Church.

kupatwa *n* (*n*) (*astron*) eclipse: *Kupatwa kwa jua,* eclipse of the sun.

kupau *n* (*n*) (*naut*) the part of the masthead that serves as a shell for the fixed double block.

kupe¹ *n* (*n*) 1. (*zool*) tick; a wingless bloodsucking insect that is *usu* parasitic on man, cattle, sheep, etc. 2. (*syn*) *Kama kupe na mkia wa ng'ombe,* like a tick and a cow's tail. This is an expression used to refer to things that are closely connected. 2. (*fig*) bloodsucker, exploiter: *Usiwe kupe; lazima ujitegemee,* don't be an exploiter; you must be self-reliant. (cf *mnyonyaji*)

kupe² *n* (*n*) a kind of saltwater fish (family Polynemidae) that is related to the mullets in body and shape, and is used extensively as food in the tropics.; threadfin.

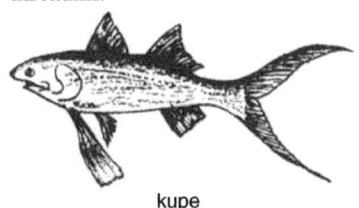

kupe
Indian thread fin. *Polynemus indicus.*

kupi.a *vt, vi* 1. wink, blink: *Alinikupia kwamba yeye alikuwa anawatania wenzake tu*, he winked at me to show that he was just playing a joke on his colleagues. 2. nod from drowsiness or sleepiness; be nodding: *Alikupia alipokuwa anasinzia*, he nodded from drowsiness. (cf *gota, pesa, pepesa*) Prep. **kupi.li.a** St. **kupi.lik.a** Cs. **kupi.sh.a** Ps. **kupi.w.a** Rp. **kupi.an.a**

kupindukia *adv* excessively, very: *Amelewa kupindukia*, he is excessively drunk.

kupita *conj* 1. than; *Wewe ni hodari kupita yeye*, you are clever than him. 2. over and above, beyond the point: *Anazungumza kupita kiasi*, he talks over and above the normal.

kuponi *n (n)* a certificate or ticket entitling the holder to a specified right; coupon. (Eng)

kupu.a *vt* 1. uproot, unroot, throw off: *Alivikupua visiki kwenye konde yake*, he uprooted the stumps in his field. (cf *ng'oa*) 2. spill. pour out: *Aliukupua wino wangu*, he spilled my ink. (cf *mwaga*) 3. hit or beat as with a stick, etc.: *Mwalimu alimkupua mwanafunzi sugu*, the teacher beat the hardened student severely. (cf *piga*) 4. snatch;

take away forcefully: *Mwizi alikikupua kipochi cha mtalii*, the thief snatched the tourist's purse (cf *nyang'anya*). Prep. **kupu.li.a** St. **kupu.k.a** and **kupu.lik.a** Cs. **kupu.lish.a** Ps. of Prep. **kupu.liw.a** Rp. **kupu.an.a** (cf *nyang'anya*)

kupuk.a *vi* bolt, hasten, dart, dash, rush: *Alikupuka alipoona amechelewa*, he dashed off when he found he was getting late. Prep. **kupuk.i.a** St. **kupuk.ik.a** Cs. **kupuk.ish.a**

kura *n (n)* vote, ballot: *Kura ya kupinga*, a no vote. *Kura ya uamuzi*, the deciding vote. *Kura ya turufu*, veto vote. *Kura ya maoni*, referendum. *Kura ya ndiyo*, yes vote. *Kura ya hapana*, no vote. *Kura ya wingi*, majority vote. *Kura fuliishi*, gallop poll. *Kura ya kuwa na imani*, vote of confidence. *Kura ya kutokuwa na imani*, vote of no-confidence. *Kura ya siri*, secret vote; secret ballot. *Kura ya shukrani*, vote of thanks. *Kura ya lawama*, vote of censure. *Piga kura*, cast a vote.

Kurani *n (n)* the Holy Koran. (cf *Msahafu*) (Ar)

kurca *n (n)* (*zool*) kingfisher (cf *mtilili, kizamidagaa, mdiria*)

kuro[1] *n (n)* (*zool*) waterbuck; a kind of African antelope (*genus Kobus*) that inhabits areas that are close to rivers and lakes in Savanna grasslands, etc.

kuro

kuro² *n* (*n*) (*mus*) a kind of big drum standing on three legs whose sides are skinned by using the hides of waterbuck; a big three-legged drum. (*syn*) *Kuro haisemi uongo*, the drum does not speak lies i.e. the drum is not beaten without any reason.

kuru¹ *n* (*n*) a cylindrical object like a cannon which is not hollowed.

kuru² *n* (*n*) the side of an ancient Zanzibar coin on which a pair of weighing scales or balances is shown.

kuruba¹ *n* (*n*) (of a road, etc). bend, corner. (cf *mzingo*)

kuruba² *n*(*n*) close relatives or friends.

kurugo (also *kuungo*) *n* (*n*) a white stone used for smoothing earthen objects. (cf *kurunge, komango, tomo*)

kurumbiza (also *kirumbizi, kurumbizi*) *n* (*n*) 1. (*zool*) golden oriole; a kind of bird with black wings, black and yellow tail, carmine bill and yellowish underparts. *Oriolus auratus*. 2. (*syn*) *Anasema kama kurumbiza*, he talks like an oriole i.e. he is very talkative.

kurumbizi *n* (*n*) see *kurumbiza*

kurunge *n* (*n*) see *kunge²*

kurungu *n* (*n*) see *kulungu*

kurunzi *n* (*n*) 1. search light. 2. electric torch. (cf *tochi*)

kurupu.a *vt, vi* (of a person, animal, bird, etc.) startle and run away; frighten away: *Mvamizi aliwakurupua ndege waliokuwa wakila mpunga kwenye konde*, the scarecrow frightened off the birds from the rice field. St. *kurupu.k.a* jump and run away; rush away, dash, bolt, dart e.g. *Mwizi alikurupuka wakati wapita njia walipopiga kelele*, the thief rushed away when the passersby shouted. Cs. *kurupu.sh.a* Ps. of Prep. *kurupu.liw.a* Rp. *kurupu.an.a*

kurupuk.a *vi* see *kurupua*. Prep. *kurupuk.i.a* St. *kurupuk.ik.a* Cs. *kurupuk.ish.a*

kurupush.a *vt* cause sby/sth to dash/run away: *Alimkurupusha paa*, he caused the deer to run away. Prep. *kurupush.i.a* St. *kurupush.ik.a* Ps. *kurupush.w.a* Ps. *kurupush.an.a* (cf *fukuza*)

kururu¹ *n* (*n*) see *kululu*

kururu² *n* (*n*) (*zool*) tiger cowrie; a solid, thick, heavy, inflated shell up to 13 cms. It is dorsally white or pale-reddish brown with large dark brown spots, and sometimes has a reddish longitudinal stripe and lives under coral and boulders in shallow or deep water. (*Cypraea tigris*)

kurusi *n* (*n*) a ripe coconut. (cf *koroma*)

kurut.a *vt* strip off sisal leaves to get fibre: *Wafanyakazi waliikuruta mikonge ili kutengeneza kamba*, the workers stripped off sisal leaves in order to make ropes. Prep. *kurut.i.a* St. *kurut.ik.a* Cs. *kurut.ish.a* Ps. *kurut.w.a*

kuruti *n* (*n*) 1. recruit. 2. a new subordinate employee. (Eng)

kuruwiji *n* (*n*) (*zool*) Zanzibar sombre bulbul; a kind of bird (family *Pycnontidae*) with a dark head, and a yellowish belly. *Andropadus insularis*.

kuruz.a¹ *vt* do sth in a disorderly manner; do sth haphazardly; bungle, mar, botch: *Ukimpa kazi ataikuruza tu*, if you give him work, he will just bungle it. Prep. *kuruz.i.a* St. *kuruz.ik.a* Cs. *kuruz.ish.a* Ps. *kuruz.w.a* Rp. *kuruz.an.a* (cf *boronga, vunda*)

kuruz.a² *vt* drag, haul, draw, pull: *Aliukuruza mkokoteni*, he pulled the push-cart. Prep. *kuruz.i.a* St. *kuruz.ik.a* Cs. *kuruz.ish.a* Ps. *kuruz.w.a* Rp. *kuruz.an.a* (cf *kokota*)

kuruz.a³ *vi* grate with a coconut grater. Prep. *kuruz.i.a* St. *kuruz.ik.a* Cs. *kuruz.ish.a* Ps. *kuruz.w.a* Rp. *kuruz.an.a* (cf *kura*)

kus.a *vt, vi* happen, meet, encounter: *Mashaka yamemkusa mwaka huu wote*, he has encountered trouble all this year. Prep. *kus.i.a* St. *kus.ik.a* Cs. *kus.ish.a* Ps. *kus.w.a* Rp. *kus.an.a* (cf *kuta, tokea*)

kusany.a *vt* collect, gather. assemble; bring together: *Alizikusanya taka zote na kisha akazitupa,* he collected all the refuse and then threw it away. Prep. **kusany.i.a** St. **kusany.ik.a,** gather, assemble e.g. *Watu wengi walikusanyika uwanjani,* many people assembled on the ground. Cs. **kusany.ish.a** Ps. **kusany.w.a** Rp. **kusany.an.a** (cf *konga, zoa, somba*)

kusanyik.a *vi* see *kusanya*. Prep. **kusanyik.i.a** St. **kusanyik.ik.a** Cs. **kusanyik.ish.a**

kusanyiko *n (ma-)* assembly, gathering, congregation: *Lilikuwa kusanyiko la wataalamu kutoka nchi mbalimbali,* that was a gathering of scholars from different countries.

kusanyo *n (ma-)* collection, gathering: *Kusanyo la stempu za zamani,* the collection of old stamps.

kushinda *prep* than: *Ahmed ni mrefu kushinda Salum,* Ahmed is taller than Salum. (cf *kuliko*)

kushoto[1] (also *shoto*) *n (n)* left: *Upande wa kushoto,* left side, leftwards.

kushoto[2] *adv* leftside: *Pita kushoto,* go to the left. (cf *kuukeni*)

kusi *n (n)* winds from the South prevailing from May to October; southernly wind: *Upepo wa kusi,* winds of this period; south monsoon wind.

kusini[1] *adv* south: *Ameenda kusini,* he has gone to the south.

kusini[2] *n (n)* south: *Kusini kuna baridi kali,* there is severe cold in the south.

kustabini *n (n)* see *kastabini*

kusudi[1] (also *kusudio*) *n (ma-)* aim, goal, purpose, intent, objective: *Kusudio lake halieleweki,* his goal is not understood. (cf *nia, lengo*) (Ar)

kusudi[2] *adv* intentionally, deliberately, purposely: *Amemchokoza ndugu yake kusudi,* he has teased his brother deliberately. (cf *makusudi*) (Ar)

kusudi[3] *conj* in order that, so that: *Amekwenda shuleni kusudi aonane na mwalimu,* he has gone to school in order to see his teacher. (cf *ili*) (Ar)

kusudi.a *vt, vi* intend, aim, determine: *Anakusudia kusafiri wiki ijayo,* he intends to travel next week. Prep. **kusudi.li.a** St. **kusudi.k.a** Cs. **kusudi.sh.a** Ps. **kusudi.w.a** Rp. **kusudi.an.a** (cf *dhamira, azimu*) (Ar)

kusudio *n (n)* see *kusudi*[1]

kusur.u[1] *vt* deny oneself of anything in order to gain an object; deprive oneself of sth in order to achieve an object; abnegate: *Mjomba wangu alijikusuru mengi ili awasaidie jamaa zake,* my uncle denied himself of many things in order to assist his relatives. Prep. **kusur.i.a** St. **kusur.ik.a** Cs. **kusur.ish.a** Ps. of Prep. **kusur.iw.a** (cf *jinyima*) (Ar)

kusur.u[2] *vt, vi* (in Islam) shorten prayers, as when someone is travelling for a long distance: *Msafiri alizikusuru sala zake,* the traveller shortened his prayers. Prep. **kusur.i.a** St. **kusur.ik.a** Cs. **kusur.ish.a** Ps. of Prep. **kusur.iw.a** (cf *fupisha, punguza*) (Ar)

kusur.u[3] *vt, vi* make a mistake; err, blunder: *Mtoto alikusuru kwa kutoamkia wageni,* the child erred in failing to greet the guests. Prep. **kusur.i.a** St. **kusur.ik.a** Cs. **kusur.ish.a** Ps. of Prep. **kusur.iw.a** (cf *kosa*) (Ar)

kut.a[1] *vt* 1. meet, encounter; come upon: *Nilimkuta nyumbani kwake,* I met him at his house. Prep. **kut.i.a** e.g. *Walimkutia akikata majani,* they met him slashing the grass. St. **kut.ik.a** Cs. **kut.ish.a** Ps. **kut.w.a,** be met, be found e.g. *Mgonjwa alikutwa katika hali mbaya,* the patient was found in a serious condition. Rp. **kuta.n.a.** 2. find, get: *Ukilisoma gazeti hili, utazikuta habari nyingi,* if you read this newspaper, you will get a lot of news. 3. blow sth with great force. Prep. **kut.i.a** St. **kut.ik.a** Cs. **kut.ish.a** Ps. **kut.w.a** Rp. **kut.an.a** (cf *pata*)

kut.a² *vi* be satisfied with food. (cf *shiba*)
kut.a³ *vt* used in the expression: *Kuta mayai*, lay eggs.
kutan.a¹ *vi* see *kuta¹*
kutan.a² *vi* 1. meet together, hold a meeting; assemble: *Bunge litakutana karibu*, parliament will meet soon. Prep. **kutan.i.a,** meet at, e.g. *Walikutania kwa nani?* At whose place did they meet? St. **kutan.ik.a** Cs. **kutan.ish.a,** cause to meet together e.g. *Anataka kuzikutanisha pande zote mbili zinazopingana*, he wants to bring together all the two contending parties. 2. converge: *Barabara zile mbili zinakutana kwenye mto*, those two roads converge at the river. Prep. **kutan.i.a** St. **kutan.ik.a** Cs. **kutan.ish.a**
kutanio *n* (*ma-*) (*math*) intercept; the part of a line, plane, etc. intercepted.
kuti¹ *n* (*ma-*) (*bot*) coconut leaf; leaf of a coconut palm; coconut frond. (cf *chanda*) 2. coconut palm leaf prepared for roofing, etc.
kuti² *n* (*n*) food (cf *chakula, riziki*)
kuti³ *n* (*n*) a square container, used for keeping gunpowder, fumigants, etc.
kutu¹ *n* (*n*) rust: *Chuma kimeshika kutu*, the iron has rusted. *Pata kutu*, get rusty. *Ingia kutu*, be rusty. (cf *kanga*)
kutu² *n* (*n*) turd; a piece of excrement: *Ona kutu*, feel obliged to defecate. (cf *shonde*)
kutu.a (also *gutua*) *vt* give a jerk to; pull suddenly; cause a shock to: *Kutua kamba*, jerk a rope. *Kutua mkono*, jerk a hand. Prep. **kutu.li.a** St. **kutu.k.a** and **kutu.lik.a**, be startled, be shaken. Cs. **kutu.sh.a** Ps. of Prep. **kutu.liw.a** Rp. **kutu.an.a**
kutukutu *adv* in a circular way.
kututu *adv* slowly and jumpily.
kutuzi *n* (*n*) 1. bad smelling perspiration like the one emanating from armpits; body odour. (cf *kikwapa*) 2. the bad smell of an animal; animal odour.
kutwa *adv* all day long: *Kutwa kucha*, day and night. *Habari za kutwa?* How have things been today?
-kuu¹ *adj* (of title, etc.) great, main, important, eminent: *Mwalimu mkuu*, headteacher. *Chakula kikuu*, main food. *Chuo kikuu*, university. *Habari kuu*, important information.
kuu² *n* (*n*) used to refer to the hole on a chessboard filled with stones at the beginning of a game.
kuu³ *n* (*ma-*) (*anat*) placenta
kuukeni *adv* on the maternal side.
-kuukuu *adj* old, worn-out, dilapidated: *Nguo kuukuu*, an old dress. *Gari kuukuu*, an old car.
kuume *n* (*n*) right hand. (cf *kuvuli*)
kuumeni *adv* on the paternal side.
kuungu *n* (*n*) see *kulungu*
kuvu *n* (*n*) mildew, mould, fungus, blight: *Kuota kuvu*, develop mould. (cf *ukungu*)
kuvuli¹ *adj* right: *Mkono wa kuvuli*, right hand. (cf *kuume, kulia*)
kuvuli² *adv* right: *Ameelekea kuvuli*, he has gone to the right side.
kuwadi (also *guwadi*) *n* (*ma-*) pimp, procure, pander, whoremonger. (cf *mtalaleshi, gambera*) (Ar)
kuwadi.a (also *guwadia*) *vt, vi* pimp, procure. Prep. **kuwadi.li.a** St. **kuwadi.k.a** Cs. **kuwadi.sh.a** Ps. **kuwadi.w.a** Rp. **kuwadi.an.a**
kuwi *n*(*n*) (*bot*) a kind of unhusked rice, which produces reddish rice.
kuyu¹ *n* (*n*) (*zool*) a kind of freshwater fish with dark scales at centres, strong and smooth dorsal spine and sometimes fleshy lips, lives in inshore waters and rivers. *Barbus altianalis*.
kuyu² *n* (*n*) (*zool*) white stork; a kind of bird (family *Ciconiidae*) which is generally white. *Ciconia ciconia*.
kuyu³ *n* (*n*) (*bot*) sycamore fig; an edible obovoid-globose fruit from the tree *mkuyu* (*Ficus sycamorus*), whose bark is useful in folk medicine.
kuz.a¹ *vt* 1. magnify, enlarge: *Aliikuza picha yake*, he enlarged his picture.

2. exaggerate, overstate: *Serikali iliikuza taarifa yenyewe*, the government exaggerated the statement. 3. develop, promote: *Lazima tuzikuze taasisi zetu za kielimu*, we must develop our educational institutions. Prep. **kuz.i.a** St. **kuz.ik.a** Cs. **kuz.ish.a** Ps. **kuz.w.a** Rp. **kuz.an.a**

kuza² *adj* having a long shape.

kuzi¹ *n* (*ma-*) an earthernware pitcher with a narrow neck, used for keeping water. (cf *nzio, balasi, gudulia*)

kuzi² *n* (*n*) (*zool*) a kind of saltwater fish (family *Atherinidae*) with silver stripes along the sides; silverside.

kuzimu *n* (*n*) life after death; the afterworld; abode of the dead. (cf *ahera*) 2. Hades, the underworld abode of the souls of the dead.

kuzumburu *n* (*n*) speckled mousebird; a kind of bird with a long thick tail, brownish underparts and a slightly crested head. *Colius striatus*. (cf *kibawanta*)

kwa *prep* 1. a word used to express an instrument used in an action; with, by: *Alipigwa kwa mawe*, he was hit by stones. *Aliandika barua kwa kalamu*, he wrote a letter with a pen. 2. used to express mode of travelling; by: *Alisafiri kwa ndege*, he travelled by plane. 3. used to express purpose or use; for: *Alikuja hapa kwa kutaka ushauri*, he came here to seek advice. 4. used to express comparison or contrast; to: *Walifungwa mabao matatu kwa mawili*, they were beaten three goals to two. 5. used to express that the use of one thing goes hand in hand with another thing: *Walikula mkate kwa mchuzi*, they ate bread with curry. *Wanawake kwa wanaume walimiminika kwenye ukumbi*, women as well as men thronged to the hall. 6. used with other words to form adverbial phrases: *Kwa bahati*, luckily. *Kwa madaha*, proudly; with airs and graces. *Kwa pupa*, in haste. *Kwa kauli moja*, unanimously. *Kwa kina*, in depth. *Kwa ghadhabu*, angrily. 7. used with other words to form interrogatives: *Kwa nini? Kwa sababu gani?* Why? 8. used in mathematical associations: *Mia kwa mia*, hundred to hundred.

kwa.a¹ *i, vt* stumble, strip. (*prov*) *Mwenda pole hajikwai*, he who goes slowly does not stumble. i.e. Haste does not bring success. Prep. **kwa.li.a** St. **kwa.lik.a** Cs. **kwa.li.sh.a** and **kwa.z.a**, cause to stumble Ps. of Prep. **kwa.liw.a** Rp. **kwa.an.a**

kwaa² *n* (*n*) act of stumbling. (*prov*) *Heri kujikwaa kwa dole kuliko kujikwaa kwa ulimi*, it is better to stumble with the toe than to stumble with the tongue. i.e. don't prattle such that it causes harm to you.

kwaam.a *vi* (of trees) cease to bear fruits.

kwaan.a *vt* compete, contest: *Timu mbili zilikwaana vikali jana*, the two teams contested bitterly yesterday. Prep. **kwaan.i.a** (cf *umana, menyana, pambana*)

kwabuk.a *vi* 1. (of a branch) break (cf *koboka*) 2. blench, blanch; lose colour, beauty, etc Prep. **kwabuk.i.a** St. **kwabuk.ik.a** Cs. **kwabuk.ish.a** (cf *kwajuka*)

kwacha *n* (*n*) (*monet*) kwacha; the monetary unit of Malawi and Zambia.

kwa heri *adv* an expletive used for bidding farewell to someone; goodbye.

kwajuk.a *vi* lose colour, beauty, etc.; fade, blench, blanch: *Mbona shati lako limekwajuka?* Why has the colour of your shirt faded? Prep. **kwajuk.i.a** St. **kwajuk.ik.a** Cs. **kwajuk.ish.a** (cf *kwabuka, pauka, chujuka*)

kwake¹ *n* (*n*) his place, her place: *Kwake ni mbali*, his place is far.

kwake² *adv* to his place, to her place, to its place: *Nilikwenda kwake*, I went to his place.

kwako¹ *n* (*n*) your place: *Kwako ni karibu*, your place is near.

kwako² *adv* to your place: *Amekuja kwako*, he has come to your place.
kwakur.a *vt* (of lion, etc.) scratch the earth: *Simba alikwakura chini*, the lion scratched the ground. Prep. **kwakur.i.a** St. **kwakur.ik.a** Cs. **kwakur.ish.a**
kwakwa *n* (*n*) (*bot*) a round edible fruit with a hard shell and triangular seeds embedded in a soft pulp from the tree *mkwakwa*. (*Strychnos innocua*)
kwale *n* (*n*) see *kware*
kwalu *n* (*n*) (*zool*) parrot (cf *kasuku*)
kwam.a *vt, vi* 1. (of spines etc.) be stuck, be jammed, be choked: *Mwiba wa samaki ulimkwama kooni mwake*, the fish bone got stuck in his throat. 2. (of vehicles, etc.) fail to pass through a place, etc.; get stuck, get mired, be bogged down: *Gari lake lilikwama matopeni*, his car got bogged down in the mud. 3. (*fig*) fail, flop; be in a fix, be stuck up: *Mipango yangu ilikwama*, my plans got stuck up. Prep. **kwam.i.a** St. **kwam.ik.a** Cs. **kwam.ish.a** Ps. **kwam.w.a**
kwamba *conj* 1. that: *Alieleza kwamba alikuwa bado anaumwa*, he stated that he was still sick. 2. used with the word *kama*, 'like' to show resemblance of things; as if, supposing: *Alizungumza kama kwamba ana habari*, he talked as if he had the information.
kwamish.a¹ *vt* see *kwama*
kwamish.a² *vt* 1. block, obstruct: *Kiongozi aliyakwamisha maendeleo ya kijiji*, the leader obstructed the development of the village. 2. cause sth to get stuck: *Aliukwamisha mshipi wangu*, he caused my fishing-line to get stuck. 3. net: *Mchezaji aliukwamisha mpira wavuni*, the player netted the ball. Prep. **kwamish.i.a** St. **kwamish.ik.a** Ps. **kwamish.w.a** Rp. **kwamish.an.a**
kwamu.a *vt* dislodge, disengage; set free from a trap, etc.: *Alimkwamua ndege mtegoni*, he set free the bird from the trap. *Viongozi hawajaweza kulikwamua tatizo la rushwa*, the leaders have not been able to solve the problem of corruption: *Nchi nyingi zimeamua kujikwamua kiuchumi*, many countries have decided to free themselves economically. Prep. **kwamu.li.a** St. **kwamu.k.a** Cs. **kwamu.lish.a** Ps. of Prep. **kwamu.liw.a** Rp. **kwamu.an.a**
kwanga *n* (*n*) (*zool*) tree dassie; a small heavily built hyrax with short and often soft coat and usually dark brown colour, living on rocky hills or among boulders. (cf *pelele, wibari*)
kwangu¹ *n* (*n*) my place: *Kwangu ni kubaya*, my place is bad.
kwangu² *adv* to my place: *Alikuja kwangu*, he came to my place.
kwangu.a (also *kwangura*) *vt* scrape, scratch; remove a coating, crust or anything adhering in a saucepan, etc.: *Mpishi alikikwangua chungu chenye ukoko wa wali*, the cook scraped the crust from the rice pot. Prep. **kwangu.li.a** St. **kwangu.k.a** and **kwangu.lik.a** Cs. **kwangu.lish.a** Ps. of Prep. **kwangu.liw.a** Rp. **kwangu.an.a** (cf *komba*)
kwangur.a *vt* see *kwangua*
kwani *conj* because, since, as, for, why: *Hakufika shuleni jana kwani alikuwa anaumwa*, he did not come to school yesterday because he was sick.
kwanja *n* (*ma-*) hand grass cutter.
kwanu.a *vt* see *kwanyua*
kwanyu.a (also *kwanua*) *vt* 1. strip off, split off, tear down: *Alilikwanyua gome la mti*, he stripped off the bark of the tree. 2. (*fig*) beat, thrash: *Timu yao iliikwanyua Real Madrid*, their team thrashed Real Madrid. Prep. **kwanyu.lia** St. **kwanyu.k.a** and **kwanyu.lik.a** Cs. **kwanyu.sh.a** Ps. of Prep. **kwanyu.liw.a** (cf *sasambua, banjua, nyuka*)
kwanza¹ *adv* 1. first, in the beginning, in the first place: *Ngoja kwanza*, wait first. *Kaa hapa kwanza*, sit here

first. *Nataka kuonana na wewe lakini kwanza mwite msarifu,* I want to see you but first call the bursar. 2. just now: *Ndio kwanza ameondoka,* he has left just now. (cf *sasa hivi*)

kwanza² *adj* first: *Hili ni tukio la kwanza,* this is the first incident.

kwao¹ *n (n) (zool)* brown-headed parrot. *Poicephalus rufiventtris.*

kwao² *n (n)* their place: *Kwao ni kuzuri,* their place is good.

kwao³ *adv* to their place, at their place: *Nilikwenda kwao,* I went to their place.

kwapa *n (ma-) (anat)* armpit

kwapajani *n (u) (bot)* axil; the upper angle formed by a leaf, twig, etc and the stem from which it grows.

kwapu.a¹ (also *kwepua*) *vt* snatch, filch; steal forcefully: *Mwizi alimkwapua mtalii kipochi,* the thief snatched the tourist's purse. Prep. **kwapu.li.a** St. **kwapu.lik.a** Cs. **kwapu.lish.a** Ps. of Prep. **kwapu.liw.a** Rp. **kwapu.an.a** (cf *pokoa, nyang'anya*)

kwapu.a² *vt* borrow without paying back. Prep. **kwapu.li.a** St. **kwapu.k.a** Cs. **kwapu.lish.a** Ps. **kwapu.liw.a** Rp. **kwapu.an.a**

kwarara *n (n)* Hadada Ibis; a kind of large wading bird (family *Threskiornithidae*) related to herons. *Hagedashia hagedash.*

kware¹ (also *kwale*) *n (n) (zool)* francolin; a kind of chicken-like terrestrial bird with a moderate or short bill. (cf *kereng'ende*)

kware² *n (n)* quarry

kwaresima *n (n)* (in Christianity) the season of Lent; the period of forty weekdays from Ash Wednesday to Easter, observed variously in Christian churches by fasting, etc.

kwaru *n (n) (zool)* gross beak weaver.

kwaruz.a *vt* scrape, scratch, grate: *Mwiba uliukwaruza mkono wake,* the thorn scratched his hand. Prep. **kwaruz.i.a** St. **kwaruz.ik.a** Cs. **kwaruz.ish.a** Ps. **kwaruz.w.a** Rp. **kwaruz.an.a** (cf *paruza, paraza*)

kwaruzan.a *vi* 1. scratch each other. 2. *(fig)* quarrel, bicker: *Nchi mbili za Kiafrika zilikwaruzana,* the two African countries quarrelled. Prep. **kwaruzan.i.a** St. **kwaruzan.ik.a** Cs. **kwaruzan.ish.a**

kwashiakoo *n (n) (med)* kwashiorkor, a severe disease of young children caused by chronic deficiency of protein and calories in the diet and characterized by stunted growth, oedema, and a protuberant belly. (Gh)

-kwasi *adj* wealth, rich, affluent, well-off: *Yeye ni mkwasi,* she is rich.

kwata *n (n)* drill, parade, manoeuvre: *Piga kwata,* parade on foot; drill. *Enda kwata,* go parading; drill. (cf *paredi, taburu*)

kwato *n (n) (zool)* the hoof of an animal.

kwatu.a¹ *vt, vi* decorate, adorn, embellish, beautify; dress elegantly, etc.: *Alijikwatua alipokwenda harusini,* she dressed elegantly when she went to the wedding. Prep. **kwatu.li.a** St. **kwatu.k.a** Cs. **kwatu.sh.a** Ps. of Prep. **kwatu.liw.a** Rp. **kwatu.an.a** (cf *remba, pamba*)

kwatu.a² *vt,vi* (in *sports*) foul sby: *Alimkwatua kwa nyuma mchezaji aliyekuwa akielekea kufunga goli,* he tackled from behind the player who was going to score the goal. Prep. **kwatu.li.a** St. **kwatu.k.a** Cs. **kwatu.sh.a** Ps. of Prep. **kwatu.liw.a** Rp. **kwatu.an.a**

kwatu.a³ *vt* make it clean by rubbing. Prep. **kwatu.li.a** St. **kwatu.k.a** Cs. **kwatu.sh.a** Ps. **kwatu.liw.a** Rp. **kwatu.an.a**

kwau *n(n) (zool)* a kind of small parrot.

kwaya *n (n)* 1. choir; a group of singers organized and trained to sing collectively. 2. the singing of this kind. (Eng)

kwazi (also *kwezi*) *n (n) (zool)* a large bird which catches and eats fish; fish-eagle.

kwe.a *vt* 1. (of coconut trees, etc.) climb, mount, ascend: *Kwea mnazi*, climb a coconut tree. Prep. **kwe.le.a** e.g. *Kamba ya kukwelea*, a rope to climb with. St. **kwe.lek.a** Cs. **kwe.z.a**, cause to go up, raise e.g. *Kweza bei*, raise the price of a commodity. *Kweza nguo*, lift the dress. Ps. **kwe.w.a** Rp. **kwe.an.a** 2. (*vul*) fuck sby. 3. (*fig*) rise with respect to position, status, etc.: *Alikwea mpaka akafika kwenye cheo cha juu serikalini*, he rose until the highest position in the government. Prep. **kwe.le.a** St. **kwe.lek.a** Cs. **kwe.z.a** Ps. **kwe.w.a**

kweche (also *kwenchi*) *n* (*n*) (*zool*) bishop; a kind of a weaver bird with a wide mouth of black plumage. (cf *pasha*)

kwekwe *n* (*ma*) (*bot*) short stiff grass: *Lima kwekwe*, remove grass of this kind.

kweli[1] *n* (*n*) see *ukweli*

-kweli[2] *adj* true, veritable, real, genuine, correct: *Amenipa taarifa kweli*, he has given me a true statement. 2. transparent, frank, candid: *Lazima tuwe wakweli*, we must be transparent

kweli[3] *adv* truly, really, genuinely: *Kweli utakuja?* Will you really come?

kwema[1] *n* (*n*) good news (cf *kuzuri*)

kwem.a[2] *vi* give a deep sound like someone suffering from wheeze asthma; gasp, wheeze. Prep. **kwem.e.a** St. **kwen.ek.a** Cs. **kwem.esh.a**

kwembe *n* (*n*) (*zool*) crowned hornbill; a kind of bird (family *Bucerotidae*) with a dusky red bill and white breast and abdomen. *Tockus alboterminatus*

kwembe

kweme *n* (*n*) (*bot*) a large flat yellowish fibre-covered seed of *mkweme*, oyster-nut plant, used for producing cooking oil and as a medicine for abdominal problems.

kwenchi *n* (*n*) see *kweche*.

kwend.a *vi, vt* see *enda*

kwenu[1] *n* (*n*) your (pl) place: *Kwenu ni kubaya*, your place is bad.

kwenu[2] *adv* to your (pl) place, at your (pl) place: *Alikuja kwenu*, he came to your place.

kwenye *prep* at, in, on: *Kwenye tundu*, in the nest. *Kwenye saa nne*, at ten o'clock. *Kwenye gari*, in the car.

kwenzi[1] *n* (*n*) (*bot*) a medium-sized gregarious bird (family *Sturnidae*) with long wings and a sharp, pointed bill; starling. (cf *kwau*)

kwenzi[2] *n* (*n*) a thin voice from someone signalling danger; screech.

kwep.a *vt, vi* see *hepa*

kwepu.a *vt* see *kwapua*

kwesh.a[1] *vi* wheeze, gasp; breathe with difficulty: *Mgonjwa wa pumu alikuwa akikwesha*, the asthmatic patient was wheezing. Prep. **kwesh.e.a** St. **kwesh.ek.a** Cs. **kwesh.ez.a** Ps. **kwesh.w.a** (cf *tuta, pwita*)

kwesh.a[2] *vt, vi* (of a handle, etc.) fix; secure firmly: *Aliukwesha mpini kwenye jembe*, he fixed the handle firmly in the hoe. Prep. **kwesh.e.a** St. **kwesh.ek.a** Cs. **kwesh.esh.a** and **kwesh.ez.a** Ps. **kwesh.w.a** Rp. **kwesh.an.a**

kwet.a *vi* shuffle along on the buttocks; move along on the buttocks as a crippled person; crawl along: *Askari majeruhi walikuwa wakikweta*, the wounded soldiers were moving along on their buttocks. Prep. **kwet.e.a** St. **kwet.ek.a** Cs. **kwet.esh.a** Ps. **kwet.w.a** (cf *sota*)

kwetu[1] *n* (*n*) our place: *Kwetu ni mbali*, our place is far.

kwetu² *adv* to our place, at our place: *Alifika kwetu*, he came to our place.

kweu (also *kweupe*) *n (n)* dawn, light, brightness; fine weather: *Mbele kweu na nyuma kweu*, brightness in front and brightness behind.

kweupe *n (n)* see *kweu*

kwezi *n (n)* see *kwazi*

kwid.a¹ *vt* 1. seize, grab: *Kwida shati*, grab by the shirt; grab by the collar. 2. pin down someone so as to force from him a confession: *Walimkwida mpaka akaitoa siri*, they pinned him down until he divulged the secret. Prep. **kwid.i.a** St. **kwid.ik.a** Cs. **kwid.ish.a** Ps. **kwid.w.a** Rp. **kwid.an.a**

kwida² *n (n)* (*zool*) myrmicine ant; a small black ant which is generally catholic in its diet but many of them are either carnivorous or granivorous. Myrmicine ants are found throughout Africa; the most common species is the "Little brown house ant."

kwikwi *n (n)* hiccup, sobbing; singultus: *Kwikwi ya kulia*, convulsive sobbing. (cf *kekefu*)

kwima *n (n)* greed, avarice, parsimony.

kwingine *adv, pron* form of *-ingine*, another place: *Sukari haipatikani kwingine*, sugar is not obtainable elsewhere.

kwingineko *adv, pron* elsewhere

kwinini *n (n)* (*med*) quinine (Eng)

kwinta *n (n)* quintal; a metric unit of weight, equal to 100 kilograms. (Eng)

L

L, 1 /l/ 1. the twelfth letter of the Swahili alphabet. 2. the sound of L or l. It is normally a voiced alveolar continuant.

la¹ *interj* No! Not so! By no means! Not at all! Absolutely not! *La! Yeye hakuja nyumbani jana!* No! he did not come home yesterday. *La sivyo*, if not; otherwise. (cf *hasha,siyo, hapana*) (Ar)

la² *prep* (used for ma- class singular nouns) of: *Daftari la mwanafunzi*, the student's exercise book; the exercise book of the student.

l.a³ *vt* 1. eat, consume, devour: *Nimekula chakula kingi leo*, I have eaten a lot of food today. Prep. ***l.i.a***, eat for (with, in, etc.) St. ***l.ik.a***, be edible, be eatable e.g. *Chakula hiki kinalika*, this food is edible. Cs. ***l.ish.a***, feed, nourish, support e.g. *Anamlisha mwanawe*, she is feeding her baby. *Anawalisha mbuzi majani*, he is feeding the goats on grass. Ps. ***l.iw.a***, be eaten e.g. *Chakula kililiwa na paka*, the food was eaten by a cat. 2. spend, use, expend: *Alikula pesa zangu zote*, he spent all of my money. Prep. ***l.i.a*** St. ***l.ik.a*** Cs. ***l.ish.a*** Ps. ***l.iw.a***, be spent e.g *Fedha zake zote zimeliwa*, all of his money has been misappropriated. 3. corrode, wear away, eat away, consume: *Kutu imekula chuma*, rust has eaten away the iron. St. ***l.ik.a*** Ps. ***l.iw.a*** (cf *haribu, punguza*) 4. lose, expend, suffer a loss: *Nilikula hasara katika biashara yangu*, I suffered a loss in my business. 5. (*idms*) *Kula njama*, conspire, intrigue, plot. *Kula rushwa*, receive bribes. Prep. ***l.i.a*** St. ***l.ik.a*** Cs. ***l.ish.a*** Ps. ***l.iw.a*** (Ar)

laab.u *vt* play, sport (cf *cheza*) (Ar)

laana *n* (*n*) curse, imprecation, condemnation, denunciation, damnation: *Utapata laana kwa Mwenyezi Mungu kama utawadharau wazee wako*, you will suffer God's curse if you neglect your parents. (cf *apizo, duizo*) (Ar)

laan.i *vt* curse, condemn, denounce, execrate, damn: *Niliwalaani watoto wale kwa kumzomea burebure mpitanjia*, I cursed those children for booing a passer-by for no reason. Prep. ***laan.i.a*** St. ***laan.ik.a*** Cs. ***laan.ish.a*** Ps. of Prep. ***laan.iw.a***, be cursed, be condemned. Rp. ***laan.i.an.a***, curse each other. (cf *apiza, duia, viza*)

-laanifu *adj* accursed, damnable: *Mtu mlaanifu*, an accursed person. (Ar)

laasiri *n* (*n*) see *alasiri*

laazizi *n* (*n*) darling, beloved, honey, sweetheart, minion, sweet: *Laazizi wake ni mkewe*, his darling is his wife. (cf *mpenzi, mwandani, mahabubu*) (Ar)

labda *adv* perhaps, probably, likely, possibly, maybe: *Labda mvua itanyesha leo*, perhaps. it will rain today. (cf *pengine, asaa, huenda, yamkini*) (Ar)

labeka *interj* At your service! Yes, sir! Yes madam! This is an answer to a call usu from a superior. (cf *abee! bee! naam!*) (Ar)

labibu *adj* sagacious, judicious, wise

labiz.i *vt* interrogate, question, enquire, quiz, probe: *Mbona unatulabizi mara kwa mara?* Why are you interrogating us over and over again? Prep. ***labiz.i.a*** St. ***labiz.ik.a*** Cs. ***labiz.ish.a*** (cf *ulizauliza*) (Ar)

labu.a *vt* 1. win easily in a game; triumph without hardships in a game: *Unaweza kulabua katika mchezo huu wa karata?* Can you win easily in this card-game? 2. clobber an opponent; hit someone decisively: *Labua kofi*, haul off a slap. *Aliweza kukulabua kwa sababu ulikuwa dhaifu*, he was

ladha   **laini¹**   **L**

able to hit you decisively because you were weak. Prep. *labu.li.a* St. *labu.k.a* Cs. *labu.sh.a* Rp. *labu.an.a* Ps. of Prep. *labu.liw.a* (Ar)

ladha *n* (*n*) taste, flavour, savour: *Haya maji ya mananasi yana ladha nzuri*, the pineapple juice has a good taste. *Keki hii haina ladha*, this cake has no taste. (cf *utamu*) (Ar)

ladu *n* (*n*) sweetmeat made up in hard round balls, consisting of flour mixed with sugar, ginger, pepper and other ingredients. (Hind)

-lafi *adj* voracious, ravenous, gluttonous, hoggish, open-mouthed: *Mtu mlafi*, a voracious person.

lafidhi *n* (*n*) see *lafudhi*

lafudhi (also *lafidhi*) *n* (*n*) accent, speech pattern; style of speaking: *Mwalimu wangu wa Kiingereza ana lafudhi nzuri*, my English teacher has a good accent. (cf *matamshi*) (Ar)

lagha.i¹ *vt* deceive, cheat, beguile, hoodwink, delude, swindle, trick: *Alinilaghai kwa maneno yake matamu*, he beguiled me with his sweet words. Prep. *lagha.i.a* St. *lagha.ik.a* Cs. *lagha.ish.a* Ps. of Prep. *lagha.iw.a*, be deceived. Rp. of Prep. *lagha.i.an.a* (cf *danganya*, *ghilibu*) (Ar)

laghai² (also *mlaghai*) *n* (*n*) swindler, cheater, trickster, rogue, crook: *Laghai yule haaminiki hata kidogo*, that crook cannot be trusted at all. (cf *ayari*, *mjanja*, *bazazi*) (Ar)

laha *n* (*n*) a piece of slate, used generally by school children for writing on with chalk; slate. (cf *sleti*)

lahaja *n* (*n*) dialect, speech pattern: *Lahaja eneo*, local dialect. *Lahaja kitabaka*, class dialect. *Lahaja maarufu*, prestige dialect. *Lahaja sanifu*, standard dialect. (Ar)

lahani (also *alhani*) *n* (*n*) tune, melody; a succession of musical tunes forming a rhythmic whole. (cf *mahadhi*, *naghama*, *tyuni*) (Ar)

lahaula¹ *interj* Oh dear! Good heavens! Good gracious! The expletive is used to express surprise over sth such as when a person blasphemes, behaves awkwardly, etc. *Lahaula! Mtu yule anamkashifu Mwenyezi Mungu*, Oh dear! That person is discrediting Almighty God. (cf *subhanallah*)

lahaula² *n* (*n*) a kind of leather sandal with ornamentation, worn usu by Muslims when going to mosques, etc.: *Viatu vya lahaula*, leather sandals of this kind. (cf *makubadhi*) (Ar)

lahik.i¹ *vt* greet, salute, address, hallo; say hallo: *Nilimlahiki mgeni wangu kwa kupeana mikono*, I greeted my guest by shaking hands. Prep. *lahik.i.a* St. *lahik.ik.a* Ps. of Prep. *lahik.iw.a* Rp. of Prep. *lahik.i.an.a* (cf *salimia*, *sabahi*, *amkia*) (Ar)

lahiki² *n* (*n*) equal status; equal position; same level: *Anashirikiana na watu wa lahiki yake tu*, he associates only with his equals. (cf *kufu*) (Ar)

laika *n* (*ma-*) body hair as on the hands, armpits, legs, etc.

laik.i¹ *vt* befit, suit; correspond to, be appropriate: *Adhabu aliyoipata inalaiki na kosa lake*, the punishment he got corresponds to his offence. (cf *lingana*) (Ar)

laiki² *n* (*n*) fitting, fitness, suitability, appropriateness, conformity: *Matendo yake si laiki ya nasaba yake*, his deeds are not in conformity with his social status. (Ar)

laiki³ *n* (*n*) 1. a person who corresponds to another with respect to status, position, etc. 2. sth that corresponds to the status, position, etc. of a person.

laili *n* (*n*) night (cf *usiku*) (Ar)

laini¹ *adj* 1. soft, delicate, tender, smooth, dainty: *Nyama laini*, soft meat. *Nguo laini*, soft clothes. *Mto laini*, a soft pillow. (cf *teketeke*, *tepetepe*) 2. (*fig*) gentle, calm, gracious, merciful, soft, good-humoured: *Ana moyo laini*, he has a soft heart. (cf *baridi*, *taratibu*) (Ar)

laini² *n* (*n*) queue, row; line of persons, etc.: *Simama kwenye laini*, stand in the queue. (cf *mlolongo, mstari*) (Eng)

lainik.a *vi* be smooth, become smooth: *Nyama ilipikwa sana mpaka ikalainika*, the meat was overcooked that it became very soft. (cf *tepetea*) 2. (*fig*) be softened, be appeased, be cool: *Alionyesha hasira nyingi mwanzoni lakini sasa amelainika*, he showed a lot of anger in the beginning but he has now cooled down. Prep. *lainik.i.a* St. *lainik.ik.a* Cs. *lainik.ish.a* (cf *poa, tulia*) (Ar)

lainish.a *vt* 1. soften, melt: *Lazima ukilainisha chuma hiki*, you must soften this iron. 2. soften, calm, pacify, cool. Prep. *lainish.i.a* St. *lainish.ik.a* Ps. *lainish.w.a* Rp. *lainish.an.a*

laiti¹ *interj* The expletive is usu used to express regret over not doing sth. It carries the equivalent meanings of "Oh that," "if only" and "would that": *Laiti ningalisikiliza ushauri wake, yasiningalifika haya yote*, if I had listened to his advice, all this would not have happened to me (cf *falaula, lau, falau*) (Ar)

laiti² *n* (*n*) see *ulaiti*

laka *n* (*n*) sealing-wax (cf *lakiri*)

lakabu *n* (*n*) nickname, sobriquet: *Jina lake ni Elizabeth lakini lakabu yake ni Liz*, her name is Elizabeth but her nickname is Liz. (Ar)

lake *adj, pron* (form of -*ake*, referring to ma- class singular nouns) his, her, its: *Ua lake*, its flower, his flower, her flower.

lak.i¹ *vt* receive, welcome; go to meet someone in a friendly or ceremonial way: *Nilikwenda uwanja wa ndege kumlaki mgeni wangu*, I went to the airport to receive my guest. Prep. *lak.i.a* St. *lak.ik.a* Cs. *lak.ish.a* Ps. of Prep. *lak.iw.a* Rp. of Prep. *lak.i.an.a* (cf *pokea, karibisha*) (Ar)

laki² *n* (*n*) a hundred thousand; one lakh: *Kiasi cha watu laki walifika kwenye mkutano*, about a hundred thousand people attended the meeting. (Hind)

lakini *adj* but, however, nevertheless: *Yeye ana pesa nyingi lakini ni bahili*, he has a lot of money but he is a miser. *Lakini wapi!* But no use! It was all useless! (Ar)

lakini.a *vt, vi* 1. (in Islam) pray for a dead body immediately after being buried. 2. pronounce words to the dead body that there is no one to be worshipped but God.

lakiri *n* (*n*) sealing-wax (cf *laka*) (Port)

lako *adj, pron* (form of -*ako* referring to ma- class singular nouns) your, yours: *Tatizo lako*, your problem. *Nanasi lako*, your pineapple. *Lako na langu ni mamoja*, yours and mine are the same

laktosi *n* (*n*) (*chem*) lactose; a type of sugar found in milk. (Eng)

lal.a¹ *vt, vi* 1. slumber, lie; go to sleep: *Lala chali*, lie on the back. *Lala kifudifudi*, lie on the stomach; lie face downwards. *Lala usingizi*, be fast asleep. *Lala fofofo*, be dead asleep. *Lala salama*, sleep peacefully. *Lala unono*, sleep peacefully. Prep. *lal.i.a*, sleep on (at, in, etc.) e.g *Lalia mkeka*, sleep on the mat. *Lalia matanga*, sleep in a house of mourning. St. *lal.ik.a* e.g. *Hapa hakulaliki kwa mbu wengi*, it is impossible to sleep here because of too many mosquitoes. Cs. *lal.ish.a* and *la.z.a*, put to bed e.g *Alimlaza mtoto wake kitandani*, she put her child to bed. Ps. of Prep. *lal.iw.a* Rp. *lal.an.a*, sleep together, sleep with each other for the purpose of sex. 2. lie, lie down, rest: *Lala hapa kwa vile umechoka*, try to rest here a little bit since you are tired. Prep. *lal.i.a* St. *lal.i.k.a* Cs. *lal.ish.a* and *la.z.a* Ps. of Prep. *lal.iw.a* Rp. of Prep. *lal.i.an.a* (cf *jinyosha, jipumzisha*) 3. collapse, fall down: *Nyumba ile imelala*, that house has collapsed. 4. (*idms*) *Lala njaa*, pass the whole night without eating,

398

Lala kihoro, sleep without eating. *Lala kingalingali*, lie on the back.

lal.a² *vt* (*vul*) fuck; have sexual intercourse with a person. Prep. ***lal.i.a*** St. ***lal.ik.a*** Cs. ***lal.ish.a*** and ***la.z.a*** Ps. of Prep. ***lal.iw.a*** Rp. ***lal.an.a*** (cf *undama, kwea, kaza, jamii*)

lalaik.a *vt, vi* cry and complain because of pain, hunger, etc.; grunt, groan: *Mtoto wangu alilalaika sana kwa vile hakupewa chakula cha mchana*, my child cried bitterly because she was not given lunch. Prep. ***lalaik.i.a*** Cs. ***lalaik.ish.a*** Ps. ***lalaik.w.a*** (cf *lalamika*)

lalam.a *vi* 1. cry loudly; complain: *Msichana alilalama kwa sababu alipigwa na kaka yake*, the girl cried loudly because she was beaten by her elder brother. (cf *lalamika*) 2. defend oneself by giving excuses: *Huna sababu ya kuchelewa kazini lakini wewe unapenda kulalama tu*, you have no reason for reporting to work late but you just like to give excuses. 3. apologize; ask pardon, beg one's pardon: *Alilalama kwangu kwa kosa alilolifanya*, he apologized to me for the mistake he had made. Prep. ***lalam.i.a*** St. ***lalam.ik.a*** Cs. ***lalam.ish.a*** Ps. ***lalam.w.a***

lalamik.a *vt* complain, protest, grumble, growl: *Alilalamika kuhusu dhamana alizopewa*, he complained about the responsibilities given to him. Prep. ***lalamik.i.a*** St. ***lalamik.ik.a*** (cf *lalama*)

lalamiki.a *vt* expostulate, remonstrate; complain about (at, against, etc.): *Unalalamikia nini?* What are you complaining about? St. ***lalamik.ik.a*** Cs. ***lalamik.ish.a***

lalamiko *n* (*ma-*) complaint, lament: *Lalamiko lake halina ukweli ndani yake*, her complaint has no truth in it.

-lalamishi *adj* quarrelsome, wranglesome: *Mchezaji mlalamishi*, a quarrelsome player.

lali.a *vt, vi* 1. sleep on, lie on. *Umelalia nini?* What have you slept on? 2. (of a hen, etc.) brood; sit on eggs to hatch them. 3. induce to lower down the price of a commodity. Prep. ***lali.k.a*** Cs. ***lali.sh.a*** Ps. ***lali.w.a*** Rp. ***lali.an.a***

lama *conj* until, till, up to, down to: *Mashindano ya kuogelea hayataanza lama saa za jioni*, the swimming competition will not start until in the afternoon. (cf *mpaka, hadi*)

lamb.a¹ *vt* see *ramba*. Prep. ***lamb.i.a*** St. ***lamb.ik.a*** Cs. ***lamb.ish.a*** Ps. ***lamb.w.a*** Rp. ***lamb.an.a***

lamba² *n* (*ma-*) (*bot*) the leaf of a banana tree. (cf *koa*)

lambo *n* (*ma-*) 1. a defensive raised structure for preventing water to spread; dyke, dam. 2. tilled land for preserving water usu rain water; catchment: *Maji ya lambo*, water for the tilled land.

lami *n* (*n*) tar, pitch, bitumen, asphalt: *Njia ya lami*, tarmac road. (Gr)

land.a¹ *vt* resemble; look like, be like: *Ninamlanda mjomba wangu*, I resemble my uncle. Prep. ***land.i.a*** St. ***land.ik.a*** Cs. ***land.ish.a*** Ps. ***land.w.a*** Rp. ***land.an.a***, resemble each other e.g *Nyumba hizi mbili zimelandana*, these two houses look alike (cf *fanana, shabihi*)

landa² *n* (*n*) see *randa*

landan.a *vi* see *landa¹*

lango *n* (*ma-*) 1. (*amplic*) a big door: *Lango la chuma*, a big iron door. 2. (in sports) goalmouth: *Lango la timu yao lilikuwa likihujumiwa tu*, the goalmouth of their team was constantly under attack.

langu *adj, pron* (form of *-angu*, referring to *ma-* class sing nouns) my, mine: *Dirisha langu*, my window. *Langu si lako*, mine is not yours.

langu.a *vt* hike prices; profiteer, extort, overcharge: *Mwenye duka alimlangua mnunuzi*, the shopkeeper overcharged the customer. Prep. ***langu.li.a*** St. ***langu.k.a*** Cs. ***langu.sh.a*** Rp. ***langu***.

an.a Ps. of Prep. *langu.liw.a,* be overcharged.
lan.i vt see *laani*
lao *adj, pron* (form of -ao referring to ma- class singular nouns) their, theirs: *Chungwa lao,* their orange. *Lao na letu halilingani,* theirs and ours is not the same.
lap.a[1] *vt* 1. gluttonize, cram, gormandize; eat ravenously, eat voraciously, eat hastily: *Alikilapa chakula kwa sababu ya njaa,* he ate the food greedily out of hunger. (cf *vongea, papia*) 2. struggle for sth, move here and there to look for sth; search high and low: *Alilapa maduka yote kijijini kutafuta sukari,* he went into every shop in the village to search for sugar. Prep. *lap.i.a* St. *lap.ik.a* Cs. *lap.ish.a* Ps. *lap.w.a* (cf *vanga, randa, wania*)
lapa[2] *n* (*ma-*) sandal, mule, mocassin, slippers. (cf *champali, ndara, kandambili*)
lapa[3] *n* (*ma-*) used in the expression: *Piga malapa,* a) ride a bicycle with pomposity b) perform an action with pomposity c) wonder aimlessly.
lasi *n* (*n*) coarse silk from the larvae of the tussah moth and related species; tussah: *Koti la lasi,* a coat made from tussore.
latami.a *vt* bring up a child, raise a child; rear, educate: *Kumlatamia mtoto ni kazi ngumu,* to bring up a child is a difficult task. (cf *lea*) (Ar)
Latifu[1] *n* (*n*) God of gentleness; God, the merciful and kind: *Ya Latifu,* Oh. God! the merciful and kind; sweet God! (Ar)
latifu[2] *adj* gentle, kind: *Yeye ni kijana latifu,* he is a gentle young man.
latitudo *n* (*n*) latitude; the distance of a place north or south of the equator measured in degrees: *Latitudo iliyoko mbali kutoka ikweta,* high latitude. (Eng)
lau *conj* if, provided, incase, supposing: *Lau ungekuja mapema hapa, ungemwona mjomba wako,* if you had come here earlier, you would have seen your uncle. (cf *kama*) (Ar)
laudispika *n* (*n*) loudspeaker (Eng)
laula *conj* if not, had it not been, unless: *Laula si msaada wako, ningeshindwa kuingia shuleni,* had it not been for your assistance, I would not have joined school. (cf *kama, lau, isingekuwa*) (Ar)
laudanumi *n* (*n*) laudanum; a narcotic painkiller. (Eng)
laum.u *vt* 1. reproach, rebuke, reprove, censure, chide, scold, blame: *Nilimlaumu ndugu yako kwa kuleta fujo darasani,* I blamed your brother for causing chaos in the class. Prep. *laum.i.a* St. *laum.ik.a,* deserve to be blamed e.g *Mtu yule halaumiki kwani kosa si lake,* that person cannot be blamed because that is not his mistake. Ps *laum.iw.a,* be blamed, be criticized. Rp. of Prep. *laum.i.an.a,* blame one another (cf *aili*). 2. accuse, charge: *Alinilaumu kwa kumchukulia kitabu chake,* he accused me of taking his book. Prep. *laum.i.a* St. *laum.ik.a* Ps. of Prep. *laum.iw.a* Rp. of Prep. *laum.i.an.a* (cf *shutumu*) (Ar)
launi *n* (*n*) 1. colour: *Launi ya kanzu yangu ni kijani,* the colour of my dress is green. (cf *rangi*) 2. kind, type, variety, form: *Launi ya lugha,* language variety. *Launi mbalimbali za vitambaa,* the different types of cloth. (Ar)
laurusi *n* (*n*) (*bot*) laurel; a kind of shrub with large glossy, aromatic leaves. (Eng)
lava *n* (*n*) (*zool*) larvae
lavani *n* (*n*) (*bot*) vannila (cf *vanila*) (Fr)
lawalawa *n* (*n*) sweetmeat, confection, sweets, bonbon, sugar candy: *Mara kwa mara, huwakirimu wageni wangu kwa lawalawa,* I often serve my guests with sweets. (cf *peremende, tamutamu*)
lawama *n* (*n*) 1. blame, censure, reproof, reproach, reprimand: *Yeye anapenda kunitupia lawama burebure,* he likes

lawaridi   **legelege**   **L**

to put the blame on me for no reason. 2. charge, accusation, indictment: *Lawama zile dhidi ya mtumishi wao hazina msingi*, those accusations against their servant are baseless. (cf *shutuma*)(Ar).
lawaridi *n* (*n*) see *halwaridi*
lawit.i *vt* sodomize; commit sodomy. Prep. *lawit.i.a* St. *lawit.ik.a* Cs *lawit.ish.a* Ps. of Prep. *lawit.iw.a* Rp. of Prep. *lawit.i.an.a* (cf *fira*) (Ar)
laz.a[1] *vt* see *lala*
laz.a[2] *vt* 1. (*naut*) careen; cause a ship to lean or lie on one side as for repairs. 2. hospitalize; admit to hospital. 3. win a game: *Tuliilaza timu yao kwa magoli mengi*, we beat their team by many goals. Prep. *laz.i.a* St. *laz.ik.a* Cs *laz.ish.a* Ps. *laz.w.a* Rp. *laz.an.a*
lazima[1] *n* (*n*) necessity, obligation, needfulness: *Hakuna lazima ya wewe kusafiri naye*, there is no necessity for you to travel with him. (cf *shuruti, sharti, wajibu*) (Ar)
lazima[2] *adv* necessarily, perforce; by force: *Lazima aifanye kazi kwa bidii*, he must do the work with diligence. (cf *sharti, inapasa*) (Ar)
lazimik.a *vi* be obliged, be compelled. Prep. *lazimik.i.a* (cf *wajibika, bidii*)
lazimish.a *vt* see *lazimu*. Prep. *lazimish.i.a* St. *lazimish.ik.a* Ps. *lazimish.w.a* Rp. *lazimish.an.a*
lazim.u *vt* be obliged, be necessary, be binding (on): *Ilimlazimu kumpeleka mtoto wake hospitali kwa haraka*, it became necessary for him to send his child to hospital urgently. Prep. *lazim.i.a* St. *lazim.ik.a*, be obliged, be compelled: e.g. *Mtu yule analazimika kulipa kodi kubwa ya mapato*, that person is obliged to pay a high excessive income tax. Cs. *lazim.ish.a,* force, compel e.g. *Walimlazimisha kuondoka mkutanoni*, they forced him to leave the meeting. Ps. of Prep. *lazim.iw.a,* be forced. (Ar)

-le (*part*) demonstrative root for non proximity: *Mwalimu yule*, that teacher. *Kitabu kile*, that book.
le.a *vt, vi* bring up, nurse, rear, raise, nurture, parent: *Lea mtoto wako vizuri*, bring up your child well. (*prov*) *Mwana umleavyo ndivyo akuavyo*, as you bring up a child, so he will be i.e. if you bring up your child well, he will have good manners, and if you don't bring him up well, he will misbehave. Prep. *le.le.a* St. *le.lek.a* Ps. *le.lew.a,* be brought up e.g *Alilelewa na shangazi yake*, she was brought up by her aunt. Rp.. *le.an.a* (cf *elimisha*)
leba[1] *n* (*n*) 1. labour office, labour department: *Ofisi ya leba*, labour office. 2. maternity ward, labour room. (Eng)
leba[2] *n* (*n*) deceit, deception, fraud, hypocricy (cf *qhiliba, udanganyifu*)
lebasi *n* (*n*) see *libasi*
lebo[1] *n*(*n*) see *lebu*
lebo[2] (*n*) label (Eng)
lebu (also *lebo*) *n* (*n*) laboratory (cf *maabara*) (Eng)
legaleg.a (also *regarega*) *vi* slack, wobble, waver, rock, shake: *Meza ile inalegalega*, that table is wobbling. Prep. *legaleg.e.a* Ps. *legaleg.ek.a* Cs. *legaleg.esh.a* (cf *cheza, yumbayumba*)
lege.a (also *regea*) *vi* 1. be loose, be weak, be soft, be pliable: *Fundo hili limelegea*, this knot is loose, (cf *dhoofu, soba*) 2. (of trees, poles, etc.) be soft, be loose, be smooth: *Nguzo za nyumba hii zimelegea*, the beams of this house are loose. 3. (of persons) be negligent, be remiss: *Mtumishi wako amelegea sana*, your worker is very slack. *Yule mgonjwa amezidi kulegea baada ya kupigwa sindano*, the patient has increasingly become weaker after being given an injection. Prep. *lege.le.a* St. *lege.k.a* Cs. *lege.z.a*
legelege *adj* loose, slack, inactive: *Chama chao sasa kimekuwa legelege*, their party has now become inactive.

401

legeni *n* (*n*) a kind of a large metal vessel used for cooking special bread known as "*mikate ya kumimina.*"

-legevu *adj* 1. slack, loose, not tight: *Fundo lilikuwa legevu*, the knot was loose. 2. (of a person) remiss, negligent, reckless, relaxed.

legez.a *vt* 1. loosen, relax, slacken: *Aliulegeza mshipi ili ampate samaki*, he loosened the fishing line in order to catch fish. 2. lower the speed of sth. Prep. *legez.e.a* St. *legez.ek.a* Ps. *legez.w.a* Rp. *legez.an.a*

lehem.u (also *lihimu*) *vt* solder; apply solder, repair with solder: *Anataka kulilehemu bati lake*, he wants to solder his roof. Prep. *lehem.i.a* St. *lehem.ik.a* Cs. *lehem.ish.a* Ps. of Prep. *lehem.iw.a* (Ar)

leja *n* (*n*) ledger book. (Eng)

lejikoo *n* (*n*) legislature, parliament. (cf *bunge*) (Eng)

leke.a *vt* see *elekea*. Prep. *leke.le.a* St. *leke.lek.a* Cs. *leke.z.a* Ps. *leke.w.a* Rp. *leke.an.a*

-lekevu *adj* see *elekevu*

lekez.a *vt* see *elekeza*

leksikografia *n* (*n*) lexicography (Eng)

leksimu *n* (*n*) (*sem*) lexeme (Eng)

lelamu *n* (*n*) see *lilamu*

lele *n* (*n*) (*mus*) the first song in a local dance serving as an introduction to an audience; prelude. (*prov*) *Mwanzo wa ngoma ni lele*, the beginning of a local dance is the first song i.e. a local dance cannot function effectively without having first an introductory song.

lelej.a *vi* prattle, twaddle, blather, babble; talk nonsense, talk foolishly: *Mwanasiasa alikuwa akileleja kutoka kwenye jukwaa*, the politician was prattling from the platform. Prep. *lelej.e.a* St. *lelej.ek.a* Cs. *lelej.esh.a* (cf *ropokwa, bwabwaja*)

leleji *n* (*n*) a lot of cold water that has precipitated in a place.

lelemama *n* (*n*) a kind of a dance which is performed by a row of singing women standing on a wooden platform holding the horn of a goat on one hand and a stick on the other hand and clicking them; women's horn dance.

lema[1] *n* (*ma-*) see *dema*[2]

lem.a[2] *vt* excel, outshine, outclass: *Amelema katika mapishi yake siku hizi*, he has excelled in cooking these days. (cf *shinda, kulula*)

lem.a[3] *vt* exorcise spirits as local witchdoctors do; drive out an evil spirit from a person: *Mganga alimlema mteja wake*, the medicineman drove out an evil spirit from his client. Prep. *lem.e.a* St. *lem.e.k.a* Cs. *lem.esh.a* Ps. *lem.w.a* Rp. *lem.an.a* Ps. of Prep. *leme.w.a* Rp. of Prep. *leme.an.a* (cf *punga*)

lema.a *vi* 1. be disfigured, be maimed, be mutilated: *Mtu yule sasa amelemaa baada ya kupata ugonjwa wa ukoma*, that person is now disfigured after having suffered from leprosy. 2. be addicted to a particular habit: *Rafiki yako sasa amelemaa katika kutumia dawa za kulevya*, your friend is now addicted to narcotics. Cs. *lema.z.a*

lemaz.a *vt* 1. cripple, maim, disable. 2. (*fig*) stifle, prevent, impede: *Huwezi kuyalemaza maendeleo yetu*, you can't impede our progress. 3. be addicted to a particular bad habit. Prep. *lemaz.i.a* St. *lemaz.ik.a* Cs. *lemaz.ish.a* Ps. *lemaz.w.a*

lemb.a[1] *vt* take sth by trickery; deceive: *Alimlemba mwenye duka*, he deceived the shopkeeper. Prep. *lemb.e.a* St. *lemb.ek.a* Cs. *lemb.esh.a* Ps. *lemb.w.a* Rp. *lemb.an.a* (cf *hadaa, danganya*)

lemba[2] *n* (*n*) (*zool*) the abdomen of an octopus. (cf *demba*)

lembalemb.a *vi* (of water) be shaking in a container because it is full. Prep. *lembalemb.e.a* St. *lembalemb.ek.a* Cs. *lembalemb.esh.a*

lembe.a¹ *vt* reach up to sth high as in the case of plucking a fruit: *Ufupi wake ulimfanya alembee mabegani mwa rafiki yake*, his state of shortness made him to climb on to his friend's shoulders.

lembe.a² *vt* aim with a rifle, etc.; zero in on; take aim. (cf *lenga*)

lembelembe¹ *adj* ripe, mature; in full bloom, in a full ripe stage: *Tunda hili liko lembelembe*, this fruit is over-ripe. *Jipu lake liko lembelembe*, her boil is about to burst.

lembelembe² *n* (*n*) ripple (cf *kiwimbi*)

leme.a *vt* see *elemea*

lembuk.a *vi* see *rembuka*

leng.a¹ *vt* 1. aim with a rifle, etc.; zero in on; take aim: *Msasi alimlenga paa*, the hunter zeroed in on the deer. 2. remove a bad portion of sth. Prep. ***leng.e.a*** St. ***leng.ek.a*** Cs. ***leng.esh.a*** Ps. ***leng.w.a*** Rp. ***leng.an.a*** (cf *elekeza*)

leng.a² *vt* cut in slices; slice, cleave, slive: *Lenga muhogo*, slice the cassava. Prep. ***leng.e.a*** St. ***leng.ek.a*** Cs. ***leng.esh.a*** Ps. ***leng.w.a*** Rp. ***leng.an.a***

lenga³ *n* (*n*) (*zool*) lagoons land crab; a large crab living in landward edge of mangrove forests and further in land, in deep burrows. *Cardisoma carnifex*

lengaleng.a *vi* begin to form tears in one's eyes; be near to crying: *Machozi yalimlengalenga*, tears began to form on her eyes. Ps. ***lengaleng.w.a***

lengelenge (also *yengeyenge*) (*ma-*) blister, pustule, blain, furuncle: *Amefanya malengelenge baada ya kuvaa viatu vipya*, he got blisters after wearing a new pair of shoes. *Lengelenge la damu*, blood blister. *Lengelenge la maji*, water blister. (cf *tutumvi*, *tutuvi*)

lenget.a¹ *vt* bisect, halve; divide into two equal parts, cut into two: *Lengeta keki hii*, cut this cake into two parts. Prep ***lenget.e.a*** St. ***lenget.ek.a*** Cs. ***lenget.esh.a*** Ps. ***lenget.w.a*** Rp. ***lenget.an.a***

lenget.a² *vt* raise a beehive on a tree by using a rope: *Aliulengeta mzinga*, he raised the beehive on to a tree by using a rope. Prep.. ***lenget.e.a***. St. ***lenget.ek.a*** Ps. ***lenget.w.a*** Rp. of Prep. ***lenget.e.an.a***

lengo *n* (*ma-*) 1. the act of zeroing in on sth with a rifle, etc. 2. aim, objective, purpose, goal, intention: *Lengo letu ni kupata ushindi kwa timu yetu*, our goal is to obtain victory for our team. (cf *dhamira*, *shabaha*)

lenu *adj*, *pron* (form of *-enu* referring to ma-class pl nouns) your, yours: *Duka lenu*, your shop. *Lenu ni mamoja*, yours is the same.

lenye *adj* (form of *-enye* for ma- class singular nouns) having, with: *Gari yenye magurudumu matatu*, a vehicle with three tyres.

lenyewe *adj*, *pron* (form of *-enyewe* referring to ma- class singular nouns) by itself: *Jambo lenyewe halijulikani*, the thing itself is unknown.

lenzi *n* (*n*) lens: *Lenzi mbinuko*, convex lens. *Lenzi mbonyeo*, concave lens. *Lenzi tawanyifu*, diverging lens. *Lenzi tufe*, spherical lens. (Eng)

leo¹ *adv* today, this day, this very day, this present day: *Mjomba atasafiri leo*, my uncle will travel today.

leo² *n* (*n*) today, this present day. *Leo ni jumapili*, today is Sunday. *Leo hii*, on this day.

lepe *n* (*ma-*) drowsiness, doziness, grogginess; a heavy slumberous condition: *Sikupata hata lepe la usingizi jana usiku*, I did not get a wink of sleep last night. (cf *gonezi*, *usingizi*)

leseni *n* (*n*) licence, permission, authority: *Leseni ya kuendesha gari*, driving licence: *Amepewa leseni ya kufanya biashara*, he has been given a licence to do business. (cf *ruhusa*, *hati*) (Eng)

leso *n* (*n*) 1. khanga; lady's wrap of cotton, usu worn around the waist, etc. which has a statement written on

let.a

it. (cf *kanga*) 2. scarf; a woman's head cloth. 3. handkerchief. (Port)
let.a *vt* bring, fetch, get, supply: *Alikileta chakula kwa haraka,* he brought the food hurriedly. *Leta maombi,* bring requests. Prep. **let.e.a**, bring for (to, at, etc) e.g. *Aliniletea kitabu changu,* he brought my book to me. Cs.. **let.esh.a** Ps.. **let.w.a** e.g. *Wameletwa hapa na baba yao,* they have been brought here by their father. Ps. of Prep. **let.ew.a** e.g. *Ameletewa maua mazuri,* he has been sent good flowers. Rp. **let.an.a** Rp. of Prep. **let.e.an.a** e.g.*Wanaleteana zawadi nzuri nzuri,* they exchange good presents. (cf *wasilisha, peleka*)
letu *adj, pron* (form of *-etu* for ma- class sing nouns) our, ours: *Jambo letu,* our issue. *Letu na lenu linatofautiana,* ours and yours are different.
leuk.a *vi* sober up. Prep. **leuk.i.a** St. **leuk.ik.a** Cs. **leuk.ish.a** Ps. **leuk.w.a**
-levi *adj* drunk, intoxicated, inebricated, drunken: *Mtu mlevi,* a drunken person.
leviathan *n* (*n*) (*Bible*) leviathani, a sea monster, variously thought of as a reptile or a whale. (Eng)
lew.a *vi* 1. be drunk, be intoxicated: *Alilewa sana mpaka akaanguka,* he was so heavily drunk that he fell down. 2. be seasick; be giddy in a sailing vessel because of the rough sea. Prep.. **lew.e.a** St.. **lew.ek.a** Cs. **lew.esh.a** and **le.vy.a** e.g. *Bahari iliyochafuka iliwalewesha abiria,* the rough sea made the passengers giddy. *Alimlewesha sana rafiki yake mpaka akapoteza fahamu,* he made his friend so drunk that he lost his consciousness.
lewalew.a *vi* stagger, reel, teeter, totter, sway, wobble, rock, shake: *Miti ilikuwa inalewalewa kwa sababu ya upepo mkali,* the trees were swaying because of the strong wind. Prep. **lewalew.e.a**

liga[1]

Cs. **lewalew.esh.a** cause to stagger (cf *pepesuka, sesereka, wayawaya*)
lewesh.a *vt* see *lewa*
li.a *vi* 1. cry, sob, weep: *Alilia sana mumewe alipofariki,* she cried very much when her husband died. Prep. **li.li.a,** cry for (at, with, etc.) e.g. *Analilia nini?* What is she crying for? St.. **li.lik.a** Cs. **li.z.a,** cause to cry e.g. *Alimliza mtoto wake mchanga kwa kuchelewa kumpa maziwa kwa wakati wake,* she made her baby cry when she failed to give it some milk in time. Rp. of Cs. **li.z.an.a,** weep together e.g. *Wanawake walikuwa wanalizana mazikoni,* the women were weeping together at the funeral. 2. ring, sound; make a sound: *Kengele ya shule imelia punde,* the school bell has just rung. *Chuma hulia kinapogongwa na nyundo,* iron rings when it is hit with a hammer. Prep. **li.li.a** St. **li.li.k.a** Cs. **li.z.a** Rp. **li.an.a**
liamba *n* (*n*) dawn (cf *alfajiri, unju*)
libasi (also *lebasi*) *n* (*n*) clothes, garments, vestments. (*prov*) *Usiku ni libasi bora,* night has good garments i.e. night offers the best cover.
licha *conj* apart from, aside from, not only: *Licha yeye, hata mimi siwezi kuunyanyua mzigo,* not only him but also I cannot lift that load. The word *licha* is commonly followed by *ya* e.g. *Licha ya hayo, kuna masuala mengine ambayo yanafaa kuzingatiwa,* besides those, there are other issues worth considering. (cf *zaidi ya, mbali na*)
lifti *n* (*n*) elevator, lift, hoist, escalator: *Jengo hili halina lifti,* this building does not have a lift. *Opereta wa lifti,* lift attendant. 2. free ride; an opportunity to travel free of charge. (Eng)
lig.a[1] *vt* poison; harm or kill someone with a poison: *Alitaka kumliga mbwa wangu,* he wanted to poison my dog. Prep. **lig.i.a** St. **lig.ik.a** Cs. **lig.ish.a** Ps. **lig.w.a** Rp. **lig.an.a**

liga² *n* (*n*) poison, venom, toxin; any medicine which makes someone get sick.

ligi *n*(*n*) (in sports) league: *Ligi kuu*, premier league. *Mini ligi*, mini league. *Ligi ya taifa*, national league. *Mashindano ya ligi*, league competition. (Eng)

ligia *n* (*n*) (*zool*) see *pale bahari*

lihamu (also *lehamu*) *n* (*n*) soldering head; solder: *Tia lihamu*, apply solder, etc. (Ar)

lihimu *n* (*n*) see *lehemu*

lijamu *n* (*n*) bit of a horse, donkey, etc.; head harness: *Seruji, lijamu na vigwe*, saddle, bit and reins. (cf *hatamu, zimamu*) (Ar)

lik.a *vi* 1. wear, cancer, degenerate: *Magurudumu ya gari langu yamelika*, the tyres of my car are worn out. 2. be edible, be eatable: *Chakula hiki hakiliki*, this food is not edible.

likiz.a *vt* (rarely used) wean; cause to give up suckling: *Likiza mtoto kunyonya*, wean a child. Prep. **likiz.i.a** Cs. **likiz.ish.a** Ps. **likiz.w.a** Rp. **likiz.an.a**

likizo *n* (*n*) holiday, vacation, respite, recess, leave: *Likizo ya kutokuwepo*, leave of absence. *Likizo bila malipo*, leave without pay. *Likizo ya lazima*, forced leave. *Likizo bila ruhusa*, French leave. *Likizo ya dharura*, emergency leave. *Likizo ya ugonjwa*, sick leave. *Amepewa likizo ndefu*, he has been given a long leave.

liko *n* (*ma-*) see *diko*

lila *n* (*n*) used in the expression: *Lila na fila havitangamani*, good and bad are incompatible.

lilahi *adv* sincerely, genuinely, wholeheartedly; for the sake of God: *Ukitaka kumsaidia mtu, fanya kwa lilahi*, if you want to help someone, do it for the sake of God. (Ar)

lilamu also (*lahamu*) *n*(*n*) auction, vendue; public sale, auction sale. (Hind)

lile *adj, pron* (demonstrative form of reference of non proximity for *ma*- class sing nouns) that: *Shamba lile*, that plantation. *Lile ni ua*, that is a flower.

lili.a *vt* 1. see *lia*. 2. want sth earnestly; yearn: *Alililia sana apewe kazi ile*, he yearned very much for that job. St. **lili.k.a** Ps. **lili.w.a** Rp. **lili.an.a**

liliwal.a *vi* forget; cease to remember Prep. **liliwal.i.a** St. **liliwal.ik.a** Cs. **liliwal.ish.a** Ps. of Prep. **liliwal.i.w.a** Rp. of Prep. **liliwal.i.an.a**

lim.a¹ *vt* 1. hoe, cultivate, farm, tilt: *Ninalima mpunga katika konde yangu*, I cultivate rice in my field. Prep. **lim.i.a,** cultivate for (with, etc) e.g. *Jembe la kulimia*, a hoe to dig with. St. **lim.ik.a** Cs. **lim.ish.a** Ps. **lim.w.a,** be cultivated (cf *katua, fyeka*) 2. (*colloq*) con someone: *Alimlima rafiki yake*, he conned his friend. 3. (*Colloq*) send: *Kiongozi alimlima barua meneja*, the leader sent a letter to the manager. Prep. **lim.i.a** St. **lim.ik.a** Cs. **lim.ish.a** Ps. **lim.w.a** Rp. of Prep. **lim.i.an.a**

lima² *n* (*n*) wedding feast, wedding reception: *Nilihudhuria lima ya harusi ya rafiki yangu*, I attended my friend's wedding feast.

limati.a¹ *vi, vt* procrastinate, delay, temporize; be late: *Mwajiri alimfukuza mfanyakazi wake kwa kulimatia kazini*, the employer sacked his worker for reporting late for work. Prep. **limati.li.a** St. **limati.k.a** Cs. **limati.sh.a** Ps. **limati.w.a** (cf *chelewa*)

limati.a² *vi, vt* be stuck, be adhered to, be clinged to, be fastened: *Nta ililimatia kwenye shati lake*, the wax got stuck to his shirt. Prep.. **limati.li.a** St.. **limati.k.a** Cs. **limati.sh.a** Ps. **limati.w.a** Rp. **limati.an.a** (cf *gandama*)

limau *n* (*ma-*) (*bot*) lemon (Hind)

limb.a¹ *vt* hit, beat, strike, smite, thwack: *Mwalimu alimlimba mwanafunzi kutokana na ukosefu wa nidhamu*, the teacher beat the student for misconduct. Prep.. **limb.i.a** St. **limb.ik.a** Cs. **limb.ish.a** Ps. **limb.w.a** Rp. **limb.an.a** (cf *piga*)

limb.a² *vt* bury itself in the ground; fall

into the ground: *Gogo lile limejilimba ardhini*, that log has buried itself deeply into the ground. Prep. **limb.i.a** St. **limb.ik.a** Cs. **limb.ish.a** Ps. **limb.w.a** (cf *jikita ardhini*)

limb.a³ *vt* fail to move either way despite pressure from both sides. Prep. **limb.i.a** St. **limb.ik.a** Cs. **limb.ish.a** Ps. **limb.w.a**

limbik.a *vt* 1. heap up, pile up, roll up, stack up, accumulate bit by bit, hoard: *Mwenyeduka alizilimbika bidhaa zake*, the shopkeeper hoarded his goods. (cf *dundukiza, tunduiza*) 2. bear with, be patient to, show consideration for: *Limbika ndizi*, wait for bananas to ripen. *Limbika nywele*, let the hair grow. *Limbika kucha*, let the nails grow. Prep. **limbik.i.a** St. **limbik.ik.a** Cs. **limbik.ish.a** and **limbik.iz.a** Ps. **limbik.w.a**

limbikiz.a¹ *vt* see *limbika*

limbikiz.a² *vt* hoard, accumulate, pile up: *Limbikiza madeni*, accumulate debts. Prep. **limbikiz.i.a** St. **limbikiz.ik.a** Cs. **limbikiz.ish.a** Ps. **limbikiz.w.a** (cf *limbika*)

limbikizo *n* (*ma-*) accumulation, reserve, backlog, stock: *Limbikizo la mshahara*, salary arrears. *Limbikizo la madeni*, accumulation of arrears.

limbiko *n* (*ma-*) see *mlimbuko*

limbu.a (also *imbua*) *vt* start a project, etc. for the first time; launch a project, etc. for the first time: *Aliulimbua mradi wa kuku kijijini*, he launched a poultry project in the village. Prep. **limbu.li.a** St. **limbu.k.a**

limbuk.a *vt* get anything for the first time; do anything for the first time; take away the first crop, etc. say in a farm, etc.: *Tulikwenda shambani kulimbuka mahindi*, we went to the farm to take away the first maize crop. Prep.. **limbuk.i.a** St. **limbuk.ik.a** Cs. **limbuk.ish.a** Ps. **limbuk.w.a**

limbukeni *n* (*ma-*) a person enjoying a thing or tasting an experience for the first time e.g. a country bumpkin. (*prov*) *Limbukeni hana siri*, a person enjoying a thing for the first time does not keep a secret i.e. a person enjoying a thing for the first time will like to show off.

limbuko *n* (*ma-*) a first taste or experience of anything: *Limbuko la kahawa*, the first taste of coffee.

limfu *n* (*n*) (*anat*) lymph: *Mzunguko wa limfu*, lymph flow. (Eng)

limk.a *vi* become conscious, become awakened; wise up: *Mtu yule hadanganyiki tena kwa vile amelimka*, that person cannot be deceived any more because he has become wise. Prep. **limk.i.a** St. **limk.ik.a** Cs. **limk.ish.a** (cf *tanabahi, erevuka*)

limk.i *vt* (rarely used) have a deficiency, have a defect, be deficient. Prep. **limk.i.a** St. **limk.ik.a** Cs. **limk.ish.a** (Ar)

limuk.a *vi* be sly, be cunning: *Mtu yule amelimuka mno*, that person is very sly.

limuzini *n* (*n*) limousine (Eng)

lind.a *vt* defend, guard, protect, shelter, shield: *Rais aliwataka raia wote kuilinda nchi yao*, the president wanted all the citizens to defend their country. Prep. **lind.i.a** St. **lind.ik.a** Ps. **lind.w.a,** be defended, be guarded e.g. *Kasri ya mfalme inalindwa na wanajeshi*, the king's palace is guarded by the army. Rp.. **lind. an.a** (cf *chunga, hami, hifadhi*)

lindi (also *dindi*) *n* (*n*) 1. pit usu of latrine; pit latrine; deep: *Lindi la choo*, cesspool, pit latrine. 2. (*idms*) *Lindi la msiba*, a great misfortune e.g. *Alipatikana na lindi la msiba alipofiwa na mkewe*, he suffered a great misfortune when his wife died. *Lindi la umasikini*, the abyss poverty. *Lindi la mashaka*, many problems.

lindo *n* (*ma-*) watching place; post to guard.

ling.a *vt* compare, assess, collate,

inspect: *Mkaguzi aliilinga kazi ya mwalimu,* the inspector assessed the teacher's work. Prep. ***ling.i.a*** St. ***ling.ik.a*** Cs. ***ling.ish.a*** Ps. ***ling.w.a*** Rp. ***ling.an.a*** (cf *pima, geza*)

lingan.a¹ *vt* 1. resemble, be like, look like: *Kijana huyu analingana kwa sura na mjomba wake,* this young man resembles his uncle in appearance. Prep. ***lingan.i.a*** St. ***lingan.ik.a*** Cs. ***lingan.ish.a,*** correlate, compare, equate e.g. *Wanafunzi waliyalinganisha maisha ya mjini na yale ya shamba,* the students compared life in town with that of the country. (cf *fanana, shabihiana*) 2. (*fig*) agree with, be in harmony with, be compatible: *Nchi zile mbili zinalingana kisiasa,* those two countries are politically compatible. Prep. ***lingan.i.a*** St. ***lingan.ik.a*** Cs. ***lingan.ish.a*** (cf *afikiana, patana*)

lingan.a² *vt* 1. pray for, invoke, supplicate, call for: *Mlinganie Mungu,* invoke God. 2. preach, sermonize, evangelize: *Alilingana dini hadharani,* he preached in public. Prep. ***lingan.i.a*** St. ***lingan.ik.a*** Cs. ***lingan.ish.a*** (cf *hubiri*)

-linganifu¹ *adj* matching, similar, suitable, comparable: *Kazi linganifu mbili,* two comparable pieces of work.

linganifu² *adj* regular

linganish.a *vt* see *lingana¹*. Prep. ***linganish.i.a*** St. ***linganish.ik.a*** Ps. ***linganish.w.a*** Rp. ***linganish.an.a***

lingo *n* (*n*) a collection of felled trees e.g. firewood, poles, etc. arranged in heaps and ready for sale.

lini *adv* (*interrog*) when? at what time? on what occasion? *Lini utasafiri?* When will you travel? (cf *siku gani*)

lip.a *vt* 1. pay, compensate, recompense, refund: *Alilipa deni langu mara moja,* he paid my debt quickly. (*prov*) *Kukopa harusi kulipa matanga,* borrowing is like a wedding, repaying is like mourning i.e. borrowing is easy but repaying is a problem. 2. return a similar action that someone has done to you; reward: *Mungu atakulipa kwa yote uliyonifanyia,* God will reward you for all you have done for me. Prep. ***lip.i.a,*** pay for (to, etc.) St. ***lip.ik.a*** Cs. ***lip.ish.a*** and ***lip.iz.a,*** force payment, settle accounts. Ps. ***lip.w.a,*** be paid. Rp. ***lip.an.a***

lipi *adj, pron* interrogative marker for ma-class singular nouns; which, what: *Jani lipi?* Which leaf? *Lipi linakusumbua?* What is bothering you?

lipi.a *vt* see *lipa.* St. ***lipi.k.a*** Cs. ***lipi.sh.a*** Ps. ***lipi.w.a*** Rp. ***lipi.an.a***

lipili *n* (*n*) (*zool*) puff adder. *Billis arietans.* (cf *kifutu, bafe*)

lipish.a (also *lipiza*) *vt* see *lipa*. Prep. ***lipish.i.a*** St. ***lipish.ik.a*** Ps. ***lipish.w.a*** Rp. ***lipish.an.a***

lipiz.a *vt* revenge, retaliate, avenge; make reprisal: *Ingawa alikukosa, lakini haifai kulipiza kisasi,* even though he offended you, it is not good to retaliate. Prep. ***lipiz.i.a*** St. ***lipiz.ik.a*** Ps. ***lipiz.w.a*** Rp. ***lipiz.an.a***

lipizi¹ *n* (*ma-*) revenge, reprisal, retribution, vengeance.

lipizi² *n* (*ma-*) extortion, exaction; enforced payment.

lipu *n* (*n*) wall plaster: *Piga lipu,* plaster a wall.

lipu.a¹ (also *ripua*) *vt* bungle, botch; do a job improperly, etc. in order to save time: *Aliilipua kazi yangu,* he did my job haphazardly in order to save time. Prep. ***lipu.li.a*** St. ***lipu.k.a*** Cs. ***lipu.sh.a*** Ps. or Prep. ***lipu.liw.a,*** be botched up. Rp. of Prep. ***lipu.li.an.a*** (cf *rasha, paraza*)

lipu.a² (also *ripua*) *vt* let off sth, let sth like a trap go off; remove a snare; blow; explode: *Majambazi walilipua bomu,* the thugs exploded a bomb. St. ***lipu.k.a,*** be exploded e.g. *Fataki zililipuka,* the crackers exploded. Cs. ***lipu.sh.a*** Ps. of Prep. ***lipu.liw.a,*** be exploded, be blown up. Rp. ***lipu.an.a***

lipuk.a (also *ripuka*) *vi* see *lipua.* 2. (*fig*) be enraged; be annoyed. Prep. ***lipuk.i.a*** St. ***lipuk.ik.a*** Ps. ***lipuk.w.a***

lipyoto *n* (*n*) 1. (*zool*) a kind of bird which spoils water e.g. in a well or fountain. 2. (*fig*) firebrand, rabble-rouser, mischief-maker; an instigator of discord; a person who incites others to discord.

lira *n* (*n*) (*monet*) the standard monetary unit of Italy: *Lira ya Italia*, Italian lira. (Ital)

lisani[1] *n* (*n*) 1. tongue. (cf *ulimi*) 2. expression; language style. (cf *lugha, usemi*) (Ar)

lisani[2] *n* (*n*) a flap in the front of a garment, *kanzu*; a strip of lining in the front of a *kanzu*. (Ar)

lisaniati *n* (*n*) linguistics. (cf *isimu, lugha wiyati*)

lish.a *vt* see *la*[2]. Prep. **lish.i.a** St. **lish.ik.a** Ps. **lish.w.a** Rp. **lish.an.a**

lishe *n*(*n*) nutrients (cf *virutubisho*)

lita *n* (*n*) litre: *Lita moja ya maziwa*, one litre of milk. (Eng)

litania *n* (*n*) (in Christianity) litany; a form of prayer in which the clergy and the congregation take part alternately with recitations and supplications and fixed responses. (Eng)

livu[1] *n* (*n*) holiday, vacation, leave: *Nikipata livu safari hii, nitaenda Ulaya kwa matembezi*, if I get leave this time, I will go to Europe for a visit. (Eng)

liv.u[2] *vt, vi* change turns in patrolling. Prep. **liv.i.a** St. **liv.ik.a** Cs. **liv.ish.a** Ps. of Prep. **liv.iw.a** Rp. of Prep. **liv.i.an.a**

liwa[1] *n* (*n*) thick gravy obtained from sweet scented sandwood and mixed with water, which is used as a perfume as well as a cooling lotion for skin; soothing lotion of sandal wood. (Ar)

liwa[2] *n* (*n*) (*bot*) hedge; trees grown on the border to separate plantations.

liwa[3] *n* (*n*) stalks of millet, used for making bird traps.

liwali *n* (*n*) a headman or governor for a particular area, found in Muslim communities. (Ar)

liwat.a *vt* trample, tread on, tramp on, stamp, stomp: *Aliziliwata nyasi kwenye bustani yangu*. he trod on the grass in my garden. Prep. **liwat.i.a** St. **liwat.ik.a** Cs. **liwat.ish.a** Ps. **liwat.w.a,** be trampled, be trodden. Rp. **liwat.an.a** (cf *vyoga, kanyaga*)

liwati *n*(*n*) sodomy (*ufiraji*)

liwato *n* (*n*) the butt of a gun: *Liwato la bunduki*, rifle butt.

liwaz.a *vt* console, comfort, solace, calm: *Nyimbo zake nzuri ziliniliwaza*, her good songs soothed me. Prep. **liwaz.i.a** St. **liwaz.ik.a** Cs. **liwaz.ish.a** Ps. **liwaz.w.a,** be consoled Rp. **liwaz.an.a** (cf *tuliza, fariji*)

liwazo *n* (*ma*-) see *maliwazo*

liz.a[1] *vi* see *lia*. 2. ring sth: *Liza kengele*, ring a bell. Prep. **liz.i.a** St. **liz.ik.a** Ps. **liz.w.a** Rp. **liz.an.a**

liza[2] *n* (*n*) see *reza*

lizi *n* (*n*) lease; the right to own a piece of land or buildings for a specified period usu in return for rent: *Pata lizi ya shamba*, get a farm lease. (Eng)

lo[1] *interj* an exclamation of horror, surprise, happiness, etc.; Oh: *Lo! Paka amekula nyama yangu*, Oh! the cat has eaten my meat.

lo[2] *pron* (*rel*) (a relative marker of *ma*- class sing nouns) meaning "which," "that": *Jambo alilolifanya lilinishangaza*, what he did surprised me. Sometimes, the particle *lo* is used indefinitely as in such phrases as *duka lo lote*, any shop and *jambo lo lote*, any issue.

lo.a (*also rowa*) *vi* get soaked, get drenched, get wet: *Aliloa chapachapa kwenye mvua*, he got thoroughly drenched in the rain. Prep.. **lo.e.a** St. **lo.ek.a** Cs. **lo.esh.a** Rp. **lo.an.a**

lodi[1] *n* (*ma*-) magnate, tycoon; a wealthy person: *Yeye sasa amekuwa lodi baada ya kupata ushindi mkubwa katika bahati nasibu*, he has now become a wealthy person after a big win in the lottery. *Lodi lofa*, a poor person who aspires to live a rich life. (Eng)

lodi² n (ma-) a field glass with a single eyepiece; monocular.
lofa n (ma-) 1. lay about, idler, loafer, slouch, sluggard, lounger: *Utapoteza wakati wako wote ukiandamana na malofa wale*, you will waste all your time if you mingle with those loafers. (cf *mzembe*) 2. pauper, a poor person; have-not, down and outer: *Lofa yule hawezi kukusaidia chochote*, that pauper can't help you in anything. (cf *fakiri, masikini*)
log.a vt, vi see *roga*
logi (also *logaridhimu*) n (n) (math) logarithm: *Logi asilia*, natural logarithm. *Logi kiziokumi*, common logarithm. *Logi naperi*, naperian logarithm. (Eng)
loho tablet; a flat, thin piece of stone, wood, metal, etc. shaped for a specific purpose. (Ar)
lokasi n (n) (math) locus (Eng)
lokisheni n (n) (in Kenya) location; administrative area below division (Eng)
lolom.a vi prattle, twaddle, twattle, blather; talk nonsense, go on speaking foolishly: *Mgonjwa aliposhikwa na homa kali, akaanza kuloloma*, when the patient was suffering from acute fever, he began to prattle. Prep. ***lolom.e.a*** St. ***lolom.ek.a*** Cs. ***lolom.esh.a*** Ps. ***lolom.w.a*** Rp. ***lolom.an.a*** (cf *bubujika, poroja, payuka, ropoka*)
loma n (n) (zool) badger, antbear. (cf *kiharara, muhanga*)
lomba n (ma-) drum beater usu for women.
londe.a vt yearn, wish, want. St. ***londe.k.a*** Cs. ***londe.sh.a*** Ps. ***londe.w.a*** Rp. ***londe.an.a***
long.a (also *ronga*) vt convene, chat, chit-chat, confubulate, talk, gossip: *Anapenda kulonga kwa muda mrefu*, he likes to talk for a long time. Prep.. ***long.e.a*** St. ***long.ek.a*** Cs. ***long.esh.a*** Ps. ***long.w.a*** Rp. ***long.an.a*** (cf *ongea, zungumza*)

longitudo n (n) longitude (Eng)
lori n (n) lorry (Eng)
lote adj, pron (form of *-ote* for ma- class singular nouns) all, the whole: *Shamba lake lote lina mikarafuu*, his whole farm has clove trees.
low.a vi see *rowa*. Prep. ***low.e.a*** St. ***low.ek.a*** Cs. ***low.esh.a*** Rp. ***low.an.a***
lowan.a vi be drenched, be wet, be waterlogged, be saturated. Prep. ***lowan.i.a*** St. ***lowan.ik.a*** Cs. ***lowan.ish.a***
lowanish.a vt drench, wet: *Amezilowanisha nguo zake*, he has wetted his clothes. Prep. ***lowanish.i.a*** St. ***lowanish.ik.a*** Ps. ***lowanish.w.a***
lowe.a vt remain in a place; linger, tarry, stay, settle: *Mzee yule amelowea vijijini miaka yote*, that old person has remained in the villages for all the years. Prep. ***lowe.le.a*** St. ***lowe.k.a*** Cs. ***lowe.sh.a*** Ps. ***lowe.w.a*** (cf *selelea, bakia*)
lowek.a vt, vi 1. drench, soak, souse: *Loweka nguo*, soak clothes. 2. be nonplussed, be stunned. Prep. ***lowek.e.a*** St. ***lowek.ek.a*** Cs. ***lowek.esh.a*** Ps. ***lowek.w.a***
lozi n (n) (bot) almond: *Lozi ya kidani*, pendant. (Ar)
lubega n (n) see *rubega*
lufufu adj numerous, many, myriad, several, very many: *Kulikuwa na watazamaji lufufu uwanjani*, there were numerous spectators at the ground. (cf *maelfu, lukuki, jamii, kaumu*) (Ar)
lugha n (n) 1. language; *Lugha ngeni*, foreign language. *Lugha matusi*, abusive language. *Lugha unde*, artificial language, constructed language. *Lugha bora*, classical language. *Lugha jumuiya*, common language. *Lugha mitaa*, colloquial language. *Lugha mnasaba*. cognate language. *Lugha mata*, extinct language. *Lugha ambishi mchanganyo*, amalgamating language, inflected

language. *Lugha tenganishi*, analytic language, isolating language. *Lugha ambishi bainishi*, agglutinating language. *Lugha ambishi*, affixing language, inflectional language. *Lugha biashara*, trade language. *Lugha unganishi*, union language. *Lugha wenyeji*, vernacular language. *Lugha chasili*, source language. *Lugha ya kwanza*, first language. *Lugha ya pili*, second language. *Lugha asili*, indigenous language. *Lugha lengwa*, target language. *Lugha rasmi*, official language. *Lugha ya taifa*, national language. *Lugha mawasiliano*, linguafranca. *Lugha ambishi awali*, prefixing language. *Lugha bainishi*, classificatory language. *Lugha kizalia*, daughter language. *Lugha tamathali*, figurative language. *Lugha ghaibu*, endophasia. *Lugha muundo gubi*, polysynthetic language, incorporating language, incapsulating language. *Lugha azali*, parent language. *Lugha kienzo*, metal language. *Lugha ya kompyuta*, computer language. *Lugha ya kale*, dead language 2. parlance; style of writing or speaking: *Alitumia lugha mbaya katika gazeti*, he used bad language in the newspaper. (Ar)

luhudi *n* (*n*) (in Islam) a shallow narrow trench in a grave where a dead body is laid to rest; inside chamber of a grave. (cf *mji, mwanandani*) (Ar)

luja[1] *n* (*n*) thief, robber, stealer: *Yeye ni luja maarufu mtaani*, he is an infamous thief in the neighbourhood. (Ar)

luja[2] *n* (*n*) excessive contemplations, deep thought: meditation: *Yumo katika luja*, he is in deep thoughts.

luja[3] *n* (*n*) (*naut*) waves of the sea. (cf *wimbi*) (Ar)

lukuki *n* (*n*) a number so large so as to be uncountable; innumerable number; endless thousands: *Maadhimisho ya kupatikana uhuru nchini yalihudhuriwa na lukuki za watu*, the anniversary on the attainment of the country's independence was attended by endless thousands of people. (Ar)

lukuma *n* (*n*) bribery, corruption: *Mkurugenzi alifukuzwa kazini kutokana na makosa ya kupokea lukuma*, the director was sacked from work on receiving bribes. (cf *rushwa, hongo*) (Ar)

lulu *n* (*n*) pearl: *Bora kama lulu*, as beautiful as a pearl. (Ar)

lulumizi *n* nacre; mother-of-pearl.

lumb.a *vt* (usu used in Rp. form) speak against someone or for the purpose of quarelling; wrangle, squabble, quarrel. Prep. *lumb.i.a* St. *lumb.ik.a* Ps. *lumb.w.a* Rp. *lumb.an.a*

lumban.a *vt* wrangle, squabble , quarrel, argue, debate: *Wanachama walikuwa wakilumbana katika kikao*, the members were arguing bitterly whilst in session. Prep. *lumban.i.a* St. *lumban.ik.a* Cs. *lumban.ish.a* Ps. *lumban.w.a*

lumbwi *n* (*n*) 1. chameleon. 2. weathercock, turncoat; a fickle person, a changeable person: *Utaweza kuiamini kauli ya lumbwi yule?* Can you trust the word of that turncoat? (cf *kinyonga, kigeugeu*)

lundik.a (also *rundika*) *vi* pile up, heap up, accumulate Prep. *lundik.i.a* St. *lundik.ik.a* Cs. *lundik.ish.a* Ps. *lundik.w.a* Rp. *lundik.an.a*

lundo (also *rundo*) *n* (*n*) see *rundo*

lung.a *vt* follow behind, go behind, go after: *Mtoto mdogo alimlunga mama yake alipokuwa anakwenda dukani*, the small child followed his mother on her way to the shop. Prep. *lung.i.a* St. *lung.ik.a* Cs. *lung.ish.a* Ps. *lung.w.a* Rp. *lung.an.a*

lungo *n* (*n*) an old word for *ungo* meaning "a winnowing basket." (cf *peku*)

luserini *n* (*n*) (*bot*) lucerne; animal grass. (Eng)

lusu *n* (*n*) 1. thief, robber, stealer. (cf *mwizi*) 2. swindler, conman, cheater, deceiver, a crooked man. (Ar)

luteka *n* (*n*) military manoeuvres, military activities.

luteni *n* (*n*) lieutenant: *Luteni-kanali*, lieutenant colonel. *Luteni jenerali*, lieutenant general. *Luteni kamanda*, lieutenant commander. (Eng)

luteni-kanali *n* (*n*) see *luteni*

luva[1] *n* (*n*) louver: *Madirisha yote yametiwa luva*, all the windows are fitted with louvers. (Fr)

luva[2] *n* (*n*) venetian blind; a window blind consisting of a number of thin horizontal adjustable slats that overlap when closed.

luvea *n* (*n*) a big horn.

M

M, m /m/ 1. the thirteenth letter of the Swahili alphabet. 2. a voiced bilabial nasal.

maabadi *n* (*ma-*) a place of worship; a mosque, church, temple, etc. (Ar)

maabara *n* (*ma-*) laboratory: *Maabara ya lugha*, language laboratory. *Maabara ya kemia*, chemistry laboratory. (Ar)

maabudu *n* (*ma-*) 1. the one who deserves to be worshipped; Almighty God. 2. things to be worshipped. 3. the followers of a particular religion. (Ar)

maada *n* (*ma-*) substance, matter. (cf *manga*)

maadamu *conj* as long as, as, since: *Maadamu atahudhuria kikao chetu, tutaweza kuonana naye*, as long as he will attend our session, we can meet him. (Ar)

maadhimisho *n* (*ma-*) commemoration, celebration: *Yale yalikuwa maadhimisho ya kupatikana kwa uhuru nchini*, those were the celebrations on the attainment of the country's independence. (cf *sherehe*) (Ar)

maadhura *adj* 1 excused, exempted, absolved. 2 insane, lunatic.

maadili *n* (*ma-*) morals, ethics; righteous behaviour: *Ukifuata maadili haya, utakuwa mtu muungwana*, if you follow these moral principles, you will be a refined person. 2. moral teaching in stories, incidents, etc. *Unaweza kujifunza maadili mema pindi ukisikiliza hadithi za wahenga*, you can learn good morals if you listen to the stories of ancient people. (cf *mafunzo*) (Ar)

maafa *n* (*ma-*) 1. disaster, calamity: *Maafa makubwa yalitokea wakati meli ilipozama kwenye ziwa*, a great disaster occurred when the ship sank in the lake. (cf *ajali, msiba*) 2. bad omen, ill-luck, jinx, misfortune: *Alituletea maafa katika biashara yetu*, he brought misfortune in our business. (cf *nuhusi, kisirani*) (Ar)

maafikiano *n* (*ma-*) agreement, concord, consensus: *Maafikiano bado hayajapatikana kati yao*, no consensus has been reached between them. (cf *itifaki, mapatano, makubaliano*) (Ar)

maafuu *n* (*ma-*) a person deserved to be pardoned because of his condition as in the case of a deranged person; a mentally sick person; lunatic, maniac: (*prov*) *Maafuu hapatilizwi*, a person who is deficient of sth such as lack of sanity, deserves to be pardoned for any reprisal of his wrongdoing.

maagizo *n* (*ma-*) instructions, orders: *Maagizo rasmi*, standing orders.

maajabu *n* (*ma-*) wonders: *Maajabu ya dunia*, the wonders of the world. (cf *mastaajabu*)

maakulati *n* (*n*) foods

maakuli[1] (also *maakulati*) *n* (*ma-*) food, victuals. (cf *mlo, chakula*) (Ar)

maakuli[2] *adj* rational, reasonable, sensible: *Fikira yako ni maakuli*, your idea is rational. (Ar)

maalumu *adj* special, particular, certain: *Alitumia vifaa maalumu kufanyia kazi yangu*, he used special instruments to do my work. (cf *hasa, mahasusi, halisi*) (Ar)

maambukizi *m* (*ma-*) see *maambukizo*

maambukizo (also *maambukizi*) *n* (*ma-*) infection: *Nchi nzima iliathiriwa vibaya na maambukizo ya ugonjwa ule*, the whole country was badly affected by infection of that disease. *Maambukizo ya virusi*, virus infection.

maamkio (also *maamkizi*) *n* (*ma-*) greetings, salutations: *Maamkio yake yalipokewa kwa heshima kubwa*, his greetings were received with great respect.

maamkizi *n* (*ma-*) see *maamkio*

maamuma *n* (*ma-*) 1. (in Islam) a mere follower of *Imam*, i.e. a person

412

conducting prayers at a particular time (cf *mfuasi*) 2. a person without experience; apprentice. 3. blockhead fool, simpleton. 4. a person who follows things blindly. (Ar)

maamuzi *n* (*ma-*) decisions, deliberations: *Maamuzi yote ya mkutano wetu lazima yatekelezwe*, all the deliberations of our meeting must be implemented.

maana *n* (*ma-*) 1. meaning: *Maana ya kimsamiati*, lexical meaning. *Nieleze maana ya neno hili*, explain to me the meaning of this word. (cf *tafsiri*) 2. reason: *Alieleza maana ya kuchukua hatua zile dhidi ya wafanyakazi*, he explained the reasons for taking those steps against the workers. (cf *sababu, kisa*) 3. goal, purpose, objective, aim: *Maana ya mimi kuondoka hapa mapema ilikuwa ni kuliwahi gari la moshi*, the purpose of my early departure here was to catch the train. (cf *lengo, azma*) 4. respect, wisdom, usefulness, use: *Mtu yule hana maana*, that person is of no use. (*syn*) *Asiyejua maana haambiwi maana*, don't argue with a fool. (cf *akili, bongo*) (Ar)

maanani *n* (*ma-*) used in the expression; *Tia maanani*, take the matter seriously.

maandalio *n* (*ma-*) see *maandalizi*

maandalizi (also *maandalio*) *n* (*ma-*) 1. preparation of food: *Maandalizi ya chakula cha wageni yalifanyika vizuri*, the preparations of food for the guests went on smoothly. 2. preparations or arrangements for receiving a guest: *Maandalizi ya kumpokea rais yamekamilika*, the arrangements for receiving the president are complete. (cf *utayarishaji, matayarisho*)

maandamano *n* (*ma-*) procession, demonstration; protest march: *Maandamano ya hamasa*, protest march. *Maandamano ya wanafunzi yaliungwa mkono na watu wengi*, the students' protest march was supported by many people. *Maandamano ya wapanda farasi*, cavalcade.

maandiko *n* (*ma-*) see *maandishi*

maandishi (also *maandiko*) *n* (*ma-*) writing, handwriting: *Maandishi haya hayasomeki*, this handwriting is not legible. *Alipeleka maombi yake kwa maandishi*, he submitted a written application. (cf *hati*)

maanga[1] *adj* transparent, shining, radiant: *Maji maanga*, transparent water.

maanga[2] *n* (*ma-*) a hole or crack in a wall where a ray of light penetrates.

maangamizi *n* (*ma-*) destruction, ruin, annihilation: *Uchezaji wa kamari ulimletea maangamizi hatimaye*, gambling eventually led to his ruin (cf *nakama, maafa, balaa*)

maangamizo *n* (*ma-*) calamity, disaster, catastrophe, tragedy: *Ajali ya ndege ililleta maangamizo makubwa*, the plane crash was a great disaster.

maanguko *n* (*ma-*) waterfall (cf *maporomoko*)

maanish.a *vt* signify, mean, imply: *Hii inamaanisha kwamba lazima apewe onyo kali*, this means that he must be given a stern warning. Prep. **maanish.i.a** St. **maanish.ik.a**. Cs. **maanish.ish.a** Ps. **maanish.w.a** Rp. **maanish.an.a** (Ar)

maarasi[1] (also *marasi*) *n* (*ma-*) 1. water carrier's pole; yoke. (cf *mzega*) 2. a measure of two buckets usu carried on the shoulders by water carriers. (Ar)

maarasi[2] *n* (*ma-*) simpleton, imbecile, fool. (cf *mjinga, juha*)

maaribu *n* (*ma-*) see *maarubu*

maarifa *n* (*ma-*) 1. strategy, tactic, technique: *Maarifa unayoyatumia hayawezi kutatua mgogoro huu*, the strategies you are using cannot solve this dispute. (cf *mbinu*) 2. experience, know-how, knowledge: *Ana maarifa makubwa katika kazi yake*, he has a lot of experience in his work. (cf *ujuzi, hekima, uzoefu*) (Ar)

maarubu (also *maaribu*) *n* (*ma*-) 1. goal, objective, intention: *Maarubu ya sisi kwenda kule ni kutaka msaada*, the purpose of our trip there is to seek assistance. (cf *nia, madhumuni, azma, kusudio*) 2. intent; sth intended. (Ar)

maarufu *adj* famous, notable, eminent: *Yeye ni daktari maarufu*, he is a famous doctor. (cf *mashuhuri*) (Ar)

maarusi *n* (*ma*-) bridal couple. (Ar)

maasi *n* (*ma*-) revolt, rebellion, mutiny, uprising: *Maasi ya wanajeshi*, army mutiny. (cf *dhambi, uhalifu, uasi*) (Ar)

maasia *n* (*ma*-) sin: *Mungu husamehe maasia ya waja wake*, God forgives the sins of his beings. (cf *makosa, dhambi*)

maasumu *adj* (of prophets, etc.) faultless, guiltless, immaculate, impeccable: *Takriban mitume wote ni maasumu*, almost all the prophets are faultless. (Ar)

maawio *n* (*ma*-) east, sunrise. (cf *mashariki*)

Maazi *n* (*ma*-) (*astron*) Mars; a planet of the solar system which is fourth in distance from the sun. (Eng)

mabadilishano *n* (*ma*-) counterchange

mabaka *n* (*ma*-) spots, stains; *Ugonjwa wa mabaka ngozini*, hives, nettle rash; urticaria.

mabaki *n* (*ma*-) remains, residue: *Mabaki ya ndege iliyopata ajali*, the remains of the plane crash.

mabano *n* (*ma*-) bracket ( ), [ ]. (cf *parandise*)

mabavu *n* (*ma*-) brute, force; coercion: *Tumia mabavu*, use force. (*cf nguvu*)

mabaya *n* (*ma*-) evils; bad deeds: *Hutakiwi kufanya mabaya kwa wenzako*, you are not supposed to do evil to others.

mabishano *n* (*ma*-) argybargy, dispute, quarrel, arguments: *Alileta mabishano mengi kwenye mkutano*, he caused a lot of arguments at the meeting. (cf *masutano, ubishi*)

mabosti *n* (*ma*-) airs, graces, pomposity. (cf *mikogo, mashobo*)

mabruki *adj* blessed, tending to succeed: *Inshallah harusi yako itakuwa mabruki*, may your wedding be blessed with success. (Ar)

machachari[1] *n* (*ma*-) 1. restiveness, fidget, restlessness. 2. disobedience, naughtiness, recalcitrance: *Aliadhibiwa kwa kufanya machachari mengi darasani*, he was punished for being naughty in the class. (cf *utundu, utukutu*)

machachari[2] *n* (*ma*-) a restless person; a jumpy person; fidget: *Yeye ni machachari*, he is a fidget. (cf *makeke, ngumbaro*).

machachari[3] *adj* skilfull, adroit: *Yeye ni mchezaji machachari*, he is a skillful player (cf *stadi, hodari*)

machafuko *n* (*ma*-) disturbance, chaos, disorder; *Machafuko ya kisiasa*, political disturbances. (cf *vurugu, fujo, ghasia*)

machagu *n* (*ma*-) fussy eater, gourmet, epicure; a dainty person: *Sikumpenda mgeni yule kwa sababu yeye ni machagu*, I didn't like that guest because he is a fussy eater. (cf *kidomo, mnywanywa, mbeuzi*)

machakuro *n* (*ma*-) 1. rummaging. 2. the act of scraping with the feet as a fowl does or as a horse with its hoofs; scratching.

machapwi (also *machubwichubwi*) *n* (*ma*-) (*med*) mumps; an acute disease characterized by the swelling of the neck, usu affecting children. (cf *matubwitubwi, matukwi*)

machaza *n* (*ma*-) 1. cooked husked maize. 2. rice. (cf *wali*) 3. porridge (*uji*)

macheche[1] *n* (*ma*-) restlessness, restiveness, fidget, uneasiness: *Ukiwa na macheche, hutaweza kuifanya kazi yako vizuri*, if you are restless, you will not be able to do your work properly. (cf *machachari*) 2. (*colloq*) sharpness, skills, adroitness: *Mchezaji alionyesha macheche yake katika mechi*, the player displayed his skills in the match. (cf *makali*)

macheche² *n* (*ma-*) a restless person; a jumpy person; fidget. (cf *machachari, ngumbaro*)

machela (also *machera*) *n* (*ma-*) hammock, litter, sling; a stretcher for carrying a corpse or a wounded or a sick person. (cf *susu*)

macheleo *n* (*ma-*) east; a place where the sun rises. (cf *maawio*)

macheo *n* (*ma-*) dawn, sunrise.

machera *n* (*ma-*) see *machela*

macheuko *n* (*ma-*) eructation, belch, belching. (cf *makovyoko*)

machezo *n* (*ma-*) 1. enjoyable activities, joyful activities: *Yeye anapenda kujishughulisha na mambo ya machezo*, he likes to involve himself in enjoyable activities. 2. juggling, conjuring; magic trick: *Jirani yetu ni hodari katika machezo*, our neighbour is good at conjuration. (cf *mazingaombwe, kiinimacho*)

Machi *n* (*ma-*) March (Eng)

machicha *n* (*ma-*) dregs, sediments.

machinga *n* (*ma-*) (*colloq*) vendor

machinjioni *n* (*ma-*) 1. the sharp side of a knife; cutting-edge. 2. abbatoir; slaughter house.

machopochopo *n* (*ma-*) different types of curry food.

machorombozi *n* (*ma-*) a reward given by someone to a person who has found lost property: *Nilimpa machorombozi kwa kuniokotea pasipoti yangu*, I gave him a reward for finding my passport. (cf *kiokosi, utotole*)

machubwichubwi *n* (*ma-*) see *machapwi*

machugachuga *n* (*ma-*) 1. uneasiness, disorder, confusion of mind: *Mwanasiasa amekuwa katika hali ya machugachuga tangu kuachiliwa na polisi*, the politician has been in a state of uneasiness since being released by the police. (cf *machulechule, wahaka, wasiwasi*) 2. the thing that causes uneasiness.

machugachuga² *n* (*ma-*) (*med*) dry dermatitis; an infection or reaction in which the skin presents swelling, maculation, vesiculation and itching.

machunga *n* (*ma-*) care, preservation. (cf *matunzo*)

machungani *n* (*ma-*) grazing area, grazing ground; pasture, range: *Mchungaji anatoka machungani sasa hivi*, the shepherd is coming from the pasture shortly. (cf *malishoni*)

machungu *n* (*ma-*) 1. bitterness, animosity: *Mateso ya gerezani yalimzidisha kuwa na machungu dhidi ya serikali*, the persecution in prison increased his bitterness against the government. 2. pang; sharp pain, severe pain. 3. great remorse, severe grief.

machwa *n* (*ma-*) see *machweo*

machweo (also *machwa*) *n* (*ma-*) time when or place where the sun sets; sunset, west.

mada¹ *n* (*ma-*) 1. a long vowel found in Arabic script signalled by the mark. (~) to show proper pronunciation in a particular word and also to show semantic difference between two morphologically related words. 2. insistence on sth. (Ar)

mada² *n* (*ma-*) topic, subject: *Mada kuu*, main theme. *Mada nyeti*, sensitive topic. *Mada za siku*, topics of the day. *Mada ilijadiliwa kwa kina*, the subject was discussed in depth. (cf *maudhui*) (Ar)

madadi¹ (also *majadi*) *n* (*ma-*) fighting spirit; bravado: *Pandwa na madadi*, be inspired by a fighting spirit. *Shikwa na madadi*, be inspired by a fighting spirit. (Ar)

madadi² *n* (*ma-*) opium rolled into pellets, ready for smoking; rolled-up opium. (cf *afyuni, bangi*)

madadi³ *n* (*ma-*) assistance, help. (cf *msaada, auni*) (Ar)

madaha *n* (*ma-*) 1. pose, pomposity, airs and graces, elegance; fascinating

M

madakata ... **maelezo**

manners: *Binti yake hutembea kwa madaha*, her daughter walks with pomposity. (cf *madoido, mbwembwe, matao*) 2. good actions depicting good manners. (Hind)

madakata *n (ma-)* dry leaves which fall by themselves; fallen dry leaves.

madaraka *n (ma-)* responsibility, obligation, duty, authority: *Amepewa madaraka makubwa serikalini*, he has been given enormous responsibilities in the government. *Gatua madaraka*, decentralize. (Ar)

madawa *n (ma-)* pharmaceuticals: *Duka la madawa*, pharmacy. (Ar)

madende *n (ma-)* (of voice) hoarseness: *Sauti ya madende*, hoarse voice.

madhabahu[1] *n (ma-)* 1. a place of sacrifice to avert evil; a place for making an offering of a sacrifice; the place of oblation. 2. abattoir; slaughtering house. (cf *machinjioni*) (Ar)

madhabahu[2] *n (ma-)* (in Christianity) altar. (cf *altare*)

madhali *conj* as long as, as, since: *Madhali yeye hajaja kufanya kazi leo, siwezi kumlipa pesa zote*, since he has not come to work today, I can't pay him all the money. (cf *maadamu*) (Ar)

madhara *n (ma-)* harm, damage: *Uvutaji sigara huleta madhara kwa binadamu*, cigarette smoking is harmful to human beings. (cf *uharibifu*)

madhehebi *n (ma-)* respect, good manners: *Omba madhehebi*, ask for apology.

madhehebu *n (ma-)* 1. religious sect; denomination: *Kuna madhehebu mbalimbali katika dini ya Kiislamu*, there are different religious sects in Islam. 2. the followers of a religious leader. 3. creeds, tenets. 4. style of doing sth.

madhii *n (ma-)* pre-ejaculatory secretion, prostatic secretion. (Ar)

madhila *n (ma-)* wretchedness, hardship, illtreatment, suffering: *Mwanamke aliweza kustahamili madhila ya mumewe*, the woman managed to bear the illtreatment from her husband. (cf *mateso, taabu*) (Ar)

madhubuti *adj* firm, reliable, strong: *Kuta za nyumba hii ni madhubuti*, the walls of this house are strong. (cf *imara, jadidi, thabiti*) (Ar)

madhumuni *n (ma-)* purpose, objective, aim: *Madhumuni ya mkutano ule ni kujadili suala la usalama nchini*, the purpose of that meeting is to discuss the question of security in the country. (cf *nia, lengo, kusudio, shabaha*) (Ar)

madigadi *n (ma-)* mudguard, fender. (Eng)

madini *n (ma-)* metal, mineral: *Madini ya zirikoni*, zircon. (Ar)

madobini *n (ma-)* a place where clothes are washed; laundry. (cf *fuo*)

madoido *n (ma-)* embellishments; frills: *Anapenda kutia madoido katika kanzu zake*, she likes to put frills on her dresses. (cf *madaha*)

madrasa *n (ma-)* Koranic school. (Ar)

maduhuli *n (ma-)* income, revenue: *Biashara yake inampatia maduhuli mazuri*, his business gives him a good income. (cf *pato*) (Ar)

maegea *n (ma-)* (*bot*) long reeds which grow in the water. (cf *mafunjo*)

maegesho[1] *n (ma-)* parking place; car park.

maegesho[2] *n (ma-)* (*naut*) mooring; the act of holding a ship to the shore by cables, chains or anchors.

maelekezo *n (ma-)* instructions, directions, guidance: *Maelekezo yako yanatatanisha*, your directions are confusing. (cf *mafunzo, mafundisho*)

maelewano *n (ma-)* consensus, agreement, understanding: *Kulikuwa hakuna maelewano kati ya pande hizi mbili*, there was no understanding between these two groups. (cf *mafahamiano*)

maelezo *n (ma-)* explanation, description, statement: *Maelezo ya polisi*, police statement. (cf *ufafanuzi, tafsiri*)

maelfu *n* (*ma-*) thousands: *Maelfu ya watu*, thousands of people.

maendeleo *n* (*ma-*) development, progress: *Maendeleo ya mjini*, urban development. *Maendeleo ya vijijini*, rural development. *Maendeleo ya jamii*, community development. *Taaluma ya maendeleo*, development studies. *Maendeleo endelevu*, continous progress. (cf *mafanikio*)

maezi (also *melezi*) *n* (*ma-*) (*naut*) roadsted, anchorage; a place to anchor.

mafa *n* (*ma-*) 1. see *mava*. 2. (*idm*) *Ingia mafa*, inherit the property or children of a deceased brother.

mafamba *n* (*ma-*) 1. gimmick, deception, ploy; underhand dealings: *Mnunuzi alimfanyia mafamba mwonye duka*, the buyer employed deception against the shopkeeper. (cf *udanganyifu, hila*) 2. disorganized affairs; disorganized activities; things done chaotically/haphazardly.

mafanikio *n* (*ma-*) success, triumph, achievement: *Mafanikio ya wazi*, éclat; brilliant or conspicuous success. *Tumepata mafanikio makubwa katika sekta ya kilimo*, we have achieved great success in the agricultural sector.

mafao *n* (*ma-*) benefits: *Mafao ya ulemavu*, invalidity benefits. *Mafao ya uzazi*, maternity benefits, *Mafao ya uzeeni*, old-age benefits.

mafasa *n* (*ma-*) (*zool*) a kind of big thick snake, which spits poison; huge spitting snake.

maficho *n* (*ma-*) covert; a thicket or woodland.

mafindofindo *n* (*ma-*) (*med*) tonsillitis; inflammation of tonsils.

mafu *n* (*ma-*) used in the expression: *Maji mafu*, neap tide.

mafua *n* (*ma-*) flu, cold: *Ana mafua*, he has a cold. *Mafua ya ndege*, bird flu.

mafunde *n* (*ma-*) see *mavunde*

mafundisho *n* (*ma-*) 1. doctrine, teachings: *Mafundisho ya Karl Marx*, Karl Marx teachings; Marxism. 2. instructions, lessons. (cf *mafunzo, maelekezo*)

mafungianyama *n* (*ma-*) the time when the cattle and other animals return from grazing and are locked in a kraal.

mafunjo *n* (*ma-*) (*bot*) reeds such as those found by the sides of lakes or in marshes. (cf *maegea*)

mafunzo *n* (*ma-*) training, instruction: *Mafunzo kazini*, inservice training, *Mafunzo ya kijeshi*, military training; drill.

mafuriko *n* (*ma-*) floods: *Mafuriko yale yaligharikisha roho za watu wengi*, the floods claimed the lives of many people. *Mafuriko ya maji*, deluge.

mafurungu *n* (*ma*) 1. warm socks. 2. ankle bells.

mafusho *n* (*ma-*) fumigants, burning incense: *Mgonjwa alifukizwa mafusho*, the patient was treated with incense burning.

mafuta *n* (*ma-*) 1. oil: *Mafuta ya nazi*, coconut oil. *Mafuta ya uto*, simsim oil. *Mafuta ya kitani*, linseed oil. *Mafuta ya mbarika*, castor oil. *Mafuta ya kupikia*, cooking oil. *Mafuta ya dizeli*, diesel oil. *Mafuta ya taa*, kerosene. *Mafuta ya petroli*, petrol. *Mafuta yasiyosafishwa*, crude oil. 2. grease, fat, lard, adipose tissue. (cf *shahamu*) 3. fuel.

mafutu[1] *n* (*ma-*) anger, bitterness, ill-temper: *Ana mafutu sana*, he has a lot of angry. (cf *hasira, uchungu*)

mafutu[2] *n* (*ma-*) the back of a knife, etc.

mafyega *n* (*ma-*) (*med*) elephantiasis (cf *matege*)

mafyongo *n* (*ma-*) 1. wrong direction. 2. zigzag; oblique line. (cf *mshadhari*)

magadi *n* (*ma-*) 1. local baking soda. 2. (*geol*) natron

magamaga *adv* astraddle, astride: *Kwenda magamaga*, walk with the legs wide apart. (cf *matagataga, mataga*)

magamgamu *n* (*ma-*) accumulation of ideas or thoughts at one time.

maganga (also *chanja maji*) n (ma-) (zool) featherstar; a free-swimming crimoid related to the sea lilies having a small disc-like body, long feathery arms for feeding and movement, and short appendages for grasping the surface.

maganga

magangao (also *magaogao*) n (ma-) ruins, relics, antiquity; the remains of a building. (cf *mahame, magofu*)

magendo¹ n (ma-) 1. blackmarket, smuggling: *Biashara ya magendo*, smuggling. *Mali ya magendo*, smuggled property. 2. bribery, corruption. (cf *rushwa, ufisadi*)

magendo² n (ma-) 1. cohabitation; the act of a man or woman living together with his opposite partner without legally getting married. 2. (idm) *Mtoto wa magendo*, a child born on the wrong side of the blanket. (cf *uhawara*)

mageuzi n (ma-) change, transformation, reform: *Mageuzi ya kikatiba*, constitutional reforms. *Kipindi cha mageuzi*, transformation period. (cf *mabadiliko*)

mageuzo n (ma-) change, transformation: *Mageuzo ya nyuklia*, nuclear transformation.

maghani n (ma-) biographical story.

magharibi n (ma-) 1. west. 2. time of sunset. (cf *machweo*) 3. the time when Muslims go for evening prayers. (Ar)

maghufira n (ma-) forgiveness from Almighty God: *Muumini aliomba maghufira kwa Mwenyezi Mungu*, the faithful asked for forgiveness from God. (cf *msamaha*) (Ar)

maghusubu n (ma-) property taken by force; seized property.

magigimo n (ma-) boastfulness, bravado, bragging, gasconade; the act of boasting or showing strength, etc.: *Magigimo yake hayafai kitu*, his bravado is useless.

magobi n (ma-) (bot) sword beans. *Canvalia ensiformis*.

magongo n (ma-) crutches, stilts: *Mpira wa magongo*, hockey.

magonjwa n (ma-) diseases: *Magonjwa ya mlipuko*, epidemic.

magoti n (ma-) knees: *Piga magoti*, kneel down.

magowe n (ma-) light clouds.

magube n (ma-) deception, subterfuge, trick: *Magube yao yaliwatia hatarini*, their subterfuges put them at risk. (cf *ulaghai, hila, ujanja*)

mahaba n (ma-) romance, love: *Ana mahaba makubwa kwa mkewe*, he has a lot of love for his wife. (cf *mapenzi*) (Ar)

mahabubu n (ma-) darling, sweetheart, beloved: *Kifo cha mahabubu wake kilimtia majonzi makubwa*, the death of his beloved wife filled him with profound grief. (cf *mpenzi*) (Ar)

mahabusi (also *mahabusu*) n (ma-) 1. remand prison. 2. a detainee or a prisoner awaiting trial; remand prisoner. 3. prisoner. (Ar)

mahabusu n (ma-) see *mahabusi*

mahadhi n (ma-) rhythm, tune, melody: *Nimeyapenda mahadhi ya wimbo ule*, I like the tune of that song. (cf *tyuni*)

mahafali n (ma-) 1. convocation, assembly; graduation ceremony, etc.: *Wanafunzi* *wengi walitunukiwa shahada katika mahafala ya mwaka huu*, many students were awarded degrees in this year's graduation. 2. short ceremonies or celebrations. (Ar)

mahakama *n (ma-)* court of law: *Mahakama kuu*, high court. *Mahakama ya rufani*, the court of appeal. *Mahakama ya mwanzo*, primary court. *Mahakama ya madai*, civil court. *Mahakama ya kijeshi*, military court. (cf *korti*) (Ar)

mahala *n (ma-)* see *mahali*

mahali (also *mahala, pahala, pahali*) *n (ma-)* 1. place, location, area: *Mahali hapa*, this place. *Mahali pabaya*, a bad place. *Kila mahali*, every place. 2. space, room. *Hakuna mahali pa kusimama*, there is no space to stand. 3. instead of, in place of: *Mahali pa kukaa kimya, wewe unaropokwa*, instead of keeping quiet, you are prattling. (Ar)

mahame *n (ma-)* a deserted place: *Vita vya wenyewe kwa wenyewe vimeifanya sehemu ile kuwa mahame*, the civil war has left that place deserted. (cf *tongo, kihame, ganjo*)

mahameli *n (ma-)* see *bahameli*

maharagwe (also *maharage*) *n (ma-)* (*bot*) French beans, kidney beans, Haricot beans. (cf *mandondo*)

maharazi *n (ma-)* a shoemaker's awl. (Ar)

mahari *n (ma-)* dowry; marriage settlement: *Mahari baada ya kutolewa, binti akaolewa*, after the dowry was offered, the girl got married. (Ar)

maharimu *n (ma-)* consanguine; a person whom you cannot marry or be married to because of the close relationship by blood, etc.: *Yeye hawezi kumwoa mtu yule kwa vile ni maharimu wake*, he cannot marry that person because he is related to him by blood. (Ar)

mahati *n (ma-)* 1. a carpenter's gauge for making lines. 2. a cord used to mark lines; marking cord. (Ar)

mahazamu *n (ma-)* girdle; a man's sash for supporting the waist. (cf *masombo*) (Ar)

mahepe[1] *n (ma-)* a kind of traditional dance played by night wizards.

mahepe[2] *n (ma-)* infrequent minor diseases. (cf *mahoka*)

mahepe[3] *n (ma-)* Newcastle disease, Fowl Pest; an acute viral disease of poultry and other birds, characterised by pneumonia and encephalomyelitis.

mahiri[1] *n (ma-)* an intelligent person; a wise person; a skilful person: *Seremala yule ni mahiri*, that carpenter is a skilful person. (Ar)

mahiri[2] *adj* clever, intelligent, skilful: *Mwanamuziki mahiri*, a skilful musician. (Ar)

mahitaji *n (ma-)* needs, necessities, requirements: *Hawezi kuyakidhi mahitaji ya mkewe*, he cannot meet his wife's needs. (cf *matakwa, matilaba*) (Ar)

mahojiano *n (ma-)* interview: *Waziri alifanya mahojiano na waandishi wa habari*, the minister held an interview with the press. (cf *mazungumzo*) (Ar)

mahoka[1] (also *masoka*) *n (ma-)* frenzy; delirium: *Alijitia mahoka*, he behaved like a half-wit.

mahoka[2] *n (ma-)* a kind of evil spirit.

mahonyo *adj* gratis, free: *Mali ya mahonyo*, free property; property given free.

mahsai *n (ma-)* see *maksai*

mahsusi *adj* see *mahususi*

mahubiri *n (ma-)* preaching, sermon, homily, pulpitry. (cf *mawaidha*)

mahuluki *n (ma-)* see *mahuluku*

mahuluku (also *mahuluki*) *n (ma-)* human being: *Kila mahuluku ana dosari zake*, every human being has his weaknesses. (cf *kiumbe*) (Ar)

mahuluti *adj* mixed, hybrid, crossbreed: *Serikali ya mahuluti*, coalition government. (Ar)

mahusiano *n* (*ma-*) relationship: *Taratibu za mahusiano*, etiquette. (cf *uhusiano, mashirikiano*)

mahususi (also *mahasusi*) *adj* particular, special, specific: *Alipewa kazi mahususi idarani*, he was given specific work in the department. (cf *hasa, maalumu*) (Ar)

mahututi *adj* critically ill, serious: *Mgonjwa alikuwa mahututi*, the patient was critically ill. *Hospitali ya wagonjwa mahututi*, hospice. (Ar)

maige *n* (*ma-*) (*zool*) young locust (cf *kimatu, tunutu*)

maikrofoni *n* (*n*) microphone (Eng)

maikroskopu *n* (*n*) microscope (Eng)

maili *n* (*n*) mile: *Maili kijiografia*, nautical mile. *Hapa ni maili kumi kutoka mjini*, here it is ten miles from town. (Eng)

maingiliano *n* (*ma-*) 1. intrusion, interruption, interference: *Kumetokea maingiliano ya simu leo*, there has been telephone interruptions today. 2. interaction: *Lazima pawepo maingiliano fulani kati ya mwalimu na wanafunzi*, there must be some interaction between a teacher and the students.

maisha¹ *n* (*ma-*) 1. period of living; life: *Aliishi maisha marefu*, she lived a long life. (cf *muda*) 2. living; mode of life: *Maisha yake yalikuwa ya anasa tupu*, his life was full of luxuries. 3. duration, permanence, lasting: *Kisu hiki hakina maisha*, this knife cannot last long. (Ar)

maisha² *adv* always, constantly, continually: *Maisha, mtu huyu anaumwa*, always, this person is sick.

maiti *n* (*ma-*) corpse; dead body: *Chumba cha maiti*, mortuary. *Sanduku la maiti*, coffin. *Zimwi la maiti*, ghoul. (*prov*) *Maiti haulizwi sanda*, a corpse does not choose a shroud, i.e. a person who is in difficulties has no freedom of choosing how he should be assisted. (cf *mfu, kimba, mzoga*) (Ar)

maiz.i *vt, vi* realize, comprehend, understand: *Nilipoona kwamba kengele ya shule haikulia, nilimaizi kwamba imeharibika*, when I found that the school bell did not ring, I realized that it was out of order. Prep. **maiz.i.a** St. **maiz.ik.a** Cs. **maiz.ish.a** Ps. **maiz.w.a** Rp. **maiz.an.a** (cf *jua, ng'amua, tambua*) (Ar)

majaaliwa *n* (*ma-*) see *majaliwa*

majadi *n* (*ma-*) see *madadi¹*

majadiliano *n* (*ma-*) discussion, debate: *Kulikuwa na majadiliano makali kwenye chumba cha mkutano*, there was a heated debate in the conference room.

majaka¹ *adv* disorderly, haphazardly: *Soma majaka*, read without following the rules; read haphazardly.

majaka² *n* (*ma-*) (bot)

majaliwa (also *majaaliwa*) *n* (*ma-*) 1. endowment, destiny; God's will: *Haya yote ni majaliwa ya Mwenyezi Mungu*, all this is all God's will. 2. fate: *Majaliwa yake hayajulikani*, his fate is unknown. (cf *takdiri, kudra*) (Ar)

majaribu *n* (*ma-*) 1. temptations: *Tutahadhari na majaribu ya dunia*, we should be careful with the temptations of the world. (cf *mitihani, vishawishi*) 2. trial; hardship, suffering, etc. that tries one's endurance as a test of his faith in religion: *Yale yalikuwa majaribu ya Mola*, those were God's trials. (cf *mitihani*)

majazi¹ *n*(*ma-*) 1. God's reward. 2. a nickname given to a person with respect to his behaviour.

majazi² *n* (*ma-*) (*lit*) synecdoche; a figure of speech in which a part is used for a whole, an individual for a class, a material for a thing, or the reverse of any of these (e.g. *mkate*; 'bread', for *chakula* 'food'; *jeshi*; 'army' for *mwanajeshi*, 'soldier'; *shaba-nyekundu*, 'copper', for peni, 'penny').

majeruhi (also *majuruhi*) n (*ma-*) casualty, injured person: *Majeruhi katika ajali ya ndege walikuwa wengi*, the casualties in the plane crash were many. (Ar)

maji n (*ma-*) water: *Maji kujaa*, high tide. *Maji kupwa*, low tide. *Maji mafu*, neap tide. *Maji magotini*, knee-deep water. *Maji kwapani*, breast-deep water. *Maji ya matunda*, fruit juice. *Maji ya zabibu*, *Maji ya kunde*, brown skinned. *Maji ya chumvi*, salt water. *Maji matamu*, fresh water. (*prov*) *Maji ukiyavulia nguo yaoge*, if you decide to undress yourself to swim, then do swim i.e. If you have decided to start doing sth, then complete it. (Ar)

majibizano n (*ma*) verbal confrontations; arguments: *Kufanya majibizano na mzee wako si jambo zuri*, to carry out arguments with your parent is not good. (cf *malumbano*)

majificho[1] n (*ma-*) camouflage, disguise.

majificho[2] n (*ma-*) hiding place; hide-out.

majigambo n (*ma-*) 1. pomposity, show off, ostentation. (cf *majisifu*) 2. braggart, show off; a person who shows off.

majikwezo n (*ma-*) superiority complex.

majili n (*ma-*) (*naut*) hanging room in a vessel.

majilio n (*ma-*) 1. Advent; the period including the four Sundays just before Christmas. 2. arrival, coming: *Majilio ya watalii*, the arrival of the tourists. (*ufujio*)

majilipo n (*ma-*) revenge, retaliation, reprisal.

majilisi (also *majlisi*) n (*ma-*) council, assembly: *Majilisi tashrii*, legislative council. (cf *bunge*) *Majilisi tanfidhi*, executive council. (cf *baraza*, *halmashauri*) (Ar)

majimaji[1] n (*ma-*) (in soccer, etc.) long cross pass.

majimaji[2] adj watery, liquid, fluid

majimaji[3] n (*n*) anything that flows like water.

majimoto n (*wa-*) (*zool*) a kind of small reddish brown ant with its abdomen having blackish bands, which makes its nests on trees by folding leaves and binding them with silk material. *Oecophylla iongonoda*. (cf *mdudumoto*, *chaki*, *koyokoyo*)

majinato n (*ma-*) arrogance, vanity, pride: *Yeye ni mtu mwenye majinato sana*, she is a person of great arrogance. (cf *majivuno*, *kiburi*)

majinuni (also *majununi*) n (*ma-*) 1. madman; maniac, lunatic: *Tahadhari na majinuni yule*, be careful of that mad man. (cf *mwehu*, *afkani*) 2. a very funny person; joker, buffon, jester. 3. simpleton, fool. (cf *fala*, *juha*) (Ar)

majira n (*ma-*) 1. season, period, time: *Majira jua*, solar time. *Majira ya mvua*, rainy season. *Majira ya joto*, hot season. 2. (of a watch) keeping time: *Saa imepotea majira*, the watch is not giving correct time. *Kutia saa majira*, to adjust a watch.

majisifu[1] n (*ma-*) boasting, brag, airs and graces, show-off, pride: *Mazungumzo yake yalijaa majisifu*, her talk was full of boastful remarks. (cf *majivuno*)

majisifu[2] n (*ma-*) a braggart; a boastful person: *Yeye ni majisifu*, he is a braggart. (cf *majigambo*)

majivuno n (*ma-*) pride, conceit, arrogance: *Ukionyesha majivuno mengi*, *watu hawatakupenda*, if you are too arrogant, people will not like you. (cf *ubora*, *maringo*, *taraghani*, *kiburi*)

majojo n (*ma-*) many big problems: *Hana raha kwa vile amezongwa na majojo*, he is not happy because he is faced with big problems. (cf *songombingo*)

majonzi n (*ma-*) grief, distress; deep sorrow: *Ana majonzi makubwa tangu kufiwa na mwanawe*, she is in profound grief since her child's death. (cf *masikitiko*, *huzuni*, *simanzi*, *jitimai*)

majungu n (*ma-*) conspiracy, machination, plot: *Mtu yule anapenda kuwapikia majungu wenzake*, that person likes to hatch plots against others. (cf *njama*, *mizengwe*)

majuni *n* (*n*) 1. opium made from Indian hemp, sugar and other ingredients. (cf *afyuni*) 2. medicine. (cf *dawa*)

majununi *n* (*ma-*) see *majinuni*

majusi *n* (*ma-*) 1. astrologer. (cf *mnajimu*) 2. people who worship fire, animals, etc.

majuto *n* (*ma-*) regret, remorse, repentance: *Kitendo chake kiovu kilimletea majuto*, his evil deed brought him regret. (*prov*) *Majuto ni mjukuu, mwisho huja kinyume*, regrets come after someone has done sth wrong. (cf *nadama*)

mak.a *vi* be nonplussed, be astounded, be dumbfounded, be astonished: *Alimaka aliposikia kwamba mdogo wake amekamatwa*, he was dumbfounded when he heard that his younger brother had been arrested. Prep. *mak.i.a* St. *mak.ik.a* Cs. *mak.ish.a* Ps. *mak.w.a* Rp. of Prep. *mak.i.an.a* (cf *duwaa, staajabu, shangaa*)

makaa *n* (*ma-*) 1. charcoal, embers: *Makaa ya mawe*, coal. 2. fuel.

makabidhiano *n* (*ma-*) handing over; bestowal: *Makabidhiano ya madaraka kati ya rais-mteule na yule wa zamani yalienda vizuri*, the handing-over of responsibilities between the president-elect and his predecessor went on smoothly.

makaburi *n* (*ma-*) cemetery, graveyard. (cf *maziara*)

makadara *n* (*ma-*) power esp of God; divine will: *Yote yaliyotokea ni makadara ya Mwenyezi Mungu*, all that happened is due to divine will. (cf *makadura, kudura*) (Ar)

makadirio *n* (*ma-*) estimates: *Waziri aliwasilisha bungeni makadirio ya matumizi ya wizara yake*, the minister presented the estimates for his ministry's expenditure to parliament. *Makadirio ya fedha*, budget. (cf *makisio, bajeti*) (Ar)

makala *n* (*ma-*) article in print in a newspaper, etc.; written article; paper for presentation in a conference, etc.: *Niliipenda makala yako katika gazeti*, I liked your article in the newspaper. (cf *maandishi*) (Ar)

makali *n* (*ma-*) 1. (of a knife, sword, etc.) cutting edge, sharp edge: *Kisu chako hakina makali*, your knife is not sharp. 2. hardships: *Makali ya maisha*, the hardships of life (cf *ukali*). 3. sharpness, adroitness: *Mchezaji alionyesha makali yake katika mechi ya kujipima nguvu*, the (cf *cheche, ukali*)

makalio *n* (*ma-*) buttocks, rump, behind.

makame *n* (*ma-*) see *mkamadume*

makamo *n* (*ma-*) 1. age: *Yeye ni mtu wa makamo yangu*, he is a person of my age. 2. used in the expression: *Mtu wa makamo*, a middle-aged person; mature age.

makamu *n* (*ma-*) deputy, vice: *Makamu wa rais*, vice president. *Makamu mwenyekiti*, vice chairman.

makani *n* (*ma-*) 1. a sitting place for talking, relaxation, etc; recreational place. 2. residence. (cf *maskani*)

makanika *n* (*ma-*) mechanic (cf *fundibomba*) (Eng)

makao *n* (*ma-*) 1. residence, dwelling-place: *Makao yake yako kijijini*, his residence is in the village. 2. a place for co-ordinating the day to day activities of a party, club, etc.; quarters: *Makao makuu ya chama tawala*, the headquarters of the ruling party.

makapi *n* (*ma-*) 1. dregs, sediment. (cf *mashata, mapepe*) 2. grain husk, cereal husk. (cf *mapute*)

makaroni *n* (*ma-*) macaroni; a variety of pasta in the shape of narrow tubes or in various other shapes, often baked with cheese, ground meat, etc. (Gr)

makasi *n* (*ma-*) see *mkasi*

makataa[1] (also *mkataa*) *n* (*ma-*) 1. agreement for payment of the wholesale work done; contract: *Kazi ya makataa*, work done on wholesale basis; contractual work. 2. final decision.

makataa[2] *adj* final; in a fixed way: *Uamuzi wangu ni makataa*, my decision is final.

makavazi *n (ma-)* 1. educational collection and displaying area. 2. archives; the place where historical documents or records are kept.

makaya *n(ma-)* (zool) acorn barnacle; a mostly conical shell fish which lives along the shore on rock surfaces mangrove trunks including on other hard subtrates.

makazi *n (ma-)* 1. residence, dwelling-place (cf *maskani*) 2. way of living: *Mtu yule hana makazi mazuri*, that person does not live a good life.

makeke *n (ma-)* 1. jumpiness, hastiness: *Makeke yake yanaweza kuiharibu kazi yako*, his hastiness can spoil your work. (cf *papara, machachari, vishindo*) 2. a restless person, a jumpy person; fidget: *Wewe ni makeke*, you are a fidget. (cf *machachari*)

makemeo *n (ma-)* harangue, tirade; a long, blustering, noisy, or scolding utterances usu. to sby.

maki *n (ma-)* thickness, width, breadth: *Kitanda hiki maki yake ni futi nne*, the width of this bed is four feet. (cf *unene, kivimbe*) (Ar)

makini[1] *n (ma-)* 1. attention, concentration: *Alinisikiliza kwa makini*, he listened to me attentively. (cf *kituo*) 2. calmness, coolness, serenity: *Sifa ya makini ni kitu adimu*, calmness is a rare quality. (cf *utulivu*) (Ar)

makini[2] *adj* calm, cool: *Yeye ni mtu makini*, he is a calm person. (Ar)

makinik.a *vi* be stable, be calm: *Amemakinika katika kazi yake*, he is stable in his work. Prep. **makinik.i.a** St. **makinik.ik.a** Cs. **makinik.ish.a** (cf *tabaradi, stakiri, poa, tua*) (Ar)

makiri *n (ma-)* 1. (*naut*) transverse spar or crosspiece for belaying the forestay. 2. cleat for fastening rope in general. (Ar)

makisio *n (ma-)* 1. estimates: *Makisio ya matumizi ya serikali yameongezeka mwaka huu*, the estimates for government expenditure have increased this year. (cf *makadirio*) 2. guess, speculation, estimation: *Makisio yetu ni kwamba watu wengi watafika harusini leo*, our estimation is that many people will come to the wedding today. (Ar)

makiwa[1] *n (ma-)* an expletive used as a kind of salutation when visitng sby's house in order to convey condolences to him because of the big misfortune he has undergone such as the death of a relative

makiwa[2] *n (ma-)* orphan: *Amekuwa makiwa tangu alipofika umri wa miaka sita*, he has been an orphan since he was six years old. (cf *yatima*)

makojozi *n (ma-)* (*bot*) a kind of thick soft plantain usu cooked by frying.

makomba *n (ma-)* millet porridge mixed with malt for brewing.

makombo *n (ma-)* 1. leftover food from the previous meal; leftovers. 2. second-hand thing; anything that remains after it has been used: *Amekuwa akivaa makombo ya ndugu yake*, he has been wearing his brother's second-hand clothes.

makopa *n (ma-)* dried cassava or bananas or potatoes.

makorokoro *n (ma-)* lumber, junk, jumble. (cf *magorogoro*)

makosi[1] *n (ma-)* (*naut*) rowlock (cf *kishwara, kileti*)

makosi[2] *n (ma-)* lines or marks drawn by a soothsayer on his divining board.

makri *n (ma-)* gimmick, intrigue, conspiracy: *Kwa nini unaambatana na mtu wa makri kama yeye?* Why do you associate yourself with a person of intrigues like him. (cf *hila*) (Ar)

maksai (also *makasai*) *n (ma-)* (*zool*) a castrated male of the cattle family; steer, bullock. (Ar)

maksi *n (n)* examination mark: *Alipata maksi nyingi kwenye fizikia*, he scored many marks in physics. (Eng)

maktaba *n (n)* 1. library. 2. a house, room, used for keeping books. 3. a collection of many books. (Ar)

maktabu n (n) military court. (Ar)
makubadhi n (ma-) a kind of leather sandal with ornamentation worn between the toes and usu used by Muslims while going for prayers, etc. (Ar)

makubadhi

makubaliano n (ma-) agreement, pact, consensus: *Makubaliano yamepatikana kati ya pande zile mbili zinazopingana*, agreement has been reached between those two conflicting parties. (cf *maafikiano, maelewano*)
makubwa n (ma-) 1. airs and graces, ostentation, show-off: *Mtu yule anapenda makubwa*, that person likes to give a show-off. (cf *makuu*) 2. serious matters or issues.
makucha n (ma-) 1. sharpness, skill: *Mchezaji aliweza kuonyesha makucha yake katika kipindi cha pili*,the player was able to exhibit his skills in the second half (cf *macheche, ukali, makali, ukali*). 2. brutality and oppression exercised by a country's leader. 3. big and sharp claws: *Makucha ya simba*, the lion's claws of this kind.
makulaji n (ma-) (colloq) food
makumbi n (ma-) see *kumbi*
makumbusho[1] n (ma-) museum: *Makumbusho ya Taifa*, National Museum. (cf *makavazi*)
makumbusho[2] n (ma-) commemoration
makumi n (ma-) tens
makungu n (ma-) anything done to strengthen traditional customs/ rituals.
makunjubo n (ma-) pandemonium, chaos, disorder: *Usilete makunjubo hapa dukani*, don't cause disorder here in the shop. (cf *fujo, ghasia*)

makupepe n (ma-) see *mapepe*[3]
makurubundi (also *makurubunji*) n (ma-) violent pressure exerted by someone to achieve sth; tantrum.
makurubunji n (n) see *makurubundi*
makuruhu n(n) disgust, abhorrence, dislike: *Kutema mate ovyoovyo ni makuruhu*, spitting here and there is disgusting. (cf *adha, maudhi, karaha*) (Ar)
makusudi[1] n (ma-) collections: *Makusanyo ya kodi*, collections of taxes.
makusudi[1] n (ma-) intention, goal, purpose: *Makusudi yake yalikuwa kuharibu mipango yetu*, his intention was to wreck our plans. (cf *madhumuni, lengo, azima*) (Ar)
makusudi[2] adv deliberately, purposely, intentionally: *Alimpiga nduguye makusudi*, he beat his brother intentionally. (Ar)
makutano n (ma-) meeting point.
makuu n (ma-) airs and graces, ostentation; high living. (prov) *Mtaka makuu hayamwachi*, he who wants high life, eventually collapses.
makuzi n (ma-) upbringing: *Mzazi ana jukumu kubwa katika makuzi ya mtoto wake*. a parent has great responsibility in the upbringing of his child. (cf *malezi*)
makwa[1] n (ma-) 1. (naut) notch or hole cut in the top of an upright post to carry a crosspiece; nock. 2. a piece of timber put in the bottom of a vessel, to prevent the cargo getting wet from the bilge.
makwa[2] n (ma-) (anat) groin (cf *mago*)
makwao n (ma-) their homes; their places: *Walikwenda makwao*,they went to their homes.
makwenu n (ma-) your homes; your places.
makwetu n (ma) our homes;our places.
malago n (ma-) camp, residence.
malai n (ma-) 1 milk cream. 2 ice-cream. (cf *aiskrimu*) (Hind)
malaika[1] n (ma-) 1. angel: *Malaika wa*

424

motoni, angel of hell. *Malaika mkuu*, archangel. 2. innocent baby. (cf *mtoto mchanga*) (Ar)

malaika² *n* (*ma-*) pl of *laika* fur; body hair. (Ar)

malaji *n* (*ma-*) diet, food, edibles. (cf *chakula*)

malalamiko *n* (*ma-*) jeremiad, complaint, lament.

malale *n* (*ma-*) (*med*) trypanosomiasis; sleeping sickness.

malalo *n* (*ma-*) place of lodging; sleeping-place.

malambo *n* (*ma-*) pl of *lambo*

malaria *n* (*ma-*) (*med*) malaria (Eng)

malau *n* (*ma-*) inquiry into an offence; court case. (cf *daawa*)

malaya *n* (*ma-*) 1. a male or female who is sexually promiscuous. 2. prostitute, whore, harlot. (cf *kahaba, asherati*)

malazi *n* (*ma-*) 1. bedding, bed clothes, 2. dwelling place, sleeping quarters: *Malazi yake hayako mbali na hapa*, his place of residence is not far from here.

malele (also *marere*) *n* (*ma-*) (*bot*) orchella weed; lichens growing on trees in mangrove formations and coastal vegetation, used as a dye. *Rocella tinctoria*.

maleleji *n* (*ma-*) 1. the period of calm or changing winds in East Africa between the monsoons and the rains (roughly between April and November) but a great deal of local variation occurs e.g. Tumbatu island having *maleleji* (also) in June. 2. shifting light winds during a calm.

malenga *n* (*ma-*) 1. professional singer. 2. an eminent poet; bard.

maleti *n* (*n*) mallet (Eng)

malezi *n* (*ma-*) upbringing, guidance, rearing: *Amepata malezi mazuri*, he has received a good upbringing. (cf *makuzi, ulezi, mafundisho*)

malhamu *n* (*ma-*) balm; a kind of ointment. (Ar)

mali *n* (*ma-*) 1. property: *Mali ya pamoja*, communal property. *Mali asili*, natural resources. *Nyumba hii ni mali yangu*. this house is my property. 2. wealth, riches: *Ana mali nyingi*, he has a lot of wealth. (*prov*) *Mali bila daftari hupotea bila habari*, money that is not accounted in books disappears i.e. a person who has no proper plans of keeping his money will find that his wealth ultimately disappears. (cf *milki, ukwasi*) (Ar)

maliasili *n* (*ma-*) see *mali*

malidadi¹ *n* (*ma-*) see *maridadi¹*

malidadi² *adj* see *maridadi²*

malighafi *n* (*n*) raw materials

maliki¹ *n* (*ma-*) (in Islam) Master (Ar)

maliki² *n* (*ma-*) see *malkia*

malikia *n* (*ma-*) see *malkia*

malimati *n* (*ma-*) a dead body's alms given on the first ten days of the third month of Swahili Calendar i.e. after the month of Ramadan. (Ar)

malimwengu *n* (*ma-*) wordly affairs; *Kushiriki kwake katika malimwengu kulimletea uharibifu mkubwa*, his involvement in worldly affairs brought him ruin.

malindi *n* (*ma-*) (*bot*) a kind of long banana that is green even when ripe.

malipo *n* (*ma-*) 1. reward or retribution from God: *Hayo ni malipo kutoka kwa Mwenyezi Mungu kwa sababu ya vitendo vyake viovu*, that is divine retribution because of his misdeeds. 2. payment: *Malipo ya mwanzo*, token payment. *Malipo yalioahirishwa*, deferred payment.

malisho *n* (*ma-*) 1. act of looking after cattle, goats, sheep, etc. in grazing; grazing, pasturage. 2. fodder; food esp hay or straw for animals such as cows and horses.

malishoni *n* (*ma-*) pasture, range; grazing area. (cf *machungani*)

maliwato *n* (*ma-*) bathroom, lavatory,

M

washroom, toilet. (cf *chooni, msalani*)

maliwazo *n* (*ma-*) words of comfort or condolence esp to one who has undergone a misfortune.

maliz.a *vt, vi* end, complete, finish. Prep. ***maliz.i.a*** complete for (at, etc.) e.g. *Aliimalizia kazi nyumbani kwake*, he completed the work from home. St ***maliz.ik.a***, be finished, be ended e.g. *Nyumba yangu bado haijamalizika*, my house is not yet finished. Ps. ***maliz.w.a***, be completed. Rp. ***maliz.an.a*** (cf *kamilisha, hitimisha, timiza*)

malizik.a *vt* see *maliza*

malkia (also *maliki, malikia*) *n* (*ma*) 1. queen. 2. female ruler. (cf *mtawala*) (Ar)

malulu *n* (*ma-*) (*bot*) Crow-feet grass. *Eleusine indica*.

malumbano *n* (*ma-*) verbal exchange, verbal confrontation: *Malumbano ya kisiasa*, political verbal confrontations.

maluuni *n* (*ma-*) an evil person; a devilish person. a cursed person. (cf *firauni, afriti*) (Ar)

mama *n* (*ma-*) mother: *Mama mkubwa*, mother's elder sister. *Mama mdogo*, mother's younger sister. *Mama wa kambo*, step-mother. *Mama mkwe*, mother-in-law.

mamajusi *n* (*n*) (*Bible*) Magi: the wise men from the East who came to do homage to the infant Jesus.

mamani.a *vt* insist, persist, be firm: *Wanafunzi walimamania waongezewe posho*, the students insisted that their allowances be increased. Prep. ***mamani.li.a*** St. ***mamani.k.a*** Cs. ***mamani.sh.a*** Ps. ***mamani.w.a*** Rp. ***mamani.an.a*** (cf *ng'ang'ania*)

mamantilie *n* (*n*) a woman who sells food at a kiosk.

mamanu.a *vt* force apart; open sth that is fixed or fastened; force open, separate: *Alizimamanua tende na kisha akazila*, he separated the dates and then ate them. Prep. ***mamanu.li.a*** St. ***mamanu.k.a*** Cs. ***mamanu.sh.a*** Ps. of Prep. ***mamanu.liw.a*** Rp. of Prep. ***mamanu.an.a*** (cf *tenganisha*)

mamba[1] *n* (*ma-*) (*zool*) crocodile, alligator. (cf *ngwena*)

mamba

mamba[2] *n* (*ma-*) (*zool*) a kind of poisonous African tree snake; black mamba. *Dendroaspis polylepis*.

mamba[3] *n* (*ma-*) (*zool*) scales of fish.

mambeta *n* (*ma-*) bran of rice, husks of rice; chaff of rice. (cf *makapi, mapepe*)

mambo[1] *n* (*ma-*) peg; a short piece of wood, metal, etc. inserted into the ground to mark a position, etc. (cf *kigingi*)

mambo[2] *n* (*ma-*) 1. affairs, matters, things: *Mambo ya kale*, antiquities. 2. (in greetings) *Mambo!* hi!

mamboleo *adj* neo-; new, different or modified way: *Ukoloni mamboleo*, neo-colonialism.

mamia[1] *n* (*ma-*) hundreds (Ar)

mamia[2] *adj* hundreds (Ar)

mami.a[3] *vi* 1. sob; weep aloud with a catch or break in the voice and short gasping breaths: *Watoto wa marehemu walikuwa wakimamia kwenye mazishi*, the children of the deceased were sobbing at the funeral. 2. interrupt an issue forcefully: *Alimamia kwenye mazungumzo ya watu*, he interrupted other people's conversation forcefully. Prep. ***mami.li.a*** St. ***mami.k.a*** Cs. ***mami.sh.a*** Ps. ***mami.w.a*** Rp. ***mami.an.a***

mamlaka *n* (*ma-*) 1. authority, mandate, jurisdiction: *Mamlaka ya mapato*, revenue authority. *Mamlaka halali*, lawful authority. *Hana mamlaka juu yetu sisi*, he has no authority over us. 2 nation, rule, dynasty. (cf *dola, enzi*) (Ar)

mamluki *n* (*ma-*) mercenary, lackey: *Mamluki wa kisiasa*, political mercenaries. (cf *mlowezi*) (Ar)

mamoja[1] *adv* all the same, all one: *Akija asije, kwetu ni mamoja*, whether he comes or not, it is all the same to us.

mamoja[2] *n* (*ma-*) unit, digit.

manamba *n* (*ma-*) big plantation workers, who are known by their number and not by names.

manane *adv* used in the phrase: *Usiku wa manane*, in the dead of night.

manani *n* (*ma-*) one of the attributes of God; the Beneficient. (Ar)

manati *n* (*ma-*) catapult, slingshot. (cf *teo, fyata, panda, kombeo*) (Ar)

manawa *n* (*ma-*) (*med*) a kind of skin disease in which there is a loss of pigment resulting in white patches; vitiligo. (cf *barasi*)

manazili *n* (*ma-*) with reference to astrology; in consultation with astrology: *Ndoa yake ilifanyika kwa manazili*, his marriage was conducted in consultation with astrology.

manda *n* (*n*) a kind of small oval bread made from maize flour. (cf *mkate wa gae*)

mandakozi *n* (*ma-*) a kind of a cage made from a log, used to imprison two or more slaves around their necks when they did manual work; slave yoke.

mandalina *n* (*n*) mandoline; a kind of musical instrument with four or five pairs of strings and a rounded back. (cf *tashkota*) (Eng)

mandalina

mandari *n* (*ma-*) jaunt, picnic, outing: *Enda mandari*, go for a picnic. (cf *pikniki*) (Hind)

mandhari *n* (*ma-*) scenery, view, landscape, setting; *Mandhari mbele*, foreground. *Mandhari nyuma*, background, *Nyumba yake ina mandhari nzuri*, his house has a good view. (Ar)

mando *n* (*ma-*) (*zool*) ape's bottom. (cf *ngoko*)

mandoji (also *mapunye*) *n* (*ma-*) (*med*) ringworm of the scalp; herpes tonsurans; tibia capitis; porrigo furfurans; a fungus infection caused by species of *Microsporum* or *Trichophyton*.

mandondo *n* (*mu-*) (*bot*) French beans, kidney beans, Haricot beans. (cf *maharagwe*)

manemane (also *manimani*) *n* (*ma-*) (*bot*) myrrh; a kind of fragrant bitter-tasting gum resin used as medicine.

manena *n* (*ma-*) (*anat*) groin; the hollow or fold where the abdomen joins either thigh

maneva[1] *n* (*ma-*) military manoeuvres. (cf *luteka*) (Eng)

maneva[2] *n* (*ma-*) practice exercises done by local dancers outside the town. (Eng)

Manga *n* (*ma-*) (*geog*) the region of Arabia esp Oman.

mangamang.a *vi* loiter, idle: *Kwa nini unamangamanga badala ya kufanya kazi?* Why are you loitering instead of working? Prep. **mangamang.i.a** St. **mangamang.ik.a** Cs. **mangamang.ish.a** (cf *zubaazubaa*)

mang'amung'amu *n* (*ma-*) confusion of mind: *Usingizi wa mang'amung'amu*, restless sleep.

manganja *n* (*ma-*) 1. rattle dance. 2. small rattles or bells worn on the legs of the dancers.

mangati *n* (*ma-*) mirage. (cf *mazigazi, sarabi*)

427

M

mangazibwe n (*ma-*) illusion, dream. (cf *ndoto*)
mangi n (*ma-*) a chief or ruler of the *Chaga* tribe in Tanzania.
mangili n (*ma-*) (*naut*) a kind of crosspiece or cat-head, used for securing a cable, anchor or rope at the bow of a dhow.
mangimeza n(*ma-*) bureaucrat
mangiriti n (*ma-*) subterfuge, tricks, gimmicks, intrigues: *Mtu yule ana mangiriti mengi*, that person is very deceptive. (cf *magube, hila*)
mangisi n (*ma-*) (*zool*) a kind of fowl with very long legs and a featherless neck; ruffled feathered fowl. (cf *kidimu, kinyanyavu*)
mango[1] n (*ma-*) a hard black stone usu rounded, used for pounding, smoothening, etc.
mango[2] n (*ma-*) solid: amorphous solid
mangrini n (*ma-*) (*naut*) a knot tied in a rope or cable of a vessel's anchor.
mangumburi n (*ma-*) dither, jittery, fidget, jumpiness, restlessness: *Mtu yule ana mangumburi kidogo*, that person is rather fidgety. (cf *machachari, matata*)
mangungumbao n (*ma-*) commotion, chaos, pandemonium: *Usinileetee mangungumbao hapa*, don't cause chaos here. (cf *fujo, ghasia*)
mani[1] n (*ma-*) a weight of about three pounds.
mani[2] n (*ma-*) (*poet*) grass
manifesto n (*n*) manifesto: *Manifesto ya chama tawala*, the manifesto of the ruling party. (Eng)
manii n(*ma-*) semen, sperm. (cf *shahawa*) (Ar)
manimani n (*ma-*) see *manemane*
manispaa n (*n*) municipality, municipal council. (Eng)
manja n (*n*) (*zool*) yellow white-eye; an East African bird (family *Zosteropidae*) with a variable plumage. *Zosterops senegalensis.*

manjali n (*ma-*) (*naut*) one of the ropes of a front sail.
manjalili n (*ma-*) a kind of local brew made from the sprouts of maize or bulrush millet. (cf *mapuya*)
manjanika n (*ma-*) (*naut*) davit, winch, crane, derrick. (cf *winchi*)
manjano n (*ma-*) 1. yellow colour. 2. turmeric.
manju n (*ma-*) an expert in composing songs in traditional dance or epic poems; maestro. (cf *malenga*)
manowari (also *manuwari*) n (*n*) main of war; battleship: *Manowari sindikizi*, frigate. *Msafara wa manowari ndogo*, flotilla. (Eng)
mansuli n (*ma-*) a kind of woollen material, used for dresses and as a bedspread. (Ar)
mantiki n (*n*) logic: *Hakuna mantiki katika hoja yake*, there is no logic in his argument. *Sio na mantiki*, illogical.
manufaa n (*ma-*) 1. benefit, use: *Kitu kile hakina manufaa kwangu*, that thing is of no use to me. (cf *faida*) 2. used in the phrase: *Kwa manufaa ya umma*, in the public interest. e.g. *Mkurugenzi alistaafishwa kwa manufaa ya umma*, the director was retired in the public interest. (Ar)
manukato n (*ma-*) perfume; anything with a sweet scent. (cf *uturi*)
manukuu n (*ma-*) 1. quotes; the words or passages quoted. 2. transcription. (cf *unukuzi*)
manung'uniko n (*ma-*) complaints, grumbles: *Manung'uniko ya wafanyikazi lazima yashughulikiwe*, the workers' complaints must be attended to. (cf *malalamiko*)
manunuzi n (*ma-*) purchases: *Manunuzi ya vitu muhimu*, purchases of essential items.
manuwari n (*n*) see *manowari*
manyago n (*ma-*) a kind of local dance

428

played during circumcision rites. (cf *unjuguu*)
manyanga *n* (*ma-*) rattle (cf *cherewa*)
manyezi *n* (*ma-*) tardiness
manyata *n* (*ma-*) a collection of houses usu built with dung; make-shift settlement/village.
manyoya *n* (*ma-*) feathers: *Manyoya ya kondoo*, fleece.
manyunyu *n* (*ma-*) light rain, shower; drizzle. (cf *rasharasha, mawaga*)
manza *n* (*ma-*) 1. crime, offence, litigation: *Kowa manza*, be litigated. 2. trouble, dispute, conflict. (cf *matatizo*)
manzili[1] *n* (*ma-*) residence, house. (Ar)
manzili[2] *n* (*ma-*) status, position. (cf *cheo, hadhi*) (Ar)
maokozi *n* (*ma-*) salvation, rescue (cf *uokoaji*)
maombezi *n* (*ma-*) supplication, plea, prayer. (cf *uombezi*)
maombi *n* (*ma-*) 1. request, petition: *Maombi yake ya kutaka nyongeza ya mshahara yamekataliwa*, his request for an increase in pay has been turned down. 2. invocation; supplication; a formal plea for God's assistance. (cf *dua*)
maombolezi *n* (*ma-*) see *maombolezo*
maombolezo (also *maombolezi*) *n* (*ma-*): *Maombolezo ya watu waliokufa kwenye tetemeko la ardhi*, the mourning of the people who died in the earthquake. 1. lamentations, mourning, dirge. 2. detailed prayer for sth.
maonevu *n* (*ma-*) bullying illtreatment, maltreatment (cf *uonevu, mateso, udhalilishaji*)
maongezi *n* (*ma-*) talk, conversation: *Maongezi yake yanachangamsha*, his conversation is entertaining. (cf *mazungumzo*)
maongozi *n* (*ma-*) instructions of ethics.
maoni *n* (*ma-*) comments, views, feelings, sentiments: *Kuna mantiki katika maoni yake*, there is logic in his arguments. (cf *ushauri, mawazo, fikira*)

maono *n* (*ma-*) vision, image. (cf *taswira*)
maonyo *n* (*ma-*) warnings (cf *makatazo, tahadhari*)
maotea *n* (*ma-*) (*bot*) volunteer; a plant growing from the seed that has fallen naturally to the ground, not planted by man. (cf *tarare, mbulia*)
mapadri *n* (*ma-*) clergy
maovu *n* (*ma-*) evils, misdeeds. (cf *mabaya*)
mapambano *n* (*ma-*) confrontation, battle, combat: *Mapambano ya mikuki mirefu kwa kutumia farasi*, joust. (cf *mashindano, harakati, vita*)
mapambazuko *n* (*ma-*) dawn. (cf *macheo, asubuhi*)
mapana[1] *n* (*ma-*) width, breadth. (*idm*) *kwa mapana na marefu*, in all aspects, in full.
mapana[2] *n* (*ma-*) freedom to do sth; latitude.
mapatano *n* (*ma-*) agreement, treaty: *Mapatano yetu sasa yamevunjika*, our agreement is now broken. (cf *makubaliano, mwafaka, ahadi, maafikiano*)
mapatilizano *n* (*ma-*) verbal exchanges: quarrel. (cf *malumbano*)
mapatilizo *n* (*ma-*) retribution from God within this world: *Hayo labda ni mapatilizo kutoka kwa Mwenyezi Mungu*, that is probably divine retribution. 2. disgrace from wrong doing.
mapato *n* (*ma-*) income, revenue, return: *Kodi ya mapato*, income tax. *Mapato ya taifa*, national income. *Mapato yake ni madogo*, his income is meagre. (cf *maduhuli*)
mapema *adv* 1. early, soon. 2. dawn, early morning. (cf *alfajiri*)
mapendano *n* (*ma-*) mutual love; endearment, affection. (cf *mapenzi, mahaba*)
mapenzi *n* (*ma-*) love, affection: *Hana mapenzi na mumewe*, she has no love for her husband. (cf *mahaba*)

mapepe¹ n (ma-) restlessness, fidget, uneasiness: *Usilete mapepe unapofanya kazi*, don't be restless when you work. (cf *machachari, mangumburi*)

mapepe² n (ma-) fidget; a restless person, a jumpy person: *Yeye ni mapepe*, he is a fidget. (cf *machachari, ngumbaro*)

mapepe³ n (ma-) grain husks damaged by the wind. (cf *makupepe*)

mapepeta n (ma-) bran, chaff, husk; outer covering of grain separated from the flour by sifting. (cf *kumvi, makapi*)

mapigano n (ma-) fight, fighting, battle: *Mapigano ya barabarani*, street fighting. *Mapigano ya karibu*, infighting. (cf *kondo, vita, ugomvi*)

mapiku¹ n (ma-) a kind of card game played by winning the trick at cards.

mapiku² n (ma-) gimmicks, deceptions. (cf *magube*)

mapindi n (ma-) coiling walk as a snake does; spirally twisting: *Nyoka alipiga mapindi*, the snake coiled itself up.

mapinduzi n (ma-) revolution: *Mapinduzi ya viwanda*, industrial revolution. *Serikali ya mapinduzi*, revolutionary government. *Baraza la mapinduzi*, revolutionary council. *Mapinduzi ya kijani*, green revolution. (cf *thaura*)

mapishi n (ma-) cuisine, cooking, cookery. (prov) *Mchele mmoja mapishi mbalimbali*, the rice grains may be the same but their way of cooking can be different i.e. everyone has his own ingenuity to make things.

mapisi n (ma-) (arch) history (cf *historia*)

mapiswa n (ma-) 1. prattle, babble; idle talk (cf *mapayo*) 2. the condition of losing one's senses; unconsciousness.

mapitio n (ma-) review of a book, etc.

mapito n (ma-) 1. traces left by a person or animal; footsteps of a person or an animal. 2 phases; different stages of anything until it is completed.

mapochopocho n (ma-) delicacies; kinds of delicious and fatty foods: *Nilikula mapochopocho harusini*, I ate various delicacies at the wedding.

mapokeo¹ n (ma-) tradition, custom: *Sarufi ya mapokeo*, traditional grammar.

mapokeo² (also *mapokezi*) n (ma-) reception room; room for receiving guests.

mapokeo³ n (ma-) welcoming of a guest, etc.; receiving of a guest, etc.

mapokezi¹ n (ma-) see *mapokeo²*

mapokezi² n (ma-) reception, welcome; the act (method, etc.) of receiving a guest, etc.: *Rais alipata mapokezi makubwa*, the president received a rousing welcome. (cf *makaribisho*)

maponea (also *maponya*) n (ma-) subsistence food.

maponya n (ma-) saviour

maponyo n (ma-) 1. rescue, cure, salvation. 2. medicine, drugs. (cf *dawa*)

mapopa n (ma-) recovery, convalescence, improvement. (cf *hujambo, nafuu, ahueni*)

maporomoko n (ma-) 1 cascade, falls, cataract, waterfalls. 2 collapse of buildings. *Maporomoko ya udongo*, soil flow; the slow movement of soil down a hill side or slope. *Maporomoko ya ardhi*, land slide; the rapid flow of a mass of loosened rocks or earth down a hill or slope.

mapozi n (ma-) pose, pomposity, airs, swaggering: *Hutembea kwa mapozi*, he walks with a swagger. (cf *maringo*)

mapumziko n (ma-) 1. rest period; break, recess, interval. 2. waiting room; rest place; lounge.

mapungufu n (ma-) defects, shortcomings, weaknesses: *Kuna mapungufu kadha katika utekelezaji wa sera ya ubinafsishaji*, there are certain shortcomings in the implementation of the policy of privatization.

mapunjo n (ma-) cuts, reductions:

Mapunjo katika mishahara ya wafanyakazi, cuts in the salary of works.
mapunye *n* (*ma-*) see *mandoji*
mapukupuku *n* (*ma-*) drops of rain that settle on the leaves of the trees and fell the branches when shaken.
mapurende *n* (*ma-*) epaulette; a shoulder ornament for certain uniforms particulalry military ones. (cf *maburende*)

mapurende

mapute *n* (*ma-*) bran, chaff, husk. (cf *makapi*)
mapuuza¹ *n* (*ma-*) a neglectful person. (cf *mbezi*)
mapuuza² *n* (*ma-*) negligence, remissness, laxity. (cf *bezo*)
mapuya *n* (*ma-*) local brew made from the sprouts of maize, bulrush millet, etc.; grain husk brew. (cf *manjililī*)
mapwa *adj* used in the expression: *Maji mapwa*, low tide water.
mara¹ *n* (*ma-*) time, times, turn, occasion; *Mara mbili*, twice. *Mara moja*, once. (Ar)
mara² *adv* then, suddenly, immediately, at once: *Nilikuwa nikimtafuta lakini mara akatokea*, I was looking for him but suddenly, he appeared. (cf *hapo hapo, ghafla*) (Ar)
maradhi *n* (*ma-*) disease: *Maradhi ya sukari*, diabetes. *Maradhi ya kupasuka vibofu vya mkojo*, the rupture of the urinary bladder. *Maradhi ya miripuko*, epidemic diseases. (cf *uwele, ugonjwa*) (Ar)
maradufu *n* (*ma-*) see *mardufu*
maraha *n* (*ma-*) excessive luxuries.

marahaba *interj* 1. a common rejoinder to the greeting of a person of a subordinate position, younger person, etc. who greets, *shikamoo*. 2. an expletive of approval, appreciation, etc.; exactly! (cf *sadakta*) 3. an expletive used to welcome a guest.
maramba *n* (*ma-*) minute particles of wood formed in sawing wood; sawdust.
marara *adj* spotted: *Simba marara*, a spotted lion.
mararuraru *n* (*ma-*) rags, tatters, shreds.
marashi *n* (*ma-*) 1. liquid perfume. 2. rose water. (Ar)
marasi *n* (*ma-*) see *maarasi¹*
marathoni *n* (*ma-*) (sports) marathon (Eng)
mardudi *adj* rejected, refuted: *Zawadi mardudi*, a rejected present. (Ar)
mardufu¹ (also *maradufu*) *n* (*ma-*) double, twofold: *Yeye ni mkubwa mardufu kuliko mimi*, she is twice older than me. (Ar)
mardufu² *n* (*ma-*) a kind of American calico, usu used to make a sail; sail cloth. (Ar)
marefu *n* (*ma-*) length
marehemu (also *marhumu*) *n* (*ma-*) the deceased, the late: *Marehemu Seif Mohamed Seif*, the late Seif Mohamed Seif. (cf *hayati*) (Ar)
marejea *n* (*ma-*) sunn hemp.
marejeo¹ *n* (*ma-*) 1. return. (*prov*) *Mwenda omo na tezi, marejeo ni ngamani*, one may go anywhere he likes to go but eventually he will return to his place of origin as long as he is alive.
marejeo² *n* (*ma-*) (in writing) references, bibliography. (cf *mapitio*)
Marekani¹ *n* (*n*) (*geog*) United States of America
marekani² *n* (*n*) a kind of plain calico cloth.
marekebisho *n* (*ma-*) adjustment, rectifications, amendments.
marenda *n* (*ma-*) see *marenderenda*

431

marendarenda (*also marenda*) *n* (*ma-*) watery substance such as watery stools, etc.; mucus.
marfaa *n* (*ma-*) see *marufaa*
marhamu *n* (*ma-*) see *malhamu*
maridadi[1] *adj* 1. dandy, smart; nicely dressed: *Kijana maridadi yule amewavutia wasichana wengi,* that dandy young man has attracted many girls. 2. impressive, attractive: *Maonyesho yalikuwa maridadi,* the show was impressive. (Pers)
maridadi[2] (*also umaridadi*) *n* (*ma-*) neatness, toppishness, smartness. (cf *ulimbwende, usafi*) (Pers)
maridhawa *adj* 1. sufficient, adequate: *Chakula kilikuwa maridhawa harusini,* the food was sufficient at the wedding. 2. (of a person) contented, gratified: *Yeye ni mtu maridhawa,* he is a contented person. (Ar)
maridhia *adj* compliant, obedient, loyal: *Mtu maridhia yule hana usumbufu kwa watu,* that obedient person is not a bother to people. (Ar)
maridhiano *n* (*ma-*) agreement, pact, detente, reconciliation: *Tume ya maridhiano,* a commission of reconciliation. (cf *maafikiano, maelewano*)
maridhio *n* (*ma-*) satisfaction (Ar)
marigedi *n* (*ma-*) a large copper cooking pot.
marijani *n* (*ma-*) 1. a red coral. 2. a kind of bead like the seeds of a plant obtained from a shoal. (Ar)
marikebu *n* (*ma-*) see *merikebu*
Marikhi *n* (*n*) (*astron*) Mars; a planet of the solar system, fourth in distance from the sun, notable for its red colour.
marimba *n* (*ma-*) 1. a kind of local xylophone; vibraphone. (cf *chondo*) 2. a stringed gourded musical instrument

marimba

marinda *n* (*ma-*) frill, fringe: *Tia marinda,* frill.
maringo *n* (*ma-*) 1. air, graces, showing off, pomposity, pose. (cf *matao, majisifu*) 2. swagger, hauteur, boastfulness
marisau (*also marisawa*) *n* (*ma-*) a small ball of metal made to be fired from a gun; pellet.
marisawa *n* (*ma-*) see *marisau*
markebu *n* (*ma-*) see *merikebu*
marmar *n* (*ma-*) see *marumaru*
maro *n* (*ma-*) 1. mob action of beating someone. 2. mob action of hunting a few people in order to beat them. (cf *kipapai, kitutu*) (Guj)
maropozi *n* (*ma-*) payment outside one's agreement
marshi *adv* fast, hurriedly, quickly: *Alikuja marshi,* he came hurriedly. (cf *haraka, upesi*) (Ar)
marudi *n* (*ma-*) 1. punishment, correction. 2. caution.
marudio[1] *n* (*ma-*) frequency: *Marudio asilia,* natural frequency. *Marudio limbikivu,* cumulative frequency. *Marudio ya chini,* low frequency. *Marudio ya juu,* high frequency
marudio[2] *n* (*ma-*) 1. repetition; *Mwanafunzi alipewa marudio katika somo lenyewe kwa vile hakufaulu,* the student repeated the course because he did not pass it. 2. return: *Katibu Mkuu alisimamia marudio ya kura za maoni,* the secretary general supervised the return of the referendum.

maruerue *n* (*ma-*) hallucination (cf *mang'amung'amu*)

marufaa (also *marfaa*) *n* (*ma-*) book rest, book stand; lectern. (Ar)

marufuku[1] *adj* prohibited, forbidden: *Amepigwa marufuku kuingia nchini*, he is non grata i.e. he is forbidden to enter the country. (Ar)

marufuku[2] *n*(*ma-*) prohibition, forbiddance, interdiction.

marugurugu *n* (*ma-*) (*med*) an inflammation of rash on the body caused by scratching oneself after being bitten by an insect; hives, nettle rash, uticaria. (cf *marimbe*)

marumaru (also *marmar*) *n* (*ma-*) marble, stone. (Ar)

marumvirumvi (also *marubwirubwi*) *n* (*ma-*) (*med*) small swellings erupted after someone has been stung by an insect such as a caterpillar, hairy leaves, etc; rash, nettle rash, uticaria.

marupurupu *n* (*ma-*) fringe benefits; allowances: *Anapata marupurupu mengi katika kazi yake mpya*, he gets many fringe benefits in his new job.

masa[1] *n* (*ma-*) evil, wickedness, vice. (cf *maovu, uovu*)

masa[2] *n* (*ma-*) court case; trial. (cf *kesi*)

masaala *n* (*ma-*) issues, problems: *Masaala yale lazima yazingatiwe*, those issues must be examined. (cf *kadhia, mambo*) (Ar)

masafa *n* (*ma-*) 1. distance: *Mwanariadha alikimbia masafa marefu*, the athlete ran a long distance. (cf *umbali*) 2. radio waves: *Masafa ya kati*, medium wave. *Masafa mafupi*, short wave. (Ar)

masahihisho *n*(*ma-*) see *sahihisho*

masaibu *n* (*ma-*) hardships, tribulations, afflictions; the trials of life: *Marehemu alipata masaibu mengi maishani mwake*, the deceased faced many hardships in his lifetime. (cf *maafa, misiba*) (Ar)

masakasaka *n* (*ma-*) 1. a combination of drugs for the sake of harming; poisonous medicinal mixture. 2. any dirt or impurities that harm.

masala *n* (*ma-*) (*bot*) masala; ground mixture of spices used in local cooking for food like pilaf. (cf *jira*) (Hind)

masalala *interj* see *masalale*

masalale (also *masalala*) *interj* an expletive of wonder; Good gracious! Good heavens! My God!

masalkheri *interj* see *msalkheri*

masalo *n* (*ma-*) 1. thick sauce. 2. overipe crushed tomatoes.

masango *n* (*ma-*) thick ornamental brass used for making rings, anklets, etc.

masao *n* (*ma-*) leftovers, remains, residue: *Paka alikula masao ya chakula chetu cha mchana*, the cat ate the remains of our lunch. (cf *mabaki, masalio*)

masazo *n* (*ma-*) leftovers, remains. (cf *masalio, mabaki*)

masengenyo *n* (*ma-*) backbiting (cf *bughudha*)

mashairi *n* (*ma-*) verse, poems: *Mashairi hafifu*, doggerel

mashaka *n* (*ma-*) difficulty, hardships, distress. (cf *udhia, kero, taabu, shida*) (Ar)

mashallah *interj* an expletive used to express wonder over sth that is exceptionally good, etc.; Good heavens! God forbid! (Ar)

mashambizo *n* (*ma-*) the clothes with which a dead body is washed with; corpse's washing clothes.

mashambulizi *n* (*ma-*) see *shambulizi*

mashamshamu *n* (*ma-*) worry, uneasiness, anxiety, excitement. (cf *wasiwasi, wahaka*) (Ar)

mashapo *n* (*ma-*) lees, dregs, sediment; the particles of solid matter that settle down at the bottom in a liquid: *Yale ni mashapo ya mafuta katika ile chupa*, those are the dregs of the oil in the bottle. (cf *mashudu, masira*)

mashariki *n* (*ma-*) east: *Mashariki ya Kati*, Middle East. (Ar)

mashata *n* (*ma-*) 1. the remains of solid matter that settle at the bottom after oil, etc. has been skimmed off or filtered; dregs, lees. 2. the remains of any liquid: *Haya ni mashata ya asali*, these are the remains of honey. 3. thick gravy; thick curry.

mashavu *n (ma-)* jowl; dewlap of cattle and other animals or gills of a fish or wattle of a fowl. (cf *shambwelele*)

mashendea *n (ma-)* gruel cooked rice; soggy cooked rice: watery cooked rice: *Mgonjwa alikula mashendea*, the patient ate gruel cooked rice. (cf *ushendea, mashaza, ubwabwa*)

mashiko *n (ma-)* grip, hold, control: *Neno lile jipya sasa limepata mashiko*, that new word has now taken roots.

mashilio *n (ma-)* necessities of life.

mashindano *n (ma-)* competition, race, contest, match; *Mashindano ya wazi*, open competition. *Mashindano ya biashara*, business competition. *Mashindano ya urembo*, beauty contest. *Mashindano ya mbio za farasi*, horse race. (cf *mapambano*)

mashine (also *mashini*) *n (ma-)* machine. *Mashine dhana*, ideal machine. *Mashine ya kuoshea*, washing machine. (Eng)

mashini *n (ma-)* see *mashine*

mashirikiano *n (ma-)* co-operation, collaboration.

mashizi *n (ma-)* see *masizi*

mashobo *n (ma-)* show off, airs, graces, pomposity: *Yeye ni mtu mwenye mashobo mengi*, he is a person of much show off. (cf *matuko, madaha, mabosti, mikogo*)

mashoni *n (ma-)* tailoring cost. (cf *ushonaji*)

mashono *n (ma-)* 1. needlework, needlecraft; style (act, method, etc.) of sewing: *Nimeyapenda mashono ya suruali yake*, I like the tailoring on his trousers. (cf *ushonaji, ufumaji*) 2. tailoring cost. (cf *ushonaji*)

mashtaka *n (ma-)* charges, accusations: *Hakimu alimsomea mshtakiwa mashtaka yake*, the judge read out the charges to the accused. (cf *daawa, kesi*) (Ar)

mashua *n (n) (naut)* plank-built transom boat, built upon a keel and not exceeding 15 or 20 tons: *Mashua ya matanga*, sailboat. *Mashua ya kasi*, speedboat. *Mashua ya mlingoti na tanga moja*, catboat. *Mashua ndogo ya fito na ngozi*, coracle. *Mashua ya uokozi*, salvation boat. (Hind)

mashudu[1] *n (ma-)* the remains of solid matter after oil has been skimmed or compressed; sediment, residue. (cf *mashata, masimbi, masira*) (Ar)

mashudu[2] *interj* an exclamation of contempt, disgust, challenge, etc.; pshaw; just you try! (cf *yaguju, mawe*) (Ar)

mashughuli *adj* busy, active: *Yeye ni mtu mashughuli*, he is a busy person.

mashuhuda *n (ma-)* eyewitness (cf *shahidi*) (Ar)

mashuhuri *adj* famous, reknown, prominent: *Mwanasiasa mashuhuri*, a prominent politician. (cf *maarufu*) (Ar)

mashumshumu *n (ma-)* ill-wishing to someone that comes back to you yourself; adverse consequences, bad repercussions: *Vitendo vyake viovu kwa watu wengine vilimletea mashumshumu*, his evil deeds have boomeranged on him. (Ar)

masi hewa *n (ma-)* air mass.

masia *adv (idm) Enda masia*, go on foot e.g. *Nilienda masia mpaka nyumbani kwake baada ya kukosa usafiri*, I went on foot up to his house after I missed transport. (Ar)

masiala *n (ma-)* 1. issues or affairs that need to be analysed: *Masiala yale yanahitaji kikao maalumu*, those issues need a special session. 2. legal problems: *Mwanasheria anataka kuyashughulikia masiala yetu*, the lawyer wants to examine our legal problems. (Ar)

Masiha (also *Masihi, Masiya*) *n (ma-)* the Messiah. (Eng)

masihara n (ma-) pun, joke, jest, fun: *Mtu wa masihara,* jester. *Yeye anapenda kunifanyia masihara,* he likes to play jokes on me. (cf *dhihaka, utani*) (Ar)

Masihi n (ma-) see *Masiha*

masika n (ma-) the monsoon rains; the season of the long rains lasting between March and June. (*prov*) *Hakuna masika yasiyo na mbu,* there is no season of heavy rainfall without mosquitoes i.e. whenever there are difficulties, there are problems.

masikilizano n (ma-) 1. accord, agreement; mutual understanding. 2. rapport; good relationship between people: *Hana masikilizano na mkewe,* he has no good relationship with his wife. (cf *mafahamiano, maelewano, mapatano, maafikiano*)

masikini[1] n (ma-) see *maskini*[1]

masikini[2] adj see *maskini*[2]

masilahi n (ma-) interests, benefits, welfare: *Bei ya masilahi,* reasonable price; a price of good bargain. *Yeye huangalia masilahi yake tu,* he looks after his interests only. (cf *manufaa, faida*)

masimbi n (ma-) dregs, lees; the remains after beer has been strained or after oil has been pressed out of seeds. (cf *mashata, wishwa*)

masimbulio (also *masimbulizi*) n (ma-) traducement, calumny, aspersion; act of shaming a person by constantly reminding him of an act of kindness shown to him when in difficulty, need, etc. (cf *bughudha*)

masimbulizi n (ma-) see *masimbulio*

masimulizi n (ma-) narratives: *Masimilizi mafupi,* idyll.

masinde n (ma-) (*bot*) nut grass, nuts edge, coco grass; a perennial herb with long rhizomes. It is a major weed of cultivated crops and of gardens and is prevalent in disturbed areas and lawns. *Cyperus rotundus.*

masira n (ma-) remains of beer, wine, etc. after they have been strained; sediment, lees. (cf *mashapo, mashata, mabaki*)

masito n (n) a person who cannot hear easily but is not deaf; a person hard of hearing; a person who is particularly deaf.

Masiya n (ma-) see *Masiha*

masizi n (ma-) soot, grime.

masjala n (ma-) registry; an office or department where registers are kept. (Ar)

maskani n (ma-) 1. abode, dwelling place, residence, living place. (cf *makao, makazi, mastakimu*) 2. (in Tanzania) a small branch of a political party. (Ar)

maskini[1] (also *masikini*) n (ma-) 1. pauper; a poor person. (*prov*) *Muskini hana muwiko,* a poor person hana no restrictions i.e. a poor person has no choice; he chooses whatever is appropriate to him. (cf *fakiri*) 2. a disabled person. (cf *mlemavu*) 3. a wretched person.

maskini[2] (also *masikini*) adj poor, impecunious. (cf *fakiri*) (Ar)

maskini[3] *interj* an expletive of sorrow, sympathy, etc. expressed to someone who has suffered a misfortune, etc.

maslahi n (ma-) see *masilahi*

masmuma adj poisonous (Ar)

masoka n (ma-) see *mahoka*

masombo n (ma-) 1. girdle, sash; a long piece of cloth worn tightly round the waist esp. by women. 2. a style of dressing from the waist, etc.

masomo n (ma-) 1 studies, lessons; *Masomo ya juu,* higher studies: *Masomo ya mbali,* overseas studies. *Nje ya masomo,* extra curricular activities. 2. different types of disciplines.

masrufu n (ma-) see *masurufu*

mastaajabu n (ma-) wonders, miracles, marvels. (cf *maajabu, shani, vioja*) (Ar)

mastahili n (ma-) one's due; merits.

mastakimu n (ma-) abode, residence, dwelling place; one's place of living:

Mastakimu yake yamezungukwa na bustani, his residence is surrounded with a garden. (cf *maskani, makazi*) (Ar)

mastamu *n (ma-) (naut)* the upper part of the prow in a canoe, boat, etc.; mast. (cf *cheleko*)

masua *n (ma-)* giddiness, dizziness: *Mgonjwa aliona masua*, the patient felt giddy. (cf *kisuunzi, kizunguzungu, kisulisuli*)

masumbuko *n (ma-)* disturbances, annoyances, sufferings: *Masumbuko makali*, agony. (cf *maudhi, kero*)

masumbwi *n (ma-)* see *sumbwi*

masuo *n (ma-)* ejected water after rinsing the mouth.

masurufu *n (ma-)* 1. travelling expenses, travelling allowances; necessaries, imprest: *Masurufu yangu yaliongezeka nilipokuwa safarini*, my travelling expenses went up during my journey. 2. daily family support; house keeping: *Masurufu ya nyumbani kwa familia yetu yamepungua sana*, the house keeping expenses for our family have gone down very much. 3. provisions taken on a journey. (Ar)

masurupwete *n (ma-)* rags, tatters, cast off. (cf *masurumbwete*)

masuto *n (ma-)* charges of wrong doing made openly against sby; accusations, incriminations. (cf *shutuma, mashutumo, mashtaka*)

mat.a[1] *vi* be dead. Prep. **mat.i.a** St. **mat.ik.a** Cs. **mat.ish.a** (Ar)

mata[2] *n (ma-)* bow (of an arrow) *(syn) Washindwao ni waume na mata*, defeat is not a strange thing. Even those who are brave have been defeated.

mataa *n (ma-)* 1. traffic lights. 2. *(idm) Acha kwenye mataa*, make a fool of sby.

mataboti *n (ma-)* see *motaboti*

matabwatabwa *n (ma-)* anything like food that has not been properly cooked; badly cooked food.

matagataga *adv* astride; used in the expression: *Enda matagataga*, walk with the legs wide apart; straddle, bestraddle.

matai *n (ma-)* pomposity, swagger, airs, pose: *Huonyesha matai anapotembea*, he shows airs and graces when he walks. (cf *mbwembwe, matao, mikogo*)

matako *n (ma-)* buttocks. *(prov) Maskini akipata, matako hulia mbwata*, if a poor person gets sth, he will inform everybody i.e. if someone who did not possess sth, then begins to possess it later, he will begin to tell everyone and even cause annoyance to people or boast infront of everybody. (cf *makalio*)

matakwa (also *takwa*) *n (ma-)* wishes, desires, wants: *Matakwa ya jamii*, social interests. (cf *matilaba, haja*)

matale *n (ma-) (min)* granite

matamanio *n (ma-)* 1. desires. wishes: *Matamanio yake hayana kikomo*, his desires have no limit. (cf *matarajio*) 2. expectations. 3. temptations: *Hakuweza kuyadhibiti matamanio yake*, he could not control his temptations. (cf *vishawishi*)

matamshi *n (ma-)* 1. pronunciation. 2. remarks: *Waziri alitoa matamshi makali dhidi ya waandishi wa habari*, the minister gave scathing remarks against the press. (cf *maneno*)

matamvua *n (ma-)* 1. fringes of a garment. 2. threads which are unspinned: *Nyuzi za matamvua*, threads of this kind. 3. *(zool)* fish gills. (cf *mashavu*)

matana *n (ma-) (med)* leprosy (cf *ukoma*)

matanda *n (ma-)* mulch; leaves, straw, etc. spread on the ground around plants to prevent evaporation; humus, compost. (cf *mboji*)

matandiko *n (ma-)* 1. caparison, trappings. 2. beddings, bed clothes

matandu *n (ma-)* the hard crust of rice formed on a cooking pot because of the charcoal fire put on the lid; top crust of cooked rice.

matanga n (ma-) 1. a formal mourning observed by people who stay at the bereaved's place for a specific period usu three days: *Vunja matanga*, go out of mourning. *Weka matanga*, remain in mourning. 2. people congregating at the bereaved's place for mourning.

matanguko n (ma-) see *matanguo*

matanguo (also *matanguko*) n (ma-) revocation, repeal: *Matanguo ya sheria yaliwaudhi wakulima*, the annulment of the law angered the farmers. (cf *ubatilifu*)

matao n (ma-) pomposity, airs and graces: *Alizungumza kwa matao mkutanoni*, he spoke with airs and graces at the meeting. (cf *maringo, madaha, mikogo*)

matapishi n (ma-) 1. vomit. 2. (fig) insults; filthy words: *Alitoa matapishi yake hadharani*, he spat his insults in public. (cf *matusi*)

matarajio n (ma-) hope, expectation. (cf *matazamio, matumaini*) (Ar)

matata n (ma-) 1. chaos, disorder. (cf *vurugu, fujo, shida, taabu*) 2. an evil person, a troublesome person; reprobate

matatizo n (ma-) 1. problems, complications: *Matatizo yake hayatatuliki*, his problems cannot be solved. (cf *mazonge, masahibu, shida*) 2. dilemma, confusion. 3. stumbling block, obstruction, impediment.

matatu n (ma-) (in Kenya) public service vehicle; commuter minibus. (cf *daladala*)

matayarisho n (ma-) preparations (cf *maandalio*) (Ar)

matazamio n (ma-) expectations, anticipations: *Matazamio yake ya kufaulu kwenye mtihani hayakusibu*, his expectations of passing the examination did not materialize. (cf *matarajio*)

matbaa n (ma-) printing press. (Ar)

mate n (ma-) saliva, spittle.

matege n (ma-) 1. (med) bow legs. *Genu valgum*. 2. a bow-legged person.

mategu n (ma-) typographical errors: *Kitabu chake cha tamthilia kina mategu*, his book on play has typographical errors.

mateka n (wa-) 1. captives, hostages. 2. booty, loot, spoils; goods captured during war.

matembele n (ma-) (bot) the leaves of a sweet potato plant, used as a kind of vegetable. (cf *mtoriro, mriba*)

matembezi n (ma-) 1. ramble, stroll, walk: *Matembezi ya hisani*, charity walk. *Matembezi ya mshikamano*, solidarity walk. *Matembezi ya hiari*, voluntary walk. 2. visit, trip: *Anataka kufanya matembezi katika nchi za Kiarabu*, he wants to pay a visit to Arab countries.

matemo n (ma-) bevel

matende n (ma-) (med) elephantiasis

matengenezo[1] n (ma-) repairs, maintenance: *Baiskeli yako inahitaji matengenezo*, your bicycle needs repairs.

matengenezo[2] n (ma-) preparations, arrangements. (cf *matayarisho*)

materesi n (ma-) (naut) curved ornaments on bows and rudder in *mtepe*. (cf *uchikichi, mauwe*)

mateso n (ma-) tribulations, sufferings, persecutions, torture, misery: *Mateso kwa kutumia jeshi*, dragonnade. *Wafungwa walipata mateso mengi*, the prisoners underwent a lot of sufferings (cf *taabu, mahangaisho, madhila, idhilali*)

mathalan adv see *mathalani*

mathalani (also *mathalan*) adv for example, for instance; an expletive used to show illustration: *Mimi ninaelewa vijana wengi waliokwenda kusoma ng'ambo, mathalani Ahmed*, I know of many young men who have gone overseas for studies, for example, Ahmed. (Ar)

mathibitisho n (ma-) confirmation,

verification. (cf *uhakika*) (Ar)
mathulubu *n* (*ma-*) 1. calumniator, slanderer. 2. insinuator. (cf *mchongezi*) (Ar)
matibabu *n* (*ma-*) medical treatment. (cf *dawa*) (Ar)
matiko *n* (*ma-*) hardening or tempering of metal: *Tia shoka matiko*, temper an axe.
matilaba (also *matulubu*) *n* (*ma-*) 1. objective, purpose: *Matilaba yake yalikuwa ni kutaka kutuangamiza*, his aim was to destroy us. (cf *lengo*, *kusudio*). 2. desires, wishes, needs, motives: *Matilaba yao yana umuhimu wa peke yake*, their desires have special significance. (cf *haja*, *matakwa*) (Ar)
matilo *n* (*ma-*) see *itilo*
matindi[1] *n* (*ma-*) (*bot*) half-grain maize; young maize; green maize.
matindi[2] *n* (*ma-*) liquor, intoxicants, alcohol. (cf *ulevi*)
matindija *n* (*ma-*) bad face; ugly face.
matini *n* (*ma-*) text (Ar)
matiti[1] *n* (*ma-*) trot: *Enda matiti*, go at a trot.
matiti[2] *n* (*ma-*) pl of *titi*, breast.
matlai *n* (*ma-*) 1. east. 2. east winds. 3. east monsoon season.
matofali *n* (*ma-*) adobe, sun-dry brick.
matokeo *n* (*ma-*) outcome, sequel, result: *Matokeo ya kushtukiza*, unexpected results. *Matokeo ya mtihani bado hayajatolewa*, the examination results have not yet been released. (cf *natija*)
matope *n* (*ma-*) mud, mire.
matu[1] *n* (*ma-*) uncooked lump of flour in maize or cassava gruel or meal. (cf *budari*, *mavumbo*)
matu[2] *n* (*ma-*) perplexity mixed with fear.
matuazi *n* (*ma-*) (*mus*) cymbal (cf *tasa*)
matubwitubwi[1] *n* (*ma-*) gruel with uncooked lumps of flour; badly cooked porridge.
matubwitubwi[2] *n* (*ma-*) (*med*) mumps (cf *perema*, *matukwi*, *machubwichubwi*)
matuko *n* (*ma-*) pomposity, airs, graces: *Aliimba kwa matuko mengi*, he sang with a lot of pomposity. (cf *madaha*, *mikogo*)
matukulele *n* (*ma-*) restlessness, distraction.
matukwi *n*(*ma-*) see *matubwitubwi*[2]
matule *n* (*ma-*) sitting room. (cf *sebule*)
matulubu *n* (*ma-*) see *matilaba*
matumaini *n* (*ma-*) hope, expectation: *Matumaini ya kuishi*, life expectancy. (cf *matarajio*)
matumatu[1] (also *kimatu*) *n* (*ma-*) (*zool*) young locusts. (cf *maige*, *tunutu*)
matumatu[2] *n* (*ma-*) 1. walking on the soles of the feet without raising the heels; tiptoe. 2. silent walk with heels high.
matumbo *n* (*ma-*) (*anat*) entrails, gut, intestines.
matumishi *n* (*ma-*) service (cf *utumaji*)
matumizi *n*(*ma-*) 1. expenditure. *Matumizi ya mapato*, revenue expenditure. *Matumizi wekezi*, capital expenditure. *Matumizi ya kawaida*, current expenditure. 2. uses, advantages: *Zana hizi zina matumizi mengi*, these implements have many uses.
matungamavi (also *mafungamavi*) *n* (*ma-*) genu valgum, knock-nee, tibia valga; a deformity marked by abduction of the leg in relation to the thigh.

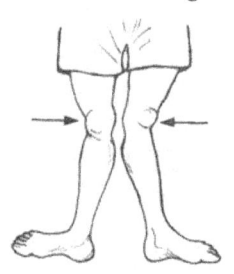

matungamavi

matungizi *n* (*ma-*) top level of a wall or of

a concrete roof. (cf *kiruguu*)
matunguu *n* (*ma-*) (*bot*) wild cardamon; a perennial herb with ginger-like stems up to 8 feet tall having yellow or yellowish-red flowers. *Afromomum angustifolium.*
matusi *n* (*ma-*) invective, vituperation, insults. (cf *matapishi*)
matwana *n* (*ma-*) a motor-omnibus for carrying passengers. *Matwana farasi*, coach.
matwi *n* (*ma-*) nervousness mixed with fear.
mauaji *n* (*ma-*) murder, massacre, slaying: *Mauaji ya halaiki*, genocide. *Mauaji ya watu wengi*, carnage. (cf *uuji*)
maudhi *n* (*ma-*) botheration, annoyance, disturbances, irksomeness. (cf *kero*) (Ar)
maudhui *n* (*ma-*) content, theme. (cf *mada*) (Ar)
mauguzi *n* (*ma-*) 1. patient care; treatment of a patient 2. the way a sick person progresses: *Mauguzi yake hayaridhishi*, his progress is not satisfactory.
mauja[1] *n* (*ma-*) dangerous affairs; hazard, chaos, misfortune.
mauja[2] (also *miuja*) *n* (*ma-*) miracles, wonders. (cf *shani, kioja, miujiza*)
maujudi *adj* available, obtainable: *Sukari imekuwa maujudi siku hizi*, sugar is available these days. (Ar)
mauko *n* (*ma-*) 1. departure, departing: *Mauko yake hayakutegemewa*, his departure was unexpected. (cf *uondokaji*) 2. death: *Mauko ya marehemu ndugu yangu yalituhuzunisha sana*, the death of my deceased brother saddened us alot. (cf *kifo*)
Maulana *n* (*ma-*) 1. the Lord; the Almighty God. 2. master, honourable. (cf *bwana, mheshimiwa*) (Ar)
Maulidi *n* (*ma-*) 1. recitation on the birthday of Prophet Muhammad. 2. congregations of Muslims for the recitation on the birthday of Prophet Muhammad. 3. birthday celebrations of Prophet Muhammad. (Ar)
maulizio *n* (*ma-*) enquiries; an office in a ministry, department, etc. incharge of giving information to visitors on the person to be visited. (cf *mapokezi*)
maulizo *n* (*ma-*) 1. questions, questionnaire: *Maulizo yake yalikuwa magumu*, his questions were difficult. (cf *masuali*) 2 enquiries.
maumbile *n* (*ma-*) nature, shape, physique. (cf *umbo*)
maumbufu *n* (*ma-*) things which bring disgrace; shame, scandal: *Vitendo vyake vimenitia maumbufu*, his evil deeds have put me into disgrace.
maumivu *n* (*ma-*) pain, anguish: *Maumivu makali*, agony. (cf *uchungu, kichomi*)
maundi *n* (*ma-*) (*naut*) boat building.
maundifu *adj* used in the expression: *Maji maundifu*, high tide.
maungio *n* (*ma-*) exchange: *Maungio ya simu*, telephone exchange.
maungo *n* (*ma-*) body, joints, organs.
maunzi *n* (*ma-*) hardware; articles made of metals such as tools, nails, etc.
mauti *n* (*ma-*) death, demise; (*prov*) *Mauti hayana kinga*, death has no shelter. (Ar)
mauwe *n* (*ma-*) (*naut*) flower design carved into *ipi* board on bows of a dhow. (cf *nakshi*)
mauzaji *n* (*ma-*) sales, marketing: *Mauzaji yake dukani yameongezeka*, his sales at the shop have risen. (cf *mauzo*)
mauzauza *n* (*ma-*) 1. juggling, conjuring tricks; illusions. (cf *kiinimacho, mazingaombwe*) 2. confusion of mind; bewilderment: *Akili yake imeingia katika mauzauza*, his mind is in a state of confusion.
mauzo *n* (*ma-*) marketing, sales: *Idara ya mauzo*, sales department. (cf *mapato, mauzaji*)
mava *n* (*ma-*) graveyard, cemetery. (cf *makaburi*)
mavani *n* (*ma-*) old and worn-out clothes.
mavi[1] *n* (*ma-*) 1. excrement, shit, dung. (cf

choo, kinyesi) 2. waste from minerals e.g. from iron, gold, etc. 3 (in card playing) *Mavi ya mbuzi*, club; any of a suit of playing cards marked with a black figure just like a clove leaf. (cf *pau*) 4. (*syn*) nonsense, rubbish, trash: *Alikuja hapa na kisha akatoa mavi yake*, he came here and then vomitted out his rubbish.

mavi² *interj* an expletive of scorn, challenge, etc. (cf *yaguju, mashudu*)

mavizio *n* (*ma-*) 1. act (method, etc) of waylaying 2 a place used inorder to waylay sby/sth.

mavu *n* (*ma-*) (*zool*) a kind of hornet known as "large paper wasp," which feeds its larvae on pieces of chewed-up caterpillar. (cf *nyigu, dondora*)

mavulia *n* (*ma-*) second-hand clothes of someone given to sby else.

mavumbo *n* (*ma-*) uncooked lump of flour in hard porridge. (cf *matu, budaa*)

mavunde (also *mafunde, mavundevunde*) *n* (*ma-*) cirrus; a formation of clouds in detached wispy filaments or feathery tufts at heights above 20,000 feet.

mavundemavunde *n* (*ma-*) see *mavunde*

mavune *n* (*ma-*) pains in the joints resulting from fatigue, etc after. doing labourious work, etc.

mavuno *n* (*ma-*) 1. harvest, yield: *Alipata mavuno makubwa sana katika msimu uliopita*, he had a bumper harvest in the previous season. 2. profit, gain, benefit: *Bidii zake zimemletea mavuno makubwa katika biashara*, his efforts have brought to him much profit in the business. (cf *faida, natija*)

mavyaa *n* (*ma-*) a name used by a wife and her husband's mother.

mawaga *n* (*ma-*) drizzle; light rain: *Haikuwa mvua kubwa; ilikuwa mawaga tu*, it was not a downpour; it was just a drizzle.

mawaidha (also *wadhi*) *n* (*ma-*) 1. sermon; religious speech. 2. advice, counsel: *Mzee alimpa bintiye mawaidha mazuri*, the parent gave his daughter good advice. (Ar)

mawanda *n* (*ma-*) scope, range, extent. (cf *wigo*)

mawano (also *mwano*) *n* (*ma-*) an oath made by using a stick, rope, etc.

mawasiliano *n* (*ma-*) 1. contact: *Kumekuwa na mawasiliano kati ya pande zile mbili*, there has been some contacts between those two sides. (cf *mazungumzo*) 2. communication: *Mawasilianoangani*, telecommunication. *Mawasiliano ya ndani*, inter-communication. (Ar)

mawazo *n* (*ma-*) see *wazo*

mawe¹ *n* (*ma-*) pl of *jiwe*, stone.

mawe² *interj* an expletive of scorn, challenge, etc.; bullshit. (cf *yaguju, mashudu*)

mawele *n* (*ma-*) (*bot*) bulrush millet. *Pennisetum malacochaete*.

mawenge¹ *n* (*ma-*) a cross-eyed person; a squinted person. (cf *makengeza*)

mawenge² *n* (*ma-*) restlessness, jumpiness, fidget: *Hafanyi kazi vizuri kwa sababu ya mawenge yake*, he does not work well because of his restlessness. (cf *mahepe, machachari*)

mawese *n* (*ma-*) used in the expression: *Mafuta ya mawese*, palm oil.

mawewa *n* (*ma-*) clean transparent water.

mawindo *n* (*ma-*) hunter's prey: *Mawindo yake kwenye usasi yalikuwa makubwa*, his prey was a big one.

mawio *n* (*ma-*) sunrise, dawn. (cf *alfajiri*)

maya *n* (*ma-*) anger, irk, rage. (cf *hasira, hamaki*)

mazalio *n* (*ma-*) hatchery, breeding place.

maziara *n* (*ma-*) cemetry, graveyard. (cf *makaburi*) (Ar)

mazidadi *n* (*ma-*) addition, supplement. (cf *nyongeza*)

maziga *n* (*ma-*) censer; an ornamented vessel for burning incense. (cf *kifukizo*)

mazigazi *n* (*ma-*) mirage (cf *mangati, sarabi*)

maziko *n* (*ma-*) funeral, burial. (cf *mazishi*)
mazingaombwe *n* (*ma-*) juggling; magic tricks, sleight of hand: *Mganga alituonyesha mazingaombwe yake*, the wizard displayed to us his magic tricks. (cf *mauzamauza, kiinimacho*)
mazao *n* (*ma-*) see *zao*
mazingara *n* (*ma-*) 1. superstition. 2. conditions, state, circumstances: *Watu watatu waliuliwa katika mazingara ya kutatanisha*, three people were killed in mysterious circumstances. *Kijana yule anafanya kazi katika mazingara magumu*, that youth is working under difficult conditions. *Mazingara hutuishi, dangerous envoronment* (cf *hali*)
mazingazi *n* (*ma-*) magic tricks, jugglery, juggling. (cf *mazingaombwe*)
mazingira *n* (*ma-*) environment surroudings: *Mazingira safi*, clean environment.
mazishi *n* (*ma-*) funeral, burial. (cf *maziko*)
maziwa *n* (*ma-*) milk: *Maziwa ya maji*, fresh milk. *Maziwa ya unga*, powdered milk.
mazoea (also *mazowea*) *n* (*ma-*) habit, custom, practice. (cf *tabia, mwenendo*)
mazoezi *n* (*ma-*) 1. pl of *zoezi*, lesson, practice, exercise. 2. practical work; exercise: *Mazoezi ya kujipima nguvu*, trial exercises. *Wachezaji walikuwa wakifanya mazoezi magumu*, the players were doing heavy exercises.
mazonge *n* (*ma-*) 1. turmoil. confusion: *Ameingia katika mazonge*, he has succumbed to confusion. (cf *mashaka, matatizo, masahibu, utata*) 2. a confused person; a perplexed person. (cf *mtingwa*)
mazowea *n* (*ma-*) see *mazoea*
mazungumzo *n* (*ma-*) talk, conversation. (cf *maongezi, gumzo*)

mba *n* (*ma-*) 1. (*med*) dandruff. 2. little scales or flakes of dead skin formed on the scalp.
mbaa *n* (*wa-*) see *mbawala*
mbaamwezi *n* (*n*) see *mbalamwezi*[1]
mbaazi *n* (*mi-* 1. (*bot*) pigeon pea. *Cajanus cajan*. (*prov*) *Mbaazi ukikosa maua husingizia jua*, if a person fails to accomplish sth and then bad consequences follow, he begins to give excuses. *Mbaazi mwitu*, a perennial herb up to 3 feet tall with triplicate leaves and bearing small yellow flowers. *Eriosema psoraleoides*. 2. the peas of this shrub.
mbabe *n* (*wa-*) 1. a strong person: *Huwezi kupigana na mbabe yule*, you can't fight that strong man. *Mbabe wa kivita*,warlord. (cf *mkota*) 2. a star in a movie, etc.; hero.
mbabekazi *n* (*wa-*) heroine; a girl or woman of outstanding courage, etc.
mbacha *n* (*mi*) an old worn-out mat. (*prov*) *Usiache mbachao kwa msala upitao*, don't leave your old mat for a praying mat i.e. dont desert your old friend for a new one who may just be a passing cloud.
mbadala *n* (*mi-*) alternative: *Mgombea mbadala*, an alternative candidate. *Njia mbadala*, alternative methods.
mbadhirifu *n* (*wa-*) an extravagant person: a spendthrift person; spendthrift; prodigal, spender: *Unajua kwamba mbadhirifu yule ameifuja mali yake yote?* Do you know that spendthrift person has squandered all his money? (cf *mfujaji*)
mbadiliko *n* (*mi-*) change: *Mbadiliko umbo*, accidence; the part of grammar that deals with the inflection of words.
mbago *adv* (*idm*) *Enda mbago*, go separately like two people who have quarrelled.
mbagombago *adv* haphazardly, disorderly, awry: *Mambo yake yalienda*

mbagombago, his affairs went awry. (cf *kombo*)
mbakaji *n* (*wa-*) rapist
mbakwaji *n* (*wa-*) a raped person.
mbalagha *n* (*n*) (*lit*) hyperbole; exaggeration for effect, not to be taken literally. (e.g *Yeye ana nguvu kama ng'ombe dume*, he is as strong as an ox.
mbalamwezi¹ *n* (*n*) bright moonlight; moonshine.
mbalamwezi² *n* (*n*) (*zool*) surf clam; a marine bivalve mollusk with shells of oval or equal sizes with a raised ridge running to posterior, and lives in eulittoral and shallow littloral mud or sand.
mbalanga *n* (*n*) (*med*) a common disorder in which there is a loss of pigment resulting in light or dark-coloured patches on the skin; vitiligo: *Mbalanga nyeusi*, dark vitiligo. (cf *manawa*)
mbale¹ *n* (*mi-*) ore; a combination of minerals.
mbale² *n* (*mi-*) (*bot*) raffia palm.
mbali¹ *adv* 1. far away, afar: *Anaishi mbali*, he lives far away. 2. (*syn*) *Tupia mbali*, throw quite away. *Achilia mbali*, forget it. *Potelea mbali*, it doesn't matter.
mbali² *adj* 1. different, dissimilar: *Rangi hii iko mbali na ile*, this colour is different from that one. (cf *tofauti*) 2. used with prepositions *na* and *ya* to form phrases: *Mbali ya hayo*, apart from that e.g. *Mbali na hayo, kuna masuala mengine ambayo yanafaa kuzingatiwa*, apart from that, there are other issues that need to be examined.
mbalimbali¹ *adj* various, different, assorted: *Vitabu mbalimbali*, different books.
mbalimbali² *adv* separately: *Mume na mke sasa wanaishi mbalimbali*, the husband and wife are now living separately.
mbalungi *n* (*mi-*) (*bot*) shaddock, pomelo;

a tree with leaves 5 to 6 inches by 2 inches with well marked wings. *Citrus maxima*.
mbamba *n* (*mi-*) a long strip of plaited straws, used for making fish traps.
mbambakofi *n* (*mi-*) 1. (*bot*) Lucky bean tree: Mahogany tree. *Afzelia quanzensis*. 2. a much-branched tree up to 60 feet tall with pinkish-white flowers and leathery black pods containing flat brown seeds. *Intsia bijuga*.
mbambangoma *n* (*mi-*) (*bot*) Hua tree; a large tree with spiny branches and trifoliate leaves and dense racemes of reddish-pink flowers and torulose pods used esp for making drums. *Erythrina sacleuxii*. 2. Flame tree; a small many branched-tree up to 25 feet tall with a very corky trunk and branches. *Erythrina tomentosa*. 3. Coral tree; a laxly branched deciduous tree with greenish-yellow bark and large scattered spines. *Erytrina variegeta*.
mbambara *n* (*mi-*) (*bot*) a deciduous shrub with compound leaves and small inconspicuous flowers. *Commiphora sp*.
mbambaro *n* (*mi-*) (*bot*) a tall forest tree with alternate ovate-oblanceolate leaves in clusters and small white flowers, used as a good timber. *Terminalia brownii*.
mbambo *n* (*mi-*) (*bot*) a scandent spiny shrub with alternate elliptic leathery leaves and small dense axillary spherical heads of white flowers, bearing a fleshy fruit when ripe. *Cardiogyne africana*.
mbamia *n* (*mi-*) (*bot*) okra: lady's fingers. *Hibiscus esculentus*. (cf *mbinda*)
mbande *n* (*u-*) used in the expression: *Maji mbande*, neap tide.
mbanduko *n* (*mi-*) cleavage, fissure, split (cf *mpasuko, mwachano*)
mbango¹ *n* (*n*) (*zool*) warthog (cf *nguta, gwase, ngiri*)

442

mbango² *n* (*n*) money (cf *pesa, fedha*)
mbanjo¹ *n* (*mi-*) cracking, breaking, splitting, cutting: *Mbanjo wa kuni*, the splitting of firewood.
mbanjo² *n* (*mi-*) present or first clothes sent to a fianceé.
mbano *n* (*mi-*) 1. squeezing, pressing, etc. 2. a stick split in the middle for holding fish or meat; cleft stick.
mbaramba *n* (*mi-*) see *mlamba*
mbarapi *n* (*n*) (*zool*) sable antelope; a large very dark-coloured antelope with conspicuous head markings and strongly ridged horns almost parallel to each other. *Hippotragus niger*. (cf *palahala*)

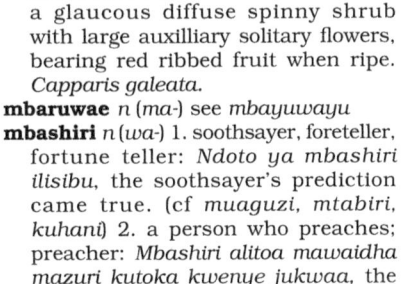

mbarapi

mbarawaji *n* (*mi-*) a kind of golden robe, made from silky material.
mbari *n* (*n*) kinsfolk, clan, family; *Yeye si mtu wa mbari yangu*, he is not a member of my family.
mbarika¹ *n* (*mi-*) 1. (*bot*) a name used in general for trees and shrubs whose fruits when ripe, open with an explosive sound. 2. lucky bean tree, mahogany bean. *Afzelia quanzensis*. 3. shoe-sole tree. *Isoberlinia scheffleri*. 4. castor oil plant. *Ricinus communis*. 5 the seeds of castor oil plant.
mbarika² *n* (*wa-*) a she-goat or cow that has not yet begotten offsprings.
mbaro *n* (used in) *Tia mbaroni*, arrest e.g. *Askari wa polisi alimtia mbaroni mwizi*, the policeman arrested the thief.
mbaruti *n* (*mi-*) 1. (*bot*) Mexican poppy; an annual herb with a yellow sap with somewhat spiny leaves and yellow poppy-like flowers, used in medicine. *Argemone mexicana*. 2. a glaucous diffuse spinny shrub with large auxilliary solitary flowers, bearing red ribbed fruit when ripe. *Capparis galeata*.
mbaruwae *n* (*ma-*) see *mbayuwayu*
mbashiri *n* (*wa-*) 1. soothsayer, foreteller, fortune teller: *Ndoto ya mbashiri ilisibu*, the soothsayer's prediction came true. (cf *muaguzi, mtabiri, kuhani*) 2. a person who preaches; preacher: *Mbashiri alitoa mawaidha mazuri kutoka kwenye jukwaa*, the preacher delivered a good sermon from the pulpit. (cf *mhubiri*)
mbasi¹ *n* (*wa-*) friend, comrade, companion. *Yeye ni mbasi wangu wa dhati*, he is my sincere friend. (cf *mgosi, sahibu, rafiki*)
mbasi² *n* (*n*) (*zool*) a kind of sailfish. similar to marlins but has a longer spike and a conspicuous large, iridescent spotted dorsal fin; bluish body. *Istiophurus pletypterus*.
mbasua *n* (*n*) giddiness, dizziness: *Alikaa kitako baada ya kuhisi mbasua*, he sat down after feeling giddy. (cf *kisunnzi, kizunguzungu, kisuli*)
mbata *n* (*n*) (*bot*) copra; dried coconut meat, the source of coconut oil. (cf *nguta*)
mbatata *n* (*n*) (*bot*) potatoes; Irish potatoes.
mbatilisho (also *mbatilizo*) *n* (*mi-*) invalidation, annulment, revocation: *Mbatilisho wa sheria*, the annulment of the law. (cf *mtanguo*)
mbatizaji *n* (*wa-*) a person who baptizes; baptizer.
mbawa *n* (*mi-*) (*zool*) bluestriped snapper; a kind of marine fish (family *Lutjanidae*) of bright yellow on back and flanks, living in coral and rocky reefs, usually deeper than 40cm. *Lutjanua kasmira*. (cf *janja, tembo*)

mbawakau *n* (*mi-*) (*zool*) beetle (Order *Coleoptera*): an insect which occupies a wide variety of habitats feeding on a wide range of food materials. Some are pests while others are beneficial to mankind. Beetles undergo a complete metamorphosis with distinct larval and papal stages. (cf *kombamwiko*)

mbawala (also *mbawara*) *n* (*n*) (*zool*) bushbuck; a small antelope (*Tragelaphus scriptus*) with large and broad ears and a long bushy tail, found in South Africa.

mbawara *n* (*n*) see *mbawala*

mbawazi (also *mbazi*) *n* (*n*) 1. mercy, clemency, forgiveness: *Mwenyezi Mungu huwapa mbawazi waja wake*, God gives mercy to his beings. (cf *rehema*) 2. kindness, pity: *Lazima uonyeshe mbawazi kwa wanyama*, you must show kindness to animals. (cf *rehema, huruma*)

mbaya *n* (*mi-*) see *mbayaya*

mbayana[1] *adj* conspicuously, obviously, openly: *Alimtukana jirani yake mbayana*, he insulted his neighbour openly. (cf *waziwazi*)

mbayana[2] *n* (*wa-*) a notorious person; a wicked person; reprobate: *Yeye ni mbayana*, he is a reprobate. (cf *mwovu*)

mbayana[3] *n* (*ma-*) conspicuousness: *Halbadiri ya mbayana*, open supplication to bring a curse or spell on someone who has done an evil.

mbayaya (also *mbaya*) *n* (*mi-*) (*bot*) hard grass; a short-lived perennial grass up to 12 feet tall with stems armed with strong somewhat stinging hairs. *Rottboelila exaltata*.

mbayuwayu (also *mbaruwae*) *n* (*mi*) (*zool*) swallow; a small swift flying insect eating bird (family *Hirundinidae*) with long, pointed wings and a forked tail, known for their regular migrations.

mbazi[1] *n* (*n*) see *mbawazi*

mbazi[2] *n* (*mi-*) parable

mbe *interj* there is nothing (cf *pepe*)

mbeberu *n* (*wa-*) imperialist (cf *mkoloni*)

mbega[1] *n* (*n*) (*zool*) colobus monkey.

mbega
Angolan black and white colobus. *Colobus angolensis*.

mbega[2] *n* (*n*) colobus monkey hair, won on the shoulders by some of the local drum players.

mbega[3] a neat person

mbege *n* (*n*) 1. local brew made by mixing ripe bananas and finger millet. 2. flour obtained from finger millet.

mbegu (also *mbeu*) *n* (*n*) 1. (*bot*) seed: *Mbegu ya mahindi*, maize seed. 2. (of people, animals, etc.) sperm, semen: *Hakupata mtoto mpaka sasa kwa vile mbegu zake ni dhaifu*, he has not yet got a child because he has a low sperm count. (cf *mbeu*)

mbeja *n* (*wa-*) a fashionable woman; a stylish woman: *Mbeja yule amewavutia wavulana wengi*, that fashionable woman has attracted many boys. (cf *mlimbwende, mtanashati*)

mbeko[1] *n* (*n*) respect, reverence, veneration: *Yeye anastahili kupewa mbeko*, he deserves to be accorded respect. (cf *staha, heshima*)

mbeko[2] *n* (*n*) savings, reserve.

mbele[1] *adv* 1. in front, forward: *Alikaa mbele kwenye mkutano*, he sat in front at the meeting. (*syn*) *Huna mbele wala nyuma*, you are a poor person; you are utterly destitute; you have no place in this world. 2. in public: *Alimkashifu mbele za watu*, he discredited him in public.

mbele[2] *n* (*n*) 1. genital organs. 2. female organs.

mbeleko (also *ubeleko*) *n* (*n*) a piece of calico used by women for carrying a baby on the back or hips during working or walking; baby carrier (cf *ubeleko*)

mbeleni[1] *adv* ahead, in future: *Serikali itaanzisha vyama vya ushirika mbeleni*, the government will introduce co-operative societies in future.

mbeleni[2] *n* (*n*) genitalia; reproductive organs.

mbelewele *n* (*n*) (*bot*) pollen (cf *chavua*)

mbembe[1] *n* (*wa-*) seducer, womanizer, lady's man. (cf *mkware. mzinifu*)

mbembe[2] *n* (*wa-*) busybody, tattler, telltale. (cf *mdaku, dukizi*)

mbembelezi *n* (*wa-*) wheedler, coaxer.

mbembeo *n* (*mi-*) (*phys*) oscillation

mbenuko *n* (*mi-*) protuberance, hump, curve, convexity: *Pana mbenuko juu ya kilima kile*, there is a hump on that hill. *Tumbo lake limeonyesha mbenuko*, his stomach shows protuberance. (cf *mwiinuko*)

mbera *n* (*mi*) (*naut*) strut in *ngalawa*, outrigger.

mberegezaji *n* (*wa-*) filibuster; a person who tries to delay business esp. in parliament by making very long speeches.

mbetuko *n* (*mi-*) inclination, incline, slope, slant: *Mbetuko wa kwenda chini ghafla*, a steep slope.

mbeu *n* (*mi-*) see *mbegu*

mbeuzi *n* (*wa-*) gourmet, epicure. (cf *machagu, kidomo*)

mbeya *n* (*wa-*) busybody, tattler, talebearer, eavesdropper, telltale: *Mbeya yule amezitangaza siri zangu zote*, that busybody has disclosed all my secrets. (cf *mdaku, dukizi*)

mbezi *n* (*wa-*) snob, egoist; a scornful person: *Usijaribu kufanya urafiki na mbezi yule*, don't befriend that snob.

mbi *adj* bad: *Tabia mbi*, bad habit. (*prov*) *Kazi mbi si mchezo mwema*, bad work is not a good game i.e. it is better to try to accomplish a task than to leave it undone.

mbia[1] *n* (*wa-*) partner: *Yeye ni mbia katika kampuni hii*, he is a partner in this company.

mbia[2] *n* (*n*) grave, tomb. (cf *kaburi*)

mbibo *n* (*mi-*) cashew nut tree. *Anacardium occidentale*.

mbigili (also *mbiliwili*) *n* (*mi-*) (*bot*) Turkey blossom; an annual spreading prostrate herb with pinnate leaves of unequal size and fruiting spiny carpels and which is common on seashows in many parts of the tropics. Its leaves are used as a vegetable and its roots are used medicinally. *Tribulus cistoides*.

mbiha *n* (*mi-*) (*bot*) a short-lived perennial herb up to 3 feet tall with leaves on long stalks and yellow flowers, and having its roots used medicinally. *Abutilon zanzibaricum*.

mbili *adj, n* two: *Mbili na mbili ni nne*, two and two is four.

mbilikimo *n* (*n*) dwarf, midget. (cf *kisheta, mbirikimo, kibete, kijima*)

mbilikizi *n* (*wa-*) bugler; a person who blows a bugle.

mbilingani *n* (*mi-*) (*bot*) egg plant. *Solanum melongena*.

mbilimbi *n* (*mi-*) see *mbirimbi*

mbiliwili[1] *n* (*mi-*) see *mbigili*

mbiliwili[2] *n* (*mi-*) flathead; a kind of elongate saltwater fish (family *Platycephalidae*) with a large mouth and fine teeth on jaws.

mbiliwili

Bartail flathead. *Platycephalus indicus*.

mbinafsi *n* (*wa-*) opportunist: *Mbinafsi wa kisiasa*, political opportunist. (Ar)

mbinda *n* (*mi-*) (*bot*) okra, lady's fingers. (cf *mbamia*)

mbinde *n* (*n*) difficulty: *Timu ilishinda kwa mbinde*, the team won with difficulty. (cf *taabu, shida*)

mbindi *n* (*mi-*) a congestion of people, etc.; squeezing of people, etc.

mbingiri *n* (*mi-*) (*bot*) a plant whose green stems are stirred with milk and yolk of an egg, and used as an aphrodisiac. (cf *tapisho*)

mbingiriko *n* (*mi-*) swirling, whirling, rolling. (cf *mfingiriko*)

mbingu *n* (*n*) sky, heavens, firmament.

mbinguni *n* (*n*) heaven

mbingusi *n* (*mi-*) (*zool*) a kind of shark belonging to rockod family, having a flattened head and greatly expanded laterally; hammerhead shark (cf *pingusi*)

mbini *n* (*wa-*) a forger of signatures.

mbinja *n* (*n*) whistle

mbinu[1] *n* (*n*) double jointed curve: *Ana mikono ya mbinu*, he has double jointed hands.

mbinu[2] *n* (*n*) 1. strategy, method, device: *Mbinu za kufundishia*, teaching methods. 2. trick: *Mbinu ya kujihami kwa miguu na mikono*, karate.

mbinuko *n* (*mi-*) protuberance, convex: *Lenzi mbinuko*, convex lens.

mbio[1] *n* (*n*) 1. speed: *Piga mbio*, run fast. *Ana mbio*, he has speed. (*prov*) *Mbio za sakafuni huishia ukingoni*, too much haste and unjustified determination to complete work will lead you nowhere. 2. sprint, race: *Mbio za kupokezana*, relay race. *Mbio za nyika*, crosscountry. *Mbio za kuruka viunzi*, hurdles. *Mbio za magari*, motor race. *mbio za langalanga* marathon.

mbio[2] *za langalanga*, marathon

mbio[3] *adv* 1. fast, hurriedly: *Alikwenda mbio*, he went fast. 2. (*idm*) *Endea mbio*, take pains e.g. *Aliyaendea mbio mambo yake*, he took pains to ensure that his affairs were given fast attention.

mbio[4] *n* (*n*) (*bot*) a kind of cassava.

mbiombio *adv* fast, hurriedly. (cf *haraka haraka, upesiupesi*)

mbirambi *n* (*n*) condolence

mbirimbi[1] *n* (*n*) see *birimbi*

mbirimbi[2] (also *mbilimbi*) *n* (*mi-*) (*bot*) cucumber tree; a small tree bearing an edible fleshy ribbed acid fruit, used in pickles, jellies, etc. *Averrhoa bilimbi.*

mbiringani (also *mbilingani*) *n* (*mi*) (*bot*) eggplant, ambergine.

mbiru *n* (*n*) income tax. (Kip)

mbishi[1] *n* (*wa-*) an argumentative person; an obstinate person. (cf *mshindani*)

mbishi[2] *n* (*wa-*) a person with whom one has a joking relationship. (cf *mtani*)

mbisho *n* (*mi-*) (*naut*) beating to windward, esp taking long tacks: *Pepo za mbisho*, headwind; contrary wind; wind blowing in the direction directly opposite the course of a ship or aircraft.

mbiu *n* (*n*) 1. an animal horn, used to make public announcements; buffalo horn: *Piga mbiu*, make a public announcement. (*prov*) *Mbiu ya mgambo ikilia, ina jambo*, if a buffalo horn is blown, then there is sth of importance i.e. Whenever there is a government announcement, then one would assume that there is a strong reason behind the public announcement. *Mpiga mbiu*, bellman. 2. a goat's or deer's horn, used in the local dance known as "lelemama."

mbiya *n* (*n*) (*bot*) seedling: *Tia mbiya*, transplant seedlings.

mbizi *n* (*n*) dive: *Piga mbizi*, dive; take a dive. *Maji ya mbizi*, deep water.

mbochi *n* (*n*) nectar

mboga[1] *n* (*n*) (*bot*) vegetable. 2. relish, side dish.

mboga[2] *n* (*n*) (*bot*) pumpkin plant. *Cucurbita maxima.*

mboga[3] *n* (*n*) (*colloq*) a person who cannot do anything; a person who has no strength to look after himself.

mboga[4] *adj* (*colloq*) simple, easy: *Hesabu hii ni mboga*, this arithmetic is easy. (cf *rahisi*)

mbogo *n* (*n*) (*zool*) buffalo (cf *nyati*)

mboji n (n) compost, humus. (cf *matanda*)

mbojo n (*wa-*) a person who wears a lion's hide so that he looks like a lion and then kills people. (cf *simba mtu*)

mboko[1] n (n) a small thin gourd for drinking water or local brew.

mboko[2] n (*mi-*) whip, lash. (cf *kiboko, mjeledi*)

mbokoko n (n) cooked jack fruit.

mbokwe n (*mi-*) (*bot*) sugar apple; sweet sop. *Annona squamosa*. (cf *mtopetope*)

mbolea n (n) manure, fertilizer: *Mbolea ya chumvichumvi*, chemical fertilizer. *Mbolea ya vunde*, compost. *Mbolea ya samadi*, animal manure.

mbolezi n (n) elegy; poem, song, etc. in a mournfully contemplative tone.

mbomoko n (*mi-*) 1. demolition, collapse, destruction: *Mbomoko wa nyumba kongwe*, the collapse of the old house. (cf *ubomokaji, mporomoko*) 2. debris, rubble.

mbona adv 1. Why? How come? Why the hell? *Mbona unafanya kelele hapa?* Why are you making noise here? 2. used as a word to express surprise: *Ulisema mahali hapa hapapitiki, mbona nimepita?* You said that this place is not passable, why then have I passed? (cf *vipi, ilikuwaje*)

mboni[1] n (n) (*anat*) pupil; the apple of one's eye.

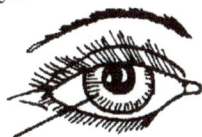

mboni[1]

mboni[2] n (n) present given to someone for sth lost; special reward; special gift. (cf *zawadi*)

mbono[1] n (*mi-*) 1. (*bot*) physic nut plant. *Jatropha curcas*. 2. castor oil plant. *Ricinus communis*. 3. *Mbono pembe*, coral plant. *Jatropha multifida*. 4. *Mbono wa kizungu*, frangipani. *Plumeria acuminata*. 5. *Mbono ndogo*, castor oil plant. *Racinus communis*.

mbono[2] n (*mi-*) (*bot*) castor oil plant seed. (cf *mbarika*)

mbono[3] n (*mi-*) (*zool*) gold striped fusilier; a marine striped fusilier (family *Caesionidae*) having a rather small, fusiform body with a blue-edged yellow stripe dorsally and lives around coral reefs and deep lagoons. *Caesio caerulaureus*.

mbonyeko (also *mbonyeo*) n (*mi-*) concavity; the quality or condition of being hollow and curved. (cf *ubonyeko*)

mbonyeo n (*mi-*) see *mbonyeko*

mboo n (n) (*anat*) penis, dick. (cf *uume, dhakari*)

mbooza adj plenty, many, abandant.

mboza[1] (also *mgoza*) n (*mi-*) 1. (*bot*) a tree up to 25 feet tall with greyish branches, bearing star-shaped fruits which split open, exposing numerous oval, black seeds with yellow arids. The bark of this tree is used for making a rope or as a tying material in hut building. *Starculia cinerea*. 2. a spreading much-branched tree up to 30 feet with nearly glabrous leaves and small yellow flowers, bearing star-shaped fruits which split open, exposing numerous seeds with arils and stinging hairs. Likewise, the bark is used as a strong fibre for making rope or as a tying material in hut building. *Starculia africana*.

mboza[2] n (n) (*zool*) a stingless bee (*Morpane bee* or *Mocca bee*) belonging to Genus *Trigona* (family: *Apidae*) which produces brood and usu nourishes honey and which are both relished by Africans.

Mbrazili n (*wa–*) Brazilian (Eng)

mbu n (n) (*zool*) mosquito: *Mbu aambukizaye malaria*, mosquito anopheles.

mbuaji *adj* murderous, savage, barbarious, cruel.

mbuai *n(n)* predator, carnivore. (cf *mgwizi*)

mbuba *n (n) (med)* fungus skin infection of the feet; tinea pedis, dermatomyocosis pedis, dermatophytosis of the feet, Hongkong foot, athletes foot, ringworm of the foot.

mbubujiko (also *bubujiko*) *n (mi-)* 1. spurting of water in large quantities; a bursting of water in large quantities: *Mbubujiko wa maji ya bomba lililopasuka uliwaudhi majirani*, the spurting of water from the broken pipe angered the neighbours. (cf *mbwabwajo, utokaji*) 2. prattling; talking of foolish words: *Mbubujiko wa mlevi ulinikera*, the prattle of the drunkard irritated me. (cf *mropoko*)

mbuda[1] *n (n)* money (cf *pesa*)

mbuda[2] *n (mi-)* a stick used for fighting; fighting stick. (cf *kigongo, kocho*)

mbuga *n (n)* savannah, grasslands: *Mbuga za wanyama*, game parks/reserve. (cf *uwanda, nyika*)

mbuge[1] *n (wa-)* nibbler, muncher; a person who is always throwing items of food into his mouth while eating. (*syn*) *Mbuge hawezi nyumba*, a nibbler knows only to nibble; he cannot eat in a house as others do.

mbuge[2] *adj* nibbling: *Mtu mbuge*, nibbler, muncher.

mbugi *n (n)* tinkle bells; ankle bells fastened to animals. (*syn*) *Ametia mbugi miguuni*, he never stops walking.

mbuguma *n (n) (zool)* a cow that continues to calve; a fecund cow.

mbuji *n (wa-)* an expert in a particular field: *Yeye ni mbuji wa kuimba*, he is an expert in singing.

mbuku *n (wa-)* miser, niggard, skinflint: *Mbuku yule hasaidii watu*, that skinflint does not help people. (cf *mroho, kisangati, bahili*)

mbukulia *n (wa-)* see *mbukuzi*

mbukuzi (also *mbukulia*) *n (wa-)* a person who discloses secrets, scandals, etc.; telltale, talebearer, gossip, scandal monger: *Siri zako zote zinaweza kufichuliwa na mbukuzi yule*, all your secrets can be disclosed by that telltale. (cf *kidomodomo, sabasi*)

mbulia *n (n) (bot)* volunteer (cf *maotea, tarare*)

mbulu *n (n)* lunacy, madness. (cf *wazimu, kichaa*)

mbumbumbu *n (ma-)* thickhead, blockhead; a stupid person: *Mwalimu wetu hampendi mbumbumbu yule*, our teacher does not like that thickhead. (cf *mpumbavu, mjinga*)

mbundungo *n (n)* medicine believed to protect someone against any bullet or weapon.

mbunge *n (wa-)* parliamentarian, legislator, law-maker; a member of parliament: *Mbunge anayejitegemea*, an independent member of parliament. *Mbunge wa kuteuliwa*, a nominated member of parliament.

mbungo[1] *n (mi-) (bot)* rubber vine tree. *Landolphia florida*.

mbung'o[2] *n (n) (zool)* tsetsefly (cf *ndorobo, chafuo*)

mbungu *n (n) (zool)* eland; a kind of a very large ox-like antelope (family *Tragelaphinae*) with thick and tightly spiralled horns. (cf *pofu*)

mbuni[1] *n (n) (zool)* ostrich

mbuni

mbuni² *n* (*mi-*) (*bot*) coffee plant. (cf *mkahawa*)

mbunju *n* (*n*) (*zool*) eland (cf *pofu*)

mbura¹ *n* (*mi-*) (*bot*) curatella plum tree; a much-branched tree having a rough grey corky bark up to 30 feet tall with simple alternate elliptic-oblong leaves and small yellow flowers. *Parinari curatellaefolium.*

mbura² *n(n)* (*bot*) an edible fleshy fruit from *curatella* plum tree, resembling plums in appearance and size and having brown roughened skins. *Curatella plum*

mburudishaji *n* (*wa-*) entertainer (cf *mkirimishaji*)

mburuga *n* (*n*) a kind of divining tool used for finding out a hidden issue: *Piga mburuga,* read the divining board.

mburukenge *n* (*mi-*) see *kenge*

mbururo (also *mburuzo, mbuuzo*) *n* (*mi-*) 1. pulling, dragging, hauling. 2. a track or marks made by pulling sth along the ground or by sth dragging itself along as in the case of a snake: *Mbururo wa nyoka,* the marks or track of a snake.

mburuzo *n* (*mi-*) see *mbururo*

mbuta *n* (*n*) 1. present, gift, souvenir, keepsake, token, tip; a present given to show gratitude to someone because of his service, etc.: *Nilimpa mbuta baada ya kunisaidia,* I gave him a present after helping me. (cf *bahashishi*) 2. anything you give to someone to assist you. 3. part of the dowry.

mbute *n* (*n*) (*bot*) boiled sweet potatoes which are later dried in the sun. 2. roasted sweet potatoes and later are eaten.

mbuuzo *n* (*mi-*) see *mbururo*

mbuya *n* (*n*) 1. companion, friend. (cf *mwenza, rafiki*) 2. concubine.

mbuyo *n* (*mi-*) (*naut*) beating to windward with long tacks. This manoeuvre brings the ship far out into the sea, but enables her voyage in a foul wind; technique of sailing in bad weather.

ˈmbuyu¹ *n* (*mi-*) 1. (*bot*) baobab tree; *Adansonia digitata.* 2. (*idm*) *Zunguka mbuyu,* bribe someone e.g. *Alipata kazi baada ya kuzunguka mbuyu,* he got the job after bribing someone.

mbuyu² *n* (*n*) (*bot*) the seeds of baobab tree.

mbuzi¹ *n* (*n*) 1. (*zool*) goat: *Mbuzi dume,* he-goat. *Mbuzi jike,* nanny goat. *Mbuzi mwitu,* ibex. 2. (*idm*) *Mkia wa mbuzi,* a useless person.

mbuzi² *n* (*n*) an instrument made up of iron with a serrated edge fixed in a board, used for grating coconut; coconut grater.

mbwa *n* (*n*) dog: *Mbwa koko,* stray dog. *Mbwa kasoro mkia,* a useless person. *Mbwa mpelelezi,* sleuth hound. *Mbwa mfuatiaji,* tracker dog. (*prov*) *Mbwa hafi maji akiwona ufuko,* i.e. if a person is on the verge of extinction, he can survive if he is given the necessary assistance.

mbwabwajo *n* (*mi-*) 1. the spurting of water: *Mbwabwajo wa maji,* the spurting of water. (cf *mbubujiko*) 2. idle talk, useless talk.

mbwago *n* (*mi-*) 1. falling; slump. 2. a decline in prices; slump.

mbwamwitu *n* (*n*) (*zool*) wolf

mbwanda *n* (*mi-*) see *mbwende*

mbwawa *n* (*wa-*) cannibal

mbwe *n* (*mi-*) a small stone or bead used by Muslims, fixed in a rosary to keep count when mentioning the names of God.

mbwedu *n* (*mi-*) 1. pah; an expletive used to scorn sth. 2. a useless person; a worthless person; good-for-nothing.

mbweha (also *bweha*) *n* (*n*) (*zool*) jackal (cf *mbwamwitu*)

mbwembwe *n* (*n*) pose, pomposity, airs, graces, boastfulness, swagger: *Tia mbwembwe,* show swagger. (cf *mikogo, mashobo, maringo*)

mbwende (also *mbwanda*) *n* (*n*) 1. (*bot*) swordbean, *Canavalia eniformis.* 2. (*idm*) *Kula mbwende,* (a) get pleasant things; gain, benefit. (cf *faidi*) (b) get problems, be in trouble. 3. any food that has not been properly cooked.

mbweu *n* (*n*) belch, hiccup, erructation: *Piga mbweu*, belch, eructate. *Enda mbweu*, belch, eructate.

mbwiji *n* (*mi-*) (*zool*) jackal-like animal.

mbwisho *n* (*mi-*) see *mgwisho*

mcha (also *mchaji*) *n* (*wa-*) a word used with another word to form a compound noun e.g. *Mcha Mungu*, a God-fearing person, (*prov*) *Mcha Mungu si mtovu*, a person who depends upon God will always have his affairs go on the right way. (cf *muogopaji*)

mchaa[1] *n* (*u*) direction, course, way. (cf *mwelekeo, njia*)

mchaa[2] *n* (*u*) (*naut*) the upper side of a canoe.

mchaa[3] *adv* directly, straight. (cf *moja kwa moja*)

mchachago *n* (*mi-*) a superficial washing of clothes; a gentle washing of clothes: *Nguo zangu hazikutakasika kutokana na mchachago wa dobi*, my clothes did not become clean because of the washerman's superficial laundering.

mchachato *n* (*mi-*) stealthily walk; stalk.

mchafu *n* (*wa-*) 1. a dirty person; an unclean person: *Yeye ni mchafu*, he is dirty. 2. an immoral person, a depraved person; reprobate: *Wao ni wachafu*, they are depraved individuals.

mchafuko *n* (*mi-*) disorder, chaos, disturbance: *Michafuko mingi hutokea mtaani kwetu baada ya watu kulewa*, a lot of disturbances occur in our neighbourhood after people get drunk. *Michafuko ya kisiasa*, political disturbances (cf *vurugu, ghasia, fujo*)

mchafukoge[1] *adj* chaotic, turbulent: *Mambo yangu yalikuwa mchafukoge*, my affairs were chaotic.

mchafukoge[2] *n* (*mi-*) chaos, pandemonium, confusion: *Mchafukoge ule uliwasumbua watu*, that confusion disturbed the people. (cf *mtafaruku*)

mchafuzi *n* (*wa-*) 1. troublemaker, trouble shooter: *Ukiwa mchafuzi, polisi watakutia nguvuni*, if you are a troublemaker, the police will arrest you. 2. a person who spoils or unsettles things or affairs; spoiler, troublemaker: *Mchafuzi aliivuruga mipango yetu*, the troublemaker messed up our plans.

mchago *n* (*mi-*) 1 the end of a bedstead where the head rests; headboard side. 2. the thing used as a support for the head to rest on in sleeping e.g. pillow.

mchaguzi *n* (*wa-*) 1. gourmet, epicure, fussy-eater: *Tabia ya mchaguzi yule iliwaudhi wageni wengi*, the habit of that groumet angered many guests. (cf *machagu*) 2. a person eligible to vote; voter: *Kila mchaguzi alipiga kura katika jimbo lake*, every voter voted in his constituency.

mchai *n* (*mi-*) 1. (*bot*) tea plant; an evergreen plant that loves subtropical areas like China and India. *Camellia sinensis*. 2. khus khus grass. *Vetiveria zizanoides*.

mchaichai (also *mzumari*) *n* (*mi-*) 1. (*bot*) lesson grass; a perennial grass; growing in thick-set clumps and its leaves yield by distillation, an essential oil which is used in perfumery and medicine. *Cymbopogon citratus*.

mchaji *n* (*wa-*) (also *mcha*) a person who is afraid of sby esp God. (cf *muogopaji*)

mchakamchaka *n* (*mi-*) an expletive used to encourage someone to do an action e.g. when soldiers are drilling.

mchakacho *n* (*mi-*) rustling sound of feet on dry grass, leaves, etc.: *Niliusikia mchakacho*, I heard the rustling sound.

mchakato *n* (*mi-*) process: *Kiongozi alihusishwa kwenye mchakato wa amani*, the leader was involved in the peace process. *Maendeleo ni mchakato*, development is a process. *Michakato ya kisiasa*, political processes.

mchambuzi n (wa-) 1 analyst: *Mchambuzi wa kisiasa*, political analyst. 2 a person who picks the grit from the grain, etc.

mchamvya n (mi-) see *mchocha*

mchana n (n) 1. day time. 2. afternoon, midday. *Mchana kutwa*, all day long. *Mchana huu*, this afternoon.

mchanga¹ n (mi-) sand: *Mchanga mwembamba*, fine sand. *Mchanga mtifu*, loose sand. *Chembe ya mchanga*, a grain of sand. *Fungu la mchanga*, sand bar.

mchanga² adj used in the expression: *Mtoto mchanga*, baby. *Mmea mchanga*, a young plant.

mchangamfu n (wa) a jolly person; a charming person; a cheerful person: *Yeye anapendwa kwa sababu ni mchangamfu*, he is liked because he is cheerful. (cf *bashasha, mpwamu*)

mchangamo adj mixed, complex: *Fikira mchangamo*, complex ideas.

mchanganuo n (mi-) 1. separation of compounded items. 2. an analysis of ideas, themes, etc. in a book, journal, etc.: *Niliufanya mchanganuo wa dhamira mbalimbali katika riwaya hii*, I did an analysis of different themes in this novel. (cf *uchambuzi*)

mchanganyiko (also *changanyiko*) n (mi-) potpourri, blend, mixture, mix, hodge podge hotch-potch, amalgam: *Mchanganyiko maalumu*, a special blend. *Mchanganyiko wa vitu*, farrago, hotch-potch.

mchanganyo (also *changanyo*) n (mi-) 1. the collection of different items into one place: *Mchanganyo wa vifaa*, the collection of different tools into one place. 2. mixture: *Huu ni mchanganyo wa kokoto na mchanga*, this is a mixture of small stones and sand.

mchangiaji n (ma-) 1. (in a discussion, meeting, etc) speaker, contributor.

mchango¹ n (mi-) contribution, donation: *Tunataka kufanya mchango kwa ajili ya kuwasaidia watoto yatima*, we want to organize fund raising for the benefit of orphans. (cf *harambe*)

mchango² (also *chango*) n (mi-) 1. (anat) intestinal worm. 2. pre-menstrual ailment. 3. gut; small intestines.

mchanguzo n (mi-) chaos, mess, confusion. (cf *vurugu, fujo*)

mchaniko n (mi-) tear, rip, rent, laceration, slash.

mchanjo (also *chanjo*) n (mi-) 1. innoculation, vaccination, immunization: *Zoezi la mchanjo dhidi ya ugonjwa wa polio lilienda vizuri*, antipolio immunization exercise progressed well. 2. medicine used as a prevention against a particular disease. 3. the splitting of firewood, etc.; chopping, cutting: *Mchanjo wa kuni ulifanyika mara moja*, the splitting of firewood went fast. (cf *ukataji*)

mchano n (mi-) act (method, style, etc.) of tearing, plaiting, etc. of sth: *Mchano wa nywele*, coiffure; a style of arranging the hair.

mchanyato¹ n (mi-) a dish of sliced bananas or cassava. 2 a mixture of bananas and raw cooked mangoes.

mchanyato² n (mi-) superficial washing of clothes; gentle washing of clothes; dab, tap, pat. (cf *mchachago*)

mchapaji n (wa-) 1. printing firm. 2. printer.

mchapakazi n (wa-) a person who works diligently at sth; a hard-working person.

mchapishaji n (wa-) publisher

mchapo¹ n (mi-) lash, whip

mchapo² n (mi-) anecdote; a short entertaining account of some happening, usu of personal or biographical nature.

mchapo³ n (m-) an instrument for mixing eggs and other ingredients in making a cake, etc. (cf *blenda*)

mchapuko n (mi-) acceleration: *Mchapuko kitovu*, centripetal acceleration.

mchapuohasi n (mi-) deceleration: *Njia*

ya mchapuo hasi, deceleration lane.

mchawi *n* (*wa-*) witch, sorcerer: *Wanavijiji walimwua mchawi*, the villagers killed the witch. (cf *mlozi*)

mche[1] *n* (*mi-*) (*bot*) seedling: *Aliipandikiza miche yake*, he transplanted his seedlings. (cf *chipukizi*)

mche[2] *n* (*mi-*) 1. bar: *Mche wa sabuni*, a bar of soap. 2. (*math*) prism: *Mche duara*, cylinder. *Mche duara mraba*, right circular cylinder. *Mche duara shazari*, oblique cylinder. *Mche mstatili*, prism. *Mche pembetatu*, triangular prism. *Mche mshazari*, oblique prism. *Mche mraba*, cube (cf *dudusawa*)

mcheche *n* (*mi-*) (*zool*) a spine or quill of a porcupine, used to pierce a hole for Swahili caps.

mchecheto *n* (*mi-*) nervousness, anxiety, panic: *Timu yao iliingiwa na mchecheto kabla ya mechi kuanza*, their team was filled with anxiety before the match. (cf *wasiwasi, kiherehere*)

mcheduara *n* (*mi-*) cylinder

mchegamo *n* (*mi-*) leaning; resting on/against sth.

mchegeleko *n* (*mi-*) the looseness or slackness of luggage, etc.: *Mchegeleko wa mzigo wangu ulivifanya vitu vyote ndani yake kuanguka*, the looseness of my luggage caused all of its contents to fall out.

mcheja *n* (*wa-*) father/mother in-law. (cf *mkwe*)

mchekecheke *n* (*mi-*) 1. (*bot*) Horse Gram; a climbing herb with tripoliolate leaves and small white pea-like flowers with small lightly curved pods. *Dolichos biflorus*. 2. a herb with pinnate trifoliolate leaves, small white pea-like flowers and flat pods. *Glycine hedysaroides*. 3. a herb with pinnate leaves and long racemes of very small pink pea-like flowers and small deflexed angled pods. *Indigofera refroflexa*.

mchekecho *n* (*mi-*) sifting, winnowing.

mchekele *n* (*mi-*) (*bot*) wild olive tree. (cf *mzaituni mwitu, mchengelevu*)

mchekeshaji *n* (*wa-*) clown, comedian, humorist; an amusing person: *Mchekeshaji aliwafurahisha watazamaji*, the clown entertained the audience. (cf *mcheshi*)

mcheko *n* (*mi-*) laughing; laughter: *Mcheko wake unachusha*, his laughter is disgusting.

mchele *n* (*mi-*) (*bot*) husked rice. (*prov*) *Mchele haukosi ndume*, where there are many people, it is possible to find a leader or a wise person who can advise on anything that has gone wrong.

mchembe[1] *n* (*n*) a lot of water.

mchembe[2] *n* (*n*) (*bot*) dried slices of sweet potatoes

mchemko *n* (*mi-*) boiling, bubbling.

mchemsho *n* (*mi-*) boiling, bubbling: *Dawa hizi za mizizi zinahitaji mchemsho*, these herbs need boiling. (cf *uchemshaji*)

mchemu[1] *n* (*mi-*) iron crow-bar. (cf *msaha*)

mchemu[2] *n*(*mi-*) boiling of a short duration.

mchengo *n* (*mi-*) the cutting of wood, trees, stalks, etc. during harvesting.

mchenza *n* (*mi-*) (*bot*) mandarine orange tree; tangarine orange tree. *Citrus nobilis*.

mchepuko *n* (*mi-*) (*phys*) refraction: *Pembe mchepuko*, angle of refraction.

mchepuo *n* (*mi-*) bias; *Mchepuo wa sayansi*, science biased. *Mchepuo wa kilimo*, agricultural biased.

mcheshi *n* (*wa-*) a cheerful person; a vivacious person; a light-hearted person: *Ukizungumza naye, utajua kwamba yeye ni mcheshi*, if you talk with him, you will know that he is a cheerful person. (cf *damisi, mfurahifu*)

mcheu *n* (*mi-*) see *mteo*

mcheza *n* (*wa-*) one who plays. (*prov*) *Mcheza kwao, hutunzwa*, a person who performs a particular task at home must be rewarded.

mchezaji n (wa-) 1. idler; loiterer. 2. (in sports) player: *Mchezaji wa kulipwa*, professional player. *Mchezaji wa ridhaa*, amateur sportsman. *Mchezaji wa nyuma*, back player. *Mchezaji wa akiba*, reserve player. *Mchezaji wa kiungo*, midfield player.

mchezo n (mi-) 1. fame, sport, amusement: *Mchezo wa mpira*, football game. *Mchezo wa ngumi*, boxing game. *Mchezo wa ng'ombe*, bullfight. *Mchezo wa kuigiza*, drama, play. *Mchezo wa vinyoya*, badminton. *Mchezo wa mishale* (*Mchezo wa datini*), darts. 2. habit, mockery, mock: *Mchezo wake wa kutania watu utamletea taabu*, his habit of deriding people will lead him into trouble.

mchi n (mi-) 1. a pole of hardwood, used for pounding grain, etc. in a wooden mortar; pestle. 2. bar: *Mchi wa sabuni*, a bar of soap.

mchicha n (mi-) (*bot*) a plant with edible leaves, used as a vegetable, like spinach and which belongs to the species of *Amaranthus*. (cf *mdwere*)

mchikichi[1] (also *mgazi*) n (mi) 1. (*bot*) camel foot tree. *Bauhinia thonningii* 2. oil palm tree, *Elaeis guineensis*.

mchikichi[2] n (mi-) a kind of motor in a well for driving water.

mchikicho[1] n (mi-) the cutting of sth such as meat by using a blunt knife, etc. (cf *uchikichaji*)

mchikicho[2] n (mi-) seasoning from a mixture of pounded things such as chillies, onions, salt, lemon, etc.

mchimba n (wa-) digger; *Mchimba migodi*, miner. *Mchimba kisima*, grave digger. *Mchimba makaa*, collier, coal miner. *Mchimba madini*, mineral miner. (*prov*) *Mchimba kaburi huingia mwenyewe*, he who stirs trouble will find himself in difficulties.

mchimvi (also *chimvi, timvi*) n (wa-) 1. a person considered an ill omen; a menace to family or neighbours; public menace: *Mchimvi yule alileta fujo mtaani*, that mischievous person caused a disturbance in the neighbourhood. 2. a person esp a child who imitates bad habits such as those related to sex, etc.: *Mchimvi yule anapenda kuzungumza mambo machafu*, that person likes to talk about dirty things. 3. intriguer, firebrand: *Usiambatane na mchimvi yule*, don't associate yourself with that firebrand.

Mchina n (wa-) Chinese: *Yeye ni Mchina*, he is a Chinese.

mchinja n (wa-) 1. butcher. 2. a cruel person; brute. 3. used in the following expressions: *Mchinja farasi*, knacker.

mchinjadamu n (mi-) (*bot*) a kind of long thick banana having an attractive bright red stem and red leaf stalks and mid-ribs.

mchinjaji n (wa-) butcher, slaughterer.

mchinjiko n (mi-) a cord made up of the fibre of the baobab tree, fastened round the breasts of some women when they are suckling a baby.

mchinjo n (mi-) 1. slaying; butchering, massacre. 2. moulding clay when making pottery vessels.

mchipwi n (n) (*bot*) marine algae, kelp; a kind of large grass found in the sea belonging to the seaweed family. (cf *mwani*)

mchiririko n (mi-) (of water, blood, etc.) trickling, trilling, flowing: *Mchiririko wa machozi*, the trickling of tears. (cf *mchiriziko*)

mchirizi n (mi-) a narrow channel along the side of a road or street to carry off water to a sewer; gutter: *Funguo zake zilianguka kwenye mchirizi*, her keys fell in the gutter. *Mchirizi wa barafu*, icicle. (cf *mlizamu*)

mchirizo *n* (*mi-*) a zigzag line.

mchobeo *n* (*mi*) the act of approaching an opposite partner in the ring usu in dancing in a circle of dancers. (cf *chambi*)

mchocha (also *mchovya*) *n* (*mi-*) (*bot*) a much - branched tree up to 70 feet tall, bearing a fleshy black edible berry. *Pachystela brevipes.*

mchochea *n* (*wa-*) a person who sitres up with a poker. (*prov*) *Mchochea moto huungua yeye*, he who stirs up fire burns himself i.e. he who stirs up trouble will find himself in difficulties.

mchocheamvua *n* (*wa-*) (*zool*) honeyguide; a drab-coloured bird of a family. (*Indicatoridae*) The bird is said to lead men and animals to bees' nests in order to eat the grubs when the honey combs are taken away. (cf *mlembe*)

mchocheaji *n* (*wa-*) inciter, firebrand, rabble-rouser, troublemaker. (cf *mchochezi*)

mchocheo *n* (*mi-*) 1. stoking; poking; stirring, etc. of fire by adding more fuel. 2. (*fig*) incitement, instigation: *Mchocheo wake umewagombanisha marafiki wawili*, his incitement has caused discord between two friends. (cf *uchochezi*)

mchochezi *n* (*wa-*) instigator, inciter, agitator: *Watu hawampendi mchochezi yule*, people don't like that firebrand. (cf *sabasi*)

mchochole *n* (*wa-*) pauper, have-not; a poor person. (cf *fukara, masikini, hawinde*)

mchochoni *n* (*mi-*) (*bot*) wild yam; a wild yam growing chiefly in forest areas. The leaves of this tree are kidney-shaped and its tubes are poisonous. *Dioscorea sansibarensis.*

mchoko *n* (*wa-*) glutton, gourmand, big eater. (cf *mlafi, mroho*)

mchokocho *n* (*mi-*) act of poking sth with a sharp stick, etc. to remove the contents in a hole.

mchokochole *n* (*mi-*) see *mchokochore*

mchokochore (also *mchokochole*) *n* (*mi-*) (*bot*) a kind of tree with leaves suitable for use as toilet paper. When its flowers are open, it is believed that the rains are over. *Triumfetta rhomboidea. Mchokochore mume*, a perennial plant with pubescent leaves and small yellow flowers. *Mchokochore jike*, a stiff erect shrubby herb with hairy leaves and pink flowers, bearing sub globose fruit.

mchokoo *n* (*mi-*) a sharp-pointed stick used for digging or for spearing fish, octopus etc. (*uchokoo, mchomo*)

mchokozi *n* (*wa-*) tease, needler; a person who teases, provokes, etc.: *Vijana walimpiga mchokozi yule*, the young men beat that tease. *Nchi ya jirani ilituhumiwa kuwa ndiyo mchokozi*, the neighbouring country was suspected to be the inciter.

mchoma *n* (*wa-*) a person whose occupation is to burn sth with fire: *Mchoma makaa*, charcoal burner.

mchomo[1] *n* (*mi-*) 1. sharp bodily pain; smarting of the body. (cf *kichomi*) 2. act (method, process, etc.) of burning sth with fire. 3. a hard shot as in the case of a football kick, etc.: *Golikipa alizuia mchomo mkali wa ana kwa ana uliopigwa na mchezaji wetu*, the goalkeeper stopped a hard shot face to face kicked by our player. 4. dash, rush; a sudden, swift movement.

mchomo *n* (*mi-*) see *mchokoo*

mchomoaji *n* (*wa-*) pickpocket (cf *kibaka*)

mchomozo *n* (*mi-*) projection

mchongaji *n* (*wa-*) carver; a person who carves.

mchongelezi *n* (*wa-*) talesbearer, tattler, gossip; a bearer of false tales. (cf *sabasi*)

mchongezi *n* (*wa-*) a person who spreads

false and malicious statements against someone in order to spoil his reputation; traducer, slanderer, calumniator: *Mchongezi alidai kwamba ati sisi tulitaka kuleta ghasia shuleni,* the slanderer claimed that we wanted to cause trouble in the school. (cf *mfitini*)

mchongo n (*mi-*) act (method, etc.) of cutting with a knife, axe, etc.: *Mchongo huu wa meza ni mzuri,* the cutting of this table is good. (cf *uchongaji*)

mchongoma n (*mi-*) (*bot*) a small tree with a spiny trunk and branches, bearing edible purple fruits and flattish seeds; Indian plum, governer's plum. *Flacourtia indica.* (*prov*) *Kupanda mchongoma, kushuka ndio ngoma,* to climb an Indian plum is easy but to get down is a problem i.e. one should be careful not to embroil himself into problems because if he does, he may find it difficult to extricate himself from them.

mchonyoto n (*mi-*) itching: *Mchonyoto wa kidonda,* the itching of the wound.

mchoo n (*mi-*) the light rains which occur roughly between July and October. (cf *kipupwe*)

mchopozi n (*wa-*) pickpocket. *Mchopozi alifikishwa mahakamani kwa kuiba kamera ya mtalii,* the pickpocket was brought before the court of law for stealing the tourist's camera. (cf *mchomoaji, mkwepuzi, mnyakuzi*)

mchoraji n (*wa-*) 1. painter, artist, cartoonist. 2. designer.

mchoro n (*mi-*) 1. sketch, drawing, scribble, scrawl: *Mchoro pacha,* isometric drawing. *Mchoro picha,* pictorial drawing. *Mchoro mtiririko,* flow diagram. *Mchoro wakilishi,* scale drawing. *Mchoro wa saketi,* circuit diagram, *Mchoro mpangilio,* flow diagram. 2. act (method, etc.) of drawing, sketching, etc.: *Mchoro wake haueleweki,* his drawing style is incomprehensible.

mchoroko n (*mi-*) (*bot*) green gram; a plant with hairy pods and yellowish flowers, bearing edible usu green seeds. *Phaseolus mungo.*

mchoto n (*mi-*) taking of a small piece, quantity, etc. of grain, water, etc.: *Mchoto wa sukari,* the taking of sugar in a small quantity by using a ladle, etc.; pinch. (cf *uchotaji*)

mchovya n (*wa-*) a person who dips sth into liquid; dipper. (*prov*) *Mchovya asali, hachovyi mara moja,* he who dips into honey does it once i.e. when you get sth good, you will never cease to go after it or pursue a similar kind of thing again and again.

mchovyo¹ n (*mi*) 1. (*cf metals*) dipping into liquid; plunging into liquid; tempering, coating, plating 2. camouflage.

mchovyo n (*mi-*)

mchoyo n (*wa-*) miser, niggard: *Mchoyo yule hatakupa kitu chake,* that miser will not give you his things. (cf *kisangati, bahili*)

mchu n (*mi-*) (*bot*) a kind of mangrove with tough wood and thin leaves and heads of small inconspicuous flowers. *Avicennia marina.*

mchuano n (*mi-*) 1. contest, match, competition: *Mchuano wa kura za maoni,* referendum. *Kulikuwepo na michuano mikali ya kandanda wiki iliyopita,* there were stiff football competitions last week. (cf *pambano, mtanange, shindano*) 2. friction, abrasion. (cf *msuguano*)

mchubuko n (*mi-*) bruise, scratch: *Alipata michubuko baada ya kuanguka kutoka kwenye ngazi,* he received bruises after falling down from the stairs.

mchujo n (*mi-*) act (method, etc.) of filtering, straining, screening, etc.: *Mchujo wa kwanza wa wagombea uraisi,* the initial screening of the presidential candidates. (cf *uchujaji*)

mchukivu n (wa-) a sulky person; splenetic, sourpuss, bête nôire.
mchukucha n (mi-) a drink with a bad taste.
mchukuzi n (wa-) porter, carrier. (cf *kuli, hamali, mpagazi*)
mchumaji n (wa-) 1. picker: *Wachumaji wa karafuu*, clove pickers. 2. earner.
mchumba n (wa-) 1. fiance. 2. fiancee.
mchumbururu (also *sambarau*) n (mi-) (zool) a kind of sword fish with a sail-like dorsal fin belonging to the family of *Hermaphidae*; half-beak. The fish is being characterized by being large and aggressive, lack of pelvic fins and gill rakers and the like. (cf *chuchunge*)
mchumi[1] n (wa-) economist
mchumi[2] n (wa-) one who picks crops, etc.
mchunaji n (wa-) (bot) a person who flays animals. (cf *kaisi*)
mchunga[1] n (mi-) (bot) a kind of plant whose sour thin leaves are used as a vegetable.
mchunga[2] n (wa-) a person who guards sth; guard, overseer.
mchungaji[1] n (wa-) 1. shepherd, herder, herdsman. 2. watchman.
mchungaji[2] n (wa-) church pastor.
mchunguaji n(wa-) 1. busybody. 2. investigator, detective. 3. winnower; a person who removes chaff from grain.
mchunguti n (wa-) see *msunguti*
mchunguzi n (wa-) 1. eavesdropper, busybody; an inquisitive person. (cf *mpelelezi*) 2. investigator, detective, fact-finder. (cf *kachero*) 3. researcher. (cf *mtafiti*)
mchungwa n (mi-) (bot) sweet orange tree. *Citrus sinensis*.
mchuuko n (mi-) cliché
mchuuzi n (wa-) vendor, monger: *Mchuuzi wa mboga/matunda* mitaani; costermonger. (cf *muuzaji, mfanyabiashara*)
mchuzi n (wa-) curry, sauce, gravy: *Mchuzi wa viungo*, curry powder. *Mchuzi wa kuku*, chicken curry.

Mchuzi wa nyama, broth.
mchwa n (n) (zool) termite; a pale-coloured social insect having an order (*Isoptera*) which is destructive to wooden structures, crops, etc.
mdaa n (mi-) 1. a shrub or small top tree up to 20 feet tall with evergreen leathery leaves and small white flowers. *Euclea bilocularis*. 2. a much-branched pubescent small tree upto 20 feet tall with alternate leaves and inconspicuous green flowers, bearing a globular fruit and producing a black dye from the roots of which are said to be poisonous. The dye is used in the treatment of snakebites. *Royena macrocalyx*. *Mdaa mwitu*, a much-branched evergreen tree upto 30 feet with alternate glossy leaves and small yellowish-green flowers, bearing a small pea-like fruit and producing a black dye, used for dying local mats. *Euclea fructuosa*. (cf *msizi*)
mdaawa n (wa-) (law) litigant (cf *mdai*)
Mdachi n (wa-) (arch) German (cf *Mjerumani*)
mdadi n (wa-) excitement, drive. (cf *hamasa, jazba*)
mdadisi n (wa-) a person who slyly elicits information by asking questions; snoop: *Mdadisi alijaribu kutaka kujua siri za majirani zake*, the snoop tried to pry into the affairs of his neighbours. (cf *mpelelezi, mtafiti, mdoya*)
mdahalo n (mi-) debate (cf *mjadala*)
mdai n (wa-) claimant, creditor. (cf *mwia, mshtaki*) (Ar)
mdaiwa n (wa-) (law) defendant, debtor: *Mdaiwa alipandishwa kizimbani*, the debtor was put in the dock. (cf *muwiwa, mdeni*) (Ar)
mdakaji n (wa-) a person who catches sth like a ball, etc.; catcher.
mdakale n (mi-) the long stem of a hookah pipe, used for smoking tobacco, etc. (cf *mburuma*)
mdakiaji n (wa-) meddler (cf *mdakulizi*)
mdakizi (also *mdakuzi*) n (wa-) eavesdropper, gossip-monger: *Siri zao*

zilifichuliwa na mdakizi, their secrets were disclosed by the eavesdropper. (cf *mbeya*)

mdako[1] *n* (*mi-*) a children's game in which they throw pebbles, etc. up and catch them; a children's game of jacks.

mdako[2] *n*(*mi-*) act (manner, method, etc.) of catching sth. (cf *udakaji*)

mdaku *n* (*wa-*) snoop, tattler. (cf *mbeya*)

mdakulizi *n* (*wa-*) a person who meddles into other people's affairs; meddler. (*mdakiaji*)

mdakuzi[1] *n* (*wa-*) a person who meddles into other people's affairs; meddler.

mdakuzi[2] *n* (*wa*) see *mdakizi*

mdalasini *n* (*mi-*) 1. (*bot*) cinnamon tree; a small tree with leathery leaves and small flowers, bearing an oval green fruit containing a brown seed. *Cinnamomun zeylanicum*. 2. cinammon bark, which is a well-known spice, used in curries, etc. (Ar)

mdambi *n* (*mi-*) (*bot*) a shrub closely resembling heather with minute leaves and tiny brownish-white flowers in clusters at the tops of the branches. These branches are used for fencing and brooms. *Phillipia mafiensis*.

mdanganyifu *n* (*wa-*) cheat, liar, fraud, phoney, swindler: *Usimwamini mdanganyifu yule*, don't trust that cheat. (cf *mnafiki, laghai, kidhabu*)

mdanzi *n* (*mi-*) (*bot*) seville orange tree; bigarade orange tree; sour orange tree; a kind of tree which produces a fruit called *danzi*, seville orange. *Citrus aurantium*.

mdarabi *n* (*mi-*) (*bot*) rose apple, pomme rose; a kind of evergreen tree of medium size bearing a round fruit consisting of a fleshy, pale yellow rose-scented pericarp surrounding a central seed. *Eugenia jambos*. (cf *mgulabi*)

mdato *n* (*mi-*) crackle, chick, snap. (cf *udataji, mualiko*)

mdau *n* (*wa-*) stakeholder: *Wadau wa michezo*, sports stakeholders.

mdeki *n* (*mi-*) ramrod; a rod used for pushing explosives, bullets, etc. into a gun that is loaded through a muzzle: *Shindilia bunduki kwa mdeki*, load a gun with a ramrod.

mdele *n* (*mi-*) see *dele*

mdema *n* (*mi-*) a kind of epic poem recited by one person from door holding a rattle.

mdengu *n* (*mi-*) (*bot*) chick pea; an erect annual plant which bears a small edible bean or pick, used extensively for making cakes, curries, etc. *Cicer arietinum*.

mdeni *n* (*wa-*) debtor (cf *mdaiwa*)

mderahani *n* (*mi-*) a kind of soft silky material.

mdhabidhabina (also *mzabizabina*) *n* (*wa-*) 1. inciter, instigator, firebrand: *Mdhabidhabina aliwayombunisha majirani zake*, the firebrand brought discord among his neighbours. (cf *mfitini, fatani*) 2. a double-faced person, a two-faced person, an underhanded person; hypocrite: *Mdhabidhabina yule haaminiki hata kidogo*, that hypocrite cannot be trusted at all. (cf *mzandiki, mnafiki*) (Ar)

mdhalilishaji *n* (*wa-*) humiliator; a person who humiliates someone else. (cf *mnyanyasaji mwoneaji*)

mdhalimu *n* (*wa-*) see *dhalimu*

mdhamini (also *dhamini*) *n* (*wa-*) guarantor, surety, sponsor: *Mshtakiwa alikosa kupata mdhamini*, the accused failed to get surety. *Timu yetu iliweza kupata mdhamini wa kugharimia mashindano yake ugenini*, our team managed to get a sponsor to meet the expenses for its matches abroad. (cf *mtadaruki*) (Ar)

mdhana *n* (*n*) bad luck, bad omen, ill luck, jinx; anything which brings bad luck or misfortune. (cf *nuhusi, kisrani*) (Ar)

mdhibiti *n* (*wa-*) protector, controller, checker: *Mdhibiti nidhamu*, disciplinarian. *Mdhibiti* (*wa*) *fedha*, financial controller. (Ar)

mdhihirisho *n* (*mi-*) evidence, proof,

verification, indication: *Huu ni mdhihirisho wa mawazo yake*, this is the indication of his ideas. (cf *mbainisho*) (Ar)

mdidimio *n* (*mi-*) submergence, sinking, submersion: *Mdidimio wa ardhi*, submersion of land. (cf *mtitio*)

mdimu *n* (*mi-*) (*bot*) lime tree. *Citrus aurantifolia*. *Mdimu mtamu*, is a monoecious glabrous shrub with alternate leathery leaves and small yellow green flowers, bearing a globose fruit. *Gelonium zanzibarense*.

mdiria *n* (*n*) (*zool*) Alcedinae kingfisher; a medium-sized bird (family *Alcedinidae*) which is brightly coloured and feeding largely upon large insects and lizards (cf *mtilili, kisharifu, kurea*)

mdirifu *n* (*wa-*) a person who is neither poor nor rich; a middle income person.

mdodoki *n* (*mi-*) 1. (*bot*) loofah; an annual climber bearing a cucumber-like fruit with 10 sharp longitudinal ridges, and is eaten young in curries, and used as a vegetable. *Luffa acutangula*. 2. an annual climber with rough leaves and yellow flowers bearing also a cucumber-like fruit, whose interior is a mass of fibrous tissue in which the seeds are embedded. The fruit is used commercially for sponges, socks, etc. *Luffa cylindrica*. *Mdodoki wa Kibaniani*, a flowering shrub. *Capparis galeata*.

mdoezi *n* (*wa-*) bum, scrounger, sponger, scrounger (cf *mdoya*).

mdogo *n* (*wa-*) junior

mdokozi *n* (*wa-*) a person who has formed the habit of stealing small things; petty thief. (cf *mdokoaji*)

mdomo (also *mdema*) *n* (*mi-*) 1. (*anat*) mouth. 2. beak of a bird; bill. 3. anything lip-like. 4. (*idms*) *Piga domo*, be garrulous; be talkative. *Ana mdomo mrefu*, he is rude. *Ana mdomo mchafu*, he is abusive. *Tia domo*, intrude; interfere in other people's affairs. *Funga mdomo*, shut your mouth.

mdomwa *n* (*n*) local dance in which people of both sexes stand in two rows facing each other, and then jump up and down at the same time clapping their hands. The opposite in the two rows are required to come down with opposite feet. In other words, if one comes down on the right foot, his opposite must come down on the left foot.

mdondoakupe *n* (*wa-*) (*zool*) a kind of bird that sticks on the back of animals esp. cattle; cattle tick bird. (cf *kongong'ombe, yangeyange*)

mdondoo *n* (*mi-*) a kind of harvest done in small quantities.

mdongea[1] *n* (*mi-*) 1. the style of throwing a cloth over the shoulders. 2. a cloth that is thrown over the shoulders; shawl. (cf *mtandio*)

mdongea[2] *n* (*mi-*) a white cap sewn by a sewing-machine.

mdoni[1] *n* (*mi-*) (*zool*) bill, beak; the bird's mouth.

mdono[1] *n* (*mi-*) (of a fish) bite; act of taking the bait or lure on the end of a fishing line into the mouth.

mdono[2] *n* (*mi-*) act of biting; bite: *Mdono wa ndege*, the bird's bite.

mdoriani (also *mduriani*) *n* (*mi-*) (*bot*) durian; a very tall and wide spreading tree with beautiful foliage and which bears a large roundish fruit with a green spiky exterior. *Durio zibethinus*. (Mly)

mdorongo *n* (*mi-*) a succession of ants e.g safari ants, small black ants, etc

mdororo *n* (*mi-*) decline, weakening, recession, deterioration, degeneration, decay, wear and tear: *Mdororo wa kiuchumi*, economic recession.

mdoshi *n* (*mi-*) a kind of pedal or treadle on a sewing machine or bicycle.

mdosi *n* (*wa-*) a well to do person; a rich person; tycoon.

mdoya *n* (*wa-*) 1. spy, secret agent. (cf *mdukizi, mbeya*) 2. sponger, scrounger.

mduara *n* (*mi-*) circumference, circle. (cf *mzingo, kivimbe*)

mdubira *n* (*mi-*) a person who always appears to have bad luck in anything he attempts; an unlucky person; jinx. (cf *mkunguru*)

mdubiri *n* (*wa-*) a person fond of superstition work; a superstitious person; voodooist, sorcerer.

mdudu *n* (*wa-*) 1. (*zool*) insect: *Mdudu wa kijamii*, social insect. 2. used in the phrase: *Mdudu wa kidoleni*, a painful pus-producing infection at the end of a finger or toe near the nail; whitlow, felon. Also called *mdudu upande*. (*kaakaa*)

mdukizi (also *dukizi*) *n* (*wa-*) eavesdropper, snoop, spy: *Mdukizi yule anaudhi*, that eavesdropper is a nuisance. (cf *mdoya*)

mdukuo (also *msukuo*) *n* (*mi-*) act of pushing someone with a finger on his face or anywhere on the head resulting from a conflict between the persons concerned.

mdumavu *n* (*wa-*) a person deficient of sth: *Mdumavu wa akili*, cretin.

mdumizi *n* (*wa-*) a person who though is able to work, depends upon others for food, money, etc.; sponger, scrounger, scrounge. (cf *doezi*)

mdundiko *n* (*mi-*) a kind of local dance which has a feature of jumping up. It is played by a certain tribe namely, Zaramo in Morogoro, Tanzania.

mdundo *n* (*mi-*) 1. drumbeat; drumming: *Mdundo ishara*, signal drumming. *Mdundo kalima*, speech drumming. *Mdundo dansa*, dancing drumming. *Piga ngoma mdundo mmoja*, hit the drum with one beat. 2. hitting sth so that it returns to its original position; bounce: *Daka mpira baada ya mdundo mmoja*, catch a ball at a first bounce. 3. pounding of sth as in a wooden mortar. 4. song or music: *Bendi yao ilipiga mdundo mmoja mzuri*, their band produced one good beat.

mdundugo *n* (*mi-*) a kind of medicine or charm that is said to make one invulnerable such that a bullet or anything of that sort cannot penetrate into him or he cannot be harmed by it when one is shot from a distance; anti-weapon charm/medicine.

mdunzi (also *mdunzidunzi*) *n* (*wa-*) investigator, spy, detective: *Mdunzi alichunguza chanzo cha mauaji*, the detective investigated the cause of the murder. (cf *mpelelezi*, *jasusi*)

mdunzidunzi *n* (*wa-*) see *mdunzi*

mdurenge *n* (*n*) a kind of local dance performed in a circle by people going round and round and at the same time holding one another.

mduriani *n* (*mi-*) see *mdoriani*

mdwere *n* (*mi-*) (*bot*) a plant with edible leaves and used as a vegetable like spinach and which belongs to the species of *Amaranthus*; local spinach. (cf *mchicha*)

me.a *vi* 1. (of plants, etc.) grow as a vegetable or plant; germinate: sprout: *Mbegu zimemea*, the seeds have germinated. (cf *ota*) 2. (of teeth, hair, nails, etc.) grow: *Kucha zimemea mno*, the nails have grown. 3. (*idms*) *Mea meno*, be arrogant, be conceited. *Mea mbawa*, boast, brag e.g. *Alimea mbawa alipopandishwa cheo kazini kwake*, he became boastful when he was promoted at his place of work. Prep. **me.le.a** St. **me.k.a** Cs. **me.sh.a** and **me.z.a**

mechi *n* (*n*) match, sporting: *Mechi ya mpira*, football match. *Mechi ya krikoti*, cricket match. *Mechi ya marudiano*, a) return match, i.e. home and away match. *Mechi ya marudiano*, a) a replay match i.e. a match played again after the abandonment of the previous game while in progress due to some technical reasons, etc. b) a second round match i.e a match that is played for the second time after the first round has been completed; home and away contest: *Mechi ya kujipima nguvu*, trial match. *Mechi za mchujo*, qualifying matches. *Mechi ya*

M

ufunguzi, opening match. *Mechi ya vuta nikuvute*, a tough match. *Mechi ya kukata na shoka*, a crucial match; a tough match; a big match. *Mechi ya kiporo*, the remaining match. (Eng)

medali *n (n)* medal: *Medali ya dhahabu*, gold medal. *Medali ya fedha*, silver medal. *Medali ya shaba*, bronze medal. (Eng)

medani *n (n)* 1. arena, battlefield. 2. *(fig)* field, circle, sphere, place: *Medani za kimataifa*, international circles. (Ar)

mede¹ *n (n)* a small bedstead, used as a seat for guests, etc.

mede² *n (n)* bay of safety in certain games such as children's game of hide-and-seek.

meg.a (also *menya*) *vt, vi* 1. (of food, etc.) break a piece; bite off a piece esp with fingers or teeth: *Aliimega keki*, he broke off a piece of cake. (cf *nofoa, nyofoa*) 2. *(fig)* break off in other ways as in the case of sea and erosion. Prep. *meg.e.a* St. *meg.ek.a* Cs. *meg.esh.a* Ps. *meg.w.a*

megawati *n (n) (elect)* megawatt (Eng)

meguk.a *vi* be fragmented, be disintegrated, be split, be divided: *Klabu yao sasa imeanza kumeguka*, their club has started to disintegrate. Prep. *meguk.i.a* St. *meguk.ik.a* Cs. *meguk.ish.a*

Mei *n (n)* the month of May. (Eng)

meja *n (n)* major in an army: *Meja jenerali*, major general. (Eng)

mekanika *n (n)* mechanic (Eng)

meko *n (n)* 1. hearth. 2. kitchen; cooking place.

melesi *n (n) (zool)* badger

melezi (also *maezi*) *n (n) (naut)* roadsted, anchorage.

meli¹ *n (n)* ship, mailboat: *Meli ya abiria*, passenger ship. *Meli ya biashara*, mercantile ship. *Meli ya shehena*, merchant ship. *Meli ya mizinga*, main-of war; battleship. *Meli ya mizigo*, cargo ship. (cf *manuwari*)

meli² *n (n)* a unit for measuring distance on land and in the sea.

melimeli *n (n)* a kind of thin white cloth usu used to stitch *kanzu;* muslin, batiste. (Hind)

memba *n (n)* 1. a person belonging to some association, society, party, etc.; member: *Memba wa bodi*, board member. (cf *mwanajumuiya, mwanachama*) 2. a distinct part or element of a whole thing; member. (Eng)

membe *n (n) (zool)* whimbrel; a large wading bird with a distinctive long down-curved bill, which allows it to probe deeply into mud for titbits. *Numenius phaeopus*. (cf *kioga, kwawa*)

memet.a *vi* see *memeteka*. Prep. *memet.e.a* St. *memet.ek.a* Cs. *memet.esh.a* Rs. *memet.w.a*

memetek.a (also *meremeta, memeta, memetuka*) *vi* sparkle, shimmer, twinkle, glitter: *Theluji ilimemeteka juani*, the snow sparkled in the sunlight. Prep. *memetek.e.a* St. *memetek.ek.a* Cs. *memetek.esh.a*

memetukaji *adj* sparkling, glimmering, shiny, shimmering

memetuk.a *vi* see *memeteka*

memsahib *n (n)* a respectful address to a rich woman or one's female employer.

men.a *vt, vi* despise, scorn, disdain. Prep. *men.e.a* St. *men.ek.a* Cs. *men.esh.a* Ps. *men.w.a* Rp. *men.an.a* (cf *dharau, beza*)

mende *n (n)* 1. *(zool)* cockroach. (cf *kombamwiki*) 2. sodomite. (cf *basha*)

meneja *n (n)* manager: *Meneja mauzo*, sales manager. *Meneja utumishi*, personal manager. *Meneja msaidizi*, assistant manager. *Meneja wa kike*, manageress. *Meneja wa kikundi cha sanaa*, impresario.

menejimenti *n (n)* management, administration. (cf *utawala*) (Eng)

meng'eny.a *vt* (of fruits such as oranges, etc.) squeeze in order to get juice; extract juice from the rind: *Aliyameng'enya machungwa*, he squeezed the oranges in order to get juice. Prep. *meng'eny.e.a* St. *meng'eny.ek.a* Cs. *meng'eny.esh.a* Ps. *meng'eny.w.a* (cf *kamua*)

meny.a¹ *vt* see *mega*

meny.a² *vt* (of fruits such as orange, cassava, etc.) peel, shell, pare, strip away: *Aliumenya muhogo*, he peeled the cassava. Prep. *meny.e.a* St. *meny.ek.a* Cs. *meny.esh.a* Ps. *meny.w.a*

menyan.a *vt, vi* contest in a game, etc.; compete: *Timu mbili zilimenyana vikali uwanjani*, the two teams contested bitterly on the ground. Prep *menyan.i.a* St. *menyan.ik.a* Cs. *menyan.ish.a* (cf *pepetana, umana, vaana, pambunu*)

menyek.a *vt, vi* 1. toil; work like a dog; go all-out: *Yeye humenyeka kazini*, he works like a dog at his place of work. (cf *chapa kazi*) 2. put a lot of efforts in doing work that has no benefit. 3. (of fruits) be peeled, be shelled. Prep. *menyek.e.a* St *menyek.ek.a* Cs *menyek.esh.a*

meremet.a *vi* see *memeteka*. Prep. *meremet.e.a* St. *meremet.ek.a* Cs. *meremet.esh.a*

meridiani *n* (*n*) (*geog*) meridian (Eng)

merikebu *n* (*n*) (*naut*) European type of sailing vessel or steamship; an ocean-going vessel. (Ar)

mesenja *n* (*n*) messenger (cf *tarishi, katikiro, mjumbe*) (Eng)

mesi *n* (*n*) dining hall. (cf *bwalo*)

Mesiya *n* (*n*) see *masihi*

met.a¹ *vi* see *memeteka*

meta² (also *mita*) *n* (*n*) 1. a device that measures the volume of electricity, gas, water, etc. passing through it; meter: *Meta ya umeme*, electricity meter. *Meta ya gesi*, gas meter. *Meta ya maji*, water meter. 2. the basic unit of length in the metric system equal to 39.37 inches; metre. (Eng)

metali *n* (*n*) metal: *Metali ya thamani*, precious metal.

methali (also *mithali*) *n* (*n*) proverb, parable, aphorism. (Ar)

metriki *adj* metric (Eng)

meya *n* (*n*) mayor: *Yeye ni meya katika jiji letu*, he is the mayor in our city. (Eng)

meza¹ *n* (*n*) 1. table: *Mtoto wa meza*, drawer. *Meza yenye saraka*, escritoire. 2. (*syn*) *Meza ya mazungumzo*, conference table e.g. *Pande mbili zinazozozana zilirudi tena kwenye meza ya mazungumzo*, the two opposing sides came back to the conference table to negotiate. (Port, Pers)

mez.a² *vt, vi* 1. swallow, gulp, guzzle: *Alimeza dawa*, he swallowed the pill. 2. (usu passive) engulf: *Nchi yao yote imemezwa*, their whole country has been engulfed. Prep. *mez.o.a* St. *mez.ek.a* Cs. *mez.esh.a* Ps. *mez.w.a*

mfaa *n* (*mi-*) centre-piece of a local door fixed to one valve to prevent one side crossing the other side i.e. *Upanga wa mlango*.

mfadhaiko *n* (*mi-*) perplexity, bewilderment, amazement, shock: *Aliingiwa na mfadhaiko aliposikia kifo cha mwanawe*, he was shocked when he heard the death of his son. (cf *mtanabahisho, mzubao*)

mfadhili *n* (*mi-*) benefactor, sponsor, philanthropist: *Timu yetu iliweza kupata mfadhili*, our team managed to get a sponsor. (cf *mhisani, mtwa*) (Ar)

mfadhiliwa *n* (*wa-*) beneficiary (cf *mkirimiwa*) (Ar)

mfadhaisho *n* (*wa-*) bewilderment, perplexity, unsettlement. (cf *uduwalifu, mzubao*) (Ar)

mfafanuzi *n* (*wa-*) interpreter, elaborator, elucidator: *Mfafanuzi aliutafsiri waraka*, the interpreter expounded the document. (cf *mfasiri*)

mfagiaji *n* (*wa-*) see *mfagizi*

mfagio *n* (*mi-*) (*bot*) a fibre plant used for brooms; broom plant. *Sida acuta*.

mfagizi (also *mfagiaji*) *n* (*wa-*) sweeper: *Mtumishi wangu ni mfagizi mzuri*, my

servant is a good sweeper.
mfalme n (wa-) king (cf *maliki*)
mfamasia n (wa-) pharmacist, apothecary, posologist. (Eng)
mfanano n (mi-) resemblance, correspondence, likeness, similarity, parallelism: *Hakuna mfanano wowote kati ya maneno yake na matendo yenyewe*, there is no correspondence between his words and the deeds. *Kuna mfanano mkubwa kati ya ndugu hawa wawili*, there is a big resemblance between these two brothers. (cf *mlingano, mshabihiano*)
mfani n (wa-) counterpart
mfano n (mi-) 1. example, parable: *Kwa mfano*, for example. *Mfano halisi*, epitome; classical example. *Mfano hai*, a living example. 2. model, pattern. (cf *sampuli, kielelezo, mithili*)
mfanyabiashara n (wa-) businessman, trader. (cf *mjasiriamali*)
mfanyakazi n (wa-) workman, worker, labourer. (cf *mwajiriwa, mtumishi*)
mfaraka n (mi-) squabble, dispute, misunderstanding, imbroglio, conflict. (cf *ugomvi, suitafahamu, mtafaruku*)
mfarakano n (mi-) estrangement, separation, split: *Palitokea mfarakano kati ya viongozi wa chama tawala*, there was a split among the leaders of the ruling party. (cf *mtengano, chamkano*) (Ar)
Mfaransa n (wa-) Frenchman (Fr)
mfariji n (wa-) consoler: *Wafariji wengi walimiminika nyumbani baada ya kusikia kifo cha mama*, many consolers thronged home after hearing of my mother's death. (cf *mliwaza*) (Ar)
mfarika n (wa-) (zool) heifer (cf *mtamba, dachia*) (Ar)
mfariki n (wa-) a person who separates himself from his home, etc.
mfarisha (also *farisha, mfarishi*) n (mi-) quilt, eiderdown; a decorative cover for a bed. (Ar)

mfarishi n (mi-) see *mfarisha*
mfaruku n (wa-) a bereaved woman; a widowed woman; widow. (cf *mjane*)
mfasa n (mi-) (bot) a tall herb with blue daisy-like flowers. *Vernonia obconica*.
mfasiri n (wa-) 1. translator, interpreter. (cf *mkalimani*) 2. elaborator, elucidator, interpreter: *Mfasiri alizifasiri sheria tata*. the interpreter elucidated the complex laws. (Ar)
mfatiliaji n (wa-) a person who makes a follow-up of sth.
mfawidhi n (wa-) the person in charge of the day-to-day activities in a department, etc.: *Mfawidhi wa sherehe*, master of ceremony. (Ar)
mfenesi n (mi-) (bot) jackfruit tree; a kind of tree which bears a large heavy greenish fruit. *Artocarpus integra*. *Mfenesi wa kizungu*, breadfruit. *Artocarpus communis*.
mfereji n (mi-) 1. irrigation ditch, water channel; a trench dug for carrying off water or for irrigation: *Mfereji ule ulichimbwa ili kuinywesha mimea*, that irrigation ditch was dug to water the plants. *Mfereji wa kupitisha maji kwenye kinu*, flume. (cf *mtaro*) 2. waterpipe. (cf *bomba*)
mfichachani n (mi-) (bot) radish; a kind of small tuberous rooted plant, whose leaves and roots are used as vegetables and eaten raw as a salad alongside with food. *Raphanus sativus*.
mfichaji n (wa-) a person who hides things.
mficho n(mi-) concealment (cf *ufichaji*)
mfigili n (mi-) (bot) radish plant. *Raphanus sativus*.
mfilisi n (wa-) 1. see *muflisi*. 2. liquidator: *Benki kuu ilimteua mfilisi ili kufunga hesabu za benki iliyofilisika*, the central bank appointed a liquidator to wind up the business of the insolvent.
mfilisiwa n (wa-) a bankrupt person; bankrupt: *Amekuwa mfilisiwa baada*

ya kushindwa katika michezo mingi ya kamari, he has become bankrupt after losing many gambles.

Mfini *n* (*wa-*) a person from Finland; Finn. (Fin)

mfiniko *n* (*mi-*) see *mfuniko*

mfinyango *n* (*mi-*) pottery, pottering: *Mfinyango wa vyungu ulifanywa na wafinyanzi wanawake*, the pottery work was done by women porters.

mfinyanzi *n* (*wa-*) a person who makes pottery; potter: *Vyungu vya mfinyanzi yule ni vizuri*, the pots of that potter are good. (*prov*) *Mfinyanzi hulia gaeni*, a porter eats off a potsherd i.e. a person may have a lot of wealth, etc, yet he may not use it for his own welfare because he is a miser, etc.

mfinyo *n* (*mi-*) pinch, nip, squeeze; act of pressing someone or sth with the fingers or nails.

mfiraji *n* (*wa-*) sodomite (cf *basha, mende*)

mfitini (also *fatani*) *n* (*wa-*) a sower of discord, a person who causes discord among people; incendiary, firebrand: *Mfitini aliwagombanisha marafiki wawili*, the firebrand caused discord between the two friends. (cf *salata, mchongezi*)

mfiwa *n* (*wa-*) a bereaved person: *Majirani walikwenda kuwafariji wafiwa*, the neighbours went to console the bereaved persons. *Haki ya mke mfiwa kutokana na mali ya mumewe*, dower.

mfiwi *n* (*mi-*) (*bot*) lima bean plant; a common variety of bean with variable leaves, creamy flowers and broad pods. *Phaseolus lunatus*.

mfo *n* (*mi-*) see *mvo*

mforsadi *n* (*mi-*) see *mfursadi*

mfu *n* (*wa-*) a dead person; corpse. (cf *maiti*)

mfua *n* (*wa-*) a word used with an object operating as a complement: *Mfuachuma*, metal worker. *Mfuadhahabu*, goldsmith. *Mfuafedha*, silver-smith. *Mfuabunduki*, gunsmith.

Mfuanazi, a person who husks coconuts; husker.

mfuanazi *n* (*wa-*) see *mfua*

mfuasi *n* (*wa-*) a follower of a particular religion, political activity, etc. (cf *mlungizi*)

mfuatano *n* (*mi-*) sequence, succession: *Mfuatano wa matukio*, sequence of events. *Mfuatano wa nyakati*, a sequence of tenses. (cf *mwandamano*)

mfuatiliaji *n* (*wa-*) monitor: *Mfuatiliaji wa mambo ya kisiasa*, political observers.

mfuatizo *n* (*mi-*) emulation, mimicry: *Mfuatizo wa tabia zake mbovu utakudhuru*, the imitation of his bad habits will harm you.

mfuauji *n* (*wa-*) dandy, coxcomb, fop; a person who is excessively concerned about smartness.

mfufu *n* (*mi-*) see *mfuru*

mfugaji *n* (*wa-*) herder, rancher; a breeder of animals: *Mfugaji wa kipanga*, falconer.

mfugo *n* (*mi-*) a livestock animal: *Daktari wa mifugo*, veterinary doctor. *Wizara yetu inashughulikia mambo ya mifugo*, our ministry takes care of livestock animals.

mfujaji *n* (*wa-*) squanderer, wastrel, spendthrift; a person who wastes money, etc.: *Yeye ni mfujaji wa pesa*, he is a spendthrift. (*mbadhirifu, mharibifu*)

mfuko *n* (*mi-*) 1. bag, sack, purse. *Mfuko wa karatasi*, paper bag. *Mfuko wa bastola*, holster. *Mfuko wa barua*, mailbag. *Mfuko wa kutia saa*, fob. (cf *mkoba*) 2. pocket, purse. 3. fund: *Mfuko wa dhamana*, trust fund. *Mfuko wa Fedha wa Kimataifa*, International Monetary Fund. *Serikali imeandaa mfuko maalumu wa kuwasaidia watoto wa barabarani*, the government has organized a special fund to assist the street children.

mfululizo[1] *n* (*mi-*) consecutiveness, succession, sequence: *Huu ni mfululizo* *wa mikasa iliyonikuta*, this is a succession of events I had encountered. (cf *mtitiriko*)

mfululizo² *n* (*mi-*) persistence, progression, succession: *Mvua ilinyesha siku tatu kwa mfululizo*, it rained three days consecutively.

mfululizo³ *n* (*mi-*) series; a number of things produced as a related group: *Hiki ni kitabu cha tatu katika mfululizo wa vitabu vya uchumi*, this is the third book on economic series.

mfumaji (also *mfumi*) *n* (*wa-*) 1. weaver: *Mfumaji wa hariri*, silk weaver. 2. a person who ornaments with needlework; embroiderer. 3. a striker with a spear or a sharp instrument.

mfumbati *n* (*mi-*) the side piece of the frame of a bed; side piece of a bedstead.

mfumbi *n* (*mi-*) a trench or channel dug to carry away rainwater; rainwater drainage. (cf *ufumbi, mvo, mchirizi*)

mfumi *n* (*wa-*) see *mfumaji*

mfumo *n* (*mi-*) 1. art (style, act, etc.) of weaving; texture. 2. system, process: *Mfumo wa kisiasa*, political system. *Mfumo wa chakula*, digestive system. *Mfumo wa mifupa*, skeletal system. *Mfumo wa metriki*, metric system. *Mfumo wa msawia*, system of simultaneous equations. *Nchi za Kiafrika zinafuata mifumo mbalimbali ya kisiasa*, African countries follow different political systems. (cf *sera, utaratibu*)

mfumuko *n* (*mi-*) hike, shoot up: *Mfumuko wa bei*, inflation; price hike. *Udhibiti wa mfumuko wa bei*, disinflation; control or reduction in the rate of inflation.

mfundo¹ *n* (*mi-*) resentment, dudgeon, umbrage: *Baada ya kugombana naye, rafiki yangu sasa ameanza kuniwekea mfundo*, after having quarrelled with him, my friend has now started to harbour resentment against me. (cf *hasira, kinyongo*)

mfundo² *n* (*mi-*) (in a race) finishing line.

mfune (also *mgude*) *n* (*mi-*) (*bot*) a tall tree upto 80 feet with a pale smooth yellow-green bark and a small rounded crown with alternate long-stalked leaves and small yellow-green flowers bearing a star-shaped fruit containing smooth black seeds. *Sterculia appendiculata*.

mfungaji *n* (*wa-*) (*sports*) scorer: *Mfungaji wa magoli*, goal scorer. *Mfungaji bora*, best scorer.

mfungo¹ *n* (*mi-*) (in Islam) fasting: *Huu ni mfungo wa mwezi wa Ramadhan*, this is the fasting month of Ramadan. (cf *saumu*)

mfungo² *n* (*mi-*) act (method, etc.) of tying sth. (cf *ufungaji*)

mfunguo *n* (*mi-*) 1. unfastening, untying, loosening, etc. 2. an expletive used to describe the nine months after the fasting month of Ramadan i.e. *Mfunguo mosi, Mfunguo pili, Mfunguo tatu*, etc.

mfungwa *n* (*wa-*) 1. prisoner: *Mfungwa wa kisiasa*, political prisoner. *Mfungwa wa vita*, prisoner of war. *Mfungwa mzoevu*, lag. *Wafungwa walitoroka gerezani*, the prisoners escaped from prison. (cf *mahabusu*) 2. a person sentenced to imprisonment.

mfuniko (also *mfiniko*) *n* (*mi-*) cover, stopper, lid: *Mfuniko wa chupa hii umepotea*, the stopper of this bottle is lost. *Mfuniko wa mlango*, hatch. (cf *kizibo*)

mfunzi *n* (*wa-*) teacher: *Mfunzi wetu anafundisha vizuri*, our teacher teaches well. (cf *mwalimu*)

mfuo¹ *n* (*mi-*) a carpenter's tool for making broad holes; a carpenter's drill.

mfuo² *n* (*mi-*) stripe, furrow, groove; a mark made by drawing a line: *Chora mifuo shambani*, make furrows on the farm.

mfuo³ (also *fuo*) *n* (*mi-*) 1. act (style, etc.) of washing clothes. 2. metal forging; smith work. 3. used in the expression:

Mfuo wa mawimbi, the beating of the waves on the shore; high-water mark as traceable on the beach.

mfupa n (mi-) (anat) bone: *Fupa la kichwa*, skull. *Fupa jororo*, cartilage. (prov) *Ulimi hauna mfupa*, a tongue has no bone i.e. a tongue is free because it can speak of anything.

mfuradi n (mi-) a line in poetry; verse.

mfuraha n (mi-) a small ornamental box, used for keeping betel nut in mixture; snuff box. (cf *kibweta, jaluba*)

mfuria n (mi-) a sort of loose garment with a collar but no sleeves; a tunic with turned-up sleeves: *Kanzu ya mfuria*, a garment of this kind. (cf *juba, bushati*)

mfuru (also *mfufu, mfuu*) n (mi-) (bot) black plum tree; a tree with glabrous, palmately compound leaves, producing small black edible berries, eaten usu by children. Its timber is used in making canoe outriggers, furniture, roof building, planks, etc. *Vitex cuneata*.

mfurufu n (mi-) a vivacious person; a humorous person; a cheerful person: *Mfurufu aliwafurahisha wasikilizaji*, the cheerful person pleased the listeners. (cf *bashashi, mchangamfu, mcheshi*)

mfurungu n (mi-) citron tree. *Citrus medica*.

mfursadi (also *mforsadi*) n (mi-) (bot) a mulberry tree. This is a small deciduous tree with broad leaves of mostly heart-shaped form genus (*Morus*) bearing the fruit with milky juice and multiple false fruits which resemble the fruits of raspberry. *Morus alba* (Ar)

mfurutangi n (mi-) (bot) a frangipani tree. (cf *msanapati, mjinga*)

mfuta n (mi-) (bot) sesame, sim-sim; a much-branched annual, which produces an edible oil obtained from its seeds. *Sesamum orientale*.

mfutafuta n (mi-) (bot) butterfly pea; a climbing herb with pea-like flowers bearing a flat pod. *Clitoria ternatea*.

mfuto[1] n (mi-) a simple plain article of anything: *Mkeka wa mfuto*, a simple plain mat. *Kofia ya mfuto*, a simple plain cap. *Mlango wa mfuto*, plain door without carving or ornamentation.

mfuto[2] n (mi-) 1. five innings in a card game. 2. act of losing all money in a gamble: *Mifuto ile mitatu ya mfululizo ilimfukarisha sana*, those three consecutive losses in gambling impoverished him very much.

mfuu n (mi-) see *mfuru*

mfuwahe n (mi-) (bot) an evergreen shrub or small tree with elliptical leaves and small axillary sessile flowers, bearing small flushy fruits. *Ludia sessilifora*.

mfyambo n (mi-) see *mtipitipi*

mfyato n (mi-) infibulation

mfyatuko (also *mfyutuko*) n (mi-) the releasing of a trap, spring, etc.; explosion, blast, shot, burst: *Ule ulikuwa mfyatuko wa risasi*, that was the bullet's shot.

mfyeko n (mi-) act of slashing grass, etc.; clearing, slashing: *Mifyeko michache inaweza kuifanya bustani yako kuwa safi*, a few slashes can make your garden clean. (cf *ufyekaji*)

mfyonyo n (mi-) tut; a click or sucking sound made with the tongue usu repeated one or more times to express annoyance, etc.: *Mifyonyo ile inaakisi waziwazi kiburi chake*, those tuts reflect clearly his annoyance. (cf *msonyo, mnyuso*)

mfyosi n (wa-) a rude person, an insolent person; churl, boor: *Tajiri wa kampuni yetu ni mfyosi*, our company's employer is a churl.

mfyuko n (mi-) the releasing of a trap, spring, etc.; explosion, burst. (cf *mfyatuko*)

mfyuo n (mi-) a kind of shorts tied around the waist with a string passed inside it.

mfyuso n (mi-) a kind of trap.

mgaagaa[1] n (mi-) (bot) a kind of tree which grows on the shore: *Mgaagaapaka*, a kind of tree, the fibre of which is used for brooms. *Sida cordifolia.*

mgaagaa² *n (wa-)* a person who moves here and there to earn his living in order to survive; beach comber. (*prov*) *Mgaagaa na upwa hali wali mkavu,* he who hunts the shore does not eat plain rice i.e. he who wanders here and there always picks up sth.

mgaagazo *n (mi-)* see *mgaragazo*

mgadenia *n (mi-)* (*bot*) gardania; a subtropical plant with glossy leaves and highly fragrant with white or yellow and waxy flowers. (Eng)

mgagani *n (mi-)* see *mkabilishemsi*

mgahawa *n (mi-)* see *mkahawa*

mgambakangu *n (mi-)* (*bot*) tuber rooted water plant.

mgambari *n (mi-)* (*bot*) a small deciduous tree up to 25 feet tall wide with alternate bi-pinnate leaves and small yellow green flowers in dense spikes. *Entada sudanica.*

mgambo *n (mi-)* 1 a meeting usu held to discuss useful matters. (*prov*) *Mbiu ya mgambo ikilia ina jambo,* if the buffalo horn is blown, then there is sth of importance. 2. used in the expression: *Kumbi la mgambo,* a place where children of over forty in number who have entered a circumcision school, are assembled. 3. guard: used in the expression: *Jeshi la mgambo,* local militia, auxillary army. *Askari wa mgambo,* militia.

mganda¹ *n (mi-)* a sheaf of rice or wheat after having been harvested.

mganda² *n (mi-)* a special walk dance played in Dar-es-Salaam or in other coastal parts of Tanzania.

mganda³ *n (mi-)* 1. a caravan of people going on foot. 2. a sound produced to signal sth either when the caravan departs or returns.

Mganda⁴ *n (wa-)* Ugandan; a person originating from Uganda.

mgandamo *n (mi-)* coagulation, clot (cf *mgando*)

mgandisho¹ *n (mi-)* gumming, coagulation:

Mgandisho wa damu, blood clot; the coagulation of blood. *Mgandisho wako wa stempu katika bahasha haukuwa madhubuti,* your gumming of the stamp on the envelope was not strong.

mgandisho² *n (mi-)* a protection charm to disable a culprit to move from the place of the action.

mgando *n (mi-)* clot, gob, mass, coagulation: *Mgando wa damu,* blood clot. (cf *mgandamo*)

mganga¹ *n (wa-)* doctor, medicine man: *Mganga wa kienyeji,* traditional doctor; herbalist. *Mganga wa meno,* dentist, *Mganga wa farasi,* farrier. (cf *tabibu, daktari*)

mganga² *n (mi-)* (*bot*) a shrub or small tree with fleshy green branches and leaves, which produce a milky juice, used as a fish poison and also for the treatment of boils or abscesses. *Synadenium carinatum.*

mgangaji *n (wa-)* (*med*) an expert in the treatment of the bones, joints, muscles, etc.; orthopaedist (cf *mhazigi*)

mgangaungo *n (mi-)* (*bot*) a tree from which the colour used for smearing sifting trays is obtained.

mgange *n (mi-)* see *mkabilishemsi*

mgango *n (mi-)* splicing, joining, mending: *Mgango wa fanicha hii ni madhubuti,* the joining of this furniture is good.

mgaragazo (also *mgangazo*) *n (mi-)* the act of rolling of one another on the ground as during fighting: *Migaragazo ya wapigaji mieleka iliwafurahisha watazamaji,* the rolling of the wrestlers against each other pleased the spectators.

mgawaji *n (wa-)* 1. distributor: *Mgawaji dawa,* dispenser. (cf *mgavi*)

mgawano *n (mi-)* sharing, allotment: property. *Mgawano wa mali,* the sharing of property.

mgawanyaji (also *mgawanyi*) *n (wa-)* divider; a person who divides things into groups, classes, etc.

mgawanyi n (wa-) see mgawanyaji
mgawanyiko n (mi-) 1. split, division: Mgawanyiko umetokea katika chama tawala, there has been a split within the ruling party. (cf mfarakano) 2. (math) divergence; the property or manner of diverging; failure to approach a limit.
mgawanyo n (mi-) division, partition, distribution, delegation: Mgawanyo mpunguo, reduction division. Mgawanyo wa madaraka, the division of powers.
mgawo n (mi-) distribution, rationing, division, allocation: Mgawo wa umeme, the rationing of electricity. Mgawo wa sehemu mbili, dichotomy. Mgawo wa fedha, the allocation of money. Mgawo wa madaraka, the distribution of responsibilities.
mgazi n (mi-) see mchikichi
mgema n (wa-) palm wine taper. (prov) Mgema akisifiwa, tembo hulitia maji, if the palm-wine tapper is praised because of his palm wine, he dilutes it with water i.e. if a person is praised too much because of his competence, etc. this can eventually produce negative effects upon him.
mgemo n (mi-) tapping of a tree, fruit, etc. (cf ugemaji)
mgeni n (wa-) 1. visitor, stranger, foreigner. 2. guest: Mgeni wa heshima, guest of honour. (prov) Akomelepo mwenyeji na mgeni koma papo, you are always at the mercy of your host when you go to visit him.
mgeuko n (mi-) turn, change: Mgeuko wa polepole, gradation.
mgeuzo n (mi-) 1. change of structure, face, condition, etc.; alteration: Mgeuzo wa hali ya maisha umewadhiki raia, the change in the living conditions has inflicted hardships on the citizens. (cf mabadiliko) 2. (math) linear transformation.
mghafala n (mi-) forgetfulness: Mghafala wake wa mara kwa mara unawaudhi wale anaowapa miadi, his attitude of forgetting frequently irks those to whom he makes promises. (cf usahaulifu) (Ar)
mghalabu n (mi-) rivalry, competition. (cf ushindani) (Ar)
mghani n (wa-) 1. singer esp of poems: Yeye ni mghani anayeweza kuyaimba mashairi vizuri, he is a singer who can sing poems well. (cf mwimbaji) 2. a good singer
mgigisi n (wa-) a chaotic person, a disorderly person; fidget, spoiler: Mgigisi aliivuruga mipango ya watu, the fidget wrecked other people's plans. (cf machachari, mahepe)
mgiligilani n (mi-) (bot) coriander plant. The plant produces oil from its seeds and the leaves and fruits are used for curries. Coriandrum sativum. (Ar)
Mgiriki n (wa-) Greek; Mgiriki wa kisasa, Hellenic. (Eng, Gr)
mgoa n (mi-) (zool) dewlap (cf shambwelele)
mgobo n (wa-) a cantankerous person, a quarrelsome person; wrangler, brawler: Mgobo yule amegombana na watu wengi, that wrangler has quarelled with many people. (cf mshari, mgomvi)
mgodi n (mi-) mine; a large excavation made in the earth from which to extract metallic ores: Mgodi wa dhahabu, gold mine.
mgogoro n (mi-) crisis, conflict, dispute, feud: Mgogoro wa kazi, trade dispute. Mgogoro wa kisiasa, political crisis. Migogoro ya ardhi, land disputes Migogoro ya uongozi katika chama chao imekithiri, leadership conflicts in their party have intensified. Waziri aliitisha kikao ili kutatua migogoro ya wafanyakazi, the minister called a meeting to solve the workers' disputes. (cf mzozo)
mgogoto n (mi-) a loud voice intended to emphasize sth: Piga mgogoto, make a loud voice of this kind.
mgogoyo n (mi-) special advice to someone so that he sticks to it; exhortation:

Walimpa mgogoyo na akausikiliza, they gave him advice and he complied with it. (cf *wasia, nasaha*)

mgoli[1] *n* (*mi-*) (*zool*) gold's cobra; a hoodless powerful snake, which is generally found in water, and which is reputed to consume a great number of frogs. *Pseudohaje geldii.*

mgoli[2] *n* (*wa-*) the wife of a traditional ruler.

mgolole (also *mgorore*) *n* (*mi-*) a long loin cloth which is worn by tucking into the shoulders.

mgomaji *n* (*wa-*) striker; sby on strike: *Wagomaji walifukuzwa kazini*, the strikers were sacked from work.

mgomba *n* (*mi-*) (*bot*) banana plant. (*syn*) *Kuwa kama mgomba, mnazi unakawia*, we wish you the best in your health.

mgombaji *n* (*wa-*) a person who forbids others to do sth because of basic reasons; forbidder.

mgombakofi (also *mtongonya*) *n* (*mi-*) (*bot*) a perennial herb with a banana-like stem with large long stalked sagittate leaves and white flower spathes, bending over in fruit to form a large cluster of many brown flattish seeds. The seeds and roots are commonly used as food particularly during the periods of food shortage. *Typhonodorum lindleyanum.*

mgombea (also *mgombezi*) *n* (*wa-*) aspirant, candidate, spokesman: *Mgombea mwenza*, a running mate candidate in presidential elections, etc. *Mgombea binafsi*, an independent candidate. *Mgombea wa kiti cha urais*, presidential candidate. *Yeye ni mgombea wa haki za binadamu*, he is defender of human rights. (cf *mtetezi*)

mgombezi *n* (*wa-*) see *mgombea*

mgombozi *n* (*wa-*) see *mkombozi*

mgomo *n* (*mi-*) strike: *Mgomo baridi*, go-slow at work; slow down; work done at a slow pace as a kind of strike; ca'canny.

mgomvi *n* (*wa-*) a quarrelsome person; wrangler, brawler: *Kwa nini unaambatana na mgomvi yule?* Why do you associate yourself with that brawler? (cf *mtesi, mshari, shabaki*)

mgonasokola *n* (*mi-*) (*bot*) a shrub with alternate simple leaves, the fibre of which is used for fishing lines and bird traps. *Acalypha sp.*

mgongaji *n* (*wa-*) 1. striker: a person who strikes things, etc. 2. (*fig*) profiteer (cf *mlanguzi*)

mgongano *n* (*mi-*) 1. clash, collision: *Mgongano wa uso kwa uso*, head-on collision. 2. used in the expression: *Mgongano wa mawazo*, a conflict of ideas (resulting from two or more people differing in views). *Mgongano wa athari*, the conflict of influences. *Mgongano wa masilahi*, conflict of interests.

mgongo *n* (*mi-*) (*anat*) the back of a person, etc.: *Uti wa mgongo*, the spine. *Kiinua mgongo*, gratuity, pension. *Nyumba ya mgongo*, the house with a ridge-roof.

mgong'oto[1] *n* (*mi-*) advice given to a person e.g. child, relative or a friend about life.

mgong'oto[2] *n* (*mi-*) a sound produced when sth like an iron is hit or when someone is knocking at the door; knock.

mgoni *n* (*wa-*) adulterer, fornicator. (cf *mzinzi*)

mgonjwa *n* (*wa-*) a sick person; patient : *Mgonjwa wa akili*, lunatic. (cf *mkongo, mwele*)

mgono *n* (*mi-*) a kind of fish-trap made from long thin pieces of sticks.

mgonzo *n* (*n*) (*med*) elephantiasis caused by philaria blocking lymphatic vessels.

mgorore *n* (*mi-*) see *mgolole*

mgosi *n* (*wa-*) friend, companion, comrade. (cf *mbasi, rafiki, sahibu*)

mgoto *n* (*mi-*) 1. the sound produced when two things knock together; click, clack, beat: *Mgoto wa makasia*, the beat of oars. (cf *mpigo*) 2. the act of beating, knocking together, etc. two things when they come into contact; clash, rattle: *Nilisikia mgoto wa chupa za soda kwenye lori*, I heard a clash of soda bottles in the lorry.

mgoza *n* (*mi-*) (*bot*) a heavily branched tree whose bark is used as a strong fibre for making ropes or as a tying material in hut building. *Sterculia africana*. (cf *mboza*)

mgude *n* (*mi-*) see *mfune*

mgulabi *n* (*mi-*) (*bot*) litchis; a much-branched evergreen tree up to 100 feet tall bearing ovoid to sub-globose crimson fruit containing a large seed. The fruit is edible. *Litchi chinensis*. (cf *mdarabi*)

mgumba *n* (*wa-*) a childless woman, a sterile woman, a barren woman; a woman who begets no children. (*syn*) *Mgumba hana kilio*, an infertile person has nothing to cry for i.e. a childless woman or man who has died cannot be remembered easily.

mgumio *n* (*mi-*) the growl of a depressed person or lion. (cf *mguno*)

mgunda (also *mnda*) *n* (*mi-*) plantation, field, farm, plot: *Amepanda mahindi kwenye mgunda wake*, he has planted maize in his farm. (cf *konde*, *shamba*)

mgunduzi *n* (*wa-*) discoverer, inventor. (cf *mvumbuzi*)

mgunga (also *mjatete*) *n* (*mi-*) (*bot*) a name used in general for species of *Acacia* trees. (cf *mjatete*)

mguno *n* (*mi-*) sound resulting from grumbling, grunting, etc. as a mark of displeasure, pain, etc. from someone: *Miguno yake ya mara kwa mara inachusha*, his frequent gruntings are disgusting. (cf *mgumio*)

mgunyo *n* (*mi-*) abrasion; act of scraping off rubbing, off af of skin, etc. (cf *mchubuko*)

mgurure *n* (*mi-*) (*bot*) a shrub or tree bearing a small straw-coloured four-winged fruit and producing a black heart-wood, used for carving. *Combretum schumannii*.

mguruto *n* (*mi-*) the act of mangling, pressing, etc.

mgusano *n* (*mi-*) contact

mguso *n* (*mi-*) 1. a special place found in a children's game when they chase one another such that if a child touches the place and holds it, that implies that he has touched him or caught whoever is being chased; homebase. 2. act (manner, etc.) of touching a thing or person. 3. touch, effect, impact: *Hotuba yake ilinipa mguso mkali*, his speech had a profound impact on me. (cf *athari*)

mguto (also *guto*) *n* (*mi-*) bawl; a shout which can be heard from a long distance. (cf *mlio*)

mgutusho *n* (*mi-*) shock, startle, fright: *Mgutusho wake aliposikia habari mbaya*, her shock on hearing the bad news. (cf *mtanabahisho*, *mshtuo*, *mkurupusho*)

mguu *n* (*mi-*) 1. (*anat*) the leg or foot of a person or any other kind of living creature. 2. anything resembling a leg in shape or use: *Mguu wa meza*, the leg of a table.

mgwaru *n* (*mi-*) (*bot*) cluster bean plant; a bushy perennial bean 2 to 4 feet high bearing clusters of slender pods 3 to 4 inches long in the axils of the leaves. *Cyamopsis psoraloides*. (cf *magwebe*)

mgwisho (also *mbwisho*) *n* (*mi-*) flywhisk (cf *mbwisho*, *usinga*, *mwengo*)

mgwizi *n* (*wa-*) (*zool*) predator, carnivore. (cf *mbwawa*)

Mhabeshi *n* (*wa-*) Ethiopian (Ar)

mhadhara *n* (*mi-*) lecture: *Ukumbi wa mihadhara*, lecture hall. *Mhadhara wa watu wote*, public lecture. *Toa mhadhara*, deliver a lecture. (Ar)

mhadhiri *n* (*wa-*) lecturer: *Mhadhiri mwandamizi*, senior lecturer. *Mhadhiri msaidizi*, assistant lecturer. (Ar)

mhafidhina n (wa-) a conservative person; diehard. (cf mkale)

mhaini n (wa-) traitor: Wahaini walinyongwa, the traitors were hanged. (cf mwasi, msaliti) (Ar)

mhajiri n (wa-) emigrant (cf mhamiaji, mguraji) (Ar)

mhakiki n (wa-) analyst, investigator, fact-sifter: Mhakiki maandishi, reviewer, critic. Mhakiki wa fasihi, literary critic. (Ar)

mhakikimali n (wa-) evaluator, assessor. (cf mtathmini)

mhali n (n) see muhali

mhalibori n (mi-) a flap in the front of a garment, kanzu; a strip of lining in the front of a garment, kanzu. (cf lisani) (Ar, Pers)

mhalifu (also mhalifu) m (wa) offender, lawbreaker, culprit. (cf mwasi, mkosaji) (Ar)

mhalili n(wa-) (In Islam) a person who recites special prayers for the dead person at the grave. 2. a person who marries a woman after being divorced three times by another person.

mhalizeti n (mi-) (bot) olive oil tree.

mhamaji n (wa-) emigrant

mhamuni n (mi-) (bot) see mhanuni

mhamasishaji n (wa-) motivator; a person who motivates others to do a particular thing.

mhamasishwaji n (wa-) a person who is motivated.

mhambarashi n (mi-) bludgeon; a short club with a thick, heavy or loaded end, used for fighting. (cf mbuda, mpweke)

mhamiaji n (wa-) immigrant (cf mhajiri)

mhandisi n (wa-) engineer: Mhandisi kemikali, chemical engineer. Mhandisi ujenzi, civil engineer. Mhandisi umeme, electrical engineer. (Ar)

mhanga[1] n (n) (zool) aadvark, antbear. (cf kibarara)

mhanga[2] n (n) act of sacrifice by killing an animal or offering to spirits; blood sacrifice: Toa mhanga, make a sacrifice of this kind. Jitolea mhanga, sacrifice one's life.

mhanga[3] n (wa-) a person who sacrifices himself or herself in a particular matter; sacrificer, martyr: Toa mhanga, sacrifice.

mhangaiko (mi-) restiveness, fuss, unrest, restlessness.

mhangi n (wa-) a toothless old person. (cf kibogoyo)

mhanuni (also mhima) n (mi-) (bot) henna plant; a woody shrub or small tree commonly grown throughout the tropics producing fragrant flowers, and used as a dye for hair and skin. Lawsonia inermis. (Ar)

mharabu n (wa-) a destructive person, a malicious person; reprobate, destroyer, scoundrel: Mharabu yule anaweza kuiharibu mipango yako, that reprobate can wreck your plans. (cf mharibifu) (Ar)

mharage n (mi-) see mharagwe

mharagwe (also mharage) n (mi-) (bot) French bean plant; kidney bean plant. Phaseolus vulgaris.

mharara n (mi-) (geog) escarpment, landslide. (cf genge)

mhardali n (mi-) (bot) mustard; a yellow-flowered Eurasian plant of the cabbage family whose seeds are used to make mustard. (Ar)

mharibifu n (wa-) a destructive person, a malicious person; reprobate, destroyer, scoundrel: Yeye ni mharibifu wa kila kitu, he is a destroyer of everything. (cf mbomoaji, mwunjaji, mwurugaji) (Ar)

mhariri n (wa-) editor: Mhariri mkuu, chief editor. Mhariri mtendaji, managing editor. Mhariri sanifu, sub-editor. Mhariri sanifu mkuu, chief sub-editor. Mhariri wa habari, news editor. Mhariri wa gazeti, newspaper editor. Yeye ni mhariri wa gazeti la chama, he is the editor of the party's newspaper. (Ar)

mharita (also mwarita) n (mi-) (bot) soapberry tree. Its seeds are used for washing clothes, etc. Sapindus saponaria.

mharuma n (mi-) a coloured woollen shawl, worn as a turban. (Ar)

mhashamu n (wa-) a prominent person; an eminent person: *Mhashamu Kadinali*, His Eminence the Cardinal. (Ar)

mhashiri (also *mwashiri*) n (mi-) (naut) wooden support of a main mast. (cf *mtwana*) (Ar)

mhasi n (wa-) a person who castrates another person or an animal; castrator.

mhasibu: accountant: *Mhasibu mkuu*, chief accountant.

mhasiwa n (wa-) a castrated man or animal; eunuch (cf *towashi*)

mhazigi n (wa-) an expert in the treatment of the bones, joints, etc.; orthopaedist. (cf *mgangaji*)

mhazili n (wa-) 1. typist. 2. office secretary. (cf *sekreteri, karani*) (Ar)

mhemshaji n (wa-) demagogue (cf *mhsisishi*)

mhemuko n (mi-) emotion, feeling, passion: *Aliingiwa na mhemuko alipokuwa anawahutubia wanavijiji walionyimwa haki zao*, he was filled with emotion when he was addressing the villagers who were deprived of their rights. (cf *jazba*)

mhenga n (wa-) 1. an ancient person; ancestor. (cf *shaibu, mkale*) 2. sage; a very wise person, esp an elderly man widely respected for his wisdom, experience, etc.: *Nilichukua ushauri kwa wahenga*, I took advice from the sages.

mhenzirani n (mi-) see *mhinzirani*

mheshimiwa n (wa-) the Honourable, Her Excellency, His Excellency. (cf *mwadhamu*)

mhifadhi n (wa-) conservationist: *Mhifadhi wa mazingira*, conservationist of the environment *Mhifadhi mkuu*, chief conservationist. (cf *mwangalizi*) (Ar)

mhimili n (mi-) 1. pillar, prop, support. (cf *mwimo*) 2. window jamb, door jamb.

3. (fig) pillar, mainstay, backbone: *Yeye ni mhimili mkuu wa chama*, he is the mainstay of the party. 4. (fig) backbone: *Zao la karafuu ni mhimili wa uchumi wa Zanzibar*, clove crop is the backbone of Zanzibar economy. (Ar)

mhimizi n (wa-) promoter (cf *promota*)

mhina n (mi-) (bot) henna plant. *Lawsonia inermis*. (cf *mhanuni*)

Mhindi¹ n (wa-) Indian, Hindu: *Mhindi mwekundu*, Red Indian. (Hind)

mhindi² n (mi-) maize plant. *Zea mais*.

mhinzirani (also *mhenzirani*) n (mi-) (bot) cane tree. (Ar)

mhisabati n (wa-) mathematician (Ar)

mhisani n (wa-) benefactor, sponsor, philanthropist: *Wahisani kadha katika nchi za nje wameahidi kusaidia miradi ya maendeleo*, several benefactors from overseas countries have promised to assist development projects. (cf *mkarimu, mfadhili*) (Ar)

mhitaji n (wa-) a person who is needy, poor, etc.: *Mhitaji aliomba msaada*, the needy person asked for assistance. (Ar)

mhitimu n (wa-) graduate. (Ar)

mhodhi n (wa-) monopolist, hoarder. (Ar)

mhogo n (mi-) see *muhogo*

mhoji n (wa-) interviewer (Ar)

mhojiwa n (wa-) interviewee (Ar)

mhonyoaji n (wa-) a person looking for free things; moocher.

mhopi n (mi-) (bot) hop; a twining climbing plant whose flowers are used in brewing beer. (Eng)

mhoro n (mi-) a spear-like pointed stick, used in game-traps, etc. (cf *mkonjo, konzo*)

Mhotento n (wa-) Hottentot; a member of the nomadic pastoral people in Southern Africa.

mhubiri n (wa-) preacher, evangelist. (cf *hatibu*) (Ar)

mhudumu n (wa-) 1. janitor, waiter, attendant: *Mhudumu wa Kanisa*, deacon. (cf *mwandikaji, mwandalizi*)

2. a person who serves people in special functions such as in weddings, feasts, etc. (Ar)

mhujumu n (wa-) saboteur; a person who engages in sabotage: *Wahujumu walifikishwa mahakamani*, the saboteurs were brought before the court of law. *Mhujumu wa uchumi*, economic saboteur. (Ar)

mhuni (also *muhuni*) n (wa-) 1. bachelor; an unmarried man. (cf *mseja*) 2. idler, loafer, vagrant. (cf *mzururaji*) 3. a disrespectful person; hooligan: *Mhuni aliwachokoza wasichana waliokuwa wakipita hapa kutoka shuleni*, the hooligan teased the girls who were passing here from the school. 4. thief, snatcher, pilferer: *Wahuni watatu waliiba mali ya mwenye duka*, three thieves stole the property of a shopkeeper. (cf *mwizi*)

mhunzi (also *muhunzi*) n (wa-) metal worker: *Mhunzi wa mawe*, stone cutter. *Mhunzi wa chuma*, blacksmith. (prov) *Mwana wa mhunzi asiposana huvuvia*, if the son of a professional is not an expert, he can still make use of the tools of his father. In other words, if you stay with a person who is skilled in one profession or another, you can glean the basic elements of his profession.

mhuri (also *muhuri*) n (mi-) 1. rubber stamp, seal: *Piga mhuri*, seal, stamp; set seal to. *Tia muhuri*, seal, set seal to; certify. *Pigwa mhuri*, be stamped. *Pata mhuri*, be approved. *Mhuri wa stakabadhi*, receipt stamp. 2. mark left by a rubber stamp. *Mhuri wa ithibati*, imprimatur. (Ar)

mhusika n (wa-) 1. (of a novel, etc.) character: *Mhusika mkuu*, main character. *Mhusika mdogo*, minor character. *Mhusika bapa*, flat character. *Mhusika mviringo*, round character. *Mhusika zuzu*, pantallon. 2. participant; a person involved in an activity, affair, etc.: *Kuna wahusika watatu katika mgogoro ule*, there are three people involved in that conflict. (Ar)

mia n (n) hundred: *Mia mbili*, two hundred. (cf *gana*) (Ar)

miadi n (n) date, appointment, promise: *Weka miadi*, make an appointment. *Timiza miadi*, keep a promise. *Vunja miadi*, break an appointment. *Yeye hana miadi*, he cannot keep a promise. (cf *makubaliano, ahadi, mapatano*) (Ar)

midabwada n (mi-) old dirty rags, old dirty clothes.

midadi n (n) ink (cf *wino*)

mie pron see *mimi*

mifugo n (mi-) livestock. *Boma la mifugo*, fold.

migongogongo n (mi-) corrugation

mihirabu n (mi-) (in Islam) the front part of a mosque where the "Imam" conducts prayers. (Ar)

Mijikenda n (mi-) the name given to refer to those coastal tribes of Kenya such as the Giriamas, Durumas, etc.

mikaha n (mi-) see *nikaha*

mikiki n (mi-) see *mkiki*

mikingamo n (mi-) unreliable information.

mikogo n (mi-) pomposity, airs and graces, show-off, boastfulness: *Hutembea kwa mikogo*, he walks with pomposity. (cf *mashobo, maringo*)

mikrofoni n (n) microphone (Eng)

mikrometa n (n) micrometer (Eng)

mikrowevu n (n) microwave (Eng)

mikwala n (n) (colloq) hindrance, obstruction.

mila n (n) culture, customs, belief: *Kila kabila ina mila zake*, every tribe has its culture. (cf *desturi*) (Ar)

milele adv forever, eternally. (cf *daima*)

milenia n (n) millennium; a period or cycle of one thousand years: *Wananchi waliingojea milenia mpya*, the people waited for the new millennium. (Eng)

mil.i vt side, incline, favour. Prep. **mil.i.a** St. **mil.ik.a** Cs. **mil.ish.a** Ps. of Prep. **mil.iw.a**

miligramu n (n) miligram (Eng)

milihoi *n* (*n*) a kind of evil spirit. (cf *shetani*)

milik.i[1] *vt, vi* possess, control, rule: *Wanamiliki mali adhimu*, they possess a lot of wealth. Prep. ***milik.i.a*** St. ***milik.ik.a*** Cs. ***milik.ish.a*** Ps. ***milik.iw.a***, be owned e.g. *Viwanda vingi vinamilikiwa nchini na watu binafsi*, many industries are owned in the country by private individuals. Rp. ***milik.i.an.a*** (cf *tawala, hozi, tamalaki*) (Ar)

miliki[2] (also *milki*) *n* (*n*) possession, control, kingdom: *Nyumba hii iko katika miliki ya serikali*, this house is under the ownership of the government. (cf *mali*) (Ar)

milikish.a 1. see milik.i 2. cause sth to be possessed by sby: *Walimikisha ardhi isiyo yake*, they made him to possess land which was not his.

milimita *n* (*n*) milimetre (Eng)

milionea *n* (*ma-*) millionaire

milioni *n* (*n*) million (Eng)

milki *n* (*n*) 1. realm, kingdom. 2. estate. (Ar)

mimba *n* (*n*) 1. pregnancy: *Shika mimba*, become pregnant; conceive. *Tia mimba*, make pregnant. *Haribu mimba*, miscarry; cause miscarriage. *Toa mimba*, carry out an abortion. *Tunga mimba*, become pregnant. *Zuia mimba*, use birth control. (cf *himila*) 2. a pregnant stomach. (*prov*) *Kulea mimba si kazi, kazi ni kulea mwana*, a pregnancy is not a problem, the real problem is to bring up the child.

mimbari *n* (*n*) pulpit, lectern: *Kiongozi wa dini alihutubia kutoka kwenye mimbari*, the religious leader preached from the pulpit. (Ar)

mimi (also *mie*) *pron* 1. me: *Mimi ni mhadhiri*, I am a lecturer. *Mimi binafsi*, I myself. *Mimi nafsi yangu*, I personally. *Mimi mwenyewe*, I myself without anybody's help.

mimin.a *vt* pour, pour out, spill: *Alimimina maziwa chomboni*, she poured milk into the vessel. Prep. ***mimin.i.a*** St. ***mimin.ik.a*** Prep. of St. ***mimin.iki.a*** Cs. ***mimin.ish.a*** Ps. ***mimin.w.a*** Rp. of Prep. ***mimin.i.an.a*** (cf *mwaga, pua*)

miminik.a *vi* be dischargeable, be capable of being poured. Prep. ***miminik.i.a*** St. ***miminik.ik.a***

minajili *conj* because of, for the sake of, for the reason: *Alikuja hapa kwa minajili ya kuonana na mimi*, he came here for the sake of seeing me. (Ar)

mindi *n* (*n*) (*zool*) Abbott's duiker; a large duiker with a dusky brown forehead and greyish chin and throat. *Cephalophus spadix*. (cf *funo*)

mindi

minenguo *n* (*mi-*) a style of dancing. (cf *miondoko*)

minghairi (also *bighairi*) *prep* without, except: *Rafiki zangu wote walifika karamuni minghairi yake yeye*, all my friends attended the party except him. (cf *pasipo*) (Ar)

ming'iny.a *vt* compress, squeeze, press: *Mvulana aliliming'inya chungwa*, the boy squeezed the orange. Prep. ***ming'iny.i.a*** St. ***ming'iny.ik.a*** Cs. ***ming'iny.ish.a*** Ps. ***ming'iny.w.a*** Rp. ***ming'iny.an.a*** (cf *bigija*).

mini *n* (*n*) miniskirt (Eng)

minibasi *n* (*n*) minibus (Eng)

mintarafu *conj* regarding, concerning, with regards to: *Mintarafu ya barua yako ya karibuni, mimi sasa nimeamua kukuunga mkono katika mzozo ule*, with regards to your recent letter, I have now decided to support you in that conflict. (Ar)

miny.a *vt* press, squeeze: *Aliliminya jipu ili atoe usaha*, he squeezed the boil to remove the pus. Prep. **miny.i.a** St. **miny.ik.a** Cs. **miny.ish.a** Ps. **miny.w.a** Rp. **miny.an.a** (cf *ming'inya, binya*)

minyoo *n* (*mi-*) see *mnyoo*

miondoko *n* (*mi-*) gait, step; style of walking or dancing, etc.: *Miondoko ya muziki*, style of music. (cf *minenguo*)

miongoni *prep* (usu followed by the particle *mwa*) among, amongst: *Miongoni mwa wageni watakaofika leo katika ufunguzi wa benki ni mawaziri*, among the guests who will arrive today for the inauguration of the bank are the ministers.

mipasho *n* (*mi-*) innuendos, insinuations: *Wabunge waliendelea na mipasho na kejeli katika kikao cha jana*, the members of parliament continued to exchange innuendos and ridicules in yesterday's session.

miraa *n* (*mi-*) a kind of stimulant herb usu used by Somali communities; khat. (cf *mrungi*)

mirathi *n* (*n*) 1. inheritance, heritage: *Suala la mirathi la jamaa wa marehemu haliko mikononi mwetu*, the issue of inheritance of the heirs of the deceased is not in our hands. (cf *urithi*) 2. Islamic inheritance laws. (Ar)

mirimo *n* (*mi-*) 1. work, profession, etc. usu inherited from parents to children. (*prov*) *Atangazaye mirimo si mwana wa liwali*, don't expect the good qualities of an ordinary person to be advertised or promoted by the son of a *liwali* or any other person in higher rank since he may be jealous of an ordinary person who is rising in status, grade, etc. 2. the secrets of the medicine men or wizards. (*prov*) *Mchawi akifichua mirimo ya wenzake, huuawa*, a traitor to his country is apt to be punished.

mirungi *n* (*mi-*) see *mrungi*

Misa *n* (*n*) 1. (in Christianity) Mass: *Misa Kuu*, High Mass. *Misa ndogo*, low Mass. 2. Mass service: *Wanavijiji walifanya misa ili kuwakumbuka marehemu*, the villagers held a Mass for the dead. (Eng)

misale *n* (*n*) missal; the official, liturgical book of the Roman rite containing all the prayers, rites, etc. used by a priest in celebrating the Mass throughout the year. (Eng)

misheni *n* (*n*) 1. church mission; the sending out of persons by a religious organization to preach, teach, etc. 2. a group of people sent by the church to spread the Christian religion esp in a foreign land. (Eng)

miski *n* (*n*) musk; a substance with a strong penetrating odour, used as a basis for numerous perfumes. (Eng)

Misri *n* (*n*) (*geog*) Egypt (Ar)

mita *n* (*n*) metre (Eng)

mitaala *n* (*n*) studies: *Mkuza mitaala*, curriculum developer. *Mitaala ya maendeleo*, development studies. (Ar)

mitabendi *n* (*n*) metreband (Eng)

mitara *n* (*n*) (used in pl form only) polygamy: *Ndoa ya mitara*, polygamous marriage.

mitembo *n* (*n*) (*med*) lymphoedema; persistent swelling of the tissues as a result of inadequate drainage from blockage or absence of the lymph channels thus ultimately causing a form of elephantiasis.

miteni *n* (*n*) two hundred: *Mia na mia ni miteni*, one hundred and one hundred is two hundred. (Ar)

mithaki *adj* reliable, firm, concrete: *Ahadi mithaki*, a firm promise. (cf *madhubuti*) (Ar)

mithali *n* (*n*) see *methali*

mithili[1] *prep* like, as, similar to: *Anazungumza mithili ya baba yake*, he talks like his father. (cf *mfano, kama*) (Ar)

mithil.i² *vt* compare; make a comparison. Prep. **mithil.i.a** St. **mithil.ik.a** Cs. **mithil.ish.a** Ps. of Prep. **mithil.iw.a** (cf *linganisha, fananisha*) (Ar)

mithilish.a *vt* compare. Prep. **mithilish.i.a** St. **mithilish.ik.a** Ps. **mithilish.w.a** (cf *linganisha, fananisha*)

mitindo *n* (*mi-*) style, fashions

mitishamba *n* (*mi-*) medicinal herbs: *Anatumia mitishamba kutibu ugonjwa wake*, she is using medicinal herbs to cure her disease.

mitu *n* (*n*) (*zool*) a kind of small parrot of yellowish and blue colour. (cf *kwau*)

mituamo *n* (*n*) (*mech*) statics; the branch of mechanics dealing with bodies, masses or forces at rest or in equilibrium.

miuja *n* (*n*) hardships, problems, tribulations, difficulties. (cf *matatizo*) (Ar)

miundombinu *n* (*mi-*) infrastructure; *Miundombinu ya usafirishaji ni muhimu katika nchi yoyote duniani*, the infrastructure of transportation is important in any country in the world. *Kuboresha miundombinu ni muhimu katika mchakato wa kuendeleza uchumi*, to improve infrastructure is essential in the process of developing the economy.

miwani *n* (*mi-*) 1. a pair of spectacles; eye-glasses: *Miwani ya jua*, sun-glasses. *Miwani yenye mpini* lorgnette. *Kifuko cha miwani*, spectacle-case. *Akisoma, huvaa miwani*, when he reads, he wears glasses. 2. (*idm*) *Vaa miwani*, (a) be drunk, (b) pretend not to have seen someone e.g. *Alinivalia miwani kwenye mkutano*, he pretended he did not see me at the meeting. (Ar)

miva *n* (*mi-*) see *msiwa*

mizani *n* (*n*) 1. weighing machine; scales, balance. (cf *kapani*) 2. (*poet*) metre, syllable: *Shairi langu lina mizani kumi na mbili kwa kila mshororo*, my poem has twelve syllables in every line. (cf *silabi*) 3. balance of ideas, etc. before doing sth: *Usiliwamie jambo lile; lazima uliwekee mizani*, don't rush into that matter, you must balance it. (Ar)

mizania *n* (*n*) balance sheet: *Karatasi ya mizania*, trial balance sheet paper. (Ar)

mizengwe *n* (*mi*) obstacles, impediments: *Serikali iliwawekea mizengwe wakulima bila ya sababu*, the government put obstacles for the farmers for no reason. (cf *vikwazo, vizuizi*)

mizungu *n* (*n*) 1. initiation secrets: *Alipovunja ungo, alifunzwa mizungu unyagoni*, when she reached the age of puberty, she was given instructions at the initiation school. 2. jugglery, juggling; magic tricks: *Mtu yule ni mzoefu katika mizungu*, that person is experienced in magic tricks. (cf *kiinimacho*) 3. smartness shown from getting out of a difficult position or danger; ruse: *Mizungu yake ilimkinga dhidi ya vitendo viovu alivyofanyiwa*, his ruses protected him against evil deeds done against him. (cf *hila*)

mja¹ *n* (*wa-*) one who comes; foreigner, new comer.

mja² *n* (*wa-*) 1. human being. (*prov*) *Ada ya mja hunena, muungwana ni kitendo*, an ordinary person talks but a gentleman shows actions. (cf *mtu, binaadamu*) 2. used in the expression: *Mja mzito*, a pregnant woman; an expectant woman.

mjadala *n* (*mi-*) debate, discussion: *Kulikuwepo na mjadala mkali kwenye mkutano*, there was a heated debate at the meeting. (cf *mdahalo, mazungumzo*) (Ar)

mjafari *n* (*mi-*) 1. (*bot*) flame tree; a small tree with dense racemes of scarlet flowers and beaded pods. *Erythrina tomentosa*. 2. *Fagara sp.*; a much-branched spiny shrub or tree with alternate glandular pinnate leaves. (Ar)

mjaji *n* (*wa-*) comer, arrival; a person who comes or arrives.

mjakazi (also *kijakazi*) *n* (*wa-*) a female slave.

mjali *n* (*mi-*) the wick of a lamp; lamp's wick.

mjakaranda *n* (*mi-*) (*bot*) jacaranda tree; a tropical American tree (family *Bignonia*) which has blue trumpet-shaped flowers, fern-like leaves and fragrant timber. (Eng)

mjamaa *n* (*wa-*) socialist: *Yeye ni mjamaa halisi*, he is a real socialist. (Ar)

mjamzito *n* (*wa-*) see *mja²*

mjane *n* (*wa-*) 1. bachelor, spinster. (cf *mseja, mhuni*) 2. widow, widower. 3. a divorced woman; divorcee.

mjango *n* (*mi-*) a fruitless trip; a useless journey: *Safari yake ya kwenda kupokea posho chuoni ilikuwa ni ya mjango*, his trip to go to the college to receive his bursary was fruitless.

mjanja *n* (*wa-*) cunning, sly; a shrewd person: *Mfanyabiashara yule ni mjanja*, that businessman is cunning. (cf *ayari, mhadaifu, mdanganyifu*)

mjao¹ *n* (*mi-*) (*math*) volume, capacity.

mjao² *n* (*mi-*) act (method, etc.) of sth filling up to the top. (cf *ujaaji*)

Mjapani *n* (*wa-*) Japanese (Jap)

mjarabu¹ (also *mujarabu*) *adj* useful, workable: *Dawa hii ni mjarabu*, this medicine can work.

mjarabu² *n* quiz, test: *huu ndio mujarabu wa muhula huu*, this is the quiz for this term.

mjarari (also *mjiari*) *n* (*mi-*) (*naut*) tiller rope in a sailing vessel such as dhow or in a sewing machine's wheel. (Ar)

mjari *n* (*mi-*) see *ujari*

mjasiri *n* (*wa-*) a fearless person; a brave person. (cf *nyamaume, simba*) (Ar)

mjasiriamali *n* (*wa-*) entrepreneur; a person who owns, manages a commercial enterprise in order to make profits.

mjatete *n* (*mi-*) see *mgunga*

mjeledi *n* (*mi-*) lash, scourge, whip: *Alimpiga mtoto wake wa kiume kwa mjeledi*, he beat his son with a whip. (Ar)

mjengo *n* (*mi-*) 1. architecture; act (style, etc.) of building: *Mjengo wa nyumba hii ni mzuri*, the architecture of this house is good. (cf *ujengaji*) 2. a pole used for constructing a house.

mjengeko *n* (*mi-*) construction, build-up, building: *Mjengeko wa sentensi*, the construction of a sentence.

mjenzi *n* (*wa-*) 1. builder, constructor. 2. contractor.

Mjerumani *n* (*wa-*) German (Germ)

mjeuri *n* (*wa-*) an insolent person, a rude person; malapert.

mji¹ *n* (*mi-*) town, city, homestead: *Mji mkuu*, capital. *Mji mkongwe*, an old town. *Mwanamji*, townsman, city dweller.

mji² *n* (*mi-*) 1. (*anat*) uterus, womb: *Mji wa uzazi*, uterus. 2. the middle part of a cloth or "khanga."

mji³ *n* (*mi-*) (in Islam) a shallow narrow trench in the grave where a dead body is laid to rest. (cf *luhudi, mwanandani*)

mjiari *n* (*mi-*) see *mjarari*

mjiko *n* (*mi-*) (*med*) piles, hemorrhoids. (cf *bawasili, futuri*)

mjima *n* (*wa-*) a person who gives friendly help in communal work esp in agriculture; a member of a communal working team.

mjinga¹ *n* (*wa-*) imbecile, idiot, simpleton, fool. (cf *mpumbavu, baradhuli*)

mjinga² *interj* an expletive of scorn, insult, etc. expressed by someone to someone else.

mjinga³ *n* (*mi-*) (*bot*) a frangipani tree; a large shrub or small tree with succulent stems and branches containing a large quantity of latex and waxy flowers of various colours, used for ceremonial garlands esp by the various Indian communities. The tree is also called *mbono wa kizungu*. *Plumeria acuminata*. (cf *mfurutangi, msanapiti*)

mjinga⁴ *n* (*mi-*) (*bot*) a kind of cassava root.

mjio *n* (*mi-*) coming, arrival: *Mjio wake hapa haukutegemewa,* his arrival here was not expected. (cf *ujio, mjo*)

mjisifu *n* (*wa-*) braggart, brag; a boastful person: *Mtu yule ni mjisifu tu lakini hana analolijua,* that person is just a braggart but he knows nothing. (cf *mjigambi*)

mjo (also *ujaji*) *n* (*mi-*) coming: *Maneno yake aliyotuambia mazuri lakini mjo wake umetutia wasiwasi,* the words he told us are good but his style of coming is suspicious. (cf *ujaji*)

mjoho *n* (*mi-*) (*bot*) velvet apple tree. *Diospyrs sp.*

mjohoro *n* (*mi-*) 1. (*bot*) iron wood tree; an exotic many branched evergreen tree up to 50 feet tall with yellow flowers and bearing black narrow flat pods. *Cassia siamea.* 2. flamboyant tree, flame tree. *Delonix regia.*

mjoja (also *mjoo*) *n* (*mi-*) a kind of hard tree, used for making canoes.

mjoli *n* (*wa-*) (*arch*) a word used to describe a fellow slave who has been freed.

mjomba¹ *n* (*wa-*) 1. a maternal uncle. 2. a male friend.

mjomba² *n* (*wa-*) a person from the coast; a Swahili person.

mjombakaka *n* (*mi-*) (*zool*) a large kind of lizard.

mjombo *n* (*mi-*) (*zool*) seabass; a kind of marine fish (family *Serranidae*) with a robust body or somewhat compressed and a large mouth, found in tropical and subtropical waters of all oceans. (cf *bokozi*)

mjoo¹ *n* (*mi-*) see *mjoja*

mjoo² *n* (*mi-*) dug-out canoe.

mjuaji *n* (*wa-*) 1. boor; quack, charlatan, mountebank (cf *baramaki*) 2. know-all; a person pretending to know everything. (cf *baramaki*)

mjuba *n* (*wa-*) an insolent person, a rude person; boor, malapert: *Majirani wanamchukia mjuba yule,* the neighbours hate that boor. (cf *mjeuri, mfyosi*)

mjukuu *n* (*wa-*) grandchild

mjumbe *n* (*wa-*) 1. delegate, representative. (cf *mwakilishi*) 2. courier; messenger: *Mjumbe alitumwa kupeleka taarifa kwa haraka,* the messenger was sent to deliver the message hurriedly. (cf *taarifa*)

mjume *n* (*wa-*) a skilled workman who executes ornamental work, engraving, inlaying, etc. on weapons, woods, etc.

mjumi *n* (*wa-*) aesthete; one who cultivates an unusually high sensitivity to beauty, as in art or nature. 2. one whose pursuit and admiration of beauty is regarded as excessive or affected.

mjumu¹ *n* (*wa-*) a person who sharpens knives. (cf *mfuavisu*)

mjumu² *n* (*mi-*) a big knife without a handle.

mjusi¹ *n* (*mi-*) 1. (*zool*) lizard. 2. a lizard-shaped ornament worked in silk stitches on the front of a *kanzu*.

mjusi

mjusi² *n* (*mi-*) (*med*) bleeding from the nose which may be caused by physical injury or may be connected with fever; nosebleed, epistaxis, nasal hermorrhage. (cf *mnoga, muhina*)

mjuu *n* (*n*) the wind which blows from the land to the sea; sea breeze.

mjuvi¹ *n* (*wa-*) know-all; a know-it-all person; a person pretending or claiming to know much about almost everything: *Yeye ni mjuvi tu lakini haelewi chochote,* he is just a know-all but he does not understand anything. (cf *mjuaji, sogora*)

mjuvi² *n* (*wa-*) a rude person, an insolent person; churl, boor: *Mjuvi aliwakashifu* *watu hadharani,* the boor discredited people in public. (cf *safihi, mjuba*)

mjuzi *n* (*wa-*) a knowledgeable person; a well-versed person; *Yeye ni mjuzi katika fani mbalimbali,* he is knowledgeable in various fields. (cf *aalimu*)

mkaa¹ *n* (*n*) see *kaa¹*

mkaa² *n* (*mi-*) (*bot*) candlenut tree; a medium-sized tree with large leaves up to 1 foot long and has creamish flowers, bearing a roundish fruit containing one or two seeds, the bark of which is used medicinally as an astringent. *Aleurites moluccana.*

mkaa³ *n* (*wa-*) see *msasi*

mkaachuma *n* (*mi-*) (*bot*) a much-branched shrub up to 12 feet tall with alternate leaves and small pinkish-white flowers. *Byrsocarpus maximus.*

mkaajabali *n* (*mi-*) (*bot*) a much-branched shrub or small tree up to twenty feet tall with alternate silvery pubescent leaves and small pinkish-white flowers. The shrub is found above high-water mark on rocky seashores and its wood is a good fuel. *Pemphis acidula.*

mkaapwani *n* (*mi-*) (*bot*) a small much branched deciduous tree up to 25 feet tall with small yellowish-green flowers, bearing small papery winged fruits. *Dodonaea viscosa.*

mkabala *n* (*mi-*) 1. opposite side: *Nyumba yangu iko mkabala na msikiti,* my house is opposite the mosque. 2. rapport, relationship: *Yeye ana mkabala mzuri na majirani zake,* he has a good relationship with his neighbours. (cf *uhusiano*) 3. encounter. (Ar)

mkabidhi *n* (*wa-*) trustee; one who holds property or money; a person to whom another's property or the management of another's property is entrusted: *Baba yake alipofariki, mkabidhi wa urithi alikuwa ami yake,* when his father died, the trustee of his inheritance was his paternal uncle. (cf *mdhamini*)

mkabilishemsi *n* (*mi-*) 1. (*bot*) Bustard Mustard. *Gynandropsis gynandra.* 2. an erect annual herb up to 3 feet tall with short palmate leaves, which are eaten as a vegetable and used in local medicine. *Cleome strigosa.* (cf *mwangani, mgagani*)

mkadamu *n* (*wa-*) a person in authority overseeing work on an estate. (Ar)

mkadi *n* (*mi-*) (*bot*) a much-branched tree up to 30 feet tall, bearing fibrous brownish yellow cone-like fruits. *Pandanus kirkii. Mkadi dume,* screw pine.

mkadiriaji *n* (*wa-*) assessor, evaluator, surveyor: *Mkadiriaji ujenzi,* quantity surveyor.

mkaguzi *n* (*wa-*) inspector: *Mkaguzi hesabu,* auditor. *Mkaguzi mkuu,* chief inspector. *Mkaguzi wa tikiti,* ticket inspector. *Yeye ni mkaguzi wa shule,* he is a school inspector. *Mkaguzi wa ndani,* internal auditor.

mkahale¹ *n* (*mi-*) a special pencil used for applying antimony to the eyes; eyeliner pencil.

mkahale² *n* (*mi-*) a devil that causes students to sleep in the class.

mkahawa¹ (also *mgahawa*) *n* (*mi-*) inn, cafe, restaurant: *Walikunywa chai kwenye mkahawa,* they drunk tea at the inn. (Ar)

mkahawa² *n* (*mi-*) (*bot*) coffee tree. *Coffee arabica.* (cf *mbuni*) (Ar)

mkaidi *n* (*wa-*) 1. a stubborn person; an obstinate person; recalcintrant, mule: *Usimpe ushauri wowote mkaidi yule,* don't give any advice to that mule. (cf *mshindani, mpinzani*) 2. a disobedient person; a rebellious person: *Mwanafunzi mkaidi aliadhibiwa na mwalimu wake,* the disobedient student was punished by his teacher. (cf *mhalifu*)

mkaja *n* (*mi-*) 1. a cloth worn by women round the body esp after childbirth. (cf *mwimba*). 2. fee or present given to the bride's mother.

mkaka *n* (*mi-*) mangrove tree. Its poles are used in buildings and its bark yields a valuable tanning. *Rhizophora mucronata*.

mkakao *n* (*mi-*) see *mkakau*

mkakasi¹(*also kasasi*) *n* (*mi-*) (*bot*) a fine soft tree but useless for timber. (*prov*) *Uzuri wa mkakasi, ukipata maji basi*, even though someone may be good in education, appearance, etc. he may have certain weaknesses and these can smear his reputation, etc.

mkakasi² *n* (*mi-*) a cylindrical metal box with a lid, used for keeping things such as perfumes.

mkakati *n* (*mi-*) strategy, technique: *Walitafuta mikakati mipya ya kumshinda adui*, they looked for new strategies of defeating the enemy. (cf *mbinu, njia*)

mkakau (also *mkakao*) *n* (*mi-*) (*bot*) cocoa tree. *Theobroma cacao*. (Eng)

mkakaya *n* (*mi-*) see *mkayakaya*

mkale *n* (*wa-*) 1. an experienced person of past events. (cf *mhenga*) 2. an old person: *Watu wengi wanamheshimu mkale yule*, many people respect that old person. (cf *mzee*) 3. a senior citizen. 4. a conservative person; diehard. (cf *mhafidhina*)

mkaliliaji *n* (*wa-*) a person who sits on the outriggers of a canoe so as to balance it. (cf *mwinukiaji, mkaliaji*)

mkalimani *n* (*wa-*) interpreter, translator: *Mkalimani yule alifanya kazi mahakamani kwa miaka mingi*, that interpreter worked at the court for many years. (cf *mtarijumani*) (Ar)

mkalio *n* (*mi-*) a customary wedding fee given to the bride's attendants during the first honeymoon days

mkalitusi *n* (*mi-*) (*bot*) gum tree

mkama *n* (*wa-*) a traditional rightful ruler in Bukoba region, Tanzania.

mkamachuma *n* (*mi-*) 1. (*bot*) a pubescent scandent shrub up to 15 feet tall with alternate, triplicate thin long-stacked leaves and small white flowers, bearing a small elliptical hairy fruit. *Allophylus stachyanthus*.

mkamadume *n* (*n*) title given to the traditional rulers in Pemba Island in Tanzania.

mkamamamba *n* (*mi-*) (*zool*) palm swift; a kind of very slim swift bird (family Apodidae) with slender wings and a deeply forked tail.

mkamasi *n* (*mi-*) (*bot*) a shrub or tree with alternate leaves bearing a round smooth apricot-coloured fruit when ripe, which contains one seed embedded in an exceedingly gluey pulp. *Cordia sp.*

mkamba¹ *n* (*mi-*) see *kamba²*

mkamba² *n* (*u*) (*med*) pneumonia; lung inflammation caused by bacterial or viral infection. (cf *nimonia, kichomi*)

mkambala *n* (*mi-*) (*bot*) a medium-sized tree with thorny trunk and branches. *Acacia nigrescens*.

mkambi *n* (*mi-*) a leg's splash during swimming.

mkamshi *n* (*mi-*) ladle; a kind of wooden spoon, used for stirring and for ladling out gravy, etc. (cf *upawa*)

mkanda¹ *n* (*mi-*) see *ukanda¹*

mkanda² *n* (*mi-*) (*naut*) channel, narrow straits. (cf *mkondo*) 2. used in the expression: *Mkanda wa jeshi*, shingles, herpes zoster; a viral infection of certain sensory nerves causing pain and an eruption of blisters along the course of the affected nerve. 3. (in sports) title: *Mwanabondia alifanikiwa kutetea mkanda wake wa kimataifa*, the boxer successfully defended his title. 4. tape: *Mkanda wa video*, video tape.

mkandaa *n* (*mi-*) 1. (*bot*) mangrove; a general term applied to different species of mangrove, the bark of which is used for tanning and furnishes a red dye. *Mkandaa dume, Lumnitzera racemosa. Mkandaa wa pwani, Ceriops Tagal. Mkandaa mwitu, Ochna thomasiana.* 2. used in the expression: *Chai ya mkandaa*, tea without milk, black tea. (cf *chai kavu*)

mkandaji *n*(*wa-*) massager; a person who massages.

mkandamizaji *n* (*wa-*) oppressor, tyrant, despot. (cf *mwonevu, dhalimu*)

mkandamizo n (mi-) pressure: *Mkandamizo wa hewa,* air pressure.
mkandamizwaji n (wa-) the oppressed.
mkandarasi n (wa-) contractor (cf *kontrakta*)
mkandi n (mi-) (bot) crowfoot grass. *Dactyloctenium aegyptium.*
mkando n (mi-) ingot; a lump or bar of cast or unwrought metal. (cf *mkuo*)
mkangaga n (mi-) (bot) a sedge with leaves up to three feet. *Cyperus distans.*
mkangaja n (mi-) (bot) a tussock herb with stems up to 3 feet with greenish flower spikes. *Cyperus rotundus.*
mkanganja n (mi-) a tree which bears a kind of manderine orange known as "tangerine." *Citrus sp.*
mkanganyiko n (mi-) confusion, bewilderment, perplexity: *Yumo katika mkanganyiko na sasa haelewi la kufanya,* he is in a state of confusion and now he does not know what to do. (cf *utatanishi*)
mkanganyo m (mi-) confusion, bewilderment: *Kaniweka katika hali ya mkanganyo,* he has put me in a state of confusion.
mkangazi n (mi-) (bot) East African mahogany. *Khaya nyasica.*
mkanju n (mi-) (bot) cashew nut tree. *Anacardium occidentale.* (cf *mbibo, mkorosho*)
mkanya n (mi-) (bot) medicinal plant bearing white flowers.
mkanyagano n (mi-) tread; the act, manner or sound of treading/tramping; stampede.
mkanyakumbwani n (mi-) (bot) a perennial herb up to 3 feet tall with dense heads of tiny greenish white flowers. *Oldenlandia bojeri.*
mkao n (mi-) act (style, etc.) of sitting. *Mkao wake kochini unavutia,* his style of sitting on the couch is impressive.
mkarafuu n (mi-) (bot) clove tree. *Eugenia aromatica. Mkarafuu maiti,* camphor. *Cinnamomum camphora.* (Ar)
mkaragazo[1] n (n) a very heavy shower of rain; downpour.

mkaragazo[2] n (n) a kind of strong tobacco.
mkarakala n (mi-) (bot) a timber tree with alternate leaves. *Bridelia sp.*
mkarambati n (mi-) (bot) a small glabrous tree with opposite ovate or lanceolate leaves and small pale yellow stalked flowers, bearing a small berry-like drupe fruit. *Canthium schimperianum.*
mkaranga n (mi-) (bot) groundnut plant; peanut plant. *Arachis hypogaea.*
mkarara n (mi-) refrain (cf *kibwagizo, kipokeo, kiitikio*)
mkarati n (mi-) (bot) a timber tree with alternate leaves. *Bridelia sp.* (cf *mkarakala*)
mkasisi mkiwa n (mi-) (bot) eucalyptus; a tall, aromatic tree of the myrtle family bearing pendent leaves and umbels of white or pink flowers and is valued for its timber, gum and oil, which is used medicinally. *Eucalyptus cinerea.*
mkasa n (mi-) 1. incident, event; good or bad luck. 2. unusual act performed by a person for the purpose of entertaining; strange event, joke: *Mtu yule ni wa mikasa mitupu,* that person is full of jokes. (cf *kituko*) (Ar)
mkasi (also *makasi*) n (mi-) a pair of scissors. (Ar)
mkasiri n (mi-) (bot) a much-branched shrub with alternate small leaves and small greenish yellow flowers, the bark of which is used for dyeing fishing lines. *Phyllanthus reticulatus.* (cf *mpesi*)
mkasisi mkiwa n (mi-) (bot) ice vine; a climbing plant with slender thread-like branches, the roots of which are used medicinally. *Cissampelos pariera.*
mkata n (wa-) a poor person; pauper: *Mkata yule anaishi maisha ya dhiki,* that pauper lives a hard life. (prov) *Mkata hana kinyongo,* a poor person is not choosy in terms of getting food, etc.; that is to say, he has to take anything for his survival. (cf *masikini, mchochole*)

mkataa n (mi-) see makataa
mkataba n (mi-) contract, agreement, treaty: *Mkataba wa kimataifa*, international agreement. *Mkataba wa ushirikiano*, a treaty of co-operation. *Kocha amefanya mkataba wa miaka miwili kuifundisha timu yetu*, the coach has signed a two-year contract to train our team. *Mkataba wa mwafaka*, a memorandum of understanding. (cf *mapatano*) (Ar)
mkatafingo n (mi-) (bot) a perennial herb with stems up to 6 feet tall, the roots of which are used medicinally. *Costus subbiflorus*.
mkatakimo n (mi-) (bot) a shrub with opposite evergreen leaves. *Memecylon* sp.
mkatale n (mi-) instrument for confining a prisoner by the feet and sometimes, his wrists; stocks. (cf *gogoo, gandalo*)
mkatani n (mi-) 1. (bot) sisal hemp plant. *Agave sisalana*. 2. blue sisal. *Agave amaniensis*. 3. Mauritius hemp, *Furcraea gigantea*; a succulent plant, at one time cultivated in East Africa for its leaves which produced a strong fibre but now abandoned in favour of sisal.
mkatavu n (wa-) a person who refuses to comply with anything he is told to do; a stubborn person; a head strong person; a defiant person; a bull-headed person; mule, recalcitrant: *Watu walikataa kumpa ushauri mkatavu yule*, people refused to give advice to that recalcitrant. (cf *mbishi, mkaidi*)
mkate n (mi-) 1. bread; loaf of bread: *Mkate wa boflo*, loaf bread. *Mkate wa mahindi*, corn pone. *Mkate wa mofa*, a kind of hard round bread made from millet flour, baked in an oven. *Mkate wa kumimina*, a kind of bread made usu from wheat flour. 2. anything that is stirred and moulded to look like a bread or cake for special use: *Mkate wa tumbaku*, tobacco cake; plug.
mkato[1] n (mi-) 1. cutting, cut, splitting: *Mkato ule wa kitambaa ni mzuri*, that cutting of the cloth is good. (cf *ukataji*) 2. section: *Mkato mtambuko*, cross-section.
mkato[2] adv, n used in the expressions: *Kwa mkato*, briefly. *Kwa njia ya mkato*, in a short cut. *Hati mkato*, short hand. *Mkato wa mzunguko wa umeme*, short circuit. *Sema kwa mkato*, speak in brief.
mkato[3] n (mi-) (gram) comma
Mkatoliki n (wa-) Catholic (Eng)
mkatu n (mi-) (bot) a scandent evergreen shrub with stems up to 15 feet long, the roots of which are said to be edible. *Synaptolepis kirkii*. *Mkatu mkubwa*, a shrub with alternate pinnate leaves and small white flowers. *Byrsocarpus* sp
mkauchi n (mi-) (bot) a parasitic shrub with small tabular flowers. *Loranthus rhamnifolius*
mkaumwa n (mi-) (bot) calumba root; a climbing perennial herb with alternate cordate three-to-five lobed leaves, the roots of which are used medicinally for dysentery and abdominal ailments. *Jateorhiza palmata*. (cf *mkando, mkuo*)
Mkawini n (wa-) (in Islam) one of the names of God that explains the attributes of his creation: *Mkawini mbingu*. the creator of the skies.
mkayakaya n (mi-) 1. iron wood tree. *Cassia siamea*. (cf *mjohoro*) 2. flamboyant tree. *Delonix regia*. (cf *mkenge, mkrismasi, mjohoro*)
mkaza n (wa-) the wife of: *Mkaza mjomba*, the wife of the uncle.
mkazahau n (wa-) wife's uncle.
mkazi n (wa-) resident, occupant: *Yeye ni mkazi wa jimbo la magharibi*, he is a resident of the western region. (cf *mkaazi, mkaaji, mwenyeji*)
mkazo n (mi-) 1. force, strength, energy: *Mlango ulifungwa kwa mkazo*, the door was closed with force. 2. (phon) stress, emphasis: *Mkazo neno*, word

481

stress. *Mkazo wa sentensi*, sentence stress. *Alitia mkazo katika kila neno alilolitamka*, he put stress on every word he uttered. (cf *shadda*)

mke *n* (*wa-*) wife: *Mke mwenza*, co-wife. *Yeye ni mke wa jirani yangu*, she is the wife of my neighbour.

mkebe *n* (*mi-*) tin, can, mug, case. (cf *kopo*)

mkeka *n* (*mi-*) mat: *Mkeka wa kazi*, a kind of mat plaited in patterns. *Mkeka wa kiwambazani*, arras.

mkeketo[1] *n* (*mi-*) used of people, things, etc. of equal size: *Wanafunzi wa kila darasa katika shule hii wamewekwa katika mkeketo mmoja*, the students of every class in this school have been put in one equal category.

mkeketo[2] *n* (*mi-*) 1. severe abdominal pains: *Tumbo lake lilikuwa na mkeketo takriban usiku wote*, he had severe abdominal pains almost the whole night. 2. the cutting of a hard thing with a blunt instrument: *Niliusikia mkeketo wa matawi ya miti jana asubuhi*, I heard the cutting of branches of trees yesterday morning. 3. The cutting of things into slices.

mkembe *n* (*mi-*) 1. a child between one and six years old. 2. a young person who has not yet married. (cf *kijana*, *ghulamu*)

mkemia *n* (*wa-*) chemist (Eng)

mkengata *n* (*mi-*) (*bot*) hop bush, hop seed bush. It is a drought-tolerant shrub with an up-right, branching form and its foliage is of bronzy-green colour. *Dodonaea viscosa*.

mkenge *n* (*mi-*) a general term applied to Albizzia trees such as *Albizzia glabrescens* and *Albizzia petersiana*. (cf *mjohoro*)

mkengeuka *n* (*wa-*) deviationist; a person who deviates from the norms of a society. (also *ukengeushi*)

mkengeuko (also *ukengeushi*) *n* (*mi*) deviation, aberration, pervesity: *Mkengeuko wa tabia zake ulimletea hasara*, the pervesity of his behaviour

brought him ruin.

Mkenya *n* (*wa-*) Kenyan

mkeraji *n* (*wa-*) a person who irritates others; harasser.

mkereketwa *n* (*wa-*) zealot, fanatic; a person who is zealous esp to an extreme or excessive degree: *Yeye ni mkereketwa wa chama tawala*, he is the ruling party zealot. (cf *mshabiki*)

mkesha[1] *n* (*mi-*) 1. eve: *Watoto arobaini walizaliwa nchini katika mkesha wa mwaka mpya*, forty children were born in the country on New Year's Eve. 2. the clearing up of the skies after it has rained or been cloudy: *Mara baada ya mkesha, watu walitawanyika*, after the rain, once the sky had cleared, people dispersed. 3. night watch; vigil.

mkesha[2] *n* (*mi-*) (*zool*) thrush; a kind of a relatively long-legged song bird (family *Turdidae*) which is brownish-grey above with a pale ashy-grey chest and a whitish breast and abdomen.

Mkhufti *n* (*wa-*) (*rel*) copt; a member of the coptic church.

mkia *n* (*mi-*) (*zool*) 1. tail: *Mkia wa mbwa*, the tail of a dog. 2. (*idm*) *Mkia wa mbuzi*, a useless thing.

mkichaa *n* (*wa-*) see *kichaa*[1]

mkiki *n* (*mi-*) the act of using force, threat, boastfulness, etc. in order to achieve or do sth: *Mtu yule amekuja kwa mikiki. Anafikiri tunamwogopa?* That person has come with threats. Does he think we fear him?

mkikimkiki *n* (*mi-*) pressure, force, exertion: *Tulifanikiwa hatimaye kumpatia pasipoti baada ya mikikimkiki mingi*, we finally succeeded in getting a passport for him after putting much pressure.

mkilua *n* (*mi-*) (*bot*) a shrub or small tree (*Annonaceae*) of *Uvaria sp*, having ovate leaves with sweet scented yellow and crimson flowers, which are used for making garlands.

mkilungwana *n* (*mi-*) (*bot*) rubbervine. *Landolphia kirkii*.

mkimbiaji *n* (*wa-*) runner, sprinter: *Alikuwa mkimbiaji hodari,* he was a good sprinter.

mkimbio *n* (*mi-*) (esp in cricket) run; a scoring point, made by a successful running of both batsmen from one wicket to the other

mkimbizi *n* (*wa-*) 1. truant, runaway. 2. refugee, fugitive: *Serikali inashughulikia tatizo la wakimbizi kwa kina,* the government is tackling the problem of refugees in depth.

mkimwa *n* (*wa-*) an impatient person; a person who cannot endure hardships, provocations, etc.: *Uzee umemfanya awe mkimwa kwani hawezi kuvumilia hata jambo dogo,* old age has made him become an impatient person because he cannot tolerate even a small thing. 2. a cheerless person; sourpuss, bete noire: *Majirani hawamchangamkii mkimwa yule,* the neighbours are not friendly to that cheerless person. (cf *bweshu*)

mkinda *n* (*mi-*) 1. a local dance used in the initiation ceremonies of young girls. 2. a local dance used in wedding ceremonies and even in the loss of someone.

mkindu *n* (*mi-*) (*bot*) wild date palm; a palm with solitary or tufted stems and small creamy flowers, bearing small oval fruits and whose young leaves are used for making mats and fine baskets. *Phoenix reclinata.*

mkingamo *n* (*mi-*) obstruction, barrier: *Njia ya mkingamo,* crossroad. (cf *njiapanda*)

mkingiri *n* (*mi-*) (*bot*) a kind of shrub or small tree found in wastelands, the pods of which are used medicinally and as an antidote to scorpion and snake bites. *Dichrostachys glomerata.*

mkingu *n* (*mi-*) (*bot*) a much-branched deciduous tree up to 40 feet tall with alternate pinnate leaves and greenish-yellow flowers, often planted as a street tree. *Albizzia lebbek.*

mkinzani *n* (*mi-*) antagonist, opponent: *Yeye alikuwa mkinzani mkubwa wa demokrasia,* he was a great opponent of democracy. (cf *mpinzani*)

mkinzano *n* (*mi-*) resistance, antagonism, opposition: *Haifai kuleta ukinzani wa bure kwenye mkutano huu,* it is not good to bring unnecessary opposition to this meeting.

mkirika *n* (*mi-*) (*bot*) a shrub or small deciduous tree with alternate leaves. *Ehertia sp.*

mkiritimba *n* (*wa-*) monopolist: *Mfanyabiashara yule ni mkiritimba,* that businessman is a monopolist.

mkite *n* (*n*) (*bot*) a kind of cowpeas which are red when raw.

mkitu *n* (*n*) (*zool*) one spot snapper; a kind of fish with black spot and yellow fins, found solitarily on coral reefs. (cf *changudoa*)

mkiwa *n* (*wa-*) 1. a bereaved person: *Nilienda nyumbani kwao kuwaliwaza wakiwa,* I went to their home to console the bereaved. 2. a solitary person; a lonely person: *Alikuwa mkiwa kwa miaka mingi kabla hajaoa,* he was lonely for so many years before getting married. (cf *mjane*) 3. a poor person. *Amekuwa mkiwa sasa tangu kufilisika,* he has now become poor since going bankrupt. (cf *masikini*)

mkizi *n* (*mi-*) (*zool*) mullet; a kind of spiny-rayed edible fish of moderately elongate body (family *Mugilidae*) with fairly large scales on the body and head and a small mouth with feeble teeth, found in fresh and salt waters. (*prov*) *Hasira ya mkizi furaha ya mvuvi,* anger of the mullet is the joy of the fisherman i.e. anger on somebody can bring a lot of harm.

mkoa[1] *n* (*mi-*) see *mkole*[1]

mkoa[2] *n* (*mi-*) region, province: *Mkoa wa magharibi,* western region. *Mkoa wa kusini,* southern region. (cf *jimbo*)

mkoa[3] (also *mkuo*) *n* (*mi-*) a rectangular bar of metal or soap: *Mkoa wa sabuni,* a bar of soap. *Mkoa wa dhahabu*, a bar of gold. *Mkoa wa shaba*, copper bar.

mkoba *n* (*mi-*) 1. purse, wallet, satchel, basket, bag: *Mkoba wa ngozi*, leatherbag. 2. a special bag used by medicine men to keep their paraphernalia: *Kifungua mkoba*, a fee paid to a medicine man to assist his client before the "treatment" work begins. *Ameachiwa mkoba*, he has inherited the work of witchraft. *Pewa mkoba*, be entrusted the work of witchraft.

mkoche (also *mkoma*) *n* (*mi-*) (*bot*) doum palms; a tropical palm with palmate arched leaves and yellowish or whitish spiny petioles bearing a polished brown fruit and its leaves when dried in the sun are used for light baskets and for making mats. *Hyphaene coriacea sp*

mkodi[1] *n* (*mi-*) a kind of evil spirit.

mkodi[2] *n* (*wa-*) renter, tenant: *Amekuwa mkodi katika nyumba yangu tangu mwanzo wa mwaka huu*, he has been my tenant since the beginning of this year. (cf *mpangaji*)

mkodisha *n* (*wa-*) see *mkodishaji*,

mkodishaji (also *mkodisha*) *n* (*wa-*) landlord, proprietor, owner.

mkodishwaji *n* (*wa-*) tenant, renter, occupier, lessee. (cf *mpangaji*)

mkoi *n* (*wa-*) the male child of a father, aunt or uncle; cousin.

mkojo *n* (*mi-*) urine: *Ugonjwa wa mkojo*, diuresis.

mkoko *n* (*mi-*) 1. (*bot*) a rambling or climbing grass, used as cut fodder for feeding cattle and for pasturage. *Panicum trichocladum*. 2. a kind of mangrove whose poles and wood are used for building and as fuel. The split stems of this tree are used to make sifting baskets and its red bark is used for dyeing. *Rhizophora mucronata*. 3. cocoa tree. *Theobroma cacao* 4 (syn) *Ndio kwanza mkoko, ualike maua*, it is just beginning (with reference to things)

mkokoa *n* (*mi-*) (*bot*) henna plant. *Lawsonia inermis*.

mkokoriko *n* (*u*) gravy.

mkokoshi *n* (*mi-*) (*bot*) red mangrove; a much-branched evergreen tree up to 60 feet tall, bearing keeled woody fruits and whose stems are used for dhow masts. *Heretiera littoralis*.

mkokoteni *n* (*mi-*) dray, pushcart: *Aliipeleka mizigo yake nyumbani kwa kukodi mkokoteni*, he sent his luggage home by hiring a pushcart. (cf *rikwama*)

mkokoto *n* (*mi-*) 1. dragging, pulling, hauling. 2. the mark of sth dragged along. (*prov*) *Mkokoto wa jembe, si bure yao*, the mark left by the dragging of a hoe has some significance i.e hardwork pays even if the results come at lower pace.

mkokotoo *n* (*mi-*) computation, calculation.

mkokwa *n* (*mi-*) (*bot*) breadfruit tree

mkole[1] *n* (*mi-*) 1. (*bot*) a much-branched shrub or small tree with small ovate alternate clusters of small yellow flowers and small red berry-like fruits, the bark of which is used for dyeing and the fibre for producing a soapy substance, which some women use to wash their hair, etc. *Grewia sp*. 2. (*syn*) *Amekwenda mkoleni*, she has completed the initiation rites at school.

mkole[2] *n* (*mi-*) see *kole*[1]

mkologwe *n* (*mi-*) (*bot*) dried banana. (cf *hangale, mchachato*)

mkoloni *n* (*wa-*) 1. colonialist. 2. a colonial-minded person. (Eng)

mkoma[1] *n* (*mi-*) see *mkoche*

mkoma[2] *n* (*wa-*) leper; a person suffering from leprosy.

mkoma[3] *n* (*wa-*) a word used to refer to a person who is suspected to be a wizard or a murderer. (*prov*) *Asiye mkoma, hujikoma mwenyewe*, if there is no one to help you in any situation, then you may have to help yourself.

mkomafi *n* (*mi-*) (*bot*) a much-branched

shrub or tree up to 25 feet tall with compound leaves and white flowers, whose globular fruits contain a large number of angular seeds. *Xyclocarpus benadirensis.*

mkomamanga n (mi-) (bot) pomegranate; a shrub or small tree bearing globular fruits about the size of an orange and which contains many seeds surrounded by a juicy pulp of a peculiar astringent, acid flavour. *Punica granatum.* (cf *mkudhumani*)

mkombo n (mi-) (naut) a bar or handle for turning a boat's rudder; tiller. (cf *kana*)

mkombozi (also *mgombozi*) n (wa-) 1. rescuer, saviour, redeemer: *Mkombozi aliwakomboa ng'ombe wake kutoka kwa mkulima*, the redeemer freed his cows from the farmer. 2. liberator, emancipator: *Wakombozi wa nchi hii*, the liberators of this country.

mkombwe n (mi-) see *mkomwe*

mkomo (also *mkomwe*) n (mi-) a kind of powder used in witchcraft and which is used to make someone faint temporarily: *Piga mkomo*, blow the powder of this kind.

mkomunisti n (wa-) 1. communist. 2. a member of the communist party. (Eng)

mkomwe[1] (also *mkombwe*) n (mi-) (bot) a scrambling shrub with very prickly stems and leaf stalks and whose greyish-white seeds are used in the local game of *bao* (draughts). *Caesalpinia crista.* (cf *msoo*)

mkomwe[2] n (mi-) see *mkomo*

mkondo n (mi-) 1. current; a flow of water in a particular direction: *Mkondo bahari*, ocean current. (prov) *Maji hufuata mkondo*, water follows the current i.e. you should adjust your behaviour, attitude, etc according to the prevailing circumstances. 2. track: *Mkondo wa nyasi*, a track through rushes, showing where people have passed. 3. current; the flow of electricity, air, etc. in a particular direction: *Mkondo wa umeme*, electric current. *Mkondo wa hewa*, current of air. 4. leg of a visit of a leader, etc.: *Rais alitembelea nchi ya jirani katika mkondo wa pili wa ziara yake*, the president visited the neighbouring country in the second leg of his visit. 5. used in other expressions: *Mkondo geu*, alternating current. *Mkondo mzunguko*, circulating current. *Mkondo mfulizo*, direct current. 6. (educ) stream: *Mwanafunzi yule yumo katika mkondo wa A*, that student is in A stream.

mkonechacha n (mi-) (bot) a much-branched shrub or tree with alternate simple leaves. *Hirtella sp.*

mkonga[1] n (mi-) (bot) a much-branched, often spiny tree, bearing slightly fleshy oval fruits with a hard-shelled seed. *Balanites wilsoniana.*

mkonga[2] n (mi-) the trunk of an elephant; tusk. (prov) *Tembo hashindwi na mkonga wake*, an elephant is never overcome by its tusk i.e one is never defeated by one's duties/responsibilities as a parent.

mkonge[1] n (mi-) 1. (bot) a large aloe-like plant whose lanceolate leaves produce fibres which are used for making strings, bags, hats, etc. *Sansevieria sp. Mkonge mume*, sisal hemp. *Agave sisalana*, also called *mkatani.* 2. lucky bean tree; Mahogany bean. *Afzelia quanzensis.*

mkonge[2] n (mi-) (zool) wolf herring; a kind of medium-sized silvery salt-fish (family *Chirocentridae*) with an elongate and highly compressed body with a belly without scales.

mkongoja n (mi-) see *mkongojo*

mkongojo (also *mkongoja*) n (mi-) a staff used as a prop or crutch for an old man, a sick person, etc.; a walking stick for an old man, a sick person, etc.: *Mkongojo mrefu unaotumiwa na wapanda milima*, alpenstock.

mkong'oto n (mi-) 1. hard beating: Waandamanaji walipata mikong'oto kutoka kwa polisi, the demonstrators received beatings from policemen. 2. (syn) Tembeza mkong'oto, beat people indiscriminately. (cf kipigo kikubwa)

mkongwa n (mi-) a kind of herb whose species can be used as a vegetable and as an antidote for majimoto (hot water) ants. Cummelina sp.

mkongwe n (wa-) 1. an old person, usu one who cannot take care of himself: Umemwona mkongwe yule akipita na wajukuu wake wawili? Have you seen that old man passing with his two grandsons? (cf mzee) 2. veteran; an old experienced person. (cf shaibu, ajuza)

mkoniferesi n (mi-) (bot) a coniferous tree; conifer; a tree that bears cones and need-like or scale-like leaves.

mkono n (mi-) 1. arm, hand; Mkono wa kulia, right hand. Mkono wa kushoto, left hand. 2. (idms) Ana mkono mrefu, (a) he is a thief (b) he likes to beat others. Mkono wa birika, a miserly person; a stingy person. Mkono mmoja, co-operatively e.g. Wanavijiji wanafanya kazi kwa mkono mmoja, the villagers work co-operatively. Ana mkono mzuri, he has a good handwriting. Ana mkono mbaya, he does not do a good job if he is given work. Ana mkono mzito, he is slow. Ana mkono mwepesi, he is fast in doing a job. 3. anything resembling an arm or works like an arm e.g. handle, etc: Mkono wa sufuria, the handle of a saucepan. Mkono wa saa, a watch hand. Mkono wa tembo, an elephant's trunk. Mkono wa ndizi, the pedicle of a banana. 4. any part or extension of a main body or system e.g. the creek of a sea or the branch of a river. Mkono wa bahari, the creek of the sea. Mikono ya mito, the branches of the rivers. Mkono wa shati, the sleeve of the shirt. (prov) Mkono mmoja haulei mwana, one hand does not bring up a child i.e. in order for us to be successful, we must cooperate. 5. cubit; a measure from finger-tip to elbow. (cf dhiraa)

mkonochuma n (mi-) (bot) a much-branched shrub up to 15 feet tall with alternate trifoliate glabrous leaves and minute yellow flowers with small glossy brown fruits. Rhus natalensis.

mkonokono n (wa-) a skillful charmer of snakes. (cf mnunguri)

mkonokono mwitu n (mi-) (bot) wild custard apple; a much branched deciduous tree bearing more or less fleshy oval fruits and whose roots are said to be poisonous. Annona chrysophylla.

mkono-wa-simba n (mi-) (bot) a shrub or small tree with alternate simple leaves. Cordia sp.

mkonzo n (mi-) a large stick with the end pointed, and hardened with fire, used as a weapon for hunting crabs or octopuses. (cf uchokoo)

mkoo n (wa-) a very dirty person; sloven.

mkopaji n (wa-) borrower (cf mkopi)

mkopeshaji n (wa-) 1. a person who lends money; money lender. 2. a person who lends money with or without an interest: Mkopeshaji fedha, money lender.

mkopi n (wa-) 1. borrower; creditor, a person who borrows money. 2. knave, swindler.

mkopo n (mi-) 1. loan, credit: Mkopo nafuu, soft loan. Ofisi ya mkopo, loan office. (cf karadha) 2. sth that has been borrowed.

mkora n (wa-) crook, thug, ruffian: Mkora alifikishwa mahakamani kwa kosa la uhalifu, the thug was brought before the court of law on criminal charges. (cf jambazi)

Mkorea n (wa-) Korean; a person originating from Korea; a citizen of Korea. (Eng)

mkorofi n (wa-) 1. an unlucky person with respect to business, marriage, etc.; an ill-omened person; an ill-fortuned person; jinx: *Mtu yule ni mkorofi kwa vile chochote anachokipata, hakikai*, that person is ill-fortuned because whatever he earns, it does not stay. (cf *kisirani, nuhusi*) 2. a troublesome person; troublemaker, reprobate: *Mkorofi yule anaweza kukuharibia mipango yako*, that troublemaker can spoil your plans.

mkorogeko *n*(*mi-*) confusion of affairs.

mkorogo *n* (*mi-*) 1. a mixture of ingredients of liquid forms. 2. disorderly affairs; chaotic matters: *Mipango yangu imo katika mikorogo*, my plans have fallen into confusion. 3. local brew for sale or given free of charge.

mkoromo (also *koromo*) *n* (*mi-*) sound made from snoring; snore.

mkoroshi *n* (*mi-*) see mkorosho

mkorosho (also *mkoroshi*) *n* (*mi-*) (*bot*) cashew nut tree. *Anacardium occidentale* (cf *mbibo, mkanju*)

mkosa *n* (*wa-*) 1. a person who misses what he wants. 2. a person who makes mistakes; wrongdoer, sinner.

mkosaji *n* (*wa-*) 1. a person who errs or makes mistakes; sinner, wrongdoer: *Mimi sikukosa lolote; mkosaji ni yeye*, I did not do anything wrong; he is the sinner. 2. a person who is always deficient in sth; a person who is always lacking sth.

mkosefu *n* (*wa-*) 1. a person who has violated a law, etc.; offender, culprit, wrongdoer: *Mkosefu wa sheria alifikishwa mahakamani kuikabili kesi*, the culprit was brought before the court of law for trial. 2. a person who is devoid of sth: *Mkosefu wa haya*, a person devoid of shyness. *Mkosefu wa heshima*, a person devoid of respect.

mkosi *n* (*mi-*) bad luck, bad omen, jinx: *Safari yao imeingia mkosi*, their journey has met a misfortune. (cf *kisirani, nuhusi*)

mkota¹ *n* (*mi-*) *Sorghum sp*; a variety of sweet stalked sorghum.

mkota² *n* (*wa-*) a strong person; a giant of a man: *Mkota anaweza kubeba vitu vizito*, a strong person can carry heavy objects. (cf *mbabe*)

mkowa *n* (*mi-*) a kind of belt usu a thick one, worn around the waist and used to keep money in; moneybelt. (cf *mkwiji*)

mkrismasi *n*(*mi-*) (*bot*) 1. iron wood tree. *Cassia Siamea*. 2. flambyonate tree *Debrix regia*. (cf *mkayakaya mjohoro*)

Mkristo *n* (*wa-*) Christian (Eng)

mkudhumani *n* (*mi-*) (*bot*) pomegranate tree. *Punica granatum*. (cf *mkomamanga*)

mkufu *n* (*mi-*) chain necklace; a chain usu of a metal form, worn generally by women as an ornament: *Msichana mrembo alivutia zaidi alipovaa mkufu*, the glamorous girl looked more attractive when she wore a necklace.

mkufunzi (also *mkufunzi*) *n* (*wa-*) tutor, instructor: *Yeye ni mkufunzi katika chuo cha ualimu*, he is a tutor at the teachers' training college.

mkugo *n* (*mi-*) debt (cf *deni*)

mkuka *n* (*mi-*) *Solacia sp.*; a shrub or tree with alternate leaves

mkuki *n* (*mi-*) 1. spear: *Chomeka mkuki*, stick a spear in the ground. *Chomoa mkuki*, extract a spear. (*prov*) *Mkuki kwa nguruwe, kwa binaadamu mchungu*, a spear is alright to the pig but is quite painful to the humanbeing i.e. You may not feel the pain of sth harmful done to sby else but if that same thing is done to you, then you feel it. 2. (*sports*) javelin.

mkuku¹ *n* (*mi-*) (*bot*) *Solacia sp*; a liane with opposite leaves and inconspicuous green or yellow flowers and globular fruits.

mkuku² *n* (*mi-*) (*naut*) the keel of a boat or ship. (cf *mastamu, cheleko*)

mkukuriko *n* (*mi-*) 1. bewilderment, pandemonium, confusion: *Mkukuriko ule ulimtia katika shida*, that confusion brought her into hardships. (cf *hangaiko*) 2. force in doing sth. (cf *msukumo*)

mkukuto n (mi-) see mkung'uto
mkule (also ngarara, ngarengare) n (mi-) (zool) needlefish; a kind of a long, pipe-like, voracious marine fish (family Belonidae) with elongated jaws and needle-like teeth.
mkulima n (wa-) 1. peasant; a person earning his living from the land he possesses. 2. a farmer usu with technical know-how. (provs) Mchagua jembe si mkulima, he who selects a hoe is not a farmer i.e. a person should not be too choosy when he is looking for a job, etc. Mkulima ni mmoja, walaji ni wengi, a farmer is one but the consumers are many i.e. one person may invent sth but those who will benefit from his invention may be many.
mkulivu n (wa-) 1. a person who bores others by deeds or words, a person who is tiresome; bore: Simpendi mtu yule kwa sababu ni mkulivu, I don't like that person because he is a bore. 2. an idle person; loafer, lounger: Nchi haiwezi kuendelea mbele kama ina wakulivu wengi, a country cannot progress if it has many idlers. (cf mzembe)
mkulo n (mi-) a strainer for straining grated coconut; coconut strainer. (cf kung'uto, kumto)
mkulu n (mi-) (bot) a much-branched shrub or tree with alternate simple leaves. Diospyros sp.
mkumbakusi n (mi-) (bot) bean tree; Mahogany bean. Afzelia quanzensis.
mkumba ng'ombe n (mi-) (bot) a tall deciduous glabrous shrub with ovate leaves and small white flowers in axillary clusters. Canthium robynsianum.
mkumbi n (mi-) (bot) a tree whose bark is used to make a yellow dye for staining ukili. (cf mwingamo)
mkumbizi n (wa-) 1. a person who cleans up; a person who sweeps; cleaner, sweeper: Wakumbizi wale hufagia mtaa wetu vizuri, those sweepers clean our neighbourhood well. 2. a person who accompanies reapers in a field and gleans whatever that has been left behind after harvesting; gleaner: Wakumbizi hawakuokota vitu vingi shambani, those gleaners did not collect many things in the farm.
mkumbo n (mi-) 1. wholesale devastation; onslaught, swoop, onrush: Mkumbo wa maji uliwagharikisha wanavijiji wote, the flood onslaught devastated all villagers. 2 (a). the sudden attack on a place or group of people in order to surround and catch them; swoop: Alichukua pesa mfukoni mwangu kwa mkumbo mmoja, he took money from my pocket in one swoop. (b) group, company, party: Wanafunzi na walimu wao wametiwa katika mkumbo mmoja kwenye basi, the students and their teachers were put in the same group. (cf kundi)
mkumbuu n (mi-) see ukumbuu
mkunaji n (wa-) coconut grater.
mkunapaa n (mi-) (bot) a shrub with alternate aromatic leaves and small white flowers in short racemes bearing a fruit of a three-lobed capsule covered with silvery scales; zebra tick, yellow-back tick. Croton pseudopulchellus.
mkunatuu n (mi-) (bot) a tree whose roots and leaves are dried and ground and used as a medicine on the wound after someone has been circumcised.
mkunazi n (mi-) (bot) jujube tree; a much-branched prickly tree with ovate leaves and small greenish-yellow flowers having fleshy fruit plum-like drupe. Ziziphus jujuba.
mkundaji (also kundaji) n (mi-) (zool) goatfish; a kind of oblong edible tropical fish (family Mullidae) with large slightly ctenoid scales having one or more long barbels on the lower jaw.
mkunde n (mi-) (bot) cowpea tree; a climbing or trailing, nearly glabrous annual plant with stout stems and trifoliate three-lobed leaves, bearing cowpeas. Vigna unguiculata.

mkundu *n (mi-) (anat)* anus. *(prov) Kufa kwa mkundu, mavi hutawanyika*, the death of the anus causes faeces to scatter i.e. when a leader departs from the scene, the followers usu get disorganized. (cf *maranda*)

mkunga¹ *n (wa-)* midwife. *(prov) Usitukane wakunga na uzazi ungalipo*, don't insult midwives when childbirth is still prevalent, don't attack or insult someone who you still need his services. *Wakunga wa jadi*, traditional midwives.

mkunga² *n (mi-) (zool)* moray, conger, eel; a kind of scaleless snake-like saltwater fish of (families *Congridae* and *Muraenidae*) characterized by brilliant colouring and a compressed tail. Zebra muray. *Echidna zebra*.

mkunga

mkunge *n (mi-) (vet)* sarcoptic mange, demodectic mange; demodicosis. This is a disease caused by a tiny and usually not directly visible parasite, the mite *Sarcoptes scarbies* which burrows under the host's skin causing intense allergic itching.

mkungu¹ *n (mi-) (bot)* Indian almond tree; a kind of tree bearing edible oval fleshy fruit up to 2 inches long with a hard-shelled seed, which is edible. The seed is called *badam*, which is very popular with local children and young people. *Terminalia catappa*.

mkungu² *n (mi-) (bot)* a bunch of bananas or plantains; the fruit stem or pedical of a banana plant carrying the whole head of the fruit.

mkungu³ *n (mi-)* 1. a large earthenware dish, used for cooking. (cf *banguu, kibia*) 2. the lid of the earthenware.

mkunguma *n (mi-) (bot)* a glabrous tree with alternate pinnate leaves and small flowers in long pendulous panicles, whose fruits are edible, oval and fleshy. *Sorindeia obtusifoliolata*.

mkungumanga *n (mi-) (bot)* nutmeg tree. *Myristica fragrans*.

mkungumanga

mkunguni¹ *n (wa-)* a lazy person; idler, loafer: *Usistaajabu kwa mtu yule kategea kazi kwa vile yeye ni mkunguni*, don't be surprised if that person dodges work because he is a loafer. (cf *mzembe*)

mkunguni² *n (mi-) (bot)* a much-branched small evergreen tree with clustered to alternate small leathery oval yellow-green leaves, whose fruits are small, oval and yellow and its wood is used for making pedles. *Terminalia fatraea*.

mkunguru¹ (also *ukunguru*) *n (mi-)* 1. the sickness of acclimatization; the fever or illness which attacks a newcomer at a place: *Alishikwa na mkunguru baada ya kuhamia katika nchi ya mbali*, he got sick after shifting to a distant country. 2. fear that someone has for a particular issue or object; phobia. (cf *hofu, woga*)

mkunguru² *n (mi-)* see *mninga*

mkungupwa *n (mi-) (bot)* zebra wood tree; a kind of tree whose timber is a useful full and also used in cabinet making. *Guettarda speciosa*.

mkung'uto (also *mkukuto*) *n (mi-)* the act of shaking off dust, chaff, etc. from a carpet, etc.; the act of dusting sth such as a carpet, etc.: *Mkung'uto wake wa zulia ulisababisha sisi tukohowe*, his dusting of the carpet made us cough a lot.

489

mkunguzi n (mi-) a name given to refer to a family of creeping plants that coil themselves around trees.

mkunjo (also *kunjo*) n (mi-) 1. the portion of a cloth, paper, etc. that has been folded, creased, wrinkled, etc.: *Mkunjo wa suruali*, the crease of the trousers. 2. wrinkling, creasing, folding; act (manner, etc.) of turning over: *Siupendi mkunjo wake wa shati*, I don't like his style of rolling the shirt sleeves.

mkuno n (mi-) act (method, etc.) of scratching with a fingernail or by grating, scraping, etc. with an appropriate instrument; scratch scape.

mkunungu n (mi-) (bot) a much branched deciduous tree with compound lemon-scented leaves and small green flowers, the branches of which are used as toothbrushes; the young fresh leaves, *pombo*, are eaten as a vegetable. *Fagara olitoria*. (cf *mnokoa*)

mkunyati n (mi-) (bot) a procumbent annual herb with opposite lancodate pubescent leaves and dense globular heads of red- to pink- and white small everlasting flowers. *Gomphrena decumbens*.

mkunyato n (mi-) (physiol) systole; the usual rhythmic contraction of the heart esp. of the ventricles.

mkunyuo n (mi-) scratching, abrasion: *Mkunyuo ule ulimletea vidonda vingi mkononi*, that scratching caused him to have a lot of wounds on the arm. (cf *mchubuo*)

mkunzo n (mi-) a bracelet of fine wire or skin, usu worn round the arm. (cf *udodi*)

mkuo n (mi-) see *mkoa*[3]

mkupa n (mi-) (bot) a much-branched evergreen tree with leathery leaves and small white flowers in much-branched small terminal panicles; the young branches are used as toothbrushes. *Dobera roxburghii*.

mkupi n (mi-) (zool) threadfin bream; a kind of yellowish salt water fish (family Nemipteridae) which lives in coastal waters.

mkupuo n (mi-) 1. one fell swoop: *Mchopozi alimnyang'anya mtalii kipochi chake kwa mkupuo mmoja*, the thief snatched the tourist's handbag in one fell swoop. (cf *mkumbo*) 2. the act of doing sth at one go and forcefully: *Alikunywa maji gilasi nzima kwa mkupuo*, he drank the whole glass of water in one gulp.

mkupuzi n (wa-) snatcher, thief, robber: *Mkupuzi alipewa kifungo kirefu*, the thief was given a long sentence. (cf *mwizi*)

mkure n (mi-) (zool) half beak; a kind of small-fish with a sail-like dorsal fin. (cf *chuchunge*)

mkuremba n (mi-) (bot) a glabrous evergreen tree with alternate lanceolate leaves and solitary inconspicuous flowers in the axils of the leaves; *Maba sp.*

mkuro[1] n (mi-) see *mkulo*

mkuro[2] n (mi-) (bot) a scandent deciduous almost glabrous shrub, the branches of which have a few scattered tendril-like branchlets with alternate leaves and short-stalked yellow scented flowers. *Hugonia castaneifolia*.

mkuruba n (mi-) nearness, closeness: *Nyumba zao zimekaa kwa mkuruba*, their houses are close to each other. (cf *ukaribu*)

mkurufunzi n (wa-) see *mkufunzi*

mkurugenzi n (wa-) 1. a person who is learned than his colleagues in the sphere of a particular profession, activity, etc.: an experienced person in a profession, activity, etc.: *Mkurugenzi ameweza kuwatibu wagonjwa wengi*, the experienced person has managed to treat many patients. 2. director: *Mkurugenzi mkuu*, director general.

mkurungu[1] n (mi-) (bot) a much-branched tree with deciduous compound leaves and paniculate small pea-like flowers and circular compressed golden hispid indehiscent fruits. *Pterocarpus chrysothrix*. (cf *mkaka*)

mkurungu² *n* (*n*) a kind of local dance for men and women.

mkurupuko *n* (*mi-*) act (method, etc.) of rushing away; dash, rush, bolt. (cf *mfyatuko*)

mkurupusho *n* (*mi-*) shock, bombshell, surprise. (cf *mshutuo, mshtusho*)

mkururo *n* (*mi-*) a string of people or things; line, queue: *Niliwona mkururo wa watu wakingojea kununua sukari dukani*, I saw a line of people waiting to buy sugar at the shop. (cf *mlolongo, foleni, mstari*)

mkuruti *n* (*mi-*) see *mkarakala*

mkuruzo¹ *n* (*mi-*) a piece of string, tape, etc. used for fastening a garment or the neck of a bag by drawing it.

mkuruzo² *n* (*mi-*) a kind of a male's pigeon cry.

mkusanyiko *n* (*mi-*) gathering, assembly, congregation: *Mkusanyiko wa watu*, the gathering of people. (cf *jumuiko*)

mkusanyo *n* (*mi-*) collection, gathering; an act of piling things together.

mkusi (also *msusu*) *n* (*mi-*) (*zool*) the tail of a hen or bird.

mkutano *n* (*mi-*) meeting, conference: *Mkutano wa hadhara*, public meeting; mass meeting. *Mkutano wa waandishi wa habari*, press conference.

mkutubi *n* (*wa-*) librarian; *Mkutubi mkuu*, chief librarian. (Ar)

mkutuo *n* (*mi-*) jerk, fright; act of making a sudden movement: *Mkutuo ule wa pazia karibu yangu ulinishtua*, that jerk of the curtain near me startled me. (cf *mshtuo, mshtuko*)

mkuu *n* (*wa-*) chief, head: *Mkuu wa shule*, head teacher, principal. *Mkuu wa wilaya*, district commissioner. *Mkuu wa mkoa*, regional commissioner, provincial commissioner. (*prov*) *Asiyesikia la mkuu huvunjika guu*, he who does not listen to elders' advice will run into trouble.

mkuwiyati *n* (*mi-*) see *mkuyati*

mkuyati (also *mkuwiyati*) *n* (*mi-*) (*med*) aphrodisiac; medicine which arouses or increases sexual desire.

mkuyu *n* (*mi-*) (*bot*) a kind of tree of several species bearing edible glabrous figs, whose bark is used in folk medicine against ringworm and other skin disorders.

mkwachuo *n* (*mi-*) act (method, etc) of scrubbing/rubbing.

mkwachuro *n* (*mi-*) a partial deformation of the coconut fruit resulting from skin damage caused by mites which feed on the outside layer of the coconut husk. (cf *pashongo*)

mkwaju¹ *n* (*mi-*) (*bot*) tamarind tree; a tree up to 60 feet tall with a rough grey and rounded crown bark and greyish green pinnate glabrous leaves. *Tamarindus indica*.

mkwaju² *n* (*mi-*) 1. cane, lash; a stick used for beating. (cf *bakora, fimbo*) 2. (in soccer, etc.) shot, kick: *Mchezaji alipiga mkwaju maridadi*, the player kicked a hard shot. 3. (in writing) stroke; a short printed or written diagonal line typically separating characters or figures. 4. (esp in golf) stroke

mkwakwa *n* (*mi-*) (*bot*) rubbervine; a creeping plant with edible orange-coloured fruit. The pulp when mixed with water and sugar makes a pleasant drink and is said to be good for curing pimples. *Landolphia florida*.

mkwakwara (also *mkwayakwaya*) *n* (*mi-*) (*bot*) prostrate hogweed; a procumbent perennial herb with sometimes glabrous leaves and small white or pink flowers, bearing small viscid conical fruits. The leaves are sometimes used as a vegetable. *Boerhaavia repens*.

mkwamba *n* (*mi-*) 1. (*bot*) a much-branched shrub or small tree up to 12 feet tall usu with erect branches and alternate elliptic leaves and small green flowers, whose fruits are slightly fleshy, the size of the pea. (*prov*) *Mkwamba hauzai zabibu*, this kind of tree does not produce grapes i.e. it is useless to expect things to occur which are impractical. *Flueggea virosa*.

mkwamo n (mi-) 1. the condition of sth becoming stuck; jam. 2. stalement, impasse, deadlock, standstill.

mkwara n (mi-) 1. (bot) a shrub or a tree with alternate pinnate leaves and small pea-like flowers, which is commonly used for firewood. *Millettia bussei*. 2 (fig) obstacle, impediment: *Alituwekea mkwara bila ya sababu*, he placed an obstacle before us for no reason. (cf *mzengwe*)

mkware n (wa-) a lascivious person either male or female; an abnormal and uncontrollable male or female for sexual desire; nymphomaniac. (prov) *Mkware hajiingilii mwenyewe*, a prostitute cannot commit adultery by herself i.e. a bad thing is usu. performed by the cooperation of another person.

mkwaruzano n (mi-) 1. friction, scratch, scraping: *Uendeshaji wake mbaya ulisababisha mikwaruzano kwenye gari yangu*, his reckless driving caused scratches on my car. 2. collision of ideas, etc.; misunderstanding: *Mkwaruzano mkali ulitokea bungeni kati ya waziri na kiongozi wa upinzani*, a heated argument occurred in parliament between the minister and the leader of opposition. (cf *mabishano*)

mkwaruzo n (mi-) a track or trail of sth scraping along; laceration, scratch: *Mkwaruzo wa nyoka*, the trail of a snake. *Mkwaruzo wa usoni*, the scratch on the face.

mkwasi n (wa-) an affluent person, a rich person; tycoon.

mkwayakwaya n (mi-) see *mkwakwara*

mkwe[1] n (wa-) in-law: *Baba mkwe*, father-in-law. *Mama mkwe*, mother-in-law.

mkwe[2] n (wa-) (bot) a glabrous tree with alternate pinnate leaves and white scented flowers, the bark of which is a useful fibre and the wood makes good charcoal. *Isoberlinia magnistipulata*.

mkweche[1] n (mi-) an old ramshackle automobile; jalopy: *Nimeamua kuuuza mkweche wangu*, I have decided to sell my jalopy. (cf *ngongongo*)

mkweche[2] n (mi-) (bot) a leafless succulent spiny tree whose branches are bruised and thrown into pools to poison fish. *Euphorbia nyikae*.

mkweme n (mi-) (bot) oysternut; a climbing perennial plant whose seeds produce oil, which is much esteemed by some tribes. *Telfairia pedala*.

mkwemo n(mi-) wheeze; an act or sound produced by breathing hard with a whistling breathy sound as in asthma.

mkwende n (mi-) (bot) swordbean. *Canaralia ensiformis*. (cf *mwinga siafu*)

mkweo n (mi-) act (manner, method, etc.) of climbing, mounting up, etc.: *Mkweo wake kwenye minazi uliangusha nazi nyingi*, his manner of climbing the coconut trees produced many coconuts.

mkwepaji n (wa-) dodger, evader, shirker; a person who evades one's responsibilities.

mkwepuzi n (wa-) 1. a person who steals by deceitfully snatching and running away; snatcher, thief. (cf *mkupuzi*) 2. a person who borrows money without returning it: *Inaonekana kwamba yeye ni mkwepuzi tu*, it seems that he is a person who borrows money without returning it.

mkwezi n (wa-) a climber esp of a coconut tree; a person who climbs esp coconut trees in order to knock them down; climber.

mkwiji n (mi-) a long narrow cylindrical cloth bag or poke used for keeping money in. (cf *anjali*)

mkwinini n (mi-) (bot) cinchona; a tree or shrub of the South American genus *Cinchona* having a medicinal bark.

mkwiro n (mi-) a stick for beating a drum; drum-stick.

mla n (wa-) a word used with another one to form a compound noun to convey different meanings: *Mla watu*, cannibal. *Mla ng'ombe*, a person who eats cows. *Mla kunde*, a person who is in the habit of eating cowpeas. *Mla mchwa*, a corrupt person. (*provs*) *Mla cha mwenziwe na chake huliwa*, he who takes away sby's property without permission will also suffer one day in the same way. *Mla ni mla leo, mla jana kala nini?* A person who owns sth today should be recognised as the one who owned in the past is no longer important.

mlaanifu *n* (*wa-*) 1. a cursed person; a condemned person: *Maanifu yule hana heri*, that accused person can bring no good. 2. a person who likes to insult others; vituperator, vilifier. (Ai)

mlaanika *n* (*wa-*) a cursed person, a damned person, a condemned person.

mlabahati *n* (*mi-*) (*bot*) Wild, *Talinum cuneifolium*.

mladi *n* (*mi-*) a thin piece of stick used by cloth weavers to tighten the threads; weaving stick.

mlafi[1] *n* (*wa-*) glutton, gourmand; a person who eats greedily: *Mlafi yule hapendi kula na wenzake*, that glutton does not like to eat with his colleagues. (cf *mmeo, mroho*)

mlafi[2] *n* (*wa-*) a person who cannot be trusted if he is given sth to keep; an untrustworthy person: *Wewe bado unataka mlafi yule akuwekee vitu vyako?* You still want that untrustworthy person to keep your things?

mlaga kuku *n* (*mi-*) (*bot*) a glabrescent shrub up to 10 feet tall with opposite narrowly ovate or elliptic leaves and terminal corymbs of small white tubular flowers. *Triainolepis hildebrandtii*.

mlaghai *n* (*wa-*) see *laghai*[2]

mlahaka *n* (*mi-*) reception, welcoming: *Mgeni alipata mlahaka mzuri kwa wenyeji*, the visitor was given a cordial reception from his host. (cf *mkuruba, ukuraba*)

mlaji *n* (*wa-*) consumer, good eater.

mlakasa *n* (*mi-*) (*bot*) a perennial vine of the tropics with long, running, fleshy stems and rose-purple convolvulus-like flowers found on sandy beaches. The plant is useful as a sand binder and its leaves are used as a vegetable. *Ipmoea pescaprae*.

mlakungu *n* (*mi-*) (*bot*) a type of antineuralgic plant/pomea.

mlakunguru *n* (*mi-*) (*bot*) a type of tree which has thorns and its black fruits are sweet.

mlakwenzi *n* (*wu-*) (*bot*) a deciduous tree bearing small papery usu two but sometimes three-winged fruits *Pteliopsis sp*.

mlala *n* (*mi-*) (*bot*) Doum palms i.e. *Hyphaene coriacea, Hyphaene crimita, Hyphaene parvula*.

mlalahoi *n* (*wa-*) the ordinary man; commoner, plebeian.

mlalaji *n* (*wa-*) 1. shirker, skiver; a person who frequently fails to report for work by giving excuses such as sickness, etc.: *Ukiwa mlalaji, tajiri wako anaweza kukufukuza kazini*, if you absent yourself from work too often by giving excuses, your employer can sack you. (cf *mkwepaji*) 2. a person who sleeps.

mlalamikaji *n* (*wa-*) 1. complainant, plaintiff; a person who brings a suit into a court of law. 2. a person who constantly complains about sth; complainer, crybaby.

mlalamikiwa *n* (*wa-*) accused, defendant: *Kitendo cha kumshtaki mlalamikiwa wa kwanza hakina msingi*, the action of suing the first accused is baseless.

mlalamishi *n* (*wa-*) 1. complainant, complainer, malcontent. 2. (in sports) a player who does not accept defeat in a game of sports; bad sport; bad loser: *Refarii alimtoa nje mlalamishi*, the referee sent a bad loser off the pitch.

mlalashi *n* (*n*) (*zool*) a kind of marine fish with a flat head, which likes to settle down in the sea in the sand.

mlalavi *n* (*wa-*) a restless sleeper; a person who turns over in his sleep or sleeps in a restless manner: *Mimi siwezi kulala na mlalavi yule*, I can't sleep with that restless sleeper.

mlale *n* (*mi-*) the cloud of a smoke (cf *mwale*)

mlaliaji *n* (*wa-*) a vendor who likes to buy goods at a cheaper price.

mlalo *n* (*mi-*) horizontal; a line parallel to the plane of the horizon; not vertical.

mlama *n*(*mi-*) a general term applied to various species which are employed to local snake-bite remedies.

mlamba¹ *n* (*mi-*) (*bot*) a kind of baobab tree.

mlamba² (also *mbaramba, mramba*) *n* (*mi-*) (*zool*) drongo; a kind of medium-sized black bird (family *Dicruridae*) with a forked tail and a red eye. *Dicrurus adsimilis*. (cf mkiapanda)

mlamba³ *n* (*wa-*) one who licks with the tongue.

mlambizu *n* (*wa-*) (*zool*) a kind of bird that likes to eat worms and grubs.

mlamu *n* (*wa-*) brother-in-law/sister-in-law.

mlandamu *n* (*mi-*) (*bot*) Banyan tree.

mlandano *n* (*mi-*) similarity, resemblance. (cf *mfanano*)

mlandege *n* (*mi-*) (*bot*) a parasitic, rumbling or bushy shrub growing often on clove trees, which may become a serious pest if left uncontrolled. *Loranthus sp.* (cf *ngurukia*)

mlanga *n* (*mi-*) (*bot*) African arrow roots; a herb with a tuberous rootstock and large glabrous leaves and brown-purple flowers, producing a starch which is obtained from the tubers. *Tacca involucrata*.

mlangalanga *n* (*mi-*) (*bot*) avocado pear tree. *Persea americana*.

mlangamia (also *mtandakanga*) 1. *n* (*mi-*) a twining parasitic perennial herb which grows on grassland and bush vegetation and often festooning tall trees; air plant. *Cassytha filformis*. 2. a leafless parasite with white or reddish stems growing on vegetation. *Cuscuta cassytoides*.

mlangilangi *n* (*mi-*) ylang ylang; a rather tall sparsely and somewhat peculiarly branched tree with ovate-oblong pointed leaves and greenish-yellow flowers which are the source of the perfume known as "Macassar oil." *Cananga odorota*.

mlango¹ *n* (*mi-*) 1. door, gate: *Mlango wa bahari*, the strait of the sea; channel. *Mlango wa mto*, estuary. *Mlango wa kizazi*, cervix. *Mlango wa fahamu*, sense organ. *Rudisha mlango*, keep the door ajar. (*prov*) *Penye wimbi pana mlango*, where there is hardship or a stumbling block, there is a way to overcome it. 2. (*idm*) *Mlango wa nyuma*, illicit ways such as bribing. (*prov*) *Kelele za mlango hazimkoseshi mwenye nyumba kulala*, the noises at the door don't make the owner become sleepless i.e. affairs that happen in the neighbourhood that don't concern the owner, don't stop him to do what he likes to perform.

mlango² *n* (*mi-*) clan, family, kinsfolk: *Anatoka katika mlango mzuri*, he comes from a good family. (cf *ukoo*)

mlango³ *n*(*mi-*) chapter, section: *Nimeanza kusoma mlango wa tatu wa kitabu hiki*, I have started reading the third chapter of this book. (cf *sura, faslu*)

mlanguzi *n* (*wa-*) 1. profiteer, price-hiker; a person who buys things from farmers at a cheaper price and inflates them when he sells them to other people in order to get a huge profit: *Serikali iliwachukulia hatua kali dhidi ya walanguzi*, the government took strong measures against the profiteers. 2. a businessman at an auction; auctioneer: *Mlanguzi alizizabuni bidhaa mnadani*, the auctioneer auctioned the goods.

mlariba *n* (*wa-*) a person who lends money with interest; usurer.

mlasa *n* (*mi-*) (*bot*) a shrubby herb with small red, pink or white flowers. *Hibiscus micranthus.*

mlaso *n* (*n*) the blood that has been preserved from an animal and then prepared as a kind of drink or cooked for food.

mlau *n* (*wa-*) a leader of convocation in a graduation ceremony.

mle *adv, pron* a demonstrative marker of non-proximity indicating the dimension of "withinness"; there in, there within: *Panya ameingia mle,* the rat has gone in there.

mlegevu *n* (*wa-*) a lazy person, a slack person; idler. (cf *goigoi, mwivu*)

mlele (also *mleli*) *n* (*mi-*) 1. the long tail-feathers of a bird usu used as a kind of adornment at local dances: *Mlele wa jogoo,* the tail-feather of a cock. 2. (*fig*) be prospering: *Yeye ametoa mlele,* he has put out a tail-feather i.e. he is prospering.

mleli *n* (*mi-*) see *mlele*

mlemavu *n* (*wa-*) a disabled person: *Chama cha walemavu,* a society for the disabled people. *Mlemavu wa ngozi,* albino; a person lacking the normal pigmentation.

mlembe[1] *n* (*mi-*) an absorbent cloth used by a woman during menstruation; sanitary napkin. (cf *uwinda, ubinda, kisodo*)

mlembe[2] *n* (*wa-*) (*zool*) honey bird; a drab-coloured bird (Family *Indicatoridae*). This bird is said to lead men and animals to bees' nests in order to eat the grubs when the honeycombs are taken away. (cf *mchochea mwua*)

mlenda *n* (*mi-*) (*bot*) a type of herb whose leaves are eaten as a vegetable. *Triumfetta annua.*

mlengaji *n* (*wa-*) marksman

mlenge *n* (*mi-*) a game played by throwing four pieces of sticks, etc. towards a particular target.

mlengwa *n* (*wa-*) target; a targeted person, etc.: *Misaada kutoka mashirika ya kimataifa hayakuwafikia walengwa,* aid from overseas organisations did not reach the targetted people.

mleoleo *n* (*mi-*) reeling, rocking, unseaworthiness; the rolling of a ship, dhow, etc. 2. the edge of a dhow, canoe, table, etc. (cf *ombe, pambizo, terebesha*)

mlete *n* (*mi-*) (*naut*) seam in a sail.

mlevi *n* (*wa-*) drunkard: *Mlevi alikuwa akipepesuka njiani,* the drunkard was staggering in the street. *Mlevi wa madawa ya kulevya,* junky; drug addict.

mlezi[1] *n* (*wa-*) guardian, patron: *Amekuwa mlezi wangu kwa miaka mingi sasa,* he has been my guardian for many years now. *Yeye alikuwa mlezi wa klabu yetu,* he was the patron of our club.

mlezi[2] *n* (*mi-*) baby's swinging cot; cradle. (cf *susu*)

mlezi[3] *n* (*n*) (*med*) goitre; a disease in which the glands swell esp around the neck; lymphadenitis. (cf *halula*)

mlezi[4] *n* (*mi-*) (*bot*) bulrush millet plant

mlezi[5] *n* (*mi-*) rope that is tied to the length of the net or seine.

mli[1] *n* (*mi-*) 1. (*naut*) a rope for hoisting and lowering a sail vessel such as a dhow; halyard. 2. a rope that is tied around the steering wheel of a vessel so as to give direction.

mli[2] *n* (*mi-*) a piece of iron with holes both sides, used to hold the rings of fetters of prisoners; shackle.

mlia[1] *n* (*mi-*) stripe of colouring surrounding a person or thing; coloured stripe: *Punda milia,* zebra.

mlia[2] *n* (*mi-*) a passage between rooms in a house.

mlifi *n* (*wa-*) one who pays or is to pay; payer. (*prov*) *Fimbo ya mnyonge, mlifi Mungu,* the weapon of a down trodden person, God is his redeemer i.e for one who has been unjustly treated, God is his redeemer.

mlima[1] *n* (*mi-*) mountain: *Mshikamano wa mlima,* mountain mass. *Mlima mrefu,* alp. *Msururu wa milima*, mountain range, mountain chain.

mlima² *n*(*wa-*) farmer (cf *mlimaji, mkulima*)

mlimaji *n* (*wa-*) farmer (cf *mlima, mkulima*)

mlimamwitu *n*(*mi-*) (*bot*) citron tree, citrus medical. (cf *mfurungu*)

mlimau (also *mlimao*) *n* (*mi-*) (*bot*) lemon tree. *Citrus limonia*.

mlimbiko (also *limbiko*) *n* (*mi-*) 1. reserve; a saving up little by little over a period of time. *Mlimbiko wa fedha*, a reserve of funds. (cf *ulimbikaji*) 2. turn, round: *Safari hii itakuwa mlimbuko wake*, this time will be his turn.

mlimbolimbo *n* (*mi-*) 1. (*bot*) a small tree, often having spine-tipped branchlets and containing much milky latex and which is often used as a hedge or boundary plant. *Euphorbia cuneata*. 2. a much-branched evergreen tree which is usu distributed from sea level to high altitudes and bearing globular fruits. *Mystroxylon aethiopicum*.

mlimbuko¹ *n* (*mi-*) 1. the first harvest; the first fruits: *Mpunga wa mlimbuko*, the first rice harvest. 2. the condition that a person is in, when he gets sth dear or sth else for the first time.

mlimbuko² *n* (*mi-*) 1. reward for waiting 2. foretaste of reward; fulfilment of hope.

mlimbwende *n* (*wa-*) a neat person, a well dressed person; dandy: *Wasichana wanamhusudu mlimbwende yule*, the girls admire that dandy. (cf *mfuauji, mangwaji, mtanashati*)

mlimi *n* (*wa-*) a talkative person, a garrulous person; babbler: *Watu wamechoka na mazungumzo ya mlimi yule*, people are tired of the conversations of that babbler. (cf *ngebe*) 2. a person who tells stories, narratives or folktales for a longtime.

mlimo *n* (*mi-*) farming, cultivation: *Mlimo wake shambani umemalizika*, his farming in the plantation has ended. (cf *ukulima*)

mlimwengu *n* (*wa-*) 1. human being. (cf *mtu, binaadamu*) 2. a person who lives in good harmony with others; a neighbourly person: *Wazee wangu wanampenda mlimwengu huyu*, my parents like this neighbourly person.

mlinda (also *mlinzi, mlindaji*) *n* (*wa-*) guardian, guard, watchman: *Mlinda mlango*, door keeper; *Mlinda goli*, goalkeeper. *Mlinda nyavu*, goalkeeper

mlindaji *n* (*wa-*) see *mlinzi*

mlinganisho *n* (*mi-*) balance: *Mlinganisho wa hesabu*, trial balance.

mlingano *n* (*mi-*) 1. sameness, resemblance, likeness, similarity: *Hakuna mlingano wowote kati ya vijana hawa wawili*, there is no resemblance at all between these two young men. (cf *mfanano*) 2. announcement, proclamation. (cf *tangazo*)

mlingoti (also *mwongoti*) *n* (*mi-*) 1. (*naut*) a tall spar or a hollow metal structure rising vertically from the keel or deck of a vessel and used to support the sails, yards, etc.: *Mlingoti wa mbele*, foremast. *Mlingoti wa galme*, mizzen mast. *Mlingoti wa maji*, bowspirit. 2. any vertical pole such as that of a flag; mast. 3. (*syn*) *Mrefu kama mlingoti*, as tall as a mast.

mlinzi (also *mlinda, mlindaji*) *n* (*wa-*) guardian, guard, watchman. (cf *gadi*)

mlio¹ *n* (*mi-*) 1. sound produced when two objects collide or trigger off: *Mlio wa bunduki*, gun shot; repart of a gun. 2. sound produced when an animal such as a lion, etc. roars: *Mlio wa mbwa*, bark; cry of a dog. *Mlio wa simba*, lion's roar. *Mlio wa punda*, bray. *Mlio wa sarafu/njuga/funguo*, jingle.

mlio² *n* (*mi-*) a stick or piece of wood used for tightening a package like that of firewood.

mlipa *n* (*wa-*) payer: *Mlipa kodi*, tax payer.

mlipaji *n* (*wa-*) rewarder, payer: *Mlipaji wa kweli ni Mwenyezi Mungu tu*, the real rewarder is God. (cf *mlifi*)

mlipu n (mi-) (bot) a herb with small leaves whose roots are used as a cure for swellings.

mlipuko n (mi-) explosion, eruption, blast, outbreak: *Mlipuko wa volkano*, volcanic explosion. *Mlipuko wa gesi*, gas explosion. *Mlipuko wa fataki*, fireworks explosion. *Mlipuko wa maradhi*, the outbreak of disease. *Mlipuko wa moto*, the outbreak of fire. *Mlipuko wa bomu*, bomb blast. *Mlipuko wa magonjwa ya kuambukiza*, the outbreak of contagious diseases. *Mlipuko wa homa ya mafua ya nguruwe*, swine flu.

mlisha n (wa-) 1. waiter/waitress. 2. herder, herdsman, shepherd. (cf *mchungaji*)

mlishaji n (wa-) 1. see *mlisha*. 2. one who feeds or takes care of animals or other creatures.

mlishi n (wa-) 1. see *mlisha*. 2. (also *mlishaji*) a person who entertains people at a feast or banquet; feaster.

mlishizi n (wa-) a person who bribes; briber.

mlishizo n (mi-) 1. the skillfulness of baiting a fish. 2. the technique of the police in trapping.

mlisho n (mi-) baiting: *Mlisho wa samaki*, the baiting of fish. *Mlisho wa mshipi*, putting bait on the fishing line. (cf *urosaji*).

mliwa n (mi-) (bot) a tree with a fragrant aromatic wood. *Spirostachys africana*.

mlizamu n (mi-) 1. funnel, duct, gutter. 2. stream, fountain.

mlizi n (wa-) 1. a person esp a child who frequently cries or makes noise; crybaby. 2. a bereaved person usu a woman: *Wanawake walikwenda kumliwaza mlizi*, the women went to console the bereaved person.

mlo n (mi-) 1. food: *Mlo wa mchana*, lunch. *Mlo wa usiku*, dinner.

mlokole n (wa-) 1. born again Christian. 2. fanatic, radical, extremist.

mlolongo n (mi-) queue, line: *Mlolongo wa wanyama au watumwa*, coffle. (cf *msururu*, *mkururu*)

mlombo n (mi-) a kind of vegetable, derived from the leaves of the baobab tree.

mlongama n (mi-) (bot) a tree from the bark of which a yellow dye is made.

mlonge n (mi-) see *mronge*

mlonje n (mi-) see *mronje*

mlowezi n (wa-) immigrant, settler; a person who visits a place and then settles there usu for good: *Walowezi waliitawala nchi yetu kwa mabavu*, the settlers ruled our country by force. (cf *setla*)

mlozi[1] n (mi-) (bot) almond tree. *Prunus amygadulus*.

mlozi[2] n (wa-) wizard, sorcerer. (cf *mchawi*)

mlumbaji n (wa-) orator; a person skilled in public speaking or in giving advice. (cf *mlumbi*)

mlumbano n (mi-) query, retort.

mlumbi n (wa-) 1. talker, speaker. 2. polyglot; a person who can speak several languages.

mlumbo n (mi-) oration, discourse.

mlungizi n (wa-) follower; a person following someone else in various contexts as in birth, etc. *Yeye ni ndugu yangu mlungizi*, he is my brother who follows after me.

mlungula n (mi-) see *mrungura*

mluzi n (mi-) see *mruzi*

mmaka n (mi-) (bot) frangipani tree. (cf *msanapati*, *mfurutangi*)

mmalizaji n (wa-) (esp in sports) a person who completes in sth e.g. in scoring a goal, etc.

Mmanga n (wa-) Omani Arab.

Mmarekani (also *Mwamerika*) n (wa-) American (Eng)

Mmasihiya n (wa-) Christian (cf *Mkristo*)

mmathali n (wa-) actor, actress. (cf *muigizaji*) (Ar)

mmavimavi n (mi-) (bot) a deciduous

mmbea

tree with small flowers containing an unpleasant smell, hence the name. *Celtis durandii.* (cf *mnukamavi*)

mmbea *n* (*wa-*) (also *mbea*) busybody, telltale, snoop, eavesdropper: *Mmbea alizifichua siri zetu*, the busybody disclosed our secrets. (cf *mpelelezi*)

mmbuji *n* (*wa-*) dandy, fop, coxcomb; a well-dressed person. (cf *mfuauji, mlimbwende*)

mmea *n* (*mi-*) (*bot*) plant: *Mmea pori*, heather. (cf *mche*)

mmego *n* (*mi-*) 1. bite, cut, piece. 2. biting, cutting; act (method, etc.) of cutting sth.

mmeguko *n* (*mi-*) split, division, divergence, difference: *Mmeguko wa kimawazo*, divergence of opinions.

mmeo *n* (*wa-*) greedy/avaricious/covetous person; glutton, gourmand: *Mmeo alikula chakula chote*, the glutton ate all the food. (cf *mroho, mlafi*)

mmemeto *n* (*mi-*) glare, flash.

mmemetuko *n* (*mi-*) phosphorescence; the giving out of light with little or no heat: *Ule ni mmemetuko wa almasi kwenye jua*, that was the sparkle of diamonds in the sunlight.

mmeng'enyo *n* (*mi-*) digestion

mmenyuko *n* (*mi-*) reaction: *Mmenyuko mfulizo*, chain reaction. *Mmenyuko pambanuzi*, critical reaction.

mmilikaji *n* (*wa-*) owner, proprietor, possessor: *Yeye ni mmilikaji wa mashamba mengi*, he is the proprietor of many plantations.

mmiliki *n* (*wa-*) owner, proprietor, possessor: *Wamiliki wa kiwanda hiki ni sisi*, we are the owners of this factory. *Mmiliki wa ardhi*, land owner. *Mmiliki wa nyumba*, the owner of the house.

mmiminiko *n* (*mi-*) influx, deluge, inrush; a flood of people, etc.: *Niliuona mmiminiko wa watu wakielekea mkutanoni*, I saw an influx of people heading towards the meeting.

mmomonyoko *n* (*mi-*) 1. erosion, deterioration; *Mmomonyoko wa udongo*, soil erosion. *Mmomonyoko wa ufukwe*, erosion of sandy beaches, *Mmomonyoko wa maadili*, moral decline. 2. (*fig*) fragmentation, split; the breaking up of a club, society, etc.: *Mmomonyoko wa chama cha upinzani uliwahuzunisha wananchi*, the breaking up of the opposition party saddened the people.

mmoyomoyo *n* (*mi-*) (*bot*) soap berry tree. *Sapindus saponaria* (cf *mwaka*)

mmumunye *n* (*mi-*) see *mmung'unye*

mmung'unye (also *mmumunye*) *n* (*mi-*) (*bot*) bottle gourd plant. *Lagenaria vulgaris.*

mmwaka *n* (*mi-*) (*bot*) soap berry tree. (cf *mmoyomoyo*)

mmwangaluchi *n* (*mi-*) (*bot*) a tree bearing small black red fruit. (cf *mtipitipi*)

mmweko *n* (*mi-*) dazzling light, flash light: *Niliuona mmweko wa kamera wakati nilipopigwa picha*, I saw a flashlight of the camera when I was photographed.

mnaa *n* (*wa-*) trouble-maker (cf *mkorofi*)

mnada[1] *n* (*mi-*) auction: *Piga mnada*, make an auction. (Ar)

mnada[2] *n*(*mi-*) a clarion call for sth.

mnadhimu *n* (*wa-*) chief of staff. (Ar)

mnadi *n* (*wa-*) 1. auctioneer. 2. announcer: *Mnadi sala*, an announcer of prayers. (Ar)

mnafiki *n* (*wa-*) impostor, hypocrite, faker, deceiver. (cf *mzandiki, fatani*) (Ar)

mnajimu *n* (*wa-*) 1. astronomer. 2. astrologer: *Utabiri wa mnajimu ulisibu*, the astrologer's prediction came true. (cf *kuhani*) (Ar)

mnajiri *n* (*mi-*) (*bot*) a kind of tree. Also called *mkono wa pongi*.

mnamo[1] *n* (*mi-*) (*naut*) edge usu of a vessel such as a dhow, canoe, etc.: *Baharia alikaa kwenye mnamo wa jahazi*, the sailor sat on the edge of the dhow. (cf *ukingo, ombe*)

mnamo[2] *prep* at, on, around: *Alifika hapa*

mnamo saa nne, he arrived here at ten o'clock. (cf *takriban*)

mnana[1] *n* (*mi*-) (*zool*) weaver; a kind of finch-like bird (family *Ploceidae*) that weaves elaborate doomed nests of sticks, grass, etc. and many of its species are highly gregarious.

mnana[2] *n* (*mi*-) a kind of yellow dye used for staining the leaf-strips (*ukili*) for making mats.

mnanaa *n* (*mi*-) 1. (*bot*) mint; a perennial herb, used for flavouring. *Mentha viridis*. 2. a herb, the scent of its leaves and flowers intoxicate someone.

mnanasi *n* (*mi*-) (*bot*) pineapple plant. *Ananas comosus*.

mnandi[1] *n* (*mi*-) (*zool*) cormorant; a large waterbird (family *Phalacrocoracidae*) with a hooked bill and webbed toes.

mnandi[2] *n* (*mi*-) (*zool*) yellow weaver bird.

mnara *n* (*mi*-) tower: *Mnara wa taa*, lighthouse. *Mnara wa saa*, clock tower. *Mnara wa kengele*, campanile.

mnasaba *n* (*mi*-) relationship (cf *uhusiano*)

mnaso *n* (*mi*-) act (condition, method, etc.) of having sth get stuck because of bird lime, etc. *Huu ni mnaso wa fenesi*, this is the jackfruit's birdlime.

mnato *n* (*mi*) 1. adhesion, stickiness. (cf *unataji, wambiso*) 2. arrogance, vanity, hauteur. (cf *maringo, majivuno*)

mnavu *n* (*mi*-) 1. (*bot*) black night-shade; an annual pubescent herb with alternate ovate or lanceolate obovate leaves and small white flowers bearing small globose black berries. *Solanum nigrum*. 2. a glabrous shrubby herb with alternate ovate acuminate leaves and umbellate cymes of small white flowers and small globose black berries. *Solanum nodiflorum*.

mnazaa *n* (*mi*-) see *nazaa*

mnazi *n* (*mi*-) (*bot*) coconut tree. *Cocus nucifera*.

mnda *n* (*mi*-) see *mgunda*

mndewa *n* (*wa*-) a leader of a person's community; pillar of a community; patriarch. (cf *jumbe*)

mndu *n* (*mi*-) matchet (cf *panga, mundu*)

mndule *n* (*mi*-) a hut built by travellers for resting in.

Mnegro *n* (*wa*-) Negro: *Yeye ni Mnegro*, he is a Negro. (Eng)

mnenaji *n* (*wa*-) a talkative person; babbler. (cf *ngebe*)

mneni *n* (*wa*-) orator; a person skilled in public speaking. (cf *msemi, msemaji*)

mnepo *n* (*mi*-) flexibility, elasticity, malleability.

mneso *n* (*mi*-) suppleness, elasticity; the quality, condition, etc. of being elastic for spring objects such as spring matresses, etc.

mng'ao (also *mng'aro*) *n* (*mi*-) dazzle, sheen, blaze, glitter, brightness: *Ule ulikuwa mng'ao wa taa kubwa za gari*, that was the dazzle of the vehicle's headlights. (cf *mwangaza*)

mngarengare *n* (*mi*-) (*zool*) crocodile needle fish, garfish; a long pipe-line slender marine fish (family Belonidae) of dark, bluish-black colour, silvery sides and whitish ventrally with elongated jaws and many sharp teeth, living in sheltered reefs and lagoons. *Tylosurus corocodililus crocodilus*.

mng'aro *n* (*mi*-) see *mng'ao*

mngogwe *n* (*mi*-) see *mtunguja*

mng'ongo *n* (*mi*-) (*bot*) a much-branched tree with yellow flowers in spicate racemes, bearing an edible roundish fruit, the seeds of which are also edible. The bark of the tree and its roots are a good medicine for treating pertussis disease. *Sclerocarya caffra*.

mnguri *n* (*mi*-) a shoe maker's mallet. (cf *pondea*)

mngurumo *n* (*mi*-) rumbling sound; rumble, growl. (cf *mrindimo*)

mnimbi (also *mnyimbi, mwanumbi*) *n* (*mi*-) (*zool*) a kind of large salt water fish with an alongate cylindrical body found in deep sea; bonefish (cf *kifimbo*).

mninga n (mi-) a much-branched deciduous tree which has useful timber for making furniture. *Pterocarpus bussei*. (cf *mkunguru, mpagata, mtumbati*)

mning'inio n (mi-) hang; the way that a thing hangs.

mnju n (mi-) (zool) cock's comb. (cf *undu, kishunzi*)

mno adv exceedingly, excessively, very much: *Yeye ni mkaidi mno*, he is very obstinate.

mnofu n (mi-) 1. fillet, a strip of boneless meat. (syn) *Uking'wafua mnofu, ukumbuke na kuguguna mfupa*, as you strip off flesh, remember to bite the bone i.e. wherever you see luxurious things, remember that they were obtained by hard work.

mnoga[1] n (mi-) the dry leaf of a tobacco plant.

mnoga[2] (also *muhina*) n (mi-) 1. (med) bleeding from the nose; nosebleed, epistaxis, nasal haemorrhage. (cf *mjusi*)

mnokoa n (mi-) see *mkunungu*

mnong'ono n (mi-) 1. whispering sound; whisper. 2. rumour, hearsay: *Nimesikia mnong'ono kwamba rais atajiuzulu*, I have heard a rumour that the president is going to resign. (cf *fununu, tetesi, uvumi*)

Mnorwei n (wa-) Norwegian (Nrw)

mnovisi n (wa-) (in Christianity) a person who has entered a religious order and is under probation. (Eng)

mnufaishwa n (wa-) (bot) beneficiary

mmukamavi n(mi-) *mnukavundo*

mnukauvundo n (mi-) (bot) stinking weed; a shrubby herb, the leaves of which if rubbed in the hands, make an unpleasant smell. The leaves of this herb are used for making medicine to bathe young children who suffer from *dege*. *Cassia occidentalis* (cf *mnukamavi*)

mnukio n (mi-) sweet smell; fragrance, aroma.

mnukisha n(wa-) see *mnukishaji*

mnukishaji (also *mnukisha*) n(wa-) a person who spreads good smell to others.

mnukizaji n(wa-) a person who spreads bad smell to others.

mnuko n(mi-) bad smell; stench, stink. (cf *ujaka, uvundo*)

mnumanuma n (wa-) 1. wizard; a person who is always playing black magic. 2. a skilful magician. 3. a naughty person; scamp, rascal.

mnuminumi n (wa-) wanderer, rambler. (cf *mzururaji*)

mnuna n (wa-) a young brother or sister.

mnume n (mi-) children's game of being silent for some time.

mnung'unikaji n (wa-) grumbler, grouch, malcontent; a discontented person.

mnung'uniko n (mi-) grumble, murmur, complaint, groan. (cf *lalamiko*)

mnunguri n(wa-) snake medicine man; snake charmer.

mnuni n (wa-) splenetic, sourpuss; a sulky person (cf *msununu*)

mnuno n (mi-) complaint, grumbling, discontent; sulkiness, moroseness. (cf *guno*)

mnunuaji n (wa-) buyer; purchaser, customer. (cf *mshtiri, mnunuzi*)

mnunurisho n(mi-) radiation: *Daktari alitumia mnunurisho kuutibu ugonjwa wake wa saratani*, the doctor used radiation to treat his cancer. *Mnunurisho wa jua*, solar radiation. *Mnunurisho mweupe*, white radiation. *Mnunurisho wa mwanga*, the radiation of light.

mnunuzi n (wa-) buyer: *Wale ni wanunuzi wa kutegemewa*, those are reliable buyers. (cf *mnunuaji*)

mnyaa n (mi-) see *muwaa*

mnyakuzi n (wa-) a person who snatches people's property such as bags, purses, etc; snatcher, pickpocket: *Mnyakuzi alifungwa jela kwa miaka miwili*, the pickpocket was imprisoned for two years. (cf *kibaka, mchopozi*)

mnyama *n* (*wa-*) 1. animal, beast: *Wanyama wa mwitu*, wild animals. *Wanyama wa kufugwa*, domesticated animals. *Wanyama-pori*, wildlife. 2. an animal-like person: *Mtu yule ni sawasawa na mnyama*, that person is like an animal.

mnyamavu *n* (*wa-*) a reticent person; a quiet person: *Yeye huwa mnyamavu katika mikutano yetu yote*, he becomes reticent in all our meetings.

mnyambuko *n* (*mi-*) stretching, lengthening.

mnyambuliko *n* (*mi-*) (*gram*) conjugation, derivation: *Mnyambuliko wa vitenzi*, verbal derivation. *Mnyambuliko wa nomino*, nominal derivation. (cf *unyambulishaji*)

mnyambuo *n* (*mi-*) (*gram*) inflexion, inflection.

mnyang'anyi *n* (*wa-*) robber, thief, highway man: *Tahadhari na wanyang'anyi*, beware of the highway men. (cf *haramia*)

mnyange *n* (*wa-*) a neat person, a well-dressed person; dandy, fop, coxcomb. (cf *mlimbwende, mfuauji*)

mnyanya *n* (*mi-*) (*bot*) tomato plant, *Solanum lycopersicum*. *Mnyanya mshumaa*, egg-plant. *Solanum melongena*. *Mnyanya wa porini, Solanum nodiflorum*.

mnyanyasaji *n* (*wa*) humiliator, molester; a person who humiliates someone else.

mnyapara *n* (*wa-*) 1. head of a caravan, expedition, etc. 2. supervisor. (cf *msimamizi*)

mnyara *n* (*mi-*) a kind of chord used for building and baiting fish.

mnyegea *n.*(*mi-*) (*bot*) sausage tree; a much-branched deciduous tree whose wood is used for making stools and its fruit is put in local beer to make it more intoxicating. *Kigelia pinnata*. (cf *mvungunya*)

mnyegeo *n* (*mi-*) itching, sensation, prickling, tickling, ticking. (cf *mnyeo*)

mnyenyekeo *n* (*mi-*) obedience, subservience, servility, humility: *Mnyenyekeo wake kwa mfalme hausemeki*, his obedience towards the king is unspeakable. (cf *utiifu*)

mnyenyekevu *n* (*wa-*) a subservient person, an obedient person; a deferential person: *Yeye ni mnyenyekevu*, he is a deferential person. (cf *mtiifu*)

mnyenyereko *n* (*mi-*) see *mnyiririko*

mnyeo *n* (*mi-*) the condition of wanting to scratch oneself. (cf *mnyegeo*)

mnyerereko *n* (*mi-*) see *mnyiririko*

myimaji *n* (*wa-*) miser, skin-flint. (cf *bahili*)

mnyimi *n* (*wa-*) miser, niggard: *Mnyimi hatakukopesha pesa zake*, a miser will not lend you his money. (cf *bahili, mchoyo*)

mnyimbi[1] *n* (*mi*) (*zool*) bonefish; a kind of marine fish (family *Albulidae*) having an elongate cylindrical body with silvery cycloid scales and a naked head. (cf *kifimbo*)

mnyimbi[2] *n* (*mi*) (*zool*) lady fish; a tropical and warm temperate marine fish having an elongated body, oval in cross section with small scales.

mnyiri (also *mnyo*) *n* (*mi-*) (*zool*) arm or tentacle of an octopus or cuttlefish. (cf *mwinyo*)

mnyiririko (also *mnyerereko*) *n* (*mi-*) slither, stealthy creep; gentle passing as in the case of a snake in the grass, etc.

mnyo *n* (*mi-*) see *mnyiri*

mnyofu *n* (*wa-*) an upright person; an honest person.

mnyonge *n* (*mi-*) 1. a weak person, a feeble person. 2. a humble person, a modest person: *Wanyonge hawapendi kuonyesha ufahari*, humble people don't like to show pride. 3. poor person; pauper: *Wanyonge hawana sauti serikalini*, poor people have no say in the government. (cf *fakiri, masikini*)

mnyonyore *n* (*mi-*) (*bot*) Barbados pride tree: a shrub with compound leaves

M mnyoo

and orange and red flowers and flat woody pods, commonly found in gardens. *Caesalpinia pulcherrima*. (*prov*) *Mnyonyore haunuki, hupendeza mauaye*, a Barbados pride tree does not stink, its flowers are attractive i.e. you may be attached to a person though he is mean to others, but because he assists you in one way or another, you are bound to associate with him even if you are aware of his meanness.

mnyoo (also *minyoo*) *n* (*mi-*) 1. intestinal worm. (cf *uchango*) 2. (*zool*) an insect which walks by coiling itself.

mnyororo (also *mnyoo*) *n* (*mi-*) chain, fetters. (cf *mkufu, silisili*)

mnyukano *n* (*mi-*) contest, fighting: *Mnyukano mkali*, bitter fighting.

mnyumbuko *n mi-*) elasticity

mnyunyizo *n* (*mi-*) spraying, sprinkle: *Mnyunyizo wa dawa za wadudu shambani ulisaidia mimea yangu*, the spraying of insecticide in the farm helped my seedlings, *Mnyunyizo wa asidi ndani ya tumbo*, the spraying of acid in the abdomen.

mnyunyuma *n* (*mi-*) see *mpendapendapo*

mnyuso *n* (*mi-*) an expression of annoyance, disapproval, etc. (cf *mfyonyo*)

mnywanywa *n* (*wa-*) 1. grumbler; a grumpy person. 2. malcontent; a person who does not value or appreciate work done by other people; a dissatisfied person. (cf *mtaaradhi*) 3. gourmet, epicure, fussy-eater (cf *machagu*)

mochari *n* (*n*) mortuary. (Eng)

modeli *n* (*n*) model; style of sth. (cf *mtaaradhi*) (Eng)

modereta *n* (*n*) moderator (Eng)

mofa *n* (*n*) a small round millet bread. (Ar)

mofimu *n* (*n*) (*gram*) morpheme: *Mofimu huru*, free morpheme. *Mofimu tegemezi*, bound morpheme. *Mofimu kapa*, zero morpheme. (Eng)

mofolojia *n* (*n*) (*ling*) morphology; the study of the structure of forms of words. (Eng)

moja *n* (*n*) one: (*idm*) *Moja kwa moja*, directly e.g. *Mgeni alikwenda moja kwa moja kwa mwenyeji wake alipowasili*, the guest went directly to his host when he arrived.

mojawapo *adj* one among: *Kiti kimojawapo*, one of the chairs. *Mti ule ni mmojawapo*, that tree is one of them.

Mola *n* (*n*) Almighty God; the Lord. (cf *Mungu*) (Ar)

moma[1] *n* (*n*) (*zool*) a kind of a large poisonous snake that requires careful handling; rhinocerous viper. (cf *piri, bafe*)

moma

mom.a[2] *vi* spread, diffuse: *Ugonjwa wa kipindupindu umemoma kijijini*, cholera has spread in the village. Prep. **mom.e.a** St. **mom.ek.a** Cs. **mom.esh.a** Ps. **mom.w.a** (cf *enea, tapakaa*)

momonyo.a (also *mong'onyoa*) *vt* erode, break off, pull off: *Aliimomonyoa sukari guru*, he broke off some brown sugar. Prep. **momonyo.le.a** St. **momonyo.k.a** and **momonyo.lek.a**, be fragmented, be falling apart e.g *Chama chao cha upinzani kinazidi kumomonyoka*, their opposition party continues to fall apart. Cs. **momonyo.sh.a** Ps. of Prep. **momonyo.lew.a** Rp **momonyo.an.a**

mondo *n* (*n*) (*zool*) serval cat: a kind of big cat with large oval ears, elongated legs and a short tail. Serval cat. *Felis serval.*

mondo

mong'onyo.a *vt* see *momonyoa.* Prep. *mong'onyo.le.a* St. *mong'onyo.k.a* and *mong'onyo.lek.a* Cs. *mong'onyo.sh.a* Ps. of Prep. *mong'onyo.lew.a*

mong'onyok.a *vi* be eroded, be broken off. Prep. **mong'onyok.e.a** St. **mong'onyok.ek.a**

monyo.a[1] *vt* eat fast esp soft food e.g. mango; gobble: *Mtazame mtoto yule anakimonyoa chakula,* look at that child gobbling the food. Prep. *monyo.le.a* St. *monyo.lek.a* Cs. *monyo.sh.a*

monyo.a[2] *vi* wiggle part of the body e.g. waist; gyrate. Prep. *monyo.le.a* St. *monyo.lek.a* Cs. *monyo.sh.a* Ps. of Prep. *monyo.lew.a* Rp. *monyo.an.a*

moo *n* (*n*) (*arch*) foot, leg: *Shika moo,* hold the leg. (cf *mguu*)

morali *n* (*n*) morale, spirit: *Timu yao ina morali kubwa ya kushinda mechi ya kesho,* their team has high morale of winning tomorrow's match. (Eng)

moramu *n* (*ma-*) murram; a form of laterite used for road surfaces. (Eng)

mori[1] *n* (*n*) 1. (zool) heifer. (cf *mtamba, mfarika*) 2. animal fat on the chest esp that of a cow used for making candles, etc.; tallow

mori[2] *n* (*n*) 1. wrath, rage, intense anger: *Shikwa na mori,* be filled with intense anger: *Pandwa na mori,* be filled with intense anger: *Ingiwa na mori,* be filled with intense anger. (cf *hasira, hamaki*) 2. a special medicine which is said to cause a person to be angry, fierce, etc.

mori[3] *n* (*n*) strong desire; yearning, longing: *Ana mori ya kutaka kuoa,* he has a strong desire to get married.

morita (also *morta*) *n* (*n*) short span i.e. a measure from the thumb to the forefinger.

morta *n* (*n*) see *morita*

moshi[1] *n* (*n*) 1. smoke. (*prov*) *Penye moshi pana moto,* where there is smoke there is fire i.e. where there is an outbreak of sth such as a disease, famine, etc. there is a cause behind it. 2. liquid from citrus fruit such as lemon, orange, etc. 3. steam; *Gari la moshi,* locomotive

moshi[2] *n* (*n*) illicit gin made from fruits or plants.

mosi *adj* first, one: *Tarehe mosi,* the first day of the month: *Mfungo mosi,* the first month after the fasting of the month of Ramadan. *Mei Mosi,* May Day.

mosia *n* (*n*) moss (Eng)

mota *n* (*n*) motor; a device that changes into movement, used to make machines work. *Mota kimstari,* linear motor. *Mota mdukizo,* induction motor: *Mota sawia,* sychronous motor. *Mota venia,* vernier motor. *Mota ya umeme,* an electric motor. (Eng)

motaboti *n* (*n*) motorboat (Eng)

motakaa *n* (*n*) see *motokaa*

motisha *n* (*n*) motivation, incentive: *Toa motisha,* give incentive. *Wafanyakazi walitaka wapewe motisha,* the workers demanded incentives. (cf *kichocheo*) (Eng)

moto[1] *n* (*mi-*) 1. fire. 2. intense heat or warmth. 3. (*fig*) anger: *Usifanye moto,* don't be angry. *Poa moto,* cool down. (*prov*) *Moto hauzai moto,* fire does not bear fire. i.e. it is not necessary for the child to inherit the good or bad characters of his parents. (cf *hasira*)

moto[2] *adj* hot: *Chakula cha moto,* hot food.

M motokaa   mpalilio

motokaa (also *motakaa*) *n* (*n*) car, automobile. (cf *gari*) (Eng)

motomoto¹ *adj* 1. hot, warm. 2. (*colloq*) hot, ardent, exited, spirited: *Habari motomoto*, exciting news.

motomoto² *interj* an expletive of encouraging sby to do sth.

moyo *n* (*mi-*) 1. heart: *Shtuko la moyo*: heart attack. *Pigo la moyo*, heart beat. *Ugonjwa wa moyo*, heart disease. 2. (*idms*) *Jipa moyo*, take courage, *Vunjika moyo*, be discouraged. *Tia moyo*, encourage. 3. courage, audacity: *Ana moyo*, he has the courage. *Piga moyo konde*, be brave; be courageous. *Moyo wa bua*, a weak heart i.e. a heart that cannot withstand hardships. etc. 4. sincerity. (*prov*) *Kutoa ni moyo, usambe ni utajiri*, to give is a question of the heart and not of the pocket i.e. a poor person can help someone or sth; yet you may find that a rich person with all the wealth at his disposal, would fail to do the same thing.

moza *n* (*n*) queue, line: *Watu wamesimama kwa moza kununua sukari*, people have stood in a queue to buy sugar. (cf *mlolongo, foleni, msururu*)

mpaazo (also *mparazo*) *n* (*mi-*) 1. the grinding of cereals. 2. the spinning of fibres to make ropes.

mpachuo *n* (*mi-*) the taking down of sth from above. (cf *mtunguo*)

mpagani *n* (*wa-*) pagan, heathen; a person who does not believe in Christianity, Islam or any other religion. (Eng)

mpagao *n* (*mi-*) hysteria, delirium, frenzy. (cf *umanyeto*)

mpagata *n* (*mi-*) (*bot*) a deciduous tree which produces good timber. *Pterocarpus bussei*. (cf *mninga, muhagata, mkunguru*)

mpagazi *n* (*wa-*) porter (cf *mchukuzi*)

mpaje *n* (*mi-*) (*bot*) the stalk of the millet, which is sweet.

mpaji *n* (*wa-*) provider, bestower, giver: *Mpaji ni Mwenyezi Mungu*, the bestower is God.

mpaka¹ *prep* until, till: *Simpi pesa mpaka aimalize kazi*, I won't give him the money until he finishes the work. (cf *hadi, hata*)

mpaka² *prep* from: *Kutoka hapa mpaka kule ni masafa marefu*, from here to there is a long distance.

mpaka³ *n* (*mi-*) 1. boundary: *Mipaka ya kikoloni*, colonial boundaries. (*prov*) *Kila mnofu una mpaka wake*, every flesh has its limits i.e. every person has got his limitations. 2. (*idms*) *Kiuka mpaka*, transgress, exceed the bounds. *Vuka mpaka*, cross the border, transgress. *Weka mpaka*, (a) lay down a limit. (b) fix a boundary.

mpaka⁴ *n* (*n*) a word used with another one to form a compound word: *Mpaka rangi*, painter. *Mpaka chokaa*, white-washer.

mpakaji *n* (*wa-*) a person whose work is to paint, whitewash, etc.

mpakani *adv* at the border; on the border: *Walifika mpakani jioni*, they arrived at the border in the afternoon.

mpakato *n* (*mi-*) act of holding anything like a baby on the lap or knee, etc.: *Mpakato wake ulimfanya mwanawe alale upesi*, her holding of the baby on the lap caused it to sleep quickly. (cf *upakataji*)

mpakizi *n* (*wa-*) one who loads; loader. (cf *mpakiaji*)

mpako *n* (*mi-*) act (style, etc.) of painting, whitewashing, etc.

mpakuaji *n* (*wa-*) 1. a person who unloads goods from a ship, vehicle, etc. 2. a person who dishes out food from the cooking pot.

mpakuzi *n* (*mi-*) 1. one who unloads a ship, train, etc.

Mpalestina *n* (*wa-*) Palestinian (Ar)

mpaliliaji *n* (*wa-*) a person who removes weeds in a land; weeder, cultivator. (cf *mpalizi*)

mpalilio *n* (*mi-*) weeding; removing of the weeds, grass, etc. from a garden, lawn, etc. (cf *upaliliaji*)

mpalizi *n* (*wa-*) a person who hoes up the soil and weeds among growing crops; weeder. (cf *mpaliliaji*)

mpamba¹ (also *mpambi*) *n* (*wa-*) 1. a person who adorns sth or someone else as in the case of a bride, etc.; equerry, decorator: *Mpamba alimremba biharusi*, the equerry adorned the bride. 2. a person who adorns the dead body after it has been washed and ready for burial.

mpamba² *n* (*n*) (*bot*) a cotton plant. *Gossypium sp.*

mpambaji *n* (*wa-*) 1. a person who adores sby/sth. 2. a person who puts ornaments in a place in order to look attractive.

mpambake *n* (*mi-*) see *mpambauke*

mpambano¹ (also *pambano*) *n* (*mi-*) confrontation, rivalry, showdown; any action or confrontation that brings matters to a climax and settles them: *Kulitokea mpambano mkali wa sare harusini kati ya makundi mawili*, there was a tough show down at the wedding between the two groups the two groups over the uniform they wore.

mpambano² *n* (*mi-*) a collection of events, topics, etc. in a discussion, etc.: *Kufika kwake kuliongeza mpambano wa mada*, his arrival added to the number of topics for discussion.

mpambauke (also *mpambake*) *n* (*mi-*) (*bot*) a much-branched shrub with very rugose aromatic leaves and small dense conical heads of greenish-yellowish flowers. *Lippia asperifolia.*

mpambe *n* (*wa-*) 1. master of ceremonies; a person who is dressed up in finery and is supposed to give information on a function such as that of a wedding; equerry: *Mpambe wa spika*, sergeant-at-arms. 2. a person fond of decorating himself or herself. 3. bridesmaid. 4. bodyguard, aide-de-camp.

mpambi *n* (*wa-*) see *mpamba¹*

mpanda *n* (*wa-*) a person who climbs a tree, etc. or mounts an animal such as a donkey, horse, etc.: *Mpanda punda*, donkey rider; cavalier. *Mpanda farasi*, horse rider. *Mpanda mlima*, mountaineer. *Askari mpanda farasi* hussar. (*prov*) *Mpanda farasi wawili, hupasuka msamba*, he who rides two horses at the same time will be split in two i.e. he who does two or more things at the same time eventually fails in his missions.

mpandaji *n* (*wa-*) 1. person who boards a sailing vessel or a vehicle; traveller. (cf *msafiri*) 2. a person who grows seeds; grower. (cf *mpanzi*)

mpande¹ *n* (*mi-*) a line drawn on the middle of the head when plaiting or combing the hair. (cf *njia*)

mpande² *n* (*mi-*) sandal wood tree.

mpande³ *n* (*wa-*) a person who farms for someone else on payment basis.

mpando¹ *n* (*mi-*) 1. act (method, style, etc.) of planting seeds. 2. time or season of planting for farmers. (*idm*) *Kimbilia mpando*, do sth at the right time before the time has expired.

mpando² *n* (*mi-*) the climbing of trees, mountains, etc.: *Mpando wake wa minazi ulikuwa holela*, his climbing of the coconut trees was haphazard.

mpandikizaji *n* (*wa-*) transplanter; a person who transplants seeds in a place.

mpangaji¹ *n* (*wa-*) lessee, tenant, renter. (cf *mkodishaji*)

mpangaji² *n* (*wa-*) a person who sets his things in order; planner: *Yeye ni mpangaji mzuri katika shughuli zote za ofisini*, he is a good planner in all the activities of the office.

mpangilio *n* (*mi-*) arrangement, order, format: *Kwa mpangilio*, by terms, in series, in proper order.

mpangishaji *n* (*wa-*) landlord, lessor, proprietor, owner.

mpango *n* (*mi-*) 1. plan; programme; arrangement: *Mpango wa dharura*, crash programme. *Mpango wa maendeleo*, development programme. *Mpango wa ishara*, programme signal, *Mpango wa safari*, itinerary. 2. order:

Lazima ufanye kazi yako kwa mpango, you must do your work in order.

mpanzi *n (wa-)* a sower of seeds; grower. (cf *mpandaji*)

mpapai (also *mpapayu*) *n (mi-) (bot)* pawpaw tree. *Carica papaya.*

mpapariko *n (mi-)* see *mpapatiko*

mpapatiko (also *mpapariko*) *n (mi-)* 1. act of fluttering because of pain, etc.: *Nilishuhudia mpapatiko wa njiwa aliyepigwa panda,* I witnessed the fluttering of the pigeon which was hit with a catapult. 2. restlessness, uneasiness, worry, confusion: *Usiifanye kazi kwa mpapatiko,* don't do the work with uneasiness. (cf *wasiwasi*)

mpapayu *n (mi-)* see *mpapai*

mpapindi *n (mi-)* 1. *(bot)* a cycad with a simple or branched stem, bearing cone-like fruits which is a common ornamental garden plant in East Africa. *Cycas thouarsii.* 2. a palm with green stems up to 40 feet tall, branching from the root, found on the island of Pemba in Tanzania. *Chrysalidocarpus sp.*

mpapuro *n (mi-)* scratching esp with nails or claws: *Mpapuro wa paka ulinitoa damu mkononi,* the cat's scratching caused my arm to bleed.

mparachichi *n (mi-) (bot)* avocado tree. *Persea americana.*

mparaganyiko *n (mi-)* jumble, tumble, muddle; a confused state of affairs. (cf *mparaganyo*)

mparaganyo *n (mi-)* clutter, jumble, hatch: *Vitu vyake viko katika mparaganyo,* his things are in a jumble. (cf *mparaganyiko*)

mparamizi *n(wa-)* a person who is fond of climbing up on a wall, tree, etc.; mounter.

mparamuzi *n (mi-)* cotton tree. *Bambax.*

mparazo *n(mi-)* act (method, etc) of scraping grain.

mpare *n (mi-)* funnel

mpareto *n (mi-) (bot)* pyrethrum; a perennial plant of the composite family, widely grown for the white, pink, red or purple flower heads.

mparuzi *n (wa-)* bungler; a person who does a job clumsily or haphazardly: *Mparuzi aliiharibu kazi yangu,* the bungler spoiled my work. (cf *mlipuaji*)

mparuzo *n (mi-)* 1. act (method, etc.) of scratching sth. 2. mark left behind after scratching; scar. 3. a scratched place.

mpasha *n (wa-)* giver of sth: *Mpasha habari,* newsman.

mpashaji *n (wa-)* informer: *Mpashaji wa habari,* news informer.

mpasi[1] *n (wa-)* a person who has the ability to acquire things without difficulties because of his good financial position: *Yeye ni mpasi ingawa si tajiri,* he is a person who can acquire things without difficulties although he is not rich.

mpasi[2] *n (wa-)* antagonist, enemy, foe, adversary. (cf *adui, mshonde*)

mpasua *n (wa-)* a person who splits wood, etc.; cutter: *Mpasua mbao,* wood cutter.

mpasuasanda *n (wa-) (zool)* night jar (cf *kirukanjia*)

mpasuko *n (mi-)* 1. explosion, blast: *Mpasuko wa gesi ulisababisha moto,* the gas explosion caused fire. 2. crack, split, tear: *Pana mpasuko katika ubao huu,* there is a crack in this wood. 3. noise caused as a result of explosion, etc. 4. (cf *ualiko*) *(fig)* split: *Mpasuko wa kisiasa,* political split.

mpasuo *n (mi-)* tearing, splitting: *Mpasuo wa shati,* the tearing of the shirt.

mpatanishaji *n (wa-)* arbitrator, negotiator. (cf *mpatanishi*)

mpatanishi *n (wa-)* arbitrator, reconciler, negotiator: *Mpatanishi wa kimataifa,* international arbitrator. *Yeye alikuwa mpatanishi maarufu kwenye migogoro mbalimbali,* he was a prominent

mpato

negotiator in different conflicts. (cf *msuluhishi*)

mpato *n* (*mi-*) see *pungu*¹

mpayukaji *n* (*wa-*) 1. chatterbox, babbler: *Mpayukaji yule hachoki kuzungumza*, that babbler is never tired of talking. (cf *mropokaji*) 2. a person who speaks without being asked.

mpea *n* (*mi-*) (*bot*) avocado pear tree. *Persea americana*.

mpekecho *n* (*mi-*) 1. act of lighting fire by rubbing two sticks together or boring a hole with a pointed instrument by twirling it between the palms of the hands. 2. act of instigating a quarrel, etc. between two or more people; instigation: *Mpekecho wake uliwatenganisha marafiki wawili*, his instigation of a quarrel alienated the two friends. 3. internal body irritation.

mpekepeke *n* (*wa-*) busybody, snoop. (cf *saatulkhabari*, *mbeya*)

mpeketevu *n* (*mi-*) a person who incites trouble, disturbance, quarrel, etc.; agitator, instigator, firebrand, troublemaker: *Tulimlaani mpeketevu yule*, we cursed that firebrand. (cf *mfitini*, *sabasi*)

mpekuzi *n* (*wa-*) 1. a person who takes too much interest in other people's affairs; busybody, snoop, eavesdropper, talebearer: *Mpekuzi alijaribu kufichua siri za watu*, the busybody tried to disclose the secrets of other people. (cf *mpelelezi*, *mchunguzi*) 2. thief: *Mtumishi wake ni mpekuzi*, his servant is a thief. 3. investigator. (cf *mpelelezi*)

mpelelezi *n* (*wa-*) 1. an inquistive person; eavesdropper: *Mpekuzi aliyachunguza mambo yetu*, the eavesdropper pried into our affairs. (cf *mpelelezi*) 2. investigator, detective: *Wapelelezi walikuja kuchunguza chanzo cha mauaji*, the detectives came to

mpepa

investigate the cause of the murder. (cf *kachero*) 3. spy: *Yule mpelelezi alifungwa jela kwa kufichua siri za nchi*, the spy was jailed on charges of revealing the country's secrets.

mpelepele *n* (*mi-*) 1. (*bot*) a pubescent shrub with obvate-oblong or elliptic leaves and white long-tubular flowers. *Pavetta mangallana*. 2. a glabrous deciduous shrub with opposite leaves and inconspicuous white small tubular flowers. *Psychotria amboniana*.

Mpemba¹ *n* (*wa-*) a Pemba resident.

mpemba² *n* (*mi-*) (*bot*) a kind of soft cassava that is easily cooked.

mpembuo *n* (*mi-*) act (method, etc.) of sifting or screening sth.

mpembuzi¹ *n* (*wa*) analyst, fact-sifter, investigator: *Mpambuzi aliitathmini taarifa yenyewe*, the analyst assessed the statement.

mpembuzi² *n* (*wa-*) sifter, winnower; a person who sifts: *Mpembuzi aliupembua mchele*, the sifter winnowed the rice.

mpenda *n* (*wa-*) a person who likes sth; lover: *Mpenda vyeo*, a lover of positions; opportunist. *Mpenda mageuzi*, reformist. *Mpenda kula*, glutton.

mpendapendapo (also *mnyunyuma*) *n* (*mi-*) (*bot*) a very common, trailing or climbing shrub, having an abundance of small white flowers and ovate or elliptic leaves and bearing edible fruits resembling coffee berries. The shrub is used in the treatment of certain diseases. *Canthium zanzibaricum*.

mpendwa *n* (*wa-*) see *mpenzi*

mpenyezo *n* (*mi-*) 1. act of passing sth through a narrow space; penetration. 2. smuggling; underhand or illicit action: *Silaha ziliingia nchini kwa mpenyezo*, the weapons entered the country by illicit means.

mpenyo *n* (*mi-*) penetration, infiltration (cf *upenyaji*)

mpenzi (also *mpendwa*) *n* (*wa-*) a beloved person; lover. (cf *laazizi*, *mbasi*)

mpepa *n* (*mi-*) (*bot*) a glabrous scandent

perennial with small white or cream flowers and small berry-like fruits, used medicinally for venereal diseases. *Flagellaria guineensis.*

mpepe *n (mi-)* 1. *(bot)* a shrubby scabrid perennial herb with pubescent leaves and long-stalked heads of yellow flowers. *Wedelia menotriche.* 2. a shrub or tree with opposite leaves and inconspicuous flowers. *Memecylon sp.*

mpepea[1] *n (mi-)* rainwater blown by the wind; sleet.

mpepea[2] n (n) air current.

mpepeaji (also *mpepezi*) *n (wa-)* a person who operates a fan so that air is circulated.

mpeperuko *n (mi-)* act (method, etc.) of sth flying away, possibly being carried away by the wind, etc.

mpepesuko *n (mi-)* staggering, swaying, reeling: *Mpepesuko wa mlevi barabarani uliwasumbua waendeshaji magari,* the drunkard's staggering on the road disturbed the motorists.

mpepetaji (also *mpeta*) *n (wa-)* sifter, winnower; one who sifts or winnows grain. (cf *mpembuzi*)

mpepezi *n (wa-)* see *mpepeaji*

mpera *n (mi-) (bot)* guava tree. *Psidium guajava.* Mpera *golabi,* rose apple. *Mpera marashi,* rose apple. *Eugenia jambos. Mpera wa kizungu,* rose apple. *Eugenia jambos. Mpera wa porini,* rubber vine. *Landolphia petersiana.*

mpesi *n (mi-) (bot)* a much-branched pubescent and scabrous tree bearing small fleshy fruits. Its bark is rubbed on to fishing lines to preserve them, making them dark-reddish brown in colour. *Trema guineensis. Mpesi dume,* a much-branched tree with alternate leaves. *Macaranga sp.* (cf *mkasiri*)

mpeta *n (mi-)* cloves which have fallen from a tree after being overripe.

mpetaji *n (wa-)* see *mpepetaji*

mpevuko *n (mi-)* maturation, maturity, ripeness (cf *upevukaji*)

mpewa *n (wa-)* recipient: *Mpewa nishani,* medalist.

mpiga *n (wa-)* a person who performs a particular action such as casting a vote, etc.: *Mpiga kura,* voter. *Mpiga muziki,* musician, instrumentalist. *Mpiga tarumbeta,* trumpet blower. *Mpiga zumari,* flageolet blower. *Mpiga ngoma,* drummer. *Mpiga picha,* photographer. *Mpiga taipu,* typist. *Mpiga mishale,* archer, bowman. *Mpiga filimbi,* flutist. *Mpiga kasia,* oarsman. *Mpiga debe,* campaigner. *Mpiga domo,* flibertigibbet.

mpigaji *n (wa-)* fighter: *Yeye ni mpigaji hodari,* he is a good fighter. (cf *mpiganaji*)

mpiga-kururu *n (mi-) (bot)* a much branched thorny tree with bright reddish-yellow bark and bright yellow flowers. *Acacia zanzibarica.*

mpigambizi *n (wa-)* 1. diver. 2. aquanaut.

mpiganaji *n (wa-)* fighter, combatant: *Wewe ni mpiganaji mzuri,* you are a good fighter.

mpigo *n (mi-)* 1. act (mode, etc.) of striking, beating, etc.: *Mpigo ule wa ngoma unapendeza,* that kind of drum beating is impressive. 2. blow, stroke, thrust: *Mpigo ule ulimwangusha chini,* that blow knocked him down. 3. concurrence: *Mshtakiwa atatumikia adhabu zote kwa mpigo,* the accused will serve all the sentences concurrently. (cf *kwa pamoja, kwa mkupuo mmoja*)

mpikaji *n (wa-)* one who cooks; cook.

mpiko *n (mi-)* 1. a stick or pole used to carry or sling loads on (cf *mtenga, mzega*) 2. lever, roller, bar. (cf *wenzo*)

mpilipili *n (mi-) (bot)* red or white paper plant. *Capsicum annuum. Mpilipili kichaa/hoho,* African pepper plant, Guinea or Bird. *Capsicum frutescens. Mpilipili manga,* Black paper plant. *Piper nigrum. Mpilipilibomba,* sweet pepper. *Capsicum annuum. Mpilipili doria, Sorinderia madagascarensis.*

mpilipilitawala *n* (*mi-*) (*bot*) a kind of tree whose small branches are used by local people as toothbrushes.

mpima (also *mpimaji*) *n* (*wa-*) 1. one who measures, etc.: *Mpima ardhi*, surveyor. *Mpima picha*, photographer. *Mpima ramani*, surveyor. 2. one who tests; tester.

mpimaji *n* (*wa-*) see *mpima*

mpindia *n* (*mi-*) a mat that shrouds a dead body after being sewn.

mpinduzi *n* (*wa-*) revolutionist: *Yeye ni mpinduzi halisi*, he is a real revolutionalist. (cf *mwanamapinduzi*)

mpingaji *n* (*wa-*) opposer (cf *mpinzani*)

mpingamaendeleo *n* (*wa-*) reactionary; a person who hampers progress in a society, etc.

mpingamapinduzi *n* (*wa-*) reactionary, conservative. (cf *mhafidhina*)

mpingani *n* (*wa-*) an argumentative person; wrangler: *Usishindane na mpingani*, don't argue with a wrangler. (cf *mbishi*)

mpingo *n* (*mi-*) 1. (*bot*) African ebony; a thorny tree, the heartwood of which is hard, heavy and black, and is for carving. *Dalbergia melanoxylon*. 2. a much-branched spiny tree with two-paired suborbicular leaflets and dense spicate racemes of small whitish flowers and jointed pods. *Entada rotundifolia*. 3. a tree with a hard black heartwood. *Disopyros sp.*

mpini *n* (*mi-*) handle: *Mpini wa shoka*, helve. *Shika mpini*, have control over sth.

mpinzani *n* (*wa-*) 1. opponent, opposer. (*mpingani*) 2. a member of the opposition in a multiparty set up; opponent: *Wapinzani waliligomea bunge*, the members of the opposition boycotted parliament. 3. a person who argues with another person about sth (cf *mshindani*)

mpira *n* (*mi-*) 1. (*bot*) rubbervine, rubber tree; the tree producing Indian rubber. *Manihot glaziovii*. 2. the sap from rubber trees. 3. (in sports) ball: *Mpira wa magongo*, hockey. *Mpira wa vikapu*, basket ball. *Mpira wa miguu*, soccer. *Mpira wa vinyoya*, badminton. *Mpira wa wavu*, volleyball. *Mpira wa meza*, ping-pong; tabletennis. *Mpira wa baiskeli*, bicycle tyre. *Mpira wa kulipwa*, professional soccer. *Mpira wa pete*, netball.

mpiripiri *n* (*mi-*) (*bot*) a small tree up to 30 feet tall with pinnate leaves. *Sorindeia sp.*

mpishi *n* (*wa-*) cook, chef.

mpitisho *n* (*mi-*) (*phys*) conduction

mpito *n* (*mi-*) transition, interim: *Utawala wa mpito*, interim administration. *Serikali ya mpito*, interim government. *Bunge la mpito*, interim parliament. *Kipindi cha mpito*, interim period.

mpo *n* (*mi-*) (*bot*) rubbervine plant bearing small avoid-globose fruits. The rubber of this plant is often used for birdlime.

mpofu *n* (*mi-*) (*bot*) a laxly branched deciduous tree with wide spreading branches and rough brown fissured bark, which produces an aromatic gum obtained from the trunk, used as incense. *Canarium liebertianum*.

mpojo *n* (*mi-*) (*bot*) black gram plant. *Phaseolus mungo*.

mpokea (also *mpokeaji*) *n* (*wa-*) receiver: *Mpokea simu*, telephonist.

mpokeaji *n* (*wa-*) 1. see *mpokea*. 2. midwife (cf *mkunga*)

mpokezi[1] *n* (*wa-*) receptionist; a person employed in a hotel, etc. to receive guests, give information, etc.

mpokezi[2] *n* (*wa-*) (*med*) recipient

mpokonyo *n* (*mi-*) snatch, grab. (cf *mkupuo*)

mpole *n* (*wa-*) a quiet person, a reticent person. (cf *mnyamavu*)

mpombo *n* (*mi-*) (*bot*) a spiny tree with small black leaves.

mpoopoo *n* (*mi-*) see *mpopoo*

mpopoo *n (mi-) (bot)* betel nut palm; a graceful, slender-stemmed palm, 50 feet or more high, leaves bearing a yellow egg-shaped fruit containing one seed about the size of a nutmeg. *Areca catechu.*

mporojo *n (mi-) (bot)* a much-branched deciduous tree whose bark is an important anthelminitic to local people. *Albizzia anthelmintica.*

mporomoko *n (mi-)* 1. collapse, sliding, drop, fall, falling, *Miporomoko ya ardhi*, landslide; the rapid fall of a mass of loosened rocks or earth down a hillside or slope. *Miporomoko ya udongo*; soil flow; the slow movement of soil down a hill side or slope 2(esp. of economy) collapse, downturn: *Mporomoko wa uchumi*, economic downturn.

mporopojo *n (mi-)* Klotsch; a scandent evergreen shrub growing over bushes and small trees with unpleasantly scented white short tubular flowers, bearing a coffee-like berry fruit. *Canthium zanzibaricum.*

mpororo[1] *n (mi-)* a succession of things or people: *Askari waliandamana kwa mpororo mbele ya mgeni wa heshima*, the policemen marched in a procession before the guest of honour. (cf *sanjari*)

mpororo[2] *n (mi-)* a line of tribal tattoo marks down the length of the nose.

mpotevu *n (wa-)* prodigal, squanderer: *Mwana mpotevu*, a prodigal son.

mpoto *n (mi-)* the twisting of the strands of flax, cotton, etc. to make a string, rope, etc.

mpotofu *n (wa-)* see *mpotevu*

mpotovu (also *mpotofu*) *n (wa-)* pervert; a person going on the wrong course: *Tabia zake mbaya zimemfanya sasa kuwa mpotovu*, his bad habits have now made him a pervert.

Mprotestanti *n (wa-)* Protestant (Eng)

mpujufu *n (wa-)* a person who uses obscene language, etc.; a foul-mouthed person: *Mpujufu aliwaudhi watu kwa sababu ya lugha yake chafu aliyoitoa hadharani*, the foul-mouthed person angered the people because of his obscene language uttered in public. (cf *mchimwi*)

mpukusaji *n (wa-)* a person who fells down fruits from the trees.

mpukutiko *n (mi-)* the spilling of sth from a container which is full. 2. the condition (state, etc.) of fruits and leaves falling in large numbers from the trees.

mpukutisho *n (mi-)* autumn season.

mpukuto *n (mi-)* shaking: *Mpukuto wa maji*, the shaking of the water.

mpumbao *n (mi-)* see *pumbao*

mpumbavu *n (wa-)* imbecile, fool, idiot. (cf *zuzu, juju, mjinga*)

mpumuo *n (mi-)* 1. breathing: *Mpumuo wa mgonjwa ulinishtua*, the patient's breathing shocked me. 2. (*gram*) aspiration: *Mpumuo wa konsonanti*, the aspiration of consonants.

mpunga *n (mi-)* 1. (*bot*) rice plant. *Oryza sativa*. When husked it is called *mchele*; when cooked, it is called *wali*. There are different kinds of rice that are known locally: *Afaa, akilimali, bungala, kibafuta, kufuli, mkarafua, sena, sindano, ushaka*, etc. 2. the rice in the husk; paddy.

mpungate *n (mi-) (bot)* prickly pear; a much-branched leafless succulent shrub whose fruit is usu pear-shaped or globose, purplish and juicy. *Opuntia dillenii.*

mpunguo *n (mi-)* decline, lessening: *Mpunguo wa idadi ya watu kazini umeleta matatizo*, the decline of the number of people at work has created problems.

mpunjaji *n (wa-)* a swindler in business.

mpupu *n (mi-)* 1. (*bot*) sword bean, *Canavalia ensiformis.* 2. buffalo bean; a climbing herb with pinnately trifoliolate leaves and small golden coloured hairs which on contact with skin cause intense irritation for several hours. *Mucuna pruriens.*

mpuririaji *n (wa-)* a person who allows things to happen in any way before he finally decides to intervene.

mpururo *n (mi-)* the stripping of a tree, plant, etc. of its leaves, bark, etc.; the pulling away of leaves, etc. from their trees, plants, etc.: *Mipurururo yake ya majani ilileta uharibifu katika mimea yangu,* his pulling of leaves caused destruction to my plants.

mpuuzaji *n(wa-)* person who neglects important things; a care-free person.

mpuuzi *n (wa-)* a person whose actions don't need to be imitated because they are valueless; wastrel: *Utakuwa mpuuzi kama utaandamana na watu wulumi,* you will become a useless person if you associate with hooligans.

mpwa *n (wa-)* nephew, niece.

mpwamu *n (wa-)* a cheerful person; a vivacious person: *Sisi tunayapenda mazungumzo ya mpwamu yule,* we like the conversation of that cheerful person. (cf *mchangamfu, bashasha, mcheshi)*

mpweke¹ *n (mi-)* 1. (*bot*) a hard kind of tree with evergreen elliptical alternate leathery leaves, used for making walking sticks. *Diospyros mespiliformis.* 2. a heavy stick made from this tree. (cf *rungu)* 3. penis. (cf *mboo)*

mpweke² *n (mi-)* a person who isolates himself from others.

Mpweke³ *adj* one of the attributes of God meaning, "unequalled."

mpwito *n (mi-)* impulse: *Mpwito wa damu,* the pulse of the blood.

mpwitompwito *n (mi-)* exhilaration obtained after victory in sports, etc. or sadness obtained from an unpleasant experience; hysteria: *Mashabiki waliingiwa na mpwitompwito wakati timu yao iliposawazisha goli,* the fans were filled with exhilaration when their team equalized a goal. (cf *furaha)*

mpyaro *n (wa-)* 1. a person fond of using filthy words; a foul-mouthed person: *Usiandamane na mpyaro yule,* don't associate with that foul-mouthed person. (*mpujufu)* 2. a person fond of exaggerating news: *Utaweza kuamini kila anachozungumza ikiwa yeye ni mpyaro?* Can you believe all he says if he is so fond of exaggerating?

mraa *n (mi-)* khat; a kind of stimulant herb. (cf *mrungu)* (Ar)

mraba¹ *n (mi-)* 1. square: *Kilometa mraba,* square kilometre. *Mraba kamilifu,* perfect square. *Mraba kizio,* unit square. 2. (*syn*) *Mtu wa miraba minne,* a person with a broad stout physique of medium stature. (Ar)

mraba² *n (mi-)* line: *Amepanda mahindi mraba mmoja mpaka mwisho,* he has grown maize on one straight line. (Ar)

mraba³ *n (mi-)* a sweet thing like honey or sugar cooked and mixed with other things so as to become hard: *Njugu za mraba,* groundnuts prepared in this way. (Ar)

mrabaha *n (mi-)* 1. business done by someone for someone else who receives some profit for the capital he has provided. 2. royalty; fee paid by a trader to a chief, etc. for the purpose of trading. 3. payment given to an author derived from the sales of his books; royalties. (Ar)

mradi¹ *n (mi-)* see *muradi*

mradi² *n (mi-)* project, venture: *Miradi ya maendeleo,* development projects. *Mradi wa mpunga,* rice project. *Mradi wa pamoja,* joint venture. (Ar)

mradi³ *n (mi-)* spindle; a thin rod on which thread is twisted or wound during spinning.

mradi⁴ *conj* provided that, on the condition that: *Yeye anaweza kutohudhuria darasa kesho mradi amwarifu mwalimu wake kabla,* he can absent from the class tomorrow provided he informs his teacher in advance. (cf *madamu*)

mrafu *n* (*wa-*) glutton, gourmand. (cf *mlafi, mchoyo, mchoko*)

mrai *n* (*n*) rye (cf *shayiri*)

mraibu *n* (*wa-*) addict: *Mraibu wa pombe*, alcoholic; a person addicted to alcohol. (cf *mshabiki*)

mrajisi *n* (*wa-*) registrar: *Mrajisi wa vyama vya ushirika*, registrar of co-operative socities. *Mrajisi wa mahakama*, registrar of court.

mrakibu *n* (*wa-*) superintendent: *Mrakibu wa polisi*, police superintendent. *Mrakibu mkuu*, chief superintendent. (Ar)

mrama *adv* astray, off-course: *Enda mrama*, roll, toss. *Chombo kilikuwa kinakwenda mrama*, the vessel was tossing. (*prov*) *Heri ya mrama kuliko kuzama*, it is better for the sailing vessel to toss than to go aground i.e. it is better to meet a small problem now and solve it rather than meeting a series of problems later on.

mramali *n* (*wa-*) horoscoper, astrologer. (cf *mnajimu*)

mramba *n* (*wa-*) see *mlamba*

mranaa *n* (*mi-*) see *mnaraha*

mranaha (also *mranaa*) *n* (*mi-*) (*bot*) thorn apple; an annual herb with unequal sided ovate leaves and trumpet-shaped flowers which are used for relieving asthma, etc. *Datura metel*.

mrao *n* (*mi-*) harvest time during cold season.

mraruasanda *n* (*mi-*) (*zool*) nightjar (cf *mpasuasanda, kirukanjia*)

mraruo *n* (*mi-*) splitting, tearing. (Ar)

mrashi *n* (*mi-*) sprinkler, sprayer. (cf *kinyunyizo*)

mrasimu[1] *n* (*wa-*) draughtsman; a person who draws plans of structures, etc. (Ar)

mrasimu[2] *n* (*wa-*) bureaucrat: *Waziri aliwakemea maofisa warasimu*, the minister reprimanded the bureaucrats. (Ar)

mrasimuramani *n* (*mi-*) cartographer; a person whose work is to make maps or charts.

mratabu *n* (*mi-*) (*bot*) sapodilla plum tree; a medium-sized evergreen tree, bearing nearly spherical or oval, thin-skinned fruit which contains sweet succulent pulp excellent for dessert. *Achras zapota*.

mratibu *n* (*wa-*) organizer, co-ordinator: *Yeye ndiye mratibu wa michezo kwa shule zote za mjini*, he is the sports co-ordinator for all the town schools. (Ar)

mrau *n* (*mi-*) 1. matchlock gun. (cf *gobori*) 2. (*syn*) *Kufuata mrau*, go to war. 3. match for lighting the powder in a matchlock gun; gunpowder match light.

mrazini *n* (*wa-*) rationalist; an advocate of the principle or practice of accepting reason as the only authority in determining one's opinions or course of action.

mregezo *n* (*mi-*) retardation

mrejeo *n* (*mi-*) 1. return; act of coming or going back as to a former place, condition, etc. 2. (*gram*) *Mrejeo sawa*, apposition; the placing of one word or phrase to another word or phrase so that the second serves as an explanation e.g. *Ndama, watoto wa ng'ombe*, heifers, the young cows. Here the phrase *watoto wa ng'ombe*, 'the young cows' is an apposition to *ndama*, heifer.

mrela *n* (*mi-*) a kind of stitching of a shirt or *kanzu* whose round bottom is broader than usual.

mrembe[1] *n* (*mi-*) a kind of a sharp-pointed wooden spear.

mrembe[2] *n* (*mi-*) a cloth used to remove body fluids after sexual intercourse between a husband and wife.

mrembeshaji *n* (*wa-*) beautician; a person who is skilled in giving cosmetic treatment.

mrembo *n* (*wa-*) a glamorous female; an attractive beautiful girl. (cf *kidosho*)

mrengu n (mi-) 1. (naut) an outrigger of a boat or canoe. 2. (fig) used in the expressions: Mrengu wa kushoto, radical position. Mrengu wa kulia, conservative position, e.g. Chama cha mrengu wa kulia kilishinda katika uchaguzi mkuu, the conservative party won the general elections.

Mreno n (wa-) Portuguese

mrera n (mi-) lines of ornamental stitching on the collar of a woman's *kanzu* or a waistcoat, usu of red silk.

mreteni n (mi-) (bot) juniper; a coniferous shrub or small tree having purple berry-like cones that yield an oil used in flavouring gin and formerly, in medicine.

mriba¹ n (mi-) (bot) the leaves of sweet potato plant, used as a kind of vegetable. *Pomea batatas*. (cf *mtortuo, matembele*)

mriba² n (mi-) (zool) the bottom part of a leg of a cow between the knee and the hoof.

mrihani (also *mrehani, mrumbamkuu*) n (mi-) (bot) basil; an erect annual much- branched herb with ovate leaves and moderately dense racemes of small white or purple tinged flowers whose leaves are used for flavouring in cooking. *Ocimum basilicum*. Mrihani wa kiunguja, *Ocimum sp.* (Ar)

mrihi (also *mtondo, mriti*) n (mi-) (bot) a tree with a rough bark and flush red or pink flowers, whose timber is used for making canoes wooden cabinets, etc. The bark is used to make ropes. *Brachystegia speciformis*. (cf *myombo*)

mrija n (mi-) 1. reed, drinking straw. 2. (fig) exploitation: Kata mrija, stop exploitation. Vunja mrija, stop exploitation. Tia mrija, exploit. Anapata faida kubwa katika kiwanda chake kwa njia ya mrija, he gets a lot of profit in his industry through exploitation.

Mrima n (n) Swahili-speaking Coast of East Africa; the coastal land of East Africa.

mrina (also *mrinaji*) n (wa-) used in the expression: Mrina asali, honey gatherer. Mrina nyuki, honeybee gatherer.

mrinaji n (wa-) see mrina

mrindimo n (mi-) booming sound; noise of thunder, heavy rains, waterfall, etc. Mrindimo wa ngoma, the booming of the drum. (cf *mngurumo*)

mripuko n (mi-) see mlipuko

Mrisho n (n) the ninth month preceding the month of "Rajab" of the Islamic calendar.

mrisi n (n) 1. a small score in card playing that makes an opponent get more than one turn. 2. (syn) Amekwenda mrisi, he has not accomplished his mission i.e. he has failed.

mrithi n (wa-) heir, inheritor, legatee. Mrithi dhahiri, heir apparent. Mrithi mstahiki, heir apparent. Mrithi mdhaniwa, presumptuous heir. Yeye ndiye mrithi wa mali ya marehemu, he is the inheritor of the property of the deceased. 2. successor: Yeye si mrithi wa kiti cha ufalme, he is not the heir of the crown. (Ar)

mriti n (mi-) see mrihi

mrogonyo n (mi-) hocuspocus, trickery.

mroho n (wa-) glutton; a voracious person: Usile na mroho yule, don't eat with that glutton. (cf *mbuku, mlafi, mmeo*)

mroma n (mi-) (bot) a deciduous tree with a branched bushy crown and rough reddish brown bark, which has useful timber and its fruits are edible. *Cordyla africana*.

mrombo n(wa-) a woman who has received teachings in an initiation school.

mronge n (mi-) (bot) horse-raddish tree; a kind of tree with pungent roots, the seeds and leaves of which are eaten as a vegetable and used in curries. *Moringa oleifera*.

mronjo (also *mironjo*) n (mi-) a large pole tied with the legs of the dancers so that they look tall; walk-on stilt.

mrundikano n (mi-) (bot) a deci

Mrwanda n (wa-) accumulation,

M mruba — msagiko

collection, backlog: *Mrundikano mkubwa wa wanafunzi*, an excessive accumulation students.

mruba *n* (*mi-*) medicine used by magicians in healings; leech.

mrufani *n* (*wa-*) appellant: *Mrufani alikataliwa rufani yake*, the appeal of the appellant was rejected.

mrugaruga *n* (*wa-*) see *rugaruga*

mrukaji *n* (*wa-*) jumper

mruko *n* (*mi-*) 1. jumping, jump, leaping, leap: *Nilifurahishwa na mruko wa mwanariadha*, I was impressed by the athlete's jumping. (cf *urukaji*) 2. flight: *Mruko wa ndege*, the flight of the plane.

mrumba¹ *n* (*wa-*) hunter (cf *mwindaji, mkaa, msasi*)

mrumba² *n* (*mi-*) (*bot*) bulrush; a perennial reed growing on the margins of lakes and ponds, whose mature flowers are used for stuffing pillows. *Typha sp.*

mrumbuzi *n* (*mi-*) (*bot*) stinking weed. *Cassia occidentalis.*

Mrundi *n* (*wa-*) a person originating from Burundi.

mrundikano *n* (*mi-*) backlog; accumulation of uncompleted work etc.: *Klabu yao imejikuta katika mrundikano wa mechi kadha*, their team is facing a backlog of several matches.

mrungi *n* (*mi-*) a kind of shrub whose leaves are chewed like an intoxicant and which is believed to make someone active so that he does not sleep; 'khat' stimulant. (cf *mraa*)

mrungura¹ *n* (*mi-*) bribe (cf *rushwa, hongo*)

mrungura² *n* (*mi-*) 1. a large wooden mortar-like drum stretched with an animal skin on one side, used to call people together; a mortar-shaped drum. (cf *mdungura, tutu*) 2. a special drumming used for this purpose.

Mrusi *n* (*wa-*) Russian (Rs)

mrututu *n* (*mi-*) sulphate of copper, bluestone, etc. often used as a caustic for sores. In other places, it is cooked with hard porridge and eaten as a medicine for yaws. (cf *muututu*)

mruzi (also *mluzi*) *n* (*mi-*) a sharp whistle; catcall: *Piga mruzi*, make a catcall. (cf *ubinja*)

msaada *n* (*mi-*) assistance, help, aid: *Msaada wa masomo*, scholarship. *Msaada wa ng'ambo*, overseas aid. *Msaada wa dharura*, emergency aid. *Msaada wa kwanza*, first aid. *Serikali ilitoa msaada kwa walemavu*, the government gave assistance to the disabled. (cf *auni, amara, muawana*) (Ar)

msabaka *n* (*mi-*) 1. horse race or race between people. 2. reading competition. (Ar)

msafa¹ *n* (*mi-*) queue, line, row. (cf *safu, mstari*) (Ar)

msafa² *n* (*mi-*) (*bot*) an annual or perennial herb with ovate acute serrate alternate leaves and small inconspicuous flowers, the leaves of which are used as a vegetable. *Corchorus acutangulus.*

msafara *n* (*mi-*) 1. caravan, expedition: *Msafara wa motokaa*, motorcade. *Msafara wa rais*, presidential entourage. *Msafara wao ulikuwa na matatizo*, their caravan had problems. 2. journey. (cf *safari, charo*) (Ar)

msafari *n* (*mi-*) (*bot*) a tuberous rooted perennial herb, the root of which is used as a poison. *Gloriosa simplex.*

msafiri *n* (*wa-*) voyager, traveller. (*prov*): *Msafiri ni aliye pwani*, a traveller is the one who is at the harbour i.e. it is necessary to prepare our things earlier than to wait at the last moment. (cf *abiria*) (Ar)

msagaji *n* (*wa-*) lesbian

msagaliwa *n* (*wa-*) 1. an effeminate person. (cf *chapapunga, dondoandume*) 2. gay, homosexual, sodomite. (cf *hanithi*)

msagiko *n* (*mi-*) breaking, break: *Msagiko wa jino*, the breaking of the tooth.

msago¹ *n* (*mi-*) grinding; act (method, etc.) of grinding grain: *Msago wa mawele*, the grinding of bulrush millet.
msago² *n* (*mi-*) 1. lesbianism; homosexuality between women. 2. a woman who practices lesbianism. (cf *msagaji*)
msaha *n* (*mi-*) iron crow bar. (cf *mchemu*) (Ar)
Msahafu *n* (*mi-*) The Holy Koran. (Ar)
msahala *n* (*mi-*) laxative, purgative. (cf *haluli*) (Ar)
msahaulifu (also *msahaulivu*) *n* (*wa-*) a forgetful person; an absent-minded person: *Msahaulifu alisahau kuninunulia vitabu*, the absent-minded person forgot to buy books for me.
msahaulivu *n* (*wa-*) see *msahaulifu*
msaidizi *n* (*wa-*) 1. assistant, samaritan, helper; a person who assists someone else in times of need, etc: *Yeye ni msaidizi mzuri kwa masikini*, he is a good helper to the poor. 2. a person who assists or serves in a subordinate position: *Msaidizi mahususi*, personal assistant. *Katibu mkuu msaidizi*, assistant secretary general.
msaili *n* (*wa-*) interviewer: *Msaili aliwahoji waombaji kazi*, the interviewer interviewed the job applicants. (Ar)
msailiwa *n* (*wa-*) interviewee (Ar)
msajaria *n* (*wa-*) (*med*) surgeon; a doctor specialized in surgery. (Eng)
msaji *n* (*mi-*) (*bot*) teak tree; a cultivated exotic tree which has a useful timber. *Tectona grandis*.
msajili *n* (*wa-*) registrar: *Msajili wa majumba*, registrar of buildings. *Msajili wa mahakama*, registrar of the high court. *Msajili wa vyama*, registrar of societies.
msako *n* (*mi-*) hunt, round-up. *Msako wa wachawi*, witchhunt. *Msako wa nyumba hadi nyumba*, in-house searching. (cf *utafutaji*)
msala¹ *n* (*mi-*) see *mswala*
msala² *n* (*mi-*) toilet, bathroom, restroom. (cf *choo*)
msalaba *n* (*mi-*) 1. cross. *Msalaba Mwekundu*, the Red Cross. 2. crucifix; a Christian symbol consisting of a cross with the figure of Jesus crucified on it.
msalani *adv* in/at the bathroom, to the bathroom: *Amekwenda msalani*, he has gone to the bathroom.
msaliti *n* (*wa-*) 1. traitor: *Msaliti aliihini nchi yake*, the traitor betrayed his country. (cf *haini, kitimbakwiri*) 2. firebrand, rabble-rouser, troublemaker: *Msaliti aliwagombanisha marafiki wawili*, the firebrand played one friend against the other. (cf *mfitini*) (Ar)
msalkheri (also *masalkheri*) *interj* an expletive of greeting used in the afternoon or evening. (Ar)
msamaha *n* (*n*) 1. apology. 2. forgiveness, pardon. 3. exemption: *Msamaha wa kodi*, tax exemption. (Ar)
Msamaria *n* (*wa-*) Samaritan; a person who comes to the aid of another: *Msamaria mwema*, a good Samaritan.
msamba *n* (*mi-*) 1. the region of the body between the thighs at the outlet of the pelvis; perineum: (*prov*) *Mpanda farasi wawili, hupasuka msamba*, he who wants to accomplish two things at the same time, may fail in his mission. In other words, you can't normally do two things simultaneously. 2. step from one leg to another: *Piga msamba mmoja*, make one step.
msambali *n* (*mi-*) (*bot*) a flowering shrub, bearing small white French beans. The plant is sometimes seen as a carpet of pretty blue flowers and it is used as a vegetable. *Lobelia fervens*. (cf *kisambare*)
msambaji *n* (*wa-*) distributor: *Yeye ni msambaji wa bidhaa mbalimbali*, he is the distributor of various goods.
msambamba *n* (*mi-*) (*math*) parallelogram
msambambasawa *n* (*mi-*) (*math*) rhombus
msambao *n* (*mi-*) diffusion, dispersion,

scatteredness, spread. (cf *uenevu*)

msambaratiko *n* (*mi-*) disarray, disorder, disorganization, confusion: *Msambaratiko katika chama tawala*, the state of disarray in the ruling party (cf *sokomoko, tandabelua, fujo*)

msambuku *n*(*mi-*) (*bot*) elder berry; a small tree or shrub with pithy stems, white flowers, and bluish-black or red berries.

msamiati *n* (*mi-*) vocabulary, word-stock: *Elimu msamiati*, lexicology. (cf *istilahi*) (Ar)

msamilo *n* (*mi-*) headboard; a wooden head-rest, used as a pillow by some people.

msana *n* (*wa-*) a person who forges, etc.: *Msana visu*, a maker of knives. *Msana majembe*, a maker of hoes; hoe-maker. (cf *mhunzi*)

msanaka *n* (*mi-*) (*bot*) screw pine; a kind of tree with lanceolate leaves, which when dry, are used to make baskets for carrying heavy articles and also for matting. *Pandanus sp.* (cf *mkadidume*)

msanapiti (also *msanapichi*) *n* (*mi-*) (*bot*) frangipani tree. *Plumeria accuminata* (cf *mfurutangi*)

msandali *n* (*mi-*) 1. sandal wood tree; an exotic tree with an aromatic wood. *Santalum album*. 2. bastard sandal wood; a much-branched tree with glabrous lanceolate leaves and greenish-yellow inconspicuous flowers, the wood of which is aromatic and exported to India for cremation purposes. *Osyris tenuifolia*. (Ar)

msandarusi *n* (*mi-*) (*bot*) gum copal tree. *Trachylobium verrucosum*. (Ar)

msangasanga *n* (*mi-*) (*bot*) a much-branched finely pubescent tree; the bark of which is boiled and the liquid is drunk for dysentry and the wood is used for local huts and bedsteads. *Heeria reticulata*.

msani *n* (*wa-*) forger; a person who forges metal. (Ar)

msanifu *n* (*wa-*) 1. artist, composer, designer: *Msanifu ujenzi*, architect. *Msanifu majengo*, architect. 2. author, writer, pen man. (cf *mtunzi, mwandishi*) (Ar)

msanii *n* (*wa-*) 1. artist. 2. composer, writer. (Ar)

msapata *n* (*mi-*) a kind of dance by men and women involving the two sexes meeting at the centre and then returning to their places in the circles or row.

msaragambo *n* (*mi-*) communal volunteer work.

msarifu *n* (*wa-*) 1. a person who uses his things, etc. carefully. 2. a person who co-ordinates programmes, etc. in an organized manner. 3. bursar, cashier: *Msarifu aliidhinisha malipo ya haraka kwa wafanyakazi*, the bursar authorized immediate payment to the workers. (cf *keshia*) (Ar)

msasa *n* (*mi-*) 1. (*bot*) a plant with rough sandpaper-like leaves used for smoothering wood. *Ficus sp.* 2. sandpaper, emery paper. 3. (*syn*) *Piga msasa*, (a) reform sby; improve someone with regards to his character, etc. e.g. *Tulijaribu sana kumpiga rafiki yetu msasa lakini tulishindwa*, we tried our best to reform our friend but we failed. (b) improve sth.

msasi *n* (*wa-*) hunter. (*prov*) *Msasi haogopi miiba*, a hunter is not afraid of the thorns i.e. if you want to do a noble cause, then ignore all the ups and downs, that is to say, difficulties. (*prov*) *Mbwa wa msasi mkali ni mkali pia*, a brave hunter also has a brave dog i.e. if a parent is a virtuous person, then his offspring will usu follow his footsteps. (cf *mkaa, mwindaji, mrumba*)

msawazo *n* (*mi-*) (*phys*) equilibrium: *Msawazo joto*, thermal equilibrium. *Msawazo thabiti*, stable equilibrium.

msawidi *n* (*wa-*) draughtsman: *Msawidi sheria*, legal draughtsman. (Ar)

mseja *n* (*wa-*) bachelor, spinster; a male

or female who is not yet married. (cf *mwanapao, mjane, mhuni*)
msemaji *n* (*wa-*) 1. orator, speaker. 2. spokesman/spokeswoman: *Msemaji mkuu wa serikali*, senior government spokesman. 3. a person who delivers a public speech.
msembe *n* (*wa-*) (*zool*) a kind of broad fish with black and yellow colour or white and black.
msemi *n* (*wa-*) a chatterbox; gabbler, a talkative person, a garrulous person. (cf *msemaji, mlimi*)
msemo *n* (*mi-*) 1. saying, idiom: *Kiswahili kina misemo mingi*, Swahili has many sayings. *Msemo mkali*, apothegem. 2. locution, logo.
msenge *n* (*wa-*) gay, a male homosexual. (cf *hanithi*)
msengenyaji (also *msengenyi*) *n* (*wa-*) backbiter; a person who speaks maliciously about an absent person; *Si vizuri kuwa msengenyaji*, it is not good to be a backbiter.
msengenyi *n* (*wa-*) see *msengenyaji*
msengenyo *n* (*mi-*) see *usengenyaji*
msepetuko *n* (*mi-*) tottering, reeling, shaking: *Msepetuko wa mlevi ulinishangaza*, the reeling of the drunkard startled me. (cf *mpepesuko*)
mserego *n* (*mi-*) a local dance performed by a group of people without proper arrangements and which usu takes place at the wedding celebrations.
msese 1. *n* (*mi-*) (*zool*) whydah; an African weaver bird (family *Ploceidae*), the male of which has a black back and a very long black tail used in display flight.
msese² *n* (*mi-*) (*bot*) mettle; a perennial herb with virulent stinging hairs on stems and leaves. *Tragia furialis*.
mseto *n* (*mi-*) 1. a kind of food made from a mixture of grains such as green gram and rice. 2. pluralism, multiracialism, coalition: *Serikali ya mseto*, coalition government.
msewe *n* (*mi-*) 1. a kind of local dance played by ankle bells or rattles fastened to the legs to make the dancers jingle. 2. ankle bells. (cf *njuga*) 3. a kind of large drum.
mshabaha *n* (*mi-*) resemblance, likeness, similarity: *Hakuna mshabaha kati ya marafiki hawa wawili*, there is no resemblance between these two friends. (cf *mlingano, mfanano, uwiano*) (Ar)
mshabiki *n* (*wa-*) 1. fanatic, enthusiast, fan; sby keen especially on sports. (cf *mraibu*) 2. a person waiting for his turn to replace those players who are going to be defeated in card-playing. (Ar)
mshadhari *n* (*mi-*) 1. a round cloth of a worked skullcap. 2. oblique line; a slanting line. (Ar)
mshahara *n* (*mi-*) salary, wage: *Mshahara wa kuanzia*, basic salary. *Kata mshahara*, deduct salary. *Wafanyakazi wamepokea mshahara wao leo*, the workers have received their salaries today.
mshairi *n* (*wa-*) poet: *Mshairi mwenye kipaji*, a poet of genius. (Ar)
mshakiki *n* (*mi-*) see *mshikaki*
mshale *n* (*mi-*) 1. arrow: *Mshale wa sumu*, a poisoned arrow. *Mshale wa manzao*, a hooked arrow. (cf *mvi*) 2. arrow; a sign (———▶) used to indicate direction or position.
mshamara *n* (*mi-*) a traditional fee given by the organizers of a show or celebration, etc. to the guests of every ward or division in order to give legitimacy to anything that may occur in that community
mshamba *n* (*wa-*) 1. a resident of rural areas. 2. a rustic person, an uncouth person; hick. 3. innocent; an innocent person; a person esp. a child who is free of evil or sin.
mshambakuche *n* (*mi-*) (*bot*) a kind of tree with thin, long and black thorny branches.
mshambo *n* (*mi-*) (*bot*) an evergreen tree with large angular seeds embedded in pulp, from which oil is obtained. *Allanblackia stuhlmannii*.
mshambuliaji *n* (*wa-*) attacker, assailer;

Mshambuliaji hatari, a dangerous attacker. *Mshambuliaji chipukizi*, upcoming attacker.
mshamo *n* (*mi-*) iron crow bar. (cf *msaha*)
mshangao *n* (*mi-*) astonishment, bewilderment, perplexity: *Pigwa na mshangao*, be struck dumb, be nonplussed. (cf *mzubao, mzinduo*)
msharafu[1] *n* (*wa-*) an esteemed person; a respected person: *Yeye ni msharafu katika kijiji chetu*, he is a respected person in our village. (cf *mheshimiwa*) (Ar)
msharafu[2] *n* (*mi-*) a kind of good mat that is spread out for respected people who come from a distance.
msharasi (also *gude*) *n* (*mi-*) awl; a small pointed tool for making holes in wood, leather, etc. (cf *gude*)
mshari *n* (*wa-*) a quarrelsome person, a cantankerous person; wrangler: *Mshari yule amemchokoza takriban kila mtu*, that wrangler has teased almost everybody. (cf *mgomvi, mgobo*) (Ar)
mshaufu *n* (*wa-*) 1. a show-off person; braggart: *Mshaufu alijisifu mbele za watu*, the braggart boasted in public. (cf *msodawi*) 2. a sexually-minded person. (Ar)
mshauri *n* (*wa-*) adviser, consultant: *Mshauri wa kisheria*, legal adviser. *Mshauri wa wanafunzi*, dean of students. *Mshauri wa rais*, president's adviser. (Ar)
mshawasha *n* (*mi-*) anxiety, eagerness; desire to do sth. (cf *shauku*)
mshawishi *n* (*wa-*) seducer, persuader; a person who tempts someone to do bad or good things. (Ar)
mshazari *n* (*wa-*) see *mshadhari*
mshelisheli[1] *n* (*mi-*) (*bot*) breadfruit tree; a handsome tree with deeply cut thick glossy leaves, bearing a nearly spherical fruit. *Artocarpus communis*.
Mshelisheli[2] *n* (*wa-*) a citizen of the Seychelles. (Sy)
Mshemali *n* (*wa-*) Omani Arab. (Ar)
mshenga *n* (*wa-*) 1. a go-between in marriage negotiations; someone who arranges a betrothal on behalf of another. 2. a messenger who brings in a special message. (cf *mjumbe*)
mshenzi *n* (*wa-*) 1. savage, barbarian; a person untouched by civilization. 2. a person with filthy habits; a person with disgusting habits; churl; boor: *Usiandamane na mshenzi yule*, don't associate yourself with that churl.
Mshihiri *n* (*wa-*) an Arab from Hadhramout and Sheher in South Arabia. (Ar)
mshika *n* (*wa-*) 1. holder: *Mshika usukani*, one who holds the tiller; steersman. *Mshika bendera*, flagman, linesman. *Mshika dau*, a person who bets. *Mshika usukani*, a person who holds the steering wheel. *Mshika fedha*, cashier. (*prov*) *Mshika mawili, moja humponyoka*, if you attempt two things at the same time, you will fail to do one of them. 2. a person engaged in a special activity.
mshikaki (also *mshakiki*) *n* (*mi-*) bits of meat roasted over embers on a skewer; a dish consisting of small chunks of meat placed over embers on a skewer.
mshikamano *n* (*mi-*) solidarity, unity, adhesion: *Matembezi ya mshikamano*, solidarity walk. *Kiongozi alisisitiza kwa wananchi kuwa na mshikamano*, the leader stressed the need of the people to have unity. (cf *umoja*)
mshikemshike *n* (*mi-*) hustle and bustle, hurly-burly; boisterous activity. (cf *pirikapirika*)
mshikizo[1] *n* (*mi-*) basting, tacking; the act of sewing with loose, temporary stitches.
mshikizo[2] *n* (*mi-*) temporary hold: *Serikali ya mshikizo*, temporary government.
mshiko *n* (*mi-*) hold
mshindaji *n* (*wa-*) victor, conquerer; a

successful candidate or competitor.
mshindani (also *mshinde*) n (*wa-*) 1. contender, opponent, rival, competitor. 2. an argumentative person: *Usishindane na mshindani*, don't argue with an argumentative person. (cf *mkaidi*)
mshinde n (*wa-*) 1. see *mshindani*. 2. a loser. 3. a person who confesses a defeat.
mshindi n (*wa-*) (of games, war, etc.) winner, victor, conquerer.
mshindikizo n (*mi-*) see *mshindilio*
mshindiliaji n (*wa-*) a person who stuffs in or rams crops into the sacks.
mshindilio (also *mshindikizo*) n (*mi-*) the act of forcefully pushing or ramming sth in a container, etc.: *Mshindilio wa nguo kwenye begi*, the ramming of clothes into a bag. *Mshindilio wa bunduki*, the charge of a gun.
mshindio¹ n (*mi-*) the act of taking one meal for the whole day: *Chakula cha mshindio*, the meal taken for the whole day.
mshindio² n (*mi-*) 1. the interlacing of plaited strips (*mashupatu*) to form a bed-stead. 2. the working of the woof or weft across the warp during weaving. 3. the woof itself.
mshindo n (*mi-*) 1. bang; loud noise explaining explosion, impact, etc.: *Mshindo wa bunduki*, the discharge of a gun. *Mshindo wa miguu*, tramp of feet. *Mshindo wa ngoma*, the noise of the drum. (*prov*) *Kimya kingi kina mshindo mkubwa*, a long silence has a mighty noise i.e. silence has a great impact. In other words, silence is more effective than much fuss. 2. (*idm*) *Kuwa na mshindo*, have awareness/ cognisance; the act of knowing or being aware of sth: *Sina mshindo*, I am not aware.
mshipa n (*mi-*) (*anat*) 1. vein, artery, nerve: *Mshipa wa damu*, blood vessel. *Mshipa wa fahamu*, nerve. *Mshipa wa ngiri*, scrotal hernia. *Mshipa wa maji*, scrotal hernia. 2. (*syn*) *Gusa mshipa*, do sth that pleases or impresses someone else.
mshipi n (*mi-*) 1. belt. 2. a fishing-line.
Mshirazi n (*wa-*) 1. Persian. 2. East African coastal person originating from Persia. (Pers)
mshirika n (*wa-*) associate, partner. (Ar)
mshiriki n (*wa-*) participant: *Wao ni washiriki katika semina*, they are participants in the seminar. 2. associate: *Profesa mshiriki*, associate professor. 3. interlocuter. (Ar)
mshirikina n (*wa-*) a superstitious person; idolater: *Mshirikina alikwenda kuonana na mganga wake*, the superstitious person went to see his magician. (Ar)
mshitiri (also *mshtiri*) n (*wa-*) buyer (cf *mnunuzi*) (Ar)
mshokishoki n (*mi-*) 1. (*bot*) rambutan tree; a glabrous evergreen tree up to 60 feet tall with alternate pinnate leaves and much-branched panicles of small greenish-yellow flowers, bearing an edible dark red spherical fruit armed with long soft spines. *Nephelium lappaceum*.
mshona n (*wa-*) sewer: *Mshona viatu*, cobbler. *Mshona sanda*, shroud maker.
mshonaji n (*wa-*) tailor; one who sews, etc. *Mshonaji mwanamke*, needle woman. (cf *mshoni*)
mshonde n (*wa-*) adversary, foe, enemy: *Ana washonde wengi kwa sababu ya kiburi chake*, he has many enemies because of his arrogance. (cf *hasimu, adui*)
mshongo n (*wa-*) nymphomaniac; a person who possesses an abnormal and uncontrolled desire of sexual intercourse. (cf *mkware*)
mshoni n (*wa-*) one who sews, etc: *Mshoni wa viatu*, shoemaker. (*prov*) *Mshoni hachagui nguo*, a tailor does not select a cloth; he will sew any cloth that comes to him i.e. Don't be too choosy for anything.

mshono *n* (*mi-*) 1. a stitched place: *Mshono wa operesheni*, an operated place. 2. seam, stitch. 3. style (method, etc.) of sewing: *Mshono wa nguo hii ni mzuri*, the style of sewing this dress is good. *Mshono mficho*, hemming stitch. (cf *ushonaji*)

mshoro *n* (*mi-*) anything that brings ill-luck or misfortune; jinx.

mshororo *n* (*mi-*) a single metrical unit consisting of a specified number of feet; a line in poetry; verse. (cf *mfuradi*)

mshtaki *n* (*wa-*) plaintiff, accuser. (cf *mdai*) (Ar)

mshtakiwa *n* (*wa-*) accused, defendant. (cf *mdaiwa*) (Ar)

mshtiri *n* (*wa-*) see *mshitiri*

mshtuko *n* (*mi-*) shock, sprain: *Goti lake lilipata mshtuko alipogongana na mchezaji kwenye mpira*, his knee got a sprain when he collided with a player in football. *Mgonjwa alipata mshtuko wa moyo*, the patient suffered a heart attack. (cf *mgutuko*)

mshtuo *n* (*mi-*) anything that causes a shock, sprain, etc.: *Mshtuo ule uliniamsha*, that shock awakened me. *Mshtuo wa umeme*, electric shock. (cf *mgutuko*)

mshubiri (also *msuburi*) *n* (*mi-*) (*bot*) aloe plant; a succulent plant with fleshy green leaves and very prickly margins. *Aloe sp.* (cf *mzimakilio*)

mshughuliko *n* (*mi-*) preoccupation

mshuko *n* (*mi-*) 1. act (method, etc.) of descending: *Mshuko wake kutoka juu ni wa taratibu*, his style of descending from the top is gentle. 2. the period after finishing an activity such as praying, etc.: *Ndoa ilifungwa mshuko wa magharibi*, the marriage ceremony was conducted after evening prayer. 3. (in drama, novels, etc.) dinoument; the outcome, solution, etc of a plot.

mshumaa *n* (*mi-*) candle. *Kinara cha mshumaa*, candlestick.

mshumbi *n* (*mi-*) a small heap of sth e.g. grain or food put inside a utensil: *Alimtilia rafiki yake mshumbi wa wali kwenye chombo*, he gave his friend a small heap of rice in a container.

mshupavu *n* (*wa-*) 1. an intransigent person; a hard person; a bold person: *Alikuwa mwanasiasa mshupavu*, he was a bold politician. 2. an obstinate person; a stubborn person; recalcitrant, mule: *Mshupavu yule hasikii lolote analoambiwa*, that recalcitrant does not listen to anything he is told. (cf *mkaidi*)

mshushio *n* (*mi-*) breath resulting from a person who is in sorrow, deep thought, etc.; sigh: *Mshushio wa pumzi wa mzee ulimshtua mwanawe*, the old man's manner of exhaling disturbed his son.

mshusho *n* (*mi-*) act of bringing sth down or causing it to descend; unloading: *Mshusho wa bidhaa kutoka kwenye basi ulichukua masaa mengi*, the unloading of goods from the bus took many hours.

msi (also *mso*) *n* (*wa-*) a person who is deficient of sth; a person who is devoid of sth: *Msi haya*, a shameless person. *Msi kwao*, a homeless person.

msia *n* (*mi-*) cloud of smoke falling on the roof of a house or wall. (cf *mwale*)

msiba *n* (*mi-*) misfortune, sorrow, blow. (*prov*) *Hakuna msiba usiokuwa na mwenziwe*, there is no misfortune without its like i.e misfortunes never come single.

msichana *n* (*wa-*) 1. girl: *Msichana wa kazi*, housegirl. (cf *mwanamwali*) 2. mistress. (cf *hawara*)

msiga *n* (*mi-*) (*bot*) a tree with small white flowers whose young branches are used as toothbrushes. *Dobera loranthifolia*.

msikiaji *n* (*wa-*) see *msikivu*

msikilizaji (also *msikizi*) *n* (*wa-*) listener

msikilizano *n* (*mi-*) silence, quietness; the condition of quietness such that everyone can hear what is being said:

Hakukuwa na msikilizano kwenye mkutano, there was no silence at the meeting.

msikita *n* (*mi-*) a strip of flesh hung up to dry in the sun or by a fire. (cf *mtanda*)

msikiti *n* (*mi-*) mosque

msikivu (also *msikiaji*) *n* (*wa-*) an obedient person; a well-disciplined person. (cf *mtiifu*)

msikizi *n* (*wa-*) see *msikilizaji*

msikundazi *n* (*mi-*) 1. (*bot*) a tree, the timber of which is used for making boats. *Xylocarpus moluccensis*. 2. red mangrove. *Heritiera littoralis*.

msimamizi *n* (*wa-*) 1. supervisor, overseer, foreman, conductor. 2. watchman. (cf *nokoa*) 3. (in educ) supervisor, advisor.

msimamo *n* (*mi-*) 1. the act of standing. 2. stand, stance, position, principles: *Mtu yule hana msimamo madhubuti*, that person hasn't got a strong stand. (cf *mtazamo*) 3. aim, purpose: *Eleza msimamo wako*, explain your purpose.

msimbo[1] *n* (*mi-*) 1. nickname. (cf *lakabu*) 2. code.

msimbo[2] *n* (*mi-*) 1. bad habit. 2. a person of bad character; reprobate: *Msimbo hapendwi na watu kwa sababu ya vitendo vyake viovu*, the reprobate is not liked by people because of his evil deeds.

msimbo[3] *n* (*mi-*) a rope which is tied to the fish that are collected in the sea.

msimo *n* (*mi-*) see *simo*

msimu (also *musimu*) *n* (*mi-*) season. *Pepo za msimu*, monsoons; seasonal winds. *Msimu wa mvua*, rain season. (Ar)

msimuliaji *n* (*wa-*) narrator, story teller, taleteller (cf *msimulizi*)

msimulizi *n* (*wa-*) narrator, storyteller: *Msimulizi wa hadithi*, storyteller. *Msimulizi wa habari*, news informer.

msindano *n* (*mi-*) (*bot*) pine tree.

msindi (also *msinzi*) *n* (*mi-*) (*bot*) mangrove; a tree with a dark bark from which poles are produced and used for building, etc. *Bruguiera gymnorhiza*.

msindikizaji (also *mshindikizaji*) *n* (*wa-*) 1. a person who sees off someone else: *Msindikizaji wa maarusi*, bridesmaid. 2. a person considered to be the weakest and the least likely to win in a competition; underdog. 3. escort: *Msindikizaji wa rais*, presidential escort.

msindikizo *n* (*mi-*) seeing off a guest, etc.; escorting: *Msindikizo wa mgeni*, the seeing off of a guest. (*ushindikizaji*)

msinduzi *n* (*mi-*) (*bot*) a kind of tree whose pounded bark is used as medicine for inflammation and its roots for colds, stomach complaints, etc. *Croton sp.*

msinga *n* (*mi*) (*bot*) a tall tree with very light wood, the roots of which are used for making a medicine for chest complaints. *Trema guineensis*.

msingaji (also *msinzi*[2]) *n* (*wa-*) massager; a person in charge of rubbing, kneading, etc. a part of the body usu with the hands, so as to stimulate circulation and make joints or muscles supple: *Msingaji mwanamume*, massaeur. *Msingaji mwanamke*, masseuse.

msingi *n* (*mi-*) 1. building foundation: *Jiwe la msingi*, stone foundation. *Weka msingi*, lay a foundation. 2. trench, ditch, etc. made in the ground round a house for carrying off water. 3. basis, origin, principle, fundamental: *Hilo ni jambo la msingi*, that is a fundamental issue. *Shule ya msingi*, primary school. (cf *chanzo, kiini, sababu*)

msingiziaji *n* (*wa-*) a person who says untrue or malicious things; calumniator. (cf *mzushi*)

msinzi[1] *n* (*mi-*) see *msindi*

msinzi[2] *n* (*wa-*) see *msingaji*

msinziaji *n* (*wa-*) dozer; a person who dozes or falls into a light sleep; a drowsy person.

msio *n* (*mi-*) a piece of soft coral stone used for massaging, etc: *Jiwe la msio*, a stone of this kind.

msira¹ n (wa-) a person who has the habit of boycotting or hating sth: *Mtu yule ni msira wa michezo*, that person, by nature, hates sports activities.

msira² n (wa-) skinflint; miser; niggard: *Msira alikataa kutoa mchango wake katika ujenzi wa shule*, the miser refused to give his contribution for the construction of a school. (cf *bahili, kisangati, mchoyo*)

msiri¹ n (wa-) confidant

msiri² n (wa-) a slow person; a remiss person; slowcoach: *Msiri yule hafai kupewa kazi*, that slowcoach should not be given work. (cf *mzito*)

msiri³ n (wa-) a person who is a bit hesitant in doing things.

msirimbo n (mi-) bad painting or white washing, etc.: *Usifanye msirimbo; paka vizuri*, don't paint badly; paint well.

msirisha n (mi-) (bot) see *msizi*

msisimko n (mi-) thrill, excitement: *Filamu ile ilijaa msisimko*, that film was full of thrills. (cf *mhemuko, jazba*)

msisitizo n (mi-) emphasis, stress. *Aliyatia msisitizo maneno yake ya mwisho*, he put emphasis on his last words. (cf *mkazo*)

msitamu n (mi-) see *mstamu*

msitari n (mi-) see *mstari*

msitiri (also *mstiri*) n (wa-) 1. a person who hides sby's scandal, etc. 2. a person who assists someone else in times of difficulty, etc.: *Awali nilikuwa katika dhiki kubwa lakini baadaye akaja msitiri kuniokoa*, in the beginning, I was in great difficulties but later, someone came to rescue me. (Ar)

msitu n (mi-) forest: *Hifadhi ya msitu*, forest reserve. *Msitu mdogo*, coppice. (cf *mwitu, pori*)

msiwa (also *masiwa*) n (mi-) (zool) cornetfish; a kind of saltwater fish (family *Fistulariidae*) with an extremely elongate body and tubular prolonged snout. The fish is common in coastal areas over soft bottoms usu at depths greater than 10 metres. Red cornet fish. *Fistularia petimba*.

msiwa

msizi (also *msirisha*) n (mi-) (bot) a plant from which black dye is made. (cf *mdaa*)

mso n (mi-) see *msi*

msoa n (mi-) an assembly of people; a group of people; crowd: *Niliuona msoa wa wawindaji wakielekea msituni*, I saw a group of hunters heading for the forest. (cf *kikundi*)

msobemsobe (also *mzobemzobe*) adv 1. haphazardly, disorderly: *Aliifanya kazi yangu msobemsobe*, he did my work haphazardly. (cf *hobelahobela, ovyoovyo*) 2. forcefully, by compulsion: *Alilima msobemsobe kufuatia amri kutoka kwa bwana wake*, he cultivated by force following an order from his master.

msokotaji n (wa-) a person who rolls tobacco, etc.

msokoto n (mi-) 1. rolling, severe twisting: *Tumbaku ya msokoto*, rolled tobacco. *Msokoto wa tumbo*, the twisting pain of the abdomen; abdominal colic; enteralgia. 2. sth made by rolling such as a cigarette, thread, etc: *Msokoto wa bangi*, the rolling of bhang.

msolo n (mi-) see *mkomwe¹*

msoma n (n) a kind of dance usu performed by women and sometimes with men by touching one another on the shoulders forming a queue while running or forming a circle.

msomaji n (wa-) 1. reader; one who reads. 2. reviewer; one who reviews books, articles, etc.

Msomali *n* (*wa-*) Somali; a person originating from Somalia.

msomeshaji *n* (*wa-*) teacher, tutor. (cf *mwalimu*)

msomewa *n* (*wa-*) a person who is the target of being prayed for ill omen or good luck.

msomi *n* (*wa-*) scholar; a well-educated person. (cf *mtaalamu*)

msondo *n* (*mi-*) 1. a kind of large long drum. 2. a kind of dance in the girls' initiation rites. 3. the big sound of a large drum, etc 4. a long kind of tarboosh.

msongamano (also *msongano*) *n* (*mi-*) congestion; a tight situation: *Msongamano wa magari*, traffic congestion. *Msongamano wa watu*, congestion of people. (cf *mbanano*)

msongano *n* (*mi-*) 1. see *msongamano*. 2. the act of people esp women to sit together in a group and plait one another's hair.

msonge *n* (*mi-*) 1. a round-shaped house or hut with a roof-like cone. 2. the rule from the top: *Utawala msonge*, top-down rule. *Mfumo msonge wa elimu*, pyramidal education system.

msongo[1] *n* (*mi-*) twisting, stirring, muddling, etc

msongo[2] *n* (*mi-*) 1. skilful art of plaiting hair; braiding 2. style of cooking; cuisine. 3. queue, line. (cf *foleni*, *mstari*)

msono *n* (*mi-*) noise made from snoring; snore. (cf *mforoto*, *mkoromo*)

msonobari *n* (*mi-*) 1. (*bot*) deal timber obtained from *pinus sp.* 2. iron-wood tree.

msononeko *n* (*mi-*) the state of being hurt or vexed; grief. (cf *uchungu*)

msonyo *n* (*mi-*) tut; act (method, etc.) of tutting. (cf *mnyuso*, *mfyonyo*)

msonzi *n* (*mi-*) see *msusi*

msoo *n* (*mi-*) see *mkomwe*[1]

mstaafu *n* (*wa-*) retiree; a retired worker: *Rais mstaafu*, a retired president. (Ar)

mstaarabu *n* (*wa-*) a refined person; a civilized person. (cf *muungwana*) (Ar)

mstafeli *n* (*mi-*) 1. (*bot*) soursop tree; a small tree bearing pleasant flavoured sweet and acid fruits, which are used for ices and cool drinks. *Annona muricata*. (cf *mdikwe*) 2. sugar apple tree; sweet sop tree. *Annona squamosa*.

mstahamilivu *n* (*wa-*) a patient person; an enduring person. (*prov*) *Mstahamilivu hula mbivu*, he who is patient will succeed. (cf *mvumilivu*) (Ar)

mstahifu *n* (*wa-*) a respectful person; a person who is respectful: *Watu walimwamkia mstahifu kwa unyenyekevu*, people greeted the respectful person with humbleness.

mstahika *n* (*wa-*) 1. a person deserving to be respected by someone else. 2. mayor's title.

mstahiki (*wa-*) a person deserving sth; a deserved person on a particular issue: *Yeye ni mstahiki kupandishwa cheo jeshini*, he is a deserved person for receiving promotion in the army. (Ar)

mstakabali (also *mustakabali*) *n* (*mi-*) prospects: *Kiongozi alizungumzia mstakabali wa taifa*, the leader talked about the prospects of the nation. (Ar)

mstamu (also *mstlumu*) *n* (*mi-*) (*naut*) mast-step, partly serving as keelson, at least in built-up ships. (Ar)

mstarehe *n* (*mi-*) see *mustarehe*

mstari (also *msitari*) *n* (*mi-*) 1. line: *Piga mstari*, draw a line. *Mstari ungwa*, broken line. *Mstari wima*, vertical line; perpendicular line. *Mstari msingi*, basic line. *Mstari wa mkazo*, line of stress. *Mstari yatima*, orphan line. 2. queue, row, line: *Panga mstari*, stand in a queue. (cf *foleni*, *mlolongo*) 3. used in the expression: *Mstari wa mbele*, frontline. e.g. *Nchi za mstari wa mbele zilikutana jana kuzingatia suala la mshikamano kati yao*, the frontline states met yesterday to discuss the question of unity between them.

mstarihi *n* (*mi-*) international date line; an

imaginary line drawn north and south through the Pacific Ocean, largely along the 180th meridian. (Ar)

mstatili *n* (*mi-*) rectangle (Ar)

mstiri *n* (*wa-*) see *msitiri*

msu *n* (*mi-*) sword (cf *upanga*)

msuaki *n* (*mi-*) see *mswaki*

msuani *n* (*mi-*) a portion of a shroud around the head and shoulders of a woman who is being buried.

msubili *n* (*mi-*) see *mshubiri*

msubukuo *n* (*mi-*) see *msukuo*

msudukishi *n* (*wa-*) a person who makes charges openly against someone else for deceit or wrongdoing; calumniator, impugner, traducer. (cf *msutaji*)

msufi *n* (*mi-*) 1. (*bot*) kapok tree, cotton tree; a tree up to 80 feet tall with a greenish bark and lightly branched crown, bearing a cigar-shaped, capsule containing numerous round black seeds. *Ceiba pentandra*. 2. *Msufi mwitu*, East African cotton tree. *Bombax rhodognaphalon*. 3. *Msufi wa bara*, cotton grass; a perennial grass with white cotton-sedge-like flowers. *Imperata cylindrica*.

msuguano *n* (*mi-*) conflict, friction, contest: *Msuguano wa pande zile mbili unaweza ukaleta matatizo*, the friction between those two sides can cause trouble. *Misuguano ya kisiasa*, political conficts.

msuka[1] *n* (*mi-*) the pointed side of a hoe or spear into which a handle is put; the spike of a hoe.

msuka[2] *n* (*wa-*) a word used with another noun to mean a person who plaits, etc. *Msuka nywele*, one who plaits hair; a plaiter of hair. *Msuka mikeka*, a plaiter of mats.

msuka[3] *n* (*mi-*) (*bot*) a shrub whose leaves are used to bathe babies in order to acquire good health.

msukaji *n* (*wa-*) a person who plaits hair, mats, nets, etc.

msuko *n* (*mi-*) 1. plaiting: *Msuko wa nywele wa binti yake unapendeza*, the hair plaiting of her daughter is impressive. 2. (in novels, etc.) plot; the plot of action of a play, novel, short story, etc. 3. a kind of swing made of ropes attached to a pole.

msukosuko *n* (*mi-*) 1. ordeal, turmoil; vicissitudes of life. 2. (of a ship, etc.) reeling, tossing, pitching: *Msukosuko wa meli uliwasumbua baadhi ya abiria*, the ship's pitch disturbed some of the passengers. *Msukosuko wa kifedha wa dunia*, global financial crisis. (cf *mtikisiko*)

msukumano *n* (*mi-*) pushing and shoving; jostling: *Kulikuwa na msukumano wa watu dukani wakati mfanyabiashara alipoanza kuuza sukari*, there was pushing and shoving of people in the shop when the businessman started to sell sugar.

msukumizi *n* (*wa-*) a person who puts blame, sickness, etc. on someone else: *Yeye hana kosa lakini wewe ni msukumizi tu*, he has not made any mistake but you are just putting the blame on him.

msukumo *n* (*mi-*) pressure, push, impetus: *Serikali iliweka msukumo mpya kwa wawekezaji*, the government put a new impetus to the investors. 2. (*med*) repulsion: *Msukumo wa kapilari*, capillary repulsion.

msukuo (also *msubukuo*) *n* (*mi-*) the act of pushing or jabbing someone with a finger on the forehead or anywhere on the head; *Alimtia msukuo bure mkutanoni*, he pushed him on the forehead at the meeting for nothing.

msukwano *n* (*mi-*) the shaft and barrel of a drill used by carpenters. (Ar)

msuli (also *musuli*) *n* (*mi-*) 1. muscle: *Misuli ya tumbo*, abdominal muscles. *Misuli ya mkono*, biceps. *Misuli ngumu*, braw. 2. (*fig*) muscle-flexing: *Utawala mpya ulitaka kuonyesha misuli yake ya utendaji kwa wapinzani wake*, the new administration wanted to flex its

muscles to its opponents. (Eng)
msuluhishaji *n* (*wa-*) see *msuluhishi*
msuluhishi (also *msuluhishaji*) *n* (*wa-*) arbitrator, arbiter, negotiator, reconciler, go-between: *Msuluhishi wa kimataifa*, international arbitrator. *Msuluhishi aliteuliwa kutatua migogoro kati ya mwajiri na wafanyakazi*, an arbitrator was appointed to solve disputes between the employer and the workers. (cf *mpatanishi*) (Ar)
msuluhivu *n* (*wa-*) 1. a person who understands issues and their ethics; a knowledgeable person. 2. know-all; a person pretending or claiming to know almost everything. quack, charlatan, mountebank: *Usimpe msuluhivu yule kuitengeneza saa yako*, don't give that know-all to repair your watch. (cf *mjuaji*)
msumari *n* (*mi-*) 1. (of carpentry) nail: *Msumari bapa*, brad. 2. (of insects, etc.) sting: *Msumari wa nyuki*, bee's sting.
msumbi *n* (*wa-*) 1. a naughty person; an unruly person; scamp: *Msumbi alinisumbua sana*, the scamp hassled me alot. (cf *mtundu, mtukutu*) 2. troublemaker.
msumbufu *n* (*wa-*) a troublesome person, a person who causes annoyance; troublemaker.
msumeno *n* (*mi-*) carpenter's saw: *Msumeno duara*, circular saw. *Msumeno uta*, bow saw. *Msumeno wa mbao*, wood saw. *Msumeno wa chuma*, iron saw. 2 (*fig*) instrument: *Tume ya uchunguzi ilikuwa msumeno mkali kwa wahalifu*, the commission of enquiry was a potent instrument to the offenders.
msungo *n* (*wa-*) 1. an uninitiated girl. 2. a woman who does not respect her womanhood.
msungululu *n* (*mi-*) (*bot*) a scandent and twining shrub, bearing woody shaggy grey fruits containing numerous golden silky ovate seeds which produce an arrow poison. *Strophantus eminii*.
msungusungu *n* (*mi-*) (*bot*) a glabrous shrub or small tree with opposite or alternate obvate-oblong to oblong acuminate leaves and white or pink flowers, producing fruits which are said to be very toxic. *Rauvolfia rosea*.
msunguti[1] *n* (*mi-*) (*bot*) an evergreen tree with acute opposite leaves and clusters of reddish-pink long-tubular flowers, bearing an edible fleshy plum-like red fruit, much liked by elephants. *Acocanthera longiflora*.
msunguti[2] *adj* 1. a word used to emphasize the sharpness, strength, etc. of sth e.g. tobacco: *Tumbaku msunguti*, strong tobacco. 2. (*syn*) *Msunguti myomba wa doti ukiingia hautoki*, someone who is always scrounging off friends, etc. will not leave them because of the benefits he is getting.
msununu *n* (*wa-*) splenetic, sourpuss, a sulky person; a person fond of showing resentment, etc. against someone else: *Usimlete msununu yule kwenye tafrija yetu*, don't bring that sulky person to our reception. (cf *mnuni*)
msuraki *n* (*mi-*) a wooden peg in a paten (thick wooden sandal or clog) used for holding the clog on the feet.
msurubwete *n* (*mi-*) overall, apron. (cf *aproni, ovaroli, msurupwete*)
msurupwenye *n* (*mi-*) overall, apron. (cf *aproni, ovaroli*)
msururu *n* (*mi-*) queue, line: *Msururu wa magari*, a line of cars. (cf *foleni*)
msusa *n* (*mi-*) (*zool*) barracuda; a kind of fierce pipe-like fish of tropical seas (family *Sphyraenidae*) with cycloid scales on the body; some species are edible. (cf *mdalia, mgalia*)
msusi[1] (also *msonzi*) *n* (*wa-*) plaiter, braider; a person usu a woman who plaits hair of other people. (cf *msonzi*)
msusi[2] *n*(*wa-*) an expert in making

domestic utensils.

msusu[1] *n* (*mi-*) (*bot*) a kind of tree whose roots are used as a medicine for syphillis.

msusu[2] *n* (*mi-*) see *mkusi*

msusumo *n* (*mi-*) compulsion, force: *Imekuwa msusumo, sio tena hiari,* that has become a force and no longer voluntariness.

msuta *n* (*wa-*) accuser, impugner, traducer.

msutaji *n* (*wa-*) a person who makes charges openly on someone else for deceit or wrongdoing; a person who confronts someone openly in order to discredit him; traducer, impugner, accuser (cf *msudukishi*)

msutano *n* (*mi-*) face-to-face confrontation on charges of wrongdoing between two or more people

msuto *n* (*mi-*) act of charging sby openly for deceit or wrongdoing; impugnation, traducement.

msutu[1] *n* (*mi-*) a piece of cloth used as a curtain for concealing a bed; bed screen.

msutu[2] *n* (*mi-*) see *kisutu*

msuuzo[1] *n* (*mi-*) a wooden handle by which the stone is turned during grinding grain, etc.

msuuzo[2] *n* (*mi-*) the final washing of anything such as that of a garment, etc.; final rinse.

Mswahili *n* (*wa-*) 1. a person whose first language is Swahili. 2. a Swahili-speaking resident of the East African Coast and the neighbouring Islands to it. 3. (*syn*) a crafty person; a tricky person. (cf *mjanja, laghai*)

mswaki (also *msuaki*) *n* (*mi-*) 1. twig; a piece of stick which when chewed at the end, is used as a toothbrush: *Piga mswaki,* brush the teeth. 2. toothbrush. 3. (*bot*) dwarf shrubs with very stiff fibrous stems whose branches are used for making toothbrushes. 4. (*syn*) a simple thing to be done: *Hesabu zile zilikuwa mswaki,* those arithmetic sums were simple. (cf *bunga*) (Ar)

mswala (also *msala*) *n* (*mi-*) prayer rug; prayer mat. (*prov*) *Usiache mbachao kwa mswala upitao,* don't leave your old friend for the sake of getting a temporary one. (Ar)

mswalihina *n* (*wa-*) a devout Muslim. (Ar)

mswele *n* (*mi-*) (*zool*) boxcrab, shy crab; a kind of crab of mottled greyish-green colour which can fold its walking legs, and lives in various soft substrates in eulittoral and shallow sublittoral, often burrowing in sand. *Cellapa hepatico.* (cf *kifukulile*)

mtaa *n* (*mi-*) town quarter, town division, avenue, street, subdivision; a block of houses,

mtaala *n* (*mi-*) studies, curriculum, (cf *masomo*) (Ar)

mtaalamu *n* (*wa-*) scholar, expert; an educated person, (cf *aalim, mjuzi*)

mtaaradhi *n* (*wa-*) 1. a person who does not value what others are doing; a discontented person; malcontent: *Mtaaradhi hataridhika na kila unalolifanya,* the person who never values what others are doing will never be contented with what you are doing. (cf *mnywanywa*) 2. a person who questions about the validity of many issues, (Ar)

mtaba *n* (*mi-*) (*bot*) the dry bark of a banana plant that is scraped and cut in order to wrap tobacco. (cf *tapa*)

mtabiri *n* (*wa-*) 1. soothsayer, foreteller, forecaster, prophet, fortune teller. (cf *mbashiri*) 2. an interpreter of dreams: *Ndoto yangu ilifasiriwa na mtabiri,* my dream was interpreted by a soothsayer. (Ar)

mtadaruki *n* (*wa-*) busybody, gossipper; *Mtadaruki alishughulika kwenye harusi ambayo haikumhusu,* the busybody involved himself in the wedding that did not concern him. (cf *kimbelembele*) (Ar)

mtafara (also *mtafura*) *n* (*mi-*) crupper; a leather strap attached to a saddle or harness and passed under the tail of a horse, donkey, etc.

mtafaruku *n* (*mi-*) pandemonium, chaos, uproar: *Mtafaruku ulitokea shuleni wakati mwalimu alipompiga mwanafunzi na kumwumiza vibaya*, pandemonium occurred in the school when the teacher beat the student and badly harmed him. (cf *fujo, ghasia*)

mtafitafi *n* (*wa-*) see *mtapitapi*

mtafiti *n* (*wa-*) researcher (cf *mchunguzi*)

mtafuno *n* (*mi-*) act (style, method, etc.) of chewing: *Mtafuno wake wa chakula unakereketa*, his way of chewing food is disgusting.

mtafura *n* (*mi-*) see *mtafara*

mtago *n* (*mi-*) 1. (of a hen, bird, etc.) act of laying eggs. 2. the period when a hen lay eggs: *Kuku wangu amemalizia mayai kumi katika mtago huu*, my hen has finished laying ten eggs this time.

mtaguso *n* (*mi-*) (in Christianity) ecumenical council.

mtahini *n* (*wa-*) examiner: *Mtahini aliutunga mtihani mgumu*, the examiner set a difficult examination. *Mtahini wa ndani*, internal examiner. *Mtahini wa nje*, external examiner. (Ar)

mtahiniwa *n* (*wa-*) examinee, candidate. (Ar)

mtai (also *mtaya*) *n* (*mi-*) a slight cut; scratch: *Piga mtai*, make a scratch; scarify. (cf *mchanjo, mkato*)

mtaimbo (also *mtarimbo*) *n* (*mi-*) iron crowbar; jemmy. *Mtarimbo kemu*, camshaft.

mtaji *n* (*mi-*) 1. (business) capital: *Mtaji geu*, floating capital. *Mtaji wa kudumu*, fixed capital. 2. assets. 3. seeds used as counters in a game of checkers. (Ar)

mtaka (also *mtakaji*) *n* (*wa-*) one who wants, asks, begs, etc. (*prov*) *Mtaka yote hukosa yote*, he who begs for everything, gets nothing.

mtakadamu *n* (*wa-*) founder, pioneer; a person who initiates sth. (cf *mwasisi*,

mtangulizi) (Ar)

mtakaji *n* (*wa-*) see *mtaka*

mtakasika *adj* (esp of God) infallible (cf *mtakata*)

mtakaso *n* (*mi-*) cleansing: *Mtakaso wa najisi ile haukukamilika*, the cleansing of that impurity was not complete.

mtakata *adj* perfect, infallible. used in the expression: *Mungu mtakata*, the infallible God.

mtakatifu *n* (*wa-*) 1. a clean person with respect to his deeds; a pure person; a holy person: *Baba mtakatifu*, Holy father. 2. a devout person; a pious person: *Mtakatifu aliwaongoza watu katika ibada*, the pious person led people in prayers. (cf *mtawa, walii*)

mtakato *n* (*wa-*) 1. cleanliness, neatness, tidiness. (cf *unadhifu*) 2. (in a game of draughts/checkers) a game which does not allow you to win the flat pieces of your opponent.

mtakawa *n* (*mi-*) (*bot*) a small tree commonly found on tropical sea shores in Zanzibar, which produces good timber used in boat building, cabinet making, gun stocks, etc. *Thespesia populnea*.

mtakwimu *n* (*wa-*) statitician: *Mtakwimu bima*, actuary; a person whose work is to calculate statistically risks, premiums, etc. for insurance. (Ar)

mtalaa *n* (*mi-*) 1. studies. (cf *masomo*) 2. continuing education; adult education. (Ar)

mtalaka *n* (*wa-*) a divorcee or a divorced husband: *Mary ni mtalaka wa Peter*, Mary is the divorcee of Peter. (Ar)

mtalaleshi[1] *n* (*wa-*) tale-bearer, tattler, eavesdropper: *Mtalaleshi alizieneza siri za watu*, the telltale spread the secrets of the people. (cf *mbeya, sabasi*)

mtalaleshi[2] *n* (*wa-*) 1. prostitute; a woman who is sexually promiscuous. (cf *malaya, hawara*) 2. pimp, procurer. (cf *kuwadi*)

mtalawanda *n* (*mi-*) see *mtarawanda*

mtale *n* (*mi-*) a very sharp knife.

mtalendu *n* (*mi-*) (*bot*) a much-branched evergreen tree, bearing small round fleshy orange fruits. *Teclea sp.*
mtali *n* (*mi-*) an anklet worn usu by women as a kind of ornament. (cf *kugesi, furungu*)
mtalii *n* (*wa-*) tourist (Ar)
mtaliki *n* (*wa-*) a man who grants a divorce. (Ar)
mtama *n* (*mi-*) 1. (*bot*) millet plant; Guinea corn. *Sorghum sp. Mtama mtindi*, young half-grown millet. *Mtama tele*, millet with grain formed but not fully ripe. Various kinds of millet are known locally. These include *felefele, fumba, kibakuli, shunzi* and *karachi.* 2. *Mtama mwitu*, wild Guinea corn plant, *Sorghum arundinacaum.* 3. grain obtained from these plants. (*prov*) *Penye kuku wengi usimwage mtama*, where there are many hens, don't distribute millet i.e. where there are many people, don't disclose your secret.
mtamalaki *n* (*wa-*) owner, possessor. (cf *mmiliki*)
mtamanifu *n* (*wa-*) 1. a covetous person; a greedy person. 2. a person who expects sth.
mtamba *n* (*mi-*) (*zool*) 1. heifer. (cf *mfarika*) 2. a person who boasts.
mtambaa (also *mtambazi*) *n* (*mi-*) (*bot*) a creeping climbing plant or liane.
mtambaachi *n* (*wa-*) (*zool*) snake (cf *nyoka*)
mtambaajongo *n* (*mi-*) (*bot*) a tree with a black trunk and small leaves used in making the handles of hoes, etc.
mtambaapanya (also *uati*) *n* (*mi-*) a pole which is placed along the roof of a house; cross beam. (cf *ndakaka*)

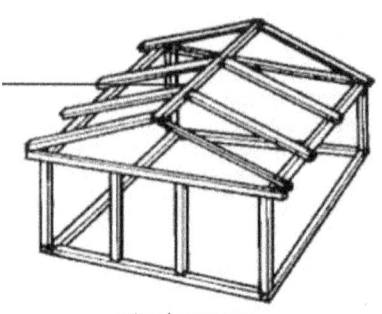

mtambaapanya

mtambaanyuki *n* (*mi-*) see *mvumanyuki*
mtambachi *n* (*mi-*) (*bot*) a short-lived succulent perennial prostrate herb, usu found in wet places and swampy ground and which produces salt. *Pentodon pentandrus.*
mtambaji *n* (*wa-*) 1. narrator. 2. a boastful person; braggart: *Mtambaji alijisifu hadharani*, the braggart boasted about himself in public. (cf *mjigambi, majisifu*)
mtambao *n* (*mi-*) act (style, etc.) of creeping; crawling.
mtambatamba *n* (*wa-*) braggart (cf *mjigambi*)
mtambo[1] *n* (*mi-*) 1. spring, trigger: *Mtambo wa saa*, watch spring. *Mtambo wa bunduki*, the lock of a gun. 2. the sides of a weaving frame. 3. engine, machine, plant; a piece of machinery or equipment: *Mtambo wa umeme*, electricity plant. *Mtambo wa nyuklia*, nuclear plant. (cf *mashine*) 4. printing press.
mtambo[2] *n* (*mi-*) delta; a deposit of sand and soil, enclosed or crossed by branches of a river.
mtambo[3] *n* (*n*) length, tallness: *Yeye ni mtambo wa kimo*, he is tall and sturdy.
mtambo[4] *n* (*wa-*) a rope for pulling nets. (cf *mlezi*)
mtambuu *n* (*mi-*) (*bot*) betel paper plant. *Piper betel.* (Hind, Pers)

mtanabahisho *n* (*mi-*) perceptiveness, awareness, alertness, attention drawing: *Mtanabahisho wako umenisaidia katika shughuli zangu*, your perceptiveness has assisted me in my activities. (cf *mzinduo*) (Ar)

mtanange *n* (*mi-*) (*colloq*) contest, match, competition. (cf *pambano*)

mtanashati *n* (*wa-*) 1. a well-dressed person, a neat person: dandy: *Angalia nguo alizovaa mtanashati yule*, look at the clothes that dandy has worn. (cf *mmbeja, mnadhifu*) 2. a cheerful person; a vivacious person: *Umeyapenda mazungumzo ya yule mtanashati?* Have you liked the conversation of the cheerful person? (cf *mchangamfu, bashasha*)

mtanato *n* (*mi-*) (*bot*) a tree or plank laid as a bridge across a stream. (cf *mtatago*)

mtanda[1] (also *mtande*) *n* (*mi-*) a strip of flesh or fish, hung up to dry in the sun or by a fire: *Nyama ya mtanda*, the meat made by this process.

mtanda[2] *n* (*mi-*) weaver's loom; threads of the warp of a loom.

mtandaji *n* (*wa-*) 1. a person who fishes by using nets. 2. a person who arranges his bed clothes by ropes.

mtandakanga *n* (*wa-*) see *mlangamia*

mtandao *n* (*mi-*) network: *Mtandao wa telefoni*, telephone network: *Mitandao ya kompyuta*, computer networks. *Mtandao wa mawasiliano*, communication network.

mtande *n* (*mi-*) see *mtanda*[1]

mtandio *n* (*mi-*) 1. shawl; a cloth worn by women as a covering for the head or shoulders. 2. a thin cloth used as a covering for oneself or for wearing over the shoulders.

mtanga *n* (*mi-*) beach sand.

Mtang'ata *n* (*n*) (*geog*) a coastal area of the South of Tanga in Tanzania where the Swahili dialect *Kimtang'ata* is spoken.

mtangawizi *n* (*mi-*) (*bot*) ginger plant; a kind of low growing herbaceous perennial plant bearing ginger which is used as a spice or perfume and in medicine, etc. *Zingiber officinale*.

mtangazaji *n* (*wa-*) broadcaster, announcer, advertiser: *Mtangazaji wa redio*, radio announcer.

mtange[1] *n* (*mi-*) the beam of a pair of scales for weighing with; the crossbar of a balance. (cf *mizani*)

mtange[2] *n* (*mi-*) see-saw game; a game played by children using a plank balanced on a support at the middle such that they ride at the ends so that when one goes up, the other comes down.

mtango *n* (*mi-*) (*bot*) cucumber plant. *Cucumis sativus*.

mtangulizi *n* (*wa-*) predecessor, precursor, forerunner; one who held a job or office before the current holder: *Rais wa sasa ni kiongozi mwadilifu pamoja na watangulizi wake*, the current president is a good leader as well as his predecessors. (cf *mtakadamu*)

mtanguo (also *mtenguo*) *n* (*mi-*) invalidation, revocation, annulment: *Mtanguo wa mkataba wa kocha wa kigeni ulitwaadhi wachezaji*, the invalidation of the contract of the foreign coach angered the players. (cf *mbatilisho*)

mtani *n* (*wa-*) a person with whom one has a joking relationship.

mtanuko *n* (*mi-*) expansion: *Mtanuko eneo*, superficial expansion. *Mtanuko unyevu*, moisture expansion.

mtanzaji *n* (*wa-*) a person or animal which is unapproachable because he or it is feared.

Mtanzania *n* (*wa-*) Tanzanian

mtanzi *n* (*wa-*) a person who fishes sardines or fish by using a selvage pulled by more than one person.

mtapa *n* (*mi-*) reed (cf *kitete, nari, kilimi*)

mtapaji *n* (*wa-*) a boastful person; braggart. (cf *mjigambi*)

mtapanyiko *n* (*mi-*) dispersion, spread: *Mtapanyiko wa watu*, the dispersion of people. (cf *mtawanyiko*)

mtapatapaji *n* (*wa-*) a person who is unstable; an unstable person. (cf *mtapitapi*)

mtapisha *n* (*mi-*) emetic; medicine or substance causing someone to vomit.

mtapisho (also *mtapishi*) *n* (*mi-*) (*bot*) a scandent shrub with alternate membranous leaves and tabular flowers, used as a medicine for vomiting. *Synaptolepis sp.*

mtapitapi (also *mtafitafi*) *n* (*wa-*) 1. a worried person, a nervous person; fidget: *Amekuwa mtapitapi tangu kuzisikia habari zenyewe*, he has become worried since he heard the news. 2. a two-faced person; chameleon, turncoat: *Wewe bado unamwamini mtapitapi yule?* You still trust that turncoat? (cf *lumbwi*)

mtapo¹ *n* (*mi-*) (*bot*) false sago palm; a cycad or a tropical shrub or tree bearing fruits which are powdered to a flour and used as porridge. *Cycas circinalis*.

mtapo² (also *kitapo*) *n* (*mi-*) body shivering because of cold, fear, illness, etc.: *Alishikwa na mtapo aliposikia mnong'ono kwamba polisi watakuja kumkamata*, he was filled with fear when he heard that the police would come to arrest him. (cf *kitapo, mtetemeko*)

mtapo³ *n* (*mi-*) ore; any combination of minerals, esp one from which a metal can be extracted. (cf *mbale*)

mtapta *n* (*wa-*) interpreter (cf *mkalimani*)

mtarawanda (also *mtalawanda, mtawanda, tarawanda*) *n* (*mi-*) a kind of thick pointed wooden sandal or clog worn indoors usu by women for going to the toilet, etc.: patten

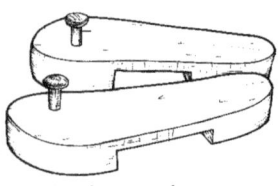

mtarawanda

mtaraza *n* (*mi-*) a mark made by drawing a line; groove, stripe, furrow. (cf *mfuo*)

mtarijumani¹ *n* (*wa-*) interpreter (cf *mkalimani*) (Ar)

mtarijumani² *n* (*wa-*) an ornamental weaver in dresses.

mtarimbo *n* (*mi-*) see *mtaimbo*

mtarizi *n* (*wa-*) weaver (cf *mfumaji, mshonaji*) (Ar)

mtaro *n* (*mi-*) ditch, trench. (cf *mfereji*)

mtasbihi *n* (*mi-*) (*bot*) 1. wild Indian shot; a perennial herb with dark green leaves and racemes of flowers, bearing black hard seeds which are the size of peas, used as beads to keep count of the names of God, etc. *Canna bidentata*. 2. a perennial grass growing in wet places, having fairly large white or grey hard-skinned oval seeds used for beads. *Coix lachryma-Jobi*.

mtashi *n* (*wa-*) a person who is need of sth very badly; beggar. (*syns*) *Mtashi hana haya*, a person who is in badly need of sth is shameless i.e if you are in need of sth very badly, you will beg. *Mtashi hana kinyongo; ajapo waswa, hakomi*, a beggar who is in need will continue to beg even if he is advised not to do so.

mtata (also *gonasokola*) *n* (*mi-*) 1. (*bot*) a shrub with alternate leaves from which good firebrands are made. *Acalypha sp.* 2. a spiny shrub or tree with aromatic pinnate alternate leaves. *Fagara sp.*

mtatago *n* (*mi-*) a tree or plank laid as a bridge across a stream. (cf *mtanato, ulalo*)

mtatizi *n* (*wa-*) a troublesome person, a person fond of causing hardships, problems, etc.; troublemaker. (cf *msumbufu*)

mtatuo *n* (*mi-*) act (method, etc.) of tearing cloth, paper, etc.; rip: *Mtatuo wa barua yake unatokana na hasira alizokuwa nazo*, the tearing up of her letter came as a result of her anger.

mtatuzi *n* (*wa-*) a person who can solve his problems when the need arises; solver.

mtawa (also *mtawaji*) *n* (*wa-*) 1. a cloistered person usu a woman; a person usu a woman living in a secluded life; stay-at-home: *Amekuwa mtawa kutokana na amri za wazee wake*, she has been living a cloistered life on orders from her parents. 2. a devout religious person; recluse, dervish. *Mtawa haandamani na anasa za ulimwengu*, a devout religious person does not hanker after worldly pleasures. (cf *walii, sufii*)

mtawafu *n* (*wa-*) a person leading those who go for pilgrimage. (Ar)

mtawaji *n* (*wa-*) see *mtawa*

mtawala *n* (*wa-*) ruler, administrator: *Mtawala wa kinasaba*, dynast (cf *mfalme, malkia*)

mtawalia (also *mtawalio*) *adv* an expletive used to describe the succession of events: *Mvua ilinyesha siku mbili mtawalia*, it rained two days continuously.

mtawaliwa *n* (*wa-*) the ruled, the governed.

mtawande *n* (*mi-*) see *mtarawanda*

mtawanyiko *n* (*mi-*) dispersion, spread: *Mtawanyiko wa watu kutoka mkutanoni ulichukua dakika chache tu baada ya kutupwa bomu la machozi*, the dispersion of the people from the meeting took only a few minutes after the tear-gas canister exploded. (cf *msambao, mtapanyiko*)

mtawanyo *n* (*mi-*) scattering, spread, dispersion. (cf *uenezaji*)

mtaya *n* (*mi-*) see *mtai*

mtazamaji *n* (*wa-*) viewer, observer, spectator: *Watazamaji walikuwa wakizishangilia timu zao*, the spectators were cheering their teams.

mtazamo *n* (*mi-*) 1. looking, watching, gazing: *Mtazamo wake kwenye darubini ulikosa utulivu*, his way of looking through the binoculars lacked concentration. 2. opinion, attitude, viewpoint: *Mtazamo hasi*, negative attitude. *Mtazamo chanya*, positive attitude. *Mtazamo wake juu ya lugha za Kiafrika si mzuri*, his attitude towards African languages is negative. (cf *msimamo, mwangalio, mwelekeo*)

mtegaji (also *mtegeaji*) *n* (*wa-*) 1. a person who avoids work deliberately; skiver, dodger; *Mtegaji alisimamishwa kazi*, the skiver was suspended from work. 2. trapper; a person who traps animals, human beings, etc.

mtegano *n* (*mi-*) act (method, etc.) of trapping one another.

mtege *n* (*wa-*) see *mteja*[1]

mtegeaji *n* (*wa-*) see *mtegaji*

mtego *n* (*mi-*) trap, snare: *Tega mtego*, set a trap. (*prov*) *Mtego wa panya huingia aliyekuwemo na asiyekuwemo*, don't get involved in matters that don't concern you because if trouble comes, you will be caught in difficulties together with those who got involved in the conflict. (cf *utegaji*)

mtegwa *n* (*wa-*) one who is trapped. (cf *mtegwaji*)

mteja (also *mtege, mteje*) *n* (*wa-*) 1. a person who is being exorcized in a local witchcraft. 2. client, customer: *Huduma zinazotolewa kwa wateja katika duka hili ni mbovu*, the services rendered to customers at this shop are poor. (cf *mshitiri, mnunuzi*)

mteji *n* (*wa-*) see *mteja*

mteka *n* (*wa-*) one who takes away: *Mteka maji*, a drawer of water. *Mteka nyara*, hijacker.

mteke *n* (*wa-*) 1. a person whose body is still soft because of his youthfulness and that he cannot do manual work.

2. coward, craven; a person who lacks courage: *Mteke hawezi kwenda kupigana vitani*, a coward cannot go to war to fight. (cf *hawafu*)
mtema¹ *n* (*wa-*) a person who makes a decision or passes a judgement; judge, magistrate.
mtema² *n* (*wa-*) used with another word to form a compound noun: *Mtema kuni*, wood cutter. (*syn*) *Utaona cha mtema kuni*, you will regret it.
mtema³ *n* (*mi-*) a cleared forest turned now to a plantation. (cf *chenge*)
mtemaji *n* (*wa-*) 1. a person who clears a forest in order to get a plantation. 2. a person who drops sth down from his mouth.
mtemba *n* (*mi-*) smoking tobacco pipe. (cf *kiko, toza*)
mtembeaji *n* (*wa-*) a street walker.
mtembezi *n* (*wa-*) 1. street walker; wanderer. (*prov*) *Mtembezi hula miguu yake*, a wanderer consumes his own legs i.e if you dont stick to one occupation, you wouldn't gain in anything. 2. prostitute, harlot. (cf *hawara, malaya*)
mtembo¹ (also *mtombo, mtombwe*) *n* (*mi-*) (*bot*) the top shoot of a coconut tree.
mtembo² *n* (*mi-*) (*med*) crack in the hard skin of the soles of the feet caused by yaws or other diseases.
mtembo³ *n* (*n*) hymen rapture causing heavy bleeding.
mtemi *n* (*wa-*) 1. the title of a local ruler in some tribes in Tanzania. 2. a giant of a man. (cf *mbabe*)
mtemo *n* (*mi-*) act (method, etc.) of cutting sth; split: *Mtemo wa kuni*, the splitting of firewood.
mtendaji *n* (*wa-*) doer, performer: *Katibu mtendaji*, executive secretary.
mtendawema *n* (*wa-*) benefactor
mtende¹ *n* (*mi-*) (*bot*) date palm tree. *Phoenix dactylifera*.
mtende² *n* (*wa-*) a handsome person; a beautiful woman: *Wavulana wengi wanataka kumwoa mtende yule*, many boys want to get married to that beautiful woman.
mtende³ *n* (*wa-*) Used in the expression: *Bahati ya mtende*, a very lucky person.
mtendikani *n* (*mi-*) (*naut*) upper thwarts esp in *mtepe*, a kind of sailing vessel.
mtenga *n* (*mi-*) a carrying stick or pole used across the shoulders for balancing heavy loads on each side; lever. (cf *mpiko, mzegazega*)
mtengano *n* (*mi-*) separation, disintegration, split, isolation. (cf *mfarakano, utengano*)
mtenge *n* (*mi-*) an outrigger of a canoe.

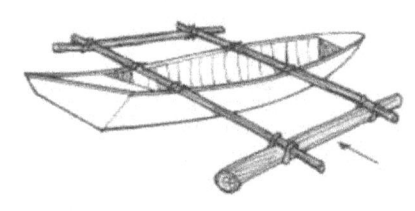

mtenge

mtengenezaji (also *mtengezaji*) *n* (*wa-*) 1. mender, repairer: *Mtengenezaji wa saa*, watch repairer. *Mtengenezaji wa baiskeli*, bicycle repairer. *Mtengenezaji wa magari*, mechanic. *Mtengenezaji sanamu*, sculptor; *Mtengenezaji wa nywele*, coiffeur. 2. producer, manufacturer, maker: *Watengenezaji wa bidhaa hizi ni watu kutoka nje*, the manufacturers of these goods are foreigners.
mtengeza *n* (*wa-*) mender, repairer, a person who repairs; a person who repairs. (*syn*) *Mtengeza jambo ni Mungu*, a person who put things in order is God. (cf *mtengenezaji*)
mtengezaji *n* (*wa-*) mender, repairer. (cf *mtengeza, mtengenezaji*)
mtengo¹ *n* (*mi-*) act (method, etc.) of separating, dividing, etc.; division, separation: *Mtengo wa wanafunzi*

katika makundi haya mawili umeinufaisha shule, the division of students into these two groups has benefitted the school. (cf *utengaji*)

mtengo² *n (mi-)* 1. a place where people sit for conversation. 2. a board where people sit on for such a purpose. 3. conversation by many people.

mtengwa¹ *n (wa-)* a person who lives by himself in a lonely or secluded life often for religious motives e.g. prophet

mtengwa² *n (wa-)* a person selected as a nominee for a particular important issue in the community.

mtenzi *n (wa-)* 1. a person who has the capacity and experience to do a particular thing: *Kama wewe ni mtenzi, basi tenda*. if you are the doer, do it. 2. a composer of poems, songs, etc. *Yeye ni mtenzi wa mashairi*, he is a composer of poems.

mteo (also *mcheu*) *n (mi-)* the act of boiling food until it is partly cooked and then removing it from the fire before it is properly done; parboil: *Pika mteo*, cook in this manner; parboil.

mtepe *n (mi-) (naut)* a kind of sewn boat of up to 30 tons, double-ended and with an upright mast, hoisting a square matting sail.

mtepetevu *n (wa-)* idler, loafer; a lazy person: *Mtepetevu yule hakuonyesha bidii katika kazi yangu*, that idler did not put effort into my work. (cf *mzembe, mkunguni*)

mterehemeshi (also *mteremezi*) *n (wa-)* a jovial person; a vivacious person; a cheerful person. (cf *bashashi*)

mterehemezi *n (mi-)* one of the names of God; the merciful.

mteremezi *n (wa-)* see *mterehemeshi*

mteremko *n (mi-)* 1. slope, incline, decline: *Pana mteremko hapo kwenye mwisho wa barabara*, there is a slope there at the end of the road. (cf *mshtuko, mwinamo*) 2. (*colloq*) easy or free thing: *Amepata mteremko kwa kitu kile*, he has obtained that thing easily.

mteremo *n (mi-)* see *nderemo*

mtesi *n (wa-)* 1. backbiter. (cf *msengenyaji, mtetaji*) 2. a hostile person, a provocative person; wrangler: *Mtesi aligombana na majirani wake wengi*, the wrangler quarrelled with many of his neighbours. (cf *mgomvi, mshari*)

mtetaji *n (wa-)* 1. a hostile person, a provocative person; wrangler (cf *mgomvi*) 2. backbiter (cf *mtesi, msengenyaji*)

mtetea¹ *n (wa-) (zool)* a hen ready to lay eggs; layer hen. (cf *tembe*)

mtetea² *adj* ready to lay eggs: *Kuku mtetea*, a hen which is ready to lay eggs.

mtetea³ (also *mtetegji*) *n (wa-)* 1. a person who fights for the rights of people. 2. (esp in sports) a person who defends his victory.

mteteaji *n (wa-)* see *mtetea³*

mtetemeko (also *mtetemo*) *n (mi-)* 1. trembling because of fear, cold, etc.; quivering: *Mtetemeko wake wa mwili mzima ulisababishwa na baridi kali*, her quivering of the whole body was caused by severe cold. (cf *mtikiso*) 2. (of earth, etc.) vibration, shaking: *Mtetemeko wa ardhi*, earthquake. (cf *zilizala*)

mtetemo¹ *n (mi-)* see *mtetemeko*

mtetemo² *n (mi-)* vibration; singing with a soft voice.

mteteo *n (mi-)* soft singing.

mtetezi *n (wa-)* 1. defendant, advocate, supporter: *Mtetezi alimtetea mshtakiwa mahakamani*, the advocate defended the accused in the court. (cf *mtetea*) 2. representative of a constituency, etc.: *Alikuwa mtetezi wetu katika jimbo hili*, he was our representative in this constituency. (cf *mgombezi*)

mteule (also *mteuliwa*) *n (wa-)* an elected person but not yet installed; nominee: *Rais mteule*, president-elect.

mteuliwa *n (wa-)* see *mteule*

mteuzi *n* (*wa-*) 1. a picky person, a fastidious person, a dainty person; a person who is choosy or fussy: *Usiwe mteuzi sana unapokuwa unatafuta kazi*, don't be too choosy when you look for an employment. (*prov*) *Mteuzi heshi tamaa*, a picky person will always crave for things i.e. if you are too choosy, you will always want to select this and that and end up getting inferior things. 2. a person who has the authority to appoint someone in a particular situation.

mthibitishaji *n* (*wa-*) affirmant, affirmer; a person who affirms sth.

mti¹ *n* (*mi-*) 1. tree: *Kilele cha mti*, tree top. *Shina la mti*, tree trunk. 2. tree material such as wood, timber, etc.: *Kijiko cha mti*, a wooden spoon. *Mlango wa mti*, a wooden door. 3. part of a tree that has been prepared for use e.g. log, pole, post, etc (*prov*) *Mti hauendi ila kwa nyenzo*, a tree does operate without the basic resources i.e for anything to acquire success, it needs good preparations.

mti² *n* (*mi-*) (*med*) dermatosclerosis, sclerosis cutanea, scleroderma; a chronic disease in which there is thickening of the skin caused by swelling of fibrous tissue, with eventual atrophy of the epidermis (cf *mafindomafindo*)

mtia¹ (also *mtiaji*) *n* (*wa-*) one who puts or applies sth else: *Mtia rangi*, painter. *Mtia dawa*, one who applies medicine, etc.

mtia² *n* (*mi-*) crest: *Mtia wa wimbi*, wave crest.

mtiaji *n* (*wa-*) see *mtia¹*

mtifuano *n* (*mi-*) contest, match, competition meet (cf *pambano, shindano, mtanange*)

mtihaki *n* (*mi-*) final decision on particular issues; final verdict.

mtihani *n* (*mi-*) 1. examination, test: *Mtihani wa taifa*, national examination. *Mtihani wa kuingilia*, entrance examination. *Mtihani wa kupima vipaji*, aptitude test. 2. trial from God; divine trial; hardship, suffering, etc. that tries one's endurance as a test of faith to his God: *Mungu amewawekea waja wake mitihani mingi*, God has given his beings many trials. (cf *msukosuko, mwonjo*)

mtii (also *mtiifu*) *n* (*wa-*) an obedient person; a dutiful person: *Mfanyakazi wangu ni mtiifu*, my worker is an obedient person.

mtiifu *n* (*wa-*) see *mtii*

mtikisa *n* (*wa-*) see *mtikisaji*

mtikisaji (also *mtikisa*) *n* (*wa-*) a person who shakes sth.

mtikisiko *n* (*mi-*) vibration, shaking, rocking, rolling, pitching: *Mtikisiko wa jahazi ulisababishwa na mawimbi makali*, the pitching of the dhow was caused by the strong waves. (cf *msukosuko*). *Mtikisiko wa kiuchumi*, economic crisis.

mtikiso *n* (*mi-*) act (style, etc.) of being pushed, shaken, etc.: *Mtikiso wa ndege ulimsumbua mgonjwa sana*, the rocking of the aircraft disturbed the patient a lot.

mtikiti *n* (*mi-*) (*bot*) water melon plant. *Citrullus vulgaris*.

mtilili *n* (*mi-*) (*zool*) bee eater; a kind of bird (family *Metropidae*) of slim and medium-sized body and brilliant plumage and a long slightly decurved bill and which feeds on bees and other insects. (cf *kidemakungu, kurea, mdiria*)

mtima *n* (*mi-*) heart (cf *moyo*)

mtimaji *n* (*mi-*) (*bot*) a tree, the seeds of which contain oil, used for cooking or for the manufacture of soap. *Trichilia emetica*. (cf *mkugwina*)

mtimbwiriko *n* (*mi-*) happiness resulting esp from a local dance: *Mtimbwiriko ulizagaa kwenye ngoma za kienyeji*, happiness prevailed in the traditional dances.

mtindapo *n* (*mi-*) (*bot*) a scandent evergreen shrub whose pliable stems are used in basket work. *Canthium gueizii*.

mtindi¹ n (mi-) 1. yoghurt. 2. butter milk; the sour liquid left after churning butter from milk. *Mtindi mtamu,* junket. 3. (syn) *Piga mtindi,* booze. (cf *pombe*)

mtindi² n (mi-) (bot) a soft tree like a pawpaw producing timber, used for making various things such as musical instruments.

mtindingilia (also *mtindigili*) n (mi-) (bot) a kind of a creeping plant bearing hard thorny short seeds.

mtindikani n (mi-) (naut) cross piece or thwart connecting the two gunwales and supporting the mast.

mtindio n (mi-) body damage: *Mtindio wa ubongo,* brain damage.

mtindo n (mi-) 1. manner of writing or speaking; style. 2. manner, social behaviour or appearance, etc.; style: *Ana mtindo mbaya wa kutukana watu hadharani,* he has a bad habit of insulting people in public. 3. fashion, esp in clothes; style: *Mtindo wa mshono huu unapendeza,* the style of this type of sewing is attractive. *Mtindo wa nywele,* hairstyle. *Mtindo wa muda,* fad.

mtingishiko n (mi-) shake, sway, jerk: *Mitingishiko ya miti ilisababishwa na upepo mkali,* the swaying of the trees was caused by the strong wind.

mtini¹ n (mi-) (bot) fig tree. *Ficus carica.*

mtini² n (wa-) an ignorant person; a rustic person, an uncouth person; philistine, bumpkin: *Mtini haelewi chochote,* the bumpkin does not understand anything. (cf *mshamba*)

mtipitipi n (mi-) (bot) a poisonous climbing plant with slender, almost thread-like stems and having pale pink pea-like flowers, bearing brilliant red and black seeds, some of which are used for beadwork and as goldsmiths' weights; crab eyes. *Abrus precatorius.* (cf *mturituri*)

mtiriri n (wa-) 1. a lascivious person; an erotic person; nymphomaniac. (cf *mkware*) 2. scamp; a naughty child: *Mtiriri alimsumbua mama yake,* the naughty child hassled her mother. (cf *mtukutu*)

mtiririko n (mi-) flow, trickle: *Mtiririko wa visa,* the flow of episodes. *Mtiririko wa maji,* the flow of water. *Mtiririko wa mambo,* the flow of events. (cf *mbubujiko*)

mti-sumu n (mi-) (bot) sausage tree. *Kigelia lanceolata.*

mti-ulaya n (mi-) (bot) iron wood tree. *Cassia siamea.*

mti wa mstari n (mi-) (bot) a perennial herb with trailing hollow stems cordate-orbicular glabrous leaves and many cymes of bright red funnel-shaped flowers. *Ipomoea repens.*

mtiririsho n (mi-) drainage

mtiti n (n-) (zool) a type of owl.

mtitigo n (mi-) the hardship that one undergoes during travelling in a car esp when there are potholes on the road; a jerk on a rough road.

mtitimo n (mi-) see *mtitio*

mtitio (also *mtitimo*) n (mi-) 1. submergence, sinking: *Mtitio wa ardhi,* the submergence of land. 2. the noise from the submerged land; hollow sound.

mto¹ n (mi-) river: *Ukingo wa mto,* river bank. *Mto mrefu,* balster. *Mkono wa mto,* tributary. *Mlango wa mto,* estuary. *Mto ule ulifurika mwaka jana,* that river flooded last year.

mto² n (mi-) pillow, cushion: *Mto wa sofa,* sofa pillow. *Mtot wa gari,* car pillow.

mtoano n (mi-) elimination, knock-out: *Mashindano ya mtoano,* knock-out competition. *Michuano ya mwisho ya Kombe la Dunia ilifanyika kwa njia ya mtoano,* the final matches of the World Cup took place on a knock-out basis.

mtobwe n (mi-) (bot) 1. a scandent shrub from which a favourite kind of walking stick is made. *Strophanthus courmuntii.* 2. a deciduous pubescent tree, the wood of which is used for making tool handles, and the bark from the young shoots is used for making rope. *Dombeya rotundifolia.*

3. a kind of a thin walking-stick.

mtofaa *n* (*mi-*) see *mtufaha*

mtoki *n* (*mi-*) (*med*) lymphadenitis; swelling of lymph nodes in the groin.

mtokoso *n* (*mi-*) boiling, broiling, seething: *Mtokoso wa muhogo ulitoa sauti kali*, the boiling of the cassava produced a lot of noise. (cf *mchemsho*)

mtokwe (also *mtopetope*) *n* (*mi-*) (*bot*) wild custard apple; a much-branched deciduous small tree or shrub whose roots are boiled with sour orange, used for stomach-ache and whose bark is pounded with water and used to dress woman's hair. *Annona chrysophylla*. (cf *mchekwa*)

mtolilo (also *mtoriro*) *n* (*mi-*) (*bot*) the leaf of a sweet potato plant, (*Ipomoea batatas*) used as green vegetable. (cf *matembele, mriba*)

mtombo[1] *n* (*mi-*) see *mtembo*[1]

mtombo[2] *n* (*mi-*) the act (style, etc.) of a man and a woman having sexual intercourse; copulation, coition. (cf *ngono*)

mtombwe *n* (*mi-*) see *mtembo*[1]

mtomeo *n* (*mi-*) a kind of mason's work of plastering a wall by using clay.

mtomo *n* (*mi-*) a kind of mason's work of reinforcing plaster work with small stones.

mtomoko[1] *n* (*mi-*) (*bot*) bullock's heart tree; a small spreading tree bearing a large brownish red round or heart-shaped fruit with sweet custard-like granular pulp. *Annona reticulata*.

mtomoko[2] *n* (*mi-*) (*bot*) a torn hole in a dress; fear, rip.

mtomondo *n* (*mi-*) 1. (*bot*) Malay apple tree; a pyramidal medium-sized tree bearing reddish pear-shaped fruit but white inside. *Eugenia malanccensis*. 2. a medium-sized much-branched tree common on the banks of streams in coastal districts having lanceolate leaves and greenish-yellow flowers whose bark is pounded to a powder and used as a fish poison. *Barringtonia racemosa*. 3. a much-branched tree with dark green glossy leathery opposite leaves and panicles of small white waxy flowers and hard globular fruits, bearing the seeds which yield oil of commercial importance. *Calophyllum inophyllum*.

mtomvi *n* (*wa-*) (*vul*) fucker (cf *mtombaji*)

mtondo[1] *n* (*mi-*) three days from today.

mtondo[2] *n* (*mi-*) see *mrihi*

mtondogoo *n* (*mi-*) three days from tomorrow; four days from today.

mtondoo[1] *n* (*mi-*) (*bot*) Alexandria laurel tree; a kind of a large evergreen tree, bearing a nut-like fruit whose seed yields a strongly-scented green oil used in medicine. Its wood is used locally for masts and planks for sailing ships and also for building purposes. *Calophyllum inophllum* (*syn*) *Mtondoo haufi maji*, Alexandrian tree never dies in water i.e. a stable or strong person never loses his integrity, position, etc.

mtondoo[2] *n* (*mi-*) (*idm*) *Piga mtondoo*, bail out water in a sinking vessel by pulling the stem and the prow.

mtondoo[3] *n* (*mi-*) a kind of old musket.

mtonesho[1] *n* (*mi-*) 1. reinjuring a sore, etc. 2. hurting, harming.

mtonesho[2] (also *utoneshaji*) *n* (*mi-*) (*phys*) condensation; the act of condensing, as the reduction of a gas to a liquid.

mtonga *n* (*mi-*) 1. (*bot*) a shrubby slightly spiny herb with stellate hairs bearing globose yellow berries. *Solanum obliquum*. 2. an erect tree with oblong opposite leaves and solitary flowers containing five to ten oblong yellow seeds. *Strychnos engleri*. 3. a glabrous tree bearing an orange shaped-like fruit whose pulp is edible. *Strychmos spinosa*.

mtonga-kima *n* (*mi-*) 1. (*bot*) mangrove. *Rhizophora mucronata*. 2. a much-branched glabrous evergreen tree having a green and white spotted fruit. *Voacanga thouarsii*.

mtongonya *n* (*mi-*) (*bot*) see *mgombakofi*

mtongotongo *n* (*mi-*) (*bot*) a kind of tree

with an abundant flow of milky latex, which causes intense irritation and temporary blindness if it enters the eye. *Eurphorbia abyssnica*.

mtopetope *n* (*mi-*) 1. see *mtokwe*. 2. sugar apple tree; sweet sop tree. *Annona squamosa*. (cf *mstafeli*)

mtori *n* (*n*) green banana soup having ground meat in it.

mtoria *n* (*mi-*) (*bot*) rubber vine; a woody climber with opposite, simple, elliptical or oblong leaves, bearing a smooth pear-shaped and apricot coloured fruit when ripe, containing about a dozen seeds covered with a sticky pulp. The vine produces a latex from which rubber may be prepared. *Landolphia petersiana*.

mtoriri *n* (*mi-*) the edge of a tarboosh or balaclava helmet.

mtoriro[1] *n* (*mi-*) (*mus*) the sound of flageolet which when blown, does not give any special song; irregular sound of a flute.

mtoriro[2] *n* (*mi-*) see *mtolilo*

mtoro *n* (*wa-*) truant, runaway.

mtoto *n* (*wa-*) 1. child, offspring; a child or animal as related to its parent: *Mtoto mchanga*, baby. *Mtoto wa batamaji*, cygnet. (*prov*) *Mtoto umleavyo ndivyo akuavyo*, if you bring up a child well, he will be a good person but if you do the opposite, your child will go astray. 2. used in the expressions: *Mtoto wa jicho*, cataract; an eye disease causing partial or total blindness. *Mtoto wa meza*, drawer. *Mtoto wa kasha*, shelf or inner compartment in a box. *Mtoto wa kitasa*, the ward of a lock. *Mtoto wa watu*, a child of good birth or a good family; a well-born child. *Mtoto wa kikopo*, an idle wandering child, an ill-mannered child; scamp. *Mtoto mwangavu*, an intelligent child. *Mtoto wa sanamu*, idol, effigy. (cf *mwanasesere*) *Mtoto wa nje*, an illegitimate child.

mtovu *n* (*wa-*) sby lacking a quality; someone deficient of a quality: *Mtovu wa haya*, sby deficient of shyness. *Mtovu wa adabu*, a person lacking in manners.

mtribu (also *mutribu*) *n* (*wa-*) singer or player of an instrument in a singing taarab group: *Mtribu aliwatumbuiza watazamaji*, the musician entertained the audience. (Ar)

mtu *n* (*wa-*) person (cf *mja*, *binaadamu*)

mtua *n* (*mi-*) see *mtunguja*

mtuatua *n* (*mi-*) see *mtunguja*

mtuchi *n* (*mi-*) (*med*) fibroid, fibroleiomyoma, leiomyofibroma; a type of benign tumour of fibrous and muscular tissue growing in the uterus of a woman causing her infertility ultimately.

mtufaa *n* (*mi-*) see *mtufaha*

mtufaha (also *mtufaa*) *n* (*mi-*) (*bot*) pommerac; a pyramidal medium-sized tree with large oblong, leathery, pointed leaves and brush-like flowers composed of many stamens and reddish, pear-shaped fruit, white inside. *Eugnia malaccensis*.

mtuhumiwa *n* (*wa-*) suspect: *Mtuhumiwa alifikishwa mahakamani kwa kosa la rushwa*, the suspect was brought before the court on charges of corruption. (cf *mshukiwa*) (Ar)

mtukufu *n* (*wa-*) 1. one of the attributes of Almighty God; the Glorious God. 2. the name given to a respected person. *Mtukufu Rais*, the honourable President; His or Her Excellency the President.

mtukutu *n* (*wa-*) a naughty person; jackanapes, scamp: *Mama alimpiga mwanawe aliye mtukutu*, the mother beat her naughty child. (*prov*) *Mwana mtukutu hali ugali mtupu*, a naughty child does not eat cooked maize meal alone i.e. without its relish. In other words, an energetic person never fails to accomplish his mission. (cf *muharabu*, *nunda*, *mtundu*)

mtukuu *n* (*wa-*) see *kitukuu*

mtula n (mi-) (bot) Indian Rennet; a spiny shrub up to 5ft tall with dense stellate hairs bearing a yellow sub-globose fruit up to 5 inches in diameter. *Solanum incanum.*

mtule¹ n (wa-) a poor person; destitute, pauper: *Majirani walimsaidia mtule yule kwa hali na mali,* the neighbours helped that poor person by all means. (cf *fukara, mkata, masikini*)

mtule² n(mi-) (bot) a kind of tree which has numerous, inconspicuous tiny flowers, whose leaves and seeds are used as a pot herb; its infusion of the leaves is used medicinally for stomach troubles by local women and the dried plant is used as a mosquito repellent. The leaves yield an essential oil by distillation. *Ocimum canum.*

mtulinga n (mi-) (anat) collarbone; clavicle: *Kazi ya mtulinga,* hard labour. (cf *sulubu*)

mtulivu n (wa-) a composed person; a calm person; a cool person: *Rais wao ni mtulivu,* their president is a composed person.

mtulwa n (mi-) see *mtunguja*

mtumba n (mi-) 1. bale, bundle: *Hii ni mitumba ya nguo,* these are bundles of clothes. (cf *furushi*) 2. (colloq) *mitumba,* second-hand clothes: *Anauza mitumba,* he sells second-hand clothes.

mtumbaku n (mi-) (bot) tobacco plant. *Nicotiana tabacum.*

mtumbati n (mi-) (bot) a much-branched deciduous tree, producing timber. *Pterocarpus bussei.* (cf *mninga, mpagata*)

mtumbwi n (mi-) kayak, dug-out canoe: *Walisafiri kwa mtumbwi,* they travelled by canoe. (cf *kihori, dau*)

mtume n (mi-) prophet: *Mtume Muhammad,* Prophet Muhammad. (cf *nabii, rasuli*)

mtumiaji n (wa-) consumer, user: *Mtumiaji madawa,* drug addict: *Mtumiaji wa bidhaa muhimu,* a consumer of essential commodities.

mtumishi n (wa-) servant: *Mtumishi wa serikali,* civil servant. *Mtumishi wa umma,* public servant. *Mtumishi wa nyumbani,* domestic servant. *Mtumishi wa kanisani,* acolyte. *Mtumishi wa kazi zote,* factotum (cf *hadimu*)

mtumwa n (wa-) slave: *Biashara ya watumwa,* slave trade.

mtundu n (wa-) 1. jackanape, scamp, rascal; an unruly person: *Mtoto wako ni mtundu,* your child is a scamp. (cf *nunda, mtukutu, msumbi*) 2. an inventive person such as a mechanic who is discovering new methods of repairing a car, etc.; a creative skilled person: *Fundi wa magari huyu ni mtundu,* this mechanic is a creative skilled workman.

mtunduizi n (wa-) guardian, trustee, supervisor, superintendent: *Mtunduizi alishughulikia mambo ya kampuni vizuri,* the supervisor oversaw the company's affairs well. (cf *kabidhi*)

mtunga n (wa-) a person who composes or writes sth. (cf *mtungaji*)

mtungaji n (wa-) 1. composer 2. author, writer. (cf *mwaandishi*)

mtungi n (mi-) clay water pot; earthen pitcher; crock: *Mtungi wangu hauna maji,* my earthen pitcher has no water in it.

mtungo n (mi-) 1. string, line, rope: *Mtungo wa shanga,* a string of beads. *Mtungo wa samaki,* a string of fish. 2. essay, composition: *Mtungo wa mwanafunzi wako ni mzuri,* your student's essay is good. (cf *insha*)

mtunguja (also *mtulwa, mtaa, mtuatua*) n (mi-) (bot) a spiny shrub, bearing a small roundish yellowish fruit when ripe. *Solanum trepidans. Mtunguja mwitu,* Indian Rennet. *Solanum incanum.* (cf *mngogwe*)

mtungule n (mi-) (bot) tomato plant. *Solanum lycopersicum.*

mtunguo n (mi-) 1. act (method, etc.) of lowering sth from the top by using a stick. 2. clothes hung in a shop for

mtunza

sale; ready-made clothes hung in a shop for sale. (cf *mpachuo*) 3. the shooting down of sth that is in the air e.g aircraft.

mtunza *n* (*wa-*) keeper, custodian.

mtunzi *n* (*wa-*) 1. composer, author; *Mtunzi wa shairi hili ni Fatuma Toti*, the composer of this poem is Fatuma Toti. (cf *mtungaji, mwandishi*) 2. author, writer: *Yeye ni mtunzi wa tamthilia nyingi*, he is the author of many plays. (cf *mtungaji*)

mtupa *n* (*mi-*) a general term applied to most plants used as fish poison: 1. a leafless succulent herb with grey-green stems which contain a milky latex. *Cynaclum sarcostemmatoides.* 2. milk bush; a leafless succulent tree with small yellow green flowers and trilocular fruits, used medicinally and as a protective hedge on account of its very caustic latex which on entering the eyes, will cause intense pain and probably injury. *Euphorbia tirucalli.* 3. fish poison plant; a shrub with greyish-greenish leaves and white or purple pea-like flowers and woody hairy pods. *Tephorsia vogellii.* 4. *Mtupa wa pori*, a shrub, used as a fish poison and which is said to be so strong that fish poisoned by it are often eaten with fatal results. *Mundulea sericea.* 5. *Mtupa wa pwani*, a shrub with silvery branches, pea-like flowers and yellow pods found on sandy sea shores in sheltered situations. The toxic contents of the leaves and stems of this plant are dissolved in the water and cause fish to float stomach upwards on the surface in an intoxicated condition. *Saphora tomentosa.*

mtupio *n* (*mi-*) 1. act (method, etc.) of throwing down a garment esp, carelessly on the shoulders; casual wrap over the shoulders: *Vazi la mtupio*, a well-known garment which is

mtwa

just thrown in any way. 2. the keeping or arrangement of things such that you leave space between them.

mtupo *n* (*mi-*) projection

mtura *n* (*mi-*) (*bot*) a shrub with ovate or elliptic leaves and purple flowers, bearing long yellowish globose fruits. The fruit pulp is applied to warts, bleeding wounds and toothaches and the fruit juice is used to clot milk by the Boran in Kenya. *Solanum bojeri.* (cf *mtunguja*)

mturituri[1] *n* (*mi-*) (*bot*) crab's eyes; a climbing plant with slender, almost thread-like stems characterised by its tiny, brilliant red and black seeds which are used locally in witchcraft along with the plant itself and as ornaments. *Abrus precatorius.* (cf *mtipitipi*)

mturituri[2] *n* (*n*) (*zool*) ballyhoo, bally; a kind of bait fish of the halfbeak (family *Hemiram phidae*) used frequently as cut balt and for trailing purposes by saltwater sportsmen. Ballyhoo can also be seen above the waters skimming the surface to escape from their protection. *Hemphiramus bransienlis.*

mtutu *n* (*mi-*) the barrel of a rifle. (*syn*) *Kwa mtutu wa bunduki*, by going to war; by fighting. *Kiongozi alishika madaraka kwa mtutu wa bunduki*, the leader assumed power by the barrel of a gun i.e. by fighting.

mtutumko *n* (*mi-*) state of swelling or leaving as in the case of bread.

mtutumo *n* (*mi*) a low distant rumbling sound like that of thunder, earthquake, waterfall, etc.; booming sound: *Ule ulikuwa mtutumo wa radi*, that was a booming sound of thunder. (cf *ngurumo*)

mtututu *n* (*mi-*) (*bot*) a shrub or tree with alternate leaves and small flowers clustered in the leaf axils. *Bridelia micrantha.* (cf *mkarakala, mkarati*)

mtwa *n* (*wa-*) 1. philanthropist. (*syn*)

Hawaachani kijibwa na mtwawe, they don't leave one another, a dog and its master i.e. they are always together like a dog and its master. 2. a title given to a traditional ruler of *Wahehe*, in Iringa, Tanzania.

mtwana[1] *n (wa-)* 1. *(arch)* a male slave. 2. a male of low class. (cf *mwanamume*)

mtwana[2] *n (mi-) (naut)* vertical spar stepped in the mast step and serving as a mast support.

mtwango *n (mi-)* 1. act (method, etc.) of pounding with a pestle and a mortar: *Mtwango wake wa mtama ulikuwa wa polepole*, her pounding of the millet was slow. (cf *utwangaji*) 2. punching; act (method, etc) of hitting hard at sby/sth; *mtwango wa bondia yule dhidi ya mpinzani wake ulikuwa mzito*, the punching of that boxer against his opponent was heavy.

mtwanzi *n (wa-)* a person who pounds grain such as millet, maize, etc. (syn) *Usijitie michini wala si mtwanzi*, don't go in the midst of pestles if you are not a pounder i.e don't involve yourself in an activity in which you are not an expert.

mtweko (also *mtwiko*) *n (mi-)* act (method, etc.) of hoisting a yard, sail, etc.: *Mtweko wa bendera*, the hoisting of a flag.

mtweto *n (mi-)* panting, gasping: *Mtweto wake ulisababishwa na kukimbia sana*, his panting was caused by running a lot. (cf *uvutaji pumvi*)

mtwiko *n (mi-)* see *mtweko*

mua (also *muwa*, (pl *muwa*) *n (mi-) (bot)* sugar cane. *Saccharum afficinarum*.

muachano *n (mi-)* variation, deviation: *Muachano sanifu*, standard deviation, *Muachano wastani*, deviation mean.

muadhamu (also *mwadhamu*) *n (wa-)* a title given to a person about his position, status, etc. in a society; honourable: *Muadhamu mwenyekiti*, the honourable chairman. *Muadhamu Kadinali Tutu*, his Eminence Cardinal Archbishop Tutu. (Ar)

muadhara *n (mi-)* disgrace, chagrin, shame. (cf *fedheha, aibu*)

muadhini *n (wa-)* see *mwadhini*

muafaka *n (mi-)* see *mwafaka*

muale (also *muali*) *n (mi-)* ray: *Miale ya jua*, rays of the sun. (cf *mwali, mwonzi*)

muali *n (mi-)* see *muale*

mualisaji *n (wa-)* nurse (cf *muuguzaji, muuguzi*)

muamala *n (n)* 1. good relations with others; rapport: *Mkurugenzi hana muamala mzuri na wafanyakazi wake*, the director does not have a good working relationship with his workers. (cf *uhusiano*) 2. business relationship (Ar)

muamana *n (n)* 1. honesty, integrity, uprightness: *Mjomba wangu aliheshimiwa sana kwa sababu ya muamana wake*, my uncle was greatly respected for his integrity. (cf *uaminifu*) 2. reliability: *Ali hana muamana*, Ali lacks reliability. 3. credit. (Ar)

muaminifu *n (wa-)* an honest person.

muaminika *n (wa-)* a reliable person; a person who cannot cheat.

muamko *n (mi-)* awareness, cognisance. (cf *ufahamu*)

muamu *n (wa-)* brother-in-law, sister-in-law. (cf *shemeji*)

muamuzi *n (wa-)* see *mwamuzi*

muanga *n (mi-)* see *mwangaza*

muarubaini *n (mi-)* see *mwarubaini*

muathirika (also *mwathirika, mwathiriwa*) *n (wa-)* victim, sufferer: *Waathiriwa wa mafuriko*, the victims of the flood. *Waathirika katika ajali ya ndege walikuwa wengi*, the victims in the plane crash were many (Ar)

muawana[1] *n (mi-)* assistance, help: *Muawana wako hautasahaulika*, your assistance will never be forgotten. (cf *msaada, auni*) (Ar)

muawana[2] *n (n)* co-operative: *Vyama vya muawana*, co-operative societies. (cf *ushirika*) (Ar)

muchanga *n (mi-)* blood sacrifice made after completing building a vessel.

muda (also *mwida*) *n* (*mi-*) 1. period of time: *Muda huu*, this time. *Muda uliopangwa*, allotted time. *Serikali ya muda*, an interim government. (cf *kipindi*) 2. chance, time: *Sina muda wa kutembea ovyoovyo*, I don't have time to loiter. (*syn*) *Muda si muda*, suddenly. (Ar)

mudiri *n* (*n*) 1. district administrator. 2. head of a department: *Yeye ni mudiri wa idara ya uchumi*, he is the head of the economics department. (Ar)

mudiria *n* (*n*) district: *Mudiria ya magharibi*, the western district. (cf (*wilaya*) (Ar)

mud.u *vt* manage, handle, master: *Unaweza kuimudu kazi hii?* Can you manage this work? Prep. *mud.i.a* St. *mud.ik.a* Cs. *mud.ish.a* Ps. of Prep. *mud.iw.a* Rp. of Prep. *mud.i.an.a* (cf *weza*) (Ar)

muflisi (also *mfilisi*) *n* (*n*) bankrupt, insolvent: *Amekuwa muflisi siku hizi baada ya biashara yake kuanguka*, he has become bankrupt these days after his business collapsed. (Ar)

mufti[1] *n* (*ma-*) 1. a scholar in Islamic law; an interpreter or expounder of islamic law in Muslim countries; mufti: *Mufti alifafanua sheria tata za Kiislamu*, the mufti expounded complex Islamic laws. 2. professor. (Ar)

mufti[2] *adj* stylish, elegant: *Amevalia nguo mufti*, she has dressed elegantly. (Ar)

muhadhara *n* (*n*) demonstration; protest march: *Wafanyakazi walifanya muhadhara dhidi ya serikali*, the workers organized a demonstration against the government. (cf *maandamano*)

muhagata *n* (*mi-*) (*bot*) a tree with good timber. *Pterocarpus bussei*. (cf *mninga, mtumbati*)

muhali[1] (also *mhali*) *n* (*mi-*) anything difficult, impossible, unreasonable, etc.: *Hayo yote anayoyataka ni muhali kwangu*, all those that he wants are impossible to me. (Ar)

muhali[2] (also *mhali*) *adj* impossible: *Ni muhali kwangu kuacha kazi kwa sasa*, it is impossible for me to leave the job now. (Ar)

muhalifu *n* (*wa-*) see *mhalifu*

Muhammad *n* (*n*) (in Islam) (570-632 AD) last prophet and messenger of God. (in Christianity) the prophet and founder of Islam. (Ar)

muhanga *n* (*n*) (*zool*) aadvark (cf *kibarara*)

Muharamu *n* (*n*) the first month of the Islamic calendar. (Ar)

muhibu *n* (*n*) darling, beloved; apple of one's eye: *Mkewe ni muhibu wake*, his wife is his darling. (cf *laazizi, hababi, mpenzi*) (Ar)

muhimu *adj* important, significant: *Ni muhimu kuudumisha umoja katika nchi yetu*, it is important to maintain unity in our country. (Ar)

muhina *n* (*n*) see *mnoga*[2]

muhogo (also *mhogo*) *n* (*mi-*) 1. (*bot*) cassava root. 2. cassava plant. *Manihot utilissima*.

muholelo *n* (*mi-*) calamity, catastrophe. (cf *balaa*)

muhtaramu *n* (*n*) a title used before a person's name as a kind of respect; honourable: *Muhtaramu Ali Mohammed anapendwa na watu wengi*, the honourable Ali Mohammed is loved by many people. (Ar)

muhtasari *n* (*mi-*) 1. summary, synopsis, highlights: *Kwa muhtasari*, in short. *Nieleze muhtasari wa maazimio ya mkutano wenu*, give me a synopsis of the resolutions of your meeting. (cf *ufupisho*) 2. syllabus: *Muhtasari wa somo la Kiingereza*, the English syllabus. (Ar)

muhtasi *adj* personal: *Katibu muhtasi*, personal secretary. (Ar)

muhu *n* (*n*) inspiration (cf *ilhamu*)

muhudi *n* (*n*) 1. a person believed that he would come towards the end of the world. 2. the period believed to be the end of the world. (Ar)

muhula *n* (*mi-*) term, semester; period of time: *Muhula wa kwanza*, first term.

Huu ni muhula wa mwisho katika shule yetu, this is the last term in our school. (prov) *Mauti hayana muhula,* death can come at any time. (Ar)

muhuni *n (wa-)* see *mhuni*

muhunzi *n (wa-)* see *mhunzi*

muhuri *n (mi-)* see *mhuri*

muhusika *n (wa-)* a person in charge: *Wahusika wa ofisi hii wametoka nje,* those in charge of this office have gone out.

mui *adj* bad, wicked: *Kijana mui,* a wicked young man. (prov) *Wimbo mui hauongolewi mwana,* a bad song should not be used to pamper a baby i.e. bad words should not be used while we are in the process of upbringing our children.

muigizaji *n (wa-)* actor in a play: *Yeye ni muigizaji mzuri,* he is a good actor. (cf *mmathili*)

mujarabu¹ *adv* at once, immediately: *Mujarabu wa kumwita, akaja kwangu,* immediately after I called him, he came to my place. (Ar)

mujarabu² *adj* (of medicine) suitable, proper, fitting, be working: *Ukitumia dawa ile, basi ni mujarabu,* if you use that medicine, it works. (Ar)

mujibu *adj* that which is according to law, custom, etc.: *Kwa mujibu wa sheria,* according to law. *Kwa mujibu wa maelezo yako, yeye si mkosa,* according to your statement, he is not guilty. (Ar)

mukafaa *n (mi-)* bonus; extra payment over and above salary given to an employer as a kind of incentive or reward: *Mfanyakazi alipewa mukafaa kufuatia kazi yake nzuri kiwandani,* the worker was given a bonus following his good work at the factory. (cf *bonasi, kifutajasho*)

mukhtari *n (n)* 1. chosen by God as in the case of a prophet. 2. used in the expression: *Hiari na mukhtari ni juu yake,* voluntariness and the choice is his. (Ar)

muktadha *n (mi-)* 1. topic: *Muktadha huu unafaa ujadiliwe vizuri,* this topic must be discussed well. 2. context: *Utalijua maana ya neno hili katika muktadha wake,* you will know the meaning of this word from its context. (Ar)

muku *n (n)* medicine used to give more strength to a person; energizer. (cf *mkuyati*)

mulik.a *vi* illuminate, light up: *Tochi hii haimuliki vizuri,* this torch does not illuminate well. (prov) *Akumulikaye mchana, usiku atakuchoma,* he who lights by day sets fire to you by night i.e. he who does a small evil to you can do a bigger one next time. Prep. **mulik.i.a,** bright light for, make a light with e.g. *Nimulikie juu,* light for me on the top. St. **mulik.ik.a** Cs. **mulik.ish.a.** Ps. **mulik.w.a** Rp. **mulik.an.a**

mulla (also *mullah*) *n (ma-)* 1. a male religious teacher or leader. 2. used as a form of address for such a man.

mullah *n (ma-)* see *mulla*

mumbi¹ *n (n)* 1. (*zool*) ground hornbill. *Bucorvus leadbeateri.* 2. (*syn*) *Utakula mumbi,* you will regret it; you shall meet with misfortune.

mumbi² *n (mi-)* water current.

mume *n (wa-)* husband. (prov) *Bamba na waume, hakuna bamba la mume, Bamba* was for men and there was no *Bamba* for a man i.e. success of the Bamba was obtained by many men and not just one person; in other words, unity is strength. (cf *bwana*)

mumiani¹ *n (n)* a dark-coloured gun-like substance or medicine used by Egyptians in the past to preserve their dead bodies. (Pers)

mumiani² *n (n)* a killer in need of blood believed to make medicine for the purpose of selling it. (Pers)

mumuch.a *vt* chew and suck the liquid as you eat sugarcane: *Muangalie kijana yule akiumumucha mua,* look at that young man chewing and sucking liquid from the sugarcane. Prep. **mumuch.i.a** St. **mumuch.ik.a** Ps. **mumuch.w.a**

mumuny.a² (also *mung'unya*) *vt* chew sth slowly in the mouth as in the case of a sweet, etc. and at the same time sucking it: *Mtoto aliimumunya peremende*, the child chewed the sweet as he was also sucking it. Prep. **mumuny.i.a** St. **mumuny.ik.a** Cs. **mumuny.ish.a** Ps. **mumuny.w.a** (cf *gurugusa*)

mumunya² *n* (*ma-*) see *mung'unye*

munda¹ *n* (*mi-*) a harpoon used to spear; a fish spear. (cf *chusa*)

munda² *n* (*mi-*) 1. (*naut*) a piece of planking put inside a sailing vessel like a dhow so as to prevent the frames and other planks from touching each other 2. a plank used on the side of a vessel during its construction.

munda³ *n* (*mi-*) twisting of an opponent's leg during wrestling. (cf *teo, gwato*)

mundu *n* (*mi-*) sickle, machete, *Panga*, billhook. (cf *panga*)

mundu

Mungu¹ *n* (*u*) Allah, Almighty God; *Mungu akipenda*, if God wishes. *Mungu wangu!* My God! *Mungu akinijalia*, God willing.

mungu² *n* (*mi-*) anything that is worshipped; god, idol: *Miungu ya masanamu*, fetish. *Mungu wa mashambani mwenye pembe na miguu ya mbuzi*, faun.

mung'unya *n* (*ma-*) see *mumunya¹*

mung'unye (also *mumunya, mumunye*) *n* (*ma-*) (*bot*) bottle gourd, calabash cucumber. (cf *bodwe*)

munkari¹ *n* (*n*) 1. a malevolent person or thing; a bad person or thing. 2. (*idm*) *Shusha munkari*, reduce one's wrath. *Pandisha munkari*, raise one's wrath (Ar)

Munkari² *n* (*n*) (in Islam) one of the names of angels supposed to interrogate a dead body immediately after being buried. (Ar)

munyamuny.a (also *mwinyamwinya*) *vt* mumble; chew gently and ineffectively like a toothless person: *Mzee alikuwa akiimunyamunya mifupa ya nyama*, the old man was mumbling meat bones. Prep. **munyamuny.i.a** St. **munyamuny.ik.a** Cs. **munyamuny.ish.a** Ps. **munyamuny.w.a**

munyu *n* (*n*) salt (cf *chumvi ya unga*)

muo *n* (*mi-*) a wooden stake fixed with an iron point, used to dig up stone, etc. or as a lever. (cf *msaha*)

muoano *n* (*mi-*) 1. harmony, congruence. 2. marriage.

muokaji *n* (*wa-*) baker; a person who bakes bread, etc

muokoaji *n* (*wa-*) saviour (cf *muokozi*)

muokozi *n* (*wa-*) see *muokoaji*

muombaji *n* (*wa-*) see *mwombaji*

muono *n* (*mi-*) (*arch*) mouth (cf *mdomo*)

mupi *pron interrog* marker for location; which?

muozi *n* (*wa-*) a person who has married in the same family.

muradi¹ (also *mradi*) *n* (*n*) objective, purpose, intention: *Muradi wake ulikuwa ni kupata msaada wetu*, his intention was to get our assistance (cf *lengo*) (Ar)

muradi² *n* (*mi-*) a piece of stick used for spinning threads in embroidery work.

muradi³ *conj* see *mradi*

muridi *n* (*n*) a student or follower of a religious order. (Ar)

muru *n* (*n*) quassia; a kind of local bitter black drug used as a medicine for abdominal pains or for putting on swellings so as to soothe them. (Ar)

murua¹ *n* (*n*) nice, pleasant character; good conduct: *Yeye ni kijana mwenye murua*, he is a young man with a pleasant character. (Ar)

murua² *adj* pleasant, meaningful: *Matamshi yake ni murua*, his statements are meaningful. (Ar)

Musa *n* (*n*) (in Islam) the apostle of God and saviour of the Jews. (in Christianity) the Hebrew prophet known as "Moses" to whom the Old Testament was revealed and who had been given the Ten commandments. (Ar)

mushkili *n* (*n*) 1. problem, difficulty: *Kuna mushkili katika suala hili*, there is a problem in this issue. (cf *tatizo*) 2. defect: *Saa yangu ina mushkili*, my watch has a defect. (cf *dosari, kasoro*) (Ar)

Mushtara *n* (*n*) (*astron*) Jupiter; the largest of the planets and the fifth from the sun. (Ar)

musimu *n* (*n*) see *msimu*

mustakabali (*also mstakabali*) *n* (*n*) prospects; further future: *Kazi hii haina mustakabali mzuri*, this work has no good future. *Mustakabali wa kiwanda hiki ni mzuri kutokana na juhudi za meneja*, the prospects of this factory are good due to the efforts of the manager. (cf *hatima*) (Ar)

mustarehe (*also mstarehe*) *adv* used in the expression: *Raha mustarehe*, great comfort; complete comfort. *Kaa raha mustarehe*, sit comfortably.

musuli *n* (*mi-*) see *msuli*

mususa *n* (*n*) see *chuchunge*

muswada (*also mswada*) *n* (*mi-*) 1. legal bill: *Muswada binafsi*, private bill. *Muswada wa umma*, public bill. *Waziri aliuwasilisha muswada wake bungeni*, the minister presented his bill in parliament. 2. manuscript. (Ar)

mutlaki *adv* categorically, completely: *Ni haramu mutlaki kwa Mwislamu kula nyama ya nguruwe*, it is completely illegal for a Muslim to eat pork. *Haramu mutlaki*, completely illegal. (Ar)

mutribu *n* (*wa-*) see *mtribu*

muuaji *n* (*wa-*) murderer, killer.

muudhi *n* (*wa-*) pesterer, nuisance, harasser.

muuguzi *n* (*wa-*) nurse: *Afisa muuguzi*, nursing officer. *Muuguzi alimpa mgonjwa dawa*, the nurse gave the patient some medicine. (cf *mwalisa, mualisaji*)

muuja *n* (*mi-*) see *muujiza*

muujiza (also *muuja, mwujiza*) *n* (*mi-*) miracle, wonder: *Ilikuwa ni muujiza kwa yeye kupona katika ajali ile*, it was a miracle for him to survive in that accident. (cf *shani, ajabu*) (Ar)

Muumba *n* (*n*) Creator (cf *Mwenyezi-Mungu*)

muumbaji *n* (*wa-*) creator (cf *Muumba*)

muumbi *n* (*mi-*) a chord made from palm leaves, usu used to tie one's luggage.

muumbuaji (also *muumbufu, muumbuzi*) *n* (*wa-*) 1. one who can uncreate; one who can destroy: *Mungu ni muumbaji na vile vile muumbuaji*, God is the creator and also capable of destroying what he has created. 2. critic: *Muumbuaji aliyafichua makosa ya viongozi wetu*, the critic exposed the mistakes of our leaders. 3. a person who likes to disclose other people's secrets; slanderer.

muumbufu *n* (*wa-*) see *muumbuaji*

muumbuzi *n* (*wa-*) see *muumbuaji*

muumbwa *n* (*wa-*) the created creature. (cf *kiumbe*)

muumikaji a professional cupper: *Muumikaji alimtibu mgonjwa*, the professional cupper treated the patient. (cf *mpiga chuku, muumisi*)

muumini *n* (*wa-*) the faithful: *Muumini mkereketwa*, fundamentalist. *Muumini mpya wa dini*, neophyte. *Yeye ni muumini wa dini ya Kikristo*, he is a Christian faithful. (Ar)

muumisi *n* (*wa-*) a professional cupper (cf *muumikaji*)

muunda (also *munda*) *n* (*mi-*) 1. a piece of planking put on the wall or sth else to prevent it from falling. 2. a kind of spear used for fishing big fishes.

muundaji *n* (*wa-*) constructor, builder, manufacturer. (cf *fundi, mtengenezaji*)

muundi *n* (*mi-*) (*anat*) shin-bone; tibia. (cf *goko*)

muundo *n* (*mi-*) 1. structure, construction, shape, form: *Muundo wa nyumba hii ni wa pekee*, the structure of this house is unique. 2. building, structuring; act (method, etc.) of constructing a building, etc. 3. (*gram*) structure: *Muundo sahili*, simple structure. *Muundo changamano*, complex structure, *Muundo ambatano*, compound structure. *Muundo wa sentensi*, the structure of a sentence. *Muundo wa kishazi*, the structure of a clause. *Muundo shurutia*, interdependent structure.

muundwaji *n* (*wa-*) creation; sth brought into existence or created: *Panapo muundwaji, kuna muundaji*, where there is a creation, there is a creator.

muungaji *n* (*wa-*) a person who joins things, etc.

muungabega *n* (*mi-*) (*anat*) humerus; the long bone of the upper arm or forelimb extending from the shoulder to the elbow.

muungamaji *n* (*wa-*) a person who admits his wrongdoing; confessor.

muungamo *n* (*wa-*) confession; acknowledgement of wrongdoing.

muungana *n* (*wa-*) a penitent person; a person who feels sorry or ashamed for having done wrong and willing to atone.

muunganishaji *n* (*wa-*) connector, tier; a person who ties or links sth with something else.

muungano *n* (*mi-*) 1. union, alliance, confederation: *Muungano wa nchi za Ulaya*, European union. *Muungano wa nchi zile mbili unataka kuvunjika*, the union of those two countries is about to break. (cf *umoja*) 2. coalition.

muungo *n* (*mi-*) 1. joint, bond; a place or part where two things are joined. 2. joining; act (method, etc.) of joining.

muungwana *n* (*wa-*) 1. a civilized person, a refined person: *Muungwana hatathubutu kumtukana mtu yeyote*, a civilized person can never dare to abuse anyone. (*prov*) *Ada ya mja hunena, muungwana ni kitendo*, an ordinary person talks but a gentleman shows actions. 2. a free man; a person who is not a slave. 3. a name of respect given to a person.

muunzi *n* (*wa-*) see *mhunzi*

muuza *n* (*wa-*) seller; salesman: *Muuza vitabu*, bookseller. *Muuza tumbaku*, tobacco seller. *Muuza samaki*, fishmonger, *Muuza kuku*, poulterer. (cf *muuzaji*)

muuzaji *n* (*wa-*) seller: *Muuzaji nguo*, haberdasher. (cf *muuza*)

muwa (also *mua*) *n* (*mi-*) (*bot*) sugarcane. *Saccharum officinarum*.

muwaa (also *myaa*) *n* (*mi-*) 1. (*bot*) brown palms; a kind of palm bearing polished brown fruits and leaves which when dry, are used for making light baskets, mats, etc. *Hyphaene sp*. 2. an annual grey pubescent procumbent herb bearing small conical fruits. *Coldenia procumbens*.

muwako[1] *n* (*mi-*) act (method, etc.) of burning: *Muwako wa moto ulizagaza nuru*, the burning of the fire radiated light everywhere.

muwako[2] *n* (*mi*) act (manner, etc.) of plastering a wall.

muwala *n* (*n*) (*poet*) balance between form and content in a poem.

muwale *n* (*mi-*) (*bot*) see *mwale*

muwele[1] *n* (*wa-*) sick person: *Muwele alikwenda hospitali*, the sick person went to hospital. (cf *mgonjwa*)

muwele[2] *n* (*mi-*) (*bot*) bulrush millet plant; a kind of annual erect grass bearing small seeds, which are a well-known cereal food. *Pennisetum malacochaete*.

muye *n* (*u*) 1. vapour (cf *mvuke*) 2. (*idm*) *Avya muye*, become angry.

muziki (also *mziki*) *n* (*n*) music: *Muziki wa dansi la yosayosa*, jig. (Eng)

mvale *n* (*mi-*) (*bot*) a much-branched tree whose young leaves are eaten by livestock in the dry season. *Lonchocarpus capassa.*

mvamizi n (*wa-*) invader, attacker: *Wavamizi waliihujumu nchi ya jirani,* the invaders attacked the neighbouring country. (cf *mhujumu*)

mvange adv haphazardly, awry, disorderly: *Mipango yangu ilienda mvange,* my plans went awry. (cf *kombo, shoto*)

mvanila n (*mi-*) (*bot*) vanilla plant; a climbing plant with fragrant greenish-yellow flowers, bearing vanilla beans. *Vanilla planifolia* (Eng)

mvao n (*mi-*) 1. act (method, etc) of wearing; dressing (cf *uvaaji*) 2. number of times one wears a garment: *Nguo hii nimeivaa mvao mmoja,* I have worn this dress once.

mvi[1] n (*n*) grey hair; white hair

mvi[2] n (*mi-*) arrow (cf *mshale*)

mviga n (*mi-*) ritual, offering. (cf *tambiko*)

mviko n (*mi-*) propitiatory offering; pacifying offering of the spirits of the dead. (cf *tambiko*)

mvilio n (*mi-*) bruise

mvimbaji n (*wa-*) thatcher; one who thatches a roof of a house, etc. with palm leaves, rushes, etc. (cf *muambaji*)

mvinje n (*mi-*) (*bot*) whistling pine, beefwood; a tall tree having scale-like leaves and flowers in small globular cone-like clusters, used as good fuel and its stems are used for making masts for dhows and boats. *Casuarina equisetifolia. Mvinje bahari,* a kind of sea plant with a thick log.

mvinyo[1] n (*mi-*) wine (cf *divai, ulevi*) (Port)

mvinyo[2] n (*mi-*) act (method, etc.) of dandling a baby. (cf *uwinyaji*)

mviringo n (*mi-*) circle, sphere: *Kitu cha mviringo,* a spherical thing.

mviru n (*mi-*) (*bot*) a much-branched shrub with opposite leaves, and its edible roots are used as anthelmintics. *Vangueria sp.*

Mvita[1] n (*n*) (*arch*) Mombasa island.

mvita[2] n (*wa-*) a brave person in fighting. (cf *shujaa*)

mvivu n (*wa-*) an idle person, a lazy person; idler: *Mvivu anamangamanga hapo nje,* the idler is loitering outside. (cf *goigoi, mzembe*)

mviza[1] n (*mi-*) a kind of evergreen tree used in magic and medicine making.

mvizaji n (*mi-*) a person who hampers progress; reactionary. (cf *mpinga maendeleo*)

mviziaji n (*wa-*) waylayer; a person who lies in wait, as in ambush.

mvo n (*mi-*) gulley; a small arrow ravine. (cf *mfoko*)

mvongonya n (*mi-*) see *mvungunya*

mvua[1] n (*n*) 1. rain: *Mvua ya mawe,* hail. (*prov*) *Aisifuye mvua imemnyia,* he who praises rain has been drenched by it i.e he who praises sby/sth must have benefitted from it (something). 2. used in the expression: *Mvua jasho,* toiler.

mvua[2] n (*wa-*) 1. a person who undresses himself. 2. fisherman; a person who fishes.

mvugulio n (*mi-*) 1. hollow compressed space e.g. air which comes out when a coconut is pierced; an outlet of air or fluid. (*syn*) *Maji ya nazi yatafuta mvugulio,* someone may look for excuses to avoid doing sth. 2. bribe, kickback: *Alishtakiwa kwa kutoa mvugulio,* he was prosecuted for offering a bribe. (cf *rushwa, hongo*)

mvuje n (*mi-*) 1. (*bot*) a tree whose gum is bad smelling and is used in local medicines but is mainly employed in charms as its strong smell is supposed to put evil spirits to flight and thus ward off sickness. *Ferula foetida.* 2. gum of asafoetida.

mvujo n (*mi-*) act (method, etc.) of oozing; leakage, oozing; *mvujo wa petroli katika tangi,* the leakage of petrol in the tank. (cf *uvujaji*)

mvuke n (*mi-*) vapour, steam: *Fanya*

mvuke, vapourize. *Mvuke-mkavu*, dry steam. (cf *muye*)
mvukizo *n* (*mi-*) evaporation
mvuko *n* (*mi-*) crossing (cf *uvukaji*)
mvukuto[1] (also *mvuo*) *n* (*mi-*) bellows used by smiths.

mvukuto

mvukuto[2] *n* (*mi-*) palpitation caused by internal pains.
mvulana *n* (*wa-*) 1. boy. 2. a young man who is unmarried; bachelor. (cf *mvuli*) 3. a regular male companion with whom one has a romantic or sexual relationship; boyfriend.
mvule *n* (*mi-*) (*bot*) a tree with a more or less flat spreading crown, producing hard timber which is used for cabinet work and building, and whose bark is used for charcoal. *Chlorophora excelsa*.
mvuli *n* (*wa-*) boy, a young man. (cf *mvulana*)
mvulia *n* (*mi-*) bee sting. (cf *uvurenje*)
mvumanyuki (also *mtambaanyuki*) *n* (*mi-*) (*bot*) a shrub whose flowers are liked very much by bees. *Premna chrysoclada*.
mvumbamkuu *n* (*mi-*) see *mrihani*
mvumburuko *n* (*mi-*) dash, a sudden swift movement; *Mvumburuko wa paa ulinishtua*, the gazelle's dash startled me.
mvumbuzi *n* (*wa-*) 1. discoverer, explorer: *Mvumbuzi wa kontinenti ya Amerika ni Columbus*, the discoverer of the continent of America is Columbus. 2. founder, pioneer, inventor: *Yeye alikuwa mvumbuzi wa chama tawala*, he was the founder of the ruling party.
mvumilivu *n* (*wa-*) a patient person; an enduring person. (cf *mstahamilivu*)
mvumishi *n* (*wa-*) gossiper, telltale, tattler, gossipmonger.
mvumo[1] *n* (*mi-*) rumble; thundering sound of bees, wind, etc.: *Ule ni mvumo wa nyuki*, that is the bees' buzz.
mvumo[2] *n* (*mi-*) 1. (*bot*) deleb palm, palmyra palm; a palm with a solitary slightly bottle-shaped stem producing brown, large and globular fruits as well as wine. *Borassus flabellifera*. 2. a tree with glossy obli-triangular leathery alternate leaves and small fig-like fruits. *Ficus lepricurii*.
mvungo *n* (*mi-*) act (method etc.) of tangling sth by covering it with something else.
mvungu *n* (*mi-*) empty space under a bed, table, etc.; cavity. (*prov*) *Mtaka cha mvunguni sharti ainame*, if you want to achieve sth, you must struggle for it.
mvungunya (also *mvogonya*) *n* (*mi-*) (*bot*) sausage tree, a much-branched tree whose wood is used for making stools, etc, *Kigelia aethiopica*. (cf *mnyegea, mwegea*)
mvunja *n* (*wa-*) a person who breaks sth: *Mvunja sheria*, law-breaker. *Mvunja fedha*, money changer.
mvunjiko *n* (*mi-*) fracture: *Mvunjiko mchanganyiko*, compound fracture. *Mvunjiko sahili*, simple fracture. (cf *uvunjikaji*)
mvunjo *n* (*mi-*) act of breaking.
mvuo[1] *n* (*mi-*) see *mvukuto*
mvuo[2] *n* (*mi-*) 1. the amount of money obtained from fishing. 2. the amount of fish taken in a single pool of net; a catch of fish; haul. 3. act (method etc.) of fishing: *Mvuo ule ulimletea pesa nyingi*, that fishing earned him a lot of money. 4. fishing ground; place of fishing.

mvuo³ n (mi-) act (method, etc.) of undressing.
mvure n (mi-) wooden bowl.
mvurugano n (mi-) 1. disharmony, dispute. 2. chaos, confusion, pandemonium. (cf *sokomoko, vurugu*)
mvurugiko n (mi-) confusion, bewilderment: *Mvurugiko wa akili*, confusion of mind.
mvurugo n (mi-) confusion, disharming, chaos. (cf *mvurugano*)
mvutano n (mi-) struggle, tussle, tug of war, tension, wrangle, quarrel, division: *Mvutano wa madaraka*, power struggle. *Pana mvutano*, (cf *mgawanyiko*) 2. (*phys*) gravity.
mvutiko (n) (mi-) tension, dilation.
mvutio n (mi-) attraction, appeal. (cf *mvuto*)
mvuto n (mi-) 1. attraction, appeal: *Hotuba yake ilileta mvuto kwa watu*, his speech attracted the people. (cf *haiba*) 2. pull (cf *uvutaji*)
mvuvi n (wa-) fisherman: *Mvuvi yule huuza samaki wake kwa bei kubwa*, that fisherman sells his fish at a high price. (*prov*) *Maji mafu na mvuvi kafu*, low tide water means fisherman dies i.e. if anything that a person depends upon heavily disappears, then that person gets into trouble.
mvyale n (wa-) a person who has the authority to speak with the ancestral spirits.
mvyazi n (wa-) dam
mvyele n (wa-) 1. father or mother of so and so; parent. 2. old woman.
mwaandamanaji n (wa-) demonstrator: *Waandamanaji walikusanyika katika kiwanja cha mpira*, the demonstrators assembled at the football ground.
mwaathirika n (wa-) see *mwaathiriwa*
mwaathiriwa (also *mwaathirika*) n (wa-) sufferer, victim: *Waathiriwa katika ajali ya ndege walikuwa wengi*, the victims in the plane crash were many. (Ar)
Mwabrania (also *Abrania*) n (wa-) old Jew.

mwabudu n (wa-) worshipper
mwachaka n (wa-) (*bot*) a kind of very hot small chillies: *Pilipili mwachaka*, chillies of this kind.
mwachano n (mi-) disjunction, separation, split.
mwadhamu (also *muadhamu*) n (wa) eminence, honourable; a title of courtesy for certain respected officials, etc.: *Mwadhamu waziri ataitembelea shule yetu karibuni*, the honourable minister will visit our school quite soon. (cf *mheshimiwa*) (Ar)
mwadhini (also *muadhini*) n (wa-) (in Islam) muezzin; a crier in a minaret, who calls the faithful to go for prayer. (*syn*) *Hasikii la mwadhini wala la mtia maji msikitini*, he does not listen neither to the muezzin nor to the water pourer in the mosque i.e. he does not listen to whatever he is told. (Ar)
mwadilifu adj see *adilifu*
mwafaka¹ n (mi-) accord, agreement, contract, harmony: *Mwafaka kati ya vyama viwili vya kisiasa*, the accord between two political parties. *Pande zote mbili zimefikia mwafaka*, both sides have come to an agreement. (cf *maafikiano, mapatano*) (Ar)
mwafaka² adj acceptable, fitting, appropriate, suitable: *Maneno yako yote ni mwafaka*, all your words are acceptable. (Ar)
mwafiki n (wa-) a seconder of motion.
Mwafrika n (wa-) African (Eng)
mwafu.a vt see *ng'wafua*. Prep. **mwafu.li.a** St. **mwafu.k.a** and **mwafu.lik.a** Cs. **mwafu.sh.a** Ps. of Prep. **mwafu.liw.a** Rp. **mwafu.an.a**
mwafulani (also *mwajimbo*) n (wa-) so and so: *Mwafulani anavaa nguo mpya siku hizi*, so and so wears new clothes these days.
mwag.a vt, vi (of milk, etc.) spill, scatter: *Mtoto wako amemwaga maziwa*, your child has spilt the milk. (*prov*) *Maji yakimwagika hayazoleki*, it is no use crying over spilt water. i.e. if something wrong has been badly

mwagi.a St. **mwag.ik.a mwag.ish.a** Ps. **mwag.w.a** Rp. of Prep. **mwag.i.an.a**

mwagi.a *vt, vi* spill/pour sth over sby/sth else: *Alinimwagia maji baridi,* she poured cold water over me. Prep. **mwagi.li.a** St. **mwagi.lik.a**

mwagik.a *vi* be scattered, be spilled. Prep. **mwagik.i.a**

mwagili.a *vt* irrigate: *Anamwagilia maji katika konde yake kila Jumamosi,* he irrigates his land every Saturday. St. **mwagili.k.a** Cs. **mwagili.sh.a** Ps. **mwagili.w.a**

mwago *n* (*mi-*) a present/gift by a husband to his wife on the eve of marrying another wife.

mwaguzi *n* (*wa-*) 1. an experienced interpreter of dreams; soothsayer: *Mwaguzi aliifasiri ndoto,* the interpreter interpreted the dream. (cf *kuhani*) 2. healer, curer.

mwairo *adj* free, gratis, without payment: *utagaiwa, na kila chako kuporwa,* you will given free, but everything will be stolen.

Mwajemi *n* (*wa-*) (*arch*) Persian (Ar)

mwajibikaji *n* (*wa-*) a person held to be accountable on a particular issue, affair, etc.

mwajificho *n* (*mi-*) a children's game of hide-and-seek. (cf *kibe*)

mwajimbo *n* (*wa-*) see *mwafulani*

mwajiri *n* (*wa-*) 1. a person who employs someone for work; employer: *Mwajiri amekubali kuniongezea mshahara wangu,* the employer has agreed to increase my salary. 2. an institution such as a ministry, firm, business, university, etc that employs someone to render services in return for wages or salary; employer. (Ar)

mwajiriwa *n* (*wa-*) employee (Ar)

mwaka *n* (*mi-*) 1. year: *Mwaka jana,* last year. *Mwaka huu,* this year. *Mwaka juzi,* two years ago. *Mwaka wa fedha,* financial year, fiscal year. *Mwaka wa masomo,* academic year. *Mwaka mrefu,* leap year. *Mwakani,* next year. *Mwaka kesho,* next year. 2. so many days. (*syn*) *Usiku mwaka,* so many things can happen in one night. 3. local annual festival in Zanzibar.

mwakani *adv* next year: *Atakuja hapa mwakani,* he will come here next year.

mwake *adj, pron* possessive adjective or pronoun for third person singular meaning 'his', 'her', 'its' 'in/at/his/her/its: *Nyumbani mwake, mna panya wengi,* in his house, there are many rats. *Nyumbani mwake, hamna wizi,* in her home, there is no theft.

mwakilishi *n* (*wa-*) 1. agent, representative. (cf *wakala, ajenti*) 2. a member of parliament; representative: *Baraza la Waakilishi,* House of Representatives.

mwakisu *n* (*mi-*) a rope bed made from dwarf palm or skin.

mwako[1] *n* (*mi-*) 1. blaze, flame, flare-up: *Mwako wa jua,* the blaze of the sun. 2. disturbance: *Akija tu, hunifanyia mwako,* as soon as he comes, he disturbs me. (cf *kero, adha*) 3. confusion, noise, chaos, pandemonium, riot: *Vijana wale hufanya mwako wanapocheza karata,* those young men make a lot of noise when they play cards. (cf *ghasia, wasiwasi*)

mwako[2] *n* (*mi-*) plastering; white washing of a wall or building.

mwako[3] *adj, pron* possessive adjective or pronoun for third person singular meaning "your" "in/at your": *Kibandani mwako, mna wadudu,* in your hut, there are insects. *Mwako, pana upepo mwingi,* at your place, it is windy.

mwalambe *n* (*mi-*) (*bot*) a tall deciduous tree branching horizontally in whorls, whose timber is yellow-brown and which is durable in saltwater. *Terminalia prunoides.*

mwalamu *n* (*mi-*) stripe; a band of colour esp in dress material. (cf *doa*)

mwale[1] (also *muwale*) *n* (*mi-*) (*bot*) raffia palm; a palm with huge, erect

549

pinnate leaves bearing oval fruits. The large mid-ribs of the leaves are used frequently to make doors etc. *Raphia kirkii*.

mwale² *n* (*mi-*) the stalk, stem, etc. of a tree.

mwale³ *n* (*mi-*) soot forming itself into dustballs as seen in a kitchen, roof of a house, etc.

mwali¹ *n* (*wa-*) see *mwari*

mwali² *n* (*mi-*) ray, beam: *Mwali ardhi*, ground ray: *Mwali mtuo*, incident ray. (cf *mwozi*)

mwalika (also *mwalikaji*) *n* (*wa-*) the person who invites; inviter.

mwalikaji *n* (*wa-*) see *mwalika*

mwaliko¹ (also *ualishi*) *n* (*mi-*) invitation: *Nilipata mwaliko wa kuhudhuria harusi ya rafiki yangu*, I got an invitation to attend my friend's wedding. (cf *karibisho*)

mwaliko² *n* (*mi-*) 1. act of confining a sick person to a house for medical treatment. (cf *utawaji*) 2. act of confining a young girl esp a virgin so that she is not seen by outsiders

mwaliko³ *n* (*mi-*) clicking, snapping. (cf *ualikaji*)

mwalikwa *n* (*wa-*) invitee, an invited person: *Waalikwa wote walifika katika karamu*, all the invitees attended the party.

mwalimu *n* (*wa-*) teacher: *Mwalimu mkuu*, headteacher. *Mwalimu wa kichwa*, experienced teacher. (cf *mfundishaji*) (Ar)

mwalisa *n* (*wa-*) see *mualisa*

mwalishi *n* (*wa-*) 1. a person who is dressed up in finery and who leads a function giving information to the guests; master of ceremonies. 2. companion.

mwaloni *n* (*mi-*) (*bot*) Holm oak; an evergreen European tree with dark green glossy leaves.

mwamana *n* (*wa-*) a trustworthy person, an honest person: *Mpe mwamana yule akuwekee pesa zako*, give that trustworthy person your money to keep it for you. (Ar)

mwamba¹ *n* (*mi-*) 1. reef: *Meli iligonga mwamba*, the ship hit a reef. 2. rock: *Mwamba geu*, metamorphic rock. *Mwamba tabaka*, sedimentary rock.

mwamba² *n* (*mi-*) a ridgepole in a building. (cf *mtambaapanya*)

mwamba³ *n* (*wa-*) (*colloq*) a strong person, a giant of a man. (cf *mbabe, mkota*)

mwamba⁴ *n* (*mi-*) (*in sports*) goalpost: *Kiki yake kali iligonga mwamba*, his hard shot hit the goalpost.

mwamba⁵ (also *mwambaji*) *n* (*wa-*) a person who stretches skin on a drum. (*prov*) *Kila mwamba ngoma ngozi, huivuta kwake*, when a person tightens and stretches the skin of a drum, he does it on his direction i.e. every human being usu first takes care of his interests before considering the interests of others.

mwambaji *n* (*wa-*) see *mwamba*

mwambao *n* (*mi-*) coast, coastline: *Sehemu za mwambao*, coastal areas. (cf *pwani*)

mwambata *n* (*wa-*) attache: *Mwambata wa kijeshi*, military attache.

mwambatano *n* (*mi-*) 1. (*gram*) compounding, compound: *Mwambatano huunganisha maneno mawili au zaidi ili kuunda neno moja*, compounding combines two or more words to form one. 2. concurrence; succession of events, etc.: *Mwambatano wa matukio yale yalimkanganya*, the concurrence of those events confused him.

mwambi *n* (*wa-*) slanderer, backbiter. (cf *msengenyaji*)

mwambo¹ *n* (*mi-*) act (manner, method, operation, etc.) of stretching sth tightly such as skin over a drum, etc.

mwambo² *n* (*n*) (*idm*) *Siku ya mwambo*, difficult days esp in the last few days of the month when the whole of a person's salary has been spent and thus nothing remains.

mwambo³ *n* (*mi-*) communal work.
mwambula *n* (*mi-*) (*bot*) a scandent shrub with ovate-oblong leaves, whose roots are used externally for swollen legs and for hookworm and whose leaves are used as a cure for sores. It is sometimes planted as an ornamental garden shrub. *Plumbago zeylanica*.
Mwamerika *n* (*wa-*) see *Mmarekani*
mwamimba *n* (*wa-*) see *mwanamimba*
mwamini *n* (*wa-*) see *muamini*
mwamizi *n* (*wa-*) a person who protects a plantation against birds, animals, etc.
mwamko (also *muamko*) *n* (*mi*) 1. awareness, consciousness: *Mwamko wa kisiasa*, political awareness. 2. flash.
mwamuzi *n* (*wa-*) 1. arbitrator, judge, negotiator, reconciler, mediator: *Serikali ilimteua mwamuzi ili kushughulikia migogoro ya ardhi nchini*, the government appointed an arbitrator to handle land disputes in the country. (*prov*) *Mwamuzi chake ni kigongo*, a person who settles a dispute ends up by being beaten with a club i.e. a person who settles a dispute usu is blamed by one of the two sides that are in conflict. (cf *msuluhishi*) 2. referee: *Mwamuzi wa kimataifa aliichezesha mechi vizuri*, the international referee officiated the match well. (cf *refa*)
mwamvuli *n* (*mi-*) see *mwavuli*
mwana¹ *n* (*wa-*) one's child; son or daughter; offspring. (*prov*) *Mwana umleavyo ndivyo akuavyo*, as you bring up your child in a particular manner that is how he will eventually be. (cf *mtoto*)
mwana² *n* (*wa-*) a name given to a woman as a sign of respect before mentioning her name: *Mwana Fatma*, Mrs Fatma/Miss Fatma.
mwanaabudu *n* (*wa-*) idol, puppet. (cf *mwanasesere*)
mwanaanga *n* (*wa-*) astronaut, aeronaut. (cf *mwanahewa*)

mwanabiolojia *n* (*wa-*) biologist
mwanachama *n* (*wa-*) party member: *Mwanachama mkereketwa*, party activist; party zealot. *Mwanachama wa chama cha siri cha kusaidiana*, freemason.
mwanachuo *n* (*wa-*) college student, university student.
mwanachuoni *n* (*wa-*) savant, scholar, educator, pundit, authority: *Yeye ni mwanachuoni wa kuheshimika*, he is a respectable scholar.
mwanadamu *n* (*wa-*) 1. human being. (cf *mtu*) 2. a humane person; a person following ethical standards, etc.: *Mwanadamu wa kweli hataacha kuwasaidia watu wengine*, a real human being will never cease to assist other people.
mwanademokrasia *n* (*wa-*) democrat (Eng)
mwanadiplomasia *n* (*wa-*) diplomat: *Mwanadiplomasia alifukuzwa nchini kwa sababu ya ujasusi*, the diplomat was expelled from the country for spying. (Eng)
mwanaelimu *n* (*wa-*) educator (Ar)
mwanafalsafa *n* (*wa-*) philosopher (Ar)
mwanafarasi *n* (*wa-*) (*zool*) colt
mwanafasihi *n* (*wa-*) a literary person; a literary man: *Mwanafasihi aliichambua riwaya kwa kina*, the literary man analysed the novel in depth. (Ar)
mwanafizikia *n* (*wa-*) physicist (Eng)
mwanafunzi *n* (*wa-*) student, pupil: *Mwanafunzi wa muda*, part-time student. *Mwanafunzi wa kike aliyepita chuo fulani*, alumna. *Mwanafunzi wa kiume aliyepita chuo fulani*, alumnus.
mwanagenzi *n* (*wa-*) 1. a woman bearing children for the first time. 2. novice, apprentice, beginner, student: *Mwanagenzi aliiharibu kazi yangu*, the apprentice spoiled my work.
mwanahabari *n* (*wa-*) newsman
mwanahalali *n* (*wa-*) a legal child; child born in wedlock. (Ar)

mwanahalmashauri *n* (*wa-*) council member.

mwanaharakati *n* (*wa-*) activist: *Wanaharakati walitaka kuleta mageuzi ya kikatiba nchini*, the activitists wanted to bring constitutional reforms in the country. (Ar)

mwanaharamu *n* (*wa-*) 1. bastard; a child whose parents are not legally married. 2. (*syn*) *Funika kombe mwanaharamu apite*, don't disclose your secrets to a telltale.

mwanahewa *n* (*wa-*) airline pilot. (Ar)

mwanahisa *n* (*wa-*) shareholder: *Mwanahisa aliongeza hisa zake katika kampuni*, the shareholder increased his shares in the company. (Ar)

mwanahistoria *n* (*wa-*) historian (Eng)

mwanaisimu *n* (*wa-*) linguist; a linguistic scholar: *Mwanaisimu huyu anazijua lugha nyingi*, this linguist knows many languages. *Mwanaisimu mapokeo*, traditional linguist. *Mwanaisimu wa kisasa*, modern linguist. (Ar)

mwanajamii *n* (*wa-*) a member of a particular society.

mwanajeshi *n* (*wa-*) soldier (cf *askari*) (Ar)

mwanajinakolojia *n* (*wa-*) gynaecologist (Eng)

mwanakamati *n* (*wa-*) committee member.

mwanakarne *n* (*wa-*) an outstanding person of a particular century.

mwanakaya *n* (*wa-*) a member of the household.

mwanakemia *n* (*wa-*) chemist (Eng)

mwanakijiji *n* (*wa-*) villager

mwanakisomo *n* (*wa-*) adult learner.

mwanakikundi *n* (*wa-*) group member.

mwanakondoo *n* (*wa-*) lamb (cf *mtoto wa kondoo*)

mwanakwaya *n* (*wa-*) chorister; a member of a choir group.

mwanakwetu *n* (*wa-*) fellow compatriot, fellow citizen, home person.

mwanaleksikografia *n* (*wa-*) lexicographer. (Eng)

mwanalugha *n* (*wa-*) language expert; language specialist.

mwanamaji *n* (*wa-*) sailor (cf *baharia*)

mwanamazingira *n* (*wa-*) environmentalist

mwanamapinduzi *n* (*wa-*) revolutionist, revolutionary.

mwanambee *n* (*wa-*) firstborn (cf *kifunguamimba*)

mwanambuzi *n* (*wa-*) kid (cf *mtoto wa mbuzi*)

mwanamchezo *n* (*wa-*) sportsman/woman.

mwanamgambo *n* (*wa-*) militiaman

mwanamimba (also *mwamimba*) *n* (*n*) (*med*) fibroid, fibroleiomyoma, leiomyofibroma (cf *mtuchi*)

mwanamize (also *nyamize*) *n* (*n*) (*zool*) ghost crab; a mostly-white crab off - white or sand - coloured and active at night living mostly in burrow in littoral fringe of sand beaches. *Ocypode ceratophthalamus*. (cf *nyamizi*)

mwanamke *n* (*wa-*) 1. woman. 2. mother; a human female creature capable of begetting children. 3. mistress; a woman who lives with a man for a period of time without being married to him: *Yeye si mkewe lakini ni mwanamke wake tu*, she is not his wife but his mistress. (cf *hawara, kimada*) 4. (*fig*) coward. (cf *hawafu*)

mwanamkiwa (pl *wanamkiwa*) *n* (*wa-*) orphan (cf *yatima*)

mwanamtandao *n* (*wa-*) internet surfer.

mwanamume *n* (*wa-*) 1. man, male (cf *rijali*) 2. lover, paramour. 3. (*fig*) a brave person; valiant, hero: *Mwanamume yule hamwogopi mtu yeyote*, that brave person is not scared of any person. (cf *shujaa, jabari*)

mwanamuziki *n* (*wa-*) musician (Eng)

mwanamwali (also *mwanamwari*) (pl *wanawali*) *n* (*wa-*) 1. maiden; a nubile girl. 2. virgin, virgo (cf *bikira*)

mwanana *adj* tranquil, serene, calm, cool: *Upepo mwanana*, cool air.

mwananchi *n* (*wa-*) nationalist, citizen. (*prov*) *Mvunjaji ni mwananchi*, the destroyer is the nationalist i.e. the real destroyer of a country is the citizen himself and not the outsider.

mwanandani *n (wa-)* (in Islam) recess in the grave into which a corpse is laid to rest. (cf *mji, luhudi*)

mwanandoa *n (wa-)* a married person.

mwanandondi *n (wa-)* boxer (cf *mwanamasumbwi*)

mwananumbi *n (n)* see *mnimbi*

mwanapaneli *n (wa-)* panelist; a member of the panel (Eng)

mwanapao *n (wa-)* an unmarried girl who has reached the age of puberty.

mwanapatholojia *n (wa-)* pathologist (Eng)

mwanapwa *n (wa-)* 1. sailor. (cf *baharia*) 2. fisherman. (cf *mvuvi*)

mwanariadha *n (wa-)* athlete: *Mwanariadha alipata medali ya fedha katika mashindano*, the athlete won a silver medal in the competition. *Mwanariadha wa kulipwa*, professional athlete. (Ar)

mwanariwaya *n (wa-)* novelist

mwanasaikolojia *n (wa-)* psychologist (Eng)

mwanasarakasi *n (wa-)* acrobat; a person who is skilled in feats of balance and agility in gymnastics.

mwanasarufi *n (wa-)* grammarian: *Mwanasarufi mapokeo*, traditional grammarian. *Mwanasarufi mamboleo*, modern grammarian. (Ar)

mwanasayansi *n (wa-)* scientist. (Eng)

mwanasemina *n (wa-)* seminar participant. (Eng)

mwanasesere *n (wa-)* doll, puppet: *Mwanasesere mweusi*, golliwog. (cf *mwanaabudu, doli, karagosi*)

mwanashanga *n (n)* north-western wind i.e. "land breeze."

mwanasheria *n (wa-)* lawyer, lawmaker: *Mwanasheria mkuu*, attorney general. *Mwanasheria wa serikali*, attorney general. (cf *wakili*) (Ar)

mwanasiasa *n (wa-)* politician: *Yeye ni mwanasiasa wa msimamo wa kati na kati*, he is a moderate politician; he is a centrist. (Ar)

mwanasoka *n (wa-)* soccer player: *Mwanasoka wa kulipwa*, professional soccer player. *Mwanasoka wa kimataifa*, international soccer player.

mwanataaluma *n (wa-)* academician, educator, specialist: *Huyu ni mwanataaluma katika tiba*, he is a specialist in medicine. (Ar)

mwanauchumi *n (wa-)* economist

mwanaviumbe *n (wa-)* naturalist; a person who studies nature, esp by direct observation of animals and plants.

mwanazuoni (also *mwanachuoni*) *n (wa)* pundit, savant, scholar; a learned person.

mwandaaji *n (wa-)* organizer: *Waandaaji wa mkutano wametayarisha ajenda ndefu*, the organisers of the meeting have prepared a long agenda. (cf *mwandazi*)

mwandalizi[1] *n (wa-)* waiter, waitress. (cf *mhudumu, mwandikaji*)

mwandalizi[2] *n (wa-)* organizer

mwandalizi[3] *adj* social: *Katibu mwandalizi*, social secretary.

mwandamano *n (mi-)* the act of persons or things moving forward as in a parade; procession, demonstration, sequence: *Mwandamano tawanyifu*, divergent sequence. (cf *mfuatano*)

mwandamizi *n (wa-)* 1. senior: *Mchunguzi mwandamizi*, senior research fellow. 2. a person with a specified position.

mwandamo *n (mi-)* used in the expression: *Mwezi mwandamo*, the new moon; crescent.

mwandani (also *mwendani*) *n (wa-)* a bosom friend; a close friend: *Yeye ni mwandani wangu wa miaka na miaka*, he is my close friend of so many years. (cf *mpenzi, sahibu, azizi*)

mwandazi *n (wa-)* 1. a person who cooks food for a special function as during a wedding, etc. (cf *mlisha*) 2. a person whose business is to provide food and service as during parties; caterer.

mwande *adv (idm) Kula mwande*, fail

to get what you were expecting e.g. *Alijaribu bahati yake kwenye mchezo wa kamari lakini alikula mwande*, he tried his luck in gambling but he failed to get what he wanted.

mwandikaji *n* (*wa*-) author, writer. (cf *mwandishi*)

mwandiko *n* (*mi*-) handwriting: *Mwandiko mbaya*, cacography. (cf *hati, maandishi*)

mwandishi *n* (*wa*-) 1. writer, author: *Mwandishi wa habari*, reporter, columnist, correspondent. *Mwandishi wa michezo*, sports writer. *Mwandishi wa insha*, essayist. *Mwandishi wa riwaya*, novelist. *Mwandishi wa tamthilia*, playwright. *Mwandishi wa historia*, historiographer. *Mwandishi mwenza*, co-author. *Mwandishi wa kumbukumbu za mkutano*, recording secretary; recorder. 2. secretary. (cf *katibu*)

mwanga[1] (also *mwangaza*) *n* (*mi*-) 1. light, brightness. (cf *nuru*) 2. (*fig*) enlightenment: *Nipe mwanga kidogo juu ya suala hili*, give me some light on this issue.

mwanga[2] *n* (*wa*-) 1. a person who performs witchcraft activities. 2. a person who works at night instead of sleeping. 3. a person who takes part in the night wizard's dance. 4. (*colloq*) a clever person; a bright-witted person.

mwanga[3] *n* (*mi*-) (*bot*) African arrow root, a tropical plant with starchy roots, bearing oval ridged fruits. *Tacca involucrata*.

mwangachaa *n* (*mi*-) (*bot*) an evergreen tree with linear-lanceolate glabrous leaves and white flowers, the stems of which contain latex. *Cerbera manghas*.

mwangajini *n* (*mi*-) (*bot*) an evergreen shrub with alternate ovate-lanceolate leathery leaves and inconspicuous small green flowers. *Popowia sp. Mwangajini mdogo*, a small evergreen tree with smooth almost black bark, opposite leaves and small bright blue flowers. *Strychnos sp.*

mwangala *n* (*mi*-) bells worn on the legs during dancing; ankle bells. (cf *njuga, msewe*)

mwangaliaji *n* (*wa*-) 1. spectator, watcher, viewer. (cf *mtazamaji*) 2. supervisor, caretaker; a person who takes care of sth such as property, etc (cf *mwangalizi*)

mwangalifu *n* (*wa*-) a cautious person; a scrupulous person: *Muuguzaji alikuwa mwangalifu katika kuviuguza vidonda vya wagonjwa wake*, the nurse was scrupulous in the treatment of her patients' wounds.

mwangalizi *n* (*wa*-) 1. caretaker; supervisor; a person taking care of sth such as property or an estate, office, child, etc. (cf *msimamizi*) 2. observer: *Waangalizi wa uchaguzi*, election observers. *Waangalizi wa kimataifa*, international observers.

mwangaluchi *n* (*mi*-) (*bot*) a kind of small black red fruit.

mwangamizi *n* (*wa*-) a destructive person, a malicious person; destroyer, devastator. (cf *mharibifu, mwurugaji*)

mwangani *n* (*mi*-) see *mkabilishemsi*

mwangao *n* (*mi*-) (*bot*) clove epiphyte; a clove plant which is parasitic.

mwangati *n* (*mi*-) (*bot*) East African cedar tree; a timber tree which is up to 140 feet tall. *Juniperus procera*.

mwangaza[1] (also *mwanga*) *n* (*mi*-) 1. light, glare, brilliance, brightness. (cf *nuru*) 2. (*fig*) enlightenment; bright idea: *Kwanza nilikuwa silielewi tatizo lenyewe lakini sasa nimepata mwangaza*, at first, I did not understand the problem but now I have found an enlightenment.

mwangaza[2] *n* (*wa*-) seeker; a person who is looking for sth. (*prov*) *Mwangaza mbili moja humponyoka*, a seeker of two things at the same time, one slips away i.e we should not do two things at the same time if we want to be successful in our daily life. Finish one thing first and then do the next one later.

mwangele n (mi-) 1. see *mgangaungo*. 2. (idm) *Piga mwangele*, put sby in suspense; confuse sby; put sby on tentahooks

mwangeni n (mi-) clover-leafed medicinal herb used also as a vegetable.

mwango¹ n (mi-) see *mlango¹*

mwango² n (mi-) a frame or bracket hung against a wall to carry a lamp; lampstand; lamp holder.

mwango³ n (mi-) (bot) 1. a kind of tree whose leaves are used as a medicine for yaws. *Rauvolfia sp.* 2. a branched shrub up to 12 feet tall with large sub-accuminate leaves.

mwanguo n (mi-) 1. (zool) great grey shrike; a kind of shrill-voiced bird. (cf *aninia, tiva, kipwe*) 2. (syn) *Mwanguo tuliu mliowe, msimuongope*, the shrike is used to make such a cry; don't fear it i.e. if a person is used to a certain habit, it is difficult to make him abandon it. In other words, habits die hard.

mwangusho n (mi-) 1. act (method, etc.) of throwing down sby/sth. 2. harvesting/reaping of crops in a farm. (cf *janguo*)

mwanguzi n (wa-) a person whose work is to knock down fruits such as coconuts or pick cloves, etc. (cf *muanguaji*)

mwangwi (also *mwengo*) n (mi-) echo; sound produced by reflecting sound waves from a surface.

mwani (pl *miani*) n (mi-) (bot) sea weed, marine, alga: *Mwani tambi*, coiled sea weed. (*Hydroclathrum clarathtus*)

mwaniaji n (wa-) contestant, contender, competitor.

mwano n (mi-) see *mawano*

mwanya n (mi-) 1. a gap esp in the front teeth. (cf *uwazi*) 2. a small opening between two things; gap. 3. loophole, chance, opportunity: *Sikupata mwanya wa kutoa fikira zangu*, I did not get an opportunity to express my views. (cf *fursa*)

mwanzaji n (wa-) see *mwanzilishi*

mwanzi n (mi-) 1. (bot) bamboo tree. *Bambusa sp.* 2. anything hollow resembling a bamboo in appearance or use such as a pipe, flute, flageolet, etc.: *Mwanzi wa pua*, nostril. *Mwanzi wa bunduki*, the barrel of a gun.

mwanzilishaji n (wa-) see *mwanzilishi*

mwanzilishi (also *mwanzaji, mwanzishaji, mwanzilishaji*) n (wa-) founder, architect, creator: *Alikuwa mwanzilishi wa klabu yetu*, he was the founder of our club.

mwanzishaji n (wa-) see *mwanzilishi*

mwanzo¹ n (mi-) 1. beginning, start. (prov) *Kila chenye mwanzo, hakikosi mwisho*, anything that has started such as play, etc has an ending. 2. (fig) source, origin, cause: *Mwanzo wa ugomvi ule haujulikani*, the cause of that conflict is unknown.

mwanzo² n (mi-) the book of Genesis.

mwanzoni adv in the beginning, at first; initially: *Mwanzoni, alikuwa mtu mzuri lakini baadaye akabadilika*, in the beginning, he was a good person, but later, he changed. (cf *awali*)

mwao¹ n (mi-) 1. awareness; state of being conscious or knowledgeable. 2. pester, annoyance, botheration. (cf *bughudha, kero*)

mwao² n (mi-) 1. (naut) slipway consisting of great many spars over which the boat is being rolled in launching. 2. planking inside the hole to protect the ceiling and the ribs against the impact of rolling cargo. 3. sth else laid on the floor e.g. matting.

mwao³ adj possessive adjective or pronoun for third plural meaning, "their", "in/at their".

mwapuza n (wa-) a negligent person, a carefree person. (cf *purukushani*)

Mwarabu n (wa-) Arab (Ar)

mwaranda n (mi-) 1. (anat) anus; the opening at the lower end of the alimentary canal. 2. anal arifice (syn) *Ukimwiga tembo kunya, utapasuka mwaranda*, if you defecate like an elephant, the hole in your anus will split i.e. if you imitate a rich or a strong person doing as he likes, you will end up in difficulties.

mwari[1] (also *mwali*) *n* (*wa-*) 1. a girl confined indoors. 2. virgin, maiden 3. bride or bridegroom during honeymoon. (*prov*) *Kwa mwari kwaliwa, kwa kungwi nako kuliwa*, don't take sth from your friend all the time without assisting him when he is in difficulties.

mwari[2] (also *mwandambize*) *n* (*wa-*) (*zool*) pelican; a large waterbird with a long hooked-tipped bill and a naked pouch.

mwari

mwaridi *n* (*mi-*) (*bot*) rose tree. *Rosa damascena*.

mwarita *n* (*mi-*) see *mharita*

mwarubaini (also *muarubaini*) *n* (*mi-*) 1. neem; a medium sized evergreen tree with white, fragrant flowers and pinnate leaves, bearing a fruit which produces an aromatic oil much used in local medicine. It is also very useful as an avenue and widely planted in Zanzibar. *Azadirachta indica* (*fig*) remedy, panaces, cure, solution: *Hiyo haiwezi kuwa mwarubaini wa matatizo yetu*, that cannot be a remedy to our problems.

mwasa (also *mwasaji*) *n* (*wa-*) a person who forbids sby to do sth.

mwasaji *n* (*wa*) see *mwasa*

mwasherati *n* (*wa-*) see *asherati*

mwashi *n* (*wa-*) mason (cf *mjenzi*)

mwashiri *n* (*mi-*) see *mhashiri*

mwasho *n* (*mi-*) irritation: *Mwasho wa upupu*, irritation from the cowitch.

mwasi *n* (*wa-*) 1. an obstinate person; bulldog (cf *mkaidi*) 2. rebel, traitor: *Askari mwasi*, insurgent. *Waasi walifanikiwa kukiteka kituo cha polisi*, the rebels succeeded in capturing a police station. (cf *mhalifu*) (Ar)

Mwasia *n* (*wa-*) Asian (Eng)

mwasisi (pl *waasisi*) *n* (*wa-*) founder, architect, creator: *Mwasisi wa chama tawala*, the founder of the ruling party. (cf *mwanzilishi*) (Ar)

mwata *n* (*n*) (*zool*) trumpet worm; a kind of coelomate worm having a swollen posterior and is plnkish-white in colour, found in coarse sand and eulittoral and used as fish bait and food.

mwatuko *n* (*mi-*) crack, split: *Mwatuko katika ukuta huu unaleta hatari*, the crack in this wall poses danger. (cf *mpasuko*)

mwavuli (also *mwamvuli*) *n* (*mi-*) umbrella: *Mwavuli wa kurukia*, parachute.

mwayamway.a *vi* loiter, loaf, idle. Prep. **mwayamway.i.a** St. **mwayamway.ik.a** Cs. **mwayamway.ish.a** Rp. **mwayamway.an.a** (cf *mangamanga*)

mwayo *n* (*mi-*) yawn

mwega *n* (*mi-*) 1. support, rop. (cf *nguzo, mwao*) 2. a person or thing that supports.

mwehu (pl *wehu*) *n* (*wa-*) an insane person, a mad person; lunatic, madman: *Usimsikilize mwehu yule*, don't listen to that madman. (cf *mapepe, afkani, mwendawazimu*)

mweka[1] *n* (*wa-*) used in the expression: *Mweka hazina*, treasurer. *Mweka fedha*, cashier. (cf *mshika fedha*)

mwek.a[2] *vi* glitter, dazzle, flash. Prep. **mwek.e.a** St. **mwek.ek.a** Cs. **mwek.esh.a** Ps. **mwek.w.a** (cf *mwesa*)

mwekevu n (wa-) see *mwelekevu*
mwekezaji (pl *wawekezaji*) n (wa-) investor: *Wawekezaji walihimizwa kuweka rasilimali zao nchini*, the investors were urged to invest their capital in the country.
mweledi (pl *weledi*) n (wa-) 1. a well-versed person; a well-informed person: *Yeye ni mweledi wa mila za watu hapa, au sivyo?* he is well-informed in the traditions of the local people around here, isn't it? (cf *mwelewa*) 2. a skilled person; expert.
mweleka (also *mwelekaji*) n (wa-) a person who carries sth with a baby's sling.
mwelekaji n (wa-) see *mweleka*
mwelekeo n (mi-) 1. stand, stance, direction, attitude: *Kiongozi wao hana mwelekeo mzuri*, their leader does not have a good stand. (cf *msimamo*) 2. direction, source, path: *Gari ilipoteza mwelekeo na baadaye kupinduka*, the vehicle lost its direction and later overturned (cf *njia*) 3. feasibility of sth to take place.
mwelekevu (also *mwelevu*) n (wa-) 1. an amenable person; a responsive person; a well-disciplined person: *Mwelekevu alifuata amri ya mwajiri wake*, the responsive person obeyed the orders of his employer. 2. a person who has a knack of sth; a person who does things in a proper way: *Mwelekevu huwafanyia insafu wake zake*, the righteous person exercises justice among his wives. (cf *mwadilifu*)
mweleko n (mi-) the carrying of a child, etc. on the back or hip, for example while at work or walking.
mwelewa n (wa-) a well-versed person; a well-informed person; savant, pundit, maven. (*mweledi*)
mwembe n (mi-) (bot) mango tree. *Mangifera indica*.
mwendachi n (mi-) (bot) a kind of yam.
mwendambize n (wa-) see *mwari²*
mwendanguu n (wa-) a person who loses hope easily; a person who despairs easily.

mwendani n (wa-) see *mwandani*
mwendawazimu (pl *wendawazimu*) n (wa-) 1. madman, lunatic; a mentally unbalanced person(cf *mkichaa*) 2. a mad person.
mwende n (mi-) (bot) a kind of tree bearing small fruits resembling dates.
mwendeleo n (mi-) progress of work, etc. in a particular sector; advancement, continuity: *Mwendeleo wake kazini si mzuri*, his progress at work is not good. (cf *uendelezaji*)
mwendelezo¹ n (mi-) (math) progression: *Mwendelezo wa jiometria*, geometric progression.
mwendelezo² n (mi-) continuation, progression: *Ule ulikuwa ni mwendelezo wa matukio yaliyotokea kabla*, that was a continuation of events that occurred earlier.
mwendesha n (wa-) a person who performs a particular duty, etc.: *Mwendesha mashtaka*, prosecutor. *Mwendesha teksi*, taxi driver. *Mwendesha baiskeli*, cyclist. *Mwendesha pikipiki*, motor cyclist.
mwendeshaji n (wa-) 1. administrator. 2. captain, pilot, navigator.
mwendo¹ n (mi-) motion, speed, movement: *Mwendo wa jua*, solar motion. *Mwendo nasibu*, random motion. *Mwendo thabiti*, rigid motion. *Mwendo wa kudumu*, perpetual motion.
mwendo² n (mi-) conduct, manners, behaviour. (cf *tabia, mwenendo*)
mwenendo n (mi-) behaviour, conduct, manner: *Mwenendo wake si mzuri*, his behaviour is not good. (cf *tabia*)
mwenge n (mi-) 1. blazing torch; firebrand: *Mwenge wa uhuru*, independence torch. 2. leaves or dried fronds that are tied together and lit at one end inorder to see what is in front.
mwengea n (mi-) (bot) sausage tree. *Kigelia pinnata*. (cf *mnyegeya, mwungunya*)
mwengele n (mi-) (bot) a climbing shrub with somewhat succulent pedate compound leaves and yellow flowers, bearing small black berries, whose leaves and fruits are used medicinally.

Cissus adenocaulis.

mwengo[1] *n (mi-)* the tail of an animal like that of a mule and giraffe; flywhisk. (cf *usinga, mgwisho*)

mwengo[2] *n (mi-)* see *mwangwi*

mwengo[3] *n (mi-)* a kind of bad scent emanating from aquatic animals such as crabs, oysters, etc; shellfish malodour.

mweni (pl *weni*) *n (wa-) (arch)* guest, visitor, stranger. (cf *mgeni*)

mwenu *adj, pron* possessive adjective or pronoun for second person plural meaning "your" "in/at your"

mwenye *n (wa-)* one who possesses; owner, possessor: *Mwenye duka*, shop owner. *Mwenye nacho*, one who has; a possessor of sth *Mwenye mali*, one who possesses wealth. *Mwenye haki*, one having the right on his side.

mwenyeji (pl *wenyeji*) *n (wa-)* 1. native, indigenous: *Wao ni wenyeji wa kisiwa hiki*, they are the natives of this island. 2. resident, inhabitant, occupant: a person resident in a particular place even if he was not born there: *Yeye si mwenyeji wa mtaa huu*, he is not a resident of this neighbourhood. 3. host: *Mwenyeji aliwakaribisha wageni wake kwa taadhima*, the host welcomed his guests warmly.

mwenyekiti *n (wa-)* chairperson; chairwoman; chairman: *Makamu mwenyekiti*, vice chairman; vice chairperson.

mwenyewe *pron* form of *-enyewe* meaning "by himself." "by herself": *Mtoto mwenyewe ameanguka*, the child fell down by himself.

Mwenyezi *n (n)* (of the quality of God) the exalted; the mighty: *Mwenyezi Mungu*, Almighty God.

mwenza *n (wa-)* see *mwenzi*

mwenzake *n (wa-)* his companion, her companion, his colleague, her colleague: *Wenzake wameondoka punde hivi*, his colleagues have just left.

mwenzi (also *mwenza*) (pl *wenzi*) *n (wa-)* friend, companion: *Mwenzi wangu ni* *mtu mpole sana*, my friend is a very quiet person. (cf *rafiki*)

mwere *n (mi-) (bot)* East African cotton tree; a kind of wild kapok tree up to 36 m with a long pole and yellow-green bark which yields a red dye. *Bombax rhodognaphalon*. (cf *msufi-mwitu*)

mwereka *n (mi-)* wrestling: *Mpigaji mwereka*, wrestler: *Angusha mwereka*, wrestle with someone. *Piga mwereka*, wrestle with someone.

mwerevu *n (wa-)* a cunning person; a shrewd person; a clever person (*provs*) *Mjinga akierevuka mwerevu yu mashakani*, if a fool wises up, the smart person is in trouble. i.e if a fool becomes enlightened, the wise man will have to seek refuge since he will be in trouble. *Mwerevu hajinyoi*, a cunning person will not last forever because one day, people will understand his deeds. (cf *mdanganyifu*)

mwerezi *n (mi-)* 1. (*bot*) a tree with alternate compound leaves. C*edreli odorata*. 2. an evergreen rain forest tree with alternate ovate lanceolate leaves with racemes of yellow flowers and fleshy fruits, which has useful timber; cedar tree. *Pygeum africanum*.

Mwethopia *n (wa-)* Ethiopian (cf *Mhabeshi*)

mwetu *adj, pron* possessive adjective or pronoun meaning "our" "at/in our."

mweuo[1] *n (mi-)* the period of high tide increasing towards full moon. (cf *maji-makuu*)

mweuo[2] *n (n)* the presentation of Virgin Mary in the temple; Purification Day.

mweuo[3] *n (mi-)* purification by observing rituals; cleansing of the body.

mwewe[1] *n (n) (zool)* hawk; a bird of prey of chicks (family *Falconidae*) characterized by short-rounded wings and a long tail.

mwewe[2] *n (n)* a kind of small to moderate-sized sea fish (family *Haemulidae*) having a fairly compressed body and moderate or small scales; sweetlips, rubber-lips.

mwezekaji *n* (*wa-*) a person who thatches a roof of a house, hut, etc. with grass, reeds or coconut leaves.

mwezi[1] *n* (*wa-*) 1. month, lunar: *Mwezi mwandamo*, the new moon. *Mwezi mchanga*, new moon. *Mwezi mpya*, new moon. *Mwezi kongo*, new moon. *Mwezi mpevu*, a full moon. *Mwezi mchimbu*, a moon having lasted between eleven and twenty days since the moon has been sighted. *Mwezi mkuu*, full moon. 2. used in the expression: *Liwa na mwezi*, getting spoiled as in the case of a cloth or coconut. (*prov*) *usigombe na mkwezi nazi imeliwa na mwezi*: do not quarrel the coconut harvester (climbers) because the coconut was eaten by the moon. i.e. you are blaming the wrong person.

mwezi[2] *n* (*mi-*) 1. a period of 28 or 29 or 30 or 31 days: *Miezi kumi na mbili inafanya mwaka mmoja*, twelve months constitute one year. 2. (*idm*) *Ingia mwezini*, menstruate. 3. date: *Leo ni mwezi ngapi?* What is the date today?

mwia[1] *n* (*ny-*) creditor (cf *mdai*)

mwia[2] (pl *nyia*) *n* (*mi-*) period, time.

mwiba *n* (*mi-*) 1. thorn: *Mti huu una miiba mingi*, this tree has many thorns. 2. spine: *Hii si miiba ya samaki*, these are not the spines of the fish. 3. sting: *Mwiba wa nyuki*, bee's sting. *Mwiba wa ng'e*, scorpion's sting.

mwibuko *n* (*mi-*) emergence: *Mwibuko wake kutoka majini ulinishtua*, his emergence from the water startled me. (cf *mzuko*)

mwida *n* (*mi-*) see *muda*

mwigaji *n* (*wa-*) one who imitates or copies someone else; actor, imitator, mimicker, copyist.

mwigizaji *n* (*wa-*) 1. actor, actress. 2. a person who imitates or copies someone else; imitator, mimicker, copyist.

mwigizo *n* (*mi-*) flywhisk. (cf *mgwisho*, *usinga*)

mwigo[1] *n* (*mi-*) mimicry, imitation, copying. (cf *wigo*)

mwigo[2] *n* (*wa-*) (*zool*) red-eyed dove; a kind of brownish grey dove having a red eye, a black collar on the hindneck, a conspicuous pale grey forehead and deep vinous-pink underparts, used for travel prediction. *Streptopelia semitorquata*.

mwijiko *n* (*mi-*) see *mjiko*

mwiko[1] *n* (*mi-*) 1. a big wooden spoon used in the kitchen: *Mwiko wa mwashi*, a mason's trowel; shovel. (cf *upawa*) 2. (*idm*) *Elekezwa mwiko*, be in a hurry to come back.

mwiko[2] *n* (*n*) 1. taboo, totem: *Ni mwiko kwa watoto wadogo kutumia maneno machafu*, it is taboo for children to use abusive words. 2. (*syn*) *Masikini hana mwiko*, a poor man knows no taboos. 3. sth that one cannot do because of principle, faith, custom, etc.: *Kutiana fitina kwetu ni mwiko*, sowing discord among ourselves is a taboo.

mwiku *n* (*u*) leftover food; food left over from evening until the next day. (cf *kilalo*, *kiporo*, *bariyo*, *uporo*)

mwili *n* (*mi-*) 1. body: -*wa na mwili*, become fat. *Ingia mwili*, become fat. *Pungua mwili*, become thin. (cf *jasadi*, *badani*) 2. the largest area of colour on a piece of cloth: *Nguo hii ina takriban mwili mwekundu*, this dress is largely red.

mwima[1] *n* (*wa-*) a person who likes to stand up instead of sitting down; a person who stands upright.

mwima[2] *n* (*wa-*) a group of women organizing a funeral function.

mwimba *n* (*mi-*) a cloth worn by women round the body esp after childbirth. (cf *mkaja*)

mwimbaji *n* (*wa-*) singer (cf *mghani*)

mwimo *n* (*mi-*) 1. pillar, prop, support. (cf *mhimili*, *nguzo*) 2. an upright or side piece of a door or window frame; door post, window jamb. (cf *kiguzo*)

mwina (pl *ngina*) *n* (*mi-*) a pit dug for catching large animals; burrow: *Mtego wa mwina*, a trap hole. (cf *rima*)

mwinamo *n* (*mi-*) 1. bending; stooping: *Mwinamo wake unaonyesha kwamba mtu yule yumo katika huzuni kubwa*, his act of bending shows that that person is in deep distress. (cf *uinamaji*) 2. slope, downslope: *Mwinamo bandia*, virtual slope. (cf *mteremko*)

mwindaji *n* (*wa-*) hunter (cf *mrumba, mkaa, msasi, msakaji*)

mwingajini (also *mhangajini*) *n* (*mi-*) (*bot*) a kind of tree that is believed to chase away evil spirits. *Cassia occidentalis.*

mwingamo *n* (*mi-*) see *mkumbi*

mwingasiafu *n* (*mi-*) (*bot*) jack bean plant, Horse bean plant, Sword bean plant. *Canavalia ensiformis.*

Mwingereza *n* (*wa-*) British, Englishman.

mwingilizi[1] (also *mwingizi*) *n* (*wa-*) a man who inherits his brother's widow according to the customs of some tribes; an inheritor of a brother's wife.

mwingilizi[2] (also *mwingizaji, mwingizi*) *n* (*wa-*) a person who introduces a new style, fashion, etc. of sth; initiator, architect, designer.

mwingine *adj, pron* form of *-ingine*, meaning "someone else": *Mtu mwingine*, another person.

mwingizaji[1] *n* (*wa-*) see *mwingilizi*[2]

mwingizaji[2] *n* (*wa-*) used with another noun to form a compound word: *Mwingizaji bidhaa*, an exporter of goods.

mwingizi *n* (*wa-*) see *mwingilizi*[1] and *mwingilizi*[2]

mwinikanguru *n* (*mi-*) a prickly climber with flat, linear, sickle-shaped leaf-branches with fragrant flowers, found in coral rocky land and on coastal areas of Zanzibar. *Asparagus falcatus.* (cf *myungiyungi, kinywele*)

mwinimba *n* (*mi-*) see *mwanamimba*

Mwinjilisti *n* (*wa-*) Evangelist (Eng)

mwinukio *n* (*mi-*) 1. state of rapid prosperity. 2. act (manner, etc.) of riding a bicycle by paddling 3. act (method, etc.) of sitting on a sailing vessel.

mwinuko *n* (*mi-*) rise, elevation, acclivity; an upward slope of ground, etc.: *Pana mwinuko wa ardhi pale*, there is an elevation of the ground over there. (cf *kilima*)

mwinyamwiny.a *vt* see *munyamunya*

mwinyi *n* (*ma-*) 1. a word carrying respect used while calling a male person; Mr: Mwinyi Ali, Mr. Ali. 2. bourgeois, lord, overlord, chief: *Wale mamwinyi wanaishi maisha ya raha na mustarehe*, those lords are living a luxurious life. (cf *bwanyenye*)

mwinyo *n* (*mi-*) (*zool*) arm or tentacle of an octopus or cuttlefish. (cf *mnyiri*)

mwiro *n* (*mi-*) elephant's trunk. (*prov*) *Ndovu hashindwi na mwirowe*, an elephant cannot be defeated by its own trunk i.e. even a weak mother will not fail to bring up her child regardless of the nature of his or her child.

mwisho *n* (*mi-*) end, conclusion: *Kila kitu kina mwisho wake*, everything has got an end. (cf *tamati*)

mwishoni (also *mwishowe*) *adv* finally, lastly, eventually. *Alikuwa anamtafuta sana binti yake lakini mwishoni, akamwona*, she was looking desperately for her daughter but eventually she found her.

mwishowe *adv* see *mwishoni*

Mwislamu *n* (*wa-*) Muslim: *Mwislamu mkereketwa*, a Muslim fundamentalist.

mwitiko[1] *n* (*mi-*) response, reply. (cf *uitikaji*)

mwitiko[2] *n* (*mi-*) refrain (cf *kibwagizo, kiitikio, mkarara*)

mwito *n* (*mi-*) 1. call, appeal: *Mwito wake wa kututaka sisi tumsaidie umepokewa vizuri*, his appeal to us to help him has been received warmly. (*prov*) *Mtu hakatai mwito, hukataa aitiwalo*, a person does not reject a call, he rejects what he is called for. 2. (act, method, style, etc.) of calling: *Mwito wake ulikuja kwa sauti ya nguvu*, his calling came in a high-pitched voice. (cf *utaji*)

mwitu[1] *n* (*mi-*) forest, bushland, bush. (cf *msitu, pori*)

mwitu[2] *adj* wild: *Mbwa mwitu*, a fox.

mwivi (pl *wevi*) *n* (*wa-*) see *mwizi*

mwivu *n* (*wa-*) 1. (in marriage matters) a jealous person: *Mke wake ni mwivu*, his wife is a jealous person; 2. an envious person; a person who does not like to see others make a progress of any kind: *Mwivu hakutaka kuona wenzake wanaendelea mbele*, the envious person did not want to see others advancing (cf *hasidi*).

mwiwa *n* (*wa-*) debtor: *Mwiwa alikubali kulimaliza deni lake*, the debtor agreed to clear his debt. (cf *mdaiwa*)

mwiza *n* (*mi-*) (*naut*) water of 15 fathoms, which is the utmost depth for safety anchoring.

mwizi (also *mwivi*) (pl *wezi*) *n* (*wa-*) thief, robber, rustler: *Wezi wa mifugo*, cattle rustlers. *Polisi waliwakamata wezi sugu*, the police arrested hardcore thieves. (*prov*) *Siku za mwizi ni arobaini*, the days of a thief are forty i.e. if you continue to steal, one day you will be caught.

mwoga *n* (*wa-*) coward. (*prov*) *Kunguru mwoga, hukimbiza ubawa wake*, a timid crow is even scared of it's own wing i.e. the coward runs at the slight sign of trouble.

mwogo *n* (*mi-*) 1. act (method, etc.) of bathing. 2. the days in which girls in initiation schools go to bathe for the first time after the ceremony.

mwogofyo *n* (*mi-*) threat, threatening.

mwoka (also *mwokaji*) *n* (*wa-*) used in conjunction with another noun to form a compound word: *Mwoka mikate*, baker. *Mwoka nyama*, meat roaster.

mwokaji *n* (*wa-*) see *mwoka*

mwokozi *n* (*wa-*) liberator, saviour: *Yeye alikuwa mwokozi wa nchi yetu*, he was the liberator of our country.

mwombaji (also *muombaji*) *n* (*wa-*) 1. beggar. (cf *masikini*) 2. applicant, petitioner: *Waombaji wa ile kazi watahojiwa wiki ijayo*, the applicants of the job will be interviewed next week.

mwombezi *n* (*wa-*) intercessor; a person who intercedes on behalf of others.

mwombi *n* (*wa-*) a person who is fond of begging.

mwombolezaji *n* (*wa-*) mourner; a person who expresses sorrow over the loss of someone, etc.: *Waombolezaji walimliwaza mfiwa*, the mourners comforted the bereaved.

mwonaji *n* (*wa-*) one who views, sees, etc.; viewer, witness.

mwondoko *n* (*mi-*) 1. gait; way of walking. 2. majestic walk.

mwonevu *n* (*wa-*) oppressor, tyrant. (cf *mkandamizaji, dhalimu*)

mwongo[1] *n* (*mi-*) 1. number; count. 2. decade.

mwongo[2] (also *mrongo*) *n* (*wa-*) cheat, liar, hypocrite: *Wewe ni mwongo nini? Kila unachosema hakiaminiki*. Are you a liar? Everything that you are saying is unbelievable. (cf *mzushi, kidhahu, mnafiki*)

mwongofu (also *mwongoka*) *n* (*wa-*) a person who follows the right path; a person who goes in the right direction; a righteous person: *Mwongofu hutenda mambo mema*, a righteous person performs good deeds. (cf *mwadilifu*)

mwongoka *n* (*wa-*) see *mwongofu*

mwongoleo *n* (*mi-*) fee given during the funeral arrangements of prominent people in the East African coastal areas and its islands; burial fee.

mwongoti *n* (*mi-*) see *mlingoti*

mwongozo *n* (*mi-*) 1. guidance, guideline: *Wanachama waliomba wapewe mwongozo madhubuti*, the members wanted to be given proper guidelines.

2. guidebook: *Mwongozo wa riwaya hii bado haujaandikwa*, the guidebook for this novel has not yet been written.

mwonjo *n* (*mi-*) 1. act (style, etc.) of tasting: *Mwonjo wake wa chakula jikoni ni wa kiajabuajabu*, his tasting of the food in the kitchen is peculiar. 2. (*fig*) taste of life; trial: *Kifo cha mama kilikuwa mwonjo katika maisha yangu*, my mother's death was a trial in my life. (cf *mtihani, jaribio*) 3. first experience or occurrence.

mwonyeshaji *n* (*wa-*) demonstrator, guide.

mwonzi *n* (*mi-*) light ray, beam: *Mianzi ya jua*, the rays of the sun. *Mwonzi tawanyifu*, divergent beam. *Mwonzi wa elektroni*, electron beam.

mwosha *n* (*wa-*) washer; one who cleans sth by washing: *Mwosha maiti*, a person engaged to wash a corpse and prepare it for burial. *Mwosha baiskeli*, a person engaged to wash bicycles. (*prov*) *Mwosha huoshwa*, the washer (of corpses) is also be washed one day when he dies.

mwosho *n* (*mi-*) act or method of washing

mwovodhaji *n* (*mi-*) a person who swims and watches carefully the fishing net under the sea so that it is not trapped and tangled; diver.

mwovu *n* (*wa-*) an evil person; devil; reprobate. (cf *muuvi, fisadi*)

mwuaji *n* (*wa-*) see *muuaji*

mwujiza *n* (*wa-*) see *muujiza*

mwumba *n* (*wa-*) see *muumba*

mwushari *n* (*mi-*) (*naut*) keelson; a longitudinal beam or set of timber or metal plates inside the hall of a ship along the keel in order to give strength and stiffness.

myaa *n* (*mi-*) palm leaves which are used to make baskets.

Myahudi *n* (*wa-*) Jew (Ar)

myeka *adj* private: *Katibu myeka*, private secretary, confidential secretary.

myegeya *n* (*mi-*) sausage tree. *Kigelia pinnata*. (cf *mwegea, mvungunya*)

myeyuko *n* (*mi-*) 1. melting: *Myeyuko wa siagi*, the melting of butter. *Myeyuko wa theluji*, the melting of snow. 2. liquid.

myeyungano *n* (*mi-*) fusion: *Myeyungano wa nyuklia*, nuclear fusion.

myeyusho *n* (*mi-*) solution

myombo *n* (*mi-*) (*bot*) a tree with flush red or pink leaves and green flowers with white filaments, whose bark is used to make ropes, boxes, crates, etc. *Brachystegia speciformis*. (cf *mtondo, mrihi*)

myugwa *n* (*mi-*) (*bot*) taro plant; coco yam plant. *Colocasia antiquorum*.

myuko *n* (*mi-*) convection

Myunani *n* (*wa-*) ancient Greek: *Myunani halisi*, Hellene; an ancient Greek (Ar)

myungiyungi *n* (*mi-*) 1. (*bot*) blue water lily. *Nymphaea capensis*. (cf *mwinikanguru*) 2. Zanzibar water lily. *Nymphaea zanzibarensis*.

myungiyungi

myunguvo *n* (*mi-*) (*bot*) a much-branched evergreen tree whose leaves and roots are very toxic. *Agauria salicifolia*.

mzaa *n* (*wa-*) parent of; one who begets or gives birth to: *Bibi mzaa baba*, paternal grandmother. *Mzaa bibi*, great grandmother.

mzabibu *n* (*mi-*) (*bot*) grape vine tree. *Vitis vinifera*. *Mzabibu mwitu*, a climbing plant with long stems, cordate leaves and small green flowers. *Ampelocissus grantii*.

mzabizabina *n* (*wa-*) see *mdhabidhabina*

mzabuni *n* (*wa-*) 1. a person offering a high bid in an auction; bidder. 2. a person who offers a tender; a formal offer to supply goods or services to an organization; tenderer.

mzagao n (mi-) diffusion, spreading, dispersion, spread, pervasion: *Mzagao wa kipindupindu nchini umeleta vifo vingi*, the spread of cholera in the country has caused a lot of deaths. (cf *uenezi*)

mzaha n (mi-) joke, mock, derision. (cf *dhihaka, utani, masihara*)

mzaituni (also *mzeituni*) n (mi-) (bot) olive tree. *Olea europea*.

mzale n (wa-) 1. a person born in a particular place; native, indigene. 2. a person given a leadership based on indigenousness. (cf *mwyale*)

mzalendo n (wa-) nationalist, patriot.

mzalia (also *kizalia, mzaliwa*) n (wa-) native; indigene: *Yeye si mzalia wa nchi hii, he is not a native of this country*.

mzaliwa n (wa-) see *mzalia*

mzama n (wa-) diver; one who dives or sinks in water.

mzamaji n (wa-) a diver by profession.

mzambarau n (mi-) (bot) Java plum tree; a large spreading evergreen tree of rather dirty appearance, having ovate to oblong leaves, bearing oval purple fruits when ripe and containing in it one large seed. *Eugenia cumini*.

mzamia n (wa-) one who dives for sth: *Mzamia lulu*, one who dives for pearls.

mzamili n (wa-) postgraduate student.

mzamio n (mi-) act (style, etc.) of diving into water for sth.

mzandiki n (wa-) hypocrite, liar: *Utamwamini mzandiki yule?* Will you trust that hypocrite? (cf *mdanganyifu, kidhabu*)

mzao n (mi-) 1. the season of special plants to bear fruits or crops. 2. act (method, etc.) of bearing: *Mzao wa mipapai hii katika msimu huu ni mzuri*, the bearing of fruits of these pawpaw trees for this season is good.

3. produce, made in one swoop.

mzawa n (wa-) 1. indigene, native. 2. descendant of.

mzazi n (wa-) 1. parent. 2. a fertile woman; a productive woman; a grand multiparous woman. 3. a woman in childbirth.

mzee n (wa-) 1. an old person. 2. a name of respect given to a man. 3. parent esp father: *Mzee wako ni mkali*, your father is strict. (cf *mzazi*) 4. a person who has a relationship with another one.

mzega (also *mzegamzega*) n (wa-) 1. water carrier; a person who carries tins of water on each end of a pole carried across the shoulders. 2. a measure of two tins carried by a water carrier. (cf *mpiko, maarasi*) 3. one of the tins so carried by such a pole.

mzegamzega n (wa-) see *mzega*

mzeituni n (mi-) see *mzaituni*

mzembe n (wa-) 1. a careless person, a negligent person. 2. a lazy person, an indolent person; loafer, idler. (cf *mvivu, mlegevu, mtepetevu*)

mzengwe n (mi-) 1. private conversations. 2. (syn) *Nendeni mzengwe*, go and talk privately. 3. intrigue, conspiracy: *Chama chao kimejaa mizengwe*, their party is full of intrigues. (cf *njama*)

mzi[1] n (mi-) see *mzizi*

mzi[2] n (mi-) (bot) a plant suitable for making ropes.

mzia n (mi-) (zool) barracuda; any pipe-like fish (family *Sphyraenidae*) with small cycloid scales, found in tropical seas.

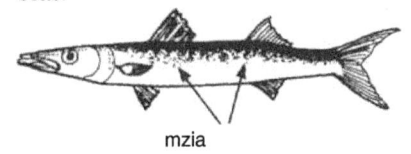

mzia

mziavu n (wa-) a stunted person; a retarded person.

mzibo n (mi-) act (method, etc.) of covering

sth such as a bottle, hole, etc.; with a cork, etc.; plugging. (*uzibaji*)
mzigo *n* (*mi-*) 1. load, luggage. (cf *shehena*) 2. (*fig*) burden: *Umenipa mtoto wako nimlee lakini huu ni mzigo kwangu*, you have given me your child to bring him up but this is a burden for me. (cf *jukumu*)
mziki *n* (*n*) see *muziki*
mzikoziko *n* (*mi-*) (*bot*) a shrub with alternate leaves, whose roots are used as an emetic. *Psychotria sp.*
mzima *n* (*wa-*) one who extinguishes, etc.: *Mzima moto*, fireman.
mzimu[1] *n* (*mi-*) 1. a place of the spirits of the dead where offerings and prayers are made. 2. a place functioning as headquarters of the big evil spirit usu located in caves, etc. 3. a grave for the ancient people.
mzimu[2] *n* (*mi-*) a kind of white soil used for smearing the face or body of *mwari* while undergoing initiation rites.
mzinduko *n* (*mi-*) sudden realization; awakening
mzinduo *n* (*mi-*) shock, astonishment, realization, awakening. (cf *mtanabahisho*)
mzinduzi *n* (*wa-*) inaugurator: *Waziri alikuwa mzinduzi katika ufunguzi wa benki mpya*, the minister was the inaugurator during the opening of the new bank.
mzinga *n* (*mi-*) 1. a large gun with a short barrel; cannon: *Piga mzinga*, fire a cannon. 2. hive: *Mzinga wa nyuki*, beehive. 3. a total victory of six rounds in card playing. 4. the frame of a drum where the animal skin is stretched; drum frame. 5. (*sl*) a bottle of booze.
mzingafuri *n* (*mi-*) see *mzingifuri*
mzingativu *n* (*wa-*) a thoughtful person; a sensitive person.
mzingi (also *mzingwi*) *n* (*mi-*) (*zool*) a kind of crane smaller than a stork.
mzingifuri (also *mzingafuri*) *n* (*mi-*) (*bot*) annato, cinnagar; a much-branched shrub which produces an orange powder, used as a dye for colouring butter, cheese, varnishes, etc. The plant is sometimes used as a hedge or screen in gardens. *Bixa orellana.*
mzingile *n* (*mi-*) 1. labyrinth, maze, puzzle: *Njia ndogondogo za mzingile*, a labyrinth of little streets. 2. (*fig*) labyrinth; a complicated situation: *Sheria zenye mzingile*, a labyrinth of laws.
mzingo[1] *n* (*mi-*) circumference, orbit, perimeter. (cf *pindamo, duara, mzunguko*)
mzingo[2] *n* (*mi-*) bad odour, rotten smell, stinking smell; malodour, putresence: *Pahala hapa pananuka kwa sababu ya mzingo wa mnyama aliyekufa*, this place is stinking because of the rotten smell of the animal that has died. (cf *kijusi, uvundo*)
mzingwa *n* (*mi-*) see *mzingi*
mzinifu *n* (*wa-*) adulterer; a sexually immoral person; a promiscuous person. (cf *mzinzi*)
mzinzi *n* (*wa-*) adulterer, fornicator, debaucher. (cf *mzinifu, asherati, mgoni*)
mzio[1] *n* (*mi-*) taboo either for medical reasons or because of totemism. (cf *mwiko*)
mzio[2] *n* (*mi-*) (*med*) allergy: *Mzio wa pua*, allergic rhinitis. *Ana mzio wa kahawa*, he has an allergy to coffee.
mzira *n* (*mi-*) a kind of fish of *Nemipteridae* family.
mzishi *n* (*wa-*) 1. a person engaged in funeral arrangements; an undertaker who manages burial arrangements. 2. a friend or brother who assists someone in difficulties.
mziwanda *n* (*wa-*) the last born child of a woman. (cf *kichinjamimba, kitindamimba*)
mziwaziwa *n* (*mi-*) 1. (*bot*) a shrub or tree with elliptic leaves and yellowish-green flowers bearing an edible glubose fruit. *Antidesma venosum.* 2. a prostrate

herb with reddish-green flowers. The herb is a very common weed in cultivations, lawns and roadsides. *Euphorbia hirta.* 3. a perennial leafless sedge with green stems up to 3 feet tall and umbels of yellow cinnamon or rust coloured spikes of flowers, found in wet and marshy places. *Cyperus flabelliformis.* 4. a much-branched glabrous evergreen tree with a milky latex with somewhat glossy opposite leaves and white tubular flowers. *Hunteria africana.*

mzizi (also *mzi*) *n* (*mi-*) 1. the root of a plant; rootlet. 2. (*gram*) radical root; the base form of a word which cannot be further analyzed without the loss of the identity i.e. it is that part of a word remaining after all affixes have been removed. In the word *mchezaji*, "player," for example, if we remove affixes *m*, *a* and *ji*, we remain with *chez*, which is the root. 3. (*syn*) *Chomekwa mzizi*, bewitched, be charmed. 4. (*fig*) source, cause, origin: *Mzizi wa ugomvi wao haujulikani*, the cause of their conflict is unknown. (cf *chanzo*, *chimbuko*)

mzizimo *n* (*mi-*) 1. chill, coldness: *Maji ya mzizimo*, cold water. 2. calmness of a place. 3. sensitivity of teeth due to coldness.

mzo[1] *n* (*mi-*) a measure of weight or dry measure of 10 frasilas or 60 *pishis* i.e. between 350-360 lbs equivalent to *jizila* or 160 kilograms.

mzo[2] *adv* abundantly, copiously, excessively: *Maziwa yalimwagika mzo*, the milk spilt excessively.

mzofafa *adv* in a show-off manner, pompously, with pomposity: *Alitembea kwa mzofafa*, he walked pompously. (cf *kwa matao*, *kwa maringo*)

mzoga *n* (*mi-*) 1. animal carcass; carrion. 2. a word used out of anger to refer to someone who has been killed unlawfully. (cf *kimba*) 3. (*fig*) a worthless thing; thingamajig, gimcrack, knick-knack.

mzomari *n* (*mi-*) see *mzumari*

mzomeo *n* (*mi-*) booing, jeering: *Mzomeo wake unachusha*, his booing is disgusting.

mzozo *n* (*mi-*) altercation, squabble, crisis, dispute: *Mzozo katika kile chama umepamba moto*, the dispute in that party has intensified. *Mzozo wa ardhi*, land dispute. *Mzozo wa kisiasa*, political crisis (cf *ugomvi*)

mzubao *n* (*mi-*) astonishment, bewilderment: *Pigwa na mzubao*, be bewildered, be nonplussed. (cf *mzinduo*, *mshtuko*)

mzuka *n* (*mi-*) goblin, apparition, ghost, evil spirit. (cf *zimwi*, *pepo*, *kizuu*)

mzukizuki *n* (*mi-*) (*bot*) a shrub or small tree with alternate oblong-elliptic leaves and small white or yellow flowers in short axillary racemes, bearing edible fruits. *Carpolobia alba.*

mzuko *n* (*mi-*) sudden appearance: *Mzuko wake kwenye mkutano ulitushangaza*, his sudden appearance at the meeting surprised us.

mzumari[1] (also *mzomari*) *n* (*mi-*) (*bot*) khuskhus grass; a perennial tossuck grass with aromatic roots and saw-toothed leaves which are used for thatching huts; vetiver oil is obtained from the roots. *Vetiveria zizanioides.* (cf *mchaichai*)

mzumari[2] *n* (*mi-*) cornet fish; a kind of ocean fish (family *Fistularidae*), orange-brown dorsally and silvery below, found on coral reefs sand flats and sea-grass beds.

mzu-moshi *n* (*mi-*) (*zool*) trumpetfish; a marine fish (family *Aulostomidac*) of elongated body with long snout and small barbel on the lower jaw and brown with pale spots near tail or completely yellow.

mzunga (also *zunga*) *n* (*mi-*) 1. an uncircumcised penis. (cf *govi*) 2. prepuce, foreskin; the fold of skin covering the end (glands) of the penis.

mzungu[1] *n* (*mi-*) 1. a device or expedient for getting out of a difficulty; strategy: *Walitafuta mizungu ya kukwepa lawama*, they looked for strategies of avoiding blame. (*prov*) *Mzungu wa kula hafundishwi mwana*, the technique of eating is not taught to a child i.e. Some of the habits are natural; they don't need to be taught to a child. (cf *mbinu*) 2. ingenuity, cleverness.

Mzungu[2] *n* (*wa-*) 1. European. 2. the name given to the picture cards in a pack of playing cards: The queen is *mzungu wa pili*; Jack is *mzungu wa tatu* and the king is *mzungu wa nne*.

mzungu[3] *n* (*mi-*) 1. sth startling, wonderful, surprizing, etc; a wonderful device. 2. the teachings given to young girls when they reach puberty or in the initiation rites. (*prov*) *Mzungu wa kula hafunzwi mwana*, the process of eating is not taught to a child i.e. not everything must be taught to a child. Something can be taught to a child but he will learn other things on his own.

mzungu[4] *n* (*mi-*) a kind of cassava.

mzungu[5] *n* (*mi-*) see *chewa*

mzunguko *n* (*mi-*) 1. rotation, revolution. 2. encirclement, besiege: *Mzunguko wa ngome*, the encirclement of the fort. 3. used in the expression: *Njia ya mzunguko*, a roundabout way; a long way. 4. (in sports, etc.) round: *Timu zote sasa zimemaliza mzunguko wa kwanza katika mashindano ya ligi*, all the teams have now completed the first round of the league tournament. 5. roundabout.

mzungumzaji (also *mzungumzi*) *n* (*wa-*) 1. a person full of entertaining talk; a person well-versed to talk on any subject. 2. spokesman. (cf *msemaji*)

mzungumzi *n* (*wa-*) see *mzungumzaji*

mzungusho *n* (*mi-*) 1. causing to go round and round; encirclement. 2. (*fig*) beating around the bush. 3. protracted bureaucracy.

mzururaji *n* (*wa-*) 1. wanderer, loiter, rambler. (cf *mtangaji, mrandaji*) 2. idler, gadabout, loafer

mzushi[1] (also *kizushi, mzuzi*) *n* (*wa-*) 1. innovator, inventor. 2. rumour-monger, rabble-rouser, liar. 3. telltale, gossipmonger, talebearer, tattler.

mzushi[2] *n* (*zool*) a kind of fish of rock-cod family having an oval body.

mzuwanda *n* (*wa-*) see *mziwanda*

mzuza (also *mzuzi*) *n* (*wa-*) an experienced person in finding the cause or the effects of a disease surrounding a particular patient by using traditional prognosis.

mzuzi[1] *n* (*wa-*) see *mzushi*

mzuzi[2] *n* (*wa-*) see *mzuza*

mzuzu *n* (*mi-*) (*bot*) a kind of plantain having a greenish stem with a faint red coloration as well as the leaf sheaths, the petioles and backs of the mid-ribs.

mzwiriri *n* (*wa-*) snake charmer.

N

N, n /n/ 1. the fourteenth letter of the Swahili alphabet. 2. it is a voiced apical nasal continuant.

na¹ *conj* and. The word *na* connects words, phrases, sentence, etc.: *Mwalimu na mwanafunzi*, the teacher and the student. *Msichana yule na mvulana huyu*, that girl and this boy.

na² *prep* by, with: *Alipigwa na mama yake*, he was beaten by his mother. *Nitasafiri na mjomba wangu*, I will travel with my uncle.

n.a³ *vt* have: *Ana mali adhimu*, she has a lot of wealth.

naam *interj* 1. a word used for responding to a call. 2. an expletive of affirmation, consent, agreement or confirmation; yes, certainly, it is so: *Naam, atakuja*, yes, he will come. 3. an expletive used by someone who is interested in seeing that the conversation by a speaker continues. (Ar)

nabihi¹ *adj* alert, vigilant, attentive, watchful: *Yeye ni nabihi wakati wote*, he is watchful all the time. (Ar)

nabih.i² *vt* remember, perceive: *Hanabihi siku yake ya kuzaliwa*, he does not remember his birthday. Prep. **nabih.i.a** St. **nabih.ik.a** Cs. **nabih.ish.a** Ps. of Prep. **nabih.iw.a** (cf *tanabahi, kumbuka, tambua*)

nabii *n* (*ma*-) prophet (cf *mtume, rasuli*) (Ar)

nachi (also *natiki*) *n* (*n*) nautch; a kind of Indian dance performed by professional dancing girls. (Hind)

nachungu *n* (*n*) see *futa⁶*

nadama *n* (*n*) repentance, remorse, contrition, penitence, sorrow: *Aliingiwa na nadama kwa kufanya vitendo viovu*, he was filled with repentance for having done evil deeds. (cf *majuto, majonzi*) (Ar)

nadhafa *n* (*n*) cleanliness, tidiness. (cf *usafi, umaridadi*)

nadhari *n* (*n*) intelligence, common sense, sound judgement. (syn) *Mtu asiye na nadhari ni kama ng'ombe*, a person without common sense is like a cow. (cf *busara, akili*) (Ar)

nadharia *n* (*n*) 1. theory: *Nadharia tete*, hypothesis. *Nadharia ya wimbi*, wave theory. *Nadharia ya mageuko ya polepole ya Darwin*, Darwin's theory of evolution. 2. guidelines. (Ar)

nadhifish.a *vt* clean, tidy: *Kila mtu lazima ajinadhifishe*, every person must be clean. Prep. **nadhifish.i.a** St. **nadhifish.ik.a** Ps. **nadhifish.w.a**

nadhifu¹ *adj* 1. clean, smart, neat: *Nguo zake ni nadhifu*, his clothes are clean. (cf *safi*) 2. impressive, good looking, well-kept: *Bustani yake ni nadhifu*, his garden is impressive. (Ar)

nadhif.u² *vt* clean; make sth tidy: *Alikinadhifu chumba chake vizuri*, he cleaned his room well. Prep. **nadhif.i.a** St. **nadhif.ik.a** Cs. **nadhif.ish.a,** make clean, make neat. Ps. of Prep. **nadhif.iw.a** Rp. of Prep. **nadhif.i.an.a** (cf *safisha*) (Ar)

nadhiri *n* (*n*) (*idms*) *Weka nadhiri*, make a solemn promise, usu in the name of God; make a vow. *Toa nadhiri*, fulfil a vow. *Ondoa nadhiri*, fulfil a vow. (Ar)

nad.i¹ *vt* 1. announce publicly, shout, proclaim: *Nadi swala*, call everyone to prayers. 2. auction; sell goods in an auction. Prep. **nad.i.a** St. **nad.ik.a** Cs. **nad.ish.a** Ps. of Prep. **nad.iw.a** Rp. of Prep. **nad.i.an.a** (cf *zabuni*) (Ar)

nadi² *n* (*n*) club, society, association. (cf *klabu*) (Ar)

nadra *n* (*n*) rarity, scarcity: *Yeye huja hapa kwa nadra*, he rarely comes here. (cf *adimu, haba*) (Ar)

nafaka *n* (*n*) (*bot*) grain, cereal. (Ar)

nafasi *n* (*n*) 1. space, place, room, vacancy. (cf *upenyu, uwazi*) 2. time, opportunity: *Hana nafasi ya kuonana na wewe leo*, he has no time to see you today. (cf *wakati*) (Ar)

nafidh.i[1] *vt* implement, execute, effect, carry out: *Kamati itanafidhi maazimio yote ya mkutano*, the committee will implement all the resolutions of the meeting. Prep. ***nafidh.i.a*** St. ***nafidh.ik.a*** Cs. ***nafidh.ish.a*** Ps. of Prep. ***nafidh.iw.a*** Rp. of Prep. ***nafidh.i.an.a*** (cf *tekeleza, timiza*) (Ar)

nafidh.i[2] *vt* help, assist: *Alininafidhi wakati wa shida*, he helped me during difficult times. Prep. ***nafidh.i.a*** St. ***nafidh.ik.a*** Cs. ***nafidh.ish.a*** Ps. ***nafidh.iw.a*** Rp. of Prep. ***nafidh.i.an.a*** (cf *saidia*) (Ar)

nafsi *n* (*n*) 1. soul, spirit. (cf *roho*) 2. ego, the self. *Yeye nafsi yake si mtu mjinga*, he himself is not an ignorant person. *Mimi nafsi yangu nilimwonya*, I personally warned him. 3. the human organism after the third month of conception; embryo. 4. in reality, in fact, in its depth: *Kwa nafsi yake, jambo lenyewe lina utata*, in its depth, the matter is complex. 5. the soul of a human being, genie or angel.

nafuu *n* (*n*) 1. (of price) profit, gain, betterment, reasonableness: *Bei nafuu*, reasonable price. 2. (of health) improvement, convalescence; feeling better: *Amepata nafuu*, he is feeling better. (cf *ahueni, hujambo*) 3. simplicity, easiness. (cf *wepesi, sahali*) (Ar)

naga *n* (*n*) a children's game of snatching a ball and then running with it; rugby. (cf *gori*)

nagana *n* (*n*)(*vet*) nagana; infectious disease affecting horses and cattle in tropical Africa. (Eng)

nage *n* (*n*) 1. a type of children's game of dismantling seven pieces of wood and then rearranging them in the original position. 2. a victory in this game; goal.

naghama *n* (*n*) timbre, voice quality: *Naghama ya mwimbaji yule ni nzuri*, the voice of that singer is good. (cf *sauti*) (Ar)

nahari *n* (*n*) 1. river. (cf *mto*) 2. daytime: *Laili wa nahari*, night and day; continuously. (cf *mfululizo*) (Ar)

nahau *n* (*n*) 1. grammar. 2. idiomatic expression. (cf *herufi*)

nahodha *n* (*ma-*) 1. captain of a ship, dhow, etc.; sailing master. (*prov*) *Manahodha wengi, chombo huenda mrama*, too many cooks spoil the broth. (cf *kapteni, rubani*) 2. a leader of a sports club e.g. football, hockey, etc. (Ar)

nai *n* (*n*) (*mus*) a long slender musical instrument like a flute, which has been in existence for a very long time now. (Ar)

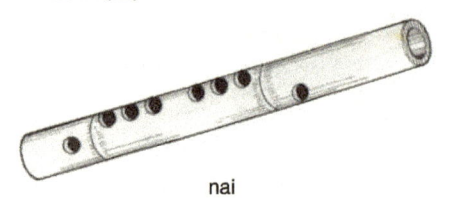

nai

naibish.a *vt* deputize; delegate authority, etc. to the person below: *Mkurugenzi alinaibisha madaraka kwa aliye chini yake*, the director delegated authority to the person below him. Prep. ***naibish.i.a*** St. ***naibish.ik.a*** Ps. ***naibish.w.a***, be deputized. (Ar)

naibu *n* (*ma-*) deputy, vice: *Naibu waziri*, deputy minister. *Naibu rais*, vice president. *Naibu mwenyekiti*, vice chairman. (Ar)

nailoni *n* (*n*) nylon (Eng)

naima *n* (*n*) happiness, peace, ecstasy: *Maisha yake yamejaa naima*, her life is full of happiness. (cf *raha, starehe*) (Ar)

nairuzi *n* (*n*) 1. the Swahili festival on the first day of the Swahili year. 2. the year of the decade. (Pers)

naitrojini n (n) (chem) nitrogen gas. (Eng)

najisi¹ (also *nitrojini*) n (n) 1. anything that makes a person become unclean unless he purifies himself by ablution, which is a special ritual washing. 2. anything that is dirty e.g. stool, urine, spit, etc.: *Nguo yake ina najisi*, her dress has dirt on it. (Ar)

najis.i² vt 1. contaminate, soil; cause religious or ritual uncleanliness; dirty. 2. rape. Prep. **najis.i.a** St. **najis.ik.a** Cs. **najis.ish.a** Ps. of Prep. **najis.iw.a** e.g. *Msichana alinajisiwa*, the girl was raped. Rp. of Prep. **najis.i.an.a** (cf *baka*) (Ar)

nakala n (n) copy, duplicate. *Ameniletea nakala ya waraka wake*, he has sent me a copy of his document. *Hii ni nakala ya pili ya kitabu chake*, this is the second edition of his book. (cf *nuskha, kopi*) (Ar)

nakama n (n) calamity, catastrophe, disaster: *Nchi yao iliingiwa na nakama kwa sababu ya matendo maovu ya watu wake*, their country met with disaster because of the evil deeds of its people. (cf *gharika, ihlaki, maangamizo*) (Ar)

nakawa adj robust, healthy, fine and strong: *Mtu nakawa*, a healthy person; a good-looking person. (Ar)

nakidi n (n) cash payment: *Malipo yake yalikuwa kwa pesa nakidi*, his payment was in cash. (Ar)

nakil.i vt duplicate, copy, transcribe. Prep. **nakil.i.a** St. **nakil.ik.a** Cs. **nakil.ish.a** Ps. of Prep. **nakil.iw.a** Rp. of Prep. **nakil.i.an.a** (Ar)

nakiri¹ vt see *ukiri*

Nakiri² n (n) (in Islam) one among the two angels believed to interrogate the dead body soon after being buried. (Ar)

nakisi¹ (also *naksi*) n (n) (of expenditure, etc.) deficit, shortage: *Waziri wa fedha alitangaza nakisi ya bajeti katika bunge*, the minister of finance announced a deficit budget in parliament. (Ar)

nakisi² (also *naksi*) adj deficient, short; of a deficient nature: *Bajeti nakisi*, a deficit budget. (Ar)

nakis.i³ (also *naksi*) vt (of expenditure, wages, etc.) reduce, deduct, rebate. Prep. **nakis.i.a** St. **nakis.ik.a** Cs. **nakis.ish.a** Ps. of Prep. **nakis.iw.a** (cf *punguza*)

nako conj and there.

nakshi¹ n (n) engraving; decoration; carved ornament: *Nakshi za milango hii zinapendeza*, the carvings of these doors are impressive. (cf *urembo, pambo*) (Ar)

naksh.i² vt embellish, adorn, decorate. Prep. **naksh.i.a** St. **naksh.ik.a** Ps. of Prep. **naksh.iw.a** Rp. of Prep. **naksh.i.an.a** (cf *pamba, tarizi*)

naksi¹ n (n) see *nakisi¹*

naksi² adj see *nakisi²*

naks.i³ vt see *nakisi³*

nam.a¹ vi 1. be flexible. *Bakora imenama*, the cane is flexible. 2. be plastic: *Udongo umenama*, the clay is plastic. 3. be sticky, be adherent. *Gundi imenama*, the glue is sticky.

nama² (also *nambari*) adj flexible, pliable.

namba (also *nambari*)n (n) number, e.g. 1, 2, 3, etc.: *Namba tasa*, a prime number. *Namba shufwa*, even number. *Namba witiri*, odd number. (Eng)

nambari n (n) see *namba*

nambo interj an expletive used to signal someone not to do a particular thing; don't! (cf *epuu!*)

nami (pron) used for *na mimi*, and I, with me, by me.

namna n (n) 1. model, design, make-up: *Ana gari jipya la namna ya Toyota*, he has a new Toyota model. 2. way, method, mode, manner. *Sielewi namna alivyopika chakula hiki*, I don't understand the way she has cooked this food. (cf *njia, jinsi*) 3. used in the expression: *Namna gani?* How? What way? What the hell is going on? (Pers)

namu *n* (*n*) a small kind of cowrie used to play in the game of checkers or draughts in British English. (cf *kete, komwe*)

namu.a *vt* 1. (used in the game of checkers or draughts) save a cowrie so that it is not won by a rival: 2. disengage, untrap, disentangle. Prep. ***namu.li.a*** Cs. ***namu.lish.a*** St. ***namu.lik.a*** Ps. of Prep. ***namu.liw.a*** Rp. ***namu.an.a***

nana *n* (*n*) madam; a word of respect used to call a woman or before mentioning her name. e.g. *Nana Hadija*, madam Hadija.

nanaa *n* (*bot*) the leaves of mint, which are used for flavouring and in medicine.

nanasi *n* (*ma-*) (*bot*) pineapple. (Pers)

nandu *n* (*n*) (*astron*) Lucifer, Venus; the morning star (cf *zuhura, ng'andu*)

nane[1] *n* (*n*) eight

nane[2] *adj* eight: *Nane na nane ni kumi na sita*, eight and eight is sixteen. *Watu wanane*, eight people.

nanga[1] *n* (*n*) (*naut*) anchor, mooring: *Tia nanga*, drop an anchor. *Ng'oa nanga*, remove the anchor. (Pers)

nanga[2] *n* (*n*) the last person holding the rope in a tug of war contest.

nang'anik.a *vi* shine as smeared with fat or other oily substance: *Uso wake ulikuwa umenang'anika kwa kupakwa mafuta*, her face was shining from being smeared with oil. Prep. ***nang'anik.i.a*** St. ***nang'anik.ik.a*** Cs. ***nang'anik.ish.a*** Ps, ***nang'anik.w.a*** (cf *ng'ara, ng'aa*)

nani *pron* (*interrog*) who?

nanigwenzula *n* (*n*) (*zool*) house gecko; a kind of tropical and subtropical lizard commonly found in houses. *Hemidactylus mabouia* (cf *mjusikafiri*)

nanigwenzula

nanu.a[1] *vt* force apart, widen, open by force: Prep. ***nanu.li.a*** St. ***nanu.lik.a*** Cs. ***nanu.lish.a*** Ps. of Prep. ***nanu.liw.a*** Rp. ***nanu.an.a*** (cf *banua*)

nanu.a[2] *vt* dislodge, untrap; let free from a trap, etc. St. ***nanu.lik.a*** Cs. ***nanu.lish.a*** Ps. ***nanu.liw.a*** Rp. ***nanu.an.a***

nargisi *n* (*n*) (*bot*) a bulb plant with clusters of white, yellow or orange flowers on a single stem; narcissus. (Ar)

nari[1] *n* (*n*) fire (cf *moto*) (Ar)

nari[2] *n* (*n*) (*mus*) reed (cf *mtapi, kilimi*) (Ar)

nas.a *vt* 1. snare, entrap; catch in a trap: *Polisi walimnasa mtuhumiwa*, the police trapped the suspect. 2. hit, beat, strike, thwack (cf *zaba, piga*) 3. tape; record sound, video material, etc.: *Tuliinasa sauti yake*, we taped his voice. 4 (*sports*) poach: *Timu ilimnasa mchezaji*, the team poached the player. Prep. ***nas.i.a*** St. ***nas.ik.a*** Cs. ***nas.ish.a*** Ps. ***nas.w.a*** Rp. ***nas.an.a***

nasaba *n* (*n*) lineage, genealogy, ancestry: *Anatoka katika nasaba ya kifalme*, he is of royal ancestry. (cf *ukoo, jadi*) (Ar)

nasaha *n* (*n*) advice, counsel. (cf *ushauri, mawaidha*) (Ar)

Nasara *n* (*ma-*) Christian: *Manasara wote wanakifuata kitabu cha Biblia*, all Christians follow the Bible. (cf *Mkristo*) (Ar)

nasi used for *na sisi*, and us, with us, by us.

nasibish.a *vt* cause oneself to be related to a person or family: *Nilimnasibisha yeye na watu wa pwani*, I related him to the people of the coast. Prep. *nasibish.i.a* St. *nasibish.ik.a* Ps. *nasibish.w.a* Rp. *nasibish.an.a* (Ar)

nasibu[1] *n (n)* pure luck, fortune. accident: *Kwa nasibu*, accidentally, by chance. (Ar)

nasib.u[2] *vt* trace one's lineage Prep. *nasib.i.a* St. *nasib.ik.a* Cs. *nasib.ish.a* Ps. of Prep. *nasib.iw.a* Rp. of Prep. *nasib.i.an.a* (Ar)

nasifish.a *vt* see *binafsisha*

nasih.i *vt* 1. advise, counsel, guide: *Nilimnasihi aishi vizuri na jirani zake*, I advised him to live peacefully with his neighbours. (cf *shauri*) 2. coax, wheedle, persuade, Prep. *nasih.i.a* St. *nasih.ik.a* Cs. *nasih.ish.a* Ps. of Prep. *nasih.iw.a* Rp. of Prep. *nasih.i.an.a* (cf *shawishi*)

nasisa *n (n)* (*bot*) narcissus; a plant with white or yellow flowers that appear in spring. (Eng)

nasu.a *vt* release from a trap, let free from a trap, etc.; dislodge, untrap. Prep. *nasu.li.a* St. *nasu.k.a* and *nasu.lik.a* Cs. *nasu.sh.a* Ps, of Prep. *nasu.liw.a* Rp. *nasu.an.a* (cf *nanua, kwamua, zongoa*)

nasuri *n (n)* (*med*) an abnormal passage leading from an abscess cavity or hollow organ to the skin or to another abscess, cavity, or organ; fistula. (Ar)

nat.a *vt, vi* be sticky, be adherent: *Gundi inanata*, the glue is sticky. Prep. *nat.i.a* St. *nat.ik.a* Cs. *nat.ish.a* Rp. *nat.an.a* (cf *ganda, shika*)

nathari *n (n)* prose (Ar)

nati *n (n)* 1. nuts and bolts. 2. head of a screw. (Eng)

natija (also *tija*) *n (n)* good outcome, good results; advantage, benefit. (cf *faida, pato*) (Ar)

natiki *n (n)* see *nachi*

naui *n (n)* type, kind, class. (cf *aina, namna*)

nauli *n (n)* charges to travellers; fare. (Ar)

naumi *n (n)* sleep, repose. (cf *usingizi*) (Ar)

naw.a *vi* 1. wash parts of the body; wash the hands and face: *Nawa mikono*, wash the hands. *Nawa uso*, wash the face. 2. (in soccer, etc.) *Nawa mpira*, handle the ball. *Mchezaji aliunawa mpira*, the player handled the ball. Prep. *naw.i.a* St. *naw.ik.a* Cs. *naw.ish.a* and *na.vy.a* Ps. of Prep. *naw.iw.a*

nawir.i *vi* 1. sparkle, dazzle, shine (cf *ng'aa, ng'ara, meremeta*) 2. become fat, grow fat: Prep. *nawir.i.a* St. *nawir.ik.a* Cs. *nawir.ish.a* (cf *tononoka, nenepa, wanda*) (Ar)

naye used for *na yeye*, and him, with him, by him.

nazaa (also *mnazaa*) *n (n)* 1. disgrace, shame: *Alinitia kwenye nazaa kutokana na sifa yake mbovu*, he put me in disgrace because of his bad conduct. (cf *aibu, fedheha*) 2. confusion, uproar, noise. (cf *ghasia, sokomoko*)

nazali *n (n)* (*phon*) nasal sound e.g. m, n,: *Sauti ya nazali*, nasal sound. (cf *king'ong'o*) (Eng)

nazi[1] *n (n)* (*bot*) coconut. (*prov*) *Nazi mbovu, harabu ya nzima*, a bad coconut spoils the good ones; one bad apple spoils good ones.

nazi[2] *n (n)* favouritism, bias, prejudice: *Akichezesha mpira, refarii yule anatumia nazi*, when he officiates a football game, that referee becomes biased. (cf *upendeleo, hatinafsi*)

Nazi[3] *n (n)* Nazi; a member of the fascist national socialist German workers. (Ger)

ncha *n (n)* tip, point, end. (*prov*) *Hakuna marefu yasiyokuwa na ncha*, every thing has an end. (cf *ukingo*)

nchi *n (n)* 1. country. 2. land. *Nchi zinazoendelea*, developing countries.

Nchi zilizoendelea, developed countries. *Nchi kavu*, dry land.
nchoro *n* (*n*) (*naut*) a small canoe.
ndafu *n* (*n*) (*zool*) wether; a castrated male sheep.
ndagano *n* (*n*) confluence; a place where two rivers flow together and become one: *Ndagano ya mito miwili*, the confluence of two rivers.
ndago *n* (*n*) (*bot*) nut grass; a pernicious weed of rapid growth, one of the terrible weeds of tropical gardens. *Cyperus rotundus*.
ndakaka *n* (*n*) long thin poles, used in roof thatching. (cf *mtambaapanya*)
ndakata *n* (*n*) (*zool*) threadfin bream; a saltwater fish. (family *Nemipteridae*)
ndama *n* (*n*) (zool) calf.
ndani[1] *n* (*n*) 1. inside, within, on the inner side. 2. a hollow space: *Geuza ndani kuwe nje*, turn inside out.
ndani[2] *adv* inside: *Amekwenda ndani*, he has gone inside.
ndara *n* (*n*) plain leather, sandal; slipper (cf *lapa, kandambili*)
ndarama (also *dirhamu*) *n* (*n*) money (cf *pesa*)
ndaraza *n* (*n*) 1. (*naut*) shallows not permitting navigation. 2. shallow water in the sea. (cf *mwamba*)
ndarire *n* (*n*) a side-track talk intended to avoid an issue; red herring: *Alitoa ndarire nyingi za upuuzi*, he gave many red herrings. (cf *porojo, pwaji*)
ndaro *n* (*n*) boasting speech; bravado, bragging: *Yeye anaonyesha ndaro zake tu lakini hawezi kufanya lolote*, he is just showing his bravado but he can't do anything. (cf *hanjamu, machachari, vitisho*)
ndau *n* (*n*) (*naut*) bailer; a vessel for bailing water out of a boat, canoe, etc.
ndaza[1] *n* (*n*) beer left to ferment.
ndaza[2] *n* (*n*) the remains of a grated coconut after the milk has been squeezed. (cf *chicha*)
ndege[1] *n* (*n*) 1. (*zool*) bird. (*prov*) *Kila ndege huruka kwa ubawa wake*, every bird flies according to the nature of its wings. i.e. do sth according to your ability. 2. (*idm*) *Ndege mbaya*, a bad omen. *Ndege mzuri*, a good omen. 3. aeroplane, plane. (cf *eropleni*)
ndege[2] *n* (*n*) a kind of local dance perfomed by women using umbrellas which are circulated round and round the dancers.
ndegechai *n* (*n*) (*zool*) a type of crane.
ndekwa *n* (*n*) plea for divorce. (cf *nyikwa*)
ndembendembe *n* (*n*) easiness, simplicity.
ndeme *n* (*n*) (*bot*) a grain of green gram that is spoilt and remains uncooked while it is boiled. (cf *ngurusumu*)
ndenge[1] *n* (*n*) (*zool*) a male goat before becoming mature; a male kid.
ndenge[2] *n* (*n*) a reception of the sorcerers.
ndeo *n* (*n*) see *ndweo*
ndere[1] *n* (*n*) a kind of powder used by medicine men to attract one of the other sex desired; love charm.
ndere[2] *n* (*n*) (*zool*) a kind of bushbaby with thick eyes and large ears.
nderemo *n* (*n*) euphoria, jubilation, elation, happiness: *Nilisikia vigelegele na nderemo harusini*, I heard ululations and elations at the wedding. (cf *hoihoi, shamrashamra, shangwe*)
nderi *n* (*n*) (*zool*) verreaux's eagle; a large black bird of prey with a long bill and white rump.
ndewe (also *njewe*) *n* (*n*) 1. the lobe of an ear; earlobe. 2. a hole pierced in the lobe of an ear. (*syn*) *Hanihusu ndewe wala sikio*, i.e. his affairs don't concern me at all. 3. the third hole of a ring pierced by women for ornamental purposes, and believed to be the largest of the three holes.
ndezi[1] *n* (*n*) (*zool*) cane rat; a big wild brownish rat with short legs and short tail. The rat is said to destroy crops esp sugarcane. *Thryonomys sp*. (cf *buku*)

ndezi

ndezi² *n* (*n*) drowsiness, grogginess, doziness.
ndi *adv* 1. an ideophone used to emphasize a forceful shutting of sth such as that of a door e.g. *Alifunga mlango ndi*, he shut the door securely. 2. used to describe the fullness of sth in a vessel or place e.g. *Watu walijaa ndi kwenye ukumbi*, people were filled to capacity in the hall (cf *tele*)
ndiga *n* (*n*) (*bot*) a climbing wild yam with prickly stems, found growing in high bush and whose fairly palatable tubers are eaten in times of food shortage. *Dioscorea dumetorum*.
ndigana *n* (*n*) (*vet*) a general term used for tick-transmitted protozoan diseases. There are two forms of these diseases: *Ndigana kali* (East Coast fever) *and Ndigana baridi* (*Anaplasmosis*). The East Coast fever is an acute cattle disease caused by *Theileria parva*. The *Anaplasmosis* is a disease of cattle caused by *Anaplasma* species and transmitted by ticks. Anaplasmosis affects domestic and wild ungulates and is spread throughout the tropics.
ndimba *n* (*n*) (*zool*) blue duiker; a small antelope with small twisted horns at the tip. *Cephalophus monticola*.
ndimi *pron* emphatic use for *ni mimi*, it is I.
ndimu *n* (*n*) (*bot*) lime; the fruit of a lime tree, which is small, round, smooth and green-fleshed.
ndinyi *pron* emphatic use for *ni nyinyi*, it is you. (pl).

ndio (also *ndiyo*) *adv* yes; a word used as an answer expressing agreement or willingness. (cf *sawa*, *naam*)
ndiposa *conj* (used usu in Mombasa and other parts of Kenya) thus, hence, therefore.
ndisi *pron* emphatic use for *ni sisi*, it is us.
ndiva *n* (*n*) a puddle, dug in order to protect water for use in farms during the hot season.
ndivyo *adv* emphatic use for *ni hivyo*, it is in this or that manner.
ndiwe *pron* emphatic use for *ni wewe*, it is you. (sing)
ndiwo *pron* emphatic use for *ni wao*, it is they.
ndiyo *adv* see *ndio*
ndizi *n* (*n*) (*bot*) banana; the fruit of a banana tree (*Musaceae*). *Ndizi kisukari*, a variety of banana that is sweet and its stems are green and rather slender. *Ndizi mzuzu*, a variety of banana with a greenish stem and a faint red coloration. *Ndizi mkono wa tembo*, is a variety of banana that is the most esteemed of all bananas and plantains for cooking purposes. *Ndizi msinyore*, a variety of banana, in which the flower stalk is reduced to an abortive stump, like that of *mkono wa tembo*. Apart from these, there are many other varieties of banana.
ndoa *n* (*n*) marriage: *Funga ndoa*, get married.
ndoana (also *ndoano*) *n* (*n*) fish hook.
ndoano *n* (*n*) see *ndoana*
ndoaro *n* (*n*) a knobbed stick like that for playing golf.
ndobe *n* (*n*) (*zool*) a kind of catfish, found in freshwater. *Cyphotilapia*.
ndogoro *n* (*n*) (*zool*) waterbuck; a kind of animal that inhabits areas that are close to water in savanna grasslands, galley forests, etc.
ndolindoli *n* (*n*) see *dandalo¹*
ndondi *n* (*n*) 1. boxing. 2. punch. (cf *konde, ngumi*)

573

ndonga¹ n (n) a stick with knobs on one side.
ndonga² n (n) a small gourd in which local medicine men keep their medicines; medicine men's calabash. (*tunguri, ndumba*)
ndongoa n (n) the custom which operates in some places of killing an ox or goat in front of the house of a dead person before the funeral takes place.
ndonya n (n) a circular plug of light wood worn on the upper lip for adornment, a practice usu performed by the Makonde women in the South of Tanzania, etc.; upper lip plug.
ndoo (*also zela*) n (n) 1. a vessel usu of calabash or metal, used to take up water from a well. 2. bucket, pail.
ndorobo n (n) (*zool*) tsetse fly. (cf *chafuo, pange, mbungo*)
ndoto n (n) dream (cf *ruya, njozi*)
ndovi n (n) cooked green plantain. (cf *ndizi*)
ndovu n (n) elephant. (*prov*) *Ndovu hashindwi na pembeze*, an elephant cannot fail to carry his tusks i.e. one may not fail to fulfil his responsibilities.
nduaro n (n) (*zool*) sailfish, a kind of fish (family *Istiophoridae*), related to swordfish and marlin.
ndubi n (n) (*zool*) an outrigger of a canoe. (cf *mrengu*)
ndude n (n) an expression used to signal sth before mentioning its name or before introducing it; thing. (cf *kidude*)
ndugu n (n) 1. brother; sister. 2. children of relatives or of the same family. 3. a close friend. 4. (in Tanzania, etc.) comrade; a person who shares interests and activities with others esp in politics and religion.
ndugubizari n (n) a kind of fishtrap with small holes; a small eyed net. (cf *uhefi, kimia, dugulizari*)
ndui n (n) (*med*) smallpox: *Uso wa ndui*, a face with smallpox.

nduli n (n) 1. a blood thirsty killer; murderer. 2. an angel of death.
ndumakuwili (also *ndumilakuwili*) n (n) 1. (*zool*) blindworm; a snake-like creature with greenish or yellow spots or stripes and very small eyes, believed by some people to have a mouth at both ends. 2. a two-faced person; a hypocritical person; turncoat, weathercock: *Bado unamwamini ndumakuwili yule?* Do you still trust that weathercock? (cf *mnafiki, kinyonga*)
ndumba n (n) 1. local witchcraft for curing a person. 2. a small gourd in which local medicine men keep their medicines; medicine man's calabash. (cf *tunguri, ndonga*)
ndume¹ n (n) 1. a strong person (cf *shujaa, simba*) 2. the character and qualities of being a strong person.
ndume² n (n) (*bot*) grains of rice that still have husks on after their barks have been stripped or pounded; chaff. (cf *kapi, wishwa*)
ndume³ n (n) (*zool*) a kind of insect that lives in the bodies of livestock; tsetse-fly. (cf *chafua*)
ndumiko n (n) a cupping instrument mostly a horn, for drawing blood or any other fluid; cupping horn.
ndumilakuwili n (n) see *ndumakuwili*
ndumo n (n) 1. a call to motivate people to ready themselves for war or celebration; inspiring call. 2. counsel.
ndumondumo n (n) gossip, rumour, grapevine. (cf *tetesi, uvumi*)
ndundu (also *ndundundu*) n (n) 1. noise emanating from a wooden mortar while pounding grain, etc. by using a pestle. 2. fees for pounding.
ndundundu n (n) see *ndundu*
nduni n (n) 1. miracle, novelty, uniqueness: *Madaktari walisema kwamba kupona kwake ilikuwa nduni tu*, the doctors said that her recovery was just a miracle. (cf *mwujiza, kioja*) 2. characteristic.
ndururu¹ adj short, small.

ndururu² *n* (*n*) a coin of small value e.g. 5 cents.

ndusi *n* (*n*) chest, box, case: *Niliziweka nguo zangu kwenye ndusi,* I put my clothes in the box. (cf *sanduku, kasha, kijaluba*)

nduu *n* (*n*) (*bot*) ground-nuts (cf *njugu*)

nduvi *n* (*n*) (*zool*) green turtle (cf *kasa*)

nduwari *n* (*n*) (*zool*) marlin; a kind of large, slender deep-sea fish (family Istiophoridae) related to sailfish and spearfish, with spear-like bill, found in all oceans. Black marlin. *Makaira indica*.

nduwari

ndwele *n* (*n*) ailment, sickness, disease. (*prov*) *Iliyopita si ndwele, ganga ijayo,* the disease that you had in the past is not important anymore, what is important is the coming disease i.e. the problems you had in the past are over but what is now really important are the forthcoming problems. (cf *ugonjwa, uele, maradhi*)

ndweo *n* (*n*) arrogance, vanity, conceit, pride: *Ndweo zake zimezidi,* his arrogance is too much. (cf *kiburi, majivuno*)

neema *n* (*n*) 1. prosperity, affluence, fortune (cf *ufanisi, ghanima*) 2. blessings from God: *Mungu ametuteremshia neema nyingi,* God has bestowed upon us many blessings. (cf *riziki, mafanikio, baraka*) (Ar)

-neemefu *adj* see *neemevu*

neemek.a *vi* 1. be prosperus, be affluent, be opulent, be rich: *Raia wote wameneemeka,* all citizens have prospered. 2. have good fortune: *Alineemeka katika shamba lake,* he got a good harvest from his farm. Prep. **neemek.e.a** St. **neemek.ek.a** Cs. **neemek.esh.a** (Ar)

neemesh.a *vt* enrich, improve, make affluent/ rich/ prosperous: *Serikali imeweza kuwaneemesha wananchi kwa mambo mengi,* the government has enabled the people to become prosperous on many matters. Prep. **neemesh.e.a** St. **neemesh.ek.a** Ps. **neemesh.w.a** Rp. **neemesh.an.a**.

-neemevu (*also neemefu*) *adj* rich, opulent, affluent, prosperous: *Nchi neemevu,* a prosperous country. (Ar)

neg.a *vi* sit properly in a bus, etc. in order to allow passage; give way to someone; make room: *Alijinega kwenye kiti ili mwenziwe apate kukaa,* he created space on the chair in order to allow his colleague to sit. Prep. **neg.e.a** St. **neg.ek.a** Cs. **neg.esh.a** Ps. **neg.w.a** (cf *pisha*)

neli *n* (*n*) tube, pipe (Hind)

nem.a *vi* 1. bend down, lean forward; crouch, slope. 2. move a neck gracefully. Prep. **nem.e.a** St. **nem.ek.a** Cs. **nem.esh.a** Ps **nem.w.a** (cf *inama*)

nembe *n* (*n*) (*zool*) a kind of freshwater fish found in large rivers and in shore areas of lakes. *Schilbe mystus*.

nembe

nembo *n* (*n*) 1. tribal mark; tattoo, incision: *Ana nembo usoni mwake,* he has tribal marks on his face. (cf *chanjo*) 2. trademark, logo; coat of arms: *Kampuni imetoa nembo yake mpya,* the company has issued its new logo.

nemedi *n* (*n*) a carpet made from feathers.

nemsi *n* (*n*) prestige, reputation, fame: *Umaarufu wake unatokana na nemsi zake nzuri,* his popularity derives from his good reputation. (Ar)

nen.a *vt* speak, say, declare: Prep. **nen.e.a** St. **nen.ek.a** Cs. **nen.esh.a** Ps. **nen.w.a** Rp. **nen.an.a**. (cf *sema, amba*)

-nene *adj* 1. fat, plump, obese: *Mtu mnene,* a fat person. 2. deep: *Sauti nene,* a deep voice.

nenep.a *vi* become fat, get fat, be fat. Prep. **nenep.e.a** St. **nenep.ek.a** Cs. **nenep.esh.a**, fatten, be fattening. Ps. **nenep.w.a** (cf *tononeka, wanda*)

nenepesh.a *vt* fatten: *Vyakula vitamu vimemnenepesha,* rich food has fattened him. Prep. **nenepesh.e.a** St. **nenepesh.ek.a** Ps. **nenepesh.w.a**

nenez.a *vt* tell sby sth. Prep. **nenez.e.a** St. **nenez.ek.a** Ps. **nenez.w.a** Ps. **nenez.an.a** (cf *semesha*)

nengu.a *vi* gyrate; dance by twisting one's hips. *Alinengua wakati midundo ya ngoma ilipolia.* She twisted her hips to the rhythm of the drum. 2. walk like a crippled person: *Ulemavu umemsababisha atembee kwa kunengua,* crippling has made him to walk by limping. (*prov*) *Utamu wa ngoma ni kunengua,* the fun of local dance is gyrating. Prep. **nengu.li.a** St. **nengu.k.a** Cs. **nengu.sh.a** Ps. of Prep. **nengu.liw.a**

neno *n* (*ma-*) 1. word, utterance, expression: *Neno halafa,* ambivalent word. *Neno mnasaba,* cognate word. *Neno tupu,* empty word. *Neno unde,* coined word. *Neno kisonde,* deictic word. *Neno mkato,* clipped word. *Neno changamano,* complex word. *Neno ambatano,* compound word. *Neno nyambuliki,* variable word. *Neno la kileksika,* content word. *Neno kuu,* headword, *Neno mkopo,* loan word. *Neno jumuishi,* superordinate word. *Neno ambatani shirikishi,* copulative compound. *Neno ambatani vumishi,* determinative compound word. *Neno amilifu,* function word; structural word. *Neno ambatani msingi,* primary compound word, fused compound word. *Neno jumla,* generic word; superordinate word. *Neno taarifa,* holo phrase. *Neno mwangwi,* echo word. *Neno geni,* alien word. *Neno potofu,* ghost word. *Neno mwigo,* imitative word. 2. message, point, advice: *Anataka kuniambia neno,* he wants to tell me something. *Hana neno,* he has no problem. *Si neno,* it doesn't matter. (cf *habari, rai, shauri*) 3. misfortune, bad luck: *Ametuletea maneno,* he has brought to us misfortune. (cf *balaa, zani*) 4. (*rel*) *Neno la Mungu,* a word of God. e.g. *Mhubiri alieneza neno la Mungu,* the preacher spread the word of God 5. (*idm*) *Mtu wa maneno mengi,* a talkative person; gabbler, babbler, prattler.

nep.a *vi* bend downwards as in the case of a twig, etc.; sag, droop, slump: *Maua kwenye mti ule yamenepa kutokana na ukosefu wa maji,* the flowers from that tree have drooped for lack of water. Prep. **nep.e.a** St. **nep.ek.a** Cs. **nep.esh.a** (cf *nesa*)

nepi *n* (*n*) nappy, diaper (Eng)

nepu.a *vi* sway, swing, oscillate, rock. *Matawi ya mti yalikuwa yakinepua kutokana na upepo mkali,* the branches of the tree were swaying because of the strong wind. Prep. **nepu.li.a** St. **nepu.k.a** Cs. **nepu.sh.a** (cf *yumba*)

nes.a[1] *vi* bend downwards; droop, slump: *Bakora yangu inanesa sana,* my stick bends very much. Prep. **nes.e.a** St. **nes.ek.a** Cs. **nes.esh.a** Ps. **nes.w.a** (cf *nepa*)

nes.a[2] *vt* beat as with a stick, etc.; flog, strike, slap: *Alininesa makofi,* he slapped me. Prep. **nes.e.a** St. **nes.ek.a** Cs. **nes.esh.a** Ps. **nes.w.a** (cf *piga*)

nesi (also *nasi*) *n* (*ma-*) nurse (cf *muuguzi*) (Eng)
neso (*also nesu*) *n* (*n*) a piece of thin calico cloth.
nesu *n* (*n*) see *neso*
netiboli *n* (*n*) (sports) netball
neva *n* (*n*) (*anat*) nerve; a rib or vein in the body (Eng)
nevi *n* (*n*) 1. navy. 2. naval personnel. (cf *askari mwanamaji*) 3. naval weapons. (Eng)
ng'a.a (*also ng'ara*) *vi* shine, shimmer, dazzle, glow. Prep. **ng'a.li.a** St. **ng'a.lik.a** Cs. **ng'az.a** (cf *meremeta, meta, memeta*)
ngabu *n* (*n*) gouge; a carpenter's tool for cutting grooves or holes in wood. (cf *bobari, sokondo*)
ngadu *n* (*n*) (*zool*) a kind of crab that lives in the banks of the seas or rivers.
ngagu *n* (*n*) (*zool*) terapon; a saltwater fish (family *Teraponidae*) having an oblong body, slightly compressed with ctenoid scales, found in inshore areas, sometimes in brackish waters. (cf *kui*)
ng'ak.a *vt* snarl, snap at, lash out at: *Mwalimu aling'aka kwa wanafunzi wake kutokana na ukosefu wa nidhamu*, the teacher snarled at his students for their misconduct. Prep. **ng'ak.i.a** St. **ng'ak.ik.a** Cs. **ng'ak.ish.a** Ps. **ng'ak.w.a** Rp. of Prep. **ng'ak.i.a.n.a** (cf *karipia, kemea*)
ngalawa (*also ng'arawa*) *n* (*n*) (*naut*) outrigger canoe.

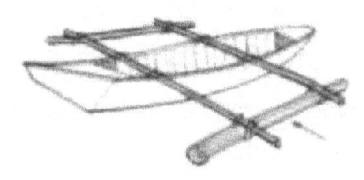

ngalawa

ngama[1] *n* (*n*) (*naut*) bilge; the bottom part of a ship, dhow, etc. (*prov*) *Mwenda tezi na omo marejeo ni ngamani*, he who goes to the front or back part of a sailing vessel will end up in the middle i.e. whoever goes anywhere in search of sth, will finally go back to his place of origin.
ngama[2] *n* (*n*) a kind of hard whitish clay resembling the one for making pottery.
ngama[3] *n* (*n*) faeces; the solid waste material passed from the bowels suddenly when someone is in the extreme or the waste which is forced out when a corpse is being washed for preparation to burial: *Toa ngama*, release faeces. *Maji ya ngama*, water that was used to wash a dead body.
ngamba *n* (*n*) 1. (*zool*) a kind of turtle from which a tortoise shell is procured and found in warmer seas; hawk's head turtle: *Chuma cha ngamba*, the shell of the hawk's head turtle. *Eretmochelys imbricata*. 2. tortoise shell from a special turtle from which objects such as combs are made. 3 slide; film plate. 4. nylon material (cf *slaidi*)
ngambi *n* (*n*) 1. an expression of consensus to act together for the common good e.g. to protect the falling coconuts and other crops from being destroyed by pests, thieves, etc.; agreement to prohibit sth. 2. shortage, scarcity, lack: *Wana ngambi ya chakula*, they have a shortage of food. (cf *upungufu*) 3. naval weapons.
ng'ambo *n* (*n*) 1. the other side, for example, of a river, road, etc.: *Ng'ambo ya mto*, the other side of the river. 2. outskirts of a city, etc.; suburbs: *Anaishi ng'ambo*, he lives in the outskirts. 3. overseas, abroad: *Ameenda kusoma ng'ambo*, he has gone to study overseas.
ngamia *n* (*n*) (*zool*) camel (cf *jamali*)
ngamiza *n* (*n*) computer (*kompyuta*)
ng'amu.a *vt, vi* realize, find out, get to know. Prep. **ng'amu.li.a** St.

N   ng'anda¹   ng'atu.a

ng'amu.k.a Ps. of Prep. **ng'amu. liw.a** Rp. **ng'amu.an.a** (cf *tanabahi, tambua, maizi*)

ng'anda¹ *n (n)* a handful of food like flour, nuts, etc.; a fistful: *Ng'anda ya unga wa ngano*, a fistful of wheat flour.

ng'anda² *n (n)* the pip on playing cards: *Ng'anda ya tano*, the five in a suit.

ng'andu *n (n)* the planet Venus; Lucifer. (cf *zuhura, nandu*)

ng'anga *adv* 1. an expression of insistence over sth: *Aling'ang'ania ng'anga*, he clung to it steadfastly. 2. an expression of defiance, resistance, etc.; never: *Kula anapenda lakini akiambiwa afanye kazi, jawabu yake ni ng'anga*. he likes to eat but when he is told to work, his answer is never.

ng'ang'ana.a *vi* 1. become stiff and dry because of dirt or because of being left in the sun or cold: *Mkate wake umeng'ang'anaa*, his bread has stiffened. Prep. **ng'ang'ana.li.a** St. **ng'ang'ana.lik.a** Cs. **ng'ang'ana. ish.a** Ps. **ng'ang'ana.w.a** (cf *kauka, kunjamana*)

ng'ang'ani *adv* unyieldingly, uncompromisingly.

ng'ang'ani.a *vt* 1. clutch; grip sth firmly so that it does not escape: *Alimng'ang'ania ndege mkononi ili asimponyoke*, he clutched the bird fastly so that it would not escape. (cf *shikilia, kazania*) 2. insist on, persist, hold; be firm, beseech persistently. Prep. **ng'ang'ani.li.a** St. **ng'ang'ani. lik.a** Cs. **ng'ang'ani.lish.a** Ps. **ng'ang'ani.w.a** Rp. **ng'ang'ani.an.a** (cf *shikilia, kazania*)

ngangari *n (n) (colloq)* vigilant, alert, firm: *Chama chao kiko ngangari*, their party is firm. (cf *chonjo*)

ngano¹ *n (n)* story, folktale, fable.

ngano² *n (n)* wheat: *Unga wa ngano*, wheat flour. (cf *nganu*)

nganu *n (n)* see *ngano²*

ngao *n (n)* 1. shield, buckler. 2. *(fig)* defence, protection, safeguard, guard: *Ile sheria ilikuwa ngao madhubuti dhidi ya wahalifu*, the law was a strong safeguard against culprits. 3. the front (face) or rear of a house.

-ngapi *(interrog) adj, pron* How much? How many? *Wanawake wangapi?* How many women? *Mara ngapi?* How many times? *Vichache vimeletwa hapa*, few (things) have been brought here.

ngara¹ *n (n) (bot)* the male blossom of the maize plant. (cf *punga, ngaa*)

ngara² *n (n)* hide or skin used for celebration esp for chiefs, etc.

ng'ar.a¹ *vi* see *ng'aa*

ng'ar.a² *vt* rejoice, become joyful: *Ameng'ara leo kwa sababu ya kupata ushindi*, he has become joyful today because of his success. Prep. **ng'ar.i.a**. St. **ng'ar.ik.a** Cs. **ng'ar.ish.a** Ps. **ng'ar.w.a** (cf *shangilia, furahi*)

ngarangare *n (n)* see *mkule*

ngarange *n (n) (bot)* the hard centre or heart of a tree; heartwood, duramen (cf *kunge*)

ngarara *n (n)* see *mkuwe*

ngarawa *n (n)* see *ngalawa*

ngariba *n (n)* a professional circumciser.

ng'arish.a *vt* brighten, shine, polish: *Aliving'arisha viatu vyangu*, he polished my shoes. Prep. **ng'arish.i.a** St. **ng'arish.ik.a** Ps. **ng'arish.w.a** Rp. of Prep. **ng'arish.i.an.a**

ng'at.a *vt* bite with the teeth; gnaw: *Mtoto yule alimng'ata kidole mwenziwe*, that child bit his mate on the finger. Prep. **ng'at.i.a** St. **ng'at.ik.a** Cs. **ng'at. ish.a** Ps. **ng'at.w.a** Rp. **ng'at.an.a** (cf *tafuna, guguna*)

ng'atu.a *vt* pull away teeth after biting; release teeth after biting: *Niliung'atua mkono wake kutoka kwenye kinywa cha mbwa*, I pulled his arm away from the dog's mouth. Prep. **ng'atu.li.a** St. **ng'atu.k.a** Cs. **ng'atu.sh.a** Rp. **ng'atu.an.a**

578

ng'atuk.a *vt* relinquish leadership, position, etc.: *Kiongozi alikubali kung'atuka madarakani*, the leader agreed to relinquish power. Prep. ***ng'atuki.a*** St. ***ng'atuk.ik.a*** Cs. ***ng'atuk.ish.a*** (cf *achilia madaraka, staafu*)

ngawa *n (n) (zool)* a kind of civet cat with black spots and a bushy tail at the base. (cf *fungo*)

ngawira *n (n)* booty; spoils of war, captured items during war. (cf *ghanima*)

ngazi *n (n)* 1. ladder, stairway, staircase. *Panda ngazi*, climb the ladder. *(prov) Mpanda ngazi hushuka*, one who climbs a staircase can also descend i.e. one can rise to power, etc. and yet fall. 2. step, stair; a single step, usu one of a series leading from one level or floor to another. 3. authority, echelon, grade, rank, status, level: *Dai lake lilipitia katika ngazi mbalimbali*, his claim was channeled through different levels. (cf *daraja, sehemu*)

Ngazija *n (n) (geog)* Comoro islands.

ng'e¹ *n (n) (zool)* scorpion

ng'e² *n (n) (astron)* Scorpio; the eighth sign of the Zodiac.

ngebe¹ *n (n)* 1. blab, gossip, prattle; endless talk: *Toa ngebe*, talk nonsense. 2. prattler; blabber; an excessive talker: *Ngebe yule hatakusikiliza kile chote unachosema*, that prattler will not listen to all that you are talking about. (cf *mlimi, kidomo, msemaji*)

ngebe² *n (n) (zool)* a fish when it has not reached its normal height.

ngebwe *n (n) (zool)* stonefish; a kind of a very venomous marine fish which is very well-camouflaged and can be expected on shallow coral reefs.

ngeda *n (n) (zool)* a kind of green locust or gregarious grasshopper (family *Acirdidae*). Locusts exist in two phases: a solitary grasshopper phase or a swarming locust phase. Africa suffers most seriously from locust swarms which devour every green vegetation.

ngedere *n (n) (zool)* vervet; a small guenon monkey; a kind of small monkey, with a moderately long, stiff tail, found in E. and S. Africa. *Cercopithecus aethiops.* (cf *tumbiri*)

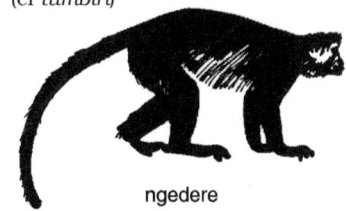

ngedere

ngegu *n (n)* a kind of red chalky earth; red ochre.

ngeja *n (n)* tartar, plaque; hard chalky deposits on the teeth. (cf *ugwagwa, ukoga*)

ngeli *n (n) (gram)* class, declension: *Ngeli nomino*, noun class. *Ngeli ya M-WA*, M-WA class. *Ngeli kiambajengo*, constituent class.

ngenga *n (n)* turmoil, pandemonium, commotion: *Alinifanyia ngenga chumbani mwangu*, he caused pandemonium in my room. (cf *kelele, ghasia*)

ngeu (also *ng'eu*) *n (n)* 1. (of colour) red. 2. blood. (cf *damu*) 3. a wound on the head caused by being hit with a stick or stone or anything without a sharp edge.

ng'eu *n (n)* see *ngeu*

ngiangia *n (n) (zool)* sea anemone; a flowerlike marine coelenterates of the class *Anthozoa*, which has a flexible cylindrical body and tentacles surrounding a central mouth.

ngiangia

ngiri¹ n (n) (zool) warthog (cf *gwase, mbango*)

ngiri² n (n) (med) hernia: *Shikwa na ngiri*, be suffering from hernia. *Ngiri ya kitovu*, umbilical hernia. *Ngiri ya tumbo*, abdominal hernia. *Mshipa wa ngiri*, hernia.

ngisha n (n) (naut) a small wave, deep in the sea.

ngisi n (n) (zool) cuttlefish. *Cephalopods. Wino wa ngisi*, cuttle dark fluid. *Kifuu cha ngisi*, cattle-fish bone.

ngizi n (n) sweet palm wine (the fermented sap of a coconut).

ng'o interj never; an expression of absolute refusal or unwillingness to offer sth: *Hakupi ng'o!* He will never give you.

ngoa n (n) 1. jealousy, illwill, envy: *Lia ngoa*, weep with jealousy. *Ana ngoa kwa kutuona sisi na gari mpya*, he is envious of seeing us with new cars. (cf *wivu*) 2. lust, desire: *Sina ngoa na chake; mwachie apate*, I have no lust for his property; let him have it. (cf *hamu*)

ng'o.a vt 1. uproot, extirpate, root out, extract, pull out, pull up: *Ng'oa jino*, extract a tooth. *Ng'oa mimea*, uproot seedlings. (cf *sikua, zidua, kongoa*) 2. (idms) *Ng'oa nanga*, start on a journey. Prep. **ng'o.le.a** St. **ng'o.k.a** Cs. **ngo.lesh.a** Ps. of Prep. **ngo.lew.a** Rp. **ng'o.an.a**.

ngoe¹ n (n) 1. (in math and ling) tree diagram. 2. hooked/forked branch or stick. (cf *kingoe, ngoeko*)

ngoe² n (n) a small swaying derived from someone attracted by sth.

ngoek.a vt take hold of anything e.g. fruit on a tree, etc. by using a forked or hooked stick: *Alingoeka maembe kwenye bustani yake*, he plucked mangoes by using a hooked stick in his garden. Prep. **ngoek.e.a** St. **ngoek.ek.a** Cs. **ngoek.esh.a** Ps. **ngoek.w.a** Rp. **ngoek.an.a**

ngoeko n (n) see *ngoe*

ng'ofo.a vt see *ng'wafua*. Prep. **ng'ofo.le.a** St. **ng'ofo.k.a** (cf *nyofoa*)

ngogo n (n) (zool) striped eel-catfish. (family *Plotosidae*)

ngogwe n (n) (bot) African eggplant; a tomato-like fruit, which is yellow, roundish and bitter. (cf *tunguja*)

ngoi n (n) a good leader of a song.

ngoj.a vi wait, remain: *Ngoja kidogo*, wait a bit. *Ngoja kikonzo*, wait for a long time. Prep. **ngoj.e.a** St. **ngoj.ek.a** Cs. **ngoj.esh.a** Ps. **ngoj.w.a** Ps. of Prep. **ngoj.e.w.a** Rp. of Prep. **ngoj.e.an.a**

ngojamaliko n (n) (zool) little bittern; a very small bird that has a black back and a buff-white wing patch. (cf *vumatiti*)

ngoje.a vi wait for sby/sth. Prep. **ngoje.le.a** St. **ngoje.lek.a** Cs. **ngoje.lesh.a** (cf *subiri*)

ng'ok.a vi 1. be uprooted, be extracted. 2. (fig) step down: *Walimtaka kiongozi ang'oke*, they wanted the leader to step down. Prep. **ng'ok.e.a** St. **ng'ok.ek.a** Cs. **ng'o.esh.a**

ngoko n (n) ape's bottom. (prov) *Nyani wanachekana ngoko*, the apes laugh at each other's bottom i.e. You may laugh at someone because of his weaknesses while you yourself have the same ones. (cf *mando*)

ngole n (n) 1. (zool) a long thin greenish non-poisonous snake. 2. the rope of a bow.

ngoma n (n) 1. drum, tambourine: *Piga ngoma*, beat the drum. *Liza ngoma*, beat the drum. (prov) *Ngoma ikilia sana, haikawii kupasuka*, when a drum sounds loud, it will soon burst, 2. tribal dance: *Ngoma ya jadi*, folk dance. *Cheza ngoma*, join in a tribal dance 3. the beat of a drum.

ng'ombe¹ n (n) (zool) cow, ox, cattle.

ng'ombe² (also *shemng'ombe*) n (n) exorcizing dance.

ng'ombe-dume n (n) bull (cf *fahali, nzao*)

ngome n (n) 1. escarpment. 2. fort,

fortress. castle: *Adui aliizunguka ngome yetu*, the enemy besieged our fort. (cf *husuni, sera, buruji*) 3. (*fig*) stronghold: *Eneo lile ni ngome ya chama cha upinzani*, that area is the stronghold of the opposition.

ng'onda *n* (*n*) (*zool*) split dried fish.

ngondo *n* (*n*) see *kondo²*

ng'ong'.a¹ *vi* make a sign of contempt or derision behind a person's back. *Baada ya wewe kuondoka tu, akaanza kukung'ong'a*, after you had just left, he started to deride you behind your back. Prep. **ng'ong'.e.a** St. **ng'ong'.ek.a** Cs. **ng'ong'.esh.a** Ps. **ng'ong'.w.a** Rp. **ng'ong.an.a**

ng'ong'.a² *vi* (of flies, etc.) fly around: *Nzi walikuwa waking'ong'a karibu na chakula*, the flies were flying around near the food. Prep. **ng'ong'.e.a** St. **ng'ong'.ek.a** Cs. **ng'ong'.esh.a** Ps. **ng'ong'.w.a** Rp. **ng'ong.an.a**

ng'ongo *n* (*n*) (*bot*) small roundish mango with a kernel; golden apple. (cf *embe sakua*)

ngongonyo *n* (*n*) 1. an old worn-out vehicle, esp lorry; jalopy. 2. freight train, cargo train.

ngonjera *n* (*n*) 1. dialogue verse; a poetic composition involving dialogue and sometimes dramatic and theatrical actions. 2. unnecessary arguments: *Kila akiambiwa kitu, basi yeye huleta ngonjera*, every time he is told of sth, he tends to argue for no reason.

ngono *n* (*n*) 1. turn for a husband to stay with one of his wives in a polygamous setting. 2. sexual intercourse; coition.

ngonzi *n* (*n*) (*zool*) sheep (cf *kondoo*)

ngoringori *n* (*n*) see *njorinjori*

ngorombwe *n* (*n*) (*zool*) bush duiker, grey duiker; a small duiker with long and broad ears, and horns standing upright. *Sylvicapra grimmia*.

ngoshi (also *ngushi*) *n* (*n*) (*naut*) one of the nether corners in the matting sail in *mitepe*, together with the attached rope.

ngosho *n* (*n*) pomposity, boastfulness, airs and graces: *Anapotembea, huonyesha ngosho zake*, when he walks, he displays his pomposity. (cf *madaha, pozi*)

ngosi *n* (*n*) see *kongoni*.

ng'ot.a *vt* 1. nibble, bite: *Nilimwona aking'ota gunzi la mahindi*, I saw him nibbling at the cob of maize. 2. tap, peck, knock: *Kigogota alikuwa aking'ota*, the woodpecker was pecking. (cf *kingota, gogota*)

ngoto *n* (*n*) closed fist; punch: *Piga ngoto*, beat with a fist; punch e.g. *Alipigwa ngoto*, he was given a punch. (cf *konzi*)

ngovi *n* (*n*) see *ngozi*

ngozi (also *ngovi*) *n* (*n*) 1. skin, leather, hide. (*syn*) *Chuna ngozi*, have sexual intercourse. (*prov*) *Mchuna ngozi huvutia kwake*, the distributor of goods, items, etc. tends to favour his side.

nguchiro *n* (*n*) (*zool*) mongoose; a flesh-eating mammal noted for its ability to kill poisonous snakes, rodents, etc.

nguchiro

ngudu *n* (*n*) an expletive used by someone in order to disassociate himself from a particular activity, esp in youth camps (cf *po simo!*)

nguli *n* (*n*) valliant, hero; a brave person: *Mwanajeshi yule alikuwa nguli*, that soldier was a hero. (cf *nyamaume, shujaa, jogoo*)

ngumbaro¹ (also *ngumbaru*) *n*(*n*) a restless person, a jumpy person, an unrelaxed person; fidget. (cf *machachari, makeke*)

ngumbaro² (*also ngumbaru*) *n* (*n*) adult; a grown-up person: *Elimu ya ngumbaro*, adult education.

ngumbi *n* (*n*) (*zool*) winged termite. (cf *kumbikumbi*).

ngumi *n* (*n*) fist, blow, hit: *Piga ngumi*, strike with the fist; give a cuff to.

ngumu *n* (*n*) (*syn*) *Wekea ngumu*, obstades sby.

ngungwe *n* (*n*) 1. a furrow made for planting seeds. 2. a portion of a field measured out for cultivation.

ngunja *n*(*n*) red dust.

nguo¹ *n*(*n*) 1. dress, gown, clothes, garment. (*prov*) *Nguo ya kuazima haisitiri matako*, a person fond of borrowing things from others can be disgraced by the owners when they take back their things. (cf *vazi, kanzu*) 2. material, cloth: *Nguo ya meza*, table cloth. *Nguo ya kitanda*, bed clothes. (cf *kitambaa*)

nguo² *n* (*n*) (*zool*) a kind of bird which is said to cause ill-omen.

nguri *n* (*n*) shoemaker's mallet.

nguru (*also nguu*) *n* (*n*) kingfish, mackerel: a kind of edible fish (family Scombridae) found in pelagic and coastal waters. King mackerel. *Scomberomorus commerson*.

nguru

ngurukia *n* (*n*) see *mlandege*

ngurum.a *vi* roar, growl, rumble, thunder: *Simba alinguruma*, the lion roared. Prep. **ngurum.i.a** St. **ngurum.ik.a** Cs. **ngurum.ish.a** Ps. **ngurum.w.a** Rp. of Prep. **ngurum.i.an.a** (cf *tutuma, rindima*)

ngurumo *n* (*n*) 1. thunder. 2. roar, rumble.

ngurunga *n* (*n*) a table or chair made of stones, clay or marble.

nguruwe *n* (*n*) (*zool*) pig, hog, swine. (*prov*) *Mkuki kwa nguruwe, kwa mwanadamu mchungu*, it is okay to spear a pig but to a human being, it is painful i.e. You may not feel pain if someone else has been injured or victimised but if that happens to you, you will really feel the pain.

nguruzi (*also nguzi*) *n* (*n*) 1. (*naut*) an opening in a ship's side to allow water to run off the deck; scupper. 2. a wooden plug to stop a leak.

ngushi *n* (*n*) see *ngoshi*.

nguta¹ *n* (*n*) copra; dried coconut. (cf *mbata*)

nguta² *n* (*n*) (*zool*) pig, hog, swine (cf *nguruwe*)

nguto *n* (*n*) a hard stirred porridge.

nguu¹ *n* (*n*) see *nguru*

nguu² *n* (*n*) the peak of a mountain; mountain top, summit. (*prov*) *Mali ilivunja nguu na vilima vikalala*, someone who is wealthy can also bribe his way through.

nguva *n* (*n*) dugong, seacow, manatee.

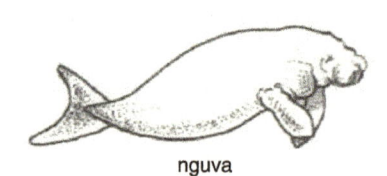

nguva

nguvu *n*(*n*) 1. strength, force, might. *Nguvu kazi*, work force, labour force; the total number of people who have ability to do work. 2. power, authority: *Yeye hana nguvu ya kutoa amri kama zile*, he has no authority to give orders of those kinds. 3. energy, power: *Nguvu za umeme*, electrical power. *Nguvu za maji*, water power. *Nguvu za upepo*, wind force.

nguvukazi *n* (*n*) 1. see *nguvu*. 2. the ability of a person to do work. 3. labour

nguyu *n* (*n*) (*anat*) ankle; the joint that connects the foot and the leg.
nguzi *n* (*n*) see *nguruzi*.
nguzo *n* (*n*) 1. prop, pillar, post: *Nguzo za taa*, lamp posts. *Nguzo za paa*, the poles of a roof. (cf *mhimili, mwimo*) 2. pillar, principle, belief: *Nguzo za dini*, the pillars (principles) of religion. *Nguzo za chama tawala*, the principles of the ruling party.
ngwa *n* (*n*) an expletive used in certain areas of Tanzania such as Tanga and Pangani to describe that sth belongs to someone else: *Mwanangwa*, sby's son. *Kofia ngwa*, sby's cap.
ng'wafu.a (*also ng'ofoa*) *vt* bite off a piece of flesh like a dog or wild animal or any other thing: *Mbwa aling'wafua pande la nyama kwenye mfupa ule*, the dog bit off a piece of flesh from that bone. Prep. **ng'wafu.li.a** St. **ng'wafu.k.a** Cs. **ng'wafu.sh.a** Ps. of Prep. **ng'wafu.liw.a** Rp. **ng'wafu.an.a** (cf *nyofoa*).
ngwamba *n* (*n*) 1. a hoe with a long handle (cf *shilanga*) 2. drudgery, hardwork: *Kula ngwamba*, work diligently. work like a dog; do the donkey work. (cf *sulubu*)
ngwara (*also ngware*) *n* (*n*) trip; a manoeuvre for causing someone to stumble or fall, as by catching his foot: *Piga ngwara*, trip sby up.
ngware *n* (*n*) a game or a manoeuvre for causing someone to stumble or fall, as by catching his foot.
ngwe[1] *n* (*n*) an allotment assigned for cultivation or which has already been tilled (cf *mraba, kuo*)
ngwe[2] *n* (*n*) a long twisted rope that has been woven from palm leaves, used in fishing.
ngwe[3] *n* (*n*) tenure; period of time someone occupies an office in civil service, etc.: *Rais anamaliza ngwe yake mwaka ujao*, the president completes his tenure of office next year.
ngwena *n* (*n*) (*zool*) crocodile (cf *mamba*)
ngwenje (*also njenje*) *n* (*n*) money usu coins; coin money.
ng'weny.a *vt* bite sth with the front teeth and then pull it; *Alikuwa aking'wenya mahindi*, he was nibbling at the maize. Prep. **ng'weny.e.a** St. **ng'weny.ek.a** Cs. **ng'weny.esh.a** Ps. **ng'weny.w.a** Rp. **ng'weny.an.a** (cf *gunya, gwenya*)
ni *vt* (*cop*) when used as a copular verb, *ni* describes the quality of a person or thing; am, is, are: *Mimi ni mwalimu*, I am a teacher. *Wewe ni nani?* Who are you?
nia *n* (*n*) intention, purpose, determination, aim, objective: *Nia yake ilikuwa ni kuharibu mipango yetu*, his intention was to disrupt our plans. (*prov*) *Penye nia pana njia*, where there is a will, there is a way. (Ar)
niaba *n* (*n*) (used in the phrase) *Kwa niaba ya*, on behalf of: *Amekuja kwa niaba ya waziri*, he has come on behalf of the minister. (cf *badala ya*) (Ar)
nibu *n* (*n*) the point of a pen; nib. (Eng)
nidhamu *n* (*n*) 1. procedure, practice, method: *Kampuni yetu haina nidhamu nzuri ya kuajiri wafanyakazi*, our company does not possess good procedures for recruiting workers. (cf *mpango, utaratibu*) 2. discipline: *Nidhamu ni kitu muhimu mahala popote*, discipline is an important thing anywhere. (Ar)
nifaki *n* (*n*) hypocrisy, fraud, deception, deceit, falseness: *Matamshi yake yamejaa nifaki*, his utterances are full of hypocricy. (cf *unafiki, udanganyifu*) (Ar).
nikaha (*also nikahi*) *n* (*n*) marriage, wedlock, matrimony: *Funga nikaha*, get married. (Ar)
nikahi *n* (*n*) see *nikaha*
niko *verb form* I am here, I am present.
nikoti *n* (*n*) (*chem*) nicotine; a poisonous,

N

water-soluble alkaloid, $C_{10}H_{14}N_2$ found in tobacco leaves. (Eng)

nikwata *n (n) (zool)* a lizard that is very fond of living in houses; house gecko; house lizard.

nili *n (n)* (of colour) blue. (cf *buluu*)

nimonia *n (n) (med)* pneumonia: inflammation of one or both lungs caused by bacteria, viruses, etc. (cf *mkamba*)

nina *n (n)* mother. (*prov*) *Mwana hufuata kisogo cha nina wake*, a daughter follows the nape of her mother i.e. a daughter follows the characters of her mother. (cf *mama*)

ninga *n (n)* 1. (*zool*) green pigeon; a kind of bird which is thickest and apple-green with coral-red cere and feet, and a greyish-white bill. *Treron australis*. 2. (*syn*) *Uko juu kwa juu kama ninga*, you are in the air like the green pigeon i.e. an expression used to describe someone who is well-off. 3. a beautiful girl.

ning'ini.a *vt, vi* dangle, swing, suspend, sag, sway: *Mtoto alikuwa akining'inia kwenye tawi la mti*, the child was hanging from the branch of a tree. Prep. **ning'ini.li.a** St. **ning'ini.k.a** Cs. **ning'ini.z.a** Rp. **ning'ini.an.a**

ning'iniz.a *vt* suspend sth; hang sth e.g. *Aliining'iniza nyama ya kondoo kwenye ndoana*, he let the mutton hung on the hook. Prep. **ning'iniz.i.a** St. **ning'iniz.ik.a** Ps. **ning'iniz.w.a** Rp. **ning'iniz.an.a**

ningu (*also ningo*) *n (n) (zool)* a kind of freshwater fish with a rounded snout and many spines all over its body, found in Lake Victoria basin; broad spined freshwater fish. *Labeo victorianus*.

ningu

nini (*interrog*) *pron* What? *Anafanya nini?* What is he doing? *Wataka nini?* What do you want? *Kwa nini?* What for?

ninyi *pron* you (pl): *Ninyi nyote*, all of you.

nipo *verb form* I am here, I am present.

nira *n (n)* yoke; a shaped piece of wood fitted around the necks of a pair of oxen, horse, etc. for harnessing them together. (cf *kitaya*) (Ar)

niru[1] *n (n)* oxygen residue.

niru[2] *n (n)* lime that has been mixed with cement, used for plastering.

nisai *n (n)* woman (cf *mwanamke*) (Ar)

nisha (also *nishaa*) *n (n)* starch (cf *uanga, wanga*) (Ar)

nishaa *n (n)* see *nisha*

nishai *n (n)* drunkenness

nishani *n (n)* medal, decoration, badge: *Nishani ya vita*, war medal. *Mpewa nishani*, medallist. (cf *tepe, medali*) (Ar)

nishati *n (n)* energy: *Nishati ya umeme*, electrical energy. *Nishati ya atomiki*, atomic energy. *Nishati ya nyuklia*, nuclear energy. *Nishati mwendo*, kinetic energy. *Nishati joto*, thermal energy. *Tia nishati*, energize. (Ar)

nitrojini *n (n) (chem)* see *naitrojini*

njaa *n (n)* 1. hunger, hungriness, appetite: *Nina njaa*, I am hungry. *Njaa imemshika*, he is hungry. 2. famine; starvation: *Nchi yote imekumbwa na njaa*, the whole country has been affected by famine. *Amekufa kwa njaa*, he has died of starvation.

njama *n (n)* 1. a secret council or meeting 2. plot, conspiracy: *Walifanya njama ya kutaka kuipindua serikali*, they plotted to overthrow the government. 3. (*idm*) *Kula njama*, hold a secret meeting for a future action; plot, scheme.

njana *n (n) (zool)* orange-striped emperor; a kind of saltwater fish (family *Lethrinidae*) with orange stripes along body, found along the east coast of Africa in shallow weedy areas. *Lethrinus ramak*.

njana

nje¹ *n* (*n*) outside, exterior: *Nje ni pahala pazuri pa kupumzikia*, outside is a good place for resting.
nje² *adv* outside, outdoors, out of the house: *Alienda nje*, he went outside.
njegere *n* (*n*) (*bot*) garden pea; a kind of round edible green pea. *Pisum sativum*. (cf *fiwi*)
njeku *n* (*n*) (*zool*) a small undersized bull.
njeli *n* (*n*) (*naut*) bow, prow; the projecting front part of a ship or other vessel. (cf *gubeti; omo*)
njema *adj* form of -*ema*, good: *Habari njema*, good news, good information.
njemba *n* (*n*) a hefty person; giant.
njenje *n* (*n*) see *ngwenje*
njeo *n* (*n*) (*gram*) tense: *Njeo sahili*, simple tense.
njewe *n* (*n*) see *ndewe*
njia *n* (*n*) **1.** road, path, way: *Njia kuu*, main road. *Njia panda*, road junction; crossroads. *Njia ya reli*, rail road. *Njia ya mkato*, a short cut. *Hakuna njia*, there is no way; no through road. (*prov*) *Penye nia pana njia*, where there is a will, there is a way. **2.** way, method, means, mode, technique: *Njia za kufundishia*, teaching methods. *Njia kuu za uchumi*, main means of production. *Njia za mawasiliano*, means of communication.
njiapanda¹ *n* (*n*) see *njia*
njiapanda² *n* (*n*) dilemma, crossroads: *Hatima ya kocha wao sasa iko njiapanda*, the fate of their coach is now at crossroads i.e. reached a point where it can go either way.
njiwa *n* (*n*) (*zool*) olive pigeon; a kind of pigeon with white-spotted underparts and bright yellow bill and legs: *Njiwa kinda*, speckled pigeon. *Njiwa manga*, feral pigeon. *Njiwa mwitu*, feral pigeon.
njombo *n* (*n*) (*zool*) a kind of fish marked with black and yellow stripes.
njongwanjongwa *adv* (of walking) softly with long stealthily steps as a tall person walks or when following a person secretly, etc.: *Alitembea njongwanjongwa*, he walked steathily (cf *kibubusa, kifichoficho*)
njoo *interj* come
njorinjori¹ (also *ngoringori*) *adj* tall, towering, lofty: *Mtu njorinjori*, a very tall person.
njorinjori² (also *ngoringori*) *n* (*n*) a very tall person; a towering person; a long-legged person.
njozi *n* (*n*) dream, vision: *Ulimwengu wa njozi*, dream land. *Niliota njozi nzuri*, I had a nice dream. (cf *ruia, ndoto*)
njuga *n* (*n*) **1.** ankle bells. (cf *kifumanzi, mbugi, mwangala*) **2.** (*idm*) *Valia njuga*, pursue sby/sth persistently or seriously e.g. *Serikali imelivalia njuga suala la rushwa*, the government is pursuing the corruption issue seriously.
njugu *n* (*n*) **1.** (*bot*) groundnut, monkey nut; an annual plant with leaves composed of leaflets and small yellow pea-like flowers, and its seeds are useful for making vegetable oil. : *Njugu nyasa*, peanut. *Arachis hypogaea*. **2.** a creeping plant which produces smooth, hard seed about $1/2$ inch diameter: *Voandezeia subterranea*. *Njugu mawe*, bambarra groundnut. *Voandzeia subterranea*.
njukuti (also *uchukuti*) *n* (*n*) **1.** sticks of coconut leaves. **2.** matchbox sticks. **3.** bicycle spokes.

585

njumu n (n) 1. stud. 2. shoe cleats.

njumu

njuti n (n) leather boots. (Hind)
njuzi n (n) (zool) a kind of wild cat fond of eating chicks. (cf *kalakonje, kala*)
nkindiza n (n) (naut) the days of neap tide; the days of decline of the tidal movement: *Watoto walienda kuogelea baharini wakati ilipokuwa nkindiza*, the children went to swim in the sea during neap tide.
nne adj (n) four
no.a[1] vt 1. sharpen, whet; make keen, put an edge on: *Alikinoa kisu chake*, he sharpened his knife. (cf *pisha, chongoa*) 2. train, coach, improve: *Wizara inatafuta kocha wa kigeni ili kuinoa timu ya taifa*, the ministry is looking for a foreign coach to train the national team. Prep. *no.le.a* St. *no.lek.a* Cs. *no.lesh.a* Ps. of Prep. *no.lew.a*.
no.a[2] vi make a bad deal; fail to get sth: *Alikuwa akitafuta sana sukari madukani lakini akanoa*, he was searching very hard for sugar in the shops but he failed to get it. Prep. *no.le.a* St. *no.lek.a* Cs. *no.lesh.a* Ps. of Prep. *no.lew.a*
noba n (n) state of working or doing sth in turns or shifts: *Vibarua waliifanya kazi yangu ya ujenzi kwa noba*, the labourers did my masonry work in shifts.
nobe n (n) a stupid person, an expletive of scorn on someone: *Ondoka hapa nobe we!* You leave here!
Noeli n (n) Christmas
nog.a vi 1. be palatable, be delicious, turn out well, be satisfying, be pleasing:

Chakula kilikuwa kimenoga, the food was palatable. 2. (in sports) thrive. Prep. *nog.e.a* St. *nog.ek.a* Cs. *nog.esh.a* Ps. of Prep. *nog.ew.a* Rp. *nog.an.a* (cf *kolea*)
nokoa n (ma-) 1. the second person in authority over plantations owned by landlords. 2. a watchman in plantations.
noma[1] n (n) identity card; work chit as proof that someone was working.
noma[2] n (n) obstacle, objection: *Una noma yoyote?* Have you any objection?
nomi adv full up to the brim, filled to the top; overflowing. (cf *pomoni, tele, topu*)
nomino n (n) (gram) noun: *Nomino dhahania*, abstract noun. *Nomino ambatani*, compound noun. *Nomino kawaida*, common noun. *Nomino mguso*, concrete noun. *Nomino idadi*, count noun. *Nomino halisi*, proper noun. *Nomino kijalizo*, object complement. *Nomino tungamo*, mass noun (cf *jina*) (Lat)
non.a vi be fat, grow fat, get fat. Prep. *non.e.a* St. *non.ek.a* Cs. *non.esh.a* (cf *tononoka, wanda, nenepa*)
nondo[1] n (n) (zool) rufous beaked grass snake; a kind of a fairly large snake with a black eye stripe and plastic-like body scales, reputed to eat insects. etc. *Rhamphiophis oxyrhynchus*. (cf *tuwanyika*)
nondo[2] n (n) (zool) a kind of brightly coloured moth, chiefly seen flying at night. Moths are of great economic importance because some are serious pests of crops and various stored commodities while others are beneficial to mankind as they are a source of food and producers of silk.
nondo[3] n (n) building iron rod; building iron bar: *Nondo za dirisha*, window iron bars.

none.a *vi* kiss a child. Prep. ***none.le.a*** St. ***none.lek.a*** Cs. ***none.sh.a*** Ps. ***non.w.a***

nong.a *vt* provoke, annoy, disturb. Prep. ***nong.e.a*** St. ***nong.ek.a*** Cs. ***nong. esh.a*** Ps. ***nong.w.a*** Rp. ***nong.an.a*** (cf *kasirisha, udhi*)

nongo[1] *n (n)* the dirt which is rubbed off the body after perspiration; body dirt.

nongo[2] *n (n)* bad luck, bad fortune. (cf *uchuro, nuksi*)

nong'on.a *vi* whisper, murmur. Prep. ***nong'on.e.a*** St. ***nong'on.ek.a*** Cs. ***nong'on.ez.a*** Ps. ***nong'on.w.a*** Ps. of Cs. ***nong'on.ez.w.a***

nong'onez.a *vt* whisper, murmur: *Alininong'oneza maneno muhimu kwenye mkutano*, he whispered to me important matters at the meeting. Prep. ***nong'onez.e.a*** St. ***nong'onez.ek.a*** Cs. ***nong'onez.esh.a*** Ps. ***nong'onez.w.a***

nong'onong'o *n (n)* rumour, gossip. (cf *uvumi, tetesi*)

nongwa (also *ging'izo*) *n (n)* 1. grudge, resentment, spite, dislike; bad feeling: *Mtu yule ana nongwa sana*, that person holds a lot of grudges. (cf *mfundo, kinyongo*) 2. a big issue; a big deal: *Akisema tu, kwao wao imekuwa nongwa*, if he just speaks, it becomes a big issue to them.

-nono *adj* 1. fat, plump. 2. fat, huge, big: *Mshahara mnono*, a fat salary.

noti[1] *n (n)* bank note. (Eng)

noti[2] *n (n)* musical note (Eng)

notisi *n (n)* 1. court summons. 2. notice, information, announcement. 3. a letter of dismissal from work; a letter of notice: *Pewa notisi*, be given notice. (Eng)

Novemba *n (n)* the month of November. (Eng)

nsi *n (n)* see *nswi*

nso *n (n)* (*anat*) kidney (cf *figo, buki*)

nswi (also *nsi, swi*) *n (n)* fish (cf *samaki*)

nsya *n (n)* (*zool*) bush duiker; grey duiker. (cf *ngorombwe*) *Sylvicapra grimmia.*

nsya

nta *n (n)* wax

nti *n (n)* ear ornament. (cf *bali*)

ntimbi *n (n)* (*naut*) shallows with one fathom at low tide. (cf *fungu*)

ntwe *n (n)* 1. stigma. 2. a horrendous event/act.

nudhumu *n (n)* (*poet*) verse (Ar)

nufaik.a *vt* profit, gain, benefit, net. *Wananchi wamenufaika kutokana na kuanzishwa kwa miradi mbalimbali*, the people have benefitted from the introduction of different projects. Prep. ***nufaik.i.a*** St. ***nufaik.ik.a*** Cs. ***nufaik.ish.a*** (Ar)

nufaish.a *vt* benefit, aid, profit: *Sera zake za kiuchumi haziwezi kuinufaisha nchi yao*, his economic policies cannot benefit their country. Prep. ***nufaish.i.a*** St. ***nufaish.ik.a*** Ps. ***nufaish.w.a*** Rp. ***nufaish.an.a***

Nuhu *n (n)* (in Islam) the first apostle of God and the father of the second generation of human beings. (in Christianity) a Hebrew patriarch known as "Noah" who saved himself, and his family, etc. from the flood by building a ship (Noah's Ark) in which they all survived. (Ar)

nuhusi *n (n)* bad luck, misfortune, jinx, spell: *Safari yao ilipata nuhusi pale gari yao ilipoharibika njiani*, their journey had a misfortune when their vehicle broke down on the way. (cf *kisirani, mkosi*) (Ar)

nui *n* (*n*) a major branch within a literary type encompassing a certain number of related genres; type, sample, model, design: *Aliandika mashairi ya kila nui*, he wrote different types of poems. (cf *namna, aina, sampuli*)

nui.a (*also nuwia*) *vt* resolve, decide, intend: *Amenuia kupanda mahindi msimu ujao*, he intends to grow maize in the next season. Prep. *nui.li.a* St. *nui.lik.a* Cs. *nui.z.a* Ps. *nui.w.a* Rp. *nui.an.a* (cf *azimu, dhamiria*) (Ar)

nuili.a *vt, vi* intend sth for sby. St. *nuili.k.a* Cs. *nuili.sh.a* Ps. *nuili.w.a*

nuio *n* (*n*) resolution, decision, intention. (cf *azma, kusudio*) (Ar)

nuiz.a¹ *vt* see *nuia*

nuiz.a² *vt* (in witchcraft, etc) used in the expression. *Nuiza uchawi*, place a spell or witchcraft on sby by wishing: *Mteja alinuiza mbele ya mchawi*, the client pronounced his wishes in front of a witchdoctor. Prep. *nuiz.i.a* St. *nuiz.ik.a*

nujumu *n* (*n*) 1. star. 2. luck, fortune; mere chance: *Ilikuwa nujumu kwake yeye kufaulu kwenye mtihani*, it was just luck for him to pass the examination. *Vuta nujumu, bewitch* (cf *bahati, fatahi*) (Ar)

nuk.a *vi* 1. stink, reck, smell. 2. detect/sense the presence of sth by using olfactory nerves; smell. (cf *nuka*) Prep. *nuk.i.a* St. *nuk.ik.a* Cs. *nuk.ish.a* Ps. *nuk.w.a*

nuki.a *vi* 1. have a sweet smell; smell nice. 2. (of sth) be nearing to appear: *Mgogoro ulianza tangu awali kunukia katika chama chao tangu awali*, the conflict began to approach their party right from the beginning (cf *karibia*) St. *nuki.k.a* Cs. *nuki.sh.a* and *nuki.z.a* Ps. of Prep. *nuki.w.a* Rp. *nuki.an.a*

nuksani *n* (*n*) 1. defect, weakness. (cf *upungufu, kasoro*) 2. squabble, feud, quarrel. (cf *ugomvi, utesi, suitafahamu*) (Ar)

nuksi *n* (*n*) see *nuhusi*

nukta *n* (*n*) 1. period; a full stop at the end of a sentence. 2. (of time) second: *Nukta kumi*, ten seconds. (cf *sekunde*) (Ar)

nuktambili *n* (*n*) colon; a mark of pronunciation (:) used before an extended quotation, explanation, example, series, etc. and after a salutation of a formal letter.

nuktamkato *n* (*n*) semicolon; a mark of pronunciation (;) indicating a degree of separation greater than that marked by the comma and less than that marked by a period, etc.

nuku.u *vt* 1. copy, quote, cite: *Askari aliyanukuu maelezo ya mashahidi*, the policeman quoted the witnesses' statements. 2. transcribe, transliterate: *Jaribu kulinukuu kifonetiki fungu hili la maneno*, try to transcribe phonetically this passage. Prep. *nuku.li.a* St. *nuku.lik.a* Cs. *nuku.lish.a* Ps. of Prep. *nuku.liw.a* Rp. of Prep. *nuku.li.an.a* (cf *nakili*) (Ar).

numbi *n* (*n*) (*zool*) emperor red snapper; a kind of saltwater fish with silver white colour body and reddish brown bands, found frequently in shallow inshore reefs and mangrove estuaries. *Lutjanus sebae*. (cf *parakanza*)

nun.a *vi* sulk; show discontent. (*prov*) *Muungwana hununa moyoni, hanuni mashavu*, a gentleman may be angry on somebody but he will not show his feelings openly. Prep. *nun.i.a* St. *nun.ik.a* Cs. *nun.ish.a* Ps. *nun.w.a* Rp. of Prep. *nun.i.an.a* (cf *kasirika*)

nunda *n* (*ma-*) 1. (*zool*) a large tomcat; a half-wild cat. (cf *gwagu, paka shume*) 2. a muscular person; a brawny person. (cf *njembe, kiboko*) 3. (*syn*) *Nunda mla watu*, man eater.

nundu¹ *n* (*n*) 1. the round projecting part on the back of a camel, etc.; hump, bump, protuberance, lump, knob. (*prov*) *Mtegemea nundu, haachi kunona*, one who relies upon someone

nundu²

who is wealthy or educated, etc. will not fail to benefit from him. 2. (*anat*) gland

nundu² *n* (*n*) (*zool*) fruit-eating bat; a small animal with a soft hairless skin, which flies like a bird at night and eats fruit. (order *Chiroptera*) (cf *popomgombo*)

nune *n* (*n*) (*zool*) horsefly; a kind of large insect that bites horses, cattle, etc.

nunge¹ *n* (*n*) leper colony, leper settlements; a settlement for those patients suffering from leprosy.

nunge² *n* (*n*) 1. stumped fingers, stubbed fingers, deformed fingers: *Ana nunge*, he has stumped fingers. 2. zero, nil: *Timu yetu ilishinda kwa mabao mawili kwa nunge.* our team won two goals to nil. (cf *sufuri*, *ziro*)

nungu¹ (also *nungunungu*) *n* (*n*) (*zool*) porcupine; a large rodent (family *Hystricidae*) having coarse hair mixed with long, stiff, sharp spines that can be erected.

nungu

nungu² *n* (*n*) (*zool*) porcupine fish, spiny globe fish; a tropical fish (family *Diodontidae*) with spines all over its body, found mostly on coral reefs and on sandy and muddy bottoms.

nungu³ *n* (*n*) (*zool*) a kind of fowl with very long legs and ruffled feathers; ruffled feathered hen; frizzled chicken. (cf *mangisi*, *kidimu*)

nung'un.a *vi*, *vt* twist the hips. Prep. **nung'un.i.a** St. **nung'un.ik.a** Cs. **nung'un.ish.a**

nus.a

nung'unika *vi* 1. speak in a low voice usu alone: *Alikuwa akinung'unika peke yake chumbani*, he was alone in the room speaking in a low voice. 2. grumble, complain, murmur: *Alinung'unika kwangu juu ya chakula alichopewa*, she complained to me about the food she was given. Prep. **nung'unik.i.a,** grumble about (about, to, etc.) St. **nung'unik.ik.a** Cs. **nungu'nik.ish.a** Ps. **nungu'nik.w.a** Rp. of Prep. **nungu'nik.an.a** (cf *lalamika*, *guna*)

nung'uniko *n* (*ma-*) complaint, grumble, murmur: *Manung'uniko ya wafanyakazi lazima yashughulikiwe*, the workers' complaints must be addressed. (cf *lalamiko*)

nunu *n* (*n*) an expletive of respect for calling a woman; madam. (cf *mwana*)

nunu.a *vt* buy, purchase, pay for: *Amenunua saa mpya*, he has bought a new watch. Prep. **nunu.li.a** St. **nunu.lik.a** Cs. **nunu.lish.a** Ps. of Prep. **nunu.liw.a.** Rp. of Prep. **nunu.li.an.a**

nunuz.a *vt* help a child to teethe by rubbing its gums. Prep. **nunuz.i.a** St. **nunuz.ik.a** Cs. **nunuz.ish.a** Ps. **nunuz.w.a.**

nuru *n* (*n*) light, brightness, illumination: *Tia nuru*, brighten, illuminate. *Toa nuru*, give out light; shine. (cf *mwangaza*, *mng'ao*) (Ar)

nururish.a *vt*, *vi* radiate, lighten: *Taa ya karabai ilinururisha chumba kizima*, the pressure lamp radiated the entire room. Prep. **nururish.i.a** St. **nururish.ik.a** Ps. **nururish.w.a** Rp. **nururish.an.a**

nus.a *vi* 1. smell; sniff; take a smell: *Mbwa alikuwa akiunusa mfupa*, the dog was sniffing at the bone. 2. (of tobacco, etc.) sniff, snuff: *Tumbaku ya kunusa*, snuff. *Alinusa tumbaku*, he sniffed tobacco. Prep. **nus.i.a** St. **nus.ik.a** Cs. **nus.ish.a** Ps. **nus.w.a**

Rp. *nus.an.a.*
nuskha *n (n)* copy, duplicate, edition: *Nuskha ya tatu ya kitabu*, the third edition of the book. (cf *nakala*) (Ar)
nusra[1] (also *nusura*) *adv* nearly, almost, narrowly, just about: *Alikuwa anaumwa sana na nusra afe*, he was so sick that he nearly died. (cf *karibu, chupuchupu*)
nusra[2] (also *nusura*) *n (n)* relief, relaxation, salvation: *Inshallah Mwenyezi Mungu atakupa nusura katika matatizo yako*, may God give you relief from your problems. (cf *tahafifu*) (Ar)
nusu *n (n)* half: *Nusu irabu*, semi-vowel. *Nusu siku*, half-day. *Nusu saa*, half an hour. *Nusu mshahara*, half pay. *Nusu peni*, half penny. (*prov*) *Heri nusu ya shari kuliko shari kamili*, it is better to face a small unpleasant problem now than to face a big one at a later stage. (Ar)
nusukaputi *n (n)* (*med*) anaesthetic, sedative, analgesic.
nusukipenyo *n (n)* the radius of a circle.
nusura *adv* see *nusra*[1] and *nusra*[2]
nusurik.a *vi* be safe, escape narrowly. Prep. *nusurik.i.a* St. *nusurik.ik.a*
nusur.u *vt* save, help, assist, defend: *Mungu atakunusuru*, God will save you. Prep. *nusur.i.a* St. *nusur.ik.a* Cs. *nusur.ish.a* Ps. of Prep. *nusur.iw.a* (cf *okoa, kinga*) (Ar)
nususi[1] *adj* strong. vigorous, intense, fierce.
nususi[2] *n (n)* an expletive used to vindicate the truth of the affairs or special words in recognized books: *Yale ni katika nususi ya mambo*, those are the realities of the affairs. (Ar)
nuwi.a *vt* see *nuia*
ny.a *vi* 1. defecate, excrete, shit; void excrement, have a bowel movement. 2. rain: *Mvua ilikunya mchana wote jana*, it rained the whole day yesterday. (*prov*) *Aisifuye mvua imemnyea*, he who praises rain has been soaked i.e. he who praises sth must have benefited from it. Prep. *ny.e.a* St. *ny.ek.a* Cs. *ny.esh.a* Ps. of Prep. *ny.ew.a* (cf *nyesha*)
nya.a *vi* (of leaves, etc.) dry up, shrivel, wither: *Maua yalinyaa kwenye bustani yake*, the flowers shrivelled up in his garden. (cf *nyauka, kauka*)
nyaenya *n (n)* (*zool*) a kind of fish.
nyafu.a *vt* strip off flesh from a bone by using fingers: *Aliinyafua nyama*, he stripped the meat with his fingers. St. *nyafu.k.a* Cs. *nyafu.sh.a* Ps. of Prep. *nyafu.liw.a* Rp. *nyafu.an.a* (cf *nyokoa*)
nyago *n (n)* 1. legs, thighs. (cf *miguu, mapaja*) 2. strides, footsteps: *Ana nyago ndefu*, he takes long strides.
nyak.a[1] *vt* 1. catch (in the hands); snatch, grip, pluck sth usu skilfully e.g. ball: *Golikipa aliunyaka mpira*, the goalkeeper caught the ball. (cf *daka, kamata*) 2. seize sth abruptly: *Alipotakwa kupigwa jiwe, mtoto alilinyaka haraka*, when he was about to be stoned, the child snatched the stone abruptly. Prep. *nyak.i.a* St. *nyak.ik.a* Cs. *nyak.ish.a* Ps. *nyak.w.a.* Rp. *nyak.an.a*
nyak.a[2] *vt* hit hard; slap with force: *Alimnyaka makofi sana usoni*, he slapped him hard on the face several times. Prep. *nyak.i.a* St. *nyak.ik.a* Cs. *nyak.ish.a* Ps. *nyak.w.a* (cf *bubuta, fufuta*)
nyakanga *n (ma-)* the chief instructor of initiation in a circumcision school or marriage.
nyakanyaka *adv* an expletive used to show sth worn-out, battered, etc.: *Alipigwa nyakanyaka*, he was battered. (cf *nyang'anyang'a*)
nyaku.a *vt* snatch sth hurriedly, grab, clutch: *Mwewe alimnyakua kifaranga cha kuku*, the hawk snatched up the chick. Prep. *nyaku.li.a* St. *nyaku.lik.a* Ps. of Prep. *nyaku.liw.a* Rp. *nyaku.an.a*

nyama[1] n (n) 1. meat, flesh: *Nyama ya ng'ombe,* beef. *Nyama ya kondoo,* mutton. *Nyama ya mbuzi,* mutton. *Nyama mbichimbichi,* raw meat. *Nyama ya kopo,* tinned meat. *Nyama ya kusaga,* minced meat. 2. (*bot*) the pulpy, usu edible part of a fruit or vegetable; flesh. 3. (*syn*) *Nyama ya ulimi,* sweet words.

nyama[2] *interj* an expletive of insult to sby.

nyama.a *vi* 1. be silent; stay quiet; stop talking; hold one's tongue: *Wanafunzi walinyamaa wakati mwalimu wao alipoingia darasani,* the students stopped talking when their teacher entered the class. (cf *sukuta, fyata*) 2. (of mental or bodily suffering, etc.) stop, cease, subside: *Kichwa chake kilikuwa kinamwuma lakini sasa kimenyamaa,* his head was aching but now the pain has stopped. Prep. **nyama.li.a** St. **nyama.lik.a** Cs. **nyama.z.a** Ps. of Cs. **nyama.z.w.a** (cf *tulia, poa*)

nyamafu (also *nyamamfu*) *n* (*n*) a dead animal. (cf *mzoga*)

nyamamfu *n* (*n*) see *nyamafu*

nyamata *n* (*n*) (*zool*) Thorny Chito; a mollusk belonging to the class of *polylacophora-Chitons* that lives in littoral fringe rock surfaces.

nyamaume *n* (*n*) hero, valiant, gallant: *Askari yule ni nyamaume,* that policeman is gallant. (cf *shujaa, nguli*)

-nyamavu *adj* silent, quiet, calm, placid, sedate, peaceful: *Mtu mnyamavu,* a quiet person. (cf *kimya, baridi*)

nyamaz.a *vt* shut up, keep quiet, be silent. Prep. **nyamaz.i.a** St. **nyamaz.ik.a** Cs. **nyamaz.ish.a**

nyamazish.a *vt* silence, quiet, shush, hush: *Aliwanyamazisha watoto waliokuwa wakifanya kelele,* he silenced the children who were making noise. Prep. **nyamazish.i.a** St. **nyamazish.ik.a** Ps. **nyamazish.wa** Rp. **nyamazish.an.a**

nyambizi *n* (*n*) (*naut*) submarine (cf *sabmarini, sapmarini*)

nyambu.a[1] *vt* disentangle, unravel, unwind: *Aliunyambua uzi ili aweze kupata vipande vipande,* he disentangled the thread in order to get its pieces. Prep. **nyambu.li.a** St. **nyambu.k.a** and **nyambu.lik.a** Cs. **nyambu.lish.a** Ps. of Prep. **nyambu.liw.a** (cf *ambua, chambua*)

nyambu.a[2] *vt* 1. stretch, lengthen, draw out: *Aliunyambua mpira,* he stretched the rubberband. 2.(*gram*) conjugate, derive: *Alikinyambua kitenzi,* he conjugated the verb. Prep. **nyambu.li.a** St. **nyambu.k.a** and **nyambu.lik.a** Cs. **nyambu.lish.a** stretch. Ps. of Prep. **nyambu.liw.a** (cf *refusha*)

nyambu.a[3] *vt* discredit, vilify, defame, humiliate, humble: *Alinimyambua hadharani,* he discredited me in public. Prep. **nyambu.li.a** St. **nyambu.lik.a** Cs. **nyambu.lish.a** Ps. of Prep. **nyambu.liwa** Rp. **nyambu.an.a** (cf *kashifu, aziri, fedhehesha*)

nyambulik.a *vi* 1. be stretchable; be capable of being extended 2. (*gram*) be conjugated, be extended. Prep. **nyambulik.i.a** St. **nyambulik.ik.a** Cs. **nyambulik.ish.a**

nyambulish.a *vt* (*gram*) cause a base form of a word to take derivative forms. Prep. **nyambulish.i.a** St. **nyambulish.ik.a** Ps. **nyambulish.w.a** Rp. **nyambulish.an.a**

nyambuo *n* (*n*) (*zool*) a small fish like sardines.

nyamburo *n* (*n*) jeweller's pliers. (cf *chamburo, pakari*)

nyamera *n* (*n*) (*zool*) topi; a large antelope with a fairly long head and striking reddish brown to purplish red coloured coat that is very glossy. *Damaliscus korrigum.*

nyamera

nyamizi n (n) see *mwanamizi*
nyamngumi n (n) see *nyangumi*
nyana n (n) the head of an arrow or spear. (cf *kigumba*)
nyanda n (n) a measure from the tip of the thumb to the tip of the little finger when the hand is stretched.
nyang'any.a vt take by force; snatch, rob, steal: *Mwizi alimnyang'anya msichana kipochi chake*, the thief snatched the girl's purse. Prep. *nyang'any.i.a* St. *nyang'any.ik.a* Cs. *nyang'any.ish.a*. Ps. *nyang'any.w.a* Rp. *nyang'any.an.a*
nyangushi n (n) see *kihalua*
nyang'anyang'a adv see *nyakanyaka*
nyangarika n (n) a person or object that is worthless; a person with physical strength but no brains, no culture, etc; blockhead, lout, clod, dolt. (cf *dude, dubwana*)
nyang'au n (n) a cruel person, savage; brute. (cf *habithi*)
nyange[1] n (n) noise, turmoil, commotion. (cf *ghasia, rabsha, kelele*)
nyange[2] n (n) moron, imbecile, simpleton, idiot: *Nyange yule haelewi chochote*, that fool does not understand anything. (cf *mjinga, mpumbavu*)
nyange[3] n (wa-) a person who grins his teeth.
nyangumi (also *nyamngumi*) (zool) n (n) whale: *Mfupa wa kinywani mwa nyangumi*, whalebone.
nyani n (ma-) (zool) baboon. (prov) *Nyani haoni kundule*, a disgraced person does not see his own weaknesses; he only sees the weaknesses of others and begins to expose them.
nyanya[1] n (n) (bot) tomato: *Nyanya chungu*, tree tomato. *Nyanya mshumaa*, tree tomato. *Cyphomandra betacea*. (cf *tungule*)
nyanya[2] n (n) grandmother (cf *bibi*)
nyanyapa.a vt show contempt to someone, avoid someone scornfully; snub: *Alininyanyapaa mkutanoni bila ya sababu*, he snubbed me at the meeting for no reason. *Usiwanyanyapae walemavu*, don't show contempt to the disabled people. Prep. *nyanyapa.li.a* St. *nyanyapa.lik.a* Cs. *nyanyapa.z.a* Ps. of Prep. *nyanyapa.liw.a* Rp. *nyanyapa.an.a* (cf *beza, dharau*)
nyanyas.a vt molest, torment, illtreat: *Aliwanyanyasa wazee wake*, she illtreated her parents. Prep. *nyanyas.i.a* St. *nyanyas.ik.a* Cs. *nyanyas.ish.a* Ps. *nyanyas.w.a* Rp. *nyanyas.an.a* (cf *dhalilisha, tesa, onea*).
nyanyaso n (ma-) illtreatment, persecution, molestation.
nyanyi.a vt 1. get sth cunningly; acquire sth by crooked means: *Yeye ana tabia ya kunyanyia vitu*, he has the habit of acquiring things by crooked means. 2. share sth among one's partners without a proper order. St. *nyanyi.k.a* Cs. *nyanyi.sh.a* Ps. *nyanyi.w.a* Rp. *nyanyi.an.a*.
nyanyu.a[1] vt, vi 1. lift, raise, elevate: *Alikinyanyua kiti*, he lifted the chair (cf *inua, beba*) 2. (fig) promote; raise to a higher position: *Meneja alimnyanyua mfanyakazi wake*, the manager promoted his worker. Prep. *nyanyu.li.a* St. *nyanyu.k.a* Cs. *nyanyu.lish.a* Ps. of Prep. *nyanyu.liw.a nyanyu.an.a*
nyanyu.a[2] vt tear, rip, rend, reave, rive: *Aliinyanyua nguo yake*, she tore her dress. (cf *chana, rarua*) Prep. *nyanyu.li.a* St. *nyanyu.k.a* Cs. *nyanyu.*

nyanyuk.a   **nyege**   **N**

lish.a Ps. of Prep. **nyanyu.liw.a** Rp. **nyanyu.an.a** Rp. of Prep. **nyanyu.li.an.a**

nyanyuk.a *vi* stand up, get up. Prep. **nyanyuk.i.a** St. **nyanyuk.ik.a** Cs. **nyanyuk.ish.a**

nyanza *n* (*n*) lake

nyap.a *vi* walk stealthily or furtively; stalk: *Msasi alinyapa alipokuwa anawinda wanyama*, the hunter stalked when he was hunting the animals. Prep. **nyap.i.a** St. **nyap.ik.a** Cs. **nyap.ish.a** Ps. **nyap.w.a**(cf *nyata, nyemelea*).

nyapuk.a *vi* go hurriedly; hasten. Prep. **nyapuk.i.a** St. **nyapuk.ik.a** Cs. **nyapuk.ish.a** (cf *chapuka*)

nyara[1] *n* (*n*) hostages, booty, loot: *Teka nyara*, take hostage e.g. *Ndege ilitekwa nyara na watu wasiojulikana*, the plane was hijacked by unknown people.

nyara[2] *adv* 1. (*idm*) *Kula nyara*, get sth easily or without effort. 2. freely, gratuitously: *Masikini alipewa nyara chakula*, the poor man was given food free of charge. (cf *bure*)

nyaraf.u *vt* avoid contact with sby or sth because of his filthiness, bad habits, etc.; shun, ignore: *Wanamnyarafu jirani yao kutokana na uchafu wake*, they ignore their neighbour because of his dirt. Prep. **nyaraf.i.a** St. **nyaraf.ik.a** Cs. **nyaraf.ish.a** Ps. **nyaraf.iw.a** Rp. of Prep. **nyaraf.i.an.a**

nyarubanja *n* (*n*) 1. a system of land lease that existed in the past in Bukoba, Tanzania. 2. a traditional system of acquiring one's land by using traditional laws.

nyasi *n* (*n*) (*bot*) long grass; reeds; rushes, sedge.

nyat.a *vi* walk stealthily or furtively; stalk. Prep. **nyat.i.a** St. **nyat.ik.a** Cs. **nyat.ish.a** Ps. of Prep. **nyat.iw.a** (cf *nyemelea, nyapa*)

nyati *n* (*n*) (*zool*) buffalo (cf *mbogo*)

nyati.a *vi* creep up to, stalk. Prep. **nyati.li.a** St. **nyati.k.a** (cf *nyapa*)

nyato *n* (*n*) nipple (cf *chuchu, nywato*)

nyatu.a *vi* walk with short uncertain steps like a child; toddle, totter: *Mtoto alikuwa akinyatua*, the child was toddling. Prep. **nyatu.li.a** St. **nyatu.k.a** Cs. **nyatu.sh.a** Ps. of Prep. **nyatu.liw.a** (cf *demadema*)

nyatunyatu *adv* stealthily, furtively, surreptitiously: *Wezi waliingia chumbani nyatunyatu*, the thieves entered the room stealthily. (cf *kinyenyere, asteaste*)

nyau *n* (*n*) 1. (*zool*) cat. (cf *paka*) 2. the mew of a cat.

-nyaufu *adj* (usu of fruits or leaves) dried up, shrivelled up, withered: *Tunda hili limekuwa nyaufu kutokana na jua kali*, this fruit has shrivelled because of the scorching sun.

nyauk.a (also *nyuuka*) (of a plant or shrub) *vi* shrivel, wither, dry up: *Majani ya mti ule yamenyauka*, the leaves of that tree have shrivelled up. Prep. **nyauk.i.a** St. **nyauk.ik.a** Cs. **nyauk.ish.a** (cf *kauka, gungumka*)

nye.a[1] *vi* see *nyaa*

nye.a[2] (also *nyegea*) *vt* prickle, itch, sting: *Nyungunyungu wanamnyea baina ya vidole*, the worms are prickling him in between his toes. Prep. **nye.le.a** St. **nye.k.a** Cs. **nye.sh.a** Ps. **nye.w.a** (cf *washa*)

nye.a[3] *vi* disappear, vanish; recede from view: *Alienda kule na hatimaye kunyea*, he went there and ultimately disappeared. Prep. **nye.le.a** St. **nye.k.a** Cs. **nye.sh.a** Ps. **nye.w.a**

nyege *n* (*n*) strong or abnormal sexual desire; prurient desire, erotic stimulation; concupiscence: *Tia nyege*, arouse strong sexual desire; cause prurient desire. (*syn*) *Nyege* *ni kunyegezana*, i.e. kindness must operate on a two-way basis. (cf *ashiki, hamu*)

nyege.a *vt* see *nyea*²

nyegere *n* (*n*) (*zool*) ratel; a relatively stout stocky animal with massive rounded ears and a short bushy tail, found in Asia and Africa. *Mellivora capensis*.

nyegere

nyegeresh.a *vt* see *nyengeresha*.

nyek.a *vi* 1. shine as though rubbed with oil or fat: *Nywele zake zilikuwa zikinyeka kwa kupakwa mafuta mengi*, her hair was shining because of applying too much oil. (cf *ng'aa, nang'anika*) 2. be moist, be wet: *Kwapa zake zimenyeka kwa jasho*, his armpits are moist with sweat. Prep. **nyek.e.a** St. **nyek.ek.a** Cs. **nyek.esh.a** Ps. **nyek.w.a**.

nyekez.a *vt* sprinkle water, etc. Prep. **nyekez.ek.a** Cs. **nyekez.esh.a**

nyemele.a (also *nyendea*) *vt, vi* walk stealthily or furtively; stalk: *Alimnyemelea paa*, he stalked the deer. St. **nyemele.k.a** Cs. **nyemele.sh.a** Ps. **nyemele.w.a** Rp. **nyemele.an.a** (cf *nyata, nyapa*)

nyemi *n* (*n*) happiness, gladness, joy: *Alikuwa katika nyemi wakati wote alipokuwa anaoa*, he was in a state of happiness throughout when he got married. (*prov*) *Kipya kinyemi ingawa kidonda*, sth that is new is enjoyable even if it has its weaknesses. (cf *furaha*)

nyende *n* (*n*) buzz, chirp; a shrill sound, chirping sound. (cf *ukemi, ukwenje*)

nyende.a *vt, vi* see *nyemelea*

nyeng.a¹ *vt* 1. deceive by using nice words; hoodwink, cheat: *Alifaulu kuninyenga nilipokubali kumwazima gari yangu*, he successfully cheated me when I agreed to lend him my car. (cf *hadaa, ghilibu*) 2. swindle by giving a short measure, less than what is due, etc.: *Mwenyeduka alimnyenga mnunuzi*, the shopkeeper swindled a customer by giving him less than what was due. Prep. **nyeng.e.a** St. **nyeng.ek.a** Cs. **nyeng.esh.a** Ps. **nyeng.w.a** Rp. **nyeng.an.a** (cf *punja*)

nyenga² *n* (*n*) (*zool*) stingray; a large wide flat fish (family *Dasyatidae*) having a long, whiplike tail with one or more usu poisonous spines that can inflict painful wounds. Honeycomb stingray. Leopard stingray (*Himantura uarnak*)

nyenga

nyengeresh.a (also *nyegeresha*) *vt* cause prurient desire to someone; arouse sexual desire in someone. Prep. **nyengeresh.e.a** St. **nyengeresh.ek.a** Ps. **nyengeresh.w.a** Rp. **nyengeresh.an.a** (cf *tekenya*)

nyenje (also *nyenze*) *n* (*n*) (*zool*) field cricket; a kind of field cricket that usually feeds on plants .(cf *chenene*)

nyeny.a *vt* interrogate sby quite

intensively on a particular issue. Prep. **nyeny.e.a** St. **nyenye.k.a** Cs. **nyenye.sh.a**

nyenyeke.a *vt, vi* 1. humble oneself in order to get sth: show humility to someone: *Alimnyenyekea mwajiri ili aweze kumpa kazi*, he degraded himself to the employer so that he could employ him. (cf *kongowea, sujudia*) 2. obey. respect, venerate, revere: *Anawanyenyekea wazee wake sana*, he respects his parents a lot. St. **nyenyeke.k.a** Cs. **nyenyeke.sh.a** Ps. **nyenyeke.w.a** Rp. **nyenyeke.an.a** (cf *heshimu, tii*)

-nyenyekevu *adj* humble, meek, servile, submissive, compliant: *Mtumishi mnyenyekevu*, a humble servant.

nyenyere *n (n)* (*zool*) a tiny black harmless ant, which is often a nuisance in the house. (cf *sisimizi*)

nyenyerek.a *vi* confuse by talking too much Prep. **nyenyerek.e.a** Cs. **nyenyerek.esh.a** Ps. **nyenyerek.ew.a**

nyenze *n (n)* see *nyenje*

nyenzo *n (n)* 1. a pole that is put under a log in order to make it easy for it to be pulled. (*prov*) *Mti hauendi ila kwa nyenzo*, a tree cannot move without a log i.e. inorder for sth to succeed, you must have the necessary tools or means. 2. instrument, means, ways: *Lazima serikali itafute nyenzo mbalimbali za kuuboresha uchumi*, the government must seek various ways of improving the economy. *Inafaa tuwape wakulima kila aina ya nyenzo*, it is important that we must give every means of support to farmers.

nyera[1] *n (n)* (*zool*) a kind of sea animal. (cf *jeta*)

nyer.a[2] *vt, vi* joke, mock, deride, ridicule; make fun of: *Anapenda kuwanyera rafiki zake*, he likes to ridicule his friends. Prep. **nyer.e.a** St. **nyer.ek.a** Cs. **nyer.esh.a** Ps. **nyer.w.a** Rp. **nyer.an.a** (cf *tania, dhihaki*)

nyerere *n (n)* brass or copper thin bangle worn round the arms and legs as an ornament by certain tribes; brass/copper bangle. (cf *uwoo*)

nyererek.a *vi* see *nyiririka*

nyererez.a *vt,vi* 1. hide one's actions so as to deceive; camouflage, disguise, cover up: *Maadui walijinyererezea kama askari kwa kuvaa nguo za namna yetu*, the enemies disguised themselves as soldiers by wearing uniforms like those of ours. 2. conceal the authenticity of sth by painting it or by other means so that it looks new; forge: *Mwenyeduka alivinyererezea baadhi ya vipuri dukani mwake*, the shopkeeper concealed the genuineness of some of the spare parts in his shop. Prep. **nyererez.e.a** St. **nyererez.ek.a** Cs. **nyererez.esh.a** Ps. **nyererez.w.a** Rp. **nyererez.an.a**

nyerezi *adj* pleasant, attractive, pleasing, charming, beautiful.

nyes.a *vi* become humid, be humid, be wet: *Ardhi yote yanyesa*, the whole ground is wet. Prep **nyes.e.a** St **nyes.ek.a** Cs **nyes.esh.a**

nyesh.a *vi* rain: *Mvua inanyesha sasa hivi*, it is raining now. Prep. **nyesh.e.a**, St. **nyesh.ek.a** Ps. of Prep. **nyesh.ew.a** (-nya)

nyet.a *vi* behave in an arrogant manner; be conceited: *Akijaribu kujinyeta, watu watamsema*, if she tries to be arrogant, people will speak ill of her. Prep. **nyet.e.a** St. **nyet.ek.a** Cs. **nyet.esh.a** and **nyet.ez.a** Ps. **nyet.w.a** (cf *deka, tamba*)

nyeti *adj* 1. sensitive: *Suala nyeti*, sensitive issue. *Nyaraka nyeti*, sensitive documents. *Habari nyeti*, sensitive information. *Eneo nyeti*, sensitive area. *Wakati nyeti*, sensitive period. *Sehemu nyeti*, sensitive place. 2. crucial, vital, important: *Pambano nyeti*, a crucial contest.

-nyevu *adj* humid, damp, wet, moist: *Udongo mnyevu*, wet soil.

nyie *pron* see *nyinyi*
nyigu *n* (*n*) (*zool*) hornet, (cf *dondora, mavu*) (*syn*) *Ana kiuno kama nyigu,* she has a small waist.

nyika *n* (*n*) open grasslands, open forest with high grass; wilderness: *Walikwenda msitu na nyika,* they went on and on through woods and forests, etc.; they had a long journey. *Mbio za nyika,* cross-country race.
nyim.a *vt* deprive, deny, refuse: *Walimnyima haki yake ya kupiga kura,* they deprived him of his right to vote. Prep. **nyim.i.a** St. **nyim.ik.a** Cs. **nyim.ish.a** Ps. **nyim.w.a** Rp. **nyim.an.a** (cf *hini, zuia, katalia*).
nyimbi (also *nyumbi*) *n* (*n*) (*zool*) a kind of saltwater fish belonging to *Mulidae* family.
nyimbo *n* (*n*) see *wimbo*
nyimifu *adj* see *nyimivu*
-nyiminyimi *adj* niggardly, stingy, miserly, skinflinty, mean: *Mtu mnyiminyimi,* a stingy person. (cf *bahili*)
-nyimivu (also *nyimifu*) *adj* stingy, miserly, mean: *Tajiri mnyimivu yule hatakusaidia chochote,* that stingy tycoon will not help you in anything.
nyinyi (also *nyie*) *pron* you there (you pl).
nyinyih.a *vi* shine as though rubbed with oil or fat. (cf *nyaa, nang'anika, nyeka*)
nyinyirik.a (also *nyenyereka*) *vt* shine after being smeared with oil, etc.; glisten, glint: *Uso wake ulinyinyirika baada ya kupakwa mafuta,* her face shone after being smeared with oil. Prep. **nyinyirik.i.a** St. **nyinyirik.ik.a** Cs. **nyinyirik.ish.a** Ps. **nyinyirik.w.a** (cf *ng'aa, nang'anika*).

nyinyoro *n* (*n*) (*bot*) a bulbous plant which produces a large head of red flowers.
nyiririk.a (also *nyerereka*) *vi* glide; move with a gliding motion like a snake or trickle of water: *Maji yalikuwa yakinyiririka kutoka kwenye paa la nyumba,* the water was trickling from the roof of the house. Prep. **nyiririk.i.a** St. **nyiririk.ik.a** Cs. **nyiririk.ish.a** Ps. **nyiririk.w.a**
nyiza *n* (*n*) dyed strips of palm leaves used for plaiting baskets, etc.
nyo.a[1] *vt* shave. *Nyoa ndevu,* shave beard. Prep. **nyo.le.a** St. **nyo.lek.a** Cs. **nyo.lesh.a** Ps. of Prep. **nyo.lew.a** Rp. **nyo.an.a** (cf *dira, chega*)
nyo.a[2] *vt* swindle, cheat: *Mfanyabiashara yule aliwanyoa wateja wake,* that businessman swindled his customers. Prep. **nyo.le.a** St. **nyo.lek.a** Cs. **nyo.lesh.a** Ps. of Prep. **nyo.lew.a** Rp. **nyo.an.a** (cf *punja, danganya*).
nyodo *n* (*n*) pomposity, arrogance, airs. (cf *maringo, majinato*)
nyofo.a *vt* pick pieces from, strip off pieces from; nibble: *Aliinyofoa keki,* he nibbled at the cake. Prep. **nyofo.le.a** St. **nyofo.k.a** Cs. **nyofo.sh.a** Ps. of Prep. **nyofo.lew.a** (cf *dokoa, nyokoa*)
-nyofu *adj* 1. straight, stretched out, uncurved, unbent, linear: *Mstari mnyofu,* a straight line. *Njia nyofu,* a straight road. 2. (*fig*) honest, upright, trustworthy: *Mwekahazina mnyofu,* an honest treasurer.
nyoka[1] *n* (*n*) (*zool*) snake, serpent. (*prov*) *Atambaaye na nyasi mtambulie ni nyoka,* he who crawls in the grass is a snake i.e. he who walks secretly to condemn you is your enemy. (cf *mtambaachi*) 2. intestinal worms.
nyok.a[2] (also *nyooka*) *vi* see *nyooka*
nyoko *n* (*n*) 1. (rarely used) your mother. 2. an expletive used with another word to convey an abusive connotation e.g. *Kuma nyoko,* your mother's cunt.
nyoko.a *vt* take a pinch of; take in pieces by using fingers: *Aliunyokoa mkate wangu,* he took a piece of my bread

by using his fingers. Prep. **nyoko.le.a** St. **nyoko.k.a** Cs. **nyoko.sh.a** Ps. of Prep. **nyoko.lew.a** (cf *nyofoa, nyotoa, nyonyora*).

nyomvi *n* (*n*) (*zool*) nightjar; a yellowish bird which builds its nest on coconut or other trees which are near houses and lives in parties.

nyonda *n* (*n*) 1. love, affection: *Hana nyonda na mkewe*, he has no love for his wife. (cf *mapenzi, mahaba*) 2. darling; sweetheart: *Nyonda wake*, his darling.

nyondenyonde *n*(*n*) a disease that does not heal quickly; a chronic disease; a prolonged illness: *Mgonjwa wangu bado anaendelea na nyondenyonde zake*, my patient is still languishing from his prolonged illness. (cf *swenene*)

nyondo.a *vt, vi* pick grains one at a time. Prep. **nyondo.e.a** St. **nyondo.ek.a** Cs. **nyondo.esh.a**

nyonga[1] *n* (*n*) hip. (*prov*) *Mwenda mbio huagana na nyonga*, he who runs comes to terms with the hip i.e. you can't do sth of significance without depending upon a solid base. For example, you cannot start a business without having the necessary capital first. (cf *gungu*)

nyong.a[2] *vt* 1. twist the neck of; strangle, throttle: *Alimnyonga kuku*, he strangled the chicken. (cf *ua, chinja*) 2. hang, bring to the gallows: *Serikali iliwanyonga wahalifu*, the government hanged the culprits. 3. (of an arm, etc.) twist: *Aliunyonga mkono wangu*, he twisted my arm. Prep. **nyong.e.a** St. **nyong.ek.a** Cs. **nyong.esh.a** Ps. **nyong.w.a** Rp. **nyong.an.a** (cf *songoa, sombogoa, popotoa*)

-nyonge *adj* weak, oppressed, poor: *Watu wanyonge*, poor people.

nyongea[1] *n* (*n*) (*med*) rickets; a disease of the skeletal system affecting children.

nyonge.a[2] *vt, vi* feel oppressed; feel humble: *Alijinyongea mbele za watu wote*, he humbled himself in front of all the people. St. **nyong.ek.a** Cs. **nyong.esh.a** Ps. **nyong.ew.a** Rp. **nyong.an.a** (cf *dhalilisha*)

nyongeza *n* (*n*) 1. increment, supplement: *Nyongeza ya mshahara*, a salary increment. (cf *ziada, ongezeko*) 2. appendix: *Nyongeza katika tasnifu*, appendices in a thesis. (cf *kiambatisho*)

nyongo[1] *n* (*n*) 1. (*anat*) bile. 2. (*idm*) *Tumbukia nyongo*, (of things), be in a mess; be in disarray.

nyongo[2] *n* (*n*) saltwater that has been collected in a pool to dry in order to get salt in it.

nyongo[3] *n* (*n*) the rolling of bhang; joint.

nyongo.a *vt* straighten out twists esp after being in a cramped or bent position: *Alivinyongoa vyuma vya kujengea*, he straightened iron bars for building. Prep. **nyongo.le.a** St. **nyongo.k.a** Cs. **nyongo.sh.a** Rp. **nyongo.an.a** (cf *nyoosha*)

nyong'ony.a *vi* be inert, be weak, be weary: *Miguu yake yote miwili ilimnyong'onya*, both his legs were weak. Prep. **nyong'ony.e.a** St. **nyong'ony.ek.a** Cs. **nyong'ony.esh.a** Ps. **nyong'ony.w.a**

nyong'onye.a *vi* be weary, be weak; languish, droop. Prep. **nyong'onye.le.a** St. **nyong'onye.k.a** Ps. **nyong'onye.sh.a** Rp. **nyong'onye.an.a**

nyono *n* (*n*) snore

nyony.a *vt, vi* 1. suck, draw into, breast feed: *Mtoto mchanga alinyonya ziwa la mama yake*, the baby sucked the breast of her mother 2. (*fig*) exploit sby; milk, profit from: *Wakoloni waliinyonya nchi yetu*, the colonialists exploited our country. Prep. **nyony.e.a** St. **nyony.ek.a** Cs. **nyony.esh.a** Ps. **nyony.w.a** Rp. **nyony.an.a**

nyonyesh.a *vt* suckle, breast-feed; feed at the breast: *Mama alimnyonyesha mwanawe*, the mother breastfed

her baby. Prep. **nyonyesh.e.a** St. **nyonyesh.ek.a** Ps. **nyonyesh.w.a** Rp. **nyonyesh.an.a** (cf *kokeza*)
nyonyo[1] *n* (*n*) (*bot*) castor nut; seeds of the castor oil plant. *Jatropha curcas.*
nyonyo[2] *n* (*n*) (*anat*) nipple, teat, tit, titty (cf *chuchu, kilembwe*).
nyonyo.a *vt* 1. pluck out hair, feathers, etc.: *Alimnyonyoa kuku wake*, he plucked out his hen's feathers. 2. (*fig*) insult, vilipend, vituperate: *Alininyonyoa bure*, he insulted me for nothing. 3. insult sby by expressing *nyoo*, an expletive of derision, contempt, etc. Prep. **nyonyo.le.a** St. **nyonyo.k.a** Cs. **nyonyo.sh.a** Ps. of Prep. **nyonyo.lew.a** Rp. **nyonyo.an.a**
nyonyor.a *vt* (of small things) take in usu furtively, take a pinch of sth furtively; pinch: *Aliunyonyora mkate wangu*, he pinched my bread. Prep. **nyonyor.e.a** St. **nyonyor.ek.a** Cs. **nyonyor.esh.a** Ps. **nyonyor.w.a**. Rp. **nyonyor.an.a**
nyonyota[1] *n* (*ma-*) a drop of light rain. *Manyonyota*, drizzle; light rain. (cf *nyunyu, nyonyoto*)
nyonyot.a[2] *vi* drizzle, sprinkle; rain lightly: *Mvua ilipoanza kunyonyota, mimi nikafungua mwavuli wangu*, when it started to drizzle, I opened my umbrella. Prep. **nyonyot.e.a** St. **nyonyot.e.k.a** Cs. **nyonyot.esh.a** Ps. **nyonyot.w.a** (cf *nyunya, chonyota, dondoka*)
nyonyotok.a *vi* be overcooked; be falling to pieces from being overcooked. Prep. **nyonyotok.e.a** St. **nyonyotok.ek.a** Cs. **nyonyotok.esh.a**
nyoo *interj* an expletive of derision, contempt, etc.
nyook.a (also *nyoka*) *vi* 1. be straight, be in a line: *Mstari umenyooka*, the line is straight. 2 (*fig*) be okay, be alright: *Mambo yake yamenyooka*, his affairs are okay. Prep. **nyook.e.a** St. **nyook.ek.a** Cs. **nyook.esh.a**
nyoosh.a (also *nyosha*) *vt* 1. straighten, unbend; make straight: *Nyoosha mgongo*, straighten the back. *Nyoosha mkono*, raise the hand 2. (*fig*) rectify, adjust: *Jaribu kuyanyoosha mambo yako*, try to rectify your affairs. Prep. **nyoosh.e.a** St. **nyoosh.ek.a** Ps. **nyoosh.w.a** Rp. **nyoosh.an.a**
nyopo.a *vt* put a bone out of its proper place in a joint; dislocate: *Mchezaji rafu aliinyopoa pia yangu*, the rough player dislocated my kneecap. Prep. **nyopo.le.a** St. **nyopo.k.a** Cs. **nyopo.sh.a** Ps. of Prep. **nyopo.lew.a** Rp. **nyopo.an.a**. (cf *tegua*)
nyoror.a *vi* become thin, be lean; become emaciated through illness, etc.: *Mwili wake sasa umenyorora baada ya kuugua kwa muda mrefu*, his body is now emaciated after suffering from a long illness. Prep. **nyoror.e.a**, St. **nyoror.ek.a** Cs. **nyoror.esh.a** Ps. **nyonyor.w.a** (cf *sinyaa, konda, dhoofika*)
nyosh.a *vi* see *nyoosha*
nyota[1] *n* (*n*) 1. (*astron*) star. 2. luck, future: *Ana nyota nzuri*, he is a lucky person. (*prov*) *Usisafirie nyota ya mwenzio*, i.e. don't rely on another's luck. (cf *bahati*) 3. (*gram*) asterisk; a star-like mark used in printing to indicate footnote references, ungrammaticality of a sentence, etc.
nyota[2] *n* (*n*) thirst. (cf *kiu*).
nyotanyot.a *vi* drizzle, sprinkle; rain lightly. (cf *nyonyota, nyunya*)
nyote *pron* used as contraction for: *Nyinyi nyote*, you all, all of you.
nyoto.a[1] *vt* nip: *Aliyanyotoa matawi ya mti*, he nipped off the branches of the tree. Prep. **nyoto.le.a** St. **nyoto.k.a** Ps. of Prep. **nyoto.lew.a**. Rp. **nyoto.an.a**
nyoto.a[2] *vt* 1. (of an illness, etc.) make thin; emaciate: *Maradhi yalimnyotoa*, the illness emaciated her. 2. smart, sting, bite: *Kidonda nilichokuwa nacho mguuni kilinyotoa*, the wound I had on the leg smarted. Prep. **nyoto.le.a** St. **nyoto.k.a** Cs. **nyoto.sh.a** Ps. of Prep. **nyoto.lew.a** Rp. **nyoto.an.a** (cf *gofua*)

nyowe *n(n)* (*zool*) a kind of long grasshopper of different colours which lives in the maize plant; a long multi-coloured grasshopper.

nyuk.a *vt* hit hard, strike hard, beat severely: *Mwalimu aliwanyuka wanafunzi watundu*, the teacher beat severely the naughty students. (cf *piga, futa*) 2.defeat overwhelmingly; thrash: *Timu yao iliinyuka yetu*, their team thrashed ours. Prep. ***nyuk.i.a***, St. ***nyuk.ik.a*** Cs. ***nyuk.ish.a*** Ps. ***nyuk.w.a*** Rp. ***nyuk.an.a*** (cf *banjua, charaza*).

nyuki *n (n)* (*zool*) bee: *Nyuki manyoya*, bumble bee. *Nyuki bambi*, bumble bee. (*prov*) *Fuata nyuki ule asali*, follow the bees that you eat honey i.e follow someone who is educated, wealthy, etc. so that you benefit from him.

nyuklia¹ *adj* nuclear: *Bomu la nyuklia*, nuclear bomb. *Silaha za nyuklia*, nuclear weapons.

nyuklia² *n (n)* (*biol*) nucleus; part of the cells containing DNA and RNA and responsible for growth and reproduction. (Eng)

nyuku.a *vt* pinch with the fingers; nip, tweak, twitch: *Alininyukua pajani*, he pinched me on the thigh. Prep. ***nyuku.li.a*** St. ***nyuku.k.a*** Ps. of Prep, ***nyuku.liw.a*** Rp. ***nyuku.an.a*** (cf *finya, bigija*)

nyuma¹ *n (n)* 1. the rear part of the human body from the neck to the buttocks; back, spine. 2. the rear part of an animal, bird, etc. that covers the tail. 3. behind in development: *Watu wale wako nyuma kimaendeleo*, those people are behind in the sphere of development. 4. back behind.

nyuma² *adv* behind, at the back of: *Siku za nyuma*, in the previous days, in the past.

nyumba *n(n)* 1. house, residence, home. 2. (*fig*) wife.

nyumbani *n (n)* at home, home

nyumbi *n (n)* see *nyimbi*

nyumbu *n (n)* mule (cf *baghala*)

nyumbu.a *vt* stretch, draw out, extend: *Mtoto aliunyumbua ubani wake*, the child stretched his chewing gum. Prep. ***nyumbu.li.a*** St. ***nyumbu.k.a*** and ***nyumbu.lik.a*** be flexible, be elastic Cs. ***nyumbu.sh.a*** Ps. of Prep. ***nyumbu.liw.a*** Rp. ***nyumbu.an.a***

-nyumbufu *adj* elastic: *Raba ni nyumbufu*, rubber is elastic.

nyumbulik.a *vi* be stretchable, be stretched, be extended. Prep. ***nyumbulik.i.a*** St. ***nyumbulik.ik.a*** Cs. ***nyumbulik.ish.a***

nyumbuk.a *vi* be stretchable, be stretched, be extended, be flexible. Prep. ***nyumbuk.ia*** St. ***nyumbuk.ik.a*** Cs. ***nyumbuk.ish.a***

nyundo *n(n)* 1. hammer: *Nyundo kubwa*, sledge hammer. *Nyundo koleo*, claw hammer. *Nyundo ya mhunzi*, sledge hammer. *Nyundo ya mawe*, stone hammer. *Nyundo ya mwashi*, stone hammer. 2. (*idm*) *Kifupi nyundo*, a very short person.

nyungu¹ *n (n)* 1. earthenware vessel for cooking; clay pot. 2. a mixture of boiled local herbs.

nyungu² *n (n)* used in the expression: *Fukiza nyungu*, treat a patient by using fumigants boiled in a sauce pan or other vessel.

nyungu³ *n (n)* an expletive used in counting the days of the month of Ramadhan: *Nyungumosi*, first day. *Nyungu pili*, second day.

nyungunyungu (also *nyungwi*) *n (n)* 1. (*zool*) a worm that causes cracks or sores on the feet, in between the toes, etc. and that may cause intense itching; gnawing worm. 2. (*med*) ringworm of the feet; athlete's foot. *Tinea pedis*.

nyungwa (also *nyungwaa, nyungwanani*) *interj* an exclamation used to alert your colleagues when you are chatting with them; attention please! (cf *jamani!*)

nyungwaa *interj* see *nyungwa*

nyungwanani *interj* see *nyungwa*
nyungwi *n* (*n*) see *nyungunyungu*
nyuni *n* (*n*) (*zool*) bird (cf *ndege*)
nyuny.a *vi* drizzle, sprinkle: *Mvua inanyunya sasa hivi*, it is drizzling now. Prep. ***nyuny.i.a***. St. ***nyuny.ik.a***. Cs. ***nyuny.iz.a***
nyunyiz.a *vt* sprinkle water, etc.; scatter drops of water, etc. Prep. ***nyunyiz.i.a*** St. ***nyunyiz.ik.a*** Cs. ***nyunyiz.ish.a*** Ps. ***nyunyiz.w.a***
nyunyizi.a[1] *vi* see *nyunya*
nyunyizi.a[2] *vt* sprinkle, water etc.; spray on or apply dust, powder, etc.: *Alinyunyizia dawa ya wadudu kwenye mazao yake*, he sprayed insecticide on his crops. Prep. ***nyunyizi.li.a*** St. ***nyunyizi.k.a*** Cs. ***nyunyizi.sh.a*** Ps. ***nyunyizi.w.a*** Rp. ***nyunyizi.an.a*** (cf *mwagia*)
nyunyu *vi* (*ma-*) (used in pl form) drizzle; light rain: *Kuna manyunyu nje*, it is drizzling outside.
nyus.a *vt* tut; make a clicking or suckling sound to express annoyance, impatience, mild rebuke, etc.: *Si vizuri kunyusa watu*, it is not good to tut people. Prep. ***nyus.i.a*** St. ***nyus.ik.a*** Cs. ***nyus.ish.a*** Ps. ***nyus.w.a*** Rp. ***nyus.an.a*** (cf *fyonya*).
nyuti (also *nyutinyuti*) *adv* slowly, gradually; carefully: *Aliyapanga mambo yake nyutinyuti*, he planned his affairs carefully.
nyuuk.a *vi* see *nyauka*
nyuzijoto *n* (*n*) degrees of heat.
nyuzisauti *n* (*n*) vocal cords. (cf *kambasauti*)
nyw.a *vt, vi* 1. drink, imbibe: *Alikunywa maji*, he drank water. 2. (*fig*) consume, absorb: *Gari lake linakunywa petroli sana*, his car consumes a lot of petrol. Prep. ***nyw.e.a*** St. ***nyw.ek.a*** Cs. ***nyw.esh.a*** Ps. ***nyw.ew.a*** Rp. of Prep. ***nyw.e.an.a***
nywe.a[1] *vi* shrivel up, dry up, wilt; lose strength: *Mimea yake imeanza kunywea kwa jua kali*, his plants are beginning to wilt because of the scorching sun. *Alinywea baada ya kumwona simba*, he shrivelled up after seeing a lion. Prep. ***nywe.le.a*** St. ***nywe.lek.a*** Cs. ***nywe.sh.a***
nywe.a[2] *vi* lose strength, become weak: *Asha amenywea siku hizi*, Asha has become weak these days. Prep. ***nywe.le.a*** St. ***nywe.lek.a*** Cs. ***nywe.sh.a***
nywele *n* (*n*) see *unywele*
nywesh.a *vt* cause sby/sth to drink water, etc. *Aliinywesha mimea yake*, he watered his plants. Prep. ***nywesh.e.a*** St. ***nywesh.ek.a*** Ps. ***nywesh.w.a***
nzaiko *n* (*n*) medicine in the form of powder, used for making someone to lose memory.
nzao *n* (*n*) (*zool*) bull (cf *fahali, ng'ombedume*)
nzi *n* (*n*) (*zool*) fly
nzige *n* (*n*) (*zool*) locust
nzigunzigu *n* (*n*) (*zool*) butterfly (cf *kurumbiza, kipepeo*)
nzio *n* (*n*) 1. a big earthen pitcher with a narrow neck. 2. a big clay jar.
nzohe *n* (*n*) (*zool*) sitatunga; a large antelope with long pointed hooves and long horns. *Tragelaphus spekei*.

nzohe

nzumari[1] (also *zumari*) *n* (*n*) (*mus*) flageolet, clarinet; a kind of musical instrument with a long wooden or metal tube and a flaring bell.
nzumari[2] *n* (*n*) see *mchaichai*

O

O, o /o/ 1. the fifteenth letter of the Swahili alphabet. 2. a mid-back vowel.
o.a *vt,vi* (used only for men) marry a wife; take a wife: *Ameoa karibuni*, he has married recently. Prep. *o.le.a* St. *o.le.ka* Cs. *o.z.a* Ps. of Prep. *o.lew.a* Rp. *o.an.a* Rp. of Prep. *o.le.an.a*
oam.a *vi* get wet, get drenched, be soaked: *Nguo zake zimeoama baada ya kunyeshewa na mvua kubwa*, his clothes are wet after being soaked by the heavy rain. Prep. *oam.i.a* St. *oam.ik.a* Cs. *oam.ish.a*
oan.a¹ *vi* see *oa*
oan.a² *vi* (of ideas, etc.) be compatible, be agreeable: *Muwuzo yao katika suala la mirathi yanaoana*, their views on the question of inheritance are compatible. (cf *lingana*)
oanish.a *vt* associate, marry, link, relate: *Jaribu kuzioanisha fikira zao*, try to marry their views. Prep. **oanish.i.a** St. **oanish.ik.a** Ps. **oanish.w.a** Rp. **oanish.an.a** (cf *patanisha, linganisha*)
oda¹ *n* (*n*) order, a single portion of some food as served in a hotel, etc.; *Umeshafanya oda yako ya chakula?* Have you placed your order for food? (Eng)
od.a² *vt, vi* request for sth such as food to be supplied, etc. (Eng)
ofisa (also *afisa*) *n* (*ma-*) officer: *Ofisa kilimo*, agricultural officer. *Ofisa uhusiano*, public relations officer. *Ofisa wa magereza*, prison officer. *Ofisa wa ngazi za juu*, senior officer. (Eng)
ofisi (also *afisi*) *n* (*n*) office: *Ofisi ya waziri kiongozi*, Chief Minister's office.
ofwe *interj* an expletive of signalling exhaustion that requires complete rest.

og.a¹ (also *koga*) *vi* bathe; take a bath: *Amekwenda msalani kuoga*, he has gone to the bathroom to take a bath. Prep. *og.e.a* St. *og.ek.a* Cs. *og.esh.a* Ps. of Cs. *og.esh.w.a*
-oga² *adj* timid, timorous, cowardly; *Mtu mwoga hawezi kutembea peke yake usiku*, a cowardly person cannot walk alone at night.
ogek.a *vi* (of a place, etc.) be fit to bathe. Prep. *ogek.e.a* St. *ogek.ek.a*
ogele.a *vi, vt* swim. St. *ogele.k.a* Cs. *ogele.sh.a* (cf *elea, ovya*)
ogesh.a *vt* cause someone to take a bath esp a child Prep. *ogesh.e.a* St. *ogesh.ek.a* Ps. *ogesh.w.a* Rp. *ogesh.un.a*
ogofy.a *vt* terrify, horrify, frighten: *Aliwaogofya wadogo zake*, he terrified his juniors. St. *ogofy.ek.a* Cs. *ogofy.esh.a* Ps. *ogofy.w.a* Rp. *ogofy.an.a* (cf *tisha, hofisha*)
ogofyo *n* (*n*) fear, terror, fright, horror (cf *tisho, hofu*)
ogop.a *vt, vi* 1. dread, be afraid, be scared; (cf *hofu*) 2. obey, respect, venerate, revere, esteem: *Lazima umwogope bosi wako kazini*, you must respect your boss at the place of work. Prep. *ogop.e.a* St. *ogop.ek.a* Cs. *ogop.esh.a* Ps. *ogop.w.a* Rp. *ogop.an.a* (cf *tii, thamini*)
ohaa *interj* an expletive of calling sby's attention; I say; hey! hallo!
oili *n* (*n*) oil (Eng)
ok.a *vt* roast, bake, grill, toast. Prep. *ok.e.a* St. *ok.ek.a* Cs. *ok.esh.a* Ps. *ok.w.a.*
oko.a *vt, vi* save, rescue, salvage. Prep. *oko.le.a* St. *oko.k.a* Ps. of Prep. *oko.lew.a* Rp. *oko.an.a* (cf *vua, ponya, nusuru*)
okot.a¹ *vt, vi* 1. pick up, take up with fingers, hands, etc.; garner, collect.

2. find: *Aliokota pesa kichochoroni*, he found money in the lane Prep. *okot.e.a* St. *okot.ek.a* Cs. *okot.esh.a* Ps. *okot.w.a* Rp. *okot.an.a* (cf *ona*)
okot.a² *vt* buy sth at a cheaper price; Prep. *okot.e.a* St. *okot.ek.a* Cs. *okot.esh.a* Ps. *okot.w.a*
okotez.a *vt* 1. do a job like an amateur; do a job without possessing professional skills; fumble, grope. 2. collect things from different sources. Prep. *okotez.e.a* St. *okotez.ek.a* Cs. *okotez.esh.a* Ps. *okotez.w.a* (cf *babia*)
oksijini *n* (*n*) oxygen (Eng)
oktavo *n* (*n*) (*mus*) an octave used in music. (Eng)
Oktoba *n* (*n*) the month of October. (Eng)
ol.a *vt* 1. (*arch*) glance, peep, glimpse, look. (cf *tazama*) 2, see, view, watch (cf *ona*) Prep. *ol.e.a* St. *ol.ek.a* Cs. *ol.esh.a* Ps. *ol.w.a* Rp. *ol.an.a*
ole *interj* an expletive used to express regret, sorrow, grief, etc.; woe: *Ole wao!* woe on to them! *Ole wangu*, woe on to me!
ole.a¹ *vi* see *elea¹*. Cs. *ole.z.a*
ole.a² *vi* marry a wife on behalf of sby who is absent during the ceremony.
olelez.a *vt* see *oleza*
olez.a (also *oleleza*) *vt* imitate, copy; follow a pattern. (cf *iga, fuatisha*)
olimpiki *n* (*n*) olympics: *Michezo ya olimpiki*, olympic games. (Eng)
omb.a *vt, vi* pray, beg, request, ask for, apply for, seek: *Aliomba kazi katika kampuni yetu*, he asked for a job in our company. *Maskini alikuwa akiomba mitaani*, the beggar was begging in the estate. *Omba radhi*, ask for apology. *Omba dua*, pray. Prep. *omb.e.a* St. *omb.ek.a* Cs. *omb.esh.a* Ps. *omb.w.a* Rp. *omb.an.a*
ombaomba *n* (*n*) beggar, pauper: *Serikali inataka kuwaondoa ombaomba katika kila mkoa*, the government wants to eliminate beggars in every region.

ombe *n* (*n*) brink, edge, bank, periphery; *Ombe la meza*, the edge of the table. (cf *pambizo, mleoleo*)
ombe.a *vt* 1. ask for sth on behalf of sby: *Nilimwombea ruhusa*, I asked for permission on his behalf. 2. curse, damn; pray sth bad for sby. St. *ombe.k.a*
ombi *n* (*ma-*) invocation, supplication, praying: *Wanavijiji walifanya ombi lao la kutaka mvua*, the villagers offered their prayer for rain.
omboje.a *vi* become soft because of being overipe or overcooked: *Usijaribu kuupika sana muhogo mpaka ukaombojea*, don't overcook the cassava until it becomes soft. St. *omboje.k.a* Cs. *omboje.sh.a* Ps. *omboje.w.a*
ombolekez.a *vt* repeat the words during oath taking or when making offering to the spirits of the dead. Prep. *ombolekez.e.a* St. *ombolekez.ek.a* Cs. *ombolekez.esh.a* Ps. *ombolekez.w.a* Rp. *ombolekez.an.a*
ombolez.a *vt, vi* mourn, lament, grieve, sorrow: *Aliomboleza kifo cha rafiki yake*, he mourned the death of his friend. Prep. *ombolez.e.a* St. *ombolez.ek.a* Ps. *ombolez.w.a* Rp. *ombolez.an.a* (cf *huzunika*)
ombwe¹ *n* (*ma-*) openness, vacuum, emptiness: *Mtungi huu hauna kitu ila ombwe*, this water jar is full of vacuums.
ombwe² *n* (*ma-*) a wall surrounding a well to prevent people who go to fetch water from falling in.
omek.a *vt* 1. put sth firmly on sth else; fix: *Aliiomeka balbu kwenye soketi*, he fixed the bulb in the socket. (cf *pachika*) 2. pile up, heap, amass: *Aliyaomeka majani kwenye gunia*, he stuffed the fodder into the sack. Prep. *omek.e.a* St. *omek.ek.a* Cs. *omek.ez.a* Ps. *omek.w.a* Rp. *omek.an.a* (cf *shindilia, sheheneza*)

omo *n* (*n*) (*naut*) prow, bow; forepart of a ship, etc. (*prov*) *Mwenda tezi na omo hurejea ngamani*, he who goes to the quarterdeck and forecastle will return to the hold eventually i.e. you may go anywhere to look for a job, etc. but as long as you are alive, one day, you will return to your homeland. (cf *gubeti, njeli*)

omo.a *vt* 1. dig up, dig out, break up: *Omoa udongo*, dig up the ground. (cf *chimba, fukua*) 2. (*fig*) pester, disturb, worry: *Aliwaomoa wazazi wake burebure*, he pestered his parents for nothing. (cf *udhi, kera, ghasi*) 3. reveal, bring to light: *Omoa vita*, bring about a war. Prep. *omo.le.a* St. *omo.k.a* Cs. *omo.sh.a* Ps. of Prep. *omo.lew.a*

omok.a *vi* (of part of a building) collapse fall down. Prep. *omok.c.a* St. *omok.ek.a* Cs. *omok.esh.a* (cf *bomoka*)

on.a *vt, vi* 1. see, watch, witness. (cf *shufu, ola*) 2. feel, sense, have feeling: *Naona baridi*, I feel cold. *Naona njaa*, I feel hungry. *Naona homa*, I feel sick. (cf *hisi*) 3. think, consider, believe, assume: *Yeye anaona kwamba mpango wetu si mzuri*, she thinks that our plan is not good. 4. discover, find out: *Tumeona kwamba wao si wakweli*, we have found that they are not honest. Prep. *on.e.a* St. *on.ek.a* Cs. *on.esh.a* Ps. *on.w.a* Rp. *on.an.a*

onan.a *vt* meet, see, accept: *Kiongozi alionana na watu wengi*, the leader met many people. Prep. *onan.i.a* St. *onan.ik.a* Cs. *onan.ish.a*

ondo *n* (*ma-*) 1. (*anat*) knee: *Ondo la mwanariadha limeteguka*, the athlete's knee is dislocated. (cf *goti*) 2. leg: *Ondo lake linamwuma*, her leg is hurting.

ondo.a *vt* 1. remove, withdraw, take off: *Ondoa vitu vyako hapa*, remove your things here. 2. abolish, repeal, annul: *Serikali iliondoa sheria ya hali ya hatari*, the government abolished the emergency law. Prep. *ondo.le.a* St. *ondo.k.a* Cs. *ondo.sh.a* Ps. of Prep. *ondo.lew.a* Ps. of Cs. *ondo.sh.w.a* be abolished. Rp. *ondo.an.a* (cf *tangua, batili*)

ondokan.a *vt* get rid of sth; stop, escape from: *Ameondokana sasa na tabia ya kuwasema watu*, he has now stopped the habit of speaking ill of people.

ondoke.a *vi* 1. recuperate, recover, improve: *Mgonjwa wangu anaondokea siku hizi*, my patient is recovering these days. (cf *pongea, inukia*) 2. be well-behaved, be descent, become disciplined: *Mtoto wake ameanza kuondokea vizuri*, his child has started to become disciplined. (cf *inukia, elekea*) 3. (used in narratives) used to be, happened to be: *Paliondokea mfalme aliyekuwa katili katika nchi yake*, there used to be a ruthless king in his country.

ondokeo[1] *n* (*ma-*) 1. starting point of a journey. 2. departure, going away, away: *Ondokeo lake lilitushangaza*, his departure surprised us.

ondokeo[2] *n* (*ma-*) prosperity; success in life: *Ondokeo lake katika biashara halikutarajiwa*, his success in business was not expected.

ondole.a *vt* remove, deprive, take away: *Ondolea heshima*, disgrace someone. *Ondolea huzuni*, comfort sby.

ondoleo *n* (*ma-*) removal, remission; taking away: *Maondoleo ya dhambi*, the remission of sins; the forgiveness of sins.

one.a *vt, vi* 1. bully, browbeat, cow, ill-treat. 2. oppress, tyrannize, suppress: *Wakoloni waliwaonea wenyeji*, the colonialists oppressed the indigenous people. Prep. *one.le.a* St. *one.lek.a* Ps. *one.w.a* Rp. *one.an.a* (cf *kandamiza, nyanyasa*)

onek.a *vi* be seable, be feasible. Prep. *onek.e.a* St. *onek.ek.a*

onekan.a *vi* 1. be seen, be visible: *Rafiki yako haonekani siku hizi*, your friend is not seen these days. 2. seen, look, appear: *Inaonekana kama mvua itanyesha*, it looks as if it will rain. Prep. **onekan.i.a** St. **onekan.ik.a** (cf *oneka*)

onele.a *vt* think, consider, assume: *Sisi tunaonelea kuwa ni bora kuivunja safari yetu*, we feel that it is better to cancel our trip. (cf *pendelea, shauri, pendekeza*)

onesh.a *vt* see *onyesha*

onesho *n* (*ma-*) see *onyesho*

-onevu¹ *adj* visible, observable, visual, bright, powerful: *Ana macho maonevu*, he has bright eyes.

-onevu² *adj* bully, oppressive: *Mtawala mwonevu*, an oppressive ruler.

onge.a¹ *vt* converse, chat, talk: *Huongea kwa muda mrefu*, he talks for a long time. Prep. **onge.le.a** St. **onge.lek.a** Cs. **onge.lesh.a** Ps. **onge.w.a** (cf *sema, zungumza, longa*)

onge.a² *vi* increase, magnify; become large: *Idadi ya watu duniani inaongea*, the world population is increasing. Ps. **onge.w.a** (cf *zidi*)

ongele.a *vt* talk about/ over sth: *Msemaji aliongelea juu ya mambo mengi*, the speaker talked about many things. St. **ongele.k.a** Cs. **ongele.sh.a** Ps. **ongele.w.a** Rp. **ongele.an.a** (cf *zungumzia*)

ongez.a *vt* add, multiply, increase: *Aliongeza juhudi katika masomo yake*, he put in more effort in his studies. Prep. **ongez.e.a** St. **ongez.ek.a** Ps. **ongez.w.a** Rp. **ongez.an.a** (cf *zidisha*)

ongezek.a *vi* be increasing, be multiplying: *Je idadi ya watoto inaongezeka?* Is the population of children increasing? Prep. **ongezek.e.a** St. **ongezek.ek.a** Cs. **ongezek.esh.a** (cf *zidi*)

ongezeko *n* (*ma-*) addition, increment, supplement: *Ongezeko la mshahara*, the salary increment. *Ongezeko la ajira*, rise in employment. (cf *nyongeza, ziada*)

-ongezo *n* (*ma-*) addition, increment. (cf *ongezeko*)

ongo¹ *n* (*n*) rheumatism (cf *baridi yabisi*)

-ongo² *adj* lying; *Mtoto mwongo*, a lying child.

ongo.a¹ *vt* show, guide, direct; lead sby the right way: *Mungu atamwongoa kijana yule*, God will lead that young man along the right path. Prep. **ongo.le.a** St. **ongo.k.a** Ps. of Prep. **ongo.lew.a** Rp. **ongo.an.a** (cf *hidi*)

ongo.a² *vt* soothe a baby usu by songs; pacify, placate: *Mama alimwongoa binti yake ambaye alikuwa akilia*, the mother sang a lullaby for her daughter who had been crying. Prep. **ongo.le.a** St. **ongo.lek.a** Cs. **ongo.lesh.a** Ps. of Prep. **ongo.lew.a** (cf *bembeleza, tuliza*)

ongo.a³ *vt* shape well pottery vessels of kneaded clay. Prep. **ongo.le.a** St. **ongo.lek.a** Cs. **ongo.lesh.a** and **ongo.lew.a**

-ongofu *adj* reformed, improved, converted: *Kijana mwongofu*, a reformed young man.

ongok.a *vi* 1. be well-behaved, be reformed: *Kijana wako ameongoka siku hizi*, your young man is behaving well these days. 2. be better than expected. Prep. **ongok.e.a** St. **ongok.ek.a** Cs. **ongok.esh.a**

ongong.a *vi* nauseate, disgorge: *Anahisi kuongonga baada ya kula chakula kibaya*, he feels nauseated after eating bad food. Prep. **ongong.e.a** St. **ongong.ek.a** Ps. **ongong.w.a**

ongop.a *vi* lie; spread lies: *Baba alimpiga bintiye kwa kuongopa*, the father beat his daughter for lying. Prep. **ongop.e.a** St. **ongop.ek.a** Cs. **ongop.esh.a** Ps. **ongop.w.a** Rp. **ongop.an.a** (cf *vunga*)

ongoz.a *vt* 1. lead, guide, direct. 2. lead a project, etc.: 3. be ahead of others as in elections, etc.; lead: *Chama* *chao mpaka sasa kinaongoza katika matokeo ya awali*, their party so far is leading in the preliminary results. Prep. *ongoz.e.a* St. *ongoz.ek.a* Ps. *ongoz.w.a* Rp. *ongoz.an.a*

ongozan.a *vi* 1. accompany each other/ one another; go together: *Watu wale watatu wameongozana kwenda kwa daktari*, those three people have gone together to the doctor. 2. advise each other/one another. (cf *elekezana*)

onj.a *vt, vi* 1. taste, savour; take a taste of sth. 2. attempt, try, taste, endeavour: *Nimeonja misukosuko mingi ya maisha*, I have tasted many trials in life. Prep. *onj.e.a* St. *onj.ek.a* Cs. *onj.esh.a* Ps. *onj.w.a* Rp. of Prep. *onj.e.an.a*

onjesh.a *vt* make sby taste sth: *Alinionjesha chumvi*, he made me taste the salt. Prep. *onjesh.e.a* St. *onjesh.ek.a* Ps. *onjesh.w.a* Rp. *onjesh.an.a*

ony.a *vt* 1. warn, admonish, reprove: *Nilimwonya asiondoke lakini akaondoka*, I warned him not to leave but he left. (cf *hadharisha, asa*) 2. advise, counsel, guide, teach: *Mama alimwonya bintiye jinsi ya kuishi vizuri*, the mother guided her daughter in the best way to live. Prep. *ony.e.a* St. *ony. ek.a* Cs. *ony.esh.a* Ps. *ony.w.a* Rp. *ony.an.a* (cf *elekeza, ongoza*)

onyesh.a *vt* 1. show, exhibit, evince, display, demonstrate: *Alinionyesha jinsi ya kuutumia mtambo*, he showed me how to operate the machine. 2. lead, guide, show the way; *Walinionyesha njia nilipokuwa nimepotea*, they showed me the way when I got lost. Prep. *onyesh.e.a* St. *onyesh.ek.a* Ps. *onyesh.w.a* Rp. *onyesh.an.a* (cf *funda, elimisha, fundisha*)

onyeshe.a *vt* (*idm*) *Onyeshea kidole* (*kwa mtu*) point an accusing finger (to sby): *Upinzani ulisinyoshea kidole serikali kwa ufisadi uliokithiri nchini*, accusing finger to the government for the rampant corruption in the country.

onyesho (also **onesho**) *n* (*ma-*) 1. demonstration, exposition, exhibition: *Mfanyabiashara alifanya maonyesho ya bidhaa zake mpya*, the businessman organized an exhibition of his new products. 2. show, scene, performance, display: *Lilikuwa onyesho la wanasanii mashuhuri*, that was a display of prominent artists.

onyo *n* (*ma-*) warning, admonition, remonstration.

onz.a *vt* disturb, hurt, bother: *Usijaribu kunionza kila mara*, don't keep pestering me all the time. Prep. *onz.e.a* St. *onz.ek.a* Ps. *onz.w.a* Rp. *onz.an.a* (cf *sumbua, umiza*)

operesheni *n* (*n*) 1. (*med*) operation: *Operesheni ya moyo*, heart operation, heart surgery. 2. operation; an exercise done for a specified time to get aid of a certain problem: *Operesheni ya kuwaondoa ombaomba mjini*, an exercise to remove beggars in town. (Eng)

opereta *n* (*n*) telephone operator. (Eng)

opo.a *vt* 1. take out, draw out, pull out, remove: *Mpishi aliopoa chinyango ya nyama kwenye mchuzi*, the cook took a piece of meat from the curry. (cf *toa*) 2. cure, treat, rescue, *Daktari alimwopoa mgonjwa wake*, the doctor cured his patient. *Mpigambizi alimwopoa mtoto mdogo aliyetaka kuzama baharini*, the diver saved a drowning child from the sea. Prep. *opo.le.a* St. *opo.lek.a* Cs. *opo.lesh.a* Ps. of Prep. *opo.lew.a* Rp. *opo.an.a* (cf *topoa, gangua, okoa*).

opok.a *vi* (of an illness) get better, recover convalesce Prep. *opok.e.a* St. *opok. ek.a* Cs. *opok.esh.a*

orodha *n* (*n*) list, inventory, catalogue.

orodhesh.a *vt* list, catalog, record. Prep. *orodhesh.e.a* St. *orodhesh.ek.a* Ps. *orodhesh.w.a* Rp. *orodhesh.an.a*

-ororo *adj* soft, delicate tender: *Muziki*

mwororo, soft music. (cf *laini*)
osh.a *vt* wash, clean: *Osha nguo zako,* wash your clothes. (*prov*) *Mwosha huoshwa*, he who washes someone is also washed i.e. he who washes and cleans a dead body will also be washed one day when he dies. Prep. *osh.e.a,* St. *osh.ek.a* Ps. *osh.w.a* Rp. *osh.an.a* (cf *safisha, nadhifisha*)

ot.a¹ *vt* germinate, sprout. Prep. *ot.e.a* St. *ot.ek.a* Cs. *ot.esh.a* Ps. *ot.w.a*, be grown. Ps. of Cs. *ot.esh.w.a,* be grown (cf *mea, chipuka, kua*)

ot.a² *vi* dream. Prep. *ot.e.a* St. *ot.ek.a* Cs. *ot.esh.a* Ps. *ot.w.a* Ps. of Cs. *ot.esh.w.a* Rp. *ot.an.a*

ot.a³ *vt* bask in the sun; sunbathe. Prep. *ot.e.a* St. *ot.ek.a* Cs. *ot.esh.a* Ps. *ot.w.a*

ot.a⁴ *vt* make marks on the body; make scars on the body: *Bakora nyingi zimemwota mwilini*, too many strokes have left scars on his body. Prep. *ot.e.a* St. *ot.ek.a* Cs. *ot.esh.a* Ps. *ot.w.a*

ot.a⁵ *vt* bend sth esp when it is dry e.g. stick, wood, etc.; flex: *Mwalimu aliota hinzirani yake*, the teacher flexed his cane. Prep. *ot.e.a* St. *ot.ek.a* Cs. *ot.esh.a* Ps. *ot.w.a*

otam.a *vi* squat. Prep. *otam.i.a* St. *otam.ik.a* Cs. *otam.ish.a* (cf *chutama, chuchumaa, totama*)

otami.a (*vi*) see *atamia*

-o-ote *adj, pron* any: *Unapenda kula chakula chochote?* Do you like to eat any food?

-ote *adj, pron* all, the whole, entire, complete: *Vitabu vyote*, all the books. *Maembe yote*, all the mangoes.

ote.a¹ *vt, vi* 1. waylay, lurk, lie in wait; lie in. (cf *vizia*) 2. wait for sth or someone 3. (in football, etc.) be offside: *Mchezaji aliotea*, the player was offside. St. *ote.k.a* Ps. *ote.w.a* Rp. *ote.an.a*

otea² *n* (*ma-*) lurking place, ambush area

othografia *n* (*n*) orthography (cf *tahajia*) (Eng)

ovaroli *n* (*-ma-*) overalls, apron. (cf *bwelasuti, msurupwenye*) (Eng)

ovataimu *n*(*n*) overtime (Eng)

ovodh.a *vi* swim so as to protect a fish trap: *Mvuvi huovodha ili aweze kunasua ngwe ya juya*, the fisherman swims over the fish trap so as to protect it. Prep. *ovodh.e.a* St. *ovodh.ek.a* Cs. *ovodh.esh.a* Ps. *ovodh.w.a*

-ovu *adj* wicked, odious, obnoxious: *Mtu mwovu*, a wicked person. (cf *thakili, dhaifu*)

ovyo¹ *adj* disorderly, recklessly, haphazardly, carelessly: *Aliifanya kazi yangu ovyo*, he did my work carelessly. (*prov*) *Mpanda ovyo hula ovyo*, i.e. as you sow, so shall you reap. (cf *shaghalabaghala, segemnege, shelabela*)

ovyo² *adj* valueless, worthless, useless. (cf *dufu, wahshi*)

oya¹ (also *woya, uoya*) *n* (*ma-*) a handful, a fistful.

oy.a² *vt* relax, repose, take a rest. (cf *pumzika, farijika*)

oyee *interj* hurray! bravo!; a shout of approval, admiration, etc. (cf *heko*)

oz.a¹ *vt, vi* marry sby off; cause sby to marry; perform the ceremony of marriage. Prep. *oz.e.a* St. *oz.ek.a* Cs. *oz.esh.a,* cause to marry e.g. *Sheikh alimwozesha binti wa jirani yangu,* the Sheik conducted the marriage of my neighbour's daughter. Ps. *oz.w.a* Rp. *oz.an.a*

oz.a² *vi* rot, decay; go bad: *Embe imeoza,* the mangoe is rotten. Prep. *oz.e.a* St. *oz.ek.a* Cs. *oz.esh.a* (cf *taghayari, vunda, haribika*)

ozesh.a *vt* see *oza¹* Prep. *ozesh.e.a* St. *ozesh.ek.a* Ps. *ozesh.w.a* Rp. *ozesh.an.a*

ozi *n* (*ma-*) (*arch*) eye (cf *jicho*)

P

P,p /p/ 1. the sixteenth letter of the Swahili alphabet. 2. it is normally a voiceless bilabial stop.
p.a¹ *vt* give, present: *Amenipa zawadi*, he has given me a present. Prep. ***p.e.a*** Ps. of Prep. ***p.ew.a*** Rp. ***ji.p.a*** Rp. of Prep. ***p.e.an.a*** (cf *toa*, *kabidhi*)
pa² *prep* (used for pa class nouns) of: *Mahala pa kulala*, a place for sleeping in.
pa.a¹ (also *para*) *vt* scrape off, scrape up; remove the scales from: *Paa samaki*, scrape the scales from a fish. Prep. ***pa.li.a*** St. of Prep. ***pa.lik.a*** Cs. of Prep. ***pa.lish.a*** Ps. of Prep. ***pa.liw.a***, be scraped. (cf *paruza*)
pa.a² *vi* ascend, rise, mount; go high: *Kishada kilipaa*, the kite flew high. (*syn*) *Sauti imenipaa*, I have lost my voice. *Usingizi ulimpaa*, sleep left him i.e. he couldn't sleep. Prep. ***pa.li.a*** St. of Prep. ***pa.lik.a*** Cs. ***pa.z.a*** and ***paa.z.a***
pa.a³ *vt* 1. used in the expression: *Paa moto*, transfer embers. 2. (*idm*) *Palia makaa*, endanger oneself; entangle oneself. (*syn*) *Umekuwa pweza wajipalia makaa*, you have changed into a cuttlefish that you cover yourself with coals i.e. you are looking for trouble yourself without being aware of the hazards because of your ignorance. Prep. ***pa.li.a*** St. of Prep. ***pa.li.ka*** Cs. of Prep. ***pa.lish.a*** Ps. of Prep. ***pa.liw.a***
pʰaa⁴ *n* (*n*) (*zool*) gazelle (cf *swala*)
paa⁵ (also *kipaa*) *n* (*ma-*) roof
paaz.a¹ *vt* see *paa²*
paaz.a² (also *paza*, *paraza*) *vt* grind grain, etc.; mill: *Alipaaza ngano katika kinu*, he ground the wheat with a pestle in the mortar. Prep. ***paaz.i.a*** St. ***paaz.ik.a*** Cs. ***paaz.ish.a*** Ps. ***paaz.w.a*** (cf *saga*)

pacha¹ *n* (*ma-*) twin: *Anatarajia kuzaa mapacha*, she is expecting twins. (*prov*) *Ng'ombe wa masikini hazai pacha*, a poor man's resources are limited and so, they cannot advance him. *Pachafanani*, identical twins.
pacha² *adj* twin, clustered, sticking together: *Ndizi pacha*, banana clusters.
pachan.a *vt* sit together in a compressed form.
pachanga *n* (*n*) a kind of local dance.
pachapacha *adj* in compressed form.
pachik.a *vt* 1. insert, stick; place sth in between: *Alipachika kisu kiunoni mwake*, he stuck a knife into the girdle around his waist. 2. bestow or give sth to someone who does not deserve it:*Amejipachika ukubwa*, he has given himself a leadership position which he does not deserve. 3. (in sports) used in the expression: *Pachika bao*, score a goal e.g. *Mchezaji alipachika bao kwa ufundi*, the player scored the goal skilfully. Prep. ***pachik.i.a*** St. ***pachik.ik.a*** Cs. ***pachik.ish.a*** Ps. ***pachik.w.a*** Rp. ***pachik.an.a***
pachikwa *n* (*n*) a place where sth can be lixed in.
pachipachi (also *patipati*) *n* (*n*) in between two things; in the space between: *Mwizi alijificha kwenye pachipachi ya magari mawili*, the thief hid himself in the space between two cars.
pachu *n* (*n*) see *pafu²*
pachu.a *vt* remove sth from the top and put it down. Prep. ***pachu.li.a*** St. ***pachu.lik.a*** Cs. ***pachu.lish.a*** Ps. ***pachu.liw.a*** (cf *tungua*)
padri *n* (*ma-*) priest, clergyman. (cf *kasisi*) (Port)
pafu¹ *n* (*ma-*) (*anat*) lung (cf *buhumu*, *yavuyavu*)
pafu² *adj* emaciated, gaunt, haggard. (cf *pachu*)

P

paga.a[1] *vt, vi* be possessed by an evil spirit. Prep. ***paga.li.a*** Cs. ***paga.z.a***, Ps. ***paga.w.a***.

paga.a[2] *vt* carry a load on the head or shoulders: *Aliupagaa mzigo wangu begani mwake*, he carried my luggage on his shoulder. Cs. ***paga.z.a***. Ps. ***paga.w.a***.

paga.a[3] *vi* (of an animal) raise ears. Prep. ***paga.li.a*** Cs. ***paga.z.a*** Ps. ***paga.w.a***

pagao *n* (*ma-*) a charm against an evil spirit or other calamity; talisman, amulet, periapt. (cf *talasimu, kago*)

pagaro[1] *n* (*n*) sash, girdle, bellyband. (cf *kibwebwe*)

pagaro[2] *n* (*n*) a stick of wood used for stoking a fire; firestick.

pagaw.a[1] *vt* see *pagaa*[1] and *pagaa*[2]

pagaw.a[2] *vi* go berserk: *Mwendawazimu amepagawa*, the madman has gone berserk. (cf *chagawa*)

pagio *n* (*ma-*) holes cut into a tree to assist someone to climb it; tree cuts for climbing. (cf *pandio*)

pagu.a[1] *vt* bypass a place in order to escape someone or sth; change route in order to avoid sth. Prep. ***pagu.li.a*** St. ***pagu.k.a*** Cs. ***pagu.sh.a*** Ps. of Prep. ***pagu.liw.a***

pagu.a[2] *vt* 1. see *pogoa*. 2. cut the legs of an animal after being slaughtered. Prep. ***pagu.li.a*** St. ***pagu.sh.a*** Cs. ***pagu.lish.a*** Ps. of Prep. ***pagu.liw.a*** Rp. ***pagu.an.a***

paguo *n* (*n*) a place that has been bypassed in order to evade sth that is on the way; diversion, detour.

pagwa *n* (*n*) 1. tip of a pole used as a rafter in the construction of a local house. 2. catapult.

pahala *n* (*pa*) see *mahali*
pahali *n* (*pa*) see *mahali*

paipu[1] *n* (*n*) siren, horn. (cf *king'ora, selo*) (Eng)

paipu[2] *n* (*n*) pipe, tube: *Paipu ya maji*, water pipe. (cf *bomba*) (Eng)

paja *n* (*ma-*) (*anat*) thigh. (*prov*) *Mwenye tende hana paja*, he who fasts as during the case of *Ramadan* will not necessarily be told that he is hungry.

pajama *n* (*ma-*) pyjama (Hind)

paje *n* (*ma-*) the bottom stalk of a plant such as that of maize, sorghum, etc., which does not have much taste; sugarless straw of maize, millet, etc. (cf *ngela*)

paji *n* (*ma-*) (*anat*) forehead: *Paji la uso*, forehead. Also *kikono cha uso*. (cf *komo*)

paka[1] *n* (*n*) (*zool*) cat: *Paka shume*, a large tomcat; stray cat. (cf *nyau*)

pak.a[2] (also *pakaa*) *vt* 1. apply, lay on, spread on, smear on: *Paka rangi*, paint. *Paka dawa*, apply ointment. 2. (*idms*) *Paka matope*, defame sby; discredit sby. *Paka mafuta kwa mgongo wa chupa*, deceive, cheat. *Paka mavi*, discredit sby. Prep. ***pak.i.a*** St. ***pak.ik.a*** Cs. ***pak.ish.a*** Ps. ***pak.w.a*** Rp. ***pak.an.a***.

paka.a *vt* see *paka*[2]

pakacha[1] *n* (*ma-*) a large basket made up of plaited coconut fronds for carrying fruits, fish, coal, etc.; palm frond basket. (*prov*) *Kuvuja kwa pakacha, nafuu kwa mchukuzi*, a leakage in a palm frond basket is a relief to a porter i.e. to reject assistance is a relief to the one who is giving you. (*syn*) *Chujua maji kwa pakacha*, do sth of no value. (cf *kachira, susu*)

pakacha[2] *n* (*ma-*) duper, swindler, conman. (cf *mzandiki, mdanganyifu*)

pakan.a *vt* 1. border on, be adjacent to, adjoin; be near to, be next to: *Nchi yetu inapakana na Kenya*, our country borders Kenya. 2. meet each other at the border. Prep. ***pakan.i.a*** St. ***pakan.ik.a*** Cs. ***pakan.ish.a*** Ps. ***pakan.w.a***.

pakanga[1] *n* (*n*) (*bot*) rue, wormwood; a type of evergreen shrub with bitter-tasting leaves and yellow flowers, used in medicine. 2. massaging lotion.

pakanga[2] *n* (*n*) 1. pain, pang, agony. (cf *uchungu*) 2. labour pains.

pakanya *n* (*ma-*) money or present given as compensation or for ending a dispute.

pakas.a (also *paraza*) *vt* twist thread, frond, string, etc; twine, weave, plait: *Msichana mrembo alizipakasa nywele zake*, the glamorous girl plaited her hair. Prep. ***pakas.i.a*** St. ***pakas.ik.a*** Cs. ***pakas.ish.a*** Ps. ***pakas.w.a*** Rp. ***pakas.an.a*** (cf *suka, pota, sokota*)

pakat.a *vt* hold sth on the thigh, lap or knee; cradle: *Alimpakata mtoto wake mchanga mapajani mwake*, he held his baby on his lap. Prep. ***pakat.i.a*** St. ***pakat.ik.a*** Cs. ***pakat.ish.a*** Ps. ***pakat.w.a*** Rp. ***pakat.an.a***

pakawa *interj* an expletive used by an audience or a listener in response to a similar call made by a narrator when he begins a story. The storyteller begins with *paukwa* and the reply from the audience or a listener is *pakawa*.

pakaz.a *vt* 1. apply medicine, oil, etc. on someone; smear, rub on: *Alimpakaza dawa mgonjwa wake mwili mzima*, he smeared his patient's body with medicine. 2. accuse someone of a bad thing: *Pakaza uovu*, accuse someone of an evil deed. Prep. ***pakaz.i.a*** St. ***pakaz.ik.a*** Cs. ***pakaz.ish.a*** Ps. ***pakaz.w.a*** Rp. ***pakaz.an.a***

pake *adj, pron* (of a place) his, her, hers: *Mahala pake*, his place. *Pake ndipo pangu*, his place is mine.

paketi *n* (*n*) see *pakiti*

pak.i *vt* park. Prep. ***pak.i.a*** St. ***pak.ik.a*** Cs. ***pak.ish.a*** Ps. of Prep. ***pak.iw.a*** (cf *egesha*) (Eng)

paki.a *vt* load up, load into, squirrel away, pile up: *Walipakia mizigo mingi kwenye jahazi*, they loaded the dhow with a lot of goods. Prep. ***paki.li.a*** St. ***paki.lik.a*** Cs. ***paki.z.a*** Ps. ***paki.w.a*** Rp. ***paki.an.a***

pakiti (also *paketi*) *n* (*n*) packet: *Pakiti ya sigareti*, a packet of cigarettes. (Eng)

paku *n* (*ma-*) spot, speak, dot, mark. (cf *baka, doa, bato*)

paku.a¹ *vt* 1. unload, off-load; remove cargo from a ship; vehicle, etc. (cf *cheleza, teremsha*) 2. dish out, serve out: *Mpishi alikipakua chakula*, the cook dished out the food. Prep. ***paku.li.a*** St. ***paku.lik.a*** Cs. ***paku.lish.a*** Ps. of Prep. ***paku.liw.a***

paku.a² *vt* (*colloq*) fuck, screw. Prep. ***paku.li.a*** St. ***paku.lik.a*** Cs. ***paku.lish.a*** Ps. of Prep. ***paku.liw.a*** Rp. ***paku.an.a***

palahala *n* (*n*) see *mbarapi*

pale *adv, pron* form of demonstrative root *-le* meaning "there," "over there," "just there," "in that spot," "just then."

pale bahari (also *ligia*) *n* (*n*) (*zool*) isopod, sea louse; it is a mainly aquatic crustacean belonging to the order of *Isopoda*. It is characterized by having a flattened body bearing seven pairs of legs and including the sow bugs and gribbles.

pale bahari

pali.a¹ *vt* choke on food; gag on sth: *Chakula kilimpalia*, the food choked him. Cs. ***pali.z.a*** Ps. ***pali.w.a***

pali.a² (also *palilia*) *vt,vi* remove weeds by using a hoe; weed out: *Alilipalilia shamba lake*, he weeded his farm. Prep. ***pali.li.a*** St. ***pali.lik.a*** Cs. ***pali.lish.a*** Ps. ***pali.w.a*** Rp. ***pali.an.a***

palili.a¹ *vt,vi* see *palia*²

palili.a² *vt* (*fig*) create a certain atmosphere for sth to take place. Prep. ***pali.li.a*** St. ***pali.lik.a*** Cs. ***pali.lish.a*** Ps. ***pali.liw.a***

palizi *n* (*n*) 1. weeding. 2. time of weeding.

pama *n* (*n*) sombrero; a kind of broad-brimmed, tall-crowned felt or straw hat usu worn by Mexicans, etc. (cf *chepeu, shepeu*)

pamamba *n* (*n*) see *paramamba*

pamba¹ *n* (*n*) (*bot*) cotton: *Mashudu ya*

pamba, cotton cake. *Mafuta ya pamba*, oil made from the seeds of a cotton plant; cotton seed oil.

pamba² *n (n)* food supplies during travels; packed meal during travels.

pamb.a³ *vt* 1. decorate, adorn, embellish, be decorated: *Aliipamba nyumba yake vizuri*, he decorated his house well. 2. dress sby in finery: *Walimpamba biharusi*, they dressed the bride in finery. (cf *remba, podoa*) 3. (used with respect to a dead body), lay out a corpse; clean and dress a corpse: *Pamba maiti*, lay out a corpse for burial. 4. (*idm*) *Pamba moto*, be red-hot, be a hit; intensify: *Mgogoro umepamba moto*, the crisis has intensified. (cf *rindima*) Prep. ***pamb.i.a*** St. ***pamb.ik.a*** Cs. ***pamb.ish.a*** Ps. ***pamb.w.a*** Rp. ***pamb.an.a*** (cf *fukuta*)

pamb.a⁴ *vt* (usu of insects) be widespread, cover, spread; be everywhere: *Wadudu wameipamba miti yote*, the insects have covered all the trees. Prep. ***pamb.i.a*** St. ***pamb.ik.a*** Cs. ***pamb.ish.a*** Ps. ***pamb.w.a*** Rp. ***pamb.an.a***

pambaja *n (n)* used in the expression: *Piga pambaja*, embrace sby; hug. (cf *kumbatia*)

pambajio *n* (n) a waiting room; reception: *Wageni walimsubiri waziri katika pambajio*, the visitors waited for the minister at the reception. (cf *mapokezi*)

pamba moto *vt* see *pamba³*

pamban.a *vt, vi* 1. contest, face, confront: *Wasemi walipambana vikali kwenye mijadala*, the speakers confronted each other bitterly in the debate. 2. confront, clash, collide; meet in conflict, meet face to face: *Wanajeshi walipambana kijasiri dhidi ya walowezi*, the soldiers confronted the settlers bravely. Prep. ***pamban.i.a*** St. ***pamban.ik.a*** Cs. ***pamban.ish.a*** Ps. ***pamban.w.a*** (cf *kumbana*)

pambanish.a *vt* 1. make two sides or more to contest each other/ one another. 2. cause a strife between two sides or more. Prep. ***pambanish.i.a*** St. ***pambanish.ik.a*** Ps. ***pambanish.w.a*** Rp. ***pambanish.an.a***

pambaniz.a (also *pambanya*) *vt* prevaricate, shrug off; brush aside; evade questions: *Waziri alipoulizwa maswala nyeti, akapambaniza*, when the minister was asked sensitive questions, he prevaricated. Prep. ***pambaniz.i.a*** St. ***pambaniz.ik.a*** Cs. ***pambaniz.ish.a*** Ps. ***pambaniz.w.a***. Rp. ***pambaniz.an.a***

pambano *n* (*ma-*) contest, match, competition: *Pambano la mchujo*, knock-out match. *Pambano la kukata na shoka*, tough contest. *Pambano la vuta nikuvute*, tough match. *Pambano la kujipima nguvu*, trial match.

pambanu.a (also *pambazua*) *vt* distinguish, differentiate, discriminate: Prep ***pambanu.li.a*** St. ***pambanu.k.a*** Cs. ***pambanu.lish.a*** Ps. of Prep. ***pambanu.liw.a*** (cf *fafanua, tofautisha*)

pambany.a *vt* see *pambaniz.a* Prep. ***pambany.i.a*** St. ***pambany.ik.a*** Cs. ***pambany.isha*** Ps. ***pambany.w.a*** Rp. ***pambany.an.a***

pambazuk.a (also *pambauka*) *vi* 1. be daylight; dawn: *Kumepambazuka*, it is daylight. 2. be clear, become visible. Prep. ***pambazuk.i.a*** St. ***pambazuk.ik.a*** Cs. ***pambazuk.ish.a***

pambazuko *n* (*ma-*) see *mapambazuko*

pambik.a¹ *vt* adorn an arrow at the end with the feathers of a bird, etc.: *Waliipambika mishale yao kwa kupendeza*, they adorned their arrows with bird feathers colourfully. Prep. ***pambik.i.a*** Ps. ***pambik.w.a***

pambik.a² *vt* soak the seeds of grain to make beer: *Alipambika kimea ili kutengeneza pombe*, he soaked the seeds of grain to make beer. Prep. ***pambik.i.a*** Ps. ***pambik.w.a***

pambik.a³ vi 1. be capable of being decorated. 2. be suitable for decoration. Prep. *pambik.i.a* St. *pambik.ik.a* Cs. *pambik.ish.a*

pambizo n (ma-) 1. edge, rim, periphery: *Alikiweka kikombe karibu na pambizo la meza*, he put the cup near the edge of the table. (cf *ukingo, terebesha*) 2. outskirts, outer areas: *Anaishi pambizoni mwa mji*, he lives in the outskirts of the city.

pambo n (ma-) decoration, finery, embellishment. *Pambo lile halinipendezi*, that decoration does not impress me. (cf *urembo, podozi*)

pambu.a¹ vt 1. remove ornaments, make-up, etc.; remove decorations; disfigure, deface: *Biharusi alijipambua sherehe zilipomalizika*, the bride removed her make-up when the celebrations were over. 2. (naut) open the sail from the main yard of the vessel. Prep. *pambu.li.a* St. *pambu.k.a* Cs. *pambu.sh.a* Ps. of Prep *pambu.liw.a* Rp. *pambu.an.a*

pambu.a² vt remove the top crust of cooked rice. Prep. *pambu.li.a* St. *pambu.k.a* Cs. *pambu.sh.a* Ps. of Prep *pambu.liw.a* Rp. *pambu.an.a*

pami.a vt collide, knock: *Kampamia mtu mzee kizani*, he has collided with an old man in the dark. St. *pami.k.a* Cs. *pami.sh.a* Ps. *pami.w.a* Rp. *pami.an.a*

pamiti n (n) permit: *Alipewa pamiti ya kuvuka mpaka*, he was given a permit to cross the border. (cf *kibali*) (Eng)

pamoja (also *pamwe*) adv 1. together with, with, in company of: *Walikuja pamoja*, they came together. 2. used in the expression: *Pamoja na*, despite e.g. *Pamoja na hoja zake, mimi bado simuungi mkono*, despite his arguments, I still don't support him.

pampu (also *pampo*) n (n) pump (Eng)

pamvu n (n) 1. a meeting to be held for giving and receiving dowry. 2. dowry to be given during that meeting.

pamwe adv see *pamoja*

-pana adj wide, broad, extensive: *Njia pana*, a wide road.

pancha (also *panchari*) n (n) puncture (Eng)

panchari n (n) see *pancha*

panchi¹ n (n) punch; a device or machine for cutting holes on leather, paper, etc. (Eng)

panchi² n (n) punch. (idm) *Piga panchi*, strike sth with a fist usu a ball. (Eng)

panda¹ n (n) 1. bifurcation, fork; the act of dividing into two parts or branches: *Njia panda*, crossroads, crossways. 2. catapult, sling-shot (cf *manati, fyata*)

panda² adj bifurcated, forked.

panda³ (also *parapanda*) n (n) bugle: *Piga panda*, blow a bugle (cf *haragumu, rewa, pembe*)

panda⁴ (also *panja*) n (ma-) (anat) temple; the two flat areas at the sides of the forehead.

panda.a⁵ vt 1. climb, mount, ascend, go up. (cf *kwea, paraga*) 2. board, go on board, enter: *Amepanda meli*, he has boarded the ship. *Panda farasi*, mount a horse; ride a horse. 3. (of mountain, etc.) be steep: *Mlima ule umepanda*, that mountain is steep. 4. (of price) go up; increase in number, amount, etc.: *Bei ya kahawa imepanda*, the price of coffee has gone up. (cf *ongezeka*) 5. (idms) *Panda cheo*, rise up in position. *Panda kichwa*, become big-headed. 6. (of a vessel) run ashore; run aground e.g. *Jahazi limepanda mwamba kwenye lundo la matope*, the dhow has run aground on a mud bank. Prep. *pand.i.a* St. *pand.ik.a* Cs. *pand.ish.a* Ps. *pand.w.a* Rp. *pand.an.a*

pand.a⁶ vt 1. grow, plant, sow, seed: *Amepanda chai*, he has grown tea. (cf *otesha, sia, melesha*) 2. bet, bid: *Unaweza kupanda kwa bei yoyote?* Can you bet any amount? Prep. *pand.i.a* St. *pand.ik.a* Cs. *pand.*

611

ish.a Ps. **pand.w.a** Rp. **pand.a.n.a**
pandarusi *n* (n) (*zool*) a kind of an insect that likes to fly and rest on the tops of the trees.

pande[1] *n* (n) (*idm*) *Piga pande*, boycott; stand aside: *Wajumbe waliupiga pande mkutano*, the delegates boycotted the meeting. (cf *chama, susia*)

pande[2] *n* (*ma-*) a large piece; block, bar: *Pande la chuma*, a bar of iron. *Pande la mti.* a block of wood. *Pande la mtu*, a giant of a man.

pandi.a *vt* sponge off, scrounge, cadge: *Mtu yule daima hupandia chakula kwa rafiki zake*, that person always sponges food off his friends. Prep. **pandi.li.a** St. **pandi.k.a** Cs. **pandi.sh.a** Ps. **pandi.w.a** Rp. **pandi.an.a** (cf *doea, rombeza*)

pandikiz.a *vt* transplant, replant, graft: *Aliipandikiza miche yake*, he transplanted his seedlings. 2. (*fig*) foment, incite; sow the seeds of: *Kiongozi alijaribu kupandikiza chuki kati ya makabila mbalimbali*, the leader tried to sow the seeds of hatred among different tribes. Prep. **pandikiz.i.a** St. **pandikiz.ik.a** Cs. **pandikiz.ish.a** Ps. **pandikiz.w.a** (cf *atika*)

pandikizi *n* (*ma-*) giant size of a person or sth else: *Pandikizi la mtu*, a giant of a man. *Pandikizi la gari*, a huge car. *Pandikizi la samaki*, a big fish.

pandio *n* (*ma-*) steps of a staircase, etc.

pandish.a[1] *vt* see *panda*[5] and *panda*[6]

pandish.a[2] *vt* 1. raise, hoist, move, lift up, lift: *Pandisha bendera*, hoist the flag. 2. breed an animal; inseminate artificially: *Anataka kumpandisha jogoo wake*, he wants to use his cock to inseminate his hen artificially. Prep. **pandish.i.a** St. **pandish.ik.a** Ps. **pandish.w.a**

pandu *n* (n) (*zool*) Talang queenfish; double-spotted queenfish; needlescale queenfish, a kind of elongate broad spiny-finned food fish (*family Carangidae*) which swims in small groups and usu frequents reefs and offshore islands.

paneli *n* (n) panel: *Paneli ya mahakimu*, a panel of judges. *Paneli ya wazungumzaji*, a panel of speakers. (cf *jopo*) (Eng)

pang.a[1] *vt* arrange, file; put in order, set in order: *Anapanga mambo yake vizuri*, he plans his affairs well. (*idm*) *Panga na kupangua*, plan and unplan. Prep. **pang.i.a** St. **pang.ik.a** Cs. **pang.ish.a** Ps. **pang.w.a** Rp. **pang.an.a** (cf *tengeneza, ratibu*)

pang.a[2] *vt* rent, hire: *Amepanga nyumba*, he has rented a house. Prep. **pang.i.a** St. **pang.ik.a** Cs. **pang.ish.a** Ps. **pang.w.a**, be rented. (cf *kodi*)

pang.a[3] *vt* arrange brotherhood, fatherhood, motherhood, friendship, etc with someone not related by blood: *Panga udugu*, arrange brotherhood. Prep. **pang.i.a** St. **pang.ik.a** Cs. **pang.ish.a** Ps. **pang.w.a** Rp. **pang.an.a**, agree to have mutual friendship e.g. *Wamepangana urafiki*, they have agreed to become friends.

pang.a[4] *vt* be someone's mistress; have a mistress; cohabit: *Yeye amepanga na msichana fulani*, he has a mistress. Prep. **pang.i.a** St. **pang.ik.a** Cs. **pang.ish.a**

panga[5] *n* (*ma-*) see *mundu*

panga[6] *n* (n) a place of spirits. (cf *mzimu*)

panga[7] *n* (n) (*zool*) a kind of a big oyster of three dimensions.

panga[8] *n* (n) a cave which has always water in it.

pangaboi *n* (*ma-*) an instrument for creating a flow of air; ceiling fan. (cf *panka*)

pangan.a *vi* 1. be sitting or standing at a place in a special format. 2. (of sides) agreeing on a special issue.

pange *n* (*ma-*) (*zool*) tsetse fly (cf *chafuo, mbung'o*)

pangik.a *vi* 1. be rentable, be rented:

Nyumba hii haipangiki kwa vile kodi yake ni kubwa, this house cannot be rented because its rent is high. (cf *pangishika*) 2. be put in a special order/system. Prep. ***pangik.i.a*** St. ***pangik.ik.a*** Cs. ***pangik.ish.a***

pangish.a *vt* rent, let, hire: *Anataka kupangisha nyumba yake mpya kwa wafanyakazi wa mashirika mbalimbali*, he wants to let his house to workers of different organisations. Prep. ***pangish.i.a*** St. ***pangish.ik.a***, be rentable. Ps. ***pangish.w.a*** Rp. ***pangish.an.a***

pangishik.a *vi* see *pangik.a*

pango *n (ma-)* cave, den, cavern. (cf *shimo*)

pangu *adj, pron* at/in my place.

pangu.a *vt* 1. replan, disarrange; change plans, etc.: *Aliipangua mipango yake*, he changed his plans. 2. deflect: *Golikipa aliipangua shuti kali*, the goalkeeper deflected a hard shot. Prep. ***pangu.li.a*** St. ***pangu.k.a*** Cs. ***pangu.lish.a*** Ps. of Prep. ***pangu.liw.a*** Rp. ***pangu.an.a*** (cf *paraganya, tapanya, vuruga*)

panguk.a *vi* be in disarray: *Mipango yake imepanguka*, his plans are in disarray, Prep. ***panguk.i.a*** St. ***panguk.ik.a*** Cs. ***panguk.ish.a***

pangus.a[1] *vt* wipe off, dust off: *Alipangusa vumbi usoni*, he wiped off the dust on the face. Prep. ***pangus.i.a*** St. ***pangus.ik.a*** Cs. ***pangus.ish.a*** Ps. ***pangus.w.a*** Rp. ***pangus.an.a*** (cf *futa, safisha*)

pangusa[2] *n (n) (med)* syphillis (cf *sekeneko, kaswende, farangi*)

pani.a *vt* 1. roll up a dress by holding its hem i.e. bottom edge; shorten a dress by folding the hem and making a new one; turn up: *Aliipania suruali yake ili aweze kukivuka kidimbwi*, he turned up his trousers in order to cross over a pond. 2. get down to serious work; intend, determine, resolve: *Nchi yetu imepania kuboresha uchumi wake*, our country is determined to improve its economy. St. ***pani.k.a*** Cs. ***pani.sh.a***

Ps. ***pani.w.a*** (cf *azimia, kusudia*)

panja *n (ma-)* 1. see *panda*[4] 2. a mode of shaving the hair leaving a tuft on the head; quiff. (cf *sekini, denge*)

panji[1] *n (n) (zool)* dolphin fish. (cf *fulusi*)

panji[2] *n (n)* a person who is boycotted by others.

panj.i[3] *vi* raise one's clothes so that it does not get wet Prep. ***panj.i.a*** St. ***panj.ik.a*** Cs. ***panj.ish.a*** Ps. ***panj.w.a***

panka *n (n)* fan (cf *pangaboi*)

pantoni *n (n)* ferry boat; pantoon. (Eng)

panu.a *vt* widen, expand, extend: *Serikali inataka kuipanua njia hii*, the government wants to expand this road. Prep. ***panu.li.a*** St. ***panu.k.a*** Cs. ***panu.lish.a*** Ps. of Prep. ***panu.liw.a*** Rp. ***panu.an.u*** (cf *tanua, papua, roromoa*)

panuk.a *vi* be extended, be widened: *Suruali yake imepanuka sasa*, his trousers have now widened. Prep. ***panuk.i.a*** St. ***panuk.ik.a*** Cs. ***panuk.ish.a***

panya *n (n) (zool)* rat, mouse. (cf *buku*)

panza[1] *n (n)* a piece of coconut remaining in the husk after it has been scraped or grated.

panza[2] *n (n)* a piece of soap left over after the whole bar has been used. (cf *kichelema*)

panzi[1] *n (n) (zool)* grasshopper

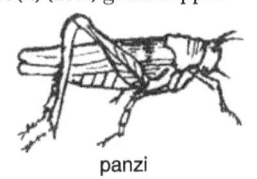

panzi

panzi[2] *n (n) (zool)* flying fish; a sea fish of elongated body with large wing-like pectoral fins (family *Exocoetide*) that make it glide through the air and is found in surface waters of both neritic and oceanic areas.

pao *adj, pron* their, theirs: *Mahala pao*,

their place. *Pao ni petu,* their place is ours.

papa¹ *adv* used for emphasising the word *hapa,* here: *Papa hapa,* just at this very place; just here; right here.

papa² *n* (*n*) (*zool*) shark: *Papa ngusi,* tiger shark. *Papa kinengwe,* thresher shark. *Papa usingizi,* short-tail nurse shark. *Papa bunshu,* silky shark. *Papa upanga,* sawfish. *Papa suruanzi,* light tip shark. *Papa marbui,* milk shark.

pap.a³ *vi* 1. throb, flutter, palpitate: used in the expression: *Moyo unampapa,* her heart is fluttering; she is worried. 2. (of pottery) ooze without having leakages or cracks. Prep. *pap.i.a* St. *pap.ik.a* Cs. *pap.ish.a*

Papa⁴ *n* (*n*) (*rel*) Pope; the bishop of Rome and head of the Roman Catholic Church.

papachi *n* (*n*) crooked teeth: *Ana papachi,* he has crooked teeth.

papai (also *papayu*) *n* (*ma-*) (*bot*) pawpaw fruit; a fruit from the tree *mpapai, Carica papaya.* (Hind)

papara *n* (*n*) rush, haste, hurry: *Mbona una papara?* Why are you in such a hurry? (cf *machachari*)

paparik.a *vi* 1. be uneasy, be unstable (cf *babaika*) 2. (esp of a bird, animal, etc.) flutter, flap, flop. Prep. *paparik.i.a* St. *paparik.ik.a* Cs. *paparik.ish.a* (cf *papatika*)

paparish.a *vt* cause sby to be uneasy or unstable. Prep *paparish.i.a* St *paparish.ik.a* Ps *paparish.w.a* Rp *paparish.an.a*

papas.a *vt* grope; touch gently, stroke with the hand: *Alimpapasa mkewe,* he touched his wife gently. Prep. *papas.i.a* St. *papas.ik.a* Cs. *papas.ish.a* Ps. *papas.w.a* Rp. *papas.an.a* (cf *tomasa, gusagusa*)

papasi¹ *n* (*n*) 1. (*zool*) spirrilum tick; a kind of wingless blood-sucking insect on humans, domestic animals, birds rodents, etc. 2. a tourist guide who conducts his activities unofficially.

papasi² (also *kipapasi*) *n* (*n*) (*zool*) antenna, feeler; either of pair of movable, jointed sense organs on the head of an insect, crab, lobster, etc.

papat.a *vt* slap; hit usu with a hand: *Alimpapata mwanawe mara nyingi usoni,* she slapped her son several times on the face. Prep. *papat.i.a* St *papat.ik.a* Cs. *papat.ish.a* Ps. *papat.w.a* Rp. *papat.an.a* (cf *zaba, piga*)

papatik.a *vi* 1. flutter, flap, flop: *Kuku alipapatika baada ya kuchinjwa,* the hen fluttered after being slaughtered. 2. be uneasy, be worried, be confused: *Alipapatika baada ya kugundua kuwa mkoba wake wenye pesa umechopolewa,* she became confused after discovering that her purse full of money had been snatched. Prep. *papatik.i.a* St. *papatik.ik.a* Cs. *papatik.ish.a* (cf *taharuki, hangaika, shughulika*)

papatiki.a *vt, vi* humble oneself before sby.

papatiko *n* (*n*) see *mpapatiko*

papatu *n* (*n*) commotion, noise. (cf *patashika*)

papatu.a (also *pepetua*) *vt* 1. wrench apart; shell; peel: *Alizipapatua njugunyasa,* he shelled the groundnuts. 2. blossom, bloom, flower: *Matumbo ya maua yale yamepapatua,* those flower buds have blossomed. Prep. *papatu.li.a* St. *papatu.k.a* Cs. *papatu.sh.a* Ps. of Prep. *papatu.liw.a* Rp. *papatu.an.a* (cf *chanua, fumbuka*)

papazi *n* (*n*) a strong south monsoon wind.

papi *n* (*n*) gusset; strip of wood/metal.

papi.a *vt, vi* be ravenous, eat or take sth greedily; gobble: *Akila, hupapia,* when he eats, he does it voraciously. Prep. *papi.li.a* St. *papi.lik.a* Cs. *papi.sh.a* Ps. *papi.w.a* (cf *lapa, haha, vongea*)

papik.a *vt* put many things together; assemble. Prep. *papik.i.a* St. *papik.*

ik.a Cs. ***papik.ish.a***
papio *n* (*n*) greediness, avarice. (cf *uroho*)
papo[1] *n* (*ma-*) palpitation of the heart due to fear, after running, etc.; throb.
papo[2] *adv* (*idm*) *Papo hapo; Papo kwa papo; Papo kwa hapo*, at that instant, just then. (*prov*) *Papo kwa papo, kamba hukata jiwe*, sooner or later a rope cuts a stone i.e. we should not be disheartened to do sth even if it is a difficult one, because eventually, we may succeed.
papu.a[1] *vt* widen, enlarge, stretch: *Mshoni aliipapua suruali yangu*, the tailor enlarged my trousers. Prep. ***papu.li.a*** St. ***papu.lik.a*** Cs. ***papu.lish.a*** Ps. of Prep. ***papu.liw.a*** (cf *tanua, panua*)
papu.a[2] *vt, vi* see *papura*.
papur.a (also *papua*) *vt, vi* scratch, claw: *Paka alimpapura mtoto*, the cat scratched the child. Prep. ***papur.i.a*** St. ***papur.ik.a*** Cs. ***papur.ish.a*** Ps. ***papur.w.a*** Rp. ***papur.an.a*** (cf *kwaruza, kwakura*)
papuri *n* (*n*) a kind of thin Indian bread made from wheat, green grams, lentils, chillies, etc.
para[1] *n* (*n*) a kind of cake or bread made from simsim; simsim cake. (Hind)
para[2] *n* (*n*) see *paa*[1]
par.a[3] *vt, vi* put on make-up; beautify oneself with cosmetics e.g. powder, perfume, etc.: *Alijipara vizuri kabla ya kwenda harusini*, she put on lots of make-up before going to the wedding. Prep. ***par.i.a*** St. ***par.ik.a*** Cs. ***par.ish.a***
parachichi *n* (*ma-*) (*bot*) avocado; a pear-shaped edible fruit having a delicate flesh, nutty flavour, rich in oil and nutritious. (cf *pea*)
parachuti *n* (*n*) parachute (Eng)
parade *n* (*n*) (*naut*) thick rope used in sailing vessels.
paradiso *n* (*n*) see *pepo*[2.]
parafujo *n* (*n*) screw; a nail with a spiral groove. (cf *skrubu, hesi*) (Port)
parag.a *vt* clamber, shinny; swarm up a tree; climb up a tree, etc. by using hands and feet: *Mkwezi aliuparaga mnazi*, the climber clambered the coconut tree. Prep. ***parag.i.a*** St. ***parag.ik.a*** Cs. ***parag.ish.a*** Ps. ***parag.w.a*** Rp. ***parag.an.a*** (cf *sombera, kwea*)
paragany.a *vt* disrupt, disarray: *Aliiparaganya mipango yangu*, he disrupted my plans. Prep. ***paragany.i.a*** St. ***paragany.ik.a*** Cs. ***paragany.ish.a*** Ps. ***paragany.w.a*** Rp. ***paragany.an.a*** (cf *vuruga, haribu*)
parago *n* (*mi-*) a kind of rope knot on the branches, of a tree as a support for a picker or climber: *Parago parago*, tie the branches of a tree such that a person can pick its fruits at its top.
paragrafu *n* (*n*) paragraph, passage. (cf *aya*) (Eng)
parakacha *n* (*n*) 1. sound like those of leaves being moved by a gentle breeze or of papers being shuffled; rustling sound; grating sound; rustle: *Alisikia parakacha msituni*, he heard a rustling sound in the forest. 2. (used to express the sudden departure of a person or animal;) stampede, dash: *Nilisikia parakacha la wanyama waliokuwa wakikimbia mbugani*, I heard a stampede of animals who were running away across the plains. (cf *mchakacho*)
parakachu.a *vt* remove sth forcefully and suddenly: *Shawishi aliiparakachua samani katika chumba changu*, the intruder removed the furniture forcefully and suddenly in my room. Prep. ***parakachu.li.a*** St. ***parakachu.k.a*** Cs. ***parakachu.sh.a*** Ps. of Prep. ***parakachu.liw.a*** (cf *paraganya*)
parakas.a *vt, vi* dash, speed, rush, scamper, scurry: *Watoto waliziparakasa mbio mpaka shuleni*, the children scampered to the school. Prep. ***parakas.i.a*** St. ***parakas.ik.a***

Cs. **parakas.ish.a**

param.a vi 1. (of organs, plants, etc) be lacking of essential nutrients for their growth: *Mnazi ule umeparama*, that coconut tree has withered. Prep. **param.i.a** St. **param.ik.a** Cs. **param.ish.a** Ps. of Prep. **param. iw.a** (cf *nyauka, pooza*) 2. (of a face) fail to shine.

paramamba (also *pamamba*) n (n) (zool) a kind of multi-coloured saltwater fish belonging to *Lutjanidae* family.

parami.a vt 1. climb up a tree, wall, etc. without wearing the necessary climbing tools; mount: *Waliparamia ukuta*, they climbed up a wall. (cf *kwea, paraza*) 2. jump into; interrupt a person in speech: *Aliniparamia nilipokuwa ninazungumza*, he interrupted me when I was talking. St. **parami.k.a** Cs. **parami.sh.a** Ps. **parami.w.a** (cf *jitia, ingilia*)

parandesi n (n) parenthesis, brackets ( ): *Maneno yaliyotiwa parandesi yanaifafanua sentensi yenyewe*, the words in the bracket explain the sentence. (cf *mabano, braketi*)

parange n (ma-) a large broad-bladed matchet or knife used for cutting trees, etc.; panga (cf *mundu, ukengee*)

parapanda n (n) see *panda³*

parapi n (n) (naut) see *mtenge*

parar.a vi (of colours) fade, bleach; lose luster: *Shati lake jekundu limeparara baada ya kufuliwa mara nyingi*, the colour of his red shirt has faded after being washed many times. Prep. **parar.i.a** St. **parar.ik.a** Cs. **parar. ish.a** (cf *pauka, chujuka, zingia*)

parare n (n) (zool) a kind of grasshopper (family *Acrididae*) with hind barbed legs; two-stripped grasshopper *Melanoplus bivittatus*

parari n (n) (arch) war horn; a horn blown to signal the beginning of war.

parati n (n) a war horn.

paraz.a¹ vt see *paaza²*

paraz.a² (also *parua*) vt botch, bungle, flub; do a job improperly: *Aliiparaza kazi ya mwalimu*, he bungled the teacher's work. Prep. **paraz.i.a** St. **paraz.ik.a** Cs. **paraz.ish.a** Ps. **paraz.w.a** (cf *lipua, bananga, rasha*)

paraz.a³ vt weave, plait. Prep. **paraz.i.a** St. **paraz.ik.a** Cs. **paraz.ish.a** Ps. **paraz.w.a** Rp. **paraz.an.a**

paraz.a⁴ vt abrade, bruise, scratch. Prep. **paraz.i.a** St. **paraz.ik.a** Cs. **paraz. ish.a** Ps. **paraz.w.a** Rp. **paraz.an.a** (cf *chubua*)

paredi n (n) parade (cf *gwaride*) (Eng)

pareto n (n) (bot) pyrethrum

pari.a vt get money or sth else by gambling. St. **pari.k.a** Ps. **pari.wa**

parishi (also *parokia*) n (n) parish; an area within a diocese having its own church and clergymen. (Eng)

paru n (n) bhang mixed with sugar, used by Indians as a kind of food; sugary bhang, sugary harshish. (Hind)

paru.a vt scrape/graze superficially. Prep. **paru.li.a** St. **paru.k.a** Cs. **paru.z.a** Rp. **paru.an.a**

parur.a vt 1. scratch, scrape, lacerate, claw: *Kuku aliniparura*, the hen scratched me. 2. (colloq) thrash, defeat; *Timu yao iliiparura Liverpool*, their team defeated Liverpool. Prep. **parur.i.a** St. **parur.ik.a** Cs. **parur. ish.a** Ps. **parur.w.a** Rp. **parur.an.a** (cf *papura, kwaruza*)

paruz.a¹ vt rasp; grate with sandpaper: *Seremala aliuparuza ubao kwa msasa*, the carpenter sandpapered the wood. Prep. **paruz.i.a** St. **paruz.ik.a** Cs. **paruz.ish.a** Ps. **paruz.w.a** Rp. **paruz.an.a**

paruz.a² vt scratch, scrape, claw: *Paka aliniparuza*, the cat scratched me. Prep. **paruz.i.a** St. **paruz.ik.a** Cs. **paruz.ish.a** Ps. **paruz.w.a** (cf *parura, papura*)

pas.a (also *paswa*) vt be obliged, be necessary, be imperative, be a duty; behove: *Inampasa awaangalie wazee*

pasaka *wake*, he is obliged to look after his parents. Prep. ***pas.i.a*** St. ***pas.ik.a*** Cs. ***pas.ish.a*** Ps. ***pas.w.a*** Rp. ***pas.an.a*** (cf *bidi, lazimu*)

Pasaka *n* (*n*) Easter

pasha[1] *n* (*n*) (*zool*) Crested malimbe; a kind of bird with a crested head and a deep red throat and chest. *Malimbus malimbicus*. (cf *kweche*)

pash.a[2] *vt* inform. (*idms*) *Pasha habari*, inform, publicize. *Pasha moto*, warm up; heat up. *Pasha adhabu*, punish. *Pasha tohara*, circumcise. Prep. ***pash.i.a*** St. ***pash.ik.a*** Ps. ***pash.w.a*** Rp. ***pash.an.a***

pash.a[3] *vi* (of paint, etc) stick properly; adhere: *Rangi ile imepasha katika ukuta wa nyumba yangu*, that paint has stuck on the wall of my house. Prep. ***pash.i.a*** St. ***pash.ik.a*** Cs. ***pash.ish.a*** Ps. ***pash.w.a*** Rp. of Prep. ***pash.i.an.a*** (cf *shaliki, bambanya*)

pashan.a *vi* exchange information between each other/one another. (cf *peana*)

pashi.a *vt* (of wood, metal, etc.) join two pieces together: *Seremala alizipashia mbao zangu*, the carpenter joined my pieces of wood together. Prep. ***pashi.li.a*** St. ***pashi.k.a*** Ps. ***pashi.w.a*** Rp. ***pashi.an.a*** (cf *shaliki, bambanya*)

pasi[1] *conj* without: *Amenitukana pasi na sababu*, he has insulted me without any reason.

pas.i[2] *vt* pass; succeed: *Aliupasi mtihani wa hesabu*, he passed the mathematics examination. St. ***pas.ik.a*** Cs. ***pas.ish.a***, cause to pass. Ps. of Cs. ***pas.ish.w.a*** e.g. *Alipasishwa kwenye mtihani*, he was made to pass the examination. (cf *fuzu, faulu*) (Eng)

pasi[3] *n* (*n*) pass; an intentional transfer of the ball, etc. to another player during play: *Mchezaji alitoa pasi maridadi kwa mwenzake*, the player gave a good pass to his teammate. (Eng)

pasi[4] *n* (*n*) iron: *Piga pasi*, iron clothes. *Pasi ya makaa*, charcoal iron. *Pasi ya umeme*, electric iron.

pasi[5] *n* (*n*) 1. permit, visa: *Aliuvuka mpaka bila ya pasi*, he crossed the border without a permit. 2. passport. (cf *paspoti*) (Eng)

Pasifiki *n* (*n*) Pacific: *Bahari ya Pasifiki*, Pacific Ocean. (Eng)

pasipoti *n* (*n*) passport: *Ofisi ya uhamiaji imempa pasipoti mpya*, the immigration office has given him a new passport. (cf *pasi*)

pasish.a *vt* 1. see *pas.i*[2] 2. verify the excellence of sth; certify, sanction: *Nani alilipasisha gari hili bovu?* Who sanctioned this ramshackle vehicle? Prep. ***pasish.i.a*** St. ***pasish.ik.a*** Ps. ***pasish.w.a*** Rp. ***pasish.an.a***

pasu.a *vt* 1. split open; chop, cut. (cf *chanja, banja*) 2. tear, rip, rend: *Aliipasua nguo yake*, she tore her dress. (cf *chana, rarua*) 3. burst: *Mtoto alilipasua bofu lake*, the child burst his balloon. 4. operate; perform surgery: *Daktari alimpasua mgonjwa*, the doctor operated on a patient. 5. (*idms*) *Pasua njia*, a) split hair. b) pass a place where there is no way as in a bush. *Pasua moyo*, be tiring; be exhausting. *Pasua maneno*, speak openly. Prep. ***pasu.li.a*** St. ***pasu.k.a*** Cs. ***pasu.sh.a*** Ps. of Prep. ***pasu.liw.a*** Rp. ***pasu.an.a***

pasuk.a *vi* burst, explode, be open: *Bofu limepasuka*, the ballon has burst. Prep. ***pasuk.i.a*** St. ***pasuk.ik.a*** Cs. ***pasuk.ish.a*** Ps. of Prep. ***pasuk.iw.a***

pat.a *vt* 1. get, obtain: *Pata homa*, get sick. *Pata ajali*, have an accident. *Pata faida*, make a profit. *Pata hasara*, make a loss. *Pata moto*, get hot. *Pata nguvu*, become strong. Prep. ***pat.i.a***, get for (by, with, in, etc.) e.g. *Amejipatia mali nyingi kwa njia ya haramu*, he has obtained a lot of wealth illegally. St. ***pat.ik.a*** Cs. ***pat.ish.a*** Ps. ***pat.w.a*** Rp. ***pat.an.a***

patan.a *vi* be reconciled, get along, work harmoniously: *Watu wale sasa* *wamepatana baada ya kugombana,* those people have now reconciled after they had quarrelled. Prep. ***patan.i.a*** St. ***patan.ik.a*** Cs. ***patan.ish.a***

patangi *n* (*n*) see *purutangi.*

patanish.a *vi* reconcile, harmonize: *Nilijaribu kuzipatanisha pande zile mbili,* I tried to reconcile those two sides. Prep. ***patanish.i.a*** St. ***patanish.ik.a*** Ps. ***patanish.w.a*** Rp. ***patanish.an.a***

patanishik.a *vi* be reconcilable, be willing to be reconciled. (cf *suluhika*)

patapotea *n* (*n*) gamble, pure luck: *Shughuli hii ni patapotea kwa vile haijaleta faida yoyote,* this business is a gamble because it has not yet brought any profit.

patashika *n* (*n*) hustle and bustle; commotion, turmoil, scramble: *Kuna patashika nyingi sokoni leo,* there is a lot of hustle and bustle in the market today. (cf *pirikapirika*)

patasi[1] *n* (*n*) wood chisel. (cf *turusi, churusi*)

patasi[2] *n* (*n*) medicine that resembles granulated salt, used as treatment for headache and abdominal pains.

Pate *n* (*n*) (*geog*) East African island north of Kenya.

patena *n* (*n*) (in Christianity) paten; a metal plate esp the plate for holding the bread in the Eucharist. (Eng)

patik.a *vi* be available, be obtained. Prep. ***patik.i.a*** St. ***patik.ik.a*** Cs. ***patik.ish.a***

patikan.a *vi* be available, be found: *Sukari inapatikana kwa wingi madukani siku hizi,* sugar is available in large quantities at the shops these days. Prep ***patikan.i.a*** St ***patikan.ik.a***

patiliz.a[1] *vt* wrap around; shroud: *Walimpatiliza maiti sanda,* they shrouded the corpse. Prep. ***patiliz.i.a*** St. ***patiliz.ik.a*** Cs. ***patiliz.ish.a*** Ps. ***patiliz.w.a*** Rp. ***patiliz.an.a*** (cf *gongomeza, zingirisha*)

patiliz.a[2] *vt* 1. have vengeance; take vengeance on; revenge: *Usipatilize hata kama amekufanyia ubaya wowote,* don't revenge even if he has wronged you of anything. 2. blame or punish sby for wrongdoing: *Mungu alimpatiliza mtu yule kwa maovu yake,* God punished that person for his misdeeds. Prep. ***patiliz.i.a*** St. ***patiliz.ik.a*** Cs. ***patiliz.ish.a*** Ps. ***patiliz.w.a*** Rp. ***patiliz.an.a*** (cf *adhibu, tesa*)

patiliz.a[3] *vt* take sby/sth seriously; pay attention, take notice of; heed: *Kwa nini unayapatiliza mambo madogo madogo kama hayo?* Why are you paying attention to trifling matters like those? Prep. ***patiliz.i.a*** St. ***patiliz.ik.a*** Cs. ***patiliz.ish.a*** Ps. ***patiliz.w.a*** Rp. ***patiliz.an.a***

patipati[1] *n* (*n*) see *pachipachi*

patipati[2] slippers (*kandambili*)

patisi *n* (*n*) a long wooden cloth wrapped round the legs like stockings and usu worn by soldiers; wrap stockings. (cf *soksi ndefu*)

pato *n* (*ma-*) income, earning, proceeds: *Pato la taifa,* national income. *Pato la ziada,* by-product. *Pato lake ni dogo,* his income is small. (cf *kipato*)

patw.a *vt, vi* be met, be stricken: *Alipatwa na malaria,* he was stricken with malaria. *Alipatwa na msiba;* he had a misfortune. *Mwezi umepatwa,* the moon is eclipsed.

pau[1] *n* (*ma-*) a long thin pole laid across the larger poles (*kombamoyo*) used to make rafters in the roof of a house. (cf *upau*)

pau[2] *n* (*n*) (in card playing) club; any of a suit of playing cards marked with a black figure like a clove leaf.

pau

pau³ n (n) a kind of big bread made from wheat flour. (cf *boflo*)
pau.a¹ vt (of colours) cause to fade, cause to bleach: *Utalipaua shati lako ukilifua sana*, you will get your shirt bleached if you overwash it. Prep. **pau.li.a** St. **pau.k.a** Cs. **pau.sh.a** Ps. of Prep. **pau.liw.a** (cf *fifia, chujuka*)
pau.a² vt (of roof) fix rafters: *Paua nyumba*, fix rafters of a house. Prep. **pau.li.a** St. **pau.k.a** Cs. **pau.sh.a** Ps. of Prep. **pau.liw.a**
pauk.a vi fade: *Suruali yake imepauka*, his pair of trousers has faded. Prep. **pauk.i.a** St. **pauk.ik.a** Cs. **pauk.ish.a** (cf *chujuka*)
paukwa interj an expletive used in narratives by a storyteller to begin a tale. see also *pakawa*.
pauni¹ n (n) (of currency) Sterling pound. (Eng)
pauni² n (n) (of weight) pound: *Pauni tatu ya dhahabu*, three pounds of gold. (Eng)
pay.a¹ vi see *payapaya*
paya² n (n) soup made from the legs of a goat, etc.
payapay.a (also *paya*) vi 1. prattle, blather; talk foolishly: *Alipolewa, akaanza kupayapaya*, when he got drunk, he started to prattle. (cf *ropokwa, payuka*) 2. be occupied, be restless: *Siku hizi mjomba anapayapaya kwenye ujenzi wa nyumba yake*, these days, my uncle is busy building his house. Prep. **payapay.i.a** St. **payapay.ik.a** Cs. **payapay.ish.a** (cf *bwata, shughulika, hangaika*)
payaya n (n) (bot) wild peanuts.
payo¹ n (n) babbling, twaddle; habit of talking nonsense.
payo² n (n) prostitution, harlotry; street walking. (cf *uzinzi, umalaya*)
payuk.a vi prattle, twaddle; spout nonsense: *Alipayuka sana kwenye mazungumzo*, he prattled alot during the conversation. Prep. **payuk.i.a** St. **payuk.ik.a** Cs. **payuk.ish.a** (cf *bwabwaja, ropoka, boboka, payapaya*)
paz.a vt cause sth to go up: *Paza sauti*, raise voice; shout. Prep. **paz.i.a** St. **paz.ik.a** Cs. **paz.ish.a**
pazi¹ n (n) (arch) chief of Zaramo.
pazi² n (n) a dented section of the head where there is no hair.
pazia n (ma-) curtain, screen. (Pers)
pe interj an expletive used to emphasize brightness or whiteness of sth: *Nguo nyeupe pe*, a very bright dress. *Kweupe pe*, it is daylight; it is a bright day; it is completely bright.
pea¹ n (ma-) (bot) a sweet juicy fruit with a rounded shape; pear. (cf *parachichi*) (Eng)
pe.a² vi (of fruits) be fully ripe; be mature: *Matunda haya yamepea*, these fruits are ripe. (cf *iva, komaa*) 2. (fig) be ripe; be reaching the boiling point; be reaching the turning point: *Mambo yake yamepea*, his affairs have reached an advanced stage. *Utundu wake umepea*, his naughtiness has reached the climax. Prep. **pe.le.a** St. **pe.k.a** Cs. **pe.sh.a**
pe.a³ vt broom, brush, sweep, clean: *Alikipea chumba chake*, he swept his room. Prep. **pe.le.a** St. **pe.k.a** Cs. **pe.sh.a** Ps. **pe.w.a**
pea⁴ n (n) pair: *Pea ya viatu*, a pair of shoes. (cf *jozi*) (Eng)
pech.a vi 1. hitch, limp, hobble; walk lamely: *Alianza kupecha baada ya kuanguka kwenye ngazi*, he started limping after falling down on the stairs. (cf *chechemea, guchia*) 2. dislocate, disarrange Prep. **pech.e.a** St. **pech.ek.a** Cs. **pech.esh.a** (cf *tegua*)
pecham.a vi (of food) be stuck in the gums of the teeth.
pechu.a vt 1. remove food that is stuck in the gums of the teeth by using a small stick. 2. remove sth that is put in the loin cloth, etc. around the waist.

P

Prep. *pechu.li.a* St. *pechu.k.a* Cs. *pechu.lish.a* Ps. *pechu.liw.a* Rp. *pechu.an.a*

pedeli *n* (*n*) 1. (of a bicycle) pedal. 2. a pedal in a machine for its operation. (Eng)

pefu *n* (*ma-*) (*zool*) side fin of a fish.

pegi[1] *n* (*n*) peg; tot of liquor: *Alipiga pegi moja*, he took a tot of liquor.

pegi[2] *n* (*n*) peg, stake (cf *kigingi*) (Eng)

peke *adv* single, alone, lonely, etc. *Peke yake*, by himself, by herself. *Peke yangu*, alone, by myself. *Anaishi peke*, he lives alone.

pekech.a *vt* 1. generate fire by twirling firesticks between the palms of the hands: *Aliwasha moto kwa kupekecha vijiti*, he lighted fire by twirling firesticks between the palms of the hands. 2. poke a fire; stoke a fire; twirl a fire: *Aliupekecha moto ili uwake vizuri*, he stoked the fire in order to burn well. 3. drill; bore a hole: *Aliupekecha ubao*, he drilled the board. (cf *toboa*) 4. search, look for: *Mtoto wako heshi kupekecha kabati langu*, your child never stops searching my cupboard. 5. (*fig*) incite, instigate, foment, provoke: *Aliupekecha ugomvi*, he instigated the quarrel. (cf *chochea*) 6. (*fig*) gnaw, ache, hurt: *Mifupa yake inampekecha*, his bones are aching. Prep. *pekech.e.a* St. *pekech.ek.a* Cs. *pekech.esh.a* Ps. *pekech.w.a*

pekecho *n* (*ma-*) 1. an instrument used for boring such as a handdrill, etc. 2. an act (method, etc.) of boring, drilling, etc.

pekechu.a *vt* search hard; search everywhere: *Alilipekechua sanduku mpaka akapata alichokitaka*, he searched hard the box until he found what he wanted. Prep. *pekechu.li.a* St. *pekechu.k.a* Cs. *pekechu.sh.a* Ps. of Prep. *pekechu.liw.a*

pekee *adj* unique, sole, lone: *Ana sifa za pekee*, he has unique characteristics.

pekenyu.a *vt* 1. separate two or more things that are fastened together in order to allow passage; disconnect: *Ingawa ua ulizibwa lakini aliupekenyua na baadaye kuingia ndani*, even though the compound was protected, he unfastened it and later entered inside. 2. take out sth by moving away things that are on it. Prep. *pekenyu.li.a* St. *pekenyu.k.a* Cs. *pekenyu.sh.a* Ps. of Prep. *pekenyu.liw.a* Rp. *pekenyu.an.a*

pekepeke *n* (*n*) intrigue, machinations; dirty tricks. *Tumechoka na pekepeke zake*, we are tired of his intrigues. (cf *fitina, chokochoko*)

peketek.a[1] *vi* be spoiled, be ruined; be in disarray: *Mipango yake ya kwenda ng'ambo imepeketeka*, his plans of going overseas are in disarray. Prep. *peketek.e.a* St. *peketek.ek.a* Cs. *peketek.esh.a* Ps. *peketek.w.a* (cf *sambaratika, haribika, vurugika*)

peketek.a[2] *vi* be arrogant, be conceited, be scornful: *Mbona amepeketeka siku hizi?* Why has he become arrogant these days? Prep. *peketek.e.a* St. *peketek.ek.a* Cs. *peketek.esh.a* (cf *jinata, jiona*)

peku (also *beku*) *n* (*n*) an old worn-out sifting basket. (*prov*) *Lililompata peku na ungo litampata*, what has happened to an old worn-out sifting basket will also happen to the winnowing basket i.e don't laugh at other people's misfortunes; the same might happen to you.

peku.a[1] *vt* 1. scratch as a hen does in the soil; scratch about. 2. search around, search diligently: *Askari wa polisi walivipekua vitu vilivyokuwemo kwenye sanduku lake*, the policemen searched the contents of his suitcase. Prep. *peku.li.a* St. *peku.k.a* Cs. *peku.sh.a* Ps. of Prep. *peku.liw.a* Rp. *peku.an.a* (cf *chakura, peleleza, chunguza*)

peku.a[2] *vi* (*colloq*) walk barefoot, go barefoot: *Alipekua mpaka shuleni*, he went to school barefoot. Prep. *peku.li.a* St. *peku.k.a* Cs. *peku.lish.a*

pekupeku[1] *adv* barefoot, shoeless, without shoes.

pekupeku² *n (n) (colloq)* an inquisitive person; busybody, telltale, tattler.

pele.a *vt* see *pogoa*

pelek.a *vt* 1. send, convey, deliver: *Nimeshapeleka mzigo wake nyumbani*, I have already sent his luggage home. (cf *fikisha, wasilisha*) 2. escort, accompany: *Alinipeleka mpaka nyumbani kwangu*, he escorted me up to my home. Prep. ***pelek.e.a***, St. ***pelek.ek.a*** Cs. ***pelek.esh.a*** Ps. ***pelek.w.a*** e.g, be sent. *Alipelekwa kwa waziri*, he was sent to the minister. Rp. ***pelek.an.a*** (cf *ongoza*)

peleke.a *vt* contribute towards; help bring about a result; act as a factor: *Kuondoka kwao kulipelekea watu wengi wasikitike*, their departure helped to bring sadness among the people.

pelele (also *perere*) *n (n) (zool)* tree hyrax, tree dassie. (cf *wibari, kwanga*)

pelele

pelelez.a *vt* 1. pry into, spy on; be inquisitive: *Alifukuzwa kwa makosa ya kuipeleleza nchi*, he was expelled from the country on charges of spying. 2. probe, investigate, research: *Makachero waliyapeleleza mauaji*, the detectives investigated the murder. Prep. ***pelelez.e.a*** St. ***pelelez.ek.a*** Ps. ***pelelez.w.a*** Rp. ***pelelez.an.a*** (cf *chunguza*)

-pelelezi *adj* investigative, inquisitive, inquiring: *Mwandishi mpelelezi*, an investigative journalist.

pelezi *n (n)* a defect in a weapon.

pemb.a¹ *vt* 1. cheat in order to get sth, deceive by trickery; dupe: *Alinipemba sana ili nimkopeshe pesa*, he struggled hard to dupe me into lending him some money. (cf *danganya, hadaa*) 2. question a person until he admits or confesses; quiz, grill, interrogate: *Nilimpemba juu ya wizi na hatimaye akakiri kushiriki kwake*, I interrogated him about the theft until he admitted his involvement. 3. pass at a distant place in order to reach a particular destination. Prep. ***pemb.e.a*** St. ***pemb.ek.a*** Cs. ***pemb.esh.a*** and ***pemb.ez.a*** Ps. ***pemb.w.a*** Rp. ***pemb.an.a*** (cf *ulizauliza*)

pemba² *vt* direct a weapon at; aim at, target on. Prep. ***pemb.e.a*** St. ***pemb.ek.a*** Cs. ***pemb.esh.a*** Ps. ***pemb.w.a*** Rp. ***pemb.an.a***

Pemba³ *n (n) (geog)* Island of Tanzania in the Indian Ocean, off the East Coast of Africa: 380 sq. m.

pembe¹ *n (n)* 1. animal horn; tusk. 2. a horn for sending signals and giving information. (cf *baragumu, parapanda*)

pembe² *n (n)* 1. corner, angle, direction, point: *Pembe za dunia*, the four points of the compass. *Pembe kali*, acute angle. *Pembe butu*, obtuse angle. *Pembe kuu*, reflex angle. *Pembe mkabala*, opposite angle. *Pembe mraba*, right angle. *Pembe tatu sawa*, equilateral triangle. *Pembe nne*, quadrilateral. *Pembe nyingi*, polygon. *Pembe nyofu*, straight angle. *Pembe sita*, hexagon. *Pembe tangamano*, adjacent angle. *Pembetatu pacha*, isosceles triangle. *Pembe za ndani*, interior angles. *Pembe za nje*, exterior angles. 2. *(idm) Pembe za chaki*, a secret place.

pembe.a¹ (also *bembea*) *vt, vi* swing, rock, sway: *Kiti cha pembea*, a rocking chair. Prep. ***pembe.le.a*** St. ***pembe.k.a*** Cs. ***pembe.z.a***

pembea² (also *bembea*) *n (n)* a swing for a child, etc.

621

pembebutu *n* (*n*) (*geom*) see *pembe²*
pembej.a (also *bembeja*) *vt* deceive with plausible statements usu implying deceit; persuade with fine words or statements in order to get sth; flatter: *Alijaribu kunipembeja lakini nikakataa kumwazima gari langu*, he tried to deceive me with fine words to lend him my car but I refused. Prep. *pembej.e.a* St. *pembej.ek.a* Cs. *pembej.esh.a* and *pembej.ez.a* Ps. *pembej.w.a* Rp. *pembej.an.a* (cf *pemba, laghai*)
pembejeo *n* (*n*) input: *Pembejeo za kilimo*, agricultural inputs.
pembejo *n* (*n*) (*anat*) the exterior part of a thigh; the lateral side of a thigh.
pembekali *n* (*n*) (*geom*) see *pembe²*
pembeni¹ *adv* aside, sideways, in a corner: *Simama pembeni*, stand sideways.
pembeni² *n* (*n*) (*bot*) a kind of small mangoe which is very sweet when ripe.
pembe mraba *n* (*n*) (*geom*) see *pembe²*
pembe nne *n* (*n*) see *pembe²*
pembe tatu *n* (*n*) see *pembe²*
pembezoni *adv* in the corner: *Amejificha pembezoni*, he has hid in the corner. *Pembezoni, kuna saa yangu*, in the corner, there is my watch.
pembu.a *vt* sift, sieve; winnow grain, etc.: *Aliupembua mchele*, he sifted the rice. Prep. *pembu.li.a* St. *pembu.k.a* Cs. *pembu.sh.a* Ps. of Prep. *pembu.liw.a* Rp. *pembu.an.a* (cf *pepeta, peta*)
pen.a *vt* (*naut*) row around; put around by rowing. *Aliupena mtumbwi wake*, he rowed around in his canoe. Prep. *pen.e.a* St. *pen.ek.a* Cs. *pen.esh.a* Ps. *pen.w.a*
penalti (also *penelti*) *n* (*n*) (in sports) penalty: *Alipiga penalti*, he took a penalty kick. (Eng)
pencheni *n* (*n*) see *pensheni*
pend.a *vt* 1. love, like. (*prov*) *Akipenda, chongo huita kengeza*, love is blind; in other words, you may love or like someone so much that you will ignore whatever the weaknesses the person may have. (cf *hibu, tamani*) 2. decide to do sth at one's wish: *Aliyafanya yale kwa kupenda kwake*, he did that out of his own accord. 3. (*syn*) *Mpende akupendaye*, love thee who loves thou. Prep. *pend.e.a* St. *pend.ek.a* Cs. *pend.ez.a* Ps. *pend.w.a* Rp. *pend.an.a*
pende.a *vt* like sby because of a particular reason. St. *pende.k.a* Cs. *pende.sh.a* Ps. *pende.w.a* Rp. *pende.an.a*
pendek.a *vt* be liked, be loved, be lovable
pendekez.a *vt, vi* 1. ingratiate; bring oneself into another's favour or good graces by conscious effort: *Anapenda kujipendekeza kwa wakubwa zake*, he likes to ingratiate himself to his superiors. 2. propose, suggest, recommend: *Alipendekeza mambo mengi kwenye mkutano*, he suggested a lot of things at the meeting. Prep. *pendekez.e.a* St. *pendekez.ek.a* Ps. *pendekez.w.a* Rp. *pendekez.an.a* (cf *shauri, rai*)
pendekezo *n* (*ma-*) 1. suggestion, proposition, idea: *Pendekezo lake halina msingi*, his suggestion is baseless. (cf *shauri, rai*) 2. (in thesis writing, etc.) proposal.
pendele.a *vt* favour, opt, prefer; be partial to: *Napendelea maisha ya vijijini kuliko ya mjini*, I prefer life in the villages to town. St. *pendele.k.a* Cs. *pendele.sh.a* Ps. *pendele.w.a* Rp. *pendele.an.a*
pendez.a *vt, vi* 1. be attractive, be pleasing; be charming: *Msichana yule anapendeza*, that girl is attractive. 2. be fitting, be attractive, become: *Nguo ile inampendeza*, that dress becomes her. 3. be pleasing, be gratifying: *Inapendeza kuona kwamba kijana huyu anawatii sana wazee wake*, it is pleasing to note that this youth obeys his parents very much. (cf *furahisha*)

St. *pendez.ek.a* Cs. *pendez.esh.a* Ps. *pendez.w.a* Rp. *pendez.an.a*
pendo *n* (*ma-*) love, affection. (cf *mapenzi, mahaba*)
penelti *n* (*n*) see *penalti*
peng.a¹ *vt* blow one's nose: *Alipenga mafua kwa sauti*, he blew his nose loudly. St. *peng.ek.a* Cs. *peng.esh.a* Ps. *peng.w.a*
penga² *n* (*n*) whistle (cf *kipenga, firimbi*)
pengine *adv* 1. perhaps, probably, maybe: *Pengine mvua itanyesha leo*, it may rain today. (cf *labda, huenda*) 2. somewhere else; elsewhere: *Hapa hakai mtu; jaribu pengine*, no one stays here; try elsewhere.
pengo *n* (*ma-*) 1. gap, hole; vacant space: *Ana mapengo kwenye meno yake ya mbele*, he has gaps in his front teeth. (cf *mwanya, uwazi*) 2. vacuum; vacant space after someone's departure or death: *Kifo chake kimeacha pengo kubwa nchini*, his death has left a big gap in the country.
peni¹ *n* (*-ma*) 1. (of currency) penny. 2. the smallest unit of currency existing in certain Commonwealth countries and elsewhere; penny. (Eng)
peni² *n* (*n*) pen, fountain pen. (cf *kalamu*) (Eng)
peninsula *n* (*n*) peninsula (Eng)
penseli *n* (*n*) pencil (Eng)
pensheni *n* (*also pencheni*) (*n*) pension: *Pensheni ya uzee*, old-age pension, *Penshoni ya urithi* inheritance pension. (Eng)
pentekoste (also *pentekote*) *n* (*n*) 1. pentecost; a Christian festival on the seventh Sunday after Easter, celebrating the descent of the Holy Spirit upon the Apostles. 2. pentecostal sect. (Eng)
pentekote *n* (*n*) see *pentekoste*
penu *adj, pron* (of a place) your (pl), yours: *Mahala penu*, your place. *Penu ni pazuri*, your place is good.
penu.a *vt* separate two parts of sth that are fastened; draw open; open a little: *Aliyapenua makuti ya ua na kisha akapenya*, he opened the palm leaves

of the fence a little and then entered immediately. Prep. **penu.li.a** St. *penu.k.a* Cs. *penu.sh.a* Ps. of Prep. *penu.liw.a*.
peny.a *vt* 1. penetrate; get inside, make a way into: *Alipenya kwenye kundi la watu*, he penetrated into the crowd. (cf *pita, ingia*) 2. penetrate, pierce; go through: *Risasi haikupenya ukutani*, the bullet never went into the wall. 3. (fig) touch, affect, influence; have an impact on: *Hotuba yake nzuri ilipenya kwenye mioyo ya watu*, his good speech touched the hearts of the people. Prep. *peny.e.a* St. *peny.ek.a* Cs. *peny.ez.a* Ps. *peny.w.a* Rp. of Cs. *peny.ez.an.a* (cf *gusa, vutia, athiri*)
penyenye *n* (*n*) rumour, gossip: *Penyenye zimezagaa nchini kwamba rais atalivunja bunge karibuni*, rumours have spread in the country that the president will soon dissolve parliament. *Pata penyenye*, hear rumours. (cf *uvumi, tetesi*)
penzi *n* (*ma-*) see *mapenzi*
peo *n* (*ma-*) broom made from palm leaves (*ufagio*)
pep.a¹ *vi* 1. totter, stagger, reel, sway: *Mlevi alikuwa anapita njiani kwa kupepa*, the drunkard was tottering on the street. (cf *yumbayumba, pepesuka*) 2. lose strength, vigour, vitality, speed, etc. Prep. *pep.e.a* St. *pep.ek.a* Cs. *pep.esh.a* Ps. *pep.w.a* (cf *pepesuka, yumbayumba*)
pepa² *interj* an expletive of gratitude to someone who has done a good thing.
pepe¹ *n* (*ma-*) chaff; empty husk of grain: *Mapepe ya ngano*, wheat chaff. (cf *kupepe*)
pepe² *adv* (of a ship, etc.) off course, be tossing, be rocking; adrift, awash: *Meli ilikuwa imekwenda pepe kutokana na mawimbi makali*, the ship went adrift because of the strong currents. (cf *mrama, upandeupande*)
pepe.a¹ *vt* 1. fan, flap; wave like a fan. 2. (of flag, etc.) wave, blow: *Bendera ilikuwa inapepea*, the flag was flapping in the breeze. Prep. **pepe.le.a** St.

pepe.k.a Cs. **pepe.sh.a** Ps. **pepe.w.a** Rp. **pepe.an.a**
pepe.a² *vi* lack strength or dynamism because of missing an important element; wither: *Mawele yamepepea*, the bull rush millet has withered. Prep. **pepe.le.a** St. **pepe.k.a** Cs. **pepe.sh.a**
pepe.a³ *vt* ripen fruits by artificial means such as covering them with sth or bury them and apply fire: *Aliyapepea maembe*, he ripened the mangoes by artificial means. Prep. **pepe.le.a** St. **pepe.k.a** Cs. **pepe.sh.a** Ps. **pepe.w.a** Rp. **pepe.an.a** (cf *vumbika, vuika*)
peperuk.a *vi* 1. be carried away by a current of air; be blown away: *Nguo zake zimepeperuka kwa upepo*, his clothes have been blown by the wind. (cf *paa, ruka*) 2. (*naut*) flap a sail in the wind. Prep. **peperuk.i.a** St. **peperuk.ik.a** Cs. **peperuk.ish.a**
peperush.a *vt* 1. blow away, waft, whiffle. 2. air news, greetings, etc.: *Alizipeperusha salamu zake kwa njia ya redio*, he sent his greetings by radio 3. sway a vehicle. Prep. **peperush.i.a** St. **peperush.ik.a** Ps. **peperush.w.a** Rp. **peperush.an.a**
pepes.a (also *pesa*) *vt* blink the eye; wink; Prep. **pepes.e.a** St. **pepes.ek.a** Cs. **pepes.esh.a** Ps. **pepes.w.a** Rp. **pepes.an.a** (cf *kopesa*)
pepesu.a *vt* sway; swing; cause sth to totter, cause sth to stagger: Prep. **pepesu.li.a** St. **pepesu.k.a**. Cs. **pepesu.sh.a** Ps. of Prep. **pepesu. liw.a** Rp. **pepesu.an.a** (cf *yumbisha*)
pepesuk.a *vi* be swaying, be tottering: *Abiria walikuwa wakipepesuka kutokana na mawimbi makali*, the passengers were swaying because of the strong waves. Prep. **pepesuk.i.a** St. **pepesuk.ik.a** Cs. **pepesuk.ish.a**
pepeta¹ *n* (*n*) grains of rice heated and then pounded to make them flat.
pepet.a² *vt* see *peta* Prep. **pepet.e.a** St. **pepet.ek.a** Cs. **pepet.esh.a** Ps. **pepet.w.a**

pepetan.a *vi* compete, battle, contest: *Timu mbili mashuhuri nchini zitapepetana kesho*, the two prominent teams in the country will contest tomorrow. Prep. **pepetan.i.a** St. **pepetan.ik.a** (cf *pambana, shindana, menyana, kwaana*)
pepetu.a¹ *vt* see *popotua*
pepetu.a² *vt* see *papatua*
pepezi *n* (*n*) a soft gentle breeze; zephyr.
pepo¹ *n* (*n*) demon, spirit. (cf *mzuka*)
pepo² (also *paradiso*) *n* (*n*) paradise, heaven.
pepopunda *n* (*n*) (*med*) tetanus, lockjaw.
pepu.a *vt* sift grain; winnow grain: Prep. **pepu.li.a** St. **pepu.k.a** Cs. **pepu.sh.a** Ps. of Prep. **pepu.liw.a** Rp. **pepu.an.a** (cf *pembua*)
pera *n* (*ma-*) (*bot*) guava (Port)
perege *n* (*n*) (*zool*) tilapia fish; a kind of freshwater fish which resembles very much a snapper. *Oreochromis jipe*.
perema *n* (*n*) (*med*) mumps (cf *machapwi, matubwitubwi*)
peremb.a *vt* 1. aim carefully with a rifle, arrow etc. (cf *lenga*) 2. walk carefully. (*syn*) *Pemba peremba ukija na winda utarudi na kilemba*, "Pemba" is a place where you need to do a lot of pampering, if you come with a loincloth, you will return with a turban i.e. Pemba is a profitable place; if you go there penniless, you will return with a lot of money. 3. look with pomposity. Prep. **peremb.e.a** St. **peremb.ek.a** Cs. **peremb.esh.a** Ps. **peremb.w.a** Rp. **peremb.an.a**
perembe *n* (*n*) a flute made from the bamboo of a millet; bamboo flute.
peremende (also *peremendi*) *n* (*n*) sweet, peppermint. (cf *pipi*) (Eng)
peremendi *n* (*n*) see *peremende*
perepes.a *vi* look right and left before crossing a road: *Aliperepesa kabla ya kuvuka barabara kuu*, he looked right and left before crossing the main road.

Prep. **perepes.e.a** St. **perepes.ek.a** Cs. **perepes.esh.a**
pesa¹ n (ma-) 1. (monet) pice; the former monetary unit and small coin of India equivalent to 1/64 of a rupee. 2. the currency worth three cents. 3. currency in general. (Hind)
pes.a² vt see *pepesa*. Prep. **pes.e.a** St. **pes.ek.a** Cs. **pes.esh.a** Ps. **pes.w.a** Rp. **pes.an.a**
pesheni n (n) (bot) passion fruit.
pet.a¹ (also *pepeta*) vt winnow grain by shaking in a tray; sift grain by shaking in a tray: *Alizipeta nafaka zake kabla ya kuzitia kwenye magunia*, he sifted his grain before packing it into the sacks. Prep. **pet.e.a** St, **pet.ek.a** Cs. **pet.esh.a** Ps. **pet.w.a** Rp. **pet.an.a** (cf *pcpcta*)
pet.a² vt bend round; fold, curve: Prep **pet.e.a** St **pet.ek.a** Cs **pet.esh.a** Ps **pet.w.a** Rp **pet.an.a** (cf *pinda, kunja*)
pet.a³ vt (in sports) win, triumph: *Timu yao ilipeta jana*, their team won yesterday. Prep. **pet.e.a** St. **pet.ek.a** Cs. **pet.esh.a** Ps. **pet.w.a** Rp. **pet.an.a** (cf *shinda*)
peta⁴ n (n) a stalk of clove flowers.
petali n (n) (bot) petal; any of the component parts, or leaves of a corolla. (Eng)
pete¹ n (n) 1. ring, hoop, staple: *Pete ya sikio*, earring. 2. (syn) *Chanda na pete*, hand in glove. e.g. *Watu wale wawili wanapendana kama chanda na pete*, those two people love each other very much.
pete² n (ma-) 1. a big hole bored through women's ears in which plugs of coloured paper are worn. 2. an adornment of this kind found in women's ears; ornamental ear-plug.
pctco n (n) a kind of roundish utensil like a winnowing basket.
peto n (ma-) bag; a matting-sack used for carrying stones, sand, etc.

petroli n (n) petrol (Eng)
petu adj, pron (of a place) our, ours: *Mahala petu*, our place. *Petu ni padogo*, our place is quite small.
petu.a vt 1. turn upside down; invert: *Alikipetua kikombe*, he inverted the cup. 2. wear sth like a shirt inside out. Prep. **petu.li.a** St. **petu.lik.a** Cs. **petu.sh.a** Ps. of Prep. **petu.liw.a** Rp. **petu.an.a**
-pevu adj 1. matured: *Binti yake amekuwa mpevu*, her daughter has matured. (cf *komavu*) 2. (of fruits, etc.) ripe, ripened: *Embe pevu*, ripe mango. (cf *tosa, bivu*)
pevu.a vt ripen. Prep. **pevu.li.a** St. **pevu.k.a** Cs. **pevu.sh.a** Ps. of Prep. **pevu.liw.a** (cf *pevush.a, ivisha, vumbisha*)
pevush.a vt 1. ripen, season. 2. be ready for delivering a baby. Prep. **pevush.i.a** St. **pevush.ik.a** Ps. **pevush.an.a**
pew.a¹ vt see *pa*
pewa² adv zigzag, askew, sideways: *Alinitupia jiwe lakini lilienda pewa*, he threw a stone at me but it went askew. (cf *kombo, upogoupogo*)
pezi n (ma-) (zool) the fin of a fish.
pi¹ (also *ti*) adv (idms) *Cheusi pi, Mweusi pi*, etc. are all expressions used to emphasize the blackness of sby/sth.
-pi² (gram) part used with personal prefixes to form interrog adjectives or pronouns meaning 'who', 'which' and 'what': *Mtu yupi?* Which person? *Kitabu kipi?* Which book?
pia¹ adv 1. also, furthermore, in addition: *Wewe pia ni mpole*, you are also calm (cf *vilevile, tena*) 2. all, the whole, complete: *Atakupa yote pia*, he will give you the whole lot.
pia² n (n) (of a toy) a top used in spinning; cone.
pia³ n (n) (idms) *Pia ya mguu, Pia ya goti*, kneecap; patella. (cf *futi, kilegesambwa*)
pia⁴ n (n) (naut) wooden ball pending from prow of *mtepe*, a kind of sailing vessel.
piano n (n) (mus) piano; a kind of musical

625

instrument played from a keyboard. (Eng)

piapi.a (also *kiakia, riaria*) *vi* be occupied, be uneasy; be restless: *Alipiapia mtoto wake alipopotea,* she was restless when her child got lost. Prep. *piapi.li.a* St. *piapi.lik.a* Cs. *piapi.lish.a* Ps. *piapi.w.a* (cf *hangaika*)

picha *n* (*n*) 1. picture, photograph: *Piga picha,* take photograph. *Picha za ngono,* pornography.(cf *taswira, sura*) 2. (*gram*) *Picha taarifa,* pictogram.

pig.a *vt* 1. hit, strike, beat, flog: *Mwalimu alimpiga mwanafunzi,* the teacher flogged the student. (cf *dunda, chapa*) 2. (*idms*) *Piga hodi,* knock at the door. *Piga honi,* hoot; sound a horn. *Piga kisi,* give a kiss. *Piga kura,* vote; cast a vote. *Piga makofi,* clap. *Piga marufuku,* ban. *Piga mbio,* run, speed off; sprint. *Piga pande,* boycott; stand aside. *Piga simu,* phone. *Piga stati,* start an engine. *Piga ngwara,* trip sby. *Piga vita,* start war. *Piga teke,* kick. *Piga zulu,* plate metal. *Piga sulu,* apply polish. *Piga pasi,* iron clothes. *Piga vigelegele,* ululate. *Piga mafunda,* take gulps. *Piga magoti,* kneel down; stoop. *Piga kinanda,* play a musical instrument such as guitar, etc. *Piga jeki,* boost someone. *Piga deki,* mop the floor. *Piga mstari,* underline. *Piga karata,* shuffle the cards so that we may play. *Piga chuku,* exaggerate. *Piga fatiha,* take the lead in offering a prayer. *Piga mbizi,* dive. *Piga-nikupige,* hit. Prep. *pig.i.a* St. *pig.ik.a* Cs. *pig.ish.a* Ps. *pig.w.a* Rp. *pig.an.a*

pigan.a *vt* 1. fight: *Nchi yetu ilipigana na adui kutoka nje,* our country fought against a foreign enemy. 2. play witchcraft against each other. Prep. *pigan.i.a* St. *pigan.ik.a* Cs. *pigan.ish.a* Ps. *pigan.w.a* Ps. of Cs. *pigan.ish.w.a.*

pigani.a *vt* fight for/over: *Anapigania masilahi ya wafanyakazi wote,* he is fighting for the interests of all workers. St. *pigan.ik.a* Cs. *pigan.* *ish.a* Ps. *pigan.w.a* Rp. *pigan.i.an.a* (cf *tetea*)

pigi[1] *n* (*n*) a small piece of wood tied with a rope usu on the leg or arm to act as medicine.

pigi[2] *n* (*n*) pieces of wood, etc. used to knock down fruits from trees. (cf *pikipiki*)

pigi.a *vt* 1. hit sth by using a special tool. 2. hit sth because of a certain reason. 3. hit sth on behalf of sby 4. (in card playing) give a signal to your partner. Prep. *pigi.li.a* St. *pigi.lik.a* Cs. *pigi.lish.a* Ps. *pigi.liw.a* Rp. *pigi.li.an.a*

pigo *n* (*ma-*) 1. blow, stroke, beat. 2. (*fig*) shock, blow: *Kifo chake kilikuwa pigo kubwa kwa familia yake,* his death was a big blow to his family. (cf *msiba, hasara*) 3. bewitching, becharming. (cf *urogaji*)

pijini *n* (*n*) pidgin; contact language resulting from trade, etc. between groups speaking different languages. (Eng)

pik.a *vt* 1. cook: *Hajui kupika chakula kizuri,* she doesnt know how to cook good food. 2. (*idm*) *Pika majungu,* hatch plot. Prep. *pik.i.a* St. *pik.ik.a* Cs. *pik.ish.a,* get someone to cook. Ps. *pik.w.a,* be cooked. Rp. of Prep. *pik.i.an.a*

pikipiki *n* (*n*) 1. motorbike (cf *tukutuku, kitututu*) 2. a stick for beautifying oneself.

pik.u *vt* 1. (in card playing) win a trick at cards. 2. surpass someone in skill, etc; excel: *Msichana yule aliwapiku wenzake katika shindano la warembo,* that girl surpassed others in the beauty contest 3. be able to do sth earlier than others. Prep. *piku.li.a* St. *piku.lik.a* Ps. of Prep. *piku.liw.a* Rp. *piku.an.a* (cf *zidi, pita*)

pilau *n* (*n*) a dish of rice boiled in a seasoned liquid and usu containing meat or fish or chicken; pilaf. (cf *kabuli*) (Pers)

pili¹ (also *piri*) n (n) (*zool*) nightadder; a kind of very poisonous snake with patches. *Causus rhombeatus*.

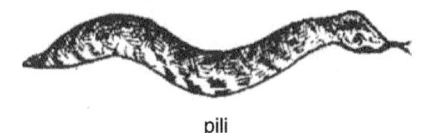

pili

pili² *adj* second, next: *Mtu wa pili*, the second person. *Mara ya pili*, the second time. *Yeye ni mtu wa pili kulalamika*, he is the second person to complain.
pilikapilika n (n) see *pirikapirika*.
pilipili n (n) (*bot*) chillies; *Pilipili hoho*, red pepper. *Capsicum frutscens*. *Pilipili manga*, black pepper, *Piper nigrum*. *Pilipili nituma*, black pepper (*prov*) *Pilipili usiyoila ya kuwashiani?* The chilly that you have not eaten, how can it irritate you? How can you be bothered with sth that does not concern you? (Pers)
piliz.a *vt* give sth to someone through sby else: *Jane alimpiliza John pesa zake kupitia Mary*, Jane gave John his money through Mary. Prep. *piliz.i.a* St. *piliz.ik.a* Ps. of Prep. *piliz.iw.a* Rp. *piliz.an.a*
pima¹ n (n) fathom, two yards; the stretch of a man's arms. (*prov*) *Ukipewa shubiri, usichukuwe pima*, if you are given little, don't take much.
pim.a² *vt* 1. measure, weigh, gauge: *Alipima upana wa chumba*, he measured the width of the room. (cf *linga, enenza*) 2. examine, evaluate, assess: *Niliyapima maneno yake lakini nikaona hayana uzito*, I assessed his words but I found that they were baseless. Prep. *pim.i.a* St. *pim.ik.a* Cs. *pim.ish.a* Ps. *pim.w.a* Rp. *pim.an.a* (cf *tathmini, chunguza*)
pimajoto n (n) thermometer.
pimamaji n (n) spirit level; an instrument for determining a horizontal plane.

pind.a *vt, vi* 1. fold, bend, twist: *Aliupinda mkono wangu*, he twisted my arm. 2. follow a crossed road. 3. (*colloq*) leave without notice; run away, flee. 4. sew a hem; hem: *Aliipinda suruali yake chini*, he hemmed down his trousers. Prep. *pind.i.a* St. *pind.ik.a* Cs. *pind.ish.a* Ps. *pind.w.a* Rp. *pind.an.a*
pindan.a¹ *vt* see *pinda*
pindan.a² *vt, vi* work hard; work diligently: *Alipindana sana kutafuta kazi bila ya mafanikio*, he looked very hard for a job without success. Prep. *pindan.i.a* St. *pindan.ik.a* Cs. *pindan.ish.a* (cf *jitahidi*)
pindi¹ n (n) a piece of sth cut from sth: *Pindi ya mua*, the piece of sugarcane. *Pindi ya mkono*, part cut from an arm. (cf *kivu, kiko*)
pindi² n (n) time; the moment; a division of time; a time of something: *Pindi za asubuhi*, morning hours. *Pindi ya chakula*, mealtime.
pindi³ n (*ma-*) an old worn-out cloth; tattered clothing; tatters, rags. (cf *tambara*)
pindi⁴ *conj* 1. although, even if: *Watakutana tu pindi mwakani*, they will meet each other although next year. 2. if: *Pindi atakapotokea, niarifu*, if he comes, inform me. (cf *ikiwa, kama, endapo, iwapo*)
pindik.a *vi* be bent, be curved. Prep. *pindik.i.a* St. *pindik.ik.a* Cs. *pindik.ish.a*
pindo n (n) the edge of a cloth or garment; hem: *Pindo jembamba*, a slim hem. *Pindo nene*, a thick hem.
pindu¹ n (n) an expletive for emphasizing somersault, overturn, etc of sth e.g. *Gari lake lilipinduka pindu*, his car overturned terribly.
pindu² *adj* erratic, aberrant, inconsistent: *Tabia pindu*, an erratic behaviour.
pindu.a *vt* 1. overturn, capsize, reverse, upset: *Aliipindua mashua*, he overturned the boat. (cf *geuza, fudikiza*) 2. overthrow, oust, depose, dethrone, unseat: *Waliipindua serikali*,

they overthrew the government. Prep. *pindu.li.a* St. *pindu.k.a* Cs. *pindu.sh.a* Ps. of Prep. *pindu.liw.a* Rp. *Pindu.an.a.*
pinduk.a *vi* overturn: *Gari lake lilipinduka jana*, his car overtuned yesterday. Prep. *pinduk.i.a* St. *pinduk.ik.a* Cs. *pinduk.ish.a*
pinduki.a *vi* transgress, exceed, go beyond: *Tabia yake imepindukia mpaka*, his habit has gone beyond the limit.
pinduli *n (n)* pendulum: *Pinduli pia*, conical pendulum.
pinduliw.a *vi* 1. be overthrown, be deposed: *Serikali yao ilipinduliwa*, their government was overthrown. 2. *(colloq)* be cuckolded.
pinduz.a *vt* invert, reverse, turn inside out. Prep. *pinduz.i.a* St. *pinduz.ik.a* Ps. *pinduz.w.a* (cf *geuza*)
ping.a¹ *vt* 1. block, bar, obstruct. 2. oppose, resist, counteract: *Alizipinga fikira zetu*, he opposed our ideas. 3. bet: *Alinipinga kama timu yetu itashinda kesho*, he betted against me that our team will win tomorrow. Prep. *ping.i.a* St. *ping.ik.a* Cs. *ping.ish.a* Ps. *ping.w.a* Rp. *ping.an.a.*
pinga² *n (n)* a holder of a spear.
pingamizi *n (n)* obstruction, obstacle, hindrance: *Alileta pingamizi nyingi kwenye maendeleo ya nchi*, he brought a lot of obstructions in the development of the country. (cf *kikwazo, kizuizi*)
pingili (also *kipingili*) *n (n)* a ring marking a knot or joint in a plant e.g. in sugarcane; a plant cutting. (cf *pingiti*)
pinginy.a *vt* see *finginya*. Prep. *pinginy.i.a* St. *pinginy.ik.a* Cs. *pinginy.ish.a* Ps. *pinginy.w.a* Rp. *pinginy.an.a.*
pingiti¹ *n (n)* see *pingili*
pingiti² *n (n)* torso; the body of a human not including the head and limbs: *Pingiti la binadamu*, torso.
pingo¹ *(ma-)* a kind of round piece or disc of wood used as an ornament, made usu from African ebony and worn by some women of some tribes in the lobes of their ears.
pingo² *n (ma-)* barrier, obstruction, bar e.g door bar.
pingu *n (n)* 1. handcuffs, fetters. 2.a cord fastened round the ankles of a climber to assist climbing a coconut tree, etc. 3. *(syn) Funga pingu za maisha*, have marriage bonds i.e. get married.
pingu.a¹ *vt* 1. cut into pieces; cut in lengths as in the case of sugarcane. 2. surrender, capitulate, give up. Prep. *pingu.li.a* St. *pingu.k.a* Cs. *pingu.lish.a* Ps. of Prep. *pingu.liw.a*
pingua² *vt* 1. unwind a rope, etc; untwist. 2. find a solution to a problem; solve. Prep. *pingu.li.a* St. *pingu.k.a* Cs. *pingu.lish.a* Ps. of Prep. *pingu.liw.a*
pinguo *n (ma-)* surrender, capitulation, submission.
pingusi *n (n)* (*zool*) hammerhead shark; a kind of shark (family *Sphyrnidae*) resembling very much caranx fish.
pingw.a¹ *vt* see *pinga*
pingwa² *n (n)* a line of things strung together like a chain or necklace; interlock: *Mkufu wake ulikatika katika pingwa tatu*, her chain broke at three joints.
pini *n (n)* pin (Eng)
pinki *n (n)* pink; a pale red colour. (Eng)
pipa *n (ma-)* cask, barrel. (Hind)
pipi *n (n)* sweet, peppermint. (cf *peremende*)
piramidi *n (n)* pyramid: *Piramidi pembetatu*, tetrahedron. (cf *haram*) (Eng)
piri *n (n)* see *pili¹*
pirikan.a *vi, vt* work diligently on a difficult task: *Kifuniko cha chupa kilipokataa kufunguka, mama akaanza kupirikana nacho*, when the cork of the bottle refused to open, my mother worked diligently on it. Prep. *pirikan.i.a* St. *pirikan.ik.a* Cs. *pirikan.ish.a* Ps. *pirikan.w.a* (cf *pindana, jitahidi*)

pirikapirika (also *pilikapilika*) *n* (*n*) scramble, hurly-burly, rush, hustle and bustle: *Pirikapirika za maisha ya jijini*, the hurly-burly of city life. (cf *patashika, hekaheka*)

piru *n* (*ma-*) (*zool*) turkey (cf *batamzinga*)

pis.a *vt* madden, derange, craze; cause mental disturbance, make mad: *Usijaribu kunipisa*, don't try to madden me. Prep. **pis.i.a** St. **pis.ik.a** Ps. **pis.w.a** Rp. **pis.an.a** (cf *wehua*)

pish.a¹ *vt, vi* let pass; allow passage; make room for: *Nipishe*, let me pass. *Wapishe*, let them pass. (*prov*) *Lipitalo hupishwa*, let bygones be bygones. *Mungu apishe mbali*, God forbid! Prep. **pish.i.a** St. **pish.ik.a** Cs. **pish.iz.a** Ps. **pish.w.a** Rp. **pish.an.a** (cf *nega*).

pish.a² *vt* sharpen; make keen, put an edge on: *Aliupisha upanga wake*, he sharpened his sword. Prep. **pish.i.a** St. **pish.ik.a** Cs. **pish.iz.a** Ps. **pish.w.a** (cf *noa, chongoa*)

pish.a³ *vt* cauterize a person, an animal, etc. with a hot iron; sear: *Alipapisha mahala alipotafunwa na nyoka*, he causterized the snake bite on his leg with a hot iron. Prep. **pish.i.a** St. **pish.ik.a** Cs. **pish.iz.a** Ps. **pish.w.a**

pishi *n* (*n*) 1. a measure of weight corresponding to 5 kilos. 2. a vessel used as a measure.

pisho *n* (*ma-*) cautery; mark or scar made by cauterizing on a person or animal.

pishori (also *pisori*) *n* (*n*) (*bot*) a kind of long-grained rice, considered to be of high quality. (Hind)

pisori *n* (*n*) see *pishori*

pit.a *vt, vi* 1. pass; go on, move past, go by: *Pita kulia*, go right. 2. (of events, etc.) pass by: *Mambo hayo sasa yamepita; kwa hivyo, hakuna haja ya kuyazungumza*, those affairs have now passed; so there is no need to discuss them. 3. beat, overtake, surpass, exceed: *Mwanariadha yule aliwapita wengine wote*, that athlete beat all others. Prep. **pit.i.a** St. **pit.ik.a** Cs. **pit.ish.a** Ps. **pit.w.a** Rp. **pit.an.a** (cf

zidi, shinda)

pitapit.a *vi, vt* pass at a place quite often; frequent a place. Prep. **pitapit.i.a** St. **pitapit.ik.a** Cs. **pitapit.ish.a** Ps. **patapit.iw.a** (cf *pitiapitia*)

pite *n* (*ma-*) simpleton, fool; a stupid person: *Pite aliuliza masuala ya kitoto*, the idiot asked childish questions. (cf *mpumbavu, mjinga, juha*)

piti.a¹ *vt* 1. pass by/at/near 2. make a brief visit Prep. **piti.li.a** St. **piti.k.a** Cs. **piti.shi.a** Ps. **piti.w.a** Rp. **piti.an.a**

piti.a² *vt* edit; read and write the necessary corrections in an article, book, etc. Prep. **piti.li.a** St. **piti.k.a** Cs. **piti.sh.a** Cs. of Prep. **piti.sh.i.a** Ps **piti.w.a** (cf *haruri*)

pitiliz.a *vi* 1. exceed, surpass, go beyond. 2. (cf a bus, etc.) pass over a station; go straight without stopping at a place: *Basi letu halikusimama kituoni; likawa limepitiliza*, our bus did not stop at the station; instead, it passed through it. Prep. **pitiliz.i.a** St. **pitiliz.ik.a** Cs. **pitiliz.ish.a**

pitio *n* (*ma-*) critical review: *Mapitio ya vitabu*, books' reviews.

pitish.a *vt* approve; pass sby/sth: *Pitisha azimio*, pass a resolution. *Pitisha hoja*, pass a motion. *Pitisha muda/wakati*, pass the time. *Pitisha sheria*, pass a law. *Kamati kuu ililipitisha jina lake kuwa mgombea ubunge*, the central committee approved his name as a parliamentary contestant. (cf *idhinisha*) 2. delay, temporize, waste time (cf *kawilisha*) Prep. **pitish.i.a** St. **pitish.ik.a** Ps. **pitish.w.a.** Rp. **pitish.an.a**

pitiw.a *vt* 1. forget; cease to remember: *Rafiki yangu alipitiwa na mambo mengi*, my friend forgot a lot of things. (cf *sahau, ghafilika*) 2. be fooled, be deceived. (cf *zugwa*)

pitu.a *vt* 1. invert, reverse, overturn; wear sth inside out: *Alilipitua shati lake wakati wa kuvaa*, he wore his shirt inside out. (cf *geuza, pindua*) 2. cause sth to fall on the other side: *Alipokuwa anaupanda ukuta, aliteleza na kupitua*, when he was climbing the

wall, he slipped and fell on the other side. Prep. *pitu.li.a* St. *pitu.k.a* Cs. *pitu.sh.a* Ps. of Prep. *pitu.liw.a* Rp. *pitu.an.a*
pituk.a *vi* pass at a place many times. Prep. *pituk.i.a* St. *pituk.ik.a* Cs. *pituk.ish.a*
piwa *n* (*n*) moonshine alcohol; illicit alcohol. (cf *gongo, moshi*)
plagi *n* (*n*) plug: *Plagi cheche*, spark plug. (Eng)
plani *n* (*n*) plan, map, chart: *Plani ya nyumba*, the plan of a house. (Eng)
plasta *n* (*n*) 1. plaster; adhesive tape: *Tia plasta*, put a plaster on. 2. gypsum; plaster of Paris. 3. a pasty preparation spread on cloth and applied to the body as a curative or counter irritant.
plastiki *n* (*n*) plastic (cf *sandarusi*) (Eng)
plau *n* (*n*) plough (Eng)
ploti *n* (*n*) plot; a piece of land (Eng)
po¹ *interj* (also *poo*) 1. an expletive of contempt. (cf *yasini! poko!*) 2. an expletive of spitting.
po² *cop. vt* (of place to indicate definiteness) be here: *Yeye yupo nyumbani*, he is at home. *Yeye hayupo*, he is not there. *Ndipo alipo*, that is where he is. *Alikuwapo*, he was there.
po³ *pron* (*rel marker*) (of time and place) when, where: *Alipokuja*, when he came. *Alipokwenda*, where he went.
po.a¹ *vi* (of food, etc.) become cool; get cool: *Chakula kimepoa*, the food has cooled. Prep. *po.le.a* St. *po.lek.a* Cs. *po.z.a* (cf *zizima*)
po.a² *vi* see *pona*. Cs. *po.z.a*
po.a³ *vt* see *pora*
po.a⁴ *vi* (of persons, etc.) become placid, get cool: *Alikuwa na hasira lakini sasa amepoa*, he was angry but now he has cooled down. Prep. *po.le.a* St. *po.lek.a* Cs. *po.z.a* (cf *stakiri, tulia, tabaradi*)
poa⁵ *interj* an expletive used to calm someone who has undergone a misfortune, etc.; cool down!
pochi¹ *n* (*ma-*) 1. purse, wallet. (cf *kibeti, kikoba*) 2. (*colloq*) money. (cf *fedha*)

pochi² *n* (*ma-*) a sort of chain bangle worn on the wrist by some women; a wide bracelet.
pochopocho *n* (*n*) see *mapochopocho*
poda (also *podari*) *n* (*n*) face powder. (Eng)
podari *n* (*n*) see *poda*
podini (also *pudini*) *n* (*n*) pudding (Eng)
podo *n* (*n*) quiver, sheath, arrow-case. (cf *pongono, ziaka*)
podo.a *vt* put on cosmetics; put make-up. Prep. *podo.le.a* St. *podo.lek.a* Cs. *podo.lesh.a* Ps. of Prep. *podo.lew.a* Rp. *podo.an.a* (cf *kwatua, para*)
pofu¹ *adj* blind, visionless, sightless: *Amekuwa pofu*, he has become blind.
pofu² *adj* (used of grain, etc.) seedless: *Iliki pofu*, seedless cardamom.
pofu³ *n* (*n*) (*zool*) eland; a kind of antelope with spirally twisted horns which grow straight back on a plane with the head. (cf *mbunju*)

pofu

pofu⁴ *adj* (of a fruit) lacking sth inside.
pofu.a *vt* 1. blind; cause blindness, spoil sight; ruin sight: *Walimpofua macho*, they blinded him. 2. (of balloon, etc.) remove air by pressing with a needle, hands, etc. against sth; deflate: *Mtoto alilipofua bofu lake*, the child deflated his balloon. 3. bleed. Prep. *pofu.li.a* St. *pofu.k.a* Cs. *pofu.sh.a* Ps. of Prep.

pofu.liw.a Rp. *pofu.an.a*
pofuk.a *vi* become blind. Prep. *pofuk.i.a* St. *pofuk.ik.a* Cs. *pofuk.ish.a*
pofush.a *vt* cause sby blindness; blind. Prep. *pofush.i.a* St. *pofush.ik.a* Ps. *pofush.w.a* Rp. *pofush.an.a*
pogo.a (also *bogoa, pagua, pelea*) *vt* lop off; prune branches or leaves off a tree: *Mfanyakazi wangu aliyapogoa matawi ya miti kwenye bustani,* my worker lopped off the branches of the trees in the garden. Prep. *pogo.le.a* St. *pogo.k.a* Cs. *pogo.lesh.a* Ps. of Prep. *pogo.lew.a* Rp. *pogo.an.a* (cf *chenga, kata*)
pogoo *n* (*ma-*) 1. a cut-off branch of a tree usu a fresh one; tree branch. 2. coconut palm leaf for making a palm leaf basket.
pointi *n* (*n*) 1. point; a scoring unit in studies, games, etc. 2. point; an impressive or telling argument, suggestion, etc: *Ametoa pointi nzuri,* he has given a good point. (Eng)
poja.a *vi* (used of a swell, etc.) shrink, contract; become smaller: *Miguu ya mgonjwa imeanza kupojaa baada ya kuvimba kwa muda kidogo,* the legs of the patient have started to shrink after they had been swollen for some time. Prep. *poja.li.a* St. *poja.lik.a* Cs. *poja.z.a* Ps. *poja.w.a* (cf *nywea, pwea*)
pojo *n* (*n*) (*bot*) green gram. (cf *choroko, chooko*)
pok.a *vt* snatch, steal, rob; take sth by force or without permission: *Wezi walipoka bidhaa nyingi dukani,* the thieves stole many goods from the shop. Prep. *pok.e.a* St. *pok.ek.a* Cs. *pok.esh.a* Ps. *pok.w.a* Rp. *pok.an.a* (cf *iba, pora*)
poke.a *vt* 1. receive, obtain, acquire: *Mwanafunzi alipokea zawadi,* the student received a present. 2. greet, welcome, bid welcome to: *Alinipokea vizuri kwake, he welcomed me warmly at his place.* (cf *karibisha, lahaki*) 3. receive sth from sby at his own

permission 4. assist someone to deliver a load, etc. Prep. *poke.le.a* St. *poke.lek.a* Cs. *poke.sh.a* and *poke.z.a* Ps. *poke.w.a* Ps. of Prep. *poke.lew.a* Rp. *poke.an.a*
pokezana *vi* 1. take turns; alternate: *Walifanya kazi ya kulinda duka kwa kupokezana,* they did the work of guarding the shop in turns. 2. pass from hand to hand; work in relay: *Mbio za kupokezana vijiti,* relay race.
poko *interj* an exclamation of contempt on sby or sth.
pokony.a *vt* snatch, rob; take sth by force: *Alinipokonya kitabu,* he snatched a book from me. Prep. *pokony.e.a* St. *pokony.ek.a* Cs. *pokony.esh.a* Ps. *pokony.w.a,* be snatched e.g. *Mtalii alipokonywa kipochi,* the tourist had her wallet snatched. Rp. *pokony.an.a* (cf *poka*)
-pole¹ *adj* gentle, soft, meek: *Yeye ni mpole,* he is gentle. (cf *rahimu, taratibu*)
pole² *interj* an expletive for expressing sorrow or condolences towards someone after an accident, bad news or other misfortune; Sorry! My sympathy! *Pole kwa kufiwa na baba yako,* my sympathy to you following the death of your father.
pole³ *n* (*n*) condolences: *Nilikwenda kuwapa pole wafiwa,* I went to send my condolences to the bereaved.
pole⁴ (also *polepole*) *adv* slowly, gradually. (*prov*) *Mwenda pole hajikwai,* he who goes slowly will not stumble i.e. he who is careful in his work, will succeed.
pole.a *vt* get the necessities of life by working casually: *Amekuwa akipolea kwa miaka mingi sasa,* he has been working casually for many years now. St. *pole.k.a* Cs. *pole.sh.a*
polepole *adv* see *pole⁴*
polio *n* (*n*) (*med*) an infectious disease esp of children caused by a virus inflammation of the spine; polio: *Ugonjwa wa polio,* polio. (Eng)

polisemi n (n) (sem) polysemy; an item that contains several meanings e.g. *panda*, climb; *panda*, grow, plant; *panda*, catapult, slingshot; *panda*, bugle, an animal's horn; *panda*, 'rise' as in the case of a price of a commodity. (Eng)

polisi n (wa-) police: *Askari polisi*, policeman/policewoman. *Kituo cha polisi*, police station. (Eng)

pombe n (n) 1. a locally brewed beer. 2. any intoxicant.

pombo n (n) (bot) the fresh green leaves of *Fagara olitoria* (*Rutac*) used as a vegetable.

pomboje.a vi (of bodily organs) become paralysed; be numbed: *Mkono wake wa kushoto umepombojea*, his left arm is paralysed. St. **pomboje.k.a** Cs. **pomboje.sh.a** Ps. **pomboje.w.a** (cf *pooza*)

pomboo n (n) (zool) dolphin (cf *fulusi, panji*)

pomo.a vt 1. pacify, calm: *Nilimpomoa alipokuwa akigombana na mwenyeduka*, I calmed him when he was quarrelling with a shopkeeper. (cf *tuliza, liwaza*) 2. disarray, disorganize, displace: *Mtoto wangu mdogo alizipomoa faili kwenye meza*, my small child disorganized the files on the table. (cf *pangua*) 3. see *ponoa*. Prep. **pomo.le.a** St. **pomo.k.a** Cs. **pomo.sh.a** Ps. of Prep. **pomo.lew.a** Rp. **pomo.an.a**.

pomoni adv filled to the brim, in abundance: *Machungwa yamejaa pomoni sokoni siku hizi*, oranges are in abundance at the market these days. (cf *chekwa, tele, nomi, belele*)

pon.a (also *poa*) vi 1. recuperate, convalesce, heal; recover from illness, get well: *Mgonjwa wangu amepona*, my patient has recovered. (cf *pongea, inukia*) 2. escape, survive; become safe, be saved, be rescued: *Abiria wachache tu walipona kwenye ajali ya ndege*, only a few passengers survived in the plane crash. (idm) *Ponea chupuchupu*, be saved narrowly. 3. make a living; subsist. Prep. **pon.e.a** St. **pon.ek.a** Cs. **pon.esh.a** Ps. **pon.w.a**

pond.a vt 1. pound, crush, squash, pulp. (cf *twanga, funda*) 2. (fig) discredit, defame, dishonour: *Aliniponda mbele za watu*, he discredited me in public. 3. (idm) *Ponda mali*, squander money; waste resources. Prep. **pond.e.a** St. **pond.ek.a** Cs. **pond.esh.a** Ps. **pond.w.a** Rp. **pond.an.a**

pondea n (n) shoe maker's mallet. (cf *mnguri, nguri*)

pondek.a vi be dented, be indented. Prep. **pondek.e.a** St. **pondek.ek.a**

ponge.a vi convalesce; recover from illness, disaster, etc: *Mgonjwa wake sasa amepongea*, his patient has now recovered, St. **ponge.k.a** Cs. **ponge.sh.a** and **ponge.z.a** Ps. **ponge.w.a**

pongez.a[1] vt see *pongea*

pongez.a[2] vt congratulate, felicitate, compliment: *Alinipongeza kwa kufaulu kwenye mtihani*, he congratulated me on passing the examination. Prep. **pongez.e.a** St. **pongez.ek.a** Ps. **pongez.w.a** Rp. **pongez.an.a** (cf *hongea*)

pongezi n (n) felicitation, congratulation, well-wishing: *Pongezi za dhati*, sincere congratulations.

pongo n (n) (zool) bushbuck (cf *mbawala, kulungu*)

pongono n (n) quiver, sheath, arrow-case. (cf *podo, riaka, ziaka*)

pongoo[1] n (n) a bracelet containing thick beads, worn by children and women.

pongoo[2] n (n) a noose of rope tied around the neck of a tame animal.

pongoo[3] n (n) coconut palm leaf for making a palm leaf basket. (cf *pogoo*)

poni[1] n (n) pawn; anything given as security as for debt, performance of an action, etc. (Eng)

poni[2] n (n) (zool) a hatched machine fowl. (cf *kukuboi*)

pono *n* (*n*) (*zool*) 1. wrasse, parrotfish; a kind of tropical ocean fish of the families *Labridae* and *Scaridae*, having various colours usu green, blue or grey, found generally on coral reefs or rocky substrate. 2. (*idm*) *Usingizi wa mnono*, a deep sleep.

pono.a¹ (also *pomoa*) *vt* bark; strip off as in the case of the bark from a tree or sisal; get the fibres out of a tree or sisal, etc.: *Aliuponoa mkonge*, he stripped off the fibres from the sisal. Prep. *pono.le.a* St *pono.k.a* Cs. *pono.sh.a* Ps. of Prep. *pono.lew.a* Rp. *pono.an.a*

pono.a² *vt* 1. clean a newly-born baby. 2. punish sby inorder to give him a lesson. Prep. *pono.lo.a* St. *pono.k.a* Cs. *pono.lesh.a* Rp. *pono.an.a*

ponuo *n* (*n*) act of stripping off the bark from a tree, etc.

ponya¹ *n* (*n*) 1. medicine that makes someone get well; cure, remedy. 2. an available fruit, obtained easily.

pony.a² *vt* cure, heal; restore to health. Prep. *pony.e.a* St. *pony.ek.a* Cs. *pony.esh.a* Ps. *pony.w.a* Rp. *pony.an.a* (cf *tibu*)

ponyeto (also *punyeto*) *n* (*n*) masturbation: *Piga ponyeto*, masturbate.

ponyaponya *adv* narrowly, nearby, just about. (cf *nusura*)

ponyok.a *vt, vi* 1. slip from grasp; slide accidentally; glide: *Ndege ameniponyoka*, the bird has slipped from my hands. 2. escape: *Mwizi ameponyoka katika mikono ya askari*, the thief has escaped from the police hands. Prep. *ponyok.e.a* St. *ponyok.ek.a* Cs. *ponyok.esh.a* Ps. *ponyok.w.a* (cf *toroka, dondoka, chopoka*)

ponz.a¹ *vt, vi* put oneself into trouble, danger, etc.; risk, imperil: *Alijiponza kwa kumkashifu rais hadharani*, he put himself into trouble by discrediting the president in public. (*prov*) *Mti huponzwa na tundale*, a person can run into problems by the actions of his child. Prep. *ponz.e.a* St. *ponz.ek.a* Cs. *ponz.esh.a* Ps. *ponz.w.a* Rp. *ponz.an.a* (cf *hizi, hatarisha*)

ponza² *n* (*n*) an issue or sth that puts someone into problems or difficulties.

poo *interj* see *po¹*

poopoo *n* (*n*) see *popoo*

pooz.a¹ *vi* 1. be paralysed; be numbed: *Mkono wake umepooza*, his arm is paralysed. (cf *pombojea*) 2. (of fruits, etc.) be spoiled, be tasteless; lose beauty, appearance, etc.: *Embe hili imepooza*, this mango is spoiled Prep. *pooz.ek.a* Cs. *pooz.esh.a* Ps. *pooz.w.a* (cf *haribika, vunda*)

pooza² *n* (*ma-*) anything such as a fruit that is spoiled or has gone awry because of losing certain vital organs: *Yale si maembe bali ni mapooza*, those are not good mangoes but are spoiled ones.

pop.a *vt* tie tightly; close tightly: *Walipopa mizigo yao ili isipate kufunguka*, they secured their luggage so that they did not fall open. Prep. *pop.e.a* St. *pop.ek.a* Cs. *pop.ez.a* Ps. *pop.w.a*. Rp. *pop.an.a*

popo *n* (*n*) 1. (*zool*) bat. 2. moth (cf *kipepeo*)

popo

popo.a (also *pupua*) *vt* 1. knock down a fruit from a tree with a stone, stick, etc.: *Alipopoa maembe mengi*, he knocked down many mangoes from the tree. (cf *angua, pukusa, lenga*) 2. hurl sth with the purpose of hitting someone: *Watoto walimpopoa mwendawazimu kwa mawe*, the children hurled stones at the madman. Prep. *popo.le.a* St. *popo.k.a* Cs. *popo.sh.a* Ps. of Prep. *popo.lew.a* Rp. *popo.an.a* (cf *rusha*)

popoo (also *poopoo*) *n* (*n*) (*bot*) betel nut, area nut; an egg-shaped fruit whose seeds are astringent and are useful in dysentry and for expelling worms in dogs. (Pers)

popot.a (also *bobota*) *vt* hit hard; beat severely: *Mwalimu alimpopota mwanafunzi kwa ukosefu wa nidhamu*, the teacher beat the student severely for misconduct. Prep. ***popot.e.a*** St. ***popot.ek.a*** Cs. ***popot.esh.a*** Ps. ***popot.w.a*** Rp. ***popot.an.a*** (cf *fufuta, kung'uta*)

popoto.a (also *pepetua*) *vt* 1. wrench, twist, strain, tear: *Mwizi aliupopotoa mkono wa mwenye nyumba*, the thief twisted the arm of the owner of the house. Prep. ***popoto.le.a*** St. ***popoto.k.a*** Cs. ***popoto.sh.a*** Ps. of Prep. ***popoto.lew.a*** Rp. ***popoto.an.a*** (cf *nyonga, sopotoa, sokota*) 2. (of the shape of the body) become spoiled because of illness.

por.a[1] (also *poa*) *vt* rob, thieve, steal by force: *Walipora bidhaa nyingi kwa mwenye duka*, they stole a lot of goods from the shopkeeper. Prep. ***por.e.a*** St. ***por.ek.a*** Cs. ***por.esh.a*** Ps. ***por.w.a*** Rp. ***por.an.a*** (cf *pokonya, nyakua, iba, nyang'anya*)

pora[2] *n* (*n*) (*zool*) cockerel; a young rooster.

porapora *n* (*ma-*) (*zool*) honey badger. (cf *nyegere*)

pori *n* (*ma-*) 1. wilderness, wasteland, wilds. 2. bush, thicket, scrub. (cf *msitu, mwitu*)

poroja *adj* watery, soggy: *Wali alioupika ulikuwa poroja*, the rice that she cooked was soggy. (cf *majimaji, chapachapa*)

porojo *n* (*n*) gossip, chitchat, rigmarole; idle chatter, idle talk. (cf *soga, gumzo*)

poromo.a (also *vomoa*) *vt* 1. demolish; pull down, tear down: *Serikali iliviporomoa vibanda vya wachuuzi*, the government demolished hawkers' huts. 2. cause things to fall down disorderly. Prep. ***poromo.le.a*** St. ***poromo.k.a*** Cs. ***poromo.sh.a*** Ps. of Prep. ***poromo.lew.a*** Rp. ***poromo.an.a*** (cf *jengua, bomoa*)

poromok.a *vi* collapse, fall down, cascade: *Jengo limeporomoka*, the building has collapsed. *Utawala wa kiongozi uliporomoka*, the regime of the leader collapsed. *Biashara yao iliporomoka vibaya mwaka jana*, their business collapsed badly last year. (cf *anguka, bomoka*) Prep.***poromok.e.a*** St. ***poromok.ek.a*** Cs. ***poromok.esh.a***

poromoko *n* (*ma-*) precipice, steep; a place of sudden descent: *Maporomoko ya maji*, water falls; cataract, cascade. *Maporomoko ya theluji na mawe*, avalanche. (cf *korongo, genge*)

poromosh.a *vt* cause/make sby/sth collapse or fall down; pull down, tear down; cause sth to tumble down: *Waliyaporomosha mabaki ya jengo chakavu*: They pulled down the remains of the decrepit building. *Jeshi liliuporomosha utawala wa kiimla*, the army toppled the dictatorial regime. Prep. ***poromosh.e.a*** St. ***poromosh.ek.a*** Ps. ***poromosh.w.a*** Rp. ***poromosh.an.a*** (cf *angusha*)

pos.a[1] *vt* propose marriage to a girl; ask in marriage; become a suitor for. Prep. ***pos.e.a*** St. ***pos.ek.a*** Cs. ***pos.esh.a*** Ps. ***pos.w.a*** (cf *chumbia*)

posa[2] (also *poso*) *n* (*n*) proposal of marriage; wooing.

pos.a[3] *vt* give food to an animal that is not free. Prep. ***pos.ea*** St. ***pos.ek.a*** Cs. ***pos.esh.a*** Ps. ***pos.w.a***

posho *n* (*n*) 1. bursary, allowance; students' grant: *Wanafunzi wa chuo kikuu bado hawajapokea posho kwa mwaka huu*, the university students have not yet received bursaries for this year. *Posho ya jamala*, entertainment allowance. *Posho ya kujikimu*, subsistence allowance. 2. lunch.

poso *n* (*n*) see *posa*[2]

posta *n* (*n*) post office. (Eng)

post.i *vt* post, mail: *Niliiposti barua yake kwa njia ya rejista*, I posted his letter by registered mail. Prep. ***post.i.a*** St. ***post.ik.a*** Cs. ***post.ish.a*** Ps. ***post.iw.a*** Rp. ***post.i.an.a*** (cf *tuma*) (Eng)

pot.a *vt* twist the strands of flax, cotton, etc.; twine: *Alizipota kamba*, he twined the ropes. Prep. ***pot.e.a*** St. ***pot.ek.a*** Cs. ***pot.esh.a*** Ps. ***pot.w.a*** Rp. ***pot.an.a*** (cf *sokota, singa*)

-pote¹ *adj, pron* form of *-ote* used for PA class meaning "everywhere." "all": *Mahala pote*, the whole place. *Pote ni pangu*, the whole place is mine.

pote² *n* (*ma-*) group, team, party: *Nililiona pote la madaktari*, I saw a team of doctors. (cf *tapo, rubaa*)

pote.a *vi* 1. be lost, be missing: *Kitabu chake kimepotea*, his book is missing. (*syn*) *Akili imempotea*, he has lost his senses. (cf *toweka, adimika*) 2. (*fig*) go astray; be ruined, be misguided: *Zamani, alikuwa kijana mzuri lakini sasa amepotea*, in the past, he was a nice young man but now he is spoilt. 3. (*idm*) *Potelea mbali*, to hell. Prep. ***pote.le.a*** St. ***pote.lek.a*** Cs. ***pote.z.a*** Rp. of Cs. ***pote.z.an.a*** Ps. of Prep. ***pote.lew.a*** Rp ***pote.an.a***

-potevu *adj* 1. depraved, misguided, misled, subverted, perverted: *Mtu mpotevu*, a perveted person. *Mwanampotevu*, stray child. 2. causing others to go astray.

potez.a *vt* lose sth: *Amepoteza kalamu yake*, he has lost his pen. *Poteza akili*, become mad. *Poteza fahamu*, lose consciousness. Prep. ***potez.e.a*** St. ***potez.ek.a*** Cs. ***potez.esh.a*** Ps. ***potez.w.a*** Rp, ***potez.an.a***

poto.a¹ *vt* 1. pervert, spoil: *Potoa maneno*, pervert words. 2. pervert, corrupt; lead astray: *Wameipotoa tabia yake*, they have ruined his character. St. ***poto.k.a*** Cs. ***poto.sh.a***, debauch, corrupt, pervert; lead astray e.g. *Walimpotosha kijana yule*, they corrupted that young man. Prep. ***poto.le.a*** St. ***poto.k.a*** Ps. ***poto.sh.a*** Cs. of Prep. ***poto.lew.a*** Rp. ***poto.an.a***

poto.a² *vt* tie poles for the construction of a ceiling or wall. Prep. ***poto.le.a*** St.

poto.k.a Cs. ***poto.sh.a*** Ps. of Prep. ***poto.lew.a*** Rp. ***poto.an.a***

-potofu *adj* see *potovu*

potok.a *vi* be misguided, be perverted, be spoiled. Prep. ***potok.e.a*** St. ***potok.ek.a*** Cs. ***potok.esh.a***

potosha *vt* see potoa¹. Prep. ***potosh.e.a*** St. ***potosh.ek.a*** Cs. ***potosh.w.a*** Rp. ***potosh.an.a***

-potovu (also *potofu*) *adj* 1. wrong, bad, misleading: *Dhana potovu*, a misleading idea. *Njia potovu*, a wrong path. *Mila potovu*, bad culture. *Kauli potovu*, a misleading statement. *Mtazamo potovu*, a misleading outlook. *Hisia potovu*, wrong feeling. *Wazo potovu*, a misleading idea. 2. spoiled, corrupted, perverted: *Kijana mpotovu*, a spoiled young man. *Yeye ni mpotovu wa mali*, he is extravagant. 3. causing others to become perverted or spoiled.

povu *n* (*ma-*) foam, froth, bubble: *Povu la sabuni*, soap lather. *Povu la bahari*, foam on the sea. *Povu la hewa*, airhole. *Fanya povu*, foam; produce froth.

poz.a¹ *vi* 1. cool, make cool. 2. comfort, soothe: *Alimpoza rafiki yake kwa kumpa maneno mazuri*, he comforted his friend by telling him nice words. Prep. ***poz.e.a*** St. ***poz.ek.a*** Ps. ***poz.w.a*** Rp. ***poz.an.a*** (cf *tuliza, liwaza*)

poza² *n* (*n*) recompense; payment given to someone to soothe him or her for having suffered a wrongdoing. (cf *jaza, fidia*)

pozi¹ *n* (*ma-*) pomposity, airs and graces, swaggering, boasting: *Hutembea kwa mapozi*, he walks with a swagger. (cf *madaha, maringo, mikogo*)

pozi² *n* (*ma-*) a string of uncooked fish. (cf *shazi*)

presha *n* (*n*) pressure, stress, hard time: *Ugonjwa wa presha*, blood pressure. (cf *shinikizo*) (Eng)

profesa *n* (*ma-*) professor: *Profesa mshiriki*, associate professor. (cf *mufti*) (Eng)

programu *n* (*n*) 1. programme; a planned series of events or performances. 2. a scheduled broadcast on radio or

television; programme. 3. (*comput*) a series of instructions that can be put into a computer in order to make it perform an operation; programme.
projekta *n* (*n*) projector (Eng)
promota *n* (*ma-*) promoter (Eng)
propaganda *n* (*n*) propaganda, rumours. (Eng)
propela *n* (*n*) propeller (cf *rafadha*) (Eng)
Protestanti *n* (*n*) Protestant (Eng)
protini *n* (*n*) protein (Eng)
protokali *n* (*n*) protocol: *Protokali ya kidiplomasia*, diplomatic protocol. (Eng)
protoni *n* (*n*) proton (Eng)
pu *interj* an exclamation expressing the act of a heavy object falling on sand, etc.
pua¹ *n* (*n*) nose: *Puani*, from the nose. (*syns*) *Kata pua uunge wajihi*, you do sth which does not help you personally but you do it for the sake of someone else. *Tokea puani*, an expression used to describe someone who has met unpleasant situation after committing a wrongdoing. *Semea puani*, speak with a nasal voice.
pua² *n* (*n*) (*naut*) reef cringle in matting sail.
pua³ *n* (*n*) (*idms*) *Chuma cha pua*, steel.
pu.a⁴ *vt* rub the body with the palm of the hand by using oil or some other ointment: *Aliupua mwili wake kwa mafuta ya karafuu*, he rubbed her body with clove oil. Prep. **pu.li.a** St. **pu.lik.a** Cs. **pu.lish.a** Ps. of Prep. **pu.liw.a** Rp. **pu.an.a**
pu.a⁵ *vt* (during eating) finish the whole lot; finish everything: *Aliupua muhogo wote aliopewa kula*, he finished all of the cassava he was given to eat. Prep. **pu.li.a** St. **pu.lik.a** Cs. **pu.lish.a** Ps. of Prep. **pu.liw.a**
puchi *n* (*n*) stucco; plaster of cement used for surfacing or smoothing walls or ceilings: *Piga puchi*, put on stucco.
puchu.a *vt* see *pujua*
pudini (*also podini*) *n* (*n*) pudding (Eng)

pufya *n* (*n*) a kind of medicine believed to strengthen someone such that his strength eventually becomes like that of a lion; energizing medicine: *Chanjia pufya*, treat someone medically so that he acquires this kind of strength
pugi *n* (*n*) (*zool*) blue-spotted wood-dove. (cf *hua*)
puju *n* (*n*) (*zool*) unicornfish; a kind of saltwater fish (subfamily *Nasinae*) having an oblong or ovoid and compressed body with a small mouth and many rays, found usu in shallow water on coral reefs or along rocky shores. (cf *kidui*)
puju.a *vt, vi* 1. deface, bruise, scratch: *Alipoanguka kwenye baiskeli, aliupujua uso wake*, when he fell from the bicycle, he bruised his face. 2. (*fig*) lead a shameful life; lead a mean life: *Alijipujua katika maisha yake baada ya kushiriki kwenye ulevi*, he led a shameful life after being involved in drinking. Prep. **puju.li.a** St. **puju.k.a** Cs. **puju.sh.a** Ps. of Prep. **puju.liw.a** Rp. **puju.an.a**
-pujufu *adj* brazen, impudent, shameless, abased, brush, mean: *Mtu mpujufu*, a shameless person.
pukachaka *interj* an expletive of contempt. (cf *po! yasini!*)
puku (also *buku*) *n* (*n*) (*zool*) a kind of big rat; cane rat.
pukuchu.a *vt* strip the grains off a cob of maize; husk the grains of a cob of maize: *Aliyapukuchua mahindi kwenye gunzi*, he stripped the grains off a cob of maize. Prep. **pukuchu.li.a** St. **pukuchu.k.a** Cs. **pukuchu.sh.a** Ps. of Prep. **pukuchu.liw.a** (cf *koboa, goboa, kokoa*)
pukupuku *adv* 1. plentifully, abundantly; in large numbers: *Vita vilipotokea, watu walikufa pukupuku*, when the war occurred, people died in large numbers. 2. jointly, together: *Maembe yalianguka pukupuku kutoka mtini*, mangoes fell together from the tree. (cf *nomi, tele*)

pukurush.a *vt* snub, disregard, brush aside: *Alilipukurusha shauri langu nililompa,* he brushed aside the advice I gave him. Prep. ***pukurush.i.a*** St. ***pukurush.ik.a*** Ps. ***pukurush.w.a*** Rp. ***purukush.an.a*** (cf *dharau*)

pukusa[1] *n* (*n*) 1. a present given to a young girl when she reaches puberty or comes out of the initiation school. 2. (*bot*) silk fig; a kind of banana with short fingers and that is inclined to be astringent unless fully ripe.

pukus.a[2] *vt* award a present; reward sby for his good deeds: *Nilimpukusa kwa kukiokota kikoba changu,* I rewarded him for picking up my wallet. Prep. ***pukus.i.a*** St. ***pukus.ik.a*** Cs. ***pukus.ish.a*** Ps. ***pukus.w.a***

pukus.a[3] *vt* (of fruits, flowers, etc.) cause to fall by shaking a tree. Prep. ***pukus.i.a*** St. ***pukus.ik.a*** Cs. ***pukus.ish.a*** Ps. ***pukus.w.a*** Rp. ***pukus.an.a***

pukus.a[4] *vt* bore as insects do in the case of grain, wood, etc. Prep. ***pukus.i.a*** St. ***pukus.ik.a*** Cs. ***pukus.ish.a*** Ps. ***pukus.w.a***

pukus.a[5] *vt* (*naut*) set the sail blow with the wind by untying the sheet. Prep. ***pukus.i.a*** St. ***pukus.ik.a*** Cs. ***pukus.ish.a*** Ps. ***pukus.w.a*** (cf *pupusa*)

pukut.a *vt* strip leaves from a tree or pluck feathers from an animal: *Aliyapukuta majani ya mbirimbi,* he stripped the leaves of a cucumber tree. Prep. ***pukut.i.a*** St. ***pukut.ik.a*** Cs. ***pukut.ish.a*** Ps. ***pukut.w.a*** Rp. ***pukut.an.a*** (cf *ondoa*)

pukute *n* (*n*) used in the expression: *Wali pukute,* rice that is cooked such that every grain is loose and separate.

pukutik.a *vi* fall, drop down: *Majani yalikuwa yanapukutika kutoka kwenye mti,* the leaves were falling from the tree. Prep. ***pukutik.ia*** St. ***pukutik.ik.a*** Cs. ***pukutik.ish.a***, let fall, drop off.

pukutish.a *vt* see *pukutika*. Prep. ***pukutish.i.a*** St. ***pukutish.ik.a*** Ps. ***pukutish.w.a*** Rp. ***pukutish.an.a***

pula *n* (*n*) simpleton, imbecile; a stupid person. (cf *fala, mjinga*)

puleki *n* (*n*) sequin, spangle; a small piece of bright metal or tinfoil or anything like scales of fish used for decoration.

pulik.a *vt* (used very often in poetry) listen. Prep. ***pulik.i.a*** St. ***pulik.ik.a*** Cs. ***pulik.iz.a*** Ps. ***pulik.w.a*** Rp. ***pulik.an.a*** (cf *sikia, sikiliza*)

puliz.a *vt* 1. blow with the mouth: *Puliza moto,* blow up a fire. (cf *pepea*) 2. spray: *Puliza dawa ya mbu,* spray mosquito killer. 3. (in fishing) play out a fishing line: *Puliza mshipi,* play out a fishing line, after a fish is hooked. Prep. ***puliz.i.a*** St. ***puliz.ik.a*** Ps. ***puliz.w.a***

pulizi.a *vt* 1. blow into, blow sth up. 2. spray on 3. play out a fishing line, etc. Prep. ***pulizi.li.a*** St. ***pulizi.k.a*** Cs. ***pulizi.sh.a*** Ps. ***pulizi.w.a*** Rp. ***pulizi.an.a***

pulizo *n* (*ma-*) balloon (cf *bofu, puto*)

pum.a *vi* 1. (of heart, pulse, etc.) throb, pulsate, pulpitate: *Moyo wake ulikuwa unampuma kwa wasiwasi,* her heart was throbbing with anxiety. (cf *hema, pwita, tweta*) 2. (of a wound, headache, etc.) smart, throb: *Jipu lake lilikuwa likimpuma usiku kucha,* his boil was throbbing with pain the whole night. (cf *pwita*)

pumba *n* (*bot*) 1. outer covering of corn, etc.; chaff, husk, shuck. (cf *kumvi, wishwa*) 2. (*med*) smegma; a cheeselike foul-smelling sebaceous secretion that accumulates under the foreskin or around the clitoris; (cf *chicha*) 3. leftovers of grains in the mouth after being chewed.

pumba.a[1] *vi* 1. be foolish; be silly; be weak-minded: *Amepumbaa sana darasani,* he is very weak in the class. 2. be speechless because of fear, astonishment, etc.; be non-plussed, be dumbfounded, be mystified: *Alipumbaa wakati sisi tulikuwa tukizungunza,*

he remained speechless while we were talking. Prep. *pumba.li.a* Cs. *pumba.z.a* (cf *zimbaa, duwaa*)
pumba.a² *vi* (of grain plant) flourish without bearing anything. Prep. *pumba.li.a* St. *pumba.lik.a*
pumbao (also *mzubao*) *n (n)* astonishment, stupefaction, amazement: *Alipigwa na pumbao*, he was stuck dumb with amazement. (cf *mzubao, mshangao*)
-pumbavu *adj* stupid, ignorant, slow-witted: *Mtu mpumbavu*, a stupid person.
pumbaz.a *vt* 1. amaze, astound, flabbergast 2. make a fool of; befool, beguile. Prep. *pumbaz.i.a* St. *pumbaz.ik.a* Cs. *pumbaz.ish.a* Ps. *pumbaz.w.a* Rp, *pumbaz.an.a*
pumbu *n (n)* 1. *(anat)* testicle, scrotum. (cf *korodani, kende, hasua*) 2. hernia, hydrocele, orchitis (cf *mshipa, busha*)
Pumbuji *n (n)* *(geog)* ancient town south of Bagamoyo, Tanzania.
pumu *n (n)* *(med)* a chronic chest illness characterized by wheezing, coughing, difficulty in breathing and a suffocating feeling; asthma.
pumu.a¹ *vi* 1. breathe; draw breath. (cf *tweta, pwita*) 2. relax, rest; find relief: *Alikuwa hana nafasi ya kupumua kwa kazi nyingi*, he had no time to rest because of excessive work. (cf *pumzika*) Prep. *pumu.li.a* St. *pumu.lik.a* Cs. *pumu.lish.a* Ps. of Prep. *pumu.liw.a* Rp. *pumu.an.a* (cf *pumzika*)
pumu.a² *vt* punish because of non-payment of fees especially in the case of students in schools. Prep. *pumu.li.a* St. *pumu.lik.a* Cs. *pumu.lish.a* Ps. of Prep. *pumu.liw.a*
pumzi *n (n)* 1. breath, respiration, breathing: *Vuta pumzi*, take breath, breathe in, draw in breath; inhale. *Shusha pumzi*, breathe out; exhale. *Kukata pumzi*, breathe with difficulty. (cf *hewa*) 2. *(idm) Pumzi juu*, breathe with fear or anxiety.
pumzik.a *vi* rest, relax; take a break. Prep. *pumzik.i.a* St. *pumzik.ik.a* Cs.

pumzik.ish.a (cf *sona, pumua*)
pumziko *n (ma-)* see *mapumziko*
pumzish.a *vt* 1. give leave/vacation, etc. 2. rest machines, etc. Prep. *pumzish.i.a* St. *pumzish.ik.a* Ps. *pumzish.w.a* Rp. *pumzish.an.a*
pun.a¹ *vt* 1. wipe off sweat; rub oneself down: *Alijipuna jasho baada ya kumaliza kucheza mpira*, he wiped off the sweat after playing soccer. 2. peel, strip off, scrape off: *Puna ganda la mti*, strip the bark off a tree. *Puna ngozi*, scrape the skin. *Puna ndizi*, strip off bananas. *Puna nywele*, cut hair. *Puna katani*, decorticate sisal. Prep. *pun.i.a* St. *pun.ik.a* Cs. *pun.ish.a* Ps. *pun.w.a* Rp. *pun.an.a*
pun.a² *vt* play with hair or beards gently. Prep. *pun.i.a* St. *pun.ik.a* Cs. *pun.ish.a*
pun.a³ *vt, vi* get sth by deception. Prep. *pun.i.a* St. *pun.ik.a* Cs. *pun.ish.a*
punda¹ *n (n)* *(zool)* donkey: *Punda kihongwe*, a kind of wild donkey, *Punda maskati*, a large white donkey. *Punda milia*, zebra.
punda² *n (n)* a long chain worn around the leg marking the accession of local chiefdom in Tanzania mainland local dances.
punda³ *n (n)* a kind of banana whose stem is tall and green with few dark markings. The bunches are usu small with few hands. (cf *bokoboko*)
punde *adv* instantly, just now: *Hivi punde*, just now. *Punde si punde*, in a jiffy; in no time at all. *Ameondoka punde hivi*, he has just left. (cf *fajaa, mara*)
punga¹ *n (n)* a cluster of flowers found in a maize plant, etc. (cf *ngaa*)
pung.a² *vt* wave, sway, flap: *Punga mkono*, wave the arm i.e. as a sign of greeting. Prep. *pung.i.a* St. *pung.ik.a* Cs. *pung.ish.a* Ps. *pung.w.a* Ps. of Prep. *pung.iw.a* Rp. of Prep. *pung.i.an.a* (cf *ashiria, salimia*)
pung.a³ *vt (idms) Punga hewa*, get some fresh air. *Punga upepo*, get some fresh

air. Prep. *pung.i.a* St. *pung.ik.a* Cs. *pung.ish.a* Ps. *pung.w.a* Rp. of Prep. *pung.i.an.a*

pung.a⁴ *vt* (in witchcraft, etc.) exorcise; drive out or away an evil spirit by ritual prayers, incantations, etc.: *Punga pepo*, exorcise a spirit. *Punga shetani*, exorcise a devil. Prep. *pung.i.a* St. *pung.ik.a* Cs. *pung.ish.a* Ps. *pung.w.a* Rp. *pung.an.a*

pung.a⁵ *vi* (of the heat of the sun, etc.) relent, subside, decrease, lessen, dwindle, wither: *Jua kali limepunga*, the heat of the hot sun has relented. Prep. *pung.i.a* St. *pung.ik.a* Cs. *pung.ish.a* (cf *pungua, fifia*)

pungu¹ (also *mpato*) *n* (*n*) (*naut*) a float or other piece of wood used to show the position of a fishing net.

pungu² (also *kipungu*) *n* (*n*) (*zool*) eagle ray; a large batoid fish. (family *Myliobatidae*)

pungu³ *n* (*n*) (*zool*) Bateleur Eagle; a kind of bird resembling a batoid fish. It has a short tail in all plumages and has a sharp barking cry. *Terathopius ecaudatus*.

pungu.a *vi, vt* 1. fall short of what is required; be less. 2. diminish, abate, subside: *Baridi sasa imepungua*, the cold weather has now subsided. Prep. *pungu.li.a* St. *pungu.k.a* Cs. *pungu.z.a*

punguani *n* (*n*) an insane person, a mentally deficient person: *Yeye ni punguani*, he is an insane person. (cf *majinuni, afkani, chakramu, mwehu*)

-pungufu *adj* deficient, lacking, incomplete: *Mpungufu wa akili*, lacking in sanity. *Mwezi mpungufu*, an incomplete month i.e. one of 29 days or 28 days.

punguk.a *vi* decrease, diminish, get less/smaller: *Idadi ya watu katika kijiji chao imepunguka*, the population in their village has decreased. Prep. *punguk.i.a* St. *punguk.ik.a* Cs.

punguk.ish.a

punguz.a *vt* reduce, shorten, diminish: *Mfanyabiashara amepunguza bei ya sukari sasa*, the businessman has now reduced the price of sugar. Prep. *punguz.i.a* St. *punguz.ik.a* Cs. *punguz.ish.a* Ps. *punguz.w.a*

punguzo *n* (*ma-*) deduction, reduction, decrease, cutback.

pungwa¹ *n* (*n*) a kind of dance used in the exorcism of spirits; exorcising dance.

pungw.a² *vt* be exorcised; be driven (of an evil spirit or spirits) out or away by ritual prayers, incantations, etc. Prep. *pungw.i.a* St. *pungw.ik.a* Cs. *pungw.ish.a*

punj.a *vt* swindle by giving short measure or less than what is due: cheat on weight or measure: *Mwenye duka alimpunja mnunuzi kwa kumuuzia sukari kwa bei ya juu*, the shopkeeper swindled the buyer by overcharging him on the price of sugar. Prep. *punj.i.a* St. *punj.ik.a* Cs. *punj. ish.a* Ps. *punj.w.a* Rp. *punj.an.a* (cf *nyenga, leba, kopa*)

punje¹ *n* (*n*) (*bot*) 1. a single grain: *Punje ya mtama*, a grain of millet. *Punje ya mpunga*, a grain of rice (*pron*) *Punje moja ya mtama ni bora kuliko almasi*, a grain of millet is better than a diamond i.e. a grain of food is better than any other valuable even if it is a diamond. (cf *chembe, tumbe*) 2. a single bead.

punje² *n* (*n*) (*med*) ring worm. (cf *choa*)

punjo *n* (*ma-*) cut, reduction.

punju (also *punyu*) *n* (*n*) a poison prepared by wizards and said to be made from the head of a black snake, lizard and chameleon entrails.

punta *n* (*n*) running stitch; makeshift tailoring; tacking.

punye *n* (*ma-*) (*med*) ringworm especially on the head. (cf *bato*)

punyeto (also *ponyeto*) *n* (*n*) masturbation

punyu n (n) see *punju*
puo n (n) gossip, idle chatter, foolish talk: *Kile chote alichozungumza ni puo tu,* all he talked about was just gossip. (cf *porojo, soga, gumzo*)
pupa n (n) haste, rush, hurry: *Ana pupa sana akifanya kazi,* he is very hasty at work. (*prov*) *Mtaka yote kwa pupa, hukosa yote,* whoever wants everything will get nothing i.e. don't look for everything at one time; look for one and when you get it, look for another and so on.
pupu.a[1] *vt* see *popoa.* Prep. ***pupu.li.a*** St. ***pupu.k.a*** Cs. ***pupu.sh.a*** Ps. of Prep. ***pupu.liw.a*** Rp. ***pupu.an.a***
pupu.a[2] *vt* strip off leaves from the plants by pulling them with the hands: *Watoto waliyapupua majani ya mimea yangu,* the children stripped off the leaves of my plants by pulling them with their hands. Prep. ***pupu.li.a*** St. ***pupu.k.a*** Cs. ***pupu.sh.a*** Ps. of Prep. ***pupu.liw.a*** Rp. ***pupu.an.a*** (cf *pura*)
pupus.a *vt* (*naut*) set the sail to blow with the wind by untying the sheet. Prep. ***pupus.i.a*** St. ***pupus.ik.a*** Cs. ***pupus.ish.a*** Ps. ***pupus.w.a*** (cf *pukusa*)
pur.a *vt* 1. strip off leaves from the plants by pulling them with the hands. *Mkulima aliyapura majani ya vitawi vya mpera,* the farmer stripped the leaves off the guava tree by pulling them with the hands. 2. beat out hard as during washing clothes; rub hard in the hand as during washing clothes; pummel: *Alizifua nguo zake chafu kwa kuzipura,* he washed his dirty clothes by rubbing them hard with the hands. 3. knock down sth such as a fruit from a tree by throwing sticks or stones: *Watoto waliyapura mapera mtini,* the children knocked down guava fruits from the tree. Prep. ***pur.i.a*** St. ***pur.ik.a*** Cs. ***pur.ish.a*** Ps. ***pur.w.a*** (cf *popoa, angusha*)
pure n (n) dish made from boiled maize and cowpeas or French beans. (cf *kande*) (Hind)
puru[1] n (n) (*med*) piles, haemorrhoids. (cf *bawasili, futuri, kikundu*)
puru[2] n (*ma-*) broad trousers.
puru.a *vt* see *purura*
puruk.a *vi* soar, fly off; take flight as of birds or winged insects when startled: *Ndege alipuruka nilipojaribu kumkamata,* the bird flew off as I tried to catch it. Prep. ***puruk.i.a*** St. ***puruk.ik.a*** Cs. ***puruk.ish.a*** Ps. ***puruk.w.a***
purukush.a *vt* disdain, ignore; treat with contempt: *Nilimwita na akasikia lakini bado akajipurukusha,* I called him and he heard me but still he ignored me. Prep. ***purukush.i.a*** St. ***purukush.ik.a*** Ps. ***purukush.w.a*** Rp. ***purukush.an.a*** (cf *dharau, beza*)
purukushani[1] n (n) negligence, contempt, laxity: *Aliifanya kazi yangu kwa purukushani,* he did my work with negligence. (cf *uvivu, ulegevu, uzembe*)
purukushani[2] n (n) squabble, imbroglio, dispute, arguments. (cf *mzozo*)
purungo n (n) see *furungu*[2]
purur.a (also *purua*) *vt* strip off in large quantities e.g. by pulling a stalk or leaves off a tree: *Aliyapurura majani ya muhogo,* he stripped the leaves of the cassava plant. Prep. ***purur.i.a*** St. ***purur.ik.a*** Cs. ***purur.ish.a*** Ps. ***purur.w.a*** Rp. ***purur.an.a***
purut.a *vi* slip on the branchless trunk of a tree during descending. Prep. ***purut.i.a*** St. ***purut.ik.a*** Cs. ***purut.ish.a*** Ps. ***purut.w.a***
purutangi (also *patangi*) n (*ma-*) a big balloon. (cf *tiara, twinga*)
pus.a *vi* stop raining; cease: *Mvua imepusa.* the rain has stopped. St. ***pus.ik.a*** Cs. ***pus.ish.a***
put.a *vt* 1. beat grain e.g. millet and rice in order to separate them from their ears; flail: *Aliuputa mtama wake ili atenganishe na mashuke,* he flailed his millet in order to separate the grain from the ears. 2. hit hard as in

the case of a ball, etc.: *Aliuputa mpira*, he hit the ball hard. Prep. *put.i.a* St. *put.ik.a* Cs. *put.ish.a* Ps. *put.w.a* (cf *piga*)

puto (also *pulizo*) *n* (*ma-*) balloon. (cf *bofu*)

puuk.a *vi* be emaciated; be enervated; be enfeebled: *Alipuuka kwa mawazo mengi*, he was enfeebled by many thoughts. Prep. *puuk.i.a* St. *puuk. ik.a* Cs. *puuk.ish.a* (cf *konda*)

puuz.a *vt* ignore, disdain, despise, scorn: *Alilipuuza shauri langu*, he ignored my advice. Prep. *puuz.i.a* St. *puuz. ik.a* Cs. *puuz.ish.a* Ps. *puuz.w.a* Rp. *puuz.an.a* (cf *beza, dharau*)

puwi *n* (*n*) (*zool*) rockcod (cf *chewa*)

puy.a[1] *n* (*n*) thick sugar that has been stirred and looking heavy like gruel, used in the preparation of brew; thick sugar solution used in brewing.

puya[2] *n* (*n*) tobacco that has been rolled; rolled tobacco.

puya[3] *n* (*n*) grapevine, gossip, idle chatter, idle talk. (cf *uzushi, uongo*)

pw.a[1] *vi* (used esp of the tide) ebb, dry out: *Maji yanakupwa*, the tide is ebbing; Prep. *pw.i.a* St. *pw.ik.a* Cs. *pw.ish.a*

pw.a[2] *interj* an expletive for expressing the sound of sth when it has fallen down.

pwaa *n* (*n*) 1. the dry place in the sea after the tide has gone out; foreshore. 2. shore, coast. (*prov*) *Mgagaa na upwa, hali wali mkavu*, a person who moves here and there along the shore will not miss his side dish of fish i.e. a person who moves here and there to look for things will not miss to get anything.

pwag.a[1] *vt* pound rice, millet, etc. in a mortar (with a pestle) to remove husks; flail, thresh: *Alipwaga mpunga*, he threshed the rice in a mortar with a pestle. Prep. *pwag.i.a* St. *pwag. ik.a* Cs. *pwag.ish.a* Ps. *pwag.w.a*

(cf *twanga*)

pwag.a[2] *vi, vt* boil, simmer, seethe, steam: *Wali ulikuwa ukipwaga chunguni*, the rice was simmering in the pot. Prep. *pwag.i.a* St. *pwag.ik.a* Cs. *pwag. ish.a* Ps. *pwag.w.a* Rp. *pwag.an.a* (cf *tokota, chemka*)

pwag.a[3] *vi* speak a lot and do it incoherently. Prep. *pwag.i.a* St. *pwag. ik.a* Cs. *pwag.ish.a* Ps. *pwag.w.a* Rp. *pwag.an.a*

pwagu *n* (*ma-*) conman, swindler, thief: *Pwagu yule haaminiki*, that conman cannot be trusted. (cf *tapeli, mwizi, bazazi*)

pwaguzi *n* (*ma-*) a thief of the highest order: *Pwagu na pwaguzi wamekutana*, an ordinary thief and one of the highest order have met.

pwaji[1] *n* (*n*) that part of the shore that only dries up at extreme low tide; lower part of the beach; foreshore. (cf *bwachi*)

pwaji[2] *n* (*n*) gossip, idle chatter, idle talk: *Amezoea kuzungumza pwaji mtaani*, he is used to having idle chatter in the neighbourhood. (cf *porojo, gumzo, soga*)

pwaju *n* (*n*) (*zool*) night jar (cf *kirukanjia*)

pwani *n* (*n*) 1. coast. (cf *mwambao*) 2. sea coast.

pway.a[1] *vi* (of clothes, ring, etc) be loose fitting, be baggy: *Suruali hii inapwaya*, this pair of trousers is baggy. Prep. *pway.i.a* St. *pway.ik.a* Cs. *pway. ish.a*

pway.a[2] *vt* pound in a mortar, etc. with a pestle, flail, etc; thresh, flail: *Alipwaya tangawazi kwenye kinu*, he flailed the ginger in the mortar. Prep. *pway.i.a* St. *pway.ik.a* Cs. *pway.ish.a* Ps. *pway.w.a* (cf *twanga*)

pway.a[3] *vi* 1. lose strength, vigour, etc. 2. be disappointed, be disheartened. Prep. *pway.i.a* St. *pway.ik.a* Cs. *pway.ish.a* Ps. *pway.w.a* (cf *gwaya*)

pwaz.a *vi* boil, stew, simmer, steam:

Aliupwaza muhogo wake, he boiled his cassava. Prep. *pwaz.i.a* St. *pwaz.ik.a* Cs. *pwaz.ish.a* (cf *chopeka, chemsha, tokosa*)

pwe.a¹ *vi* see *pwa*

pwe.a² *vi* (of a wound, etc.) subside, decline, abate, decrease: *Uvimbe katika mkono wake sasa umepwea*, the swelling in his arm has now subsided. Prep. *pwe.le.a* St. *pwe. lek.a* Cs. *pwe.lesh.a* and *pwe.z.a* (cf *pojaa, nywea*)

pwek.a *vi* be opening and shutting.

pweke¹ *adj* lonely, lone, solitary.

pweke² *adv* alone; without any companion: *Alikuwa akiishi pweke*, she was living alone. (cf *peke*)

pwele.a *vt, vi* 1. lose voice; dry up: *Sauti yake imempwelea*, her voice has gone. (cf *kauka*) 2. go aground, go ashore: *Meli ilipwelea kwenye mwamba*, the ship went aground on the reef. St. *pwele.k.a* Cs. *pwele.z.a* Ps. *pwele.w.a*

pwelew.a *vi* 1. be left by the water 2. be unknowing what to do; be confused. Prep. *pwelew.e.a* St. *pwelew.ek.a* Cs. *pwelew.esh.a*

pwet.a *vt, vi* be abashed, become disgraced, be ashamed: *Alipweta baada ya kugunduliwa anakopi kwenye mtihani*, he was in disgrace after being caught copying in the examination. Prep. *pwet.e.a* St. *pwet.ek.a* Cs. *pwet.esh.a* (cf *aibika, fedheheka*)

pwete *interj* an expletive signalling the sound of sitting down. *Alijipweteka pwete kwenye kochi*. He sat down heavily on the couch.

pwetek.a *vt, vi* throw oneself down carefully in a sitting position; slump down: *Alijipweteka kwenye kochi kwa sababu ya uchovu*, he slumped down onto the sofa because of fatigue. *pwetek.e.a* St. *pwetek.ek.a* Cs. *pwetek.esh.a* (cf *jitupa*)

pwetepwete *adj* 1. (of fruits, etc.) watery, soft, squishy, squashy: *Tunda hili ni pwetepwete*, this fruit is squashy. (cf *majimaji, tepetepe, chege*) 2. (of a person, etc.) lazy, loose. *Alikuwa pwetepwete kazini kwake*, he was lazy in his place of work.

pweza¹ *n* (*n*) (*zool*) octopus. (*prov*) *Umekuwa pweza wajipalia makaa*, you have become an octopus and now you are burning yourself i.e. you want to involve yourself into problems unnecessarily because of your sheer ignorance.

pwez.a² *vt* (*naut*) cause a ship to be grounded. Prep. *pwez.e.a* St. *pwez. ek.a* Ps. *pwez.w.a*

pwezu.a *vt* (*naut*) launch a ship, etc into the water: *Mabaharia waliipwezua mashua yao bila ya shida*, the sailors launched their boat into the water without any difficulty. Prep. *pwezu. li.a* St. *pwezu.k.a* Cs. *pwezu.sh.a* Ps. of Prep. *pwezu.liw.a*

pwit.a *vi* 1. pant, pulse, throb, pulsate, beat: *Baada ya kuzipanda ngazi, akasimama juu akipwita*, after climbing the stairs, he stood panting. (cf *tweta, puma, hema*) 2. (of a boil, wound, etc.) throb painfully: *Jipu lake lilikuwa likipwita*, his boil was throbbing painfully. Prep. *pwit.i.a* St. *pwit.ik.a* Cs. *pwit.ish.a* Ps. *pwit.w.a* Rp. *pwit.an.a* (cf *fukuta*)

-pya *adj* 1. new, modern: *Amenionyesha kitabu chake kipya*, he has shown me his new book. 2. strange, novel: *Vituko vyake vipya vinatushangaza*, her new eccentricities shock us.

pyor.a *vt* insult, affront, offend: *Alinipyora hadharani*, he insulted me in public. Prep. *pyor.e.a* St. *pyor.ek.a* Cs. *pyor. esh.a* Ps. *pyor.w.a* Rp. *pyor.an.a* (cf *tukana, chamba*)

-pyoro (also *pyororo*) *adj* offensive, affronting, insulting, insolent.

pyororo *adj* see *pyoro*

R

R,r /r/ 1. the seventeenth letter of the Swahili alphabet. 2. an alveolar trill.
raara.a *vi* be confused in giving a point of argument; be bewildered. Prep. ***raara.ik.a*** St. ***raara.ik.a*** Cs. ***raara.ish.a*** Ps of Prep. ***raara.iw.a*** (cf *babaika*)
raba *n (n)* 1. rubber; a kind of eraser used for rubbing out pencil or ink marks. (cf *kifutio*) 2. rubber shoes; sneakers. (Eng)
rabana[1] *adv* nakedly, nudely: *Mwendawazimu alitembea rabana*, the madman walked nakedly. (cf *utupu*) (Ar)
Rabana[2] *n (n)* see *rabi*
Rabi (also *Rabana*) *n (n)* Almighty God; the Almighty; Divine Being; *Ya Rabi*, Oh God! (Ar)
rabsha *n (n)* row, melee, brawl, chaos, confusion, tussle: *Wachezaji walileta rabsha kubwa uwanjani*, the players caused a lot of chaos on the ground. (cf *vurugu, fujo, zahama*)
Rabuka *n (n)* your Almighty God.
rada[1] *n (n)* punishment from God to someone who has done an evil deed; divine retribution: *Ile ilikuwa rada kutoka kwa Mwenyezi Mungu kwa sababu ya maovu yake*, that was divine retribution because of his evil deeds. (Ar)
rada[2] *n (n)* radar (Eng)
radhi *n (n)* 1. blessing, benediction: *Amekosa radhi kwa wazee wake*, he has lost the blessings of his parents. 2. pardon, apology: *Ninaomba radhi*, I beg your pardon. *Wia radhi*, ask for an apology. *Omba radhi*, ask for an apology. 3. satisfaction, contentment: *Je uko radhi?* Are you satisfied? (cf *msamaha*) (Ar)
radi *n (n)* thunder bolt. (Ar)
radid.i *vt, vi* repeat, reiterate; do an action again: *Anapenda kuliradidi jambo lile kwa lile*, he likes to repeat that issue every now and again. Prep. ***radid.i.a*** St. ***radid.ik.a*** Cs. ***radid.ish.a*** Ps. of Rep. ***radid.iw.a*** (cf *kariri*) (Ar)
rafadha *n (n)* propeller of a ship, boat, plane, etc.: *Rafadha ya ndege*, the propeller of a plane.
rafi *adj* (used in business) irreducible, fixed: *Bei rafi*, fixed price. *Kipimo rafi*, fixed measure.
rafiki *n (n)* (*ma-*) friend, companion, comrade: *Yeye ni rafiki mzuri*, he is a good friend. (cf *sahibu*) (Ar)
rafu[1] *n (n)* 1. shelf, rack. 2. an open cupboard used for keeping things such as books, utensils, etc. (Ar)
rafu[2] *n (n)* (in sports, etc.) roughness: *Cheza rafu*, play rough. *Wachezaji walifanya rafu kwenye mechi*, the players played in a rough manner during the match. (Eng)
raghba *n (n)* anxiety, enthusiasm, zeal, interest: *Yeye hana raghba na kazi anayoifanya hivi sasa*, he has no interest in the work he is currently doing. (cf *hamu, mapenzi*) (Ar)
raghibish.a *vt* motivate, prompt, rouse, encourage. Prep. ***raghibish.i.a*** St. ***raghibish.ik.a*** Ps. ***raghibish.w.a*** Rp. ***raghibish.an.a***
raghib.u *vt* motivate, rouse, encourage: *Baba aliniraghibu kwenye masomo yangu*, my father encouraged me in my studies. Prep. ***raghib.i.a*** St. ***raghib.ik.a*** Cs. ***raghib.ish.a*** Ps. of Prep. ***raghib.iw.a*** Rp. of Prep. ***raghib.i.an.a*** (cf *hamasisha, shajiisha*)
rago *n (n)* see *ago*[1]
raha *n (n)* comfort, happiness, respite, calmness: *Ona raha*, feel happy. *Ona mustarehe*, feel happy. *Mtu yule ana mali nyingi lakini hana raha*, that person has a lot of wealth but he is not happy. (cf *furaha, starehe, buraha*) (Ar)
rahani[1] (also *rehani*) *n (n)* pawn, mortgage, security: *Weka rahani*. pawn; place in pawn. *Mshika rahani*, pawn-broker. (cf *poni*) (Ar)

643

rahani² (also *rehani*) n (n) (*naut*) a special store in a house or sailing vessel such as a ship, dhow, etc. for keeping valuable things. (Ar)

rahi n (n) health; physical fitness, good condition: *Mtu yule amekuwa hana rahi tangu kurudi vitani*, that person is not healthy since returning from war. (cf *afya, siha*)

Rahimu¹ n (n) (in Islam) God the merciful: *Mungu Rahimu karimu*, the merciful and bountiful God. (Ar)

rahimu² adj merciful, gentle, kind: *Yeye ni mtu rahimu*, he is a gentle person. (cf *baridi*) (Ar)

rahisi¹ adj 1. cheap, inexpensive, low-priced: *Mchele umekuwa rahisi siku hizi*, rice has become cheap these days. 2. easy, simple: *Hesabu hii ni rahisi*, this sum is easy. (cf *sahili*) 3. (of a woman, etc.) cheap, loose: *Mwanamke alijifanya rahisi*, the woman made herself loose. 4. humble, modest, simple: *Waziri alijifanya rahisi mbele za watu*, the minister made himself humble in public. (Ar)

rahis.i² (usu *rahisisha*) vt humiliate: *Mbona anajirahisisha hivyo?* Why is she cheapening herself like that? Prep. *rahis.i.a* St. *rahis.ik.a* Cs. *rahis.ish.a* Ps. of Prep. *rahis.iw.a* (cf *thakilisha, tweza, dunisha*) (Ar)

rahisish.a vt 1. see *rahisi²*. 2. simplify: *Jaribu kuyarahisisha mambo yako*, try to simplify your matters. Prep. *rahisish.i.a* St. *rahisish.ik.a* Ps. of Prep. *rahisish.iw.a* Rp. of Prep. *rahisish.i.an.a*

ra.i¹ vt advise, counsel, guide: *Nilimru asisafiri lakini akasafiri*, I advised him not to travel but he travelled. Prep. *ra.i.a* St. *ra.ik.a* Ps. of Prep. *ra.iw.a* Rp. of Prep. *ra.i.an.a* (cf *shawishi, sihi, usia*) (Ar)

rai² n (n) opinion, viewpoint, suggestion: *Alinipa rai kwamba nisiache shule*, he suggested to me that I should not leave school. (cf *ushauri, wazo, fikira*) (Ar)

ra.i³ vt put food into the mouth as a sign of affection, etc.; feed sby as a sign of affection: *Mke wangu alinirai kidogo chakula*, my wife fed me some food. Prep. *ra.i.a* St. *ra.ik.a* Cs. *ra.ish.a* Ps. *ra.iw.a* Rp. of Prep. *ra.i.an.a* (cf *lisha*) (Ar)

raia n (n) 1. citizen, subject, nationalist: *Raia wa heshima*, honorary citizen. 2. civilian; an ordinary person who is not a member of the armed forces or police force. (Ar)

raira.i vt blandish, cajole; pursuade sby to do sth by flattery or deceit: *Alinirairai sana nimwazime gari yangu*, he cajoled me very much by deceit to lend him my car. Prep. *raira.i.a* Cs. *raira.ish.a* Ps. *raira.iw.a* (cf *bembeleza*)

rais (also *raisi*) n (n) 1. president of a republic: *Rais mstaafu*, the retired president. *Rais mteule*, the president elect. *Rais wa mpito*, interim president. 2. president of a company, corporation, party, etc.: *Rais wa klabu yetu anataka kujiuzulu*, the president of our club wants to resign. (Ar)

Rajabu n (n) (in Islam) the seventh month according to the Islamic calendar. This month is regarded as one among the holy months on account of being the month of the Prophet Muhammad's journey to heaven. (Ar)

rajamu n (n) emblem, stamp, trademark. (cf *chapa*) (Ar)

rajimi adj (in reference to Satan) deserving to be cursed: *Shetani rajimi*, the cursed Satan. (Ar)

rajis.i vt see *sajili*. Prep. *rajis.i.a* St. *rajis.ik.a* Cs. *rajis.ish.a* Ps. of Prep. *rajis.iw.a* (Ar)

rajua¹ n (n) hope, expectation, anticipation: *Hana rajua ya kupata kazi yoyote*, he has no hope of getting a job. (cf *tumaini*) (Ar)

raju.a² *vt* hope, expect, anticipate, foresee: *Anarajua kufaulu vizuri kwenye mtihani,* he is expecting to pass well in the examination. (cf *tumaini*)

rakaa *n (n)* (in Islam) the act of bowing with the hands on the knees while a Muslim prays. The number of *rakaas* performed is determined by the exact time he is praying. (Ar)

rakaateni¹ *n (n)* two times in bowing while praying; two bows. (Ar)

rakaateni² *n (n) (syn)* a small event that takes a short time to be accomplished. (Ar)

rakadha *n (n)* compulsion, force, insistence. *Fanya rakadha,* make a compulsion; force, compel e.g, *Alinifanyia rakadha ili nimkopeshe pesa,* he forced me to lend him some money. (Ar)

rakamu *n (n)* number, numeral e.g. 1, 2, 3, 4 ... (cf *nambari, mwongo*) (Ar)

raketi *n (n)* racket (Eng)

rakibish.a *vt* see *rekebisha*

rakib.u *vt* ride a horse, donkey, etc.; bestraddle, mount, bestride, straddle: *Alirakibu farasi,* he mounted a horse. Prep. *rakib.i.a* St. *rakib.ik.a* Cs. *rakib.ish.a* Ps. of Prep. *rakib.iw.a* Rp. of Prep. *rakib.i.an.a* (Ar)

rala *n (n)* a port whose goods are preserved for exportation to other countries; harbour.

Ramadhani *n (n)* Ramadan; the month of fasting for Muslims, which is the ninth month according to the Islamic calendar. (Ar)

ramani *n (n)* 1. map, chart: *Ramani ya Afrika,* the map of Africa. 2. plan, drawings: *Ramani ya nyumba,* the plan of a house. (Ar)

ramba¹ *n (n)* a kind of curved knife used by shoemakers. (cf *kotama, upumba*)

ramba² *n (n)* a kind of Madagascar dress of fine plaited grass with coloured stripes, worn from the waist to the bottom; grass skirt.

ramb.a³ (also *lamba*) *vt* 1. lick, lap; pass the tongue over sth: *Aliviramba vidole vyake baada ya kula chakula kitamu,* she licked her fingers after eating delicious food. 2. *(idm) Ramba kisogo,* ignore by symbolism what a person has said after he goes away. Prep. **ramb.i.a** St. **ramb.ik.a** Cs. **ramb.ish.a** Ps. **ramb.w.a**

rambaz.a¹ *vt* 1. troll; fish with a moving line esp one with a revolving lure trailed behind a moving boat: *Walikuwa wanarambaza samaki,* they were trolling for fish. 2. trawl; catch fish at night with a trawl holding a torch or a light. Prep. **rambaz.i.a** St. **rambaz.ik.a** Cs. **rambaz.ish.a** Ps. **rambaz.w.a** Rp. **rambaz.an.a**

rambaz.a² *vt* go whoring around; look for a prostitute for sexual intercourse. Prep. **rambaz.i.a** St. **rambaz.ik.a** Cs. **rambaz.ish.a** Ps. **rambaz.w.a** Rp. **rambaz.an.a**

rambirambi *n (n)* 1. (always used in pl) condolences conveyed to the bereaved person, family, etc.: *Nilimpelekea rambirambi zangu kutokana na kifo cha mkewe,* I conveyed my condolences to him following the death of his wife.

rambit.a *vt* desire to taste sth or eat it. Prep. **rambit.i.a** St. **rambit.ik.a** Cs. **rambit.ish.a** Ps. of Prep. **rambit.w.a** Rp. **rambit.an.a**

rambuza *n (ma-)* an effeminate male. (cf *hanithi, shoga*)

ramia *n (n)* 1. a clip of cartridges. 2. an enclosed form of bait in a hook. (Ar)

ramis.i *vt, vi* enjoy oneself; amuse oneself: *Watazamaji waliramisi kwenye tamasha la sanaa,* the audience enjoyed itself at the art festival. Prep. **ramis.i.a** St. **ramis.ik.a** Cs. **ramis.ish.a** Ps. of Prep. **ramis.iw.a** (cf *furahi, sherehekea*) (Pers)

ramli *n (n)* soothsaying, augury, prophecy: *Piga ramli,* read the divining board. (cf *bao, utabiri*)

645

ramramu n (n) procession, multitude, flock, crowd: *Niliona ramramu ya watu mazikoni*, I saw a multitude of people at the funeral. (cf *rubaa, afwaji*)

ramsa n (n) euphoria, exultation; jubilation resulting from celebration of sth: *Kulikuwa na ramsa kubwa kwenye sherehe za harusi*, there was great jubilation during the wedding celebrations. (cf *furaha, nderemo*) (Pers)

ramu n (n) house plot.

ramuk.a vi attack each other in war. Prep. ***ramuk.i.a*** St. ***raruk.ik.a*** Cs. ***ramuk.ish.a***

ranchi n (n) ranch (Eng)

randa¹ (also *landa*) n (n) carpenter's plane: *Piga randa*, smooth a rough surface by using a plane. *Randa ya kuwingiria*, spoke shave plane. (Pers)

rand.a² vt plane; smooth a rough surface: *Aliuranda ubao vizuri*, he planed the wood well. Prep. ***rand.i.a*** St. ***rand.ik.a*** Cs. ***rand.ish.a*** Ps. ***rand.w.a*** (Pers)

rand.a³ (also *ranga*) vi 1. wander, roam, stray, idle; walk around aimlessly: *Anapenda kuranda mjini lakini kazi hataki kufanya*, he likes to wander in town but he doesn't want to work. (cf *zurura, tanga*) 2. brag, boast, show off: *Aliranda kwamba yeye ni mchezaji bora kabisa katika timu*, he boasted that he is the best player in the team. Prep. ***rand.i.a*** St. ***rand.ik.a*** Cs. ***rand.ish.a*** (cf *tamba, tamba, hanja*)

randarand.a vt loiter; walk around aimlessly. Prep. ***randarand.i.a*** St. ***randarand.ki.a*** Cs. ***randarand.ish.a***

rang.a vi see *randa³*

rangaito n (n) chaos, confusion, unrest: *Kulikuwa na rangaito nyingi hapo mnadani*, there was a lot of chaos at the auction. (cf *fujo, zahama*)

rangi n (n) 1. colour: *Rangi nyeusi*, black colour. *Rangi nyeupe*, white colour. *Chai ya rangi*, black tea. 2. dye, paint, pigment. *Tia/paka rangi*, paint, dye, stain. (Hind, Pers)

rapu¹ n (n) (mus) a kind of popular music of US Black origin in which words are recited rapidly and rhythimically over an instrumental backing.

rap.u² vi (mus) perform rap music Prep. ***rap.i.a*** St. ***rap.ik.a*** Cs. ***rap.ish.a*** Ps. of Prep. ***rap.iw.a*** Rp. of Prep. ***rap.i.an.a***

rapu³ interj an expletive indicating the sound of someone being whipped.

rapu.a vt whip someone unexpectedly. Prep. ***rapu.i.a*** St. ***rapu.ik.a*** Cs. ***rapu.ish.a*** Ps. of Prep. ***rapu.iw.a***

raru.a vt 1. tear, rip. (cf *chana, pasua*) 2. (colloq) boot sby: *Beki alimrarua mfungaji*, the backplayer booted the scorer. 3. (fig) defeat, thrash, beat: *Timu ya nyumbani iliirarua ile ya wageni*, the home team thrashed the foreign one. 4. (colloq) attack severely; castigate, rebuke: *Bunge liliirarua serikali wiki jana*, parliament attacked severely the government last week. Prep. ***raru.li.a*** St. ***raru.k.a*** Cs. ***raru.sh.a*** Ps. of Prep. ***raru.liw.a*** Rp. ***raru.an.a*** (cf *nyuka, vurumisha, bamiza*)

raruk.a vi get torn, be torn, be tattered: *Nguo yako imeraruka*, your dress is torn. Prep. ***raruk.i.a*** St. ***raruk.ik.a*** Cs. ***raruk.ish.a***

rash.a vt bungle; do a job improperly: *Nilimpa kazi kuifanya lakini akairasha*, I gave him the work to do but he bungled it. Prep. ***rash.i.a*** St. ***rash.ik.a*** Cs. ***rash.ish.a*** Ps. ***rash.w.a*** (cf *boronga, lipua, kuruza*) (Ar)

rasharasha n (n) drizzle; light rain: (cf *manyunyu, manyonyota*) (Ar)

rashi.a vt 1. sprinkle. 2. do sth superficially. Prep ***rashi.li.a*** St ***rashi.k.a*** Ps ***rashi.w.a*** Rp ***rashi.an.a***

rasi¹ n (n) (geog) cape, peninsula. (Ar)

rasi² n (n) head of a human being. (cf *kichwa*) (Ar)

rasiberi n (n) (bot) raspberry; a plant, of the rose family bearing the fruit, which is small, juicy and edible. (Eng)

rasilmali n (n) capital, assets, property: *Kampuni ilianzishwa huku kukiwa* na rasilmali ndogo, the company was started with limited capital. (Ar)

rasimish.a *vt* institutionalize: *Serikali imerasimisha sheria mpya za ndoa nchini*, the government has institutionalized new marriage laws in the country. Prep. ***rasimish.i.a*** St. ***rasimish.ik.a*** Ps. ***rasimish.w.a*** (Ar)

rasim.u[1] *vt* 1. plan, organize: *Meneja yule anazirasimu shughuli zake vizuri*, that manager organizes his activities well. 2. draft. Prep. ***rasim.i.a*** St. ***rasim.ik.a*** Cs. ***rasim.ish.a*** Ps. of Prep. ***rasim.iw.a***, be planned (cf *ratibu, panga*)

rasim.u[2] *vt* write, inscribe: *Aliirasimu insha yake vizuri*, he wrote his essay well. Prep. ***rasim.i.a*** St. ***rasim.ik.a*** Cs. ***rasim.ish.a*** Ps. of Prep. ***rasim.iw.a*** Rp. of Prep. ***rasim.i.an.a*** (cf *andika*) (Ar)

rasimu[3] *n* (*n*) draft, sketch, outline. *Rasimu ya katiba*, the draft of the constitution. *Rasimu ya mkataba*, the draft of the contract.

rasis.i *vt* plate with tin: *Aliirasisi sufuria yangu*, he plated my saucepan with tin. Prep. ***rasis.i.a*** St. ***rasis.ik.a*** Cs. ***rasis.ish.a*** Ps. of Prep. ***rasis.iw.a*** (Ar)

rasmi *adj* official, formal, functional: *Ziara rasmi*, official visit. *Nguo rasmi*, official dress. *Mwaliko rasmi*, official invitation. *Maziko rasmi*, state funeral. *Mpokezi rasmi*, official receiver. (Ar)

rasta *n* (*n*) raster (Eng)

rasua *n* (*n*) see *rasuli*

rasuli (also *rasua*) *n* (*n*) prophet, apostle; God's messenger. (cf *mtume*) (Ar)

ratiba *n* (*n*) programme, timetable, schedule: *Ratiba ya mtihani*, examination timetable. *Ratiba ya michezo*, sports programme. (cf *mpango*) (Ar)

ratib.u[1] *vt* plan, co-ordinate: *Mwalimu mkuu anaratibu shughuli zote za shule vizuri*, the headmaster co-ordinates well all the activities of the school. Prep. ***ratib.i.a*** St. ***ratib.ik.a*** Cs. ***ratib.ish.a*** Ps. of Prep. ***ratib.iw.a*** Rp. of Prep. ***ratib.i.an.a*** (cf *panga*) (Ar)

ratib.u[2] *vt* collect, gather: *Rais aliteua kamati ili kuratibu maoni ya wananchi kuhusu suala la katiba*, the president appointed a committee to gather the views from the people regarding the constitution. Prep. ***ratib.i.a*** St. ***ratib.ik.a*** Cs. ***ratib.ish.a*** Ps. of Prep. ***ratib.iw.a*** Rp. of Prep. ***ratib.i.an.a*** (cf *kusanya*) (Ar)

ratil.i[1] *vt* peruse; read carefully, read thoroughly: *Aliiratili riwaya kabla ya kuihakiki*, he perused the novel before reviewing it. Prep. ***ratil.i.a*** St. ***ratil.ik.a*** Cs. ***ratil.ish.a*** Ps. of Prep. ***ratil.iw.a*** (Ar)

ratil.i[2] *vt* 1. weigh, measure; put on the scales in the balance: *Aliuratili mchele kwenye mizani*, he weighed the rice on the weighing machine. 2. assess, evaluate (cf *pima, tathmini*) Prep. ***ratil.i.a*** St. ***ratil.ik.a*** Cs. ***ratil.ish.a*** Ps. of Prep. ***ratil.iw.a*** (cf *pima*) (Ar)

ratili[3] (also *ratli*) *n* (*n*) one pound weight. (Ar)

Raufu[1] *n* (*n*) (of Almighty God) the quality of being gentle. (Ar)

raufu[2] *adj* gentle, gracious: *Yule ni kijana raufu*, that is a gentle young man.

rauk.a *vi* get up early in the morning; wake up at dawn: *Itakubidi kurauka kesho ili uliwahi gari la moshi*, you will have to wake up early tomorrow morning in order to catch the train. Prep. ***rauk.i.a*** St. ***rauk.ik.a*** Cs. ***rauk.ish.a*** Ps. ***rauk.w.a*** (cf *damka, jihimu*)

raundi *n* (*n*) round: *Raundi ya mtoano*, knockout round. (Eng)

raun.i *vi,vt* stroll, saunter, perambulate, amble, ramble; take a walk: *Anapenda kurauni nyakati za jioni*, he likes to stroll in the evenings. Prep. ***raun.i.a*** St. ***raun.ik.a*** Cs. ***raun.ish.a*** Ps. of Prep. ***raun.iw.a*** (cf *tembea, zurura*)

rauni.a *vt* see *rauni*

raus.i *vt* (*naut*) trim a sail; straighten a sail. Prep. ***raus.i.a*** St. ***raus.ik.a*** Cs. ***raus.ish.a*** Ps. of Prep. ***raus.iw.a*** (Ar)

razini *adj* sane, rational: *Mtu razini*, a sane person. (Ar)

re.a *vi* be annoyed; be vexed; be angry:

Jirani yangu alirea baada ya mimea yake kuliwa na mbuzi, my neighbour got angry after his plants were eaten by goats. Prep. **re.le.a** St. **re.k.a** Cs. **re.sh.a** Ps. **re.w.a** Rp. **re.an.a** (cf *hamaki, kasirika*)

redio *n* (*n*) 1. radio. 2. radio station. (Eng)

rediokaseti *n* (*n*) radio cassette. (Eng)

rediolojia *n* (*n*) radiology (Eng)

ree *n* (*n*) 1. (in card playing) the ace. (cf *dume*) 2. homosexual actor. (cf *basha, mende*) (Port)

refa (also *refarii, rifarii*) *n* (*n*) referee (Eng)

refarii *n* (*n*) see *refa*

-refu *adj* 1. tall, high, long: *Mtu mrefu*, a tall person. (cf *tawili, ronjo*) 2. distant, far: *Masafa marefu*, long distance. (cf *baidi*)

refuk.a *vt* be lengthened; be elongated; grow tall. Prep. **refuk.i.a** St. **refuk.ik.a** Cs. **refuk.ish.a**

refush.a *vt* prolong heighten, lengthen: *Usijaribu kuyarefusha mazungumzo yetu*, don't try to prolong our conversation. *Wanasayansi wanajaribu kutafuta mbinu mbalimbali za kurefusha maisha ya binadamu*, scientists are trying to devise different methods of lengthening the life of a human being. Prep. **refush.i.a** St. **refush.ik.a** Ps. **refush.w.a** Rp. **refush.an.a**

regareg.a *vi* see *legalega*

rege.a *vi* see *rejea*

rehani[1] *n* (*n*) see *rahani*[1]

rehani[2] *n* (*n*) see *rahani*[2]

rehani[3] *n* (*n*) a red or brown striped cloth usu of silk. (*prov*) *Bura yangu sibadili kwa rehani*, i.e. your own thing that serves you however inferior it is, is better than sby's property that is superior in quality. (cf *debwani*) (Ar)

rehema *n* (*n*) mercy, grace, compassion: *Mtu yule anaishi vizuri kutokana na rehema za Mwenyezi Mungu*, that person lives well by the mercy of God. (Ar)

rehem.u *vt* 1. (of God) give grace to; have mercy on; commiserate: *Mungu huwarehemu waja wake*, God gives mercy to his beings. 2. give prosperity, give comfort. Prep. **rehem.e.a** St. **rehem.ek.a** Cs. **rehem.esh.a** Ps. of Prep. **rehem.ew.a** Rp. of Prep. **rehem.e.an.a** (Ar)

rej.a[1] *vt* prattle, babble, jabber Prep. **rej.e.a** St. **rej.ek.a** Cs. **rej.esh.a** (cf *ropoka, bwata*)

reja[2] *n* (*n*) prattle, babble, small talk. (cf *porojo*)

reja[3] *adj* loose in fastening.

rejareja *adv* on retail: *Duka la rejareja*, retail shop. *Biashara ya rejareja*, retail business. *Alinunua nguo kwa bei ya rejareja*, he bought clothes on retail price.

reje.a (also *regea*) *vt, vi* 1. return; go back: *Aliondoka lakini alirejea mara moja*, he left but he came back immediately. 2. (used in correspondences,etc.) refer: *Rejea barua yangu iliyopita*, refer to my previous letter. 3. remarry a wife after having divorced her. 4. read a book in order to get a particular information. Prep. **reje.le.a** St. **reje.k.a** and **reje.lek.a** Cs. **reje.sh.a** and **reje.z.a** Ps. **reje.w.a** Rp. **reje.an.a** (Ar)

rejesh.a *vt* return, send back, reinstate: *Wamemrejesha kazini*, they have reinstated him at the place of work. Prep. **rejesh.e.a** St. **rejesh.ek.a** Ps. **rejesh.w.a** Rp. **rejesh.an.a**

rejesho *n* (*ma-*) (*math*) integral: *Rejesho halisi*, proper integral.

rejesta[1] (also *rejista*) *n* (*n*) 1. registered envelope. 2. register; a book containing a list or record of names of people, items, etc. (Eng)

rejesta[2] (also *rejista*) *n* (*n*) (*ling*) register; a speech variety used by a particular group of people. (Eng)

rekebish.a (also *rakibisha*) *vt* 1. (of things) rectify, adjust, fix, repair: *Aliirekebisha saa yake*, he adjusted his watch. 2. (of habits, etc.) change, modify, alter: *Lazima urekebishe tabia yako*, you must reform your character.

Prep. *rekebish.i.a* St. *rekebish.ik.a* Ps. *rekebish.w.a* Rp. *rekebish.an.a* (cf *badilisha*) (Ar)
rekebisho (also *rakibisho*) *n* (*ma-*) repair, change, reform, amendment: *Kocha alifanya marekebisho fulani kuhusu mbinu za ushambulizi*, the coach made certain changes in the attack strategies. (cf *sawazisho, tengenezo*) (Ar)
reki *n* (*n*) rack (Eng)
rekodi[1] *n* (*n*) gramophone record. (Eng)
rekodi[2] *n* (*n*) record; a written statement of facts, events, etc. (cf *kumbukumbu*) (Eng)
rekodi[3] (also *rikodi*) *n* (*n*) (in sports, etc.) record; the best performance, highest rate, etc. achieved esp when officially recorded: *Mwanariadha alivunja rekodi ya kukimbia masafa marefu*, the athlete broke the record for the marathon. *Rekodi ya dunia*, world record. (Eng)
rekod.i[4] (also *rikodi*) *vt* record, document, post: *Polisi waliyarekodi maelezo ya mtuhumiwa*, the police recorded the statement of the accused. Prep. *rekod.i.a* St. *rekod.ik.a* Cs. *rekod.ish.a* Ps. of Prep. *rekod.iw.a* Rp. of Prep. *rekod.i.an.a* (Eng)
rekodiplea (also *rikodiplea*) *n* (*n*) record player. (Eng)
reli *n* (*n*) railway, rail: *Njia ya reli*, railway track. (Eng)
remb.a *vt* decorate, embellish, beautify: *Marehemu alikuwa akiiremba nyumba yake*, the deceased used to decorate his house. Prep. *remb.e.a* St. *remb. ek.a* Cs. *remb.esh.a* Ps. *remb.w.a* Rp. *remb.an.a* (cf *pamba*)
rembesh.a *vt* beautify, decorate, embellish. Prep. *rembesh.e.a* St. *rembesh.ek.a* Ps. *rembesh.w.a* Rp. *rembesh.an.a*
rembo[1] *n* (*n*) decoration, adornment, embellishment. (cf *pambo*)

-rembo[2] *adj* glamorous, attractive, beautiful: *Msichana mrembo*, a beautiful girl.
rembu.a *vt* 1. remove make-up, etc.; spoil the beauty of; disfigure, deface, disfeature: *Alijirembua baada ya kurudi kutoka harusini*, she removed her make-up after returning from the wedding. 2. (*idm*) *Rembua macho*, make eyes at; show the whites of the eyes; as a seducing sign. Prep. *rembu. li.a* St. *rembu.k.a* Cs. *rembu.sh.a* Ps. of Prep. *rembu.liw.a* Rp. *rembu.an.a* (cf *pambua, haribu*)
rembwer.a *vt,vi* do sth with airs and graces. Prep. *rembwer.e.a* St. *rembwer.ek.a* Cs. *rembwer.esh.a* Ps. *rembwer.w.a*
reng.a *vt* treat as a fool; make a fool of: *Jirani yangu amemrenga mumewe; kila analomwambia, mume hukubali*; my neighbour has bewitched her husband; everything she tells him, he agrees. Prep. *reng.e.a* St. *reng. ek.a* Cs. *reng.e.sh.a* Ps. *reng.w.a* Rp. *reng.an.a* (cf *zuzua*)
renge[1] *n* (*ma-*) simpleton, idiot, imbecile: *Renge yule hataielewa kazi yoyote utakayompa*, that idiot will not understand any work you give him. (cf *zuzu*)
renge[2] *n* (*n*) a kind of local dance performed in a circle, played by young men who go round and round, and then approach their partner on the opposite side.
repa *n* (*ma-*) (*mus*) a musician.
rerej.a *vi* prattle, twattle, blather; go on speaking foolishly; talk nonsense: *Homa kali ilimfanya kurereja*, the acute fever caused him to talk nonsense. Prep. *rerej.e.a* St. *rerej.ek.a* Cs. *rerej.esh.a* Ps. *rerej.w.a* (cf *ropokwa, bwata*)
reresh.a *vt* 1. be in the habit of performing sexual intercourse with everyone; be adulterous; fornicate. 2. wander here

649

and there in search of conversation; loiter: *Yeye hupenda kureresha kwa majirani*, he likes to wander here and there in search of conversation with the neighbours. Prep. *reresh.e.a* St. *reresh.ek.a* Ps. *reresh.w.a* (cf *zurura, randa*)
rewa n (n) 1. a large signal drum intended to congregate people for a particular purpose. 2. the sound or beat produced by the drum intended for this purpose.
reza¹ (also *liza, riza*) n (n) door ring through which an iron fastener is fixed to fasten a door.
reza² look (cf. *tazama*)
ria n (n) pomp; pretentious show, pompous display: *Unapowasaidia masikini, usifanye kwa ria*, when you help the poor, don't do it for show-off. (Ar)
riadha n (n) athletics (Ar)
riahi n (n) 1. (*med*) dyspepsia, indigestion. 2. flatulence; excessive gas in the stomach. (Ar)
riaka n (n) see *ziaka*
riale (also *riali*) n (n) the monetary unit and a coin in some Arab countries such as Saud Arabia and Oman. Its value against an American dollar varies from one country to another; rial. (Ar)
riari.a (also *kiakia, piapia*) vi be unsettled, be busy, be occupied, be uneasy: fret: *Mama aliriaria wakati wa harusi ya bintiye*, the mother was busy during the wedding of her daughter. (*prov*) *Mwenye kijungu mekoni, haachi kuriaria*, whoever is engrossed in sth, will be restless. Prep. *riari.li.a* St. *riari.k.a* Cs. *riari.sh.a* Ps. *riari.w.a*
riba n (n) interest, usury: *Kula riba*, earn interest, practice usury: *Toza riba*, make sby pay interest. *Riba sahili*, simple interest. *Riba peu*, compound interest. *Riba mchanganyiko*, compound interest. *Riba maalumu*, fixed interest. *Riba halisi*, actual interest: *Benki yangu inatoa riba nzuri kwa wateja wake*, my bank gives good interest to its customers. (Ar)
ribiz.a vt syllabify; place a vowel between consonants to form a syllable. Prep. *ribiz.i.a* St. *ribiz.ik.a* Cs. *ribiz.ish.a* Ps. *ribiz.w.a* Rp. *ribiz.an.a*
riboni n (n) 1. ribbon; a narrow strip of inked cloth against which type characters strike for printing, as in a typewriter. 2. a narrow strip of silk, rayon, velvet etc. finished at the edges and of various widths, used for decoration, tying things, etc.; ribbon. (Eng)
riboribo¹ n (n) jubilation, euphoria: *Kulikuwa na riboribo baada ya chama chetu kutangazwa ndicho mshindi katika uchaguzi mdogo*, there was jubilation after our party was declared as the winner in the by-election. (cf *shangwe, furaha*)
riboribo² (also *ripuripu*) interj an expletive used to express happiness, jubilation, etc.; hurray! hooray!
ridhaa n (n) consent, assent, approval, permission: *Walioana bila ya ridhaa ya wazee wao*, they got married without the consent of their parents. (cf *kibali, idhini, ruhusa*) (Ar)
ridh.i vt consent, accept, comply: *Ameridhi kila analoambiwa na mkewe*, he complies with everything he is told by his wife. Prep. *ridh.i.a* St. *ridh.ik.a* Cs. *ridh.ish.a,* be satisfactory e.g. *Kazi yake hairidhishi*, his work is not satisfactory. Ps. of Prep. *ridh.iw.a* Rp. of Prep. *ridh.i.an.a* (cf *kubali, afiki*) (Ar)
ridhi.a vt agree, accept, approve, consent: *Aliridhia matakwa yangu yote*, he accepted all my requests. Prep. *ridhi.li.a* St. *ridhi.k.a* Cs. *ridhi.sh.a* Ps. *ridhi.w.a* Rp. *ridhi.an.a* (cf *idhinisha, kubali*)
ridhik.a vt, vi be contented, be satisfied. Prep. *ridhik.i.a* St. *ridhik.ik.a* Cs. *ridhik.ish.a* Rp. *ridhik.an.a* (cf *ridhika*)

ridhish.a vt, vi cause to be satisfied/contented: *Ameniridhisha na kazi zake*, he has satisfied me with his work. Prep. **ridhish.i.a** St. **ridhish.ik.a** Ps. **ridhish.w.a** Rp. **ridhish.an.a** (cf *tosheleza*)

rifarii n (n) see *refa*

riha n (n) see *rihi*

rihani n (n) (*bot*) a sweet scented flower from the sweet basil herb, *mrihani* used as incense; basil flower. (Ar)

rihi (also *riha*) n (n) scent, smell: *Takataka zile zimeleta rihi mbaya*, that garbage has caused bad smell. (Ar)

rijali n (n) macho man, he-man; a real man; a man with sexual powers. (cf *mwanamume*) (Ar)

rika¹ n (n) (*mus*) tambourine; a kind of small drum with jungling metal disks in the rim, used in local cultural activities, etc.

rika

rika² n (n) contemporary, age-mate, peer; of the same age: *Yeye si mtu wa rika langu*, he is not my contemporary. (cf *jirimu, hirimu*)

rikabu n (n) (*zool*) an animal used for riding such as a horse, camel, donkey, etc. (Ar)

rikodi n (n) see *rekodi*³ and *rekodi*⁴

rikoriko n (n) side dish; anything eaten as a relish with the main food e.g. curry.

riksho (also *ringsho*) n (ma-) rickshaw; a small two-wheeled carriage with a hood pulled by one or two men. (Jap)

rikwama (also *rukwana*) n (ma-) handcart; cart. (cf *mkokoteni*)

rilab.a vt deny, refute, negate. Prep. **rilab.i.a** St. **rilab.ik.a** Cs. **rilab.ish.a** Ps. of Prep. **rilab.iw.a** Rp. of Prep. **rilab.i.an.a**

rima¹ n (n) pit-trap; a pit dug for catching animals.

rima² n (n) pushcart (cf *mkokoteni*)

rimbwata n (n) a kind of special medicine, made from meat, usually liver, which is believed to have great impact on love for the person intended to be loved; love medicine.

rin.a vt gather honey: *Mfuga nyuki alienda porini kurina asali*, the apiarist went to the bush to collect honey. Prep. **rin.i.a** St. **rin.ik.a** Cs. **rin.ish.a** Ps. **rin.w.a**

rinda¹ n (ma-) a flat double fold in cloth or other material, of uniform width and pressed or stitched in place, pleat.

rinda² n (ma-) a broad lady's dress. (cf *gauni*)

rindim.a vi,vt 1. resonate, rumble, resound: roar as in the case of thunder, etc.: *Mizinga ilirindima, rais wa nchi ya jirani alipowasili*, the guns thundered when the president from the neighbouring country arrived. (cf *nguruma, dunda*) 2. (*fig*) hit, pound, beat: *Bondia alimrindima mpinzani wake*, the boxer pounded his opponent. 3. prevail, pervade: *Ufisadi umerindima katika jamii zetu*, corruption has prevailed in our societies. *Michuano ya kandanda ya kutafuta klabu bingwa ilirindima juma lililopita*, club soccer championship competitions dominated last week. Prep. **rindim.i.a** St. **rindim.ik.a** Cs. **rindim.ish.a** Ps. **rindim.w.a** (cf *dunda*)

rindimo n (n) see *mrindimo*

ring.a¹ vi 1. boast, brag, show off. (cf *hanja, tamba*) 2. be conceited, be arrogant, be proud: *Mwanafunzi yule anaringa siku hizi kutokana na ushindi wake mkubwa kwenye mtihani*, that student is proud these days because of his great success in the examination. Prep. *ring.i.a* St. *ring.ik.a* Cs. *ring.ish.a* Ps *ring.w.a* Rp *ring.an.a* (cf *jivuna, jiona, takabari*)

ring.a² *vt* impregnate a girl before legally getting married to her. Prep. *ring.i.a* St. *ring.ik.a* Cs. *ring.ish.a* Ps. *ring.w.a*

ripe.a *vt* repair, mend. (cf *tengeneza, karabati*) (Eng)

ripoti¹ *n* (*n*) report, account, story: *Ripoti ya mwaka*, annual report. *Ripoti ya kesi*, law report. *Toa ripoti*, make a report. (cf *taarifa*) (Eng)

ripot.i² *vt, vi* report, account, tell. Prep. *ripot.i.a* St. *ripot.ik.a* Cs. *ripot.ish.a* Ps. *ripot.iw.a* Rp. of Prep. *ripot.i.an.a* (cf *arifu, eleza*) (Eng)

ripu¹ *n* (*n*) plaster

ripu² *interj* an expletive of a sound of an exploded thing.

ripu.a *vt* 1. see *lipua¹* and *lipua²*. 2. do sth hapharzadly. Prep. *ripu.li.a* St. *ripu.lik.a* Cs. *repu.lish.a* Ps. *repu.liw.a* Rep of Prep. *ripu.li.an.a*

ripuk.a (also *lipuka*) *vi* 1. be exploded, be burst: *Bomu liliripuka jana mtaani*, the bomb exploded yesterday in the neighbourhood. 2. (*fig*) be annoyed, be vexed. Prep. *ripuk.i.a* St. *ripuk.ik.a* Cs. *ripuk.ish.a*

ripuripu¹ *interj* an expletive used to express happiness usu after completing or after achieving sth; hip hip!

ripuripu² *n* (*n*) see *riboribo²*

risala *n* (*n*) 1. message; communication: short speech: *Tulifurahikiwa na risala ya waziri*, we were impressed by the minister's short speech. (cf *hotuba, ujumbe*) 2. letter; a written message: *Aliniandikia risala ndefu*, he wrote to me a long letter. (cf *barua*) (Ar)

risasi¹ *n* (*n*) bullet, pellet: *Piga risasi*, shoot a bullet. *Fyatua risasi*, fire a bullet; open fire. (Ar)

risasi² *n* (*n*) solder, lead, tin: *Tia risasi*, solder sth. (Ar)

rishafu *n* (*n*) blotting paper. (cf *kikausho*) (Ar)

risha.i *vi* 1 be wet, be moist, be damp: *Nguo zangu zimerishai baada ya kunyeshewa na mvua kubwa*, my clothes have become wet after being soaked with heavy rain. (cf *roa*) 2. exude moisture. Prep. *risha.i.a* St. *risha.ik.a* Cs. *risha.ish.a* Ps. of Prep. *risha.iw.a* Rp. of Prep. *risha.i.an.a* (cf *nyekeza*) (Ar)

risimu *n* (*n*) the first price given in an auction; first bidding, opening bid: *Alitoa risimu yake kwenye mnada*, he gave his first bidding in the auction. (Ar)

risiti *n* (*n*) receipt: *Kitabu cha risiti*, receipt book. *Alipokea risiti kutoka kwa mwenye duka*, he received a receipt from the shopkeeper. (cf *stakabadhi*) (Eng)

ritad.i *vi* desert Islamic religion; renegade Islamic religion; apostatize from Islam: *Muumini aliritadi*, the faithful apostatized from Islam. Prep. *ritad.i.a* St. *ritad.ik.a* Cs. *ritad.ish.a* (cf *tanasari*) (Ar)

rith.i *vt* 1. inherit; become heir to: *Alirithi mali adhimu baba yake alipokufa*, he inherited a lot of wealth when his father died. (cf *halifu*) 2. resemble sby in character, etc.; take after sby: *Msichana yule amemrithi mama yake namna anavyocheka*, that girl takes after her mother in the way she laughs. (cf *fanana, randa*) 3. acquire skills from parents, etc.: *Amemrithi baba yake kazi ya useremala*, he has inherited the skill of carpentry from his father. Prep. *rith.i.a* St. *rith.ik.a* Cs. *rith.ish.a* Ps. of Prep. *rith.iw.a* Rp. of Prep. *rith.i.an.a* (Ar)

riwaya¹ *n* (*n*) novel: *Riwaya pendwa*, popular novel. *Riwaya sira*, biographical novel. *Riwaya tendi*, epic novel. *Riwaya teti*, picaresque novel. *Riwaya ya kihistoria*, historical novel. *Riwaya ya upepelezi*, detective novel. *Riwaya ya vitisho*, gothic novel. *Riwaya-chuku*, romance. *Riwaya barua*, epistolary novel. (Ar)

riwaya² *n* (*n*) narration, tradition; transmission of "hadith": *Riwaya za mitume*, "traditions" of prophets. (Ar)

riza *n* (*n*) see *reza*
rizavu[1] *n* (*n*) (*sports*) reserve (Eng)
rizavu[2] *n* (*n*) reserve; a piece of land set aside for wild animals, plants occupation, etc. (Eng)
riziki *n* (*n*) 1. sustenance, daily needs; means of subsistence: *Vibarua wale huenda gatini kutafuta riziki zao*, those labourers go to the harbour in search of their means of subsistence. 2. earnings; means of living: *Riziki haipatikani ila kwa jasho*, nothing is obtained without hard work. 3. God's blessings, God's providence (cf *majaaliwa*) 4. (*syn*) *Riziki na maji imekuwa si riziki*, time of death has come. (Ar)
robo *n* (*n*) one quarter; a fourth: *Ameifuja robo ya mali yake*, he has squandered one quarter of his wealth. *Robo tatu*, three quarters. *Roboduara*, quadrant. (Ar)
roboo *n* (*n*) a currency worth half-rupee or one shilling. (Ar)
robota (*ma-*) bale, bundle, package: *Pamba ilifungwa kwa marobota*, cotton was packed in bales. *Nimeuza marobota ya makatani leo*, I have sold bales of sisal today. *Robota la pamba*, cotton bale. (cf *mtumba, mtita, furushi*) (Ar)
roda *n* (*n*) pulley: *Roda fuasi*, driven pulley. (cf *kapi, abedari*) (Port)
rog.a (also *loga*) *vt* bewitch, charm; place black magic against someone with the intention of doing harm: *Alimroga jirani yake*, he bewitched his neighbour. Prep. **rog.e.a** St. **rog.ek.a** Cs. **rog.esh.a** Ps. **rog.w.a** be witched, be charmed. Rp. **rog.an.a** (cf *cheza*)
rogony.a *vi* gabble; speak quite fast special words which cannot be understood during witchcraft or when offering to proptitiate the spirits of the dead: *Waganga hutumia lugha ya kurogonya wakati wanapofanya shughuli zao za uganga*, the medicine men gabble when they perform their magical activities. Prep. **rogony.e.a** St. **rogony.ek.a** Cs. **rogony.esh.a** Ps. **rogony.w.a** Rp. **rogony.an.a**
rogw.a *vi* see *roga*
roho *n* (*n*) 1. soul, spirit, life; breath of life: *Kila roho itaonja mauti*, every soul will taste death. 2. (*idms*) *Kata roho*, die. *Kaza roho*, tolerate; be patient. *Kaba roho*, strangle, throttle. *Roho mkononi*, be nervous. *Roho dafafa*, the attitude of being hasty. 3. character, attitude, personality, individuality: *Ana roho nzuri*, he is kind-hearted. *Ana roho mbaya*, he is evil-hearted. 4. greediness, ravenousness, voraciousness: *Ana roho sana*, he is very greedy. 5. used in the expression: *Roho Mtakatifu*, the Holy Spirit.
rojo (also *rojorojo*) *n* (*n*) 1. thick gravy; sauce: *Mpishi amepika wali na rojo la mchuzi*, the cook has cooked rice and curry sauce. 2. thick liquid stuff like mud.
rojorojo[1] *n* (*n*) see *rojo*
rojorojo[2] *adj* juicy, succulent: *Mchuzi wa rojorojo*, succulent curry. *Nyama ya rojorojo*, succulent meat.
roketi *n* (*n*) rocket: *Kambi ya roketi*, rocket base. (Eng)
rombez.a *vt, vi* hang around hoping to be invited for food; sponge for food, drinks, etc.; scrounge: *Kazi yake ni kurombeza tu vyakula kwa majirani*, his job is just to sponge food from the neighbours. Prep. **rombez.e.a** St. **rombez.ek.a** Ps. **rombez.w.a** (cf *doea, rondea*)
ronda *n* (*n*) (*zool*) a kind of fish like a sardine.
ronde.a[1] *vt* rummage; search thoroughly, rifle through: *Alikuwa akirondea kipochi chake kwenye kabati*, she was rummaging for her purse in the cupboard. Prep. **ronde.le.a** St. **ronde.k.a** Cs. **rond.esh.a** Ps. **ronde.w.a** Rp. **ronde.an.a** (cf *chakura, pekua*)

653

ronde.a² *vt* sponge, scrounge, mooch, cadge: *Hurondea vyakula kwa rafiki zake*, he sponges food from his friends. Prep. ***ronde.le.a*** St. ***ronde.k.a*** Cs. ***ronde.sh.a*** Ps. ***ronde.w.a*** Rp. ***ronde. an.a*** (cf *buga, rombeza*)

rondo *n* (*ma-*) (*zool*) the fleshy back part of an animal between the knee and the hoof; leg

rong.a *vi* see *longa*. Prep. ***rong.e.a*** St. ***rong.ek.a*** Cs. ***ronge.sh.a*** Ps. ***rong.w.a*** Rp. ***rong,an.a***

rongarong.a *vt* see *engaenga²*

rongera *n* (*n*) sweet local beer or brew before it is fermented; unfermented local beer/brew.

-rongo *adj* deceitful, false, untruthful, lying: *Usimwamini mtu mrongo*, don't trust an untruthful person.

ronjo *adj* tall, towering: *Mtu ronjo*, a tall person.

ropok.a *vt, vi* blather, prattle; talk nonsense: *Watu humcheka akiropoka kwenye jukwaa*, people laugh at him when he prattles on the platform. Prep. ***ropok.e.a*** St. ***ropok.ek.a*** Cs. ***ropok. esh.a*** Ps. ***ropok.w.a*** (cf *bwabwaja, payuka, boboka*)

roromo.a *vi* (of wound, etc) expand, deepen, spread, stretch: *Kidonda kwenye mguu wake kimeroromoa*, the wound on his leg has deepened. Prep. ***roromo.le.a*** St. ***roromo.k.a*** Cs. ***roromo.sh.a*** Ps. of Prep. ***roromo. lew.a*** Rp. ***roromo.an.a***

roshani *n* (*n*) balcony: *Roshani yake inaelekea pwani*, his balcony faces the sea. (Pers)

rovu *n* (*n*) (*med*) goitre (cf *tezi, mlezi*)

rovurovu *adj* squishy, soggy, sodden, soaked, wet. (cf *chapachapa*)

rovyo *adj* succulent, sappy, soft: *Embe rovyo*, a succulent mango. (cf *teketeke, laini*)

row.a (also *loa*) *vi* get soaked; be drenched; get wet: *Alirowa baada ya kunyeshewa na mvua*, he got wet after it had rained on him. Prep. ***row.e.a*** St. ***row.ek.a***. Cs. ***row.esh.a*** Ps. of St. ***row.ek.w.a*** be soaked Rp. ***row.an.a***

rowan.a (also *lowana*) *vt, vi* get totally wet; be water logged: *Nguo zake zote zimerowana kufuatia mvua kubwa*, all of his clothes got wet because of the heavy rain. Prep. ***rowan.i.a*** St. ***rowan.ik.a*** Cs. ***rowanish.a*** wet, soak, damp e.g. *Jaribu kuzirowanisha nguo zako kabla hujazifua*, try to soak your clothes before you wash them.

rowanisha *vt* see *rowana*

rowek.a *vi* put sth in water for some time; soak, wet: *Mtumishi aliziroweka nguo zangu kabla ya kuzifua*, the servant soaked my clothes before washing them. Prep. ***rowek.e.a*** St. ***rowek. ek.a***

rowesh.a *vt, vi* cause sby/sth to get wet; soak, wet. Prep. ***rowesh.e.a*** St. ***rowesh.ek.a*** Ps. ***rowesh.w.a***

rozari *n* (*n*) rosary; a string of beads. (Eng)

ruba *n* (*n*) (*zool*) leech; a small bloodsucking worm living in wet places. (cf *mwata*)

rubaa *n* (*n*) clique, coterie, set; a group of people who share common interests: *Rubaa la waandishi*, literary coterie. (Ar)

rubani *n* (*ma-*) 1. pilot, aviator, flier, captain: *Rubani wa meli*, the ship's captain. *Rubani wa ndege*, air pilot. (cf *nahodha*) 2. leader, head, chief: *Yeye ni rubani wa shughuli zote za harusi hii*, he is the leader of all the activities of this wedding. (cf *kiongozi*) (Ar)

rubega (also *lubega*) *n* (*n*) a kind of dressing, clothing, etc. like that of a loin cloth, which involves passing the ends between the legs and tucking them into the fold round the waist.

rubun.i¹ *vt* swindle, fleece, deceive: *Alinirubuni kwa kuniuzia mchele mbaya*, he cheated me by selling me bad rice. Prep. ***rubun.i.a*** St. ***rubun. ik.a*** Cs. ***rubun.ish.a*** Ps. of Prep.

rubun.iw.a Rp. of Prep. ***rubun.i.an.a*** (cf *hadaa, ghilibu, danganya*) (Ar)
rubuni² *n* (*n*) see *arbuni*
rud.i¹ *vt, vi* return, go back, come back: *Alirudi kutoka Urusi wiki iliyopita*, he returned from Russia last week. Prep. ***rud.i.a*** St. ***rud.ik.a*** Cs. ***rud.ish.a*** return sth, send back e.g. *Rudisha mlango*, keep the door ajar. Ps. of Prep. ***rud.iw.a*** Rp. ***rud.i.an.a***, reunite, have a return match e.g. *Timu zile mbili zitarudiana baada ya kwenda sare*, those two teams will go for a replay after having drawn. (cf *rejea*) (Ar)
rud.i² *vt* pay back in money for the thing one has taken: *Alinirudi pesa kwa sababu ya kalamu aliyoichukua*, he paid me back in money for the pen he had taken. Prep. ***rud.i.a*** St. ***rud.ik.a*** Cs. ***rud.ish.a*** Ps. of Prep. ***rud.iw.a*** Ps. of Cs. ***rud.ish.iw.a*** be returned e.g. *Alirudishiwa kitabu chake alipozitoa pesa*, he had his book returned to him when he paid the money.
rud.i³ *vt* discipline, punish, warn, caution: *Alimrudi mtoto wake kwa kutowaamkia wageni*, he punished his child for failing to greet the visitors. Prep. ***rud.i.a*** St. ***rud.ik.a*** Cs. ***rud.ish.a*** Ps. of Prep. ***rud.iw.a***. Rp. of Prep. ***rud.i.an.a*** (cf *adhibu, onya*)
rud.i⁴ *vi* shrink, contract; become smaller: *Nguo yangu mpya imerudi baada ya kufuliwa*, my new dress has shrunk after being washed. Prep. ***rud.i.a*** St. ***rud.ik.a*** Cs. ***rud.ish.a*** (cf *ruka*)
rudi.a *vt vi* repeat, reiterate. Prep. ***rudi.li.a*** St. ***rudi.k.a*** Cs. ***rudi.w.a*** Ps. ***rudi.w.a*** (cf *ruka*)
rudian.a *vt* see *rudi¹* and *rudi³*
rudish.a *vt* 1. see *rudi¹*. 2. refund: *Rudisha pesa*, refund the money. Prep. ***rudish.i.a*** St. ***rudish.ik.a*** Ps. ***rudish.w.a*** Rp. of Prep. ***rudish.i.an.a***
rudishi.a *vt* replace. St. ***rudishi.k.a*** Ps of Prep. ***rudishi.w.a*** Rp. of Prep. ***rudishi.an.a***

ruduf.u *vt* 1. strengthen sth by doubling it; harden; make strong: *Walizirudufu kamba kwa kuzisonga mbilimbili*, they strengthened the ropes by weaving them in twos. 2. duplicate, replicate, copy: *Alilirudufu jarida*, he duplicated the magazine. Prep. ***ruduf.i.a*** St. ***ruduf.ik.a*** Cs. ***ruduf.ish.a*** Ps. of Prep. ***ruduf.iw.a*** (Ar)
rufaa¹ *n* (*n*) see *rufani*
rufaa² *n* (*n*) cargo, freight, lading: *Meli ilipakua rufaa*, the ship unloaded the cargo. (cf *shehena*) (Ar)
rufa.i *vt* elevate, raise, lift. Prep ***rufa.i.a*** St. ***rufa.ik.a*** Cs. ***rufa.ish.a*** Ps. of Prep. ***rufa.iw.a*** (Ar)
rufaish.a *vt* cause to ascend. Prep. ***rufaish.i.a*** St. ***rufaish.ik.a*** Ps. ***rufaish.w.a*** (Ar)
rufani (also *rufaa¹*) *n* (*n*) legal appeal: *Rufani dhidi ya rufani*, counter appeal. *Kata rufani*, lodge an appeal.
rugaruga *n* (*ma-*) a subordinate workman working under a chief: *Chifu alimtaka rugaruga wake kuwakaribisha wageni*, the chief wanted his subordinate to welcome the guests.
ruhani *n* (*ma-*) a kind of benign genie; a kind of supernatural being that can take human or animal form and influence human affairs. (Ar)
ruhusa *n* (*n*) permission, authority, sanction: *Omba ruhusa*, ask for permission. *Nyima ruhusa*, refuse permission. *Toa ruhusa*, give permission. *Serikali ilimpa ruhusa ya kuondoka*, the government gave him permission to leave. (cf *idhini, kibali*) (Ar)
ruhus.u *vt* allow, permit, authorise. Prep. ***ruhus.i.a*** St. ***ruhus.ik.a*** Cs. ***ruhus.ish.a*** Ps. of Prep. ***ruhus.iw.a*** Rp. of Prep. ***ruhus.i.an.a*** (cf *idhinisha, ridhia, kubali*) (Ar)
rui *n* (*ma-*) fraud, crook, swindler, rogue: *Nilimwamini bila ya kujua kwamba yeye ni rui*, I trusted him without knowing that he is a crook. (cf *tapeli*) (Ar)

ruiya *n* (*n*) see *ruya*.
rujum.u *vt* attack by stoning; kill by stoning. Prep. *rujum.i.a* St. *rujum.ik.a* Cs. *rujum.ish.a* Ps. of Prep. *rujum. iw.a* Rp. of Prep. *rujum.i.an.a* (Ar)
ruk.a¹ *vt, vi* 1. jump, hop, spring, skip (cf *chupa, kiuka, tambuka*) 2. (*idm*) *Rukwa na akili*, lose one's mind. 3. fly up; pass through the air: *Niliiona ndege ikiruka*, I saw the aeroplane flying up. (*prov*) *Kila ndege huruka kwa ubawa wake*, every bird flies according to its wing i.e. every person operates according to his capability. 4. by-pass an officer in the chain of command in an organization: *Mfanyakazi alimruka mkurugenzi wake alipokwenda moja kwa moja kuonana na meneja mkuu*, the worker bypassed his director when he went straight to see the general manager. Prep. *ruk.i.a* St. *ruk.ik.a* Cs. *ruk.ish.a* Ps. *ruk.w.a* Rp. *ruk.an.a*
ruk.a² *vi* deny, reject, dispute, refuse: *Nilimwambia kwamba yeye alivichukua viatu vyangu lakini akaruka haraka*, I told him that he had taken my shoes but he denied it immediately. Prep. *ruk.i.a* St. *ruk.ik.a* Cs. *ruk.ish.a* (cf *kana, kataa*)
ruk.a³ *vi* shrink, contract; become smaller: *Shati langu sasa limeruka baada ya kufuliwa sana*, my shirt has now shrunk after being washed many times. Prep. *ruk.i.a* St. *ruk.ik.a* Cs. *ruk.ish.a* (cf *rudi, chupa*)
ruki.a *vt, vi* 1. catch sth by jumping at it. 2. jump into a vehicle, etc. (cf *dandia*) 3. intrude, snoop, pry, meddle: *Mbona unapenda kurukia katika mazungumzo yetu?* Why do you like to meddle in our conversation? (cf *ingilia*)
ruku.u *vi* (in Islam) bow with hands on the knees while praying so that the back and the head become straight line. Prep. *ruku.i.a* St. *ruku.ik.a* Cs. *ruku.ish.a* Ps. of Prep. *ruku. iw.a* (Ar)
rukwama *n* (*n*) see *rikwama*

rula *n* (*n*) ruler (Eng)
ruma *n* (*n*) rumour, gossip. (cf *uvumi, tetesi*) (Eng)
rumada *n* (*n*) (*naut*) gudgeon; a pivot on which a rudder is swung. (Port)
rumande *n* (*n*) remand: *Weka rumande*, put someone in remand. (Eng)
rumani¹ *n* (*n*) the nipples of a breast of a young girl; tit, teat. (cf *chuchu, kilembwe, tombo*)
rumani² *n* (*n*) (*bot*) pomegranate (cf *komamanga*)
rumba *n* (*n*) a kind of dance of Cuban Negro origin having a complex rhythm; rumba. (Eng)
rumbi *n* (*n*) a kind of large water jar.
rumenya *n* (*n*) 1. gigolo, ladykiller; the illicit sexual partner of a mistress: *Wekwa rumenya*, be kept at a woman's place. 2. cohibition at a woman's place.
rund.a *vi* be stunted in growth; be dwarfed; fail to get full development: *Watoto wale wawili wamerunda kwa sababu ya utapiamlo*, those two children are stunted because of malnutrition. St. *rund.ik.a* Cs. *rund. ish.a* Ps. *rund.w.a* Rp. *rund.an.a* (cf *via, dumaa*)
rundik.a (also *lundika*) *vt* be piled up on top of the other; accumulate, heap up: *Amerundika bidhaa nyingi dukani*, he has piled up a lot of goods at the shop. Prep. *rundik.i.a* St. *rundik.ik.a* Cs. *rundik.ish.a* Ps. *rundik.w.a* Rp. *rundik.an.a*, be piled up in one place in large numbers. (cf *kusanya*)
rundikan.a *vi* see *rundika*
rundo (also *lundo*) *n* (*ma-*) heap, pile, stock, bulk: *Rundo la taka*, a heap of garbage. *Rundo la karatasi*, a heap of papers. *Rundo la sarafu*, a stack of coins.
rung.a *vt, vi* gather esp for the purpose of hunting; assemble, convoke: *Wasasi walirunga ili kwenda kuwinda wanyama wa porini*, the hunters gathered together in order to go hunting wild animals. Prep. *rung.i.a*

St. **rung.ik.a** Cs. **rung.ish.a**
rungu n (ma-) knobkerrie, club, cudgel, bludgeon: *Askari alitumia rungu kumpiga mwizi*, the policeman used a club to beat the thief. (cf *gongo, kibarango*)
runinga n (n) television (cf *televisheni*)
rupia n (n) 1. rupee; currency used in India, Pakistan and some other countries in Asia. 2. (*syn*) *Rupia kwa ya pili*, as alike as two rupees, i.e. as alike as two twins; exactly the same. (Hind)
rus.a vt seduce, lure; tempt someone to have sexual intercourse: *Alimrusa msichana mrembo*, he seduced a glamorous girl. Prep. **rus.i.a** St. **rus.ik.a** Cs. **rus.ish.a** Ps. **rus.w.a** Rp. **rus.an.a** (cf *tongoza*)
rush.a[1] vt deny (sth) outright. Prep. **rush.i.a** St. **rush.ik.a**
rush.a[2] vt 1. throw, hurl, fling, sling: *Alirusha mkuki*, he threw a spear. (cf *tupa*) 2. see *ruka*[2]. 3. used in the expression: *Rusha kichwa*, frogwalk sby. *Rusha roho*, put someone in a state of anxiety. St. **rush.ik.a** Ps. **rush.w.a** Rp. **rush.an.a** Rp. of Prep. **rush.i.an.a**
rushwa n (n) bribe, kickback: *Kula rushwa*, take a bribe. *Pokea rushwa*, receive a bribe. *Toa rushwa*, give a bribe; offer a bribe. (cf *hongo, chai*) (Ar)
rusu[1] n (n) tier, row, rank: *Zipange mbegu hizi katika rusu tatu*, plant these seeds in three rows.
rus.u[2] vt arrange in tiers/layers. Prep. **rus.i.a** St. **rus.ik.a** Cs. **rus.ish.a** Ps. **rus.w.a**
rusu[3] n (n) (*zool*) pinworm; a small nematode worm (*Enterobius vermicularis*) found as a parasite in the human rectum and large intestine esp in children.
rutuba n (n) soil fertility, soil productiveness; fecundity: *Ardhi hii haina rutuba*, this land is not fertile. (Ar)

-rutubifu adj fertile, productive: *Ardhi rutubifu*, fertile land. (Ar)
rutubik.a vi (of soil) be fertile, become fertile: *Ardhi yangu sasa imerutubika*, my land has now become fertile. Prep. **rutubik.i.a** St. **rutubik.ik.a** Cs. **rutubik.ish.a** (Ar)
rutubish.a vt 1. apply nutrients. 2. enrich, develop, improve. Prep. **rutubish.i.a** St. **rutubish.ik.a** Ps. **rutubish.w.a** Rp. **rutubish.an.a**
rutubisho n (ma-) soil fertility; soil productiveness. (Ar)
ruwaza n (n) 1. example, model: *Fuata ruwaza ya wazee wako*, follow the example of your parents. (cf *mfano, kigezo*) 2. (*phon*) *Ruwaza ya kiimbo*, intonation pattern. (Ar)
ruya n (n) vision, dream. (Ar)
ruz.u vi become impoverished; become very poor; be in financial difficulties *Tangu kufukuzwa kazini hivi karibuni, mtu yule sasa ameruzu*, since being dismissed from work recently, that person has now become impoverished Prep. **ruz.i.a** St. **ruz.ik.a** Cs. **ruz.ish.a** (Ar)
ruzuk.u[1] vt, vi (of God) bestow blessings; provide daily needs: *Mungu amemruzuku mwanamke yule kwa kupata watoto wengi*, God has blessed that woman with many children. Prep. **ruzuk.i.a** St. **ruzuk.ik.a** Cs. **ruzuk.ish.a** Ps. of Prep. **ruzuk.iw.a**, be blessed. (Ar)
ruzuku[2] n (n) grants usu given by the government to a particular organization, etc. to meet the necessary needs; subsidy: *Serikali ilivipa vyama vya upinzani ruzuku zao*, the government gave the opposition parties the grants due to them. (Ar)
ruzuna n (n) herbal medicine which is supposed to cure madness or children's cough: *Anataka kufanyiwa ruzuna*, he needs to be treated to cure his madness. (Ar)

S,s /s/ 1. the eighteenth letter of the Swahili alphabet. 2 it is a voiceless fricative.

saa[1] *n (n)* 1. hour, time: *Saa ngapi sasa hivi?* What is the time now? (cf *muda, wakati)* 2. watch, clock: *Saa ya mkono.* wristwatch. *Saa ya ukutani,* wall clock. *Saa za mauzo,* shop hours. (Ar)

saa[2] *interj* an expletive used to express amazement or urge someone to do sth: *Sema saa!* tell me! *Wacha saa!* don't tell me!

sa.a[3] (also *salia*) *vt, vi* remain, be left. Prep. ***sa.li.a*** Ps. of Prep. ***sa.li.w.a*** (cf *baki, selekea*) (Ar)

saada *n (n)* luck, fortune; happy chance: *Alipata saada ya kushinda kwenye bahati nasibu,* he was lucky to win in the lottery. (cf *fuluki, futahi, sudi*) (Ar)

saari *n (n)* price, value. (cf *bei, thamani*) (Ar)

saba (also *sabaa*) *adj* 1. seven. 2. the number of days a person is confined for a particular purpose as in the case of treatment, circumcision, etc. 3. honeymoon. (*cf fungate*) (Ar)

sababish.a *vt* cause, be the cause of, be the reason for: *Alisababisha ugomvi kati yetu,* he caused a quarrel between us. Prep. ***sababish.i.a*** St. ***sababish.ik.a*** Ps. ***sababish.w.a*** (cf *anzisha*) (Ar)

sababu *n (n)* 1. cause, reason, basis: *Sababu zisizo na msingi,* baseless reasons. *Sababu zisizozuilika,* unavoidable circumstances. (cf *chanzo, kisa*) 2. reason, grounds: *Toa sababu zako kwa nini umemtaliki mkeo,* give your reasons why you have divorced your wife. (cf *hoja, maelezo*) 3. motive, goal, purpose, intent, aim: *Alikwenda kule kwa sababu gani?* For what reason did he go there? (cf *madhumuni, lengo*) (Ar)

sabah.i *vt* greet someone in the morning: *Alinisabahi nilipokuwa ninakula staftahi yangu,* he greeted me while I was taking my breakfast. Prep. ***sabah.i.a*** St. ***sabah.ik.a*** Cs. ***sabah.ish.a*** Ps. of Prep. ***sabah.iw.a*** Rp. of Prep. ***sabah.i.an.a*** (cf *amkia, lahiki*) (Ar)

sabalkheri (also *subalkheri*) *interj* Good morning. (Ar)

Sabasaba *n (n)* 1. the day on which the ruling party, *Tanu* was founded in Tanganyika. 2. Trade Fair Day in Tanzania is observed on 7th july of every year.

sabasi *n (n)* incendiary, firebrand, trouble-maker: *Majirani wamemlaani sabasi yule,* the neighbours have cursed that firebrand. (cf *fatani, chakubimbi*) (Ar)

sabatashara *adj* seventeen (Ar)

sabatele *n (n)* (*bot*) a low quality unhusked rice seed.

sabato *n (n)* (in Christianity) the Sabbath; the seventh day of the week, namely Saturday set aside for worship: *Waadventista wa Sabato,* Seventh Day Adventists. (Eng)

sabid.i *vt* arrange; put in order. Prep. ***sabid.i.a*** St. ***sabid.ik.a*** Cs. ***sabid.ish.a*** Ps. of Prep ***sabid.iw.a*** (cf *panga, tengeneza*) (Ar)

sabih.i *vt* glorify the name of God. Prep. ***sabih.i.a*** St. ***sabih.ik.a*** Cs. ***sabih.ish.a*** Ps. of Prep. ***sabih.iw.a*** Rp. of Prep. ***sabih.i.an.a*** (Ar)

sabik.i *vt* lead the way, go before; precede: *Alisabiki shuleni na baadaye nikafika mimi,* he led the way to school and later I followed him. Prep. ***sabik.i.a*** St. ***sabik.ik.a*** Cs. ***sabik.ish.a*** Ps. of Prep. ***sabik.iw.a*** (cf *takadamu, tangulia*) (Ar)

sabiini[1] (*also sabini*) *n (n)* seventy (Ar)
sabiini[2] (*also sabini*) *adj* seventy (Ar)

sabili¹ n (n) (*poet*) path, road. (cf *njia*) (Ar)
sabili² n (n) used in the expression: *Toa sabili*, 1. give sth for the sake of God. 2. give sth free: *Jitolea sabili*, sacrifice. (Ar)
sabili³ adj free, gratuitous. (Ar)
sabili.a vt offer sth freely to be used to someone. Cs. *sabili.sh.a* Ps. of Prep. *sabili.w.a* (Ar)
sabini¹ n (n) see *sabiini¹* (Ar)
sabini² adj see *sabiini²*
sabmarini n (n) submarine (cf *nyambizi*) (Eng)
sabuni n (n) soap: *Mchi wa sabuni*, bar of soap. *Sabuni ya kufulia*, laundry soap. *Sabuni ya kuogea*, bath soap. (syn) *Kujikaza kisabuni*, suffer while you are enduring the hardships at the same time. (Ar)
sachi¹ n (n) search, inspection: *Fanya sachi*, conduct a search. (cf *upekuzi*, *speksheni*) (Eng)
sach.i² vt search, inspect, investigate: *Waliisachi nyumba yangu bila ya kuona chochote*, they searched my home without seeing anything. Prep. *sach.i.a* St. *sach.ik.a* Cs. *sach.ish.a* Ps. of Prep. *sach.iw.a* Rp. of Prep. *sach.i.an.a* (cf *pekua*, *speksheni*) (Eng)
sadaka n (n) 1. religious offering; alms: *Alitoa sadaka kuwapa masikini*, he gave alms to the poor. (cf *zaka*) 2. ritual sacrifice: *Walitoa sadaka kwa mizimu*, they offered their sacrifices to the spirits of the dead. (Ar)
sadakta interj an expletive of approval, appreciation, etc. to someone. (cf *vizuri*, *barabara*) (Ar)
sadfa n (n) simultaneous occurrence of two events; coincidence, fluke, chance: *Ilikuwa sadfa tu kukutana naye mnadani*, it was just a coincidence that I met him at the auction. (Ar)
sadif.u¹ vt turn out to be accidental; turn out to be a coincidence: *Ilisadifu harusi yake siku ya Krismasi*, his wedding coincided with Christmas. Prep. *sadif.i.a* St. *sadif.ik.a* (Ar)

sadifu² adj suitable, proper: *Teknolojia sadifu*, suitable technology.
sadik.i vt,vi believe, trust, count on; have confidence in: *Usiyasadiki maneno yake*, don't trust his words. Prep. *sadik.i.a* St. *sadik.ik.a*, be credible Cs. *sadik.ish.a* Ps. of Prep. *sadik.iw.a*, be accepted, be trusted e.g. *Maelezo yake yalisadikiwa na polisi*, his statement was accepted by the police. Ps. of Cs. *sadik.ish.w.a*, become verified, become convinced (cf *amini*, *kubali*)
sadikifu adj trustworthy, credible, responsible: *Taarifa yake ni sadikifu*, his statement is credible. (Ar)
sadikik.a vi see *sadiki*
sadiri n (n) (*poet*) 1. chest. (cf *kifua*) 2. heart (cf *moyo*) (Ar)
safa n (n) a kind of big and deep trough, used for taking a bath.
safari¹ n (n) journey, trip, tour. (syn) *Safari ni hatua*, a journey is by steps i.e. one may encounter a lot of problems when one is travelling. (cf *ziara*, *matembezi*) (Ar)
safari² n (n) occasion, time, turn: *Safari ya mwisho*, last time. (cf *zamu*, *mara*) (Ar)
safi¹ adj 1. clean, neat, spotless: *Nguo zake ni safi*, his clothes are clean. (cf *nadhifu*) 2. pure, clean: *Moyo wake ni safi*, his heart is clean i.e. he is a good hearted person. (cf *rahimu*) 3. correct, accurate: *Ametoa maelezo safi*, he has given a clear statement. (cf *sahihi*) (Ar)
saf.i² vt see *safisha*
safi³ interj an exclamation of approval, admiration, etc.: *Safi sana!* Wonderful! Great!
safihi¹ (also *safii*) n (ma-) 1. a rude person; a discourteous person; boor, churl: *Safihi yule anaweza kukuadhiri mbele za watu*, that churl can discredit you in public. (cf *sodai*) 2. a reticent person. (Ar)
safihi² (also *safii*) adj rude, impolite, brazen, bad mannered: *Mwanafunzi*

safihi, a rude student. (Ar)
safih.i³ (also *safii*) *vt, vi* be rude to sby; be impolite to sby: *Alinisafihi burebure*, he was rude to me for no reason. Prep. *safih.i.a* St. *safih.ik.a* Cs. *safih.ish.a* Ps. of Prep. *safih.iw.a*
safii¹ *n (n)* see *safihi¹*
safii² *adj* see *safihi²*
safi.i *vt,vi* see *safihi³*
safina *n (n)* 1. Noah's ark. 2 dhow, ship. (Ar)
safir.i *vt, vi* travel, voyage, tour: *Hajawahi kusafiri kwenda Ulaya*, he has never travelled to Europe. Prep. *safir.i.a* St. *safir.ik.a* Cs. *safir.ish.a* Ps. of Prep. *safir.iw.a* (cf *abiri, ondoka*) (Ar)
safiri.a *vt* 1. travel for (in, by, with, etc.): *Utasafiria chombo gani?* By what means will you travel? 2. rely/depend on sby's luck: *Usisafirie nyota ya mwenzio*, don't depend on sby's luck.
safirish.a *vt* send off: *Alimsafirisha mgeni wake*, he sent off his guest. Prep. *safirish.i.a* St. *safirish.ik.a* Ps. *safirish.w.a* Rp. *safirish.an.a*
safish.a (also *safi*) *vt, vi* 1. clean, purify; make clean: *Mtumishi alikisafisha chumba changu*, the servant cleaned my room. 2. (*fig*) clean one's heart: *Lazima ujisafishe moyo*, you must clean your heart. Prep. *safish.i.a* St. *safish.ik.a* Ps. *safish.w.a* Rp. *safish.an.a* (Ar)
safu *n (n)* 1. row, queue, range: *Safu ya milima*, mountain range. *Safu ya ushambuliaji*, offensive line of players. (cf *msafa*) 2. rank, grade; the plan of arranging things in order: *Mwenye duka alizipanga bidhaa zake kwa safu*, the shopkeeper arranged his goods in order. (Ar)
safura *n (n)* 1. (*med*) hookworm disease. (cf *kung'uta*) 2. parasitic hookworms (family *Ancylostomatidae*) with hooks around the mouth, infesting the small intestine of man and other animals, esp in tropical climates. (Ar)

sag.a *vt* 1. grind, mill, crush: *Alizisaga dengu*, she ground the lentils. (cf *ponda, twanga*) 2. rub two objects together by applying friction or pressure: *Gurudumu lilisaga madigadi*,the wheel rubbed on the mudguard. 3. (of women) practise an erotic role between two members of the same sex; practise lesbianism. Prep. *sag.i.a* St. *sag.i.k.a* Cs. *sag.ish.a* Ps. *sag.w.a* Rp. *sag.an.a*
sagai¹ *n (n)* a short stabbing spear used by Zulus and kindred tribes. (*mkuki, fumo*)
sagai² *n (n)* a kind of ceremony marking the consent of the bride's parents after a proposal for marriage has been submitted to them.
sagamba *n (n)* callus, induration; the hardness on a skin: *Mikono yake imefanya sagamba kwa sababu ya kukata miti*, his hands have developed calluses for felling trees. (cf *suguru*)
saghiri *adj* (*poet*) small, little. (cf *dogo*) (Ar)
sagik.a *vi* be ground, be milled. Prep. *sagik.i.a* St. *sagik.ik.a* (cf *pondeka*)
sago¹ *n (n)* (*bot*) 1. a dry banana stem cover; leaf vine. (cf *sapatu*) 2. a dry leaf of banana plant. (cf *koa*) 3. the breadth of a strip plaited palm leaf.
sago² *n (n)* used in the expression: *Kula sago*, play traditional dance and to enjoy it.
sagu.a *vt,vi* mock, ridicule; make fun of: *Watoto wadogo waliwasagua walemavu*, the small children mocked the crippled. Prep. *sagu.li.a* St. *sagu.lik.a* Cs. *sagu.lish.a* Ps. of Prep. *sagu.liw.a* Rp. *sagu.an.a* (cf *tania, dhihaki*)
saguo *n (n)* 1. mockery, ridicule; teasing; act (method, etc.) of teasing. 2. an expletive used in ridiculing someone.
sahaba *n (n)* one of the companions of Prophet Muhammad who embraced

sahala¹ ... **sail.i**

Islam, saw the Prophet and accompanied him even for a short period. (Ar)
sahala¹ n (n) see *sahali¹*
sahala² adj see *sahali²*
sahali¹ (also *sahala, sahili*) n (n) easiness, smoothness: *Safari yake ilikuwa ya sahali tangu mwanzo mpaka mwisho*, his trip was smooth right from the beginning to the end. (cf *wepesi*)
sahali² (also *sahala, sahili*) adj easy, simple: *Mambo yake yalikuwa sahali kabisa*, his affairs turned out to be completely simple. (Ar) (cf *rahisi*)
sahani n (n) 1. plate, dish. (cf *kombe*) 2. gramophone record. (Ar)
sahari n (n) a kind of cloth made from silk or cotton, used to make a turban; turban cloth. (Ar)
saha.u¹ vt forget, overlook; fail to remember: *Nimelisahau jina lake*, I have forgotten his name. (prov) *Usisahau ubaharia kwa kupata unahodha*, don't forget the work of being a sailor by becoming a captain i.e. don't despise those who are low in rank or forget the bottom place where you started, now that you have gained a big position. Prep. *sahau.li.a* St. *sahau.lik.a* Cs. *sahau.lish.a* Ps. of Prep. *sahau.liw.a*, be forgotten. (cf *ghafilika*) (Ar)
sahau² n (n) forgetfulness, obliviousness, absent-mindedness: *Ana sahau nyingi*, he is very forgetful. (cf *mghafala*)
-sahaulifu adj forgetful, absent-minded, oblivious: *Mtu msahaulifu*, an absent-minded person. (Ar)
sahibu n (n) friend, companion: *Yeye ni sahibu yangu wa miaka mingi*, he has been my friend for many years. (cf *mwandani, rafiki, mwenzi*) (Ar)
sahifa n (n) page or leaf of a book. (cf *ukurasa*) (Ar)
sahih.i¹ vt see *sahihisha*
sahihi² adj correct, right, true: *Hesabu sahihi*, correct calculation. (Ar)
sahihi³ n (n) signature: *Tia sahihi*, sign sth. (cf *saini*) (Ar)

sahihish.a (also *sahihi*) vt 1. correct, rectify; set right: *Wachezaji waliyasahihisha makosa yao*, the players rectified their mistakes. (cf *rekebisha, sawazisha*) 2. mark, correct: *Mwalimu alizisahihisha karatasi za mtihani*, the teacher marked the examination papers. Prep. *sahihish.i.a* St. *sahihish.ik.a* Ps. *sahihish.w.a* Rp. *sahihish.an.a*
sahihisho n (ma-) correction, adjustment, rectification. (cf *rekebisho*) (Ar)
sahili¹ adj *sahali²*
sahili² (usu *sahilisha*) vt simplify, make easier. Prep. *sahil.i.a* St. *sahil.ik.a* Cs. *sahil.ish.a* Ps. of Prep *sahil.iw.a* (cf *rahisisha*) (Ar)
sahilish.a vt see *sahili²* Prep. *sahilish.i.a* St. *sahilish.ik.a* Ps. *sahilish.w.a* Rp. *sahilish.an.a*
sa.i¹ vt 1. provoke someone so as to make him fight: *Alimsai rafiki yangu*, he provoked my friend to the point of fighting. (cf *chokoza, udhi*) 2. challenge or invite a person to compete in a game: *Walimsai katika mashindano ya farasi*, they challenged him to compete in the horse race. Prep. *sa.i.a* St. *sa.ik.a* Cs. *sa.ish.a* Ps. *sa.iw.a* Rp. of Prep. *sa.i.an.a* (Ar)
sa.i² vt (in Islam) go hurriedly while perfoming pilgrimage around the mountains of "As-Safa" and "Al-Marwah" Prep. *sa.i.a* St. *sa.ik.a* Cs. *sa.ish.a* Ps. *sa.iw.a* Rp. *sa.i.an.a*
saidi n (n) see *sayidi*
saidi.a vt assist, aid, help: *Alinisaidia wakati wa dhiki*, he helped me in time of difficulties. St. *saidi.k.a* Cs. *saidi.sh.a* Ps. *saidi.w.a* Rp. *saidi.an.a* (cf *auni, nafidhi*) (Ar)
saikolojia n (n) psychology: *Saikolojia ya elimu*, educational psychology. *Saikolojia ya kiisimu*, linguistic psychology. (Eng)
sail.i vt interrogate, question, ask, quiz: *Polisi walimsailijuu ya wizi*, the police

interrogated him about the theft. Prep. **sail.i.a** St. **sail.ik.a** Cs. **sail.ish.a** Ps. **sail.iw.a** Rp. **sail.i.an.a** (cf *uliza, hoji*) (Ar)

saini[1] *n* (n) signature: *Tia saini*, sign; put your signature. (cf *sahihi*) (Eng)

sain.i[2] *vt* sign; put one's signature on sth: *Aliusaini mkataba*, he signed the contract. Prep. **sain.i.a** St. **sain.ik.a** Cs. **sain.ish.a** Ps. **sain.iw.a** Rp. of Prep. **sain.i.an.a** (cf *idhinisha*) (Eng)

sair.i[1] *vt* coddle, cossett, pamper; sooth someone esp a child: *Mama alimsairi binti yake alipolia*, the mother soothed her daughter when she cried. Prep. **sair.i.a** St. **sair.ik.a** Cs. **sair.ish.a** Ps. **sair.iw.a** Rp. of Prep. **sair.i.an.a** (cf *sihi, bembeleza, rai*)

sair.i[2] *vt* (*naut*) hug the shoreline in a vessel such as a ship, dhow, etc. Prep. **sair.i.a**. St. **sair.ik.a** Cs. **sair.ish.a** Ps. **sair.iw.a** Rp. of Prep. **sair.i.an.a**

sair.i[3] *vt* pound in a mortar by using a pestle, etc; thresh: *Alivisairi vitunguu thaumu kwenye kinu*, he threshed the garlic in the mortar. Prep. **sair.i.a** St. **sair.ik.a** Cs. **sair.ish.a** Ps. **sair.iw.a** Rp. of Prep. **sair.i.an.a** (cf *twanga, ponda*) (Ar)

sairi[4] *n* (n) (in Islam) a name given to one of the hell-fires; burning fire. (Ar)

saisi *n* (n) a person in charge of horses, etc. groom. (Ar)

saizi *n* (n) size, measurement: *Shati hili si saizi yangu*, this shirt is not of my size. (cf *kadiri, cheo, kipimo*) (Eng)

sajil.i (also *rajisi*) *vt* register, record: *Walikisajili chama chao cha siasa*, they registered their political party. Prep. **sajil.i.a** St. **sajil.ik.a** Cs. **sajil.ish.a** Ps. **sajil.iw.a**, be registered Rp. of Prep. **sajil.i.an.a** (cf *orodhesha*) (Ar)

sajini *n* (n) sergeant: *Sajini meja*, sergeant major. (cf *bimbashi*) (Eng)

sak.a *vt* hunt, search for, look for: *Polisi walikuwa bado wanawasaka majambazi sugu*, the police were still hunting the hardcore criminals. Prep. **sak.i.a** St. **sak.ik.a** Cs. **sak.ish.a** Ps. **sak.w.a** Rp. **sak.an.a** (cf *tafuta*)

sakafi.a *vt* put a floor for sby. Prep. **sakafi.li.a** St. **sakafi.k.a** Cs. **sakafi.sh.a** Ps. **sakafi.shw.a**

sakafu[1] *n* (n) 1. floor: *Sakafu ya zege*, cement floor, floor board. 2. flat roof. (*prov*) *Mbio za sakafuni huishia ukingoni*, running on a roof finishes at the edge i.e. one may rush very fast for a particular assignment, project, etc., yet, the final results may not be good for him.

sakaf.u[2] (also *sakifu*) *vt* lay cement floor: *Nilisakafu nyumba yangu*, I cemented the floor of my house. Prep. **sakaf.i.a** St. **sakaf.ik.a** Cs. **sakaf.ish.a** Ps. of Prep. **sakaf.iw.a** Rp. of Prep. **sakaf.i.an.a**

sakam.a[1] *vt* be stuck as in the case of food in a throat; be jammed, be choked: *Chakula kilimsakama kooni*, the food choked him in the throat. Prep. **sakam.i.a** St. **sakam.ik.a** Cs. **sakam.ish.a** and **sakam.iz.a** Ps. **sakam.w.a** Rp. **sakam.an.a** (cf *kwama, data*)

sakam.a[2] *vt* 1. rankle, pester, irk, annoy: *Maneno yake yalinisakama moyoni*, his words rankled in my heart. (cf *udhi, kera, choma*) 2 (in sports, etc.) attack continuously: *Wachezaji wao walilisakama goli la timu yetu katika dakika za mwisho*, their players attacked the goalmouth of our team in the dying minutes. 3. insist on sby to sth. Prep. **sakam.ia** St. **sakam.ik.a** Cs. **sakam.ish.a** and **sakam.iz.a** Ps. **sakam.w.a** Rp. **sakam.an.a**

sakamw.a *vi* be chased, be hunted: *Kiongozi alisakamwa na wapinzani wake*, the leader was hunted by his opponents.

sakarani *adv* in a state of unconsciousness because of being drunk: *Hali yake ilikuwa sakarani*, he was unconscious because of being drunk. (Ar)

sakat.a¹ *vt* hit; go at it, eat up everything, do sth wonderfully well: *Alikisakata chakula*, he ate up everything. *Alimsakata ngumi*, he punched him hard. *Alisakata disko usiku kucha*, he pounded out a disco dance the whole night. *Yeye anajua kulisakata gozi*, he knows how to play soccer skilfully. Prep. *sakat.i.a* St. *sakat.ik.a* Cs. *sakat.ish.a* Ps. *sakat.w.a* Rp. *sakat.an.a*

sakata² *n (n)* 1. chaos, pandemonium, disorder: *Sakata ilitokea ndani ya basi wakati abiria alipokataa kulipa nauli*, pandemonium broke out inside the bus when a passenger refused to pay for the bus fare. (cf *sokomoko, fujo, ghasia*) 2. controversy, dispute (cf *mzozo*)

sak.i *vt, vi* 1. (of clothes, stopper of a bottle, etc.) be crammed together, be tight, be stuck: *Kizibo kilisaki kwenye mdomo wa chupa*, the cork got stuck in the neck of the bottle. 2. stick well in a place; be firm. Prep. *sak.i.a* St. *sak.ik.a* Cs. *sak.ish.a* and *sak.iz.a* Ps. *sak.iw.a* (cf *kwama*)

sakim.u *vi* be sick, be ill: *Amesakimu kwa kiasi cha mwezi mmoja sasa*, she has been ill for one month now. Prep. *sakim.i.a* St. *sakim.ik.a* (Ar)

sakin.i¹ *vt, vi* dwell, domicile, reside, live at. Prep. *sakin.i.a* St. *sakin.ik.a* Cs. *sakin.ish.a* Ps. *sakin.iw.a* (Ar)

sakin.i² *vt* see *sikini*

sakramenti *n (n)* (in Christianity) sacrament; any of certain rites ordained by Jesus and regarded as a means of grace. (Eng)

saksafoni *n (n)* (*mus*) saxophone; a keyed wood wind instrument having a single reed, conical, and metal body, usu curved.

saksafoni

sakubimbi (also *shakubimbi*) *n (n)* incendiary, firebrand, troublemaker: *Sakubimbi yule heshi kugombanisha watu*, that firebrand never stops creating discord among people. (cf *salata, mfitini, subusi*)

sala (also *swala*) *n (n)* 1. prayer: *Sala ya sunna*, optional prayer. *Sala ya jamaa*, congregational prayer. 2. ceremonial prayer. (Ar)

salaam *n (n)* see *salamu*

saladi *n (n)* salad: *Saladi ya matunda*, fruit salad. (Eng)

salala¹ *interj* an expletive of wonder: *Salala! Itakuwaje mwanamke yule kuzaa watoto watano?* Incredible! How can that woman bear five children? (cf *afanalayek! du!*) (Ar)

salala² *n (n)* see *sarara*

salama¹ *n (n)* peace, security, safety: *Nchi ile haina salama*, that country is not peaceful. (cf *usalama, amani, utulivu*)

salama² (also *salaam*) *adv* peacefully, safely: *Fika salama*, have a safe trip. *Lala salama*, sleep well. *Nenda salama*, go safely. (Ar)

salamati *n (n)* (*naut*) top-mast rope in a vessel such as a dhow, etc.

salamu *n (n)* 1. greetings, compliments, best wishes: *Pokea salamu za dhati*, receive sincere greetings. *Peleka salamu*, convey greetings. *Toa salamu*, send greetings. (cf *maamkizi*) 2. message: *Salamu aliyonipa ni kwamba umpelekee kitabu chake kwa haraka*, the message he has given me is that you should send him his book as soon as possible. (cf *ujumbe, maagizo*) 3. used while Muslims greet one another: *Salamu aleikum,* peace be with you. (Ar)

salata *n (n)* a sower of discord; firebrand, incendiary, troublemaker, rabble-rouser: *Usifanye urafiki na salata,* don't make friendship with a troublemaker. (cf *mchonganishi, sabasi, mfitini*) (Ar)

sal.i *vt, vi* pray; recite prayers: *Alisali kwa unyenyekevu,* he prayed with humbleness. Prep. *sal.i.a* St. *sal.ik.a* Cs. *sal.ish.a* Ps. *sal.iw.a* (Ar)

sali.a¹ *vt* see *sali*

sali.a² *vt, vi* see *saa³*

sali.a³ *vi* be left over, be extra. (cf *baki, bakia*)

salili *n (n)* (*zool*) Cape teal, Cape wigeon; a small pale white and brownish duck with a bright pink bill and a pale crown. *Anas capensis.* (cf *kotwe*)

salimi.a¹ *vt* send greetings St. *salimi.k.a* Cs. *salimi.sh.a* Ps. *salimi.w.a* Rp. of Prep. *salimi.an.a*

salimia² *n (n)* a kind of liniment used for relieving muscular pains, sprains, cramps, aching joints, etc.

salimi.k.a *vi* 1. be safe, be rescued; survive: *Alisalimika katika ajali ya gari,* he survived in the car accident. 2. be in a state of peacefulness. Prep. *salimik.i.a* St. *salimik.ik.a*

salimini *adv* used in the expression: *Salama wa salimini,* safe and sound. (Ar)

salimish.a *vt* 1. surrender, capitulate, give up: *Waasi walikubali kusalimisha silaha zao,* the rebels agreed to give up their weapons. 2. rescue, save. (cf *okoa*) Prep. *salimish.i.a* St. *salimish.ik.a* Ps. *salimish.w.a* Rp. *salimish.an.a*

salim.u¹ (also *salimia*) *vt* 1. send regards; express good wishes. 2. greet, salute: *Nilimsalimu kwa mbali nilipomwona barabarani,* I greeted him from far when I saw him on the road. Prep. *salim.i.a* St. *salim.ik.a* Cs. *salim.ish.a* Ps. of Prep. *salim.iw.a* Rp. of Prep. *salim.i.an.a* (Ar)

salim.u² *vt* used in the expression: *Salimu amri,* surrender. Prep. *salim.i.a* St. *salim.ik.a* Cs. *salim.ish.a.* Ps. of Prep. *salim.iw.a* (cf *chicha, kai*) (Ar)

salio *n* (*ma-*) residue, remains; leftovers: *Salio la chakula,* the leftover food. (cf *sazo, bakaa*) (Ar)

salish.a *vt* conduct prayers. Prep. *salish,i.a* St. *salish.ik.a* Ps. *salish.w.a* Rp. *salish.an.a*

salit.i¹ *vt* 1. betray one's country, etc.: *Aliisaliti nchi yake,* he betrayed his country. (cf *hini, asi*) 2. stir up trouble between people; calumniate, instigate: *Aliwasaliti majirani zake wawili,* he stirred up trouble between his two neighbours. Prep. *salit.i.a* St. *salit.ik.a* Cs. *salit.ish.a* Ps. *salit.iw.a* Rp. of Prep. *salit.i.an.a* (cf *gombanisha, fitini, chonganisha*) (Ar)

salit.i² *vt* adulterate, mix, blend; put together: *Aliusaliti unga na mayai na baadaye akatengeneza keki,* he blended the flour and eggs and then prepared cakes. Prep. *salit.i.a* St. *salit.ik.a* Cs. *salit.ish.a* Ps. *salit.iw.a* (cf *changanya*) (Ar)

salitik.a *vt* be enamoured of; be captivated by: *Amesalitika sana na msichana mwanafunzi,* he is too enamoured with the female student. Prep. *salitik.i.a* Cs. *salitik.ish.a* (cf *rengwa, oza, vutiwa*)

salua *n (n)* history, account. (cf *mapisi, historia*)

saluni *n (n)* salon; an establishment where women go for hairdressing. (Eng)

saluti (also *soluti*) *n (n)* 1. salute; a special gesture of respect to the army, navy, etc.: *Piga saluti,* salute. *Toa saluti,* salute. *Pokea saluti,* take the salute. 2. (*fig*) compliment, congratulations, salute. (cf *pongezi, hongera*) (Eng)

sama *n (n)* summer (Eng)

samadari *n* (*n*) a kind of Zanzibar wooden bed with thick decorated legs. (Hind)
samadi *n* (*n*) animal dung used as manure. (Ar)
samahani[1] *interj* an expletive for asking someone's apology; excuse me! sorry! (Ar)
samahani[2] *n* (*n*) apology, forgiveness: *Omba samahani*, seek forgiveness. (cf *kumradhi*) (Ar)
samai[1] *n* (*n*) a kind of music involving the use of a flute and tambourine, found in Muslim functions; instrumental religious music. (Ar)
samai[2] *n* (*n*) skies (cf *mbingu*) (Ar)
samaki *n* (*n*) (*zool*) fish. (*prov*) *Samaki mmoja akioza ni mtungo pia*, if one fish gets spoilt, the whole string will also get spoilt i.e. if one person in a group is bad, he spoils the image of the rest of the members in that group; that is to say, the rest of the members are also considered to be bad. (Ar)
samani *n* (*n*) furniture: *Seremala amemaliza kunitengenezea samani yangu*, the carpenter has finished making my furniture. (cf *fanicha*) (Pers, Hind)
samawari *n* (*n*) a kind of long urn with a receptacle for keeping charcoal beneath, used usu by coffee sellers. (cf *mdele*)
samawati[1] *n* (*n*) sky blue colour. (Ar)
samawati[2] *n* (*n*) skies (cf *mbingu*)
samba.a *vt* be scattered, be dispersed; spread about: *Wakimbizi wamesambaa katika nchi za jirani*, the refugees are scattered in the neighbouring countries. Prep. *samba.li.a* St. *samba.lik.a* Cs. *samba.z.a* (cf *tapakaa, zagaa*)
sambamba *adv* abreast; side by side, bumper to bumper: *Magari yamefuatana sambamba barabarani*, the cars are going side by side on the highway. (cf *sanjari*)
sambaratik.a *vi* be in disarray, be disorderly, be in a state of confusion: *Miradi yake ilisambaratika*, his projects were in disarray. *Taifa lao lilisambaratika*, their nation was in disarray. Prep. *sambaratik.i.a* Cs. *sambarat.ish.a*
sambaratish.a *vt* disorder, unsettle, destabilize: *Serikali ilivisambaratisha vyama vya upinzani*, the government destabilized the opposition parties. Prep. *sambaratish.i.a* St. *sambaratish.ik.a* Ps. *sambaratish.w.a* Rp. *sambaratish.an.a*.
sambarik.a *vi* see *tambarika*. Prep. *sambarik.i.a* St. *sambarik.ik.a* Cs. *sambarik.ish.a* Ps. *sambarik.w.a*
sambasamb.a *vi* be uneasy; be restless: be occupied: *Alikuwa akisambasamba mitaani akimtafuta binti yake*, she was restless looking for her daughter in the neighbourhood. Prep. *sambasamb.i.a* St. *sambasamb.ik.a* Cs. *sambasamb.ish.a* (cf *hangaika, hamanika*)
samberuru *n* (*n*) see *mchumbururu*
sambik.a *vt* compel to do sth; force, pressurize: *Mwenye nyumba alimsambika mtumishi wake kukata nyasi*, the landlord forced his servant to slash the grass. Prep. *sambik.i.a* St. *sambik.ik.a* Cs. *sambik.iz.a* Ps. *sambik.w.a*, be compelled. Rp. *sambik.an.a* (cf *lazimisha, kalifisha*)
sambiz.a *vt* purify a dead body by washing: *Walimsambiza maiti na baadaye wakamzika*, they purified the dead body by washing and later buried it. Prep. *sambiz.i.a* St. *sambiz.ik.a* Cs. *sambiz.ish.a* Ps. *zambiz.w.a*
sambo[1] *n* (*n*) sailing vessel e.g. dhow, boat. (*prov*) *Kila muacha samboye huenda ali mwanamaji*, he who abandons his sailing vessel is still a sailor i.e. whoever abandons to practise his profession will still be identified or recognized by his previous work.
sambo[2] *n* (*n*) blood (cf *ngeu, damu*)
sambusa *n* (*n*) samosa; an Indian three-sided pastry case filled up with chopped meat, onions, chillies, vegetables, etc. and cooked in hot fat. (Pers)

sameh.e vt, vi 1. forgive, pardon, remit: *Alinisamehe kwa kosa nililolifanya,* he forgave me for the mistake I had committed. (cf *ghofiri*) 2. (of debts, etc.) say that sby needs not repay the money owed; forgive: *Walikuwa wakimdai pesa nyingi lakini sasa wamemsamehe,* they used to owe him a lot of money but they have now released him from the debt. Prep. **sameh.e.a** St. **sameh.ek.a** Cs. **sameh.esh.a** Ps. **sameh.ew.a** Rp. of Prep. **sameh.e.an.a** (Ar)

samesame n (n) 1. red bead. 2. (*zool*) a kind of reddish brown ant. 3. (*bot*) a kind of small red fruit.

samli n (n) ghee (Ar)

samoni[1] n (n) (*law*) summons; a notice summoning a defendant to appear in a court. (Eng)

samon.i[2] vt, vi summons; order sby to appear in court by the issuance of a summons. (Eng)

sampuli n (n) 1. sample, kind, sort. (cf *aina, namna*) 2. new design; new fashion. (cf *mtindo*) (Eng)

samsuli n (n) see *sansuli*

sana[1] adv very much, very: *Alikuwa anaumwa sana,* she was very sick. (cf *mno*)

san.a[2] vt (cf hammers, shoes, etc.) forge, beat, hammer out: *Aliusana mnyororo,* he forged the chain. (*prov*) *Mtoto wa mhunzi asiposana huvukuta,* if the son of a professional is not an expert, he can still make use of the tools of his father. (Ar)

sanaa n (n) arts, fine arts, skilled handicraft: *Sanaa za maonyesho,* theatre arts. *Sanaa za jadi,* traditional art. *Sanaa pendwa,* popular art. *Sanaa ya masimulizi,* narrative art. *Kazi ya sanaa,* craftwork. (Ar)

sanamaki n (n) (*bot*) senna; dried leaves from a tropical plant (*Genus Cassia*) used as a laxative. (Ar)

sanamu n (n) statue, idol. (Ar)

sanda[1] n (n) a cloth covering a dead body for burial; shroud. (cf *katani*)

sanda[2] n (n) a customary fee given to the bereaved in order to meet burial expenses. (cf *ubani*)

sandali n (n) 1. (*bot*) sandalwood obtained from the tree *msandali* (*Santalum album*). 2. a kind of perfume made from sandal wood. (Ar)

sandarusi n (n) (*bot*) gumcopal obtained from the tree *msandarusi. Trachylobium verrucosum.* (Ar)

sanduku n (*ma-*) box, suitcase, trunk, case: *Sanduku la maiti,* coffin. *Sanduku la kura,* ballot box. *Sanduku la Agano,* Ark of the covenant. *Sanduku la bahari,* boxfish; a kind of fish of yellowish with hexagonal plates and having two prominent spines pointing forward from above eyes. (Ar)

sangara[1] n (n) (*zool*) a kind of small red ant that bites very much and goes in parties, and is usu found in plantations, trees, etc. *Oecophylla longnoda* (cf *mdudumoto, chaki, maji moto, koyokoyo*)

sangara[2] n (n) (*zool*) Nile Perch.

sange n (n) (*zool*) true shrew; mouse like mammal (*family Soricidae*) with soft, brown fur and a long, pointed snout.

sange

sanid.i vt construct, make: *Alisanidi ngalawa,* he constructed a canoe. *Alisanidi mtungi,* he made a water jar. *Alisanidi sanamu,* he constructed a statue. Prep. **sanid.i.a** St. **sanid.ik.a** Cs. **sanid.ish.a** Ps. **sanid.iw.a** Rp. of Prep. **sanid.i.an.a** (cf *unda, tengeneza*) (Ar)

sanifish.a vt, vi (*gram*) standardize; make standard or uniform: *Lazima* *tuisanifishe lugha yetu*, we must standardize our language. Prep. *sanifish.ia* St. *sanifish.ik.a* Ps. *sanifish.w.a* Rp. of Prep. *sanifish.ian.a*

sanif.u¹ *vt* compose; do an artful job, do a job with skill: *Yeye ni hodari katika kusanifu picha za binaadamu*, he is good at drawing human beings. Prep. *sanif.i.a* St. *sanif.ik.a* Cs. *sanif.ish.a* Ps. of Prep. *sanif.iw.a* (Ar)

sanif.u² *vt* mock, ridicule: *Hupenda kuwasanifu rafiki zake*, he likes to ridicule his friends. Prep. *sanif.i.a* St. *sanif.ik.a* Cs. *sanif.ish.a* Ps. of Prep. *sanif.iw.a* Rp. of Prep. *sanif.i.an.a* (cf *kejeli, kebehi, tania*) (Ar)

-sanifu³ *adj* 1. entertaining, amusing, pleasing: *Mtu msanifu*, an amusing person. 2. standard, official, acceptable: *Lugha sanifu*, standard language. (Ar)

sani.i *vt* produce work of art; compose artistic work: *Alilisanii shairi la ukombozi*, he skilfully composed a poem on liberation. Prep. *sani.li.a* St. *sani.lik.a* Cs. *sani.sh.a* Ps. *sani.w.a*

sanjari (also *chanjari*) *adv* side by side, abreast, cheek by jowl: *Waliandamana sanjari mpaka kazini kwao*, they went to their place of work side by side. (cf *sambamba*) (Ar)

sansuli (also *samsuli*) *n* (*n*) (*zool*) a kind of fish of the families Xiphidae and Istiophoridae having a sail-like dorsal fin and with the upper jawbone extending in a swordlike projection, found mainly in oceanic but sometimes coastal waters as well; marlin, sail-fish, sword fish. Striped marlin. *Tetrapturus audax*.

sansuli

sansuri *n* (*n*) a kind of knife like a sword with a blunt point.

santuri *n* (*n*) (*mus*) gramophone, record player: *Sahani ya santuri*, gramophone disc. (cf *gramafoni, kinanda*) (Ar)

sanzu.a *vt* steal; take away sth without the permission of the owner; *Alizisanzua nyanya sokoni wakati mwenyewe alipokuwa hayupo*, he stole the tomatoes at the market when the owner was away. Prep. *sanzu.li.a* St. *sanzu.lik.a* Cs. *sanzu.lish.a* Ps. *sanzu.liw.a*

sanzuk.a *vi* leave, depart. Prep. *sanzuk.i.a* St. *sanzuk.ik.a* Cs. *sanzuk.ish.a* (cf *ondoka*)

sap.a¹ *vt* deplete all of sby's wealth; declare bankrupt; make insolvent: *Walitsapa mali yake yote*, they bankrupted all of his property. Prep. *sap.i.a* St. *sap.ik.a* Cs. *sap.ish.a* Ps. *sap.w.a* (cf *filisi, komba*)

sapa² *n* (*n*) an old worn-out thing still in use e.g. basket, cloth, etc.: *Aliniletea sapa langu*, he sent me my old worn-out thing.

sapasap.a *vi* see *tapatapa*.

sapatu¹ *n* (*n*) slippers, sandals. (cf *koshi*) (Port)

sapatu² *n* (*n*) a kind of reed rope plaited from palm leaves and used for making baskets, mats, etc. (Port)

sar.a *vt* spread mud, blood, etc. everywhere; smear completely. Prep. *sar.i.a* St. *sar.ik.a* Cs. *sar.ish.a* Ps. *sar.w.a* Rp. *sar.an.a*

sarabi *n* (*n*) mirage. (cf *mazigazi*) (Ar)

saradani *n* (*n*) see *seredani*

sarafu *n* (*n*) 1. coin; small change: *Sarafu hizi hazina thamani*, these coins have no value. 2. small metal plate worn as an ornament by women round their neck or on the head. (Ar)

sarahangi (also *serehangi*) *n* (*n*) second in-command after a captain in a sailing vessel such as a dhow, etc.

saraka *n* (*n*) drawer of a table. (cf *dawati, almari*) (Pers)

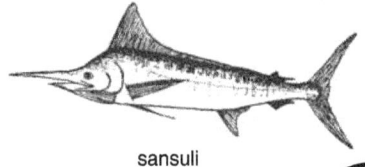

sarakasi n (n) circus; travelling company comprising of entertainers including acrobats, riders, clowns, animals, etc. (Eng)
saramala n (ma-) see *seremala*
sarara (also *salala*) n (n) meat containing part of the backbone; chine, sirloin steak.
Saratani[1] n (n) 1. (*astron*) Saturn; the second largest planet in the solar system with nine known satellites, sixth in distance from the sun. 2. Crab; the constellation and fourth sign of the Zodiac. (Eng)
saratani[2] n (n) (*med*) cancer: *Saratani ya damu*, cancer of the blood; leukaemia. *Saratani ya matiti*, breast cancer. *Saratani ya kibofu*, prostate cancer. *Saratani ya mapafu*, lung cancer. (cf *kensa*) (Ar)
sarataṅji n (n) see *sataranji*
sare[1] *adv* 1. uniformly, exactly the same: *Walivaa sare*, they wore exactly the same. 2. (in sports) a draw in scoring; tie: *Timu zile mbili zilienda sare*, those two teams drew. (cf *suluhu*) (Ar)
sare[2] n (n) a special cloth won esp by Indians in a wedding, etc.
sarifik.a *vt, vi* be contented, be satisfied: *Mvulana yule hasarifiki*, that boy is never satisfied.
sarif.u[1] *vt* compose sth elegantly esp in language; use words well with style, etc. Prep. *sarif.i.a* St. *sarif.ik.a* Cs. *sarif.ish.a* Ps. of Prep. *sarif.iw.a* (Ar)
sarif.u[2] *vt* organize; arrange in order: *Mtu yule anajua kuyasarifu mambo yake*, that person knows how to organize his affairs. Prep. *sarif.i.a* St. *sarif.ik.a* Cs. *sarif.ish.a* Ps. of Prep. *sarif.iw.a* (cf *panga, ratibu*)
sarufi n (n) grammar: *Sarufi mapokeo*, traditional grammar. *Sarufi fafanuzi*, descriptive grammar. *Sarufi bia*, general grammar, universal grammar. *Sarufi zalishi*, generative grammar. *Sarufi maumbo*, formal grammar. *Sarufi uhusika*, case grammar. *Sarufi muundo virai*, phrase structure grammar. *Sarufi muundo virai changamano*, generalized phrase structure grammar. *Sarufi geuza maumbo zalishi*, transformational generative grammar. *Sarufi egemezi*, dependency grammar. *Sarufi elekezi*, prescriptive grammar. *Sarufi msonge*, systematic grammar. *Sarufi linganishi*, comparative grammar. *Sarufi miundo ukomo*, finite state grammar. *Sarufi kanuni*, formal grammar. *Sarufi huru*, context free grammar. *Sarufi muktadha*, context sensitive grammar. *Sarufi miundo ambajengo*, constituent structure grammar. (Ar)
saruji[1] n (n) 1. cement. (cf *simenti, simiti*) 2. rubble; debris of demolition (cf *kifusi*) (Ar)
saruji[2] n (n) saddle of a horse or donkey. (Ar)
saruni n (n) sarong; a kind of loin-cloth usu coloured and worn by Muslims of the various areas as in Malay, Arabia, etc. (cf *shuka*) (Mly)
sasa[1] *adv.* 1. now, at present, at this time: *Sasa ataondoka*, now he will leave. 2. used in the construction: *Sasa hivi*, just now; right now.
sasa[2] n (n) present period, up to date, modern.
sasa[3] n (n) nest, roost. (cf *kiota*)
sasa[4] n (n) (*bot*) a kind of green leafy plant like spinach used as vegetables. (cf *kibwando*)
sasambu.a *vt* defeat overwhelmingly; thrash: *Timu yao iliisasambua Arsenal kwa mabao mawili*, their team thrashed Arsenal by two goals. Prep. *sasambu.li.a* St. *sasambu.k.a* Cs. *sasambu.lish.a* Ps. of Prep. *sasambu.liw.a* Rp. *sasambu.an.a* (cf *bamiza, nyuka*)
sasamlanda n (n) (*bot*) a kind of herb used as a vegetable after being pounded and cooked.

satalaiti n (n) satellite: *Kituo cha satalaiti,* satellite station.
sataranji[1] (also *sarataṇji*) n (n) the game of chess.
sataranji[2] n (n) a kind of sleeping mat usu made of broad plaited leaf-strips.
satini n (n) a kind of glossy fabric having a smooth finish, made from cotton threads, etc.; satin. (Eng)
sato n (n) (*zool*) a kind of freshwater fish resembling very much a snapper, found mostly in inshore waters in Lake Victoria, etc.; Tilapia nilotica. Oreochromis niloticus. (cf *ngege*)
satua n (n) authority, power, capacity, influence: *Hana satua juu ya jambo hili,* he has no authority over this issue. (cf *ushawishi*) (Ar)
saujik.a vi see *sawijika*
saumu[1] n (n) fasting, fast: *Saumu ya sunna,* optional fast. *Saumu ya faradhi,* obligatory fast. *Funga saumu,* fast; observe fasting. (Ar)
saumu[2] (also *thomo*) n (n) (*bot*) garlic: *Kitunguu saumu,* garlic. (Ar)
sauti n (n) voice, sound: *Sauti bubu,* mute. *Sauti dhahania,* absolute sound. *Sauti mitindo,* phonosylistics. *Sauti nong'ono,* breathy voice. *Sauti zoloto,* creaky voice. *Sauti halisi,* concrete sound. *Sauti peke,* tone of voice. *Sauti pambizo,* marginal element. *Paza sauti,* raise the voice. (cf *mlio, ukemi*) 2. used in the expression: *Sema kwa sauti moja,* speak in unison; speak with one voice. 3. used in the expression: *Kuwa na sauti,* have a say; have authority. (Ar)
savana n (n) (*geog*) savannah; an open flat area of treeless grassy plains in tropical and subtropical regions. (Eng)
sawa[1] (also *sawasawa*) adj 1. accurate, precise, correct, alright: *Maneno yake yako sawa,* his words are accurate. (cf *barabara*) 2. equal, same, alike. (Ar)

sawa[2] (also *sawasawa*) adv properly, well: *Aliifanya kazi sawa,* he did the work well. (cf *vizuri, barabara*) (Ar)
sawa[2] *interj* exactly ! okay !
sawanyish.a vt see *sawazisha*
sawasawa[1] adj see *sawa*[1]
sawasawa[2] adv see *sawa*[2]
sawazish.a (also *sawanyisha*) vt 1. rectify, sort out, square: *Kiongozi alisawazisha makosa yake,* the leader rectified his mistakes. 2. equalize: *Mchezaji alisawazisha goli katika dakika za mwisho,* the player equalized the goal in the last minutes. Prep *sawazish.i.a* St *sawazish.ik.a* Ps *sawazish.w.a* Rp *sawazish.an.a* (cf *rekebisha*)
sawia adv at the same time, simultaneously: *Kufika kwake na kuja kwetu kulitokea sawia,* his coming and our arrival occurred simultaneously.
sawid.i[1] vt draft, draw up, write: *Aliusawidi wasia,* he drafted the will. Prep. *sawid.i.a* St. *sawid.ik.a* Cs. *sawid.ish.a* Ps. *sawid.iw.a* Rp. of Prep. *sawid.i.an.a* (Ar)
sawid.i[2] vt dishonour, discredit, defame, degrade: *Walitusawidi bila ya msingi wowote,* they discredited us for no reason. Prep. *sawid.i.a* St. *sawid.ik.a* Cs. *sawid.ish.a* Ps. *sawid.iw.a* (cf *aziri, kashifu*) (Ar)
sawijik.a (also *saujika*) vi 1. be disfigured; be marred; be emaciated from illness, disease, famine, etc.: *Uso wake ulisawijika baada ya kupata ugonjwa wa ukoma,* his face became disfigured after contracting leprosy. (cf *haribika, fujika*) 2. (*fig*) be in a mess; be in disarray; be spoiled: *Mipango yake imesawijika,* her plans are in disarray. Prep. *sawijik.i.a* Cs. *sawiji.sh.a* (cf *vurugika, haribika*) (Ar)
sawir.i vt 1. draw a picture; paint a picture: *Msanii aliisawiri sura yangu,* the artist drew my face. 2. ponder, think, meditate: *Alisawiri juu ya matatizo mbalimbali,* he pondered over

669

many problems. Prep. *sawir.i.a* St. *sawir.ik.a* Cs. *sawir.ish.a* Ps. *sawir. iw.a* (cf *fikiri, waza*) (Ar)
sayansi *n* (*n*) science: *Sayansi kimu,* domestic science. *Sayansi asilia,* natural science. *Sayansi ya elimu viumbe,* biological science, *Sayansi jamii,* social science. *Sayansi ya kiisimu,* linguistic science. *Sayansi umbile,* physical science. *Sayansi ya uchumi wa kilimo,* agronomy.
sayari *n* (*n*) 1. planet: *Sayari ndogo,* planetoid. 2. anything that rotates around the planet. (Ar)
sayidi (also *saidi, seyyid*) *n* (*n*) lord, master, king, majesty: *Sayidi yangu,* my lord. (Ar)
saz.a (also *saa*) *vt, vi* leave over, leave unfinished, cause to remain: *Mpishi alikisaza chakula,* the cook left the food behind. Prep. *saz.i.a* St. *saz.ik.a* Cs. *saz.ish.a* Ps. *saz.w.a*
sazo *n* (*ma-*) remains, leftover. (cf *baki, salio*)
sebeh.a *n* (*n*) breakfast; take a morning meal: *Alisebeha kwa kunywa chai na mayai ya kuchemsha,* he took his breakfast of tea and boiled eggs. Prep. *sebeh.e.a* St. *sebeh.ek.a* Cs. *sebeh. esh.a* (cf *staftahi*)
sebule *n* (*n*) sitting room; reception room; waiting room; lounge. (cf *ukumbi*) (Ar)
sedek.a *vi* be ill for a long time; be suffering from a long illness: *Mgonjwa amekuwa akisedeka kitandani kwa muda mrefu,* the patient has been bed-ridden for a long time. Prep. *sedek.e.a* St. *sedek. ek.a* Ps. *sedek.w.a* (cf *ugua*)
sefle *n* (*n*) see *sefule.*
sefu[1] *n* (*ma-*) a strong lockable box or cupboard with thick metal sides, used for storing valuables; safe. (Eng)
sefu[2] *n* (*n*) sword, matchet. (cf *upanga*) (Ar)
sefule (also *sefle*) *n* (*ma-*) a disgusting person; a stupid person: *Watu wengi wanambeza sefule yule,* many people ignore that stupid person. (cf *mpuuzi, baradhuli*) (Ar)

sega[1] *n* (*ma-*) honeycomb (cf *kambaa*)
seg.a[2] *vt* roll up a dress by holding its bottom edge; shorten a dress by folding the bottom edge and making a new hem; turn up: *Alisega kanzu yake kabla ya kuanza kulima kondeni,* she turned up her garment before beginning to work in the field. Prep. *seg.e.a* St. *seg.ek.a* Cs. *seg.esh.a* Ps. *seg.w.a* Rp. *seg.an.a* (cf *kweza, kunja, pania*)
seg.a[3] *vi* sit by being packed tightly together; sit by being squeezed or crammed together. Prep. *seg.e.a* St. *seg.ek.a* Cs. *seg.esh.a* Ps. *seg.w.a* Rp. *seg.an.a*
segele *n* (*n*) see *shegele*
segemnege *adv* awry, haphazardly, disorderly: *Mambo yake yamekwenda segemnege,* his affairs have gone haphazardly. (cf *shelabela, ovyoovyo*)
segu.a *vt* see *sekua* Prep. *segu.li.a* St. *segu.k.a* and *segu.lik.a* Cs. *segu. lish.a* Ps. of Prep. *segu.liw.a*
sehele.a *vi* see *selea*
sehemu *n* (*n*) 1. portion, segment, fraction, section, part: *Sehemu guni,* improper fraction. *Sehemu halisi,* proper fraction. *Sehemu kawaida,* common factor. *Sehemu moja,* unit fraction. *Sehemu mtambuko,* cross-section. *Sehemu sahili,* simple fraction. *Sehemu ya desimali,* decimal fraction. (cf *fungu, kasama, kundi*) 2. side, part: *Wakimbizi walipelekwa katika sehemu mbalimbali,* the refugees were sent to different places. (cf *upande, janibu*) 3. (*gram*) component: *Sehemu msingi,* base component. (Ar)
sehewa *n* (*n*) (*zool*) bonito, tuna; a kind of saltwater fish (family *Scombridae*) having an elongate and fusiform body with strong teeth and jaws, found in coastal waters and far offshore.
sekanti *n* (*n*) (*math*) secant; any straight line intersecting a curve at two or more points. (Eng)

sekasek.a *vi* walk with difficulties; traipse. Prep. *sekasek.e.a* St. *sekasek.ek.a* Cs. *sekasek.esh.a* (cf *jikongoja*)

sekenek.a *vi* have syphillis: *Mgonjwa wangu alikuwa akisekeneka kwa muda mrefu*, my patient had syphillis for a long period. Prep. *sekenek.e.a* St. *sekenek.ek.a* Cs. *sekenek.esh.a*

sekeneko *n* (*n*) (*med*) syphillis (cf *kaswende, farangi*)

sekenene *n* (*n*) sty; an inflamed swelling of a sebaceous gland on the rim of an eyelid. (cf *chekea, chokea*)

sekeseke *n* (*n*) confusion: *Sekeseke ilisababishwa na watazamaji walipouvamia uwanja*, confusion was caused by the spectators when they invaded the pitch. (cf *fujo, ghasia*)

sekini *n* (*n*) a kind of shaving leaving a tuft of hair on the crown; quiff. (cf *denge, panja, bwenzi*)

sekondari *n* (*n*) secondary school: *Sekondari ya juu*, upper secondary school. *Sekondari ya awali*, lower secondary school. (Eng)

sekretari *n* (*n*) secretary (cf *mhazili*) (Eng)

sekretarieti *n* (*n*) secretariat (Eng)

sekta *n* (*n*) sector, area: *Sekta ya uchumi*, economic sector. *Sekta ya utalii*, tourism sector. *Sekta ya elimu*, education sector. *Sekta ya kilimo*, agricultural sector. *Sekta binafsi*, private sector. *Sekta ya umma*, public sector. (Eng)

seku.a (also *sikua, sukua*) *vt* uproot, extirpate, unroot: *Mkulima aliisekua miche yake*, the farmer uprooted his seedlings. Prep. *seku.li.a* St. *seku.k.a* Cs. *seku.lish.a* Ps. of Prep. *seku.liw.a* Rp. *seku.an.a* (cf *ng'oa, tekua, futua, zidua*)

sekunde *n* (*n*) (of time) second: *Sekunde ishirini*, twenty seconds. (cf *nukta*) (Eng)

sele.a (also *sehelea, selehea, selelea*) *vt* stay at; remain in a place for quite long. Prep. *sele.le.a* St. *sele.k.a* Ps. *sele.w.a* (cf *baki*)

selehe.a *vt* see *selea*

selele.a *vt* see *selea*

seli[1] *n* (*n*) sale; a special disposal of goods at lowered prices. (Eng)

seli[2] *n* (*n*) a small room in a prison where a particular prisoner is kept; cell. (Eng)

seli[3] *n* (*n*) cell; a piece of equipment for producing electricity from chemicals, heat or light. (Eng)

selo (also *sero*) *n* (*n*) 1. siren, honker, horn. (cf *king'ora, honi*) 2. signal of the arrival or departure of a sailing vessel.

selwa *n* (*n*) see *surwa*

sem.a *vt, vi* 1. speak, utter, say: *Alisema maneno machafu*, he uttered obscene words. (cf *umba, nena, tamka*) 2. speak against: *Walinisema nilipokuwa sipo*, they spoke against me when I was away. (cf *sengenya*) 3. advise, counsel. Prep. *sem.e.a* St. *sem.ek.a* Cs. *sem.esh.a* and *sem.ez.a* Ps. *sem.w.a* Rp. *sem.an.a*

semantiki (also *simantiki*) *n* (*n*) semantics; the study of meaning in language: *Semantiki miundo*, structural semantics. *Uchunguzi wa kisemantiki*, semantic analysis. (Eng)

sembe *n* (*n*) (*bot*) maize flour, corn flour.

sembuse *adv* let alone, not to mention: *Dada yako alishindwa kuwapiga watoto wale sembuse wewe*, your elder sister couldn't beat those children let alone you. (cf *fakaifa, kaifa, kefu, seuze*)

semekan.a *vt* be said, be claimed, be asserted: *Inasemekana kwamba wao hawakuwa raia wa nchi hii*, it is said that they were not the citizens of this country.

sementi (also *simenti, simiti*) *n* (*n*) cement (Eng)

semezan.a *vi* 1. converse; talk /speak to each other: *Walikuwa wanasemezana*

kwenye mkutano, they were talking to each other at the meeting. 2 start reconciling after a period of non-communication between the parties. Prep. *semezan.i.a* St. *semezan.ik.a* Cs. *semezan.ish.a*
semina n (n) 1. seminar, workshop: *Semina ya waandishi*, writer's workshop. (Eng)
seminari n (n) seminary (Eng)
semitiki adj semitic: *Lugha za semitiki*, semitic languages. (Eng)
sena[1] n (n) a word used to describe the good quality of sth; beautiful.
sena[2] n (n) (bot) a kind of thin sweet potato leaves.
sene.a vi (of knife, tool, etc.) be blunt: *Kisu chake kimesenea*, his knife is blunt. St. *sene.k.a* Cs. *sene.z.a*
senene[1] n (n) (zool) edible grasshopper; a kind of grasshopper usu green (family *Tettigoniidae*) used as food. The adults of this kind fly in swarms during the rainy season. They are sporadically serious pests in many cereal crops at the milky stage.

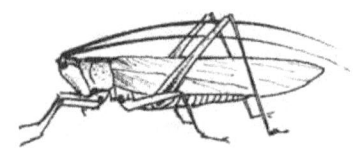

senene

senene[2] n (n) (med) long illness.
seneta n (n) 1. senator; a member of a university council. 2. a member of the legislative assembly in U.S. (Eng)
seneti n (n) 1. senate; a supreme governing or advisory council in a university or college. 2. a supreme legislative assembly in U.S.
senezo n (n) adze; a tool like an axe having a blade at right angles, used for trimming and smoothing wood, etc. (cf *tezo*)

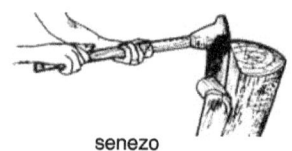

senezo

seng.a vt cut with a sharp instrument such as a knife: *Aliisenga miti kwa panga kali*, he cut the trees with a sharp matchet. Prep. *seng.e.a* St. *seng.ek.a* Cs. *seng.esh.a* Ps. *seng.w.a* Rp. *seng.an.a*
seng'enge (also *senyenge*) n (n) barbed wire with sharp points on it, used for fences, etc.
sengeny.a vt backbite: *Alinisengenya burebure*, he backbited me for nothing. Prep. *sengeny.e.a* St. *sengeny.ek.a* Cs. *sengey.esh.a* Ps. *sengeny.w.a* Rp. *sengeny.an.a* (cf *teta, simbulia*)
sens.a[1] vt censor; examine a book, film, etc. and remove unacceptable parts of it. (cf *kagua*) (Eng)
sensa[2] n (n) census; an official count or survey, esp of a population. (Eng)
senta n (n) centre (cf *katikati*) (Eng)
sentafowadi n (n) (in soccer, etc.) centreforward (Eng)
sentahafu n (n) (in soccer, etc) centrehalf
sentensi n (n) (gram) sentence: *Sentensi sahili*, simple sentence. *Sentensi changamano*, complex sentence. *Sentensi ambatano*, compound sentence. *Sentensi zalishwa*, derived sentence. *Sentensi msingi*, kernel sentence; basic sentence. *Sentensi solo*, matrix sentence. *Sentensi yakinishi*, declarative sentence; affirmative sentence. *Sentensi funge*, bound sentence. *Sentensi ambajengo*, constituent sentence. (Eng)
senti n (n) cent (Eng)
sentigramu n (n) centigram (Eng)
sentimita n (n) centimetre (Eng)
senturi n (n) see *santuri*
sepetu n (n) shovel, spade. (cf *beleshi, pauro, shepe*)

sepetu

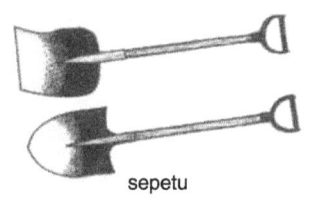

sepetuk.a *vi* walk unsteadily as if drunk; totter, stagger: *Mlevi alikuwa akisepetuka barabarani*, the drunkard was staggering along the road. Prep. **sepetuk.i.a** St. **sepetuk.ik.a** Cs. **sepetuk.i.sh.a** Ps. of Prep. **sepetuk.iw.a** (cf *pepesuka, sesereka*)

Septemba *n (n)* September (Eng)

sera[1] *n(n)* fort, fortress, castle, stronghold. (cf *boma, ngome, burují*)

sera[2] *n (n)* bees' wax. (cf *nta*) (Ar)

sera[3] *n (n)* 1. policy: *Sera ya lugha*, language policy. *Sera ya kilimo*, agriculture policy. *Sera ya uwekezaji*, investment policy. 2. behaviour; mode of life: *Fuata sera nzuri ya wazazi wako*, follow the good behaviour of your parents. (cf *mwenendo, mpango, siasa*) (Ar)

seredani (also *saradani*) *n (n)* 1. brazier; a metal pan, bowl, etc. used to hold burning charcoal as for warming a room or grilling food. 2. a metal vessel containing burning charcoal for warming black coffee, etc. (Pers)

serehangi *n (n)* see *sarahangi*

seraji *n (n)* a kind of lantern. (Ar)

seremala (also *saramala*) *n (n)* carpenter.

serena *n (n)* (*bot*) a kind of millet which ripens in a short time.

sererek.a *vi* glide, slip, slide: *Alisererekα alipolikanyaga ganda la ndizi mbivu*, he slipped when he trod on the rind of a ripe banana. Prep. **sererek.e.a** St. **sererek.ek.a** Cs. **sererek.esh.a** Ps. **sererek.w.a** (cf *teleza*)

serikali *n (n)* government: *Serikali kuu*, central government. *Serikali ya mseto*, coalition government. *Serikali ya mpito*, transition government. *Serikali ya kijeshi*, military government. *Serikali ya mitaa*, local government. *Serikali ya muda*, interim government. *Serikali ya muda*, caretaker government. *Serikali ya watawala wawili*, diarchy. *Serikali shirikishi*, coalition government. (cf *dola*) (Pers)

sero *n (n)* see *selo*

serwa *n (n)* see *surwa*

sesa *n (n)* non-terrace farming; agriculture flat planting i.e. planting without beds: *Lima sesa*, plant in this manner.

seserek.a *vt, vi* walk unsteadily as if drunk: stagger, reel, totter, sway: *Mzee alikuwa akisosereka njiani*, the old man was staggering along the street. Prep. **seserek.o.a** St. **seserek.ek.a** Cs. **seserek.esh.a** (cf *sepetuka, yumbayumba*)

set.a (also *sheta*) *vt* 1. crush, squash, mash, pound, break up: *Mwanamke alikuwa akiviseta vitunguu saumu*, the woman was pounding garlic (to a paste). (cf *ponda, twanga*) 2. mix different kinds of corn for cooking: *Mpishi aliuseta mchele na kunde kwa sababu ya chakula cha mchana*, the cook mixed rice and cow peas for the preparation of the lunch. Prep. **set.e.a** St. **set.ek.a** Cs. **set.esh.a** Ps. **set.w.a**

setaset.a *vt* see *shetasheta*

setek.a *vi* be dented, be pressed in. Prep. **setek.e.a** Cs. **setek.esh.a** (cf *bonyeka, pondeka*)

seti[1] *n (n)* (in card playing) the sevens in a pack of playing cards. (cf *jike*) (Eng)

seti[2] *n(n)* set, pair, couplet, duo, twosome. *Seti ya vyombo vya kulia*, dining set. *Seti sawa*, equal sets. *Seti tengeka*, disjoint set. *Seti toshelezi*, solution set. *Seti tupu*, empty set. (Eng)

seti[3] *n (n)* set

setir.i *vt* see *sitiri*

setla *n* (*ma-*) immigrant settler, squatter. (cf *mlowezi*) (Eng)
seuze *adv* let alone; not to mention. (cf *kefu, sembuse, kaifa*)
seyyid *n* (*n*) see *sayidi*
sez.a *vt* smooth a surface by using a carpenter's adze: *Seremala aliuseza ubao*, the carpenter smoothed the wood by using a jack plane. Prep. *sez.e.a* St. *sez.ek.a* Cs. *sez.esh.a* Ps. *sez.w.a*
sha *interj* an exclamation of disgust or annoyance.
sha.a[1] *vt* used in the expression: *Utashaa*, you will face the music. (cf *koma, juta*)
shaa[2] *n* (*ma-*) (also *shaha*) the white soft inside part of the shoot of a coconut tree which can easily be chewed; pith of a coconut tree; heart of a coconut tree.
Shaabani (also *Shaban*) *n* (*n*) the eighth month of the Islamic calendar, the month which is preceding the fasting month of Ramadan. (Ar)
shaba[1] *n* (*n*) copper: *Shaba nyeupe*, brass. *Shaba nyekundu*, copper. *Kebo ya shaba*, copper cable.
shaba[2] *n* (*n*) the bullet of a gun.
shababi[1] (also *shababu*) *n* (*n*) youth, sprig; adolescent instead of a man. (cf *kijana, ghulamu*) (Ar)
shababi[2] (also *shababu*) *adj* young, teenager, adolescent; in the teens: *Mtu shababi*, a young person. (Ar)
shababu[1] *n* (*n*) see *shababi*[1]
shababu[2] *adj* see *shababi*[2]
shabaha *n* (*n*) 1. target; sth to be fired at as by means of a gun, spear, arrow, etc. 2. accuracy in hitting a target. 3. goal, objective, aim, purpose: *Shabaha ya serikali ni kuboresha uchumi wa nchi*, the objective of the government is to develop the country's economy. (cf *lengo, kusudio*) (Ar)
shabaki *n* (*n*) a cantankerous person, a cross-grained person, a quarrelsome person; wrangler: *Usifanye urafiki na shabaki yule*, don't befriend that wrangler. (cf *mgobo, mgomvi*) (Ar)
Shabani *n* (*n*) see *Shaabani*
shabashi *interj* an expletive of praise, joy or wonder for someone who has done sth of remarkable nature; wonderful! wow! (Ar)
shabih.i *vt* resemble, look like, appear like, sound like: *Anamshabihi mjomba wake*, he resembles his uncle. Prep. *shabih.i.a* St. *shabih.ik.a* Cs. *shabih.ish.a* Ps. *shabih.iw.a* Rp. of Prep. *shabih.i.an.a,* look like; resemble e.g. *Watu wale wawili wameshabihiana*, those two people look alike. (cf *fanana, randa*) (Ar)
shabihian.a *vi* see *shabihi*
shabiki (also *mshabiki*) *n* (*ma-*) 1. fan, enthusiast, aficionado, devotee: *Yeye ni shabiki wa mchezo wa ngumi*, he is a boxing fan. (cf *mraibu, mpenzi*) 2. (in card playing) a person waiting to participate in the game being played: *Yule shabiki anasubiri kwa hamu kushiriki kwenye mashindano ya karata*, the would-be card player is waiting anxiously to participate in the competition. (Ar)
shabiki.a *vt* side a party, etc.; be partisan: *Rais aliwakataza wananchi kushabikia chama chochote katika utendaji-kazi serikalini*, the president forbade the people to side any party when they perform government business. St. *shabik.i.a* Cs. *shabik.ish.a* Ps. *shabik.iw.a* (Ar)
shabu *n* (*n*) alum; white mineral salt, used in medicine, dyeing, etc. (cf *magadi*) (Ar)
shabuka *n* (*n*) difficulty, trouble, hassle; difficult time: *Yeye yumo katika shabuka siku hizi*, he is in difficulties these days. (cf *dhiki, taabu*) (Ar)
shada *n* (*ma-*) 1. (of flowers, beads, etc.) cluster, bunch, string: *Shada la maua*, a bunch of flowers; garland. *Shada la shanga*, a string of beads. 2. (*gram*) cluster: *Shada kitenzi*, verb cluster. (Ar)

shadda *n* (*n*) (*phon*) stress: *Alitia shadda katika neno la pili*, he put stress on the second word. *Shadda funge*, bound accent (cf *mkazo*) (Ar)

shadid.i[1] *vt, vi* 1. hold fast; become strong; become intense: *Joto limeshadidi siku hizi*, the heat has itensified these days. 2. insist on sth; persist. e.g. *Alishadidia kuwachongea wenzake*, he was persistently giving negative reports about his colleagues. St. *shadid.ik.a* Cs. *shadid.ish.a* Ps. *shadid.iw.a* (Ar)

shadidi[2] *adj* extreme, severe: *Kulikuwa na baridi shadidi jana*, there was severe cold yesterday. (Ar)

shafti *n* (*n*) a revolving rod that transmits motion or power in a machine. (Eng)

shaghalabaghala *adv* disorderly, awry, helter-skelter, topsy-turvy; in disarray: *Mambo yake yalienda shaghalabaghala*, his affairs went awry. (cf *shelabela, hobelahobela, trivyogo, ovyoovyo*) (Ar)

shaha[1] *n* (*ma-*) 1. minstrel, epict poet; writer of songs. 2. a king of the game of chess. (Pers)

shaha[2] *n* (*ma-*) see *sheha*

shaha[3] *n* (*n*) (*bot*) pith of a coconut tree; heart of a coconut tree. (cf *kilele*)

shahada[1] (also *stashahada*) *n* (*n*) 1. certificate, document: *Alipomaliza masomo yake ya sekondari, alitunukiwa shahada*, when he completed his secondary education, he was given a certificate. (cf *cheti, hati*) 2. degree: *Alipata shahada ya udaktari wa falsafa katika Chuo Kikuu cha Melbourne*, she got a doctoral degree in philosophy at Melbourne University. (cf *digrii*) (Ar)

shahada[2] *n* (*n*) an expression of faith by Muslims that there is no one to be worshipped except Almighty God and that Prophet Muhammad is his messenger. *Kidole cha shahada*, forefinger. *Maji ya shahada*, water given to a person on the verge of dying. Also water used for washing a dead body. (Ar)

shahadi.a *vi* pronounce the statement that there is no one to be worshipped except the Almighty God. Prep. *shahadi.li.a* St. *shahadi.k.a* Cs. *shahadi.sh.a* Ps. *shahadi.w.a*

shahamu *n* (*n*) 1. animal fat used in painting the quickwork of a dhow, boat, etc. to prevent the vessel from being "eaten" by insects. 2. lard, grease, adipose, fat. (Ar)

shahari *n* (*n*) one month. (cf *mwezi*) (Ar)

shahawa *n* (*n*) sperm, semen. (cf *manii*) (Ar)

shahidi[1] (also *shuhuda*) *n* (*ma-*) witness; a person who saw or can give a first-hand account of sth: *Shahidi wa serikali*, government witness. *Alikuwa shahidi katika kesi ya mauaji*, he was a witness in the murder case. (cf *mshuhudiaji*) (Ar)

shahidi[2] *n* (*ma-*) martyr: *Alikufa shahidi kwa kupigania dini yake*, he died a martyr for fighting for his religion. (Ar)

shahiri *adv* an expletive used to emphasize the transparency of sth: *Dhahiri shahiri*, clearly, evidently, vividly, openly: *Siku hizi, mvulana yule amekuwa anamsimanga mzee wake dhahiri shahiri*, these days, that boy has been putting his parent down openly. (cf *waziwazi, bayana*)

shaibu *n* (*ma-*) a very old man: *Lazima umheshimu shaibu yule*, you must respect that old man. (cf *buda*) (Ar)

shairi *n* (*ma-*) poem: *Shairi la mapigo matano*, pentameter. *Shairi la ukombozi wa mwanamke*, a poem on the liberation of a woman. *Shairi la mapenzi*, a poem on love. (cf *abiyati*) (Ar)

shaitani *n* (*ma-*) see *shetani*

shaj.a *vi* roam, ramble, rove, meander, range, wander; amble aimlessly: *Tangu kufukuzwa kazini, amekuwa*

shajaa

akishaja mitaani, since being sacked from work, he has been roaming about in the neighbourhood. Prep. ***shaj.i.a*** St. ***shaj.ik.a*** Cs. ***shaj.ish.a*** (cf *zurura, randa*)
shajaa *n* (*n*) see *ushujaa*
shajara *n* (*n*) 1. a book containing a daily record of events, appointments, etc.; diary. 2. a chart or recorded history of the descent of a person or family from past to present; genealogy: *Shajara ya nasaba*, genealogy tree. (Ar)
shajari *n* (*n*) tree (cf *mti*) (Ar)
shajiik.a *vi* be motivated, be encouraged, be inspired. Cs. ***shajiik.ish.a***
shajiish.a *vt* motivate, encourage, enhearten, inspire: *Mwalimu aliwashajiisha wanafunzi wake kusema ukweli*, the teacher encouraged his students to speak the truth. Prep. ***shajiish.i.a*** St. ***shajiish.ik.a*** Ps. ***shajiish.w.a***, be encouraged Rp. ***shajiish.an.a*** (cf *hamasisha, raghibu*) (Ar)
shaka[1] *n* (*n*) suspicion, doubt, doubtfulness, misgiving: *Tia shaka*, give rise to doubt. *Bila ya shaka*, without doubt. *Usiwe na shaka*, don't worry. *Ana shaka juu ya kuja kwake kesho*, he is doubtful whether he will come tomorrow. (cf *wasiwasi, dukuduku*) (Ar)
shak.a[2] *vt* chase, go after, drive away, send away. Prep. ***shak.i.a*** St. ***shak.ik.a*** Cs. ***shak.ish.a*** Ps. ***shak.w.a*** Rp. ***shak.an.a*** (cf *winga, shunga*)
shakawa *n* (*n*) tribulation, difficulty, trouble, hardships: *Familia ile imekuwa katika shakawa tangu kufa kwa mzee wao*, that family has been facing hardships since their father's death. (cf *shida, dhiki, usumbufu, taabu*) (Ar)
shake *n* (*n*) used in the expression: *Ingiwa na shake*, be silently sobbing. (Ar)
shakevale *n* (*n*) (*zool*) common buzzard; a kind of hawk (family *Acciptindae*) that is slow and heavy in flight: *Shakevale mweupe*, augur buzzard. *Shakevale misitu*, forest buzzard. *Shakevale mlaasali*, honey buzzard.
shakii *adj* 1. courageous, brave, valiant, fearless: *Yeye ni shakii kama simba*, he is as courageous as a lion. (cf *jabari*) 2. wicked, evil, perverted: *Usifanye urafiki na mtu shakii*, don't make friendship with a perverted person.
shakir.i[1] *vi* be satisfied esp of food: *Alishakiri na chakula tulichompa*, he was satisfied with the food we gave him. Prep. ***shakir.i.a*** St. ***shakir.ik.a*** Cs. ***shakir.ish.a*** Ps. ***shakir.iw.a***
shakiri[2] *adj* 1. courageous. 2. mannerless.
shakiz.a *vt* give instructions or a signal to someone or a dog to arrest or chase someone else. Prep. ***shakiz.i.a*** St. ***shakiz.ik.a*** Cs. ***shakiz.ish.a*** Ps. ***shakiz.w.a*** (cf *tomeza*)
shakwe *n* (*n*) (*zool*) gull; a common water bird (family *Laridae*) with large wings, slender legs and a strong hooked bill. *Shakwe kijivu*, herring gull. *Shakwe mweusi*, sooty gull.
shalaka *n* (*n*) 1. (*naut*) a hole in the gunwale of a vessel such as a boat, made to secure the loop of a rope used as a rowlock. (cf *kileti*) 2. a rope eye or grommet serving as a rowlock.
shali *n* (*n*) shawl; a large heavy woollen material worn round the shoulders usu by Muslim clerics and teachers. (cf *kashida*) (Pers)
shalik.i[1] *vt* repair, mend, fix: *Aliishaliki mashua yake*, he repaired his boat. Prep. ***shalik.i.a*** St. ***shalik.ik.a*** Cs. ***shalik.ish.a*** Ps. ***shalik.w.a*** (Ar)
shalik.i[2] *vt* used in the expression: *Shaliki makasia*, put the oars in the grommets i.e. start rowing a boat. Prep. ***shalik.i.a*** St. ***shalik.ik.a*** Cs. ***shalik.ish.a*** Ps. ***shalik.w.a***
shamasi *n* (*n*) see *shemasi*
shamba *n* (*ma-*) 1. farm, plantation, field, allotment: *Shamba la kuku*, poultry

farm. *Shamba la mpunga*, paddy field. *Shamba la kahawa*, coffee plantation. *Shamba la Wanyama*, Animals' Farm. *Amepanda mahindi kwenye shamba lake*, he has grown maize in his farm. (cf *mgunda, kore, kande*) 2. countryside. (*prov*) *Jogoo la shamba haliwiki mjini*, the country cock does not crow in town i.e. when you are at home, you can do as you wish but when you are at a foreign place, you can't have that liberty. *Anaishi shamba*, he lives in the countryside.

shambiro¹ *n* (*n*) brothel, bordello, bagnio, whorehouse; a house of prostitution or theft. (cf *danguro*)

shambiro² *adv* idly; without work: *Siku hizi amejikalia shambiro barazani, these days, he sits idly on the verandah. Jendea shambiro*, roam; walk aimlessly. (cf *bure, ovyo*)

shambu.a *vt* see *chambua¹* and *chambua²*

shambuli.a *vt* 1. attack, invade, raid, storm: *Adui aliishambulia ngome*, the enemy attacked the fort. St. *shambuli.k.a* Ps. *shambuli.w.a*, be attacked, be stormed e.g. *Duka lilishambuliwa na wezi*, the shop was attacked by thieves. Rp. *shambuli.an.a* attack one another (cf *hujumu, vamia*) 2. insult, affront, offend: *Alitushambulia kwa maneno makali*, he insulted us with harsh words. St. *shambuli.k.a* Ps. *shambuli.w.a* Rp. *shambuli.an.a* (cf *tusi, tukana, chamba*)

shambulio *n* (*ma-*) attack, invasion, offensive, assault, raid: *Shambulio la anga*, air strike. *Shambulio la adui lilizimwa*, the enemy's attack was halted. (cf *shambulizi, hujuma, vamio, uvamizi*)

shambulizi *n* (*ma-*) attack, invasion, raid: *Timu yao ilifanya mashambulizi makali katika dakika za majeruhi*, their team made a scathing attack during the injury time. *Mashambulizi ya adui nchini yalikuja bila ya kutegemewa*, the enemy's attack in the country came unexpectedly. (cf *uvamizi, shambulio, vamio*)

shambwelele *n* (*n*) (*zool*) dewlap; a loose fold of skin hanging from the throat of cattle and some other animals.

shambwelele

shamia *n* (*n*) see *kishamia*

shamili *n* (*n*) ear ornament worn by women; earring.

shamir.i¹ *vi* spread; be rife, be widespread: *Tetesi zimeshamiri nchini kwamba rais ataunda baraza jipya la mawaziri*, rumours are rife in the country that the president will form a new cabinet. Prep. *shamir.i.a* St. *shamir.ik.a* Cs. *shamir.ish.a* Ps. *shamir.iw.a* (cf *enea, tapakaa, zagaa*) (Ar)

shamir.i² *vi* prosper, thrive, flourish, boom, develop: *Uchumi wa nchi yetu umeshamiri kutokana na jitihada za viongozi*, the economy of our country has prospered following the efforts of our leaders. Prep. *shamir.i.a* St. *shamir.ik.a* Cs. *shamir.ish.a* Ps. *shamir.iw.a* (cf *tengemaa, endelea, kua*) (Ar)

shamir.i³ *vt* 1. load a gun: *Mwanajeshi alizishamiri risasi nyingi kwenye mzinga*, the soldier loaded many bullets into the cannon. 2. put together e.g. fix the legs of a bedstead, table, chair, etc. or hammer into something as in the case of nails, etc; assemble: *Seremala aliishamiri miguu ya meza*, the carpenter fixed the legs of the table. Prep. *shamir.i.a* St. *shamir.*

ik.a Cs. ***shamir.ish.a*** Ps. ***shamir.iw.a*** Rp. of Prep. ***shamir.i.an.a*** (cf *pachika, gongomelea*) (Ar)
shamirisho *n* (*ma-*) (*gram*) complement, object: *Ali alipokea zawadi*, Ali received a prize. Here, the word *zawadi* is referred to in grammar as complement. (cf *yambwa*)
shamiana *n* (*n*) a tent that protects people from the sun or rain at a special function or event.
shamla *n* (*n*) a multitude of people gathering for a particular purpose e.g. meeting, etc.: *Niliiona shamla kwenye mkutano wa kisiasa*, I saw a multitude of people in a political rally. (Ar)
shamrashamra *n* (*n*) celebrations, jubilations, razzmatazz: *Kulikuwa na shamrashamra nyingi kwenye harusi*, there was a lot of razzmatazz at the wedding. (cf *hekaheka, shangwe, nderemo*)
shamsi (also *shemsi*) *n* (*n*) sun (cf *jua*) (Ar)
Shamu *n* (*n*) Syria: *Bahari ya Shamu*, Red Sea. (Ar)
shanga.a *vt, vi* be amazed, be stunned, be astonished, be shocked: *Nilishangaa niliposikia kwamba rafiki yangu amemwacha mkewe*, I was shocked when I heard that my friend had divorced his wife. Prep. ***shanga.li.a*** St. ***shanga.lik.a*** Cs. ***shanga.z.a*** Ps. ***shanga.w.a*** Rp. ***shanga.an.a*** (cf *staajabu, shtuka*)
shangama *n* (*n*) 1. a kind of unstitched short-sleeved shirt with a hole for the head to pass through. 2. a house with a ridge roof i.e. a house with two roofs.
shangaz.a *vt* astonish, astound, amaze: *Kujiuzulu kwake kulitushangaza sote*, his resignation astounded us. Prep. ***shangaz.i.a*** St. ***shangaz.ik.a*** Ps. ***shangaz.w.a*** Rp. ***shangaz.an.a*** (cf *staajabisha, ajaabisha*)
shangazi *n* (*ma-*) paternal aunt, father's sister.
shangili.a (also *shangiria*) *vt* cheer, acclaim, clap; give an ovation: *Walikuwa wakiishangilia timu yao*, they were cheering their team. St. ***shangili.k.a*** Ps. ***shangili.w.a*** be cheered e.g. *Alishangiliwa na watazamaji*, he was cheered by the spectators. Rp. ***shangili.an.a*** (cf *furahia, chapukia*)
shangingi[1] *n* (*ma-*) (*colloq*) prostitute, harlot. (cf *changudoa*)
shangingi[2] *n* (*ma-*) (*colloq*) a big luxurious four-wheel drive car.
shangiri.a *vt* see *shangilia*
shangwe *n* (*n*) festivity, razzmatazz, jubilation: *Kulikuwa na shangwe nyingi kwenye ngoma za jadi*, there was a lot of jubilation at the traditional dances. (cf *shamrashamra, nderemo*)
shani *n* (*n*) novelty, curiosity, strangeness, miracle, peculiarity: *Ni shani kwa mwanamke yule kutoka Afrika ya magharibi kuzaa watoto wanane pacha*, it is a miracle for that woman from West Africa to give birth to octuplets. (cf *muujiza, kiroja, kioja*) (Ar)
shanjari *n* (*n*) see *sanjari*
shanta *n* (*n*) haversack, knapsack, backpack, kitbag. (Ar)
shanua *n* (*n*) surf; waves or swell of the sea breaking on the shore or a reef.
shanuo[1] *n* (*ma-*) a big plastic comb used by women.
shanuo[2] *n* (*n*) (*zool*) sea urchin; a marine echinoderm having a spherical or flattened shell covered in mobile spines, with a mouth on the underside and calcareous jaws. (cf *urumba*)

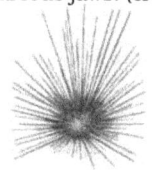

shanuo

sharabu[1] *n* (*n*) an intoxicating drink such as beer, wine, etc. (cf *kileo, ulevi*) (Ar)
sharab.u[2] *vt, vi* drink, absorb, saturate. Prep. ***sharab.i.a*** St. ***sharab.ik.a*** Cs.

sharab.ish.a Ps. of Prep. **sharab. iw.a** (cf -*nywa*) (Ar)
sharafa *n* (*ma*-) (*anat*) the hair on a man's face, just in front of the ears up to the cheeks, esp when the rest of the beard is cut off; sideburns. (Ar)
sharafu *n* (*n*) glory, dignity, eminence. (cf *utukufu*) (Ar)
shari *n* (*n*) 1. adversity, evil, iniquity, vice, wickedness. (*prov*) *Heri nusu ya shari kuliko shari kamili*, better half an evil than a complete evil i.e. it is better to face a small problem than a big one. (cf *uovu, ukorofi, balaa*) 2. mischief, misconduct, squabble, feud, quarrel. *Yeye ni mtu wa shari, he is a person fond of quarrelling. Tumechoka na shari zako*, we are tired of your mischief. (cf *ugomvi, utesi*) (Ar)
sharia *n* (*n*) see *sheria*
sharid.i *vi* flee, run away. Prep. **sharid.i.a** St. **sharid.ik.a** Cs. **sharid.ish.a** (cf *kimbia*) (Ar)
sharifu[1] *n* (*n*) 1. (*in Islam*) a descendant of Prophet Muhammad from his daughter's side, Fatma. 2. any noble religious leader; an honourable religious person. (Ar)
sharif.u[2] *vt* respect, venerate, revere, esteem: *Huwasharifu viongozi wa dini*, he respects religious leaders. Prep. **sharif.i.a** St. **sharif.ik.a** Cs. **sharif.ish.a** Ps. of Prep. **sharif.iw.a** (cf *tukuza, heshimu*) (Ar)
sharti[1] *n* (*n*) (*naut*) a rope used for tightening a sail in a vessel. (Ar)
sharti[2] (also *shuruti*) *n* (*n*) condition, regulation, requirement, term, obligation: *Niliyakataa masharti yake*, I rejected his terms. *Alikubali kwa masharti fulani*, he agreed under certain conditions. *Waliwekeana masharti fulani*, they set certain conditions among themselves. (cf *kanuni, mkataba*) (Ar)
sharti[3] (also *shuruti*) *n* (*n*) necessity, must, obligation: *Sharti amtake radhi rafiki yake*, he must apologize to his friend. (cf *lazima, wajibu*) (Ar)
sharubati *n* (*n*) a special drink usu made of milk, sugar and other aromatic substances; sherbet. (Ar)
sharubu *n* (*ma*-) (*anat*) the hair on the upper lip of men; moustache. (Ar)
sharutish.a *vt, vi* see *shurutisha*
shashi *n* (*n*) a kind of thin light muslin or tissue paper. (Ar)
shashimamishi *n* (*n*) a debased person, a scorned person; bastard: *Ondoka hapa shashimamishi!* Get out of here you bastard! (Ar)
shata[1] *n* (*ma*-) lees of coconut oil; dregs of coconut oil; sediment. (cf *mashudu, masimbi*)
shata[2] *n* (*ma*-) shutter; a piece of glass or wood on a door or window that can be closed for security or privacy. (Eng)
shatashata *adv* juicy; full of coconut milk or coconut oil: *Viazi vilitiwa tui shatashata*, the potatoes were full of milk from grated coconut. (cf *rikoriko, rojorojo, majimaji*)
shati *n* (*ma*-) shirt: *Shati la mikono mirefu*, a long-sleeved shirt. *Shati la mikono mifupi*, a short-sleeved shirt. (Eng)
shatoruma *n* (*n*) a shawl usu worn round the waist as a belt by Muslims, etc. (Pers)
shau.a *vt,vi* 1. laud, extol, praise: *Alimshaua rafiki yake na sasa amekuwa na kichwa kikubwa*, he praised his friend and now he has become big-headed. (*prov*) *Apendwaye akajua, haachi, kujishaua*, a person who is loved by people and comes to know that he is loved, will not fail to feel good i.e. We should not show someone that we openly love him. (cf *sifu, tukuza*) 2. boast, brag, vaunt: *Anapenda kujishaua mbele ya wanawake*, he likes to boast in front of women. Prep. **shau.li.a** St. **shau.k.a** Cs. **shau.lish.a** Ps. of Prep. **shau.liw.a** Rp.

shau.an.a (cf *takabari, hanja*) (Ar)

-shaufu *adj* proud, boastful: *Usichanganyike na mtu mshaufu kama yeye,* don't associate with such a boastful person like him. (cf *sodawi*)

shauku *n* (*n*) craving, yearn, longing; strong desire: *Ana shauku ya kutaka kuoa,* he has a strong desire to get married. (cf *uchu, hamu, utashi*) (Ar)

shaunge *n* (*n*) (*bot*) a kind of flower with strong odour from a large shrub (*Frangipan*) with thick, succulent stems and branches.

shauri[1] *n* (*n*) 1. discussion, debate: *Wanafanya shauri kama wamchukulie hatua yoyote kijana yule,* they are still having a discussion on whether they should take any action against that young man.(cf *mjadala*) 2. advice, counsel: *Toa shauri,* give advice. *Nipe shauri,* give me advice. *Ametupa shauri zuri,* he has given us a good advice. 3. used in many expressions to give different meanings: *Fanya shauri,* make a decision; decide. *Kata shauri,* make a decision; decide. *Sina shauri,* I have no advice to give; I have no say in this. (Ar)

shaur.i[2] *vt* advise. counsel: *Meneja alishauri kwamba wafanyakazi waongezewe mshahara,* the manager advised that the salaries of workers should be increased. Prep. **shaur.i.a** St. **shaur.ik.a** Cs. **shaur.ish.a** Ps. **shaur.iw.a,** be advised e.g *Alishauriwa na daktari aache kula pilipili,* he was advised by the doctor to stop eating chillies. Rp. **shaur.i.an.a,** make consultations, consult together e.g. *Wanashauriana juu ya suala la wakimbizi,* they are consulting each other on the question of refugees. (cf *nasihi.*) (Ar)

shaurian.a *vt see shauri*[2]. Prep. **shaurian.i.a**

shaushi *n* (*n*) see *bishaushi*.

shavu *n* (*ma-*) (*anat*) cheek: *Shavu la samaki,*the gill of a fish, *Shavu la mguu,* the calf of a leg. *Shavu la jogoo,* the wattles of a cock.

Shawali *n* (*n*) the tenth month according to the Islamic calendar. (Ar)

shawish.i[1] *vt* 1. persuade, tempt, induce: *Alinishawishi nimwazime baiskeli yangu,* he persuaded me to lend him my bicycle. Prep. **shawish.i.a** St. **shawish.ik.a,** be tempted, be persuaded e.g. *Mtu yule hashawishiki,* that person cannot be persuaded. Ps. **shawish.iw.a,** be tempted. Rp. **shawish.i.an.a** (cf *rai, bembeleza*) 2. entice, allure, tempt, lure: *Alimshawishi msichana mrembo,* he enticed a glamorous girl. Prep. **shawish.i.a** St. **shawish.ik.a** Ps. **shawish.iw.a** Rp. **shawish.i.an.a** (cf *tongoza*) (Ar)

shawishi[2] *n* (*n*) busybody. meddler, eavesdropper, snoop, gossip: *Mimi nimechoka na vitendo vya shawishi yule,* I am tired of the activities of that busybody. (cf *kimbelembele*) (Ar)

shawishi[3] *adj* meddlesome, officious, impertinent, pushing.

shawishik.a *vi see shawishi.* Prep. **shawishik.i.a**

shayiri *n* (*n*) (*bot*) barley (Ar)

shaza *n* (*n*) see *chaza*

shazasi *n* (*n*) a kind of medicine with a pungent smell, used to enable a person who has fainted regain consciousness; salvolatile. *Ammonium carbonate.*

shazia[1] *n* (*n*) see *kishazi*

shazia[2] *n* (*n*) a long big copper or brass needle, used in sewing mats, mattresses, etc.; bodkin, sailmaker's needle.

shazilla *n* (*ma-*) (*bot*) inflorescence, flowering; the producing of blossoms.

shegele (also *segele*) *n* (*n*) a garment used for children consisting of beads worn round the loins to cover the front part of the body; beaded loinbelt.

sheha (also *shaha*) *n* (*ma-*) 1. councillor, chief, headman. 2. a head of a village or party. (cf *jumbe, balozi*) 3. (in

Zanzibar) ward executive officer. (Ar)
shehe[1] (also *shekhe, sheikh*) *n* (*ma-*) 1. a Muslim teacher; sheik. 2. a Muslim reverend; sheik. (Ar)
shehe[2] *n* (*ma-*) a respectable wise man; patriarch: *Wanavijiji humwendea shehe wao wanapokuwa na matatizo*, the villagers go to see their patriarch when they have problems. (cf *shaibu*) (Ar)
shehe[3] *n* (*n*) demon's drum.
shehelez.a *vt* present sth before the people for discussion. Prep. **shehelez.e.a** St. **shehelez.ek.a** Cs. **shehelez.esh.a** Ps. **shehelez.ew.a**
shehena *n* (*n*) cargo, freight, lading, shipment, load; *Makuli waliipakua shehena kutoka kwenye meli*, the coolies unloaded cargo from the ship. (cf *kago*) (Ar)
shehenez.a *vt* load cargo. Prep. **shehenez.e.a** St. **shehenez.ek.a** Ps. **shehenez.w.a**
shehen.i *vt* have cargo on board; load cargo: *Walizisheheni bidhaa zao katika jahazi*, they loaded their goods into the dhow. *Tuliisheheni mizigo yetu kwenye paa la basi*, we loaded our cargo on the roof of the bus. Prep. **shehen.i.a** St. **shehen.ik.a** Cs. **shehen.ish.a** Ps. **shehen.iw.a** (cf *pakia*) (Ar)
sheikh *n* (*ma-*) see *shehe*[1]
sheitani *n* (*ma-*) see *shetani*
shekhe *n* (*ma-*) see *shehe*[1]
shela[1] *n* (*n*) 1. a large woman's veil worn over the head. (cf *dusumali, utaji, barakoa*) 2. a bride's dress of light material. (Ar)
shela[2] *n* (*n*) a kind of Arab sword dance. (cf *tari, hanzua*) (Ar)
shelabela *adv* haphazardly, awry, topsy-turvy, chaotically; in a mess, in disarray: *Waliifanya kazi yetu shelabela*, they did our work haphazardly. (cf *ndivyosivyo, segemnege*) (Ar)
shelel.i *vt* sew a seam. Prep. **shelel.i.a** St. **shelel.ik.a** Cs. **shelel.ish.a** Ps. of Prep. **shelel.iw.a** (Ar)
shelisheli *n* (*n*) (*bot*) bread-fruit; a large round seedless fruit with a starchy pulp, and may be eaten either boiled or roasted or in soups.
shemali *n* (*n*) see *shimali*
shemasi *n* (*ma-*) deacon; a minister ranking below a priest. (Ar)
shembeu *n* (*n*) see *chembeu*[1]
shemegi *n* (*n*) see *shemeji*
shemeji *n* (*n*) 1. sister/brother in law. 2. wife/husband's friend.
shemere *n* (*n*) 1. nose ring of an ox. (cf *hazamu*) 2. (*idm*) *Tia mtu shemere*, have sby under your thumb; control sby fully e.g. *Ingawa kijana yule awali alikuwa mtukutu lakini baba yake sasa ameweza kumtia shemere*, even though that young man was naughty in the beginning, his father now has him under his thumb.
shemngo'mbe *n* (*n*) see *ng'ombe*[2]
shemsi *n* (*n*) see *shamsi*
shemvi *n* (*n*) a person in a joking relationship. (cf *mtani*)
shenez.a *vt* load cargo in a vessel, vehicle, etc.: *Aliisheneza mizigo yake kwenye lori*, he loaded his cargo in the lorry. Prep. **shenez.e.a** St. **shenez.ek.a** Cs. **shenez.esh.a** Ps. **shenez.w.a** (Ar)
-shenzi *adj* barbarous, savage, uncouth, unrefined, uncivil: *Zile zilikuwa tabia za kishenzi*, those were barbarous manners.
shepe *n* (*ma-*) shovel, spade. (cf *sepetu, beleshi*)
sherasi *n* (*ma-*) the leader of a local dance; dance leader.
shere *n* (*n*) joke, fun, ridicule: *Cheza shere*, play a joke on; make a fool of.
sherehe[1] *n* (*n*) celebration, festivity, ceremony: *Nilizihudhuria sherehe za harusi jana*, I attended the wedding celebrations yesterday. (cf *shangwe, tafrija, maadhimisho, tamasha*) (Ar)
sherehe[2] *n* (*n*) 1. an analysis or report of a book or article by someone else; review: *Niliipenda sherehe yake juu ya riwaya hii*, I liked his review on this novel. 2. blurb; a promotional

description, as on a book, jacket, esp one that is highly laudatory. (Ar)
sherehe³ *n (n)* glossary (cf *faharasa*)
sherehek.a *vi* be happy, be joyful. (cf *furahi*)
shereheke.a *vt* celebrate, commemorate: *Waislamu waliisherehekea sikukuu ya Idd*, the Muslims celebrated Idd holiday. Ps. **shereheke.w.a,** be celebrated e.g. *Sikukuu ya Krismasi ilisherehekewa na Wakristo wote duniani*, Christmas holiday was celebrated by all the Christians in the world. (Ar)
shereh.i *vt* analyse, review, critique, criticize: *Waliisherehi tamthilia yangu*, they reviewed my play. Prep. **shereh.i.a** St. **shereh.ik.a** Ps. of Prep. **shereh.iw.a** (cf *chambua, fafanua*)
sheresi *n (n)* see *sherisi*
sheria¹ *n (n)* 1. law, bill: *Sheria za nchi*, laws of the land. *Sheria za mila*, customary laws. (*prov*) *Sheria ni msumeno; hukata mbele na nyuma*, the law is just like a cutting saw; it cuts forwards and backwards i.e. law applies to everybody. *Sheria ndogo-ndogo*. by-laws. 2. tradition. 3. (*ling*) *Sheria panuzi*, expansion rule. 4. regulations. (Ar)
sheria² (also *sharia*) *n (n)* Literally, *Sheria* means "the way to a watering place." In its applied context, it means the law, including both the teaching of the Holy Koran and of the traditional sayings or the practices of Prophet Mohammad.
sherisi (also *sheresi*) *n (n)* glue used by carpenters; carpenter's glue. (cf *ambo*)
sheshe¹ *adj* good, nice, beautiful: *Kitu sheshe*, a beautiful thing; a good thing. (cf *jamali,-zuri*)
sheshe² *n (n)* (*zool*) puku; a medium-sized antelope with rather short thick strongly ringed horns, curving outwards and backwards and then forwards.

sheshe

sheshi *n (n)* 1. a kind of thin white paper 2 a kind of thin white muslin (cf *bushashi*)
shet.a *vt* see *seta* Prep. **shet.e.a** St. **shet.ek.a** Cs. **shet.esh.a** Ps. **shet.w.a** Rp. **shet.an.a**
shetani (also *shaitani*) *(n) (ma-)* 1. satan, devil. (cf *pepo, ibilisi*) 2. a wicked person; reprobate, monster, devil: *Usiandamane na shetani yule*, don't associate with that devil. (*prov*) *Shetani wa mtu ni mtu*, the greatest enemy of a human being is his fellow human being. (cf *gwagu, mwovu*)
shetashet.a (also *setaseta*) *vi* stroll by taking a stick in the armpit: *Hutembea kwa kushetasheta*, he strolls with a walking-stick under his arm. Prep. **shetashet.e.a** St. **shetashet.ek.a**
shetri *n (n)* (*naut*) the stern of a ship, dhow, etc.; poop. (Ar)
shevule *n (n)* (*zool*) zebra fish, zebra dsamio; a kind of fish with barred zebra-markings, some of whom live in fresh water and others in marine waters.
Shia *n (n)* 1. (in Islam) one amongst the Muslim religious sects which considers Ali as the rightful successor of Prophet Mohammad. 2. a follower of this sect.
shib.a *vi* 1. eat to one's fill; have enough to eat; have a full meal: *Amekula sana na sasa ameshiba*, he has eaten a lot and now he can't eat any more. 2. (*fig*) used to describe full trust among two or more friends but used

in the reciprocal form: *Marafiki wale wawili wameshibana*, those two friends trust each other completely. Prep. *shib.i.a* St. *shib.ik.a* Cs. *shib.ish.a* Ps. *shib.w.a* Rp. *shib.an.a* (Ar)

shiban.a *vi* be contented among each other, be trusting each other. (cf *kinaiana*)

shibe *n* (*n*) fullness, satiety, repletion; the point of satisfaction: *Nimekula shibe yangu*, I have eaten to my satisfaction; I have eaten my fill. (*prov*) *Shibe mwana malevya njaa mwana malegeza*, a person who is full of food in his stomach gets drunk while the one who is hungry, slacks i.e. a person who has the means of anything such as wealth, power, etc. becomes arrogant, powerful, etc. on the other hand, a person who has no such means, becomes weak and thus can't do anything.

shibiri *n* (*n*) see *shubiri*

shibish.a *vt* feed someone to the maximum; satisfy sby: *Alinishibisha aliponialika kwenye karamu yake*, he fed me to the full when he invited me at his party. Prep. *shibish.i.a* St. *shibish.ik.a* Ps. *shibish.w.a* Rp. *shibish.an.a*

shibli *n* (*n*) (*zool*) the young of a lion; lion's cub. (Ar)

shida *n* (*n*) problem, hardship, difficulty, trouble: *Hatukupata shida yoyote katika safari yetu*, we did not have any problem during our journey. *Wana shida gani?* What is their problem? *Hapa, kuna shida tupu*, here, there are a lot of problems. (cf *uzito, adha, taabu, dhiki*)

shifaa¹ *n* (*n*) see *shufaa¹*

shifaa² *n* (*n*) see *shufaa²*

shifta *n* (*n*) (in Kenya) pirate, highway robber, brigand (cf *haramia*)

shifti¹ *n* (*n*) shift: *Mshono wa shifti*, shift style. (Eng)

shifti² *n* (*n*) shift: *Wafanyakazi wa shifti ya mchana*, daytime workers. (Eng)

shige *n* (*n*) see *manja*

shigi *n* (*n*) see *sigi*

shik.a *vt, vi* 1. hold, arrest, apprehend, catch: *Askari alimshika mwizi*, the policeman caught the thief. (cf *kamata, gwia, bamba*) 2. hold fast; stick: *Gundi imeshika katika bahasha hii*, the glue sticks firm on this envelope. Prep. *shik.i.a* St. *shik.ik.a* Cs. *shik.ish.a* Ps. *shik.w.a* Rp. *shik.an.a* (cf *ganda, nata*) 3. used in various expressions to convey different meanings: *Shika adabu*, be polite. *Shika maneno*, think. *Shika amri*, obey an order. *Shika lako*, mind your own business. *Shika mkia*, trail behind. *Shika hatamu*, assume leadership. *Shika mguu*, stoop; condescend. It is used in the expression: *Patashika*, disorder, confusion, pandemonium e.g. *Kulikuwa na patashika kubwa kwenye mashindano ya mpira*, there was a great pandemonium during the football match. (cf *fujo, ghasia*)

shikaman.a *vt, vi* be fast together; be united: *Nchi zao zimeshikamana kisiasa*, their countries are politically cohesive. (*prov*) *Ushikwapo shikamana*, if you are pressed, hold together i.e. be firm when you are in difficulties.

shikamoo *interj* a respectful greeting to someone older than yourself.

shikan.a *vi* 1. be in co-operation, be together in all aspects: *Vijana wale wawili wameshikana*, those two young men are together in all respects. 2. hold together, stick together: *Stempu hii imeshikana vizuri kwenye bahasha hii*, this stamp is well stuck on this envelope. Prep. *shikan.i.a* St. *shikan.ik.a* Cs. *shikan.ish.a*

shikili.a *vt* 1. hold fast to; hold on to: *Alishikilia kwenye kiguzo ili asianguke*, he held fast to a post so that he does not fall. (cf *kamata*) 2 insist on, persist, keep on, cling to: *Yeye akitoa wazo, hushikilia hilo hilo*, if he gives a suggestion, he clings to it. St.

shikili.k.a Ps. ***shikili.w.a*** Rp. ***shikili.an.a*** (cf *kazania, ng'ang'ania*)

shikio[1] *n (ma-)* 1. handle, hilt: *Shikio la kikapu*, the handle of a basket. 2. a wooden or metal blade at the back of a ship, dhow, boat, etc. used for steering; rudder. (cf *sukani*)

shikio[2] *n (ma-)* see *sikio*

shikiz.a *vt* 1. use sth as a makeshift; use sth as a temporary expedient: *Anajishikiza nalo tu gari bovu lile*, he is only using that worn-out vehicle temporarily. 2. make sth be allied with another. Prep. ***shikiz.i.a*** St. ***shikiz.ik.a*** Ps. ***shikiz.w.a*** Rp. ***shikiz.an.a***

shikizo *n (ma-)* tack, baste. (cf *bandi*)

shilamu *n (n)* the stem of a hookah pipe. (cf *digali, bori*) (Hind)

shilanga *n (n)* 1. a hoe with a long handle. (cf *gwamba*) 2 a wooden standing hoe.

shilingi *n (n)* 1. shilling; a monetary unit used in East African countries worth 100 cents. 2. the value of money worth 100 cents. (Eng)

shimali (also *shemali*) *n (n)* 1. north (cf *kaskazini*) 2. left side: *Amekwenda upande wa shimali*, he has gone to the left side. (Ar)

shime *n (n)* a word used in encouraging someone to do a particular thing; keep it up! good work! *Tia shime*, encourage; give an encouragement. *Shime jamani! Tuimalize kazi yetu kabla ya jua halijakuchwa*, hurry up! let us complete our work before sunset.

shimizi (also *shumizi*) *n (n)* a loose fitting undergarment worn by a woman, somewhat like a loose short slip; chemise. (cf *kamisi*) (Fr)

shimo *n (ma-)* 1. hole, pit, cavity, hollow 2 hollow, deep: *Nilinunua sahani ya shimo*, I bought a deep plate.

shimoni *n (ma-)* in /at / on /to the hole or pit, etc.: *Panya ameingia shimoni*, the rat has gone into the hole.

shina[1] *n (ma-]* 1. *(bot)* the stem of a tree comprising all parts from the rootlets to the branches. 2 *(gram)* the root of a word and its affix or affixes: *Shina sahili*, simple stem e.g. *taa*, 'lamp'. *Shina ambatano*, compound stem e.g. *pakamwitu*, 'wild cat'. *Shina ulimi*, back of the tongue.

shina[2] *n (ma-)* (in politics) cell: *Kiongozi wa shina*, cell leader.

shind.a[1] *vt, vi* 1. win, conquer, triumph, overcome, subdue: *Alishinda kwenye pambano la ndondi*, he won the boxing bout. (cf *faulu, fanikiwa*) 2. excel, exceed; be bigger, be fatter, etc: *Rafiki yangu amenishinda kwa unene*, my friend is fatter than me. (cf *zidi*) 3. pass, succeed: *Alishinda kwenye mtihani*, he passed the examination. Prep. ***shind.i.a*** St. ***shind.ik.a*** Cs. ***shind.ish.a*** Ps. ***shind.w.a*** Rp. ***shind.an.a*** (cf *faulu, pita*)

shind.a[2] *vt* 1. go to stay at a particular place for the whole day; spend a day away: *Nilishinda kwake jana*, I spent the whole day yesterday at his place. 2. used to express the state of affairs of the whole day: *Umeshindaje?* How was your day? *Habari za kushinda?* How was the day? *Ameshinda na njaa leo*, he has stayed hungry the whole day today.

shinda[3] *adj* semifull, not completely full; half-full *(prov)* *Debe shinda haliachi kutika*, an empty tin never stops making noise i.e. a person may talk a lot about sth without being knowledgeable about it.

shindan.a *vt, vi* 1. compete, contest, be rivals: *Walishindana vikali katika mbio za baiskeli*, they competed seriously in the cycling race. 2. haggle, argue, debate: *Watu wale walishindana juu ya chaguzi za serikali za mitaa*, those people haggled over the elections of the local government. Prep. ***shindan.i.a,*** compete over, haggle over e.g *Wanashindania bei*, they are haggling over price. St.

-shindani   **shirika²**   **S**

shindan.ik.a Cs. *shindan.ish.a* Rp. of Prep. *shindan.i.an.a* e.g. *Walikuwa wakishindaniana kwa jambo la upuuzi*, they were haggling over a petty issue.
-shindani *adj* argumentative, contentious, opposing, competing: *Usishindane na mtu mshindani*, don't argue with an argumentative person.
shindano¹ *n* (*ma-*) contest, competition: *Lile lilikuwa shindano la kuogelea*, that was a swimming competition. *Shindano la urembo*, beauty contest.
shindano² *n* (*n*) see *sindano*
shindano³ *n* (*n*) (*zool*) pipefish; a relatively long, narrow body-scaled fish (family *Syngnathidae*) with a tube-like snout.
-shinde *adj* 1. defeated, conquered, vanquished, subdued: *Alistahili pongezi ingawa alikuwa mshinde*, he deserved praise even though he was defeated. 2. competing, rival, competitive, combative.
shindik.a (also *sindika*) *vt* (of door, window, etc.) close without applying a latch, etc.; close but not fasten; set ajar: *Aliushindika mlango wangu*, he left my door ajar. Prep. *shindik.i.a* St. *shindik.ik.a* Cs. *shindik.iz.a* Ps. *shindik.w.a* (cf *vugaza, bana*)
shindikan.a *vt, vi* be unsuccessful, be fruitless, be impossible: *Ilishindikana kumshawishi aivunje safari yake*, it was not possible to persuade him to cancel his trip.
shindikiz.a¹ *vt* see *shindika*
shindikiz.a² *vt* see *sindikiza*
shindikiz.a³ *vt* see *shinikiza*
shindikizo *n* (*n*) see *shinikizo*
shindili.a *vt* press, compress, ram in, force into, stuff in: *Alishindilia nguo zake kwenye begi*, he rammed his clothes into the suitcase. *Alishindilia chakula kinywani*, he stuffed the food into his mouth. Ps. *shindili.w.a*, be compressed, be pressed. (cf *sheheneza, sheneza*)

shingo *n* (*n*) 1. (*anat*) (of a human organ) neck. 2. the narrowest part of any object considered to be like a neck: *Shingo ya chupa*, the neck of a bottle. 3. (*idm*) *Shingo upande*, reluctantly e.g. *Alikubali shingo upande*, he agreed reluctantly.
shinikiz.a (also *shindikiza*) *vt* pressurize, press, force, compel: *Wanafunzi wa chuo kikuu waliushinikiza utawala kuwaongezea posho*, the university students pressurized the administration to increase the bursary. Prep. *shinikiz.i.a* St. *shinikiz.ik.a* Ps. *shinikiz.w.a*, be pressurized e.g. *Serikali ilishinikizwa na wabunge kuchukua hatua kali dhidi ya wabakaji*, the government was pressurized by members of parliament to take strong measures against rapists. Rp. *shinikiz.an.a* (cf *chagiza*)
shinikizo (also *shindikizo*) *n* (*n*) 1. pressure, force, compulsion: *Shinikizo la raia kwa serikali yao lilizaa matunda*, public pressure on the government bore fruit. (cf *chagizo*) 2. used in the expression: *Shinikizo la damu*, blood pressure.
shira¹ *n* (*n*) syrup (Ar)
shira² *n* (*n*) (*naut*) sail of a vessel. (Ar)
shiraa *n* (*n*) a kind of veil that does not show the other side of the face, worn by women. (Ar)
shirika¹ *n* (*ma-*) corporation, organization, parastatal, partnership: *Shirika la umma*, public corporation. *Shirika la umeme*, electricity corporation. *Shirika la posta*, post office corporation. *Shirika la Fedha Duniani*, International Monetary Fund. *Shirika la Afya Duniani*, World Health Organization. *Shirika la reli*, railway corporation. *Shirika la usagishaji*, milling corporation. *Shirika la habari*, news agency. *Shirika la hiari*, voluntary organization. *Shirika mama*, sister corporation. *Mashirika ya kimataifa*, international organizations. (Ar)
shirika² *adj* (used of joint ownership) corporate, combined, united: *Nyumba*

hii ni shirika mimi na dada yangu, this house belongs jointly to me and my sister. (cf *bia*) (Ar)
shirika³ *adv* together, in unison, as a group: *Walilima shirika*, they farmed together. (cf *pamoja*)
shirik.i *vt* 1. participate, take part, cooperate, share in: *Alishiriki katika mashindano ya mpira*, he participated in the football tournament. 2. be addicted, be obsessed with: *Mtu yule anashiriki sana katika uvutaji wa bangi*, that person is very much addicted to bhang smoking. Prep. ***shirik.i.a*** St. ***shirik.ik.a*** Cs. ***shirik.ish.a*** Ps. ***shirik.iw.a*** Ps. of Cs. ***shirik.ish.w.a*** Rp ***shirik.i.an.a*** (Ar)
shirik.i² *vt* (in Christianity) receive Holy Communion (Ar)
shirikish.a¹ *vt* see *shiriki¹*
shirikish.a² *vt* associate one thing with the other; equate: *Ni dhambi kwa Mwislamu kumshirikisha Mwenyezi Mungu*, it is a sin for a Muslim to associate God with any partners. Prep. ***shirikish.i.a*** St. ***shirikish.ik.a*** Ps. ***shirikish.w.a*** (Ar)
shirikisho *n* (*ma-*) federation, union, community, association: *Shirikisho la wakulima*, a union of farmers. *Shirikisho la wafanyakazi*, a union of workers. *Shirikisho la nchi mbalimbali*, a federation of different states. (Ar)
shisha *n* (*n*) hour glass; an instrument for measuring time by the trickling of sand, mercury, water, etc. (Ar)

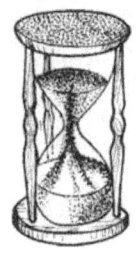

shisha

shitad.i *vi* 1. exceed, transcend, escalate, intensify, increase: *Baridi imeshitadi leo*, it is very cold today. *Joto lilishitadi jana*, the heat had intensified yesterday. (cf *kithiri, zidi*) 2. continue without a stop; persist: *Vitimbi vyake vimeshitadi siku hizi*, his wiles have persisted these days. Prep. ***shitad.i.a*** St. ***shitad.ik.a*** Cs. ***shitad.ish.a***
shitaka *n* (*ma-*) see *shtaka*
shitak.i *vt* see *shtaki*
shiti *n* (*ma-*) bed sheet; a large, rectangular piece of cotton, etc. used on a bed, usu in pairs. (Eng)
shitu.a *vt* see *shtua*
shizi *n* (*n*) brew made from coconut, cashew apple, etc. (cf *tembo*)
shoga¹ *n* (*ma-*) (used by women of one another) close woman friend: *Yeye ni shoga yangu*, she is my friend.
shoga² *n* (*ma-*) (in reference to males) gay, homosexual. (cf *hanithi, msenge*)
shogi¹ (also *sogi*) *n* (*n*) a pit, etc. inside a vessel in which slaves were hidden when they were being searched for or transported.
shogi² (also *shoji, sogi*) *n* (*n*) a donkey's pannier; pack-saddle.
shoji *n* (*n*) see *shogi²*
shojo.a *vt* see *shonoa*
shoka *n* (*ma-*) axe: *Shoka la bapa*, adze.
shokishoki *n* (*n*) (*bot*) rambutan; a maroon, red yellow or green spiny egg-shaped fruit with pleasant acid-sweet seed and somewhat transparent pulp.
shokoa¹ *n* (*n*) used in the expression: *Shika shokoa*, compel someone to do sth he does not like e.g. *Alihamaki kwa sababu tulimshika shokoa*, he got angry because we compelled him to do something he did not want to do.
shokoa² *n* (*n*) compulsory work, forced labour; corvee: *Fanyisha shokoa*, compel someone to work. (Pers)
shokoa³ *n* (*n*) a farm that has been cultivated and later abandoned thus resulting in for long grass to grow; abandoned farmland. (cf *vuwe*)

shokomzoba *n (n) (engin)* shock absorber; a device, as on the springs of a car, that lessens the effect or absorbs the force of shocks and jarring. (Eng)

shombe *n (ma-)* mongrel, hybrid, half-cast, half-blood. (cf *chotara, suriama, hafukasti*)

shombo *n (n)* a nasty smell of fish after it has been caught; fish smell. (cf *vumba*)

shomoro *n (n)* see *shore¹*

shon.a *vt* sew, stitch, tailor: *Aliishona nguo yangu vizuri,* he stitched my garment nicely. *Daktari alimshona mgonjwa baada ya kumfanyia operesheni,* the doctor stitched the patient after operating on him. Prep. *shon.e.a* e.g. *Sindano ya kushonea,* a sewing needle. St. *shon.ek.u* Cs. *shon.esh.a* e.g. *Ameshonesha suti mpya,* he has had his new suit made. Ps. *shon.w.a* Rp. of Prep. *shon.e.an.a* (cf *fuma*)

shonan.a *vi* be crammed, be congested: *Magari yameshonana barabarani,* the cars are in a traffic jam on the road. Prep. *shonan.i.a* St. *shonan.ik.a* Cs. *shonan.ish.a*

shonde¹ *n (n)* a mass of animal dung or human excrement: *Shonde la mavi,* turd. (cf *kutu*)

shonde² *n (n)* a state of non-communication between two people who have quarrelled: *Wekea shonde,* be in a state of non communication with each other; hold a grudge against sby.

shondi *n (n)* see *shundi*

shonga *n (n)* 1. curse, imprecation, malediction: *Shonga imempata mtoto yule,* a curse has fallen upon that child. (cf *laana, apizo*) 2. insanity, derangement, lunacy, madness: *Mzee ana shonga na ndiyo maana watu wanamkwepa,* the old man is mad and that is why people avoid him. (cf *kichaa, wehu, wazimu*) 3. used in the expression: *Tia shonga,* madden someone by inciting him to do sth.

shono.a *vt* unstitch, unweave, unravel, unseam, undo: *Aliishonoa nguo yake ilipokuwa ndogo,* she unstitched her tight frock. Prep. *shono.le.a* St. *shono.lek.a* Ps. of Prep. *shono.lew.a* (cf *fumua, fudua*)

shopo.a *vt* see *chopoa*

shore¹ *n (n) (zool)* flycatcher; a small or medium sized bird (family *Muscicapidae*) with a flattened bill, which catches insects in flight.

shore² *n (n)* a lock of hair growing above the forehead; forelock: *Funga shore,* keep a forelock.

shorekishungi *n (n) (zool)* paradise flycatcher; a kind of bird with an extremely long tail and a blue-black head and back. *Terpsiphone viridis.*

shorewanda *n (n) (zool)* grey-headed sparrow; a kind of a rather short-tailed greyish-brown bird with a pale dove-grey cap. *Pseudonigrita arnaudii.*

shoro¹ *adv* chaotically, awry, disorderly; in disarray: *Mipango yake ilienda shoro,* his plans went awry. (cf *kombo, ovyoovyo*)

shoro² *n (n) (zool)* warbler, a kind of song bird (family *Sylviidae*) having a small bill and cryptic plumage: *Shoro miraba,* barred warbler. *Shoro kijivu,* garden warbler. *Sharo manjano,* icterine warbler. (cf *chiriku*)

shoti¹ *n (n)* short; used in the expression: *Enda shoti,* run speedily, run fast e.g. *Farasi wake alienda shoti,* his horse ran fast. *Alienda shoti baada ya kufukuzwa,* he ran fast after being chased.

shoti² *n (n)* used in business activities to signal loss: *Ingia shoti,* run into a loss e.g. *Aliingia shoti katika biashara yake ya jana,* he suffered a loss in his yesterday's business. (cf *hasara*)

shoto¹ *n (n)* see *kushoto*

shoto² *adv* chaotically, disorderly, awry, haphazardly: *Shughuli zangu zilienda* *shoto,* my activities went awry. (cf *kombo, ovyoovyo*)

shtaka (also *shitaka*) *n* (*n*) charge, accusation, complaint: *Alikabiliwa na shtaka la kuhujumu uchumi nchini,* he was faced with the charge of economic sabotage in the country. (cf *daawa, manza, kesi*) (Ar)

shtak.i (also *shitaki*) *vt* accuse, charge, indict, complain: *Polisi walimshtaki kwa kuendesha gari bila ya hadhari,* the police charged him for careless driving. Prep. **shtak.i.a**, complain to (for, at, etc.) e.g. *Alimshtakia baba yangu,* he complained to my father. St. **shtak.ik.a** Ps. **shtak.iw.a,** be accused e.g. *Alishtakiwa kwa kosa la jinai,* he was accused of a criminal offence. Rp. of Prep. **shtak.i.an.a** (cf *ripoti, lalamika*) (Ar)

shtu.a (also *shitua, stua*) *vt* 1. (of person, animal, bird, etc.) scare off, frighten, affright, startle, shock: *Tulipomshtua ndege, akaruka,* when we scared the bird, it flew off. St. **shtu.k.a,** be startled, be shocked e.g. *Nilishtuka kusikia kifo cha ghafla cha jirani yangu,* I was shocked to hear of the sudden death of my neighbour. Cs. **shtu.sh.a,** startle, shock. Ps. of Prep. **shtu.liw.a** Ps. of Cs. **shtu.sh.w.a,** be shocked, be startled e.g. *Nilishtushwa na vitendo vyake viovu,* I was shocked by his evil deeds. Rp. **shtu.an.a** (cf *shangaza*) 2. (of a joint in the body, etc.) sprain, dislocate: *Alilishtua goti langu aliponiumiza kwenye mazoezi ya kabumbu,* he sprained my knee during football practice. St. **shtu.k.a** Cs. **shtu.sh.a** Ps. of Prep. **shtu.liw.a** Rp. **shtu.an.a** (cf *tegua, gutua*)

shtuk.a *vi* see *shtua.* Prep. **shtuk.i.a,** be caught in surprise e.g. *Nilipoamka, nilishtukia saa nne,* when I woke up, I found by surprise that it was ten o'clock. St. **shtuk.ik.a** Cs. **shtuk.ish.a**

shtuko *n* (*ma-*) shock, attack: *Shtuko la moyo,* heart attack; myocardial infarction.

shtush.a *vt* see *shtua* Prep. **shtush.i.a** St. **shtush.ik.a** Ps. **shtush.w.a** Rp. **shtush.an.a**

shu.a *vt* (*naut*) launch a vessel e.g. ship, dhow, boat, etc. into the water: *Aliishua mashua yake maji yalipojaa,* he launched his boat into the water when the tide was high. (*prov*) *Usishue dau na maji yajaa,* don't launch your canoe when the tide is high i.e. don't rush to do sth when other people are in the process of doing the same thing. Prep. **shu.li.a** St. **shu.lik.a** Cs. **shu.sh.a** Ps. of Prep. **shu.liw.a**

shuari *n* (*n*) see *shwari*

shubaka *n* (*ma-*) bay, alcove, niche; a recess or hollow in a wall to keep things. (cf *daka, rafu*) (Ar)

shubiri[1] (also *shabiri*) *n* (*n*) a span from the thumb to the little finger of the open hand of roughly nine inches. (Ar)

shubiri[2] *n* (*n*) (*bot*) bitter aloes: *Chungu kama shubiri,* as bitter as aloes. (Ar)

shuduza *n* (*n*) (*bot*) coconut palm's shoot.

shufa *n* (*n*) see *shufwa*

shufaa *n* (*n*) 1. pardon, clemency, forgiveness: *Mshtakiwa alipewa shufaa na rais,* the accused was granted clemency by the president. (cf *msamaha*) 2. improvement, convalescence: *Mgonjwa wake amepata shufaa,* his patient has got some improvement. (cf *afueni, ahueni, nafuu*) (Ar)

shufaka *n* (*n*) compassion, pity, tenderness. (cf *huruma, kite*) (Ar)

shuf.u *vt* look, glance, glimpse, watch Prep. **shuf.i.a** St. **shuf.ik.a** Cs. **shuf.ish.a** Ps. **shuf.w.a** Rp. **shuf.an.a** (cf *tazama*) (Ar)

shufwa *n* (*n*) even number: *Mbili, nne na sita ni nambari shufwa,* two, four and six are even numbers. (cf *kifuasi*) (Ar)

shughuli *n* (*n*) 1. activity, business, enterprise, engagement, work: *Shughuli za biashara*, commercial enterprises. *Ana shughuli nyingi ofisini leo*, he has a lot of work in the office today. (cf *kazi, amali*) 2. reception, party: *Shughuli yake ilikuwa bulbul*, his reception was superb. (cf *karamu*)

shughulik.a¹ *vi* 1. be busy, be occupied, be engaged: *Wanawake wameshughulika na matayarisho ya harusi*, the women are busy with preparations for the wedding. (cf *hangaika*) 2. be uneasy, be unsettled: *Bibi yule alishughulika baada ya kupoteza kipochi chake*, that lady became restless after losing her purse. Prep. *shughulik.i.a* (cf *hamanika*)

shughulika² *interj* (used in army parade) a command given to look right and then one step forward and then back by footing on the ground in order to be on the line making sure that the line is straight; be in a straight line!

shughuliki.a *vt* attend to: *Alinishughulikia nilipokwenda ofisini mwake*, he attended to me when I went to his office Ps *shughuliki.w.a*

shughulish.a *vt* 1. disturb/irk sby: *Mwanangu alinishughulisha nilipokuwa ninaandika*, my daughter disturbed me when I was writing. 2. engage sby; keep sby busy: *Nilimwambia anishughulishe kwa namna fulani kwa vile nilikuwa sina kazi*, I told him to keep me busy in some way or another as I was not doing anything then. Prep. *shughulish.i.a* Ps. *shughulish.w.a* Rp. *shughulish.an.a*

shuhuda *n* (*ma-*) see *shahidi*

shuhudi.a *vt* testify, witness, attest; bear witness: *Alishuhudia mauaji ya kikatili*, he witnessed a brutal murder. Prep. *shuhudi.li.a* St. *shuhudi.lik.a* Ps. *shuhudi.w.a*, be witnessed e.g. *Ajali ilishuhudiwa na wapita njia*, the accident was witnessed by the passers-by. Rp. *shuhudi.an.a* (cf *ona*) (Ar)

shuhudiani *n* (*n*) a commission or present given to someone who witnesses a transaction between the parties concerned. (Ar)

shujaa *n* (*ma-*) hero, stalwart; a brave person: *Yeye alikuwa shujaa vitani*, he was a hero in the war. (cf *jabari, simba*) (Ar)

shuk.a¹ *vi, vt* 1. descend, debark, disembark, alight; go down, come down: *Alishuka haraka kutoka kwenye gari*, he alighted hurriedly from the car. (*prov*) *Mpanda ngazi hushuka*, he who climbs a ladder, also comes down. 2. (of price, etc.) go down: *Bei ya sukari imeshuka siku hizi*, the price of sugar has gone down these days. Prep. *shuk.i.a* St. *shuk.ik.a* Cs. *shuk.ish.a*

shuka² *n* (*ma-*) bedsheet, loin-cloth. (cf *shiti*)

shuke (also *suke*) *n* (*n*) (*bot*) ear of corn or grain.

shuki.a¹ *vt* get off at, land at: *Walishukia kwenye kituo cha reli*, they got off at the railway station.

shuki.a² *vt* accuse sby falsely for an evil deed; asperse, traduce, calumniate. Prep. *shuki.li.a*, be suspicious of. St. *shuki.lik.a* Ps. *shuki.liw.a*

shukrani (also *shukurani*) *n* (*n*) thanks, gratitude, acknowledgment: *Toa shukrani*, give thanks to someone: *Alinipa shukrani zake*, he gave me his thanks. (cf *ahsante*) (Ar)

shuk.u *vt* suspect, disbelieve; have doubts, be skeptical, be suspicious: *Nilimshuku kuwa yeye ndiye mwizi mwenyewe*, I suspected him to be the real thief. Prep. *shuk.i.a*, be suspicious of. St. *shuk.ik.a* Ps. of Prep. *shuk.iw.a*, be suspected of Rp. of Prep. *shuk.i.an.a* (cf *tuhumu, shtumu, dhani*)

shukurani *n* (*n*) see *shukrani*

shukur.u *vt* thank, acknowledge; be

grateful: *Nilimshukuru kwa msaada wake,* I thanked her for her assistance. *Shukuru Mungu kwa lile ulilolifanya.* thank God for what you have done. Prep. ***shukur.i.a*** St. ***shukur.ik.a*** Cs. ***shukur.ish.a*** Ps. ***shukur.iw.a*** Rp. of Prep. ***shukur.i.an.a*** (Ar)
shule (also *skuli*) *n* (*n*) 1. school: *Shule za binafsi,* private schools. *Shule ya msingi,* primary school. *Shule ya upili,* secondary school. *Shule ya chekechea,* kindergarten. *Shule ya vidudu,* nursery school. *Shule ya bweni,* boarding school. (cf *skuli*) 2. institute. (Germ)
shuli *n* (*n*) the back part of a house; backyard.
shulu¹ *n* (*n*) see *shuru¹*
shulu² *vt* see *shuru²*
shumari *n* (*n*) (*bot*) a kind of light-yellowish dill, used as a seasoning agent in food; fennel seeds. (Ar)
shumbi *n* (*n*) 1. a deep channel; deep water. (cf *kilindi*) 2. a heap of sand.
shumburere *n* (*n*) sombrero (cf *pama*) (Sp)

shumburere

shume *n* (*n*) 1. used in the expression: *Paka shume,* a semi-wild cat; a large male cat. (cf *nunda, duzi*) 2. a wicked person, an evil person; reprobate, devil, monster.
shumizi *n* (*n*) see *shimizi*
shundi *n* (*n*) (*zool*) black coucal; a kind of bird with oily-black plumage, which lives in swamps and marshes. *Centropus grillii.* (cf *dudumizi*)
shundwa *n* (*n*) (*zool*) hyena (cf *kingugwa, fisi*)
shung.a *vt* 1. shoo off, drive away, drive off: *Aliwashunga ndege ili wasije kula mtama wake,* he drove the birds away so that they did not eat his millet. (cf *fukuza, winga*) 2. look after, take care of: *Aliwashunga ng'ombe wake vizuri,* he looked after his cattle well. (cf *linda, tunza*) Prep. ***shung.i.a*** St. ***shung.ik.a*** Cs. ***shung.ish.a*** Ps. ***shung.w.a***
shungi *n* (*ma-*) forelock, tress; a lock of hair or a bird's crest: *Anapenda kufuga shungi la nywele,* he likes to keep a forelock. (cf *shore, denge, panja*)
shuo *n* (*n*) ability, deftness, ableness.
shupa.a *vi* 1. (of things) be hard, be compact: *Aliutia mafuta usukani wa baiskeli ulioshupaa,* he oiled the bicycle's handle which had become stiff. (cf *kauka, gungumka*) 2. (of persons) be hard, be tough, be rigid, be headstrong: *Kiongozi alishupaa katika msimamo wake,* the leader was tough in his stance. Prep. ***shupa.i.a*** St. ***shupa.lik.a*** Cs. ***shupa.z.a*** Ps. of Prep. ***shupa.liw.a*** Rp. ***shupa.an.a*** (cf *kakamaa, kaidi, chachamaa*)
shupali.a *vt* insist, assert. Prep. ***shupali.li.a*** St. ***shupali.k.a*** Cs. ***shupali.sh.a*** Ps. ***shupali.w.a*** Rp. ***shupali.an.a***
shupatu *n* (*n*) 1. a narrow strip of plaited grass or palm leaves, used for lacing bedstead or for sewing mats. 2. a kind of shoes, sewn by a rope of plaited leaf strips.
-shupavu *adj* 1. hard, stiff, solid: *Usukani huu wa baiskeli ni shupavu,* this bicycle's handle is stiff. (cf *-gumu*) 2. unyielding, obstinate, obdurate, tough, firm: *Mwanasiasa yule ni mshupavu,* that politician is firm.
shupaza¹ *n* (*n*) (in cards) spade; a black figure marking one of the four suits of playing cards. (Port)

shupaza

shupaz.a² *vt* 1. harden, stiffen. 2. cause to become obstinate. Prep. ***shupaz.i.a*** St. ***shupaz.ik.a*** Cs. ***shupaz.ish.a*** Ps. ***shupaz.w.a*** Rp. ***shupaz.an.a***
shupi *n* (*ma-*) a plaited palm leaf make-shift basket; straw make-shift basket.
shura *n* (*n*) a kind of chemical resembling salt which is used for making gunpowder; saltpetre. (Pers)
shuru¹ *n* (*n*) a kind of sewing in embroidery; tack.
shur.u² *vi* tack, baste; sew with long loose stitches so as to keep the parts together until properly sewed. Prep. ***shur.i.a*** St. ***shur.ik.a*** Cs. ***shur.ish.a*** Ps. of Prep. ***shur.iw.a***
shurua (also *surua*) *n* (*n*) (*med*) an acute infectious communicable virus disease which is characterized by red-spots on the skin, high fever, nasal discharge, etc.; measles. (Pers)
shuruka (also *magenge*) *n* (*n*) (*zool*) hermit crab; a kind of crab that belongs to a superfamily esp *Paguroidea*, having asymmetrical, soft abdomen and lives in the empty shells of certain mollusks, as snails.

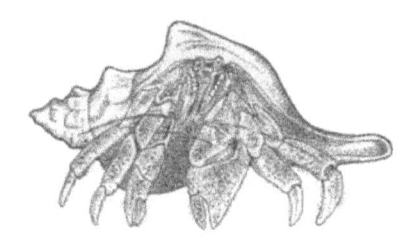

shuruka

shuruti *n* (*n*) see *sharti*² and *sharti*³
shurutish.a *vt* compel, force, coerce, press: *Nilimshurutisha kuifanya kazi yangu kwa mara ya pili*, I forced him to do my work for the second time. Prep. ***shurutish.i.a*** St. ***shurutish.ik.a*** Ps. ***shurutish.w.a***, be compelled, e.g. *Alishurutishwa kujiunga na Jeshi la Kujenga Taifa*, he was compeled to join the National Service. Rp. ***shurutish.an.a*** (cf *lazimisha*)
shush.a *vt* 1. ejaculate; discharge sperm from the penis. 2. discharge cargo, etc.; unload, offload, let down: *Aliushusha mzigo wangu kutoka kwenye basi*, he offloaded my luggage from the bus. (cf *teremsha*) 3. used in the expression: *Shusha pumzi*, breathe out, exhale. Prep. ***shush.i.a*** St. ***shush.ik.a*** Ps. ***shush.w.a*** Rp. of Prep. ***shush.i.an.a***
shushi.a *vi* fornicate, copulate; commit coition; have sexual intercourse with someone.
shushu *n* (*ma-*) (*bot*) husk, peel, rind: *Shushu la ndizi*, banana peel, *Shushu la chungwa*, orange peel. *Shushu la mtama*, millet husk. *Shushu la mpunga*, rice husk.
shushu.a *vt* discredit, defame: *Kiongozi aliweza kuwashushua hadharani wale wasioamini kuwa demokrasia haiwezi kusitawi katika Afrika*, the leader managed to discredit in public those who didn't believe that democracy can't flourish in Africa. Prep. ***shushu.li.a*** St. ***shushu.k.a*** Cs. ***shushu.sh.a*** Ps. of Prep. ***shushu.liw.a*** Rp. ***shushu.an.a***
shut.a *vi* fart; break wind: *Alishuta mbele za watu*, he farted in public. Prep. ***shut.i.a*** St. ***shut.ik.a*** Cs. ***shut.ish.a***
shuti *n* (*ma-*) (in soccer, etc.) kick, shot: *Alipiga shuti kali*, he kicked a hard shot. (cf *kiki*) (Eng)
shutuma *n* (*n*) accusation, reprimand, censure, blame, criticism: *Shutuma kali*, wild accusation.
shutum.u *vt* reprove, blame, reproach, scold, chide, rebuke: *Mzazi alimshutumu bintiye bila ya sababu*, the parent scolded her daughter for no reason. Prep. ***shutum.i.a*** St. ***shutum.ik.a*** Cs. ***shutum.ish.a*** Ps. of Prep. ***shutum.iw.a*** Rp. of Prep. ***shutum.i.an.a*** (cf *karipia, laumu, aili*) (Ar)

shuu *n* (*ma-*) a wave that breaks into foam against a shore or reef; breaker, foamy sea wave.
shuwari *adj* see *shwari*
shuzi (also *ushuzi*) *n* (*ma-*) an intestinal gas emitted from the anus.
shwari (also *shuari, shuwari*) *adj* calm, quiet, tranquil, serene, placid, undisturbed: *Bahari iko shwari leo*, the sea is calm today. (cf *nyamavu, kimya*)
si *vt* (*cop*) negative copular verb meaning not: *Yeye si mjinga*, he is not a fool. *Usifanye kelele*, don't make noise.
si.a¹ *vt* sow seeds by dibbling; dibble: *Mkulima alisia mbegu za mpunga kwenye shamba lake*, the farmer dibbled rice seeds in his farm. Prep. *si.li.a* St. *si.lik.a* Cs. of Prep. *si.lish.a* Ps. of Prep. *si.liw.a* (cf *otesha, melesha*)
si.a² *vt* drive away doryline ants (*siafu*) by burning them: *Niliwasia siafu walipoingia chumbani mwangu*, I burnt the doryline ants when they entered my room. Prep. *si.li.a* St. *si.lik.a* Cs. of Prep. *si.lish.a* Ps. of Prep. *si.liw.a*
siafu *n* (*n*) (*zool*) doryline ants; they are commonly known as "driver ants" (family *Dorylidae*) which are forced to live a nomadic life as they are hunters.
siagi *n* (*n*) butter (Ar)
siahi *n* (*n*) yell, scream; a loud cry: *Piga siahi*, cry out loudly. (Ar)
siasa *n* (*n*) 1. politics: *Elimu ya siasa*, political education. *Siasa ya ubepari*, capitalism. *Siasa ya ubaguzi wa rangi*, apartheid. *Siasa ya mrengu wa kulia*, conservatism. *Siasa ya mrengu wa kushoto*, leftism; radicalism. (cf *itikadi*) 2. organization, plan, system, policy: *Siasa ya serikali ya kuwaelimisha watu wote vijijini ni nzuri*, the government's policy of educating all people in the villages is good. (cf *mpango, sera*) 3. diplomacy, judiciousness, common sense: *Alitumia siasa katika kusuluhisha ugomvi wetu*, he used diplomacy to settle our dispute. *Fanya mambo kwa siasa*, do things diplomatically. (cf *busara, maarifa*) 4. (*gram*) *Siasa lugha*, glotto politics. (Ar)
sibab.i *vt* 1. abuse, revile, affront, vituperate; heap abuse on: *Alitusibabi mbele za watu*, he abused us in public. (cf *tukana, tusi*) 2. calumniate, asperse, slander; accuse falsely: *Walimsibabi burebure*, they cast aspersion on him for no reason. Prep. *sibab.i.a* St. *sibab.ik.a* Cs. *sibab.ish.a* Ps. of Prep. *sibab.iw.a* Rp. of Prep. *sibab.i.an.a* (cf *teta, simbulia*) (Ar)
siborio *n* (*n*) (in Christianity) ciborium; a covered cup for holding the consecrated waters of the Eucharist. (Eng)
sib.u¹ *vi* happen, materialize; come true: *Utabiri wa mganga ulisibu*, the soothsayer's prediction came true. (Ar)
sib.u² *vt* afflict; bring misfortune upon: *Maafa yamemsibu*, some misfortune has fallen upon him. *Mauti yamemsibu*, death has occurred upon him. (cf *patwa, tokea*) (Ar)
sidiria *n* (*n*) a woman's undergarment worn to support her breasts; woman's bra, brassiere. (cf *kanchiri*) (Ar)
sie *pron* see *sisi*
sifa¹ *n* (*n*) fish oil made from shark, kingfish, etc. used in coating the hull strakes. (Ar)
sifa² *n* (*n*) 1. trait, attribute, characteristic, qualification: *Walinipa sifa zote juu ya kiongozi wao*, they gave me all the full qualifications of their leader. (cf *wasifu, maelezo*) 2. reputation, repute, name: *Ana sifa mbaya*, he has a bad reputation. 3. (*gram*) *Sifa bainifu*, distinctive features. *Sifa jumuiya*, common features. *Sifa kichemba*,

sifongo   sijida   **S**

cavity features. *Sifa kiarudhi,* supra segmental features. *Sifa kisemantiki,* semantic features. *Sifa kuu pambanuzi,* major class features. *Sifa ya uwiano,* mark of correlation. *Sifa akustiki,* acoustic features. (Ar)

sifongo (also *sponji*) *n (n)* sponge (Ar)

sif.u *vt* praise, commend, extol, laud: *Wageni wetu walikisifu chakula,* our guests praised the meal. *Nilimsifu daktari kwa ushujaa wake,* I praised the doctor for his courage. Prep. *sif.i.a* St. *sif.ik.a* Cs. *sif,ish.a* Ps. of Prep. *sif.iw.a,* be praised e.g. *Alisifiwa na kila mtu,* he was praised by everyone. Rp. of Prep. *sif.i.an.a*

sifuri[1] (also *sufuri*) *n (n)* white brass. (Ar)

sifuri[2] (also *sufuri*) *n (n)* number 0; zero, nil, naught: *Mwanafunzi aliandika alama ya sifuri ubaoni,* the student wrote a mark of zero on the blackboard. (cf *nunge*)

sig.a[1] *vi* (of the colour of sth) get changed because of dirt; soil: *Kanzu yake ilisiga kwa sababu ya uchafu mwingi,* her dress was very soiled. Prep. *sig.i.a* St. *sig.ik.a* Cs. *sig.ish.a* Ps. *sig.w.a*

sig.a[2] *vt* differ, oppose, gainsay, contradict: *Tulimpa ushauri lakini yeye akausiga,* we gave him a suggestion but he opposed it. *Wazo lake kuhusu siasa ya ubepari linasiga lile langu,* his idea on the policy of capitalism contradicts with mine. Prep. *sig.i.a* St. *sig.ik.a* Cs. *sig.ish.a* Ps. *sig.w.a* Rp. *sig.an.a* (cf *pingana*)

sigara (also *sigareti*) *n (n)* cigarette, cigar: *Vuta sigara,* smoke a cigarette. *Sokota sigara,* roll a cigarette. *Kishika sigara,* cigar lighter. (Eng)

sigareti *n (n)* see *sigara*

sigi (also *usisi*) *n (n) (zool)* bronze mannikin; a kind of small bird with black feathers on the head and chest, a small tail and a blackish head. *Lonchura cucullata.* (cf *chigi*)

sigishan.a *vt, vi* quarrel between two or more sides: *Waliposigishana, uhusiano kati yao ukazidi kudorora,* when they quarrelled, the relation between them worsened further. Prep. *sigishan.i.a* St. *sigishan.ik.a* Ps. *sigishan.w.a*

siha *n (n)* health, strength: *Hana siha siku hizi,* he is not healthy these days. *Sina siha ya kuweza kuifanya kazi,* I have no strength to do the work. (cf *afya, nguvu*) (Ar)

sih.i[1] *vt* beseech, implore, plead: *Nilimsihi asisafiri lakini akasafiri,* i beseeched him not to travel but he did. Prep. *sih.i.a* St. *sih.ik.a* Cs. *sih.ish.a* Ps. of Prep. *sih.iw.a* Rp. of Prep. *sih.i.an.a* (cf *bembeleza, rai, omba, tafadhalisha*) (Ar)

sih.i[2] *vt, vi* be fit, be proper, be suitable: *Haisihi mume yule kumnyanyasa mkewe,* it is not befitting for that husband to ill-treat his wife. Prep. *sih.i.a* St. *sih.ik.a* Cs. *sih.ish.a* Ps. of Prep. *sih.iw.a* Rp. of Prep. *sih.i.an.a* (cf *faa*)

sihir.i[1] *vt* bewitch, hex. *Alimsihiri jirani yake na hatimaye akafariki,* she bewitched her neighbour and in the end, he died. Prep. *sihir.i.a* St. *sihir. ik.a* Cs. *sihir.ish.a* Ps. of Prep. *sihir. iw.a* Rp. of Prep. *sihir.i.an.a* (cf *roga, cheza, anga*) (Ar)

sihiri[2] *n (n)* witchcraft, sorcery: *Anaamini sana mambo ya sihiri,* he believes very much in witchcraft. (cf *uramali, uchawi, amali, ulozi*) (Ar)

sijafu *n (n)* an internal cuff or wristband of a coat or a long garment, that is *kanzu.* (Pers)

sijambo *adv* an expletive used by someone to indicate that he is in good health; I am fine.

sijida *n (n)* 1. (in Islam) a callus or black patch on the forehead resulting from prostration during praying. 2. prostration; act of laying with the face downward on the ground during praying as a highest manifestation

693

of humility and self-surrender to Almighty God. By this act, all the limbs, forehead, two hands, two knees, two ends of feet and nose are brought to submission. (Ar)

sijiko *n* (*ma-*) grief, sadness. (cf *majonzi, simanzi, huzuni*)

siki *n* (*n*) vinegar (Pers)

siki.a *vt, vi* 1. hear; perceive sound, receive sound: *Nilisikia mlio wa bunduki kutoka mbali,* I heard a gunshot from a distance. 2. obey, comply, observe, heed. (*prov*) *Asiyesikia la mkuu huvunjika guu,* i.e. he who does not listen to advice from an elder, will suffer in the end. 3. sense, feel: *Anasikia njaa,* he feels hungry. *Anasikia usingizi,* he feels sleepy. *Anajisikia vibaya,* he feels unwell. *Hajisikii vizuri,* he does not feel well. Prep. **siki.li.a** St. **siki.k.a** Cs. **siki.z.a** Ps. **siki.w.a** Rp. **siki.an.a** (cf *hisi, ona*) (Ar)

sikik.a *vi* (of sound) be audible, be heard

sikilizan.a *vt, vi* get along well, understand each other: *Vijana wale wanasikilizana sana,* those young men get along very well. Prep. **sikilizan.i.a** St. **sikilizan.ik.a** Cs. **sikilizan.ish.a**

sikini *n* (*n*) a special kind of hair cutting for a person, that leaves a tuft on the forehead; quiff. (Ar)

sikio (also *shikio*) *n* (*n*) 1. (*anat*) ear: *Sikio la ndani,* labyrinth. 2. (*idm*) *Tega sikio,* listen attentively. (*prov*) *Sikio la kufa halisikii dawa,* an ear that is approaching its death, does not have a remedy i.e. if a person is heading for a disaster, there is nothing that can be done to save him however much assistance is given to him.

sikitik.a *vi* regret, grieve; be sad, be sorry, feel pity: *Tulisikitika sana kwa kitendo chake kiovu,* we were very sad for his misdeed. Prep. **sikitik.i.a** St. **sikitik.ik.a** Cs. **sikitik.ish.a** Rp. of Prep. **sikitik.i.an.a** (cf *huzunika*)

sikitiko *n* (*ma-*) melancholy, sadness, grief, sorrow. (cf *jitimai, huzuni, simanzi*)

sikitish.a *vt* disappoint, sadden: *Inasikitisha kusikia habari zile,* it is saddening to hear those news. Prep. **sikitish.i.a** St. **sikitish.ik.a** Ps. **sikitish.w.a** Rp. **sikitish.an.a**

-sikivu *adj* compliant, obedient, docile, attentive: *Mtumishi msikivu,* an obedient servant.

siku *n* (*n*) day: *Siku kwa siku,* day after day. *Siku za usoni,* in future. *Siku zote,* always. (*prov*) *Siku za mwizi ni arobaini,* the days of a thief are forty i.e. you may commit an evil deed and escape with it, but one day, you will be caught if you continue doing the same thing.

siku.a *vt* see *sekua*

sikukuu *n* (*n*) holiday, vacation, festival: *Sikukuu ya kuzaliwa,* birthday. *Sikukuu ya Krismasi,* Christmas holiday. *Sikukuu ya Idi,* Idd festival.

sila *n* (*n*) dipper; bailer; a vessel for bailing water out of a canoe, boat, etc. (cf *upo, zila, ndau*) (Pers)

silabasi (also *silibasi*) *n* (*n*) syllabus, curriculum: *Silabasi ya shule,* school syllabus. (Eng)

silabi *n* (*n*) a unit in speech which is quite often longer than one sound and smaller than a word; syllable: *Silabi wazi,* open syllable. *Silabi huru,* free syllable. *Silabi funge,* closed syllable; blocked syllable. *Silabi sisitizi,* accented syllable. (cf *mizani, pigo*) (Eng)

silaha *n* (*n*) weapon, arms: *Silaha za maangamizi,* weapons of destruction. *Silaha za jadi,* traditional weapons e.g axes, pangas, etc. *Twaa silaha,* take up arms. (cf *zana*) (Ar)

silesi *n* (*n*) slice of bread. (Eng)

sili.a *vt* leave someone to take care of sth while you are away; entrust sth to sby while away: *Alinisilia watoto wake alipokwenda ng'ambo kwa masomo,* he entrusted me with the care of his

children when he went abroad for further studies. St. *sili.k.a* Cs. *sili.sh.a* Ps. *sili.w.a* Rp. *sili.an.a*
silika *n* (*n*) character, behaviour, conduct: *Ana silika nzuri*, he has a good character. (cf *tabia, mwenendo*) (Ar)
silim.u *vi* be converted to Islam; become a Muslim. Prep. *silim.i.a* St. *silim.ik.a* Cs. *silim.ish.a* Ps. of Cs. *silim.ish.w.a* (Ar)
silinda *n* (*n*) 1. cylinder: *Silinda kipimio*, measuring cylinder. 2. (*geom*) cylinder; a surface formed by a line moving round a closed plane curve at a fixed angle to it (cf *mcheduara*) (Eng)
silingi *n* (*n*) winch, crane, derrick. (Eng)
silisila *n* (*n*) see *silisili*
silisili (also *silisila*) *n* (*n*) shackles, chain, fetter. (cf *mnyororo*)
sima *n* (*n*) cooked maize meal or cassava or millet made by stirring the flour of these ingredients in boiling water; hard porridge. (cf *ugali*)
simaku *n* (*n*) see *sumaku*
simam.a *vi* 1. stand, rise; remain upright: *Kwanza alisimama, kisha akakaa kitako*, first he stood up and then he sat down. (cf *inuka*) 2. stop doing sth; cease: *Gari lilipoharibika, ilibidi isimame*, when the car broke down, it had to stop. (cf *sita*) 3. be erect, be upright: *Askari jeshi walisimama imara katika paredi*, the soldiers stood upright in the parade. 4. (*idms*) *Simama dede*, stand uncertainly. *Simama kidete*, stand firm; stand without fear. *Simama tanda*, stand upright. *Simama tisti*, stand firm. Prep. *simam.i.a* St. *simam.ik.a* Cs. *simam.ish.a* Ps. of Prep. *simam.iw.a* Rp. of Prep. *simam.i.an.a*
simami.a¹ *vi* see *simama*
simami.a² *vt* 1. supervise, preside, sponsor: *Niliisimamia kazi yake*, I supervised his work. 2. depend, rely: *Alisimamia mguu mmoja*, he depended on one leg. St. *simami.k.a* Cs. *simami.sh.a* Ps. *simami.w.a* (cf *tegemea*)
simamish.a¹ *vt* see *simama* Prep. *simamish.i.a* St. *simamish.ik.a* Ps. *simamish.w.a* Rp. *simamish.an.a*
simamish.a² *vt* 1. suspend someone from work: *Meneja alimsimamisha kazi mfanyakazi*, the manager suspended an employer from work. 2. stop, halt: *Aliisimamisha gari barabarani*, he stopped the car on the road. 3. field/ uphold a candidate: *Chama kitasimamisha watetezi wengi katika uchaguzi ujao*, the party will field many candidates in the forthcoming elections. 4. keep up to do sth; maintain: *Lazima usimamishe sala*, you must maintain your prayers. Prep. *simamish.i.a* St. *simamish.ik.a* Ps. *simamish.w.a* Rp. *simamish.an.a*
simang.a *vt* remind sby constantly of what you have done to help him when in trouble, etc.; rub it in; put sby down. Prep. *simang.i.a* St. *simang.ik.a* Cs. *simang.ish.a* Ps. *simang.w.a* Rp. *simang.an.a* (cf *sengenya, simbulia*)
simango *n* (*n*) humiliation; act of putting sby down: *Simango lolote ni baya*, any form of humiliation is bad.
simantiki *n* (*n*) see *semantiki*
simanzi *n* (*n*) sadness, melancholy, grief: *Alijaa na simanzi*, he was filled with profound sorrow. (cf *sikitiko, huzuni, majonzi*)
simba¹ *n* (*n*) 1. (*zool*) lion. *Simba mwenda pole ndiye mla nyama*, a lion who walks secretly eats meat i.e. he who does his actions silently and carefully, always succeeds. 2 (*fig*) a courageous person, a brave person; hero: *Watu wanamhusudu simba yule*, people admire that courageous person. (cf *shujaa, fahali, jabari*)
simb.a² *vt* code a language. Prep. *simb.i.a* St. *simb.ik.a* Cs. *simb.ish.a* Ps. *simb.w.a*

simbamarara n (n) (zool) a kind of large spotted hyena.
simbauranga n (bot) a kind of red barked mangroove, used as beams for building.
simbi n (n) a small cowry shell used for playing certain games and formerly used as a currency. (cf *kaure*)
simbik.a (also *sumbika*) vt (*naut*) hook or entangle a fishing-line: *Baada ya kusimbika ndoana katika mshipi, rafiki yangu akaanza kuvua samaki*, after he had hooked a fishing-line, my friend started to fish. Prep. **simbik.i.a** St. **simbik.ik.a** Cs. **simbik.iz.a** Ps. **simbik.w.a**
simbiko (also *sumbiko*) n (*ma-*) the act of hooking or entangling a fishing line.
simbo n (n) thimble (cf *dopa*) (Eng)
simbu.a vt decode; translate a coded message) into ordinary, understandable language. Prep. **simbu.li.a** St. of Prep. **simbu.lik.a** Cs. of Prep. **simbu.lish.a** Ps. of Prep. **simbu.liw.a**
simbuli.a vt humiliate; remind sby constantly of what you have done to help him when in trouble, etc.; rub it in, put sby down: *Alitusimbulia mbele za watu kwa chakula alichotupa*, he rubbed it in publicly that he gave us food. St **simbuli.k.a** Cs **simbuli.sh.a** Ps **simbuli.w.a** Rp **simbuli.an.a** (cf *simanga, sengenya*)
simbulio n (*ma-*) the act of reminding someone constantly of what you have done for him when in trouble, etc (cf *simango*)
sime n (n) a large double-edged bush knife. (cf *shembea*)
simenti n (n) see *sementi*
simik.a¹ vi (of the penis, etc.) be erect; have an erection. Prep. **simik.i.a** St. **simik.ik.a** Cs. **simik.iz.a** Ps. **simik.w.a** Rp. **simik.an.a** (cf *kita, dinda*)
simik.a² vt instal someone in office: *Askofu alimsimika padri mpya*, the bishop installed the new clergy.

Prep **simik.i.a** St. **simik.ik.a** Ps. **simik.w.a** Rp. **simik.an.a**
simile *interj* see *sumile*
simiti n (n) see *sementi*
simo¹ n (n) jargon, argot, patois.
sim.o² vi (*cop*) I am not in it; I am out of it; I am not responsible.
simsim (*bot*) sesame; the seeds of sesame: *Mafuta ya simsim*, sesame oil.
simu¹ n (n) 1. telephone, telegram, telex: *Simu ya mbali*, trunk call. *Piga simu*, make a phone call. *Peleka simu*, send telex, etc. *Simu ya mdomo*, phone call. *Simu ya mkono*, mobile phone. 2. message or information obtained through telephone, telegram, etc.: *Simu ya upepo*, telegraph. 3. a message or information to be transmitted by telephone, telegram, etc. (Pers)
simu² n (n) (zool) a kind of small fish of the family of sardines.
simuli.a vt narrate, novelize; tell a story in writing or speech. *Alinisimulia hadithi yote*, he narrated to me the whole story. St. **simuli.k.a** Cs. **simuli.sh.a** and **simuli.z.a** Ps. **simuli.w.a** Rp. **simuli.an.a** (cf *eleza, hadithia*)
-simulizi n (n) narrative, story: *Fasihi simulizi*, oral literature.
sin.a¹ vi see *sinasina*
sin.a *verb form* I haven't: *Sina watoto*, I don't have children. *Sina kazi*, I don't have work. *Sina nafasi*, I am busy.
sinasin.a (also *sina*) vi be in an emotional state after having cried; be on the verge of tears: *Msichana yule alisinasina baada ya kulaumiwa*, that girl shed tears after being blamed. Prep. **sinasin.i.a** St. **sinasin.ik.a** Cs. **sinasin.ish.a**
sindano¹ (also *shindano*) n (n) 1. sewing needle. *Tunga sindano*, thread a needle. (cf *shazia*) 2. a stylus used in playing gramophone records. 3a. injection: *Piga sindano*, give an injection. *Pigwa sindano*, get an injection. *Dunga sindano*, get an injection. b) a small slender implement used for surgical

suturing. 4. (idm) *Toka kwenye tundu ya sindano*, survive miraculously.
sindano² *n* (*n*) (*bot*) a kind long thin rice.
sindano³ *n* (*n*) (*bot*) a kind of small thin mango.
sindik.a¹ *vt* see *shindika*
sindik.a² *vt* extract or press out seeds, fruits, etc. in order to get liquid: *Sindika mafuta*, extract oil by pressure. 2. mill: *Aliusindika unga wake kwenye kinu*, he milled his flour in the milling machine. Prep. *sindik.i.a* St. *sindik.ik.a* Cs. *sindik.ish.a* Ps. *sindik.w.a* (cf *saga*)
sindikiz.a (also *shindikiza²*) *vt* accompany a departing guest a little way; give a send-off to a departing guest; escort, see off: *Alimsindikiza mgeni wake mpaka kwenye kituo cha basi*, he escorted his guest to the bus-stand. Prep. *sindikiz.i.a* St. *sindikiz.ik.a* Cs. *sindikiz.ish.a* Ps. *sindikiz.w.a* Rp. *sindikiz.an.a* (cf *ongoza, adi, safirisha*)
sindu.a *vt, vi* 1. open a door or window without putting a stopper. 2. remove the residue of grain in a mortar during pounding. Prep. *sindu.li.a* St. of Prep. *sindu.lik.a* Cs. of Prep. *sindu.lish.a* Ps. of Prep. *sindu.liw.a*
sine¹ (also *sini*) *n* (*ma-*) (*anat*) gum of the teeth. (cf *ufizi*) (Ar)
sine² *n* (*n*) face or body usu of a person.
sinema *n* (*n*) 1. cinema, theatre building. 2. film show at the cinema. (Eng)
sing.a¹ *vt* massage with oil, etc.: *Alinisinga kwa mafuta baada ya misuli kuniuma*, he massaged me with oil following muscle pains. Prep. *sing.i.a* St. *sing.ik.a* Cs. *sing.ish.a* Ps. *sing.w.a* Rp. *sing.an.a* (cf *chua, sugua*)
singa² *n* (*n*) long straight hair: *Nywele za singa*, straight hair.
Singasinga *n* (*n*) Sikh; a member of the Hindu religious sect founded in Northern India that rejects the cast system and idolatry. (Hind)

singe *n* (*n*) bayonet: *Choma kwa singe*, bayonet someone or sth.
singizi.a *vt* 1. make a fictitious charge against someone, insinuate falsely, accuse falsely; asperse, traduce, calumniate: *Alinisingizia mimi kuwa nilimchukulia kalamu yake*, he accused me falsely of taking his pen. (cf *zulia, binia*) 2. make a pretence, pretend to be ill, etc. in order to escape duty or work; malinger, feign: *Alisingizia kwamba anaumwa*, he feigned that he was sick. Prep. *singizi.li.a* St. *singizi.k.a* Cs. *singizi.sh.a* Ps. *singizi.w.a* Rp. *singizi.an.a*
singizio *n* (*ma-*) 1. aspersion; false insinuation, false accusation. 2. feigning: *Singizio lake la kwamba alikuwa mgonjwa lilimponza kazini mwako*, his feigning illness led him to problems at his place of work.
sini¹ (also *sine*) *n* (*ma-*) (*anat*) gum of the teeth. (cf *ufizi*) (Ar)
sini² *n* (*n*) china ware, porcelain.
sini³ *n* (*n*) feature, complexion.
sini⁴ *adv* never, not at all.
sinia *n* (*n*) a large round metal tray, used for carrying food, etc.; platter. (Ar)
siniguse *n* (*n*) a kind of hollow bead made of very thin glass usu of gold or silver colour, worn by women around the waist; fragile glass beads.
sinki *n* (*ma-*) sink (Eng)
sinodi *n* (*n*) church synod. (Eng)
sinonimu *n* (*n*) synonym; a word having the same or nearly the same meaning in one or more senses as another in the same language. (Eng)
sintaksia *n* (*n*) syntax; the arrangement of words as elements in a sentence to show their relationship to one another. (Eng)
sinu.a *vt* push over, make a bend over; make sby or sth fall by pushing: *Alinisinua wakati nilipotaka kufunga goli*, he pushed me over when I wanted to score a goal. Prep. *sinu.li.a* St. *sinu.k.a* Cs. *sinu.sh.a* and *sinu.lish.a* Ps. of Prep. *sinu.liw.a* Rp. *sinu.an.a*

siny.a vt hate, loathe, abhor, dislike: *Sisi sote tunavisinya vitendo vyake viovu*, we all abhor his evil deeds. Prep. ***siny.i.a*** St. ***siny.ik.a*** Cs. ***sinyi.z.a*** Ps. of Prep. ***siny.w.a*** Rp. ***siny.an.a*** (cf *kunyaa, chukia, zia*)

sinya.a vi shrivel up, wilt, curl up, wither: *Mwili wake umesinyaa baada ya kuugua kwa muda mrefu*, his body has shrivelled up after a long illness. Prep. ***sinya.li.a*** St. ***sinya.lik.a*** Cs. ***sinya.z.a*** Ps. ***sinya.liw.a*** (cf *kunyaa, konda, nywea*)

sinzi.a[1] vi doze, catnap, drowse. Prep. ***sinzi.li.a*** be sleepy about; fail to pay attention e.g. *Walitutazama kwa kusinzilia*, they looked at us with dreamy eyes. *Macho ya kusinzilia*, dreamy eyes. St. ***sinzi.lik.a*** Cs. ***sinzi.lish.a*** Ps. ***sinzi.w.a*** (cf *gotea*)

sinzia[2] n (n) pickpocket

sio[1] n (n) powder formed by grinding up broken cooking pots, etc. and then mixed with other clay to make new pots.

si.o[2] vt (cop) they are not: *Wao sio wakulima*, they are not farmers.

sipo vt (cop) I am not here. I am not involved.

sira n (n) see *masira*

siraji n (n) lamp, torch. (cf *taa*) (Ar)

sirati n (n) 1. (in Islam) it means the "right way" of religion. In Muslim traditions and other writings, it is commonly used for the bridge across the infernal fire, which has been described as thinner than a hair and sharper than a sword, and is beset on each side with briars and cooked horns. 2. road, path. (Ar)

siri[1] n (n) secret, private affair, confidential matter: *Sehemu za siri*, sex organs; private parts. *Barua ya siri*, confidential letter. *Kwa siri*, secretly e.g. *Hufanya mambo yake kwa siri*, he carries out his affairs secretly. (prov) *Siri ya mtungi iulize kata*, the secret of a clay water pot is known by a laddle i.e. if we want to get information of a particular person or thing, then we need to approach the right sources. (Ar)

sir.i[2] vt (of an issue, etc.) change dramatically into, become, prove: (prov) *Asili haisiri ila kwa kustajiri*, the character of a parent is inherited by one/his offsprings. Prep. (cf *geuka, badilika*) Prep. ***sir.i.a*** St. ***sir.ik.a*** Cs. ***sir.ish.a*** (Ar)

sirib.a (also *sirima*) vt 1. build a wall, floor or ceiling by using clay or mortar so as to give a smooth surface; smear, plaster: *Alizisiriba kuta za nyumba yangu*, he plastered the walls of my house. (cf *taliza*) 2. scatter liquid substance; sprinkle, splash, sparge: *Walimsiriba rafiki yao tope*, they sprinkled their friend with mud. Prep. ***sirib.i.a*** St. ***sirib.ik.a*** Cs. ***sirib.ish.a*** Ps. ***sirib.w.a*** Rp. ***sirib.an.a***

siridado n (n) (*zool*) silverfish, fishmoths, bristletails; these are wingless insects which are found in cupboards with starched linen, among stored papers, on bookshelves, underneath wall papers and behind pictures on the wall. They feed on starch and may cause considerable damage by gnawing holes in the mentioned materials.

sirim.a[1] vt see *siriba*. Prep. ***sirim.i.a*** St. ***sirim.ik.a*** Cs. ***sirim.ish.a*** Ps. ***sirim.w.a***

sirim.a[2] vi despair, despond; lose hope: *Alisirima baada ya kusikia kwamba wakuu wa uhamiaji hawatampa viza ya kusafiria*, he despaired after learning that the immigration officers would not grant him a visa to travel. Prep. ***sirim.i.a*** St. ***sirim.ik.a*** Cs. ***sirim.ish.a*** Ps. ***sirim.w.a*** (cf *angema*)

sirinji n (n) syringe; an instrument for taking blood from someone's body, for washing out wounds, etc.

sisi pron we: *Sisi sote*, all of us, we all. *Sisi wenyewe*, we ourselves.

sisimizi n (n) (zool) sugar ant; small black ant. (cf *nyenyere*)
sisimk.a vi cause the blood to run cold; raise hairs. Prep. ***sisimk.i.a*** Ps. ***sisimk.w.a***
sisimu.a vt 1. be exciting; thrill, excite: *Riwaya ile ilikuwa inasisimua*, that novel was exciting. (cf *hamasisha, chechemua*) 2. (of ideas, etc.) be stimulating; enkindle, enflame, arouse, touch off: *Hotuba yake kali iliwasisimua wasikilizaji*, his fiery speech aroused the audience. Prep. ***sisimu.li.a*** St. ***sisimu.k.a*** Cs. ***sisimu.sh.a*** Ps. of Prep. ***sisimu.liw.a*** Rp. ***sisimu.an.a*** (cf *hamasisha*)
sisisi¹ adv compact, fully packed, well-crammed; filled to capacity: *Wanachama walyaa sisisi kwenye ukumbi wa mkutano*, the members were fully-packed at the assembly hall. (cf *pamojapamoja*)
sisisi² adv literal, verbatim, word-for-word: *Tafsiri sisisi*, literal translation.
sisitiz.a vt stress, emphasize, underscore, underlie: *Rais alisisitiza umuhimu wa mshikamano nchini*, the president stressed the importance of unity in the country. Prep. ***sisitiz.i.a*** St. ***sisitiz.ik.a*** Ps. ***sisitiz.w.a*** Rp. ***sisitiz.an.a*** (cf *shadidia*)
sisitizo n (ma-) emphasis, stress: *Sisitizo lake halina mantiki*, his emphasis is illogical.
sista n (ma-) 1. (in Christianity) a member of a female religious order; sister. 2. senior hospital nurse. (Eng)
sita¹ adj, n 1. six. (cf *tandatu*) 2. (in Islam) the optional six days of fasting after the Holy month of Ramadan. (Ar)
sit.a² vt, vi 1. hesitate, hang back, pause, hold off: *Alisita kumpiga bintiye*, she hesitated to beat her daughter. (cf *chelea, hofu*) 2. stop, cease, discontinue, quit, leave off: *Mvua ilikuwa ikinyesha lakini sasa imesita*, it was raining but now it has stopped. Prep. ***sit.i.a*** St. ***sit.ik.a*** Cs. ***sit.ish.a*** (cf *koma, acha*)
sitaha¹ (also *staha*) n (n) (naut) forward deck or after deck of a vessel e.g. dhow, canoe, etc.
sitaha² n (n) see *staha*
sitah.i vt see *stahi*
sitara¹ (also *stara*) n (n) 1. concealment of a scandal; cover-up: *Sitara ya kashfa ile ilimhifadhi waziri*, the cover-up of that scandal protected the minister. 2. secluded place: *Alikwenda mahala pa sitara kujisaidia*, he went to a secluded place to relieve himself. 3. respectability in marriage, etc.: *Mwanamke alitafuta sitara katika ndoa ili kuhifadhi jina lake*, the woman looked for respectability in marriage in order to preserve her dignity. (Ar)
sitara² n (n) curtain (cf *pazia*)
sitaw.i vi see *stawi*
sitawish.a vt see *stawisha*
siti n (ma-) a respectful form of address to a woman preceding her actual name; madam, lady. (cf *bibi, mwana*)
sitiari n (n) (lit) metaphor; a figure of speech. (Ar)
sitima n (n) see *stima*
sitini n (n) sixty (Ar)
sitir.i (also *setiri, stiri*) vt 1. conceal, cover-up, hide. (cf *ficha*) 2. protect, safeguard: *Alivaa sweta zito ili ajisitiri na baridi kali*, he wore a heavy sweater to protect himself from severe cold. Prep. ***sitir.i.a*** St. ***sitir.ik.a*** Cs. ***sitir.ish.a*** Ps. ***sitir.iw.a*** Rp. of Prep. ***sitir.i.an.a*** (cf *hifadhi, hama*) (Ar)
sitish.a vt prevent, stop, preclude, hinder: *Huwezi kusitisha maendeleo ya miradi yetu*, you can't stop the development of our projects. Prep. ***sitish.i.a*** St. ***sitish.ik.a*** Ps. ***sitish.w.a*** (cf *zuia, komesha*)
sivyo adv a common form of negative meaning *Isn't it so? That is not so. Not that way.*

siye *pron* negative of third person singular; not him, not her.
siyo *adv* a common form of negative meaning *Isn't it so?; It is not so; no. Au siyo?* Is it not so? *Ndiyo au siyo?* Yes or no? *Siyo hivyo,* that is not right, not that way.
siwa *n (ma-)* 1. a kind of big horn used as a trumpet and usu made from wood or ivory and used in the past in big celebrations esp of national nature. (cf *baragumu, pembe, parapanda*) 2. mace (Ar, Pers)
skauti[1] *n (ma-)* scout (Eng)
skauti[2] *n (ma-)* a person sent out to get information about the enemy's position, strength, movements, etc.; scout. (Eng)
skeli *n (n)* scale; either of the shallow dishes or pans of a balance. (Eng)
sketi *n (n)* skirt (Eng)
skonzi *n (n)* scones, bun, roll (Eng)
skrubu *n (n)* screw (cf *hesi, parafujo*) (Eng)
skrudreva *n (n)* screwdriver (Eng)
skuli *n (n)* see *shule*
skuta *n (n)* scooter (Eng)
sleti *n (n)* writing slate. (cf *kibao*) (Eng)
slipa *n (n)* slippers (Eng)
smaku *n (n)* see *sumaku*
so.a *vt* see *sora*. Prep. **so.le.a** St. **so.lek.a** Cs. **so.lesh.a** Ps. **so.w.a** Rp. **so.an.a**
sob.a *vi* 1. be loose, be untied, be infirm: *Fundo hilo limesoba,* that knot is loose. (cf *legea*) 2. be soft, be starchy, be pulpy, be watery: *Aliupika muhogo sana mpaka ukasoba,* he cooked the cassava so much that it became soft. (cf *lainika*) Prep. **sob.e.a** St. **sob.ek.a** Cs. **sob.esh.a**
soda[1] *n (n)* soda (Eng)
soda[2] *n (n)* lunacy, madness. (cf *kichaa*)
sodai (also *sodawi*) *n (n)* an arrogant person; a conceited person; braggart, coxcomb, snob: *Sodai yule hapendi kuingiliana na watu wengine,* that snob does not like to mix with other people. (cf *mfyosi, majivuno*)
sodo *n (n)* sanitary pad or napkin. (cf *ufyambo*)
sofa *n (n)* sofa (Eng)
soga *n (n)* idle gossip, idle chatter, small talk; palaver, prattle, conversation: *Piga soga,* chatter, gossip; indulge in idle gossip. (cf *porojo, pwaji*)
soge.a (also *songea*) *vi* 1. move oneself; come nearer: *Alisogea karibu nami ili tuweze kuzungumza kwa siri,* he moved closer to me so that we could talk in secret. 2. used in the expressions: *Sogeza mbele,* push forward. e.g. *Mahakama ilikataa kusogeza mbele tarehe iliyopangwa juu ya kesi yangu,* the court refused to push forward the date fixed for my case. *Sogeza nyuma,* push back. Prep. **soge.le.a** St. **soge.lek.a** Cs. **soge.z.a** Ps. of Prep. **soge.lew.a** Rp. of Prep. **soge.le.an.a** (cf *jongea, karibia*)
sogelean.a[1] *vi* see *sogea*
sogelean.a[2] *vi* have sex
sogi[1] *n (n)* see *shogi*
sogi[2] *n (n)* donkey's pannier
sogo.a *vi* natter, chat, converse, talk. Prep. **sogo.le.a** St. **sogo.lek.a** Cs. **sogo.lesh.a** (cf *ongoa*)
sogon.a *vt, vi* clean oneself with grass, leaves, etc after evacuation. Prep. **sogon.e.a** St. **sogon.ek.a** Cs. **sogon.esh.a** Ps. **sogon.w.a** (cf *kokona*)
sogora *n (ma-)* 1. an expert at playing the drum for local dances, etc. 2. a person pretending to know sth while infact he does not know it; charlatan, mountebank: *Yeye si mshoni ingawa anajifanya ni sogora,* he is not a tailor although he pretends to be one. (cf *mjuaji, msuluhivu*)
soji *n (n)* see *shogi*[1]
soka *n (n)* soccer: *Soka la kulipwa,* professional soccer. (cf *kambumbu, gozi, kandanda*) (Eng)
soketi *n (n)* socket (Eng)
soko *n (ma-)* market, emporium, mart:

Soko la dunia, world market. *Soko huru*, free market. *Soko huria*, free market. *Meneja masoko*, marketing manager. *Soko la hisa*, stock exchange. *Soko la mali kwa mali*, swop market. *Soko la kimataifa*, international market. *Soko la nje*, external market. (Ar)

soko.a *vt* prise, detach, untwine; separate sth adhering closely: *Vibarua walizisokoa mbata kutoka kwenye vifuu kwa kutumia chembeu*, the labourers prised copra from their shells with a caulking chisel. Prep. *soko.le.a* St. *soko.lek.a* Cs. *soko.lesh.a* Ps. of Prep. *soko.lew.a* (cf *gandua, ambua*)

sokomez.a *vt* force sth into place; ram, stuff in, compress, cram, overload: *Alizisokomeza pamba kwenye gunia*, he rammed cotton into the sack. Prep. *sokomez.e.a* St. *sokomez.ek.a* Cs. *sokomez.esh.a* Ps. *sokomez.w.a* Rp. *sokomez.an.a* (cf *sheheni, shindilia, jaza*)

sokomoko *n* (*n*) turmoil, chaos, confusion: *Sokomoko ilitokea jela baada ya wafungwa kutoroka*, confusion broke out in jail after the prisoners escaped. (cf *fujo, ghasia*)

sokondo *n* (*n*) gouge (cf *bobari, ngabu*)

sokondo

sokot.a[1] *vt* 1. twist, twine, spin; roll in the hands: *Sokota kamba*, spin fibres to make rope. *Sokota sigara*, roll cigarettes. (cf *zingirisha, zongomeza*) 2. spin, roll; make round by means of turning a whipping top: *Mvuvi aliusokota mshipi wake kwa kutumia pia*, the fisherman spinned his fishing-line by means of a whipping top. Prep. *sokot.e.a* St. *sokot.ek.a* Cs. *sokot.esh.a* Ps. *sokot.w.a* Rp. *sokot.an.a*

sokot.a[2] *vi* have stomach cramps; have colic; have acute abdominal pains caused by various abnormal conditions in the bowels: *Tumbo lake linamsokota*, his stomach is aching. Prep *sokot.e.a* St. *sokot.ek.a* Cs. *sokot.esh.a* Ps. *sokot.w.a* Rp. *sokot.an.a* (cf *uma*)

soksi *n* (*n*) 1. socks, stockings. 2. (*colloq*) condom. (Eng)

sokwe *n* (*n*) (*zool*) chimpanzee. *Pan troglodytes*.

sokwe

soli[1] *n* (*n*) sole of a shoe. (Eng)
soli[2] *n* (*n*) (*arch*) a term used to refer to the rank of a sergeant during the colonial period in former Tanganyika.
solo[1] *n* (*n*) the seeds of the *Msolo* tree (*Caesalpinia crista*) used as counters in the local game of *bao*, that is draughts or checkers.
solo[2] *n* (*n*) terraces dug to block the flow of water to prevent erosion.
solo[3] *n* (*n*) (*math*) matrix; a set of numbers or terms arranged in rows and columns

between parentheses or double lines: Solo gumba, identity matrix. Solo shani, singular matrix. Solo kinyume, inverse matrix.
som.a[1] *vt* read, study, peruse: *Aliisoma barua yote*, he read the whole letter. Prep. **som.e.a,** read for (to, etc.) St. **som.ek.a** Cs. **som.esh.a** Ps. **som.w.a** Rp. **som.an.a** (cf *fyoma, tali*)
som.a[2] *vt, vi* study; attend school: *Hakusoma shuleni*, he did not attend school. Prep. **som.e.a** St. **som.ek.a** Cs. **som.esh.a**, Ps. **som.w.a** Rp. **som.an.a** (cf *jifunza*)
somb.a[1] *vt* take things in a heap; gather together; collect, heap: *Alisomba mawe kwa ajili ya ujenzi wa nyumba yake*, he gathered stones for the construction of his house. Prep. **somb.e.a** St. **somb.ek.a** Cs. **somb.esh.a** Ps. **somb.w.a** (cf *soza, kusanya*)
somba[2] *n* (*n*) (*zool*) fish (cf *samaki*)
sombe.a *vt, vi* see *sombera*. Prep. **sombe.le.a** St. **sombe.lek.a** Cs. **sombe.lesh.a** Ps. **sombe.w.a**
somber.a (also *sombea*) *vt* move oneself by means of the hands in climbing a tree, etc.; shin up, shinny up, clamber: *Aliusombera mnazi ili aweze kuangusha nazi*, he shinned up the coconut tree in order to bring down the coconuts. Prep. **somber.e.a** St. **somber.ek.a** Cs. **somber.esh.a** Ps. **somber.w.a** (cf *paraga*)
sombogo.a *vi* twist the body; wriggle: *Mchezaji aliusombogoa mwili wake kifundi*, the player twisted her body artistically. Prep. **sombogo.le.a** St. **sombogo.lek.a** Cs. **sombogo.lesh.a** Ps. of Prep. **sombogo.lew.a** (cf *jinyonganyonga*)
some.a[1] *vt* see *soma*[1]
some.a[2] *vt* 1. study (for): *Alisomea udaktari*, he studied medicine. 2. read sth on behalf of sby. 3. read the Holy Quran to pray for a sick person to get recovery. Ps. **some.w.a**

somek.a *vi* be readable, be legible, be decipherable: *Hati hizi hazisomeki*, this handwriting is not legible. Prep. **somek.e.a** St. **somek.ek.a**
somesh.a *vt* 1. teach: *Anasomesha katika shule ya msingi*, he is teaching in a primary school. (cf *fundisha*) 2. educate: *Rafiki yako anamsomesha mtoto wake ng'ambo*, your friend is educating his son overseas. Prep. **somesh.e.a** St. **somesh.ek.a** Ps. **somesh.w.a** Rp. **somesh.an.a** (cf *elimisha*)
somo[1] *n* (*ma-*) 1. study, subject, course, discipline: *Somo la Kiingereza*, English subject. 2. lesson, reading: *Somo hili ni gumu*, this lesson is difficult. (cf *tamrini, zoezi*) 3. teaching period. 4. (*fig*) an experience or event that serves as a warning or encouragement; lesson: *Lile litakuwa somo kubwa kwa mtoto mtundu yule*, that will be a big lesson to that naughty child.
somo[2] *n* (*n*) 1. a person with the same name as another; namesake. 2. friend. (cf *rafiki, sahibu*)
somo[3] *n* (*n*) a person usu a woman who initiates a young bride into the ways of married life esp during consummation or advise them when they reach puberty; initiation instructor. (cf *kungwi*)
son.a *vi* relax, repose, rest: *Nilipohisi nimechoka, nikaamua kusona kwenye kochi*, when I felt I was tired, I decided to relax on the couch Prep. **son.e.a** St. **son.ek.a** Cs. **son.esh.a** (cf *pumzika*)
sonara *n* (*ma-*) goldsmith, silversmith; jeweller. (Hind)
sondo[1] (also *sondomti*) *n* (*n*) (*zool*) wood borer; a white stinging insect with a red head. (cf *duduvule*)
sondo[2] *n* (*n*) (*zool*) sillago; a marine fish (family *Silloginidae*) with a rather elongate cylindrical body and fairly small scales.
sondoge.a *vt, vi* sit on a dirty place. Prep.

sondoge.le.a St. *sondoge.lek.a* Cs. *sondoge.lesh.a* Ps. *sondoge.lew.a* (cf *sogonea*)
sondomti *n* (*n*) see *sondo*[1]
song.a[1] *vt* (during cooking, plaiting, etc) stir up a solid mass of food, etc: *Mama alikuwa akisonga ugali*, the mother was stirring hard porridge during cooking. Prep. *song.e.a* St. *song.ek.a* Cs. *song.esh.a* Ps. *song.w.a* Rp. *song.an.a*
song.a[2] *vt, vi* press forward, move ahead, push ahead; advance: *Jeshi linasonga mbele*, the army is advancing. Prep. *song.e.a* St. *song.ek.a* Cs. *song.esh.a* Ps. *song.w.a* Rp. *song.an.a* (cf *clokea, leken*)
song.a[3] *vt* squeeze, block, throng, choke: *Maji yalimsonga kooni alipokunywa kwa haraka*, the water choked him when he was drinking it hurriedly. *Waandamanaji waliyasonga magari barabarani*, the demonstrators blocked the cars on the highway. Prep. *song.e.a* St. *song.ek.a* Cs. *song.esh.a* Ps. *song.w.a* Rp. *song.an.a* (cf *bana*)
song.a[4] *vt* see *songoa*. Prep. *song.e.a* St. *song.ek.a* Cs. *song.esh.a* Ps. *song.w.a* Rp. *song.an.a* (cf *bana*)
songaman.a *vt, vi* be jammed together; be crammed, be pressed: *Abiria katika basi walikuwa wamesongamana*, the passengers were jammed together. Prep. *songaman.i.a* St. *songaman.ik.a* Cs. *songaman.ish.a* (cf *banana, minyana*)
songe.a *vi* see *sogea*
songo.a (also *songa, songonyoa*) *vt* wrench, wrest, twist together: *Alizisongoa nguo zake kabla hajazianika*, he wrung his clothes before putting them to dry. Prep. *songo.le.a* St. *songo.k.a* Cs. *songo.sh.a* Ps. of Prep. *songo.lew.a* Rp. *songo.an. a* (cf *minya, bing'inya*)
-songofu *adj* twisted, wrenched, wrung, strangled: *Nilimkataza kula nyama songofu*, I forbade him to eat the meat of the strangled animal.
songombingo *n* (*n*) turmoil, imbroglio, complexity, difficulty. (cf *matata, utatanishi*)
songomez.a *vi* (of snake, etc.) squirm, writhe, wriggle; twist about: *Nyoka alijisongomeza alipomwagiwa mafuta ya taa*, the snake writhed when paraffin oil was poured on it. St. *songomez.ek.a* Ps. *songomez.w.a*
songonyo.a *vt* 1. see *songoa*. 2. throttle, strangle, choke; twist the neck: *Alimsongonyoa kuku*, he strangled the chicken. Prep. *songonyo.le.a* St. *songonyo.lek.a* Cs. *songonyo.lesh.a* Ps. of Prep. *songonyo.lew.a* Rp. *songonyo.an.a*
songoro *n* (*n*) (*zool*) cobia; a large voracious game fish (family *Rachycentridae*) with an elongate body and minute scales, found in warm seas.
songosongo *adj* twisted, twirled, whirled: *Fimbo songosongo*, a twisted stick.
songwe[1] *n* (*n*) (*zool*) black-mouthed mamba; a highly venomous and fairly fast moving mamba, whose prey consists mainly of rodents and birds. *Dendroaspis polylepis*.

songwe

songwe[2] *n* (*n*) (*zool*) scorpion fish.
soni *n* (*n*) 1. shame, disgrace, dishonour, ill repute: *Ona soni*, feel ashamed. *Kuwa na soni*, be ashamed. *Patwa na soni*, be ashamed. 2. shyness: *Ona*

soni, feel shy. *Kuwa na soni*, be shy.
sono.a *vt* harm, hurt, damage: *Kuingiza bidhaa kimagendo nchini kumeusonoa uchumi*, entering goods illegally in the country has damaged the country's economy. Prep. **sono.le.a** St. **sono.k.a** and **sono.lek.a** Cs. **sono.lesh.a** Ps. of Prep. **sono.lew.a** Rp. **sono.an.a** (cf *haribu, hasiri*)
sonon.a[1] *vi* (of food) overboil, overcook, overstew, oversimmer: *Muhogo ulikuwa unasonona chunguni*, the cassava was overboiling in the pot. Prep. **sonon.e.a** St. **sonon.ek.a** Cs. **sonon.esh.a** Ps. of Prep. **sonon.ew.a** (cf *tokota, cheuka*)
sonon.a[2] *vi* grieve, mourn; be sorry: *Anasonona kutokana na kifo cha baba mkwe*, he is grieving for the death of his father in-law. Prep. **sonon.e.a** St. **sonon.ek.a** Cs. **sonon.esh.a** Ps. **sonon.w.a** (cf *sononeka, huzunika*)
sonon.a[3] *vi* see *sononeka*
sononek.a (also *sonona*) *vi* be grieved, be vexed, be hurt. Prep. **sononek.e.a** Cs. **sononek.esh.a** (cf *huzunika*)
sononeko *n* (*n*) the state of being hurt or vexed, etc.; grief: *Ana sononeko*, he is grieved. (cf *sonono, uchungu*)
sononesh.a *vt* hurt, cause pain: *Ananisononesha kwa maudhi yake ya mara kwa mara*, he hurts me because of his frequent irritations. Prep. **sononesh.e.a** St. **sononesh.ek.a** Ps. **sononesh.w.a** (cf *umia*)
sonono *n* (*n*) grief (cf *sononeko, uchungu*)
sony.a (also *fyonya*) *vi* express contempt or displeasure over someone by curling the upper lips; tut: *Alinisonya hadharani*, he tutted at me in public. Prep. **sony.e.a** St. **sony.ek.a** Cs. **sony.esh.a** Ps. **sony.w.a** Rp. **sony.an.a** (cf *fyonya, shonya*)
sonyo *n* (*n*) rolled tobacco; rolled cigarette.
sor.a (also *soa*) *vt* cohabit; live with a woman without legally getting married: *Amemsora mwanamume yule kwa muda mrefu*, she has been cohabiting with that man for years. Prep. **sor.e.a** St. **sor.ek.a** Cs. **sor.esh.a** Ps **sor.w.a** Rp. **sor.an.a**
soro *n* (*n*) bridegroom's dish.
soroveya *n* (*n*) surveyor (Eng)
soseji *n* (*n*) sausage (Eng)
soshalisti *n* (*n*) socialist: *Yeye ni soshalisti mkereketwa*, he is a radical socialist. (Eng)
sosholojia *n* (*n*) sociology (Eng)
sosi *n* (*n*) sauce (Eng)
soson.a *vt, vi* clean oneself with leaves, grass, stones, etc. after evacuation; wipe one's private parts by using leaves, grass, stones, etc. Prep. **soson.e.a** St. **soson.ek.a** Cs. **soson.esh.a** Ps. **soson.w.a** (cf *kokona, sogona*)
sot.a[1] *vi* 1. crawl along on the buttocks as a crippled person: *Kiwete alisota upesi upesi*, the crippled person moved along on his buttocks hurriedly. 2. have a rough time. Prep. **sot.e.a** St. **sot.ek.a** Cs. **sot.esh.a** (cf *kweta, sowera*)
sota[2] *n* (*n*) (*zool*) cutworm; any of various types of catepillars that feed on young plants like cabbage, corn, etc.
sote *adj* form of *-ote* "all," used in agreement with the personal pronoun: *Sisi sote*, all of us. *Twende sote*, let us all go.
sote.a *vt, vi* counsel, wheedle, woo, coax. Prep. **sote.le.a** St. **sote.k.a** Cs. **sote.sh.a** Rp. **sote.an.a** (cf *bembeleza, sihi, bembejea*)
sotoka *n* (*n*) (*vet*) rinderpest; an acute infectious disease of cattle, sheep, etc. characterized by fever and inflammation of the mucuous membrane of the intestines.
sower.a[1] *vi, vt* 1. crawl along: *Mlemavu alikuwa anasowera*, the handicapped person was crawling. (cf *sota, kweta*) 2. (*fig*) depend, count on: *Masikini yule husowera kwa majirani zake kwa ajili ya kupata maisha*, that poor person

depends upon his neighbours for his survival. Prep. *sower.e.a* St. *sower. ek.a* Cs. *sower.esh.a* Ps. *sower.w.a*
sower.a² *vi* dance about flamboyantly; jump and jive: *Alisowera huku akipiga ngoma*, he jumped and jived while beating the drum. Prep *sower.e.a sower.ek.a* Cs *sower.esh.a*
soz.a¹ *vt* 1. (*naut*) (of a vessel) bring ashore; beach; come to land: *Waliisoza ngalawa yao karibu na bandari baada ya kuvua*, they beached their vessel after fishing. 2. (of a vessel) crash into another ship. Prep. *soz.e.a* St. *soz.ek.a* Cs. *soz.esh.a* Ps. *soz.w.a*
soz.a² *vt* squander, lose, waste: *Amezisoza pesa zake zote*, he has squandered all his money. Prep. *soz.e.a* St. *soz.ek.a* Cs. *soz.esh.a* Ps. *soz.w.a* (cf *angamiza*, *poteza*)
soz.a³ *vt* collect people or things in large quantities; arrest massively; round up, swoop: *Polisi waliwasoza wachezaji kamari*, the police rounded up the gamblers. Prep. *soz.e.a* St. *soz.ek.a* Cs. *soz.esh.a* Ps. *soz. w.a* Rp. *soz.an.a* (cf *somba*, *kusanya*)
spaki *n* (*n*) spark (cf *umeme*) (Eng)
spana (also *supana*) *n* (*n*) spanner (Eng)
spanaboi *n* (*n*) mechanic's assistant.
spea (also *speapati*) *n* (*n*) spare part. (Eng)
speapati *n* (*n*) see *spea*
speksheni¹ *n* (*n*) inspection, examination: *Fanya speksheni*, make an inspection. (cf *ukaguzi*, *upekuzi*) (Eng)
spekshen.i² *vt* inspect, examine, probe. Prep. *spekshen.i.a* St. *spekshen. ik.a* Cs. *spekshen.ish.a* Ps. of Prep. *spekshen.iw.a* Rp. of Prep. *spekshen.i.an.a* (cf *kagua*, *sachi*) (Eng)
spekta *n* (*n*) see *inspekta*
spidi *n* (*n*) speed, fastness. (cf *kasi*) (Eng)
spika¹ *n* (*n*) speaker of parliament. (Eng)
spika² *n* (*n*) loudspeaker (cf *kipazasauti*)

spinachi *n* (*n*) (*bot*) spinach (Eng)
spiriti *n* (*n*) 1. distilled alcohol for industrial use e.g. methylated spirit, white spirit, etc. 2. strong distilled alcoholic drink e.g. whisky, gin, brandy, etc. (Eng)
spishi *n* (*n*) (*biol*) species; a taxonomic group into which a plant or an animal is said to share a high degree of similarity among its members: *Spishi za wanyama*, animal species. (Eng)
spitali *n* (*n*) see *hospitali*
sponji *n* (*n*) sponge (cf *michezo*) (Eng)
spoti¹ *n* (*ma*-) a stylish person, a natty person; dandy: *Umevutiwa na spoti yule?* Are you impressed by that dandy? (cf *maridadi*, *mtanashati*)
spoti² *n* (*n*) sports (cf *michezo*) (Eng)
springi *n* (*n*) 1. a coiled metal or wire that is put under the couches, beds, etc. to make the seats more comfortable; spring. 2. a kind of large coiled wire put under the body of a vehicle to act as shock absorbers. (Eng)
staafish.a *vt*, *vi* see *staafu*
staaf.u *vi* retire from work; stop working because of old age, etc.: *Hakimu alistaafu alipofika miaka sabini*, the judge retired after reaching seventy years of age. Prep. *staaf.i.a* St. *staaf.ik.a* Cs. *staaf.ish.a* Ps. of Cs. *staaf.ish.w.a* be forced to retire e.g. *Mkuu wa polisi alistaafishwa kwa manufaa ya umma*, the police chief was retired in the public interest. Rp. of Cs. *staaf.ish.an.a* (cf *ng'atuka*) (Ar)
staajabi.a *vt* be astonished of sth; be amazed of sth: *Unaastajabia nini?* What are you astounded of? Prep *staajabi.li.a* Cs *staajabi.sh.a* Ps *staajabi.w.a* Rp *staajabi.an.a* (cf *taajabia*) (Ar)
staajabish.a *vt* astonish, amaze, surprise: *Inastaajabisha kuona kwamba watoto wengi hawawatii wazee wao siku hizi*, it is surprising to note that many

staajab.u

children don't obey their parents these days. Prep. *staajabish.i.a* St. *staajabish.ik.a* Ps. *staajabish.w.a* Rp. *staajabish.an.a* (cf *shangaza, taajabisha*) (Ar)

staajab.u (also *taajabu*) *vt* be surprised, be amazed, be shocked; be stunned: *Nilistaajabu kusikia kwamba amempa talaka mkewe*, I was surprised to learn that he has divorced his wife. Prep. *staajab.i.a* St. *staajab.ik.a* Cs. *staajab.ish.a* Ps. of Prep. *staajab.iw.a* (cf *shangaa, shtuka*) (Ar)

staarabik.a *vi* be civilised, be polished, be refined; *Amestaarabika sasa baada ya kutembelea nchi mbalimbali*, he has now become civilized after visiting different countries. Prep. *staarabik.i.a* St. *staarabik.ik.a* (cf *suluhia*) (Ar)

staarabish.a *vt* civilize, acculturize. Prep. *staarabish.i.a* St. *staarabish.ik.a* Ps. *staarabish.w.a* Rp. *staarabish.an.a* (Ar)

-staarabu *adj* civilized, refined polished: *Mtu mstaarabu*, a civilized person. (Ar)

stadi[1] *n (ma-)* expert, master, specialist. (cf *bingwa, fundi*) (Ar)

stadi[2] *n (n)* skill: *Stadi za lugha*, language skills. *Stadi ya kiisimu*, linguistic skill. (Ar)

stadi[3] *adj* skilful, expert, masterful: *Mwanamuziki stadi*, a skilful musician.

stafeli *n (ma-)* (*bot*) soursoup; a kind of fruit from the tree, *mstafeli* (*Annona squamosa*) (Ar)

staftahi[1] *n(n)* breakfast (cf *chemshakinywa, kiamshakinywa*) (Ar)

staftah.i[2] *vi* take breakfast: *Alistaftahi kwa chai na mayai*, He had tea and eggs for breakfast. Prep. *staftah.i.a* St. *staftah.ik.a* Cs. *staftah.ish.a* Ps. *staftah.iw.a* (cf *sebeha*) (Ar)

staha[1] *n (n)* respect, veneration: *Mtu yule hana staha hata kidogo*, that person has no respect at all. (cf *heshima, utiifu*)

staha[2] *n (n)* see *sitaha*[1]

stahab.u *vt* prefer, opt, choose: *Nilistahabu kusafiri kwa ndege kuliko kwa meli*, I preferred to travel by air rather than by ship. Prep. *stahab.i.a* St. *stahab.ik.a* Cs. *stahab.ish.a* Ps. of Prep. *stahab.iw.a* Rp. of Prep. *stahab.i.an.a* (cf *pendelea*) (Ar)

stahamala *n (n)* see *ustahamilivu*

stahamil.i (also *stahimili*) *vt* persevere, endure, tolerate, be patient, put up with: *Alistahamili matatizo yote wakati wa safari yake*, he endured all the hardships during his journey. Prep. *stahamil.i.a* St. *stahamil.ik.a* Cs. *stahamil.ish.a* Ps. *stahamil.iw.a* Rp. of Prep. *stahamil.i.an.a* (cf *vumilia, subiri, chukulia*) (Ar)

-stahamilivu (also *stahimilivu*) *adj* patient, relaxed, tolerant: *Alikuwa mke mstahamilivu*, she was a tolerant wife. (Ar)

staharak.i *vi* see *taharaki*

stah.i *vt* respect, honour, venerate, esteem: *Mwanafunzi yule hawastahi walimu wake*, that student does not respect his teachers. Prep. *stah.i.a* St. *stah.ik.a* Cs. *stah.ish.a* Ps. *stah.iw.a* Rp. of Prep. *stah.i.an.a*, respect one another. (cf *heshimu, tii*) (Ar)

-stahifu *adj* respectful, dutiful, obedient: *Kijana mstahifu*, a respectful young man. *Mstahifu meya*, the honourable mayor. (Ar)

stahik.i[1] *vt* merit, deserve; be worthy of, be qualified for, be eligible. *Alistahiki kupata zawadi*, he deserved to get a prize. Prep. *stahik.i.a* St. *stahik.ik.a* Cs. *stahik.ish.a* Ps. *stahik.iw.a* (Ar)

stahik.i[2] *adj* deserved, appropriate, suitable, right: *Sifa stahiki*, suitable qualifications.

stahil.i[1] *vt* deserve, merit: *Alistahili kupandishwa cheo*, he deserved to be promoted. Prep. *stahil.i.a* St. *stahil.ik.a* Cs. *stahil.ish.a*, make worthy, declare good, render deserving. Ps. *stahil.iw.a* (Ar)

stahili² *n* (*n*) merit, worthiness: *Ni stahili yake kufukuzwa kazini kwa sababu ya ukosefu wake wa nidhamu,* he deserved dismissal from work because of his misconduct. (cf *ustahiki, ustahabu*) (Ar)
-stahimilivu *adj* see *stahamilivu*
staili *n* (*n*) style, vogue, fashion. (cf *mtindo, fesheni*) (Eng)
stajir.i¹ *vi* seek assistance; ask for assistance: *Chama chao cha siasa kilistajiri kwa wafadhili kutoka nje,* their political party sought assistance from the overseas donors. Prep. *stajir.i.a* St. *stajir.ik.a* Cs. *stajir.ish.a* Ps. of Prep. *stajir.iw.a* Rp. of Prep. *stajir.i.an.a* (cf *taradhia*) (Ar)
stajir.i² *vi* be settled, be calm, be stable. Prep. *stajir.i.a* St. *stajir.ik.a* Cs. *stajir.ish.a* Ps. of Prep. *stajir.iw.a* (cf *tulia, makinika*)
staka *n* (*n*) leather sandal. (Ar)
stakabadhi¹ *n* (*n*) receipt, acknowledgement: *Mweka hazina alinipa stakabadhi baada ya kutoa mchango wangu kwa klabu,* the treasurer issued a receipt to me after I offered my contribution to the club. (cf *risiti, cheti*)
stakabadh.i² *vt* entrust to, hand over. Prep. *stakabadh.i.a* St. *stakabadh.ik.a* Cs. *stakabadh.ish.a* Ps. of Prep. *stakabadh.iw.a* Rp. of Prep. *stakabadh.i.an.a* (cf *kabidhi*)
stakim.u *vt, vi* 1. live, stay, reside: *Pale ndipo anapostakimu,* that is where he lives. (cf *ishi, kaa*) 2. prosper, thrive flourish: *Mfanyabiashara amestakimu,* the businessman has prospered. (cf *stawi, neemeka*) 3. be proved; be established; be justified: *Maelezo yake yamestakimu kuwa yeye si mkosa,* his statement has proved that he is not guilty. Prep. *stakim.i.a* St. *stakim.ik.a* Cs. *stakim.ish.a* Ps. of Prep. *stakim.iw.a* (cf *thibiti*)
stakir.i *vi* be settled; be stable; be calm: *Mtu yule alikuwa na matatizo mengi lakini sasa amestakiri,* that person had a lot of problems but now he is settled. Prep. *stakir.i.a* St. *stakir.ik.a* Cs. *stakir.ish.a* Ps. of Prep. *stakir.iw.a* (cf *stajiri, tulia, makinika*) (Ar)
stala *n* (*n*) stole; a long decorated strip of cloth worn round the neck with the ends hanging down and used by some clergymen during services (Eng)
stampu *n* (*n*) see *stempu*
stara *n* (*n*) see *sitara¹*
stareh.e¹ *vt, vi* 1. be comfortable; have a pleasant life. (cf *pumzika, burudika, sona*) 2. repose, have a luxurious life. Prep. *stareh.e.a* St. *stareh.ek.a* Cs. *stareh.esh.a* Ps. of Prep. *stareh.esh.w.a* Rp. of Prep. *stareh.e.an.a* (Ar)
starehe² *n* (*n*) 1. comfort, rest, repose: *Anaishi kwa starehe,* he lives comfortably. (cf *raha, furaha*) 2. a life of luxury; voluptuousness, self-indulgence: *Aliishi maisha ya starehe,* he led a life of luxury. *Maisha ya starehe,* life of luxury. (cf *anasa*) (Ar)
stashahada *n* (*n*) see *shahada¹*
stati *n* (*n*) starter; a device for starting a motorcar engine or other machine. (Eng)
staw.i (also *stawul*) *vi* prosper, thrive, flourish: *Uchumi wa nchi yetu umestawi,* our country's economy has prospered. Prep. *staw.i.a* St. *staw.ik.a* Cs *staw.ish.a* Ps. of Cs. *stawish.w.a* (cf *neemeka, endelea*) (Ar)
steki *n* (*n*) steak (Eng)
stempu (also *stampu*) *n* (*n*) postage stamp. (Eng)
stendi *n* (*n*) 1. stand; a parking for vehicles and for carrying passengers to various places. 2. a bicycle carrier or any other two-wheeled vehicle. (Eng)
stesheni *n* (*n*) station (Eng)
steshenimasta *n* (*n*) station master. (Eng)
stihiza.i¹ *vt* ridicule, mock, insult, dishonour. Prep. *stihiza.i.a* St.

stihiza.ik.a Cs. ***stihiza.ish.a*** Ps. of Prep. ***stihiza.iw.a*** Rp. of Prep. ***stihiza.i.an.a*** (cf *kejeli, tania, dhihaki*) (Ar)
stihizai² (also *istihizai*) *n* (*n*) ridicule, derision, mockery, fun: *Fanyia stihizai*, ridicule, tease, mock; make fun. (cf *tashtiti, mzaha*) (Ar)
stima¹ *n* (*n*) (*naut*) a ship driven by steampower; steamer. (Eng)
stima² (also *stovu*) *n* (*n*) an apparatus contaning one or more ovens used for cooking; stove. (Eng)
stima³ *n* (*n*) see *stimu¹*
stima⁴ *n* (*n*) gas cooker.
stimu¹ *n* (*n*) electricity (cf *umeme*) (Eng)
stimu² *n* (*n*) 1. used in the expression: *Taa ya stimu*, a) pressure lamp. (cf *karabai*) b) bulb, globe. (Eng)
stir.i *vt* see *sitiri*
stoo *n* (*n*) store, warehouse, godown, storeroom: *Ameviweka vifaa vyake kwenye stoo*, he has kept his farming equipments in the store. (cf *ghala, bohari*) (Eng)
stovu *n* (*n*) see *stima²*
stu.a *vt* see *shtua*
studio *n* (*n*) 1. studio; a room or rooms where radio or television programs are produced or where recordings are made. 2. studio; an establishment where motion pictures are made. 3. studio; a room or rooms where an artist or photographer does his work. (Eng)
stuli *n* (*n*) 1. stool. 2. a single seat having three or four legs and no back or arms. (cf *kibago*) (Eng)
su.a *vi* 1. eject water from the mouth. 2. spit phlegm from the throat due to flu, etc.: *Alisua kwa sauti kubwa*, he spat phlegm loudly. Prep. ***su.li.a*** St. ***su.lik.a*** Cs. ***su.lish.a*** Ps. of Prep. ***su.liw.a*** Rp. ***su.an.a***
suala (also *swala*) *n*(*ma-*) issue, question: *Suala nyeti*, sensitive question. *Suala sugu*, chronic issue. *Suala zima*, the whole issue. (cf *jambo, kadhia*) (Ar)

suali *n* (*ma-*) see *swali*
suasu.a *vt, vi* falter; move unsteadily: *Wanachama wa klabu walikuwa wakisuasua katika kugombea uongozi*, the members of the club were still moving unsteadily to contest for leadership. *Uandikishaji wa kupiga kura ulianza kwa kusuasua hapa kituoni*, the registration for voting started on a low key. *Timu mashuhuri zilikuwa zikisuasua mwanzoni*, the prominent teams were faltering in the beginning. Prep. ***suasu.li.a*** St. ***suasu.lik.a*** Cs. ***suasu.lish.a*** Ps. of Prep. ***suasu.liw.a*** Rp. ***suasu.an.a***
subalkheri *interj* see *sabalkheri*
subana *n* (*n*) thimble (cf *kastabini, tondoo*)
Subhana¹ *n* (*n*) (of God) the exalted: *Subhana Allah*, Allah the exalted; the Almighty. (Ar)
Subhana² *interj* used in the expression *Subhana Allah*, to express profound wonder over sth. (Ar)
subiana *n* (*n*) a kind of evil spirit; fiend. (Ar)
subili *n* (*n*) see *shubili²*
subira *n* (*n*) patience, endurance, tolerance: *Mzee yule alionyesha subira alipopata matatizo*, that old man showed tolerance when he had problems. (*prov*) *Subira huvuta heri*, patience brings happiness i.e. Patience can be a key to success. (cf *uvumilivu, ustahamilivu*) (Ar)
subir.i *vt* 1. wait, stay: *Alinisubiri kwa muda mrefu*, he waited for me for a long time. 2. be patient; wait patiently: *Ni vizuri kusubiri unapopata misukosuko*, it is better to be patient when you have problems. (*prov*) *Mwenye kusubiri hajuti*, he who remains patient does not regret. Prep. ***subir.i.a*** St. ***subir.ik.a*** Cs. ***subir.ish.a*** Ps. of Prep. ***subir.iw.a*** Rp. of Prep. ***subir.i.an.a*** (cf *vumilia, stahamili*) (Ar)
subu¹ *n* (*n*) see *kalibu¹*
sub.u² *vt* see *kalibu²*

sub.u³ *vt* vilipend, insult, affront, offend: *Alitusubu kwa kosa dogo*, he insulted us for a small mistake. Prep. ***sub.i.a*** St. ***sub.ik.a*** Cs. ***sub.ish.a*** Ps. of Prep. ***sub.iw.a*** Rp. of Prep. ***sub.i.an.a*** (cf *apiza, tukana, tusi*)

subuku.a *vt* poke someone with a finger as a sign of anger, contempt, etc.: *Alinisubukua na kisha kunitusi bila ya sababu*, he poked me with his finger contemptuously and then insulted me for no reason. Prep. ***subuku.li.a*** St. ***subuku.k.a*** Cs. ***subuku.sh.a*** Ps. of Prep. ***subuku.liw.a*** Rp. ***subuku.an.a***

subutu¹ *interj* see *thubutu¹*

subutu² *interj* see *thubutu²*

sudi *n* (*n*) luck, chance, fortune: *Msichana yule hana sudi na jambo lolote*, that girl has no luck in anything. (cf *bahati, saada*)

suduk.u *vt* 1. substantiate, verify, confirm, ascertain: *Unaweza kusuduku dai lako?* Can you substantiate your claim? 2. taunt, refute: *Unamsuduku rafiki yako mbele za watu?* Are you taunting your friend in public? Prep. ***suduk.i.a*** St. ***suduk.ik.a*** Cs. ***suduk.ish.a*** Ps. ***suduk.w.a*** Rp. ***suduk.an.a***

suduri *n* (*n*) see *sadiri*

sudusi *n* (*n*) a sixth part ($\frac{1}{6}$). (Ar)

suezi *n* (*n*) soft steel.

sufi¹ (also *usufi*) *n* (*n*) cotton-like material for stuffing cushions, etc.; kapok. (Ar)

sufi² *n* (*n*) see *sufu*

sufii *n* (*n*) (esp in Islam) a person dedicated to the worship of God; dervish, hermit, recluse, eremite: *Sufii wa kike*, anchoress. *Kiongozi yule wa dini ni sufii*, that religious leader is a dervish. (cf *mtawa, walii*) (Ar)

sufu (also *sufi, usufu*) *n* (*n*) wool; the soft curly or crisped hair esp of a sheep: *Sufu ya mwanakondoo*, lamb's wool. (Ar)

sufufu *adj* plenty, copious, abundant: *Ana mali sufufu*, he has plenty of wealth. (Ar)

sufuri¹ *n* (*n*) see *sifuri¹*

sufuri² *n* (*n*) see *sifuri²*

sufuria *n* (*n*) metal cooking pot. (Ar)

sugu¹ *n* (*n*) area of hardened skin; callosity, callus, wart: *Kidole chake cha gumba kina sugu*, his thumb is callous. (cf *sagamba*)

sugu² *n* (*n*) 1. a hard person; a hard character: *Mwanafunzi wako ni sugu*, your student is a hard character. (cf *sui, kiduku, kiloo*) 2. chronic: *Maradhi sugu*, chronic disease.

sugu³ *adj* hardened, callus, impervious, unfeeling: *Jambazi sugu*, a hardened criminal.

sugu.a *vt* rub, scrub, massage: *Aliisugua sakafu vizuri*, he scrubbed the floor thoroughly. Prep. ***sugu.li.a*** St. ***sugu.lik.a*** Cs. ***sugu.lish.a*** Ps. of Prep. ***sugu.llw.u*** Rp. ***sugu.an.a*** (cf *chua, singa*)

suguru *n* (*n*) callus, induration. (cf *sagamba*)

suheli *n* (*n*) south (cf *kusini*) (Ar)

suhuba *n* (*n*) friendship, companionship, comradeship. (cf *usahibu, urafiki*) (Ar)

suhubian.a *vi* be friends with; form a friendship with: *Vijana wale wawili walisuhubiana tangu udogoni*, those two young men had been friends since childhood. Prep. ***suhubian.i.a*** St. ***suhubian.ik.a*** Cs. ***suhubian.ish.a*** (Ar)

sui *n* (*n*) a patient person, a hardened person; a person who is able to endure hardships: *Yeye ni sui*, he is a hard character. (cf *sugu, kiduku*)

suitafahamu *n* (*n*) misunderstanding: *Kuna suitafahamu kati ya marafiki wale wawili*, there is some misunderstanding between those two friends. (cf *mzozo*) (Ar)

sujudi.a *vi, vt* 1. (in Islam) bow down before God during praying. 2. (*fig*) adore, revere, venerate, respect: *Anamsujudia sana mkubwa wake kazini*, he respects his boss very much at the place of work. Prep. ***sujudi.li.a*** St. ***sujudi.k.a*** Cs. ***sujudi.sh.a*** Ps. of Prep. ***sujudi.liw.a*** Rp. ***sujudi.an.a***

sujud.u *vt, vi* 1. (in Islam) bow down while praying with the forehead touching the ground; prostrate: *Walisujudu kwa unyenyekevu mkubwa*, they prostrated themselves with much humility. 2. (*fig*) adore; respect very much: *Anamsujudia sana mkubwa wake kazini*, he respects his boss very much at the place of work. Prep. *sujud.i.a* St. *sujud.ik.a* Cs. *sujud.ish.a* Ps. of Prep. *sujud.iw.a* Rp. of Prep. *sujud.i.an.a* (cf *enzi, abudu*)

suk.a¹ 1. plait hair; weave a basket, etc. (cf *fuma, sokota, songa*) 2. frame, concoct, compose, construct: *Aliusuka uwongo ule kwa ufundi*, he concocted those lies cleverly. Walisuka mikakati mipya kumwengua kiongozi wao aliyekuwa madarakani, kwa kipindi kirefu, *they devised new strategies of dislodging their leader who was at the helon for a long period*. Prep. *suk.i.a* St. *suk.ik.a* Cs. *suk.ish.a* Ps. *suk.w.a* Rp. *suk.an.a* (cf *tunga*)

suk.a² (also *sukasuka*) *vt* shake, wag, wobble, churn; move sth to and fro: *Mbwa aliusuka mkia wake*, the dog wagged its tail. *Aliisuka chupa ya mtoto yenye maziwa*, he shook the baby's feeding bottle. Prep. *suk.i.a* St. *suk.ik.a* Cs. *suk.ish.a* Ps. *suk.w.a* Rp. *suk.an.a* (cf *tingisha, tikisa*)

suk.a³ (also *tondo*) *n* (*n*) (*zool*) a thick heavy conical shell with long pointed spire and lives in upper eulittoral mud or in mangrove swamps; mangrove whalk, mud creeper (cf *tondo*)

sukani *n* (*n*) see *usukani*

sukari *n* (*n*) sugar: *Sukari guru*, brown sugar; molasses. *Sukari ya mawe*, sugar blocks. *Sukari mchanga*, granulated sugar. *Sukari ya unga*, castor sugar. (Ar)

sukasuk.a *vt* 1. see *suka²*. 2. put sby into problems; entangle sby. Prep. *sukasuk.i.a* St. *sukasuk.ik.a* Cs. *sukasuk.ish.a* Ps. *sukasuk.w.a* Rp. *sukasuk.an.a*

suke *n* (*n*) see *shuke*

suko *n* (*ma-*) a big whetting stone; grindstone.

suku.a *vt* 1. see *sekua*. 2. prise, pry apart, untwist: *Aliisukua nazi kutoka kwenye kifuu chake*, he prised the coconut from its shell. Prep. **suku.li.a** St. **suku.k.a** Cs. **suku.sh.a** Ps. **suku.w.a**

sukum.a *vt* 1. push, drive, trundle, thrust: *Alimsukuma rafiki yake na kisha kuanguka matopeni*, he pushed his friend and then fell into the mud. (cf *vuta*) 2. (*fig*) encourage, push: *Mwalimu wa darasani alimsukuma mwanafunzi wake mzito kwenda darasa la juu*, the class teacher pushed his dull student to the upper class. 3. used in the expressions: *Sukuma maisha*, continue to live without concrete means of livelihood. *Sukuma mambo*, push the affairs forward. *Sukuma soga*, chat, converse. Prep. **sukum.i.a** St. **sukum.ik.a** Cs. **sukum.iz.a** Ps. **sukum.w.a** Rp. **sukum.an.a**

sukumawiki *n* (*n*) (*bot*) kale; a kind of hardy spinach with loose, curled spreading leaves.

sukumi.a *vt* leave sth entirely on sby else for action. Prep. **sukumi.li.a** St. **sukumi.lik.a** Cs. **sukumi.lish.a** Ps. **sukumi.w.a**

sukumiz.a¹ *vt* see *sukuma*

sukumiz.a² *vt* throw, thrust away; give a vigorous push or impulse to: *Sukumiza rungu*, throw a club; *Sukumiza jiwe*, throw a stone. *Sukumiza maradhi*, avert sickness. *Sukumiza pepo*, propitiate evil spirits. Prep. **sukumiz.i.a** St. **sukumiz.ik.a** Ps. **sukumiz.w.a** Rp. **sukumiz.an.a** (cf *tupa*)

sukut.u¹ *vi* be silent; remain silent. Prep. **sukut.i.a** St. **sukut.ik.a** Cs. **sukut.ish.a** (cf *nyamaza*) (Ar)

sukutu² *n* (*n*) (*zool*) tree snake.

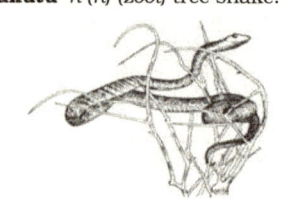

sukutu

sukutu.a *vi* 1. rinse the mouth with water; gargle: *Alisukutua kwa maji ya chumvi*, he rinsed his mouth with salt water. 2. (*fig*) eat, consume: *Alisukutua samaki wote*, he ate all the fish. Prep. ***sukutu.li.a*** St. ***sukutu.k.a*** Cs. ***sukutu.sh.a*** Ps. ***sukutu.w.a***
suli *n* (*n*) a very red garment; rimson garment.
sulib.i (also *sulubisha*) *vt* crucify: *Wafalme wa Kirumi waliwasulibi mateka wao*, the Roman emperors crucified their captives. Prep. ***sulib.i.a*** St. ***sulib.ik.a*** Cs. ***sulib.ish.a*** Ps. of Prep. ***sulib.iw.a***, be crucified. Rp. of Prep. ***sulub.i.an.a*** (Ar)
sulik.a *vi* be dizzy, become giddy: *Alisulika wakati alipokuwa anasafiri kwenye bahari iliyochafuka*, he felt dizzy when he was travelling in the rough sea. Prep. ***sulik.i.a*** St ***sulik.ik.a*** Cs ***sulik.ish.a*** Ps. of Prep. ***sulik.iw.a***
sulisuli *n* (*n*) (*zool*) a kind of large slender deep-sea fish of *Istiophoridae* family; sword fish.
sultani *n* (*ma-*) sultan (cf *mfalme*) (Ar)
sulu *adv* used in the expression: *Piga sulu*, polish sth hard until it shines; clean sth hard.
sulubi *n* (*n*) perpendicular
sulubish.a *vt* 1. crucify. 2. torture. Prep. ***sulubish.i.a*** St. ***sulubish.ik.a*** Ps. ***sulubish.w.a*** Rp. ***sulubish.an.a***
sulubu[1] *n* (*n*) 1. hard labour, hard work: *Kazi ya sulubu*, hard labour. (Ar)
sulub.u[2] *vt* 1. crucify, kill: *Walimsulubu katika mazingira ya kutatanisha*, they crucified him in mysterious circumstances. 2. (*fig*) torture; punish severely. Prep. ***sulub.i.a*** St. ***sulub.ik.a*** Cs. ***sulub.ish.a*** Ps. of Prep. ***sulub.iw.a*** be tortured e.g. *Kibaka alikuwa akisulubiwa na kundi la watu*, the pickpocket was being tortured by a crowd. Rp. of Prep. ***sulub.i.an.a*** (Ar)
suluhi.a *vi* 1. behave according to norms; be gentle, be calm: *Mvulana wako amesuluhia kutokana na malezi bora*, your boy has become gentle as a result of good upbringing.

2. be civilized, be refined: *Vijana wa sasa wamesuluhia katika mavazi wanayoyavaa*, the young men of today show sophistication in the style of dressing. Prep. ***suluhi.li.a*** St. ***suluhi.k.a*** Cs. ***suluhi.sh.a*** Ps. ***suluhi.w.a*** (cf *staarabika*) (Ar)
suluhish.a *vt* 1. mediate, reconcile, conciliate, compromise, settle; resolve differences: *Niliweza kusuluhisha ugomvi wao*, I was able to resolve their conflict. (cf *patanisha*) 2. streamline, revamp, restructure, overhaul, sort out, straighten out: *Tumesuluhisha kasoro kadha za uzalishaji-mali katika kiwanda chetu*, we have sorted out certain discrepancies in production in our industry. Prep. ***suluhish.i.a*** St. ***suluhish.ik.a*** Ps. ***suluhish.w.a*** ***suluhish.an.a*** (cf *sawuzisha*) (Ar)
suluhishik.a *vi* be reconcilable. Prep. ***suluhishik.i.a*** St. ***suluhishik.ik.a***
suluhisho *n* (*ma-*) 1. solution, arbitration, mediation, compromise: *Suluhisho la kisiasa*, political solution. 2. solution, answer: *Wanavijiji sasa wamepata suluhisho la uhaba wa madawa kwenye zahanati*, the villagers have now found a solution to the shortage of drugs in the dispensaries. (Ar)
suluhu[1] *n* (*n*) compromise, reconciliation, arbitration; *Suluhu sasa imepatikana kati ya pande zile mbili*, reconciliation has now been reached between those two sides. (cf *mapatano, masikilizano*) (Ar)
suluhu[2] *adv* (in sports) used in the expression: *Toka suluhu*, draw; bring a game to a tie e.g. *Timu mbili zilitoka suluhu*, the two teams drew. (Ar)
sulula *n* (*n*) (*zool*) water-dikkop, stone-curlew. (cf *chekeamwezi, kipila*)
sululu *n* (*n*) see *sururu*[2]
suluti *n* (*n*) see *saluti*
sumaku (also *smaku*) *n* (*n*) 1. magnetism. 2. magnet: *Sumaku umeme*, electric magnet. *Sumaku aushi*, permanent magnet. *Sumaku ncha mbili*, magnetic dipole. *Sumaku ncha moja*, magnetic monopole. *Sumaku pao*, bar magnet. *Sumaku ya muda*, temporary magnet. (Ar)

sumb.a¹ *vi* 1. be worried, be confused; fret: *Alisumba baada ya kusikia kwamba mtoto wake mdogo alikuwa akioga pwani*, she fretted learning that her son was swimming in the sea. (cf *hangaika, shughulika*). 2. (of vessels, etc.) be uneasy, be unsettled, be unrelaxed; pitch and toss: *Chombo kilipoenda mrama, abiria wengi walisumba*, when the vessel pitched and tossed, many passengers became unsettled. 3. ignore older people for not paying attention to their problems. Prep. *sumb.i.a* St. *sumb.ik.a* Cs. *sumb.ish.a* Ps. *sumb.w.a*

sumb.a² *vt* sell off goods at a throw-away price in order to clear the stock, etc.: *Mfanyabiashara alizisumba bidhaa zake sokoni*, the businessman sold off goods at a throw-away price in order to clear the shop. Prep. *sumb.i.a* St. *sumb.ik.a* Cs. *sumb.ish.a* Ps. *sumb.w.a*

sumba³ *n* (*n*) 1. (*bot*) banana tree pad. 2. the fibres of a coconut husk. (cf *tojo*)

sumbik.a *vt* see *simbika* Prep. *sumbik.i.a* St. *sumbik.ik.a* Cs. *sumbik.ish.a* Ps. *sumbik.w.a*

sumbiko *n* (*ma-*) see *simbiko*

sumbu.a *vt* harass, hassle, hector, annoy, bother, vex, disturb: *Alinisumbua wakati nilipokuwa ninaandika*, he disturbed me while I was writing. Prep. *sumbu.li.a* St. *sumbu.k.a* Cs. *sumbu.sh.a* Ps. of Prep. *sumbu.liw.a* Rp. *sumbu.an.a* (cf *hangaisha, taabisha, udhi*)

-sumbufu *adj* troublesome, fretful, bothersome, harassing: *Kijana msumbufu*, a troublesome young man.

sumbuk.a *vi* be disturbed, be bothered, waste time. Prep. *sumbuk.i.a* St. *sumbuk.ik.a* Cs. *sumbuk.ish.a* (cf *taabika, hangaika*)

sumbuli.a *vt* see *simbulia* Prep. *sumbuli.li.a* St. *sumbuli.k.a* Cs. *sumbu.li.lish.a* Ps. of Prep. *sumbuli.w.a* Rp. *sumbuli.an.a*

sumbwi *n* (*ma-*) fist, box, punch: *Mpigaji-ndondi alipigwa masumbwi*, the boxer received punches. (cf *konde, ngumi*)

sumi.a *vt* abominate, abhor, loathe, detest, hate: *Anatusumia bila ya sababu*, he hates us for no reason. Prep. *sumi.li.a* St. *sumi.k.a* Cs. *sumi.sh.a* Ps. *sumi.w.a* Rp. *sumi.an.a* (cf *chukia*)

sumile (also *simile*) *interj* an exclamation of warning from someone to allow him to pass. (cf *habadari! heria!*)

sumsumu *adj* robust, energetic, strong: *Barubaru sumsumu*, a strong young man. (Ar)

sumu¹ *n* (*n*) poison, toxin: *Lisha sumu*, give poison to someone. *Gesi ya sumu*, poisonous gas. *Silaha za sumu*, poisonous weapons. (cf *liga*) (Ar)

sum.u² *vt* poison; give poison to someone: *Alijisumu kwa kula tembe nyingi za dawa*, he poisoned himself with an overdose of medicine. *Walijisumu kwa kuwashambulia viongozi wa serikali*, they committed political suicide by attacking government leaders. Prep. *sum.i.a* St. *sum.ik.a* Cs. *sum.ish.a* Ps. of Prep. *sum.iw.a* Rp. of Prep. *sum.i.an.a* (Ar)

suna¹ (also *sunna*) *n* (*n*) (in Islam) supererogatory religious activities found in praying, fasting, etc; unobligatory religious rituals. (Ar)

suna² *n* (*n*) used in the expression: *Tia suna*, circumcise. (Ar)

sundusi *n* (*n*) a kind of cloth made from high quality soft silk.

sungu.a *vt* gather chaff, etc. when winnowing: *Alizisungua taka za mahindi na kisha kuzitupa*, he gathered the chaff of the corn and later threw it away. Prep. *sungu.li.a* St. *sungu.lik.a* Cs. *sungu.sh.a* Ps. of Prep. *sungu.liw.a*

sungura n (n) 1. (zool) rabbit, hare. (cf *kititi, kitungule*) 2. (fig) a cunning person.
sungusungu¹ n (n) (zool) a small black ant that travels in large swarms and bites severely. (cf *majimoto*)
sungusungu² n (n) 1. vigilante: *Askari wa sungusungu waliyalinda majengo ya serikali*, the vigilantes guarded government buildings. 2. homeguard.
Suni n (n) the large sect of Muslims who acknowledge the first four caliphs to have been the rightful successors of Prophet Muhammad; sunnite. (Ar)
sunobari n (n) (bot) pinewood (Ar)
sunz.a¹ vt give sth reluctantly; let go of sth reluctantly: *Niliisunza kalamu yangu kwake lakini hana shukrani hata kidogo*, I gave him my pen reluctantly but he is completely thankless. Prep. *sunz.i.a* St. *sunz.ik.a* Cs. *sunz.ish.a* Ps. *sunz.w.a* Rp. *sunz.an.a*
sunz.a² vt, vi (usu during darkness) put the foot or arm forward to feel if anything is on the way; move along blindly, grope about: *Kipofu alitembea kwa kusunza*, the blindman walked along his way by groping. Prep. *sunz.i.a* St. *sunz.ik.a* Cs. *sunz.ish.a* (cf *papasa*)
sunz.a³ vt 1. throw sth such as a stone by using a catapult or sling: *Mvulana alisunza jiwe kwa njiwa*, the boy catapulted a stone at the pigeon. 2. throw one's arms to and fro while walking, etc.: *Kijana alisunza mikono yake kwa maringo alipokuwa anatembea*, the young man swung his arms flamboyantly while he was walking. Prep. *sunz.i.a* St. *sunz.ik.a* Cs. *sunz.ish.a* Ps. *sunz.w.a*
sunz.a⁴ vt hassle, bother, vex, disturb: *Nilimpiga mwanangu kwa sababu alikuwa akinisunza*, I beat my child because he was disturbing me. Prep. *sunz.i.a* St. *sunz.ik.a* Cs. *sunz.ish.a* Ps. *sunz.w.a* Rp. *sunz.an.a* (cf *hangaisha, udhi,*

ghasi)
sunz.a⁵ vt stir, mix: *Aliusunza uji ili usifanye madongedonge ya unga*, he stirred the porridge so that it does not form lumps. Prep. *sunz.i.a* St. *sunz.ik.a* Cs. *sunz.ish.a* Ps. *sunz.w.a* (cf *koroga*)
sunzu n (n) tuft of hair on the forehead.
supamaketi n (n) supermarket (Eng)
supu n (n) soup (Eng)
sura¹ n (n) 1. appearance, look, feature, form, face: *Ana sura nzuri*, she has a good face. (cf *wajihi, uso*) 2. feature, shape, form: *Ukoloni mamboleo hujitokeza katika sura mbalimbali*, neocolonialism comes in different forms. 3. different facial expressions: *Sura yake haikuonyesha kama alikuwa anadanganya*, his facial expression did not show that he was cheating. (Ar)
sura² n (n) chapter, section, part: *Niliisoma sura ya tano ya kitabu*, I read the fifth chapter of the book. (cf *faslu, babu, mlango*) (Ar)
sur.a³ vi fart; break wind. Prep. *sur.i.a* St. *sur.ik.a* Cs. *sur.ish.a* Rp. of Prep. *sur.i.an.a* (cf *jamba, shuta*)
suri¹ n (n) a pair of scissors used for cutting betel nuts; nut crackers.
suri¹ n (n) horn, bungle. (cf *baragumu, parapanda*)
suria n (n) concubine but usu one who is a slave. (Ar)
suriama n (n) mongrel, half blood, halfcast; a half-breed person: *Ameolewa na suriama*, she is married to a halfcast. (cf *chotara, hafukasti*) (Ar)
surua n (n) (also *shurua*) (med) measles
suruali (also *suruale*) n (n) trousers, pants, slacks, drawers: *Suruali ya kipande*, shorts. *Suruali ndefu*, long trousers. (Ar)
surupwenye n (n) 1. baggy trousers; trousers hanging loosely. 2. overall, overcoat. (cf *ovaroli, bwelasuti*)
sururu¹ n (n) (zool) thumb print monocle

S

bream; a kind of saltwater fish (family *Nempiteridae*) of greyish colour and elongate body with blackish patch on the upper part of it. *Scolopsis bimaculatus.*

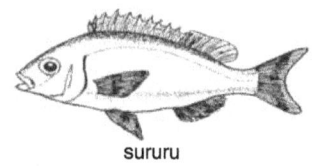

sururu

sururu² (also *sululu*) *n* (*n*) (*zool*) painted snipe; a kind of more brightly coloured bird (family *Rostratula*) with chestnut on back of neck and throat, a white ring eye and a slightly decurved bill. *Rostratula benghalensis.*

sururu³ *n* (*n*) (*zool*) rhinoceros beetle; a kind of tropical beetle which attacks coconut palms; a severely attacked palm will die and remain standing but lifeless.

sururu⁴ *n* (*n*) pickaxe

sururu

surwa (also *serwa*) *n* (*n*) extra soup free of charge that is given to someone in a hotel, etc.; additional broth. (Ar)

sus.a¹ *vt* 1. boycott, refuse: *Walimu wamesusa kufundisha leo*, the teachers have boycotted teaching today. (cf *gahamu, goma*) 2. refuse to co-operate with someone: *Siku hizi, jirani yangu amenisusa*, these days, my neighbour has refused to co-operate with me. Prep. *sus.i.a* St. *sus.ik.a* Cs. *sus.ish.a* Ps. *sus.w.a* Ps. of Prep. *sus.*

iw.a Rp. *sus.an.a*
sus.a² *vt* shake: *Aliisusa chupa kabla hajainywa dawa*, she shook the bottle before taking the medicine. Prep. *sus.i.a* St. *sus.ik.a* Cs. *sus.ish.a* Ps. *sus.w.a* Rp. *sus.an.a* (cf *tikisa, tingisha*)

susa³ *n* (*n*) (*zool*) blowfly larva; a two-winged fly (family *Calliphoridae*), majority of which cause myiasis when their larva develop in or on the living tissues of animals including man.

susa⁴ *n* (*n*) (*med*) yellowish chalky deposits on the teeth consisting of saliva proteins, food deposits, etc.; tooth stain, tartar, dental calculus.

susa⁵ *n* (*n*) the upper part of sugarcane which is not sweet; unsweet tip of a sugarcane.

susi *n* (*n*) (*zool*) the dried root of a perennial plant used in medicine for chest problems, etc.; liquorice, licorice. (cf *urukususu*)

susi.a *vt* boycott: *Wajumbe waliususia mkutano*, the delegates boycotted the meeting. Prep. *susi.li.a* St. *susi.k.a* Cs. *susi.sh.a* Ps. *susi.w.a* Rp. *susi.an.a* (cf *goma, susa*)

susu *n* (*ma-*) 1. a long piece of strong cloth hung up by the ends to rock babies to sleep; hammock. 2. a baby's swinging cot; hammock. (cf *mlezi*) 3. a crate made from plaited palm leaves, etc and used for preserving food so that it is not eaten by insects, cats, etc. (cf *tenga, kachira*)

susu.a *vt, vi* refute, rebute, oppugn, impugn, disprove. Prep. *susu.li.a* St. *susu.k.a* Cs. *susu.lish.a* Ps. of Prep. *susu.liw.a*

susuaz.a *vt* refute, disprove, deny. Prep. *susuaz.i.a* St. *susuaz.ik.a* Cs. *susuaz.ish.a* Ps. *susuaz.w.a* (cf *kataa, kanusha*)

susum.a¹ *vt* gather sth in large quantities: *Mke wangu alikwenda porini kususuma kuni*, my wife went to the bush to gather firewood. Prep. *susum.i.a* St. *susum.ik.a* Cs. *susum.ish.a* Ps. *susum.w.a* (cf *tikita*)

susum.a² *vi* walk or wander aimlessly. Prep. *susum.i.a* St. *susum.ik.a* Cs.

susum.ish.a Ps. *susum.w.a*
susurik.a *vi* range, roam, ramble, wander about: *Amezoea kususurika mitaani mwetu siku za Jumapili,* he is used to roaming around in our neighbourhood on Sundays. Prep. *susurik.i.a* St. *susurik.ik.a* Cs. *susurik.ish.a* Ps. *susurik.w.a* (cf *tanga, zurura, ranga*)
susuwa.a *vi* 1. become dry and hard; shrivel up, droop, wilt: *Maua yangu yamesusuwaa kondeni kutokana na ukosefu wa mvua,* my flowers have drooped in the field because of lack of rain. (cf *nywea, kauka*) 2. be disgraced, be ashamed: *Alisusuwaa alipogundulikana akipokea hongo,* he became disgraced when he was caught taking bribes. Prep. *susuwa.li.a* St. *susuwu.lik.a* Cs. *susuwa.s.a* (cf *fedheheka, aibika*)
sut.a¹ *vt* impugn, oppugn, charge someone openly with deceit or wrong doing, etc.; show sby openly what he really is: *Nilimsuta mbele za watu kwamba hakuwa anasema la kweli,* I charged him in public that he was not speaking the truth. Prep. *sut.i.a* St. *sut.ik.a* Cs. *sut.ish.a* Ps. *sut.w.a* Rp. *sut.an.a* (cf *susua, susuaza, kadhibisha*)
suta² *n* (*n*) bankrupt; a poor person unable to pay his debts: *Amekuwa suta sasa baada ya kupoteza pesa zake zote katika kamari,* he has now become bankrupt after losing all his money in gambling. (cf *muflisi*)
sut.a³ *vt* push, shove. Prep. *sut.i.a* St. *sut.ik.a* Cs. *sut.ish.a* Ps. *sut.w.a*
suti *n* (*n*) suit; a suit of clothing. (cf *sukuma*) (Eng)
suto *n* (*ma-*) charges of wrongdoing made in public against someone; taunting, impugnment, oppugnancy, twitting: *Suto lake juu yetu sisi halina msingi,* his charge against us in public is baseless.
suunz.a *vt* see *suuza*. Prep. *suunz.i.a* St *suunz.ik.a* Cs *suunz.ish.a* Ps *suunz.w.a*
suuz.a (also *suunza, suza*) *vt* wash clothes or utensils for the last time; swill, souse: *Alivisuuza kwanza vyombo vyake kabla ya kupakua chakula,* she first washed her dishes before serving the food. Prep. *suuz.i.a* St. *suuz.ik.a* Cs. *suuz.ish.a* Ps. *suuz.w.a* (cf *safisha, osha*)
suz.a *vt* see *suuza*
swag.a *vt* drive cattle, goats, etc. along quite fast: *Aliwaswaga ng'ombe wake kwa kuwapeleka malishoni,* he drove his cattle to the pasture. Prep. *swag.i.a* St. *swag.ik.a* Cs. *swag.ish.a* Ps. *swag.w.a*
swala¹ (also *sala*) *n* (*n*) prayers, invocation, supplication: *Swala yake ilichukua muda mrefu,* his prayers took a long time. (Ar)
swala² (also *suala*) *n* (*ma-*) issue, point, matter: *Swala sugu,* a chronic issue. *Swala hili lazima lizingatiwe,* this issue must be addressed. (Ar)
swala³ *n* (*n*) see *swara*
swali¹ (also *suali*) *n* (*n*) question, query. (cf *ulizo*) (Ar)
swal.i² (also *sali*) *vt, vi* pray, invoke, supplicate; *Aliswali msikitini,* he prayed in the mosque. Prep. *swal.i.a* St. *swal.ik.a* Cs. *swal.ish.a* Ps. of Prep. *swal.iw.a* (Ar)
swalish.a (also *salisha*) *vt, vi* conduct prayers in a congregation. Prep. *swalish.i.a* St. *swalish.ik.a* Ps. *swalish.w.a* Rp. *swalish.an.a*
swara (also *swala*) *n* (*n*) (*zool*) grants gazelle; a kind of a very large gazelle with very long horns and stout r base and strongly ringed. (*granti*. 2. deer: *Anaruka kama* he jumps like a deer. (cf *paa*)
sweta *n* (*n*) sweater (Eng)
swi (also *nswi*) *n* (*n*) fish (cf *samaki*)
swichi *n* (*n*) switch; a device used to open, close or divert an electric current, etc.: *Swichibodi,* switchboard. *Swichi ya mlangoni,* door switch. *Swichi pewa,* centrifugal switch. (Eng)
swila¹ *n* (*n*) (*zool*) spitting cobra. (cf *fira*)
swila² *n* (*n*) hammock

T

T, t /t/ 1. the nineteenth letter of the Swahili alphabet. 2. it is a voiceless stop.
t.a¹ *vt* hit, beat. Prep. *t.i.a* St. *t.ik.a* Cs. *t.ish.a* (cf *piga*)
t.a² *vi* lay eggs. (*prov*): *Kuku wa mkata hatagi na akitaga, hufa*, a poor person's hen does not lay eggs and if it does it will die i.e. as long as you are a poor person, your chances of success in this world are limited. Prep. *t.i.a* St. *t.ik.a* Cs. *t.ish.a* Ps. *t.w.a*
-ta-³ part a tense marker for futurity; will: *Atakuja kesho*, he will come tommorow.
ta⁴ *adv* completely, entirely. (cf *kabisa*)
taa¹ *n* (*n*) lamp: *Taa ya kandili*, lantern. *Taa ya karabai*, pressure lamp. *Taa ya kibatari*, a small oil lamp. *Washa taa*, turn on the light/lights. *Zima taa*, turn off the light/lights.
taa² *n* (*n*) (*zool*) skate, ray; a kind of fish of the families *Gymnuridae, Rajidae* and *Dasyatidae*, having a broad flat body and a short spineless whiplike tail with two dorsal fins. *Taa chui*, manta ray. *Taa usinga*, sting ray. *Taa kilimawe*, electric ray.
taa³ *n* (*n*) obedience, loyalty, respect: *Lazima uonyeshe taa kwa Mwenyezi Mungu*, you must show obedience to God. (cf *utii, unyenyekevu*) (Ar)
taa⁴ *adj* exalted, sacred, holy (Ar)
taabani *adj* (because of exhaustion or sickness, etc.) in dire straits; in distress; in a critical state: *Mgonjwa wake sasa ni taabani*, his patient is now in a critical state. (cf *hoi, chordo*) (Ar)
taabanik.a *vi* be extremely exhausted, be very tired.
taabik.a *vi* be troubled, be in distress; be in dire straits: *Siku hizi, bibi yule anataabika sana tangu kufa kwa mumewe*, these days, that lady is very distressed following her husband's death. Prep. *taabik.i.a* St. *taabik.ik.a* Cs. *taabik.ish.a* (cf *dhikika, teseka, sumbuka, hangaika*) (Ar)
taabini *n* (*n*) eulogy, a speech or writing in praise of a person who has died, performed usu forty days after his death: *Walimfanyia marehemu taabini wiki iliyopita*, they gave an eulogy for the deceased last week. (cf *arobaini*) (Ar)
taabish.a *vt* trouble, hassle, pester: *Alikuwa akinitaabisha sana*, he used to trouble me alot. Prep. *taabish.i.a* St. *taabish.ik.a* Ps. *taabish.w.a* Rp. *taabish.an.a* (cf *hangaisha, dhidi, tesa*)
taabu *n* (*n*) see *tabu*
taadab.u *vi* be well-mannered; be respectful: *Baba alimwambia mwanawe ataadabu mbele za watu*, the father ordered his son to behave himself in front of the public. Prep. *taadab.i.a* St. *taadab.ik.a* Cs. *taadab.ish.a* (Ar)
taadhamish.a *vt* extol, praise, laud. Prep. *taadhamish.i.a* St. *taadhamish.w.a* Rp. of Prep. *taadhimish.i.an.a*
taadhima *n* (*n*) respect, esteem, honour: *Waziri alipokewa kwa heshima na taadhima*, the minister was received with respect and honour. (cf *utukufu, unyenyekevu, adabu*) (Ar)
taadhim.u *vt* honour, respect, venerate, revere, adore: *Yeye anapenda kuwataadhimu wakubwa zake*, he likes to respect his elders. Prep. *taadhim.i.a* St. *taadhim.ik.a* Cs. *taadhim.ish.a* Ps. of Prep. *taadhim.iw.a* (cf *heshimu, tii*) (Ar)
taadi¹ *n* (*n*) see *tadi¹*
taadi² *vi* see *tadi²*
taahar.i *vi* delay; be belated, be late: *Alitaahari kwa masaa matatu na hivyo*

akalikosa basi, she was late by three hours and therefore, she missed the bus. Prep. **taahar.i.a** St. **taahar.ik.a** Cs. **taahar.ish.a**, delay; cause to be late. (cf *limatia, chelewa, kawia*) (Ar)
taahira[1] *n (n)* delay, tardiness, lateness: *Taahira ya daktari kumhudumia mgonjwa hatimaye ilisababisha kifo*, the doctor's delay in attending to the patient ultimately lead to his death. (cf *ulimatiaji, ukawiaji, ucheleweshaji*) (Ar)
taahira[2] *adj* retarded, deficient: *Akili taahira*, mental retardation. *Watoto taahira*, retarded children, (Ar)
taahira[3] *n (n)* a mentally retarded person.
taajab.u *vi* see *staajabu*
taala *adj* sacred, holy, consecrated, sanctified: *Subhana wa taala*, God is exalted and glorified. *Inshallah taala*, if God (the glorified) wishes.
taalak.i *vt* be associated with, be related to: *Tukio lile limetaalaki na mambo ya dini*, that incident is related to religion. Prep. **taalak.i.a** St. **taalak.ik.a** Cs. **taalak.ish.a** Ps. of Prep. **taalak.iw.a**
taalamik.a (also *taalamu*) *vt* be educated in, be trained in, be specialized in: *Ametaalamika katika uhandisi*, he has specialized in engineering. Prep. **taalamik.i.a** St. **taalamik.ik.a** Cs. **taalamik.ish.a**
taalam.i *vt* see *taalamika*
taal.i *vi* come. Prep. **taal.i.a** St. **taal.ik.a** Cs. **taal.ish.a** (cf *njoo*) (Ar)
taalimu *n (n)* education, knowledge: *Alikwenda ng'ambo kutafuta taalimu*, he went abroad to seek education. (cf *elimu*) (Ar)
taaluma *n (n)* academic field, discipline: *Taaluma za kisayansi zimepewa umuhimu sana katika taasisi zetu*, scientific disciplines have been given great importance in our institutions. *Uhuru wa kitaaluma*, academic freedom. *Afisa mkuu wa taaluma*, chief academic officer. (Ar)

taamal.i *vt* think, contemplate, ponder: *Daktari alitaamali juu ya operesheni ngumu atakayomfanyia mgonjwa wake*, the doctor contemplated the difficult operation he was going to perform on his patient. Prep. **taamal.i.a** St. **taamal.ik.a** Cs. **taamal.ish.a** Ps. of Prep. **taamal.iw.a** (cf *tafakari, zingatia*) (Ar)
taamuli *n (n)* contemplation, meditation: *Ni bora kulifanyia taamuli suala nyeti kama hili*, it is better to give consideration to such a sensitive issue like this. (cf *tafakuri, uzingativu*) (Ar)
taamul.i *vt* contemplate, meditate. Prep. **taamul.i.a** St. **taamul.ik.a** Cs. **taamul.ish.a** Ps. **taamul.iw.a** Rp. **taamul.i.an.a**
taanis.i (also *anisi*) *vt* please, gratify, entertain: *Tamasha la jahazi liliwataanisi watazamaji*, the dhow festival entertained the audience. Prep. **taanis.i.a** St. **taanis.ik.a** Cs. **taanis.ish.a** (cf *furahisha, pendeza*)
taanusi *adj* thrilling, fascinating, attractive: *Tamasha taanusi*, an exciting festival. (Ar)
taarabu *n (n)* see *tarabu*
taaradh.i *vt, vi* 1. pry, meddle, interfere; poke one's nose in: *Mbona unapenda kutaaradhi katika mambo ya watu?* Why do you like to pry into other people's affairs? 2. inquire, investigate, question: *Amezoea kuwataaradhi watu katika mambo yasiyomhusu*, he is used to questioning people on matters that don't concern him. Prep. **taaradh.i.a** St. **taaradh.ik.a** Cs. **taaradh.ish.a** Ps. **taaradh.iw.a** Rp. **taaradh.i.an.a** (cf *dadisi, ulizauliza*) (Ar)
taarifa *n (n)* statement, report, communique, information: *Taarifa ya pamoja*, joint communique. *Taarifa ya ikulu*, state house statement. *Taarifa ya mwaka*, annual report. *Taarifa rasmi*, official statement. *Taarifa ya habari*, news bulletin. (cf *ujumbe, habari, ripoti*) (Ar)

taarif.u *vt* see *arifu*. Prep. ***taarif.i.a*** St. ***taarif.ik.a*** Cs. ***taarif.ish.a*** Ps. of Prep. ***taarif.iw.a***

taashira (also *ishara*) *n* (*n*) 1. indication, symbol, clue. (cf *ishara, dalili*) 2. (*lit*) metonymy; a figure of speech in which one word or phrase is substituted for another with which it is closely associated (e.g. *mvi*, grey hair, to substitute *uzee*, old age (Ar)

taasisi *n* (*n*) institute: *Taasisi ya Uchunguzi*, Institute for Research. *Taasisi ya Elimu ya Watu Wazima*, Institute for Adult Education. *Taasisi ya Lugha za Kigeni*, Institute for Foreign Languages. (Ar)

taasubi *n* (*n*) fanaticism, dogmaticism; excessive and unreasonable zeal: *Taasubi zake zilileta athari mbaya katika chama*, his fanaticism brought adverse effects on the party. (Ar)

taata.a (also *tayataya*) *vt, vi* fret, be uneasy; be worried; be restless: *Alitaataa baada ya kusikia kwamba mwanawe amewekwa korokoroni*, she was worried after learning that her son had been detained. Prep. ***taata.li.a*** St. ***taata.lik.a*** Cs. ***taata.lish.a*** Ps. of Prep. ***taata.liw.a*** (cf *hangaika, shughulika*)

taathira *n* (*n*) 1. scar. 2. relic, vestige, trace: *Wareno waliwacha taathira za ujenzi wao katika Afrika Mashariki*, the Portuguese left behind their architectural style in East Africa. (cf *alama, baki*) 3. defect, fault, weakness: *Gari mpya ile ina taathira kidogo*, that new car is slightly defective. (cf *dosari, kasoro, ila*) 4. influence, impact: *Mwanasiasa yule ana taathira mbaya kwa wafuasi wake*, that politician has bad influence on his followers. (cf *athari*) 5. used in the expression: *Taathira ya akili*, mental retardation. (Ar)

taazia *n* (*n*) see *tanzia*

tabahar.i *vt,vi* excel in a particular activity, etc; be well versed in. Prep. ***tabahar.i.a*** St. ***tabahar.ik.a*** Cs. ***tabahar.ish.a*** (cf *topea, bobea*) (Ar)

tabaini *n* (*n*) (*lit*) antithesis; a figure of speech in which contrasting words or ideas are expressed: *Macho yanacheka, moyo unalia*, the eyes laugh, the heart cries. (Ar)

tabaka¹ (also *tabaki*) *n* (*ma-*) stratum, level, layer: *Alizichukua bidhaa zake kutoka kwenye tabaka zajuu*, he took his goods from the top layer. (Ar)

tabaka² *n* (*ma-*) class, rank, grade, position: *Tabaka tawala*, the ruling class. *Tabaka la wafanyakazi*, the working class. *Tabaka la wanyonge*, the oppressed. (Ar)

tabakero (also *tabakero*) *n* (*n*) a small, ornamented box for holding snuff; snuffbox, tobacco case. (Port)

tabaki *n* (*n*) see *tabaka¹*

taban.a *vt* (of a witchdoctor, etc.) weave a spell; chant magical words/formula to a patient in an attempt to cure him; conjure: *Mchawi alitabana kwa mgonjwa wake lakini hakupona*, the witchdoctor chanted incantations to his patient but he did not recover. Prep. ***taban.i.a*** St. ***taban.ik.a*** Cs. ***taban.ish.a*** Ps. ***taban.w.a*** (Pers)

tabang.a *vt* spoil, destroy, ruin: *Aliitabanga mipango yangu*, he spoiled my plans. Prep. ***tabang.i.a*** St. ***tabang.ik.a*** Cs. ***tabang.ish.a*** Ps. ***tabang.w.a*** Rp. ***tabang.an.a*** (cf *vuruga, haribu*)

tabano *n* (*n*) special magical words or formula chanted by a witchdoctor to heal a patient; conjuration, incantation. (Pers)

tabarad.i *vi* calm down; relax, become cool: *Alitabaradi baada ya kusikia kwamba mambo yake yamenyoka*, he relaxed after learning that his affairs are sorted out. Prep. ***tabarad.i.a*** St. ***tabarad.ik.a*** Cs. ***tabarad.ish.a*** (cf *stakiri, burudika, poa*) (Ar)

tabaruk.u *vt* seek God's blessings by participating in special activities such as marriage, circumcision, etc.: *Wanavijiji walitabaruku katika kusherehekea harusi ya jirani yao*, the villagers sought God's blessings by celebrating the wedding of their neighbour. Prep. *tabaruk.i.a* St. *tabaruk.ik.a* Cs. *tabaruk.ish.a* Ps. of Prep. *tabaruk.iw.a* (Ar)

tabasam.u¹ *vi* smile, beam: *Alitabasamu aliponiona*, she smiled when she saw me. Prep. *tabasam.i.a* St. *tabasam.ik.a* Cs. *tabasam.ish.a* Ps. of Prep. *tabasam.iw.a* Rp. of Prep. *tabasam.i.an.a* (cf *cheka*) (Ar)

tabasamu² *n* (*n*) smile, cheerfulness. (cf *uchangamfu*)

tabasur.i *vi* be wise in contemplating, etc.: *Angalia jinsi mzee yule alivyotabasuri kwenye maamuzi yake*, see how that old man is wise in his decisions. Prep. *tabasur.i.a* St. *tabasur.ik.a* Cs. *tabasur.ish.a* (Ar)

tabawal.i *vi* urinate: *Mama alimpeleka mtoto wake chooni kutabawali*, the mother took her child to the toilet to urinate. Prep. *tabawal.i.a* St. *tabawal.ik.a* Cs. *tabawal.ish.a* Ps. *tabawal.iw.a* (Ar)

tabenakulo *n* (*n*) 1. tabernacle; the Jewish Temple. 2 a cabinet like enclosure for consecrated Hosts, usu in the centre of the altar at the back.

tabia *n* (*n*) 1. habit, conduct, custom, character: *Ana tabia mbovu*, he has bad habits (cf *hulka, mwenendo*) 2. property: *Tabia bainika*, transitive property. *Tabia kinyume*, inverse property.

tabibi.a *vt* treat medically. (Ar)

tabibu *n* (*n*) healer, doctor: *Tabibu maungo*, chiropractor. *Tabibu wangu ana uzoefu mkubwa katika kazi yake*, my doctor has a lot of experience in his profession. (cf *mganga, daktari*) (Ar)

tabi.i *vt* emulate; be like, become like: *Lengo lake ni kumtabii baba yake kuwa wakili*, his goal is to become a lawyer like his father. Prep. *tabi.li.a* St. *tabi.k.a* Cs. *tabi.sh.a* Ps. *tabi.w.a* Rp *tabi.an.a* (cf *iga, fuata*)

tabir.i *vt* predict, forecast, foretell: *Alitabiri kwamba chama tawala kitashinda katika uchaguzi*, he predicted that the ruling party would win in the elections. Prep. *tabir.i.a* St. *tabir.ik.a* Cs. *tabir.ish.a* Ps. *tabir.iw.a* (Ar)

tabu (also *taabu*) *n* (*n*) trouble, difficulty, distress, hardship, (cf *kero, udhi, shida, dhiki*) (Ar)

tabu.a *vt* soften sth e.g sisal by constant beating in order to get fibres: *Aliyatabua makumbi ya nazi*, he softened the coconut husks by constant beating. Prep. *tabu.li.a* St. *tabu.k.a* Cs. *tabu.sh.a* Ps. of Prep. *tabu.liw.a*

taburu *n* (*n*) 1. (of soldiers) drill. (cf *kwata*) 2. additional drill given to a soldier when he makes mistakes. (Ar)

tabwarik.a *vi* see *tebwereka*

tabwatabwa *adj* (of cooked rice, etc.) watery, soggy; soppy: *Mgonjwa alikula wali tabwatabwa*, the sick person ate soggy rice. (cf *majimaji*)

tadarak.i¹ (also *tadaruki*) *vt* undertake or assume responsibility to do sth: *Raisimteule alitadaraki hatimaye katika uongozi wa nchi*, the president-elect eventually assumed the leadership of the country. *Mtoto alitadaraki kulipa madeni ya marehemu mzee wake*, the son took the responsibility to clear the debts of his late father. Prep. *tadarak.i.a* St. *tadarak.ik.a* Cs. *tadarak.ish.a* Ps. *tadarak.iw.a* Rp. *tadarak.i.an.a*

tadarak.i² (also *tadaruki*) *vt* come to realize; recollect, remember: *Alitadaraki sala zote zilizompita*, he remembered all his unsaid prayers. Prep. *tadarak.i.a* St. *tadarak.ik.a* Cs. *tadarak.ish.a* Ps. *tadarak.iw.a* Rp. of Prep. *tadarak.i.an.a* (cf *kumbuka, tanabahi*) (Ar)

tadaruk.i *vt* see *tadaraki¹* and *tadaraki²*

tadbiri *n* (*n*) good planning; good organisation: *Fanya tadbiri*, make

T   tad.i[1]

good plans. *Huzifanya shughuli zake kwa tadbiri*, he plans his activities well. (Ar)
tad.i[1] (also *taadi*) *vi* be very rude, be very offensive: *Ana tadi kwa vile yeye ni tajiri*, he is excessively rude because he is rich. (*prov*) *Akutadiye nawe mtadiye*, be rude to he who is rude to you. (Ar)
tadi[2] *n* (*n*) rudeness, discourteousness, impoliteness: *Meneja alionyesha tadi kwa wafanyakazi wake*, the manager was rude to his workers. (cf *ujeuri, ufidhuli*)
tadubiri *n* (*n*) see *tadbiri*
tafadhal.i[1] *vt* be good to, please: *Hutafadhali ukanitengezea chai?* Can you please prepare tea for me? Cs. *tafadhal.ish.a* (Ar)
tafadhali[2] *interj* an expletive used for politeness in requests or commands to people "be obliging enough (to)"; "please"; "for goodness sake": *Tafadhali niletee chakula changu*, please bring my food. (Ar)
tafadhalish.a *vt* request kindly. Prep. *tafadhalish.i.a* St. *tafadhalish.ik.a* Ps. *tafadhalish.w.a* Rp. *tafadhalish.an.a*
tafakar.i (also *tafakuri*) *vt* think over carefully; contemplate, ponder: *Alilitafakari wazo nililompa*, he pondered over the suggestion 1 gave him. Prep. *tafakar.i.a* St. *tafakar.ik.a* Cs. *tafakar.ish.a* Ps. *tafakar.iw.a* (cf *taamuli, zingatia*) (Ar)
tafakur.i[1] *vt* see *tafakari*
tafakuri[2] *n* (*n*) contemplation, cogitation, meditation: *Tafakuri zake za mara kwa mara zilimkondesha hatimaye*, his recurrent thoughts wore him out finally. (cf *fikira, taamuli*) (Ar)
tafaraj.i (also *tafaruji*) *vt, vi* comfort, entertain, gratify: *Walijitafaraji kwa kusikiliza muziki wa asili*, they entertained themselves by listening to classical music. Prep. *tafaraj.i.a*

tafsida

St. *tafaraj.ish.a* Ps. *tafaraj.iw.a* Rp. of Prep. *tafaraj.i.an.a* (cf *faraji, burudisha*) (Ar)
tafaruj.i *vt, vi* see *tafaraji*
tafauti[1] *n* (*n*) see *tofauti*[1]
tafauti[2] *adj* see *tofauti*[2]
tafautik.a *vi* see *tofautika*
tafautish.a *vt* see *tofautisha*
tafi *n* (*n*) see *chafi*
tafir.i *vt* harass, irritate, annoy: *Alitutafiri tulipokuwa tunazungumza*, he irritated us when we were conversing. Prep. *tafir.i.a* St. *tafir.ik.a* Cs. *tafir.ish.a* Ps. *tafir.iw.a* Rp. of Prep. *tafir.i.an.a* (cf *tafishi, sumbua, ghasi*) (Ar)
tafish.i *vt* hassle, disturb, annoy: *Tafadhali usinitafishi*, please don't disturb me. Prep. *tafish.i.a* St. *tafish.ik.a* Cs. *tafish.ish.a* Ps. *tafish.iw.a* Rp. of Prep. *tafish.i.an.a* (cf *tafiri, ghasia, kera*) (Ar)
tafit.i *vt* 1. research, look into. 2. pry, snoop; be inquisitive: *Amezoea kutafiti mambo ya watu*, he is used to prying into other people's affairs. Prep. *tafit.i.a* St. *tafit.ik.a* Cs. *tafit.ish.a* Ps. *tafit.iw.a* Rp. of Prep. *tafit.i.an.a* (cf *dadisi, chungua, peleleza*)
taflisi *n* (*n*) the act of confiscating a debtor's property in order to clear his debt; the seizure of goods in order to pay a person's debt; confiscation, attachment; *Tia taflisi*, seize goods in this manner. (Ar)
tafrani *n* (*n*) disturbance, annoyance, vexation, harassment: *Tafrani zake hazishi*, his vexations are endless. (cf *kero, udhia*) (Ar)
tafrija *n* (*n*) reception, party: *Tafrija kabambe ilifanywa na rais katika ikulu*, a grandeur reception was held by the president at the state house. (cf *sherehe*) (Ar)
tafsida *n* (*n*) (*lit*) euphemism; the use of a word that is less expressive or direct but considered less offensive, etc. than another. (e.g. *Ni mja mzito*, "she is pregnant," instead of *Ana mimba*.)

tafsili¹ *n (n)* exposition, elaborate explanation; detailed information: *Alinipa tafsili ya insha yake*, he gave me an exposition of his essay. (cf *fusuli, timamu*) (Ar)
tafsili² *adv* in detail; in an elaborate way: *Mwandishi wa habari aliiandika ripoti yake kwa tafsili*, the news reporter wrote his report in detail. (Ar)
tafsir.i¹ (also *fasiri*) *vt* 1. translate: *Aliitafsiri tamthilia kwa lugha ya Kiingereza*, he translated the play into English. 2. paraphrase, interpret: *Aliitafsiri ndoto yangu*, he interpreted my dream. Prep. *tafsir.i.a* St. *tafsir.ik.a* Cs. *tafsir.ish.a* Ps. *tafsir.iw.a* Rp. of Prep. *tafsir.i.an.a* (cf *fafanua, eleza*) (Ar)
tafsiri² *n (n)* 1. translation. 2 interpretation, paraphrase: *Tafsiri potofu*, a misleading interpretation; a wrong interpretation. (cf *tarjumi*) (Ar)
taftishi *n (n)* annoyance, disturbance, nuisance: *Tumechoka na taftishi zake*, we are fed up with his disturbances.
tafu *n (n)* (*anat*) a collection of fibres forming a tendon.
tafun.a *vt* nibble, chew, masticate, gnaw: *Mtoto alitafuna uhani*, the child chewed a gum. *Mbwa alimtafuna jirani yangu*, the dog bit my neighbour. Prep. *tafun.i.a* St. *tafun.ik.a* Cs. *tafun.ish.a* Ps. *tafun.w.a* Rp. *tafun.an.a* (cf *cheua, guguna*)
tafut.a *vt* 1. search, seek, look for, hunt through. 2. paraphrase, find out. Prep. *tafut.i.a* St. *tafut.ik.a* Cs. *tafut.ish.a* Ps. *tafut.w.a* Rp. *tafut.an.a* (cf *angalia*)
tag.a¹ *vt,vi* (of birds) lay eggs. Prep. *tag.i.a* St. *tag.ik.a* Cs. *tag.ish.a* Ps. *tag.w.a* (cf *ta, kuta*)
taga² *n (n)* a branch of a tree, commonly used by women to hold their cooking pots firmly when preparing hard porridge (*ugali*); bifurcated branch.
taga.a¹ *vi* walk with the legs wide apart; waddle, straddle: *Anapotembea,*

hutagaa, when he walks, he waddles. Prep. *taga.li.a* St. *taga.lik.a* Cs. *taga.lish.a*
tagaa² *n (ma-)* (*bot*) branch of a tree: *Alilikata tagaa la mgomba kwa kutumia panga*, he cut down the branch of a banana tree with a slasher. (cf *tawi*)
taghafal.i¹ *vi* see *ghafilika*. Prep. *taghafal.i.a* Cs. *taghafal.ish.a* Ps. *taghafal.iw.a*
taghafal.i² *vt* attack by surprise; make a sudden violent attack; storm: *Wezi walilitaghafali duka*, the thieves stormed the shop suddenly. Prep. *taghafal.i.a* St. *taghafal.ik.a* Cs. *taghafal.ish.a* Ps. *taghafal.iw.a* (Ar)
taghayar.i *vi* decompose, decay, putrefy; go bad: *Nyama imetaghayari*, the meat has decayed. Prep. *taghayar.i.a* St *taghayar.ik.a* Cs *taghayar.ish.a* Ps *taghayar.iw.a* (cf *oza*) (Ar)
tagh.i *vt* be arrogant, be conceited, be proud. Prep. *tagh.i.a* St. *tagh.ik.a* Cs. *tagh.ish.a* (cf *takabari*) (Ar)
tahabibu *n (n)* velocity accrued from shaking a sword, etc.: *Mwanajeshi aliutia tahabibu upanga wake kwenye paredi*, the soldier brandished his sword at the parade. (Ar)
tahadhar.i¹ *vt* be wary, be cautious, be careful; beware. (*prov*) *Tahadhari kabla ya athari*, beware before an evil befalls you. Prep. *tahadhar.i.a* St. *tahadhar.ik.a* Cs. *tahadhar.ish.a* warn, caution e.g. *Alinitahadharisha nisifanye kelele*, he warned me not to make noise. Ps. *tahadhar.iw.a* (cf *busuri, hadhari*) (Ar)
tahadhari² (also *hadhari*) *n(n)* readiness: preparedness: *Jeshi lilikuwa katika hali ya tahadhari*, the army was on the alert. (Ar)
tahadharish.a *vt* see *tahadhari*. Prep. *tahadharish.i.a* St. *tahadharish.ik.a* Ps. *tahadharish.w.a* Rp. *tahadharish.an.a*

tahafifu¹ n (n) (of sickness, etc.) recovery, relief; getting better: *Mgonjwa amepata tahafifu sasa*, the patient is now improving. (cf *nafuu, ahueni*) (Ar)
tahafifu² *adj* (of prices, etc.) reasonable, modest: *Bei tahafifu*, reasonable price. (cf *nafuu*)
tahajia n (n) 1. alphabet letter. (cf *abtathi, alfabeti*) 2. orthography, spelling. (Ar)
tahajudi n (n) (in Islam) an optional prayer after midnight usu after someone has woken up from sleep, which is intended to show the faithful's entire self-surrender to Almighty God. (Ar)
tahakiki (also *uhakiki*) n (n) critique, review. (cf *uhakiki*)
tahalili (also *halili*) n (n) (in Islam) prayer for the departed by reciting the name of God a fixed number of times; dirge. (Ar)
tahamak.i *vt* realize suddenly: *Nilikuwa nikiandika, nikitahamaki ni saa nane za mchana*, I was writing and suddenly, I realized it was 2.00 p.m. Prep. *tahamak.i.a* St. *tahamak.ik.a* Cs. *tahamak.ish.a* (Ar)
tahanani n (n) (*idm*) *Tenge tahanani*, great chaos that cannot be rectified. (Ar)
tahania n (n) congratulations, felicitations, compliments: *Mkono wa tahania*, congratulations. (cf *pongezi*) (Ar)
taharak.i (also *taharuki*) *vt, vi* 1. be busy, be occupied; bustle: *Rafiki yangu ametaharaki katika kupokea wageni leo*, my friend is busy receiving guests today. (cf *shughulika*) 2. be excited, be shaken, be uneasy, worry: *Alitaharaki alipasikia kwamba jahazi yao iliyochukua abiria wengi imezama*, he was shaken when he heard that their dhow with a full load of passengers has sunk. Prep. *taharak.i.a* St. *taharak.ik.a* Cs. *taharak.ish.a* (cf *babaika*) (Ar)
tahariri n (n) editorial: *Tahariri katika gazeti la jana iliwashambulia viongozi wabovu*, yesterday's editorial in the newspaper castigated bad leaders.

taharizi n (n) side-pieces of a *kanzu*, robe. (Ar)
taharuki¹ *vt, vi* see *taharaki*
taharuki² n (n) 1. apprehension, restlessness, anxiety: *Aliingiwa na taharuki aliposikia kwamba nimewekwa rumande*, she was in a state of anxiety when she heard that I had been detained. (cf *papatiko, mbabaiko, wasiwasi*) 2. (*lit*) suspence; the growing interest and excitement felt while awaiting a climax or resolution in a novel, play and the like. (Ar)
tahayar.i *vt, vi* feel ashamed, become ashamed, be abashed: *Alitahayari watu walipomgundua kwamba alikuwa akisema uwongo*, she felt ashamed when people discovered that she was lying. Prep. *tahayar.i.a* St. *tahayar. ik.a* Cs. *tahayar.ish.a*, disgrace e.g. *Alitutahayarisha mbele za watu*, he disgraced us in public. (cf *fedheheka, azirika*) (Ar)
tahayarish.a *vt, vi* see *tahayari*. Prep. *tahayarish.i.a* St. *tahayarish.ik.a* Ps. *tahayarish.w.a* Rp. *tahayarish. an.a*
tahayuri n (n) dishonour, shame, disgrace: *Waliingiwa na tahayuri walipokamatwa papo hapo wakiiba vitu vya jirani*, they were embarrassed when they were caught red-handed stealing the neighbour's belongings. (cf *fedheha, aibu, haya*) (Ar)
tahin.i *vt* examine, evaluate, assess, test. Prep. *tahin.i.a* St. *tahin.ik.a* Cs. *tahin.ish.a* Ps *tahin.iw.a* Rp. of Prep. *tahin.i.an.a* (cf *tathmini, pima*) (Ar)
tahir.i *vt* 1. circumcise. 2. (of a female) cut off the clitoris. (cf *keketa*) Prep. *tahir.i.a* St. *tahir.ik.a* Cs. *tahir.ish.a* Ps. *tahir.iw.a* (Ar)
tahiyatu n (n) (in Islam) a sitting posture during prayer in which the worshipper makes a salutation to prophet Mohammad and that may God bestow his blessings on him: *Kaa tahiyatu*, sit in this manner during prayer. (Ar)

tai¹ *n* (*n*) (*zool*) eagle; a large, strong flesh-eating bird of prey of the falcon family. (*prov*) *Makuukuu ya tai si mapya ya kengewa*, the secrets of an eagle are not new to a kite i.e. the deeds and misdeeds of person are best known to a person who is close to the doer.

tai² *n* (*n*) necktie, tie. (Eng)

taibu¹ (also *twaibu*) *interj* an expletive of approval or of a common rejoinder for being impressed by sby esp during conversation, greeting, etc.; exactly, okay (cf *naam*) (Ar)

taibu² *adj* good, splendid, magnificent: *Tabia yake ni taibu*, his character is good. (Ar)

taifa *n* (*ma-*) nation: *Taifa changa*, a young nation. (Ar)

taifish.a *vt* nationalize: *Serikali iliitaifisha kampuni ya meli*, the government nationalized the shipping company. Prep. *taifish.i.a* St. *taifish.ik.a* Ps. *taifish.w.a* (Ar)

taifodi *n* (*n*) (*med*) typhoid (Eng)

tail.i *vt*, *vi* see *talii¹*

taipu¹ (also *taipureta*) *n* (*n*) typewriter (Eng)

taip.u² *vt* type. Prep. *taip.i.a* St. *taip.ik.a* Cs. *taip.ish.a* Ps of Prep. *taip.iw.a* Rp. of Prep. *taip.i.an.a*

taipureta *n* (*n*) see *taipu¹*

taire (also *tawire*) *interj* 1. an expletive used by a medicine man to make people listen to him at a place where spirits are exorcized. 2. an expletive of assent from the people in response to the utterances of the medicine man in soothsaying; exactly, okay.

tairi *n* (*n*) tyre (Eng)

taiti¹ *n* (*n*) a tight dress. (Eng)

taiti² *adj* (*colloq*) financially pressed; not having enough money: *Yeye yuko taiti leo*, he doesn't have enough money today.

taj.a *vt* mention, name; speak of: *Walilitaja jina lake kwenye mkutano*, they mentioned his name at the meeting. Prep. *taj.i.a* St. *taj.ik.a* Cs. *taj.ish.a* Ps. *taj.w.a* Rp. *taj.an.a*

tajamala *n* (*n*) favour, kindness. (Ar)

tajamal.i *vt* do a favour; show kindness to: *Alitajamali kwa kutukaribisha katika nyumba yake*, he showed hospitality by inviting us to his house. Prep. *tajamal.i.a* St. *tajamal.ik.a* Cs. *tajamal.ish.a* Ps. of Prep. *tajamal.iw.a* (cf *fadhili*)

taji *n* (*ma-*) 1. crown, diadem: *Taji la mfalme*, the king's crown. 2. used in the expression: *Taji la maua*, chaplet. 3. championship. (Ar)

tajinisi (also *tajnisi*) *n* (*n*) naturalization; the process of acquiring citizenship: *Kukata tajinisi*, naturalization; seek citizenship of a country. (Ar)

tajiri¹ *n* (*ma-*) 1. a rich person; tycoon, magnate (cf *kizito, lodi, bepari, mkwasi*). 2. trader, merchant; a business person 3. employer: *Tajiri wangu anupendwa sana na wafanyakazi wake*, my employer is liked very much by his workers. (cf *mwajiri, bosi*) (Ar)

tajiri² *adj* affluent, wealthy, prosperous: *Yeye si mtu tajiri sana*, he is not a very rich person. (Ar)

tajiriba *n* (*n*) experience (cf *uzoefu*) (Ar)

tajirik.a *vi* become rich; be wealthy, *Alikuwa mtu masikini lakini sasa ametajirika*, he was a poor person but now he has become rich. Prep. *tajirik.i.a* St. *tajirik.ik.a* Ps. *tajirik.ish.a* (cf *neemeka*)

tajirish.a *vt* 1. enhance, enrich: *Sera mpya ya uchumi imeitajirisha nchi yetu*, the new economic policy has enriched our country. 2. make sby rich; enrich. Prep. *tajirish.i.a* St. *tajirish.ik.a* Ps. *tajirish.w.a*

tajiwidi *n* (*n*) see *tajuwidi*

tajuwidi (also *tajiwidi*) *n* (*n*) a recitation of verses from the HolyQoran and other sources with rhythmical information: *Soma tajuwidi*, recite in this manner. (Ar)

taka¹ (also *takataka*) *n* (*n*) junk, rubbish, refuse, garbage, dirt. (cf *uchafu, uchama*)

tak.a² *vt* want, wish, need, yearn. (*prov*) *Mtaka yote hukosa yote*, he who wants everything gets nothing. Prep. ***tak.i.a*** pray for sby to get sth. St. ***tak.ik.a*** Cs. ***tak.ish.a*** Ps. ***tak.w.a*** Ps. of Prep. ***tak.iw.a*** Rp. ***tak.an.a*** Rp. of Prep. ***tak.i.an.a*** Rp. of St. ***tak.ik an.a***

tak.a³ *vt* be on the verge of; have a tendency to: *Mtoto mdogo alitaka kuzama*, the small child was about to be drowned.

takabal.i *vt* (*of God*) accept, approve, agree: *Inshallah Mwenyezi Mungu atakabali dua yetu*, may God answer our prayer. Prep. ***takabal.i.a*** St. ***takabal.ik.a*** Ps. ***takabal.iw.a***, be approved. (cf *kubali*) (Ar)

takabar.i *vi* be arrogant, be conceited, be proud: *Tangu kuteuliwa kuwa meneja, mtu yule amekuwa anatakabari*, since being appointed as a manager, that person has become arrogant. Prep. ***takabar.i.a*** St. ***takabar.ik.a*** Cs. ***takabar.ish.a*** (cf *taghi, jitapa, jigamba*) (Ar)

takadam.u *vi* precede; go before, lead the way: *Umeme ulitakadamu kwanza na halafu ikafuatia radi*, the flash of lightning preceded the thunder. Prep. ***takadam.i.a*** St. ***takadam.ik.a*** Cs. ***takadam.ish.a*** (cf *ongoza, tangulia*) (Ar)

takalifu *n* (*n*) see *takilifu*

takariri *n* (*n*) 1. tautology, repetition. 2. chorus. (Ar)

takas.a *vt* 1. purify, cleanse, sanctify, clean. 2. (*fig*) clean, purify: *Lazima uutakase moyo wako kwa rafiki zako*, you must show a good heart to your friends. Prep. ***takas.i.a*** St. ***takas.ik.a*** Cs. ***takas.ish.a*** Ps. ***takas.w.a*** Rp. ***takas.an.a*** (cf *safisha, toharisha*)

takat.a¹ *vi* be clean; be cleansed; be bright: *Suruali yake imetakata baada ya kufuliwa*, his pair of trousers is clean after having been washed. *Mbingu zimetakata*, the sky is clear. Prep. ***takat.i.a*** St. ***takat.ik.a*** Cs. ***takat.ish.a*** Ps. ***takat.w.a*** (cf *safika*)

takat.a² *vt* (used in the game of draughts) distribute *komwe* (used as counters) into its holes to facilitate victory for a player. Prep. ***takat.i.a*** St. ***takat.ik.a*** Cs. ***takat.ish.a*** Ps. ***takat.w.a***

takataka *n* (*n*) see *taka¹*

-takatifu *adj* sacred, holy, sanctified: *Msikiti mtakatifu*, a sacred mosque. *Kurani takatifu*, the Holy Koran. *Biblia takatifu*, the Holy Bible. *Roho mtakatifu*, Holy Spirit. *Papa Mtakatifu*, the Holy Pope.

takbira *n* (*n*) see *takbiri*

takbiri (also *takbira*) *n* (*n*) (in Islam) an expletive of invocation for glorifying God by saying "God is great": *Soma takbiri*, read invocation of this kind. *Leta takbiri*, recite invocation of this kind. *Toa takbiri*, recite invocation of this kind. (Ar)

takdiri (also *kadari*) *n* (*n*) God's power (Ar)

taki *n* (*n*) the residue of a coconut after it has been grated and squeezed; coconut dregs. (cf *chicha*)

taki.a¹ *vt* see *taka²*

takia² *n* (*ma-*) a large cushion. (cf *chegemeo*)

takikan.a *vi* be needed, be wanted. Prep. ***takikan.i.a*** St. ***takikan.ik.a*** Cs. ***takikan.ish.a*** (cf *hitajika*)

takilifu (also *takalifu*) *n* (*n*) strain, exertion, struggle, discomfort: *Fanya/Chukua takilifu*, take the trouble e.g. *Alichukua takilifu ya kuja kunitembelea*, he took the trouble of coming to visit me. (cf *shida, usumbufu*)

takirima (also *takrima*) *n* (*n*) 1. warm welcome; reception: *Aliwakaribisha wageni wake kwenye karamu kwa takirima*, he gave his guests a warm welcome at the party. (cf *wema, ukarimu*) 2. festive entertainment. 3. gift, present: *Je takrima ni rushwa?* Is the giving of gifts equivalent to corruption? (Ar)

tako *n* (*ma-*) 1. (*anat*) buttock, posterior. 2. the butt-end of anything such as gun, bowl, etc.; the base of anything: *Tako la bunduki*, rifle butt. *Tako la bakuli*, the base of a bowl.

takriban *adv* almost, nearly, approximately: *Aliteleza na takriban aanguke*, she slipped and almost fell. (cf *nusura*, *karibu*) (Ar)

takrima *n* (*n*) see *takirima*

takriri (also *takariri*) *n* (*n*) 1. repetition, tautology: *Alifanya takriri nyingi katika mada ya elimu kwenye hotuba yake*, he made many repetitions in his speech. *Nitakufa usiponioa nitakufa*, I will die if you don't marry me, I will die. 2. (*lit*) alliteration, the repetition of the same sounds or of the same kinds of sounds at the beginning of words or in stressed syllables: *Kitu kipi kikusikitichasho?* What bothers you? *Hasira hasara*, anger leads someone to a disaster.

taksiri *n* (*n*) 1. defect, weakness, deficiency: *Kila binadamu ana taksiri zake*, every human being has his weaknesses. (cf *upungufu*, *ila*, *dosari*) 2. mistake, error, fault: *Alifanya taksiri kwa kutomtembelea mjomba wake hospitali*, he made a mistake by not visiting his uncle at the hospital. (cf *kosa*) (Ar)

takua (also *takwa*) *n* (*n*) piety, piousness: *Huwezi kupata utulivu wa kiroho bila ya takua*, you can't achieve spiritual calm without piety. (cf *uchaji*) (Ar)

takwa[1] *n*(*ma-*) see *matakwa*

takwa[2] *n* (*n*) see *takua*

takwimu *n* (*n*) statistics: *Takwimu za serikali*, government statistics. *Takwimu ijielezayo*, descriptive statistics. (Ar)

talaka *n* (*n*) divorce: *Batilisha talaka*, nullify a divorce. (Ar)

talasimu *n* (*n*) talisman, charm, amulet: *Mganga alimpa mgonjwa wake talasimu ili ajikinge na ubaya wowote*, the medicine man gave a talisman to his patient to protect himself against any evil. (cf *hirizi*, *kinga*, *kago*)

talibisi *n* (*n*) (*naut*) matting bulwark aboard a vessel to prevent waves from washing in. (Ar)

tali.i[1] (also *taili*) *vt* revise, review: *Mwanafunzi aliyatalii masomo yake*, the student revised his lessons. Prep. *tali.i.a* St. *tali.k.a* Cs. *tali.sh.a* Ps. *tali.w.a* (cf *durusu*) (Ar)

tali.i[2] *vt* visit, tour: *Wageni waliitalii nchi yetu*, the tourists visited our country. Prep. *tali.i.a* St. *tali.k.a* Cs. *tali.sh.a* Ps. *tali.w.a* (cf *zuru*) (Ar)

talik.i[1] *vt* divorce. Prep. *talik.i.a* St. *talik.ik.a* Cs. *talik.ish.a* Ps. *talik.w.a* (Ar)

taliki[2] *n* (*n*) (*naut*) rope used to lift cargo or the foot of a sail. (Ar)

taliz.a *vt* build a wall, floor, etc. of a house by using clay or mortar in order to give a smooth surface; daub, bedaub, smear, plaster. Prep. *taliz.i.a* St. *taliz.ik.a* Cs. *taliz.ish.a* Ps. *taliz.w.a* (cf *siriba*)

talkini *n* (*n*) (in Islam) a recitation or an exhortation offered by a religious person to a dead body just after being buried. (Ar)

talo *n* (*n*) 1. a kind of game resembling cricket, made of two teams using a bat. The player of one team hits a piece of wood while the other team struggles hard to catch it to avoid that team scoring many innings. 2. a piece of wood of not less than 15 centimetres, used for this game.

tama[1] *adj* an expletive used in ascertaining the truth of sth; truly, infact: *Tamko lake ni tama*, his utterance is a fact. (cf *kweli*) (Ar)

tama[2] *n* (*n*) see *tamati*

tama[3] *n* (*n*) used in the expression: *Shika tama, rest the cheek on the hand* as a sign of deep thought, etc.; brood, ponder. (Ar)

tama⁴ n (n) used in the expression: *Piga tama*, fill fluid into the mouth. (Ar)
tamaa n (n) 1. craving, lust, strong desire. (prov) *Tamaa mbele mauti nyuma*, if you desire sth so much, this can bring great disaster to you such as death. 2. hope, expectation, greediness: *Kata tamaa*, despair; lose hope. *Weka tamaa*, keep hope. *Ana tamaa* (a) he is hopeful. (b) he is greedy. (cf *matamanio, matarajio*)
tamadunik.a vi be acculturated, be civilized: *Ametamadunika sasa baada ya kuishi ugenini kwa muda mrefu*, he has now become civilized after living abroad for quite a long time. Prep. **tamadunik.i.a** St. **tamadunik.ik.a** Cs. **tamadunik.ish.a**
tamakan.i vt be well settled in a place: *Mjomba ametamakani huko kijijini*, my uncle is now settled in the village. Prep **tamakan.i.a** St **tamakan.ik.a** Cs **tamakan.ish.a** Ps **tamakan.iw.a** (Ar)
tamalak.i vt 1. possess, own: *Ametamalaki shamba kubwa*, he owns a big plantation. (cf *miliki, hozi*) 2. govern, rule: *Malkia ameitamalaki Uingereza tangu 1953*, the queen has ruled Great Britain since 1953. (cf *tawala*) 3. master; become proficient: *Seremala yule ameitamalaki kazi yake*, that carpenter has mastered his profession. (cf *weza, dhibiti*) Prep. **tamalak.i.a** St. **tamalak.ik.a** Cs. **tamalak.ish.a** Ps. **tamalak.iw.a** Rp. of Prep. **tamalak.i.an.a**
taman.i vt wish for, covet, yearn. Prep. **taman.i.a** St. **taman.ik.a** Cs. **taman.ish.a** Ps. **taman.iw.a** Rp. of Prep. **taman.i.an.a** (cf *taka*)
tamanio n (ma-) expectation, wish, desire: *Tamanio lake la kutaka kujenga nyumba kubwa halikusibu*, his hope of building a big house did not materialize.
tamanish.a vt cause sby to have an anxiety or desire, on sth. Prep.

tamanish.i.a St. **tamanish.ik.a** Ps. **tamanish.w.a** Rp. **tamanish.an.a**
tamari n (n) the first milk of an animal immediately after it has produced an offspring. (cf *uvugua*)
tamasha n (n) festival, gala, show: *Tamasha la jahazi*, the dhow festival. (cf *sherehe, burudani, onyesho, tafrija*) (Ar)
tamathali n (n) used in the expression: *Tamathali za usemi*, figures of speech.
tamati (also *tama*) n (n) end, ending, conclusion: *Tamati ya mchezo ilikuwa inasikitisha*, the end of the game was tragic. (cf *kikomo, mwisho*) (Ar)
tamauk.a vi despond, despair; lose hope: *Alitamauka baada ya kushindwa kwa mfululizo kupata kazi*, he despaired after repeated failures to get a job. Prep. **tamauk.i.a** St. **tamauk.ik.a** Cs. **tamauk.ish.a** Ps. **tamauk.w.a** (cf *sirima, angema*) (Ar)
tamb.a¹ vi 1. roam, meander, rove, wander: *Vijana wengi wanatamba siku hizi kutokana na ukosefu wa ajira*, many young men wander these days because of lack of employment. (cf *zurura, randa*) 2. brag, boast, show off: *Anapenda kutamba kwa vile ana mali nyingi*, he likes to brag because he has a lot of wealth. Prep. **tamb.i.a** St. **tamb.ik.a** Cs. **tamb.ish.a** Ps. **tamb.w.a** Rp. of Prep. **tamb.i.an.a** (cf *hanja, jisifu, jibodoa*)
tamb.a² vt narrate, tell, account: *Ni hodari katika kutamba hadithi za kale*, he is good at narrating ancient tales. Prep. **tamb.i.a** St. **tamb.ik.a** Cs. **tamb.ish.a** Ps. **tamb.w.a** (cf *simulia, elezea*)
tamb.a³ vi see *chamba¹*. Prep. **tamb.i.a** St. **tamb.ik.a** Cs. **tamb.ish.a** Ps. **tamb.w.a**
tamba.a¹ vi crawl, glide; inch along: *Nyoka alikuwa akitambaa*, the snake was crawling. Prep. **tamba.li.a** St. **tamba.lik.a** Cs. **tamba.lish.a** Ps. of

Prep. *tamba.liw.a* Rp. *tamba.an.a* (cf *jikokota, sombera*)
tamba.a² *vi* be spread out; be extended; have space: *Habari ilitambaa kwamba rais atalivunja bunge*, the news spread that the president would dissolve parliament. Prep. *tamba.li.a* St. *tamba.lik.a* Cs. *tamba.lish.a* Ps. of Prep. *tamba.liw.a* Rp. of Prep. *tamba.i.an.a* (cf *enea, zagaa*)
tamba.a³ (also *tambara*) *n* (*ma-*) rag, tatters, cast-offs; tattered clothing, old cloth: *Alitumia tambaa kufuta maziwa yaliyomwagika*, she used a rag to wipe off the spilt milk. (cf *mararu*)
tambara *n* (*n*) see *tambaa*
tambarajik.a *vi* see *tambarika*. Prep. *tambarajik.i.a* St. *tambarajik.ik.a* Cs. *tambarajik.ish.a*
tambarare *adj* used to refer to a country, area, etc. *Nchi tambarare*, a flat country. *Eneo tambarare*, a flat area.
tambarik.a (also *sambarika, tambarajika*) *vi* be weak because of sickness, oldage, etc.; be worn-out: *Gari yake imetambarika baada ya kutumika kwa muda mrefu*, his car is worn-out with long use. Prep. *tambarik.i.a* St. *tambarik.ik.a* Cs. *tambarik.ish.a* (cf *chakaa*)
tambavu *n* (*n*) shoulder-strap; a broad belt worn over one shoulder and across the chest with pockets used to carry ammunition, etc.
tambaz.a *vt* drawl words; slur: *Tambaza maneno*, slur one's words e.g. *Mzee akizungumza, hutambaza maneno*, when an old person talks, he slurs his words. Prep. *tambaz.i.a* St. *tambaz.ik.a* Cs. *tambaz.ish.a* Ps. *tambaz.w.a* Rp *tambaz.an.a* (cf *gogoteza*)
tambazi *n* (*n*) (*med*) a disease involving the inflammation of connective tissue especially of subcutaneous tissue; cellulitits.

tambi¹ *n* (*n*) pasta made in the form of long, thin strings cooked by boiling, etc.; spaghetti, vermicelli, noodles.
tambi² *n* (*ma-*) branch (cf *tawi*)
tambian.a *vi* boast or brag between each other: *Timu mbili zilikuwa zinatambiana kupata ushindi*, the two teams were bragging that each side would win. Prep. *tambian.i.a*
tambik.a *vt* perform rituals to appease the dead; make an offering to propitiate the spirits of the dead: *Alitambika ili ajikinge na maovu*, he made a propitiatory offering to protect himself against evil. Prep. *tambik.i.a* St. *tambik.ik.a* Cs. *tambik.ish.a* Ps. *tambik.w.a* (cf *kaga, hasa*)
tambiko *n* (*ma*) peace offering to the spirits of the dead; a propitiatory offering: *Tambiko lake dhidi ya maadui lilisaidia*, his propitiatory offering against the enemies helped. (cf *kago, edaha, mviko*)
tambo¹ *n* (*n*) puzzle; a game, toy or problem for testing cleverness, skill or ingenuity.
tambo² *n* (*ma-*) size, amplitude; condition of being well-built: *Tambo la mtu*, a well-built person; a stockily built person. (cf *gimba, jitrimu, kimba*)
tambo³ *n* (*ma-*) loop, noose. (cf *kitanzi*)
tamboa *n* (*n*) (*anat*) testicles (cf *pumbu*)
tambu.a *vt,vi* 1. recognize, realize, recall, understand, mark: *Aliponiona akanitambua*, when he saw me, he recognized me. (cf *fahamu*) 2. used in the expression: *Utanitambua*, you will see me i.e. I will treat you harshly such that you will not like it. Prep. *tambu.li.a* St. *tambu.lik.a* Cs. *tambu.lish.a* Ps. of Prep. *tambu.liw.a* Rp. *tambu.an.a*
tambuk.a *vt* jump over, leap over, sail over: *Nilikitambuka kizingiti cha mlango wangu*, I jumped over the threshold of my door. Prep. *tambuk.i.a* St. *tambuk.ik.a* Cs. *tambuk.ish.a* Ps. *tambuk.w.a* (cf *kiuka, ruka*)

tambuu n (n) 1. chewing mix in betel leaf. 2. betel leaf. (Hind)

tambuz.a vt weld, forge: *Mhunzi alizitambuza zana za jikoni,* the blacksmith forged kitchen utensils. Prep. *tambuz.i.a* St. *tambuz.ik.a* Cs. *tambuz.ish.a* Ps. *tambuz.w.a* (cf *fua*)

-tambuzi adj intelligent, perceptive, quickwitted: *Ana akili tambuzi,* he is intelligent.

tambuzo n (n) welding, forging.

tami.a¹ vt, vi (of hens or birds) sit on eggs; brood, incubate, hatch: *Kuku wangu alitamia mayai mengi mwaka jana,* my hen incubated many eggs last year. Prep. *tami.li.a* St. *tami.k.a* Cs. *tami.sh.a* Ps. *tami.w.a*

tami.a² vt please, gratify: *Tamasha lile lilitutamia sana,* that festival pleased us very much. Prep. *tami.li.a* St. *tami.k.a* Cs. *tami.sh.a* Ps. *tami.w.a* (cf *pendeza, furahisha, starehesha*)

tamimu n (n) a name of respect given to some traditional rulers of some tribes in Tanzania.

tamk.a vt articulate, pronounce; speak esp in a formal way: *Mwanasiasa alitamka maneno ya busara,* the politician spoke words of wisdom. Prep. *tamk.i.a* St. *tamk.ik.a* Cs. *tamk.ish.a* Ps. *tamk.w.a* (cf *tongoa, nena, sema*)

tamko (also *tamshi*) n (ma-) 1. pronunciation, articulation, utterance. (cf *sauti, lafudhi*) 2. promise, statement: *Serikali ilitoa tamko rasmi kuhusu suala la wakimbizi nchini,* the government issued an official statement regarding the question of refugees in the country. (cf *kauli, kalima*)

tamrini n (n) 1. exercise: *Tamrini za ufahamu,* comprehension exercises. *Tamrini za sarufi,* grammatical exercises. 2. formality: *Alikamilisha tamrini zote za kujaza maombi ya kuagiza gari kutoka ng'ambo,* he completed all the formalities of filling the application forms relating to the importation of a car. (Ar)

tamshi n (n) see *tamko*

tamthilia n (n) 1. play: *Tamthilia-bubu,* mime. 2. drama. (Ar)

-tamu adj 1. (of sugar-like taste) sweet, delicious: *Umekula machungwa matamu leo,* you have eaten sweet oranges today. 2. (of other kinds of food) nice, sweet, delicious, pleasant: *Nyama ya kuchoma ilikuwa tamu,* the roast meat was delicious. 3. melodious, pleasant, sweet-sounding: *Muziki wako ulikuwa mtamu,* your music was melodious. *Maneno matamu,* sweet words.

tamutamu n (n) bonbons, sweets, confectionary.

tamviri n (n) (bot) branch of a tree. (cf *tawi, utagaa*)

tamvua n (ma-) see *matamvua*

tamw.a vi feel happy; be glad: *Alitamwa kwa kutumbuizwa na mwanamuziki maarufu,* he was happy to be entertained by a popular musician. Prep. *tamw.i.a* St. *tamw.ik.a* Cs. *tamw.ish.a* (cf *faidi*)

tanabah.i vt, vi 1. recollect, realize: *Alipofika kwenye barabara kuu, alitanabahi ghafla kwamba alikisahau kipochi chake nyumbani,* when she reached the highway, she suddenly realized that she had forgotten her purse at home. (cf *gundua, maizi*) 2. beware, be on the alert: *Tanabahi na matapeli,* beware of thugs. Prep. *tanabah.i.a* St. *tanabah.ik.a* Cs. *tanabah.ish.a* Ps. of Cs. *tanabah.ish.w.a* (cf *tahadhari*) (Ar)

tanabahish.a vt 1. alert sby, caution sby. (cf *zindua*) 2. remind; put in mind. (cf *kumbusha*) Prep. *tanabahish.i.a* St. *tanabahish.ik.a* Ps. *tanabahish.w.a* Rp. *tanabahish.an.a* (Ar)

tanadhar.i vi beware, be careful: *Lazima utanadhari unapovuka barabara kuu,*

you must be careful when you cross the highway. Prep. *tanadhar.i.a* St. *tanadhar.ik.a* Cs. *tanadhar.ish.a* Ps. *tanadhar.iw.a* (cf *hadhari*) (Ar)
tanasar.i *vi* become a Christian after being a Muslim: *Muumini alitanasari,* the faithful became a Christian convert. Prep. *tanasar.i.a* St. *tanasar.ik.a* Cs. *tanasar.ish.a* Ps. *tanasar.iw.a* (cf *ritadi*) (Ar)
-tanashati *adj* clean, neat, well-dressed: *Kijana mtanashati,* a well-dressed young man. (Ar)
tanbihi *n* (*n*) footnote, notabene. (Ar)
tanchi *n* (*n*) see *tanji*
tand.a[1] (also *tanza*) *vt* 1. spread ropes interlaced within a bed frame; cover a bedstead with ropes interlaced: *Fundi seremala aliyutanda matendegu ili anitengenezee kitanda changu,* the carpenter covered the bedstead with ropes interlaced so as to construct a bed for me. 2. spread out, be dispersed, be overcast: *Mawingu yametanda,* the clouds have spread everywhere; it is clouded. 3. used in the expression: *Tanda dagaa,* catch sardines by spreading a large piece of calico in the water. Prep. *tand.i.a* St. *tand.ik.a* Cs. *tand.ish.a* and *tand.az.a* Ps. *tand.w.a*
tand.a[2] *vt* (of a plant) flourish, prosper. Prep. *tand.ik.a* Cs. *tand.ish.a* and *tand.az.a* Ps. *tand.w.a* (cf *wanda*)
tandaa *n* (*n*) (*mus*) clarinet (cf *nzumari*)
tandabelua *n* (*n*) uproar, chaos, disorder, turmoil: *Wanafunzi watukutu walileta tandabelua chuoni,* the troublesome students brought chaos at the college. (cf *vurugu, fujo, ghasia*) (Hind)
tandabui *n* (*n*) (*zool*) spider's web.
tandala *n* (*n*) (*zool*) kudu; a kind of African antelope with stripes and spots on the body and spirally twisted horns.
tandam.a *vi* (of a crocodile, etc.) be stretched out; be spread out; be in an extended position: *Mamba alijitandama aliposhiba,* the crocodile stretched

itself out when his stomach was full. Prep. *tandam.i.a* St. *tandam.ik.a* Cs. *tandam.ish.a* (cf *tandawaa, jieneza*)
tandatu *n* (*n*) six (cf *sita*)
tandawa.a *vi* (of a person reclining, lolling, etc.) be stretched right out; be spread: *Alijitandawaa kwenye basi hata kuwazuia abiria kushuka,* he spread himself right out in the bus such that he prevented passengers from alighting. Prep. *tandawa.li.a* St. *tandawa.lik.a* Cs. *tandawa.z.a* and *tandawa.lish.a* (cf *enea, zagaa*)
tandaz.a[1] *vt* see *tanda*
tandaz.a[2] *vt, vi* 1. spread out, stretch: *Tandaza mkeka,* stretch out the mat. *Tandaza nguo,* stretch out the garment. 2. reveal. 3. (*colloq*) (esp in sports) play superbly: *Mchezaji alitandaza gozi safi,* the player played soccer well. Prep. *tandaz.i.a* St. *tandaz.ik.a* Cs. *tandaz.ish.a* Ps. *tandaz.w.a*
tandik.a[1] *vt* lay a cover; lay out; spread out: *Tandika mkeka kitandani,* spread a mat on the bed. *Tandika kitanda,* make the bed. *Tandika meza,* lay a table. Prep. *tandik.i.a* St. *tandik.ik.a* Cs. *tandik.ish.a* Ps. *tandik.w.a*
tandik.a[2] *vt* beat, thrash, strike, smack: *Mzazi alimtandika mwanawe,* the parent beat his son. Prep. *tandik.i.a* St. *tandik.ik.a* Cs. *tandik.ish.a* Ps. *tandik.w.a* Rp. *tandik.an.a* (cf *piga, charaza, chapa*)
tandiko *n* (*ma-*) bedding, bedclothes: *Usitumie matandiko machafu haya ya kulalia,* don't use these dirty bedclothes for sleeping.
tando[1] *n* (*n*) a kind of fish trap which has two long ends and which is made from sticks. (cf *uzio, wando*)
tando[2] *n* (*n*) used in the expression: *Tando la buibui,* spider's web.
tandu *n* (*n*) (*zool*) centipede
tandu.a *vt* remove what is laid on; spread out, etc.: *Alizitandua bedshiti kutoka kwenye kitanda,* he removed

tanga¹

the bedsheets from the bed. Prep. *tandu.li.a* St. *tandu.lik.a* Cs. *tandu.lish.a* and *tandu.z.a* Ps. of Prep. *tandu.liw.a* Rp *tandu.an.a*
tanga¹ *n* (*n*) (of a vessel) sail: *Tua tanga*, lower sail. *Tweka tanga*, hoist sail. *Kunja tanga*, reef sail. (cf *shira*)
tanga² *n* (*ma-*) see *matanga*
tang.a³ *vi, vt* loiter, roam, wander; walk aimlessly: *Anapotoka kazini, hutanga katika mitaa yetu*, when he comes out from work, he wanders about in our neighbourhood. Prep. *tang.i.a* St. *tang.ik.a* Cs. *tang.ish.a* Ps. *tang.w.a* (cf *zurura*)
tanga.a *vt, vi* 1. become generally known; be revealed. *Habari zenyewe zimetangaa*, the news have spread. 2. be widespread. Prep. *tanga.li.a* St. *tanga.lik.a* Cs. *tanga.z.a* (cf *zagaa*)
tangalachi *n* (*n*) a kind of mat made from plaited palm leaves, used for burying a dead body; burial mat.
tangaman.a *vi* 1. be mixed up; be together: *Matunda yote aliyoyachuma yametangamana katika pakacha hili*, all the fruits that he has plucked have been mixed up in this plaited coconut palm-leaves basket. (cf *changamana, changanyika*) 2. co-operate, collaborate, interact: *Nchi za Afrika ya Mashariki zinatangamana katika sekta ya uchumi*, the East African countries co-operate with one another in the economic sector. (cf *shirikiana, ingiliana*)
tangamano *n* (*n*) 1. the state of being mixed up. (cf *changamano, fungamano*) 2. harmony, collaboration, co-operation: *Waziri aliwahimiza wanavijiji kuishi kwa moyo wa tangamano*, the minister urged the villagers to live in the spirit of co-operation. (cf *uelewano, ushirikiano*)
tangawizi *n* (*n*) 1. (*bot*) ginger: *Tangawizi mbichi*, raw ginger. 2. a drink made from boiled ginger powder mixed with water and sugar

tangaz.a¹ *vt* see *tangaa*
tangaz.a² *vt* announce, advertise. Prep. *tangaz.i.a* St. *tangaz.ik.a* Cs. *tangaz.ish.a* Ps. *tangaz.w.a*, Rp. of Prep. *tangaz.i.an.a* (cf *lingania*)
tangazo *n* (*ma-*) announcement, notice, proclamation, commentary, advertisement: *Tangazo la serikali*, government notice. *Tangazo rasmi*, official announcement. *Tangazo la biashara*, advertisement. *Tangazo mfululizo*, running commentary. *Tangazo la ndoa*, marriage banns. *Tangazo la redio*, radio announcement (cf *ilani, taarifa, notisi*)
tange *n* (*n*) a cleared forest in preparation for farming. (cf *mtema*)
tangi *n* (*ma-*) tank, cistern: *Tangi la maji*, water tank. *Tangi la petroli*, petrol tank. (Eng)
tango¹ (also *tangopepeta*) *n* (*ma-*) 1. (*bot*) wild melon. 2. cucumber. 3. *Tango mung'unye*, melon. *Cucumis melo*.
tango² *n* (*ma-*) wandering, roaming, roving; aimless walking.
tangopepeta *n* (*ma-*) see *tango¹*
tangu¹ *conj* since, ever since: *Tangu amefika hapa, amekuwa akitukera tu*, ever since he arrived here, he has just been bothering us. *Tangu lini alipokuja hapa?* Since when did he come here?
tangu² *prep* since, from: *Amekusubiri tangu asubuhi*, he has been waiting for you since morning. (cf *toka, kuanzia*)
tangu³ *n* (*n*) see *changu¹*
tangu.a (also *tengua*) *vt* invalidate, revoke, annul, repeal: *Tangua ndoa*, annul a marriage. *Tangua sheria*, rescind a law. *Tangua udhu*, make ablution null and void. *Tangua saumu*, break a fast. *Tangua ahadi*, break a promise. *Tangua urafiki*, break off a friendship. Prep. *tangu.li.a* St. *tangu.k.a* Cs. *tangu.z.a* Ps. of Prep. *tangu.liw.a* Rp. *tangu.an.a* (cf *haramisha, batilisha, vunja*)
tanguli.a *vt, vi* precede; go before, set off first. St. *tanguli.k.a* Cs. *tanguli.z.a*

Ps. *tanguli.w.a* Rp. *tangu.li.an.a* (cf *ongoza, takadamu*)
tanguliz.a *vt, vi* 1. send sby/sth in advance: *Kwanza aliwatanguliza watoto wake na baadaye akasafiri yeye mwenyewe*, first he sent his children in advance and later he travelled himself. 2. precede to do sth before the other one follows: *Alitanguliza kuoga kabla ya kula chakula chake cha mchana*, he started to take a bath first before taking his lunch. Prep. ***tanguliz.i.a*** St. ***tanguliz.ik.a*** Ps. ***tanguliz.w.a*** Rp. ***tanguliz.an.a***
tani[1] *n* (*n*) 1. ton: *Tani mbili za shehena*, two tons of cargo. *Tani metriki*, metric ton. 2. strength of the body: *Hakuuweza kupigana nawe kwa vile si tani yako*, he could not fight you because he is not as strong as you. 3. capacity, ability, strength: *Kula tani yako*, eat your fill; eat as much as you possibly can. (Eng)
tani[2] *adv* (of position) on the back: *Lala tani*, lie on the back.
tani.a *vt* mock, deride, ridicule: *Mbona Sarah anapenda kukutania?* Why does Sarah like to tease you? Prep. ***tani.li.a*** St. ***tani.k.a*** Cs. ***tani.sh.a*** Ps. ***tani.w.a*** Rp. ***tani.an.a*** (cf *dhihaki*)
taniaba *n* (*n*) (*lit*) antonomasia; the substitution of a personal name for a common noun to designate a member of group or class (e.g. *Yesu wa kwanza wa Afrika alikuwa Kwame Nkurmah*, the first Jesus in Africa was Kwame Nkrumah). Here, the word *Yesu*, Jesus is used to substitute *mkombozi*, liberator (Ar).
taniboi *n* (*ma-*) a lad who works on buses, etc.; tout, turnboy. (cf *utingo, kondakta*) (Eng)
tanji (also *tanchi*) *n* (*n*) (*leg*) confiscation of property by a government, institution, etc., to clear sby's debt; attachment: *Piga tanji*, confiscate in this manner.
tanjiti *n* (*n*) (*math*) tangent; a tangent line, curve or surface. (Eng)
tanki *n* (*n*) see *tangi*

tano *adj,n* five: *Watu watano*, five people: *Tano na Tano ni kumi*, five and five is ten.
tanu[1] *n* (*n*) used in the expression: *Mkungu wa tanu; Kibia cha tanu*, the lid of a cooking pot that has been made from an earthenware. (cf *kiana*)
tanu[2] *n* (*n*) 1. a collection of firewood or logs that have been burnt to get charcoal. 2. a collection of firewood, coconut empty shells, etc. burnt together with stones to get lime.
tanu.a *vt* 1. stretch apart; widen, expand: *Tanua miguu*, stretch your legs apart. (cf *panua*) 2. (*idm*) *Tanua kifua*, boast about oneself. (cf *jigamba*). Prep. ***tanu.li.a*** St. ***tanu.k.a*** Cs. ***tanu.sh.a*** Ps. of Prep. ***tanu.liw.a*** Rp. ***tanu.an.a***
tanuk.a *vi* be expanded, be wide open: *Kibofu changu kimetanuka*, my balloon has expanded Prep. ***tanuk.i.a*** St. ***tanuk.ik.a*** Cs. ***tanuk.ish.a*** (cf *panuka*)
tanuri (also *tanuu*) *n* (*ma-*) kiln, furnace. (Ar)
tanuu *n* (*n*) see *tanuri*
tanuwini *n* (*n*) (*gram*) nunation; the process of doubling the final vowel of a word esp those of indefinite pronouns and adjectives so that a nasalized sound "n" is heard: The objective of using nunation is mainly to make the words in question. (whether it is a noun or adjective) as indefinuite: *Tia tanuwini*, put nasalized "n" at the end of the word such as *kalbu* 'dog' to read as *kalbun* or *kitabu*, 'book', to read as *kitabun*.
tanz.a[1] *vt* baffle, perplex, confuse: *Shairi lake limenitanza na kwa hivyo, ningependa unifafanulie*, his poem has baffled me and so I would like you to explain it to me. Prep. ***tanz.i.a*** St. ***tanz.ik.a*** Cs. ***tanz.ish.a*** Ps. ***tanz.w.a*** Rp. ***tanz.an.a*** (cf *tatanisha, tatiza, tinga*)
tanz.a[2] *vt* see *tanda*. Prep. ***tanz.i.a*** St. ***tanz.ik.a*** Cs. ***tanz.ish.a*** Ps. ***tanz.w.a***
tanzi *n* (*ma-*) loop, noose: *Tia tanzi, noose. Tanzi la roho*, halter
tanzia (also *taazia*) *n* (*n*) 1. obituary notice;

news of a death: *Pokea tanzia*, receive condolences. *-pa mkono wa tanzia*, give condolences. 2. tragedy. *Tanzia ramsa*, tragic comedy. (cf *msiba*)
tanzu¹ *n* (*n*) see *utanzu*
tanzu² *interj* an expletive for emphasizing the solving of a problem, etc.
tanzu.a *vt* 1. disentangle, solve; clear up: *Ameweza kulitanzua tatizo lake*, he has managed to solve his problem. (cf *dadavua, tatua, zongoa*) 2. clarify, elaborate: *Serikali iliutanzua msimamo wake juu ya suala la haki za binadamu*, the government clarified its position on the question of human rights. Prep. *tanzu.li.a* St. *tanzu.k.a* Cs. *tanzu.sh.a* Ps. of Prep. *tanzu.liw.a* Rp. *tanzu.an.a* (cf *eleza, fafanua*)
tanzuk.a *vi* 1. be solved, be clarified: *Mgogoro umetanzuka*, the conflict is solved. 2. (of weather, etc) be clear: *Kumetanzuka*, the clouds have dispersed i.e. it is clear. Prep. *tanzuk.i.a* St. *tanzuk.ik.a* Cs. *tanzuk.ish.a*
tao *n* (*ma-*) 1. a curve like that of an arc or bend of a river or hem of a dress: *Fanya matao*, be curved. *Piga matao*, be curved. *Njia imefanya matao*, the road is curved. *Kanzu yake imefanya matao*, his garment is hemmed. 2. used in the expression: *Enda kwa matao*, walk with pomposity.
tapa¹ (also *dapa*) *n* (*ma-*) (*bot*) the broad frond of a Deleb or palmyra palm.
tapa² *n* (*ma-*) the dry fibre of a banana tree that is scraped and cut in order to wrap tobacco powder.
tap.a³ *vi* see *tapatapa*
tapaka.a *vt, vi* be spread all over; be scattered about; be here and there; be dotted about; be everywhere: *Habari za kifo chake zimetapakaa mjini*, the news about her death has spread all over town. Prep. *tapaka.li.a* St. *tapaka.lik.a* Cs. *tapaka.z.a* Ps. of Cs. *tapaka.z.w.a* (cf *shamiri, zaga*a)
tapakaz.a *vt* 1. spread, diffuse: *Alitapakaza matope hapa*, he spread mud here. 2. Prep. *tapakaz.i.a* St. *tapakaz.ik.a* Ps. *tapakaz.w.a* Rp. *tapakaz.an.a*

tapany.a *vt* 1. scatter about, dispense; throw away things indiscriminately in all directions: *Alizitapanya karatasi nyingi chumbani mwake*, he scattered many papers in his room. (cf *tupa*) 2. squander, misuse, waste: *Walizitapanya pesa zao*, they squandered their money. Prep. *tapany.i.a* St. *tapany.ik.a* Cs. *tapany.ish.a* Ps. *tapany.w.a* (cf *fuja*)
tapatap.a (also *tapa*) *vi* fret, be worried, be uneasy: *Ameanza kutapatapa baada ya kusikia kwamba serikali itamshtaki*, he has started to fret after learning that the government will sue him. (*prov*) *Mfa maji haishi kutapa*, a drowning man never stops for his survival i.e. a person whose business, etc. is on the verge of decline will do his utmost to make sure that his enterprise does not collapse. Prep. *tapatap.i.a* St. *tapatap.ik.a* Cs. *tapatap.ish.a*
tapeli¹ *n* (*n*) conman, swindler, duper: *Usimwamini tapeli yule*, don't trust that conman. (cf *shambenga, jambazi, bazazi*)
tapel.i² *vt* swindle; con someone: *Alishindwa kunitapeli*, he failed to con me. Prep. *tapel.i.a* St. *tapel.ik.a* Cs. *tapel.ish.a* Ps. of Prep. *tapel.iw.a* Rp. of Prep. *tapel.i.an.a* (cf *danganya*)
tapi.a *vt* want sth hurriedly; be avid for sth; be extremely eager: *Mtu mwenye njaa alitapia kula*, the hungry man was avid for food. Prep. *tapi.li.a* St. *tapi.k.a* Cs. *tapi.sh.a* Ps. *tapi.w.a* (cf *rapia, wania*)
tapik.a *vi* vomit. Prep. *tapik.i.a* St. *tapik.ik.a* Cs. *tapi.sh.a*, cause to vomit (cf *cheuka*)
tapish.a¹ *vi* see *tapika* Prep. *tapish.i.a* St. *tapish.ik.a* Ps. *tapish.w.a*
tapish.a² *vt* finalize ritual teachings to young girls in the initiation. Prep. *tapish.i.a* St. *tapish.ik.a* Ps. *tapish.w.a*
tapish.a³ *vt* empty the faeces, etc. in a toilet/latrine: *Wafanyakazi walikitapisha choo*, the workers emptied the faeces

in a toilet. Prep. ***tapish.i.a*** St. ***tapish.ik.a*** Ps. ***tapish.w.a***
tapishi (*used in the pl*) *n* (*ma-*) 1. vomit: *Matapishi haya lazima yaondolewe,* this vomit must be removed. 2. (*colloq*) filthy words.
tapisho[1] *n* (*n*) a special fee given during the ceremonies connected with initiation of young girls.
tapisho[2] *n* (*n*) medicine given to someone to vomit; emetic: *Alikula tapisho baada ya kupewa chakula chenye sumu,* he took an emetic after being given poisonous food.
tapo[1] *n* (*ma-*) group, troupe, party: *Tapo la watu lilikuwa likimngojea bwana harusi nje,* a group of people was waiting for the bridegroom outside. *Tapo la waandishi,* a group of writers.
tapo[2] *n* (*n*) (*bot*) false sago; a kind of edible fruit usu white and if powdered to flour, can be used to make porridge: *Uji wa tapo,* porridge from this powdered fruit.
tapo[3] *n* (*n*) a kind of net made from dwarf-palm leaves joined in the middle of two strings, used for catching fish; dragnet.
tapo[4] *n* (*n*) (*lit*) used in the expression: *Tapo la fasihi,* literary movement.
tapo[5] *n* (*ma-*) pride, arrogance, boastfulness (cf *majivuno, maringo*)
tara *n* (*n*) intrigue, plot: *Toa tara,* intrigue; hatch a plot.
taraa *conj* if, provided, in case: *Taraa akija hapa, nitampa pesa zake,* if he comes here, I will give him his money. (cf *pindi, endapo*)
tarabe *n* (*n*) a double-valve door or window; a door or window consisting of two halves: *Mlango wa tarabe,* a door of two halves.
tarabizuna *n* (*n*) a kind of perfume made from different kinds of flowers and mixed with water; perfume made from potpourri. (Ar)

tarabu (also *taarabu*) *n* (*n*) traditional coastal Swahili orchestra with vocals. (Ar)
tarabushi *n* (*n*) see *tarbushi*
taradad.i *vi* 1. hesitate, pause: *Mwanafunzi alitaradadi kuchukua somo gumu,* the student hesitated to take a difficult subject. 2. be restless, be occupied, be busy: *Rafiki yangu anataradadi kutafuta nyumba ya kuishi,* my friend is busy looking for a house to live in. Prep. ***taradad.i.a*** St. ***taradad.ik.a*** Cs. ***taradad.ish.a*** Ps. ***taradad.iw.a*** (cf *hangaika, haha*) (Ar)
taaridh.i 1. *vt* encroach sby's freedom in order to fulfil one's objectives. 2. spy; observe sby's activities, etc. Prep ***taaradh.i.a*** St ***taaradh.ik.a*** Cs ***taaradh.ish.u*** Ps ***taaradh.iw.a*** Rp of Prep ***taaradh.i.an.a***
taradhi.a *vt* beg; beseech, implore, entreat: *Nilimtaaradhia meneja anipatie kazi kwenye kiwanda chake,* I implored the manager to give me a job in his factory. Prep. ***taradhi.li.a*** St. ***taradhi.lik.a*** Cs. ***taradhi.lish.a*** Ps. of Prep. ***taradhi.liw.a*** (cf *omba, taka, sihi*) (Ar)
tarafa *n* (*n*) (of an administrative area) division: *Katibu tarafa,* divisional secretary. *Mkuu wa tarafa,* divisional head. (Ar)
taraghani *n* (*n*) arrogance, vanity, conceit, pride: *Taraghani zake hazitamsaidia kitu,* his arrogance will not help him. (cf *kiburi, majivuno*) (Ar)
taraj.i (also *tarajia*) *vt, vi* expect, anticipate, hope: *Anataraji kupata mtoto karibu,* she is expecting a baby soon. Prep. ***taraj.i.a*** St. ***taraj.ik.a*** Cs. ***taraj.ish.a*** Ps. ***taraj.iw.a***, Rp. of Prep. ***taraj.i.an.a*** (cf *rajua, tumai*) (Ar)
taraji.a *vt* see *taraji.* Prep. ***taraji.li.a*** St. ***taraji.k.a*** Cs. ***taraji.sh.a***
tarajio *n* (*ma-*) hope, expectation. (cf *tumaini, tegemeo, tazamio*)(Ar)

tarakany.a (also *taranya*) *vt* 1. spoil, wreck, undermine: *Aliitarakanya mipango yangu ya kuoa*, he spoiled my marriage plans. (cf *vuruga*) 2. talk senselessly so as not to be understood; confuse: *Aliitarakanya taarifa yake ili kuwakanganya polisi*, he talked senselessly so as to confuse his statement to the police. Prep. *tarakany.i.a* St. *tarakany.ik.a* Cs. *tarakany.ish.a* Ps. *tarakany.w.a* Rp. *tarakany.an.a*
tarakilishi *n* (*n*) computer (cf *kompyuta*)
tarakimu *n* (*n*) numeral, digit: *Tarakimu aushi*, significant figures. *Tarakimu kadiri*, significant figures. *Tarakimu za Kiarabu*, Arabic numerals. *Tarakimu za Kirumi*, Roman numerals. (Ar)
taranya *n* (*n*) see *tarakanya*
tarare *n* (*n*) (*bot*) a plant growing on its own accord in a garden, etc that is, without seeds having been planted; volunteer. (cf *maotea, mbulia*)
taratibu[1] *n* (*n*) procedure, formality, practice, convention: *Mwombaji alikamilisha taratibu zote za kupata paspoti*, the applicant completed all the formalities of getting a passport. (cf *kaidi*) (Ar)
taratibu[2] *adv* carefully, orderly, cautiously: *Meli ilikuwa inaingia bandarini taratibu*, the ship was sailing into the port slowly. (cf *polepole, asteaste*) (Ar)
-taratibu[3] *adj* calm, quiet, serene: *Kijana mtaratibu*, a quiet young man. (Ar)
tarawanda *n* (*n*) see *mtarawanda*
tarawehe (also *tarawehi*) *n* (*n*) (In Islam) a long optional prayer said at night after *Isha* prayers during the month of Ramadan. (Ar)
tarawehi *n* (*n*) see *tarawehe*
taraza[1] *n* (*n*) border or edging of a garment that has been ornamented or decorated; embroidered hem. (Ar)
taraza[2] *n* (*n*) a kind of strip of plaited palm leaf ready for work.
tarazak.i *vi* earn a living; work in order to get the necessities of life: *Kuli yule anatarazaki bandarini*, that coolie works at the port in order to earn his living. Prep. *tarazak.i.a* St. *tarazak.ik.a* Cs. *tarazak.ish.a* (Ar)
tarazia *n* (*n*) coastal dance played by men and women who go round a circle in turns. (Ar)
tarazo *n* (*n*) terrazzo; flooring of small chips of marble set in cement and polished. (Eng)
tarbushi *n* (*n*) fez, tarboosh; a brimless red cap with a tassel usu worn by Muslims. (cf *tunga, kitunga*) (Ar)
tardidi (also *uradidi, tarididi*) (*gram*) reduplication; a process of repeating a syllable or other linguistic element.
tarehe *n* (*n*) 1. date. 2. history, chronicle, annals. (cf *mapisi, historia*) (Ar)
tari[1] *n* (*n*) tambourine, timbrel, a kind of shallow single-headed hand drum with a stretched skin on one side and usu having jingling metal disks in the rim. (cf *tafi, kigoma*)
tari[2] *n* (*n*) 1. a drum used in exorcising spirits. 2. a kind of coastal dance played by males using sticks and swords.
tari[3] *n* (*n*) a condition of having an absence of a pupil in an eye thus causing partial or total blindness; cataract (cf *mtoto wa jicho*).
tarididi *n* (*n*) see *tardidi*
tarijama *n* (*n*) autobiography (cf *tawasifu*)
tarika *n* (*n*) 1. Islamic teachings conducted by a religious leader or sheikh, based on the fundamental principles of the religion. 2. disciples of these kinds of teachings. (Ar)
tariki *n* (*n*) road, path, way: *Fuata tariki hii*, follow this path. (cf *njia*) (Ar)
tariku *n* (*n*) used in the expression: *Tariku swalati*, a person who abandons praying. (Ar)
tarishi *n* (*ma-*) a messenger sent in haste or on a regular schedule with important messages; courier. (cf *katikiro, mjumbe*) (Ar)
tariz.i[1] (also *darizi*) *vt* ornament fabric with a special design; embroider;

weave a border: *Niliitarizi nguo yangu kwa nyuzi za hariri*, I embroidered my dress with silk thread. Prep. *tariz.i.a* St. *tariz.ik.a* Cs. *tariz.ish.a* Ps. *tariz.iw.a* Rp. of Prep. *tariz.i.an.a* (Ar)
tariz.i² *vt* (*naut*) spin a fishing-line or net: *Nitarizie mshipi wangu*, spin for me the fishing-line. Prep. *tariz.i.a* St. *tariz.ik.a* Cs. *tariz.ish.a* Ps. *tariz.iw.a* (Ar)
tarjum.i¹ *vt* translate: *Walikitarjumi kifungu cha habari kwa Kiarabu*, they translated the passage into Arabic. Prep. *tarjum.i.a* St. *tarjum.ik.a* Cs. *tarjum.ish.a* Ps. *tarjum.iw.a* (cf *fasiri, tafsiri*) (Ar)
tarjumi² *n* (*n*) translation: *Tarjumi ile ilikuwa potofu*, that translation was misleading. (cf *tafsiri*) (Ar)
taruma *n* (*ma-*) 1. a piece of wood used to stiffen or strengthen a structure or framework e.g. rib, frame, including filling-timbers and square-body frames: *Dau la mataruma*, flat-bottomed *dau*. 2. a railway sleeper; a railway tie; crosstie 3. tatoo, incision.
tarumbeta *n* (*ma-*) trumpet (Eng, Port)

tarumbeta

tasa¹ *n* (*n*) a sterile female creature; a barren female creature.
tasa² *adj* sterile, barren, infertile: *Mwanamke tasa*, a barren woman. *Ng'ombe tasa*, a sterile cow. *Mchungwa tasa*, a barren orange tree.
tasa³ *n* (*n*) a number that cannot be divided into two; odd number. (cf *witri*)
tasa⁴ (also *toasi, tuwazi*) *n* (*n*) a large metal vessel for spitting, washing hands before and after meals.
tas.a⁵ *vt* baffle, confuse, entangle: *Methali hii imenitasa*, this proverb has baffled me. Prep. *tas.i.a* St. *tas.ik.a* Cs. *tas.ish.a* Ps. *tas.w.a* Rp. *tas.an.a* (cf *tatiza, tatanisha*)
tasa⁶ *n* (*n*) a round silver dish-shaped gong used in music and traditional dances. (cf *matuazi*)
tasa⁷ *n* (*ma-*) bamboo basket. (cf *tenga, susu*)
tasaufi (also *tasaufu*) *n* (*n*) mysticism, suficism; a religious system that believes in the unity of God and purifies a person from secular affairs and also makes him totally devout in religious tenets. (Ar)
tasaufu *n* (*n*) see *tasaufi*
tasawar.i *vi* 1. be credible, be reliable: *Taarifa yake haitasawari hata kidogo*, his statement is not reliable at all. (cf *aminika, sadikika*) 2. (of affairs, etc.) be in good form, shape well; improve: *Siku hizi, mambo yake yanatasawari*, these days his affairs are shaping up well. Prep. *tasawar.i.a* St. *tasawar.ik.a* Cs. *tasawar.ish.a* Ps. *tasawar.iw.a* (Ar)
tasbihi *n* (*n*) 1. a string of beads, used to keep count of the names of God, etc.; rosary. 2. (in Islam) an optional prayer in Islam prayed usu at night to seek God's forgiveness requesting a person as advised by Prophet Mohammad, to pray at least once in his life time. (Ar)
tasfida *n* (*n*) see *tasifida*
tashdidi *n* (*n*) see *tashididi*
tashibiha (also *tashbihi*) *n* (*n*) (*lit*) a figure of speech in which one thing is likened to another; simile: *Yeye ni shujaa kama simba*, he is as brave as a lion. (Ar)
tashididi (also *tashdidi*) *n* (*n*) (*phonet*) stress (cf *mkazo*) (Ar)

tashihisi (*also tasihisi*) *n* (*n*) (*lit*) personification; a figure of speech in which a thing, quality or idea is represented as a person. (eg: *Nyota zilikuwa zikitabasamu huku zikimzunguka mama yao, Mwezi, ambaye aliuachia mwili wake wote uchi kabisa*, The stars were smiling, and embracing their mother, Moon, which left its body completely naked) (*Ar*).

tashkota *n* (*n*) (*mus*) an old kind of musical instrument with four pairs of strings, originating from Japan and China; mandolin. (cf *mandolina*)

tashtiti *n* (*n*) 1. derision, satire, mockery, joke: *Anapenda kunifanyia tashtiti*, he likes to play jokes on me. (cf *stihizai, chagizo*) 2. (in *poet*) satire. (Ar)

tashwishi *n* (*n*) uncertainty, anxiety, doubt: *Alishikwa na tashwishi aliposikia kwamba huenda asiajiriwe kwenye kampuni*, she was filled with anxiety when she heard that she might not be employed in the company. (cf *wasiwasi, wahaka*) (Ar)

tasi[1] *n* (*n*) see *chafi*

tasi[2] *n* (*n*) a kind of oil used for cleaning a rope or fishing-line in order to make them firm.

tasifida (*also tasfida*)*n*(*n*) (*lit*) euphemism; the use of a word or phrase that is less expressive or direct but considered less offensive e.g. *Amekwenda msalani*, he has gone to the bathroom. (cf *usafidi*) (Ar)

tasihili (*also tashili*) *adv* hurriedly, fast, swiftly: *Mambo yake yanatendeka kwa tasihili*, his affairs operate quite fast. (Ar)

tashihisi *n* (*n*) (*lit*) personification; a figure of speech in which a thing, quality or idea is represented as a person. (Ar)

tasinifu (*also tasnifu*)*n* (*n*) thesis, dissertation. (Ar)

tasilita *n* (*n*) intrigue, michief: *Fanya tasilita*, do mischief. (cf *fitina*) (Ar)

tasilit.i *vt* make mischief. Prep. *tasilit.i.a* St. *tasilit.ik.a* Cs. of Prep. *tasilit.ish.a* Ps. *tasilit.iw.a*

taslimu *adj* used in the expression: *Fedha taslimu*, cash payment; cash in hand, spot cash. (Ar)

tasliti *n* (*n*) excessive love, excessive like. (syn) *Tasliti hushinda beluwa*, excessive love of sth is more serious than a mere hardship i.e. if you love someone such as a girl, you can suffer more than a mere hardship like hunger; in other words, the strength of love is greater than a mere hardship like hunger. (Ar)

tasnia *n* (*n*) industry: *Tasnia ya chuma*, the steel industry. (Ar)

tasu.a *vt* 1. unravel, disentangle, resolve, solve: *Siwezi kulitasua tatizo lenu*, I can't solve your problem. (cf *tanzua, tatua, zongoa*) 2. clarify, elaborate, explain: *Nilijaribu kuyatasua maelezo yangu kwake na baadaye akaelewa*, I tried to clarify my statement to him and later he understood. Prep. *tasu.li.a* St. *tasu.k.a* Cs. *tasu.sh.a* Ps. of Prep. *tasu.liw.a* (cf *dadavua, fafanua*)

taswira *n* (*n*) 1. image, imagery: *Taswira bandia*, virtual image. *Taswira halisi*, real image. *Taswira tobwe*, pinhole image. *Mshairi alitumia taswira zake vizuri*, the poet employed his imagery effectively. 2. picture, drawing: *Taswira yake ya jahazi inapendeza*, his drawing of the dhow is attractive. (cf *mchoro, sanamu*) (Ar)

tat.a[1] *vi* be complicated, be tangled, be snarled: *Uzi wangu umetata*, my string is tangled. Prep. *tat.i.a* St. *tat.ik.a* Cs. *tat.iz.a* Rp. *tat.an.a*

tata[2] *adj* (*gram*) complex, ambiguous: *Tungo tata*, complex construction. *Sentensi tata*, ambiguous sentence. *Nadharia tata*, abstruse theory.

tata[2] *n* (*n*) toddle; an unsteady walk.

tatag.a *vt* walk precariously as on a rope: *Mwanasarakasi alitataga kwenye kamba*, the acrobat walked precariously on the rope. Prep. *tatag.i.a* St. *tatag.ik.a* Cs. *tatag.ish.a*

tatalik.a *vi* see *tatarika*

tatanish.a (also *tatiza*) *vt, vi* be puzzling, be perplexing, be confusing: *Taarifa yako inatatanisha*, your statement is confusing. Prep. *tatanish.i.a* St. *tatanish.ik.a* Ps. *tatanish.w.a* Rp. *tatanish.an.a* (cf *kanganya, zonga, tinga*)

tatanisho *n* (*ma-*) difficulty, problem: *Tatanisho hili halitatuliki*, this problem is insoluble. (cf *tatizo, shida*)

tatanu.a *vt* force a hard thing apart as in the case of bars of iron window; widen: *Wezi walizitatanua nondo za dirisha ili waweze kuingia ndani ya nyumba*, the thieves forced the bars of the iron window apart in order to enter the house. Prep. *tatanu.li.a* St. *tatanu.k.a* Ps. *tatanu.sh.a* Ps. of Prep. *tatanu.liw.a* (cf *panua*)

tatarik.a (also *tatalika*) *vi* 1. be rattled, be spluttered; hop about: *Bisi zilikuwa zikitatarika kwenye kikaango*, the popcorns were spluttering in the frying pan. (cf *rukaruka, papatika*) 2. be restless, be uneasy; fret, writhe: *Alitatarika alipogundua kwamba kipochi chake kimepotea*, she became restless when she found that her purse was missing. Prep. *tatarik.i.a* St. *tatarik.ik.a* Cs. *tatarik.ish.a* Ps. *tatarik.w.a* (cf *hangaika, mahanika*)

tatas.a *vi* feel or search blindly as in a dark place or like a blindman; grope, grabble, fumble. Prep. *tatas.i.a* St. *tatas.ik.a* Cs. *tatas.ish.a* Ps. *tatas.w.a* (cf *susuma*)

tathmin.i[1] *vt* evaluate, assess, estimate: *Aliitathmini kazi yangu*, he evaluated my work. Prep. *tathmin.i.a* St. *tathmin.ik.a* Cs. *tathmin.ish.a* Ps. *tathmin.iw.a* (cf *kadiria, pima*) (Ar)

tathmini[2] *n* (*n*) evaluation, assessment, evaluation, estimate: *Fanya tathmini*, make an assessment. (cf *ukadiriaji, ukadirifu*)

tatiz.a[1] *vi, vt* see *tatanisha*. Prep. *tatiz.i.a* St. *tatiz.ik.a* Cs. *tatiz.ish.a* Ps. *tatiz.w.a* Rp. *tatiz.an.a*

tatiz.a[2] *vt* wrap a cloth round the waist, shoulders, etc. as women do when they intend to work or dance: *Alijitatiza kanga mbili alipokwenda shambani kulima*, she wrapped herself with two pieces of 'khangas' when she went to the farm to cultivate. Prep. *tatiz.i.a* St. *tatiz.ik.a* Cs. *tatiz.ish.a* Ps. *tatiz.w.a* Rp. *tatiz.an.a*

tatizo *n* (*ma-*) problem, difficulty, complexity, dilemma: *Tatizo sugu*, a chronic problem. *Ana matatizo mengi*, she has many problems.

tatu *adj, n* three: *Tatu na tatu ni sita*, three and three is six. *Tatutatu*, triple.

tatu.a[1] *vt* 1. solve, resolve, work out: *Mbunge aliweza kuyatatua matatizo ya jimbo lake*, the member of parliament managed to solve the problems of his constituency. (cf *dadavua, tanzua, tasua*) 2. unwind, unravel, undo: *Alilitatua fundo*, he undid the knot. Prep. *tatu.li.a* St. *tatu.k.a* Ps. of Prep. *tatu.liw.a* (cf *zongomoa, fundua*)

tatu.a[2] *vt* tear, rip, rend, rive; pull apart: *Aliitatua barua yake vipandevipande baada ya kuisoma*, she tore her letter in pieces after reading it. *Aliitatua nguo yangu burebure*, she tore my dress for no reason. Prep. *tatu.li.a* St. *tatu.k.a* Ps. of Prep. *tatu.liw.a* (cf *pasua, chana*)

taufiki *n* (*n*) acceptance by God of sby's supplication: *Wabilahi taufiki*, the ability for someone to do what he likes rests upon God. (Ar)

tauhidi (also *tawhidi*) *n* (*n*) the unity of God, which is the great fundamental basis of the Islamic religion; monotheism: *Tauhidi sadifu*, systematic theology. (Ar)

taulo *n* (*n*) towel (Eng)

taumu *n* (*ma-*) (*naut*) block to support the keel of a vessel under construction.

tauni *n* (*n*) (*med*) bubonic plague: *Ugonjwa wa tauni uliwaua watu wengi*, the

bubonic plague claimed the lives of many people.
Taurati (also *torati*) n (n) the sacred book which God gave to Moses; the Torah. (Ar)
tausi n (n) (zool) peacock, peahen: *Tausi dume*, peacock.
taw.a¹ vi 1. live in seclusion; remain indoors: *Msichana alitawa alipobaleghe*, the girl remained in seclusion after she reached puberty. 2. lead a hermitic life; live in seclusion for religious purposes: *Ameanza kutawa kwa kufuata maadili ya Mwenyezi Mungu*, he has started to live a hermitic life in compliance with the teachings of God. Prep. *taw.i.a* St. *taw.ik.a* Cs. *taw.ish.a* (Ar)
-tawa² adj devout, pious, religious: *Mwanamke mtawa*, a pious woman.
tawa³ n (n) metal frying pan. (Ar)
tawadh.a (also *tawaza*) vi 1. take ablutions before praying: *Alitawadha kabla ya kusali*, he performed ablutions before praying. 2. wash legs, hands, private parts, etc. with water, etc.; cleanse, clean: *Mvulana alitawadha baada ya kujisaidia*, the boy cleaned his private parts after relieving himself. Prep. *tawadh.i.a* St. *tawadh.ik.a* Cs. *tawadh.ish.a* Ps. of Cs. *tawadh.ish.w.a* (Ar)
tawaf.u¹ vt circumambulate the Kaaba seven times: *Alitawafu alipokwenda kuhiji Maka*, he circumambulated seven times when he went on a pilgrimage to Mecca. Prep. *tawaf.i.a* St. *tawaf.ik.a* Cs. *tawaf.ish.a* Ps. of Prep. *tawaf.iw.a* (Ar)
tawafu² n (n) circumambulation of the Kaaba.
tawakal.i vt put trust in God; rely on God; have confidence in God: *Walitawakali kwa Mwenyezi mungu walipokuwa kwenye safari*, they relied upon God's mercy when they were on a journey. Prep. *tawakal.i.a* St. *tawakal.ik.a* Cs. *tawakal.ish.a* Ps. *tawakal.iw.a* (Ar)

tawal.a vt 1. rule, govern, colonize: *Tabaka tawala*, the ruling class. (cf *tamalaki, miliki*) 2. master; be competent: *Mtaalamu yule ameutawala uwanja wa fasihi-simulizi*, that scholar has mastered the field of oral literature. 3. (fig) dominate, control: *Wachezaji wetu waliutawala mchezo tangu mwanzo mpaka mwisho*, our players dominated the game from the beginning up to the end. Prep. *tawal.i.a* St. *tawal.ik.a* Cs. *tawal.ish.a* Ps. of Prep. *tawal.iw.a*
tawany.a vt distribute, allocate, disperse: *Askari wa polisi waliwatawanya waandamanaji*, the police dispersed the demonstrators. Prep. *tawany.i.a* St. *tawany.ik.a* Cs. *tawany.ish.a* Ps. *tawany.w.a* (cf *tapanya*) (Ar)
tawanyik.a vi be dispersed, be scattered: *Watu walitawanyika katika sehemu mbalimbali baada ya mkutano*, people scattered in different places after the meeting. Prep. *tawanyik.i.a* St. *tawanyik.ik.a* Cs. *tawanyik.ish.a* (cf *fumukana*)
tawasal.i vt pray to God by using some of his names: *Walitawasali mvua kwa Mwenyezi Mungu*, they prayed to God for rain. Prep. *tawasal.i.a* St. *tawasal.ik.a* Cs. *tawasal.ish.a* Ps. *tawasal.iw.a* (Ar)
tawasifu n (n) autobiography; the story of one's own life written or dictated by oneself. (Ar)
tawasuli n (n) pray to God by a person of rank.
tawaz.a vt enthrone, install in office: *Walimtawaza rais-mteule wiki iliyopita*, they inaugurated the president-elect to office last week. 2. see *tawadha*. Prep. *tawaz.i.a* St. *tawaz.ik.a* Cs. *tawaz.ish.a* Ps. *tawaz.w.a* (Ar)
tawhidi (also *tauhidi*) n (n) oneness of God; monotheism. (Ar)
tawi (also *utawi*) n (ma-) 1. branch of a tree: *Hili ni tawi la mpapai*, this is the branch of a pawpaw tree. (cf *utanzu, utagaa, tamviri*) 2. branch of a party, organization, etc.: *Tawi*

738

tawili   tebwerek.a T

la chama tawala, the branch of the ruling party.
tawili (also *tuili*) *adj* long, lofty, towering: *Umri tawili*, a long life. (Ar)
tawire *interj* see *taire*
tawish.a *vt* confine sby indoors; schedule sby such that he is not seen by the public. Prep. **tawash.i.a** St. **tawash.ik.a** Ps. **tawish.w.a** Rp. **tawish.an.a**
tawiz.a *vt* curse sby for an evil deed. Prep. **tawiz.i.a** St. **tawiz.ik.a** Cs. **tawiz.ish.a** Ps. **tawiz.w.a** (cf *patiliza*)
taya[1] *n* (*ma-*) (*anat*) jaw: *Taya la chini*, submaxilla, mandibula: *Taya la juu*, upper jaw bone, maxilla.
taya[2] *n* (*n*) 1. (*naut*) a vertical strip of cloth, a number of which form the total sail. (cf *fatika*) 2. length of a sail cloth.
tay.a[3] *vt* reproach, rebuke, scold, censure: *Tajiri alimtaya mfanyakazi wake kwa ukosefu wa nidhamu*, the employer scolded his worker for misconduct. Prep. **tay.i.a** St. **tay.ik.a** Cs. **tay.ish.a** Ps. **tay.w.a** Rp. **tay.an.a** (cf *karipia*, *laumu*)
tayari *adv* ready, prepared; all set: *Kaa tayari*, be ready. *Kazi yako iko tayari*, your work is ready. (cf *ange*) (Ar)
tayarish.a *vt* prepare, ready, arrange: *Tayarisha safari yako*, prepare your journey. *Tayarisha bili yangu*, prepare my bill. *Tayarisha chakula*, prepare food (for eating); Prep. **tayarish.i.a** St. **tayarish.ik.a** Ps. **tayarish.w.a**, be prepared. (cf *tengeneza*) (Ar)
tayo *n* (*ma-*) reproach, censure, blame, rebuke, criticism: *Tayo la mzazi kwa mwanawe halina msingi*, the parent's blame on his child is baseless.
tayu (also *tayupau*) *n* (*n*) steelyard; a type of weighing machine. (cf *mizani*)
tayupau *n* (*n*) see *tayu*
tazam.a (also *tizama*) *vt, vi* 1. watch, look, gaze, see, view: *Tazama moto*

mkubwa ule, look at that big fire. (cf *angalia, ona*) 2. look after; take care of; provide basic necessities: *Kijana yule anawatazama wazee wake vizuri*, that young man looks after his parents well. (cf *angalia*) 3. beware, be cautious, be careful: *Tazama magari unapovuka barabara kuu*, be careful of vehicles when you cross the main road. (cf *tahadhari*) Prep. **tazam.i.a** St. **tazam.ik.a** Cs. **tazam.ish.a** Ps. **tazam.w.a** Rp. **tazam.an.a** (cf *tahadhari*)
tazaman.a *vi* 1. look at each other/one another: *Vijana wale wawili, wanatazamana*, those two youths look at each other. 2. be opposite, face each other: *Nyumba hizi mbili zinatazamana*, these two houses face each other.
tazami.a *vi* 1. consult a divining board; read the omens; see in the stars; tell fortunes: *Amekwenda kwa mganga kutazamia*, he has gone to the sorcerer to read the omens. 2. expect, hope; look forward: *Nilimtazamia mgeni wangu kufika hapa jana*, I expected my guest to arrive here yesterday. Ps. **tazami.w.a** (cf *tarajia, tumainia*)
tebo *n* (*n*) numerical table. (cf *jedwali*) (Eng)
tebwere[1] *adj* soft, squashy, pulpy, pappy, mushy, overripe: *Mimi sipendi kula ndizi tebwere*, I don't like to eat overripe bananas. (cf *tepetepe, laini*)
tebwere[2] *adv* used to emphasize the softness of sth: *Wametebwereka tebwere*, they are too soft.
tebwerek.a *vi* 1. be weak, be feeble, be frail: *Mtoto ametebwereka kwa njaa*, the child has become weak because of hunger. (cf *legea, fusika, lainika*) 2. be soft, be mushy: Prep. **tebwerek.e.a** St. **tebwerek.ek.a** Cs. **tebwerek.esh.a,** soften sth (cf *lainika*)

-tefutefu *adj* 1. (of food) soft, squashy, pulpy: *Alikula chakula kilicho kitefutefu,* she ate soft food. (cf *laini, tebwere*) 2. (of persons) soft, lenient, meek: *Usiwe mtefutefu mpaka watu wakakuchezea,* don't be so soft that people make fun of you.

teg.a¹ *vt* 1. snare, trap, enmesh, entrap, plant: *Tega mtego,* set a trap. *Tega bomu,* plant a bomb. *Tega saa,* set a watch. (cf *nasisha*) 2. used in the expressions: *Tega sikio,* cock an ear; listen attentively, pay attention: *Tega kazi,* shirk work. *Tega kitendawili,* propound a riddle. Prep. *teg.e.a* St. *teg.ek.a* Cs. *teg.esh.a* Ps. *teg.w.a* Rp. *teg.an.a* Rp. of Prep. *teg.e.an.a*

teg.a² (also *tegea*) *vt* (*fig*) deceive, cheat, beguile, swindle, hoodwink. Prep. *teg.e.a* St. *teg.ek.a* Cs. *teg.esh.a* Ps. *teg.w.a* Rp. *teg.an.a*

tega³ *interj* an expletive used during the uttering of a riddle.

tege (also *chege*) *adj* bowed, bending, twisted, bent: *Yeye ni matege,* he is bow-legged.

tege.a¹ (also *tega*) *vt* lay a trap for (against, etc.), trip up: *Alinitegea mguu nilipokuwa ninapita,* he tripped me with his leg when I was passing. St. *tege.k.a* Cs. *tege.sh.a* Ps. *tege.w.a* Rp. *tege.an.a*

tege.a² *vt, vi* shirk work, etc.: *Alikuwa hategei kazi yake abadan,* she never shirked her work. St. *tege.k.a* Cs. *tege.sh.a* Ps. *tege.w.a* Rp. *tege.an.a* (cf *zembea*)

tegeme.a *vt* 1. rely, depend, count on: *Nchi yetu inategemea utalii,* our country depends upon tourism. *Shule yao inajitegemea,* their school is self-reliant. (cf *angukia, egama*) 2. expect, hope, anticipate: *Ameanguka kwenye mtihani bila ya kutegemea,* he has failed the examination unexpectedly. *Ninategemea kusafiri karibu,* I hope to travel soon. *Inategemea,* it depends, (cf *tazamia, taraji, tumai*) 3. used in the expression: *Tegemea nundu,* be dependent upon someone who is wealthier, more capable, etc (than yourself). Prep. *tegeme.le.a* St. *tegeme.k.a* Cs. *tegeme.sh.a* Ps. *tegeme.w.a* Rp. *tegeme.an.a*

tegemeo *n* (*ma-*) 1. trust, dependence, protection: *Tegemeo lake liko kwa Mungu tu,* his trust lies in God only. 2. hope, expectation, anticipation: *Lipo tegemeo kwamba uchaguzi utafanyika karibu nchini,* there is hope that elections will soon take place in the country. (cf *tumaini, tarajio*)

-tegemevu *adj* honest, upright, upstanding: *Mtu mtegemevu,* an honest person.

-tegemezi *adj* dependent, relying: *Nchi tegemezi,* a dependent country. *Bajeti tegemezi,* a dependent budget. *Kishazi tegemezi,* a dependent clause. *Sentensi tegemezi,* a dependent sentence.

tego¹ *n* (*n*) (*med*) sexually transmitted diseases e.g. syphilis, gonorrhoea, etc.

tego² *n* (*n*) a piece of wood used by a circumciser while performing the operation; a circumciser's board.

tego³ *n* (*n*) charm protection by a wife.

tegu *n* (*ma-*) tapeworm

tegu.a¹ *vt* 1. disassemble a trap; defuse a bomb, etc.: *Askari wa polisi walilitegua bomu kwenye gari,* the policemen defused a bomb in the car. (cf *nasua, namua*) 2. (of a joint, etc.) sprain, dislocate: *Alilitegua bega lake kwenye mechi ya mpira,* he dislocated his shoulder during a soccer match. (cf *shtua, gutusha*) 3. (of a witchcraft) remove a magic spell; cast out a magic spell. Prep. *tegu.li.a* St. *tegu.k.a* Cs. *tegu.sh.a* Ps. of Prep. *tegu.liw.a* Rp. *tegu.an.a*

tegu.a² *vt* take off sth from the fire; remove sth like a pot from a stove, etc.: *Alilitegua birika la chai lilipoanza kuchemka,* he removed the kettle from the fire when the tea started to boil. Prep. *tegu.li.a* St. *tegu.k.a* Cs. *tegu.sh.a* Ps. of Prep. *tegu.liw.a* Rp. *tegu.an.a* (cf *ipua, telekua*)

teguk.a *vi* be dislocated, be sprained: *Goti lake limeteguka*, his knee is dislocated. Prep. *teguk.i.a* St. *teguk.ik.a* Cs. *teguk.ish.a*

tehem.u *vt* 1. disgrace, dishonour, discredit: *Kwa nini ulimtehemu rafiki yako hadharani?* Why did you disgrace your friend in public? (cf *aziri, aibisha*) 2. feel shy, feel bashful: *Hutehemu mbele za wanawake*, he feels shy in the presence of women. Prep. *tehem.i.a* St. *tehem.ik.a* Cs. *tehem.ish.a* Ps. *tehem.w.a* Rp. of Prep. *tehem.i.an.a*

teitei *n* (*ma-*) wide loose pants tucked around the waist and usu made of soft materials; loose pants.

tek.a¹ *vt* scoop up, take up, carry off, fetch: *Teka maji*, fetch water. Prep *tek.e.a* St. *tek.ek.a* Cs. *tek.esh.a* Ps. *tek.w.a* Rp. of Prep. *tek.e.an.a* (cf *chota, chopa*)

tek.a² *vt* 1. capture, ransack, seize, kidnap: *Adui aliuteka mji*, the enemy captured the town. (cf *kamata, shika, bemba*) 2. used in other expressions: *Teka nyara*, hijack, kidnap: *Teka mtu bakunja*, (a) fool someone (b) catch someone by surprise doing sth. *Teka akili*, fool someone. Prep. *tek.e.a* St. *tek.ek.a* Cs. *tek.esh.a* Ps. *tek.w.a*, Rp. *tek.an.a*

teka³ *n* (*n*) a small living room; a small sitting room; mini sitting room.

teke¹ *n* (*ma-*) 1. kick: *Piga teke*, kick someone or sth. (*prov*) *Teke la kuku halimwumizi mwewe*, a hen's kick cannot harm a hawk i.e. a parent's punishment cannot harm his child. It only teaches him to behave well. 2. (*idm*) *Piga teke*, expel someone; abandon someone.

teke² *adj* (of fruits, etc.) soft, squashy, squishy: *Embe teke*, a soft mango. *Papai teke*, a squashy pawpaw. (cf *laini*)

tekele.a *vt* be complete, be ready. Prep. *tekele.k.a* Cs. *tekele.sh.a* Ps. *tekele.w.a*

tekelez.a (also *tekeza*) *vt* fulfil, implement, execute: *Kamati iliyatekeleza maazimio yote*, the committee fulfilled all the resolutions. Prep. *tekelez.e.a* St. *tekelez.ek.a* Cs. *tekelez.esh.a* Ps. *tekelez.w.a*, (cf *timiza*)

tekelezo *n* (*ma-*) fulfilment, execution, implementation. (cf *kamilisho, timizo*)

tekeny.a¹ *vt* tickle, titillate, twiddle, stroke: *Alihamaki nilipomtekenya*, he became annoyed when I tickled him. Prep. *tekeny.e.a* St. *tekeny.ek.a* Cs. *tekeny.esh.a* Ps. *tekeny.w.a* Rp. *tekeny.an.a* (cf *nyegeza, nyega*)

tekenya² *n* (*n*) (*zool*) jigger, maggot, grub. (cf *funza*)

tekete.a *vi* 1. be devastated because of fire, flood, etc.; be ruined, be ravaged, be burnt down: *Nyaraka zote ziliteketea wakati jengo liliposhika moto*, all the documents were destroyed when the building caught fire. Prep. *tekete.le.a* St. *tekete.k.a* Cs. *tekete.z.a* Ps. of Cs. *tekete.z.w.a*, be destroyed, be annihilated. (cf *angamia, haribu*)

teketeke *adj* soft, marshy, boggy: *Papai teketeke*, a soft pawpaw. (cf *laini, tepetepe*)

teketez.a *vi* 1. (esp. of fire) destroy, ruin, burn, ravage: *Watu wasiojulikana walilliteketeza shambu kubwa*, unknown people burnt a big farm. 2. destroy, wreck, ruin: *Hawezi kuiteketeza mipango yetu*, he can't wreck our plans. Prep. *teketez.e.a* St. *teketez.ek.a* Cs. *teketez.esh.a* Ps. *teketez.w.a* Rp. *teketez.an.a* (cf *haribu, boronga, vuruga, angamiza*)

tekew.a *vi* be overwhelmed, be helpless, be indecisive: *Baada ya kuporwa mali yake yote, mwenye duka sasa ametekewa*, after being robbed of all his property, the shopkeeper has now become helpless. Prep. *tekew.e.a* St. *tekew.ek.a* Cs. *tekew.esh.a* (cf *hemewa*)

tekez.a *vt* see *tekeleza*

teknolojia *n* (*n*) technology: *Teknolojia tekelezi*, applied technology. *Teknolojia*

ya kisasa, modern technology. (Eng)
teksi n 1. taxi, cab: *Teksi bubu*, a taxi operating unofficially. 2. motorcar; a small car. (Eng)
teku.a vt 1. bring down sth with one shot e.g. a fruit off a tree with a stone or a stick: *Watoto waliyatekua maembe kwa mawe kutoka kwenye mwembe*, the children knocked down mangoes with stones from the mangoe tree. (cf *dengua, tengua, dekua*) 2. (of plants, etc.) uproot, unroot, pull out, root out: *Aliitekua baadhi ya mimea katika shamba lake*, he uprooted some of the seedlings in his farm. Prep. *teku.li.a* St. *teku.k.a* Cs. *teku.lish.a* and *teku.z.a* Ps. of Prep. *teku.liw.a* Rp. *teku.an.a* (cf *ng'oa, zidua, sekua*)
tele[1] adj filled to the brim; abundant, much, many: *Niletee gilasi tele ya maji*, bring me a full glass of water.
tele[2] adv in abundance, filled to, fully, overflowing; crowded, overloaded: *Watazamaji walijaa tele kwenye uwanja wa michezo*, the spectators were fully packed at the sports ground. (cf *pomoni, topu, kochokocho*)
telegramu n (n) telegram (Eng)
telek.a[1] vt (of cooking pot and the food in it) put on to cook; put on the fire: *Ameteleka chungu jikoni*, he has placed a cooking pot on the fire. Prep. *telek.e.a* St. *telek.ek.a* Cs. *telek.esh.a* Ps. *telek.w.a* (cf *injika*)
teleka[2] (also *telekatui*) n (n) (zool) swift; a kind of bird (family Apodidae) with a short tail and long, slender wings resembling the swallow. (cf *kizelele*)
telekatui n (n) see *teleka*[2]
telekevu adj obedient, compliant, servile, subservient: *Yeye ni mtumishi telekevu*, he is an obedient servant. (cf *nyenyekevu*)
telekez.a[1] vt 1. leave a project, etc after having started it; abandon, forsake: *Aliitelekeza gari yake ilipoharibika barabarani*, he abandoned his car when it broke down on the road.

2. leave sby to take some responsibilities for you. Prep. *telekez.e.a* St. *telekez.ek.a* Ps. *telekez.w.a* Rp. *telekez.an.a*
telekez.a[2] vt get cooking done; cook a meal: *Alikwenda jikoni na kutelekeza*, he went to the kitchen to cook food. Prep. *telekez.e.a* St. *telekez.ek.a* Ps. *telekez.w.a* Rp. *telekez.an.a*
teleksi n (n) telex (Eng)
teleprinta n (n) teleprinter (Eng)
televisheni n (n) television (cf *runinga*) (Eng)
telez.a vi 1. (of liquids) be slippery: *Grisi hii inateleza*, this grease is slippery. (cf *nyiririka*) 2. slip, skid, fall: *Aliumia vibaya alipoteleza*, he was badly injured when he slipped. (cf *serereka, sepetuka*) 3. be slippery: *Pahala hapa panateleza*, this place is slippery. 4. (fig) go astray; go askew. 5. (idm) *Teleza ulimi*, prattle.
teli n (n) gold or silver thread.
telki (also *dalki*) n (n) the quick ambling gait of a horse or donkey: *Enda telki*, amble in this way; trot. (Hind)
tem.a[1] vt chop, cut: *Tema kuni*, cut firewood. Prep. *tem.e.a* St. *tem.ek.a* Cs. *tem.esh.a* Ps. *tem.w.a* Rp. *tem.an.a* (cf *kata, chenga*)
tem.a[2] vt, vi 1. spit, expectorate: *Tema mate*, spit. 2. (in sports) fumble: *Golikipa aliutema mpira kutokana na shuti kali la mchezaji*, the goalkeeper fumbled the ball following a hard shot from the player. 3. drop: *Timu ilimtema kipa wao*, the team dropped their goalkeeper. Prep. *tem.e.a* St. *tem.ek.a* Cs. *tem.esh.a* Ps. *tem.w.a* Rp. *tem.an.a*
tembe[1] n (n) (zool) a hen ready to lay eggs; a layer hen. (cf *mtamba, mtetea*)
tembe[2] n (n) a flat-roofed house.
tembe[3] n (n) pill, tablet: *Tembe ya vitamini*, vitamin tablet. *Tembe ya aspirini*, an aspirin tablet. (cf *chembe, punje, kidonge*)
tembe[4] adj little, small: *Kuna maji tembe*

tembe.a tendeti

bakulini, there is little water in the bowl. (cf *chache, kidogo*)
tembe.a *vi* 1. walk, stroll; move around. (*prov*) *Chema chajiuza kibaya chajitembeza*, a good thing sells itself, a bad one advertises itself for sale i.e a good thing attracts, a bad one forces its way for publicity, recognition, etc. (cf *zunguka, randa, zurura*) 2. move around for sex; womanize. (cf *zini*) Prep. ***tembe.le.a*** St. ***tembe.lek.a*** Cs. ***tembe.z.a*** Ps. of Prep. ***tembe.lew.a*** Rp. of Prep. ***tembe.le.an.a*** (cf *zini*)
tembele.a *vt* 1. visit: *Aliitembelea Ugiriki mwaka jana*, he visited Greece last year. 2. walk with: *Tembelea kwa mkongojo*, walk with a stick. St. ***tembele.k.a*** Cs. ***tembele.sh.a*** Ps. ***tembele.w.a*** Rp. ***tembele.an.a***
tembez.a *vt* 1. take sby around, show sby around. Prep. ***tembez.e.a*** St. ***tembez.ek.a*** Ps. ***tembez.w.a*** Ps. ***tembez.an.a***
tembo[1] *n* (*n*) (*zool*) elephant: (*prov*) *Ukimwiga tembo kunya, utapasuka mwaranda*, if you imitate an elephant defecating, your anus will burst i.e. don't imitate things of which you are not capable. *Mkono wa tembo*, a kind of plantain, which is long and big.
tembo[2] *n* (*n*) coconut palmwine, i.e. the fermented sap of a coconut tree. (*prov*) *Mgema akisifiwa tembo hulitia maji*, if the palmwine tapper is praised, he dilutes the palmwine with water i.e. if a person is praised too much for sth, he may lose his qualities as an expert.
tembo[3] (also *kitembwe*) *n* (*n*) (*zool*) blackspot snapper; a kind of saltwater fish (family *Lutjanidae*) with horizontal golden stripes and a black blotch. (cf *janja*)
temsi *n* (*n*) filigree, arabesque; an ornamental work or design made on the handle of a knife, sword, etc. (Pers)
temu.a *vt* make a hole in a tree e.g. when preparing to make a beehive or mortar; hollow out a log, etc. Prep. ***temu.li.a*** St. ***temu.k.a*** Cs. ***temu.sh.a*** Ps. of Prep. ***temu.liw.a***

tena[1] *conj* besides, in addition, furthermore: *Yeye ni mjeuri; tena ni mgomvi*, he is rude; in addition, he is quarrelsome. (cf *isitoshe, vilevile*)
tena[2] *adv* again, still: *Alifika hapa jana na atakuja tena leo*, he came here yesterday and he will come again today.
tena[3] *adv* an expletive used to confirm sth usu unexpected: a) *Alitaka kutuhujumu*, he wanted to attack us. b) *Tena iliishiaje?* So how did it end?
tend.a[1] *vt* 1. do, act, perform: *Tenda vizuri*, perform well. (cf *fanya, tekeleza*) 2. commit an evil act; mistreat: *Yeye amenitenda*, he has wronged me. (*prov*) *Akutendaye mtende, mche asiyekutenda*, do harm to him who harms you and fear him who harms you not. Prep. ***tend.e.a***, do for (to, etc.) St. ***tend.ek.a*** Ps. ***tend.w.a*** Rp. ***tend.an.a*** Rp. of Prep. ***tend.e.an.a***
tenda[2] *n* (*n*) tender, bid. (cf *zabuni*) (Eng)
tende[1] *n* (*ma-*) (*med*) elephantiasis
tende[2] *n* (*n*) (*bot*) date fruit; fruit of the datepalm, *mtende*.
tendegu (also *tendeguu*) *n* (*ma-*) the leg of a bed; bed's leg.
tendeguu *n* (*ma-*) see *tendegu*
tendek.a *vi* be accomplished, be done: *Kazi hii inatendeka*, this work can be done. Prep. ***tendek.e.a*** St. ***tendek.ek.a*** Cs. ***tendek.ez.a***
tendekez.a[1] *vt* see *endekeza*
tendekez.a[2] *vi* pretend to be sick; malinger: *Mwanafunzi yule haumwi; anajitendekeza tu*, that student is not sick; he only malingers. Prep. ***tendekez.e.a*** St. ***tendekez.ek.a*** Cs. ***tendekez.esh.a*** Ps. ***tendekez.w.a*** Rp. ***tendekez.an.a***
tendes.a *vt* exceed, overstep, go beyond the limit: *Mtu yule ametendesa kwa kupenda kucheza kamari*, that person is obsessed with gambling. Prep. ***tendes.e.a*** St. ***tendes.ek.a*** Cs. ***tendes.esh.a*** (cf *kithiri, zidi*)
tendeti *n* (*n*) a kind of small doughnut

made from wheat flour or rice and sugar mixed in coconut juice.
tendo *n* (*n*) act, action, deed. (cf *kitendo, amali*)
tendwa *n* (*n*) remedy, cure; any medicine or treatment that cures, heals or relieves a disease, etc.: *Maradhi yake hayana tendwa*, her disease has no treatment.
teng.a¹ *vt* isolate, excommunicate, exclude, bar, separate: *Jamii yake imemtenga kijana yule*, his society has ostracized that young person. *Niliyatenga mayai mabovu na yale yaliyo mazima*, I separated the bad eggs from the good ones. Prep. **teng.e.a** St. **teng.ek.a** Cs. **teng.esh.a** Ps. **teng.w.a** Rp. **teng.an.a**
tenga² *n* (*ma-*) crate, case; a hamper of wickerwork or a container made from palm leaf stalks, used for carrying things: *Katika tenga hili, mna mapapai mengi*, in this crate, there are many pawpaws. (cf *susu, dohani*)
tenga³ *n* (*n*) (*zool*) a very large kind of batoid fish (family *Mobulidae/Myliobatidae*) with a long tail.
tenga⁴ *n* (*ma-*) a kind of snare for trapping birds and some wild animals.
tengan.a *vi* 1. be separated, be isolated. 2. be estranged, be separated: *Mume na mkewe sasa wametengana*, the husband and his wife are now separated. Prep. **tengan.i.a** St. **tengan.ik.a** Cs. **tengan.ish.a**
tenganish.a *vt* 1. separate: *Kwa nini unayatenganisha mayai haya katika kikapu hiki?* Why are you separating the eggs in this basket? 2 separate, estrange: *Kijana yule aliwatenganisha mume na mkewe bila ya kukusudia*, that youth estranged the husband and his wife unintentionally. Prep. **tenganish.i.a** St. **tenganish.ik.a** Ps. **tenganish.w.a**
tenge¹ *adv* astray, afield, awry, adrift, off the track: *Mambo yake yamekwenda tenge*, her affairs have gone awry. (cf *kombo, shoto, ndivyosivyo*)
tenge² *n* (*n*) chaos, confusion, disorder, uproar, broil, turmoil: *Tenge ilitokea wakati mpigaji-kura alipozuiliwa kupiga kura kituoni*, chaos erupted when a voter was stopped from voting at the polling station. (cf *ghasia, fujo*)
tenge.a¹ *vi* see *tengemaa*
tenge.a¹ *vt, vi* keep sth aside for sby. Prep. **tenge.le.a**
tengema.a (also *tengea, tengenea*) *vi* be back to normal after a country, etc. has experienced famine, war, etc.; be at peace; settle down: *Uchumi wa nchi ya jirani sasa umetengemaa baada ya kuanguka kwa kipindi kirefu*, the economy of the neighbouring country has now improved after a long period of recession. Prep. **tengem.ek.a** Cs. **tengem.ez.a** (cf *nyooka*)
tengene.a *vi* see *tengemaa*
tengenez.a (also *tengeza*) *vt* 1. manufacture, construct, make, build: *Kiwanda chao kinatengeneza gari*, their factory manufactures cars. (cf *fanya, unda*) 2. repair, mend, patch up: *Aliitengeneza saa yangu*, he repaired my watch. Prep. **tengenez.e.a** St. **tengenez.ek.a** Cs. **tengenez.esh.a** Ps. **tengenez.w.a** (cf *sahihisha, rekebisha, sawazisha*)
tengenezo *n* (*ma-*) 1. manufacture, construction, production, building. (cf *uundaji, matengenezo, utengenezaji*) 2. repairs, mending, maintenance.
tengez.a *vt* see *tengeneza*
tengu.a¹ (also *tangua*) *vt* 1. rescind, revoke, annul, invalidate, repeal, abrogate: *Mahakama iliutengua ubunge wa mwakilishi katika jimbo letu*, the court nullified the parliamentarianship of the representative in our constituency. (cf *batilisha*) 2. differentiate, distinguish. Prep. **tengu.li.a** St. **tengu.k.a** Cs. **tengu.lish.a** Ps. of Prep. **tengu.liw.a** Rp. **tengu.an.a** (cf *tofautisha*)
tengu.a² *vt* release a trap, spring, etc.; remove sth with a shot or blow:

Aliyatengua maembe kutoka kwenye kitawi cha mti kwa pigo moja, he knocked down the mangoes from the branch of the tree with only one shot. Prep. ***tengu.li.a*** St. ***tenguk.a*** Cs. ***tengu.sh.a*** Ps. of Prep. ***tengu.liw.a*** Rp. ***tengu.an.a*** (cf *tekua, tegua, dengua*)
tenisi *n* (*n*) tennis: *Kiwanja cha tenisi*, tennis court. (Eng)
teo *n* (*n*) a sling for throwing stones, etc. consisting of a piece of leather or rope that is whirled by hand for releasing the missile. (cf *kumbwewe, manati, kombeo*)
tepe (also *utepe*) *n* (*n*) medal, decoration; badge of honour: *Askari alitunukiwa tepe kwa kazi yake nzuri*, the policeman was given a medal for his good work. (cf *nishani*)
tepet.a *vi* see *tepetea*
tepete.a (also *tepeta*) *vi* be weak, be lazy: *Mfanyakazi wako ametepetea*, your worker is lazy. St. ***tepete.k.a*** Cs. ***tepete.sh.a*** (cf *bweteka, zorota, regea*)
tepetepe[1] *adj* soft, squashy, mushy: *Tunda tepetepe*, a mushy fruit. (cf *laini, tebwere*)
tepetepe[2] *adj* plentiful, many, a lot: *Ana habari tepetepe*, he has a lot of news.
tepetepe[3] *adv* fast, hurriedly. (cf *wanguwangu*)
-tepetevu *adj* weak, loose, limp, lazy, indolent: *Yeye ni mtumishi mtepetevu*, he is a lazy servant.
tepo *n* (*n*) pride, arrogance, conceit, boastfulness: *Watu hawampendi mtu yule kutokana na tepo zake*, people don't like that person because of his arrogance. (cf *majivuno, maringo*)
tepu (also *tepurekoda*) *n* (*n*) tape, tapemeasure; an instrument for measuring the length of sth.
tepu.a *vt* tire, enervate, fatigue, wear: *Vitendo viovu vya mtoto vilimtepua hatimaye mzazi wake*, the child's evil deeds eventually tired his parent. Prep. ***tepu.li.a*** St. ***tepu.k.a*** Cs. ***tepu.sh.a*** Ps. of Prep. ***tepu.liw.a*** Rp. ***tepu.an.a***
terafini *n* (*n*) turpentine (Eng)
terebesha *n* (*n*) brink, edge, rim, border, margin: *Baharia alikaa kwenye terebesha ya jahazi*, the sailor sat on the edge of the dhow. (cf *pambizo, mleoleo, ukingo*)
terekta (also *trekta*) *n* (*n*) tractor (cf *tingatinga*) (Eng)
terem.a (also *teremea*) *vi* be cheerful, be happy, be lively: *Aliterema aliposikia kwamba ameshinda kwenye bahati nasibu*, he was happy when he heard that he had won the lottery. Prep. ***terem.e.a*** St. ***terem.ek.a*** Cs. ***terem.esh.a*** Ps. ***terem.w.a*** (cf *changamka, furahi*)
tereme.a *vi* see *terema*
teremk.a (also *teremua*) *vt* descend, alight, dismount, disembark; come down, go down. Prep. ***teremk.i.a*** St. ***teremk.ik.a*** Cs. ***terem.sh.a*** (cf *shuka*)
teremsh.a *vt* 1. offload, unload: *Makuli waliiteremsha mizigo kutoka kwenye meli*, the coolies unloaded the goods from the ship. (cf *shusha*) 2. (of prices, etc.) lower down: *Wafanyabiashara waliiteremsha bei ya sukari*, the businessmen lowered the price of sugar. Prep. ***teremsh.i.a*** St. ***teremsh.ik.a*** Ps. ***teremsh.w.a*** Rp. ***teremsh.an.a***
teremu.a *vt,vi* see *teremka*
tes.a *vt, vi* torture, persecute, torment: *Wanajeshi waliwatesa wafungwa*, the soldiers tortured the prisoners. Prep. ***tes.e.a*** St. ***tes.ek.a*** Cs. ***tes.esh.a*** Ps. ***tes.w.a*** Rp. ***tes.an.a*** (cf *adhibu, dhili, kandamiza*)
tet.a *vi* 1. quarrel, wrangle, dispute: *Waliteta kwa mambo ya upuuzi*, they quarrelled on flimsy grounds. (cf *gombana, bishana*) 2. speak against;

talk about someone behind his back; backbite: *Aliteta dhidi yangu kwa vile nilikataa kumwazima gari yangu,* he talked about me behind my back because I refused to lend him my car. St. *tet.ek.a* Cs. *tet.esh.a* Ps. *tet.w.a* Rp. *tet.an.a* (cf *sengenya*)
tete¹ *n* (*ma-*) reed, *Arundo phragmites. Mabua ya matete,* the stalks of reeds.
tete² *adj* used in expression: *Enda tete,* walk unsteadily.
tete⁴ *adj* sensitive, explosive, serious, critical: *Hali tete,* sensitive situation. *Suala tete,* sensitive issue.
tete⁴ *n* (*n*) slag; waste matter that remains after iron has been extracted from ore.
tete⁵ *n* (*n*) see *tetekuwanga*
tete.a¹ *vi* 1. cackle like a hen: *Kuku alitetea alipokuwa anataka kutaga,* the hen cackled when it was about to lay eggs. 2. recite or sing a poem, etc. by heart and with pomposity: *Watoto wa shule walilisoma shairi kwa kutetea,* the school children recited the poem in a melodious voice. Ps. *tete.w.a*
tete.a² *vt* defend, speak for: *Wakili alimtetea mshtakiwa kwenye kosa la jinai,* the lawyer defended the accused on criminal charges. Prep. *tete.le.a* St. *tete.k.a* Ps. *tete.w.a* Rp. *tete.an.a*
tetekuwanga (also *tete, tetemaji*) *n* (*n*) (*med*) chicken pox. (cf *tetewanga*)
tetelek.a *vi* see *tetereka*
tetem.a *vi* tremble, shiver, shudder, shake: *Alikuwa akitetema kwa baridi,* he was trembling with cold. Prep. *tetem.e.a* St. *tetem.ek.a* Cs. *tetem.esh.a* Ps. *tetem.w.a* (cf *tikisika, taharuki, gwaya*)
tetemaji *n* (*n*) see *tetekuwanga*
tetemek.a (also *tetema*) *vi* tremble, shake, quiver, shiver: *Mgonjwa alikuwa akitetemeka kwa baridi,* the sick person was trembling with cold. Prep. *tetemek.e.a* St. *tetemek.ek.a* Cs. *tetemek.esh.a* Ps. *tetemek.ew.a*
tetemeko *n* (*n*) earthquake, tremor, seism: *Tetemeko la ardhi,* earthquake. *Tetemeko lilipotokea nchini, watu wengi walikufa,* when the earthquake occurred in the country, many people died. (cf *zilizala*)
tetere *n* (*n*) (*zool*) ring-necked dove; a kind of dove with a black collar on the hind neck and pale-grey and white underparts. (*Streptopelia capicola*)
teterek.a (also *teteleka*) *vi* 1. stagger, wobble, sway: *Alitetereka njiani alipolewa sana,* he staggered along the road while he was very drunk. (cf *pepesuka, sesereka*) 2. be slightly disabled; be sprained a little: *Mkono wake umetetereka,* his arm is slightly sprained. (cf *teguka, teuka*) 3. (*fig*) be spoiled, be ruined: *Maisha yake yametetereka,* his life is ruined. Prep. *teterek.e.a* St. *teterek.ek.a* Cs. *teterek.esh.a* Ps. of Prep. *teterek. ew.a* (cf *haribika, vurugika*)
teteresh.a *vt* make sby/sth restless, uneasy etc; make sby/sth lose the necessary stability; shake waver: *Huwezi kabisa kumteteresha kiongozi yule kwa kumwekea vikwazo vya kiuchumi,* you don't at all make that leader waver by imposing on him economic sanctions. Prep. *teteresh.e.a* St. *teteresh.ek.a* St. *teteresh.ek.a* Ps. *teteresh.w.a* Rp. *teteresh.an.a*
tetesi *n* (*n*) rumour, gossip: *Kuna tetesi kwamba serikali itaongeza mishahara ya wafanyakazi wake,* there are rumours that the government will increase the salaries of its workers. (cf *penyenye, mnong'ono, fununu, uvumi*)
teu.a *vt* select, appoint, nominate, designate: *Walimteua kuwa kiranja wa shule yao,* they appointed him as their school prefect. Prep. *teu.li.a* St. *teu.lik.a* Cs. *teu.lish.a* Ps. of Prep. *teu.liw.a,* be appointed, be selected Rp. *teu.an.a* (cf *chagua*)
teuk.a¹ *vi* belch, eructate; expel gas through the mouth from the stomach: *Aliposhiba, akateuka,* when his stomach was full, he belched. Prep.

teu.ki.a St. **teuk.ik.a** Cs. **teu.sh.a** (cf *cheuka*)
teuk.a² *vi* be sprained a little. Prep. **teuk.i.a** St. **teuk.ik.a** Cs. **teu.sh.a** (cf *tetereka*)
-teule *adj* elected, chosen: *Rais mteule, president-elect. Mwenyekiti mteule*, the chairman elect.
teushi *n* (*n*) odorous belching, halitosis; a gas that usually comes out during belching. (cf *tombovu*)
tewengu *n* (*n*) worry, anxiety, fright: *Alimtia tewengu*, he frightened her. (cf *wahaka, dududuku, wasiwasi*)
tezi¹ *n* (*ma-*) (*naut*), stern of a ship, dhow, etc. (Pers)
tezi² *n* (*n*) (*med*) glandular swelling; wen: *Tezi ya kikoromeo*, swelling of the thyroid. *Tezi ya shingo*, cervical lymphadenopathy; lymphedonosis. *Tezi ya mate*, swelling of the salivary gland.
tezi³ *n* (*n*) an organ that separates certain elements from the blood and secretes them in a form for further use.
tezo *n* (*n*) adze; an axe like tool with a curved blade at right angles to the handle, used to shape wood in boat building, masonry, etc.
thabiti *adj* 1. firm, resolute, steadfast, determined: *Ana moyo thabiti*, he has a firm stand. *Moyo wake ni thabiti*, his stand is firm. (cf *imara, hadidi*) 2. true, actual, real: *Kauli yake ni thabiti*, his statement is true. (cf *sahihi*) (Ar)
thakala *n* (*n*) difficulty, complexity, problem. (cf *takilifa, taabu, shida*)
thakili¹ *adj* 1. difficult, hard, tough: *Inahitaji kuwa na subira kuifanya kazi thakili kama ile*, it requires patience to do a difficult job like that one. 2. mean, wicked, evil: *Mtu thakili yule hatakusaidia kitu*, that mean person will not help you in anything. (Ar)
thakili² *n* (*n*) difficulty, hardships: *Naona thakili kumchukulia hatua*, I find it difficult to take action against him. (cf *taabu, dhiki*) (Ar)
thakilish.a *vt* hassle, harass, hector, mistreat, bother: *Tajiri aliwathakilisha sana wafanyakazi wake*, the employer mistreated very much his workers. Prep. **thakilish.i.a** St. **thakilish.ik.a** Ps. **thakilish.w.a** Rp. **thakilish.an.a** (cf *nyanyasa, taabisha*) (Ar)
thalathini (also *thelathini*) *adj, n* (*n*) thirty: *Watu thalathini*, thirty people. (Ar)
thama *conj* (rarely used) except, but, save: *Asingefika hapa thama alikuwa na shida*, he would not have come here save that he had problems. (cf *ila, isipokuwa*) (Ar)
thamani *n* (*n*) value, price, cost: *Thamani ya nyumba hii ni shilingi milioni kumi*, the value of this house is ten million shillings. *Thamani halisi*, absolute value. *Thamani rejeo*, definite integral. (cf *bei, gharama*) (Ar)
thamanini¹ (also *themanini*) *adj, n* (*n*) eighty: *Viti thamanini*, eighty chairs. (Ar)
thamanini² *n* (*n*) a kind of light cotton material white in colour. (Ar)
thamin.i *vt* 1. value, evaluate, estimate: *Wakaguzi walilithamini shamba langu*, the inspectors valued my farm. (cf *kadirisha, tathmini*) 2. respect, revere, adore, venerate: *Simthamini mtu yule kwa sababu ya unafiki wake*, I don't respect that person because of his hypocrisy. (*prov*) *Asiyekujua hakuthamini*, he who does not know you, will not value you. (cf *heshimu, stahi, tii*) (Ar) Prep. **thamin.i.a** St. **thamin.ik.a** Cs. **thamin.ish.a** Ps. **thamin.iw.a** Rp. of Prep. **thamin.i.an.a**, respect each other (Ar)
thamomita *n* (*n*) see *themomita*
thamra *n* (*n*) (*bot*) young cloves when just beginning to form. (Ar)
thaura *n* (*n*) revolution: *Kulikuwa na thaura katika nchi ya jirani*, there was a revolution in the neighbouring country. (cf *mapinduzi*) (Ar)
thawabu *n* (*n*) reward from God; blessings: *Ukiwasaidia masikini, utapata thawabu kwa Mwenyezi Mungu*, if you help the poor, you will

get rewards from God. (cf *jaza*) (Ar)
thelathini n (n) see *thalathini*
theluji n (n) snow: *Bonge la theluji*, snowball. (Ar)
theluthi (also *thuluthi*) n (n) one third: *Theluthi moja ya watu katika mtaa huu ni wanaume*, one third of the people in this neighbourhood are men. (Ar)
themanini n (n) see *thamanini*
themometa (also *thamomita*) n (n) thermometer (cf *kipimajoto*) (Eng)
thenashara n (n) see *thinashara*
theolojia (also *thiolojia*) n (n) theology; the study of the nature of God and religious truth. (Eng)
thibit.i vt be established, be proved, be confirmed: *Imethibiti kwamba maelezo ya mshtakiwa ni ya kweli*, it has proved that the statement of the accused is true. Prep. **thibit.i.a** St. **thibit.ik.a** Cs. **thibit.ish.a**
thibitik.a vi be confirmed, be proved: *Imethibitika kwamba mchezaji wa kiungo alimpiga refarii kwa makusudi*, it is confirmed that the midfield player beat the referee deliberately. Prep. **thibitik.i.a** St. **thibitik.ik.a** Rp. **thibitik.an.a** (cf *sadikika*)
thibitish.a vt prove, confirm, ratify: *Anaweza kuithibitisha kauli yake?* Can he verify his statement?. Prep **thibitish.i.a** St **thibitish.ik.a** Ps **thibitish.w.a**, be confirmed e.g. *Taarifa yake imethibitishwa na msemaji wa serikali*, his statement has been confirmed by the government's spokesman. (cf *sadikisha*, *yakinisha*) (Ar)
thibitisho n (ma-) proof, evidence, validation, confirmation: *Hakuna thibitisho lolote kwamba yeye aliiba pesa za benki*, there is no evidence that she stole the bank's money. (cf *hakikisho*, *ithibiti*) (Ar)
thieta n (n) 1. theatre; a place where plays, operas, etc. are presented: *Thieta ya majaribio*, experimental theatre. *Thieta ya umma*, popular theatre. 2. a surgical clinic. (Eng)
thinashara (also *thenashara*) adj, n (n)

twelve. (Ar)
thiolojia n (n) see *theolojia*
thomo n (n) see *saumu*²
thori n (n) (of men) unable to perform a sexual act; an impotent person. (cf *hanithi*, *msenge*) (Ar)
thubut.u¹ (also *subutu*) vt dare, venture, brave, hazard: *Alithubutu kumkabili simba*, he dared to face the lion. St. **thubut.ik.a** Cs. **thubut.ish.a** Ps. of Prep. **thubut.iw.a** (cf *jasiri*, *diriki*) (Ar)
thubutu² (also *subutu*) interj an expletive used to show contempt or to challenge someone to do sth he has boasted about; Just you try! I dare you! (cf *mashudu*) (Ar)
thubut.u³ vt come true, confirm, prove, show: *Maelezo yake yamethubutu kwamba yeye ni mtu mkweli*, his statement has confirmed that he is an honest person. St. **thubut.ik.a** Cs. **thubut.ish.a** Ps of Prep. **thubut.iw.a** (cf *dhihirika*, *bainika*) (Ar)
thuluthi n (n) see *theluthi*
thumni n (n) 1. one eighth of a section, etc. 2. (*arch*) one eighth of a riyal. 3. a fifty cent coin.
thurea n (n) (*astron*) constellation (Pleiades); a cluster of stars which predict the arrival of rain. (cf *kilimia*) (Ar)
ti adv used to emphasize the total blackness of an object; a deep lustrous black; jet black: *Nyeusi ti*, jet black.
ti.a vt put in, insert; *Ametia sukari nyingi katika chai*, he has put a lot of sugar in the tea (cf *weka*, *ingiza*, *penyeza*) 2. (*idms*) *Tia chumvi*, exaggerate. *Tia fora*, be outstanding. *Tia hasara*, cause a loss. *Tia hofu*, frighten. *Tia moyo*, encourage. *Tia aibu*, disgrace. *Tia rangi*, paint; put a paint. *Tia nanga*, drop an anchor. *Tia risasi*, solder; join things with solder. *Tia sahihi*, sign. *Tia huruma*, cause sympathy. *Tia uchungu*, cause sadness. *Tia hatiani*, implicate; be judged guilty. *Tia wasiwasi*, cause anxiety. *Tia dawa*, apply medicine. *Tia adabu*, punish. *Tia makali*, sharpen. *Tia mimba*, impregnate. Prep. **ti.li.a**

St *ti.lik.a* Cs. *ti.lish.a* Ps. of Prep. *ti.liw.a* Rp. of Prep. *ti.li.an.a*
tiabu *n* (*n*) a game played by throwing bits of sticks and watching how they fall; a stick throwing game.
tiara[1] *n* (*n*) kite (cf *kishada, kisulisuli*)
tiara[2] *n* (*n*) crown (cf *taji*)
tiba *n* (*n*) 1. medicine as a discipline: *Kitivo cha tiba*, faculty of medicine. *Tiba mifupa*, orthopaedics. *Tiba maungo*, physiotherapy. *Tiba kemikali*, chemotherapy. 2. medical treatment: *Alipata tiba nzuri kwa daktari*, he got good medical treatment from the doctor. (cf *matibabu, dawa*) (Ar)
tib.u *vt* treat medically; cure, heal. Prep. *tib.i.a* St. *tib.ik.a, ugonjwa ule unatibika*, that disease is curable. Cs. *tib.ish.a* Ps. of Prep. *tib.iw.a* Rp. of Prep. *tib.i.an.a* (cf *ganga, opoa*) (Ar)
tibu.a *vt* unsettle, mess up, stir up: *Watoto waliyatibua maji kwenye kidimbwi*, the children stirred up water in the pond. Prep. *tibu.li.a* St. *tibu.lik.a* Cs. *tibu.lish.a* Ps. of Prep. *tibu.liw.a* Rp. *tibu.an.a* (cf *vuruga, paraganya*)
tibuk.a *vi* be unsettled, be messed up.
tibwatibwa *n* (*n*) see *tipwatipwa*
tibwirik.a *vi* 1. shake the body like someone dancing: *Nilimwona akitibwirika katika ngoma*, I saw her shaking her body at the local dance. 2. (*of body*) be weak, be loose. Prep. *tibwirik.i.a* St. *tibwirik.ik.a* Cs. *tibwirik.ish.a*
tifu[1] *adj* dusty
tifu[2] *n* (*ma-*) chaos, pandemonium. (cf *vurugu, fujo*)
tifu.a *vt* 1. raise dust; stir up dust: *Farasi alitifua vumbi alipopita kwa kasi*, the horse raised dust when it passed fast. 2. loosen soil; soften soil. Prep. *tifu.li.a* St. *tifu.k.a*, be capable of raising dust. Cs. *tifu.sh.a* Ps. of Prep. *tifu.liw.a*
tifuk.a[1] *vi* see *tifua*
tifuk.a[2] *vi* be cultivable with easiness; be easily suitable for cultivation; be easily arable. Prep. *tifuk.i.a* St. *tifuk.ik.a* Cs. *tifuk.ish.a* (cf *limika*)

-tifutifu *adj* (of sand, etc.) powdery, loose: *Huu ni mchanga tifutifu*, this is powdery sand.
tig.a *vt* pound sth like clay, sand, etc by using hands or legs: *Aliyatiga madonge ya mchanga kwa miguu*, he pounded the lumps of sand with his feet. Prep. *tig.i.a* St. *tig.ik.a* Cs. *tig.ish.a* Ps. *tig.w.a* Rp. *tig.an.a*
ti.i[1] *vt* revere, obey, observe, comply with, respect: *Anawatii wazee wake sana*, he respects his parents a lot. Prep. *ti.i.a* St. *ti.ik.a* Cs. *ti.ish.a* Ps. *ti.iw.a* Rp. of Prep. *ti.i.an.a* (cf *fuata, heshimu*) (Ar)
tii[2] *intcrj* an expletive for emphasing the blackness of sth. (cf *tititi*)
-tiifu *adj* obedient, respectful, subservient: *Mtumishi mtiifu*, an obedient servant. (cf *maridhia, -sikivu*) (Ar)
tija *n* (*n*) see *natija*
tijara *n* (*n*) 1. profit, surplus (cf *faida*) 2. wealth, riches (cf *ukwasi, utajiri*) (Ar)
tik.a *vi* rattle, chatter, rock. (*prov*) *Debe shinda haliachi kutika*, an empty tin never stops sounding, i.e. a useless person never stops talking nonsense. Prep. *tik.i.a* St. *tik.ik.a* Cs. *tik.ish.a* Ps. *tik.w.a* (cf *dugika*)
tikatik.a *vi* be rattling, be rocking. (cf *tika, dugika*)
tiki *adv* completely, an expletive used to emphasize the complete state of exhaustion or laxity: *Amechoka tiki*, he is completely exhausted.
tikinyik.a *vi* laugh foolishly until one's body shakes: *Alipopata habari nzuri alitikinyika*, when he got good news, his body shook with laughter. Prep. *tikinyik.i.a* St. *tikinyik.ik.a* Cs. *tikinyik.ish.a*
tikis.a (also *tingisha*) *vt* 1. shake, wave: *Aliitikisa chupa*, he shook the bottle. 2. (colloq) Prep. *tikis.i.a* St. *tikis.ik.a* Cs. *tikis.ish.a* Ps. *tikis.w.a* Rp. *tikis.an.a* (cf *suka, tukusa*)
tikisik.a *vi* be shaken: *Eneo lote limetikisika kufuatia tetemeko la ardhi*,

the entire area vibrated following the earthquake. Prep. *tikisik.i.a* St. *tikisik.ik.a* Cs. *tikisik.ish.a*
tikit.a¹ *vt* enjoy sleep: *Ameutikita usingizi*, he is sleeping soundly. Prep. *tikit.i.a* St. *tikit.ik.a* Cs. *tikit.ish.a* Ps. *tikit.w.a* Rp. *tikit.an.a*
tikit.a² *vt* see *chikicha*
tikiti¹ (also *tiketi*) *n* (*n*) ticket, pass: *Mkusanyaji wa tiketi*, ticket collector. *Mkaguzi wa tiketi*, ticket inspector. *Tikiti bandia*, fake ticket. (cf *nauli*) (Eng)
tikiti² *n* (*bot*) water melon; a kind of edible fruit with a hard, green rind and juicy, pink or red pulp containing many seeds. (cf *tikimaji*)
tikitiki *adj* soft, squashy: *Mtama wake umekuwa tikitiki baada ya kusagwa*, his millet has been ground to powder. (cf *teketeke, tepetepe*)
tilifik.a *vi* be lost, be destroyed. Prep. *tilifik.i.a* St. *tilifik.ik.a* Cs. *tilifik.ish.a* (cf *angamia, hiliki*)
tilif.u *vi* be weary, be exhausted. Prep. *tilif.i.a* St. *tilif.ik.a* Cs. *tilif.ish.a*
timamu *adj* complete, sound: *Ana akili timamu*, he has a sound mind. (cf *kamilifu, timilifu*) (Ar)
timasi *n* (*n*) see *timazi*
timazi (also *timasi*) *n* (*ma-*) mason's plummet; plumb. (cf *bildi, chubwi*) (Ar)
timb.a¹ *vt* 1. trod on mud, excrement, etc and get them stuck: *Aliyatimba matope alipokuwa anapita usiku mitaani*, he trod on the mud when he was walking at night in the neighbourhood. (cf *kanyaga, vyoga*) 2. spend lavishly: *Alizitimba fedha zake zote*, he spent all his money lavishly. 3. hassle, pester, hector, bother (cf *sumbua, taabisha*) Prep. *timb.i.a* St. *timb.ik.a* Cs. *timb.ish.a* Ps. *timb.w.a* Rp. *timb.an.a*
timba² *n* (*n*) a string of beads or cowries.
timba³ *n* (*n*) (*bot*) cereal grain used to make local beer; malt.
timbe *n* (*n*) a lump of cast or unwrought metal. (cf *mkuo*)

timbi *n* (*n*) bracelet, armlet, bangle (cf *udodi, bangili, kikuku*)
timi.a (also *timia*) *vi* be complete; be ready; be accomplished: *Zana zake zote zimetimia*, all his tools are complete. 2. be concluded. Prep. *timi.li.a* St. *timi.lik.a* Cs. *timi.z.a* Ps. of Cs. *timi.zw.a* Ps. *timi.liw.a* (cf *kamilika, malizika*) (Ar)
-timilifu *adj* completed, finished, perfect: *Kazi timilifu*, a complete work.
timiry.a *vt* assist, help, aid: *Alinitimirya wakati wa shida*, he helped me during difficult times. Prep. *timiry.i.a* St. *timiry.ik.a* Cs. *timiry.ish.a* Ps. *timiry.w.a* Rp. *timiry.an.a* (cf *saidia, auni*) (Gir)
timiz.a *vt* fulfil, complete: *Timiza ahadi*, fulfil a promise. Prep. *timiz.i.a* St. *timiz.ik.a* Cs. *timiz.ish.a* Ps. *timiz.w.a*
timk.a *vi* 1. run away, run off, flee. 2. (of hair, feathers, etc.) be messy, be tousled, be dishevelled, be ruffled: *Nywele zake zimetimka*, his hair is tousled. Prep. *timk.i.a* St. *timk.ik.a* Cs. *timk.ish.a* Ps. *timk.w.a*.
timtimu *adj* disorganized; shuffled: *Alifika hapa nywele timtimu*, she came here with her dishevelled hair. (cf *ovyoovyo*)
tim.u¹ *vi* see *timia*
timu² *n* (*n*) team in a sports game. (Eng)
timu.a¹ *vt* scare away, evict, sack; make a human or any creature run away; awaken someone or an animal suddenly; frighten away: *Watoto waliwatimua ndege*, the children scared away the birds. *Mwajiri alimtimua mfanyakazi wake*, the employer sacked his worker. Prep. *timu.li.a* St. *timu.k.a* Cs. *timu.sh.a* Ps. of Prep. *timu.liw.a* Rp. *timu.an.a* (cf *amsha, kurupusha*)
timu.a² *vt* disorganize, mix up, disturb: *Aliyatimua maji kwenye kidimbwi*, he disturbed the water in the puddle. Prep. *timu.li.a* St. *timu.k.a* Cs. *timu.*

timvi

sh.a Ps. of Prep. ***timu.liw.a*** Rp. ***timu. an.a*** (cf *paraganya, pangua, vuruga*)
timvi *n* (*n*) see *chimvi*
tindi[1] (also *unane*) *n* (*n*) joint in a body or in a sugarcane.
tindi[2] (also *njukuti*) *n* (*n*) spoke (of a bicycle wheel)
tindi.a *vi* (of an organ in the body) get hurt after falling down; be paining: *Mguu wake umetindia baada ya kuanguka ngazini,* her leg is paining after having fallen from the stairs. Prep. ***tindi.li.a*** St. ***tindi.ik.a*** Cs. ***tindi.sh.a*** Ps. ***tindi.w.a*** Rp. ***tindi.an.a***
tindiga *n* (*n*) (*bot*) a kind of marsh grass.
tindigi.a *vt* (of blood) stagnate; stop flowing. Prep. ***tindigi.li.a*** St. ***tindigi.k.a*** Cs. ***tindigi.sh.a***
tindija *n* (*n*) a decorative scar made on a woman's arm, by using cashewnut's sap or burnt powder of a coconut.
tindikali *n* (*n*) 1. a substance, as borax or rosin, used to help metals fuse together; flux: *Tindikali ya kulehemia,* soldering flux. 2. acid. (cf *asidi*)
tindikiw.a *vi* be lacking, be wanting for.
tindiwa.a *vi* swell, expand, dilate: *Mkono wake ulikuwa umekwisha kutindiwaa baada ya kuamka,* her arm had already swollen after she woke up.
tindo *n* (*n*) cold chisel, punch.
tine *n* (*n*) (*anat*) penis glands; circumcized glands of the penis.
ting.a[1] *vi* bob, shake, swing, rock, sway: *Ngalawa yao ilitinga kutokana na mawimbi makali,* their canoe was rocked by the strong waves. Prep. ***ting.i.a*** St. ***ting.ik.a*** Cs. ***ting.ish.a.*** Ps. ***ting.w.a*** (cf *chezacheza, rukaruka, yumba*)
ting.a[2] *vt* puzzle, baffle, bewilder: *Taarifa yake imenitinga,* his information has baffled me. Prep. ***ting.i.a*** St. ***ting.ik.a*** Cs. ***ting.ish.a*** Ps. ***ting.w.a*** Rp. ***ting.an.a*** (cf *zonga, tatanisha*)
ting.a[3] *vt* defeat, overcome: *Vitendo vyake viovu vilitutinga sote,* his evil deeds

tiny.a **T**

defeated all of us. Prep. ***ting.i.a*** St. ***ting.ik.a*** Cs. ***ting.ish.a*** Ps. ***ting.w.a***
ting.a[4] *vt* 1. (in sports) get into the net/goal: *Mpira umetinga golini,* the ball has gone into the net. 2. cruise: *Timu yao ilitinga fainali kwa mbinde,* their team cruised to final with difficulty. Prep. ***ting.i.a*** St. ***ting.ik.a*** Cs. ***ting.ish.a*** Ps. ***ting.w.a***
tingatinga[1] *n* (*ma-*) 1. a bridge across a river usu made of wood or rope. (cf *daraja*) 2. marsh area.
tingatinga[2] *n* (*ma-*) 1. tractor. (cf *trekta*) 2.

tingatinga

tinge *n* (*n*) a competition in leaping in which the participants attempt to keep to a particular order in which they bring their feet to the ground and at the same time they clap their hands.
tingi[1] *n* (*n*) (*naut*) a rope used in changing a sail.
ting.i[2] *vi* (*naut*) sail with a following wind. Prep. ***ting.i.a*** St. ***ting.ik.a*** Cs. ***ting.ish.a*** Ps. ***ting.w.a***
tingish.a *vt* 1. shake. (cf *tikisa, tikisha*) 2. (in sports) score: *Mchezaji alitingisha wavu,* the player kicked the ball into the net. Prep. ***tingish.i.a*** St. ***tingish.ik.a*** Ps. ***tingish.w.a*** Rp. ***tingish.an.a***
tini *n* (*n*) (*bot*) fig; a pear-shaped fruit of the fig tree with sweet pulpy flesh containing numerous tiny seeds. (Ar)
tiny.a *vt* cut a small piece such as meat, etc.; take in pieces by using fingers: *Aliitinya nyama ya kondoo iliyowekwa mezani na kuila,* he cut a piece of mutton that was put on the table and

ate it. Prep. *tiny.i.a* St. *tiny.ik.a* Cs. *tiny.ish.a* Ps. *tiny.w.a* Rp. *tiny.an.a* (cf *nyofoa, nyokoa*)

tinyango *n* (*n*) see *chinyango*

tipitipi *n* (*n*) (*zool*) white-browed coucal; a mainly chestnut-plummed bird (*family Cucculidae*) with a long slender body and a long black tail. (cf *dudumizi, shundi*)

tipwatipwa *adj* 1. plump, stocky; heavily built: *Kijana tipwatipwa*, a plump young man. 2. robust, healthy; good shape: *Amekuwa tipwatipwa kutokana na mazoezi yake kemkem*, he has become healthy because of the numerous exercises he performs.

tirir.i *vt* torment; provoke someone continuously. Prep. *tirir.i.a* St. *tirir.ik.a* Cs. *tirir.ish.a* Ps. *tirir.iw.a* Rp. of Prep. *tirir.i.an.a* (cf *kirihi*)

tiririk.a[1] (also *chiririka*) *vi* trickle; flow gently: *Damu ilikuwa ikitiririka mguuni mwake*, blood was trickling from his leg. Prep. *tiririk.i.a* St. *tiririk.ik.a* Cs. *tirir.ish.a* (cf *churuzika, vuja*)

tiririk.a[2] *n* (*n*) a kind of plaited leaf-strip ready for use.

tisa[1] *adj, n* (*n*) nine (cf *kenda*) (Ar)

tis.a[2] *vt* 1. soften a ripe fruit. 2. cause pain in a swollen part.

tish.a *vt* frighten, horrify, terrify. Prep. *tish.i.a* St. *tish.ik.a*, be easily frightened. Ps. *tish.w.a* Rp. *tish.an.a* (cf *ogofya, hofisha*)

tishali *n* (*ma-*) (*naut*) a large low flat-bottomed boat used in loading and unloading vessels; barge, lighter.

tishi.a *vt* threaten, frighten: *Tishia uhai wa mtu*, threaten the life of sby. St. *tishi.k.a* Ps. *tishi.w.a* Rp. *tishi.an.a*

tishik.a *vi* be threatened, be terrified. St. *tishi.k.a* Ps. *tishi.w.a* Rp. *tishi.an.a* (cf *ogopa*)

tishio *n* (*n*) menace, threat, danger: *Kijiji kinakabiliwa na tishio kubwa la kupata ugonjwa wa kipindupindu*, the village is faced with a big threat of getting cholera.

tishu *n* (*n*) cartilage (cf *gegedu*) (Eng)

tisik.a *vi* 1. (of a fruit) become soft inside without bursting as a result of falling down or being hit by sth. 2. contuse, bruise; injure without breaking the skin. Prep. *tisik.i.a* St. *tisik.ik.a* Cs. *tisik.ish.a*

tisini *adj, n* (*n*) ninety (Ar)

tisti *adv* firm, steadfast: *Simama tisti*, stand firm.

tita *n* (*n*) a bundle of wood; a clump of grass; bunch of grass: *Tita la kuni*, a bundle of firewood.

titi *n* (*ma-*) 1. breast, teat, tit, titty. (*prov*) *Titi la mama litamu jingine halishi hamu*, the nipple of the mother is sweet, the others do not satisfy i.e. an original thing is better than an improvised one. (cf *chuchu, ziwa*) 2. part of an animal corresponding to the human breast where milk is obtained.

titi.a (also *tittima*) *vt, vi* sink down in mud, etc: *Alititia matopeni kutokana na mvua kubwa*, he sank down in the mud due to the downpour. 2. (of land, etc.) push in, be submerged: *Eneo lote limetitia baada ya volkano kutokea*, the whole area is submerged after the volcano had errupted. (cf *didimia*) Prep. *titi.li.a* St. *titi.k.a* Cs. *titi.sh.a*

titig.a *vt* beat sby or sth with hands, sticks, etc. for the purpose of inflicting harm, etc: *Watu walimtitiga mwizi mpaka akawa hoi*, the people beat up the thief severely until he was almost dead. Prep. *titig.i.a* St. *titig.ik.a* Cs. *titig.ish.a* Ps. *titig.w.a* Rp. *titig.an.a* (cf *piga*)

titigik.a *vi* be shaking, be shaky. (cf *tikisika*) Prep. *titigik.i.a* St. *titigik.ik.a* Cs. *titigik.ish.a*

titik.a *vt* accumulate, heap up: *Walititika matunda mengi sokoni*, they heaped a lot of fruits at the market. Prep. *tikik.i.a* Cs. *titik.ish.a* and

titik.iz.a (cf *susuma, kusanya*)
titim.a¹ *vt, vi* see *titia*
titim.a² (also *tutuma*) *vi* rumble, roll, thunder: *Mawingu yalititimua baada ya radi kupiga*, the clouds rumbled after it had thundered. Prep. ***titim.i.a*** St ***titim.ik.a*** Cs ***titim.ish.a*** and ***titim.iz.a*** (cf *rindima*)
titimu.a¹ *vt* 1. run fast after a fright or a call from someone in danger; flee from danger: *Alizititimua mbio aliposikia kwamba askari kanzu walikuwa wakimtafuta*, he ran fast after learning that the plainclothes policemen were looking for him. 2. squander, waste Prep. ***titimu.li.a*** St. ***titimu.k.a*** Cs. ***titimu.sh.a*** Ps. of Prep. ***titimu.liw.a***
titimu.a² *vt* 1. pull out a tree and its roots 2. carry heavy loads. Prep. ***titimu.li.a*** St. ***titimu.k.a*** Cs. ***titimu.sh.a*** Ps. of Prep. ***titimu.liw.a***
tititi *adj* very black.
tiva *n* (*n*) (*zool*) Zanzibar boubou; a medium-sized bird with strong hooked bill: *Tiva mweusi*, Fuleborn's black boubou: *Laniarius fulleborni*. *Tiva mwekundu*, Papyrus gonolek: *Laniarius mufumbiri*. *Tiva dume*, Zanzibar boubou: *Laniarius ferrugineus*. *Tiva mke*, Zanzibar puffback: *Dryoscopus affinis*.
tizam.a *vt, vi* see *tazama*
to *part* negative particle used for futurity. It is used interchangeably with the *-ta-* marker: *Hatafika kesho*, he will not come tomorrow.
to.a *vt* 1. remove, extract: *Toa meno*, extract teeth. 2. give sth to someone. (*prov*): *Kutoa ni moyo usambe ni utajiri*, a poor man even if he has little, may help someone else while a rich person may not do so even if he has so much wealth at his disposal. 3. (*idms*) *Toa habari*, give information; publicize. *Toa hoja*, give an argument. *Toa hotuba*, give a speech. *Toa idhini*, give one's consent. *Toa jefule*, be rude to someone. *Toa maagizo*, give instructions. *Toa macho*, be nonplussed; be stunted. *Toa mavi*, speak nonsense. *Toa mhanga*, sacrifice. *Toa moyoni*, carry out. *Toa mtu jasho*, give someone a hard time. *Toa mpya*, say sth new; give new information. *Toa mfano*, exemplify; give an example. *Toa mimba*, procure an abortion. *Toa pumzi*, (a) exhale. (b) deflate as in the case of a bicycle tyre. *Toa sauti*, speak loudly. *Toa maoni*, give ideas. *Toa rambirambi*, convey condolences. *Toa mfano*, give an example. Prep. ***to.le.a*** St. ***to.k.a*** Cs. ***to.z.a*** and ***to.lesh.a*** Ps. of Prep. ***to.lew.a*** Rp. ***to.an.a***
toasi *n* (*n*) see *tasa⁴*
toasi *n* (*ma-*) 1. cymbal; a concave, large caotanet that makes a loud clashing time when hit with a drumstick or when used in pairs 2. see *tasa⁴* (cf *tuwazi*)

toasi

toba¹ *n* (*n*) repentance, remorse, forgiveness: *Mwenyezi mungu hupokea toba kutoka kwa waja wake*, God grants forgiveness to his beings. *Omba toba*, ask for divine forgiveness. *Vuta toba*, ask for forgiveness. (cf *msamaha*) (Ar)
toba² *interj* used as an expletive in the expression: *Toba we!* God save us! Mercy sake! (Ar)
tobi¹ *n* (*n*) see *topi³*
tobi² (also *topi*) *adv* to the brim, filled to the top; overflowing: *Maji yalijaa tobi kisimani*, the well was filled to the brim. (cf *pomoni, nomi*)
tobo *n* (*ma-*) hole, cavity, opening. (cf *tundu, toma*)

tobo.a *vt* drill, pierce; bore a hole: *Alitoboa tundu katika ukuta*, he drilled a hole in the wall. Prep. ***tobo.le.a*** St. ***tobo.k.a***. Cs. ***tobo.lesh.a*** Ps. of Prep. ***tobo.lew.a***, be holed, be drilled. Rp. ***tobo.an.a*** (cf *tomoa, dopoa, dunga*)

tobok.a *vi* be holed, be punctured: *Mfuko wa karatasi umetoboka*, the paper bag has holes in it. Prep. ***tobok.e.a*** St. ***tobok.ek.a*** Cs. ***tobok.esh.a***

tobosha *n* (*ma-*) a kind of dish made from flour, honey or sugar, sweet palm wine and coconut juice.

tobwe[1] *n* (*ma-*) 1. tunnel; an opening. 2. hole

tobwe[2] *adj* 1. (*colloq*) stupid, imbecile, silly: *Yeye ni tobwe*, he is stupid. 2. unskilled.

tobwe[3] *n* (*ma-*) 1. a stupid person; fool, nincompoop, imbecile, idiot. (cf *zuzu, zumbukuku*) 2. an unskilled person.

tochi *n* (*n*) a small electric light that is carried in the hand; torch. (Eng)

tofaa *n* (*ma-*) see *tufaha*

tofali (also *tufali*) *n* (*ma-*) brick, cement block. (*Ar*)

tofauti[1] (also *tafauti*) *n* (*n*) difference, contrast: *Kuna tofauti yoyote kati ya vitu hivi viwili?* Is there any difference between these two things?

tofauti[2] (also *tafauti*) *n* (*n*) misunderstanding, discord, controversy: *Kumetokea tofauti kati ya marafiki wale*, there has been some misunderstanding between those friends. (cf *hitilafu, suitafahamu*)

tofauti[3] (also *tafauti*) *adj* different, unlike: *Mambo haya mawili ni tofauti*, these two issues are different.

tofautian.a *vi* be different, differ: *Vitu vile viwili vinatofautiana*, those two things are different. Prep. ***tofautian.i.a*** St. ***tofautian.ik.a*** Cs. ***tofautian.ish.a***

tofautik.a *vi* be different, be dissimilar. Cs. ***tofauti.sh.a*** (cf *hitilafiana*)

tofautish.a *vt, vi* differentiate, distinguish: *Unaweza ukatofautisha kati ya aina hizi mbili za mchele?* Can you differentiate between these two types of rice? Prep. ***tofautish.i.a*** St. ***tofautish.ik.a*** Ps. ***tofautish.w.a***

tofi *n* (*n*) toffee, toffy. (Eng)

tofy.a *vt* touch gently; press gently; squeeze lightly: *Alilitofya papai kuangalia kama limeiva*, he squeezed the pawpaw gently to see if it was ripe. Prep. ***tofy.e.a*** St. ***tofy.ek.a*** Cs. ***tofy.esh.a*** Ps. ***tofy.w.a*** Rp. ***tofy.an.a*** (cf *bofya, tomasa, binyabinya*)

tog.a *vt* pierce the ear, etc.; have ears, etc. pierced: *Toga sikio*, pierce an ear. *Toga ndonya*, pierce between the nose and the upper or lower lip. *Toga mapete*, pierce through sby's ear usu a woman in order to put in an earring. Prep. ***tog.e.a*** St. ***tog.ek.a*** Cs. ***tog.esh.a*** Ps. ***tog.w.a***. Rp. ***tog.an.a*** (cf *toboa*)

togwa *n* (*n*) sweet unfermented brew made from millet flour, sugar, etc.; sweet malt drink.

tohara *n* (*n*) circumcision, purity, cleanliness, cleansing: *Tohara yake ilikamilika baada ya kuoga*, his ablution was completed after taking a bath. *Zoezi la tohara kwa wanawake limepingwa vikali nchini*, the exercise on women circumcision has been condemned bitterly in the country. (Ar)

toharani *n* (*n*) (*rel*)purgatory (Ar)

toharik.a *vi* be in the state of purity; be clean, be cleansed: *Nguo yake imetoharika baada ya kuoshwa*, his dress is cleansed after being washed. Prep. ***toharik.i.a*** Cs. ***tohari.sh.a*** (Ar)

toharish.a *vt* purify, cleanse, clean. Prep. ***toharish.i.a*** St. ***toharish.ik.a*** Ps. ***toharish.w.a*** Rp. ***toharish.an.a***

tohe *n* (*n*) (*zool*) reedbuck; a kind of African antelope with thick ringed horns at their base, a short tail and white underparts.

toho.a *vt* 1. dilute, extenuate, weaken: *Aliitohoa kahawa yake nyeusi kwa kuongeza maji ya moto*, he diluted his black coffee by adding hot water.

(cf *zimua*) 2. adapt a word from one language to another language e.g. *pencil* in English to *penseli* in Swahili. Prep. *toho.le.a* St. *toho.lek.a* Cs. *toho.lesh.a* Ps. of Prep. *toho.lew.a*
toj.a *vt* 1. incise, tatoo; make incisions; scarify, tattoo. 2. make a trademark: *Alizitoja bidhaa zake zote*, he put trade marks on all of his goods. Prep. *toj.e.a* St. *toj.ek.a* Cs. *toj.esh.a* Ps. *toj.w.a* Rp *toj.an.a*
tojo *n* (*ma-*) 1. incision, tattoo, cut, slash (cf *chanjo, chale*) 2. trademark, brand: *Bidhaa zao zina tojo*, their goods have trademarks.
toka[1] *prep* since, from. (cf *tangu*)
toka[2] *conj* ever since, since. (cf *tangu*)
tok.a[3] *vt* get out, go out; leave: *Toka jasho*, sweat, *Toka machozi*, weep. *Toka damu*, bleed. Prep. *tok.e.u* St. *tok.ek.a* Cs. *tok.esh.a*
tokan.a *vi* 1. stem from, result from, be caused by. 2. part, split, break, leave. 2. *Ameshatokana naye*, he has already parted her. Prep. *tokan.i.a* St. *tokan.ik.a* Cs. *tokan.ish.a*
toke.a *vt* happen, emerge, become: St. *tok.ek.a* Cs. *toke.z.a* Ps. of Cs. *toke.z.e.a* (cf *bainika, jiri, sadifu*)
tokeo (also *tukio*) *n* (*ma-*) 1. outcome, result. 2. incident: *Tokeo lile halisahauliki*, that incident is unforgettable. (cf *tukio*)
tokez.a *vi* protrude, project, jut out: *Shati lako limetokeza nje*, your shirt has jutted out. Prep. *tokez.e.a* St. *tokez.ek.a* (cf *chomoza*)
tokeze.a *vt* 1. bulge at, jut at. 2. happen without being expected: *Ilitokezea kwamba yeye alikuwa akisema uwongo*, it happened unexpectedly that he was lying. St. *tokeze.k.a* Cs. *tokeze.sh.a*
tokome.a *vi, vt* 1. vanish, disappear; recede from view. (cf *yoyoma*) 2. be destroyed completely; perish. (cf *angamia*) Prep. *tokome.le.a* St. *tokome.lek.a* Cs. *tokome.z.a*
tokomez.a *vt* eradicate, annihilate,

destroy, abolish: *Serikali yao ilijaribu sana kutokomeza malaria*, their government tried its best to eradicate malaria. Prep *tokomez.e.a* St. *tokomez.ek.a* Cs. *tokomez.esh.a* Ps. *tokomez.w.a* Rp. *tokomez.an.a*
tokomire *n* (*n*) a kind of local dance played by *Wazaramu*, a tribe from Tanzania.
tokoni (also *tokono*) *n* (*n*) (*anat*) pelvis
tokono *n* (*n*) see *tokoni*
tokonyasi *n* (*n*) (*zool*) larva, caterpillar.
tokos.a *vt* (of food, etc.) boil; seethe: *Tokosa muhogo*, boil cassava. Prep. *tokos.e.a* St. *tokos.ek.a* Ps. *tokos.w.a*
tokot.a *vi* 1. (of food, etc.) be boiling; be boiled (cf *pwaza*) 2. (*fig*) heighten, simmer, intensify, deepen: *Mgogoro umeanza kutokota katika chama*, the crisis has started to simmer in the party. Prep. *tokot.e.a* St. *tokot.ek.a* Cs. *tokot.esh.a* (cf *fukuta*)
tola *n* (*n*) a weight of about $\frac{1}{2}$ ounce, used for weighing silver, gold, oil, perfumes, etc. (Hind)
tolatola[1] *n* (*n*) different types.
tolatola[2] *adj* different, various: *Vyakula tolatola*, different types of food.
toleo *n* (*ma-*) edition, issue: *Hili ni toleo la kwanza la kitabu*, this is the first edition of the book. 2. offering.
tom.a *vt* burst into; enter suddenly or forcefully: *Alijitoma katika karamu ingawa yeye hakualikwa*, he burst into the reception although he was not invited. Prep. *tom.e.a* St. *tom.ek.a* Cs. *tom.esh.a* Ps. *tom.w.a* Rp. *tom.an.a*
tomas.a *vt* squeeze lightly; press gently: *Alilitomasa embe*, he squeezed the mango gently. Prep. *tomas.i.a* St. *tomas.ik.a* Cs. *tomas.ish.a* Ps. *tomas.w.a* Rp. *tomas.an.a* (cf *bofya, tofya, papasa*)
tomba *vt* (*taboo*) fuck, lay, copulate. Prep. *tomb.e.a* St. *tomb.ek.a* Cs. *tomb.esh.a* Ps. *tomb.w.a* Rp. *tomb.an.a* (cf *jamii, undama*)

tombo¹ n (ma-) teat, nipple, tit. (cf *titi, chuchu*)
tombo² (also *tomboo, tamboro*) n (n) (*zool*) Harlequin quail; a kind of bird (family *Phasianidae*) with mainly black underparts and black and white throat markings. *Coturnix delegorguei.*
tombola n (n) a kind of gambling game somewhat like bingo, in which people pick tickets out of a revolving drum and certain tickets win immediate prizes, usu played at a fair or fete. (Eng)
tombovu n (n) 1. odorous belching; halitosis; a gas that usu comes out during belching; offensive breath; foul-smelling breath. (cf *teushi*). 2. dirty words that are spoken by someone; abusive words. (cf *porojo, upuuzi*)
tome.a¹ vt (used of mason's work) apply small stones or clay on a new wall, etc. in order to bring it to a surface and also strengthen it; do retouching: *Anatomea viambaza vya nyumba yake kwa kokoto*, he is applying final touches on the walls of his house. Prep. **tome.le.a** St. **tome.k.a** Cs. **tome.sh.a** Ps. **tome.w.a** (cf *aka*)
tome.a² vt 1. stuff in grains in a sack to fill to the top. 2. (*lex*) write dictionary entries. Prep. **tome.le.a** St. **tome.k.a** Cs. **tome.sh.a** Ps. **tome.w.a**
tomo n (n) a stone used to smoothen pottery instruments; smoothing stone. (cf *kirugo, komango*)
tomoko n (ma-) (*bot*) sweetsop, sugar apple; an edible greenish yellow fruit from the *mtomoko* tree (bullock's heart) with a powdery bloom and with many black seeds inside.
tomondo n (ma-) (*bot*) a pear-shaped edible fruit which is white inside; Malay apple.
ton.a¹ vi drip, trickle. Prep. **ton.e.a** St. **ton.ek.a** Cs. **ton.esh.a** Ps. **ton.w.a** Rp. **ton.an.a**
ton.a² vt decorate sby with coloured spots: *Alimtona biharusi miguu na mikono*, she decorated the bride's feet and hands. Prep. **ton.e.a** St. **ton.ek.a** Cs. **ton.esh.a** Ps. **ton.w.a** Rp. **ton.an.a**
tona³ n (n) yam (cf *tongonya*)
tonado n (n) tornado; a violent and destructive storm occurring in a small area (cf *kimbunga, chamchela*) (Eng)
tondo n (n) 1. (*zool*) see *suka* 2 a shell used as an inkwell.
tondoo¹ n (n) (*bot*) a kind of fruit which is nut-like and a little larger than marbles and comes from a tree, *mtondoo*; Alexandrian laurel.
tondoo² n (n) thimble (cf *kastabini, subana*)
tondozi n (n) panegyric; a formal speech or writing praising a person or event.
tone¹ n (ma-) a drop of liquid; drip.
tone² n (n) harmful effect like that of a disease or pain caused by the action of someone else; defect. weakness: *Ingiwa na tone*, have a defect. *Tangu apate ajali ya gari, afya yake sasa imeingia tone*, since he had a car accident, his health is now impaired. (cf *kovu, jeraha*)
tone.a vt plait temporarily in preparation for the actual plaiting by the hairdresser: *Msichana alitonea nywele zake kabla hajaenda kwa msusi*, the girl plaited her hair temporarily in preparation for the actual plaiting by the hairdresser. Prep. **tone.le.a** St. **tone.lek.a** Cs. **tone.sh.a** Ps. **tone.w.a** Rp. **tone.an.a**
tones.a vt see *tonesa*
tonesh.a (also *tonesa*) vt 1. re-injure a sore; hurt a sore by knocking against it; reopen a wound: *Alikitonesha kidole changu aliponisukuma*, he hurt my sore when he pushed me. (cf *umiza*) 2. (*fig*) hurt, harm; affect adversely: *Hatua za serikali ziliutonesha uchumi wa nchi*, the government's steps harmed the country's economy. Prep. **tonesh.e.a**

tonesho

St. *tonesh.ek.a* Ps. *tonesh.w.a* Rp. *tonesh.an.a* (cf *umiza*)
tonesho n (*ma-*) 1. the re-injuring of a sore, etc.: *Tonesho la jipu lake lilimfanya asilale takriban usiku wote*, the hurting of her wound kept her sleepless almost the whole night. 2. adverse effect of sth that is harmful.
tonga¹ n (*ma-*) 1. (*bot*) a globose fruit one inch in diameter containing five to ten oblong yellow seeds from the tree. *Strychnos engleri*. 2. a globose yellow berry from the tree, *Solanum obliquum*.
tonga² n (*n*) the size of a coconut or *dafu* i.e. when the nutty part is well set and tough: *Dafu la tonga*, a big coconut full of milk.
tonge n (*ma-*) a small lump of food, a ball of food; goblet: *Tonge la wali*, a ball of rice. *Tonge la ugali*, a ball of hard porridge.
tongo¹ (also *tongotongo, utongo*) n (*ma-*) eye discharge; discharge from the eyes. (cf *makopokopo*)
tongo² n (*n*) a deserted place. (cf *mahame, kihame, ganjo*)
tongo³ n (*ma-*) (*zool*) a flock of small birds.
tongo.a vt explicate, elucidate, elaborate; explain clearly: *Aliitongoa hotuba yake*, he elucidated his speech. Prep. *tongo.le.a* St. *tongo.lek.a* Cs. *tongo.lesh.a* and *tongo.lez.a* Ps. of Prep. *tongo.lew.a* (cf *fafanua, sema, eleza*)
tongonya n (*ma-*) (*bot*) a fruit from a tree *mtongonya*, Giant aroid. *Typhonodorum lindleyanum*.
tongonya n (*n*) (*bot*) 1. the fruit of. *Mtongonya*, Giant avoid, a perrenial herb with a banana-like stem. 2. the seeds of a yam.
tongotongo n (*ma-*) see *tongo¹*
tongoz.a vt seduce, lure, entice, beguile: *Alimtongoza msichana mrembo*, he seduced a beautiful girl. Prep. *tongoz.e.a* St. *tongoz.ek.a* Cs. *tongoz.*

tope.a²

esh.a Ps. *tongoz.w.a* Rp. *tongoz.an.a* (cf *rusa, bemba*)
toni n (*n*) (*phon*) tone; sound with reference to quality, pitch or volume. (Eng)
tonobari n (*n*) see *turubai*
tononok.a vi 1. fatten; get fat; become obese: *Ametononoka kwa kula vyakula vya mafuta*, he has become obese because of eating fatty foods. (cf *nenepa*) 2. be in fine shape; get new health and strength: *Umetononoka kwa kufanya mazoezi ya kuogelea*, you have become healthy and strong because of doing swimming exercises. Prep. *tononok.e.a* St. *tononok.ek.a* Cs. *tonono.sh.a* (cf *nawiri, sitawi*)
tony.a vt narrate; tell, state: *Alitonya kuwamba askari wa jela walimpiga alipokuwa kizuizini*, he stated that the prison warders beat him when he was in detention. Prep. *tony.e.a* St. *tony.ek.a* Cs. *tony.esh.a* Ps. *tony.w.a*
topa¹ n (*n*) see *chopa²*
top.a² vt ladle, lade, scoop up; take a little at a time with the hand or with an instrument: *Alitopa unga wa ngano kutoka kwenye gunia*, he scooped up wheat flour out of the sack. Prep. *top.e.a* St. *top.ek.a* Cs. *top.esh.a* Ps. *top.w.a* Rp. *top.an.a* (cf *chota, mega*)
topasi n (*ma-*) scavenger, street-sweeper, street cleaner. (cf *chura*)
tope¹ n (*ma-*) 1. mud, muck, mire: *Viatu vyangu vilijaa matope kutokana na mvua kubwa*, my shoes were full of mud following the heavy downpour. 2. (*idm*) *Paka mtu matope*, slander someone; sling mud at sby.
tope² n see *topi*
tope.a¹ vi trod on the mud at a place where your leg sinks; sink on the mud: *Alitopea alipopita wakati wa usiku mitaani*, he trod on the mud while passing at night in the neighbourhood. St. *tope.k.a* Cs. *tope.z.a* Ps. *tope.w.a* (cf *kanyaga*)
tope.a² vt excel in, outshine, surpass: *Mvulana yule ametopea katika muziki*, that boy has excelled in music. (cf

757

T topo.a³

bobea) St. ***tope.k.a*** Cs. ***tope.z.a*** Ps. ***tope.w.a*** (cf *bobea, komaa*)
tope.a³ *vt, vi* 1. (of a thorn or nail) go deep into the body. 2. (of a load) lie heavily on the head or shoulders.
topetope *n* (*ma-*) (*bot*) custard apple; an edible heart-shaped orange-fruit from the wild custard apple tree. (*Annona chyrysophylla*)
topi¹ *adv* see *tobi²*
topi² *n* (*n*) a hat without a brim; a brimless hat; top hat.
topi³ (also *tobi*) *n* (*n*) (*zool*) hartebeest. *Alcelaphus cokii*. (cf *kongoni, ngosi*)

topi

topito *n* (*n*) torpedo (Eng)
topo.a¹ *vt* 1. remove magic spell or poison from the body in order to cure; heal, treat: *Daktari aliyatopoa maradhi yangu, opoa*) 2. rescue, save: *Alimtopoa mtoto mdogo aliyetaka kuzama*, he rescued a small child from drowning. Prep. ***topo.le.a*** St. ***topo.k.a*** Cs. ***topo.sh.a*** Ps. of Prep. ***topo.lew.a*** Rp. ***topo.an.a*** (cf *okoa, nusuru*)
topo.a² *vt* mark boundaries of a farm, etc so that it is not taken by someone else; demark, demarcate: *Alilitopoa shamba lake*, he demarked his farm. Prep ***topo.le.a*** St ***topo.k.a*** Cs ***topo.sh.a*** Ps of Prep ***topo.lew.a*** Rp ***topo.an.a*** (cf *aua*)
topolojia *n* (*n*) topology (Eng)

tos.a²

topozi *n* (*ma-*) a remedy to counteract a poison or treat a disease; antidote. (cf *kiuasumu*)
topu *interj* full to the brim; completely: *Maji yamejaa topu kwenye pipa*, the cask is full to the brim. *Amelewa topu*, he is completely drunk. (Eng)
tora *n* (*n*) a kind of small spear.
Torati *n* (*n*) see *Taurati*
torok.a *vi* flee, escape, run away. Prep. ***torok.e.a*** St. ***torok.ek.a*** Cs. ***toro.sh.a*** Ps. ***torok.w.a*** Rp. ***torok.an.a*** (cf *kimbia, timuka*)
toroli (also *troli*) *n* (*n*) 1. a small vehicle that runs on the railroad by being pushed; trolley. 2. a small locomotive; wheelbarrow. (cf *kiberenge*) (Eng)

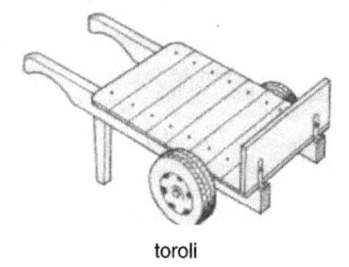

toroli

torosh.a *vt* assist sby/sth to run away; elope: *Aliwatorosha wafungwa wote*, he made the prisoners to run away. Prep. ***torosh.e.a*** St. ***torosh.ek.a*** Ps. ***torosh.w.a*** Rp. ***torosh.an.a***
tos.a¹ *vt* 1. dip, immerse, plunge. throw overboard: *Alivitosa viatu vyake vibovu baharini*, he dipped his worn-out shoes into the sea 2. (*fig*) put sby into problems; ensnarl, befuddle, entangle, embroil: *Alimtosa rafiki yake katika mfululizo wa misuguano*, he entangled his friend in a series of conflicts (cf *zamisha*) Prep ***tos.e.a*** St ***tos.ek.a*** Cs ***tos.esh.a*** Ps ***tos.w.a*** Rp ***tos.an.a***
tosa² *adj* (*bot*) (of fruits) nearly ripe: *Papai tosa*, a nearly ripe pawpaw. *Embe tosa*, a nearly ripe mango.

tosh.a¹ *vt, vi* suffice; be sufficient, be adequate, be enough: *Chakula kile kiliwatosha wageni wangu*, that food was enough for my guests. Prep. *tosh.e.a* St. *tosh.ek.a* Ps. *tosh.w.a* (cf *tosheleza, faa*)

tosha² *adj* sufficient, adequate: *Ule ulikuwa ushahidi tosha kwamba mshtakiwa alishiriki katika wizi wa nguvu*, that was sufficient evidence that the accused was involved in the violent robbery.

toshek.a *vi* be satisified, be contented: *Nimetosheka na kazi yake*, I am satisfied with his work. Prep. *toshek.e.a* St. *toshek.ek.a* (cf *kinai*)

toshelevu *adj* adequate, sufficient: *Fasili toshelevu*, an adequate explanation.

toshelez.a *n (n)* be adequate, satisfy: *Maelezo yake peke yake hayatoshelezi*, his explanation alone is not adquate. Prep. *toshelez.e.a* St. *toshelez.ek.a* Ps. *toshelez.w.a* Rp. *toshelez.an.a* (cf *kidhi*)

toshelezi *adj* sufficient, adequate: *Ushahidi toshelezi*, sufficient evidence

tosti *n (n)* a kind of hard small bread.

tosi *n (n)* toast; sliced bread made brown and crisp by heat. (Eng)

tot.a *vt, vi* be drenched, be soaked, sink: *Alitota kwa mvua kubwa*, he was drenched in heavy rain. *Karatasi hii imetota kwa mafuta*, this paper is drenched with oil. Prep. *tot.e.a* St. *tot.ek.a* Cs. *tot.esh.a* and *tos.a* (cf *rowa, risha*)

totam.a *vi* squat on the hunches or heels; hunker, crouch: *Alitotama alipokuwa anakula*, he crouched when he was eating. Prep. *totam.i.a* St. *totam.ik.a* Cs. *totam.ish.a* Ps. *totam.w.a* (cf *chutama*)

toto.a *vi* hatch eggs: *Kuku wangu alitotoa jana*, my hen hatched eggs yesterday. Prep. *toto.le.a* St. *toto.lek.a* Cs. *toto.sh.a* Ps. of Prep. *toto.lew.a* (cf *angua*)

totom.a¹ *vi* see *yoyoma*

totom.a² *vi* stich a cloth in a mattress. Prep. *totom.e.a* St. *totom.ek.a* Cs. *totom.esh.a*

totoro *adv* an expletive used to emphasize complete blackness: *Giza totoro*, blackest night; terribly dark; completely dark.

totov.a *vi* be speechless, be dumbfounded, be astonished, be stunned: *Alitotova alipohukumiwa kwamba ana hatia ya mauaji*, he was stunned when he was convicted of murder. Prep. *totov.i.a* St. *totov.ik.a* Cs. *totov.ish.a* (cf *duwaa, zubaa*)

totovu *n (n)* (*zool*) white-spotted pufferfish; a kind of saltwater fish belonging to *Tretraodontidae* family, which has greyish-brown body with white or light blue spots and swells when touched.

tovi *n (n)* (*zool*) a male animal selected for its good breed; breeding bull.

tovu¹ *n (ma-)* metal decoration such as that of gold or brass put on a door; knob: *Mlango wa matovu*, knobbed door.

tovu² *adj* used in the expression: *Mtovu wa adabu*, deficient in manners. *Mtovu wa haya*, shameless. *Mtovu wa imani*, lacking in belief; heathen. (*prov*) *Mcha Mungu si mtovu*, one who fears or believes in God does not transgress his laws i.e he who fears God is likely to succeed in life.

tovu³ *n (n)* a kind of thick short bananas which are ripe or raw when cooked. (cf *punda*)

tovuti (also *wavuti*) *n (n)* website; a location connected to the internet that maintains one or more pages on the World Wide Web. *Tovuti ya www*, world wide website.

towashi *n (ma-)* a castrated person; eunuch. (Pers)

towe *n (n)* 1. porter's clay for making pottery vessels. 2. manufactured clay.

towe.a *vt* use sth as a relish while eating

food: *Alitowea mboga ya mchicha alipokuwa anakula wali,* he used spinach as a relish to eat with rice. Prep. *towe.le.a* St. *towe.lek.a* Cs. *towe.z.a* Ps. *towe.w.a*
towek.a *vi* 1. disappear, vanish: *Sijui kwa nini rafiki yangu ametoweka siku hizi,* I don't know why my friend has disappeared these days (cf *potea, tokomea).* 2. go to an undisclosed destination. Prep. *towek.e.a* St. *towek.ek.a* Cs. *towek.esh.a* Ps. *towek.w.a* (cf *yoyoma, potea)*
toza *n* (n) tobacco pipe. (cf *mtemba, kiko)*
trafiki[1] *n* (n) traffic (Eng)
trafiki[2] *n* (n) traffic; a congestion of automobiles, ships, etc. along a road or sea. (Eng)
transfoma *n* (n) transformer: *Transfoma ya umeme,* electric transformer. *Transfoma ya nguvu,* power transformer. (Eng)
trei *n* (n) tray (Eng)
trekta *n* (ma-) tractor (cf *tingatinga)* (Eng)
trela *n* (ma-) trailer (Eng)
treni *n* (n) train (cf *garimoshi)* (Eng)
trignomia *n* (n) (math) trigonometry (Eng)
tropiki *n* (n) tropic: *Nchi za tropiki,* tropical countries. (Eng)
tu *adj* alone, only, just: *Wajumbe watano tu walifika kwenye mkutano,* only five delegates attended the meeting.
tu.a[1] *vi* 1. land, stop at, stop over: *Ndege ilitua polepole,* the plane landed slowly. (cf *teremka)* 2. (of the view) set go down: *Jua limetua,* the sun has set. 3. lower, put down: *Tua mzigo,* put down the load. *Tua tanga,* lower a sail. Prep. *tu.li.a* St. *tu.lik.a* Ps. of Prep. *tu.liw.a*
tu.a[2] (also *tulia) vi* be calm, be settled; be quiet: *Mwanafunzi mtukutu ametua siku hizi baada ya kupewa adhabu kali,* the naughty student is quiet these days after being punished severely. Prep. *tu.li.a,* be calm. St. *tu.lik.a* (cf *makinika, tabaradi)*
tua[3] *n* (n) disgrace, shame, scandal. (syn) *Talaka si tua,* divorce is not a disgrace.
tua[4] *n* (n) thicket, copse, undergrowth. (cf *kichaka).*
tuam.a *vi* stay calm, be calm, be nice: *Maji yametuama,* the water has stayed calm. Prep. *tuam.i.a* St. *tuam.ik.a* Cs. *tuam.ish.a* Ps. *tuam.w.a*
tubakero *n* (n) see *tabakero*
tubi.a *vi* repent for. St. *tub.ik.a* Cs. *tub.ish.a* (cf *staghafiru)*
tub.u *vi, vt* repent, regret for, feel remorse: *Alitubu kwa Mola wake,* he repented to his God. *Nilitubu kwa mzee wangu kwa makosa niliyoyafanya,* I apologised to my parent for the mistakes I had committed. Prep. *tub.i.a* St. *tub.ik.a* Cs. *tub.ish.a* Ps. of Prep. *tub.iw.a* (Ar)
tubwiki.a *vi* tumble/sink in the water and make a splash: *Alitubwikia chubwi!* he sank with a splash in the water. Prep. *tubwiki.li.a* St. *tubwiki.lik.a* Cs. *tubwiki.z.a* Ps. *tubwiki.w.a* (cf *zama, tumbukia)*
tubwish.a *vt* throw up a baby and catch it during playing. Prep. *tubwish.i.a* St. *tubwish.ik.a* Ps. *tubwish.w.a*
tufaa *n* (ma-) see *tufaha*
tufaha (also *tufaa) n* (ma-) apple; an edible pear-shaped fruit which is usu ripe and is white inside. The fruit comes from the pomerac tree. (*Eugenia malaccensis)* (Ar)
tufali (also *tofali) n* (ma-) brick, cement block: *Matufali ya kuchoma,* burnt bricks. *Matufali ya udongo,* mud bricks.
tufani *n* (n) typhoon, hurricane, cyclone: *Ilipotokea tufani, watu wengi waliangamia,* when the typhoon occurred, many people perished. (cf *kimbunga, chemchela)* (Ar)

tufe *n (ma-)* sphere, globe; any round body or figure having the surface equally distant from the centre at all points: *Tufe mango,* solid ball. *Chungwa lina umbo la tufe,* an orange has the shape of a sphere. (cf *puto, purutangi*)

tuf.u *vt* (in Islam) go round the *Kaaba* seven times as part of the pilgrimage; circumambulate. *Mahujaji waliitufu Kaaba,* the pilgrims circumambulated *Kaaba.* Prep. *tuf.i.a* St. *tuf.ik.a* Cs. *tuf.ish.a* Ps. of Prep. *tuf.iw.a* (Ar)

tuguu¹ *n (ma-)* a kind of spherical mat on which women usu dry food in the sun; grain-drying mat. (cf *utanga, kitanga*)

tuguu² *n (n) (zool)* circular bat fish; a marine fish (*family Ephippidae*) f deep, almost circular body having a short head, small mouth and lives around reefs and lagoons.

tuguu³ *n (ma-) (bot)* a kind of fruit.

tuhuma *n (n)* suspicion, mistrust, doubt: *Tuhuma zake juu yetu sisi hazina msingi,* his suspicions on us are baseless. (cf *shaka, dhana*)

tuhum.u *vt* accuse, suspect, doubt: *Polisi walimtuhumu kuwa alishiriki katika mauaji,* the police suspected him that he was involved in the murder. Prep. *tuhum.i.a* St. *tuhum.ik.a* Cs. *tuhum.ish.a* Ps. of Prep. *tuhum.iw.a* Rp. of Prep. *tuhum.i.an.a* (cf *shuku, fikiria*) (Ar)

tui *n (ma-)* milk from grated coconut; coconut milk.

tuili¹ *adj* see *tawili*

tuil.i² *vi* delay; be late. Prep. *tuil.i.a* St. *tuil.ik.a* Cs. *tuil.ish.a* Ps. of Prep. *tuil.iw.a* (cf *kawia, chelewa*)

tuk.a¹ (also *tukia*) *vt* happen, occur: *Pametuka mambo ya ajabu leo,* strange incidents have happened today. Prep. *tuk.i.a* St. *tuk.ik.a* Cs. *tuk.ish.a* Ps. of Prep. *tuk.iw.a* (cf *tokea, awa*)

tuka² *n (n)* a post supporting the projecting eaves of a verandah; verandah post.

tuka³ *n (n)* 1. a small bunch of seedlings that have been uprooted and later used for transplanting. 2. dry land.

tukan.a *vt* vituperate, abuse, insult; use abusive language Prep. *tukan.i.a* St. *tukan.ik.a* Cs. *tukan.ish.a* Ps. *tukan.w.a* Rp. *tukan.an.a* (cf *tusi, chamba*)

tukano *n (ma-)* vituperation, insult, abuse: *Sikutegemea tukano lile kwa mtu kama yeye,* I did not expect that insult from a person like him (cf *tusi*)

tuki.a *vt* see *tuka¹*

tukio (also *tuko*) *n (ma-)* incident, event, occurrence: *Tukio hilo halisahauliki,* that incident is unforgettable. (cf *kadhia*)

tukizi *n (n)* rareness, seldomness, unusualness: *Ni tukizi kwake kupewa zawadi shuleni,* it is a rare thing for her to be given a prize in school. (cf *nadra*)

tuko *n (ma-)* see *tukio*

tuku *n (n) (zool)* mahsena emperor; a kind of saltwater fish with a red blotch on the forehead. *Lenthrinus mahsena.*

tuku

-tukufu *adj* sacred, holy, glorious, honourable: *Kuran tukufu,* the Holy Koran. *Rais Mtukufu,* his/her the excellency the president. *Siku tukufu,* a sacred day. (cf *adhimu, takatifu*)

tukuk.a *vi* be revered; be exalted; be glorious: *Mwenyezi Mungu ametukuka,* God is exalted. Prep. *tukuk.i.a* St. *tukuk.ik.a* Cs. *tukuk.ish.a*

tukut.a¹ *vt* shake: *Aliitukuta nazi kama ni nzima,* he shook the coconut to find out if it was good. Prep. *tukut.i.a* St. *tukut.ik.a* Cs. *tukut.ish.a* Ps. *tukut.w.a* Rp. *tukut.an.a* (cf *tikisa, suka*)

tukut.a² *vi* be restless; be jumpy; be always on the move: *Kijana yule ametukuta kwani siku zote yuko*

mbioni, that man is restless since he is always moving. Prep. ***tukut.i.a*** St. ***tukut.ik.a*** Cs. ***tukut.ish.a*** Ps. ***tukut.w.a*** Rp. ***tukut.an.a***
tukutiko (also *tukuto*) *n* (*ma-*) restlessness, nervousness, uneasiness: *Tukutiko la moyo*, the palpitation of the heart.
tukuto *n* (*ma-*) see *tukutiko*
-tukutu *adj* (esp of a child) mischievous, naughty: *Mtoto mtukutu*, a naughty child.
tukutuku *n* (*ma-*) see *pikipiki*
tukuz.a *vt* glorify, exalt, dignify: *Waumini walimtukuza Mwenyezi Mungu*, the faithfuls glorified the Almighty God. Prep. ***tukuz.i.a*** St. ***tukuz.ik.a*** Cs. ***tukuz.ish.a*** Ps. ***tukuz.w.a*** Rp. ***tukuz.an.a*** (cf *heshimu*, *thamini*)
tukuzo *n* (*ma-*) laudatory songs.
tukwa *n* (*-ma*) (*anat*) thyroid gland; endocrine gland situated in the neck like a bow tie across the front of the upper part of the windpipe.
tule[1] *adj* 1. bad, wicked, evil: *Ana tabia tule*, he has bad habits. (cf *dhaifu*) 2. poor, penurious, needy: *Hana pesa za kulipia karo kwa vile wazee wake ni tule*, he has no money to pay for the school fees because his parents are poor. (cf *masikini*)
tule[2] *adj* (*bot*) a kind of boiled herb used by a dental patient as waterwash.
tuli *adv* used to emphasize the state of calmness: *Ametulia tuli*, he is completely calm. *Amesimama tuli*, he is standing completely motionless. (cf *kimya*)
tuli.a *vi* be stable, be calm, be quiet, be settled: *Mtoto wako ametulia*, your child is calm. *Maji yale baharini yametulia*, that water in the sea is calm. St. ***tuli.k.a*** Cs. ***tuli.z.a*** (cf *poa*, *tabaradi*)
-tulivu (also *tuvu*) *adj* quiet, serene, calm: *Mwanafunzi mtulivu*, a quiet student. *Bahari ni tulivu leo*, the sea is calm today.
tuliz.a *vt* calm, soothe, placate, mollify:

Walimtuliza mwenye duka aliyekuwa na hasira, they calmed the shopkeeper who was angry. Prep. ***tuliz.i.a*** St. ***tuliz.ik.a*** Cs. ***tuliz.ish.a*** Ps. ***tuliz.w.a*** Rp. ***tuliz.an.a***
tulizan.a *vt* be stable, be settled: *Ametulizana sana katika kazi yake*, he is very stable in his work. Prep. ***tulizan.i.a*** St. ***tulizan.ik.a*** Cs. ***tulizan.ish.a***
tulizo *n* (*ma-*) a thing that gives someone comfort, relief, etc.: *Kufanikiwa kupata kazi kumekuwa sasa tulizo kwake*, his success in getting a job has now given him comfort.
tum.a *vt* 1. send e.g. a letter, a message, etc. Prep. ***tum.i.a.*** St. ***tum.ik.a*** Cs. ***tum.ish.a*** Ps. ***tum.w.a*** Rp. ***tum.an.a***
tuma.i *vt* see *tumaini*
tumain.i[1] (also *tumai*, *amania*) *vt* hope, expect, anticipate: *Anatumaini kupata mtoto karibu*, she expects to get a baby soon. Prep. ***tumain.i.a*** St. ***tumain.ik.a*** Cs. ***tumain.ish.a*** Ps. ***tumain.iw.a***. Rp. ***tumain.i.an.a*** (cf *tegemea*, *taraji*, *rajua*)
tumaini[2] *n* (*ma-*) hope, expectation, anticipation: *Tumaini lake la kupata msaada kwa watu mbalimbali sasa limefifia*, his hope of getting assistance from various people has now diminished. (cf *tegemeo*, *tarajio*, *tazamio*)
tumba[1] *n* (*ma-*) (*bot*) a single grain or seed of fruit: *Tumba la mtama*, a grain of millet. *Tumba la kunde*, a seed of cowpea. *Tumba la chungwa*, a seed of an orange.
tumba[2] *n* (*ma-*) unopened bud of a flower: *Tumba la ua*, flower bud. *Tumba la waridi*, rosebud. (cf *fumbu*)
tumba[3] *n* (*mi-*) bale, bundle: *Tumba la nguo*, a bale of cloth.
tumba[4] *n* (*n*) the halo surrounding and encasing the moon; the moon's halo.
tumba[5] *n* (*n*) a kind of a small hand drum used by musical dancers.

tumbaku *n* (*n*) (*bot*) 1. tobacco. 2. the leaves of this plant, prepared for smoking, chewing or snuffing. (Eng)
tumbasi *n* (*n*) see *tambazi*
tumbawe *n* (*ma-*) coral: *Tumbawe gumu,* hard coral; inidaria. *Tumbawe laini,* soft coral; octocoral. (cf *chaawe, fufuwele*)
tumbi[1] *n* (*n*) a big flat basket made from plaited palm leaves, used by fishermen for carrying fish. (cf *pakacha*)
tumbi[2] *adv* an expletive used to describe the preponderance of things, people or affairs: *Amenunua machungwa tumbi nzima,* he has bought lots of oranges.
tumbiri *n* (*n*) (*zool*) velvet monkey; a guenan monkey. (*prov*) *Tumbiri akisha miti, huju mwilini,* a velvet monkey when it finishes to hide in the trees, comes to the body i.e. don't ignore sby who is inferior because when he is desperate, he can come and fight by all means. *Cercopithecus aethiops.* (cf *ngedere*)
tumbo[1] *n* (*n*) literary work e.g. poetry.
tumbo[2] *n* (*ma-*) 1. abdomen; the part of the body between the diaphragm and the pelvis containing the stomach, intestines, etc.: *Ana tumbo kubwa,* he has a big abdomen. (cf *batini*) 2. stomach 3. protrusion 4. used in the expression: *Tumbo la kuhara,* diarrhoea.
tumbu.a[1] *vt* 1. disembowel, lance, slit; cut open: *Alilitumbua jipu lake,* he lanced his boil. Prep. *tumbu.li.a* St. *tumbu.k.a.* Cs. *tumbu.lish.a* and *tumbu.z.a* Ps. of Prep. *tumbu.liw.a* Rp. *tumbu.an.a* (*tungua, toboa*) 2. (*idm*) *Tumbua macho,* stare at with wide open eyes.
tumbu.a[2] *vt, vi* spend money on luxuries. Prep. *tumbu.li.a* St. *tumbu.lish.a* and *tumbu.z.a* Ps. of Prep. *tumbu.liw.a*
tumbuiz.a *vt* entertain by singing, etc.: *Wanamuziki waliwatumbuiza wageni,* the musicians entertained the guests. Prep. *tumbuiz.ia* St. *tumbuiz.ik.a* Ps. *tumbuiz.w.a* Rp. *tumbuiz.an.a* (cf *furahisha, liwaza, burudisha*)
tumbuk.a *vi* burst out, break or cut open: *Jipu limetumbuka,* the abscess has broken open. Prep. *tumbuk.i.a* St. *tumbuk.ik.a* Cs. *tumbuk.ish.a*
tumbuki.a *vt* 1. fall into a pit, etc. or water; tumble into a pit, etc. or water: 2. (*fig*) fall into a disaster; fall into a trap: *Alitumbukia katika janga,* he fell into the disaster. St. *tumbuki.k.a* Cs. *tumbuki.z.a*
tumbukiz.a *vt* 1. drop sby/sth into a liquid. *Aliutumbukiza mshipi wake majini,* he dropped his fishing line into the water. 2. (*fig*) put sby into trouble; entangle: *Alimtumbukiza rafiki yake shimoni,* she put her friend into problems. Prep. *tumbukiz.i.a* St. *tumbukiz.ik.a* Cs. *tumbukiz.ish.a* Ps. *tumbukiz.w.a* Rp. *tumbukiz.an.a*
tumburujik.a *vi* (of tomatoes, puss, etc.) be completely rotten such that a liquid comes out; rot: *Tungule zake zimetumburujika,* his tomatoes are completely rotten. *Jipu lake lilitumburujika,* his boil burst. Prep. *tumburujik.i.a* St. *tumburujik.ik.a* Cs. *tumburujik.ish.a*
tumbuu *n* (*n*) hasp; a hinged metal fastening for a door, window, esp a metal piece fitted over a staple and fastened by a bolt or padlock.

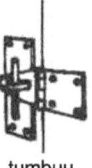

tumbuu

tume[1] *n* (*n*) commission: *Tume ya kudumu,* permanent commission. *Tume ya taifa ya uchaguzi,* national electoral commission. *Tume ya bei,* price commission. *Tume ya uchunguzi,*

T tume²   tundu.a

commission of inquiry. *Tume ya rais*, presidential commission. *Tume ya upatanishi*, a commission of reconciliation. *Tume ya ukweli na maridhiano*, commission of truth and reconciliation.

tume² *n* (*n*) anxiety, worry, nervousness: *Yeye amekuwa na tume sana tangu kukamatwa na polisi*, he has been in great worry since being apprehended by the police. (*prov*) *Ng'ombe mwenye tume ndiye achinjwaye*, the cow with anxiety is the one which will be slaughtered first i.e. anyone who is troublesome should be dealt with immediately.

tume³ *n* (*n*) service, activity, work. (cf *kazi, utumishi, shughuli*)

tumi.a *vt* 1. use, apply, employ: *Walitumia silaha za kisasa katika vita*, they employed modern weapons in the war. St. ***tum.ik.a*** Cs. ***tum.ish.a*** Ps. ***tum.iw.a***. Rp. of Prep. ***tum.i.an.a*** 2. (*idms*) *Tumia mabavu*, use force; use iron fist. *Tumia akili*, use intelligence.

tumik.a *vt, vi* 1. be relevant, be applicable: *Sheria ile bado inatumika*, that law is still applicable. 2. be serving for, be at the service of: *Mfanyakazi huyu anatumika kwa tajiri wake vizuri*, this servant serves well his employer. Prep. ***tumik.i.a*** St. ***tumik.ik.a*** Cs. ***tumik.ish.a***

tumiki.a *vt* serve; be at the service of: *Tuliwatumikia wakoloni kwa muda mrefu*, we served the colonialists for quite long. St. ***tumik.ik.a*** Cs. ***tumik.ish.a*** Ps. ***tumik.iw.a*** Rp. ***tumik.i.an.a***

tumili.a¹ *vt* exploit, use: *Yeye huwatumilia watu wale kwa manufaa yake*, he uses those people for his own benefit. St. ***tumili.k.a*** Ps. ***tumili.w.a*** Rp. ***tumili.an.a***

tumili.a² *vt* eat or drink. St. ***tumili.k.a*** Ps. ***tumili.w.a*** Rp. ***tumili.an.a***

tun.a *vi* swell, puff out, bloat, dilate, blow up: *Uso wake umetuna kwa hasira*, his face is swollen with anger. *Bofu lake limetuna kwa kupulizwa*, his balloon has swollen by being blown. Prep. ***tun.i.a*** St. ***tun.ik.a*** Cs. ***tun.ish.a*** Ps. ***tun.w.a*** (cf *vuvumka, tononoka, fura, vimba*).

tund.a¹ *vt* pluck fruits, flowers, etc.: *Watoto waliyatunda machungwa ingawa yalikuwa bado mabichi*, the children plucked oranges though they were still unripe. Prep. ***tund.i.a*** St. ***tund.ik.a*** Cs. ***tund.ish.a*** Ps. ***tund.w.a*** (cf *chuma, tungua*)

tunda² *n* (*ma-*) (*bot*) 1. fruit. 2. (*idm*) *Zaa matunda*, bear fruit e.g. *Juhudi zake zitazaa matunda*, his efforts will bear fruit.

tundik.a (also *tungika*) *vt* hang, suspend, sling: *Alilitundika koti lake ukutani*, he hung his coat on the wall. Prep. ***tundik.i.a*** St. ***tundik.ik.a*** Cs. ***tundik.ish.a*** Ps. ***tundik.w.a*** Rp. ***tundik.an.a*** (cf *angika, ning'iniza*)

tundiz.a *vt* accumulate, heap up, amass, pile up: *Anatundiza pesa zake ili aweze kununua gari*, he is accumulating his money so that he can buy a car. Prep. ***tundiz.i.a*** St. ***tundiz.ik.a*** Cs. ***tunduz.ish.a*** Ps. ***tundiz.w.a*** (cf *lundika, limbika*)

tundu¹ *n* (*ma-*) 1. hole, cavity, hollow: *Kijiti hiki hakiwezi kupita katika tundu hili*, this stick cannot pass through this hole (cf *tobo, tomo, shimo, genge*) 2. used in the expression: *Tundu ya pua*, nostril. 3. (*fig*) loophole: *Kuna matundu mengi katika sheria za klabu yao*, there are many loopholes in the regulations of their club.

tundu² *n* (*ma-*) nest, den, roost: *Tundu la kuku*, hencoop. *Hili ni tundu la ndege*, this is a bird's nest. (cf *kirimba, kizimba*)

tundu³ *adj* naughty, impish, selfish: *Mtoto mtundu*, a naughty child.

tundu.a *vt* take down anything that has been hung up or suspended: *Alivitundua vitabu vyake kutoka* *kwenye rafu*, he removed his books from the shelf. Prep. ***tundu.li.a*** St. ***tundu.k.a*** Cs. ***tundu.ish.a*** Ps. of Prep. ***tundu.liw.a*** Rp. of Prep. ***tundu.li.an.a***

tundui.a *vt* 1. guard, look after, oversee: *Mzazi yule anajua namna ya kuwatunduia watoto wake*, that parent knows how to look after her children. (cf *tunza, angalia*) 2. spy, observe. Prep. ***tundui.li.a*** St. ***tundui.k.a*** Cs. ***tundui.z.a*** Ps. ***tundui.w.a*** Rp. ***tundui.an.a*** (cf *peleleza*)

-tunduizi *adj* 1. watchful, sharp-eyed, eagle-eyed: *Mzazi mtunduizi*, a watchful parent. 2. curious, inquisitive: *Kwa nini yu mtunduizi kama vile?* Why is he so inquisitive like that?

tunduwa.a *vi* be nonplussed, be dumbfounded, be stunned, be startled; be taken aback: *Nilitunduwaa niliposikia akitamka maneno machafu hadharani*, I was dumbfounded when I heard her uttering nasty words in public. Prep. ***tunduwa.li.a*** St. ***tunduwa.lik.a*** Cs. ***tunduwa.lish.a*** Ps. ***tunduwa.liw.a*** (cf *duwaa, shangaa*)

tung.a[1] *vt* string together; bring materials or ingredients together. *Tunga ushanga*, string beads. *Tunga samaki*, string fish together. Prep. ***tung.i.a*** St. ***tung.ik.a*** Cs. ***tung.ish.a*** Ps. ***tung.w.a*** Rp. ***tung.an.a*** (cf *dunga*)

tung.a[2] (also *tunza*) *vt* 1. (of an abscess, etc.) fester, suppurate, maturate, gather: *Tunga usaha*, from pus; fester suppurate. 2. (*idm*) *Tunga mimba*, get pregnant; conceive, form embryo. Prep. ***tung.i.a*** St. ***tung.ik.a*** Cs. ***tung.ish.a*** Ps. ***tung.w.a*** Rp. ***tung.an.a***

tung.a[3] *vt* compose, construct, arrange: *Tunga shairi*, compose a poem. *Tunga wimbo*, compose a song. *Tunga kitabu*, write a book. *Tunga hotuba*, compose a speech. *Tunga uwongo*, lie; concoct lies. *Tunga hadithi*, (a) compose a story. (b) lie, concoct. Prep. ***tung.i.a*** St. ***tung.ik.a*** Cs. ***tung.ish.a*** Ps. ***tung.w.a*** Rp. ***tung.an.a*** (cf *buni, unda*)

tung.a[4] *vt* target, aim at, focus on: *Tunga shabaha*, make a target on sth. Prep. ***tung.i.a*** St. ***tung.ik.a*** Cs. ***tung.ish.a*** Ps. ***tung.w.a*** Rp. ***tung.an.a***

tung.a[5] *n* (*n*) tarboosh, fez. (cf *tarbushi*)

tunga[6] *n* (*ma-*) hamper; a large basket fitted with a cover (cf *jamanda, tenga*)

tungaman.a *vi* be connected; be stuck together: *Ukwaju huu umetungamana*, this tamarind is stuck together. *Nchi zile mbili zimetungamana*, those two countries are united. Prep. ***tungaman.i.a*** St. ***tungaman.ik.a*** Cs. ***tungaman.ish.a*** (cf *fungamana, shikana, gandana*)

tungamo *n* (*n*) mass

tungas.a *vt* suspend an injured hand in a string. Prep. ***tungas.i.a*** Cs. ***tungas.ish.a*** Ps. ***tungas.w.a***

tungat.a (also an*gata*) *vt* carry on the shoulders: *Wapagazi walitungata magunia ya karafuu*, the porters carried the cloves' sacks on their shoulders. Prep. ***tungat.i.a*** St. ***tungat.ik.a*** Cs. ***tungat.ish.a*** Ps. ***tungat.w.a*** Rp. ***tungat.an.a*** (cf *beba, chukua*)

tungazi *n* (*ma-*) ridge, terrace.

tungi *n* (*ma-*) chimney of an oil lamp; lamp chimney. (cf *chemni*)

tungik.a *vt* see *tundika*

tungo *n* (*n*) composition, construction e.g. of poems, songs, etc. (*gram*) *Tungo sahili*, simple construction. *Tungo tata*, complex construction. *Tungo ambatano*, compound construction. *Tungo shurutia*, interdependent construction.

tungu.a *vt* 1. take down, let down; remove: *Alizitungua nguo zake kwenye kamba*, he took his clothes down from the line. (cf *pachua, teremsha, tundua*) 2. knock down, shoot down: *Waliitungua ndege ya adui*, they shot down the enemy's plane. Prep. ***tungu.li.a*** St. ***tungu.k.a*** Cs. ***tungu.lish.a*** Ps. of Prep. ***tungu.liw.a*** Rp. ***tungu.an.a*** (cf *dengua, angusha*)

tunguja n (n) (bot) yellow roundish tomato from the plant, *mtunguja, Solanum trepidans*. (cf *ngongwe*)
tungule n (n) (bot) tomato (cf *nyanya*)
tunguri n (n) a small gourd in which local medicine men keep their medicine; medicine man's gourd. (cf *ndonga, ndumba*)
tunguridi n (n) (zool) Cord on-bleu, Green-winged pytilia. This is a common species of *estridid finch* found in Africa, South of the Sahara. It is a beautiful bird in both feather and character. It is also characterized by being not overtly aggressive to other finches. *Pytilia melba.*
tunguru n (n) (zool) spadefish, batfish; a disc-shaped food fish with sharp spined fins.
tuni n (n) tune, melody. (cf *lahani*) (Eng)
tunu[1] n (n) a special gift given to sth as a symbol of affection, etc.: *Nilimpa tunu rafiki yangu alipoenda ng'ambo kwa masomo*, I gave my friend a present when he went overseas for studies. (cf *zawadi*)
tunu[2] n (n) rarity, momento, souvenir; sth rare to be found: *Sukari imekuwa tunu madukani siku hizi kwa vile haipatikani kwa urahisi*, sugar has become a rare commodity in the shops these days since it is not easily available. (cf *azizi*)
tunuk.a vt 1. treasure, prize; set one's heart on, have a special affection: *Ninazitunuka barua zake sana*, I treasure his letters very much. (cf *enzi, thamini*) 2. award, present: *Walimtunuka zawadi nzuri*, they awarded him a good present. Prep. *tunuk.i.a* St. *tunuk.ik.a* Cs. *tunuk. ish.a* Ps. *tunuk.w.a* Rp. *tunuk.an.a*
tunuki.a vt award; present to; make a present of. St. *tunuki.k.a* Cs. *tunuki. sh.a* Ps. *tunuki.w.a,* be awarded e.g. *Alitunukiwa zawadi kutokana na kazi zake nzuri*, he was awarded a present following his good services. Rp. *tunuki.an.a* (cf *tunza, zawadia*)

tunuk.u vt award. Prep. *tunuk.i.a* St. *tunuk.ik.a* Cs. *tunuk.ish.a* Ps. *tunuk.iw.a* Rp. *tunuk.i.an.a*
tunutu (also *kimatu, matumatu*) n (n) (zool) young locusts.
tunz.a[1] vt care for, look after; preserve, conserve, maintain, sustain: *Aliwatunza watoto wangu nilipokuwa masomoni*, she looked after my children when I was on studies. Prep. *tunz.i.a* St. *tunz.ik.a* Cs. *tunz.ish.a* Ps. *tunz.w.a* Rp. *tunz.an.a* (cf *hifadhi, linda*)
tunz.a[2] (also *tuza*) vt 1. award, present; bestow a gift: *Nilimtunza mwimbaji kwenye jukwaa*, I awarded the singer a present on the stage. (cf *zawadia*) 2. (syn) *Mcheza kwao hutunzwa*, he who dances at his home is rewarded i.e. he who does a good thing esp at home deserves to be rewarded. Prep. *tunz.i.a* St. *tunz.ik.a* Cs. *tunz.ish.a* Ps. *tunz.w.a* Rp. *tunz.an.a*
tunzo (also *tuzo*) n (n) gift, present, reward: *Mfanyakazi mwenye nidhamu alipewa tunzo*, a disciplined worker was given a gift. (cf *zawadi*)
tupa[1] n (n) file; a tool with a rough ridge surface for smoothing, grinding or sharpening: *Tupa duara*, round file. *Tupa pembetatu*, triangular file.
tup.a[2] vt 1. throw away, fling, hurl: *Alilitupa jiwe kwa nguvu*, he threw the stone with force. (cf *rusha, gea*) 2. abandon or throw sth unwanted such as refuse; dump: *Alizitupa taka*, he dumped the garbage. (cf *acha, tenga*) 3. discard, ignore, abandon: *Mzee yule amewatupa watoto wake na sasa majirani wanamsema*, that old person has abandoned his children and now the neighbours speak ill of him. (cf *telekeza*) 4. (idms) *Tupa jicho*, glance at. *Tupa mkono*, die. *Tupa mashtaka*, drop the suit. *Tupa wajibu*, ignore your responsibilities. *Tupa maneno*, exchange harsh words. *Tupa jongoo na mti wake*, forget someone or sth completely. Prep. *tup.i.a* St. *tup.*

ik.a Cs. **tup.ish.a** Ps. **tup.w.a** Rp. **tup.an.a** Prep. **tup.i.li.a** Rp. of Prep. **tup.i.an.a**
tupa³ n (n) (zool) file snake; a non-venomous triangular snake with juxtaposed dorsal scales. *Mehelya capensis.*
tupi.a vt, vi 1. put things in a disorderly manner. 2. put clothes on your shoulders. 3. put one thing on another by throwing them at different places 4. (idm) *Tupia macho,* look after sth; guard. (cf *tunza*)
-tupu¹ adj 1. empty, bare, void, hollow, vacant: *Nyumba hii ni tupu,* this house is vacant. (prov) *Mkono mtupu haurambwi,* an empty hand is not licked i.e. if someone wants to get sth or the services of someone else, he must also be prepared to be generous. In other words, we must also be prepared to offer sth to people. 2. only, mere, bare, by itself: *Waliokuja harusini, walikuwa wanaume watupu,* those who attended the wedding were only men.
-tupu² adj naked, nude, undressed: *Yeye yu mtupu,* he is naked.
tupu³ n (n) private organs, private parts; external sex organs. *Tupu ya mbele,* penis or vagina. *Tupu ya nyuma,* anus.
tura n (n) (bot) wild tomato; a long yellowish globose fruit from the tree, *mtura, Solanum incanum.* (cf *tunguja*)
turu n (n) see *turuturu*
turubai (also *turubali, tonobari*) n (ma-) tarpaulin; a piece of material serving as waterproof canvas to protect exposed objects.
turubali n (n) see *turubai*
turufu n (n) (in card games) trump; a particular card chosen out of a pack representing a suit which must be followed by the players: *Kura ya turufu,* veto. (Port)
turuhani¹ n (n) 1. allowance made in weighing for package, vehicle, etc.; tare. 2. sth given extra in a sale, bonus:
Mchuuzi alinipa turuhani niliponunua tungule kwake, the retailer gave me some extra bonus when I bought tomatoes from him. (Ar)
turuhani² n (n) prestige, reverence, honour: *Utajitoa turuhani ukisema mambo ya upuuzi hadharani,* you will lose respect if you speak nonsense in public. *Toa turuhani,* dishonour. (cf *hadhi, heshima*) (Ar)
turusi n (n) a wooden chisel. (cf *patasi*)
turuturu (also *turu*) n (n) (med) simple acne. (cf *kivimbe*)
tushi n (n) see *tusi¹*
tusi¹ (also *tushi*) n (ma-) insult, abuse, affront. (cf *tukano*)
tus.i² vt insult, abuse, affront: *Walimtusi bila ya sababu,* they insulted him for no reason. Prep. **tus.i.a** St. **tus.ik.a** Cs. **tus.ish.a** Ps. **tus.iw.a,** be insulted. Rp. **tus.i.an.a** (cf *tukana, nyonyoa*)
tusi³ n (ma-) bier, coffin, casket. (cf *kitanda, jeneza*)
tuta¹ n (ma-) flower-bed: *Piga tuta,* make a flower-bed. *Tuta la waridi,* rosebed.
tut.a² (also *tutusa*) vi (of the heart, etc.) throb, pulpitate, pulse, beat: *Moyo wake ulikuwa ukimtuta baada ya kukimbia masafa marefu,* his heart was throbbing after running for a long distance. Prep. **tut.i.a** St. **tut.ik.a** Cs. **tut.ish.a** Ps. **tut.w.a** (cf *tweta, tutusa*)
tut.a³ (also *tutika*) vt 1. carry heavy loads from one place to another; *Yeye ni hodari wa kututa mizigo,* he is good at carrying heavy loads. 2. take things in a disorderly manner: *Alikuja hapa na kututa vitu vya watu,* he came here and took away people's things in a disorderly manner. Prep. **tut.i.a** St. **tut.ik.a** Cs. **tut.ish.a** Ps. **tut.w.a** Rp. **tut.an.a**
tuta⁴ (also *tutamavi*) n (n) (zool) scavenger beetle. (cf *dundu*)
tutamavi n (n) see *tuta⁴*
tuti.a vt fill up; fill in a hole, etc.: *Walilitutia shimo ili wanavijiji wasije*

wakatumbukia ndani yake, they filled up the pit so that the villagers might not fall into it. St. *tuti.k.a* Cs. *tuti.sh.a* Ps. *tuti.w.a*, be filled up. Rp. *tuti.an.a* (cf *fukia*)

tutik.a *vt* 1. see *tuta³*. 2. pile or put many things together; accumulate: *Alitutika kuni kichakani ili aende kupikia*, he collected firewood from the forest to use for cooking. Prep. *tutik.i.a* St. *tutik.ik.a* Cs. *tutik.iz.a* and *tutik.ish.a* Ps. *tutik.w.a* Rp. *tutik.an.a* (cf *rundika, kusanya*)

tutu¹ *n* (*n*) (*med*) acne; a small hard swelling, usu black that protrudes on the body. (cf *chunusi, mavimbevimbe*)

tutu² *n* (*n*) (*zool*) red-eyed dove. (cf *fumvu*)

tutu³ *n* (*n*) a dish of cowpeas that have been boiled with maize or millet and sometimes mixed with grated coconut juice.

tutuk.a *vi* be swollen; be puffed out; be bellied: *Ngozi yake usoni ilitutuka baada ya kuumwa na nyuki*, his skin on the face swelled after he was stung by bees. St. *tutuk.i.a* St. *tutuk.ik.a* Cs. *tutuk.ish.a* Ps. *tutuk.w.a* Rp. *tutuk.an.a* (cf *duduika*)

tutum.a¹ *vi* 1. see *titima²*. 2. (of a sailing vessel) make a low sound. Prep. *tutum.i.a* St. *tutum.ik.a* Cs. *tutum.ish.a* Ps. *tutum.w.a* Rp. *tutum.an.a*

tutum.a² *vi* grumble, moan, complain: *Raia walitutuma kwa sababu ya kuongezeka bei kwa bidhaa*, the citizens complained over the price hike in commodities. Prep. *tutum.i.a* St. *tutum.ik.a* Cs. *tutum.ish.a* Ps. of Prep. *tutum.w.a* (cf *nung'unika, guna*)

tutumu.a¹ *vt* 1. blow up, swell up. (cf *furisha, vimbisho*) 2. (*fig*) brag, be swollen-headed, be boastful: *Anapenda kujitutumua*, he likes to brag. Prep. *tutumu.li.a* St *tutumu.k.a* Cs. *tutumu.sh.a* and *tutumu.z.a* Ps. of Prep. *tutumu.liw.a*

tutumu.a² *vt* 1. carry heavy loads. 2. uproot sth stuck deep in the soil by holding it firmly at the stem position. Prep. *tutumu.li.a* St. *tutumu.k.a* Cs. *tutumu.sh.a* Ps. *tutumu.liw.a*

tutumuk.a *vt* become swollen, be dilated, be filled with: *Uso wake ulitutumuka alipotukanwa hadharani*, his face was filled with indignation when he was insulted in public. Prep. *tutumuk.i.a* St. *tutumuk.ik.a* Cs. *tutumuk.ish.a* (cf *vimba, tuna*)

tutumvi (also *tuutuu*) *n* (*n*) (*med*) allergic rash; swollen pimples resulting from insect bite or contact with itchy leaves; eczema. (cf *ukurutu*)

tutuo *n* (*mi-*) haste, fidgetiness, impatience: *Mitutuo mingi haina maana*, too much haste is useless. (cf *kishindo, papara, pupa*)

tutus.a¹ *vi* see *tuta²*. Prep. *tutus.i.a* St. *tutus.ik.a* Cs. *tutus.ish.a* Ps. *tutus.w.a* Rp. *tutus.an.a*

tutus.a² *vi* walk by groping like a blind man or a person in the dark; grope, grabble, fumble, scrabble: *Nilikuwa nikitutusa chumbani wakati taa zilipozimwa*, I was groping in the room when the lights went off. Prep. *tutus.i.a* St. *tutus.ik.a* Cs. *tutus.ish.a* Ps. *tutus.w.a* Rp. *tutus.an.a*

tutusa³ *n* (*n*) a stupid person; fool, imbecile. (cf *zuzu, mpumbavu*)

tutuuk.a *vi* swell, bloat, expand. Prep. *tutuuk.i.a* St. *tutuuk.ik.a* (cf *vimba, fura*)

tutwe *adv* quietly, idly; without doing or saying anything because of being astounded, etc.: *Kaa tutwe*, sit idly. *Yeye hukaa tutwe siku zote*, he always sits idly.

tuutuu *n* (*ma-*) see *tutumvi*

tuvu *adj* see *tulivu*

tuwanyika *n* (*n*) sharp beaked grass snake. (cf *nondo*)

tuwazi *n* (*n*) see *tasa⁴*

tuz.a *vt* see *tunza³*

tuzo *n* (*n*) see *tunzo*

tuzu.a *vt* disgrace, humiliate, besmirch:

Alinituzua mbele ya kundi kubwa la watu, he disgraced me in front of a large group of people. Prep. ***tuzu.i.a*** St. ***tuzu.ik.a*** Cs. ***tuzu.ish.a*** Ps. ***tuzu.w.a*** Rp. ***tuzu.an.a*** (cf *aibisha, tahayarisha, kashifu, fedhehesha*)

twa.a *vt* take, capture, occupy: *Alikitwaa kitabu changu bila ya ruhusa*, he took my book without permission. Prep. ***twa.li.a*** St. ***twa.lik.a*** Cs. ***twa.lish.a*** Ps. of Prep. ***twa.liw.a*** Rp. ***twa.an.a*** (cf *chukua, beba*)

twaibu *interj* see *taibu*

twali.a[1] *vt* take up for (from, with, etc.) sby; rob of; seize from.

twali.a[2] *vt* (in mat sewing) sew two eyes simultaneously. St. ***twali.k.a*** Cs. ***twali.sh.a*** Ps. ***twali.w.a*** Rp. of Prep. ***twali.an.a***

twang.a *vt* 1. pound sth in a mortar such as wheat, millet, etc. in order to get off the husks: *Aliyatwanga mahindi yake kwenye kinu*, he pounded his maize in a mortar. (cf *ponda*) 2. (*fig*) hit hard; punch hard: *Alinitwanga ngumi*, he punched me hard. Prep. ***twang.i.a*** St. ***twang.ik.a*** Cs. ***twang.ish.a*** Ps. ***twang.w.a*** Rp ***twang.an.a***

twaz.a *vi* vaunt oneself; be arrogant, be conceited: *Siku hizi rafiki yako anajitwaza*, these days your friend is becoming arrogant. Prep. ***twaz.i.a*** St. ***twaz.ik.a*** Cs. ***twaz.ish.a*** Ps. ***twaz.w.a*** Rp. ***twaz.an.a*** (cf *jigamba, jinata*)

twek.a[1] (also *twika*) *vt* hoist, raise, elevate, uplift: *Aliitweka bendera ya taifa*, he hoisted the national flag. *Wavuvi walilitweka tanga*, the fishermen hoisted the sail. Prep. ***twek.e.a*** St. ***twek.ek.a*** Cs. ***twek.esh.a*** Ps. ***twek.w.a*** Rp. ***twek.an.a*** (cf *pandisha, kweza*)

twek.a[2] *vt* carry, take: *Aliutweka mzigo wetu*, he carried out luggage. Prep. ***twek.e.a*** St. ***twek.ek.a*** Cs. ***twek.esh.a*** Ps. ***twek.w.a*** Rp. ***twek.an.a*** (cf *beba, chukua*)

tweka[3] (also *twesha*) *n* (*n*) burden, hardship: *Kazi uliyonipa ni tweka kwangu*, the work you have given me is a burden to me. (cf *mzigo*)

twesh.a[1] *vt* 1. greet esp the elders, parents, etc.: *Mtoto aliwatwesha wazee wake*, the child greeted his parents. 2. (usu occurs in polygamous communities) visit a wife just to greet her, when her turn to stay with the husband is not ready. Prep. ***twesh.e.a*** St. ***twesh.ek.a*** Cs. ***twesh.esh.a*** Rp. ***twesh.an.a***

twesha[2] *n* (*n*) see *tweka*[3]

twet.a *vi* gasp, pant, wheeze; breathe with difficulty: *Mgonjwa alikuwa akitweta*, the patient was wheezing. Prep. ***twet.e.a*** St. ***twet.ek.a*** Cs. ***twet.esh.a*** Ps. ***twet.w.a*** (cf *puma, hema*)

twez.a *vt* humiliate, besmirch, discredit: *Mwanafunzi aliadhibiwa baada ya kumtweza mwalimu wake*, the student was punished for humiliating his teacher. Prep. ***twez.e.a*** St. ***twez.ek.a*** Cs. ***twez.esh.a*** Ps. ***twez.w.a*** Rp. ***twez.an.a*** (cf *beza, dharau*)

twiga *n* (*n*) (*zool*) giraffe

twik.a[1] *vt* load cargo, freight (cf *shehena, mzigo*)

twik.a[2] *vt* (of loads, etc.) lift to the head; carry on the head: *Alijitwika gunia lenye mahindi*, he carried a sack of maize on his head. Prep. ***twik.i.a*** St. ***twik.ik.a*** Cs. ***twi.sh.a*** Ps. ***twik.w.a*** Rp. ***twik.an.a***

twik.a[3] *vt* see *tweka*[1]

twinga *n* (*n*) a big balloon. (cf *purutangi, tiara*)

twish.a *vt* raise a load and put it on sby's head or shoulders. Prep. ***twish.i.a*** St. ***twish.ik.a*** Ps. ***twish.w.a*** Rp. ***twish.an.a***

tyubu *n* (*n*) tube (Eng)

U

U, u/*u*/ 1. the twentieth letter of the Swahili alphabet. 2. a high back vowel.
u *vt cop. v* 1. (used for 2nd person sing) you are: *Wewe u tajiri*, you are rich. 2. (used with m-mi class singular nouns) it is: *Mlango u wazi*, the door is open. 3. (used with u class singular nouns) it is: *Ukuta u mkubwa*, the wall is big.
ua¹ *n* (*ma-*) 1. flower: *Ua la waridi*, rose flower. *Kitalu cha maua*, flower bed. 2. (*idm*) *Hana maua*, he has nothing; she has nothing. *Ua la uzazi*, uterus.
ua² (pl *nyua*) *n* (*u*) fence, enclosure, compound: *Ua wake umejaa miti*, his compound contains many trees. (cf *uga, kiwanja, kitalu*)
u.a³ *vt* kill, murder. Prep. **u.li.a** St. **u.lik.a** Cs. **u.lish.a** Ps. of Prep. **u.liw.a**, be killed, be murdered e.g. *Mwanasiasa aliuliwa katika mazingara ya kutatanisha*, the politician was killed in mysterious circumstances. Rp. **u.an.a**. kill one another.
uadhimishaji *n* (*u*) commemoration, celebrations, observance: *Uadhimishaji wa siku ya kupata uhuru*, the commemoration of independence day. (cf *usherehekeaji*) (Ar)
uadilifu *n* (*u*) impartiality, justice, integrity, uprightness: *Hakimu alitumia uadilifu katika kuihukumu kesi*, the judge exercised impartiality in trying the case. (cf *usawa, haki*) (Ar)
uadimikaji *n* (*u*) scarcity, dearth, paucity, lack. (cf *uhaba*)
uadui¹ (also *adawa*) *n* (*u*) enmity, hostility. (cf *uhasama, utesi*) (Ar)
uadui² (also *adawa*) *n* (*u*) cruelty (*unyama*) (Ar)
uagizaji *n* (*u*). act (method, etc.) of ordering; command: *Uagizaji wao ni mbaya*, their manner of ordering about is unpleasant. 2. work of ordering.

uagiziaji *n* (*u*) ordering, requesting.
uagizishaji *n* (*u*) importation
uaguaji *n* (*u*) see *uaguzi*
uaguzi (also *uaguaji*) *n* (*u*) 1. divination, prophesy, prediction, foretelling: *Uaguzi wake ulisibu*, her prediction came true. (cf *utazamiaji, utabiri, ubashiri*) 2. medical treatment, medication. 3. removal of a spell.
uahirishaji *n* (*u*) postponment, adjournment: *Uahirishaji wa mkutano*, the postponement of the meeting.
uaili *n* (*u*) blame, censure. (Ar)
uainishaji *n* (*u*) act (method, etc.) of classifying; classification, categorization. (cf *ubanishaji*)
uainisho *n* (*u*) classification (cf *uainishaji, ubainishi*)
Uajemi *n* (*u*) (*geog*) Persia (Ar)
uajenti *n* (*u*) agency; the act of serving as an agent for a particular company, person, etc.
uajibikaji *n* (*u*) accountability, answerability, responsibility, liability, obligation: *Kila mtu ana uajibikaji maalumu kwa nchi yake*, every person has special responsibility to his country. (Ar)
uajibishaji *n* (*u*) the act (method, etc) of shouldering responsibilities to sby. (Ar)
uajiri *n* (*u*) employment, recruitment. (Ar)
uajizi *n* (*u*) delay, lateness, slowness. (cf *uchelewaji*) (Ar)
uajuza *n* (*u*) old womanhood. (cf *ukongwe*) (Ar)
uake *n* (*u*) (*lit*) feminism; a sociological approach to literature which takes into consideration the female's viewpoint in the course of analysing literary issues.
uakiaji *n* (*u*) gulping, swallowing; the act of putting food into the mouth: *Uakiaji wake unachusha*, his style of throwing

food into the mouth is disgusting. (cf *ubwakiaji, uvunganyiaji*)
uakida *n (u) (arch)* 1.the office of the head of the army. 2. the office of the assistant to a district officer in East Africa during the colonial period. 3. the office of the head in charge of cultural affairs in some tribes of the Swahili community.
uakuaji *n (u)* 1. snatching, grabbing, seizing. *Uakuaji wa mikoba ya wanawake umeongezeka nchini*, the snatching of purses from women has become common in the country. (cf *unyakuaji, ukamataji*.) 2. marking of areas that are to be cultivated.
ualikaji¹ *n (u)* clicking, snapping, checking, cracking.
ualikaji² *n (u)* invitation; the act of inviting people for a particular activity e.g wedding. (cf *mwaliko*)
ualikaji³ *n (u)* act (method, etc.) of confining a sick person for medical treatment or a young person for initiation rites.
ualimikaji *n (u)* the act (method, etc.) of being educated. (cf *upataji-elimu*)
ualimu *n (u)* teaching profession. (cf *usomeshaji, ufunzaji*)
ualisaji *n (u)* nursing; the act of looking after sick people: *Ualisaji ni kazi ngumu*, nursing is a difficult job. (cf *uuguzi, unasi*)
ualishi *n (u)* see *mwaliko¹*
uambaji¹ *n (u)* 1. speaking, talking: *Uambaji wake kwenye jukwaa uliwavutia watu wengi*, his style of talking on the platform attracted many people. (cf *usemaji*) 2. speaking ill of sby. (cf *usengenyaji*)
uambaji *n (u)* 1 the stretching of skin over a drum. 2. the filling of walls of a hut.
uambishaji *n (u) (gram)* affixation; the adding of affixes or roots or bases in order to vary function, modify meaning, etc.

uambuaji *n (u)* stripping of bark, leaves etc.; peeling (cf *uchambuaji, uchambuzi, umenyaji*)
uambukizaji *n (u)* contagion, infection; the spreading of a disease from one individual to another. (cf *uenezaji*)
uamiaji *n (u)* 1 protection of a plantation, garden, etc. 2 the laying of eggs to produce chicks.
uamilifu *n (u)* 1. the ability to wake. 2. the act (method, etc.) of providing services to people. (cf *utumikiaji watu*)
uaminifu *n (u)* honesty, rectitude, integrity: *Meneja amemsifu msarifu kwa uaminifu wake*, the manager has praised the bursar for his honesty. (cf *muamana*)
uamiri *n (u)* commandership: *Uamirijeshi*, the commandership of an army. (cf *uongozi*) (Ar)
uamirishaji *n (u)* consolidation, solidification, strengthening. (Ar)
uamuaji *n (u)* 1. arbitration, reconciliation, intervention. (cf *usuluhishi, uamuaji*) 2. judgement: *Uamuaji wa kesi yao umeleta ubishi mwingi*, the judgement of their case has brought a lot of arguments.
uamuzi *n (u)* 1. judgement, ruling, decision: *Uamuzi wa pamoja*, unanimous decision. *Uamuzi wa wengi*, majority decision. 2. arbitration, reconciliation. (cf *usuluhishi*)
uana *n (u)* sexism: *Uana katika lugha*, sexism in language.
uanaadamu (also *uanadamu*) *n (u)* humanity, kindness, sympathy. (cf *ubinadamu*)
uanamama *n (u)* womanhood
uanaanga *n (u)* 1. astronautics; the science that deals with spacecraft and with travel in outer space. 2. the work of astronautics.
uanachama *n (u)* 1. membership: *Uanachama wake umesimamishwa*, his membership has been suspended. 2. the condition of being a member.

uanachuoni (also *uanazuoni*) *n* (*u*) erudition, scholarship, academic learning: *Uanachuoni wake umempa heshima kubwa*, his scholarship has earned him great respect.
uanadamu *n* (*u*) see *uanaadamu*
uanafunzi *n* (*u*) studentship
uanagenzi *n* (*u*) ameteurism, apprenticeship.
uanahabari *n* (*u*) act (method, etc.) of reporting.
uanahalali *n* (*u*) 1. legitimacy, legality, lawfulness: *Uanahalali wa sheria ile uko mashakani*, the legality of that law is questionable. 2. legitimacy: *Uanahalali wa kijana yule ulithibitishwa mahakamani*, the legality of that youth was proved in the court. (Ar)
uanaharamu *n* (*u*) 1. illegitimacy, bastardy; the state of being born of parents not married to each other: *Mtoto hana uanaharamu wowote kwa vile wazee wake walioana*, the boy is not a bastard at all because his parents were legally married. 2. impishness, puckishness, buffoonery, naughtiness, mischievouness: *Uanaharamu wa mwanafunzi yule umewachosha walimu wote*, the naughtiness of that student has tired all the teachers. 3. waggishness, elfishness, funniness, humour: *Uanaharamu wake umempatia watu wengi*, his humour has won him many people.
uanahewa *n* (*u*) 1. aviation. 2. aviation work.
uanamaji *n* (*u*) 1. navigation, seamanship. 2. navigation work; marine activity. (cf *ubaharia, uanapwa*)
uanamapinduzi *n* (*u*) revolutionary fervour, revolutionary spirit; the state of being revolutionary.
uananchi *n* (*u*) citizenship, nationhood.
uanapwa *n* (*u*) 1. seamanship, navigation, helmenship. (cf *ubaharia, uanamaji*) 2. marine activity.
uanasheria *n* (*u*) 1. law. 2. legal profession: *Ana maarifa makubwa katika kazi ya uanasheria*, he has vast experience in legal work. (cf *uwakili*)
uanasiasa *n* (*u*) political skill, political ingenuity: *Uanasiasa wake ni wa kupigiwa mfano*, his political ingenuity is exemplary.
uanasoka *n* (*u*) qualities and behaviour befitting soccer: *Uanasoka bora*, qualities and behaviour befitting good soccer
uanauke *n* (*u*) 1. womanhood; the condition of being a woman: *Uanauke wake umemchosha mumewe*, her womanhood has tired her husband. 2. womanhood; female tastes.
uanaume *n* (*u*) manhood; the state of being a man. 2. (*fig*) bravery, valiance, courage: *Kazi hii inataka uanaume*, this work requires courage. (cf *ushujaa, ujabari.*)
uanazuoni (also *uanachuoni*) *n* (*u*) scholarship, erudition, punditry, learning.
uandaaji (also *uandazi*) *n* (*u*) preparation, arrangement, planning: *Uandaaji wa mkutano umemalizika*, the preparation of the meeting is complete.
uandamanaji *n* (*u*) 1. succession, sequence, progression. 2. demonstration, rally. protest. (cf *maandamano*)
uandazi *n* (*u*) see *uandaaji*
uandikaji (also *uandishi*) *n* (*u*) 1. writing, penmanship. 2. the art of composing sth. *Uandikaji wa insha*, essay writing.
uandikishaji *n* (*u*) registration, enrollment, enlistment: *Uandikishaji wa wapiga-kura*, the registration of voters. (cf *usajili, uorodheshaji*)
uandikishwaji *n* (*u*) the state of being registered, enrolled, etc.
uandishi *n* (*u*) authorship, writing: *Uandishi wa riwaya*, the writing of novels. (cf *uandikaji*)
uanga[1] *n* (*u*) the act of bewitching at night; wizardry, witchery.
uanga[2] *n* (*u*) see *uwanga*

uangaliaji n (u) observation. watching, inspection, watching. (cf *uangalizi*)
uangalifu n (u) care, attention, caution: *Kazi yake ilifanywa kwa uangalifu*, his work was done with care. (cf *umakini, hadhari, utunduivu*)
uangalizi n (u) 1. responsibility, care, protection, guardianship. (cf *ulinzi, utazamaji*) 2. supervision, management, control, surveillance: *Aliwekwa chini ya uangalizi wa polisi*, he was kept under surveillance by the police. (cf *ulinzi, udhamini*)
uangamizaji n (u) 1. destruction, ruin, devastation: *Uangamizaji wa wanyama wa pori*, the destruction of wild animals. (cf *uhilikishaji, uteketezaji, uharibifu*) 2. ruin, downfall: *Uangamizaji wake ulisababishwa na malezi mabaya*, his ruin was brought by bad upbringing.
uangavu n (u) 1. (of water, etc.) clearness, purity, transparency: *Uangavu wa bahari umemfanya mvuvi aone samaki vizuri*, the clearness of the sea has enabled the fishermen to see fish clearly. (cf *weupe*.) 2. (fig) shrewdness, intelligence, ingenuity, cleverness: *Uangavu wa mwanasiasa yule umeziunganisha kabila mbalimbali*, the shrewdness of that politician has caused different tribes to unite. (cf *ufahamu*) 3. the simplicity of sth to be understood.
uani n (u) 1. back yard. 2. toilet, restroom. (idm) *Enda uani*, go to the toilet to relieve oneself. (cf *msalani*)
uanzishaji (also *uanzilishaji*) n (u) introduction, commencement, opening, establishment, formation: *Uanzishaji wa huduma za afya umewasaidia watu wengi vijijini*, the establishment of health services has helped a number of people in the villages.
uanzishwaji n (u) the state of being introduced, commenced, established, formed, etc.: *Uanzishwaji wa serikali ya mseto*, the introduction of a coalition government.
uapaji n (u) swearing; oath taking: *Uapaji*

wake ni wa dhati, his oath is genuine. *Uapaji wa uwongo*, perjury. (cf *ulajiyamini*)
uapizaji n (u) cursing, curse, imprecation, denunciation. (cf *apizo*)
uapo n (u) see *kiapo*
Uarabu n (u) Arab character, origin, etc. (Ar)
Uarabuni n (u) geog Arabia (Ar)
uasherati n (u) promiscuity, prostitution, harlotry: *Uasherati umezagaa nchini*, prostitution is prevalent in the country. (cf *uzinzi, umalaya*) (Ar)
uashi n (u) brick-laying, masonry: *Uashi wa kutumia vipande vya mawe na matofali*, rubble masonry.
uasi n (u) rebellion, mutiny, insurgence: *Wanujeshi walifanya uasi*, the soldiers staged a mutiny. (cf *upinzani, uhalifu*) (Ar)
uasili n (u) origin, nativity, ethnicity: *Sielewi uasili wa mtu yule*, i don't know the origin of that person (cf *usuli, chimbuko, chanzo, kiini*) (Ar)
uasilia n (u) naturalism; action or thought based on natural desires or instincts. (cf *tanakala*) (Ar)
uaskari n (u) the work of a policeman; police work: *Rafiki yangu anaipenda kazi ya uaskari wa polisi*, my friend likes police work. (Ar)
uaskofu n (u) episcopacy; the work of bishops. (Eng)
uati (pl *mbati*) n (u) see *mtambaapanya*
uatikaji n (u) (bot) transplanting
uatilifu n (u) incapacitation, disability; physical handicap: *Ajali ya gari ilimsababisha kupata uatilifu mdogo wa mkono*, the motor accident caused a slight incapacitation on her arm. (cf *mvunjiko, uharibikaji*)
uayari n (u) cunningness, deceit, slyness, craftiness, trickery: *Uayari wake wa mara kwa mara utamtia mashakani*, his habitual cunningness will cause him problems. (cf *ujanja, udanganyifu*) (Ar)
ubaba n (u) fatherhood

ubabaikaji n (u) the act, (method, etc.) of being puzzled; puzzling, puzzle, perplexity. (cf *fazaa*)

ubabaishaji[1] n (u) deceit, deception; bogus way: *Alichukua fomu za maombi ya viza kwa njia ya ubabaishaji*, he took the application forms for visa in a deceptive way.

ubabaishaji[2] n (u) the act (method, etc.) of deceiving sby; deceit.

ubabe n (u) heroism, boldness, derring-do, toughness, muscles: *Watu wale wanapenda kuonyeshana ubabe*, those people like to show each other's muscles. *Sera za ubabe*, the policies of flexing each other's muscles.

ubadhirifu n (u) extravagance, prodigality, lavishness: *Ubadhirifu wa fedha*, extravagance of money. (cf *ufujaji, upotevu*) (Ar)

ubadilifu n (u) 1. change, mutation. (cf *ugeuzi*) 2. fickleness, capriciousness. (cf *ugeugeu*)

ubadilikaji n (u) change, transformation, permutation. (cf *ugeukaji*)

ubadilishaji n (u) exchange, interchange: *Ubadilishaji wa wafungwa kati ya nchi zile mbili sasa umeanza*, the exchange of prisoners between those two countries has now started. (Ar)

ubaguzi n (u) discrimination, segregation: *Ubaguzi wa rangi*, racism. *Meneja alitumia ubaguzi wakati wa kuwaajiri watu*, the manager exercised discrimination when employing people. (cf *hatinafsi, upendeleaji*)

ubahaimu (also *ubahau*) n (u) 1. cruelty, brutality, inhumanity. (cf *ukatili, unyama*) 2. insanity, madness: *Ubahaimu wake umemfanya adharauliwe*, his insanity has led him to be despised. (cf *ujahili*) (Ar)

ubahaluli (also *ubahalulu*) n (u) ignorance, stupidity. (cf *ujinga, upumbavu*)

ubahalulu n (u) see *ubahaluli*

ubaharia n (u) seamanship, navigation. (cf *uanapwa, uanamaji*) (Ar)

ubahau[1] n (u) see *ubahaimu*

ubahau[2] n (u) foolishness, ignorance, stupidity: *Ubahau wake unatokana na kutojua kuandika na kusoma*, his ignorance comes from from illiteracy. (cf *ubahaimu, upumbavu*)

ubahili n (u) miserliness, meanness: *Ubahili ni sifa mbaya*, miserliness is a bad trait. (cf *ugomo, uchoyo, ukavu*) (Ar)

ubainifu n (u) 1. elucidation, explication, explanation. (cf *uchambuzi, ufafanuzi*) 2. recognition: perception, understanding: *Nilipata ubainifu wa hesabu ile kutokana na maelezo ya mwalimu*, I was able to understand that sum from the explanation of the teacher. (cf *utambuzi*) (Ar)

ubakaji n (u) 1. catching, grabbing, grasping. 2. raping, defilement: *Ubakaji wa wasichana*, the raping of girls.

ubakwaji n (u) 1. the act of being caught, grabbed, etc. in sth. 2. the act of being raped, defiled, etc.

ubale (pl *mbale*) n (u) 1. slice, piece, chunk. 2. middle strips of palm leaves called *miyaa*.

ubalehe n (u) puberty, young adulthood: *Msichana yule amefikia ubalehe*, that girl has reached puberty. (cf *upevu*) (Ar)

ubalighishaji n (u) conveyance, transmission, deliverance. (cf *uwasilishaji, upelekaji, ufikaji*) (Ar)

ubalozi (pl *balozi*) n (u) 1. ambassadorial work: *Ana uzoefu mkubwa wa kazi ya ubalozi*, he has a lot of diplomatic experience. 2. embassy, consulate: *Alikwenda kwenye ubalozi kutengeneza viza yake*, he went to the embassy to process his visa.

ubamba[1] n (u) a flat thin piece of anything such as metal, corrugated iron, etc.; a flake of sth.

ubamba[2] n (u) a board for collecting refuse. (cf *bango*)

ubambikaji n (u) soaking, dipping, drenching. (cf *urowekaji*)

ubambo n (u) (vet) wingborne.

ubanaji n (u) a the cutting down of sth; reduction: *Ubanaji wa matumizi*, the cutting down of expenses.
ubanangaji n (u) destruction, havoc, devastation, ruin. (cf *uborongaji, uharibifu, uvurugaji*)
ubango¹ n (u) 1. the leathery sheath of a betel nut. 2. (*bot*) a kind of reed.
ubango² n (u) (in Christianity) the cross of Saint Andrew.
ubango³ n (u) (*naut*) the edge of a sailing vessel.
ubanyaji n (u) 1. rectification, correction, repairment. 2. confusion, mess, disorder.
ubani n (u) 1. (*bot*) frankincense, incense. (*idms*) *Peleka ubani*, send contribution e.g. money to the bereaved family. *Tia ubani*, pray for the dead. 2. (*fig*) customary fee given to a trainer or teacher when beginning or completing his instruction. 3. used in the expression: *Wangu wa ubani*, the one I really love most. 4. a kind of sweet that is elastic like rubber. (Ar)
ubano (also *mbano*) n (u) see *kibaniko*
ubao¹ n (u) 1. plank, wood, board. 2. bench, settle; long seat (cf *benchi*) 3. blackboard, chalkboard.
ubao² n (u) 1. (*naut*) used in the expressions: *Ubao wa maliki*, the first bottom strake adjoining the keel. *Ubao wa chanda*, equerry serving as half keelson and supporting both apron and mass foot. 2. used in the expression: *Piga ubao*, float in the water.
ubapa (also *bapa*) n (u) 1. flatness; flat surface: *Huu ni ubapa wa kisu*, this is the flat surface of the knife. 2. flat blade of a knife, etc. 3. (*math*) plane: *Ubapa nambari*, number plane.
ubaradhuli n (u) 1. rudeness, impoliteness: *Mzee alimpiga mwanawe kwa ajili ya ubaradhuli wake*, the parent beat his child for rudeness. (cf *usafihi, ufidhuli*) 2. ignorance, dullness, stupidity, imbecility, foolishness: *Ubaradhuli wake kwenye masomo hausemeki*, his dullness in the studies is beyond description. (cf *ujinga*) 3. gayness, faggism, homosexuality. (cf *ushoga, uhanithi*) (Ar)
ubaramaki n (u) 1. the tendency to think that one knows a lot; a know-all attitude. 2. deceit, juggery. (cf *ujanja, uayari, udanganyifu*) (Pers, Ar)
ubaridi¹ n (u) 1. coldness, coolness. 2. gentleness, calmness, quietness. (Ar)
ubaridi² n (u) the dryness of a skin. (cf *uyabisi*) (Ar)
ubarobaro n (u) see *ubarubaru*
ubarubaru (also *ubarobaro*) n (u) adolescence, youth. (cf *ushababi, ujana*)
ubasha n (u) sodomy, pederasty; the practice of a man having sexual relations with a male (cf *uafandi, ulawiti, ufiraji, umende*.)
ubashasha (also *ubashahi*) n (u) cheerfulness, gaiety, blithness. (cf *ucheshi, uchangamfu*)
ubashashi n (u) see *ubashasha*
ubashiri n (u) 1. preaching, propagation, sermonizing. (cf *utabiri, uaguzi*) 2. prediction, prophecy, foretelling. (Ar)
ubashiru n (u) (in Islam) a chunk of meat given to a muezzin when an animal is slaughtered and the meat is given to people for charity purposes.
ubati¹ n (u) out-house, lean-to wing, out-building. (cf *kipenu*)
ubati² (pl *mbati*) n (u) a thin cane for flogging children; a thin small whip. (cf *mkwaju, uchapu*)
ubati³ n (u) a piece of corrugated iron for roofing a house, etc. (cf *bati*)
ubatilifu n (u) 1. the act of performing an illegal matter. 2. abolition, nullity, emptiness. (Ar)
ubatilikaji n (u) the act (method, etc.) of nullifying sth.
ubatizaji n (u) baptizing (Eng)

ubatizo *n* (*u*) baptism, christening; the act of baptizing. (Eng)
ubavu[1] (pl *mbavu*) *n* (*u*) 1. (*anat*) rib. 2. side: *Lala ubavu*, lie on the side. *Ngalawa imelala ubavu*, the canoe lies on the side. (cf *upande*) 3 (*idm*) *Hana ubavu*, he has no guts.
ubavu[2] *adv* on the side
ubawa (pl *mbawa*) *n* (*u*) 1. wing of a bird or insect. (*prov*) *Kila ndege huruka kwa ubawa wake*, every bird flies according to its wings i.e. cut your coat according to your cloth. 2. sth that looks like a wing in appearance, function or position relative to the main body: *Ubawa wa eropleni*, the wing of an aeroplane.
ubawabu *n* (*u*) doorkeeping; the work of a doorkeeper. (Ar)
ubaya *n* (*u*) wickedness, badness, evil. (cf *ubovu, uovu, udhaifu*)
ubazazi *n* (*u*) 1 dishonesty, deceit, trickery, hypocrisy: *Ubazazi wake umemtia hatarini*, his cheating has put him in danger. (cf *ulaghai, udanganyifu*) 2. the habit of wandering. (cf *utangaji*) (Ar)
ubeberu *n* (*u*) imperialism, colonialism. (cf *istiimari*)
ubedui *n* (*u*) cruelty, barbarity, ruthlessness. (cf *udhalimu, ukatili*)
ubele (pl *mabele*) *n* (*u*) (of bird or hen) feather: *Niliuokota ubele wa kuku karibu na nyumbani*, I picked up the feather of a hen near my house.
ubeleko (pl *mbeleko*) *n* (*u*) a piece of calico used usu by women for carrying a child on the back or hip. (*prov*) *Usikate ubeleko, mtoto hajazaliwa*, i.e. don't count the dress before a child is born i.e don't opt for sth ahead before you know all the relevant items required for your choice. (cf *uweleko*)
ubembe *n* (*u*) 1. prying, snooping. (cf *umbeya*) 2. wheedling, seduction, coaxing: *Msichana mrembo alighadhibika kwa sababu ya ubembe wa mzee yule*, the glamorous girl was annoyed because of that old man's seductive behaviour (cf *utongozaji*) 3. prostitution. (cf *uzinzi*)
ubenibeni *n* (*u*) disorientation; loss of direction.
ubepari *n* (*u*) capitalism; free enterprise, laissezfaire. (Hind)
ubereuzaji *n* (*u*) inattentiveness, the act (method, etc.) of paying least attention to sth because of lack of interest in it.
uberu (pl *mberu*) *n* (*u*) (*naut*) a small cloth hung on a mast in a dhow or boat.
ubeti (pl *beti*) *n* (*u*) (*poet*) verse, stanza: *Shairi lake lina beti nyingi*, his poem has many stanzas. (Ar)
ubia[1] (pl *mbia*) *n* (*u*) a special pan or pot for frying *vitumbua*, a kind of fritter.
ubia[2] *n* (*u*) partnership; joint venture: *Ubia wenye ukomo*, limited partnership. *Serikali yetu imeingia katika ubia na kampuni ya binafsi*, our government has joined partnership with a private company. (cf *ushirika*)
ubibi (also *ubibiye*) *n* (*u*) the state of regarding oneself as a good lady. (cf *ubibiye*)
ubibiye *n* (*u*) see *ubibi*
ubichi *n* (*u*) 1. greenness, rawness, freshness. 2. moistness, dampness. (cf *umajimaji*) 3. (of meat, etc) rawness, uncookedness. 4. immaturity, inexperience.
ubigoubigo pl (*mbigombigo*) *n* (*u*) 1. bank, edge, margin: *Alisimama kwenye ubigoubigo wa mto*, he stood on the bank of the river (cf *ukingo, terebesha, ugenge, mleoleo*) 2. (*fig*) verge, brink: *Mfanyabiashara yumo katika ubigoubigo wa kufilisika*, the businessman is on the verge of bankruptcy.
ubikira *n* (*u*) virginity (cf *uzinda, uanawari*) (Ar)
ubinaadamu *n* (*u*) humanity, kindness: *Ubinaadamu ni kitu azizi*, humanity is a precious thing. (cf *utu, unaadamu*)
ubinafsi *n* (*u*) individualism, self-

centredness, egotism, selfishness. (Ar)

ubinafsishaji n (u) privatization: *Mfumo wa ubinafsishaji*, the system of privatization. (Ar)

ubinda (pl *mbinda*) n (u) 1. the act of girding up a loin-cloth by passing the ends between the thighs and tucking it to the front or back position of the waist. 2. a small piece of cloth used to dress a baby in its private parts; napkin. (cf *nepi, winda*)

ubingwa n (u) 1. expertise, proficiency, mastery (cf *umahiri, ustadi*) 2. championship, title: *Timu yao inaendelea kutetea ubingwa wake vizuri*, their team continues to defend its title well.

ubini[1] n (u) relationship with someone on the father's side. (Ar)

ubini[2] n (u) forgery: *Alifungwa kwa kosa la ubini*, he was imprisoned for forgery. (Ar)

ubinja n (u) see *mbinja*

ubishanaji n (u) provocation, instigation. (cf *uchokozanaji*)

ubishani n (u) argument, debate.

ubishi n (u) 1. argument, dispute: *Usilete ubishi wa bure hapa*, don't bring arguments here unnecessarily. (cf *ukinzani, ushindani, upinzani*) 2. obstinacy, obduracy: *Ubishi mwingi hauna maana*, excessive obstinacy is useless. (cf *ukaidi, ushupavu*)

ubivu n (u) ripeness, mellowness.

uboharia n (u) 1 the work of looking after goods in a godown. 2 the discipline of looking after goods in a godown.

uboho n (u) (*anat*) 1. bone marrow 2. brain.

uboi n (u) the work of a houseboy; houseboy work.

ubomoaji n (u) demolition; pulling down of a building, etc.: *Ubomoaji wa nyumba*, the destruction of houses.

ubongo (also *bongo*) n (u) 1. (*anat*) brain: *Ubongo wa nyuma*, hind brain, after brain; rhombencephalon.

2. intelligence.

ubora n (u) 1. superiority, greatness. 2. excellence, fineness,

uboreshaji n (u) improvement, amelioration: *Uboreshaji wa huduma*, improvement of services.

uboreshwaji n (u) the act (method, etc.) of being improved: *Uboreshwaji wa huduma za umma*, the act of social services being improved.

uborongaji n (u) destruction, devastation, damage, harm. (cf *uharibifu, ubanangaji*)

ubovu n (u) 1. weakness, badness. (cf *udhaifu*) 2. rotteness, badness: *Ubovu wa tunda hili labda umesababishwa na mdudu*, the rottenness of this fruit has probably been caused by an insect. (cf *ubaya*)

ubozi n (u) stupidity, foolishness, ignorance: *Ubozi wake kwenye masomo umemhuzunisha mwalimu*, his stupidity in the lessons has saddened the teacher. (cf *udubu, ubaradhuli*)

ubua n (u) see *bua*[1]

ububu[1] (also *ububwi*) n (u) 1. dumbness, muteness. 2. reticence, taciturnity: *Ububu wake unadhihirika waziwazi pale watu wanapoongea*, his taciturnity becomes evident when people talk.

ububu[2] n (u) a kind of small black bead.

ububwi n (u) see *ububu*[1]

ubuda n (u) senescence, agedness, old age. (cf *utuuzima, ukongwe, uzee*)

ubuge n (u) frequent nibbling.

ubugu (pl *mbugu*) n (u) (*bot*) a creeping plant which can be used as a substitute for cord.

ubuku n (u) the act of eating food in the kitchen before being dished out.

ubukuzi[1] n (u) swotting; studying hard esp when examinations are near.

ubukuzi[2] n (u) discovery, finding: *Ubukuzi wa kashfa ile umemfedhehesha waziri*, the discovery of that scandal has embarrassed the minister. (cf *ugunduzi, uvumbuzi*)

ubunge n (u) parliamentarianship; the work, office, etc of a member of parliament: *Alipigania ubunge kwa vishindo*, he contested for parliamentarianship with vigour.

ubunifu n (u) creativity: *Walimu wanatakiwa kukuza ubunifu darasani*, teachers are required to promote creativity in the class.

ubutu n (u) bluntness, dullness.

ubuyu n (u) (*bot*) 1. pulp of a baobab kernel. 2. the stone of a baobab tree.

ubwabwa n (u) 1. soggy rice prepared for a baby or a sick person. (cf *mashendea*) 2. gruel of rice prepared for a baby; rice pap.

ubwana n (u) mastership, lordship, overlordship.

ubwanyenye n (u) a bourgeois outlook; a lordly outlook; lordliness. (cf *ulodi, umwinyi*)

ubwege n (u) stupidity, imbecility, foolishness. (cf *ubozi, ujinga, upumbavu*)

ubwete n (u) laziness, idleness: *Piga ubwete*, be lazy. (cf *ugoigoi, ukunguni, uvivu*)

ubwiri n (u) (*bot*) mildew; a fungus like a white powder that grows on plants and other surfaces when they are wet.

ucha¹ n (u) see *ncha*

ucha² n (u) see *uchaji*

uchaaza n (u) brightness after downpour. (cf *kichaaza, uchechea*)

uchache n (u) paucity, shortage, dearth, scarcity: *Uchache wa fedha*, the shortage of money (cf *uchechefu, ukufi, uhaba*)

uchachu n (u) 1. sourness, acidity, tartness: *Mchuzi huu umeshaingia uchachu*, this curry is already sour. 2. (of fruits) tartness, acerbity, sourness: *Embe hili lina uchachu*, this mango is sour. (cf *ugwadu*)

uchafu n (u) 1. dirt, grime, squalor, smudge, stain: *Nguo zake zina uchafu mwingi*, his clothes are too dirty. (cf *ukoo, uchama*)

2. dirt, filth, garbage. (cf *taka*)

uchafuzi n (u) dirt, pollution, filth: *Uchafuzi wa mazingira*, environmental pollution. *Uchafuzi wa hewa*, air pollution.

uchaga (pl *chaga*) n (u) a drying rack; a raised stage for storing grain, etc. (cf *kichaga*)

uchago (also *chago, mchago*) n (u) part of a bedstead on which the head rests; headboard side.

uchaguzi n (u) 1. election: *Uchaguzi ulikuwa huru na wa haki*, the election was free and fair: *Uchaguzi mdogo*, bye election. *Uchaguzi wa mitaa*, local elections. (cf *upigaji-kura*) 2. selection, choosing, picking; the act of choosing or selecting. (cf *uteuzi, utengaji*)

uchaji (also *ucha*) n (u) (of God, etc.) fear, respect, veneration. (cf *ucha, kicho, uogopaji*)

uchakavu¹ n (u) decrepitude, depreciation, deterioration; wear and tear: *Gari lile imeanza kuharibika kutokana na uchakavu*, that vehicle has started to be out of order because of wear and tear. *Uchakavu wa majengo*, the decrepitude of buildings. *Uchakavu wa miundombinu*, dilapidated infrastructure.

uchakachuaji n (u) (*colloq*) the practice of making adulteration or mixing sth with something else inorder to deceive e.g. petrol with diesel or milk with water; malpractice: *Uchakuchuaji wa mafuta*, fuel adulteration. (cf *ughushaji*)

uchakavu² n (u) the condition of a cloth to lose its original colour due to washing, etc.

uchakubimbi n (u) tattling, gossiping, tellbearing.

uchale¹ (also *usare*) n (u) 1. gash, cut; *Chanja uchale*, have an incision. *Pigwa chale*, be given an incision 2. blood brotherhood: *Kula uchale*, have blood brotherhood.

uchale² n (u) clownishness, humour, joke: *Uchale wako ulitufurahisha*

uchama   **uchechefu**   **U**

sana. your clownish antics entertained us very much. (cf *uchepe, udamisi, uchekeshaji*)

uchama *n* (*u*) dirt, grime, squalor: *Shati lake lina uchama mwingi,* his shirt is too dirty. (cf *uchafu, ukoo*)

uchambuzi¹ *n* (*u*) 1. selection, choice: *Uchambuzi wake wa mboga sokoni haukuwa mzuri,* his selection of vegetables at the market was not good. 2. (of publications, etc.) analysis, critique, review: *Uchambuzi wa kina,* intensive analysis. *Uchambuzi wa sentensi ulifanywa na mwanasarufi,* the analysis of the sentences was done by a grammarian. (cf *ufafanuzi, uhakiki*) 3. (*ling*) *Uchambuzi msamiati,* lexicology. (cf *elimu msamiati*)

uchambuzi² *n* (*u*) snooping, prying, the act of enquiring into other people's affairs: *Uchambuzi wake wa mambo ya watu wengine ulimponza,* her habit of snooping into other people's affairs put her into danger. (cf *udadisi, uchunguzi, upelelezi*)

uchamungu *n* (*u*) spirituality, pietism, religiousness, godliness, piety; extreme religious devotion. (cf *utawa, uwalii*)

uchane¹ *n* (*u*) (*bot*) a strip of palm leaf, etc.

uchane² *n* (*u*) (*bot*) a bunch of bananas held under its stalk.

uchanga *n* (*u*) 1. (of fruits, etc.) immaturity. unripeness. 2. (of human beings) immaturity, youthfulness. (cf *ukembe, utoto*)

uchangamfu *n* (*u*) joviality, vivacity, cheerfulness. (cf *ukunjufu, ucheshi*)

uchangaji *n* (*u*) splitting of firewood. cf *uchanjaji, upasuaji-kuni*

uchangiaji *n* (*u*) the act (method, etc.) of contributing towards sth: *Uchangiaji wake katika mjadala,* his contribution in the debate. *Uchangiaji wake wa Mfuko wa Fedha wa Kimataifa,* his contribution in International Monetary Fund.

uchangishaji *n* (*u*) act (method, etc.) of collecting money, etc from various sources.

uchangishwaji *n* (*u*) the act (method, etc.) of money, etc. being collected.

uchango *n* (*u*) (*anat*) small intestine. (cf *uchengelele, ujengelele*)

uchanguaji *n* (*u*) act (method, etc) of dissecting sth such as parts of an animal, plant, etc for purposes of study, etc; dissection.

uchangudoa *n* (*u*) (*colloq*) harlotry, prostitution, street walking. (cf *umalaya, uasherati*)

uchanjaa *n* (*u*) field, open ground, wilderness. (cf *ua, uwanja*)

uchanjaji *n* (*u*) 1. act (method, etc.) of splitting legs for firewood. 2. vaccination; the act or practice of vaccinating.

uchapaji¹ *n* (*u*) printing

uchapaji² *n* (*u*) beating, hitting, striking. (cf *upigaji*)

uchapakazi *n* (*u*) the act (method, etc of working diligently at sth

uchapasi *n* (*u*) cleverness or swiftness in doing sth; dexterity, adroitness.

uchapishaji *n* (*u*) publishing: *Uchapishaji ofisini,* desktop publishing.

uchapu *n* (*u*) (also *uchuapu*) *n* (*u*) a thin cane.

uchapwa *n* (*u*) tastelessness

ucharazaji *n* (*u*) flogging, whipping. (cf *uchapaji*)

uchavushaji *n* (*u*) pollination: *Uchavushaji mtambuko,* cross pollination.

uchawi *n* (*u*) 1. witchcraft, sorcery, magic. 2. tools used in witchcraft.

uche¹ *n* (*u*) see *wiche*

uche² *n* (*u*) see *uchechea*

uchechea *n* (*u*) dawn; brightness after cloudiness: *Kumeanza kutokea uchechea baada ya mvua kubwa kuanuka,* it has started to become bright after the heavy rain has stopped. (cf *uchaaza*)

uchechefu *n* (*u*) paucity, scarcity, shortage: *Uchechefu wa mchele nchini umewapa shida raia wengi,*

U   uchekaji

the scarcity of rice in the country has inflicted hardships on many citizens. (cf *upungufu, uhaba, ukosefu*)

uchekaji *n* (*u*) laughing, smiling; the act (manner, style, etc.) of laughing: *Uchekaji wake unachusha*, his laughing style is disgusting. (cf *mcheko*)

uchekechaji *n* (*u*) act (method, etc.) of sifting; sieving, winnowing. (cf *upembuzi, uchungaji*)

uchekechea *n* (*u*) a collection of small things which are of no significance. *Ule pale ni uchekechea wa matumatu*, that is a collection of young locusts.

uchekeleaji *n* (*u*) the act (method, etc.) of rejoicing for sth.

uchekeshaji *n* (*u*) act (method, etc.) of causing sby to laugh. (cf *udamisi, uchale*)

ucheleweshaji *n* (*u*) delay: *Kulikuwa na ucheleweshaji katika safari za ndege jana*, there was a delay in air services yesterday.

uchemkaji *n* (*u*) boiling

uchengelele (also *ujengelele*) *n* (*u*) small intestines; bowels. (cf *chengelele*)

ucheo *n* (*u*) see *macheo*²

uchepe *n* (*u*) 1. vagabondage, mischief, vagrancy, hooliganism, ruffianism: *Mwalimu alimpiga mwanafunzi kwa sababu alifanya uchepe darasani*, the teacher beat the student because he played pranks in the class. (cf *uhuni, uanaharamu*)
2. clownishness, buffoonery, funniness; joke, humour: *Mimi ninampenda kijana yule kwa uchepe wake*, I like that young man because of his humour. (cf *uchekeshaji, udamisi, uchale*)

uchepechepe *n* (*u*) wetness, moisture, dampness: *Nguo zake bado zina uchepechepe*, his clothes are still wet. (cf *umajimaji*)

uchepukaji (also *uchepuzi*) *n* (*u*) refraction: *Kosa la uchepukaji*, error of refraction.

uchepuzi *n* (*u*) see *uchepukaji*

uchimvi

ucheshi *n* (*u*) gaiety, humour, cheerfulness: *Ucheshi wake umewavutia watu wengi*, his humour has attracted a lot of people. (cf *uchangamfu*)

ucheu *n* (*u*) tilth, a tilled land; a piece of land cultivated ready for planting. (cf *weu*)

uchezaji *n* (*u*) 1. style of playing; playing: *Uchezaji wake katika mechi ulikuwa mzuri*, his style of playing in the match was good. 2. lack of seriousness: *Alianguka kwenye mitihani kutokana na uchezaji wake*, he failed in the examinations because of his lack of seriousness. 3. wobbling; moving unsteadily: *Uchezaji wa meza hii ni tishio kubwa kwa watoto wadogo*, the wobbling of this table is a big threat to small children.

uchezeshaji *n* (*u*) (in sports) refereeing, officiating, umpiring, judging: *Uchezeshaji wake kwenye Kombe la Dunia ulikuwa mbovu*, his refereeing in the World Cup was poor. 2. the act or practice of causing others to play.

uchi¹ *n* (*u*) 1. sex organs; private organs: *Uchi wa mnyama*, stark naked.
2. nakedness, nudity, undress. (cf *utupu*)

uchi² *adv* naked, nude: *Alikaa uchi*, he stayed naked. (cf *utupu*)

uchikichi *n* (*u*) (*naut*) carving on the front of a dhow, etc.

uchikichaji *n* (*u*) the cutting of sth by using a blunt knife.

uchikichia *n* (*u*) infancy; early childhood: *Uchikichia wao umewafanya wasiweze kuingia shuleni*, their infancy has made them ineligible for schooling. (cf *udogo*)

uchikichiaji *n* (*u*) patience, endurance. (cf *uvumiliaji*)

uchimbaji *n* (*u*) digging: *Uchimbaji wa madini*, mining. *Uchimbaji wa dhahabu*, gold mining. *Uchimbaji wa migodi*, mining.

uchimvi (also *utimbi*) *n*(*u*) mischievousness, selfishness, naughtiness: *Mzazi*

780

alimtaka mwanawe aache uchimvi, the parent wanted his child to stop being naughty. (cf *utukutu, ufisadi*)
Uchina *n* (*u*) (*geog*) China
uchinjo[1] *n* (*u*) a fee given to a butcher for slaughtering a goat, sheep, etc; slaughter's fee.
uchinjo[2] *n* (*u*) a slice of sth. (cf *chinjo*)
uchocheo *n* (*u*) connotation (cf *kidokezo*)
uchochezi *n* (*u*) incitement, provocation: *Uchochezi wa nchi ya jirani haustahamiliki*, the provocation of the neighbouring country is unbearable. (cf *chokochoko, uchonganishi, ufitinishaji*)
uchochole *n* (*u*) poverty, penury, impecunousness, mendicity, pauperism: *Uchochole umemfanya aishi kwa dhiki*, poverty has made her live in misery. (cf *ukata, umaskini, ufukara*)
uchochoro (also *kichochoro*) *n* (*u*) 1. alley, lane, back street, byway: *Wezi walijificha kwenye uchochoro huu*, the thieves hid themselves in this alley. 2. narrow path. (cf *ujia, kichochoro*)
uchofu *n* (*u*) see *uchovu*
uchokoo *n* (*u*) see *mchokoo*
uchokonozi *n* (*u*) scrutiny, unearthing, examination, digging, investigation, inquiring: *Uchokonozi ni sehemu muhimu ya waandishi-habari*, investigation is an important part of journalist.
uchokozi *n* (*u*) provocation, incitement: *Alijihami kutokana na uchokozi*, he defended himself out of provocation. (cf *ugobo, ushari*)
uchomaji *n* (*u*) burning, blazing: *Uchomaji moto wa nyumba*, the burning of houses; arson.
uchomoaji *n* (*u*) 1. extraction; the act, process etc. of pulling out sth: *Uchomoaji wa kisu*, the drawing out of a knife. 2. the act (process, etc.) of doing sth in a haste.
uchomozi[1] *n* (*u*) rising, coming out: *Uchomozi wa jua*, the rising of the sun;

bursting out of the sun. *Uchomozi wa mwezi*, the rising of the moon.
uchomozi[2] *n* (*u*) 1. see *ukomozi*. 2. a kind of local witchcraft supposedly believed to enter the body of the bewitched person.
uchonganishi *n* (*u*) incitement, instigation, formentation, provocation: *Uchonganishi wake uliwagombanisha marafiki wawili*, his incitement caused misunderstanding between two friends. (cf *uchochezi*)
uchongeaji (also *uchongezi*) *n* (*u*) the act of reporting against someone so as to hurt his reputation, etc.; calumny, traducement, false reporting: *Uchonqeaji uliopo mashuleni umeleta uhasama baina ya wanafunzi*, the false reporting that exists in the schools has brought discord amongst the students.
uchongezi (also *uchongeaji*) *n* (*u*) false accusation; calumny, traducement. (cf *ufitini*)
uchopozi *n* (*u*) 1. pickpocketing 2. extraction; pulling out of sth (cf *uchomoaji*)
uchoraji *n* (*u*) drawing, sketching, designing, painting, tracing: *Kazi yake ya uchoraji imempatia pesa nyingi*, his work in drawing has earned him a lot of money.
uchotara *n* (*u*) hybridism; the state, condition etc. of being a crossbreed person. (cf *usuriama, uhafukasti*)
uchovu (also *uchofu*) *n* (*u*) fatigue, exhaustion, weariness, tiredness: *Amekwenda kupumzika kutokana na uchovu mwingi wa kazi*, he has gone to rest because of too much exhaustion from work. (cf *unyong'onyevu*)
uchoyo *n* (*u*) see *choyo*
uchu *n* (*u*) 1. strong desire to eat fish or meat. 2. craving, hankering, yearning; strong desire: *Ana uchu wa kuoa mke wa tatu*, he has a strong desire to have

781

a third wife. (cf *hamu, kiu, shauku*)
uchujaji *n (u)* filtering, sieving, screening: *Uchujaji wa wagombea-ubunge*, the screening of the parliamentary candidates.
uchukivu *n (u)* disgust, dislike, hatred: *Ana uchukivu mkubwa na kazi ile*, he has a strong dislike of that job. (cf *karaha*)
uchuku *n (u)* exaggeration, lie, fish story, untruth, falsehood: *Anapenda kupiga uchuku anapozungumza*, he likes to exaggerate matters when he talks. (cf *uongo, uzandiki*)
uchukuaji *n (u)* act (method, etc.) of taking or carrying sth.
uchukuti (pl *chukuti*) *n (u)* see *ujukuti*
uchukuzi *n (u)* transportation, freightage, shipment, truckage: *Wizara ya uchukuzi*, the ministry for transport. *Amenunua gari ili afanye kazi ya uchukuzi*, he has bought a car to do transport work.
uchumaji *n (u)* 1. act (method, etc.) of plucking fruits, flowers, etc. 2. the act (method, etc.) of using resources economically to increase production.
uchumba *n (u)* courtship, engagement, betrothal, espousal, betrothment: *Funga uchumba*, engage someone for marriage. *Amefunga uchumba na msichana wa kabila lake*, he is engaged to a girl of his tribe.
uchumi *n (u)* economics, economy: *Uchumi tegemezi*, dependent economy. *Uchumi huria*, free enterprise. *Idara ya uchumi*, the department of economics. *Serikali inataka kuboresha uchumi wa nchi*, the government wants to improve the country's economy. (cf *iktisadi*)
uchumiaji *n (u)* act (method, etc.) of providing basic needs to a person.
uchumishaji *n (u)* act (method, etc.) of hiring people to pluck fruits in a plantation.
uchungu[1] *n (u)* 1. sadness, resentment, bitterness, anger: *Ameingiwa na uchungu baada ya kutukanwa burebure*, he has become bitter after being insulted for no reason. (cf *kichomi, hasira, maumivu*) 2. uterine contractions occuring in birth child; labour pains; birth pain. (*prov*) *Uchungu wa mwana aujua mzazi*, the pains of childbirth are known to the mother i.e. the difficulty of sth is best known to the sufferer. 3. pain; a sensation of hurting or strong discomfort in some of the body caused by an injury, disease, etc.
uchungu[2] *n (u)* (of fruits, medicine, etc.) bitterness, sourness, acridity, sharp pain: *Siwezi kulila chungwa hili kwa sababu ya uchungu wake*, I can't eat this orange because it is sour. *Mgonjwa amekataa kula dawa hii kwa sababu ya uchungu wake*, the patient has refused to take this medicine because of its bitterness.
uchunguzi *n (u)* 1. investigation, inquiry, probe, inquest: *Uchunguzi juu ya mauaji ya mwanakijiji sasa umemalizika*, the investigation of the murder of the villager is now complete. (cf *upekuzi, upelelezi, udadisi*) 2. inquiry, snooping: *Uchunguzi wake juu ya mambo ya watu wengine utamtia taabuni*, his prying into other people's affairs will lead him into problems. (cf *upelelezi*) 3. research, study, examination: *Uchunguzi wa uwezekano*, feasibility study. *Uchunguzi wa kitabibu*, medical examination. *Madaktari bado wanafanya uchunguzi juu ya tiba ya Ukimwi*, doctors are still carrying out research on the treatment of AIDS. (cf *utafiti*)
uchuro *n (u)* a bad omen, ill-omen; jinx: *Kabla hatujafunga safari, mzee yule akaanza kutuletea uchuro*, before we set out on the journey, that old man started to bring to us ill-omen. (cf *mkosi, nuhusi, ukorofi*)
uchusa *n (u)* sulkiness, sullenness,

grumpiness: the condition of showing resentment and ill-humour by sullen and withdrawn behaviour: *Msichana atakosa marafiki wengi kwa sababu ya uchusa wake,* the girl will miss many friends because of her sullenness.

uchusichusi *n (u)* darkness, lightlessness: *Uchusichusi ulipoingia, shangazi akawapeleka kuku wake bandani,* when darkness fell, my aunt sent her hens to the shed. (cf *giza*)

uchuuzi *n (u)* hawking, retail business: *Ameingia katika kazi ya uchuuzi siku hizi,* he has gone into retail business these days.

uchwara *adj* inferior, worthless, insignificant: *Nyumba ile ni uchwara,* that house is worthless. *Ukabaila ni uchwaru kijijini mwao,* lordohip has no value in their village. *Ubwanyenye uchwara,* petty bourgeoisie. (cf *duni*)

Udachi *n (u)* Germany (Eng)

udadisi *n (u)* inquisitiveness, curiosity, acquisitiveness: *Udadisi wake umewaudhi majirani,* his inquisitive behaviour has annoyed the neighbours. (cf *umbeya, usabasi, upelelezi*)

udagaa *n (u)* see *dagaa*

udago *n (u)* see *dagaa*

udaha *n (u) (bot)* a kind of chilly that is long and hot; cayenne pepper.

udakaji *n (u)* catching of a ball etc: *Udakaji wa mpira wa kipa wetu unapendeza,* the goalkeeping of our goal keeper is impressive.

udakiaji *n (u)* meddling, intrusion. (cf *udakuzi*)

udakizi *n (u)* interruption, interjection.

udaktari *n (u)* 1. medicine. 2. medical profession; medical practice: *Kazi ya udaktari ina heshima kubwa,* medical profession carries great respect. (cf *utabibu*) 3. doctorate, doctoral degree: *Ana shahadu ya udaktari katika isimu,* he has a doctoral degree in linguistics.

udaku *n (u)* snooping, intrusiveness, inquisitiveness, curiosity, inquiring: *Udaku mwingi unaweza kusababisha ugomvi kati ya watu,* too much inquisitiveness can cause misunderstanding between people. (cf *umbeya*)

udakuzi *n (u)* the habit of interfering in the discussions of other people; interloping, interruption, meddling, intrusion: *Nilimwambia asiyaingilie maneno ya watu wengine wanapozungumza kwani huo ni udakuzi,* I told him not to interfere in the discussion of other people when they are talking because that is intrusion. (cf *udakiaji, udaku*)

udalali *n (u)* auctioneering, brokerage.

udamisi *n (u)* clownishness, humour, joke: *Usimfanyie rafiki yako udamisi wowote,* don't crack jokes at your friend's expense. (cf *uchekeshaji, uchepe utani, mzaha*)

udanganyifu *n (u)* deceit, fraud, hypocrisy, cheating: *Alipata pesa kwa njia ya udanganyifu,* he obtained money by fraud. (cf *ulaghai, ujanja, ubabaishaji*)

udara *n (u)* see *ndara*

udekaji *n (u)* 1. (of a child) act (method, etc.) of behaving in a manner calculated to induce elders to pamper him. 2. conceitedness, haughtiness.

udekani (also *udekoni*) *n (u)* (in Christianity) the office of a deacon; deaconship.

udekoni *n (u)* see *udekani*

udekuaji (also *udenguaji*) *n (u)* 1. (of a fruit, bird, etc.) the act of knocking down; felling: *Udekuaji wa maembe ulifanywa na watoto wadogo,* the knocking down of the mangoes from the tree was done by the children. (cf *uangushaji*) 2. abrupt turning up of the head to look at sth that is passing, etc.: *Udekuaji wa kichwa wa kijana yule ulitokea pale alipopitwa na msichana mrembo,* the abrupt turning of the head of that young man occurred

when a beautiful girl passed him.
udenda *n (u)* drool from the mouth; drivel, slaver: *Udenda ulimtoka alipokuwa amelala,* he was drooling at the mouth when he was asleep. (cf *dovuo, ute, uderere*)
udenguaji *n (u)* see *udekuaji*
uderembwe *n (u)* smallness (cf *upunje*)
uderere *n (u)* drool, drivel; saliva from the mouth. (cf *udenda*)
udererekaji *n (u)* act (method, etc.) of performing an act lazily.
udererezi *n (u)* trickling, trilling: *Udererezi wa mate ya mtu yule aliyelala, ulinichusha,* the trickling of saliva from the person sleeping disgusted me.
udereva *n (u)* driving; the way one drives in an automobile, etc.
udevu (pl *ndevu*) *n (u)* beard: *Anapenda kufuga ndevu,* he likes to wear a beard.
udhahania *n (u)* abstraction: *Kiwango cha udhahania,* level of abstraction.
udhaifu *n (u)* 1. (of health) feebleness, frailty, debility, weakness. 2. poverty, penury: *Alishindwa kumwoa binti mzuri yule kutokana na udhaifu wake wa kipesa,* he failed to get married to that beautiful girl because of lack of money. (cf *ukata*) 3. evil, wickedness, meanness: *Hawezi kukusaidia kwa sababu ya udhaifu wake wa moyo,* he cannot help you because of his evil heart. (cf *ubaya*) (Ar)
udhalili *n (u)* inferiority, baseness, humiliation: *Kutawaliwa na nchi nyingine ni udhalili mkubwa,* to be ruled by another country is a great humiliation. (cf *unyonge*) (Ar)
udhalilishaji *n (u)* humiliation, mortification, humble pie: *Udhalilishaji wowote dhidi ya raia wake ni mbaya,* any humiliation against its citizens is bad. (cf *unyanyasaji*) (Ar)
udhalilishwaji *n (u)* the act (method, etc.) of being humiliated, humbled, etc. (cf *unyanyaswaji*)

udhalimu *n (u)* oppression, persecution, brutality: *Udhalimu wa serikali ya kijeshi kwa raia zake hauwezi kusahaulika,* the military government's brutality upon its citizens cannot be forgotten. (cf *uonevu, utesaji*) (Ar)
udhamini *n (u)* sponsorship, patnership, financial backing: *Timu yao inatafuta udhamini ili iweze kushiriki katika mashindano ya kimataifa,* their team is looking for sponsorship so that it can participate in international competitions. (cf *usimamiaji*) (Ar)
udhanifu *n (u)* suspicion, doubt, mistrust: *Udhanifu wake juu yangu mimi hauna msingi,* his suspicion on me is baseless. (cf *tuhuma, shaka*)
udh.i *vt, vi* 1. disturb, annoy, hector. (cf *ghasi, sumbua*) 2. provoke, enrage, exasperate, huff, anger: *Ukimuudhi baba yako, atakupiga,* if you anger your father, he will beat you. Prep. *udh.i.a* St. *udh.ik.a* Cs. *udh.ish.a* Ps. *udh.iw.a* Rp. *udh.i.an.a* (cf *ghadhibisha, kasirisha, hamakisha*) (Ar)
udhia *n (u)* 1. annoyance, disturbance, nuisance; pain in the neck: *Udhia wake unachusha,* his disturbance is disgusting. (cf *kero, adha, tafrani, usumbufu*) 2. provocation, annoyance: *Wanafunzi watukutu walikuwa wakimletea udhia mwalimu wao,* the naughty students were causing irritation to their teacher. (cf *hamaki*) (Ar)
udhibiti *n (u)* 1. control: *Udhibiti wa fedha za kigeni,* foreign exchange control. *Udhibiti husishi,* integrated control.
2. supervision. (Ar)
udhik.a *vi* be annoyed, be angry. *Ameudhika bila ya sababu,* he is annoyed for no reason. Prep. *udhik.i.a* St. *udhik.ik.a* Cs. *udhik.ish.a* (cf *kasirika*)
udhoofu *n (u)* weakness, frailty, feebleness: *Maradhi yake ya muda*

mrefu yamemtia udhoofu wa mwili, his long illness has caused him bodily weakness. (cf *udhaifu, ufefe.*)
udhu *n (u)* (in Islam) ablution; a washing of the body excluding private organs, done for religious purposes esp for praying: *Ana udhu,* he has taken ablution. *Hana udhu,* he has not taken ablution. (Ar)
udhuru *n (u)* 1. pretext; alleged reason. (cf *kisingizio, sababu*) 2. dire need; want: *Alikuja kwako kwa vile alikuwa ana udhuru wa kutaka kuonana na wewe,* he came to your place because he had a dire need of seeing you. (cf *dharura, haja*)
udi¹ *n (u)* 1. aloe wood; aromatic substance which derives from the heartwood of a special form. 2. (*idm*) *Kwa udi na uvumba,* in any possible means; by hook or by crook. (Ar)
udi² *n (u)* (*mus*) lute; an old stringed musical instrument related to the guitar having a short neck with a body shaped like a half pear and six to thirteen strings stretched along the fretted neck, which is often bent to form a share angle. (cf *gambusi*) (Ar)

udi

udikteta *n (u)* dictatorship: *Udikteta wa watu wachache,* oligarchy. *Udikteta hauwezi kukubalika katika ulimwengu wa leo,* dictatorship is unacceptable in the present world.

udini *n (u)* religiousness; religious bias: *Udini ni marufuku katika chama chetu,* religious bigotry is forbidden in our party.
udiwani *n (u)* councillorship (Ar)
udobi *n (u)* laundering; the work of a washerman or washerwoman: *Anaijua vizuri kazi ya udobi kwa vile nguo anozozifua ni safi,* he knows well how to launder because the clothes he washes are clean.
udodi *n (u)* a bracelet of fine wire or leather, usu worn round the arm. (cf *mkunzo*)
udodosaji *n (u)* 1. drawling; the act of hesitating in speech or writing: *Udodosaji wake katika kusoma ulimkasirisha mwalimu,* his manner of hesitating while reading annoyed the teacher. 2. cross-examination, interrogation: *Udodosaji wa mshtakiwa ulichukua masaa machache,* the cross-examination of the accused took a few hours. 3. investigation, research, study: *Udodosaji wa mtafiti uliwaudhi wasailiwa,* the investigation of the researcher annoyed the respondents. (cf *udadisi, uduhushi*)
udogo *n (u)* smallness, littleness, insignificance: *Tatizo lile halina udogo,* that problem is not a small one. (cf *usaghiri*)
udogoshaji *n (u)* the act of lowering the status, position, value, etc. of sby/sth; debasement, devaluation, humiliation. (cf *udunishaji, udhalilishaji*)
udogoshi *n (u)* dimunitiveness; the act of making sth to become small.
udohoudoho *n (u)* munchies, snacks: *Anapenda kula udohoudoho,* he likes to eat munchies.
udokozi *n (u)* pilfering, pilferage, filching, stealing.
udole *n (u)* strength: (*syn*) *Hana udole,* he is weak; he is not strong.
udondoshaji *n (u)* (*gram*) deletion, ellipsis: *Udondoshaji wa nomino,* nominal ellipsis. *Udondoshaji wa kitenzi,* verbal ellipsis. *Udondoshaji*

785

wa kishazi, clausal ellipsis.
udongo *n (u)* soil, earth: *Udongo mzito*, heavy soil. *Udongo mahuluku*, organic soil. *Udongo tifutifu*, loam soil. *Udongo wa mfinyanzi*, clay. (*prov*) *Udongo upate ulimaji*, soil needs cultivation. i.e. Act in time and don't wait until it is already late.
udugu *n (u)* 1. brotherhood, blood relationship: *Hana udugu na mimi*, he has no brotherly relationship with me. 2. comradeship.
udui *n u* see *ndui*
udukuzi¹ *n (u)* curiosity, inquisitiveness: *Udukuzi wake unaweza ukamharibia jina lake*, his inquisitiveness can spoil his name. (cf *umbeya, udadisi*)
udukuzi² *n (u)* the act (method, etc.) of taking things in small quantities.
uduni *n (u)* inferiority, lowness, cheapness: *Uduni wa kazi hii haustahamiliki*, the poor quality of this work is intolerable. (cf *udhaifu, uhafifu, ubaya*)
udumishaji *n (u)* act (method, etc) of sustaining, prolonging sth so that it lasts longer.
udunishaji *n (u)* humiliation, devaluation. (cf *unyanyasaji, udhalilishaji*)
uduvi *n (u)* (*zool*) a kind of small prawn found in shallow waters; shrimp. (cf *uruso, ushimba*)

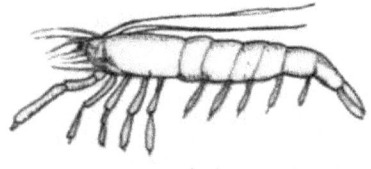

uduvi

uegemeaji *n (u)* the act (method, etc.) of leaning over sth; inclination.
uegemeshaji *n (u)* act (method, etc.) of parking.
uegeshaji *n (u)* parking: *Uegeshaji mbaya*, poor parking.
uele *n (u)* see *uwele*
uelewa *n (u)* see *uelewaji*

uelewaji (also *uelewa*) *n (u)* understanding, comprehension, knowledge: *Uelewaji wake katika jambo lile ulikuwa mdogo*, his understanding on that matter was little (cf *ufahamu*)
uelekeo *n (u)* tendency, direction: *Uelekeo wa lazima wa magari*, obligatory direction of traffic. *Uelekeo kati*, central tendency.
uelekevu *n (u)* see *wekevu*
uelewano *n (u)* understanding, relationship, rapport: *Uelewano wake na wafanyakazi ni mbaya*, his relationship with the workers is bad.
uendaji *n (u)* style of walking, moving, etc.
uendekezaji *n (u)* the method or practice of pampering esp. a child.
uendelezaji *n (u)* 1. development, growth, extension: *Uendelezaji wa elimu ya watu wazima nchini ni jambo zuri*, the development of adult education in the country is a good thing. (cf *usitawi, uamirishaji*) 2. spelling, orthography; the way in which a word is spelt.
uendelezwaji *n (u)* the state of being developed, extended, improved, etc.
uendeshaji *n (u)* 1. administration, management: *Uendeshaji wake wa ofisi ni mbaya*, his running of the office is poor. 2. driving: *Uendeshaji mbovu wa magari umekuwa tishio kubwa kwa watembea kwa miguu*, careless driving has become a big threat to the pedestrians. 3. proceedings: *Uendeshaji wa kesi mahakamani una dosari nyingi*, court proceedings have many flaws.
uendeshwaji *n (u)* the act (method, etc.) of sth being administered or managed: *Uendeshwaji wa chaguzi za mitaa*, the administration of local government elections.
ueneaji *n (u)* spread, diffusion, expansion.
uenezaji *n (u)* distribution, allocation.
uenezi *n (u)* 1. dissemination, propagation.

786

2. publicity: *Uenezi wa habari*, dissemination of information.
uenyeji *n (u)* the state, condition, etc. of being a host.
uenyeketi *n (u)* chairmanship: *Nafasi ya uenyekiti iko wazi katika chama chetu*, the position of chairmanship is vacant in our party.
ufa (pl *nyufa*) *n (u)* crack, split, slit. (*prov*) *Usipoziba ufa utajenga ukuta*, if you ignore a small thing now, you will have to pay a heavy price later; a stitch in time saves nine. *Bonde la ufa*, the rift valley.
ufafanuzi *n (u)* interpretation, elaboration, clarification, explication, explanation: *Ufafanuzi wa sheria ulifanywa na wakili mkuu wa serikali*, the interpretation of the law was done by the attorney general. (cf *sherehe*)
ufagio (also *peo*) *n (u)* broom, sweeper, besom: *Hassan amenunua ufagio mpya*. Hassan has bought a new broom.
ufagizi (also *ufyagizi*) *n (u)* sweeping, cleaning, brushing: *Anapenda kazi ya ufagizi barabarani*, he likes sweeping the streets.
ufahamu *n (u)* 1. comprehension, understanding: *Ufahamu wake wa dunia ni mdogo*, his understanding of the world is limited. (cf *uelewaji*, *ujuzi*) 2. comprehension lesson: *Wanafunzi wangu wanalipenda somo la ufahamu*, my students like comprehension lesson. (Ar)
ufahari *n (u)* 1. pride, haughtiness, hauteur, arrogance: *Ushindi kwa timu yetu utaleta ufahari nchini*, victory for our team will bring pride to the country. (cf *riya*) 2. the condition or tendency to enjoy living in luxuries.
ufakiri *n (u)* poverty, indigence. (cf *uchochole*, *ukata*, *umasikini*)
ufalme (pl *falme*) *n (u)* 1. kingdom, empire: *Ufalme wa Uingereza*, British Empire. 2. realm, dominion. 3. crown.
ufanani *n (u)* similarity, resemblance, likeness. (cf *ushabihiano*) (Ar)
ufanifu *n (u)* success, prosperity, good life: *Ufanifu wao ulikuja kwa haraka*, their prosperity came quick. (Ar)
ufanisi *n (u)* success, achievement, efficiency: *Waziri aliwahimiza wafanyakazi kuongeza ufanisi katika kazi*, the minister urged the workers to increase efficiency at work. (cf *fanaka*, *mafanikio*, *usitawi*)
Ufaransa *n (u)* (*geog*) France (Fr)
ufarisi *n (u)* 1. expertise, proficiency: *Yeye hana ufarisi wowote katika uendeshaji-magari*, he is not an expert driver. 2. expertise in horse riding. (Ar)
ufasaha *n (u)* eloquence, articulation, elocution: *Alizungumza kwenye mjadala kwa ufasaha mkubwa*, he spoke in the debate with great eloquence. (cf *usemaji*, *ulumbaji*)
ufashisti *n (u)* fascism (Eng)
ufasiki *n (u)* prostitution, harlotry: *Ufasiki si kitu kizuri kuwepo katika jamii yetu*, prostitution is not a good thing to exist in our society. (cf *ufuska*, *uasherati*, *uzinzi*) (Ar)
ufatiliaji (also *ufuatiliaji*) *n (u)* follow-up: *Ufatiliaji wa maazimio yetu ya mkutano bado haujafanyika*, the follow-up of the resolutions of our meeting has not been made. *Ufuatiliaji duni*, poor follow-up.
ufawidhi *n (u)* adjutancy; the work of serving as an assistant (cf *upambe*) (Ar)
ufefe *n (u)* see *ufyeufye* [1] and *ufyeufye* [2]
ufichuaji *n (u)* the act (method, etc of revealing sby/sth; disclosure, exposure, revelation (cf *ufichuzi*)
ufichuzi *n (u)* exposure, revelation, disclosure (cf *ufichuaji*)
ufidhuli (also *ufedhuli*) *n (u)* rudeness, contempt, disrespect: *Ufidhuli wake kwa wazee unazidi kila siku*, his rudeness towards his parents increases every day. (cf *usafihi*, *ufyosi*, *upeketevu*)
ufifi *n (u)* rumour, gossip, clue, hint: *Hajapata ufifi wowote juu ya watu*

waliozama baharini, he has not got at all over the people who were drowned in the sea. (cf *fununu, uvumi, tetesi*)

ufifiaji *n (u)* decline, deterioration, fading: *Ufifiaji wa mwanga*, the fading of the light.

ufifilizi¹ *n (u)* dilution, weakening, attenuation, adulteration: *Ufifilizi wa maziwa*, the dilution of the milk. (cf *ufifiaji*)

ufifilizi² *n (u)* swindling or cheating for personal benefit.

ufikichaji *n (u)* act (method, etc) of stripping off grains, etc.; husking, skinning, paring.

ufilipino *n (u) (geog)* Philippine

ufinga (also *ufunga*) (pl *finga*) *n (u)* verandah, porch; a stone bench or seat of masonry erected in front of a house for resting, etc.

Ufini *n (u) (geog)* Finland

ufinyanzi *n (u)* pottery, ceramics, crockery, earthenware: *Anapenda kazi ya ufinyanzi*, he likes pottery.

ufiraji *n (u)* pederasty; sodomy between males (cf *ulawiti*)

ufisadi *n (u)* 1. vice, indecency, viciousness, immorality: *Ufisadi wake wa kuiba mali ya umma umezidi*, his vice of stealing public property has increased. (cf *ulaji-rushwa, uovu, uharibifu)* 2. prostitution, whoredom (cf *umalaya, uasherati*) 3. (esp used in Kenya) corruption. (Ar)

ufite *n (u)* gore, gusset; a long narrow piece of cloth cut from a dress. (cf *upapi, utepe*)

ufitini *n (u)* act (method, etc) of malicious reporting against sby; calumny, traducement, aspersion, slandering (cf *uchongeaji, uchongezi*)

ufito¹ (pl *fito*) *n (u)* a long thin piece of stick, rod, etc. used for building purposes.

ufito² (pl *fito*) *n (u)* a present given by a parent to a teacher when entering his child to a Koranic school.

ufizi (pl *fizi*) *n (u)* (*anat*) (of the jaw) gum. (cf *sine*)

ufu¹ *n (u)* deadness; the state of being dead.

ufu² (pl nyufu) *n (u)* (*bot*) grated coconut.

ufuasi *n (u)* the act of following a particular ideology, system; adherence to a particular ideology, system, etc: *Ufuasi wao katika siasa ya ujamaa uko madhubuti*, their adherence to socialist ideas is firm.

ufuatiliaji *n (u)* see *ufatiliaji*

ufufuaji *n (u)* 1. resurrection, reincarnation, revival: *Ufufuaji wa binaadamu ni kitu cha lazima*, the resurrection of a human being is a must (cf *ufufuo*) 2. (*fig*) revival, renewal, revitalization: *Uchumi wa nchi yetu unahitaji ufufuaji wa haraka*, the economy of our country calls for urgent revival.

ufufuo *n (u)* resurrection, reincarnation: *Siku ya ufufuo*, the day of resurrection.

ufugaji *n (u)* animal husbandry: *Ufugaji bora*, livestock management. *Ufugaji wa ng'ombe*, domestication of cattle. *Ufugaji wa wanyama*, livestock.

ufujaji *n (u)* waste, misappropriation: *Ufujaji wa mali ya umma*, misappropriation of public funds.

ufukara *n (u)* 1. poverty, indigence, penury, impoverishment: *Ufukara wa ghafla umenitia katika shida kubwa*, the sudden poverty has landed me in great difficulties. (cf *uchochole*) 2. worthlessness, wretchedness, abjectness, meanness: *Watu wanambeza kwa sababu ya ufukara wake*, people despise him because of his wretchedness. (cf *unyonge, uduni*) (Ar)

ufukizaji *n (u)* act (method, etc.) of burning incense, etc.

ufukiziaji *n (u)* act (method, etc.) of exorcizing spirits.

ufukizo *n (u)* the burning of incense; the burning of aromatics, etc.

ufuko¹ (also *ufukwe, ufuo*) *n (u)* shoreline,

sandy beach; the sandy margin of the seashore, the edge of the body of water: *Waliziweka mashua zao kwenye ufuko*, they anchored their boats on the shoreline. (cf *pwaa*)
ufuko² n (u) see *ufuo²*
ufukufuku n (u) incitement, formentation, provocation: *Ufukufuku wake ulimletea uhasama kwa rafiki zake*, his provocation caused hatred to his friends. (cf *uchokozi, uchochezi, ufitini*)
ufukwe n (u) see *ufuko¹*
ufumaji n (u) act (method, etc.) of weaving; knitting, interlacing 2. stabbing, spearing, piercing, goring.
ufumaniaji n (u) see *ufumanizi*
ufumanizi (also *ujamaniaji*) n (u) act (method, etc.) of catching sby red-handed, committing an evil deed esp that of adultery.
ufumbati (pl *fumbati*) n (u) see *mfumbati*
ufumbi (pl *fumbi*) n (u) see *mfumbi*
ufumbuzi n (u) 1. elucidation, interpretation, explanation: *Kahini alitoa ufumbuzi wa ndoto yangu*, the soothsayer made an interpretaton of my dream. (cf *ufafanuzi, ubainifu*) 2. solution, denouement, revelation: *Ufumbuzi wa kudumu*, permanent solution. *Viongozi walijaribu sana kutafuta ufumbuzi wa kisiasa wa mgogoro wenyewe*, the leaders tried their best to seek the political solution to the conflict. (cf *utatuzi, suluhisho*)
ufumi n (u) act (method etc.) of weaving; knitting, interlacing. (cf *ufumaji*)
ufumwele (pl *fumwele*) n (u) (*bot*) fibre from raffia palm, etc.
ufundi¹ n (u) expertise, skilfulness, artistry: *Ana ufundi mkubwa wa kuimba hadharani*, he has great skill of singing in public. (cf *uhodari, ubingwa, utaalamu*)
ufundi² n (u) craftmanship, artisanship: *Ufundi magari*, motor mechanics. *Ufundi mchundo*, basic technology.

Ufundi sadifu, qualified craftmanship. *Ufundi stadi*, expert workmanship. *Ufundi taaluma*, high technology. *Shule ya ufundi*, technical school.
ufundishaji n (u) teaching, lecturing, training: *Ufundishaji soka*, the training of soccer. (cf *usomeshaji*)
ufunga (pl *funga*) n (u) see *ufinga*
ufungaji n (u) 1. scoring: *Mchezaji wetu anaongoza katika ufungaji wa magoli*, our player is leading in goal scoring. 2. closing, shutting: *Ufungaji wake wa mlango kwa nguvu ulitukera*, his act of closing the door forcefully angered us.
ufungu (pl *fungu*) n (u) family, kinship, ancestry; blood ties. (cf *uzawa, mlango, ukoo*)
ufunguo¹ (pl *funguo*) n (u) key, opener: *Tundu la ufunguo*, key hole. *Ufunguo malaya*, master key; skeleton key.
ufunguo² (pl *funguo*) n (u) (of a watch) winder, knob.
ufunguo³ n (u) key; a thing that explains or solves something else, as a book of answers, the explanations on a map, etc.
ufunguzi n (u) inauguration, installation: *Waziri alishiriki katika ufunguzi wa zahanati*, the minister took part in the inauguration of the dispensary. 2. act (method, etc.) of opening sth that is closed.
ufuniko n (u) stopper, lid, cover. (cf *kifuniko*)
Ufunuo n (u) (in Christianity) Revelation; the Book of Revelation: *Ufunuo wa Yohana Mbatizaji*, the Revelation of St. John the Divine.
ufuo¹ (pl *fuo*) n (u) see *ufuko¹*
ufuo² (also *ufuko*) (pl *fuo*) n (u) a hollow made beneath the bed on which a corpse is laid to allow the water to pass through the hollow, when the corpse is washed.
ufuo³ (pl *fuo*) n (u) drainage, channel.
ufuo⁴ n (u) origin, source, beginning (cf *chanzo, chimbuko*)
ufupi n (u) brevity, briefness, shortness:

U ufupishaji

Kwa ufupi, in short. *Sikuielewa taarifa ile kutokana na ufupi wake*, I did not understand that statement because of its brevity.
ufupishaji *n* (*u*) act (method, etc.) of reducing sth.
ufupisho *n* (*u*) 1. abbreviation, synopsis: *Ufupisho wa shahada ya* Master of Arts *ni* M.A., the abbreviation for the degree of Master of Arts is M.A. 2. summary, precis writing: *Wanafunzi walifanya zoezi la ufupisho*, the students did an exercise on precis writing. (cf *muhtasari*)
ufurufuru *n* (*u*) 1. anger, ire, bitterness, wrath: *Ufurufuru mwingi husababisha hasara*, excessive anger causes damage. (cf *hasira, hamaki*) 2. cloudiness, haziness: *Sitaendesha gari yangu leo kwa sababu kuna ufurufuru*, I will not drive my car today because it is misty. (cf *utusitusi, giza*)
ufusa *n* (*u*) fart: a gas that comes out as a result of farting noiselessly (cf *ushuzi*)
ufusaji *n* (*u*) act (method, etc) of farting noiselessly.
ufusio[1] *n* (*u*) the act of filling in a hole; the act of sprinkling small stones on the foundation of a building.
ufusio[2] *n* (*u*) fart; breaking wind without a noise.
ufuska *n* (*u*) prostitution, harlotry, whoredom. (cf *ufasiki*)
ufuso *n* (*u*) fart (cf *ushuzi*)
ufuta *n* (*u*) (*bot*) 1. sesmum, simsim. *Sesamum orientale*. 2. the seeds of this plant.
ufyambo (pl *fyambo*) *n* (*u*) pad, sanitary napkin. (cf *sodo*)
ufyeufye[1] *n* (*u*) a kind of reed toy used by children.
ufyeufye[2] (also *unane*) *n* (*u*) 1. emaciation, leanness, frailty, weakness, thinness: *Ufyeufye wake umesababishwa na maradhi*, his weakness has been caused by sickness. (cf *ufefe, udhaifu*) 2. poverty, penury, impecuniousness:

uganga

Ufyeufye umezagaa, duniani, poverty is widespread in the world. (cf *umaskini, ufakiri*)
ufyosi *n* (*u*) josh, jest, absurdity: *Mzee alimpiga bintiye kwa sababu ya ufyosi wake*, the parent beat his daughter because of her absurdity. (cf *utani, masihara*)
uga[1] *n* (*u*) an open field; an open ground. (cf *uchanjaa, uwanja*)
ug.a[2] *vi* bellow, blare, roar: *Fahali aliuga kwa hasira*, the bull bellowed angrily. Prep. *ug.i.a* St. *ug.ik.a* Cs. *ug.ish.a* Ps. *ug.w.a*
ugaga also *ugavu* *n* (*u*) dental calculus, tartar; a hard deposit formed around the teeth, consisting of saliva proteins, food deposits, etc.
ugagundi *n* (*u*) (*bot*) adhesive flowery cover of the florescent coconut.
ugaidi[1] *n* (*u*) terrorism, brigandage, banditry: *Ugaidi wa kimataifa*, international terrorism. *Ugaidi wa kisiasa*, political terrorism.
ugaidi[2] *n* (*u*) the work of guiding tourists in a city, town, etc.
ugale (pl *gale*) *n* (*u*) the soft part of the trunk of a tree; pith, core. (cf *moyo*)
ugali *n* (*u*) hard porridge; stiff porridge made of maize, millet or cassava flour.
ugandamizaji (also *ukandamizaji*) *n* (*u*) 1. pressure, compression; the act of applying pressure; force, etc. on sth: *Ugandamizaji wa vipuri uliyavunja mayai kwenye mkoba*, the weight of the spare parts broke the eggs in the basket. 2. oppression, persecution, suppression: *Ugandamizaji wa serikali kwa raia wake umeleta machafuko nchini*, the government's oppression on its citizens has brought chaos in the country. (cf *utesaji, uonevu*)
uganga *n* (*u*) 1. medicine, medical practice: *Alisomea taaluma ya uganga katika nchi za ng'ambo*, he studied medicine abroad. (cf *utibabu, utabibu*) 2. treatment, healing: *Uganga wake*

haukugangua, his treatment did not heal. (cf *tiba*) 3. witchcraft, sorcery, magic: *Anashiriki sana katika uganga*, he indulges a lot in sorcery. (cf *ulozi, uchawi*)
ugavi *n* (*u*) distribution, supply: *Ugavi wa umeme*, the supply of electricity. *Ugavi wa maji*, the supply of water. *Ugavi na utashi*, supply and demand. (cf *ugawaji, usambazaji*)
ugavu[1] *n* (*u*) see *ugaga*
ugavu[2] (pl *ngavu*) *n* (*u*) a net for trapping animals or fish.
ugawaji *n* (*u*) 1. distribution centre. 2. distribution, allotment: *Ugawaji wa madaraka*, the distribution of responsibilities. *Ugawaji kwa masikini haukufanyika vizuri*, the distribution of dates to the poor was not done properly (cf *usambazaji, utoaji*)
ugawanaji *n* (*u*) sharing, distribution, division, allocation: *Ugawanaji wa madaraka*, the sharing of responsibilities.
ugaya (also *ugavu, ugaga, ugwaugwa*) *n* (*u*) tartar, dental calculus; calcium deposits, etc. formed around the teeth consisting of food deposits, saliva proteins, etc. (cf *ukoga, ngeja*)
ugea *n* (*u*) a kind of relish made from shark or batoid fish (ray) first boiled and then mixed with its liver.
ugege *n* (*u*) sensitivity on the teeth caused by eating acidic fruits, etc. (cf *ugwadu, uyeye*)
ugele *n* (*u*) (*bot*) the stalk of millet.
ugelegele *n* (*u*) see *kigelegele*
ugema *n* (*u*) 1. the cutting or lopping of a tree esp from its top so as to remove its sap, which is usu preserved in a container.
ugemaji *n* (*u*) see *ugemi*
ugemi (also *ugemaji*) *n* (*u*) 1. the collection of palm wine; tapping. 2. the collection of sap. 3. the collection of oil by a pipe in a vehicle having a tank inside.
ugeni *n* (*u*) 1. strangeness, novelty, freshness: *Ugeni wao umewafanya wawe wanyonge kwa wenyeji*, their state of being new strangers had made them humble to their hosts. (cf *upya, uzungu*) 2. visitation. 3. official visitor.
ugenini *adv* abroad, in a foreign place: *Amekwenda ugenini*, he has gone abroad.
ugeugeu *n* (*u*) fickleness, instability, unsteadiness, unpredictability: *Ugeugeu wa baadhi ya wanasiasa umewafanya wasipendwe na watu*, the unpredictable behaviour of some politicians has made them unpopular to the people. (cf *undumakuwili*)
ugeuzaji *n* (*u*) see *ugeuzi*
ugeuzi (also *ugeuzaji*) *n* (*u*) change, alteration, variation: *Ugeuzi wake wa kazi wa mara kwa mara umewafanya waajiri wasimpende*, his behaviour of changing jobs often has made him unpopular to the employers. (cf *ugeuzaji, ubadilishaji*)
ughaibuni *n* (*u*) overseas; foreign places: *Amekwenda ughaibuni kwa mapumziko*, she has gone overseas for holidays. (cf *ng'ambo*) (Ar)
ughali *n* (*u*) expensiveness, costliness: *Ughali wa bidhaa hizi hausemeki*, the expensiveness of these goods is beyond description.
ugharimiaji *n* (*u*) the costs or expenses for bearing sth; defrayment: *Ugharimiaji wa bwawa la kuogelea*, the costs for the construction of the swimming pool. (Ar)
ughushaji *n* (*u*) see *ughushi*
ughushi *n* (*u*) 1. adulteration; the act of adding sth of lower quality to sth else in order to make it look genuine. (cf *uchakuchuaji*) 2. forgery: *Ughushi wa hundi ya benki*, bank cheque forgery. (Ar)
ugimbi *n* (*u*) brew, alcohol, beverage; intoxicating liquour: *Ugimbi umemdhoofisha mtu yule sana*, alcohol has weakened that person very much. (cf *ulevi*)

ugingisi n (u) the act of exasperating a co-wife in order to break her marriage.
Ugiriki n (u) (geog) Greece (Eng)
ugo (also *nyugo*) n (u) enclosure, courtyard. (cf *ua, kitalu*)
ugobo n (u) hostility, animosity, antagonism, ill will, ill feeling, unfriendliness: *Anapenda kuleta ugobo na majirani zake*, he likes to cause hostilities between his neighbours. (cf *ushari, uchokozi, ugomvi*)
ugoe (pl *ngoe*) n (u) 1. hooking a foot by bending it in order to trip someone up: *Piga ugoe*, trip up. 2. a hooked or forged stick or pole used for pulling down branches of trees in order to pluck fruits. (cf *kigoe, kigovya*)
ugogomozi n (u) gargling
ugoigoi (pl *ngoe*) n (u) laziness, idleness, laxity: *Ugoigoi wa mfanyakazi wangu haustahamiliki*, the laziness of my worker is unbearable. (cf *ubwete, uzembe, uvivu*)
ugomba n (u) friendship between young people. (cf *usuhuba*)
ugombezaji n (u) act (method, etc.) of censuring sby; reprimand, scold, rebuke, reproof (cf *ukemeaji, ukatazaji, ukaripiaji*)
ugombezi n (u) 1. contention, contest: *Ugombezi wake wa kutaka uongozi katika chama umeleta sokomoko*, his contest for leadership in the party has brought chaos. 2. the act of defending another person's rights.
ugombo n (u) a kind of banjo made from wood, with one or more strings which are plucked with the fingers.
ugomvi n (u) quarrel, feud, discord: *Ugomvi wa ndani*, internal dispute. *Niliweza kuutatua ugomvi wao*, I managed to solve their dispute. (cf *utesi, mzozo, suitafahamu*)
ugonezi n (u) the act of interpreting information by examining a dream; divination by dream analysis.
ugoni n (u) 1. licentiousness, adultery, libertinism. (cf *uzinzi, uzinifu, ukware*) 2. a fine paid by an adulterer to the husband or wife affected; fine paid for commiting adultery.
ugonjwa n (u) disease, illness: *Ugonjwa wa kuharisha*, diarrhoea. *Ugonjwa wa kiharusi*, paralysis. *Ugonjwa wa akili*, mental disease. *Ugonjwa wa njano*, hepatitis. *Ugonjwa wa sukari*, diabetes. *Ugonjwa wa uti wa mgongo*, meningitis. *Ugonjwa wa tauni*, plague. *Ugonjwa wa mapafu*, pneumonia. *Ugonjwa wa mifupa*, arthritis. *Ugonjwa wa zinaa*, veneral disease. *Ugonjwa wa mkojo*, diueresis; an increased or excessive secretion or flow of urine. *Ugonjwa wa mafua ya ndege*, bird flu. *Ugonjwa wa bonde la ufa*, Rift valley fever. *Ugonjwa wa matumba*, bud disease.
ugoro n (u) 1. snuff. (cf *tumbaku*) 2. (fig) nonsense.
ugoya (pl *ngoya*) n (u) a fibre of wool; feather, quill. (cf *unyoya*)
ugozi n (u) see *ngozi*
ugu.a vi be ill; be sick; be ailing: *Amekuwa akiugua ugonjwa wa saratani kwa muda mrefu*, he has been suffering from cancer for a long time. (syn) *Kuugua si kufa*, to fall sick does not mean dying. Prep. **ugu.li.a** St. **ugu.lik.a** Cs. **ugu.z.a** Ps. of Prep. **ugu.liw.a** (cf *sononeka*)
ugumba n (u) sterility, childlessness, barrenness, infecundity, infertility: *Ugumba wake umemfanya mwanamke yule kutafuta mtoto wa kulea*, her infertility has made that woman to adopt a child.
ugumu n (u) 1. (of things) hardness, dryness, rigidity: *Ugumu wa mkate huu umeufanya usilike*, the hardness of this bread has made it inedible. 2. (of problems, etc.) dryness, difficulty: *Ugumu wa hesabu ile umemfanya mwanafunzi atake msaada kwa mwalimu*, the difficulty of that mathematical problem has made the

student to seek assistance from the teacher. 3. miserliness, stinginess, meanness: *Ugumu wake unamfanya avae nguo mbovu,* his stinginess makes him wear worn-out clothes. (cf *uchoyo, ubahili*)

ugundi *n (u)* a kind of brown powder made from the leaf-stem of coconut palm and used as a cure for sores; coconut husk balm.

ugunduzi *n (u)* discovery, invention, realization: *Ugunduzi wa dawa ya ugonjwa wa kifua kikuu umepunguza idadi ya vifo duniani,* the discovery of medicine for tuberculosis has reduced the death rate in the world. (cf *ufumbuzi, ugunduaji*)

uguz.a *vt* nurse the sick; attend to a sick person: *Shangazi anamwuguza bintiye siku hizi,* my aunt is nursing her sick daughter. Prep. *uguz.i.a* St. *uguz. ik.a* Cs. *uguz.ish.a* Ps. *uguz.w.a* Rp. *uguz.an.a*

ugwadu *n (u)* the acidity found in certain fruits esp when they are not ripe; acerbity, sourness: *Ugwadu wa embe hili umelifanya lisifae kuliwa,* the acidity of this mango has made it inedible. (cf *ukakasi, ukali*)

ugwagwa *n (u) see ngayo*

ugwe (pl *nyugwe*) *n (u)* string; a small cord, etc. (cf *uzi, kamba*)

uhaba *n (u)* scarcity, paucity, shortage: *Uhaba wa maji umeleta shida kubwa kwa watu,* the scarcity of water has brought great hardships to the people. (cf *upungufu, uchechefu, uadimikaji, uchache*)

Uhabeshi *n (u) (geog)* Ethiopia (Ar)

uhafifu *n (u)* 1. inferiority, lowness, cheapness. (cf *uduni, urahisi*) 2. poorness, meanness, wretchedness: *Uhafifu wa rafiki yako umemfanya adharauliwe,* the meanness of your friend has caused him to be ignored. (cf *unyonge, udhaifu*) 3. unheaviness, weightlessness, lightness: *Uhafifu wa mzigo wangu umeniwezesha kuuchukua bila ya shida,* the light weight of my luggage has enabled me to carry it without any difficulty. (cf *wepesi*) (Ar)

uhai *n (u)* 1. life, existence, lifetime: *Kuna uhai na mauti,* there is life and death. 2. *(fig)* survival, viability: *Uhai wa chama chetu uko mashakani,* the survival of our party is at stake. (cf *uzima*) 3. sth that allows a person, an animal, etc. to live. (Ar)

uhaini *n (u)* treason, betrayal: *Uhaini mkubwa,* high treason. *Aliifanyia uhaini nchi yake,* he betrayed his country. (cf *usaliti, utimbakwiri*) (Ar)

uhaji *n (u)* 1. *(idms) Ingia uhaji,* convert to the Muslim faith; become a Muslim e.g. *Alipoingia katika uhaji, akaitwa Ali Mohamed,* when he became a Muslim, he was named Ali Mohamed. 2. *Ingia uhaji,* be circumcised as a condition for becoming a Muslim. (Ar)

uhakika *n (u)* certainty, assurance, doubtlessness. *Hana uhakika wa habari yenyewe,* he is not sure of the news. (cf *usahihi, uyakini, ithibati*) (Ar)

uhakiki *n (u)* 1. verification, evidence, authenticity, truth, genuineness. (cf *uyakini, ukweli*) 2. critique, review: *Uhakiki wa fasihi,* literary criticism. (cf *ukweli, uchambuzi, tahakiki*) (Ar)

uhakikishaji *n (u)* act (method, etc.) of verifying sth; verification, establishment, confirmation. (cf *uthibitishaji*)

uhakikisho *n (u)* assurance, pledge, promise. (cf *uthibitisho*) (Ar)

uhakimu *n (u)* judgeship, adjudication, refereeing: *Ana uzoefu mkubwa katika kazi ya uhakimu,* he has a lot of experience as a judge. (cf *ujaji, urefa*) (Ar)

uhalali *n (u)* legality, legitimacy; the quality or state of being legitimate: *Uhalali wa serikali ile uko mashakani,* the legitimacy of that government is in doubt. *Mahakama ilithibitisha uhalali wa kijana yule*, the court proved the legitimacy of that child. (Ar)

uhalalishaji *n (u)* act (method, etc.) of verifying sth; verification, establishment. (cf *uthibitishaji*)

uhalifu *n (u)* lawlessness, crime: *Wanajeshi walifanya uhalifu nchini*, the soldiers staged a rebellion in the country. (cf *uasi*) (Ar)

uhalisi *n (u)* reality, actuality, authenticity: *Uhalisi wa taarifa yake una mashaka*, the genuineness of his statement is in doubt. (Ar)

uhamaji *n (u)* emigration, shifting, movement: *Uhamaji wa wasomi*, brain drain; depletion of the intellectuals, etc. through emigration.

uhamasishaji *n (u)* act (method, etc) of motivating sby/sth; motivation, encouragement.

uhamiaji *n (u)* immigration: *Idara ya uhamiaji*, department of immigration. *Ofisa wa uhamiaji*, immigration officer. *Uhamiaji haramu*, illegal immigration.

uhamisho *n (u)* transfer: *Mfanyakazi alipata uhamisho*, the worker got a transfer. *Uhamisho wa kimataifa*, international transfer.

uhamishoni *adv* exile: *Mwanasiasa alirudi nchini kutoka uhamishoni*, the politician returned to the country from exile.

uhandisi *n (u)* engineering: *Uchoraji wa uhandisi*, engineering drawing. *Kazi ya uhandisi ina mustakabala mzuri*, the engineering profession has good prospects. *Uhandisi mitambo*, mechanical engineering. *Uhandisi ujenzi*, civil engineering. (Ar)

uhanithi *n (u)* 1. impotence, infecundity. 2. gayness, rakishness. (cf *ushoga, ubaradhuli, usenge*) 3. *(colloq)* nonsense. (Ar)

uharamia *n (u)* piracy, banditry. (cf *unyang'anyi*)

uharamu *n (u)* illegality, illegitimacy; the quality or state of being illegitimate: *Uharamu wa mtoto yule bado haujathibitishwa*, the illegitimacy of that child has not yet been proved. (Ar)

uharibifu *n (u)* sabotage, destruction, ruin, harm: *Uharibifu wa mazingira*, environmental destruction. *Alitaka kuleta uharibifu wa uchumi katika nchi yetu*, he wanted to bring economic sabotage to our country. (cf *uangamizaji, uwurugaji*) (Ar)

uhariri *n (u)* editorship, editorial work. (Ar)

uharo *n (u)* liquid stool; liquid faeces; liquid waste matter. (cf *mavi ya majimaji*)

uhasama (also *hasama, uhasimu*) *n (u)* antagonism, animosity, hostility, unfriendliness: *Uhasama uliokuwepo kati ya mume na mke uliwafanya hatimaye kutengana*, the enmity that existed between the wife and the husband led eventually to their separation. (cf *utesi, uadui*) (Ar)

uhasibu *n (u)* accountancy (Ar)

uhasidi (also *husuda*) *n (u)* jealousy, envy, resentment: *Anamwonea uhasidi jirani yangu kwa sababu ya cheo chake kizuri*, he is jealous of my neighbour because of his good position. (cf *wivu, kijicho*) (Ar)

uhasimu *n (u)* see *uhasama*

uhawara *n (u)* concubinage; the state of being a concubine: *Uhawara wake umewafanya watu wamdharau*, her concubinage has made people to shun her. (cf *ugoni, uzinzi, uasherati*)

uhayawani *n (u)* 1. brutality, cruelty, ruthlessness, barbarity: *Alimfanyia uhayawani mbwa wa jirani yake*, he showed cruelty towards his neighbour's dog. (cf *unyama, ukatili*) 2. stupidity, imbecility, ignorance: *Kila mtu anaelewa uhayawani wake darasani*, everybody knows her dullness in the class. (cf *ujinga, uzembe*) (Ar)

uhazigi *n (u) (med)* surgery; the branch of medicine dealing with the operations on the body to treat diseases, injuries or deformities. (cf *jabara*)

uheke *n (u)* gossip, hypocricy. (cf *uzandiki, uongo*)

uhenga *n (u)* possession of knowledge of the past; sageness, wisdom: *Mtu yule anaheshimika sana kutokana na uhenga wake*, that person is very well-respected because of his sageness. (cf *ukale*)

uhifadhi *n (u)* preservation, conservation, protection: *Uhifadhi wa mazingira*, environmental protection. *Uhifadhi wa misitu*, forestry conservation. (Ar)

Uhispania (also *Hispania*) *n (u)* Spain (Eng)

uhistorishaji *n (u) (drm)* a technique in epic theatre whereby episodes are dramatized in such a way so as to illuminate current social problems and underscore the possibility of change for the better. (Eng)

uhitaji *n (u)* 1. requirement, need, want: *Masikini yule ana uhitaji wa chakula na pesa*, that poor man needs food and money. (cf *haja*) 2. the condition of not possessing anything.

uhodari *n (u)* 1. cleverness, skilfulness, brilliance, sharpness: *Uhodari wake katika kutunga mashairi ni mkubwa*, his skill in composing poems is great. (cf *ubingwa*) 2. courage, bravery: *Alionyesha uhodari alipopigana na simba*, he showed courage when he fought with the lion. (cf *ushujaa*)

Uholanzi *n (u) (geog)* Holland (Eng)

uhondo *n (u)* 1. sweet stuff; dainty: *Anapenda kula uhondo*, he likes to eat sweet stuff. 2. feast, reception, party: *Alikwenda kwenye uhondo wa harusi*, she went to a wedding party. 3. (*fig*) satisfaction, pleasures: *Anapenda kula uhondo*, he likes pleasures i.e. he likes a luxurious life. 4. ecstatic beauty; appeal: *Uhondo wa riwaya ile ni mkubwa*, the ecstatic beauty of that novel is high.

uhonyoaji *n (u)* extravagance, lavishness: *Amefilisika kutokana na uhonyoaji wa mali yake*, he has become bankrupt because of his extravagance. (cf *ufujaji, ubadhirifu*)

uhudumiaji *n (u)* servicing, running: *Uhudumiaji wa maji vijijini ni mbovu*, water service in the villages is poor.

uhuni *n (u)* 1. hooliganism, vagrancy; irresponsible way of life: *Uhuni wake haustahamiliki sasa*, his hooliganism is now becoming unbearable. (cf *ukora*) 2. bachelorhood: *Amekuwa akiishi maisha ya uhuni mpaka hivi karibuni alipooa*, he has been living the life of a bachelor until recently when he got married. (*useja, ukapera*)

uhunzi *n (u)* metalwork; smithing. (cf *usani*)

uhuru *n (u)* liberty, freedom, independence. (cf *istiklali*) (Ar)

uhururishaji *n (u)* liberalization; *Uhururishaji wa biashara*, liberalization of trade.

uhusiano *n (u)* 1. relationship: *Uhusiano wa kibalozi*, diplomatic relations. *Uhusiano kati ya nchi zile mbili ni mbaya*, the relationship between those two countries is bad. 2. connection, relationship, relevance, link: *Hakuna uhusiano wowote kati ya jambo hili na lile*, there is no relationship between this matter and that one. (Ar)

uhusika *n (u) (gram)* case: *Uhusika yambwa*, accusative case. *Sarufi uhusika*, case grammar. (Ar)

uigaji *n (u)* imitation, mimicry: *Uigaji wake wa jinsi mjomba anavyozungumza ni sahihi*, his mimicry of my uncle's style of speaking is accurate. (cf *mwigo, wigo*)

uigizaji *n (u)* dramatization

uimara *n (u)* firmness, stability, soundness, reliability: *Uimara wa nguzo hizi umeweza kuidumisha nyumba yetu*, the soundness of these pillars has enabled our house to

U   uimarishaji

last for a long time. (cf *uthabiti, umadhubuti*)
uimarishaji *n* (*u*) strengthening, consolidation: *Rais amesisitiza uimarishaji wa majeshi ya nchi yetu*, the president has emphasized the consolidation of our country's armed forces.
uimla *n* (*u*) dictatorship (cf *udikteta*)
Uingereza *n* (*u*) (*geog*) Great Britain, England.
uingiaji *n* (*u*) penetration, entering, coming in: *Uingiaji wake chumbani haukutegemewa*, his coming into the room came unexpectedly.
uingiliaji *n* (*u*) 1. meddlesomeness, intrusion, interference. 2. penetration of a man's penis into a woman's vagina.
uingizaji *n* (*u*) 1. importation: *Uingizaji wa bidhaa katika bandari umeshuka sana*, the importation of goods at the port has declined a lot. 2. sneaking: *Uingizaji wa silaha katika eneo lenyewe*, the sneaking of weapons into the area.
Uislamu (also *Islamu*) *n* (*u*) Islam (Ar)
uitaji *n* (*u*) act (method, etc.) of calling sby/sth.
uitikiaji *n* (*u*) act (method, etc.) of responding to sby/sth.
uizi *n* (*u*) see *wizi*
uja *n* (*u*) humanity, kindness, goodness: *Ikiwa hoja yake ni suala la uja, basi mimi ni mja*, if his argument is the issue of humanity, I am also a human. (cf *utu, ubinaadamu*)
ujabari *n* (*u*) valour courage. (cf *ujasiri*)
ujahili[1] (also *ujuhula*) *n* (*u*) brutality, cruelty, ruthlessness: *Alimfanyia ujahili mtoto wake wa kambo kwa kumpiga sana*, he showed cruelty to his stepchild by beating him severely. (cf *ubedui, ukatili, unyama*)
ujahili[2] *n* (*u*) dull-wittedness, ignorance, stupidity, imbecility: *Ujahili wake uko wazi*, her dull-wittedness is obvious.

ujangili

(cf *upumbavu, ujinga, upofu*)
ujaji[1] *n* (*u*) see *mjo*
ujaji[2] *n* (*u*) judgeship; the position, work, etc of a judge: *Kazi ya ujaji ina heshima*, judge's profession carries respect. (cf *uhakimu*)
ujaka[1] *n* (*u*) (*bot*) a kind of leaves used as vegetables; a kind of spinach. (cf *mchicha*)
ujaka[2] *n* (*u*) small mushrooms.
ujaka[3] *n* (*u*) stench, stink; bad smell: *Pana harufu ya ujaka hapo karibu na takataka*, there is a stench near the refuse. (cf *mzingo, kijusi, uvundo*)
ujali *n* (*u*) 1. the wick of a small oil lamp. 2. the thin rolling of a cloth. (Hind)
ujalidi *n* (*u*) book binding.
ujalivu *n* (*u*) (of food) satiety, fullness.
ujamaa *n* (*u*) 1. family, relationship, family ties: *Ujamaa kati yao na sisi uko mbali*, the relationship between them and us is a distant one. (cf *udugu, uhusiano*) 2. socialism: *Cuba inafuata siasa ya ujamaa*, Cuba follows the policy of socialism.
ujambazi *n* (*u*) gangsterism, thuggery; armed robbery: *Serikali itachukua hatua kali kukomesha ujambazi nchini*, the government will take strong measures to stop thuggery in the country. (cf *ujangili, uharamia*)
ujana *n* (*u*) youth, adolescence, teenage: *Alikuwa mchezaji hodari wa mpira wakati wa ujana wake*, he was a good football player during his youth. (cf *ushababi, ubarubaru*)
ujanajike *n* (*u*) womanhood: *Kaonyesha ujeuri wa ujanajike*, she has shown the pride of her womanhood.
ujane *n* (*u*) widowerhood, widowhood; a single life after having lost a spouse: *Amekuwa katika hali ya ujane tangu kufiwa na mkewe mwaka jana*, he has been living as a widow since his wife's death last year. (cf *ukapera, useja*)
ujangili (also *ujangiri*) (*u*) 1. poaching. 2. thuggery, rowdiness.

ujangiri *n* (*u*) see *ujangili*
ujanja *n* (*u*) cunning, craft, trickery, slyness, trick. (cf *werevu, uayari, hadaa, ghiliba*)
Ujapani *n* (*u*) (*geog*) Japan
ujapojapo (pl *japojapo*) *n* (*u*) alley; a lane between a row of buildings or between two rows of buildings that face each other on adjacent streets: *Mwizi alionekana amejificha katika ujapojapo,* the thief was found hiding in the alley. (cf *uchochoro, ujia, usita*)
ujapongo *n* (*u*) enormous appetite esp after illness; ravenousness, voracity: *Alionyesha ujapongo mbele za watu wakati wa kula,* he showed enormous appetite in public while eating. (cf *ulafi, uroho*)
ujari[1] (also *jari*) *n* (*u*) (*naut*) rudder tackle; a rope used for steering a vessel.
ujari[2] *n* (*u*) the state, condition, etc. of being a virgin; virginity, maidenhood, chastity, spinsterhood. (cf *ubikira*)
ujasiri (also *jasara*) *n* (*u*) audacity, courage, bravery, gallantry: *Ujasiri wako umekupa sifa jeshini,* your bravery has earned you respect in the army. (cf *ujabari, ushujaa, uhodari*) (Ar)
ujasiriamali *n* (*u*) enterpreneurship; the practice of owning or managing a business enterprise in order to make profits.
ujasusi *n* (*u*) espionage, spying; intelligence gathering: *Alifungwa kwa kosa la ujasusi,* he was imprisoned for spying. (cf *upelelezi*) (Ar)
ujauzito *n* (*u*) gestation, pregnancy. (cf *himila, mimba*)
ujazi *n* (*u*) bountifulness, blessings, prosperity. (cf *neema*) (Ar)
ujazo *n* (*u*) volume, capacity. (cf *mjazo*)
ujengaji *n* (*u*) masonry, building, construction: *Ujengaji wake wa nyumba za kisasa unavutia,* his style of constructing modern houses is attractive. (cf *ujenzi*)

ujengelele *n* (*u*) see *uchengelele*
ujenzi *n* (*u*) masonry, building, construction: *Ujenzi holela,* haphazard construction. (cf *ujengaji*)
Ujerumani *n* (*u*) (*geog*) Germany (Eng)
ujeuri (also *jeuri*) *n* (*u*) insolence, rudeness, arrogance: *Alifukuzwa kazini kwa sababu ya ujeuri wake,* he was sacked from work because of being rude. (cf *tadi, usodawi, ujuba, usafihi*) (Ar)
uji *n* (*u*) 1. gruel, porridge: *Uji wa mapande,* gruel made from rice. *Uji wa ngano,* gruel made from wheat. 2. (*idm*) *Mfua uji,* dandy; a neat person. a well-dressed person. (cf *mtanashati, mlimbwende*)
ujia *n* (*u*) alley, lane, back street: *Kuna uchafu mwingi katika ujia huu,* there is a lot of dirt in this alley. (cf *uchochoro, usita*)
ujifunzaji *n* (*u*) learning: *Ujifunzaji lugha,* language learning.
ujima *n* (*u*) communalism, communal work: *Wakulima walifanya kazi ya ujima katika konde zao,* the workers did communal work in their fields. *Lima kwa ujima,* farm communally.
ujinga *n* (*u*) ignorance, stupidity: *Ujinga wake unawajanya watu wamdharau,* his stupidity makes people ignore him. (cf *ubozi, upumbavu, uzuzu, ujuha*)
ujini *n* (*u*) the act of a socerer or any other person performing evil deed..
ujio *n* (*u*) coming, arrival, advent: *Ujio wake haukutegemewa,* his coming was unexpected.
ujira *n* (*u*) wage, salary: *Hajapewa ujira wake mpaka sasa ingawa kazi ameimaliza,* he has not received his wages until now although he has completed his work. (cf *ijara, malipo*)
ujirani *n* (*u*) 1. neighbourhood, vicinity: *Ujirani wetu umetuletea masikilizano mema,* our neighbourhood has brought us good understanding. (cf *ukaribu*) 2. neighbourliness: *Mawaziri wawili kutoka nchi zao walikutana ili*

kufanikisha misingi ya ujirani mwema, the two ministers from their respective countries met as a gesture of good neighbourliness.
ujiti (also *kijiti*) (pl *njiti*) n (*u*) twig
ujoli n (*u*) the status of an offspring of a slave who was freed; free slave lineage.
ujomba n (*u*) the relation between one's mother and her brother; the relation between a child and a maternal uncle.
ujombani n (*u*) 1. (*arch*) areas where Swahili-speaking people live, esp the coast. 2. the maternal side.
ujuaji n (*u*) 1. knowledge, awareness, understanding: *Hana ujuaji wa jambo lile*, he is not knowledgeable about that issue. (cf *ujuzi, maarifa*) 2. know-all attitude; the tendency for someone to know everything: *Anajitia ujuaji wa kila kitu*, he pretends to know everything. (cf *usogora, ubaramaki*)
ujuba n (*u*) insolence, rudeness, arrogance: *Haifai kuonyesha ujuba kwa wazee wako*, it is not good to be rude to your parents. (cf *ujeuri, usafihi*)
ujuha n (*u*) imbecility, stupidity, ignorance. (cf *uzuzu, ubozi*)
ujuhula n (*u*) see *ujahili*[1] and *ujahili*[2]
ujukuti (also *uchukuti*) (pl *njukuti*) n (*u*) 1. the midriff of a coconut palm leaf. 2. the spoke of a bicycle wheel; bicycle spoke.
ujumbe n (*u*) 1. message, information: *Aliniletea ujumbe muhimu kutoka kwa mwajiri wetu*, he brought an important message for me from our employer. (cf *habari*) 2. delegation: *Ujumbe wa watu wawili ulipelekwa nchi ya jirani kuonana na rais*, a delegation of two people was sent to the neighbouring country to see the president.
ujumi n (*u*) aesthetics; the branch of philosophy concerned with the study of such concepts as beauty, taste, etc.

ujusi n (*u*) 1. postnatal defilement of a mother *usu* lasting for forty days and requiring her to be washed ceremoniously. 2. the unpleasant smell emanating from a mother after delivery; postnatal odour.
ujuvi[1] n (*u*) knowingness, awareness, understanding: *Yeye haelewi chochote katika jambo lile ingawa anajaribu kuonyesha ujuvi wake*, he does not understand anything on that issue although he pretends to be knowledgeable about it. (cf *ujuaji*)
ujuvi[2] n (*u*) impertinence, insolence, rudeness: *Ujuvi wake umemfanya akose marafiki wengi*, her rudeness has lost her many friends. (cf *ujeuri, ufidhuli, usafihi, ujuba*)
ujuzi n (*u*) skill, expertise, knowledge: *Hana ujuzi wowote katika kazi ya useremala*, he has no skills in carpentry. (cf *ustadi, maarifa*)
uk.a[1] *vi* depart, leave, go away. Prep. *uk.i.a* St. *uk.ik.a* Cs. *uk.ish.a* Ps. *uk.w.a* (cf *enda, ondoka*)
uk.a[2] *vt* hate sth without any reason; abhor, loathe, dislike: *Sarah anamwuka mwalimu wake wa kemia bure*, Sarah hates her chemistry teacher for no reason. Prep. *uk.i.a* St. *uk.ik.a* Cs. *uk. ish.a* Ps. *uk.w.a* (cf *zia, chukia*)
ukaaji n (*u*) 1. mode of sitting: *Siupendi ukaaji wake katika kiti*, I don't like the way he sits on the chair. (cf *mkao, ukazi*) 2. stay; dwelling; mode of residing: *Ukaaji wake mtaani ulipendwa na majirani wengi*, his stay in the neighbourhood was liked by many neighbours. (cf *ukazi, makazi, maskani*)
ukaala n (*u*) (*bot*) the small branch of a coconut palm leaf.
ukaango[1] n (*u*) a very large cooking pot *usu* used for cooking rice at a feast.
ukaango[2] n (*u*) (*bot*) coconut flower stem sheath.
ukabaila n (*u*) 1. exploitation; the unethical

use of sby's labour for one's own advantage: *Tajiri yule aliwanyanyasa sana wafanyakazi kutokana na ukabaila wake*, that tycoon mistreated the workers very much as a result of his exploitation. (cf *unyonyaji*) 2. feudalism: *Ukabaila umezagaa nchini*, feudalism is widespread in the country. (cf *ubwanyenye, ulodi, umwinyi*) (Ar)

ukabidhi¹ *n* (*u*) trusteeship; the work of administering money or property for someone's benefit under the laws of inheritance, etc. (Ar)

ukabidhi² *n* (*u*) 1 economy, saving, keeping. 2 stinginess, miserliness. (cf *ubahili*) (Ar)

ukabila *n* (*u*) tribalism, racism: *Serikali inajaribu kuondosha ukabila nchini*, the government is trying to abolish racism in the country. (Ar)

ukabili *n* (*u*) the work of blowing a clarinet.

ukabiliano *n* (*u*) confrontation, showdown, face-off.

ukachero *n* (*u*) detective work.

ukada *n* (*u*) cadre system; the system of having cadres in an organization, etc.: *Ukada umezagaa katika chama tawala*, the system of having cadres is widespread in the ruling party.

ukadamu *n* (*u*) the work of superintending an estate: foremanship. (Ar)

ukadhi *n* (*u*) the work, position, profession, etc of a judge in Islamic courts; Islamic judgeship. (Ar)

ukafiri *n* (*u*) blasphemy, apostasy, sacrilege. (Ar)

ukafu¹ *n* (*u*) froth, foam, sud: *Sabuni yake ina ukafu mwingi*, his soap has a lot of suds. (cf *povu*)

ukafu² *n* (*u*) the dryness of the teeth after one has eaten unripe acid fruits, etc.; acid taste. (cf *ukakafu, ukakasi, ukamwu*)

ukaguzi *n* (*u*) inspection, examination: *Ukaguzi hesabu*, auditing. (cf *upekuzi,*

uchunguzi)

ukahaba *n* (*u*) prostitution, whoredom: *Ukahaba umezagaa duniani*, prostitution has spread in the world. (cf *uasherati, uhawara*) (Ar)

ukaidi *n* (*u*) bullheadedness, obduracy, stubbornness, obstinacy: *Ukaidi wake umemletea maafa*, his stubbornness has brought him disaster. (cf *ushupavu, ubishi*)

ukaimu¹ *n* (*u*) deputyship; the work of serving as an acting head of an institution when the head is away. (Ar)

ukaimu² *n* (*u*) the act of exorcizing spirits.

ukakafu *n* (*u*) acid taste as found on the teeth after someone has eaten unripe fruits, etc.: *Ndizi hizi zina ukakafu kwa vile hazijaiva*, these bananas have a sour taste because they are not yet ripe. (cf *ukamwi, ukakasi*)

ukakamavu *n* (*u*) determination, firmness, endurance, patience: *Wafanyakazi walishinda kwenye mgomo wao kutokana na ukakamavu wao*, the workers won the strike because of their determination. (cf *lengo, azma*)

ukakasi *n* (*u*) acid taste as one found on the teeth after someone has eaten unripe fruits, etc. (cf *ukakafu, ukamwu*)

ukale *n* (*u*) ancientness, antiquity, oldness: *Ukale wake umemfanya aheshimike kijijini*, his old age has earned him respect in the village. (cf *uhenga*)

ukali *n* (*u*) 1. (of persons) temper, anger, harshness: *Alisema kwa ukali*, he spoke with anger. (cf *hamaki, hasira*) 2. (of fruits) sourness, bitterness, tartness, acidity: *Chungwa hili lina ukali mwingi*, this orange is very sour. 3. (of other things) hot, intense, vehement, severe: *Sijatoka nje leo kutokana na ukali wa jua*, I have not gone out today because of the scorching sun. *Ukali wa maisha*, the hardships of life; the high cost of living (cf *ugumu*)

ukalifashaji *n* (*u*) act (method, etc.) of forcing sby/sth; coercisim.

ukalifu *n* (*u*) inconvenience, annoyance, disturbance: *Jambo lile limeniletea ukalifu*, that issue has caused me inconvenience. (cf *usumbufu, dhiki*) (Ar)

ukalili *n* (*u*) scarcity, shortage, paucity. (cf *uchache, uhaba, upungufu*) (Ar)

ukambaa (pl *kambaa*) *n* (*u*) a thick cord of plaited leaf strips of tobacco, etc. (cf *ukindu, usumba*)

ukambe *n* (*u*) see *ukambi*

ukambi (also *ukambe*) *n* (*u*) (*med*) measles, morbilli, rubeola. (cf *surua*)

ukame *n* (*u*) famine, drought; dry spell. (cf *ukiwa, ukavu*)

ukamilifu *n* (*u*) completeness, entirety, perfection, fullness: *Aliifanya kazi yangu kwa ukamilifu*, he did my work with perfection. (cf *utimilifu*) (Ar)

ukamilisho *n* (*u*) completion, finish, end, accomplishment: *Ukamilisho wa taratibu zote za safari yake umetangazwa*, the completion of all the formalities for his journey has been announced. (cf *utimizaji*) (Ar)

ukamvu *n* (*u*) the dryness of the teeth found after someone has eaten unripe acid fruits. (cf *ukakasi, ukakafu, ugwadu*)

ukanda[1] (also *mkanda*), (pl *kanda*) *n* (*u*) 1. a belt worn around the waist to hold clothing up, support tools, etc.; strap, band. 2. tape; a magnetic substance on which sound can be recorded and played back on a tape recorder.

ukanda[2] (pl *kanda*) *n* (*u*) 1. zone, area: *Ukanda wa magharibi*, west zone. *Ukanda wa kati*, central zone. (cf *sehemu, upande*) 2. (*pol*) regionalism; the (method, practice, etc) of advocating, promoting, etc regional issues, etc.

ukandamizaji (also *ugandamizaji*) *n* (*u*) suppression; oppression, persecution; the act of suppressing people, etc.

ukandamizwaji *n* (*u*) the act of being suppressed; oppressed, persecuted, etc; tyranny: *Ukandamizwaji wowote dhidi ya raia ni mbaya*, any kind of oppression against its citizens is bad.

ukandarasi *n* (*u*) the work (position, etc) of a contractor

ukano (pl *kano*) *n* (*u*) (*anat*) sinew; tendon.

ukapera *n* (*u*) bachelorhood: *Anapenda kuishi maisha ya ukapera*, he likes to live the life of being a bachelor. (cf *uhuni, useja*)

ukarabati *n* (*u*) rehabilitation, renovation: *Wizara ya elimu inataka kufanya ukarabati wa shule zote za umma*, the ministry of education wants to make renovations on all public schools. (cf *utengenezaji, urekebishaji*)

ukarafati *n* (*u*) preventive maintenance.

ukaramkaji *n* (*u*) deceit mixed with lack of shamefulness.

ukaramshi *n* (*u*) trickery, deceit, craft, tricks: *Ukaramshi wake ulimtia hatarini*, his deceitful ways got him into trouble. (cf *upwamu, ujanja*)

ukarani *n* (*u*) clerical work. (Pers)

ukarara *n* (*u*) (*bot*) the tough leathery sheath of a cocounut flower-stem.

ukaria *n* (*u*) ochre

ukaribiano *n* (*u*) approach, proximity, closeness: *Sina ukaribiano naye*, I am not close to him. (Ar)

ukarimu *n* (*u*) hospitality, generosity, nobleness, goodness: *Sisi sote tunampenda Badru kwa ukarimu wake*, we all like *Badru* because of his generosity. (cf *fadhili, wema*) (Ar)

ukasi (pl *kasi*) *n* (*u*) a ladle from a coconut shell fixed on a short stick, used as a handle for use in the kitchen; coconut shell ladle. (cf *upawa*)

ukasisi *n (u)* priesthood, chaplainship. (cf *upadre*)

ukaskazini *n (u)* the state, etc. of being in the north.

ukasuku *n (u)* the habit of behaving like a parrot i.e. mechanically repeating the words or acts of others usu without full understanding.

ukata *n (u)* poverty, penury, impecuniousness: *Ukata umezaga katika nchi za Kiafrika*, poverty is widespread in African countries. (cf *umasikini, ufukara*)

ukataji *n (u)* 1. cutting, splitting: *Ukataji kuni*, the splitting of firewood. *Serikali imechukua hatua kadha kuzuia ukatajimiti wa ovyo*, the government has taken several measures to stop the indiscriminate cutting of trees. 2. (of ticket, cloth materials, etc.) buying: *Ukataji wa nguo mpya umepungua siku hizi kwa sababu ya mitumba*, the buying of new clothes has declined these days because of second-hand clothes.

ukatibu *n (u)* 1. secretarial work. 2. the work of a secretary.

ukatili *n (u)* brutality, cruelty, ruthlessness: *Mkuu wa magereza aliwafanyia ukatili wafungwa*, the commissioner of prisons was cruel to the prisoners. (cf *ubedui, unyama, uhabithi*) (Ar)

ukavu[1] *n (u)* dryness, drought, barreness: *Ardhi yote ina ukavu*, the whole land is dry. (cf *ukame, ukiwa*)

ukavu[2] *n (u)* brazenness, impudence, shamelessness: *Ukavu wake unamfanya amuadhiri mtu yoyote*, his impudence causes him to disgrace any person.

ukawa (also *ukawio*) *n (u)* lateness, tardiness, procrastination.

ukawafi *n (u)* (*poet*) a poem of 3 verses of varying *mizani* (syllable) per stanza.

ukawiaji *n (u)* delay, procrastination, tardiness (cf *ucheleweshaji*)

ukawilishaji *n (u)* act (method, etc.) of causing a delay. (cf *ucheleweshaji*)

ukawio *n (u)* see *ukawa*

ukaya (pl *kaya*) *n (u)* a long thin light cloth rolled up and wound round the head and under the chin, worn by women; veil, yashmak.

uke *n (u)* 1. (*anat*) vagina 2. womanhood, female condition, status, etc.

ukeketaji *n (u)* 1. circumcision esp of a woman: *Ukeketaji wa wanawake*, the circumcision of women. 2. act (method, etc.) of cutting sth into slices.

ukelele *n (u)* scream, noise, shout, yell: *Ukelele wake ulinishtua*, his yelling startled me. (cf *ukwenzi, ukemi, usiyahi*)

ukembe *n (u)* infancy, early childhood: *Yeye bado yuko katika hali ya ukembe*, he is still in the stage of childhood. (cf *uchanga*)

ukembwa (also *utembwa*) *n (u)* 1. a soft thing which cannot be held by the palms of the hands. 2. (of persons, fruits, etc.) immaturity, childishness, unripeness: *Usiniletee ukembwa*, don't be childish. (cf *uchanga*)

ukemeaji *n (u)* act (method, etc) of disapproving sby/sth; disapproval, scolding, chiding.

ukemi *n (u)* 1. scream, yell, shout, yap: *Nilisikia ukemi wake kutoka mbali*, I heard his yell from a far. 2. plaint, diatribe, complaint, gripe, reproof.

ukemia *n (u)* 1. pharmacy; the art or profession of preparing and dispensing drugs and medicines. 2. the work of a pharmacist.

ukenekaji *n (u)* (*chem*) distillation; the process of purifying a liquid by vapourizing it and later condensing its vapour (cf *utoneshaji*)

ukengee *n (u)* an old kind of knife without a handle; a handless knife. (cf *jumu*)

ukengeushi (also *mkengeuko*) *n (u)* alienation, aversion, aberration, digression, divergence, pervesity; departure from the proper or expected course.

ukereketwa *n* (*u*) fanatism, extremism; radical political policies, etc.: *Ukereketwa wake katika chama tawala umezidi*, his extremism in the ruling party is too much.
uketo[1] *n* (*u*) depth, abyss: *Uketo wa sehemu hii ya bahari unatisha*, the depth of this part of the sea is frightening.
uketo[2] *n* (*u*) (*poet*) final rhyme.
uketo[3] *n* (*u*) popcorn: *Mtoto wangu anapenda kula uketo*, my child likes to eat popcorn. (cf *bisi*)
uketuzi *n* (*u*) the cutting of trees in preparation for a new farm: *Uketuzi wa pori hili haukufanyika vizuri*, the cutting down of trees in this forest was not properly done.
ukewenza *n* (*u*) the state of having more than one wife sharing the same husband: *Ukewenza unampa shida rafiki yangu*, the state of having more than one wife sharing the same husband is giving problems to my friend.
ukigo (pl *kigo*) *n* (*u*) fence, hedge, enclosure, compound. (cf *wigo*)
ukili *n* (*u*) a narrow strip of plaited leaves from the wild date palms, sewn together to make baskets, etc.
ukili.a *vt* determine, intend, decide, resolve: *Serikali imeukilia kuondosha rushwa nchini*, the government intends to eliminate corruption in the country. (cf *dhamiria, nuia, azimu, kusudia*)
ukimbizaji *n* (*u*) act (method, etc) of assisting sby to escape so as to seek refuge elsewhere 2 (esp in sports) act (method, etc) of assisting sby to run.
ukimbizi *n* (*u*) refuge, shelter, protection: *Kufuatia vita vya wenyewe kwa wenyewe, watu wengi waliondoka nchini kutafuta ukimbizi*, following the civil war, many people left the country to seek refuge.
ukimwa[1] *n* (*u*) boredoom, fatigue, weariness, tiredness. (cf *uchovu, ukinaifu*)

ukimwa[2] *n* (*u*) arrogance, vanity, pride: *Watu hawapendi kuchanganyika naye kwa sababu ya ukimwa wake*, people don't like to mingle with him because of his arrogance. (cf *usununu, kiburi*)
UKIMWI *n* (*u*) (of a disease) AIDS.
ukimya *n* (*u*) quiteness, calmness, serenity: *Ukimya wa kijana yule hausemeki*, that young man's quietness is beyond description. (cf *upole, ubaridi*)
ukinaifu *n* (*u*) 1. satiety, contentment; the point of satisfaction: *Nimekuwa nikila wali kila siku na sasa umenitia ukinaifu*, I have been eating rice everyday and now I am contented with it. 2. monotony, tediousness: *Ukinaifu wa maisha ya kijijini umemfanya aende mjini kuishi*, the monotonous life in the village has caused him to move to town to live there. (cf *ukiwa*) (Ar)
ukindu (pl *kindu*) *n* (*u*) (*bot*) the leaf of the wild date palm. (*Phoenix reclinata*)
ukingo (pl *kingo*) *n* (*u*) edge, brink, bank, rim, margin: *Ukingo mnyofu*, straight edge. *Alisimama karibu na ukingo wa mto*, he stood near the bank of the river. (cf *chambochambo, pambizo*)
ukinzani *n* (*u*) resistance, opposition, objection: *Ukinzani wa ndani*, internal resistance. *Ukinzani mgusano*, contact resistance. (cf *upinzani*)
ukipa *n* (*u*) goalkeeping: *Mchezaji wetu anaweza vizuri nafasi ya ukipa*, our player can be a good goalkeeper.
ukiri *n* (*u*) confession, admission, recognition: *Alitoa kauli ya ukiri kwa kosa la jinai alilolifanya*, he made his confession to the crime he committed. (cf *ungamo, ukubalifu*)
ukiri.i *vt* deny, refute. Prep. **ukiri.a** St. **ukiri.k.a** Cs. **ukiri.sh.a**
ukiritimba *n* (*u*) monopoly, control: *Wafanyabiashara wale watatu wamechukua ukiritimba katika usafirishaji wa kahawa*, those

three businessmen have acquired a monopoly in the exportation of coffee. (cf *uhozi*)
ukiukaji *n* (*u*) act of violating a law, right, etc.; violation, transgression.
ukiukwaji *n* (*u*) act of being violated; violation, transgression: *Ukiukwaji wa haki za binaadamu duniani ni jambo la kusikitisha*, the violation of human rights in the world is a sad thing.
ukiwa *n* (*u*) solitude; loneliness, separateness: *Amekuwa katika hali ya ukiwa tangu kufiwa na mumewe*, she has been in a state of solitude since her husband's death. (cf *kivumvu, upweke, huzuni*)
uk.o (*cop*) *vt* you are, it is: *Mlango uko wazi*, the door is open. *Usalama uko wapi?* Where is the security?
ukoa *n* (*u*) a band of thin metal plate worn as an ornament on the neck, arm, etc.
ukocha *n* (*u*) (*sports*) coaching
ukoga¹ *n* (*u*) dental calculus; tartar; accretions of hard deposits on the teeth consisting of food deposits, saliva proteins, etc.: *Ana ukoga kwenye meno yake kwa sababu hapigi msuwaki*, he has tartar on his teeth because he does not brush them. (cf *koya, ugagu, nyeju*)
ukoga² *n* (*u*) accretions of scum on water.
ukogo *n* (*u*) see *kogo²*
ukoja (pl *koja*) *n* (*u*) a necklace of beads. (cf *kidani*)
ukoka *n* (*u*) 1. (*bot*) a perennial mat grass up to 1 foot tall; grass used as fodder for horses, cattle, etc. *Sacciolepis curvata*. 2. (*idm*) *Vika kilemba cha ukoka*, give sby undue praise; flatter sby.
ukoko¹ *n* (*u*) a crust of food found in a pot or other vessel, which is often dry and scorched.
ukoko² *n* (*u*) seborrhoeic dermatitis; severe dandruff. 2. rash, seborrhoea sicca.

ukoloni *n* (*u*) colonialism: *Ukoloni mkongwe*, old colonialism. *Ukoloni mamboleo*, neocolonialism. (Eng)
ukoma *n* (*u*) (*med*) leprosy (cf *jedhamu, matana*)
ukomaji *n* (*u*) the reaching point of sth.
ukomavu *n* (*u*) maturity, ripeness, mellowness: *Ukomavu wa kisiasa*, political maturity. *Matunda haya yamefika katika hali ya ukomavu*, these fruits have reached the stage of ripeness. (cf *ubivu*)
ukomba *n* (*u*) (*bot*) a young coconut consisting of a soft kernel.
ukombaji *n* (*u*) act (method, etc) of taking curry by using a ball of food.
ukombati (also *uwati*), (pl *kumbati*) *n* (*u*) 1. a small building pole tied on the wall. 2. (*bot*) a long thin tree.
ukombe *n* (*u*) 1. a curved tool used for hollowing out by cutting and scraping sth e.g. for mortars, drums, etc. 2. a small wooden or earthenware spoon.
ukombozi *n* (*u*) liberation, emancipation: *Kamati ya ukombozi*, liberation committee. *Jeshi la ukombozi*, liberation army. *Harakati za ukombozi*, liberation movements. *Ukombozi wa mwanamke*, the liberation of a woman.
ukomeshaji *n* (*u*) prevention, banning, prohibition: *Ukomeshaji wa biashara ya haramu*, the banning of illicit trade.
ukomo *n* (*u*) end, limit, apex: *Siwezi kukusaidia tena kwa vile nimefika ukomo wa juhudi zangu*, I can't help you anymore because I have reached the limit of my ability. *Ukomo wa njia*, the end of the road. (cf *mwisho, tamati*)
ukomozi (also *uchomozi*) *n* (*u*) 1. act (method, etc.) of making someone suffer the consequences. 2. act of driving out an evil spirit from a person's head. 3. act of removing witchcraft where it exists.

ukomunisti *n* (*u*) 1. communism: *Nchi nyingi zimeacha siasa za ukomunisti,* many countries have abondoned communism. 2. a political party run along communist lines. 3. a government run along communist lines.
ukomwe (pl *komwe*) *n* (*u*) see *kete*
ukonavi (also *ukondavi*) *n* (*u*) a present given by the bridegroom to his bride if he finds that she is a virgin. (cf *jazua, kipamkono, kipakasa*)
ukongo *n* (*u*) ailment, disease, sickness: *Ukongo wake umemdhoofisha,* his disease has weakened him. (cf *ugonjwa, maradhi, uwele*)
ukongojo *n* (*u*) see *mkongojo*
ukongonyanzi (also *ukungunyanzi*) *n* (*u*) a thin black fibre from the dwarf palm or cocunut husk.
ukongwe *n* (*u*) senescence, agedness, old age, oldness, elderliness: *Bibi yule anasahau mambo mengi kwa sababu ya ukongwe wake,* that woman forgets many things because of her old age. (cf *uzee, ubuda*)
ukonyezaji *n* (*u*) act (method, etc.) of blinking; blink, wink.
ukonyezo *n* (*u*) blinking, winking.
ukonyoaji *n* (*u*) (of grains, etc.) plucking, extracting: *Ukonyoaji wake wa mahindi kutoka kwenye magunzi yale ni wa haraka,* his method of plucking maize from their cobs is fast.
ukonzo (pl *konzo*) *n* (*u*) a large stick, stack, etc. with the end printed and hardened with fire, used for hunting fish, etc.; hunting/fishing spear.
ukoo¹ (pl *koo*) *n* (*u*) kinship, ancestry: *Dr. Khalid ana ukoo mkubwa,* Dr. Khalid has a large family. (cf *ufungu, mlango, familia, ali*)
ukoo² *n* (*u*) filth, dirt, uncleanliness: *Kuna ukoo mwingi katika chumba chake,* there is a lot of dirt in his room. (cf *uchafu*)
ukopaji *n* (*u*) act (method, etc.) of borrowing money, etc.

ukope (pl *kope*) *n* (*u*) eyelash, cilium; one of the stiff hairs projecting from the tarsal margin of the eyelid. 2. (*syn*) *Anadaiwa hata kope si zake,* he has many debts.
ukopeshaji *n* (*u*) lending.
ukopi *n* (*u*) act (method, etc.) of borrowing of sth and promising to pay it later.
ukora *n* (*u*) vagrancy, thuggery, hooliganism: *Alifungwa kwa sababu ya ukora wake,* he was jailed for hooliganism. (cf *uhuni*)
ukorofi *n* (*u*) 1. jinx, misfortune, bad omen: *Aliniletea ukorofi kazini mwangu,* he caused me a misfortune at my place of work. (cf *nuksi, balaa*) 2. evil mindedness.
ukosefu *n* (*u*) lack, deficiency, shortage: *Ukosefu wa adabu,* lack of manners. *Ukosefu wa haya,* lack of shame. *Ukosefu wa umeme umewatia raia katika dhiki,* lack of electricity supply has caused inconvenience to people. (cf *upungufu, ukosekano*)
ukosekanaji *n* (*u*) absence, lack, unavailability: *Ukosekanaji wa mchele mjini ulisababishwa na uzembe wa viongozi,* the unavailability of rice in the town was caused by the irresponsibility of leaders. (cf *ukosefu*)
ukosi *n* (*u*) the collar of a garment; nape: *Ukosi wa shati lake haukukaa sawa,* the collar of his shirt is not straight. (cf *kola*)
ukozi *n* (*u*) (*naut*) fixed forestay in a sailing vessel, *mtepe.*
Ukristo *n* (*u*) Christianity (Eng)
ukuaji *n* (*u*) growth, development: *Ukuaji wa mimea ile umekuwa kwa haraka,* the growth of those plants has been rapid. *Ukuaji wa uchumi,* the growth of the economy
ukuba¹ *n* (*u*) jinx; bad omen, badluck: *Usituletee ukuba,* don't jinx us. (cf *ukorofi*)
ukuba² *n* (*u*) stench, stink; bad smell: *Kuna ukuba jaani,* there is a stench at the garbage heap. (cf *ujaka, mzingo,*

uvundo)
ukuba³ *n* (*u*) big sin.
ukubaliano *n* (*u*) agreement, consensus: *Hapajapatikana ukubaliano wowote kwenye mkutano*, no consensus has been reached at the meeting.
ukubalifu *n* (*u*) acceptability, acceptance, approval, acknowledgement. *Lugha yoyote lazima ipate ukubalifu kutoka kwa wasemaji wake*, any language must gain acceptability from its speakers. (cf *idhini, ridhaa*)
ukubwa *n* (*u*) 1. size, largeness: *Siwezi kuibeba meza hii kutokana na ukubwa wake*, I can't carry this table because of its size. 2. high position, high status; prestige, fame: *Akipewa ukubwa kazini, mtu yule atazidi kuwa na kiburi*, if he is promoted to a higher position at work, that person will become more arrogant. 3. seniority; the state or quality of being senior.
ukucha *n* (*u*) fingernail, toe nail; claw.
ukufi (pl *kufi*) *n* (*u*) handful, fistful: *Alichota ukufi mmoja wa kunde dukani*, he scooped up a handful of cowpeas at the shop. (cf *konzi, woya*)
ukukwi *n* (*u*) (*zool*) green bush snake; a kind of non-venomous snake, found in bushes, which is well-known to eat tree lizards, geckos and frogs. *Philothamnus semivariegatus*.
ukuli *n* (*u*) portership; the worker of a caravan porter. (cf *upagazi*)
ukulima *n* (*u*) (*bot*) husbandry, agriculture, farming: *Ukulima wa jadi*, traditional agriculture. *Ukulima wa kisasa*, modern agriculture. *Ukulima wa mazao*, crop husbandry. *Ukulima wa ufugaji* (*wanyama*), animal husbandry.
ukumbi (pl *kumbi*) *n* (*u*) 1. hall, gallery, lobby, waiting room: *Ukumbi wa mihadhara*, lecture hall. *Ukumbi wa mji*, city hall. 2. parlour; a room in a private home set apart for the entertainment of visitors. (cf *bwalo, sebule, ukumbizo*)

ukumbiri *n* (*u*) (*bot*) fibrous sheath or leaf of a coconut, etc. used for building.
ukumbizaji *n* (*u*) sweeping of refuse by a broom.
ukumbizaji *n* (*u*) sweeping
ukumbizo¹ *n* (*u*) verendah, gallery. (cf *ufinga*)
ukumbizo² *n* (*u*) dump, junkyard; a place for dumping rubbish, etc.
ukumbusho *n* (*u*) memorial, remembrance, commemoration: *Sala ya ukumbusho ilifanywa kwa wale waliouawa vitani*, a memorial service was held for those who died in the war.
ukumbuu (also *mkumbuu*) *n* (*u*) sash; a kind of cloth used as a belt usu worn over the shoulder or around the waist.
ukumvi (pl *kumvi*) *n* (*u*) (*bot*) empty ear, spike, etc. of rice, maize, coconut, etc.; chaff, husk.
ukunde *n* (*u*) (*bot*) outer covering of a runner bean; pod.
ukunga *n* (*u*) 1. obstetrics, tocology. 2. the work of a midwife; midwifery. (*prov*) *Usitukane ukunga na uzazi ungalipo*, don't speak ill of midwives while childbirth still continues i.e. don't abuse people whose work is needed.
ukungu¹ *n* (*u*) 1. mildew, mist, haziness: *Kuna ukungu nje*, there is mist outside. (cf *utusiutusi, kungungu*) 2. dampness, fog: *Majani yana ukungu katika bustani yangu*, the grass in my garden is damp. (cf *unyevu*)
ukungu² *n* (*u*) mold; a downy or furry growth on the surface of organic matter, caused by fungus, esp in the presence of dampness or decay: *Kuota ukungu*, development of mold.
ukunguni *n* (*u*) indolence, laziness, idleness: *Hawezi kufanya kazi yoyote kutokana na ukunguni wake*, he can't do any work because of his laziness. (cf *ugoigoi, uvivu, uzembe*)
ukungunyanzi *n* (*u*) see *ukongonyanzi*
ukunguru *n* (*u*) see *mkunguru*

805

ukungwi *n (u)* the work of a person usu a woman who initiates young brides into the ways of married life and advises young girls on how to cope with menstruation, etc.
ukuni (pl *kuni*) *n (u)* a stick of firewood; fuelwood.
ukunjaji *n (u)* act (method, etc.) of folding/wrapping sth. (cf *mkunjo*)
ukunjo *n (u)* 1. folding in a cloth; crease, wrinkle, crimp. (cf *upeto*) 2. a portion of sth that is rolled up; crease, band.
ukunjufu *n (u)* cheerfulness, gaiety, humour, charm: *Ukunjufu wake kwenye mazungumzo umempa umaarufu*, his charm in conversations has earned him fame. (cf *ucheshi, bashasha, uchangamfu*)
ukupe[1] *n (u)* leeching, sponging; the act of living at the expense of another or others without making any useful contribution or return: *Anaishi maisha ya ukupe*, he lives at the expense of others.
ukupe[2] *n (u)* stealing by jugglery: *Mwizi wa ukupe naye anastahili adhabu*, a person who steals from someone by using jugglery deserves punishment.
ukura[1] (also *ukuta*) *n (u)* the sides of a fish-trap; wicker trap's cover.
ukura[2] *n (u)* (*bot*) a kind of millet, usu grown in barren places.
ukurasa (pl *kurasa*) *n (u)* 1. page. (cf *sahifu*) 2. (*idm*) *Fungua ukurasa mpya*, turn over a new leaf; open a new chapter.
ukurati *n (u)* see *ukurutu*
ukurugenzi *n (u)* directorship; the work of a director. (cf *udairekta*)
ukurutu (also *ukurati*) *n (u)* (*med*) skin eruptions; small pimples; eczema, tetter, dry tetter, scaly tetter. (cf *machuguchugu*)
ukusanyaji *n (u)* collection, amassment, accumulation: *Serikali imesisitiza umuhimu wa kusimamia ukusanyaji mzuri wa kodi nchini*, the government has emphasized the importance of good supervision of tax collection in the country. (cf *usombaji*)
ukusini *n (u)* the state, etc of being in the south.
ukuta[1] *n (u)* see *ukura*[1]
ukuta[2] (pl *kuta*) *n (u)* wall. (*prov*) *Usipoziba ufa utajenga ukuta*, if you don't fill a crack now, you will erect a wall later i.e. if you ignore a small thing now, it can cost you a lot later on.
ukuti[1] (pl *kuti*) *n (u)* a side frond of a coconut tree; a leaf of a coconut tree.
ukuti[2] *n (u)* ring around the rosy; a children's game in which they join hands and go round in a circle quite fast.
ukutubi *n (u)* librarianship (Eng)
ukuu[1] *n (u)* 1. headship, leadership: *Alipopewa ukuu, akatabakari*, when he was given the headship, he became arrogant. 2. greatness, largeness.
ukuu[2] *n (u)* labour pains, birth pain. (cf *uchungu*)
ukuukuu *n (u)* oldness, agedness. (cf *uchakavu, ukale*)
ukuzaji *n (u)* enhancement, advancement, promotion: *Ukuzaji wa soko la biashara*, the promotion of the business market.
ukwaju (pl *kwaju*) *n (u)* (*bot*) tamarind fruit.
ukwapi *n (u)* (*poet*) mid-rhyme.
ukware *n (u)* hyper sexual drive; nymphomania; lascivious love, carnal lust. (cf *ashiki*)
ukwasi *n (u)* richness, opulence, wealth. (cf *utajiri*)
ukwasu *n (u)* rash; small pimples usu of frickling kind, spreading all over the body or part of it.
ukwato (pl *kwato*) *n (u)* (*zool*) hoof of a donkey, horse, camel, etc.
ukwe *n (u)* father-in law or mother-in law relationship.
ukweli (also *kweli*) *n (u)* truth, fact, reality. (*prov*) *Kweli ikidhihiri, uwongo hujitenga*, if truth prevails, lies stay aside. *Ukweli usiopingika*, undisputable truth. (cf *uyakini, yakini*)

ukweni *n* (*u*) the side a person has married or is married; in-law relationship.
ukwenje *n* (*u*) noise, shout. (cf *ukemi*)
ukwenzi *n* (*u*) shout, noise, yell, call. (cf *ukemi, ukwenje*)
ukwezi *n* (*u*) 1. the act of climbing a tree esp a coconut tree. 2. the work of climbing a tree.
ulaanifu *n* (*u*) cursing, denunciation. (cf *apizo, duizo*) (Ar)
ulafi (also *ulafu*) *n* (*u*) gluttony, ravenousness, voracity: *Alikula ndizi kwa ulafi,* he ate the bananas voraciously. (cf *uroho, umero*).
ulafu *n* (*u*) see *ulafi*
ulaghai *n* (*u*) deceit, trickery. (cf *ughushi, udanganyifu, ujanja, uayari*)
ulaika *n* (*u*) body hair grown on the hands, armpits, etc.
ulaini *n* (*u*) 1. softness, tenderness, smoothness. (cf *uteketeke*) 2. (of a person) calmness, gentleness, softness.
ulaiti (also *ulafu*) *n* (*u*) a kind of light cotton material: *Sindano ulaiti,* a kind of soft rice seedling.
ulaji *n* (*u*) 1. act (method, etc.) of eating. 2. the maximum capacity a person can eat. 3. food. (cf *chakula*) 4. used in the expression: *Ulaji rushwa,* bribing, bribery.(cf *ufisadi*)
ulalaji *n* (*u*) 1. act (method, etc.) of sleeping. 2. the attitude of sleeping.
ulalamikaji *n* (*u*) the act (method, etc.) of complaining; complaint, grumble.
ulaka *n* (*u*) see *uraka*
ulalamishi *n* (*u*) quarrelsomeness, complaint, grumble. (cf *ubishi, ushindani*)
ulalo *n* (*u*) 1. camping-place, bivouac. 2. a sheltered place where ships can anchor at night.
ulamaa (pl of *alimu*) *n* (*u*) 1. religious scholars. 2. scholars, pundits; the learned. (cf *wanavyuoni*) (Ar)
ulanga *n* (*u*) mica; a transparent mineral used as an electrical insulator, etc.
ulanguzi *n* (*u*) 1. price-hiking; overcharging of items in business. 2. black marketing.
ulanifu *n* (*u*) the habit of eating indiscriminately.
ulanzi *n* (*u*) wine from bamboo sap; bamboo wine.
ulawiti *n* (*u*) pederasty, sodomy; sexual intercourse between two males. (Ar)
Ulaya *n* (*u*) (*geog*) Europe
ule *adj, pron* form of *-le,* 'that' used for **mi-** and **u** classes singular nouns: *Mzigo ule,* that luggage. *Wembe ule,* that razor.
uleaji *n* (*u*) upbringing
uledi *n* (*u*) (*naut*) cabin boy in a sailing vessel; kitchen servant in a sailing vessel; a servant of low class in a sailing ship.
ulegevu *n* (*u*) 1. slackness, laziness, looseness. (cf *uzembe, utepetevu, ugoigoi*) 2. looseness, weakness. (cf *udhaifu*)
ulegezaji *n* (*u*) 1. relaxation, loosening: *Ulegezaji wa kamba shingoni mwake ulimtorosha mbuzi yule,* the loosening of the rope around its neck caused the goat to escape. 2. liberalization: *Ulegezaji masharti ya biashara umeboresha uchumi wa nchi yao,* the trade liberalization has improved their country's economy.
ulemavu *n* (*u*) lameness, maim, crippling; physical disability. *Ulemavu wa ngozi,* lack of normal pigmentation on the skin. *Ulemavu wa kudumu,* permanent physical disability.
uleoleo *n* (*u*) staggering, reeling, rocking, wavering.
ulevi *n* (*u*) 1. intoxicant, alcohol. 2. drunkness, alcoholism. (cf *ugimbi*)
ulezi[1] *n* (*ma-*) upbringing, rearing, raising.
ulezi[2] (also *wimbi*) *n* (*u*) 1. (*bot*) finger millet. *Eleusine coracana.* 2. the seeds of this plant.
ulifi *n* (*u*) payment, paying. (cf *ulipaji*)
ulili *n* (*u*) 1. stretcher, litter, etc. (cf *machela*) 2. a kind of platform.
ulimaji *n* (*u*) method (process, etc.) of cultivating.

U   ulimbikizaji   ulokole

ulimbikizaji n (u) accumulation heap, hoard: *Ulimbikizaji mali*, the accumulation of wealth.

ulimbo n (u) birdlime; thick substance spread to catch birds.

ulimbwende n (u) dandyism, foppishness. (cf *umbuji, umaridadi, utanashati*)

ulimi¹ n (u) 1. tongue. (*prov*) *Ulimi hauna mfupa*, a tongue has no limits; it can speak about anything. 2. (*idms*) *Ulimi mkali*, a tongue that possesses fierce words. *Ulimi wa upanga*, a tongue that possesses fierce words. *Ulimi mrefu*, loose tongue e.g. *Mwanamke yule ana ulimi mrefu*, that woman has a loose tongue. 3. anything that resembles a tongue; a tongue-like object.

ulimi² (pl *ndimi*) n (u) a tongue of flame esp from a distance.

ulimikaji n (u) the cultivability of land; the fertility of a land to allow seeds to be planted.

ulimwengu n (u) 1. world, universe. (cf *dunia*) 2. worldly affairs: *Mambo ya dunia*, pleasures of life.

ulindaji n (u) protection, defence. (cf *ulinzi, hifadhi*)

ulindi n (u) a stick used for poking fire while cooking, etc.; poker.

ulinganaji n (u) the act (method, etc.) of comparing items; comparison. (cf *ulinganifu*)

ulinganifu n (u) correspondence, analogy, comparison, parallelism. (cf *urari, uwiano, ulingano*)

ulingano n (u) comparison, resemblance, correspondence, likeness, connection: *Kuna ulingano mkubwa kati ya maneno yake na matendo*, there is a big correspondence between his words and actions. (cf *mshabaha, urari*)

ulingo n (u) 1. observation platform for a watchman in charge of crops in a plantation. 2. boxing ring, wrestling mat. 3. (*fig*) arena: *Kiongozi ameamua kung'atuka katika ulingo wa siasa*, the leader has decided to abandon the political arena.

ulinzi n (u) 1. defence, protection, guard, custody: *Ulinzi wa sungusungu*, vigilante defence. *Ulinzi shirikishi*, community policing; a kind of defence involving different categories of people e.g. villagers, farmers, etc. (cf *polisi jamii*) *Ulinzi wa doria*, patrolling in turns. *Ulinzi wa taifa umepewa kipaumbele hapa nchini kwetu*, national defence has been given top priority in our country. *Aliwekwa chini ya ulinzi wa polisi*, he was kept under police surveillance (cf *hifadhi, himaya*) 2. method (means, etc.) of guarding: *Ulinzi wake ni mzuri*, his method of guarding is good. (cf *ulindaji*)

ulipaji n (u) payment, paying. (cf *ulifi*)

ulipuaji n (u) explosion, burst: *Ulipuaji wa mabomu*, bomb explosion.

ulipwaji n (u) the act (method, etc.) of being paid.

ulitima n (u) recession, depression, unemployment: *Nchi yao iliingia katika kipindi cha ulitima*, their country entered a period of recession. (*idm*) *Shika ulitima*, contest in the last round of the trump card.

uliwali n (u) governorship, headmanship, etc. in a Muslim community. (Ar)

uliz.a vt ask, query, question. Prep. *uliz.i.a* St. *uliz.ik.a* Cs. *uliz.ish.a* Ps. *uliz.w.a*, be asked. Rp. *uliz.an.a*, ask one another. (cf *dadisi, hoji, saili*)

ulizi (also *ulizo*) n (u) interrogative marker; question mark.

ulizi.a vt ask for, enquire. Ps. *uliz.iw.a* Rp. *uliz.i.an.a*

ulizo n (u) 1. question, quiz, querry, 2. see *ulizi*.

ulodi n (u) lordship, mastership: *Ulodi wake umewafanya wafanyakazi wamchukie*, his bossism has made the workers hate him. (cf *umwinyi, useti*) (Eng)

ulokole n (u) revivalism; the fervid spirit or methods characteristic of religious revivals.

808

uloo n (u) an iron stick with a knob on the end like a hook, used by fishermen to pull large fish for packing them in a vessel; gaff.
ulumbanaji n (u) the act (method, etc.) of liking to argue. (cf *ushindanaji*)
ulumbi n (u) *(ling)* multilingualism; a linguistic situation where a society speaks more than two languages.
uluwa n (u) prestige, celebrity, reputation: *Mtu yule anapenda uluwa*, that person likes to be given prestige. (cf *utukufu, hadhi*) (Ar)
um.a¹ (pl *nyuma*) n (u) fork .
um.a² vt,vi 1. pain, hurt, ache, wound: *Jino langu la juu linaniuma*, my upper tooth is paining. 2. *(fig)* hurt, pain: *Maneno yake machafu yaliniuma*, his dirty words hurt me. Prep. *um.i.a* Cs. *um.iz.a* Ps. *um.w.a* Rp. of Cs. *um.iz.w.a* Rp. of Cs. *um.iz.an.a* (cf *kang'ata, wanga*)
um.a³ vt,vi bite, sting: *Mbwa wako anauma?* Does your dog bite? *Nyigu aliniuma*, the wasp bit me. *(prov)* *Meno ya mbwa hayaumani*, the teeth of a dog don't lock together i.e. brothers don't harm one another even if they fight. Prep *um.i.a* St. *um.i.ka* Cs. *um.iz.a* Ps. *um.w.a* Rp. *um.an.a*
umaarufu n (u) fame, celebrity, renown: *Ujabari wake umempa umaarufu*, his daring has earned him fame. (cf *umashuhuri*) (Ar)
umadinishaji n (u) mineralization; act (method, etc) of converting organic matter into a mineral.
umafia n (u) the act (practice, etc) of exercising hostility and criminal methods to law and goverment (Eng)
umagharibi n (u) the state, etc. of being in the west.
umahiri n (u) intellect, intelligence, ingenuity: *Umahiri wake umemfanya afaulu vizuri kwenye mtihani*, her intelligence has made her pass the examination well. (cf *uhodari*) (Ar)
umajimaji n (u) dampness, moisture, wetness: *Nguo zile bado zina umajimaji*, those clothes are still damp. (cf *uowevu, uchepechepe*)
umajimbo n (u) regionalism, regional patriotism.
umajinuni¹ n (u) imbecility, stupidity, foolishness. (cf *ujinga, upumbavu*)
umajinuni² n (u) insaness, madness, lunacy. (cf *uwandaazimu*)
umakamu n (u) the work (office etc) of serving as a deputy in an institution, etc
umakanika n (u) mechanics; the work, etc. of repairing vehicles. (Eng)
umaksisti n (u) Marxism (Eng)
umalaya n (u) prostitution, whoredom. (cf *ukahaba, uasherati*)
umale n (u) sea depth.
umalizaji n (u) finishing: *Timu yetu ilifungwa kwa sababu umalizaji wake ulikuwa mbovu*, our team was defeated because its finishing power was poor.
umamluki n (u) the work of a mercenary; mercenariness: *Mbunge alifanyiwa umamluki na watu wasiojulikana*, the member of parliament was made a mercenary by unknown people. (Ar)
uman.a vi contest usu bitterly between two sides: *Timu mbili ziliumana vikali jana*, the two teams contested bitterly yesterday. (cf *umana, pepetana, kwaana*)
umande n (u) dew, brume, fog: *Umande wa theluji*, hoar-frost. (cf *ukungu*)
umanyeto n (u) hysteria (cf *mpagao*)
umaridadi n (u) 1. dandyism, neatness, smartness. (cf *umbeja, ulimbwende. usafi*) 2. *(fig)* perfectness: *Alifanya kazi yangu kwa umaridadi zaidi*, he did my work with greater perfection. (Pers)
umashariki n (u) the state, etc. of being in the east.
umashuhuri n (u) notability, fame, renown, distinction: *Umashuhuri wake unatokana na tabia yake nzuri*, his fame comes from his good manners. (cf *umaarufu*) (Ar)

umasikini n (u) poverty, penury. (cf *ufukara, ukata*) (Ar)
umati n (u) 1. crowd, throng, mass: *Umati mkubwa wa watu ulimiminika mjini kuhudhuria mazishi ya mwanasiasa mkongwe*, a huge crowd of people flocked to the town to attend the veteran politician's funeral. (cf *halaiki*) 2. followers, disciples; a people of one religious belief: *Umati wa Mtume Muhammad*, the followers of Prophet Muhammad.
umayamaya n (u) crowd, horde, mass: *Niliuona umayamaya wa watu wakingojea kumlaki rais*, I saw a crowd of people waiting to welcome the president.
umb.a¹ vt 1. create, make. (cf *huluku*) 2. make, construct: *Msanii aliwaumba wahusika wake kiufundi*, the writer created his characters artistically. Prep. **umb.i.a** St. **umb.ik.a** Cs. **umb.ish.a** Ps. **umb.w.a** (cf *sawiri, unda*)
umba² n (u) (med) failure to thrive; a kind of medical condition affecting infants and children esp those mentally retarded ones, who without evident cause, fail to gain weight and often lose weight as a result of phychosocial circumstances.
umbali n (u) 1. distance, farness: *Pana umbali wa kilomita 100 kutoka hotelini*, there is a distance of 100 kilometres from the hotel. 2. (maths) *Umbali sawa*, equidistant. (cf *kitalifa, masafa*)
umbeja n (u) chic, dandyism, neatness, smartness: *Msichana anapendeza kwa sababu ya umbeja wake*, the girl looks attractive because of her chic. (cf *umaridadi, usafi*)
umbelembele n (u) meddlesomeness, intrusiveness; the act (method, etc) of taking part in other people's affairs without being asked or needed (cf *ushawishi*)
umbeya n (u) curiosity, inquisitiveness, taletelling, talebearing, snooping: *Umbeya wake unachusha*, his inquisitiveness is disgusting. (cf *udaku, udukuzi, usabasi*)
umbi.a¹ vi (of a bird, etc.) hover; glide, fly in the air like a bird without using wings: *Ndege aliumbia kwa masaa mengi*, the bird glided for hours. Prep. **umbi.li.a** St. **umbi.lik.a** Cs. **umbi.lish.a** Ps. of Prep. **umbi.liw.a**
umbi.a² vt, vi (of fire) burn very much such that it gives out flames. Prep. **umbi.li.a** St. **umbi.lik.a** Cs. **umbi.lish.a** Ps. **umbi.liw.a**
umbijani n (u) (bot) chlorophyl; green substance found in certain plant cells. (cf *klorofili*)
umbile¹ n (ma-) 1. (used usu in pl) nature, character: *Ni maumbile yake kuwasema watu*, it is his nature to speak ill of people.
umbile² n (ma-) physique, shape, figure, form: *Mtu yule ana umbile zuri*, that person has a good physique. (cf *umbo*)
umbo n (ma-) shape, figure, physique, form: *Mtu yule hana umbo la kupendeza*, that person does not have a good figure. (cf *jisimu, umbile*)
umbu n (u) sister or brother. (cf *dada, kaka*)
umbu.a vt 1. belittle, degrade, debase, downgrade: *Mwanafunzi alimwumbua mwalimu wake darasani*, the student belittled his teacher in the class. (cf *tweza, hizi, aibisha*) 2. disfigure, deform, deface, spoil the look of. (prov) *Asiyeweza kutuumba, kutuumbua hawezi*, he who cannot create us, cannot degrade us. 3. harrow; break up clods in a land by using a harrow. (cf *buruga*) Prep. **umbu.li.a** St. **umbu.k.a** and **umbu.lik.a** Cs. **umbu.lish.a** Ps. of Prep. **umbu.liw.a** Rp. **umbu.an.a**
umbuji n (u) oratory, eloquence; power of speech: *Umbuji wake wa kuweza kuhutubia hadharani hauelezeki*, his eloquence of speaking in public is beyond description. (cf *ufasaha, ulumbaji*)
umbuya n (u) friendship, comradeship: *Kuendeleza umbuya kati ya mataifa*

ni jambo zuri, to develop friendship between countries is a good thing. (cf *urafiki, udugu*)
umeme *n* (*u*) 1. lightning: *Mti ulipigwa na umeme*, the tree was struck by lightning. 2. electricity: *Serikali inataka kueneza umeme vijijini*, the government wants to spread electricity in the villages. (cf *umeta, spaki*)
umeng'enyaji *n* (*u*) digestion; the process by which food is converted into substances that can be absorbed and assimilated by the body.
umero *n* (*u*) voracity, raveousness, gluttony, greed: *Umero wake ulionekana waziwazi wakati wa kula*, his voracity was clearly manifested during meals. (cf *ulafi, uroho*)
umi.a *vi* be hurt; be injured; get hurt: *Aliumia wakati wa kucheza mpira wa magongo*, he was injured while playing hockey. Prep. **umi.li.a** St. **umi.lik.a** Cs. **umi.z.a** (cf *dhurika, tindia*)
umik.a *vt* cup blood. Prep. **umik.i.a** St. **umik.ik.a** Cs. **umik.ish.a** Ps. **umik.w.a** Rp. **umik.an.a**
umilikaji (also *umiliki*) *n* (*u*) possession, ownership, proprietorship: *Umilikaji wa ardhi*, land ownership.
umiliki (also *umilikaji*) *n* (*u*) ownership, possession: *Umiliki wa nyumba*, house ownership. *Umiliki wa ardhi*, land ownership.
umilikishaji *n* (*u*) an act (method, etc) of bestowing ownership of sth (e.g property) upon sby.
umilisi *n* (*u*) competence, mastery: *Umilisi wa lugha*, language competence.
umio *n* (*u*) (*anat*) pharynx; the joint opening of the gullet and windpipe, the upper expanded portion of the digestive tube, between esophagus below and the mouth and nasal cavities above and in front. (cf *koromeo*)
umito *n* (*u*) 1. the swelling of the feet and ankles of a pregnant woman due to excessive fluid retention; pre-eclampsia. It occurs after the 20th week of gestation but may develop before this time in the presence of trophoblastic disease. It is predominantly a disorder of primigravidas. 2. idleness of a man supposedly thought to be caused by the condition of a pregnant woman.
umiz.a *vt, vi* hurt, injure: *Ameniumiza*, he has injured me. Prep. **umiz.i.a** St. **umiz.ik.a** Ps. **umiz.w.a** Rp. **umiz.an.a**
umma *n* (*u*) mass, people, public: *Mali ya umma*, public property. *Jeshi la umma*, people's army.
umoja *n* (*u*) 1. union, unity: *Umoja wa mataifa*, United Nations Organisation. *Umoja wa Nchi Huru za Afrika*, Organization of African Unity. *Umoja wa Soko Nafuu*, Preferential Trade Area. (*prov*) *Umoja ni nguvu*, unity is strength. 2. (*gram*) singular: *Umoja wa 'viti'ni 'kiti'* the singular of 'chairs' is 'chair'.
umoto *n* (*u*) hotness, gravity, seriousness.
umri *n* (*u*) age, oldness; stage of life: *Ana umri gani?* how old is he? *Umri wa kuishi*, life expectancy. (Ar)
umu.a[1] *vt* leaven dough; put yeast or leaven into flour in order to make it rise: *Aliumua unga wa mkate*, she leavened the dough in order to make bread. Prep. **umu.li.a** St. **umu.k.a**. Cs. **umu.sh.a** Ps. of Prep. **umu.liw.a**
umu.a[2] *vt* 1. steal a woman from her husband. 2. steal honey from bees. Prep. **umu.li.a** St. **umu.k.a** and **umu.lik.a** Cs. **umu.lish.a** Ps. of Prep. **umu.liw.a**
umu.a[3] *vt* cast metal in a mould: *Alimpelekea mhunzi ufunguo ili apate kuumua*, he sent the key to the iron-smith in order to get it cast. Prep. **umu.li.a** St. **umu.k.a** and **umu.lik.a** Cs. **umu.lish.a** Ps. of Prep. **umu.liw.a**
umu.a[4] *vt* disentangle, disjoin, dismember Prep. **umu.li.a** St. **umu.k.a** Cs. **umu.sh.a** Ps. of Prep. **umu.liw.a**
umuhimu *n* (*u*) importance, significance, greatness, urgency: *Wao hawaelewi*

umuhimu wa jambo hili, they do not understand the importance of this issue. (cf *uzito, ubora, maana*) (Ar)
umuk.a¹ *vi* be leavened, be raised. Prep. *umuk.i.a* St. *umuk.ik.a* Cs. *umuk.ish.a*
umuk.a² *vi* be disjoined, be dismembered. Prep. *umuk.i.a* St. *umuk.ik.a* Cs. *umuk.ish.a*
umuk.a³ *vi* work hard, work diligently. Prep. *umuk.i.a* St. *umuk.ish.a*
umw.a¹ *vi* be sick, be ill, be in pain: *Yeye anaumwa siku hizi*, she is sick these days.
umw.a² *vi* (of a woman) be pregnant, be expecting a baby.
umwagaji *n* (*u*) pouring, spilling: *Umwagaji-damu*, bloodshed.
umwagiaji *n* (*u*) act (method, etc.) of pouring out water on sth else.
umwagiliaji *n* (*u*) irrigation, watering: *Mradi wa umwagiliaji*, irrigation project. *Kilimo cha umwagiliaji*, irrigation by farming (cf *unyunyizi*)
umwamba *n* (*u*) toughness; the act of flexing one's muscles: *Kila timu ilijaribu kuonyesha umwamba wake uwanjani*, every team tried to flex its muscles on the ground. (cf *ubabe*)
umwinyi *n* (*u*) a bourgeois outlook, lordly outlook; lordliness. (cf *ubwanyenye*)
una *n* (*u*) (*zool*) mackerel, fusilier, scad; a kind of striped edible salt fish. (cf *kibua*)
unaa (also *unai*) *n* (*u*) calumny, aspersion; malicious falsehood: *Unaa wake ulisababisha suitafahamu mtaani*, her malicious lies caused misunderstanding in the neighbourhood. (cf *fitina, usabasi, uchongezi*)
unabii *n* (*u*) prophecy; the work of a prophet. (cf *utume*)
unadhifu *n* (*u*) cleanliness, neatness, tidiness: *Unadhifu ni kitu muhimu kwa mwanadamu*, cleanliness is an essential thing for a human being. (cf *usafi*) (Ar)
unafiki *n* (*u*) hypocrisy, false profession: *Unafiki wake unawafanya wanachama wasimwamini*, her hypocrisy makes the members to distrust her. (cf *uzandiki, ujanja, ulaghai*) (Ar)
unafuu *n* (*u*) improvement, relief: *Wafanyakazi wamepata unafuu wa kodi*, the workers have got tax relief. (Ar)
unahodha *n* (*u*) 1. (in a sailing vessel) captainship, helmship, commandership: *Ameshika kazi ile ya unahodha katika jahazi kwa miaka mingi*, he has been in that position of being a captain of the dhow for many years. 2. leadership in a sports team: *Timu yake iliweza kupata ushindi kwa mara nyingi alipoeshika unahodha*, his team was able to clinch many victories under his captainship. (cf *ukapteni*)
unaibu *n* (*u*) deputyship: *Kazi ya unaibu serikalini imempa umaarufu nchini*, the work of serving as a deputy in the government has earned him fame in the country. (cf *usaidizi*) (Ar)
unajimu *n* (*u*) 1. astrology. 2. astronomy. (Ar)
unajisi¹ *n* (*u*) impurity, uncleanness, contamination: *Aliifua nguo ile kwa sababu ya unajisi wake*, he washed that dress because it was unclean for religious use. (Ar)
unajisi² *n* (*u*) defilement, defloration, rape: *Alifungwa jela kwa sababu ya kosa la unajisi*, he was imprisoned on charges of rape. (Ar)
unamu *n* (*u*) (in soil, text, etc.) texture.
unamuaji *n* (*u*) act (method, etc.) of dislodging sby/sth; untrapping. (cf *unamuzi*)
unamuzi *n* (*u*) dislodging, disengagement, untrapping, disentanglement: *Unamuzi wa chombo kilichopanda mwamba baharini ulichukua siku nyingi*, the dislodging of the sailing vessel that hit a cliff in the sea took many days. (cf *unamuaji*)
unane¹ *n* (*u*) see *tindi¹*
unane² *n* (*u*) see *ufyeufye²*
unanuaji *n* (*u*) act (method) of dislodging,

unasi

an animal from a trap. (cf *unanuza*)
unasi *n (u)* many people. (Ar)
und.a¹ *vt* 1. construct, make, build, set: *Waliiunda ndege kubwa*, they constructed a big plane. (cf *tengeneza, sanii, sana*) 2. (*idm*) tread on, trample, run over, crush: *Gari liliimwunda mtoto mdogo*, the car crushed a small child. Prep. **und.i.a** St. **und.ik.a** Cs. **und.ish.a** Ps. **und.w.a** Rp. **und.an.a** (cf *kanyaga*)
und.a² *vt* remove honey from a beehive: gather honey: *Aliunda asali nyingi ndani ya mzinga*, he removed a lot of honey from the beehive. Prep **und.i.a** St **und.ik.a** Cs **und.ish.a** Ps **und.w.a**
undam.a *vt* have sex with a woman. Prep **undam.i.a** St. **undam.ik.a** Cs. **undam.ish.a** Ps. **undam.w.a** (cf *jamii*)
undani¹ *n (u)* grudge, umbrage, resentment: *Mtu yule huweka undani hata kwa jambo dogo*, that person harbours a grudge even for a small matter. (cf *kinyongo, mfundo*)
undani² *n (u)* confirmation, authenticity: *Bado hatujapata undani wa habari yenyewe*, we have not yet received the confirmation of the news. *Kwa undani*, in depth e.g. *Alilizingatia jambo lenyewe kwa undani*, he considered the issue in depth. (cf *uhakika, uthabiti*)
undu (pl *nyundu*) *n (u)* (*zool*) cock's comb (cf *shunzi, kilemba*)
undugu *n (u)* brotherhood, kinship: *Yeye na mimi hatuna undugu*, he and me are not brothers. *Undugu wa kuchanjana*, blood brotherhood (cf *mlango, ukoo*)
undumakuwili *n (u)* hypocrisy, duplicity: *Undumakuwili si sifa nzuri*, hypocrisy is not a good quality.
uneemevu *n (u)* prosperity, fortune, wealth: *Uneemevu wa nchi yao unatokana na uongozi bora*, the prosperity of their country emanates from good leadership. (cf *ufanisi, usitawi*) (Ar)

ungam.a   **U**

unenaji *n (u)* art (manner, practice, etc) of speaking: *Unenaji wake ni wa kifasaha*, her manner of speaking demonstrates eloquence.
unene *n (u)* 1. obesity, fatness, corpulence, overweight. *Unene ule ulikuwa chanzo cha maradhi yangu*, that obesity was the cause of my disease. 2. thickness: *Unene wa ubao huu*, the thickness of this wood.
uneni¹ *n (u)* feud, vendetta, hostility: *Uneni ulioko kati yao umezifanya familia zao zitengane*, the enmity that exists between them has estranged their families. (cf *utesi, uhasama*)
uneni² *n (u)* 1. speaking, articulation (cf *utamkaji*) 2. backbiting; speaking slanderously about sby.
unga¹ *n (u)* 1. flour: *Unga wa ngano*, wheat flour *Unga wa mahindi*, maize flour. 2. powder: *Unga wa hamira*, yeast powder. *Unga wa ndere*, powder made by witchdoctors for bewitching people. *Unga wa mbao* (*ungambao*), sawdust. (cf *maramba*)
ung.a² *vt* join, combine, unite: *Walijiunga na chama chetu*, they joined our party. *Aliziunga waya mbili*, he joined two wires. Prep **ung.i.a**, join with (by, etc) St **ung.ik.a** Cs **ung.ish.a** Ps **ung.w.a**, be joined Rp **ung.an.a** St **ung.am.an.a**. Cs of Rp **ung.an.ish.a** (cf *shikamanisha*)
ung.a³ *vt* 1. season food; make food more tasty by adding ingredients such as salt, spices, etc: *Mpishi alikiunga chakula*, the cook seasoned the food. Prep **ung.i.a** St **ung.ik.a** Cs **ung.ish.a** Ps **ung.w.a** 2. (*idms*) *Unga mkono*, support e.g *Aliliunga mkono wazo langu*, he supported my idea. *Unga hesabu*, add, total, mix together.
ungam.a *vt* concede, admit, confess, acknowledge: *Mshtakiwa aliungama kosa lake la jinai mbele ya hakimu*, the accused confessed his crime before the judge. Prep **ungam.i.a** St **ungam.ik.a** Cs **ungam.ish.a**, induce to confess,

813

force to confess. Ps *ungam.w.a* (cf *kiri)*
ungami.a *vt* confess to, concede to. Prep *ungami.li.a* Cs of Prep *ungami.lish.a* Rp of Cs *ungami.sh.an.a*
ungamish.a *vt* make sby agree to confess; persuade sby to confess. Prep *ungamish.i.a* St *ungamish.ik.a* Ps *ungamish.w.a*
ungamo[1] *n* (*ma-*) 1. confession, admission, acknowledgement: *Ungamo lake kwenye kesi lilimpeleka kifungoni*, his confession in the case sent him to jail. 2. act (method, etc) of confessing. *Ungamo la shahidi*, the confession of the witness.
ungamo[2] *n* (*u*) yellow stuff, used as a dye from a shrub.
ungan.a *vt* 1. unite, be united, be joined: *Nchi zetu zimeungana*, our countries are united. 2. cooperate on an issue (cf *shirikiana*) Prep *ungan.i.a* St *ungan.ik.a* Cs *ungan.ish.a*
ung'ang'anizi *n* (*u*) inflexibility; the act of being tough or rigid: *Usichukulie mambo kwa ung'ang'anizi sana*, don't be too tough; be flexible.
unganik.a *vi* be united, be joined. Prep *unganik.i.a* St *unganik.ik.a* Cs *unganik.ish.a*
unganish.a *vt* connect, join, unite, amalgamate: *Aliweza kuziunganisha pande mbili zilizokuwa zikizozana*, he was able to unite two warring sides. *Timu ilipata bao la kuongoza baada ya mchezaji wetu wa kiungo kuunganisha krosi yangu*, the team managed to secure a leading goal after our midfield player connected a cross from me. Prep. *unganish.i.a* St. *unganish.ik.a* Ps. *unganish.w.a*, be linked, be joined e.g. *Aliunganishwa katika kesi ya uchochezi iliyowakabili wanachama wengine*, he was linked to the seditious case facing

other members.
ungio-sahili *n* (*u*) (*gram*) the process of linking items of equal status, typically introduced by words such as 'ina' *and*, 'lakini' *but*, etc.; parataxis, coordination. (cf *uambatishaji*)
ungiotegemezi *n* (*u*) (*gram*) hypotaxis, subordination; the process of linking items of unequal status, typically introduced by words such as 'tangu' since 'kwa vile' because, etc (cf *utegemezaji*)
ungo[1] *n* (*u*) (used in) *Vunja ungo*, begin to menstruate; have first menses, enter a virgin.
ungo[2] (pl *nyungo*) *n* (*u*) a winnowing tray; a round flat tray used for sifting grain. (cf *uteo*)
ungo[3] *n* (*u*) (*zool*) the shell of a crab; crab's shell.
ung'oaji *n* (*u*) uprooting: *Ung'oaji wa mimea*, the uprooting of plants.
ung'ongo (pl *ng'ongo*) *n* (*u*) a strip of leaf esp of the wild date palm, used for sewing the plaits of a mat or for fastening things. (*prov*) *Aliyeumwa na nyoka akiona ung'ongo hushtuka*, he who is bitten by a snake is startled even if he sees *ung'ongo*, a strip of palm-leaf i.e. once beaten twice shy. (cf *utengule*)
ung'ong'o *n* (*u*) speaking nasally.
ungoyo *n* (*u*) see *unyoya*
ungu.a *vt,vi* be burnt, be scorched, be scalded: *Aliungua ulimi alipokuwa anakunywa chai moto*, he scalded his tongue when he was drinking hot tea. Prep. *ungu.li.a* St. *ungu.lik.a* Cs. *ungu.z.a*. Ps. of Prep. *ungu.liw.a*, be burnt. (cf *teketea*)
Unguja *n* (*u*) (*geog*) Zanzibar
unguz.a *vt,vi* burn, char, scorch: *Aliliunguza shati langu alipokuwa anapiga pasi*, he burnt my shirt when

he was ironing. Prep. *unguz.i.a* St. *unguz.ik.a* Ps. *unguz.w.a* Rp. *unguz. an.a* (cf *teketeza*)

unju[1] *n* (*u*) a person considered to be very tall: *Yu mrefu kama unju*, he is very tall.

unju[2] *n* (*u*) dawn (cf *alfajiri*)

unjuguu *n* (*u*) a kind of local dance used during circumcision rites.

unonaji *n* (*u*) the condition of an animal having a lot of fatness in its body.

unong'onezaji *n* (*u*) act (method, etc.) of whispering; whisper, murmur undertone. (cf *unong'onezi*)

unong'onezi *n* (*u*) whisper, murmur, undertone. (cf *unong'onezaji*)

unono *n* (*u*) 1. richness, prosperity, wealth; *Lala unono*, sleep well. 2. luxury, comfort, indulgence: *Yeye hapendi kuishi maisha ya unono*, he doesn't like to live a luxurious life. (cf *starehe*)

unukuzi *n* (*u*) (*phon*) transcription: *Maandishi ya unukuzi*, phonetic transription.

ununu *n* (*u*) (*bot*) fibre from the inner skin of the stalk of a coconut leaf. *Puna ununu*, strip the fibre of this kind.

ununuaji *n* (*u*) purchasing, buying: *Ununuaji wa jumla*, wholesale buying. (cf *ununuzi*)

ununurifu *n* (*u*) radiance, brightness; the quality or state of being radiant. (cf *mng'aro*)

ununuzi *n* (*u*) purchasing, buying. (cf *ununuaji*)

unusukaputi *n* (*u*) anaesthesia; a loss of sensation induced by an anaesthetic and limited to a specific area or involving a loss of consciousness.

unyaa *n* (*u*) 1. filth, excrement: *Matopasi waliuondoa unyaa mtaani*, the scavengers removed the filth from the neighbourhood. (cf *kinyesi, kinyaa*) 2. (*fig*) anything of disgust.

unyafuzi *n* (*u*) (*med*) kwashiorkor; a disease of young children caused by chronic deficiency of protein, etc. (cf *chirwa*)

unyago *n* (*u*) 1. initiation of young brides. 2. dancing and other activities connected with the initiation ceremony.

unyaji *n* (*u*) act (method, etc.) of defecating.

unyakanga *n* (*u*) the work of a chief instructor in initiation rites.

unyakuzi *n* (*u*) grabbing, snatching, clutching. 2. theft, pilferage, stealing; *Alikamatwa kwa kosa la unyakuzi*, he was arrested for stealing.

unyalio *n* (*u*) a stick placed inside, at the bottom of a container of fish, etc to prevent them from getting stuck in it.

unyama *n* (*u*) 1. inhumanity, cruelty, brutality: *Wafungwa walifanyiwa unyama walipokuwa gerezani*, the prisoners were treated with brutality while in jail. (cf *ukatili, uovu*) 2. abnormal activities by an animal.

unyamavu *n* (*u*) quietness, calmness, peacefulness: *Unyamavu wake umempa mke mzuri*, his calmness has made him to get a beautiful wife. (cf *ukimya, upole*)

unyamazaji *n* (*u*) act (method, etc.) of remaining quiet.

unyambi *n* (*u*) 1. insensitivity; lack of concern for others; the practice of being a dog in the manger: *Unyambi wake umemfanya akatae kuazima watu vitu vyake*, his insensitivity has made him reluctant to lend his things to other people. (cf *inda, tadi*) 2. audacity to pry into other people's affairs.

unyambuaji *n* (*u*) act (method, etc.) of stretching sth.

unyambulishaji *n* (*u*) (*gram*) conjugation

unyang'anyi *n* (*u*) robbery, theft, stealing. (cf *upokaji, unyakuzi*)

unyange (also *nyange*) *n* (*u*) scream,

noise, yell, roar: *Tulisikia unyange kutoka upande wa mashariki*, we heard a yell from the eastern side. (cf *ukelele, ukemi, yowe*)
unyanya¹ *n* (*u*) 1. dislike of sth or someone who is filthy; dislike of unclean environment: *Unyanya wake umemfanya avae nguo safi*, his dislike of a filthy environment has made him wear clean clothes. 2. feeling of arrogance, superiority, etc. over sth and ultimately remaining aloof; standoffishness. *Watu wanamsema kwa sababu ya unyanya wake*, people speak ill of him because of his arrogance. (cf *unyarafu*)
unyanya² *n* (*u*) old womanhood.
unyanyapaa *n* (*u*) disdain, scorn, contempt: *Unyanyapaa ni sifa mbaya*, contempt is a bad trait. *Unyanyapaa wa kijinsia*, sexual contempt. *Unyanyapaa wa walemavu*, the contempt of the disabled people.
unyanyasaji *n* (*u*) persecution, oppression, humiliation: *Unyanyasaji wowote ni mbaya*, any oppression is bad. *Unyanyasaji wa kijinsia*, sexual humiliation.
unyarafu *n* (*u*) 1. disdain, contempt, scorn: *Mimi simpendi kijana yule kwa sababu ya unyarafu wake*, I dont like that young man because he is scornful. (cf *dharau*) 2. arrogance. *Unyarafu ni kitu kibaya*, arrogance is a bad thing. (cf *unyambi*)
unyarubanja *n* (*u*) a feudal condition of which a system of land tenure in Bahaya, Tanzania existed; feudalism.
unyataji *n* (*u*) act (method, etc. of sth being sticky.
unyaufu *n* (*u*) the condition of being dried up, wasted away, shrivelled, etc.; pining away: *Unyaufu wake ulisababishwa na maradhi*, her pining away was caused by the disease.
unyayo (pl *nyayo*) *n* (*u*) see *wayo*

unyegezi (also *kinyenyezi*) *n* (*u*) 1. blindness from glare; glare, dazzle: *Macho yake yaliingiwa na unyegezi kutokana na miale ya jua*, his eyes were dazzled by the rays of the sun. 2. the condition of being dazzled. (cf *kiwi*)
unyeleaji *n* (*u*) the condition of being soft.
unyeleo (also *unyeo*) (p1 *nyeleo*) *n* (*u*) (*anat*) the pore of a skin; skin pore.
unyende (also *nyende*) *n* (*u*) scream; a loud cry esp because of fear, etc.: *Piga unyende*, make a loud cry because of fear. (cf *ukwenzi*)
unyenyefu *n* (*u*) 1. tingling of the blood with passion, etc.; goose bumps, goose flesh: *Aliingiwa na unyenyefu alipoguswa na majani ya mti ule*, her body tingled when it was touched by the leaves of that tree. (cf *msisimko, mtambalio, kimbimbi* 2. the condition of feeling cold. 3. act (method, etc.) of being subservient, humble, etc.
unyenyekeaji *n* (*u*) act (method, etc.) of being subservient, humble, etc.
unyenyekeo *n* (*u*) see *unyenyekevu*
unyenyekevu (also *unyenyekeo*) *n* (*u*) submission, humility, subservience. *Mtumishi alimwamkia rais kwa unyenyekevu*, the servant greeted the president with humility. (cf *utu, heshima*)
unyenyezi *n* (*u*) 1. tingling of the blood with passion, etc.; goose flesh, goose bumps, goose skin, goose pimples: *Niliingiwa na unyenyezi mdudu aliponitambaa mwilini*, my body tingled when an insect crawled on it. (cf *msisimko, kimbimbi, mtambalio, unyenyefu*) 2. haziness, mistiness.
unyeti *n* (*u*) 1. coddling; act (manner, attitude, etc of tenderly treating a person esp. a baby, invalid, etc: *Mvulana yule alilelewa kwa unyeti*, that boy was brought up in a coddling manner. 2. sensitivity: *Unyeti wa suala lile*, the sensitivity of that issue. *Unyeti wa habari yenyewe*, the sensitivity of the information.

unyevu (also *unyevunyevu*) *n* (*u*) moisture, dampness, wetness: *Nguo hizi zina unyevu*, these clothes are damp. (cf *umajimaji, uowevu*)
unyevunyevu *n* (*u*) see *unyevu*
unyimwaji *n* (*u*) deprivation: *Unyimwaji wa haki za binaadamu kwa raia*, the deprivation of human rights to its citizens.
unyofu *n* (*u*) uprightness, integrity, honesty: *Unyofu wa kiongozi wenu umemfanya apendwe na raia*, the uprightness of your leader has made him to be loved by the citizens. (cf *ikhlasi, uadilifu*)
unyogovu *n* (*u*) weariness, exhaustion, fatigue: *Amelala kwa sababu ya unyogovu*, he has slept because of exhaustion. (cf *uchofu, unyong'anyevu*)
unyonge *n* (*u*) 1. misery, wretchedness, abjectness, tribulation: *Umasikini umeyatia maisha yake katika unyonge*, poverty has made her life a misery. (cf *simanzi, huzuni*) 2. loneliness, solitude: *Unyonge wangu umesababisha niwe na mawazo mengi*, my loneliness has caused me to have many thoughts. (cf *upweke*) 3. inability to meet the basic needs of living
unyong'onyevu *n* (*u*) fatigue, exhaustion, languid: *Hakuweza kwenda kulima jana kwa sababu ya unyong'anyevu*, he could not go to cultivate yesterday because of fatigue. (cf *unyogovu*)
unyong'onyeaji *n* (*u*) act (method, etc.) of undergoing weariness.
unyonyaji *n* (*u*) 1. suckling, feeding at breast: *Unyonyaji wa mtoto mdogo yule kutoka kwenye ziwa la mama yake ulichukua dakika kumi*, the suckling of that baby from its mother's breast took ten minutes. (cf *ufyonzaji*) 2. exploitation: *Kuna unyonyaji mwingi katika mfumo wa kibepari*, there is a lot of exploitation in the capitalist system.
unyonyeshaji *n* (*u*) breastfeeding

unyounyo *n* (*u*) closely (used in the expression) *Fuata unyounyo*, follow sby very closely. (cf *karibukaribu*)
unyoya *n* (*ma-*) (*zool*) animal's or bird's hair but usu with reference to the later; quill, feather.
unyumba *n* (*u*) 1. married life; relation of husband and wife; *Vunja unyumba*, divorce or separate husband from wife. 2. living together of a woman and a man even if not legally married; cohabitation: *Wanaishi kwa unyumba ijapokuwa hawajaoana*, they live together even though they are not legally married.
unyusi (pl *nyusi*) *n* (*u*) (*anat*) supercilium, eyebrow; the crescentic line of hairs at the superior edge of the orbit.
unywaji *n* (*u*) act (method, etc.) of drinking, absorbing liquid, moisture etc.: *Unywaji wake wa pombe hausemeki*, his manner of drinking beer is beyond description. *Unywaji pombe*, beer drinking.
unywanywa *n* (*u*) upset stomach, nausea; sickness in the stomach, with an impulse to vomit: *Niliingiwa na unywanywa nilipouona uchafu njiani*, 1 was filled with nausea when I saw filth on the road. (cf *kichefucheju, kinyaa*)
unywele (pl *nywele*) *n* (*u*) hair: *Nywele za singa*, long straight soft hair. *Nywele za kipilipili*, curly hair. (*prov*) *Akili ni nywele, kila mtu ana zake*, brains are like hair; everyone has his/her own kind i.e. intelligence is not the same among individuals.
unyweleo *n* (*u*) a hair grown in the pore of a skin. (cf *ulaika*)
unywelevu *n* (*u*) porosity; the state or property of being porous.
uo (pl *nyuo*) *n* (*u*) sheath, scabbard, cover: *Uo wa kisu*, the sheath of a knife. *Uo wa upanga*, the sheath of a sword. *Uo wa jambia*, the sheath of a dagger. (cf *ala*)

U

uoanishaji n (u) act (method, etc) of amking two or more things agree with one another.
uoga n (u) see woga
uogopaji n (u) fear, cowardice: *Uogopaji wake kwa mwalimu mkuu hauna maana* his fear of the school head is baseless. (cf *hofu, uchaji*)
uokoaji n (u) an act of rescuing; salvation, rescue: *Kazi za uokoaji ziliendelea kwa masaa mengi*, rescue efforts continued for many hours.
uokosi n (u) jealousy; the feeling of being jealous to others who have succeeded in life.
uokotaji n (u) act (method, etc.) of picking up sth.
uokovu n (u) see wokovu
uombaji n (u) begging, praying, request. (cf *utakaji*)
uombeaji n (u) act (method, etc.) of interceding for sby.
uonaji n (u) sight seeing: *Uonaji karibu*, short sight. *Uonaji mbali*, long sight.
uondoshaji n (u) displacement, removal
uonevu n (u) oppression, bullying, unjust treatment: *Uonevu wake umekithiri*, his bullying is too much. (cf *utesaji, udhalimu*)
uongo n (u) lie, untruth, falsehood. (cf *uchuku, uzandiki*) 2. a false statement.
uongofu n (u) see wongofu
uongozi n (u) leadership, management: *Uongozi wa juu*, higher authorities. *Uongozi wake ni mzuri*, his leadership is good. (cf *unahodha, ukuu*)
uono n (u) (zool) short head anchovy, buccaneer anchovy; a small fish of subcylindirical body with a rounded belly, found in pelagic coastal waters.
uopoaji n (u) rescuing, saving: *Uopoaji wa maiti*, the rescuing of corpses.
uotaji n (u) 1. germination. (cf *umeaji*) 2. the plants of an area or of a region.
uoto n (u) growth of plants; vegetation.
uovu n (u) evil, vice, wickedness. (cf *ubaya, unyama*)

uowevu n (u) moisture, wetness: *Soksi hizi zina uowevu*, these socks are damp. (cf *umajimaji, uchepechepe*)
uoya n (u) see oya
uoza n (u) 1. decay, rottenness, putrefaction, rot, decomposition: *Uoza wa nyama hii umesababishwa na nzi*, the rotting of this meat has been caused by flies. 2. (fig) decline, degeneration, collapse, weakness: *Uoza katika mfumo wa kisiasa kwenye chama tawala*, the weakness in the political system of the ruling party.
uozaji n (u) 1. act (method, etc.) of marrying. 2. act (method, etc.) of decaying.
uozi n (u) marrying: *Uozi wa msichana yule ulichukua muda mfupi*, that girl's marriage took a short time.
uozo n (u) 1.the stench of sth that has gone bad. 2. any person or thing that has decomposed.
upaa n (u) see upara
upachikaji n (u) 1. inserting. 2. scoring: *Upachikaji wa mabao*, goal scoring.
upadiri (also *upadre*) n (u) priesthood, chaplaincy (cf *ukasisi*) (Port)
upadirisho n (u) priestly ordination. (Port)
upadre n (u) see upadiri
upagazi[1] n (u) the work of a caravan porter; portership.
upagazi[2] n (u) spirit possession; witchcraft; being bewitched or possessed by a spirit. (cf *ukuli*)
upaji[1] n (u) endowment, talent: gift esp from God. (cf *kipaji, kipawa*)
upaji[2] n (u) giving, donation, offering.
upakasaji n (u) act (method, etc.) of plaiting leaf-strips of the wide-date palm.
upakataji n (u) act (method, etc.) of holding sby/sth in the lap.
upakiaji (also *upakizi*) n (u) the loading in a ship, train, etc. (cf *upakizaji*)
upakizaji (also *upakizi*) n (u) freightage, shipment, loading. (cf *upakiaji*)

818

upakizi *n (u)* see *upakiaji*
upakuaji (also *upakuzi*) *n (u)* 1. unloading. 2. act (method, etc.) of dishing out food.
upakuzi *n (u)* see *upakuaji*
upamba¹ *n (u)* a small bit of raw cotton such as cotton wool, lint, etc. used medicinally esp for children.
upamba² (pl *pamba*) *n (u)* billhook; a knife with a broad, flat, thin blade used in tapping palmwine or for plaiting baskets. (cf *kotama, ramba*)
upamba³ (pl *pamba*) *n (u)* (*zool*) tusk of a boar, warthog, etc.
upambaji *n (u)* decoration, adornment. (cf *upambi, urembo*)
upambanuaji *n (u)* differentiation, discrimination. (cf *upambanuzi*)
upambanuzi *n (u)* differentiation, discrimination, distinguishing. (cf *upambanuaji, ufafanuzi, tafsili*)
upana *n (u)* width, breadth. (cf, *mapana*)
upandaji¹ *n (u)* planting, growing: *Upandaji miti*, the planting of trees. (cf *uoteshaji*)
upandaji² *n (u)* 1. climbing, ascending. (cf *uparamiaji*) 2. embarkment, boarding.
upande¹ *n (u)* 1 side, direction section. *Upande wa kulia*, right side. *Upande wa kushoto*, left side. 2. (*syn*) *Mdudu upande*, whitlow, felon.
upande² *adv* aside, askew, on one side: *Weka upande*, put aside. *Mambo yake yamekwenda upande*, her affairs have gone askew.
upandikizaji *n (u)* grafting; the act or process of inserting a bud or shoot of one plant or tree into the stem or trunk of another, where it continues to grow, becoming a permanent part; scion
upanga *n (u)* 1. sword. 2. (*syn*) *Upanga wa jogoo*, a cock's comb. (*prov*) *Amani haiji ila kwa ncha ya upanga*, peace cannot be obtained without a tip of a sword i.e. if you want peace, prepare for war. 2. a flat, wooden, sword-shaped instrument used for weaving. 3. used in the expression: *Upanga wa suruali*, crease of trousers.
upangaji¹ *n (u)* arrangement, grouping, organization: *Upangaji wao wa kazi unastahili sifa*, the organization of their work is commendable. (cf *utaratibu, uendeshaji*)
upangaji² *n (u)* 1. renting, hiring; the act (method, etc.) of renting a house, etc. 2. fixing: *Upangaji wa bei*, the fixing of prices.
upangiliaji *n (u)* act (method, etc.) of arranging one thing on top of another; arrangement.
upangishaji *n (u)* the act (method, etc.) of renting a house, etc.
upanuaji *n (u)* expansion, extension; the act (method, etc.) of expanding sth. (cf *upanuzi*)
upanuzi *n (u)* expansion, extension, enlargement: *Upanuzi wa njia hii utawafurahisha waendeshaji magari*, the expansion of this road will please motorists. (cf *upanuaji*)
upanukaji *n (u)* the (act, method, etc) of expanding an area of sth; expansion, extension. (cf *upanuzi*)
upanzi *n (u)* planting; sowing seeds.
upao (also *pau, upau*) *n (u)* 1. bar, rod: *Upao wa chuma*, iron bar. 2. a long thin pole, used in the construction of a hut, etc.
upapa *n (u)* popedom; the office, position, etc of a pope.
upapasa *n (u)* a kind of bread made from cassava flour and coconut milk; cassava bread.
upapi (pl *papi*) *n (u)* 1. a long narrow piece of cloth cut from a dress; gusset, gore. (cf *ufito, ufite*) 2. a long narrow strip, flat or rounded, of wood or metal used for decorating, etc.; beading.
upara (also *upaa*) *n (u)* baldness; hairless condition. (cf *kidazi*)
uparara *n (u)* (*arch*) a short spear used during a war.

upashaji n (u) the act (method, etc.) of informing sth: *Upashaji-habari*, dissemination of information.
upasi n (u) enmity, animosity, ill-will, hostility: *Upasi kati yao umewatenganisha*, the hostility between them has separated them. (cf *utesi, uhasama*)
upasishaji n (u) 1. licensing, inspection, examination: *Upasishaji wa magari*, the inspection of vehicles valid licenses. 2. (of an examiner, etc) an act (method, etc) of making a candidate pass an examination by cheating in the examinee's favour.
upasuaji n (u) 1. cutting down, chopping: *Tulimsaidia katika upasuaji wa kuni*, we helped him in the splitting of firewood. 2. surgery, operation: *Upasuaji wa mgonjwa uliwachukua madaktari masaa machache*, the surgery of the patient took the doctors a few hours. *Upasuaji wa moyo*, cardiac surgery. *Upasuaji wa kubadilisha sura*, cosmetic surgery.
upataji n (u) acquisition: *Upataji lugha*, language acquisition.
upatanishaji (also *upatanishi, upatanisho*) n (u) reconciliation, compromise, settlement, arbitration: *Upatanishaji kati ya meneja na wafanyakazi wake haukufanikiwa*, the arbitration between the manager and his workers did not succeed. (cf *usuluhishaji*)
upatanishi n (u) see *upatanishaji*
upatanisho n (u) see *upatanishaji*
upati (pl *pati*) n (u) 1. a loin-cloth tucked up between the legs to form a kind of loose trousers. (cf *ubinda, winda*) 2. sanitary napkin; a cloth used by women during menstruation. (cf *sodo.*)
upatiara n (u) deception, trickery, subterfuge, false pretence: *Amekosa marafiki wengi kwa sababu ya upatiara wake*, he has lost a number of friends because of his deceitful practice. (cf *ujanja, udanganyifu*)
upatikaji n (u) availability (cf *upatikanaji*)
upatikanaji n (u) availability; the quality or condition of being available: *Upatikanaji wa mchele madukani ni adimu sasa*, the availability of rice in the shops is now rare. *Upatikanaji wa ajira*, the availability of employment. *Upatikanaji wa malighafi*, the availability of natural resources.
upatilivu (also *upatilizo*) n (u) reproach, damnation, censure: *Upatilivu wake ulisababishwa na kiburi chake*, his damnation was due to his arrogance.
upatilizo n (u) see *upatilivu*
upatu[1] (also *patu*) n (u) 1. a round metal dish-shaped gong usu of copper with its edges turned up. 2. a vessel such as a plate used during celebrations, ceremonies, etc. for collecting gifts such as money.
upatu[2] n (u) 1. gifts put in the vessel during festivities. (cf *zawadi, bahashishi*) 2. money received on rotational basis by a person usu a woman who is a member of a particular group. 3. a system of collecting money on a rotational basis: *Cheza upatu*, put money in for saving purposes along rotational basis. *Piga upatu*, make an announcement in public.
upau n (u) see *upao*
upaukaji n (u) the fading of colour.
upawa (pl *pawa*) n (u) a flat shallow ladle or dipper usu part of it is made from a coconut shell, and used for stirring or scooping curry, gruel, etc.
upayukaji n (u) prattling, gibbering, ranting: *Upayukaji wake mbele za watu haukutarajiwa*, his prattle in the public was unexpected. (cf *uropokaji, ubwataji*)
upekecho[1] (pl *pekecho*) n (u) an instrument usu a stick used for twirling fire, etc.
upekecho[2] n (u) 1. twirling, spinning, whirling, rotating. 2. (fig) incitement, formentation, provocation: *Ana desturi ya kufanya upekecho*, he is given to causing provocation. (cf *uchochezi*)
upekepeke[1] n (u) treason, betrayal;

violation of faith: *Upekepeke wake nchini hautasahaulika*, her betrayal of the country will not be forgotten. (cf *uhaini, usaliti*)

upekepeke² *n* (*u*) 1. idiosyncrasy; the temperament or mental constitution peculiar to a person or group. 2. prying, eavesdropping, snooping; the habit of investigating other people's affairs.

upeketevu *n* (*u*) 1. incitement, provocation, instigation: *Upeketevu wake uliwagombanisha marafiki wawili*, his instigation estranged two friends. (cf *uchokozi*) 2. rudeness, disrespect: *Mwanafunzi aliadhibiwa kutokana na upeketevu wake*, the student was punished because of his rudeness. (cf *ujeuri, ufidhuli*)

upekuzi *n* (*u*) investigation, probe, inquiry: *Upekuzi wa maofisa wa forodha uliwasumbua wasafiri*, the search by custom officials bothered the travellers.

upele *n* (*u*) (*med*) scabies, scabs, pimples, eczema, psoriasis: *Ana upele mwingi mwilini*, he has a lot of scabs on the body. (cf *ukurutu*)

upelekaji *n* (*u*) 1. sending, transmission, conveyance: *Upelekaji sambamba*, parallel transmission. (cf *utumaji*) 2. delivery, transportation, freightage: *Kampuni ile itashughulikia upelekaji wa bidhaa zetu ng'ambo*, that company will deal with the transportation of our goods overseas. (cf *usafirishaji*)

upelelezi *n* (*u*) 1. investigation, probe: *Idara ya upelelezi*, department of investigation. (cf. *uchunguzi*) 2. prying, snooping: *Upelelezi wake juu ya mambo ya watu wengine umezidi siku hizi*, his snooping into other people's affairs has worsened these days. (cf *udakuzi, umbeya*) 3. spying, espionage. (cf *ujasusi*)

upembe¹ (pl *pembe*) *n* (*u*) (*anat*) horn; a hard bony outgrowth on the head of cattle, sheep, goats and other hoofed animals.

upembe² (pl *pembe*) *n* (*u*) (*naut*) upper corner of lateen sail.

upembuzi *n* (*u*) discrimination; the act (method, etc) of distinguishing sby/sth.

upembo (pl *pembo*) *n* (*u*) a hooked stick, etc. for pulling down fruits from a tree or flowers. (cf *kingowe, chovyo, hangwe*)

upendano *n* (*u*) mutual love, affection, liking. (cf *mapenzi, huba*)

upendeleaji *n* (*u*) act (method, etc.) of favouring sby/sth; favouritism, partiality.

upendeleo *n* (*u*) favouritism, partiality, prejudice: *Mwamuzi aliuchezesha mchezo kwa upendeleo*, the referee officiated the game with favouritism.

upendezaji (also *upondozi*) *n* (*u*) glamour, attraction, fascination, charm: *Vipodozi viliongeza upendezaji wake*, the make-up enhanced her glamour.

upendezi *n* (*u*) see *upendezaji*

upendo *n* (*u*) love, affection fondness, liking: *Upendo wa kisiasa*, political likeness. *Kuna upendo mkubwa kati ya mume yule na mkewe*, there is a great love between that husband and his wife. (cf *mapenzi, huba, upendano*)

upenu (pl *penu*) *n* (*u*) 1. eaves, lean-to, overhang of a roof; the lower edge of a roof usu projecting beyond the sides of a building: *Alijificha kwenye upenu wakati mvua iliponyesha sana*, he hid himself under the eaves when it rained heavily. 2. a small space in a house used as a room, etc.; an appendage to a house. (cf *kipesa*) 3. (*fig*) loophole, a means of escape: *Mfungwa aliugundua upenu wa kutokea*, the thief found a way of escaping.

upenyaji *n* (*u*) act (method, etc.) of passing into a narrow space.

upenyenye (pl *penyenye*) *n* (*u*) 1. rumour, information, word, news: *Sijapata* *upenyenye wowote juu ya idadi ya watu waliozama baharini*, I have not yet received any information on the number of people who drowned in the sea. 2. a small outlet through which sth is passed.

upenyezaji *n (u)* penetration, permeation, inflow: *Polisi walizuia upenyezaji wa bidhaa mipakani kutoka nchi ya jirani*, the police stopped the inflow of goods from the neighbouring country at the border. (cf *uingizaji*)

upenyezi *n (u)* an underhand illicit action of allowing goods, etc. to pass through; smuggling, contraband: *Walifikishwa kortini kwa upenyezi wa madawa ya kulevya kutoka ng'ambo*, they were taken to court for charges of smuggling drugs from overseas. (cf *uingizaji*)

upenyo (pl *penyo*) *n (u)* 1. penetration. 2. a place to pass through, a way of escape; outlet, way out: *Panya alipata upenyo wa kukimbia*, the rat found a way out and ran away. (cf *upenyu*)

upenyu (pl *penyu*) *n (u)* 1. outlet, exit, passage: *Wezi walishindwa kupata upenyu wa kukimbilia*, the thieves could not get a safe exit. (cf *upenyo*) 2. gap in the teeth.

upenzi *n (u)* an inclination to like one side e.g. a soccer team

upeo *n (u)* climax, optimum, zenith: *Ule ulikuwa upeo wa riwaya*, that was the climax of the novel. *Upeo wa macho*, the horizon. 2. (a) vision; the ability to perceive sth not actually visible, as through mental acuteness or keen foresight (b) force or power of imagination: *Mwanasiasa mwenye upeo mkubwa*, a politician of great vision.

upepe (pl *pepe*) *n (u)* (*bot*) the part of the axis, or stem, below the cotyledons in the embryo of a plant; hypocotyl.

upepea *n (u)* the rain that goes into a house usu by passing through the window because of the wind; slashing rain. (cf *mpepea*)

upepeaji (also *upepezi*) *n (u)* fanning, ventilating: *Upepeaji wake ulilipunguza joto nililokuwa nikilihisi*, his fanning reduced the amount of heat I was feeling.

upepeo *n (u)* fan, punkah, aerator.

upepepe *n (u)* (*bot*) cotyledon (cf *ghalambegu, kotiledoni*)

upepezi *n (u)* see *upepeaji*

upepo (pl *pepo*) *n (u)* wind, breeze, fresh air, draft: *Upepo mwanana*, light wind, sea breeeze. *Pepo za pwani*, coastal winds.

upera *n (u)* a string, etc. obtained from a plant, etc. used to tie the navel of a newly-born child.

upesi *adv* quickly, fast, rapidly, immediately, at once. *Aliimaliza kazi upesi*, he completed the work fast. (cf *haraka, chapuchapu*)

upeto (pl *peto*) *n (u)* fold, wrinkle, bend: *Nguo ile ina peto tatu*, that cloth has three wrinkles. (cf *ukunjo, upindo*)

upevu *n (u)* maturity, ripeness, mellowness: *Upevu wa matunda haya yamenifanya niyale haraka*, the ripeness of these fruits has made me eat them immediately. *Msichana yule amefika katika hali ya upevu*, that girl has reached the stage of maturity. (cf *ubivu, ukomavu*)

upi *adj, pron* an interrogative for u class nouns meaning "Which": *Uzi upi?* Which thread? *Upi ni uzi wako?* Which is your thread?

upigaji *n (u)* the act of beating, hitting, etc. The nature of action is determined by the noun that co-occurs with it. *Upigaji-kura*, voting. *Upigaji makasia*, rowing.

upiganaji *n (u)* fighting, contesting: *Niliupenda upiganaji wa bondia yule*, I liked the fighting style of that boxer. (cf *utwangaji, udundaji*)

upiganiaji *n u* act (method, etc.) of defending sby/sth; defence. (cf *utetezi*)

upikaji *n (u)* act (method, etc.) of cooking;

cuisine, cookery, cooking. (cf *upishi*)
upimaji *n* (*u*) survey, valuation, measurement: *Idara ya upimaji*, department of survey. *Upimaji ardhi*, surveying. *Upimaji kazi*, work measurement. *Upimaji fichu*, indirect measurement. *Upimaji UKIMWI*, AIDS testing.
upinda *adv* naturally: (*idm*) *Kufa upinda* die naturally.
upindaji *n* (*u*) refraction; the changing direction of light when passing through at an angle.
upinde *n* (*u*) 1. bow of an arrow. 2. anything that resembles a bow: *Upinde wa mvua*, rainbow. (cf *ukole*)
upindo¹ (pl *pinda*) *n* (*u*) 1. the hem of a garment; fringe, purl: *Mshoni aliufumua upindo wa suruali yangu*, the tailor unstitched the hem of my trousers. 2. the border or edge of anything. (cf *ufite*)
upindo² (pl *pindo*) *n* (*u*) a garment like a loincloth, used for catching sardines.
upinduzi *n* (*u*) see *mapinduzi*
upingaji *n* (*u*) act (method, etc.) of opposing sth.
upingamapinduzi *n* (*u*) counter revolution: *Upingamapinduzi haukufanikiwa katika nchi ya jirani*, counter revolution did not succeed in the neighbouring country.
upinzani *n* (*u*) 1 opposition, resistance: *Chama cha upinzani*, opposition party. *Kiongozi wa upinzani*, leader of the opposition. 2. a group of people opposing sth.
upishi *n* (*u*) cuisine, cookery; the art of cooking. (cf *upikaji*)
upitishaji *n* (*u*) 1 act (method, etc.) of goods, etc. being passed from one place to another. 2. (*phys*) conduction: *Upitishaji joto*, thermal conductivity.
upitishwaji *n* (*u*) passing of goods, etc. from one place to another; transportation: *Upitishwaji wa vitu vya magendo mpakani umezidi siku*

hizi, the conveying of smuggled goods through the border has increased these days.
upo¹ (pl *nyupo*) *n* (*u*) bailer, a dipper for bailing water out of a boat, canoe etc. (cf *zila, ndau*)
up.o² *cop vt* you are here, it is here: *Upo?* Are you here?
upofu¹ *n* (*u*) day blindness, sightlessness, hemeralopia: *Upofukiza*, night blindness; nyctophilia.
upofu² *n* (*u*) imbecilify, stupidity. (cf *ubwege, ujinga, upumbavu*)
upogo *n* (*u*) awry, askew, skant: *Mambo yake yamekwenda upogo*, her affairs have gone awry.
upogoaji *n* (*u*) act (method, etc) of pruning the unnecessary parts of a plant e.g. branches.
upokaji *n* (*u*) snatching, stealing, pilfering: *Alishtakiwa kwa kosa la upokaji*, he was charged with stealing. (cf *unyang'anyi, uporaji*)
upokeaji *n* (*u*) reception, welcoming, receiving: *Upokeaji wa wageni ulikwenda vizuri*, the reception of the guests progressed well. (cf *upokezi*)
upokezi *n* (*u*) reception, welcoming, receiving. (cf *upokeaji*)
upokonyaji *n* (*u*) seizure, stealing, pilfering: *Upokonyaji wa vipochi vya wasichana umezagaa mjini*, the snatching of girls' purses is common in the town. (cf *upokaji, unyakuzi*)
upole¹ *n* (*u*) gentleness, calmness, kindness. (cf *uraufu, ukimya*)
upole² *n* (*u*) madness, lunacy. (cf *wazimu*)
upondo (pl *pondo*) *n* (*u*) 1. a pole for punting; a punting pole for pushing a boat, canoe, etc. along shallow waters. (*prov*) *Maji ya pondo hayataki tanga*, shallow water does not need a sail. i.e. a small thing cannot usu serve a big purpose.
2. a pole for vaulting; a pole for leaping over a barrier, etc.

upongoo (pl *pongoo*) *n* (*u*) 1. (*bot*) central rib or stem of a coconut leaf, etc. 2. any long stick usu of a coconut tree used for making palm leaves.

uponyaji *n* (*u*) act (method, etc) of curing sby/sth: *Huduma za uponyaji*, curing services.

upoozaji *n* (*u*) 1. (of disease) paralysis, numbness. 2. (of work, etc.) paralysis, standstill, halt: *Upoozaji wa kazi katika kiwanda umeathiri uzalishaji mali*, the halting of work at the industry has affected production.

uporaji *n* (*u*) embezzlement, stealing: *Uporaji wa fedha za umma*, embezzlement of public funds. (cf *wizi*)

uporo *n* (*u*) leftovers; food left over from the previous evening until the next day. (cf *kiporo, kilalo, mwiku*)

uposaji *n* (*u*) engagement, espousal, betrothal; proposal of marriage.

upote (pl *pote*) *n* (*u*) thong, bowstring; a cord stretched from one end of an archer's bow to the other.

upoteaji (also *upotevu*) *n* (*u*) losing one's way; disorientation: *Watalii walipata taabu kutokana na upoteaji wao wa njia*, the tourists got problems because of having lost their way.

upotevu¹ *n* (*u*) 1. perversion, aberration, waywardness; the act of departing from what is right or good. 2. prodigality, profligacy, waste, wastefulness.

upotevu² *n* (*u*) see *upoteaji*

upotofu *n* (*u*) see *upotovu*

upotovu (also *upotofu*) *n* (*u*) perversion, ruin, depravity: *Upotovu wa mwanafunzi ulisababishwa na umasikini*, the student's ruin was caused by poverty.

uprofesa *n* (*u*) professorship: *Uprofesa mshiriki*, associate professorship.

upumba *n* (*u*) a kind of thin braced-bladed knife. (cf *ramba, kotama*)

upumbao *n* (*u*) see *upumbavu*

upumbavu (also *upumbao*) *n* (*u*) 1. stupidity, imbecility, foolishness. (cf *upofu, ujinga, ujahili, ujuha*) 2. senselessness.

upumuaji *n* (*u*) respiration: *Upumuaji wa nje*, external respiration: *Upumuaji wa tishu*, tissue respiration.

upumuo *n* (*u*) drawing in breath; breathing, respiration: *Ana matatizo ya upumuo*, he has breathing problems.

upunga (pl *punga*) *n* (*u*) (*bot*) stage in the growth of a fruit-bearing tree or plant, when the flowers are in full bloom and the embryo fruit begins to emerge; blossoming.

upungaji *n* (*u*) 1. act (method, etc.) of blowing sth. 2. exorcism; act (method, etc.) of driving out an evil spirit by ritual prayers, incantations, etc.

upungufu *n* (*u*) shortage, dearth, deficiency, paucity: *Upungufu wa chakula*, shortage of food. *Upungufu wa akili*, mental retardation. *Kuna upungufu wa vipuri madukani siku hizi*, there is a shortage of spare parts in the shops these days.

upunguzaji *n* (*u*) alleviation, reduction, remission: *Upunguzaji wa umasikini*, poverty alleviation.

upunjaji *n* (*u*) swindling by giving short measure or less than what is due.

upupu *n* (*u*) (*bot*) cowage, cowhage; a kind of strong climber with hairy stems, trifoliate, long-stalked leaves which are very irritating when in contact with the skin. *Mucuna pruriens*. 2. a kind of dust derived from grain, which is irritating on the body; stinging rash from grain dust. (cf *wage*)

upurukushani *n* (*u*) negligence, dereliction: *Waliifanya kazi yetu kwa upurukushani, kinyume na maagizo yetu*, they did our work with negligence, contrary to our directives.

upuuzi (also *upuzi*) *n* (*u*) 1. hogwash, nonsense, absurdity, absurdness. 2. words or actions that convey an absurd meaning by someone who is ignored; hogwash.

upuzi *n* (*u*) see *upuuzi*

upwa¹ (pl *pwaa*) *n* (*u*) a place on the shore where the tide gets high or low; seashore, coast.

upwa² *n* (*u*) nephew or niece relationship.

upwamu *n* (*u*) 1. trickery, deceit, jugglery: *Upwamu huweza kumtia mtu matatani*, deceit can put someone in problems. (cf *ujanja, ukaramshi*) 2. impudence, shamelessness; impedinence, insolence: *Upwamu wake unabainika wazi kwa matamshi yake ya kifidhuli kwa mumewe*, her impudence manifests itself clearly by her rude utterances to her husband.

upweke *n* (*u*) 1. isolation, solitude, loneliness. (cf *ukiwa*) 2. sadness, sorrowfulness, sorrow: *Amekuwa katika upweke tangu kufiwa na mkewe*, he has been living in sorrow since the demise of his wife. (cf *huzuni, majonzi*)

upya¹ *n* (*u*) newness, freshness, greenness. (cf *uzungu*)

upya² *adv* afresh, anew, again; *Serikali ilitarajiwa kuangalia upya sera yake ya mambo ya nje*, the government was expected to look afresh at its foreign policy.

uradi *n* (*u*) (in Islam) a religious recitation involving the counting of prayer beads by an individual or groups usu held after the daily prayers: *Vuta uradi*, recite in this manner. (Ar)

uradidi *n* (*u*) occ *tardidi*

urafiki *n* (*u*) friendship, comradeship. cf *usuhuba, udugu*) (Ar)

urahisi *n* (*u*) 1. easiness, facileness, simpleness, simplicity. (cf *sahali*) 2. cheapness, inexpensiveness: *Niliweza kuinunua shati hili kwa sababu ya urahisi wake*, I was able to buy this shirt because of its cheapness. (Ar)

uraia *n* (*u*) 1. citizenship, nationality: *Uraia wa heshima*, honorary citizenship. *Uraia wa nchi mbili*, dual citizenship 2. civics. (Ar)

uraibu *n* (*u*) the practice of doing sth that one is acustomed to and cannot do without. it e.g. drinking alcohol, coffee, chewing betel leaves, etc.; addiction, habituation: *Ana uraibu wa kutafuna tambuu kila siku*, he has the habit of chewing betel leaves evryday. (cf *ushabiki*) (Ar)

urais *n* (*u*) presidency (Ar)

uraka *n* (*u*) local brew made from cashew apples.

uramali *n* (*u*) black magic usu intended to harm others; witchcraft, sorcery. (cf *sihiri, uchawi, ulozi*) (Ar)

uramberambe *n* (*u*) (*bot*) soft substance inside a young coconut i.e. when the nutty part is just forming; coconut kernel.

urari *n* (*u*) (*min*) uranium

urari *n* (*u*) balance, uniformity: *Urari wa biashara*, balance of trade. *Urari wa hesabu*, the balance of accounts, trial balance. *Urari tuli*, static balance. (cf *uwiano, ulinganifu, usawa*)

urasharasha *n* (*u*) occ *rasharasha*

urasimu¹ *n* (*u*) bureaucracy: *Urasimu umezagaa katika utumishi wa serikali*, bureaucracy is prevalent in the civil service. (Ar)

urasimu² *n* (*u*) technical drawing: *Urasimu ramani*, cartography, (Ar)

uratibu *n* (*u*) co-ordination, organization. (cf *upangaji*) (Ar)

uraufu *n* (*u*) 1. gentleness, kindness, compassion: *Uraufu wake umempa heshima*, his gentleness has earned him respect. (cf *upole, ukimya*). (Ar) 2. reasonableness in a price.

urazini *n* (*u*) 1 rationalism; the principle and practice of accepting reason as the only authority in determining one's opinions or actions. 2. rationale; reason for doing or taking an action.

ureda *n* (*u*) happiness, enjoyment, joy, comfort: *Yule kijana anapenda ureda sana*, the young man likes comfort, very much. (cf *raha*)

urefu *n* (*u*) 1. length, tallness, height, depth: *Urefu wa bomba*, the length of a pipe. 2. extent or distance from beginning to end: *Urefu wa riwaya ile*. the length of that novel.

urejeaji n (u) repetition: *Urejeaji wa faridi ya kileksika katika sentensi*, the repetition of a lexical, item.
urejeshaji n (u) act (method of returning sth/sby to another place; submission: *Urejeshaji wa fomu za wapiga-kura* the submission of the voters forms.
urekebishaji (also *urekebisho*) n (u) adjustment, rectification, correction, streamlining, straightening. (cf *usahihishaji*)
urekebisho n (u) see *urekebishaji*
urembo n (u) 1. decoration, beautification, adornment, embellishment. (cf *pambo*) 2. chic, neatness, dandyism. 3. fashion, style. (cf *umaridadi*) 4. beauty, glamour, elegance.
Ureno n (u) (*geog*) Portugal
urimbo n (u) see *ulimbo*
urithi n (u) 1. inheritance, heirship: *Suala la urithi limeleta mgogoro katika ukoo wao*, the question of inheritance has brought a dispute in their family. (cf *mirathi*) 2. heritage: *Urithi wa kiutamaduni*, cultural heritage. *Urithi wa kitaifa*, national heritage. (Ar)
uroho n (u) voracity, ravenousness, edacity, gluttony, greed: *Uroho wake wa kukusanya mali nyingi hausemeki*, her greed for accumulating a lot of wealth is beyond description. (cf *umero, ulafi*)
urongo n (u) see *uongo*
uru[1] (also *huru*) n (u) (in card playing) a red lozenge-shaped figure on a playing card.
uru[2] n (*ma-*) (*zool*) monitor lizard. (cf *kenge, bomla*)
urudishaji n (u) return: *Urudishaji wa fomu za wagombea ubunge ulienda vizuri*, the return of election forms of parliamentary candidates went smoothly.
urudufu (also *urudufushaji*) n (u) (*gram*) reduplication; a process of repeating a syllable or other linguistic element.
urudufushaji n (u) see *urudufu*
uruhanga (pl *ruhanga*) n (*ma-*) (*bot*) the seed of a wild banana plant.
urujuani n (u) (of colour) violet: *Urujuanimno*, ultraviolet.

urukaji n (u) act (method, etc.) of jumping, leaping, etc.; jump.
urukususu n (u) (*med*) a herbal cough medicine; cough expectorant, cough linctus.
urumba n (u) (*zool*) sea urchin. (cf *shanuo*)
urumo n (u) poverty, penury: *Pigwa na urumo*, be in a state of poverty; be financially handicapped.
urushaji n (u) 1. the flying of an object such as a kite, rocket. (cf *urukaji*) 2. (of tapes, etc) airing: *Urushaji wa kanda za kashfa zinazomhusu kiongozi wao ziliaibisha nchi nzima*, the airing of scandal tapes concerning their leader disgraced the whole nation. 3. denial of a statement, claim, etc.: *Urushaji wa tamko lake la awali ulitushangaza*, the denial of his earlier statement surprized us. 4. overcharging.
urusi[1] (pl *rusi*) n (u) (*zool*) a calf of one-month old.
Urusi[2] n (u) (*geog*) Russia (Rs)
urutubishaji n (u) enrichment, development, improvement: *Urutubishaji wa madini ya uraniam*, uranium enrichment.
usa n (u) (*naut*) halyard; a rope or tackle for raising a sail.
usaa n (u) see *usaha*
usafi n (u) sanitation, hygiene, cleanliness, neatness: *Usafi wa mazingira*, environmental cleanliness. (cf *unadhifu*) (Ar)
usafidi n (u) (*lit*) euphemism; the use of a word or phrase that is less expressive or direct but considered less distateful, less offensive, etc. than another.
usafihi n (u) rudeness, impoliteness, disrespect: *Usafihi wake kwa walimu ulimtia matatani*, his rudeness towards the teachers put him into problems. (cf *ujeuri, ufidhuli*) (Ar)
usafiri n (u) travel, transport: *Usafiri wa angani*, air transport. *Usafiri wa malori*, lorry transport. (Ar)
usafirishaji n (u) 1. transportation. 2. freightage: *Usafirishaji wa bidhaa uligharimu pesa nyingi*, the freightage cost a lot of money.

usafishaji n (u) refining, cleaning: *Usafishaji elektrolitia*, electrolytic refining. *Usafishaji wa mafuta ya karafuu unafanywa katika kiwanda hiki*, the refining of clove oil is done in this factory.
usagaji[1] n (u) milling, grinding: *Usagaji wa mahindi*, the milling of maize.
usagaji[2] n (u) lesbianism; female homosexuality.
usagishaji n (u) milling: *Shirika la usagishaji*, milling corporation.
usaha (also *usaa*) n (u) (med) pus; a usu yellowish white fluid that builds up at a site of infection. (Ar)
usahaulifu (also *usahaulivu*) n (u) forgetfulness, obliviousness, absent-mindedness: *Usahaulifu ni sifa ya binadamu wote*, forgetfulness is a trait that all human beings possess. (cf *mghafala, chechele*) (Ar)
usahaulivu n (u) see *usahaulifu*
usahibu (also *usuhuba*) n (u) friendship, comradeship, companionship: *Usahibu ni kitu azizi*, friendship is a precious thing. (cf *urafiki, umbuya*) (Ar)
usahihi n (u) 1. accuracy, precision: *Hakuna usahihi katika takwimu zako*, there is no accuracy in your statistics. (cf *uthabiti*) 2. truth, reality, validity: *Ushahidi wa mshtakiwa haukuwa na usahihi*, the evidence of the accused contained no truth. (cf *ukweli, yakini*)
usahihishaji n (u) correction. *Usahihishaji mno*, hypercorrection; the use of an erroneous word form or pronunciation based on a false analogy with a correct or prestigious form. (cf *rekebisho, sahihisho*)
usaili n (u) interview, questioning, cross examining, interrogation. (cf *uulizaji*) (Ar)
usajili n (u) registration, enrollment. *Usajili mkuu*, central registration. *Usajili wa kudumu*, permanent registration. *Usajili wa wachezaji*, the registration of players. *Usajili wa wapiga kura*, registration of voters. *Usajili wa dirisha dogo la wachezaji*, minor registration of players (cf *urajisi, uandikishaji*) (Ar)
usakataji n (u) act (method, etc.) of doing sth skillfully:*Usakataji wake katika kabumbu hausemeki*, his perfomance in soccer is beyond description.
usalama n (u) 1. security, safety, peace: *Ofisa wa usalama*, security officer. *Usalama barabarani*, road safety. (cf *amani*) 2. police work. (Ar)
usalata n (u) 1. incitement, instigation, intrigue: *Usalata wake umewachosha majirani zake*, his instigation has tired his neighbours. (cf *upekepeke*) 2. treason, treachery, betrayal: *Sisi hatutawasahau watu wale kwa sababu ya usalata dhidi ya nchi yao*, we will not forget those people because of the betrayal against their country. (cf *uhaini, uasi, usaliti*) (Ar)
usalimishaji n (u) surrender, capitulation, submission: *Usalimishaji wa silaha za maangamizi*, the surrendering of weapons of mass destruction.
usaliti n (u) 1. incitement, instigation, dissension: *Ukiwafanyia usaliti wenzako, watu watakusema*, if you cause dissension amongst your colleagues, people will speak ill of you. (cf *ufitini*) 2. treachery, treason, betrayal: *Usaliti kwa nchi yako ni kosa kubwa*, betrayal to your country is a great crime. (cf *uhaini*) (Ar)
usambao n (u) circulation, propagation, diffusion. (cf *usambazaji*)
usambazaji n (u) circulation, propagation, dissemination, diffusion: *Usambazaji wa habari*, the dissemination of information.
usambiko n (u) force, coercion; the act of forcing someone to do a particular thing: *Tendo lolote la usambiko haliwezi kukubalika*, any act of coercion cannot be accepted. (cf *ulazimishaji*)
usana n (u) see *usani*

usani (also *usana*) *n* (*u*) metal work, smithery, smithing: *Amechukua shahada katika usani*, he has taken a degree in metal work. (cf *uhunzi*) (Ar)
usanifu *n* (*u*) 1. the art of composing esp language; skill in writing a language: *Usanifu wake wa lugha unajitokeza kwenye insha zake*, his skill in writing is evident in his essays.
2. standardization: *Usanifu wa lugha*, standardization of language. (Ar)
usanii *n* (*u*) art, artistry, skill: *Ninauhusudu usanii wa mchoraji katika picha hii*, I admire the painter's artistry in this picture. (Ar)
usanisi *n* (*u*) synthesis
usaramala *n* (*u*) see *useremala*
usarakasi *n* (*u*) acrobatics; the art, skill or performance of an acrobat.
usare *n* (*u*) see *uchale*[1]
usasa *n* (*u*) modernity, modernism, novelty: *Usasa wa usanifu majengo wa nyumba hii unavutia*, the novelty of the architecture of this house is impressive.
usasi *n* (*u*) hunting (cf *uwindaji*)
usawa *n* (*u*) 1. equality, parity: *Usawa wa binaadamu*, equality among human beings: *Haki na usawa*, justice and equality. 2. level: *Usawa wa jinsia*, gender equality. *Usawa bahari wastani*, mean sea level. *Usawa macho*, eye level.
usawidi *n* (*u*) the drafting of a law, etc.: *Usawidi kamusi*, lexicography. (Ar)
useja[1] *n* (*u*) bachelorhood, celibacy. (cf *ukapera*)
useja[2] *n* (*u*) a collar of beads. (cf *ushanga*)
usemaji (also *usemi*) *n* (*u*) 1. speaking, talking; act (style, etc.) of talking: *Usemaji wake ni mzuri sana*, his style of talking is excellent.
usemeaji *n* (*u*) 1. the act of reporting on someone; calumny, traducement, hostile report: *Usemeaji wake kwa mwalimu mkuu uliwaudhi wanafunzi*, his hostile report given to the headteacher enraged the students. (cf *uchongeaji*)
2. defence, defending: *Jukumu la usemeaji kwa mshtakiwa wa kosa la jinai ni kubwa*, the responsibility of defending an accused on charges of felony is big. (cf *utetezi, uteteaji*)
usemi[1] *n* (*u*) see *usemaji*
usemi[2] (pl *semi*) *n* (*u*) 1. utterance, speech, articulation. 2. expression, saying: *Kuna usemi kwamba "Akili ni mali,"* there is a saying that "Intelligence is wealth." 3. language, dialect.
usena[1] *n* (*u*) (*zool*) a bee sting. (cf *uvurenje*)
usena[2] *n* (*u*) friendship, companionship, fraternity: *Usena wao sasa umevunjika*, their friendship is now broken. (cf *usuhuba, urafiki*)
usenge *n* (*u*) gayness, homosexuality. (cf *uhanithi*)
usengenyaji (also *usengenyo*) *n* (*u*) backbiting; speaking ill of an absent person: *Usengenyaji kama ule wa rafiki zake unachusha*, that kind of backbiting against her friends is disgusting.
useremala (also *usaramala*) *n* (*u*) carpentry, woodwork.
ush.a[1] *vi* (of milk, etc.) give bubbles and make a thundering sound like a wave. Prep. **ush.i.a** St. **ush.ik.a** Cs. **ush.ish.a** Ps. **ush.w.a**
ush.a[2] *vt* remove sth from a place. Prep. **ush.i.a** St. **ush.ik.a** Cs. **ush.ish.a** Ps. **ush.w.a**
ushababi *n* (*u*) youthfulness, boyhood, adolescence: *Amekuwa mtundu kwa sababu ya ushababi wake*, he has become mischievous because of his adolescence. (cf *ujana, utoto*) (Ar)
ushabaki *n* (*u*) 1. cunningness, slyness, deceit, trickery: *Ushabaki si kitu kizuri*, deceit is not a good thing (cf *ujanja, udanganyifu*) 2. quarrel, feud, discord. (cf *ugomvi, ushari*) (Ar)
ushabiki *n* (*u*) fanaticism, devotion,

enthusiasm: *Ushabiki wa kisiasa,* political fanaticism. *Ushabiki wake katika kandanda ni mkubwa,* his level of enthusiasm for soccer is high. (Ar)

ushahidi *n (u)* evidence, testimony, proof, exhibit: *Ushahidi wa kuandikwa,* documentary evidence. *Ushahidi wa moja kwa moja,* direct evidence. *Hakimu aliukataa ushahidi wa mshtakiwa,* the judge rejected the evidence from the accused. *Toa ushahidi,* give evidence. (cf *ithibati*) (Ar)

ushaibu *n (u)* senescence, old age, agedness, oldness: *Ushaibu umemfanya asahau mambo mengi,* he has made him forget many things because of old age. (cf *ubuda, uzee*) (Ar)

ushairi *n (u)* poetry: *Ushairi wake hauna vina,* his poetry has no rhyme.

ushakii[1] *n (u)* bravery, gallantry, courage. (cf *ujabari, ujasiri*) (Ar)

ushakii[2] *n (u)* bad character; evil, wickedness: *Mimi simpendi mtu yule kwa sababu ya ushakii wake,* I don't like that person because of his bad character. (cf *uovu*)

ushamba *n (u)* uncouthness, unsophistication: *Ushamba wa kisiasa,* political unsophistication.

ushanga (pl *shanga*) *n (u)* bead, rosary. (cf *useja*)

ushangiliaji *n (u)* act (method, etc of cheering sby/sth; cheering, applause.

ushari *n (u)* provocation, wrangle, quarrelsomeness, discord: *Ushari wake umewatenganisha yeye na mkewe,* his quarrelsome behaviour has separated him from his wife. (cf *utesi, ugobo, ugomvi*) (Ar)

usharifu *n (u)* 1. ancestry of Prophet Muhammad. 2. nobility, high birth. 3. respectability, dignity. (Ar)

usharika (pl *sharika*) *n (u)* parish

ushaufu[1] *n (u)* flirtation, promiscuous behaviour; feeling of indulging in casual and indiscriminate sexual relationships: *Usishirikiane naye kwa sababu ya tabia yake ya ushaufu,* don't associate with him because of his promiscuous behaviour. (Ar)

ushaufu[2] *n (u)* bad behaviour. (cf *ushakii*)

ushauri *n (u)* 1. advice, counsel, guidance. (cf *nasaha*) 2. consultancy. (Ar)

ushawishi[1] *n (u)* temptation, coaxing, persuasion. 2. influence, pressure, power: *Ushawishi wake katika sera za nchi ulikuwa mkubwa,* his influence on the country's policies was great.

ushawishi[2] *n (u)* intrusiveness, meddlesomeness, busybody attitude: *Ushawishi wake umewaudhi rafiki zake,* his meddlesome behaviour has irritated his friends. (cf *umbelembele*) (Ar)

usheha[1] *n (u)* headmanship, councillorship.

usheha[2] *n (u)* a multitude of people. (cf *umati, halaiki*)

ushei *adv* a little more: *Alinipa shilingi elfu na ushei,* he gave me one thousand shillings plus a little more. (Ar)

ushemasi *n (u)* deaconry, diaconate; the work, office, etc. of a deacon.

ushenzi *n (u)* savagery, barbarism, brutality, uncoothness. (cf *unyama, ukatili*)

ushikamano *n (u)* solidarity, unity. (cf *mshikamano*)

ushi *n (u)* 1. (*anat*) eyebrow, supercilium. 2. any ridge representing an eyebrow e.g. hedge, cornice, etc.

ushimba *n (u)* (*zool*) shrimp; a kind of small prawn found in shallow waters. (cf *ukamba, uduvi*)

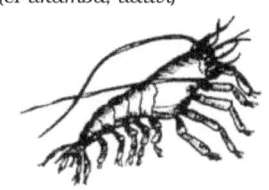

ushimba

ushindani *n* (*u*) competition, argument, rivalry, debate, discussion. (cf *ubishi*)
ushinde *n* (*u*) defeat, loss: *Asiyekubali ushinde si mshindani*, he who does not accept defeat is not a competitor.
ushindi *n* (*u*) 1. victory, conquest, triumph: *Ushindi mwembamba*, a narrow victory. *Ushindi wa kishindo*, landslide victory. 2. point of dispute; cause of contention. (cf *mafanikio*)
ushindwaji *n* (*u*) defeat, conquest; act (method, etc.) of being defeated.
ushiri *n* (*u*) tenth
Ushirika[1] *n* (*u*) (in Christianity) Holy Communion; the sacrament of the Eucharist, or the Lord's supper: *Ushiriki mtakatifu*, Holy Communion. (Ar)
ushirika[2] *n* (*u*) co-operative, union: *Vyama vya ushirika*, co-operative societies. (cf *muawana*)
ushiriki *n* (*u*) union, community, partnership. (cf *umoja, ujima, muawana*)
ushirikiano *n* (*u*) co-operation, co-ordination; mutual pact: *Ushirikiano wa kiulimwengu*, global cooperation. (Ar)
ushirikina *n* (*u*) superstition: *Watu wa kijiji kile wanaamini sana mambo ya ushirikina*, people of that village believe very much in superstition. (cf *uchawi*) (Ar)
ushirikishaji *n* (*u*) mobilization, involvement. (Ar)
ushirikishwaji *n* (*u*) the practice of involving people in communal activities, etc.: *Ushirikishwaji wa watu katika miradi ya maendeleo*, the involvement of people in development projects.
ushoga[1] *n* (*u*) friendship usu between women. (cf *urafiki*)
ushoga[2] *n* (*u*) gayness, homosexuality. (cf *usenge, uhanithi*)
ushoni (also *uchono*) *n* (*u*) 1. sewing, tailoring: *Ushoni wa ghali*, expensive tailoring.

2. style (method, etc.) of sewing: *Ushoni huu ni mzuri*, this type of needlework is good. 3. payment given to tailor for the cost of sewing; tailor's wage.
ushoroba *n* (*u*) alleyway, passage-way, backstreet. (cf *kichochoro, ujia*)
ushughulikiaji *n* (*u*) the act (method, etc.) of paying attention to a particular issue, etc.: *Ushughulikiaji wa matatizo ya wanavijiji*, the paying of the attention to the problems of the villagers.
ushuhuda *n* (*u*) testimony, evidence. (cf *ushahidi, uthibitisho*) (Ar)
ushujaa *n* (*u*) heroism, courage, bravery, gallantry. (cf *ujasiri, ujabari, uhodari*) (Ar)
ushumbi *n* (*u*) (*naut*) makeshift sail of any cloth. e.g. loincloth, etc. spread between two upright poles, and usu used by fishermen in canoes, etc. (cf *uberu*)
ushungi[1] *n* (*u*) 1. veil; a covering of thin material worn esp by women on the head or in front of the face. (cf *utaji*) 2. crest, plume; a tuft of feathers. 3. cock's comb
ushungi[2] *n* (*u*) prepuce, foreskin. (cf *govi*)
ushupavu *n* (*u*) 1. determination, resoluteness, firmness. (cf *ukakamavu, uimara*) 2. obduracy, obstinacy, stubbornness. (cf *ukaidi, ubishi*)
ushuri *n* (*u*) a tenth of sth. (Ar)
ushuru *n* (*u*) 1. customs duty, customs levy: *Ushuru wa forodha*, customs duty. 2. fee paid by a trader in an open market; market dues.
ushushushu *n* (*u*) 1. investigation, inquiry, probe. (cf *upelelezi*) 2. espionage, spying, undercover work.
ushuzi *n* (*u*) fart; breaking wind. (cf *ufusa*)
ushwa *n* (*u*) (*bot*) chaff, bran, husk (cf *wishwa*)
usi *n* (*u*) (*bot*) grass like that of rice but its flowers blossom like cotton.
usia[1] *n* (*u*) see *wasia*
usi.a[2] (also *wasia*) *vt* express dying

wishes; make a will, advise solemnly: *Aliusia kwamba azikwe kwenye makaburi yao,* he expressed dying wishes that he should be buried at their graveyard. Prep. *usi.a* St. *usi.k.a* Cs. *usi.sh.a* Ps. *usi.w.a* Rp. *usi.an.a* (cf *agiza, nasihi*)
usiasa *n (u)* politicization
usichana *n (u)* girlhood (cf *uanawali*)
usikilikaji *n (u)* audibility
usikivu (also *usikizi*) *n (u)* 1. obedience, compliance, subservience. (cf *utiifu*) 2. reception, hearing, attention.
usikizi *n (u)* see *usikivu*
usiku *n (u)* night. *Usiku wa manane,* dead of night; depth of night; midnight.
usimamizi *n (u)* supervision, management, control: *Usimamizi wa mazingira,* environmental control. *Usimamizi wa fedha,* financial management. (cf *uangalizi*)
usimeme *n (u)* firmness, stability, strength.
usimu *n (u)* see *simu²*
usimulizi *n (u)* see *simulizi*
usindikaji *n (u)* extraction: *Usindikaji wa mafuta,* oil extraction.
usinga¹ *n (u)* 1. long hairs of certain animals such as a mule, horse, etc. worn around the wrist as a kind of bangle. 2. the tail of certain animals such as a mule, giraffe, etc. which was cut and parched, then used in the hand while playing local drums; flywhisk. (cf *mwengo, mgwisho*)
usinga² *n (u)* a kind of witchcraft cast on adulterers.
usingizi *n (u)* sleep, drowziness.
usiniguse *n (u)* see *siniguse*
usira *n (u)* powder made from the burnt skin of an animal, used for making talisman to protect a person against the animal.
usiri *n (u)* 1. laziness, laxity, indolence, idleness. (cf *uvivu, uzembe*) 2. procrastination, lateness, slowness, delay: *Usiri wake umetumahanisha,* his procrastination irritated us. (cf *ucheleweshaji, uzohali*) 3. secrecy: *Usiri wa mazungumzo,* the secrecy of the conversation.
usisi *n (u)* see *sigi*
usita *n (u)* alley, lane, backstreet; narrow passage. (cf *uchochoro*)
usitawi *n (u)* see *ustawi*
usitishaji *n (u)* cessation, stoppage, suspension: *Usitishaji wa huduma muhimu,* the suspension of essential services. *Usitishaji wa mapigano,* the cessation of fighting.
usito *n (u)* deafness (cf *uziwi*)
usirisiri *n (u)* mystery, puzzle: *Kifo cha mwanasiasa yule bado kipo katika usirisiri,* the death of that politician is still a mystery.
uso (pl *nyuso*) *n (u)* 1. (anat) face. (cf *wajihi*) 2. surface, face: *Uso wa dunia,* the face of the earth. 3. (*idm*) *Uso kwa uso,* face to face. e.g *Walitukanana uso kwa uso,* they insulted each other face to face.
usodai (also *usodawi*) *n (u)* pride, conceit, arrogance, hauteur. (cf *kiburi, utadi*) (Ar)
usodawi *n (u)* see *usodai*
usogora *n (u)* 1. know-all attitude; the tendency for someone to know everything: *Usogora wake umezidi,* his know-all attitude is too much. (cf *ujuaji, kimbelembele*) 2. expertness in playing drums, etc.: *Usogora wake kwenye ngoma hauelezeki,* his expertise in playing drums is beyond description.
usomeshaji *n (u)* teaching, instruction: *Usomeshaji wake unachukiza,* his teaching method is disgusting. (cf *uelimishaji, ufundishaji*)
usongombwingo *n (u)* hypocrisy, pretense; false profession: *Usimwamini mtu yule kwa sababu ya usongombwingo wake,* don't trust that person because of his hypocrisy. (cf *unafiki, uzandiki*)
usono¹ *n (u)* rest, repose, sleep: *Hana usono,* he has no rest. (cf *liwazo*)
usono² *n (u)* friendship, amity, rapport.

usoshalisti n (u) socialism (Eng)
usoto n (u) remissness; lack of ability to do sth swiftly.
uspika n (u) the office, work, etc. of a speaker. (Eng)
ustaarabu n (u) civilization, refinement, civility. (cf *utamaduni*)
ustadi n (u) mastery, expertness, skill, skilfulness. (cf *ufundi, ubingwa*)
ustahamilivu n (u) patience, tolerance, forebearance, endurance. (cf *subira, uvumilivu*) (Ar)
ustahiki n (u) worthiness, merit, excellence: *Askari alipewa nishani kutokana na ustahiki wake*, the policeman was awarded a medal on the basis of his merit. (cf *ustahili*)
ustawi (also *usitawi*) n (u) development, success, prosperity, growth, welfare. *Ustawi wa jamii*, social welfare. (Ar)
ustawishaji n (u) development, growth, evolution: *Ustawishaji wa mimea*, the growth of plants.
usu *interj* shush, hush, keep quiet!, shut up!; an expletive of scorn or anger of asking someone to keep quiet. (cf *chup!, chub!*)
usubi n (u) (*zool*) biting midge, gnat; a tiny two-winged insect, several of which are parasites specific to different insects and a few are regular blood suckers on vertebrates.
usubuhi n (u) see *asubuhi*
usufi n (u) see *sufi¹*
usufii n (u) sufism, piousness; the practice of living a lonely life with the object of showing total worship to Almighty God. (cf *uwalii, utawa, uchamungu*) (Ar)
usufu n (u) see *sufu*
usugu n (u) calluousness, induration; the quality of being inured, insensitive, unfeeling, etc. to hardships: *Usugu umempa mwanafunzi yule sifa shuleni*, his inured attitude to hardships has earned that student fame in school. 2. resistance: *Usugu wa wadudu wa malaria, uliwahangaisha madaktari*, the resistance of malaria parasites worried the doctors.
usuguano n (u) (*mech*) friction (cf *msuguano*)
usuhuba n (u) see *usahibu*
usukani (pl *sukani*) n (u) 1. steering gear, steering wheel; rudder of a ship, motorcar, etc. 2. (*fig*) leadership: *Alishika usukani na kuongoza nchi vizuri*, he assumed leadership and led the country well. (cf *unahodha, uongozi*)
usukumo (also *usukumizi*) n (u) propulsion, impulse, drive.
usukumizi n (u) see *usukumo*
usuli n (u) 1. cause, reason, source: *Usuli wa kufukuzwa kwake kazini ni uzembe*, the cause of his dismissal from work is laziness. (cf *sababu, chanzo*) 2. origin, source: *Usuli wa neno* kitabu, 'book' ni 'kitab' *kwa lugha ya Kiarabu*, the origin of the word *kitabu* 'book' is kitab in Arabic language. 3. (*lit*) background.
usultani n (u) the rule, work, etc. of a Sultan; sultanate. (cf *ufalme*) (Ar)
usulubu n (u) hardwork; arduous work: *Usulubu umemchosha*, ardous work has tired him.
usuluhishaji n (u) act (method,etc) of reconciling between persons, etc; reconcilliation, arbitration.
usuluhishi n (u) 1. the act (method, etc.) of reconciling warring sides; reconciliation, mediation, compromise. (cf *upatanishaji, upatanishi*) 2. solution, mediation, pacification. (cf *ufumbuzi*)
usumaku n (u) magnetism: *Usumaku ardhi*, geomagnetism. *Usumaku chuma*, ferro magnetism.
usumba n (u) coconut fibre; coir.
usumbi n (u) naughtiness, mischief, disobedience: *Mwalimu alimwadhibu mwanafunzi kutokana na usumbi wake*, the teacher punished the student for his naughtiness. (cf *uharabu, utukutu, utundu*)

usumbufu *n (u)* bother, disturbance, nuisance. (cf *kero, udhia, adha*)
usungo *n (u)* 1. state of being innocent or naive or inexperienced in sexual affairs or initiation rites. 2. unsophistication, primitiveness, uncouthness. (cf *ushamba*)
usununu *n (u)* 1. arrogance, pride, conceit. (*kiburi, ujeuri*) 2. sulkiness, sullenness.
usuria *n (u)* the state of being a concubine; concubinage. (cf *upakasaji*) (Ar)
ususi *n (u)* hair plaiting. (cf *usukaji*)
ususu *n (u)* 1. passage in a house; corridor, passage-way, hallway. 2. lane, alley, backstreet: *Ususu huu ni mwembamba sana,* this alley is very narrow.
ususuani *n (u)* uprightness, honesty, cleanness; firmness to temptations, etc. *Ususuani wao hauelezeki,* their uprightness is beyond description. (cf *unyofu, uadilifu*)
ususuavu *n (u)* procrastination, delay, hesitation, indecisiveness: *Ususuavu wa nchi katika kutoa maamuzi yake,* the country's delay to make its decisions.
usutu *n (u)* a narrow length of plaited wild date palm leaf which, when sewn with other strips makes mats, baskets, etc.
uswa *n (u)* see *wishwa*[1]
uswagaji *n (u)* the driving of livestock esp cattle along the road, etc.: *Serikali imepiga marufuku uswagaji wa mifugo kwenye barabara kuu,* the government has prohibited the driving of livestock along the main roads.
Uswahili *n (u)* 1. Swahilism; state of being a Swahili speaker. 2. (*syn*) good language: *Uswahili unamtoka kama lugha yake,* he speaks Swahili eloquently like his native language.
Uswisi *n (u)* (*geog*) Switzerland
uta (pl *nyuta*) *n (u)* bow of an arrow. (cf *upinde, mata*)
utaa (pl *taa*) *n (u)* a godown or a hut for storing grain or firewood; storage. (cf *uchaga, ghala*)
utaabishaji *n (u)* bother, distress, affliction, trouble: *Utaabishaji wake wa mara kwa mara ulituchosha,* her frequent bother tired us. (cf *utesaji, usumbufu*)
utaadi *n (u)* see *tadi*
utaalamu *n (u)* professionalism, expertise, specialization, scholarship. (cf *uanachuoni*) (Ar)
utaba *n (u)* the act (manner, etc.) of pulling down a fruit from the branch of its tree; plucking. (cf *ukonyoaji*)
utabaka *n (u)* stratification, level, class distinction: *Jamii yetu ina utabaka,* our society has class distinctions. (Ar)
utabibu *n (u)* 1. medical treatment, medications. 2. medicine. 3. (*ling*) *Utabibu lugha,* speech therapy. (Ar)
utabiri *n (u)* 1. prediction; the thing predicted or foretold. 2. prediction, prophecy, forecast; the act of foretelling: *Alitoa utabiri kwamba serikali itaanguka,* he made a prediction that the government would collapse. (cf *uaguzi, ubashiri, ukuhani*)
utabwa *n (u)* softness, smoothness, tenderness: *Mgonjwa aliweza kula wali bila ya shida kutokana na utabwa wake,* the patient could eat the rice without any difficulty because of its softness. (cf *uteketeke, ulaini*)
utadi (also *utaadi*) *n (u)* rudeness, impoliteness, incivility, disrespect: *Watu wanamsema kwa sababu ya utadi wake,* people speak ill of him because of his rudeness. (cf *ufyosi, ufidhuli*)
utafiti *n (u)* research, search, investigation. (cf *uchunguzi*)
utafutaji *n (u)* the act (method, etc.) of seeking sby/sth; quest, search: *Utafutaji wa suluhu,* the search for reconciliation.
utagaa (pl *tagaa*) *n (u)* (*bot*) the branch of a tree. (cf *utanzu, utamviri*)

833

utago n (u) broom grass.
utaifa n (u) nationality, nationhood. (Ar)
utaiti n (u) poverty, impecuniousness: *Utaiti husababisha maisha kuwa magumu*, poverty causes life to be difficult. (cf *umasikini, ufukara*)
utaji n (u) veil; a piece of cloth usu coloured, used by women as a covering for the head and face. (cf *ushungi, dusumali*)
utajiri n (u) richness, wealth, affluence. (cf *ukwasi*) (Ar)
utakaso n (u) purification, sanctification. (cf *utakasaji*)
utakatifu n (u) holiness, sanctity, sacredness.
utako[1] n (u) see *tako*
utako[2] n (u) (*naut*) keel; flat bottom of a ship, dhow, etc.
utalaleshi[1] n (u) prostitution, whoredom, harlotry, street-walking. (cf *ukahaba, uasherati, umalaya*)
utalaleshi[2] n (u) inquisitiveness, tale-bearing. (cf *udukuzi, umbeya*)
utalii u (u) tourism (Ar)
utamaduni (pl *tamaduni*) n (u) culture (cf *mila, ustaarabu*) (Ar)
utamaradi n (u) cosmetics (cf *vipodozi*)
utambaa n (u) rag; tattered cloth; a waste piece of cloth that is old or torn. (cf *tambara, kitema*)
utambaaji n (u) see *utambaazi*
utambaazi (also *utambaaji*) n (u) act (method, etc.) of creeping; crawling: *Utambaazi wa mtoto unaweza ukachukua siku nyingi*, a child's crawling may last for many days.
utambi[1] (pl *tambi*) n (u) 1. the wick of a candle, etc. 2. the cotton wool that is used to apply medicine to an open or broken wound or abscess; lint. 3. (*idm*) *Tia/choma, utambi*, incite, instigate.
utambi[2] n (u) (*anat*) membrane enclosing the bowels.
utambo[1] (pl *tambo*) n (u) the swinging handle of a bucket, iron pot, etc.

utambo[2] n (u) see *kitambo*
utamboni n (u) (*arch*) in the war; state of being at war. (cf *vitani*)
utambulishaji n (u) act (method, etc) of identifying people, things, etc 2. act (method, etc.) of introducing people, things, etc.
utambulisho n (u) identification, recognition, detection: *Utambulisho wake haujulikani*, his identity is unknown i.e. he cannot be identified. 2. introduction: *Ule ulikuwa mkutano wa utambulisho wa mgombea-urais*, that was a meeting to introduce the presidential candidate.
utambuzi n (u) realization, perception, comprehension, understanding: *Utambuzi wake juu ya mambo mbalimbali ya kitaaluma umempa sifa*, his understanding of various academic issues has earned him respect. (cf *ubainifu, ugunduzi*)
utamu n (u) sweetness, deliciousness. (cf *ladha*)
utamviri (pl *tamviri*) n (u) branch of a tree. (cf *tawi, tagaa*)
utamvua (pl *matamvua*) n (u) a thread hanging loose or tied in bunches; fringe, tassle, lappet.
utanashati n (u) dandyism, neatness, smartness: *Utanashati wake umewapendeza walimu*, his neatness has impressed the teachers. (cf *umaridadi, usafi*) (Ar)
utandabui (also *utando*) n (u) spider's web.
utandaridhi n (u) see *utandawazi*
utandawazi (also *utandaridhi*) n (u) globalization
utando n (u) 1. see *utandabui* . 2. membrane, film, coating: *Utando wa maziwa*, milk cream; film. *Utando wa mlishano*, grazing layer.
utanga[1] (pl *tanga*) n (u) the top or bottom of a wicker trap.
utanga[2] n (u) see *kitanga[1]*
utangazaji n (u) 1. broadcasting.

2. advertising, publicity.
utango n (u) (naut) a piece of wood used as a seat in a canoe or *dau*, a kind of small fishing vessel.
utangule (pl *tangule*) n (u) the leaves of the wide date palm cut into narrow strips for plaiting mats, etc. (cf *ung'ongo*)
utangulizi (pl *tangulizi*) n (u) 1. proceeding, advancing; going ahead in a journey, etc. 2. (in a book, etc.) introduction, foreward. (cf *dibaji*)
utanguzi n (u) annulment, invalidation, abolishment: *Utanguzi wa sheria zile umewafurahisha raia*, the annulment of those laws has pleased the citizens.
utani n (u) 1. a system where some tribes in Tanzania can joke with one another freely without harbouring resentment; joking relationship. 2. joke: *Alinifanyia utani, he made a joke on me.* (cf *mzaha, masihara*)
utaniboi n (u) the work of serving as a conductor in a public vehicle used to transport people from one place to another; bus conducting (cf *utingo*)
utanuzi n (u) expansion, extension: *Utanuzi wa barabara zetu umesaidia usafirishaji*, the expansion of our roads has facilitated transportation.
utanzu (pl *tanzu*) n (u) 1. branch of a tree. (cf *tawi*) 2. genre, branch: *Fasihi imegawika katika tanzu mbalimbali*, literature is divided into different genres.
utapeli n (u) fraudulence, confidence trick, swindling. (cf *ujambazi*)
utapiamlo n (u) malnutrition: *Watoto wengi wanakufa kutokana na utapiamlo*, many children die of malnutrition.
utapishi¹ n (u) the act of inculcating tribal customs, etc. to young girls when they reach puberty or are in the initiation rites.
utapishi² n (u) 1. vomiting: *Utapishi wa mgonjwa ulitushtua*, the patient's vomiting shocked us. 2. (fig) prattling, babbling; talking excessively: *Utapishi*

wake unachusha, his prattling is disgusting.
utaratibu (pl *taratibu*) n (u) formality, system, procedure, routine: *Utaratibu wa kibalozi*, diplomatic formalities. *Utaratibu wa biashara*, business routine. (cf *sera, kanuni*) (Ar)
utari (pl *tari*) n (u) 1. (naut) cable, etc. to haul a ship if it is grounded. 2. cable, rope, etc. of a sailing vessel. 3. rope, cable, etc. of an instrument.
utasa n (u) (of a woman) sterility, barreness, infertility: *Mwanamke alishindwa kupata watoto kutokana na utasa wake*, the woman could not have children because of her infertility. (cf *ugumba*)
utashi n (u) desire, wish, will, anxiety, hunger: *Ana utashi mkubwa wa kuoa*, he has a strong desire to get married. (cf *uchu, tamaa*)
utasi (also *utatu*) n (u) inability to speak because of being tongue-tied; lisp. speech impediment.
utata¹ n (u) see *utasi*
utata² (pl *tata*) n (u) complication, complexity, difficulty, ambiguity: *Utata wa maelezo yako bado unatinga*, the complexity of your statement is still baffling. (cf *ugumu*)
utatizaji n (u) act (method, etc.) of complicating matters; complexness, complication.
utatu n (u) 1. (in Christianity) trinity; the union of three personalities as one God i.e. Father, Son and Holy Spirit or Holy Ghost: *Utatu Mtakatifu*, the Holy Trinity. 2. three, three foldness; being triple. 3. a third part.
utatuaji n (u) act (method, etc.) of solving a problem, etc.: *Utatuaji wa mgogoro wao hautakuwa rahisi*, the solving of their problem will not be easy.
utatuzi¹ n (u) the habit usu of small children to tear clothes very often.
utatuzi² n (u) solution, resolution, disentanglement. (cf *ufumbuzi, suluhisho*)

utawa n (u) 1. religious devotion and seclusion; spirituality, monasticism, piety: (cf *uchamungu, uwalii*) 2. seclusion; staying in the house: *Alianza kuishi maisha ya utawa, alipobaleghe*, she started to live in seclusion when she reached the age of puberty. (cf *upweke*)

utawala n (u) administration, rule, regime, government: *Utawala wa mpito*, transitional government. *Utawala wa mabavu*, iron fist rule. *Utawala wa kijeshi*, military rule. *Utawala wa makabaila*, aristocracy. *Utawala huria*, anarchism. *Utawala wa kiimla*, dictatorial rule. *Utawala wa makasisi*, hierocracy. *Utawala bora*, good governance. *Utawala wa sheria*, rule of law.

utawi n (u) see *tawi*

utaya (pl *taya*) n (u) (*anat*) jaw, jawbone.

utayarishaji n (u) preparation, planning: *Utayarishaji wa somo la kemia*, the preparation of the chemistry lesson. (cf *upangaji*)

utazamaji n (u) observation, watching, viewing, spectatorship. (cf *uangaliaji*)

ute (pl *nyute*) n (u) 1. thick sticky fluid saliva coming from the mouth while someone is asleep or when someone sees food that he is keen to eat; drool, slaver, drivel, dribble, lather. (cf *udenda, uderere*) 2. anything resembling saliva coming from the mouth: *Ute wa yai*, white of an egg; eggwhite. *Utemaji*, aqueous humour.

utegaji[1] n (u) trapping, snaring, cornering, hunting: *Ule ni utegaji wa panya*, that is the snaring of the rats. (cf *unasaji*)

utegaji[2] n (u) shirking from work, etc.: *Alifukuzwa kazini kwa sababu ya tabia yake ya utegaji*, he was sacked from work because of shirking duty. (cf *ukwepaji-kazi*)

utegemezaji n (u) (*gram*) hypotaxis, subordination; the process of linking items of unequal status, typically introduced by words such as *ijapokuwa*, 'although', *kwa vile*, 'because', etc.

utegemezi n (u) dependence, reliance.

uteja n (u) clientship; the act, method, etc. of serving as a customer, victim, etc.: *Timu ilipania kufuta uteja kwa mpinzani wake*, the team was determined to make sure that it did not always become a loser.

utekelezaji n (u) implementation: *Utekelezaji wa maazimio ya mkutano huu utakuwa mgumu*, the implementation of the resolutions of this meeting will be difficult.

uteketeke n (u) smoothness, softness. (cf *wororo, utabwa, ulaini*)

uteketevu n (u) see *uteketezaji*

uteketezaji (also *uteketevu*) n (u) (of fire, etc.) destruction, annihilation, ruin, burning. (cf *uangamizaji*)

utelezi n (u) 1. slipperiness, iciness, oiliness. 2. a slippery place.

utembeaji[1] n (u) see *utembezi*

utembeaji[2] n (u) act (method, etc) of assisting sby esp. a visitor, etc. to visit important places. 2. (in business) act (method, etc) of advertising or hawking a product, etc.

utembezi (also *utembeaji*) n (u) 1. perambulation, travelling, touring 2. womanising; the act of being sexually promiscuous with women.

utembo (also *utembwe*) n (u) fibre from the leaf-stalk of various palms, used for making ropes, strings, etc.

utembwe[1] n (u) see *utembo*

utembwe[2] n (u) see *ukembwa*

utendaji n (u) perfomance, executive action: *Utendaji wake kazini si mzuri*, his performance at work is not good.

utendi (also *utenzi*) n (u) (*poet*) epic poem.

utendwa u (u) (*gram*) passive voice.

utengaji n (u) separation, exclusion, isolation; act (method, etc.) of separating things, people, etc.

utenganisho n (u) separation, split,

isolation: *Utenganisho wa kisheria*, judicial separation.
utengano *n* (*u*) separation, exclusion, isolation.
utengemano *n* (*u*) peace, security, tranquility, calmness: *Utengemano nchini uko mashakani*, security in the country is at stake. (cf *utulivu, amani*)
utengenezaji (also *utengezaji*) *n* (*u*) manufacture, construction, production: *Utengenezaji wa magari unafanyika katika kiwanda hiki*, the manufacture of cars is done in this factory. (cf *uundaji*)
utengeneshaji *n* (*u*) the act of separating sby from his society etc; alienation, separation. (cf *mfarakano*)
utengezaji *n* (*u*) see *utengenezaji*
utenguo (also *mtanguo*) *n* (*u*) invalidation, annulment, repeal: *Utenguo wa sheria uliwafurahisha raia*, the repeal of the law pleased the citizens. (cf *utenguzi, ubatilishaji*)
utenguzi *n* (*u*) 1. nullification, annulment: *Utenguzi wa matokeo ya uchaguzi katika eneo letu haukutegemewa*, the nullification of the results of the elections in our constituency was not expected. (cf *ubatilishaji*) 2. destruction, spoil: *Utenguzi wa mipango yangu ulifanywa makusudi*, the destruction of my plans was done deliberately.
utenzi[1] *n* (*u*) performance, execution, accomplishment. (cf *utendaji*)
utenzi[2] (pl *tenzi*) *n* (*u*) (*poet*) epic poem
uteo[1] (pl *teo*) *n* (*u*) a tray made of plaited leaf strips used for sifting grain, flour, etc.; winnowing basket: *Uteo wa mfiwa*, a special winnowing basket, containing food sent to the bereaved person from a neighbour. (cf *ungo*)
uteo[2] *n* (*u*) a thin board used in the weaving of a mat. (cf *kiwao*)
utepe[1] (pl *tepe*) *n* (*u*) 1. a narrow strip of cloth etc.; band, ribbon, fillet: *Utepe wa marudio*, frequency band. *Utepe wa mawasiliano* communication

band. 2. see *tepe*.
utepe[2] *n* (*u*) tape; a narrow plastic material with a magnetic substance, used for recording sound and playing it back.
utepetevu *n* (*u*) apathy, lethargy, laziness: *Utepetevu ni kitu kibaya*, laziness is a bad thing. (cf *uzembe, ulegevu, ugoigoi, uvivu*)
uteremkaji *n* (*u*) 1. disembarkment, disembarkation, landing: *Uteremkaji wa abiria kutoka kwenye meli ulikuwa na fujo*, the disembarking of the passengers from the ship was chaotic. (cf *ushukaji*) 2. descent; the act of coming down or going down: *Uteremkaji wake kutoka juu ulichukuwa dakika chache tu*, his descent from the top took only a few minutes. 3. (of prices, etc.) falling down: *Uteremkaji wa bei ya vitu muhimu uliwafurahisha wananchi*, the falling down of prices of essential commodities pleased the people.
utesaji *n* (*u*) torment, torture, persecution: *Utesaji wa wafungwa wa kisiasa ulilaaniwa na jumuiya ya kimataifa*, the ill treatment of political prisoners was condemned by the international community.
utesi[1] *n* (*u*) rumour, grapevine, gossip.
utesi[2] *n* (*u*) squabble, quarrel. (cf *ugomvi*)
utete[1] *n* (*u*) stalk or stem of a reed or grass used as a pipe or musical instrument.
utete[1] *n* (*u*) cowardice, timidity, weak knees. (cf *uoga*)
uteteaji *n* (*u*) defence; act (method, etc) of defending as in a court of law.
utetezi *n* (*u*) 1. defence arguments 2. defence; the method, etc. of defending: *Utetezi wa mshtakiwa ulifanyika vizuri*, the defence of the accused was done well.
uteule *n* (*u*) appointment, nomination: *Uteule wa rais ulifanyika wiki iliyopita*, the appointment of the president was done last week.

uteuzi n (u) nomination, election, appointment.
uthabiti n (u) 1. stability, firmness, validity: *Uthabiti wa msimamo wake hauelezeki*, the firmness of his stand is beyond description. (cf *uimara*) 2. truth, reality, genuineness: *Uthabiti wa kauli yake una mashaka*, the truth of his statement is doubtful. (cf *ukweli*) (Ar)
uthibitisho n (u) confirmation, assurance, verification (cf *hakikisho*) (Ar)
uti n (u) 1. stem, trunk, etc. of a tree. 2. spine, backbone: *Uti wa mgongo*, spinal cord. *Ugonjwa wa uti wa mgongo*, meningitis.
utiaji n (u) putting in, fixing: *Utiaji-saini*, signing; putting of one's signature.
utibabu n (u) medical treatment, medication. cf *utabibu* (Ar)
utifu n (u) tilth; cultivation of land. (cf *ucheu, weu*)
utifutifu n (u) loam; rich soil composed of clay, sand and some organic matter, used for enriching plants.
utii n (u) loyalty, obedience, subservience, respect. (cf *utiifu*)
utiifu n (u) obedience, subservience, respect (cf *utii*)
utiko (pl *mitiko*) n (u) roofridge of a house.
utimbakwiri n (u) treachery, treason, betrayal: *Utimbakwiri wake nchini hautasahaulika*, his betrayal of the country will not be forgotten. (cf *uhaini, usalata*)
utimbi n (u) see *uchimbi*
utimilifu n (u) perfection, completeness, fullness: *Aliifanya kazi yangu kwa utimilifu*, he did my work with perfection. (cf *ukamilifu*)
utimizaji n (u) fulfilment, accomplishment: *Utimizaji wa ahadi zake umo mashakani*, the fulfilment of his promises is doubtful. (cf *ukamilishaji, ukamilisho*)
utingo n (u) 1. a bus conductor who usu hangs out of the door to serve the passengers; tout, loader, unloader; (cf *taniboi*) 2. the work of this type. i.e the work of serving as a conductor in a public vehicle used to transport people from one place to another; bus conducting (cf *utaniboi*)
utiriri[1] (also *utiririkaji*) n (u) 1. (of liquid) flowing, trickling, dripping: *Angalia utiriri wa maji kutoka kwenye paa la nyumba*, look at the trickling of water from the roof of the house. (cf *mchiriziko*) 2 an influx of people or things: a huge crowd: *Niliuona utiriri wa watu ukielekea kwenye uwanja wa mpira*, I saw a huge crowd of people going towards the football ground. 3. constant coming of people.
utiriri[2] n (u) the habit of someone esp a child to insist on sth provocatively; pervesity, pique, pestering: *Dada yangu hapendi kufuatana na mtoto yule madukani kwa sababu ya utiriri wake*, my sister does not like to go shopping with that child because of his pestering behaviour. (cf *inda*)
utiririkaji n (u) see *utiriri*[1]
utishaji n (u) the act (method, etc.) of frightening sby.
utisho n (u) frightening, scaring, terrifying: *Utisho wake kwa wanafunzi wa darasani utamtia matatani*, his habit of frightening pupils in the class will put him into problems. (cf *mwogofyo, utishaji*)
utitiri[1] n (u) (zool) nit; the egg or young form of a louse or other parasitic insect.
utitiri[2] n (u) a large number of people or things; abundance. (idms) *Utitiri wa mambo*, many issues. *Utitiri wa watu*, many people. *Utitiri wa vyama vya upinzani*, the proliferation of opposition parties. *Niliuona utitiri wa askari wa polisi katika mtaa wetu*, I saw a large number of policemen in our neighbourhood.

uto *n* (*u*) 1. any thick oily fluid: *Mafuta ya uto*, sesame oil: *Uto wa tui la nazi*, oil from coconut juice. 2. anything pure which is the source of another thing; pure essence. *Uto wa chuma*, molten, iron.

utoaji *n* (*u*) 1. the act of giving out/ removing of sth: *Utoaji wa madawa*, the dispensing of drugs. *Utoaji-rushwa* corruption; the giving out of bribes. *Utoaji mimba*, abortion. *Utoaji vibali*, the issuing of permits. *Utoaji fomu*, the issuing of forms. 2. (*phon*) *Utoaji lugha*, speech production.

utobwe *n* (*u*) ignorance esp in playing draughts i.e. the game of checkers. (cf *upofu, ujuha*)

utohara *n* (*u*) (in Islam) purification of the body, etc; cleansing, cleanliness: *Utohara wa mwili wake ulimwezesha kusali*, the cleansing of his body enabled him to pray. (Ar)

utokazi *n* (*u*) a kind of white wax like clay, used to fill in cracks of earthenware.

utokezaji *n* (*u*) the act (method, etc.) of sth protruding, appearing, etc.

utokezo *n* (*u*) protrusion; anything protruding.

utoko *n* (*u*) vaginal secretion; the normal uterine discharge of mucus, blood and tissue from the vagina after childbirth; lochia.

utokomezaji *n* (*u*) eradication, elimination, removal: *Utokomezaji wa magonjwa ya mlipuko*, the eradication of epidemic diseases. *Utokomezaji wa umasikini*, the eradication of poverty.

utomondo *n* (*u*) (*bot*) fibre from a poisonous fish tree (*Barringtonia racemosa*), used to make fishing lines or threads of a guitar, etc.

utomvu *n* (*u*) sap of a plant.

utondoti[1] (pl *tondoti*) *n* (*u*) a silver ornament like a big necklace, worn by some women on the chest; a big silver pendant.

utondoti[2] (pl *tondoti*) *n* (*u*) long statement; long explanation.

utoneo[1] *n* (*u*) temporary plaiting of hair; braiding.

utoneo[2] *n* (*u*) dripping, trickling.

utoneshaji *n* (*u*) 1, see *mtonesho* 2. (*chem*) distillation (cf *ukenekaji*)

utongo[1] (also *tongo*) *n* (*u*) (*med*) eye discharge due to conjunctivitis i.e inflsmmstion of conjunctiva: *Jicho lake moja lina utongo*, he has eye discharge in one eye.

utongo[2] *n* (*u*) see *tongo*[3]

utongozaji (also *utongozi*) *n* (*u*) 1. seduction usu of women. 2. persuasion, enticement; honeyed-words.

utongozi *n* (*u*) see *utongozaji*

utoro *n* (*u*) the act of someone escaping from danger, etc.; flight from danger, etc.; truancy: *Utoro wake nchini ulisababishwa na vita vya wenyewe kwa wenyewe*, his fleeing from the country was caused by the civil war.

utoshelevu *n* (*u*) sufficiency, adequacy, utility: *Kila lugha ina utosholevu kwa aina yake*, every language is adequate in its own way.

utosi (pl *tosi*) *n* (*u*) crown of the head; top of the head.

utoto *n* (*u*) 1. childhood, infancy. (cf *ukembe, ujana*) 2. used in the expression: *Achа utoto*, don't be childish.

utotole *n* (*u*) a reward given for finding sth that has been lost by another person: *Nilimpa utotole aliponiletea paspoti yangu iliyopotea*, I gave him a reward for finding my lost passport. (cf *kiokosi , kiangazamacho*)

utovu *n* (*u*) lack, absence: *Utovu wa adabu*, lack of manners. *Utovu wa shukrani*, ingratitude. *Utovu wa nidhamu*, lack of discipline; indiscipline.

utu *n* (*u*) human value, humanity, altruism, goodness. *Utu uzima*, adulthood, maturity, old age e.g. *Utu uzima wake umemletea mvi nyingi*, his old age has brought him a lot of grey hair. (cf *ubinaadamu*)

utukufu *n* (*u*) glory, magnificence,

splendor. (cf *uadhama*)
utukutu *n (u)* prankishness, impishness, naughtiness. (cf *usumbi, utundu*)
utukuzo *n (u)* glory, eminence.
utulivu *n (u)* equanimity, peace, peacefulness, serenity. (cf *amani*)
utulizo *n (u)* comfort, solace. tranquility: *Mgonjwa wangu alipata utulizo baada ya kupewa dawa mwafaka*, my patient obtained relief after being given proper medicine.
utumaji *n (u)* 1. delivery, sending: *Utumaji wa barua kwa njia ya rejista ni madhubuti*, the sending of letters by registered mail is reliable. 2. the sending of an errand to a place for a particular purpose.
utumbo *n (u)* intestine: *Utumbo mwembamba*, small intestine. (*intestinum tenue*); jejenum *Utumbo mpana*, large intestine (*Intestinum crassum*); colon

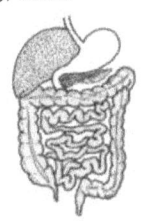

utumbo

utumbuizaji *n (u)* act (method, etc.) of entertaining by means of songs, dances, etc.; enterertainment.
utumbuizo (pl *tumbuizo*) *n (u)* 1. act (method, etc.) of entertaining sby by means of songs, lullabies, dances, etc.: *Utumbuizo wa waimbaji wale uliwavutia wageni*, the entertainment provided by those singers attracted the guests. (cf *uburudishaji*) 2. happiness obtained from singing, dancing, etc.: *Tulipata utumbuizo mkubwa kwenye tamasha*, we had a lot of entertainment at the festival. 3. a long measure of Swahili poetic form usu with many lines (more than four) per

stanza and generally sung to entertain people on special occasions as in weddings, etc.
utume[1] *n (u)* service, job, duty: *Alinipa utume wake na nikaufanya haraka*, he gave me a job and I did it immediately. (cf *kazi*)
utume[2] *n (u)* prophethood, apostolate. (cf *unabii*)
utumiaji *n (u)* use, usage, application, employment: *Utumiaji wake wa kifaa hiki ni mbaya*, his use of this equipment is bad.
utumishi *n (u)* 1. service, personnel: *Ofisa utumishi*, personnel officer. *Idara ya utumishi*, department of civil service. 2. civil service department.
utumizi *n (u)* use, usage, usefulness.
utumwa[1] *n (u)* service
utumwa[2] *n (u)* slavery, bondage: *Utumwa uliwadunisha*, slavery degraded them. (*prov*) *Hewala si utumwa*, acceptance is not slavery i.e. To accept or be contented with sth does not mean that you are now surrendering. (cf *utwana*)
utunda *n (u)* a string of beads, worn by some women around their loins; waist beads. (cf *ukama, kogo*)
utundu *n (u)* naughtiness, prankishness, impishness. (cf *utukutu, usumbi*)
utunduivu *n (u)* see *utunduizi*
utunduizi (also *utunduivu*) *n (u)* good care, careful handling: *Redio yake imeweza kudumu kwa sababu ya utunduizi wake*, his radio has been able to last because of his careful handling. 2. the practice of collecting little by little; accumulation.
utungaji *n (u)* composition, construction: *Utungaji wa insha*, the construction of essays; essay writing.
utungishaji (also *utungisho*) *n (u)* insemination, fertilization: *Utungishaji nje*, external fertilization.
utungisho *n (u)* see *utungishaji*
utungo *n (u)* 1. composition; anything composed; line of ideas, objects, etc. 2. literary work such as a novel, poetry, essay.

utunzaji¹ n (u) care, caring; looking after: *Utunzaji wa wanyama ni jambo muhimu*, the care of animals is important.
utunzaji² n (u) the awarding of prizes, etc.
utunzi¹ n (u) authorship
utunzi² n (u) caring for, looking after: *Utunzi wa watoto*, child care.
utupa n (u) 1. a kind of fish poison, used in pods on the reefs and derived from a spiny leafless tree, *mkweche, Eurphobia nyikae*. 2. the leaves of this tree.
utupaji n (u) throwing away: *Utupaji wa vifurushi vya takataka kiholela umeyachafua mandhari*, the indiscriminate throwing of rubbish parcels has spoiled the scenery.
utupu n (u) 1. nudity, nakedness. *Sehemu za utupu*, private parts, sex organs. 2. hollowness, emptiness: *Utupu wa debe hili ulifanya lilete kelele tupu lilipoanguka*, the emptiness of this tinbox made it emit a lot of noise when it fell down.
uturi n (u) attar, perfume, scent, aroma: *Msichana yule anapenda kujipaka uturi mwilini anapokwenda harusini, that girl likes to apply perfume on her body when she goes to a wedding.* (cf *manukato*)
Uturuki n (u) (*geog*) Turkey
utusitusi (also *uchechea*) n (u) darkness, mistiness, cloudiness, penumbra: *Dereva aliendesha gari polepole kutokana na utusitusi uliozagaa*, the driver drove the car slowly because of the prevailing mist.
utuvu n (u) see *utulivu*
utwaaji n (u) seizure, grabbing: *Utwaaji wa mashamba yale kiholela, ulilaaniwa na jumuia ya kimataifa*, the indiscriminate seizure of those farms, was condemned by the international community. *Utwaaji wa madaraka*, the seizing of power.

utwalio (pl *twalio*) n (u) the corner of a cloth such as that of a loin cloth, which is held when wearing it.
utwana¹ n (u) slavery, bondage, servitude, serfdom.
utwana² n (u) youthfulness, boyhood.
utweshi¹ n (u) greeting: *Utweshi wowote kwa mtu mwingine ni jambo la hiari*, any greeting to another person is a voluntary thing. (cf *maamkizi*)
utweshi² n (u) the hoisting of a flag or sail.
uuaji n (u) murder, slaying: *Alinyongwa kwa kosa la uuaji*, he was hanged for murder. (cf *mauaji*)
uuguzi n (u) nursing; the act of attending to the sick, injured or aged people: *Hakupata uuguzi mzuri katika hospitali*, he did not get good nursing in the hospital. (cf *unasi*)
uumbuaji n (u) 1. act (method, etc) of discrediting or debasing sby/sth 2. disfiguration; the act (method, etc) of spoiling the attractiveness of sth.
uume n (u) 1. manhood. 2. penis, phallus. (cf *zubu, mboo, dhakari*) 3. male's nakedness. 4. the ability to look after a wife.
uumikaji (also *uumisi*) n (u) the drawing of blood to the surface by using glass cups; blood-letting by cupping: *Uumikaji ulimpatia mgonjwa ahueni*, blood-letting by cupping improved the patient's health.
uumizi n (u) see *uumikaji*
uundaji n (u) construction, building, manufacture, production: *Uundaji wa meli unagharimu pesa nyingi*, ship-building costs a lot of money. *Uundaji wa istilahi*, terminology coinage. (cf *utengenezaji*)
uundwaji n (u) formation, construction: *Uundwaji wa serikali mpya*, the formation of a new government.
uungaji n (u) the act (method, etc.) of supporting sby/sth: *Uungaji-mkono*, the act of supporting sby on a particular issue; support.

841

U

uungamaji *n* (*u*) confession, admission: *Mshtakiwa alipelekwa gerezani kutokana na uungamaji wake juu ya kosa la jinai*, the accused was sent to prison after his confession of the crime. (cf *ukiri, ukubalifu*)

Uungu *n* (*u*) divinity, godliness: *Suala lile linahusu uungu wa Yesu*, that issue has to do with the divinity of Jesus.

uungwaji *n* (*u*) the act (method, etc.) of being joined or supported: *Uungwaji-mkono*, the act of being supported: *Uungwaji-mkono wa azimio la wapinzani*, the support of the resolution of the opposition.

uungwana *n* (*u*) gentleness, courtesy: *Uungwana ni kitu adimu*, gentleness is a precious thing. (cf *ustaarabu, utu, ubinadamu*)

uunzi *n* (*u*) formation, workmanship, construction, make: *Uunzi wa meza hii ni mzuri sana*, the workmanship of this table is exquisite. (cf *uundaji*)

uuzaji *n* (*u*) sale, salesmanship: *Uuzaji wa jumla*, wholesale. *Uuzaji wa rejareja*, retail sale.

uvamizi *n* (*u*) invasion, assault, occupation: *Uvamizi wa adui nchini ulilaaniwa na jumuiya ya kimataifa*, the enemy's invasion of the country was condemned by the international community. (cf *shambulio, hujuma*)

uvati *n* (*u*) (*naut*) gunwale or rubbing strake surrounding top of a hull.

uvimbe *n* (*u*) inflammation, swelling: *Uvimbechungu*, infection. *Uvimbe wa ini*, hepatitis. *Uvimbe wa figo*, nephritis. *Ana uvimbe mguuni*, he has a swelling on the leg. (cf *jeraha, kidonda*)

uviringaji *n* (*u*) act (method, etc.) of making sth spherical.

uviringo *n* (*u*) sphericity, roundness: *Uviringo wa dunia zamani ulikuwa haujulikani*, the roundness of the world in the past was unknown. (cf *uduwara*)

uvivu *n* (*u*) laziness, idleness: *Uvivu si sifa nzuri kwa mwanadamu*, laziness is not a good trait for a human being. (cf *ugoigoi, uzembe*)

uvoo *n* (*u*) an armlet of ivory or beads. (cf *kikuku*)

uvuguvugu *n* (*u*) 1. lukewarm, tepedity, warmth, mildness: *Niliyanywa maziwa wakati bado yana uvuguvugu*, I drank the milk while it had still some warmth. (cf *fufutende*) 2. excitement, thrill, ferment. (cf *msisimko*)

uvujaji *n* (*u*) 1. (of containers, etc.) leakage, leaking, seepage; *Uvujaji wa mafuta*, oil leakage 2. (of examinations, etc.) leakage: *Uvujaji wa mitihani katika shule ulimwaibisha mwalimu mkuu*, the leakage of the examinations in the school disgraced the headteacher.

uvukizo *n* (*u*) see *ufukizo*

uvukuto *n* (*u*) see *fukuto*

uvulana *n* (*u*) youthfulness, youth, boyhood: *Alikuwa mwanariadha mzuri wakati wa uvulana wake*, he was a good athlete in his youth. (cf *ushababi*)

uvule *n* (*u*) see *uvuli*[1]

uvuli[1] (also *uvule*) *n* (*u*) the firmness, courage, etc. of a person; manhood: *Uvuli si kitu cha kudumu katika maisha*, manhood cannot last forever. (cf *uanaume, utuume*)

uvuli[2] *n* (*u*) shadiness, shade: *Uvuli wa mti ulimpa bikizee yule buraha*, the shadiness of the tree gave that old woman some comfort.

uvumba *n* (*u*) odoriferous gum used for perfume and incense.

uvumbi *n* (*u*) see *vumbi*

uvumbuaji *n* (*u*) discovery (cf *uvumbuzi*)

uvumbuzi (also *uvumbuaji*) *n* (*u*) 1. discovery, exploration. 2. invention; the act (method, etc.) of starting anything for the first time (cf *ugunduzi, uanzishaji*)

uvumi[1] *n* (*u*) rumour, gossip. (cf *upenyenye, fununu, tetesi*)

uvumi² *n* (*u*) (of bees, flies, wind, etc.) wheezing, humming, buzzing, murmur: *Nilisikia uvumi wa nyuki nje ya nyumba yangu*, I heard the buzzing of bees outside my house.

uvumilivu *n* (*u*) patience, tolerance, endurance: *Lazima uonyeshe uvumilivu unapopata matatizo*, you must show patience when you get problems. (cf *subira, ustahamilivu*)

uvunaji *n* (*u*) harvesting, reaping: *Uvunaji wa pamba*, the harvesting of cotton.

uvundaji *n* (*u*) putrefaction: *Uvundaji wa nyama uliwavutia nzi*, the putrefaction of the meat attracted the flies.

uvundikaji *n* (*u*) fermentation: *Uvundikaji wa hamira*, the fermentation of yeast.

uvundivu *n* (*u*) 1. decay, rot, putrefaction: *Uvundivu wa ndizi ulitoa harufu kali*, the rotting of the bananas produced a strong smell. 2. spoiling, destroying, breaking: *Uvundivu ni rahisi kuliko ujenzi*, destroying is easier than constructing.

uvundo *n* (*u*) stink, stench, effluvium; rotten smell. (cf *mzingo*)

uvunjaji *n* (*u*) 1. breaking, violation, breach: *Uvunjaji wa haki za binaadamu*, violation of human rights. *Uvunjaji wa sheria*, breach of the law. 2. breaking, cutting, splitting: *Uvunjaji wa vyombo vya kupikia*, the breaking of cooking utensils.

uvunjifu *n* (*u*) breach, violation: *Uvunjifu wa amani*, breach of peace

uvunjwaji *n* (*u*) (of law, etc.) the act of being broken, violated, etc.: *Uvunjwaji wa sheria*, the violation of laws.

uvurungu *n* (*u*) concave or hollow in a stone, coconut, pawpaw, etc.: *Mwanzi huu una uvurungu*, this bamboo is hollow.

uvushi *n* (*u*) see *uvusho*

uvusho (also *uvushi*) *n* (*u*) ferrying across; crossing a road, etc.

uvutaji *n* (*u*) 1. smoking: *Uvutaji (wa) sigara*, cigarette smoking. *Uvutaji wa bangi*, bhang smoking. 2. dragging, drawling, pulling.

uvutano *n* (*u*) gravitation, attraction, influence. (cf *mvutano*)

uvuvi *n* (*u*) fishing, fisheries: *Uvuvi haramu*, illicit fishing. *Uvuvi wa sumu*, fishing using poison. *Uvuvi unampa pato zuri*, fishing gives him a good income.

uvuvio *n* (*u*) blowing fire with the mouth or bellows; puffing, stoking. (cf *mpulizio*)

uvuzi *n* (*u*) see *vuzi*

uvyalio *n* (*u*) birthplace (cf *uzalio*)

uvyausaji *n* (*u*) hybridization

uvyauso *n* (*u*) midwifery, obstetrics. (cf *uzalishaji*)

uvyazi *n* (*u*) (*med*) delivery, parturition, childbirth. (cf *uzaaji, uzazi*)

uwadhijini *n* (*u*) (*naut*) face of a ship i.e. portion of bows around oculus.

uwajibikaji *n* (*u*) 1. accountability; a condition of being responsible: *Uwajibikaji ni muhimu kwa watumishi wote wa serikali*, accountability is vital for all civil servants. 2. the act of doing sth that is necessary (Ar)

uwakili *n* (*u*) 1. attorneyship; legal advocacy. 2. agency, representation, spokesmanship: *Uwakili wake unahusu kushughulikia masilahi ya kampuni yetu*, his agency is to look after the interests of our company. (cf *uajenti, uwakilishi*)

uwakilishaji *n* (*u*) see *uwakilishi*

uwakilishi (also *uwakilishaji*) *n* (*u*) 1. representation: *Uwakilishi wa picha*, pictorial representation. *Uwakilishi wa uwiano*, proportional representation. *Uwakilishi wake kutoka jimbo hili uko mashakani*, his representation in this area is in doubt. 2. (*gram*) substitution: *Uwakilishi wa kishazi*, clausal substitution. *Uwakilishi wa nomino*, nominal substitution. *Uwakilishi wa kitenzi*, verbal substitution.

uwalisho *n* (*u*) incarnation; an instance of being alive in human form.

uwalii n (u) 1. spirituality, piety, piousness, extreme religious devotion: *Uwalii wake umemfanya asahau anasa za dunia*, his piety has made him forget worldly pleasures. (cf *utawa, uchamungu*) 2. guardianship; the practice of legally looking after a minor or someone incapable of managing his own affairs.

uwalio¹ (pl *nyalio*) n (u) fish trap barring a river mouth; river-mouth fish trap.

uwalio² (pl *nyalio*) n (u) a chair for enthroning local chiefs.

uwambo¹ (pl *mawambo*) n (u) act (manner, etc.) of stretching over, etc.

uwambo² n (u) (*zool*) the bone of a bird's wing; wingbone.

uwanafunzi n (u) studentship: *Alionyesha juhudi sana wakati wa uwanafunzi wake*, he showed great diligence during his studentship.

uwanambee n (u) primogeniture; the condition or fact of being the firstborn of the same parents.

uwaandaazimu n (u) madness, lunacy, craziness (cf *kichaa, umajinuni*)

uwanda (pl *nyanda*) n (u) 1. an open space. (cf *uchanjaa*) 2. plateau, plain: *Uwanda huu ni mkubwa*, this plateau is big. 3. flat land, level place. 4. a place for doing research.

uwandwe n (u) (*bot*) a coarse perennial grass growing in dense tussocks by the road side. *Panicum maximum*.

uwanga (also *uanga*) (pl *wanga*) n (u) 1. (*bot*) arrow root; a perennial tropical plant having smooth, whitish underground stems. *Maranta arundinacea*. 2. powder obtained from this plant. 3. white powder obtained from some roots and grain, eaten by people.

uwanja (also *kiwanja*) n (u) 1. ground, pitch, field: *Uwanja una maji*, the ground is water-logged. 2.(*pe nyanja*) area; field of study: *Mtafiti amechagua uwanja mpana*, the researcher has chosen a broad area.

uwasa (pl *wasa*) n (u) a thin soft board used by masons to prevent cracks, expansions, etc.

uwashio n (u) fuel

uwasii¹ n (u) 1. the act (method, etc.) of giving a will.

uwasii² n (u) trustee appointment.

uwasilishaji n (u) submission, presentation: *Uwasilishaji wa ripoti ya uchunguzi*, the submission of the report of inquiry.

uwati¹ (pl *mbati*) n (u) see *ukombati*

uwati² n (u) (*med*) skin eruption; demartitis, eczema. (cf *uwawati, upele*)

uwatu n (u) (*bot*) an erect annual herb with obovate leaflets whose seeds are used for flavouring curries; fenugreek. *Trigonella foenum-graecum*.

uwawati n (u) skin erruption, dermatitis, eczema. (cf *uwati, upele*)

uwayo n (u) see *wayo¹*

uwazi n (u) 1. openness, emptiness, space. 2. clarity, frankness, openness, candidness: *Alitoa hoja zake kwa uwazi*, he expressed his arguments with clarity. (cf *ukweli, ubayana*) 3. the condition of sth to remain without a cover or lid.

uwaziri n (u) ministerial portfolio: *Uwaziri mkuu*, premiership. *Anaipenda kazi ya uwaziri*, he likes ministerial work.

uwekaji n (u) putting, placing: *Uwekaji-saini*, signing.

uwekevu n (u) economy (cf *ukabidhi*)

uwekezaji n (u) investment: *Uwekezaji wa rasilimali nchini umepamba moto*, the investment of capital in the country has intensified.

uwele¹ n (u) (*bot*) bulrush millet. *Pennisetum typhoides*.

uwele² n (u) sickness, illness, disease. (cf *ugonjwa, maradhi*)

uweza n (u) power usu of God: *Uweza wa Mungu*, omnipotence of God; power of God.

uwezekano *n* (*u*) 1. possibility, probability, chance: *Uko uwezekano kwamba mvua itanyesha baadaye*, there is a possibility that it will rain afterwards. 2. (*math*) *Uwezekano sharti*, conditional probability.

uwezo *n* (*u*) 1. ability, capability, power: *Uwezo wake wa kulibeba gunia hili la mahindi ni finyu*, his ability to carry this sack of maize is limited. (cf *nguvu*) 2. power, authority: *Meneja wetu ana uwezo wa kuajiri wafanyakazi wengine*, our manager has the authority to employ other workers. (cf *mamlaka, madaraka*) 3. (*math*) *Uwezo wa mvutiko*, tensile strength.

uwi *n* (*u*) evil, wickedness (cf *ubaya, uovu*)

uwiano *n* (*u*) proportion, correlation, correspondence, ratio: *Uwiano wa hesabu*, balance of accounts: *Uwiano rudio*, common ratio. *Uwiano wa jinsia*, balance of gender. *Hakuna uwiano wowote kabisa kati ya maneno yake na matendo*, there is no correlation at all between his words and deeds. (cf *usawa, urari*)

uwinda *n* (*u*) see *ubinda*

uwindaji *n* (*u*) hunting (cf *usasi*)

uwingu (pl *mbingu*) *n* (*u*) sky, cloud, upper air.

uwinja *n* (*u*) see *mbinja*

uwongo *n* (*u*) see *uongo*

uy.a *vi* return from a place; come back. Prep. *uy.i.a* St. *uy.ik.a* Cs. *uy.ish.a* Ps. *uy.w.a* cf *rejea*

uyabisi *n* (*u*) 1. dryness, hardness, stiffness: *Uyabisi wa tumbo* constipation. *Uyabisi wa viungo au mifupa*, rheumatism. 2. small flakes of dead skin formed usu on the scalp; dandruff. (cf *mba*) (Ar)

Uyahudi *n* (*u*) 1. (*geog*) Israel. 2. the state of being a Jew. (Ar)

uyoga *n* (*u*) (*bot*)mushroom

uz.a *vt* 1. sell. Prep. *uz.i.a* St, *uz.ik.a* e.g. *Maembe yake hayauziki upesiupesi*, his mangoes do not sell well Cs. *uz.ish.a* Ps. *uz.w.a* Rp. *uz.an.a* 2. (*fig*) (of an idea, etc) sell; persuade sby of the value of sth: *Chamatawala kiliweza kuuza sera zake kwa wananchi*, the ruling party managed to sell its policies to the people 3. (fig) betrays sellout, doublecross: *Mwanasiasa aliwauza wanavijiji wake*, the politician sold out his villagers. Prep. *uz.i.a* St. *uz.ik.a* Ps. *uz.w.a* Rp *uz.an.a* Rp of Prep. *uz.i.an.a*

uzalendo *n* (*u*) 1. nativeness, indigenousness; the state of being born in a particular place or having naturalized: *Uzalendo pofu*, chauvinism. (cf *uananchi, utaifa*) 2. patriotism, nationalism; love and devotion to one's country.

uzaliano *n* (*u*) reproduction: *Uzaliano kijinsia*, sexual reproduction: *Uzaliano vuvumshi*, vegetative reproduction

uzalio *n* (*n*) labour room, labour ward, delivery room: breeding place.

uzalishaji *n* (*u*) production, breeding: *Uzalishaji wa ziada*, surplus production. *Uzalishaji mali*, production of wealth. *Uzalishaji kwa chupa*, test tube production. *Uzalishaji menyu*, inbreeding. *Uzalishaji bora*, better breeding.

uzamili *n* (*u*) postgraduate studentship, postgraduate studies: *Anachukua masomo ya uzamili katika Chuo Kikuu cha NewYork*, he is doing postgraduate studies at New York University. (Ar)

uzandiki *n* (*u*) hypocrisy, falsehood. (cf *uongo, uchukuu*) (Ar)

uzani *n* (*u*) weight: *Uzani atomia*, atomic weight. *Uzani halisi*, net weight. *Uzani jumla*, gross weight. *Uzani mahususi*, specific weight. (cf *uzito*) (Ar)

uzao *n* (*u*) offspring, progeny, offshoots, new generation.

uzawa[1] *n* (*u*) family, kinfolk, relatives, ancestry. (cf *uzazi*)

uzawa[2] *n* (*u*) indigenousness, nativeness: *Suala la uzawa sasa limeanza kujitokeza waziwazi katika chama chao cha siasa*, the question of indigenousness has now started to manifest itself openly in their political party. (cf *uzalendo*)

845

uzazi *n* (*u*) 1. childbearing, child birth, birth control: *Uzazi wa majira*, family planning, birth control. *Uzazi wa mpango*, family planning. *Elimu-uzazi*, gynaecology. *Via vya uzazi*, reproductive organs. *Chango la uzazi*, umbilical cord. 2. fertility, reproductive power. *Kukosa uzazi ni tatizo lake kubwa*, infertility is her main problem. *Mwanamke yule hana uzazi*, that woman is not fertile. 3. the act (process, etc.) of giving birth to children; parturition, delivery, childbearing: *Uzazi wake una matatizo*, her delivery has problems.
uzee *n* (*u*) senescence, aged, old age (cf *ubuda, ushaibu, ukongwe*)
uzembe *n* (*u*) idleness, laziness, sluggishness, negligence, remissness: *Uzembe wake kazini umezidi*, his laziness at his place of work is beyond the limit. (cf *uvivu, ugoigoi*)
uzi (*pl nyuzi*) *n* (*u*) thread, string: *Nyuzinyuzi*, fibre.
uzidishaji *n* (*u*) (*math*) multiplication: *Uzidishaji kirefu*, long multiplication, *Uzidishaji mtambuko*, cross multiplication
uziduzi *n* (*u*) (in science, etc.) extraction: *Uziduzi wa chuma*, the extraction of iron.
uzima *n* (*u*) health, life, wellbeing: *Mtu yule hana uzima wowote*, that person is not healthy at all. (cf *afya, rai*)
uzimbezimbe *n* (*u*) idleness, laziness, sluggishness: *Uzimbezimbe ni sifa mbaya*, laziness is a bad trait. (cf *uvivu, ugoigoi*)
uzinda *n* (*u*) virginity, celibacy, maidenhood. (cf *ubikira*)
uzinduzi[1] *n* (*u*) inauguration: *Rais alishiriki kikamilifu katika uzinduzi wa zahanati*, the president participated fully in the inauguration of the dispensary. (cf *ufunguzi*)
uzinduzi[2] *n* (*u*) awareness, awakening: *Uzinduzi wake umemwelimisha mambo mengi*, his awakening has enlightened him in many matters. (cf *uamkaji*)
uzingatiaji *n* (*u*) the act method, etc of examining sby/sth; examination, observation: *Uzingatiaji wa maadili*, the observation of ethics.
uzinge *n* (*u*) see *uzingo*
uzingo (also *uzinge*) *n* (*u*) 1. anything that surrounds: *Uzingo wa mwezi*, a halo round the moon. 2. siege, blockade, encirclement.
uzinifu *n* (*u*) see *uzinzi*
uzinzi (also *uzinifu*) *n* (*u*) adultery, fornication, debauchery. (cf *uasherati, zinaa*) (Ar)
uzio (*pl nyuzio*) *n* (*u*) 1. a fish trap consisting of a wattle fence of upright sticks fastened together, used to prevent fish from escaping when the tide falls; a fish trap jutting out from the beach. (cf *tando, boma*) 2. fence, hedge.
uzito (also *uzani*) *n* (*u*) 1. weight, heaviness. 2. importance, concern: *Lazima ulipe uzito suala hili*, you must give importance to this issue. 3. difficulty, complexity perplexity: *Uzito wa tatizo lako uko bayana*, the complexity of your problem is evident. (cf *ugumu*)
uziwi *n* (*u*) 1. deafness. (cf *komangu*) 2. (*fig*) naughtiness. (cf *uharabu*)
uzoaji *n* (*u*) act (method, etc) of collecting sth from the floor, etc; gathering, collection: *Uzoaji-taka*, the collection of garbage/refuse.
uzoefu *n* (*u*) experience, knowledge: *Uzoefu wa kimataifa*, International experience. *Ana uzoefu mkubwa katika kazi yake*, he has a lot of experience in his work.
uzohali *n* (*u*) procrastination, delay; slowness in doing sth. (cf *usiri, ulegevu*) (Ar)
uzoroteshaji *n* (*u*) degeneration, declension, declension, decline.
uzu.a (*usu uzulu*) *vi* dethrone, depose; remove from office: Prep. **uzu.li.a** St.

uzu.lik.a Cs. ***uzu.lish.a*** Ps. of Prep. ***uzu.liw.a***
uzuiliaji *n* (*u*) hindrance, blocking, obstruction, prevention: *Uzuiliaji wa watu kuvuka mpaka kiholela umepunguza biashara haramu*, the act of preventing people from crossing the border illegally has reduced illicit trade.
uzuio (also *uzuizi*) *n* (*u*) hindrance, blocking, prevention.
uzuizi *n* (*u*) see *uzuio*
uzuka *n* (*u*) (in Islam) the state of a widow living in seclusion after her husband's death. This seclusion prevents the widow from seeing distant people except her relatives: *Uzuka umemtia katika huzuni*, widowhood has put her into a sorrowful condition.
uzul.u *vi* see *uzua*
uzulufu *n* (*u*) dotage, caducity, senility; condition of experiencing weaknesses due to old age: *Uzulufu umemvaa*, senility has attacked him.
uzungu *n* (*u*) novelty, newness; strangeness. (cf *ugeni, upya*)
uzunguni *n* (*u*) European quarters, European area: *Alikwenda kutembea uzunguni*, he went to visit the European quarters.
uzuri[1] *n* (*u*) goodness, beauty. (cf *ubora*)
uzuri[2] *n* (*u*) cosmetic things like perfume, powder, etc.; cosmetics: *Alijitia uzuri mwilini kabla ya kwenda harusini*, she applied on cosmetics on her body before she went to the wedding. (cf *urembo*)
uzuri[3] *adv* fine, well, okay.
uzururaji *n* (*u*) act (method, etc.) of wandering; roaming, rambling, roving.
uzushi (also *uzuzi*) *n* (*u*) 1. invention, innovation. 2. falsehood, untruthfulness. (cf *uongo*)
uzuzi[1] *n* (*u*) see *uzushi*
uzuzi[2] *n* (*u*) unearthing; bringing to light sth that has been hidden.
uzuzu *n* (*u*) 1. amateurism, apprenticeship; the state of being a novice or inexperienced in a particular profession, work, etc.: *Uzuzu wake katika useremala ulikuwa wazi*, his inexperience in carpentry was evident. 2. ignorance, stupidity, imbecility, dull-wittedness. (cf *ujinga, upumbavu*)

V/v/v/ 1. the twenty first letter of the Swahili alphabet. 2. a voiced labiodental fricative.

va.a[1] *vt* 1. (a) wear, dress, garb, cloth; get dressed: *Amevaa nguo mpya*, he has worn new clothes. 2. wear things other than a cloth: *Vaa saa*, wear a watch. *Vaa mkufu*, wear a chain. 3. (fig) attack, invade, offend: *Umeanza kunivaa tangu ufike hapa*, you have started attacking me since your arrival here. 4. (fig) (in sports) compete; play against: *Timu yetu itaivaa chelsea katika mchezo wa kirafiki*, our team will paly against Chelsea in a friendly match. Prep. *va.li.a* St. *va.lik.a* Ps. of Prep. *va.liw.a* Rp. *va.an.a* Ps. of Cs. *va.lish.w.a* (cf *vamia*)

vaa[2] *n* (*n*) (*naut*) yard brace; a rope passed through a block at the end of a yard, by which the yard is swung from the deck.

vaan.a *vi* engage in a fight. *Vijana wale wawili wanataka kuwaana*, those two young men are about to come to blows: *Timu zile mbili mashuhuri zitavaana karibu*, those two prominent teams will contest bitterly quite soon. Prep. *vaan.i.a* St. *vaan.ik.a* Cs. *vaan.ish.a* (cf *pepetana, menyana, umana*)

valensi *n* (*n*) valency: *Valensitatu* trivalent. (Eng)

vali *n* (*n*) valve: *Valivutaji*, induction valve. (Eng)

vali.a *vi* 1. dress up smartly: *Rafiki yako amevalia leo*, your friend has dressed up smartly today. 2. put on with (for, in, etc.): *Mshipi wa kuvalia nguo*, a belt to secure one's clothes with. St. *vali.k.a* Cs. *vali.sh.a*

valio *n* (*ma*-) extra apparel, fine attire; ornaments. (cf *pambo, urembo*)

valish.a *vt* 1. assist sby to dress: *Walimvalisha biharusi*, they dressed the bride. 2. buy clothes for sby. Prep. *valish.i.a* St. *valish.w.a* Rp *valish.an.a*

vam.a *vt* be firmly obsessed, be firmly established; take deep roots: *Mapenzi yamemwama*, love has overwhelmed him. Prep. *vam.i.a* St. *vam.ik.a* Cs. *vam.ish.a* Ps. *vam.w.a* (cf *zama, topea*)

vami.a *vt* 1. attack, invade, raid, storm: *Adui aliivamia nchi yetu*, the enemy attacked our country. (cf *shambulia*) 2. rush; dash recklessly or rashly: *Alilivamia jambo lenyewe bila ya kwanza kulipima*, he rushed into the matter without first weighing it. Prep. *vami.li.a* St. *vami.k.a* Cs. *vami.sh.a* Ps. *vami.w.a* Rp. *vami.an.a* (cf *rukia, ingilia*)

vamio *n* (*ma*-) onslaught, invasion, attack. (cf *shambulizi, shambulio*)

vang.a *vi* be restless; be uneasy; be occupied: *Mama alikuwa amevanga kabla ya harusi ya bintiye*, the mother was restless before her daughter's wedding. Prep. *vang.i.a* St. *vang.ik.a* Cs. *vang.ish.a* Ps. *vang.w.a* (cf *hangaika, shughulika*)

vangavang.a *vt* distort information, news, statement, etc.: garble, warp: *Alikuwa akivanganga tu badala ya kutoa ukweli wa mambo*, he was just distorting the information instead of telling the plain truth. Prep. *vangavang.i.a* St. *vangavang.ik.a* Cs. *vangavang.ish.a* Ps. *vangavang.w.a* (cf *vungavunga)*

vania *n* (*n*) see *venia*

vanila *n* (*n*) (*bot*) vanilla (cf *lavani*) (Eng)

varanda *n* (*n*) verandah (cf *baraza*) (Eng)

varanga[1] *n* (*n*) disturbance, disorder, chaos, unrest: *Watu walipokuwa wanazungumza, yeye alijaribu kuleta varanga zake za kawaida*,when the people were talking, he tried to cause his usual disturbances. (cf *zogo, fujo, ghasia*)

varang.a[2] *vt* snoop, meddle; interfere rudely in other people's affairs: *Kwa nini anavaranga katika mambo*

yasiyomhusu? Why is he meddling in other people's affairs? Prep. *varang.i.a* St. *varang.ik.a* Cs. *varang.ish.a* Ps. *varang.w.a* Rp *varang.an.a* (cf *jidukiza, mamia, jiingiza*)
varange *n* (ma-) deceit, deception, hypocricy. (cf *ubabaishaji, hadaa, ghiliba*)
vavaga.a *vt, vi* spread out, circulate; be here and there: *Habari kwamba Jane ameachwa zimevavagaa mjini*, the news that Jane is divorced has spread in the town. Prep. *vavaga.li.a* St. *vavaga.lik.a* Cs. *vavaga.z.a*, spread, diffuse. Ps. of Prep. *vavaga.liw.a* (cf *zagaa, tapakaa, enea*)
vazi *n* (ma-)dress, costume, gown, outfit: *Vazi la asubuhi*, morning dress. *Vazi la jioni*, evening dress. *Vazi la taifa* national dress. *Mavazi rasmi*, full dress. *Vazi lile linampendeza* that dress becomes her. (cf *libasi, nguo*)
veli *n* (n) veil; a kind of white dress worn by a bride during the wedding. (Eng)
vema *adv* see *vyema*
vena *n* (n) (*anat*) vein (Eng)
vengeny.a *vt* bore a hole by gnawing. Prep. *vengeny.e.a* St. *vengeny.ek.a* Cs. *vengeny.esh.a* Ps. *vengeny.w.a*
venia (aloo *vania*) *n* (n) vernier; an auxiliary device intended to give accurate measurements. (Eng)
ventrikali *n* (u) (*anat, zool*) a) ventricle; each of the two main chambers of the heart which receive blood from the atria and pump it into the arteries. b) any of the four small continuous cavities within the brain; ventricle. (Eng)
vetebra *n* (u) (*anat*) any of the single bones or segments of the spinal column; vertebra.

vetebra

vetebrata *n* (u) (*zool*) vertebrate; any of a large subphylum of chordate animals, including all animals, fishes, birds, reptiles and amphibians, characterized by a segmented spinal column and a brain enclosed in a brainpain or cranium. (Eng)
veto *n* (n) veto; the power to prevent legislation or action proposed by others.
vi.a *vi* 1. (of persons, fruits, etc) be stunted in growth; be dwarfed; be underdone: *Kijana yule amevia kwa sababu ya utapiamlo*, that young man is stunted because of malnutrition. *Tunda hili limevia*, this fruit is stunted. (cf *dumaa, runda, kundaa*) 2. (*fig*) fail, be fruitless: *Mapinduzi yalivia*, the revolution failed. Prep. *vi.li.a* St. *vi.lik.a* Cs. *vi.z.a*
vibaya *adv* 1. badly, terribly, miserably: *Aliumia vibaya aliposhambuliwa na simba*, he was badly injured when he was attacked by the lion. 2. wrongfully, improperly, incorrectly: *Amelijibu suala vibaya*, he has answered the question incorrectly.
video *n* (n) video (Eng)
viereje *adv* (*interrog*) How (cf *iweje*)
vifijo *n* (ki-vi) applause, cheer, ovation: *Bibi harusi alipokewa kwa vifijo na vigelegele*, the bride was received with standing ovation and ululations. (cf *shangwe, shamrashamra*)
vigavig.a *vt* disturb, hassle, harass: *Wanafunzi walimvigaviga mwalimu*

wao darasani, the students hassled their teacher in class. Prep. ***vigavig.i.a*** St. ***vigavig.ik.a*** Cs. ***vigavig.ish.a*** Ps. ***vigavig.w.a*** Rp. ***vigavig.an.a*** (cf *sumbua, taabisha*)

vigumu *adv* hard, difficult: *Ni vigumu kumfurahisha mtu yule*, It is difficult to please that person. (cf *taabu, taklifu*)

vije *adv* an expletive used for questioning made by someone in order to know the state of affairs; How are things? How is it going?

vijuk.a *vi* nauseate; have a feeling of sickness in the stomach characterized by an urge to vomit. Prep. ***vijuk.i.a*** St. ***vijuk.ik.a*** Cs. ***vijuk.ish.a***

vikapu *n* (*ki-vi*) used in: *Mchezo wa vikapu*, basketball.

vikorokoro *n* (*ki-vi*) junk, rubbish, trash, garbage, clutter; items usu of less importance: *Mbona kumejaa vikorokoro chumbani mwako?* Why is there so much junk in your room? (cf *vigorogoro, takataka*)

vilasi *n* (*n*) (*anat*) intestinal worm. (Eng)

vile[1] *adj, pron* form of *-le* for ki-vi- class pl nouns: *Vitabu vile*, those books. *Viatu vile*, those shoes. *Vile ni vyangu*, those are mine.

vile[2] *adv* as, like: *Kama vile*, like that. *Alifanya vile makusudi*, he did that deliberately.

vilevile *adv* also, likewise, moreover, over and above, in addition: *Yeye ni mwanamuziki hodari. Vile vile, yeye ni mchezaji mzuri wa kandanda*, he is a good musician. Also, he is a good soccer player. (cf *tena, waidha*)

vili.a *vi* bruise: *Kidole chake kilivilia baada ya kiganja chake kujibana kwenye bawabu*, his finger was bruised after his hand was caught up between the hinges. Prep. ***vili.li.a*** St. ***vili.k.a*** Cs. ***vili.sh.a*** Ps. ***vili.w.a***

viliz.a *vt* cause sth to fail to be implemented. Prep. ***viliz.i.a*** St. ***viliz.ik.a***

vimb.a[1] *vi* 1. expand, swell, dilute, bloat, inflate, puff out: *Uso wangu ulivimba baada ya kuumwa na nyuki*, my face swelled after being stung by bees. *Jipu lake sasa limevimba*, his boil is now swollen. (cf *fura, tuna*) 2. (fig) be angry, be annoyed; swell in anger: *Uso wake ulivimba baada ya kukemewa na mwalimu*, his face was swollen with anger after being scolded by the teacher. (cf *hamaki, kasirika*) Prep. ***vimb.i.a*** St. ***vimb.ik.a*** Cs. ***vimb.ish.a*** caused to swell, e.g. *Umenivimbisha kwa kunipa chakula kingi*, you have caused my stomach to swell by giving me too much food. Ps. ***vimb.w.a*** Rp. ***vimb.an.a***

vimb.a[2] *vt* thatch; cover a house or a hut with palm leaves, stems etc.: *Alilivimba paa langu la nyumba kwa makuti*, he thatched the roof of my house with coconut palm leaves. Prep. ***vimb.i.a*** St. ***vimb.ik.a*** Cs. ***vimb.ish.a*** Ps. ***vimb.w.a*** (cf *ezeka*)

vimbish.a *vt* see *vimba* Prep. ***vimbish.i.a***, St. ***vimbish.ik.a*** Ps. ***vimbish.w.a*** Rp. ***vimbish.an.a***

vimbiw.a *vi* be crammed with food; be stuffed with food in the stomach; be gorged with food: *Alikula sana mpaka akavimbiwa*, he ate so much that his stomach swelled; he overate. (cf *shiba*)

vimbizi *n* (*n*) breathing problems caused by overeating; breathing pains caused by eating greedily; gastric pains caused by indigestion: *Amepata vimbizi*, he has gastric pains caused by indigestion.

vin.a *vt* see *vinya*

vinani *n* (*ki-vi*) pl of *vina*

vindimk.a *vi* be swollen, be enlarged. Prep. ***vindimk.i.a*** St. ***vindimk.ik.a*** Cs. ***vindimk.ish.a***

ving.a *vt* take sth and throw it up. Prep. ***ving.i.a*** St. ***ving.ik.a*** Cs. ***ving.ish.a*** Ps. ***ving.w.a***

vingine[1] (also *vinginevyo*) *conj* if not,

otherwise or else: *Fanya kama ulivyoambiwa; vingine, utaingia matatani,* do as you were told; otherwise you will be in trouble.
vingine² *adj, pron* form of *-ingine;* 'other' used for ki-vi class pl nouns: *Vitu vingine,* other things. *Vingine, havitanifaa,* others will not suit me.
vinginevyo¹ *conj* see *vingine¹*
vinginevyo² *adj, pron* form of *-ingine* used for ki-vi class pl nouns: *Vitabu vinginevyo,* other books.
vinginy.a (also *finginya*) *vi* 1. wriggle; twist from side to side with rapid short movements: *Nyoka alivinginya wakati watu walipompiga kwa fimbo,* the snake wriggled as the people beat it with a stick. (cf *jinyonga*) 2. wiggle, waggle; shake the hips and backside during dancing or walking: *Msichana alivinginya kifundi kwenye ngoma,* the girl wiggled skilfully during dancing. Prep. *vinginy.i.a* St. *vinginyi.k.a* Cs. *vinginy.ish.a* Ps. *vinginy.w.a* Rp. *vinginy.an.a*
vingirik.a (also *fingirika*) *vi* roll round, swirl, twirl; go round and round like a grinding stone: *Mchezaji alivingirika mbele za watazamaji,* the dancer swirled before the audience. Prep. *vingirik.i.a* St. *vingirik.ik.a* Cs. *vingirik.ish.a* (cf *bingirika*)
vingirish.a *vt* cause sth to roll around like a grinding stone. Prep. *vingirish.i.a* St. *vingirish.ik.a* Ps. *vingirish.w.a* Rp. *vingirish.an.a* (cf *bingirisha*)
vingiz.a *vt* hassle, hector, disturb. Prep. *vingiz.i.a* St. *vingiz.ik.a* Cs. *vingiz.ish.a* Ps. *vingiz.w.a* Rp. *vingiz.an.a* (cf *kera, sumbua, ghasi*)
vinjar.i *vt, vi* 1. cruise around, make the rounds; patrol: *Sungusungu walikuwa wakivinjari mtaani ili kuhakikisha kama kuna usalama,* the local vigilantes were patrolling the neighbourhood to ensure that there was security. 2. stand firm; be resolute: *Wananchi wamevinjari katika kupigania haki zao,* the people have stood firm in the fight for their rights. Prep. *vinjar.i.a* St. *vinjar.ik.a* Cs. *vinjar.ish.a* Ps. *vinjar.iw.a* (cf *zatiti*)

viny.a (also *vina*) *vt* 1. dandle a child, etc.; dance a child, etc.; toss sth up and down: *Mara tu alipofika nyumbani, mzee akamvinya mwanawe,* soon after he arrived home, the parent dandled his child. 2. (of lip, eyelid, muscle, etc.) tremble due to illness, anger, etc.: *Mdomo wake ulivinya kutokana na homa kali,* her lip trembled due to acute fever. (cf *tetema, tikisika*) Prep. *viny.i.a* St. *viny.ik.a* Cs. *viny.ish.a* Ps. *viny.w.a*
vinyuk.a *vt* swirl, whirl, revolve, spin around. Prep. *vinyuk.i.a* St. *vinyuk.ik.a* Cs. *vinyuk.ish.a* (cf *fingirita*)
vipi *adv interrog* a word used for questioning or describing the manner or state of affairs; How? "How are things"? *Kwa vipi?* How? *Alifika hapa vipi?* How did he arrive here? *Vipi atakuja hapa bila ya yeye kuonana na mimi?* How could he come here without seeing me?
virigiz.a *vt* disturb, harass, hector, pester, hassle: *Mbwa wako aliniwirigiza usiku wote,* your dog disturbed me throughout the night. Prep. *virigiz.i.a* St. *virigiz.ik.a* Cs. *virigiz.ish.a* Ps. *virigiz.w.a* Rp. *virigiz.an.a* (cf *sumbua, ghasi*)
viring.a *vt* roll up; make round; form a curve or bend: *Aliuviringa unga katika madonge,* he formed the dough into balls. Prep. *viring.i.a* St. *viring.ik.a* Cs. *viring.ish.a* Ps. *viring.w.a* Rp. *viring.an.a* (cf *burunga, petemanisha*)
viringan.a *vi* 1. become round; coil: *Unga umeviringana,* the dough has coiled itself. 2. (*syn*) *Ameviringana,* he is well-built.
viringe¹ *n* (*n*)(*bot*) a kind of small round mango. (cf *pembeni*)
viringe² *n* (*n*) a spherical shape.
viringik.a *vi* 1. be in a spherical shape. 2. turn by rotation. St. *viring.ik.a* Cs.

viringikish.a
viringish.a *vt* wrap up, circle around: *Watoto waliwaviringisha udongo wenzi wao*, the children wrapped their mates with clay. Prep. ***viringish.i.a*** St. ***viringish.ik.a*** Ps. ***viringish.w.a*** Rp. ***viringish.an.a***
viru *n (ma-) (bot)* a kind of custard apple about the size of a pomegranate.
virusi *n (ki-vi)* virus: *Virusi vya UKIMWI*, AIDS viruses. (Eng)
vish.a *vt* dress sby/sth: *Alimwisha nguo mtoto wake*, she dressed up her child. Prep. ***vish.i.a*** St. ***vish.ik.a*** Ps. ***vish.w.a*** Rp. ***vish.an.a***
visivyo *adv* erroneously: *Alinielewa visivyo*, he misunderstood me. *Alikwenda visivyo*, he took the wrong direction.
visuguru *n (ki-vi) (bot)* corn
vita *n (n)* war, battle: *Vita baridi*, cold war. *Vita vya Kwanza vya Dunia*, First World War. *Vita vya Pili vya Dunia*, Second World War. *Vita vya msituni*, guerrilla war. *Vita vya wenyewe kwa wenyewe*, civil war. *(prov) Vita vya panzi ni neema ya kunguru*, a fight between grasshoppers is a joy to crows i.e. a quarrel between two relatives, countries, etc. is a benefit to an outsider who may be their common enemy. (cf *kitali, bangu*)
vitamini *n (n)* vitamin: *Vitamini B-tata*, vitamin B-complex. *Vitamini A*, vitamin A. *Vitamini C*, vitamin C.
vitimbi *n (ki-vi)* intrigues, conspiracies, machinations. (cf *vituko, visa*)
vivi *adv* used in the expression: *Vivi hivi* a) in this way only; just like that e.g. *Alifanya vivi hivi*, he did it just like that. b) without: *Alikula vivi hivi; hakutumia kijiko au uma*, he ate without using a spoon or fork.
vivi.a *vt* see *vuvia* Prep. ***vivi.li.a*** St. ***vivi.lik.a*** Cs. ***vivi.lish.a*** Ps. ***vivi.w.a*** Rp. ***vivi.an.a***
vivinyuk.a *vi* wriggle like a worm or maggot: *Funza alikuwa akivivinyuka*, the maggot was wriggling. Prep. ***vivinyuk.i.a*** St. ***vivinyuk.ik.a*** Cs. ***vivinyuk.ish.a***
vivizi.a *vi* heave and release spewed spittle around as when a medicineman is weaving a spell on his client. Prep. ***vivizi.li.a*** St. ***vivizi.lik.a*** Cs. ***vivizi.sh.a*** Ps. ***vivizi.w.a***
-vivu *adj* lazy, indolent, slothful, idle: *Mwalimu wetu hampendi mwanafunzi mvivu*, our teacher does not like a lazy student. (cf *goigoi*)
vivyo *adv* in the same way; in the manner mentioned; exactly.
viz.a¹ *vi* 1. stunt, underdevelop, retard. 2. curse, destroy: *Mungu akuvize*, May God curse you. 3. delay sth to be implemented. Prep. ***viz.i.a*** St. ***viz.ik.a*** Cs. ***viz.ish.a*** Ps. ***viz.w.a*** Rp. ***viz.an.a***
viza² *adj* rotten, bad, spoiled: *Hili ni yai viza*, this is a rotten egg.
viza³ *n (n)* visa; an endorsement on a passport allowing a person to enter a particular country or region. (Eng)
vizi.a *vt,vi* 1. waylay, lurk; wait in ambush. 2. stalk, still-hunt, tip-toe; follow stealthily: *Alimwizia paa mpaka akamkamata*, he followed the deer stealthily until he caught it. Prep. ***vizi.li.a*** St. ***vizi.k.a*** and ***vizi.lik.a*** Cs. ***vizi.sh.a*** Ps. ***vizi.w.a*** Rp. ***vizi.an.a*** (cf *nyatia, nyapa, nyemelea*)
vizuri *adv* well, properly, correctly, smoothly. *Fanya kazi vizuri*, do the work properly. *Hafla yake ilienda vizuri*, his reception proceeded smoothly. (cf *barabara, sawa*)
vocha *n (n)* voucher (Eng)
vogome.a *vi* disappear; vanish from sight, recede from view: *Ndege ilivogomea mara tu baada ya kuruka*, the plane disappeared immediately after take-off. Prep. ***vogome.le.a*** St. ***vogome.k.a*** Cs. ***vogome.z.a*** (cf *yoyoma, tokomea, toweka, potea*)

vokali *n* (*n*) vowel: *Mfumo wa vokali*, vowel system. (cf *irabu*) (Eng)
volkano *n* (*n*) volcano: *Volkano lala*, dormant volcano. *Milima ya volkano*, volcanic mountains. (cf *zaha*) (Eng)
volteji *n* (*n*) voltage: *Volteji dukizwa*, induced voltage. *Volteji fuasi*, secondary voltage. (Eng)
vondomok.a *vi* come out abruptly and fast from a place. Prep. *vondomok.e.a* St. *vondomok.ek.a* Cs. *vondomok.esh.a*
vonge.a *vt,vi* gluttonize; eat voraciously, eat ravenously: *Alikula kwa kuvongea*, he ate voraciously. Prep. *vonge.le.a* St. *vonge.k.a* and *vonge.lek.a* Cs. *vonge.sh.a* and *vonge.lesh.a* Ps. *vonge.w.a* cf *fakamia, papia*
vongonya[1] *n* (*ma-*) see *vungunya*
vongony.a[2] *vt* bore hy twirling from inside. Prep. *vongony.e.a* St. *vongony.ek.a* Cs. *vongony.esh.a* Ps. *vongony.w.a*
vongonyo.a *vt* disclose or uncover sth that is wrapped and hidden inside. Prep. *vongonyo.le.a* St. *vongonyo.k.a* Cs. *vongonyo.lesh.a* Ps. *vongonyo.lew.a* Rp. *vongonyo.an.a*
vono *n* (*n*) used in the expression: *Kitanda cha vono*, spring bed.
voromo.a *vt* see *poromoa*
vot.a *vt,vi* (in discussions, etc.) win, beat, triumph: *Smith amemvota rafiki yake katika majadiliano*, Smith has beaten his friend in the debate. Prep. *vot.e.a* St. *vot.ek.a* Cs. *vot.esh.a* Ps. *vot.w.a* (cf *shinda, faulu*)
vu.a[1] *vt* 1. undress, strip, take off clothes: *Vua shati lako*, take off your shirt. *Vua kofia*, take off the cap. *Alimvua mtoto wake nguo*, she undressed her child. 2. used in the expression: *Vua madaraka*, strip sby of powers, authority, etc.: *Baraza la Chuo Kikuu lilimvua madaraka mkuu wa kitivo*, the University Council stripped of the powers of the faculty dean. Prep. *vu.li.a* St. *vu.k.a*, Cs. *vu.sh.a* Ps. of Prep. *vu.liw.a*, Rp. *vu.an.a*

vu.a[2] *vt* save, rescue; save from the jaws of death, etc.: *Alimvua rafiki yake kwenye janga*, he saved his friend from the disaster. Prep. *vu.li.a* St. *vu.k.a* Cs. *vu.sh.a* Ps. of Prep. *vu.liw.a* Rp. *vu.an.a* (cf *okoa, opoa, nusuru*)
vu.a[3] *vt* fish; go fishing, catch fish. Prep. *vu.li.a* St. *vu.k.a* Cs. *vu.sh.a* Ps. of Prep. *vu.liw.a* Rp. *vu.an.a*
vu.a[4] *vt* used in the expression: *Vua macho*, glance, glimpse, raise the eyes. Prep. *vu.li.a* St. *vu.lik.a*
vuam.a *vi* get into the water and remain there.
vuat.a *vt* 1. (of tobacco, etc.) put or hold between the teeth and the lower lip: *Usivuate tumbaku kwenye mkutano*, don't put a quid of tobacco in your mouth during the meeting. 2. (*idm*) *Vuata ulimi*, keep quiet; be silent; refrain from making noise. (cf *nyamaza, nyamaa*) 3. dry a place by using a cloth, etc. Prep. *vuat.i.a* Cs. *vuat.ik.a* Ps. *vuat.ish.a* Ps. *vuat.w.a*
vuaz.a[1] *vt* 1. (by using an instrument with a sharp edge such as a knife, razor, etc.) mark, etch: *Alilivuaza jina lake kwenye gogo la mti*, he etched his name on the trunk of a tree. 2. (*fig*) wound the feelings; hurt, scathe, pain: *Maneno yake makali yalituvuaza ndani kwa ndani*, his blunt words hurt us deeply. Prep. *vuaz.i.a* St. *vuaz.ik.a* Cs. *vuaz.ish.a* Ps. *vuaz.w.a* Rp. *vuaz.an.a* (cf *choma, umiza*)
vuaz.a[2] *vt* soak sth in water. Prep. *vuaz.i.a* St. *vuaz.ik.a* Cs. *vuaz.ish.a* Ps. *vuaz.w.a* Rp. *vuaz.an.a*
vue *n* (*ma-*) (*bot*) a thicket of long grass.
vug.a[1] *vt* preserve food by using smoke or putting salt in it. Prep. *vug.i.a* St. *vug.ik.a* Cs. *vug.ish.a* Ps. *vug.w.a* Rp. *vug.an.a*
vug.a[2] *vt* pass at a place and tramp on it. Prep. *vug.i.a* St. *vug.ik.a* Cs. *vug.ish.a* Ps. *vug.w.a* Rp. *vug.an.a*

V vugaz.a

vugaz.a *vt* close a door without putting on a lock or a latch of wood; close but not fasten; set ajar: *Aliivugaza milango ya nyumba yake*, he closed the doors of his house without locking them. Prep. *vugaz.i.a* St. *vugaz.ik.a* Cs. *vugaz.ish.a* Ps. *vugaz.w.a* (cf *shindika, sindika*)
vugo *n* (*ma-*) 1. a local dance of using horns by beating them up, performed by the women of East African Coast. 2. a horn usu from a bull, used for this purpose.
vugu.a¹ *vt* pass through to the other side of a forest, bush, roadblock, etc.; break through the forest, bush, etc.: *Alikivugua kizuizi barabarani na kuendelea na safari yake*, he removed the roadblock and continued with his journey. Prep. *vugu.li.a* St. *vugu.lik.a* Cs. *vugu.lish.a* Ps. of Prep. *vugu.liw.a*
vugu.a² *vt* undergo menstruation after failing to conceive. Prep. *vugu.li.a* St. *vugu.lik.a* Cs. *vugu.lish.a* Ps. of Prep. *vugu.liw.a*
vugut.a *vi* see *fukuta*
vuguto *n* (*n*) see *fukuto*
vuguvugu¹ *adj* tepid, lukewarm, temperate: *Maji ya vuguvugu*, tepid water.
vuguvugu² *n* (*n*) activity, movement, agitation, turmoil, fever: *Vuguvugu la kisiasa*, political turmoil. *Vuguvugu la mapinduzi*, revolutionary movement. *Vuguvugu la uchaguzi mkuu linazidi kupamba moto*, general election fever continues to become hot.
vuik.a *vi* see *vumika*
vuj.a *vi* leak, seep, ooze, drip: *Ndoo yangu inavuja*, my bucket is leaking. Prep. *vuj.i.a* St. *vuj.ik.a* Cs. *vuj.ish.a* Ps. *vuj.w.a* (cf *churura, churuzika, derereka*)
vuk.a¹ *vt, vi* 1. cross over, sail over, travel across: *Vuka barabara*, cross the road. 2. (*idm*) *Vuka mpaka*, go too far; go beyond the limit. Prep. *vuk.i.a* St.

vumaik.a

vuk.ik.a Cs. *vu.sh.a* and *vuk.ish.a* Ps. *vuk.w.a* Rp. *vuk.an.a*
vuk.a² *vi* become undressed. Prep. *vuk.i.a* St. *vuk.ik.a* Cs. *vuk.ish.a*
vukut.a *vi* see *fukuta*
vukuto *n* (*n*) see *fukuto*
vuli *n* (*n*) the short rains beginning in October and ending in December. *Mvua za vuli*, the short rains during this period.
vulio *n* (*ma-*) 1. cast-off clothing; old clothes: *Masikini wale walipewa mavulio*, those poor people were given old clothes. (cf *vazi, kukuu*) 2. the slough of a snake; the skin of a snake esp the outer layer that is periodically cast off; the snake's cast skin.
vum.a¹ *vi* 1. roar, bellow, buzz, rumble; make a loud sound like that of wild animals, bees, drums, wind, etc.: *Upepo unavuma vibaya*, the wind is blowing hard. (*prov*) *Ngoma ivumayo haikawii kupasuka*, the drum that vibrates a lot soon ruptures i.e. if a bad person exceeds his evil deeds, his ending will be disastrous. (cf *rindima, nguruma*)
2. be in the air, be a subject of common talk, be the talk of the town; spread, circulate: *Habari kwamba Ramla anaolewa zinavuma mtaani*, the news that Ramla is getting married has spread in the neighbourhood. (cf *enea, zagaa*) 3. become famous; become widely known: *Mwanasiasa yule anavuma nchini kwa sera zake*, that politician is reknown in the country for his policies. Prep. *vum.i.a* St. *vum.ik.a* Cs. *vum.ish.a* Ps. *vum.w.a* (cf *julikana*)
vum.a² *vt* jeer, flout, boo: *Walimvuma alipovaa nguo za kike*, they jeered at him when he wore women's clothes. Prep. *vum.i.a* St. *vum.ik.a* Cs. *vum.w.a* Ps. *vum.w.a* (cf *zomea*)
vumaik.a *vi* be preoccupied in looking for sth which is not easily available; strive, toil: *Ilinibidi kuvumaika madukani*

854

kutokana na uhaba wa mchele, it was necessary for me to toil to get rice in the shops because of its scarcity. Prep. *vumaik.i.a* St. *vumaik.ik.a* Cs. *vumaik.ish.a* Ps. *vumaik.w.a* (cf *hangaika, sumbuka*)

vumatiti *n* (*n*) (*zool*) dwarf bittern; a kind of wading bird of the heron family with slate-grey neck and underparts. *Ardeirralus sturmii.* (cf *ngojamaliko*)

vumba *n* (*n*) fish smell (cf *shombo*)

vumbi *n* (*ma-*) dust, soot; powdery dirt: *Tifua vumbi*, stir up dust. *Vumbi la ulimwengu*, cosmic dust. *Vumbi zaha*, volcanic dust. *Vumbi la volkano*, volcanic dust.

vumbik.a (also *vuika*) *vt* 1. cover food such as fruits and then keep it somewhere in order to ripen it; bury fruit in order to ripen it: *Nilizimimbika ndizi zangu pahala penye jotojoto*, I kept my bananas in a hot place in order to ripen them. 2. make milk sour by artificial means e.g. in a vessel; curdle, coagulate; clot. Prep. *vumbik.i.a* St. *vumbik.ik.a* Cs. *vumbik.ish.a* Ps. *vumbik.w.a* (cf *pepea*)

vumbo *n* (*ma-*) lump in flour esp wheat flour formed during cooking; flour lump: *Uji wangu umejaa mavumbo kwa vile sijaukoroga vizuri*, my gruel is full of lumps of flour because I have not stirred it properly.

vumbu.a *vt* 1. discover, explore, invent: *Madaktari wanajaribu sana kuvumbua tiba ya UKIMWI*, scientists are trying hard to discovers a cure for AIDS. (cf *gundua, fichua*) 2. find, discover, devise; create sth not in existence: *Alijaribu kuvumbua mbinu mpya za kumshinda adui*, he tried to find new tactics of defeating the enemy. Prep. *vumbu.li.a* St. *vumbu.lik.a* Cs. *vumbu.lish.a* Ps. of Prep. *vumbu.liw.a* (cf *anzisha, asisi*)

vumburuk.a (also *bumburuka*) *vi* be startled and run away as in the case of birds, etc.; be frightened away.

Paa alivumburuka aliposikia mlio wa bunduki, the deer was startled and ran away when it heard a gunshot. Prep. *vumburuk.i.a* St. *vumburuk.ik.a* Cs. *vumburuk.ish.a* (cf *kimbia*)

vumi *n* (*n*) a kind of drum skinned on one side; one-sided drum.

vumili.a *vt* tolerate, endure, persevere, withstand: *Amevumilia sana matatizo ya mumewe*, she has tolerated a lot the hardships from her husband. St. *vumili.k.a* Cs. *vumili.sh.a* Ps. *vumili.w.a* Rp. *vumili.an.a* (cf *stahamili, subiri*)

vumo *n* (*ma-*) (*bot*) a large brown globular edible fruit from the tree *mvumo*, deleb palm. (*Borassus flabellifera*)

vun.a¹ *vt* 1. (of harvest) reap, harvest (*syn*) *Utavuna ulichokipanda*, you will harvest what you have grown. 2. (of evils, etc.) reap, gain Prep. *vun.i.a* St. *vun.ik.a* Cs. *vun.ish.a* Ps. *vun.w.a* (cf *chuma, barikiwa*)

vuna² *n* (*ma-*) honeycomb (cf *sega la asali*)

vunan.a¹ *vi* be ripe; be seasoned: *Ndizi hizi zimevunana*, these bananas are ripe. Prep. *vunan.i.a* St. *vunan.ik.a* Cs. *vunan.ish.a* Ps. *vunan.w.a* (cf *iva, pea, komaa*)

vunana² *n* (*n*) rice or any food which has been cooled and can be eaten but its water has not dried properly: *Mimi ninapenda kula wali vunana*, I like to eat moist rice.

vund.a *vi* 1. (of beans, peas, etc.) go stale: *Kunde zilivunda baada ya kushinda kutwa nzima bila ya kupashwa moto*, the cowpeas had gone stale after staying the whole day without being warmed. 2. stink, reek; smell to high heaven: *Nyama hii imevunda*, this meat is stinking. (*prov*) *La kuvunda halina ubani*, there is no incense for sth rotting i.e. there is no way to rectify an already spoiled thing. 3. (*fig*) get spoiled, get ruined; be in disarray.

V   vundag.a

Prep. *vund.i.a* St. *vund.ik.a*, Cs. *vund.ish.a* (cf *haribika, vurugika*)
vundag.a *vt* see *vunjaga* Prep. *vundag.i.a* St. *vundag.ik.a* Cs. *vundag.ish.a* Ps. *vundag.w.a*
vundareg.a *vt* break through the forest as animals do or get into a plantation to destroy crops by stamping, etc. Prep. *vundareg.e.a* St. *vundareg.ek.a* Cs. *vundareg.esh.a* Ps. *vundareg.w.a*
vundarere *n* (*n*) see *fundarere*
vunde *adj* rotten, decayed, spoiled.
vundemeka *n* (*ma-*) clouds that signal the arrival of rain.
vundevunde *n* (*n*) mist, haze, gaze, cloud: *Ilibidi niendeshe gari polepole kwa sababu kulikuwa na vundevunde*, I was obliged to drive the car slowly because it was misty. (cf *ukungu, utusitusi*)
vundo *n* (*ma-*) stench, stink, fetor, malodor, bad smell: (*prov*) *Vundo la kinyasi ni malazi ya paka*, a cat usu likes to stay in a dirty and stinking place i.e. things that we ignore may be useful to other people.
vundumk.a *vi* become swollen, become enlarged: Prep. *vundumk.i.a* St. *vundumk.ik.a* Cs. *vundumk.ish.a* (cf *vuvumka*)
vunga[1] *n* (*ma-*) a tuft of hair on the crown; a thick crop of hair: *Vunga lake linavutia*, his thick hair is fascinating. (cf *denge, panja, sakini*)
vung.a[2] *vt* cheat, deceive, lie: *Wewe usimwamini mtu mwenye kuvunga wengine*, don't trust a person who deceives others. Prep. *vung.i.a* St. *vung.ik.a* Cs. *vung.ish.a* Ps. *vung.w.a* Rp. *vung.an.a* (cf *babaisha, danganya, hadaa*)
vung.a[3] *vt* confuse by covering, circling, sth; mix sth up; tangle: *Tulipata shida kukiona kitabu kile kwa vile mwanafunzi mtukutu alikuwa amekivungavunga*, we had problems in locating the book because the naughty student had mixed it with other things.

vungany.a *vt* do a job haphazardly; botch, bungle. Prep. *vungany.i.a* St. *vungany.ik.a* Cs. *vungany.ish.a* Ps. *vungany.w.a*
vunganyi.a *vt* put the whole food in the mouth all at once.
vunganyiz.a *vt* mess up esp work; botch, muff, bungle, spoil: *Aliivunganyiza kazi yangu*, he bungled my work. Prep. *vunganyiz.i.a* St. *vunganyiz.ik.a* Ps. *vunganyiz.w.a* (cf *haribu*)
vungumiz.a *vt* see *vurumiza*. Prep. *vungumiz.i.a* St. *vungumiz.ik.a* Ps. *vungumiz.w.a* Rp. *vungumiz.an.a*
vungunya[1] (also *vongonya*) *n* (*ma-*) (*bot*) a kind of fruit from the tree *mvugunya* sausage tree (*Kigelia pinnata*) whose fruit is put in local beer to make it more intoxicating; sausage tree fruit.
vunguny.a[2] *vi* 1. boil over, deepen: *Mgogoro unavungunya katika chama chao*, the crisis is deepening in their party. (cf *fukuta*) 2. burn internally. Prep *vunguny.i.a* St. *vunguny.ik.a* Cs. *vunguny.ish.a* Ps. *vunguny.w.a*
vungwi *n* (*n*) (*zool*) white spotted grouped; a kind of rockod of moderately clongate body having rounded fin and large and fleshy pectoral fins. *Epineohelus caeruleopuntatus*.
vunj.a *vt* 1. break, smash, wreck: *Mtoto amekivunja kikombe*, the child has broken the cup. (cf *kata, pasua, tema*). 2. (*idms*) *Vunja baraza*, end a meeting. *Vunja heshima*, disrespect. *Vunja jungu*, celebrate calendar years of various types. *Vunja kikao*, close a session. *Vunja mbavu*, die laughing. *Vunja mkataba*, break a contract. *Vunja moyo*, despond, dishearten; break one's heart. *Vunja mwiko*, break the taboo. *Vunja nyumba*, a) break a marriage. b) pull down a house. *Vunja pesa*, give change for large notes. *Vunja safari*, cancel a trip. *Vunja sheria*, break a law. *Vunja ungo*, have first menses; enter a virgin. *Vunja rekodi*, break a record. *Vunja ukimya*, break silence and begin to speak out. Prep. *vunj.i.a* St. *vunj.ik.a*, Cs. *vunj.ish.a* Ps. *vunj.w.a* Rp. *vunj.an.a*

vunjajungu *n* (*n*) see *kivunjajungu*
vunjang.a (also *vundaga*) *vt* mess sth such as work etc.; botch, bungle, muddle: *Waliivunjanga kazi yetu*, they bungled our work. Prep. *vunjang.i.a* St. *vunjang.ik.a* Cs. *vunjang.ish.a* Ps. *vunjang.w.a* (cf *haribu, fuja*)
-vunjifu *adj* destructive, ruinous, malicious.
vunjik.a *vi* 1. be broken: *Kikombe kimevunjika*, the cup is broken 2. (*idm*) *Vunjika moyo*, lose hope; be despondent. Prep. *vunjik.i.a* St. *vunjik.ik.a* Cs. *vunjik.ish.a*
vunju *n* (*ma-*) colloid; a solid, liquid or gaseous substance made up of very small, insoluble non-diffusible particles.
vuno *n* (*ma-*) harvest, yield, produce, output. (cf *pato, chumo*)
vunzu *n* (*ma-*) a kind of dust found from the disturbed water. (cf *vinzu*)
vuo[1] *n* (*n*) steeped leaves and roots whose vapour is inhaled to relieve a patient.
vuo[2] *n* (*ma-*) 1. the total amount of fish caught on a particular day. 2. the place where a person fishes
vura *n* (*n*) a kind of devil.
vurug.a *vt* 1. stir up, stir round, commix. (cf *koroga*) 2. (*fig*) sabotage, ruin, wreck, scuttle, distrupt, spoil: *Wapinzani walitaka kuuvuruga uchaguzi mkuu*, the opposition wanted to sabotage the general election. Prep. *vurug.i.a* St. *vurug.ik.a*, Cs. *vurug.ish.a*, Ps. *vurug.w.a* (cf *tibua, haribu*)
vurugik.a *vi* be in disarray, be chaotic, be mixed up: *Mipango yake imevurugika*, his plans are in disarray. Prep. *vurugik.i.a* St. *vurugik.ik.a* Ps. *vuruguk.iw.a* Rp. *vurugik.an.a* (cf *haribika, chafuka, paraganyika*)
vurugu *n* (*n*) chaos, pandemonium, disorder: *Usilete vurugu hapa*, don't cause chaos here. (cf *zogo, fujo, ghasia*)
vuruju.a *vt* (of food, etc.) soften, bray. Prep. *vuruju.li.a* St. *vuruju.lik.a* Cs. *vuruju.lish.a* Ps. of Prep. *vuruju.liw.a* (cf *lainisha, pondaponda*)
vurumai *n* (*n*) pandemonium, chaos, disorder. (cf *vurugu, fujo*)
vurumish.a *vt* see *vurumiza*
vurumiz.a (also *vurumisha*) *vt* throw sth forcefully such as a stone, stick, etc; hurl: *Waandamanaji walikuwa wakivurumisha mawe kwa askari wa polisi*, the demonstrators were hurling stones at the police. Prep. *vurumiz.i.a* St. *vurumiz.ik.a* Cs. *vurumiz.ish.a* Ps. *vurumiz.w.a* Rp. *vurumiz.an.a* (cf *tupa*)
vurund.a *vt* spoil, wreck: *Walijaribu kuivurunda mipango yetu bila ya mafanikio*, they tried unsuccessfully to wreck our plans, Prep. *vurund.i.a* St. *vurund.ik.a* Cs. *vurund.ish.a* Ps. *vurund.w.a* (cf *horonga, vunjuga*)
vush.a *vt* 1. cause sby to cross a river, lake, road, etc. 2. extricate sby from hardships, etc. Prep *vush.i.a* St. Ps. *vush.w.a* Rp. *vush.an.a*
vut.a[1] *vt* 1. pull, drag, draw. (cf *burura, kokota*) 2. attract, lure, influence. (at, with, etc.) Prep. *vut.i.a* St. *vut.ik.a* Cs. *vut.ish.a* Ps. *vut.w.a* Ps. of Prep. *vut.iw.a* be impressed by, be fascinated by e.g. *Nilivutiwa na kazi yake nzuri*, I was impressed by his good work. Rp. *vut.an.a* (cf *shawishi*)
vut.a[2] *vt* (*idms*) *Vuta sigara*, smoke a cigarette. *Vuta kamasi*, sniffle. *Vuta pumzi*, breathe in. *Vuta maji*, bail out water. *Vuta wakati*, allow yourself to think. *Vuta subira*, endure. Prep. *vut.i.a* St. *vut.ik.a* Cs. *vut.ish.a* Ps. *vut.w.a*
vuti.a *vi* be impressive, be attractive: *Msichana yule anavutia*, that girl is impressive. St. *vuti.k.a* Ps. *vuti.w.a* (cf *pendeza*)
vutian.a *vi* be competing among themselves, be interesting among themselves. (cf *gombania, wiliana*)

vuu *adv* suddenly, abruptly, hurriedly: *Mambo yale yalitokea vuu*, those incidents took place suddenly. (cf *ghafla, fajaa*)

vuu.a *vt* 1. take out sth sunk in the water. 2. take out sth from the cooking pot still on fire.

vuvi *n* (*n*) (*zool*) a kind of grey venomous spitting snake.

vuvi.a (*also vivia*) *vt* blow sth with the mouth or bellows; fan sth: *Mpishi aliuvuvia moto ili uwake vizuri*, the cook fanned the fire in order to make it burn well. Prep. **vuvi.li.a** St. **vuvi.lik.a** Cs. **vuvi.lish.a** Ps. of Prep. **vuvi.liw.a** Rp. **vuvi.an.a** (cf *vukuta*)

vuvumk.a *vi* be swollen, be enlarged, magnified. Prep. **vuvumk.i.a** (cf *vundumka*)

vuvumu.a *vt* magnify, exaggerate: *Vuvumua habari*, exaggerate news. Prep. **vuvumu.li.a** St. **vuvumu.k.a**, Cs. **vuvumu.sh.a** Ps. of Prep. **vuvumu.liw.a**

vuvuwa.a *vi* 1. (of liquids), be lukewarm; be slightly warmed: *Kahawa ilipovuvuwaa, nikainywa*, when the coffee was lukewarm, I drank it. (cf *chemka*) 2. be silent as a person who has no thoughts or opinion on the subject under discussion: *Alivuvuwaa wakati wote wa mazungumzo ingawa sisi tulimhimiza aseme japo kidogo*, he kept silent throughout the conversation although we urged her to talk a little bit. Prep. **vuvuwa.li.a** St. **vuvuwa.lik.a** Cs. **vuvuwa.lish.a** Ps. **vuvuwa.w.a** (cf *totovaa, nyamaa, sukutu*)

vuzi (*also uwuzi*) *n* (*ma-*) hair that is in the genital area.

vya *prep* (used for ki-vi class pl nouns) of, for: *Vitabu vya shule*, school books.

vya.a *vi* see *zaa*. Prep. **vya.li.a** St. **vya.lik.a** Cs. **vya.lish.a** and **vya.z.a** Ps. **vya.w.a** Rp. **vya.an.a**

vyake *adj pron* form of -*ake*, his, her, hers, used for ki-vi class pl nouns: *Vitu vyake*, his things, her things.

vyako *adj, pron* form of *ako*, your, yours (singular) used for ki-vi class pl nouns: *Vikombe vyako*, your cups.

vyangu *adj, pron* form of *angu*, my, mine, used for ki-vi class pl nouns: *Vijiko vyangu*, my spoons.

vyao *adj, pron* of *ao* their, theirs used for Ki-Vi class pl nouns: *Viatu vyao*, their shoes.

vyaus.a *vt* hybridize, crossbreed; produce or cause to produce hybrids. Prep. **vyaus.i.a** St. **vyaus.ik.a** Cs. **vyaus.ish.a** Ps. of Prep. **vyaus.iw.a**

vyema (*also vema*) *adv* 1. well, nicely, properly, rightly: *Umefanya vyema kuja hapa leo*, you have done the right thing to come here today. (cf *vizuri, barabara*) 2. it is used as a rejoinder of assent; fine, okay.

vyenu *adj, pron* form of *enu*, your, yours (pl) used for ki-vi class pl nouns : *Viti vyenu*, your chairs.

vyero *n* (*n*) wickerwork, fish-trap; a kind of fish trap with upright sticks fastened together, used to prevent fish from escaping when the tide falls. (cf *tando, uzio*)

vyetu *adj, pron* form of *etu*, our, ours (pl) used for ki-vi pl nouns: *Vitabu vyetu*, our books. *Vyetu ni vyenu*, ours is yours.

vyog.a *vt* tread upon; trample Prep. **vyog.e.a** St. **vyog.ek.a** Cs. **vyog.esh.a** Ps. **vyog.w.a** Rp. **vyog.an.a** (cf *vuga, kanyaga*)

vyote *adj, pron* form of -*ote*, all, used for ki-vi pl nouns: *Vitu vyote*, all things; everything.

vyovyote[1] *adv* any means; by whatever means, at any rate: *Kwa vyovyote*, by any means e.g. *Kwa vyovyote vile, Shangazi yangu atakuja leo*, at any rate, my aunt will come today.

vyovyote[2] *adj, pron* form of *ote*, 'any' used for ki-vi pl nouns: *Visu vyovyote*, any knives.

W

W, w/w/ 1. represents the twenty-second letter of the Swahili alphabet. 2. represents the sound of **W** or **w** and is classified as a semi-vowel.

wa¹ *prep* (used for wa-,mi- and u- classes singular nouns) for, of: *Mtoto wa jirani yangu*, my neighbour's child. *Mtego wa samaki*, fish trap.

-wa² *vt cop* 1. be, become, occur, happen: *Mkulima yule amekuwa mzee*, that farmer has become old. 2. functions as a copular verb agreeing with the plural of the wa- class. Prep. ***w.i.a*** and ***w.e.a***

wa.a¹ *vi* 1. glitter, blaze, shimmer. (cf *ng'aa*) 2. spread, pervade, diffuse: *Habari imewaa kwamba Fatuma ameposwa*, news has spread that Fatuma is engaged. St. ***wa.k.a*** Cs. ***wa.sh.a*** (cf *zagaa, enea*)

waa² *n* (*ma-*) spot, blotch, mark. (cf *paku, bato*)

waa³ *adv* (*colloq*) exactly, alright. (cf *barabara*)

waa⁴ *interj* an expletive used to describe the sound of a spilling liquid.

waadhi (also *mawaidha*) *n* (*n*) sermon, advice, counsel. (cf *mawaidha, wasaha, ushauri*) (Ar)

waadhi *n* (*n*) see *uwudi*

waadi *n* (*n*) promise, pledge, word of honour. (cf *ahadi, miadi*)

waaidha *n* (*n*) see *aidha¹*

waama (also *waima*) *conj* indeed; as a matter of fact; truly, infact; actually: *Waama, tukio lile lilinifurahisha sana*, indeed, that incident pleased me very much. (cf *hakika*)

waba *n* (*n*) (*med*) cholera (cf *kipindupindu*)

wabaadu *n* (*n*) an expletive used usu in letter writing to convey meanings such as "after this" "next": *Salamu nyingi kutoka kwangu; wabaadu napenda kukuarifu kuwa sisi sote ni wazima, compliments from me and next, I wish* to inform you that we are all fine (Ar)

wach.a *vt* see *acha*

wadhifa *n* (*n*) post, position, rank, status, standing: *Amepata wadhifa mkubwa serikalini*, he has got a big post in the government. (cf *madaraka, cheo*) (Ar)

wadhiha¹ *adv* openly, clearly, plainly, overtly: *Aliwatukana majirani zake wadhiha*, he insulted his neighbours openly. (cf *dhahiri, waziwazi*)

wadhiha² *n* (*u*) period, time, era. (cf *kipindi, muda*)

wadi¹ (also *wodi*) *n* (*n*) a large room in a hospital usu for people undergoing medical treatment; ward. (Eng)

wadi² *n* (*n*) see *kata²*

wadi³ (*arch*) son of (cf *bin*)

wadi⁴ *n* (*n*) (*arch*) watercourse; bed of a torrent.

wadi.a *vi* arrive finally; be in good time for: *Wakati wa kuondoka sasa umewadia*, the time to depart has finally come. Prep. ***wadi.li.a*** St. ***wadi.k.a*** Cs. ***wadi.sh.a*** Ps. ***wadi.w.a*** (Ar)

wadinasi *n* (*u*) a child of a prominent family.

wafik.i (also *afiki*) *vt, vi* 1. agree with; accord, concur: *Sisi tunawafiki na wazo lako*, we agree with your suggestion. (cf *kubali*) 2. support, agree with: *Je, wewe unauwafiki msimamo wake?* Do you support his stand? 3. suit, match: *Bei ya shati hili litakuwafiki*, the price of this shirt will suit you. Prep. ***wafik.i.a*** St. ***wafik.ik.a*** Ps. ***wafik.iw.a*** Rp. ***wafik.i.an.a*** (cf *faa, pendeza*)

wafikian.a *vt* reconcile, compromise: *Hawajawafikiana bado katika suala lenyewe*, they have not compromised on the issue. Prep. ***wafikian.i.a*** St. ***wafikian.ik.a*** Cs. ***wafikian.ish.a***

wage (also *wambe*) *n* (*u*) (*bot*) nettle, cowhage, cowage; a stinging rash which comes from plants, which cause skin irritation on contact. (cf *upupu*)

W

wagivu *n* (*u*) charm, allure, attraction, applied: *Nguo nzuri alizozivaa zilimletea wagivu zaidi*, the smart clothes she wore gave her extra attraction. (cf *haiba*)

wahaka *n* (*u*) worry, anxiety, uneasiness, fretfulnes: *Usiwe na wahaka*, don't worry. (cf *wasiwasi, wahasha, dukuduku*)

wahedi[1] *adj*, (*n*) one: *Wahedi arobaini*, forty one. (Ar)

wahedi[2] *interj* an expletive used to stress the quality possessed by someone esp if it is a bad one.

wahenga *n* (*u*) ancestors, forefathers.

wah.i *vt* 1. be on time; happen to be; be in time; prompt to act: *Aliwahi kuipanda meli kabla haijaondoka*, she was able to board the ship before it left. (cf *mudu, diriki*) 2. manage to do sth before it goes amiss. (*prov*) *Udongo uwahi ungali maji* i.e. you must rush to save sth before it is too late. Prep. ***wah.i.a*** St. ***wah.ik.a*** Cs. ***wah.ish.a*** Ps. ***wah.iw.a*** Rp. ***wah.i.an.a*** (Ar)

Wahidi *n* (*n*) one of the names of God that describes his uniqueness. (Ar)

wahshi *adj* useless, valueless, worthless: good-for-nothing: *Kazi wahshi*, useless work. *Mtu yule ni wahshi*, that person is useless.

wahyi *n* (*u*) special inspiration given by God to his prophets. (Ar)

waidha *conj* see *aidha*

waidh.i *vt* deliver a speech on religious matters; homilize. Prep. ***waidh.i.a*** St. ***waidh.ik.a*** Cs. ***waidh.ish.a*** Ps. ***waidh.iw.a*** Rp. ***waidh.i.an.a*** (cf *hotubu, hubiri*) (Ar)

wainish.a *vt* rationalize: *Wainisha asili*, rationalize the denominator. Prep. ***wainish.i.a*** St. ***wainish.ik.a*** Ps. ***wainish.w.a***

wajibik.a *vt, vi* 1. be obliged: *Niliwajibika kumsaidia mdogo wangu*, I was obliged to help my younger brother. 2. be accountable, be answerable, be responsible: *Kila kiongozi anawajibika kwa watu wake*, every leader is accountable to his people. Prep. ***wajibik.i.a*** St. ***wajibik.ik.a*** Cs. ***wajibik.ish.a*** Ps. ***wajibik.iw.a***

wajibish.a *vt* 1. cause sby to be accountable: *Meneja aliwajibisha wafanyakazi wake wazembe watatu*, the manager held his three employees responsible 2. cause sth to be necessary. Prep. ***wajibish.i.a*** St. ***wajibish.ik.a*** Ps. ***wajibish.w.a*** Rp. ***wajibish.an.a***

wajibu *n* (*u*) obligation, necessity: *Ana wajibu wa kulilipa deni lake*, he has an obligation to pay his debt. (cf *jukumu, dhamana*) (Ar)

wajih.i[1] *vt* meet, encounter, come across. Prep. ***wajih.i.a*** Cs. ***wajih.ish.a*** Ps. ***wajih.iw.a*** Rp. ***wajih.i.an.a*** (Ar)

wajihi[2] face, feature: *Ana wajihi mzuri*, he has a good face. (*prov*) *Kata pua uunge wajihi*, a bad thing may serve a useful purpose later. (cf *uso*)

wajihian.a *vt, vi* meet sby/sth face to face.

wak.a *vi* 1. blaze; burn brightly: *Moto unawaka*, the fire is burning. 2. (of machines) start: *Gari limewaka*, the car has started. Prep. ***wak.i.a*** St. ***wak.ik.a*** Cs. ***wa.sh.a***

waki.a *vi* (of machines, etc.) be burnt, be destroyed. Prep. ***wak.i.a*** St. ***wak.ik.a*** Cs. ***wa.sh.a*** (cf *teketea, ungua*)

wakaa (*pl nyakaa*) *n* (*u*) time, period, occasion. (cf *wakati*)

wakala *n* (*ma-*) 1. agent, representative: *Wakala wa safari*, travel agent.(cf *mwakilishi*) 2. agency, representation.

wakatabahu *n* (*u*) (in letter writing) yours. (Ar)

wakati (*pl nyakati*) *n* (*u*) time, period: *Hana wakati*, he does not have the time. (cf *kipindi, majira*)

wake *adj, pron* form of -ake, "his", "her," used for *m-* and *wa-* classes pl nouns.

860

wakfu *n* (*u*) sth that has been set aside for religious purposes, consecrated and devoted to holy use: *Pesa za wakfu*, money set apart for religious purposes. (Ar)

wakia *n* (*u*) an ounce in weight. (Ar)

wakif.u[1] (also *akifu*) *vt* satisfy, gratify, please. Prep. *wakif.i.a* St. *wakif.ik.a* Cs. *wakif.ish.a* (cf *kifu, tosheleza, ridhisha*) (Ar)

wakifu[2] *n* (*u*) cost, price, value. (cf *gharama, thamani*) (Ar)

wakili *n* (*ma-*) 1. lawyer, attorney, barrister: *Wakili mkuu*, attorney general. *Wakili wa serikali*, state attorney. *Wakili wa kujitegemea* independent lawyer. (cf *mwanasheria*) 2. representative, agent, proxy: *Wakili yule anashughulikia masuala ya kampuni ya tumbaku*, that agent takes care of the interests of the tobacco company. (cf *mwakilishi*) (Ar)

wakilish.a[1] *vt* 1. represent, symbolize; stand for: *Waziri yule alimwakilisha rais kwenye sherehe za uhuru wa nchi jirani*, that minister represented the president in the independence celebrations of the neighbouring country 2. entrust to as an agent; appoint sby as a agent: *Anaposafiri kwenda nje huniwakilisha nyumba yake*, when he travels abroad, he entrusts me his house. Prep. *wakilish.i.a* St. *wakilish.ik.a* Ps. *wakilish.w.a* Rp. *wakilish.an.a* (Ar)

wakilish.a[2] *vt* illustrate, represent, exhibit, symbolize: *Sielewi michoro hii inawakilisha kitu gani*, I don't understand what these drawings represent for. Prep. *wakilish.i.a* St. Ps. *wakilish.w.a* Rp.

wako *adj, pron* form of -ako, your, yours, used for **n, mi-** and **wa-** classes, singular and pl nouns: *Mbwa wako*, your dog. *Wako ni mdogo*, mine is a small one.

wala *conj* an expletive used to imply negation of both parts of a statement; neither, nor: *Havuti sigara wala hanywi pombe*, he neither smokes cigarettes nor drinks beer. *Sipendi chai wala kahawa*, I like neither tea nor coffee. (Ar)

waladi (pl *auladi*) *n* (*n*) boy, youth, sprig. (cf *mvulana*) (Ar)

walakini[1] *n* (*u*) defect, weakness: *Yeye ni mtu mzuri ingawa vilevile ana walakini zake*, he is a good person although he has his weaknesses. (cf *ila, dosari, kasoro*)

walakini[2] (also *lakini*) *conj* but, nevertheless, however.

walau (also *alau*) *conj* at least, even: *Kama huwezi kumpa malazi nyumbani kwako, basi mpe walau pesa kidogo*, if you cannot give him accommodation at your house, at least give him some money. (cf *angalau, japo*)

wale *adj, pron* form of -le 'that', used for class pl nouns: *Watu wale*, those people.

wali (pl *nyali*) *n* (*u*) cooked rice. (cf *ubwabwa, machaza*)

wali.a[1] *vt* enthrone, crown, royalize; install as a ruler, set on the throne. Prep. *wali.li.a* St. *wali.k.a* Cs. *wali.sh.a* and *wali.z.a* Ps. *wali.w.a*. (cf *tawaza*)

wali.a[2] *vt* call for a special assignment; call for a special purpose: *Rafiki yangu aliniwalia kwenye karamu yake*, my friend invited me to his party. Prep *wali.li.a* St *wali.k.a* Cs *wali.sh.a* and *wali.z.a* Ps *wali.w.a*

walii (*ma-*) 1. dervish, pietist, a devout person: *Walii humwogopa Mungu*, a dervish fears God (cf *mtawa, sufii*) 2. guardian, trustee, caretaker: *Walii wa mtoto huyu mdogo ni mimi*, the guardian of this small child is me. (cf *mlezi*) (Ar)

walio[1] (*pl nyalio*) *n* (*u*) usu used in the pl form) bits of sticks put crosswise underneath; bits of sticks put at the bottom of a cooking pot to prevent the contents from burning. (cf *unyalio*)

walio² (*pl nyalio*) *n* (*u*) a kind of wattle fence, used for trapping fish.

Wallahi *interj* a common oath among Muslims intended to strengthen the view that what is said by a speaker is genuine; Swear to God; in God's name. (Ar)

wam.a *vt* (*usu wamia*) stretch oneself on the ground or before a fire; bend over a fire. Prep. *wam.i.a* St. *wam.ik.a* Cs. *wam.ish.a*

wamb.a¹ *vt* stretch over, overlay, overspread. (*prov*) *Mwamba ngoma huvutia kwake*, he who makes the drum pulls to his side i.e. every person will favour his own side. Prep. *wamb.i.a* St. *wamb.ik.a* Cs. *wamb. ish.a* Ps. *wamb.w.a* Rp. *wamb.an.a* (cf *tandaza*)

wamb.a² *vi* go bankrupt; become insolvent; become financially ruined, be wiped out: *Mfanyabiashara aliwamba baada ya kampuni yake kutaifishwa*, the businessman went bankrupt after his company was nationalized. Prep. *wamb.i.a* St. *wamb.ik.a* Cs. *wamb.ish.a* Ps. *wamb.w.a* (cf *filisika, fusika*)

wamb.a³ *vi* be widespread, spread, diffuse: *Ukungu umewamba*, the mist has spread. Prep. *wamb.i.a* St. *wamb. ik.a* Cs. *wamb.ish.a* Ps. *wamb.w.a* (cf *enea, zagaa*)

wamb.a⁴ *n* (*ma-*) (*bot*) the frond of a deleb palm/palmyra palm.

wambe *n* (*u*) see *wage*

wan.a¹ *vt* (*arch*) fight, Prep. *wan.i.a*, St. *wan.ik.a* Cs. *wan.ish.a* Ps. *wan.w.a* (cf *pigana*)

wan.a² *verb form* they have: *Wana mali nyingi*, they have a lot of wealth.

wand.a¹ *vi* get fat, become fat, become stout. Prep. *wand.i.a* St. *wand.ik.a* Cs. *wand.ish.a* (cf *nawiri, nenepa, tononoka*)

wanda² (*pl nyanda*) *n* (*u*) a finger's breadth of about one inch.

wand.a³ *vt* cut small branches of a fallen tree. Prep. *wand.i.a* St. *wandiik.a* Cs. *wand.ish.a* Ps. *wand.w.a*

wando (also *tando*) *n* (*u*) wickerwork, fishtrap; a kind of fishtrap (cf *tando, uzio*)

wang.a¹ *vi* pain, hurt, pinch: *Kichwa kinamwanga*, his head is paining him. Prep. *wang.i.a* St. *wang.ik.a* Cs. *wang.ish.a* Ps. *wang.w.a* cf *uma*

wang.a² (also *anga*) *vt* find the total of sth; count, calculate, reckon up: *Waliwawanga abiria wote waliosalimika katika ajali ya ndege*, they counted all the passengers who survived in the plane crash. Prep. *wang.i.a* St. *wang.ik.a* Cs. *wang. ish.a* Ps. *wang.w.a* Rp. *wang.an.a* (cf *hesabu*)

wang.a³ *vt* practise witchcraft at night. Prep. *wang.i.a* St. *wang.ik.a* Cs. *wang.ish.a*

wanga⁴ *n* (*u*) see *uwanga*

wango *n* (*ma-*) computation, counting, enumeration. (cf *idadi*)

wangu *adj, pron* form of *-angu*, "my" "mine" used for *wa-* class pl nouns, *wa-, mi-* and *u-* classes singular nouns.

wanguwangu *adv* hurriedly, quickly, speedily: *Waliondoka hapa wanguwangu ili wayawahi mazishi*, they left here hurriedly so that they could be in time for the funeral. (cf *upesiupesi, yosayosa*)

wangwa (*pl nyangwa*) *n* (*u*) 1. lagoon, shoal; an area of shallow salt water separated from the sea by sand dunes and usu surrounded by mangrove trees. 2. sandy wilderness, bare ground. (cf *jangwa, ongwa*)

wani.a *vt* contest, compete, fight: *Timu yetu ilikuwa inawania ubingwa wa soka nchini* our, the team was contesting for soccer championship at home. (cf *gombania, shindania*)

wanja *n* (*u*) kohl, mascara, antimony; a black cosmetic preparation, used by women for colouring or darkening eyebrows, eyelashes, etc. (*prov*) *Wanja wa manga si dawa ya chongo*, the antimony you put on the eyes is not a remedy i.e. a thing that is heading for destruction cannot be rescued.

wano[1] *n* (*ma-*) the shaft of a spear or an arrow or a harpoon. (cf *mpini*)

wano[2] *n* (*ma-*) a stick used along with three others for arresting a thief. (cf *kibano*)

wanzuki *n* (*u*) honey beer.

wao *adj, pron* form of *-ao*, "they" "them" used for *wa-* class pl nouns : *Watoto wao*, their children. *Wao ni wengi*, they are many.

wapi *adv, pron* It is an interrogative word for place meaning "where": *Wapi unakwenda?* Where are you going? It also means "never", "nothing" e.g. *Alijaribu sana lakini wapi!* he tried hard but nothing had come out. Sometimes, the word *wapi* is shortened to *-api* and *pi* and then suffixed to verbs for questioning e.g. *Amekwendapi?*, where has he gone?

wapili.a *vi* (of scent), smell strongly; be heavily scented; aromatize: *Marashi yanawapilia*, the liquid perfume is smelling strongly. (cf *nukia*)

wap.o *vt cop* there are, they are here, they are there: *Wakaguzi wapo*, the inspectors are there.

waragi (also *wargi*) *n* (*u*) a type of distilled alcohol.

waraka[1] (pl *nyaraka*) *n* (*u*) 1. letter, epistle, missive (cf *barua*) 2. document, certificate, record 3. invoice, bill of sale. (cf *ankra*) (Ar)

waraka[2] (pl *nyaraka*) *n* (*u*) a small piece of paper, used for rolling tobacco to make cigarettes; cigarrette paper. (cf *chupri*) (Ar)

warakatamvu *n* (*u*) spreadsheet; a sheet of paper used for computation and analysis of data of a particular problem.

waranti *n* (*u*) 1. warrant; a written authority or sanction by a court of law to do sth: *Alipelekewa waranti ya kukamatwa*, he was issued a warrant of arrest. 2. warrant; a document that entitles you to get special services without paying cash money e.g. in the case of travelling. (Eng)

wardi *n* (*ma-*) see *warigi*

wari *n* (*u*) yard; a measure equal to two cubits. (cf *dhiraa, mikono*)

waria *n* (*ma-*) a skilled workman; artisan.

waridi (also *la waridi, lawaridi, wardi*) *n* (*ma-*) (*bot*) rose; a kind of fragrant flower of red, pink, white, yellow, etc. having many stamens: *Ua la waridi*, rose flower. *Rangi ya waridi*, pink.

warsha *n* (*u*) workshop, seminar, discussion group. *Warsha ya kitaifa*, national workshop. *Warsha ya waandishi*, writers' workshop. (Ar)

wasa[1] *n* (*u*) a small stick or lath which is put in to reduce spaces between larger ones in the construction of a well or roof of a house. (Ar)

was.a[2] (also *asa*) *vt* 1. forbid, prohibit, inhibit, taboo (cf *kataza*) 2. prevent, stop: *Alimwasa mwanawe kunyonya alipoanza kuwa mkubwa*, she stopped her baby suckling when she started to grow bigger. Prep. **was.i.a** St. **was.ik.a** Cs. **was.ish.a** Ps. **was.w.a** Rp. **was.an.a** (cf *zuia*) (Ar)

wasa[3] *n* (*ma-*) drizzle, sprinkle, light rain: *Wasa la mvua*, light rain.

wasaa *n* (*u*) free time, good time, chance: *Sina wasaa wa kuandika vitabu vingi*, I don't have free time to write many books. (cf *nafasi, muda*) (Ar)

wasalaam *adv* see *wasalaamu*

wasalaamu (also *wasalaam*) *adv* a style employed in letter writing to mark the ending. The word *wasalaam* is used to mean "with best wishes." (Ar)

wash.a[1] *vt* ignite, kindle, light, switch: *Washa taa*, switch on the lights. Prep.

wash.i.a St. **wash.ik.a** Ps. **wash.w.a** Rp. **wash.an.a**

wash.a² vt, vi itch, prickle, tickle: *Mwili unaniwasha*, my body is itching. *Kidonda kinaniwasha*, the wound itches me. *Majani haya yanawasha sana*, these leaves sting badly. Prep. **wash.i.a** St. **wash.ik.a** Ps. **wash.w.a** (cf *choma, wawa*)

wasia (also **usia**) n (u) 1 parting advice of a dying person, etc.; earnest wish of a dying person, etc.; religious exhortation involving a will: *Andika wasia*, write a will. *Mzee aliacha wasia kabla hajafa*, the old man left a will before he died. (cf *maagizo*) 2. any advice intended for good guidance on life.

wasifu¹ n (u) biography, memoirs; description about a person's life: *Wasifu wa Kwame Nkurumah*, the biography of Kwame Nkurumah. (Ar)

wasifu² n (u) feature, shape, figure. (cf *haiba*)

wasil.i vi arrive, reach, come: *Mgeni wangu alichelewa kuwasili*, my guest arrived late. Prep. **wasil.i.a** St. **wasil.ik.a** Cs. **wasil.ish.a** Ps of Prep. **wasil.iw.a** Rp. **wasil.i.an.a** (cf *fika*) (Ar)

wasilian.a vt, vi communicate, give one to understand: *Umewasiliana na ndugu yako tangu alipoondoka hapa?* Have you communicated with your brother since he left here?

wasilish.a vt submit, deliver, send: *Mwanafunzi aliiwasilisha tasnifu yake kwa mhadhiri wake*, the student submitted his thesis to his lecturer. Prep. **wasilish.i.a** St. **wasilish.ik.a** Ps. **wasilish.w.a** Rp. **wasilish.an.a**

wasiojiweza n (wa) the disabled; the handicapped people.

wasionacho n (wa-) the have-nots: *Wale wasionacho hupata shida nyingi duniani*, the have-nots get many problems in this world.

wasiwasi n (u) 1. worry, anxiety, uneasiness: *Ana wasiwasi mkubwa juu ya mwanawe aliyepotea*, she is very worried about her son who is missing. (cf *hatihati, wahaka, dukuduku*) 2. a kind of mental sickness. (Ar)

wasta n (u) 1. arbitrator, go-between, middleman: *Wasta alizipatanisha pande mbili*, the intermediary reconciled the two sides. (cf *mpatanishi*.) 2. auctioneer, vendue, broker. (Ar)

wasta² n (u) influence: *Bila ya wasta, huwezi kupata kazi nzuri*, without influence, you can't get a good job. (cf *ushawishi*) (Ar)

wastani¹ n (u) average, mean: *Wastani wa kihesabu*, arithmetic mean. *Wastani wa 6, 8 na10 ni 8*, the average of 6, 8 and 10 is 8. (Ar)

wastani² adj average, moderate, normal: *Wanafunzi wenye akili za wastani walifuzu kwenye mtihani*, the students of average intelligence passed the examination. (Ar)

watani n (u) country, nation, kingdom: *Kila watani ina bendera yake* every country has its flag. (cf *nchi, dola*) (Ar)

wavu (pl *nyavu*) n (u) net, mesh; a trap for fish, etc: *Huu ni wavu wa kuvulia samaki*, this is a net for fishing. (cf *neti, kimia, jarife*)

wavuti (esp in Kenya) n (u) see *tovuti*

waw.a vt, vi (of body, etc) itch, sting, prickle: *Mwili wake unawawa wakati wote*, his body itches all the time. Prep. **waw.i.a** St. **waw.ik.a** Cs. **waw.ish.a**

wawe n (u) a kind of Swahili song used during the celebrations of the burning of heaps of plantation rubbish to prepare for the cultivation of a farm.

waya¹ (pl *nyaya*) n (u) wire: *Waya wa simu*, telephone wire. *Waya wa umeme*, electric wire; live wire. (Eng)

waya² n (u) an earthenware baking dish.

wayaway.a vi be confused, be restless, be uneasy, be perplexed: *Alikuwa anawayawaya aliposikia kwamba*

mwanawe amegongwa na gari, she was restless when she heard that her son has been knocked down by a car. Prep. **wayaway.i.a** St. **wayaway.ik.a** Cs. **wayaway.ish.a** (cf *changanyikiwa, gaagaa*)
wayo[1] (also *uwayo*) (pl *nyayo*) n (u) 1. the sole of a foot. 2. footprint, footstep, footmark; tract of a foot. (*idm*) *Kununua wayo ng'ombe*, to buy sth that you have not seen before.
wayo[2] (also *galagala*) n (u) (*zool*) spiny turbot, flounder; a kind of flat fish (families *Psettodidae* and *Bothidae*) which is usu caught for food and which is found in all tropical and temperate seas. (cf *gaogao*)
wayowayo n (u) anxiety, worry, uneasiness: *Bibi aliingiwa na wayowayo aliposikia kwamba mumewe ametiwa korokoroni*, the wife was in a state of uneasiness when she heard that her husband has been detained. (cf *wasiwasi, hangaiko*)
waz.a vt think, imagine, contemplate, ponder. Prep. **waz.i.a** St. **waz.ik.a** Cs. **waz.ish.a** Ps. **waz.w.a** Rp. **waz. an.a** (cf *zingatia, fikiri, dhani*)
wazi[1] (also *waziwazi*) adv clearly, openly, plainly: *Tukio hili limezidi kuonyesha wazi kwamba yeye ni mwongo*, this incident has further shown that he is a liar. (cf *dhahiri, bayana*)
wazi[2] adj clear, vivid, plain: *Maamrisho yake yako wazi kabisa*, his instructions are very clear. (cf *bayana*)
wazi[3] adj (of a door, etc.) open, unclosed, unshut, ajar: *Mlango uko wazi*, the door is open.
wazimu n (u) lunacy, insanity, madness: *Tia wazimu*, make mad. *Fanya wazimu*, become mad. *Ingiliwa na wazimu go* mad. (cf *wehu, kichaa, uafkani*)
waziri n (*ma*-) government minister, secretary of state: *Waziri mkuu*, prime minister. *Waziri mkuu wa muda*, caretaker prime minister. *Waziri mwandamizi*, senior minister. *Waziri*

msaidizi, assistant minister. *Waziri bila wizara maalum*, minister without portfolio. (Ar)
waziwazi adv see *wazi*[1]
wazo n (*ma*-) idea, opinion, view. (cf *fikira*)
wazu.a vt, vi used in the expression: *Kuwaza na kuwazua*, consider from all angles e.g. *Aliwazua juu ya suala lile na hatimaye akapata ufumbuzi*, he considered the matter from all angles, and eventually, he found the solution.
wazumi n (u) (*drm*) chorus; that part of a drama, song, etc. performed by a group.
wee *interj* an exclamation for calling someone usu scornfully or for warning him: *Wee! Ukifanya kelele nitakuchapa* You there! if you make noise, I will beat you.
wehu n (u) madness, lunacy, insanity. (cf *wazimu*)
wehu.a (also *ehua*) vt madden someone, make sby mad; craze: *Watoto walikuwa wakimwehua mzee mmoja kwa kumchokoza*, the children were maddening an old person by teasing him. Prep. **wehu.li.u** St. **wehu.k.a** Co. **wehu.sh.a** Ps. of Prep. **wehu.liw.a** Rp. **wehu.an.a**
wek.a vt 1. put, place, set, lay: *Weka chakula mezani*, put the food on the table. (cf *ika, tua*) 2. store, accumulate: *Mfanyabiashara ameweka bidhaa nyingi ghalani*, the businessman has stored a lot of goods in the warehouse. cf *limbikiza* 3. (*idms*) *Weka ahadi*, keep promise. *Weka akiba*, save up. *Weka amana*, put in trust; mortgage. *Weka deko*, revenge. *Weka desturi*, establish a custom. *Weka dhamana*, find bail. *Weka kifua*, make oneself a brave person. *Weka sheria*, enact a law. *Weka wakfu*, consecrate. *Weka uporo*, do things in halves; do things in piecemeals. *Weka nia*, make an intention; intend, determine. *Weka*

msingi, lay a foundation. *Weka chini ya ulinzi*, arrest. Prep. **wek.e.a** St. **wek.ek.a** Cs. **wek.esh.a** Ps. **wek.w.a** Ps. of Prep. **wek.ew.a** Rp. **wek.an.a** Rp. of Prep. **wek.e.an.a**
wekevu (also *welelevu*) *n* (*u*) 1. intelligence, awareness, knowledge; capability of understanding: *Wekevu wake katika uhusiano wa mambo ya kimataifa umemfanya achaguliwe kuwa balozi*, his grasp of international affairs has led to his appointment as an ambassador. 2. obedience, loyalty, allegiance: *Ninampenda mtumishi yule kwa sababu ya wekevu wake*, I like that servant because of his obedience. (cf *utiifu*)
wekez.a *vt* invest: *Serikali inawataka wafanyabiashara kutoka nje kuwekeza vitegauchumi nchini*, the government wants overseas businessmen to invest in the country. Prep. **wekez.e.a** St. **wekez.ek.a** Cs. **wekez.esh.a** Ps. **wekez.w.a**, be invested Rp. **wekez.an.a**
weku.a *vt* see *ekua*
wekundu *n* (*u*) redness
weledi *n* (*u*) intelligence, skill, cleverness: *Weledi wake katika uhunzi ni mkubwa*, his skill in metalwork is great. (cf *ufahamu*, *uelewaji*)
welekeo *n* (*u*) direction 2. attitude, behaviour.
welekevu *n* (*u*) see *wekevu*
wema *n* (*u*) goodness, kindness, virtuousness: *Wema wake hautasahaulika*, his kindness will never be forgotten. (*prov*) *Wema hauozi*, kindness is never forgotten.
wembamba *n* (*u*) slenderness, slimness skinniness, thinness. (cf *ukondefu*, *ufinyu*)
wembe (pl *nyembe*) *n* (*u*) 1. razor (*prov*) *Mtoto akililia wembe mpe*, if a child wants something, give it to him as this is a "test" for him. 2. razor blade; shaving blade.
wembembe *n* (*u*) (*zool*) a kind of very small stingless bee that nests in holes, walls or rocks, door-locks, hollow tree trunks and other small apertures in houses; mocca bee, mopane bee.
wembezi *n* (*u*) (*med*) funnel chest, pectus excavatum; a hollow at the lower part of the chest caused by a backward displacement of the xiphoid cartilage.
wendo (pl *nyendo*) *n* (*u*) movement, process, step, sequence.
weng.a¹ *vt*, *vi* come out in a rash after eating certain kinds of fish, meat, etc.; come out in skin erruption; be allergic to certain kinds of food: *Alikula pweza na baadaye akaja kumwenga*, he ate an octopus and later, his skin erupted in a rash. Prep. **weng.e.a** St. **weng.ek.a** Cs. **weng.esh.a** Ps. **weng.w.a** Rp. **weng.an.a** (cf *dhuru*)
weng.a² *vt* dislike, hate, mislike, disfavour. Prep. **weng.e.a** St. **weng.ek.a** Cs. **weng.esh.a** Ps. **weng.w.a** (cf *chukia*)
wengi *adj*, *pron* form of -*ingi*, 'many' used for **wa**- class pl nouns: *Watu wengi*, many people. (*prov*) *Wengi wape au watajichukulia*, if the majority of people are in favour of sth, then give it to them; if not, they will revolt.
wengo *n* (*u*) a kind of curved knife.
wengu *n* (*ma*-) (*anat*) spleen (cf *bandama*)
weni (*bot*) a stinging plant, which serves as a cure for sores.
wenu *adj*, *pron* form of -*enu*, 'your.' 'yours' used for **wa**- class pl and **u**- class singular nouns: *Watoto wenu*, your children. *Wajibu wenu*, your duty.
wenye *adj* form of -*enye* 'with' 'having' used for **mi**-, **u**- classes sing and **ma**- class pl nouns: *Mti wenye miiba mingi*, a tree with many thorns. *Ua wenye sengenge*, a compound enclosed with barbed wire. *Mume mwenye matatizo mengi*, a husband with many problems.

wenyewe *adj, pron* form of *-enyewe* 'itself' 'themselves' used for **mi-, u** classes singular and **wa-** class pl nouns: *Sisi wenyewe tuna makosa*, we ourselves have mistakes.

wenzi *n* (*u*) 1. friendship, friendliness, comradeship: *Wenzi wao umedumu kwa miaka mingi*, their friendship has lasted for many years. (cf *uelewano, urafiki*) 2. pl of *mwenzi*, companion.

wenzo (pl *nyenzo*) *n* (*u*) 1. lever, roller, bar. (*prov*) *Mti wako hawendi ila kwa nyenzo*, your piece of wood cannot be moved without the help of rollers i.e. for sth to succeed, you must have the necessary materials or resources. (cf *mpiko*) 2. appliance.

wepesi *n* (*u*) 1. agility, swiftness, suppleness, lightness. (cf *uhafifu*) 2. easiness, simplicity, facileness: *Wepesi wa hesabu hizi zimewafanya wanafunzi wengi kupata alama nzuri*, the simpleness of these sums has made many students to get good marks. (cf *sahali, urahisi*)

werevu *n* (*u*) shrewdness, cunning, guile: *Alitumia werevu kuwahadaa watu*, he employed cunning to deceive others. (cf *ujanja, uhodari*)

wetu *adj, pron* form of *-etu*, our, ours used for **wa-** class and some **n** class nouns.

weu (pl *nyeu*) *n* (*u*) a piece of cultivated land ready for planting; tilth (cf *sesa, ucheu*)

weupe *n* (*u*) 1. whiteness: *Nimeupenda weupe wa kanzu hii*, I like the whiteness of this dress. 2. cleanliness, spotlessness: *Weupe wa barabara hii umewafurahisha watalii*, the cleanliness of this road has impressed the tourists. 3 brightness, lightness (cf *mwangaza*) 4. (*fig*) purity: *Weupe wa roho yake*, the purity of his heart.

weusi *n* (*u*) 1. blackness; black or dark colour: *Suti hii inavutia sana kwa sababu ya weusi wake*, this suit is too attractive because it is black. 2. (*fig*)

evil-heartedness: *Ana weusi wa roho* he is evil-hearted.

wewe (also *weye*) *pron* (second person singular) you: *Wewe na sisi*, you and we. *Wewe ni mpole*, you are gentle.

wewesek.a (also *weweteka*) *vi* talk in one's sleep; talk in delirium; talk unconsciously: *Niliweweseka usiku kutokana na filamu ya kutisha niliyoiona*, I talked in my sleep at night following the horror film I saw at the cinema. Prep. ***wewesek.e.a*** St. ***wewesek.ek.a*** Cs. ***wewesek.esh.a*** Ps. ***wewesek.w.a*** (cf *hohosa*)

wewetek.a *vi* see *weweseka*

weye *pron* you

wez.a *vt* (*aux*) be able, be capable; can: *Anaweza kupika chakula kizuri*, she can cook good food. *Unaweza kuzungumza kama unataka*, you can talk if you want. *Ameniweza*, he has got the better of me. Prep. ***wez.e.a*** St. ***wez.ek.a*** Cs. ***wez.esh.a*** Ps. ***wez.w.a*** Rp. ***wez.an.a*** Rp. of St. ***wez.ek.an.a*** (cf *mudu*)

wezekan.a *vt* be possible: *Inawezekana mvua ikanyesha leo*, it is possible that it may rain today. Prep. ***wezekan.i.a*** St. ***wezekan.ik.a*** Cs. ***wezekan.ish.a***

-wi *adj* (*arch*) bad, wicked, satanic: *Mtu yule ni mwi sana*, that person is very wicked. (cf *ovu, baya*)

wi.a[1] *vt* be owed by; be creditor of; have a claim on: *Ninamwia pesa nyingi*, he owes me a lot of money. Prep. ***wi.li.a*** St. ***wi.lik.a*** Cs. ***wi.sh.a*** Ps. ***wi.w.a*** Rp. ***wi.an.a*** (cf *dai*)

wi.a[2] *vi* (of water, etc.) seethe, get warm: *Maji yanawia mekoni*, the water is seething at the hearth. Prep. ***wi.li.a*** St. ***wi.lik.a*** Cs. ***wi.sh.a*** Ps. ***wi.w.a*** Rp. ***wi.an.a***

wia[3] *vt* return, come back. Prep. ***wi.li.a*** St. ***wi.lik.a*** Cs. ***wi.sh.a*** Ps. ***wi.w.a*** Rp. ***wi.an.a*** (cf *rudi, rejea*)

wia[4] (pl *nyia*) *n* (*u*) song, melody. (cf *wimbo*)

wianish.a vt rationalize. Prep. *wianish.i.a* St. *wianish.ik.a* Ps. *wianish.w.a*
wianisho n (u) ratio
wibari[1] n (u) (zool) dassie, hyrax. *kwanga, perere* (Ar)
wibari[2] n (u) an expletive used to describe a man's dress that is clean; man's clean dress esp the one worn at prayers.
wiche (also *uche, wito*) n (u) (of disease, habit, etc.) infection: *Tia wiche*, cause an infection; infect. *Pata wiche*, get an infection.
wifi n (n) (a word used only by women) a woman's female in-law.
wigo[1] n (u) 1. fence, hedge, enclosure, compound. (cf *ukigo*) 2. (fig) extent, avenue, scope: *Lazima tupanue wigo wa shughuli zetu za uchumi*, we must expand the scope of our economic activities.
wigo[2] n (u) mimicry, imitation; the act (method, etc.) of imitating.
wik.a (also *ika*) vi 1. crow like a cock. (prov) *Likiwika lisiwika kutakucha*, whether it crows or not, it will dawn. 2. triumph, reign, dominate, overtop, outshine: *Mwanafunzi yule ndiye anayewika darasani*, that student is the one who outshines others in the class. Prep. *wik.i.a* St. *wik.ik.a* Cs. *wik.ish.a* Ps. *wik.w.a* (cf *tamba, tawala*)
wiki n (u) week; seven days. (cf *juma, fungate*) (Eng)
wilaya n (u) district; administrative area: *Mkuu wa wilaya*, district commissioner. *Wilaya ya kaskazini*, northern district. *Wilaya ya magharibi*, western district. (Ar)
-wili[1] adj, pron two: *Vikapu viwili*, two baskets. *Miaka miwili*, two years.
wili[2] n (n) wheel (cf *gurudumu*) (Eng)
wima adv upright, perpendicular: *Alisimama wima akiangalia mpira*, he stood upright watching soccer.
wimbi[1] n (ma-) 1. (of sea) wave, breaker. (prov) *Penye wimbi na milango i papo*, where there are strong waves, there are outlets i.e. even where there are difficulties and problems, there is a way to get your thing accomplished. 2. (of light) wave: *Wimbi ardhi*, ground wave. *Wimbi redio*, radio wave. *Wimbi endelevu*, continuous wave. *Wimbi sauti*, sound wave. 3. (idms) *Wimbi la watu*, a multitude of people. *Wimbi la ghasia*, a wave of violence. *Wimbi la ujambazi*, a wave of thuggery.
wimbi[2] n (u) see *ulezi*[2]
wimbo (pl *nyimbo*) n (u) song, hymn: *Wimbo wa huzuni*, elegy. *Wimbo wa mazishi*, threnody, dirge, funeral song. *Wimbo wa kazi*, work song. (prov) *Wimbo waimbwa huja ngomani*, a song is found in a traditional dance i.e. everything has got a context in which it can be found or obtained.
wimbowimbo n (u) a stick with a hole twirled by rubbing between the palms of the hands to produce fire.
winchi (also *winji*) n (n) winch, crane. (cf *manjanika*) (Eng)
winda[1] n (u) a loincloth usu worn by Hindus who wear it by passing the ends between the legs and tucking them into a fold round the waist.
wind.a[2] vt 1. (of wild animals, birds, etc.) hunt. (cf *saka*) 2. (of people) track down. Prep. *wind.i.a* St. *wind.ik.a* Cs. *wind.ish.a* Ps. *wind.w.a* Rp. *wind.an.a* (cf *saka, vizia*)
windo n (ma-) booty, prey, game, quarry; what is obtained from hunting: *Wasasi waligawana mawindo yao baada ya usasi*, the hunters divided their quarry after the hunt. (cf *vuno, pato*)
wing.a vt drive away, send away, chase: *Aliwawinga ndege waliokuwa wakila mtama wake*, he drove away the birds which were eating his sorghum. (prov) *Mavi usiyoyala wayawangiani kuku?* Why do you interfere in matters that don't concern you? In other words, mind your business. Prep. *wing.i.a* St. *wing.ik.a* Cs. *wing.ish.a* Ps. *wing.w.a* Rp. *wing.an.a* (cf *inga*)
wingi[1] n (u) 1. abundance, bounty, vast number: *Wingi wa watu*, a large

number of people. 2. (*gram*) plural.
wingi² *n* (*u*) (in football, hockey, etc.) a position played forward and right or left of centre; wing: *Wingi wa kulia*, right wing. *Wingi wa kushoto*, left wing. (Eng)
wingu *n* (*ma-*) cloud, haze: *Mawingu yametanda*, it is all clouded. (*prov*) *Dalili ya mvua ni mawingu*, there is no smoke without fire. (cf *furufuru*)
winji *n* (*u*) see *winchi*
wino *n* (*u*) ink: *Wino mwekundu*, red ink. *Kidau cha wino*, inkpot; inkstand. *Chupa ya wino*, inkpot. cf *midadi*
wishwa¹ (also *ushwa*) *n* (*u*) chaff, bran, husk; outer seed cover separated from grain before it is used as food (cf *kapi, pumba*)
wishwa² *n* (*u*) an instrument used by masons, blacksmiths etc. when making archs for buildings and ornaments in the case of the latter; roller, lever.
witiri¹ (also *witri*) *n* (*u*) odd number such as 1, 3, 5, 7....; number that cannot be divided by two. (cf *kitangulizi*)
witiri² (also *witri*) *n* (*u*) (in Islam) optional prayers prayed after *Isha* that is, last prayer of the day, which operates along odd number dimensions.
wito¹ *n* (*u*) see *wiche*
wito² *n* (*u*) liquid derived from molten iron: casting.
wito³ *n* (*u*) call, calling, invitation: *Wananchi waliitikia wito wa kiongozi wao wa kujenga nchi*, the people responded to the call of their leader to build the nation. (cf *agizo*)
witri¹ *n* (*u*) see *witiri¹*
witri² *n* (*u*) see *witiri²*
wiv.a *vi* see *iva*
wivi *n* (*u*) see *wizi*
wivu¹ *n* (*u*) 1. feeling or showing of fear or resentment of possible rivals in love or affection; jealousy: *Mwanamke yule ana wivu sana*, that woman is very jealous. 2. feeling or showing of resentment of someone's advantages; envy, enviousness; *Yeye anamwonea wivu rafiki yako kwa sababu ya mali yake*, he feels envious of your friend because of his wealth. (*syn*) *Wivu hauna dawa*, jealousy has no medicine i.e. You can't treat someone who is jealous or envious. (cf *kijicho, husuda*)
-wivu² *adj* 1. jealous: *Mke mwivu*, a jealous wife. 2 envious: *Mtu mwivu*, an envious person.
wizani *n* (*u*) rhythm, *Aliupata wizani wa shairi barabara*, he captured the rhythm of the poem precisely. (Ar)
wizara *n* (*ma-*) government ministry: *Wizara ya utalii*, ministry of tourism. *Wizara ya kilimo*, ministry of agriculture. (Ar)
wizi (also *wivi*) *n* (*u*) theft, robbery, stealing: *Wizi wa nguvu*, violent robbery; robbery with violence. *Wizi wa mifugo*, rustling. *Alifungwa kwa kosa la wizi*, he was imprisoned for theft. (cf *uchopozi, wibaji*)
wodi (also *wadi*) *n* (*u*) ward; a room or division of a hospital set apart for a specific class or group of patients: *Wodi ya uzazi*, a maternity ward.
woga (also *uoga*) *n* (*u*) cowardice, fear, timidity: *Ana tabia ya woga*, he has a timid nature. (cf *hofu, ukunguru*)
wokovu (also *uokovu*) *n* (*u*) salvation esp from God; redemption, rescue: *Jeshi la Wokovu*, Salvation Army.
wongofu (also *uogofu*) *n* (*u*) righteousness, uprightness, decency: *Anaishi maisha ya wongofu*, he is living a descent life. (cf *uadilifu*)
wororo *n* (*u*) smoothness, tenderness, softness: *Wororo wa godoro hili umekuwa jambo zuri kwa mgonjwa*, the softness of this mattress has been good for the patient.
woto¹ *n* (*u*) vegetation, germination, growth: *Woto wa mbegu*, the germination of seeds.
woto² *n* (*u*) basking, warmth: *Woto wa jua*, the basking in the sun.
woya *n* (*u*) as much as will lie on the flat side of the hand; fistful, handful. (cf *ukufi, konzi*)

Y

Y, y, /j/ 1. represents the twenty-third letter of the Swahili alphabet. 2. represents the sound of Y or y and is classified as a semi-vowel.

ya *prep* 1. (used for *u* and *ma-* class pl countable and uncountable nouns as well as n- class singular nouns) of, for: *Mikuki ya wasasi,*, hunters' spears. *Majumba ya mawe,* stone buildings. *Maji ya baridi,* cold water. *Ngoma ya jadi,* traditional dance. 2. the *ya* particle is also used for indefinite and general reference: *Ya nini?* Why so? *Ya Rabi!* My God! 3. used with conjunctions *kuwa* and *kwamba* to introduce a subordinate clause e.g. *Alieleza ya kuwa hatafika kwenye mkutano leo,* he stated that he would not come to the meeting today.

y.a *vt cop* 1. they are: *Madirisha ya wazi,* the windows are open.

ya.a *vi* see *lala.* Prep. **ya.li.a** St. **ya.lik.a** Cs. **ya.z.a** (cf *jinyosha*)

yaani *conj* an expletive used for exemplification or elucidation of sth; that is to say; I mean; that is, namely: *Mwanafunzi wangu hakufika darasani jana, yaani Tom,* my student was absent in the class yesterday, namely Tom. (cf *tuseme*)

yabisi *adj* 1. dry, hard: *Udongo yabisi,* dry earth; parched earth. 2 used in the expression *Baridi yabisi,* rheumatism. (Ar)

yabisik.a *vi* become dry; become stiff: *Udongo huu umeyabisika,* this soil has become dry. Prep. **yabisik.i.a** St. **yabisik.ik.a** Cs. **yabisik.ish.a** (cf *kauka, kakamaa*)

yadi *n* (*n*) yard; a measure of 36 inches or 3 feet. (Eng)

yahe (also *yakhe*) *n* (*n*) 1. companion, chum, comrade, brother. (cf *rafiki, mpenzi*) 2. used in the expression: *Kina yahe,* the common man; commoner e.g. *Akina yahe wanataka kugoma leo,* the ordinary people want to strike today. (cf *makabwela*)

yahomu *interj* (*naut*) an expletive of joy on the arrival of a vessel. 2. straight ahead!

yai *n* (*ma-*) 1. egg, ovum: female reproducing cell: *Yai la kuku,* hen's egg. *Yai la kuchemsha,* boiled egg. *Yai la kukaanga,* fried egg. *Yai viza,* rotten egg. 2. zero, nil, naught: *Alipata yai katika mtihani wa kemia,* he got zero in the chemistry examination. (cf *zero, sufuri*)

yake *adj, pron* form of *-ake,* 'his', 'her', 'hers', 'its' used for *u* and *ma-* classes pl count and uncountable nouns as well as *n* class singular nouns: *Minazi yake,* his coconut trees, her coconut trees. *Mali yake,* his wealth, her wealth. *Nyama yake,* his meat, her meat. *Yake na yangu ni mamoja,* his and mine are the same.

yakhe *n* (*n*) see *yahe*

yakini[1] *n* (*n*) certainty, truth, fact, actuality: *Hakuna yakini kama mjomba wangu atakuja leo au la,* there is no certainty whether my uncle will come today or not. (cf *hakika, ukweli*) (Ar)

yakini[2] *adj* certain, actual, true: *Ni yakini kwamba Elizabeth ameachwa,* it is certain that Elizabeth has been divorced. (cf *sahihi, kweli*) (Ar)

yakin.i[3] (also *yakinisha*) *vt, vi* certify, confirm, validate, verify, affirm: *Alijaribu kuuyakini ukweli wa mambo,* he tried to verify the truth of the matter. Ps. **yakin.i.a** St. **yakin.ik.a** be certain. Cs. **yakin.ish.a** Ps. **yakin.iw.a** (cf *hakikisha, sadikisha*) (Ar)

yakini.a *vt, vi* resolve to. Prep. **yakini.li.a** St. **yakini.k.a** Cs. **yakini.sh.a**

yakinifu *adj* 1. actual, correct, real: *Taarifa yakinifu,* a correct statement. 2. empirical. (Ar)

yakinish.a (also *yakini*) *vt, vi* verify, certify, confirm: *Jaribu kuyakinisha kama yeye atakuja kesho*, try to confirm if he will be coming tomorrow. Prep. *yakinish.i.a* St. *yakinish.ik.a* Ps. *yakinish.w.a*

yako *adj, pron* form of *-ako*, 'your', 'yours' used for **u** and **ma-** classes pl count and uncountable nouns as well as **n** class singular nouns: *Miche yako* your seedlings. *Makosa yako*, your mistakes. *Maziwa yako*, your milk. *Nazi yako*, your coconut.

yakuti *n* (*n*) ruby, saphire. (cf *johari*) (Ar)

yale *adj, pron* form of *-le*, 'that', 'those' used for **ma-** class pl count and uncountable nouns: *Mananasi yale*, those pineapples. *Mafuta yale*, that oil.

yaliyomo *n* (*ma-*) table of contents; contents. (cf *faharisi*)

yambiwa *n* (*n*) (*gram*) object: *Shamirisho yambiwa*, indirect object.

yambwa *n* (*n*) (*gram*) object, complement: *Yambwa tendwa*, object complement. *Yambwa tendewa*, indirect object. *Yambwa kihusishi*, prepositional object. *Yambwa mnasaba*, cognate object.

yamini *n* (*n*) 1. the right hand. (cf *kulia, kuumeni*) 2. oath, vow, avowal: *Kula yamini*, swear solemnly. *Walimlisha yamini*, they made him swear an oath. (cf *kiapo, halafa*) (Ar)

yamkini¹ (also *yumkini*) *adv* possibly, probably, most likely: *Yamkini mvua ikanyesha leo*, probably, it will rain today. (cf *yawezekana, labda, huenda*)

yamkini² *n* (*n*) (*math*) probability; the branch in mathematics dealing with the extent to which an event is likely to occur, measured on a scale from zero (impossibility) to one (certainty).

yangeyange *n* (*n*) (*zool*) little egret; a heron family *Ardeidae* with black legs and conspicuous yellow toes, which lives in marshes, swamps, shallow lakes, flood plains, seashore, etc. *Egretta garzetta*. (cf *dandala*)

yangu *adj, pron* form of *-angu* 'my', 'mine' used for **mi-** and **ma-** class pl count and uncountable nouns as well as **n** class singular nouns: *Miguu yangu*, my legs. *Matango yangu*, my cucumbers. *Maji yangu*, my water. *Konde yangu*, my field. *Yangu ni yako*, mine is yours.

yao *adj, pron* form of *-ao* 'their', 'theirs' used for **mi-** and **ma-** class pl count and uncountable nouns as well as n-class singular nouns: *Mifuko yao*, their bags. *Mapendekezo yao*, their suggestions. *Mali yao*, their wealth. *Kamba yao*, their rope.

Yarabi *interj* Oh God! an expletive used by Muslims in direct address, to draw attention to His Almighty God for support, etc. (Ar)

yasini¹ *n* (*n*) (in Islam) the thirty sixth chapter from the Holy Koran, which is the heart of this holy book. (Ar)

yasini² *interj* an exclamation of scornful, disdainful and vituperative remark, used by both males and females in conversations, etc.; To hell! (Ar)

yasini³ *interj* an expletive for expressing wonder (cf *salale!*) (Ar)

yasmini *n* (*n*) see *asumini*

yaspi *n* (*u*) (*min*) jasper (Eng)

yatima *n* (*n*) orphan; a fatherless person, a motherless person: *Nyumba ya yatima* orphanage. (cf *kiokote, mwanamkiwa*) (Ar)

yavuyavu *n* (*ma-*) 1. lungs. (cf *pafu, buhumu*) 2. sponge.

yaya¹ *n* (*ma-*) ayah; a child's nurse usu a female; babysitter. (Port, Hind)

yay.a² *vt* burn completely, be on fire completely; be devastated. Prep. *yay.i.a* St. *yay.ik.a* Cs. *yay.ish.a* (cf *teketea*)

Y

yegayega n (ma-) a loose luggage; a luggage which is on an awkward position.
yegeya n (ma-) (bot) a kind of fruit from the Sausage tree (*Kigelia pinnata*),having a grey-brown colour when ripe; sausage fruit. (cf *vungunya*)
yengeyenge n (ma-) see *lengelenge*
yenu adj, pron form of *enu*, 'your' 'yours' used for **mi-** and **ma-** classes pl count and uncountable nouns and **n** class singular nouns: *Miavuli yenu*, your umbrellas. *Mashamba yenu*, your farms. *Mapenzi yenu*, your love.
yenyewe adj, pron form of *-enyewe*, 'itself' 'themselves' used for **mi-** and **ma-** classes pl count and uncountable nouns as well as nclass singular nouns: *Misumeno yenyewe*, the saws themselves. *Maua yenyewe*, the flowers themselves. *Sahani yenyewe*, the plate itself.
Yesu n (n) Christ: *Yesu Kristo*, Jesus Christ. *Mtoto Yesu*, Christ child.
yetu adj, pron form of *etu*, 'our', 'ours', used for **mi-** and **ma-** classes pl count and uncountable nouns as well as n-class sing nouns: *Mimea yetu*, our plants. *Maduka yetu*, our shops. *Maziwa yetu*, our milk. *Meza yetu*, our table.
yeye pron he, she, him, her: *Yeye ni mrefu*, he is tall, she is tall.
yeyote adj, pron form of *-o-ote* 'any', used for **wa-** class singular nouns: *Yeyote kati yenu aje hapa*, anyone of you should come here.
yeyuk.a vi melt away; dissolve: *Barafu imeyeyuka*, the ice has melted. Prep. **yeyuk.i.a** St. **yeyuk.ik.a** Cs. **yeyuk.ish.a**
yeyush.a vt dissolve, melt: *Aliiyeyusha samli*, she melted the ghee. Prep. **yeyush.i.a** St. **yeyush.ik.a** Ps. **yeyush.w.a** Rp. **yeyush.an.a**
yombiyombi n (n) (*zool*) grossbeak; a kind of a large, heavy swamp-haunting weaver family *Ploceidae* with a thick bill. *Amblyospiza albifrons*.
yong.a vi sway due to weakness, weight etc.; swing, stagger, teeter, rock, reel: *Mlevi alikuwa anayonga barabarani*, the drunkard was staggering along the road. *Jahazi lilikuwa linayonga*, the dhow was rocking. Prep. **yong.e.a** St. **yong.ek.a** Cs. **yong.esh.a** Ps. **yong.w.a** (cf *pepesuka*, *yumbayumba*)
yongo.a vt carry sby shoulder high or on sby's back as during initiation rites, marriage ceremonies, etc.: *Watazamaji walimyongoa mshindi*, the spectators carried the victor shoulder high. Prep. **yongo.e.a** St. **yongo.ek.a** Cs. **yongo.esh.a** Ps. **yongo.w.a** (cf *jitwika*)
yongoy.a vi sway due to weakness, weight, etc. Prep. **yongoy.e.a** St. **yongoy.ek.a** Cs. **yongoy.esh.a** cf *yonga*
yosayosa adv hurriedly, quickly, speedily: *Alikuja yosayosa*, he came hurriedly. (cf *harakaharaka*, *chapuchapu*)
yowe n (ma-) 1. a loud cry esp that for calling help; scream, yell, shriek: *Piga yowe*, shout loudly; yell, scream. 2 noise: *Anapenda kupiga mayowe*, he likes to make noises. (cf *unyange*, *unyende*, *siyahi*)
yoyom.a vi (of plans, etc.) 1. go without direction; go haphazardly, go awry, be in disarray: *Mipango yake iliyoyoma*, his plans went awry. 2. recede from view; disappear, vanish, perish: *Alikuwepo hapa punde hivi lakini sasa ameyoyoma*, he was here a while ago but now he has disappeared. *Wakati unayoyoma*, time is running out (cf *tokomea*). Prep. **yoyom.e.a** St. **yoyom.ek.a** Cs. **yoyom.esh.a** Ps. **yoyom.w.a** (cf *tokomea*)
yu vt cop he is, she is: *Yeye yu hodari*, he is clever, she is clever.
yu.a vi wobble, tip, tilt: *Mshale uliyua*, the

arrow wobbled i.e. the arrow did not fly straight.Prep. *yu.i.a* St. *yu.ish.a* Ps. of Prep. *yu.iw.a*

yuga n (*ma-*) see *yugwa*

yugayug.a *vi* be restless, be uneasy, be confused: *Mama aliyugayuga aliposikia kwamba binti yake amepotea*, the mother became restless when she heard that her daughter was missing. Prep. *yugayug.i.a* St. *yugayug.ik.a* Cs. *yugayug.ish.a* Ps. *yugayug.w.a* (cf *babaika, hangaika*)

yugwa (also *yuga*) n (*ma-*) (*bot*) cocoyam; eddo, taro. *Colocasia antiquarum*

yule *adj, pron* form of *-le* 'that' is used for *wa-* class singular nouns to signal remoteness of an object: *Mtu yule* that person. *Yule ni mgeni*, that is a guest.

yumb.a *vi* 1. sway, swing, stagger; move to and fro: *Miti ilikuwa ikiyumba kwa sababu ya upepo mkali*, the trees were swaying in the strong wind. 2. struggle, labour: *Vijana wengi wanayumba mjini siku hizi kwa ajili ya kutafuta kazi*, many young men are struggling in the city these days in search of jobs. (*prov*) *Mti mkuu ukianguka wana wa ndege huyumba*, if a big tree falls down, the chicks of the bird disintegrate i.e. if a person looking after his family dies, that family suffers a lot. Prep. *yumb.i.a* St. *yumb.ik.a* Cs. *yumb.ish.a*

yumbish.a[1] *vt* see *yumba*

yumbish.a[2] *vt* misguide, mislead: *Kiongozi aliweza kuwayumbisha wananchi*, the leader managed to mislead the people. Prep. *yumbish.i.a* St. *yumbish.ik.a* Ps. *yumbish.w.a* Rp. *yumbish.an.a*

yumkini *adj* see *yamkini*

yungi (also *yungiyungi*) n (*ma-*) (*bot*) blue water-lily; a flower with a wide range of colours having large, flat and floating leaves. *Nymphaea capensis*.

yungiyungi n (*n*) see *yungi*

yunifomu n (*n*) uniform: *Unifomu za shule*, school uniforms (Eng)

yupi *adj, pron* form of *-pi* 'which', used for *wa-* class singular nouns: *Mtu yupi?* Which person? *Paka yupi?* Which cat? *Kipi kinakukera?* What is bothering you? Which thing is bothering you?

yurea n (*n*) urea; a highly crystalline solid, $CO(NH_3)_2$ found in urine and other body fluids of mammals or produced synthetically; it is used as a fertilizer, in making plastics, etc.

Z

Z, z /z/ 1. the twenty fourth letter of the Swahili alphabet. 2. the sound of Z or z is normally a voiced palatal fricative.

za.a *vt, vi* 1. give birth, produce children, have children; beget: *Amezaa watoto wengi,* she has many children. Prep. *za.li.a,* give birth at (in, at, etc.) e.g. *Alizalia nyumbani,* she gave birth at home. St. *za.lik.a* Cs. *za.lish.a,* assist at birth e.g. *Mkunga alimzalisha mwanamke yule,* the midwife assisted birth for that woman. Ps. *za.w.a* Ps. of Prep. *za.liw.a,* be born e.g. *Alizaliwa mwaka jana,* he was born last year. Rp. *za.an.a* Rp. of Prep. *za.li.an.a,* reproduce, multiply e.g. *Panya wale wanazaliana tu,* those rats reproduce in large numbers. 2. bear fruit, produce fruit: *Mti huu umezaa mapapai mengi,* this tree has produced many pawpaws. Prep. *za.li.a* St. *za.lik.a* Cs. *za.lish.a* Ps. *za.w.a* Rp. *za.an.a*

zaan.a *vi, vt* reproduce, breed, multiply. Prep. *zaan.i.a* St. *zaan.ik.a* Cs. *zaan.ish.a* (cf *zaliana*)

zaatari *n* (*n*) (*bot*) a kind of herb, put in the tea, milk, etc in order to give it a pleasant flavour and smell; thyme. (Ar)

zab.a *vt* slap, flap, hit, beat: *Alimzaba makofi mdogo wake,* he slapped his younger brother. Prep. *zab.i.a* St. *zab.ik.a* Cs. *zab.ish.a* Ps. *zab.w.a,* be slapped e.g. *Mwanafunzi alizabwa makofi na mwalimu,* the student was slapped by the teacher. Rp. *zab.an.a,* slap one another. (cf *ezeka, charaza*)

zabadi *n* (*n*) a substance with a strong penetrating odour obtained from the civet and otter, which is used to make some perfumes; musk. (Ar)

zabarijadi *n* (*n*) a precious stone or gem that resembles ruby or sapphire. (Ar)

zabibu (*bot*) raisin, grape.

zabun.i[1] *vi* 1. bid at an auction; offer a bid at an auction: *Ilibidi azabuni alipokuwa anataka kununua vitu mnadani,* he was obliged to offer a bid when he wanted to buy things at the auction. 2. assess, value. Prep. *zabun.i.a* St. *zabun.ik.a* Cs. *zabun.ish.a* Ps. of Prep. *zabun.iwa* (Ar)

zabuni[2] *n* (*n*) 1. tender notice. 2. tender. (Ar)

Zaburi[1] *n* (*n*) 1. Psalter hymns. 2. Psalms; a book of the Bible consisting of the 150 psalms. 3. a holy book which Muslims believe God delivered to Prophet Daud (David).

zaburi[2] *adj* unpalatable, unsavoury, savourless, unappetizing: *Chakula zaburi,* unpalatable food. (cf *chapwa*)

zafa (also *zefe*) *n* (*n*) a procession by Muslims held before or after the commemoration of the birthday of Prophet Muhammad. (Ar)

zafarani *n* (*n*) 1. saffron; the dried, aromatic stigmas of the saffron plant, used in flavouring and colouring foods, and formerly in medicine. 2. orange yellow colour. (Ar)

zafe *n* (*n*) slippery mud; slime: *Barabara ile ina zafe,* that road has slime.

zaga.a *vi* be spread all over; diffuse, pervade: *Habari imezagaa nchini kwamba rais atalihutubia bunge,* news has spread all over the country that the president will address the parliament. Prep. *zaga.li.a* St. *zaga.lik.a* Cs. *zaga.z.a* Ps. *zaga.w.a* (cf *tapakaa, enea*)

zaha *n* (*n*) melted rock issuing from a volcano; lava (Ar)

zahama *n* (*n*) hustle, commotion, turmoil, turbulence, confusion, pandemonium, chaos: *Kulikuwa na zahama kiwanjani baada ya wachezaji kumpiga ngumi*

rifarii, there was pandemonium at the stadium after the players punched the referee. (cf *fujo, ghasia*) (Ar)
zahanati *n* (*n*) dispensary, clinic. (cf *kliniki*) (Pers)
zaibaki¹ (also *zebaki*) *n* (*n*) mercury. (*syn*) *Zaibaki ya uso imemtoka*, he is shameless. (Ar)
zaibaki² *n* (*n*) see *zebaki*²
zaidi *adv.* 1. more, in addition, to a greater extent: *Hataki zaidi*, he doesn't want more. (*prov*) *Hakuna zaidi mbovu*, there is no addition which is bad i.e. an increase can serve a useful purpose to a person. 2. used to show a difference between two conditions or things: *Amelima zaidi mwaka huu kuliko mwaka jana*, he has cultivated more this year than last year. 3. extra, more: *Nipe chakula zaidi*, give me more food. 4. used with *ya* and a demonstrative to give the meanings of 'besides' 'furthermore' e.g. *Zaidi ya hayo, yeye ni mkaidi*, furthermore, he is stubborn. (Ar)
zailemu (also) *zilemu n* (*n*) (*bot*) xylem; the woody vascular tissue of a plant. (Eng)
zain.i¹ *vt* 1. persuade someone to do wrong; mislead, misguide, tempt: *Shetani alimzaini kuiba vitu dukani*, the devil tempted him to steal things from the shop. 2. decorate, embellish. Prep. *zain.i.a* St. *zain.ik.a* Cs. *zain.ish.a* Ps. of Prep. *zain.iw.a* Rp. of Prep. *zain.i.an.a* (Ar)
zain.i² *vt, vi* decorate, embellish Prep. *zain.i.a* St. *zain.ik.a* Cs. *zain.ish.a* Ps. of Prep. *zain.iw.a* Rp. of Prep. *zain.i.an.a*
zaituni (also *zeituni*) *n* (*n*) (*bot*) olive; an egg-shaped edible fruit with a small bitter taste, which is green when unripe. *Olea europea*. (Ar)
zaka¹ (also *zakati*) *n* (*n*) alms, tithe: offerings for religious purposes:

Kila Mwislamu mwenye kujiweza, anawajibika kutoa zaka, every able Muslim of means is obliged to give alms. (Ar)
zaka² *n* (*n*) a quiver of arrows; a container for carrying arrows; arrow-case. (cf *podo, pongono*) (Ar)
zakati *n* (*n*) see *zaka*¹
zake *adj, pron* form of -*ake*, 'his' 'her' 'hers' 'its' used for *n* class pl nouns: *Safari zake*, his journeys.
zako *adj, pron* form of -*ako*, 'your' 'yours' used for *n* class pl nouns: *Nguo zako*, your clothes.
zalbia (also *zelbia*) *n* (*n*) a kind of light pastry made in the form of a horseshoe. Its main ingredients are flour, ghee and sugar.
zalian.a *vi* multiply in the production of the same offsprings; reproduce, breed.
zalio *n* (*ma*-) the membrane enclosing a foetus; caul. (cf *tandabui*)
zalish.a *vt* 1. aid/assist at childbirth 2. produce, manufacture: *Kiwanda kilizalisha bidhaa za kiwango cha juu*, the factory produced goods of high quality. Prep. *zalish.i.a* St. *zalish. ik.a* Ps. *zalish.w.a* Rp. *zalish.an.a*
zama¹ (also *zamani*) *n* (*n*) era, age, epoch, eon, period; *Zama za kale*, in early days, old age. *Zama za kati*, Middle Ages. *Zama zile*, in those times. *Zama za mwisho*, late period.
zam.a² *vt, vi* 1. sink in a fluid; be drowned; be submerged; be immersed: *Alizama baharini*, he was drowned in the sea. Prep. *zam.i.a*, dive for e.g. *Alizamia lulu*, he dived for pearls. St. *zam.ik.a* Cs. *zam.ish.a* 2. disappear, wane; be lost from sight, recede from view: *Jua limezama*, the sun has disappeared i.e. it is sunset. (cf *toweka, tokomea*) 3. (*fig*) hide; go underground: *Mwanasiasa alizama baada ya serikali kuamrisha msako mkali juu yake*, the politician went into hiding after the government

875

ordered an intensive hunt for him. Prep. *zam.i.a* St. *zam.ik.a* Cs. *zam.ish.a*

zamani[1] *n (n)* see *zama*[1]

zamani[2] *adv* 1. in the past; formerly, in ancient times: *Zamani, wazee wetu walikuwa wakiishi kwa amani,* in the past, our forefathers used to live in peace. 2. used to express different periods: *Zamani za leo,* nowadays. *Zamani zijazo,* in future. (Ar)

zambarau *n (n)* 1. (*bot*) Java plum; the fruit of a java plum tree (*Syzygium jambolanum*) which is fleshy oval and purple-like in colour. 2. purple colour.

zamda (also *zimda*) *n (n)* (*med*) an aromatic, crystalline compound used as an antiseptic, esp in mouthwashes and nose and throat sprays and in perfumery, embalming, etc.; thymol. (Ar)

zamu *n (n)* turn, innings, workshift; time when each one in a group must or may do sth. *Alingojea zamu yake ili aendeshe gari,* he waited for his turn in order to drive the vehicle. *Shika zamu,* take one's turn. (cf *duru, mzunguko*)

zana[1] *n (n)* implement, tool, instrument, utensil, appliance, apparatus, gadget, etc.: *Zana za vita,* weaponry for war; ammunitions for war; arms for war. (cf *nyenzo*)

zana[2] (also *jana*) *n (n)* honeycomb

zangu *adj, pron* form of *-angu,* 'my' 'mine,' used for **n** class pl nouns: *Nguo zangu,* my clothes.

zani *n (n)* calamity, disaster, difficulty, affliction, anguish, sadness: *Kulitokea zani mjini baada ya bomu kulipuka katika nyumba ya ubalozi,* there had been a disaster in the town after a bomb explosion in the embassy. (*idm*) *Bwaga zani,* cause a calamity. (cf *janga, balaa, janga*)

zanuba *n (n)* (*zool*) skipjack tuna; a kind of marine food fish having small conical teeth belonging to the genus *Euthynnus.*

zao[1] *n (ma-)* 1. seedling, plant: *Zao la pamba,* cotton plant. 2. crop, harvest, product, produce, yield: *Zao sehemu,* partial product. *Zaotuka,* by-product. (cf *zao la ziada*) *Zaotokeo,* output. *Zao mtambuko,* cross product. *Zao la kahawa limeshamiri nchini mwaka huu,* the coffee harvest has boomed in the country this year. (cf *vuno, pato*)

zao[2] *adj, pron* form of *-ao,* 'their,' 'theirs' used for **n** class pl nouns: *Bendera zao,* their flags.

zaraa *n (n)* agriculture, farming: *Kazi ya zaraa ni ngumu,* agricultural work is difficult. (cf *kilimo*) (Ar)

zarambo *n (n)* spirit distilled from palm wine; distilled palm wine.

zari *n (n)* golden embroidery thread; braid, brocade. (Pers)

zarniki *n (n)* a silvery-white poisonous chemical element, compounds of which are used in making medicines, glass, etc and used to exterminate insects, rats, etc; arsenic. (cf *aseniki*)

zartari *n (n)* see *zaatari*

zatit.i *vt* 1. prepare, ready; make ready, make preparations for : *Nchi yetu imejizatiti vizuri katika kuzikabili hujuma za adui,* our country is fully prepared to meet the enemy's aggression. Prep. *zatit.i.a* St. *zatit.ik.a* Cs. *zatit.ish.a* Ps. of Prep. *zatit.iw.a* (cf *andaa, imarisha*) (Ar)

zawadi *n (n)* gift, present, prize, keepsake: *Msichana alipata zawadi katika mashindano ya kuimba,* the girl won a prize in the singing competition. (cf *tunzo, hidaya, bahashishi*)

zawadi.a *vt* give a present; award: *Mkuu wa shule aliwazawadia wanafunzi waliofuzu vizuri kwenye mitihani yao,* the headmaster gave presents to students who did well in their examinations. St. *zawadi.k.a* Cs. *zawadi.sh.a* Ps. *zawadi.w.a* Rp. *zawadi.an.a* (cf *tunza*)

zawaridi *n (n)* (*zool*) melba finch; a kind of bird (family *Estrididae*) having a green

back and wings, a red tail with red face and throat. *Pytilia melba*.
zawij.i *vt,vi* marry, wed, wife, espouse; tie the knot: *Alizawiji mke wa ukoo wake*, he married a woman of his clan. Prep. ***zawij.i.a*** St. ***zawij.ik.a*** Cs. ***zawij.ish.a*** Ps. of Prep. ***zawij.iw.a*** (cf *oa*) (Ar)
-zazi *adj* productive, fertile, fruitful, fecund: *Mwanamke mzazi*, a fertile woman; a grand multiparous woman. *Kuku huyu ni mzazi*, this hen is productive.
zebaki[1] (also *zaibaki*) *n (n) (chem)* mercury (Ar)
Zebaki[2] *n (n) (astron)* Mercury; the smallest planet in the solar system and the one nearest to the sun
zebe *n (ma-)* fool, simpleton, imbecile, idiot: *Zebe yule atasadiki lolote unalomwambia*, that idiot will believe in anything you tell him. (cf *fala, bozi, baradhuli, bwege*)
zebu *n (n) (zool)* zebu; a big long-horned ox-like domestic animal

zebu

-zee *adj* old, aged, ageing: *Mwanamke mzee yule haoni vizuri*, that old woman does not see properly.
zeek.a *vi* become old, grow old, get on in years: *Bibi yake amezeeka siku hizi*, her grandmother has become old these days. (cf *konga*) Prep. ***zeek.e.a*** St. ***zeek.ek.a*** Cs. ***zeek.esh.a*** (cf *chakaa, konga*)
zefe *n (n)* see *zafa*
zege *(n) (ma-)* 1. concrete used for construction purposes: *Zege imara* reinforced concrete. (cf *kangiriti*) 2. dome, cupola. (cf *kuba*)
zeituni *n (n)* see *zaituni*
zela[1] *n (n)* see *ndoo*
zela[2] *n (n)* see *zila*
zelbia *n (n)* see *zalbia*
-zembe *adj* lazy, indolent, slothful, idle: *Mfanyakazi mzembe*, a lazy worker. *Mwanafunzi mzembe*, a lazy student. (cf *goigoi*)
zembe.a *vi* work lazily, work indolently; idle: *Alifukuzwa kazini kwa sababu alikuwa akizembea*, he was sacked from work because he was idling. Prep. ***zembe.le.a*** St. ***zembe.lek.a*** Cs. ***zembe.sh.a*** Ps. ***zembe.w.a*** Rp. ***zembe.an.a*** (cf *zigia, zorota, bweteka*)
zenge.a *vt* search for, hunt; follow or come near sby/sth usu with the aim of getting sth or commiting a crime. Prep. ***zenge.k.a*** St. ***zenge.lek.a*** Ps. ***zenge.w.a*** Rp. ***zenge.an.a*** (cf *tafuta*)
zengwe *n (mi-)* intrigue, machination, plot consipiracy. (cf *mzengwe*)
zenu *adj, pron* form of *enu*, 'your' 'yours.' (pl) used for **n** class pl nouns: *Ndizi zenu*, your bananas.
zenye *adj* form of *-enye*, 'with' 'having' used for **n** class pl nouns: *Nyumba zenye ghorofa nyingi*, houses with many floors.
zenyewe *adj, pron* form of *-enyewe*, 'themselves' used for **n** class pl nouns: *Benki zenyewe*, the banks themselves.
zeri *n (n)* balm (cf *malhamu*)
zeriba *n (n)* cowshed, byre, stable; a building in which cattle are sheltered and fed. (cf *chaa*)
zeru *n (ma-)* see *zeruzeru*
zeruzeru (also *zeru*) *n (ma-)* albino; a person or animal born with no colouring pigment in the skin and hair. (cf *albino*)
zeti *n (n)* a kind of olive oil.

877

zetu *adj, pron* form of *-etu*, 'our' 'ours' used for **n** class pl nouns: *Taarifa zetu,* our statements.
zeze *n (n) (mus)* 1. a kind of an old stringed musical instrument related to the guitar; lute. 2. *(syn) Kazi ya zeze,* a useless work.

zeze

zezeta¹ *n (n)* restiveness, fidget, restlessness, jumpiness, unquietness: *Zezeta ni kitu kisichokubalika katika jamii yoyote,* restiveness ia an unacceptable thing in any society (cf *machachari, makeke*)
zezet.a² *adj* restive, restless, fidgety, unquiet: *Yeye ni mtu wa zezeta,* he is a restless person. (cf *wasiwasi*)
zi.a (also *zira*) *vi* 1. abhor, abominate, shudder, loathe, hate: *Mwanafunzi anamzia mwalimu wake bure,* the student hates his teacher for nothing. (cf *chukia*) 2. stop or refrain from eating a certain kind of food because of illness, etc.: *Ugonjwa wake wa kisukari umemfanya kuzia vyakula vingi vitamu,* his diabetes has made him allergic to many kinds of sweet foods. Prep. *zi.li.a* St. *zi.lik.a* Cs. *zi.lish.a* Ps. of Prep. *zi.liw.a*
ziada *n(n)* 1. excess, surplus, supplement, extra, more: *Kitabu cha ziada,* a supplementary book. *Kazi ya ziada,* extra work e.g. *Vibarua walifanya kazi ya ziada ili kuongeza pato lao,* the labourers did extra work to raise their income. *Timu yao ilifanya kazi ya ziada wakati tulipolisakama goli lao,* their team did extra work when we constantly attacked their goalmouth. (cf *nyongeza*) 2. remainder after part of the total has been spent balance: *Nilitumia baadhi ya pesa zangu na hizi ni ziada,* I spent part of my money and this is the remainder. (Ar)
ziaka (also *riaka*) *n (n)* quiver, sheath, arrow-case. *(prov) Mshale mzuri haukai ziakani* a good arrow never stays in its case i.e. a good thing will always advertise itself. (cf *pongono, riaka*)
ziara¹ *n (n)* 1. visit, tour: *Rais wetu alifanya ziara katika nchi za Ulaya mwaka jana,* our president paid a visit to Europe last year. 2. (in Islam) a gathering in which the name of God is recited rhythmetically and repeatedly (Ar)
ziara² *n (n)* 1. an act of visiting sacred places such as shrines, etc. to pray for the dead. 2. tomb, grave. (Ar)
zib.a *vt* 1. stop up, cork, plug, peg, wedge, spike, fill in: *Aliiziba tundu kwenye paipu ya maji,* he plugged the hole in the water-pipe. *(prov) Usipoziba ufa, utajenga ukuta,* if you don't fill up a crack, you will have to build a wall i.e. if you ignore to repair now sth small, you will find that eventually that thing worsens. In other words, a stitch in time saves nine. 2. cover, shelter, shield; put up a screen, etc.: *Aliiziba ile sehemu kwa kitambaa kikubwa ili watu wa ndani wasionekane,* he put up a big screen so that the people inside would not be seen. Prep. *zib.i.a* St. *zib.ik.a* Cs. *zib.ish.a* Ps. *zib.w.a,* e.g. *Njia imezibwa kwa sababu ya matengenezo,* the road is blocked for repairs. Rp *zib.an.a* Ps. of Prep. *zib.iw.a* (cf *funika*)
zibu.a *vt* uncover, uncork, unplug, unstop; unclose an opening: *Aliizibua chupa,* he uncorked the bottle. Prep. *zibu.li.a* St. *zibu.k.a* Cs. *zibu.lish.a* Ps. of Prep. *zibu.liw.a* Rp. *zibu.an.a* (cf *fungua*)

zid.i *vt* 1. exceed the limit, target, etc.: *Utundu wake umezidi siku hizi,* his naughtiness has worsened these days. Prep. **zid.i.a** St. **zid.ik.a** Cs. **zid.ish.a** Ps. of Prep. **zid.iw.a** become worse, be overwhelmed, be hard-pressed. Rp. **zid.i.an.a** e.g. *Watu huzidiana kiakili na kimaarifa,* people outshine one another in intelligence and experience. 2. increase, multiply: *Wageni wanazidi kufika kwenye karamu,* the guests are increasing in number at the party. Prep. **zid.i.a** St. **zid.ik.a** Cs. **zid.ish.a,** cause to increase. Ps. **zid.iw.a** Rp. of Prep. **zid.i.an.a** (cf *kithiri, ongezeka*) (Ar)

zidish.a[1] *vt* see *zidi*

zidish.a[2] *vt* 1. (*math*) multiply: *Alizidisha sita kwa tatu na akapata kumi na nane,* he multiplied six by three and got eighteen. 2. (*fig*) increase, multiply, redouble, intensify, step-up: *Lazima tuzidishe juhudi zetu kama tunataka tufanikiwe,* we must redouble our efforts if we want to succeed. Prep. **zidish.i.a** St. **zidish.ik.a** Ps. **zidish.w.a** Rp. **zidish.an.a**

zidishi.a *vt* add more and more; give more and more: *Mungu atakuzidishia kila la heri,* God will give you more and more blessings. Prep. **zidishi.li.a** St. **zidishi.lik.a** Ps. **zidishi.w.a** Rp. **zidishi.an.a** (cf *ongezea*)

zidiw.a *vt* 1. be overwhelmed: *Nilizidiwa na kazi,* I was overwhelmed with work. 2. be in a critical situation; be very ill; worsen, deteriorate: *Mgonjwa alizidiwa,* the patient's is condition bacame worse.

zidu.a *vt* uproot, extract, extirpate, unroot, outroot, pull out: *Niliizidua misumari,* I pulled out the nails. Prep. **zidu.li.a** St. **zidu.k.a** and **zidu.lik.a** Cs. **zidu.sh.a** Ps. of Prep. **zidu.liw.a** Rp. **zidu.an.a** (cf *ng'oa, sekua*)

ziga *n* (*ma-*) thurible, censer; a container in which incense, etc. is burned to warm a sick person or to perform religious rites. (cf *chetezo*)

zigi.a *vi* be lazy, become less active; idle: *Mfanyakazi wangu amezigia siku hizi,* my worker has become less active these days. Prep. **zigi.a** St. **zigi.lik.a** Cs. **zigi.lish.a** (cf *bweteka, zembea*)

zigizaga[1] *adv* crookedly, haphazardly, disorderly, unsystematically, awry: *Mambo yake yalikwenda zigizaga,* his affairs went awry. (cf *kombo, ovyo*)

zigizaga[2] *n* (*n*) a kind of stitching with a pattern like the blade of a saw.

zihi *n* (*n*) 1. strength, force, power, energy: *Ijapokuwa yeye ni mwembamba lakini ana zihi,* even though he is slim, he has strength. (cf *hima, motisha, kani, shime*) 2. stubbornness, firmness: *Mbona umeshika zihi kama hivyo?* Why are you stubborn like that?

zii *interj* 1. an exclamation used to express scorn, disapproval, etc.; boo! 2. (*idm*) *Pigwa zii,* be rejected; thumb down.

zik.a[1] *vt* bury, inter, inhume: *Walimzika marehemu jana,* they buried the deceased yesterday. Prep. **zik.i.a,** bury for (in, at, etc) e.g. *Hakuwa na fedha za kuzikia,* he had no money for burial expenses. St. **zik.ik.a** Cs. **zik.ish.a** Ps. **zik.w.a,** be buried e.g. *Alizikwa mbali kutoka hapa,* he was buried far from here. Rp. **zik.an.a** (cf *fukia*)

zik.a[2] *vt* cheat, doublecross; betray someone by doing sth the opposite: *Walimzika rafiki yao,* they cheated their friend. Prep. **zik.i.a** St. **zik.ik.a** Cs. **zik.ish.a** Ps. **zik.w.a** Rp. **zik.an.a**

ziki *n* (*n*) white embroidered stitching usu round the neck of a gent's garment known as *kanzu;* extra stitching at neckline.

ziku.a *vt* disinter, exhume, disentomb, disinhume, dig up: *Mahakama iliiamuru polisi kuuzikua mwili wa marehemu,* the court ordered the police to exhume the body of the deceased. Prep. *ziku.li.a* St. *ziku.k.a* Cs. *ziku.lish.a* Ps. of Prep. *ziku.liw.a*, be exhumed. Rp. *ziku.an.a* (cf *fukua, zua*)

zila (also *zela*) n (n) an instrument for bailing out water from a canoe, dhow, etc.; bailer, bailing scoop. (cf *upo, ndau*)

zile adj, pron form of *-le*, 'that' used for **n** class pl nouns to signal non-proximity: *Ndoto zile*, those dreams.

zilizala n (n) earthquake, seism, earth tremor: *Zilizala ilipotokea, watu wengi wakafariki*, when the earthquake occurred, many people died. (cf *tetemeko*) (Ar)

-zima¹ adj 1. complete, whole, entire: *Siku nzima*, the whole day. *Samaki mzima*, the whole fish. 2. healthy, well, salubrious, fine, physically-fit: *Wewe ni mzima*, you are healthy. 3. (idm) *Mtu mzima*, adult.

zim.a² vt 1. switch off, turn off: *Zima taa*, switch off the lights, turn off the lights. 2. (of an engine car, etc.) switch off, put out: *Zima swichi ya gari*, switch off the car engine. *Zima moto*, put out the fire. 3. (fig) quell, crush, repress, suppress: *Walilizima jaribio la kutaka kuiangusha serikali*, they quelled the attempt to overthrow the government. Prep. *zim.i.a* St. *zim.ik.a* Cs. *zim.ish.a* Ps. *zim.w.a* (cf *zuia*)

zimamu n (n) bridle; leather bands put on a horse's head to control its movements. (cf *hatamu, lijamu*)

zimba.a vi be dumbfounded, be astounded, be nonplussed, be floored: *Mbakaji alizimbaa aliposikia kwamba amepewa kifungo cha maisha*, the rapist was dumbfounded when he heard that he was given a life sentence. Prep. *zimba.li.a* St. *zimba.lik.a* Cs. *zimba.lish.a* Ps. *zimb.w.a* (cf *pumbaa*)

zimda n (n) see *zamda*

zimi.a vi faint, swoon; loose consciousness: *Mwanajeshi alizimia wakati wa paredi*, the soldier fainted during the parade Prep. *zimi.li.a* St. *zimi.lik.a* Cs. *zimi.sh.a* (cf *zirai, zulu*)

zimik.a vi be extinguished, go out: *Moto umezimika*, the fire has gone out. Prep. *zimik.i.a* Cs. *zimik.ish.a*

zimu.a vt 1. dilute; allow hot water, etc: cool; thin down sth by mixing it with water or other liquid: *Aliizimua tindikali*, he diluted the acid. 2 warm cold water or some other cold liquid; allow cold water or some other liquid so as to make it lukewarm: *Maji haya ni baridi sana; jaribu kuyazimua*, this water is very cold; try to make it lukewarm. Prep. *zimu.li.a* St. *zimu.k.a* Cs. *zimu.sh.a* Ps. of Prep. *zimu.liw.a*

-zimwe adj 1. burnt out, extinguished, lifeless: *Makaa zimwe*, dead coals; burnt-out embers. 2. empty, hollow: *Nazi zimwe*, a hollow coconut i.e. a coconut without milk or kernel.

zimwi n (ma-) ogre, goblin, demon, ghost. (prov) *Zimwi likujualo halikuli likakwisha*, a ghost that knows you will not devour you completely i.e. Better the devil you know than the one you don't.

zinaa n (n) adultery, fornication, affair: *Ugonjwa wa zinaa*, venereal disease. (cf *fuska*)

zinara n (n) water mark in a ship, etc.: plimsoll line/mark.

zind.a vi be firm; stand firm; stick fast: *Alijaribu kumshawishi kufanya mapenzi naye lakini akajizinda*, she tried to seduce him but he stood firm. Prep. *zind.i.a* St. *zind.ik.a* Cs. *zind.ish.a* Ps. *zind.w.a* (cf *jikaza, dinda*)

zindik.a¹ vi see *zinda*

zindik.a² vt protect by magic means; protect with a spell or charm; keep away evil spirits: *Mganga alimzindika mgonjwa wake kwa kumpa hirizi*, the medicineman protected his patient

with the talisman. Prep. *zindik.i.a* St. *zindik.ik.a* Cs *zindik.ish.a* Ps. *zindik.w.a* Rp. *zindik.an.a*
zindiko *n* (*ma-*) magic charm; magic protection: *Nyumba yake inalindwa na zindiko aliloliweka*, his house is protected by the magic charm he has kept. (cf *kago, fingo*)
zindu.a¹ *vt* 1. enlighten, awaken, remind; open the eyes for sby: *Nilikuwa nimeshasahau ujumbe wake lakini wewe ukanizindua*, I had already forgotten his message but you reminded me. (cf *tanabahisha, amsha*) 2. guide, direct: *Kama isingekuwa yeye kunizindua, ningefanya kazi ile ovyovyo*, had it not been for him, I would have done that work haphazardly. Prep. *zindu.li.a* St. *zindu.k.u* Cs. *zindu.sh.a* Ps. of Prep. *zindu.liw.a* Rp. *zindu.an.a* (cf *ongoza*)
zindu.a² *vt* inaugurate, launch, kick off: *Marais wawili waliizindua rasmi ujenzi wa barabara*, the two presidents officially inaugurated the construction of a road. *Balozi mdogo alizindua awamu ya pili ya chanjo dhidi ya polio*, the charge d'affaires inaugurated the second phase of inoculation against polio. Prep. *zindu.li.a* St. *zindu.k.a* Cs. *zindu.sh.a* Ps. of Prep. *zindu. liw.a* (cf *fungua*)
zinduk.a *vt* 1. wake up, gain consciousness: *Alizinduka ghafla baada ya kulala kwa muda mrefu*, he woke up suddenly after sleeping for a long time. 2. become awakened/conscious / aware: *Wananchi wamezinduka kisiasa*, the people are politically awakened. Prep. *zinduk.i.a* St. *zinduk.ik.a* Cs. *zinduk.ish.a* Ps. *zinduk.w.a*
zinduko *n* (*ma-*) realization; awakening from sleep, etc.: *Yumo katika zinduko la maasi yake*, he has awakened to the extent of his evil deeds.
zinduna *n* (*n*) fossil gum-copal. (cf *kaharabu*) (Ar)

zinduo¹ *n* (*ma-*) realization from forgetfulness, etc.: *Zinduo la kisiasa liliwawezesha wananchi kuikomboa nchi yao*, the political awakening enabled the people to liberate their country. (cf *tanbihi, indhari*)
zinduo² *n* (*ma-*) inauguration, launching, kick off: *Zinduo la posta mpya lilihudhuriwa na watu wengi*, the inauguration of the new post office was attended by many people. (cf *ufunguzi*)
zing.a *vi* 1. roam, wander, range, rove, meander, stray: *Tangu amesimamishwa kazi, amekuwa akizinga tu mitaani*, since being suspended from work, he has been wandering in the neighbourhood. (cf *zunguka, vanga*) 2. stroll, saunter, amble, ramble: *Anapenda kuzinga sehemu za pwani nyakati za jioni*, he likes to stroll around the seashore in the evenings. (cf *tembea*) 3. (of winds, etc.) veer, swerve, shift; change direction: *Upepo mkali ulikuwa ukivuma upande wa mashariki lakini sasa umezinga*, the strong wind was blowing towards the east but now it has changed its direction. 4. go after women; womanize: *Baada ya kumwacha mkewe, akaanza kuzinga*, after his divorcing his wife, he started to womanize. Prep. *zing.i.a* and *zingir.a* St. *zing.ik.a* Cs. *zing.ish.a* Ps. *zing.w.a* (cf *tembea*)
zingati.a *vt* bear in mind, take into account; examine, observe, consider: *Aliizingatia nasaha niliyompa*, he considered the advice I gave him. Prep. *zingati.li.a* St. *zingati.k.a* Cs. *zingati.sh.a* Ps. *zingati.w.a*, be examined e.g. *Wazo lake lilizingatiwa kwa makini kwenye mkutano*, his suggestion was seriously considered at the meeting. Rp. *zingati.an.a* (cf *fikiria, tafakari, waza*)
zingatio *n* (*ma-*) consideration, examination. (cf *tafakuri*)

-zingativu *adj* thoughtful, pensive: *Mwanasiasa mzingativu*, a thoughtful politician.
zingi.a¹ *vt* surround, encircle, endorse: *Walimzingia adui*, they surrounded the enemy. Prep. *zingi.li.a* St. *zingi.k.a* Cs. *zingi.sh.a* Ps. *zingi.w.a* Rp. *zingi.an.a* (cf *zingira*)
zingi.a² *vi* (of colour, etc.) fade away, die out, dribble away; pine, wane: *Fulana yangu ya buluu imeanza kuzingia*, the colour of my blue vest has started to fade. Prep. *zingi.li.a* St. *zingi.k.a* Cs. *zingi.sh.a* (cf *fifia, parara*)
zingifuri *n* (*n*) 1. (*bot*) a kind of edible bright red fruit containing numerous round seeds covered with orange powder, used as a dye for colouring food products, varnishes; annato fruit. 2. cinnabar.
zingio¹ *n* (*ma-*) siege, blockade, beleagurment, encirclement: *Zingio la ngome*, the siege of the fort.
zingio² *n* (*ma-*) (of colour, etc.) fade-out; dying away: *Zingio la rangi ya suruali*, the fading out of the trousers' colour.
zingir.a *vt* surround, besiege, enclose: *Adui aliuzingira mji*, the enemy besieged the town. Prep. *zingir.i.a* St. *zingir.ik.a* Cs. *zingir.ish.a*, e.g. *Alimzingirisha mwizi kwa kamba*, he tied up the thief with a rope. Ps. *zingir.w.a*, be besieged e.g. *Jeshi lilizingirwa*, the army was surrounded. Rp. *zingir.an.a* (cf *zingia*)
zingizi¹ *n* (*n*) 1. (*med*) dysmenorrhoea; difficult and painful menstruation the pains which women undergo at the beginning of menstruation. 2. uterine contraction, labour pains; the pains that a woman undergo during and after delivery: *Tumbo la zingizi*, the abdominal pains of these kinds.
zingizi² *n* (*n*) 1. (*anat*) the section of the gut in the naval of a baby; umbilical cord.

2. the substance that comes out from the uterus through the vagina afterbirth in the pregnant woman, locally called *kondo ya nyuma*; placenta. 3. a customary fee or present given to old women who render their services at a birth.
zingu.a¹ (also *zungua*) *vt* exorcize esp by reading verses of Holy Quran; relieve someone from anxiety, illness, etc. by reciting prayers over him or her: *Shehe alimzingua mgonjwa wake kwa kumsomea aya mbalimbali*, the sheik relieved his patient from anxiety by reading different verses. Prep. *zingu.li.a* St. *zingu.lik.a* Cs. *zingu.lish.a* Ps. of Prep. *zingu.liw.a* Rp. *zingu.an.a*
zingu.a² *vt* unwrap, unroll: *Aliizingua kamba*, he unrolled the rope. Prep. *zingu.li.a* St. *zingu.lik.a* Cs. *zingu.lish.a* Ps. of Prep. *zingu.liw.a* Rp. *zingu.an.a* (cf *kunjua, fungua*)
zingu.a³ *vt* (*colloq*) cheat, deceive. Prep. *zingu.li.a* St. *zingu.lik.a* Cs. *zingu.lish.a* Ps. of Prep. *zingu.liw.a* Rp. *zingu.an.a* (cf *hadaa, danganya*)
zinguo (also *zunguo*) *n* (*ma-*) exorcism, disenchantment; riddance of a malign influence esp by reading Koranic verses: *Zinguo lilimpa ahueni*, the exorcism gave him some relief.
zin.i *vi* commit adultery; fornicate: *Dini zote zinakataza kuzini*, all religions forbid adultery. Prep. *zin.i.a* St. *zin.ik.a* Cs. *zin.ish.a* (Ar)
-zinifu *adj* lecherous, adulterous, prurient, concupiscent, lascivious: *Mwanamke mzinifu*, a lecherous woman.
zinki *n* (*n*) (min) zinc (Eng)
zinz.a¹ *vt* 1. (*idm*) *Zinza kichwa*, be arrogant, be conceited; brag, boast: *Tangu kupandishwa cheo kazini, amekuwa akizinza kichwa*, since being promoted, he has become arrogant.

2. display goods for sale. 3. place a patient on a special diet. Prep. *zinz.i.a* St. *zinz.ik.a* Cs. *zinz.ish.a* Ps. *zinz.w.a* (cf *jitapa, jivuna*)

zinz.a² *vt* disgrace a culprit in public. Prep. *zinz.i.a* St. *zinz.ik.a* Cs. *zinz.ish.a* Ps. *zinz.w.a*

zio *n* (*ma-*) a post or pole used in making the sides of a local hut.

zipi *adj, pron* form of *-pi*, 'which', used for **n** and **u** classes pl nouns: *Nguo zipi?* Which clothes? *Kuta zipi?* Which walls? *Zipi zako?* Which are yours?

zipu *n* (*n*) zip; zipper; fastener: *Suruali yangu haina zipu*, my trousers does not have a zip. (Eng)

zir.a *vt* see *zia*. Prep. *zir.i.a* St. *zir.ik.a* Cs. *zir.ish.a* Ps. *zir.w.a* Rp. *zir.an.a*

zira.i *vi* faint, swoon; loose consciousness: *Mwanariadha alizirai wakati wa kufanya mazoezi*, the athlete fainted during work-out. Prep. *zira.i.a* St. *zira.ik.a* Cs. *zira.ish.a* (cf *zimia*)

zirifu *adj* feeling sick by touching or eating sth.

ziro *n* (*n*) zero, nil: *Alipata ziro katika hesabu*, he got zero in arithmetic.

-zito *adj* 1. heavy, hefty, weighty: *Mzigo huu ni mzito*, this load is heavy. 2. intricate, crucial, sensitive, difficult: *Hilo ni suala zito*, that is a difficult issue. 3. sluggish, slow: *Ana mkono mzito*, he is slow. 4. bad, wicked: *Ana tabia nzito*, he has a bad habit. 5. depressed, sad: *Ana moyo mzito siku hizi*, he is sad these days. 6. dull, stupid: *Yeye ni mwanafunzi mzito*, he is a dull student. 7. deaf: *Ana masikio mazito*, he is deaf; he can't hear properly. 8. slow in speaking: *Mtoto yule ana ulimi mzito*, that child has taken long to speak.

ziwa¹ *n* (*ma-*) lake: *Ziwa la Viktoria*, Lake Victoria. *Ziwa la Nyasa*, Lake Nyasa. *Maziwa Makuu*, the Great Lakes. *Nchi za Maziwa Makuu*, the Great Lakes

Countries. (cf *bwawa*)

ziwa² *n* (*ma-*) breast, bosom: *Ziwa la mwanamke*, a woman's breast. (cf *chuchu*)

zizi *n* (*ma-*) kraal, corral, pen: *Zizi la ng'ombe*, a cattle pen; byre, cowshed. (cf *faja*)

zizim.a *vi* (of body, water, etc.) be cold, become cold: *Mwili wake wote umezizima*, his whole body has become cold. *Chai yako ilikuwa i moto sana lakini sasa imezizima*, your tea was very hot but now it has become cold. Prep. *zizim.i.a* St. *zizim.ik.a* Cs. *zizim.ish.a* Ps. *zizim.w.a*

zizimi.a *vt* sink in the ground. Prep. *sisimi.li.a* St. *zizimi.lik.a* Cs. *zizimi.sh.a* Ps. *zizimi.w.a*

zizimish.a entangle sby; tangle, embroil, muddle Prep. *zizimish.i.a* St. *zizimish.ik.a* Ps. *zizimish.w.a* Ps. *zizimish.an.a*

zo *pron* (*rel*) a relative pronoun for **n** and **u** classes pl nouns: *Nyumba alizozijenga ni nyingi*, the houses he has built are many. *Nyakati zilizokusudiwa sasa zimewadia*, the periods that were set have finally come.

zo.a *vt* 1. sweep up, sweep away; gather up; pick up: *Alizoa taka*, he gathered up the rubbish. *Zoa mtama uliomwagika*, pick up the millet that is scattered all over. Prep. *zo.le.a*, sweep up for e.g. *Ufagio wa kuzolea*, a broom for cleaning up rubbish. St. *zo.lek.a* e.g. *Maji yaliyomwagika hayazoleki*, the water that has spilt cannot be gathered up i.e. You cannot rectify sth that is terribly spoilt. Cs. *zo.lesh.a* Ps. of Prep. *zo.lew.a,* be picked up. Rp. *zo.an.a* 2. (*fig*) collect, garner: *Mwanariadha alizizoa medali nne*, the athlete swept four medals. Prep. *zo.le.a* St. *zo.lek.a* Cs. *zo.lesh.a* Ps. of Prep. *zo.lew.a*

zoe.a *vt* be used to; be accustomed to, become used: *Amezoea kula wali* *kila siku*, he is used to eating rice every day. *Amezoea kuomba*, he is accustomed to begging. Prep. *zoe.le.a* St. *zoe.lek.a* Cs. *zoe.sh.a* and *zoe.z.a* Ps. *zoe.w.a* Rp. *zoe.an.a*, be accustomed to one another e.g. *Vijana wale wawili wamezoeana*, those two young men are friendly and familiar to each other.

-zoefu (also *zoevu*) *adj* experienced, seasoned, skillful: *Mhunzi mzoefu*, an experienced blacksmith.

zoelek.a *vt* become accustomed, be familiar. Prep. *zoelek.e.a* St. *zoelek.ek.a* Cs. *zoelek.esh.a*

zoesh.a (also *zoeza*) *vt* accustom: *Kanizoesha kunywa kahawa kila siku*, he has made me accustomed to drinking coffee everyday. Prep. *zoesh.e.a* St. *zoesh.ek.a* Ps. *zoesh.w.a* Rp. *zoesh.an.a*

-zoevu *adj* see *zoefu*

zoezi *n* (*ma*-) (of studies, sports, etc.) lesson, practice, practical exercise: *Zoezi la pili*, lesson two. *Zoezi la lugha*, language practice. *Zoezi la mpira*, football practice. *Mazoezi ya mkono*, manual exercises. *Wananchi walilipinga zoezi la kupunguza wafanyakazi katika sekta za umma*, the people opposed the exercise of reducing workers in the public sectors.

zog.a *vt* pound, crush, smash, mash. Prep. *zog.e.a* St. *zog.ek.a* Cs. *zog.esh.a* Ps. *zog.w.a*

zogo *n* (*n*) commotion, disturbance, confusion, hubbub, hullabaloo, uproar: *Usilete zogo hapa wakati sisi tunadurusu masomo yetu*, don't create disturbances here while we are revising our lessons. (cf *vurugu, zahama, ghasia, rabsha*)

Zohali[1] *n* (*n*) (*astron*) Uranus; a planet of the solar system, seventh in distance from the sun, having five satellites. (Ar)

zohali[2] *n* (*n*) sluggishness, slackness, laxity, remissness, delay: *Zohali zake zimemfanya afukuzwe kazini*, his laxities have caused him to be sacked from work. (cf *ajizi*)

zoloto *n* (*n*) (*anat*) larynx, voicebox, Adam's apple (cf *koo, koromeo, kongomeo*)

zom.a see *zomea*. Prep. *zom.e.a* St. *zom.ek.a* Cs. *zom.esh.a* Ps. of Prep. *zom.ew.a* Rp. *zom.an.a*

zome.a (also *zoma*) *vt* gibe, jeer, boo, fleer, scoff: *Wasikilizaji walimzomea msemaji*, the audience jeered at the speaker. Prep. *zome.le.a* St. *zome.k.a* Cs. *zome.sh.a* Ps. *zome.w.a*, be booed, e.g. *Mchezaji alizomewa na watazamaji*, the player was booed by the spectators. Rp. *zome.an.a*

zong.a *vt* 1. coil round, knot, entangle: *Kamba ilimzonga mbuzi miguuni mwake*, the rope entangled the goat's legs. (cf *songa*) 2. (*fig*) puzzle, confuse, bewilder, overwhelm: *Matatizo yamemzonga*, problems have overwhelmed him. Prep. *zong.e.a* St. *zong.ek.a* Cs. *zong.esh.a* Ps. *zong.w.a*, be hard-pressed, be pressed up e.g. *Nimezongwa na kazi*, I am up to the neck with work. Rp. *zong.an.a* (cf *tatiza, tinga*)

zongapingu *n* (*n*) (*zool*) sea slug, beche-de-mer; worm of the sea resembling a millipede. (cf *kojokojo*)

zongo *n* (*n*) (*med*) a condition where the abdomen gets swollen esp in the cases of children, where this may be due to *Hirchspring's* disease (congenital megacolon), kidney failure, etc. In traditional thinking, the concept of "zongo" is usu. associated with a "look of envy".

zongo.a *vt* 1. unwind, uncoil, untie, unfurl, uncurl, undo: *Aliizongoa kamba*, he unwound the rope. (cf *nasua*) 2. (*fig*) disentangle, disembroil, solve, resolve: *Aliweza kulizongoa*

tatizo lake, he managed to solve his problem. Prep. ***zongo.le.a*** St. ***zongo. lek.a*** Cs. ***zongo.lesh.a*** Ps. of Prep. ***zongo.lew.a*** Rp. ***zongo.an.a*** (cf *tatua, dadavua*)
zongomez.a *vt. vi* (of a cloth, turban, etc.) wrap around; coil around; tie round: *Mzee alijizongomeza kilemba kichwani mwake*, the old man wrapped a turban round his head. Prep. ***zongomez.e.a*** St. ***zongomez.ek.a*** Cs. ***zongomez.esh.a*** Ps. ***zongomez.w.a*** Rp. ***zongomez.an.a***
zongomi *adj* springy, bouncy.
zongomo *n* (*ma-*) a coiled thing usu a wire or a metal coil; spring.
zongon (*ma-*)**o.a** *vt, vi* unwind, unravel: *Aliuzongomoa uzi*, he unwound the string. Prep. ***zongomo.le.a*** St. ***zongomo.k.a*** Cs. ***zongomo.sh.a*** Ps. of Prep ***zongomo.lew.a***
zoni *n* (*n*) zone; an area or a region with a particular feature or use. (cf *eneo*) (Eng)
zorot.a *vi* slow down, slacken, deteriorate, taper off: *Uchumi wa nchi yetu umezorota*, the economy of our country has deteriorated. Prep. ***zorot.e.a*** St. ***zorot.ek.a*** Cs. ***zorot.esh.a***, Ps. ***zorot.w.a***, be delayed. Rp. of Prep. ***zorot.e.an.a*** (cf *legalega, suasua*)
zorotesh.a *vt* slacken, retard; *Kiongozi alishutumiwa kwa kuuzorotesha uchumi wa nchi*, the leader was accused of slackening the country's economy. Prep. ***zorotesh.e.a*** St. ***zorotesh.ek.a*** Ps. ***zorotesh.w.a*** Rp. ***zorotesh.an.a***
zote *adj, pron* form of *-ote*, 'all', used for **n** and **u** class pl nouns: *Ngome zote*, all the forts. *Nyavu zote*, all the nets. *Zote ni zangu*, all is mine.
zoz.a *vi* wrangle, bicker, spat, jangle, quarrel, dispute, nag. Prep. ***zoz.e.a*** St. ***zoz.ek.a*** Cs. ***zoz.esh.a*** Ps. ***zoz.w.a*** Rp. ***zoz.an.a***, nag at each other e.g. *Wakewenza wawili walikuwa wakizozana*, the co-wives were nagging

at each other. (cf *bishana, shindana*)
zozan.a *vi* see *zoza*
zu.a¹ *vt* 1. invent lies, rumours, etc; make up lies, etc; concoct lies. etc.; cook up stories: *Alizua uwongo*, he made up lies. Prep. ***zu.li.a***, invent lies for (against, with, etc.) e.g. *Walimzulia hadithi za uwongo*, they invented fake stories against him. St. ***zu.k.a*** and ***zu.lik.a*** Cs. ***zu.sh.a*** Cs. of Prep. ***zu.lish.a*** Ps. of Prep. ***zu.liw.a*** (cf *singizia, binia*) 2. initiate, invent, start, trigger off: *Waliuzua mtindo mpya wa nywele*, they invented a new hair style. Prep. ***zu.li.a*** St. ***zu.k.a*** and ***zu.lik.a*** Cs. ***zu.sh.a*** Ps. of Prep. ***zu.liw.a*** Rp. of Prep. ***zu.li.an.a*** (cf *anzisha*)
zu.a² *vt* unearth, dig out, dig up, bring to surface: *Mwizi alipazua pale pahala ili avichukue vitu alivyovuba*, the thief unearthed the spot inorder to take out the things he had stolen. Prep. ***zu.li.a*** St. ***zu.k.a*** and ***zu.lik.a*** Cs. ***zu.sh.a*** Ps. of Prep. ***zu.liw.a*** (cf *fukua*)
zuakulu *n* (*n*) (*zool*) black-collared barbet; a kind of tropical bird (family *Capitonidae*) having a strong bill with a red head, a black band across the breast and a yellowish belly. *Lybius*

zuakulu

zuba.a *vi* 1. stand around gawking; goggle, gape, gawk: *Acha kuzubaa*,stop gawking. 2. be dumbfounded; be nonplussed; be shocked: *Nilizubaa nilipopata taarifa mbaya ile*, I was nonplussed when I got that sad news.

Prep. *zuba.i.a* St. *zuba.ik.a* Cs. *zuba.ish.a* and *zuba.za* (cf *duwaa, zimbaa*)
zubu *n* (*n*) penis (cf *dhakari, mboo*) (Ar)
zubu.a *vt* see *zibua*. Prep. *zubu.li.a* St. *zubu.k.a* Cs. *zubu.sh.a* Ps of Prep. *zubu.liw.a*
zug.a *vt* befool someone to the point of agreeing with anything that he is told; bamboozle, hoodwink: *Bibi yule amemzuga mumewe*, that woman has fooled her husband. Prep. *zug.i.a* St. *zug.ik.a* Cs. *zug.ish.a* Ps. *zug.w.a*, be fooled e.g. *Amezugwa sana na rafiki yake; kila kitu anaitikia hewallah*, he has been often fooled by his friend; everything he is told, he says "yes". Rp. *zug.an.a*. (cf *renga, hadaa*)
zuge (also *zugezuge*) *n* (*ma-*) dupe, halfwit; a befooled person, a witless person: *Zuge alichekwa na watu*, the half-wit was laughed at by the people.
zugezuge *n* (*ma-*) see *zuge*
zugma *n* (*n*) (*gram*) zeugma; a figure of speech in which a word applies to two others in different senses. (Ex: Mr. John took his hat and his pen, *Bwana John alichukua kofia yake na kalamu yake*). (Eng)
Zuhura *n* (*n*) (*astron*) Venus; the most brilliant planet in the solar system, second in distance from the sun. (cf *ng'andu*) (Ar)
zui.a *vt* 1. prevent, stop, bar, hinder, impede: *Huwezi kuzuia maendeleo ya nchi yetu*, you cannot stop the development of our country. *Ofisa wa uhamiaji alinizuia nisivuke mpaka*, the immigration officer stopped me from crossing the border. Prep. *zui.li.a* e.g. *Alimzuilia urithi wake*, he barred her from her inheritance. St. *zui. lik.a* Cs. *zui.lish.a* Ps. *zui.w.a*, be prevented e.g. *Mwanasiasa alizuiwa na serikali asisafiri nje*, the politician was prevented by the government from travelling abroad. Rp. *zui.an.a* (cf *kataza, komesha*) 2. prevent from falling: *Kibao hiki kinazuia meza hii isicheze*, this piece of wood prevents the table from wobbling. Prep. *zui. li.a* St. *zui.lik.a* Cs. *zui.lish.a* Ps. *zui.w.a* Rp. of Prep. *zui.liw.a* Rp. *zui.an.a*
zuk.a¹ *vt* see *zua*
zuk.a² *vi* emerge, appear, come, surface: *Baada ya kupotea kwa muda mrefu, mtu yule sasa amezuka*, after disappearing for quite long, that person has now resurfaced. Prep. *zuk.i..a* St. *zuk.ik.a* Cs. *zuk.ish.a* (cf *ibuka, chomoza*)
zuka³ *n* (*ma-*) apparition, ghost, spirit. (cf *zimwi*)
zuli.a¹ *vt* see *zua*
zulia² *n* (*ma-*) carpet (Ar)
zul.u *vi* 1. feel dizzy, befuddled, be flustered; reel: *Kichwa chake kilizulu mara tu alipoamka*, his head reeled as soon as he got up Prep. *zul.i.a*, St. *zul.ik.a* Cs. *zul.ish.a*, cause someone to feel dizzy e.g. *Pombe ilimzulisha kichwa*, beer caused him to become dizzy. Ps. *zul.iw.a*. (cf *sulika*) 2. become senile because of old age; become less sane: *Maneno yake ya ovyoovyo yanaonyesha waziwazi kwamba yeye sasa amezulu*, her useless talk shows that she has now become senile. Prep. *zul.i.a* St. *zul. ik.a* Cs. *zul.ish.a* Ps. of Prep. *zul. iw.a*
zumari *n* (*n*) see *nzumari*
zumaridi *n* (*n*) (*min*) aquamarine, emerald; a transparent pale bluish-green variety of beryl, used in jewelry. (Pers)
zumbu.a *vt* 1. have the means to get the daily necessities of livelyhood: *Ingawa sukari imeadimika sana mjini, lakini jirani yangu ameweza kuizumbua*, even though sugar has become very scarce in the town, my neighbour has managed to get it. (cf *pata*) 2. devise, invent, discover: *Alizumbua mtindo mpya wa kuwadanganya wateja wake*, he invented a new

scheme of deceiving his customers. *Ameshazumbua balaa nyingine sasa, he has now already devised some other mischief.* Prep. **zumbu.li.a** St. **zumbu. lik.a** Cs. **zumbu.sh.a** Ps. of Prep. **zumbu.liw.a.** (cf *vumbua, anzisha*)

zumbukuku n (*ma-*) nincompoop; a very ignorant person; a real witless person.

zumburu (also *dumbwara*) n (*ma-*) (*zool*) emperor red snapper; a kind of salt water fish (family *Lutjanidae*) having a moderately elongate body and usu with a deep coloration of the body among the adults, found on coral or rocky reefs. *Lutjanus sebae.*

zumo n (n) 1. songs of victory, etc.; paean. 2. noises of joy as in wedding celebrations; ululations. (cf *vifijo, vigelegele*)

zunga n (*ma-*) 1. the fold of skin that covers the end of the penis and is removed when performing circumcision; foreskin, prepuce 2. an uncircumcised person. (cf *govi, chamburere*)

zungu.a [1] *vt* see *zingua*

zungu.a² *vt* spin, rotate; cause to go round, turn round: *Alilizungua gurudumu la baiskeli, he span the bicycle wheel.* St. **sungu.k.a,** go round, circle around, move around; gyrate e.g. : *Aliuzunguka uwanja wa mpira mara moja, he went round the football pitch once.* Cs. **zungu. sh.a,** put round, surround with e.g. *Alizungusha senyenge kwenye nyumba yake, he surrounded his house with a barbed wire.* Ps. of St. **zungu.k.w.a,** be surrounded e.g. *Jeshi lilizungukwa na adui, the army was surrounded by the enemy.*

zunguk.a¹ *vt* see *zungua²*

zunguk.a² *vi* 1. wander, roam, range, rive: *Anapenda kuzunguka hapa na pale,* he likes to wander here and there. 2. (*fig*) betray; rat on, stab in the back: *Tulifanya mpango pamoja lakini baadaye akanizunguka,* we made the plan together but later, he betrayed

me. Prep. **zunguk.i.a** St. **zunguk.ik.a** Cs. **zunguk.ish.a** Ps. **zunguk.w.a** (cf *hini, saliti, laghai*) 3. (*idms*) *Zunguka mbuyu,* bribe someone e.g. *Aliipata kazi kwa kuzunguka mbuyu,* he got the job by bribing. *Zunguka vuruvuru,* go round continuously.

zungumz.a¹ *vt, vi* talk, converse, chitchat, discuss, speak, chat: *Alizungumza juu ya nidhamu mashuleni,* he spoke about discipline in schools. Prep. **zungumz.i.a,** talk about, discuss, speak about e.g. *Alizungumzia mada ile kwa ufasaha,* he spoke about that topic with eloquence. St. **zungumz. ik.a** Cs. **zungumz.ish.a,** e.g. *Nilijaribu kukaa kimya kwenye mkutano lakini yeye akawa ananizungumzisha,* I tried to remain silent at the meeting but he made me talk. Ps. **zungumz.w.a** be talked e.g. *Ulikuwa ukizungumzwa na sisi,* you were being talked about by us. Rp. **zungumz.an.a** (cf *ongea, longa*)

zungumz.a² *vt (colloq)* bribe Prep. **zungumz.i.a** St. **zungumz.ik.a** Cs. **zungumz.ish.a** Ps. **zungumz.w.a**

zungumzi.a *vt* see *zungumza*. Prep. **zungumzi.li.a** St. **zungumzi.k.a,** be discussed, be talked e.g. *Mada hiyo inazungumzika,* that topic can be discussed. Cs. **zungumzi.sh.a** Ps. **zungumzi.w.a**

zunguo n (*ma-*) see *zinguo*

zungush.a *vt* 1. waste the time of someone; bother, trouble: *Yeye ananizungusha tu kwa kunipa ahadi zake za uwongo,* he is just putting me off with his false promises. Ps. **zungush.w.a** e.g. *Mtu yule anazungushwa tu; Sifikiri kwamba atarejeshewa vitu vyake,* that person has just been taken for a ride; I don't think he will get his things back Rp. **zungush.an.a** 2. take round: *Walijaribu kunizungusha mjini ingawa mimi sikutaka,* they tried to make me wander round the town even though I did not want. 3. make sth to go

round; circle, rotate: *Walilizungusha gurudumu,* they rotated the wheel Prep. *zungush.i.a* St. *zungush.ik.a* Ps. *zungush.w.a* Rp. *zungush.an.a*
zungushi.a *vt* encircle, surround, enclose: *Aliuzungushia ua wake kwa senyenge,* he enclosed his fence with berbed wire. Prep. *zungushi.li.a* St. *zungushi.ki.a* Ps. *zungushi.w.a* Rp. *zungushi.an.a*
zuolojia *n* (*n*) (*zool*) zoology; the scientific study of animals and animals life. (Eng)
-zuri¹ *adj* good, nice, pleasant, beautiful, handsome, pretty: *Msichana mzuri,* a beautiful girl. *Kitabu kizuri,* a good book (cf *sheshe, jamili*)
zuri² *n* (*n*) 1. false evidence 2. perjury; false swearing: *Hakimu alimtia shahidi hatiani kwa kosa la zuri,* the judge convicted the accused for perjury.
zur.u 1. visit, tour, call upon: *Niliizuru Ufaransa mwaka jana,* I visited France last year. Prep. *zur.i.a* St. *zur.ik.a* Cs. *zur.ish.a* Ps. of Prep. *zur.iw.a,* be visited e.g. *Rais alizuriwa na viongozi mbalimbali,* the president was visited by different leaders. (cf *tembea*) 2. used in the expression: *Zuru makaburi,* visit tombs to pray for the dead e.g. *Aliyazuru makaburi ili kuwaombea dua maiti,* he visited the graves to pray for the dead. Prep. *zur.i.a* St. *zur.ik.a* Cs. *zur.ish.a* Ps. of Prep. *zur.iw.a*
zurur.a *vi* meander, wander, range, roam around: *Anataka kuzurura tu lakini hapendi kufanya kazi,* he just wants to roam around but he does not like to work. Prep. *zurur.i.a* St. *zurur.ik.a* Cs. *zurur.ish.a* Ps. of Prep. *zurur.iw.a* (cf *tanga, renga*)
zush.a *vt* 1. start up, 2. fabricate, concoct, invent: *Tafadhali usizushe uwongo hapa,* please don't invent lies here. Prep. *zush.i.a* St. *zush.ik.a*

Ps. of Prep. *zush.iw.a* Rp. *zush.an.a* (cf *zua*)
zuumu *vt* determine, intend, resolve, decide: *Amezuumu kuoa mke mwingine,* he has decided to marry a second wife. Prep. *zuum.i.a* St. *zuum.ik.a* Cs. *zuum.ish.a* Ps. of Prep. *zuum.iw.a* (cf *dhamiria, kusudia*) (Ar)
zuwarde *n* (*n*) (*zool*) melba finch; a red-billed green finch-like bird with a red face and trail. *Pytilia melba.*
zuzu *n* (*ma-*) bumpkin, fool, simpleton, imbecile, idiot: *Yeye ni zuzu kabisa,* he is a real bumpkin. (cf *bozi, dubu*)
zuzu.a *vt* 1. waste time for no reason: *Naona anajizuzua bure kwani hana atakalolipata kwangu,* I feel that he is just wasting his time because there is nothing he will gain from me. 2. fool, befool; make a fool of: *Rafiki yake hakusoma na ndio maana anamzuzua,* his friend is not educated and that is why he is fooling him. (cf *pumbaza, danganya*) 3. make sby become big-headed; make sby swollen-headed: *Usimzuzue ili asije akatakabari,* don't make him swollen-headed lest he becomes vain. Prep. *zuzu.li.a* St. *zuzu.k.a,* become swollen headed/ big headed Cs. *zuzu.sh.a* Ps. of Prep. *zuzu.liw.a* Rp. *zuzu.an.a*
zuzuk.a¹ *vt* see *zuzua.* Prep. *zuzuk.i.a* St. *zuzuk.ik.a* Cs. *zuzuk.ish.a*
zuzuk.a² *vi* vaunt or fool oneself without reason as the result of being praised too much for sth: *Amezuzuka siku hizi kwa kuambiwa kuwa yeye ni mwanafunzi hodari,* he has become vaunted these days for being told that he is a clever student. Prep. *zuzuk.i.a* St. *zuzuk.ik.a* Cs. *zuzuk.ish.a*
zuzuwa.a *vi* be foolish, be ignorant, be weak-minded: *Mbona umezuzuwaa hivyo?* Why are you foolish like that? Prep. *zuzuwa.li.a* St. *zuzuwa.lik.a* Cs. *zuzuwa.lish.a* (cf *pumbaa*)

Bibliography

Bakhressa, S.K.	*Kamusi ya Maana na Matumizi*, Oxford University Press, 1992
Beentje, H.	*Flora of Tropical East Africa, Cambridge International Dictionary of English*, Cambridge University Press, 1995
Child, R.	*Coconuts*, Longman, 1976
Doi, A.I.	*Shariah the Islamic Law*, Taha Publishers, London U.K. 1984
Dorset, J. and Dandelot, P.	*A Field Guide to the larger Mammals of Africa*, Collins, London (edition 1990)
Eccles, D.H.	*Field Guide To The Freshwater Fishes of Tanzania*, Food and Agriculture Organisation of the United Nations, rome 1992
Elias, A.E.	*Elias' Pocket Dictionary English-Arabia*, Edward Elias Elias, Cairo, 1973
FAO	*Field Guide Commercial Marine and Brackish Water Species of Tanzania*
Farsi, S.S.	*Swahili Sayings*, Eastern African Publications, Arusha (edition, 1981)
Greenway, P.J.	*A Swahili-Botanical English Dictionary of Plant Names*, E.A. Agri. Res Station Amani, Tanganyika Territory, Dar es laam, 1940
Gurnalik, D. (ed)	*Webster's New World Dictionary*, Second College Edition, 1972
Hedges, N.G.	*Reptiles Amphibians of East Africa*, Kenya Literature Bureau, 1983
Hornby, A.S.	*Oxford Advanced Learners' Dictionary* Oxford University Press (ed. 1992)
Ifedha, A.S.	*Semi za Kiswahili: Maana na Matumizi*, Oxford University Press, 1987
Irira, S.D.	*Kamusi Awali ya Sayansi na Teknolojia*, Ben and Company Limited, Dar es salaam, 1995
Jahadhmy, A.A.	*Learner's Swahili-English Dictionary* Evans Brothers, Nairobi, 1981
Johnson, F.	*Kamusi Ya Kiswahili*, Oxford University Press, Nairobi, 1939

Johnson, F.	*A Standard Swahili-English Dictionary*, Oxford University Press Nairobi, (ed. 1997)
Johnson, F.	*A Standard English-Swahili Dictionary*, Oxford Unversity Press Nairobi (ed 1989)
Koenders, L.	*Fauna of Pemba Island, Wildlife Conservation Society of Tanzania*, Publication No. 1, 1992
Koenders, L.	*Flora of Pemba Island, Wildlife Conservation Society of Tanzania*, Publication No. 2, 1992
Leskine, N. J. et al	*Woody Biomass Inventory of Zanzibar Island*, Tech. paper No. 10, Ministry of Agriculture National Resources, Zanzibar, 1997
Livingstone, C.	*Medical Dictionary*, The Royal Society of Medicine, NewYork (ed. 1998), *Longman Dictionary of Contemporary English*, Longman, U.K. (ed. 1992)
Maimu, M.	*Kamusi ya Ndege wa Tanzania*, Tanzania Publishing House, Dar es Salaam, 1982
Maimu, M.	*Kamusi ya Wanyama na Nyoka wa Tanzania*, Tanzania Publishing House Dar es Salaam 1982
Malaika, B.	*The Friendly Modern Swahili-English Dictionary*, Denmark (ed 1994)
Martin, E.A. (ed)	*Concise Medical Dictionary*, Oxford University Press, U.K. (ed 1994)
Mc Colaugh, D.W.	*Wild Lives, Profiles of East African Mammals*, 1989
Mlingwa, C.D.F.	*Birds of Tanzania: Provisional List of Bird Names in Kiswahili*, Africa Study Monographs, Vol. 18(2), 1997
Mohamed, A.M. and Mohamed, S.A.	*Kamusi ya Visawe*, East African Educational Publishers, Nairobi, 1998
Ndalu, A. and King'ei, K.G.	*Kamusi ya Semi za Kiswahili*, East African Educational Publishers Nairobi, 1988
Pakenham, R.H.W.	*The Birds of Zanzibar and Pemba: an annonated check-list*. Brit. Orn. Union checklist No. 2, London
Prons, A.H.J.	*A Nautical Swahili-English Dictionary*
Rodale, J.I.	*The Synonym Finder*, Rodal Press, 1981

Ruffo, C.K. et al	*Useful Trees and Shrubs in Tanzania*, Regional Soil Conservation Unit (RSCU) Swedish Interntional Development Authority (SIDA) Embassy of Sweden, Nairobi
Safari, J and Akida, H.	*English-Swahili; Pocket Dictionary*, Mkuki na Nyota Publishers, 1991
Smith, M.M and Heemstra (eds)	*Smiths' Sea Fishes*, Springs-Verlag Berlin Heideberg, NewYork 1986
Tuki	*Kamusi Ya Kiswahili Sanifu*, Oxford University Press (ed. 1988)
Tuki	*English-Swahili Dictionary*, Institute of Kiswahili Research University of Dar es salaam, 1996
Tuki	*Kamusi Sanifu ya Isimu na Lugha*, Institute of Kiswahili Research, University of Dar es salaam.
Vaughan, J.H.	"*The Birds of Zanzibar and Pemba*". The Ibis Ser 12(5) 1929
Williams, J.G. and Arloh, N.	*A Field Guide to the Birds of East Africa*, Collins, London (ed. 1992)
Williams, R.O.	*The Useful and Ornamental Plants in Zanzibar and Pemba*. St Ann's Press, Temperly, Altrincham, 1949
Ziadeh, F. and Winder, R.B.	*An Introducton To Modern Arabic*, Princeton University Press, Princeton, New Jersey, 1957